SOLUTIONS MANUAL for CHEMISTRY A MOLECULAR APPROACH

by Nivaldo J. Tro

Kathleen Thrush Shaginaw • Mary Beth Kramer

Custom Edition for the University of Vermont

Taken from:
Solutions Manual for *Chemistry: A Molecular Approach* by Nivaldo J. Tro, Second Edition
by Kathleen Thrush Shaginaw and Mary Beth Kramer

Learning Solutions

New York Boston San Francisco
London Toronto Sydney Tokyo Singapore Madrid
Mexico City Munich Paris Cape Town Hong Kong Montreal

Cover Art: Courtesy of PhotoDisc/Getty Images

Taken from:

Solutions Manual for *Chemistry: A Molecular Approach* by Nivaldo J. Tro, Second Edition
by Kathleen Thrush Shaginaw and Mary Beth Kramer

Published by Prentice Hall
Upper Saddle River, New Jersey 07458

This special edition published in cooperation with Pearson Learning Solutions.

Pearson Learning Solutions, 501 Boylston Street, Suite 900, Boston, MA 02116
A Pearson Education Company
www.pearsoned.com

Printed in the United States of America

3 4 5 6 7 8 9 10 V0ZN 15 14 13 12 11

000200010270591291

LR

PEARSON

ISBN 10: 0-558-76255-7
ISBN 13: 978-0-558-76255-1

Contents

Student Guide to Using This Solutions Manual

The vision of this solutions manual is to give guidance that is useful for both the struggling student and the advanced student.

An important feature of this solutions manual is that answers for the review questions are given. This will help in the review of the major concepts in the chapter.

The format of the solutions very closely follows the format seen in the textbook. Each mathematical problem includes **Given**, **Find**, **Conceptual Plan**, **Solution**, and **Check** sections.

Given and Find: Many students struggle with taking the written problem, parsing the information into categories, and determining the goal of the problem. It is also important to know which pieces of information in the problem are not necessary to solve the problem and if addition information needs to be gathered from sources, such as tables in the textbook.

Conceptual Plan: The conceptual plan shows a step-by-step method to solve the problem. In many cases, the given quantities need to be converted to a different unit. Under each of the arrows is the equation, constant, or conversion factor needed to complete this portion of the problem. In the "Problems by Topic" section of the end of chapter exercises, the odd-numbered and even-numbered problems are paired. This will allow you to use a conceptual plan from an odd-numbered problem in this manual as a starting point to solve the following even-numbered problem. Students should keep in mind that the examples shown are one way to solve the problems. Other, mathematically equivalent solutions may be possible.

5.49 **Given:** $m\ (CO_2) = 28.8$ g, $P = 742$ mmHg, and $T = 22$ °C **Find:** V

Conceptual Plan: °C $\rightarrow$ K and mmHg $\rightarrow$ atm and g $\rightarrow$ mol then $n, P, T \rightarrow V$

$$\text{K} = {}^{\circ}\text{C} + 273.15 \qquad \frac{1\ \text{atm}}{760\ \text{mm Hg}} \qquad \frac{1\ \text{mol}}{44.01\ \text{g}} \qquad PV = nRT$$

Solution: $T_1 = 22\ ^{\circ}\text{C} + 273.15 = 295\ \text{K}$, $P = 742\ \cancel{\text{mmHg}} \times \dfrac{1\ \text{atm}}{760\ \cancel{\text{mmHg}}} = 0.976316\ \text{atm}$,

$n = 28.8\ \cancel{\text{g}} \times \dfrac{1\ \text{mol}}{44.01\ \cancel{\text{g}}} = 0.654397\ \text{mol}$ $PV = nRT$ Rearrange to solve for V.

$$V = \frac{nRT}{P} = \frac{0.654397\ \cancel{\text{mol}} \times 0.08206\ \dfrac{\text{L} \cdot \cancel{\text{atm}}}{\cancel{\text{mol}} \cdot \cancel{\text{K}}} \times 295\ \cancel{\text{K}}}{0.976316\ \cancel{\text{atm}}} = 16.2\ \text{L}$$

Check: The units (L) are correct. The magnitude of the answer (16 L) makes sense because one mole of an ideal gas under standard conditions (273 K and 1 atm) occupies 22.4 L. Although these are not standard conditions, they are close enough for a ballpark check of the answer. Since this gas sample contains 0.65 moles, a volume of 16 L is reasonable.

Solution: The solution section will walk you through solving the problem following the conceptual plan. Equations are rearranged to solve for the appropriate quantity. Intermediate results are shown with additional digits to minimize round-off error. The units are cancelled in each appropriate step.

Check: The check section confirms that the units in the answer are correct. This section also challenges the student to think about whether the magnitude of the answer makes sense. Thinking about what is a reasonable answer can help to uncover errors, such as calculation errors.

1 Matter, Measurement, and Problem Solving

Review Questions

1.1 "The properties of the substances around us depend on the atoms, ions, or molecules that compose them" means that the specific types of atoms and molecules that compose something tell us a great deal about which properties to expect from a substance. A material composed of only sodium and chloride ions will have the properties of table salt. A material composed of molecules with one carbon atom and two oxygen atoms will have the properties of the gas carbon dioxide. If the atoms and molecules change, so do the properties that we expect the material to have.

1.2 The main goal of chemistry is to seek to understand the behavior of matter by studying the behavior of atoms and molecules.

1.3 The scientific approach to knowledge is based on observation and experiment. Scientists observe and perform experiments on the physical world to learn about it. Observations often lead scientists to formulate a hypothesis, a tentative interpretation or explanation of their observations. Hypotheses are tested by experiments, highly controlled procedures designed to generate such observations. The results of an experiment may support a hypothesis or prove it wrong—in which case the hypothesis must be modified or discarded. A series of similar observations can lead to the development of scientific law, a brief statement that summarizes past observations and predicts future ones. One or more well-established hypotheses may form the basis for a scientific theory. A scientific theory is a model for the way nature is and tries to explain not merely what nature does, but why.

The Greek philosopher Plato (427 – 347 B.C.) took an opposite approach. He thought that the best way to learn about reality was not through the senses, but through reason. He believed that the physical world was an imperfect representation of a perfect and transcendent world (a world beyond space and time). For him, true knowledge came, not through observing the real physical world, but through reasoning and thinking about the ideal one.

1.4 A hypothesis is a tentative interpretation or explanation of the observed phenomena. A law is a concise statement that summarizes observed behaviors and observations and predicts future observations. A theory attempts to explain why the observed behavior is happening.

1.5 Antoine Lavoisier studied combustion and made careful measurements of the mass of objects before and after burning them in closed containers. He noticed that there was no change in the total mass of material within the container during combustion. Lavoisier summarized his observations on combustion with the law of conservation of mass, which states that, "In a chemical reaction, matter is neither created nor destroyed."

1.6 John Dalton formulated the atomic theory of matter. Dalton explained the law of conservation of mass, as well as other laws and observations of the time, by proposing that matter was composed of small, indestructible particles called atoms. Since these particles were merely rearranged in chemical changes (and not created or destroyed), the total amount of mass would remain the same.

1.7 The statement "that is just a theory" is generally taken to mean that there is no scientific proof behind the statement. This statement is the opposite of the meaning in the context of the scientific theory, where theories are tested again and again.

1.8 Matter can be classified according to its state—solid, liquid, or gas—and according to its composition.

1.9 In solid matter, atoms or molecules pack close to each other in fixed locations. Although the atoms and molecules in a solid vibrate, they do not move around or past each other. Consequently, a solid has a fixed volume and rigid shape.

In liquid matter, atoms or molecules pack about as closely as they do in solid matter, but they are free to move relative to each other, giving liquids a fixed volume but not a fixed shape. Liquids assume the shape of their container.

In gaseous matter, atoms or molecules have a lot of space between them and are free to move relative to one another, making gases compressible. Gases always assume the shape and volume of their container.

1.10 Solid matter may be crystalline, in which case its atoms or molecules are arranged in patterns with long-range, repeating order, or it may be amorphous, in which case its atoms or molecules do not have any long-range order.

1.11 A pure substance is composed of only one type of atom or molecule. In contrast, a mixture is a substance composed of two or more different types of atoms or molecules that can be combined in variable proportions.

1.12 An element is a pure substance which cannot be decomposed into simpler substances. A compound is composed of two or more elements in fixed proportions.

1.13 A homogeneous mixture has the same composition throughout, while a heterogeneous mixture has different compositions in different regions.

1.14 If a mixture is composed of an insoluble solid and a liquid, the two can be separated by filtration, in which the mixture is poured through filter paper (usually held in a funnel).

1.15 Mixtures of miscible liquids (substances that easily mix) can usually be separated by distillation, a process in which the mixture is heated to boil off the more volatile (easily vaporizable) liquid. The volatile liquid is then recondensed in a condenser and collected in a separate flask.

1.16 A physical property is one that a substance displays without changing its composition, whereas a chemical property is one that a substance displays only by changing its composition via a chemical change.

1.17 Changes that alter only state or appearance, but not composition, are called physical changes. The atoms or molecules that compose a substance *do not change* their identity during a physical change. For example, when water boils, it changes its state from a liquid to a gas, but the gas remains composed of water molecules, so this a physical change. When sugar dissolves in water, the sugar molecules are separated from each other, but the molecules of sugar and water remain intact.

In contrast, changes that alter the composition of matter are called chemical changes. During a chemical change, atoms rearrange, transforming the original substances into different substances. For example, the rusting of iron, the combustion of natural gas to form carbon dioxide and water, and the denaturing of proteins when an egg is cooked are examples of chemical changes.

1.18 In chemical and physical changes, matter often exchanges energy with its surroundings. In these exchanges, the total energy is always conserved; energy is neither created nor destroyed. Systems with high potential energy tend to change in the direction of lower potential energy, releasing energy into the surroundings.

1.19 Chemical energy is potential energy. It is the energy that is contained in the bonds that hold the molecules together. This energy arises primarily from electrostatic forces between the electrically charged particles (protons and electrons) that compose atoms and molecules. Some of these arrangements—such as the one within the molecules that compose gasoline—have a much higher potential energy than others. When gasoline undergoes combustion the arrangement of these particles changes, creating molecules with much lower potential energy and transferring a great deal of energy (mostly in the form of heat) to the surroundings. A raised weight has a certain amount of potential energy (dependent on the height the weight is raised) that can be converted to kinetic energy when the weight is released.

1.20 The SI base units include the meter (m) for length, the kilogram (kg) for mass, the second (s) for time, and the Kelvin (K) for temperature.

1.21 The three different temperature scales are Kelvin (K), Celsius (°C), and Fahrenheit (°F). The size of the degree is the same in the Kelvin and the Celsius scales, and they are 1.8 times larger than the degree size for the Fahrenheit scale.

1.22 Prefix multipliers are used with the standard units of measurement to change the value of the unit by powers of 10.

For example, the kilometer has the prefix "kilo," meaning 1000 or 10^3. Therefore:

1 kilometer = 1000 meters = 10^3 meter

Similarly, the millimeter has the prefix "milli," meaning 0.001 or 10^{-3}.

1 millimeter = 0.001 meters = 10^{-3} meters

1.23 A derived unit is a combination of other units. Examples of derived units include: speed in meters per second (m/s), volume in meters cubed (m^3), and density in grams per cubic centimeter (g/cm^3).

1.24 The density (d) of a substance is the ratio of its mass (m) to its volume (V):

$$\text{Density} = \frac{\text{mass}}{\text{Volume}} \text{ or } d = \frac{m}{V}$$

The density of a substance is an example of an intensive property, one that is independent of the amount of the substance. Mass is one of the properties used to calculate the density of a substance. Mass, in contrast, is an extensive property, one that depends on the amount of the substance.

1.25 An intensive property is a property that is independent of the amount of the substance. An extensive property is a property that depends on the amount of the substance.

1.26 Measured quantities are reported so that the number of digits reflects the uncertainty in the measurement. The non-place-holding digits in a reported number are called significant figures.

1.27 In multiplication or division, the result carries the same number of significant figures as the factor with the fewest significant figures.

1.28 In addition or subtraction, the result carries the same number of decimal places as the quantity with the fewest decimal places.

1.29 When rounding to the correct number of significant figures, round down if the last (or left-most) digit dropped is four or less; and round up if the last (or left-most) digit dropped is five or more.

1.30 Accuracy refers to how close the measured value is to the actual value. Precision refers to how close a series of measurements are to one another or how reproducible they are. A series of measurements can be precise (close to one another in value and reproducible) but not accurate (not close to the true value).

1.31 Random error is error that has equal probability of being too high or too low. Almost all measurements have some degree of random error. Random error can, with enough trials, average itself out. Systematic error is error that tends towards being either too high or too low. Systematic error does not average out with repeated trials.

1.32 Using units as a guide to solving problems is often called dimensional analysis. Units should always be included in calculations; they are multiplied, divided, and canceled like any other algebraic quantity.

The Scientific Approach to Knowledge

1.33 (a) This statement is a theory because it attempts to explain why. It is not possible to observe individual atoms.

(b) This statement is an observation.

(c) This statement is a law because it summarizes many observations and can explain future behavior.

(d) This statement is an observation.

1.34 (a) This statement is a law because it summarizes many observations and can explain future behavior.

(b) This statement is a law because it summarizes many observations and can explain future behavior.

(c) This statement is a law because it summarizes many observations and can explain future behavior.

(d) This statement is a theory because it attempts to explain why.

1.35 (a) If we divide the mass of the oxygen by the mass of the carbon the result is always 4/3.

(b) If we divide the mass of the oxygen by the mass of the hydrogen the result is always 16.

(c) These observations suggest that the masses of elements in molecules are ratios of whole numbers (4 and 3; and 16 and 1, respectively).

(d) Atoms combine in small whole number ratios and not as random weight ratios.

1.36 There are many hypotheses that may be developed. One hypothesis is that a large explosion generated galaxies with fragments that are still moving away from each other.

The Classification and Properties of Matter

1.37 (a) Sweat is a homogeneous mixture of water, sodium chloride, and other components.

(b) Carbon dioxide is a pure substance that is a compound (two or more elements bonded together).

(c) Aluminum is a pure substance that is an element (element 13 in the periodic table).

(d) Vegetable soup is a heterogeneous mixture of broth, chunks of vegetables, and extracts from the vegetables.

1.38 (a) Wine is a generally homogeneous mixture of water, ethyl alcohol, and other components from the grapes. In some cases, there may be sediment present and so it would be a heterogeneous mixture.

(b) Beef stew is a heterogeneous mixture of thick broth and chunks of vegetables.

(c) Iron is a pure substance that is an element (element 26 in the periodic table).

(d) Carbon monoxide is a pure substance that is a compound (two or more elements bonded together).

1.39

substance	pure or mixture	Type (element or compound)
aluminum	pure	element
apple juice	mixture	neither – mixture
hydrogen peroxide	pure	compound
chicken soup	mixture	neither – mixture

1.40

substance	pure or mixture	Type (element or compound)
water	pure	compound
coffee	mixture	neither – mixture
ice	pure	compound
carbon	pure	element

1.41 (a) pure substance that is a compound (one type of molecule that contains two different elements)

(b) heterogeneous mixture (two different molecules that are segregated into regions)

(c) homogeneous mixture (two different molecules that are randomly mixed)

(d) pure substance that is an element (individual atoms of one type)

1.42 (a) pure substance that is an element (individual atoms of one type)

(b) homogeneous mixture (two different molecules that are randomly mixed)

(c) pure substance that is a compound (one type of molecule that contains two different elements)

(d) pure substance that is a compound (one type of molecule that contains two different elements)

1.43 (a) physical property (color can be observed without making or breaking chemical bonds)

(b) chemical property (must observe by making or breaking chemical bonds)

(c) physical property (the phase can be observed without making or breaking chemical bonds)

(d) physical property (density can be observed without making or breaking chemical bonds)

(e) physical property (mixing does not involve making or breaking chemical bonds, so this can be observed without making or breaking chemical bonds)

1.44 (a) physical property (color can be observed without making or breaking chemical bonds)

(b) physical property (odor can be observed without making or breaking chemical bonds)

(c) chemical property (must observe by making or breaking chemical bonds)

(d) chemical property (decomposition involves breaking bonds, so bonds must be broken to observe this property)

(e) physical property (the phase of a substance can be observed without making or breaking chemical bonds)

1.45 (a) chemical property (burning involves breaking and making bonds, so bonds must be broken and made to observe this property)

(b) physical property (shininess is a physical property and so can be observed without making or breaking chemical bonds)

(c) physical property (odor can be observed without making or breaking chemical bonds)

(d) chemical property (burning involves breaking and making bonds, so bonds must be broken and made to observe this property)

1.46 (a) physical property (vaporization is a phase change and so can be observed without making or breaking chemical bonds)

(b) physical property (sublimation is a phase change and so can be observed without making or breaking chemical bonds)

(c) chemical property (rusting involves the reaction of iron with oxygen to form iron oxide; observing this process involves making and breaking chemical bonds)

(d) physical property (color can be observed without making or breaking chemical bonds)

1.47 (a) chemical change (new compounds are formed as methane and oxygen react to form carbon dioxide and water)

(b) physical change (vaporization is a phase change and does not involve the making or breaking of chemical bonds)

(c) chemical change (new compounds are formed as propane and oxygen react to form carbon dioxide and water)

(d) chemical change (new compounds are formed as the metal in the frame is converted to oxides)

1.48 (a) chemical change (new compounds are formed as the sugar burns)

(b) physical change (dissolution is a phase change and does not involve the making or breaking of chemical bonds)

(c) physical change (this is simply the rearrangement of the atoms)

(d) chemical change (new compounds are formed as the silver converts to an oxide)

1.49 (a) physical change (vaporization is a phase change and does not involve the making or breaking of chemical bonds)

(b) chemical change (new compounds are formed)

(c) physical change (vaporization is a phase change and does not involve the making or breaking of chemical bonds)

1.50 (a) physical change (vaporization of butane is a phase change and does not involve the making or breaking of chemical bonds)

(b) chemical change (new compounds are formed as the butane combusts)

(c) physical change (vaporization of water is a phase change and does not involve the making or breaking of chemical bonds)

Units in Measurement

1.51 (a) To convert from °F to °C, first find the equation that relates these two quantities. $°C = \frac{°F - 32}{1.8}$ Now substitute °F into the equation and compute the answer. Note: The number of digits reported in this answer follow significant figure conventions, covered in Section 1.6. $°C = \frac{°F - 32}{1.8} = \frac{0.}{1.8} = 0.\ °C$

(b) To convert from K to °F, first find the equations that relate these two quantities.
$K = °C + 273.15$ and $°C = \frac{°F - 32}{1.8}$
Since these equations do not directly express K in terms of °F, you must combine the equations and then solve the equation for °F. Substituting for °C:
$K = \frac{°F - 32}{1.8} + 273.15$ rearrange $K - 273.15 = \frac{°F - 32}{1.8}$
rearrange $1.8\,(K - 273.15) = (°F - 32)$ finally $°F = 1.8\,(K - 273.15) + 32$ Now substitute K into the equation and compute the answer.
$°F = 1.8\,(77 - 273.15) + 32 = 1.8\,(-196) + 32 = -353 + 32 = -321\ °F$

(c) To convert from °F to °C, first find the equation that relates these two quantities. $°C = \frac{°F - 32}{1.8}$ Now substitute °F into the equation and compute the answer.

$$°C = \frac{-109\,°F - 32\,°F}{1.8} = \frac{-141}{1.8} = -78.3\,°C$$

(d) To convert from °F to K, first find the equations that relate these two quantities.

$K = °C + 273.15$ and $°C = \frac{°F - 32}{1.8}$

Since these equations do not directly express K in terms of °F, you must combine the equations and then solve the equation for K. Substituting for °C: $K = \frac{°F - 32}{1.8} + 273.15$

Now substitute °F into the equation and compute the answer.

$$K = \frac{(98.6 - 32)}{1.8} + 273.15 = \frac{66.6}{1.8} + 273.15 = 37.0 + 273.15 = 310.2\,K$$

1.52 (a) To convert from °F to °C, first find the equation that relates these two quantities. $°C = \frac{°F - 32}{1.8}$ Now substitute °F into the equation and compute the answer. Note: The number of digits reported in this answer follow significant figure conventions, covered in Section 1.6.

$$°C = \frac{212\,°F - 32\,°F}{1.8} = \frac{180.}{1.8} = 100.\,°C$$

(b) Begin by finding the equation that relates the quantity that is given (°C) and the quantity you are trying to find (K). $K = °C + 273.15$ Since this equation gives the temperature in K directly, simply substitute in the correct value for the temperature in °C and compute the answer.
$K = 22\,°C + 273.15 = 295\,K$

(c) To convert from K to °F, first find the equations that relate these two quantities: $K = °C + 273.15$ and $°C = \frac{°F - 32}{1.8}$ Since these equations do not directly express K in terms of °F, you must combine the equations and then solve the equation for °F. Substituting for °C: $K = \frac{°F - 32}{1.8} + 273.15$, rearrange $K - 273.15 = \frac{°F - 32}{1.8}$, rearrange $1.8(K - 273.15) = (°F - 32)$, rearrange $°F = 1.8\,(K - 273.15) + 32$. Now substitute K into the equation and compute the answer.
$°F = 1.8(0.00K - 273.15) + 32 = 1.8\,(-273.15\,K) + 32 = -491.67 + 32 = -459.67\,°F$

(d) Begin by finding the equation that relates the quantity that is given (°C) and the quantity you are trying to find (K). $K = °C + 273.15$ Since this equation does not directly express °C in terms of K, you must solve the equation for °C. $°C = K - 273.15$. Now substitute K into the equation and compute the answer. $°C = 2.735 - 273.15 = -270.42\,°C$

1.53 To convert from °F to °C, first find the equation that relates these two quantities. $°C = \frac{°F - 32}{1.8}$ Now substitute °F into the equation and compute the answer. Note: The number of digits reported in this answer follow significant figure conventions, covered in Section 1.6. $°C = \frac{-80.\,°F - 32\,°F}{1.8} = \frac{-112}{1.8} = -62.2\,°C$

Begin by finding the equation that relates the quantity that is given (°C) and the quantity you are trying to find (K). $K = °C + 273.15$. Since this equation gives the temperature in K directly, simply substitute in the correct value for the temperature in °C and compute the answer. $K = -62.2\,°C + 273.15 = 210.9\,K$

1.54 To convert from °F to °C, first find the equation that relates these two quantities. $°C = \frac{°F - 32}{1.8}$ Now substitute °F into the equation and compute the answer. Note: The number of digits reported in this answer follow significant figure conventions, covered in Section 1.6.

$$°C = \frac{134\,°F - 32\,°F}{1.8} = \frac{102}{1.8} = 56.\underline{6}667\,°C = 56.7\,°C$$

Begin by finding the equation that relates the quantity that is given (°C) and the quantity you are trying to find (K). $K = °C + 273.15$ Since this equation gives the temperature in K directly, simply substitute in the correct value for the temperature in °C and compute the answer. $K = 56.\underline{6}667\,°C + 273.15 = 329.8\,K$

1.55 Use Table 1.2 to determine the appropriate prefix multiplier and substitute the meaning into the expressions.

(a) 10^{-9} is equivalent to "nano" so 1.2 $\times 10^{-9}$ m = 1.2 nanometers = 1.2 nm

(b) 10^{-15} is equivalent to "femto" so 22 $\times 10^{-15}$ s = 22 femtoseconds = 22 fs

(c) 10^{9} is equivalent to "giga" so 1.5 $\times 10^{9}$ g = 1.5 gigagrams = 1.5 Gg

(d) 10^{6} is equivalent to "mega" so 3.5 $\times 10^{6}$ L = 3.5 megaliters = 3.5 ML

1.56 Use Table 1.2 to determine the appropriate prefix multiplier and substitute the meaning into the expressions.

(a) 38.8 $\times 10^{5}$ g = 3.88 $\times 10^{6}$ g; 10^{6} is equivalent to "mega" so 3.88 $\times 10^{6}$ g = 3.88 megagrams = 3.88 Mg

(b) 55.2 $\times 10^{-10}$ s = 5.52 $\times 10^{-9}$ s; 10^{-9} is equivalent to "nano" so 5.52 $\times 10^{-9}$ s = 5.52 nanoseconds = 5.52 ns

(c) 23.4 $\times 10^{11}$ m = 2.34 $\times 10^{12}$ m; 10^{12} is equivalent to "tera" so 2.34 $\times 10^{12}$ m = 2.34 terameters = 2.34 Tm

(d) 87.9 $\times 10^{-7}$ L = 8.79 $\times 10^{-6}$ L; 10^{-6} is equivalent to "micro" so 8.79 $\times 10^{-6}$ L = 8.79 microliters = 8.79 μL

1.57 Use Table 1.2 to determine the appropriate prefix multiplier and substitute the meaning into the expressions.

(a) 10^{-9} is equivalent to "nano" so 4.5 ns = 4.5 nanoseconds = 4.5 $\times 10^{-9}$ s

(b) 10^{-15} is equivalent to "femto" so 18 fs = 18 femtoseconds = 18 $\times 10^{-15}$ s = 1.8 $\times 10^{-14}$ s
Remember that in scientific notation the first number should be smaller than 10.

(c) 10^{-12} is equivalent to "pico" so 128 pm = 128 $\times 10^{-12}$ m = 1.28 $\times 10^{-10}$ m
Remember that in scientific notation the first number should be smaller than 10.

(d) 10^{-6} is equivalent to "micro" so 35 μm = 35 micrograms = 35 $\times 10^{-6}$ g = 3.5 $\times 10^{-5}$ m
Remember that in scientific notation the first number should be smaller than 10.

1.58 Use Table 1.2 to determine the appropriate prefix multiplier and substitute the meaning into the expressions.

(a) "μ" is equivalent to "micro" or 10^{-6} so 35 μL = 35 microliters = 35 $\times 10^{-6}$ L = 3.5 $\times 10^{-5}$ L
Remember that in scientific notation the first number should be smaller than 10.

(b) "M" is equivalent to "mega" or 10^{6} so 225 Mm = 225 megameters = 225 $\times 10^{6}$ m = 2.25 $\times 10^{8}$ m
Remember that in scientific notation the first number should be smaller than 10.

(c) "T" is equivalent to "tera" or 10^{12} so 133 Tg = 133 teragrams = 133 $\times 10^{12}$ g = 1.33 $\times 10^{14}$ g
Remember that in scientific notation the first number should be smaller than 10.

(d) "c" is equivalent to "centi" or 10^{-2} so 1.5 cg = 1.5 centigrams = 1.5 $\times 10^{-2}$ g

1.59 (b) **Given:** 515 km **Find:** dm

Conceptual Plan: **km → m → dm**

$$\frac{1000\ \text{m}}{1\text{km}} \qquad \frac{10\ \text{dm}}{1\text{m}}$$

Solution: $515\ \cancel{\text{km}} \times \frac{1000\ \cancel{\text{m}}}{1\cancel{\text{km}}} \times \frac{10\ \text{dm}}{1\cancel{\text{m}}} = 5.15 \times 10^{6}\ \text{dm}$

Check: The units (dm) are correct. The magnitude of the answer (10^6) makes physical sense because a decimeter is a much smaller unit than a kilometer.

Given: 515 km **Find:** cm

Conceptual Plan: **km → m → cm**

$$\frac{1000\ \text{m}}{1\text{km}} \qquad \frac{100\ \text{cm}}{1\text{m}}$$

Solution: $515\ \cancel{\text{km}} \times \frac{1000\ \cancel{\text{m}}}{1\cancel{\text{km}}} \times \frac{100\ \text{cm}}{1\cancel{\text{m}}} = 5.15 \times 10^{7}\ \text{cm}$

Check: The units (cm) are correct. The magnitude of the answer (10^7) makes physical sense because a centimeter is a much smaller unit than either a kilometer or a decimeter.

(c) **Given:** 122.355 s **Find:** ms

Conceptual Plan: **s → ms**

$$\frac{1000\text{ ms}}{1\text{s}}$$

Solution: $122.355\text{ s} \times \frac{1000\text{ ms}}{1\text{ s}} = 1.22355 \times 10^5\text{ ms}$

Check: The units (ms) are correct. The magnitude of the answer (10^5) makes physical sense because a millisecond is a much smaller unit than a second.

Given: 122.355 s **Find:** ks

Conceptual Plan: **s → ks**

$$\frac{1\text{ ks}}{1000\text{ s}}$$

Solution: $122.355\text{ s} \times \frac{1\text{ ks}}{1000\text{ s}} = 1.22355 \times 10^{-1}\text{ ks} = 0.122355\text{ ks}$

Check: The units (ks) are correct. The magnitude of the answer (10^{-1}) makes physical sense because a kilosecond is a much larger unit than a second.

(d) **Given:** 3.345 kJ **Find:** J

Conceptual Plan: **kJ → J**

$$\frac{1000\text{ J}}{1\text{kJ}}$$

Solution: $3.345\text{ kJ} \times \frac{1000\text{ J}}{1\text{kJ}} = 3.345 \times 10^3\text{ J}$

Check: The units (J) are correct. The magnitude of the answer (10^3) makes physical sense because a joule is a much smaller unit than a kilojoule.

Given: 3.345×10^3 J (from above) **Find:** mJ

Conceptual Plan: **J → mJ**

$$\frac{1000\text{ mJ}}{1\text{ J}}$$

Solution: $3.345 \times 10^3\text{ J} \times \frac{1000\text{ mJ}}{1\text{J}} = 3.345 \times 10^6\text{ mJ}$

Check: The units (mJ) are correct. The magnitude of the answer (10^6) makes physical sense because a millijoule is a much smaller unit than a joule.

1.60 (a) **Given:** 355 km/s **Find:** cm/s

Conceptual Plan: **km/s → m/s → cm/s**

$$\frac{1000\text{ m}}{1\text{km}} \qquad \frac{100\text{ cm}}{1\text{m}}$$

Solution: $\frac{355\text{ km}}{1\text{ s}} \times \frac{1000\text{ m}}{1\text{km}} \times \frac{100\text{ cm}}{1\text{m}} = 3.55 \times 10^7\,\frac{\text{cm}}{\text{s}}$

Check: The units (cm/s) are correct. The magnitude of the answer (10^7) makes physical sense because a centimeter is a much smaller unit than a kilometer.

Given: 355 km/s **Find:** m/ms

Conceptual Plan: **km/s → m/s → m/ms**

$$\frac{1000\text{ m}}{1\text{km}} \qquad \frac{1\text{ s}}{1000\text{ ms}}$$

Solution: $\frac{355\text{ km}}{1\text{s}} \times \frac{1000\text{ m}}{1\text{km}} \times \frac{1\text{ s}}{1000\text{ ms}} = 355\,\frac{\text{m}}{\text{ms}}$

Check: The units (m/ms) are correct. The magnitude of the answer (10^2) makes physical sense because the conversion to meters increases the magnitude by a factor of 1000 and the conversion from seconds to milliseconds decreases the magnitude by a factor of 1000.

(b) **Given:** 1228 g/L **Find:** g/mL

Conceptual Plan: **g/L → g/mL**

$$\frac{1\text{ L}}{1000\text{ mL}}$$

Solution: $\frac{1228\text{ g}}{1\text{L}} \times \frac{1\text{ L}}{1000\text{ mL}} = 1.228\,\frac{\text{g}}{\text{mL}}$

Check: The units (g/mL) are correct. The magnitude of the answer (1) makes physical sense because a milliliter is a much smaller unit than a liter.

Given: 1228 g/L **Find:** kg/ML

Conceptual Plan: **g/L → kg/L → kg/ML**

$$\frac{1\text{ kg}}{1000\text{ g}} \qquad \frac{10^6\text{ L}}{1\text{ML}}$$

Solution: $\frac{1228\ \cancel{g}}{1\ \cancel{L}} \times \frac{1\ kg}{1000\ \cancel{g}} \times \frac{10^6\ \cancel{L}}{1\ ML} = 1.228 \times 10^6 \frac{kg}{ML}$

Check: The units (g/ML) are correct. The magnitude of the answer (10^6) makes physical sense because the conversion to kilograms decreases the magnitude by a factor of 1000 and the conversion from liters to megaliters increases the magnitude by a factor of 10^6.

(c) **Given:** 554 mK/s **Find:** K/s

Conceptual Plan: mK/s $\rightarrow$ K/s

$\frac{1\ K}{1000\ mK}$

Solution: $\frac{554\ \cancel{mK}}{1\ s} \times \frac{1\ K}{1000\ \cancel{mK}} = 0.554 \frac{K}{s}$

Check: The units (K/s) are correct. The magnitude of the answer (10^{-1}) makes physical sense because a millikelvin is a much smaller unit than a kelvin.

Given: 554 mK/s **Find:** μK/ms

Conceptual Plan: mK/s $\rightarrow$ K/s $\rightarrow$ μK/s $\rightarrow$ μK/ms

$\frac{1\ K}{1000\ mK}$ $\quad \frac{10^{-6}\ \mu K}{1\ K}$ $\quad \frac{1\ s}{1000\ ms}$

Solution: $\frac{554\ \cancel{mK}}{1\ s} \times \frac{1\ \cancel{K}}{1000\ \cancel{mK}} \times \frac{10^6\ \mu K}{1\ \cancel{K}} \times \frac{1\ \cancel{s}}{1000\ ms} = 554 \frac{\mu K}{ms}$

Check: The units (μK/ms) are correct. The magnitude of the answer (10^2) makes physical sense because the conversion to microkelvins increases the magnitude by a factor of 1000 and the conversion from seconds to milliseconds decreases the magnitude by a factor of 1000.

(d) **Given:** 2.544 mg/mL **Find:** g/L

Conceptual Plan: mg/mL $\rightarrow$ g/mL $\rightarrow$ g/L

$\frac{1\ g}{1000\ mg}$ $\quad \frac{1000\ mL}{1\ L}$

Solution: $\frac{2.554\ \cancel{mg}}{1\ mL} \times \frac{1\ g}{1000\ \cancel{mg}} \times \frac{1000\ \cancel{mL}}{1\ L} = 2.554 \frac{g}{L}$

Check: The units (g/L) are correct. The magnitude of the answer (3) makes physical sense because the conversion to grams decreases the magnitude by a factor of 1000 and the conversion from milliliters to liters increases the magnitude by a factor of 1000.

Given: 2.544 mg/mL **Find:** μg/mL

Conceptual Plan: mg/mL $\rightarrow$ g/mL $\rightarrow$ μg/mL

$\frac{1\ g}{1000\ mg}$ $\quad \frac{10^6\ \mu g}{1\ g}$

Solution: $\frac{2.554\ \cancel{mg}}{1\ mL} \times \frac{1\ \cancel{g}}{1000\ \cancel{mg}} \times \frac{10^6\ \mu g}{1\ \cancel{g}} = 2.554 \times 10^3 \frac{\mu g}{mL}$

Check: The units (μg/mL) are correct. The magnitude of the answer (10^3) makes physical sense because a microgram is a much smaller unit than a milligram.

1.61 (a) **Given:** 254,998 m **Find:** km

Conceptual Plan: m $\rightarrow$ km

$\frac{1\ km}{1000\ m}$

Solution: $254{,}998\ \cancel{m} \times \frac{1\ km}{1000\ \cancel{m}} = 2.54998 \times 10^2\ km = 254.998\ km$

Check: The units (km) are correct. The magnitude of the answer (10^2) makes physical sense because a kilometer is a much larger unit than a meter.

(b) **Given:** 254,998 m **Find:** Mm

Conceptual Plan: m $\rightarrow$ Mm

$\frac{1\ Mm}{10^6\ m}$

Solution: $254{,}998\ \cancel{m} \times \frac{1\ Mm}{10^6\ \cancel{m}} = \ = 2.54998 \times 10^{-1}\ Mm = 0.254998\ Mm$

Check: The units (Mm) are correct. The magnitude of the answer (10^{-1}) makes physical sense because a megameter is a much larger unit than a meter or kilometer.

(c) **Given:** 254,998 m **Find:** mm
Conceptual Plan: m → mm
$$\frac{1000\text{ mm}}{1\text{ m}}$$
Solution: $254{,}998\text{ m} \times \frac{1000\text{ mm}}{1\text{ m}} = 2.54998 \times 10^8\text{ mm}$
Check: The units (mm) are correct. The magnitude of the answer (10^8) makes physical sense because a millimeter is a much smaller unit than a meter.

(d) **Given:** 254,998 m **Find:** cm
Conceptual Plan: m → cm
$$\frac{100\text{ cm}}{1\text{ m}}$$
Solution: $254{,}998\text{ m} \times \frac{100\text{ cm}}{1\text{ m}} = 2.54998 \times 10^7\text{ cm}$
Check: The units (cm) are correct. The magnitude of the answer (10^7) makes physical sense because a centimeter is a much smaller unit than a meter, but larger than a millimeter.

1.62 (a) **Given:** 556.2×10^{-12} s **Find:** ms
Conceptual Plan: s → ms
$$\frac{1000\text{ ms}}{1\text{ s}}$$
Solution: $556.2 \times 10^{-12}\text{ s} \times \frac{1000\text{ ms}}{1\text{ s}} = 5.562 \times 10^{-7}\text{ ms}$
Check: The units (ms) are correct. The magnitude of the answer (10^{-7}) makes physical sense because a millisecond is a much smaller unit than a second.

(b) **Given:** 556.2×10^{-12} s **Find:** ns
Conceptual Plan: s → ns
$$\frac{10^9\text{ ns}}{1\text{ s}}$$
Solution: $556.2 \times 10^{-12}\text{ s} \times \frac{10^9\text{ ns}}{1\text{ s}} = 0.5562\text{ ns}$
Check: The units (ns) are correct. The magnitude of the answer (0.6) makes physical sense because a nanosecond is a much smaller unit than a second.

(c) **Given:** 556.2×10^{-12} s **Find:** ps
Conceptual Plan: s → ps
$$\frac{10^{12}\text{ ns}}{1\text{ s}}$$
Solution: $556.2 \times 10^{-12}\text{ s} \times \frac{10^{12}\text{ ps}}{1\text{ s}} = 556.2\text{ ps}$
Check: The units (ps) are correct. The magnitude of the answer (10^2) makes physical sense because a picosecond is a much smaller unit than a second.

(d) **Given:** 556.2×10^{-12} s **Find:** fs
Conceptual Plan: s → fs
$$\frac{10^{15}\text{ fs}}{1\text{ s}}$$
Solution: $556.2 \times 10^{-12}\text{ s} \times \frac{10^{15}\text{ fs}}{1\text{ s}} = 5.562 \times 10^5\text{ fs}$
Check: The units (fs) are correct. The magnitude of the answer (10^5) makes physical sense because a femtosecond is a much smaller unit than a second.

1.63 **Given:** 1 m square 1 m^2 **Find:** cm^2
Conceptual Plan: 1 m^2 → cm^2
$$\frac{100\text{ cm}}{1\text{ m}}$$
Notice that for squared units, the conversion factors must be squared.
Solution: $1\text{ m}^2 \times \frac{(100\text{ cm})^2}{(1\text{ m})^2} = 1 \times 10^4\text{ cm}^2$
Check: The units of the answer are correct and the magnitude makes sense. The unit centimeter is smaller than a meter, so the value in square centimeters should be larger than in square meters.

1.64 **Given:** 4 cm on each edge cube **Find:** cm^3
Conceptual Plan: Read the information given carefully. The cube is 4 cm on each side.

$$l, w, h \rightarrow V$$
$$V = l\,w\,h \quad \text{in a cube } l = w = h$$

Solution: 4 cm x 4 cm x 4 cm = $(4\text{ cm})^3 = \underline{6}4\text{ cm}^3 = 60\text{ cm}^3$
Check: The units of the answer are correct and the magnitude makes sense. The unit 4 centimeters is larger than 1 centimeter, so the value in cubic centimeters should be larger.

Density

1.65 **Given:** $m = 2.49$ g, $V = 0.349\text{ cm}^3$ **Find:** d in g/cm^3 and compare to pure copper.
Conceptual Plan: $m, V \rightarrow d$ ($d = m/V$)
Compare to the published value. d (pure copper) = 8.96 g/cm^3 (This value is in Table 1.4.)

Solution: $d = \dfrac{2.49\text{ g}}{0.349\text{ cm}^3} = 7.13\dfrac{\text{g}}{\text{cm}^3}$

The density of the penny is much smaller than the density of pure copper (7.13 g/cm^3; 8.96 g/cm^3) so the penny is not pure copper.
Check: The units (g/cm^3) are correct. The magnitude of the answer seems correct. Many coins are layers of metals, so it is not surprising that the penny is not pure copper.

1.66 **Given:** $m = 1.41$ kg, $V = 0.314$ L **Find:** d in g/cm^3 and compare to pure titanium.
Conceptual Plan: $m, V \rightarrow d$ **then kg** $\rightarrow$ **g then L** $\rightarrow$ **cm^3**

$$d = m/V \qquad \frac{1000\text{ g}}{1\text{ kg}} \qquad \frac{1000\text{ cm}^3}{1\text{ L}}$$

Compared to the published value. d (pure titanium) = 4.51 g/cm^3 (This value is in Table 1.4.)

Solution: $d = \dfrac{1.41\text{ kg}}{0.314\text{ L}} \times \dfrac{1000\text{ g}}{1\text{ kg}} \times \dfrac{1\text{ L}}{1000\text{ cm}^3} = 4.49\dfrac{\text{g}}{\text{cm}^3}$

Check: The units (g/cm^3) are correct. The magnitude of the answer seems correct. The density of the frame is almost exactly the density of pure titanium (4.49 g/cm^3 versus 4.51 g/cm^3) so the frame could be titanium.

1.67 **Given:** $m = 4.10 \times 10^3$ g, $V = 3.25$ L **Find:** d in g/cm^3
Conceptual Plan: $m, V \rightarrow d$ **then L** $\rightarrow$ **cm^3**

$$d = m/V \qquad \frac{1000\text{ cm}^3}{1\text{ L}}$$

Solution: $d = \dfrac{4.10 \times 10^3\text{ g}}{3.25\text{ L}} \times \dfrac{1\text{ L}}{1000\text{ cm}^3} = 1.26\dfrac{\text{g}}{\text{cm}^3}$

Check: The units (g/cm^3) are correct. The magnitude of the answer seems correct.

1.68 **Given:** $m = 371$ grams, $V = 19.3$ mL **Find:** d in g/cm^3 and compare to pure gold.
Conceptual Plan: $m, V \rightarrow d$ $\quad d = m/V$
Compare to the published value. d (pure gold) = 19.3 g/mL (This value is in Table 1.4.)

Solution: $d = \dfrac{371\text{ g}}{19.3\text{ mL}} = 19.2\dfrac{\text{g}}{\text{mL}}$

The density of the nugget is essentially the same as the density of pure gold (19.2 g/mL versus 19.3 g/mL) so the nugget could be gold.
Check: The units (g/cm^3) are correct. The magnitude of the answer seems correct and is essentially the same as the density of pure gold.

1.69 (a) **Given:** $d = 1.11$ g/cm^3, $V = 417$ mL **Find:** m
Conceptual Plan: $d, V \rightarrow m$ **then cm^3** $\rightarrow$ **mL**

$$d = m/V \qquad \frac{1\text{ mL}}{1\text{ cm}^3}$$

Solution: $d = m/V$ Rearrange by multiplying both sides of equation by V. $m = d \times V$

$$m = 1.11\frac{\text{g}}{\text{cm}^3} \times \frac{1\text{ cm}^3}{1\text{ mL}} \times 417\text{ mL} = 4.63 \times 10^2\text{ g}$$

Check: The units (g) are correct. The magnitude of the answer seems correct considering the value of the density is about 1 g/cm^3.

(b) **Given:** $d = 1.11\ g/cm^3$, $m = 4.1\ kg$ **Find:** V in L
Conceptual Plan: $d, V \rightarrow m$ **then kg** $\rightarrow$ **g and** $cm^3 \rightarrow$ **L**

$d = m/V$ $\quad \frac{1000\ g}{1\ kg} \quad \frac{1\ L}{1000\ cm^3}$

Solution: $d = m/V$ Rearrange by multiplying both sides of equation by V and dividing both sides of the equation by d.

$$V = \frac{m}{d} = \frac{4.1\ \cancel{kg}}{1.11\ \frac{\cancel{g}}{cm^3}} \times \frac{1000\ \cancel{g}}{1\ \cancel{kg}} = 3.7 \times \cancel{10^3\ cm^3} \times \frac{1\ L}{\cancel{1000\ cm^3}} = 3.7\ L$$

Check: The units (L) are correct. The magnitude of the answer seems correct considering the value of the density is about 1 g/cm^3.

1.70 (a) **Given:** $d = 0.7857\ g/cm^3$, $V = 28.56\ mL$ **Find:** m
Conceptual Plan: $d, V \rightarrow m$

$d = m/V$

Solution: $d = m/V$ Rearrange by multiplying both sides of equation by V. $m = d \times V$

$$m = \left(0.7857\ \frac{g}{\cancel{cm^3}}\right) \times \frac{1\ \cancel{cm^3}}{1\ \cancel{mL}} \times (28.56\ \cancel{mL}) = 22.44\ g$$

Check: The units (g) are correct. The magnitude of the answer seems correct considering the value of the density is less than 1 g/cm^3.

(b) **Given:** $d = 0.7857\ g/cm^3$, $m = 6.54\ g$ **Find:** V
Conceptual Plan: $d, m \rightarrow V$ **then** $cm^3 \rightarrow$ **mL**

$d = m/V$ $\quad \frac{1\ mL}{1\ cm^3}$

Solution: $d = m/V$ Rearrange by multiplying both sides of equation by V and dividing both sides of the equation by d.

$$V = \frac{m}{d} = \frac{6.54\ \cancel{g}}{0.7857\ \frac{\cancel{g}}{cm^3}} = 8.32\ \cancel{cm^3} \times \frac{1\ mL}{1\ \cancel{cm^3}} = 8.32\ mL$$

Check: The units (mL) are correct. The magnitude of the answer seems correct considering the value of the density is less than 1 g/cm^3.

1.71 **Given:** $V = 245\ L$ $d = 0.821\ g/mL$, **Find:** m
Conceptual Plan: **g/mL** $\rightarrow$ **g/L then** $d, V \rightarrow m$

$\frac{1000\ mL}{1\ L}$ $\quad d = m/V$

Solution: $d = m/V$ Rearrange by multiplying both sides of equation by V. $m = d \times V$

$$m = 245\ \cancel{L} \times \frac{1000\ \cancel{mL}}{1\ \cancel{L}} \times \left(0.821\ \frac{g}{\cancel{mL}}\right) = 2.01 \times 10^5\ g$$

Check: The units (g) are correct. The magnitude of the answer seems correct considering the value of the density is less than 1 g/mL and the volume is very large.

1.72 **Given:** $d = 0.918\ g/cm^3$, $m = 10.0\ lbs$ **Find:** V
Conceptual Plan: **lb** $\rightarrow$ **g then** $d, m \rightarrow V$

$\frac{453.59\ g}{1\ lb}$ $\quad d = m/V$

Solution: $10.0\ \cancel{lbs} \times \frac{453.59\ g}{1\ \cancel{lbs}} = 4.5\underline{3}59 \times 10^3\ g$ then $d = m/V$ Rearrange by multiplying both sides of equation by V and dividing both sides of the equation by d.

$$V = \frac{m}{d} = \frac{4.5\underline{3}59 \times 10^3\ \cancel{g}}{0.918\ \frac{\cancel{g}}{cm^3}} = 4.94 \times 10^3\ cm^3$$

Check: The units (mL) are correct. The magnitude of the answer seems correct considering the value of the density is less than 1 g/cm^3.

The Reliability of a Measurement and Significant Figures

1.73 In order to obtain the readings, look to see where the bottom of the meniscus lies. Estimate the distance between two markings on the device.

(a) 73.0 mL – the meniscus appears to be sitting on the 73 mL mark.

(b) 88.2 °C – the mercury is between the 84 °C mark and the 85 °C mark, but it is closer to the lower number.

(c) 645 mL – the meniscus appears to be just above the 640 mL mark.

1.74 In order to obtain the readings, look to see where the bottom of the meniscus lies. Estimate the distance between two markings on the device. Use all digits on a digital device.

(a) 4.50 mL – the meniscus appears to be on the 4.5 mL mark.

(b) 27.43 °C – the mercury is just above the 27.4 °C mark. Note that the 10s digit is only labeled every 10 °C.

(c) 0.873 g – read all the places on the digital display.

1.75 Remember that

1. interior zeroes (zeroes between two numbers) are significant.
2. leading zeroes (zeroes to the left of the first non-zero number) are not significant. They only serve to locate the decimal point.
3. trailing zeroes (zeroes at the end of a number) are categorized as follows:
   - Trailing zeroes after a decimal point are always significant.
   - Trailing zeroes before an implied decimal point are ambiguous and should be avoided by using scientific notation or by inserting a decimal point at the end of the number.

(a) 1,050,501 km

(b) 0.0020 m

(c) 0.0000000000000002 s

(d) 0.001090 cm

1.76 Remember that

1. interior zeroes (zeroes between two numbers) are significant.
2. leading zeroes (zeroes to the left of the first non-zero number) are not significant. They only serve to locate the decimal point.
3. trailing zeroes (zeroes at the end of a number) are categorized as follows:
   - Trailing zeroes after a decimal point are always significant.
   - Trailing zeroes before an implied decimal point are ambiguous and should be avoided by using scientific notation or by inserting a decimal point at the end of the number.

(a) 180,701 mi

(b) 0.001040 m

(c) 0.005710 km

(d) 90,201 m

1.77 Remember all of the rules from Section 1.7.

(a) Three significant figures. The 3, 1, and the 2 are significant (rule 1). The leading zeroes only mark the decimal place and are therefore not significant (rule 3).

(b) Ambiguous. The 3, 1, and the 2 are significant (rule 1). The trailing zeroes occur before an implied decimal point and are therefore ambiguous (rule 4). Without more information, we would assume 3 significant figures. It is better to write this as 3.12×10^5 to indicate three significant figures or as 3.12000×10^5 to indicate six (rule 4).

(c) Three significant figures. The 3, 1, and the 2 are significant (rule 1).

(d) Five significant figures. The 1s, 3, 2, and 7 are significant (rule 1).

(e) Ambiguous. The 2 is significant (rule 1). The trailing zeroes occur before an implied decimal point and are therefore ambiguous (rule 4). Without more information, we would assume one significant figure. It is better to write this as 2×10^3 to indicate one significant figure or as 2.000×10^3 to indicate four (rule 4).

1.78 Remember all of the rules from Section 1.7.

(a) Four significant figures. The 1s are significant (rule 1). The leading zeroes only mark the decimal place and are therefore not significant (rule 3).

(b) One significant figure. The 7 is significant (rule 1). The leading zeroes only mark the decimal place and are therefore not significant (rule 3).

(c) Ambiguous. The 1, 8, and the 7 are significant (rule 1). The first 0 is significant, since it is an interior 0 (rule 2). The trailing zeroes occur before an implied decimal point and are therefore ambiguous (rule 4). Without more information, we would assume 4 significant figures. It is better to write this as 1.087×10^5 to indicate 4 significant figures or as 1.08700×10^5 to indicate six (rule 4).

(d) Seven significant figures. The 1, 5, 6, and 3s are significant (rule 1). The trailing zeros are significant because they are to the right of the decimal point and non-zero numbers (rule 4).

(e) Ambiguous. The 3 and 8 are significant (rule 1). The first 0 is significant because the first one is an interior zero. The trailing zeroes occur before an implied decimal point and are therefore ambiguous (rule 4). Without more information, we would assume three significant figures. It is better to write this as 3.08×10^4 to indicate three significant figures or as 3.0800×10^4 to indicate five (rule 4).

1.79 (a) This is not exact because π is an irrational number. The number 3.14 only shows three of the infinite number of significant figures that π has.

(b) This is an exact conversion because it comes from a definition of the units, and so has an unlimited number of significant figures.

(c) This is a measured number and so it is not an exact number. There are two significant figures.

(d) This is an exact conversion because it comes from a definition of the units, and so has an unlimited number of significant figures.

1.80 (a) This is a measured number and so it is not an exact number. There are nine significant figures.

(b) This is a an exact conversion, so it has an unlimited number of significant figures.

(c) This is a measured number and so it is not an exact number. There are three significant figures.

(d) This is an exact conversion because it comes from a definition of the units and so has an unlimited number of significant figures.

1.81 (a) 156.9 – The 8 is rounded up since the next digit is a 5.

(b) 156.8 – The last two digits are dropped since 4 is less than 5.

(c) 156.8 – The last two digits are dropped since 4 is less than 5.

(d) 156.9 – The 8 is rounded up since the next digit is a 9, which is greater than 5.

1.82 (a) 7.98×10^4 – The last digits are dropped since 4 is less than 5.

(b) 1.55×10^7 – The 8 is rounded up since the next digit is a 9, which is greater than 5.

(c) 2.35 – The 4 is rounded up since the next digit is a 9, which is greater than 5.

(d) 4.54×10^{-5} – The 3 is rounded up since the next digit is an 8, which is greater than 5.

Significant Figures in Calculations

1.83 (a) $9.15 \div 4.970 = 1.84$ – Three significant figures are allowed to reflect the three significant figures in the least precisely known quantity (9.15).

(b) $1.54 \times 0.03060 \times 0.69 = 0.033$ – Two significant figures are allowed to reflect the two significant figures in the least precisely known quantity (0.69). The intermediate answer (0.03251556) is rounded up since the first non-significant digit is a 5.

(c) $27.5 \times 1.82 \div 100.04 = 0.500$ – Three significant figures are allowed to reflect the three significant figures in the least precisely known quantity (27.5 and 1.82). The intermediate answer (0.50029988) is truncated since the first non-significant digit is a 2, which is less than 5.

(d) $(2.290 \times 10^6) \div (6.7 \times 10^4) = 34$ – Two significant figures are allowed to reflect the two significant figures in the least precisely known quantity (6.7×10^4). The intermediate answer (34.17910448) is truncated since the first non-significant digit is a 1, which is less than 5.

1.84 (a) $89.3 \times 77.0 \times 0.08 = 6 \times 10^2$ – One significant figure is allowed to reflect the one significant figure in the least precisely known quantity (0.08). The intermediate answer (5.50088×10^2) is rounded up since the first non-significant digit is a 5.

(b) $(5.01 \times 10^5) \div (7.8 \times 10^2) = 6.4 \times 10^2$ – Two significant figures are allowed to reflect the two significant figures in the least precisely known quantity (7.8×10^2). The intermediate answer (6.423076923×10^2) is truncated since the first non-significant digit is a 2, which is less than 5.

(c) $4.005 \times 74 \times 0.007 = 2$ – One significant figure is allowed to reflect the one significant figure in the least precisely known quantity (0.007). The intermediate answer (2.07459) is truncated since the first non-significant digit is a 0, which is less than 5.

(d) $453 \div 2.031 = 223$ – Three significant figures are allowed to reflect the three significant figures in the least precisely known quantity (453). The intermediate answer (223.042836) is truncated since the first non-significant digit is a 0, which is less than 5.

1.85 (a)

$$\begin{array}{r} 43.7 \\ \underline{-\,2.341} \\ 41.359 = 41.4 \end{array}$$

Round the intermediate answer to one decimal place to reflect the quantity with the fewest decimal places (43.7). Round the last digit up since the first non-significant digit is 5.

(b)

$$\begin{array}{r} 17.6 \\ +\,2.838 \\ +\,2.3 \\ \underline{+\,110.77} \\ 133.508 = 133.5 \end{array}$$

Round the intermediate answer to one decimal place to reflect the quantity with the fewest decimal places (2.3). Truncate non-significant digits since the first non-significant digit is 0.

(c)
$$\begin{array}{r} 19.6 \\ +\ 58.33 \\ \underline{-\ 4.974} \\ 72.956 = 73.0 \end{array}$$

Round the intermediate answer to one decimal place to reflect the quantity with the fewest decimal places (19.6). Round the last digit up since the first non-significant digit is 5.

(d)
$$\begin{array}{r} 5.99 \\ \underline{-\ 5.572} \\ 0.418 = 0.42 \end{array}$$

Round the intermediate answer to two decimal places to reflect the quantity with the fewest decimal places (5.99). Round the last digit up since the first non-significant digit is 8.

1.86 (a)
$$\begin{array}{r} 0.004 \\ \underline{+\ 0.09879} \\ 0.10279 = 0.103 \end{array}$$

Round the intermediate answer to three decimal places to reflect the quantity with the fewest decimal places (0.004). Round the last digit up since the first non-significant digit is 9.

(b)
$$\begin{array}{r} 1239.3 \\ +\ 9.73 \\ \underline{+\ 3.42} \\ 1252.45 = 1252.5 \end{array}$$

Round the intermediate answer to one decimal place to reflect the quantity with the fewest decimal places (1239.3). Round the last digit up since the first non-significant digit is 5.

(c)
$$\begin{array}{r} 2.4 \\ \underline{-\ 1.777} \\ 0.623 = 0.6 \end{array}$$

Round the intermediate answer to one decimal place to reflect the quantity with the fewest decimal places (2.4). Truncate non-significant digits since the first non-significant digit is 2.

(d)
$$\begin{array}{r} 532 \\ +\ 7.3 \\ \underline{-\ 48.523} \\ 490.777 = 491 \end{array}$$

Round the intermediate answer to zero decimal places to reflect the quantity with the fewest decimal places (532). Round the last digit up since the first non-significant digit is 7.

1.87 Perform operations in parentheses first. Keep track of significant figures in each step, by noting which is the last significant digit in an intermediate result.

(a)
$$\begin{array}{rr} (24.6681 \times 2.38) + 332.58 = & 58.\underline{7}10078 \\ & \underline{+\ 332.58\quad\ \ } \\ & 391.290078 = 391.3 \end{array}$$

The first intermediate answer has one significant digit to the right of the decimal, because it is allowed three significant figures (reflecting the quantity with the fewest significant figures (2.38)). Underline the most significant digit in this answer. Round the next intermediate answer to one decimal place to reflect the quantity with the fewest decimal places (58.7). Round the last digit up since the first non-significant digit is 9.

(b) $\dfrac{(85.3 - 21.489)}{0.0059} = \dfrac{63.\underline{8}11}{0.0059} = 1.\underline{0}81542 \times 10^4 = 1.1 \times 10^4$

The first intermediate answer has one significant digit to the right of the decimal, to reflect the quantity with the fewest decimal places (85.3). Underline the most significant digit in this answer. Round the next intermediate answer to two significant figures to reflect the quantity with the fewest significant figures (0.0059). Round the last digit up since the first non-significant digit is 8.

(c) $(512 \div 986.7) + 5.44 = 0.51\underline{8}9014$

$$\begin{array}{r} 0.51\underline{8}9014 \\ \underline{+\ 5.44} \\ 5.9589014 = 5.96 \end{array}$$

The first intermediate answer has three significant figures and three significant digits to the right of the decimal, reflecting the quantity with the fewest significant figures (512). Underline the most significant digit in this answer. Round the next intermediate answer to two decimal places to reflect the quantity with the fewest decimal places (5.44). Round the last digit up since the first non-significant digit is 8.

(d) $[(28.7 \times 10^5) \div 48.533] + 144.99 = 59\underline{1}35.01$

$$\begin{array}{r} 59\underline{1}35.01 \\ \underline{+\ \ 144.99} \\ 59280.01 = 59300 = 5.93 \times 10^4 \end{array}$$

The first intermediate answer has three significant figures, reflecting the quantity with the fewest significant figures (28.7×10^5). Underline the most significant digit in this answer. Since the number is so large this means that when the addition is performed, the most significant digit is the 100's place. Round the next intermediate answer to the 100's places and put in scientific notation to remove any ambiguity. Note that the last digit is rounded up since the first non-significant digit is 8.

1.88 Perform operations in parentheses first. Keep track of significant figures in each step, by noting which is the last significant digit in an intermediate result.

(a) $[(1.7 \times 10^6) \div [(2.63 \times 10^5)] + 7.33 = 6.\underline{4}63878$

$$\begin{array}{r} 6.\underline{4}63878 \\ \underline{+\ 7.33} \\ 13.793878 = 13.8 \end{array}$$

The first intermediate answer has one significant digit to the right of the decimal, because it is allowed two significant figures (reflecting the quantity with the fewest significant figures (1.7×10^6)). Underline the most significant digit in this answer. Round the next intermediate answer to one decimal place to reflect the quantity with the fewest decimal places (6.5). Round the last digit up since the first non-significant digit is 9.

(b) $(568.99 - 232.1) \div 5.3 = 336.\underline{8}9 \div 5.3 = 63.564151 = 64$

The first intermediate answer has one significant digit to the right of the decimal, to reflect the quantity with the fewest decimal places (232.1). Underline the most significant digit in this answer. Round the next intermediate answer to two significant figures to reflect the quantity with the fewest significant figures (5.3). Round the last digit up since the first non-significant digit is 5.

(c) $(9443 + 45 - 9.9) \times 8.1 \times 10^6 = = 947\underline{8}.1 \times 8.1\times 10^6 = 7.67726 \times 10^{10} = 7.7 \times 10^{10}$

The first intermediate answer only has significant digits to the left of the decimal, reflecting the quantity with the fewest significant figures (9443 and 45). Underline the most significant digit in this answer. Round the next intermediate answer to two significant figures to reflect the quantity with the fewest significant figures (8.1×10^6). Round the last digit up since the first non-significant digit is 7.

(d) $(3.14 \times 2.4367) - 2.34 = 7.6\underline{5}1238$

$$\begin{array}{r} 7.6\underline{5}1238 \\ \underline{-\ 2.34} \\ 5.311238 = 5.31 \end{array}$$

The first intermediate answer has three significant figures, reflecting the quantity with the fewest significant figures (3.14). Underline the most significant digit in this answer. This number has two significant digits to the right of the decimal point. Round the next intermediate answer to two significant digits to the right of the decimal point, since both numbers have two significant digits to the right of the decimal point. Note that the last digit is truncated since the first non-significant digit is 1.

Unit Conversions

1.89 (a) **Given:** 154 cm **Find:** in

Conceptual Plan: **cm → in**

$\frac{1 \text{ in}}{2.54 \text{ cm}}$

Solution: $154 \text{ cm} \times \frac{1 \text{ in}}{2.54 \text{ cm}} = 60.62992 \text{ in} = 60.6 \text{ in}$

Check: The units (in) are correct. The magnitude of the answer (60.6) makes physical sense because an inch is a larger unit than a cm. Three significant figures are allowed because 154 cm has three significant figures.

(b) **Given:** 3.14 kg **Find:** g

Conceptual Plan: **kg → g**

$\frac{1000 \text{ g}}{1 \text{ kg}}$

Solution: $3.14 \text{ kg} \times \frac{1000 \text{ g}}{1 \text{ kg}} = 3.14 \times 10^3 \text{ g}$

Check: The units (g) are correct. The magnitude of the answer (10^3) makes physical sense because a kg is a much larger unit than a gram. Three significant figures are allowed because 3.14 kg has three significant figures.

(c) **Given:** 3.5 L **Find:** qt

Conceptual Plan: **L → qt**

$\frac{1.057 \text{ qt}}{1 \text{ L}}$

Solution: $3.5 \text{ L} \times \frac{1.057 \text{ qt}}{1 \text{ L}} = 3.6995 \text{ qt} = 3.7 \text{ qt}$

Check: The units (qt) are correct. The magnitude of the answer (3.7) makes physical sense because a L is a smaller unit than a qt. Two significant figures are allowed because 3.5 L has two significant figures.

Round the last digit up because the first non-significant digit is a 9.

(d) **Given:** 109 mm **Find:** in

Conceptual Plan: **mm → m → in**

$\frac{1 \text{ m}}{1000 \text{ mm}}$ $\frac{39.37 \text{ in}}{1 \text{ m}}$

Solution: $109 \text{ mm} \times \frac{1 \text{ m}}{1000 \text{ mm}} \times \frac{39.37 \text{ in}}{1 \text{ m}} = 4.29133 \text{ in} = 4.29 \text{ in}$

Check: The units (in) are correct. The magnitude of the answer (4) makes physical sense because a mm is a much smaller unit than an inch. Three significant figures are allowed because 109 mm has three significant figures.

1.90 (a) **Given:** 1.4 in **Find:** mm

Conceptual Plan: **in → cm → m → mm**

$\frac{2.54 \text{ cm}}{1 \text{ in}}$ $\frac{1 \text{ m}}{100 \text{ cm}}$ $\frac{1000 \text{ mm}}{1 \text{ m}}$

Solution: $1.4 \text{ in} \times \frac{2.54 \text{ cm}}{1 \text{ in}} \times \frac{1 \text{ m}}{100 \text{ cm}} \times \frac{1000 \text{ mm}}{1 \text{ m}} = 35.56 \text{ mm} = 36 \text{ mm}$

Check: The units (mm) are correct. The magnitude of the answer (36) makes physical sense because a mm is smaller than an inch. Two significant figures are allowed because 1.4 in has two significant figures. Round the last digit up because the first non-significant digit is a 5.

(b) **Given:** 116 ft **Find:** cm

Conceptual Plan: **ft → in → cm**

$\frac{12 \text{ in}}{1 \text{ ft}}$ $\frac{2.54 \text{ cm}}{1 \text{ in}}$

Solution: $116 \text{ ft} \times \frac{12 \text{ in}}{1 \text{ ft}} \times \frac{2.54 \text{ cm}}{1 \text{ in}} = 3.5357 \times 10^3 \text{ cm} = 3.54 \times 10^3 \text{ cm}$

Check: The units (cm) are correct. The magnitude of the answer (10^3) makes physical sense because a ft is a much larger unit than a cm. Three significant figures are allowed because 116 ft has three significant figures. Round the last digit up because the first non-significant digit is a 5.

(c) **Given:** 1845 kg **Find:** lb

Conceptual Plan: kg → g → lb

$$\frac{1000\ g}{1\ kg} \quad \frac{1\ lb}{453.6\ g}$$

$$\textbf{Solution: } 1845\ \cancel{kg} \times \frac{1000\ \cancel{g}}{1\ \cancel{kg}} \times \frac{1\ lb}{453.6\ \cancel{g}} = 4.06\underline{7}5 \times 10^3\ lb = 4.067 \times 10^3\ lb$$

Check: The units (lb) are correct. The magnitude of the answer (10^3) makes physical sense because a lb is a smaller unit than a kg. Four significant figures are allowed because 1845 kg and 453.6 g/lb each have four significant figures. Round the last digit up because the first non-significant digit is a 5.

(d) **Given:** 815 yd **Find:** km

Conceptual Plan: yd → m → km

$$\frac{1\ m}{1.094\ yd} \quad \frac{1\ km}{1000\ m}$$

$$\textbf{Solution: } 815\ \cancel{yd} \times \frac{1\ \cancel{m}}{1.094\ \cancel{yd}} \times \frac{1\ km}{1000\ \cancel{m}} = 0.74\underline{4}9726\ km = 0.745\ km$$

Check: The units (km) are correct. The magnitude of the answer (0.7) makes physical sense because a yd is a much smaller unit than a km. Three significant figures are allowed because 815 yd has three significant figures. Round the last digit up because the first non-significant digit is a 9.

1.91 **Given:** 10.0 km **Find:** minutes **Other:** running pace = 7.5 miles per hour

Conceptual Plan: km → mi → hr → min

$$\frac{0.6214\ mi}{1\ km} \quad \frac{1hr}{7.5\ mi} \quad \frac{60\ min}{1\ hr}$$

$$\textbf{Solution: } 10.0\ \cancel{km} \times \frac{0.6214\ \cancel{mi}}{1\ \cancel{km}} \times \frac{1\cancel{hr}}{7.5\ \cancel{mi}} \times \frac{60\ min}{1\cancel{hr}} = 4\underline{9}.712\ min = 50.\ min = 5.0 \times 10^1\ min$$

Check: The units (min) are correct. The magnitude of the answer (50) makes physical sense because she is running almost 7.5 miles (which would take her 60 min = 1 hr). Two significant figures are allowed because of the limitation of 7.5 mi/hr (two significant figures). Round the last digit up because the first non-significant digit is a 7.

1.92 **Given:** 212 km **Find:** hours **Other:** riding pace = 18 miles per hour

Conceptual Plan: km → mi → hr

$$\frac{0.6214\ mi}{1\ km} \quad \frac{1hr}{18\ mi}$$

$$\textbf{Solution: } 212\ \cancel{km} \times \frac{0.6214\ \cancel{mi}}{1\ \cancel{km}} \times \frac{1hr}{18\ \cancel{mi}} = 7.\underline{3}18711\ hr = 7.3\ hr$$

Check: The units (hr) are correct. The magnitude of the answer (7) makes physical sense because she is riding over 100 miles (which would take her over 4 hr). Two significant figures are allowed because of the limitation of 24 mi/hr (two significant figures). Truncate after the last digit up because the first non-significant digit is a 1.

1.93 **Given:** 17 km/L **Find:** miles per gallon

Conceptual Plan: $\frac{\textbf{km}}{\textbf{L}} \rightarrow \frac{\textbf{mi}}{\textbf{L}} \rightarrow \frac{\textbf{mi}}{\textbf{gal}}$

$$\frac{0.6214\ mi}{1\ km} \quad \frac{3.785\ L}{1\ gallon}$$

$$\textbf{Solution: } \frac{17\ \cancel{km}}{1\ \cancel{L}} \times \frac{0.6214\ mi}{1\ \cancel{km}} \times \frac{3.785\ \cancel{L}}{1\ gallon} = 3\underline{9}.98398\ \frac{miles}{gallon} = 40.\ \frac{miles}{gallon}$$

Check: The units (mi/gal) are correct. The magnitude of the answer (40) makes physical sense because the dominating factor is that a L is much smaller than a gallon, so the answer should go up. Two significant figures are allowed because of the limitation of 17 km/L (two significant figures). Round the last digit up because the first non-significant digit is a 9.

1.94 **Given:** 5.0 gallons **Find:** cm^3

Conceptual Plan: **gal → L → cm³**

$$\frac{3.785\text{ L}}{1\text{ gallon}} \quad \frac{1000\text{ cm}^3}{1\text{ L}}$$

Solution: $5.0\ \cancel{\text{gallons}} \times \frac{3.785\ \cancel{\text{L}}}{1\ \cancel{\text{gallon}}} \times \frac{1000\text{ cm}^3}{1\ \cancel{\text{L}}} = 1.8925 \times 10^4\text{ cm}^3 = 1.9 \times 10^4\text{ cm}^3$

Check: The units (cm^3) are correct. The magnitude of the answer (10^4) makes physical sense because cm^3 is much smaller than a gallon, so the answer should go up several orders of magnitude. Two significant figures are allowed because of the limitation of 15.0 gallons (two significant figures). Round the last digit up because the first non-significant digit is a 9.

1.95 (a) **Given:** 195 m^2 **Find:** km^2

Conceptual Plan: $\mathbf{m^2 \rightarrow km^2}$

$$\frac{(1\text{ km})^2}{(1000\text{ m})^2}$$

Notice that for squared units, the conversion factors must be squared.

Solution: $195\ \cancel{\text{m}^2} \times \frac{(1\text{ km})^2}{(1000\ \cancel{\text{m}})^2} = 1.95 \times 10^{-4}\text{ km}^2$

Check: The units (km^2) are correct. The magnitude of the answer (10^{-4}) makes physical sense because a kilometer is a much larger unit than a meter.

(b) **Given:** 195 m^2 **Find:** dm^2

Conceptual Plan: $\mathbf{m^2 \rightarrow dm^2}$

$$\frac{(10\text{ dm})^2}{(1\text{ m})^2}$$

Notice that for squared units, the conversion factors must be squared.

Solution: $195\ \cancel{\text{m}^2} \times \frac{(10\text{ dm})^2}{(1\ \cancel{\text{m}})^2} = 1.95 \times 10^4\text{ dm}^2$

Check: The units (dm^2) are correct. The magnitude of the answer (10^4) makes physical sense because a decimeter is a much smaller unit than a meter.

(c) **Given:** 195 m^2 **Find:** cm^2

Conceptual Plan: $\mathbf{m^2 \rightarrow cm^2}$

$$\frac{(100\text{ cm})^2}{(1\text{ m})^2}$$

Notice that for squared units, the conversion factors must be squared.

Solution: $195\ \cancel{\text{m}^2} \times \frac{(100\text{ cm})^2}{(1\ \cancel{\text{m}})^2} = \quad = 1.95 \times 10^6\text{ cm}^2$

Check: The units (cm^2) are correct. The magnitude of the answer (10^6) makes physical sense because a centimeter is a much smaller unit than a meter.

1.96 (a) **Given:** 115 m^3 **Find:** km^3

Conceptual Plan: $\mathbf{m^3 \rightarrow km^3}$

$$\frac{(1\text{ km})^3}{(1000\text{ m})^3}$$

Notice that for cubed units, the conversion factors must be cubed.

Solution: $115\ \cancel{\text{m}^3} \times \frac{(1\text{ km})^3}{(1000\ \cancel{\text{m}})^3} = 1.15 \times 10^{-7}\text{ km}^3$

Check: The units (km^3) are correct. The magnitude of the answer (10^{-7}) makes physical sense because a kilometer is a much larger unit than a meter.

(b) **Given:** 115 m^3 **Find:** dm^3

Conceptual Plan: $\mathbf{m^3 \rightarrow mm^3}$

$$\frac{(10\text{ dm})^3}{(1\text{ m})^3}$$

Notice that for cubed units, the conversion factors must be cubed.

Solution: $115\ \cancel{\text{m}^3} \times \frac{(10\text{ dm})^3}{(1\ \cancel{\text{m}})^3} = 1.15 \times 10^5\text{ dm}^3$

Check: The units (dm^3) are correct. The magnitude of the answer (10^5) makes physical sense because a decimeter is a much smaller unit than a meter.

(c) **Given:** 115 m^3 **Find:** cm^3
Conceptual Plan: $m^3 \rightarrow cm^3$

$$\frac{(100\ cm)^3}{(1\ m)^3}$$

Notice that for cubed units, the conversion factors must be cubed.

Solution: $115\ m^3 \times \frac{(100\ cm)^3}{(1\ m)^3} = 1.15 \times 10^8\ cm^3$

Check: The units (cm^3) are correct. The magnitude of the answer (10^8) makes physical sense because a centimeter is a much smaller unit than a meter.

1.97 **Given:** 435 acres **Find:** square miles **Other:** 1 acre = 43,560 ft^2, 1 mile = 5280 ft
Conceptual Plan: acres $\rightarrow ft^2 \rightarrow mi^2$

$$\frac{43560\ ft^2}{1\ acre} \quad \frac{(1\ mi)^2}{(5280\ ft)^2}$$

Notice that for squared units, the conversion factors must be squared.

Solution: $435\ acres \times \frac{43560\ ft^2}{1\ acre} \times \frac{(1\ mi)^2}{(5280\ ft)^2} = 0.6796875\ mi^2 = 0.680\ mi^2$

Check: The units (mi^2) are correct. The magnitude of the answer (0.7) makes physical sense because an acre is much smaller than a mi^2, so the answer should go down several orders of magnitude. Three significant figures are allowed because of the limitation of 435 acres (three significant figures). Round the last digit up because the first non-significant digit is a 7.

1.98 (a) **Given:** 954 million acres **Find:** square miles **Other:** 1 acre = 43,560 ft^2, 1 mile = 5280 ft
Conceptual Plan: Substitute 10^6 for million then acres $\rightarrow ft^2 \rightarrow mi^2$

$$\frac{43560\ ft^2}{1\ acre} \quad \frac{(1\ mi)^2}{(5280\ ft)^2}$$

Notice that for squared units, the conversion must be squared.
Solution: 954 million acres = 954 x 10^6 acres

$954 \times 10^6\ acres \times \frac{43560\ ft^2}{1\ acre} \times \frac{(1\ mi)^2}{(5280\ ft)^2} = 1.490625 \times 10^6\ mi^2 = 1.49 \times 10^6\ mi^2$

Check: The units (mi^2) are correct. The magnitude of the answer (10^6) makes physical sense because an acre is much smaller than a mi^2, so the answer should go down several orders of magnitude. Three significant figures are allowed because of the limitation of 435 acres (three significant figures). Truncate the last digit up because the first non-significant digit is a 0.

(b) **Given:** 3.537 million square miles **Find:** percentage of U.S. land is farmland
Conceptual Plan: Substitute 10^6 for million then % farm = $\frac{\textbf{farmland}}{\textbf{total land}}$ x 100%

Note - units of farmland and total land must be the same.

Solution: 3.537 million mi^2 = 3.537 x 10^6 mi^2

$\%\ farmland = \frac{1.49 \times 10^6\ mi^2}{3.537 \times 10^6\ mi^2} \times 100\ \% = 42.1437659\ \%\ farmland = 42.1\ \%\ farmland$

Check: The units (%) are correct. The magnitude of the answer (4%) makes physical sense because less and less of our land is devoted to farmland. Three significant figures are allowed because of the limitation of 435 acres (three significant figures). Truncate the last digit up because the first non-significant digit is a 4.

1.99 **Given:** 14 lbs **Find:** mL **Other:** 80 mg/0.80 mL and 15 mg/kg body
Conceptual Plan: lb $\rightarrow$ kg body $\rightarrow$ mg $\rightarrow$ mL

$$\frac{1\ kg\ body}{2.205\ lb} \quad \frac{15\ mg}{1\ kg\ body} \quad \frac{0.80\ mL}{80\ mg}$$

Solution: $14\ lb \times \frac{1\ kg\ body}{2.205\ lb} \times \frac{15\ mg}{1\ kg\ body} \times \frac{0.80\ mL}{80\ mg} = 0.9523809524\ mL = 0.95\ mL$

Check: The units (cm^3) are correct. The magnitude of the answer (1 mL) makes physical sense because it is reasonable amount of liquid to give to a baby. Two significant figures are allowed because of the statement in the problem. Truncate the last digit because the first non-significant digit is a 2.

1.100 **Given:** 18 lbs **Find:** mL **Other:** 100 mg/5.0 mL and 10 mg/kg body
Conceptual Plan: **lb** $\rightarrow$ **kg body** $\rightarrow$ **mg** $\rightarrow$ **mL**

$$\frac{1\text{ kg body}}{2.205\text{ lb}} \qquad \frac{10\text{ mg}}{1\text{ kg body}} \quad \frac{5.0\text{ mL}}{100\text{ mg}}$$

Solution: $18\ \cancel{\text{lb}} \times \frac{1\ \cancel{\text{kg body}}}{2.205\ \cancel{\text{lb}}} \times \frac{10\ \cancel{\text{mg}}}{1\ \cancel{\text{kg body}}} \times \frac{5.0\text{ mL}}{100\ \cancel{\text{mg}}} = 4.\underline{0}81632653\text{ mL} = 4.1\text{ mL}$

Check: The units (cm^3) are correct. The magnitude of the answer (4 mL) makes physical sense because it is reasonable amount of liquid to give to a baby.

Two significant figures are allowed because of the statement in the problem. Round up the last digit because the first non-significant digit is an 8.

Cumulative Problems

1.101 **Given:** solar year **Find:** seconds
Other: 60 seconds/minute; 60 minutes/ hour; 24 hours/solar day; and 365.24 solar days/solar year
Conceptual Plan: **yr** $\rightarrow$ **day** $\rightarrow$ **hr** $\rightarrow$ **min** $\rightarrow$ **sec**

$$\frac{365.24\text{ day}}{1\text{ solar yr}} \quad \frac{24\text{ hr}}{1\text{ day}} \quad \frac{60\text{ min}}{1\text{ hr}} \quad \frac{60\text{ sec}}{1\text{ min}}$$

Solution: $1\cancel{\text{solar yr}} \times \frac{365.24\ \cancel{\text{day}}}{1\ \cancel{\text{solar yr}}} \times \frac{24\ \cancel{\text{hr}}}{1\cancel{\text{day}}} \times \frac{60\ \cancel{\text{min}}}{1\ \cancel{\text{hr}}} \times \frac{60\text{ sec}}{1\ \cancel{\text{min}}} = 3.155\underline{6}736 \times 10^7\text{ sec} = 3.1557 \times 10^7\text{ sec}$

Check: The units (seconds) are correct. The magnitude of the answer (10^7) makes physical sense because each conversion factor increases the value of the answer—a second is many orders of magnitude smaller than a year. Five significant figures are allowed because all conversion factors are assumed to be exact, except for the 365.24 days/ solar year (five significant figures). Round up the last digit because the first non-significant digit is a 7.

1.102 (a) "Million" translates to 10^6 in Table 1.2. Substitute this quantity into the expression and move the decimal point to be in proper scientific notation. Fifty million Frenchmen = 50×10^6 Frenchmen = 5×10^7 Frenchmen (assuming one significant figure in fifty.)

(b) This can be expressed as two different ratios: 10 jokes / 100 enemies $= 1.0 \times 10^{-1}$ jokes per enemy or 100 enemies / 10 jokes = 1×10^1 enemies per joke.

(c) "Hundred" translates as 10^{-2} (since this modifies millionth, something less than 1) and "millionth" translates to 10^{-6} in Table 1.2. Substitute this quantity into the expression and move the decimal point to be in proper scientific notation. $1.8 \times 10^{-2} \times 10^{-6}$ cm = 1.8×10^{-8} cm

(d) "Thousand" translates to 10^3 in Table 1.2. Substitute this quantity into the expression and move the decimal point to be in proper scientific notation. Sixty thousand dollars = 60×10^3 dollars = 6×10^4 dollars (assuming one significant figure in sixty).

(e) The density of platinum (Table 1.4) = 21.4 g/mL = 2.14×10^1 g/mL moving the decimal point to be in proper scientific notation.

1.103 (a) Extensive – The volume of a material depends on how much there is present.

(b) Intensive – The boiling point of a material is independent of how much material you have, so these values can be published in reference tables.

(c) Intensive – The temperature of a material depends on how much there is present.

(d) Intensive – The electrical conductivity of a material is independent of how much material you have, so these values can be published in reference tables.

(e) Extensive – The energy contained in material depends on how much there is present. Many times energy is expressed in terms of Joules/mole, which then turns this quantity into an intensive property.

1.104 **Given:** $°C = \frac{°F - 32}{1.8}$ **Find:** temperature where °F = °C

Conceptual Plan: $°C = \frac{°F - 32}{1.8}$ **set °C = °F = x and solve for x**

Solution: $x = \frac{x - 32°F}{1.8} \rightarrow 1.8\ x = x - 32 \rightarrow 1.8\ x - x = -32 \rightarrow 0.8\ x = -32 \rightarrow x = -32/0.8 = -40. \rightarrow$ $-40.\ °F = -40.\ °C$

Check: The units (°F and °C) are correct. Plugging the result back into the equation confirms that the calculations were done correctly. The magnitude of the answer seems correct, since it is known that the result is not between 0°C and 100 °C. The numbers are getting closer together as the temperature is dropped.

1.105 **Given:** 130 °X = 212 °F and 10 °X = 32 °F **Find:** temperature where °X = °F.

Conceptual Plan: Use data to derive an equation relating °X and °F. Then set °F = °X = z and solve for z.

Solution: Assume a linear relationship between the two temperatures (y = mx + b).

Let y = °F and let x = °X.

The slope of the line (m) is the relative change in the two temperature scales:

$$m = \frac{\Delta\ °F}{\Delta\ °X} = \frac{212\ °F - 32\ °F}{130\ °X - 10\ °X} = \frac{180\ °F}{120\ °X} = 1.5$$

Solve for intercept (b) by plugging one set of temperatures into the equation:

$y = 1.5\ x + b \rightarrow 32 = (1.5)(10) + b \rightarrow 32 = 15 + b \rightarrow b = 17 \rightarrow °F = (1.5)\ °X + 17$

Set °F = °X = z and solve for z.

$z = 1.5\ z + 17 \rightarrow -17 = 1.5\ z - z \rightarrow -17 = 0.5\ z \rightarrow z = -34 \rightarrow -34°F = -34\ °X$

Check: The units (°F and °X) are correct. Plugging the result back into the equation confirms that the calculations were done correctly. The magnitude of the answer seems correct, since it is known that the result is not between 32°F and 212 °F. The numbers are getting closer together as the temperature is dropped.

1.106 **Given:** 17 °J = 0 °H and 97 °J = 120 °H **Find:** temperature where methyl alcohol boils in °J

Other: methyl alcohol boils at 84° H

Conceptual Plan: Use data to derive an equation relating °J and °H. Then set °H = 84 °H and solve for °J.

Solution: Assume a linear relationship between the two temperatures (y = mx + b).

Let y = °J and let x = °H.

The slope of the line (m) is the relative change in the two temperature scales.

$$m = \frac{\Delta\ °J}{\Delta\ °H} = \frac{97\ °J - 17\ °J}{120\ °H - 0\ °H} = \frac{80\ °J}{120\ °H} = 0.667$$

Solve for intercept (b) by plugging one set of temperatures into the equation:

$y = 0.6\underline{6}7\ x + b \rightarrow 17 = (0.6\underline{6}7)(0) + b \rightarrow b = 17 \rightarrow °J = (0.6\underline{6}7)\ °H + 17$

Set °H = 84 °H and solve for °J.

$°J = (0.6\underline{6}7)(84) + 17 \rightarrow °J = 56 + 17 = 73\ °J$

Check: The units (°J) are correct. Plugging the original data points back into the equation confirms that the calculations were done correctly. The magnitude of the answer seems correct, since the result should be between 17°J and 97 °J, and closer to 97°J than 17°J.

1.107 1G. F = ma = kg(m/s^2). Let's call it N for Newton. Ten tons = 20,000 lb = (1 kg/2.2 lb) x 20,000 lb = 4.4 x 10 x 10^4 kg, deceleration = 55 mi x .6 km/mi x 10^3 m/km x 1/3.6 x 10^3 s^2. Exponents = 10^4 x10^3 x 10^{-3} = 10^4. So the kN is convenient.

For one molecule, the mass is 10^{-20} kg and deceleration is 3 x 10^8 m/s^2. So Exponents = 10^{-20} x 10^8 = 10^{-12}. So the pN is convenient.

1.108 **Given:** 25 °C and –196 °C **Find:** Why significant figures are 3 and 2, respectively.
Conceptual plan: The problem is stated in units of °C, so it must be converted to another temperature unit to see if the significant figures can change. Try K. Begin by finding the equation that relates the quantity that is given (°C) and the quantity you are trying to find (K). $K = °C + 273.15$

K = 25 °C + 273.15 = 298 K → K = –196 °C + 273.15 = 77 K

A small positive temperature in °C gains significant figures because of the rules of addition for significant figures—going from 2 to 3. A very negative temperature in °C loses significant figures because of the rules of addition for significant figures—going from 3 to 2.

1.109 (a) 1.76 x 10–3/8.0 x 102 = 2.2×10^{-6} Two significant figures are allowed to reflect the quantity with the fewest significant figures (8.0×10^2).

(b) Write all figures so that the decimal points can be aligned:

0.0187
+ 0.0002 All quantities are known to four places to the right of the decimal place,
– 0.0030 so the answer should be reported to four places to the right of the
0.0159 decimal place or three significant figures.

(c) [(136000)(0.000322)/0.082)](129.2) = $6.899910244 \times 10^4 = 6.9 \times 10^4$ Round the intermediate answer to two significant figures to reflect the quantity with the fewest significant figures (0.082). Round up the last digit since the first non-significant digit is 9.

1.110 **Given:** one gallon of gasoline **Find:** US dollars **Other:** 1 Euro = $1.35 US and 1 liter of gasoline in France = 0.97 Euro

Conceptual Plan: gal → L → Euro → $ US

$$\frac{3.785\ \text{L}}{1\ \text{gallon}} \quad \frac{0.97\ \text{Euro}}{1\ \text{L}} \quad \frac{\$1.35\ \text{US}}{1\ \text{Euro}}$$

Solution: $$1\ \text{gallon} \times \frac{3.785\ \text{L}}{1\ \text{gallon}} \times \frac{0.97\ \text{Euro}}{1\ \text{L}} \times \frac{\$1.35\ \text{US}}{1\ \text{Euro}} = \$4.956458\ \text{US} = \$5.0\ \text{US}$$

Check: The units ($ US) are correct. The magnitude of the answer ($5 US) makes physical sense because the dominating conversion factor is ~4. Two significant figures are allowed because of the limitation of 0.97 Euro/L. Round up the last significant digit because the first non-significant digit is a 5.

1.111 (a) **Given:** cylinder dimensions: length = 22 cm, radius = 3.8 cm, d(gold) = 19.3 g/cm^3 and d(sand) = 3.00 g/cm^3 **Find:** m(gold) and m(sand)
Conceptual Plan: $l, r \rightarrow V$ **then** $d, V \rightarrow m$

$$V = l\pi r^2 \qquad d = m/V$$

Solution: $V(\text{gold}) = V(\text{sand}) = (22\ \text{cm})(\pi)(3.8\ \text{cm})^2 = 998.0212\ \text{cm}^3$ $d = m/V$
Rearrange by multiplying both sides of equation by V. → $m = d \times V$

$$m(\text{gold}) = \left(19.3\frac{\text{g}}{\text{cm}^3}\right) \times (998.0212\ \text{cm}^3) = 1.926181 \times 10^4\ \text{g} = 1.9 \times 10^4\ \text{g}$$

Check: The units (g) are correct. The magnitude of the answer seems correct considering the value of the density is ~20 g/cm^3. Two significant figures are allowed to reflect the significant figures in 22 cm and 3.8 cm. Truncate the non-significant digits because the first non-significant digit is a 2.

$$m(\text{sand}) = \left(3.00\frac{\text{g}}{\text{cm}^3}\right) \times (998.0212\ \text{cm}^3) = 2.99206 \times 10^3\ \text{g} = 3.0 \times 10^3\ \text{g}$$

Check: The units (g) are correct. The magnitude of the answer seems correct considering the value of the density is 3 g/cm^3. This number is much lower than the gold mass. Two significant figures are allowed to reflect the significant figures in 22 cm and 3.8 cm. Round the last digit up because the first non-significant digit is a 9.

(b) Comparing the two values 1.9×10^4 g versus 3.0×10^3 g shows a difference in weight of almost a factor of 10. This difference should be enough to trip the alarm and alert the authorities to the presence of the thief.

1.112 **Given:** $r = 1.0 \times 10^{-13}$ cm, $m = 1.7 \times 10^{-24}$ g **Find:** density **Other:** $V = (4/3)\,\pi\, r^3$

Conceptual Plan: $r \rightarrow V$ **then** $m, V \rightarrow d$

$$r \xrightarrow{V = (4/3)\pi r^3} V \qquad m, V \xrightarrow{d = m/V} d$$

Solution: $V = (4/3)\,\pi\, r^3 = (4/3)(\pi)(1.0 \times 10^{-13}\ \text{cm})^3 = 4.\underline{1}88790205 \times 10^{-39}\ \text{cm}^3$

$$d = \frac{m}{V} = \frac{1.7 \times 10^{-24}\ \text{g}}{4.\underline{1}88790205 \times 10^{-39}\ \text{cm}^3} = 4.\underline{0}58451049 \times 10^{14}\ \frac{\text{g}}{\text{cm}^3} = 4.1 \times 10^{14}\ \frac{\text{g}}{\text{cm}^3}$$

Check: The units (g/cm^3) are correct. The magnitude of the answer seems correct considering how small a nucleus is compared to an atom. Two significant figures are allowed to reflect the significant figures in 1.0×10^{-13} cm. Round the last digit up because the first non-significant digit is a 5.

1.113 **Given:** 3.5 lb of titanium **Find:** volume in in^3 **Other:** density of titanium is 4.51 g/cm^3

Conceptual Plan: **lb** $\rightarrow$ **g then** $m, d \rightarrow V$ **then** $\text{cm}^3 \rightarrow \text{in}^3$

$$\text{lb} \xrightarrow{\frac{453.6\ \text{g}}{1\ \text{lb}}} \text{g} \qquad m, d \xrightarrow{d = m/V} V \qquad \text{cm}^3 \xrightarrow{\frac{(1\ \text{in})^3}{(2.54\ \text{cm})^3}} \text{in}^3$$

Solution: $3.5\ \text{lb} \times \dfrac{453.6\ \text{g}}{1\ \text{lb}} = 1.\underline{5}876 \times 10^3\ \text{g}$

$d = m/V$ Rearrange by multiplying both sides of the equation by V and dividing both sides of the equation by d.

$$V = \frac{m}{d} = \frac{1.\underline{5}876 \times 10^3\ \text{g}}{4.51\ \frac{\text{g}}{\text{cm}^3}} = 3.\underline{5}20 \times 10^2\ \text{cm}^3 = 3.5 \times 10^2\ \text{cm}^3 \times \frac{(1\ \text{in})^3}{(2.54\ \text{cm})^3} = 21\ \text{in}^3$$

Check: The units (in^3) are correct. The magnitude of the answer seems correct considering many grams we have. Two significant figures are allowed to reflect the significant figures in 3.5 lb. Truncate the non-significant digits because the first non-significant digit is a 2.

1.114 **Given:** density (g/cm^3) **Find:** density (lb/in^3) **Other:** density of iron is 7.86 g/cm^3

Conceptual Plan:

$$\frac{\text{g}}{\text{cm}^3} \xrightarrow{\frac{1\ \text{lb}}{453.6\ \text{g}}} \frac{\text{lb}}{\text{cm}^3} \xrightarrow{\frac{(2.54\ \text{cm})^3}{(1\ \text{in})^3}} \frac{\text{lb}}{\text{in}^3}$$

Solution:

$$\frac{7.86\ \text{g}}{\text{cm}^3} \times \frac{1\ \text{lb}}{453.6\ \text{g}} \times \frac{(2.54\ \text{cm})^3}{(1\ \text{in})^3} = 0.28\underline{3}9557386\ \frac{\text{lb}}{\text{in}^3} = 0.284\ \frac{\text{lb}}{\text{in}^3}$$

Check: The units (lb/in^3) are correct. The magnitude of the answer seems correct considering that the dominating factor is that a gram is smaller than a pound, so the answer should go down. Three significant figures are allowed to reflect the significant figures in 7.86 lb. Round the last digit up because the first non-significant digit is a 9.

1.115 **Given:** cylinder dimensions: length = 2.16 in, radius = 0.22 in, m= 41 g **Find:** density (g /cm^3)

Conceptual Plan: **in** $\rightarrow$ **cm then** $l, r \rightarrow V$ **then** $m, V \rightarrow d$

$$\text{in} \xrightarrow{\frac{2.54\ \text{cm}}{1\ \text{in}}} \text{cm} \qquad l, r \xrightarrow{V = l\pi r^2} V \qquad m, V \xrightarrow{d = m/V} d$$

Solution: $2.16\ \text{in} \times \dfrac{2.54\ \text{cm}}{1\ \text{in}} = 5.\underline{4}864\ \text{cm} = l$ $\qquad 0.22\ \text{in} \times \dfrac{2.54\ \text{cm}}{1\ \text{in}} = 0.5\underline{5}88\ \text{cm} = r$

$V = l\,\pi\, r^2 = (5.4\underline{8}64\ \text{cm})(\pi)(0.5\underline{5}88\ \text{cm})^2 = 5.\underline{3}820798\ \text{cm}^3$

$$d = \frac{m}{V} = \frac{41\ \text{g}}{5.\underline{3}820798\ \text{cm}^3} = 7.\underline{6}178729\ \frac{\text{g}}{\text{cm}^3} = 7.6\ \frac{\text{g}}{\text{cm}^3}$$

Check: The units (g/cm^3) are correct. The magnitude of the answer seems correct considering the value of the density of iron (a major component in steel) is 7.86 g/cm^3. Two significant figures are allowed to reflect the significant figures in 0.22 in and 41 g. Truncate the non-significant digits because the first non-significant digit is a 2.

1.116 **Given:** $m = 85$ g **Find:** radius of the sphere (inches)

Other: density (aluminum) = 2.7 g /cm^3

Conceptual Plan: $m, d \rightarrow V$ **then** $V \rightarrow r$ **then cm** $\rightarrow$ **in**

$$m, d \xrightarrow{d = m/V} V \qquad V \xrightarrow{V = (4/3)\pi r^3} r \qquad \text{cm} \xrightarrow{\frac{1\ \text{in}}{2.54\ \text{cm}}} \text{in}$$

Solution: $d = m/V$ Rearrange by multiplying both sides of the equation by V and dividing both sides of the equation by d.

$$V = \frac{m}{d} = \frac{85\ \cancel{g}}{2.7\ \frac{\cancel{g}}{cm^3}} = 31.48148148\ cm^3$$

$V = (4/3)\pi r^3$ Rearrange by dividing both sides of the equation by $(4/3)\ \pi$. $r^3 = \frac{3V}{4\pi}$
Take the cube root of both sides of the equation.

$$r = \left(\frac{3V}{4\pi}\right)^{1/3} = \left(\frac{(3)\ (31.48148148\ cm^3)}{4\pi}\right)^{1/3} = (7.51565009\ cm^3)^{1/3} = 1.958794386\ cm$$

$$1.958794386\ \cancel{cm} \times \frac{1\ in}{2.54\ \cancel{cm}} = 0.7711788923\ in = 0.77\ in$$

Check: The units (in) are correct. The magnitude of the answer seems correct. The magnitude of the volume is about a third of the mass (density is about 3 g/cm^3). The radius in cm seems right considering the geometry involved. The magnitude goes down when we convert from cm to inches because an inch is bigger than a cm. Two significant figures are allowed to reflect the significant figures in 2.7 g/cm^3 and 85 g. Truncate the non-significant digits because the first non-significant digit is a 1.

1.117 **Given:** 185 cubic yards (yd^3) of H_2O **Find:** mass of the H_2O (pounds)
Other: d(H_2O) = 1.00 g/cm^3 at 0°C
Conceptual Plan: $yd^3 \rightarrow m^3 \rightarrow cm^3 \rightarrow g \rightarrow lb$

$$\frac{(1\ m)^3}{(1.094\ yd)^3} \quad \frac{(100\ cm)^3}{(1m)^3} \quad \frac{1.00\ g}{1.00\ cm^3} \quad \frac{1\ lb}{453.59\ g}$$

Solution: $185\ \cancel{yd^3} \times \frac{(1\cancel{m})^3}{(1.094\ \cancel{yd})^3} \times \frac{(100\ \cancel{cm})^3}{(1\cancel{m})^3} \times \frac{1.00\ \cancel{g}}{1.00\ \cancel{cm^3}} \times \frac{1\ lb}{453.59\ \cancel{g}} = 3.114987377 \times 10^5\ lbs = 3.11 \times 10^5\ lbs$

Check: The units (lb) are correct. The magnitude of the answer (10^5) makes physical sense because a pool is not a small object. Three significant figures are allowed because the conversion factor with the least precision is the density (1.00 g/cm^3 – 3 significant figures) and the initial size has three significant figures. Truncate after the last digit because the first non-significant digit is a 4.

1.118 **Given:** 7655 cubic feet (ft^3) of ice **Find:** mass of the ice (kg) **Other:** 1.00 cm^3 ice = 0.917 g ice
Conceptual Plan: $ft^3 \rightarrow cm^3 \rightarrow g \rightarrow kg$

$$\frac{(30.48\ cm)^3}{(1\ ft)^3} \quad \frac{0.917\ g}{1.00\ cm^3} \quad \frac{1\ kg}{1000\ g}$$

Solution: $7655\ \cancel{ft^3} \times \frac{(30.48\ \cancel{cm})^3}{(1\ \cancel{ft})^3} \times \frac{0.917\ \cancel{g}}{1.00\ \cancel{cm^3}} \times \frac{1\ kg}{1000\ \cancel{g}} = 1.987739274 \times 10^5\ kg = 1.99 \times 10^5\ kg$

Check: The units (kg) are correct. The magnitude of the answer (10^5) makes physical sense because an iceberg is a large object. Three significant figures are allowed because the conversion factor with the least precision is the density (0.917 g/cm^3 – 3 significant figures). Round up the last digit because the first non-significant digit is a 7.

1.119 **Given:** 15 liters of gasoline **Find:** kilometers **Other:** 52 mi/gal in the city
Conceptual Plan: $L \rightarrow gal \rightarrow mi \rightarrow km$

$$\frac{1\ gallon}{3.785\ L} \quad \frac{52\ mi}{1.0\ gallon} \quad \frac{1\ km}{0.6214\ mi}$$

Solution: $15\ \cancel{L} \times \frac{1\ \cancel{gallon}}{3.785\ \cancel{L}} \times \frac{52\ \cancel{mi}}{1.0\ \cancel{gallon}} \times \frac{1\ km}{0.6214\ \cancel{mi}} = 3.316327941 \times 10^2\ km = 3.3 \times 10^2\ km$

Check: The units (km) are correct. The magnitude of the answer (10^2) makes physical sense because the dominating conversion factor is the mileage, which increases the answer. Two significant figures are allowed because the conversion factor with the least precision is 52 mi/gallon (2 significant figures) and the initial volume (15 L) has 2 significant figures. Truncate the last digit because the first non-significant digit is a 1. It is best to put the answer in scientific notation so that it is unambiguous how many significant figures are expressed.

1.120 **Given:** 355 mL of gasoline **Find:** kilometers **Other:** 57 mi/gal in the city
Conceptual Plan: $mL \rightarrow L \rightarrow gal \rightarrow mi \rightarrow km$

$$\frac{1\ L}{1000\ mL} \quad \frac{1\ gallon}{3.785\ L} \quad \frac{57\ mi}{1.0\ gallon} \quad \frac{1\ km}{0.6214\ mi}$$

Solution: $355\ \text{mL} \times \frac{1\ \text{L}}{1000\ \text{mL}} \times \frac{1\ \text{gallon}}{3.785\ \text{L}} \times \frac{57\ \text{mi}}{1.0\ \text{gallon}} \times \frac{1\ \text{km}}{0.6214\ \text{mi}} = 8.603319984\ \text{km} = 8.6\ \text{km}$

Check: The units (km) are correct. The magnitude of the answer (8.6) makes physical sense because the dominating conversion factor is the conversion from mL to L, which decreases the answer. Two significant figures are allowed because the conversion factor with the least precision is 57 mi/gallon (2 significant figures). Truncate the last digit because the first non-significant digit is a 0.

1.121 **Given:** radius of nucleus of the hydrogen atom = 1.0×10^{-13} cm; radius of the hydrogen atom = 52.9 pm.
Find: percent of volume occupied by nucleus (%)
Conceptual Plan: cm → m then pm → m then r → V then V_{atom}, $V_{nucleus}$ → % $V_{nucleus}$

$\frac{1\ \text{m}}{100\ \text{cm}}$ $\quad$ $\frac{1\ \text{m}}{10^{12}\ \text{pm}}$ $\quad$ $V = (4/3)\pi r^3$ $\quad$ $\%V_{nucleus} = \frac{V_{nucleus}}{V_{atom}} \times 100\%$

Solution: $1.0 \times 10^{-13}\ \text{cm} \times \frac{1\ \text{m}}{100\ \text{cm}} = 1.0 \times 10^{-15}\ \text{m}$ and $52.9\ \text{pm} \times \frac{1\ \text{m}}{10^{12}\ \text{pm}} = 5.29 \times 10^{-11}\ \text{m}$

$V = (4/3)\pi r^3$ Substitute into %V equation.

$\%V_{nucleus} = \frac{V_{nucleus}}{V_{atom}} \times 100\% \rightarrow \%V_{nucleus} = \frac{(4/3)\pi r^3_{nucleus}}{(4/3)\pi r^3_{atom}} \times 100\%$ Simplify equation.

$\%V_{nucleus} = \frac{r^3_{nucleus}}{r^3_{atom}} \times 100\%$ Substitute numbers and calculate result.

$\%V_{nucleus} = \frac{(1.0 \times 10^{-15}\ \text{m})^3}{(5.29 \times 10^{-11}\ \text{m})^3} \times 100\% = (1.890359168 \times 10^{-5})^3 \times 100\% = 6.755118685 \times 10^{-13} = 6.8 \times 10^{-13}$

Check: The units (none) are correct. The magnitude of the answer seems correct (10^{-15}), since a proton is so small. Two significant figures are allowed to reflect the significant figures in 1.0×10^{-13} cm. Round up the last digits because the first non-significant digit is a 5.

1.122 **Given:** radius of neon = 69 pm; 2.69×10^{22} atoms per liter **Find:** percent of volume occupied by neon (%)
Conceptual Plan: Assume 1L total volume.
pm → m → cm then r → V then cm^3 → L then L/atom → L then V_{Ne}, V_{Total} → %V_{Ne}

$\frac{1\ \text{m}}{10^{12}\ \text{pm}}$ $\frac{100\ \text{cm}}{1\ \text{m}}$ $\quad$ $V = (4/3)\pi r^3 = 1\ atom$ $\quad$ $\frac{1\ \text{L}}{1000\ \text{cm}^3}$ $\quad$ 2.69×10^{22} atoms $\quad$ $\%V_{Ne} = \frac{V_{Ne}}{V_{Total}} \times 100\%$

Solution: $69\ \text{pm} \times \frac{1\ \text{m}}{10^{12}\ \text{pm}} \times \frac{100\ \text{cm}}{1\ \text{m}} = 6.9 \times 10^{-9}\ \text{cm}$

$V = (4/3)\ \pi\ r^3 = (4/3)\ \pi\ (6.9 \times 10^{-9}\ \text{cm})^3 = 1.37605528 \times 10^{-24}\ \text{cm}^3$

$1.37605528 \times 10^{-24}\ \text{cm}^3 \times \frac{1\ \text{L}}{1000\ \text{cm}^3} = 1.37605528 \times 10^{-27}\ \text{L}$

$\frac{1.37605528 \times 10^{-27}\ \text{L}}{\text{atom}} \times 2.69 \times 10^{22}\ \text{atoms} = 3.701588707 \times 10^{-5}\ \text{L}$ Substitute into %V equation.

$\%V_{Ne} = \frac{V_{Ne}}{V_{Total}} \times 100\% = \frac{3.701588707 \times 10^{-5}\ \text{L}}{1\ \text{L}} \times 100\% = 3.701588707 \times 10^{-3}\ \% = 3.7 \times 10^{-3}\ \%$

Check: This says that the separation between atoms is very large in the gas phase.
The units (%) are correct. The magnitude of the answer seems correct (10^{-3} %), it is known that gases are primarily empty space. Two significant figures are allowed to reflect the significant figures in 69 pm. Truncate the non-significant digits because the first non-significant digit is a 0.

1.123 **Given:** radius of hydrogen = 212 pm; radius of ping pong ball = 4.0 cm, 6.02×10^{23} atoms and balls in a row
Find: row length (km)
Conceptual Plan: atoms → pm → m → km and ball → cm → m → km

$\frac{212\ \text{pm}}{1\ \text{atom}}$ $\frac{1\ \text{m}}{10^{12}\ \text{pm}}$ $\frac{1\ \text{km}}{1000\ \text{m}}$ $\quad$ $\frac{4.0\ \text{cm}}{1\ \text{ball}}$ $\frac{100\ \text{cm}}{1\ \text{m}}$ $\frac{1\ \text{km}}{1000\ \text{m}}$

Solution: $6.02 \times 10^{23}\ \cancel{\text{atoms}} \times \frac{212\ \cancel{\text{pm}}}{1\ \cancel{\text{atom}}} \times \frac{1\ \cancel{\text{m}}}{10^{12}\ \cancel{\text{pm}}} \times \frac{1\ \text{km}}{1000\ \cancel{\text{m}}} = 1.28 \times 10^{11}\ \text{km}$

$6.02 \times 10^{23}\ \cancel{\text{balls}} \times \frac{4.0\ \cancel{\text{cm}}}{1\ \cancel{\text{ball}}} \times \frac{1\ \cancel{\text{m}}}{100\ \cancel{\text{cm}}} \times \frac{1\ \text{km}}{1000\ \cancel{\text{m}}} = 2.4 \times 10^{19}\ \text{km}$

Check: The units (km) are correct. The magnitude of the answers seem correct (10^{11} and 10^{19}). The answers are driven by the large number of atoms or balls. The ping pong ball row is 10^8 times longer. Three significant figures are allowed to reflect the significant figures in 212 pm. Two significant figures are allowed to reflect the significant figures in 4.0 cm.

1.124 **Given:** 100 m in 9.69 s; 100 yards in 9.21 s **Find:** miles/hr

Conceptual Plan: speed is distance/time; m/s → km/s → miles/s → miles/hr → miles/hr and

$\frac{1\ \text{km}}{1000\ \text{m}}$ $\frac{0.62137\ \text{mi}}{1\ \text{km}}$ $\frac{60\ \text{s}}{1\ \text{min}}$ $\frac{60\ \text{min}}{1\ \text{hr}}$

yd/s → m/s → km/s → miles/s → miles/hr → miles/hr and

$\frac{1\ \text{m}}{1.0936\ \text{yd}}$ $\frac{1\ \text{km}}{1000\ \text{m}}$ $\frac{0.62137\ \text{mi}}{1\ \text{km}}$ $\frac{60\ \text{s}}{1\ \text{min}}$ $\frac{60\ \text{min}}{1\ \text{hr}}$

Solution: $\frac{100\ \cancel{\text{m}}}{9.69\ \cancel{\text{s}}} \times \frac{1\ \cancel{\text{km}}}{1000\ \cancel{\text{m}}} \times \frac{0.62137\ \cancel{\text{mi}}}{1\ \cancel{\text{km}}} \times \frac{60\ \cancel{\text{s}}}{1\ \cancel{\text{min}}} \times \frac{60\ \cancel{\text{min}}}{1\ \text{hr}} = 23.\underline{0}84954\ \text{mi/hr} = 23.1\ \text{mi/hr}$

$\frac{100\ \cancel{\text{yd}}}{9.21\ \cancel{\text{s}}} \times \frac{1\ \cancel{\text{m}}}{1.0936\ \cancel{\text{yd}}} \times \frac{1\ \cancel{\text{km}}}{1000\ \cancel{\text{m}}} \times \frac{0.62137\ \text{mi}}{1\ \cancel{\text{km}}} \times \frac{60\ \cancel{\text{s}}}{1\ \cancel{\text{min}}} \times \frac{60\ \cancel{\text{min}}}{1\ \text{hr}} = 22.\underline{2}09289\ \text{mi/hr} = 22.2\ \text{mi/hr}$

Check: The units (mi/hr) are correct. The magnitude of the answers seem correct (23 and 22) and they are close to each other. Assuming that 100 m and 100 yd have three significant figures, three significant figures are allowed to reflect the significant figures in the times.

1.125 **Given:** 39.33 g sodium/100 g salt; 1.25 g salt/100 g snack mix; FDA maximum 2.40 g sodium/day **Find:** g snack mix

Conceptual Plan: g sodium → g salt → g snack mix

$\frac{100\ \text{g salt}}{39.33\ \text{g sodium}}$ $\frac{100\ \text{g snack mix}}{1.25\ \text{g salt}}$

Solution: $\frac{2.40\ \cancel{\text{g sodium}}}{1\ \text{day}} \times \frac{100\ \cancel{\text{g salt}}}{39.33\ \cancel{\text{g sodium}}} \times \frac{100\ \text{g snack mix}}{1.25\ \cancel{\text{g salt}}} = 48\underline{8}.1770\ \text{g snack mix/day}$

$= 488\ \text{g snack mix/day}$

Check: The units (g) are correct. The magnitude of the answer seems correct (500) since salt is less than half sodium and there is a little over a gram of salt per 100 grams of snack mix. Three significant figures are allowed to reflect the significant figures in the FDA maximum and in the amount of salt in the snack mix.

1.126 **Given:** 86.6 g lead/100 g galena; 68.5 g galena/100 g ore; 92.5 g lead extracted/100 g lead available; 1.500 cm radius sphere **Other:** d(lead) = 11.4 g/cm³ **Find:** g ore

Conceptual Plan:

$r_{\text{sphere}} \rightarrow V_{\text{sphere}}$ **then** $V_{\text{sphere}}, d_{\text{sphere}} \rightarrow m_{\text{sphere}}$**(g lead) → g lead available → g galena → g ore**

$V = (4/3)\pi r^3$ $d = m/V$ $\frac{100\ \text{g lead available}}{92.5\ \text{g lead extracted}}$ $\frac{100\ \text{g galena}}{86.6\ \text{g lead}}$ $\frac{100\ \text{g ore}}{68.5\ \text{g galena}}$

Solution: Calculate m_{sphere} $V_{\text{sphere}} = (4/3)\ \pi\ r^3_{\text{sphere}} = (4/3)\ \pi\ (5.00\ \text{cm})^3 = 52\underline{3}.5988\ \text{cm}^3$

$d = m/V$ Solve for m by multiplying both sides of the equation by V. $m = V \times d$

$$m = 52\underline{3}.5988\ \cancel{\text{cm}^3} \times \frac{11.4\ \text{g lead}}{1\ \cancel{\text{cm}^3}} = 59\underline{6}9.026\ \text{g lead}$$

$$5\underline{9}69.026\ \cancel{\text{g lead}} \times \frac{100\ \cancel{\text{g lead available}}}{92.5\ \cancel{\text{g lead extracted}}} \times \frac{100\ \cancel{\text{g galena}}}{86.6\ \cancel{\text{g lead available}}} \times \frac{100\ \text{g ore}}{68.5\ \cancel{\text{g galena}}}$$

$$= 1.0\underline{8}7811 \times 10^4\ \text{g ore} = 1.09 \times 10^4\ \text{g ore}$$

Check: The units (g) are correct. The magnitude of the answer seems correct (10^4) since lead is so dense and the sphere is not small. Three significant figures are allowed to reflect the significant figures in all of the information given.

1.127   **Given:** d(liquid nitrogen) = 0.808 g/mL; d(gaseous nitrogen) = 1.15 g/L; 175 L liquid nitrogen; 10.00 m x 10.00 m x 2.50 m room   **Find:** fraction of room displaced by nitrogen gas

Conceptual Plan: L → mL then V_{liquid}, d_{liquid} → m_{liquid} **then set** $m_{liquid} = m_{gas}$ **then** m_{gas}, d_{gas} → V_{gas} **then**

$$\frac{1000\ mL}{1\ L} \qquad\qquad d = m/V \qquad\qquad d = m/V$$

Calculate the V_{room} → cm^3 → **L then calculate the fraction displaced**

$$V = l \times w \times h \quad \frac{(100\ cm)^3}{(1\ m)^3} \quad \frac{1\ L}{1000\ cm^3} \qquad\qquad \frac{V_{gas}}{V_{room}}$$

Solution: $175\ \cancel{L} \times \dfrac{1000\ mL}{1\ \cancel{L}}$ = 1.75×10^5 mL. Solve for m by multiplying both sides of the equation by V.

$$m = V \times d = 1.75 \times 10^5\ \cancel{mL} \times \frac{0.808\ g}{1\ \cancel{mL}} = 1.4\underline{1}4 \times 10^5\ g\ \text{nitrogen liquid} = 1.4\underline{1}4 \times 10^5\ g\ \text{nitrogen gas}$$

$d = m/V$. Rearrange by multiplying both sides of the equation by V and dividing both sides of the equation by d.

$$V = \frac{m}{d} = \frac{1.4\underline{1}4 \times 10^5\ \cancel{g}}{1.15\ \dfrac{\cancel{g}}{L}} = 1.2\underline{2}9565 \times 10^5\ \text{L nitrogen gas}$$

$$V_{room} = l \times w \times h = 10.00\ \cancel{m} \times 10.00\ \cancel{m} \times 2.50\ \cancel{m} \times \frac{(100\ \cancel{cm})^3}{(1\ \cancel{m})^3} \times \frac{1\ L}{1000\ \cancel{cm^3}} = 2.50 \times 10^5\ L$$

$$\frac{V_{gas}}{V_{room}} = \frac{1.2\underline{2}9565 \times 10^5\ \cancel{L}}{2.50 \times 10^5\ \cancel{L}} = 0.49\underline{1}8272 = 0.492$$

Check: The units (none) are correct. The magnitude of the answer seems correct (0.5) since there is a large volume of liquid and the density of the gas is about a factor of 1000 less than the density of the liquid. Three significant figures are allowed to reflect the significant figures in the densities and the volume of the liquid given.

1.128   **Given:** d(mercury at 0.0 °C) = 13.596 g/cm³; d(mercury at 25.0 °C) = 13.534 g/cm³; 3.380 g; 0.200 mm diameter capillary   **Find:** distance mercury rises

Conceptual Plan: at each temperature m, d → V **then mm → m → cm then** V, r → h

$$d = m/V \qquad \frac{1\ m}{1000\ mm}\quad \frac{100\ cm}{1\ m} \qquad V = \pi r^2 h$$

then calculate the difference between the two heights

Solution: $d = m/V$. Rearrange by multiplying both sides of the equation by V and dividing both sides of the equation by d. $V = \dfrac{m}{d}$

at 0.0 °C: $V = \dfrac{m}{d} = \dfrac{3.380\ \cancel{g}}{13.596\ \dfrac{\cancel{g}}{cm^3}} = 0.248\underline{6}0253\ cm^3$

and at 25.0 °C: $V = \dfrac{m}{d} = \dfrac{3.380\ \cancel{g}}{13.534\ \dfrac{\cancel{g}}{cm^3}} = 0.249\underline{7}41392\ cm^3$

$r = 0.220\ \cancel{mm} \times \dfrac{1\ \cancel{m}}{1000\ \cancel{mm}} \times \dfrac{100\ cm}{1\ \cancel{m}} = 0.0220\ cm$ then $V = \pi r^2 h$.

Rearrange by dividing both sides of the equation by πr^2. $h = \dfrac{V}{\pi r^2}$

at 0.0 °C: $h = \dfrac{V}{\pi r^2} = \dfrac{0.248\underline{6}0253\ cm^3}{\pi\ (0.0220\ cm)^2} = 163.\underline{4}97196\ cm$

and at 25.0 °C: $h = \dfrac{V}{\pi r^2} = \dfrac{0.249\underline{7}41392\ cm^3}{\pi\ (0.0220\ cm)^2} = 164.\underline{2}46186\ cm$

the difference in height is $164.\underline{2}46186\ cm\ -\ 163.\underline{4}97196\ cm = 0.7\underline{4}8990\ cm = 0.7\ cm$

Check: The units (cm) are correct. The magnitude of the answer seems correct (0.7) since there is a relatively small change in temperature and the two densities are very close to each other. Only one significant figure is allowed because the heights have four significant figures and so the error is in the tenths place.

Challenge Problems

1.129 Force = (mass) x (acceleration) or $F = ma$ and Pressure = force / area. So if a force of 2.31×10^4 N is applied on an area of 125 cm^2, the

$$\text{Pressure} = \frac{2.31 \times 10^4 \text{ N}}{125 \text{ cm}^2 \times \frac{(1 \text{ m})^2}{(100 \text{ cm})^2}} = 1.8\underline{4}6 \times 10^6 \frac{\text{N}}{\text{m}^2}.$$

Referring to Chapter 5, 1 N/m^2 = 1 Pa and

$$1 \text{ atm} = 101{,}325 \text{ Pa, so } 1.8\underline{4}6 \times 10^6 \frac{\text{N}}{\text{m}^2} = 1.8\underline{4}6 \times 10^6 \text{ Pa} \times \frac{1 \text{ atm}}{101{,}325 \text{ Pa}} = 18.2 \text{ atm}$$

1.130 A Newton (N) has units of kg·m/s^2. If a dyne has mass measured in units of grams, this will make a dyne a factor of 10^3 larger than a Newton (N). To get the additional factor of 10^2 needed to get to a factor of 10^5, the length must be in centimeters (cm) $1 \text{ dyne} = 1\frac{\text{g} \cdot \text{cm}}{\text{s}^2} \times \frac{1 \text{ kg}}{1000 \text{ g}} \times \frac{1 \text{ m}}{100 \text{ cm}} = 10^{-5} \frac{\text{kg} \cdot \text{m}}{\text{s}^2} = 10^{-5} \text{ N}.$

1.131 Referring to the definition of energy in Chapter 6, 1 Joule = 1J = kg·m^2/s^2. For kinetic energy, if the units of mass are the kilogram (kg) and the units of the velocity are meters/second (m/s) then

kinetic energy units $= mv^2 = \text{kg}\left(\frac{\text{m}}{\text{s}}\right)^2 = \frac{\text{kg} \cdot \text{m}^2}{\text{s}^2} = \text{J}$. Since a Newton (N) is a unit of force and has units of kg·m/s^2. Pressure = force / area and has units of N/m^2, and Force = (mass) x (acceleration) or $F = ma$, then

$$3/2 \text{ PV units} = \frac{\text{N}}{\text{m}^2} \cdot \text{m}^3 = \frac{\text{kg} \cdot \text{m}}{\text{s}^2} \cdot \text{m} = \frac{\text{kg} \cdot \text{m}^2}{\text{s}^2} = \text{J}.$$

1.132 **Given:** mass of black hole (BH) = 1x 10^3 suns; radius of black hole = one-half the radius of our moon
Find: density (g/cm^3) **Other:** radius of our sun = 7.0×10^5 km; average density of our sun = 1.4×10^3 kg/m^3; diameter of the moon = 2.16×10^3 miles
Conceptual Plan: $d_{BH} = m_{BH}/V_{BH}$
Calculate m_{BH} **:** $r_{sun} \rightarrow V_{sun}$ km$^3_{sun} \rightarrow$ m$^3_{sun}$ $V_{sun}, d_{sun} \rightarrow m_{sun}$ **then** $m_{sun} \rightarrow m_{BH}$ **kg** $\rightarrow$ **g**

$V = (4/3)\pi r^3$ $\qquad \frac{(1000 \text{ m})^3}{(1 \text{ km})^3}$ $\qquad d_{sun} = \frac{m_{sun}}{V_{sun}}$ $\qquad m_{BH} = (1 \times 10^3) \times m_{sun}$ $\qquad \frac{1000 \text{ g}}{1 \text{ kg}}$

Calculate V_{BH}**:** $d_{moon} \rightarrow r_{moon} \rightarrow r_{BH}$ **mi** $\rightarrow$ **km** $\rightarrow$ **m** $\rightarrow$ **cm then** $r \rightarrow V$

$r_{moon} = 1/2\, d_{moon}$ $\quad r_{BH} = 1/2\, r_{moon}$ $\quad \frac{1 \text{ km}}{0.6214 \text{ mi}}$ $\quad \frac{1000 \text{ m}}{1 \text{ km}}$ $\quad \frac{100 \text{ cm}}{1 \text{ m}}$ $\qquad V = (4/3)\pi r^3$

Substitute into $d_{BH} = m_{BH}/ V_{BH}$
Solution: Calculate m_{BH}: $V_{sun} = (4/3)\ \pi\ r^3_{sun} = (4/3)\ \pi\ (7.0 \times 10^5 \text{ km})^3 = 1.\underline{4}3675504 \times 10^{18} \text{ km}^3$

$$1.\underline{4}3675504 \times 10^{18} \text{ km}^3 \times \frac{(1000 \text{ m})^3}{(1 \text{ km})^3} = 1.\underline{4}3675504 \times 10^{27} \text{ m}^3$$

$d_{sun} = m_{sun}/V_{sun}$. Solve for m by multiplying both sides of the equation by V_{sun}. $\quad m_{sun} = V_{sun} \times d_{sun}$

$m_{sun} = (1.\underline{4}3675504 \times 10^{27} \text{ m}^3)(1.4 \times 10^3 \text{ kg/m}^3) = 2.\underline{0}11457056 \times 10^{30} \text{ kg}$

$m_{BH} = (1 \times 10^3) \times m_{sun} = (1 \times 10^3) \times (2.\underline{0}11457056 \times 10^{30} \text{ kg}) = 2.\underline{0}11457056 \times 10^{33} \text{ kg}$

$$2.\underline{0}11457056 \times 10^{33} \text{ kg} \times \frac{1000 \text{ g}}{1 \text{ kg}} = 2.\underline{0}11457056 \times 10^{36} \text{ g}$$

Calculate V_{BH}: $r_{moon} = \frac{1}{2} d_{moon} = \frac{1}{2}(2.16 \times 10^3 \text{ miles}) = 1.08 \times 10^3$ miles

$r_{BH} = \frac{1}{2} r_{moon} = \frac{1}{2}(1.08 \times 10^3 \text{ miles}) = 540.$ miles

$$540.\ \text{miles} \times \frac{1\ \text{km}}{0.6214\ \text{mi}} \times \frac{1000\ \text{m}}{1\ \text{km}} \times \frac{100\ \text{cm}}{1\ \text{m}} = 8.69\underline{0}0547 \times 10^{7}\ \text{cm}$$

$$V = (4/3)\ \pi\ r^3 = (4/3)\ \pi\ (8.69\underline{0}0547 \times 10^7\ \text{cm})^3 = 2.7\underline{4}888228 \times 10^{24}\ \text{cm}^3$$

$$\text{Substitute into } d_{BH} = \frac{m_{BH}}{V_{BH}} = \frac{2.\underline{0}11457056 \times 10^{36}\ \text{g}}{2.7\underline{4}888228 \times 10^{24}\ \text{cm}^3} = 7.\underline{3}1737339 \times 10^{11} \frac{\text{g}}{\text{cm}^3} = 7.3 \times 10^{11} \frac{\text{g}}{\text{cm}^3}$$

Check: The units (g/cm^3) are correct. The magnitude of the answer seems correct (10^{12}), since we expect extremely high numbers for black holes. Two significant figures are allowed to reflect the significant figures in the radius of our sun (7.0×10^5 km) and the average density of the sun ($1.4 \times 10^3\ kg/m^3$). Truncate the non-significant digits because the first non-significant digit is a 4.

1.133 **Given:** 15.0 ppm CO; eight hour period **Find:** milligrams of carbon monoxide
Other: 0.50 L of air per breath; 20 breaths per minute; carbon monoxide has a density of 1.2 g/L; and 15.0 ppm CO means 15.0 L CO per 10^6 L air
Conceptual plan: hr → min → breaths → L_{air} → L_{CO} → g_{CO} → mg_{CO}

$$\frac{60\ \text{min}}{1\ \text{hr}} \quad \frac{20\ \text{breath}}{1\ \text{min}} \quad \frac{0.50\ L_{air}}{1\ \text{breath}} \quad \frac{15.0\ L_{CO}}{1 \times 10^6\ L_{air}} \quad \frac{1.2\ g_{CO}}{1\ L_{CO}} \quad \frac{1000\ mg_{CO}}{1\ g_{CO}}$$

Solution:

$$8\ \text{hr} \times \frac{60\ \text{min}}{1\ \text{hr}} \times \frac{20\ \text{breath}}{1\ \text{min}} \times \frac{0.50\ L_{air}}{1\ \text{breath}} \times \frac{15.0\ L_{CO}}{1 \times 10^6\ L_{air}} \times \frac{1.2\ g_{CO}}{1\ L_{CO}} \times \frac{1000\ mg_{CO}}{1\ g_{CO}} = \underline{8}6.4\ mg_{CO} = 9 \times 10^1\ mg_{CO}$$

Check: The units (mg) are correct. The magnitude of the answer (10^2) makes physical sense because there are more than 6 powers of 10 visible in these conversion factors in the numerator and one factor of 10^6 in the denominator. This means that most of the conversions cancel each other out, but there is still some left in the numerator. One significant figure is allowed because the conversion factor with the least precision is 20 breaths/minute (1 significant figure) and the starting time (8 hours) also has one significant figure. Round up the last digit because the first non-significant digit is a 6.

1.134 **Given:** cubic nanocontainers with an edge length = 25 nanometers
Find: a) volume of one nanocontainer; b) grams of oxygen could be contained by each nanocontainer; c) grams of oxygen inhaled per hour; d) minimum number of nanocontainers per hour; and e) minimum volume of nanocontainers.
Other: (pressurized oxygen) = 85 g/L; 0.28 g of oxygen per liter; average human inhales about 0.50 L of air per breath and takes about 20 breaths per minute; and adult total blood volume = ~5 L
Conceptual Plan:

(a) **nm → m → cm then l → V then cm3 → L**

$$\frac{1\ \text{m}}{10^9\ \text{nm}} \quad \frac{100\ \text{cm}}{1\ \text{m}} \qquad V = l^3 \qquad \frac{1\ \text{L}}{1000\ \text{cm}^3}$$

(b) **L → g pressurized oxygen**

$$\frac{85\ \text{g oxygen}}{1\ \text{L nanocontainers}}$$

(c) **hr → min → breaths → L_{air} → g_{O2}**

$$\frac{60\ \text{min}}{1\ \text{hr}} \quad \frac{20\ \text{breath}}{1\ \text{min}} \quad \frac{0.50\ L_{air}}{1\ \text{breath}} \quad \frac{0.28\ g_{CO}}{1\ L_{air}}$$

(d) **grams oxygen → number nanocontainers**

$$\frac{1\ \text{nanocontainer}}{\text{part (b) grams of oxygen}}$$

(e) **number nanocontainers → volume nanocontainers**

$$\frac{\text{part (a) volume}}{\text{of 1 nanocontainer}}$$

Solution:

(a) $$25\ \cancel{\text{nm}} \times \frac{1\ \cancel{\text{m}}}{10^9\ \cancel{\text{nm}}} \times \frac{100\ \text{cm}}{1\ \cancel{\text{m}}} = 2.5 \times 10^{-6}\ \text{cm}$$

$$V = l^3 = (2.5 \times 10^{-6}\ \text{cm})^3 = 1.\underline{5}625 \times 10^{-17}\ \cancel{\text{cm}^3} \times \frac{1\ \text{L}}{1000\ \cancel{\text{cm}^3}} = 1.\underline{5}625 \times 10^{-20}\ \text{L} = 1.6 \times 10^{-20}\ \text{L}$$

(b) $$1.\underline{5}625 \times 10^{-20}\ \cancel{\text{L}} \times \frac{85\ \text{g oxygen}}{1\ \cancel{\text{L}}\ \text{nanocontainers}} = 1.\underline{3}28125 \times 10^{-18}\ \frac{\text{g pressurized } O_2}{\text{nanocontainer}}$$

$$= 1.3 \times 10^{-18}\ \frac{\text{g pressurized } O_2}{\text{nanocontainer}}$$

(c) $$1\ \cancel{\text{hr}} \times \frac{60\ \cancel{\text{min}}}{1\ \cancel{\text{hr}}} \times \frac{20\ \cancel{\text{breath}}}{1\ \cancel{\text{min}}} \times \frac{0.50\ \cancel{\text{L}_{\text{air}}}}{1\ \cancel{\text{breath}}} \times \frac{0.28\ \text{g}O_2}{1\ \cancel{\text{L}_{\text{air}}}} = 1.\underline{6}8 \times 10^2\ \text{g oxygen} = 1.7 \times 10^2\ \text{g oxygen}$$

(d) $$1.\underline{6}8 \times 10^2\ \cancel{\text{g oxygen}} \times \frac{1\ \text{nanocontainer}}{1.3 \times 10^{-18}\ \cancel{\text{g of oxygen}}} = 1.\underline{2}92307692 \times 10^{20}\ \text{nanocontainers}$$

$$= 1.3 \times 10^{20}\ \text{nanocontainers}$$

(e) $$1.\underline{2}92307692 \times 10^{20}\ \cancel{\text{nanocontainers}} \times \frac{1.5625 \times 10^{-20}\ \text{L}}{\cancel{\text{nanocontainer}}} = 2.\underline{0}19230769\ \text{L} = 2.0\ L$$

This volume is much too large to be feasible, since the volume of blood in the average human is 5 L.

Check:

(a) The units (L) are correct. The magnitude of the answer (10 – 20) makes physical sense because these are very, very tiny containers. Two significant figures are allowed, reflecting the significant figures in the starting dimension (25 nm – 2 significant figures). Round up the last digit because the first non-significant digit is a 6.

(b) The units (g) are correct. The magnitude of the answer (10^{-18}) makes physical sense because these are very, very tiny containers and very few molecules can fit inside. Two significant figures are allowed, reflecting the significant figures in the starting dimension (25 nm) and the given concentration (85 g/L) – 2 significant figures in each. Truncate the non-significant digits because the first non-significant digit is a 2.

(c) The units (g oxygen) are correct. The magnitude of the answer (10^2) makes physical sense because of the conversion factors involved and the fact that air is not very dense. Two significant figures are allowed because it is stated in the problem. Round up the last digit because the first non-significant digit is an 8.

(d) The units (nanocontainers) are correct. The magnitude of the answer (10^{20}) makes physical sense because these are very, very tiny containers and we need a macroscopic quantity of oxygen in these containers. Two significant figures are allowed, reflecting the significant figures in both of the quantities in the calculation – 2 significant figures. Round up the last digit because the first non-significant digit is a 9.

(e) The units (L) are correct. The magnitude of the answer (2) makes physical sense because, the magnitudes of the numbers in this step. Two significant figures are allowed reflecting the significant figures in both of the quantities in the calculation – 2 significant figures. Truncate the non-significant digits because the first non-significant digit is a 1.

1.135 Since the person weighs 155 lbs and has a density of 1.0 g/cm^3, the volume of the person can be calculated as $155\ \cancel{\text{lbs}} \times \frac{453.59\ \cancel{\text{g}}}{1\ \cancel{\text{lb}}} \times \frac{1\ \text{cm}^3}{1.0\ \cancel{\text{g}}} = 7.\underline{0}30645 \times 10^4\text{cm}^3$.

Approximating the volume of a person as a cylinder 4.0 feet tall, $V = l\,\pi\,r^2$. Rearranging the equation, solving for r.

$$r = \left(\frac{V}{l\pi}\right)^{\frac{1}{2}} = \sqrt{\frac{7.030645 \times 10^4\,\text{cm}^3}{4.0\,\text{ft} \times \frac{30.48\,\text{cm}}{1\,\text{ft}} \times \pi}} = 13.54831\ \text{cm}.$$

The circumference is $2\,\pi\,r = 2\pi(13.54831\ \text{cm}) = 85.12655\ \text{cm}$. When the person gains 40.0 lbs of fat the volume increase is $40.0\ \text{lbs} \times \frac{453.59\ \text{g}}{1\ \text{lb}} \times \frac{1\ \text{cm}^3}{0.918\ \text{g}} = 1.97643 \times 10^4\text{cm}^3$.

Thus the new volume is $7.030645 \times 10^4\text{cm}^3 + 1.97643 \times 10^4\text{cm}^3 = 9.00707 \times 10^4\ \text{cm}^3$. So the new radius is

$$r = \left(\frac{V}{l\pi}\right)^{\frac{1}{2}} = \sqrt{\frac{9.00707 \times 10^4\,\text{cm}^3}{4.0\,\text{ft} \times \frac{30.48\,\text{cm}}{1\,\text{ft}} \times \pi}} = 15.33485\ \text{cm}$$ and the new circumference is

$$2\,\pi\,r = 2\pi(15.33485\ \text{cm}) = 96.35167\ \text{cm}.$$

The percent increase in circumference $\frac{96.35167\ \text{cm} - 85.12655\ \text{cm}}{85.12655\ \text{cm}} \times 100\ \% = 13.1864\ \% = 13\ \%$.

1.136 Assume that all of the spheres are the same size. Let x = the percentage of spheres that are copper (expressed as a fraction) and so the volume of copper = $(427\ \text{cm}^3)x$ and the volume of lead = $(427\ \text{cm}^3)(1 - x)$. Since the density of copper is 8.96 g/cm^3, the mass of copper $= (427\ \text{cm}^3)x \times \frac{8.96\ \text{g}}{\text{cm}^3} = 3825.92(x)\ \text{g}$. Since the density of lead is 11.4 g/cm^3, the mass of lead $= (427\ \text{cm}^3)(1 - x) \times \frac{11.46\ \text{g}}{\text{cm}^3} = 4893.42\ (1 - x)\ \text{g}$. Since the total mass is 4.36 kg = 4360 g, $4360\ \text{g} = 3825.92(x)\ \text{g} + 4893.42\ (1 - x)\ \text{g}$. Solving for x, $1067.5(x)\ \text{g} = 533.6\ \text{g} \rightarrow x = 0.499859$ or 50.% of the spheres are copper.

Check: This answer makes sense, since the average density of the spheres = 4360 g/427 cm^3 = 10.2 g/cm^3 and the average of the density of copper and the density of lead = (8.96 + 11.4)/2 g/cm^3 = 10.2 g/cm^3.

Conceptual Problems

1.137 No. Since the container is sealed the atoms and molecules can move around, but they cannot leave. If no atoms or molecules can leave, the mass must be constant.

1.138 (c) is the best representation. When solid carbon dioxide (dry ice) sublimes, it changes phase from a solid to a gas. Phase changes are physical changes, so no molecular bonds are broken. This diagram shows molecules with one carbon atom and two oxygen atoms bonded together in every molecule. The other diagrams have no carbon dioxide molecules.

1.139 This problem is similar to Problem 64, only the dimension is changed to 7 cm on each edge.
Given: 7 cm on each edge cube **Find:** cm^3
Conceptual plan: Read the information given carefully. The cube is 7 cm on each side.
l, w, h → *V*

$V = l\,w\,h$

in a cube $l = w = h$

Solution: 7 cm x 7 cm x 7 cm = (7 cm)^3 = = 343 cm^3 or 343 cubes

1.140 In order to determine which number is large, the units need to be compared. There is a factor of 1000 between grams and kg, in the numerator. There is a factor of (100)^3 or 1,000,000 between cm^3 and m^3. This second factor more than compensates for the first factor. Thus Substance A with a density of 1.7 g/cm^3 is denser than Substance B with a density of 1.7 kg/m^3.

1.141 Remember that density = mass/volume.

(a) The darker colored box has a heavier mass, but a smaller volume, so it is denser than the lighter-colored box.

(b) The lighter colored box is heavier than the darker colored box and both boxes have the same volume, so the lighter colored box is denser.

(c) The larger box is the heavier box, so it cannot be determined with this information which box is denser.

1.142 Remember that an observation is the information collected when studying phenomena. A law is a concise statement that summarizes observed behaviors and observations and predicts future observations. A theory attempts to explain why the observed behavior is happening.

(a) This statement is most like a law because it summarizes many observations and can explain future behavior—many places and many days.

(b) This statement is a theory because it attempts to explain why (gravitational forces).

(c) This statement is most like an observation because it is information collected in order to understand tidal behavior.

(d) This statement is most like a law, because it summarizes many observations and can explain future behavior—many places and many days and months.

2 Atoms and Elements

Review Questions

2.1 Scanning tunneling microscopy is a technique that can image, and even move, individual atoms and molecules. A scanning tunneling microscope works by moving an extremely sharp electrode over a surface and measuring the resulting tunneling current, the electrical current that flows between the tip of the electrode, and the surface even though the two are not in physical contact.

2.2 The first people to propose that matter was composed of small, indestructible particles were Leucippus and Democritus. These Greek philosophers theorized that matter was ultimately composed of small, indivisible particles called *atomos*. In the sixteenth century modern science began to emerge. A greater emphasis on observation brought rapid advancement as the scientific method became the established way to learn about the physical world. By the early 1800s certain observations led the English chemist John Dalton to offer convincing evidence that supported the early atomic ideas of Leucippus and Democritus. The theory that all matter is composed of atoms grew out of observations and laws. The three most important laws that led to the development and acceptance of the atomic theory were the law of conservation of mass, the law of definite proportions, and the law of multiple proportions. John Dalton explained the laws with his atomic theory.

2.3 The law of conservation of mass states the following: In a chemical reaction, matter is neither created nor destroyed. In other words, when you carry out any chemical reaction, the total mass of the substances involved in the reaction does not change.

2.4 The law of definite proportions states the following: All samples of a given compound, regardless of their source or how they were prepared, have the same proportions of their constituent elements. This means that elements composing a given compound always occur in fixed (or definite) proportions in all samples of the compound.

2.5 The law of multiple proportions states the following: When two elements (call them A and B) form two different compounds, the masses of element B that combine with 1 g of element A can be expressed as a ratio of small whole numbers. This means that when two atoms (A and B) combine to form more than one compound, the ratio of B in one compound to B in the second compound will be a small whole number.

2.6 The main ideas of John Dalton's atomic theory are as follows: 1) Each element is composed of tiny, indestructible particles called atoms. 2) All atoms of a given element have the same mass and other properties that distinguish them from the atoms of other elements. 3) Atoms combine in simple, whole number ratios to form compounds. 4) Atoms of one element cannot change into atoms of another element. In a chemical reaction, atoms change the way that they are bound together with other atoms to form a new substance. The law of conservation of mass is explained by the fourth idea. Since the atoms cannot change into another element, and just change how they are bound together, the total mass will remain constant. The law of constant composition is supported by idea 2 and 3. Since the atoms of a given element always have the same mass and other distinguishing properties, and they combine in simple whole number ratios, different samples of the same compound will have the same properties and the same composition. The law of multiple proportions is also supported by ideas 2 and 3 since the atoms can combine in simple whole number ratios; the ratio of the mass of B in one compound to the mass of B in a second compound will also be a small whole number.

2.7 In the late 1800s, an English physicist named J.J. Thomson performed experiments to probe the properties of cathode rays. Thomson found that these rays were actually streams of particles with the following properties: They traveled in straight lines; they were independent of the composition of the material from which they originated; and they carried a negative electrical charge. He measured the charge to mass ratio of the particles and found that the cathode ray particle was about 2000 times lighter than hydrogen.

2.8 In Millikan's oil drop experiment, oil was sprayed into fine droplets using an atomizer. The droplets were allowed to fall under the influence of gravity through a small hole into the lower portion of the apparatus where they could be viewed. During their fall, the drops would acquire electrons that had been produced by the interaction of high energy radiation with air. These charged drops interacted with two electrically charged plates within the apparatus. The negatively charged plate at the bottom of the apparatus repelled the negatively charged drops. By varying the voltage on the plates, the fall of the charged drops could be slowed, stopped, or even reversed. From the voltage required to halt the free fall of the drops, and from the masses of the drops themselves, Millikan calculated the charge of each drop. He then reasoned that, since each drop must contain an integral number of electrons, the charge of each drop must be a whole number multiple of the electron's charge. The magnitude of the charge of the electron is of tremendous importance because it determines how strongly an atom holds its electrons.

2.9 The plum-pudding model of the atom, proposed by J.J. Thomson hypothesized that the negatively charged electrons were small particles electrostatically held within a positively charged sphere.

2.10 Rutherford's gold foil experiment directed positively charged α particles at an ultrathin sheet of gold foil. These particles were to act as probes of the gold atoms' structures. If the gold atoms were indeed like plum pudding—with their mass and charge spread throughout the entire volume of the atom—these speeding probes should pass right through the gold foil with minimum deflection. A majority of the particles did pass directly through the foil, but some particles were deflected, and some even bounced back. He realized that to account for the deflections, the mass and positive charge of an atom must all be concentrated in a space much smaller than the size of the atom itself.

2.11 Rutherford's nuclear model of the atom has three basic parts: 1) Most of the atom's mass and all of its positive charge are contained in a small core called the **nucleus.** 2) Most of the volume of the atom is empty space, throughout which tiny negatively charged electrons are dispersed. 3) There are as many negatively-charged electrons outside the nucleus as there are positively-charged particles within the nucleus, so that the atom is electrically neutral. The revolutionary part of this theory is the idea that matter, at its core, is much less uniform than it appears.

2.12 Matter appears solid because the variation in its density is on such a small scale that our eyes cannot see it.

2.13 The three subatomic particles that compose atoms are as follows:

Protons, which have a mass of 1.67262×10^{-27} kg or 1.00727 amu and a relative charge of +1

Neutrons, which have a mass of 1.67493×10^{-27} kg or 1.00866 amu and a relative charge of 0

Electrons, which have a mass of 0.00091×10^{-27} kg or 0.00055 amu and a relative charge of – 1

2.14 The number of protons in the nucleus defines the identity of an element.

2.15 The atomic number, Z, is the number of protons in an atom's nucleus. The atomic mass number (A) is the sum of the neutrons and protons in an atom.

2.16 The names of the elements were often given to describe their properties. For example, argon originates from the Greek word argos meaning inactive. Other elements were named after figures from Greek or Roman mythology or astronomical bodies. Still others were named for the places where they were discovered or where their discoverer was born. More recently, elements have been named after scientists.

2.17 Isotopes are atoms with the same number of protons but different numbers of neutrons. The percent natural abundance is the relative amount of each different isotope in a naturally occurring sample of a given element.

2.18 Isotopes can be symbolized as ${}^{A}_{Z}X$, where A is the mass number, Z is the atomic number, and X is the chemical symbol. A second notation is the chemical symbol (or chemical name) followed by a dash and the mass number of the isotope, such as

X-A, where X is the chemical symbol or name and A is the mass number. The carbon isotope with a mass of 12 would have the symbol ${}^{12}_{6}C$ or C-12.

2.19 An ion is a charged particle. Positively charged ions are called cations. Negatively charged ions are called anions.

2.20 The periodic law states the following: When elements are arranged in order of increasing mass, certain sets of properties recur periodically. Mendeleev organized all the known elements in a table consisting of a series of rows in which mass increased from left to right. The rows were arranged so that elements with similar properties were aligned in the same vertical column.

2.21 Metals are found on the left side and the middle of the periodic table. They are good conductors of heat and electricity; they can be pounded into flat sheets (malleable), they can be drawn into wires (ductile), they are often shiny, and they tend to lose electrons when they undergo chemical changes.

Nonmetals are found on the upper-right side of the periodic table. Their properties are more varied: Some are solids at room temperature, while others are liquids or gases. As a whole they tend to be poor conductors of heat and electricity and they all tend to gain electrons when they undergo chemical changes.

Metalloids lie along the zigzag diagonal line that divides metals and nonmetals. They show mixed properties. Several metalloids are also classified as semiconductors because of their intermediate and temperature-dependent electrical conductivity.

2.22 (a) Noble gases are in group 8A and are mostly unreactive. As the name implies, they are all gases in their natural state.

(b) Alkali metals are in group 1A and are all reactive metals.

(c) Alkaline earth metals are in group 2A and are also fairly reactive.

(d) Halogens are in group 7A and are very reactive nonmetals.

2.23 Main group metals tend to lose electrons, forming cations with the same number of electrons as the nearest noble gas. Main group nonmetals tend to gain electrons, forming anions with the same number of electrons as the nearest following noble gas.

2.24 Atomic mass represents the average mass of the isotopes that compose that element. The average calculated atomic mass is weighted according to the natural abundance of each isotope.

$$\text{Atomic mass} = \sum_{n} (\text{fraction of isotope n}) \times (\text{mass of isotope n})$$

2.25 In a mass spectrometer, the sample is injected into the instrument and vaporized. The vaporized atoms are then ionized by an electron beam. The electrons in the beam collide with the vaporized atoms, removing electrons from the atoms and creating positively charged ions. Charged plates with slits in them accelerate the positively charged ions into a magnetic field, which deflects them. The amount of deflection depends on the mass of the ions—lighter ions are deflected more than heavier ones. Finally, the ions strike a detector and produce an electrical signal that is recorded.

2.26 The result of the mass spectrometer is the separation of the atoms in the sample according to their mass, producing a mass spectrum. The position of each peak on the x-axis gives the mass of the isotope, and the intensity (indicated by the height of the peak) gives the relative abundance of that isotope.

2.27 A mole is an amount of material. It is defined as the amount of material containing 6.0221421×10^{23} particles (Avogadro's number). The numerical value of the mole is defined as being equal to the number of atoms in exactly 12 grams of pure carbon-12. It is useful for converting number of atoms to moles of atoms and moles of atoms to number of atoms.

2.28 The mass corresponding to a mole of one element is different from the mass corresponding to a mole of another element because the mass of the atom of each element is different. A mole is a specific number of atoms, so the heavier the mass of each atom, the heavier the mass of one mole of atoms.

Problems by Topic

The Laws of Conservation of Mass, Definite Proportions, and Multiple Proportions

2.29 **Given:** 1.50 g hydrogen; 12.0 g oxygen **Find:** grams water vapor
Conceptual Plan: total mass reactants = total mass products
Solution: Mass of reactants = 1.50 g hydrogen + 12.0 g oxygen = 13.5 grams
Mass of products = mass of reactants = 13.5 grams water vapor.
Check: According to the law of conservation of mass, matter is not created or destroyed in a chemical reaction, so, since water vapor is the only product, the masses of hydrogen and oxygen must combine to form the mass of water vapor.

2.30 **Given:** 21 kg gasoline; 84 kg oxygen **Find:** mass of carbon dioxide and water
Conceptual Plan: total mass reactants = total mass products
Solution: Mass of reactants = 21 kg gasoline + 84 kg oxygen = 105 kg mass
Mass of products = mass of reactants = 105 kg of mass of carbon dioxide and water.
Check: According to the law of conservation of mass, matter is not created or destroyed in a chemical reaction, so, since carbon dioxide and water are the only products, the masses of gasoline and oxygen must combine to form the mass of carbon dioxide and water.

2.31 **Given:** sample 1: 38.9 g carbon, 448 g chlorine; sample 2: 14.8 g carbon, 134 g chlorine
Find: consistent with definite proportions
Conceptual Plan: determine mass ratio of sample 1 and 2 and compare

$$\frac{\text{mass of chlorine}}{\text{mass of carbon}}$$

Solution: Sample 1: $\frac{448\text{ g chorine}}{38.9\text{ g carbon}} = 11.5$ Sample 2: $\frac{134\text{ g chlorine}}{14.8\text{ g carbon}} = 9.05$

Results are not consistent with the law of definite proportions because the ratio of chlorine to carbon is not the same.
Check: According to the law of definite proportions, the mass ratio of one element to another is the same for all samples of the compound.

2.32 **Given:** sample 1: 6.98 grams sodium, 10.7 grams chlorine; sample 2: 11.2 g sodium, 17.3 grams chlorine
Find: consistent with definite proportions
Conceptual Plan: determine mass ratio of sample 1 and 2 and compare

$$\frac{\text{mass of chlorine}}{\text{mass of sodium}}$$

Solution: Sample 1: $\frac{10.7\text{ g chorine}}{6.98\text{ g sodium}} = 1.53$ Sample 2: $\frac{17.3\text{ g chlorine}}{11.2\text{ g sodium}} = 1.54$

Results are consistent with the law of definite proportions.
Check: According to the law of definite proportions, the mass ratio of one element to another is the same for all samples of the compound.

2.33 **Given:** mass ratio sodium to fluorine = 1.21:1; sample = 28.8 g sodium **Find:** g fluorine
Conceptual Plan: g sodium $\rightarrow$ g fluorine

$$\frac{\text{mass of fluorine}}{\text{mass of sodium}}$$

Solution: $28.8\,\text{g}\,\cancel{\text{sodium}} \times \frac{1\text{ g fluorine}}{1.21\,\text{g}\,\cancel{\text{sodium}}} = 23.8\text{ g fluorine}$

Check: The units of the answer (g fluorine) are correct. The magnitude of the answer is reasonable since it is less than the grams of sodium.

2.34 **Given:** sample 1: 1.65 kg magnesium, 2.57 kg fluorine; sample 2: 1.32 kg magnesium
Find: g fluorine in sample 2
Conceptual Plan: mass magnesium and mass fluorine → mass ratio → mass fluorine(kg) → mass fluorine(g)

$$\frac{\text{mass of fluorine}}{\text{mass of magnesium}} \qquad \frac{1000\text{ g}}{\text{kg}}$$

Solution: $\text{mass ratio} = \dfrac{2.57\text{ kg fluorine}}{1.65\text{ kg magnesium}} = \dfrac{1.56\text{ kg fluorine}}{1.00\text{ kg magnesium}}$

$$1.32\,\cancel{\text{kg magnesium}} \times \frac{1.56\text{ kg fluorine}}{1.00\,\cancel{\text{kg magnesium}}} \times \frac{1000\text{ g}}{\text{kg}} = 2.06 \times 10^3\text{ g fluorine}$$

Check: The units of the answer (g fluorine) are correct. The magnitude of the answer is reasonable since it is greater than the mass of magnesium and the ratio is greater than 1.

2.35 **Given:** 1 gram osmium: sample 1 = 0.168 g oxygen; sample 2 = 0.3369 g oxygen
Find: consistent with multiple proportions
Conceptual Plan: determine mass ratio of oxygen

$$\frac{\text{mass of oxygen sample 2}}{\text{mass of oxygen sample 1}}$$

Solution: $\dfrac{0.3369\text{ g oxygen}}{0.168\text{ g oxygen}} = 2.00$ Ratio is a small whole number. Results are consistent with multiple proportions

Check: According to the law of multiple proportions, when two elements form two different compounds, the masses of element B that combine with 1 g of element A can be expressed as a ratio of small whole numbers.

2.36 **Given:** 1 g palladium: compound A: 0.603 g S; compound B: 0.301 g S; compound C: 0.151 g S
Find: consistent with multiple proportions
Conceptual Plan: determine mass ratio of sulfur in the three compounds

$$\frac{\text{mass of sulfur sample A}}{\text{mass of sulfur sample B}} \quad \frac{\text{mass of sulfur sample A}}{\text{mass of sulfur sample C}} \quad \frac{\text{mass of sulfur sample B}}{\text{mass of sulfur sample C}}$$

Solution: $\dfrac{0.603\text{ g S in compound A}}{0.301\text{ g S in compound B}} = 2.00 \qquad \dfrac{0.603\text{ g S in compound A}}{0.151\text{ g S in compound C}} = 3.99 \sim 4$

$$\frac{0.301\text{ g S in compound B}}{0.151\text{ g S in compound C}} = 1.99 \sim 2$$

Ratio of each is a small whole number. Results are consistent with multiple proportions.

Check: According to the law of multiple proportions, when two elements form two different compounds, the masses of element B that combine with 1 g of element A can be expressed as a ratio of small whole numbers.

2.37 **Given:** sulfur dioxide = 3.49 g oxygen and 3.50 g sulfur; sulfur trioxide = 6.75 g oxygen and 4.50 g sulfur
Find: mass oxygen per g S for each compound and then determine the mass ratio of oxygen

$$\frac{\text{mass of oxygen in sulfur dioxide}}{\text{mass of sulfur in sulfur dioxide}} \quad \frac{\text{mass of oxygen in sulfur trioxide}}{\text{mass of sulfur in sulfur trioxide}} \quad \frac{\text{mass of oxyen in sulfur trioxide}}{\text{mass of oxyen in sulfur dioxide}}$$

Solution: $\text{sulfur dioxide} = \dfrac{3.49\text{ g oxygen}}{3.50\text{ g sulfur}} = \dfrac{0.997\text{ g oxygen}}{1\text{ g sulfur}} \quad \text{sulfur trioxide} = \dfrac{6.75\text{ g oxygen}}{4.50\text{ g sulfur}} = \dfrac{1.50\text{ g oxygen}}{1\text{ g sulfur}}$

$$\frac{1.50\text{ g oxygen in sulfur trioxide}}{0.997\text{ g oxygen in sulfur dioxide}} = \frac{1.50}{1} = \frac{3}{2}$$

Ratio is in small whole numbers and is consistent with multiple proportions.

Check: According to the law of multiple proportions, when two elements form two different compounds, the masses of element B that combine with 1 g of element A can be expressed as a ratio of small whole numbers.

2.38 **Given:** sulfur hexafluoride = 4.45 g fluorine and 1.25 g sulfur; sulfur tetrafluoride = 4.43 g fluorine and 1.87 g sulfur
Find: mass fluorine per g S for each compound and then determine the mass ratio of fluorine

$$\frac{\text{mass of fluorine in sulfur hexafluoride}}{\text{mass of sulfur in sulfur hexafluoride}} \quad \frac{\text{mass of fluorine in sulfur tetrafluoride}}{\text{mass of sulfur in sulfur tetrafluoride}} \quad \frac{\text{mass of oxyen in sulfur hexafluoride}}{\text{mass of oxyen in sulfur tetrafluoride}}$$

Solution:

$$\text{sulfur hexafluoride} = \frac{4.45\,\text{g fluorine}}{1.25\,\text{g sulfur}} = \frac{3.56\,\text{g fluorine}}{1\,\text{g sulfur}}$$

$$\text{sulfur tetrafluoride} = \frac{4.43\,\text{g fluorine}}{1.87\,\text{g sulfur}} = \frac{2.36\underline{9}\,\text{g fluorine}}{1\,\text{g sulfur}}$$

$$\frac{3.56\,\text{g fluorine in sulfur hexafluoride}}{2.3\underline{6}9\,\text{g fluorine in sulfur tetrafluoride}} = \frac{1.50}{1} = \frac{3}{2}$$

Ratio is in small whole numbers and is consistent with multiple proportions.

Check: According to the law of multiple proportions, when two elements form two different compounds, the masses of element B that combine with 1 g of element A can be expressed as a ratio of small whole numbers.

Atomic Theory, Nuclear Theory, and Subatomic Particles

2.39 (a) Sulfur and oxygen atoms have the same mass. INCONSISTENT with Dalton's atomic theory because only atoms of the same element have the same mass.

(b) All cobalt atoms are identical. CONSISTENT with Dalton's atomic theory because all atoms of a given element have the same mass and other properties that distinguish them from atoms of other elements.

(c) Potassium and chlorine atoms combine in a 1:1 ratio to form potassium chloride. CONSISTENT with Dalton's atomic theory because atoms combine in simple, whole-number ratios to form compounds.

(d) Lead atoms can be converted into gold. INCONSISTENT with Dalton's atomic theory because atoms of one element cannot change into atoms of another element.

2.40 (a) All carbon atoms are identical. CONSISTENT with Dalton's atomic theory because all atoms of a given element have the same mass and other properties that distinguish them from atoms of other elements.

(b) An oxygen atom combines with 1.5 hydrogen atoms to form a water molecule. INCONSISTENT with Dalton's atomic theory because atoms combine in simple, whole-number ratios to form compounds. An oxygen atom actually combines with 2 hydrogen atoms to form a water molecule.

(c) Two oxygen atoms combine with a carbon atom to form a carbon dioxide molecule. CONSISTENT with Dalton's atomic theory because atoms combine in simple, whole-number ratios to form compounds.

(d) The formation of a compound often involves the destruction of one or more atoms. INCONSISTENT with Dalton's atomic theory. Atoms change the way that they are bound together with other atoms when they form a new substance, but are neither created nor destroyed.

2.41 (a) The volume of an atom is mostly empty space. CONSISTENT with Rutherford's nuclear theory because most of the volume of the atom is empty space, throughout which tiny, negatively-charged electrons are dispersed.

(b) The nucleus of an atom is small compared to the size of the atom. CONSISTENT with Rutherford's nuclear theory because most of the atom's mass and all of its positive charge are contained in a small core called the nucleus.

(c) Neutral lithium atoms contain more neutrons than protons. INCONSISTENT with Rutherford's nuclear theory because it did not distinguish where the mass of the nucleus came from other than from the protons.

d) Neutral lithium atoms contain more protons than electrons. INCONSISTENT with Rutherford's nuclear theory because there are as many negatively charged particles outside the nucleus as there are positively charged particles within the nucleus.

2.42 (a) Since electrons are smaller than protons, and since a hydrogen atom contains only one proton and one electron, it must follow that the volume of a hydrogen atom is mostly due to the proton.

INCONSISTENT with Rutherford's nuclear theory because most of the volume of the atom is empty space, throughout which tiny, negatively charged electrons are dispersed.

(b) A nitrogen atom has seven protons in its nucleus and seven electrons outside of its nucleus. CONSISTENT with Rutherford's nuclear theory because there are as many negatively charged particles outside the nucleus as there are positively charged particles within the nucleus.

(c) A phosphorus atom has 15 protons in its nucleus and 150 electrons outside of its nucleus. INCONSISTENT with Rutherford's nuclear theory because there are as many negatively charged particles outside the nucleus as there are positively charged particles within the nucleus.

(d) The majority of the mass of a fluorine atom is due to its nine electrons. INCONSISTENT with Rutherford's nuclear theory because most of the atom's mass and all of its positive charge are contained in a small core called the nucleus.

2.43 **Given:** drop A = -6.9×10^{-19} C; drop B = -9.2×10^{-19}C; drop C = -11.5×10^{-19}C; drop D = -4.6×10^{-19} C
Find: The charge on a single electron
Conceptual Plan: determine the ratio of charge for each set of drops

$$\frac{\text{charge on drop 1}}{\text{charge on drop 2}}$$

Solution: $\dfrac{-6.9 \times 10^{-19}\text{C drop A}}{-4.6 \times 10^{-19}\text{ C drop D}} = 1.5 \quad \dfrac{-9.2 \times 10^{-19}\text{C drop B}}{-4.6 \times 10^{-19}\text{ C drop D}} = 2 \quad \dfrac{-11.5 \times 10^{-19}\text{C drop C}}{-4.6 \times 10^{-19}\text{ C drop D}} = 2.5$

The ratios obtained are not whole numbers, but can be converted to whole numbers by multiplying by 2.
Therefore, the charge on the electron has to be 1/2 the smallest value experimentally obtained. The charge on the electron = -2.3×10^{-19}C.
Check: The units of the answer (Coulombs) are correct. The magnitude of the answer is reasonable since all the values experimentally obtained are integer multiples of -2.3×10^{-19}.

2.44 **Given:** drop A = -4.8×10^{-9}z; drop B = -9.6×10^{-9}z; drop C = -6.4×10^{-9}z; drop D = -12.8×10^{-9} z
Find: The charge on a single electron
Conceptual Plan: determine the ratio of charge for each set of drops, determine the charge on an electron,

$$\frac{\text{charge on drop 1}}{\text{charge on drop 2}}$$

and then determine the number of electrons in each drop

$$\frac{\text{charge on drop}}{\text{charge on one electron}}$$

Solution: $\dfrac{-9.6 \times 10^{-9}\text{z drop B}}{-4.8 \times 10^{-9}\text{ z drop A}} = 2 \quad \dfrac{-6.4 \times 10^{-9}\text{z drop C}}{-4.8 \times 10^{-9}\text{ z drop A}} = 1.33 \quad \dfrac{-12.8 \times 10^{-9}\text{z drop B}}{-4.8 \times 10^{-9}\text{ z drop A}} = 2.66$

The ratios obtained are not all whole numbers, but can be converted to whole numbers by multiplying by 3. Therefore, the charge on the electron has to be 1/3 the smallest value experimentally obtained. The charge on the electron = $\dfrac{1}{3} \times -4.8 \times 10^{-9}\text{ z} = -1.6 \times 10^{-9}$ z.

Number of electrons in

Drop A: $\dfrac{-4.8 \times 10^{-9}\text{ z}}{-1.6 \times 10^{-9}\text{ z}} = 3$ electrons Drop B: $\dfrac{-9.6 \times 10^{-9}\text{ z}}{-1.6 \times 10^{-9}\text{ z}} = 6$ electrons

Drop C: $\dfrac{-6.4 \times 10^{-9}\text{ z}}{-1.6 \times 10^{-9}\text{ z}} = 4$ electrons Drop D: $\dfrac{-12.8 \times 10^{-9}\text{ z}}{-1.6 \times 10^{-9}\text{ z}} = 8$ electrons

Check: The units of the answer (zorg) are correct. The magnitude of the answer is reasonable since all the values experimentally obtained are integer multiples of -1.6×10^{-9}.

2.45 **Given:** charge on body = $-15\ \mu$C **Find:** number of electrons, mass of the electrons
Conceptual Plan: μC → C → number of electrons → mass of electrons

$$\frac{1\text{ C}}{10^6\,\mu\text{C}} \quad \frac{1\text{ electron}}{-1.60 \times 10^{-19}\text{C}} \quad \frac{9.10 \times 10^{-28}\text{ g}}{1\text{ electron}}$$

Solution: $-15\ \mu C \times \frac{1\ C}{10^6\ \mu C} \times \frac{1\ \text{electron}}{-1.60 \times 10^{-19}\ C} = 9.375 \times 10^{13}\ \text{electrons} = 9.4 \times 10^{13}\ \text{electrons}$

$9.375 \times 10^{13}\ \text{electrons} \times \frac{9.10 \times 10^{-28}\ g}{1\ \text{electron}} = 8.5 \times 10^{-14}\ g$

Check: The units of the answers (number of electrons and grams) are correct. The magnitude of the answers is reasonable since the charge on an electron and the mass of an electron are very small.

2.46 **Given:** charge = – 1.0 C **Find:** number of electrons, mass of the electrons
Conceptual Plan: C → number of electrons → mass of electrons

$\frac{1\ \text{electron}}{-1.60 \times 10^{-19} C}$ $\frac{9.10 \times 10^{-28}\ g}{1\ \text{electron}}$

Solution: $-1.0\ C \times \frac{1\ \text{electron}}{-1.60 \times 10^{-19}\ C} = 6.25 \times 10^{18}\ \text{electrons} = 6.3 \times 10^{18}\ \text{electrons}$

$6.25 \times 10^{18}\ \text{electrons} \times \frac{9.10 \times 10^{-28}\ g}{1\ \text{electron}} = 5.7 \times 10^{-9}\ g$

Check: The units of the answers (number of electrons and grams) are correct. The magnitude of the answers are reasonable since the charge on an electron and the mass of an electron are very small.

2.47 (a) True: Protons and electrons have equal and opposite charges.

(b) True: Protons and electrons have opposite charge so they will attract each other.

(c) True: The mass of the electron is much less than the mass of the neutron.

(d) False: The mass of the proton and the mass of the neutron are about the same.

2.48 (a) True: Protons and electrons have equal and opposite charges.

(b) True: The mass of the proton and the mass of the neutron are about the same.

(c) False: All atoms contain protons. The lightest element, hydrogen, contains 1 proton.

(d) False: Protons have a positive charge, while neutrons are neutral.

2.49 **Given:** mass of proton **Find:** number of electron in equal mass
Conceptual Plan: mass of protons → number of electrons

$\frac{1.67262 \times 10^{-27}\ kg}{1\ \text{proton}}$ $\frac{1\ \text{electron}}{9.10938 \times 10^{-31}\ kg}$

Solution: $1.67262 \times 10^{-27}\ kg \times \frac{1\ \text{electron}}{9.10938 \times 10^{-31}\ kg} = 1.83615 \times 10^{3}\ \text{electrons}$

Check: The units of the answer (electrons) are correct. The magnitude of the answer is reasonable since the mass of the electron is much less than the mass of the proton.

2.50 **Given:** helium nucleus **Find:** number of electrons in equal mass
Conceptual Plan:
 # protons → mass of protons and # neutrons → mass of neutrons → total mass → number of electrons

$\frac{1.67262 \times 10^{-27}\ kg}{1\ \text{proton}}$ $\frac{1.67493 \times 10^{-27}\ kg}{1\ \text{neutron}}$ mass protons + mass neutrons $\frac{1\ \text{electron}}{0.00091 \times 10^{-27}\ kg}$

Solution: $2\ \text{protons} \times \frac{1.67262 \times 10^{-27}\ kg}{\text{proton}} = 3.34524 \times 10^{-27}\ kg$

$2\ \text{neutrons} \times \frac{1.67493 \times 10^{-27}\ kg}{\text{neutron}} = 3.34986 \times 10^{-27}\ kg$

$(3.34524 \times 10^{-27}\ kg + 3.34986 \times 10^{-27}\ kg) \times \frac{1\ \text{electron}}{9.10938 \times 10^{-31}\ kg} = 7.34968 \times 10^{3}\ \text{electrons}$

Check: The units of the answer (electrons) are correct. The magnitude of the answer is reasonable since the mass of the electrons is much less than the mass of the proton and neutron.

Isotope and Ions

2.51 For each of the isotopes determine Z (the number of protons) from the periodic table and determine A (protons + neutrons). Then, write the symbol in the form $^{A}_{Z}X$.

(a) The copper isotope with 34 neutrons: Z = 29; A = 29 + 34 = 63; $^{63}_{29}Cu$

(b) The copper isotope with 36 neutrons: Z = 29; A = 29 + 36 = 65; $^{65}_{29}Cu$

(c) The potassium isotope with 21 neutrons: Z = 19; A = 19 + 21 = 40; $^{40}_{19}K$

(d) The argon isotope with 22 neutrons: Z = 18; A = 18 + 22 = 40; $^{40}_{18}Ar$

2.52 For each of the isotopes determine Z (the number of protons) from the periodic table and determine A (protons + neutrons). Then, write the symbol in the form X-A.

(a) The silver isotope with 60 neutrons: Z = 47; A = 47 + 60 = 107; Ag-107

(b) The silver isotope with 62 neutrons: Z = 47; A = 47 + 62 = 109; Ag-109

(c) The uranium isotope with 146 neutrons: Z = 92; A = 92 + 146 = 238; U-238

(d) The hydrogen isotope with 1 neutrons: Z = 1: A = 1 + 1 = 2; H-2

2.53 (a) $^{14}_{7}N$: Z = 7 ; A = 14; protons = Z = 7; neutrons = A – Z = 14 – 7 = 7

(b) $^{23}_{11}Na$: Z = 11; A = 23; protons = Z = 11; neutrons = A – Z = 23 – 11 = 12

(c) $^{222}_{86}Rn$: Z = 86; A = 222; protons = Z = 86; neutrons = A – Z = 222 – 86 = 136

(d) $^{208}_{82}Pb$: Z = 82; A = 208; protons = Z = 82; neutrons = A – Z = 208 – 82 = 126

2.54 (a) $^{40}_{19}K$: Z = 19; A = 40; protons = Z = 19; neutrons = A – Z = 40 – 19 = 21

(b) $^{226}_{88}Ra$: Z = 88; A = 226; protons = Z = 88; neutrons = A – Z = 226 – 88 = 138

(c) $^{99}_{43}Tc$: Z = 43; A = 99; protons = Z = 43; neutrons = A – Z = 99 – 43 = 56

(d) $^{33}_{15}P$: Z = 15; A = 33; protons = Z = 15; neutrons = A – Z = 33 – 15 = 18

2.55 Carbon – 14: A = 14, Z = 6: $^{14}_{6}C$ # protons = Z = 6 # neutrons = A – Z = 14 – 6 = 8

2.56 Uranium – 235: A = 235, Z = 92: $^{235}_{92}U$ # protons = Z = 92 # neutrons = A – Z = 235 – 92 = 143

2.57 In a neutral atom the number of protons = the number of electrons = Z. For an ion, electrons are lost (cations) or gained (anions)

(a) Ni^{2+}: Z = 28 = protons; Z – 2 = 26 = electrons

(b) S^{2-}: Z = 16 = protons; Z + 2 = 18 = electrons

(c) Br^{-} : Z = 35 = protons; Z + 1 = 36 = electrons

(d) Cr^{3+}: Z = 24 = protons; Z – 3 = 21 = electrons

2.58 In a neutral atom the number of protons = the number of electrons = Z. For an ion, electrons are lost (cations) or gained (anions)

(a) Al^{3+}: Z = 13 = protons; Z – 3 = 10 = electrons

(b) Se^{2-}: Z = 34 = protons; Z + 2 = 36 = electrons

(c) Ga^{3+}: Z = 31 = protons; Z – 3 = 28 = electrons

(d) Sr^{2+}: Z = 38 = protons; Z – 2 = 36 = electrons

2.59 Main group metal atoms will lose electrons to form a cation with the same number of electrons as the nearest, previous noble gas.

Nonmetal atoms will gain electrons to form an anion with the same number of electrons as the nearest noble gas.

(a) O^{2-} O is a nonmetal and has 8 electrons. It will gain electrons to form an anion. The nearest noble gas is neon with 10 electrons, so O will gain 2 electrons.

(b) K^{+} K is a main group metal and has 19 electrons. It will lose electrons to form a cation. The nearest noble gas is argon with 18 electrons, so K will lose 1 electron.

(c) Al^{3+} Al is a main group metal and has 13 electrons. It will lose electrons to form a cation. The nearest noble gas is neon with 10 electrons, so Al will lose 3 electrons.

(d) Rb^{+} Rb is a main group metal and has 37 electrons. It will lose electrons to form a cation. The nearest noble gas is krypton with 36 electrons, so Rb will lose 1 electron.

2.60 Main group metal atoms will lose electrons to form a cation with the same number of electrons as the nearest, previous noble gas.

Nonmetal atoms will gain electrons to form an anion with the same number of electrons as the nearest noble gas.

(a) Mg^{2+} Mg is a main group metal and has 12 electrons. It will lose electrons to form a cation. The nearest noble gas is neon with 10 electrons, so Mg will lose 2 electrons.

(b) N^{3-} N is a nonmetal and has 7 electrons. It will gain electrons to form an anion. The nearest noble gas is neon with 10 electrons, so N will gain 3 electrons.

(c) F^{-} F is a nonmetal and has 9 electrons. It will gain electrons to form an anion. The nearest noble gas is neon with 10 electrons, so F will gain 1 electron.

(d) Na^{+} Na is a main group metal and has 11 electrons. It will lose electrons to form a cation. The nearest noble gas is neon with 10 electrons, so Na will lose 1 electron.

2.61 Main group metal atoms will lose electrons to form a cation with the same number of electrons as the nearest, previous noble gas. Atoms in period 4 and higher lose electrons to form the same ion as the element at the top of the group.

Nonmetal atoms will gain electrons to form an anion with the same number of electrons as the nearest noble gas.

Symbol	Ion Formed	Number of Electrons in Ion	Number of Protons in Ion
Ca	Ca^{2+}	**18**	**20**
Be	Be^{2+}	2	**4**
Se	Se^{2-}	**36**	34
In	In^{3+}	**46**	49

2.62 Main group metal atoms will lose electrons to form a cation with the same number of electrons as the nearest, previous noble gas.

Nonmetal atoms will gain electrons to form an anion with the same number of electrons as the nearest noble gas.

Symbol	Ion Formed	Number of Electrons in Ion	Number of Protons in Ion
Cl	Cl^{-}	18	17
Te	Te^{2-}	54	52
Br	Br^{-}	36	35
Sr	Sr^{2+}	36	38

The Periodic Table and Atomic Mass

2.63	(a)	K	Potassium is a metal
	(b)	Ba	Barium is a metal
	(c)	I	Iodine is a nonmetal
	(d)	O	Oxygen is a nonmetal
	(e)	Sb	Antimony is a metalloid
2.64	(a)	gold	Au is a metal
	(b)	fluorine	F is a nonmetal
	(c)	sodium	Na is a metal
	(d)	tin	Sn is a metal
	(e)	argon	Ar is a nonmetal
2.65	(a)	tellurium	Te is in group 6A and is a main group element
	(b)	potassium	K is in group 1A and is a main group element
	(c)	vanadium	V is in group 5B and is a transition element
	(d)	manganese	Mn is in group 7B and is a transition element
2.66	(a)	Cr	Chromium is in group 6B and is a transition element
	(b)	Br	Bromine is in group 7A and is a main group element
	(c)	Mo	Molybdenum is in group 6B and is a transition element
	(d)	Cs	Cesium is in group 1A and is a main group element
2.67	(a)	sodium	Na is in group 1A and is an alkali metal
	(b)	iodine	I is in group 7A and is a halogen
	(c)	calcium	Ca is in group 2A and is an alkaline earth metal
	(d)	barium	Ba is in group 2A and is an alkaline earth metal
	(e)	krypton	Kr is in group 8A and is a noble gas
2.68	(a)	F	Fluorine is in group 7A and is a halogen
	(b)	Sr	Strontium is in group 2A and is an alkaline earth metal
	(c)	K	Potassium is in group 1A and is an alkali metal
	(d)	Ne	Neon is in group 8A and is a noble gas
	(e)	At	Astatine is in group 7A and is a halogen

2.69 (a) N and Ni would not be similar. Nitrogen is a nonmetal, nickel is a metal.

(b) Mo and Sn would not be most similar. Although both are metals, molybdenum is a transition metal and tin is a main group metal.

(c) Na and Mg would not be similar. Although both are main group metals, sodium is in group 1A and magnesium is in group 2A.

(d) Cl and F would be most similar. Chlorine and fluorine are both in group 7A. Elements in the same group have similar chemical properties.

(e) Si and P would not be most similar. Silicon is a metalloid and phosphorus is a nonmetal.

2.70 (a) Nitrogen and oxygen would not be most similar. Although both are nonmetals, N is in group 5A and O is in group 6A.

(b) Titanium and gallium would not be most similar. Although both are metals, Ti is a transition metal and Ga is a main group metal.

(c) Lithium and sodium would be most similar. Li and Na are both in group 1A. Elements in the same group have similar chemical properties.

(d) Germanium and arsenic would not be the most similar. Ge and As are both metalloids and would share some properties, but Ge is in group 4A and As is in group 5A.

(e) Argon and bromine would not be most similar. Although both are nonmetals, Ar is in group 8A and Br is in group 7A.

2.71 **Given:** Ga-69; mass = 68.92558 amu; 60.108%: Ga-71; mass = 70.92470 amu; 39.892 % **Find:** atomic mass Ga
Conceptual Plan: % abundance → fraction and then find atomic mass

$$\frac{\%\text{abundance}}{100} \qquad \text{Atomic mass} = \sum_n (\text{fraction of isotope n}) \times (\text{mass of isotope n})$$

Solution: Fraction Ga-69 $= \frac{60.108}{100} = 0.60108$ Fraction Ga-71 $= \frac{39.892}{100} = 0.39892$

$$\text{Atomic mass} = \sum_n (\text{fraction of isotope n}) \times (\text{mass of isotope n})$$

$$= 0.60108(68.92588 \text{ amu}) + 0.39892(70.92470 \text{ amu}) = 69.723 \text{ amu}$$

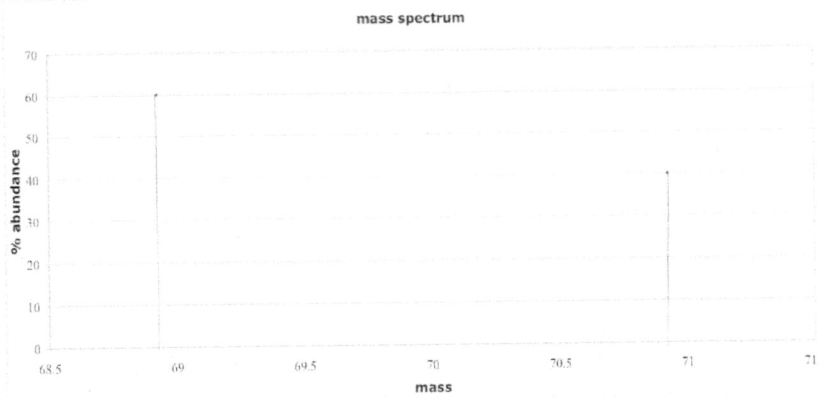

Check: Units of the answer (amu) are correct. The magnitude of the answer is reasonable because it lies between 68.92588 amu and 70.92470 amu and is closer to 68.92588, which has the higher % abundance. The mass spectrum is reasonable because it has two mass lines corresponding to the two isotopes and the line at 68.92588 is about 1.5 times larger than the line at 70.92470.

2.72 **Given:** Mg-24: mass = 23.9850 amu; 78.99%: Mg-25; mass = 24.9858 amu; 10.00%: Mg-26: mass = 25.9826 amu; 11.01%
Find: atomic mass Mg
Conceptual Plan: % abundance → fraction and then find atomic mass

$$\frac{\%\text{abundance}}{100} \qquad \text{Atomic mass} = \sum_n (\text{fraction of isotope n}) \times (\text{mass of isotope n})$$

Solution: Fraction Mg-24 $= \frac{78.99}{100} = 0.7899$ Fraction Mg-25 $= \frac{10.00}{100} = 0.1000$

Fraction Mg-26 $= \frac{11.01}{100} = 0.1101$

$$\text{Atomic mass} = \sum_n (\text{fraction of isotope n}) \times (\text{mass of isotope n})$$

$$= 0.7899(23.9850 \text{ amu}) + 0.1000(24.9858 \text{ amu}) + 0.1101(25.9826 \text{ amu}) = 24.31 \text{ amu}$$

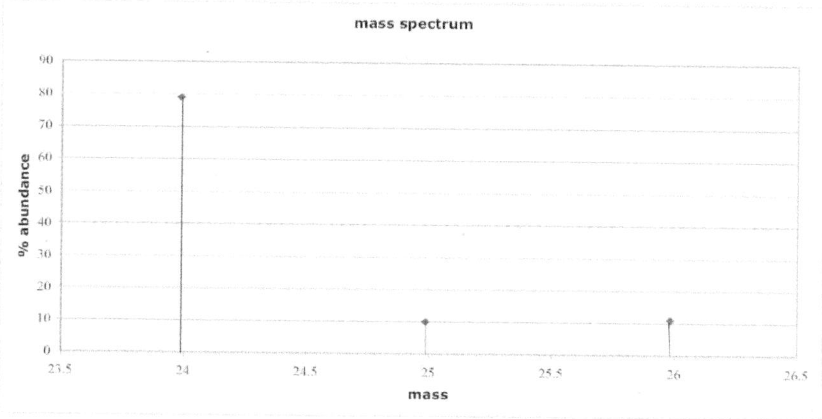

Check: The units of the answer (amu) are correct. The magnitude of the answer is reasonable because it lies between 23.9850 amu and 25.9826 amu and is closer to 23.9850, which has the highest % abundance. The mass spectrum is reasonable because it has three mass lines corresponding to the three isotopes and the line at 23.9850 is about eight times larger than the other two lines.

2.73 Fluorine has an isotope F-19 with a very large abundance so that the mass of fluorine is very close to the mass of the isotope and the line in the mass spectrum reflects the abundance of F-19. Chlorine has two isotopes Cl-35 and Cl-37 and the mass of 35.45 amu is the weighted average of these two isotopes, so there is no line at 35.45 amu.

2.74 Copper would have no isotope with a mass of 63.546 amu. Since the mass of the isotope comes primarily from the sum of the protons and neutrons, the mass of the isotope has to have a value close to a whole number. Copper must be composed of two or more isotopes, one with a mass less than 63.546 amu and one with a mass greater than 63.546 amu.

2.75 **Given:** Isotope – 1 mass = 120.9038 amu, 57.4%. Isotope – 2 mass = 122.9042 amu.
Find: atomic mass of the element and identify the element
Conceptual Plan:
% abundance Isotope 2 → and then % abundance → fraction and then find atomic mass

$$100\% - \%\text{abundance Isotope 1} \qquad \frac{\%\text{abundance}}{100} \qquad \text{Atomic mass} = \sum_n (\text{fraction of isotope n}) \times (\text{mass of isotope n})$$

Solution: 100.0% – 57.4 % Isotope 1 = 42.6 % Isotope 2

$$\text{Fraction Isotope 1} = \frac{57.4}{100} = 0.574 \qquad \text{Fraction Isotope 2} = \frac{42.6}{100} = 0.426$$

$$\text{Atomic mass} = \sum_n (\text{fraction of isotope n}) \times (\text{mass of isotope n})$$

$$= 0.574(120.9038 \text{ amu}) + 0.426(122.9042 \text{ amu}) = 121.8 \text{ amu}$$

From the periodic table Sb has a mass of 121.757 amu, so it is the closest mass and the element is antimony.
Check: The units of the answer (amu) are correct. The magnitude of the answer is reasonable because it lies between 120.9038 and 122.9042 and is slightly less than halfway between the two values because the lower value has a slightly greater abundance.

2.76 **Given:** Isotope – 1 mass = 135.90714 amu, 50.19%; Isotope – 2 mass = 137.90599 amu, 0.25%; Isotope – 3 mass = 139.90543 amu, 88.43%; Isotope – 4, mass = 141.90924, 11.13%.
Find: atomic mass of the element and identify the element
Conceptual Plan: % abundance → fraction and then find atomic mass

$$\frac{\%\text{abundance}}{100} \qquad \text{Atomic mass} = \sum_n (\text{fraction of isotope n}) \times (\text{mass of isotope n})$$

Solution: Fraction Isotope 1 $= \frac{0.19}{100} = 0.0019$ Fraction Isotope 2 $= \frac{0.25}{100} = 0.0025$

Fraction Isotope 3 $= \frac{88.43}{100} = 0.8843$ Fraction Isotope 4 $= \frac{11.13}{100} = 0.1113$

$$\text{Atomic mass} = \sum_n (\text{fraction of isotope n}) \times (\text{mass of isotope n})$$

$= 0.0019(135.90714 \text{ amu}) + 0.0025(137.90599 \text{ amu}) + 0.8843(139.90543 \text{ amu}) + 0.1113(141.90924 \text{ amu})$

$= 140.1 \text{ amu}$

From the periodic table Ce has a mass of 140.12 amu, so it is the closest mass and the element is cerium.
Check: The units of the answer (amu) are correct. The magnitude of the answer is reasonable because it lies between 135.90714 and 141.90924 and is closer to the higher value because Isotopes 3 and 4 make up most of the mass of the element with a combined abundance of 99.56%.

2.77 **Given:** Br-81; mass = 80.9163 amu; 49.31 %: atomic mass Br = 79.904 amu **Find:** mass and abundance
Conceptual Plan: % abundance Br-79 → then % abundance → fraction → mass Br-79

$100\% - \%\text{Br-81}$ $\frac{\%\text{abundance}}{100}$ $\text{Atomic mass} = \sum_n (\text{fraction of isotope n}) \times (\text{mass of isotope n})$

Solution: 100.00% – 49.31 % = 50.69%

Fraction Br-79 $= \frac{50.69}{100} = 0.5069$ Fraction Br-81 $= \frac{49.31}{100} = 0.4931$

Let X be the mass of Br-79

$$\text{Atomic mass} = \sum_n (\text{fraction of isotope n}) \times (\text{mass of isotope n})$$

$79.904 \text{ amu} = 0.5069(\text{X amu}) + 0.4931(80.9163 \text{ amu})$

$\text{X} = 78.92 \text{ amu} = \text{mass Br-79}$

Check: The units of the answer (amu) are correct. The magnitude of the answer is reasonable because it is less than the mass of the atom and the second isotope (Br-81) has a mass greater than the mass of the atom.

2.78 **Given:** Si-28; mass = 27.9769 amu; 92.2%: Si-29; mass = 28.9765 amu; 4.67%: atomic mass Si = 28.09 amu
Find: mass and abundance Si-30
Conceptual Plan: % abundance Si-30 → then % abundance → fraction → mass Si-30

$100\% - \%\text{Si-30}$ $\frac{\%\text{abundance}}{100}$ $\text{Atomic mass} = \sum_n (\text{fraction of isotope n}) \times (\text{mass of isotope n})$

Solution: 100.00% – 92.2 % – 4.67% = 3.1% Si-30

Fraction Si-28 $= \frac{92.2}{100} = 0.922$ Fraction Si-29 $= \frac{4.67}{100} = 0.0467$ Fraction Si-30 $= \frac{3.1}{100} = 0.031$

Let X be the mass of Si-30

$$\text{Atomic mass} = \sum_n (\text{fraction of isotope n}) \times (\text{mass of isotope n})$$

$28.09 \text{ amu} = 0.922(27.9769 \text{ amu}) + 0.0467(28.9765 \text{ amu}) + 0.031(\text{X})$

$\text{X} = 30 \text{ amu} = \text{mass Si-30}$

Check: The units of the answer (amu) are correct. The magnitude of the answer is reasonable because it is greater than the mass of the second isotope (Si-29), which has a mass greater than the mass of the atom.

The Mole Concept

2.79 **Given:** 3.8 mol sulfur **Find:** atoms of sulfur
Conceptual Plan: mol S → atoms S

$\frac{6.022 \times 10^{23} \text{ atoms}}{\text{mol}}$

Solution: $3.8 \text{ ~~mol S~~} \times \frac{6.022 \times 10^{23} \text{ atoms S}}{\text{~~mol S~~}} = 2.3 \times 10^{24} \text{ atoms S}$

Check: The units of the answer (atoms S) are correct. The magnitude of the answer is reasonable since there is more than 1 mole of material present.

2.80 **Given:** 5.8×10^{24} aluminum atoms **Find:** mol Al

Conceptual Plan: atoms Al $\rightarrow$ mol Al

$$\frac{1\,\text{mol}}{6.022 \times 10^{23}\,\text{atoms}}$$

Solution: $5.8 \times 10^{24}\,\cancel{\text{atoms Al}} \times \dfrac{1\text{ mol Al}}{6.022 \times 10^{23}\,\cancel{\text{atoms Al}}} = 9.6\text{ mol Al}$

Check: The units of the answer (mol Al) are correct. The magnitude of the answer is reasonable since there is greater than Avogadros number of atoms present.

2.81 (a) **Given:** 11.8 g Ar **Find:** mol Ar

Conceptual Plan: g Ar $\rightarrow$ mol Ar

$$\frac{1\,\text{mol Ar}}{39.95\,\text{g Ar}}$$

Solution: $11.8\,\cancel{\text{g Ar}} \times \dfrac{1\text{ mol Ar}}{39.95\,\cancel{\text{g Ar}}} = 0.295\text{ mol Ar}$

Check: The units of the answer (mol Ar) are correct. The magnitude of the answer is reasonable since there is less than the mass of 1 mol present.

(b) **Given:** 3.55 g Zn **Find:** mol Zn

Conceptual Plan: g Zn $\rightarrow$ mol Zn

$$\frac{1\,\text{mol Zn}}{65.41\,\text{g Zn}}$$

Solution: $3.55\,\cancel{\text{g Zn}} \times \dfrac{1\text{ mol Zn}}{65.41\,\cancel{\text{g Zn}}} = 0.0543\text{ mol Zn}$

Check: The units of the answer (mol Zn) are correct. The magnitude of the answer is reasonable since there is less than the mass of 1 mol present.

(c) **Given:** 26.1 g Ta **Find:** mol Ta

Conceptual Plan: g Ta $\rightarrow$ mol Ta

$$\frac{1\,\text{mol Ta}}{180.95\,\text{g Ta}}$$

Solution: $26.1\,\cancel{\text{g Ta}} \times \dfrac{1\text{ mol Ta}}{180.95\,\cancel{\text{g Ta}}} = 0.144\text{ mol Ta}$

Check: The units of the answer (mol Ta) are correct. The magnitude of the answer is reasonable since there is less than the mass of 1 mol present.

(d) **Given:** 0.211 g Li **Find:** mol Li

Conceptual Plan: g Li $\rightarrow$ mol Li

$$\frac{1\,\text{mol Li}}{6.941\,\text{g Li}}$$

Solution: $0.211\,\cancel{\text{g Li}} \times \dfrac{1\text{ mol Li}}{6.941\,\cancel{\text{g Li}}} = 0.0304\text{ mol Li}$

Check: The units of the answer (mol Li) are correct. The magnitude of the answer is reasonable since there is less than the mass of 1 mol present.

2.82 (a) **Given:** 2.3×10^{-3} mol Sb **Find:** grams Sb

Conceptual Plan: mol Sb $\rightarrow$ g Sb

$$\frac{121.76\text{ g Sb}}{1\,\text{mol Sb}}$$

Solution: $2.3 \times 10^{-3}\,\cancel{\text{mol Sb}} \times \dfrac{121.76\text{ g Sb}}{1\,\cancel{\text{mol Sb}}} = 0.28\text{ grams Sb}$

Check: The units of the answer (grams Sb) are correct. The magnitude of the answer is reasonable since there is less than 1 mol of Sb present.

(b) **Given:** 0.0355 mol Ba **Find:** grams Ba

Conceptual Plan: mol Ba $\rightarrow$ g Ba

$$\frac{137.33\text{ g Ba}}{1\,\text{mol Ba}}$$

Solution: $0.0355\,\cancel{\text{mol Ba}} \times \dfrac{137.33\text{ g Ba}}{1\,\cancel{\text{mol Ba}}} = 4.88\text{ grams Ba}$

Check: The units of the answer (grams Ba) are correct. The magnitude of the answer is reasonable since there is less than 1 mol of Ba present.

(c) **Given:** 43.9 mol Xe **Find:** grams Xe
Conceptual Plan: mol Xe → g Xe

$$\frac{131.29 \text{ g Xe}}{1 \text{ mol Xe}}$$

Solution: $43.9 \cancel{\text{mol Xe}} \times \frac{131.29 \text{ g Xe}}{1 \cancel{\text{mol Xe}}} = 5.76 \times 10^3$ grams Xe

Check: The units of the answer (grams Xe) are correct. The magnitude of the answer is reasonable since there is much more than 1 mol of Xe present.

(d) **Given:** 1.3 mol W **Find:** grams W
Conceptual Plan: mol W → g W

$$\frac{183.84 \text{ g W}}{1 \text{ mol W}}$$

Solution: $1.3 \cancel{\text{mol W}} \times \frac{183.84 \text{ g W}}{1 \cancel{\text{mol W}}} = 2.4 \times 10^2$ grams W

Check: The units of the answer (grams W) are correct. The magnitude of the answer is reasonable since there is slightly over 1 mol of W present.

2.83 **Given:** 3.78 g silver **Find:** atoms Ag
Conceptual Plan: g Ag → mol Ag → atoms Ag

$$\frac{1 \text{ mol Ag}}{107.87 \text{ g Ag}} \qquad \frac{6.022 \times 10^{23} \text{ atoms}}{\text{mol}}$$

Solution: $3.78 \cancel{\text{g Ag}} \times \frac{1 \cancel{\text{mol Ag}}}{107.87 \cancel{\text{g Ag}}} \times \frac{6.022 \times 10^{23} \text{ atoms Ag}}{1 \cancel{\text{mol Ag}}} = 2.11 \times 10^{22}$ atoms Ag

Check: The units of the answer (atoms Ag) are correct. The magnitude of the answer is reasonable since there is less than the mass of 1 mol of Ag present.

2.84 **Given:** 4.91×10^{21} Pt atoms **Find:** g Pt
Conceptual Plan: atoms Pt → mol Pt → g Pt

$$\frac{1 \text{ mol}}{6.022 \times 10^{23} \text{ atoms}} \qquad \frac{195.08 \text{ g Pt}}{1 \text{ mol Pt}}$$

Solution: $4.91 \times 10^{21} \cancel{\text{atoms Pt}} \times \frac{1 \cancel{\text{mol Pt}}}{6.022 \times 10^{23} \cancel{\text{atoms Pt}}} \times \frac{195.08 \text{ g Pt}}{1 \cancel{\text{mol Pt}}} = 1.59$ g Pt

Check: The units of the answer (g Pt) are correct. The magnitude of the answer is reasonable since there is less than 1 mol of Pt atoms present.

2.85 (a) **Given:** 5.18 g P **Find:** atoms P
Conceptual Plan: g P → mol P → atoms P

$$\frac{1 \text{ mol P}}{30.97 \text{ g P}} \qquad \frac{6.022 \times 10^{23} \text{ atoms}}{\text{mol}}$$

Solution: $5.18 \cancel{\text{g P}} \times \frac{1 \cancel{\text{mol P}}}{30.97 \cancel{\text{g P}}} \times \frac{6.022 \times 10^{23} \text{ atoms P}}{1 \cancel{\text{mol P}}} = 1.01 \times 10^{23}$ atoms P

Check: The units of the answer (atoms P) are correct. The magnitude of the answer is reasonable since there is less than the mass of 1 mol of P present.

(b) **Given:** 2.26 g Hg **Find:** atoms Hg
Conceptual Plan: g Hg → mol Hg → atoms Hg

$$\frac{1 \text{ mol Hg}}{200.59 \text{ g Hg}} \qquad \frac{6.022 \times 10^{23} \text{ atoms}}{\text{mol}}$$

Solution: $2.26 \cancel{\text{g Hg}} \times \frac{1 \cancel{\text{mol Hg}}}{200.59 \cancel{\text{g Hg}}} \times \frac{6.022 \times 10^{23} \text{ atoms Hg}}{1 \cancel{\text{mol Hg}}} = 6.78 \times 10^{21}$ atoms Hg

Check: The units of the answer (atoms Hg) are correct. The magnitude of the answer is reasonable since there is much less than the mass of 1 mol of Hg present.

(c) **Given:** 1.87 g Bi **Find:** atoms Bi

Conceptual Plan: g Bi → mol Bi → atoms Bi

$$\frac{1\text{ mol Bi}}{208.98\text{ g Bi}} \quad \frac{6.022\times10^{23}\text{ atoms}}{\text{mol}}$$

Solution: $1.87\ \cancel{\text{g Bi}} \times \frac{1\ \cancel{\text{mol Bi}}}{208.98\ \cancel{\text{g Bi}}} \times \frac{6.022\times10^{23}\text{ atoms Bi}}{1\ \cancel{\text{mol Bi}}} = 5.39\times10^{21}\text{ atoms Bi}$

Check: The units of the answer (atoms Bi) are correct. The magnitude of the answer is reasonable since there is less than the mass of 1 mol of Bi present.

(d) **Given:** 0.082 g Sr **Find:** atoms Sr

Conceptual Plan: g Sr → mol Sr → atoms Sr

$$\frac{1\text{ mol Sr}}{87.62\text{ g Sr}} \quad \frac{6.022\times10^{23}\text{ atoms}}{\text{mol}}$$

Solution: $0.082\ \cancel{\text{g Sr}} \times \frac{1\ \cancel{\text{mol Sr}}}{87.62\ \cancel{\text{g Sr}}} \times \frac{6.022\times10^{23}\text{ atoms Sr}}{1\ \cancel{\text{mol Sr}}} = 5.6\times10^{20}\text{ atoms Sr}$

Check: The units of the answer (atoms Sr) are correct. The magnitude of the answer is reasonable since there is less than the mass of 1 mol of Sr present.

2.86 (a) **Given:** 14.955 g Cr **Find:** atoms Cr

Conceptual Plan: g Cr → mol Cr → atoms Cr

$$\frac{1\text{ mol Cr}}{52.00\text{ g Cr}} \quad \frac{6.022\times10^{23}\text{ atoms}}{\text{mol}}$$

Solution: $14.955\ \cancel{\text{g Cr}} \times \frac{1\ \cancel{\text{mol Cr}}}{52.00\ \cancel{\text{g Cr}}} \times \frac{6.022\times10^{23}\text{ atoms Cr}}{1\ \cancel{\text{mol Cr}}} = 1.732\times10^{23}\text{ atoms Cr}$

Check: The units of the answer (atoms Cr) are correct. The magnitude of the answer is reasonable since there is less than the mass of 1 mol of Cr present.

(b) **Given:** 39.733 g S **Find:** atoms S

Conceptual Plan: g S → mol S → atoms S

$$\frac{1\text{ mol S}}{32.07\text{ g S}} \quad \frac{6.022\times10^{23}\text{ atoms}}{\text{mol}}$$

Solution: $39.733\ \cancel{\text{g S}} \times \frac{1\ \cancel{\text{mol S}}}{32.07\ \cancel{\text{g S}}} \times \frac{6.022\times10^{23}\text{ atoms S}}{1\ \cancel{\text{mol S}}} = 7.461\times10^{23}\text{ atoms S}$

Check: The units of the answer (atoms S) are correct. The magnitude of the answer is reasonable since there is slightly more than the mass of 1 mol of S present.

(c) **Given:** 12.899 g Pt **Find:** atoms Pt

Conceptual Plan: g Pt → mol Pt → atoms Pt

$$\frac{1\text{ mol Pt}}{195.08\text{ g Pt}} \quad \frac{6.0221\times10^{23}\text{ atoms}}{\text{mol}}$$

Solution: $12.899\ \cancel{\text{g Pt}} \times \frac{1\ \cancel{\text{mol Pt}}}{195.08\ \cancel{\text{g Pt}}} \times \frac{6.0221\times10^{23}\text{ atoms Pt}}{1\ \cancel{\text{mol Pt}}} = 3.9819\times10^{22}\text{ atoms Pt}$

Check: The units of the answer (atoms Pt) are correct. The magnitude of the answer is reasonable since there is less than the mass of 1 mol of Pt present.

(d) **Given:** 97.552 g Sn **Find:** atoms Sn

Conceptual Plan: g Sn → mol Sn → atoms Sn

$$\frac{1\text{ mol Sn}}{118.71\text{ g Sn}} \quad \frac{6.0221\times10^{23}\text{ atoms}}{\text{mol}}$$

Solution: $97.552\ \cancel{\text{g Sn}} \times \frac{1\ \cancel{\text{mol Sn}}}{118.71\ \cancel{\text{g Sn}}} \times \frac{6.0221\times10^{23}\text{ atoms Sn}}{1\ \cancel{\text{mol Sn}}} = 4.948\times10^{23}\text{ atoms Sn}$

Check: The units of the answer (atoms Sn) are correct. The magnitude of the answer is reasonable since there is slightly less than the mass of 1 mol of Sn present.

2.87 (a) **Given:** 1.1×10^{23} gold atoms **Find:** grams Au

Conceptual Plan: atoms Au → mol Au → g Au

$$\frac{1\text{ mol}}{6.022\times10^{23}\text{ atoms}} \quad \frac{196.97\text{ g Au}}{1\text{ mol Au}}$$

Solution: $1.1\times10^{23}\ \cancel{\text{atoms Au}} \times \frac{1\ \cancel{\text{mol Au}}}{6.022\times10^{23}\ \cancel{\text{atoms Au}}} \times \frac{196.97\text{ g Au}}{1\ \cancel{\text{mol Au}}} = 36\text{ g Au}$

Check: The units of the answer (g Au) are correct. The magnitude of the answer is reasonable since there are fewer than Avogadro's number of atoms in the sample.

(b) **Given:** 2.82×10^{22} helium atoms **Find:** grams He
Conceptual Plan: atoms He → mol He → g He

$$\frac{1\text{ mol}}{6.022\times10^{23}\text{ atoms}} \qquad \frac{4.002\text{ g He}}{1\text{ mol He}}$$

Solution: $2.82 \times 10^{22}\ \cancel{\text{atoms He}} \times \dfrac{1\ \cancel{\text{mol He}}}{6.022 \times 10^{23}\ \cancel{\text{atoms He}}} \times \dfrac{4.002\text{ g He}}{1\ \cancel{\text{mol He}}} = 0.187\text{ g He}$

Check: The units of the answer (g He) are correct. The magnitude of the answer is reasonable since there are fewer than Avogadro's number of atoms in the sample.

(c) **Given:** 1.8×10^{23} lead atoms **Find:** grams Pb
Conceptual Plan: atoms Pb → mol Pb → g Pb

$$\frac{1\text{ mol}}{6.022\times10^{23}\text{ atoms}} \qquad \frac{207.2\text{ g Pb}}{1\text{ mol Pb}}$$

Solution: $1.8 \times 10^{23}\ \cancel{\text{atoms Pb}} \times \dfrac{1\ \cancel{\text{mol Pb}}}{6.022 \times 10^{23}\ \cancel{\text{atoms Pb}}} \times \dfrac{207.2\text{ g Pb}}{1\ \cancel{\text{mol Pb}}} = 62\text{ g Pb}$

Check: The units of the answer (g Pb) are correct. The magnitude of the answer is reasonable since there are fewer than Avogadro's number of atoms in the sample.

(d) **Given:** 7.9×10^{21} uranium atoms **Find:** grams U
Conceptual Plan: atoms U → mol U → g U

$$\frac{1\text{ mol}}{6.022\times10^{23}\text{ atoms}} \qquad \frac{238.029\text{ g U}}{1\text{ mol U}}$$

Solution: $7.9 \times 10^{21}\ \cancel{\text{atoms U}} \times \dfrac{1\ \cancel{\text{mol U}}}{6.022 \times 10^{23}\ \cancel{\text{atoms U}}} \times \dfrac{238.029\text{ g U}}{1\ \cancel{\text{mol U}}} = 3.1\text{ g U}$

Check: The units of the answer (g U) are correct. The magnitude of the answer is reasonable since there are fewer than Avogadro's number of atoms in the sample.

2.88 (a) **Given:** 7.55×10^{26} cadmium atoms **Find:** kg Cd
Conceptual Plan: atoms Cd → mol Cd → g Cd → kg Cd

$$\frac{1\text{ mol}}{6.022\times10^{23}\text{ atoms}} \qquad \frac{112.41\text{ g Cd}}{1\text{ mol Cd}} \qquad \frac{1\text{ kg}}{1000\text{ g}}$$

Solution:

$7.55 \times 10^{26}\ \cancel{\text{atoms Cd}} \times \dfrac{1\ \cancel{\text{mol Cd}}}{6.022 \times 10^{23}\ \cancel{\text{atoms Cd}}} \times \dfrac{112.41\text{ g Cd}}{1\ \cancel{\text{mol Cd}}} \times \dfrac{1\text{ kg Cd}}{1000\ \cancel{\text{g Cd}}} = 141\text{ kg Cd}$

Check: The units of the answer (kg Cd) are correct. The magnitude of the answer is reasonable since there are many more than Avogadro's number of atoms in the sample.

(b) **Given:** 8.15×10^{27} nickel atoms **Find:** kg Ni
Conceptual Plan: atoms Ni → mol Ni → g Ni → kg Ni

$$\frac{1\text{ mol}}{6.022\times10^{23}\text{ atoms}} \qquad \frac{58.69\text{ g Ni}}{1\text{ mol Ni}} \qquad \frac{1\text{ kg}}{1000\text{ g}}$$

Solution:

$8.15 \times 10^{27}\ \cancel{\text{atoms Ni}} \times \dfrac{1\ \cancel{\text{mol Ni}}}{6.022 \times 10^{23}\ \cancel{\text{atoms Ni}}} \times \dfrac{58.69\text{ g Ni}}{1\ \cancel{\text{mol Ni}}} \times \dfrac{1\text{ kg Ni}}{1000\ \cancel{\text{g Ni}}} = 794\text{ kg Ni}$

Check: The units of the answer (kg Ni) are correct. The magnitude of the answer is reasonable since there are many more than Avogadro's number of atoms in the sample.

(c) **Given:** 1.22×10^{27} manganese atoms **Find:** kg Mn
Conceptual Plan: atoms Mn → mol Mn → g Mn → kg Mn

$$\frac{1\text{ mol}}{6.022\times10^{23}\text{ atoms}} \qquad \frac{54.94\text{ g Mn}}{1\text{ mol Mn}} \qquad \frac{1\text{ kg}}{1000\text{ g}}$$

Solution:

$1.22 \times 10^{27}\ \cancel{\text{atoms Mn}} \times \dfrac{1\ \cancel{\text{mol Mn}}}{6.022 \times 10^{23}\ \cancel{\text{atoms Mn}}} \times \dfrac{54.94\text{ g Mn}}{1\ \cancel{\text{mol Mn}}} \times \dfrac{1\text{ kg Mn}}{1000\ \cancel{\text{g Mn}}} = 111\text{ kg Mn}$

Check: The units of the answer (kg Mn) are correct. The magnitude of the answer is reasonable since there are many more than Avogadro's number of atoms in the sample.

(d) **Given:** 5.48×10^{29} lithium atoms **Find:** kg Li
Conceptual Plan: atoms Li → mol Li → g Li → kg Li

$$\frac{1\text{ mol}}{6.022 \times 10^{23}\text{ atoms}} \quad \frac{6.941\text{ g Li}}{1\text{ mol Li}} \quad \frac{1\text{ kg}}{1000\text{ g}}$$

Solution: $5.48 \times 10^{29}\ \cancel{\text{atoms Li}} \times \frac{1\ \cancel{\text{mol Li}}}{6.022 \times 10^{23}\ \cancel{\text{atoms Li}}} \times \frac{6.941\text{ g Li}}{1\ \cancel{\text{mol Li}}} \times \frac{1\text{ kg Li}}{1000\ \cancel{\text{g Li}}} = 6.32 \times 10^{3}\text{ kg Li}$

Check: The units of the answer (kg Li) are correct. The magnitude of the answer is reasonable since there are many more than Avogadro's number of atoms in the sample.

2.89 **Given:** 52 mg diamond (carbon) **Find:** atoms C
Conceptual Plan: mg C → g C → mol C → atoms C

$$\frac{1\text{ g C}}{1000\text{ mg C}} \quad \frac{1\text{ mol C}}{12.011\text{ g C}} \quad \frac{6.022 \times 10^{23}\text{ atoms}}{\text{mol}}$$

Solution: $52\ \cancel{\text{mg C}} \times \frac{1\ \cancel{\text{g C}}}{1000\ \cancel{\text{mg C}}} \times \frac{1\ \cancel{\text{mol C}}}{12.011\ \cancel{\text{g C}}} \times \frac{6.022 \times 10^{23}\text{ atoms C}}{1\ \cancel{\text{mol C}}} = 2.6 \times 10^{21}\text{ atoms C}$

Check: The units of the answer (atoms C) are correct. The magnitude of the answer is reasonable since there is less than the mass of 1 mol of C present.

2.90 **Given:** 536 kg helium **Find:** atoms He
Conceptual Plan: kg He → g He → mol He → atoms He

$$\frac{1000\text{ g He}}{1\text{ kg He}} \quad \frac{1\text{ mol He}}{4.0026\text{ g He}} \quad \frac{6.022 \times 10^{23}\text{ atoms}}{\text{mol}}$$

Solution: $536\ \cancel{\text{kg He}} \times \frac{1000\ \cancel{\text{g He}}}{1\ \cancel{\text{kg He}}} \times \frac{1\ \cancel{\text{mol He}}}{4.0026\ \cancel{\text{g He}}} \times \frac{6.022 \times 10^{23}\text{ atoms He}}{1\ \cancel{\text{mol He}}} = 8.06 \times 10^{28}\text{ atoms He}$

Check: The units of the answer (atoms He) are correct. The magnitude of the answer is reasonable since there is much more than the mass of 1 mol of He present.

2.91 **Given:** 1 atom platinum **Find:** g Pt
Conceptual Plan: atoms Pt → mol Pt → g Pt

$$\frac{1\text{ mol}}{6.022 \times 10^{23}\text{ atoms}} \quad \frac{195.08\text{ g Pt}}{1\text{ mol Pt}}$$

Solution: $1\ \cancel{\text{atom Pt}} \times \frac{1\ \cancel{\text{mol Pt}}}{6.022 \times 10^{23}\ \cancel{\text{atoms Pt}}} \times \frac{195.08\text{ g Pt}}{1\ \cancel{\text{mol Pt}}} = 3.239 \times 10^{-22}\text{ g Pt}$

Check: The units of the answer (g Pt) are correct. The magnitude of the answer is reasonable since there is only 1 atom in the sample.

2.92 **Given:** 35 atoms xenon **Find:** g Xe
Conceptual Plan: atoms Xe → mol Xe → g Xe

$$\frac{1\text{ mol}}{6.022 \times 10^{23}\text{ atoms}} \quad \frac{131.29\text{ g Xe}}{1\text{ mol Xe}}$$

Solution: $35\ \cancel{\text{atom Xe}} \times \frac{1\ \cancel{\text{mol Xe}}}{6.022 \times 10^{23}\ \cancel{\text{atoms Xe}}} \times \frac{131.29\text{ g Xe}}{1\ \cancel{\text{mol Xe}}} = 7.631 \times 10^{-21}\text{ g Xe}$

Check: The units of the answer (g Xe) are correct. The magnitude of the answer is reasonable since there are only 35 atoms in the sample.

Cumulative Problems

2.93 **Given:** 7.83 g HCN sample 1: 0.290 g H; 4.06 g N. 3.37 g HCN sample 2 **Find:** g C in sample 2
Conceptual Plan: g HCN sample 1 → g C in HCN sample 1 → ratio g C to g HCN → g C in HCN sample 2

$$\text{g HCN} - \text{g H} - \text{g N} \qquad \frac{\text{g C}}{\text{g HCN}} \qquad \text{g HCN} \times \frac{\text{g C}}{\text{g HCN}}$$

Solution: 7.83 g HCN − 0.290 g H − 4.06 g N = 3.48 g C

$$3.37\ \cancel{\text{g HCN}} \times \frac{3.48\ \text{g C}}{7.83\ \cancel{\text{g HCN}}} = 1.50\ \text{g C}$$

Check: The units of the answer (g C) are correct. The magnitude of the answer is reasonable since the sample size is about half the original sample size, the g C are about half the original g C.

2.94 (a) **Given:** mass ratio S:O = 1.0:1.0 in SO_2 **Find:** mass ratio S:O in SO_3

Conceptual Plan: determine the ratio of O:O in SO_3 and SO_2 then determine g O per g S in SO_3

Solution: For a fixed amount of S, the ratio of O is $\frac{3\ \text{O}}{2\ \text{O}} = 1.5$. So, for 1 gram S, SO_3 would have 1.5 g O. The mass ratio of S:O = 1.0:1.5, that is 2.0:3.0, in SO_3.

Check: The answer is reasonable since the ratio is smaller than the ratio for SO_2 and SO_3 has to contain more O per gram of S.

(b) **Given:** mass ratio S:O = 1.0:1.0 in SO_2 **Find:** mass ratio S:O in S_2O

Conceptual Plan: determine the ratio of S:S in S_2O and SO_2 then determine g O per g S in S_2O

Solution: For a fixed amount of O, the ratio of S is $\frac{2\ \text{S}}{0.5\ \text{S}} = 4.0$. So, for 1 gram O, S_2O would have 4 gram S. The mass ratio of S:O = 4.0:1.0 in S_2O.

Check: The answer is reasonable since the ratio is larger than the ratio for SO_2 and S_2O has to contain more S per gram of O.

2.95 **Given:** In CO mass ratio O:C = 1.33:1; in compound X, mass ratio O:C = 2:1. **Find:** formula of X

Conceptual Plan: determine the mass ratio of O:O in the two compounds

Solution: For 1 gram of C $\frac{2\ \text{g O in compound X}}{1.33\ \text{g O in CO}} = 1.5$

So, the ratio of O to C in compound X has to be 1.5:1 and the formula is C_2O_3.

Check: The answer is reasonable since it fulfills the criteria of multiple proportions and the mass ratio of O:C is 2:1.

2.96 **Given:** mass ratio 1 atom N:1 atom ^{12}C = 7:6; mass ratio 2 mol N:1 mol O in N_2O = 7:4

Find: mass of 1 mol O

Conceptual Plan: determine the mass ratio of O to ^{12}C from the mass ratio of N to ^{12}C and the mass ratio of N to O and then determine the mol ratio of ^{12}C to O; then use the mass of 1 mol ^{12}C to determine mass 1 mol O

$$\frac{12.00\ \text{g}\ ^{12}\text{C}}{1\ \text{mol}\ ^{12}\text{C}}$$

Solution: From the mass ratios, for every 7 grams N there are 6 grams ^{12}C and for every 7 grams N there are 4 grams O. So, the mass ratio of O^{12}, C is 4:6.

$$\frac{1\ \cancel{\text{atom}\ ^{12}\text{C}}}{1\ \cancel{\text{atom N}}} \times \frac{6.022 \times 10^{23}\ \cancel{\text{atom N}}}{1\ \cancel{\text{mol N}}} \times \frac{1\ \text{mol}\ ^{12}\text{C}}{6.022 \times 10^{23}\ \cancel{\text{atom}\ ^{12}\text{C}}} \times \frac{2\ \cancel{\text{mol N}}}{1\ \text{mol O}} = \frac{2\ \text{mol}\ ^{12}\text{C}}{1\ \text{mol O}}$$

$$\frac{2\ \cancel{\text{mol}\ ^{12}\text{C}}}{1\ \text{mol O}} \times \frac{12.00\ \cancel{\text{g}\ ^{12}\text{C}}}{1\ \cancel{\text{mol}\ ^{12}\text{C}}} \times \frac{4\ \text{g O}}{6\ \cancel{\text{g}\ ^{12}\text{C}}} = 16.00\ \text{g O/ mol O}$$

Check: The units of the answer (g O/mol O) are correct. The magnitude of the answer is reasonable since it is close to the value on the periodic table.

2.97 **Given:** $^4He^{2+}$ = 4.00151 amu **Find:** charge to mass ratio C/kg

Conceptual Plan: determine total charge on $^4He^{2+}$ and then amu $^4He^{2+}$ → g $^4He^{2+}$ → kg $^4He^{2+}$

$$\frac{+\ 1.60218 \times 10^{-19}\text{C}}{\text{proton}} \qquad \frac{1\ \text{g}}{1.66054 \times 10^{-24}\ \text{amu}} \qquad \frac{1\ \text{kg}}{1000\ \text{g}}$$

Solution:

$$\frac{2\ \cancel{\text{protons}}}{1\ \text{atom}\ ^4\text{He}^{2+}} \times \frac{+\ 1.60218 \times 10^{-19}\ \text{C}}{\cancel{\text{proton}}} = \frac{3.20436 \times 10^{-19}\ \text{C}}{\text{atom}\ ^4\text{He}^{2+}}$$

$$\frac{4.00151\ \cancel{\text{amu}}}{1\ \text{atom}\ ^4\text{He}^{2+}} \times \frac{1.66054 \times 10^{-24}\ \cancel{\text{g}}}{1\ \cancel{\text{amu}}} \times \frac{1\ \text{kg}}{1000\ \cancel{\text{g}}} = \frac{6.64466742 \times 10^{-27}\ \text{kg}}{1\ \text{atom}\ ^4\text{He}^{2+}}$$

$$\frac{3.20436 \times 10^{-19}\ \text{C}}{\cancel{\text{atom}\ ^4\text{He}^{2+}}} \times \frac{1\ \cancel{\text{atom}\ ^4\text{He}^{2+}}}{6.64466742 \times 10^{-27}\ \text{kg}} = 4.82245 \times 10^{7}\ \text{C/kg}$$

Check: The units of the answer (C/kg) are correct. The magnitude of the answer is reasonable when compared to the charge to mass ratio of the electron.

2.98 **Given:** 12.3849 g sample I; atomic mass I = 126.9045 amu; 1.00070g ^{129}I; mass ^{129}I = 128.9050 amu
Find: mass of contaminated sample
Conceptual Plan: total mass of sample → fraction I and ^{129}I in the sample → apparent "atomic mass"

$$\text{mass I} + \text{mass } ^{129}\text{I} \qquad \frac{\text{g I}}{\text{g sample}}, \frac{\text{g } ^{129}\text{I}}{\text{g sample}} \qquad \text{Atomic mass} = \sum_n (\text{fraction of isotope n}) \times (\text{mass of isotope n})$$

Solution: 12.3849 g I + 1.00070 g ^{129}I = 13.3856 g sample

$$\frac{12.3849\text{ g}}{13.3856\text{ g}} = 0.925240557 \text{ fraction I} \qquad \frac{1.00070\text{ g}}{13.3856\text{ g}} = 0.07475944 \text{ fraction } ^{129}\text{I}$$

$$\begin{aligned}\text{Atomic mass} &= \sum_n (\text{fraction of isotope n}) \times (\text{mass of isotope n}) \\ &= (0.925240557)(126.9045\text{ amu}) + (0.07475944)(128.9050\text{ amu}) \\ &= 127.055\text{ amu}\end{aligned}$$

Check: The units of the answer (amu) are correct. The magnitude of the answer is reasonable because it is between 126.9045 and 128.9050 and only slightly higher than the naturally occurring value.

2.99 $^{236}_{90}$Th A – Z = number of neutrons. 236 – 90 = 146 neutrons. So, any nucleus with 146 neutrons is an isotone of $^{236}_{90}$Th.

Some would be $^{238}_{92}$U; $^{239}_{93}$Np; $^{241}_{95}$Am; $^{237}_{91}$Pa; $^{235}_{89}$Ac; $^{244}_{98}$Cf etc.

2.100

Symbol	Z	A	Number protons	Number electrons	Number neutrons	Charge
Si	14	**28**	**14**	14	14	**0**
S^{2-}	**16**	32	**16**	**18**	**16**	2 –
Cu^{2+}	**29**	**63**	**29**	**27**	34	2+
P	15	**31**	**15**	15	16	**0**

2.101

Symbol	Z	A	Number protons	Number electrons	Number neutrons	Charge
O^{2-}	8	**16**	**8**	**10**	8	2 –
Ca^{2+}	20	**40**	**20**	**18**	20	**2+**
Mg^{2++}	**12**	25	**12**	**10**	13	**2+**
N^{3-}	7	14	7	10	**7**	**3 –**

2.102 **Given:** r (neutron) = 1.0 x 10^{-13}cm; r(star piece) = 0.10 mm **Find:** density of neutron, mass (kg) of star piece
Conceptual Plan: r (neutron) → vol (neutron) → density (neutron) and then r (star piece) → vol (star piece) → mass (star piece)

$$V = \frac{4}{3}\pi r^3 \qquad d = \frac{m}{V} \qquad V = \frac{4}{3}\pi r^3 \qquad m = dv$$

Solution:

For the neutron:

$$\text{Vol(neutron)} = \frac{4}{3}\pi(1.0\text{x}10^{-13}\text{cm})^3 = 4.19\text{x}10^{-39}\text{cm}^3 \qquad d = \frac{1.00727\,\cancel{\text{amu}}}{4.19\text{x}10^{-39}\text{cm}^3}\text{x}\frac{1.661\text{x}10^{-24}\text{g}}{\cancel{\text{amu}}} = 3.99\text{x}10^{14}\text{g/cm}^3$$

For the star piece:

$$\text{Vol(star piece)} = \frac{4}{3}\pi(0.10\,\cancel{\text{mm}})^3 \frac{(1\,\text{cm})^3}{(10\,\cancel{\text{mm}})^3} = 4.19 \times 10^{-4}\,\text{cm}^3 \qquad m = 4.19 \times 10^{-4}\,\cancel{\text{cm}^3} \times \frac{3.99 \times 10^{14}\,\cancel{\text{g}}}{\cancel{\text{cm}^3}} \times \frac{1\,\text{kg}}{1000\,\cancel{\text{g}}} = 1.7 \times 10^8\,\text{kg}$$

Check: The units of the answer (kg) are correct. The magnitude of the answer shows the great mass of the neutron star.

2.103 **Given:** r(nucleus) = 2.7 fm; r(atom) = 70 pm (assume two significant figures)
Find: vol(nucleus); vol(atom); % vol(nucleus)
Conceptual Plan:
r(nucleus)(fm) → r(nucleus)(pm) → vol(nucleus) and then r(atom) → vol(atom) and then % vol

$$\frac{10^{-15}\,\text{m}}{1\,\text{fm}}\ \frac{1\,\text{pm}}{10^{-12}\,\text{m}} \qquad V = \frac{4}{3}\pi r^3 \qquad V = \frac{4}{3}\pi r^3 \qquad \frac{\text{vol(nucleus)}}{\text{vol(atom)}} \times 100$$

Solution:

$$2.7\,\cancel{\text{fm}} \times \frac{10^{-15}\,\cancel{\text{m}}}{\cancel{\text{fm}}} \times \frac{1\,\text{pm}}{10^{-12}\,\cancel{\text{m}}} = 2.7 \times 10^{-3}\,\text{pm} \qquad V_{\text{nucleus}} = \frac{4}{3}\pi\,(2.7 \times 10^{-3}\,\text{pm})^3 = 8.2 \times 10^{-8}\,\text{pm}^3$$

$$V_{\text{atom}} = \frac{4}{3}\pi\,(70\,\text{pm})^3 = 1.4 \times 10^6\,\text{pm}^3 \qquad \frac{8.2 \times 10^{-8}\,\cancel{\text{pm}^3}}{1.4 \times 10^6\,\cancel{\text{pm}^3}} \times 100\% = 5.9 \times 10^{-12}\%$$

Check: The units of the answer (% vol) are correct. The magnitude of the answer is reasonable because the nucleus only occupies a very small % of the vol of the atom.

2.104 **Given:** 1 penny = 1.0 mm **Find:** height in km of Avogadro's number of pennies
Conceptual Plan: height of 1 penny → height of Avogadro's number of pennies

$$6.022 \times 10^{23}$$

Solution: $\frac{1.0\,\text{mm}}{\cancel{\text{penny}}} \times 6.022 \times 10^{23}\,\cancel{\text{pennies}} \times \frac{1\,\cancel{\text{m}}}{1000\,\cancel{\text{mm}}} \times \frac{1\,\text{km}}{1000\,\cancel{\text{m}}} = 6.0 \times 10^{17}\,\text{km}$

Check: The units of the answer (km) are correct. The magnitude of the answer shows just how large Avogadro's number is.

2.105 **Given:** 6.022×10^{23} pennies **Find:** the amount in dollars; the dollars/person
Conceptual Plan: pennies → dollars → dollars/person

$$\frac{1\,\text{dollar}}{100\,\text{pennies}} \qquad \text{6.5 billion people}$$

Solution:

$$6.022 \times 10^{23}\,\cancel{\text{pennies}} \times \frac{1\,\text{dollar}}{100\,\cancel{\text{pennies}}} = 6.022 \times 10^{21}\,\text{dollars} \qquad \frac{6.022 \times 10^{21}\,\text{dollars}}{6.5 \times 10^9\,\text{people}} = 9.3 \times 10^{11}\,\text{dollars/person}$$

They are billionaires.

2.106 **Given:** 1 mol blueberries, m = 0.75 g; m(automobile) = 2.0×10^3 kg **Find:** number of autos for 1 mol blueberries
Conceptual Plan:
mol blueberries → mass blueberries (g) → mass blueberries (kg) → number of automobiles

$$\frac{0.75\,\text{g}}{\text{blueberry}} \qquad \frac{\text{kg}}{1000\,\text{g}} \qquad \frac{1\,\text{automobile}}{2.0 \times 10^3\,\text{kg}}$$

Solution:

$$1\,\cancel{\text{mol blueberries}} \times \frac{6.022 \times 10^{23}\,\cancel{\text{blueberries}}}{\cancel{\text{mol blueberries}}} \times \frac{0.75\,\cancel{\text{g}}}{\cancel{\text{blueberry}}} \times \frac{1\,\cancel{\text{kg}}}{1000\,\cancel{\text{g}}} \times \frac{1\,\text{automobile}}{2.0 \times 10^3\,\cancel{\text{kg}}} = 2.3 \times 10^{17}\,\text{automobiles}$$

Check: The units of the answer (automobiles) are correct. The magnitude of the answer is reasonable because Avogadro's number is so large.

2.107 **Given:** O = 16.00 amu when C = 12.01 amu **Find:** mass O when C = 12.000 amu
Conceptual Plan: determine ratio O:C for ^{12}C system then use the same ratio when C = 12.00

$$\frac{\text{mass O}}{\text{mass C}}$$

Solution: Based on $^{12}C = 12.00$, O = 15.9994 and C = 12.011 so, $\frac{\text{mass O}}{\text{mass C}} = \frac{16.00\text{ amu}}{12.01\text{ amu}} = \frac{1.3322\text{ amu O}}{1\text{ amu C}}$

Based on C = 12.00, the ratio has to be the same,

$$12.000\ \cancel{\text{amu C}} \times \frac{1.3322\text{ amu O}}{1\ \cancel{\text{amu C}}} = 15.986\text{ amu O} = 15.99\text{ amu O}$$

Check: The units of the answer (amu O) are correct. The magnitude of the answer is reasonable because the value for the new mass basis is smaller then the original mass basis, therefore, the mass of O should be less.

2.108 **Given:** Ti cube: d = 4.50 g/cm^3; e = 2.78 in **Find:** number Ti atoms

Conceptual Plan: e in inch → e in cm → vol cube → g Ti → mol Ti → atoms Ti

$\frac{2.54\text{ cm}}{1\text{ inch}}$ $V = e^3$ $\frac{4.50\text{ g}}{\text{cm}^3}$ $\frac{1\text{ mol Ti}}{47.87\text{ g}}$ $\frac{6.022 \times 10^{23}\text{ atoms}}{\text{mol}}$

Solution: $2.78\ \cancel{\text{in}} \times \frac{2.54\text{ cm}}{\cancel{\text{in}}} = 7.061\text{ cm}$

$$(7.061\ \cancel{\text{cm}})^3 \times \frac{4.50\ \cancel{\text{g}}}{\cancel{\text{cm}^3}} \times \frac{1\ \cancel{\text{mol Ti}}}{47.87\ \cancel{\text{g}}} \times \frac{6.022 \times 10^{23}\text{ atoms Ti}}{1\ \cancel{\text{mol Ti}}} = 1.99 \times 10^{25}\text{ atoms Ti}$$

Check: The units of the answer (atoms Ti) are correct. The magnitude of the answer is reasonable because there is about 30 mol of Ti in the cube.

2.109 **Given:** Cu sphere: r = 0.935 in; d = 8.96 g/cm^3 **Find:** number of Cu atoms

Conceptual Plan: r in inch → r in cm → vol sphere → g Cu → mol Cu → atoms Cu

$\frac{2.54\text{ cm}}{1\text{ inch}}$ $V = \frac{4}{3}\pi r^3$ $\frac{8.96\text{ g}}{\text{cm}^3}$ $\frac{1\text{ mol Cu}}{63.546\text{ g}}$ $\frac{6.022 \times 10^{23}\text{ atoms}}{\text{mol}}$

Solution: $0.935\ \cancel{\text{in}} \times \frac{2.54\text{ cm}}{\cancel{\text{in}}} = 2.3749\text{ cm}$

$$\frac{4}{3}\pi(2.3749\ \cancel{\text{cm}})^3 \times \frac{8.96\ \cancel{\text{g}}}{\cancel{\text{cm}^3}} \times \frac{1\ \cancel{\text{mol Cu}}}{63.546\ \cancel{\text{g}}} \times \frac{6.022 \times 10^{23}\text{ atoms Cu}}{1\ \cancel{\text{mol Cu}}} = 4.76 \times 10^{24}\text{ atoms Cu}$$

Check: The units of the answer (atoms Cu) are correct. The magnitude of the answer is reasonable because there are about 8 mol Cu present.

2.110 **Given:** B-10 = 10.01294 amu; B-11 = 11.00931 amu; B = 10.81 amu **Find:** % abundance B-10 and B-11

Conceptual Plan: Let x = fraction B-10 then 1 – x = fraction B-11 → abundances

$\text{Atomic mass} = \sum_n (\text{fraction of isotope n}) \times (\text{mass of isotope n})$

Solution: $\text{Atomic mass} = \sum_n (\text{fraction of isotope n}) \times (\text{mass of isotope n})$

$10.81 = (x)(10.01294\text{ amu}) + (1 - x)(11.00931\text{ amu})$

$0.19931 = 0.99637\,x$

$x = 0.200 \quad 1 - x = 0.800$

B-10 = 0.200 x 100 = 20. % and B-11 = 0.800 x 100 = 80. %

Check: The units of the answer (%, which gives the relative abundance of each isotope) are correct. The relative abundances are reasonable because B has an atomic mass closer to the mass of B-11 than to B-10.

2.111 **Given:** Li-6 = 6.01512 amu; Li-7 = 7.01601 amu; B = 6.941 amu

Find: % abundance Li-6 and Li-7

Conceptual Plan: Let x = fraction Li-6 then 1 – x = fraction Li-7 → abundances

$\text{Atomic mass} = \sum_n (\text{fraction of isotope n}) \times (\text{mass of isotope n})$

Solution: $\text{Atomic mass} = \sum_n (\text{fraction of isotope n}) \times (\text{mass of isotope n})$

$6.941 = (x)(6.01512\text{ amu}) + (1 - x)(7.01601\text{ amu})$

$0.07501 = 1.00089\,x$

$x = 0.07494 \quad 1 - x = 0.92506$

Li-6 = 0.07494 x 100 = 7.494 % and Li-7 = 0.92506 x 100 = 92.506 %

Check: The units of the answer (%, which gives the relative abundance of each isotope) are correct. The relative abundances are reasonable because Li has an atomic mass closer to the mass of Li-7 than to Li-6.

2.112 **Given:** Brass: 37.0% Zn, d = 8.48g/cm^3, volume = 112.5 cm^3 **Find:** atoms of Zn and Cu
Conceptual Plan: Volume sample → g sample → g Zn → mole Zn → atoms Zn

$$\frac{8.48\,g}{cm^3} \quad \frac{37.0\,g\,Zn}{100.0\,g\,sample} \quad \frac{65.41\,g\,Zn}{mol\,Zn} \quad \frac{6.022 \times 10^{23}\,atoms}{mol}$$

→ g Cu → moles Cu → atoms Cu

$$g\,sample - g\,Zn \quad \frac{63.55\,g\,Cu}{mol\,Cu} \quad \frac{6.022 \times 10^{23}\,atoms}{mol}$$

Solution: $112.5\,\cancel{cm^3} \times \frac{8.48\,g}{\cancel{cm^3}} = 95\underline{4}.0\,g\,sample \qquad 95\underline{4}.0\,\cancel{g\,sample} \times \frac{37.0\,g\,Zn}{100.0\,\cancel{g\,sample}} = 35\underline{2}.98\,g\,Zn$

$$35\underline{2}.98\,\cancel{g\,Zn} \times \frac{1\,\cancel{mol\,Zn}}{65.41\,\cancel{g\,Zn}} \times \frac{6.022 \times 10^{23}\,atoms\,Zn}{\cancel{mol\,Zn}} = 3.2\underline{4}97 \times 10^{24}\,atoms\,Zn = 3.25 \times 10^{24}\,atoms\,Zn$$

$$95\underline{4}.0\,g\,sample - 35\underline{2}.98\,g\,Zn = 60\underline{1}.02\,g\,Cu$$

$$60\underline{1}.01\,\cancel{g\,Cu} \times \frac{1\,\cancel{mol\,Cu}}{63.55\,\cancel{g\,Cu}} \times \frac{6.022 \times 10^{23}\,atoms\,Cu}{\cancel{mol\,Cu}} = 5.6\underline{9}52 \times 10^{24}\,atoms\,Cu = 5.70 \times 10^{24}\,atoms\,Cu$$

Check: The units of the answer (atoms of Zn and atoms of Cu) are correct. The magnitude is reasonable since there is more than 1 mole of each element in the sample.

2.113 **Given:** Alloy of Au and Pd = 67.2 g; 2.49 x 10^{23} atoms **Find:** % composition by mass
Conceptual Plan: atoms Au and Pd → mol Au and Pd → g Au and Pd → g Au

$$\frac{1\,mol}{6.022 \times 10^{23}\,atoms} \quad \frac{196.97\,g\,Au}{1\,mol\,Au};\ \frac{106.42\,g\,Pd}{1\,mol\,Pd}$$

Solution: Let X = atoms Au and Y = atoms Pd, develop expressions that will permit atoms to be related to moles and then to grams.

$$(X\,\cancel{atoms\,Au})\left(\frac{1\,mol\,Au}{6.022 \times 10^{23}\,\cancel{atoms\,Au}}\right) = \frac{X}{6.022 \times 10^{23}}\,mol\,Au$$

$$(Y\,\cancel{atoms\,Pd})\left(\frac{1\,mol\,Pd}{6.022 \times 10^{23}\,\cancel{atoms\,Pd}}\right) = \frac{Y}{6.022 \times 10^{23}}\,mol\,Pd$$

X + Y = 2.49 x 10^{23} atoms; Y = 2.49 x 10^{23} - X

$$\left(\frac{X}{6.022 \times 10^{23}}\,\cancel{mol\,Au}\right)\left(\frac{196.97\,g\,Au}{\cancel{mol\,Au}}\right) = \frac{196.97X}{6.022 \times 10^{23}}\,g\,Au$$

$$\left(\frac{2.49 \times 10^{23} - X}{6.022 \times 10^{23}}\,\cancel{mol\,Pd}\right)\left(\frac{106.42\,g\,Pd}{\cancel{mol\,Pd}}\right) = \frac{106.42(2.49 \times 10^{23} - X)}{6.022 \times 10^{23}}\,g\,Pd$$

g Au + g Pd = 67.2 g total

$$\frac{196.97X}{6.022 \times 10^{23}}\,g\,Au + \frac{106.42(2.49 \times 10^{23} - X)}{6.022 \times 10^{23}}\,g\,Pd = 67.2\,g$$

X = 1.5$\underline{4}$26 x 10^{23} atoms Au

$$(1.54 \times 10^{23}\,\cancel{atoms\,Au})\left(\frac{1\,\cancel{mol\,Au}}{6.022 \times 10^{23}\,\cancel{atoms\,Au}}\right)\left(\frac{196.97\,g\,Au}{\cancel{mol\,Au}}\right) = 50.\underline{3}7\,g\,Au$$

$$\left(\frac{50.\underline{3}7\,g\,Au}{67.2\,g\,sample}\right) \times 100 = 74.\underline{9}5\%\,Au = 75.0\%\,Au$$

% Pd = 100.0% − 75.0% Au = 25.0% Pd
Check: Units of the answer (% composition) is correct.

2.114 **Given:** Cl-35, mass = 34.9688 amu, 75.76%; Cl-37, mass = 36.9659 amu, 24.24%; O-16, mass = 15.9949 amu, 99.57%; O-17, mass = 16.9991 amu, 0.038%; O-18, mass = 17.9991, 0.205%
Find: number of different masses of Cl_2O, the mass of the three most abundant

Conceptual Plan: Determine the different combinations of Cl and O. Use the % abundance to determine the most abundant. Determine the mass of the molecule.

Mass = $\sum$ mass of each isotpe

Solution: Possible combinations: $^{35}Cl^{35}Cl^{16}O$ $^{35}Cl^{35}Cl^{17}O$ $^{35}Cl^{35}Cl^{18}O$
$^{35}Cl^{37}Cl^{16}O$ $^{35}Cl^{37}Cl^{17}O$ $^{35}Cl^{37}Cl^{18}O$
$^{37}Cl^{37}Cl^{16}O$ $^{37}Cl^{37}Cl^{17}O$ $^{37}Cl^{37}Cl^{18}O$

So, there are nine possible combination and nine different masses of Cl_2O.
O-17 and O-18 are both less than 1% naturally occurring, so molecules containing these isotopes will not be very abundant, therefore, the three most abundant molecules will be the ones that contain O-16; $^{35}Cl^{35}Cl^{16}O$, $^{35}Cl^{37}Cl^{16}O$, $^{37}Cl^{37}Cl^{16}O$.

Mass $^{35}Cl^{35}Cl^{16}O$ = 34.9688 amu + 34.9688 amu + 15.9949 amu = 85.9325 amu
Mass $^{35}Cl^{37}Cl^{16}O$ = 34.9688 amu + 36.9659 amu + 15.9949 amu = 87.9296 amu
Mass $^{37}Cl^{37}Cl^{16}O$ = 36.9659 amu + 36.9659 amu + 15.9949 amu = 89.9267 amu

Check: The units of the answer (amu) are correct.

2.115 **Given:** Ag-107, 51.839%, Ag-109, $\frac{\text{mass Ag-109}}{\text{mass Ag-107}} = 1.0187$ **Find:** mass Ag-107

Conceptual Plan: % abundance Ag-107 → % abundance Ag-109 → fraction → mass Ag-107

$100\% - (\%\text{Ag-107})$ $\qquad \frac{\%\text{ abundance}}{100}$

$$\text{Atomic mass} = \sum_n (\text{fraction of isotope n}) \times (\text{mass of isotope n})$$

Solution: 100.00% – 51.839 % = 48.161% Ag – 109

$$\text{Fraction Ag-107} = \frac{51.839}{100.00} = 0.51839 \qquad \text{Fraction Ag-109} = \frac{48.161}{100.00} = 0.48161$$

Let X be the mass of Ag-107 then mass Ag-109 = 1.0187X

$$\text{Atomic mass} = \sum_n (\text{fraction of isotope n}) \times (\text{mass of isotope n})$$

$$107.87\text{ amu} = 0.51839(X\text{ amu}) + 0.48161(1.0187X\text{ amu})$$

$$X = 106.9\underline{0}7\text{ amu} = 106.91\text{ amu mass Ag-107}$$

Check: The units of the answer (amu) are correct. The answer is reasonable since it is close to the atomic mass number of Ag-107.

2.116 **Given:** Air contains 1.5 μg Pb/m^3; lung volume = 5.50L **Find:** atoms of Pb in lungs

Conceptual Plan: Lung in L → mL → cm^3 → m^3 → μg Pb → g Pb → mol Pb → atoms Pb

$\frac{1000\text{mL}}{\text{L}}$ $\frac{1\text{cm}^3}{\text{mL}}$ $\frac{1\text{m}^3}{(100\text{cm})^3}$ $\frac{1.5\mu\text{g Pb}}{\text{m}^3}$ $\frac{1\text{g Pb}}{10^6\mu\text{g Pb}}$ $\frac{1\text{ mol Pb}}{207.2\text{g Pb}}$ $\frac{6.022\times10^{23}\text{atoms Pb}}{1\text{mol Pb}}$

Solution: $5.50\cancel{\text{L}} \times \left(\frac{1000\cancel{\text{mL}}}{\cancel{\text{L}}}\right) \times \left(\frac{1\cancel{\text{cm}^3}}{1\cancel{\text{mL}}}\right) \times \left(\frac{1\cancel{\text{m}^3}}{(100\cancel{\text{cm}})^3}\right) \times \left(\frac{1.5\cancel{\mu\text{g Pb}}}{\cancel{\text{m}^3}}\right) \times \left(\frac{1\cancel{\text{g Pb}}}{10^6\cancel{\mu\text{g Pb}}}\right)$

$$\times \left(\frac{1\cancel{\text{mol Pb}}}{207.2\cancel{\text{g Pb}}}\right) \times \left(\frac{6.022\times10^{23}\text{atoms Pb}}{1\cancel{\text{mol Pb}}}\right) = 2.\underline{3}97 \times 10^{13}\text{atoms Pb} = 2.4 \times 10^{13}\text{atoms Pb}$$

Check: The units of the answer (atoms Pb) are correct. The magnitude of the answer is reasonable since there is about 400 nmol of Pb present.

2.117 **Given:** 0.255 ounce 18K Au **Find:** atoms Au

Conceptual Plan: Ounces 18K Au → ounces pure Au → g Au → mol Au → atoms Au

$\frac{75\text{ oz Au}}{100\text{ oz 18K Au}}$ $\frac{453.59\text{ g Au}}{16\text{ oz Au}}$ $\frac{1\text{ mol Au}}{196.97\text{ g Au}}$ $\frac{6.022\times10^{23}\text{atoms Au}}{1\text{ mol Au}}$

Solution: $0.255\cancel{\text{oz 18K Au}} \times \left(\frac{75\cancel{\text{oz pure Au}}}{100\cancel{\text{oz 18K Au}}}\right) \times \left(\frac{453.59\cancel{\text{g}}}{16\cancel{\text{oz}}}\right) \times \left(\frac{1\cancel{\text{mol Au}}}{196.97\cancel{\text{g Au}}}\right) \times \left(\frac{6.022\times10^{23}\text{atoms Au}}{1\cancel{\text{mol Au}}}\right)$

$$= 1.\underline{6}57 \times 10^{22}\text{atoms Au} = 1.7 \times 10^{22}\text{atoms Au}$$

Check: The units of the answer (atoms Au) are correct. The magnitude of the answer is reasonable since there is less than 1 mol of Au in the sample.

Challenge Problems

2.118   **Given:** 1 mol sand grains; cube edge (e) = 0.10 mm; area Texas = 268,601 sq mi **Find:** height of sand ft
          Conceptual Plan:
          mol sand $\rightarrow$ grains sand $\rightarrow$ vol sand mm^3 $\rightarrow$ vol sand ft^3 and then area Texas mi^2 $\rightarrow$ area ft^2

$$\frac{6.022 \times 10^{23}\,\text{grains}}{\text{mol}} \qquad V = e^3 \qquad mm^3 \times \left(\frac{cm}{10\,mm}\right)^3 \left(\frac{1\,in}{2.54\,cm}\right)^3 \left(\frac{1\,ft}{12\,in}\right)^3 \qquad \left(\frac{5280\,ft}{1\,mi}\right)^2$$

          and then $\rightarrow$ **height ft**

$$h = \frac{\text{Volume}}{\text{Area}}$$

          Solution:

$$1\;\cancel{\text{mol sand grains}} \times \frac{6.022 \times 10^{23}\;\cancel{\text{grains}}}{\cancel{\text{mol}}} \times \frac{(0.10\;\cancel{mm})^3}{\cancel{\text{grain}}} \times \left(\frac{\cancel{cm}}{10\;\cancel{mm}}\right)^3 \times \left(\frac{1\;\cancel{in}}{2.54\;\cancel{cm}}\right)^3 \times \left(\frac{1\,ft}{12\;\cancel{in}}\right)^3 = 2.1266 \times 10^{13}\,\text{ft}^3\,\text{sand}$$

$$\frac{2.1266 \times 10^{13}\,\text{ft}^3\,\text{sand}}{268,601\;\cancel{mi^2}} \times \left(\frac{1\;\cancel{mi}}{5280\;\cancel{ft}}\right)^2 = 2.8\,\text{ft of sand}$$

          Check: The units of the answer (ft sand) are correct. The magnitude of the answer seems reasonable.

2.119   **Given:** sun: d = 1.4 g/cm^3, r = 7 $\times$ 10^8 m; 100 billion stars/galaxy; 10 billion galaxies/universe
          Find: number of atoms in the universe
          Conceptual Plan: r (star) in m $\rightarrow$ r (star) in cm $\rightarrow$ vol (star) $\rightarrow$ g H/star $\rightarrow$ mol H star $\rightarrow$ atoms H/star

$$\frac{100\,cm}{m} \qquad\qquad V = \frac{4}{3}\pi r^3 \qquad \frac{1.4\,g\,H}{cm^3} \qquad \frac{1\,mol\,H}{1.008\,g} \qquad \frac{6.022 \times 10^{23}\,atoms}{mol}$$

          $\rightarrow$ **atoms H/galaxy** $\rightarrow$ **atoms H/universe**

$$\frac{100 \times 10^9\,\text{stars}}{\text{galaxy}} \qquad \frac{10 \times 10^9\,\text{galaxies}}{\text{universe}}$$

          Solution: $7 \times 10^8\;\cancel{m} \times \dfrac{100\,cm}{\cancel{m}} = 7 \times 10^{10}\,cm$

$$\frac{4}{3}\pi \frac{(7 \times 10^{10}\;\cancel{cm})^3}{\cancel{\text{star}}} \times \frac{1.4\;\cancel{g\,H}}{\cancel{cm^3}} \times \frac{1\;\cancel{mol\,H}}{1.008\;\cancel{g\,H}} \times \frac{6.022 \times 10^{23}\;\cancel{\text{atoms H}}}{\cancel{mol\,H}} \times \frac{100 \times 10^9\;\cancel{\text{stars}}}{\cancel{\text{galaxy}}} \times \frac{10 \times 10^9\;\cancel{\text{galaxies}}}{\text{universe}}$$

          $= 1 \times 10^{78}$ atoms/universe
          Check: The units of the answer (atoms/universe) are correct.

2.120   (a)   **Given:** 36 Wt-296; 2 Wt-297; 12 Wt-298 **Find:** % abundance of each
                  Conceptual Plan: total atoms $\rightarrow$ fraction of each isotope $\rightarrow$ % abundance

$$\text{Sum of atoms} \qquad \frac{\text{number of each isotope}}{\text{total atoms}} \qquad \text{fraction} \times 100$$

                  Solution: Total atoms = 36 + 2 + 12 = 50

$$\frac{36}{50} \times 100 = 72\%\,\text{Wt-296}, \quad \frac{2}{50} \times 100 = 4\%\,\text{Wt-297}, \quad \frac{12}{50} \times 100 = 24\%\,\text{Wt-298}$$

                  Check: The units of the answers (% abundance) are correct. The values of the answers are reasonable since they add up to 100 %

(b)

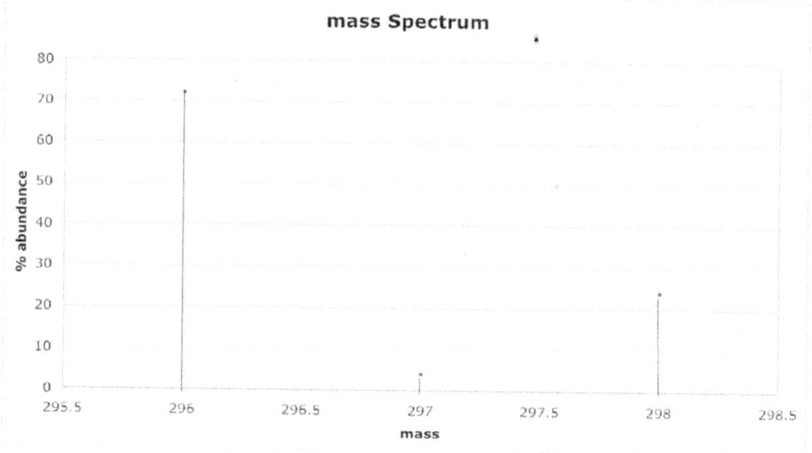

(c) **Given:** Wt-296 m = 24.6630 x mass ^{12}C, 72.55%: Wt-297 m = 24.7490 x mass ^{12}C, 3.922%: Wt-298 m = 24.8312 x mass ^{12}C; 23.53 %.
Find: atomic mass Wt
Conceptual Plan: mass of isotope relative to ^{12}C → mass of isotope and then % abundance →

(Mass relative to ^{12}C)(12.00 amu) $\qquad \frac{\%\text{ abundance}}{100}$

fraction abundance then determine atomic mass

$$\text{Atomic mass} = \sum_n (\text{fraction of isotope n}) \times (\text{mass of isotope n})$$

Solution:
Wt-296 = 24.6630 x 12.00 amu = 295.956 amu; Wt-297 = 24.7490 x 12.00 amu = 296.988 amu;
Wt-298 = 24.8312 x 12.00 amu = 297.974 amu

$$\text{fraction Wt-296} = \frac{72}{100} = 0.72 \quad \text{fraction Wt-297} = \frac{4}{100} = 0.04 \quad \text{fraction Wt-298} = \frac{24}{100} = 0.24$$

$$\begin{aligned}\text{Atomic mass} &= \sum_n (\text{fraction of isotope n}) \times (\text{mass of isotope n}) \\ &= (0.72)(295.956\text{ amu}) + (0.04)(296.988\text{ amu}) + (0.24)(297.974\text{ amu}) \\ &= 296.482\text{ amu}\end{aligned}$$

Check: The units of the answer (amu) are correct. The magnitude of the answer is reasonable because it lies between 295.956 and 297.974 and is closer to 296, which has the highest abundance.

2.121 **Given:** $\frac{\text{mass 2 O}}{\text{mass 1 N}} = \frac{2.29}{1.00}; \frac{\text{mass 3 F}}{\text{mass 1 N}} = \frac{4.07}{1.00}$ **Find:** $\frac{\text{mass O}}{\text{mass 2 F}}$
Conceptual Plan: Mass O/N and mass F/N ⟶ mass O/F → mass O/2F

$\frac{\text{mass 2 O}}{\text{mass 1 N}} \quad \frac{\text{mass 3 F}}{\text{mass 1 N}} \quad \frac{\text{mass 2 O}}{\text{mass 3 F}}$

Solution: $\frac{\text{mass 2 O}}{\text{mass 1 N}} = \frac{2.29}{1.00}; \frac{\text{mass 3 F}}{\text{mass 1 N}} = \frac{4.07}{1.00} \quad \left(\frac{2.29\text{ mass }\cancel{2\text{ O}}}{4.07\text{ mass }\cancel{3\text{ F}}}\right)\left(\frac{1\text{O}}{\cancel{2\text{O}}}\right)\left(\frac{\cancel{3\text{F}}}{2\text{ F}}\right) = \frac{0.422\text{ mass O}}{\text{mass 2 F}}$
Check: Mass ratio of O to F is reasonable since the mass of O is slightly less than the mass of fluorine.

2.122 **Given:** Sample = 1.5886 g, ^{59}Co = 58.9332 amu, ^{60}Co = 59.9338 amu, apparent mass = 58.9901 amu
Find: mass of ^{60}Co in sample
Conceptual Plan: apparent mass → fraction ^{60}Co → mass ^{60}Co

$$\text{Atomic mass} = \sum_n (\text{fraction of isotope n}) \times (\text{mass of isotope n})$$

Solution: Let X = fraction of ^{60}Co, so: 1.00 – X = fraction ^{59}Co

$$58.9901\text{ amu} = (1.00 - X)(58.9332\text{ amu}) + (X)(59.9338\text{ amu})$$

$$X = 0.056\underline{8}6$$

$$1.5886\text{ g sample} \times 0.056\underline{8}6 = 0.090\underline{3}37\text{ g }^{60}Co = 0.0903\text{ g }^{60}Co$$

Check: The units of the answer (g ^{60}Co) are correct. The magnitude of the answer is reasonable since the apparent mass is very close to the mass ^{59}Co.

2.123 **Given:** 7.36 g Cu, 0.51 g Zn **Find:** atomic mass of sample
Conceptual Plan: fraction Cu and Zn $\rightarrow$ atomic mass

$$\text{Atomic mass} = \sum_n (\text{fraction of atom n}) \times (\text{mass of atom n})$$

Solution: 7.36 g Cu + 0.51 g Zn = 7.87 g sample

$$\left(\frac{7.36 \text{ g Cu}}{7.87 \text{ g sample}}\right)\left(\frac{63.55 \text{ g Cu}}{\text{mol Cu}}\right) + \left(\frac{0.51 \text{ g Zn}}{7.87 \text{ g sample}}\right)\left(\frac{65.41 \text{ g Zn}}{\text{mol Zn}}\right) = 63.67 \text{ g/mol}$$

Check: Units of the answer (g/mol) are correct. The magnitude of the answer is reasonable since it is between the mass of Cu (63.55g/mol) and Zn (65.41 g/mol) and is closer to the mass of Cu.

2.124 **Given:** $N_2O_3 = \frac{\text{mass O}}{\text{mass N}} = \frac{12}{7}$; sample $X = \frac{\text{mass O}}{\text{mass N}} = \frac{16}{7}$ **Find:** Formula of X, next in series
Conceptual Plan: ratio O/N for N_2O_3 $\rightarrow$ ratio O/N for X $\rightarrow$ ratio if O/O

Solution: $\frac{\text{mass O}}{\text{mass N}} = \frac{12}{7} = \frac{3 \text{ O mass O}}{2 \text{ N mass N}} = \frac{16}{7} = \frac{\text{X O mass O}}{2 \text{ N mass O}} = \frac{16}{12} = \frac{\text{X O}}{3 \text{ O}} X = 4$

Therefore, formula is N_2O_4

The next member of the series would be N_2O_5

$\frac{\text{mass O}}{\text{mass O}} = \frac{5 \text{ O}}{3 \text{ O}} = \frac{Y}{12} Y = 20$

So, $\frac{\text{mass O}}{\text{mass N}} = \frac{20}{7}$

2.125 **Given:** Mg = 24.312 amu, ^{24}Mg = 23.98504, 78.99%, ^{26}Mg = 25.98259 amu, $\frac{\text{abundance } ^{25}Mg}{\text{abundance } ^{26}Mg} = \frac{0.9083}{1}$
Find: mass ^{25}Mg
Conceptual Plan: Abundance of ^{24}Mg and ratio $^{25}Mg/^{26}Mg$ $\rightarrow$ abundance ^{25}Mg and ^{26}Mg $\rightarrow$ mass ^{25}Mg

$$\text{Atomic mass} = \sum_n (\text{fraction of isotope n}) \times (\text{mass of isotope n})$$

Solution: 100.00% – % abundance ^{24} = % abundance ^{25}Mg and ^{26}Mg

100.00% – 78 99% = 21.01% ^{25}Mg and ^{26}Mg

fraction ^{25}Mg and $^{26}Mg = \frac{21.01}{100.0} = 0.2101$

$\frac{\text{abundance } ^{25}Mg}{\text{abundance } ^{26}Mg} = \frac{0.9083}{1}$

Let X = fraction ^{26}Mg, 0.9083X = fraction ^{25}Mg

fraction ^{25}Mg and ^{26}Mg = X + 0.9083X = 0.2101

X = ^{26}Mg = 0.1101, 0.9083X = ^{25}Mg = 0.1000

$$\text{Atomic mass} = \sum_n (\text{fraction of isotope n}) \times (\text{mass of isotope n})$$

24.312 = (0.7899)(23.98504 amu) + (0.1000)(mass ^{25}Mg) + (0.1101)(25.98259 amu)

mass ^{25}Mg = 25.0$\underline{5}$6 amu = 25.06 amu

Check: The units of the answer (amu) are correct. The magnitude of the answer is reasonable since it is between the masses of ^{24}Mg and ^{26}Mg.

Conceptual Problems

2.126 (a) This is the law of definite proportions: All samples of a given compound, regardless of their source or how they were prepared, have the same proportions of their constituent elements.

(b) This is the law of conservation of mass: In a chemical reaction, matter is neither created nor destroyed.

(c) This is the law of multiple proportions: When two elements form two different compounds, the masses of element B that combine with 1 g of element A can be expressed as a ratio of small whole numbers. In this example the ratio of O from hydrogen peroxide to O from water = 16:8 $\rightarrow$ 2:1, a small whole number ratio.

2.127 If the amu and mole were not based on the same isotope, the numerical values obtained for an atom of material and a mole of material would not be the same. If, for example, the mole was based on the number of particles in C – 12 but the amu was changed to a fraction of the mass of an atom of Ne – 20 the number of particles and the number of amu that make up one mole of material would no longer be the same. We would no longer have the relationship where the mass of an atom in amu is numerically equal to the mass of a mole of those atoms in grams.

2.128 **Given:** a. Cr: 55.0 g, atomic mass = 52 g/mol; b. Ti: 45.0 g, atomic mass = 48 g/mol; and c. Zn: 60.0 g, atomic mass = 65 g/mol
Find: which has the greatest mol, and which has the greatest mass
Conceptual Plan: without calculation, compare grams of material to g/mol for each
Solution: Cr would have the greatest mole amount of the elements. It is the only one whose mass is greater than the molar mass. Zn would be the greatest mass amount because it is the largest mass value.

2.129 The different isotopes of the same element have the same number of protons and electrons, so the attractive forces between the nucleus and the electrons is constant and there is no difference in the radii of the isotopes. Ions, on the other hand, have a different number of electrons than the parent atom from which they are derived. Cations have fewer electrons than the parent atom. The attractive forces are greater because there is a larger positive charge in the nucleus than the negative charge in the electron cloud. So, cations are smaller than the parent atom from which they are derived. Anions have more electrons than the parent. The electron cloud has a greater negative charge than the nucleus, so the anions have larger radii than the parent.

3 Molecules, Compounds, and Chemical Equations

Review Questions

3.1 The properties of compounds are generally very different from the properties of the elements that compose them. When two elements combine to form a compound, an entirely new substance results.

3.2 Chemical bonds are the result of interactions between charged particles—electrons and protons—that compose atoms. Ionic bonds, which occur between metals and nonmetals, involve the transfer of electrons from one atom to another. Covalent bonds, which occur between two or more nonmetals, involve the sharing of electrons between two atoms.

3.3 Chemical compounds can be represented by chemical formulas and molecular models. The type of formula or model you use depends on how much information you have about the compound and how much you want to communicate. An empirical formula gives the relative number of atoms of each element in the compound. It contains the smallest whole number ratio of the elements in the compound. A molecular formula gives the actual number of atoms of each element in the compound. A structural formula shows how the atoms are connected. A ball and stick model shows the geometry of the compound. A space-filling model shows the relative sizes of the atoms and how they merge together.

3.4 An empirical formula gives the relative number of atoms of each element in a compound.

A molecular formula gives the actual number of atoms of each element in a molecule of a compound.

3.5 Atomic elements are those that exist in nature with single atoms as their base units. Neon (Ne), gold (Au), and potassium (K) are a few examples of atomic elements.

Molecular elements do not normally exist in nature with single atoms as their base unit, rather they exist as molecules, two or more atoms of the same element bonded together. Most exist as diatomic molecules, for example hydrogen (H_2), nitrogen (N_2), and oxygen (O_2). Some exist as polyatomic molecules: phosphorus (P_4) and sulfur (S_8).

Ionic compounds are generally composed of a one or more metal cations (usually one type of metal) and one or more nonmetal anions bound together by ionic bonds. Sodium chloride ($NaCl$), potassium sulfate (Na_2SO_4) would be examples of ionic compounds.

Molecular compounds are composed of two or more covalently bonded nonmetals. Examples would be water (H_2O), sulfur dioxide (SO_2), and nitrogen dioxide (NO_2).

3.6 To write a formula for an ionic compound: 1) Write the symbol for the metal cation and its charge followed by the symbol for the nonmetal or polyatomic anion and its charge. 2) Adjust the subscript on each cation and anion to balance the overall charge. 3) Check that the sum of the charges of the cations equals the sum of the charges of the anions.

3.7 Binary ionic compounds are named by using the name of the cation (metal) and the base name of the anion (nonmetal) + the suffix *-ide*. Ionic compounds that contain a polyatomic anion are named by using the name of the cation (metal) and the name of the polyatomic anion.

3.8 Ionic compounds formed from metals that can form more than one cation must include the charge of the cation in the name. The charge is indicated by putting the charge of the metal in roman numerals in parentheses after the metal name. Metals that can form only one cation do not need the charge specified.

3.9 To name a binary molecular inorganic compound list the name of the first element with a prefix to indicate the number of atoms in the compound if there is more than one, followed by the base name of the second element with a prefix to indicate the number of atoms in the compound if there is more than one, followed by the suffix *-ide*.

3.10 The prefix mono = 1; di = 2; tri = 3; tetra = 4; penta = 5; hexa = 6.

3.11 Binary acids are composed of hydrogen and a nonmetal. The names for binary acids have the form: hydro plus the base name of the nonmetal + ic acid. Oxyacids contain hydrogen and an oxyanion. The names of oxyacids depend on the ending of the oxyanion and have the following forms: oxyanions ending with *-ate*: base name of the oxyanion + *ic* acid; oxyanions ending with *-ite*: base name of the oxyanion + *ous* acid.

3.12 The formula mass is the average mass of the molecule (or formula unit) of a compound. The formula mass allows the conversion between the mass of molecules and the number of molecules present.

3.13 The chemical formula indicates the elements present in the compound and the relative number of atoms of each type. The chemical formula gives the conversion factor between the kind of element and the formula; it also allows the determination of mass percent composition.

3.14 Mass percent composition is the mass of an element of the compound divided by the total mass of the compound times 100. Mass percent composition is used as a conversion factor between the mass of the element and the mass of the compound.

3.15 Chemical formulas contain within them inherent relationships between atoms (or moles of atoms) and molecules (or moles of molecules). For example, the formula CCl_2F_2 tells us that one mole of CCl_2F_2 contains one mole of C atoms, two moles of Cl atoms, and two moles of F atoms.

3.16 The experimental data showing the relative masses of the elements in a compound can be used to obtain an empirical formula.

3.17 The molecular formula is a whole-number multiple of the empirical formula. To find the molecular formula the molar mass of the compound must be known. The molecular molar mass divided by the empirical molar mass gives the whole number multiple used to convert the empirical formula to the molecular formula.

3.18 In combustion analysis, the unknown compound undergoes combustion (burning) in the presence of pure oxygen. All of the carbon in the sample is converted to CO_2 and all of the hydrogen is converted to H_2O.

3.19 Organic compounds are composed of carbon, hydrogen and a few other elements including nitrogen, oxygen, and sulfur.

3.20 An alkane is a hydrocarbon containing only single C to C bonds. An alkene contains at least one double C to C bond and an alkyne contains at least one triple C to C bond.

3.21 Functionalized hydrocarbons are hydrocarbons in which a functional group—a characteristic atom or group of atoms—has been incorporated into the hydrocarbon. The family or organic compounds known as alcohols have an –OH functional group.

3.22 (a) alcohol: R — O — H

(b) ethers: R — O — R'

(c)   aldehyde:

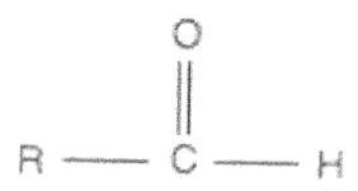

$$R - \overset{\overset{\textstyle O}{\|}}{C} - H$$

    (d)   ketone:

$$R - \overset{\overset{\textstyle O}{\|}}{C} - R'$$

    (e)   carboxylic acid:

$$R - \overset{\overset{\textstyle O}{\|}}{C} - OH$$

    (f)   ester:

$$R - \overset{\overset{\textstyle O}{\|}}{C} - OR'$$

    (g)   amines: RNH_2

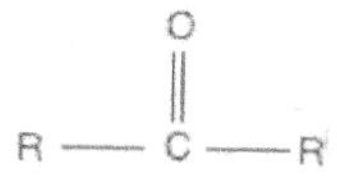

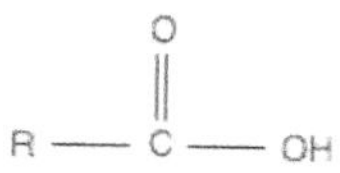

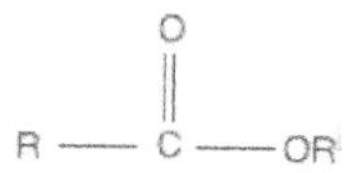

Problems by Topic

Chemical Formulas and Molecular View of the Elements

3.23   The chemical formula gives you the kind of atom and the number of each atom in the compound.

    (a) $Mg_3(PO_4)_2$ contains: 3 magnesium atoms, 2 phosphorus atoms, and 8 oxygen atoms

    (b) $BaCl_2$ contains: 1 barium atom and 2 chlorine atoms

    (c) $Fe(NO_2)_2$ contains: 1 iron atom, 2 nitrogen atoms, and 4 oxygen atoms

    (d) $Ca(OH)_2$ contains: 1 calcium atom, 2 oxygen atoms, and 2 hydrogen atoms

3.24   The chemical formula gives you the kind of atom and the number of each atom in the compound.

    (a) $Ca(NO_2)_2$ contains: 1 calcium atom, 2 nitrogen atoms, and 4 oxygen atoms

    (b) $CuSO_4$ contains: 1 copper atom, 1 sulfur atom, and 4 oxygen atoms

    (c) $Al(NO_3)_3$ contains: 1 aluminum atom, 3 nitrogen atoms, and 9 oxygen atoms

    (d) $Mg(HCO_3)_2$ contains: 1 magnesium atom, 2 hydrogen atoms, 2 carbon atoms, and 6 oxygen atoms

3.25   (a)   1 blue = nitrogen, 3 white = hydrogen: NH_3

    (b)   2 black = carbon, 6 white = hydrogen: C_2H_6

    (c)   1 yellow – green = sulfur, 3 red = oxygen: SO_3

3.26   (a)   1 blue = nitrogen, 2 red = oxygen: NO_2

    (b)   1 yellow – green = sulfur, 2 white = hydrogen: SH_2

    (c)   1 black = carbon, 4 white = hydrogen: CH_4

3.27   (a)   Neon is an element and it is not one of the elements that exist as diatomic molecules, therefore it is an atomic element.

    (b)   Fluorine is one of the elements that exist as diatomic molecules, therefore it is a molecular element.

    (c)   Potassium is not one of the elements that exist as diatomic molecules, therefore it is an atomic element.

    (d)   Nitrogen is one of the elements that exist as diatomic molecules, therefore it is a molecular element.

3.28 (a) Hydrogen is one of the elements that exist as diatomic molecules, therefore it has a molecule as its basic unit.

(b) Iodine is one of the elements that exist as diatomic molecules, therefore it has a molecule as its basic unit.

(c) Lead is not one of the elements that exist as a diatomic molecule, therefore it does not have a molecule as its basic unit.

(d) Oxygen is one of the elements that exist as diatomic molecules, therefore it has a molecule as its basic unit.

3.29 (a) CO_2 is a compound composed of a nonmetal and a nonmetal, therefore it is a molecular compound.

(b) $NiCl_2$ is a compound composed of a metal and a nonmetal, therefore it is an ionic compound.

(c) NaI is a compound composed of a metal and a nonmetal, therefore it is an ionic compound.

(d) PCl_3 is a compound composed of a nonmetal and a nonmetal, therefore it is a molecular compound.

3.30 (a) CF_2Cl_2 is a compound composed of a nonmetal and 2 other nonmetals, therefore it is a molecular compound.

(b) CCl_4 is a compound composed of a nonmetal and a nonmetal, therefore it is a molecular compound.

(c) PtO_2 is a compound composed of a metal and a nonmetal, therefore it is an ionic compound.

(d) SO_3 is a compound composed of a nonmetal and a nonmetal, therefore it is a molecular compound.

3.31 (a) white – hydrogen: a molecule composed of two of the same element, therefore it is a molecular element.

(b) blue – nitrogen, white – hydrogen: a molecule composed of a nonmetal and a nonmetal, therefore it is a molecular compound.

(c) purple – sodium: a substance composed of all the same atoms, therefore it is an atomic element.

3.32 (a) green – chlorine, purple – sodium: a compound composed of metal and nonmetal, therefore it is an ionic compound.

(b) green – chlorine: a molecule composed of two of the same element, therefore it is a molecular element.

(c) red – oxygen, black – carbon, white – hydrogen: a molecule composed of nonmetals, therefore it is a molecular compound.

Formulas and Names for Ionic Compounds

3.33 To write the formula for an ionic compound do the following: 1) Write the symbol for the metal cation and its charge and the symbol for the nonmetal anion and its charge. 2) Adjust the subscript on each cation and anion to balance the overall charge. 3) Check that the sum of the charges of the cations equals the sum of the charges of the anions.

(a)	calcium and oxygen:	Ca^{2-}	O^{2-}	CaO	cations 2+, anions 2–
(b)	zinc and sulfur:	Zn^{2+}	S^{2-}	ZnS	cations 2+, anions 2–
(c)	rubidium and bromine:	Rb^{+}	Br^{-}	RbBr	cation +, anions –
(d)	aluminum and oxygen:	Al^{3+}	O^{2-}	Al_2O_3	cation 2(3+) = 6+, anions 3(2–) = 6–

3.34 To write the formula for an ionic compound do the following: 1) Write the symbol for the metal cation and its charge and the symbol for the nonmetal anion and its charge. 2) Adjust the subscript on each cation and anion to balance the overall charge. 3) Check that the sum of the charges of the cations equals the sum of the charges of the anions.

(a)	silver and chlorine:	Ag^+	Cl^-	$AgCl$	cation +, anions –
(b)	sodium and sulfur:	Na^+	S^{2-}	Na_2S	cation 2(1+) = 2+, anion 2–
(c)	aluminum and sulfur:	Al^{3+}	S^{2-}	Al_2S_3	cation 2(3+) = 6+, anions 3(2–) = 6–
(d)	potassium and chlorine:	K^+	Cl^-	KCl	cation +, anion –

3.35 To write the formula for an ionic compound do the following: 1) Write the symbol for the metal cation and its charge and the symbol for the polyatomic anion and its charge. 2) Adjust the subscript on each cation and anion to balance the overall charge. 3) Check that the sum of the charges of the cations equals the sum of the charges of the anions.

Cation = calcium: Ca^{2+}

(a)	hydroxide:	OH^-	$Ca(OH)_2$	cation 2+, anion 2(1–) = 2–
(b)	chromate:	CrO_4^{2-}	$CaCrO_4$	cation 2+, anion 2–
(c)	phosphate:	PO_4^{3-}	$Ca_3(PO_4)_2$	cation 3(2+) = 6+, anion 2(3–) = 6–
(d)	cyanide:	CN^-	$Ca(CN)_2$	cation 2+, anion 2(1–) = 2–

3.36 To write the formula for an ionic compound do the following: 1) Write the symbol for the metal cation and its charge and the symbol for the nonmetal anion and its charge. 2) Adjust the subscript on each cation and anion to balance the overall charge. 3) Check that the sum of the charges of the cations equals the sum of the charges of the anions.

Cation = potassium: K^+

(a)	carbonate:	CO_3^{2-}	K_2CO_3	cation 2(1+) = 2+, anion 2–
(b)	phosphate:	PO_4^{3-}	K_3PO_4	cation 3(1+) = 3+, anion 3–
(c)	hydrogen phosphate:	HPO_4^{2-}	K_2HPO_4	cation 2(1+) = 2+, anion 2–
(d)	acetate:	$C_2H_3O_2^-$	$KC_2H_3O_2$	cation 1+, anion 1–

3.37 To name a binary ionic compound name the metal cation followed by the base name of the anion + *-ide*.

(a) Mg_3N_2: The cation is magnesium; the anion is from nitrogen, which becomes nitride: magnesium nitride.

(b) KF: The cation is potassium; the anion is from fluorine, which becomes fluoride: potassium fluoride.

(c) Na_2O: The cation is sodium; the anion is from oxygen, which becomes oxide: sodium oxide.

(d) Li_2S: The cation is lithium; the anion is from sulfur, which becomes sulfide: lithium sulfide.

(e) CsF: The cation is cesium; the anion is fluorine, which becomes fluoride: cesium fluoride.

(f) KI: The cation is potassium; the anion is iodine, which becomes iodide: potassium iodide.

(g) $SrCl_2$: The cation is strontium; the anion is chlorine, which becomes chloride: strontium chloride.

(h) $BaCl_2$: The cation is barium; the anion is chlorine, which becomes chloride: barium chloride.

3.38 To name an ionic compound with a metal cation that can have more than one charge, name the metal cation followed by parentheses with the charge in roman numerals followed by the base name of the anion + *-ide*.

(a) $SnCl_4$: The charge on Sn must be 4+ for the compound to be charge neutral: The cation is tin(IV); the anion is from chlorine, which becomes chloride: tin(IV) chloride.

(b) PbI_2: The charge on Pb must be 2+ for the compound to be charge neutral: The cation is lead(II); the anion is from iodine, which becomes iodide: lead(II) iodide.

(c) Fe_2O_3: The charge on Fe must be 3+ for the compound to be charge neutral: The cation is iron(III); the anion is from oxygen, which becomes oxide: iron(III) oxide.

(d) CuI_2: The charge on Cu must be 2+ for the compound to be charge neutral: The cation is copper(II); the anion is from iodine, which becomes iodide: copper(II) iodide.

(e) SnO_2: The charge on Sn must be 4+ for the compound to be charge neutral: The cation is tin(IV); the anion is from oxygen, which becomes oxide: tin(IV) oxide.

(f) $HgBr_2$: The charge of Hg must be 2+ for the compound to charge neutral: The cation is mercury(II); the anion is from bromine, which becomes bromide: mercury(II) bromide.

(g) $CrCl_2$: The charge on Cr must be 2+ for the compound to be charge neutral: The cation is chromium(II); the anion is from chlorine, which becomes chloride: chromium(II) chloride.

(h) $CrCl_3$: The charge on Cr must be 3+ for the compound to be charge neutral: The cation is chromium(III); the anion is from chlorine, which becomes chloride: chromium(III) chloride.

3.39 To name these compounds you must first decide if the metal cation is invariant or can have more than one charge. Then, name the metal cation followed by the base name of the anion + *-ide*.

(a) SnO: Sn can have more than one charge. The charge on Sn must be 2+ for the compound to be charge neutral: The cation is tin(II); the anion is from oxygen, which becomes oxide: tin(II) oxide.

(b) Cr_2S_3: Cr can have more than one charge. The charge on Cr must be 3+ for the compound to be charge neutral: The cation is chromium(III); the anion is from sulfur, which becomes sulfide: chromium(III) sulfide.

(c) RbI: Rb is invariant: The cation is rubidium; the anion is from iodine, which becomes iodide: rubidium iodide.

(d) $BaBr_2$: Ba is invariant: The cation is barium; the anion is from bromine, which becomes bromide: barium bromide.

3.40 To name these compounds you must first decide if the metal cation is invariant or can have more than one charge. Then, name the metal cation followed by the base name of the anion + *-ide*.

(a) BaS: Ba is invariant: The cation is barium; the anion is from sulfur, which becomes sulfide: barium sulfide.

(b) $FeCl_3$: Fe can have more than one charge. The charge on Fe must be 3+ for the compound to be charge neutral: The cation is iron(III); the anion is from chlorine, which becomes chloride: iron(III) chloride.

(c) PbI_4: Pb can have more than one charge. The charge on Pb must be 4+ for the compound to be charge neutral: The cation is lead(IV); the anion is from iodine, which becomes iodide: lead(IV) iodide.

(d) $SrBr_2$: Sr is invariant: The cation is strontium; the anion is from bromine, which becomes bromide: strontium bromide.

3.41 To name these compounds you must first decide if the metal cation is invariant or can have more than one charge. Then, name the metal cation followed by the name of the polyatomic anion.

(a) $CuNO_2$: Cu can have more than one charge. The charge on Cu must be 1+ for the compound to be charge neutral: The cation is copper(I); the anion is nitrite: copper(I) nitrite.

(b) $Mg(C_2H_3O_2)_2$: Mg is invariant: The cation is magnesium; the anion is acetate: magnesium acetate.

(c) $Ba(NO_3)_2$: Ba is invariant: The cation is barium; the anion is nitrate: barium nitrate.

(d) $Pb(C_2H_3O_2)_2$: Pb can have more than one charge. The charge on Pb must be 2+ for the compound to be charge neutral: The cation is lead(II); the anion is acetate: lead(II) acetate.

(e) $KClO_3$: K is invariant: The cation is potassium; the anion is chlorate: potassium chlorate.

(f) $PbSO_4$: Pb can have more than one charge. The charge on Pb must be 2+ for the compound to be charge neutral: The cation is lead(II); the anion is sulfate: lead(II) sulfate.

3.42 To name these compounds you must first decide if the metal cation is invariant or can have more than one charge. Then, name the metal cation followed by the name of the polyatomic anion.

(a) $Ba(OH)_2$: Ba is invariant: The cation is barium; the anion is hydroxide: barium hydroxide.

(b) NH_4I: The cation is ammonium; the anion is from iodine, which becomes iodide: ammonium iodide.

(c) $NaBrO_4$: Na is invariant: The cation is sodium; the anion is perbromate: sodium perbromate.

(d) $Fe(OH)_3$: Fe can have more than one charge. The charge on Fe must be 3+ for the compound to be charge neutral: The cation is iron(III); the anion is hydroxide: iron(III) hydroxide.

(e) $CoSO_4$: Co can have more than one charge. The charge on Co must be 2+ for the compound to be charge neutral: The cation is cobalt(II); the anion is sulfate: cobalt(II) sulfate.

(f) $KClO$: K is invariant: The cation is potassium; the anion is hypochlorite: potassium hypochlorite.

3.43 To write the formula for an ionic compound do the following: 1) Write the symbol for the metal cation and its charge and the symbol for the nonmetal anion or polyatomic anion and its charge. 2) Adjust the subscript on each cation and anion to balance the overall charge. 3) Check that the sum of the charges of the cations equals the sum of the charges of the anions.

(a)	sodium hydrogen sulfite:	Na^+	HSO_3^-	$NaHSO_3$	cation 1+, anion 1–
(b)	lithium permanganate:	Li^+	MnO_4^-	$LiMnO_4$	cation 1+, anion 1–
(c)	silver nitrate:	Ag^+	NO_3^-	$AgNO_3$	cation 1+, anion 1–
(d)	potassium sulfate:	K^+	SO_4^{2-}	K_2SO_4	cation 2(1+) = 2+, anion 2–
(e)	rubidium hydrogen sulfate:	Rb^+	HSO_4^-	$RbHSO_4$	cation 1+, anion 1–
(f)	potassium hydrogen carbonate:	K^+	HCO_3^-	$KHCO_3$	cation 1+, anion 1–

3.44 To write the formula for an ionic compound do the following: 1) Write the symbol for the metal cation and its charge and the symbol for the nonmetal anion or polyatomic anion and its charge. 2) Adjust the subscript on each cation and anion to balance the overall charge. 3) Check that the sum of the charges of the cations equals the sum of the charges of the anions.

(a)	copper(II) chloride:	Cu^{2+}	Cl^-	$CuCl_2$	cation 2+, anion 2(1–) = 2–
(b)	copper(I) iodate:	Cu^+	IO_3^-	$CuIO_3$	cation 1+, anion 1–
(c)	lead(II) chromate:	Pb^{2+}	CrO_4^{2-}	$PbCrO_4$	cation 2+, anion 2–
(d)	calcium fluoride:	Ca^{2+}	F^-	CaF_2	cation 2+, anion 2(1–) = 2–
(e)	potassium hydroxide:	K^+	OH^-	KOH	cation 1+, anion 1–
(f)	iron(II) phosphate:	Fe^{2+}	PO_4^{3-}	$Fe_3(PO_4)_2$	cation 3(2+) = 6+, anion 2(3–) = 6–

3.45 Hydrates are named the same way as other ionic compounds with the addition of the term *prefix*hydrate, where the prefix is the number of water molecules associated with each formula unit.

(a)	$CoSO_4 \cdot 7H_2O$	cobalt(II) sulfate heptahydrate
(b)	iridium(III) bromide tetrahydrate	$IrBr_3 \cdot 4H_2O$
(c)	$Mg(BrO_3)_2 \cdot 6H_2O$	magnesium bromate hexahydrate
(d)	potassium carbonate dihydrate	$K_2CO_3 \cdot 2H_2O$

3.46 Hydrates are named the same way as other ionic compounds with the addition of the term *prefix*hydrate, where the prefix is the number of water molecules associated with each formula unit.

(a)	cobalt(II) phosphate octahydrate	$Co_3(PO_4)_2 \cdot 8H_2O$
(b)	$BeCl_2 \cdot 2H_2O$	beryllium chloride dihydrate
(c)	chromium(III) phosphate trihydrate	$CrPO_4 \cdot 3H_2O$
(d)	$LiNO_2 \cdot H_2O$	lithium nitrite monohydrate

Formulas and Names for Molecular Compounds and Acids

3.47 (a) CO The name of the compound is the name of the first element, *carbon*, followed by the base name of the second element, *ox*, prefixed by *mono-* to indicate one and given the suffix *-ide*: carbon monoxide.

(b) NI_3 The name of the compound is the name of the first element, *nitrogen*, followed by the base name of the second element, *iod*, prefixed by *tri-* to indicate three and given the suffix *-ide*: nitrogen triiodide.

(c) $SiCl_4$ The name of the compound is the name of the first element, *silicon*, followed by the base name of the second element, *chlor*, prefixed by *tetra-* to indicate four and given the suffix *-ide*: silicon tetrachloride.

(d) N_4Se_4 The name of the compound is the name of the first element, *nitrogen*, prefixed by *tetra-* to indicate four followed by the base name of the second element, *selen*, prefixed by *tetra-* to indicate four and given the suffix *-ide*: tetranitrogen tetraselenide.

(e) I_2O_5 The name of the compound is the name of the first element, *iodine*, prefixed by *di-* to indicate two followed by the base name of the second element, *ox*, prefixed by *penta-* to indicate five and given the suffix *-ide*: diiodine pentaoxide.

3.48 (a) SO_3 The name of the compound is the name of the first element, *sulfur*, followed by the base name of the second element, *ox*, prefixed by *tri-* to indicate three and given the suffix *-ide*: sulfur trioxide.

(b) SO_2 The name of the compound is the name of the first element, *sulfur*, followed by the base name of the second element, *ox*, prefixed by *di-* to indicate two and given the suffix *-ide*: sulfur dioxide.

(c) BrF_5 The name of the compound is the name of the first element, *bromine*, followed by the base name of the second element, *fluor*, prefixed by *penta-* to indicate five and given the suffix *-ide*: bromine pentafluoride.

(d) NO The name of the compound is the name of the first element, *nitrogen*, followed by the base name of the second element, *ox*, prefixed by *mono-* to indicate one and given the suffix *-ide*: nitrogen monoxide.

(e) XeO_3 The name of the compound is the name of the first element, *xenon*, followed by the base name of the second element, *ox*, prefixed by *tri-* to indicate three and given the suffix *-ide*: xenon trioxide.

3.49 (a) phosphorus trichloride: PCl_3

(b) chlorine monoxide: ClO

(c) disulfur tetrafluoride: S_2F_4

(d) phosphorus pentafluoride: PF_5

(e) diphosphorus pentasulfide: P_2S_5

3.50 (a) boron tribromide: BBr_3

(b) dichlorine monoxide: Cl_2O

(c) xenon tetrafluoride: XeF_4

(d) carbon tetrabromide: CBr_4

(e) diboron tetrachloride: B_2Cl_4

3.51 (a) HI: The base name of I is *iod* so the name is hydroiodic acid.

(b) HNO_3: The oxyanion is *nitrate,* which ends in *-ate;* therefore, the name of the acid is nitric acid.

(c) H_2CO_3: The oxyanion is *carbonate,* which ends in *-ate;* therefore, the name of the acid is carbonic acid.

(d) $HC_2H_3O_2$: The oxyanion is *acetate,* which ends in *-ate;* therefore, the name of the acid is acetic acid.

3.52 (a) HCl: The base name of Cl is *chlor,* so the name is hydrochloric acid.

(b) $HClO_2$: The oxyanion is *chlorite,* which ends in *-ite;* therefore, the name of the acid is chlorous acid.

(c) H_2SO_4: The oxyanion is *sulfate,* which ends in *-ate;* therefore, the name of the acid is sulfuric acid.

(d) HNO_2: The oxyanion is *nitrite,* which ends in *-ite;* therefore, the name of the acid is nitrous acid.

3.53 (a) hydrofluoric acid: HF

(b) hydrobromic acid: HBr

(c) sulfurous acid: H_2SO_3

3.54 (a) phosphoric acid: H_3PO_4

(b) hydrocyanic acid: HCN

(c) chlorous acid: $HClO_2$

Formula Mass and the Mole Concept for Compounds

3.55 To find the formula mass, we sum the atomic masses of each atom in the chemical formula.

(a) NO_2 formula mass
$= 1 \text{ x (atomic mass N)} + 2 \text{ x (atomic mass O)}$
$= 1 \text{ x } (14.01 \text{ amu}) + 2 \text{ x } (16.00 \text{ amu})$
$= 46.01 \text{ amu}$

(b) C_4H_{10} formula mass
$= 4 \text{ x (atomic mass C)} + 10 \text{ x (atomic mass H)}$
$= 4 \text{ x } (12.01 \text{ amu}) + 10 \text{ x } (1.008 \text{ amu})$
$= 58.12 \text{ amu}$

(c) $C_6H_{12}O_6$ formula mass
$= 6 \text{ x (atomic mass C)} + 12 \text{ x (atomic mass H)} + 6 \text{ x (atomic mass O)}$
$= 6 \text{ x } (12.01 \text{ amu}) + 12 \text{ x } (1.008 \text{ amu}) + 6 \text{ x } (16.00 \text{ amu})$
$= 180.16 \text{ amu}$

(d) $Cr(NO_3)_3$ formula mass = 1 x (atomic mass Cr) + 3 x (atomic mass N) + 9 x (atomic mass O)
= 1 x (52.00 amu) + 3 x (14.01 amu) + 9 x (16.00 amu)
= 238.03 amu

3.56 To find the formula mass, we sum the atomic masses of each atom in the chemical formula.

(a) $MgBr_2$ formula mass = 1 x (atomic mass Mg) + 2 x (atomic mass Br)
= 1 x (24.31 amu) + 2 x (79.90 amu)
= 184.11 amu

(b) HNO_2 formula mass = 1 x (atomic mass H) + 1 x (atomic mass N) + 2 x (atomic mass O)
= 1 x (1.008 amu) + 1 x (14.01 amu) + 2 x (16.00 amu)
= 47.02 amu

(c) CBr_4 formula mass = 1 x (atomic mass C) + 4 x (atomic mass Br)
= 1 x (12.01 amu) + 4 x (79.90 amu)
= 331.61 amu

(d) $Ca(NO_3)_2$ formula mass = 1 x (atomic mass Ca) + 2 x (atomic mass N) + 6 x (atomic mass O)
= 1 x (40.08 amu) + 2 x (14.01 amu) + 6 x (16.00 amu)
= 164.10 amu

3.57 (a) **Given:** 25.5 g NO_2 **Find:** number of moles

Conceptual Plan: g NO_2 → mole NO_2

$$\frac{1 \text{ mol}}{46.01 \text{ g } NO_2}$$

Solution: $25.5 \cancel{\text{g } NO_2} \times \frac{1 \text{ mol } NO_2}{46.01 \cancel{\text{g } NO_2}} = 0.554 \text{ mol } NO_2$

Check: The units of the answer (mole NO_2) are correct. The magnitude is appropriate because it is less than 1 mole of NO_2.

(b) **Given:** 1.25 kg CO_2 **Find:** number of moles

Conceptual Plan: kg CO2 → g CO2 → mole CO2

$$\frac{1000 \text{ g } CO_2}{\text{kg } CO_2} \qquad \frac{1 \text{ mol}}{44.01 \text{ g } NO_2}$$

Solution: $1.25 \cancel{\text{kg } CO_2} \times \frac{1000 \cancel{\text{g } CO_2}}{\cancel{\text{kg } CO_2}} \times \frac{1 \text{ mol } CO_2}{44.01 \cancel{\text{g } CO_2}} = 28.4 \text{ mol } CO_2$

Check: The units of the answer (mole CO_2) are correct. The magnitude is appropriate because there is over a kg of CO_2 present.

(c) **Given:** 38.2 g KNO_3 **Find:** number of moles

Conceptual Plan: g KNO_3 → mole KNO_3

$$\frac{1 \text{ mol}}{101.11 \text{ g } KNO_3}$$

Solution: $38.2 \cancel{\text{g } KNO_3} \times \frac{1 \text{ mol } KNO_3}{101.11 \cancel{\text{g } KNO_3}} = 0.378 \text{ mol } KNO_3$

Check: The units of the answer (mole KNO_3) are correct. The magnitude is appropriate because there is less than 1 mole of KNO_3.

(d) **Given:** 155.2 kg Na_2SO_4 **Find:** number of moles

Conceptual Plan: kg Na_2SO_4 → g Na_2SO_4 → mole Na_2SO_4

$$\frac{1000 \text{ g } Na_2SO_4}{\text{kg } Na_2SO_4} \qquad \frac{1 \text{ mol}}{142.05 \text{ g } Na_2SO_4}$$

Solution: $155.2 \cancel{\text{kg } Na_2SO_4} \times \frac{1000 \cancel{\text{g } Na_2SO_4}}{\cancel{\text{kg } Na_2SO_4}} \times \frac{1 \text{ mol } Na_2SO_4}{142.05 \cancel{\text{g } Na_2SO_4}} = 1092 \text{ mol } Na_2SO_4$

Check: The units of the answer (mole Na_2SO_4) are correct. The magnitude is appropriate because there is over 100 kg of Na_2SO_4 present.

3.58 (a) **Given:** 55.98 g CF_2Cl_2 **Find:** number of moles

Conceptual Plan: g CF_2Cl_2 → mole CF_2Cl_2

$$\frac{1 \text{ mol}}{120.91 \text{ g } CF_2Cl_2}$$

Solution: $55.98 \text{ g } CF_2Cl_2 \times \frac{1 \text{ mol } CF_2Cl_2}{120.91 \text{ g } CF_2Cl_2} = 0.46298 \text{ mol } CF_2Cl_2 = 0.4630 \text{ mol } CF_2Cl_2$

Check: The units of the answer (mole CF_2Cl_2) are correct. The magnitude is appropriate because it is less than 1 mole of CF_2Cl_2.

(b) **Given:** 23.6 kg $Fe(NO_3)_2$ **Find:** number of moles

Conceptual Plan: kg $Fe(NO_3)_2$ → g $Fe(NO_3)_2$ → mole $Fe(NO_3)_2$

$\frac{1000 \text{ g } Fe(NO_3)_2}{\text{kg } Fe(NO_3)_2}$ $\frac{1 \text{ mol}}{179.87 \text{ g} Fe(NO_3)_2}$

Solution: $23.6 \text{ kg } Fe(NO_3)_2 \times \frac{1000 \text{ g } Fe(NO_3)_2}{\text{kg } Fe(NO_3)_2} \times \frac{1 \text{ mol } Fe(NO_3)_2}{179.87 \text{ g } Fe(NO_3)_2} = 131 \text{ mol } Fe(NO_3)_2$

Check: The units of the answer (mole $Fe(NO_3)_2$) are correct. The magnitude is appropriate because there is over a kg of $Fe(NO_3)_2$ present.

(c) **Given:** 0.1187g C_8H_{18} **Find:** number of moles

Conceptual Plan: g C_8H_{18} → mole C_8H_{18}

$\frac{1 \text{ mol}}{114.22 \text{ g } C_8H_{18}}$

Solution: $0.1187 \text{ g } C_8H_{18} \times \frac{1 \text{ mol } C_8H_{18}}{114.22 \text{ g } C_8H_{18}} = 1.039 \times 10^{-3} \text{ mol } C_8H_{18}$

Check: The units of the answer (mole C_8H_{18}) are correct. The magnitude is appropriate because it is much less than 1 mole of C_8H_{18}.

(d) **Given:** 195 kg CaO **Find:** number of moles

Conceptual Plan: kg CaO → g CaO → mole CaO

$\frac{1000\text{g CaO}}{\text{kg CaO}}$ $\frac{1 \text{ mol}}{56.08 \text{ g CaO}}$

Solution: $195 \text{ kg CaO} \times \frac{1000 \text{ g CaO}}{\text{kg CaO}} \times \frac{1 \text{ mol CaO}}{56.08 \text{ CaO}} = 3477 \text{ mol CaO} = 3.48 \times 10^3 \text{ mol CaO}$

Check: The units of the answer (mole CaO) are correct. The magnitude is appropriate because there is over a kg of CaO present.

3.59 (a) **Given:** 6.5 g H_2O **Find:** number of molecules

Conceptual Plan: g H_2O → mole H_2O → number H_2O molecules

$\frac{1 \text{ mol}}{18.02 \text{ g } H_2O}$ $\frac{6.022 \times 10^{23} \text{ } H_2O \text{ molecules}}{\text{mol } H_2O}$

Solution: $6.5 \text{ g } H_2O \times \frac{1 \text{ mol } H_2O}{18.02 \text{ g } H_2O} \times \frac{6.022 \times 10^{23} \text{ } H_2O \text{ molecules}}{\text{mol } H_2O} = 2.2 \times 10^{23} \text{ } H_2O \text{ molecules}$

Check: The units of the answer (H_2O molecules) are correct. The magnitude is appropriate: it is smaller than Avogadro's number, as expected, since we have less than 1 mole of H_2O.

(b) **Given:** 389 g CBr_4 **Find:** number of molecules

Conceptual Plan: g CBr_4 → mole CBr_4 → number CBr_4 molecules

$\frac{1 \text{ mol}}{331.6 \text{ g } CBr_4}$ $\frac{6.022 \times 10^{23} \text{ } CBr_4 \text{ molecules}}{\text{mol } CBr_4}$

Solution: $389 \text{ g } CBr_4 \times \frac{1 \text{ mol } CBr_4}{331.6 \text{ g } CBr_4} \times \frac{6.022 \times 10^{23} \text{ } CBr_4 \text{ molecules}}{\text{mol } CBr_4} = 7.06 \times 10^{23} \text{ } CBr_4 \text{ molecules}$

Check: The units of the answer (CBr_4 molecules) are correct. The magnitude is appropriate: it is larger than Avogadro's number, as expected, since we have more than 1 mole of CBr_4.

(c) **Given:** 22.1 g O_2 **Find:** number of molecules

Conceptual Plan: g O_2 → mole O_2 → number O_2 molecules

$\frac{1 \text{ mol}}{32.00 \text{ g } O_2}$ $\frac{6.022 \times 10^{23} \text{ } O_2 \text{ molecules}}{\text{mol } O_2}$

Solution: $22.1 \text{ g } O_2 \times \frac{1 \text{ mol } O_2}{32.00 \text{ g } O_2} \times \frac{6.022 \times 10^{23} \text{ } O_2 \text{ molecules}}{\text{mol } O_2} = 4.16 \times 10^{23} \text{ } O_2 \text{ molecules}$

Check: The units of the answer (O_2 molecules) are correct. The magnitude is appropriate: it is smaller than Avogadro's number, as expected, since we have less than 1 mole of O_2.

(d) **Given:** 19.3 g C_8H_{10} **Find:** number of molecules
Conceptual Plan: g C_8H_{10} → mole C_8H_{10} → number C_8H_{10} molecules

$$\frac{1 \text{ mol}}{106.16 \text{ g } C_8H_{10}} \qquad \frac{6.022 \times 10^{23} \; C_8H_{10} \text{ molecules}}{\text{mol } C_8H_{10}}$$

Solution:

$$19.3 \text{ g } C_8H_{10} \times \frac{1 \text{ mol } C_8H_{10}}{106.16 \text{ g } C_8H_{10}} \times \frac{6.022 \times 10^{23} \; C_8H_{10} \text{ molecules}}{\text{mol } C_8H_{10}} = 1.09 \times 10^{23} \; C_8H_{10} \text{ molecules}$$

Check: The units of the answer (C_8H_{10} molecules) are correct. The magnitude is appropriate: it is smaller than Avogadro's number, as expected, since we have less than 1 mole of C_8H_{10}.

3.60 (a) **Given:** 85.26 g CCl_4 **Find:** number of molecules
Conceptual Plan: g CCl_4 → mole CCl_4 → number CCl_4 molecules

$$\frac{1 \text{ mol}}{153.81 \text{ g } CCl_4} \qquad \frac{6.022 \times 10^{23} \; CCl_4 \text{ molecules}}{\text{mol } CCl_4}$$

Solution: $85.26 \text{ g } CCl_4 \times \frac{1 \text{ mol } CCl_4}{153.81 \text{ g } CCl_4} \times \frac{6.022 \times 10^{23} \; CCl_4 \text{ molecules}}{\text{mol } CCl_4}$

$= 3.33\underline{8}1 \times 10^{23} \; CCl_4 \text{ molecules} = 3.338 \times 10^{23} \; CCl_4 \text{ molecules}$

Check: The units of the answer (CCl_4 molecules) are correct. The magnitude is appropriate: it is smaller than Avogadro's number, as expected, since we have less than 1 mole of CCl_4.

(b) **Given:** 55.93 kg $NaHCO_3$ **Find:** number of molecules
Conceptual Plan: kg $NaHCO_3$ → g $NaHCO_3$ → mole $NaHCO_3$ → number $NaHCO_3$ molecules

$$\frac{1000 \text{ g}}{\text{kg}} \qquad \frac{1 \text{ mol}}{84.01 \text{ g } NaHCO_3} \qquad \frac{6.022 \times 10^{23} \; NaHCO_3 \text{ molecules}}{\text{mol } NaHCO_3}$$

Solution:

$$55.93 \text{ kg } NaHCO_3 \times \frac{1000 \text{ g } NaHCO_3}{\text{kg } NaHCO_3} \times \frac{1 \text{ mol } NaHCO_3}{84.01 \text{ g } NaHCO_3} \times \frac{6.022 \times 10^{23} \; NaHCO_3 \text{ molecules}}{\text{mol } NaHCO_3}$$

$= 4.009 \times 10^{26} \; NaHCO_3 \text{ molecules}$

Check: The units of the answer ($NaHCO_3$ molecules) are correct. The magnitude is appropriate: it is more than Avogadro's number, as expected, since we have many moles of $NaHCO_3$.

(c) **Given:** 119.78 g C_4H_{10} **Find:** number of molecules
Conceptual Plan: g C_4H_{10} → mole C_4H_{10} → number C_4H_{10} molecules

$$\frac{1 \text{ mol}}{58.12 \text{ g } C_4H_{10}} \qquad \frac{6.022 \times 10^{23} \; C_4H_{10} \text{ molecules}}{\text{mol } C_4H_{10}}$$

Solution:

$$119.78 \text{ g } C_4H_{10} \times \frac{1 \text{ mol } C_4H_{10}}{58.12 \text{ g } C_4H_{10}} \times \frac{6.022 \times 10^{23} \; C_4H_{10} \text{ molecules}}{\text{mol } C_4H_{10}} = 1.241 \times 10^{24} \; C_4H_{10} \text{ molecules}$$

Check: The units of the answer (C_4H_{10} molecules) are correct. The magnitude is appropriate: it is larger than Avogadro's number, as expected, since we have more than 1 mole of C_4H_{10}.

(d) **Given:** 4.59×10^5 g Na_3PO_4 **Find:** number of molecules
Conceptual Plan: g Na_3PO_4 → mole Na_3PO_4 → number Na_3PO_4 molecules

$$\frac{1 \text{ mol}}{163.94 \text{ g } Na_3PO_4} \qquad \frac{6.022 \times 10^{23} \; Na_3PO_4 \text{ molecules}}{\text{mol } Na_3PO_4}$$

Solution: $4.59 \times 10^5 \text{ g } Na_3PO_4 \times \frac{1 \text{ mol } Na_3PO_4}{163.94 \text{ g } Na_3PO_4} \times \frac{6.022 \times 10^{23} \; Na_3PO_4 \text{ molecules}}{\text{mol } Na_3PO_4}$

$= 1.6\underline{8}6 \times 10^{27} \; Na_3PO_4 \text{ molecules} = 1.69 \times 10^{27} \; Na_3PO_4 \text{ molecules}$

Check: The units of the answer (Na_3PO_4 molecules) are correct. The magnitude is appropriate: it is larger than Avogadro's number, as expected, since we have more than 1 mole of Na_3PO_4.

3.61 (a) **Given:** 5.94×10^{20} SO_3 molecules **Find:** mass in g
Conceptual Plan: number SO_3 molecules → mole SO_3 → g SO_3

$$\frac{1 \text{ mol } SO_3}{6.022 \times 10^{23} \; SO_3 \text{ molecules}} \qquad \frac{80.07 \text{ g } SO_3}{1 \text{ mol } SO_3}$$

Solution: $5.94 \times 10^{20}\ \text{SO}_3\ \text{molecules} \times \dfrac{1\ \text{mol SO}_3}{6.022 \times 10^{23}\ \text{SO}_3\ \text{molecules}} \times \dfrac{80.07\ \text{g SO}_3}{1\ \text{mol SO}_3} = 0.0790\ \text{g SO}_3$

Check: The units of the answer (grams SO_3) are correct. The magnitude is appropriate: there is less than Avogadro's number of molecules so we have less than 1 mole of SO_3.

(b) **Given:** 2.8×10^{22} H_2O molecules **Find:** mass in g

Conceptual Plan: number H_2O molecules $\rightarrow$ mole H_2O $\rightarrow$ g H_2O

$$\frac{1\ \text{mol H}_2\text{O}}{6.022 \times 10^{23}\ \text{H}_2\text{O molecules}} \qquad \frac{18.02\ \text{g H}_2\text{O}}{1\ \text{mol H}_2\text{O}}$$

Solution: $2.8 \times 10^{22}\ \text{H}_2\text{O molecules} \times \dfrac{1\ \text{mol H}_2\text{O}}{6.022 \times 10^{23}\ \text{H}_2\text{O molecules}} \times \dfrac{18.02\ \text{g H}_2\text{O}}{1\ \text{mol H}_2\text{O}} = 0.84\ \text{g H}_2\text{O}$

Check: The units of the answer (grams H_2O) are correct. The magnitude is appropriate: there is less than Avogadro's number of molecules so we have less than 1 mole of H_2O.

(c) **Given:** 1 $C_6H_{12}O_6$ molecule **Find:** mass in g

Conceptual Plan: number $C_6H_{12}O_6$ molecules $\rightarrow$ mole $C_6H_{12}O_6$ $\rightarrow$ g $C_6H_{12}O_6$

$$\frac{1\ \text{mol C}_6\text{H}_{12}\text{O}_6}{6.022 \times 10^{23}\ \text{C}_6\text{H}_{12}\text{O}_6\ \text{molecules}} \qquad \frac{180.16\ \text{g C}_6\text{H}_{12}\text{O}_6}{1\ \text{mol C}_6\text{H}_{12}\text{O}_6}$$

Solution:

$$1\ \text{C}_6\text{H}_{12}\text{O}_6\ \text{molecule} \times \frac{1\ \text{mol C}_6\text{H}_{12}\text{O}_6}{6.022 \times 10^{23}\ \text{C}_6\text{H}_{12}\text{O}_6\ \text{molecules}} \times \frac{180.16\ \text{g C}_6\text{H}_{12}\text{O}_6}{1\ \text{mol C}_6\text{H}_{12}\text{O}_6} = 2.992 \times 10^{-22}\ \text{g C}_6\text{H}_{12}\text{O}_6$$

Check: The units of the answer (grams $C_6H_{12}O_6$) are correct. The magnitude is appropriate: there is much less than Avogadro's number of molecules so we have much less than 1 mole of $C_6H_{12}O_6$.

3.62 (a) **Given:** 4.5×10^{25} O_3 molecules **Find:** mass in g

Conceptual Plan: number O_3 molecules $\rightarrow$ mole O_3 $\rightarrow$ g O_3

$$\frac{1\ \text{mol O}_3}{6.022 \times 10^{23}\ \text{O}_3\ \text{molecules}} \qquad \frac{48.00\ \text{g O}_3}{1\ \text{mol O}_3}$$

Solution: $4.5 \times 10^{25}\ \text{O}_3\ \text{molecules} \times \dfrac{1\ \text{mol O}_3}{6.022 \times 10^{23}\ \text{O}_3\ \text{molecules}} \times \dfrac{48.00\ \text{g O}_3}{1\ \text{mol O}_3} = 3.6 \times 10^{3}\ \text{g O}_3$

Check: The units of the answer (grams O_3) are correct. The magnitude is appropriate: there is more than Avogadro's number of molecules so we have more than 1 mole of O_3.

(b) **Given:** 9.85×10^{19} CCl_2F_2 molecules **Find:** mass in g

Conceptual Plan: number CCl_2F_2 molecules $\rightarrow$ mole CCl_2F_2 $\rightarrow$ g CCl_2F_2

$$\frac{1\ \text{mol O}_3}{6.022 \times 10^{23}\ \text{O}_3\ \text{molecules}} \qquad \frac{120.91\ \text{g CCl}_2\text{F}_2}{1\ \text{mol CClF}_2}$$

Solution:

$$9.85 \times 10^{19}\ \text{CCl}_2\text{F}_2\ \text{molecules} \times \frac{1\ \text{mol CCl}_2\text{F}_2}{6.022 \times 10^{23}\ \text{CCl}_2\text{F}_2\ \text{molecules}} \times \frac{120.91\ \text{g CCl}_2\text{F}_2}{1\ \text{mol CCl}_2\text{F}_2} = 1.98 \times 10^{-2}\ \text{g CCl}_2\text{F}_2$$

Check: The units of the answer (grams CCl_2F_2) are correct. The magnitude is appropriate: there is less than Avogadro's number of molecules so we have less than 1 mole of CCl_2F_2.

(c) **Given:** 1 H_2O molecule **Find:** mass in g

Conceptual Plan: number H_2O molecules $\rightarrow$ mole H_2O $\rightarrow$ g H_2O

$$\frac{1\ \text{mol H}_2\text{O}}{6.022 \times 10^{23}\ \text{H}_2\text{O molecules}} \qquad \frac{18.02\ \text{g H}_2\text{O}}{1\ \text{mol H}_2\text{O}}$$

Solution: $1\ \text{H}_2\text{O molecule} \times \dfrac{1\ \text{mol H}_2\text{O}}{6.022 \times 10^{23}\ \text{H}_2\text{O molecules}} \times \dfrac{18.02\ \text{g H}_2\text{O}}{1\ \text{mol H}_2\text{O}} = 2.992 \times 10^{-23}\ \text{g H}_2\text{O}$

Check: The units of the answer (grams H_2O) are correct. The magnitude is appropriate: there is much less than Avogadro's number of molecules so we have much less than 1 mole of H_2O.

3.63 **Given:** 1.8×10^{17} $C_{12}H_{22}O_{11}$ molecule **Find:** mass in mg

Conceptual Plan: number $C_{12}H_{22}O_{11}$ molecules → mole $C_{12}H_{22}O_{11}$ → g $C_{12}H_{22}O_{11}$ → mg $C_{12}H_{22}O_{11}$

$$\frac{1 \text{ mol } C_{12}H_{22}O_{11}}{6.022 \times 10^{23} \; C_{12}H_{22}O_{11} \text{ molecules}} \qquad \frac{342.3 \text{ g } C_{12}H_{22}O_{11}}{1 \text{ mol } C_{12}H_{22}O_{11}} \qquad \frac{1 \times 10^{3} \text{ mg } C_{12}H_{22}O_{11}}{1 \text{ g } C_{12}H_{22}O_{11}}$$

Solution:

$$1.8 \times 10^{17} \; \cancel{C_{12}H_{22}O_{11} \text{ molecules}} \times \frac{1 \; \cancel{\text{mol } C_{12}H_{22}O_{11}}}{6.022 \times 10^{23} \; \cancel{C_{12}H_{22}O_{11} \text{ molecules}}} \times \frac{342.3 \; \cancel{\text{g } C_{12}H_{22}O_{11}}}{1 \; \cancel{\text{mol } C_{12}H_{22}O_{11}}} \times \frac{1 \times 10^{3} \; \cancel{\text{mg } C_{12}H_{22}O_{11}}}{1 \; \cancel{\text{g } C_{12}H_{22}O_{11}}}$$

$$= 0.10 \text{ mg } C_{12}H_{22}O_{11}$$

Check: The units of the answer (milligrams $C_{12}H_{22}O_{11}$) are correct. The magnitude is appropriate: there is much less than Avogadro's number of molecules so we have much less than 1 mole of $C_{12}H_{22}O_{11}$.

3.64 **Given:** 0.12 mg NaCl **Find:** number of formula units

Conceptual Plan: mg NaCl → g NaCl → mole NaCl → number of formula units NaCl

$$\frac{1 \text{ g NaCl}}{1 \times 10^{3} \text{ mg NaCl}} \qquad \frac{1 \text{ mol NaCl}}{58.44 \text{ g NaCl}} \qquad \frac{6.022 \times 10^{23} \text{ NaCl formula units}}{1 \text{ mol NaCl}}$$

Solution:

$$0.12 \; \cancel{\text{mg NaCl}} \times \frac{1 \; \cancel{\text{g NaCl}}}{1 \times 10^{3} \; \cancel{\text{mg NaCl}}} \times \frac{1 \; \cancel{\text{mol NaCl}}}{58.44 \; \cancel{\text{g NaCl}}} \times \frac{6.022 \times 10^{23} \text{ formula units NaCl}}{1 \; \cancel{\text{mol NaCl}}} = 1.2 \times 10^{18} \text{ formula units NaCl}$$

Check: The units of the answer (formula units NaCl) are correct. The magnitude is appropriate: there is less than 1 mole of NaCl so we have less than Avogadro's number of formula units.

Composition of Compounds

3.65 (a) **Given:** CH_4 **Find:** mass percent C

Conceptual Plan: $\text{mass } \%C = \dfrac{1 \times \text{molar mass C}}{\text{molar mass } CH_4} \times 100$

Solution:

$$1 \times \text{molar mass C} = 1(12.01 \text{g/mol}) = 12.01 \text{ g C}$$
$$\text{molar mass } CH_4 = 1(12.01 \text{ g/mol}) + 4(1.008 \text{ g/mol}) = 16.04 \text{ g/mol}$$
$$\text{mass } \% \text{ C} = \frac{1 \times \text{molar mass C}}{\text{molar mass } CH_4} \times 100\%$$
$$= \frac{12.01 \; \cancel{\text{g/mol}}}{16.04 \; \cancel{\text{g/mol}}} \times 100\%$$
$$= 74.87 \; \%$$

Check: The units of the answer (%) are correct. The magnitude is reasonable because it is between 0 and 100% and carbon is the heaviest element.

(b) **Given:** C_2H_6 **Find:** mass percent C

Conceptual Plan: $\text{mass } \%C = \dfrac{2 \times \text{molar mass C}}{\text{molar mass } C_2H_6} \times 100$

Solution:

$$2 \times \text{molar mass C} = 2(12.01 \text{g/mol}) = 24.02 \text{ g C}$$
$$\text{molar mass } C_2H_6 = 2(12.01 \text{ g/mol}) + 6(1.008 \text{ g/mol}) = 30.07 \text{ g/mol}$$
$$\text{mass } \% \text{ C} = \frac{2 \times \text{molar mass C}}{\text{molar mass } C_2H_6} \times 100\%$$
$$= \frac{24.02 \; \cancel{\text{g/mol}}}{30.07 \; \cancel{\text{g/mol}}} \times 100\%$$
$$= 79.89 \; \%$$

Check: The units of the answer (%) are correct. The magnitude is reasonable because it is between 0 and 100% and carbon is the heaviest element.

(c) **Given:** C_2H_2 **Find:** mass percent C

Conceptual Plan: $\text{mass } \%C = \dfrac{2 \times \text{molar mass C}}{\text{molar mass } C_2H_2} \times 100$

Solution:

$$2 \text{ x molar mass C} = 2(12.01\text{g/mol}) = 24.02 \text{ g C}$$
$$\text{molar mass } C_2H_2 = 2(12.01 \text{ g/mol}) + 2(1.008 \text{ g/mol}) = 26.04 \text{ g/mol}$$
$$\text{mass \% C} = \frac{2 \text{ x molar mass C}}{\text{molar mass } C_2H_2} \text{ x } 100\%$$
$$= \frac{24.02 \cancel{\text{g/mol}}}{26.04 \cancel{\text{g/mol}}} \text{ x } 100\%$$
$$= 92.26 \text{ \%}$$

Check: The units of the answer (%) are correct. The magnitude is reasonable because it is between 0 and 100% and carbon is the heaviest element.

(d) **Given:** C_2H_5Cl **Find:** mass percent C

Conceptual Plan: $\text{mass \%C} = \frac{2 \text{ x molar mass C}}{\text{molar mass } C_2H_5Cl} \text{ x } 100$

Solution:

$$2 \text{ x molar mass C} = 2(12.01\text{g/mol}) = 24.02 \text{ g C}$$
$$\text{molar mass } C_2H_5Cl = 2(12.01 \text{ g/mol}) + 5(1.008 \text{ g/mol}) + 1(35.45 \text{ g/mol}) = 64.51 \text{ g/mol}$$
$$\text{mass \% C} = \frac{2 \text{ x molar mass C}}{\text{molar mass } C_2H_5Cl} \text{ x } 100\%$$
$$= \frac{24.02 \cancel{\text{g/mol}}}{64.51 \cancel{\text{g/mol}}} \text{ x } 100\%$$
$$= 37.23 \text{ \%}$$

Check: The units of the answer (%) are correct. The magnitude is reasonable because it is between 0 and 100% and chlorine is heavier than carbon.

3.66 (a) **Given:** N_2O **Find:** mass percent N

Conceptual Plan: $\text{mass \%N} = \frac{2 \text{ x molar mass N}}{\text{molar mass } N_2O} \text{ x } 100$

Solution:

$$2 \text{ x molar mass N} = 2(14.01\text{g/mol}) = 28.02 \text{ g N}$$
$$\text{molar mass } N_2O = 2(14.01 \text{ g/mol}) + (16.00 \text{ g/mol}) = 44.02 \text{ g/mol}$$
$$\text{mass \% N} = \frac{2 \text{ x molar mass N}}{\text{molar mass } N_2O} \text{ x } 100\%$$
$$= \frac{28.02 \cancel{\text{g/mol}}}{44.02 \cancel{\text{g/mol}}} \text{ x } 100\%$$
$$= 63.65 \text{ \%}$$

Check: The units of the answer (%) are correct. The magnitude is reasonable because it is between 0 and 100% and there are 2 nitrogens per molecule.

(b) **Given:** NO **Find:** mass percent N

Conceptual Plan: $\text{mass \%N} = \frac{1 \text{ x molar mass N}}{\text{molar mass NO}} \text{ x } 100$

Solution:

$$1 \text{ x molar mass N} = 1(14.01\text{g/mol}) = 14.01 \text{ g N}$$
$$\text{molar mass NO} = (14.01 \text{ g/mol}) + (16.00 \text{ g/mol}) = 30.01 \text{ g/mol}$$
$$\text{mass \% N} = \frac{1 \text{ x molar mass N}}{\text{molar mass NO}} \text{ x } 100\%$$
$$= \frac{14.01 \cancel{\text{g/mol}}}{30.01 \cancel{\text{g/mol}}} \text{ x } 100\%$$
$$= 46.68 \text{ \%}$$

Check: The units of the answer (%) are correct. The magnitude is reasonable because it is between 0 and 100% and the mass of nitrogen is less than the mass of oxygen.

(c) **Given:** NO_2 **Find:** mass percent N

Conceptual Plan: $\text{mass \%N} = \frac{1 \text{ x molar mass N}}{\text{molar mass } NO_2} \text{ x } 100$

Solution:

$$1 \text{ x molar mass N} = 1(14.01\text{g/mol}) = 14.01 \text{ g N}$$
$$\text{molar mass } NO_2 = (14.01 \text{ g/mol}) + 2(16.00 \text{ g/mol}) = 46.01 \text{ g/mol}$$
$$\text{mass \% N} = \frac{1 \text{ x molar mass N}}{\text{molar mass } NO_2} \text{ x } 100\%$$
$$= \frac{14.01 \cancel{\text{g/mol}}}{46.01 \cancel{\text{g/mol}}} \text{ x } 100\%$$
$$= 30.45\ \%$$

Check: The units of the answer (%) are correct. The magnitude is reasonable because it is between 0 and 100%. The mass of nitrogen is less than the mass of oxygen and there are 2 oxygens per molecule.

(d) **Given:** HNO_3 **Find:** mass percent N

Conceptual Plan: $\text{mass \% N} = \frac{1 \text{ x molar mass N}}{\text{molar mass } HNO_3} \text{ x } 100$

Solution:

$$1 \text{ x molar mass N} = 1(14.01\text{g/mol}) = 14.01 \text{ g N}$$
$$\text{molar mass } HNO_3 = (1.008 \text{ g/mol}) + (14.01 \text{ g/mol}) + 3(16.00 \text{ g/mol}) = 63.02 \text{ g/mol}$$
$$\text{mass \% N} = \frac{1 \text{ x molar mass N}}{\text{molar mass } HNO_3} \text{ x } 100\%$$
$$= \frac{14.01 \cancel{\text{g/mol}}}{63.02 \cancel{\text{g/mol}}} \text{ x } 100\%$$
$$= 22.23\ \%$$

Check: The units of the answer (%) are correct. The magnitude is reasonable because it is between 0 and 100%. The mass of nitrogen is less than the mass of oxygen and there are 3 oxygens per molecule.

3.67 **Given:** NH_3 **Find:** mass percent N

Conceptual Plan: $\text{mass \% N} = \frac{1 \text{ x molar mass N}}{\text{molar mass } NH_3} \text{ x } 100$

Solution:

$$1 \text{ x molar mass N} = 1(14.01\text{g/mol}) = 14.01 \text{ g N}$$
$$\text{molar mass } NH_3 = 3(1.008 \text{ g/mol}) + (14.01 \text{ g/mol}) = 17.03 \text{ g/mol}$$
$$\text{mass \% N} = \frac{1 \text{ x molar mass N}}{\text{molar mass } NH_3} \text{ x } 100\%$$
$$= \frac{14.01 \cancel{\text{g/mol}}}{17.03 \cancel{\text{g/mol}}} \text{ x } 100\%$$
$$= 82.27\ \%$$

Check: The units of the answer (%) are correct. The magnitude is reasonable because it is between 0 and 100% and nitrogen is the heaviest atom present.

Given: $CO(NH_2)_2$ **Find:** mass percent N

Conceptual Plan: $\text{mass \% N} = \frac{2 \text{ x molar mass N}}{\text{molar mass } CO(NH_2)_2} \text{ x } 100$

Solution:

$$2 \text{ x molar mass N} = 1(14.01\text{g/mol}) = 28.02 \text{ g N}$$
$$\text{molar mass } CO(NH_2)_2 = (12.01 \text{ g/mol}) + (16.00 \text{ g/mol}) + 2(14.01 \text{ g/mol}) + 4(1.008 \text{ g/mol}) = 60.06 \text{ g/mol}$$
$$\text{mass \% N} = \frac{2 \text{ x molar mass N}}{\text{molar mass } CO(NH_2)_2} \text{ x } 100\%$$
$$= \frac{28.02 \cancel{\text{g/mol}}}{60.06 \cancel{\text{g/mol}}} \text{ x } 100\%$$
$$= 46.65\ \%$$

Check: The units of the answer (%) are correct. The magnitude is reasonable. It is between 0 and 100% and there are two nitrogens and only one carbon and one oxygen per molecule.

Given: NH_4NO_3 **Find:** mass percent N

Conceptual Plan: $\text{mass \% N} = \dfrac{2 \times \text{molar mass N}}{\text{molar mass } NH_4NO_3} \times 100$

Solution:

$$2 \times \text{molar mass N} = 2(14.01 \text{g/mol}) = 28.02 \text{ g N}$$
$$\text{molar mass } NH_4NO_3 = 2(14.01 \text{ g/mol}) + 4(1.008 \text{ g/mol}) + 3(16.00 \text{ g/mol}) = 80.05 \text{ g/mol}$$
$$\text{mass \% N} = \frac{2 \times \text{molar mass N}}{\text{molar mass } NH_4NO_3} \times 100\%$$
$$= \frac{28.02 \text{ g/mol}}{80.05 \text{ g/mol}} \times 100\%$$
$$= 35.00\ \%$$

Check: The units of the answer (%) are correct. The magnitude is reasonable because it is between 0 and 100%. The mass of nitrogen is less than the mass of oxygen and there are two nitrogens and three oxygens per molecule.

Given: $(NH_4)_2SO_4$ **Find:** mass percent N

Conceptual Plan: $\text{mass \% N} = \dfrac{2 \times \text{molar mass N}}{\text{molar mass } (NH_4)_2SO_4} \times 100$

Solution:

$$2 \times \text{molar mass N} = 2(14.01 \text{g/mol}) = 28.02 \text{ g N}$$
$$\text{molar mass } (NH_4)_2SO_4 = 2(14.01 \text{ g/mol}) + 8(1.008 \text{ g/mol}) + (32.07 \text{ g/mol}) + 4(16.00 \text{ g/mol}) = 132.15 \text{ g/mol}$$
$$\text{mass \% N} = \frac{2 \times \text{molar mass N}}{\text{molar mass } (NH_4)_2SO_4} \times 100\%$$
$$= \frac{28.02 \text{ g/mol}}{132.15 \text{ g/mol}} \times 100\%$$
$$= 21.20\ \%$$

Check: The units of the answer (%) are correct. The magnitude is reasonable because it is between 0 and 100% and the mass of nitrogen is less than the mass of oxygen and sulfur.

The fertilizer with the highest nitrogen content is NH_3 with a N content of 82.27% N.

3.68 **Given:** Fe_2O_3 **Find:** mass percent Fe

Conceptual Plan: $\text{mass \% Fe} = \dfrac{2 \times \text{molar mass Fe}}{\text{molar mass } Fe_2O_3} \times 100$

Solution:

$$2 \times \text{molar mass Fe} = 2(55.85 \text{g/mol}) = 111.7 \text{ g Fe}$$
$$\text{molar mass } Fe_2O_3 = 2(55.85 \text{ g/mol}) + 3(16.00 \text{ g/mol}) = 159.7 \text{ g/mol}$$
$$\text{mass \% Fe} = \frac{2 \times \text{molar mass Fe}}{\text{molar mass } Fe_2O_3} \times 100\%$$
$$= \frac{111.7 \text{ g/mol}}{159.7 \text{ g/mol}} \times 100\%$$
$$= 69.94\ \%$$

Check: The units of the answer (%) are correct. The magnitude is reasonable because it is between 0 and 100% and iron provides most of the formula mass.

Given: Fe_3O_4 **Find:** mass percent Fe

Conceptual Plan: $\text{mass \% Fe} = \dfrac{3 \times \text{molar mass Fe}}{\text{molar mass } Fe_3O_4} \times 100$

Solution:

$$3 \times \text{molar mass Fe} = 3(55.85 \text{g/mol}) = 167.6 \text{ g Fe}$$
$$\text{molar mass } Fe_3O_4 = 3(55.85 \text{ g/mol}) + 4(16.00 \text{ g/mol}) = 231.6 \text{ g/mol}$$
$$\text{mass \% Fe} = \frac{3 \times \text{molar mass Fe}}{\text{molar mass } Fe_3O_4} \times 100\%$$
$$= \frac{167.6 \text{ g/mol}}{231.6 \text{ g/mol}} \times 100\%$$
$$= 72.37\ \%$$

Check: The units of the answer (%) are correct. The magnitude is reasonable because it is between 0 and 100% and iron provides most of the formula mass.

Given: $FeCO_3$ **Find:** mass percent Fe

Conceptual Plan: $\text{mass \% Fe} = \dfrac{1 \text{ x molar mass Fe}}{\text{molar mass } FeCO_3} \text{ x } 100$

Solution:

$$1 \text{ x molar mass Fe} = (55.85 \text{ g/mol}) = 55.85 \text{ g Fe}$$
$$\text{molar mass } FeCO_3 = 1(55.85 \text{ g/mol}) + 1(12.01 \text{ g/mol}) + 3(16.00 \text{ g/mol}) = 115.86 \text{ g/mol}$$
$$\text{mass \% Fe} = \frac{1 \text{ x molar mass Fe}}{\text{molar mass } FeCO_3} \text{ x } 100\% = \frac{55.85 \cancel{\text{g/mol}}}{115.86 \cancel{\text{g/mol}}} \text{ x } 100\% = 48.20\ \%$$

Check: The units of the answer (%) are correct. The magnitude is reasonable because it is between 0 and 100% and iron provides slightly less than half of the formula mass.

The ore with the highest iron content is Fe_3O_4 with an Fe content of 72.37% Fe.

3.69 **Given:** 55.5 g CuF_2: 37.42 % F **Find:** g F in CuF_2
Conceptual Plan: **g CuF_2 → g F**

$$\frac{37.42 \text{ g F}}{100.0 \text{ g } CuF_2}$$

Solution: $55.5 \cancel{\text{g } CuF_2} \text{ x } \dfrac{37.42 \text{ g F}}{100.0 \cancel{\text{g } CuF_2}} = 20.77 = 20.8 \text{ g F}$

Check: The units of the answer (g F) are correct. The magnitude is reasonable because it is less than the original mass.

3.70 **Given:** 155 mg Ag; 75.27 % Ag in AgCl **Find:** mg AgCl
Conceptual Plan: **mg Ag → g Ag → g AgCl → mg AgCl**

$$\frac{1 \text{ g Ag}}{1000 \text{ mg Ag}} \quad \frac{100.0 \text{ g AgCl}}{75.27 \text{ g Ag}} \quad \frac{1000 \text{ mg AgCl}}{1 \text{ g AgCl}}$$

Solution: $155 \cancel{\text{mg Ag}} \text{ x } \dfrac{1 \cancel{\text{g Ag}}}{1000 \cancel{\text{mg Ag}}} \text{ x } \dfrac{100.0 \cancel{\text{g AgCl}}}{75.27 \cancel{\text{g Ag}}} \text{ x } \dfrac{1000 \text{ mg AgCl}}{1 \cancel{\text{g AgCl}}} = 206 \text{ mg AgCl}$

Check: The units of the answer (g AgCl) are correct. The magnitude is reasonable because it is greater than the original mass.

3.71 **Given:** 150 μg I; 76.45% I in KI **Find:** μg KI
Conceptual Plan: **μg I → g I → g KI → μg KI**

$$\frac{1 \text{ g I}}{1 \text{ x } 10^6 \ \mu\text{g I}} \quad \frac{100.0 \text{ g KI}}{76.45 \text{ g I}} \quad \frac{1 \text{ x } 10^6 \ \mu\text{g KI}}{1 \text{ g KI}}$$

Solution: $150 \cancel{\mu\text{g I}} \text{ x } \dfrac{1 \cancel{\text{g I}}}{1\text{x}10^6 \cancel{\mu\text{g I}}} \text{ x } \dfrac{100.0 \cancel{\text{g KI}}}{76.45 \cancel{\text{g I}}} \text{ x } \dfrac{1 \text{ x } 10^6 \ \mu\text{g KI}}{1 \cancel{\text{g KI}}} = 196 \ \mu\text{g KI}$

Check: The units of the answer (μg KI) are correct. The magnitude is reasonable because it is greater than the original mass.

3.72 **Given:** 3.0 mg F; 45.24 % F in NaF **Find:** mg NaF
Conceptual Plan: **mg F → g F → g NaF → mg NaF**

$$\frac{1 \text{ g F}}{1000 \text{ mg F}} \quad \frac{100.0 \text{ g NaF}}{45.24 \text{ g F}} \quad \frac{1000 \text{ mg NaF}}{1 \text{ g NaF}}$$

Solution: $3.0 \cancel{\text{mg F}} \text{ x } \dfrac{1 \cancel{\text{g F}}}{1000 \cancel{\text{mg F}}} \text{ x } \dfrac{100.0 \cancel{\text{g NaF}}}{45.24 \cancel{\text{g NaF}}} \text{ x } \dfrac{1000 \text{ mg NaF}}{1 \cancel{\text{g NaF}}} = 6.6 \text{ mg NaF}$

Check: The units of the answer (mg NaF) are correct. The magnitude is reasonable because it is greater than the original mass.

3.73 (a) red – oxygen, white – hydrogen: 2H:O H_2O

(b) black – carbon, white – hydrogen: 4H:C CH_4

(c) black – carbon, white – hydrogen, red – oxygen: 2C:O:6H CH_3CH_2OH or C_2H_6O

3.74 (a) black – carbon, red – oxygen: 2O:C CO_2

(b) red – oxygen, white – hydrogen: 2H:2O H_2O_2

(c) red – oxygen, white – hydrogen: 2H:O H_2O

3.75 (a) **Given:** 0.0885 mol C_4H_{10} **Find:** mol H atoms

Conceptual Plan: mol C_4H_{10} → mole H atom

$$\frac{10 \text{ mol H}}{1 \text{ mol } C_4H_{10}}$$

Solution: $0.0885 \cancel{\text{mol } C_4H_{10}} \times \frac{10 \text{ mol H}}{1 \cancel{\text{mol } C_4H_{10}}} = 0.885 \text{ mol H atoms}$

Check: The units of the answer (mol H atoms) are correct. The magnitude is reasonable because it is greater than the original mol C_4H_{10}.

(b) **Given:** 1.3 mol CH_4 **Find:** mol H atoms

Conceptual Plan: mol CH_4 → mole H atom

$$\frac{4 \text{ mol H}}{1 \text{ mol } CH_4}$$

Solution: $1.3 \cancel{\text{mol } CH_4} \times \frac{4 \text{ mol H}}{1 \cancel{\text{mol } CH_4}} = 5.2 \text{ mol H atoms}$

Check: The units of the answer (mol H atoms) are correct. The magnitude is reasonable because it is greater than the original mol CH_4.

(c) **Given:** 2.4 mol C_6H_{12} **Find:** mol H atoms

Conceptual Plan: mol C_6H_{12} → mole H atom

$$\frac{12 \text{ mol H}}{1 \text{ mol } C_6H_{12}}$$

Solution: $2.4 \cancel{\text{mol } C_6H_{12}} \times \frac{12 \text{ mol H}}{1 \cancel{\text{mol } C_6H_{12}}} = 29 \text{ mol H atoms}$

Check: The units of the answer (mol H atoms) are correct. The magnitude is reasonable because it is greater than the original mol C_6H_{12}.

(d) **Given:** 1.87 mol C_8H_{18} **Find:** mol H atoms

Conceptual Plan: mol C_8H_{18} → mole H atom

$$\frac{18 \text{ mol H}}{1 \text{ mol } C_8H_{18}}$$

Solution: $1.87 \cancel{\text{mol } C_8H_{18}} \times \frac{18 \text{ mol H}}{1 \cancel{\text{mol } C_8H_{18}}} = 33.7 \text{ mol H atoms}$

Check: The units of the answer (mol H atoms) are correct. The magnitude is reasonable because it is greater than the original mol C_8H_{18}.

3.76 (a) **Given:** 4.88 mol H_2O_2 **Find:** mol O atoms

Conceptual Plan: mol H_2O_2 → mole O atom

$$\frac{2 \text{ mol O}}{1 \text{ mol } H_2O_2}$$

Solution: $4.88 \cancel{\text{mol } H_2O_2} \times \frac{2 \text{ mol O}}{1 \cancel{\text{mol } H_2O_2}} = 9.76 \text{ mol O atoms}$

Check: The units of the answer (mol O atoms) are correct. The magnitude is reasonable because it is greater than the original mol H_2O_2.

(b) **Given:** 2.15 mol N_2O **Find:** mol O atoms

Conceptual Plan: mol N_2O → mole O atom

$$\frac{1 \text{ mol O}}{1 \text{ mol } N_2O}$$

Solution: $2.15\ \cancel{\text{mol N}_2\text{O}} \times \dfrac{1\ \text{mol O}}{1\ \cancel{\text{mol N}_2\text{O}}} = 2.15\ \text{mol O atoms}$

Check: The units of the answer (mol O atoms) are correct. The magnitude is reasonable because it is the same as the original mol N_2O.

(c) **Given:** 0.0237 mol H_2CO_3 **Find:** mol O atoms

Conceptual Plan: mol H_2CO_3 → mole O atom

$\dfrac{3\ \text{mol O}}{1\ \text{mol H}_2\text{CO}_3}$

Solution: $0.0237\ \cancel{\text{mol H}_2\text{CO}_3} \times \dfrac{3\ \text{mol O}}{1\ \cancel{\text{mol H}_2\text{CO}_3}} = 0.0711\ \text{mol O atoms}$

Check: The units of the answer (mol O atoms) are correct. The magnitude is reasonable because it is greater than the original mol H_2CO_3.

(d) **Given:** 24.1 mol CO_2 **Find:** mol O atoms

Conceptual Plan: mol CO_2 → mole O atom

$\dfrac{2\ \text{mol O}}{1\ \text{mol CO}_2}$

Solution: $24.1\ \cancel{\text{mol CO}_2} \times \dfrac{2\ \text{mol O}}{1\ \cancel{\text{mol CO}_2}} = 48.2\ \text{mol O atoms}$

Check: The units of the answer (mol O atoms) are correct. The magnitude is reasonable because it is greater than the original mol CO_2.

3.77 (a) **Given:** 8.5 g NaCl **Find:** g Na

Conceptual Plan: g NaCl → mole NaCl → mol Na → g Na

$\dfrac{1\ \text{mol NaCl}}{58.44\ \text{g NaCl}} \qquad \dfrac{1\ \text{mol Na}}{1\ \text{mol NaCl}} \qquad \dfrac{22.99\ \text{g Na}}{1\ \text{mol Na}}$

Solution: $8.5\ \cancel{\text{g NaCl}} \times \dfrac{1\ \cancel{\text{mol NaCl}}}{58.44\ \cancel{\text{g NaCl}}} \times \dfrac{1\ \cancel{\text{mol Na}}}{1\ \cancel{\text{mol NaCl}}} \times \dfrac{22.99\ \text{g Na}}{1\ \cancel{\text{mol Na}}} = 3.3\ \text{g Na}$

Check: The units of the answer (g Na) are correct. The magnitude is reasonable because it is less than the original g NaCl.

(b) **Given:** 8.5 g Na_3PO_4 **Find:** g Na

Conceptual Plan: g Na_3PO_4 → mole Na_3PO_4 → mol Na → g Na

$\dfrac{1\ \text{mol Na}_3\text{PO}_4}{163.94\ \text{g Na}_3\text{PO}_4} \qquad \dfrac{3\ \text{mol Na}}{1\ \text{mol Na}_3\text{PO}_4} \qquad \dfrac{22.99\ \text{g Na}}{1\ \text{mol Na}}$

Solution: $8.5\ \cancel{\text{g Na}_3\text{PO}_4} \times \dfrac{1\ \cancel{\text{mol Na}_3\text{PO}_4}}{163.94\ \cancel{\text{g Na}_3\text{PO}_4}} \times \dfrac{3\ \cancel{\text{mol Na}}}{1\ \cancel{\text{mol Na}_3\text{PO}_4}} \times \dfrac{22.99\ \text{g Na}}{1\ \cancel{\text{mol Na}}} = 3.6\ \text{g Na}$

Check: The units of the answer (g Na) are correct. The magnitude is reasonable because it is less than the original g Na_3PO_4.

(c) **Given:** 8.5 g $NaC_7H_5O_2$ **Find:** g Na

Conceptual Plan: g $NaC_7H_5O_2$ → mole $NaC_7H_5O_2$ → mol Na → g Na

$\dfrac{1\ \text{mol NaC}_7\text{H}_5\text{O}_2}{144.10\ \text{g NaC}_7\text{H}_5\text{O}_2} \qquad \dfrac{1\ \text{mol Na}}{1\ \text{mol NaC}_7\text{H}_5\text{O}_2} \qquad \dfrac{22.99\ \text{g Na}}{1\ \text{mol Na}}$

Solution: $8.5\ \cancel{\text{g NaC}_7\text{H}_5\text{O}_2} \times \dfrac{1\ \cancel{\text{mol NaC}_7\text{H}_5\text{O}_2}}{144.10\ \cancel{\text{g NaC}_7\text{H}_5\text{O}_2}} \times \dfrac{1\ \cancel{\text{mol Na}}}{1\ \cancel{\text{mol NaC}_7\text{H}_5\text{O}_2}} \times \dfrac{22.99\ \text{g Na}}{1\ \cancel{\text{mol Na}}} = 1.4\ \text{g Na}$

Check: The units of the answer (g Na) are correct. The magnitude is reasonable because it is less than the original g $NaC_7H_5O_2$.

(d) **Given:** 8.5 g $Na_2C_6H_6O_7$ **Find:** g Na

Conceptual Plan: g $Na_2C_6H_6O_7$ → mole $Na_2C_6H_6O_7$ → mol Na → g Na

$\dfrac{1\ \text{mol Na}_2\text{C}_6\text{H}_6\text{O}_7}{236.1\ \text{g Na}_2\text{C}_6\text{H}_6\text{O}_7} \qquad \dfrac{2\ \text{mol Na}}{1\ \text{mol Na}_2\text{C}_6\text{H}_6\text{O}_7} \qquad \dfrac{22.99\ \text{g Na}}{1\ \text{mol Na}}$

Solution:

$8.5\ \cancel{\text{g Na}_2\text{C}_6\text{H}_6\text{O}_7} \times \dfrac{1\ \cancel{\text{mol Na}_2\text{C}_6\text{H}_6\text{O}_7}}{236.1\ \cancel{\text{g Na}_2\text{C}_6\text{H}_6\text{O}_7}} \times \dfrac{2\ \cancel{\text{mol Na}}}{1\ \cancel{\text{mol Na}_2\text{C}_6\text{H}_6\text{O}_7}} \times \dfrac{22.99\ \text{g Na}}{1\ \cancel{\text{mol Na}}} = 1.7\ \text{g Na}$

Check: The units of the answer (g Na) are correct. The magnitude is reasonable because it is less than the original g $Na_2C_6H_6O_7$.

3.78 (a) **Given:** 25 kg CF_2Cl_2 **Find:** kg Cl

Conceptual Plan: **kg CF_2Cl_2 → g CF_2Cl_2 → mole CF_2Cl_2 → mol Cl → g Cl → kg Cl**

$$\frac{1000 \text{ g } CF_2Cl_2}{1 \text{ kg } CF_2Cl_2} \quad \frac{1 \text{ mol } CF_2Cl_2}{120.91 \text{ g } CF_2Cl_2} \quad \frac{2 \text{ mol Cl}}{1 \text{ mol } CF_2Cl_2} \quad \frac{35.45 \text{ g Cl}}{1 \text{ mol Cl}} \quad \frac{1 \text{ kg Cl}}{1000 \text{ g Cl}}$$

Solution: $25 \text{ kg } CF_2Cl_2 \times \frac{1000 \text{ g } CF_2Cl_2}{1 \text{ kg } CF_2Cl_2} \times \frac{1 \text{ mol } CF_2Cl_2}{120.91 \text{ g } CF_2Cl_2} \times \frac{2 \text{ mol Cl}}{1 \text{ mol } CF_2Cl_2} \times \frac{35.45 \text{ g Cl}}{1 \text{ mol Cl}} \times \frac{1 \text{ kg Cl}}{1000 \text{ g Cl}}$

$= 15 \text{ kg Cl}$

Check: The units of the answer (kg Cl) are correct. The magnitude is reasonable because it is less than the original kg CF_2Cl_2.

(b) **Given:** 25 kg $CFCl_3$ **Find:** kg Cl

Conceptual Plan: **kg $CFCl_3$ → g $CFCl_3$ → mole $CFCl_3$ → mol Cl → g Cl → kg Cl**

$$\frac{1000 \text{ g } CFCl_3}{1 \text{ kg } CFCl_3} \quad \frac{1 \text{ mol } CFCl_3}{137.4 \text{ g } CFCl_3} \quad \frac{3 \text{ mol Cl}}{1 \text{ mol } CFCl_3} \quad \frac{35.45 \text{ g Cl}}{1 \text{ mol Cl}} \quad \frac{1 \text{ kg Cl}}{1000 \text{ g Cl}}$$

Solution: $25 \text{ kg } CFCl_3 \times \frac{1000 \text{ g } CFCl_3}{1 \text{ kg } CFCl_3} \times \frac{1 \text{ mol } CFCl_3}{137.4 \text{ g } CFCl_3} \times \frac{3 \text{ mol Cl}}{1 \text{ mol } CFCl_3} \times \frac{35.45 \text{ g Cl}}{1 \text{ mol Cl}} \times \frac{1 \text{ kg Cl}}{1000 \text{g Cl}}$

$= 19 \text{ kg Cl}$

Check: The units of the answer (kg Cl) are correct. The magnitude is reasonable because it is less than the original kg CF_2Cl_2.

(c) **Given:** 25 kg $C_2F_3Cl_3$ **Find:** kg Cl

Conceptual Plan: **kg $C_2F_3Cl_3$ → g $C_2F_3Cl_3$ → mole $C_2F_3Cl_3$ → mol Cl → g Cl → kg Cl**

$$\frac{1000 \text{ g } C_2F_3Cl_3}{1 \text{ kg } C_2F_3Cl_3} \quad \frac{1 \text{ mol } C_2F_3Cl_3}{187.4 \text{ g } C_2F_3Cl_3} \quad \frac{3 \text{ mol Cl}}{1 \text{ mol } C_2F_3Cl_3} \quad \frac{35.45 \text{ g Cl}}{1 \text{ mol Cl}} \quad \frac{1 \text{ kg Cl}}{1000 \text{ g Cl}}$$

Solution: $25 \text{ kg } C_2F_3Cl_3 \times \frac{1000 \text{ g } C_2F_3Cl_3}{1 \text{kg } C_2F_3Cl_3} \times \frac{1 \text{ mol } C_2F_3Cl_3}{187.4 \text{ g } C_2F_3Cl_3} \times \frac{3 \text{ mol Cl}}{1 \text{ mol } C_2F_3Cl_3} \times \frac{35.45 \text{ g Cl}}{1 \text{ mol Cl}} \times \frac{1 \text{ kgCl}}{1000 \text{ g Cl}}$

$= 14 \text{ kg Cl}$

Check: The units of the answer (kg Cl) are correct. The magnitude is reasonable because it is less than the original kg $C_2F_3Cl_3$.

(d) **Given:** 25 kg CF_3Cl **Find:** kg Cl

Conceptual Plan: **kg CF_3Cl → g CF_3Cl → mole CF_3Cl → mol Cl → g Cl → kg Cl**

$$\frac{1000 \text{ g } CF_3Cl}{1 \text{ kg } CF_3Cl} \quad \frac{1 \text{ mol } CF_3Cl}{104.46 \text{ g } CF_3Cl} \quad \frac{1 \text{ mol Cl}}{1 \text{ mol } CF_3Cl} \quad \frac{35.45 \text{ g Cl}}{1 \text{ mol Cl}} \quad \frac{1 \text{ kg Cl}}{1000 \text{ g Cl}}$$

Solution: $25 \text{ kg } CF_3Cl \times \frac{1000 \text{ g } CF_3Cl}{1 \text{ kg } CF_3Cl} \times \frac{1 \text{ mol } CF_3Cl}{104.46 \text{ g } CF_3Cl} \times \frac{1 \text{ mol Cl}}{1 \text{ mol } CF_3Cl} \times \frac{35.45 \text{ g Cl}}{1 \text{ mol Cl}} \times \frac{1 \text{ kg Cl}}{1000 \text{ g Cl}}$

$= 8.5 \text{ kg Cl}$

Check: The units of the answer (kg Cl) are correct. The magnitude is reasonable because it is less than the original kg CF_3Cl.

Chemical Formulas from Experimental Data

3.79 (a) **Given:** 1.651 g Ag; 0.1224 g O **Find:** empirical formula

Conceptual Plan:

convert mass to mol of each element → write pseudoformula → write empirical formula

$$\frac{1 \text{ mol Ag}}{107.9 \text{ g Ag}} \quad \frac{1 \text{ mol O}}{16.00 \text{ g O}}$$

divide by smallest number

Solution: $1.651 \text{ g Ag} \times \frac{1 \text{ mol Ag}}{107.9 \text{ g Ag}} = 0.01530 \text{ mol Ag}$

$0.1224 \text{ g O} \times \frac{1 \text{ mol O}}{16.00 \text{ g O}} = 0.007650 \text{ mol O}$

$Ag_{0.01530}O_{0.007650}$

$Ag_{\frac{0.01530}{0.007650}}O_{\frac{0.007650}{0.007650}} \rightarrow Ag_2O$

The correct empirical formula is Ag_2O.

(b) **Given:** 0.672 g Co; 0.569 g As; 0.486 g O **Find:** empirical formula

Conceptual Plan:

convert mass to mol of each element → write pseudoformula → write empirical formula

$\frac{1 \text{ mol Co}}{58.93 \text{ g Co}}$ $\frac{1 \text{ mol As}}{74.92 \text{ g As}}$ $\frac{1 \text{ mol O}}{16.00 \text{ g O}}$ divide by smallest number

Solution: $0.672 \cancel{\text{g Co}} \times \frac{1 \text{ mol Co}}{58.93 \cancel{\text{g Co}}} = 0.0114 \text{ mol Co}$

$0.569 \cancel{\text{g As}} \times \frac{1 \text{ mol As}}{74.92 \cancel{\text{g As}}} = 0.00759 \text{ mol O}$

$0.486 \cancel{\text{g O}} \times \frac{1 \text{ mol O}}{16.00 \cancel{\text{g O}}} = 0.0304 \text{ mol O}$

$Co_{0.0114}As_{0.00759}O_{0.0304}$

$Co_{\frac{0.0114}{0.00759}}As_{\frac{0.00759}{0.00759}}O_{\frac{0.0304}{0.00759}} \rightarrow Co_{1.5}As_1O_4$

$Co_{1.5}As_1O_4 \times 2 \rightarrow Co_3As_2O_8$

The correct empirical formula is $Co_3As_2O_8$.

(c) **Given:** 1.443 g Se; 5.841 g Br **Find:** empirical formula

Conceptual Plan:

convert mass to mol of each element → write pseudoformula → write empirical formula

$\frac{1 \text{ mol Se}}{78.96 \text{ g Se}}$ $\frac{1 \text{ mol Br}}{79.90 \text{ g Br}}$ divide by smallest number

Solution: $1.443 \cancel{\text{g Se}} \times \frac{1 \text{ mol Se}}{78.96 \cancel{\text{g Se}}} = 0.01828 \text{ mol Se}$

$5.841 \cancel{\text{g Br}} \times \frac{1 \text{ mol Br}}{79.90 \cancel{\text{g Br}}} = 0.07310 \text{ mol Br}$

$Se_{0.01828}Br_{0.07310}$

$Se_{\frac{0.01828}{0.01828}}Br_{\frac{0.07310}{0.01828}} \rightarrow SeBr_4$

The correct empirical formula is $SeBr_4$.

3.80 (a) **Given:** 1.245 g Ni; 5.381 g I **Find:** empirical formula

Conceptual Plan:

convert mass to mol of each element → write pseudoformula → write empirical formula

$\frac{1 \text{ mol Ni}}{58.69 \text{ g Ni}}$ $\frac{1 \text{ mol I}}{126.9 \text{ g I}}$ divide by smallest number

Solution: $1.245 \cancel{\text{g Ni}} \times \frac{1 \text{ mol Ni}}{58.69 \cancel{\text{g Ni}}} = 0.02121 \text{ mol Ni}$

$5.381 \cancel{\text{g I}} \times \frac{1 \text{ mol I}}{126.9 \cancel{\text{g I}}} = 0.04240 \text{ mol I}$

$Ni_{0.02121}I_{0.04240}$

$Ni_{\frac{0.02121}{0.02121}}I_{\frac{0.04240}{0.02121}} \rightarrow NiI_2$

The correct empirical formula is NiI_2.

(b) **Given:** 2.677 g Ba; 3.115 g Br **Find:** empirical formula

Conceptual Plan:

convert mass to mol of each element → write pseudoformula → write empirical formula

$\frac{1 \text{ mol Ba}}{137.3 \text{ g Ba}}$ $\frac{1 \text{ mol Br}}{79.90 \text{ g Br}}$ divide by smallest number

Solution: $2.677 \cancel{\text{g Ba}} \times \frac{1 \text{ mol Ba}}{137.3 \cancel{\text{g Ba}}} = 0.01950 \text{ mol Ba}$

$3.115 \cancel{\text{g Br}} \times \frac{1 \text{ mol Br}}{79.90 \cancel{\text{g Br}}} = 0.03899 \text{ mol Br}$

$Ba_{0.01950}Br_{0.03899}$

$Ba_{\frac{0.01950}{0.01950}}Br_{\frac{0.03899}{0.01950}} \rightarrow BaBr_2$

The correct empirical formula is $BaBr_2$.

(c) **Given:** 2.128 g Be; 7.557 g S; 15.107 g O **Find:** empirical formula
Conceptual Plan:
convert mass to mol of each element → write pseudoformula → write empirical formula

$\frac{1 \text{ mol Be}}{9.012 \text{ g Be}}$ $\frac{1 \text{ mol S}}{32.07 \text{ g S}}$ $\frac{1 \text{ mol O}}{16.00 \text{ g O}}$ divide by smallest number

Solution: $2.128 \cancel{\text{g Be}} \times \frac{1 \text{ mol Be}}{9.012 \cancel{\text{g Be}}} = 0.2361 \text{ mol Be}$

$7.557 \cancel{\text{g S}} \times \frac{1 \text{ mol S}}{32.07 \cancel{\text{g S}}} = 0.2356 \text{ mol S}$

$15.107 \cancel{\text{g O}} \times \frac{1 \text{ mol O}}{16.00 \cancel{\text{g O}}} = 0.9442 \text{ mol O}$

$Be_{0.2361}S_{0.2356}O_{0.9442}$

$Be_{\frac{0.2361}{0.2356}}S_{\frac{0.2356}{0.2356}}O_{\frac{0.9442}{0.2356}} \rightarrow BeSO_4$

The correct empirical formula is $BeSO_4$.

3.81 (a) **Given:** In a 100 g sample: 74.03 g C, 8.70 g H, 17.27 g N **Find:** empirical formula
Conceptual Plan:
convert mass to mol of each element → write pseudoformula → write empirical formula

$\frac{1 \text{ mol C}}{12.01 \text{ g C}}$ $\frac{1 \text{ mol H}}{1.008 \text{ g H}}$ $\frac{1 \text{ mol N}}{14.01 \text{ g N}}$ divide by smallest number

Solution: $74.03 \cancel{\text{g C}} \times \frac{1 \text{ mol C}}{12.01 \cancel{\text{g C}}} = 6.164 \text{ mol C}$

$8.70 \cancel{\text{g H}} \times \frac{1 \text{ mol H}}{1.008 \cancel{\text{g H}}} = 8.63 \text{ mol H}$

$17.27 \cancel{\text{g N}} \times \frac{1 \text{ mol N}}{14.01 \cancel{\text{g N}}} = 1.233 \text{ mol N}$

$C_{6.164}H_{8.63}N_{1.233}$

$C_{\frac{6.164}{1.233}}H_{\frac{8.63}{1.233}}N_{\frac{1.233}{1.233}} \rightarrow C_5H_7N$

The correct empirical formula is C_5H_7N.

(b) **Given:** In a 100 g sample: 49.48 g C, 5.19 g H, 28.85 g N, 16.48 g O **Find:** empirical formula
Conceptual Plan:
convert mass to mol of each element → write pseudoformula → write empirical formula

$\frac{1 \text{ mol C}}{12.01 \text{ g C}}$ $\frac{1 \text{ mol H}}{1.008 \text{ g H}}$ $\frac{1 \text{ mol N}}{14.01 \text{ g N}}$ $\frac{1 \text{ mol O}}{16.00 \text{ g O}}$ divide by smallest number

Solution: $49.48 \cancel{\text{g C}} \times \frac{1 \text{ mol C}}{12.01 \cancel{\text{g C}}} = 4.120 \text{ mol C}$

$5.19 \cancel{\text{g H}} \times \frac{1 \text{ mol H}}{1.008 \cancel{\text{g H}}} = 5.15 \text{ mol H}$

$28.85 \cancel{\text{g N}} \times \frac{1 \text{ mol N}}{14.01 \cancel{\text{g N}}} = 2.059 \text{ mol N}$

$16.48 \cancel{\text{g O}} \times \frac{1 \text{ mol O}}{16.00 \cancel{\text{g O}}} = 1.030 \text{ mol O}$

$C_{4.120}H_{5.15}N_{2.059}O_{1.030}$

$C_{\frac{4.120}{1.030}}H_{\frac{5.15}{1.030}}N_{\frac{2.059}{1.030}}O_{\frac{1.030}{1.030}} \rightarrow C_4H_5N_2O$

The correct empirical formula is $C_4H_5N_2O$.

3.82 (a) **Given:** In a 100 g sample: 58.80 g C, 9.87 g H, 31.33 g O **Find:** empirical formula
Conceptual Plan:
convert mass to mol of each element → write pseudoformula → write empirical formula

$\frac{1 \text{ mol C}}{12.01 \text{ g C}}$ $\frac{1 \text{ mol H}}{1.008 \text{ g H}}$ $\frac{1 \text{ mol O}}{16.00 \text{ g O}}$ divide by smallest number

Solution: $58.80\ \cancel{g\,C} \times \dfrac{1\text{ mol C}}{12.01\ \cancel{g\,C}} = 4.896\text{ mol C}$

$9.87\ \cancel{g\,H} \times \dfrac{1\text{ mol H}}{1.008\ \cancel{g\,H}} = 9.79\text{ mol H}$

$31.33\ \cancel{g\,O} \times \dfrac{1\text{ mol O}}{16.00\ \cancel{g\,O}} = 1.958\text{ mol O}$

$C_{4.896}H_{9.79}O_{1.958}$

$C_{\frac{4.896}{1.958}}H_{\frac{9.79}{1.958}}O_{\frac{1.958}{1.958}} \rightarrow C_{2.5}H_5O$

$C_{2.5}H_5O \times 2 = C_5H_{10}O_2$

The correct empirical formula is $C_5H_{10}O_2$.

(b) **Given:** In a 100 g sample: 63.15 g C, 5.30 g H, 31.55 g O **Find:** empirical formula

Conceptual Plan:

convert mass to mol of each element → write pseudoformula → write empirical formula

$\dfrac{1\text{ mol C}}{12.01\text{ g C}}$ $\dfrac{1\text{ mol H}}{1.008\text{ g H}}$ $\dfrac{1\text{ mol O}}{16.00\text{ g O}}$ divide by smallest number

Solution: $63.15\ \cancel{g\,C} \times \dfrac{1\text{ mol C}}{12.01\ \cancel{g\,C}} = 5.258\text{ mol C}$

$5.30\ \cancel{g\,H} \times \dfrac{1\text{ mol H}}{1.008\ \cancel{g\,H}} = 5.26\text{ mol H}$

$31.55\ \cancel{g\,O} \times \dfrac{1\text{ mol O}}{16.00\ \cancel{g\,O}} = 1.972\text{ mol O}$

$C_{5.258}H_{5.26}O_{1.972}$

$C_{\frac{5.258}{1.972}}H_{\frac{5.26}{1.972}}O_{\frac{1.972}{1.972}} \rightarrow C_{2.67}H_{2.67}O$

$C_{2.67}H_{2.67}O \times 3 = C_8H_8O_3$

The correct empirical formula is $C_8H_8O_3$.

3.83 **Given:** In a 100 g sample: 75.69 g C, 8.80 g H, 15.51 g O **Find:** empirical formula

Conceptual Plan:

convert mass to mol of each element → write pseudoformula → write empirical formula

$\dfrac{1\text{ mol C}}{12.01\text{ g C}}$ $\dfrac{1\text{ mol H}}{1.008\text{ g H}}$ $\dfrac{1\text{ mol O}}{16.00\text{ g O}}$ divide by smallest number

Solution: $75.69\ \cancel{g\,C} \times \dfrac{1\text{ mol C}}{12.01\ \cancel{g\,C}} = 6.302\text{ mol C}$

$8.80\ \cancel{g\,H} \times \dfrac{1\text{ mol H}}{1.008\ \cancel{g\,H}} = 8.73\text{ mol H}$

$15.51\ \cancel{g\,O} \times \dfrac{1\text{ mol O}}{16.00\ \cancel{g\,O}} = 0.9694\text{ mol O}$

$C_{6.302}H_{8.73}O_{0.9694}$

$C_{\frac{6.302}{0.9694}}H_{\frac{8.73}{0.9694}}O_{\frac{0.9694}{0.9694}} \rightarrow C_{6.50}H_{9.01}O$

$C_{6.50}H_{9.01}O \times 2 = C_{13}H_{18}O_2$

The correct empirical formula is $C_{13}H_{18}O_2$.

3.84 **Given:** In a 100 g sample: 40.92 g C, 4.58 g H, 54.50 g O **Find:** empirical formula

Conceptual Plan:

convert mass to mol of each element → write pseudoformula → write empirical formula

$\dfrac{1\text{ mol C}}{12.01\text{ g C}}$ $\dfrac{1\text{ mol H}}{1.008\text{ g H}}$ $\dfrac{1\text{ mol O}}{16.00\text{ g O}}$ divide by smallest number

Solution: $40.92\ \cancel{g\,C} \times \dfrac{1\text{ mol C}}{12.01\ \cancel{g\,C}} = 3.407\text{ mol C}$

$4.58\ \cancel{g\,H} \times \dfrac{1\text{ mol H}}{1.008\ \cancel{g\,H}} = 4.54\text{ mol H}$

$54.50\ \cancel{g\,O} \times \dfrac{1\text{ mol O}}{16.00\ \cancel{g\,O}} = 3.406\text{ mol O}$

$C_{3.407}H_{4.54}O_{3.406}$

$C_{\frac{3.407}{3.406}}H_{\frac{4.54}{3.406}}O_{\frac{3.406}{3.406}} \rightarrow C_{1.00}H_{1.33}O_{1.00}$

$C_{1.00}H_{1.33}O_{1.00} \times 3 = C_3H_4O_3$

The correct empirical formula is $C_3H_4O_3$.

3.85 **Given:** 0.77 mg N, 6.61 mg N_xCl_y **Find:** empirical formula

Conceptual Plan:

Find mg Cl → convert mg to g for each element → convert mass to mol of each element →

mg N_xCl_y – mg N $\quad \frac{1\text{ g}}{1000\text{ mg}} \quad \frac{1\text{ mol N}}{14.01\text{ g N}} \quad \frac{1\text{ mol Cl}}{35.45\text{ g Cl}}$

write pseudoformula → write empirical formula

divide by smallest number

Solution: 6.61 mg N_xCl_y – 0.77 mg N = 5.84 mg Cl

$$0.77\ \text{mg N} \times \frac{1\ \text{g N}}{1000\ \text{mg N}} \times \frac{1\ \text{mol N}}{14.01\ \text{g N}} = 5.5 \times 10^{-5}\ \text{mol N}$$

$$5.84\ \text{mg Cl} \times \frac{1\ \text{g Cl}}{1000\ \text{mg Cl}} \times \frac{1\ \text{mol Cl}}{35.45\ \text{g Cl}} = 1.6 \times 10^{-4}\ \text{mol Cl}$$

$N_{5.5 \times 10^{-5}}Cl_{1.6 \times 10^{-4}}$

$N_{\frac{5.5\times10^{-5}}{5.5\times10^{-5}}}Cl_{\frac{1.6\times10^{-4}}{5.5\times10^{-5}}} \rightarrow NCl_3$

The correct empirical formula is NCl_3.

3.86 **Given:** 45.2 mg P, 131.6 mg P_xSe_y **Find:** empirical formula

Conceptual Plan: Find mg Se → convert mg to g for each element → convert mass to mol of each element

mg P_xSe_y – mg P $\quad \frac{1\text{ g}}{1000\text{ mg}} \quad \frac{1\text{ mol P}}{30.97\text{ g P}} \quad \frac{1\text{ mol Se}}{78.96\text{ g Se}}$

→ write pseudoformula → write empirical formula

divide by smallest number

Solution: 131.6 mg P_xSe_y – 45.2 mg P = 86.4 mg Se

$$45.2\ \text{mg P} \times \frac{1\ \text{g P}}{1000\ \text{mg P}} \times \frac{1\ \text{mol P}}{30.97\ \text{g P}} = 0.00146\ \text{mol P}$$

$$86.4\ \text{g Se} \times \frac{1\ \text{g Se}}{1000\ \text{mg Se}} \times \frac{1\ \text{mol Se}}{78.96\ \text{g Se}} = 0.00109\ \text{mol Se}$$

$P_{0.00146}Se_{0.00109}$

$P_{\frac{0.00146}{0.00109}}Se_{\frac{0.00109}{0.00109}} \rightarrow P_{1.33}Se$

$P_{1.33}Se \times 3 = P_4Se_3$

The correct empirical formula is P_4Se_3.

3.87 (a) **Given:** empirical formula = C_6H_7N, molar mass = 186.24 g/mol **Find:** molecular formula

Conceptual Plan: molecular formula = empirical formula x n $\quad n = \frac{\text{molar mass}}{\text{empirical formula mass}}$

Solution: empirical formula mass = 6(12.01 g/mol) + 7(1.008 g/mol) + 1(14.01 g/mol) = 93.13 g/mol

$$n = \frac{\text{molar mass}}{\text{formula molar mass}} = \frac{186.24\ \text{g/mol}}{93.13\ \text{g/mol}} = 1.998 = 2$$

molecular formula $= C_6H_7N \times 2$

$= C_{12}H_{14}N_2$

(b) **Given:** empirical formula = C_2HCl, molar mass = 181.44 g/mol **Find:** molecular formula

Conceptual Plan: molecular formula = empirical formula x n $\quad n = \frac{\text{molar mass}}{\text{empirical formula mass}}$

Solution: empirical formula mass = 2(12.01 g/mol) + 1(1.008 g/mol) + 1(35.45 g/mol) = 60.48 g/mol

$$n = \frac{\text{molar mass}}{\text{formula molar mass}} = \frac{181.44\ \text{g/mol}}{60.48\ \text{g/mol}} = 3$$

molecular formula $= C_2HCl \times 3$

$= C_6H_3Cl_3$

(c) **Given:** empirical formula = $C_5H_{10}NS_2$, molar mass = 296.54 g/mol **Find:** molecular formula

Conceptual Plan: molecular formula = empirical formula x n $n = \frac{\text{molar mass}}{\text{empirical formula mass}}$

Solution: empirical formula mass = 5(12.01 g/mol) + 10(1.008 g/mol) + 1(14.01 g/mol) + 2(32.07) = 148.28 g/mol

$$n = \frac{\text{molar mass}}{\text{formula molar mass}} = \frac{296.54 \text{ g/mol}}{148.28 \text{ g/mol}} = 2$$

molecular formula = $C_5H_{10}NS_2$ x 2 = $C_{10}H_{20}N_2S_4$

3.88 (a) **Given:** empirical formula = C_4H_9, molar mass = 114.22 g/mol **Find:** molecular formula

Conceptual Plan: molecular formula = empirical formula x n $n = \frac{\text{molar mass}}{\text{empirical formula mass}}$

Solution: empirical formula mass = 4(12.01 g/mol) + 9(1.008 g/mol) = 57.11 g/mol

$$n = \frac{\text{molar mass}}{\text{formula molar mass}} = \frac{114.22 \text{ g/mol}}{57.11 \text{ g/mol}} = 2$$

molecular formula = C_4H_9 x 2 = C_8H_{18}

(b) **Given:** empirical formula = CCl, molar mass = 284.77 g/mol **Find:** molecular formula

Conceptual Plan: molecular formula = empirical formula x n $n = \frac{\text{molar mass}}{\text{empirical formula mass}}$

Solution: empirical formula mass = 1(12.01 g/mol) + 1(35.45 g/mol) = 47.46 g/mol

$$n = \frac{\text{molar mass}}{\text{formula molar mass}} = \frac{284.77 \text{ g/mol}}{47.46 \text{ g/mol}} = 6$$

molecular formula = CCl x 6 = C_6Cl_6

(c) **Given:** empirical formula = C_3H_2N, molar mass = 312.29 g/mol **Find:** molecular formula

Conceptual Plan: molecular formula = empirical formula x n $n = \frac{\text{molar mass}}{\text{empirical formula mass}}$

Solution: empirical formula mass = 3(12.01 g/mol) + 2(1.008 g/mol) + 1(14.01 g/mol) = 52.06 g/mol

$$n = \frac{\text{molar mass}}{\text{formula molar mass}} = \frac{312.29 \text{ g/mol}}{52.06 \text{ g/mol}} = 6$$

molecular formula = C_3H_2N x 6 = $C_{18}H_{12}N_6$

3.89 **Given:** 33.01 g CO_2, 13.51 g H_2O **Find:** empirical formula

Conceptual Plan:

mass CO_2, H_2O → mol CO_2, H_2O → mol C, mol H → pseudoformula → empirical formula

$\frac{1 \text{ mol } CO_2}{44.01 \text{ g } CO_2}$ $\frac{1 \text{ mol } H_2O}{18.02 \text{ g } H_2O}$ $\frac{1 \text{ mol C}}{1 \text{ mol } CO_2}$ $\frac{2 \text{ mol H}}{1 \text{ mol } H_2O}$ divide by smallest number

Solution:

$$33.01 \cancel{\text{g } CO_2} \times \frac{1 \text{ mol } CO_2}{44.01 \cancel{\text{g } CO_2}} = 0.7500 \text{ mol } CO_2$$

$$13.51 \cancel{\text{g } H_2O} \times \frac{1 \text{ mol } H_2O}{18.02 \cancel{\text{g } H_2O}} = 0.7497 \text{ mol } H_2O$$

$$0.7500 \cancel{\text{mol } CO_2} \times \frac{1 \text{ mol C}}{1 \cancel{\text{mol } CO_2}} = 0.7500 \text{ mol C}$$

$$0.7497 \cancel{\text{mol } H_2O} \times \frac{2 \text{ mol H}}{1 \cancel{\text{mol } H_2O}} = 1.499 \text{ mol H}$$

$C_{0.7500}H_{1.499}$

$C_{\frac{0.7500}{0.7500}}H_{\frac{1.499}{0.7500}} \rightarrow CH_2$

The correct empirical formula is CH_2.

3.90 **Given:** 8.80 g CO_2, 1.44 g H_2O **Find:** empirical formula

Conceptual Plan:

mass CO_2, H_2O → mol CO_2, H_2O → mol C, mol H → pseudoformula → empirical formula

$$\frac{1 \text{ mol } CO_2}{44.01 \text{ g } CO_2} \quad \frac{1 \text{ mol } H_2O}{18.02 \text{ g } H_2O} \quad \frac{1 \text{ mol C}}{1 \text{ mol } CO_2} \quad \frac{2 \text{ mol H}}{1 \text{ mol } H_2O} \quad \text{divide by smallest number}$$

Solution:

$$8.80\ \cancel{\text{g } CO_2} \times \frac{1 \text{ mol } CO_2}{44.01\ \cancel{\text{g } CO_2}} = 0.200 \text{ mol } CO_2$$

$$1.44\ \cancel{\text{g } H_2O} \times \frac{1 \text{ mol } H_2O}{18.02\ \cancel{\text{g } H_2O}} = 0.0799 \text{ mol } H_2O$$

$$0.200\ \cancel{\text{mol } CO_2} \times \frac{1 \text{ mol C}}{1\ \cancel{\text{mol } CO_2}} = 0.200 \text{ mol C}$$

$$0.0799\ \cancel{\text{mol } H_2O} \times \frac{2 \text{ mol H}}{1\ \cancel{\text{mol } H_2O}} = 0.160 \text{ mol H}$$

$C_{0.200}H_{0.160}$

$C_{\frac{0.200}{0.160}}H_{\frac{0.160}{0.160}} \rightarrow C_{1.25}H_1$

$C_{1.25}H_1 \times 4 = C_5H_4$

The correct empirical formula is C_5H_4.

3.91 **Given:** 4.30 g sample, 8.59 g CO_2, 3.52 g H_2O **Find:** empirical formula

Conceptual Plan:

mass CO_2, H_2O → mol CO_2, H_2O → mol C, mol H → mass C, mass H, mass O → mol O →

$$\frac{1 \text{ mol } CO_2}{44.01 \text{ g } CO_2} \quad \frac{1 \text{ mol } H_2O}{18.02 \text{ g } H_2O} \quad \frac{1 \text{ mol C}}{1 \text{ mol } CO_2} \quad \frac{2 \text{ mol H}}{1 \text{ mol } H_2O} \quad \frac{12.01 \text{ g C}}{1 \text{ mol C}} \quad \frac{1.008 \text{ g H}}{1 \text{ mol H}} \quad \text{g sample} - \text{gC} - \text{g H} \quad \frac{1 \text{ mol O}}{16.00 \text{ g O}}$$

pseudoformula → empirical formula

divide by smallest number

Solution:

$$8.59\ \cancel{\text{g } CO_2} \times \frac{1 \text{ mol } CO_2}{44.01\ \cancel{\text{g } CO_2}} = 0.195 \text{ mol } CO_2$$

$$3.52\ \cancel{\text{g } H_2O} \times \frac{1 \text{ mol } H_2O}{18.02\ \cancel{\text{g } H_2O}} = 0.195 \text{ mol } H_2O$$

$$0.195\ \cancel{\text{mol } CO_2} \times \frac{1 \text{ mol C}}{1\ \cancel{\text{mol } CO_2}} = 0.195 \text{ mol C}$$

$$0.195\ \cancel{\text{mol } H_2O} \times \frac{2 \text{ mol H}}{1\ \cancel{\text{mol } H_2O}} = 0.390 \text{ mol H}$$

$$0.195\ \cancel{\text{mol CO}} \times \frac{12.01 \text{ mol C}}{1\ \cancel{\text{mol CO}}} = 2.34 \text{ g C}$$

$$0.390\ \cancel{\text{mol } H_2O} \times \frac{1.008 \text{ g H}}{1\ \cancel{\text{mol H}}} = 0.393 \text{ g H}$$

4.30 g – 2.34 g – 0.393 g = 1.57 g O

$$1.57\ \cancel{\text{g O}} \times \frac{1 \text{ mol O}}{16.00\ \cancel{\text{g O}}} = 0.0979 \text{ mol O}$$

$C_{0.195}H_{0.390}O_{0.0979}$

$C_{\frac{0.195}{0.0979}}H_{\frac{0.390}{0.0979}}O_{\frac{0.0979}{0.0979}} \rightarrow C_2H_4O$

The correct empirical formula is C_2H_4O.

3.92 Given: 12.01 g sample, 14.08 g CO_2, 4.32 g H_2O **Find:** empirical formula

Conceptual Plan:

mass CO_2, H_2O → mol CO_2, H_2O → mol C, mol H → mass C, mass H, mass O → mol O →

$$\frac{1 \text{ mol } CO_2}{44.01 \text{ g } CO_2} \quad \frac{1 \text{ mol } H_2O}{18.02 \text{ g } H_2O} \quad \frac{1 \text{ mol C}}{1 \text{ mol } CO_2} \quad \frac{2 \text{ mol H}}{1 \text{ mol } H_2O} \quad \frac{12.01 \text{ g C}}{1 \text{ mol C}} \quad \frac{1.008 \text{ g H}}{1 \text{ mol H}} \quad \text{g sample} - \text{gC} - \text{g H} \quad \frac{1 \text{ mol O}}{16.00 \text{ g O}}$$

pseudoformula → empirical formula

divide by smallest number

Solution:

$$14.08\ \cancel{g\ CO_2} \times \frac{1\ mol\ CO_2}{44.01\ \cancel{g\ CO_2}} = 0.3199\ mol\ CO_2$$

$$4.32\ \cancel{g\ H_2O} \times \frac{1\ mol\ H_2O}{18.02\ \cancel{g\ H_2O}} = 0.2397\ mol\ H_2O$$

$$0.3199\ \cancel{mol\ CO_2} \times \frac{1\ mol\ C}{1\ \cancel{mol\ CO_2}} = 0.3199\ mol\ C$$

$$0.2397\ \cancel{mol\ H_2O} \times \frac{2\ mol\ H}{1\ \cancel{mol\ H_2O}} = 0.4795\ mol\ H$$

$$0.3199\ \cancel{mol\ C} \times \frac{12.01\ g\ C}{1\ \cancel{mol\ C}} = 3.842\ g\ C$$

$$0.4795\ \cancel{mol\ H} \times \frac{1.008\ g\ H}{1\ \cancel{mol\ H}} = 0.4833\ g\ H$$

$$12.01\ g - 3.842\ g - 0.4833\ g = 7.68\ g\ O$$

$$7.68\ \cancel{g\ O} \times \frac{1\ mol\ O}{16.00\ \cancel{g\ O}} = 0.480\ mol\ O$$

$$C_{0.3199}H_{0.4795}O_{0.480}$$

$$C_{\frac{0.3199}{0.3199}}H_{\frac{0.4795}{0.3199}}O_{\frac{0.480}{0.3199}} \rightarrow CH_{1.5}O_{1.5}$$

$$CH_{1.5}O_{1.5} \times 2 = C_2H_3O_3$$

The correct empirical formula is $C_2H_3O_3$.

Writing and Balancing Chemical Equations

3.93 **Conceptual Plan: write a skeletal reaction → balance atoms in more complex compounds → balance elements that occur as free elements → clear fractions**

Solution:

Skeletal reaction:	$SO_2(g) + O_2(g) + H_2O(l) \rightarrow H_2SO_4(aq)$	
Balance O:	$SO_2(g) + 1/2O_2(g) + H_2O(l) \rightarrow H_2SO_4(aq)$	
Clear fraction:	$2SO_2(g) + O_2(g) + 2H_2O(l) \rightarrow 2H_2SO_4(aq)$	

Check:

left side	right side
2 S atoms	2 S atoms
8 O atoms	8 O atoms
4 H atoms	4 H atoms

3.94 **Conceptual Plan: write a skeletal reaction → balance atoms in more complex compounds → balance elements that occur as free elements → clear fractions**

Solution:

Skeletal reaction:	$NO_2(g) + O_2(g) + H_2O(l) \rightarrow HNO_3(aq)$
Balance H:	$NO_2(g) + O_2(g) + H_2O(l) \rightarrow 2HNO_3(aq)$
Balance N:	$2NO_2(g) + O_2(g) + H_2O(l) \rightarrow 2HNO_3(aq)$
Balance O:	$2NO_2(g) + 1/2O_2(g) + H_2O(l) \rightarrow 2HNO_3(aq)$
Clear fraction:	$4NO_2(g) + O_2(g) + 2H_2O(l) \rightarrow 4HNO_3(aq)$

Check:

left side	right side
4 N atoms	4 N atoms
12 O atoms	12 O atoms
4 H atoms	4 H atoms

3.95 **Conceptual Plan: write a skeletal reaction → balance atoms in more complex compounds → balance elements that occur as free elements → clear fractions**

Solution:

Skeletal reaction:	$Na(s) + H_2O(l) \rightarrow H_2(g) + NaOH(aq)$
Balance H:	$Na(s) + H_2O(l) \rightarrow 1/2H_2(g) + NaOH(aq)$
Clear fraction:	$2Na(s) + 2H_2O(l) \rightarrow H_2(g) + 2NaOH(aq)$

Check:

left side	right side
2 Na atoms	2 Na atoms
4 H atoms	4 H atoms
2 O atoms	2 O atoms

3.96 **Conceptual Plan: write a skeletal reaction → balance atoms in more complex compounds → balance elements that occur as free elements → clear fractions**

Solution: Skeletal reaction: $Fe(s) + O_2(g) \rightarrow Fe_2O_3(s)$

Balance O: $Fe(s) + 3O_2(g) \rightarrow 2Fe_2O_3(s)$

Balance Fe: $4Fe(s) + 3O_2(g) \rightarrow 2Fe_2O_3(s)$

Check:

left side	right side
4 Fe atoms	4 Fe atoms
6 O atoms	6 O atoms

3.97 **Conceptual Plan: write a skeletal reaction → balance atoms in more complex compounds → balance elements that occur as free elements → clear fractions**

Solution: Skeletal reaction: $C_{12}H_{22}O_{11}(aq) + H_2O(l) \rightarrow C_2H_5OH(aq) + CO_2(g)$

Balance H: $C_{12}H_{22}O_{11}(aq) + H_2O(l) \rightarrow 4C_2H_5OH(aq) + CO_2(g)$

Balance C: $C_{12}H_{22}O_{11}(aq) + H_2O(l) \rightarrow 4C_2H_5OH(aq) + 4CO_2(g)$

Check:

left side	right side
12 C atoms	12 C atoms
24 H atoms	24 H atoms
12 O atoms	12 O atoms

3.98 **Conceptual Plan: write a skeletal reaction → balance atoms in more complex compounds → balance elements that occur as free elements → clear fractions**

Solution: Skeletal reaction: $CO_2(g) + H_2O(l) \rightarrow C_6H_{12}O_6(aq) + O_2(g)$

Balance C: $6CO_2(g) + H_2O(l) \rightarrow C_6H_{12}O_6(aq) + O_2(g)$

Balance H: $6CO_2(g) + 6H_2O(l) \rightarrow C_6H_{12}O_6(aq) + O_2(g)$

Balance O: $6CO_2(g) + 6H_2O(l) \rightarrow C_6H_{12}O_6(aq) + 6O_2(g)$

Check:

left side	right side
6 C atoms	6 C atoms
18 O atoms	18 O atoms
12 H atoms	12 H atoms

3.99 (a) **Conceptual Plan: write a skeletal reaction → balance atoms in more complex compounds → balance elements that occur as free elements → clear fractions**

Solution: Skeletal reaction: $PbS(s) + HBr(aq) \rightarrow PbBr_2(s) + H_2S(g)$

Balance Br: $PbS(s) + 2HBr(aq) \rightarrow PbBr_2(s) + H_2S(g)$

Check:

left side	right side
1 Pb atom	1 Pb atom
1 S atom	1 S atom
2 H atoms	2 H atoms
2 Br atoms	2 Br atoms

(b) **Conceptual Plan: write a skeletal reaction → balance atoms in more complex compounds → balance elements that occur as free elements → clear fractions**

Solution: Skeletal reaction: $CO(g) + H_2(g) \rightarrow CH_4(g) + H_2O(l)$

Balance H: $CO(g) + 3H_2(g) \rightarrow CH_4(g) + H_2O(l)$

Check:

left side	right side
1 C atom	1 C atom
1 O atom	1 O atom
6 H atoms	6 H atoms

(c) **Conceptual Plan: write a skeletal reaction → balance atoms in more complex compounds → balance elements that occur as free elements → clear fractions**

Solution: Skeletal reaction: $HCl(aq) + MnO_2(s) \rightarrow MnCl_2(aq) + H_2O(l) + Cl_2(g)$

Balance Cl: $4HCl(aq) + MnO_2(s) \rightarrow MnCl_2(aq) + H_2O(l) + Cl_2(g)$

Balance O: $4HCl(aq) + MnO_2(s) \rightarrow MnCl_2(aq) + 2H_2O(l) + Cl_2(g)$

Check:

left side	right side
4 H atoms	4 H atoms
4 Cl atoms	4 Cl atoms
1 Mn atom	1 Mn atom
2 O atoms	2 O atoms

(d) **Conceptual Plan: write a skeletal reaction → balance atoms in more complex compounds → balance elements that occur as free elements → clear fractions**

Solution: Skeletal reaction: $C_5H_{12}(l) + O_2(g) \rightarrow CO_2(g) + H_2O(l)$

Balance C: $C_5H_{12}(l) + O_2(g) \rightarrow 5CO_2(g) + H_2O(l)$

Balance H: $C_5H_{12}(l) + O_2(g) \rightarrow 5CO_2(g) + 6H_2O(l)$

Balance O: $C_5H_{12}(l) + 8O_2(g) \rightarrow 5CO_2(g) + 6H_2O(l)$

Check:

left side	right side
5 C atoms	5 C atoms
12 H atoms	12 H atoms
16 O atoms	16 O atoms

3.100 (a) **Conceptual Plan: write a skeletal reaction → balance atoms in more complex compounds → balance elements that occur as free elements → clear fractions**

Solution: Skeletal reaction: $Cu(s) + S(s) \rightarrow Cu_2S(s)$

Balance Cu: $2Cu(s) + S(s) \rightarrow Cu_2S(s)$

Check:

left side	right side
2 Cu atoms	2 Cu atoms
1 S atom	1 S atom

(b) **Conceptual Plan: write a skeletal reaction → balance atoms in more complex compounds → balance elements that occur as free elements → clear fractions**

Solution: Skeletal reaction: $Fe_2O_3(s) + H_2(g) \rightarrow Fe(s) + H_2O(l)$

Balance O: $Fe_2O_3(s) + H_2(g) \rightarrow Fe(s) + 3H_2O(l)$

Balance Fe: $Fe_2O_3(s) + H_2(g) \rightarrow 2Fe(s) + 3H_2O(l)$

Balance H: $Fe_2O_3(s) + 3H_2(g) \rightarrow 2Fe(s) + 3H_2O(l)$

Check:

left side	right side
2 Fe atoms	2 Fe atoms
3 O atoms	3 O atoms
6 H atoms	6 H atoms

(c) **Conceptual Plan: write a skeletal reaction → balance atoms in more complex compounds → balance elements that occur as free elements → clear fractions**

Solution: Skeletal reaction: $SO_2(g) + O_2(g) \rightarrow SO_3(g)$

Balance O: $SO_2(g) + 1/2O_2(g) \rightarrow SO_3(g)$

Clear fraction: $2SO_2(g) + O_2(g) \rightarrow 2SO_3(g)$

Check:

left side	right side
2 S atoms	2 S atoms
6 O atoms	6 O atoms

(d) **Conceptual Plan: write a skeletal reaction → balance atoms in more complex compounds → balance elements that occur as free elements → clear fractions**

Solution: Skeletal reaction: $NH_3(g) + O_2(g) \rightarrow NO(g) + H_2O(g)$

Balance H: $2NH_3(g) + O_2(g) \rightarrow NO(g) + 3H_2O(g)$

Balance O: $2NH_3(g) + 5/2O_2(g) \rightarrow 2NO(g) + 3H_2O(g)$

Clear fraction: $4NH_3(g) + 5O_2(g) \rightarrow 4NO(g) + 6H_2O(g)$

Check:

left side	right side
4 N atoms	4 N atoms
6 H atoms	6 H atoms
10 O atoms	10 O atoms

3.101 (a) **Conceptual Plan: balance atoms in more complex compounds → balance elements that occur as free elements → clear fractions**

Solution: Skeletal reaction: $CO_2(g) + CaSiO_3(s) + H_2O(l) \rightarrow SiO_2(s) + Ca(HCO_3)_2(aq)$

Balance C: $2CO_2(g) + CaSiO_3(s) + H_2O(l) \rightarrow SiO_2(s) + Ca(HCO_3)_2(aq)$

Check:

left side	right side
2 C atoms	2 C atoms
8 O atoms	8 O atoms
1 Ca atom	1 Ca atom
1 Si atom	1 Si atom
2 H atoms	2 H atoms

(b) **Conceptual Plan: balance atoms in more complex compounds → balance elements that occur as free elements → clear fractions**

Solution: Skeletal reaction: $Co(NO_3)_3(aq) + (NH_4)_2S(aq) \rightarrow Co_2S_3(s) + NH_4NO_3(aq)$

Balance S: $Co(NO_3)_3(aq) + 3(NH_4)_2S(aq) \rightarrow Co_2S_3(s) + NH_4NO_3(aq)$

Balance Co: $2Co(NO_3)_3(aq) + 3(NH_4)_2S(aq) \rightarrow Co_2S_3(s) + NH_4NO_3(aq)$

Balance N: $2Co(NO_3)_3(aq) + 3(NH_4)_2S(aq) \rightarrow Co_2S_3(s) + 6NH_4NO_3(aq)$

Check:

left side	right side
2 Co atoms	2 Co atoms
12 N atoms	12 N atoms
18 O atoms	18 O atoms
24 H atoms	24 H atoms
3 S atoms	3 S atoms

(c) **Conceptual Plan: balance atoms in more complex compounds → balance elements that occur as free elements → clear fractions**

Solution: Skeletal reaction: $Cu_2O(s) + C(s) \rightarrow Cu(s) + CO(g)$

Balance Cu: $Cu_2O(s) + C(s) \rightarrow 2Cu(s) + CO(g)$

Check:

left side	right side
2 Cu atoms	2 Cu atoms
1 O atom	1 O atom
1 C atom	1 C atom

(d) **Conceptual Plan: balance atoms in more complex compounds → balance elements that occur as free elements → clear fractions**

Solution: Skeletal reaction: $H_2(g) + Cl_2(g) \rightarrow HCl(g)$

Balance Cl: $H_2(g) + Cl_2(g) \rightarrow 2HCl(g)$

Check:

left side	right side
2 H atoms	2 H atoms
2 Cl atoms	2 Cl atoms

3.102 (a) **Conceptual Plan: balance atoms in more complex compounds → balance elements that occur as free elements → clear fractions**

Solution: Skeletal reaction: $Na_2S(aq) + Cu(NO_3)_2(aq) \rightarrow NaNO_3(aq) + CuS(s)$

Balance Na: $Na_2S(aq) + Cu(NO_3)_2(aq) \rightarrow 2NaNO_3(aq) + CuS(s)$

Check:

left side	right side
2 Na atoms	2 Na atoms
1 S atom	1 S atom
1 Cu atom	1 Cu atom
2 N atoms	2 N atoms
6 O atoms	6 O atoms

(b) **Conceptual Plan: balance atoms in more complex compounds → balance elements that occur as free elements → clear fractions**

Solution: Skeletal reaction: $N_2H_4(l) \rightarrow NH_3(g) + N_2(g)$

Balance H: $3N_2H_4(l) \rightarrow 4NH_3(g) + N_2(g)$

Check:

left side	right side
6 N atoms	6 N atoms
12 H atoms	12 H atoms

(c) **Conceptual Plan: balance atoms in more complex compounds → balance elements that occur as free elements → clear fractions**

Solution: Skeletal reaction: $HCl(aq) + O_2(g) \rightarrow H_2O(l) + Cl_2(g)$

Balance Cl: $2HCl(aq) + O_2(g) \rightarrow H_2O(l) + Cl_2(g)$

Balance O: $2HCl(aq) + 1/2O_2(g) \rightarrow H_2O(l) + Cl_2(g)$

Clear fraction: $4HCl(aq) + O_2(g) \rightarrow 2H_2O(l) + 2Cl_2(g)$

Check:

left side	right side
4 H atoms	4 H atoms
4 Cl atoms	4 Cl atoms
2 O atoms	2 O atoms

(d) **Conceptual Plan: balance atoms in more complex compounds → balance elements that occur as free elements → clear fractions**

Solution: Skeletal reaction: $FeS(s) + HCl(aq) \rightarrow FeCl_2(aq) + H_2S(g)$

Balance Cl: $FeS(s) + 2HCl(aq) \rightarrow FeCl_2(aq) + H_2S(g)$

Check:

left side	right side
1 Fe atom	1 Fe atom
1 S atom	1 S atom
2 H atoms	2 H atoms
2 Cl atoms	2 Cl atoms

Organic Compounds

3.103 (a) composed of metal cation and polyatomic anion – inorganic compound

(b) composed of carbon and hydrogen – organic compound

(c) composed of carbon, hydrogen, and oxygen – organic compound

(d) composed of metal cation and nonmetal anion – inorganic compound

3.104 (a) composed of carbon and hydrogen – organic compound

(b) composed of carbon, hydrogen, and nitrogen – organic compound

(c) composed of metal cation and nonmetal anion – inorganic compound

(d) composed of metal cation and polyatomic anion – inorganic compound

3.105 (a) contains a double bond – alkene

(b) contains only single bonds – alkane

(c) contains triple bond – alkyne

(d) contains only single bonds – alkane

3.106 (a) contains triple bond – alkyne

(b) contains double bond – alkene

(c) contains only single bonds – alkane

(d) contains triple bond – alkyne

3.107 (a) prop = 3 C, ane = single bonds: $CH_3CH_2CH_3$

(b) 3 C = prop, single bonds = ane: propane

(c) oct = 8 C, ane = single bonds: $CH_3CH_2CH_2CH_2CH_2CH_2CH_2CH_3$

(d) 5 C = pent, single bonds = ane: pentane

3.108 (a) 2 C = eth, single bonds = ane: ethane

(b) pent = 5 C, and = single bonds: $CH_3CH_2CH_2CH_2CH_3$

(c) 6 C = hex, single bonds = ane: hexane

(d) hept = 7 C, ane = single bonds: $CH_3CH_2CH_2CH_2CH_2CH_2CH_3$

3.109 (a) contains O: functionalized hydrocarbon: alcohol

(b) contains only C and H: hydrocarbon

(c) contains O: functionalized hydrocarbon: ketone

(d) contains N: functionalized hydrocarbon: amine

3.110 (a) contains O: functionalized hydrocarbon: carboxylic acid

(b) contains O: functionalized hydrocarbon: aldehyde

(c) contains only C and H: hydrocarbon

(d) contains O: functionalized hydrocarbon: ether

Cumulative Problems

3.111 **Given:** 145 mL C_2H_5OH, d = 0.789g/cm^3 **Find:** number of molecules

Conceptual Plan: $\text{cm}^3 \rightarrow \text{mL}$: $\text{mL } C_2H_5OH \rightarrow \text{g } C_2H_5OH \rightarrow \text{mol } C_2H_5OH \rightarrow \text{molecules } C_2H_5OH$

$$\frac{1\text{ cm}^3}{1\text{ mL}} \qquad \frac{1\text{ mL } C_2H_5OH}{0.789\text{ g } C_2H_5OH} \qquad \frac{1\text{ mol } C_2H_5OH}{46.07\text{ g } C_2H_5OH} \qquad \frac{6.022 \times 10^{23}\text{ molecules } C_2H_5OH}{1\text{ mol } C_2H_5OH}$$

Solution:

$$145\ \cancel{\text{mL } C_2H_5OH} \times \frac{0.789\ \cancel{\text{g } C_2H_5OH}}{\cancel{\text{cm}^3}} \times \frac{1\ \cancel{\text{cm}^3}}{1\ \cancel{\text{mL}}} \times \frac{1\text{ mol } C_2H_5OH}{46.07\ \cancel{\text{g } C_2H_5OH}} \times \frac{6.022 \times 10^{23}\text{ molecules } C_2H_5OH}{1\ \cancel{\text{mol } C_2H_5OH}}$$

$= 1.50 \times 10^{24}$ molecules C_2H_5OH

Check: The units of the answer (molecules C_2H_5OH) are correct. The magnitude is reasonable because we had more than 2 moles of C_2H_5OH and we have more than 2 times Avogadro's number of molecules.

3.112 **Given:** 0.05 mL H_2O, d = 1.0 g/cm^3 **Find:** number of molecules

Conceptual Plan: $\text{cm}^3 \rightarrow \text{mL}$: $\text{mL } H_2O \rightarrow \text{g } H_2O \rightarrow \text{mol } H_2O \rightarrow \text{molecules } H_2O$

$$\frac{1\text{ cm}^3}{1\text{ mL}} \qquad \frac{1\text{ mL } H_2O}{1.0\text{ g } H_2O} \qquad \frac{1\text{ mol } H_2O}{18.02\text{ g } H_2O} \qquad \frac{6.022 \times 10^{23}\text{ molecules } H_2O}{1\text{ mol } H_2O}$$

Solution:

$$0.05\ \cancel{\text{mL } H_2O} \times \frac{1\ \cancel{\text{cm}^3}}{1\ \cancel{\text{mL}}} \times \frac{1.0\ \cancel{\text{g}}}{\cancel{\text{cm}^3}} \times \frac{1\ \cancel{\text{mol } H_2O}}{18.02\ \cancel{\text{g } H_2O}} \times \frac{6.022 \times 10^{23}\text{ molecules } H_2O}{1\ \cancel{\text{mol } H_2O}} = 2 \times 10^{21}\text{ molecules } H_2O$$

Check: The units of the answer (molecules H_2O) are correct. The magnitude is reasonable because we have less then 1 mole H_2O and we have less than Avogadro's number of molecules.

3.113 (a) To write the formula for an ionic compound do the following: 1) Write the symbol for the metal cation and its charge and the symbol for the nonmetal anion or polyatomic anion and its charge. 2) Adjust the subscript on each cation and anion to balance the overall charge. 3) Check that the sum of the charges of the cations equals the sum of the charges of the anions.

potassium chromate: K^+ CrO_4^{2-}; K_2CrO_4 cation 2(1+) = 2+; anion 2–

Given: K_2CrO_4 **Find:** mass percent of each element

Conceptual Plan: %K, then %Cr, then %O

$\text{mass \%K} = \frac{2 \text{ x molar mass K}}{\text{molar mass } K_2CrO_4} \text{ x } 100$ $\text{mass \%Cr} = \frac{1 \text{ x molar mass Cr}}{\text{molar mass } K_2CrO_4} \text{ x } 100$ $\text{mass \%O} = \frac{4 \text{ x molar mass O}}{\text{molar mass } K_2CrO_4} \text{ x } 100$

molar mass of K = 39.10 g/mol, molar mass Cr = 52.00 g/mol, molar mass O = 16.00 g/mol

Solution: molar mass K_2CrO_4 = 2(39.10 g/mol) + 1(52.00 g/mol) + 4(16.00 g/mol) = 194.20 g/mol

$$2 \text{ x molar mass K} = 2(39.10 \text{ g/mol}) = 78.20 \text{ g K}$$

$$\text{mass \% K} = \frac{2 \text{ x molar mass K}}{\text{molar mass } K_2CrO_4} \text{ x } 100\% = \frac{78.20 \cancel{\text{g/mol}}}{194.20 \cancel{\text{g/mol}}} \text{ x } 100\% = 40.27\ \%$$

$$1 \text{ x molar mass Cr} = 1(52.00 \text{ g/mol}) = 52.00 \text{ g Cr}$$

$$\text{mass \% Cr} = \frac{1 \text{ x molar mass Cr}}{\text{molar mass } K_2CrO_4} \text{ x } 100\% = \frac{52.00 \cancel{\text{g/mol}}}{194.20 \cancel{\text{g/mol}}} \text{ x } 100\% = 26.78\ \%$$

$$4 \text{ x molar mass O} = 4(16.00 \text{ g/mol}) = 64.00 \text{ g O}$$

$$\text{mass \% O} = \frac{4 \text{ x molar mass O}}{\text{molar mass } K_2CrO_4} \text{ x } 100\% = \frac{64.00 \cancel{\text{g/mol}}}{194.20 \cancel{\text{g/mol}}} \text{ x } 100\% = 32.96\ \%$$

Check: The units of the answer (%) are correct. The magnitude is reasonable because each is between 0 and 100% and the total is 100%.

(b) To write the formula for an ionic compound do the following: 1) Write the symbol for the metal cation and its charge and the symbol for the nonmetal anion or polyatomic anion and its charge. 2) Adjust the subscript on each cation and anion to balance the overall charge. 3) Check that the sum of the charges of the cations equals the sum of the charges of the anions.

Lead(II)phosphate: Pb^{2+} PO_4^{3-}; $Pb_3(PO_4)_2$ cation 3(2+) = 6+; anion 2(3–) = 6–

Given: $Pb_3(PO_4)_2$ **Find:** mass percent of each element

Conceptual Plan: %Pb, then % P, then %O

$\text{mass \%PB} = \frac{3 \text{ x molar mass Pb}}{\text{molar mass } Pb_3(PO_4)_2} \text{ x } 100$ $\text{mass \%P} = \frac{2 \text{ x molar mass P}}{\text{molar mass } Pb_3(PO_4)_2} \text{ x } 100$ $\text{mass \%O} = \frac{8 \text{ x molar mass O}}{\text{molar mass } Pb_3(PO_4)_2} \text{ x } 100$

Solution: molar mass $Pb_3(PO_4)_2$ = 3(207.2 g/mol) + 2(30.97 g/mol) + 8(16.00 g/mol) = 811.5 g/mol

$$3 \text{ x molar mass Pb} = 3(207.2 \text{ g/mol}) = 621.6 \text{ g Pb}$$

$$\text{mass \% Pb} = \frac{3 \text{ x molar mass Pb}}{\text{molar mass } Pb_3(PO_4)_2} \text{ x } 100\% = \frac{621.6 \cancel{\text{g/mol}}}{811.5 \cancel{\text{g/mol}}} \text{ x } 100\% = 76.60\ \%$$

$$2 \text{ x molar mass P} = 2(30.97 \text{ g/mol}) = 61.94 \text{ g P}$$

$$\text{mass \% P} = \frac{2 \text{ x molar mass P}}{\text{molar mass } Pb_3(PO_4)_2} \text{ x } 100\% = \frac{61.94 \cancel{\text{g/mol}}}{811.5 \cancel{\text{g/mol}}} \text{ x } 100\% = 7.632\ \%$$

$$4 \text{ x molar mass O} = 8(16.00 \text{ g/mol}) = 128.0 \text{ g O}$$

$$\text{mass \% O} = \frac{8 \text{ x molar mass O}}{\text{molar mass } Pb_3(PO_4)_2} \text{ x } 100\% = \frac{128.0 \cancel{\text{g/mol}}}{811.5 \cancel{\text{g/mol}}} \text{ x } 100\% = 15.77\ \%$$

Check: The units of the answer (%) are correct. The magnitude is reasonable because each is between 0 and 100% and the total is 100%.

(c) sulfurous acid: H_2SO_3

Given: H_2SO_3 **Find:** mass percent of each element

Conceptual Plan: %H, then %S, then %O

$\text{mass \%H} = \frac{2 \text{ x molar mass H}}{\text{molar mass } H_2SO_3} \text{ x } 100$ $\text{mass \%S} = \frac{1 \text{ x molar mass S}}{\text{molar mass } H_2SO_3} \text{ x } 100$ $\text{mass \%O} = \frac{3 \text{ x molar mass O}}{\text{molar mass } H_2SO_3} \text{ x } 100$

Solution: molar mass H_2SO_3 = 2(1.008 g/mol) + 1(32.07 g/mol) + 3(16.00 g/mol) = 82.0$\underline{8}$6 g/mol

2 x molar mass H = 1(1.008 g/mol) = 2.016 g H   1 x molar mass S = 1(32.07 g/mol) = 32.07 g S

$$\text{mass \%H} = \frac{2 \text{ x molar mass H}}{\text{molar mass } H_2SO_3} \text{ x } 100\% = \frac{2.016 \cancel{\text{g/mol}}}{82.0\underline{8}6 \cancel{\text{g/mol}}} \text{ x } 100\% = 2.456\ \%$$

$$\text{mass \% S} = \frac{1 \text{ x molar mass S}}{\text{molar mass } H_2SO_3} \text{ x } 100\% = \frac{32.07 \cancel{\text{g/mol}}}{82.0\underline{8}6 \cancel{\text{g/mol}}} \text{ x } 100\% = 39.07\ \%$$

3 x molar mass O = 3(16.00 g/mol) = 48.00 g O

$$\text{mass \% O} = \frac{3 \text{ x molar mass O}}{\text{molar mass } H_2SO_3} \text{ x } 100\% = \frac{48.00 \cancel{\text{g/mol}}}{82.0\underline{8}6 \cancel{\text{g/mol}}} \text{ x } 100\% = 58.48\ \%$$

Check: The units of the answer (%) are correct. The magnitude is reasonable because each is between 0 and 100% and the total is 100%.

(d) To write the formula for an ionic compound do the following: 1) Write the symbol for the metal cation and its charge and the symbol for the nonmetal anion or polyatomic anion and its charge. 2) Adjust the subscript on each cation and anion to balance the overall charge. 3) Check that the sum of the charges of the cations equals the sum of the charges of the anions.

cobalt(II)bromide: Co^{2+} Br^-; $CoBr_2$ cation 2+ = 2+; anion 2(1–) = 2–

Given: $CoBr_2$ **Find:** mass percent of each element

Conceptual Plan: %Co, then %Br

$$\text{mass \%Co} = \frac{1 \text{ x molar mass Co}}{\text{molar mass } CoBr_2} \text{ x } 100 \qquad \text{mass \%Br} = \frac{2 \text{ x molar mass Br}}{\text{molar mass } CoBr_2} \text{ x } 100$$

Solution: molar mass $CoBr_2$ = (58.93 g/mol) + 2(79.90 g/mol) = 218.73 g/mol

2 x molar mass Co = 1(58.93 g/mol) = 58.93 g Co   1 x molar mass Br = 2(79.90 g/mol) = 159.80 g Br

$$\text{mass \% Co} = \frac{1 \text{ x molar mass Co}}{\text{molar mass } CoBr_2} \text{ x } 100\% = \frac{58.93 \cancel{\text{g/mol}}}{218.73 \cancel{\text{g/mol}}} \text{ x } 100\% = 26.94\ \%$$

$$\text{mass \% Br} = \frac{2 \text{ x molar mass Br}}{\text{molar mass } CoBr_2} \text{ x } 100\% = \frac{159.80 \cancel{\text{g/mol}}}{218.73 \cancel{\text{g/mol}}} \text{ x } 100\% = 73.058\ \%$$

Check: The units of the answer (%) are correct. The magnitude is reasonable because each is between 0 and 100% and the total is 100%.

3.114 (a) perchloric acid: $HClO_4$

Given: $HClO_4$ **Find:** mass percent of each element

Conceptual Plan: %H, then %Cl, then %O

$$\text{mass \%H} = \frac{1 \text{ x molar mass H}}{\text{molar mass } HClO_4} \text{ x } 100 \qquad \text{mass \%Cl} = \frac{1 \text{ x molar mass Cl}}{\text{molar mass } HClO_4} \text{ x } 100 \qquad \text{mass \%O} = \frac{4 \text{ x molar mass O}}{\text{molar mass } HClO_4} \text{ x } 100$$

Solution: molar mass $HClO_4$ = 1(1.008 g/mol) + 1(35.45 g/mol) + 4(16.00 g/mol) = 100.46 g/mol

1 x molar mass H = 1(1.008 g/mol) = 1.008 g H   1 x molar mass Cl = 1(35.45 g/mol) = 35.45 g Cr

$$\text{mass \%H} = \frac{1 \text{ x molar mass H}}{\text{molar mass } HClO_4} \text{ x } 100\% = \frac{1.008 \cancel{\text{g/mol}}}{100.46 \cancel{\text{g/mol}}} \text{ x } 100\% = 1.003\ \%$$

$$\text{mass \% Cl} = \frac{1 \text{ x molar mass Cl}}{\text{molar mass } HClO_4} \text{ x } 100\% = \frac{35.45 \cancel{\text{g/mol}}}{100.46 \cancel{\text{g/mol}}} \text{ x } 100\% = 35.29\ \%$$

4 x molar mass O = 4(16.00 g/mol) = 64.00 g O

$$\text{mass \% O} = \frac{4 \text{ x molar mass O}}{\text{molar mass } HSO_3} \text{ x } 100\% = \frac{64.00 \cancel{\text{g/mol}}}{100.46 \cancel{\text{g/mol}}} \text{ x } 100\% = 63.71\ \%$$

Check: The units of the answer (%) are correct. The magnitude is reasonable because each is between 0 and 100% and the total is 100%.

(b) phosphorus pentachloride: PCl_5
Given: PCl_5 **Find:** mass percent of each element
Conceptual Plan: %P, then %Cl

$$\text{mass }\%H = \frac{1 \text{ x molar mass P}}{\text{molar mass PCl}_5} \text{ x } 100 \qquad \text{mass }\%H = \frac{5 \text{ x molar mass Cl}}{\text{molar mass PCl}_5} \text{ x } 100$$

Solution: molar mass PCl_5 = 1(30.97 g/mol) + 5(35.45 g/mol) = 208.2 g/mol

$$1 \text{ x molar mass P} = 1(30.97 \text{ g/mol}) = 30.97 \text{ g P} \qquad 5 \text{ x molar mass Cl} = 5(35.45 \text{ g/mol}) = 177.25 \text{ g Cl}$$

$$\text{mass }\%P = \frac{1 \text{ x molar mass P}}{\text{molar mass PCl}_5} \text{ x } 100\% = \frac{30.97 \text{ g/mol}}{208.2 \text{ g/mol}} \text{ x } 100\% = 14.87\ \%$$

$$\text{mass }\%\ Cl = \frac{5 \text{ x molar mass Cl}}{\text{molar mass PCl}_5} \text{ x } 100\% = \frac{177.25 \text{ g/mol}}{208.2 \text{ g/mol}} \text{ x } 100\% = 85.13\ \%$$

Check: The units of the answer (%) are correct. The magnitude is reasonable because each is between 0 and 100% and the total is 100%.

(c) nitrogen triiodide: NI_3
Given: NI_3 **Find:** mass percent of each element
Conceptual Plan: %N, then %I

$$\text{mass }\%N = \frac{1 \text{ x molar mass N}}{\text{molar mass NI}_3} \text{ x } 100 \qquad \text{mass }\%I = \frac{3 \text{ x molar mass I}}{\text{molar mass NI}_3} \text{ x } 100$$

Solution: molar mass NI_3 = 1(14.01 g/mol) + 3(126.9 g/mol) = 394.7 g/mol

$$1 \text{ x molar mass N} = 1(14.01 \text{ g/mol}) = 14.01 \text{ g N} \qquad 1 \text{ x molar mass I} = 3(126.9 \text{ g/mol}) = 380.7 \text{ g I}$$

$$\text{mass }\%N = \frac{1 \text{ x molar mass N}}{\text{molar mass NI}_3} \text{ x } 100\% = \frac{14.01 \text{ g/mol}}{394.7 \text{ g/mol}} \text{ x } 100\% = 3.549\ \%$$

$$\text{mass }\%\ I = \frac{3 \text{ x molar mass I}}{\text{molar mass NI}_3} \text{ x } 100\% = \frac{380.7 \text{ g/mol}}{394.7 \text{ g/mol}} \text{ x } 100\% = 96.45\ \%$$

Check: The units of the answer (%) are correct. The magnitude is reasonable because each is between 0 and 100% and the total is 100%.

(d) carbon dioxide: CO_2
Given: CO_2 **Find:** mass percent of each element
Conceptual Plan: %C, then %O

$$\text{mass }\%C = \frac{1 \text{ x molar mass C}}{\text{molar mass CO}_2} \text{ x } 100 \qquad \text{mass }\%O = \frac{2 \text{ x molar mass O}}{\text{molar mass CO}_2} \text{ x } 100$$

Solution: molar mass CO_2 = 1(12.01 g/mol) + 2(16.00 g/mol) = 44.01 g/mol

$$1 \text{ x molar mass C} = 1(12.01 \text{ g/mol}) = 12.01 \text{ g C} \qquad 2 \text{ x molar mass O} = 2(16.00 \text{ g/mol}) = 32.00 \text{ g O}$$

$$\text{mass }\%C = \frac{1 \text{ x molar mass C}}{\text{molar mass CO}_2} \text{ x } 100\% = \frac{12.01 \text{ g/mol}}{44.01 \text{ g/mol}} \text{ x } 100\% = 27.29\ \%$$

$$\text{mass }\%\ O = \frac{2 \text{ x molar mass O}}{\text{molar mass CO}_2} \text{ x } 100\% = \frac{32.00 \text{ g/mol}}{44.01 \text{ g/mol}} \text{ x } 100\% = 72.71\ \%$$

Check: The units of the answer (%) are correct. The magnitude is reasonable because each is between 0 and 100% and the total is 100%.

3.115 **Given:** 25 g CF_2Cl_2/mo. **Find:** g Cl /yr.
Conceptual Plan: g CF_2Cl_2/mo → g Cl/mo → g Cl/yr.

$$\frac{70.90 \text{ g Cl}}{120.91 \text{ g CF}_2\text{Cl}_2} \qquad \frac{12 \text{ mo.}}{1 \text{ yr.}}$$

Solution: $\dfrac{25 \text{ g CF}_2\text{Cl}_2}{\text{mo.}} \text{ x } \dfrac{70.90 \text{ g Cl}}{120.91 \text{ g CF}_2\text{Cl}_2} \text{ x } \dfrac{12 \text{ mo.}}{1 \text{ yr.}} = 1.8 \text{ x } 10^2 \text{ g Cl/yr.}$

Check: The units of the answer (g Cl) is correct. Magnitude is reasonable because it is less than the total CF_2Cl_2 /yr.

3.116 **Given:** 12 kg CHF_2Cl/mo. **Find:** kg Cl /yr.
Conceptual Plan: kg CHF_2Cl/mo → kg Cl/mo → kg Cl/yr.

$$\frac{35.45 \text{ g Cl}}{86.47 \text{ g CHF}_2\text{Cl}} = \frac{35.45 \text{ kg Cl}}{86.47 \text{ kg CHF}_2\text{Cl}} \qquad \frac{12 \text{ mo.}}{1 \text{ yr.}}$$

Solution: $$\frac{12 \text{ kg CHF}_2\text{Cl}}{\text{mo.}} \times \frac{35.45 \text{ kg Cl}}{86.47 \text{ kg CHF}_2\text{Cl}} \times \frac{12 \text{ mo.}}{1 \text{ yr.}} = 59 \text{ kg Cl/yr.}$$

Check: The units of the answer (kg Cl) is correct. Magnitude is reasonable because it is less than the total CHF_2Cl /yr.

3.117 **Given:** MCl_3, 65.57% Cl **Find:** identify M
Conceptual Plan: g Cl → mol Cl → mol M → atomic mass M

$$\frac{1 \text{ mol Cl}}{35.45 \text{ g Cl}} \qquad \frac{1 \text{ mol M}}{3 \text{ mol Cl}} \qquad \frac{\text{g M}}{\text{mol M}}$$

Solution: in 100 g sample: 65.57 g Cl, 34.43 g M

$$65.57 \text{ g Cl} \times \frac{1 \text{ mol Cl}}{35.45 \text{ g Cl}} \times \frac{1 \text{ mol M}}{3 \text{ mol Cl}} = 0.6165 \text{ mol M} \qquad \frac{34.43 \text{ g M}}{0.6165 \text{ mol M}} = 55.84 \text{ g/mol M}$$

molar mass of 55.84 = Fe
The identity of M = Fe.

3.118 **Given:** M_2O, 16.99% O **Find:** identify M
Conceptual Plan: g O → mol O → mol M → atomic mass M

$$\frac{1 \text{ mol O}}{16.00 \text{ g O}} \qquad \frac{2 \text{ mol M}}{1 \text{ mol O}} \qquad \frac{\text{g M}}{\text{mol M}}$$

Solution: in 100 g sample: 16.99 g O, 83.01 g M

$$16.99 \text{ g O} \times \frac{1 \text{ mol O}}{16.00 \text{ g O}} \times \frac{2 \text{ mol M}}{1 \text{ mol O}} = 2.124 \text{ mol M} \qquad \frac{83.01 \text{ g M}}{2.124 \text{ mol M}} = 39.08 \text{ g/mol M}$$

molar mass of 39.08 = K
The identity of M = K.

3.119 **Given:** In a 100 g sample: 79.37 g C, 8.88 g H, 11.75 g O, molar mass = 272.37g/mol
Find: molecular formula
Conceptual Plan:
convert mass to mol of each element → pseudoformula → empirical formula → molecular formula

$$\frac{1 \text{ mol C}}{12.01 \text{ g C}} \qquad \frac{1 \text{ mol H}}{1.008 \text{ g H}} \qquad \frac{1 \text{ mol O}}{16.00 \text{ g O}}$$

divide by smallest number   empirical formula x n

Solution: $$79.37 \text{ g C} \times \frac{1 \text{ mol C}}{12.01 \text{ g C}} = 6.609 \text{ mol C}$$

$$8.88 \text{ g H} \times \frac{1 \text{ mol H}}{1.008 \text{ g H}} = 8.81 \text{ mol H}$$

$$11.75 \text{ g O} \times \frac{1 \text{ mol O}}{16.00 \text{ g O}} = 0.7344 \text{ mol O}$$

$C_{6.609}H_{8.81}O_{0.7344}$

$C_{\frac{6.609}{0.7344}}H_{\frac{8.81}{0.7344}}O_{\frac{0.7344}{0.7344}} \rightarrow C_9H_{12}O$

The correct empirical formula is $C_9H_{12}O$.
empirical formula mass = 9(12.01 g/mol) + 12(1.008 g/mol) + 1(16.00 g/mol) = 136.19 g/mol

$$n = \frac{\text{molar mass}}{\text{formula molar mass}} = \frac{272.37 \text{ g/mol}}{136.19 \text{ g/mol}} = 2$$

molecular formula = $C_9H_{12}O \times 2 = C_{18}H_{24}O_2$

3.120 **Given:** In a 100 g sample: 40.00 g C, 6.72 g H, 53.28 g O, molar mass = 180.16 g/mol
Find: molecular formula
Conceptual Plan:
convert mass to mol of each element → pseudoformula → empirical formula → molecular formula

$$\frac{1 \text{ mol C}}{12.01 \text{ g C}} \qquad \frac{1 \text{ mol H}}{1.008 \text{ g H}} \qquad \frac{1 \text{ mol O}}{16.00 \text{ g O}}$$

divide by smallest number   empirical formula x n

Solution: $40.00\ \cancel{g\ C} \times \frac{1\ mol\ C}{12.01\ \cancel{g\ C}} = 3.331\ mol\ C$

$6.72\ \cancel{g\ H} \times \frac{1\ mol\ H}{1.008\ \cancel{g\ H}} = 6.67\ mol\ H$

$53.28\ \cancel{g\ O} \times \frac{1\ mol\ O}{16.00\ \cancel{g\ O}} = 3.330\ mol\ O$

$C_{3.331}H_{6.67}O_{3.330}$

$C_{\frac{3.331}{3.331}}H_{\frac{6.67}{3.331}}O_{\frac{3.330}{3.330}} \rightarrow CH_2O$

The correct empirical formula is CH_2O.

empirical formula mass = 1(12.01 g/mol) + 2(1.008 g/mol) + 1(16.00 g/mol) = 30.03 g/mol

$n = \frac{\text{molar mass}}{\text{formula molar mass}} = \frac{180.16\ g/mol}{30.03\ g/mol} = 6$

molecular formula $= CH_2O \times 6 = C_6H_{12}O_6$

3.121 **Given:** 13.42 g sample, 39.61 g CO_2, 9.01 g H_2O, molar mass = 268.34 g/mol
Find: molecular formula
Conceptual Plan:
mass CO_2, H_2O → mol CO_2, H_2O → mol C, mol H → mass C, mass H, mass O → mol O →

$\frac{1\ mol\ CO_2}{44.01\ g\ CO_2}$ $\frac{1\ mol\ H_2O}{18.02\ g\ H_2O}$ $\frac{1\ mol\ C}{1\ mol\ CO_2}$ $\frac{2\ mol\ H}{1\ mol\ H_2O}$ $\frac{12.01\ g\ C}{1\ mol\ C}$ $\frac{1.008\ g\ H}{1\ mol\ H}$ g sample – gC – g H $\frac{1\ mol\ O}{16.00\ g\ O}$

pseudoformula → empirical formula → molecular formula

divide by smallest number empirical formula x n

$39.61\ \cancel{g\ CO_2} \times \frac{1\ mol\ CO_2}{44.01\ \cancel{g\ CO_2}} = 0.9000\ mol\ CO_2$

$9.01\ \cancel{g\ H_2O} \times \frac{1\ mol\ H_2O}{18.02\ \cancel{g\ H_2O}} = 0.5000\ mol\ H_2O$

$0.9000\ \cancel{mol\ CO_2} \times \frac{1\ mol\ C}{1\ \cancel{mol\ CO_2}} = 0.9000\ mol\ C$

$0.5000\ \cancel{mol\ H_2O} \times \frac{2\ mol\ H}{1\ \cancel{mol\ H_2O}} = 1.000\ mol\ H$

$0.9000\ \cancel{mol\ C} \times \frac{12.01\ g\ C}{1\ \cancel{mol\ C}} = 10.81\ g\ C$

$1.000\ \cancel{mol\ H_2O} \times \frac{1.008\ g\ H}{1\ \cancel{mol\ H}} = 1.008\ g\ H$

$13.42\ g - 10.81\ g - 1.008\ g = 1.60\ g\ O$

$1.60\ \cancel{g\ O} \times \frac{1\ mol\ O}{16.00\ \cancel{g\ O}} = 0.100\ mol\ O$

$C_{0.9000}H_{1.000}O_{0.100}$

$C_{\frac{0.9000}{0.100}}H_{\frac{1.000}{0.100}}O_{\frac{0.100}{0.100}} \rightarrow C_9H_{10}O$

The correct empirical formula is $C_9H_{10}O$.

empirical formula mass = 9(12.01 g/mol) + 10(1.008 g/mol) + 1(16.00 g/mol) = 134.2 g/mol

$n = \frac{\text{molar mass}}{\text{formula molar mass}} = \frac{268.34\ g/mol}{134.2\ g/mol} = 2$

molecular formula $= C_9H_{10}O \times 2 = C_{18}H_{20}O_2$

3.122 **Given:** 1.893 g sample, 5.545 g CO_2, 1.388 g H_2O, molar mass = 270.36 g/mol
Find: molecular formula
Conceptual Plan:
mass CO_2, H_2O → mol CO_2, H_2O → mol C, mol H → mass C, mass H, mass O → mol O →

$\frac{1\ mol\ CO_2}{44.01\ g\ CO_2}$ $\frac{1\ mol\ H_2O}{18.02\ g\ H_2O}$ $\frac{1\ mol\ C}{1\ mol\ CO_2}$ $\frac{2\ mol\ H}{1\ mol\ H_2O}$ $\frac{12.01\ g\ C}{1\ mol\ C}$ $\frac{1.008\ g\ H}{1\ mol\ H}$ g sample – gC – g H $\frac{1\ mol\ O}{16.00\ g\ O}$

pseudoformula → empirical formula → molecular formula

divide by smallest number empirical formula x n

Solution:

$$5.545\ \text{g CO}_2 \times \frac{1\ \text{mol CO}_2}{44.01\ \text{g CO}_2} = 0.1260\ \text{mol CO}_2$$

$$1.388\ \text{g H}_2\text{O} \times \frac{1\ \text{mol H}_2\text{O}}{18.02\ \text{g H}_2\text{O}} = 0.07703\ \text{mol H}_2\text{O}$$

$$0.1260\ \text{mol CO}_2 \times \frac{1\ \text{mol C}}{1\ \text{mol CO}_2} = 0.1260\ \text{mol C}$$

$$0.07703\ \text{mol H}_2\text{O} \times \frac{2\ \text{mol H}}{1\ \text{mol H}_2\text{O}} = 0.1541\ \text{mol H}$$

$$0.1260\ \text{mol C} \times \frac{12.01\ \text{g C}}{1\ \text{mol C}} = 1.513\ \text{g C}$$

$$0.1541\ \text{mol H}_2\text{O} \times \frac{1.008\ \text{g H}}{1\ \text{mol H}} = 0.1553\ \text{g H}$$

$$1.893\ \text{g} - 1.513\ \text{g} - 0.1553\ \text{g} = 0.2247\ \text{g O}$$

$$0.2247\ \text{g O} \times \frac{1\ \text{mol O}}{16.00\ \text{g O}} = 0.01404\ \text{mol O}$$

$C_{0.1260}H_{0.1541}O_{0.01404}$

$C_{\frac{0.1260}{0.01404}}H_{\frac{0.1541}{0.01404}}O_{\frac{0.01404}{0.01404}} \rightarrow C_9H_{11}O$

The correct empirical formula is $C_9H_{11}O$

empirical formula mass = 9(12.01 g/mol) + 11(1.008 g/mol) + 1(16.00 g/mol) = 135.2 g/mol

$$n = \frac{\text{molar mass}}{\text{formula molar mass}} = \frac{270.36\ \text{g/mol}}{135.2\ \text{g/mol}} = 2$$

molecular formula $= C_9H_{11}O \times 2$

$= C_{18}H_{22}O_2$

3.123 **Given:** 4.93 g $MgSO_4 \cdot xH_2O$, 2.41 g $MgSO_4$ **Find:** value of x

Conceptual Plan: g $MgSO_4$ → mol $MgSO_4$ g H_2O → mol H_2O Determine mole ratio

$$\frac{1\ \text{mol MgSO}_4}{120.38\ \text{g MgSO}_4} \qquad \frac{1\ \text{mol H}_2\text{O}}{18.02\ \text{g H}_2\text{O}} \qquad \frac{\text{mol HO}_2}{\text{mol MgSO}_4}$$

Solution:

$$2.41\ \text{g MgSO}_4 \times \frac{1\ \text{mol MgSO}_4}{120.38\ \text{g MgSO}_4} = 0.0200\ \text{mol MgSO}_4$$

Determine g H_2O: 4.93 g $MgSO_4 \cdot xH_2O$ – 2.41 g $MgSO_4$ = 2.52 g H_2O

$$2.52\ \text{g H}_2\text{O} \times \frac{1\ \text{mol H}_2\text{O}}{18.02\ \text{g H}_2\text{O}} = 0.140\ \text{mol H}_2\text{O}$$

$$\frac{0.140\ \text{mol H}_2\text{O}}{0.0200\ \text{mol MgSO}_4} = 7$$

x = 7

3.124 **Given:** 3.41 g $CuCl_2 \cdot xH_2O$, 2.69 g $CuCl_2$ **Find:** value of x

Conceptual Plan: g $CuCl_2$ → mol $CuCl_2$ g H_2O → mol H_2O Determine mole ratio

$$\frac{1\ \text{mol CuCl}_2}{134.45\ \text{g CuCl}_2} \qquad \frac{1\ \text{mol H}_2\text{O}}{18.02\ \text{g H}_2\text{O}} \qquad \frac{\text{mol HO}_2}{\text{mol CuCl}_2}$$

Solution:

$$2.69\ \text{g CuCl}_2 \times \frac{1\ \text{mol CuCl}_2}{134.45\ \text{g CuCl}_2} = 0.0200\ \text{mol CuCl}_2$$

Determine g H_2O: 3.41 g $CuCl_2 \cdot xH_2O$ – 2.69 g $CuCl_2$ = 0.72 g H_2O

$$0.72\ \text{g H}_2\text{O} \times \frac{1\ \text{mol H}_2\text{O}}{18.02\ \text{g H}_2\text{O}} = 0.040\ \text{mol H}_2\text{O}$$

$$\frac{0.040\ \text{mol H}_2\text{O}}{0.0200\ \text{mol CuCl}_2} = 2$$

x = 2

3.125 **Given:** molar mass = 177 g/mol, g C = 8(g H) **Find:** molecular formula

Conceptual Plan: C_xH_yBrO

Solution: in 1 mol compound, let x = mol C and y = mol H, assume mol Br = 1, assume mol O = 1

$$177 \text{ g/mol} = x(12.01 \text{ g/mol}) + y(1.008 \text{ g/mol}) + 1(79.90 \text{ g/mol}) + 1(16.00 \text{ g/mol})$$
$$x(12.01 \text{ g/mol}) = 8\{y(1.008 \text{ g/mol})\}$$
$$177 \text{ g/mol} = 8y(1.008 \text{ g/mol}) + y(1.008 \text{ g/mol}) + 79.90 \text{ g/mol} + 16.00 \text{ g/mol}$$
$$81 = 9y(1.008)$$
$$y = 9 = \text{mol H}$$
$$x(12.01) = 8 \times 9(1.008)$$
$$x = 6 = \text{mol C}$$

molecular formula = C_6H_9BrO

Check: molar mass = 6(12.01 g/mol) + 9(1.008 g/mol) + 1(79.90 g/mol) + 1(16.00 g/mol) = 177.0 g/mol

3.126 **Given:** 3.54 g sample yields 8.49 g CO_2 and 2.14 g H_2O; 2.35 g sample yields 0.199 g N; molar mass = 165

Find: molecular formula

Conceptual Plan:

mass N → mol N; then mass CO_2, H_2O → mol CO_2, H_2O → mol C, mol H → mass C, mass H;

$\frac{1 \text{ mol N}}{14.01 \text{ g N}}$ $\frac{1 \text{ mol } CO_2}{44.01 \text{ g } CO_2}$ $\frac{1 \text{ mol } H_2O}{18.02 \text{ g } H_2O}$ $\frac{1 \text{ mol C}}{1 \text{ mol } CO_2}$ $\frac{2 \text{ mol H}}{1 \text{ mol } H_2O}$ $\frac{12.01 \text{ g C}}{1 \text{ mol C}}$ $\frac{1.008 \text{ g H}}{1 \text{ mol H}}$

mass O → mol O → pseudoformula → empirical formula → molecular formula

g sample − gC − g H; $\frac{1 \text{ mol O}}{16.00 \text{ g O}}$; divide by smallest number; empirical formula x n

Solution:

$$\frac{0.199 \text{ g N}}{2.35 \text{ g sample}} = \frac{x \text{ g N}}{3.54 \text{ g sample}};\ x = 0.300 \text{ g N}$$
$$0.300 \text{ g N} \times \frac{1 \text{ mol N}}{14.01 \text{ g N}} = 0.0214 \text{ mol N}$$
$$8.49 \text{ g } CO_2 \times \frac{1 \text{ mol } CO_2}{44.01 \text{ g } CO_2} = 0.193 \text{ mol } CO_2$$
$$2.14 \text{ g } H_2O \times \frac{1 \text{ mol } H_2O}{18.02 \text{ g } H_2O} = 0.119 \text{ mol } H_2O$$
$$0.193 \text{ mol } CO_2 \times \frac{1 \text{ mol C}}{1 \text{ mol } CO_2} = 0.193 \text{ mol C}$$
$$0.119 \text{ mol } H_2O \times \frac{2 \text{ mol H}}{1 \text{ mol } H_2O} = 0.238 \text{ mol H}$$
$$0.193 \text{ mol C} \times \frac{12.01 \text{ g C}}{1 \text{ mol C}} = 2.32 \text{ g C}$$
$$0.238 \text{ mol } H_2O \times \frac{1.008 \text{ g H}}{1 \text{ mol H}} = 0.240 \text{ g H}$$
$$3.54 \text{ g} - 2.32 \text{ g C} - 0.240 \text{ g H} - 0.300 \text{ g N} = 0.680 \text{ g O}$$
$$0.680 \text{ g O} \times \frac{1 \text{ mol O}}{16.00 \text{ g O}} = 0.0425 \text{ mol O}$$
$$C_{0.193}H_{0.238}N_{0.0214}O_{0.0425}$$
$$C_{\frac{0.193}{0.0214}}H_{\frac{0.238}{0.0214}}N_{\frac{0.0214}{0.0214}}O_{\frac{0.0425}{0.0214}} \rightarrow C_9H_{11}NO_2$$

The correct empirical formula is $C_9H_{11}NO_2$.

empirical formula mass =

9(12.01 g/mol) + 11(1.008 g/mol) + 1(14.01 g/mol) + 2(16.00 g/mol) = 165.19 g/mol

$$n = \frac{\text{molar mass}}{\text{formula molar mass}} = \frac{165 \text{ g/mol}}{165.19 \text{ g/mol}} = 1$$

molecular formula $= C_9H_{11}NO_2 \times 1$

$= C_9H_{11}NO_2$

3.127 **Given:** 23.5 mg $C_{17}H_{22}ClNO_4$ **Find:** total number of atoms

Conceptual Plan: mg compound → g compound → mol compound → mol atoms → number of atoms

$\frac{1\ g}{1000\ mg}$ $\frac{1\ mol}{339.8\ g}$ $\frac{45\ mol\ atoms}{1\ mol\ compound}$ $\frac{6.022 \times 10^{23}\ atoms}{1\ mol\ atoms}$

Solution: $23.5\ \cancel{mg} \times \frac{1\ \cancel{g}}{1000\ \cancel{mg}} \times \frac{1\ \cancel{mol\ cpd}}{339.8\ \cancel{g}} \times \frac{45\ \cancel{mol\ atoms}}{1\ \cancel{mol\ cpd}} \times \frac{6.022 \times 10^{23}\ atoms}{\cancel{mol}} = 1.87 \times 10^{21}\ atoms$

Check: The units of the answer (number of atoms) is correct. The magnitude of the answer is reasonable since the molecule is so complex.

3.128 **Given:** In a 100 g sample: 76 g V, 24 g O **Find:** formula and name

Conceptual Plan:

convert mass to mol of each element → write pseudoformula → write empirical formula

$\frac{1\ mol\ V}{50.94\ g\ V}$ $\frac{1\ mol\ O}{16.00\ g\ O}$ divide by smallest number

Solution:

$76\ \cancel{g\ V} \times \frac{1\ mol\ V}{50.94\ \cancel{g\ V}} = 1.5\ mol\ V$

$24\ \cancel{g\ O} \times \frac{1\ mol\ O}{16.00\ \cancel{g\ O}} = 1.5\ mol\ O$

$V_{1.5}O_{1.5}$

$V_{\frac{1.5}{1.5}}O_{\frac{1.5}{1.5}} \rightarrow VO$

The correct formula is VO: vanadium(II) oxide.

Given: In a 100 g sample: 68 g V, 32 g O **Find:** formula and name

Conceptual Plan:

convert mass to mol of each element → write pseudoformula → write empirical formula

$\frac{1\ mol\ V}{50.94\ g\ V}$ $\frac{1\ mol\ O}{16.00\ g\ O}$ divide by smallest number

Solution:

$68\ \cancel{g\ V} \times \frac{1\ mol\ V}{50.94\ \cancel{g\ V}} = 1.33\ mol\ V$

$32\ \cancel{g\ O} \times \frac{1\ mol\ O}{16.00\ \cancel{g\ O}} = 2\ mol\ O$

$V_{1.33}O_2$

$V_{\frac{1.33}{1.33}}O_{\frac{2}{1.33}} \rightarrow VO_{1.5} \rightarrow V_2O_3$

The correct formula is V_2O_3: vanadium(III) oxide.

Given: In a 100 g sample: 61 g V, 39 g O **Find:** formula and name

Conceptual Plan:

convert mass to mol of each element → write pseudoformula → write empirical formula

$\frac{1\ mol\ V}{50.94\ g\ V}$ $\frac{1\ mol\ O}{16.00\ g\ O}$ divide by smallest number

Solution:

$61\ \cancel{g\ V} \times \frac{1\ mol\ V}{50.94\ \cancel{g\ V}} = 1.2\ mol\ V$

$39\ \cancel{g\ O} \times \frac{1\ mol\ O}{16.00\ \cancel{g\ O}} = 2.4\ mol\ O$

$V_{1.2}O_{2.4}$

$V_{\frac{1.2}{1.2}}O_{\frac{2.4}{1.2}} \rightarrow VO_2$

The correct formula is VO_2: vanadium(IV) oxide.

Given: In a 100 g sample: 56 g V, 44 g O **Find:** formula and name

Conceptual Plan:

convert mass to mol of each element → write pseudoformula → write empirical formula

$\frac{1\ mol\ V}{50.94\ g\ V}$ $\frac{1\ mol\ O}{16.00\ g\ O}$ divide by smallest number

Solution:

$$56\ \text{g V} \times \frac{1\ \text{mol V}}{50.94\ \text{g V}} = 1.1\ \text{mol V}$$

$$44\ \text{g O} \times \frac{1\ \text{mol O}}{16.00\ \text{g O}} = 2.75\ \text{mol O}$$

$V_{1.1}O_{2.75}$

$V_{\frac{1.1}{1.1}}O_{\frac{2.75}{1.1}} \rightarrow VO_{2.5} \rightarrow V_2O_5$

The correct formula is V_2O_5: vanadium(V) oxide.

3.129 **Given:** MCl_3, 2.395 g sample, 3.606×10^{-2} mol Cl **Find:** atomic mass M

Conceptual Plan: mol Cl $\rightarrow$ g Cl $\rightarrow$ g X

$\frac{35.45\ \text{g Cl}}{1\ \text{mol Cl}}$ g sample – g Cl = g M

mol Cl $\rightarrow$ **mol M** $\rightarrow$ **atomic mass M**

$\frac{1\ \text{mol M}}{3\ \text{mol Cl}}$ $\frac{\text{g M}}{\text{mol M}}$

Solution:

$$3.606 \times 10^{-2}\ \text{mol Cl} \times \frac{35.45\ \text{g}}{1\ \text{mol Cl}} = 1.278\ \text{g Cl}$$

$$2.395\ \text{g} - 1.278\ \text{g} = 1.117\ \text{g M}$$

$$3.606 \times 10^{-2}\ \text{mol Cl} \times \frac{1\ \text{mol M}}{3\ \text{mol Cl}} = 1.202 \times 10^{-2}\ \text{mol M}$$

$$\frac{1.117\ \text{g M}}{0.01202\ \text{mol M}} = 92.93\ \text{g/mol M}$$

molar mass of M = 92.93 g/mol

3.130

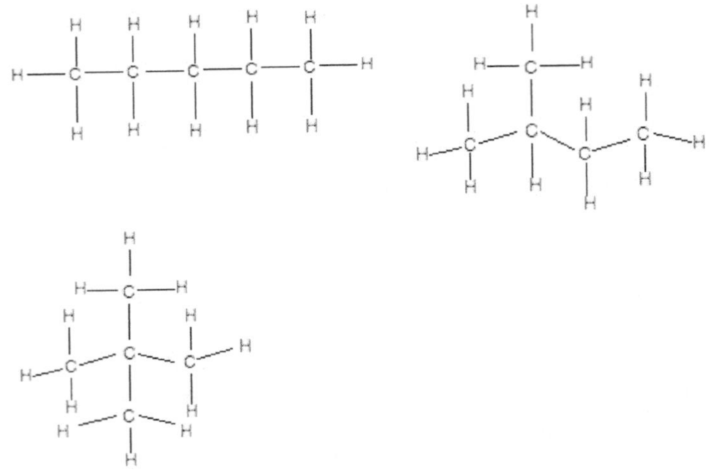

3.131 **Given:** $Fe_xCr_yO_4$; 28.59% O **Find:** x and y

Conceptual Plan: %O $\rightarrow$ **molar mass** $Fe_xCr_yO_4$ $\rightarrow$ **mass Fe + Cr**

$\frac{\text{mass O}}{\text{molar mass compound}} \times 100 = \%O$ mass cpd – mass O = mass Fe+Cr

Solution: $\frac{28.59\ \text{g O}}{100.0} = \frac{64.00\ \text{g O}}{\text{molar mass cpd}}$ molar mass $= 223.8$ g/mol

Mass Fe + Cr = molar mass – (4x molar mass O) = 223.8 – 64.00 = 159.8 g

Molar mass Fe = 55.85, molar mass Cr = 52.00

Since the mass of the two metals is close, the average mass can be used to determine the total moles of Fe and Cr present in the compound. Average mass of Fe and Cr = 53.5. $\frac{159.8\text{g}}{53.5\text{g/mol}} = 2.96 = 3$ mol metal.

Let x = mol Fe and y = mol Cr

x mol Fe + y mol Cr = 3 mol total

x mol Fe(55.85 g Fe/mol) + y mol Cr(52.00 g/ mol) = 159.8

y mol Cr = 3 – x mol Fe
x(55.85) + (3-x)(52.00) = 159.8
So x = 1 and y = 2.

Check: Formula = $FeCr_2O_4$ would have a molar mass of Fe + 2Cr + 4O = 55.85 + 2(52.00) + 4(16.00) = 223.85 and the molar mass of the compound is 223.8.

3.132 **Given:** X_3P_2; 34.00% P, 100 g sample contains 34.00 g P **Find:** X

Conceptual Plan: g P → mol P → mol X

$$\frac{1\text{ mol P}}{30.97\text{ g P}} \quad \frac{3\text{ mol X}}{2\text{ mol P}}$$

and then g P → g X → molar mass X

$$100.00\text{ g sample} - 34.00\text{ g P} \quad \frac{\text{grams X}}{\text{mol X}}$$

Solution: $34.00\ \cancel{\text{g P}} \times \frac{1\ \cancel{\text{mol P}}}{30.97\ \cancel{\text{g P}}} \times \frac{3\text{ mol X}}{2\ \cancel{\text{mol P}}} = 1.647\text{ mol X}$

100.00 g sample – 34.00 g P = 66.00 g X

$$\frac{66.00\text{ g X}}{1.647\text{ mol X}} = 40.08\text{ g/mol} = \text{Ca}$$

Check: The units (g/mol) are correct. The answer, Ca, is reasonable because Ca_3P_2 is a molecule that exists.

3.133 **Given:** 0.0552% $NaNO_2$; 8.00 oz bag **Find:** mass Na in bag

Conceptual Plan: oz. bag → g bag → g NaNO2 → g Na

$$\frac{453.6\text{ g}}{16.00\text{ oz}} \quad \frac{0.0552\text{ g NaNO}_2}{100.0\text{ g bag}} \quad \frac{22.99\text{ g Na}}{69.00\text{ g NaNO}_2}$$

Solution: $8\ \cancel{\text{oz bag}} \times \frac{453.6\ \cancel{\text{g bag}}}{16.00\ \cancel{\text{oz bag}}} \times \frac{0.0552\ \cancel{\text{g NaNO}_2}}{100.0\ \cancel{\text{g bag}}} \times \frac{22.99\ \cancel{\text{g Na}}}{69.00\ \cancel{\text{g NaNO}_2}} \times \frac{1000\text{ mg Na}}{\cancel{\text{g Na}}} = 41.7\text{ mg Na}$

Check: The units of the answer (mg Na) are correct. The magnitude of the answer is reasonable because only a small % of the total mass is Na.

3.134 **Given:** ore is 57.8% $Ca_3(PO_4)_2$ **Find:** mass of ore to get 1.00 kg P

Conceptual Plan: mass ore → mass $Ca_3(PO_4)_2$ → mass P

Solution: Assume a 100.0 gram sample of ore.

$$100.0\ \cancel{\text{g ore}} \times \frac{57.8\ \cancel{\text{g Ca}_3\text{(PO}_4)_2}}{100.0\ \cancel{\text{g ore}}} \times \frac{61.94\text{ g P}}{310.18\ \cancel{\text{g Ca}_3\text{(PO}_4)_2}} = 11.54\text{ g P}$$

$$1.00\ \cancel{\text{kg P}} \times \frac{1000\ \cancel{\text{g P}}}{\cancel{\text{kg P}}} \times \frac{100.0\ \cancel{\text{g ore}}}{11.54\ \cancel{\text{g P}}} \times \frac{1\text{k g ore}}{1000\ \cancel{\text{g ore}}} = 8.6\underline{6}5\text{ kg ore} = 8.67\text{ kg ore}$$

Check: The units of the answer (kg ore) are correct. The magnitude of the answer is reasonable since the amount is greater than 1 kg.

Challenge Problems

3.135 **Given:** g NaCl + g NaBr = 2.00 g, g Na = 0.75 g **Find:** g NaBr

Conceptual Plan:

Let x = mol NaCl, y = mol NaBr, then x(molar mass NaCl) = g NaCl, y(molar mass NaBr) = g NaBr

Solution: x(58.4) + y(102.9) = 2.00
x(23.0) + y(23.0) = 0.75 y = 0.0326 –x
58.4x + 102.9(0.0326-x) = 2.00
58.4x + 3.354 – 102.9x = 2.00
44.5x = 1.354
x = 0.03043 mol NaCl
y = 0.0326 – 0.03043 = 0.00217 mol NaBr
g NaBr = (0.00217)(102.9g/mol) = 0.223 g NaBr

Check: The units of the answer (g NaBr) are correct. The magnitude is reasonable since it is less than the total mass.

3.136 **Given:** Sample 1:1.00 g X, 0.472 g Z, X_2Z_3; Sample 2: 1.00 g X, 0.630 g Z; Sample 3: 1.00 g X, 0.789 g Z
Find: empirical formula for samples 2 and 3
Conceptual Plan: moles X remains constant, determine relative moles of Z for three samples.
Solution: Let X = atomic mass X, Z = atomic mass Z

$$n_X = \frac{1.00 \text{ g X}}{X} \quad n_Z = \frac{0.472 \text{ g Z}}{Z}$$

$$\text{for sample 1: } \frac{n_X}{n_Z} = \frac{2}{3}$$

$$\text{for sample 2: } \frac{0.630 \text{ g}}{0.472 \text{ g}} = 1.33, \text{ so, mol } = 1.33n_Z$$

$$\text{mol ratio: } \frac{n_X}{1.33n_Z} = \frac{2}{(1.33)3} = \frac{2}{4} = \frac{1}{2}$$

Empirical formula sample 2: XZ_2

$$\text{for sample 3: } \frac{0.789 \text{ g}}{0.472 \text{ g}} = 1.67, \text{ so, mol } = 1.67n_Z$$

$$\text{mol ratio: } \frac{n_X}{1.67n_Z} = \frac{2}{(1.67)3} = \frac{2}{5}$$

Empirical formula sample 3: X_2Z_5

3.137 **Given:** Sample of $CaCO_3$ and $(NH_4)_2CO_3$ is 61.9% $CO_3^{\ 2-}$ **Find:** % $CaCO_3$
Conceptual Plan: Let x = $CaCO_3$, y = $(NH_4)_2CO_3$, then x(molar mass $CaCO_3$) = g $CaCO_3$, y(molar mass $(NH_4)_2CO_3$) = g $(NH_4)_2CO_3$
then, a 100.0 g sample contains: x(100.0) g $CaCO_3$; y(96.1) g $(NH_4)_2CO_3$; and 61.9 g $CO_3^{\ 2-}$
Solution:

$$x(100.0) + y(96.1) = 100.0$$
$$x(60.0) + y(60.0) = 61.9 \qquad y = 1.03\underline{1}67 - x$$
$$100.0x + 96.1(1.032\text{-}x) = 100$$
$$100.0x + 99.14 - 96.1x = 100$$
$$3.9x = 0.96$$
$$x = 0.22 \text{ mol } CaCO_3$$
$$y = 1.032 - 0.22 = 0.81 \text{ mol } (NH_4)_2CO_3$$

g $CaCO_3$ = (0.22 mol)(100.0g/mol) = 22.0 g $CaCO_3$ in a 100 g sample:
mass % $CaCO_3$ = 22.0%

Check: The units of the answer (mass % $CaCO_3$) are correct. The magnitude is reasonable since it is between 0 and 100%.

3.138 **Given:** 50.0 g S, 1.00 x 10^2 g Cl_2, 150. g mixture S_2Cl_2 and SCl_2 **Find:** g S_2Cl_2
Conceptual Plan: total mol S = 2(mol S_2Cl_2) + mol SCl_2; mol S_2Cl_2 → g S_2Cl_2

$$\frac{135.04 \text{ g}}{1 \text{ mol } S_2Cl_2} \times 100$$

then, S_2Cl_2 = 135.04 g/mol, SCl_2 = 103.0 g/mol, let x = mol S_2Cl_2, y = mol SCl_2
x(135.04) = g S in S_2Cl_2, y(103.0) = g S in SCl_2

Solution:

$$\text{mol S} = 50.0 \text{ g S} \times \frac{1 \text{ mol S}}{32.1 \text{ g S}} = 1.56 \text{ mol}$$

2x = mol S in S_2Cl_2, y = mol S in SCl_2

$$2x + y = 1.56$$
$$x(135.04) + y(103.0) = 150.0$$
$$135.04x + 103.0(1.56 - 2x) = 150.0$$
$$71.1x = 10.68$$
$$x = 0.150$$
$$y = 1.25$$

$$0.150 \text{ mol } S_2Cl_2 \times \frac{135.04 \text{ g } S_2Cl_2}{1 \text{ mol } S_2Cl_2} = 20.2 \text{ g } S_2Cl_2$$

Check: The units of the answer (g S_2Cl_2) are correct. Magnitude is reasonable since there would be fewer moles of S_2Cl_2 than SCl_2.

3.139 **Given:** 1.1 kg CF_2Cl_2/automobile, 25% leak/year, 100 x 10^6 automobiles **Find:** kg Cl/yr

Conceptual Plan: **kg CF_2Cl_2 /auto → kg CF_2Cl_2 leaked/yr → kg Cl/yr/auto → kg Cl**

$$\frac{25 \text{ kg } CF_2Cl_2}{100 \text{ kg } CF_2Cl_2} \qquad \frac{70.9 \text{ g Cl}}{120.91 \text{ g } CF_2Cl_2} \qquad 100 \times 10^6 \text{ auto}$$

Solution: $$\frac{1.1 \text{ kg } CF_2Cl_2}{\text{auto}} \times \frac{25 \text{ kg } CF_2Cl_2}{100 \text{ kg } CF_2Cl_2} \times \frac{70.9 \text{ kg Cl}}{120.91 \text{ kg } CF_2Cl_2} \times 100 \times 10^6 \text{ auto} = 1.6 \times 10^7 \text{ kg Cl/yr}$$

Check: The units of the answer (kg Cl) are correct. The magnitude is reasonable because it is less than the kg CF_2Cl_2 leaked per year.

3.140 **Given:** coal = 2.55%S, H_2SO_4,1.0 metric ton coal **Find:** metric ton H_2SO_4 produced

Conceptual Plan: H_2SO_4 → %S

$$\frac{32.07 \text{ g S}}{98.09 \text{ g } H_2SO_4} \times 100$$

Solution: $$\frac{32.07 \text{ g S}}{98.09 \text{ g } H_2SO_4} \times 100 = 32.69\% \text{ S}$$

Conceptual Plan: metric ton coal → kg coal → kg S → kg H_2SO_4 → metric ton H_2SO_4

$$\frac{1000 \text{ kg}}{\text{metric ton}} \qquad \frac{2.55 \text{ kg S}}{100 \text{ kg coal}} \qquad \frac{100 \text{ kg } H_2SO_4}{32.69 \text{ kg S}} \qquad \frac{\text{metric ton}}{1000 \text{ kg}}$$

Solution: $$1.0 \text{ metric ton coal} \times \frac{1000 \text{ kg coal}}{1 \text{metric ton coal}} \times \frac{2.55 \text{ kg S}}{100 \text{ kg coal}} \times \frac{100 \text{ kg } H_2SO_4}{32.69 \text{ kg S}} \times \frac{1 \text{ metric ton } H_2SO_4}{1000 \text{ kg } H_2SO_4}$$

$$= 0.078 \text{ metric ton } H_2SO_4$$

Check: The units of the answer (metric ton H_2SO_4) are correct. Magnitude is reasonable since it is more than 2.55% of a metric ton and the mass of H_2SO_4 is greater than the mass of S.

3.141 **Given:** rock contains: 38.0% PbS, 25.0% $PbCO_3$, 17.4% $PbSO_4$ **Find:** kg rock needed for 5.0 metric ton Pb

Conceptual Plan: determine kg Pb/ 100 kg rock then ton Pb → kg Pb → kg rock

$$\frac{1000 \text{ kg}}{\text{metric ton}} \qquad \frac{100 \text{ kg rock}}{64.2 \text{ kg rock}}$$

Solution: in 100 kg rock:

$$\left(38.0 \text{ kg PbS} \times \frac{207.2 \text{ kg Pb}}{239.3 \text{ kg PbS}}\right) + \left(25.0 \text{ kg } PbCO_3 \times \frac{207.2 \text{ kg Pb}}{267.2 \text{ kg } PbCO_3}\right) + \left(17.4 \text{ kg } PbSO_4 \times \frac{207.2 \text{ kg Pb}}{303.1 \text{ kg } PbSO_4}\right)$$

$$= 64.2 \text{ kg Pb}$$

$$5.0 \text{ metric ton Pb} \times \frac{1000 \text{ kg Pb}}{\text{metric ton Pb}} \times \frac{100 \text{ kg rock}}{64.2 \text{ kg Pb}} = 7.8 \times 10^3 \text{ kg rock}$$

Check: The units of the answer (kg rock) are correct. Magnitude is reasonable since it is greater than the amount of Pb needed.

3.142 **Given:** Sample 1: 2.52 g sample, 4.23 g CO_2, 1.01 g H_2O; Sample 2: 4.14 g, 2.11 g SO_3; Sample 3: 5.66 g, 2.27 g HNO_3

Find: empirical formula of the compound

Conceptual Plan: g CO_2 → g C → %C; g H_2O → g H → %H; g SO_2 → g S → %S;

$$\frac{12.01 \text{ g C}}{44.01 \text{ g } CO_2} \quad \frac{\text{g C}}{\text{g sample}} \times 100 \qquad \frac{1.01 \text{ g H}}{18.02 \text{ g } H_2O} \quad \frac{\text{g H}}{\text{g sample}} \times 100 \qquad \frac{32.07 \text{ g S}}{80.07 \text{ g } SO_2} \quad \frac{\text{g S}}{\text{g sample}} \times 100$$

g HNO_3 → g N → % N and the → % O and the % composition → mol of each atom →

$$\frac{14.01 \text{ g N}}{63.02 \text{ g } HNO_3} \quad \frac{\text{g N}}{\text{g sample}} \times 100 \qquad 100\text{-}\%C\text{-}\%H\text{-}\%N\text{-}\%S = \%O$$

pseudoformula → empirical formula

divide by smallest number

Solution: $$4.23 \text{ g } CO_2 \times \frac{12.01 \text{ g C}}{44.01 \text{ g } CO_2} = 1.154 \text{ g C} \qquad \frac{1.154 \text{ g C}}{2.52 \text{ g sample}} \times 100 = 45.81\% \text{ C}$$

$$1.01 \text{ g } H_2O \times \frac{2.02 \text{ g H}}{18.02 \text{ g } H_2O} = 0.1132 \text{ g H} \qquad \frac{0.1132 \text{ g H}}{2.52 \text{ g sample}} \times 100 = 4.49\% \text{ H}$$

$$2.11 \text{ g } SO_3 \times \frac{32.07 \text{ g S}}{80.07 \text{ g } SO_3} = 0.8451 \text{ g S} \qquad \frac{0.8451 \text{ g S}}{4.14 \text{ g sample}} \times 100 = 20.41\% \text{ S}$$

$2.27\ \cancel{g\ HNO_3} \times \frac{14.01\ g\ N}{63.02\ \cancel{g\ HNO_3}} = 0.5046\ g\ N \qquad \frac{0.5046\ g\ N}{5.66\ g\ sample} \times 100 = 8.92\%\ N$

% O = 100 – 45.81 – 4.49 – 20.41 – 8.92 = 20.37 % O

Assume a 100 g sample:

$45.81\ \cancel{g\ C} \times \frac{1\ mol\ C}{12.01\ \cancel{g\ C}} = 3.814\ mol\ C \qquad 4.49\ \cancel{g\ H} \times \frac{1\ mol\ H}{1.01\ \cancel{g\ H}} = 3.445\ mol\ H$

$20.41\ \cancel{g\ S} \times \frac{1\ mol\ S}{32.07\ \cancel{g\ S}} = 0.6364\ mol\ S \qquad 8.92\ \cancel{g\ N} \times \frac{1\ mol\ N}{14.01\ \cancel{g\ N}} = 0.6367\ mol\ N$

$20.37\ \cancel{g\ O} \times \frac{1\ mol\ O}{16.00\ \cancel{g\ O}} = 1.273\ mol\ O$

$C_{3.814}H_{4.445}S_{0.6364}N_{0.6367}O_{1.273}$

$C_{\frac{3.814}{0.6364}}H_{\frac{4.445}{0.6364}}S_{\frac{0.6364}{0.6364}}N_{\frac{0.6367}{0.6364}}O_{\frac{1.273}{0.6364}} \rightarrow C_6H_7SNO_2$

3.143 **Given:** molar mass = 229 g/mol, 6 times mass C as H, **Find:** molecular formula
Conceptual Plan: Let x = mass of C, then 6x = mass of C
Solution: in 1 mol of the compound: g C + g H + g S + g I = 229 g

Since the molar mass of I = 127, there can not be more than 1 mol of I in the compound, so

x + 6x + g S + 127 = 229

x + 6x + g S = 102

If the compound contains 1 mol S, then 7x = 102 – 32 = 70 and x = 10 g H and 6x = 60 g C

$10\ \cancel{g\ H} \times \frac{1\ mol\ H}{1.0\ \cancel{g\ H}} = 10\ mol\ H$

$60\ \cancel{g\ C} \times \frac{1\ mol\ C}{12\ \cancel{g\ C}} = 5\ mol\ C$

1 mol I and 1 mol S, so empirical formula is $C_5H_{10}SI$

Check: Molar mass of $C_5H_{10}SI$ = 5(12) + 10(1.0) + 32 + 127 = 229 g/mol which is the mass given.

3.144 **Given:** Compound is 40% X and 60% Y, atomic mass X = 2(atomic mass Y) **Find:** empirical formula
Conceptual Plan: mass X and Y → mass ratio X:Y and then g X → mol X and g Y → mol Y and then mole ratio

$\frac{g\ X}{atomic\ mass\ X} \qquad \frac{g\ Y}{atomic\ mass\ Y}$

Solution: $\frac{mass\ X}{mass\ Y} = \frac{40}{60} = \frac{2}{3} \quad mol\ X = \frac{2\ g}{atomic\ mass\ X}$ and $mol\ Y = \frac{3\ g}{atomic\ mass\ Y}$

But: atomic mass X = 2(atomic mass Y)

$mol\ X = \frac{2\ g}{2(atomic\ mass\ Y)}$ and $mol\ Y = \frac{3\ g}{atomic\ mass\ Y}$

$\frac{mol\ X}{mol\ Y} = \frac{\frac{\cancel{2}\ \cancel{g}}{\cancel{2}(\cancel{atomic\ mass\ Y})}}{\frac{3\ \cancel{g}}{\cancel{atomic\ mass\ Y}}} = \frac{1}{3}$ Empirical Formula: XY_3

3.145 **Given:** Compound is 1/3 X by mass, atomic mass X is 3/4 atomic mass Y **Find:** empirical formula
Conceptual Plan: mass X and Y → mass ratio X:Y and then g X → mol X and g Y → mol Y and then

$\frac{g\ X}{atomic\ mass\ X} \qquad \frac{g\ Y}{atomic\ mass\ Y}$

mole ratio

Solution: $\frac{mass\ X}{mass\ Y} = \frac{\frac{1}{3}}{\frac{2}{3}} = \frac{1}{2} \quad mol\ X = \frac{1\ g}{atomic\ mass\ X}$ and $mol\ Y = \frac{2\ g}{atomic\ mass\ Y}$

But atomic mass X = 3/4 atomic mass Y so:

$mol\ X = \frac{1\ g}{3/4(atomic\ mass\ Y)}$ and $mol\ Y = \frac{2\ g}{atomic\ mass\ Y}$

$$\frac{\text{mol X}}{\text{mol Y}} = \frac{\dfrac{1\ \cancel{g}}{3/4(\cancel{\text{atomic mass Y}})}}{\dfrac{2\ \cancel{g}}{\cancel{\text{atomic mass Y}}}} = \frac{2}{3} \qquad \text{Empirical Formula} = X_2Y_3$$

3.146 **Given:** 9.0 g sample of C and S, 23.3 g mixture of CO_2 and SO_2 **Find:** mass of S in sample
Conceptual Plan: Let x = g C and y = g S and then x g C → mol C → mol CO_2 → g CO_2 and the

$$\frac{x\ g\ C}{12.01\ g\ C} \quad \frac{1\ mol\ CO_2}{1\ mol\ C} \quad \frac{44.01\ g\ CO_2}{1\ mol\ CO_2}$$

y g S → mol S → mol SO_2 → g SO_2

$$\frac{y\ g\ S}{32.01\ g\ S} \quad \frac{1\ mol\ SO_2}{1\ mol\ S} \quad \frac{64.01\ g\ SO_2}{1\ mol\ SO_2}$$

Solution: $(x\ g\ C) \times \frac{1\ \cancel{mol\ C}}{12.01\ \cancel{g\ C}} \times \frac{1\ \cancel{mol\ CO_2}}{1\ \cancel{mol\ C}} \times \frac{44.01\ g\ CO_2}{1\ \cancel{mol\ CO_2}} = 3.66 \times g\ CO_2$

$(y\ g\ S) \times \frac{1\ \cancel{mol\ S}}{32.07\ \cancel{g\ S}} \times \frac{1\ \cancel{mol\ SO_2}}{1\ \cancel{mol\ S}} \times \frac{64.07\ g\ SO_2}{1\ \cancel{mol\ SO_2}} = 2.00\ y\ g\ SO_2$

$x + y = 9.0$
$3.66x + 2.00y = 23.3$
$3.66x + (9-x)2.00 = 23.3$
$x = 3.2$ g C and $y = 5.8$ g S

Check: The units of the answer (g S) is correct. The magnitude is reasonable since it is less than 9.0 g.

Conceptual Problems

3.147 The sphere in the molecular models represents the electron cloud of the atom. On this scale, the nucleus would be too small to see.

3.148 (a) Atomic mass O > atomic mass C, % O would be higher.

(b) Atomic mass N and O close, molecule contains 2N to 1 O, % N would be higher.

(c) Atomic mass O > atomic mass C, same number of atoms, % O would be higher.

(d) Atomic mass N much greater than atomic mass H, % N would be higher.

3.149 The statement is incorrect because a chemical formula is based on the ratio of atoms combined, not the ratio of grams combined. The statement should read the following: The chemical formula for ammonia (NH_3) indicates that ammonia contains three hydrogen atoms to each nitrogen atom.

3.150 The statement is incorrect because equations are balanced based on the number and kind of atoms, not molecules. The statement should read the following: When a chemical equation is balanced, the number of atoms of each type on both sides of the equation will be equal.

3.151 H_2SO_4: Atomic mass S is approximately twice atomic mass O, both are much greater than atomic mass H. The order of % mass is % O > % S > % H.

4 Chemical Quantities and Aqueous Reactions

Review Questions

4.1 Reaction stoichiometry is the numerical relationships between chemical amounts in a balanced chemical equation. The coefficients in a chemical reaction specify the relative amounts in moles of each of the substances involved in the reaction.

4.2 The limiting reactant is the reactant that is completely consumed in a chemical reaction and limits the amount of product. The theoretical yield is the amount of product that can be made in a chemical reaction based on the amount of limiting reactant. The percent yield is calculated as $\frac{\text{actual yield}}{\text{theoretical yield}} \times 100$. The reactant in excess is any reactant that occurs in a quantity greater than that required to completely react with the limiting reactant. Some of this reactant will be left over when the reaction is complete.

4.3 No, the percent yield would not be different if the actual yield and theoretical yield were calculated in moles. The relationship between grams and moles is the molar mass. This would be the same value for the actual yield and the theoretical yield.

4.4 An aqueous solution is a solution in which water acts as the solvent. The solvent is the majority component of the mixture, and the solute is the minority component in the mixture.

4.5 Molarity is a concentration term. It is the amount of solute (in moles) divided by the volume of solution (in liters). The molarity of a solution can be used as a conversion factor between moles of the solute and liters of the solution.

4.6 Substances that completely dissociate into ions when they dissolve in water are called strong electrolytes and conduct electricity easily. Substances that do not completely dissociate in water are called weak electrolytes and conduct electricity only weakly. Compounds that do not dissociate into ions when dissolved in water are called non-electrolytes and do not conduct electricity.

4.7 Acids are molecular compounds that ionize—form ions—when they dissolve in water. A strong acid is one that completely ionizes in solution. A weak acid is one that does not completely ionize in water. A solution of a weak acid is composed mostly of the non-ionized acid.

4.8 A compound is termed soluble if it dissolves in water. A compound is insoluble if it does not dissolve in water.

4.9 The solubility rules are a set of empirical rules that have been inferred from observations on many ionic compounds. The solubility rules allow us to predict if a compound is soluble or insoluble.

4.10 Cations that usually form soluble compounds are Li^+, Na^+, K^+, and NH_4^+. The anions that usually form soluble compounds are NO_3^- and $C_2H_3O_2^-$, which have no exceptions; Cl^-, Br^-, I^- except when these ions pair with Ag^+, Hg_2^{2+}, or Pb^{2+}, which result in insoluble compounds; and SO_4^{2-} except with Sr^{2+}, Ba^{2+}, Pb^{2+}, Ag^+ or Ca^{2+}, which form insoluble compounds. The anions that usually form insoluble compounds are OH^- and S^{2-} except with Li^+, Na^+, K^+, and NH_4^+, which form soluble compounds and when S^{2-} pairs with Ca^{2+},Sr^{2+} or Ba^{2+} the compounds are soluble; CO_3^{2-} and PO_4^{3-} are insoluble except when paired with Li^+, Na^+, K^+, and NH_4^+.

4.11 A precipitation reaction is one in which a solid or precipitate forms upon mixing two solutions. An example is $2\ KI(aq) + Pb(NO_3)_2(aq) \rightarrow PbI_2(s) + 2\ KNO_3(aq)$.

4.12 The key to predicting precipitation reactions is to understand that only insoluble compounds form precipitates. In a precipitation reaction, two solutions containing soluble compounds combine and an insoluble compound precipitates.

4.13 A molecular equation is an equation showing the complete neutral formulas for each compound in the reaction as if they existed as molecules. Equations that list individually all of the ions present as either reactants or products in a chemical reaction are complete ionic equation. Equations that show only the species that actually change during the reaction are net ionic equations.

4.14 An Arrhenius acid is a substance that produces H^+ ions in aqueous solutions. An Arrhenius base is a substance that produces OH^- ions in aqueous solutions.

4.15 When an acid and base are mixed, the $H^+(aq)$ from the acid combines with the OH^- from the base to form $H_2O(l)$. An example is $HCl(aq) + NaOH(aq) \rightarrow H_2O(l) + NaCl(aq)$.

4.16 In a titration, a substance in a solution of known concentration is reacted with another substance in a solution of unknown concentration. The acid-base titration is continued until the neutralization is complete. At the equivalence point, the point when the number of moles of OH^- equals the number of moles of H^+, the titration is complete. An indicator is a dye whose color depends on the acidity or basicity of the solution.

4.17 Aqueous reactions that form a gas upon mixing two solutions are called gas-evolution reactions. An example is $H_2SO_4(aq) + Li_2S(aq) \rightarrow H_2S(g) + Li_2SO_4(aq)$.

4.18 The reactant types that give rise to gas-evolution reactions are sulfides, carbonates, bicarbonate, sulfites, bisulfites, and ammonium compounds.

4.19 Oxidation–reduction reactions or redox reactions are reactions in which electrons are transferred from one reactant to the other. An example is $4\ Fe(s) + 3\ O_2(g) \rightarrow 2\ Fe_2O_3(s)$.

4.20 The oxidation state or oxidation number is a number given to each atom based on the electron assignments. It is the charge an atom would have if all shared electrons were assigned to the atom with a greater attraction for those electrons.

4.21 To identify redox reactions by using oxidation states, begin by assigning oxidation states to each atom in the reaction. A change in oxidation state for the atoms indicates a redox reaction.

4.22 When a substance is oxidized it loses electrons and there is an increase in oxidation state. When a substance is reduced it gains electrons and there is a reduction in oxidation state.

4.23 A substance that causes the oxidation of another substance is called an oxidizing agent. A substance that causes the reduction of another substance is called a reducing agent.

4.24 Combustion reactions are characterized by the reaction of a substance with O_2 to form one or more oxygen containing compounds, often including water. Combustion reactions emit heat. Combustion reactions are important because most of our society's energy is derived from them. An example is $CH_4(g) + 2\ O_2(g) \rightarrow CO_2(g) + 2\ H_2O(g)$.

Problems by Topic

Reaction Stoichiometry

4.25 **Given:** 7.2 moles C_6H_{14} **Find:** balanced reaction, moles O_2 required

Conceptual Plan: balance the equation then mol C_6H_{14} → mol O_2

$2\ C_6H_{14}(g) + 19\ O_2(g) \rightarrow 12\ CO_2(g) + 14\ H_2O(g)$ $\qquad \frac{19 \text{ mol } O_2}{2 \text{ mol } C_6H_{14}}$

Solution: $7.2 \text{ mol } C_6H_{14} \times \frac{19 \text{ mol } O_2}{2 \text{ mol } C_6H_{14}} = 68.4 \text{ mol } O_2 = 68 \text{ mol } O_2$

Check: The units of the answer (mol O_2) are correct. The magnitude is reasonable because much more O_2 is needed than C_6H_{14}.

4.26 **Given:** 0.461 moles $HC_2H_3O_2$ **Find:** balanced reaction, moles $Ba(OH)_2$ required

Conceptual Plan: balance the reaction then mol $HC_2H_3O_2$ → mol $Ba(OH)_2$

$2\ HC_2H_3O_2\ (aq) + Ba(OH)_2(aq) \rightarrow 2\ H_2O(l) + Ba(C_2H_3O_2)_2(aq)$ $\qquad \frac{1 \text{ mol } Ba(OH)_2}{2 \text{ mol } HC_2H_3O_2}$

Solution: $0.461 \text{ mol } HC_2H_3O_2 \times \frac{1 \text{ mol } Ba(OH)_2}{2 \text{ mol } HC_2H_3O_2} = 0.2305 \text{ mol } Ba(OH)_2 = 0.231 \text{ mol } Ba(OH)_2$

Check: The units of the answer (mol $Ba(OH)_2$) are correct. The magnitude is reasonable because much less $Ba(OH)_2$ is needed than $HC_2H_3O_2$.

4.27 (a) **Given:** 2.5 mol N_2O_5 **Find:** mol NO_2

Conceptual Plan: mol N_2O_5 → mol NO_2

$\frac{4\ NO_2}{2\ N_2O_5}$

Solution: $2.5 \text{ mol } N_2O_5 \times \frac{4 \text{ mol } NO_2}{2 \text{ mol } N_2O_5} = 5.0 \text{ mol } NO_2$

Check: The units of the answer (mol NO_2) are correct. The magnitude is reasonable since it is greater than mol N_2O_5.

(b) **Given:** 6.8 mol N_2O_5 **Find:** mol NO_2

Conceptual Plan: mol N_2O_5 → mol NO_2

$\frac{4\ NO_2}{2\ N_2O_5}$

Solution: $6.8 \text{ mol } N_2O_5 \times \frac{4 \text{ mol } NO_2}{2 \text{ mol } N_2O_5} = 13.6 \text{ mol } NO_2 = 14 \text{ mol } NO_2$

Check: The units of the answer (mol NO_2) are correct. The magnitude is reasonable since it is greater than mol N_2O_5.

(c) **Given:** 15.2 g N_2O_5 **Find:** mol NO_2

Conceptual Plan: g N_2O_5 → mol N_2O_5 → mol NO_2

$\frac{1 \text{ mol } N_2O_5}{108.02 \text{ g } N_2O_5} \qquad \frac{4\ NO_2}{2\ N_2O_5}$

Solution: $15.2 \text{ g } N_2O_5 \times \frac{1 \text{ mol } N_2O_5}{108.02 \text{ g } N_2O_5} \times \frac{4 \text{ mol } NO_2}{2 \text{ mol } N_2O_5} = 0.2814 \text{ mol } NO_2 = 0.281 \text{ mol } NO_2$

Check: The units of the answer (mol NO_2) are correct. The magnitude is reasonable since 15 g is about 0.13 mol N_2O_5 and the answer is greater than mol N_2O_5.

(d) **Given:** 2.87 kg N_2O_5 **Find:** mol NO_2

Conceptual Plan: kg N_2O_5 → g N_2O_5 → mol N_2O_5 → mol NO_2

$\frac{1000 \text{ g } N_2O_5}{\text{kg } N_2O_5} \qquad \frac{1 \text{ mol } N_2O_5}{108.02 \text{ g } N_2O_5} \qquad \frac{4\ NO_2}{2\ N_2O_5}$

Solution:

$$2.87\ \cancel{\text{kg } N_2O_5} \times \frac{1000\ \cancel{\text{g } N_2O_5}}{\cancel{\text{kg } N_2O_5}} \times \frac{1\ \cancel{\text{mol } N_2O_5}}{108.02\ \cancel{\text{g } N_2O_5}} \times \frac{4\ \text{mol } NO_2}{2\ \cancel{\text{mol } N_2O_5}} = 53.1\underline{4}\ \text{mol } NO_2 = 53.1\ \text{mol } NO_2$$

Check: The units of the answer (mol NO_2) are correct. The magnitude is reasonable since 2.87 kg is about 27 mol N_2O_5 and the answer is greater than mol N_2O_5.

4.28 (a) **Given:** 2.6 mol N_2H_4 **Find:** mol NH_3

Conceptual Plan: mol N_2H_4 → mol NH_3

$$\frac{4\ NH_3}{3\ N_2H_4}$$

Solution: $2.6\ \cancel{\text{mol } N_2H_4} \times \frac{4\ \text{mol } NH_3}{3\ \cancel{\text{mol } N_2H_4}} = 3.\underline{4}6\ \text{mol } NH_3 = 3.5\ \text{mol } NH_3$

Check: The units of the answer (mol NH_3) are correct. The magnitude is reasonable since it is greater than mol N_2H_4.

(b) **Given:** 3.55 mol N_2H_4 **Find:** mol NH_3

Conceptual Plan: mol N_2H_4 → mol NH_3

$$\frac{4\ NH_3}{3\ N_2H_4}$$

Solution: $3.55\ \cancel{\text{mol } N_2H_4} \times \frac{4\ \text{mol } NH_3}{3\ \cancel{\text{mol } N_2H_4}} = 4.7\underline{3}3\ \text{mol } NH_3 = 4.73\ \text{mol } NH_3$

Check: The units of the answer (mol NH_3) are correct. The magnitude is reasonable since it is greater than mol N_2H_4.

(c) **Given:** 65.3 g N_2H_4 **Find:** mol NH_3

Conceptual Plan: g N_2H_4 → mol N_2H_4 → mol NH_3

$$\frac{1\ \text{mol } N_2H_4}{32.05\ \text{g } N_2H_4} \qquad \frac{4\ NH_3}{3\ N_2H_4}$$

Solution: $65.3\ \cancel{\text{g } N_2H_4} \times \frac{1\ \cancel{\text{mol } N_2H_4}}{32.05\ \cancel{\text{g } N_2H_4}} \times \frac{4\ \text{mol } NH_3}{3\ \cancel{\text{mol } N_2H_4}} = 2.7\underline{1}6\ \text{mol } NH_3 = 2.72\ \text{mol } NH_3$

Check: The units of the answer (mol NH_3) are correct. The magnitude is reasonable since there is about 2 mol N_2H_4 and the answer is greater than mol N_2H_4.

(d) **Given:** 4.88 kg N_2H_4 **Find:** mol NH_3

Conceptual Plan: kg N_2H_4 → g N_2H_4 → mol N_2H_4 → mol NH_3

$$\frac{1000\ \text{g } N_2H_4}{\text{kg } N_2H_4} \qquad \frac{1\ \text{mol } N_2H_4}{32.05\ \text{g } N_2H_4} \qquad \frac{4\ NH_3}{3\ N_2H_4}$$

Solution:

$$4.88\ \cancel{\text{kg } N_2H_4} \times \frac{1000\ \cancel{\text{g } N_2H_4}}{\cancel{\text{kg } N_2H_4}} \times \frac{1\ \cancel{\text{mol } N_2H_4}}{32.05\ \cancel{\text{g } N_2H_4}} \times \frac{4\ \text{mol } NH_3}{3\ \cancel{\text{mol } N_2H_4}} = 20\underline{3}.0\ \text{mol } NH_3 = 203\ \text{mol } NH_3$$

Check: The units of the answer (mol NH_3) are correct. The magnitude is reasonable since 4.88 kg is about 150 mol N_2H_4 and the answer is greater than mol N_2H_4.

4.29 **Given:** 3 mol SiO_2 **Find:** mol C, mol SiC, mol CO

Conceptual Plan: mol SiO_2 → mol C → mol SiC → mol CO

$$\frac{3\ C}{SiO_2} \qquad \frac{SiC}{SiO_2} \qquad \frac{2\ CO}{SiO_2}$$

Solution: $3\ \cancel{\text{mol } SiO_2} \times \frac{3\ \text{mol C}}{\cancel{\text{mol } SiO_2}} = 9\ \text{mol C}$ $\qquad 3\ \cancel{\text{mol } SiO_2} \times \frac{\text{mol SiC}}{\cancel{\text{mol } SiO_2}} = 3\ \text{mol SiC}$

$$3\ \cancel{\text{mol } SiO_2} \times \frac{2\ \text{mol CO}}{\cancel{\text{mol } SiO_2}} = 6\ \text{mol CO}$$

Given: 6 mol C **Find:** mol SiO_2, mol SiC, mol CO

Conceptual Plan: mol C → mol SiO_2 → mol SiC → mol CO

$$\frac{SiO_2}{3\ C} \qquad \frac{SiC}{3\ C} \qquad \frac{2\ CO}{3\ C}$$

Solution: $6\ \cancel{\text{mol C}} \times \dfrac{\text{mol SiO}_2}{3\ \cancel{\text{mol C}}} = 2\ \text{mol SiO}_2$ $\quad 6\ \cancel{\text{mol C}} \times \dfrac{\text{mol SiC}}{3\ \cancel{\text{mol C}}} = 2\ \text{mol SiC}$

$6\ \cancel{\text{mol C}} \times \dfrac{2\ \text{mol CO}}{3\ \cancel{\text{mol C}}} = 4\ \text{mol CO}$

Given: 10 mol CO **Find:** mol SiO_2, mol C, mol SiC

Conceptual Plan: **mol CO → mol SiO_2 → mol C → mol SiC**

$\dfrac{\text{SiO}_2}{2\ \text{CO}} \qquad \dfrac{3\ \text{C}}{2\ \text{CO}} \qquad \dfrac{\text{SiC}}{2\ \text{CO}}$

Solution: $10\ \cancel{\text{mol CO}} \times \dfrac{\text{mol SiO}_2}{2\ \cancel{\text{mol CO}}} = 5.0\ \text{mol SiO}_2$ $\quad 10\ \cancel{\text{mol C}} \times \dfrac{3\ \text{mol C}}{2\ \cancel{\text{mol CO}}} = 15\ \text{mol C}$

$10\ \cancel{\text{mol CO}} \times \dfrac{\text{mol SiC}}{2\ \cancel{\text{mol CO}}} = 5.0\ \text{mol SiC}$

Given: 2.8 mol SiO_2 **Find:** mol C, mol SiC, mol CO

Conceptual Plan: **mol SiO_2 → mol C → mol SiC → mol CO**

$\dfrac{3\ \text{C}}{\text{SiO}_2} \qquad \dfrac{\text{SiC}}{\text{SiO}_2} \qquad \dfrac{2\ \text{CO}}{\text{SiO}_2}$

Solution: $2.8\ \cancel{\text{mol SiO}_2} \times \dfrac{3\ \text{mol C}}{\cancel{\text{mol SiO}_2}} = 8.4\ \text{mol C}$ $\quad 2.8\ \cancel{\text{mol SiO}_2} \times \dfrac{\text{mol SiC}}{\cancel{\text{mol SiO}_2}} = 2.8\ \text{mol SiC}$

$2.8\ \cancel{\text{mol SiO}_2} \times \dfrac{2\ \text{mol CO}}{\cancel{\text{mol SiO}_2}} = 5.6\ \text{mol CO}$

Given: 1.55 mol C **Find:** mol SiO_2, mol SiC, mol CO

Conceptual Plan: **mol C → mol SiO_2 → mol SiC → mol CO**

$\dfrac{\text{SiO}_2}{3\ \text{C}} \qquad \dfrac{\text{SiC}}{3\ \text{C}} \qquad \dfrac{2\ \text{CO}}{3\ \text{C}}$

Solution: $1.55\ \cancel{\text{mol C}} \times \dfrac{1\ \text{mol SiO}_2}{3\ \cancel{\text{mol C}}} = 0.517\ \text{mol SiO}_2$ $\quad 1.55\ \cancel{\text{mol C}} \times \dfrac{\text{mol SiC}}{3\ \cancel{\text{mol C}}} = 0.517\ \text{mol SiC}$

$1.55\ \cancel{\text{mol C}} \times \dfrac{2\ \text{mol CO}}{3\ \cancel{\text{mol C}}} = 1.03\ \text{mol CO}$

SiO_2	C	SiC	CO
3	9	3	6
2	**6**	2	4
5.0	15	5.0	**10**
2.8	8.4	2.8	5.6
0.517	**1.55**	0.517	1.03

4.30 **Given:** 2 mol N_2H_4 **Find:** mol N_2O_4, mol N_2, mol H_2O

Conceptual Plan: **mol N_2H_4 → mol N_2O_4 → mol N_2 → mol H_2O**

$\dfrac{\text{N}_2\text{O}_4}{2\ \text{N}_2\text{H}_4} \qquad \dfrac{3\ \text{N}_2}{2\ \text{N}_2\text{H}_4} \qquad \dfrac{4\ \text{H}_2\text{O}}{2\ \text{N}_2\text{H}_4}$

Solution: $2\ \cancel{\text{mol N}_2\text{H}_4} \times \dfrac{1\ \text{mol N}_2\text{O}_4}{2\ \cancel{\text{mol N}_2\text{H}_4}} = 1\ \text{mol N}_2\text{O}_4$ $\quad 2\ \cancel{\text{mol N}_2\text{H}_4} \times \dfrac{3\ \text{mol N}_2}{2\ \cancel{\text{mol N}_2\text{H}_4}} = 3\ \text{mol N}_2$

$2\ \cancel{\text{mol N}_2\text{H}_4} \times \dfrac{4\ \text{mol H}_2\text{O}}{2\ \cancel{\text{mol N}_2\text{H}_4}} = 4\ \text{mol H}_2\text{O}$

Given: 5 mol N_2O_4 **Find:** mol N_2H_4, mol N_2, mol H_2O

Conceptual Plan: **mol N_2O_4 → mol N_2H_4 → mol N_2 → mol H_2O**

$\dfrac{2\ \text{N}_2\text{H}_4}{\text{N}_2\text{O}_4} \qquad \dfrac{3\ \text{N}_2}{\text{N}_2\text{O}_4} \qquad \dfrac{4\ \text{H}_2\text{O}}{\text{N}_2\text{O}_4}$

Solution: $5\ \cancel{\text{mol N}_2\text{O}_4} \times \dfrac{2\ \text{mol N}_2\text{H}_4}{\cancel{\text{mol N}_2\text{O}_4}} = 10\ \text{mol N}_2\text{H}_4$ $\quad 5\ \cancel{\text{mol N}_2\text{O}_4} \times \dfrac{3\ \text{mol N}_2}{\cancel{\text{mol N}_2\text{O}_4}} = 15\ \text{mol N}_2$

$5\ \cancel{\text{mol N}_2\text{O}_4} \times \dfrac{4\ \text{mol H}_2\text{O}}{\cancel{\text{mol N}_2\text{O}_4}} = 20\ \text{mol H}_2\text{O}$

Given: 10 mol H_2O **Find:** mol N_2O_4, mol N_2O_4, mol N_2
Conceptual Plan: **mol H_2O → mol N_2H_4 → mol N_2 → mol N_2O_4**

$$\frac{2\,N_2H_4}{4\,H_2O} \qquad \frac{3\,N_2}{4\,H_2O} \qquad \frac{1\,N_2O_4}{4\,H_2O}$$

Solution: $10\ \cancel{mol\ H_2O} \times \frac{2\ mol\ N_2H_4}{4\ \cancel{mol\ H_2O}} = 5.0\ mol\ N_2H_4 \qquad 10\ \cancel{mol\ H_2O} \times \frac{3\ mol\ N_2}{4\ \cancel{mol\ H_2O}} = 7.5\ mol\ N_2$

$$10\ \cancel{mol\ H_2O} \times \frac{1\ mol\ N_2O_4}{4\ \cancel{mol\ H_2O}} = 2.5\ mol\ N_2O_4$$

Given: 2.5 mol N_2H_4 **Find:** mol N_2O_4, mol N_2, mol H_2O
Conceptual Plan: **mol N_2H_4 → mol N_2O_4 → mol N_2 → mol H_2O**

$$\frac{N_2O_4}{2\,N_2H_4} \qquad \frac{3\,N_2}{2\,N_2H_4} \qquad \frac{4\,H_2O}{2\,N_2H_4}$$

Solution: $2.5\ \cancel{mol\ N_2H_4} \times \frac{1\ mol\ N_2O_4}{2\ \cancel{mol\ N_2H_4}} = 1.3\ mol\ N_2O_4 \quad 2.5\ \cancel{mol\ N_2H_4} \times \frac{3\ mol\ N_2}{2\ \cancel{mol\ N_2H_4}} = 3.8\ mol\ N_2$

$$2.5\ \cancel{mol\ N_2H_4} \times \frac{4\ mol\ H_2O}{2\ \cancel{mol\ N_2H_4}} = 5.0\ mol\ H_2O$$

Given: 4.2 mol N_2O_4 **Find:** mol N_2H_4, mol N_2, mol H_2O
Conceptual Plan: **mol N_2O_4 → mol N_2H_4 → mol N_2 → mol H_2O**

$$\frac{2\,N_2H_4}{N_2O_4} \qquad \frac{3\,N_2}{N_2O_4} \qquad \frac{4\,H_2O}{N_2O_4}$$

Solution:

$4.2\ \cancel{mol\ N_2O_4} \times \frac{2\ mol\ N_2H_4}{\cancel{mol\ N_2O_4}} = 8.4\ mol\ N_2H_4 \quad 4.2\ \cancel{mol\ N_2O_4} \times \frac{3\ mol\ N_2}{\cancel{mol\ N_2O_4}} = 12.6\ mol\ N_2 = 13\ mol\ N_2$

$$4.2\ \cancel{mol\ N_2O_4} \times \frac{4\ mol\ H_2O}{\cancel{mol\ N_2O_4}} = 16.8\ mol\ H_2O = 17\ mol\ H_2O$$

Given: 11.8 mol N_2 **Find:** mol N_2H_4, mol N_2O_4, mol H_2O
Conceptual Plan: **mol N_2 → mol N_2H_4 → mol N_2O_4 → mol H_2O**

$$\frac{2\,N_2H_4}{3\,N_2} \qquad \frac{1\,N_2O_4}{3\,N_2} \qquad \frac{4\,H_2O}{3\,N_2}$$

Solution: $11.8\ \cancel{mol\ N_2} \times \frac{2\ mol\ N_2H_4}{3\ \cancel{mol\ N_2}} = 7.87\ mol\ N_2H_4 \quad 11.8\ \cancel{mol\ N_2} \times \frac{mol\ N_2O_4}{3\ \cancel{mol\ N_2}} = 3.93\ mol\ N_2$

$$11.8\ \cancel{mol\ N_2} \times \frac{4\ mol\ H_2O}{3\ \cancel{mol\ N_2}} = 15.7\ mol\ H_2O$$

N_2H_2	N_2O_4	N_2	H_2O
2	1	3	4
10	**5**	15	20
5	2.5	7.5	**10**
2.5	1.3	3.8	5.0
8.4	**4.2**	13	17
7.87	3.93	**11.8**	15.7

4.31 **Given:** 3.2 g Fe **Find:** g HBr; g H_2
Conceptual Plan: **g Fe → mol Fe → mol HBr → g HBr**

$$\frac{mol\ Fe}{55.8\ g\ Fe} \qquad \frac{2\ mol\ HBr}{mol\ Fe} \qquad \frac{80.9\ g\ HBr}{mol\ HBr}$$

g Fe → mol Fe → mol H_2 → g H_2

$$\frac{mol\ Fe}{55.8\ g\ Fe} \qquad \frac{1\ mol\ H_2}{mol\ Fe} \qquad \frac{2.02\ g\ H_2}{mol\ H_2}$$

Solution: $3.2\ \cancel{g\ Fe} \times \frac{1\ \cancel{mol\ Fe}}{55.8\ \cancel{g\ Fe}} \times \frac{2\ \cancel{mol\ HBr}}{1\ \cancel{mol\ Fe}} \times \frac{80.9\ g\ HBr}{1\ \cancel{mol\ HBr}} = 9.3\ g\ HBr$

$$3.2\ \cancel{g\ Fe} \times \frac{1\ \cancel{mol\ Fe}}{55.8\ \cancel{g\ Fe}} \times \frac{1\ \cancel{mol\ H_2}}{1\ \cancel{mol\ Fe}} \times \frac{2.02\ g\ H_2}{1\ \cancel{mol\ H_2}} = 0.12\ g\ H_2$$

Check: The units of the answers (g HBr, g H_2) are correct. The magnitude of the answers is reasonable because molar mass HBr is greater than Fe and molar mass H_2 is much less than Fe.

4.32 **Given:** 15.2 g Al **Find:** g H_2SO_4; g H_2

Conceptual Plan: **g Al → mol Al → mol H_2SO_4 → g H_2SO_4**

$$\frac{\text{mol Al}}{26.98 \text{ g Al}} \quad \frac{3 \text{ mol } H_2SO_4}{2 \text{ mol Al}} \quad \frac{98.09 \text{ g } H_2SO_4}{\text{mol } H_2SO_4}$$

g Al → mol Al → mol H_2 → g H_2

$$\frac{\text{mol Al}}{26.98 \text{ g Al}} \quad \frac{3 \text{ mol } H_2}{2 \text{ mol Al}} \quad \frac{2.016 \text{ g } H_2}{\text{mol } H_2}$$

Solution: $$15.2 \cancel{\text{g Al}} \times \frac{1 \cancel{\text{mol Al}}}{26.98 \cancel{\text{g Al}}} \times \frac{3 \cancel{\text{mol } H_2SO_4}}{2 \cancel{\text{mol Al}}} \times \frac{98.09 \text{ g } H_2SO_4}{1 \cancel{\text{mol } H_2SO_4}} = 82.9 \text{ g } H_2SO_4$$

$$15.2 \cancel{\text{g Al}} \times \frac{1 \cancel{\text{mol Al}}}{26.98 \cancel{\text{g Al}}} \times \frac{3 \cancel{\text{mol } H_2}}{2 \cancel{\text{mol Al}}} \times \frac{2.016 \text{ g } H_2}{1 \cancel{\text{mol } H_2}} = 1.70 \text{ g } H_2$$

Check: The units of the answers (g H_2SO_4, g H_2) are correct. The magnitude of the answers is reasonable because molar mass H_2SO_4 is greater than Al and molar mass H_2 is much less than Al.

4.33 (a) **Given:** 3.67 g Ba **Find:** g $BaCl_2$

Conceptual Plan: **g Ba → mol Ba → mol $BaCl_2$ → g $BaCl_2$**

$$\frac{\text{mol Ba}}{137.33 \text{ g Ba}} \quad \frac{1 \text{ mol } BaCl_2}{1 \text{ mol Ba}} \quad \frac{208.23 \text{ g } BaCl_2}{1 \text{ mol } BaCl_2}$$

Solution: $$3.67 \cancel{\text{g Ba}} \times \frac{1 \cancel{\text{mol Ba}}}{137.33 \cancel{\text{g Ba}}} \times \frac{1 \cancel{\text{mol } BaCl_2}}{1 \cancel{\text{mol Ba}}} \times \frac{208.23 \text{ g } BaCl_2}{1 \cancel{\text{mol } BaCl_2}} = 5.5\underline{6}47 \text{ g } BaCl_2 = 5.56 \text{ g } BaCl_2$$

Check: The units of the answer (g $BaCl_2$) are correct. The magnitude of the answer is reasonable because it is larger than grams Ba.

(b) **Given:** 3.67 g CaO **Find:** g $CaCO_3$

Conceptual Plan: **g CaO → mol CaO → mol $CaCO_3$ → g $CaCO_3$**

$$\frac{\text{mol CaO}}{56.08 \text{ g CaO}} \quad \frac{\text{mol } CaCO_3}{1 \text{ mol CaO}} \quad \frac{100.09 \text{ g } CaCO_3}{\text{mol } CaCO_3}$$

Solution:

$$3.67 \cancel{\text{g CaO}} \times \frac{1 \cancel{\text{mol CaO}}}{56.08 \cancel{\text{g CaO}}} \times \frac{1 \cancel{\text{mol } CaCO_3}}{1 \cancel{\text{mol CaO}}} \times \frac{100.09 \text{ g } CaCO_3}{1 \cancel{\text{mol } CaCO_3}} = 6.5\underline{5}0 \text{ g } CaCO_3 = 6.55 \text{ g } CaCO_3$$

Check: Units of answer (g $CaCO_3$) are correct. The magnitude of the answer is reasonable because it is larger than grams CaO.

(c) **Given:** 3.67 g Mg **Find:** g MgO

Conceptual Plan: **g Mg → mol Mg → mol MgO → g MgO**

$$\frac{\text{mol Mg}}{24.30 \text{ g Mg}} \quad \frac{\text{mol MgO}}{\text{mol Mg}} \quad \frac{40.30 \text{ g MgO}}{\text{mol MgO}}$$

Solution: $$3.67 \cancel{\text{g Mg}} \times \frac{1 \cancel{\text{mol Mg}}}{24.30 \cancel{\text{g Mg}}} \times \frac{1 \cancel{\text{mol MgO}}}{1 \cancel{\text{mol Mg}}} \times \frac{40.30 \text{ g MgO}}{1 \cancel{\text{mol MgO}}} = 6.0\underline{8}6 \text{ g MgO} = 6.09 \text{ g MgO}$$

Check: The units of the answer (g MgO) are correct. The magnitude of the answer is reasonable because it is larger than grams Mg.

(d) **Given:** 3.67 g Al **Find:** g Al_2O_3

Conceptual Plan: **g Al → mol Al → mol Al_2O_3 → g Al_2O_3**

$$\frac{\text{mol Al}}{26.98 \text{ g Al}} \quad \frac{2 \text{ mol } Al_2O_3}{4 \text{ mol Al}} \quad \frac{101.96 \text{ g } Al_2O_3}{\text{mol } Al_2O_3}$$

Solution: $$3.67 \text{ g Al} \times \frac{1 \cancel{\text{mol Al}}}{26.98 \cancel{\text{g Al}}} \times \frac{2 \cancel{\text{mol } Al_2O_3}}{4 \cancel{\text{mol Al}}} \times \frac{101.96 \text{ g } Al_2O_3}{1 \cancel{\text{mol } Al_2O_3}} = 6.9\underline{3}4 \text{ g } Al_2O_3 = 6.93 \text{ g } Al_2O_3$$

Check: The units of the answer (g Al_2O_3) are correct. The magnitude of the answer is reasonable because it is larger than grams Al.

4.34 (a) **Given:** 15.39 g Cl_2 **Find:** g KCl

Conceptual Plan: g Cl_2 → mol Cl_2 → mol KCl → g KCl

$$\frac{\text{mol } Cl_2}{70.90 \text{ g } Cl_2} \qquad \frac{2 \text{ mol KCl}}{1 \text{ mol } Cl_2} \qquad \frac{74.55 \text{ g KCl}}{\text{mol KCl}}$$

Solution: $15.39 \text{ g } Cl_2 \times \frac{1 \text{ mol } Cl_2}{70.90 \text{ g } Cl_2} \times \frac{2 \text{ mol KCl}}{1 \text{ mol } Cl_2} \times \frac{74.55 \text{ g KCl}}{1 \text{ mol KCl}} = 32.3\underline{6}4 \text{ g KCl} = 32.36 \text{ g KCl}$

Check: The units of the answer (g KCl) are correct. The magnitude of the answer is reasonable because it is larger than grams Cl_2.

(b) **Given:** 15.39 g Br_2 **Find:** g KBr

Conceptual Plan: g Br_2 → mol Br_2 → mol KBr → g KBr

$$\frac{\text{mol } Br_2}{159.8 \text{ g } Br_2} \qquad \frac{2 \text{ mol KBr}}{1 \text{ mol } Br_2} \qquad \frac{119.00 \text{ g KBr}}{\text{mol KBr}}$$

Solution: $15.39 \text{ g } Br_2 \times \frac{1 \text{ mol } Br_2}{159.80 \text{ g } Br_2} \times \frac{2 \text{ mol KBr}}{1 \text{ mol } Br_2} \times \frac{119.00 \text{ g KBr}}{1 \text{ mol KBr}} = 22.9\underline{2}1 \text{ g KBr} = 22.92 \text{ g KBr}$

Check: The units of the answer (g KBr) are correct. The magnitude of the answer is reasonable because it is larger than grams Br_2.

(c) **Given:** 15.39 g O_2 **Find:** g Cr_2O_3

Conceptual Plan: g O_2 → mol O_2 → mol Cr_2O_3 → g Cr_2O_3

$$\frac{\text{mol } O_2}{32.00 \text{ g } O_2} \qquad \frac{2 \text{ mol } Cr_2O_3}{3 \text{ mol } O_2} \qquad \frac{152.00 \text{ g } Cr_2O_3}{\text{mol } Cr_2O_3}$$

Solution:

$15.39 \text{ g } O_2 \times \frac{1 \text{ mol } O_2}{32.00 \text{ g } O_2} \times \frac{2 \text{ mol } Cr_2O_3}{3 \text{ mol } O_2} \times \frac{152.00 \text{ g } Cr_2O_3}{1 \text{ mol } Cr_2O_3} = 48.7\underline{3}5 \text{ g } Cr_2O_3 = 48.74 \text{ g } Cr_2O_3$

Check: The units of the answer (g Cr_2O_3) are correct. The magnitude of the answer is reasonable because it is larger than g Cr.

(d) **Given:** 15.39 g Sr **Find:** g SrO

Conceptual Plan: g Sr → mol Sr → mol SrO → g SrO

$$\frac{\text{mol Sr}}{87.62 \text{ g Sr}} \qquad \frac{2 \text{ mol SrO}}{2 \text{ mol Sr}} \qquad \frac{103.62 \text{ g SrO}}{\text{mol SrO}}$$

Solution: $15.39 \text{ g Sr} \times \frac{1 \text{ mol Sr}}{87.62 \text{ g Sr}} \times \frac{2 \text{ mol SrO}}{2 \text{ mol Sr}} \times \frac{103.62 \text{ g SrO}}{1 \text{ mol SrO}} = 18.2\underline{0}0 \text{ g SrO} = 18.20 \text{ g SrO}$

Check: The units of the answer (g SrO) are correct. The magnitude of the answer is reasonable because it is larger than g Sr.

4.35 (a) **Given:** 4.85 g NaOH **Find:** g HCl

Conceptual Plan: g NaOH → mol NaOH → mol HCl → g HCl

$$\frac{\text{mol NaOH}}{40.01 \text{ g NaOH}} \qquad \frac{1 \text{ mol HCl}}{1 \text{ mol NaOH}} \qquad \frac{36.46 \text{ g HCl}}{1 \text{ mol HCl}}$$

Solution: $4.85 \text{ g NaOH} \times \frac{1 \text{ mol NaOH}}{40.01 \text{ g NaOH}} \times \frac{1 \text{ mol HCl}}{1 \text{ mol NaOH}} \times \frac{36.46 \text{ g HCl}}{1 \text{ mol HCl}} = 4.42 \text{ g HCl}$

Check: The units of the answer (g HCl) are correct. The magnitude of the answer is reasonable since it is less than g NaOH.

(b) **Given:** 4.85 g $Ca(OH)_2$ **Find:** g HNO_3

Conceptual Plan: g $Ca(OH)_2$ → mol $Ca(OH)_2$ → mol HNO_3 → g HNO_3

$$\frac{\text{mol } Ca(OH)_2}{74.10 \text{ g } Ca(OH)_2} \qquad \frac{2 \text{ mol } HNO_3}{1 \text{ mol } Ca(OH)_2} \qquad \frac{63.02 \text{ g } HNO_3}{1 \text{ mol } HNO_3}$$

Solution: $4.85 \text{ g } Ca(OH)_2 \times \frac{1 \text{ mol } Ca(OH)_2}{74.10 \text{ g } Ca(OH)_2} \times \frac{2 \text{ mol } HNO_3}{1 \text{ mol } Ca(OH)_2} \times \frac{63.02 \text{ g } HNO_3}{1 \text{ mol } HNO_3} = 8.25 \text{ g } HNO_3$

Check: The units of the answer (g HNO_3) are correct. The magnitude of the answer is reasonable since it is more than g $Ca(OH)_2$.

(c) **Given:** 4.85 g KOH **Find:** g H_2SO_4

Conceptual Plan: **g KOH → mol KOH → mol H_2SO_4 → g H_2SO_4**

$$\frac{\text{mol KOH}}{56.11\text{ g KOH}} \quad \frac{1\text{ mol }H_2SO_4}{2\text{ mol KOH}} \quad \frac{98.09\text{ g }H_2SO_4}{1\text{ mol }H_2SO_4}$$

Solution: $4.85\ \cancel{\text{g NaOH}} \times \frac{1\ \cancel{\text{mol KOH}}}{56.11\ \cancel{\text{g KOH}}} \times \frac{1\ \cancel{\text{mol }H_2SO_4}}{2\ \cancel{\text{mol KOH}}} \times \frac{98.09\text{ g }H_2SO_4}{1\ \cancel{\text{mol }H_2SO_4}} = 4.24\text{ g }H_2SO_4$

Check: The units of the answer (g H_2SO_4) are correct. The magnitude of the answer is reasonable since it is less than g KOH.

4.36 (a) **Given:** 55.8 g $Pb(NO_3)_2$ **Find:** g KI

Conceptual Plan: **g $Pb(NO_3)_2$ → mol $Pb(NO_3)_2$ → mol KI → g KI**

$$\frac{\text{mol }Pb(NO_3)_2}{331.2\text{ g }Pb(NO_3)_2} \quad \frac{2\text{ mol KI}}{1\text{ mol }Pb(NO_3)_2} \quad \frac{166.00\text{ g KI}}{1\text{ mol KI}}$$

Solution: $55.8\ \cancel{\text{g }Pb(NO_3)_2} \times \frac{1\ \cancel{\text{mol }Pb(NO_3)_2}}{331.2\ \cancel{\text{g }Pb(NO_3)_2}} \times \frac{2\ \cancel{\text{mol KI}}}{1\ \cancel{\text{mol }Pb(NO_3)_2}} \times \frac{166.00\text{ g KI}}{1\ \cancel{\text{mol KI}}} = 55.9\text{ g KI}$

Check: The units of the answer (g KI) are correct. The magnitude of the answer is reasonable since there are 2 mol KI for each $Pb(NO_3)_2$.

(b) **Given:** 55.8 g $CuCl_2$ **Find:** g Na_2CO_3

Conceptual Plan: **g $CuCl_2$ → mol $CuCl_2$ → mol Na_2CO_3 → g Na_2CO_3**

$$\frac{\text{mol }CuCl_2}{134.45\text{ g }CuCl_2} \quad \frac{1\text{ mol }Na_2CO_3}{1\text{ mol }CuCl_2} \quad \frac{106.01\text{ g }Na_2CO_3}{1\text{ mol }Na_2CO_3}$$

Solution: $55.8\ \cancel{\text{g }CuCl_2} \times \frac{1\ \cancel{\text{mol }CuCl_2}}{134.45\ \cancel{\text{g }CuCl_2}} \times \frac{1\ \cancel{\text{mol }Na_2CO_3}}{1\ \cancel{\text{mol }CuCl_2}} \times \frac{106.01\text{ g }Na_2CO_3}{1\ \cancel{\text{mol }Na_2CO_3}} = 44.0\text{ g }Na_2CO_3$

Check: The units of the answer (g Na_2CO_3) are correct. The magnitude of the answer is reasonable since it is less than g $CuCl_2$.

(c) **Given:** 55.8 g $Sr(NO_3)_2$ **Find:** g K_2SO_4

Conceptual Plan: **g $Sr(NO_3)_2$ → mol $Sr(NO_3)_2$ → mol K_2SO_4 → g K_2SO_4**

$$\frac{\text{mol }Sr(NO_3)_2}{211.64\text{ g }Sr(NO_3)_2} \quad \frac{1\text{ mol }K_2SO_4}{1\text{ mol }Sr(NO_3)_2} \quad \frac{174.27\text{ g }K_2SO_4}{1\text{ mol }K_2SO_4}$$

Solution: $55.8\ \cancel{\text{g }Sr(NO_3)_2} \times \frac{1\ \cancel{\text{mol }Sr(NO_3)_2}}{211.64\ \cancel{\text{g }Sr(NO_3)_2}} \times \frac{1\ \cancel{\text{mol }K_2SO_4}}{1\ \cancel{\text{mol }Sr(NO_3)_2}} \times \frac{174.27\text{ g }K_2SO_4}{1\ \cancel{\text{mol }K_2SO_4}} = 45.9\text{ g }K_2SO_4$

Check: The units of the answer (g K_2SO_4) are correct. The magnitude of the answer is reasonable since it is less than g $Sr(NO_3)_2$.

Limiting Reactant, Theoretical Yield, and Percent Yield

4.37 (a) **Given:** 2 mol Na; 2 mol Br_2 **Find:** Limiting reactant

Conceptual Plan: **mol Na → mol NaBr**

$$\frac{2\text{ mol NaBr}}{2\text{ mol Na}}$$

→ smallest mol amount determines limiting reactant

mol Br_2 → mol NaBr

$$\frac{2\text{ mol NaBr}}{1\text{ mol }Br_2}$$

Solution: $2\ \cancel{\text{mol Na}} \times \frac{2\text{ mol NaBr}}{2\ \cancel{\text{mol Na}}} = 2\text{ mol NaBr}$

$2\ \cancel{\text{mol }Br_2} \times \frac{2\text{ mol NaBr}}{1\ \cancel{\text{mol }Br_2}} = 4\text{ mol NaBr}$

Na is limiting reactant

Check: The answer is reasonable since Na produced the smallest amount of product.

(b) **Given:** 1.8 mol Na; 1.4 mol Br_2 **Find:** Limiting reactant

Conceptual Plan: mol Na → mol NaBr

$$\frac{2\text{ mol NaBr}}{2\text{ mol Na}}$$ **→ smallest mol amount determines limiting reactant**

mol Br_2 → mol NaBr

$$\frac{2\text{ mol NaBr}}{1\text{ mol Br}_2}$$

Solution: $1.8\ \cancel{\text{mol Na}} \times \frac{2\text{ mol NaBr}}{2\ \cancel{\text{mol Na}}} = 1.8\text{ mol NaBr}$

$1.4\ \cancel{\text{mol Br}_2} \times \frac{2\text{ mol NaBr}}{1\ \cancel{\text{mol Br}_2}} = 2.8\text{ mol NaBr}$

Na is limiting reactant

Check: The answer is reasonable since Na produced the smallest amount of product.

(c) **Given:** 2.5 mol Na; 1 mol Br_2 **Find:** Limiting reactant

Conceptual Plan: mol Na → mol NaBr

$$\frac{2\text{ mol NaBr}}{2\text{ mol Na}}$$ **→ smallest mol amount determines limiting reactant**

mol Br_2 → mol NaBr

$$\frac{2\text{ mol NaBr}}{1\text{ mol Br}_2}$$

Solution: $2.5\ \cancel{\text{mol Na}} \times \frac{2\text{ mol NaBr}}{2\ \cancel{\text{mol Na}}} = 2.5\text{ mol NaBr}$

$1\ \cancel{\text{mol Br}_2} \times \frac{2\text{ mol NaBr}}{1\ \cancel{\text{mol Br}_2}} = 2\text{ mol NaBr}$

Br_2 is limiting reactant

Check: The answer is reasonable since Br_2 produced the smallest amount of product.

(d) **Given:** 12.6 mol Na; 6.9 mol Br_2 **Find:** Limiting reactant

Conceptual Plan: mol Na → mol NaBr

$$\frac{2\text{ mol NaBr}}{2\text{ mol Na}}$$ **→ smallest mol amount determines limiting reactant**

mol Br_2 → mol NaBr

$$\frac{2\text{ mol NaBr}}{1\text{ mol Br}_2}$$

Solution: $12.6\ \cancel{\text{mol Na}} \times \frac{2\text{ mol NaBr}}{2\ \cancel{\text{mol Na}}} = 12.6\text{ mol NaBr}$

$6.9\ \cancel{\text{mol Br}_2} \times \frac{2\text{ mol NaBr}}{1\ \cancel{\text{mol Br}_2}} = 13.8\text{ mol NaBr}$

Na is limiting reactant

Check: The answer is reasonable since Na produced the smallest amount of product.

4.38 (a) **Given:** 1 mol Al; 1 mol O_2 **Find:** Limiting reactant

Conceptual Plan: mol Al → mol Al_2O_3

$$\frac{2\text{ mol Al}_2\text{O}_3}{4\text{ mol Al}}$$ **→ smallest mol amount determines limiting reactant**

mol O_2 → mol Al_2O_3

$$\frac{2\text{ mol Al}_2\text{O}_3}{3\text{ mol O}_2}$$

Solution: $1\ \cancel{\text{mol Al}} \times \frac{2\text{ mol Al}_2\text{O}_3}{4\ \cancel{\text{mol Al}}} = 0.5\text{ mol Al}_2\text{O}_3$

$1\ \cancel{\text{mol O}_2} \times \frac{2\text{ mol Al}_2\text{O}_3}{3\ \cancel{\text{mol O}_2}} = 0.67\text{ mol Al}_2\text{O}_3$

Al is limiting reactant

Check: The answer is reasonable since Al produced the smallest amount of product.

(b) **Given:** 4 mol Al; 2.6 mol O_2 **Find:** Limiting reactant

Conceptual Plan: mol Al → mol Al_2O_3

$$\frac{2 \text{ mol } Al_2O_3}{4 \text{ mol Al}}$$ → **smallest mol amount determines limiting reactant**

mol O_2 → mol Al_2O_3

$$\frac{2 \text{ mol } Al_2O_3}{3 \text{ mol } O_2}$$

Solution: $4 \cancel{\text{mol Al}} \times \frac{2 \text{ mol } Al_2O_3}{4 \cancel{\text{mol Al}}} = 2 \text{ mol } Al_2O_3$

$2.6 \cancel{\text{mol } O_2} \times \frac{2 \text{ mol } Al_2O_3}{3 \cancel{\text{mol } O_2}} = 1.7 \text{ mol } Al_2O_3$

O_2 is limiting reactant

Check: The answer is reasonable since O_2 produced the smallest amount of product.

(c) **Given:** 16 mol Al; 13 mol O_2 **Find:** Limiting reactant

Conceptual Plan: mol Al → mol Al_2O_3

$$\frac{2 \text{ mol } Al_2O_3}{4 \text{ mol Al}}$$ → **smallest mol amount determines limiting reactant**

mol O_2 → mol Al_2O_3

$$\frac{2 \text{ mol } Al_2O_3}{3 \text{ mol } O_2}$$

Solution: $16 \cancel{\text{mol Al}} \times \frac{2 \text{ mol } Al_2O_3}{4 \cancel{\text{mol Al}}} = 8.0 \text{ mol } Al_2O_3$

$13 \cancel{\text{mol } O_2} \times \frac{2 \text{ mol } Al_2O_3}{3 \cancel{\text{mol } O_2}} = 8.67 \text{ mol } Al_2O_3$

Al is limiting reactant

Check: The answer is reasonable since Al produced the smallest amount of product.

(d) **Given:** 7.4 mol Al; 6.5 mol O_2 **Find:** Limiting reactant

Conceptual Plan: mol Al → mol Al_2O_3

$$\frac{2 \text{ mol } Al_2O_3}{4 \text{ mol Al}}$$ → **smallest mol amount determines limiting reactant**

mol O_2 → mol Al_2O_3

$$\frac{2 \text{ mol } Al_2O_3}{3 \text{ mol } O_2}$$

Solution: $7.4 \cancel{\text{mol Al}} \times \frac{2 \text{ mol } Al_2O_3}{4 \cancel{\text{mol Al}}} = 3.7 \text{ mol } Al_2O_3$

$6.5 \cancel{\text{mol } O_2} \times \frac{2 \text{ mol } Al_2O_3}{3 \cancel{\text{mol } O_2}} = 4.3 \text{ mol } Al_2O_3$

Al is limiting reactant

Check: The answer is reasonable since Al produced the smallest amount of product.

4.39 The greatest number of Cl_2 molecules will be formed from reaction mixture b and would be 3 molecules Cl_2.

(a) **Given:** 7 molecules HCl, 1 molecule O_2 **Find:** Theoretical yield Cl_2

Conceptual Plan: molecules HCl → molecules Cl_2

$$\frac{2 \text{ molecules } Cl_2}{4 \text{ molecules HCl}}$$ → **smallest molecule amount determines limiting reactant**

molecules O_2 → molecules Cl_2

$$\frac{2 \text{ molecules } Cl_2}{1 \text{ molecules } O_2}$$

Solution: $7 \cancel{\text{molecules HCl}} \times \frac{2 \text{ molecules } Cl_2}{4 \cancel{\text{molecules HCl}}} = 3 \text{ molecules } Cl_2$

$1 \cancel{\text{molecules } O_2} \times \frac{2 \text{ molecules } Cl_2}{1 \cancel{\text{molecules } O_2}} = 2 \text{ molecules } Cl_2$

Theoretical Yield = 2 molecules Cl_2

(b) **Given:** 6 molecules HCl, 3 molecules O_2 **Find:** Theoretical yield Cl_2

Conceptual Plan: molecules HCl → molecules Cl_2

$$\frac{2 \text{ molecules } Cl_2}{4 \text{ molecules HCl}}$$ **→ smallest molecule amount determines limiting reactant**

molecules O_2 → molecules Cl_2

$$\frac{2 \text{ molecules } Cl_2}{1 \text{ molecules } O_2}$$

Solution: $6 \text{ molecules HCl} \times \frac{2 \text{ molecules } Cl_2}{4 \text{ molecules HCl}} = 3 \text{ molecules } Cl_2$

$3 \text{ molecules } O_2 \times \frac{2 \text{ molecules } Cl_2}{1 \text{ molecules } O_2} = 6 \text{ molecules } Cl_2$

Theoretical Yield = 3 molecules Cl_2

(c) **Given:** 4 molecules HCl, 5 molecules O_2 **Find:** Theoretical yield Cl_2

Conceptual Plan: molecules HCl → molecules Cl_2

$$\frac{2 \text{ molecules } Cl_2}{4 \text{ molecules HCl}}$$ **→ smallest molecule amount determines limiting reactant**

molecules O_2 → molecules Cl_2

$$\frac{2 \text{ molecules } Cl_2}{1 \text{ molecules } O_2}$$

Solution: $4 \text{ molecules HCl} \times \frac{2 \text{ molecules } Cl_2}{4 \text{ molecules HCl}} = 2 \text{ molecules } Cl_2$

$5 \text{ molecules } O_2 \times \frac{2 \text{ molecules } Cl_2}{1 \text{ molecules } O_2} = 10 \text{ molecules } Cl_2$

Theoretical Yield = 2 molecules Cl_2

Check: The units of the answer (molecules Cl_2) are correct. The answer is reasonable based on the limiting reactant in each mixture.

4.40 The greatest number of CO_2 molecules will be formed from reaction mixture a, and would be 2 molecules CO_2.

(a) **Given:** 3 molecules CH_3OH, 3 molecules O_2 **Find:** Theoretical yield CO_2

Conceptual Plan: molecules CH_3OH → molecules CO_2

$$\frac{2 \text{ molecules } CO_2}{2 \text{ molecules } CH_3OH}$$ **→ smallest molecule amount determines limiting reactant**

molecules O_2 → molecules CO_2

$$\frac{2 \text{ molecules } CO_2}{3 \text{ molecules } O_2}$$

Solution: $3 \text{ molecules } CH_3OH \times \frac{2 \text{ molecules } CO_2}{2 \text{ molecules } CH_3OH} = 3 \text{ molecules } CO_2$

$3 \text{ molecules } O_2 \times \frac{2 \text{ molecules } CO_2}{3 \text{ molecules } O_2} = 2 \text{ molecules } CO_2$

Theoretical Yield = 2 molecules CO_2

(b) **Given:** 1 molecules CH_3OH, 6 molecules O_2 **Find:** Theoretical yield CO_2

Conceptual Plan: molecules CH_3OH → molecules CO_2

$$\frac{2 \text{ molecules } CO_2}{2 \text{ molecules } CH_3OH}$$ **→ smallest molecule amount determines limiting reactant**

molecules O_2 → molecules CO_2

$$\frac{2 \text{ molecules } CO_2}{3 \text{ molecules } O_2}$$

Solution: $1 \text{ molecules } CH_3OH \times \frac{2 \text{ molecules } CO_2}{2 \text{ molecules } CH_3OH} = 1 \text{ molecules } CO_2$

$6 \text{ molecules } O_2 \times \frac{2 \text{ molecules } CO_2}{3 \text{ molecules } O_2} = 4 \text{ molecules } CO_2$

Theoretical Yield = 1 molecules CO_2

(c) **Given:** 4 molecules CH_3OH, 2 molecules O_2 **Find:** Theoretical yield CO_2
Conceptual Plan: molecules CH_3OH → molecules CO_2

$$\frac{2 \text{ molecules } CO_2}{2 \text{ molecules } CH_3OH}$$ → **smallest molecule amount determines limiting reactant**

molecules O_2 → molecules CO_2

$$\frac{2 \text{ molecules } CO_2}{3 \text{ molecules } O_2}$$

Solution: $4 \text{ molecules } CH_3OH \times \frac{2 \text{ molecules } CO_2}{2 \text{ molecules } CH_3OH} = 4 \text{ molecules } CO_2$

$2 \text{ molecules } O_2 \times \frac{2 \text{ molecules } CO_2}{3 \text{ molecules } O_2} = 1.3 \text{ molecules } CO_2 = 1 \text{ molecules } CO_2$ since you can not have a fraction of a molecule

Theoretical Yield = 1 molecules CO_2

Check: The units of the answer (molecules CO_2) are correct. The answer is reasonable based on the limiting reactant in each mixture.

4.41 (a) **Given:** 4 mol Ti, 4 mol Cl_2 **Find:** Theoretical yield $TiCl_4$
Conceptual Plan: mol Ti → mol $TiCl_4$

$$\frac{1 \text{ mol } TiCl_4}{1 \text{ mol Ti}}$$ → **smallest mol amount determines limiting reactant**

mol Cl_2 → mol $TiCl_4$

$$\frac{1 \text{ mol } TiCl_4}{2 \text{ mol } Cl_2}$$

Solution: $4 \text{ mol Ti} \times \frac{1 \text{ mol } TiCl_4}{1 \text{ mol Ti}} = 4 \text{ mol } TiCl_4$

$4 \text{ mol } Cl_2 \times \frac{1 \text{ mol } TiCl_4}{2 \text{ mol } Cl_2} = 2 \text{ mol } TiCl_4$

Theoretical Yield = 2 mol $TiCl_4$

Check: The units of the answer (mol $TiCl_4$) are correct. The answer is reasonable since Cl_2 produced the smallest amount of product and is the limiting reactant.

(b) **Given:** 7 mol Ti, 17 mol Cl_2 **Find:** Theoretical yield $TiCl_4$
Conceptual Plan: mol Ti → mol $TiCl_4$

$$\frac{1 \text{ mol } TiCl_4}{1 \text{ mol Ti}}$$ → **smallest mol amount determines limiting reactant**

mol Cl_2 → mol $TiCl_4$

$$\frac{1 \text{ mol } TiCl_4}{2 \text{ mol } Cl_2}$$

Solution: $7 \text{ mol Ti} \times \frac{1 \text{ mol } TiCl_4}{1 \text{ mol Ti}} = 7 \text{ mol } TiCl_4$

$17 \text{ mol } Cl_2 \times \frac{1 \text{ mol } TiCl_4}{2 \text{ mol } Cl_2} = 8.5 \text{ mol } TiCl_4$

Theoretical Yield = 7 mol $TiCl_4$

Check: The units of the answer (mol $TiCl_4$) are correct. The answer is reasonable since Ti produced the smallest amount of product and is the limiting reactant.

(c) **Given:** 12.4 mol Ti, 18.8 mol Cl_2 **Find:** Theoretical yield $TiCl_4$
Conceptual Plan: mol Ti → mol $TiCl_4$

$$\frac{1 \text{ mol } TiCl_4}{1 \text{ mol Ti}}$$ → **smallest mol amount determines limiting reactant**

mol Cl_2 → mol $TiCl_4$

$$\frac{1 \text{ mol } TiCl_4}{2 \text{ mol } Cl_2}$$

Solution: $12.4 \text{ mol Ti} \times \frac{1 \text{ mol TiCl}_4}{1 \text{ mol Ti}} = 12.4 \text{ mol TiCl}_4$

$18.8 \text{ mol Cl}_2 \times \frac{1 \text{ mol TiCl}_4}{2 \text{ mol Cl}_2} = 9.40 \text{ mol TiCl}_4$

Theoretical Yield = 9.40 mol $TiCl_4$

Check: The units of the answer (mol $TiCl_4$) are correct. The answer is reasonable since Cl_2 produced the smallest amount of product and is the limiting reactant.

4.42 (a) **Given:** 3 mol Mn, 3 mol O_2 **Find:** Theoretical yield MnO_2

Conceptual Plan: mol Mn → mol MnO_2

$\frac{2 \text{ mol MnO}_2}{2 \text{ mol Mn}}$ **→ smallest mol amount determines limiting reactant**

mol O_2 → mol MnO_2

$\frac{2 \text{ mol MnO}_2}{2 \text{ mol O}_2}$

Solution: $3 \text{ mol Mn} \times \frac{1 \text{ mol MnO}_2}{1 \text{ mol Mn}} = 3 \text{ mol MnO}_2$

$3 \text{ mol O}_2 \times \frac{1 \text{ mol MnO}_2}{1 \text{ mol O}_2} = 3 \text{ mol MnO}_2$

Theoretical Yield = 3 mol MnO_2

Check: The units of the answer (mol MnO_2) are correct. The answer is reasonable since equal mol are produced for both reactants.

(b) **Given:** 4 mol Mn, 7 mol O_2 **Find:** Theoretical yield MnO_2

Conceptual Plan: mol Mn → mol MnO_2

$\frac{2 \text{ mol MnO}_2}{2 \text{ mol Mn}}$ **→ smallest mol amount determines limiting reactant**

mol O_2 → mol MnO_2

$\frac{2 \text{ mol MnO}_2}{2 \text{ mol O}_2}$

Solution: $4 \text{ mol Mn} \times \frac{2 \text{ mol MnO}_2}{2 \text{ mol Mn}} = 4 \text{ mol MnO}_2$

$7 \text{ mol O}_2 \times \frac{2 \text{ mol MnO}_2}{2 \text{ mol O}_2} = 7 \text{ mol MnO}_2$

Theoretical Yield = 4 mol MnO_2

Check: The units of the answer (mol MnO_2) are correct. The answer is reasonable since Mn produced the smallest amount of product and is the limiting reactant.

(c) **Given:** 27.5 mol Mn, 43.8 mol O_2 **Find:** Theoretical yield MnO_2

Conceptual Plan: mol Mn → mol MnO_2

$\frac{2 \text{ mol MnO}_2}{2 \text{ mol Mn}}$ **→ smallest mol amount determines limiting reactant**

mol O_2 → mol MnO_2

$\frac{2 \text{ mol MnO}_2}{2 \text{ mol O}_2}$

Solution: $27.5 \text{ mol Mn} \times \frac{2 \text{ mol MnO}_2}{2 \text{ mol Mn}} = 27.5 \text{ mol MnO}_2$

$43.8 \text{ mol O}_2 \times \frac{2 \text{ mol MnO}_2}{2 \text{ mol O}_2} = 43.8 \text{ mol MnO}_2$

Theoretical Yield = 27.5 mol MnO_2

Check: The units of the answer (mol MnO_2) are correct. The answer is reasonable since Mn produced the smallest amount of product and is the limiting reactant.

4.43 **Given:** 4.2 mol ZnS, 6.8 mol O_2 **Find:** Mole amount of excess reactant left

Conceptual Plan: mol ZnS → mol ZnO $\frac{2 \text{ mol ZnO}}{2 \text{ mol ZnS}}$ **→ smallest mol amount determines limiting reactant**

mol O_2 → mol ZnO $\frac{2 \text{ mol ZnO}}{3 \text{ mol } O_2}$

then: mol limiting reactant → mol excess reactant required → mol excess reactant left $\frac{2 \text{ mol ZnS}}{3 \text{ mol } O_2}$

Solution: $4.2 \text{ mol ZnS} \times \frac{2 \text{ mol ZnO}}{2 \text{ mol ZnS}} = 4.2 \text{ mol ZnO}$

$6.8 \text{ mol } O_2 \times \frac{2 \text{ mol ZnO}}{3 \text{ mol } O_2} = 4.5 \text{ mol ZnO}$

ZnS is the limiting reactant, therefore, O_2 is the excess reactant.

$4.2 \text{ mol ZnS} \times \frac{3 \text{ mol } O_2}{2 \text{ mol ZnS}} = 6.3 \text{ mol } O_2 \text{ required}$

$6.8 \text{ mol } O_2 - 6.3 \text{ mol } O_2 = 0.5 \text{ mol } O_2 \text{ left}$

Check: The units of the answer (mol O_2) are correct and the magnitude is reasonable since it is less than the original amount of O_2.

4.44 **Given:** 0.223 mol FeS, 0.652 mol HCl **Find:** Mole amount of excess reactant left

Conceptual Plan: mol FeS → mol $FeCl_2$ $\frac{1 \text{ mol } FeCl_2}{1 \text{ mol FeS}}$ **→ smallest mol amount determines limiting reactant**

mol HCl → mol $FeCl_2$ $\frac{1 \text{ mol } FeCl_2}{2 \text{ mol HCl}}$

then: mol limiting reactant → mol excess reactant required → mol excess reactant left $\frac{1 \text{ mol FeS}}{2 \text{ mol HCl}}$

Solution: $0.223 \text{ mol FeS} \times \frac{1 \text{ mol } FeCl_2}{1 \text{ mol FeS}} = 0.223 \text{ mol } FeCl_2$

$0.652 \text{ mol HCl} \times \frac{1 \text{ mol } FeCl_2}{2 \text{ mol HCl}} = 0.326 \text{ mol } FeCl_2$

FeS is the limiting reactant, therefore, HCl is the excess reactant.

$0.223 \text{ mol ZFeS} \times \frac{2 \text{ mol HCl}}{1 \text{ mol FeS}} = 0.446 \text{ mol HCl required}$

$0.652 \text{ mol HCl} - 0.446 \text{ mol HCl} = 0.206 \text{ mol HCl left}$

Check: The units of the answer (mol HCl) are correct and the magnitude is reasonable since it is less than the original amount of HCl.

4.45 (a) **Given:** 2.0 g Al, 2.0 g Cl_2 **Find:** Theoretical yield in g $AlCl_3$

Conceptual Plan: g Al → mol Al → mol $AlCl_3$ $\frac{1 \text{ mol Al}}{26.98 \text{ g Al}}$ $\frac{2 \text{ mol } AlCl_3}{2 \text{ mol Al}}$ **→ smallest mol amount determines limiting reactant**

g Cl_2 → mol Cl_2 → mol $AlCl_3$ $\frac{1 \text{ mol } Cl_2}{70.90 \text{ g } Cl_2}$ $\frac{2 \text{ mol } AlCl_3}{3 \text{ mol } Cl_2}$

then: mol $AlCl_3$ → g $AlCl_3$ $\frac{133.3 \text{ g } AlCl_3}{\text{mol } AlCl_3}$

Solution: $2.0 \text{ g Al} \times \frac{1 \text{ mol Al}}{26.98 \text{ g Al}} \times \frac{2 \text{ mol } AlCl_3}{2 \text{ mol Al}} = 0.074 \text{ mol } AlCl_3$

$$2.0\ \cancel{g\ Cl_2} \times \frac{1\ \cancel{mol\ Cl_2}}{70.90\ \cancel{g\ Cl_2}} \times \frac{2\ mol\ AlCl_3}{3\ \cancel{mol\ Cl_2}} = 0.0188\ mol\ AlCl_3$$

$$0.0188\ mol\ AlCl_3 \times \frac{133.3\ g\ AlCl_3}{mol\ AlCl_3} = 2.5\ g\ AlCl_3$$

Check: The units of the answer (g $AlCl_3$) are correct. The answer is reasonable since Cl_2 produced the smallest amount of product and is the limiting reactant.

(b) **Given:** 7.5 g Al, 24.8 g Cl_2 **Find:** Theoretical yield in g $AlCl_3$

Conceptual Plan: g Al → mol Al → mol $AlCl_3$

$$\frac{1\ mol\ Al}{26.98\ g\ Al} \quad \frac{2\ mol\ AlCl_3}{2\ mol\ Al}$$ → **smallest mol amount determines limiting reactant**

g Cl_2 → mol Cl_2 → mol $AlCl_3$

$$\frac{1\ mol\ Cl_2}{70.90\ g\ Cl_2} \quad \frac{2\ mol\ AlCl_3}{3\ mol\ Cl_2}$$

then: mol $AlCl_3$ → g $AlCl_3$

$$\frac{133.3\ g\ AlCl_3}{mol\ AlCl_3}$$

Solution:
$$7.5\ \cancel{g\ Al} \times \frac{1\ \cancel{mol\ Al}}{26.98\ \cancel{g\ Al}} \times \frac{2\ mol\ AlCl_3}{2\ \cancel{mol\ Al}} = 0.2780\ mol\ AlCl_3$$

$$24.8\ \cancel{g\ Cl_2} \times \frac{1\ \cancel{mol\ Cl_2}}{70.90\ \cancel{g\ Cl_2}} \times \frac{2\ mol\ AlCl_3}{3\ \cancel{mol\ Cl_2}} = 0.2332\ mol\ AlCl_3$$

$$0.2332\ mol\ AlCl_3 \times \frac{133.3\ g\ AlCl_3}{mol\ AlCl_3} = 31.1\ g\ AlCl_3$$

Check: The units of the answer (g $AlCl_3$) are correct. The answer is reasonable since Cl_2 produced the smallest amount of product and is the limiting reactant.

(c) **Given:** 0.235 g Al, 1.15 g Cl_2 **Find:** Theoretical yield in g $AlCl_3$

Conceptual Plan: g Al → mol Al → mol $AlCl_3$

$$\frac{1\ mol\ Al}{26.98\ g\ Al} \quad \frac{2\ mol\ AlCl_3}{2\ mol\ Al}$$ → **smallest mol amount determines limiting reactant**

g Cl_2 → mol Cl_2 → mol $AlCl_3$

$$\frac{1\ mol\ Cl_2}{70.90\ g\ Cl_2} \quad \frac{2\ mol\ AlCl_3}{3\ mol\ Cl_2}$$

then: mol $AlCl_3$ → g $AlCl_3$

$$\frac{133.34\ g\ AlCl_3}{mol\ AlCl_3}$$

Solution:
$$0.235\ \cancel{g\ Al} \times \frac{1\ \cancel{mol\ Al}}{26.98\ \cancel{g\ Al}} \times \frac{2\ mol\ AlCl_3}{2\ \cancel{mol\ Al}} = 0.008710\ mol\ AlCl_3$$

$$1.15\ \cancel{g\ Cl_2} \times \frac{1\ \cancel{mol\ Cl_2}}{70.90\ \cancel{g\ Cl_2}} \times \frac{2\ mol\ AlCl_3}{3\ \cancel{mol\ Cl_2}} = 0.01081\ mol\ AlCl_3$$

$$0.008710\ mol\ AlCl_3 \times \frac{133.34\ g\ AlCl_3}{mol\ AlCl_3} = 1.16\ g\ AlCl_3$$

Check: The units of the answer (g $AlCl_3$) are correct. The answer is reasonable since Al produced the smallest amount of product and is the limiting reactant.

4.46 (a) **Given:** 5.0 g Ti, 5.0 g F_2 **Find:** Theoretical yield in g TiF_4

Conceptual Plan: g Ti → mol Ti → mol TiF_4

$$\frac{1\ mol\ Ti}{47.87\ g\ Ti} \quad \frac{1\ mol\ TiF_4}{1\ mol\ Ti}$$ → **smallest mol amount determines limiting reactant**

g F_2 → mol F_2 → mol TiF_4

$$\frac{1\ mol\ F_2}{38.00\ g\ F_2} \quad \frac{1\ mol\ TiF_4}{2\ mol\ F_2}$$

then: mol TiF_4 → g TiF_4

$$\frac{123.87\ g\ TiF_4}{mol\ TiF_4}$$

Solution: $5.0\ \cancel{g\ Ti} \times \dfrac{1\ \cancel{mol\ Ti}}{47.87\ \cancel{g\ Ti}} \times \dfrac{1\ mol\ TiF_4}{1\ \cancel{mol\ Ti}} = 0.10\underline{4}\ mol\ TiF_4$

$5.0\ \cancel{g\ F_2} \times \dfrac{1\ \cancel{mol\ F_2}}{38.00\ \cancel{g\ F_2}} \times \dfrac{1\ mol\ TiF_4}{2\ \cancel{mol\ F_2}} = 0.06\underline{5}8\ mol\ TiF_4$

$0.06\underline{5}8\ mol\ TiF_4 \times \dfrac{123.87\ g\ TiF_4}{mol\ TiF_4} = 8.1\ g\ TiF$

Check: The units of the answer (g TiF_4) are correct. The answer is reasonable since F_2 produced the smallest amount of product and is the limiting reactant.

(b) **Given:** 2.4 g Ti, 1.6 g F_2 **Find:** Theoretical yield in g TiF_4

Conceptual Plan: **g Ti → mol Ti → mol TiF_4**

$\dfrac{1\ mol\ Ti}{47.87\ g\ Ti}$ $\dfrac{1\ mol\ TiF_4}{1\ mol\ Ti}$ → **smallest mol amount determines limiting reactant**

g F_2 → mol F_2 → mol TiF_4

$\dfrac{1\ mol\ F_2}{38.00\ g\ F_2}$ $\dfrac{1\ mol\ TiF_4}{2\ mol\ F_2}$

then: mol TiF_4 → g TiF_4

$\dfrac{123.87\ g\ TiF_4}{mol\ TiF_4}$

Solution: $2.4\ \cancel{g\ Ti} \times \dfrac{1\ \cancel{mol\ Ti}}{47.87\ \cancel{g\ Ti}} \times \dfrac{1\ mol\ TiF_4}{1\ \cancel{mol\ Ti}} = 0.0501\ mol\ TiF_4$

$1.6\ \cancel{g\ F_2} \times \dfrac{1\ \cancel{mol\ F_2}}{38.00\ \cancel{g\ F_2}} \times \dfrac{1\ mol\ TiF_4}{2\ \cancel{mol\ F_2}} = 0.02\underline{1}0\ mol\ TiF_4$

$0.02\underline{1}0\ mol\ TiF_4 \times \dfrac{123.87\ g\ TiF_4}{mol\ TiF_4} = 2.6\ g\ TiF_4$

Check: The units of the answer (g TiF_4) are correct. The answer is reasonable since F_2 produced the smallest amount of product and is the limiting reactant.

(c) **Given:** 0.233 g Ti, 0.288 g F_2 **Find:** Theoretical yield in g TiF_4

Conceptual Plan: **g Ti → mol Ti → mol TiF_4**

$\dfrac{1\ mol\ Ti}{47.87\ g\ Ti}$ $\dfrac{1\ mol\ TiF_4}{1\ mol\ Ti}$ → **smallest mol amount determines limiting reactant**

g F_2 → mol F_2 → mol TiF_4

$\dfrac{1\ mol\ F_2}{38.00\ g\ F_2}$ $\dfrac{1\ mol\ TiF_4}{2\ mol\ F_2}$

then: mol TiF_4 → g TiF_4

$\dfrac{123.87\ g\ TiF_4}{mol\ TiF_4}$

Solution: $0.233\ \cancel{g\ Ti} \times \dfrac{1\ \cancel{mol\ Ti}}{47.87\ \cancel{g\ Ti}} \times \dfrac{1\ mol\ TiF_4}{1\ \cancel{mol\ Ti}} = 0.0048\underline{6}7\ mol\ TiF_4$

$0.288\ \cancel{g\ F_2} \times \dfrac{1\ \cancel{mol\ F_2}}{38.00\ \cancel{g\ F_2}} \times \dfrac{1\ mol\ TiF_4}{2\ \cancel{mol\ F_2}} = 0.0037\underline{8}9\ mol\ TiF_4$

$0.0037\underline{8}9\ mol\ TiF_4 \times \dfrac{123.87\ g\ TiF_4}{mol\ TiF_4} = 0.469\ g\ TiF_4$

Check: The units of the answer (g TiF_4) are correct. The answer is reasonable since F_2 produced the smallest amount of product and is the limiting reactant.

4.47 **Given:** 22.55 Fe_2O_3, 14.78 g CO **Find:** Mole amount of excess reactant left

Conceptual Plan: **g Fe_2O_3 → mol Fe_2O_3 → mol Fe**

$\dfrac{1\ mol\ Fe_2O_3}{159.7\ g\ Fe_2O_3}$ $\dfrac{2\ mol\ Fe}{1\ mol\ Fe_2O_3}$ → **smallest mol amount determines limiting reactant**

g CO → mol CO → mol Fe

$\dfrac{1\ mol\ CO}{28.01\ g\ CO}$ $\dfrac{2\ mol\ Fe}{3\ mol\ CO}$

then: mol limiting reactant → mol excess reactant required → mol excess reactant left → g excess reactant left

$\frac{1\text{ mol }Fe_2O_3}{3\text{ mol CO}}$ $\frac{159.7\text{ g }Fe_2O_3}{1\text{ mol }Fe_2O_3}$ or $\frac{28.01\text{g CO}}{1\text{ mol CO}}$

Solution: $22.55\text{ g }\cancel{Fe_2O_3} \times \frac{1\text{ mol }Fe_2O_3}{159.7\cancel{\text{g }Fe_2O_3}} \times \frac{2\text{ mol Fe}}{1\cancel{\text{ mol }Fe_2O_3}} = 0.2824\text{ mol Fe}$

$14.78\cancel{\text{ g CO}} \times \frac{1\cancel{\text{ mol CO}}}{28.01\cancel{\text{ g CO}}} \times \frac{2\text{ mol Fe}}{3\cancel{\text{ mol CO}}} = 0.3518\text{ mol Fe}$

Fe_2O_3 is the limiting reactant, therefore, CO is the excess reactant.

$22.55\text{ g }\cancel{Fe_2O_3} \times \frac{1\cancel{\text{ mol }Fe_2O_3}}{159.7\cancel{\text{g }Fe_2O_3}} \times \frac{3\cancel{\text{ mol CO}}}{1\cancel{\text{ mol }Fe_2O_3}} \times \frac{28.01\text{ g CO}}{1\cancel{\text{mol CO}}} = 11.8\underline{6}5\text{ g CO required}$

$14.78\text{ g CO} - 11.87\text{ g CO} = 2.91\text{ g CO left}$

Check: The units of the answer (g CO) is correct and the magnitude is reasonable since it is less than the original amount of CO.

4.48 **Given:** 45.69g P_4, 131.3 g Cl_2 **Find:** Mole amount of excess reactant left

Conceptual Plan: g P_4 → mol P_4 → mol PCl_3

$\frac{1\text{ mol }P_4}{123.88\text{ g }P_4}$ $\frac{4\text{ mol }PCl_3}{1\text{ mol }P_4}$ → **smallest mol amount determines limiting reactant**

g Cl_2 → mol Cl_2 → mol PCl_3

$\frac{1\text{ mol }Cl_2}{70.90\text{ g }Cl_2}$ $\frac{1\text{ mol }PCl_3}{6\text{ mol }Cl_2}$

then: mol limiting reactant → mol excess reactant required → mol excess reactant left → g excess reactant left

$\frac{6\text{ mol }Cl_2}{1\text{ mol }P_4}$ $\frac{123.88\text{ g }P_4}{1\text{ mol }P_4}$ or $\frac{70.90\text{ g }Cl_2}{1\text{ mol }Cl_2}$

Solution: $45.69\text{ g }\cancel{\text{mol }P_4} \times \frac{1\cancel{\text{ mol }P_4}}{123.88\cancel{\text{ g }P_4}} \times \frac{4\text{ mol }PCl_3}{1\cancel{\text{ mol }P_4}} = 1.475\text{ mol }PCl_3$

$131.3\cancel{\text{ g }Cl_2} \times \frac{1\cancel{\text{ mol }Cl_2}}{70.90\cancel{\text{ g }Cl_2}} \times \frac{4\text{ mol }PCl_3}{6\cancel{\text{ mol }Cl_2}} = 1.235\text{ mol }PCl_3$

Cl_2 is the limiting reactant, therefore, P_4 is the excess reactant.

$131.3\cancel{\text{ g }Cl_2} \times \frac{1\cancel{\text{ mol }Cl_2}}{70.90\cancel{\text{ g }Cl_2}} \times \frac{1\cancel{\text{ mol }P_4}}{6\cancel{\text{ mol }Cl_2}} \times \frac{123.88\text{ g }P_4}{1\cancel{\text{ mol }P_4}} = 38.2\underline{3}6\text{ g }P_4\text{ required}$

$45.69\text{ g }P_4 - 38.2\underline{3}6\text{ g }P_4 = 7.45\text{ g }P_4\text{ left}$

Check: Units of the answer (g P_4) is correct and the magnitude is reasonable since it is less than the original amount of P_4.

4.49 **Given:** 28.5 g KCl; 25.7 g Pb^{2+}; 29.4 g $PbCl_2$ **Find:** limiting reactant, theoretical yield $PbCl_2$, % yield

Conceptual Plan: g KCl → mol KCl → mol $PbCl_2$

$\frac{1\text{ mol KCl}}{74.55\text{ g KCl}}$ $\frac{1\text{ mol }PbCl_2}{2\text{ mol KCl}}$ → **smallest mol amount determines limiting reactant**

g Pb^{2+} → mol Pb^{2+} → mol $PbCl_2$

$\frac{1\text{ mol }Pb^{2+}}{207.2\text{ g }Pb^{2+}}$ $\frac{1\text{ mol }PbCl_2}{1\text{ mol }Pb^{2+}}$

then: mol $PbCl_2$ → g $PbCl_2$ **then: determine % yield**

$\frac{278.1\text{ g }PbCl_2}{\text{mol }PbCl_2}$ $\frac{\text{actual yield g }PbCl_2}{\text{theoretical yield g }PbCl_2} \times 100$

Solution: $28.5\cancel{\text{ g KCl}} \times \frac{1\cancel{\text{ mol KCl}}}{74.55\cancel{\text{ g KCl}}} \times \frac{1\text{ mol }PbCl_2}{2\cancel{\text{ mol KCl}}} = 0.19\underline{1}1\text{ mol }PbCl_2$

$25.7\cancel{\text{ g }Pb^{2+}} \times \frac{1\cancel{\text{ mol }Pb^{2+}}}{207.2\cancel{\text{ g }Pb^{2+}}} \times \frac{1\text{ mol }PbCl_2}{1\cancel{\text{ mol }Pb^{2+}}} = 0.1240\text{ mol }PbCl_2$ Pb^{2+} is the limiting reactant.

$$0.1240 \text{ mol PbCl}_2 \times \frac{278.1 \text{ g PbCl}_2}{1 \text{ mol PbCl}_2} = 34.5 \text{ g PbCl}_2$$

$$\frac{29.4 \text{ g PbCl}_2}{34.5 \text{ g PbCl}_2} \times 100 = 85.2\%$$

Check: The theoretical yield has the correct units (g $PbCl_2$) and has a reasonable magnitude compared to the mass of Pb^{2+}, the limiting reactant. The % yield is reasonable, under 100%.

4.50 **Given:** 10.1 g Mg; 10.5 g O_2; 11.9 g MgO **Find:** limiting reactant, theoretical yield MgO, % yield

Conceptual Plan: g Mg → mol Mg → mol MgO

$$\frac{1 \text{ mol Mg}}{24.31 \text{ g Mg}} \quad \frac{2 \text{ mol MgO}}{2 \text{ mol Mg}}$$

→ smallest mol amount determines limiting reactant

g O_2 → mol O_2 → mol MgO

$$\frac{1 \text{ mol O}_2}{32.00 \text{ g O}_2} \quad \frac{2 \text{ mol MgO}}{1 \text{ mol O}_2}$$

then: mol MgO → g MgO **then: determine % yield**

$$\frac{40.31 \text{ g MgO}}{1 \text{ mol MgO}} \qquad \frac{\text{actual yield g MgO}}{\text{theoretical yield g MgO}} \times 100$$

Solution:

$$10.1 \text{ g Mg} \times \frac{1 \text{ mol Mg}}{24.31 \text{ g Mg}} \times \frac{2 \text{ mol MgO}}{2 \text{ mol Mg}} = 0.4156 \text{ mol MgO}$$

Mg is the limiting reactant.

$$10.5 \text{ g O}_2 \times \frac{1 \text{ mol O}_2}{32.00 \text{ g O}_2} \times \frac{2 \text{ mol MgO}}{1 \text{ mol O}_2} = 0.6562 \text{ mol MgO}$$

$$0.4156 \text{ mol MgO} \times \frac{40.31 \text{ g MgO}}{1 \text{ mol MgO}} = 16.75 \text{ g MgO}$$

$$\frac{11.9 \text{ g MgO}}{16.75 \text{ g MgO}} \times 100 = 71.0\%$$

Check: The theoretical yield has the correct units (g MgO) and has a reasonable magnitude compared to the mass of Mg, the limiting reactant. The % yield is reasonable, under 100%.

4.51 **Given:** 136.4 kg NH_3; 211.4 kg CO_2; 168.4 kg CH_4N_2O

Find: limiting reactant, theoretical yield CH_4N_2O, % yield

Conceptual Plan: kg NH_3 → g NH_3 → mol NH_3 → mol CH_4N_2O

$$\frac{1000 \text{ g}}{1 \text{ kg}} \quad \frac{1 \text{ mol NH}_3}{17.03 \text{ g NH}_3} \quad \frac{1 \text{ mol CH}_4\text{N}_2\text{O}}{2 \text{ mol NH}_3}$$

→ smallest amount determines limiting reactant

kg CO_2 → g CO_2 → mol CO_2 → mol CH_4N_2O

$$\frac{1000 \text{ g}}{1 \text{ kg}} \quad \frac{1 \text{ mol CO}_2}{44.01 \text{ g CO}_2} \quad \frac{1 \text{ mol CH}_4\text{N}_2\text{O}}{1 \text{ mol CO}_2}$$

then: mol CH_4N_2O → g CH_4N_2O → kg CH_4N_2O **then: determine % yield**

$$\frac{60.06 \text{ g CH}_4\text{N}_2\text{O}}{1 \text{ mol CH}_4\text{N}_2\text{O}} \quad \frac{1 \text{ kg}}{1000 \text{ g}} \qquad \frac{\text{actual yield kg CH}_4\text{N}_2\text{O}}{\text{theoretical yield kg CH}_4\text{N}_2\text{O}} \times 100$$

Solution:

$$136.4 \text{ kg NH}_3 \times \frac{1000 \text{ g}}{\text{kg}} \times \frac{1 \text{ mol NH}_3}{17.03 \text{ g NH}_3} \times \frac{1 \text{ mol CH}_4\text{N}_2\text{O}}{2 \text{ mol NH}_3} = 4004.7 \text{ mol CH}_4\text{N}_2\text{O}$$

$$211.4 \text{ kg CO}_2 \times \frac{1000 \text{ g}}{\text{kg}} \times \frac{1 \text{ mol CO}_2}{44.01 \text{ g CO}_2} \times \frac{1 \text{ mol CH}_4\text{N}_2\text{O}}{1 \text{ mol CO}_2} = 4803.4 \text{ mol CH}_4\text{N}_2\text{O}$$

NH_3 is the limiting reactant

$$4004.7 \text{ mol CH}_4\text{N}_2\text{O} \times \frac{60.06 \text{ g CH}_4\text{N}_2\text{O}}{1 \text{ mol CH}_4\text{N}_2\text{O}} \times \frac{\text{kg}}{1000 \text{ g}} = 240.52 \text{ kg CH}_4\text{N}_2\text{O}$$

$$\frac{168.4 \text{ kg CH}_4\text{N}_2\text{O}}{240.52 \text{ kg CH}_4\text{N}_2\text{O}} \times 100 = 70.01\%$$

Check: The theoretical yield has the correct units (kg CH_4N_2O) and has a reasonable magnitude compared to the mass of NH_3, the limiting reactant. The % yield is reasonable, under 100%.

4.52 **Given:** 155.8 kg SiO_2; 78.3 kg C; 66.1 kg Si **Find:** limiting reactant, theoretical yield Si, % yield

Conceptual Plan: write and balance the reaction, then

kg SiO_2 → g SiO_2 → mol SiO_2 → mol Si

$$\frac{1000\text{ g}}{1\text{ kg}} \quad \frac{1\text{ mol SiO}_2}{60.09\text{ g SiO}_2} \quad \frac{1\text{ mol Si}}{2\text{ mol SiO}_2}$$ → **smallest amount determines limiting reactant**

kg C → g C → mol C → mol Si

$$\frac{1000\text{ g}}{1\text{ kg}} \quad \frac{1\text{ mol CO}_2}{44.01\text{ g CO}_2} \quad \frac{1\text{ mol Si}}{2\text{ mol C}}$$

then: mol Si → g Si → kg CH_4N_2O then: determine % yield

$$\frac{28.09\text{ g Si}}{1\text{ mol Si}} \quad \frac{1\text{ kg}}{1000\text{ g}} \qquad \frac{\text{actual yield kg Si}}{\text{theoretical yield kg Si}} \times 100$$

Solution: $SiO_2(l) + 2C(s) \rightarrow Si(l) + 2CO(g)$

$$155.8\text{ kg SiO}_2 \times \frac{1000\text{ g}}{\text{kg}} \times \frac{1\text{ mol SiO}_2}{60.09\text{ g SiO}_2} \times \frac{1\text{ mol Si}}{1\text{ mol SiO}_2} = 2592.8\text{ mol Si}$$

$$78.3\text{ kg C} \times \frac{1000\text{ g}}{\text{kg}} \times \frac{1\text{ mol C}}{12.01\text{ g C}} \times \frac{1\text{ mol Si}}{2\text{ mol C}} = 3259.8\text{ mol Si.}$$ SiO_2 is the limiting reactant

$$2592.8\text{ mol Si} \times \frac{28.09\text{ g Si}}{1\text{ mol Si}} \times \frac{\text{kg}}{1000\text{ g}} = 72.831\text{ kg Si}$$

$$\frac{66.1\text{ kg Si}}{72.83\text{ kg Si}} \times 100 = 90.8\%$$

Check: The theoretical yield has the correct units (kg Si) and has a reasonable magnitude compared to the mass of SiO_2, the limiting reactant. The % yield is reasonable, under 100%.

Solution Concentration and Solution Stoichiometry

4.53 (a) **Given:** 3.25 mol LiCl; 2.78 L solution **Find:** Molarity LiCl

Conceptual Plan: mol LiCl, L solution → Molarity

$$\text{molarity (M)} = \frac{\text{amount of solute (in moles)}}{\text{volume of solution (in L)}}$$

Solution: $$\frac{3.25\text{ mol LiCl}}{2.78\text{ L solution}} = 1.169\text{ M} = 1.17\text{ M}$$

Check: The units of the answer (M) are correct. The magnitude of the answer is reasonable. Concentrations are usually between 0 M and 18 M.

(b) **Given:** 28.33 g $C_6H_{12}O_6$; 1.28 L solution **Find:** Molarity $C_6H_{12}O_6$

Conceptual Plan: g $C_6H_{12}O_6$ → mol $C_6H_{12}O_6$, L solution → Molarity

$$\frac{\text{mol C}_6\text{H}_{12}\text{O}_6}{180.16\text{ g C}_6\text{H}_{12}\text{O}_6} \qquad \text{molarity (M)} = \frac{\text{amount of solute (in moles)}}{\text{volume of solution (in L)}}$$

Solution: $$28.33\text{ g C}_6\text{H}_{12}\text{O}_6 \times \frac{1\text{ mol C}_6\text{H}_{12}\text{O}_6}{180.16\text{ g C}_6\text{H}_{12}\text{O}_6} = 0.15724\text{ mol C}_6\text{H}_{12}\text{O}_6$$

$$\frac{0.15724\text{ mol C}_6\text{H}_{12}\text{O}_6}{1.28\text{ L solution}} = 0.1228\text{ M} = 0.123\text{ M}$$

Check: The units of the answer (M) are correct. The magnitude of the answer is reasonable. Concentrations are usually between 0 M and 18 M.

(c) **Given:** 32.4 mg NaCl; 122.4 mL solution **Find:** Molarity NaCl

Conceptual Plan: mg NaCl → g NaCl → mol NaCl, and mL solution → L solution then Molarity

$$\frac{\text{g NaCl}}{1000\text{ mg NaCl}} \quad \frac{\text{mol NaCl}}{58.45\text{ g NaCl}} \qquad \frac{\text{L solution}}{1000\text{ mL solution}} \quad \text{molarity (M)} = \frac{\text{amount of solute (in moles)}}{\text{volume of solution (in L)}}$$

Solution: $$32.4\text{ mg NaCl} \times \frac{1\text{ g}}{1000\text{ mg}} \times \frac{1\text{ mol NaCl}}{58.45\text{ g NaCl}} = 5.543 \times 10^{-4}\text{ mol NaCl}$$

$$122.4 \text{ ~~mL solution~~} \times \frac{1 \text{ L}}{1000 \text{ ~~mL~~}} = 0.1224 \text{ L}$$

$$\frac{5.543 \times 10^{-4} \text{ mol NaCl}}{0.1224 \text{ L}} = 0.0045287 \text{ M NaCl} = 0.00453 \text{ M NaCl}$$

Check: The units of the answer (M) are correct. The magnitude of the answer is reasonable. Concentrations are usually between 0 M and 18 M.

4.54 (a) **Given:** 0.38 mol $LiNO_3$; 6.14 L solution **Find:** Molarity $LiNO_3$

Conceptual Plan: mol $LiNO_3$, L solution → Molarity

$$\text{molarity (M)} = \frac{\text{amount of solute (in moles)}}{\text{volume of solution (in L)}}$$

Solution: $\frac{0.38 \text{ mol } LiNO_3}{6.14 \text{ L solution}} = 0.06189 \text{ M} = 0.062 \text{ M}$

Check: The units of the answer (M) are correct. The magnitude of the answer is reasonable. Concentrations are usually between 0 M and 18 M.

(b) **Given:** 72.8 g C_2H_6O; 2.34 L solution **Find:** Molarity $C_6H_{12}O_6$

Conceptual Plan: g C_2H_6O → mol C_2H_6O, L solution → Molarity

$$\frac{\text{mol } C_2H_6O}{46.068 \text{ g } C_2H_6O} \qquad \text{molarity (M)} = \frac{\text{amount of solute (in moles)}}{\text{volume of solution (in L)}}$$

Solution: $72.8 \text{ ~~g } C_2H_6O~~ \times \frac{1 \text{ mol } C_2H_6O}{46.068 \text{ ~~g } C_2H_6O~~} = 1.580 \text{ mol } C_2H_6O$

$$\frac{1.580 \text{ mol } C_2H_6O}{2.34 \text{ L solution}} = 0.6753 \text{ M} = 0.675 \text{ M}$$

Check: The units of the answer (M) are correct. The magnitude of the answer is reasonable. Concentrations are usually between 0 M and 18 M.

(c) **Given:** 12.87 mg KI; 112.4 mL solution **Find:** Molarity KI

Conceptual Plan: mg KI → g KI → mol KI, and mL solution → L solution then Molarity

$$\frac{\text{g KI}}{1000 \text{ mg KI}} \qquad \frac{\text{mol KI}}{166.00 \text{ g KI}} \qquad \frac{\text{L solution}}{1000 \text{ mL solution}} \qquad \text{molarity (M)} = \frac{\text{amount of solute (in moles)}}{\text{volume of solution (in L)}}$$

Solution: $12.87 \text{ ~~mg KI~~} \times \frac{1 \text{ ~~g~~}}{1000 \text{ ~~mg~~}} \times \frac{1 \text{ mol KI}}{166.00 \text{ ~~g KI~~}} = 7.7530 \times 10^{-5} \text{ mol KI}$

$$112.4 \text{ ~~mL solution~~} \times \frac{1 \text{ L}}{1000 \text{ ~~mL~~}} = 0.1124 \text{ L}$$

$$\frac{7.7530 \times 10^{-5} \text{ mol KI}}{0.1124 \text{ L}} = 6.8977 \times 10^{-4} \text{ M KI} = 6.898 \times 10^{-4} \text{ M}$$

Check: The units of the answer (M) are correct. The magnitude of the answer is reasonable. Concentrations are usually between 0 M and 18 M.

4.55 (a) **Given:** 0.556 L; 2.3 M KCl **Find:** mol KCl

Conceptual Plan: volume solution x M = mol

$$\text{volume solution (L)} \times \text{M} = \text{mol}$$

Solution: $0.556 \text{ ~~L solution~~} \times \frac{2.3 \text{ mol KCl}}{\text{~~L solution~~}} = 1.3 \text{ mol KCl}$

Check: The units of the answer (mol KCl) are correct. The magnitude is reasonable since it is less than 1 L solution.

(b) **Given:** 1.8 L; 0.85 M KCl **Find:** mol KCl

Conceptual Plan: volume solution x M = mol

$$\text{volume solution (L)} \times \text{M} = \text{mol}$$

Solution: $1.8 \text{ ~~L solution~~} \times \frac{0.85 \text{ mol KCl}}{\text{~~L solution~~}} = 1.5 \text{ mol KCl}$

Check: The units of the answer (mol KCl) are correct. The magnitude is reasonable since it is less than 2 L solution.

(c) **Given:** 114 mL; 1.85 M KCl **Find:** mol KCl
Conceptual Plan: mL solution → L solution, then volume solution x M = mol

$$\frac{1\ \text{L}}{1000\ \text{mL}} \qquad \text{volume solution (L)} \times \text{M} = \text{mol}$$

Solution: $114\ \cancel{\text{mL solution}} \times \frac{1\ \cancel{\text{L}}}{1000\ \cancel{\text{mL}}} \times \frac{1.85\ \text{mol KCl}}{\cancel{\text{L solution}}} = 0.211\ \text{mol KCl}$

Check: The units of the answer (mol KCl) are correct. The magnitude is reasonable since it is less than 1 L solution.

4.56 (a) **Given:** 0.45 mol C_2H_5OH, 0.200 M C_2H_5OH **Find:** volume solution
Conceptual Plan: mol C_2H_5OH → volume solution

$$\frac{\text{mol } C_2H_5OH}{\text{M } C_2H_5OH}$$

Solution:

$$\frac{0.45\ \cancel{\text{mol } C_2H_5OH}}{0.200\ \frac{\cancel{\text{mol } C_2H_5OH}}{\text{L solution}}} = 2.3\ \text{L } C_2H_5OH$$

Check: The units of the answer (L C_2H_5OH) are correct. The magnitude is reasonable for the amount and volume of solution.

(b) **Given:** 1.22 mol C_2H_5OH, 0.200 M C_2H_5OH **Find:** volume solution
Conceptual Plan: mol C_2H_5OH → volume solution

$$\frac{\text{mol } C_2H_5OH}{\text{M } C_2H_5OH}$$

Solution:

$$\frac{1.22\ \cancel{\text{mol } C_2H_5OH}}{0.200\ \frac{\cancel{\text{mol } C_2H_5OH}}{\text{L solution}}} = 6.10\ \text{L } C_2H_5OH$$

Check: The units of the answer (L C_2H_5OH) are correct. The magnitude is reasonable for the amount and volume of solution.

(c) **Given:** 1.2×10^{-2} mol C_2H_5OH, 0.200 M C_2H_5OH **Find:** volume solution
Conceptual Plan: mol C_2H_5OH → volume solution

$$\frac{\text{mol } C_2H_5OH}{\text{M } C_2H_5OH}$$

Solution:

$$\frac{1.2 \times 10^{-2}\ \cancel{\text{mol } C_2H_5OH}}{0.200\ \frac{\cancel{\text{mol } C_2H_5OH}}{\text{L solution}}} = 0.060\ \text{L } C_2H_5OH$$

Check: The units of the answer (L C_2H_5OH) are correct. The magnitude is reasonable for the amount and volume of solution.

4.57 **Given:** 400.0 mL; 1.1 M $NaNO_3$ **Find:** g $NaNO_3$
Conceptual Plan: mL solution → L solution, then volume solution x M = mol $NaNO_3$

$$\frac{\text{L solution}}{1000\ \text{mL solution}} \qquad \text{volume solution (L)} \times \text{M} = \text{mol}$$

then mol $NaNO_3$ → g $NaNO_3$

$$\frac{85.01\ \text{g } NaNO_3}{\text{mol } NaNO_3}$$

Solution: $400.0\ \cancel{\text{mL solution}} \times \frac{1\ \cancel{\text{L}}}{1000\ \cancel{\text{mL}}} \times \frac{1.1\ \cancel{\text{mol } NaNO_3}}{\cancel{\text{L solution}}} \times \frac{85.01\ \text{g}}{\cancel{\text{mol } NaNO_3}} = 37\ \text{g } NaNO_3$

Check: The units of the answer (g $NaNO_3$) are correct. The magnitude is reasonable for the concentration and volume of solution.

4.58 **Given:** 5.5 L; 0.300 M $CaCl_2$ **Find:** g $CaCl_2$

Conceptual Plan: volume solution x M = mol $CaCl_2$ then mol $CaCl_2$ → g $CaCl_2$

$$\text{volume solution (L)} \times M = \text{mol} \qquad \frac{110.98 \text{ g } CaCl_2}{\text{mol } CaCl_2}$$

Solution: $5.5 \text{ L solution} \times \frac{0.300 \text{ mol } CaCl_2}{\text{L solution}} \times \frac{110.98 \text{ g}}{\text{mol } CaCl_2} = 1.8 \times 10^2 \text{ g } CaCl_2$

Check: The units of the answer (g $CaCl_2$) are correct. The magnitude is reasonable for the concentration and volume of solution.

4.59 **Given:** V_1 = 123 mL; M_1 = 1.1 M; V_2 = 500.0 mL **Find:** M_2

Conceptual Plan: mL → L then V_1, M_1, V_2 → M_2

$$\frac{1 \text{ L}}{1000 \text{ mL}} \qquad V_1M_1 = V_2M_2$$

Solution: $123 \text{ mL} \times \frac{1 \text{ L}}{1000 \text{ mL}} = 0.123 \text{ L} \qquad 500.0 \text{ mL} \times \frac{1 \text{ L}}{1000 \text{ mL}} = 0.5000 \text{ L}$

$$M_2 = \frac{V_1M_1}{V_2} = \frac{(0.123 \text{ L})(1.1 \text{ M})}{(0.5000 \text{ L})} = 0.27 \text{ M}$$

Check: The units of the answer (M) are correct. The magnitude of the answer is reasonable since it is less than the original concentration.

4.60 **Given:** V_1 = 3.5 L; M_1 = 4.8 M; V_2 = 45 L **Find:** M_2

Conceptual Plan: V_1, M_1, V_2 → M_2

$$V_1M_1 = V_2M_2$$

Solution: $M_2 = \frac{V_1M_1}{V_2} = \frac{(3.5 \text{ L})(4.8 \text{ M})}{(45 \text{ L})} = 0.37 \text{ M}$

Check: The units of the answer (M) are correct. The magnitude of the answer is reasonable since it is less than the original concentration.

4.61 **Given:** V_1 = 50 mL; M_1 = 12 M; M_2 = 0.100 M **Find:** V_2

Conceptual Plan: mL → L then V_1, M_1, M_2 → V_2

$$\frac{1 \text{ L}}{1000 \text{ mL}} \qquad V_1M_1 = V_2M_2$$

Solution: $50 \text{ mL} \times \frac{1 \text{ L}}{1000 \text{ mL}} = 0.050 \text{ L}$

$$V_2 = \frac{V_1M_1}{M_2} = \frac{(0.050 \text{ L})(12 \text{ M})}{(0.100 \text{ M})} = 6.0 \text{ L}$$

Check: The units of the answer (L) are correct. The magnitude of the answer is reasonable since the new concentration is much less than the original; the volume must be larger.

4.62 **Given:** V_1 = 25 mL; M_1 = 10.0 M; M_2 = 0.150 M **Find:** V_2

Conceptual Plan: mL → L then V_1, M_1, M_2 → V_2

$$\frac{1 \text{ L}}{1000 \text{ mL}} \qquad V_1M_1 = V_2M_2$$

Solution: $25 \text{ mL} \times \frac{1 \text{ L}}{1000 \text{ mL}} = 0.025 \text{ L}$

$$V_2 = \frac{V_1M_1}{M_2} = \frac{(0.025 \text{ L})(10.0 \text{ M})}{(0.150 \text{ M})} = 1.7 \text{ L}$$

Check: The units of the answer (L) are correct. The magnitude of the answer is reasonable since the new concentration is much less than the original; the volume must be larger.

4.63 **Given:** 95.4 mL, 0.102 M $CuCl_2$; 0.175 M Na_3PO_4 **Find:** volume Na_3PO_4

Conceptual Plan: mL $CuCl_2$ → L $CuCl_2$ → mol $CuCl_2$ → mol Na_3PO_4 → L Na_3PO_4 → mL Na_3PO_4

$$\frac{1 \text{ L}}{1000 \text{ mL}} \qquad \frac{0.102 \text{ mol } CuCl_2}{\text{L}} \qquad \frac{2 \text{ mol } Na_3PO_4}{3 \text{ mol } CuCl_2} \qquad \frac{1 \text{ L}}{0.175 \text{ mol } Na_3PO_4} \qquad \frac{1000 \text{ mL}}{\text{L}}$$

Solution: $95.4 \text{ mL } CuCl_2 \times \frac{1 \text{ L}}{1000 \text{ mL}} \times \frac{0.102 \text{ mol } CuCl_2}{1 \text{ L}} \times \frac{2 \text{ mol } Na_3PO_4}{3 \text{ mol } CuCl_2} \times \frac{1 \text{ L}}{0.175 \text{ mol } Na_3PO_4} \times \frac{1000 \text{ mL}}{1 \text{ L}}$

$= 37.1 \text{ mL } Na_3PO_4$

Check: The units of the answer (mL Na_3PO_4) are correct. The magnitude of the answer is reasonable since the concentration of Na_3PO_4 is greater.

4.64 **Given:** 125 mL, 0.150 M $Co(NO_3)_2$; 0.150 M Li_2S **Find:** volume Li_2S

Conceptual Plan: mL $Co(NO_3)_2$ → L $Co(NO_3)_2$ → mol $Co(NO_3)_2$ → mol Li_2S → L Li_2S → mL Li_2S

$$\frac{1 \text{ L}}{1000 \text{ mL}} \quad \frac{0.150 \text{ mol } Co(NO_3)_2}{\text{L}} \quad \frac{1 \text{ mol } Li_2S}{1 \text{ mol } Co(NO_3)_2} \quad \frac{1 \text{ L}}{0.155 \text{ mol } Li_2S} \quad \frac{1000 \text{ mL}}{\text{L}}$$

Solution:

$$125 \text{ mL } Co(NO_3)_2 \times \frac{1 \text{ L}}{1000 \text{ mL}} \times \frac{0.150 \text{ mol } Co(NO_3)_2}{1 \text{ L}} \times \frac{1 \text{ mol } Li_2S}{1 \text{ mol } Co(NO_3)_2} \times \frac{1 \text{ L}}{0.150 \text{ mol } Li_2S} \times \frac{1000 \text{ mL}}{1 \text{ L}}$$

$= 125 \text{ mL } Li_2S$

Check: The units of the answer (mL Li_2S) are correct. The magnitude of the answer is reasonable since the concentrations are the same and the mole ratio is 1:1.

4.65 **Given:** 25.0 g H_2; 6.0 M H_2SO_4 **Find:** volume H_2SO_4

Conceptual Plan: g H_2 → mol H_2 → mol H_2SO_4 → L H_2SO_4

$$\frac{2.016 \text{ g } H_2}{1 \text{ mol } H_2} \quad \frac{3 \text{ mol } H_2SO_4}{3 \text{ mol } H_2} \quad \frac{1 \text{ L}}{6.0 \text{ mol } H_2SO_4}$$

Solution: $25.0 \text{ g } H_2 \times \frac{1 \text{ mol } H_2}{2.016 \text{ g } H_2} \times \frac{3 \text{ mol } H_2SO_4}{3 \text{ mol } H_2} \times \frac{1 \text{ L}}{6.0 \text{ mol } H_2SO_4} = 2.1 \text{ L } H_2SO_4$

Check: The units of the answer (L H_2SO_4) are correct. The magnitude is reasonable since there are approximately 12 mol H_2 and the mole ratio is 1:1.

4.66 **Given:** 25.0 g Zn, 275 mL solution **Find:** M $ZnCl_2$

Conceptual Plan: g Zn → mol Zn → mol $ZnCl_2$ → M $ZnCl_2$

$$\frac{65.41 \text{ g Zn}}{1 \text{ mol Zn}} \quad \frac{1 \text{ mol } ZnCl_2}{1 \text{ mol Zn}} \quad \frac{\text{mol } ZnCl_2}{\text{volume solution}}$$

Solution:

$$25.0 \text{ g Zn} \times \frac{1 \text{ mol Zn}}{65.41 \text{ g Zn}} \times \frac{1 \text{ mol } ZnCl_2}{1 \text{ mol Zn}} = 0.38\underline{2}2 \text{ mol } ZnCl_2$$

$$\frac{0.38\underline{2}2 \text{ mol } ZnCl_2}{275 \text{ mL}} \times \frac{1000 \text{ mL}}{\text{L}} = 1.39 \text{ M } ZnCl_2$$

Check: The units of the answer (M $ZnCl_2$) are correct. The magnitude is reasonable because the stoichiometry is 1:1 and the mol Zn is less than 0.5.

Types of Aqueous Solutions and Solubility

4.67 (a) CsCl is an ionic compound. An aqueous solution is an electrolyte solution, so it conducts electricity.

(b) CH_3OH is a molecular compound that does not dissociate. An aqueous solution is a nonelectrolyte solution, so it does not conduct electricity.

(c) $Ca(NO_3)_2$ is an ionic compound. An aqueous solution is an electrolyte solution, so it conducts electricity.

(d) $C_6H_{12}O_6$ is a molecular compound that does not dissociate. An aqueous solution is a nonelectrolyte solution, so it does not conduct electricity.

4.68 (a) $MgBr_2$ is an ionic compound. An aqueous solution is a strong electrolyte.

(b) $C_{12}H_{22}O_{11}$ is a molecular compound that does not dissociate. An aqueous solution is a nonelectrolyte.

(c) Na_2CO_3 is an ionic compound. An aqueous solution is a strong electrolyte.

(d) KOH is a strong base. An aqueous solution is a strong electrolyte.

4.69 (a) $AgNO_3$ is soluble. Compounds containing NO_3^- are always soluble with no exceptions. The ions in the solution are $Ag^+(aq)$ and $NO_3^-(aq)$.

(b) $Pb(C_2H_3O_2)_2$ is soluble. Compounds containing $C_2H_3O_2^-$ are always soluble with no exceptions. The ions in the solution are $Pb^{2+}(aq)$ and $C_2H_3O_2^-(aq)$.

(c) KNO_3 is soluble. Compounds containing K^+ are always soluble with no exceptions. The ions in solution are $K^+(aq)$ and $NO_3^-(aq)$.

(d) $(NH_4)_2S$ is soluble. Compounds containing NH_4^+ are always soluble with no exceptions. The ions in solution are $NH_4^+(aq)$ and $S^{2-}(aq)$.

4.70 (a) AgI is insoluble. Compounds containing I^- are normally soluble but Ag^+ is an exception.

(b) $Cu_3(PO_4)_2$ is insoluble. Compounds containing PO_4^{3-} are normally insoluble and Cu^{2+} is not an exception.

(c) $CoCO_3$ is insoluble. Compounds containing CO_3^{2-} are normally insoluble and Co^{2+} is not an exception.

(d) K_3PO_4 is soluble. Compounds containing PO_4^{3-} are normally insoluble, but K^+ is an exception. The ions in solution are $K^+(aq)$ and $PO_4^{3-}(aq)$.

Precipitation Reactions

4.71 (a) $LiI(aq) + BaS(aq) \rightarrow$ Possible products: Li_2S and BaI_2. Li_2S is soluble. Compounds containing S^{2-} are normally insoluble but Li^+ is an exception. BaI_2 is soluble. Compounds containing I^- are normally soluble and Ba^{2+} is not an exception. $LiI(aq) + BaS(aq) \rightarrow$ No Reaction

(b) $KCl(aq) + CaS(aq) \rightarrow$ Possible products: K_2S and $CaCl_2$. K_2S is soluble. Compounds containing S^{2-} are normally insoluble but K^+ is an exception. $CaCl_2$ is soluble. Compounds containing Cl^- are normally soluble and Ca^{2+} is not an exception. $KCl(aq) + CaS(aq) \rightarrow$ No Reaction

(c) $CrBr_2(aq) + Na_2CO_3(aq) \rightarrow$ Possible products: $CrCO_3$ and NaBr. $CrCO_3$ is insoluble. Compounds containing CO_3^{2-} are normally insoluble and Cr^{2+} is not an exception. NaBr is soluble. Compounds containing Br^- are normally soluble and Na^+ is not an exception.
$CrBr_2(aq) + Na_2CO_3(aq) \rightarrow CrCO_3(s) + 2\ NaBr(aq)$

(d) $NaOH(aq) + FeCl_3(aq) \rightarrow$ Possible products NaCl and $Fe(OH)_3$. NaCl is soluble. Compounds containing Na^+ are normally soluble, no exceptions. $Fe(OH)_3$ is insoluble. Compounds containing OH^- are normally insoluble and Fe^{3+} is not an exception.
$3\ NaOH(aq) + FeCl_3(aq) \rightarrow 3\ NaCl(aq) + Fe(OH)_3(s)$

4.72 (a) $NaNO_3(aq) + KCl(aq) \rightarrow$ Possible products: NaCl and KNO_3. NaCl is soluble. Compounds containing Na^+ are always soluble, no exceptions. KNO_3 is soluble. Compounds containing K^+ are always soluble, no exceptions. $NaNO_3(aq) + KCl(aq) \rightarrow$ No Reaction

(b) $NaCl(aq) + Hg_2(C_2H_3O_2)_2(aq) \rightarrow$ Possible products: $NaC_2H_3O_2$ and Hg_2Cl_2. $NaC_2H_3O_2$ is soluble. Compounds containing Na^+ are always soluble, no exceptions. Hg_2Cl_2 is insoluble. Compounds containing Cl^- are normally soluble but Hg_2^{2+} is an exception.
$2\ NaCl(aq) + Hg_2(C_2H_3O_2)_2(aq) \rightarrow 2\ NaC_2H_3O_2(aq) + Hg_2Cl_2(s)$

(c) $(NH_4)_2SO_4(aq) + SrCl_2(aq) \rightarrow$ Possible products: NH_4Cl and $SrSO_4$. NH_4Cl is soluble. Compounds containing NH_4^+ are always soluble, no exceptions. $SrSO_4$ is insoluble. Compounds containing SO_4^{2-} are normally soluble but Sr^{2+} is an exception. $(NH_4)_2SO_4(aq) + SrCl_2(aq) \rightarrow 2\ NH_4Cl(aq) + SrSO_4(s)$

(d) $NH_4Cl(aq) + AgNO_3(aq) \rightarrow$ Possible products: NH_4NO_3 and AgCl. NH_4NO_3 is soluble. Compounds containing NH_4^+ are always soluble, no exceptions. AgCl is insoluble. Compounds containing Cl^- are normally soluble, but Ag^+ is an exception. $NH_4Cl(aq) + AgNO_3(aq) \rightarrow NH_4NO_3(aq) + AgCl(s)$

4.73 (a) $K_2CO_3(aq) + Pb(NO_3)_2(aq) \rightarrow$ Possible products: KNO_3 and $PbCO_3$. KNO_3 is soluble. Compounds containing K^+ are always soluble, no exceptions. $PbCO_3$ is insoluble. Compounds containing CO_3^{2-} are normally insoluble and Pb^{2+} is not an exception.
$K_2CO_3(aq) + Pb(NO_3)_2(aq) \rightarrow 2\ KNO_3(aq) + PbCO_3(s)$

(b) $Li_2SO_4(aq) + Pb(C_2H_3O_2)_2(aq) \rightarrow$ Possible products: $LiC_2H_3O_2$ and $PbSO_4$. $LiC_2H_3O_2$ is soluble. Compounds containing Li^+ are always soluble, no exceptions. $PbSO_4$ is insoluble. Compounds containing $SO_4^{\ 2-}$ are normally soluble but, Pb^{2+} is an exception.
$Li_2SO_4(aq) + Pb(C_2H_3O_2)_2(aq) \rightarrow 2\ LiC_2H_3O_2(aq) + PbSO_4(s)$

(c) $Cu(NO_3)_2(aq) + MgS(s) \rightarrow$ Possible products: CuS and $Mg(NO_3)_2$. CuS is insoluble. Compounds containing S^{2-} are normally insoluble and Cu^{2+} is not an exception. $Mg(NO_3)_2$ is soluble. Compounds containing NO_3^- are always soluble, no exceptions. $Cu(NO_3)_2(aq) + MgS(s) \rightarrow CuS(s) + Mg(NO_3)_2(aq)$

(d) $Sr(NO_3)_2(aq) + KI(aq) \rightarrow$ Possible products: SrI_2 and KNO_3. SrI_2 is soluble. Compounds containing I^- are normally soluble and Sr^{2+} is not an exception. KNO_3 is soluble. Compounds containing K^+ are always soluble, no exceptions. $Sr(NO_3)_2(aq) + KI(aq) \rightarrow$ No Reaction

4.74 (a) $NaCl(aq) + Pb(C_2H_3O_2)_2(aq) \rightarrow$ Possible products $NaC_2H_3O_2$ and $PbCl_2$. $NaC_2H_3O_2$ is soluble. Compounds containing Na^+ are always soluble, no exceptions. $PbCl_2$ is insoluble. Compounds containing Cl^- are normally soluble but Pb^{2+} is an exception.
$2\ NaCl(aq) + Pb(C_2H_3O_2)_2(aq) \rightarrow 2\ NaC_2H_3O_2(aq) + PbCl_2(s)$

(b) $K_2SO_4(aq) + SrI_2(aq) \rightarrow$ Possible products: KI and $SrSO_4$. KI is soluble. Compounds containing K^+ are always soluble, no exceptions. $SrSO_4$ is insoluble. Compounds containing SO_4^{2-} are normally soluble, but Sr^{2+} is an exception. $K_2SO_4(aq) + SrI_2(aq) \rightarrow 2\ KI(aq)$ and $SrSO_4(s)$

(c) $CsCl(aq) + CaS(aq) \rightarrow$ Possible products: Cs_2S and $CaCl_2$. Cs_2S is soluble. Compounds containing S^{2-} are normally insoluble but Cs^+ is an exception. $CaCl_2$ is soluble. Compounds containing Cl^- are normally soluble and Ca^{2+} is not an exception. $CsCl(aq) + CaS(aq) \rightarrow$ No Reaction

(d) $Cr(NO_3)_3(aq) + Na_3PO_4(aq) \rightarrow$ Possible products: $CrPO_4$ and $NaNO_3$. $CrPO_4$ is insoluble. Compounds containing PO_4^{3-} are normally insoluble and Cr^{3+} is not an exception. $NaNO_3$ is soluble. Compounds containing Na^+ are always soluble, no exceptions.
$Cr(NO_3)_3(aq) + Na_3PO_4(aq) \rightarrow CrPO_4(s) + 3\ NaNO_3(aq)$

Ionic and Net Ionic Equations

4.75 (a) $H^+(aq) + \cancel{Cl}^-(aq) + \cancel{Li}^+(aq) + OH^-(aq) \rightarrow H_2O(l) + \cancel{Li}^+(aq) + \cancel{Cl}^-(aq)$
$H^+(aq) + OH^-(aq) \rightarrow H_2O(l)$

(b) $\cancel{Mg}^{2+}(aq) + S^{2-}(aq) + Cu^{2+}(aq) + 2\ \cancel{Cl}^-(aq) \rightarrow CuS(s) + \cancel{Mg}^{2+}(aq) + 2\ \cancel{Cl}^-(aq)$
$Cu^{2+}(aq) + S^{2-}(aq) \rightarrow CuS(s)$

(c) $\cancel{Na}^+(aq) + OH^-(aq) + H^+(aq) + \cancel{NO_3}^-(aq) \rightarrow H_2O(l) + \cancel{Na}^+(aq) + \cancel{NO_3}^-(aq)$
$H^+(aq) + OH^-(aq) + \rightarrow H_2O(l)$

(d) $6\ \cancel{Na}^+(aq) + 2\ PO_4^{\ 3-}(aq) + 3\ Ni^{2+}(aq) + 6\ \cancel{Cl}^-(aq) \rightarrow Ni_3(PO_4)_2(s) + 6\ \cancel{Na}^+(aq) + 6\ \cancel{Cl}^-(aq)$
$3\ Ni^{2+}(aq) + 2\ PO_4^{\ 3-}(aq) \rightarrow Ni_3(PO_4)_2(s)$

4.76 (a) $2\ \cancel{K}^+(aq) + SO_4^{\ 2-}(aq) + Ca^{2+}(aq) + 2\ \cancel{I}^-(aq) \rightarrow CaSO_4(s) + 2\ \cancel{K}^+(aq) + 2\ \cancel{I}^-(aq)$
$Ca^{2+}(aq) + SO_4^{\ 2-}(aq) \rightarrow CaSO_4(s)$

(b) $NH_4^+(aq) + \cancel{Cl}^-(aq) + \cancel{Na}^+(aq) + OH^-(aq) \rightarrow H_2O(l) + NH_3(g) + \cancel{Na}^+(aq) + \cancel{Cl}^-(aq)$
$NH_4^+(aq) + OH^-(aq) \rightarrow H_2O(l) + NH_3(g)$

(c) $Ag^+(aq) + \cancel{NO_3}^-(aq) + \cancel{Na}^+(aq) + Cl^-(aq) \rightarrow AgCl(s) + \cancel{Na}^+(aq) + \cancel{NO_3}^-(aq)$
$Ag^+(aq) + Cl^-(aq) \rightarrow AgCl(s)$

(d) $2H^+(aq) + \cancel{2C_2H_3O_2^-}(aq) + \cancel{2K^+}(aq) + CO_3^{2-}(aq) \rightarrow H_2O(l) + CO_2(g) + \cancel{2K^+}(aq) + \cancel{2C_2H_3O_2^-}(aq)$
$2H^+(aq) + CO_3^{2-}(aq) \rightarrow H_2O(l) + CO_2(g)$

4.77 $Hg_2^{2+}(aq) + \cancel{2NO_3^-}(aq) + \cancel{2Na^+}(aq) + 2\,Cl^-(aq) \rightarrow Hg_2Cl_2(s) + \cancel{2Na^+}(aq) + \cancel{2NO_3^-}(aq)$
$Hg_2^{2+}(aq) + 2\,Cl^-(aq) \rightarrow Hg_2Cl_2(s)$

4.78 $Pb^{2+}(aq) + \cancel{2NO_3^-}(aq) + \cancel{2K^+}(aq) + SO_4^{2-}(aq) \rightarrow PbSO_4(s) + \cancel{2K^+}(aq) + \cancel{2NO_3^-}(aq)$
$Pb^{2+}(aq) + SO_4^{2-}(aq) \rightarrow PbSO_4(s)$

Acid-Base and Gas-Evolution Reactions

4.79 Skeletal reaction: $HBr(aq) + KOH(aq) \rightarrow H_2O(l) + KBr(aq)$
acid base water salt
Net ionic equation: $H^+(aq) + OH-(aq) \rightarrow H_2O(l)$

4.80 Skeletal reaction: $HNO_3(aq) + Ca(OH)_2(aq) \rightarrow H_2O(l) + Ca(NO_3)_2(aq)$
acid base water salt
Balanced reaction: $2\,HNO_3(aq) + Ca(OH)_2(aq) \rightarrow 2\,H_2O(l) + Ca(NO_3)_2(aq)$
Net ionic equation: $H^+(aq) + OH^-(aq) \rightarrow H_2O(l)$

4.81 (a) Skeletal reaction: $H_2SO_4(aq) + Ca(OH)_2(aq) \rightarrow H_2O(l) + CaSO_4(s)$
acid base water salt
Balanced reaction: $H_2SO_4(aq) + Ca(OH)_2(aq) \rightarrow 2\,H_2O(l) + CaSO_4(s)$

(b) Skeletal reaction: $HClO_4(aq) + KOH(aq) \rightarrow H_2O(l) + KClO_4(aq)$
acid base water salt
Balanced reaction: $HClO_4(aq) + KOH(aq) \rightarrow H_2O(l) + KClO_4(aq)$

(c) Skeletal reaction: $H_2SO_4(aq) + NaOH(aq) \rightarrow H_2O(l) + Na_2SO_4(aq)$
acid base water salt
Balanced reaction: $H_2SO_4(aq) + 2\,NaOH(aq) \rightarrow 2\,H_2O(l) + Na_2SO_4(aq)$

4.82 (a) Skeletal reaction: $HI(aq) + LiOH(aq) \rightarrow H_2O(l) + LiI(aq)$
acid base water salt
Balanced reaction: $HI(aq) + LiOH(aq) \rightarrow H_2O(l) + LiI(aq)$

(b) Skeletal reaction: $HC_2H_3O_2(aq) + Ca(OH)_2(aq) \rightarrow H_2O(l) + Ca(C_2H_3O_2)_2(aq)$
acid base water salt
Balanced reaction: $2\,HC_2H_3O_2(aq) + Ca(OH)_2(aq) \rightarrow 2\,H_2O(l) + Ca(C_2H_3O_2)_2(aq)$

(c) Skeletal reaction: $HCl(aq) + Ba(OH)_2(aq) \rightarrow H_2O(l) + BaCl_2(aq)$
acid base water salt
Balanced reaction: $2\,HCl(aq) + Ba(OH)_2(aq) \rightarrow 2\,H_2O(l) + BaCl_2(aq)$

4.83 **Given:** 22.62 mL, 0.2000 M NaOH solution; 25.00 mL $HClO_4$ solution **Find:** M $HClO_4$ solution
Conceptual Plan: mL NaOH $\rightarrow$ L NaOH $\rightarrow$ mol NaOH $\rightarrow$ mol $HClO_4$

$$\frac{1\text{ L}}{1000\text{ mL}} \qquad \frac{0.200\text{ mol NaOH}}{\text{L NaOH}} \qquad \frac{1\text{ mol }HClO_4}{1\text{ mol NaOH}}$$

mol $HClO_4$, volume $HClO_4$ solution $\rightarrow$ M

$$M = \frac{1\text{ mol }HClO_4}{\text{L }HClO_4\text{ solution}}$$

Solution: $$22.62\,\cancel{\text{mL NaOH}} \times \frac{1\,\cancel{\text{L}}}{1000\,\cancel{\text{mL}}} \times \frac{0.2000\,\cancel{\text{mol NaOH}}}{\cancel{\text{L}}\text{ NaOH}} \times \frac{1\text{ mol }HClO_4}{1\,\cancel{\text{mol NaOH}}} = 0.00452\underline{4}\text{ mol }HClO_4$$

$$\frac{0.00452\underline{4}\text{ mol }HClO_4}{25.00\,\cancel{\text{mL}}\text{ }HClO_4} \times \frac{1000\,\cancel{\text{mL}}}{1\text{ L}} = 0.180\underline{9}6\text{ M }HClO_4 = 0.1810\text{ M }HClO_4$$

Check: The units of the answer (M $HClO_4$) are correct. The magnitude of the answer is reasonable since it is less than the M of NaOH.

4.84 **Given:** 26.38 mL, 0.100 M NaOH solution; 30.00 mL H_3PO_4 solution **Find:** M H_3PO_4 solution

Conceptual Plan: mL NaOH → L NaOH → mol NaOH → mol H_3PO_4

$$\frac{1\text{ L}}{1000\text{ mL}} \quad \frac{0.100\text{ mol NaOH}}{\text{L NaOH}} \quad \frac{1\text{ mol }H_3PO_4}{3\text{ mol NaOH}}$$

mol H_3PO_4, volume H_3PO_4 solution → M

$$M = \frac{1\text{ mol }H_3PO_4}{\text{L }H_3PO_4\text{ solution}}$$

Solution: $26.38\ \text{mL NaOH} \times \frac{1\text{ L}}{1000\text{ mL}} \times \frac{0.100\text{ mol NaOH}}{\text{L NaOH}} \times \frac{1\text{ mol }H_3PO_4}{3\text{ mol NaOH}} = 0.00087\underline{9}33\text{ mol }H_3PO_4$

$$\frac{0.00087\underline{9}33\text{ mol }H_3PO_4}{30.00\text{ mL }H_3PO_4} \times \frac{1000\text{ mL}}{1\text{ L}} = 0.029\underline{3}1\text{ M }H_3PO_4 = 0.0293\text{ M }H_3PO_4$$

Check: The units of the answer (M H_3PO_4) are correct. The magnitude of the answer is reasonable since it is less than the concentration of the NaOH.

4.85 (a) Skeletal reaction: $HBr(aq) + NiS(s) \rightarrow NiBr_2(aq) + H_2S(g)$
gas

Balanced reaction: $2\ HBr(aq) + NiS(s) \rightarrow NiBr_2(aq) + H_2S(g)$

(b) Skeletal reaction: $NH_4I(aq) + NaOH(aq) \rightarrow NH_4OH(aq) + NaI(aq) \rightarrow H_2O(l) + NH_3(g) + NaI(aq)$
decomposes gas

Balanced reaction: $NH_4I(aq) + NaOH(aq) \rightarrow H_2O(l) + NH_3(g) + NaI(aq)$

(c) Skeletal reaction: $HBr(aq) + Na_2S(aq) \rightarrow NaBr(aq) + H_2S(g)$
gas

Balanced reaction: $2\ HBr(aq) + Na_2S(aq) \rightarrow 2\ NaBr(aq) + H_2S(g)$

(d) Skeletal reaction:
$HClO_4(aq) + Li_2CO_3(aq) \rightarrow H_2CO_3(aq) + LiClO_4(aq) \rightarrow H_2O(l) + CO_2(g) + LiClO_4(aq)$
decomposes gas

Balanced reaction: $2\ HClO_4(aq) + Li_2CO_3(aq) \rightarrow H_2O(l) + CO_2(g) + 2\ LiClO_4(aq)$

4.86 (a) Skeletal reaction:
$HNO_3(aq) + Na_2SO_3(aq) \rightarrow H_2SO_3(aq) + NaNO_3(aq) \rightarrow H_2O(l) + SO_2(g) + NaNO_3(aq)$
decomposes gas

Balanced reaction: $2\ HNO_3(aq) + Na_2SO_3(aq) \rightarrow H_2O(l) + SO_2(g) + 2\ NaNO_3(aq)$

(b) Skeletal reaction: $HCl(aq) + KHCO_3(aq) \rightarrow H_2CO_3(aq) + KCl(aq) \rightarrow H_2O(l) + CO_2(g) + KCl(aq)$
decomposes gas

Balanced reaction: $HCl(aq) + KHCO_3(aq) \rightarrow H_2O(l) + CO_2(g) + KCl(aq)$

(c) Skeletal reaction:
$HC_2H_3O_2(aq) + NaHSO_3(aq) \rightarrow NaC_2H_3O_2(aq) + H_2SO_3(aq) \rightarrow H_2O(l) + SO_2(g) + NaC_2H_3O_2(aq)$
decomposes gas

Balanced reaction: $HC_2H_3O_2(aq) + NaHSO_3(aq) \rightarrow H_2O(l) + SO_2(g) + NaC_2H_3O_2(aq)$

(d) Skeletal reaction:
$(NH_4)_2SO_4(aq) + Ca(OH)_2(aq) \rightarrow NH_4OH(aq) + CaSO_4(s) \rightarrow H_2O(l) + NH_3(g) + CaSO_4(s)$
decomposes gas

Balanced reaction: $(NH_4)_2SO_4(aq) + Ca(OH)_2(aq) \rightarrow 2H_2O(l) + 2NH_3(g) + CaSO_4(s)$

Oxidation-Reduction and Combustion

4.87 (a) Ag. The oxidation state of Ag = 0. The oxidation state of an atom in a free element is 0.

(b) Ag^+. The oxidation state of Ag^+ = +1. The oxidation state of a monatomic ion is equal to its charge.

(c) CaF_2. The oxidation state of Ca = +2, and the oxidation state of F = – 1. The oxidation state of a group 2A metal always has an oxidation state of +2, the oxidation of F is – 1 since the sum of the oxidation states in a neutral formula unit = 0.

(d) H_2S. The oxidation state of H = + 1, and the oxidation state of S = – 2. The oxidation state of H when listed first is +1, the oxidation state of S is – 2 since S is in group 6A and the sum of the oxidation states in a neutral molecular unit = 0.

(e) CO_3^{2-}. The oxidation state of C = +4, and the oxidation state of O = – 2. The oxidation state of O is normally – 2, and the oxidation state of C is deduced from the formula since the sum of the oxidation states must equal the charge on the ion. (C ox state) + 3(O ox state) = – 2; (C ox state) + 3(– 2) = – 2, so C ox state = + 4.

(f) CrO_4^{2-}. The oxidation state of Cr = +6, and the oxidation state of O = – 2. The oxidation state of O is normally –2, and the oxidation state of Cr is deduced from the formula since the sum of the oxidation states must equal the charge on the ion. (Cr ox state) + 4(O ox state) = – 2; (Cr ox state) + 4(– 2) = – 2, so Cr ox state = + 6.

4.88 (a) Cl_2. The oxidation of both Cl atoms = 0. Since Cl_2 is a free element, the oxidation state of Cl = 0.

(b) Fe^{3+}. The oxidation of Fe = +3. The oxidation state of a monatomic ion is equal to its charge.

(c) $CuCl_2$. The oxidation state of Cu = +2, and the oxidation state of each Cl = – 1. The oxidation state of group 7A atoms is normally – 1, and the oxidation state of Cu is deduced from the formula since the sum of the oxidation states in a neutral formula unit = 0.

(d) CH_4. The oxidation state of C = – 4, and the oxidation state of H = +1. The oxidation state of H is normally +1, and the oxidation state of C is deduced for the formula since the sum of the oxidation states in a neutral molecular unit = 0. (C ox state) + 4(H ox state) = 0; (C ox state) + 4(+ 1) = 0, so C ox state = – 4.

(e) $Cr_2O_7^{2-}$. The oxidation state of Cr = +6, and the oxidation state of O = – 2. The oxidation state of O is normally – 2, and the oxidation state of Cr is deduced from the formula since the sum of the oxidation states must equal the charge of the ion. 2(Cr ox state) + 7(O ox state) = – 2; 2(Cr ox state) + 7(– 2) = – 2, so Cr ox state = +6.

(f) HSO_4^-. The oxidation state of H = +1, the oxidation state of S = +6, and the oxidation state of O = – 2. The oxidation state of H is normally +1, the oxidation state of O is normally – 2, and the oxidation state of S is deduced from the formula since the sum of the oxidation states must equal the charge of the ion.
(H ox state) + (S ox state) + 4(O ox state) = – 1;
(+1) + (S ox state) + 4(– 2) = – 1, so S ox state = +6.

4.89 (a) CrO. The oxidation state of Cr = +2, and the oxidation state of O = – 2. The oxidation state of O is normally – 2, and the oxidation state of Cr is deduced from the formula since the sum of the oxidation states must = 0.
(Cr ox state) + (O ox state) = 0; (Cr ox state) + (– 2) = 0, so Cr = +2.

(b) CrO_3. The oxidation state of Cr = +6, and the oxidation state of O = – 2. The oxidation state of O is normally – 2, and the oxidation state of Cr is deduced from the formula since the sum of the oxidation states must = 0.
(Cr ox state) + 3(O ox state) = 0; (Cr ox state) +3 (– 2) = 0, so Cr = +6.

(c) Cr_2O_3. The oxidation state of Cr = +3, and the oxidation state of O = – 2. The oxidation state of O is normally – 2, and the oxidation state of Cr is deduced from the formula since the sum of the oxidation states must = 0.
2(Cr ox state) +3 (O ox state) = 0; 2(Cr ox state) + 3(– 2) = 0, so Cr = +3.

4.90 (a) ClO^-. The oxidation state of Cl = +1, and the oxidation state of O = – 2. The oxidation state of O is normally – 2, and the oxidation state of Cl is deduced from the formula since the sum of the oxidation states must equal the charge of the ion. (Cl ox state) + (O ox state) = – 1; (Cl ox state) + (– 2) = – 1, so Cl = +1.

(b) ClO_2^-. The oxidation state of Cl = +3, and the oxidation state of O = – 2. The oxidation state of O is normally – 2, and the oxidation state of Cl is deduced from the formula since the sum of the oxidation states must equal the charge of the ion. (Cl ox state) + 2(O ox state) = – 1; (Cl ox state) + 2(– 2) = – 1, so Cl = +3.

(c) ClO_3^-. The oxidation state of Cl = +5, and the oxidation state of O = – 2. The oxidation state of O is normally – 2, and the oxidation state of Cl is deduced from the formula since the sum of the oxidation states must equal the charge of the ion. (Cl ox state) + 3(O ox state) = – 1; (Cl ox state) + 3(– 2) = – 1, so Cl = +5.

(d) ClO_4^-. The oxidation state of Cl = +7, and the oxidation state of O = – 2. The oxidation state of O is normally – 2, and the oxidation state of Cl is deduced from the formula since the sum of the oxidation states must equal the charge of the ion. (Cl ox state) + 4(O ox state) = – 1; (Cl ox state) + 4(– 2) = – 1, so Cl = +7.

4.91 (a) $4\,Li(s) + O_2(g) \rightarrow 2\,Li_2O(s)$

Oxidation states; 0 0 +1 – 2

This is a redox reaction since Li increases in oxidation number (oxidation) and O decreases in number (reduction). O_2 is the oxidizing agent, and Li is the reducing agent.

(b) $Mg(s) + Fe^{2+}(aq) \rightarrow Mg^{2+}(aq) + Fe(s)$

Oxidation states; 0 +2 +2 0

This is a redox reaction since Mg increases in oxidation number (oxidation) and Fe decreases in number (reduction). Fe^{2+} is the oxidizing agent, and Mg is the reducing agent.

(c) $Pb(NO_3)_2(aq) + Na_2SO_4(aq) \rightarrow PbSO_4(s) + 2\,NaNO_3(aq)$

Oxidation states; +2 +5 – 2 +1 +6 – 2 +2 +6 –2 +1 +5 –2

This is a not a redox reaction since none of the atoms undergoes a change in oxidation number.

(d) $HBr(aq) + KOH(aq) \rightarrow H_2O(l) + KBr(aq)$

Oxidation states;+1 – 1 +1 – 2 +1 +1 –2 +1 –2

This is a not a redox reaction since none of the atoms undergoes a change in oxidation number.

4.92 (a) $Al(s) + 3\,Ag^+(aq) \rightarrow Al^{3+}(aq) + 3\,Ag(s)$

Oxidation states; 0 +1 +3 0

This is a redox reaction since Al increases in oxidation number (oxidation) and Ag decreases in number (reduction). Ag^+ is the oxidizing agent, and Al is the reducing agent.

(b) $SO_3(g) + H_2O(l) \rightarrow H_2SO_4(aq)$

Oxidation states; +6 –2 +1 – 2 +1 +6 –2

This is a not a redox reaction since none of the atoms undergoes a change in oxidation number.

(c) $Ba(s) + Cl_2(g) \rightarrow BaCl_2(s)$

Oxidation states; 0 0 +2 –1

This is a redox reaction since Ba increases in oxidation number (oxidation) and Cl decreases in number (reduction). Cl_2 is the oxidizing agent, and Ba is the reducing agent.

(d) $Mg(s) + Br_2(l) \rightarrow MgBr_2(s)$

Oxidation states; 0 0 +2 –1

This is a redox reaction since Mg increases in oxidation number (oxidation) and Br decreases in number (reduction). Br_2 is the oxidizing agent, and Mg is the reducing agent.

4.93 (a) Skeletal reaction: $S(s) + O_2(g) \rightarrow SO_2(g)$

Balanced reaction: $S(s) + O_2(g) \rightarrow SO_2(g)$

(b) Skeletal reaction: $C_3H_6(g) + O_2(g) \rightarrow CO_2(g) + H_2O(g)$

Balance C: $C_3H_6(g) + O_2(g) \rightarrow 3CO_2(g) + H_2O(g)$

Balance H: $C_3H_6(g) + O_2(g) \rightarrow 3CO_2(g) + 3H_2O(g)$

Balance O: $C_3H_6(g) + 9/2\,O_2(g) \rightarrow 3CO_2(g) + 3H_2O(g)$

Clear fraction: $2C_3H_6(g) + 9O_2(g) \rightarrow 6CO_2(g) + 6H_2O(g)$

(c) Skeletal reaction: $Ca(s) + O_2(g) \rightarrow CaO(s)$

Balance O: $Ca(s) + O_2(g) \rightarrow 2CaO(s)$

Balance Ca: $2Ca(s) + O_2(g) \rightarrow 2CaO(s)$

(d) Skeletal reaction: $C_5H_{12}S(l) + O_2(g) \rightarrow CO_2(g) + H_2O(g) + SO_2(g)$
Balance C: $C_5H_{12}S(l) + O_2(g) \rightarrow 5CO_2(g) + H_2O(g) + SO_2(g)$
Balance H: $C_5H_{12}S(l) + O_2(g) \rightarrow 5CO_2(g) + 6H_2O(g) + SO_2(g)$
Balance S: $C_5H_{12}S(l) + O_2(g) \rightarrow 5CO_2(g) + 6H_2O(g) + SO_2(g)$
Balance O: $C_5H_{12}S(l) + 9O_2(g) \rightarrow 5CO_2(g) + 6H_2O(g) + SO_2(g)$

4.94 (a) Skeletal reaction: $C_4H_6(g) + O_2(g) \rightarrow CO_2(g) + H_2O(g)$
Balance C: $C_4H_6(g) + O_2(g) \rightarrow 4CO_2(g) + H_2O(g)$
Balance H: $C_4H_6(g) + O_2(g) \rightarrow 4CO_2(g) + 3H_2O(g)$
Balance O: $C_4H_6(g) + 11/2\ O_2(g) \rightarrow 4CO_2(g) + 3H_2O(g)$
Clear fraction: $2C_4H_6(g) + 11\ O_2(g) \rightarrow 8CO_2(g) + 6H_2O(g)$

(b) Skeletal reaction: $C(s) + O_2(g) \rightarrow CO_2(g)$
Balanced reaction: $C(s) + O_2(g) \rightarrow CO_2(g)$

(c) Skeletal reaction: $CS_2(s) + O_2(g) \rightarrow CO_2(g) + SO_2(g)$
Balance C: $CS_2(s) + O_2(g) \rightarrow CO_2(g) + SO_2(g)$
Balance S: $CS_2(s) + O_2(g) \rightarrow CO_2(g) + 2SO_2(g)$
Balance O: $CS_2(s) + 3O_2(g) \rightarrow CO_2(g) + 2SO_2(g)$

(d) Skeletal reaction: $C_3H_8O(l) + O_2(g) \rightarrow CO_2(g) + H_2O(g)$
Balance C: $C_3H_8O(l) + O_2(g) \rightarrow 3CO_2(g) + H_2O(g)$
Balance H: $C_3H_8O(l) + O_2(g) \rightarrow 3CO_2(g) + 4H_2O(g)$
Balance O: $C_3H_8O(l) + 9/2\ O_2(g) \rightarrow 3CO_2(g) + 4H_2O(g)$
Clear fraction: $2C_3H_8O(l) + 9O_2(g) \rightarrow 6CO_2(g) + 8H_2O(g)$

Cumulative Problems

4.95 **Given:** In 100 g solution, 20.0 g $C_2H_6O_2$; density of solution = 1.03 g/mL **Find:** M of solution
Conceptual Plan: **g $C_2H_6O_2$ → mol $C_2H_6O_2$ and g solution → mL solution → L solution**

$$\frac{1\ \text{mol}\ C_2H_6O_2}{62.06\ \text{g}\ C_2H_6O_2} \qquad \frac{1.00\ \text{mL}}{1.03\ \text{g}} \qquad \frac{1\ \text{L}}{1000\ \text{mL}}$$

then M $C_2H_6O_2$

$$M = \frac{\text{mol}\ C_2H_6O_2}{\text{L solution}}$$

Solution:

$$20.0\ \text{g}\ C_2H_6O_2 \times \frac{1\ \text{mol}\ C_2H_6O_2}{62.06\ \text{g}\ C_2H_6O_2} = 0.3222\ \text{mol}\ C_2H_6O_2$$

$$100.0\ \text{g solution} \times \frac{1.00\ \text{mL solution}}{1.03\ \text{g solution}} \times \frac{1\ \text{L}}{1000\ \text{mL}} = 0.09708\ \text{L}$$

$$M = \frac{0.3222\ \text{mol}\ C_2H_6O_2}{0.09708\ \text{L}} = 3.32\ M$$

Check: The units of the answer (M $C_2H_6O_2$) are correct. The magnitude of the answer is reasonable since the concentration of solutions is usually between 0 and 18 M.

4.96 **Given:** 1.35 M NaCl; density of solution = 1.05 g /mL **Find:** % NaCl by mass
Conceptual Plan: **mol NaCl → g NaCl and L solution → mL solution → g solution then % NaCl**

$$\frac{58.45\ \text{g NaCl}}{1\ \text{mol NaCl}} \qquad \frac{1000\ \text{mL}}{1\ \text{L}} \qquad \frac{1.05\ \text{g}}{1.00\ \text{mL}} \qquad \frac{\text{g NaCl}}{\text{g solution}} \times 100$$

Solution: $1.35\ M = \dfrac{1.35\ \text{mol NaCl}}{1\ \text{L solution}}$

$1.35 \text{ mol NaCl} \times \frac{58.45 \text{ g NaCl}}{1 \text{ mol NaCl}} = 78.91 \text{ g NaCl}$ $1 \text{ L solution} \times \frac{1000 \text{ mL}}{\text{L}} \times \frac{1.05 \text{ g solution}}{\text{mL solution}} = 1050 \text{ g solution}$

$\frac{78.91 \text{ g NaCl}}{1050 \text{ g solution}} \times 100 = 7.52\ \%\ \text{NaCl}$

Check: The units of the answer (% NaCl) are correct. The magnitude of the answer is reasonable for the concentration of the solution.

4.97 **Given:** 2.5 g $NaHCO_3$ **Find:** g HCl

Conceptual Plan: g $NaHCO_3$ → mol $NaHCO_3$ → mol HCl → g HCl

$\frac{1 \text{ mol } NaHCO_3}{84.02 \text{ g } NaHCO_3}$ $\frac{1 \text{ mol HCl}}{1 \text{ mol } NaHCO_3}$ $\frac{36.46 \text{ g HCl}}{1 \text{ mol HCl}}$

Solution: $HCl(aq) + NaHCO_3(aq) \rightarrow H_2O(l) + CO_2(g) + NaCl(aq)$

$$2.5 \text{ g } NaHCO_3 \times \frac{1 \text{ mol } NaHCO_3}{84.02 \text{ g } NaHCO_3} \times \frac{1 \text{ mol HCl}}{1 \text{ mol } NaHCO_3} \times \frac{36.46 \text{ g HCl}}{1 \text{ mol HCl}} = 1.1 \text{ g HCl}$$

Check: The units of the answer (g HCl) are correct. The magnitude of the answer is reasonable since the molar mass of HCl is less than the molar mass of $NaHCO_3$.

4.98 **Given:** 3.8 g HCl **Find:** g $CaCO_3$

Conceptual Plan: g HCl → mol HCl → mol $CaCO_3$ → g $CaCO_3$

$\frac{1 \text{ mol HCl}}{36.46 \text{ g HCl}}$ $\frac{1 \text{ mol } CaCO_3}{2 \text{ mol HCl}}$ $\frac{100.09 \text{ g } CaCO_3}{1 \text{ mol } CaCO_3}$

Solution: $2\ HCl(aq) + CaCO_3(s) \rightarrow H_2O(l) + CO_2(g) + CaCl_2(aq)$

$$3.8 \text{ g HCl} \times \frac{\text{mol HCl}}{36.46 \text{ g HCl}} \times \frac{1 \text{ mol } CaCO_3}{2 \text{ mol HCl}} \times \frac{100.09 \text{ g } CaCO_3}{\text{mol } CaCO_3} = 5.2 \text{ g } CaCO_3$$

Check: The units of the answer (g $CaCO_3$) are correct. The magnitude of the answer is reasonable since the molar mass of $CaCO_3$ is greater than the molar mass of HCl.

4.99 **Given:** 1.0 kg C_8H_{18} **Find:** kg CO_2

Conceptual Plan: kg C_8H_{18} → g C_8H_{18} → mol C_8H_{18} → mol CO_2 → g CO_2 → kg CO_2

$\frac{1000 \text{ g}}{\text{kg}}$ $\frac{1 \text{ mol } C_8H_{18}}{114.22 \text{ g } C_8H_{18}}$ $\frac{16 \text{ mol } CO_2}{2 \text{ mol } C_8H_{18}}$ $\frac{44.01 \text{ g } CO_2}{1 \text{ mol } CO_2}$ $\frac{\text{kg}}{1000 \text{ g}}$

Solution: $2\ C_8H_{18}(g) + 25\ O_2(g) \rightarrow 16\ CO_2(g) + 18\ H_2O(g)$

$$1.0 \text{ kg } C_8H_{18} \times \frac{1000 \text{ g}}{\text{kg}} \times \frac{1 \text{ mol } C_8H_{18}}{114.22 \text{ g } C_8H_{18}} \times \frac{16 \text{ mol } CO_2}{2 \text{ mol } C_8H_{18}} \times \frac{44.01 \text{ g } CO_2}{1 \text{ mol } CO_2} \times \frac{\text{kg}}{1000 \text{ g}} = 3.1 \text{ kg } CO_2$$

Check: The units of the answer (kg CO_2) are correct. The magnitude of the answer is reasonable since the ratio of CO_2 to C_8H_{18} is 8:1.

4.100 **Given:** 18.9 L C_3H_8, d = 0.621 g/mL **Find:** kg CO_2

Conceptual Plan: L C_3H_8 → mL C_3H_8 → g C_3H_8 → mol C_3H_8 → mol CO_2 → g CO_2 → kg CO_2

$\frac{1000 \text{ mL}}{\text{L}}$ $\frac{0.621 \text{ g}}{\text{mL}}$ $\frac{1 \text{ mol } C_3H_8}{44.09 \text{ g } C_3H_8}$ $\frac{3 \text{ mol } CO_2}{1 \text{ mol } C_3H_8}$ $\frac{44.01 \text{ g } CO_2}{1 \text{ mol } CO_2}$ $\frac{\text{kg}}{1000 \text{ g}}$

Solution: $C_3H_8(g) + 5\ O_2(g) \rightarrow 3\ CO_2(g) + 4\ H_2O(g)$

$$18.9 \text{ L } C_3H_8 \times \frac{1000 \text{ mL}}{\text{L}} \times \frac{0.621 \text{ g}}{\text{mL}} \times \frac{1 \text{ mol } C_3H_8}{44.09 \text{ g } C_3H_8} \times \frac{3 \text{ mol } CO_2}{1 \text{ mol } C_3H_8} \times \frac{44.01 \text{ g } CO_2}{\text{mol } CO_2} \times \frac{\text{kg}}{1000 \text{ g}}$$

$= 35.1 \text{ kg } CO_2$

Check: The units of the answer (kg CO_2) are correct. The magnitude of the answer is reasonable since the molar mass of CO_2 and C_3H_8 are close and there is a mole ratio of 1:3.

4.101 **Given:** 3.00 mL $C_4H_6O_3$, d = 1.08 g/mL; 1.25 g $C_7H_6O_3$; 1.22 g $C_9H_8O_4$ **Find:** limiting reactant, theoretical yield $C_9H_8O_4$ and % yield $C_9H_8O_4$

Conceptual Plan: **mL $C_4H_6O_3$ → g $C_4H_6O_3$ → mol $C_4H_6O_3$ → mol $C_9H_8O_4$**

$$\frac{1.08 \text{ g } C_4H_6O_3}{1.00 \text{ mL } C_4H_6O_3} \quad \frac{1 \text{ mol } C_4H_6O_3}{102.09 \text{ g } C_4H_6O_3} \quad \frac{1 \text{ mol } C_9H_8O_4}{1 \text{ mol } C_4H_6O_3}$$

→ smallest amount determines limiting reactant

g $C_7H_6O_3$ → mol $C_7H_6O_3$ → mol $C_9H_8O_4$

$$\frac{1 \text{ mol } C_7H_6O_3}{138.12 \text{ g } C_7H_6O_3} \quad \frac{1 \text{ mol } C_9H_8O_4}{1 \text{ mol } C_7H_6O_3}$$

then: mol $C_9H_8O_4$ → g $C_9H_8O_4$

$$\frac{180.1 \text{ g } C_9H_8O_4}{\text{mol } C_9H_8O_4}$$

then: determine % yield

$$\frac{\text{actual yield g } C_9H_8O_4}{\text{theoretical yield g } C_9H_8O_4} \times 100$$

Solution:

$$3.00 \text{ mL } C_4H_6O_3 \times \frac{1.08 \text{ g } C_4H_6O_3}{\text{mL } C_4H_6O_3} \times \frac{1 \text{ mol } C_4H_6O_3}{102.09 \text{ g } C_4H_6O_3} \times \frac{1 \text{ mol } C_9H_8O_4}{1 \text{ mol } C_4H_6O_3} = 0.03174 \text{ mol } C_9H_8O_4$$

$$1.25 \text{ g } C_7H_6O_3 \times \frac{1 \text{ mol } C_7H_6O_3}{138.12 \text{ g } C_7H_6O_3} \times \frac{1 \text{ mol } C_9H_8O_4}{1 \text{ mol } C_7H_6O_3} = 0.009050 \text{ mol } C_9H_8O_4$$

Salicylic acid is the limiting reactant.

$$0.009050 \text{ mol } C_9H_8O_4 \times \frac{180.1 \text{ g } C_9H_8O_4}{1 \text{ mol } C_9H_8O_4} = 1.630 \text{ g } C_9H_8O_4$$

$$\frac{1.22 \text{ g } C_9H_8O_4}{1.630 \text{ g } C_9H_8O_4} \times 100 = 74.8\%$$

Check: The theoretical yield has the correct units (g $C_9H_8O_4$) and has a reasonable magnitude compared to the mass of $C_7H_6O_3$, the limiting reactant. The % yield is reasonable, under 100%.

4.102 **Given:** 4.62 mL C_2H_5OH, d = 0.789 g/mL; 15.55 g O_2; 3.72 mL H_2O, d = 1.00g/mL
Find: limiting reactant, theoretical yield H_2O and % yield H_2O

Conceptual Plan: **mL C_2H_5OH → g C_2H_5OH → mol C_2H_5OH → mol H_2O**

$$\frac{0.789 \text{ g } C_2H_5OH}{1.00 \text{ mL } C_2H_5OH} \quad \frac{1 \text{ mol } C_2H_5OH}{46.07 \text{ g } C_2H_5OH} \quad \frac{3 \text{ mol } H_2O}{1 \text{ mol } C_2H_5OH}$$

→ smallest amount determines limiting reactant

g O_2 → mol O_2 → mol H_2O

$$\frac{1 \text{ mol } O_2}{32.00 \text{ g } O_2} \quad \frac{3 \text{ mol } H_2O}{3 \text{ mol } O_2}$$

then: mol H_2O → g H_2O

$$\frac{18.02 \text{ g } H_2O}{\text{mol } H_2O}$$

then: determine % yield

$$\frac{\text{actual yield g } C_9H_8O_4}{\text{theoretical yield g } C_9H_8O_4} \times 100$$

Solution:

$$C_2H_5OH(l) + 3\ O_2(g) \rightarrow 2\ CO_2(g) + 3\ H_2O(l)$$

$$4.62 \text{ mL } C_2H_5OH \times \frac{0.789 \text{ g } C_2H_5OH}{\text{mL } C_2H_5OH} \times \frac{1 \text{ mol } C_2H_5OH}{46.07 \text{ g } C_2H_5OH} \times \frac{3 \text{ mol } H_2O}{1 \text{ mol } C_2H_5OH} = 0.2374 \text{ mol } H_2O$$

C_2H_5OH is the limiting reactant.

$$15.55 \text{ g } O_2 \times \frac{1 \text{ mol } O_2}{32.00 \text{ g } O_2} \times \frac{1 \text{ mol } H_2O}{1 \text{ mol } O_2} = 0.48593 \text{ mol } H_2O$$

$$0.2374 \text{ mol } O_2 \times \frac{18.02 \text{ g } H_2O}{1 \text{ mol } O_2} = 4.278 \text{ g } H_2O$$

$$\frac{3.72 \text{ g } H_2O}{4.278 \text{ g } H_2O} \times 100 = 87.0\%$$

Check: The theoretical yield has the correct units (g H_2O) and has a reasonable magnitude compared to the mass of C_2H_5OH, the limiting reactant. The % yield is reasonable, under 100%.

4.103 **Given:** (a) 11 molecules H_2, 2 molecules O_2; (b) 8 molecules H_2, 4 molecules O_2; (c) 4 molecules H_2, 5 molecules O_2; (d) 3 molecules H_2, 6 molecules O_2 **Find:** loudest explosion based on equation
Conceptual Plan: loudest explosion will occur in the balloon with the mol ratio closest to the balanced equation and that contains the most H_2
Solution: $2H_2(g) + O_2(g) \rightarrow H_2O(l)$
Balloon (a) has enough O_2 to react with 4 molecules H_2; balloon (b) has enough O_2 to react with 8 molecules H_2; balloon (c) has enough O_2 to react with 10 molecules H_2; and balloon (d) has enough O_2 for 3 molecules of H_2 to react. Therefore, balloon (b) will have the loudest explosion because it has the most H_2 that will react.
Check: Answer seems correct since it has the most H_2 with enough O_2 in the balloon to completely react.

4.104 **Given:** Beaker containing 4 ions H^+, 4 ions Cl^- **Find:** which NaOH beaker will just neutralize HCl beaker
Conceptual Plan: molecules H^+ $\rightarrow$ molecules OH^- then compare to four beakers.

$$\frac{1 \text{ ion OH}^-}{1 \text{ ion H}^+}$$

Solution: $HCl(aq) + NaOH(aq) \rightarrow NaCl(aq) + H_2O(l)$
Net Ionic: $H^+(aq) + OH^-(aq) \rightarrow H_2O(l)$

$$4 \cancel{\text{ions H}^+} \times \frac{1 \text{ ion OH}^-}{1 \cancel{\text{ion H}^+}} = 4 \text{ ions OH}^-$$

Beaker (a) contains 2 ions OH^-; beaker (b) contains 4 ions OH^-;
beaker (c) contains 5 ions OH^-; beaker (d) contains 8 ions OH^-.
Beaker (b) will completely neutralize the HCl beaker with no excess.
Check: The answer is correct because it will completely neutralize the H^+ with no excess OH^-.

4.105	(a)	Skeletal reaction:	$HCl(aq) + Hg_2(NO_3)_2(aq) \rightarrow Hg_2Cl_2(s) + HNO_3(aq)$
		Balance Cl:	$2HCl(aq) + Hg_2(NO_3)_2(aq) \rightarrow Hg_2Cl_2(s) + 2HNO_3(aq)$
	(b)	Skeletal reaction:	$KHSO_3(aq) + HNO_3(aq) \rightarrow H_2O(l) + SO_2(g) + KNO_3(aq)$
		Balanced reaction:	$KHSO_3(aq) + HNO_3(aq) \rightarrow H_2O(l) + SO_2(g) + KNO_3(aq)$
	(c)	Skeletal reaction:	$NH_4Cl(aq) + Pb(NO_3)_2(aq) \rightarrow PbCl_2(s) + NH_4NO_3(aq)$
		Balance Cl:	$2NH_4Cl(aq) + Pb(NO_3)_2(aq) \rightarrow PbCl_2(s) + NH_4NO_3(aq)$
		Balance N:	$2NH_4Cl(aq) + Pb(NO_3)_2(aq) \rightarrow PbCl_2(s) + 2NH_4NO_3(aq)$
	(d)	Skeletal reaction:	$NH_4Cl(aq) + Ca(OH)_2(aq) \rightarrow NH_3(g) + H_2O(l) + CaCl_2(aq)$
		Balance Cl:	$2NH_4Cl(aq) + Ca(OH)_2(aq) \rightarrow NH_3(g) + H_2O(l) + CaCl_2(aq)$
		Balance N:	$2NH_4Cl(aq) + Ca(OH)_2(aq) \rightarrow 2NH_3(g) + H_2O(l) + CaCl_2(aq)$
		Balance H:	$2NH_4Cl(aq) + Ca(OH)_2(aq) \rightarrow 2NH_3(g) + 2H_2O(l) + CaCl_2(aq)$

4.106	(a)	Skeletal reaction:	$H_2SO_4(aq) + HNO_3(aq) \rightarrow$ No Reaction
	(b)	Skeletal reaction:	$Cr(NO_3)_3(aq) + LiOH(aq) \rightarrow Cr(OH)_3(s) + LiNO_3(aq)$
		Balance OH:	$Cr(NO_3)_3(aq) + 3LiOH(aq) \rightarrow Cr(OH)_3(s) + LiNO_3(aq)$
		Balance Li:	$Cr(NO_3)_3(aq) + 3LiOH(aq) \rightarrow Cr(OH)_3(s) + 3LiNO_3(aq)$
	(c)	Skeletal reaction:	$C_5H_{12}O(l) + O_2(g) \rightarrow CO_2(g) + H_2O(g)$
		Balance C:	$C_5H_{12}O(l) + O_2(g) \rightarrow 5CO_2(g) + H_2O(g)$
		Balance H:	$C_5H_{12}O(l) + O_2(g) \rightarrow 5CO_2(g) + 6H_2O(g)$
		Balance O:	$C_5H_{12}O(l) + 15/2\ O_2(g) \rightarrow 5CO_2(g) + 6H_2O(g)$
		Clear fraction:	$2C_5H_{12}O(l) + 15O_2(g) \rightarrow 10CO_2(g) + 12H_2O(g)$
	(d)	Skeletal reaction:	$SrS(aq) + CuSO_4(aq) \rightarrow SrSO_4(s) + CuS(s)$
		Balanced reaction:	$SrS(aq) + CuSO_4(aq) \rightarrow SrSO_4(s) + CuS(s)$

4.107 **Given:** 1.5 L solution, 0.050 M $CaCl_2$, 0.085 M $Mg(NO_3)_2$ **Find:** g Na_3PO_4
Conceptual Plan: V,M $CaCl_2$ $\rightarrow$ mol $CaCl_2$ and V,M $Mg(NO_3)_2$ $\rightarrow$ mol $Mg(NO_3)_2$

$$V \times M = \text{mol} \qquad\qquad V \times M = \text{mol}$$

then (mol $CaCl_2$ + mol $Mg(NO_3)_2$) → Na_3PO_4 → g Na_3PO_4

$$\frac{2\text{ mol }Na_3PO_4}{3\text{ mol }(CaCl_2 + Mg(NO_3)_2)} \qquad \frac{163.97\text{ g }Na_3PO_4}{1\text{ mol }Na_3PO_4}$$

Solution: $3CaCl_2(aq) + 2Na_3PO_4(aq) \rightarrow Ca_3(PO_4)_2(s) + 6\,NaCl(aq)$

$3\,Mg(NO_3)_2(aq) + 2Na_3PO_4(aq) \rightarrow Mg_3(PO_4)_2(s) + 6\,NaCl(aq)$

$1.5\text{ L} \times 0.050\text{ M }CaCl_2 = 0.07\underline{5}\text{ mol }CaCl_2$

$1.5\text{ L} \times 0.085\text{ M }Mg(NO_3)_2 = 0.1\underline{2}75\text{ mol }Mg(NO_3)_2$

$$0.2\underline{0}25\ \cancel{\text{mol }CaCl_2\text{ and }Mg(NO_3)_2} \times \frac{2\ \cancel{\text{mol }Na_3PO_4}}{3\text{ mol }\cancel{CaCl_2\text{ and }Mg(NO_3)_2}} \times \frac{163.97\text{ g mol }Na_3PO_4}{\cancel{\text{mol }Na_3PO_4}} = 22\text{ g mol }Na_3PO_4$$

Check: The units of the answer (g Na_3PO_4) are correct. The magnitude of the answer is reasonable since it is needed to remove both the Ca and Mg ions.

4.108 **Given:** 500.0 mL 0.100 M HCl and 0.200 M H_2SO_4; 0.150 M KOH **Find:** volume KOH to neutralize the acid
Conceptual Plan:
mL → L, then VM(HCl) → mol HCl → mol H^+ and VM(H_2SO_4) → mol H_2SO_4 → mol H^+

$$\frac{1\text{ L}}{1000\text{ mL}} \qquad V \times M = \text{mol} \qquad \frac{\text{mol }H^+}{\text{mol HCl}} \qquad V \times M = \text{mol} \qquad \frac{2\text{ mol }H^+}{\text{mol }H_2SO_4}$$

Total mol H^+ → mol OH^- → mol KOH → volume KOH

$$\frac{\text{mol }OH^-}{\text{mol }H^+} \qquad \frac{\text{mol KOH}}{\text{mol }OH^-} \qquad V = \frac{\text{mol KOH}}{\text{M KOH}}$$

Solution: $500.0\ \cancel{\text{mL}} \times \frac{1\ \cancel{\text{L}}}{1000\ \cancel{\text{mL}}} \times \frac{0.100\ \cancel{\text{mol HCl}}}{1\ \cancel{\text{L}}} \times \frac{1\text{ mol }H^+}{1\ \cancel{\text{mol HCl}}} = 0.050\underline{0}0\text{ mol }H^+$

$$500.0\ \cancel{\text{mL}} \times \frac{1\ \cancel{\text{L}}}{1000\ \cancel{\text{mL}}} \times \frac{0.200\ \cancel{\text{mol }H_2SO_4}}{1\ \cancel{\text{L}}} \times \frac{2\text{ mol }H^+}{1\ \cancel{\text{mol }H_2SO_4}} = 0.20\underline{0}0\text{ mol }H^+$$

$$(0.20\underline{0}0 + 0.050\underline{0}0)\text{ mol }H^+ \times \frac{1\ \cancel{\text{mol }OH^-}}{1\ \cancel{\text{mol }H^+}} \times \frac{1\ \cancel{\text{mol KOH}}}{1\ \cancel{\text{mol }OH^-}} \times \frac{1\text{ L solution}}{0.150\ \cancel{\text{mol KOH}}} = 1.67\text{ L KOH solution}$$

Check: The units of the answer (L KOH) are correct. The magnitude of the answer is reasonable because the average concentration of acid is greater than the concentration of base.

4.109 **Given:** 1.0 L, 0.10 M OH^- **Find:** g Ba
Conceptual Plan: VM → mol OH^- → mol $Ba(OH)_2$ → mol BaO → mol Ba → g Ba

$$V \times M = \text{mol} \qquad \frac{1\text{ mol }Ba(OH)_2}{2\text{ mol OH}} \qquad \frac{1\text{ mol BaO}}{1\text{ mol }Ba(OH)_2} \qquad \frac{1\text{ mol Ba}}{1\text{ mol BaO}} \qquad \frac{137.3\text{ g Ba}}{1\text{ mol Ba}}$$

Solution: $BaO(s) + H_2O(l) \rightarrow Ba(OH)_2(aq)$

$$1.0\ \cancel{\text{L}} \times \frac{0.10\ \cancel{\text{mol }OH^-}}{\cancel{\text{L}}} \times \frac{1\ \cancel{\text{mol }Ba(OH)_2}}{2\ \cancel{\text{mol }OH^-}} \times \frac{1\ \cancel{\text{mol BaO}}}{1\ \cancel{\text{mol }Ba(OH)_2}} \times \frac{1\ \cancel{\text{mol Ba}}}{1\ \cancel{\text{mol BaO}}} \times \frac{137.3\text{ g Ba}}{1\text{ mol Ba}} = 6.9\text{ g Ba}$$

Check: The units of the answer (g Ba) are correct. The magnitude is reasonable since the molar mass of Ba is large and there are 2 moles hydroxide per mole Ba.

4.110 **Given:** 1.00 L, 1.51 M NaF; 49.6 g sample; mixture Cr^{3+} and Mg^{2+} **Find:** g Cr^{3+}
Conceptual Plan: V,M NaF → mol NaF → mol F^- and let x = mol CrF_3 and y = mol MgF_2 → mol F

$$V \times M = \text{mol} \qquad \frac{1\text{ mol }F^-}{1\text{ mol NaF}} \qquad \frac{3\text{ mol F}}{\text{mol }CrF_3} \quad \frac{2\text{ mol F}}{\text{mol }MgF_2}$$

and → g sample then solve for x = mol CrF_3 → mol Cr^{3+} → g Cr^{3+}

$$x\text{ (molar mass }CrF_3) = \text{g }CrF_3 \quad y\text{ (molar mass }MgF_2) = \text{g }MgF_2 \qquad \frac{1\text{ mol }Cr^{3+}}{1\text{ mol }CrF_3} \qquad \frac{52.00\text{ g }Cr^{3+}}{1\text{ mol }Cr^{3+}}$$

Solution: $1.00\ \cancel{\text{L}} \times \frac{1.51\ \cancel{\text{mol NaF}}}{\cancel{\text{L}}} \times \frac{1\text{ mol }F^-}{1\ \cancel{\text{mol NaF}}} = 1.51\text{ mol }F^-$

Let x = mol CrF_3 and y = mol MgF_2;

3x = mol F^- from CrF_3 ; 2y = mol F^- from MgF_2

$3x + 2y = 1.51\text{ mol }F^-$

$2y = 1.51 - 3x$

$y = 0.755 - 3/2x$

$$x \text{ mol CrF}_3 \times \frac{109.00 \text{ g CrF}_3}{\text{mol CrF}_3} = \text{g CrF}_3$$

$$y \text{ mol MgF}_2 \times \frac{62.30 \text{ g MgF}_2}{\text{mol MgF}_2} = \text{g MgF}_2$$

$$x(109.00) + y(62.30) = 49.6 \text{ g sample}$$

$$y = 0.755 - \frac{3}{2x}$$

Solve simultaneous equations by substituting for y: x = 0.16$\underline{4}$8 = mol CrF_3

$$0.16\underline{4}8 \text{ mol CrF}_3 \times \frac{1 \text{ mol Cr}^{3+}}{1 \text{ mol CrF}_3} \times \frac{52.00 \text{ g Cr}^{3+}}{1 \text{ mol Cr}^{3+}} = 8.57 \text{ g Cr}^{3+}$$

Check: Units of answer (g Cr^{3+}) are correct. The magnitude of the answer is reasonable since it is less than the mass of the sample.

4.111 **Given:** 30.0% $NaNO_3$, \$9.00/ 100 lb; 20.0 % $(NH_4)_2SO_4$, \$8.10/ 100 lb **Find:** cost / lb N
Conceptual Plan: mass fertilizer → mass $NaNO_3$ → mass N → cost/lb N

$$\frac{30.0 \text{ lb NaNO}_3}{100 \text{ lb fertilizer}} \quad \frac{16.48 \text{ lb N}}{100 \text{ lb NaNO}_3} \quad \frac{\$9.00}{100 \text{ lb fertilizer}}$$

and: mass fertilizer → mass $(NH_4)_2SO_4$ → mass N → cost/lb N

$$\frac{20.0 \text{ lb (NH}_4)_2\text{SO}_4}{100 \text{ lb fertilizer}} \quad \frac{21.2 \text{ lb N}}{100 \text{ lb (NH}_4)_2\text{SO}_4} \quad \frac{\$8.10}{100 \text{ lb fertilizer}}$$

Solution:

$$100 \text{ lb fertilizer} \times \frac{30.0 \text{ lb NaNO}_3}{100 \text{ lb fertilizer}} \times \frac{16.48 \text{ lb N}}{100 \text{ lb NaNO}_3} = 4.9\underline{4}4 \text{ lb N}$$

$$\frac{\$9.00}{100 \text{ lb fertilizer}} \times \frac{100 \text{ lb fertilizer}}{4.9\underline{4}4 \text{ lb N}} = \$1.82/\text{ lb N}$$

$$100 \text{ lb fertilizer} \times \frac{20.0 \text{ lb (NH}_4)_2\text{SO}_4}{100 \text{ lb fertilizer}} \times \frac{21.2 \text{ lb N}}{100 \text{ lb (NH}_4)_2\text{SO}_4} = 4.2\underline{4}0 \text{ lb N}$$

$$\frac{\$8.10}{100 \text{ lb fertilizer}} \times \frac{100 \text{ lb fertilizer}}{4.2\underline{4} \text{ lb N}} = \$1.91/\text{ lb N}$$

The more economical fertilizer is the $NaNO_3$ because it costs less/ lb N.

Check: The units of the cost (\$/lb N) are correct. The answer is reasonable because you compare the cost/lb N directly.

4.112 **Given:** 0.110 M HCl; 1.52 g $Al(OH)_3$ **Find:** volume HCl needed to neutralize
Conceptual Plan: g $Al(OH)_3$ → mol $Al(OH)_3$ → mol HCl → vol HCL

$$\frac{\text{mol Al(OH)}_3}{78.00 \text{ g Al(OH)}_3} \quad \frac{3 \text{ mol HCl}}{1 \text{ mol Al(OH)}_3} \quad \frac{\text{mol HCl}}{\text{M HCl}}$$

Solution: 3 HCl(*aq*) + $Al(OH)_3$(*aq*) → 3 H_2O(*l*) + $AlCl_3$(*aq*)

$$1.52 \text{ g Al(OH)}_3 \times \frac{1 \text{ mol Al(OH)}_3}{78.00 \text{ g Al(OH)}_3} \times \frac{3 \text{ mol HCl}}{1 \text{ mol Al(OH)}_3} \times \frac{1 \text{ L}}{0.110 \text{ mol HCl}} = 0.531 \text{ L HCl}$$

Check: Units of the answer (L HCl) are correct. The magnitude of the answer is reasonable since the mole ratio of HCl to $Al(OH)_3$ is 3:1.

4.113 **Given:** 24.5 g Au, 24.5 g BrF_3, 24.5 g KF **Find:** g $KAuF_4$
Conceptual Plan: g Au → mol Au → mol $KAuF_4$

$$\frac{1 \text{ mol Au}}{196.97 \text{ g Au}} \quad \frac{2 \text{ mol KAuF}_4}{2 \text{ mol Au}}$$

g BrF_3 → mol BrF_3 → mol $KAuF_4$ **→ smallest mol amount determines limiting reactant**

$$\frac{1 \text{ mol BrF}_3}{136.9 \text{ g BrF}_3} \quad \frac{2 \text{ mol KAuF}_4}{2 \text{ mol BrF}_3}$$

g KF → mol KF → mol $KAuF_4$

$$\frac{1 \text{ mol KF}}{58.10 \text{ g KF}} \quad \frac{2 \text{ mol KAuF}_4}{2 \text{ mol KF}}$$

then: mol $KAuF_4$ → g $KAuF_4$

$$\frac{312.07 \text{ g KAuF}_4}{\text{mol KAuF}_4}$$

$$2\,Au(s) + 2BrF_3(l) + 2KF(s) \rightarrow Br_2(l) + 2KAuF_4(s)$$

Oxidation states; 0 + 3– 1 +1 – 1 0 +1 +3 – 1

This is a redox reaction since Au increases in oxidation number (oxidation) and Br decreases in number (reduction). BrF_3 is the oxidizing agent, and Au is the reducing agent.

Solution:

$$24.5\ \text{g Au} \times \frac{1\ \text{mol Au}}{196.97\ \text{g Au}} \times \frac{2\ \text{mol KAuF}_4}{2\ \text{mol Au}} = 0.1244\ \text{mol KAuF}_4$$

$$24.5\ \text{g BrF}_3 \times \frac{1\ \text{mol BrF}_3}{136.90\ \text{g BrF}_3} \times \frac{2\ \text{mol KAuF}_4}{2\ \text{mol BrF}_3} = 0.1790\ \text{mol KAuF}$$

$$24.5\ \text{g KF} \times \frac{1\ \text{mol KF}}{58.10\ \text{g KF}} \times \frac{2\ \text{mol KAuF}_4}{2\ \text{mol KF}} = 0.4217\ \text{mol KAuF}_4$$

$$0.1244\ \text{mol KAuF}_4 \times \frac{312.07\ \text{g KAuF}_4}{1\ \text{mol KAuF}_4} = 38.8\ \text{g KAuF}_4$$

Check: Units of the answer (g $KAuF_4$) are correct. The magnitude of the answer is reasonable compared to the mass of the limiting reactant Au.

4.114 **Given:** 0.10 L, 0.12 M NaCl; 0.23 L, 0.18 M $MgCl_2$; 0.20 M $AgNO_3$ **Find:** volume $AgNO_3$ to precipitate all the Cl^-

Conceptual Plan: VM(NaCl) → mol NaCl → mol Cl^- and VM($MgCl_2$) → mol $MgCl_2$ → mol Cl^-

vol x M = mol; $\frac{1 \text{ mol Cl}^-}{1 \text{ mol NaCl}}$; vol x M = mol; $\frac{2 \text{ mol Cl}^-}{1 \text{ mol MgCl}_2}$

Then: total mol Cl^- → mol Ag^+ → mol $AgNO_3$ → vol $AgNO_3$

$\frac{1 \text{ mol Ag}^+}{1 \text{ mol Cl}^-}$; $\frac{1 \text{ mol AgNO}_3}{1 \text{ mol Ag}^+}$; $\frac{1 \text{ L AgNO}_3}{0.20 \text{ mol AgNO}_3}$

Solution:

$$0.10\ \text{L NaCl} \times \frac{0.12\ \text{mol NaCl}}{\text{L NaCl}} \times \frac{1\ \text{mol Cl}^-}{1\ \text{mol NaCl}} = 0.012\ \text{mol Cl}^-$$

$$0.23\ \text{L NaCl} \times \frac{0.18\ \text{mol MgCl}_2}{\text{L MgCl}_2} \times \frac{2\ \text{mol Cl}^-}{1\ \text{mol MgCl}_2} = 0.0828\ \text{mol Cl}^-$$

$$\text{Total Cl}^- = 0.012\ \text{mol Cl}^- + 0.0828\ \text{mol Cl}^- = 0.0948\ \text{mol Cl}^-$$

$$0.0948\ \text{mol Cl}^- \times \frac{1\ \text{mol Ag}^+}{1\ \text{mol Cl}^-} \times \frac{1\ \text{mol AgNO}_3}{1\ \text{mol Ag}^+} \times \frac{\text{L AgNO}_3}{0.20\ \text{mol AgNO}_3} = 0.47\ \text{L AgNO}_3$$

Check: Units of the answer (L $AgNO_3$) are correct. The magnitude of the answer is reasonable since the Cl^- comes from two sources.

4.115 **Given:** solution may contain Ag^+, Ca^{2+}, and Cu^{2+} **Find:** determine which ions are present

Conceptual Plan: test the solution sequentially with NaCl, Na_2SO_4, and Na_2CO_3 and see if precipitates form

Solution: Original solution + NaCl yields no reaction: Ag^+ is not present since chlorides are normally soluble, but Ag^+ is an exception.

Original solution with Na_2SO_4 yields a precipitate and solution 2. The precipitate is $CaSO_4$, so Ca^{2+} is present. Sulfates are normally soluble but Ca^{2+} is an exception.

Solution 2 with Na_2CO_3 yields a precipitate. The precipitate is $CuCO_3$, so Cu^{2+} is present. All carbonates are insoluble.

NET IONIC EQUATIONS:

$$Ca^{2+}(aq) + SO_4^{\,2-}(aq) \rightarrow CaSO_4(s)$$

$$Cu^{2+}(aq) + CO_3^{\,2-}(aq) \rightarrow CuCO_3(s)$$

Check: The answer is reasonable since two different precipitates formed and all the Ca^{2+} was removed before the carbonate was added.

4.116 **Given:** solution may contain $Hg_2^{\,2+}$, Ba^{2+}, and Fe^{2+} **Find:** determine which ions are present

Conceptual Plan: test the solution sequentially with KCl, K_2SO_4, and K_2CO_3 and see if precipitates form

Solution: Original solution + KCl yields a precipitate and solution 2: The precipitate is Hg_2Cl_2, so Hg_2^{2+} is present. Chlorides are normally soluble, but Hg_2^{2+} is an exception.
Solution 2 with K_2SO_4 yields no precipitate, so Ba^{2+} is not present. Sulfates are normally soluble, but Ba^{2+} is an exception.
Solution 2 with K_2CO_3 yields a precipitate. The precipitate is $FeCO_3$, so Fe^{2+} is present. All carbonates are insoluble.
NET IONIC EQUATIONS:

$$Hg_2^{2+}(aq) + 2Cl^-(aq) \rightarrow Hg_2Cl_2(s)$$
$$Fe^{2+}(aq) + CO_3^{2-}(aq) \rightarrow FeCO_3(s)$$

Check: The answer is reasonable since two different precipitates formed and all the Hg_2^{2+} was removed before the carbonate was added.

4.117 **Given:** 1.00 g NH_3 **Find:** g PH_3
Conceptual Plan: Determine reaction sequence, then g NH_3 → mol NH_3 → mol PH_3 → g PH_3

$$\frac{1\ \text{mol NH}_3}{17.04\ \text{g NH}_3} \qquad \frac{34.00\ \text{g PH}_3}{1\ \text{mol PH}_3}$$

Solution: Balance the reaction sequence:

$$6NH_3 + 71/2\ O_2 \rightarrow \cancel{6NO} + 9H_2O$$
$$\cancel{6NO} + P_4 \rightarrow \cancel{P_4O_6} + 3\ N_2$$
$$\cancel{P_4O_6} + 6H_2O \rightarrow \cancel{4H_3PO_3}$$
$$\cancel{4H_3PO_3} \rightarrow PH_3 + 3H_3PO_4$$

Therefore, 6 mol NH_3 produces 1 mol PH_3

$$1.00\ \cancel{\text{g NH}_3} \times \frac{1\ \cancel{\text{mol NH}_3}}{17.04\ \cancel{\text{g NH}_3}} \times \frac{1\ \cancel{\text{mol PH}_3}}{6\ \cancel{\text{mol NH}_3}} \times \frac{34.00\ \text{g PH}_3}{1\ \cancel{\text{mol PH}_3}} = 0.333\ \text{g PH}_3$$

Check: The answer is g PH_3, which is correct. The magnitude is reasonable. Even though the molar mass of PH_3 is greater than NH_3, 6 mol of NH_3 are required to produce 1 mol PH_3.

4.118 **Given:** 910 kg Fe **Find:** kg Fe_2O_3 and kg CO_2
Conceptual Plan: kg Fe → g Fe → mol Fe → mol Fe_2O_3 → g Fe_2O_3 → kg Fe_2O_3

$$\frac{1000\ \text{g Fe}}{\text{kg Fe}} \qquad \frac{1\ \text{mol Fe}}{55.85\ \text{g Fe}} \qquad \frac{1\ \text{mol Fe}_2\text{O}_3}{2\ \text{mol Fe}} \qquad \frac{159.70\ \text{g Fe}_2\text{O}_3}{1\ \text{mol Fe}_2\text{O}_3} \qquad \frac{1\ \text{kg Fe}_2\text{O}_3}{1000\ \text{g Fe}_2\text{O}_3}$$

and then mol Fe → mol CO_2 → g CO_2 → kg CO_2

$$\frac{3\ \text{mol CO}_2}{2\ \text{mol Fe}} \qquad \frac{44.01\ \text{g CO}_2}{1\ \text{mol CO}_2} \qquad \frac{1\ \text{kg CO}_2}{1000\ \text{g CO}_2}$$

Solution: Balanced Reaction: $Fe_2O_3 + 3CO \rightarrow 2Fe + 3CO_2$

$$910\ \cancel{\text{kg Fe}} \times \frac{1000\ \cancel{\text{g Fe}}}{1\ \cancel{\text{kg Fe}}} \times \frac{1\ \cancel{\text{mol Fe}}}{55.85\ \cancel{\text{g Fe}}} \times \frac{1\ \cancel{\text{mol Fe}_2\text{O}_3}}{2\ \cancel{\text{mol Fe}}} \times \frac{159.70\ \cancel{\text{g Fe}_2\text{O}_3}}{1\ \cancel{\text{mol Fe}_2\text{O}_3}} \times \frac{1\ \text{kg Fe}_2\text{O}_3}{1000\ \cancel{\text{g Fe}_2\text{O}_3}}$$

$$= 1.3\underline{0}1 \times 10^3\ \text{kg Fe}_2\text{O}_3 = 1.30 \times 10^3\ \text{kg Fe}_2\text{O}_3$$

$$910\ \cancel{\text{kg Fe}} \times \frac{1000\ \cancel{\text{g Fe}}}{1\ \cancel{\text{kg Fe}}} \times \frac{1\ \cancel{\text{mol Fe}}}{55.85\ \cancel{\text{g Fe}}} \times \frac{3\ \cancel{\text{mol CO}_2}}{2\ \cancel{\text{mol Fe}}} \times \frac{44.01\ \cancel{\text{g CO}_2}}{1\ \cancel{\text{mol CO}_2}} \times \frac{1\ \text{kg CO}_2}{1000\ \cancel{\text{g CO}_2}}$$

$$= 1.0\underline{7}5 \times 10^3\ \text{kg CO}_2 = 1.08 \times 10^3\ \text{kg CO}_2$$

Check: The answers (kg Fe_2O_3 and kg CO_2) are correct. The magnitudes are reasonable since the molar mass of Fe_2O_3 is greater than the molar mass of Fe and the mole of CO_2 is greater than the mole of Fe.

4.119 **Given:** 10.0 kg mixture, 30.35% hexane, 15.85% heptane, 53.80% octane **Find:** Total mass CO_2
Conceptual Plan: kg hexane → kmol hexane → kmol CO_2 → kg CO_2

$$\frac{1\ \text{kmol C}_6\text{H}_{14}}{86.20\ \text{kg C}_6\text{H}_{14}} \qquad \frac{12\ \text{kmol CO}_2}{2\ \text{kmol C}_6\text{H}_{14}} \qquad \frac{44.01\ \text{kg CO}_2}{1\ \text{kmol CO}_2}$$

kg heptane → kmol heptane → kmol CO_2 → kg CO_2

$$\frac{1\ \text{kmol C}_7\text{H}_{16}}{100.23\ \text{kg C}_7\text{H}_{16}} \qquad \frac{7\ \text{kmol CO}_2}{1\ \text{kmol C}_7\text{H}_{16}} \qquad \frac{44.01\ \text{kg CO}_2}{1\ \text{kmol CO}_2}$$

kg octane → kmol octane → kmol CO_2 → kg CO_2

$$\frac{1\ \text{kmol C}_8\text{H}_{18}}{114.26\ \text{kg C}_8\text{H}_{18}} \qquad \frac{16\ \text{kmol CO}_2}{2\ \text{kmol C}_8\text{H}_{18}} \qquad \frac{44.01\ \text{kg CO}_2}{1\ \text{kmol CO}_2}$$

Solution: Balanced Reactions:

$$2C_6H_{14}(l) + 19O_2(g) \rightarrow 12CO_2(g) + 14H_2O(l)$$
$$C_7H_{16}(l) + 11O_2(g) \rightarrow 7CO_2(g) + 8H_2O(l)$$
$$2C_8H_{18}(l) + 25O_2(g) \rightarrow 16CO_2(g) + 18H_2O(l)$$

$$10.0\ \cancel{\text{kg mix}} \times \frac{30.35\ \cancel{\text{kg } C_6H_{14}}}{100.0\ \cancel{\text{kg mix}}} \times \frac{1\ \cancel{\text{kmol } C_6H_{14}}}{86.20\ \cancel{\text{kg } C_6H_{14}}} \times \frac{12\ \cancel{\text{kmol } CO_2}}{2\ \cancel{\text{kmol } C_6H_{14}}} \times \frac{44.01\text{kg } CO_2}{1\cancel{\text{kmol } CO_2}} = 9.2\underline{9}7 \text{ kg } CO_2$$

$$10.0\ \cancel{\text{kg mix}} \times \frac{15.85\ \cancel{\text{kg } C_7H_{16}}}{100.0\ \cancel{\text{kg mix}}} \times \frac{1\ \cancel{\text{kmol } C_7H_{16}}}{100.23\ \cancel{\text{kg } C_7H_{16}}} \times \frac{7\ \cancel{\text{kmol } CO_2}}{1\ \cancel{\text{kmol } C_7H_{16}}} \times \frac{44.01\text{kg } CO_2}{1\cancel{\text{kmol } CO_2}} = 4.8\underline{7}1 \text{ kg } CO_2$$

$$10.0\ \cancel{\text{kg mix}} \times \frac{53.80\ \cancel{\text{kg } C_8H_{18}}}{100.0\ \cancel{\text{kg mix}}} \times \frac{1\ \cancel{\text{kmol } C_8H_{18}}}{114.26\ \cancel{\text{kg } C_8H_{18}}} \times \frac{16\ \cancel{\text{kmol } CO_2}}{2\ \cancel{\text{kmol } C_8H_{18}}} \times \frac{44.01\text{kg } CO_2}{1\cancel{\text{kmol } CO_2}} = 16.\underline{5}78 \text{ kg } CO_2$$

Total CO_2 = 9.30 kg + 4.87 kg + 16.6 kg = 30.8 kg CO_2

Check: The units of the answer (kg CO_2) are correct. The magnitude of the answer is reasonable since a large amount of CO_2 is produced per mole of hydrocarbon.

4.120 **Given:** 1.00 kg sand, 22.8% ilemite ($FeTiO_3$) **Find:** g Ti

Conceptual Plan: kg sand → g sand → g $FeTiO_3$ → mol $FeTiO_3$ → mol $TiCl_4$ → mol Ti → g Ti

$$\frac{1000 \text{ g sand}}{1 \text{ kg sand}} \quad \frac{22.8 \text{ g } FeTiO_3}{100 \text{ g sand}} \quad \frac{151.72 \text{ g } FeTiO_3}{1 \text{ mol } FeTiO_3} \quad \frac{0.908 \text{ mol } TiCl_4}{1 \text{ mol } FeTiO_3} \quad \frac{0.859 \text{ mol Ti}}{1 \text{ mol } TiCl_4} \quad \frac{47.87 \text{ g Ti}}{1 \text{ mol Ti}}$$

Solution: $$1.00\ \cancel{\text{kg sand}} \times \frac{1000\ \cancel{\text{g sand}}}{1\ \cancel{\text{kg sand}}} \times \frac{22.8\ \cancel{\text{g } FeTiO_3}}{100\ \cancel{\text{g sand}}} \times \frac{1\ \cancel{\text{mol } FeTiO_3}}{151.72\ \cancel{\text{g } FeTiO_3}} \times \frac{0.908\cancel{\text{mol } TiCl_4}}{1\cancel{\text{mol } FeTiO_3}} \times \frac{0.859\cancel{\text{mol Ti}}}{1\cancel{\text{mol } TiCl_4}}$$
$$\times \frac{47.87 \text{ g Ti}}{1\cancel{\text{mol Ti}}} = 56.\underline{1}09 \text{ g Ti} = 56.1 \text{ g Ti}$$

Check: The units of the answer (g Ti) are correct. The magnitude is reasonable since the % of ilemite in the sand is small.

Challenge Problems

4.121 **Given:** g C_3H_8 + C_2H_2 = 2.0 g; mol CO_2 = 1.5 mol H_2O **Find:** original g C_2H_2

Conceptual Plan: mol C_3H_8 → mol CO_2 and mol H_2O and mol C_2H_2 → mol CO_2 and mol H_2O

Solution: Let a = mol C_3H_8 and b = mol C_2H_2

$C_3H_8 + 5O_2 \rightarrow 3CO_2 + 4H_2O$ (a, 3a, 4a) $\quad$ $C_2H_2 + 3/2O_2 \rightarrow 2CO_2 + H_2O$ (b, 2b, b)

Total mol CO_2 = 3a + 2b and total mol H_2O = 4a + b

mol CO_2 = 1.5(mol H_2O)

So: 3a + 2b = 1.5(4a + b)

$$\text{And} \left(a\ \cancel{\text{mol } C_3H_8} \times \frac{44.11\ C_3H_8}{1\ \cancel{\text{mol } C_3H_8}}\right) + \left(b \text{ mol } C_2H_2 \times \frac{26.01\ C_2H_2}{\cancel{\text{mol } C_2H_2}}\right) = 2.0 \text{ g}$$

Solve simultaneous equations: a = $9.\underline{9}8 \times 10^{-3}$ mol C_3H_8 and b = $0.05\underline{9}9$ mol C_2H_2

Substitute for b and solve for grams C_2H_2.

$$0.06\underline{0} \text{ mol } C_2H_2 \times \frac{26.01\ C_2H_2}{\cancel{\text{mol } C_2H_2}} = 1.\underline{5}6 \text{ g } C_2H_2 = 1.6 \text{ g } C_2H_2$$

Check: The units of the answer (g C_2H_2) are correct. The magnitude is reasonable since it is less than the total mass.

4.122 **Given:** 20.6 g P; 79.4 g Cl_2 **Find:** g PCl_3

Conceptual Plan: g P → mol P

$$\frac{1 \text{ mol P}}{30.97 \text{ g P}}$$

g Cl_2 → mol Cl_2 →

$$\frac{1 \text{ mol } Cl_2}{70.90 \text{ g } Cl_2}$$

then: mol PCl_3 → g PCl_3

$$\frac{137.32 \text{ g } PCl_3}{1 \text{ mol } PCl_3}$$

Solution: $20.6 \text{ g P} \times \frac{1 \text{ mol P}}{30.97 \text{ g P}} = 0.6652 \text{ mol P}$

$79.4 \text{ g } Cl_2 \times \frac{1 \text{ mol } Cl_2}{70.90 \text{ g } Cl_2} \times \frac{2 \text{ mol Cl}}{1 \text{ mol } Cl_2} = 2.240 \text{ mol } Cl_2$

mol P = mol PCl_3 + mol PCl_5 and mol Cl = 3(mol PCl_3) + 5(mol PCl_5)

let x = mol PCl_3 therefore, 0.6652 − x = mol PCl_5

mol Cl = 3x + 5(0.6652 − x) = 2.240

3x + 3.326 − 5x = 2.240

x = 0.543 = mol PCl_3

0.6652 − x = 0.122 = mol PCl_5

$0.543 \text{ mol } PCl_3 \times \frac{137.32 \text{ g } PCl_3}{1 \text{ mol } PCl_3} = 74.56 \text{ g} = 74.6 \text{ g } PCl_3$

Check: The units of the answer (g PCl_3) are correct. The magnitude is reasonable since it is less than the total mass of P and Cl_2.

4.123 **Given:** 0.100L, 1.22M NaI; total mass = 28.1 g **Find:** g AgI

Conceptual Plan: vol, M → mol NaI → mol I^-; total mol I^- → mol AgI and HgI_2

Solution: $0.100 \text{ L soln} \times \frac{1.22 \text{ mol NaI}}{\text{L soln}} \times \frac{1 \text{ mol } I^-}{\text{mol NaI}} = 0.122 \text{ mol } I^-$

Let x = mol AgI and y = mol HgI_2

x + 2y = 0.122 mol I^- so y = 0.061 − 0.5x

$$\left(x \text{ mol AgI} \times \frac{234.77 \text{ g AgI}}{1 \text{ mol AgI}}\right) + \left(y \text{ mol } HgI_2 \times \frac{454.39 \text{ g } HgI_2}{\text{mol } HgI_2}\right) = 28.1 \text{ g}$$

Solve the simultaneous equations and x = 0.0504 mol AgI

$0.0504 \text{ mol AgI} \times \frac{234.77 \text{ g AgI}}{1 \text{ mol AgI}} = 11.8 \text{ g AgI}$

Check: The units of the answer (g AgI) are correct. The magnitude is reasonable since it is less than the total mass.

4.124 **Given:** 15.2 billion L lake water, 1.8×10^{-5} M H_2SO_4, 8.7×10^{-6} M HNO_3 **Find:** kg $CaCO_3$ needed to neutralize

Conceptual Plan: Vol lake → mol H_2SO_4 → mol H^+ and vol lake → mol HNO_3 → mol H^+

vol x M = mol; $\frac{2 \text{ mol } H^+}{1 \text{ mol } H_2SO_4}$; vol x M = mol; $\frac{1 \text{ mol } H^+}{1 \text{ mol } HNO_3}$

Then: total mol H^+ → mol CO_3^{2-} → mol $CaCO_3$ → g $CaCO_3$ → kg $CaCO_3$

$\frac{1 \text{ mol } CO_3^{2-}}{2 \text{ mol } H^+}$; $\frac{1 \text{ mol } CaCO_3}{1 \text{ mol } CO_3^{2-}}$; $\frac{100.09 \text{ g } CaCO_3}{1 \text{ mol } CaCO_3}$; $\frac{\text{kg}}{1000 \text{ g}}$

Solution: $2H^+(aq) + CO_3^{2-}(aq) \rightarrow H_2O(l) + CO_2(g)$

$15.2 \times 10^9 \text{ L} \times \frac{1.8 \times 10^{-5} \text{ mol } H_2SO_4}{\text{L soln}} \times \frac{2 \text{ mol } H^+}{\text{mol } H_2SO_4} = 547200 \text{ mol } H^+$

$15.2 \times 10^9 \text{ L} \times \frac{8.7 \times 10^{-6} \text{ mol } HNO_3}{\text{L soln}} \times \frac{1 \text{ mol } H^+}{\text{mol } HNO_3} = 132240 \text{ mol } H^+$

Total H^+ = 547200 mol H^+ + 132240 mol H^+ = 679440 mol H^+

$679440 \text{ mol } H^+ \times \frac{1 \text{ mol } CO_3^{2-}}{2 \text{ mol } H^+} \times \frac{1 \text{ mol } CaCO_3}{\text{mol } CO_3^{2-}} \times \frac{100.09 \text{ g } CaCO_3}{1 \text{ mol } CaCO_3} \times \frac{\text{kg}}{1000 \text{ g}} = 3.4 \times 10^4 \text{ kg } CaCO_3$

Check: The units of the answer (kg $CaCO_3$) are correct. The magnitude of the answer is reasonable based on the size of the lake.

4.125 **Given:** 3.5×10^{-3} M Ca^{2+}. 1.1×10^{-3} M Mg^{2+}, 19.5 gal H_2O; 0.65 kg detergent/load **Find:** % by mass Na_2CO_3

Conceptual Plan: gal H_2O → L H_2O then VM → mol Ca^{2+} and VM → mol Mg^{2+}

$$\frac{3.785\text{ L}}{1\text{ gal}} \qquad \text{vol x M} = \text{mol} \qquad \text{vol x M} = \text{mol}$$

Then total moles ions → mol CO_3^{2-} → mol Na_2CO_3 → g Na_2CO_3 → kg Na_2CO_3 → % Na_2CO_3

$$\frac{1\text{ mol }CO_3^{2-}}{1\text{ mol ion}} \quad \frac{1\text{ mol }Na_2CO_3}{1\text{ mol }CO_3^{2-}} \quad \frac{106.01\text{ g }Na_2CO_3}{1\text{ mol }Na_2CO_3} \quad \frac{\text{kg}}{1000\text{ g}} \quad \frac{\text{kg }Na_2CO_3}{\text{kg detergent x 100}}$$

Solution: $$19.5\text{ gal} \times \frac{3.785\text{ L}}{1\text{ gal}} \times \frac{3.5 \times 10^{-3}\text{ mol }Ca^{2+}}{\text{L}} = 0.2\underline{5}8\text{ mol }Ca^{2+}$$

$$19.5\text{ gal} \times \frac{3.785\text{ L}}{1\text{ gal}} \times \frac{1.1 \times 10^{-3}\text{ mol }Mg^{2+}}{\text{L}} = 0.08\underline{1}19\text{ mol }Mg^{2+}$$

$$0.\underline{3}392\text{ mol ions} \times \frac{1\text{ mol }CO_3^{2-}}{\text{mol ions}} \times \frac{1\text{ mol }Na_2CO_3}{\text{mol }CO_3^{2-}} \times \frac{106.01\text{ g }Na_2CO_3}{1\text{ mol }Na_2CO_3} \times \frac{\text{kg }Na_2CO_3}{1000\text{ g }Na_2CO_3} = 0.03\underline{5}96\text{ kg }Na_2CO_3$$

$$\frac{0.03\underline{5}96\text{ kg }Na_2CO_3}{0.65\text{ kg detergent}} \times 100 = 5.5\ \%\ Na_2CO_3$$

Check: The units of the answer (% Na_2CO_3) are correct. The magnitude of the answer is reasonable. The percent is less than 100 %.

4.126 **Given:** 45 μg Pb/dL blood, Vol = 5.0 L, 1 mol succimer($C_4H_6O_4S_2$) = 1 mol Pb **Find:** mass $C_4H_6O_4S_2$ in mg

Conceptual Plan: Volume blood L → Volume blood dL → μg Pb → g Pb → mol Pb →

$$\frac{10\text{ dL}}{\text{L}} \quad \frac{45\ \mu\text{g}}{\text{dL}} \quad \frac{10^6\ \mu\text{g}}{\text{g}} \quad \frac{\text{mol Pb}}{207.2\text{ g Pb}} \quad \frac{1\text{ mol succimer}}{1\text{ mol Pb}}$$

mol succimer → g succimer → mg succimer

$$\frac{182.23\text{ g succimer}}{1\text{ mol succimer}} \quad \frac{1000\text{ mg succimer}}{1\text{ g succimer}}$$

Solution:

$$5.0\text{ L blood} \times \frac{10\text{ dL}}{\text{L}} \times \frac{45\ \mu\text{g}}{\text{dL}} \times \frac{1\text{ g}}{10^6\ \mu\text{g}} \times \frac{1\text{ mol Pb}}{207.2\text{ g}} \times \frac{1\text{ mol succimer}}{1\text{ mol Pb}} \times \frac{182.23\text{ g succimer}}{1\text{ mol succimer}} \times \frac{1000\text{ mg}}{\text{g}}$$

$$= 2.0\text{ mg succimer}$$

Check: The units of the answer (mg succimer) are correct. The magnitude is reasonable for the volume of blood and the concentration.

4.127 In designing the unit you would need to consider the theoretical yield and % yield of the reaction, how changing the limiting reactant would affect the reaction, and the stoichiometry between KO_2 and O_2 in order to determine the mass of KO_2 required to produce enough O_2 for 10 minutes. You might also consider the speed of the reaction and whether or not the reaction produced heat. Additionally, because your body does not use 100% of the oxygen taken in with each breath, the apparatus would only need to replenish the oxygen used. The percentage of oxygen in air is about 20% and the percentage in exhaled air is about 16%, so we will assume that 4% of the air would need to be replenished with oxygen. (NOTE: The problem can also be solved by finding the amount of KO_2 that would be required to react with all of the exhaled CO_2.)

Given: air = 4% O_2, volume = 5 – 8 L/ min, 1 mol gas = 22.4 L gas **Find:** O_2 for 10 min breathing time

Conceptual Plan: 10 min → vol air → vol O2 → mol O2 → mol KO2 → g KO2

$$\frac{8\text{ L air}}{1\text{ min}} \quad \frac{4\text{ L }O_2}{100\text{ L air}} \quad \frac{1\text{ mol }O_2}{22.4\text{ L }O_2} \quad \frac{4\text{ mol }KO_2}{3\text{ mol }O_2} \quad \frac{71.10\text{ g }KO_2}{1\text{ mol }KO_2}$$

Solution: $$10\text{ min.} \times \frac{8\text{ L air}}{\text{min}} \times \frac{4\text{ L }O_2}{100\text{ L air}} \times \frac{1\text{ mol }O_2}{22.4\text{ L }O_2} \times \frac{4\text{ mol }KO_2}{3\text{ mol }O_2} \times \frac{71.10\text{ g }KO_2}{1\text{ mol }KO_2} = 14\text{ g }KO_2$$

Check: The units of the answer (g KO_2) are correct. The magnitude of the answer is reasonable since it is an amount that could be carried in a portable device.

4.128 **Given:** 250 g sample, 67.2 mol % Al **Find:** Theoretical yield in g of Mn
Conceptual Plan: mol % Al → g Al and mol % MnO_2 → g MnO_2, then mass % Al

$$\frac{26.98 \text{ g Al}}{\text{mol Al}} \qquad \frac{86.94 \text{ g } MnO_2}{\text{mol } MnO_2} \qquad \frac{\text{g Al}}{\text{total g}} \times 100$$

then: sample → g Al → mol Al → mol Mn

$$\frac{38.86 \text{ g Al}}{100 \text{ g sample}} \quad \frac{\text{mol Al}}{26.98 \text{ g Al}} \quad \frac{3 \text{ mol Mn}}{4 \text{ mol Al}}$$ **→ smallest mol amount determines limiting reactant**

sample → g MnO_2 → mol MnO_2 → mol Mn

$$\frac{61.14 \text{ g } MnO_2}{100 \text{ g sample}} \quad \frac{\text{mol } MnO_2}{86.94 \text{ g } MnO_2} \quad \frac{1 \text{ mol Mn}}{\text{mol } MnO_2}$$

then mol Mn → g Mn

$$\frac{54.94 \text{ g Mn}}{\text{mol Mn}}$$

Solution: $4Al(s) + 3\,MnO_2(s) \rightarrow 3Mn + 2Al_2O_3(s)$

Assume 1 mole: $0.672 \text{ mol Al} \times \frac{26.98 \text{ g Al}}{\text{mol Al}} = 18.13 \text{ g Al}$

$$0.328 \text{ mol } MnO_2 \times \frac{86.94 \text{ g } MnO_2}{\text{mol } MnO_2} = 28.52 \text{ g } MnO_2$$

$$\frac{18.13 \text{ g Al}}{(18.13 \text{ g Al} + 28.52 \text{ g } MnO_2)} \times 100 = 38.86\ \%\text{ Al}$$ So: 61.14 % MnO_2

$$250 \cancel{\text{g sample}} \times \frac{38.86 \cancel{\text{g Al}}}{100 \cancel{\text{g sample}}} \times \frac{\cancel{\text{mol Al}}}{26.98 \cancel{\text{g Al}}} \times \frac{3 \text{ mol Mn}}{4 \cancel{\text{mol Al}}} = 2.7\underline{0}1 \text{ mol Mn}$$

$$250 \cancel{\text{g sample}} \times \frac{61.14 \cancel{\text{g } MnO_2}}{100 \cancel{\text{g sample}}} \times \frac{\cancel{\text{mol } MnO_2}}{86.94 \cancel{\text{g } MnO_2}} \times \frac{1 \text{ mol Mn}}{1 \cancel{\text{mol } MnO_2}} = 1.7\underline{5}8 \text{ mol Mn}$$

$$1.7\underline{5}8 \cancel{\text{mol Mn}} \times \frac{54.94 \text{ g Mn}}{1 \cancel{\text{mol Mn}}} = 96.6 \text{ g Mn}$$

Check: The units of the answer (g Mn) are correct. The magnitude of the answer is reasonable based on the amount of the limiting reactant, MnO_2.

4.129 **Given:** 151 g $Na_2B_4O_7$ **Find:** g B_5H_9
Conceptual Plan: g $Na_2B_4O_7$ → mol $Na_2B_4O_7$ → mol B_5H_9 → g B_5H_9

$$\frac{\text{mol } Na_2B_4O_7}{201.22 \text{ g } Na_2B_4O_7} \quad \frac{4 \text{ mol } B_5H_9}{5 \text{ mol } Na_2B_4O_7} \quad \frac{63.13 \text{ g } B_5H_9}{\text{mol } B_5H_9}$$

Solution: All the B in B_5H_9 goes to the $Na_2B_4O_7$ so the mole ratio between the two can be used.

$$151 \cancel{\text{g } Na_2B_4O_7} \times \frac{1 \cancel{\text{mol } Na_2B_4O_7}}{201.22 \cancel{\text{g } Na_2B_4O_7}} \times \frac{4 \cancel{\text{mol } B_5H_9}}{5 \cancel{\text{mol } Na_2B_4O_7}} \times \frac{63.13 \text{ g } B_5H_9}{1 \cancel{\text{mol } B_5H_9}} = 37.9 \text{ g } B_5H_9$$

Check: The units of the answer (g B_5H_9) are correct. The magnitude of the answer is reasonable since the molar mass of B_5H_9 is less than the molar mass of $Na_2B_4O_7$.

4.130 The correct answer is d. The molar mass of K and O_2 are comparable. Since the stoichiometry has a ratio of 4 mol K to 1 mol O_2, K will be the limiting reactant when mass of K is less than 4 times the mass of O_2.

4.131 **Given:** 5 mol NO, 10 mol H_2 **Find:** conditions of product mixture
Conceptual Plan: mol H_2 → mol NO and mol H_2 → mol NH_3 and mol H_2 → mol H_2O
Solution: The correct answer is a. Since the mol ratio of H_2 to NO is 5:2, the 10 mol of H_2 will require 4 mol NO and H_2 is the limiting reactant. This eliminates answers b and c. Since there is excess NO, this eliminates d, leaving answer a.

4.132 **Given:** 1 M solution contains 8 particles **Find:** amount of solute or solvent needed to obtain new concentration
Conceptual Plan: determine amount of solute particles in each new solution, then determine if solute (if the number is greater) or solvent (if the number is less) needs to be added to obtain the new concentration
Solution: Solution (a) contains 12 particles solute. Concentration is greater than the original, so solute needs

to be added. $12 \text{ particles} \times \frac{1 \text{ mol}}{8 \text{ particles}} = 1.5 \text{ mol}$ $(1.5 \text{ mol} - 1.0 \text{ mol}) = 0.5$ mol solute added.

$$0.5 \text{ mol solute} \times \frac{8 \text{ particles}}{1 \text{ mol solute}} = 4 \text{ solute particles added}$$

Solution (a) is obtained by adding 4 particles solute to 1 L of original solution.

Solution (b) contains 4 particles. Concentration is less than the original so solvent needs to be added.

$4 \text{ particles} \times \frac{1 \text{ mol}}{8 \text{ particles}} = 0.5 \text{ mol solute}$ So, 1 L solution contains 0.5 mol = 0.5M

$(1 \text{ M})(1 \text{ L}) = (0.5 \text{ M})(x)$ $x = 2 \text{ L}$

Solution (b) is obtained by diluting 1 L of the original solution to 2 L.

Solution (c) contains 6 particles. Concentration is less than the original, so solvent needs to be added.

$6 \text{ particles} \times \frac{1 \text{ mol}}{8 \text{ particles}} = 0.75 \text{ mol solute}$ So, 1 L solution contains 0.75 mol = 0.75M

$(1 \text{ M})(1 \text{ L}) = (0.75 \text{ M})(x)$ $x = 1.3 \text{ L}$

Solution (c) is obtained by diluting 1 L of the original solution to 1.3 L.

4.133 **Given:** 6 molecules N_2H_4; 4 molecules N_2O_4; (a) contains 9 molecules N_2, 12 molecules H_2O, and 1 molecule N_2O_4; solution (b) contains 12 molecules N_2, 16 molecules H_2O , and 2 molecules N_2O_4; solution (c) contains 9 molecules N_2, 12 molecules H_2O **Find:** theoretical yield N_2, H_2O

Conceptual Plan: molecules N_2H_4 → molecules N_2

$$\frac{3 \text{ molecules } N_2}{2 \text{ molecules } N_2H_4}$$

→ smallest molecules amount determines limiting reactant

molecules N_2O_4 → molecules N_2

$$\frac{3 \text{ molecules } N_2}{1 \text{ molecules } N_2O_4}$$

molecules N_2H_4 → molecules H_2O

$$\frac{4 \text{ molecules } H_2O}{2 \text{ molecules } N_2H_4}$$

molecules N_2H_4 → molecules N_2O_4

$$\frac{1 \text{ molecules } N_2O_4}{2 \text{ molecules } N_2H_4}$$

Solution: $6 \text{ molecules } N_2H_4 \times \frac{3 \text{ molecules } N_2}{2 \text{ molecules } N_2H_4} = 9 \text{ molecules } N_2$

$$6 \text{ molecules } N_2O_4 \times \frac{3 \text{ molecules } N_2}{1 \text{ molecules } N_2O_4} = 18 \text{ molecules } N_2$$

Limiting reactant = N_2H_4 because it produced the least molecules of N_2

$$6 \text{ molecules } N_2H_4 \times \frac{4 \text{ molecules } H_2O}{2 \text{ molecules } N_2H_4} = 12 \text{ molecules } H_2O$$

$$6 \text{ molecules } N_2H_4 \times \frac{1 \text{ molecules } N_2O_4}{2 \text{ molecules } N_2H_4} = 3 \text{ molecules } N_2O_4 \text{ used}$$

Reaction mixture should contain 9 molecules N_2, 12 molecules H_2O, and 1 molecule N_2O_4; this is best represented by (a).

5 Gases

Review Questions

5.1 Pressure is the force exerted per unit area by gas molecules as they strike the surfaces around them. Pressure is caused by collisions of gas molecules with surfaces or other gas molecules.

5.2 When you inhale, the muscles that surround your chest cavity expand the volume of your lungs. The expanded volume results in a lower concentration of gas molecules (the number of gas molecules does not change, but since the volume increases, the concentration goes down). This in turn results in fewer molecular collisions, which results in lower pressure. The external pressure (the pressure outside of your lungs) remains relatively constant and is now higher than the pressure in your lungs. As a result, gas molecules flow into your lungs, from the region of higher pressure to the region of lower pressure.

5.3 When you exhale, you reverse the process of inhalation. The chest cavity muscles relax, which decreases the lung volume, increasing the pressure within the lungs and forcing the air out of the lungs.

5.4 101,325 Pa = 760 torr = 760 mmHg = 29.92 in Hg = 14.7 psi = 1 atm

5.5 A manometer is a U-shaped tube containing a dense liquid, usually mercury. In an open-ended manometer, one end of the tube is open to atmospheric pressure and the other is attached to a flask containing the gas sample. If the pressure of the gas sample is exactly equal to atmospheric pressure, then the mercury levels on both sides of the tube are the same. If the pressure of the sample is greater than atmospheric pressure, the mercury level on the sample side of the tube is lower than on the side open to the atmosphere. If the pressure of the sample is less than atmospheric pressure, the mercury level on the sample side is higher than on the side open to the atmosphere. This type of manometer always measures the pressure of the gas sample relative to atmospheric pressure. The difference in height between the two levels is equal to the pressure difference from atmospheric pressure.

5.6 Boyle's law states that the volume of the gas varies inversely to the pressure on the gas, while temperature and number of moles are kept constant ($P_1 V_1 = P_2 V_2$). Charles' law states that the volume of a gas is directly proportional to the temperature of the gas, while pressure and number of moles are kept constant ($V_1 / T_1 = V_2 / T_2$). All temperatures must be in kelvins when used in gas law calculations. Avagadro's Law states that the volume of a gas is directly proportional to the number of moles of the gas, while pressure and temperature are kept constant ($V_1 / n_1 = V_2 / n_2$).

5.7 This pain is caused by air-containing cavities within your ear. When you ascend a mountain, the external pressure (the pressure that surrounds you) drops, while the pressure within your ear cavities (the internal pressure) remains the same. This creates an imbalance—the greater internal pressure forces your eardrum to bulge outward, causing pain. With time, and the help of a yawn or two, the excess air within your ear cavities escapes, equalizing the internal and external pressure and relieving the pain.

5.8 For every 10 m of depth that a diver descends in water, they experience an additional 1 atm of pressure due to the weight of the water above her. The pressure regulator used in scuba diving delivers air at a pressure that matches the external pressure; otherwise the diver could not inhale the air. For example, when a diver is at a depth of 20 m below the surface, the regulator delivers air at a pressure of 3 atm to match the 3 atm of pressure around the diver (1 atm due to normal atmospheric pressure and 2 additional atmospheres due to the weight of the water at 20 m). Suppose that a diver inhaled a lungful of air at a pressure of 3 atm and swam quickly to the surface (where the pressure drops to 1 atm) while holding this breath. What would happen to the volume of air in the diver's lungs? Since the pressure decreases by a factor of 3, the volume of the air in the diver's lungs would increase by a factor of 3, severely damaging the diver's lungs and possibly killing the diver.

5.9 When we breathe, we expand the volume of our chest cavity, reducing the pressure on the outer surface of the lungs to less than 1 atm (Boyle's law). Because of this pressure differential, the lungs expand, the pressure in them falls, and air from outside our lungs then flows into them. Extra-long snorkels do not work because of the pressure exerted by water at an increased depth. A diver at 10 m experiences an external pressure of 2 atm. This is more than the muscles of the chest cavity can overcome—the chest cavity and lungs are compressed, resulting in an air pressure within them of more than 1 atm. If the diver had a snorkel that went to the surface—where the air pressure is 1 atm—air would flow out of his lungs, not into them. It would be impossible to breathe.

5.10 Charles's law explains why a hot-air balloon can take flight. The gas that fills a hot air balloon is warmed with a burner increasing its volume and lowering its density, and causing it to float in the colder, denser surrounding air. Charles's law also explains why the second floor of a house is usually a bit warmer than the ground floor because when air is heated its volume increases, resulting in a lower density. The warm, less dense air tends to rise in a room filled with colder, denser air.

5.11 The ideal gas law ($PV = nRT$) combines all of the relationships between the four variables relevent to gases (pressure, volume, number of moles, and temperature (in kelvin's)) in one simple expression.

5.12 We know that $V \propto 1/P$ (Boyle's law) $V \propto T$ (Charles's law) $V \propto n$ (Avogadro's law).

Combining these three expressions we get $V \propto nT/P$. Replace the proportional sign with an equal sign by incorporating R (the ideal gas constant) $V = RnT/P$. Rearranging, we get $PV = nRT$.

5.13 The molar volume of an ideal gas is the volume occupied by one mole of gas at T = 0 °C (273 K) and P = 1.00 atm. Substituting these values into the ideal gas law, one can calculate this value as 22.414 L.

5.14 Since $d = \frac{P\mathcal{M}}{RT}$ this means that the density will decrease as temperature increases. It will increase as pressure increases or as the molar mass of the gas increases.

5.15 The pressure due to any individual component in a gas mixture is called the partial pressure (P_n) of that component and can be calculated from the ideal gas law by assuming that each gas component acts independently. The sum of the partial pressures of the components in a gas mixture must equal the total pressure: $P_{total} = P_a + P_b + P_c + \ldots$ where P_{total} is the total pressure and P_a, P_b, $P_c \ldots$ are the partial pressures of the components.

5.16 Too much oxygen can also cause physiological problems. Scuba divers breathe pressurized air. At 30 m, a scuba diver breathes air at a total pressure of 4.0 atm, making P_{O_2} about 0.84 atm. This elevated partial pressure of oxygen raises the density of oxygen molecules in the lungs, resulting in a higher concentration of oxygen in body tissues. When P_{O_2} increases beyond 1.4 atm, the increased oxygen concentration in body tissues causes a condition called oxygen toxicity, which results in muscle twitching, tunnel vision, and convulsions.

5.17 No, when collecting a gas over water, it will contain some water molecules. The vapor pressure of water can be gotten from Table 5.4. Therefore, $P_{Gas} = P_{Total} - P_{H_2O}$.

5.18 In Chapter 4, we learned how the coefficients in chemical equations can be used as conversion factors between number of moles of reactants and number of moles of products in a chemical reaction; and that the molar mass can be used to convert the number of moles to the mass. At STP, each mole of gas occupies 22.414 L. The mass of the product will be as follows:

$$\text{Volume of limiting reagent (L)} \times \frac{1 \text{ mol limiting reagent}}{22.414 \text{ L}} \times \frac{c \text{ mol product}}{a \text{ mol limiting reagent}} \times \frac{\text{g product}}{1 \text{ mol product}}$$

for the reaction:
a A + b B $\rightarrow$ c C + d D, where A is the limiting reagent and C is the product of interest.

5.19 The basic postulates of kinetic molecular theory are as follows: (1) The size of a particle is negligibly small, (2) the average kinetic energy of a particle is proportional to the temperature in kelvins, and (3) the collision of one particle with another (or with the walls) is completely elastic. Pressure is defined as force divided by area. According to kinetic molecular theory, a gas is a collection of particles in constant motion. The motion results in collisions between the particles and the surfaces around them. As each particle collides with a surface, it exerts a force upon that surface. The result of many particles in a gas sample exerting forces on the surfaces around them is constant pressure.

5.20 Boyle's law states that, for a constant number of particles at constant temperature, the volume of a gas is inversely proportional to its pressure. If you decrease the volume of a gas, you force the gas particles to occupy a smaller space. It follows from kinetic molecular theory that, as long the temperature remains the same, the result is a greater number of collisions with the surrounding surfaces and therefore a greater pressure.

Charles's law states that, for a constant number of particles at constant pressure, the volume of a gas is proportional to its temperature. According to kinetic molecular theory, when you increase the temperature of a gas, the average speed, and thus the average kinetic energy, of the particles increases. Since this greater kinetic energy results in more frequent collisions and more force per collision, the pressure of the gas would increase if its volume were held constant (Gay-Lussac's law). The only way for the pressure to remain constant is for the volume to increase. The greater volume spreads the collisions out over a greater area, so that the pressure (defined as force per unit area) is unchanged.

Avogadro's law states that, at constant temperature and pressure, the volume of a gas is proportional to the number of particles. According to kinetic molecular theory, when you increase the number of particles in a gas sample, the number of collisions with the surrounding surfaces increases. Since the greater number of collisions would result in a greater overall force on surrounding surfaces, the only way for the pressure to remain constant is for the volume to increase so that the number of particles per unit volume (and thus the number of collisions) remains constant.

Dalton's law states that the total pressure of a gas mixture is the sum of the partial pressures of its components. In other words, according to Dalton's law, the components in a gas mixture act identically to, and independently of, one another. According to kinetic molecular theory, the particles have negligible size and they do not interact. Consequently, the only property that would distinguish one type of particle from another is its mass. However, even particles of different masses have the same average kinetic energy at a given temperature, so they exert the same force upon a collision with a surface. Consequently, adding components to a gas mixture—even different *kinds* of gases—has the same effect as simply adding more particles. The partial pressures of all the components sum to the overall pressure.

5.21 Postulate 2 of kinetic molecular theory states that the average kinetic energy is proportional to the temperature in kelvins. The root mean square velocity of a collection of gas particles is inversely proportional to the square root of the molar mass of the particles in kilograms per mole.

5.22 Gaseous particles travel at tremendous speeds along very haphazard paths. To a perfume molecule, the path from the perfume bottle in the bathroom to your nose 2 m away is much like the path through a busy shopping mall during a clearance sale. The molecule travels only a short distance before it collides with another molecule, changes direction, only to collide again, and so on. The average distance that a molecule travels between collisions is called its mean free path.

5.23 The process by which gas molecules spread out in response to a concentration gradient is called diffusion. Effusion is the process by which a gas escapes from a container into a vacuum through a small hole. The rate of effusion is inversely proportional to the square root of the molar mass of the gas.

5.24 Gases behave ideally when both of the following are true: (a) The volume of the gas particles is small compared to the space between them; and b) The forces between the gas particles are not significant. At high pressures the number of molecules increases, so the volume of the gas particles becomes larger; and since the spacing between the particles is smaller, the interactions become more significant. At low temperatures, the molecules are not moving as fast as at higher temperatures, so the when they collide they have a greater opportunity to interact.

5.25 Sulfur oxides (SO_x): Sulfur oxides include SO_2 and SO_3, which are produced chiefly during coal-fired electricity generation and industrial metal refining. Carbon monoxide (CO): Carbon monoxide is formed by the incomplete combustion of fossil fuels (petroleum, natural gas, and coal). It is emitted mainly by motor vehicles. Nitrogen oxides (NO_x): Nitrogen oxides include NO and NO_2, which are emitted by motor vehicles, by fossil-fuel based electricity generation plants, and by any high temperature combustion process that occurs in air. Ozone (O_3): Ozone is produced when some of the products of fossil-fuel combustion, especially nitrogen oxides and unburned volatile organic compounds (VOCs), react in the presence of sunlight. The levels of all of these pollutants are decreasing over U.S. cities.

5.26 Ground-level ozone (in the lower atmospheres) is an eye and lung irritant and prolonged exposure has been shown to cause permanent lung damage. Stratospheric ozone (in the upper atmosphere) is a natural part of our environment that protects the Earth from harmful ultraviolet light. Stratospheric ozone does not harm us because we are not directly exposed to it.

5.27 Chlorofluorocarbons (CFCs) are blamed for destroying stratospheric ozone. When CFCs reach the stratosphere, UV light (which is less abundant below the ozone layer because the ozone absorbs it) breaks a carbon-chlorine bond in the CFC, generating a very reactive chlorine atom. This chlorine atom then reacts with ozone in a cyclic reaction that destroys two ozone molecules and regenerates itself to repeat the process. In this way, a single chlorine atom can destroy hundreds of ozone molecules. Legislation has been passed in many nations calling for a complete ban on CFC production beginning in 1996.

5.28 When the sun rises in the Antarctic spring (October), sunlight breaks the relatively weak Cl-Cl bond, releasing chlorine atoms into the stratosphere. The chlorine atoms then deplete ozone through a catalytic cycle. Normally the chlorine that enters our atmosphere from chlorofluorocarbons is neutralized in atmospheric chemical reservoirs. Conditions at the South Pole in the month of October happen to be just right for releasing that chlorine from its reservoirs, allowing it to continue to destroy ozone.

Converting Between Pressure Units

5.29 (a) **Given:** 24.9 in Hg **Find:** atm

Conceptual Plan: in Hg → atm

$$\frac{1\text{ atm}}{29.92\text{ in Hg}}$$

Solution: $24.9\,\cancel{\text{in Hg}} \times \dfrac{1\text{ atm}}{29.92\,\cancel{\text{in Hg}}} = 0.832\text{ atm}$

Check: The units (atm) are correct. The magnitude of the answer (<1) makes physical sense because we started with less than 29.92 in Hg.

(b) **Given:** 24.9 in Hg **Find:** mmHg

Conceptual Plan: Use answer from part (a) then convert atm → mmHg

$$\frac{760\text{ mm Hg}}{1\text{ atm}}$$

Solution: $0.832\,\cancel{\text{atm}} \times \dfrac{760\text{ mmHg}}{1\,\cancel{\text{atm}}} = 632\text{ mmHg}$

Check: The units (mmHg) are correct. The magnitude of the answer (< 760 mmHg) makes physical sense because we started with less than 1 atm.

(c) **Given:** 24.9 in Hg **Find:** psi

Conceptual Plan: Use answer from part (a) then convert atm → psi

$$\frac{14.7\text{ psi}}{1\text{ atm}}$$

Solution: $0.832\,\cancel{\text{atm}} \times \dfrac{14.7\text{ psi}}{1\,\cancel{\text{atm}}} = 12.2\text{ psi}$

Check: The units (psi) are correct. The magnitude of the answer (< 14.7 psi) makes physical sense because we started with less than 1 atm.

(d) **Given:** 24.9 in Hg **Find:** Pa
Conceptual Plan: Use answer from part (a) then convert atm → Pa

$$\frac{101{,}325\ \text{Pa}}{1\ \text{atm}}$$

Solution: $0.832\ \cancel{\text{atm}} \times \dfrac{101{,}325\ \text{Pa}}{1\ \cancel{\text{atm}}} = 8.43 \times 10^4\ \text{Pa}$

Check: The units (mmHg) are correct. The magnitude of the answer (< 101,325 Pa) makes physical sense because we started with less than 1 atm.

5.30 (a) **Given:** 235 mmHg **Find:** torr
Conceptual Plan: mmHg → torr

$$\frac{1\ \text{torr}}{1\ \text{mm Hg}}$$

Solution: $235\ \cancel{\text{mmHg}} \times \dfrac{1\ \text{torr}}{1\ \cancel{\text{mmHg}}} = 235\ \text{torr}$

Check: The units (torr) are correct. The magnitude of the answer (235) makes physical sense because both units are of the same size.

(b) **Given:** 235 mmHg **Find:** psi
Conceptual Plan: mmHg → atm → psi

$$\frac{760\ \text{mmHg}}{1\ \text{atm}} \quad \frac{14.7\ \text{psi}}{1\ \text{atm}}$$

Solution: $235\ \cancel{\text{mmHg}} \times \dfrac{1\ \cancel{\text{atm}}}{760\ \cancel{\text{mmHg}}} \times \dfrac{14.7\ \text{psi}}{1\ \cancel{\text{atm}}} = 4.55\ \text{psi}$

Check: The units (psi) are correct. The magnitude of the answer (< 14.7 psi) makes physical sense because we started with less than 760 mmHg = 1 atm.

(c) **Given:** 235 mmHg **Find:** in Hg
Conceptual Plan: mmHg → in Hg

$$\frac{1\ \text{in Hg}}{25.4\ \text{mmHg}}$$

Solution: $235\ \cancel{\text{mmHg}} \times \dfrac{1\ \text{in Hg}}{25.4\ \cancel{\text{mmHg}}} = 9.25\ \text{in Hg}$

Check: The units (in Hg) are correct. The magnitude of the answer (9) makes physical sense because inches are larger than mm.

(d) **Given:** 235 mmHg **Find:** atm
Conceptual Plan: mmHg → atm

$$\frac{760\ \text{mmHg}}{1\ \text{atm}}$$

Solution: $235\ \cancel{\text{mmHg}} \times \dfrac{1\ \text{atm}}{760\ \cancel{\text{mmHg}}} = 0.309\ \text{atm}$

Check: The units (atm) are correct. The magnitude of the answer (< 1) makes physical sense because we started with less than 760 mmHg.

5.31 (a) **Given:** 31.85 in Hg **Find:** mmHg
Conceptual Plan: in Hg → mmHg

$$\frac{25.4\ \text{mmHg}}{1\ \text{in Hg}}$$

Solution: $31.85\ \cancel{\text{inHg}} \times \dfrac{25.4\ \text{mmHg}}{1\ \cancel{\text{inHg}}} = 809.0\ \text{mmHg}$

Check: The units (mmHg) are correct. The magnitude of the answer (809) makes physical sense because inches are larger than mm.

(b) **Given:** 31.85 in Hg **Find:** atm
Conceptual Plan: Use answer from part (a) then convert mmHg → atm

$$\frac{1\ \text{atm}}{760\ \text{mmHg}}$$

Solution: $809.0\ \cancel{\text{mmHg}} \times \dfrac{1\ \text{atm}}{760\ \cancel{\text{mmHg}}} = 1.064\ \text{atm}$

Check: The units (atm) are correct. The magnitude of the answer (>1) makes physical sense because we started with more than 760 mmHg.

(c) **Given:** 31.85 in Hg **Find:** torr

Conceptual Plan: Use answer from part (a) then convert mmHg → torr

$$\frac{1\ \text{torr}}{1\ \text{mmHg}}$$

Solution: $809.0\ \cancel{\text{mmHg}} \times \frac{1\ \text{torr}}{1\ \cancel{\text{mmHg}}} = 809.0\ \text{torr}$

Check: The units (torr) are correct. The magnitude of the answer (809) makes physical sense because both units are of the same size.

(d) **Given:** 31.85 in Hg **Find:** kPa

Conceptual Plan: Use answer from part b) then convert atm → Pa → kPa

$$\frac{101{,}325\ \text{Pa}}{1\ \text{atm}} \quad \frac{1\ \text{kPa}}{1000\ \text{Pa}}$$

Solution: $1.064\ \cancel{\text{atm}} \times \frac{101{,}325\ \cancel{\text{Pa}}}{1\ \cancel{\text{atm}}} \times \frac{1\ \text{kPa}}{1000\ \cancel{\text{Pa}}} = 107.8\ \text{kPa}$

Check: The units (kPa) are correct. The magnitude of the answer (108) makes physical sense because we started with more than 1 atm and there are ~101 kPa in an atm.

5.32 (a) **Given:** 652.5 mmHg **Find:** torr

Conceptual Plan: mmHg → torr

$$\frac{1\ \text{torr}}{1\ \text{mmHg}}$$

Solution: $652.5\ \cancel{\text{mmHg}} \times \frac{1\ \text{torr}}{1\ \cancel{\text{mmHg}}} = 652.5\ \text{torr}$

Check: The units (torr) are correct. The magnitude of the answer (653) makes physical sense because both units are of the same size.

(b) **Given:** 652.5 mmHg **Find:** atm

Conceptual Plan: mmHg → atm

$$\frac{760\ \text{mmHg}}{1\ \text{atm}}$$

Solution: $652.5\ \cancel{\text{mmHg}} \times \frac{1\ \text{atm}}{760\ \cancel{\text{mmHg}}} = 0.8586\ \text{atm}$

Check: The units (psi) are correct. The magnitude of the answer (< 14.7 psi) makes physical sense because we started with less than 760 mmHg = 1 atm.

(c) **Given:** 652.5 mmHg **Find:** in Hg

Conceptual Plan: mmHg → in Hg

$$\frac{1\ \text{in Hg}}{25.4\ \text{mmHg}}$$

Solution: $652.5\ \cancel{\text{mmHg}} \times \frac{1\ \text{in Hg}}{25.4\ \cancel{\text{mmHg}}} = 25.69\ \text{in Hg}$

Check: The units (in Hg) are correct. The magnitude of the answer (26) makes physical sense because inches are larger than mm.

(d) **Given:** 652.5 mmHg **Find:** psi

Conceptual Plan: Use answer from part b) then convert atm → psi

$$\frac{14.70\ \text{psi}}{1\ \text{atm}}$$

Solution: $0.8586\ \cancel{\text{atm}} \times \frac{14.70\ \text{psi}}{1\ \cancel{\text{atm}}} = 12.62\ \text{psi}$

Check: The units (psi) are correct. The magnitude of the answer (< 14.7 psi) makes physical sense because we started with less than 1 atm.

5.33 (a) **Given:** P_{bar} = 762.4 mm Hg and figure **Find:** P_{gas}

Conceptual plan: Measure height difference then convert cm Hg → mm Hg → mm Hg

$$\frac{10\ \text{mm Hg}}{1\ \text{cm Hg}} \qquad P_{gas} = h + P_{bar}$$

Solution:

$h = 7.0\ \cancel{\text{cm Hg}} \times \frac{10\ \text{mm Hg}}{1\ \cancel{\text{cm Hg}}} = 70.\ \text{mm Hg}$ $\quad P_{\text{gas}} = 70.\ \text{mm Hg} + 762.4\ \text{mm Hg} = 832\ \text{mm Hg}$

Check: The units (mm Hg) are correct. The magnitude of the answer (832 mm Hg) makes physical sense because the mercury column is higher on the right, indicating that the pressure is above barometric pressure. No significant figures to the right of the decimal point can be reported since the mercury height is known only to the 1's place.

(b) **Given**: $P_{bar} = 762.4$ mm Hg and figure **Find**: P_{gas}
Conceptual plan: **Measure height difference then convert cm Hg → mm Hg → mm Hg**

$$\frac{10\,mm\,Hg}{1\,cm\,Hg} \qquad P_{gas} = h + P_{bar}$$

Solution:

$$h = -4.4\,\cancel{cm\,Hg} \times \frac{10\,mm\,Hg}{1\,\cancel{cm\,Hg}} = -44\,mm\,Hg \quad P_{gas} = -44\,mm\,Hg + 762.4\,mm\,Hg = 718\,mm\,Hg$$

Check: The units (mm Hg) are correct. The magnitude of the answer (718 mm Hg) makes physical sense because the mercury column is higher on the left, indicating that the pressure is below barometric pressure. No significant figures to the right of the decimal point can be reported since the mercury height is known only to the 1's place.

5.34 (a) **Given**: $P_{bar} = 751.5$ mm Hg and figure **Find**: P_{gas}
Conceptual plan: **Measure height difference then convert cm Hg → mm Hg → mm Hg**

$$\frac{10\,mm\,Hg}{1\,cm\,Hg} \qquad P_{gas} = h + P_{bar}$$

Solution:

$$h = -2.2\,\cancel{cm\,Hg} \times \frac{10\,mm\,Hg}{1\,\cancel{cm\,Hg}} = -22\,mm\,Hg \quad P_{gas} = -22\,mm\,Hg + 751.5\,mm\,Hg = 730.\,mm\,Hg$$

Check: The units (mm Hg) are correct. The magnitude of the answer (730 mm Hg) makes physical sense because the mercury column is higher on the left, indicating that the pressure is below barometric pressure. No significant figures to the right of the decimal point can be reported since the mercury height is known only to the 1's place.

(b) **Given**: $P_{bar} = 751.5$ mm Hg and figure **Find**: P_{gas}
Conceptual plan: **Measure height difference then convert cm Hg → mm Hg → mm Hg**

$$\frac{10\,mm\,Hg}{1\,cm\,Hg} \qquad P_{gas} = h + P_{bar}$$

Solution:

$$h = 6.8\,\cancel{cm\,Hg} \times \frac{10\,mm\,Hg}{1\,\cancel{cm\,Hg}} = 68\,mm\,Hg \quad P_{gas} = 68\,mm\,Hg + 751.5\,mm\,Hg = 820.\,mm\,Hg$$

Check: The units (mm Hg) are correct. The magnitude of the answer (820 mm Hg) makes physical sense because the mercury column is higher on the right, indicating that the pressure is above barometric pressure. No significant figures to the right of the decimal point can be reported since the mercury height is known only to the 1's place.

Simple Gas Laws

5.35 **Given**: $V_1 = 5.6$ L, $P_1 = 735$ mmHg, and $V_2 = 9.4$ L **Find**: P_2
Conceptual Plan: $V_1, P_1, V_2 \rightarrow P_2$

$$P_1 V_1 = P_2 V_2$$

Solution:

$P_1 V_1 = P_2 V_2$ Rearrange to solve for P_2.

$$P_2 = P_1 \frac{V_1}{V_2} = 735\,mmHg \times \frac{5.6\,\cancel{L}}{9.4\,\cancel{L}} = 437.872\,mmHg = 4.4 \times 10^2\,mmHg$$

Check: The units (mmHg) are correct. The magnitude of the answer (440 mmHg) makes physical sense because Boyle's Law indicates that as the volume increases, the pressure decreases.

5.36 **Given**: $V_1 = 13.9$ L, $P_1 = 1.22$ atm, and $V_2 = 10.3$ L **Find**: P_2
Conceptual Plan: $V_1, P_1, V_2 \rightarrow P_2$

$$P_1 V_1 = P_2 V_2$$

Solution: $P_1 V_1 = P_2 V_2$ Rearrange to solve for P_2.

$$P_2 = P_1 \frac{V_1}{V_2} = 1.22\,atm \times \frac{13.9\,\cancel{L}}{10.3\,\cancel{L}} = 1.646408\,atm = 1.65\,atm$$

Check: The units (atm) are correct. The magnitude of the answer (2 atm) makes physical sense because Boyles Law indicates that as the volume decreases, the pressure increases.

5.37 **Given:** $V_1 = 48.3$ mL, $T_1 = 22$ °C, and $T_2 = 87$ °C **Find:** V_2

Conceptual Plan: °C → K then $V_1, T_1, T_2 \rightarrow V_2$

$K = °C + 273.15$ $\quad \frac{V_1}{T_1} = \frac{V_2}{T_2}$

Solution: $T_1 = 22$ °C + 273.15 = 295 K and $T_2 = 87$ °C + 273.15 = 360. K

$\frac{V_1}{T_1} = \frac{V_2}{T_2}$ Rearrange to solve for V_2. $V_2 = V_1 \frac{T_2}{T_1} = 48.3 \text{ mL} \times \frac{360 \text{ K}}{295 \text{ K}} = 58.9 \text{ mL}$

Check: The units (mL) are correct. The magnitude of the answer (59 mL) makes physical sense because Charles's Law indicates that as the volume increases, the temperature increases.

5.38 **Given:** $V_1 = 1.55$ mL, $T_1 = 95.3$ °C, and $T_2 = 0.0$ °C **Find:** V_2

Conceptual Plan: °C → K then $V_1, T_1, T_2 \rightarrow V_2$

$K = °C + 273.15$ $\quad \frac{V_1}{T_1} = \frac{V_2}{T_2}$

Solution: $T_1 = 95.3$ °C + 273.15 = 368.5 K and $T_2 = 0.0$ °C + 273.15 = 273.2 K

$\frac{V_1}{T_1} = \frac{V_2}{T_2}$ Rearrange to solve for V_2. $V_2 = V_1 \frac{T_2}{T_1} = 1.55 \text{ mL} \times \frac{273.2 \text{ K}}{368.5 \text{ K}} = 1.15 \text{ mL}$

Check: The units (mL) are correct. The magnitude of the answer (1.15 mL) makes physical sense because Charles's Law indicates that as the volume decreases, the temperature decreases.

5.39 **Given:** $V_1 = 2.46$ L, $n_1 = 0.158$ mol, and $\Delta n = 0.113$ mol **Find:** V_2

Conceptual Plan: $n_1 \rightarrow n_2$ then $V_1, n_1, n_2 \rightarrow V_2$

$n_1 + \Delta n = n_2$ $\quad \frac{V_1}{n_1} = \frac{V_2}{n_2}$

Solution: $n_2 = 0.158$ mol + 0.113 mol = 0.271 mol

$\frac{V_1}{n_1} = \frac{V_2}{n_2}$ Rearrange to solve for V_2. $V_2 = V_1 \frac{n_2}{n_1} = 2.46 \text{ L} \times \frac{0.271 \text{ mol}}{0.158 \text{ mol}} = 4.21937 \text{ L} = 4.22 \text{ L}$

Check: The units (L) are correct. The magnitude of the answer (4 L) makes physical sense because Avogadro's Law indicates that as the number of moles increases, the volume increases.

5.40 **Given:** $V_1 = 253$ mL, $n_1 = 0.553$ mol, and $\Delta n = 0.365$ mol **Find:** V_2

Conceptual Plan: $n_1 \rightarrow n_2$ then $V_1, n_1, n_2 \rightarrow V_2$

$n_1 + \Delta n = n_2$ $\quad \frac{V_1}{n_1} = \frac{V_2}{n_2}$

Solution: $n_2 = 0.553$ mol + 0.365 mol = 0.918 mol

$\frac{V_1}{n_1} = \frac{V_2}{n_2}$ Rearrange to solve for V_2. $V_2 = V_1 \frac{n_2}{n_1} = 253 \text{ mL} \times \frac{0.918 \text{ mol}}{0.553 \text{ mol}} = 419.989 \text{ mL} = 4.20 \times 10^2 \text{ mL}$

Check: The units (mL) are correct. The magnitude of the answer (420 L) makes physical sense because Avogadro's Law indicates that as the number of moles increases, the volume increases.

Ideal Gas Law

5.41 **Given:** $n = 0.118$ mol, $P = 0.97$ atm, and $T = 305$ K **Find:** V

Conceptual Plan: $n, P, T \rightarrow V$

$PV = nRT$

Solution: $PV = nRT$ Rearrange to solve for V. $V = \frac{nRT}{P} = \frac{0.118 \text{ mol} \times 0.08206 \frac{\text{L} \cdot \text{atm}}{\text{mol} \cdot \text{K}} \times 305 \text{ K}}{0.97 \text{ atm}} = 3.0 \text{ L}$

The volume would be the same for argon gas because the ideal gas law does not care about the mass of the gas, only the number of moles of gas.

Check: The units (L) are correct. The magnitude of the answer (3 L) makes sense because, as you will see in the next section, one mole of an ideal gas under standard conditions (273 K and 1 atm) occupies 22.4 L. Although these are not standard conditions, they are close enough for a ballpark check of the answer. Since this gas sample contains 0.118 moles, a volume of 3 L is reasonable.

5.42 **Given:** 12.5 g argon or 12.5 g helium, $P = 1.05$ atm, and $T = 322$ K **Find:** V

Conceptual Plan: g → n then $n, P, T \rightarrow V$

$\frac{1 \text{ mol}}{39.95 \text{ g}}$ or $\frac{1 \text{ mol}}{4.003 \text{ g}}$ $\quad PV = nRT$

Solution: $12.5\,\cancel{g\,Ar} \times \frac{1\text{ mol Ar}}{39.95\,\cancel{g\,Ar}} = 0.3128911\text{ mol Ar}$ $PV = nRT$ Rearrange to solve for V.

$$V = \frac{nRT}{P} = \frac{0.3128911\,\cancel{mol\,Ar} \times 0.08206\,\frac{L\cdot \cancel{atm}}{\cancel{mol}\cdot \cancel{K}} \times 322\,\cancel{K}}{1.05\,\cancel{atm}} = 7.87\text{ L Ar}$$

$$12.5\,\cancel{g\,He} \times \frac{1\text{ mol He}}{4.003\,\cancel{g\,He}} = 3.122658\text{ mol He}$$ $PV = nRT$ Rearrange to solve for V.

$$V = \frac{nRT}{P} = \frac{3.122658\,\cancel{mol\,He} \times 0.08206\,\frac{L.\,\cancel{atm}}{\cancel{mol}\,.\,\cancel{K}} \times 322\,\cancel{K}}{1.05\,\cancel{atm}} = 78.6\text{ L He}$$

Check: The units (L) are correct. The magnitude of the answer (8 L and 80 L) makes sense because, as you will see in the next section, one mole of an ideal gas under standard conditions (273 K and 1 atm) occupies 22.4 L. Although these are not standard conditions, they are close enough for a ballpark check of the answer. Since the molar mass of the two gases are different by a factor of ten, the resulting volumes will differ by a factor of ten.

5.43 **Given:** $V = 10.0$ L, $n = 0.448$ mol, and $T = 315$ K **Find:** P

Conceptual Plan: $n, V, T \rightarrow P$

$PV = nRT$

Solution:

$PV = nRT$ Rearrange to solve for P. $$P = \frac{nRT}{V} = \frac{0.448\,\cancel{mol} \times 0.08206\,\frac{\cancel{L}\cdot atm}{\cancel{mol}\cdot \cancel{K}} \times 315\,\cancel{K}}{10.0\,\cancel{L}} = 1.16\text{ atm}$$

Check: The units (atm) are correct. The magnitude of the answer (~1 atm) makes sense because, as you will see in the next section, one mole of an ideal gas under standard conditions (273 K and 1 atm) occupies 22.4 L. Although these are not standard conditions, they are close enough for a ballpark check of the answer. Since this gas sample contains 0.448 moles in a volume of 10 L, a pressure of 1 atm is reasonable.

5.44 **Given:** $V = 15.0$ L, 32.7 g oxygen, and $T = 302$ K **Find:** P

Conceptual Plan: g $\rightarrow$ n then $n, P, T \rightarrow V$

$\frac{1\text{ mol}}{32.00\text{ g}}$ $PV = nRT$

Solution: $32.7\,\cancel{g\,O_2} \times \frac{1\text{ mol }O_2}{32.00\,\cancel{g\,O_2}} = 1.021875\text{ mol }O_2$ $PV = nRT$ Rearrange to solve for P.

$$P = \frac{nRT}{V} = \frac{1.021875\,\cancel{mol} \times 0.08206\,\frac{\cancel{L}\cdot atm}{\cancel{mol}\cdot \cancel{K}} \times 302\,\cancel{K}}{15.0\,\cancel{L}} = 1.688282\text{ atm} = 1.69\text{ atm}$$

Check: The units (atm) are correct. The magnitude of the answer (~1.7 atm) makes sense because, as you will see in the next section, one mole of an ideal gas under standard conditions (273 K and 1 atm) occupies 22.4 L. Although these are not standard conditions, they are close enough for a ballpark check of the answer. Since this gas sample contains ~ 1 mole in a volume of 15 L, a pressure of 1.7 atm is reasonable.

5.45 **Given:** $V = 28.5$ L, $P = 1.8$ atm, and $T = 298$ K **Find:** n

Conceptual Plan: $V, P, T \rightarrow n$

$PV = nRT$

Solution: $PV = nRT$ Rearrange to solve for n. $$n = \frac{PV}{RT} = \frac{1.8\,\cancel{atm} \times 28.5\,\cancel{L}}{0.08206\,\frac{\cancel{L}\cdot \cancel{atm}}{mol\cdot \cancel{K}} \times 298\,\cancel{K}} = 2.1\text{ mol}$$

Check: The units (mol) are correct. The magnitude of the answer (2 mol) makes sense because, as you will see in the next section, one mole of an ideal gas under standard conditions (273 K and 1 atm) occupies 22.4 L. Although these are not standard conditions, they are close enough for a ballpark check of the answer. Since this gas sample has a volume of 28.5 L, and a pressure of 1.8 atm, ~ 2 mol is reasonable.

5.46 **Given:** $V = 11.8$ L, $P = 1.3$ atm, and $n = 0.52$ mol **Find:** T

Conceptual Plan: $V, P, n \rightarrow T$

$PV = nRT$

Solution: $PV = nRT$ Rearrange to solve for T. $T = \frac{PV}{nR} = \frac{1.3 \text{ atm} \times 11.8 \text{ L}}{0.52 \text{ mol} \times 0.08206 \frac{\text{L} \cdot \text{atm}}{\text{mol} \cdot \text{K}}} = 360 \text{ K}$

Check: The units (T) are correct. The magnitude of the answer (360 K) makes sense because, as you will see in the next section, one mole of an ideal gas under standard conditions (273 K and 1 atm) occupies 22.4 L. Although these are not standard conditions, they are close enough for a ballpark check of the answer. Since this gas sample has 0.52 mol, a volume of 11.8 L, and a pressure of 1.3 atm, 360 K is reasonable.

5.47 **Given:** $P_1 = 36.0$ psi (gauge P), $V_1 = 11.8$ L, $T_1 = 12.0$ °C, $V_2 = 12.2$ L, and $T_2 = 65.0$ °C
Find: P_2 and compare to $P_{max} = 38.0$ psi (gauge P)
Conceptual Plan: °C → K and gauge P → psi → atm then $P_1, V_1, T_1, V_2, T_2 \rightarrow P_2$

K = °C + 273.15 ; psi = gauge P + 14.7 ; $\frac{1 \text{ atm}}{14.7 \text{ psi}}$; $\frac{P_1V_1}{T_1} = \frac{P_2V_2}{T_2}$

Solution: $T_1 = 12.0$ °C + 273.15 = 285.2 K and $T_2 = 65.0$ °C + 273.15 = 338.2 K

$$P_1 = 36.0 \text{ psi (gauge P)} + 14.7 = 50.7 \text{ psi} \times \frac{1 \text{ atm}}{14.7 \text{ psi}} = 3.44\underline{8}98 \text{ atm}$$

$$P_{max} = 38.0 \text{ psi (gauge P)} + 14.7 = 52.7 \text{ psi} \times \frac{1 \text{ atm}}{14.7 \text{ psi}} = 3.59 \text{ atm}$$

$\frac{P_1V_1}{T_1} = \frac{P_2V_2}{T_2}$ Rearrange to solve for P_2. $P_2 = P_1 \frac{V_1}{V_2}\frac{T_2}{T_1} = 3.44\underline{8}98 \text{ atm} \times \frac{11.8 \text{ L}}{12.2 \text{ L}} \times \frac{338.2 \text{ K}}{285.2 \text{ K}} = 3.96 \text{ atm}$

This exceeds the maximum tire rating of 3.59 atm or 38.0 psi (gauge P).
Check: The units (atm) are correct. The magnitude of the answer (3.95 atm) makes physical sense because the relative increase in T is greater than the relative increase in V, so P should increase.

5.48 **Given:** $P_1 = 748$ mmHg, $V_1 = 28.5$ L, $T_1 = 28.0$ °C, $P_2 = 385$ mmHg, and $T_2 = -15.0$ °C **Find:** V_2
Conceptual Plan: °C → K then $P_1, V_1, T_1, V_2, T_2 \rightarrow P_2$

K = °C + 273.15 ; $\frac{P_1V_1}{T_1} = \frac{P_2V_2}{T_2}$

Solution: $T_1 = 28.0$ °C + 273.15 = 301.2 K and $T_2 = -15.0$ °C + 273.15 = 258.2 K

$\frac{P_1V_1}{T_1} = \frac{P_2V_2}{T_2}$ Rearrange to solve for V_2. $V_2 = V_1 \frac{P_1}{P_2}\frac{T_2}{T_1} = 28.5 \text{ L} \times \frac{748 \text{ mmHg}}{385 \text{ mmHg}} \times \frac{258.2 \text{ K}}{301.2 \text{ K}} = 47.5 \text{ L}$

Check: The units (L) are correct. The magnitude of the answer (47 L) makes physical sense because the relative decrease in P is greater than the relative decrease in T, so V should increase.

5.49 **Given:** m (CO_2) = 28.8 g, $P = 742$ mmHg, and $T = 22$ °C **Find:** V
Conceptual Plan: °C → K and mmHg → atm and g → mol then $n, P, T \rightarrow V$

K = °C + 273.15 ; $\frac{1 \text{ atm}}{760 \text{ mm Hg}}$; $\frac{1 \text{ mol}}{44.01 \text{ g}}$; $PV = nRT$

Solution: $T_1 = 22$ °C + 273.15 = 295 K, $P = 742 \text{ mmHg} \times \frac{1 \text{ atm}}{760 \text{ mmHg}} = 0.97\underline{6}316 \text{ atm}$,

$n = 28.8 \text{ g} \times \frac{1 \text{ mol}}{44.01 \text{ g}} = 0.65\underline{4}397 \text{ mol}$ $PV = nRT$ Rearrange to solve for V.

$$V = \frac{nRT}{P} = \frac{0.65\underline{4}397 \text{ mol} \times 0.08206 \frac{\text{L} \cdot \text{atm}}{\text{mol} \cdot \text{K}} \times 295 \text{ K}}{0.97\underline{6}316 \text{ atm}} = 16.2 \text{ L}$$

Check: The units (L) are correct. The magnitude of the answer (16 L) makes sense because one mole of an ideal gas under standard conditions (273 K and 1 atm) occupies 22.4 L. Although these are not standard conditions, they are close enough for a ballpark check of the answer. Since this gas sample contains 0.65 moles, a volume of 16 L is reasonable.

5.50 **Given:** 1.0 L of liquid N_2 w/$d = 0.807$ g/mL, $T = 25.0$ °C, $P = 1.0$ atm, and closet is 1.0 m x 1.0 m x 2.0 m
Find: V% of closet displaced by evaporated liquid
Conceptual Plan: °C → K and L → mL → g → mol then $n, P, T \rightarrow V_{evap}$

K = °C + 273.15 ; $\frac{1000 \text{ mL}}{1 \text{ L}}$; $d = m/V$; $\frac{1 \text{ mol}}{28.02 \text{ g}}$; $PV = nRT$

then l, w, h → V_{closet} m³ → cm³ → L finally V_{evap}, V_{closet} → % V displaced

$V = lwh$; $\frac{(100 \text{ cm})^3}{(1 \text{ m})^3}$; $\frac{1 \text{ L}}{1000 \text{ mL}}$; $\% V displaced = \frac{V_{evap}}{V_{closet}} \times 100\%$

Solution: $T_1 = 25.0\ °C + 273.15 = 298.2\ K$, $1.0\ \cancel{L} \times \frac{1\,000\ mL}{1\ \cancel{L}} = 1.0 \times 10^3\ mL$, $d = m/V$ Rearrange to solve for m. $m = d \times V = 0.807 \frac{g}{\cancel{mL}} \times 1.0 \times 10^3\ \cancel{mL} = 8.07 \times 10^2\ \cancel{g} \times \frac{1\ mol}{28.02\ \cancel{g}} = 28.801\ mol$ $PV = nRT$ Rearrange to solve for V.

$$V_{evap} = \frac{nRT}{P} = \frac{28.801\ \cancel{mol} \times 0.08206 \frac{L \cdot \cancel{atm}}{\cancel{mol} \cdot \cancel{K}} \times 298.2\ \cancel{K}}{1.0\ \cancel{atm}} = 7.0477 \times 10^2\ L$$

$$V_{closet} = l\,w\,h = 1.0\ m \times 1.0\ m \times 2.0\ m = 2.0\ m^3 \quad V_{closet} = 2.0\ \cancel{m^3} \times \frac{(100\ \cancel{cm})^3}{(1\ \cancel{m})^3} \times \frac{1\ L}{1000\ \cancel{cm^3}} = 2.0 \times 10^3\ L$$

$$\%\ V\ displaced = \frac{V_{evap}}{V_{closet}} \times 100\% = \frac{7.0477 \times 10^2\ L}{2.0 \times 10^3\ L} \times 100\% = 35\ \%$$

Check: The units (%) are correct. The magnitude of the answer (35 %) makes sense because it should be between 0 and 100 %. Looking at the two volumes, when a liquid evaporates, the volume increases by several orders of magnitude; when converting from cubic meters to L, there is an increase of 3 orders of magnitude.

Molar Volume, Density, and Molar Mass of a Gas

5.51 **Given:** 26.0 g argon, $V = 55.0$ mL, and $T = 295$ K **Find:** P

Conceptual Plan: g → n and mL → L then n, V, T → P

$\frac{1\ mol}{39.95\ g}$ $\frac{1\ L}{1000\ mL}$ $PV = nRT$

Solution: $26.0\ \cancel{g\ Ar} \times \frac{1\ mol\ Ar}{39.95\ \cancel{g\ Ar}} = 0.6508135\ mol\ Ar$ $\quad 55.0\ \cancel{mL} \times \frac{1\ L}{1000\ \cancel{mL}} = 0.0550\ L$

$PV = nRT$ Rearrange to solve for P.

$$P = \frac{nRT}{V} = \frac{0.6508135\ \cancel{mol} \times 0.08206 \frac{\cancel{L} \cdot atm}{\cancel{mol} \cdot \cancel{K}} \times 295\ \cancel{K}}{0.0550\ \cancel{L}} = 286.44906\ atm = 286\ atm$$

Check: The units (atm) are correct. The magnitude of the answer (300 atm) makes sense because, as you will see in the next section, one mole of an ideal gas under standard conditions (273 K and 1 atm) occupies 22.4 L. Although these are not standard conditions, they can be used for a ballpark check of the answer. Since the volume is ~ 1/400th the molar volume and we have ~2/3 of a mole, the resulting pressure should be (400)(2/3) = 270 atm.

Given: $V_1 = 55.0$ mL, $P_1 = 286$ atm, and $P_2 = 1.20$ atm **Find:** V_2 (number of 750 mL-bottles)

Conceptual Plan: V_1, P_1, P_2 → V_2

$P_1 V_1 = P_2 V_2$

Solution: $P_1 V_1 = P_2 V_2$ Rearrange to solve for V_2.

$$V_2 = V_1 \frac{P_1}{P_2} = 55.0\ mL \times \frac{286.44906\ \cancel{atm}}{1.20\ \cancel{atm}} = 1.31289 \times 10^4\ \cancel{mL} \times \frac{1\ bottle}{750.0\ \cancel{mL}} = 17.5\ bottles$$

Check: The units (bottles) are correct. The magnitude of the answer (18 bottles) makes physical sense because Boyle's Law indicates that as the volume decreases, the pressure increases. The pressure is decreasing by a factor of ~ 250 and so the volume should increase by this factor.

5.52 **Given:** 16.0 g CO_2, $V = 3.45$ L, and $T = 298$ K **Find:** P (psi)

Conceptual Plan: g → n then n, V, T → P then atm → psi (absolute) → psi (gauge)

$\frac{1\ mol}{44.01\ g}$ $PV = nRT$ $\frac{14.7\ psi}{1\ atm}$ subtract 14.7 psi (atmospheric pressure)

Solution: $16.0\ \cancel{g} \times \frac{1\ mol}{44.01\ \cancel{g}} = 0.3635537\ mol$ $\quad 55.0\ \cancel{mL} \times \frac{1\ L}{1000\ \cancel{mL}} = 0.0550\ L$

$PV = nRT$ Rearrange to solve for P.

$$P = \frac{nRT}{V} = \frac{0.3635537\ \cancel{mol} \times 0.08206 \frac{\cancel{L} \cdot atm}{\cancel{mol} \cdot \cancel{K}} \times 298\ \cancel{K}}{3.45\ \cancel{L}} = 2.576898\ \cancel{atm} \times \frac{14.7\ psi}{1\ \cancel{atm}} = 37.9\ psi\ (absolute)$$

or 23.2 psi (gauge) after subtracting 14.7 psi.

Check: The units (psi) are correct. The magnitude of the answer (23 psi) makes sense because, as you will see in the next section, one mole of an ideal gas under standard conditions (273 K and 1 atm) occupies 22.4 L.

Although these are not standard conditions, they can be used for a ballpark check of the answer. Since the volume is almost $1/7^{th}$ the molar volume and we have ~1/3 of a mole, the resulting pressure should be just under (7)(1/3) = 3 atm.

5.53 **Given:** sample a = 5 gas particles, sample b = 10 gas particles, and sample c = 8 gas particles, with all temperatures and volumes the same **Find:** sample with largest P
Conceptual Plan: $n, V, T \rightarrow P$

$$PV = nRT$$

Solution: $PV = nRT$ Since V and T are constant, this means that $P \alpha n$. The sample with the largest number of gas particles will have the highest P. $P_b > P_c > P_a$.

5.54 **Given:** $P_1 = 1$ atm, $V_1 = 1$ L, $T_1 = 25$ °C, $V_2 = 0.5$ L, and $T_2 = 250.$ °C
Find: Draw picture and P_2
Conceptual Plan: °C $\rightarrow$ K then $P_1, V_1, T_1, V_2, T_2 \rightarrow P_2$

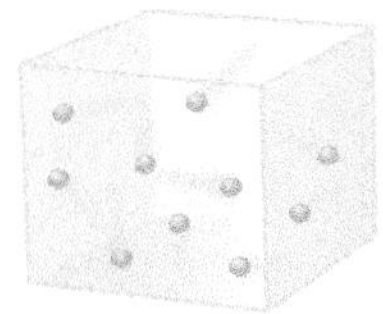

$$\text{K} = {}^\circ\text{C} + 273.15 \qquad \frac{P_1V_1}{T_1} = \frac{P_2V_2}{T_2}$$

Solution: $T_1 = 25$ °C + 273.15 = 298 K and $T_2 = 250.$ °C + 273.15 = 523. K

$\frac{P_1V_1}{T_1} = \frac{P_2V_2}{T_2}$ Rearrange to solve for P_2. $P_2 = P_1 \frac{V_1}{V_2}\frac{T_2}{T_1} = 1 \text{ atm} \times \frac{1 \text{ L}}{0.5 \text{ L}} \times \frac{523. \text{ K}}{298 \text{ K}} = 4 \text{ atm}$

Check: The units (atm) are correct. The magnitude of the answer (3 atm) makes physical sense because there is an increase in T and a decrease in V, both of which increase P.

5.55 **Given:** $P_1 = 755$ mmHg, $T_1 = 25$ °C, and $T_2 = 1155$ °C **Find:** P_2
Conceptual Plan: °C $\rightarrow$ K and mmHg $\rightarrow$ atm then $P_1, T_1, T_2 \rightarrow P_2$

$$\text{K} = {}^\circ\text{C} + 273.15 \qquad \frac{1 \text{ atm}}{760 \text{ mmHg}} \qquad \frac{P_1}{T_1} = \frac{P_2}{T_2}$$

Solution: $T_1 = 25$ °C + 273.15 = 298 K and $T_2 = 1155$ °C + 273.15 = 1428 K

$P = 755 \text{ mmHg} \times \frac{1 \text{ atm}}{760 \text{ mmHg}} = 0.993421 \text{ atm}$ $\frac{P_1}{T_1} = \frac{P_2}{T_2}$ Rearrange to solve for P_2.

$P_2 = P_1 \frac{T_2}{T_1} = 0.993421 \text{ atm} \times \frac{1428 \text{ K}}{298 \text{ K}} = 4.76 \text{ atm}$

Check: The units (atm) are correct. The magnitude of the answer (5 atm) makes physical sense because there is a significant increase in T, which will increase P significantly.

5.56 **Given:** $V_1 = 1.75$ L, $P_1 = 1.35$ atm, $T_1 = 25$ °C, $V_2 = 1.75$ L, and $T_2 = 355$ °C **Find:** P_2
Conceptual Plan: °C $\rightarrow$ K then $P_1, T_1, T_2 \rightarrow P_2$

$$\text{K} = {}^\circ\text{C} + 273.15 \qquad \frac{P_1}{T_1} = \frac{P_2}{T_2}$$

Solution: $T_1 = 25$ °C + 273.15 = 298 K and $T_2 = 355$ °C + 273.15 = 628 K

$\frac{P_1}{T_1} = \frac{P_2}{T_2}$ Rearrange to solve for P_2. $P_2 = P_1 \frac{T_2}{T_1} = 1.35 \text{ atm} \times \frac{628 \text{ K}}{298 \text{ K}} = 2.84 \text{ atm}$

Check: The units (atm) are correct. The magnitude of the answer (3 atm) makes physical sense because there is a significant increase in T, which will increase P significantly.

5.57 **Given:** STP and m (Ne) = 33.6 g **Find:** V
Conceptual Plan: g $\rightarrow$ mol $\rightarrow$ V

$$\frac{1 \text{ mol}}{20.18 \text{ g}} \qquad \frac{22.414 \text{ L}}{1 \text{ mol}}$$

Solution: $33.6 \text{ g} \times \frac{1 \text{ mol}}{20.18 \text{ g}} \times \frac{22.414 \text{ L}}{1 \text{ mol}} = 37.3 \text{ L}$

Check: The units (L) are correct. The magnitude of the answer (37 L) makes sense because one mole of an ideal gas under standard conditions (273 K and 1 atm) occupies 22.4 L and we have about 1.7 mol.

5.58 **Given:** STP and N_2 **Find:** d
Conceptual Plan: mol $\rightarrow$ g then $m, V \rightarrow d$

$$\frac{28.02 \text{ g}}{1 \text{ mol}} \qquad d = \frac{m}{V}$$

Solution: $1\ \text{mol} \times \dfrac{28.02\ \text{g}}{1\ \text{mol}} = 28.02\ \text{g} = \text{m at STP}\ V = 22.414\ \text{L}\ d = \dfrac{m}{V} = \dfrac{28.02\ \text{g}}{22.414\ \text{L}} = 1.250\ \text{g/L}$

Check: The units (g/L) are correct. The magnitude of the answer (1 g/L) is reasonable for a gas density.

5.59 **Given:** H_2, P = 1655 psi, and T = 20.0 °C **Find:** d

Conceptual Plan: °C → K and psi → atm then $P, T, \mathcal{M}$ → d

$K = °C + 273.15 \qquad \dfrac{1\ \text{atm}}{14.70\ \text{psi}} \qquad d = \dfrac{P\mathcal{M}}{RT}$

Solution: $T = 20.0\ °C + 273.15 = 293.2\ \text{K} \qquad P = 1655\ \text{psi} \times \dfrac{1\ \text{atm}}{14.70\ \text{psi}} = 112.\underline{5}85\ \text{atm}$

$$d = \frac{P\mathcal{M}}{RT} = \frac{112.\underline{5}85\ \text{atm} \times 2.016\ \dfrac{\text{g}}{\text{mol}}}{0.08206\dfrac{\text{L atm}}{\text{K mol}} \times 293.2\ \text{K}} = 9.434\ \frac{\text{g}}{\text{L}}$$

Check: The units (g/L) are correct. The magnitude of the answer (9 g/L) makes physical sense because this is a high pressure, so the gas density will be on the high side.

5.60 **Given:** N_2O, d = 2.85 g/L, and T = 298 K **Find:** P (mmHg)

Conceptual Plan: $d, T, \mathcal{M}$ → d then atm → mmHg

$d = \dfrac{P\mathcal{M}}{RT} \qquad \dfrac{760\ \text{mmHg}}{1\ \text{atm}}$

Solution: $d = \dfrac{P\mathcal{M}}{RT}$ Rearrange to solve for P. $P = \dfrac{dRT}{\mathcal{M}} = \dfrac{2.85\ \dfrac{\text{g}}{\text{L}} \times 0.08206\dfrac{\text{L atm}}{\text{K mol}} \times 298\ \text{K}}{60.02\ \dfrac{\text{g}}{\text{mol}}} = 1.1\underline{6}117\ \text{atm}$

$$P = 1.1\underline{6}117\ \text{atm} \times \frac{760\ \text{mmHg}}{1\ \text{atm}} = 882\ \text{mmHg}$$

Check: The units (mmHg) are correct. The magnitude of the answer (1200 mmHg) makes physical sense because the gas density is reasonable and so we expect a P ~1 atm.

5.61 **Given:** V = 248 mL, m = 0.433 g, P = 745 mmHg, and T = 28 °C **Find:** $\mathcal{M}$

Conceptual Plan: °C → K mmHg → atm mL → L then V, m → d then d, P, T → $\mathcal{M}$

$K = °C + 273.15 \qquad \dfrac{1\ \text{atm}}{760\ \text{mmHg}} \qquad \dfrac{1\ \text{L}}{1000\ \text{mL}} \qquad d = \dfrac{m}{V} \qquad d = \dfrac{P\mathcal{M}}{RT}$

Solution: $T = 28\ °C + 273.15 = 301\ \text{K} \quad P = 745\ \text{mmHg} \times \dfrac{1\ \text{atm}}{760\ \text{mmHg}} = 0.98\underline{0}263\ \text{atm}$

$V = 248\ \text{mL} \times \dfrac{1\ \text{L}}{1000\ \text{mL}} = 0.248\ \text{L}\ \ d = \dfrac{m}{V} = \dfrac{0.433\ \text{g}}{0.248\ \text{L}} = 1.7\underline{4}597\ \text{g/L}\ \ d = \dfrac{P\mathcal{M}}{RT}$ Rearrange to solve for $\mathcal{M}$.

$$\mathcal{M} = \frac{dRT}{P} = \frac{1.7\underline{4}597\ \dfrac{\text{g}}{\text{L}} \times 0.08206\dfrac{\text{L} \cdot \text{atm}}{\text{K} \cdot \text{mol}} \times 301\ \text{K}}{0.98\underline{0}263\ \text{atm}} = 44.0\ \text{g/mol}$$

Check: The units (g/mol) are correct. The magnitude of the answer (44 g/mol) makes physical sense because this is a reasonable number for a molecular weight of a gas.

5.62 **Given:** V = 113 mL, m = 0.171 g, P = 721 mmHg, and T = 32 °C **Find:** $\mathcal{M}$

Conceptual Plan: °C → K mmHg → atm mL → L then V, m → d then d, P, T → $\mathcal{M}$

$K = °C + 273.15 \qquad \dfrac{1\ \text{atm}}{760\ \text{mmHg}} \qquad \dfrac{1\ \text{L}}{1000\ \text{mL}} \qquad d = \dfrac{m}{V} \qquad d = \dfrac{P\mathcal{M}}{RT}$

Solution: $T = 32\ °C + 273.15 = 305\ \text{K} \quad P = 721\ \text{mmHg} \times \dfrac{1\ \text{atm}}{760\ \text{mmHg}} = 0.94\underline{8}684\ \text{atm}$

$V = 113\ \text{mL} \times \dfrac{1\ \text{L}}{1000\ \text{mL}} = 0.113\ \text{L}\ \ d = \dfrac{m}{V} = \dfrac{0.171\ \text{g}}{0.113\ \text{L}} = 1.5\underline{1}327\ \text{g/L}\ \ d = \dfrac{P\mathcal{M}}{RT}$ Rearrange to solve for $\mathcal{M}$.

$$\mathcal{M} = \frac{dRT}{P} = \frac{1.5\underline{1}327\ \dfrac{\text{g}}{\text{L}} \times 0.08206\dfrac{\text{L atm}}{\text{K mol}} \times 305\ \text{K}}{0.94\underline{8}684\ \text{atm}} = 39.9\ \text{g/mol}$$

Check: The units (g/mol) are correct. The magnitude of the answer (40 g/mol) makes physical sense because this is a reasonable number for a molecular weight of a gas.

5.63 **Given:** m = 38.8 mg, V = 224 mL, T = 55 °C, and P = 886 torr **Find:** $\mathcal{M}$
Conceptual Plan: mg → g mL → L °C → K torr → atm then V, m → d then d, P, T → $\mathcal{M}$

$\frac{1\text{ g}}{1000\text{ mg}}$ $\frac{1\text{ L}}{1000\text{ mL}}$ $K = °C + 273.15$ $\frac{1\text{ atm}}{760\text{ torr}}$ $d = \frac{m}{V}$ $d = \frac{P\mathcal{M}}{RT}$

Solution: $m = 38.8\text{ mg} \times \frac{1\text{ g}}{1000\text{ mg}} = 0.0388\text{ g}$ $V = 224\text{ mL} \times \frac{1\text{ L}}{1000\text{ mL}} = 0.224\text{ L}$ $T = 55\text{ °C} + 273.15 = 328\text{ K}$

$P = 886\text{ torr} \times \frac{1\text{ atm}}{760\text{ torr}} = 1.165789\text{ atm}$ $d = \frac{m}{V} = \frac{0.0388\text{ g}}{0.224\text{ L}} = 0.173214\text{ g/L}$ $d = \frac{P\mathcal{M}}{RT}$

Rearrange to solve for $\mathcal{M}$. $\mathcal{M} = \frac{dRT}{P} = \frac{0.173214\frac{\text{g}}{\text{L}} \times 0.08206\frac{\text{L atm}}{\text{K mol}} \times 328\text{ K}}{1.165789\text{ atm}} = 4.00\text{ g/mol}$

Check: The units (g/mol) are correct. The magnitude of the answer (4 g/mol) makes physical sense because this is a reasonable number for a molecular weight of a gas, especially since the density is on the low side.

5.64 **Given:** m = 0.555 g, V = 117 mL, T = 85 °C, and P = 753 mmHg **Find:** → $\mathcal{M}$
Conceptual Plan: mL → L °C → K mmHg → atm then V, m → d then d, P, T → $\mathcal{M}$

$\frac{1\text{ L}}{1000\text{ mL}}$ $K = °C + 273.15$ $\frac{1\text{ atm}}{760\text{ mmHg}}$ $d = \frac{m}{V}$ $d = \frac{P\mathcal{M}}{RT}$

Solution: $V = 117\text{ mL} \times \frac{1\text{ L}}{1000\text{ mL}} = 0.117\text{ L}$ $T = 85\text{ °C} + 273.15 = 358\text{ K}$

$P = 753\text{ mmHg} \times \frac{1\text{ atm}}{760\text{ mmHg}} = 0.9907895\text{ atm}$ $d = \frac{m}{V} = \frac{0.555\text{ g}}{0.117\text{ L}} = 4.74359\text{ g/L}$ $d = \frac{P\mathcal{M}}{RT}$

Rearrange to solve for $\mathcal{M}$. $\mathcal{M} = \frac{dRT}{P} = \frac{4.74359\frac{\text{g}}{\text{L}} \times 0.08206\frac{\text{L}\cdot\text{atm}}{\text{K}\cdot\text{mol}} \times 358\text{ K}}{0.9907895\text{ atm}} = 141\text{ g/mol}$

Check: The units (g/mol) are correct. The magnitude of the answer (141 g/mol) makes physical sense because this is a reasonable number for a molecular weight of a gas, especially since the density is on the high side.

Partial Pressure

5.65 **Given:** P_{N_2} = 215 torr, P_{O_2} = 102 torr, P_{He} = 117 torr, V = 1.35 L, and T = 25.0 °C
Find: $P_{Total}, m_{N_2}, m_{O_2}, m_{He}$
Conceptual Plan: °C → K and torr → atm and P, V, T → n then mol → g

$K = °C + 273.15$ $\frac{1\text{ atm}}{760\text{ torr}}$ $PV = nRT$ $\mathcal{M}$

and P_{N_2}, P_{O_2}, P_{He} → P_{Total}

$P_{Total} = P_{N_2} + P_{O_2} + P_{He}$

Solution: $T_1 = 25.0\text{ °C} + 273.15 = 298.2\text{ K}$, $PV = nRT$ Rearrange to solve for n.

$n = \frac{PV}{RT}$ $P_{N_2} = 215\text{ torr} \times \frac{1\text{ atm}}{760\text{ torr}} = 0.2828947\text{ atm}$ $n_{N_2} = \frac{0.2828947\text{ atm} \times 1.35\text{ L}}{0.08206\frac{\text{L}\cdot\text{atm}}{\text{mol}\cdot\text{K}} \times 298.2\text{ K}} = 0.01560700\text{ mol}$

$0.01560700\text{ mol} \times \frac{28.02\text{ mol}}{1\text{ mol}} = 0.437\text{ g } N_2$

$P_{O_2} = 102\text{ torr} \times \frac{1\text{ atm}}{760\text{ torr}} = 0.1342105\text{ atm}$ $n_{O_2} = \frac{0.1342105\text{ atm} \times 1.35\text{ L}}{0.08206\frac{\text{L}\cdot\text{atm}}{\text{mol}\cdot\text{K}} \times 298.2\text{ K}} = 0.007404252\text{ mol}$

$0.007404252\text{ mol} \times \frac{32.00\text{ mol}}{1\text{ mol}} = 0.237\text{ g } O_2$

$P_{He} = 117\text{ torr} \times \frac{1\text{ atm}}{760\text{ torr}} = 0.1539474\text{ atm}$ $n_{He} = \frac{0.1539474\text{ atm} \times 1.35\text{ L}}{0.08206\frac{\text{L}\cdot\text{atm}}{\text{mol}\cdot\text{K}} \times 298.2\text{ K}} = 0.008493113\text{ mol}$

$0.008493113\text{ mol} \times \frac{4.003\text{ mol}}{1\text{ mol}} = 0.0340\text{ g He}$ and

$P_{Total} = P_{N_2} + P_{O_2} + P_{He} = 0.283\text{ atm} + 0.134\text{ atm} + 0.154\text{ atm} = 0.571\text{ atm}$ or
$P_{Total} = P_{N_2} + P_{O_2} + P_{He} = 215\text{ torr} + 102\text{ torr} + 117\text{ torr} = 434\text{ torr}$

Check: The units (g and atm) are correct. The magnitude of the answer (1 g) makes sense because gases are not very dense and these pressures are < 1 atm. Since all of the pressures are small, the total is < 1 atm.

5.66 **Given:** $P_{\text{Total}} = 745$ mmHg, $P_{CO_2} = 125$ mmHg, $P_{Ar} = 214$ mmHg, $P_{O_2} = 187$ mmHg, $V = 12.0$ L, and $T = 273$ K
Find: P_{He} and m_{He}
Conceptual Plan: $P_{\text{Total}}, P_{CO_2}, P_{Ar}, P_{O_2} \rightarrow P_{He}$ **then mmHg** $\rightarrow$ **atm then** $P, V, T \rightarrow n$ **then mol** $\rightarrow$ **g**

$P_{\text{Total}} = P_{CO_2} + P_{Ar} + P_{O_2} + P_{He}$ $\quad \frac{1 \text{ atm}}{760 \text{ mmHg}}$ $\quad V = nRT$ $\quad \frac{4.003 \text{ g}}{1 \text{ mol}}$

Solution: $P_{\text{Total}} = P_{CO_2} + P_{Ar} + P_{O_2} + P_{He}$ Rearrange to solve for P_{He}.
$P_{He} = P_{\text{Total}} - P_{CO_2} + P_{Ar} + P_{O_2} = 745 \text{ mmHg} - 125 \text{ mmHg} - 214 \text{ mmHg} - 187 \text{ mmHg} = 219 \text{ mmHg}$

$$P_{He} = 219 \text{ mmHg} \times \frac{1 \text{ atm}}{760 \text{ mmHg}} = 0.288 \text{ atm} \quad PV = nRT \text{ Rearrange to solve for } n. \; n = \frac{PV}{RT}$$

$$n_{He} = \frac{0.288 \text{ atm} \times 12.0 \text{ L}}{0.08206 \frac{\text{L} \cdot \text{atm}}{\text{mol} \cdot \text{K}} \times 273 \text{ K}} = 0.15\underline{4}3539 \text{ mol} \quad 0.15\underline{4}3539 \text{ mol} \times \frac{4.003 \text{ g}}{1 \text{ mol}} = 0.618 \text{ g He}$$

Check: The units (g) are correct. The magnitude of the answer (1 g) makes sense because gases are not very dense and these pressures are < 1 atm.

5.67 **Given:** $m\,(CO_2) = 1.20$ g, $V = 755$ mL, $P_{N_2} = 725$ mmHg, and $T = 25.0$ °C **Find:** P_{Total}
Conceptual Plan: mL $\rightarrow$ **L and °C** $\rightarrow$ **K and g** $\rightarrow$ **mol and** $n, P, T \rightarrow V$ **then atm** $\rightarrow$ **mmHg**

$\frac{1 \text{ L}}{1000 \text{ mL}}$ $\quad K = °C + 273.15$ $\quad \frac{1 \text{ mol}}{44.01 \text{ g}}$ $\quad PV = nRT$ $\quad \frac{760 \text{ mmHg}}{1 \text{ atm}}$

finally $P_{CO_2}, P_{N_2} \rightarrow P_{\text{Total}}$

$P_{\text{Total}} = P_{CO_2} + P_{N_2}$

Solution: $V = 755 \text{ mL} \times \frac{1 \text{ L}}{1000 \text{ mL}} = 0.755 \text{ L} \quad T = 25.0\text{ °C} + 273.15 = 298.2 \text{ K},$

$$n = 1.20 \text{ g} \times \frac{1 \text{ mol}}{44.01 \text{ g}} = 0.027\underline{2}665 \text{ mol}, \quad PV = nRT \text{ Rearrange to solve for } P.$$

$$P = \frac{nRT}{V} = \frac{0.027\underline{2}665 \text{ mol} \times 0.08206 \frac{\text{L} \cdot \text{atm}}{\text{mol} \cdot \text{K}} \times 298.2 \text{ K}}{0.755 \text{ L}} = 0.88\underline{3}735 \text{ atm}$$

$$P_{CO_2} = 0.88\underline{3}735 \text{ atm} \times \frac{760 \text{ mmHg}}{1 \text{ atm}} = 672 \text{ mmHg}$$

$$P_{\text{Total}} = P_{CO_2} + P_{N_2} = 672 \text{ mmHg} + 725 \text{ mmHg} = 1397 \text{ mmHg or } 1397 \text{ torr} \times \frac{1 \text{ atm}}{760 \text{ torr}} = 1.84 \text{ atm}$$

Check: The units (mmHg) are correct. The magnitude of the answer (1400 mmHg) makes sense because it must be greater than 725 mmHg.

5.68 **Given:** $V_{1He} = 275$ mL, $P_{1He} = 752$ torr, $V_{1Ar} = 475$ mL, and $P_{1Ar} = 722$ torr **Find:** P_{2He}, P_{2Ar}, and P_{Total}
Conceptual Plan: $V_{1He}, V_{1Ar} \rightarrow V_2$ $V_1, P_1, V_2 \rightarrow P_2$ **then** $P_{2He}, P_{2Ar} \rightarrow P_{\text{Total}}$

$V_{1He} + V_{1Ar} = V_2$ $\quad P_1V_1 = P_2V_2$ $\quad P_{\text{Total}} = P_{2He} + P_{2Ar}$

Solution: $V_{1He} + V_{1Ar} = V_2 = 275 \text{ mL} + 475 \text{ mL} = 750. \text{ mL}$, $P_1 V_1 = P_2 V_2$ Rearrange to solve for P_2.

$$P_2 = P_1 \frac{V_1}{V_2} \quad P_{2He} = P_{1He} \frac{V_{1He}}{V_2} = 752 \text{ torr} \times \frac{275 \text{ mL}}{750. \text{ mL}} = 27\underline{5}.733 \text{ torr} = 276 \text{ torr He}$$

$$P_{2Ar} = P_{1Ar} \frac{V_{1Ar}}{V_2} = 722 \text{ torr} \times \frac{475 \text{ mL}}{750. \text{ mL}} = 45\underline{7}.267 \text{ torr} = 457 \text{ torr Ar}$$

$P_{\text{Total}} = P_{2He} + P_{2Ar} = 27\underline{5}.733 \text{ torr} + 45\underline{7}.267 \text{ torr} = 733$ torr total pressure
Check: The units (torr) are correct. The magnitude of the answers makes physical sense because Boyles Law indicates that as the volume increases, the pressure decreases. Since both initial pressures are ~700 torr, the final total pressure should be about the same pressure.

5.69 **Given:** $m\,(N_2) = 1.25$ g, $m\,(O_2) = 0.85$ g, $V = 1.55$ L, and $T = 18$ °C **Find:** $\chi_{N_2}, \chi_{O_2}, P_{N_2}, P_{O_2}$
Conceptual Plan: g $\rightarrow$ **mol then** $n_{N_2}, n_{O_2} \rightarrow \chi_{N_2}$ **and** $n_{N_2}, n_{O_2} \rightarrow \chi_{O_2}$ **°C** $\rightarrow$ **K**

$\mathcal{M}$ $\quad \chi_{N_2} = \frac{n_{N_2}}{n_{N_2} + n_{O_2}}$ $\quad \chi_{O_2} = \frac{n_{O_2}}{n_{N_2} + n_{O_2}}$ $\quad K = °C + 273.15$

then $n, V, T \rightarrow P$

$PV = nRT$

Solution: $n_{N_2} = 1.25\ \text{g} \times \frac{1\ \text{mol}}{28.02\ \text{g}} = 0.0446110\ \text{mol}$, $n_{O_2} = 0.85\ \text{g} \times \frac{1\ \text{mol}}{32.00\ \text{g}} = 0.026563\ \text{mol}$,

$T = 18\ °C + 273.15 = 291\ K$, $\chi_{N_2} = \frac{n_{N_2}}{n_{N_2} + n_{O_2}} = \frac{0.0446110\ \text{mol}}{0.0446110\ \text{mol} + 0.026563\ \text{mol}} = 0.626792 = 0.627$,

$\chi_{O_2} = \frac{n_{O_2}}{n_{N_2} + n_{O_2}} = \frac{0.026563\ \text{mol}}{0.0446110\ \text{mol} + 0.026563\ \text{mol}} = 0.373212$ We can also calculate this as

$\chi_{O_2} = 1 - \chi_{N_2} = 1 - 0.626792 = 0.373208 = 0.373$ $PV = nRT$ Rearrange to solve for P. $P = \frac{nRT}{V}$

$$P_{N_2} = \frac{0.044611\ \text{mol} \times 0.08206 \frac{\text{L}\cdot\text{atm}}{\text{mol}\cdot\text{K}} \times 291\ \text{K}}{1.55\ \text{L}} = 0.687\ \text{atm}$$

$$P_{O_2} = \frac{0.026563\ \text{mol} \times 0.08206 \frac{\text{L}\cdot\text{atm}}{\text{mol}\cdot\text{K}} \times 291\ \text{K}}{1.55\ \text{L}} = 0.409\ \text{atm}$$

Check: The units (none and atm) are correct. The magnitude of the answers makes sense because the mole fractions should total 1 and since the weight of N_2 is greater than O_2, its mole fraction is larger. The number of moles is <<1, so we expect the pressures to be <1 atm, given the V (1.55 L).

5.70 **Given:** Table 5.3, $m\ (O_2) = 10.0$ g, $T = 273$ K, and $P = 1.00$ atm **Find:** χ_{O_2} and V_{air}

Conceptual Plan: $\%V \rightarrow \chi_{O_2}$ **and g** $\rightarrow$ **mol** $\rightarrow V_{O_2} \rightarrow V_{air}$

$\frac{1}{100\ \%}$; $\frac{1\ \text{mol}}{32.00\ \text{g}}$; $\frac{22.414\ \text{L}}{1\ \text{mol}}$; $\frac{100\ \text{L air}}{21\ \text{L}\ O_2}$

Solution: from Table 5.3 $\%V_{O_2} = 21\ \%$ $\quad 21\ \% \times \frac{1}{100\ \%} = 0.21 = \chi_{O_2}$

$10.0\ \text{g} \times \frac{1\ \text{mol}}{32.00\ \text{g}} \times \frac{22.414\ \text{L}}{1\ \text{mol}} = 7.00\ \text{L} = V_{O_2}$ finally $7.00\ \text{L}\ O_2 \times \frac{100\ \text{L air}}{21\ \text{L}\ O_2} = 33\ \text{L air}$

Check: The units (none and L) are correct. The magnitude of the answer (0.21) makes sense because most of air is nitrogen. The magnitude of the answer (33 L) makes sense because one mole of an ideal gas under standard conditions (273 K and 1 atm) occupies 22.4 L and we have about 1/3 mol of O_2 and so over a mole of air.

5.71 **Given:** $T = 30.0$ °C, $P_{Total} = 732$ mmHg, and $V = 722$ mL **Find:** P_{H_2} and m_{H_2}

Conceptual Plan: $T \rightarrow P_{H_2O}$ **then** $P_{Total}, P_{H_2O} \rightarrow P_{H_2}$ **then mmHg** $\rightarrow$ **atm and mL** $\rightarrow$ **L**

Table 5.4 ; $P_{Total} = P_{H_2O} + P_{H_2}$; $\frac{1\ \text{atm}}{760\ \text{mmHg}}$; $\frac{1\ \text{L}}{1000\ \text{mL}}$

and °C $\rightarrow$ **K** $P, V, T \rightarrow n$ **then mol** $\rightarrow$ **g**

$K = °C + 273.15$; $PV = nRT$; $\frac{2.016\ \text{g}}{1\ \text{mol}}$

Solution: Table 5.4 states that at 30° C, $P_{H_2O} = 31.86$ mmHg $P_{Total} = P_{H_2O} + P_{H_2}$
Rearrange to solve for P_{H_2}. $P_{H_2} = P_{Total} - P_{H_2O} = 732\ \text{mmHg} - 31.86\ \text{mmHg} = 700.\ \text{mmHg}$

$P_{H_2} = 700.\ \text{mmHg} \times \frac{1\ \text{atm}}{760\ \text{mmHg}} = 0.921052\ \text{atm}$ $\quad V = 722\ \text{mL} \times \frac{1\ \text{L}}{1000\ \text{mL}} = 0.722\ \text{L}$,

$T = 30.0\ °C + 273.15 = 303.2\ K$, $PV = nRT$ Rearrange to solve for n. $n = \frac{PV}{RT}$

$$n_{H_2} = \frac{0.921052\ \text{atm} \times 0.722\ \text{L}}{0.08206 \frac{\text{L}\cdot\text{atm}}{\text{mol}\cdot\text{K}} \times 303.2\ \text{K}} = 0.0267277\ \text{mol then } 0.0267277\ \text{mol} \times \frac{2.016\ \text{g}}{1\ \text{mol}} = 0.0539\ \text{g}\ H_2$$

Check: The units (g) are correct. The magnitude of the answer (<< 1 g) makes sense because gases are not very dense, hydrogen is light, the volume is small, and the pressure is ~1 atm.

5.72 **Given:** $T = 25$ °C, $V = 5.45$ L, and $P_{Total} = 745$ mmHg **Find:** n

Conceptual Plan: $T \rightarrow P_{H_2O}$ **then** $P_{Total}, P_{H_2O} \rightarrow P_{air}$ **then mmHg** $\rightarrow$ **atm and °C** $\rightarrow$ **K**

Table 5.4 ; $P_{Total} = P_{H_2O} + P_{air}$; $\frac{1\ \text{atm}}{760\ \text{mmHg}}$; $K = °C + 273.15$

$P, V, T \rightarrow n$

$PV = nRT$

Solution: Table 5.4 states that at 25°C $P_{H_2O} = 23.78$ mmHg $P_{Total} = P_{H_2O} + P_{air}$ Rearrange to solve for P_{air}. $P_{air} = P_{Total} - P_{H_2O} = 745\ \text{mmHg} - 23.78\ \text{mmHg} = 721\ \text{mmHg}$

$$P_{air} = 721 \text{ mmHg} \times \frac{1 \text{ atm}}{760 \text{ mmHg}} = 0.948684 \text{ atm} \quad T = 25\ °C + 273.15 = 298 \text{ K}, \quad PV = nRT$$

Rearrange to solve for n. $n = \dfrac{PV}{RT} = \dfrac{0.948684 \text{ atm} \times 5.45 \text{ L}}{0.08206 \frac{\text{L} \cdot \text{atm}}{\text{mol} \cdot \text{K}} \times 298 \text{ K}} = 0.211 \text{ mol}$

Check: The units (mol) are correct. The magnitude of the answer (0.2 mol) makes sense because 22.4 L of a gas at STP contains 1 mol. We have only 5.45 L, so the answer makes sense.

5.73 **Given:** $T = 25\ °C$, $P_{Total} = 748$ mmHg, and $V = 0.951$ L **Find:** P_{H_2} and m_{H_2}

Conceptual Plan: $T \rightarrow P_{H_2O}$ **then** $P_{Total}, P_{H_2O} \rightarrow P_{H_2}$ **then mmHg → atm and mL → L**

Table 5.4 $\quad P_{Total} = P_{H_2O} + P_{H_2} \quad \dfrac{1 \text{ atm}}{760 \text{ mmHg}} \quad \dfrac{1 \text{ L}}{1000 \text{ mL}}$

and °C → K $P, V, T \rightarrow n$ **then mol → g**

$K = °C + 273.15 \quad PV = nRT \quad \dfrac{2.016 \text{ g}}{1 \text{ mol}}$

Solution: Table 5.4 states that at 25° C, $P_{H_2O} = 23.78$ mmHg $P_{Total} = P_{H_2O} + P_{H_2}$

Rearrange to solve for P_{H_2}. $P_{H_2} = P_{Total} - P_{H_2O} = 748 \text{ mmHg} - 23.78 \text{ mmHg} = 724 \text{ mmHg}$

$$P_{H_2} = 724 \text{ mmHg} \times \frac{1 \text{ atm}}{760 \text{ mmHg}} = 0.952632 \text{ atm} \quad T = 25\ °C + 273.15 = 298 \text{ K}, \quad PV = nRT$$

Rearrange to solve for n. $n_{H_2} = \dfrac{PV}{RT} = \dfrac{0.952632 \text{ atm} \times 0.951 \text{ L}}{0.08206 \frac{\text{L} \cdot \text{atm}}{\text{mol} \cdot \text{K}} \times 298 \text{ K}} = 0.0370474 \text{ mol}$

$$0.0370474 \text{ mol} \times \frac{2.016 \text{ g}}{1 \text{ mol}} = 0.0747 \text{ g } H_2$$

Check: The units (g) are correct. The magnitude of the answer (<< 1 g) makes sense because gases are not very dense, hydrogen is light, the volume is small, and the pressure is ~1 atm.

5.74 **Given:** $m\ (O_2) = 2.0$ g, m (He) $= 98.0$ g, $P_{Total} = 8.5$ atm **Find:** P_{O_2}

Conceptual Plan: g → mol then $n_{O_2}, n_{He} \rightarrow \chi_{O_2}$ **then** $\chi_{O_2}, P_{Total} \rightarrow P_{O_2}$

$\mathcal{M} \quad \chi_{O_2} = \dfrac{n_{O_2}}{n_{O_2} + n_{He}} \quad P_{O_2} = \chi_{O_2} P_{Total}$

Solution: $n_{O_2} = 2.0 \text{ g} \times \dfrac{1 \text{ mol}}{32.00 \text{ g}} = 0.0625 \text{ mol}, \; n_{He} = 98.0 \text{ g} \times \dfrac{1 \text{ mol}}{4.003 \text{ g}} = 24.4816 \text{ mol},$

$$\chi_{O_2} = \frac{n_{O_2}}{n_{O_2} + n_{He}} = \frac{0.0625 \text{ mol}}{0.0625 \text{ mol} + 24.4816 \text{ mol}} = 0.0025464,$$

$$P_{O_2} = \chi_{O_2} P_{Total} = 0.0025464 \times 8.5 \text{ atm} = 0.022 \text{ atm}$$

Check: The units (atm) are correct. The magnitude of the answer (0.22 atm) makes sense because, at these depths, high oxygen pressures can cause toxicity.

Reaction Stoichiometry Involving Gases

5.75 **Given:** m (C) $= 15.7$ g, $P = 1.0$ atm, and $T = 355$ K **Find:** V

Conceptual Plan: g C → mol C → mol H_2 then n (mol H_2), P, T → V

$\dfrac{1 \text{ mol}}{12.01 \text{ g C}} \quad \dfrac{1 \text{ mol } H_2}{1 \text{ mol C}} \quad PV = nRT$

Solution: $15.7 \text{ g C} \times \dfrac{1 \text{ mol C}}{12.01 \text{ g C}} \times \dfrac{1 \text{ mol } H_2}{1 \text{ mol C}} = 1.30724 \text{ mol } H_2, \quad PV = nRT$ Rearrange to solve for V.

$$V = \frac{nRT}{P} = \frac{1.30724 \text{ mol} \times 0.08206 \frac{\text{L} \cdot \text{atm}}{\text{mol} \cdot \text{K}} \times 355 \text{ K}}{1.0 \text{ atm}} = 38 \text{ L}$$

Check: The units (L) are correct. The magnitude of the answer (38 L) makes sense because we have more than one mole of gas, and so we expect more than 22 L.

5.76 **Given:** $V_{O_2} = 1.4$ L, $T = 315$ K, $P_{O_2} = 0.957$ atm **Find:** g H_2O

Conceptual Plan: P(mol O_2), V(mol O_2), T → n(mol O_2) then mol O_2 → mol H_2O → g H_2O

$PV = nRT \quad \dfrac{2 \text{ mol } H_2O}{1 \text{ mol } O_2} \quad \dfrac{18.02 \text{ g } H_2O}{1 \text{ mol } H_2O}$

Solution: $PV = nRT$ Rearrange to solve for n. $n = \frac{PV}{RT} = \frac{0.957\ \text{atm} \times 1.4\ \text{L}}{0.08206\ \frac{\text{L}\cdot\text{atm}}{\text{mol}\cdot\text{K}} \times 315\ \text{K}} = 0.05\underline{1}832\ \text{mol } O_2$

$0.05\underline{1}832\ \text{mol } O_2 \times \frac{2\ \text{mol } H_2O}{1\ \text{mol } O_2} \times \frac{18.02\ \text{g } H_2O}{1\ \text{mol } H_2O} = 1.9\ \text{g } H_2O$

Check: The units (g) are correct. The magnitude of the answer (2 g) makes sense because we have much less than a mole of oxygen.

5.77 **Given:** $P = 748$ mmHg, $T = 86$ °C, and m (CH_3OH) = 25.8 g, and **Find:** V_{H_2} and V_{CO}

Conceptual Plan: g CH_3OH → mol CH_3OH → mol H_2 and mmHg → atm and °C → K

$\frac{1\ \text{mol } CH_3OH}{32.04\ \text{g } CH_3OH}$ $\frac{2\ \text{mol } H_2}{1\ \text{mol } CH_3OH}$ $\frac{1\ \text{atm}}{760\ \text{mmHg}}$ K = °C + 273.15

then n (mol H_2), P, T → V and mol H_2 → mol CO then n (mol CO), P, T → V

$PV = nRT$ $\frac{1\ \text{mol CO}}{2\ \text{mol } H_2}$ $PV = nRT$

Solution: $25.8\ \text{g } CH_3OH \times \frac{1\ \text{mol } CH_3OH}{32.04\ \text{g } CH_3OH} \times \frac{2\ \text{mol } H_2}{1\ \text{mol } CH_3OH} = 1.6\underline{1}049\ \text{mol } H_2$,

$P_{H_2} = 748\ \text{mmHg} \times \frac{1\ \text{atm}}{760\ \text{mmHg}} = 0.98\underline{4}211$ atm, $T = 86$ °C + 273.15 = 359 K, $PV = nRT$

Rearrange to solve for V. $V = \frac{nRT}{P}$ $V_{H_2} = \frac{1.6\underline{1}049\ \text{mol} \times 0.08206\ \frac{\text{L}\cdot\text{atm}}{\text{mol}\cdot\text{K}} \times 359\ \text{K}}{0.98\underline{4}211\ \text{atm}} = 48.2\ \text{L } H_2$

$1.6\underline{1}049\ \text{mol } H_2 \times \frac{1\ \text{mol CO}}{2\ \text{mol } H_2} = 0.80\underline{5}25\ \text{mol CO}$, $V_{CO} = \frac{0.80\underline{5}25\ \text{mol} \times 0.08206\ \frac{\text{L}\cdot\text{atm}}{\text{mol}\cdot\text{K}} \times 359\ \text{K}}{0.98\underline{4}211\ \text{atm}} = 24.1\ \text{L CO}$

Check: The units (L) are correct. The magnitude of the answer (48 L and 24 L) makes sense because we have more than one mole of hydrogen gas and half that of CO and so we expect significantly more than 22 L for hydrogen and half that for CO.

5.78 **Given:** $P = 782$ mmHg, $T = 25$ °C, and m (Al) = 53.2 g **Find:** V_{O_2}

Conceptual Plan: g Al → mol Al → mol O_2 and mmHg → atm and °C → K then

$\frac{1\ \text{mol Al}}{26.98\ \text{g Al}}$ $\frac{3\ \text{mol } O_2}{4\ \text{mol Al}}$ $\frac{1\ \text{atm}}{760\ \text{mmHg}}$ K = °C + 273.15

n (mol O_2), P, T → V

$PV = nRT$

Solution: $53.2\ \text{g Al} \times \frac{1\ \text{mol Al}}{26.98\ \text{g } O_2} \times \frac{3\ \text{mol } O_2}{4\ \text{mol Al}} = 1.4\underline{7}8873\ \text{mol } O_2$,

$P_{O_2} = 782\ \text{mmHg} \times \frac{1\ \text{atm}}{760\ \text{mmHg}} = 1.0\underline{2}8947$ atm, $T = 25$ °C + 273.15 = 298 K, $PV = nRT$

Rearrange to solve for V. $V_{O_2} = \frac{nRT}{P} = \frac{1.4\underline{7}8873\ \text{mol} \times 0.08206\ \frac{\text{L}\cdot\text{atm}}{\text{mol}\cdot\text{K}} \times 298\ \text{K}}{1.0\underline{2}8947\ \text{atm}} = 35.1\ \text{L } O_2$

Check: The units (L) are correct. The magnitude of the answer (35 L) makes sense because we have more than one mole of oxygen gas and more than 1 atm, so we expect significantly more than 22 L.

5.79 **Given:** $V = 11.8$ L, and STP **Find:** m (NaN_3)

Conceptual Plan: V_{N_2} → mol N_2 → mol NaN_3 → g NaN_3

$\frac{1\ \text{mol } N_2}{22.414\ \text{L } N_2}$ $\frac{2\ \text{mol } NaN_3}{3\ \text{mol } N_2}$ $\frac{65.03\ \text{g } NaN_3}{1\ \text{mol } NaN_3}$

Solution: $11.8\ \text{L } N_2 \times \frac{1\ \text{mol } N_2}{22.414\ \text{L } N_2} \times \frac{2\ \text{mol } NaN_3}{3\ \text{mol } N_2} \times \frac{65.03\ \text{g } NaN_3}{1\ \text{mol } NaN_3} = 22.8\ \text{g } NaN_3$

Check: The units (g) are correct. The magnitude of the answer (23 g) makes sense because, we have about a half a mole of nitrogen gas, which translates to even fewer moles of NaN_3 and so we expect significantly less than 65 g.

5.80 **Given:** $V = 58.5$ mL, and STP **Find:** m (Li)

Conceptual Plan: $\mathbf{mL_{N_2} \rightarrow L_{N_2} \rightarrow mol\ N_2 \rightarrow mol\ Li \rightarrow g\ Li}$

$\frac{1\,L}{1000\,mL}$ $\frac{1\,mol\,N_2}{22.414\,L\,N_2}$ $\frac{6\,mol\,Li}{1\,mol\,N_2}$ $\frac{6.941\,g\,Li}{1\,mol\,Li}$

Solution: $58.5\ \cancel{mL\ N_2} \times \frac{1\ \cancel{L\ N_2}}{1000\ \cancel{mL\ N_2}} \times \frac{1\ \cancel{mol\ N_2}}{22.414\ \cancel{L\ N_2}} \times \frac{6\ \cancel{mol\ Li}}{1\ \cancel{mol\ N_2}} \times \frac{6.941\ g\ Li}{1\ \cancel{mol\ Li}} = 0.109\ g\ Li$

Check: The units (g) are correct. The magnitude of the answer (0.1 g) makes sense because we have such a small volume, which translates to a small fraction of a mole of Li, and so we expect significantly less than 6.9 g.

5.81 **Given:** $V_{CH_4} = 25.5$ L, $P_{CH_4} = 732$ torr, and $T = 25$ °C; mixed with $V_{H_2O} = 22.8$ L, $P_{H_2O} = 702$ torr, and $T = 125$ °C; forms $P_{H_2} = 26.2$ L at STP **Find:** % Yield

Conceptual Plan: $\mathbf{CH_4}$**: torr → atm and °C → K and** $\boldsymbol{P, V, T \rightarrow n_{CH_4} \rightarrow n_{H_2}}$

$\frac{1\,atm}{760\,torr}$ $K = °C + 273.15$ $PV = nRT$ $\frac{3\,mol\,H_2}{1\,mol\,CH_4}$

$\mathbf{H_2O}$**: torr → atm and °C → K and** $\boldsymbol{P, V, T \rightarrow n_{H_2O} \rightarrow n_{H_2}}$

$\frac{1\,atm}{760\,torr}$ $K = °C + 273.15$ $PV = nRT$ $\frac{3\,mol\,H_2}{1\,mol\,CH_4}$

Select smaller $\mathbf{n_{H_2}}$ **as theoretical yield,**

then $\boldsymbol{L_{H_2}}$ **→ mol** $\mathbf{H_2}$ **(actual yield) finally actual yield, theoretical yield → % Yield**

$\frac{1\,mol\,H_2}{22.414\,L\,H_2}$ $\%\ Yield = \frac{actual\ yield}{theoretical\ yield} \times 100\%$

Solution: CH_4: $P_{CH_4} = 732\ \cancel{torr} \times \frac{1\ atm}{760\ \cancel{torr}} = 0.963158\ atm$, $T = 25\ °C + 273.15 = 298\ K$, $PV = nRT$

Rearrange to solve for n. $n = \frac{PV}{RT}$ $n_{CH_4} = \frac{0.963158\ \cancel{atm} \times 25.5\ \cancel{L}}{0.08206\ \frac{\cancel{L \cdot atm}}{mol \cdot \cancel{K}} \times 298\ \cancel{K}} = 1.00436\ mol\ CH_4$

$1.00436\ \cancel{mol\ CH_4} \times \frac{3\ mol\ H_2}{1\ \cancel{mol\ CH_4}} = 3.01308\ mol\ H_2$

H_2O: $P_{H_2O} = 702\ \cancel{torr} \times \frac{1\ atm}{760\ \cancel{torr}} = 0.923684\ atm$, $T = 125\ °C + 273.15 = 398\ K$, $n = \frac{PV}{RT}$

$n_{H_2O} = \frac{0.923684\ \cancel{atm} \times 22.8\ \cancel{L}}{0.08206\ \frac{\cancel{L \cdot atm}}{mol \cdot \cancel{K}} \times 398\ \cancel{K}} = 0.644828\ mol\ H_2O$ $0.644828\ \cancel{mol\ H_2O} \times \frac{3\ mol\ H_2}{1\ \cancel{mol\ H_2O}} = 1.93448\ mol\ H_2$

Water is the limiting reagent since the moles of hydrogen generated is lower.

Theoretical yield = 1.93448 mol H_2.

$26.2\ \cancel{L\ H_2} \times \frac{1\ mol\ H_2}{22.414\ \cancel{L\ H_2}} = 1.16891\ mol\ H_2 = actual\ yield$

$\%\ Yield = \frac{actual\ yield}{theoretical\ yield} \times 100\ \% = \frac{1.16891\ \cancel{mol\ H_2}}{1.93448\ \cancel{mol\ H_2}} \times 100\ \% = 60.4\ \%$

Check: The units (%) are correct. The magnitude of the answer (60 %) makes sense because it is between 0 and 100 %.

5.82 **Given:** $P = 25.0$ mmHg, $T = 225$ K, and m (CF_3Cl) = 15.0 g; and 10 cycles **Find:** V_{O_3}

Conceptual Plan: $\mathbf{g\ CF_3Cl \rightarrow mol\ CF_3Cl \rightarrow mol\ O_3 \rightarrow mol\ O_3}$ **and mmHg → atm then**

$\frac{1\,mol\,CF_3Cl}{104.46\,g\,CF_3Cl}$ $\frac{2\,mol\,O_3/\,cycle}{1\,mol\,CF_3Cl}$ 10 cycles $\frac{1\,atm}{760\,mmHg}$

$\boldsymbol{n, P, T \rightarrow V}$

$PV = nRT$

Solution: $15.0\ \cancel{g\ CF_3Cl} \times \frac{1\ \cancel{mol\ CF_3Cl}}{104.46\ \cancel{g\ CF_3Cl}} \times \frac{2\ mol\ O_3\ /\cancel{cycle}}{1\ \cancel{mol\ CF_3Cl}} \times 10\ \cancel{cycles} = 2.871913\ mol\ O_3$,

$P_{O_3} = 25.0\ \cancel{torr} \times \frac{1\ atm}{760\ \cancel{torr}} = 0.0328947\ atm$, $PV = nRT$ Rearrange to solve for V. $V = \frac{nRT}{P}$

$V_{O_3} = \frac{2.871913\ \cancel{mol} \times 0.08206\ \frac{L \cdot \cancel{atm}}{\cancel{mol} \cdot \cancel{K}} \times 225\ \cancel{K}}{0.0328947\ \cancel{atm}} = 1.61 \times 10^3\ L\ O_3$

Check: The units (L) are correct. The magnitude of the answer (1600 L) makes sense because we have ~ 3 moles of ozone gas and the pressure is so low (0.03 atm), so we expect a large volume.

Kinetic Molecular Theory

5.83 (a) Yes, since the average kinetic energy of a particle is proportional to the temperature in kelvins and the two gases are at the same temperature, they have the same average kinetic energy.

(b) No, since the helium atoms are lighter, they must move faster to have the same kinetic energy as argon atoms.

(c) No, since the Ar atoms are moving slower to compensate for their larger mass, they will exert the same pressure on the walls of the container.

(d) Since He is lighter, it will have the faster rate of effusion.

5.84 (a) Since both gases have a mole fraction of 0.5, they will have the same partial pressure.

(b) The nitrogen molecules will have a greater velocity since they are lighter than Xe atoms.

(c) Since the average kinetic energy of a particle is proportional to the temperature in kelvins and the two gases are at the same temperature, they have the same average kinetic energy.

(d) Since nitrogen is lighter, it will have the faster rate of effusion.

5.85 **Given:** F_2, Cl_2, Br_2, and $T = 298$ K **Find:** u_{rms} KE_{avg} for each gas and relative rates of effusion
Conceptual Plan: $\mathcal{M}, T \rightarrow u_{rms} \rightarrow KE_{avg}$

$$u_{rms} = \sqrt{\frac{3RT}{\mathcal{M}}} \qquad KE_{avg} = \frac{1}{2}N_A m u_{rms}^2 = \frac{3}{2}RT$$

Solution:

$$F_2: \mathcal{M} = \frac{38.00\ \text{g}}{1\ \text{mol}} \times \frac{1\ \text{kg}}{1000\ \text{g}} = 0.03800\ \text{kg/mol},\ u_{rms} = \sqrt{\frac{3RT}{\mathcal{M}}} = \sqrt{\frac{3 \times 8.314\frac{\text{J}}{\text{K}\cdot\text{mol}} \times 298\ \text{K}}{0.03800\frac{\text{kg}}{\text{mol}}}} = 442\ \text{m/s}$$

$$Cl_2: \mathcal{M} = \frac{70.90\ \text{g}}{1\ \text{mol}} \times \frac{1\ \text{kg}}{1000\ \text{g}} = 0.07090\ \text{kg/mol},\ u_{rms} = \sqrt{\frac{3RT}{\mathcal{M}}} = \sqrt{\frac{3 \times 8.314\frac{\text{J}}{\text{K}\cdot\text{mol}} \times 298\ \text{K}}{0.07090\frac{\text{kg}}{\text{mol}}}} = 324\ \text{m/s}$$

$$Br_2: \mathcal{M} = \frac{159.80\ \text{g}}{1\ \text{mol}} \times \frac{1\ \text{kg}}{1000\ \text{g}} = 0.15980\ \text{kg/mol},\ u_{rms} = \sqrt{\frac{3RT}{\mathcal{M}}} = \sqrt{\frac{3 \times 8.314\frac{\text{J}}{\text{K}\cdot\text{mol}} \times 298\ \text{K}}{0.15980\frac{\text{kg}}{\text{mol}}}} = 216\ \text{m/s}$$

All molecules have the same kinetic energy:

$$KE_{avg} = \frac{3}{2}RT = \frac{3}{2} \times 8.314\frac{\text{J}}{\text{K}\cdot\text{mol}} \times 298\ \text{K} = 3.72 \times 10^3\ \text{J/mol}$$

Since rate of effusion is proportional to $\sqrt{\frac{1}{\mathcal{M}}}$, F_2 will have the fastest rate and Br_2 will have the slowest rate.

Check: The units (m/s) are correct. The magnitude of the answer (200 – 450 m/s) makes sense because it is consistent with what was seen in the text, and the heavier the molecule, the slower the molecule.

5.86 **Given:** CO, CO_2, SO_3, and $T = 298$ K
Find: u_{rms} KE_{avg} for each gas, and rate greatest u_{rms} KE_{avg} and rates of effusion
Conceptual Plan: $\mathcal{M}, T \rightarrow u_{rms} \rightarrow KE_{avg}$

$$u_{rms} = \sqrt{\frac{3RT}{\mathcal{M}}} \qquad KE_{avg} = \frac{1}{2}N_A m u_{rms}^2 = \frac{3}{2}RT$$

Solution:

$$CO: \mathcal{M} = \frac{28.01\ \text{g}}{1\ \text{mol}} \times \frac{1\ \text{kg}}{1000\ \text{g}} = 0.02801\ \text{kg/mol},$$

$$u_{rms} = \sqrt{\frac{3RT}{\mathcal{M}}} = \sqrt{\frac{3 \times 8.314\frac{\text{J}}{\text{K}\cdot\text{mol}} \times 298\ \text{K}}{0.02801\frac{\text{kg}}{\text{mol}}}} = 515\ \text{m/s}$$

CO_2: $\mathcal{M} = \frac{44.01\ \cancel{g}}{1\ \text{mol}} \times \frac{1\ \text{kg}}{1000\ \cancel{g}} = 0.04401\ \text{kg/mol},$

$$u_{rms} = \sqrt{\frac{3RT}{\mathcal{M}}} = \sqrt{\frac{3 \times 8.314 \frac{\text{J}}{\cancel{\text{K}} \cdot \cancel{\text{mol}}} \times 298\ \cancel{\text{K}}}{0.04401 \frac{\text{kg}}{\cancel{\text{mol}}}}} = 411\ \text{m/s}$$

SO_3: $\mathcal{M} = \frac{80.07\ \cancel{g}}{1\ \text{mol}} \times \frac{1\ \text{kg}}{1000\ \cancel{g}} = 0.08007\ \text{kg/mol},$

$$u_{rms} = \sqrt{\frac{3RT}{\mathcal{M}}} = \sqrt{\frac{3 \times 8.314 \frac{\text{J}}{\cancel{\text{K}} \cdot \cancel{\text{mol}}} \times 298\ \cancel{\text{K}}}{0.08007 \frac{\text{kg}}{\cancel{\text{mol}}}}} = 305\ \text{m/s}$$

All molecules have the same kinetic energy:

$KE_{avg} = \frac{3}{2}RT = \frac{3}{2} \times 8.314 \frac{\text{J}}{\cancel{\text{K}} \cdot \text{mol}} \times 298\ \cancel{\text{K}} = 3.72 \times 10^3\ \text{J/mol}$. CO has the fastest speed; all molecules have the same kinetic energy; and since rate of effusion is proportional to $1/\sqrt{\mathcal{M}}$, CO will have the fastest rate.

Check: The units (m/s) are correct. The magnitude of the answer (300 – 520 m/s) makes sense because it is consistent with what was seen in the text, and the heavier the molecule, the slower the molecule.

5.87 **Given:** $^{238}UF_6$ and $^{235}UF_6$ U-235 = 235.054 amu, U-238 = 238.051 amu
Find: ratio of effusion rates $^{238}UF_6$ / $^{235}UF_6$
Conceptual Plan: $\mathcal{M}(^{238}UF_6)$, $\mathcal{M}(^{235}UF_6)$ → **Rate ($^{238}UF_6$)/Rate ($^{235}UF_6$)**

$$\frac{Rate(^{238}UF_6)}{Rate(^{235}UF_6)} = \sqrt{\frac{\mathcal{M}(^{235}UF_6)}{\mathcal{M}(^{238}UF_6}}$$

Solution: $^{238}UF_6$: $\mathcal{M} = \frac{352.05\ \cancel{g}}{1\ \text{mol}} \times \frac{1\ \text{kg}}{1000\ \cancel{g}} = 0.35205\ \text{kg/mol},$

$^{235}UF_6$: $\mathcal{M} = \frac{349.05\ \cancel{g}}{1\ \text{mol}} \times \frac{1\ \text{kg}}{1000\ \cancel{g}} = 0.34905\ \text{kg/mol},$

$$\frac{Rate(^{238}UF_6)}{Rate(^{235}UF_6)} = \sqrt{\frac{\mathcal{M}(^{235}UF_6)}{\mathcal{M}(^{238}UF_6)}} = \sqrt{\frac{0.34905\ \cancel{\text{kg/mol}}}{0.35205\ \cancel{\text{kg/mol}}}} = 0.99574$$

Check: The units (none) are correct. The magnitude of the answer (<1) makes sense because the heavier molecule has the lower effusion rate since it moves slower.

5.88 **Given:** Ar and Kr **Find:** ratio of effusion rates Ar/Kr
Conceptual Plan: $\mathcal{M}$**(Ar),** $\mathcal{M}$**(Kr)** → **Rate (Ar)/Rate (Kr)**

$$\frac{Rate(Ar)}{Rate(Kr)} = \sqrt{\frac{\mathcal{M}(Kr)}{\mathcal{M}(Ar)}}$$

Solution: Ar: $\mathcal{M} = \frac{39.95\ \cancel{g}}{1\ \text{mol}} \times \frac{1\ \text{kg}}{1000\ \cancel{g}} = 0.03995\ \text{kg/mol}$, Kr: $\mathcal{M} = \frac{83.80\ \cancel{g}}{1\ \text{mol}} \times \frac{1\ \text{kg}}{1000\ \cancel{g}} = 0.08380\ \text{kg/mol},$

$$\frac{Rate(Ar)}{Rate(Kr)} = \sqrt{\frac{\mathcal{M}(Kr)}{\mathcal{M}(Ar)}} = \sqrt{\frac{0.08380\ \cancel{\text{kg/mol}}}{0.03995\ \cancel{\text{kg/mol}}}} = 1.448$$

Check: The units (none) are correct. The magnitude of the answer (>1) makes sense because the lighter molecule has the higher effusion rate since it moves faster.

5.89 **Given:** Ne and unknown gas; and Ne effusion in 76 s and unknown in 155 s
Find: identify unknown gas
Conceptual Plan: $\mathcal{M}$**(Ne), Rate (Ne), Rate (Unk)** → $\mathcal{M}$**(Kr)**

$$\frac{Rate(Ne)}{Rate(Unk)} = \sqrt{\frac{\mathcal{M}(Unk)}{\mathcal{M}(Ne)}}$$

Solution: Ne: $\mathcal{M} = \frac{20.18\ \cancel{g}}{1\ \text{mol}} \times \frac{1\ \text{kg}}{1000\ \cancel{g}} = 0.02018\ \text{kg/mol},$ $\frac{Rate(Ne)}{Rate(Unk)} = \sqrt{\frac{\mathcal{M}(Unk)}{\mathcal{M}(Ne)}}$ Rearrange to solve for $\mathcal{M}(Unk)$. $\mathcal{M}(Unk) = \mathcal{M}(Ne)\left(\frac{Rate(Ne)}{Rate(Unk)}\right)^2$ Since Rate α 1/(effusion time),

$$\mathcal{M}(Unk) = \mathcal{M}(Ne)\left(\frac{Time\,(Unk)}{Time\,(Ne)}\right)^2 = 0.02018\frac{\text{kg}}{\text{mol}} \times \left(\frac{155\,\cancel{\text{s}}}{76\,\cancel{\text{s}}}\right)^2 = 0.084\frac{\cancel{\text{kg}}}{\text{mol}} \times \frac{1000\,\text{g}}{1\,\cancel{\text{kg}}} = 84\,\text{g/mol or Kr.}$$

Check: The units (g/mol) are correct. The magnitude of the answer (>Ne) makes sense because, Ne effused faster and so must be lighter.

5.90 **Given:** N_2O and I_2 gas; and NO_2 effusion in 42 s **Find:** effusion time for I_2 gas
Conceptual Plan: $\mathcal{M}(NO_2)$, $\mathcal{M}(Kr)$, Rate (NO_2), → Rate (I_2)

$$\frac{Rate\,(N_2O)}{Rate\,(I_2)} = \sqrt{\frac{\mathcal{M}(I_2)}{\mathcal{M}(N_2O)}}$$

Solution: N_2O: $\mathcal{M} = \frac{44.02\,\cancel{\text{g}}}{1\text{ mol}} \times \frac{1\text{ kg}}{1000\,\cancel{\text{g}}} = 0.04402$ kg/mol, I_2: $\mathcal{M} = \frac{253.8\,\cancel{\text{g}}}{1\text{ mol}} \times \frac{1\text{ kg}}{1000\,\cancel{\text{g}}} = 0.2538$ kg/mol,

$\frac{Rate\,(N_2O)}{Rate\,(I_2)} = \sqrt{\frac{\mathcal{M}(I_2)}{\mathcal{M}(N_2O)}}$ Since Rate α 1/(effusion time) $\frac{Time\,(I_2)}{Time\,(N_2O)} = \sqrt{\frac{\mathcal{M}(I_2)}{\mathcal{M}(N_2O)}}$ Rearrange to solve for $Time\,(I_2)$. $Time\,(I_2) = Time\,(N_2O) \times \sqrt{\frac{\mathcal{M}(I_2)}{\mathcal{M}(N_2O)}} = 42\,\text{s} \times \sqrt{\frac{0.2538\,\cancel{\text{kg/mol}}}{0.04402\,\cancel{\text{kg/mol}}}} = 1.0 \times 10^2\,\text{s}$

Check: The units (s) are correct. The magnitude of the answer (100 s) makes sense because the mass ratio of I_2 to N_2O is ~6, so the time should be over twice as long.

5.91 Gas A has the higher molar mass, since it has the slower average velocity. Gas B will have the higher effusion rate, since it has the higher velocity.

5.92 T_2 is the higher temperature, since it has the higher average velocity.

Real Gases

5.93 The postulate that the volume of the gas particles is small compared to the space between them breaks down at high pressure. At high pressures the number of molecules per unit volume increases, so the volume of the gas particles becomes more significant. Since the spacing between the particles is reduced, the molecules themselves occupy a significant portion of the volume.

5.94 The postulate that the forces between the gas particles are not significant breaks down at low temperatures. At low temperatures, the molecules are not moving as fast as at higher temperatures, so when they collide they have a greater opportunity to interact.

5.95 **Given:** Ne, n = 1.000 mol, P = 500.0 atm, and T = 355.0 K **Find:** V(ideal) and V(van der Waals)
Conceptual Plan: $n, P, T \rightarrow V$ and $n, P, T \rightarrow V$

$$PV = nRT \qquad \left(P + \frac{an^2}{V^2}\right)(V - nb) = nRT$$

Solution: $PV = nRT$ Rearrange to solve for V.

$$V = \frac{nRT}{P} = \frac{1.000\,\cancel{\text{mol}} \times 0.08206\frac{\text{L}\cdot\cancel{\text{atm}}}{\cancel{\text{mol}}\cdot\cancel{\text{K}}} \times 355.0\,\cancel{\text{K}}}{500.0\,\cancel{\text{atm}}} = 0.05826\text{ L}$$

$\left(P + \frac{an^2}{V^2}\right)(V - nb) = nRT$ Rearrange to solve to $V = \frac{nRT}{\left(P + \frac{an^2}{V^2}\right)} + nb$

Using a = 0.211 L^2 atm/mol^2 and b = 0.0171 L/mol from Table 5.5, and the V from the ideal gas law calculation above, solve for V by successive approximations.

$$V = \frac{1.000\,\cancel{\text{mol}} \times 0.08206\frac{\text{L}\cdot\cancel{\text{atm}}}{\cancel{\text{mol}}\cdot\cancel{\text{K}}} \times 355.0\,\cancel{\text{K}}}{500.0\,\cancel{\text{atm}} + \frac{0.211\frac{\cancel{\text{L}^2}\cdot\cancel{\text{atm}}}{\cancel{\text{mol}^2}} \times (1.000\,\cancel{\text{mol}})^2}{(0.05826\,\cancel{\text{L}})^2}} + \left(1.000\,\cancel{\text{mol}} \times 0.0171\frac{\text{L}}{\cancel{\text{mol}}}\right) = 0.06\underline{8}915\text{L}$$

Plug in this new value.

$$V = \frac{1.000\,\text{mol} \times 0.08206\,\frac{\text{L}\cdot\text{atm}}{\text{mol}\cdot\text{K}} \times 355.0\,\text{K}}{500.0\,\text{atm} + \frac{0.211\,\frac{\text{L}^2\cdot\text{atm}}{\text{mol}^2} \times (1.000\,\text{mol})^2}{(0.068915\,\text{L})^2}} + \left(1.000\,\text{mol} \times 0.0171\,\frac{\text{L}}{\text{mol}}\right) = 0.070\underline{6}09\text{ L}$$

Plug in this new value.

$$V = \frac{1.000\,\text{mol} \times 0.08206\,\frac{\text{L}\cdot\text{atm}}{\text{mol}\cdot\text{K}} \times 355.0\,\text{K}}{500.0\,\text{atm} + \frac{0.211\,\frac{\text{L}^2\cdot\text{atm}}{\text{mol}^2} \times (1.000\,\text{mol})^2}{(0.070609\,\text{L})^2}} + \left(1.000\,\text{mol} \times 0.0171\,\frac{\text{L}}{\text{mol}}\right) = 0.070\underline{8}17\text{ L}$$

Plug in this new value.

$$V = \frac{1.000\,\text{mol} \times 0.08206\,\frac{\text{L}\cdot\text{atm}}{\text{mol}\cdot\text{K}} \times 355.0\,\text{K}}{500.0\,\text{atm} + \frac{0.211\,\frac{\text{L}^2\cdot\text{atm}}{\text{mol}^2} \times (1.000\,\text{mol})^2}{(0.070817\,\text{L})^2}} + \left(1.000\,\text{mol} \times 0.0171\,\frac{\text{L}}{\text{mol}}\right) = 0.070\underline{8}42\text{ L} = 0.0708\text{ L}$$

The two values are different because we are at very high pressures. The pressure is corrected from 500.0 atm to 542.1 atm and the final volume correction is 0.0171 L.

Check: The units (L) are correct. The magnitude of the answer (~0.06 L) makes sense because we are at such a high pressure and have one mole of gas.

5.96 **Given:** Cl_2, n = 1.000 mol, L = 5.000 L, and T = 273.0 K **Find:** P(ideal) and P(van der Waals)

Conceptual Plan: $n, V, T \rightarrow P$ **and** $n, V, T \rightarrow P$

$PV = nRT$ $\quad \left(P + \frac{an^2}{V^2}\right)(V - nb) = nRT$

Solution: $PV = nRT$ Rearrange to solve for P.

$$P = \frac{nRT}{V} = \frac{1.000\,\text{mol} \times 0.08206\,\frac{\text{L}\cdot\text{atm}}{\text{mol}\cdot\text{K}} \times 273.0\,\text{K}}{5.000\,\text{L}} = 4.480\text{ atm}$$

$\left(P + \frac{an^2}{V^2}\right)(V - nb) = nRT$ Rearrange to solve for P. $P = \frac{nRT}{(V - nb)} - \frac{an^2}{V^2}$

Using a = 6.49 L^2 atm/mol^2 and b = 0.0562 L/mol from Table 5.5,

$$P = \frac{1.000\,\text{mol} \times 0.08206\,\frac{\text{L}\cdot\text{atm}}{\text{mol}\cdot\text{K}} \times 273.0\,\text{K}}{5.000\,\text{L} - \left(1.000\,\text{mol} \times 0.0562\,\frac{\text{L}}{\text{mol}}\right)} - \frac{6.49\,\frac{\text{L}^2\cdot\text{atm}}{\text{mol}^2} \times (1.000\,\text{mol})^2}{(5.000\,\text{L})^2} = 4.272\text{ atm}$$

The pressure values differ slightly because of the non-ideal behavior of chlorine (a large molecule) at a slightly elevated temperature.

Check: The units (atm) are correct. The magnitude of the answers (4.5 atm and 4.3 atm) makes sense because we are at such a low temperature and small volume with one mole of gas; we expect a difference in two pressures of less than 1 atm and a P >1 atm.

Cumulative Problems

5.97 **Given:** m (penny) = 2.482 g, T = 25 °C, V = 0.899 L, and P_{Total} = 791 mmHg **Find:** % Zn in penny

Conceptual Plan: $T \rightarrow P_{H_2O}$ **then** $P_{Total}, P_{H_2O} \rightarrow P_{H_2}$ **then mmHg** $\rightarrow$ **atm and °C** $\rightarrow$ **K**

Table 5.3 $\quad P_{Total} = P_{H_2O} + P_{H_2}$ $\quad \frac{1\text{ atm}}{760\text{ mmHg}}$ $\quad K = °C + 273.15$

and $P, V, T \rightarrow n_{H_2} \rightarrow n_{Zn} \rightarrow g_{Zn} \rightarrow$ **% Zn**

$PV = nRT$ $\quad \frac{1\text{ mol Zn}}{1\text{ mol H}_2}$ $\quad \frac{65.39\text{ g Zn}}{1\text{ mol Zn}}$ $\quad \%Zn = \frac{g_{Zn}}{g_{penny}} \times 100\%$

Solution: Table 5.4 states that P_{H_2O} = 23.78 mmHg at 25 °C $P_{Total} = P_{H_2O} + P_{H_2}$ Rearrange to solve for P_{H_2}.

$P_{H_2} = P_{Total} - P_{H_2O}$ = 791 mmHg – 23.78 mmHg = 767 mmHg $P_{H_2} = 767\ \cancel{mmHg} \times \dfrac{1\ atm}{760\ \cancel{mmHg}} = 1.0\underline{0}95$ atm

then T = 25 °C + 273.15 = 298 K, $PV = nRT$

Rearrange to solve for n. $n_{H_2} = \dfrac{PV}{RT} = \dfrac{1.0\underline{0}95\ \cancel{atm} \times 0.899\ \cancel{L}}{0.08206\ \dfrac{\cancel{L}\cdot\cancel{atm}}{mol\cdot\cancel{K}} \times 298\ \cancel{K}} = 0.037\underline{1}123$ mol

$$0.037\underline{1}123\ \cancel{mol\ H_2} \times \frac{1\ \cancel{mol\ Zn}}{1\ \cancel{mol\ H_2}} \times \frac{65.39\ g\ Zn}{1\ \cancel{mol\ Zn}} = 2.4\underline{2}677\ g\ Zn$$

$$\%Zn = \frac{g_{Zn}}{g_{penny}} \times 100\ \% = \frac{2.4\underline{2}677\ \cancel{g}}{2.482\ \cancel{g}} \times 100\ \% = 97.8\ \%\ Zn$$

Check: The units (% Zn) are correct. The magnitude of the answer (98 %) makes sense because it should be between 0 and 100 %. We expect about 1/22 a mole of gas, since our conditions are close to STP and we have ~ 1 L of gas.

5.98 **Given:** m (CFC) = 2.85 g, V = 564 mL, P = 752 mmHg, and T = 298 K **Find:** % Cl in CFC

Conceptual Plan: mmHg → atm and mL → L and $P, V, T \rightarrow n_{Cl_2} \rightarrow g_{Cl}$

$\dfrac{1\,atm}{760\,mmHg}$ $\quad \dfrac{1\,L}{1000\,mL}$ $\quad PV = nRT$ $\quad \dfrac{70.90\ g\ Cl}{1\ mol\ Cl_2}$

then g_{Cl}, g_{CFC} → % Cl

$\%\ Cl = \dfrac{g_{Cl}}{g_{CFC}} \times 100\%$

Solution: $P_{Cl_2} = 752\ \cancel{mmHg} \times \dfrac{1\ atm}{760\ \cancel{mmHg}} = 0.98\underline{9}47$ atm, $V_{Cl_2} = 564\ \cancel{mL} \times \dfrac{1\ L}{1000\ \cancel{mL}} = 0.564$ L,

$PV = nRT$ Rearrange to solve for n. $n_{Cl_2} = \dfrac{PV}{RT} = \dfrac{0.98\underline{9}47\ \cancel{atm} \times 0.564\ \cancel{L}}{0.08206\ \dfrac{\cancel{L}\cdot\cancel{atm}}{mol\cdot\cancel{K}} \times 298\ \cancel{K}} = 0.022\underline{8}21\ mol\ Cl_2$

$$0.022\underline{8}21\ \cancel{mol\ Cl_2} \times \frac{70.90\ g\ Cl}{1\ \cancel{mol\ Cl_2}} = 1.6\underline{1}80\ g\ Cl,\ \%\ Cl = \frac{g_{Cl}}{g_{CFC}} \times 100\ \% = \frac{1.6\underline{1}80\ \cancel{g}}{2.85\ \cancel{g}} \times 100\ \% = 56.8\ \%\ Cl$$

Check: The units (% Cl) are correct. The magnitude of the answer (57 %) makes sense because it should be between 0 and 100 %. Since there will also be carbon and flourine in the compound, we do not expect it to be extremely close to 100 %.

5.99 **Given:** V = 255 mL, m (flask) = 143.187 g, m (flask + gas) = 143.289 g, P = 267 torr, and T = 25 °C **Find:** $\mathcal{M}$

Conceptual Plan: °C → K torr → atm mL → L m (flask), m (flask + gas) → m (gas)

$K = °C + 273.15$ $\quad \dfrac{1\,atm}{760\,torr}$ $\quad \dfrac{1\,L}{1000\,mL}$ $\quad m\ (gas) = m\ (flask + gas) - m\ (flask)$

then $V, m \rightarrow d$ then $d, P, T, \rightarrow \mathcal{M}$

$d = \dfrac{m}{V}$ $\quad d = \dfrac{P\mathcal{M}}{RT}$

Solution: T = 25 °C + 273.15 = 298 K, $P = 267\ \cancel{torr} \times \dfrac{1\ atm}{760\ \cancel{torr}} = 0.35\underline{1}316$ atm,

$V = 255\ \cancel{mL} \times \dfrac{1\ L}{1000\ \cancel{mL}} = 0.255$ L,

$m\ (gas) = m\ (flask + gas) - m\ (flask) = 143.289\ g - 143.187 g = 0.102\ g$,

$d = \dfrac{m}{V} = \dfrac{0.102\ g}{0.255\ L} = 0.400\ g/L,\ d = \dfrac{P\mathcal{M}}{RT}$ Rearrange to solve for $\mathcal{M}$.

$$\mathcal{M} = \frac{dRT}{P} = \frac{0.400\ \dfrac{g}{\cancel{L}} \times 0.08206\ \dfrac{\cancel{L}\ \cancel{atm}}{\cancel{K}\ mol} \times 298\ \cancel{K}}{0.35\underline{1}316\ \cancel{atm}} = 27.8\ g/mol$$

Check: The units (g/mol) are correct. The magnitude of the answer (28 g/mol) makes physical sense because this is a reasonable number for a molecular weight of a gas.

5.100 **Given:** V = 118 mL, m (flask) = 97.129 g, m (flask + gas) = 97.171 g, P = 768 torr, and T = 35 °C

Find: Is gas pure?

Conceptual Plan: °C → K torr → atm mL → L m (flask), m (flask + gas) → m (gas)

$K = °C + 273.15$ $\quad \dfrac{1\,atm}{760\,torr}$ $\quad \dfrac{1\,L}{1000\,mL}$ $\quad m\ (gas) = m\ (flask + gas) - m\ (flask)$

then $V, m \rightarrow d$ then $d, P, T, \rightarrow \mathcal{M}$

$d = \frac{m}{V}$ $\quad d = \frac{P\mathcal{M}}{RT}$

Solution: $T = 35\ °C + 273.15 = 308\ K$, $P = 768\ \text{torr} \times \frac{1\ \text{atm}}{760\ \text{torr}} = 1.01053\ \text{atm}$,

$V = 118\ \text{mL} \times \frac{1\ \text{L}}{1000\ \text{mL}} = 0.118\ \text{L}$

$m\ (gas) = m\ (flask + gas) - m\ (flask) = 97.171\ \text{g} - 97.129\ \text{g} = 0.042\ \text{g}$,

$d = \frac{m}{V} = \frac{0.042\ \text{g}}{0.118\ \text{L}} = 0.35593\ \text{g/L}$, $d = \frac{P\mathcal{M}}{RT}$ Rearrange to solve for $\mathcal{M}$.

$$\mathcal{M} = \frac{dRT}{P} = \frac{0.35593\ \frac{\text{g}}{\text{L}} \times 0.08206 \frac{\text{L atm}}{\text{K mol}} \times 308\ \text{K}}{1.01053\ \text{atm}} = 8.9\ \text{g/mol}$$

The gas is not pure He, since the molar mass is not 4.003 g/ml.

Check: The units (g/mol) are correct. The magnitude of the answer (9 g/mol) makes physical sense because this is a reasonable number for a molecular weight of a gas.

5.101 **Given:** $V = 158$ mL, m (gas) = 0.275 g, $P = 556$ mmHg, $T = 25$ °C, gas = 82.66 % C and 17.34 % H
Find: Molecular formula

Conceptual Plan: °C → K mmHg → atm mL → L then V, m → d

$K = °C + 273.15$ $\quad \frac{1\ \text{atm}}{760\ \text{mmHg}}$ $\quad \frac{1\ \text{L}}{1000\ \text{mL}}$ $\quad d = \frac{m}{V}$

then $d, P, T, \rightarrow \mathcal{M}$ then % C, % H, $\mathcal{M}$ → formula

$d = \frac{P\mathcal{M}}{RT}$ $\quad \#C = = \frac{\mathcal{M} 0.8266 g\ C}{12.01 \frac{g\ C}{mol\ C}}$ $\quad \#H = \frac{\mathcal{M} 0.1734 g H}{1.008 \frac{g H}{mol\ H}}$

Solution: $T = 25\ °C + 273.15 = 298\ K$, $P = 556\ \text{mmHg} \times \frac{1\ \text{atm}}{760\ \text{mmHg}} = 0.731579\ \text{atm}$,

$V = 158\ \text{mL} \times \frac{1\ \text{L}}{1000\ \text{mL}} = 0.158\ \text{L}$, $d = \frac{m}{V} = \frac{0.275\ \text{g}}{0.158\ \text{L}} = 1.74051\ \text{g/L}$, $d = \frac{P\mathcal{M}}{RT}$ Rearrange to solve for $\mathcal{M}$.

$$\mathcal{M} = \frac{dRT}{P} = \frac{1.74051\ \frac{\text{g}}{\text{L}} \times 0.08206 \frac{\text{L atm}}{\text{K mol}} \times 298\ \text{K}}{0.731579\ \text{atm}} = 58.2\ \text{g/mol},$$

$$\#C = \frac{\mathcal{M} \times 0.8266\ g\ C}{12.01 \frac{g\ C}{mol\ C}} = \frac{58.2 \frac{\text{g HC}}{\text{mol HC}} \times \frac{0.8266\ \text{g C}}{1\ \text{g HC}}}{12.01 \frac{\text{g C}}{\text{mol C}}} = 4.00 \frac{\text{mol C}}{\text{mol HC}}$$

$$\#H = \frac{\mathcal{M} \times 0.1734\ g\ H}{1.008 \frac{g\ H}{mol\ H}} = \frac{58.2 \frac{\text{g HC}}{\text{mol HC}} \times \frac{0.1734\ \text{g H}}{1\ \text{g HC}}}{1.008 \frac{\text{g H}}{\text{mol H}}} = 10.0 \frac{\text{mol H}}{\text{mol HC}}$$ Formula is C_4H_{10} or butane.

Check: The answer came up with integer number of C and H atoms in the formula and a molecular weight (58 g/mol) that is reasonable for a gas.

5.102 **Given:** STP, $V = 258$ mL, m (gas) = 0.646 g, gas = 85.63 % C and 14.37 % H. **Find:** $\mathcal{M}$

Conceptual Plan: mL → L then $V, m \rightarrow d$ then $d, P, T, \rightarrow \mathcal{M}$

$\frac{1\ \text{L}}{1000\ \text{mL}}$ $\quad d = \frac{m}{V}$ $\quad d = \frac{P\mathcal{M}}{RT}$

then % C, % H, $\mathcal{M}$ → formula

$\#C = = \frac{\mathcal{M} 0.8563 g\ C}{12.01 \frac{g\ C}{mol\ C}}$ $\quad \#H = \frac{\mathcal{M} 0.1437 g H}{1.008 \frac{g H}{mol\ H}}$

Solution: $V = 258\ \text{mL} \times \frac{1\ \text{L}}{1000\ \text{mL}} = 0.258\ \text{L}$, $d = \frac{m}{V} = \frac{0.646\ \text{g}}{0.258\ \text{L}} = 2.50388\ \text{g/L}$, $d = \frac{P\mathcal{M}}{RT}$ Rearrange to solve for $\mathcal{M}$. $\mathcal{M} = \frac{dRT}{P} = \frac{2.50388\ \frac{\text{g}}{\text{L}} \times 0.08206 \frac{\text{L atm}}{\text{K mol}} \times 273.15\ \text{K}}{1\ \text{atm}} = 56.12\ \text{g/mol}$,

$$\#C = \frac{\mathcal{M} \times 0.8563\ g\ C}{12.01\ \frac{g\ C}{mol\ C}} = \frac{56.12\ \frac{\cancel{g\ HC}}{mol\ HC} \times \frac{0.8563\ \cancel{g\ C}}{1\ \cancel{g\ HC}}}{12.01\ \frac{\cancel{g\ C}}{mol\ C}} = 4.00\ \frac{mol\ C}{mol\ HC}$$

$$\#H = \frac{\mathcal{M} \times 0.1437\ g\ H}{1.008\ \frac{g\ H}{mol\ H}} = \frac{56.12\ \frac{\cancel{g\ HC}}{mol\ HC} \times \frac{0.1437\ \cancel{g\ H}}{1\ \cancel{g\ HC}}}{1.008\ \frac{\cancel{g\ H}}{mol\ H}} = 8.00\ \frac{mol\ H}{mol\ HC}$$ Formula is C_4H_8 or butene.

Check: The answer came up with integer number of C and H atoms in the formula and a molecular weight (56 g/mol) that is reasonable for a gas.

5.103 **Given:** m (NiO) = 24.78 g, T = 40.0 °C, and P_{Total} = 745 mmHg **Find:** V_{O_2}

Conceptual Plan: $T \rightarrow P_{H_2O}$ **then** $P_{Total}, P_{H_2O} \rightarrow P_{O_2}$ **then mmHg → atm and °C → K**

Table 5.4 ; $P_{Total} = P_{H_2O} + P_{O_2}$; $\frac{1\ atm}{760\ mmHg}$; K = °C + 273.15

and $g_{NiO} \rightarrow n_{NiO} \rightarrow n_{O_2}$ **then** $P, V, T \rightarrow n_{O_2}$

$\frac{1\ mol\ NiO}{74.69\ g\ NiO}$; $\frac{1\ mol\ O_2}{2\ mol\ NiO}$; $PV = nRT$

Solution: Table 5.4 states that P_{H_2O} = 55.40 mmHg at 40°C $P_{Total} = P_{H_2O} + P_{O_2}$ Rearrange to solve for P_{O_2}.

$P_{O_2} = P_{Total} - P_{H_2O}$ = 745 mmHg – 55.40 mmHg = 689.6 mmHg

$$P_{O_2} = 689.6\ \cancel{mmHg} \times \frac{1\ atm}{760\ \cancel{mmHg}} = 0.907368\ atm \quad T = 40.0\ °C + 273.15 = 313.2\ K,$$

$$24.78\ \cancel{g\ NiO} \times \frac{1\ \cancel{mol\ NiO}}{74.69\ \cancel{mol\ NiO}} \times \frac{1\ mol\ O_2}{2\ \cancel{mol\ NiO}} = 0.1658857\ mol\ O_2 \quad PV = nRT$$

Rearrange to solve for V. $$V_{O_2} = \frac{nRT}{P} = \frac{0.1658857\ \cancel{mol} \times 0.08206\ \frac{L \cdot \cancel{atm}}{\cancel{mol} \cdot \cancel{K}} \times 313.2\ \cancel{K}}{0.907368\ \cancel{atm}} = 4.70\ L$$

Check: The units (L) are correct. The magnitude of the answer (5 L) makes sense because we have much less than 0.5 mole of NiO, so we get less than a mole of oxygen. Thus we expect a volume much less than 22 L.

5.104 **Given:** m (Ag) = 15.8 g, T = 25 °C, and P_{Total} = 752 mmHg **Find:** V_{O_2}

Conceptual Plan: $T \rightarrow P_{H_2O}$ **then** $P_{Total}, P_{H_2O} \rightarrow P_{O_2}$ **then mmHg → atm and °C → K**

Table 5.3 ; $P_{Total} = P_{H_2O} + P_{O_2}$; $\frac{1\ atm}{760\ mmHg}$; K = °C + 273.15

and $g_{Ag} \rightarrow n_{Ag} \rightarrow n_{O_2}$ **then** $P, V, T \rightarrow n_{O_2}$

$\frac{1\ mol\ Ag}{107.9\ g\ Ag}$; $\frac{1\ mol\ O_2}{4\ mol\ Ag}$; $PV = nRT$

Solution: Table 5.4 states that P_{H_2O} = 23.78 mmHg at 25 °C $P_{Total} = P_{H_2O} + P_{O_2}$ Rearrange to solve for P_{O_2}.

$P_{O_2} = P_{Total} - P_{H_2O}$ = 752 mmHg – 23.78 mmHg = 728.22 mmHg

$$P_{O_2} = 728.22\ \cancel{mmHg} \times \frac{1\ atm}{760\ \cancel{mmHg}} = 0.958184\ atm \quad T = 25\ °C + 273.15 = 298\ K,$$

$$15.8\ \cancel{g\ Ag} \times \frac{1\ \cancel{mol\ Ag}}{107.9\ \cancel{mol\ Ag}} \times \frac{1\ mol\ O_2}{4\ \cancel{mol\ Ag}} = 0.03660780\ mol\ O_2 \quad PV = nRT$$ Rearrange to solve for V.

$$V_{O_2} = \frac{nRT}{P} = \frac{0.03660780\ \cancel{mol} \times 0.08206\ \frac{L \cdot \cancel{atm}}{\cancel{mol} \cdot \cancel{K}} \times 298\ \cancel{K}}{0.958184\ \cancel{atm}} = 0.934\ L$$

Check: The units (L) are correct. The magnitude of the answer (1 L) makes sense because, we have ~ 0.1 mole of Ag, so we get less than 0.5 mol of oxygen. Thus we expect a volume much, much less than 22 L.

5.105 **Given:** HCl, K_2S to H_2S, V_{H_2S} = 42.9 mL, P_{H_2S} = 752 mmHg, and T = 25.8 °C **Find:** $m(K_2S)$

Conceptual Plan: read description of reaction and convert words to equation then °C → K

K = °C + 273.15

and mmHg → atm and mL → L then $P, V, T \rightarrow n_{H_2S} \rightarrow n_{K_2S} \rightarrow g_{K_2S}$

$\frac{1\ atm}{760\ mmHg}$; $\frac{1\ L}{1000\ mL}$; $PV = nRT$; $\frac{1\ mol\ K_2S}{1\ mol\ H_2S}$; $\frac{1\ mol\ K_2S}{110.27\ g\ K_2S}$

Solution: $2\ HCl\ (aq) + K_2S\ (s) \rightarrow H_2S\ (g) + 2\ KCl\ (aq)$

$T = 25.8\ °C + 273.15 = 299.0\ K$, $P_{H_2S} = 752\ mmHg \times \frac{1\ atm}{760\ mmHg} = 0.989474\ atm$,

$V_{H_2S} = 42.9\ mL \times \frac{1\ L}{1000\ mL} = 0.0429\ L$ $\quad PV = nRT$ Rearrange to solve for n_{H_2S}.

$$n_{H_2S} = \frac{PV}{RT} = \frac{0.989474\ atm \times 0.0429\ L}{0.08206 \frac{L \cdot atm}{mol \cdot K} \times 299.0\ K} = 0.00173005\ mol$$

$$0.00173005\ mol\ H_2S \times \frac{1\ mol\ K_2S}{1\ mol\ H_2S} \times \frac{110.27\ g\ K_2S}{1\ mol\ K_2S} = 0.191\ g\ K_2S$$

Check: The units (g) are correct. The magnitude of the answer (0.1 g) makes sense because we have such a small volume of gas generated.

5.106 (a) **Given:** $T = 315\ K$, $P = 50.0\ mmHg$, $V_{SO_2} = 285.5\ mL$, $V_{O_2} = 158.9\ mL$
Find: limiting reagent and theoretical yield
Conceptual Plan: mmHg → atm and mL$_{SO_2}$ → L $_{SO_2}$ then $P, V_{SO_2}, T \rightarrow n_{SO_2} \rightarrow n_{SO_3}$

$\frac{1\ atm}{760\ mmHg}$ $\quad \frac{1\ L}{1000\ mL}$ $\quad PV = nRT$ $\quad \frac{2\ mol\ SO_3}{2\ mol\ SO_2}$

and mL$_{O2}$ → L$_{SO_2}$ then $P, V_{SO_2}, T \rightarrow n_{O_2} \rightarrow n_{SO_3}$

$\frac{1\ L}{1000\ mL}$ $\quad PV = nRT$ $\quad \frac{2\ mol\ SO_3}{1\ mol\ O_2}$

Solution: $50.0\ mmHg \times \frac{1\ atm}{760\ mmHg} = 0.0657895\ atm$ and $285.5\ mL\ SO_2 \times \frac{1\ L\ SO_2}{1000\ mL\ SO_2} = 0.2855\ L$

then $PV = nRT$ Rearrange to solve for n.

$$n_{SO_2} = \frac{PV}{RT} = \frac{0.0657895\ atm \times 0.2855\ L}{0.08206 \frac{L \cdot atm}{mol \cdot K} \times 315\ K} = 7.26642 \times 10^{-4}\ mol\ SO_2$$

$$7.26642 \times 10^{-4}\ mol\ SO_2 \times \frac{2\ mol\ SO_3}{2\ mol\ SO_2} = 7.26642 \times 10^{-4}\ mol\ SO_3$$

then $158.9\ mL\ O_2 \times \frac{1\ L\ O_2}{1000\ mL\ O_2} = 0.1589\ L\ O_2$ then $PV = nRT$ Rearrange to solve for n.

$$n_{O_2} = \frac{PV}{RT} = \frac{0.0657895\ atm \times 0.1589\ L}{0.08206 \frac{L \cdot atm}{mol \cdot K} \times 315\ K} = 4.04425 \times 10^{-4}\ mol\ O_2 \text{ then}$$

$4.04425 \times 10^{-4}\ mol\ O_2 \times \frac{2\ mol\ SO_3}{1\ mol\ O_2} = 8.08851 \times 10^{-4}\ mol\ SO_3$ Since the amount generated from the SO_2 is less, it is the limiting reagent and the theoretical yield is $7.27 \times 10^{-4}\ mol\ SO_3$.
Check: The units (mol) are correct. The magnitude of the answer (0.0007 mol) makes sense because we have small volumes of gas involved (compared to 22 L).

(b) **Given:** preceding info and $V_{SO_3} = 187.2\ mL$, $T = 315\ K$, and $P = 50.0\ mmHg$ **Find:** % Yield
Conceptual Plan: mmHg → atm and mL$_{SO_3}$ → L $_{SO_3}$ then $P, V_{SO_2}, T \rightarrow n_{SO_2} \rightarrow n_{SO_3}$

$\frac{1\ atm}{760\ mmHg}$ $\quad \frac{1\ L}{1000\ mL}$ $\quad PV = nRT$

then actual yield, theoretical yield → % yield

$$\%\ Yield = \frac{actual\ yield}{theoretical\ yield} \times 100\%$$

Solution: $50.0\ mmHg \times \frac{1\ atm}{760\ mmHg} = 0.0657895\ atm$ and

$187.2\ mL\ SO_3 \times \frac{1\ L\ SO_3}{1000\ mL\ SO_3} = 0.1872\ L\ SO_3$ then $PV = nRT$ Rearrange to solve for n.

$$n_{SO_3} = \frac{PV}{RT} = \frac{0.0657895\ atm \times 0.1872\ L}{0.08206 \frac{L \cdot atm}{mol \cdot K} \times 315\ K} = 4.76453 \times 10^{-4}\ mol\ SO_3$$

then $\% \text{ Yield} = \frac{\text{actual yield}}{\text{theoretical yield}} \times 100\,\% = \frac{4.76453 \times \cancel{10^{-4}\ \text{mol SO}_3}}{7.26642 \times \cancel{10^{-4}\ \text{mol SO}_3}} \times 100\,\% = 65.6\,\%$

Check: The units (%) are correct. The magnitude of the answer (66 %) makes sense because it should be between 0 and 100 %. Since the volume of product is a bit over half of the volume of the limiting reagent and there is a 2:2 mole ratio of the reactant and product, we expect a number a bit over 50 %.

5.107 **Given:** $T = 22\ °C$, $P = 1.02$ atm, and $m = 11.83$ g **Find:** V_{Total}

Conceptual Plan: °C → K and g $(NH_4)_2CO_3$ → n $(NH_4)_2CO_3$ → n Gas then P, n, T → V

$K = °C + 273.15$ $\quad \frac{1\ \text{mol}\ (NH_4)_2CO_3}{96.09\ \text{g}\ (NH_4)_2CO_3}$ $\quad \frac{(2 + 1 + 1 = 4)\ \text{mol gas}}{1\ \text{mol}\ NH_4CO_3}$ $\quad PV = nRT$

Solution: $T = 22\ °C + 273.15 = 295$ K,

$$11.83\ \cancel{\text{g}\ NH_4CO_3} \times \frac{1\ \cancel{\text{mol}\ (NH_4)_2CO_3}}{96.09\ \cancel{\text{g}\ (NH_4)_2CO_3}} \times \frac{4\ \text{mol gas}}{1\ \cancel{\text{mol}\ (NH_4)_2CO_3}} = 0.492455\ \text{mol gas}$$

$PV = nRT$ Rearrange to solve for V_{Gas}.

$$V_{Gas} = \frac{nRT}{P} = \frac{0.492455\ \cancel{\text{mol gas}} \times 0.08206\ \frac{\text{L} \cdot \cancel{\text{atm}}}{\cancel{\text{mol}} \cdot \cancel{\text{K}}} \times 295\ \cancel{\text{K}}}{1.02\ \cancel{\text{atm}}} = 11.7\ \text{L}$$

Check: The units (L) are correct. The magnitude of the answer (12 L) makes sense because we have about a half a mole of gas generated.

5.108 **Given:** $T = 125\ °C$, $P = 748$ mmHg, and $m = 1.55$ kg **Find:** V_{Total}

Conceptual Plan: °C → K and mmHg → atm and kg NH_4NO_3 → g NH_4NO_3 → n NH_4NO_3 → n Gas

$K = °C + 273.15$ $\quad \frac{1\ \text{atm}}{760\ \text{mmHg}}$ $\quad \frac{1000\ \text{g}}{1\ \text{kg}}$ $\quad \frac{1\ \text{mol}\ NH_4NO_3}{80.05\ \text{g}\ NH_4NO_3}$ $\quad \frac{(2 + 1 + 47)\ \text{mol gas}}{2\ \text{mol}\ NH_4NO_3}$

then P, n, T → V

$PV = nRT$

Solution: $T = 125\ °C + 273.15 = 398$ K, $748\ \cancel{\text{mmHg}} \times \frac{1\ \text{atm}}{760\ \cancel{\text{mmHg}}} = 0.984211$ atm

$$1.55\ \cancel{\text{kg}\ NH_4NO_3} \times \frac{1000\ \cancel{\text{g}\ NH_4NO_3}}{1\ \cancel{\text{kg}\ NH_4NO_3}} \times \frac{1\ \cancel{\text{mol}\ NH_4NO_3}}{80.05\ \cancel{\text{g}\ NH_4NO_3}} \times \frac{7\ \text{mol gas}}{2\ \cancel{\text{mol}\ NH_4NO_3}} = 67.7701\ \text{mol gas}$$

$PV = nRT$ Rearrange to solve for V_{Gas}.

$$V_{Gas} = \frac{nRT}{P} = \frac{67.7701\ \cancel{\text{mol gas}} \times 0.08206\ \frac{\text{L} \cdot \cancel{\text{atm}}}{\cancel{\text{mol}} \cdot \cancel{\text{K}}} \times 398\ \cancel{\text{K}}}{0.984211\ \cancel{\text{atm}}} = 2250\ \text{L}$$

Check: The units (L) are correct. The magnitude of the answer (2250 L) makes sense because we have about 67 moles of gas generated, so we expect a volume a bit above 67 x 22 L.

5.109 **Given:** He and air; $V = 855$ mL, $P = 125$ psi, $T = 25\ °C$, → (air) = 28.8 g/mol **Find:** $\Delta = m(\text{air}) - m(\text{He})$

Conceptual Plan: mL → L and psi → atm and °C → K then P, T, $\mathcal{M}$ → d

$\frac{1\ \text{L}}{1000\ \text{mL}}$ $\quad \frac{1\ \text{atm}}{14.7\ \text{psi}}$ $\quad K = °C + 273.15$ $\quad d = \frac{P\mathcal{M}}{RT}$

then d, V → m then m(air), m(He) → Δ

$d = \frac{m}{V}$ $\quad \Delta = m(air) - m(He)$

Solution: $V = 855\ \cancel{\text{mL}} \times \frac{1\ \text{L}}{1000\ \cancel{\text{mL}}} = 0.855\ \text{L}$, $P = 125\ \cancel{\text{psi}} \times \frac{1\ \text{atm}}{14.7\ \cancel{\text{psi}}} = 8.50340\ \text{atm}$,

$$T = 25\ °C + 273.15 = 298\text{K},\ d_{air} = \frac{P\mathcal{M}}{RT} = \frac{8.50340\ \cancel{\text{atm}} \times 28.8\ \frac{\text{g air}}{\cancel{\text{mol air}}}}{0.08206\ \frac{\text{L} \cdot \cancel{\text{atm}}}{\cancel{\text{K}} \cdot \cancel{\text{mol}}} \times 298\ \cancel{\text{K}}} = 10.0147\ \frac{\text{g air}}{\text{L}},\ d = \frac{m}{V}$$

Rearrange to solve for m. $m = dV$

$$m_{air} = 10.0147\ \frac{\text{g air}}{\cancel{\text{L}}} \times 0.8554\ \cancel{\text{L}} = 8.56657\ \text{g air},\ d_{He} = \frac{P\mathcal{M}}{RT} = \frac{8.50340\ \cancel{\text{atm}} \times 4.03\ \frac{\text{g He}}{\cancel{\text{mol He}}}}{0.08206\ \frac{\text{L} \cdot \cancel{\text{atm}}}{\cancel{\text{K}} \cdot \cancel{\text{mol}}} \times 298\ \cancel{\text{K}}} = 1.40136\ \frac{\text{g He}}{\text{L}},$$

$$m_{He} = 1.40136\ \frac{\text{g He}}{\cancel{\text{L}}} \times 0.855\ \cancel{\text{L}} = 1.19816\ \text{g He},$$

$\Delta = m(air) - m(He) = 8.56657 \text{ g air} - 1.19816 \text{ g He} = 7.37 \text{ g}$

Check: The units (g) are correct. We expect the difference to be less than the difference in the molecular weights since we have less than a mole of gas.

5.110 **Given:** $V_1 = 2.95$ L, $P = 0.998$ atm, $T_1 = 25.0$ °C, and $T_2 = -196$ °C **Find:** V_2 and compare to 0.61 L

Conceptual Plan: °C → K then $V_1, T_1, T_2 \rightarrow V_2$ and then compare to 0.61 L

$K = °C + 273.15$ $\quad \frac{V_1}{T_1} = \frac{V_2}{T_2}$

Solution: $T_1 = 25\ °C + 273.15 = 298 K$, $T_2 = -196\ °C + 273.15 = 77$ K, $\frac{V_1}{T_1} = \frac{V_2}{T_2}$ Rearrange to solve for V_2.

$V_2 = V_1 \times \frac{T_2}{T_1} = 2.95 \text{ L} \times \frac{77 \text{ K}}{298 \text{ K}} = 0.76 \text{ L}$ This is 25 % larger than the measured volume. We expect gases to behave non-ideally as the temperature drops. We are at the boiling point of the material, so the velocity dramatically decreases and some nitrogen will be condensing.

Check: The units (L) are correct. We expect the volume to dramatically decrease since the temperature has dropped significantly.

5.111 **Given:** flow = 335 L/s, P_{NO} = 22.4 torr, T_{NO} = 955 K, P_{NH_3} = 755 torr, and T_{NO} = 298 K, and NH_3 purity = 65.2 % **Find:** Flow_{NH_3}

Conceptual Plan: torr → atm then $P_{NO}, V_{NO}/s, T_{NO} \rightarrow n_{NO}/s \rightarrow n_{NH_3}/s$ (pure)

$\frac{1 \text{ atm}}{760 \text{ torr}}$ $\quad PV = nRT$ $\quad \frac{4 \text{ mol } NH_3}{4 \text{ mol NO}}$

then n_{NH_3}/s (pure) → n_{NH_3}/s (impure) then n_{NH_3}/s (impure), $P_{NH_3}, T_{NH_3} \rightarrow V_{NH_3}/s$

$\frac{100 \text{ mol } NH_3 \text{ impure}}{65.2 \text{ mol } NH_3 \text{ pure}}$ $\quad PV = nRT$

Solution: $P_{NO} = 22.4 \text{ torr} \times \frac{1 \text{ atm}}{760 \text{ torr}} = 0.0294737 \text{ atm}$, $P_{NH_3} = 755 \text{ torr} \times \frac{1 \text{ atm}}{760 \text{ torr}} = 0.993421 \text{ atm}$

$PV = nRT$ Rearrange to solve for n_{NO}. Note that we can substitute V/s for V and get n/s as a result.

$$\frac{n_{NO}}{s} = \frac{PV}{RT} = \frac{0.0294737 \text{ atm} \times 335 \text{ L/s}}{0.08206 \frac{\text{L} \cdot \text{atm}}{\text{mol} \cdot \text{K}} \times 955 \text{ K}} = 0.125992 \frac{\text{mol NO}}{\text{s}}$$

$$0.125992 \frac{\text{mol NO}}{\text{s}} \times \frac{4 \text{ mol } NH_3}{4 \text{ mol NO}} \times \frac{100 \text{ mol } NH_3 \text{ impure}}{65.2 \text{ mol } NH_3 \text{ pure}} = 0.193240 \frac{\text{mol } NH_3 \text{ impure}}{\text{s}} \quad PV = nRT$$

Rearrange to solve for V_{NH_3}. Note that we can substitute n/s for n and get V/s as a result.

$$\frac{V_{NH_3}}{s} = \frac{nRT}{P} = \frac{0.193240 \frac{\text{mol } NH_3 \text{ impure}}{\text{s}} \times 0.08206 \frac{\text{L} \cdot \text{atm}}{\text{mol} \cdot \text{K}} \times 298 \text{ K}}{0.993421 \text{ atm}} = 4.76 \frac{\text{L}}{\text{s}} \text{ impure } NH_3$$

Check: The units (L) are correct. The magnitude of the answer (5 L/s) makes sense because we expect it to be less than for the NO. The NO is at a very low concentration and a high temperature, when this converts to a much higher pressure and lower temperature this will go down significantly, even though the ammonia is impure. From a practical standpoint, you would like a low flow rate to make it economical.

5.112 **Given:** Flow_{NO} = 2.55 L/s, P_{NO} = 12.4 torr, T_{NO} = 655 K, and 8.0 hours **Find:** m (urea)

Conceptual Plan: torr → atm and hr → min → s then $P_{NO}, V_{NO}/s, T_{NO} \rightarrow n_{NO}/s$

$\frac{1 \text{ atm}}{760 \text{ torr}}$ $\quad \frac{60 \text{ s}}{1 \text{ min}}$ $\quad \frac{60 \text{ min}}{1 \text{ hr}}$ $\quad PV = nRT$

$n_{NO}/s \rightarrow n_{urea}/s$ then s → $n_{urea} \rightarrow g_{urea}$

$\frac{2 \text{ mol urea}}{4 \text{ mol NO}}$ $\quad n_{urea} = (n_{urea}/s)(s)$ $\quad \frac{60.06 \text{ g urea}}{1 \text{ mol urea}}$

Solution: $P_{NO} = 12.4 \text{ torr} \times \frac{1 \text{ atm}}{760 \text{ torr}} = 0.01631579 \text{ atm}$, $8.0 \text{ hr} \times \frac{60 \text{ min}}{1 \text{ hr}} \times \frac{60 \text{s}}{1 \text{ min}} = 28800 \text{ s}$

$PV = nRT$ Rearrange to solve for n_{NO}. Note that we can substitute V/s for V and get n/s as a result.

$$\frac{n_{NO}}{s} = \frac{PV}{RT} = \frac{0.01631579 \text{ atm atm} \times 2.55 \text{ L/s}}{0.08206 \frac{\text{L} \cdot \text{atm}}{\text{mol} \cdot \text{K}} \times 655 \text{ K}} = 0.000774061 \frac{\text{mol NO}}{\text{s}},$$

$$0.000774061 \frac{\text{mol NO}}{\text{s}} \times \frac{2 \text{ mol urea}}{4 \text{ mol NO}} = 0.000387031 \frac{\text{mol urea}}{\text{s}},$$

$$28800 \text{ s} \times 0.000387031 \frac{\text{mol urea}}{\text{s}} \times \frac{60.06 \text{ g urea}}{1 \text{ mol urea}} = 670 \text{ g urea}$$

Check: The units (g) are correct. The magnitude of the answer (670 g) is not unreasonable mass to add to a car because many more grams of gasoline are burned in 8 hours of driving.

5.113 **Given:** l = 30.0 cm, w = 20.0 cm, h = 15.0 cm, 14.7 psi **Find:** Force (lbs)
Conceptual Plan: ***l, w, h*** → **Surface Area, *SA* (cm^2)** → **Surface Area(in^2)** → **Force**

$SA = 2(lh) + 2(wh) + 2(lw)$ $\quad \frac{(1 \text{ in})^2}{(2.54 \text{ cm})^2}$ $\quad \frac{14.7 \text{ lbs}}{1 \text{ in}^2}$

Solution: $SA = 2(lh) + 2(wh) + 2(lw) = 2(30.0 \text{ cm} \times 15.0 \text{ cm}) + 2(20.0 \text{ cm} \times 15.0 \text{ cm}) + 2(30.0 \text{ cm} \times 20.0 \text{ cm}) = 2700 \text{ cm}^2$

$$2700 \text{ cm}^2 \times \frac{(1 \text{ in})^2}{(2.54 \text{ cm})^2} = 418.50 \text{ in}^2,\ 418.50 \text{ in}^2 \times \frac{14.7 \text{ lbs}}{1 \text{ in}^2} = 6150 \text{ lbs}.$$ The can would be crushed.

Check: The units (lbs) are correct. The magnitude of the answer (6150 lbs) is not unreasonable since there is a large surface area.

5.114 **Given:** l = 20.0 cm, r = 10.0 cm, 25 mL with d = 0.807 g/ml, P_1 = 760.0 mmHg = 1.000 atm
Find: Force (lbs)
Conceptual Plan: mL → **g** → **mol then *l, r*** → ***V*(cm^3)** → ***V*(L) then *V, n, T*** → P_{N_2} **then**

$d = \frac{m}{V}$ $\quad \frac{1 \text{ mol}}{28.02 \text{ g}}$ $\quad V = \pi r^2 l$ $\quad \frac{1 \text{ L}}{1000 \text{ cm}^3}$ $\quad PV = nRT$

P_{N_2}, P_{atm} → P_{Total} **then atm** → **psi *l, r*** → **Surface Area(cm^2)** → **Surface Area(in^2)** → **Force**

$P_{Total} = P_{atm} + P_{N_2}$ $\quad \frac{14.7 \text{ lbs}}{1 \text{ atm}}$ $\quad SA = 2\pi rl + 2\pi r^2$ $\quad \frac{(1 \text{ in})^2}{(2.54 \text{ cm})^2}$ $\quad P = \frac{F}{A}$

Solution: $d = \frac{m}{V}$ Rearrange to solve for m. $m = dV = 0.807 \frac{\text{g}}{\text{mL}} \times 25 \text{ mL} = 20.175 \text{ g}$,

$$20.175 \text{ g} \times \frac{1 \text{ mol}}{28.02 \text{ g}} = 0.72002 \text{ mol},\ V = \pi r^2 l = \pi \times (10.0 \text{ cm})^2 \times 20.0 \text{ cm} = 6283.19 \text{ cm}^3,$$

$$6283.19 \text{ cm}^3 \times \frac{1 \text{ L}}{1000 \text{ cm}^3} = 6.28319 \text{ L},\ PV = nRT$$ Rearrange to solve for P.

$$P_{N_2} = \frac{nRT}{V} = \frac{0.72002 \text{ mol} \times 0.08206 \frac{\text{L} \cdot \text{atm}}{\text{mol} \cdot \text{K}} \times 298 \text{ K}}{6.28319 \text{ L}} = 2.80229 \text{ atm},$$

$$P_{Total} = P_{atm} + P_{N_2} = 1.000 \text{ atm} + 2.80229 \text{ atm} = 3.80229 \text{ atm},\ 3.80229 \text{ atm} \times \frac{14.7 \text{ psi}}{1 \text{ atm}} = 55.894 \text{ psi}$$

$$SA = 2\pi rl + 2\pi r^2 = (2 \times \pi \times 10.0 \text{ cm} \times 20.0 \text{ cm}) + (2 \times \pi \times (10.0 \text{ cm})^2) = 1884.956 \text{ cm}^2,$$

$$1884.956 \text{ cm}^2 \times \frac{(1 \text{ in})^2}{(2.54 \text{ cm})^2} = 292.169 \text{ in}^2,\ P = \frac{F}{A}$$ Rearrange to solve for F.

$$292.169 \text{ in}^2 \times \frac{55.894 \text{ lbs}}{1 \text{ in}^2} = 1.6 \times 10^4 \text{ lbs}$$

Check: The units (lbs) are correct. The magnitude of the answer (16,000 lbs) is not unreasonable since there is a large surface area and this is a high pressure.

5.115 **Given:** V_1 = 160.0 L, P_1 = 1855 psi, 3.5 L/balloon, P_2 = 1.0 atm = 14.7 psi, and T = 298 K **Find:** # balloons
Conceptual Plan: V_1, P_1, P_2 → V_2 **then L** → **# balloons**

$P_1V_1 = P_2V_2$ $\quad \frac{1 \text{ balloon}}{3.5 \text{ L}}$

Solution: $P_1V_1 = P_2V_2$ Rearrange to solve for V_2. $V_2 = \frac{P_1}{P_2}V_1 = \frac{1855 \text{ psi}}{14.7 \text{ psi}} \times 160.0 \text{ L} = 20190.5 \text{ L}$,

$$20190.5 \text{ L} \times \frac{1 \text{ balloon}}{3.5 \text{ L}} = 5800 \text{ balloons}$$

Check: The units (balloons) are correct. The magnitude of the answer (5800) is reasonable since a store does not want to buy a new helium tank very often.

5.116 **Given:** 11.5 mL with d = 0.573 g/ml, T = 28.5 °C, P = 892 torr **Find:** V

Conceptual Plan: mL → g → mol and °C, → K and torr → atm then $P, n, T \rightarrow V$

$d = \frac{m}{V}$ $\frac{1\text{ mol}}{58.12\text{ g}}$ K = °C + 273.15 $\frac{1\text{ atm}}{760\text{ torr}}$ $PV = nRT$

Solution: $d = \frac{m}{V}$ Rearrange to solve for m. $m = dV = 0.573\frac{\text{g}}{\text{mL}} \times 11.5\text{ mL} = 6.5895\text{ g}$,

$6.5895\text{ g} \times \frac{1\text{ mol}}{58.12\text{ g}} = 0.113377\text{ mol}$, T = 28.5C + 273.15 = 301.7 K, $892\text{ torr} \times \frac{1\text{ atm}}{760\text{ torr}} = 1.17368\text{ atm}$

$PV = nRT$ Rearrange to solve for V.

$$V = \frac{nRT}{P} = \frac{0.113377\text{ mol} \times 0.08206\frac{\text{L}\cdot\text{atm}}{\text{mol}\cdot\text{K}} \times 301.7\text{ K}}{1.17368\text{ atm}} = 2.39\text{ L}$$

Check: The units (L) are correct. The magnitude of the answer (1 L) is reasonable since there is a lot less than one mole of butane.

5.117 **Given:** r_1 = 2.5 cm, P_1 = 4.00 atm, T = 298 K, and P_2 = 1.00 atm **Find:** r_2

Conceptual Plan: $r_1 \rightarrow V_1$ $V_1, P_1, P_2 \rightarrow V_2$ then $V_2 \rightarrow r_2$

$V = \frac{4}{3}\pi r^3$ $P_1V_1 = P_2V_2$ $V = \frac{4}{3}\pi r^3$

Solution: $V = \frac{4}{3}\pi r^3 = \frac{4}{3} \times \pi \times (2.5\text{ cm})^3 = 65.450\text{ cm}^3$ $P_1V_1 = P_2V_2$ Rearrange to solve for V_2.

$V_2 = \frac{P_1}{P_2}V_1 = \frac{4.00\text{ atm}}{1.00\text{ atm}} \times 65.450\text{ cm}^3 = 261.80\text{ cm}^3$, $V = \frac{4}{3}\pi r^3$

Rearrange to solve for r. $r = \sqrt[3]{\frac{3V}{4\pi}} = \sqrt[3]{\frac{3 \times 261.80\text{ cm}^3}{4 \times \pi}} = 4.0\text{ cm}$

Check: The units (cm) are correct. The magnitude of the answer (4 cm) is reasonable since the bubble will expand as the pressure is decreased.

5.118 **Given:** max SA = 1257 cm^2, V_1 = 3.0 L, P_1 = 755 torr, T_1 = 298 K, T_2 = 273 K **Find:** P_2 to burst balloon

Conceptual Plan: torr → atm and $A \rightarrow r \rightarrow V$ (cm^3) → V (L) then

$\frac{1\text{ atm}}{760\text{ torr}}$ $SA = 4\pi r^2$ $V = \frac{4}{3}\pi r^3$ $\frac{1\text{ L}}{1000\text{ cm}^3}$

$P_1, V_1, P_2, T_1, V_2, T_2 \rightarrow P_2$

$\frac{P_1V_1}{T_1} = \frac{P_2V_2}{T_2}$

Solution: $P_1 = 755\text{ torr} \times \frac{1\text{ atm}}{760\text{ torr}} = 0.993421\text{ atm}$, $SA = 4\pi r^2$ Rearrange to solve for r.

$r = \sqrt{\frac{SA}{4\pi}} = \sqrt{\frac{1257\text{cm}^2}{4\pi}} = 10.00144\text{ cm}$, $V = \frac{4}{3}\pi r^3 = \frac{4}{3} \times \pi \times (10.00144\text{ cm})^3 = 4190.600\text{ cm}^3$

$4190.600\text{ cm}^3 \times \frac{1\text{ L}}{1000\text{ cm}^3} = 4.190600\text{ L}$ $\frac{P_1V_1}{T_1} = \frac{P_2V_2}{T_2}$ Rearrange to solve for P_2.

$$P_2 = P_1\frac{V_1}{V_2}\frac{T_2}{T_1} = 0.993421\text{ atm} \times \frac{3.00\text{ L}}{4.190600\text{ L}} \times \frac{273\text{ K}}{298\text{ K}} = 0.652\text{ atm}$$

Check: The units (atm) are correct. The magnitude of the answer (0.65 atm) is reasonable since the pressure must decrease in order for the balloon to expand.

5.119 **Given:** 2.0 mol CO : 1.0 mol O_2, V = 2.45 L, P_1 = 745 torr, P_2 = 552 torr, and T = 552 °C

Find: % reacted

Conceptual Plan: from $PV = nRT$ we know that $P \propto n$, looking at the chemical reaction we see that 2 + 1 = 3 moles of gas gets converted to 2 moles of gas. If all the gas reacts, P_2 = 2/ 3 P_1.

Calculate $-\Delta P$ for 100 % reacted and for actual case. Then calculate % reacted.

$-\Delta P\ 100\ \%\ reacted = P_1 - \frac{2}{3}P_1$ $-\Delta P\ actual = P_1 - P_2$ $\%\ reacted = \frac{\Delta P\ actual}{\Delta P\ 100\%\ reacted} \times 100\ \%$

Solution: $-\Delta P$ 100 % *reacted* $= P_1 - \frac{2}{3}P_1 = 745\text{ torr} - \frac{2}{3}745\text{ torr} = 24\underline{8}.333\text{ torr}$,

$-\Delta P\text{ actual} = P_1 - P_2 = 745\text{ torr} - 552\text{ torr} = 193\text{ torr}$,

$$\%\ reacted = \frac{\Delta P\ actual}{\Delta P\ 100\%\ reacted} \times 100\% = \frac{193\ \cancel{\text{torr}}}{24\underline{8}.333\ \cancel{\text{torr}}} \times 100\% = 77.7\ \%$$

Check: The units (%) are correct. The magnitude of the answer (78 %) makes sense because the pressure dropped most of the way to the pressure if all of the reactants had reacted. **Note: There are many ways to solve this problem, including calculating the moles of reactants and products using *PV* = *nRT*.**

5.120 **Given:** N_2, $V_1 = 1.0$ L, $P_1 = 1.0$ atm, $T_1 = 300.$ K, and $V_2 = 3.0$ L, **Find:** d_2
Conceptual Plan: $\mathcal{M}, V_1, P_1, T_1 \rightarrow d_1 \rightarrow d_2$

$$d = \frac{P\mathcal{M}}{RT} \qquad d = \frac{m}{V}$$

Solution: $$d_1 = \frac{P\mathcal{M}}{RT} = \frac{1.0\ \cancel{\text{atm}} \times 28.02\ \frac{\text{g}}{\cancel{\text{mol}}}}{0.08206\ \frac{\text{L}\ \cancel{\text{atm}}}{\cancel{\text{K}}\ \cancel{\text{mol}}} \times 300.\ \cancel{\text{K}}} = 1.\underline{1}3819\ \frac{\text{g}}{\text{L}},\ d = \frac{m}{V}$$

Since we have a sealed container, $m_1 = m_2$. Rearrange to solve for m. $m = dV$ or $m = d_1V_1 = d_2V_2$

Rearrange to solve for d_2. $$d_2 = d_1\frac{V_1}{V_2} = 1.\underline{1}3819\ \frac{\text{g}}{\text{L}} \times \frac{1.0\ \cancel{\text{L}}}{3.0\ \cancel{\text{L}}} = 0.38\ \frac{\text{g}}{\text{L}}$$

Check: The units (g/L) are correct. The magnitude of the answer (0.4 g/L) is a typical gas density. The density dropped as the volume went up.

5.121 **Given:** $P(\text{Total})_1 = 2.2$ atm = CO + O_2, $P(\text{Total})_2 = 1.9$ atm = CO + O_2 + CO_2, $V = 1.0$ L, $T = 1.0 \times 10^3$ K
Find: mass CO_2 made
Conceptual Plan: $P(\text{Total})_1 = 2.2\text{ atm} = P(\text{CO})_1 + P(\text{O}_2)_1$, $P(\text{Total})_2 = 1.9\text{ atm} = P(\text{CO})_2 + P(\text{O}_2)_2 + P(\text{CO}_2)_2$. Let x = amount of $P(\text{O}_2)$ reacted. From stoichiometry: $P(\text{CO})_2 = P(\text{CO})_1 - 2x$, $P(\text{O}_2)_2 = P(\text{O}_2)_1 - x$, $P(\text{CO}_2)_2 = 2x$. Thus $P(\text{Total})_2 = 1.9\text{ atm} = P(\text{CO})_1 - 2x + P(\text{O}_2)_1 - x + 2x = P(\text{Total})_1 - x$. Using the initial conditions: 1.9 atm = 2.2 atm – x. So x = 0.3 atm and since $2x = P(\text{CO}_2)_2 = 0.6$ atm, then $P, V, T \rightarrow n \rightarrow$ g.

$$PV = nRT \qquad \frac{44.01\text{ g}}{1\text{ mol}}$$

Solution: $PV = nRT$ Rearrange to solve for n.

$$n = \frac{PV}{RT} = \frac{0.6\ \cancel{\text{atm}} \times 1.0\ \cancel{\text{L}}}{0.08206\ \frac{\cancel{\text{L}} \cdot \cancel{\text{atm}}}{\text{mol} \cdot \cancel{\text{K}}} \times 1000\ \cancel{\text{K}}} = 0.00\underline{7}3117\text{ mol}$$

$$0.00\underline{7}3117\ \cancel{\text{mol}} \times \frac{44.01\text{ g}}{1\ \cancel{\text{mol}}} = 0.\underline{3}21789\text{ g }CO_2 = 0.3\text{ g }CO_2$$

Check: The units (g) are correct. The magnitude of the answer (0.3 g) makes sense because we have such a small volume, at a very high temperature and such a small pressure. This leads us to expect a very small number of moles.

5.122 **Given:** $r = 1.3 \times 10^{-8}$ cm, $V = 100.$ mL, $P = 1.0$ atm, $T_1 = 273$ K **Find:** V fraction occupied by Xe atoms
Conceptual Plan: mL $\rightarrow$ L then $V \rightarrow n \rightarrow$ atoms then $r \rightarrow V$ (cm^3)/atom

$$\frac{1\text{ L}}{1000\text{ mL}} \qquad \frac{1\text{ mol}}{22.414\text{ L}}\text{ at STP} \qquad 6.022 \times 10^{23}\text{ atoms/mol} \qquad V = \frac{4}{3}\pi r^3$$

then atoms, V (cm^3)/atom $\rightarrow$ V(Xe) then V(Xe), V(container) $\rightarrow$ Fraction Xe

$$V(Xe) = (V/atom)(atoms) \qquad \%V(Xe) = \frac{V(Xe)}{V(container)} \times 100\%$$

Solution: $$100\ \cancel{\text{mL}} \times \frac{1\text{ L}}{1000\ \cancel{\text{mL}}} = 0.100\text{ L},$$

$$0.100\ \cancel{\text{L}} \times \frac{1\text{ mol}}{22.414\ \cancel{\text{L}}} = 0.00\underline{4}46149\ \cancel{\text{mol}} \times 6.022 \times 10^{23}\ \frac{\text{atoms}}{\cancel{\text{mol}}} = 2.\underline{6}8671 \times 10^{21}\text{ atoms}$$

$$V = \frac{4}{3}\pi r^3 = \frac{4}{3} \times \pi \times (1.3 \times 10^{-8}\text{ cm})^3 = 9.\underline{2}028 \times 10^{-24}\text{ cm}^3/\text{atom},$$

$$V(Xe) = (V/atom)(atoms) = \frac{9.\underline{2}028 \times 10^{-24}\text{cm}^3}{\cancel{\text{atom}}} \times 2.\underline{6}8671 \times 10^{21}\ \cancel{\text{atoms}} = 0.02\underline{4}725\text{ cm}^3$$

$$\%\ V(Xe) = \frac{V(Xe)}{V(container)} \times 100\ \% = \frac{0.02\underline{4}725\ \cancel{\text{cm}^3}}{100\ \cancel{\text{cm}^3}} \times 100\ \% = 0.025\ \%V$$

Check: The units (%V) are correct. The magnitude of the answer (0.025 %V) is reasonable since we expect the molecules to take up very little of the volume of a container of a gas.

5.123 **Given:** $h_1 = 22.6$ m, $T_1 = 22$ °C, and $h_2 = 23.8$ m **Find:** T_2

Conceptual Plan: °C → K since $V_{cylinder} \alpha h$ we do not need to know r to use $V_1, T_1, T_2 \rightarrow V_2$

$K = °C + 273.15$ $\quad V = \pi r^2 h$ $\quad \frac{V_1}{T_1} = \frac{V_2}{T_2}$

Solution: $T_1 = 22\ °C + 273.15 = 295K$, $\frac{V_1}{T_1} = \frac{V_2}{T_2}$ Rearrange to solve for T_2.

$$T_2 = T_1 \times \frac{V_2}{V_1} = T_1 \times \frac{\pi r^2 h_2}{\pi r^2 h_1} = 295\ K \times \frac{23.8\ m}{22.6\ m} = 311\ K$$

Check: The units (K) are correct. We expect the temperature to increase since the volume increased.

5.124 **Given:** m (CH_4) = 8.0 g, m (Xe) = 8.0 g, $P_{Total} = 0.44$ atm **Find:** P_{CH_4}

Conceptual Plan: g → mol then $n_{CH_4}, n_{Xe} \rightarrow \chi_{CH_4}$ then $\chi_{CH_4}, P_{Total} \rightarrow P_{CH_4}$

$\mathcal{M}$ $\quad \chi_{CH_4} = \frac{n_{CH_4}}{n_{CH_4} + n_{Xe}}$ $\quad P_{CH_4} = \chi_{CH_4} P_{Total}$

Solution: $n_{CH_4} = 8.0\ g \times \frac{1\ mol}{16.04\ g} = 0.49869$ mol, $n_{Xe} = 8.0\ g \times \frac{1\ mol}{131.3\ g} = 0.060929$ mol,

$$\chi_{CH_4} = \frac{n_{CH_4}}{n_{CH_4} + n_{Xe}} = \frac{0.49869\ mol}{0.49869\ mol + 0.060929\ mol} = 0.89112,$$

$$P_{CH_4} = \chi_{CH_4} P_{Total} = 0.89112 \times 0.44\ atm = 0.39\ atm$$

Check: The units (atm) are correct. The magnitude of the answer (0.22 atm) makes sense because the molecular weight of methane is so much lower than xenon, so we have many more moles of methane. The partial pressure of methane is almost as large as the total pressure.

5.125 **Given:** He, $V = 0.35$ L, $P_{max} = 88$ atm, and $T = 299$ K **Find:** m_{He}

Conceptual Plan: $P, V, T \rightarrow n$ then mol → g

$PV = nRT$ $\quad \mathcal{M}$

Solution: $PV = nRT$ Rearrange to solve for n.

$$n_{He} = \frac{PV}{RT} = \frac{88\ atm \times 0.35\ L}{0.08206 \frac{L \cdot atm}{mol \cdot K} \times 299\ K} = 1.2553\ mol,\ 1.2553\ mol \times \frac{4.003\ g}{1\ mol} = 5.0\ g\ He$$

Check: The units (g) are correct. The magnitude of the answer (5 g) makes sense because the high pressure and the low volume cancel out (remember 22 L / mol at STP) and so we expect ~ 1 mol and so ~ 4 g.

5.126 **Given:** NaH + water, $V = 0.490$ L, $P_{Total} = 758$ mmHg, and $T = 35$ °C **Find:** m_{H_2} and m_{NaH}

Other: $P_{H_2O} = 42.23$ mmHg at 35 °C

Conceptual Plan: °C → K and P_{Total}(mmHg) → P_{H_2}(mmHg) → P_{H_2}(atm) then

$K = °C + 273.15$ $\quad P_{Total} = P_{H_2O} + P_{H_2}$ $\quad \frac{1\ atm}{760\ mm\ Hg}$

Write balanced reaction

$NaH\ (s) + H_2O\ (l) \rightarrow NaOH\ (aq) + H_2\ (g)$

$P, V, T \rightarrow n_{H_2}$ then mol $_{H_2}$ → g $_{H_2}$ then mol $_{H_2}$ → mol $_{NaH}$ → g $_{NaH}$

$PV = nRT$ $\quad \frac{2.016\ g}{1\ mol}$ $\quad \frac{1\ mol\ NaH}{1\ mol\ H_2}$ $\quad \frac{24.0\ g}{1\ mol}$

Solution: $T = 35°C + 273.15 = 308$ K, $P_{Total} = P_{H_2O} + P_{H_2}$ Rearrange to solve for P_{H_2}.

$$P_{H_2} = 758\ mmHg - 42.23\ mmHg = 715.77\ mmHg,\ 715.77\ mmHg \times \frac{1\ atm}{760\ mm\ Hg} = 0.941803\ atm\quad PV = nRT$$

Rearrange to solve for n. $n_{H_2} = \frac{PV}{RT} = \frac{0.941803\ atm \times 0.490\ L}{0.08206 \frac{L \cdot atm}{mol \cdot K} \times 308\ K} = 0.0182589$ mol,

$$0.0182589\ mol \times \frac{2.016\ g}{1\ mol} = 0.0368\ g\ H_2 \text{ and } 0.0182589\ mol\ H_2 \times \frac{1\ mol\ NaH}{1\ mol\ H_2} = 0.0182589\ mol\ NaH,$$

$$0.0182589\ mol\ NaH \times \frac{24.0\ g}{1\ mol} = 0.438\ g\ NaH$$

Check: The units (g) are correct. The magnitude of the answer (0.04 g and 0.4 g) makes sense because we have much less than a mole of each material (remember 22 L / mol at STP), so we expect < 2 g gas and < 24 g solid.

5.127 **Given:** 15.0 mL HBr in 1.0 min; and 20.3 mL unknown hydrocarbon gas in 1.0 min
Find: formula of unknown gas
Conceptual Plan: Since these are gases under the same conditions $V \alpha n$, V, time → Rate then

$$Rate = \frac{V}{time}$$

$\mathcal{M}$(HBr), Rate (HBr), Rate (Unk) → $\mathcal{M}$(Unk)

$$\frac{Rate(HBr)}{Rate(U)} = \sqrt{\frac{\mathcal{M}(U)}{\mathcal{M}(HBr)}}$$

Solution: $Rate(HBr) = \frac{V}{time} = \frac{15.0\ \text{mL}}{1.0\ \text{min}} = 15.0\frac{\text{mL}}{\text{min}}$, $Rate(Unk) = \frac{V}{time} = \frac{20.3\ \text{mL}}{1.0\ \text{min}} = 20.3\frac{\text{mL}}{\text{min}}$,

$\frac{Rate(HBr)}{Rate(Unk)} = \sqrt{\frac{\mathcal{M}(Unk)}{\mathcal{M}(HBr)}}$ Rearrange to solve for $\mathcal{M}(Unk)$.

$$\mathcal{M}(Unk) = \mathcal{M}(HBr)\left(\frac{Rate(HBr)}{Rate(Unk)}\right)^2 = 80.91\frac{\text{g}}{\text{mol}} \times \left(\frac{15.0\frac{\text{mL}}{\text{min}}}{20.3\frac{\text{mL}}{\text{min}}}\right)^2 = 44.2\frac{\text{g}}{\text{mol}}$$ The formula is C_3H_8, propane.

Check: The units (g/mol) are correct. The magnitude of the answer (< HBr) makes sense because the unknown diffused faster and so must be lighter.

5.128 Since $N_2O_3\ (g) \rightarrow NO_2\ (g) + NO\ (g)$ undergoes a complete reaction, according to Avogadro's law the pressure will double since one mole of gas decomposes to two moles of gas. According to Charles law, when the temperature in kelvins doubles the pressure doubles. Thus, the pressure will increase by a factor of four or 4 x 0.017 atm = 0.068 atm.

5.129 **Given:** 0.583 g neon, $V = 8.00 \times 10^2\ \text{cm}^3$, $P_{Total} = 1.17$ atm, and $T = 295$ K **Find:** g argon
Conceptual Plan: g → n and mL → L then n, V, T → P_{Ne} then P_{Ne}, P_{Total} → P_{Ar} then

$$\frac{1\ \text{mol}}{20.18\ \text{g}} \qquad \frac{1\ \text{L}}{1000\ \text{mL}} \qquad PV = nRT \qquad P_{Total} = P_{Ne} + P_{Ar}$$

P_{Ar}, V, T → n → g

$$PV = nRT \qquad \frac{39.95\ \text{g}}{1\ \text{mol}}$$

Solution: $0.583\ \text{g Ne} \times \frac{1\ \text{mol Ne}}{20.18\ \text{g Ne}} = 0.02888999\ \text{mol Ne}$ $\quad 8.00 \times 10^2\ \text{mL} \times \frac{1\ \text{L}}{1000\ \text{mL}} = 0.800\ \text{L}$

$PV = nRT$ Rearrange to solve for P.

$$P = \frac{nRT}{V} = \frac{0.02888999\ \text{mol} \times 0.08206\frac{\text{L}\cdot\text{atm}}{\text{mol}\cdot\text{K}} \times 295\ \text{K}}{0.800\ \text{L}} = 0.874200\ \text{atm Ne}$$

$P_{Total} = P_{Ne} + P_{Ar}$ Rearrange to solve for P_{Ar}. $P_{Ar} = P_{Total} - P_{Ne} = 1.17\ \text{atm} - 0.874200\ \text{atm} = 0.295800\ \text{atm}$

$PV = nRT$ Rearrange to solve for n. $n_{Ar} = \frac{PV}{RT} = \frac{0.295800\ \text{atm} \times 0.800\ \text{L}}{0.08206\frac{\text{L}\cdot\text{atm}}{\text{mol}\cdot\text{K}} \times 295\ \text{K}} = 0.00977539\ \text{mol Ar}$

$$0.00977539\ \text{mol Ar} \times \frac{39.95\ \text{g Ar}}{1\ \text{mol Ar}} = 0.390527\ \text{g Ar} = 0.39\ \text{g Ar}$$

Check: The units (g) are correct. The magnitude of the answer (0.4 g) makes sense because the pressure and volume are small.

5.130 **Given:** helium + argon density 0.670 g/L, $P = 755$ mmHg, and $T = 298$ K **Find:** composition
Solution: Assume 22.414 L, so number of moles of gas = 755 mmHg/760 mmHg = 0.9934721 moles of gas and the mass of the gas $= \frac{0.670\ \text{g}}{1\ \text{L}} \times 22.414\ \text{L} = 15.01738$ g total. Let $x = n_{He}$, so

$$m_{Total} = 15.01738\ \text{g total} = x\frac{4.003\ \text{g}}{1\ \text{mol}} + (0.9934721 - x)\frac{39.95\ \text{g}}{1\ \text{mol}}$$ Solve for x.

$$x\ \text{mol}\left(\frac{39.95\ \text{g}}{1\ \text{mol}} - \frac{4.003\ \text{g}}{1\ \text{mol}}\right) = (39.68921 - 15.01738)\ \text{g} \rightarrow x\ \text{mol} = \frac{(24.67183)\ \text{g}}{\left(\frac{35.947\ \text{g}}{1\ \text{mol}}\right)} = 0.6863391\ \text{mol He}$$

and (0.9934721 – 0.6863391) mol Ar = 0.3071330 mol Ar. The composition on a volume basis is the same as the composition on a molar basis.

$$\frac{0.6863391 \text{ mol He}}{0.9934721 \text{ mol total}} \times 100\ \% = 69.1\ \%\ \text{He and } 100\ \% - 69.1\ \%\ \text{Ar} = 30.9\ \%\ \text{Ar}$$

Check: The units (%) are correct. The magnitude of the answer (70 % He) makes sense because, the average molar mass is ~15 g/mol, which is closer to the molar mass of He than to Ar.

5.131 **Given:** 75.2 % by mass nitrogen + 24.8 % by mass krypton, $P_{Total} = 745$ mmHg **Find:** P_{Kr}
Solution: Assume 100 g total, so we have 75.2 g N_2 and 24.8 g Kr. Converting these masses to moles,

$$75.2 \text{ g } N_2 \times \frac{1 \text{ mol } N_2}{28.02 \text{ g } N_2} = 2.683797 \text{ mol } N_2 \text{ and } 24.8 \text{ g Kr} \times \frac{1 \text{ mol Kr}}{83.80 \text{ g Kr}} = 0.2959427 \text{ mol Kr.}$$

$$P_{Kr} = \chi_{Kr} P_{Total} = \frac{0.2959427 \text{ mol Kr}}{2.683797 \text{ mol } N_2 + 0.2959427 \text{ mol Kr}} 745 \text{ mmHg Kr} = 74.0 \text{ mmHg Kr}$$

Check: The units (mmHg) are correct. The magnitude of the answer (74 mmHg) makes sense because, the mixture is mostly nitrogen by mass, and this dominance is magnified since the molar mass of krypton is larger than the molar mass of nitrogen.

Challenge Problems

5.132 **Given:** $V = 10$ L, 0.10 mol H_2 initially, $T = 3000$ K, $P_{Final} = 3.0$ atm **Find:** P_H
Conceptual Plan: Write balanced reaction to determine change in moles of gas.

$H_2\,(g) \rightarrow 2\,H\,(g)$ thus $\frac{2 \text{ mol H}}{1 \text{ mol } H_2 \text{ reacted}}$. Since $P_{H_2} \propto n_{H_2}$, the pressure will increase 1 atm for every 1 atm of H_2 that reacts.

$n, T, V \rightarrow P_{initial}$ $\quad P_{initial}, P_{final} \rightarrow \Delta P$ $\quad$ write expression for P_H

$PV = nRT \qquad \Delta P = P_{final} - P_{initial} \qquad P_H = \Delta P \frac{2 \text{ mol H}}{1 \text{ atm reacted}}$

Solution: $PV = nRT$ Rearrange to solve for P.

$$P = \frac{nRT}{V} = \frac{0.10 \text{ mol} \times 0.08206 \frac{\text{L}\cdot\text{atm}}{\text{mol}\cdot\text{K}} \times 3000 \text{ K}}{10 \text{ L}} = 2.4618 \text{ atm } H_2$$

$\Delta P = P_{final} - P_{initial} = 3.0 \text{ atm} - 2.4618 \text{ atm} = 0.5382$ atm, and

$$P_H = \Delta P \frac{2 \text{ mol H}}{1 \text{ atm reacted}} = 0.5382 \text{ atm} \times \frac{2 \text{ mol H}}{1 \text{ atm reacted}} = 1.0764 \text{ atm} = 1.1 \text{ atm H}$$

Check: The units (atm) are correct. The magnitude of the answer (1 atm) makes sense because if all the hydrogen dissociated, the final pressure would have been 5 atm. Since we are closer to the initial pressure than this maximum pressure, less than half of the hydrogen has dissociated.

5.133 **Given:** $2\,NH_3\,(g) \rightarrow N_2\,(g) + 3\,H_2\,(g)$; $N_2H_4\,(g) \rightarrow N_2\,(g) + 2\,H_2\,(g)$; initially $P = 0.50$ atm, $T = 300$ K, finally $P = 4.5$ atm, $T = 1200$ K **Find:** N_2H_4 percent initially
Conceptual Plan: $P_{initial}, T_{initial}, T_{final} \rightarrow P_{final}$ then determine change in moles of gas

$\frac{P_{initial}}{T_{initial}} = \frac{P_{final}}{T_{final}} \qquad \frac{3 \text{ atm added gas}}{1 \text{ atm } NH_3 \text{ reacted}}$ and $\frac{2 \text{ atm added gas}}{1 \text{ atm } N_2H_4 \text{ reacted}}$

$P_1, P_2 \rightarrow \Delta P$ write expression for ΔP then solve for $P_{1N_2H_4}$ and P_{1NH_3} finally $P_{1N_2H_4}, P_{1NH_3} \rightarrow \%\ N_2H_4$

$\Delta P = P_2 - P_1 \quad \Delta P = P_{1NH_3} \frac{3 \text{ atm added gas}}{2 \text{ atm reacted}} + P_{1N_2H_4} \frac{2 \text{ atm added gas}}{1 \text{ atm reacted}}$ where $P_{1,1200K} = P_{1NH_3} + P_{1N_2H_4}$ $\quad \%N_2H_4 = \frac{P_{N_2H_4}}{P_{N_2H_4} + P_{NH_3}} \times 100\%$

Solution: $\frac{P_{initial}}{T_{initial}} = \frac{P_{final}}{T_{final}}$ Rearrange to solve for P_{final}. $P_2 = P_1 \times \frac{T_2}{T_1} = 0.50 \text{ atm} \times \frac{1200 \text{ K}}{300 \text{ K}} = 2.0$ atm if no reaction occurred.

$\Delta P = P_{final} - P_{initial} = 4.5 \text{ atm} - 2.0 \text{ atm} = 2.5$ atm, and $P_{1,1200K} = 2.0 \text{ atm} = P_{1NH_3} + P_{1N_2H_4}$ or

$P_{1NH_3} = 2.0 \text{ atm} - P_{1N_2H_4}$.

Substitute this into $\Delta P = P_{1NH_3} \frac{3 \text{ atm added gas}}{2 \text{ atm reacted}} + P_{1N_2H_4} \frac{2 \text{ atm added gas}}{1 \text{ atm reacted}}$ and solve for $P_{1N_2H_4}$.

$$\Delta P = 2.5 \text{ atm} = (2.0 \text{ atm} - P_{1N_2H_4}) \frac{3 \text{ atm added gas}}{2 \text{ atm reacted}} + P_{1N_2H_4} \frac{2 \text{ atm added gas}}{1 \text{ atm reacted}} \rightarrow$$

$P_{1N_2H_4} = 3.0 \text{ atm} - 2.5 \text{ atm} = 0.5$ atm and $P_{NH_3} = 2.0 \text{ atm} - 0.5 \text{ atm} = 1.5$ atm finally

$$\%N_2H_4 = \frac{P_{N_2H_4}}{P_{N_2H_4} + P_{NH_3}} \times 100\% = \frac{0.5 \text{ atm}}{0.5 \text{ atm} + 1.5 \text{ atm}} \times 100\% = 25\%\ N_2H_4 = 30\%\ N_2H_4$$

Check: The units (%) are correct. The magnitude of the answer (30 %) makes sense because if it were all N_2H_4 the final pressure would have been 6 atm. Since we are closer to the initial pressure than this maximum pressure, less than half of the gas is N_2H_4.

5.134 **Given:** CO gas, Initial: V = 0.48 L, P = 1.0 atm, and T = 275 K; Final: V = 1.3 L **Find:** Final gas density

Conceptual Plan: $P, V, T \rightarrow n \rightarrow m$ then m, V $\rightarrow d$

$PV = nRT$ $\quad \frac{28.01 \text{ g}}{1 \text{ mol}}$ $\quad d = m/V$

Solution: $PV = nRT$ Rearrange to solve for n. $n = \frac{PV}{RT} = \frac{1.0 \text{ atm} \times 0.48 \text{ L}}{0.08206 \frac{\text{L} \cdot \text{atm}}{\text{mol} \cdot \text{K}} \times 275 \text{ K}} = 0.02127047 \text{ mol}$,

$0.02127047 \text{ mol} \times \frac{28.01 \text{ g}}{1 \text{ mol}} = 0.5957858 \text{ g}$ then $d = \frac{m}{V} = \frac{0.5957858 \text{ g}}{1.3 \text{ L}} = 0.4582968 \text{ g/L} = 0.46 \text{ g/L}$

Check: The units (g/L) are correct. The magnitude of the answer (0.5 g/L) makes sense because this is typical for a gas density.

5.135 **Given:** $2\ CO_2\ (g) \rightarrow 2\ CO\ (g) + O_2\ (g)$; initially P = 10.0 atm, T = 701 K, finally P = 22.5 atm, T = 1401 K **Find:** mole percent decomposed

Conceptual Plan: $P_{initial}, T_{initial}, T_{final} \rightarrow P_{final}$ then determine change in moles of gas

$\frac{P_{initial}}{T_{initial}} = \frac{P_{final}}{T_{final}}$ $\quad \frac{1 \text{ atm added gas}}{2 \text{ atm } CO_2 \text{ reacted}}$

$P_1, P_2 \rightarrow \Delta P$ write expression for ΔP then solve for $P_{CO_2 \text{ reacted}}$ finally

$\Delta P = P_2 - P_1$ $\quad \Delta P = P_{CO_2 \text{ reacted}} \frac{1 \text{ atm added gas}}{2 \text{ atm } CO_2 \text{ reacted}}$

$P_{final}, P_{CO2 \text{ reacted}} \rightarrow \%\ CO_2$ decomposed

$\%CO_2 \text{ decomposed} = \frac{P_{CO_2 \text{ reacted}}}{P_{final}} \times 100\%$

Solution: $\frac{P_{initial}}{T_{initial}} = \frac{P_{final}}{T_{final}}$ Rearrange to solve for P_{final}. $P_2 = P_1 \times \frac{T_2}{T_1} = 10.0 \text{ atm} \times \frac{1401 \text{ K}}{701 \text{ K}} = 19.985735 \text{ atm}$

$\Delta P = P_{final} - P_{initial} = 22.5 \text{ atm} - 19.985735 \text{ atm} = 2.514265 \text{ atm}$,

$\Delta P = P_{CO_2 \text{ reacted}} \frac{1 \text{ atm added gas}}{2 \text{ atm } CO_2 \text{ reacted}}$ or the pressure increases 1 atm for each 2 atm of gas decomposed, so 5.02853 atm decomposes and then

$\%CO_2 \text{ decomposed} = \frac{P_{CO_2 \text{ reacted}}}{P_{final}} \times 100\% = \frac{5.02853 \text{ atm}}{19.875735 \text{ atm}} \times 100\% = 25.1606\%\ CO_2 \text{ decomposed} =$

25% CO_2 decomposed

Check: The units (%) are correct. The magnitude of the answer (11 %) makes sense because if all of the gas decomposed the final pressure would have been 40 atm. Since we are much closer to the initial pressure than this maximum pressure, much less than half of the gas decomposed.

5.136 **Given:** 9.0 x 10^{12} kg/yr octane; atm = 387 ppm CO_2 by volume; atm thickness = 15 km; r_{Earth} = 6371 km; P_{atm} = 381 torr; T_{atm} = 275 K **Find:** $m(CO_2)$ and % increase in CO_2

Conceptual Plan: Write a balanced chemical reaction kg $C_3H_8 \rightarrow$ g $C_3H_8 \rightarrow$ mol$_{C_3H_8} \rightarrow$ mol$_{CO_2}$

$2\ C_3H_8\ (g) + 25\ O_2\ (g) \rightarrow 16\ CO_2\ (g) + 18\ H_2O\ (l)$ $\quad \frac{1000 \text{ g}}{1 \text{ kg}}$ $\quad \frac{1 \text{ mol}}{114.22 \text{ g}}$ $\quad \frac{16 \text{ mol } CO_2}{2 \text{ mol } C_3H_8}$

then mol$_{CO_2} \rightarrow$ g$_{CO_2}$ and ppm$_{CO_2} \rightarrow \chi_{CO_2} \rightarrow P_{CO_2}$ torr $\rightarrow$ atm then $r_{Earth} \rightarrow V_{Earth}$ and

$\frac{44.01 \text{ g}}{1 \text{ mol}}$ $\quad \frac{1 \text{ part}}{10^6 \text{ parts}}$ $\quad P_{CO_2} = \chi_{CO_2} P_{atm}$ $\quad \frac{1 \text{ atm}}{760 \text{ torr}}$ $\quad V = \frac{4}{3}\pi r^3$

r_{Earth}, atm thickness $\rightarrow r_{Earth+atm}$ then $r_{Earth+atm} \rightarrow V_{Earth+atm}$ $V_{Earth+atm}, V_{Earth} \rightarrow V_{atm}$ then

$r_{Earth+atm} = r_{Earth} + r_{atm}$ $\quad V = \frac{4}{3}\pi r^3$ $\quad V_{atm} = V_{Earth+atm} - V_{Earth}$

km$^3 \rightarrow$ m$^3 \rightarrow$ cm$^3 \rightarrow$ L then $V_{atm}, P_{CO_2}, T_{atm} \rightarrow n_{CO_2} \rightarrow$ g$_{CO_2}$ and

$\left(\frac{1000 \text{ m}}{1 \text{ km}}\right)^3 \left(\frac{100 \text{ cm}}{1 \text{ m}}\right)^3 \frac{1 \text{ L}}{1000 \text{ cm}^3}$ $\quad PV = nRT$ $\quad \frac{44.01 \text{ g}}{1 \text{ mol}}$

g$_{CO_2 \text{added}}$, g$_{CO_2 \text{initially}} \rightarrow$ % increase$_{CO_2}$

$\%\ increase = \frac{added}{initial} \times 100\%$

Solution: $9.0 \times 10^{12}\ \cancel{kg} \times \frac{1000\ \cancel{g}}{1\ \cancel{kg}} \times \frac{1\ \cancel{mol}}{114.22\ \cancel{g}} \times \frac{16\ \cancel{mol\ CO_2}}{2\ \cancel{mol\ C_8H_{18}}} \times \frac{44.01\ g}{1\ \cancel{mol}} = 2.7742 \times 10^{16}\ g\ CO_2$ added,

$387\ \text{parts}\ CO_2 \frac{1\ \text{part}}{10^6\ \text{parts}} = 3.87 \times 10^{-4} = \chi_{CO_2},\ P_{CO_2} = \chi_{CO_2} P_{atm} = 3.87 \times 10^{-4} \times 381\ \text{torr} = 0.147447\ \text{torr},$

$0.147447\ \cancel{torr} \times \frac{1\ atm}{760\ \cancel{torr}} = 0.00019401\ atm,\ V_{Earth} = \frac{4}{3}\pi r^3 = \frac{4}{3} \times \pi \times (6371\ km)^3 = 1.08321 \times 10^{12} km^3,$

$r_{Earth+atm} = r_{Earth} + r_{atm} = 6371\ km + 15\ km = 6386\ km,$

$V_{Earth+atm} = \frac{4}{3}\pi r^3 = \frac{4}{3} \times \pi \times (6386\ km)^3 = 1.09086 \times 10^{12} km^3,$

$V_{atm} = V_{Earth+atm} - V_{Earth} = 1.09086 \times 10^{12} km^3 - 1.08321 \times 10^{12} km^3 = 7.666 \times 10^{9} km^3,$

$7.666 \times 10^9\ \cancel{km^3} \times \left(\frac{1000\ \cancel{m}}{1\ \cancel{km}}\right)^3 \times \left(\frac{100\ \cancel{cm}}{1\ \cancel{m}}\right)^3 \times \frac{1\ L}{1000\ \cancel{cm^3}} = 7.666 \times 10^{21}\ L,\ PV = nRT$

Rearrange to solve for n. $n_{CO_2\ initial} = \frac{PV}{RT} = \frac{0.00019401\ \cancel{atm} \times 7.666 \times 10^{21}\ \cancel{L}}{0.08206 \frac{\cancel{L} \cdot \cancel{atm}}{mol \cdot \cancel{K}} \times 275\ \cancel{K}} = 6.591 \times 10^{16}\ mol,$

$6.591 \times 10^{16}\ \cancel{mol} \times \frac{44.01\ g}{1\ \cancel{mol}} = 2.9005 \times 10^{18}\ g\ CO_2$

$\%\ increase = \frac{added}{initial} \times 100\ \% = \frac{2.7742 \times 10^{16}\ g\ CO_2}{2.9005 \times 10^{18}\ g\ CO_2} \times 100 = 1\ \%\ \text{increase}$

Check: The units (g and %) are correct. The magnitude of the answer (10^{16} g) is reasonable since we started with so much octane, and the mass of CO_2 will be larger than the original octane weight since there is so much added oxygen. The % increase is reasonable since the volume of the atmosphere is so large.

5.137 **Given:** CH_4: V = 155 mL at STP; O_2: V = 885 mL at STP; NO: V = 55.5 mL at STP; mixed in a flask: V = 2.0 L, T = 275 K, and 90.0 % of limiting reagent used. **Find:** Ps of all components and P_{Total}.

Conceptual Plan: CH_4: mL → L → mol_{CO_4} → mol_{CO_2} and
$\frac{1\ L}{1000\ mL}$ $\frac{1\ mol}{22.414\ L}$ $\frac{1\ mol\ CO_2}{5\ mol\ NO}$

O_2: mL → L → mol_{O_2} → mol_{CO_2} and NO: mL → L → mol_{NO} → mol_{CO_2}
$\frac{1\ L}{1000\ mL}$ $\frac{1\ mol}{22.414\ L}$ $\frac{1\ mol\ CO_2}{5\ mol\ O_2}$ $\frac{1\ L}{1000\ mL}$ $\frac{1\ mol}{22.414\ L}$ $\frac{1\ mol\ CO_2}{5\ mol\ NO}$

the smallest yield determines the limiting reagent then initial mol_{NO} → reacted mol_{NO} → final mol_{NO}
NO is the limiting reagent 90.0% 0.100 x initial mol_{no}

reacted mol_{NO} → reacted mol_{CH_4} then initial mol_{CH_4}, reacted mol_{CH_4} → final mol_{CH_4} then
$\frac{1\ mol\ CH_4}{5\ mol\ NO}$ initial mol_{CH_4} – reacted mol_{CH_4} = final mol_{CH_4}

final mol_{CH_4}, V, T → final P_{CH_4} and reacted mol_{NO} → reacted mol_{O_2} then
$PV = nRT$ $\frac{5\ mol\ O_2}{5\ mol\ NO}$

initial mol_{O_2}, reacted mol_{O_2} → final mol_{O_2} then final mol_{O_2}, V, T → final P_{O_2} and
initial mol_{O_2} – reacted mol_{O_2} = final mol_{O_2} $PV = nRT$

final mol_{NO}, V, T → final P_{NO} and theoretical mol_{CO_2} from NO → final mol_{CO_2}
$PV = nRT$ 90.0%

final mol_{CO_2}, V, T → P_{CO_2} then final mol_{CO_2} → mol_{H_2O} then mol_{H_2O}, V, T → P_{H_2O} and
$PV = nRT$ $\frac{1\ mol\ H_2O}{1\ mol\ CO_2}$ $PV = nRT$

final mol_{CO_2} → mol_{NO_2} then mol_{NO_2}, V, T → P_{NO_2} and final mol_{CO_2} → mol_{OH} then
$\frac{1\ mol\ NO_2}{1\ mol\ CO_2}$ $PV = nRT$ $\frac{2\ mol\ OH}{1\ mol\ CO_2}$

mol_{OH}, V, T → P_{OH} finally P_{CH_4}, P_{O_2}, P_{NO}, P_{CO_2}, P_{H_2O}, P_{NO_2}, P_{OH} → P_{Ttotal}
$PV = nRT$ $P_{Total} = \sum P$

Solution: CH_4: $155\ \cancel{mL} \times \frac{1\ \cancel{L}}{1000\ \cancel{mL}} \times \frac{1\ \cancel{mol\ CH_4}}{22.414\ \cancel{L}} \times \frac{1\ mol\ CO_2}{1\ \cancel{mol\ CH_4}} = 0.00691532\ mol\ CO_2,$

$$O_2\text{: } 885\ \cancel{\text{mL}} \times \frac{1\ \cancel{\text{L}}}{1000\ \cancel{\text{mL}}} \times \frac{1\ \cancel{\text{mol } O_2}}{22.414\ \cancel{\text{L}}} = 0.0394842\ \text{mol } O_2 \times \frac{1\ \cancel{\text{mol } CO_2}}{5\ \cancel{\text{mol } O_2}} = 0.00789685\ \text{mol } CO_2$$

$$\text{NO: } 55.5\ \cancel{\text{mL}} \times \frac{1\ \cancel{\text{L}}}{1000\ \cancel{\text{mL}}} \times \frac{1\ \cancel{\text{mol NO}}}{22.414\ \cancel{\text{L}}} \times \frac{1\ \text{mol } CO_2}{5\ \cancel{\text{mol NO}}} = 0.000495226\ \text{mol } CO_2.$$

0.000495226 mol CO_2 is the smallest yield, so NO is the limiting reagent.

$$55.5\ \cancel{\text{mL}} \times \frac{1\ \cancel{\text{L}}}{1000\ \cancel{\text{mL}}} \times \frac{1\ \text{mol NO}}{22.414\ \cancel{\text{L}}} = 0.00247613\ \text{mol NO}$$

$$\textit{reacted mol NO} = 0.900 \times \textit{mol NO} = 0.900 \times 0.00247613\ \text{mol NO} = 0.00222852\ \text{mol NO},$$

$$\textit{unreacted mol NO} = 0.100 \times \textit{mol NO} = 0.100 \times 0.00247613\ \text{mol NO} = 0.000247613\ \text{mol NO},$$

$$0.00222852\ \cancel{\text{mol NO}} \times \frac{1\ \text{mol } CH_4}{5\ \cancel{\text{mol NO}}} = 0.000445704\ \text{mol } CH_4\ \text{reacted},$$

$$0.00691532\ \text{mol } CH_4 - 0.000445704\ \text{mol } CH_4\ \text{reacted} = 0.00646962\ \text{mol } CH_4\ \text{then } PV = nRT$$

Rearrange to solve for P. $$P = \frac{nRT}{V} = \frac{0.00646962\ \cancel{\text{mol}} \times 0.08206\ \frac{\cancel{\text{L}}\cdot\text{atm}}{\cancel{\text{mol}}\cdot\cancel{\text{K}}} \times 275\ \cancel{\text{K}}}{2.0\ \cancel{\text{L}}} = 0.0730\ \text{atm } CH_4$$

remaining

$$0.00222852\ \cancel{\text{mol NO}} \times \frac{5\ \text{mol } O_2}{5\ \cancel{\text{mol NO}}} = 0.00222852\ \text{mol } O_2\ \text{reacted},$$

$$0.0394842\ \text{mol } O_2 - 0.00222852\ \text{mol } O_2\ \text{reacted} = 0.0372557\ \text{mol } O_2$$

$$P = \frac{nRT}{V} = \frac{0.0372557\ \cancel{\text{mol}} \times 0.08206\ \frac{\cancel{\text{L}}\cdot\text{atm}}{\cancel{\text{mol}}\cdot\cancel{\text{K}}} \times 275\ \cancel{\text{K}}}{2.0\ \cancel{\text{L}}} = 0.420\ \text{atm } O_2\ \text{remaining}$$

$$P = \frac{nRT}{V} = \frac{0.000247613\ \cancel{\text{mol}} \times 0.08206\ \frac{\cancel{\text{L}}\cdot\text{atm}}{\cancel{\text{mol}}\cdot\cancel{\text{K}}} \times 275\ \cancel{\text{K}}}{2.0\ \cancel{\text{L}}} = 0.00279\ \text{atm NO remaining}$$

$$0.00222852\ \cancel{\text{mol NO}} \times \frac{1\ \text{mol } CO_2}{5\ \cancel{\text{mol NO}}} = 0.000445704\ \text{mol } CO_2$$

$$P = \frac{nRT}{V} = \frac{0.000445704\ \cancel{\text{mol}} \times 0.08206\ \frac{\cancel{\text{L}}\cdot\text{atm}}{\cancel{\text{mol}}\cdot\cancel{\text{K}}} \times 275\ \cancel{\text{K}}}{2.0\ \cancel{\text{L}}} = 0.00503\ \text{atm } CO_2\ \text{produced}$$

$$0.00222852\ \cancel{\text{mol NO}} \times \frac{1\ \text{mol } H_2O}{5\ \cancel{\text{mol NO}}} = 0.000445704\ \text{mol } H_2O$$

$$P = \frac{nRT}{V} = \frac{0.000445704\ \cancel{\text{mol}} \times 0.08206\ \frac{\cancel{\text{L}}\cdot\text{atm}}{\cancel{\text{mol}}\cdot\cancel{\text{K}}} \times 275\ \cancel{\text{K}}}{2.0\ \cancel{\text{L}}} = 0.00503\ \text{atm } H_2O\ \text{produced}$$

$$0.00222852\ \cancel{\text{mol NO}} \times \frac{5\ \text{mol } NO_2}{5\ \cancel{\text{mol NO}}} = 0.00222852\ \text{mol } NO_2$$

$$P = \frac{nRT}{V} = \frac{0.00222852\ \cancel{\text{mol}} \times 0.08206\ \frac{\cancel{\text{L}}\cdot\text{atm}}{\cancel{\text{mol}}\cdot\cancel{\text{K}}} \times 275\ \cancel{\text{K}}}{2.0\ \cancel{\text{L}}} = 0.0251\ \text{atm } NO_2\ \text{produced}$$

$$0.00222852\ \cancel{\text{mol NO}} \times \frac{2\ \text{mol OH}}{5\ \cancel{\text{mol NO}}} = 0.000891408\ \text{mol OH}$$

$$P = \frac{nRT}{V} = \frac{0.000891408\ \cancel{\text{mol}} \times 0.08206\ \frac{\cancel{\text{L}}\cdot\text{atm}}{\cancel{\text{mol}}\cdot\cancel{\text{K}}} \times 275\ \cancel{\text{K}}}{2.0\ \cancel{\text{L}}} = 0.0101\ \text{atm OH produced}$$

$$P_{Total} = \sum P$$
$$= 0.0730\,\text{atm} + 0.420\,\text{atm} + 0.00279\,\text{atm} + 0.00503\,\text{atm} + 0.00503\,\text{atm} + 0.0251\,\text{atm} + 0.0101\,\text{atm}$$
$$= 0.541\ \text{atm}$$

Check: The units (atm) are correct. The magnitude of the answers is reasonable. The limiting reagent has the lowest pressure. The product pressures are in line with the ratios of the stoichiometric coefficients.

5.138 **Given:** He and air **Find:** % He diffused through balloon wall

Conceptual Plan: $\mathcal{M}(N_2)$, $\mathcal{M}(O_2)$ → $\mathcal{M}$(air) then $\mathcal{M}$(air), $\mathcal{M}$(He), % air diffused → % He diffused

$$\mathcal{M}(air) = \chi(N_2)\mathcal{M}(N_2) + \chi(O_2)\mathcal{M}(O_2) \qquad \frac{Rate(He)}{Rate(air)} = \sqrt{\frac{\mathcal{M}(air)}{\mathcal{M}(He)}}$$

Solution:

$$\mathcal{M}(air) = \chi(N_2)\mathcal{M}(N_2) + \chi(O_2)\mathcal{M}(O_2) = \left(\frac{4}{5} \times 28.02\,g/mol\right) + \left(\frac{1}{5} \times 32.00\,g/mol\right) = 28.82\,g/mol$$

$\frac{Rate\,(He)}{Rate\,(air)} = \sqrt{\frac{\mathcal{M}(air)}{\mathcal{M}(He)}}$ Since rate α % diffused, substitute % diffused for rate and rearrange to solve for % He diffused. $\%He\ diffused = \%air\ diffused\sqrt{\frac{\mathcal{M}(air)}{\mathcal{M}(He)}} = 5.0\%\sqrt{\frac{28.82\,\cancel{g/mol}}{4.003\,\cancel{g/mol}}} = 13\%$

Check: The units (%) are correct. The magnitude of the answer (>5%) makes sense because He is lighter, so it has the higher diffusion rate.

5.139 **Given:** $P_{CH_4} + P_{C_2H_6} = 0.53$ atm, $P_{CO_2} + P_{H_2O} = 2.2$ atm **Find:** χ_{CH_4}
Conceptual Plan: Write balanced reactions to determine change in moles of gas for CH_4 and C_2H_6.

$2\,CH_4\,(g) + 4\,O_2\,(g) \rightarrow 4\,H_2O\,(g) + 2\,CO_2\,(g)$ and $2\,C_2H_6\,(g) + 7\,O_2\,(g) \rightarrow 6\,H_2O\,(g) + 4\,CO_2\,(g)$ thus $\frac{6\text{ mol gases}}{2\text{ mol }CH_4}$ $\frac{10\text{ mol gases}}{2\text{ mol }C_2H_6}$

write expression for final pressure, substituting in data given $\rightarrow$ χ_{CH_4}

$$\chi_{CH_4} = \frac{n_{CH_4}}{n_{CH_4} + n_{C_2H_6}} \text{ and } \chi_{C_2H_6} = 1 - \chi_{CH_4}$$

$$P_{CH_4} = \chi_{CH_4}P_{Total} \quad P_{C_2H_6} = \chi_{C_2H_6}P_{Total} \quad P_{Final} = \left(\chi_{CH_4}P_{Total} \times \frac{6\text{ mol gases}}{2\text{ mol }CH_4}\right) + \left((1 - \chi_{CH_4})P_{Total} \times \frac{10\text{ mol gases}}{2\text{ mol }C_2H_6}\right)$$

Solution:

$$P_{Final} = \left(\chi_{CH_4} \times 0.53\,atm \times \frac{6\text{ mol gases}}{2\text{ mol}CH_4}\right) + \left((1 - \chi_{CH_4}) \times 0.53\text{ atm} \times \frac{10\text{ mol gases}}{2\text{ mol }C_2H_6}\right) = 2.2\,atm$$

Substitute as above for $\chi_{C_2H_6}$, then to solve for $\chi_{CH_4} = 0.42$.

Check: The units (none) are correct. The magnitude of the answer (0.42) makes sense because if it were all methane the final pressure would have been 1.59 atm, and if it were all ethane the final pressure would have been 2.65 atm. Since we are closer to the latter pressure, we expect the mole fraction of methane to be less than 0.5.

5.140 **Given:** $P_{C_2H_2} = 7.8$ kPa initially, $P_{C_2H_2} + P_{C_6H_6} = 3.9$ kPa **Find:** fraction of C_2H_2 reacted
Conceptual Plan: Write balanced reaction to determine change in moles of gas.

$3C_2H_2\,(g) \rightarrow C_6H_6\,(g)$ thus $\frac{1\text{ mol }C_6H_6}{3\text{ mol }C_2H_2\,reacted}$ Since $P_{C_2H_2}\ \alpha\ n_{C_2H_2}$, the pressure will drop 2 kPa for every 3 kPa of ethylene that reacts.

$P_{initial}$, P_{final} $\rightarrow$ P_{drop} write expression for reacted $P_{C_2H_2}$, then

$$P_{drop} = P_{initial} - P_{final} \qquad reacted\ P_{C_2H_2} = \Delta P\frac{3\text{ kPa }C_2H_2\text{ reacted}}{2\text{ kPa pressure drop}}$$

reacted $P_{C_2H_2}$, initial $P_{C_2H_2}$ $\rightarrow$ % C_2H_2 reacted

$$\%C_2H_2\ reacted = \frac{reacted\ P_{C_2H_2}}{initial\ P_{C_2H_2}} \times 100\%$$

Solution: $P_{drop} = P_{initial} - P_{final} = 7.8\,kPa - 3.9\,kPa = 3.9\,kPa$,

$$reacted\ P_{C_2H_2} = \Delta P\frac{3\text{ kPa }C_2H_2\,reacted}{2\text{ kPa}\,pressure\,drop} = 3.9\,kPa \times \frac{3\,\cancel{kPa}\,C_2H_2\ reacted}{2\,\cancel{kPa}\ pressure\ drop} = 5.\underline{8}5\,kPa$$

$$\%C_2H_2\,reacted = \frac{reacted\ P_{C_2H_2}}{initial\ P_{C_2H_2}} \times 100\% = \frac{5.\underline{8}5\,\cancel{kPa}}{7.8\,\cancel{kPa}} \times 100\,\% = 75\%$$

Check: The units (%) are correct. The magnitude of the answer (75 %) makes sense because if all the ethylene reacted, the final pressure would have been 2.6 kPa. Since we are most of the way to that, we expect the amount reacted to be higher than 50 %.

Conceptual Problems

5.141 Since the passengers have more mass than the balloon, they have more momentum than the balloon. The passengers will continue to travel in their original direction longer. The car is slowing so the relative position of the passengers is to move forward and the balloon to move backwards. The opposite happens upon acceleration.

5.142 If a liquid is 10 times denser than water, the force needed to move it will be 10 times greater per unit volume. This means that the straw will be 1/10 the maximum length of a straw that can be used for water.

5.143 B is the limiting reactant (2.0 L of B requires 1.0 L A to completely react). The final container will have 0.5 L A and 2.0 L C, so the final volume will be 2.5 L. The change will be ((2.5 L/3.5 L) x 100 %) – 100 % = – 29 %.

5.144 Since each gas will occupy 22.414 L / mole at STP and we have 2 moles of gas, we will have a volume of 44.828 L.

5.145 (a) False – All gases have the same average kinetic energy at the same temperature.

(b) False – The gases will have the same partial pressures since we have the same number of moles of each.

(c) False – The average velocity of the B molecules will be less than that of the A molecules since the Bs are heavier.

(d) True – Since B molecules are heavier they will contribute more to the density ($d = m/V$).

5.146 Br_2 would deviate the most from ideal behavior since it is the largest of the three.

6 Thermochemistry

Review Questions

6.1 Thermochemistry is the study of the relationship between chemistry and energy. It is important because energy and its uses are critical to our society. It is important to understand how much energy is required or released in a process.

6.2 Energy is the capacity to do work. Work is the result of a force acting through a distance. Examples of energy are kinetic energy, heat energy, electrical energy, chemical energy, and light or radiant energy. Examples of work are moving an object, expansion of a cylinder, and running a marathon.

6.3 Kinetic energy is energy associated with the motion of an object. Potential energy is energy associated with the position or composition of an object. Examples of kinetic energy are a moving billiard ball, gas molecules, and a raging river. Examples of potential energy are a billiard ball raised above the surface of a billiard table, a compressed spring, and molecules.

6.4 The law of conservation of energy states that energy can neither be created nor destroyed. Energy can be transferred from one object to another, and it can assume different forms. In an energy exchange, energy is transferred between the system and the surroundings. If the system loses energy, the surroundings gain energy, and vice versa.

6.5 The SI unit of energy is $kg\frac{m^2}{s^2}$, defined as the joule (J), named after the English scientist James Joule. Other units of energy are the kilojoule (kJ), the calorie (cal), the Calorie (Cal), and the kilowatt-hour (kWh).

6.6 The first law of thermodynamics is the law of energy conservation, stated as follows: The total energy of the universe is constant. In other words, because energy is neither created nor destroyed, and the universe does not exchange energy with anything else; its energy content does not change. The first law has many implications, the most important of which is that with energy you do not get something for nothing. The best we can do with energy is break even—there is no free lunch.

6.7 According to the first law, a device that would continually produce energy with no energy input, sometimes known as a perpetual motion machine, cannot exist because the best we can do with energy is break even.

6.8 A state function is a function whose value depends only on the state of the system, not on how the system arrived at that state. Examples are pressure, volume, and internal energy.

6.9 The internal energy (E) of a system is the sum of the kinetic and potential energies of all of the particles that compose the system. Internal energy is a state function.

6.10 If energy is flowing out of the system it is like a withdrawal from a checking account, and therefore carries a negative sign.

6.11 If the reactants have a lower internal energy than the products, ΔE_{sys} is positive and energy flows into the system from the surroundings.

6.12 Heat is the flow of thermal energy caused by a temperature difference. Thermal energy is actually a type of kinetic energy because it arises from the motions of atoms or molecules within a substance. The higher the temperature, the greater the motion of atoms and molecules. Heat is measured in units of energy: joules, calories, kilowatt-hours, etc. while temperature is measured in units of Kelvins, degrees Celsius, and degrees Fahrenheit.

6.13 The internal energy (E) of a system is the sum of the kinetic and potential energies of all of the particles that compose the system. The change in the internal energy of the system (ΔE) must be the sum of the heat transferred (q) and the work done (w): $\Delta E = q + w$.

6.14 According to the first law of thermodynamics, the change in the internal energy of the system (ΔE) must be the sum of the heat transferred (q) and the work done (w): $\Delta E = q + w$. The total change in internal energy (ΔE) is the difference between its initial energy and its final energy. The amount of work done and the amount of heat transferred is dependent on the details of the path. In one path more energy may be transferred through conversion to heat energy (if, for example there is more friction). In another path more energy may be transferred through work. Work and heat are not state functions, but their sum (ΔE) is constant.

6.15 The heat capacity of a system is usually defined as the quantity of heat required to change its temperature by 1 °C. Heat capacity (C) is a measure of the system's ability to hold thermal energy without undergoing a large change in temperature. The difference between heat capacity (C) and specific heat capacity (C_s) is that the specific heat capacity is the amount of heat required to raise the temperature of *1 gram* of the substance by 1 °C.

6.16 Since water has such a high heat capacity, it can moderate temperature changes. This keeps coastal temperatures more constant. Changing the temperature of water absorbs or releases large quantities of energy for a relatively small change in temperature. This serves to keep the air temperature of coastal areas more constant than the air temperature in inland areas.

6.17 When two objects of different temperatures come in direct contact heat flows from the higher temperature object to the lower temperature object. The amount of heat lost by the warmer object is equal to the amount of heat gained by the cooler object. The warmer object's temperature will drop and the cooler object's temperature will rise until they reach the same temperature. The magnitude of these temperature changes depends on the mass and heat capacities of the two objects.

6.18 The work caused by an expansion of volume is simply the negative of the pressure that the volume expands against multiplied by the change in volume that occurs during the expansion: $w = -P\,\Delta V$.

6.19 In calorimetry, the thermal energy exchanged between the reaction (defined as the system) and the surroundings is measured by observing the change in temperature of the surroundings. A bomb calorimeter is used to measure the ΔE_{rxn} for combustion reactions. The calorimeter includes a tight fitting, sealed container that forces the reaction to occur at constant volume. A coffee-cup calorimeter is used to measure ΔH_{rxn} for many aqueous reactions. The calorimeter consists of two Styrofoam® coffee cups, one inserted into the other, to provide insulation from the laboratory environment. Since the reaction happens under conditions of constant pressure (open to the atmosphere), $q_{rxn} = q_p = \Delta H_{rxn}$.

6.20 ΔH is the heat exchanged with the surroundings under conditions of constant pressure. ΔH is equal to q_p, the heat at constant pressure. Conceptually (and often numerically), ΔH and ΔE are similar: They both represent changes in a state function for the system. However, ΔE, is a measure of all of the energy (heat and work) exchanged with the surroundings. $\Delta H = \Delta E + P\Delta V$.

6.21 An endothermic reaction has a positive ΔH and absorbs heat from the surroundings. An endothermic reaction feels cold to the touch. An exothermic reaction has a negative ΔH and gives off heat to the surroundings. An exothermic reaction feels warm to the touch.

6.22 The internal energy of a chemical system is the sum of its kinetic energy and its potential energy. It is this potential energy that is the energy source in an exothermic chemical reaction. Under normal circumstances, chemical potential energy (or simply chemical energy) arises primarily from the electrostatic forces between the protons and electrons that compose the atoms and molecules within the system. In an exothermic reaction, some bonds break and new ones form, and the protons and electrons go from an arrangement of higher potential energy to one of lower potential energy. As they rearrange, their potential energy is converted into kinetic energy, the heat emitted in the reaction. This increase in kinetic energy is detected as an increase in temperature.

6.23 The internal energy of a chemical system is the sum of its kinetic energy and its potential energy. It is this potential energy that absorbs the energy in an endothermic chemical reaction. In an endothermic reaction, as some bonds break and others form, the protons and electrons go from an arrangement of lower potential energy to one of higher potential energy, absorbing thermal energy in the process. This absorption of thermal energy reduces the kinetic energy of the system. This is detected as a drop in temperature.

6.24 ΔH_{rxn} is an extensive property; therefore it depends on the quantity of reactants undergoing reaction. ΔH_{rxn} is usually reported for a reaction involving stoichiometric amounts of reactants and is dependent on the specific chemical reaction. For example, for a reaction A + 2 B $\rightarrow$ C, ΔH_{rxn} is usually reported as the amount of heat emitted or absorbed when 1 mole A reacts with 2 mole B to form 1 mole C.

6.25 (a) If a reaction is multiplied by a factor, the ΔH is multiplied by the same factor.

(b) If a reaction is reversed, the sign of ΔH is reversed.

The relationships hold because H is a state function. Twice as much energy is contained in twice the quantity of reactants or products. If the reaction is reversed, the final and initial states have been switched and the direction of heat flow is reversed.

6.26 Hess's law states that if a chemical equation can be expressed as the sum of a series of steps, then ΔH_{rxn} for the overall equation is the sum of the heats of reactions for each step. This makes it possible to determine ΔH for a reaction without directly measuring it in the laboratory. If you can find related reactions (with known ΔH) that sum to the reaction of interest, you can find ΔH for the reaction of interest.

6.27 The standard state is defined as follows: for a gas, the pure gas at a pressure of exactly 1 atmosphere; for a liquid or solid, the pure substance in its most stable form at a pressure of 1 atm and the temperature of interest (often taken to be 25 °C); and for a substance in solution, a concentration of exactly 1 M. The standard enthalpy change (ΔH°) is the change in enthalpy for a process when all reactants and products are in their standard states. The superscript degree sign indicates standard states.

6.28 The standard enthalpy of formation (ΔH_f°) for a pure compound is the change in enthalpy when 1 mole of the compound forms from its constituent elements in their standard states. For a pure element in its standard state $\Delta H_f^\circ = 0$.

6.29 To calculate ΔH_{rxn}°, subtract the heats of formations of the reactants multiplied by their stoichiometric coefficients from the heats of formation of the products multiplied by their stoichiometric coefficients. In the form of an equation:

$$\Delta H_{rxn}^\circ = \sum n_p \Delta H_f^\circ(\text{products}) - \sum n_R \Delta H_f^\circ(\text{reactants})$$

6.30 Most U.S. energy comes from the combustion of fossil fuels, which include petroleum, natural gas, and coal.

6.31 One of the main problems associated with the burning of fossil fuels is that, even though they are abundant in the Earth's crust, they are a finite and non-renewable energy source. The other major problems associated with fossil fuel use are related to the products of combustion. Three major environmental problems associated with the emissions of fossil fuel combustion are air pollution, acid rain, and global warming. One of the main products of fossil fuel combustion is carbon dioxide (CO_2), which is a greenhouse gas.

6.32 One of the main products of fossil fuel combustion is carbon dioxide (CO_2). Carbon dioxide is a greenhouse gas, meaning that it allows visible light from the sun to enter Earth's atmosphere, but prevents heat (in the form of infrared light) from escaping. The result is that carbon dioxide acts as a blanket, keeping Earth warm. However, because of fossil-fuel combustion, carbon dioxide levels in the atmosphere have been steadily increasing. This increase is expected to raise Earth's average temperature. Current observations suggest that Earth has already warmed by about 0.6 °C in the last century, due to an increase of about 25 percent in atmospheric carbon dioxide. Computer models suggest that the warming could worsen if carbon dioxide emissions are not curbed. The possible effects of this warming include heightened storm severity, increasing numbers of floods and droughts, major shifts in agricultural zones, rising sea levels and coastal flooding, and profound changes in habitats that could result in the extinction of some plant and animal species.

Energy Units

6.33 (a) **Given:** 534 kWh **Find:** J

Conceptual Plan: kWh → J

$$\frac{3.60 \times 10^6\ \text{J}}{1\ \text{kWh}}$$

Solution: $534\ \cancel{\text{kWh}} \times \frac{3.60 \times 10^6 \text{J}}{1\ \cancel{\text{kWh}}} = 1.92 \times 10^9\ \text{J}$

Check: The units (J) are correct. The magnitude of the answer (10^9) makes physical sense because a kWh is much larger than a Joule, so the answer increases.

(b) **Given:** 215 kJ **Find:** Cal

Conceptual Plan: kJ → J → Cal

$$\frac{1000\ \text{J}}{1\ \text{kJ}} \quad \frac{1\ \text{Cal}}{4184\ \text{J}}$$

Solution: $215\ \cancel{\text{kJ}} \times \frac{1000\ \cancel{\text{J}}}{1\ \cancel{\text{kJ}}} \times \frac{1\ \text{Cal}}{4184\ \cancel{\text{J}}} = 51.4\ \text{Cal}$

Check: The units (Cal) are correct. The magnitude of the answer (51) makes physical sense because a Calorie is about $\frac{1}{4}$ of a kJ, so the answer decreases by a factor of about four.

(c) **Given:** 567 Cal **Find:** J

Conceptual Plan: Cal → J

$$\frac{4184\ \text{J}}{1\ \text{Cal}}$$

Solution: $567\ \cancel{\text{Cal}} \times \frac{4184\ \text{J}}{1\ \cancel{\text{Cal}}} = 2.37 \times 10^6\ \text{J}$

Check: The units (J) are correct. The magnitude of the answer (10^6) makes physical sense because a Calorie is much larger than a Joule, so the answer increases.

(d) **Given:** 2.85×10^3 J **Find:** cal

Conceptual Plan: J → cal

$$\frac{1\ \text{cal}}{4.184\ \text{J}}$$

Solution: $2.85 \times 10^3\ \cancel{\text{J}} \times \frac{1\ \text{cal}}{4.184\ \cancel{\text{J}}} = 681\ \text{cal}$

Check: The units (cal) are correct. The magnitude of the answer (680) makes physical sense because a J is about $\frac{1}{4}$ the size of a calorie, so the answer decreases by a factor of about four.

6.34 (a) **Given:** 231 cal **Find:** kJ

Conceptual Plan: cal → J → kJ

$$\frac{4.184\ \text{J}}{1\text{cal}} \quad \frac{1\ \text{kJ}}{1000\ \text{J}}$$

Solution: $231\ \cancel{\text{cal}} \times \frac{4.184\ \cancel{\text{J}}}{1\ \cancel{\text{cal}}} \times \frac{1\ \text{kJ}}{1000\ \cancel{\text{J}}} = 0.967\ \text{kJ}$

Check: The units (kJ) are correct. The magnitude of the answer (1) makes physical sense because a kJ is much larger than a cal, so the answer decreases.

(b) **Given:** 132×10^4 kJ **Find:** kcal

Conceptual Plan: kJ → J → cal → kcal

$$\frac{1000\ \text{J}}{1\text{k J}} \quad \frac{1\ \text{cal}}{4.184\ \text{J}} \quad \frac{1\ \text{kcal}}{1000\ \text{cal}}$$

Solution: $132 \times 10^4\ \cancel{\text{kJ}} \times \frac{1000\ \cancel{\text{J}}}{1\ \cancel{\text{kJ}}} \times \frac{1\ \cancel{\text{cal}}}{4.184\ \cancel{\text{J}}} \times \frac{1\ \text{kcal}}{1000\ \cancel{\text{cal}}} = 3.15 \times 10^5\ \text{kcal}$

Check: The units (kcal) are correct. The magnitude of the answer (10^5) makes physical sense because a kcal is smaller than a kJ, so the answer increases.

(c) **Given:** 4.99×10^3 kJ **Find:** kWh

Conceptual Plan: kJ → J → kWh

$$\frac{1000\ \text{J}}{1\ \text{kJ}} \quad \frac{1\ \text{kWh}}{3.60 \times 10^6\ \text{J}}$$

Solution: $4.99 \times 10^3\ \text{kJ} \times \frac{1000\ \text{J}}{1\ \text{kJ}} \times \frac{1\ \text{kWh}}{3.60 \times 10^6\ \text{J}} = 1.39\ \text{kWh}$

Check: The units (kWh) are correct. The magnitude of the answer (1) makes physical sense because a kWh is much smaller than a Joule, so the answer increases.

(d) **Given:** 2.88×10^4 J **Find:** Cal

Conceptual Plan: J → Cal

$$\frac{1\ \text{Cal}}{4184\ \text{J}}$$

Solution: $2.88 \times 10^4\ \text{J} \times \frac{1\ \text{Cal}}{4184\ \text{J}} = 6.88\ \text{Cal}$

Check: The units (Cal) are correct. The magnitude of the answer (7) makes physical sense because a J is much smaller than a Cal, so the answer decreases.

6.35 (a) **Given:** 2387 Cal **Find:** J

Conceptual Plan: Cal → J

$$\frac{4184\ \text{J}}{1\ \text{Cal}}$$

Solution: $2387\ \text{Cal} \times \frac{4184\ \text{J}}{1\ \text{Cal}} = 9.987 \times 10^6\ \text{J}$

Check: The units (J) are correct. The magnitude of the answer (10^7) makes physical sense because a Calorie is much larger than a Joule, so the answer increases.

(b) **Given:** 2387 Cal **Find:** kJ

Conceptual Plan: Cal → J → kWh

$$\frac{4184\ \text{J}}{1\ \text{Cal}} \quad \frac{1\ \text{kJ}}{1000\ \text{J}}$$

Solution: $2387\ \text{Cal} \times \frac{4184\ \text{J}}{1\ \text{Cal}} \times \frac{1\ \text{kJ}}{1000\ \text{J}} = 9.987 \times 10^3\ \text{kJ}$

Check: The units (kJ) are correct. The magnitude of the answer (10^4) makes physical sense because a Calorie is larger than a kJ, so the answer increases.

(c) **Given:** 2387 Cal **Find:** kWh

Conceptual Plan: Cal → J → kWh

$$\frac{4184\ \text{J}}{1\ \text{Cal}} \quad \frac{1\ \text{kWh}}{3.60 \times 10^6\ \text{J}}$$

Solution: $2387\ \text{Cal} \times \frac{4184\ \text{J}}{1\ \text{Cal}} \times \frac{1\ \text{kWh}}{3.60 \times 10^6\ \text{J}} = 2.774\ \text{kWh}$

Check: The units (kWh) are correct. The magnitude of the answer (3) makes physical sense because a Calorie is much smaller than a kWh, so the answer decreases.

6.36 (a) **Given:** 745 kWh **Find:** J

Conceptual Plan: kWh → J

$$\frac{3.60 \times 10^6\ \text{J}}{1\ \text{kWh}}$$

Solution: $745\ \text{kWh} \times \frac{3.60 \times 10^6\ \text{J}}{1\ \text{kWh}} = 2.68 \times 10^9\ \text{J}$

Check: The units (J) are correct. The magnitude of the answer (10^9) makes physical sense because a kWh is much larger than a Joule, so the answer increases.

(b) **Given:** 745 kWh **Find:** kJ

Conceptual Plan: kWh → J → kJ

$$\frac{3.60 \times 10^6\ \text{J}}{1\ \text{kWh}} \quad \frac{1\ \text{kJ}}{1000\ \text{J}}$$

Solution: $745 \text{ kWh} \times \frac{3.60 \times 10^6 \text{ J}}{1 \text{ kWh}} \times \frac{1 \text{ kJ}}{1000 \text{ J}} = 2.68 \times 10^6 \text{ kJ}$

Check: The units (J) are correct. The magnitude of the answer (10^6) makes physical sense because a kWh is much larger than a Joule, so the answer increases.

(c) **Given:** 745 kWh **Find:** Cal

Conceptual Plan: kWh → J → Cal

$\frac{3.60 \times 10^6 \text{ J}}{1 \text{ kWh}}$ $\frac{1 \text{ Cal}}{4184 \text{ J}}$

Solution: $745 \text{ kWh} \times \frac{3.60 \times 10^6 \text{ J}}{1 \text{ kWh}} \times \frac{1 \text{ Cal}}{4184 \text{ J}} = 6.41 \times 10^5 \text{ Cal}$

Check: The units (Cal) are correct. The magnitude of the answer (10^5) makes physical sense because a kWh is much larger than a Cal, so the answer increases.

Internal Energy, Heat, and Work

6.37 (d) $\Delta E_{sys} = -\Delta E_{surr}$ If energy change of the system is negative, energy is being transferred from the system to the surroundings, decreasing the energy of the system and increasing the energy of the surroundings. The amount of energy lost by the system must go somewhere, so the amount gained by the surroundings is equal and opposite to that lost by the system.

6.38 The sign is positive since the energy is being taken in by or deposited into the system.

6.39 (a) The energy exchange is primarily heat since the skin (part of the surroundings) is cooled. There is a small expansion (work) since water is being converted from a liquid to a gas. The sign of ΔE_{sys} is positive since the surroundings cool.

(b) The energy exchange is primarily work. The sign of ΔE_{sys} is negative since the system is expanding (doing work on the surroundings).

(c) The energy exchange is primarily heat. The sign of ΔE_{sys} is positive since the system is being heated by the flame.

6.40 (a) The energy exchange is primarily work since there is a lot of motion. There is a small amount of heat transferred since there is some friction as the balls roll. The sign of ΔE_{sys} is negative since the kinetic energy of the first ball is transferred to the second ball.

(b) The energy exchange is primarily work. The sign of ΔE_{sys} is negative since the potential energy of the book decreases as it falls.

(c) The energy exchange is primarily work. The sign of ΔE_{sys} is positive since the father is doing work to move the girl and the swing.

6.41 **Given:** 622 kJ heat released; 105 kJ work done on surroundings **Find:** ΔE_{sys}

Conceptual Plan: interpret language to determine the sign of the two terms then $q, w \rightarrow \Delta E_{sys}$

$\Delta E = q + w$

Solution: Since heat is released from the system to the surroundings, $q = -622$ kJ; since the system is doing work on the surroundings, $w = -105$ kJ. $\Delta E = q + w = -622 \text{ kJ} - 105 \text{ kJ} = -727 \text{ kJ} = -7.27 \times 10^2 \text{ kJ}$

Check: The units (kJ) are correct. The magnitude of the answer (– 730) makes physical sense because both terms are negative.

6.42 **Given:** 196 kJ heat absorbed; surroundings do 117 kJ work **Find:** ΔE_{sys}

Conceptual Plan: interpret language to determine the sign of the two terms then $q, w \rightarrow \Delta E_{sys}$

$\Delta E = q + w$

Solution: Since heat is absorbed by the system, $q = +196$ kJ; since the surroundings are doing work on the system, $w = +117$ kJ. $\Delta E = q + w = 196 \text{ kJ} + 117 \text{ J} = 313 \text{ kJ} = 3.13 \times 10^2 \text{ kJ}$.

Check: The units (kJ) are correct. The magnitude of the answer (+300) makes physical sense because both terms are positive.

6.43 **Given:** 655 J heat absorbed; 344 J work done on surroundings **Find:** ΔE_{sys}
Conceptual Plan: interpret language to determine the sign of the two terms then $q, w \rightarrow \Delta E_{sys}$
$\Delta E = q + w$

Solution: Since heat is absorbed by the system, $q = +655$ J; since the system is doing work on the surroundings, $w = -344$ J. $\Delta E = q + w = 655\text{ J} - 344\text{ J} = 311\text{ J}$.
Check: The units (J) are correct. The magnitude of the answer (+300) makes physical sense because heat term dominates over the work term.

6.44 **Given:** 155 J heat absorbed; 77 kJ work done on surroundings **Find:** ΔE_{sys}
Conceptual Plan: interpret language to determine the sign of the two terms J $\rightarrow$ kJ then $q, w \rightarrow \Delta E_{sys}$
$\frac{1\text{ kJ}}{1000\text{ J}}$ $\Delta E = q + w$

Solution: Since heat is absorbed by the system, $q = +155$ J; since the system is doing work on the surroundings, $w = -77$ kJ. Thus $-77\text{ kJ} \times \frac{1000\text{ J}}{1\text{ kJ}} = -77000\text{ J}$ and
$\Delta E = q + w = 155\text{ J} - 77000\text{ J} = -77000\text{ J} = -77\text{ kJ}$.
Check: The units (kJ) are correct. The magnitude of the answer (– 77 kJ) makes physical sense because the work term dominates over the heat term. In fact the heat term is negligible compared to the work term.

Heat, Heat Capacity, and Work

6.45 Cooler A had more ice after 3 hours because most of the ice in cooler B was melted in order to cool the soft drinks that started at room temperature. In cooler A the drinks were already cold and so the ice only needed to maintain this cool temperature.

6.46 Since the specific heat capacity of water is much larger than the specific heat capacity of aluminum, much more heat needs to be released by the water than the aluminum for each 1 **°C** of temperature drop. This means that more heat is stored in each kg of water than aluminum.

6.47 **Given:** 1.50 L water, $T_i = 25.0$ °C, $T_f = 100.0$ °C, d = 1.0 g/mL **Find:** q
Conceptual Plan: L $\rightarrow$ mL $\rightarrow$ g and pull C_s from Table 6.4 and $T_i, T_f \rightarrow \Delta T$ then $m, C_s, \Delta T \rightarrow q$
$\frac{1000\text{ mL}}{1\text{ L}}$ $\frac{1.0\text{ g}}{1.0\text{ mL}}$ $4.18\frac{\text{J}}{\text{g}\cdot{}^\circ\text{C}}$ $\Delta T = T_f - T_i$ $q = mC_s\Delta T$

Solution: $1.50\text{ L} \times \frac{1000\text{ mL}}{1\text{ L}} \times \frac{1.0\text{ g}}{1.0\text{ mL}} = 1500\text{ g}$ and $\Delta T = T_f - T_i = 100.0\text{ °C} - 25.0\text{ °C} = 75.0\text{ °C}$
then $q = mC_s\Delta T = 1500\text{ g} \times 4.18\frac{\text{J}}{\text{g}\cdot{}^\circ\text{C}} \times 75.0\text{ °C} = 4.7 \times 10^5\text{ J}$
Check: The units (J) are correct. The magnitude of the answer (10^6) makes physical sense because there is such a large mass, a significant temperature change, and a high specific heat capacity material.

6.48 **Given:** 1.50 kg sand, $T_i = 25.0$ °C, $T_f = 100.0$ °C **Find:** q
Conceptual Plan: kg $\rightarrow$ g and pull C_s from Table 6.4 and $T_i, T_f \rightarrow \Delta T$ then $m, C_s, \Delta T \rightarrow q$
$\frac{1000\text{ g}}{1\text{ g}}$ $0.84\frac{\text{J}}{\text{g}\cdot{}^\circ\text{C}}$ $\Delta T = T_f - T_i$ $q = mC_s\Delta T$

Solution: $1.50\text{ L} \times \frac{1000\text{ mL}}{1\text{ L}} \times \frac{1.0\text{ g}}{1.0\text{ mL}} = 1500\text{ g}$ and $\Delta T = T_f - T_i = 100.0\text{ °C} - 25.0\text{ °C} = 75.0\text{ °C}$
then $q = mC_s\Delta T = 1500\text{ g} \times 0.84\frac{\text{J}}{\text{g}\cdot{}^\circ\text{C}} \times 75.0\text{ °C} = 9.5 \times 10^4\text{ J}$
Check: The units (J) are correct. The magnitude of the answer (~10^5) makes physical sense because there is such a large mass and a significant temperature change.

6.49 (a) **Given:** 25 g gold, $T_i = 27.0$ °C, $q = 2.35$ kJ **Find:** T_f
Conceptual Plan: kJ $\rightarrow$ J and pull C_s from Table 6.4 then $m, C_s, q \rightarrow \Delta T$ then $T_i, \Delta T \rightarrow T_f$
$\frac{1000\text{ J}}{1\text{ kJ}}$ $0.128\frac{\text{J}}{\text{g}\cdot{}^\circ\text{C}}$ $q = mC_s\Delta T$ $\Delta T = T_f - T_i$

Solution: $2.35\ \text{kJ} \times \frac{1000\ \text{J}}{1\ \text{kJ}} = 2350\ \text{J}$ then $q = mC_s\Delta T$. Rearrange to solve for ΔT.

$$\Delta T = \frac{q}{mC_s} = \frac{2350\ \text{J}}{25\ \text{g} \times 0.128 \frac{\text{J}}{\text{g} \cdot {}^\circ\text{C}}} = 734.375\ {}^\circ\text{C}$$ finally $\Delta T = T_f - T_i$. Rearrange to solve for T_f.

$T_f = \Delta T + T_i = 734.375\ {}^\circ\text{C} + 27.0\ {}^\circ\text{C} = 760\ {}^\circ\text{C}$

Check: The units (°C) are correct. The magnitude of the answer (760) makes physical sense because there is such a large amount of heat absorbed, such a small mass, and specific heat capacity. The temperature change should be very large.

(b) **Given:** 25 g silver, $T_i = 27.0\ {}^\circ\text{C}$, $q = 2.35$ kJ **Find:** T_f

Conceptual Plan: kJ → J and pull C_s from Table 6.4 then m, C_s, q → ΔT then T_i, ΔT → T_f

$\frac{1000\ \text{J}}{1\ \text{kJ}}$ $\quad 0.235 \frac{\text{J}}{\text{g} \cdot {}^\circ\text{C}}$ $\quad q = mC_s\Delta T$ $\quad \Delta T = T_f - T_i$

Solution: $2.35\ \text{kJ} \times \frac{1000\ \text{J}}{1\ \text{kJ}} = 2350\ \text{J}$ then $q = mC_s\Delta T$. Rearrange to solve for ΔT.

$$\Delta T = \frac{q}{mC_s} = \frac{2350\ \text{J}}{25\ \text{g} \times 0.235 \frac{\text{J}}{\text{g} \cdot {}^\circ\text{C}}} = 400\ {}^\circ\text{C}$$ finally $\Delta T = T_f - T_i$. Rearrange to solve for T_f.

$T_f = \Delta T + T_i = 400\ {}^\circ\text{C} + 27.0\ {}^\circ\text{C} = 430\ {}^\circ\text{C}$

Check: The units (°C) are correct. The magnitude of the answer (430) makes physical sense because there is such a large amount of heat absorbed, such a small mass, and specific heat capacity. The temperature change should be very large. The temperature change should be less than that of the gold because the specific heat capacity is greater.

(c) **Given:** 25 g aluminum, $T_i = 27.0\ {}^\circ\text{C}$, $q = 2.35$ kJ **Find:** T_f

Conceptual Plan: kJ → J and pull C_s from Table 6.4 then m, C_s, q → ΔT then T_i, ΔT → T_f

$\frac{1000\ \text{J}}{1\ \text{kJ}}$ $\quad 0.903 \frac{\text{J}}{\text{g} \cdot {}^\circ\text{C}}$ $\quad q = mC_s\Delta T$ $\quad \Delta T = T_f - T_i$

Solution: $2.35\ \text{kJ} \times \frac{1000\ \text{J}}{1\ \text{kJ}} = 2350\ \text{J}$ then $q = mC_s\Delta T$. Rearrange to solve for ΔT.

$$\Delta T = \frac{q}{mC_s} = \frac{2350\ \text{J}}{25\ \text{g} \times 0.903 \frac{\text{J}}{\text{g} \cdot {}^\circ\text{C}}} = 104.10{}^\circ\text{C}$$ finally $\Delta T = T_f - T_i$. Rearrange to solve for T_f.

$T_f = \Delta T + T_i = 104.10\ {}^\circ\text{C} + 27.0\ {}^\circ\text{C} = 130\ {}^\circ\text{C}$

Check: The units (°C) are correct. The magnitude of the answer (130) makes physical sense because there is such a large amount of heat absorbed, and such a small mass. The temperature change should be less than that of the silver because the specific heat capacity is greater.

(d) **Given:** 25 g water, $T_i = 27.0\ {}^\circ\text{C}$, $q = 2.35$ kJ **Find:** T_f

Conceptual Plan: kJ → J and pull C_s from Table 6.4 then m, C_s, q → ΔT then T_i, ΔT → T_f

$\frac{1000\ \text{J}}{1\ \text{kJ}}$ $\quad 4.18 \frac{\text{J}}{\text{g} \cdot {}^\circ\text{C}}$ $\quad q = mC_s\Delta T$ $\quad \Delta T = T_f - T_i$

Solution: $2.35\ \text{kJ} \times \frac{1000\ \text{J}}{1\ \text{kJ}} = 2350\ \text{J}$ then $q = mC_s\Delta T$. Rearrange to solve for ΔT.

$$\Delta T = \frac{q}{mC_s} = \frac{2350\ \text{J}}{25\ \text{g} \times 4.18 \frac{\text{J}}{\text{g} \cdot {}^\circ\text{C}}} = 22.488{}^\circ\text{C}$$ finally $\Delta T = T_f - T_i$. Rearrange to solve for T_f.

$T_f = \Delta T + T_i = 22.488\ {}^\circ\text{C} + 27.0\ {}^\circ\text{C} = 49\ {}^\circ\text{C}$

Check: The units (°C) are correct. The magnitude of the answer (130) makes physical sense because there is such a large amount of heat absorbed, and such a small mass. The temperature change should be less than that of the aluminum because the specific heat capacity is greater.

6.50 (a) **Given:** Pyrex glass, $q = 1.95 \times 10^3$ J, $T_i = 23.0\ {}^\circ\text{C}$, $T_f = 55.4\ {}^\circ\text{C}$ **Find:** m

Conceptual Plan: pull C_s from Table 6.4 and T_i, T_f → ΔT then ΔT, C_s, q → m

$0.75 \frac{\text{J}}{\text{g} \cdot {}^\circ\text{C}}$ $\quad \Delta T = T_f - T_i$ $\quad q = mC_s\Delta T$

Solution: $\Delta T = T_f - T_i = 55.4\ °C - 23.0\ °C = 32.4\ °C$ and $q = mC_s\Delta T$. Rearrange to solve for m.

$$m = \frac{q}{C_s\Delta T} = \frac{1.95 \times 10^3\ \text{J}}{0.75\frac{\text{J}}{\text{g} \cdot °\text{C}} \times 32.4\ °\text{C}} = 80.\ \text{g or } 8.0 \times 10^1\ \text{g}$$

Check: The units (g) are correct. The magnitude of the answer (80) makes physical sense because there is such a large amount of heat absorbed, a moderate temperature rise, and specific heat capacity.

(b) **Given:** sand, $q = 1.95 \times 10^3$ J, $T_i = 23.0$ °C, $T_f = 62.1$ °C **Find:** m

Conceptual Plan: pull C_s from Table 6.4 and $T_i, T_f \rightarrow \Delta T$ then $\Delta T, C_s, q \rightarrow m$

$0.84\frac{\text{J}}{\text{g} \cdot °\text{C}}$ $\quad \Delta T = T_f - T_i \quad q = mC_s\Delta T$

Solution: $\Delta T = T_f - T_i = 62.1\ °C - 23.0\ °C = 39.1\ °C$ then $q = mC_s\Delta T$. Rearrange to solve for m.

$$m = \frac{q}{C_s\Delta T} = \frac{1.95 \times 10^3\ \text{J}}{0.84\frac{\text{J}}{\text{g} \cdot °\text{C}} \times 39.1\ °\text{C}} = 59\ \text{g}$$

Check: The units (g) are correct. The magnitude of the answer (60) makes physical sense because there is such a large amount of heat absorbed, a moderate temperature rise, and specific heat capacity.

(c) **Given:** ethanol, $q = 1.95 \times 10^3$ J, $T_i = 23.0$ °C, $T_f = 44.2$ °C **Find:** m

Conceptual Plan: pull C_s from Table 6.4 and $T_i, T_f \rightarrow \Delta T$ then $\Delta T, C_s, q \rightarrow m$

$2.42\frac{\text{J}}{\text{g} \cdot °\text{C}}$ $\quad \Delta T = T_f - T_i \quad q = mC_s\Delta T$

Solution: $\Delta T = T_f - T_i = 44.2\ °C - 23.0\ °C = 21.2\ °C$ then $q = mC_s\Delta T$. Rearrange to solve for m.

$$m = \frac{q}{C_s\Delta T} = \frac{1.95 \times 10^3\ \text{J}}{2.42\frac{\text{J}}{\text{g} \cdot °\text{C}} \times 21.2\ °\text{C}} = 38.0\ \text{g}$$

Check: The units (g) are correct. The magnitude of the answer (40) makes physical sense because there is such a large amount of heat absorbed, a small temperature rise, and specific heat capacity.

(d) **Given:** water, $q = 1.95 \times 10^3$ J, $T_i = 23.0$ °C, $T_f = 32.4$ °C **Find:** m

Conceptual Plan: pull C_s from Table 6.4 and $T_i, T_f \rightarrow \Delta T$ then $\Delta T, C_s, q \rightarrow m$

$4.18\frac{\text{J}}{\text{g} \cdot °\text{C}}$ $\quad \Delta T = T_f - T_i \quad q = mC_s\Delta T$

Solution: $\Delta T = T_f - T_i = 32.4\ °C - 23.0\ °C = 9.4\ °C$ then $q = mC_s\Delta T$. Rearrange to solve for m.

$$m = \frac{q}{C_s\Delta T} = \frac{1.95 \times 10^3\ \text{J}}{4.18\frac{\text{J}}{\text{g} \cdot °\text{C}} \times 9.4\ °\text{C}} = 50.\ \text{g or } 5.0 \times 10^1\ \text{g}$$

Check: The units (g) are correct. The magnitude of the answer (50) makes physical sense because there is such a large amount of heat absorbed, a small temperature rise, and very specific heat capacity.

6.51 **Given:** $V_i = 0.0$ L, $V_f = 2.5$ L, $P = 1.1$ atm **Find:** w (J)

Conceptual Plan: $V_i, V_f \rightarrow \Delta V$ then $P, \Delta V \rightarrow w$ (L atm) $\rightarrow w$ (J)

$\Delta V = V_f - V_i \quad w = -P\Delta V \quad \frac{101.3\ \text{J}}{1\ \text{L} \cdot \text{atm}}$

Solution: $\Delta V = V_f - V_i = 2.5\text{L} - 0.0\text{L} = 2.5\text{L}$ then

$$w = -P\Delta V = -1.1\ \text{atm} \times 2.5\ \text{L} \times \frac{101.3\ \text{J}}{1\ \text{L} \cdot \text{atm}} = -280\ \text{J}$$

Check: The units (J) are correct. The magnitude of the answer (–280) makes physical sense because this is an expansion (negative work) and we have ~ atmospheric pressure and a small volume of expansion.

6.52 **Given:** $\Delta V = 0.50$ L, $P = 1.0$ atm **Find:** w (J)

Conceptual Plan: $P, \Delta V \rightarrow w$ (L atm) $\rightarrow w$ (J)

$w = -P\Delta V \quad \frac{101.3\ \text{J}}{1\ \text{L} \cdot \text{atm}}$

Solution: $w = -P\Delta V = -1.0\ \text{atm} \times 0.50\ \text{L} \times \frac{101.3\ \text{J}}{1\ \text{L} \cdot \text{atm}} = -51\ \text{J}$

Check: The units (J) are correct. The magnitude of the answer (–51) makes physical sense because this is a small expansion (negative work) and we do not expect breathing to take much energy.

6.53 **Given:** $q = 565$ J absorbed, $V_i = 0.10$ L, $V_f = 0.85$ L, $P = 1.0$ atm **Find:** ΔE_{sys}

Conceptual Plan: $V_i, V_f \rightarrow \Delta V$ **and interpret language to determine the sign of the heat**

$\Delta V = V_f - V_i$ $\quad q = +565$ J

then $P, \Delta V \rightarrow w$ **(L atm)** $\rightarrow w$ **(J) finally** $q, w \rightarrow \Delta E_{sys}$

$w = -P\Delta V \quad \frac{101.3\text{ J}}{1\text{ L atm}} \quad \Delta E = q + w$

Solution: $\Delta V = V_f - V_i = 0.85\text{ L} - 0.10\text{ L} = 0.75\text{ L}$ then

$w = -P\Delta V = -1.0\text{ atm} \times 0.75\text{ L} \times \frac{101.3\text{ J}}{1\text{ L}\cdot\text{atm}} = -75.975\text{ J}$ $\Delta E = q + w = +565\text{ J} - 75.975\text{ J} = 489\text{ J}$

Check: The units (J) are correct. The magnitude of the answer (500) makes physical sense because the heat absorbed dominated the small expansion work (negative work).

6.54 **Given:** $q = 124$ J released, $V_i = 5.55$ L, $V_f = 1.22$ L, $P = 1.00$ atm **Find:** ΔE_{sys}

Conceptual Plan: $V_i, V_f \rightarrow \Delta V$ **and interpret language to determine the sign of the heat**

$\Delta V = V_f - V_i$ $\quad q = -124$ J

then $P, \Delta V \rightarrow w$ **(L atm)** $\rightarrow w$ **(J) finally** $q, w \rightarrow \Delta E_{sys}$

$w = -P\Delta V \quad \frac{101.3\text{ J}}{1\text{ L}\cdot\text{atm}} \quad \Delta E = q + w$

Solution: $\Delta V = V_f - V_i = 1.22\text{ L} - 5.55\text{ L} = -4.33\text{ L}$ then

$w = -P\Delta V = -1.00\text{ atm} \times (-4.33\text{ L}) \times \frac{101.3\text{ J}}{1\text{ L}\cdot\text{atm}} = +438.629\text{ J}$ then

$\Delta E = q + w = -124\text{ J} + 438.629\text{ J} = 315\text{ J}$

Check: The units (J) are correct. The magnitude of the answer (300) makes physical sense because the compression work dominated the small heat released.

Enthalpy and Thermochemical Stoichiometry

6.55 **Given:** 1 mol fuel, 3452 kJ heat produced; 11 kJ work done on surroundings **Find:** ΔE_{sys}, ΔH

Conceptual Plan: interpret language to determine the sign of the two terms

then $q \rightarrow \Delta H$ **and** $q, w \rightarrow \Delta E_{sys}$

$\Delta H = q_p \quad \Delta E = q + w$

Solution: Since heat is produced by the system to the surroundings, $q = -3452$ kJ; since the system is doing work on the surroundings, $w = -11$ kJ. $\Delta H = q_p = -3452$ kJ and

$\Delta E = q + w = -3452\text{ kJ} - 11\text{ kJ} = -3463\text{ kJ}$.

Check: The units (kJ) are correct. The magnitude of the answer (–3500) makes physical sense because both terms are negative. We expect significant amounts of energy from fuels.

6.56 **Given:** 1 mol octane, $P = 1.0$ atm, $\Delta E_{sys} = 5084.3$ kJ; $\Delta H = 5074.1$ kJ **Find:** w

Conceptual Plan: interpret language to determine the sign of the two terms then $q \rightarrow \Delta H$ **and** $q, \Delta E_{sys} \rightarrow w$

$\Delta E_{sys} = -5084.3$ kJ; $\Delta H = -5074.1$ kJ $\quad \Delta H = q_p \quad \Delta E = q + w$

Solution: Since heat is produced by the system to the surroundings, $\Delta H = q_p = -5074.1$ kJ;

$\Delta E_{sys} = -5084.3$ kJ $\Delta E = q + w$. Rearrange to solve for w.

$w = \Delta E - q = -5084.3\text{ kJ} - -5074.1\text{ kJ} = -10.2\text{ kJ}$

Check: The units (kJ) are correct. The magnitude of the answer (–10) makes physical sense because the work should be negative in an expansion. We expect more heat than work in an engine.

6.57 (a) Combustion is an exothermic process; ΔH is negative.

(b) Evaporation requires an input of energy, so it is endothermic; ΔH is positive.

(c) Condensation is the reverse of evaporation, so it is exothermic; ΔH is negative.

6.58 (a) Sublimation requires an input of energy, so it is endothermic; ΔH is positive.

(b) Combustion is an exothermic process; ΔH is negative.

(c) Since the temperature drops this is an endothermic process; ΔH is positive.

6.59 **Given:** 177 mL acetone (C_3H_6O), $\Delta H^\circ_{rxn} = -1790$ kJ; d = 0.788 g/mL **Find:** q
Conceptual Plan: mL acetone → g acetone → mol acetone → q

$$\frac{0.788\text{ g}}{1\text{ mL}} \quad \frac{1\text{ mol}}{58.08\text{ g}} \quad \frac{-1790\text{ kJ}}{1\text{ mol}}$$

Solution: $177\ \cancel{\text{mL}} \times \frac{0.788\ \cancel{\text{g}}}{1\ \cancel{\text{mL}}} \times \frac{1\ \cancel{\text{mol}}}{58.08\ \cancel{\text{g}}} \times \frac{-1790\text{ kJ}}{1\ \cancel{\text{mol}}} = -4.30 \times 10^3$ kJ or 4.30×10^3 kJ released

Check: The units (kJ) are correct. The magnitude of the answer (-10^3) makes physical sense because the enthalpy change is negative and we have more than a mole of acetone. We expect more than 1790 kJ to be released.

6.60 **Given:** natural gas (CH_4), $\Delta H^\circ_{rxn} = -802.3$ kJ; $q = 267$ kJ **Find:** m
Conceptual Plan: q → mol natural gas → g natural gas

$$\frac{1\text{ mol}}{-802.3\text{ kJ}} \quad \frac{16.04\text{ g}}{1\text{ mol}}$$

Solution: $-267\ \cancel{\text{kJ}} \times \frac{1\ \cancel{\text{mol}}}{-802.3\ \cancel{\text{kJ}}} \times \frac{16.04\text{ g}}{1\ \cancel{\text{mol}}} = 5.34$ g

Check: The units (g) are correct. The magnitude of the answer (5) makes physical sense because the enthalpy change per mole is so large and we need to burn less than a mole.

6.61 **Given:** pork roast, $\Delta H^\circ_{rxn} = -2217$ kJ; q needed = 1.6×10^3 kJ, 10 % efficiency **Find:** $m(CO_2)$
Conceptual Plan: q used → q generated → mol CO_2 → g CO_2

$$\frac{100\text{ kJ generated}}{10\text{ kJ used}} \quad \frac{3\text{ mol}}{2217\text{ kJ}} \quad \frac{44.01\text{ g}}{1\text{ mol}}$$

Solution: $1.6 \times 10^3\ \cancel{\text{kJ}} \times \frac{100\ \cancel{\text{kJ generated}}}{10\ \cancel{\text{kJ used}}} \times \frac{3\ \cancel{\text{mol CO}_2}}{2217\ \cancel{\text{kJ}}} \times \frac{44.01\text{ g CO}_2}{1\ \cancel{\text{mol CO}_2}} = 950\text{ g CO}_2$

Check: The units (g) are correct. The magnitude of the answer (~1000) makes physical sense because the process is not very efficient and a lot of energy is needed.

6.62 **Given:** carbon, $\Delta H^\circ_{rxn} = -393.5$ kJ; q needed = 5.00×10^2 kJ **Find:** $m(CO_2)$
Conceptual Plan: q needed → mol CO_2 → g CO_2

$$\frac{1\text{ mol}}{393.5\text{ kJ}} \quad \frac{44.01\text{ g}}{1\text{ mol}}$$

Solution: $5.00 \times 10^2\ \cancel{\text{kJ}} \times \frac{1\ \cancel{\text{mol CO}_2}}{393.5\ \cancel{\text{kJ}}} \times \frac{44.01\text{ g CO}_2}{1\ \cancel{\text{mol CO}_2}} = 55.9\text{ g CO}_2$

Check: The units (g) are correct. The magnitude of the answer (~60) makes physical sense as there is a 1:1 mol ratio between the carbon burned and the carbon dioxide produced.

Thermal Energy Transfer

6.63 **Given:** silver block, $T_{Agi} = 58.5$ °C, 100.0 g water, $T_{H_2Oi} = 24.8$ °C, $T_f = 26.2$ °C **Find:** mass of silver block
Conceptual Plan: pull C_s values from table then H_2O: m, C_s, T_i, T_f → q Ag: C_s, T_i, T_f → m

$$\text{Ag: } 0.235\frac{\text{J}}{\text{g}\cdot{}^\circ\text{C}} \quad \text{H}_2\text{O: } 4.18\frac{\text{J}}{\text{g}\cdot{}^\circ\text{C}} \qquad q = mC_s(T_f - T_i) \text{ then set } q_{Ag} = -q_{H_2O}$$

Solution: $q = mC_s(T_f - T_i)$ substitute in values and set $q_{Ag} = -q_{H_2O}$.

$$q_{Ag} = m_{Ag}C_{Ag}(T_f - T_{Agi}) = m_{Ag} \times 0.235\frac{\text{J}}{\text{g}\cdot\cancel{{}^\circ\text{C}}} \times (26.2\ \cancel{{}^\circ\text{C}} - 58.5\ \cancel{{}^\circ\text{C}}) =$$

$$-q_{H_2O} = -m_{H_2O}C_{H_2O}(T_f - T_{H_2Oi}) = -100.0\ \cancel{\text{g}} \times 4.18\frac{\text{J}}{\cancel{\text{g}}\cdot\cancel{{}^\circ\text{C}}} \times (26.2\ \cancel{{}^\circ\text{C}} - 24.8\ \cancel{{}^\circ\text{C}})$$

Rearrange to solve for m_{Ag}.

$$m_{Ag} \times \left(-7.5\underline{9}05\frac{\text{J}}{\text{g}}\right) = -58\underline{5}.2\text{ J} \rightarrow m_{Ag} = \frac{-58\underline{5}.2\ \cancel{\text{J}}}{-7.5\underline{9}05\frac{\cancel{\text{J}}}{g}} = 77.\underline{0}964\text{ g Ag} = 77.1\text{ g Ag}$$

Check: The units (g) are correct. The magnitude of the answer (77 g) makes physical sense because the heat capacity of water is much greater than the heat capacity of silver.

6.64 **Given:** 32.5 g iron rod, T_{Fei} = 22.7 °C, T_{H_2Oi} = 63.2 °C, T_f = 59.5 °C **Find:** mass of water
Conceptual Plan: pull C_s values from table then Fe: $m, C_s, T_i, T_f \rightarrow q$ H_2O: $C_s, T_i, T_f \rightarrow m$

$$\text{Fe: } 0.449\,\frac{J}{g\cdot °C}\quad H_2O{:}\,4.18\,\frac{J}{g\cdot °C}\qquad q = mC_s(T_f - T_i) \text{ then set } q_{Fe} = -q_{H_2O}$$

Solution: $q = mC_s(T_f - T_i)$ substitute in values and set $q_{Fe} = -q_{H_2O}$.

$$q_{Fe} = m_{Fe}C_{Fe}(T_f - T_{Fei}) = 32.5\,\text{g} \times 0.449\,\frac{J}{g\cdot °C} \times (59.5\,°C - 22.7\,°C) =$$

$$-q_{H_2O} = -m_{H_2O}C_{H_2O}(T_f - T_{H_2Oi}) = -m_{H_2O} \times 4.18\,\frac{J}{g\cdot °C} \times (59.5\,°C - 63.2\,°C)$$

Rearrange to solve for m_{H2O}.

$$537.004\,J = -m_{H_2O} \times \left(15.466\,\frac{J}{g}\right) \rightarrow m_{H_2O} = \frac{537.004\,J}{15.466\,\frac{J}{g}} = 34.72158\,g\,H_2O = 34.7\,g\,H_2O$$

Check: The units (g) are correct. The magnitude of the answer (35 g) makes physical sense because the heat capacity of water is much greater than the heat capacity of iron.

6.65 **Given:** 31.1 g gold, T_{Aui} = 69.3 °C, 64.2 g water, T_{H_2Oi} = 27.8 °C **Find:** T_f
Conceptual Plan: pull C_s values from table then $m, C_s, T_i \rightarrow T_f$

$$\text{Au: } 0.128\,\frac{J}{g\cdot °C}\quad H_2O{:}\,4.18\,\frac{J}{g\cdot °C}\qquad q = mC_s(T_f - T_i) \text{ then set } q_{Au} = -q_{H_2O}$$

Solution: $q = mC_s(T_f - T_i)$ substitute in values and set $q_{Au} = -q_{H_2O}$.

$$q_{Au} = m_{Au}C_{Au}(T_f - T_{Aui}) = 31.1\,\text{g} \times 0.128\,\frac{J}{g\cdot °C} \times (T_f - 69.3\,°C) =$$

$$-q_{H_2O} = -m_{H_2O}C_{H_2O}(T_f - T_{H_2Oi}) = -64.2\,\text{g} \times 4.18\,\frac{J}{g\cdot °C} \times (T_f - 27.8\,°C)$$

Rearrange to solve for T_f.

$$3.9808\,\frac{J}{°C} \times (T_f - 69.3\,°C) = -268.356\,\frac{J}{°C} \times (T_f - 27.8\,°C) \rightarrow$$

$$3.9808\,\frac{J}{°C}\,T_f - 275.8694\,J = -268.356\,\frac{J}{°C}\,T_f + 7460.2967\,J \rightarrow$$

$$268.356\,\frac{J}{°C}\,T_f + 3.9808\,\frac{J}{°C}\,T_f = 275.8694\,J + 7460.2967\,J \rightarrow 272.3368\,\frac{J}{°C}\,T_f = 7736.1661\,J \rightarrow$$

$$T_f = \frac{7736.1661\,J}{272.3368\,\frac{J}{°C}} = 28.4\,°C$$

Check: The units (°C) are correct. The magnitude of the answer (28) makes physical sense because the heat transfer is dominated by the water (larger mass and larger specific heat capacity). The final temperature should be closer to the initial temperature of water than of gold.

6.66 **Given:** 2.85 g lead, T_{Pbi} = 10.3 °C, 7.55 g water, T_{H_2Oi} = 52.3 °C, **Find:** T_f
Conceptual Plan: pull C_s values from table then $m, C_s, T_i \rightarrow T_f$

$$\text{Pb: } 0.128\,\frac{J}{g\cdot °C}\quad H_2O{:}\,4.18\,\frac{J}{g\cdot °C}\qquad q = mC_s(T_f - T_i) \text{ then set } q_{Pb} = -q_{H_2O}$$

Solution: $q = mC_s(T_f - T_i)$ substitute in values and set $q_{Pb} = -q_{H_2O}$.

$$q_{Pb} = m_{Pb}C_{Pb}(T_f - T_{Pbi}) = 2.85\,\text{g} \times 0.128\,\frac{J}{g\cdot °C} \times (T_f - 10.3\,°C) =$$

$$-q_{H_2O} = -m_{H_2O}C_{H_2O}(T_f - T_{H_2Oi}) = -7.55\,\text{g} \times 4.18\,\frac{J}{g\cdot °C} \times (T_f - 52.3\,°C)$$

Rearrange to solve for T_f.

$$0.3648\,\frac{J}{°C} \times (T_f - 10.3\,°C) = -31.559\,\frac{J}{°C} \times (T_f - 52.3\,°C) \rightarrow$$

$$0.3648\,\frac{J}{°C}\,T_f - 3.75744\,J = -31.559\,\frac{J}{°C}\,T_f + 1650.5357\,J \rightarrow$$

$$0.3648\,\frac{J}{°C}\,T_f + 31.559\,\frac{J}{°C}\,T_f = 3.75744\,J + 1650.5357\,J \rightarrow 31.9238\,\frac{J}{°C}\,T_f = 1654.2931\,J \rightarrow$$

$$T_f = \frac{1654.2931\ \text{J}}{31.9238\ \frac{\text{J}}{°\text{C}}} = 51.8\ °\text{C}$$

Check: The units (°C) are correct. The magnitude of the answer (52) makes physical sense because the heat transfer is dominated by the water (larger mass and larger specific heat capacity). The final temperature should be closer to the initial temperature of water than of lead.

6.67 **Given:** 6.15 g substance A, T_{Ai} = 20.5 °C, 25.2 g substance B, T_{Bi} = 52.7 °C, C_s = 1.17 J/g ·°C, T_f = 46.7 °C
Find: specific heat capacity of substance A
Conceptual Plan: A: $m, T_i, T_f \rightarrow q$ B: $m, C_s, T_i, T_f \rightarrow q$ and solve for C

$q = mC_s(T_f - T_i)$ then set $q_A = -q_B$

Solution: $q = mC_s(T_f - T_i)$ substitute in values and set $q_A = -q_B$.

$q_A = m_AC_A(T_f - T_{Ai}) = 6.15\ \text{g} \times C_A \times (46.7\ °\text{C} - 20.5\ °\text{C}) =$

$-q_B = -m_BC_B(T_f - T_{Bi}) = -25.2\ \text{g} \times 1.17\ \frac{\text{J}}{\text{g} \cdot °\text{C}} \times (46.7\ °\text{C} - 52.7\ °\text{C})$

Rearrange to solve for C_A.

$$C_A \times (161.13\text{g} \cdot °\text{C}) = 176.904\ \text{J} \rightarrow C_A = \frac{176.904\ \text{J}}{161.13\text{g} \cdot °\text{C}} = 1.097896\ \frac{\text{J}}{\text{g} \cdot °\text{C}} = 1.10\ \frac{\text{J}}{\text{g} \cdot °\text{C}}$$

Check: The units (J/g ·°C) are correct. The magnitude of the answer (1 J/g ·°C) makes physical sense because the mass of substance B is greater than the mass of substance A by a factor of ~4.1, and the temperature change for substance A is greater than the temperature change of substance B by a factor of ~4.4, so the heat capacity of substance A will be a little smaller.

6.68 **Given:** 2.74 g substance that may be gold, $T_{Au?i}$ = 72.1 °C, 15.2 g water, T_{H_2Oi} = 24.7 °C, T_f = 26.3 °C
Find: heat capacity of substance that may be gold, and could it be gold
Conceptual Plan: pull C_s values from Table 6.4 substance: $m, T_i, T_f \rightarrow q$ H_2O: $m, C_s, T_i, T_f \rightarrow q$

Au: $0.128\ \frac{\text{J}}{\text{g} \cdot °\text{C}}$ H_2O: $4.18\ \frac{\text{J}}{\text{g} \cdot °\text{C}}$ $q = mC_s(T_f - T_i)$ then set $q_{Au?} = -q_{H_2O}$.

and solve for C

Solution: $q = mC_s(T_f - T_i)$ substitute in values and set $q_{Au?} = -q_{H_2O}$.

$q_{Au?} = m_{Au?}C_{Au?}(T_f - T_{Au?i}) = 2.74\text{g} \times C_{Au?} \times (26.3\ °\text{C} - 72.1°\text{C}) =$

$-q_{H_2O} = -m_{H_2O}C_{H_2O}(T_f - T_{H_2Oi}) = -15.2\ \text{g} \times 4.18\ \frac{\text{J}}{\text{g} \cdot °\text{C}} \times (26.3\ °\text{C} - 24.7\ °\text{C})$

Rearrange to solve for $C_{Au?}$.

$$C_{Au?} \times (-125.492\ \text{g} \cdot °\text{C}) = -101.6576\ \text{J} \rightarrow C_{Au?} = \frac{-101.6576\ \text{J}}{-125.492\ \text{g} \cdot °\text{C}} = 0.8100724\ \frac{\text{J}}{\text{g} \cdot °\text{C}} = 0.81\ \frac{\text{J}}{\text{g} \cdot °\text{C}}$$

Since the specific heat capacity of gold is 0.128 J/g ·°C, this substance is not gold.

Check: The units (J/g ·°C) are correct. The magnitude of the answer (1 J/g ·°C) makes physical sense because the mass of the substance is much less than the mass of the water by a factor of ~5.5, and the temperature change for the substance is greater than the temperature change of the water by a factor of ~29, so the heat capacity of the unknown substance will be a factor of ~5.2 smaller than the water, but not as low as 0.128 J/g ·°C.

Calorimetry

6.69 $\Delta H_{rxn} = q_p$ and $\Delta E_{rxn} = q_V = \Delta H - P\Delta V$. Since combustions always involve expansions, expansions do work and therefore have a negative value. Combustions are always exothermic and therefore have a negative value. This means that ΔE_{rxn} is more negative than ΔH°_{rxn} and so A (– 25.9 kJ) is the constant volume process and B (– 23.3 kJ) is the constant pressure process.

6.70 Constant volume conditions should be used. Since $\Delta E = q + w$ *and* $w = -P\ \Delta V$, this means that at constant V, $w = 0$ and all of the energy is released at heat ($\Delta E_{rxn} = q_V$). At constant P, $\Delta H_{rxn} = q_p$ and $\Delta E_{rxn} = q_p = \Delta H - P\Delta V$. Since combustions always involve expansions; expansions do work and so have a negative value. Combustions are always exothermic and so have a negative value. This means that ΔE_{rxn} is more negative than ΔH°_{rxn} and so more heat will be generated in a constant V process.

6.71 **Given:** 0.514 g biphenyl ($C_{12}H_{10}$), bomb calorimeter, $T_i = 25.8\ °C$, $T_f = 29.4\ °C$, $C_{cal} = 5.86\ kJ/°C$ **Find:** ΔE_{rxn}

Conceptual Plan: $T_i, T_f \rightarrow \Delta T$ **then** $\Delta T, C_{cal} \rightarrow q_{cal} \rightarrow q_{rxn}$ **then g** $C_{12}H_{10} \rightarrow$ **mol** $C_{12}H_{10}$

$\Delta T = T_f - T_i$ $\quad q_{cal} = C_{cal}\Delta T \quad q_{cal} = -q_{rxn} \quad \frac{1\ mol}{154.20\ g}$

then q_{rxn}, **mol** $C_{12}H_{10} \rightarrow \Delta E_{rxn}$

$\Delta E_{rxn} = \frac{q_V}{mol\ C_{12}H_{10}}$

Solution: $\Delta T = T_f - T_i = 29.4\ °C - 25.8\ °C = 3.6\ °C$ then $q_{cal} = C_{cal}\Delta T = 5.86 \frac{kJ}{°C} \times 3.6\ °C = 21.096\ kJ$

then $q_{cal} = -q_{rxn} = -21.096\ kJ$ and $0.514\ g\ C_{12}H_{10} \times \frac{1\ mol\ C_{12}H_{10}}{154.20\ g\ C_{12}H_{10}} = 0.00333333\ mol\ C_{12}H_{10}$ then

$$\Delta E_{rxn} = \frac{q_V}{mol\ C_{12}H_{10}} = \frac{-21.096\ kJ}{0.00333333\ mol\ C_{12}H_{10}} = -6.3 \times 10^3\ kJ/mol$$

Check: The units (kJ/mol) are correct. The magnitude of the answer (– 6000) makes physical sense because there is such a large heat generated from a very small amount of biphenyl.

6.72 **Given:** 1.025 g naphthalene ($C_{10}H_8$), bomb calorimeter, $T_i = 24.25\ °C$, $T_f = 32.33\ °C$, $C_{cal} = 5.11\ kJ/°C$ **Find:** ΔE_{rxn}

Conceptual Plan: $T_i, T_f \rightarrow \Delta T$ **then** $\Delta T, C_{cal} \rightarrow q_{cal} \rightarrow q_{rxn}$ **then g** $C_{10}H_8 \rightarrow$ **mol** $C_{10}H_8$

$\Delta T = T_f - T_i$ $\quad q_{cal} = C_{cal}\Delta T \quad q_{cal} = -q_{rxn} \quad \frac{1\ mol}{128.16\ g}$

then q_{rxn}, **mol** $C_{10}H_8 \rightarrow \Delta E_{rxn}$

$\Delta E_{rxn} = \frac{q_V}{mol\ C_{10}H_8}$

Solution: $\Delta T = T_f - T_i = 32.33\ °C - 24.25\ °C = 8.08\ °C$ then

$q_{cal} = C_{cal}\Delta T = 5.11 \frac{kJ}{°C} \times 8.08\ °C = 41.2888\ kJ$ then $q_{cal} = -q_{rxn} = -41.2888\ kJ$ and

$1.025\ g\ C_{10}H_8 \times \frac{1\ mol\ C_{10}H_8}{128.16\ g\ C_{10}H_8} = 0.007997815\ mol\ C_{10}H_8$ then

$$\Delta E_{rxn} = \frac{q_V}{mol\ C_{10}H_8} = \frac{-41.2888\ kJ}{0.007997815\ mol\ C_{10}H_8} = -5.16 \times 10^3\ kJ/mol$$

Check: The units (kJ/mol) are correct. The magnitude of the answer (– 5000) makes physical sense because there is such a large heat generated from a very small amount of naphthalene.

6.73 **Given:** 0.103 g zinc, coffee-cup calorimeter, $T_i = 22.5\ °C$, $T_f = 23.7\ °C$, 50.0 mL solution, d (solution) = 1.0 g/mL, $C_{soln} = 4.18\ kJ/g\ °C$ **Find:** ΔH_{rxn}

Conceptual Plan: $T_i, T_f \rightarrow \Delta T$ **and mL soln** $\rightarrow$ **g soln then** $\Delta T, C_{cal} \rightarrow q_{cal} \rightarrow q_{rxn}$ **then**

$\Delta T = T_f - T_i \quad \frac{1.0\ g}{1.0\ mL} \quad q_{cal} = m\ C_{soln}\ \Delta T \quad q_{soln} = -q_{rxn}$

g Zn $\rightarrow$ **mol Zn then** q_{rxn}, **mol Zn** $\rightarrow \Delta H_{rxn}$

$\frac{1\ mol}{65.37\ g} \quad \Delta H_{rxn} = \frac{q_P}{mol\ Zn}$

Solution: $\Delta T = T_f - T_i = 23.7\ °C - 22.5°C = 1.2°C$ and $50.0\ mL \times \frac{1.0\ g}{1.0\ mL} = 50.0\ g$ then

$q_{soln} = m\ C_{soln}\ \Delta T = 50.0\ g \times 4.18 \frac{J}{g \cdot °C} \times 1.2\ °C = 250.8\ J$ then $q_{soln} = -q_{rxn} = -250.8\ J$ and

$0.103\ g\ Zn \times \frac{1\ mol\ Zn}{65.37\ g\ Zn} = 0.00157565\ mol\ Zn$ then

$$\Delta H_{rxn} = \frac{q_P}{mol\ Zn} = \frac{-250.8\ J}{0.00157565\ mol\ Zn} = -1.6 \times 10^5\ J/mol = -1.6 \times 10^2\ kJ/mol$$

Check: The units (kJ/mol) are correct. The magnitude of the answer (–160) makes physical sense because there is such a large heat generated from a very small amount of zinc.

6.74 **Given:** 1.25 g NH_4NO_3, coffee-cup calorimeter, $T_i = 25.8\ °C$, $T_f = 21.9\ °C$, 25.0 mL solution, d (solution) = 1.0 g/mL, $C_{soln} = 4.18\ kJ/g\ °C$ **Find:** ΔH_{rxn}

Conceptual Plan: $T_i, T_f \rightarrow \Delta T$ **and mL soln** $\rightarrow$ **g soln then** $\Delta T, C_{cal} \rightarrow q_{cal} \rightarrow q_{rxn}$ **then**

$\Delta T = T_f - T_i \quad \frac{1.0\ g}{1.0\ mL} \quad q_{cal} = m\ C_{soln}\ \Delta T \quad q_{soln} = -q_{rxn}$

g NH_4NO_3 → mol NH_4NO_3 then q_{rxn}, mol NH_4NO_3 → ΔH_{rxn}

$\frac{1\text{ mol}}{80.05\text{ g}}$ $\qquad \Delta H_{rxn} = \frac{q_P}{mol\ NH_4NO_3}$

Solution: $\Delta T = T_f - T_i = 21.9\ °C - 25.8\ °C = -3.9\ °C$ and $25.0\ \text{mL} \times \frac{1.0\text{ g}}{1.0\text{ mL}} = 25.0\text{ g}$ then

$q_{soln} = mC_{soln}\Delta T = 25.0\text{ g} \times 4.18\frac{\text{J}}{\text{g}\cdot °\text{C}} \times (-3.9\ °\text{C}) = -40\underline{7}.55\text{ J}$ then $q_{soln} = -q_{rxn} = 40\underline{7}.55\text{ J}$ and

$1.25\text{ g } NH_4NO_3 \times \frac{1\text{ mol } NH_4NO_3}{80.05\text{ g } NH_4NO_3} = 0.015\underline{6}152\text{ mol } NH_4NO_3$ then

$\Delta H_{rxn} = \frac{q_P}{\text{mol } NH_4NO_3} = \frac{40\underline{7}.55\text{ J}}{0.015\underline{6}152\text{ mol } NH_4NO_3} = 2.6\text{x}10^4\text{ J/mol} = 26\text{ kJ/mol}$

Check: The units (kJ/mol) are correct. The magnitude of the answer (26) makes physical sense because there is such a small amount of heat absorbed.

Quantitative Relationships Involving ΔH and Hess's Law

6.75 (a) Since A + B → 2 C has ΔH_1 then 2 C → A + B will have a $\Delta H_2 = -\Delta H_1$. When the reaction direction is reversed, it changes from exothermic to endothermic (or vice versa), so the sign of ΔH changes.

(b) Since A + $\frac{1}{2}$ B → C has ΔH_1 then 2 A + B → 2 C will have a $\Delta H_2 = 2\ \Delta H_1$. When the reaction amount doubles, the amount of heat (or ΔH) doubles.

(c) Since A → B + 2 C has ΔH_1 then $\frac{1}{2}$ A → $\frac{1}{2}$ B + C will have a $\Delta H_{1'} = \frac{1}{2}\ \Delta H_1$. When the reaction amount is cut in half, the amount of heat (or ΔH) is cut in half. Then $\frac{1}{2}$ B + C → $\frac{1}{2}$ A will have a $\Delta H_2 = -\Delta H_{1'} = -\frac{1}{2}\ \Delta H_1$. When the reaction direction is reversed, it changes from exothermic to endothermic (or vice versa), so the sign of ΔH changes.

6.76 (a) Since A + 2 B → C + 3 D has ΔH = 155 kJ then 3A + 6 B → 3 C + 9 D will have a $\Delta H' = 3\ \Delta H$ = 3 (155 kJ) = 465 kJ. When the reaction amount triples, the amount of heat (or ΔH) triples.

(b) Since A + 2 B → C + 3 D has ΔH = 155 kJ then C + 3 D → 3A + 6 B will have a $\Delta H' = -\Delta H$ = – 155 kJ. When the reaction direction is reversed, it changes from endothermic to exothermic, so the sign of ΔH changes.

(c) Since A + 2 B → C + 3 D has ΔH = 155 kJ then $\frac{1}{2}$ A + B → $\frac{1}{2}$ C + 3/2 D will have a $\Delta H' = \frac{1}{2}\ \Delta H = \frac{1}{2}$ (155 kJ) = 77.5 kJ. When the reaction amount is cut in half, the amount of heat (or ΔH) is cut in half. Then $\frac{1}{2}$ C + 3/2 D → $\frac{1}{2}$ A + B will have a $\Delta H'' = -\Delta H'$ = – 77.5 kJ. When the reaction direction is reversed, the sign of it changes from endothermic to exothermic, so the sign of ΔH changes.

6.77 Since the first reaction has Fe_2O_3 as a product and the reaction of interest has it as a reactant, we need to reverse the first reaction. When the reaction direction is reversed, ΔH changes.

$Fe_2O_3\ (s) \rightarrow 2\ Fe\ (s) + 3/2\ O_2\ (g)$ $\qquad \Delta H = +824.2\text{ kJ}$

Since the second reaction has 1 mole CO as a reactant and the reaction of interest has 3 moles of CO as a reactant, we need to multiply the second reaction and the ΔH by 3.

$3[CO\ (g) + 1/2\ O_2\ (g) \rightarrow CO_2\ (g)]$ $\qquad \Delta H = 3(-282.7\text{ kJ}) = -848.1\text{ kJ}$

Hess's Law states the ΔH of the net reaction is the sum of the ΔH of the steps.

The rewritten reactions are as follows:

$Fe_2O_3\ (s) \rightarrow 2\ Fe\ (s) + \cancel{3/2\ O_2\ (g)}$ $\qquad \Delta H = +824.2\text{ kJ}$

$3\ CO\ (g) + \cancel{3/2\ O_2\ (g)} \rightarrow 3\ CO_2\ (g)$ $\qquad \Delta H = -848.1\text{ kJ}$

$Fe_2O_3\ (s) + 3\ CO\ (g) \rightarrow 2\ Fe\ (s) + 3\ CO_2\ (g)$ $\qquad \Delta H_{rxn} = -23.9\text{ kJ}$

6.78 Since the first reaction has $CaCO_3$ as a product and the reaction of interest has it as a product, we simply write the first reaction and the ΔH unchanged.

$Ca\ (s) + CO_2\ (g) + 1/2\ O_2\ (g) \rightarrow CaCO_3\ (s)$ $\qquad \Delta H = -812.8\text{ kJ}$

Since the second reaction has 2 moles CaO as a product and the reaction of interest has 1 mole of CaO as a reactant, we need to reverse the direction of the reaction of the second reaction and multiply it by $\frac{1}{2}$. The sign of the ΔH in the second reaction is changed and is multiplied by $\frac{1}{2}$.

$1/2[2\ CaO\ (s) \rightarrow 2\ Ca\ (s) + O_2\ (g)]$ $\qquad \Delta H = -1/2(-1269.8\text{ kJ}) = +634.9\text{ k}$

Hess's Law states the ΔH of the net reaction is the sum of the ΔH of the steps.
The rewritten reactions are as follows:

~~$Ca\ (s)$~~ + $CO_2\ (g)$ + ~~$1/2\ O_2\ (g)$~~ $\rightarrow CaCO_3\ (s)$	$\Delta H = -\ 812.8$ kJ
$CaO\ (s) \rightarrow$ ~~$Ca\ (s)$~~ + ~~$1/2\ O_2\ (g)$~~	$\Delta H = +\ 634.9$ kJ
$CaO\ (s) + CO_2\ (g) \rightarrow CaCO_3\ (s)$	$\Delta H_{rxn} = -\ 177.9$ kJ

6.79 Since the first reaction has C_5H_{12} as a reactant and the reaction of interest has it as a product, we need to reverse the first reaction. When the reaction direction is reversed, ΔH changes.

$5\ CO_2\ (g) + 6\ H_2O\ (g) \rightarrow C_5H_{12}\ (l) + 8\ O_2\ (g)$ $\qquad \Delta H = +\ 3505.8$ kJ

Since the second reaction has 1 mole C as a reactant and the reaction of interest has 5 moles of C as a reactant, we need to multiply the second reaction and the ΔH by 5.

$5[C\ (s) + O_2\ (g) \rightarrow CO_2\ (g)]$ $\qquad \Delta H = 5(-\ 393.5\ kJ) = -\ 1967.5$ kJ

Since the third reaction has 2 moles H_2 as a reactant and the reaction of interest has 6 moles of H_2 as a reactant, we need to multiply the third reaction and the ΔH by 3.

$3[2\ H_2\ (g) + O_2\ (g) \rightarrow 2\ H_2O\ (g)]$ $\qquad \Delta H = 3(-\ 483.5\ kJ) = -\ 1450.5$ kJ

Hess's Law states the ΔH of the net reaction is the sum of the ΔH of the steps.
The rewritten reactions are as follows:

~~$5\ CO_2\ (g)$~~ + ~~$6\ H_2O\ (g)$~~ $\rightarrow C_5H_{12}\ (l)$ + ~~$8\ O_2\ (g)$~~	$\Delta H = +\ 3505.8$ kJ
$5\ C\ (s)$ + ~~$5\ O_2\ (g)$~~ $\rightarrow$ ~~$5\ CO_2\ (g)$~~	$\Delta H = -\ 1967.5$ kJ
$6\ H_2\ (g)$ + ~~$3\ O_2\ (g)$~~ $\rightarrow$ ~~$6\ H_2O\ (g)$~~	$\Delta H = -\ 1450.5$ kJ
$5\ C\ (s) + 6\ H_2\ (g) \rightarrow C_5H_{12}\ (l)$	$\Delta H_{rxn} = +\ 87.8$ kJ

6.80 Since the first reaction has CH_4 as a product and the reaction of interest has it as a reactant, we need to reverse the first reaction. When the reaction direction is reversed, ΔH changes.

$CH_4\ (g) \rightarrow C\ (s) + 2\ H_2\ (g)$ $\qquad \Delta H = +\ 74.6$ kJ

Since the first reaction has CCl_4 as a product and the reaction of interest has it as a product, we simply write the first reaction and the ΔH unchanged.

$C\ (s) + 2\ Cl_2\ (g) \rightarrow CCl_4\ (g)$ $\qquad \Delta H = -\ 95.7$ kJ

Since the third reaction has 2 moles HCl as a product and the reaction of interest has 4 moles of HCl as a product, we need to multiply the third reaction and the ΔH by 2.

$2[H_2\ (g) + Cl_2\ (g) \rightarrow 2\ HCl\ (g)]$ $\qquad \Delta H = 2(-\ 92.3\ kJ) = -\ 184.6$ k

Hess's Law states the ΔH of the net reaction is the sum of the ΔH of the steps.
The rewritten reactions are as follows:

$CH_4\ (g) \rightarrow$ ~~$C\ (s)$~~ + ~~$2\ H_2\ (g)$~~	$\Delta H = +\ 74.6$ kJ
~~$C\ (s)$~~ + $2\ Cl_2\ (g) \rightarrow CCl_4\ (g)$	$\Delta H = -\ 95.7$ kJ
~~$2\ H_2\ (g)$~~ + $2\ Cl_2\ (g) \rightarrow 4\ HCl\ (g)$	$\Delta H = -\ 184.6$ kJ
$CH_4\ (g) + 4\ Cl_2\ (g) \rightarrow CCl_4\ (g) + 4HCl\ (g)$	$\Delta H_{rxn} = -\ 205.7$ kJ

6.81 (a) $\frac{1}{2} N_2\ (g) + \frac{3}{2} H_2\ (g) \rightarrow NH_3\ (g)$ $\qquad \Delta H_f^\circ = -\ 45.9$ kJ/mol

(b) $C\ (s) + O_2\ (g) \rightarrow CO_2\ (g)$ $\qquad \Delta H_f^\circ = -\ 393.5$ kJ/mol

(c) $2\ Fe\ (s) + \frac{3}{2} O_2\ (g) \rightarrow Fe_2O_3\ (s)$ $\qquad \Delta H_f^\circ = -\ 824.2$ kJ/mol

(d) $C\ (s) + 2\ H_2\ (g) \rightarrow CH_4\ (g)$ $\qquad \Delta H_f^\circ = -\ 74.6$ kJ/mol

6.82 (a) $\frac{1}{2} N_2\ (g) + O_2\ (g) \rightarrow NO_2\ (g)$ $\qquad \Delta H_f^\circ = 33.2$ kJ/mol

(b) $Mg\ (s) + C\ (s) + \frac{3}{2} O_2\ (g) \rightarrow MgCO_3\ (s)$ $\qquad \Delta H_f^\circ = -\ 1095.8$ kJ/mol

(c) $2\ C\ (s) + 2\ H_2\ (g) \rightarrow C_2H_4\ (g)$ $\qquad \Delta H_f^\circ = 52.4$ kJ/mol

(d) $C\ (s) + 2\ H_2\ (g) + \frac{1}{2} O_2\ (g) \rightarrow CH_3OH\ (l)$ $\qquad \Delta H_f^\circ = -\ 238.6$ kJ/mol

6.83 **Given:** $N_2H_4\ (l) + N_2O_4\ (g) \rightarrow 2\ N_2O\ (g) + 2\ H_2O\ (g)$ **Find:** ΔH°_{rxn}
Conceptual Plan: $\Delta H^\circ_{rxn} = \sum n_P \Delta H^\circ_f(products) - \sum n_R \Delta H^\circ_f(reactants)$
Solution:

Reactant/Product	ΔH°_f(kJ/mol from Appendix IIB)
$N_2H_4\ (l)$	50.6
$N_2O_4\ (g)$	11.1
$N_2O\ (g)$	81.6
$H_2O\ (g)$	− 241.8

Be sure to pull data for the correct formula and phase.

$$\begin{aligned}\Delta H^\circ_{rxn} &= \sum n_P \Delta H^\circ_f(products) - \sum n_R \Delta H^\circ_f(reactants)\\ &= [2(\Delta H^\circ_f(N_2O\ (g))) + 2(\Delta H^\circ_f(H_2O\ (g)))] - [1(\Delta H^\circ_f(N_2H_4\ (l))) + 1(\Delta H^\circ_f(N_2O_4\ (g)))]\\ &= [2(81.6\ kJ) + 2(-241.8\ kJ)] - [1(50.6\ kJ) + 1(11.1\ kJ)]\\ &= [-320.4\ kJ] - [61.7\ kJ]\\ &= -382.1\ kJ\end{aligned}$$

Check: The units (kJ) are correct. The answer is negative, which means that the reaction is exothermic. The answer is dominated by the negative heat of formation of water.

6.84 **Given:** $C_5H_{12}\ (l) + 8\ O_2\ (g) \rightarrow 5\ CO_2\ (g) + 6\ H_2O\ (g)$ **Find:** ΔH°_{rxn}
Conceptual Plan: $\Delta H^\circ_{rxn} = \sum n_P \Delta H^\circ_f(products) - \sum n_R \Delta H^\circ_f(reactants)$
Solution:

Reactant/Product	ΔH°_f(kJ/mol from Appendix IIB)
$C_5H_{12}\ (l)$	− 146.8
$O_2\ (g)$	0.0
$CO_2\ (g)$	− 393.5
$H_2O\ (g)$	− 241.8

Be sure to pull data for the correct formula and phase.

$$\begin{aligned}\Delta H^\circ_{rxn} &= \sum n_P \Delta H^\circ_f(products) - \sum n_R \Delta H^\circ_f(reactants)\\ &= [5(\Delta H^\circ_f(CO_2\ (g))) + 6(\Delta H^\circ_f(H_2O\ (g)))] - [1(\Delta H^\circ_f(C_5H_{12}\ (l))) + 8(\Delta H^\circ_f(O_2\ (g)))]\\ &= [5(-393.5\ kJ) + 6(-241.8\ kJ)] - [1(-146.8\ kJ) + 8(0.0\ kJ)]\\ &= [-3418.3\ kJ] - [-146.8\ kJ]\\ &= -3271.5\ kJ\end{aligned}$$

Check: The units (kJ) are correct. The answer is negative, which means that the reaction is exothermic, which is typical for combustion reactions.

6.85 (a) **Given:** $C_2H_4\ (g) + H_2\ (g) \rightarrow C_2H_6\ (g)$ **Find:** ΔH°_{rxn}
Conceptual Plan: $\Delta H^\circ_{rxn} = \sum n_P \Delta H^\circ_f(products) - \sum n_R \Delta H^\circ_f(reactants)$
Solution:

Reactant/Product	ΔH°_f(kJ/mol from Appendix IIB)
$C_2H_4\ (g)$	52.4
$H_2\ (g)$	0.0
$C_2H_6\ (g)$	− 84.68

Be sure to pull data for the correct formula and phase.

$$\begin{aligned}\Delta H^\circ_{rxn} &= \sum n_P \Delta H^\circ_f(products) - \sum n_R \Delta H^\circ_f(reactants)\\ &= [1(\Delta H^\circ_f(C_2H_6\ (g)))] - [1(\Delta H^\circ_f(C_2H_4\ (g))) + 1(\Delta H^\circ_f(H_2\ (g)))]\\ &= [1(-84.68\ kJ)] - [1(52.4\ kJ) + 1(0.0\ kJ)]\\ &= [-84.68\ kJ] - [52.4\ kJ]\\ &= -137.1\ kJ\end{aligned}$$

Check: The units (kJ) are correct. The answer is negative, which means that the reaction is exothermic. Both hydrocarbon terms are negative, so the final answer is negative.

(b) **Given:** $CO\ (g) + H_2O\ (g) \rightarrow H_2\ (g) + CO_2\ (g)$ **Find:** ΔH°_{rxn}
Conceptual Plan: $\Delta H^\circ_{rxn} = \sum n_P \Delta H^\circ_f(products) - \sum n_R \Delta H^\circ_f(reactants)$

Solution:

Reactant/Product	ΔH_f°(kJ/mol from Appendix IIB)
CO (*g*)	− 110.5
H_2O (*g*)	− 241.8
H_2 (*g*)	0.0
CO_2 (*g*)	− 393.5

Be sure to pull data for the correct formula and phase.

$$\begin{aligned}\Delta H^\circ_{rxn} &= \sum n_P \Delta H_f^\circ(products) - \sum n_R \Delta H_f^\circ(reactants)\\ &= [1(\Delta H_f^\circ(H_2\,(g))) + 1(\Delta H_f^\circ(CO_2\,(g)))] - [1(\Delta H_f^\circ(CO\,(g))) + 1(\Delta H_f^\circ(H_2O\,(g)))]\\ &= [1(0.0\text{ kJ}) + 1(-393.5\text{ kJ})] - [1(-110.5\text{ kJ}) + 1(-241.8\text{ kJ})]\\ &= [-393.5\text{ kJ}] - [-352.3\text{ kJ}]\\ &= -41.2\text{ kJ}\end{aligned}$$

Check: The units (kJ) are correct. The answer is negative, which means that the reaction is exothermic.

(c) **Given:** $3\,NO_2\,(g) + H_2O\,(l) \rightarrow 2\,HNO_3\,(aq) + NO\,(g)$ **Find:** ΔH°_{rxn}
Conceptual Plan: $\Delta H^\circ_{rxn} = \sum n_P \Delta H_f^\circ(products) - \sum n_R \Delta H_f^\circ(reactants)$
Solution:

Reactant/Product	ΔH_f°(kJ/mol from Appendix IIB)
NO_2 (*g*)	33.2
H_2O (*l*)	− 285.8
HNO_3 (*aq*)	− 207
NO (*g*)	91.3

Be sure to pull data for the correct formula and phase.

$$\begin{aligned}\Delta H^\circ_{rxn} &= \sum n_P \Delta H_f^\circ(products) - \sum n_R \Delta H_f^\circ(reactants)\\ &= [2(\Delta H_f^\circ(HNO_3\,(aq))) + 1(\Delta H_f^\circ(NO\,(g)))] - [3(\Delta H_f^\circ(NO_2\,(g))) + 1(\Delta H_f^\circ(H_2O\,(l)))]\\ &= [2(-207\text{ kJ}) + 1(91.3\text{ kJ})] - [3(33.2\text{ kJ}) + 1(-285.8\text{ kJ})]\\ &= [-32\underline{2}.7\text{ kJ}] - [-186.2\text{ kJ}]\\ &= -137\text{ kJ}\end{aligned}$$

Check: The units (kJ) are correct. The answer is negative, which means that the reaction is exothermic.

(d) **Given:** $Cr_2O_3\,(s) + 3\,CO\,(g) \rightarrow 2\,Cr\,(s) + 3\,CO_2\,(g)$ **Find:** ΔH°_{rxn}
Conceptual Plan: $\Delta H^\circ_{rxn} = \sum n_P \Delta H_f^\circ(products) - \sum n_R \Delta H_f^\circ(reactants)$
Solution:

Reactant/Product	ΔH_f°(kJ/mol from Appendix IIB)
Cr_2O_3 (*s*)	− 1139.7
CO (*g*)	− 110.5
Cr (*s*)	0.0
CO_2 (*g*)	− 393.5

Be sure to pull data for the correct formula and phase.

$$\begin{aligned}\Delta H^\circ_{rxn} &= \sum n_P \Delta H_f^\circ(products) - \sum n_R \Delta H_f^\circ(reactants)\\ &= [2(\Delta H_f^\circ(Cr\,(s))) + 3(\Delta H_f^\circ(CO_2\,(g)))] - [1(\Delta H_f^\circ(Cr_2O_3\,(s))) + 3(\Delta H_f^\circ(CO\,(g)))]\\ &= [2(0.0\text{ kJ}) + 3(-393.5\text{ kJ})] - [1(-1139.7\text{ kJ}) + 3(-110.5\text{ kJ})]\\ &= [-1180.5\text{ kJ}] - [-1471.2\text{ kJ}]\\ &= 290.7\text{ kJ}\end{aligned}$$

Check: The units (kJ) are correct. The answer is positive, which means that the reaction is endothermic.

6.86 (a) **Given:** $2\,H_2S\,(g) + 3\,O_2\,(g) \rightarrow 2\,H_2O\,(l) + 2\,SO_2\,(g)$ **Find:** ΔH°_{rxn}
Conceptual Plan: $\Delta H^\circ_{rxn} = \sum n_P \Delta H_f^\circ(products) - \sum n_R \Delta H_f^\circ(reactants)$
Solution:

Reactant/Product	ΔH_f°(kJ/mol from Appendix IIB)
H_2S (*g*)	− 20.6
O_2 (*g*)	0.0
H_2O (*l*)	− 285.8
SO_2 (*g*)	− 296.8

Be sure to pull data for the correct formula and phase.

$\Delta H^\circ_{rxn} = \sum n_P \Delta H^\circ_f(products) - \sum n_R \Delta H^\circ_f(reactants)$
$= [2(\Delta H^\circ_f(H_2O\,(l))) + 2(\Delta H^\circ_f(SO_2\,(g)))] - [2(\Delta H^\circ_f(H_2S\,(g))) + 3(\Delta H^\circ_f(O_2\,(g)))]$
$= [2(-\,285.8\text{ kJ}) + 2(-\,296.8\text{ kJ})] - [2(-\,20.6\text{ kJ}) + 3(0.0\text{ kJ})]$
$= [-\,1165.2\text{ kJ}] - [-\,41.2\text{ kJ}]$
$= -\,1124.0\text{ kJ}$

Check: The units (kJ) are correct. The answer is negative, which means that the reaction is exothermic.

(b) **Given:** $SO_2\,(g) + 1/2\,O_2\,(g) \rightarrow SO_3\,(g)$ **Find:** ΔH°_{rxn}
Conceptual Plan: $\Delta H^\circ_{rxn} = \sum n_P \Delta H^\circ_f(products) - \sum n_R \Delta H^\circ_f(reactants)$
Solution:

Reactant/Product	ΔH°_f(kJ/mol from Appendix IIB)
$SO_2\,(g)$	− 296.8
$O_2\,(g)$	0.0
$SO_3\,(g)$	− 395.7

Be sure to pull data for the correct formula and phase.

$\Delta H^\circ_{rxn} = \sum n_P \Delta H^\circ_f(products) - \sum n_R \Delta H^\circ_f(reactants)$
$= [1(\Delta H^\circ_f(SO_3\,(g)))] - [1(\Delta H^\circ_f(SO_2\,(g))) + 1/2(\Delta H^\circ_f(O_2\,(g)))]$
$= [1(-\,395.7\text{ kJ})] - [1(-\,296.8\text{ kJ}) + 1/2(0.0\text{ kJ})]$
$= [-\,395.7\text{ kJ}] - [-\,296.8\text{ kJ}]$
$= -\,98.9\text{ kJ}$

Check: The units (kJ) are correct. The answer is negative, which means that the reaction is exothermic. The SO_3 has a lower heat of formation than SO_2, so we expect an exothermic reaction.

(c) **Given:** $C\,(s) + H_2O\,(g) \rightarrow CO\,(g) + H_2\,(g)$ **Find:** ΔH°_{rxn}
Conceptual Plan: $\Delta H^\circ_{rxn} = \sum n_P \Delta H^\circ_f(products) - \sum n_R \Delta H^\circ_f(reactants)$
Solution:

Reactant/Product	ΔH°_f(kJ/mol from Appendix IIB)
$C\,(s)$	0.0
$H_2O\,(g)$	− 241.8
$CO\,(g)$	− 110.5
$H_2\,(g)$	0.0

Be sure to pull data for the correct formula and phase.

$\Delta H^\circ_{rxn} = \sum n_P \Delta H^\circ_f(products) - \sum n_R \Delta H^\circ_f(reactants)$
$= [1(\Delta H^\circ_f(CO\,(g))) + 1(\Delta H^\circ_f(H_2\,(g)))] - [1(\Delta H^\circ_f(C\,(s))) + 1(\Delta H^\circ_f(H_2O\,(g)))]$
$= [1(-\,110.5\text{ kJ}) + 1(0.0\text{ kJ})] - [1(0.0\text{ kJ}) + 1(-\,241.8\text{ kJ})]$
$= [-\,110.5\text{ kJ}] - [-\,241.8\text{ kJ}]$
$= 131.3\text{ kJ}$

Check: The units (kJ) are correct. The answer is positive, which means that the reaction is endothermic. The CO has a smaller (less negative) heat of formation than H_2O, so we expect an endothermic reaction.

(d) **Given:** $N_2O_4\,(g) + 4\,H_2\,(g) \rightarrow N_2\,(g) + 4\,H_2O\,(g)$ **Find:** ΔH°_{rxn}
Conceptual Plan: $\Delta H^\circ_{rxn} = \sum n_P \Delta H^\circ_f(products) - \sum n_R \Delta H^\circ_f(reactants)$
Solution:

Reactant/Product	ΔH°_f(kJ/mol from Appendix IIB)
$N_2O_4\,(g)$	11.1
$H_2\,(g)$	0.0
$N_2\,(g)$	0.0
$H_2O\,(g)$	− 241.8

Be sure to pull data for the correct formula and phase.

$\Delta H^\circ_{rxn} = \sum n_P \Delta H^\circ_f(products) - \sum n_R \Delta H^\circ_f(reactants)$
$= [1(\Delta H^\circ_f(N_2\,(g))) + 4(\Delta H^\circ_f(H_2O\,(g)))] - [1(\Delta H^\circ_f(N_2O_4\,(g))) + 4(\Delta H^\circ_f(H_2\,(g)))]$
$= [1(0.0\text{ kJ}) + 4(-\,241.8\text{ kJ})] - [1(11.1\text{ kJ}) + 4(0.0\text{ kJ})]$
$= [-\,967.2\text{ kJ}] - [11.1\text{ kJ}]$
$= -\,978.3\text{ kJ}$

Check: The units (kJ) are correct. The answer is negative, which means that the reaction is exothermic. The H_2O has a lower heat of formation than N_2O_4, so we expect an exothermic reaction.

6.87 **Given:** form glucose ($C_6H_{12}O_6$) and oxygen from sunlight, carbon dioxide, and water **Find:** ΔH°_{rxn}

Conceptual Plan: write balanced reaction then $\Delta H^\circ_{rxn} = \sum n_P \Delta H^\circ_f(products) - \sum n_R \Delta H^\circ_f(reactants)$

Solution: $6\ CO_2\ (g) + 6\ H_2O\ (l) \rightarrow C_6H_{12}O_6\ (s) + 6\ O_2\ (g)$

Reactant/Product	ΔH°_f(kJ/mol from Appendix IIB)
$CO_2\ (g)$	− 393.5
$H_2O\ (l)$	− 285.8
$C_6H_{12}O\ (s)$	− 1273.3
$O_2\ (g)$	0.0

Be sure to pull data for the correct formula and phase.

$$\begin{aligned}\Delta H^\circ_{rxn} &= \sum n_P \Delta H^\circ_f(products) - \sum n_R \Delta H^\circ_f(reactants)\\ &= [1(\Delta H^\circ_f(C_6H_{12}O\ (s))) + 6(\Delta H^\circ_f(O_2\ (g)))] - [6(\Delta H^\circ_f(CO_2\ (g))) + 6(\Delta H^\circ_f(H_2O\ (l)))]\\ &= [1(-\ 1273.3\ kJ) + 6(0.0\ kJ)] - [6(-\ 393.5\ kJ) + 6(-\ 285.8\ kJ)]\\ &= [-\ 1273.3\ kJ] - [-\ 4075.6\ kJ]\\ &= +\ 2802.5\ kJ\end{aligned}$$

Check: The units (kJ) are correct. The answer is positive, which means that the reaction is endothermic. The reaction requires the input of light energy, so we expect that this will be an endothermic reaction.

6.88 **Given:** ethanol (C_2H_5OH) combustion **Find:** ΔH°_{rxn}

Conceptual Plan: write balanced reaction then $\Delta H^\circ_{rxn} = \sum n_P \Delta H^\circ_f(products) - \sum n_R \Delta H^\circ_f(reactants)$

Solution: Combustion is the combination with oxygen to form carbon dioxide and water:

$C_2H_5OH\ (l) + 3\ O_2\ (g) \rightarrow 2\ CO_2\ (g) + 3\ H_2O\ (g)$

Reactant/Product	ΔH°_f(kJ/mol from Appendix IIB)
$C_2H_5OH\ (l)$	− 277.6
$O_2\ (g)$	0.0
$CO_2\ (g)$	− 393.5
$H_2O\ (g)$	− 241.8

Be sure to pull data for the correct formula and phase.

$$\begin{aligned}\Delta H^\circ_{rxn} &= \sum n_P \Delta H^\circ_f(products) - \sum n_R \Delta H^\circ_f(reactants)\\ &= [2(\Delta H^\circ_f(CO_2\ (g))) + 3(\Delta H^\circ_f(H_2O\ (g)))] - [1(\Delta H^\circ_f(C_2H_5OH\ (l))) + 3(\Delta H^\circ_f(O_2\ (g)))]\\ &= [2(-\ 393.5\ kJ) + 3(-\ 241.8\ kJ)] - [1(-\ 277.6\ kJ) + 3(0.0\ kJ)]\\ &= [-\ 1512.4\ kJ] - [-\ 277.6\ kJ]\\ &= -\ 1234.8\ kJ\end{aligned}$$

Check: The units (kJ) are correct. The answer is negative, which means that the reaction is exothermic; this is typical for combustion reactions.

6.89 **Given:** $2\ CH_3NO_2\ (l) + 3/2\ O_2\ (g) \rightarrow 2\ CO_2\ (g) + 3\ H_2O\ (g) + N_2\ (g)$ and $\Delta H^\circ_{rxn} = -\ 709.2$ kJ/mol

Find: $\Delta H^\circ_f\ (CH_3NO_2\ (l))$

Conceptual Plan: fill known values into $\Delta H^\circ_{rxn} = \sum n_P \Delta H^\circ_f(products) - \sum n_R \Delta H^\circ_f(reactants)$ **and rearrange to solve for** $\Delta H^\circ_f\ (CH_3NO_2\ (l))$

Solution:

Reactant/Product	ΔH°_f(kJ/mol from Appendix IIB)
$O_2\ (g)$	0.0
$CO_2\ (g)$	− 393.5
$H_2O\ (g)$	− 241.8
$N_2\ (g)$	0.0

Be sure to pull data for the correct formula and phase.

$\Delta H^\circ_{rxn} = \sum n_P \Delta H^\circ_f(products) - \sum n_R \Delta H^\circ_f(reactants)$

$= [2(\Delta H^\circ_f(CO_2\ (g))) + 3(\Delta H^\circ_f(H_2O\ (g))) + 1(\Delta H^\circ_f(N_2\ (g)))] - [2(\Delta H^\circ_f(CH_3NO_2\ (l))) + 3/2(\Delta H^\circ_f(O_2\ (g)))]$

$2(-\ 709.2\ kJ) = [2(-\ 393.5\ kJ) + 3(-\ 241.8\ kJ) + 1(0.0\ kJ)] - [2(\Delta H^\circ_f(CH_3NO_2(l)) + 3/2(0.0\ kJ)]$

$-\ 1418.4\ kJ = [-\ 1512.4\ kJ] - [2(\Delta H^\circ_f(CH_3NO_2(l))]$

$\Delta H^\circ_f(CH_3NO_2(l)) = -\ 94.0$ kJ/mol

Check: The units (kJ/mol) are correct. The answer is negative (but not as negative as water and carbon dioxide), which is consistent with an exothermic combustion reaction.

6.90 **Given:** 4 $C_3H_5N_3O_9$ (l) $\rightarrow$ 12 CO_2 (g) + 10 H_2O (g) + 6 N_2 (g) + O_2 (g) and $\Delta H^\circ_{rxn} = -5678$ kJ/mol
Find: ΔH°_f ($C_3H_5N_3O_9$ (l))
Conceptual Plan: fill known values into $\Delta H^\circ_{rxn} = \sum n_P \Delta H^\circ_f(products) - \sum n_R \Delta H^\circ_f(reactants)$ **and rearrange to solve for** ΔH°_f **($C_3H_5N_3O_9$ (l))**
Solution:

Reactant/Product	ΔH°_f(kJ/mol from Appendix IIB)
CO_2 (g)	− 393.5
H_2O (g)	− 241.8
N_2 (g)	0.0
O_2 (g)	0.0

Be sure to pull data for the correct formula and phase.

$$H^\circ_{rxn} = \sum n_P \Delta H^\circ_f(products) - \sum n_R \Delta H^\circ_f(reactants)$$
$$= [12(\Delta H^\circ_f(CO_2\,(g))) + 10(\Delta H^\circ_f(H_2O\,(g))) + 6(\Delta H^\circ_f(N_2\,(g))) + 1(\Delta H^\circ_f(O_2\,(g)))]$$
$$- [4(\Delta H^\circ_f(C_3H_5N_3O_9(l)))]$$
$$4(-5678\text{ kJ}) = [12(-393.5\text{ kJ}) + 10(-241.8\text{ kJ}) + 6(0.0\text{ kJ}) + 1(0.0\text{ kJ})] - [4(\Delta H^\circ_f(C_3H_5N_3O_9\,(l)))]$$
$$-22712\text{ kJ} = [-7140.\text{ kJ}] - [4(\Delta H^\circ_f(C_3H_5N_3O_9\,(l))]$$
$$\Delta H^\circ_f(CH_3NO_2(l)) = 3893\text{ kJ/mol}$$

Check: The units (kJ/mol) are correct. The answer is positive, which is not surprising since this is a complex molecule with very high potential energy.

Energy Use and the Environment

6.91 (a) **Given:** methane, $\Delta H^\circ_{rxn} = -802.3$ kJ; $q = 1.00 \times 10^2$ kJ **Find:** $m(CO_2)$
Conceptual Plan: $q \rightarrow$ **mol** $CO_2 \rightarrow$ **g** CO_2

$$\frac{1\text{ mol}}{-802.3\text{ kJ}} \qquad \frac{44.01\text{ g}}{1\text{ mol}}$$

Solution: $-1.00 \times 10^2\text{ kJ} \times \dfrac{1\text{ mol }CO_2}{-802.3\text{ kJ}} \times \dfrac{44.01\text{ g }CO_2}{1\text{ mol }CO_2} = 5.49\text{ g }CO_2$

Check: The units (g) are correct. The magnitude of the answer (~5) makes physical sense because less than a mole of fuel is used.

(b) **Given:** propane, $\Delta H^\circ_{rxn} = -2217$ kJ; $q = 1.00 \times 10^2$ kJ **Find:** $m(CO_2)$
Conceptual Plan: $q \rightarrow$ **mol** $CO_2 \rightarrow$ **g** CO_2

$$\frac{3\text{ mol}}{-2217\text{ kJ}} \qquad \frac{44.01\text{ g}}{1\text{ mol}}$$

Solution: $-1.00 \times 10^2\text{ kJ} \times \dfrac{3\text{ mol }CO_2}{-2217\text{ kJ}} \times \dfrac{44.01\text{ g }CO_2}{1\text{ mol }CO_2} = 5.96\text{ g }CO_2$

Check: The units (g) are correct. The magnitude of the answer (~6) makes physical sense because less than a mole of fuel is used.

(c) **Given:** octane, $\Delta H^\circ_{rxn} = -5074.1$ kJ; $q = 1.00 \times 10^2$ kJ **Find:** $m(CO_2)$
Conceptual Plan: $q \rightarrow$ **mol** $CO_2 \rightarrow$ **g** CO_2

$$\frac{8\text{ mol}}{-5074.1\text{ kJ}} \qquad \frac{44.01\text{ g}}{1\text{ mol}}$$

Solution: $-1.00 \times 10^2\text{ kJ} \times \dfrac{8\text{ mol }CO_2}{-5074.1\text{ kJ}} \times \dfrac{44.01\text{ g }CO_2}{1\text{ mol }CO_2} = 6.94\text{ g }CO_2$

Check: The units (g) are correct. The magnitude of the answer (~7) makes physical sense because less than a mole of fuel is used.
The methane generated the least carbon dioxide for the given amount of heat, while the octane generated the most carbon dioxide for the given amount of heat.

6.92 **Given:** methanol (CH_3OH) combustion **Find:** ΔH°_{rxn}, $m(CO_2)$/kJ for methane and octane (using Problem 91)
Conceptual Plan: write balanced reaction then $\Delta H^\circ_{rxn} = \sum n_P \Delta H^\circ_f(products) - \sum n_R \Delta H^\circ_f(reactants)$
then $q \rightarrow$ **mol** $CO_2 \rightarrow$ **g** CO_2 **then for octane** $m(CO_2)$/ 1.00×10^2 **kJ** $\rightarrow$ $m(CO_2)$/ **kJ**

$$\frac{1\text{ mol}}{\Delta H^\circ_{rxn}(\text{kJ})} \qquad \frac{44.01\text{ g}}{1\text{ mol}} \qquad \div 100$$

Solution: Combustion is the combination with oxygen to form carbon dioxide and water:

$CH_3OH\ (l) + 3/2\ O_2\ (g) \rightarrow CO_2\ (g) + 2\ H_2O\ (g)$

Reactant/Product	ΔH°_f(kJ/mol from Appendix IIB)
$CH_3OH\ (l)$	− 238.6
$O_2\ (g)$	0.0
$CO_2\ (g)$	− 393.5
$H_2O\ (g)$	− 241.8

Be sure to pull data for the correct formula and phase.

$$\begin{aligned}\Delta H^\circ_{rxn} &= \sum n_P \Delta H^\circ_f(products) - \sum n_R \Delta H^\circ_f(reactants)\\ &= [1(\Delta H^\circ_f(CO_2\ (g)) + 2(\Delta H^\circ_f(H_2O\ (g))] - [1(\Delta H^\circ_f(CH_3OH\ (l)) + 3/2(\Delta H^\circ_f(O_2(g))]\\ &= [1(-393.5\text{ kJ}) + 2(-241.8\text{ kJ})] - [1(-238.6\text{ kJ}) + 3/2(0.0\text{ kJ})]\\ &= [-877.1\text{ kJ}] - [-238.6\text{ kJ}]\\ &= -638.5\text{ kJ}\end{aligned}$$

$$-1\ \cancel{\text{kJ}} \times \frac{1\ \cancel{\text{mol CO}_2}}{-638.5\ \cancel{\text{kJ}}} \times \frac{44.01\text{ g CO}_2}{1\ \cancel{\text{mol CO}_2}} = 0.06893\text{ g CO}_2 \text{ for methanol and}$$

$$\frac{6.94\text{ g CO}_2}{-1.00 \times 10^2\ \cancel{\text{kJ}}} \times -1\ \cancel{\text{kJ}} = 0.0694\text{ g CO}_2 \text{ for octane}$$

Methanol contributes less CO_2 / kJ than octane, contributing less to global warming.

Check: The units (g) are correct. The magnitude of the answer (~7) makes physical sense because less than a mole of fuel is used.

6.93 **Given:** 7×10^{12} kg/yr octane (C_8H_{18}), $\Delta H^\circ_{rxn} = -5074.1$ kJ (using Problem 91), 3×10^{15} kg CO_2 in the atmosphere,
Find: $m(CO_2)$ in kg and time to double atmospheric CO_2

Conceptual Plan: use reaction from Problem 91 $C_8H_{18}\ (l) + 25/2\ O_2\ (g) \rightarrow 8\ CO_2\ (g) + 9\ H_2O\ (g)$

kg (C_8H_{18}) → g (C_8H_{18}) → mol (C_8H_{18}) → mol CO_2 → g CO_2 → kg CO_2 produced

$$\frac{1000\text{ g}}{1\text{ kg}} \quad \frac{1\text{ mol } C_8H_{18}}{114.22\text{ g}} \quad \frac{8\text{ mol } CO_2}{1\text{ mol } C_8H_{18}} \quad \frac{44.01\text{ g}}{1\text{ mol}} \quad \frac{1\text{ kg}}{1000\text{ g}}$$

then kg CO_2 → yr

$$\frac{3 \times 10^{15}\text{ kg CO}_2}{\left(\dfrac{\text{kg CO}_2\text{ produced}}{\text{yr}}\right)}$$

Solution:

$$7 \times 10^{12}\ \cancel{\text{kg}} \times \frac{1000\ \cancel{\text{g}}}{1\ \cancel{\text{kg}}} \times \frac{1\ \cancel{\text{mol C}_8\text{H}_{18}}}{114.22\ \cancel{\text{g}}} \times \frac{8\ \cancel{\text{mol CO}_2}}{1\ \cancel{\text{mol C}_8\text{H}_{18}}} \times \frac{44.01\ \cancel{\text{g CO}_2}}{1\ \cancel{\text{mol CO}_2}} \times \frac{1\text{ kg}}{1000\ \cancel{\text{g}}} = \underline{2}.158 \times 10^{13}\text{ kg CO}_2$$

$$= 2 \times 10^{13}\text{ kg CO}_2 \text{ per year}$$

$$\frac{3 \times 10^{15}\ \cancel{\text{kg CO}_2}}{\left(\dfrac{\underline{2}.158 \times 10^{13}\ \cancel{\text{kg CO}_2\text{ produced}}}{\text{yr}}\right)} = \underline{1}39\text{ yr} = 100\text{ yr}$$

Check: The units (kg and yr) are correct. The magnitude of the answer (10^{13} kg) makes physical sense because the mass of CO_2 is larger than the hydrocarbon mass in a combustion (since O is much heavier than H). The time is consistent with earlier Chapter 5 problems where ~1 % of the atmospheric carbon dioxide is generated each year.

6.94 **Given:** sunlight power density = 1 kW/m^2, solar cell efficiency = 15 %, home usage = 385 kWh/month
Find: m^2 solar cells needed

Conceptual Plan:

power density available → power density generated → kWh/ m^2 · 24 hr → kWh/m^{2}day

$$\frac{15\text{ kW generated}}{100\text{ kW available}} \quad \frac{8\text{ hr power generation}}{24\text{ hr}} \quad \frac{24\text{ hr}}{1\text{ day}}$$

then kWh/ m^{2}day → kWh/ m^{2}month generated then power needed/month → m^2 needed

$$\frac{30\text{ days}}{1\text{ month}} \qquad \div\ \text{kWh/ m}^2\text{ month generated}$$

Solution:

$$\frac{1\ \cancel{\text{kW available}}}{1\text{ m}^2} \times \frac{15\text{ kW generated}}{100\ \cancel{\text{kW available}}} \times \frac{8\text{ hr power generation}}{24\ \cancel{\text{hr}}} \times \frac{24\ \cancel{\text{hr}}}{1\ \cancel{\text{day}}} \times \frac{30\ \cancel{\text{day}}}{1\text{ month}} = \underline{3}6\ \frac{\text{kWh generated}}{\text{m}^2\text{ month}}$$

$$\frac{385\frac{\text{kWh needed}}{\text{month}}}{\left(36\frac{\text{kWh generated}}{\text{m}^2\ \text{month}}\right)} = 1\underline{0}.694\ \text{m}^2 = 10\ \text{m}^2$$

Check: The units (m^2) are correct. The magnitude of the answer (10) makes physical sense because this could fit on the roof of a house.

Cumulative Problems

6.95 **Given:** billiard ball$_A$ = system: $m_A = 0.17$ kg, $v_{A1} = 4.5$ m/s slows to $v_{A2} = 3.8$ m/s and $v_{A3} = 0$; ball$_B$: $m_B = 0.17$ kg, $v_{B1} = 0$ and $v_{B2} = 3.8$ m/s, and $KE = \frac{1}{2}mv^2$ **Find:** w, q, ΔE_{sys}

Conceptual Plan: $m, v \rightarrow KE$ **then** $KE_{A3}, KE_{A1} \rightarrow \Delta E_{sys}$ **and** $KE_{A2}, KE_{A1} \rightarrow q$ **and** $KE_{B2}, KE_{B1} \rightarrow w_B$

$KE = \frac{1}{2}mv^2$ $\qquad \Delta E_{sys} = KE_{A3} - KE_{A1}$ $\qquad q = KE_{A2} - KE_{A1}$ $\qquad w_B = KE_{B2} - KE_{B1}$

$\Delta E_{sys}, q \rightarrow w_A$ **verify that** $w_A = -w_B$ **so that no heat is transferred to ball$_B$**

$\Delta E = q + w$

Solution: $KE = \frac{1}{2}mv^2$ since m is in kg and v is in m/s, KE will be in kg·m^2/s^2, which is joule.

$$KE_{A1} = \frac{1}{2}(0.17\ \text{kg})\left(4.5\frac{\text{m}}{\text{s}}\right)^2 = 1.\underline{7}213\frac{\text{kg}\cdot\text{m}^2}{\text{s}^2} = 1.\underline{7}213\ \text{J},$$

$$KE_{A2} = \frac{1}{2}(0.17\ \text{kg})\left(3.8\frac{\text{m}}{\text{s}}\right)^2 = 1.\underline{2}274\frac{\text{kg}\cdot\text{m}^2}{\text{s}^2} = 1.\underline{2}274\ \text{J},$$

$$KE_{A3} = \frac{1}{2}(0.17\ \text{kg})\left(0\frac{\text{m}}{\text{s}}\right)^2 = 0\frac{\text{kg}\cdot\text{m}^2}{\text{s}^2} = 0\ \text{J},\ KE_{B1} = \frac{1}{2}(0.17\ \text{kg})\left(0\frac{\text{m}}{\text{s}}\right)^2 = 0\frac{\text{kg}\cdot\text{m}^2}{\text{s}^2} = 0\ \text{J and}$$

$$KE_{B2} = \frac{1}{2}(0.17\ \text{kg})\left(3.8\frac{\text{m}}{\text{s}}\right)^2 = 1.\underline{2}274\frac{\text{kg}\cdot\text{m}^2}{\text{s}^2} = 1.\underline{2}274\ \text{J}.$$

$\Delta E_{sys} = KE_{A3} - KE_{A1} = 0\ \text{J} - 1.\underline{7}213\ \text{J} = -1.\underline{7}213\ \text{J} = -1.7\ \text{J}$,
$q = KE_{A2} - KE_{A1} = 1.\underline{2}274\ \text{J} - 1.\underline{7}213\ \text{J} = -0.\underline{4}939\ \text{J} = -0.5\ \text{J}$,
$w_B = KE_{B2} - KE_{B1} = 1.\underline{2}274\ \text{J} - 0\ \text{J} = 1.\underline{2}274\ \text{J}$ and
$w = \Delta E - q = -1.\underline{7}213\ \text{J} - -0.\underline{4}939\ \text{J} = -1.\underline{2}274\ \text{J} = -1.2\ \text{J}$.
Since $w_A = -w_B$ no heat is transferred to ball$_B$.

Check: The units (J) are correct. Since the ball is initially moving and is stopped at the end, it has lost energy (negative ΔE_{sys}). As the ball slows due to friction, it is releasing heat (negative q). The kinetic energy is transferred to a second ball, so it does work (w negative).

6.96 **Given:** 100-W lightbulb in a piston; bulb on for 0.015 hr, $V_i = 0.85$ L, $V_f = 5.88$ L, $P = 1.0$ atm
Find: w, q, ΔE_{sys}

Conceptual Plan: bulb wattage, time $\rightarrow \Delta E_{sys}$**(Wh)** $\rightarrow \Delta E_{sys}$**(Wh)** $\rightarrow \Delta E_{sys}$**(J) and** $V_i, V_f \rightarrow \Delta V$ **then**

$\Delta E = (wattage)(time)$ $\qquad \frac{1\ \text{kW}}{1000\ \text{W}}$ $\qquad \frac{3.60 \times 10^6\ \text{J}}{1\ \text{kWh}}$ $\qquad \Delta V = V_f - V_i$

$P, \Delta V \rightarrow w$ **(L atm)** $\rightarrow w$ **(J) finally** $\Delta E_{sys}, w \rightarrow q$

$w = -P\Delta V$ $\qquad \frac{101.3\ \text{J}}{1\ \text{L atm}}$ $\qquad \Delta E = q + w$

Solution: $\Delta E = (wattage)(time) = (100\text{W})(0.015\ \text{hr}) = 1.5\ \text{Wh} \times \frac{1\ \text{kW}}{1000\ \text{W}} \times \frac{3.60 \times 10^6\ \text{J}}{1\ \text{kWh}} = 5400\ \text{J}$ and
$\Delta V = V_f - V_i = 5.88\ \text{L} - 0.85\ \text{L} = 5.03\ \text{L}$ then
$w = -P\Delta V = -1.0\ \text{atm} \times 5.03\ \text{L} \times \frac{101.3\ \text{J}}{1\ \text{L atm}} = -5\underline{0}9.539\ \text{J} = -5.1 \times 10^2\ \text{J}$ $\qquad \Delta E = q + w$
Rearrange to solve for q. $\qquad q = \Delta E_{sys} - w = +5\underline{4}00\ \text{J} - (-5\underline{0}9.539\ \text{J}) = 5900\ \text{J}$

Check: The units (J) are correct. Electricity is added so energy is added (positive ΔE_{sys}). The piston expands and so does work (negative work). In order for the lightbulb to generate light, it must be heated or it must absorb energy (positive q).

6.97 **Given:** H_2O (l) $\rightarrow$ H_2O (g) $\Delta H^\circ_{rxn} = +44.01$ kJ/mol; $\Delta T_{body} = -0.50$ °C, $m_{body} = 95$ kg, $C_{body} = 4.0$ J/g °C
Find: m_{H_2O}

Conceptual Plan: kg $\rightarrow$ g then m_{body}, ΔT, C_{body} $\rightarrow$ q_{body} $\rightarrow$ q_{rxn} (J) $\rightarrow$ q_{rxn} (kJ) $\rightarrow$ mol H_2O $\rightarrow$ g H_2O

$\frac{1000\text{ g}}{1\text{ kg}}$ $\quad q_{body} = m_{body}C_{body}\Delta T_{body}$ $\quad q_{rxn} = -q_{body}$ $\quad \frac{1\text{ kJ}}{1000\text{ J}}$ $\quad \frac{1\text{ mol}}{44.01\text{ kJ}}$ $\quad \frac{18.01\text{ g}}{1\text{ mol}}$

Solution: $95\text{ kg} \times \frac{1000\text{ g}}{1\text{ kg}} = 95000\text{ g}$ then

$q_{body} = m_{body}C_{body}\Delta T_{body} = 95000\text{ g} \times 4.0 \frac{\text{J}}{\text{g}\cdot{}^\circ\text{C}} \times (-0.50\,{}^\circ\text{C}) = -190000\text{ J}$ then

$q_{rxn} = -q_{body} = 190000\text{ J} \times \frac{1\text{ kJ}}{1000\text{ J}} \times \frac{1\text{ mol}}{44.01\text{ kJ}} \times \frac{18.01\text{ g}}{1\text{ mol}} = 78\text{ g } H_2O$

Check: The units (g) are correct. The magnitude of the answer (78) makes physical sense because a person can sweat this much on a hot day.

6.98 **Given:** LP gas combustion, $\Delta H^\circ_{rxn} = -2044$ kJ; 1.5 L water, $T_{H_2Oi} = 25.0\,{}^\circ$C, $T_{H_2Of} = 100.0\,{}^\circ$C, 15 % efficiency
Find: $m_{LP\ gas}$
Conceptual Plan: L $\rightarrow$ mL $\rightarrow$ g and T_i, T_f $\rightarrow$ ΔT then m_{H_2O}, ΔT_{H_2O}, C_{H_2O} $\rightarrow$ q_{H_2O} $\rightarrow$ q_{rxn}

$\frac{1000\text{ mL}}{1\text{ L}}$ $\quad \frac{1.0\text{ g}}{1.0\text{ mL}}$ $\quad \Delta T = T_f - T_i$ $\quad q_{H_2O} = m_{H_2O}C_{H_2O}\Delta T_{H_2O}$ $\quad q_{rxn} = -q_{H_2O}$

then q_{rxn} needed $\rightarrow$ q_{rxn} generated (J) $\rightarrow$ q_{rxn} (kJ) $\rightarrow$ mol LP gas $\rightarrow$ g LP gas

$\frac{100\text{ J generated}}{15\text{ J needed}}$ $\quad \frac{1\text{ kJ}}{1000\text{ J}}$ $\quad \frac{1\text{ mol}}{-2044\text{ kJ}}$ $\quad \frac{44.09\text{ g}}{1\text{ mol}}$

Solution: $1.5\text{ L} \times \frac{1000\text{ mL}}{1\text{ L}} \times \frac{1.0\text{ g}}{1.0\text{ mL}} = 1500\text{ g}$ and $\Delta T = T_f - T_i = 100.0\,{}^\circ\text{C} - 25.0\,{}^\circ\text{C} = 75.0\,{}^\circ\text{C}$ then

$q_{H_2O} = m_{H_2O}C_{H_2O}\Delta T_{H_2O} = 1500\text{ g} \times 4.184 \frac{\text{J}}{\text{g}\cdot{}^\circ\text{C}} \times (75.0\,{}^\circ\text{C}) = 470700\text{ J}$ then

$q_{rxn} = -q_{H_2O} = -470700\text{ J needed} \times \frac{100\text{ J generated}}{15\text{ J needed}} \times \frac{1\text{ kJ}}{1000\text{ J}} \times \frac{1\text{ mol}}{-2044\text{ kJ}} \times \frac{44.09\text{ g}}{1\text{ mol}} = 68\text{ g LP gas}$

Check: The units (g) are correct. The magnitude of the answer (68) makes physical sense because a tank of LP gas contains many orders of magnitude more than this amount.

6.99 **Given:** H_2O (*s*) $\rightarrow$ H_2O (*l*) ΔH°_f (H_2O (*s*)) = – 291.8 kJ/mol; 355 mL beverage $T_{Bevi} = 25.0\,{}^\circ$C, $T_{Bevf} = 0.0\,{}^\circ$C, $C_{Bev} = 4.184$ J/g °C, $d_{Bev} = 1.0$ g/mL **Find:** ΔH°_{rxn} (ice melting) and m_{ice}
Conceptual Plan: $\Delta H^\circ_{rxn} = \sum n_P \Delta H^\circ_f(products) - \sum n_R \Delta H^\circ_f(reactants)$ mL $\rightarrow$ g and T_i, T_f $\rightarrow$ ΔT then

$\frac{1.0\text{ g}}{1.0\text{ mL}}$ $\quad \Delta T = T_f - T_i$

m_{H_2O}, ΔT_{H_2O}, C_{H_2O} $\rightarrow$ q_{H_2O} $\rightarrow$ q_{rxn} (J) $\rightarrow$ q_{rxn} (kJ) $\rightarrow$ mol ice $\rightarrow$ g ice

$q_{Bev} = m_{Bev}C_{Bev}\Delta T_{Bev}$ $\quad q_{rxn} = -q_{Bev}$ $\quad \frac{1\text{ kJ}}{1000\text{ J}}$ $\quad \frac{1\text{ mol}}{\Delta H^\circ_{rxn}}$ $\quad \frac{18.01\text{ g}}{1\text{ mol}}$

Solution:

Reactant/Product	ΔH°_f(kJ/mol from Appendix IIB)
H_2O (*s*)	– 291.8
H_2O (*l*)	– 285.8

Be sure to pull data for the correct formula and phase.

$$\begin{aligned}\Delta H^\circ_{rxn} &= \sum n_P \Delta H^\circ_f(products) - \sum n_R \Delta H^\circ_f(reactants)\\ &= [1(\Delta H^\circ_f(H_2O\ (l)))] - [1(\Delta H^\circ_f(H_2O\ (s)))]\\ &= [1(-285.8\text{ kJ})] - [1(-291.8\text{ kJ})]\\ &= +6.0\text{ kJ}\end{aligned}$$

$355\text{ mL} \times \frac{1.0\text{ g}}{1.0\text{ mL}} = 355\text{ g}$ and $\Delta T = T_f - T_i = 0.0\,{}^\circ\text{C} - 25.0\,{}^\circ\text{C} = -25.0\,{}^\circ\text{C}$ then

$q_{Bev} = m_{Bev}C_{Bev}\Delta T_{Bev} = 355\text{ g} \times 4.184 \frac{\text{J}}{\text{g}\cdot{}^\circ\text{C}} \times (-25.0\,{}^\circ\text{C}) = -37133\text{ J}$ then

$q_{rxn} = -q_{Bev} = -37133\text{ J} \times \frac{1\text{ kJ}}{1000\text{ J}} \times \frac{1\text{ mol}}{-6.0\text{ kJ}} \times \frac{18.01\text{ g}}{1\text{ mol}} = 110\text{ g ice}$

Check: The units (kJ and g) are correct. The answer is positive, which means that the reaction is endothermic. We expect an endothermic reaction because we know that heat must be added to melt ice. The magnitude of the answer (110 g) makes physical sense because it is much smaller than the weight of the beverage and it would fit in a glass with the beverage.

6.100 **Given:** $CO_2(s) \rightarrow CO_2(g)$ $\Delta H_f^\circ (CO_2(s)) = -427.4$ kJ/mol; 15.0 L water $T_{H_2Oi} = 85$ °C, $T_{H_2Of} = 25$ °C
Find: ΔH_{rxn}° (dry ice sublimation) and m_{dryice}
Conceptual Plan: $\Delta H_{rxn}^\circ = \sum n_P \Delta H_f^\circ(products) - \sum n_R \Delta H_f^\circ(reactants)$ **L → mL → g and T_i, T_f → ΔT then**

$$\frac{1000\text{ mL}}{1\text{ L}} \quad \frac{1.00\text{ g}}{1.00\text{ mL}} \qquad \Delta T = T_f - T_i$$

$m_{H_2O}, \Delta T_{H_2O}, C_{H_2O} \rightarrow q_{H_2O} \rightarrow q_{rxn}$ **(J) →** q_{rxn} **(kJ) → mol ice → g ice**

$$q_{H_2O} = m_{H_2O}C_{H_2O}\Delta T_{H_2O} \quad q_{rxn} = -q_{H_2O} \quad \frac{1\text{ kJ}}{1000\text{ J}} \quad \frac{1\text{ mol}}{\Delta H_{rxn}^\circ} \quad \frac{44.01\text{ g}}{1\text{ mol}}$$

Solution:

Reactant/Product	ΔH_f°(kJ/mol from Appendix IIB)
$CO_2(s)$	− 427.4
$CO_2(g)$	− 393.5

Be sure to pull data for the correct formula and phase.

$$\begin{aligned}\Delta H_{rxn}^\circ &= \sum n_P \Delta H_f^\circ(products) - \sum n_R \Delta H_f^\circ(reactants)\\ &= [1(\Delta H_f^\circ(CO_2(g)))] - [1(\Delta H_f^\circ(CO_2(s)))]\\ &= [1(-393.5\text{ kJ})] - [1(-427.4\text{ kJ})]\\ &= +33.9\text{ kJ}\end{aligned}$$

$$15.0\text{ L} \times \frac{1000\text{ mL}}{1\text{ L}} \times \frac{1.00\text{ g}}{1.00\text{ mL}} = 15\underline{0}00\text{ g and } \Delta T = T_f - T_i = 25\text{ °C} - 85\text{ °C} = -60.\text{ °C then}$$

$$q_{H_2O} = m_{H_2O}C_{H_2O}\Delta T_{H_2O} = 15\underline{0}00\text{ g} \times 4.184\frac{\text{J}}{\text{g}\cdot\text{°C}} \times (-60.\text{ °C}) = -3\underline{7}65600\text{ J then}$$

$$q_{rxn} = -q_{H_2O} = 3\underline{7}65600\text{ J} \times \frac{1\text{ kJ}}{1000\text{ J}} \times \frac{1\text{ mol}}{33.9\text{ kJ}} \times \frac{44.01\text{ g}}{1\text{ mol}} = 4900\text{ g dry ice}$$

Check: The units (kJ and g) are correct. The answer is positive, which means that the reaction is endothermic. We expect an endothermic reaction because we know that heat must be added to sublime dry ice. The magnitude of the answer (4900 g) makes physical sense because the temperature change of the water is fairly large, and the volume of water is large. It is a reasonable amount to put in a cooler.

6.101 **Given:** 25.5 g aluminum, $T_{Ali} = 65.4$ °C, 55.2 g water, $T_{H_2Oi} = 22.2$ °C **Find:** T_f
Conceptual Plan: pull C_s values from table then m, C_s, T_i → T_f

$$\text{Al: } 0.903\frac{\text{J}}{\text{g}\cdot\text{°C}} \text{ H}_2\text{O: } 4.18\frac{\text{J}}{\text{g}\cdot\text{°C}} \qquad q = mC_s(T_f - T_i) \text{ then set } q_{Al} = -q_{H_2O}$$

Solution: $q = mC_s(T_f - T_i)$ substitute in values and set $q_{Al} = -q_{H_2O}$.

$$q_{Al} = m_{Al}C_{Al}(T_f - T_{Ali}) = 25.5\text{ g} \times 0.903\frac{\text{J}}{\text{g}\cdot\text{°C}} \times (T_f - 65.4\text{ °C}) =$$

$$-q_{H_2O} = -m_{H_2O}C_{H_2O}(T_f - T_{H_2Oi}) = -55.2\text{ g} \times 4.18\frac{\text{J}}{\text{g}\cdot\text{°C}} \times (T_f - 22.2\text{ °C})$$

Rearrange to solve for T_f.

$$23.\underline{0}265\frac{\text{J}}{\text{°C}} \times (T_f - 65.4\text{ °C}) = -23\underline{0}.736\frac{\text{J}}{\text{°C}} \times (T_f - 22.2\text{ °C}) \rightarrow$$

$$23.\underline{0}265\frac{\text{J}}{\text{°C}}T_f - 15\underline{0}5.93\text{ J} = -23\underline{0}.736\frac{\text{J}}{\text{°C}}T_f + 51\underline{2}2.34\text{ J} \rightarrow$$

$$-51\underline{2}2.34\text{ J} - 15\underline{0}5.93\text{ J} = -23\underline{0}.736\frac{\text{J}}{\text{°C}}T_f - 23.\underline{0}265\frac{\text{J}}{\text{°C}}T_f \rightarrow 66\underline{2}8.27\text{ J} = 25\underline{3}.7625\frac{\text{J}}{\text{°C}}T_f \rightarrow$$

$$T_f = \frac{66\underline{2}8.27\text{ J}}{25\underline{3}.7625\frac{\text{J}}{\text{°C}}} = 26.1\text{°C}$$

Check: The units (°C) are correct. The magnitude of the answer (26) makes physical sense because the heat transfer is dominated by the water (larger mass and larger specific heat capacity). The final temperature should be closer to the initial temperature of water than of aluminum.

6.102 **Given:** ethanol: 50.0 mL; $d = 0.789$ g/mL, $T_{EtOHi} = 7.0$ °C, water: 50.0 mL; $d = 1.0$ g/mL $T_{H_2Oi} = 28.4$ °C **Find:** T_f
Conceptual Plan: pull C_s values from Table 6.4 mL → g then m, C_s, T_i → T_f

$$\text{EtOH: } 2.42\frac{\text{J}}{\text{g}\cdot\text{°C}} \text{ H}_2\text{O: } 4.18\frac{\text{J}}{\text{g}\cdot\text{°C}} \quad \text{EtOH: }\frac{0.789\text{ g}}{1.0\text{ mL}} \text{ H}_2\text{O: }\frac{1.0\text{ g}}{1.0\text{ mL}} \quad q = mC_s(T_f - T_i) \text{ then set } q_{EtOH} = -q_{H_2O}$$

Solution: $50.0\ \text{mL} \times \frac{0.789\ g}{1.0\ \text{mL}} = 39.4\underline{5}\ g$ EtOH and $50.0\ \text{mL} \times \frac{1.0\ g}{1.0\ \text{mL}} = 50.0\ g\ H_2O$ then

$q = mC_s(T_f - T_i)$ substitute in values and set $q_{EtOH} = -q_{H_2O}$.

$q_{EtOH} = m_{EtOH}C_{EtOH}(T_f - T_{EtOHi}) = 39.4\underline{5}\ g \times 2.42 \frac{J}{g \cdot °C} \times (T_f - 7.0\ °C) =$

Rearrange to solve for T_f.

$-q_{H_2O} = -m_{H_2O}C_{H_2O}(T_f - T_{H_2Oi}) = -50.0\ g \times 4.18 \frac{J}{g \cdot °C} \times (T_f - 28.4\ °C)$

$95.\underline{4}69 \frac{J}{°C} \times (T_f - 7.0\ °C) = -20\underline{9}.0 \frac{J}{°C} \times (T_f - 28.4\ °C) \rightarrow$

$95.\underline{4}69 \frac{J}{°C} T_f - 6\underline{6}8.283\ J = -20\underline{9}.0 \frac{J}{°C} T_f + 59\underline{3}5.6\ J \rightarrow$

$-6\underline{6}8.283\ J - 59\underline{3}5.6\ J = -20\underline{9}.2 \frac{J}{°C} T_f - 95.\underline{4}69 \frac{J}{°C} T_f \rightarrow 66\underline{0}3.883\ J = 30\underline{4}.669 \frac{J}{°C} T_f \rightarrow$

$$T_f = \frac{66\underline{0}3.783\ J}{30\underline{4}.669 \frac{J}{°C}} = 21.7\ °C$$

Check: The units (°C) are correct. The magnitude of the answer (22) makes physical sense because the heat transfer is dominated by the water (larger mass and larger specific heat capacity). The final temperature should be closer to the initial temperature of water than of ethanol.

6.103 **Given:** palmitic acid ($C_{16}H_{32}O_2$) combustion ΔH_f° ($C_{16}H_{32}O_2$ (s)) = – 208 kJ/mol; sucrose ($C_{12}H_{22}O_{11}$) combustion ΔH_f° ($C_{12}H_{22}O_{11}$ (s)) = – 2226.1 kJ/mol **Find:** ΔH°_{rxn} in kJ/mol and Cal/g

Conceptual Plan: write balanced reaction then $\Delta H^\circ_{rxn} = \sum n_P \Delta H_f^\circ(\textit{products}) - \sum n_R \Delta H_f^\circ(\textit{reactants})$ **then kJ/mol → J/mol → Cal/mol → Cal/g**

$\frac{1000\ J}{1\ kJ}$ $\frac{1\ Cal}{4184\ J}$ PA: $\frac{1\ mol}{256.42\ g}$ S: $\frac{1\ mol}{342.30\ g}$

Solution: Combustion is the combination with oxygen to form carbon dioxide and water (*l*):

$C_{16}H_{32}O_2\ (s)\ +\ 23\ O_2\ (g) \rightarrow 16\ CO_2\ (g) + 16\ H_2O\ (l)$

Reactant/Product	ΔH_f°(kJ/mol from Appendix IIB)
$C_{16}H_{32}O_2$ (s)	– 208
O_2 (g)	0.0
CO_2 (g)	– 393.5
H_2O (l)	– 285.8

Be sure to pull data for the correct formula and phase.

$$\begin{aligned}\Delta H^\circ_{rxn} &= \sum n_P \Delta H_f^\circ(\textit{products}) - \sum n_R \Delta H_f^\circ(\textit{reactants}) \\ &= [16(\Delta H_f^\circ(CO_2\ (g))) + 16(\Delta H_f^\circ(H_2O\ (l)))] - [1(\Delta H_f^\circ(C_{16}H_{32}O_2\ (s))) + 23(\Delta H_f^\circ(O_2\ (g)))] \\ &= [16(-393.5\ kJ) + 16(-285.8\ kJ)] - [1(-208\ kJ) + 23(0.0\ kJ)] \\ &= [-10868.8\ kJ] - [-208\ kJ] \\ &= -10{,}66\underline{0}.8\ kJ/mol = -10{,}661\ kJ/mol\end{aligned}$$

$$-10{,}66\underline{0}.8 \frac{kJ}{mol} \times \frac{1000\ J}{1\ kJ} \times \frac{1\ Cal}{4184\ J} \times \frac{1\ mol}{256.42\ g} = -9.9378\ Cal/g$$

$C_{12}H_{22}O_{11}\ (s)\ +\ 12\ O_2\ (g) \rightarrow 12\ CO_2\ (g) + 11\ H_2O\ (l)$

Reactant/Product	ΔH_f°(kJ/mol from Appendix IIB)
$C_{12}H_{22}O_{11}$ (s)	– 2226.1
O_2 (g)	0.0
CO_2 (g)	– 393.5
H_2O (l)	– 285.8

Be sure to pull data for the correct formula and phase.

$$\begin{aligned}\Delta H^\circ_{rxn} &= \sum n_P \Delta H_f^\circ(\textit{products}) - \sum n_R \Delta H_f^\circ(\textit{reactants}) \\ &= [12(\Delta H_f^\circ(CO_2\ (g))) + 11(\Delta H_f^\circ(H_2O\ (l)))] - [1(\Delta H_f^\circ(C_{12}H_{22}O_{11}\ (s))) + 12(\Delta H_f^\circ(O_2\ (g)))] \\ &= [12(-393.5\ kJ) + 11(-285.8\ kJ)] - [1(-2226.1\ kJ) + 12(0.0\ kJ)] \\ &= [-7865.8\ kJ] - [-2226.1\ kJ] \\ &= -5639.7\ kJ/mol\end{aligned}$$

$$-5639.7\frac{\text{kJ}}{\text{mol}} \times \frac{1000\text{ J}}{1\text{ kJ}} \times \frac{1\text{ Cal}}{4184\text{ J}} \times \frac{1\text{ mol}}{342.30\text{ g}} = -3.938\text{ Cal/g}$$

Check: The units (kJ/mol and Cal/g) are correct. The magnitudes of the answers are consistent with the food labels we see every day. Palmitic acid gives more Cal/g than sucrose.

6.104 **Given:** hydrogen, methanol (CH_3OH), and octane combustion **Find:** q released in kJ/kg

Conceptual Plan: write balanced reaction then $\Delta H^\circ_{rxn} = \sum n_P \Delta H^\circ_f(products) - \sum n_R \Delta H^\circ_f(reactants)$ **then kJ/mol → kJ/g → kJ/kg**

H_2: $\frac{1\text{ mol}}{2.016\text{ g}}$ MeOH: $\frac{1\text{ mol}}{32.04\text{ g}}$ O: $\frac{1\text{ mol}}{114.22\text{ g}}$ $\frac{1000\text{ g}}{1\text{ kg}}$

Solution: Combustion is the combination with oxygen to form carbon dioxide and water:

$H_2(g) + \frac{1}{2}O_2(g) \rightarrow H_2O(g)$. This reaction is the heat of formation of gaseous water, so

$\Delta H^\circ_{rxn} = -241.8$ kJ/mol.

$$-241.8\frac{\text{kJ}}{\text{mol}} \times \frac{1\text{ mol}}{2.016\text{ g}} \times \frac{1000\text{ g}}{1\text{ kg}} = -1.199 \times 10^5\text{ kJ/g } H_2 \text{ and}$$

$CH_3OH(l) + 3/2\,O_2(g) \rightarrow CO_2(g) + 2\,H_2O(g)$

Reactant/Product	ΔH°_f(kJ/mol from Appendix IIB)
$CH_3OH(l)$	− 238.6
$O_2(g)$	0.0
$CO_2(g)$	− 393.5
$H_2O(g)$	− 241.8

Be sure to pull data for the correct formula and phase.

$$\begin{aligned}\Delta H^\circ_{rxn} &= \sum n_P \Delta H^\circ_f(products) - \sum n_R \Delta H^\circ_f(reactants)\\ &= [1(\Delta H^\circ_f(CO_2(g))) + 2(\Delta H^\circ_f(H_2O(g)))] - [1(\Delta H^\circ_f(CH_3OH(l))) + 3/2(\Delta H^\circ_f(O_2(g)))]\\ &= [1(-393.5\text{ kJ}) + 2(-241.8\text{ kJ})] - [1(-238.6\text{ kJ}) + 3/2(0.0\text{ kJ})]\\ &= [-877.1\text{ kJ}] - [-238.6\text{ kJ}]\\ &= -638.5\text{ kJ}\end{aligned}$$

$$-638.5\frac{\text{kJ}}{\text{mol}} \times \frac{1\text{ mol}}{32.04\text{ g}} \times \frac{1000\text{ g}}{1\text{ kg}} = -1.993 \times 10^4\text{ kJ/kg } CH_3OH \text{ and}$$

$$-5074.1\frac{\text{kJ}}{\text{mol}} \times \frac{1\text{ mol}}{114.22\text{ g}} \times \frac{1000\text{ g}}{1\text{ kg}} = -4.4424 \times 10^4\text{ kJ/kg } C_8H_{18}$$ This result is from problem 91.

Hydrogen delivers the most energy per weight of fuel. This is not surprising since hydrogen is so light. Octane delivers more energy per gram than methanol.

Check: The units (kJ/kg fuel) are correct. The magnitude of the answers ($10^4 - 10^5$) makes physical sense because there are many moles of fuel in a kg and the heat of reactions are high.

6.105 At constant P $\Delta H_{rxn} = q_P$ and at constant V $\Delta E_{rxn} = q_V = \Delta H_{rxn} - P\Delta V$. $PV = nRT$ at constant P, and a constant number of moles of gas, as we change the T the only variable that can change is V, so $P\Delta V = nR\Delta T$. Substituting into the equation for ΔE_{rxn} we get $\Delta E_{rxn} = \Delta H_{rxn} - nR\Delta T$ or $\Delta H_{rxn} = \Delta E_{rxn} + nR\Delta T$.

6.106 **Given:** $SO_2(g) + 1/2\,O_2(g) \rightarrow SO_3(g)$, $\Delta H_{rxn} = +89.5$ kJ, and $\Delta H_f(SO_3(g)) = -204.2$ kJ

Find: $\Delta H_{rxn}(SO_2(g))$

Conceptual Plan: fill known values into $\Delta H^\circ_{rxn} = \sum n_P \Delta H^\circ_f(products) - \sum n_R \Delta H^\circ_f(reactants)$ **and rearrange to solve for ΔH°_f ($SO_2(g)$)**

Solution:

Reactant/Product	ΔH°_f(kJ/mol)
$O_2(g)$	0.0
$SO_3(g)$	− 204.2

$$\begin{aligned}\Delta H^\circ_{rxn} &= \sum n_P \Delta H^\circ_f(products) - \sum n_R \Delta H^\circ_f(reactants)\\ &= [1(\Delta H^\circ_f(SO_3(g)))] - [1(\Delta H^\circ_f(SO_2(g))) + 1/2(\Delta H^\circ_f(O_2(g)))]\\ &= [1(-204.2\text{ kJ})] - [1(\Delta H^\circ_f(SO_2(g))) + 1/2(0.0\text{ kJ})]\end{aligned}$$

$+89.5\text{ kJ} = [-204.2\text{ kJ}] - [\Delta H^\circ_f(SO_2(g)]$

$\Delta H^\circ_f(SO_2(g)) = -293.7$ kJ

Check: The units (kJ) are correct. The answer is more negative than ΔH_f (SO_3 (*g*)), which makes sense since the reaction is endothermic.

6.107 **Given:** 16 g peanut butter, bomb calorimeter, $T_i = 22.2$ °C, $T_f = 25.4$ °C, $C_{cal} = 120.0$ kJ/°C
Find: calories in peanut butter
Conceptual Plan: $T_i, T_f \rightarrow \Delta T$ **then** $\Delta T, C_{cal} \rightarrow q_{cal} \rightarrow q_{rxn}$ **(kJ)** $\rightarrow q_{rxn}$ **(kJ)** $\rightarrow q_{rxn}$ **(Cal)**

$\Delta T = T_f - T_i$ $\quad q_{cal} = -C_{cal}\Delta T \quad q_{rxn} = -q_{cal} \quad \frac{1000\text{ J}}{1\text{ kJ}} \quad \frac{1\text{ Cal}}{4184\text{ J}}$

then q_{rxn} **(Cal)** $\rightarrow$ **Cal/g**

÷ 16 g peanut butter

Solution: $\Delta T = T_f - T_i = 25.4\text{ °C} - 22.2\text{ °C} = 3.2\text{ °C}$ then $q_{cal} = C_{cal}\Delta T = 120.0\frac{\text{kJ}}{\text{°C}} \times 3.2\text{ °C} = 384\text{ kJ}$

then $q_{rxn} = -q_{cal} = -384\text{ kJ} \times \frac{1000\text{ J}}{1\text{ kJ}} \times \frac{1\text{ Cal}}{4184\text{ J}} = 91.778\text{ Cal}$ then $\frac{91.778\text{ Cal}}{16\text{ g}} = 5.7\text{ Cal/g}$

Check: The units (Cal/g) are correct. The magnitude of the answer (6) makes physical sense because there is a significant percentage of fat and sugar in peanut butter. The answer is in line with the answers in Problem 103.

6.108 **Given:** 2.0 mol H_2 (*g*) + 1.0 mol O_2 (*g*) at 25 °C **Find:** temperature of water
Conceptual Plan: write balanced reaction then $\Delta H^\circ_{rxn} = \sum n_P \Delta H^\circ_f(products) - \sum n_R \Delta H^\circ_f(reactants)$
then kJ/mol $\rightarrow q$**(kJ)** $\rightarrow q$**(J) then 2.0 mol** H_2 **+ 1.0 mol** $O_2 \rightarrow$ **mol** $H_2O \rightarrow$ **g** H_2O **then**

x mol of limiting reagent $\quad \frac{1000\text{ J}}{1\text{ kJ}} \quad \frac{1\text{ mol } H_2O}{1\text{ mol } H_2} \quad \frac{18.01\text{ g}}{1\text{ mol}}$

$q_{rxn} \rightarrow q_{H_2O}$ **then pull** C_s **for** H_2O **(*l*) then** $q, m, C_s, T_i \rightarrow T_f$

$q_{rxn} = -q_{H_2O} \quad 4.18\frac{\text{J}}{\text{g}\cdot\text{°C}} \quad q = mC_s(T_f - T_i)$

Solution: Combustion is the combination with oxygen to form water; choose liquid water because $T = 25$ °C.
$H_2 (g) + \frac{1}{2} O_2 (g) \rightarrow H_2O (l)$. This reaction is the heat of formation of gaseous water, so
$\Delta H^\circ_{rxn} = -285.8$ kJ/mol. The two reactants are in the stoichiometric ratio, so either amount can be used.

$-285.8\frac{\text{kJ}}{1\text{ mol } H_2} \times 2.0\text{ mol } H_2 \times \frac{1000\text{ J}}{1\text{ kJ}} = -571600\text{ J}$ and $q_{H_2O} = -q_{rxn} = 571600\text{ J}$

$2.0\text{ mol } H_2 \times \frac{1\text{ mol } H_2O}{1\text{ mol } H_2} \times \frac{18.01\text{ g}}{1\text{ mol } H_2O} = 36.02\text{ g } H_2O$ then $q = mC_s(T_f - T_i)$. Rearrange to solve for T_f.

$$T_f = \frac{mC_sT_i + q}{mC_s} = \frac{\left(36.02\text{ g} \times 4.18\frac{\text{J}}{\text{g}\cdot\text{°C}} \times 25\text{ °C}\right) + 571600\text{ J}}{36.02\text{ g} \times 4.18\frac{\text{J}}{\text{g}\cdot\text{°C}}} = 3821\text{ °C}.$$ This is much higher than the boiling point of water. The heat needed to raise the water to 100 °C is

$q = mC_s(T_f - T_i) = 36.02\text{ g} \times 4.18\frac{\text{J}}{\text{g}\cdot\text{°C}} \times (100\text{ °C} - 25\text{ °C}) = 11292\text{ J}$ so $571600\text{ J} - 11292\text{ J} = 560308\text{ J}$ is still available. 2.0 moles H_2O utilizes 88,000 J (= 44 kJ/mol) so 472308 J (= 560308 J – 88000 J) is available to heat steam. Note: C_s (steam) = 2.04 J/g·°C.

Using equation from above $$T_f = \frac{mC_sT_i + q}{mC_s} = \frac{\left(36.02\text{ g} \times 2.04\frac{\text{J}}{\text{g}\cdot\text{°C}} \times 100.\text{ °C}\right) + 472308\text{ J}}{36.02\text{ g} \times 2.04\frac{\text{J}}{\text{g}\cdot\text{°C}}} = 6500\text{ °C}$$

Check: The units (°C) are correct. The temperature is extremely high. A large amount of heat is liberated and only a relatively small amount of mass absorbs it.

6.109 **Given:** $V_1 = 20.0$ L at $P_1 = 3.0$ atm; $P_2 = 1.5$ atm let expand at constant T **Find:** $w, q, \Delta E_{sys}$
Conceptual Plan: $V_1, P_1, P_2 \rightarrow V_2$ **then** $V_1, V_2 \rightarrow \Delta V$ **then** $P, \Delta V \rightarrow w$ **(L atm)** $\rightarrow w$ **(J)**

$P_1V_1 = P_2V_2 \quad \Delta V = V_2 - V_1 \quad w = -P\Delta V \quad \frac{101.3\text{ J}}{1\text{ L atm}}$

for an ideal gas $\Delta E_{sys}\ \alpha\ T$**, so since this is a constant temperature process** $\Delta E_{sys} = 0$ **finally** $\Delta E_{sys}, w \rightarrow q$

$\Delta E = q + w$

Solution: $P_1V_1 = P_2V_2$. Rearrange to solve for V_2. $V_2 = V_1 \dfrac{P_1}{P_2} = (20.0\text{ L}) \times \dfrac{3.0\ \cancel{\text{atm}}}{1.5\ \cancel{\text{atm}}} = 40.\text{L}$ and

$\Delta V = V_2 - V_1 = 40.\text{ L} - 20.0\text{ L} = 20.\text{ L}$ then

$w = -P\Delta V = -1.5\ \cancel{\text{atm}} \times 20.\ \cancel{\text{L}} \times \dfrac{101.3\text{ J}}{1\ \cancel{\text{L}}\cdot\cancel{\text{atm}}} = -3\underline{0}39\text{ J} = -3.0 \times 10^3\text{ J} \qquad \Delta E = q + w$

Rearrange to solve for q. $q = \Delta E_{sys} - w = +0\text{ J} - (-3\underline{0}39\text{ J}) = 3.0 \times 10^3\text{ J}$

Check: The units (J) are correct. Since there is no temperature change, we expect no energy change (ΔE_{sys} = 0). The piston expands and so does work (negative work) and so heat is absorbed (positive q).

6.110 **Given:** 10.00 g $P_4\ (s) + O_2\ (g)$ to form $P_4O_{10}(s)$; q released heats 2950 g water from $T_i = 18.0\ °C$ to $T_f = 38.0\ °C$
Find: $\Delta H_f^\circ\ (P_4O_{10}\ (s))$
Conceptual Plan: write balanced reaction then $\Delta H^\circ_{rxn} = \sum n_P \Delta H^\circ_f(products) - \sum n_R \Delta H^\circ_f(reactants)$ **then** $m, C_s, T_i, T_f \rightarrow q_{H_2O} \rightarrow q_{rxn}$ **(J)** $\rightarrow q$**(kJ) then g** $(P_4) \rightarrow$ **mol** (P_4) **finally**

$q = mC_s(T_f - T_i) \quad q_{rxn} = -q_{H_2O} \quad \dfrac{1\text{ kJ}}{1000\text{ J}} \quad \dfrac{123.90\text{ g}}{1\text{ mol}}$

q**(kJ), mol** $(P_4) \rightarrow \Delta H^\circ_f\ (P_4O_{10}\ (s))$

$\Delta H^\circ_f(P_4O_{10}\ (s)) = \dfrac{q}{\text{mol } P_4}$

Solution: $P_4\ (s) + 5\ O_2\ (g) \rightarrow P_4O_{10}\ (s)$. This reaction is the heat of formation of $P_4O_{10}\ (s)$, so

$\Delta H^\circ_{rxn} = \Delta H^\circ_f(P_4O_{10}\ (s))$ then $q = mC_s(T_f - T_i) = 2950\ \cancel{\text{g}} \times 4.18 \dfrac{\text{J}}{\cancel{\text{g}}\cdot\cancel{°\text{C}}} \times (38.0\ \cancel{°\text{C}} - 18.0\ \cancel{°\text{C}}) = 24\underline{6}620\text{ J}$

$q_{rxn} = -q_{H_2O} = -24\underline{6}620\ \cancel{\text{J}} \times \dfrac{1\text{ kJ}}{1000\ \cancel{\text{J}}} = -24\underline{6}.620\text{ kJ}$ then $10.00\ \cancel{\text{g } P_4} \times \dfrac{1\text{ mol } P_4}{123.90\ \cancel{\text{g } P_4}} = 0.08071\underline{0}\text{ mol } P_4$

then $\Delta H^\circ_f(P_4O_{10}\ (s)) = \dfrac{q}{\text{mol } P_4} = \dfrac{-24\underline{6}.620\text{ kJ}}{0.08071\underline{0}\text{ mol}} = -3060\text{ kJ/mol}$

Check: The units (kJ/mol) are correct. The negative sign is consistent with the fact that there was heat released to heat a large amount of water. The magnitude (3000) is not surprising since a small amount of phosphorous heated a lot of water (a high heat capacity material).

6.111 The oxidation of $S\ (g)$ to SO_3 can be written as follows:
$S\ (g) + 3/2\ O_2\ (g) \rightarrow SO_3\ (g) \qquad \Delta H = -204\text{ kJ}$
The oxidation of $SO_2\ (g)$ to SO_3 can be written as follows:
$SO_2\ (g) + 1/2\ O_2\ (g) \rightarrow SO_3\ (g) \qquad \Delta H = +89.5\text{ kJ}$
The enthalpy of formation reaction for $SO_2\ (g)$ under these conditions can be written as follows:
$S\ (g) + O_2\ (g) \rightarrow SO_2\ (g) \qquad \Delta H = ??$
Since the second reaction has 1 mole SO_2 as a reactant and the reaction of interest has 1 mole of SO_2 as a product, we need to reverse the second reaction. When the reaction direction is reversed, ΔH changes sign.
$SO_3\ (g) \rightarrow SO_2\ (g) + 1/2\ O_2\ (g) \qquad \Delta H = -89.5\text{ kJ}$
Hess's Law states the ΔH of the net reaction is the sum of the ΔH of the steps.
The rewritten reactions are as follows:
$S\ (g) + \cancel{3/2}\ O_2\ (g) \rightarrow \cancel{SO_3\ (g)} \qquad \Delta H = -204\text{ kJ}$
$\cancel{SO_3\ (g)} \rightarrow SO_2\ (g) + \cancel{1/2\ O_2\ (g)} \qquad \Delta H = -89.5\text{ kJ}$
$S\ (g) + O_2\ (g) \rightarrow SO_2\ (g) \qquad \Delta H = -294\text{ kJ} = \Delta H_f$
Note that this is not under standard conditions, since S is not a solid.

6.112 The heat of formation of $TiI_3\ (s)$ can be written as follows:
$Ti\ (s) + 3/2\ I_2\ (s) \rightarrow TiI_3\ (s) \qquad \Delta H = -328\text{ kJ}$
The reaction of Ti (s) with $I_2\ (g)$ can be written as follows:
$2\ Ti\ (s) + 3\ I_2\ (g) \rightarrow 2\ TiI_3\ (s) \qquad \Delta H = -839\text{ kJ}$
The sublimation of $I_2\ (s)$ can be written as follows:
$I_2\ (s) \rightarrow I_2\ (g) \qquad \Delta H = ??$
Since the first reaction has 3/2 moles $I_2\ (s)$ as a reactant and the reaction of interest has 1 mole of $I_2\ (s)$ as a reactant, we need to multiply it by 2/3.
$2/3\ Ti\ (s) + I_2\ (s) \rightarrow 2/3\ TiI_3\ (s) \qquad \Delta H = (2/3)(-328\text{ kJ}) = -21\underline{8}.667\text{ kJ}$

Since the second reaction has 3 moles I_2 (*g*) as a reactant and the reaction of interest has 1 mole of I_2 (*g*) as a product, we need to reverse the second reaction and divide it by 3. When the reaction direction is reversed, ΔH changes sign.

$2/3\ TiI_3\ (s) \rightarrow 2/3\ Ti\ (s) + I_2\ (g)$ $\quad \Delta H = (-1/3)(-839\ kJ) = +27\underline{9}.667\ kJ$

Hess's Law states that the ΔH of the net reaction is the sum of the ΔH of the steps.

The rewritten reactions are as follows:

$\cancel{2/3\ Ti\ (s)} + I_2\ (s) \rightarrow \cancel{2/3\ TiI_3\ (s)}$ $\quad \Delta H = (2/3)(-328\ kJ) = -21\underline{8}.667\ kJ$

$\cancel{2/3\ TiI_3\ (s)} \rightarrow \cancel{2/3\ Ti\ (s)} + I_2\ (g)$ $\quad \Delta H = (-1/3)(-839\ kJ) = +27\underline{9}.667\ kJ$

$I_2\ (s) \rightarrow I_2\ (g)$ $\quad \Delta H = +61.0\ kJ = \Delta H_{sub}$

Note that this is endothermic, as expected.

6.113 **Given:** 25.3% methane (CH_4), 38.2% ethane (C_2H_6), and the rest propane (C_3H_8) by volume; $V = 1.55$ L tank, $P = 755$ mmHg, and $T = 298$ K **Find:** heat for combustion

Conceptual Plan: percent composition → mmHg → atm then *P, V, T* → *n* then

Dalton's Law of Partial Pressures; $\frac{1\ atm}{760\ mmHg}$; $PV = nRT$

use data in Problem 91 for methane, and calculate heat of combustion for ethane and propane

$\Delta H^\circ_{rxn}(CH_4) = -802.3$ kJ; $\Delta H^\circ_{rxn}(C_3H_8) = -2217$ kJ write balanced reaction then $\Delta H^\circ_{rxn} = \sum n_P \Delta H^\circ_f(products) - \sum n_R \Delta H^\circ_f(reactants)$

then *n*, ΔH → *q*

Solution: $P_{CH_4} = \frac{25.3\ \cancel{mmHg\ CH_4}}{100\ \cancel{mmHg\ gas}} \times 755\ \cancel{mmHg\ gas} \times \frac{1\ atm\ CH_4}{760\ \cancel{mmHg}} = 0.25\underline{1}3355\ atm\ CH_4,$

$$P_{C_2H_6} = \frac{38.2\ \cancel{mmHg\ C_2H_6}}{100\ \cancel{mmHg\ gas}} \times 755\ \cancel{mmHg\ gas} \times \frac{1\ atm\ C_2H_6}{760\ \cancel{mmHg}} = 0.37\underline{9}48684\ atm\ C_2H_6,$$

$$P_{C_3H_8} = \frac{100 - (25.3 + 38.2)\ \cancel{mmHg\ C_3H_8}}{100\ \cancel{mmHg\ gas}} \times 755\ \cancel{mmHg\ gas} \times \frac{1\ atm\ C_3H_8}{760\ \cancel{mmHg}} = 0.36\underline{2}59868\ atm\ C_3H_8$$

$PV = nRT$ Rearrange to solve for n.

$$n_{CH_4} = \frac{PV}{RT} = \frac{0.25\underline{1}3355\ \cancel{atm\ CH_4} \times 1.55\ \cancel{L}}{0.08206 \frac{\cancel{L} \cdot \cancel{atm}}{mol \cdot \cancel{K}} \times 298\ \cancel{K}} = 0.015\underline{9}3081\ mol\ CH_4,$$

$$n_{C_2H_6} = \frac{PV}{RT} = \frac{0.37\underline{9}48684\ \cancel{atm\ C_2H_6} \times 1.55\ \cancel{L}}{0.08206 \frac{\cancel{L} \cdot \cancel{atm}}{mol \cdot \cancel{K}} \times 298\ \cancel{K}} = 0.024\underline{0}5363\ mol\ C_2H_6$$

$$n_{C_2H_6} = \frac{PV}{RT} = \frac{0.36\underline{2}59868\ \cancel{atm\ C_3H_8} \times 1.55\ \cancel{L}}{0.08206 \frac{\cancel{L} \cdot \cancel{atm}}{mol \cdot \cancel{K}} \times 298\ \cancel{K}} = 0.022\underline{9}83181\ mol\ C_3H_8$$

$C_2H_6\ (g) + 7/2\ O_2\ (g) \rightarrow 2\ CO_2\ (g) + 3\ H_2O\ (g)$

Reactant/Product	ΔH°_f(kJ/mol from Appendix IIB)
$C_2H_6\ (g)$	− 84.68
$O_2\ (g)$	0.0
$CO_2\ (g)$	− 393.5
$H_2O\ (g)$	− 241.8

Be sure to pull data for the correct formula and phase.

$$\begin{aligned}\Delta H^\circ_{rxn} &= \sum n_P \Delta H^\circ_f(products) - \sum n_R \Delta H^\circ_f(reactants)\\ &= [2(\Delta H^\circ_f(CO_2\ (g))) + 3(\Delta H^\circ_f(H_2O\ (g)))] - [1(\Delta H^\circ_f(C_2H_6\ (g))) + 7/2(\Delta H^\circ_f(O_2\ (g)))]\\ &= [2(-393.5\ kJ) + 3(-241.8\ kJ)] - [1(-84.68\ kJ) + 7/2(0.0\ kJ)]\\ &= [-1512.4\ kJ] - [-84.68\ kJ]\\ &= -1427.7\ kJ\end{aligned}$$

$C_3H_8\ (g) + 5\ O_2\ (g) \rightarrow 3\ CO_2\ (g) + 4\ H_2O\ (g)$

Reactant/Product	ΔH°_f(kJ/mol from Appendix IIB)
$C_3H_8\ (g)$	− 103.85
$O_2\ (g)$	0.0
$CO_2\ (g)$	− 393.5
$H_2O\ (g)$	− 241.8

Be sure to pull data for the correct formula and phase.

$$\Delta H^\circ_{rxn} = \sum n_P \Delta H^\circ_f(products) - \sum n_R \Delta H^\circ_f(reactants)$$
$$= [3(\Delta H^\circ_f(CO_2(g))) + 4(\Delta H^\circ_f(H_2O(g)))] - [1(\Delta H^\circ_f(C_3H_8(g))) + 5(\Delta H^\circ_f(O_2(g)))]$$
$$= [3(-393.5 \text{ kJ}) + 4(-241.8 \text{ kJ})] - [1(-103.85 \text{ kJ}) + 5(0.0 \text{ kJ})]$$
$$= [-2147.7 \text{ kJ}] - [-103.85 \text{ kJ}]$$
$$= -2043.9 \text{ kJ}$$

$$0.01593081 \cancel{\text{mol } CH_4} \times \frac{-802.3 \text{ kJ}}{1 \cancel{\text{mol } CH_4}} = -12.781289 \text{ kJ},$$

$$0.02405363 \cancel{\text{mol } C_2H_6} \times \frac{-1427.7 \text{ kJ}}{1 \cancel{\text{mol } C_2H_6}} = -34.34137 \text{ kJ, and}$$

$$0.022983181 \cancel{\text{mol } C_3H_8} \times \frac{-2043.9 \text{ kJ}}{1 \cancel{\text{mol } C_3H_8}} = -46.97417 \text{ kJ}$$

The total heat is $-12.781289 \text{ kJ} - 34.34137 \text{ kJ} - 46.97417 \text{ kJ} = -94.09683 \text{ kJ} = -94.0 \text{ kJ}$

Check: The units (kJ) are correct. The magnitude of the answer (–100 kJ) makes sense because heats of combustion are typically large and negative.

6.114 **Given:** methane (CH_4) + propane (C_3H_8); $V = 11.7$ L, $P = 745$ mmHg, and $T = 298$ K, 769 kJ released
Find: mole fraction of methane in mixture

Conceptual Plan: let x = mole fraction methane → mmHg → atm then $P, V, T \rightarrow n$ then

Dalton's Law of Partial Pressures; $\frac{1 \text{ atm}}{760 \text{ mmHg}}$; $PV = nRT$

use data in Problem 113 for methane and propane, then $q, \Delta H \rightarrow x$

$\Delta H^\circ_{rxn}(CH_4) = -802.3$ kJ; $\Delta H^\circ_{rxn}(C_3H_8) = -2043.9$ kJ

Solution: Let x = mole fraction methane, then

$$P_{CH_4} = \chi_{CH_4} P_{Total} = x \times 745 \cancel{\text{mmHg gas}} \times \frac{1 \text{ atm } CH_4}{760 \cancel{\text{mmHg}}} = x(0.98026315) \text{ atm } CH_4,$$

$$P_{C_3H_8} = = \chi_{C_3H_8} P_{Total} = (1 - x) \times 745 \cancel{\text{mmHg gas}} \times \frac{1 \text{ atm } C_3H_8}{760 \cancel{\text{mmHg}}} = (0.98026315 - 0.98026315x) \text{ atm } C_3H_8$$

$PV = nRT$. Rearrange to solve for n.

$$n_{CH_4} = \frac{PV}{RT} = \frac{x(0.98026315) \cancel{\text{atm } CH_4} \times 11.7 \cancel{\text{L}}}{0.08206 \frac{\cancel{\text{L}} \cdot \cancel{\text{atm}}}{\text{mol} \cdot \cancel{\text{K}}} \times 298 \cancel{\text{K}}} = x(0.46900855) \text{ mol } CH_4,$$

$$n_{C_2H_6} = \frac{PV}{RT} = \frac{(0.98026315 - 0.98026315x) \cancel{\text{atm } C_3H_8} \times 11.7 \cancel{\text{L}}}{0.08206 \frac{\cancel{\text{L}} \cdot \cancel{\text{atm}}}{\text{mol} \cdot \cancel{\text{K}}} \times 298 \cancel{\text{K}}} = (0.46900855 - 0.46900855x) \text{ mol } C_3H_8$$

The total heat is the sum of the combustion of the two components.

$$\Delta H = -769 \text{ kJ} = x(0.46900855) \cancel{\text{mol } CH_4} \times \frac{-802.3 \text{ kJ}}{1 \cancel{\text{mol } CH_4}} + (0.46900855 - 0.46900855x) \cancel{\text{mol } C_3H_8} \times \frac{-2043.9 \text{ kJ}}{1 \cancel{\text{mol } C_3H_8}}$$

Solve for x. $-769 \text{ kJ} = x(-376.2856) \text{ kJ} + (-958.6066 \text{ kJ}) + x(958.6066 \text{ kJ}) \rightarrow$

$$+189.6066 \text{ kJ} = x(+582.3209 \text{ kJ}) \rightarrow x = \frac{+189.6066 \cancel{\text{kJ}}}{+582.3209 \cancel{\text{kJ}}} = 0.325605 = 0.326 \text{ mole fraction methane}$$

Check: The units (none) are correct. The magnitude of the answer (0.3) makes sense because if the mixture were all methane the amount of heat would have been –376 kJ, and if the mixture were all propane the amount of heat would have been –1040 kJ. Since the heat released is closer to the all-propane amount, the mixture must be mostly propane.

6.115 **Given:** 1.55 cm copper cube and 1.62 cm aluminum cube, $T_{Metalsi} = 55.0$ °C, 100.0 mL water, $T_{H_2Oi} = 22.2$ °C
Other: density (water) = 0.998 g/mL **Find:** T_f

Conceptual Plan: pull d values from Table 1.4 then edge length → $V \rightarrow m$ then

Cu: 8.96 g/mL Al: 2.70 g/mL; $V = l^3$ $d = m/V$

pull C_s values from Table 6.4 then $m, C_s, T_i \rightarrow T_f$

Cu: $0.385 \frac{\text{J}}{\text{g} \cdot °\text{C}}$ Al: $0.903 \frac{\text{J}}{\text{g} \cdot °\text{C}}$ H_2O: $4.18 \frac{\text{J}}{\text{g} \cdot °\text{C}}$; $q = mC_s(T_f - T_i)$ then set $q_{Cu} + q_{Al} = -q_{H_2O}$

Solution: $V_{Cu} = l^3 = (1.55 \text{ cm})^3 = 3.723875 \text{ cm}^3 = 3.723875$ mL and
$V_{Al} = l^3 = (1.62 \text{ cm})^3 = 4.251528 \text{ cm}^3 = 4.251528$ mL then $d = m/V$. Rearange to solve for m. $m = d\,V$

$m_{Cu} = 8.96 \frac{g}{\cancel{mL}} \times 3.7\underline{2}3875\ \cancel{mL} = 33.\underline{3}6592\ g\ Cu,$

$m_{Al} = 2.70 \frac{g}{\cancel{mL}} \times 4.2\underline{5}1528\ \cancel{mL} = 11.\underline{4}791256\ g\ Al$ and $m_{H_2O} = 0.998 \frac{g}{\cancel{mL}} \times 100.0\ \cancel{mL} = 99.8\ g\ H_2O$

$q = mC_s(T_f - T_i)$ substitute in values and set $q_{Cu} + q_{Al} = -q_{H_2O}$.

$q_{Cu} + q_{Al} = m_{Cu}C_{Cu}(T_f - T_{Cui}) + m_{Al}C_{Al}(T_f - T_{Ali}) =$

$$33.\underline{3}6592\ \cancel{g} \times 0.385 \frac{J}{\cancel{g} \cdot °C} \times (T_f - 55.0\ °C) + 11.\underline{4}791256\ \cancel{g} \times 0.903 \frac{J}{\cancel{g} \cdot °C} \times (T_f - 55.0\ °C) =$$

$$-q_{H_2O} = -m_{H_2O}C_{H_2O}(T_f - T_{H_2Oi}) = -99.8\ \cancel{g} \times 4.18 \frac{J}{\cancel{g} \cdot °C} \times (T_f - 22.2\ °C)$$

Rearrange to solve for T_f.

$$12.\underline{8}4588 \frac{J}{°C} \times (T_f - 55.0\ °C) + 10.\underline{3}6565 \frac{J}{°C} \times (T_f - 55.0\ °C) = -41\underline{7}.164 \frac{J}{°C} \times (T_f - 22.2\ °C) \rightarrow$$

$$12.\underline{8}4588 \frac{J}{°C} T_f - 70\underline{6}.5234\ J + 10.\underline{3}6565 \frac{J}{°C} T_f - 57\underline{0}.1108\ J = -41\underline{7}.164 \frac{J}{°C} T_f + 92\underline{6}1.041\ J \rightarrow$$

$$12.\underline{8}4588 \frac{J}{°C} T_f + 10.\underline{3}6565 \frac{J}{°C} T_f + 41\underline{7}.164 \frac{J}{°C} T_f = +70\underline{6}.5234\ J + 57\underline{0}.1108\ J + 92\underline{6}1.041\ J \rightarrow$$

$$44\underline{0}.3755 \frac{J}{°C} T_f = 105\underline{3}7.675\ J \rightarrow T_f = \frac{105\underline{3}7.675\ \cancel{J}}{44\underline{0}.3755 \frac{\cancel{J}}{°C}} = 23.\underline{9}2884\ °C = 23.9\ °C$$

Check: The units (°C) are correct. The magnitude of the answer (24) makes physical sense because the heat transfer is dominated by the water (larger mass and larger specific heat capacity). The final temperature should be closer to the initial temperature of water than of copper and aluminum.

6.116 **Given:** mass (gold + silver) = 14.9 g, $T_{Metalsi}$ = 62.0 °C, 15.0 mL water, T_{H_2Oi} = 23.5 °C, T_f = 25.0 °C
Other: density (water) = 0.998 g/mL **Find:** mass of each ring
Conceptual Plan: $V \rightarrow m$ **then pull C_s values from Table 6.4 then**

$d = m/V$

pull C_s values from Table 6.4, then let x = mass of gold ring, and then m, C_s, T_i, T_f $\rightarrow$ m

Au: $0.128 \frac{J}{g \cdot °C}$ Ag: $0.235 \frac{J}{g \cdot °C}$ H_2O: $4.18 \frac{J}{g \cdot °C}$ $q = mC_s(T_f - T_i)$ then set $q_{Au} + q_{Ag} = -q_{H_2O}$

Solution: $d = m/V$. Rearange to solve for m. $m = d\ V$ so $m_{H_2O} = 0.998 \frac{g}{\cancel{mL}} \times 15.0\ \cancel{mL} = 14.\underline{9}7 g\ H_2O$

Let x = mass of the gold ring. $q = mC_s(T_f - T_i)$ substitute in values and set $q_{Au} + q_{Ag} = -q_{H_2O}$.

$q_{Au} + q_{Ag} = m_{Au}C_{Au}(T_f - T_{Aui}) + m_{Ag}C_{Ag}(T_f - T_{Agi}) =$

$$x \times 0.128 \frac{J}{g \cdot \cancel{°C}} \times (25.0\ \cancel{°C} - 62.0\ \cancel{°C}) + (14.9\ g - x) \times 0.235 \frac{J}{g \cdot \cancel{°C}} \times (25.0\ \cancel{°C} - 62.0\ \cancel{°C}) =$$

$$-q_{H_2O} = -m_{H_2O}C_{H_2O}(T_f - T_{H_2Oi}) = -14.\underline{9}7\ \cancel{g} \times 4.18 \frac{J}{\cancel{g} \cdot \cancel{°C}} \times (25.0\ \cancel{°C} - 23.5\ \cancel{°C})$$

Rearrange to solve for mass of Au.

$$x\left(-4.7\underline{3}6 \frac{J}{g}\right) - 12\underline{9}.5555\ J + x\left(-8.6\underline{9}5 \frac{J}{g}\right) = -17\underline{5}.2089\ J \rightarrow$$

$$x\left(-4.7\underline{3}6 \frac{J}{g}\right) + x\left(-8.6\underline{9}5 \frac{J}{g}\right) = +12\underline{9}.5555\ J - 17\underline{5}.2089\ J \rightarrow x\left(-13.4\underline{3}1 \frac{J}{g}\right) = -4\underline{5}.6534\ J \rightarrow$$

$$x = \frac{-4\underline{5}.6534\ \cancel{J}}{-13.4\underline{3}1 \frac{\cancel{J}}{g}} = 3.\underline{3}9911\ g\ Au = 3.40\ g\ Au \text{ and } 14.9\ g - 11.\underline{5}009\ g = 3.\underline{3}9911\ g\ Ag = 11.5\ g\ Ag$$

Check: The units (g) are correct. The magnitude of the answer (12 g and 3 g) makes physical sense because the heat transfer is dominated by the larger specific heat capacity of water. The mass is mostly silver: the temperature change of the metals is large compared to the temperature change of the water, indicating a low metal specific heat.

Challenge Problems

6.117 **Given:** 655 kWh/yr, coal is 3.2 % S, remainder is C, S emitted as SO_2 (*g*) and gets converted to H_2SO_4 when reacting with water **Find:** *m* (H_2SO_4)/yr

Conceptual Plan: write balanced reaction then $\Delta H^\circ_{rxn} = \sum n_P \Delta H^\circ_f(products) - \sum n_R \Delta H^\circ_f(reactants)$ **(since the form of sulfur is not given, assume all heat is from combustion of only carbon) then kWh → J → kJ → mol (C) → g (C) → g (S) → mol (H_2SO_4) → mol (H_2SO_4) → g (H_2SO_4)**

$\frac{3.60 \times 10^6 J}{1 kWh}$ $\frac{1 kJ}{1000 J}$ $\frac{mol C}{\Delta H^\circ_f(CO_2(g))}$ $\frac{12.01 g}{1 mol}$ $\frac{3.2 g S}{(100.0 - 3.2) g C}$ $\frac{1 mol}{32.06 g}$ $\frac{1 mol H_2SO_4}{1 mol S}$ $\frac{98.09 g}{1 mol}$

Solution: C (*s*) + O_2 (*g*) → CO_2 (*g*). This reaction is the heat of formation of CO_2 (*g*), so $\Delta H^\circ_{rxn} = \Delta H^\circ_f(CO_2(g)) = -393.5$ kJ/mol then

$$655 \text{ kWh} \times \frac{3.60 \times 10^6 \text{ J}}{1 \text{ kWh}} \times \frac{1 \text{ kJ}}{1000 \text{ J}} \times \frac{\text{mol C}}{393.5 \text{ kJ}} \times \frac{12.01 \text{ g C}}{1 \text{ mol C}} \times \frac{3.2 \text{ g S}}{(100.0 - 3.2) \text{ g C}} \times \frac{1 \text{ mol S}}{32.07 \text{ g S}} \times \frac{1 \text{ mol } H_2SO_4}{1 \text{ mol S}} \times \frac{98.09 \text{ g } H_2SO_4}{1 \text{ mol } H_2SO_4} = 7.3 \times 10^3 \text{ g } H_2SO_4$$

Check: The units (g) are correct. The magnitude (7300) is reasonable, considering this is just 1 home.

6.118 **Given:** 2.5 x 10^3 kg SUV, v_1 = 0.0 mph, v_2 = 65.0 mph, octane combustion, 30 % efficiency **Find:** *m* (CO_2)

Conceptual Plan: mi/hr → m/hr → m/min → m/s then *m*, *v* → *KE* then

$\frac{1000 m}{0.6214 mi}$ $\frac{1 hr}{60 min}$ $\frac{1 min}{60 sec}$ $KE = \frac{1}{2}mv^2$

***KE*$_1$, *KE*$_2$ → Δ*E* used → Δ*E* generated**

$\Delta E_{sys} = KE_2 - KE_1$ $\frac{100 \text{ J generated}}{30 \text{ J used}}$

use reaction from Problem 91 C_8H_{18} (*l*) + 25/2 O_2 (*g*) → 8 CO_2 (*g*) + 9 H_2O (*g*)

with $\Delta H^\circ_{rxn} = -5074.1$ kJ

Δ*E* generated (J) → kJ → mol (C_8H_{18}) → mol CO_2 → g CO_2

$\frac{1 kJ}{1000 J}$ $\frac{1 mol C_8H_{18}}{5074.1 kJ}$ $\frac{8 mol CO_2}{1 mol C_8H_{18}}$ $\frac{44.01 g}{1 mol}$

Solution: v_1 = 0.0 m/s, $65.0 \frac{\text{mi}}{\text{hr}} \times \frac{1000 \text{ m}}{0.6214 \text{ mi}} \times \frac{1 \text{ hr}}{60 \text{ min}} \times \frac{1 \text{ min}}{60 \text{ sec}} = 29.0563 \frac{\text{m}}{\text{s}}$ then $KE = \frac{1}{2}mv^2$

$$KE_1 = \frac{1}{2}(2.5 \times 10^3 \text{ kg})(0)^2 = 0$$

$$KE_2 = \frac{1}{2}(2.5 \times 10^3 \text{ kg})\left(29.0563\frac{\text{m}}{\text{s}}\right)^2 = 1.05533 \times 10^6 \frac{\text{kg m}^2}{\text{s}^2} = 1.05533 \times 10^6 \text{ J}$$

$$\Delta E_{sys} = KE_2 - KE_1 = 1.05533 \times 10^6 \text{ J} - 0 \text{ J} = 1.05533 \times 10^6 \text{ J used} \times \frac{100 \text{ J generated}}{30 \text{ J used}} =$$

$= 3.51777 \times 10^6$ J generated

$$3.51777 \times 10^6 \text{ J generated} \times \frac{1 \text{ kJ}}{1000 \text{ J}} \times \frac{1 \text{ mol } C_8H_{18}}{5074.1 \text{ kJ}} \times \frac{8 \text{ mol } CO_2}{1 \text{ mol } C_8H_{18}} \times \frac{44.01 \text{ g } CO_2}{1 \text{ mol } CO_2} = 240 \text{ g } CO_2$$

Check: The units (g) are correct. The magnitude (240) is reasonable, considering the vehicle is so heavy and we generate 8 moles of CO_2 for each mole of octane.

6.119 **Given:** methane combustion, 100 % efficiency, Δ*T* = 10.0 °C, house = 30.0 m x 30.0 m x 3.0 m, C_s (air) = 30 J/K·mol, 1.00 mol air = 22.4 L **Find:** *m* (CH_4)

Conceptual Plan: *l*, *w*, *h* → *V*(m^3) → *V*(cm^3) → *V*(L) → mol (air) then *m*, C_s, Δ*T* → q_{air} (J)

$V = lwh$ $\frac{(100 cm)^3}{(1 m)^3}$ $\frac{1 L}{1000 cm^3}$ $\frac{1 mol air}{22.4 L}$ $q = mC_s\Delta T$

then q_{air} (J) → q_{rxn} (J) → *q*(kJ), then write balanced reaction for methane combustion,

$q_{rxn} = -q_{air}$ $\frac{1 kJ}{1000 J}$

then $\Delta H^\circ_{rxn} = \sum n_P \Delta H^\circ_f(products) - \sum n_R \Delta H^\circ_f(reactants)$, **and then *q*(kJ) → mol (CH_4) → g (CH_4)**

ΔH°_{rxn} $\frac{16.04g}{1 mol}$

Solution: $V = l w h = 30.0 \text{ m} \times 30.0 \text{ m} \times 3.0 \text{ m} = 2700 \text{ m}^3$, then

$$2700\ \cancel{m^3} \times \frac{(100\ \cancel{cm})^3}{(1\ \cancel{m})^3} \times \frac{1\ \cancel{L}}{1000\ \cancel{cm^3}} \times \frac{1\ \text{mol air}}{22.4\ \cancel{L}} = 1.20536 \times 10^5\ \text{mol air, and then}$$

$$q = mC_s\Delta T = 1.20536 \times 10^5\ \cancel{mol} \times 30\ \frac{J}{\cancel{mol} \cdot \cancel{°C}} \times 10.0\ \cancel{°C} = 3.6161 \times 10^7\ \cancel{J} \times \frac{1\ kJ}{1000\ \cancel{J}} = 3.6161 \times 10^4\ \text{J needed}$$

$CH_4\ (g) + 2\ O_2\ (g) \rightarrow CO_2\ (g) + 2\ H_2O\ (g)$

Reactant/Product	ΔH_f°(kJ/mol from Appendix IIB)
$CH_4\ (g)$	− 74.6
$O_2\ (g)$	0.0
$CO_2\ (g)$	− 393.5
$H_2O\ (g)$	− 241.8

Be sure to pull data for the correct formula and phase.

$$\begin{aligned}\Delta H_{rxn}^\circ &= \sum n_P \Delta H_f^\circ(products) - \sum n_R \Delta H_f^\circ(reactants)\\ &= [1(\Delta H_f^\circ(CO_2\ (g))) + 2(\Delta H_f^\circ(H_2O\ (g)))] - [1(\Delta H_f^\circ(CH_4\ (g))) + 2(\Delta H_f^\circ(O_2\ (g)))]\\ &= [(-393.5\ kJ) + 2(-241.8\ kJ)] - [1(-74.6\ kJ) + 2(0.0\ kJ)]\\ &= [-877.1\ kJ] - [-74.6\ kJ]\\ &= -802.5\ kJ\end{aligned}$$

$$q_{rxn} = -q_{air} = -3.6161 \times 10^4\ \cancel{kJ} \times \frac{1\ \cancel{mol\ CH_4}}{-802.5\ \cancel{kJ}} \times \frac{16.04\ g\ CH_4}{1\ \cancel{mol\ CH_4}} = 722.8\ g\ CH_4 = 700\ g\ CH_4$$

Check: The units (g) are correct. The magnitude (700) is not surprising since the volume of a house is large.

6.120 **Given:** water: $V = 35$ L, $T_i = 25.0$ °C, $T_f = 100.0$ °C; fuel = C_7H_{16}, 15 % efficiency, $d = 0.78$ g/ml

Find: V (fuel)

Conceptual Plan: write balanced reaction then $\Delta H_{rxn}^\circ = \sum n_P \Delta H_f^\circ(products) - \sum n_R \Delta H_f^\circ(reactants)$ **then L → mL → g then T_i, T_f → ΔT then m, C_s, ΔT → q_{H_2O} (J) → q_{H_2O} (kJ) → q_{rxn} (kJ)**

$\frac{1000\ mL}{1\ L}$ $\frac{1.0\ g}{1.0\ mL}$ $\Delta T = T_f - T_i$ $q_{H_2O} = m_{H_2O}C_{H_2O}\Delta T_{H_2O}$ $\frac{1\ kJ}{1000\ J}$ $q_{rxn} = -q_{H_2O}$

then q_{rxn} generated (J) → q_{rxn} used (kJ) → mol C_7H_{16} → g C_7H_{16} → mL C_7H_{16}

$\frac{100\ J\ generated}{15\ J\ needed}$ $\frac{1\ mol\ C_7H_{16}}{\Delta H_{rxn}^\circ}$ $\frac{100.21\ g}{1\ mol}$ $\frac{1.0\ mL}{0.78\ g}$

Solution: Combustion is the combination with oxygen to form carbon dioxide and water:

$C_7H_{16}\ (l) + 11\ O_2\ (g) \rightarrow 7\ CO_2\ (g) + 8\ H_2O\ (g)$

Reactant/Product	ΔH_f°(kJ/mol from Appendix IIB)
$C_7H_{16}\ (l)$	− 224.4
$O_2\ (g)$	0.0
$CO_2\ (g)$	− 393.5
$H_2O\ (g)$	− 241.8

Be sure to pull data for the correct formula and phase.

$$\begin{aligned}\Delta H_{rxn}^\circ &= \sum n_P \Delta H_f^\circ(products) - \sum n_R \Delta H_f^\circ(reactants)\\ &= [7(\Delta H_f^\circ(CO_2\ (g))) + 8(\Delta H_f^\circ(H_2O\ (g)))] - [1(\Delta H_f^\circ(C_7H_{16}\ (l))) + 11(\Delta H_f^\circ(O_2\ (g)))]\\ &= [7(-393.5\ kJ) + 8(-241.8\ kJ)] - [1(-224.4\ kJ) + 11(0.0\ kJ)]\\ &= [-4688.9\ kJ] - [-224.4\ kJ]\\ &= -4464.5\ kJ\end{aligned}$$

$$35\ \cancel{L} \times \frac{1000\ \cancel{mL}}{1\ \cancel{L}} \times \frac{1.0\ g}{1.0\ \cancel{mL}} = 35000\ g \text{ then } \Delta T = T_f - T_i = 100.0\ °C - 25.0\ °C = 75.0\ °C\text{s then}$$

$$q_{H_2O} = m_{H_2O}C_{H_2O}\Delta T_{H_2O} = 35000\ \cancel{g} \times 4.18\ \frac{J}{\cancel{g} \cdot \cancel{°C}} \times 75.0\ \cancel{°C} = 1.09725 \times 10^7\ \cancel{J} \times \frac{1\ kJ}{1000\ \cancel{J}} = 1.09725 \times 10^4\ kJ$$

$$q_{rxn} = -q_{H_2O} = -1.09725 \times 10^4\ \cancel{kJ} \times \frac{100\ \cancel{kJ\ generated}}{15\ \cancel{kJ\ used}} \times \frac{1\ \cancel{mol\ C_7H_{16}}}{-4467.3\ \cancel{kJ}} \times \frac{100.21\ \cancel{g\ C_7H_{16}}}{1\ \cancel{mol\ C_7H_{16}}} \times \frac{1.0\ mL\ C_7H_{16}}{0.78\ \cancel{g\ C_7H_{16}}} =$$

$$= 2100\ mL\ C_7H_{16} = 2.1\ L\ C_7H_{16}$$

Check: The units (mL) are correct. The magnitude (2 L) is a reasonable volume to have to take on a back-packing trip.

6.121 **Given:** m (ice) = 9.0 g; coffee: T_1 = 90.0 °C, m = 120.0 g, $C_s = C_{H_2O}$, ΔH°_{fus} = 6.0 kJ/mol **Find:** T_f of coffee

Conceptual Plan: $q_{ice} = -q_{coffee}$ **so g (ice) → mol (ice) →** q_{fus}**(kJ) →** q_{fus} **(J) →** q_{coffee} **(J) then**

$\frac{1\text{ mol}}{18.01\text{ g}}$ $\frac{6.0\text{ kJ}}{1\text{ mol}}$ $\frac{1000\text{ J}}{1\text{ kJ}}$ $q_{coffee} = -q_{ice}$

$q, m, C_s \rightarrow \Delta T$ **then** $T_i, \Delta T \rightarrow T_2$ **now we have slightly cooled coffee in contact with 0.0 °C water**

$q = mC_S\Delta T$ $\Delta T = T_2 - T_i$

so $q_{ice} = -q_{coffee}$ **with** $m, C_s, T_i \rightarrow T_f$

$q = mC_s(T_f - T_i)$ then set $q_{ice} = -q_{coffee}$

Solution: $9.0\text{ g} \times \frac{1\text{ mol}}{18.01\text{ g}} \times \frac{6.0\text{ kJ}}{1\text{ mol}} \times \frac{1000\text{ J}}{1\text{ kJ}} = 2.9983 \times 10^3\text{ J}$, $q_{coffee} = -q_{ice} = -2.9983 \times 10^3\text{ J}$

$q = mC_S\Delta T$ Rearrange to solve for ΔT. $\Delta T = \frac{q}{mC_S} = \frac{-2.9983 \times 10^3\text{ J}}{120.0\text{ g} \times 4.18\frac{\text{J}}{\text{g}\cdot°\text{C}}} = -5.9775\text{ °C}$ then

$\Delta T = T_2 - T_i$. Rearrange to solve for T_2. $T_2 = \Delta T + T_i = -5.9775\text{ °C} + 90.0\text{ °C} = 84.0225\text{ °C}$

$q = mC_s(T_f - T_i)$ substitute in values and set $q_{H_2O} = -q_{coffee}$.

$q_{H_2O} = m_{H_2O}C_{H_2O}(T_f - T_{H_2Oi}) = 9.0\text{ g} \times 4.18\frac{\text{J}}{\text{g}\cdot°\text{C}} \times (T_f - 0.0\text{ °C}) =$

$-q_{coffee} = -m_{coffee}C_{coffee}(T_f - T_{coffee2}) = -120.0\text{ g} \times 4.18\frac{\text{J}}{\text{g}\cdot°\text{C}} \times (T_f - 84.0225\text{ °C})$

Rearrange to solve for T_f.

$9.0\text{ g } T_f = -120.0\text{ g }(T_f - 84.0225\text{ °C}) \rightarrow 9.0\text{ g } T_f = -120.0\text{ g } T_f + 10082.7\text{ g} \rightarrow$

$-10082.7\text{ g} = -129.0\frac{\text{g}}{°\text{C}}T_f \rightarrow T_f = \frac{-10082.7\text{ g}}{-129.0\frac{\text{g}}{°\text{C}}} = 78.2\text{ °C}$

Check: The units (°C) are correct. The temperature is closer to the original coffee temperature since the mass of coffee is so much larger than the ice mass.

6.122 **Given:** liquid water at – 10.0 °C, C_s (ice) = 2.04 J/g · °C; ΔH°_{fus} = – 332 J/g (@ 0.0 °C)

Find: ΔH, ΔE, q, and w for freezing at –10.0 °C

Conceptual Plan: Assume exactly 1 g H_2O for all calculations (report answers as J/g) and constant P = 1 atm. Construct the following path: According to Hess's Law $\Delta H_1 + \Delta H_2 + \Delta H_3 = \Delta H_4$ $= \Delta H^\circ_{fus}$ @ –10.0 °C

	step 2		
Liquid @ 0.0 °C	**→**	**solid @ 0.0 °C**	
↑ step 1		**↓ step 3**	**at constant P, $\Delta H = q$**
Liquid @ –10.0 °C	**→**	**solid @ –10.0 °C**	**For steps 1 and 3 $q = mC_s\Delta T$**
	step 4		

Look up the density of liquid and solid water at 0.0 °C. (Assume the density of each phase does not change significantly at – 10.0 °C.)

d_L = 0.9998 g/mL and d_S = 0.917 g/mL

g → mL → L then V_L, V_S → ΔV then P, ΔV → w (L atm) → w (J) then q, w → ΔE

L: $\frac{1\text{ mL}}{0.9998\text{ g}}$ S: $\frac{1\text{ mL}}{0.917\text{ g}}$ $\frac{1\text{ L}}{1000\text{ mL}}$ $\Delta V = V_S - V_L$ $w = -P\Delta V$ $\frac{101.3\text{ J}}{1\text{ L atm}}$ $\Delta E = q + w$

Solution: $\Delta H_1 = q_1 = mC_S\Delta T = 1\text{ g} \times 4.18\frac{\text{J}}{\text{g}\cdot°\text{C}} \times (0.00\text{ °C} - (-10.0\text{ °C})) = +41.8\text{ J}$,

$\Delta H_2 = q_2 = m\Delta H = 1\text{ g} \times -332\frac{\text{J}}{\text{g}} = -332\text{ J}$,

$\Delta H_3 = q_3 = mC_S\Delta T = 1\text{ g} \times 2.04\frac{\text{J}}{\text{g}\cdot°\text{C}} \times (-10.00\text{ °C} - 0.0\text{ °C}) = -20.4\text{ J}$

so $\Delta H_4 = q_4 = \Delta H_1 + \Delta H_2 + \Delta H_3 = +41.8\text{ J} - 332\text{ J} - 20.4\text{ J} = -310.6\text{ J} = -311\text{ J/g}$.

$V_L = 1\text{ g} \times \frac{1\text{ mL}}{0.9998\text{ g}} \times \frac{1\text{ L}}{1000\text{ mL}} = 0.00100020004\text{ L}$ and $V_S = 1\text{ g} \times \frac{1\text{ mL}}{0.917\text{ g}} \times \frac{1\text{ L}}{1000\text{ mL}} = 0.0010905\text{ L}$

then $\Delta V = V_S - V_L = 0.0010905\text{ L} - 0.00100020004\text{ L} = 9.02999 \times 10^{-5}\text{ L}$

then, $w = -P\Delta V = -1\ \text{atm} \times 9.02999 \times 10^{-5}\ \text{L} \times \frac{101.3\ \text{J}}{1\ \text{L atm}} = -0.009147\ \text{J} = -0.009\ \text{J/g}$

and $\Delta E = q + w = -310.6\ \text{J} - 0.009147\ \text{J} = -311\ \text{J/g}$

Check: The units (J/g) are correct. We expect freezing to release less energy at – 10 °C because we are below the normal freezing point. The work is negligible since the volume change is so small.

6.123 $KE = \frac{1}{2}mv^2$, for an ideal gas $v = u_{rms} = \sqrt{\frac{3RT}{\mathcal{M}}}$ and so $KE_{avg} = \frac{1}{2}N_A m u_{rms}^2 = \frac{3}{2}RT$ then

$\Delta E_{sys} = KE_2 - KE_1 = \frac{3}{2}RT_2 - \frac{3}{2}RT_1 = \frac{3}{2}R\Delta T$. At constant V $\Delta E_{sys} = C_V\Delta T$ so $C_V = \frac{3}{2}R$.

At constant P, $\Delta E_{sys} = q + w = q_P - P\Delta V = \Delta H - P\Delta V$, but since $PV = nRT$, for one mole of an ideal gas at constant P $P\Delta V = R\Delta T$, so $\Delta E_{sys} = q + w = q_P - P\Delta V = \Delta H - P\Delta V = \Delta H - R\Delta T$ then

$\frac{3}{2}R\Delta T = \Delta H - R\Delta T$ or $\Delta H = \frac{5}{2}R\Delta T = C_P\Delta T$ so $C_P = \frac{5}{2}R$.

6.124 **Given:** fixed amount of an ideal gas; step 1: V_1 = 12.0 L to V_2 = 24.0 L at constant P = 1.0 atm; step 2: gas cooled at constant V = 24.0 L to original T; step 3: V_1 = 24.0 L to V_2 = 12.0 L **Find:** q for entire process

Solution: For the expansion: $w_1 = -(24.0\ \text{L} - 12.0\ \text{L})(1.0\ \text{atm}) = -12.0\ \text{L atm}$; for the constant V step: $w_2 = 0$ since there is no PV work at constant volume; for the contraction: $w_3 = -nRT \ln(V_2/V_1) = -PV \ln(V_2/V_1) = -(1.0\ \text{atm})(12.0\ \text{L}) \ln(12.0\ \text{L}/24.0\ \text{L}) = 8.3\ \text{L} \cdot \text{atm}$, then $w_{total} = w_1 + w_2 + w_3 = -12.0\ \text{L atm} + 0 + 8.3\ \text{L atm}$

$w_{total} = -3.7\ \text{L} \cdot \text{atm} \times \frac{101\ \text{J}}{\text{L} \cdot \text{atm}} = -370\ \text{J}$. Since the system ends where it started $\Delta E = 0$ and, therefore, $q = -w = 370\ \text{J}$.

Check: The units (J) are correct. The total energy change over the entire cycle is 0 since we end where we started, but this does not mean that q has to be 0.

6.125 $q = \Delta H = 454\ \text{g} \times \frac{1\ \text{mol}}{18.02\ \text{g}} \times \frac{40.7\ \text{kJ}}{1\ \text{mol}} = 1025.405\ \text{kJ} = 1030\ \text{kJ}$ and $w = -P\Delta V$. Assume that P = 1 atm (exactly) and $\Delta V = V_G - V_L$, where $V_L = 454\ \text{g} \times \frac{1\ \text{mL}}{0.9998\ \text{g}} \times \frac{1\ \text{L}}{1000\ \text{mL}} = 0.4540908\ \text{L}$ and $PV = nRT$.

Rearrange to solve for V_G. $V_G = \frac{nRT}{P} = \frac{454\ \text{g} \times \frac{1\ \text{mol}}{18.02\ \text{g}} \times 0.08206 \frac{\text{L} \cdot \text{atm}}{\text{mol} \cdot \text{K}} \times 373\ \text{K}}{1\ \text{atm}} = 771.1545\ \text{L}$

$\Delta V = V_G - V_L = 771.1545\ \text{L} - 0.4540908\ \text{L} = 770.7004\ \text{L}$ and so

$w = -P\Delta V = -1.0\ \text{atm} \times 770.7004\ \text{L} \times \frac{101.3\ \text{J}}{1\ \text{L atm}} = -78071.9539\ \text{J} = -7.81 \times 10^4\ \text{J} = -78.1\ \text{kJ}$.

Finally $\Delta E = q + w = 1025.405\ \text{kJ} - 78.0719539\ \text{kJ} = 947.333\ \text{kJ} = 950\ \text{kJ}$.

6.126 $q = q_1 + q_2 + q_3 = \Delta H$, where

$q_1 = nC\Delta T = 1.0\ \text{mol} \times 75.3 \frac{\text{J}}{\text{mol} \cdot {}^\circ\text{C}} \times (100\ {}^\circ\text{C} - 80\ {}^\circ\text{C})) = +1506\ \text{J}$,

$q_2 = n\Delta H = 1.0\ \text{mol} \times 40.7 \times 10^3 \frac{\text{J}}{\text{mol}} = 4.07 \times 10^4\ \text{J}$ and

$q_3 = nC\Delta T = 1.0\ \text{mol} \times 25.0 \frac{\text{J}}{\text{mol} \cdot {}^\circ\text{C}} \times (110\ {}^\circ\text{C} - 100\ {}^\circ\text{C})) = +250\ \text{J}$, so

$q = q_1 + q_2 + q_3 = \Delta H = +1506\ \text{J} + 4.07 \times 10^4\ \text{J} + 250\ \text{J} = 42456\ \text{J} = 42500\ \text{J} = 42.5\ \text{kJ}$

and $w = -P\Delta V$. Assume that P = 1 atm (exactly) and $\Delta V = V_G - V_L$ where

$V_L = 1.0\ \text{mol} \times \frac{18.02\ \text{g}}{1\ \text{mol}} \times \frac{1\ \text{mL}}{0.9998\ \text{g}} \times \frac{1\ \text{L}}{1000\ \text{mL}} = 0.01802\ \text{L}$ and $PV = nRT$. Rearrange to solve for V_G.

$V_G = \frac{nRT}{P} = \frac{1.0\ \text{mol} \times 0.08206 \frac{\text{L} \cdot \text{atm}}{\text{mol} \cdot \text{K}} \times (110 + 273)\ \text{K}}{1\ \text{atm}} = 31.4290\ \text{L}$ and so

$\Delta V = V_G - V_L = 31.4290\text{ L} - 0.01802\text{ L} = 31.410976\text{ L}$ and

$w = -P\Delta V = -1.0\text{ atm} \times 31.410976\text{ L} \times \frac{101.3\text{ J}}{1\text{ L}\cdot\text{atm}} = -3181.932\text{ J} = -3200\text{ J} = -3.2\text{ kJ}.$

Finally $\Delta E = q + w = 5826\text{ J} - 3181.932\text{ J} = 2644.068\text{ J} = 2600\text{ J} = 2.6\text{ kJ}.$

6.127 $C_8H_{18}\,(l) + 25/2\,O_2\,(g) \rightarrow 8\,CO_2\,(g) + 9\,H_2O\,(l)$; $q = \Delta H = -1303\text{ kJ/mol}$, and $w = -P\Delta V$. Assume that $P = 1$ atm (exactly) and $\Delta V = \Delta V_G$ since the gas volumes are so much larger than the liquid volumes. The change in the number of moles of gas $\Delta n_G = 8\text{ mol} - \frac{25}{2}\text{mol} = -4.5\text{ mol}$ and $P\Delta V = \Delta nRT$. Rearrange to solve for ΔV_G. $\Delta V_G = \frac{\Delta nRT}{P} = \frac{-4.5\text{ mol} \times 0.08206\frac{\text{L}\cdot\text{atm}}{\text{mol}\cdot\text{K}} \times 298\text{ K}}{1\text{ atm}} = -110.0425\text{ L}$ and so

$w = -P\Delta V = -1.0\text{ atm} \times (-110.0425\text{ L}) \times \frac{101.3\text{ J}}{1\text{ L}\cdot\text{atm}} = +11147.30\text{ J} = +11000\text{ J} = +11\text{ kJ}.$

Finally $\Delta E = q + w = -1303\text{ kJ} + 11.14730\text{ kJ} = -1291.8527\text{ kJ} = -1292\text{ kJ}.$

6.128 $C_2H_6O\,(l) + 3\,O_2\,(g) \rightarrow 2\,CO_2\,(g) + 3\,H_2O\,(l)$;

$q_{Cal} = C\Delta T = 34.65\frac{\text{kJ}}{\text{K}} \times (295.84\text{ K} - 294.33\text{ K}) = 52.3215\text{ kJ} = -q_{rxn} = -\Delta E_{rxn}$ and

$n = 1.765\text{ g} \times \frac{1\text{ mol}}{46.07\text{ g}} = 0.038312929\text{ mol}.$

There is no work, since $w = -P\Delta V$ and there is no volume change in a bomb calorimeter. On a per mole basis, $q_{rxn} = \Delta E_{rxn} = \frac{-52.3215\text{ kJ}}{0.038312929\text{ mol}} = -1365.6356\text{ kJ/mol} = -1370\text{ kJ/mol}$. Since this is not a constant pressure problem, $\Delta E_{rxn} \neq \Delta H_{rxn}$. In fact, $\Delta H_{rxn} = \Delta E_{rxn} + \Delta nRT$. In this case the change in the number of moles of gas $\Delta n_G = 2\text{ mol} - 3\text{ mol} = -1\text{ mol}$ and so

$$\Delta H_{rxn} = \Delta E_{rxn} + \Delta nRT = -1365.6356\text{ kJ/mol} + \left(-1\text{ mol} \times 0.08206\frac{\text{L}\cdot\text{atm}}{\text{mol}\cdot\text{K}} \times 295\text{ K} \times \frac{101.3\text{ J}}{1\text{ L}\cdot\text{atm}} \times \frac{1\text{ kJ}}{1000\text{ J}}\right) =$$
$$-1368.0878\text{ kJ/mol} = -1370\text{ kJ/mol}.$$

This answer is in the same ballpark as the answer in Problem 88, which had gaseous water as a product.

Conceptual Problems

6.129 (d) Only one answer is possible. $\Delta E_{sys} = -\Delta E_{surr}$.

6.130 (a) False. An isothermal process has $\Delta E_{sys} = 0$.

(b) False. $w < 0$ for expansions.

(c) True. If $\Delta E_{sys} = 0$ and $\Delta E_{sys} = q + w$ and $w < 0$, then $q > 0$.

(d) False. An isothermal process has $\Delta E_{sys} = 0$.

6.131 (a) At constant P, $\Delta E_{sys} = q + w = q_P + w = \Delta H + w$ so $\Delta E_{sys} - w = \Delta H = q$.

6.132 Refrigerator A contains only air,which will cool quickly, but will not stabilize the temperature. Refrigerator B contains containers of water, which require a great deal of energy to cool on day 1, but which will remain stable at a cold temperature on day 2.

6.133 The aluminum cylinder will be cooler after 1 hour because it has a lower heat capacity than water (less heat needs to be pulled out for every °C temperature change).

6.134 Since $q = mC_S\Delta T$, $m_A = 2\ m_B$, $C_B = 4\ C_A$, $q_A = -\ q_B$ we can substitute into the equation to get $q_A = m_AC_A\Delta T_A = -q_B = -\ m_BC_B\Delta T_B \rightarrow (2\ m_B)C_A\Delta T_A = -m_B(4\ C_A)\Delta T_B$

$\rightarrow \Delta T_A = \dfrac{-\cancel{m_B}(4\ \cancel{C_A})}{(2\ \cancel{m_B})\cancel{C_A}}\Delta T_B = \dfrac{-4}{2}\Delta T_B = -2\Delta T_B$ or the temperature change for substance A is twice the magnitude of the temperature change for substance B.

6.135 **Given:** 2418 J heat produced; 5 J work done on surroundings at constant P **Find:** ΔE, ΔH, q, and w
Conceptual Plan: interpret language to determine the sign of the two terms then $q, w \rightarrow \Delta E_{sys}$

$\Delta E = q + w$

Solution: Since heat is released from the system to the surroundings, $q = -\ 2418$ J since the system is doing work on the surroundings, $w = -\ 5$ kJ. At constant P, $\Delta H = q = -\ 2.418$ kJ; $\Delta E = q + w = -\ 2418\ \text{J} - 5\ \text{J} = -\ 2423\ \text{J} = -\ 2\ \text{kJ}$.
Check: The units (kJ) are correct. The magnitude of the answer (–2) makes physical sense because both terms are negative and the amount of work done is negligibly small.

6.136 The internal energy of a chemical system is the sum of its kinetic energy and its potential energy. It is this potential energy that is the energy source in an exothermic chemical reaction. Under normal circumstances, chemical potential energy (or simply chemical energy) arises primarily from the electrostatic forces between the protons and electrons that compose the atoms and molecules within the system. In an exothermic reaction, some bonds break and new ones form, and the protons and electrons go from an arrangement of higher potential energy to one of lower potential energy. As they rearrange, their potential energy is converted into kinetic energy. Heat is emitted in the reaction and so it feels hot to the touch.

6.137 (b) If ΔV is positive then $w = -\ P\,\Delta V < 0$. Since $\Delta E_{sys} = q + w = q_P + w = \Delta H + w$ if w is negative then $\Delta H > \Delta E_{sys}$.

7 The Quantum-Mechanical Model of the Atom

Review Questions

7.1 When a particle is absolutely small it means that you cannot observe it without disturbing it. When you observe the particle, it behaves differently than when you do not observe it. Electrons fit this description.

7.2 You can measure the position of a baseball by observing the light that strikes the ball, bounces off it, and enters your eye. The baseball is so large in comparison to the disturbance caused by the light that it is virtually unaffected by your observation. By contrast, if you attempt to measure the position of an electron using light, the light itself disturbs the electron. The interaction of the light with the electron changes its position.

7.3 The quantum-mechanical model of the atom is important because it explains how electrons exist in atoms and how those electrons determine the chemical and physical properties of elements.

7.4 Light is electromagnetic radiation, a type of energy embodied in oscillating electric and magnetic fields. Light in a vacuum travels at 3.00×10^8 m/s.

7.5 The wavelength (λ) of the wave is the distance in space between adjacent crests and is measured in units of distance. The amplitude of the wave is the vertical height of a crest. The more closely spaced the waves, that is, the shorter the wavelength, the more energy there is. The amplitude of the electric and magnetic field waves in light determine the intensity or brightness of the light. The higher the amplitude, the more energy the wave has.

7.6 The frequency, (ν), is the number of cycles (or wave crests) that pass through a stationary point in a given period of time. The units of frequency are cycles per second. The frequency is inversely proportional to the wavelength (λ). Frequency and wavelength are related by the equation $\nu = \frac{c}{\lambda}$.

7.7 For visible light, wavelength determines the color. Red light has a wavelength of 750 nm, the longest wavelength of visible light, and blue has a wavelength of 500 nm.

7.8 The presence of a variety of wavelengths in white light is responsible for the way we perceive colors in objects. When a substance absorbs some colors while reflecting others, it appears colored. Grass appears green because it reflects primarily the wavelength associated with green light and absorbs the others.

7.9 (a) Gamma rays(γ) – the wavelength range is 10^{-11} to 10^{-15} m. Gamma rays are produced by the sun, other stars, and certain unstable atomic nuclei on Earth. Human exposure to gamma rays is dangerous because the high energy of gamma rays can damage biological molecules.

(b) X-rays – the wavelength range is 10^{-8} to 10^{-11} m. X-rays are used in medicine. X-rays pass through many substances that block visible light and are therefore used to image bones and internal organs. X-rays are sufficiently energetic to damage biological molecules so, while several yearly exposures to X-rays are harmless, excessive exposure increases cancer risk.

(c) Ultraviolet radiation (UV) – the wavelength range is 0.4 x 10^{-6} to 10^{-8} m. Ultraviolet radiation is most familiar as the component of sunlight that produces a sunburn or suntan. While not as energetic as gamma rays or X-rays, ultraviolet light still carries enough energy to damage biological molecules. Excessive exposure to ultraviolet light increases the risk of skin cancer and cataracts and causes premature wrinkling of the skin.

(d) Visible light – the wavelength range is 0.75 x 10^{-6} to 0.4 x 10^{-6} m (750 nm to 400 nm). Visible light, as long as the intensity is not too high, does not carry enough energy to damage biological molecules. It does, however, cause certain molecules in our eyes to change their shape, sending a signal to brains that results in vision.

(e) Infrared radiation (IR) – the wavelength range is 0.75 x 10^{-6} to 10^{-3} m. The heat you feel when you place your hand near a hot object is infrared radiation. All warm objects, including human bodies, emit infrared light. Although infrared light is invisible to our eyes, infrared sensors can detect it and are often used in night vision technology to "see" in the dark.

(f) Microwave radiation – the wavelength range is 10^{-3} to 10^{-1} m. Microwave radiation is used in radar and in microwave ovens. Microwave radiation is efficiently absorbed by water and can therefore heat substances that contain water.

(g) Radio waves – the wavelength range is 10^{-1} to 10^{5} m. Radio waves are used to transmit the signals responsible for AM and FM radio, cellular telephones, television, and other forms of communication.

7.10 Waves interact with each other in a characteristic way called interference: They can cancel each other out or build each other up, depending on their alignment upon interaction. Constructive interference occurs if waves of equal amplitude from two sources are in phase (they align with overlapping crests) and a wave with twice the amplitude results. Destructive interference occurs if the waves are completely out of phase—they align so that the crest from one source overlaps the trough form the other source—and the waves cancel each other.

7.11 Diffraction occurs when a wave encounters an obstacle or a slit that is comparable in size to its wavelength. The wave bends around the slit. The diffraction of light through two slits separated by a distance comparable to the wavelength of the light results in an interference pattern. Each slit acts as a new wave source, and the two new waves interfere with each other. This results in a pattern of bright and dark lines.

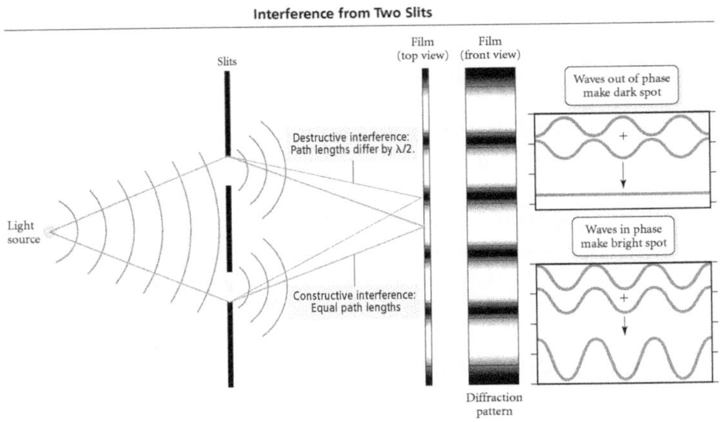

7.12 The photoelectric effect was the observation that many metals emit electrons when light shines on them. Classical electromagnetic theory attributed this effect to the transfer of energy from the light to an electron in the metal, dislodging the electron. In this description, changing either the wavelength (color) or the amplitude (intensity) of the light should affect the emission of electrons. So, the rate at which electrons were emitted from a metal due to the photoelectric effect could be increased by using either light of shorter wavelength or light of higher intensity. With dim light there should be a lag time between the initial shining of the light and the emission of an electron. This time would be needed for the transfer of sufficient energy to the electron to dislodge. However, experiments showed that the light used to dislodge electrons had a threshold frequency below which no electrons were emitted from the metal, no matter how long the light shone on the metal. Low-frequency light would not eject electrons from a metal regardless of intensity or duration. But high-frequency light would eject electrons even at low intensity without any lag time.

7.13 Because of the results of the experiments with the photoelectric effect, Einstein proposed that light energy must come in packets. The amount of energy in a light packet depends on its frequency (wavelength). The emission of electrons depends on whether or not a single photon has sufficient energy to dislodge a single electron.

7.14 A photon is a packet of light. The energy of the photon can be expressed in terms of wavelength as $E = \frac{hc}{\lambda}$ or in terms of frequency as $E = h\nu$.

7.15 An emission spectrum occurs when an atom absorbs energy and re-emits that energy as light. The light emitted contains distinct wavelengths for each element. The emission spectrum of a particular element is always the same and can be used to identify the element. A white light spectrum is continuous, meaning that there are no sudden interruptions in the intensity of the light as a function of wavelengths. It consists of all wavelengths. Emission spectra are not continuous. They consist of bright lines at specific wavelengths, with complete darkness in between.

7.16 In the Bohr model electrons travel around the nucleus in circular orbits. Bohr's orbits could exist only at specific, fixed distances form the nucleus. The energy of each orbit was also fixed, or quantized. Bohr called these orbits stationary states and suggested that, although they obeyed the laws of classical mechanics, they also possessed "a peculiar, mechanically unexplainable, stability." Bohr further proposed that, in contradiction to classical electromagnetic theory, no radiation was emitted by an electron orbiting the nucleus in a stationary state. It was only when an electron jumped, or made a transition, from one stationary state to another that radiation was emitted or absorbed. The emission spectrum of an atom consisted of discrete lines because the stationary states existed only at specific, fixed energies. The energy of the photon created when an electron made a transition from one stationary state to another was simply the energy difference between the two stationary states.

7.17 Electron diffraction occurs when an electron beam is aimed at two closely spaced slits, and a series of detectors is arranged to detect the electrons after they pass through the slits. An interference pattern similar to that observed for light is recorded behind the slits. Electron diffraction is evidence of the wave nature of electrons.

7.18 The de Broglie wavelength is the wavelength associated with an electron traveling through space. It is related to its kinetic energy. The wavelength, λ, associated with an electron of mass, m, moving at velocity, v, is given by the de Broglie relation: $\lambda = \frac{h}{mv}$.

7.19 Complementary properties are those that exclude one another. The more you know about one, the less you know about the other. Which of two complementary properties you observe depends on the experiment you perform. In electron diffraction, when you try to observe which hole the electron goes through (particle nature) you lose the interference pattern (wave nature). When you try to observe the interference pattern, you cannot determine which hole the electron goes through.

7.20 Heisenberg's uncertainty principle states that the product of Δx and $m\Delta v$ must be greater than or equal to a finite number. In other words, the more accurately you know the position of an electron (the smaller Δx) the less accurately you can know its velocity (the bigger Δv) and vice versa. The complementarity of the wave nature and particle nature of the electron results in the complementarity of velocity and position. Heisenberg solved the contradiction of an object as both a particle and a wave by introducing complementarity—an electron is observed as either a particle or a wave, but never both at once.

7.21 A trajectory is a path that is determined by the particle's velocity (the speed and direction of travel), its position, and the forces acting on it. Both position and velocity are required to predict a trajectory.

7.22 Because the uncertainty principle says that you cannot know both the position and velocity of the electron simultaneously, you cannot predict the trajectory.

7.23 Deterministic means that the present determines the future. That means that under the identical condition, identical results will occur.

7.24 The indeterminate behavior of an electron means that under identical conditions, the electron does not have the same trajectory and does not "land" in the same spot each time.

7.25 A probability distribution map is a statistical map that shows where an electron is likely to be found under a given set of conditions.

7.26 Using the Schrödinger equation we describe the probability distribution maps for electron states. In these the electron has a well-defined energy, but not a well-defined position. In other words, for each state, we can specify the energy of the electron precisely, but not its location at a given instant. The electron's position is described in terms of an orbital.

7.27 An orbital is a probability distribution map showing where the electron is likely to be found.

7.28 The mathematical derivation of energies and orbitals for electrons in atoms comes from solving the Schrödinger equation. The general form of the Schrödinger equation is $\mathcal{H}\Psi = E\Psi$. The symbol $\mathcal{H}$ stands for the Hamiltonian operator, a set of mathematical operations that represent the total energy (kinetic and potential) of the electron within the atom. The symbol E is the actual energy of the electron. The symbol ψ is the wave function, a mathematical function that describes the wavelike nature of the electron. A plot of the wave function squared (Ψ^2) represents an orbital, a position probability distribution map of the electron.

7.29 The principal quantum number (n) is an integer and has possible values of 1,2,3, etc. The principal quantum number determines the overall size and energy of an orbital.

7.30 The angular momentum quantum number (l) is an integer and has possible values of 0,1,2,3, etc. The angular momentum quantum number determines the shape of the orbital.

7.31 The magnetic quantum number (m_l) is an integer ranging from $-l$ to $+l$. For example, if $l = 1$, $m_l = -1, 0, +1$. The magnetic quantum number specifies the orientation of the orbital.

7.32 (a) $n = 1, l = 0, m_l = 0$

(b) $n = 2, l = 0, m_l = 0$; $n = 2, l = 1, m_l = -1$; $n = 2, l = 1, m_l = 0$; $n = 2, l = 1, m_l = +1$

(c) $n = 3, l = 0, m_l = 0$; $n = 3, l = 1, m_l = -1$; $n = 3, l = 1, m_l = 0$; $n = 3, l = 1, m_l = +1$; $n = 3, l = 2, m_l = -2$; $n = 3, l = 2, m_l = -1$; $n = 3, l = 2, m_l = 0$; $n = 3, l = 2, m_l = +1$; $n = 3, l = 2, m_l = +2$

(d) $n = 4, l = 0, m_l = 0$; $n = 4, l = 1, m_l = -1$; $n = 4, l = 1, m_l = 0$; $n = 4, l = 1, m_l = +1$; $n = 4, l = 2, m_l = -2$; $n = 4, l = 2, m_l = -1$; $n = 4, l = 2, m_l = 0$; $n = 4, l = 2, m_l = +1$; $n = 4, l = 2, m_l = +2$; $n = 4, l = 3, m_l = -3$; $n = 4, l = 3, m_l = -2$; $n = 4, l = 3, m_l = -1$; $n = 4, l = 3, m_l = 0$; $n = 4, l = 3, m_l = +1$; $n = 4, l = 3, m_l = +2$; $n = 4, l = 3, m_l = +3$

7.33 The probability density is the probability per unit volume of finding the electron at a point in space. The radial distribution function represents the total probability of finding the electron within a thin spherical shell at a distance r from the nucleus. In contrast to probability density, which has a maximum at the nucleus for an s orbital, the radial distribution function has a value of zero at the nucleus. It increases to a maximum and then decreases again with increasing r.

7.34

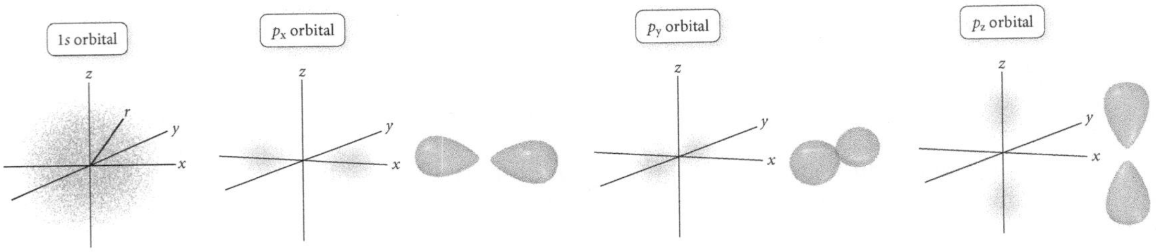

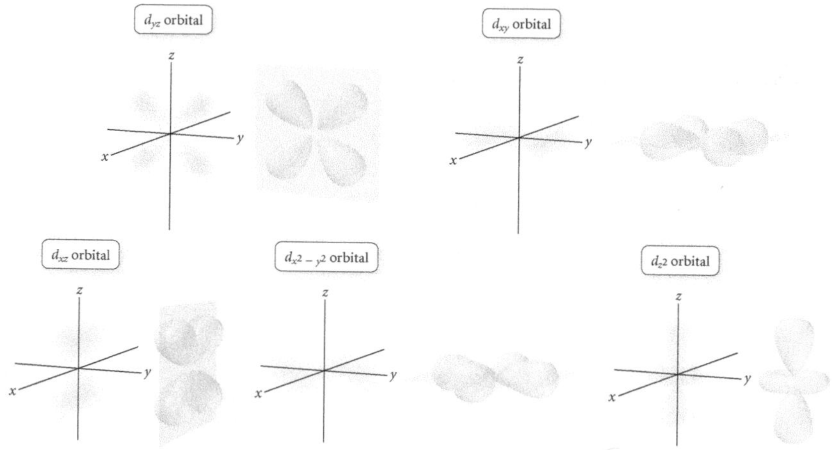

7.35 The sublevels are s (l=0), which can hold a maximum of 2 electrons; p (l = 1), which can hold a maximum of 6 electrons; d (l = 2), which can hold a maximum of 10 electrons; and f (l = 3), which can hold a maximum of 14 electrons.

7.36 Atoms are usually drawn as spheres because most atoms contain many electrons occupying a number of different orbitals. Therefore, the shape of an atom is obtained by superimposing all of its orbitals. If the s, p, and d orbitals are superimposed, they have a spherical shape.

Problems by Topic

Electromagnetic Radiation

7.37 **Given:** distance to sun = 1.496×10^8 km **Find:** time for light to travel from sun to Earth
Conceptual Plan: distance km → distance m → time

$$\frac{1000\ \text{m}}{\text{km}} \qquad \text{time} = \frac{\text{distance}}{3.00 \times 10^8\ \text{m/s}}$$

Solution: $1.496 \times 10^8\ \cancel{\text{km}} \times \frac{1000\ \cancel{\text{m}}}{\cancel{\text{km}}} \times \frac{\text{s}}{3.00 \times 10^8\ \cancel{\text{m}}} = 499\ \text{s}$

Check: The units of the answer, seconds, are correct. The magnitude of the answer is reasonable, since it corresponds to about 8 min.

7.38 **Given:** 4.3 light years to star **Find:** distance in km
Conceptual Plan: light years → days → hours → seconds → m → km

$$\frac{365\ \text{days}}{\text{yr}} \quad \frac{24\ \text{hr}}{\text{day}} \quad \frac{3600\ \text{s}}{\text{hr}} \quad \frac{3.00 \times 10^8\ \text{m}}{\text{s}} \quad \frac{\text{km}}{1000\ \text{m}}$$

Solution: $4.3\ \text{light}\ \cancel{\text{yr}} \times \frac{365\ \cancel{\text{days}}}{\cancel{\text{yr}}} \times \frac{24\ \cancel{\text{hrs}}}{\cancel{\text{day}}} \times \frac{3600\ \cancel{\text{s}}}{\cancel{\text{hr}}} \times \frac{3.00 \times 10^8\ \cancel{\text{m}}}{\cancel{\text{s}}} \times \frac{\text{km}}{1000\ \cancel{\text{m}}} = 4.1 \times 10^{13}\ \text{km}$

Check: The units of the answer, km, are correct. The magnitude of the answer is reasonable since it takes much longer for the light to reach Earth from Proxima Centauri than from the sun, so the distance should be much greater.

7.39 (i) By increasing wavelength the order is d) ultraviolet < c) infrared < b) microwave < a) radio waves.

(ii) By increasing energy the order is a) radio waves < b) microwaves < c) infrared < d) ultraviolet.

7.40 (i) By increasing frequency the order is b) radio waves < c) microwaves < d) visible light < a) gamma rays.

(ii) By decreasing energy the order is a) gamma rays > d) visible light > c) microwaves > b) radio waves.

7.41 (a) **Given:** λ = 632.8 nm **Find:** frequency (ν)

Conceptual Plan: nm $\rightarrow$ m $\rightarrow$ ν

$\frac{m}{10^9\ nm}$ $\nu = \frac{c}{\lambda}$

Solution: $632.8\ \cancel{nm} \times \frac{m}{10^9\ \cancel{nm}} = 6.328 \times 10^{-7}\ m \quad \nu = \frac{3.00 \times 10^8\ \cancel{m}}{s} \times \frac{1}{6.328 \times 10^{-7}\ \cancel{m}} = 4.74 \times 10^{14}\ s^{-1}$

Check: The units of the answer, s^{-1}, are correct. The magnitude of the answer seems reasonable since wavelength and frequency are inversely proportional.

(b) **Given:** λ = 503 nm **Find:** frequency (ν)

Conceptual Plan: nm $\rightarrow$ m $\rightarrow$ ν

$\frac{m}{10^9\ nm}$ $\nu = \frac{c}{\lambda}$

Solution: $503\ \cancel{nm} \times \frac{m}{10^9\ \cancel{nm}} = 5.03 \times 10^{-7}\ m \quad \nu = \frac{3.00 \times 10^8\ \cancel{m}}{s} \times \frac{1}{5.03 \times 10^{-7}\ \cancel{m}} = 5.96 \times 10^{14}\ s^{-1}$

Check: The units of the answer, s^{-1}, are correct. The magnitude of the answer seems reasonable since wavelength and frequency are inversely proportional.

(c) **Given:** λ = 0.052 nm **Find:** frequency (ν)

Conceptual Plan: nm $\rightarrow$ m $\rightarrow$ ν

$\frac{m}{10^9\ nm}$ $\nu = \frac{c}{\lambda}$

Solution: $0.052\ \cancel{nm} \times \frac{m}{10^9\ \cancel{nm}} = 5.2 \times 10^{-9}\ m \quad \nu = \frac{3.00 \times 10^8\ \cancel{m}}{s} \times \frac{1}{5.2 \times 10^{-9}\ \cancel{m}} = 5.8 \times 10^{18}\ s^{-1}$

Check: The units of the answer, s^{-1}, are correct. The magnitude of the answer seems reasonable since wavelength and frequency are inversely proportional.

7.42 (a) **Given:** ν = 100.2 MHz **Find:** wavelength (λ)

Conceptual Plan: MHz $\rightarrow$ Hz $\rightarrow$ s^{-1} $\rightarrow$ λ

$\frac{10^6\ Hz}{MHz}$ $1\ Hz = 1\ s^{-1}$ $\lambda = \frac{c}{\nu}$

Solution: $100.2\ \cancel{MHz} \times \frac{10^6\ \cancel{Hz}}{\cancel{MHz}} \times \frac{s^{-1}}{\cancel{Hz}} = 1.002 \times 10^8\ s^{-1} \quad \lambda = \frac{3.00 \times 10^8\ m}{\cancel{s}} \times \frac{\cancel{s}}{1.002 \times 10^8} = 2.99\ m$

Check: The units of the answer, m, are correct. The magnitude of the answer is reasonable because FM wavelengths are generally in the 3–8 m range.

(b) **Given:** ν = 1070 kHz **Find:** wavelength (λ)

Conceptual Plan: kHz $\rightarrow$ Hz $\rightarrow$ s^{-1} $\rightarrow$ λ

$\frac{10^3\ Hz}{kHz}$ $1\ Hz = 1\ s^{-1}$ $\lambda = \frac{c}{\nu}$

Solution: $1070\ \cancel{kHz} \times \frac{10^3\ \cancel{Hz}}{\cancel{kHz}} \times \frac{s^{-1}}{\cancel{Hz}} = 1.070 \times 10^6\ s^{-1} \quad \lambda = \frac{3.00 \times 10^8\ m}{\cancel{s}} \times \frac{\cancel{s}}{1.070 \times 10^6} = 280.\ m$

Check: The units of the answer, m, are correct. The magnitude of the answer is reasonable because AM wavelengths are generally in the 100–1000 m range.

(c) Given: ν = 835.6 MHz **Find:** wavelength (λ)

Conceptual Plan: MHz $\rightarrow$ Hz $\rightarrow$ s^{-1} $\rightarrow$ λ

$\frac{10^6\ Hz}{MHz}$ $1\ Hz = 1\ s^{-1}$ $\lambda = \frac{c}{\nu}$

Solution: $835.6\ \cancel{MHz} \times \frac{10^6\ \cancel{Hz}}{\cancel{MHz}} \times \frac{s^{-1}}{\cancel{Hz}} = 8.356 \times 10^8\ s^{-1} \quad \lambda = \frac{3.00 \times 10^8\ m}{\cancel{s}} \times \frac{\cancel{s}}{8.356 \times 10^8} = 3.59 \times 10^{-1}\ m$

Check: The units of the answer, m, are correct. The magnitude of the answer is reasonable because cell phone wavelengths are generally in the 0.1–0.5 m range.

7.43 (a) **Given:** frequency (ν) from 5 a. = $4.74 \times 10^{14}\ s^{-1}$ **Find:** Energy

Conceptual Plan: ν $\rightarrow$ E

$E = h\nu \quad h = 6.626 \times 10^{-34}\ J\ s$

Solution: $6.626 \times 10^{-34}\ J\ \cancel{s} \times \frac{4.74 \times 10^{14}}{\cancel{s}} = 3.14 \times 10^{-19}\ J$

Check: The units of the answer, J, are correct. The magnitude of the answer is reasonable since we are talking about the energy of one photon.

(b) **Given:** frequency (ν) from 5 b. = $5.96 \times 10^{14}\ s^{-1}$ **Find:** Energy
Conceptual Plan: $\nu \rightarrow E$

$E = h\nu \quad h = 6.626 \times 10^{-34}$ J s

Solution: $6.626 \times 10^{-34}\ \text{J}\ \cancel{\text{s}} \times \dfrac{5.96 \times 10^{14}}{\cancel{\text{s}}} = 3.95 \times 10^{-19}\ \text{J}$

Check: The units of the answer, J, are correct. The magnitude of the answer is reasonable since we are talking about the energy of one photon.

(c) **Given:** frequency (ν) from 5 c. = $5.8 \times 10^{18}\ s^{-1}$ **Find:** Energy
Conceptual Plan: $\nu \rightarrow E$

$E = h\nu \quad h = 6.626 \times 10^{-34}$ J s

Solution: $6.626 \times 10^{-34}\ \text{J}\ \cancel{\text{s}} \times \dfrac{5.8 \times 10^{18}}{\cancel{\text{s}}} = 3.8 \times 10^{-15}\ \text{J}$

Check: The units of the answer, J, are correct. The magnitude of the answer is reasonable since we are talking about the energy of one photon.

7.44 (a) **Given:** frequency (ν) from 6 a. = 100.2 MHz **Find:** Energy
Conceptual Plan: MHz $\rightarrow$ Hz $\rightarrow$ s^{-1} $\rightarrow$ E

$\dfrac{10^6\ \text{Hz}}{\text{MHz}} \quad 1\ \text{Hz} = 1\ s^{-1} \quad E = h\nu \quad h = 6.626 \times 10^{-34}$ J s

Solution: $100.2\ \cancel{\text{MHz}} \times \dfrac{10^6\ \cancel{\text{Hz}}}{\cancel{\text{MHz}}} \times \dfrac{s^{-1}}{\cancel{\text{Hz}}} = 1.002 \times 10^8\ s^{-1} \quad 6.626 \times 10^{-34}\ \text{J}\ \cancel{\text{s}} \times \dfrac{1.002 \times 10^8}{\cancel{\text{s}}} = 6.639 \times 10^{-26}\ \text{J}$

Check: The units of the answer, J, are correct. The magnitude of the answer is reasonable since we are talking about the energy of one photon and have a relatively long wavelength.

(b) **Given:** ν = 1070 kHz **Find:** Energy
Conceptual Plan: kHz $\rightarrow$ Hz $\rightarrow$ s^{-1} $\rightarrow$ E

$\dfrac{10^3\ \text{Hz}}{\text{kHz}} \quad 1\ \text{Hz} = 1\ s^{-1} \quad E = h\nu \quad h = 6.626 \times 10^{-34}$ J s

Solution:

$1070\ \cancel{\text{kHz}} \times \dfrac{10^3\ \cancel{\text{Hz}}}{\cancel{\text{kHz}}} \times \dfrac{s^{-1}}{\cancel{\text{Hz}}} = 1.070 \times 10^6\ s^{-1} \quad 6.626 \times 10^{-34}\ \text{J}\ \cancel{\text{s}} \times \dfrac{1.070 \times 10^6}{\cancel{\text{s}}} = 7.090 \times 10^{-28}\ \text{J}$

Check: The units of the answer, J, are correct. The magnitude of the answer is reasonable since we are talking about the energy of one photon and have a relatively long wavelength.

(c) **Given:** ν = 835.6 MHz **Find:** Energy
Conceptual Plan: MHz $\rightarrow$ Hz $\rightarrow$ s^{-1} $\rightarrow$ E

$\dfrac{10^6\ \text{Hz}}{\text{MHz}} \quad 1\ \text{Hz} = 1\ s^{-1} \quad E = h\nu \quad h = 6.626 \times 10^{-34}$ J s

Solution: $835.6\ \cancel{\text{MHz}} \times \dfrac{10^6\ \cancel{\text{Hz}}}{\cancel{\text{MHz}}} \times \dfrac{s^{-1}}{\cancel{\text{Hz}}} = 8.356 \times 10^8\ s^{-1} \quad 6.626 \times 10^{-34}\ \text{J}\ \cancel{\text{s}} \times \dfrac{8.356 \times 10^8}{\cancel{\text{s}}} = 5.537 \times 10^{-25}\ \text{J}$

Check: The units of the answer, J, are correct. The magnitude of the answer is reasonable since we are talking about the energy of one photon and have a relatively long wavelength.

7.45 **Given:** λ = 532 nm and E_{pulse} = 3.85 mJ **Find:** number of photons
Conceptual Plan: nm $\rightarrow$ m $\rightarrow$ E_{photon} $\rightarrow$ number of photons

$\dfrac{\text{m}}{10^9\ \text{nm}} \quad E = \dfrac{hc}{\lambda};\ h = 6.626 \times 10^{-34}\ \text{J s} \quad \dfrac{E_{pulse}}{E_{photon}}$

Solution: $532\ \cancel{\text{nm}} \times \dfrac{\text{m}}{10^9\ \cancel{\text{nm}}} = 5.32 \times 10^{-7}\ \text{m} \quad E = \dfrac{6.626 \times 10^{-34}\ \text{J}\ \cancel{\text{s}} \times \dfrac{3.00 \times 10^8\ \cancel{\text{m}}}{\cancel{\text{s}}}}{5.32 \times 10^{-7}\ \cancel{\text{m}}} = 3.73\underline{6}4 \times 10^{-19}\ \text{J/photon}$

$3.85\ \cancel{\text{mJ}} \times \dfrac{\cancel{\text{J}}}{1000\ \cancel{\text{mJ}}} \times \dfrac{1\ \text{photon}}{3.73\underline{6}4 \times 10^{-19}\ \cancel{\text{J}}} = 1.03 \times 10^{16}\ \text{photons}$

Check: The units of the answer, number of photons, are correct. The magnitude of the answer is reasonable for the amount of energy involved.

7.46 **Given:** $\lambda = 6.5\ \mu m$; power = 32.8 watts **Find:** photons/second
Conceptual Plan: $\mu m \rightarrow m \rightarrow E_{photon}$ **and then watts** $\rightarrow$ **J/s** $\rightarrow$ **number of photons**

$$\frac{m}{10^6\ \mu m} \quad E = \frac{hc}{\lambda};\ h = 6.626 \times 10^{-34}\ J\ s \qquad \frac{J/sec}{watt} \quad \frac{J/sec}{J/photon}$$

Solution: $6.5\ \cancel{\mu m} \times \frac{m}{10^6\ \cancel{\mu m}} = 6.5 \times 10^{-6}\ m \quad E = \frac{6.626 \times 10^{-34}\ J\ \cancel{s} \times \frac{3.00 \times 10^8\ \cancel{m}}{\cancel{s}}}{6.5 \times 10^{-6}\ \cancel{m}} = 3.0\underline{5}8 \times 10^{-20}\ J/photon$

$$32.8\ \cancel{watts} \times \frac{\cancel{J}/s}{1\ \cancel{watt}} \times \frac{1\ photon}{3.0\underline{5}8 \times 10^{-20}\ \cancel{J}} = 1.1 \times 10^{21}\ photons/s$$

Check: The units of the answer, photons/s, are correct. The magnitude of the answer is reasonable for the amount of energy involved.

7.47 (a) **Given:** $\lambda = 1500$ nm **Find:** E for 1 mol photons
Conceptual Plan: $nm \rightarrow m \rightarrow E_{photon} \rightarrow E(J)_{mol} \rightarrow E(kJ)_{mol}$

$$\frac{m}{10^9\ nm} \quad E = \frac{hc}{\lambda};\ h = 6.626 \times 10^{-34}\ J\ s \quad \frac{mol}{6.022 \times 10^{23}\ photons} \quad \frac{kJ}{1000\ J}$$

Solution:

$$1500\ \cancel{nm} \times \frac{m}{10^9\ \cancel{nm}} = 1.500 \times 10^{-6}\ m \quad E = \frac{6.626 \times 10^{-34}\ J\ \cancel{s} \times \frac{3.00 \times 10^8\ \cancel{m}}{\cancel{s}}}{1.500 \times 10^{-6}\ \cancel{m}} = 1.3\underline{2}52 \times 10^{-19}\ J/photon$$

$$\frac{1.3\underline{2}52 \times 10^{-19}\ \cancel{J}}{\cancel{photon}} \times \frac{6.022 \times 10^{23}\ \cancel{photons}}{mol} \times \frac{kJ}{1000\ \cancel{J}} = 79.8\ kJ/mol$$

Check: The units of the answer, kJ/mol, are correct. The magnitude of the answer is reasonable for a wavelength in the infrared region.

(b) **Given:** $\lambda = 500$ nm **Find:** E for 1 mol photons
Conceptual Plan: $nm \rightarrow m \rightarrow E_{photon} \rightarrow E_{mol} \rightarrow E(kJ)_{mol}$

$$\frac{m}{10^9\ nm} \quad E = \frac{hc}{\lambda};\ h = 6.626 \times 10^{-34}\ J\ s \quad \frac{mol}{6.022 \times 10^{23}\ photons} \quad \frac{kJ}{1000\ J}$$

Solution:

$$500\ \cancel{nm} \times \frac{m}{10^9\ \cancel{nm}} = 5.00 \times 10^{-7}\ m \quad E = \frac{6.626 \times 10^{-34}\ J\ \cancel{s} \times \frac{3.00 \times 10^8\ \cancel{m}}{\cancel{s}}}{5.00 \times 10^{-7}\ \cancel{m}} = 3.9\underline{7}56 \times 10^{-19}\ J/photon$$

$$\frac{3.9\underline{7}56 \times 10^{-19}\ \cancel{J}}{\cancel{photon}} \times \frac{6.022 \times 10^{23}\ \cancel{photons}}{mol} \times \frac{kJ}{1000\ \cancel{J}} = 239\ kJ/mol$$

Check: The units of the answer, kJ/mol, are correct. The magnitude of the answer is reasonable for a wavelength in the visible region.

(c) **Given:** $\lambda = 150$ nm **Find:** E for 1 mol photons
Conceptual Plan: $nm \rightarrow m \rightarrow E_{photon} \rightarrow E_{mol} \rightarrow E(kJ)_{mol}$

$$\frac{m}{10^9 nm} \quad E = \frac{hc}{\lambda};\ h = 6.626 \times 10^{-34}\ J\ s \quad \frac{mol}{6.022 \times 10^{23}\ photons} \quad \frac{kJ}{1000\ J}$$

Solution:

$$1.50\ \cancel{nm} \times \frac{m}{10^9\ \cancel{nm}} = 1.50 \times 10^{-7}\ m \quad E = \frac{6.626 \times 10^{-34}\ J\ \cancel{s} \times \frac{3.00 \times 10^8\ \cancel{m}}{\cancel{s}}}{1.50 \times 10^{-7}\ \cancel{m}} = 1.3\underline{2}52 \times 10^{-18}\ J/photon$$

$$\frac{1.3\underline{2}52\ \times 10^{-18}\ \cancel{J}}{\cancel{photon}} \times \frac{6.022 \times 10^{23}\ \cancel{photons}}{mol} \times \frac{kJ}{1000\cancel{J}} = 798\ kJ/mol$$

Check: The units of the answer, kJ/mol, are correct. The magnitude of the answer is reasonable for a wavelength in the ultraviolet region. Note: The energy increases from the IR to the Vis to the UV as expected.

7.48 (a) **Given:** $\lambda = 0.135$ nm **Find:** E for 1 mol photons
Conceptual Plan: $nm \rightarrow m \rightarrow E_{photon} \rightarrow E_{mol} \rightarrow E(kJ)_{mol}$

$$\frac{m}{10^9\ nm} \quad E = \frac{hc}{\lambda};\ h = 6.626 \times 10^{-34}\ J\ s \quad \frac{mol}{6.022 \times 10^{23} photons} \quad \frac{kJ}{1000\ J}$$

Solution:

$$0.135\ \text{nm} \times \frac{\text{m}}{10^{9}\ \text{nm}} = 1.35 \times 10^{-10}\text{m} \quad E = \frac{6.626 \times 10^{-34}\ \text{J s} \times \dfrac{3.00 \times 10^{8}\ \text{m}}{\text{s}}}{1.35 \times 10^{-10}\ \text{m}} = 1.4\underline{7}2 \times 10^{-15}\ \text{J/photon}$$

$$\frac{1.4\underline{7}2 \times 10^{-15}\ \text{J}}{\text{photon}} \times \frac{6.022 \times 10^{23}\ \text{photons}}{\text{mol}} \times \frac{\text{kJ}}{1000\ \text{J}} = 8.86 \times 10^{5}\ \text{kJ/mol}$$

Check: The units of the answer, kJ/mol, are correct. The magnitude of the answer is reasonable for a wavelength in the X-ray region.

(b) **Given:** $\lambda = 2.15 \times 10^{-5}$ nm **Find:** E for 1 mol photons
Conceptual Plan: nm $\rightarrow$ m $\rightarrow$ E_{photon} $\rightarrow$ E_{mol} $\rightarrow$ $E(kJ)_{mol}$

$$\frac{\text{m}}{10^{9}\ \text{nm}} \quad E = \frac{hc}{\lambda};\ h = 6.626 \times 10^{-34}\ \text{J s} \quad \frac{\text{mol}}{6.022 \times 10^{23}\ \text{photons}} \quad \frac{\text{kJ}}{1000\ \text{J}}$$

Solution:

$$2.15 \times 10^{-5}\ \text{nm} \times \frac{\text{m}}{10^{9}\ \text{nm}} = 2.15 \times 10^{-14}\ \text{m} \quad E = \frac{6.626 \times 10^{-34}\ \text{J s} \times \dfrac{3.00 \times 10^{8}\ \text{m}}{\text{s}}}{2.15 \times 10^{-14}\ \text{m}} = 9.2\underline{4}6 \times 10^{-12}\ \text{J/photon}$$

$$\frac{9.2\underline{4}6 \times 10^{-12}\ \text{J}}{\text{photon}} \times \frac{6.022 \times 10^{23}\ \text{photons}}{\text{mol}} \times \frac{\text{kJ}}{1000\ \text{J}} = 5.57 \times 10^{9}\ \text{kJ/mol}$$

Check: The units of the answer, kJ/mol, are correct. The magnitude of the answer is reasonable for a wavelength in the gamma ray region.

The Wave Nature of Matter and the Uncertainty Principle

7.49 The interference pattern would be a series of light and dark lines.

7.50 Since the interference pattern is caused by single electrons interfering with themselves, the pattern remains the same even when the rate of the electrons passing through the slits is one electron per hour. It will simply take longer for the full pattern to develop. When a laser is placed behind the slits in order to determine which hole the electron passes through, the laser flashes when a photon is scattered at the point of crossing indicating the slit used, but the interference pattern is now absent. With the laser on, the electrons hit positions directly behind each slit, as if they were ordinary particles.

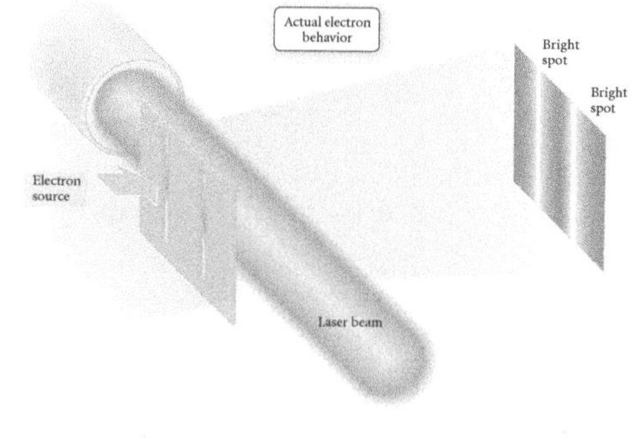

7.51 **Given:** $m = 9.109 \times 10^{-31}$ kg, $\lambda = 0.20$nm **Find:** v
Conceptual Plan: m, $\lambda \rightarrow$ v

$$v = \frac{h}{m\lambda}$$

Solution:
$$\frac{6.626 \times 10^{-34} \dfrac{\text{kg} \cdot \text{m}^2}{\text{s}^2} \cdot \text{s}}{(9.109 \times 10^{-31}\ \text{kg})(0.20\ \text{nm})\left(\dfrac{1\text{m}}{1 \times 10^{9}\ \text{nm}}\right)} = 3.6 \times 10^{6}\ \text{m/s}$$

Check: The units of the answer, m/s are correct. The magnitude of the answer is large as would be expected for the speed of the electron.

7.52 **Given:** m = 1.673×10^{-27} kg; v = 475 m/s **Find:** λ
Conceptual Plan: **m,v** $\rightarrow$ $\boldsymbol{\lambda}$

$$\lambda = \frac{h}{mv}$$

Solution: $$\frac{6.626 \times 10^{-34}\,\frac{\text{kg}\cdot\text{m}^2}{\text{s}^2}\cdot\text{s}\left(\frac{1 \times 10^{12}\ \text{pm}}{\text{m}}\right)}{(1.673 \times 10^{-27}\ \text{kg})\left(\frac{475\ \text{m}}{\text{s}}\right)} = 833\ \text{pm}$$

Check: The units of the answer, pm, are correct. The magnitude of the wavelength is small as expected.

7.53 **Given:** m = 9.109×10^{-31} kg; v = 1.35×10^{5} m/s **Find:** λ
Conceptual Plan: **m,v** $\rightarrow$ $\boldsymbol{\lambda}$

$$\lambda = \frac{h}{mv}$$

Solution: $$\frac{6.626 \times 10^{-34}\,\frac{\text{kg}\cdot\text{m}^2}{\text{s}^2}\cdot\text{s}}{(9.109 \times 10^{-31}\ \text{kg})\left(\frac{1.35 \times 10^{5}\ \text{m}}{\text{s}}\right)} = 5.39 \times 10^{-9}\ \text{m} = 5.39\ \text{nm}$$

Check: The units of the answer, m, are correct. The magnitude is reasonable since we are looking at an electron.

7.54 **Given:** m = 1.673×10^{-27} kg; λ = 122pm **Find:** v
Conceptual Plan: **m,** $\boldsymbol{\lambda}$ $\rightarrow$ **v**

$$v = \frac{h}{m\lambda}$$

Solution: $$\frac{6.626 \times 10^{-34}\,\frac{\text{kg}\cdot\text{m}^2}{\text{s}^2}\cdot\text{s}}{\left(1.673 \times 10^{-27}\ \text{kg}\right)(122\ \text{pm})\left(\frac{\text{m}}{1 \times 10^{12}\ \text{pm}}\right)} = 3.25 \times 10^{3}\ \text{m/s}$$

Check: The units of the answer, m/s, are correct. The magnitude of the is reasonable since it is smaller than the speed of an electron.

7.55 **Given:** m = 143 g; v = 95 mph **Find:** λ
Conceptual Plan: **m,v** $\rightarrow$ $\boldsymbol{\lambda}$

$$\lambda = \frac{h}{mv}$$

Solution: $$\frac{6.626 \times 10^{-34}\,\frac{\text{kg}\cdot\text{m}^2}{\text{s}^2}\cdot\text{s}}{(143\ \text{g})\left(\frac{\text{kg}}{1000\ \text{g}}\right)\left(\frac{95\ \text{mi}}{\text{hr}}\right)\left(\frac{1.609\ \text{km}}{\text{mi}}\right)\left(\frac{1000\ \text{m}}{\text{km}}\right)\left(\frac{\text{hr}}{3600\ \text{s}}\right)} = 1.1 \times 10^{-34}\ \text{m}$$

The value of the wavelength, 1.1×10^{-34} m, is so small it will not have an effect on the trajectory of the baseball.

Check: The units of the answer, m, are correct. The magnitude of the answer is very small as would be expected for the de Broglie wavelength of a baseball.

7.56 **Given:** m = 27 g; v = 765 m/s **Find:** λ
Conceptual Plan: **m,v** $\rightarrow$ $\boldsymbol{\lambda}$

$$\lambda = \frac{h}{mv}$$

Solution: $$\frac{6.626 \times 10^{-34}\,\frac{\text{kg}\cdot\text{m}^2}{\text{s}^2}\cdot\text{s}}{(27\ \text{g})\left(\frac{\text{kg}}{1000\ \text{g}}\right)\left(\frac{765\ \text{m}}{\text{s}}\right)} = 3.2 \times 10^{-35}\ \text{m}$$

The value of the wavelength, 3.2×10^{-35} m, is so small it will not have an effect on the trajectory of the bullet. The wave nature of matter is irrelevant to bullets.

Check: The units of the answer, m, are correct. The magnitude of the answer is very small as would be expected for the de Broglie wavelength of a bullet.

7.57 **Given:** $\Delta x = 552\text{pm}$, $m = 9.109 \times 10^{-31}$ kg **Find:** Δv
Conceptual Plan: Δx, m $\rightarrow$ Δv

$$\Delta x \times m\Delta v \geq \frac{h}{4\pi}$$

Solution:
$$\frac{6.626 \times 10^{-34} \frac{\text{kg} \cdot \text{m}^2}{\text{s}^2} \cdot \text{s}}{4(3.141)(9.109 \times 10^{-31} \text{ kg})(552 \text{ pm})\left(\frac{\text{m}}{1 \times 10^{12} \text{ pm}}\right)} = 1.05 \times 10^5 \text{ m/s}$$

Check: The units of the answer, m/s, are correct. The magnitude is reasonable for the uncertainty in the speed of an electron.

7.58 **Given:** $m = 9.109 \times 10^{-31}$ kg, $v = 3.7 \times 10^5$m/s, $\Delta v = 1.88 \times 10^5$m/s **Find:** Δx
Conceptual Plan Δv, m $\rightarrow$ Δx

$$\Delta x \times m\Delta v \geq \frac{h}{4\pi}$$

Solution:
$$\frac{6.626 \times 10^{-34} \frac{\text{kg} \cdot \text{m}^2}{\text{s}^2} \cdot \text{s}\left(\frac{1 \times 10^{12} \text{ pm}}{\text{m}}\right)}{4(3.141)(9.109 \times 10^{-31} \text{ kg})\left(\frac{1.88 \times 10^5 \text{ m}}{\text{s}}\right)} = 308 \text{ pm}$$

Check: The units of the answer, pm, are correct. The magnitude is reasonable when compared to the speed of the electron.

Orbitals and Quantum Numbers

7.59 Since the size of the orbital is determined by the *n* quantum, with the size increasing with increasing *n*, an electron in a 2*s* orbital is closer, on average, to the nucleus than an electron in a 3*s* orbital.

7.60 Since the size of the orbital is determined by the *n* quantum, with the size increasing with increasing *n*, an electron in a 4*p* orbital is further away, on average, from the nucleus than an electron in a 3*p* orbital.

7.61 The value of l is an integer that lies between 0 and $n - 1$.

(a) When $n = 1$, l can only be $l = 0$.

(b) When $n = 2$, l can be $l = 0$ or $l = 1$.

(c) When $n = 3$, l can be $l = 0$, $l = 1$, or $l = 2$.

(d) When $n = 4$, l can be $l = 0$, $l = 1$, $l = 2$, or $l = 3$.

7.62 The value of m_l is an integer that lies between $-l$ and $+l$.

(a) When $l = 0$, m_l can only be $m_l = 0$.

(b) When $l = 1$, m_l can be $m_l = -1$, $m_l = 0$, or $m_l = +1$.

(c) When $l = 2$, m_l can be $m_l = -2$, $m_l = -1$, $m_l = 0$, $m_l = +1$, or $m_l = +2$.

(d) When $l = 3$, m_l can be $m_l = -3$, $m_l = -2$, $m_l = -1$, $m_l = 0$, $m_l = +1$, $m_l = +2$, or $m_l = +3$.

7.63 Set c cannot occur together as a set of quantum numbers to specify an orbital. l must lie between 0 and $n - 1$, so for $n = 3$, l can only be as high as 2.

7.64 (a) 1*s* is a real orbital, $n = 1$, $l = 0$.

(b) 2*p* is a real orbital, $n = 2$, $l = 1$.

(c) 4*s* is a real orbital, $n = 4$, $l = 0$.

(d) 2*d* is an impossible representation. $n = 2$, $l = 2$ is not allowed. l must lie between 0 and $n - 1$, so for $n = 2$ l can only be as high as 1(*p*).

7.65 The 2*s* orbital would be the same shape as the 1*s* orbital but would be larger in size and the 3*p* orbitals would have the same shape as the 2*p* orbitals but would be larger in size. Also, the 2*s* and 3*p* orbitals would have more nodes.

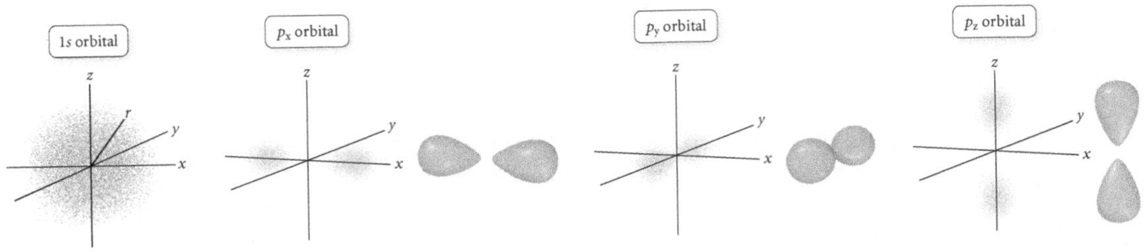

7.66 The 4*d* orbitals would be the same shape as the 3*d* orbitals but would be larger in size and the 4*d* orbital would have more nodes.

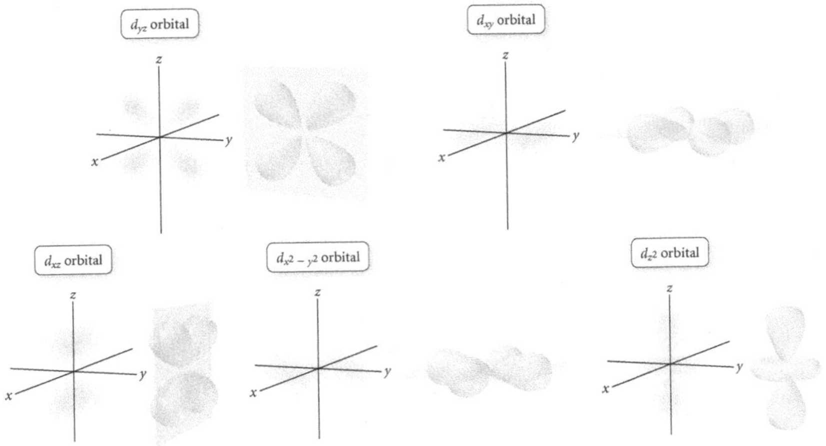

Atomic Spectroscopy

7.67 When the atom emits the photon of energy that was needed to raise the electron to the $n = 2$ level, the photon has the same energy as the energy absorbed to move the electron to the excited state. Therefore, the electron has to be in $n = 1$ (the ground state) following the emission of the photon.

7.68 (a) From $n = 3 \rightarrow n = 1$, the electron is moving to a lower energy, therefore, there is an emission of energy.

(b) From n = 2 → n = 4, the electron is moving to a higher energy, therefore, there is an absorption of energy.

(c) From n = 4 → n = 3, the electron is moving to a lower energy, therefore, there is an emission of energy.

7.69 According to the quantum-mechanical model, the higher the n level the higher the energy. So, the transition from 3*p* → 1*s* would be a greater energy difference than a transition from 2*p* → 1*s*. The lower energy transition would have the longer wavelength. Therefore, the 2*p* → 1*s* transition would produce a longer wavelength.

7.70 According to the quantum-mechanical model, the higher the n level the higher the energy and the higher in energy, the closer the levels are to each other. So, the transition from 3*p* → 2*s* would be a greater energy difference than the transition from 4*p* → 3*p*. The lower energy transition would have the longer wavelength. Therefore, the 4*p* → 3*p* transition would produce a longer wavelength.

7.71 (a) **Given:** $n = 2 \rightarrow n = 1$ **Find:** λ

Conceptual Plan: $n = 1, n = 2 \rightarrow \Delta E_{atom} \rightarrow \Delta E_{photon} \rightarrow \lambda$

$\Delta E_{atom} = E_1 - E_2$ $\quad \Delta E_{atom} \rightarrow -\Delta E_{photon}$ $\quad E = \frac{hc}{\lambda}$

Solution:

$$\Delta E = E_1 - E_2$$
$$= -2.18 \times 10^{-18}\,J\left(\frac{1}{1^2}\right) - \left[-2.18 \times 10^{-18}\left(\frac{1}{2^2}\right)\right] = -2.18 \times 10^{-18}\,J\left[\left(\frac{1}{1^2}\right) - \left(\frac{1}{2^2}\right)\right] = -1.6\underline{3}5 \times 10^{-18}\,J$$

$$\Delta E_{photon} = -\Delta E_{atom} = 1.6\underline{3}5 \times 10^{-18}\,J \qquad \lambda = \frac{hc}{E} = \frac{(6.626 \times 10^{-34}\,\cancel{J}\cdot\cancel{s})(3.00 \times 10^8\,m/\cancel{s})}{1.6\underline{3}5 \times 10^{-18}\,\cancel{J}} = 1.22 \times 10^{-7}\,m$$

This transition would produce a wavelength in the UV region.

Check: The units of the answer, m, are correct. The magnitude of the answer is reasonable since it is in the region of UV radiation.

(b) **Given:** $n = 3 \rightarrow n = 1$ **Find:** λ

Conceptual Plan: $n = 1, n = 3 \rightarrow \Delta E_{atom} \rightarrow \Delta E_{photon} \rightarrow \lambda$

$\Delta E_{atom} = E_1 - E_3$ $\quad \Delta E_{atom} \rightarrow -\Delta E_{photon}$ $\quad E = \frac{hc}{\lambda}$

Solution:

$$\Delta E = E_1 - E_3$$
$$= -2.18 \times 10^{-18}\,J\left(\frac{1}{1^2}\right) - \left[-2.18 \times 10^{-18}\left(\frac{1}{3^2}\right)\right] = -2.18 \times 10^{-18}\,J\left[\left(\frac{1}{1^2}\right) - \left(\frac{1}{3^2}\right)\right] = -1.9\underline{3}8 \times 10^{-18}\,J$$

$$\Delta E_{photon} = -\Delta E_{atom} = 1.9\underline{3}8 \times 10^{-18}\,J \qquad \lambda = \frac{hc}{E} = \frac{(6.626 \times 10^{-34}\,\cancel{J}\cdot\cancel{s})(3.00 \times 10^8\,m/\cancel{s})}{1.9\underline{3}8 \times 10^{-18}\,\cancel{J}} = 1.03 \times 10^{-7}\,m$$

This transition would produce a wavelength in the UV region.

Check: The units of the answer, m, are correct. The magnitude of the answer is reasonable since it is in the region of UV radiation.

(c) **Given:** $n = 4 \rightarrow n = 2$ **Find:** λ

Conceptual Plan: $n = 2, n = 4 \rightarrow \Delta E_{atom} \rightarrow \Delta E_{photon} \rightarrow \lambda$

$\Delta E_{atom} = E_2 - E_4$ $\quad \Delta E_{atom} \rightarrow -\Delta E_{photon}$ $\quad E = \frac{hc}{\lambda}$

Solution:

$$\Delta E = E_2 - E_4$$
$$= -2.18 \times 10^{-18}\,J\left(\frac{1}{2^2}\right) - \left[-2.18 \times 10^{-18}\left(\frac{1}{4^2}\right)\right] = -2.18 \times 10^{-18}\,J\left[\left(\frac{1}{2^2}\right) - \left(\frac{1}{4^2}\right)\right] = -4.0\underline{8}7 \times 10^{-19}\,J$$

$$\Delta E_{photon} = -\Delta E_{atom} = 4.0\underline{8}7 \times 10^{-19}\,J \qquad \lambda = \frac{hc}{E} = \frac{(6.626 \times 10^{-34}\,\cancel{J}\cdot\cancel{s})(3.00 \times 10^8\,m/\cancel{s})}{4.0\underline{8}7 \times 10^{-19}\,\cancel{J}} = 4.86 \times 10^{-7}\,m$$

This transition would produce a wavelength in the visible region.

Check: The units of the answer, m, are correct. The magnitude of the answer is reasonable since it is in the region of visible light.

(d) **Given:** $n = 5 \rightarrow n = 2$ **Find:** λ

Conceptual Plan: $n = 2, n = 5 \rightarrow \Delta E_{atom} \rightarrow \Delta E_{photon} \rightarrow \lambda$

$\Delta E_{atom} = E_2 - E_5$ $\quad \Delta E_{atom} \rightarrow -\Delta E_{photon}$ $\quad E = \frac{hc}{\lambda}$

Solution:

$$\Delta E = E_2 - E_5$$
$$= -2.18 \times 10^{-18}\,J\left(\frac{1}{2^2}\right) - \left[-2.18 \times 10^{-18}\left(\frac{1}{5^2}\right)\right] = -2.18 \times 10^{-18}\,J\left[\left(\frac{1}{2^2}\right) - \left(\frac{1}{5^2}\right)\right] = -4.5\underline{7}8 \times 10^{-19}\,J$$

$$\Delta E_{photon} = -\Delta E_{atom} = 4.5\underline{7}8 \times 10^{-19}\,J \qquad \lambda = \frac{hc}{E} = \frac{(6.626 \times 10^{-34}\,\cancel{J}\cdot\cancel{s})(3.00 \times 10^8\,m/\cancel{s})}{4.5\underline{7}8 \times 10^{-19}\,\cancel{J}} = 4.34 \times 10^{-7}\,m$$

This transition would produce a wavelength in the visible region.

Check: The units of the answer, m, are correct. The magnitude of the answer is reasonable since it is in the region of visible light.

7.72 (a) **Given:** $n = 4 \rightarrow n = 3$ **Find:** ν

Conceptual Plan: $n = 3, n = 4 \rightarrow \Delta E_{atom} \rightarrow \Delta E_{photon} \rightarrow \nu$

$\Delta E_{atom} = E_3 - E_4 \qquad \Delta E_{atom} \rightarrow -\Delta E_{photon} \qquad E = h\nu$

Solution:

$$\Delta E = E_3 - E_4$$

$$= -2.18 \times 10^{-18}\,\text{J}\left(\frac{1}{3^2}\right) - \left[-2.18 \times 10^{-18}\left(\frac{1}{4^2}\right)\right] = -2.18 \times 10^{-18}\,\text{J}\left[\left(\frac{1}{3^2}\right) - \left(\frac{1}{4^2}\right)\right] = -1.0\underline{6}0 \times 10^{-19}\,\text{J}$$

$$\Delta E_{photon} = -\Delta E_{atom} = 1.0\underline{6}0 \times 10^{-19}\,\text{J} \qquad \nu = \frac{E}{h} = \frac{(1.0\underline{6}0 \times 10^{-19}\,\text{J})}{6.626 \times 10^{-34}\,\text{J} \cdot \text{s})} = 1.60 \times 10^{14}\,\text{s}^{-1}$$

Check: The units of the answer, s^{-1}, are correct. The magnitude of the answer is reasonable since it is a transition between two close levels and the levels become closer as the n value increases. Therefore, the energy difference is smaller and the frequency is smaller.

(b) **Given:** $n = 5 \rightarrow n = 1$ **Find:** ν

Conceptual Plan: $n = 1, n = 5 \rightarrow \Delta E_{atom} \rightarrow \Delta E_{photon} \rightarrow \nu$

$\Delta E_{atom} = E_1 - E_5 \qquad \Delta E_{atom} \rightarrow -\Delta E_{photon} \qquad E = h\nu$

Solution:

$$\Delta E = E_1 - E_5$$

$$= -2.18 \times 10^{-18}\,\text{J}\left(\frac{1}{1^2}\right) - \left[-2.18 \times 10^{-18}\left(\frac{1}{5^2}\right)\right] = -2.18 \times 10^{-18}\,\text{J}\left[\left(\frac{1}{1^2}\right) - \left(\frac{1}{5^2}\right)\right] = -2.0\underline{9}3 \times 10^{-18}\,\text{J}$$

$$\Delta E_{photon} = -\Delta E_{atom} = 2.0\underline{9}3 \times 10^{-18}\,\text{J} \qquad \nu = \frac{E}{h} = \frac{2.0\underline{9}3 \times 10^{-18}\,\text{J}}{6.626 \times 10^{-34}\,\text{J} \cdot \text{s}} = 3.16 \times 10^{15}\,\text{s}^{-1}$$

Check: The units of the answer, s^{-1}, are correct. The magnitude of the answer is reasonable since it is a transition that will produce a wavelength in the UV region, and the frequency is correct for the UV region.

(c) **Given:** $n = 5 \rightarrow n = 4$ **Find:** ν

Conceptual Plan: $n = 4, n = 5 \rightarrow \Delta E_{atom} \rightarrow \Delta E_{photon} \rightarrow \nu$

$\Delta E_{atom} = E_4 - E_5 \qquad \Delta E_{atom} \rightarrow -\Delta E_{photon} \qquad E = h\nu$

Solution:

$$\Delta E = E_4 - E_5$$

$$= -2.18 \times 10^{-18}\,\text{J}\left(\frac{1}{4^2}\right) - \left[-2.18 \times 10^{-18}\left(\frac{1}{5^2}\right)\right] = -2.18 \times 10^{-18}\,\text{J}\left[\left(\frac{1}{4^2}\right) - \left(\frac{1}{5^2}\right)\right] = -4.9\underline{0}5 \times 10^{-20}\,\text{J}$$

$$\Delta E_{photon} = -\Delta E_{atom} = 4.9\underline{0}5 \times 10^{-20}\,\text{J} \qquad \nu = \frac{E}{h} = \frac{4.9\underline{0}5 \times 10^{-20}\,\text{J}}{6.626 \times 10^{-34}\,\text{J} \cdot \text{s}} = 7.40 \times 10^{13}\,\text{s}^{-1}$$

Check: The units of the answer, s^{-1}, are correct. The magnitude of the answer is reasonable since it is a transition between two close levels and the levels become closer as the n value increases. Therefore, the energy difference is smaller and the frequency is smaller.

(d) **Given:** $n = 6 \rightarrow n = 5$ **Find:** ν

Conceptual Plan: $n = 5, n = 6 \rightarrow \Delta E_{atom} \rightarrow \Delta E_{photon} \rightarrow \nu$

$\Delta E_{atom} = E_5 - E_6 \qquad \Delta E_{atom} \rightarrow -\Delta E_{photon} \qquad E = h\nu$

Solution:

$$\Delta E = E_5 - E_6$$

$$= -2.18 \times 10^{-18}\,\text{J}\left(\frac{1}{5^2}\right) - \left[-2.18 \times 10^{-18}\left(\frac{1}{6^2}\right)\right] = -2.18 \times 10^{-18}\,\text{J}\left[\left(\frac{1}{5^2}\right) - \left(\frac{1}{6^2}\right)\right] = -2.6\underline{6}4 \times 10^{-20}\,\text{J}$$

$$\Delta E_{photon} = -\Delta E_{atom} = 2.6\underline{6}4 \times 10^{-20}\,\text{J} \qquad \nu = \frac{E}{h} = \frac{2.6\underline{6}4 \times 10^{-20}\,\text{J}}{6.626 \times 10^{-34}\,\text{J} \cdot \text{s}} = 4.02 \times 10^{13}\,\text{s}^{-1}$$

Check: The units of the answer, s^{-1}, are correct. The magnitude of the answer is reasonable since it is a transition between two close levels and the levels become closer as the n value increases. Therefore, the energy difference is smaller and the frequency is smaller.

7.73 **Given:** n(initial) = 7 λ = 397 nm **Find:** n(final)

Conceptual Plan: $\lambda \rightarrow \Delta E_{photon} \rightarrow \Delta E_{atom} \rightarrow n = x, n = 7$

$E = \frac{hc}{\lambda}$ $\quad \Delta E_{photon} \rightarrow -\Delta E_{atom}$ $\quad \Delta E_{atom} = E_x - E_7$

Solution: $E = \frac{hc}{\lambda} = \frac{(6.626 \times 10^{-34}\ J \cdot s)(3.00 \times 10^8\ m/s)}{(397\ nm)\left(\frac{m}{10^9\ nm}\right)} = 5.007 \times 10^{-19}\ J$

$\Delta E_{atom} = -\Delta E_{photon} = -5.007 \times 10^{-19}\ J$

$\Delta E = E_x - E_7 = -5.007 \times 10^{-19} = -2.18 \times 10^{-18}\ J\left(\frac{1}{x^2}\right) - \left[-2.18 \times 10^{-18}\left(\frac{1}{7^2}\right)\right] = -2.18 \times 10^{-18}\ J\left[\left(\frac{1}{x^2}\right) - \left(\frac{1}{7^2}\right)\right]$

$0.2297 = \left(\frac{1}{x^2}\right) - \left(\frac{1}{7^2}\right)$ $\quad 0.25229 = \left(\frac{1}{x^2}\right)$ $\quad x^2 = 3.998 \quad x = 2$

Check: The answer is reasonable since it is an integer less than the initial value of 7.

7.74 **Given:** n(final) = 4, ν = 11.4 THz **Find:** n(initial)

Conceptual Plan: $\nu \rightarrow \Delta E_{photon} \rightarrow \Delta E_{atom} \rightarrow n = 4, n = x$

$E = h\nu$ $\quad \Delta E_{photon} \rightarrow -\Delta E_{atom}$ $\quad \Delta E_{atom} = E_4 - E_x$

Solution: $E = h\nu = (6.626 \times 10^{-34}\ J \cdot s)(114\ THz)\left(\frac{10^{12}\ Hz}{T}\right)\left(\frac{s^{-1}}{Hz}\right) = 7.553 \times 10^{-20}\ J$

$\Delta E_{atom} = -\Delta E_{photon} = -7.553 \times 10^{-20}\ J$

$\Delta E = E_4 - E_x = -7.553 \times 10^{-20}\ J = -2.18 \times 10^{-18}\ J\left(\frac{1}{4^2}\right) - \left[-2.18 \times 10^{-18}\left(\frac{1}{x^2}\right)\right] = -2.18 \times 10^{-18}\ J\left[\left(\frac{1}{4^2}\right) - \left(\frac{1}{x^2}\right)\right]$

$0.03465 = \left(\frac{1}{4^2}\right) - \left(\frac{1}{x^2}\right)$ $\quad 0.02785 = \left(\frac{1}{x^2}\right); x^2 = 35.9 = 36 \text{ so } x = 6$

Check: The answer is reasonable since it is an integer greater than the final value of 4.

Cumulative Problems

7.75 **Given:** 348 kJ/mol **Find:** λ

Conceptual Plan: kJ/mol $\rightarrow$ kJ/molec $\rightarrow$ J/molec $\rightarrow$ λ

$\frac{6.022 \times 10^{23}\ C-C\ bonds}{mol\ C-C\ bonds}$ $\quad \frac{1000\ J}{kJ}$ $\quad E = \frac{hc}{\lambda}$

Solution: $\frac{348\ kJ}{mol\ C-C\ bonds} \times \frac{mol\ C-C\ bonds}{6.022 \times 10^{23}\ C-C\ bonds} \times \frac{1000\ J}{kJ} = 5.779 \times 10^{-19}\ J$

$\lambda = \frac{(6.626 \times 10^{-34}\ J \cdot s)(3.00 \times 10^8\ m/s)}{5.779 \times 10^{-19}\ J} = 3.44 \times 10^{-7} m = 344\ nm$

Check: The units of the answer, m or nm, are correct. The magnitude of the answer is reasonable since this wavelength is in the UV region.

7.76 **Given:** 164 kJ/mol **Find:** λ

Conceptual Plan: kJ/mol $\rightarrow$ kJ/molec $\rightarrow$ J/molec $\rightarrow$ λ

$\frac{6.022 \times 10^{23}\ molec}{mol}$ $\quad \frac{1000\ J}{kJ}$ $\quad E = \frac{hc}{\lambda}$

Solution: $\frac{164\ kJ}{mol} \times \frac{mol}{6.022 \times 10^{23}\ molecules} \times \frac{1000\ J}{kJ} = 2.723 \times 10^{-19}\ J$

$\lambda = \frac{(6.626 \times 10^{-34}\ J \cdot s)(3.00 \times 10^8\ m/s)}{2.723 \times 10^{-19}\ J} = 7.30 \times 10^{-7}\ m = 730\ nm$

Check: The units of the answer, m or nm, are correct. The magnitude of the answer is reasonable since this wavelength is in the red region of visible light.

7.77 **Given:** E_{pulse} = 5.0 watts; d = 5.5 mm; hole = 1.2 mm; λ = 532 nm **Find:** photons/s

Conceptual Plan: fraction of beam through hole → fraction of power and then E_{photon} → number photons/s

$\frac{\text{area hole}}{\text{area beam}}$ fraction x power $E = \frac{hc}{\lambda}$ $\frac{\text{power/s}}{\text{E/photon}}$

Solution: $A = \pi r^2 \frac{\pi(0.60\text{ mm})^2}{\pi(2.75\text{ mm})^2} = 0.0476$ $\quad 0.0476 \times 5.0 \text{ watts} \times \frac{\text{J/s}}{\text{watt}} = 0.2\underline{3}8 \text{ J/s}$

$$E_{photon} = \frac{(6.626 \times 10^{-34}\text{ J}\cdot\text{s})(3.00 \times 10^8 \text{ m/s})}{(532 \text{ nm})\left(\frac{\text{m}}{10^9\text{ nm}}\right)} = 3.7\underline{3}6 \times 10^{-19}\text{ J/photon}$$

$$\frac{0.2\underline{3}8 \text{ J/s}}{3.7\underline{3}6 \times 10^{-19}\text{ J/photon}} = 6.4 \times 10^{17}\text{ photons/s}$$

Check: The units of the answer, number of photons/s, are correct. The magnitude of the answer is reasonable.

7.78 **Given:** A_{leaf} = 2.50 cm^2; E_{rad} = 1000 W/m^2; λ = 504 nm **Find:** photons/s

Conceptual Plan: E_{rad}/s → E_{leaf}/s and then E_{photon} → number photons/s

$E_{rad} \times A_{leaf}$ $E = \frac{hc}{\lambda}$ $\frac{E_{leaf}/s}{\text{E/photon}}$

Solution: $E_{rad} = 2.50 \text{ cm}^2 \times \frac{1000 \text{ W}}{\text{m}^2} \times \frac{\text{m}^2}{(100 \text{ cm})^2} \times \frac{\text{J/s}}{\text{W}} = 0.250 \text{ J/s}$

$$E_{photon} = \frac{hc}{\lambda} = \frac{(6.626 \times 10^{-34}\text{ J}\cdot\text{s})(3.00 \times 10^8 \text{ m/s})}{(504 \text{ nm})\left(\frac{\text{m}}{10^9\text{ nm}}\right)} = 3.9\underline{4}4 \times 10^{-19}\text{ J/photon}$$

$$\frac{E_{rad}}{E_{photon}} = \frac{0.250 \text{ J/s}}{3.9\underline{4}4 \times 10^{-19}\text{ J/photon}} = 6.34 \times 10^{17}\text{ photons/s}$$

Check: The units of the answer, photons/s, are correct. The magnitude of the answer is reasonable compared to the radiation from the sun.

7.79 **Given:** KE = 506 eV **Find:** λ

Conceptual Plan: KE_{ev} → KE_J → v → λ

$\frac{1.602 \times 10^{-19}\text{ J}}{\text{eV}}$ $KE = 1/2\, mv^2$ $\lambda = \frac{h}{mv}$

Solution:

$$506 \text{ eV}\left(\frac{1.602 \times 10^{-19}\text{ J}}{\text{eV}}\right)\left(\frac{\frac{\text{kg}\cdot\text{m}^2}{\text{s}^2}}{\text{J}}\right) = \frac{1}{2}(9.11 \times 10^{-31}\text{ kg})\, v^2$$

$$v^2 = \frac{506 \text{ eV}\left(\frac{1.602 \times 10^{-19}\text{ J}}{\text{eV}}\right)\left(\frac{\frac{\text{kg}\cdot\text{m}^2}{\text{s}^2}}{\text{J}}\right)}{\frac{1}{2}(9.11 \times 10^{-31}\text{ kg})} = 1.7796 \times 10^{14}\,\frac{\text{m}^2}{\text{s}^2}$$

$$v = 1.33 \times 10^7 \text{ m/s} \qquad \lambda = \frac{h}{mv} = \frac{6.626 \times 10^{-34}\,\frac{\text{kg}\cdot\text{m}^2}{\text{s}^2}\cdot\text{s}}{(9.11 \times 10^{-31}\text{ kg})(1.33 \times 10^7 \text{ m/s})} = 5.47 \times 10^{-11}\text{ m} = 0.0547 \text{ nm}$$

Check: The units of the answer, m or nm, are correct. The magnitude of the answer is reasonable because a de Broglie wavelength is usually a very small number.

7.80 **Given:** λ = 0.989 nm; KE = 969 eV **Find:** BE/mol

Conceptual Plan: λ → E_{photon} → BE_{photon} → BE_{mol}

$E = \frac{hc}{\lambda}$ $BE_{photon} = E_{photon} - KE$ $\frac{\text{mol}}{6.022 \times 10^{23}\text{ photons}}$

Solution: $E_{photon} = \frac{hc}{\lambda} = \frac{(6.626 \times 10^{-34}\ J \cdot \cancel{s})(3.00 \times 10^{8}\ \cancel{m}/\cancel{s})}{(0.989\ \cancel{nm})(\frac{\cancel{m}}{10^{9}\ \cancel{nm}})} = 2.0\underline{1}0 \times 10^{-16}\ J/photon$

$$BE_{photon} = 2.0\underline{1}0 \times 10^{-16}\ J/photon - \left[(969\ \cancel{eV})\left(\frac{1.602 \times 10^{-19}\ J}{\cancel{eV}}\right)\right] = 4.5\underline{7}6 \times 10^{-17}\ J/photon$$

$$\frac{4.5\underline{7}6 \times 10^{-17}\ \cancel{J}}{\cancel{photon}} \times \frac{6.022 \times 10^{23}\ \cancel{photons}}{mol} \times \frac{kJ}{1000\ \cancel{J}} = 2.76 \times 10^{4}\ kJ/mol$$

Check: The units of the answer, kJ/mol, are correct. The magnitude of the answer is reasonable since it should require a large amount of energy to remove an electron from a metal surface.

7.81 **Given:** $n = 1 \rightarrow n = \infty$ **Find:** E; λ

Conceptual Plan: $n = \infty, n = 1 \rightarrow \Delta E_{atom} \rightarrow \Delta E_{photon} \rightarrow \lambda$

$\Delta E_{atom} = E_{\infty} - E_1$ $\qquad \Delta E_{atom} \rightarrow \Delta E_{photon}$ $\qquad E = \frac{hc}{\lambda}$

Solution: $\Delta E = E_{\infty} - E_1 = 0 - \left[-2.18 \times 10^{-18}\left(\frac{1}{1^2}\right)\right] = +2.18 \times 10^{-18}\ J$

$$\Delta E_{photon} = -\Delta E_{atom} = +2.18 \times 10^{-18} J$$

$$\lambda = \frac{hc}{E} = \frac{(6.626 \times 10^{-34}\ \cancel{J} \cdot \cancel{s})(3.00 \times 10^{8}\ m/\cancel{s})}{2.18 \times 10^{-18}\ \cancel{J}} = 9.12 \times 10^{-8}\ m = 91.2\ nm$$

Check: The units of the answers, J for E and m or nm for part 1, are correct. The magnitude of the answer is reasonable because it would require more energy to completely remove the electron than just moving it to a higher n level. This results in a shorter wavelength.

7.82 **Given:** E = 496 kJ/mol **Find:** ν

Conceptual Plan: kJ/mol $\rightarrow$ kJ/molecule $\rightarrow$ J/molecule $\rightarrow$ ν

$\frac{6.022 \times 10^{23}\ molecules}{mol}$ $\qquad \frac{1000\ J}{kJ}$ $\qquad E = h\nu$

Solution: $\nu = \frac{E}{h} = \frac{\left(\frac{496\ \cancel{kJ}}{\cancel{mol}}\right)\left(\frac{\cancel{mol}}{6.022 \times 10^{23}\ atom}\right)\left(\frac{1000\ \cancel{J}}{\cancel{kJ}}\right)}{6.626 \times 10^{-34}\ \cancel{J} \cdot} = 1.24 \times 10^{15}\ s^{-1}$

Check: The units of the answer, s^{-1}, are correct. The magnitude of the answer is reasonable because the frequency is slightly higher than the visible region of the spectrum and this is expected because the excitation of sodium produces a line in the visible region.

7.83 (a) **Given:** $n = 1$ **Find:** number of orbitals if $l = 0 \rightarrow n$

Conceptual Plan: value n $\rightarrow$ values l $\rightarrow$ values m_l $\rightarrow$ number of orbitals

$l = 0 \rightarrow n$ $\qquad m_l = -1 \rightarrow +1$ total m_l

Solution:

$n =$	1	
$l =$	0	1
$m_l =$	0	- 1, 0, +1

total 4 orbitals

Check: The total orbitals will be equal to the number of l sublevels^2.

(b) **Given:** $n = 2$ **Find:** number of orbitals if $l = 0 \rightarrow n$

Conceptual Plan: value n $\rightarrow$ values l $\rightarrow$ values m_l $\rightarrow$ number of orbitals

$l = 0 \rightarrow n$ $\qquad m_l = -1 \rightarrow +1$ total m_l

Solution:

$n =$	2		
$l =$	0	1	2
$m_l =$	0	- 1, 0, +1	- 2,- 1,0,1,2

total 9 orbitals

Check: The total orbitals will be equal to the number of l sublevels^2.

(c) **Given:** $n = 3$ **Find:** number of orbitals if $l = 0 \rightarrow n$

Conceptual Plan: value n $\rightarrow$ **values** l $\rightarrow$ **values** m_l $\rightarrow$ **number of orbitals**

$l = 0 \rightarrow n$ $\qquad$ $m_l = -1 \rightarrow +1$ total m_l

Solution:

$n =$	3			
$l =$	0	1	2	3
$m_l =$	0	- 1, 0, +1	- 2,- 1,0,1,2	- 3,- 2,- 1,0,1,2,3

total 16 orbitals

Check: The total orbitals will be equal to the number of l sublevels^2.

7.84 (a) **Given:** s sublevel **Find:** number of orbital if $m_l = -l - 1 \rightarrow l + 1$

Conceptual Plan: values l $\rightarrow$ **values** m_l $\rightarrow$ **number of orbitals**

$m_l = -l - 1 \rightarrow +l + 1$ $\qquad$ total m_l

Solution: sublevel $s \rightarrow l = 0$

$m_l = -1, 0, +1$

total 3 orbitals

(b) **Given:** p sublevel **Find:** number of orbital if $m_l = -l - 1 \rightarrow l + 1$

Conceptual Plan: values l $\rightarrow$ **values** m_l $\rightarrow$ **number of orbitals**

$m_l = -l - 1 \rightarrow +l + 1$ $\qquad$ total m_l

Solution: sublevel $p \rightarrow l = 1$

$m_l = -2, -1, 0, +1, +2$

total 5 orbitals

(c) **Given:** d sublevel **Find:** number of orbital if $m_l = -l - 1 \rightarrow l + 1$

Conceptual Plan: values l $\rightarrow$ **values** m_l $\rightarrow$ **number of orbitals**

$m_l = -l - 1 \rightarrow +l + 1$ $\qquad$ total m_l

Solution: sublevel $d \rightarrow l = 2$

$m_l = -3, -2, -1, 0, +1, +2, +3$

total 7 orbitals

7.85 **Given:** $\lambda = 1875$ nm; 1282 nm; 1093 nm **Find:** equivalent transitions

Conceptual Plan: $\lambda \rightarrow E_{photon} \rightarrow E_{atom} \rightarrow n$

$E = \frac{hc}{\lambda}$ $\qquad$ $E_{photon} = -E_{atom}$ $\qquad$ $E = -2.18 \times 10^{-18}\,J\left(\frac{1}{n_f^2} - \frac{1}{n_i^2}\right)$

Solution: Since the wavelength of the transitions are longer wavelengths than those obtained in the visual region, the electron must relax to a higher n level. Therefore, we can assume that the electron returns to the n = 3 level.

For $\lambda = 1875$ nm: $E = \dfrac{(6.626 \times 10^{-34}\,J \cdot \cancel{s})(3.00 \times 10^8\,\cancel{m}/\cancel{s})}{1875\,\cancel{nm}\left(\dfrac{\cancel{m}}{10^9\,\cancel{nm}}\right)} = 1.060 \times 10^{-19}\,J \quad 1.060 \times 10^{-19}\,J = -1.060 \times 10^{-19}\,J$

$$-1.060 \times 10^{-19}\,J = -2.18 \times 10^{-18}\left(\frac{1}{3^2} - \frac{1}{n^2}\right);\ n = 4$$

For $\lambda = 1282$ nm: $E = \dfrac{(6.626 \times 10^{-34}\,J \cdot \cancel{s})(3.00 \times 10^8\,\cancel{m}/\cancel{s})}{1282\,\cancel{nm}\left(\dfrac{\cancel{m}}{10^9\,\cancel{nm}}\right)} = 1.551 \times 10^{-19}\,J \quad 1.551 \times 10^{-19}\,J = -1.551 \times 10^{-19}\,J$

$$-1.551 \times 10^{-19} = -2.18 \times 10^{-18}\left(\frac{1}{3^2} - \frac{1}{n^2}\right);\ n = 5$$

For $\lambda = 1093$ nm: $E = \dfrac{(6.626 \times 10^{-34}\,J \cdot \cancel{s})(3.00 \times 10^8\,\cancel{m}/\cancel{s})}{1093\,\cancel{nm}\left(\dfrac{\cancel{m}}{10^9\,\cancel{nm}}\right)} = 1.819 \times 10^{-19}\,J \quad 1.819 \times 10^{-19}\,J = -1.819 \times 10^{-19}\,J$

$$-1.819 \times 10^{-19}\,J = -2.18 \times 10^{-18}\left(\frac{1}{3^2} - \frac{1}{n^2}\right);\ n = 6$$

Check: The values obtained are all integers, which is correct. The values of n: 4,5,6, are reasonable. The values of n increase as the wavelength decreases because the two n levels involved are further apart and more energy is released as the electron relaxes to the $n = 3$ level.

7.86 **Given:** λ = 121.5 nm; 102.6 nm; 97.23 nm **Find:** equivalent transitions
Conceptual Plan: $\lambda \rightarrow E_{photon} \rightarrow E_{atom} \rightarrow n$

$$E = \frac{hc}{\lambda} \qquad E_{photon} = -E_{atom} \qquad E = -2.18 \times 10^{-18} J\left(\frac{1}{n_f^2} - \frac{1}{n_i^2}\right)$$

Solution: Since the wavelengths of the transitions are shorter wavelengths than those obtained in the visual region, the electron must relax to a lower n level. Therefore, we can assume that the electron returns to the $n = 1$ level.

$$\text{For } \lambda = 121.5 \text{ nm: } E = \frac{(6.626 \times 10^{-34} \text{ J}\cdot\text{s})(3.00 \times 10^8 \text{ m/s})}{121.5 \text{ nm}\left(\frac{\text{m}}{10^9 \text{ nm}}\right)} = 1.636 \times 10^{-18} \text{ J} \quad 1.636 \times 10^{-18} \text{ J} = -1.636\text{x}10^{-18} \text{J}$$

$$-1.636 \times 10^{-18} \text{ J} = -2.18 \times 10^{-18}\left(\frac{1}{1^2} - \frac{1}{n^2}\right); n = 2$$

$$\text{For } \lambda = 102.6 \text{ nm: } E = \frac{(6.626 \times 10^{-34} \text{ J}\cdot\text{s})(3.00 \times 10^8 \text{ m/s})}{102.6 \text{ nm}\left(\frac{\text{m}}{10^9 \text{ nm}}\right)} = 1.937 \times 10^{-18} \text{ J} \quad 1.937 \times 10^{-18} \text{ J} = -1.937 \times 10^{-18} \text{ J}$$

$$-1.937 \times 10^{-18} \text{ J} = -2.18 \times 10^{-18}\left(\frac{1}{1^2} - \frac{1}{n^2}\right); n = 3$$

$$\text{For } \lambda = 97.23 \text{ nm: } E = \frac{(6.626 \times 10^{-34} \text{ J}\cdot\text{s})(3.00 \times 10^8 \text{ m/s})}{97.23 \text{ nm}\left(\frac{\text{m}}{10^9 \text{ nm}}\right)} = 2.044 \times 10^{-18} \text{ J} \quad 2.044 \times 10^{-18} \text{ J} = -2.044 \times 10^{-18} \text{ J}$$

$$-2.044 \times 10^{-18} \text{ J} = -2.18 \times 10^{-18}\left(\frac{1}{1^2} - \frac{1}{n^2}\right); n = 4$$

Check: The values obtained are all integers, which is *correct*. The values of n: 2,3,4, are reasonable. The values of n increase as the wavelength decreases because the two n levels involved are further apart and more energy is released as the electron relaxes to the $n = 1$ level.

7.87 **Given:** Φ = 193 kJ/mol **Find:** threshold frequency(ν)
Conceptual Plan: Φ **kJ/ mol** $\rightarrow$ Φ **kJ/ atom** $\rightarrow$ Φ **J/ atom** $\rightarrow$ ν

$$\frac{6.022 \times 10^{23} \text{ atoms}}{\text{mol}} \qquad \frac{1000 \text{ J}}{\text{kJ}} \qquad \Phi = h\nu$$

$$\textbf{Solution: } \nu = \frac{\Phi}{h} = \frac{\left(\frac{193 \text{ kJ}}{\text{mol}}\right)\left(\frac{\text{mol}}{6.022 \times 10^{23} \text{ atoms}}\right)\left(\frac{1000 \text{ J}}{\text{kJ}}\right)}{6.626 \times 10^{-34} \text{ J}\cdot\text{s}} = 4.84 \times 10^{14} \text{ s}^{-1}$$

Check: The units of the answer, s^{-1}, are correct. The magnitude of the answer puts the frequency in the infrared range and is a reasonable answer.

7.88 **Given:** m = 2 amu; v = 1 x 10^6 m/s **Find:** λ
Conceptual Plan: **m(amu)** $\rightarrow$ **m(g)** $\rightarrow$ **m(kg) and then m, v** $\rightarrow \lambda$

$$\frac{1.661 \times 10^{-24} \text{ g}}{\text{amu}} \qquad \frac{\text{kg}}{1000 \text{ g}} \qquad \lambda = \frac{h}{mv}$$

$$\textbf{Solution: } \frac{6.626 \times 10^{-34} \frac{\text{kg}\cdot\text{m}^2}{\text{s}^2}\cdot\text{s}}{(2 \text{ amu})\left(\frac{1.661 \times 10^{-24} \text{ g}}{\text{amu}}\right)\left(\frac{\text{kg}}{1000 \text{ g}}\right)(1 \times 10^6 \text{ m/s})} = 2 \times 10^{-13} \text{ m}$$

Check: The units of the answer, m, are correct. The magnitude of the answer is reasonable since it is a smaller wavelength than for an electron and a deuteron has a much larger mass than an electron.

7.89 **Given:** $\nu_{low} = 30\text{s}^{-1}$ $\nu_{hi} = 1.5 \times 10^4 \text{ s}^{-1}$; speed = 344 m/s **Find:** $\lambda_{low} - \lambda_{hi}$
Conceptual Plan: $\nu_{low} \rightarrow \lambda_{low}$ **and** $\nu_{hi} = \lambda_{hi}$ **then** $\lambda_{low} - \lambda_{hi}$

$$\lambda\nu = \text{speed}$$

$$\textbf{Solution: } \lambda = \frac{\text{speed}}{\nu} \quad \lambda_{low} = \frac{344 \text{ m/s}}{30 \text{ s}^{-1}} = 11 \text{ m} \quad \lambda_{hi} = \frac{344 \text{ m/s}}{1.5 \times 10^4 \text{ s}^{-1}} = 0.023 \text{ m} \quad 11 \text{ m} - 0.023 \text{ m} = 11 \text{ m}$$

Check: The units of the answer, m, are correct. The magnitude is reasonable since the value is only determined by the low frequency value because of significant figures.

7.90 **Given:** d = 1.5×10^8 km, $\nu = 1.0 \times 10^{14}\ s^{-1}$ **Find:** number of wave crests

Conceptual Plan: $\nu \rightarrow \lambda$ and then d(km) $\rightarrow$ d(m) $\rightarrow$ number of waves $\rightarrow$ number of crests

$$\nu = \frac{c}{\lambda} \qquad \frac{1000\ m}{km} \qquad \frac{d}{\lambda}$$

Solution: $$\frac{3.00 \times 10^8\ m/s}{1.0 \times 10^{14}\ s^{-1}} = 3.0 \times 10^{-6}\ m \qquad \frac{1.5 \times 10^8\ km \times \frac{1000\ m}{km}}{3.0 \times 10^{-6}\ m} = 5.0 \times 10^{16}\ \text{waves}$$

Since wavelength is measured crest to crest, the number of wave crests would be $5.0 \times 10^{16} + 1$.

Check: The answer is reasonable since the wavelength is small and the distance traveled is large.

7.91 **Given:** λ = 792 nm, V = 100.0 mL, P = 55.7 mtorr, T = 25°C **Find:** E to dissociate 15.0%

Conceptual Plan: λ $\rightarrow$ E/molecule and then P.V.T $\rightarrow$ n $\rightarrow$ molecules

$$E = \frac{hc}{\lambda} \qquad n = \frac{PV}{RT} \qquad \frac{6.022 \times 10^{23}\ \text{molecules}}{\text{mole}}$$

Solution: $$E = \frac{(6.626 \times 10^{-34}\ J \cdot s)(3.00 \times 10^8\ m/s)}{792\ nm\left(\frac{m}{10^9\ nm}\right)} = 2.51 \times 10^{-19}\ J/\text{molecule}$$

$$\frac{(55.7\ mtorr)\left(\frac{1\ torr}{1000\ mtorr}\right)\left(\frac{1\ atm}{760\ torr}\right)(100.0\ mL)\left(\frac{L}{1000\ mL}\right)\left(\frac{6.022 \times 10^{23}\ \text{molecules}}{mol}\right)}{\left(\frac{0.0821\ L\,atm}{mol\,K}\right)(298\ K)} = 1.80 \times 10^{17}\ \text{molecules}$$

$(1.80 \times 10^{17}\ \text{molecules})(0.15\%) = 2.70 \times 10^{16}$ molecules dissociated

$(2.51 \times 10^{-19}\ J/\text{molecule})(2.70 \times 10^{16}\ \text{molecules}) = 6.777 \times 10^{-3}\ J = 6.78 \times 10^{-3}\ J$

Check: The units of the answer, J, are correct. The magnitude is reasonable since it is for a part of a mole of molecules.

7.92 **Given:** 5.00 mL, 0.100 M, E = 15.5 J, λ = 349 nm **Find:** % molecules emitting a photon

Conceptual Plan: mL, M $\rightarrow$ mol $\rightarrow$ molecules and then λ $\rightarrow$ E/molecule and then E $\rightarrow$ % molecules

$$VM \qquad \frac{6.022 \times 10^{23}\ \text{molecules}}{\text{mole}} \qquad E = \frac{hc}{\lambda} \qquad (\text{E given}/(\text{E x molecules})) \times 100$$

Solution: $$(5.00\ mL)\left(\frac{1\ L}{1000\ mL}\right)\left(\frac{0.100\ mol}{L}\right)\left(\frac{6.022 \times 10^{23}\ \text{molecules}}{mol}\right) = 3.0\underline{1}1 \times 10^{20}\ \text{molecules}$$

$$E = \frac{(6.626 \times 10^{-34}\ J \cdot s)(3.00 \times 10^8\ m/s)}{349\ nm\left(\frac{m}{10^9\ nm}\right)} = 5.6\underline{9}6 \times 10^{-19}\ J/\text{molecule}$$

$(3.01 \times 10^{20}\ \text{molecules})(5.70 \times 10^{-19}\ J/\text{molecule}) = 17\underline{1}.57\ J = 172\ J$

$$\frac{15.5\ J}{172\ J} \times 100 = 9.01\%$$

Check: The units of the answer are correct; the magnitude is reasonable since it is less than 100%.

7.93 **Given:** 20.0 mW, 1.00 hr., 2.29×10^{20} photons **Find:** λ

Conceptual Plan: mW $\rightarrow$ W $\rightarrow$ J $\rightarrow$ J/photon $\rightarrow$ λ

$$\frac{W}{1000\ mW} \qquad E = W \times s \qquad \frac{E}{\text{number of photons}} \qquad \lambda = \frac{hc}{E}$$

Solution: $$(20.0\ mW)\left(\frac{1\ W}{1000\ mW}\right)\left(\frac{\frac{J}{s}}{W}\right)\left(\frac{3600\ s}{2.29 \times 10^{20}\ \text{photons}}\right) = 3.14 \times 10^{-19}\ J/\text{photon}$$

$$\frac{(6.626 \times 10^{-34}\ \text{J}\cdot\text{s})(3.00 \times 10^{8}\ \text{m/s})\left(\frac{10^9\ \text{nm}}{\text{m}}\right)}{3.14 \times 10^{-19}\ \text{J}} = 632\ \text{nm}$$

Check: The units of the answer, nm, are correct. The magnitude is reasonable because it is in the red range.

7.94 **Given:** 150.0 W, 1.33×10^{19} photons/s, $\lambda = 1064$ nm **Find:** % efficiency

Conceptual Plan: $\lambda \rightarrow$ E/photon $\rightarrow$ E $\rightarrow$ W $\rightarrow$ %

$E = \frac{hc}{\lambda}$ x Photons $\frac{E}{s}$ $(W/W_{total}) \times 100$

Solution:

$$E = \frac{(6.626 \times 10^{-34}\ \frac{\text{J}}{\text{photon}}\cdot\text{s})(3.00 \times 10^{8}\ \text{m/s})\left(1.33 \times 10^{19}\frac{\text{photon}}{\text{s}}\right)\left(\frac{\text{W}}{\text{J/s}}\right)}{1064\ \text{nm}\left(\frac{\text{m}}{10^9\ \text{nm}}\right)} = 2.4\underline{8}4\ \text{W}$$

$$\frac{2.48\ \text{W}}{150.0\ \text{W}} \times 100 = 1.65\%$$

Check: The units of the answer, %, are correct. The magnitude is reasonable since it is less than 100%.

Challenge Problems

7.95 (a) **Given:** $n = 1, n = 2, n = 3$, L = 155 pm **Find:** E_1, E_2, E_3

Conceptual Plan: $n \rightarrow$ E

$E_n = \frac{n^2h^2}{8\,m\,L^2}$

Solution:

$$E_1 = \frac{1^2(6.626 \times 10^{-34}\ \text{J}\cdot\text{s})^2}{8(9.11 \times 10^{-31}\ \text{kg})(155\ \text{pm})^2\left(\frac{\text{m}}{10^{12}\ \text{pm}}\right)^2} = \frac{1(6.626 \times 10^{-34})^2\ \text{J}^2\,\text{s}^2}{8(9.11\text{x}10^{-31}\ \text{kg})(155 \times 10^{-12})^2\ \text{m}^2}$$

$$= \frac{1(6.626 \times 10^{-34})^2\left(\frac{\text{kg}\cdot\text{m}^2}{\text{s}^2}\right)\text{J}\,\text{s}^2}{8(9.11 \times 10^{-31}\ \text{kg})(155 \times 10^{-12})^2\ \text{m}^2} = 2.51 \times 10^{-18}\ \text{J}$$

$$E_2 = \frac{2^2(6.626 \times 10^{-34}\ \text{J}\cdot\text{s})^2}{8(9.11 \times 10^{-31}\ \text{kg})(155\ \text{pm})^2\left(\frac{\text{m}}{10^{12}\ \text{pm}}\right)^2} = \frac{4(6.626 \times 10^{-34})^2\ \text{J}^2\,\text{s}^2}{8(9.11\text{x}10^{-31}\ \text{kg})(155 \times 10^{-12})^2\text{m}^2}$$

$$= \frac{4(6.626 \times 10^{-34})^2\left(\frac{\text{kg}\cdot\text{m}^2}{\text{s}^2}\right)\text{J}\,\text{s}^2}{8(9.11 \times 10^{-31}\ \text{kg})(155 \times 10^{-12})^2\ \text{m}^2} = 1.00 \times 10^{-17}\ \text{J}$$

$$E_3 = \frac{3^2(6.626 \times 10^{-34}\ \text{J}\cdot\text{s})^2}{8(9.11 \times 10^{-31}\ \text{kg})(155\ \text{pm})^2\left(\frac{\text{m}}{10^{12}\ \text{pm}}\right)^2} = \frac{9(6.626 \times 10^{-34})^2\ \text{J}^2\,\text{s}^2}{8(9.11 \times 10^{-31}\ \text{kg})(155 \times 10^{-12})^2\ \text{m}^2}$$

$$= \frac{9(6.626 \times 10^{-34})^2\left(\frac{\text{kg}\cdot\text{m}^2}{\text{s}^2}\right)\text{J}\,\text{s}^2}{8(9.11 \times 10^{-31}\ \text{kg})(155 \times 10^{-12})^2\ \text{m}^2} = 2.26 \times 10^{-17}\ \text{J}$$

Check: The units of the answers, J, are correct. The answers seem reasonable since the energy is increasing with increasing n level.

(b) **Given:** $n = 1 \rightarrow n = 2$ and $n = 2 \rightarrow n = 3$ **Find:** λ

Conceptual Plan: $n = 1, n = 2 \rightarrow \Delta E_{atom} \rightarrow \Delta E_{photon} \rightarrow \lambda$

$\Delta E_{atom} = E_2 - E_1$ $\Delta E_{atom} \rightarrow -\Delta E_{photon}$ $E = \frac{hc}{\lambda}$

Solution: Using the energies calculated in part a

$E_2 - E_1 = (1.00 \times 10^{-17}\ \text{J} - 2.51 \times 10^{-18}\ \text{J}) = 7.49 \times 10^{-18}\ \text{J}$

$$\lambda = \frac{(6.626 \times 10^{-34}\ \cancel{J} \cdot \cancel{s})(3.00 \times 10^{8}\ m/\cancel{s})}{7.49 \times 10^{-18}\ \cancel{J}} = 2.65 \times 10^{-8}\ m = 26.5\ nm$$

$E_3 - E_2 = (2.26 \times 10^{-17}\ J - 1.00 \times 10^{-17}\ J) = 1.26 \times 10^{-17}\ J$

$$\lambda = \frac{(6.626 \times 10^{-34}\ \cancel{J} \cdot \cancel{s})(3.00 \times 10^{8}\ m/\cancel{s})}{1.26 \times 10^{-17}\ \cancel{J}} = 1.58 \times 10^{-8}\ m = 15.8\ nm$$

These wavelengths would lie in the UV region.

Check: The units of the answers, m, are correct. The magnitude of the answers is reasonable based on the energies obtained for the levels.

7.96 **Given:** $n = 1$, $\nu = 8.85 \times 10^{13}\ s^{-1}$ **Find:** E, λ

Conceptual Plan: $n, \nu \rightarrow E \rightarrow \lambda$

$$E = \left(n + \frac{1}{2}\right)h\nu \quad E = \frac{hc}{\lambda}$$

Solution:

$$E = \left(1 + \frac{1}{2}\right)(6.626 \times 10^{-34}\ J \cdot \cancel{s})(8.85 \times 10^{13}\ \cancel{s^{-1}}) = 8.80 \times 10^{-20}\ J$$

$$\lambda = \frac{hc}{E} = \frac{(6.626 \times 10^{-34}\ \cancel{J} \cdot \cancel{s})(3.00 \times 10^{8}\ m/\cancel{s})}{8.80 \times 10^{-20}\ \cancel{J}} = 2.26 \times 10^{-6}\ m$$

Check: The units of the answer, J and m, are correct. The magnitude of the answer puts the vibrational frequency in the infrared region, which is reasonable.

7.97 For the 1s orbital in the Excel spreadsheet, call column A: r; and column B: Ψ(1s). Make the values for r column A: 0–200. In column B, put the equation for the wave function written as follows: =(POWER(1/3.1415,1/2))*(1/POWER(53,3/2))*(EXP(-A2/53)). Go to make chart, choose xy scatter.

e.g., sample values

r	Ψ (1s)
0	7.000146224
1	7.000143491
2	7.000140809
3	7.000138177
4	7.000135594
5	7.00013306
6	7.000130573

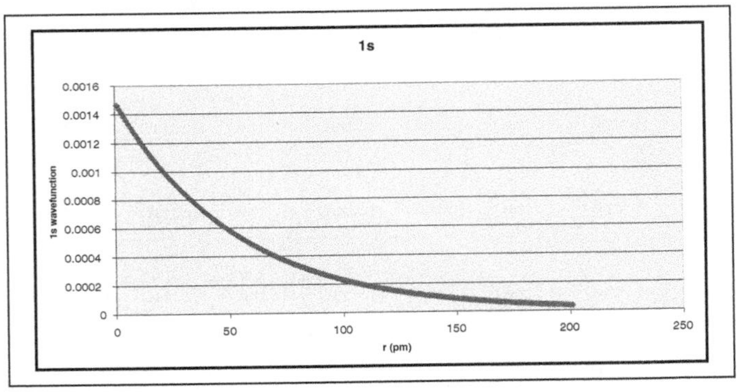

For the 2s orbital in the same Excel spreadsheet, call column A: r; and column C: Ψ(2s). Use the same values for r in column A: 0–200. In column C, put the equation for the wave function written as follows: =(POWER(1/((32)*(3.1415)),1/2))*(1/POWER(53,3/2))*(2-(A2/53))*(EXP(-A2/53)). Go to make chart, choose xy scatter.

e.g., sample values

r	Ψ (2s)
0	7.0000516979
1	7.000050253
2	7.0000488441
3	7.0000474702
4	7.0000461307
5	7.0000448247
6	7.0000435513

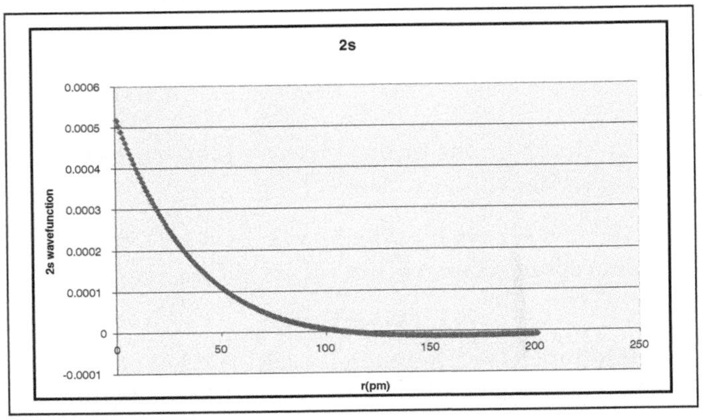

Note: The plot for the 2s orbital extends below the x axis. The x-intercept represents the radial node of the orbital.

7.98 **Given:** $\Delta E = E_m - E_n = -2.18 \times 10^{-18}(1/m^2) - [-2.18 \times 10^{-18}(1/n^2)]$; $E = hc/\lambda$ **Find:** $1/\lambda = R(1/m^2 - 1/n^2)$
Conceptual Plan: $\Delta E_{atom} \rightarrow E_{photon} \rightarrow 1/\lambda$

$\Delta E_{atom} = E_m - E_n \Delta E_{atom} \rightarrow -\Delta E_{photon}$ $E = \frac{hc}{\lambda}$

Solution:

$$\Delta E = E_m - E_n = -2.18 \times 10^{-18}\left(\frac{1}{m^2}\right) - \left[-2.18 \times 10^{-18}\left(\frac{1}{n^2}\right)\right] = -2.18 \times 10^{-18}\left(\frac{1}{m^2} - \frac{1}{n^2}\right)$$

$\Delta E_{atom} = -\Delta E_{photon}$

$$E_{photon} = -\left(-2.18 \times 10^{-18}\left(\frac{1}{m^2} - \frac{1}{n^2}\right)\right) = \frac{hc}{\lambda}\frac{1}{\lambda} = \frac{2.18 \times 10^{-18}}{hc}\left(\frac{1}{m^2} - \frac{1}{n^2}\right) = 1.1 \times 10^{7}\left(\frac{1}{m^2} - \frac{1}{n^2}\right)$$

$$\frac{1}{\lambda} = R\left(\frac{1}{m^2} - \frac{1}{n^2}\right)$$

7.99 **Given:** threshold frequency $= 2.25 \times 10^{14}\ s^{-1}$; $\lambda = 5.00 \times 10^{-7}$ m **Find:** v of electron
Conceptual Plan: $\nu \rightarrow \Phi$ **and then** $\lambda \rightarrow E$ **and then** $\rightarrow KE \rightarrow v$

$\Phi = h\nu$ $E = \frac{hc}{\lambda}$ $KE = E - \Phi$ $KE = 1/2\ mv^2$

Solution:

$$\Phi = (6.626 \times 10^{-34}\ J \cdot s)(2.25 \times 10^{14}\ s^{-1}) = 1.491 \times 10^{-19}\ J \quad E = \frac{(6.626 \times 10^{-34}\ J \cdot s)(3.00 \times 10^{8}\ m/s)}{5.00 \times 10^{-7}\ m} = 3.976 \times 10^{-19}\ J$$

$$KE = 3.976 \times 10^{-19}\ J - 1.491 \times 10^{-19}\ J = 2.485 \times 10^{-19}\ J \quad v^2 = \frac{2.485 \times 10^{-19}\ \frac{kg \cdot m^2}{s^2}}{\frac{1}{2}(9.11 \times 10^{-31}\ kg)} = 5.455 \times 10^{11}\ \frac{m^2}{s^2}$$

$v = 7.39 \times 10^5$ m/s

Check: The units of the answer, m/s, are correct. The magnitude of the answer is reasonable for the speed of an electron.

7.100 **Given:** $\lambda = 2.8 \times 10^{-4}$ cm; m = 2.0 g; $\Delta T = 2.0$ K **Find:** number of photons
Conceptual Plan: $\lambda(cm) \rightarrow \lambda(m) \rightarrow E_{photon}$ **and** $m, \Delta T \rightarrow q_{water}$ **and then** $\rightarrow$ **number photons**

$\frac{m}{100\ cm}$ $E = \frac{hc}{\lambda}$ $q = mC_s\Delta T$ $\frac{q_{water}}{E_{photon}}$

Solution: $$E_{photon} = \frac{(6.626 \times 10^{-34}\ J \cdot s)(3.00 \times 10^{8}\ m/s)}{(2.8 \times 10^{-4}\ cm)\left(\frac{m}{100\ cm}\right)} = 7.1 \times 10^{-20}\ J/photon$$

$$q = (2.0\ g)\left(4.18\frac{J}{g \cdot {}^\circ C}\right)\left(\frac{{}^\circ C}{K}\right)(2.0\ K) = 16.7\ J \quad \text{number of photons} = \frac{16.7\ J}{7.1 \times 10^{-20}\ J/photon} = 2.4 \times 10^{20}\ \text{photons}$$

Check: The units of the answer, photons, are correct. The magnitude of the answer seems reasonable because a large amount of heat energy is needed to raise the temperature of the water.

7.101 **Given:** t = 5.0 fs, $\lambda_{low} = 722$ nm **Find:** ΔE, and λ_{high}
Conceptual Plan: $t \rightarrow \Delta E$ **and then** $\lambda_{low} \rightarrow E_{high} \rightarrow E_{low} \rightarrow \lambda_{high}$

$\Delta t \times \Delta E \geq \frac{h}{4\pi}$ $E = \frac{hc}{\lambda}$ $E - \Delta E$ $\lambda = \frac{hc}{E}$

Solution: $$\frac{6.626 \times 10^{-34}\ J \cdot s}{4(3.141)(5.0\ fs)\left(\frac{s}{1 \times 10^{15}\ fs}\right)} = 1.055 \times 10^{-20}\ J$$

$$E = \frac{(6.626 \times 10^{-34}\ J \cdot s)(3.00 \times 10^{8}\ m/s)}{722\ nm\left(\frac{m}{10^{9}\ nm}\right)} = 2.75 \times 10^{-19}\ J$$

$2.75 \times 10^{-19}\,\text{J} - 1.06 \times 10^{-20}\,\text{J} = 2.64 \times 10^{-19}\,\text{J}$

$$\frac{(6.626 \times 10^{-34}\,\text{J}\cdot\text{s})(3.00 \times 10^{8}\,\text{m/s})\left(\frac{10^9\,\text{nm}}{\text{m}}\right)}{(2.64 \times 10^{-19}\,\text{J})} = 751.8\text{ nm} = 7.5 \times 10^2\text{ nm}$$

Check: The units of the answer, nm, are correct. The magnitude of the answer is reasonable since it is a longer wavelength but it is close to the original wavelength.

7.102 **Given:** threshold $\nu = 6.71 \times 10^{14}\,\text{s}^{-1}$, $v = 6.95 \times 10^5$ m/s, $\nu = 1.01 \times 10^{15}\,\text{s}^{-1}$ **Find:** mass of electron

Conceptual Plan: threshold $\nu \rightarrow \Phi$ and then $\nu \rightarrow$ E and then KE $\rightarrow$ m

$\Phi = h\nu$ $\qquad$ $E = h\nu$ $\qquad$ $KE = E - \Phi$ $\quad$ $m = \frac{2KE}{v^2}$

Solution: $\Phi = (6.626 \times 10^{-34}\,\text{J s})(6.71 \times 10^{14}\,\text{s}^{-1}) = 4.45 \times 10^{-19}\,\text{J}$

$E = (6.626 \times 10^{-34}\,\text{J s})(1.01 \times 10^{15}\,\text{s}^{-1}) = 6.69 \times 10^{-19}\,\text{J}$

$KE = E - \Phi = 2.24 \times 10^{-19}\,\text{J}$

$$m = \frac{2\left(2.24 \times 10^{-19}\,\frac{\text{kg m}^2}{\text{s}^2}\right)}{\left(6.95 \times 10^5\,\frac{\text{m}}{\text{s}}\right)^2} = 9.27 \times 10^{-31}\text{ kg}$$

Check: The units of the answer, kg, are correct. The magnitude of the answer is reasonable since it is very close to the accepted mass of an electron.

7.103 **Given:** r = 1.8 m **Find:** λ

Conceptual Plan: r $\rightarrow$ C

$C = 2\pi r$

Solution: (2)(3.141)(1.8m) = 11.3 m = the circumference of the orbit. So the largest wavelength that would fit the orbit would be 11 m.

Check: The units of the answer, m, are correct. The magnitude of the wave is about the circumference of the orbit.

7.104 **Given:** $\Delta H_{fusion} = 6.00$ kJ/mol, $\lambda = 6.42 \times 10^{-6}$ m, 1.00 g ice **Find:** number of photons

Conceptual Plan: ΔH kJ/mol $\rightarrow$ ΔH J/mol $\rightarrow$ ΔH J/g and then $\lambda \rightarrow$ E/photon $\rightarrow$ photons

$\frac{1000\text{ J}}{\text{kJ}}$ $\qquad$ $\frac{1\text{ mol } H_2O}{18.0\text{ g}}$ $\qquad$ $E = \frac{hc}{\lambda}$

Solution: $\left(\frac{6.00\,\text{kJ}}{\text{mol}}\right) \times \left(\frac{1000\,\text{J}}{\text{kJ}}\right) \times \left(\frac{1\,\text{mol}}{18.0\,\text{g}}\right) \times (1.00\text{ g}) = 333\text{ J}$

$$E = \frac{(6.626 \times 10^{-34}\,\text{J}\cdot\text{s})(3.00 \times 10^{8}\,\text{m/s})}{6.42 \times 10^{-6}\,\text{m}} = 3.10 \times 10^{-20}\text{ J/photon}$$

$$\frac{333\,\text{J}}{3.10 \times 10^{-20}\,\text{J/photon}} = 1.08 \times 10^{22}\text{ photons}$$

Check: The units of the answer, number of photons, are correct. The magnitude is reasonable since you will need a fairly large number of photons to melt 1 gram of ice.

Conceptual Problems

7.105 In the Bohr model of the atom, the electron travels in a circular orbit around the nucleus. It is a 2-dimensional model. The electron is constrained to move only from one orbit to another orbit. But, the electron is treated as a particle that behaves according to the laws of classical physics. The quantum-mechanical model of the atom is 3-dimensional. In this model, we treat the electron, an absolutely small particle, differently than we treat particles with classical physics. The electron is in an orbital, which gives us the probability of finding the electron within a volume of space.

Because the electron in the Bohr model is constrained to a circular orbit, it would theoretically be possible to know both the position and the velocity of the electron simultaneously. This contradicts the Heisenberg uncertainty principle, which states that position and velocity are complementary terms that cannot both be known with precision.

7.106 The transition from $n = 3 \rightarrow n = 2$ would cause the photoelectric effect, while the transition from $n = 4 \rightarrow n = 3$ would not. Because the n levels get closer together as n increases, the energy difference between the 4 and 3 level would be less than the energy difference between the 3 and 2 levels. Therefore, the energy of the photon emitted when the electron moves from 4 to 3 would not be above the threshold energy for the metal. The energy of the photon emitted when the electron makes the transition from $n = 3$ to $n = 2$ is larger and surpasses the threshold energy, thus causing the photoelectric effect.

7.107 (a) Since the interference pattern is caused by single electrons interfering with themselves, the pattern remains the same even when the rate of the electrons passing through the slits is one electron per minute. It will simply take longer for the full pattern to develop.

(b) When a light is placed behind the slits, it flashes to indicate which hole the electron passed through, but the interference pattern is now absent. With the laser on, the electrons hit positions directly behind each slit, as if they were ordinary particles.

(c) Diffraction occurs when a wave encounters an obstacle of a slit that is comparable in size to its wavelength. The wave bends around the slit. The diffraction of light through two slits separated by a distance comparable to the wavelength of the light results in an interference pattern. Each slit acts as a new wave source, and the two new waves interfere with each other, which results in a pattern of bright and dark lines.

(d) Since the mass of the bullets and their particle size are not absolutely small, the bullets will not produce an interference pattern when they pass through the slits. The de Broglie wavelength produced by the bullets will not be sufficiently large enough to interfere with the bullet trajectory and no interference pattern will be observed.

8 Periodic Properties of the Elements

Review Questions

8.1 A periodic property is one that is predictable based on the element's position within the periodic table.

8.2 The relative size of the sodium and potassium ions is important to nerve signal transmission. The pumps and channels within cell membranes are so sensitive that they can distinguish between the sizes of these two ions and selectively allow only one or the other to pass. The movement of ions is the basis for the transmission of nerve signals in the brain and throughout the body.

8.3 The first attempt to organize the elements according to similarities in their properties was made by the German chemist Johann Dobereiner. He grouped elements into triads; three elements with similar properties. A more complex approach was attempted by the English chemist John Newlands. He organized elements into octaves, analogous to musical notes. When arranged this way, the properties of every eighth element were similar.

8.4 The modern periodic table is credited primarily to the Russian chemist Dmitri Mendeleev. Mendeleev's table is based on the periodic law, which states that when elements are arranged in order of increasing mass, their properties recur periodically. Mendeleev arranged the elements in a table in which mass increased from left to right and elements with similar properties fell in the same columns.

8.5 Meyer proposed an organization of the known elements based on some periodic properties. Moseley listed elements according to the atomic number rather than atomic mass. This resolved the problems in Mendeleev's table where an increase in atomic mass did not correlate with similar properties.

8.6 The periodic law was based on the observations that the properties of elements recur and certain elements have similar properties. The theory that explains the existence of the periodic law is quantum-mechanical theory.

8.7 Electron spin is a fundamental property of electrons. It is more correctly expressed as saying the electron has inherent angular momentum. The value m_s is the spin quantum number. An electron with $m_s = +1/2$ has a spin opposite of an electron with $m_s = -1/2$.

8.8 In the Stern–Gerlach experiment a beam of silver atoms is split into two separate trajectories by a magnet. The spin of the electrons within the atoms creates a tiny magnetic field that interacts with the external field. One spin orientation causes the deflection of the beam in one direction, while the other orientation causes a deflection in the opposite direction. Since there were only two trajectories, the spin of the electron is quantized, that is, it can have one of two values and nothing in between.

8.9 An electron configuration shows the particular orbitals that are occupied by electrons in an atom. Some examples are H = $1s^1$, He = $1s^2$, and Li = $1s^22s^1$.

8.10 Coulomb's law states that the potential energy (E) of two charged particles depends of their charges (q_1 and q_2) and on their separation, (r). $E = \frac{1}{4\pi\epsilon_o}\frac{q_1 q_2}{r}$. The potential energy is positive for charges of the same sign and negative for charges of opposite sign. The magnitude of the potential energy depends inversely on the separation between the charged particles.

8.11 Shielding or screening occurs when one electron is blocked from the full effects of the nuclear charge so that the electron experiences only a part of the nuclear charge. It is the inner (core) electrons that shield the outer electrons from the full nuclear charge.

8.12 Penetration occurs when an electron penetrates the electron cloud of the 1s orbital and experiences the charge of the nucleus more fully because it is less shielded by the intervening electrons. As the outer electron undergoes penetration into the region occupied by the inner electrons, it experiences a greater nuclear charge and therefore, according to Coulomb's law, a lower energy.

8.13 The sublevels within a principle level split in multielectron atoms because of penetration of the outer electrons into the region of the core electrons. The sublevels in hydrogen are not split because they are empty in the ground state.

8.14 An orbital diagram is a different way to show the electron configuration of an atom. It symbolizes the electron as an arrow in a box that represents the orbital.

The orbital diagram for a hydrogen atom: $\underset{1s}{\boxed{\uparrow}}$ H

8.15 The Pauli exclusion principle states the following: No two electrons in an atom can have the same four quantum numbers.

Since two electrons occupying the same orbital have three identical quantum numbers (n, l, m_l), they must have different spin quantum numbers. The Pauli exclusion principle implies that each orbital can have a maximum of only two electrons, with opposing spins.

8.16 Degenerate orbitals are orbitals of the same energy. In a multielectron atom, the orbitals in a sublevel are degenerate. Hund's rule states that when filling degenerate orbitals, electrons fill them singly first, with parallel spins. This is a result of an atom's tendency to find the lowest energy state possible.

8.17 In order of increasing energy the orbitals are 1s < 2s < 2p < 3s < 3p < 4s < 3d < 4p < 5s. The 4s orbital fills before the 3d and the 5s fills before the 4d. They are lower in energy because of greater penetration of the 4s and 5s orbitals.

8.18 Valence electrons are those that are important in chemical bonding. For main-group elements, the valence electrons are those in the outermost principal energy level. For transition elements, we also count the outermost d electrons among the valence even though they are not in the outermost principal energy level. The chemical properties of an element depend on its valence electrons, which are important in bonding because they are held most loosely. This is why the elements in a column of the periodic table have similar chemical properties: they have the same number of valence electrons.

8.19

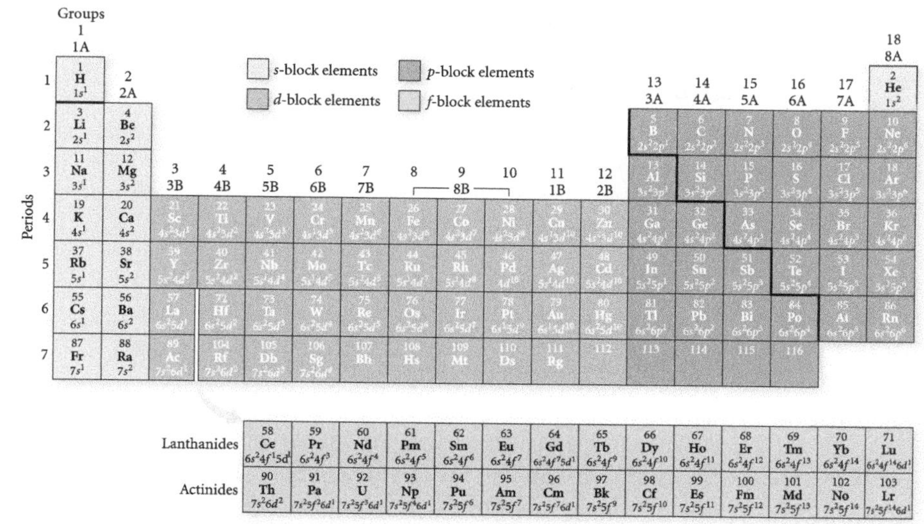

8.20 The number of columns in a block corresponds to the maximum number of electrons that can occupy the particular sublevel of that block. The s block has two columns corresponding to one s orbital holding a maximum of two electrons. The p block has six columns corresponding to the three p orbitals with two electrons each.

8.21 The rows in the periodic table grow progressively longer because you are adding sublevels as the n level increases.

8.22 The lettered group number of a main-group element is equal to the number of valence electrons for that element.

8.23 The row number of a main-group element is equal to the highest principal quantum number of that element. However, the principal quantum number of the d orbital being filled across each row in the transition series is equal to the row number minus one. For the inner transition elements, the principal quantum number of the f orbital being filled across each row is the row number minus two.

8.24 In the first transition series of the d block, Cr and Cu have anomalous electron configurations. Cr is expected to be $[Ar]4s^2 3d^4$, but is found to be $[Ar]4s^1 3d^5$; and Cu is expected to be $[Ar]4s^2 3d^9$, but is found to be $[Ar]4s^1 3d^{10}$.

8.25 To use the periodic table to write the electron configuration find the noble gas that precedes the element. The element has the inner electron configuration of that noble gas. Place the symbol for the noble gas in [ ]. Obtain the outer electron configuration by tracing the element across the period and assigning electrons in the appropriate orbitals.

8.26 The chemical properties of elements are largely determined by the number of valence electrons they contain. Their properties are periodic because the number of valence electrons is periodic. Since elements within a column in the periodic table have the same number of valence electrons, they also have similar chemical properties.

8.27 (a) The alkali metals (group 1A) have 1 valence electron, are among the most reactive metals because their outer electron configuration (ns^1) is one electron beyond a noble gas configuration. They react to lose the ns^1 electron, obtaining a noble gas configuration. This is why the group 1A metals tend to form 1+ cations.

(b) The alkaline earth metals (group 2A) have 2 valence electrons, have an outer electron configuration of ns^2, and also tend to be reactive metals. They lose their ns^2 electrons to form 2+ cations.

(c) The halogens (group 7A) have 7 valence electrons and have an outer electron configuration of ns^2np^5. They are among the most reactive nonmetals. They are only one electron short of a noble gas configuration and tend to react to gain that one electron, forming 1– anions.

(d) The oxygen family (group 6A) has 6 valence electrons and has an outer electron configuration of ns^2np^4. They are 2 electrons short of a noble gas configuration and tend to react to gain those two electrons, forming 2– anions.

8.28 One way to define atomic radii is to consider the distance between nonbonding atoms in molecules or atoms that are touching each other but are not bonded together. An atomic radius determined in this way is called the nonbonding atomic radius or the van der Waals radius. The van der Waals radius represents the radius of an atom when it is not bonded to another atom.

Another way to define the size of an atom, called bonding an atomic radius or covalent radius, is defined differently for nonmetals and metals as follows:

Nonmetals: one-half the distance between two of the atoms bonded together

Metal: one-half the distance between two of the atoms next to each other in a crystal of the metal

A more general term, the atomic radius, refers to a set of average bonding radii determined from measurements on a large number of elements and compounds. The atomic radius represents the radius of an atom when it is bonded to another atom and is always smaller than the van der Waals radius.

(a) As you move to the right across a period in the periodic table, atomic radius decreases.

(b) As you move down a column in the periodic table, atomic radius increases.

8.29 The effective nuclear charge (Z_{eff}) is the average or net charge from the nucleus experienced by the electrons in the outermost levels. Shielding is the blocking of nuclear charge from the outermost electrons. The shielding is primarily due to the inner (core) electrons although there is some interaction and shielding from the electron repulsions of the outer electrons with each other.

8.30 As you move to the right across a row in the periodic table, the n level stays the same. However, the nuclear charge increases and the amount of shielding stays about the same since the number of inner electrons stays the same. So, the effective nuclear charge experienced by the electrons in the outermost principal energy level increases, resulting is a stronger attraction between the outermost electrons and the nucleus and therefore, smaller atomic radii.

8.31 (a) The radii of transition elements stay roughly constant across each row instead of decreasing in size as in the main group elements. The difference is that, across a row of transition elements, the number of electrons in the outermost principal energy level is nearly constant. As another proton is added to the nucleus with each successive element, another electron is added as well, but the electron goes into an $n_{highest} - 1$ orbital. The number of outermost electrons stays constant and they experience a roughly constant effective nuclear charge, keeping the radius approximately constant.

(b) As you go down the first two rows of a column within the transition metals, the elements follow the same general trend in atomic radii and the main-group elements; i.e., the radii get larger because you are adding outermost electrons into higher n levels.

8.32 The electron configuration of a main-group monatomic ion can be deduced from the electron configuration of the neutral atom and the charge of the ion. For anions, we simply add the number of electrons required by the magnitude of the charge of the anion. The electron configuration of cations is obtained by subtracting the number of electrons required by the magnitude of the charge.

8.33 An important exception to simply subtracting the number of electrons occurs for transition metal cations. When writing the electron configuration of a transition metal cation, remove the electrons in the highest n-value orbitals first, even if this does not correspond to the reverse order of filling. Normally, even though the d orbital electrons add after the s orbital electrons, the s orbital electrons are lost first. This is because 1) the ns and (n – 1)d orbitals are extremely close in energy and depending on the exact configuration can vary in relative energy ordering; and 2) as the (n – 1)d orbitals begin to fill in the first transition series, the increasing nuclear charge stabilizes the (n – 1)d orbitals relative to the ns orbitals. This happens because the (n – 1)d orbitals are not outermost orbitals and are therefore not effectively shielded from the increasing nuclear charge by the ns orbitals.

8.34 (a) In general, cations are much smaller than their corresponding parent. This is because the outermost electrons are shielded from the nuclear charge in the atom and contribute greatly to the size of the atom. When these electrons are removed to form the cation, the same nuclear charge is now acting only on the core electrons.

(b) In general, anions are much larger than their corresponding atoms. This is because the extra electrons are added to the outermost electrons but no additional protons are added to increase the nuclear charge. The extra electrons increase the repulsions among the outermost electrons resulting in an anion that is larger than the atom.

8.35 The ionization energy (IE) of an atom or ion is the energy required to remove an electron from the atom or ion in the gaseous state. The ionization energy is always positive because removing an electron always takes energy. The energy required to remove the first electron is called the first ionization energy (IE_1). The energy required to remove the second electron is called the second ionization energy (IE_2). The second IE is always greater than the first IE.

8.36 Ionization energy generally decreases as you move down a column in the periodic table because electrons in the outermost principal level become farther away from the positively charged nucleus and are therefore held less tightly.

Ionization energy generally increases as you move to the right across a period in the periodic table because electrons in the outermost principal energy level generally experience a greater effective nuclear charge and therefore the electrons are closer to the nucleus.

8.37 Exceptions occur with elements Be, Mg, and Ca in group 2A having a higher first ionization energy than elements B, Al, and Ga in group 3A. This exception is caused by the change in going from the s block to the p block. The result is that the electrons in the s orbital shield the electron in the p orbital from nuclear charge making it easier to remove.

Another exception occurs with N, P, and As in group 5A having a higher first ionization energy than O, S, and Se in group 6A. This exception is caused by the repulsion between electrons when they must occupy the same orbital. Group 5A has 3 p electrons while group 6A has 4 p electrons. In the group 5A elements the p orbitals are half-filled, which makes the configuration particularly stable. The fourth group 6A electron must pair with another electron making it easier to remove.

8.38 The second ionization energy of Mg involves removing the second outermost electron leading to an ion with a noble gas configuration for the core electrons. The third ionization energy requires removing a core electron from an ion with a noble gas configuration. This requires a tremendous amount of energy making IE_3 very high.

For Al, IE_3 involves removing the third outermost electron for Al, leaving the ion with a noble gas configuration of the core electrons. IE_4 then requires removing a core electron from an ion with a noble gas configuration. This requires a tremendous amount of energy and makes IE_4 very high.

You can predict whether the IE energy is going to be very high by looking for the ionization that requires removing a core electron.

8.39 The electron affinity (EA) of an atom or ion is the energy change associated with the gaining of an electron by the atom in the gaseous state. The electron affinity is usually—though not always—negative because an atom or ion usually releases energy when it gains an electron. The trends in electron affinity are not as regular as trends in other properties. For main-group elements, electron affinity generally becomes more negative as you move to the right across a row in the periodic table. There is not a corresponding trend in electron affinity going down a column.

8.40 Metals are good conductors of heat and electricity, they can be pounded into flat sheets (malleability), they can be drawn into wires (ductility), they are often shiny, and they tend to lose electrons in chemical reactions. As you move to the right across a period in the periodic table, metallic character decreases. As you move down a column in the periodic table, metallic character increases.

8.41 (a) The reactions of the alkali metals with halogens result in the formation of metal halides.
$2\ M(s) + X_2 \rightarrow 2\ MX(s)$

(b) Alkali metals react with water to form the dissolved alkali metal ion, the hydroxide ion, and hydrogen gas.
$2\ M(s) + 2\ H_2O(l) \rightarrow 2\ M^+(aq) + 2\ OH^-(aq) + H_2(g)$

8.42 All of the halogens are powerful oxidizing agents.
(a) The halogens react with metals to form metal halides.
$2\ M(s) + n\ X_2 \rightarrow 2\ MX_n(s)$

(b) The halogens react with hydrogen to form hydrogen halides.
$H_2(g) + X_2 \rightarrow 2\ HX(g)$

(c) The halogens react with each other to form interhalogen compounds.
e.g. $Br_2(l) + F_2(g) \rightarrow 2\ BrF(g)$

Problems by Topic

Electron Configurations

8.43 (a) Si Silicon has 14 electrons. Distribute two of these into the 1*s* orbital, two into the 2*s* orbital, six into the 2*p* orbital, two into the 3*s* orbital, and two into the 3*p* orbital. $1s^22s^22p^63s^23p^2$

(b) O Oxygen has 8 electrons. Distribute two of these into the 1*s* orbital, two into the 2*s* orbital, and four into the 2*p* orbital. $1s^22s^22p^4$

(c) K Potassium has 19 electrons. Distribute two of these into the 1*s* orbital, two into the 2*s* orbital, six into the 2*p* orbital, two into the 3*s* orbital, six into the 3*p* orbital, and one into the 4s orbital. $1s^22s^22p^63s^23p^64s^1$

(d) Ne Neon has 10 electrons. Distribute two of these into the 1*s* orbital, two into the 2*s* orbital, and six into the 2*p* orbital. $1s^22s^22p^6$

8.44 (a) C Carbon has 6 electrons. Distribute two of these into the 1*s* orbital, two into the 2*s* orbital, and two into the 2*p* orbital. $1s^22s^22p^2$

(b) P Phosphorus has 15 electrons. Distribute two of these into the 1s orbital, two into the 2*s* orbital, six into the 2*p* orbital, two into the 3s orbital, and three into the 3*p* orbital. $1s^22s^22p^63s^23p^3$

(c) Ar Argon has 18 electrons. Distribute two of these into the 1*s* orbital, two into the 2*s* orbital, six into the 2*p* orbital, two into the 3*s* orbital, and six into the 3*p* orbital. $1s^22s^22p^63s^23p^6$

(d) Na Sodium has 11 electrons. Distribute two of these into the 1s orbital, two into the 2*s* orbital, six into the 2*p* orbital, and one into the 3*s* orbital. $1s^22s^22p^63s^1$

8.45 (a) N Nitrogen has 7 electrons and has the electron configuration $1s^22s^22p^3$. Draw a box for each orbital, putting the lowest energy orbital (1s) on the far left and proceeding to orbitals of higher energy to the right. Distribute the 7 electrons into the boxes representing the orbitals, allowing a maximum of two electrons per orbital and remembering Hund's rule. You can see from the diagram that nitrogen has 3 unpaired electrons.

↓↑	↓↑	↑ ↑ ↑
1*s*	2*s*	2*p*

(b) F Fluorine has 9 electrons and has the electron configuration $1s^22s^22p^5$. Draw a box for each orbital, putting the lowest energy orbital (1s) on the far left and proceeding to orbitals of higher energy to the right. Distribute the 9 electrons into the boxes representing the orbitals, allowing a maximum of two electrons per orbital and remembering Hund's rule. You can see from the diagram that fluorine has 1 unpaired electron.

[↓↑] [↓↑] [↓↑|↓↑|↑]
1*s* 2*s* 2*p*

(c) Mg Magnesium has 12 electrons and has the electron configuration $1s^22s^22p^63s^2$. Draw a box for each orbital, putting the lowest energy orbital (1s) on the far left and proceeding to orbitals of higher energy to the right. Distribute the 12 electrons into the boxes representing the orbitals, allowing a maximum of two electrons per orbital and remembering Hund's rule. You can see from the diagram that magnesium has no unpaired electrons.

[↓↑] [↓↑] [↓↑|↓↑|↓↑] [↓↑]
1*s* 2*s* 2*p* 3*s*

(d) Al Aluminum has 13 electrons and has the electron configuration $1s^22s^22p^63s^23p^1$. Draw a box for each orbital, putting the lowest energy orbital (1s) on the far left and proceeding to orbitals of higher energy to the right. Distribute the 13 electrons into the boxes representing the orbitals, allowing a maximum of two electrons per orbital and remembering Hund's rule. You can see from the diagram that aluminum has 1 unpaired electron.

[↓↑] [↓↑] [↓↑|↓↑|↓↑] [↓↑] [↑| |]
1*s* 2*s* 2*p* 3*s* 3*p*

8.46 (a) S Sulfur has 16 electrons and has the electron configuration $1s^22s^22p^63s^23p^4$. Draw a box for each orbital, putting the lowest energy orbital (1s) on the far left and proceeding to orbitals of higher energy to the right. Distribute the 16 electrons into the boxes representing the orbitals, allowing a maximum of two electrons per orbital and remembering Hund's rule. You can see from the diagram that sulfur has 2 unpaired electrons.

[↓↑] [↓↑] [↓↑|↓↑|↓↑] [↓↑] [↓↑|↑|↑]
1*s* 2*s* 2*p* 3*s* 3*p*

(b) Ca Calcium has 20 electrons and has the electron configuration $1s^22s^22p^63s^23p^64s^2$. Draw a box for each orbital, putting the lowest energy orbital (1s) on the far left and proceeding to orbitals of higher energy to the right. Distribute the 20 electrons into the boxes representing the orbitals, allowing a maximum of two electrons per orbital and remembering Hund's rule. You can see from the diagram that nitrogen has no unpaired electrons.

[↓↑] [↓↑] [↓↑|↓↑|↓↑] [↓↑] [↓↑|↓↑|↓↑] [↓↑]
1*s* 2*s* 2*p* 3*s* 3*p* 4*s*

(c) Ne Neon has 10 electrons and has the electron configuration $1s^22s^22p^6$. Draw a box for each orbital, putting the lowest energy orbital (1s) on the far left and proceeding to orbitals of higher energy to the right. Distribute the 10 electrons into the boxes representing the orbitals, allowing a maximum of two electrons per orbital and remembering Hund's rule. You can see from the diagram that neon has no unpaired electrons.

[↓↑] [↓↑] [↓↑|↓↑|↓↑]
1*s* 2*s* 2*p*

(d) He Helium has 2 electrons and has the electron configuration $1s^2$. Draw a box for each orbital, putting the lowest energy orbital (1s) on the far left and proceeding to orbitals of higher energy to the right. Distribute the 2 electrons into the boxes representing the orbitals, allowing a maximum of two electrons per orbital and remembering Hund's rule. You can see from the diagram that helium has no unpaired electrons.

[↓↑]
1*s*

8.47 (a) P The atomic number of P is 15. The noble gas that precedes P in the periodic table is neon, so the inner electron configuration is [Ne]. Obtain the outer electron configuration by tracing the elements between Ne and P and assigning electrons to the appropriate orbitals. Begin with [Ne]. Because P is in row 3, add two 3*s* electrons. Next add three 3*p* electrons as you trace across the *p* block to P, which is in the third column of the p block.

P [Ne]$3s^23p^3$

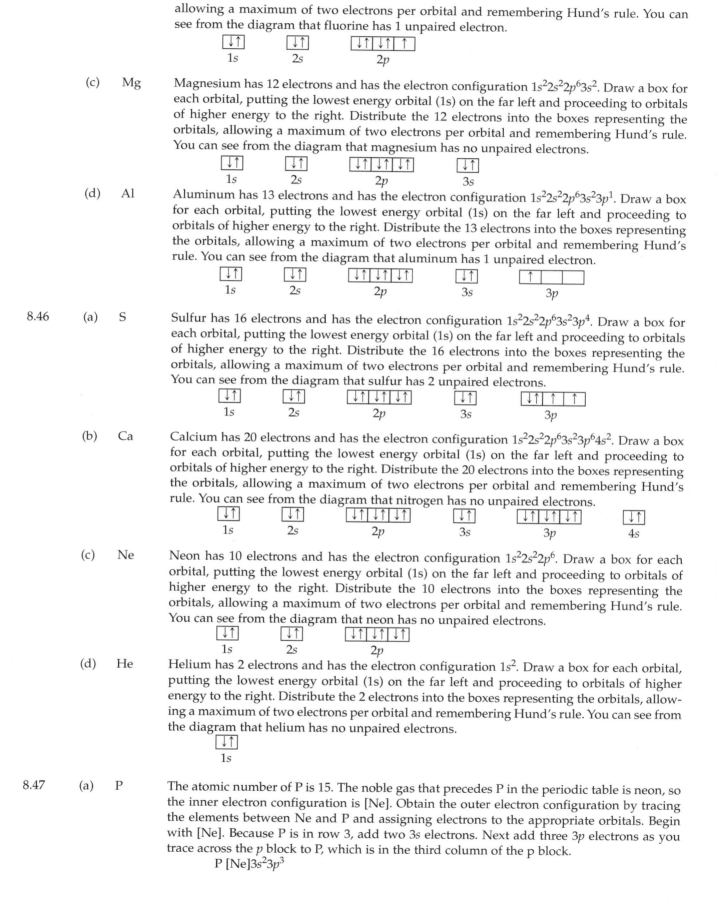

(b) Ge The atomic number of Ge is 32. The noble gas that precedes Ge in the periodic table is argon, so the inner electron configuration is [Ar]. Obtain the outer electron configuration by tracing the elements between Ar and Ge and assigning electrons to the appropriate orbitals. Begin with [Ar]. Because Ge is in row 4, add two 4*s* electrons. Next, add ten 3*d* electrons as you trace across the *d* block. Finally add two 4*p* electrons as you trace across the *p* block to Ge, which is in the second column of the *p* block.

Ge $[Ar]4s^23d^{10}4p^2$

(c) Zr The atomic number of Zr is 40. The noble gas that precedes Zr in the periodic table is krypton, so the inner electron configuration is [Kr]. Obtain the outer electron configuration by tracing the elements between Kr and Zr and assigning electrons to the appropriate orbitals. Begin with [Kr]. Because Zr is in row 5, add two 5*s* electrons. Next, add two 4*d* electrons as you trace across the *d* block to Zr, which is in the second column.

Zr $[Kr]5s^24d^2$

(d) I The atomic number of I is 53. The noble gas that precedes I in the periodic table is krypton, so the inner electron configuration is [Kr]. Obtain the outer electron configuration by tracing the elements between Kr and I and assigning electrons to the appropriate orbitals. Begin with [Kr]. Because I is in row 5, add two 5*s* electrons. Next, add ten 4*d* electrons as you trace across the d block. Finally add five 5*p* electrons as you trace across the *p* block to I which is in the fifth column of the *p* block.

I $[Kr]5s^24d^{10}5p^5$

8.48 (a) $[Ar]\ 4s^23d^{10}4p^6$ To determine the element corresponding to the electron configuration, begin with Ar then trace across the 4*s* block, the 3*d* block, and then the 4*p* block until you come to the sixth column. The element is Kr.

(b) $[Ar]\ 4s^23d^2$ To determine the element corresponding to the electron configuration, begin with Ar then trace across the 4*s* block, and then 3*d* block until you come to the second column. The element is Ti.

(c) $[Kr]\ 5s^24d^{10}5p^2$ To determine the element corresponding to the electron configuration, begin with Kr then trace across the 5*s* block, the 4*d* block, and then the 5*p* block until you come to the second column. The element is Sn.

(d) $[Kr]\ 5s^2$ To determine the element corresponding to the electron configuration, begin with Kr then trace across the 5*s* block to the second column. The element is Sr.

8.49 (a) Li is in period 2, and the first column in the *s* block so Li has one 2*s* electron.

(b) Cu is in period 4, and the ninth column in the *d* block (n – 1) so Cu should have nine 3*d* electrons, however, it is one of our exceptions, so it has ten 3*d* electrons.

(c) Br is in period 4, and the fifth column of the *p* block, so Br has five 4*p* electrons.

(d) Zr is in period 5, and the second column of the *d* block (n – 1), so Zr has two 4*d* electrons.

8.50 (a) Mg is in period 3, and the second column of the *s* block, so Mg has two 3*s* electrons.

(b) Cr is in period 4, and the fourth column of the *d* block (n – 1), so Cr should have four 3*d* electrons, however, Cr is one of our exceptions, so it has five 3*d* electrons.

(c) Y is in period 5, and the first column of the *d* block (n – 1), so Y has one 4*d* electron.

(d) Pb is in period 6, and the second column of the *p* block, so Pb has two 6*p* electrons.

8.51 (a) In period 4, an element with five valence electrons could be V or As.

(b) In period 4, an element with four 4*p* electrons would be in the fourth column of the *p* block, and is Se.

(c) In period 4, an element with three $3d$ electrons would be in the third column of the d block (n – 1) and is V.

(d) In period 4, an element with a complete outer shell would be in the sixth column of the p block and is Kr.

8.52 (a) In period 3, an element with three valence electrons would be in the first column of the p block and is Al.

(b) In period 3, an element with four $3p$ electrons would be in the fourth column of the p block and is S.

(c) In period 3, an element with six $3p$ electrons would be in the sixth column of the p block and is Ar.

(d) In period 3, an element with two $3s$ electrons and no $3p$ electrons would be in the second column of the s block and is Mg.

Valence Electrons and Simple Chemical Behavior form the Periodic Table

8.53 (a) Ba is in column 2A, so it has two valence electrons.

(b) Cs is in column 1A, so it has one valence electron.

(c) Ni is in column 8 of the d block, so it has 10 valence electrons (8 from the d block and 2 from the s block).

(d) S is in column 6A, so it has six valence electrons.

8.54 (a) Al is in column 3A, so it has three valence electrons. Al is a metal and will tend to lose the three valence electrons to achieve the noble gas configuration of Ne.

(b) Sn is in column 4A, so it has four valence electrons. Sn is a metal and will tend to lose the valence electrons to obtain a completely filled $n = 3$ level.

(c) Br is in column 7A, so it has seven valence electrons. Br is a nonmetal and will tend to gain an electron to achieve the noble gas configuration of Kr.

(d) Se is in column 6A, so it has six valence electrons. Se is a nonmetal and will tend to gain electrons to achieve the noble gas configuration of Kr.

8.55 (a) The outer electron configuration ns^2 would belong to a reactive metal in the alkaline earth family.

(b) The outer electron configuration ns^2np^6 would belong to an unreactive nonmetal in the noble gas family.

(c) The outer electron configuration ns^2np^5 would belong to a reactive nonmetal in the halogen family.

(d) The outer electron configuration ns^2np^2 would belong to an element in the carbon family. If $n = 2$, the element is a nonmetal, if $n = 3$ or 4, the element is a metalloid, and if $n = 5$ or 6, the element is a metal.

8.56 (a) The outer electron configuration ns^2 would belong to a metal in the alkaline earth family for period n = 2 and greater. He is a noble gas with a 1s2 electron configuration.

(b) The outer electron configuration ns^2np^6 would belong to a nonmetal in the noble gas family.

(c) The outer electron configuration ns^2np^5 would belong to a nonmetal in the halogen family.

(d) The outer electron configuration ns^2np^2 would belong to an element in the carbon family. If $n = 2$, the element is a nonmetal, if $n = 3$ or 4, the element is a metalloid, and if $n = 5$ or 6, the element is a metal.

Effective Nuclear Charge and Atomic Radius

8.57 The valence electrons in nitrogen would experience a greater effective nuclear charge. Be has four protons and N has seven protons. Both atoms have two core electrons that predominately contribute to the shielding, while the valence electrons will contribute a slight shielding effect. So, Be has an effective nuclear charge of slightly more than 2+ and N has an effective nuclear charge of slightly more than 5+.

8.58 S(16) = [Ne]$3s^2 3p^4$ Mg(12) = [Ne]$3s^2$ Al(13) = [Ne]$3s^2 3p^1$ Si(14) = [Ne]$3s^2 3p^2$
All four atoms have the same number of core electrons that contribute to shielding. So, the effective nuclear charge will decrease with decreasing number of protons. S > Si > Al > Mg

8.59 (a) K(19) [Ar]$4s^1$ Z_{eff} = Z – core electrons = 19 – 18 = 1+

(b) Ca(20) [Ar]$4s^2$ Z_{eff} = Z – core electrons = 20 – 18 = 2+

(c) O(8) [He]$2s^2 2p^4$ Z_{eff} = Z – core electrons = 8 – 2 = 6+

(d) C(6) [He]$2s^2 2p^2$ Z_{eff} = Z – core electrons = 6 – 2 = 4+

8.60 B has an electron configuration of $1s^2 2s^2 2p^1$. To estimate the effective nuclear charge experienced by the outer electrons we need to distinguish between two different types of shielding: (1) the shielding of the outermost electrons by the core electrons and (2) the shielding of the outermost electrons by each other. The three outermost electrons in boron experience the 5+ charge of the nucleus through the shield of the two 1*s* core electrons. We can estimate that the shielding experienced by any one of the outermost electrons due to the core electrons is nearly 2. For the 2*s* electrons the shielding due to the other 2*s* electron is nearly zero. For the 2*p* electron however, we would expect that the 2s electrons would contribute some shielding because although the 2*p* orbital penetrates the 2*s* orbital to some degree most of the 2*p* orbital lies outside the 2*s* orbital. So the effective nuclear charge would be slightly greater than 3+ and the effective nuclear charge felt by the 2*s* electrons would be greater than the effective nuclear charge felt by the 2*p* electrons.

8.61 (a) Al or In In atoms are larger than Al atoms because as you trace the path between Al and In on the periodic table you move down a column. Atomic size increases as you move down a column because the outermost electrons occupy orbitals with a higher principal quantum number that are therefore larger, resulting in a larger atom.

(b) Si or N Si atoms are larger than N atoms because as you trace the path between N and Si on the periodic table you move down a column (atomic size increases) and then to the left across a period (atomic size increases). These effects add together for an overall increase.

(c) P or Pb Pb atoms are larger than P atoms because as you trace the path between P and Pb on the periodic table you move down a column (atomic size increases) and then to the left across a period (atomic size increases). These effects add together for an overall increase.

(d) C or F C atoms are larger than F atoms because as you trace the path between C and F on the periodic table you move to the right within the same period. As you move to the right across a period, the effective nuclear charge experienced by the outermost electrons increase, which results in a smaller size.

8.62 (a) Sn or Si Sn atoms are larger than Si atoms because as you trace the path between Si and Sn on the periodic table you move down a column. Atomic size increases as you move down a column because the outermost electrons occupy orbitals with a higher principal quantum number that are therefore larger, resulting in a larger atom.

(b) Br or Ga Ga atoms are larger than Br atoms because as you trace the path between Ga and Br on the periodic table you move to the right within the same period. As you move to the right across a period, the effective nuclear charge experienced by the outermost electrons increases, which results in a smaller size.

(c) Sn or Bi Based on periodic trends alone, you cannot tell which atom is larger because as you trace the path between Sn and Bi you go to the right across a period (atomic size decreases) and then down a column (atomic size increases). These effects tend to oppose each other, and it is not easy to tell which will predominate.

(d) Se or Sn Sn atoms are larger than Se atoms because as you trace the path between Se and Sn on the periodic table you move down a column (atomic size increases) and then to the left across a period (atomic size increases). These effects add together for an overall increase.

8.63 Ca, Rb, S, Si, Ge, F F is above and to the right of the other elements, so we start with F as the smallest atom. As you trace a path from F to S you move to the left (size increases) and down (size increases), next you move left from S to Si (size increases), then down to Ge (size increases), next move to the left to Ca (size increases), and then to the left and down to Rb (size increases). So, in order of increasing atomic radii F < S < Si < Ge < Ca < Rb.

8.64 Cs, Sb, S, Pb, Se Cs is below and to the left of the other elements, so we start with Cs as the largest atom. As you trace a path from Cs to Pb you move to the right in the same period (size decreases), next, going from Pb to Sb you move up a column and then to the right (size decreases), from Sb to Se you move up the column and then to the right (size decreases), and finally from Se to S you move up the column (size decreases). So, in order of decreasing radii Cs > Pb > Sb > Se > S.

Ionic Electron Configurations, Ionic Radii, Magnetic Properties, and Ionization Energy

8.65 (a) O^{2-} Begin by writing the electron configuration of the neutral atom.
O $1s^2 2s^2 2p^4$
Since this ion has a 2 – charge, add two electrons to write the electron configuration of the ion.
O^{2-} $1s^2 2s^2 2p^6$ This is isoelectronic with Ar.

(b) Br^- Begin by writing the electron configuration of the neutral atom.
Br $[Ar]4s^2 3d^{10} 4p^5$
Since this ion has a 1 – charge, add one electron to write the electron configuration of the ion.
Br^- $[Ar]4s^2 3d^{10} 4p^6$ This is isoelectronic with Kr.

(c) Sr^{2+} Begin by writing the electron configuration of the neutral atom.
Sr $[Kr]5s^2$
Since this ion has a 2+ charge, remove two electrons to write the electron configuration of the ion.
Sr^{2+} [Kr]

(d) Co^{3+} Begin by writing the electron configuration of the neutral atom.
Co $[Ar]4s^2 3d^7$
Since this ion has a 3+ charge, remove three electrons to write the electron configuration of the ion. Since it is a transition metal, remove the electrons from the 4*s* orbital before removing electrons from the 3*d* orbitals.
Co^{3+} $[Ar]4s^0 3d^6$

(e) Cu^{2+} Begin by writing the electron configuration of the neutral atom. Remember, Cu is one of our exceptions.
Cu $[Ar]4s^1 3d^{10}$
Since this ion has a 2+ charge, remove two electrons to write the electron configuration of the ion. Since it is a transition metal, remove the electrons from the 4*s* orbital before removing electrons from the 3*d* orbitals.
Cu^{2+} $[Ar]4s^0 3d^9$

8.66 (a) Cl^- Begin by writing the electron configuration of the neutral atom.
Cl $[Ne]3s^2 3p^5$
Since this ion has a 1 – charge, add one electron to write the electron configuration of the ion.
Cl^- $[Ne]3s^2 3p^6$ This is isoelectronic with Ar.

(b) P^{3-} Begin by writing the electron configuration of the neutral atom.
P $[Ne]3s^2 3p^3$
Since this ion has a 3 – charge, add three electrons to write the electron configuration of the ion.
P^{3-} $[Ne]3s^2 3p^6$ This is isoelectronic with Ar.

(c) K^+ Begin by writing the electron configuration of the neutral atom.
K [Ar]$4s^1$
Since this ion has a 1+ charge, remove one electron to write the electron configuration of the ion.
K^+ [Ar]

(d) Mo^{3+} Begin by writing the electron configuration of the neutral atom. Remember, Mo is one of our exceptions.
Mo [Kr]$5s^1 4d^5$
Since this ion has a 3+ charge, remove three electrons to write the electron configuration of the ion. Since it is a transition metal, remove the electrons from the 5*s* orbital before removing electrons from the 4*d* orbitals.
Mo^{3+} [Kr]$5s^0 4d^3$

(e) V^{3+} Begin by writing the electron configuration of the neutral atom.
V [Ar]$4s^2 3d^3$
Since this ion has a 3+ charge, remove three electrons to write the electron configuration of the ion. Since it is a transition metal, remove the electrons from the 4*s* orbital before removing electrons from the 3*d* orbitals.
V^{3+} [Ar]$4s^0 3d^2$

8.67 (a) V^{5+} Begin by writing the electron configuration of the neutral atom.
V [Ar]$4s^2 3d^3$
Since this ion has a 5+ charge, remove five electrons to write the electron configuration of the ion. Since it is a transition metal, remove the electrons from the 4*s* orbital before removing electrons from the 3*d* orbitals.
V^{5+} [Ar]$4s^0 3d^0$ = [Ne]$3s^2 3p^6$

	3*s*	3*p*		
[Ne]	↓↑	↓↑	↓↑	↓↑

V^{5+} is diamagnetic.

(b) Cr^{3+} Begin by writing the electron configuration of the neutral atom. Remember, Cr is one of our exceptions.
Cr [Ar]$4s^1 3d^5$
Since this ion has a 3+ charge, remove three electrons to write the electron configuration of the ion. Since it is a transition metal, remove the electrons from the 4*s* orbital before removing electrons from the 3*d* orbitals.
Cr^{3+} [Ar]$4s^0 3d^3$

	4*s*	3*d*				
[Ar]		↑	↑	↑		

Cr^{3+} is paramagnetic.

(c) Ni^{2+} Begin by writing the electron configuration of the neutral atom.
Ni [Ar]$4s^2 3d^8$
Since this ion has a 2+ charge, remove two electrons to write the electron configuration of the ion. Since it is a transition metal, remove the electrons from the 4*s* orbital before removing electrons from the 3*d* orbitals.
Ni^{2+} [Ar]$4s^0 3d^8$

	4*s*	3*d*				
[Ar]		↓↑	↓↑	↓↑	↑	↑

Ni^{2+} is paramagnetic.

(d) Fe^{3+} Begin by writing the electron configuration of the neutral atom.
Fe [Ar]$4s^2 3d^6$
Since this ion has a 3+ charge, remove three electrons to write the electron configuration of the ion. Since it is a transition metal, remove the electrons from the 4s orbital before removing electrons from the 3d orbitals.

Fe^{3+} [Ar]$4s^0 3d^5$

[Ar] [ ] [↑][↑][↑][↑][↑]

4s 3d

Fe^{3+} is paramagnetic.

8.68 (a) Cd^{2+} Begin by writing the electron configuration of the neutral atom.

Cd [Kr]$5s^2 4d^{10}$

Since this ion has a 2+ charge, remove two electrons to write the electron configuration of the ion. Since it is a transition metal, remove the electrons from the 5*s* orbital before removing electrons from the 4*d* orbitals.

Cd^{2+} [Kr]$5s^0 4d^{10}$

[Kr] [ ] [↓↑][↓↑][↓↑][↓↑][↓↑]

5*s* 4*d*

Cd^{2+} is diamagnetic.

(b) Au^+ Begin by writing the electron configuration of the neutral atom. Remember Au is one of our exceptions.

Au [Xe]$6s^1 4f^{14} 5d^{10}$

Since this ion has a + charge, remove one electron to write the electron configuration of the ion. Since it is a transition metal, remove the electrons from the 6*s* orbital before removing electrons from the 5*d* or 4*f* orbitals.

Au^+ [Xe]$6s^0 4f^{14} 5d^{10}$

[Xe] [ ] [↓↑][↓↑][↓↑][↓↑][↓↑][↓↑][↓↑] [↓↑][↓↑][↓↑][↓↑][↓↑]

6*s* 4*f* 5*d*

Au^+ is diamagnetic.

(c) Mo^{3+} Begin by writing the electron configuration of the neutral atom. Remember, Mo is one of our exceptions.

Mo [Kr]$5s^1 4d^5$

Since this ion has a 3+ charge, remove three electrons to write the electron configuration of the ion. Since it is a transition metal, remove the electrons from the 5*s* orbital before removing electrons from the 4*d* orbitals.

Mo^{3+} [Kr]$5s^0 4d^3$

[Kr] [ ] [↑][↑][↑][ ][ ]

5*s* 4*d*

Mo^{3+} is paramagnetic.

(d) Zr^{2+} Begin by writing the electron configuration of the neutral atom.

Zr [Kr]$5s^2 4d^2$

Since this ion has a 2+ charge, remove two electrons to write the electron configuration of the ion. Since it is a transition metal, remove the electrons from the 5*s* orbital before removing electrons from the 4*d* orbitals.

Zr^{2+} [Kr]$5s^0 4d^2$

[Kr] [ ] [↑][↑][ ][ ][ ]

5*s* 4*d*

Zr^{2+} is paramagnetic.

8.69 (a) Li or Li^+ A Li atom is larger than Li^+ because cations are smaller than the atoms from which they are formed.

(b) I^- or Cs^+ An I^- ion is larger than a Cs^+ ion because, although they are isoelectronic, I^- has two fewer protons than Cs^+, resulting in a lesser pull on the electrons and therefore a larger radius.

(c) Cr or Cr^{3+} A Cr atom is larger than Cr^{3+} because cations are smaller than the atoms from which they are formed.

(d) O or O^{2-} An O^{2-} ion is larger than an O atom because anions are larger than the atoms from which they are formed.

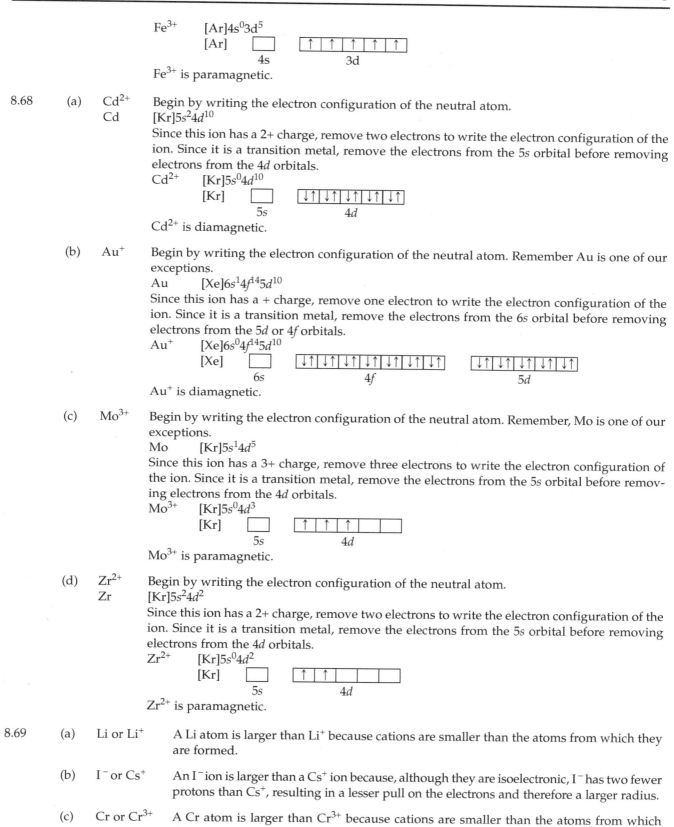

8.70 (a) Sr or Sr^{2+} A Sr atom is larger than Sr^{2+} because cations are smaller than the atoms from which they are formed.

(b) N or N^{3-} An N^{3-} ion is larger than an N atom because anions are larger than the atoms from which they are formed.

(c) Ni or Ni^{2+} A Ni atom is larger than Ni^{2+} because cations are smaller than the atoms from which they are formed.

(d) S^{2-} or Ca^{2+} An S^{2-} ion is larger than a Ca^{2+} ion because, although they are isoelectronic, S^{2-} has four fewer protons than Ca^{2+}, resulting in a lesser pull on the electrons and therefore a larger radius.

8.71 Since all the species are isoelectronic, the radius will depend on the number of protons in each species. The fewer the protons the larger the radius.
F: Z = 9; Ne: Z = 10; O: Z = 8; Mg: Z = 12; Na: Z = 11
So: $O^{2-} > F^{-} > Ne > Na^{+} > Mg^{2+}$

8.72 Since all the species are isoelectronic, the radius will depend on the number of protons in each species. The fewer the protons, the larger the radius.
Se: Z = 34; Kr: Z = 36; Sr: Z = 38; Rb: Z = 37; Br: Z = 35
So: $Sr^{2+} < Rb^{+} < Kr < Br^{-} < Se^{2-}$

8.73 (a) Br or Bi Br has a higher ionization energy than Bi because, as you trace the path between Br and Bi on the periodic table, you move down a column (ionization energy decreases) and then to the left across a period (ionization energy decreases). These effects sum together for an overall decrease.

(b) Na or Rb Na has a higher ionization energy than Rb because, as you trace a path between Na and Rb on the periodic table, you move down a column. Ionization energy decreases as you go down a column because of the increasing size of orbitals with increasing n.

(c) As or At Based on periodic trends alone, it is impossible to tell which has a higher ionization energy because as you trace the path between As and At you go to the right across a period (ionization energy increases) and then down a column (ionization energy decreases). These effects tend to oppose each other, and it is not obvious which will dominate.

(d) P or Sn P has a higher ionization energy than Sn because as you trace the path between P and Sn on the periodic table you move down a column (ionization energy decreases) and then to the left across a period (ionization energy decreases). These effects sum together for an overall decrease.

8.74 (a) P or I Based on periodic trends alone, it is impossible to tell which has a higher ionization energy because as you trace the path between P and I you go to the right across a period (ionization energy increases) and then down a column (ionization energy decreases). These effects tend to oppose each other, and it is not obvious which will dominate.

(b) Se or Cl Cl has a higher ionization energy than Se because as you trace the path between Cl and Se on the periodic table you move down a column (ionization energy decreases) and then to the left across a period (ionization energy decreases). These effects sum together for an overall decrease.

(c) P or Sb P has a higher ionization energy than Sb because as you trace a path between P and Sb on the periodic table you move down a column. Ionization energy decreases as you go down a column because of the increasing size of orbitals with increasing n.

(d) Ga or Ge Ge has a higher ionization energy than Ga because as you trace a path between Ga and Ge on the periodic table you move to the right within the same period. Ionization energy increases as you go to the right because of increasing effective nuclear charge.

8.75 Since ionization energy increases as you move to the right across a period and increases as you move up a column, the element with the smallest first ionization energy would be the element farthest to the left and lowest down on the periodic table. So, In has the smallest ionization energy; as you trace a path to the right and up on the periodic table, the next element reached is Si; continuing up and to the right you reach N; and then continuing to the right you reach F. So, in the order of increasing first ionization energy the elements are In < Si < N < F.

8.76 Since ionization energy increases as you move to the right across a period and increases as you move up a column, the element with the largest first ionization energy would be the element farthest to the right and highest up on the periodic table. So, Cl has the largest ionization energy; as you trace a path to the left on the periodic table you reach Sp; as you move down a column and to the left you reach Sn; and then moving down the column you reach Pb. So, in the order of decreasing first ionization energy the elements are Cl > S > Sn > Pb.

8.77 The jump in ionization energy occurs when you change from removing a valence electron to removing a core electron. To determine where this jump occurs you need to look at the electron configuration of the atom.

(a) Be $1s^22s^2$ The first and second ionization energies involve removing 2*s* electrons, while the third ionization energy removes a core electron, so the jump will occur between the second and third ionization energies.

(b) N $1s^22s^22p^3$ The first five ionization energies involve removing the 2*p* and 2*s* electrons, while the sixth ionization energy removes a core electron, so the jump will occur between the fifth and sixth ionization energies.

(c) O $1s^22s^22p^4$ The first six ionization energies involve removing the 2*p* and 2*s* electrons, while the seventh ionization energy removes a core electron, so the jump will occur between the sixth and seventh ionization energies.

(d) Li $1s^22s^1$ The first ionization energy involves removing a 2*s* electron, while the second ionization energy removes a core electron, so the jump will occur between the first and second ionization energies.

8.78 The jump occurs between IE_3 and IE_4, so removing the first three electrons involves removing valence electrons and the fourth electron is a core electron, so the valence electron configuration would be ns^2np^1; this puts the element in column 3A and would be Al.

Electron Affinities and Metallic Character

8.79 (a) Na or Rb Na has a more negative electron affinity than Rb. In column 1A electron affinity becomes less negative as you go down the column.

(b) B or S S has a more negative electron affinity than B. As you trace from B to S in the periodic table you move to the right, which shows the value of the electron affinity becoming more negative. Also, as you move from period 2 to period 3 the value of the electron affinity becomes more negative. Both of these trends sum together for the value of the electron affinity to become more negative.

(c) C or N C has the more negative electron affinity. As you trace from C to N across the periodic table you would normally expect N to have the more negative electron affinity. However, N has a half-filled p sublevel, which lends it extra stability, therefore it is harder to add an electron.

(d) Li or F F has the more negative electron affinity. As you trace from Li to F on the periodic table you move to the right in the period. As you go to the right across a period the value of the electron affinity generally becomes more negative.

8.80 (a) Mg or S S has the more negative electron affinity. As you trace from Mg to S on the periodic table you move to the right in the period. As you go to the right across a period the value of the electron affinity generally becomes more negative.

(b) K or Cs — K has the more negative electron affinity. In column 1A, as you go down the column the electron affinity becomes less negative.

(c) Si or P — Si has the more negative electron affinity. As you trace from Si to P across the periodic table you would normally expect P to have the more negative electron affinity. However, P has a half-filled p sublevel, which lends extra stability, therefore it is harder to add an electron.

(d) Ga or Br — Br has the more negative electron affinity. As you trace from Ga to Br on the periodic table you move to the right in the period. As you go to the right across a period the value of the electron affinity generally becomes more negative.

8.81 (a) Sr or Sb — Sr is more metallic than Sb because as we trace the path between Sr and Sb on the periodic table we move to the right within the same period. Metallic character decreases as you go to the right.

(b) As or Bi — Bi is more metallic because as we trace a path between As and Bi on the periodic table we move down a column in the same family (metallic character increases).

(c) Cl or O — Based on periodic trends alone, we cannot tell which is more metallic because as we trace the path between O and Cl we go to the right across a period (metallic character decreases) and then down a column (metallic character increases). These effects tend to oppose each other and it is not easy to tell which will predominate.

(d) S or As — As is more metallic than S because as we trace the path between S and As on the periodic table we move down a column (metallic character increases) and then to the left across a period (metallic character increases). These effects add together for an overall increase.

8.82 (a) Sb or Pb — Pb is more metallic than Sb because as we trace the path between Sb and Pb on the periodic table we move down a column (metallic character increases) and then to the left across a period (metallic character increases). These effects add together for an overall increase.

(b) K or Ge — K is more metallic than Ge because as we trace the path between K and Ge on the periodic table we move to the right within the same period. Metallic character decreases as you go to the right.

(c) Ge or Sb — Based on periodic trends alone, we cannot tell which is more metallic because as we trace the path between Ge and Sb we go to the right across a period (metallic character decreases) and then down a column (metallic character increases). These effects tend to oppose each other and it is not easy to tell which will predominate.

(d) As or Sn — Sn is more metallic than As because as we trace the path between As and Sn on the periodic table we move down a column (metallic character increases) and then to the left across a period (metallic character increases). These effects add together for an overall increase.

8.83 The order of increasing metallic character is S $<$ Se $<$ Sb $<$ In $<$ Ba $<$ Fr.
Metallic character decreases as you move left to right across a period and decreases as you move up a column, therefore, the element with the least metallic character will be to the top right of the periodic table. So, of these elements, S has the least metallic character. As you move down the column the next element is Se; as you continue down and then to the right you reach Sb; continuing to the right goes to In; going down the column and then to the right comes to Ba; and then down the column and to the right is Fr.

8.84 The order of decreasing metallic character is Sr $>$ Ga $>$ Al $>$ Si $>$ P $>$ N.
Metallic character decreases as you move left to right across a period and decreases as you move up a column, therefore, the element with the greatest metallic character will be at the bottom left of the periodic table. So, of these elements, Sr has the most metallic character. As you trace up the column and then to the right across the period the next element is Ga; trace up the column to Al; then to the right to Si and then P; and finally trace up the column to N.

8.85 Alkaline earth metals react with halogens to form metal halides. Write the formulas for the reactants and the metal halide product.

$$Sr(s) + I_2(g) \rightarrow SrI_2(s)$$

8.86 Fr would be the alkali metal with the smallest ionization energy so it should have the most exothermic reaction with chlorine gas.

$$2\ Fr(s) + Cl_2(g) \rightarrow 2\ FrCl(s)$$

8.87 Alkali metals react with water to form the dissolved metal ion, the hydroxide ion, and hydrogen gas. Write the skeletal equation including each of these and then balance it.

$$Li(s) + H_2O(l) \rightarrow Li^+(aq) + OH^-(aq) + H_2(g)$$
$$2\ Li(s) + 2\ H_2O(l) \rightarrow 2\ Li^+(aq) + 2\ OH^-(aq) + H_2(g)$$

8.88 Alkali metals react with water to form the dissolved metal ion, the hydroxide ion, and hydrogen gas. Write the skeletal equation including each of these and then balance it.

$$K(s) + H_2O(l) \rightarrow K^+(aq) + OH^-(aq) + H_2(g)$$
$$2\ K(s) + 2\ H_2O(l) \rightarrow 2\ K^+(aq) + 2\ OH^-(aq) + H_2(g)$$

8.89 The halogens react with hydrogen to form hydrogen halides. Write the skeletal reaction with each of the halogen and hydrogen as the reactants and the hydrogen halide compound as the product and balance the equation.

$$H_2(g) + Br_2(g) \rightarrow HBr(g)$$
$$H_2(g) + Br_2(g) \rightarrow 2\ HBr(g)$$

8.90 Halogens react with each other to form interhalogen compounds. Write the skeletal reaction with each of the halogens as the reactants and the interhalogen compound as the product and balance the equation.

$$Cl_2(g) + F_2(g) \rightarrow ClF(g)$$
$$Cl_2(g) + F_2(g) \rightarrow 2\ ClF(g)$$

Cumulative Problems

8.91 Br: $1s^22s^22p^63s^23p^64s^23d^{10}4p^5$

Kr: $1s^22s^22p^63s^23p^64s^23d^{10}4p^6$

Krypton has a completely filled *p* sublevel giving it chemical stability. Bromine needs one electron to achieve a completely filled *p* sublevel and therefore has a highly negative electron affinity. It therefore easily takes on an electron and is reduced to the bromide ion, giving it the added stability of the filled *p* sublevel.

8.92 K: $1s^22s^22p^63s^23p^64s^1$

Ar: $1s^22s^22p^63s^23p^6$

Argon has a completely filled *p* sublevel giving it chemical stability. Potassium has one electron in the 4*s* sublevel and can easily lose this electron so it has a low first ionization energy. It therefore loses the 4*s* electron to achieve an argon electron configuration, giving it the added stability of the filled p sublevel.

8.93 Write the electron configuration of vanadium.

V: [Ar] $4s^23d^3$

Since this ion has a 3+ charge, remove three electrons to write the electron configuration of the ion. Since it is a transition metal, remove the electrons from the 4*s* orbital before removing electrons from the 3*d* orbitals.

V^{3+}: [Ar] $4s^03d^2$

Both vanadium and the V^{3+} ion have unpaired electrons and are paramagnetic.

8.94 Begin by writing the electron configuration of the neutral atom. Remember, Cu is one of our exceptions.

Cu: [Ar]$4s^13d^{10}$

Since this ion has a 1+ charge, remove one electron to write the electron configuration of the ion. Since it is a transition metal, remove the electrons from the 4*s* orbital before removing electrons from the 3*d* orbitals.

Cu^+: [Ar]$4s^03d^{10}$

Cu contains one unpaired electron in the 4*s* orbital and is paramagnetic; Cu^+ has all paired electrons in the 3*d* orbitals and is diamagnetic.

8.95 Since K^+ has a 1+ charge you would need a cation with a similar size and a 1+ charge. Looking at the ions in the same family, Na^+ would be too small and Rb^+ would be too large. If we then consider Ar^+ and Ca^+ we would have ions of similar size and charge. Between these two Ca^+ would be the easier to achieve because the first ionization energy of Ca is similar to that of K, while the first ionization energy of Ar is much larger. However, the second ionization energy of Ca is relatively low, making it easy to lose the second electron.

8.96 Since Na^+ has a 1+ charge you would need a cation with a similar size and a 1+ charge. Looking at the ions in the same family, Li^+ would be too small and K^+ would be too large. If we then consider Ne^+ and Mg^+ we would have ions of similar size and charge. Between these two Mg^+ would be the easier to achieve because the first ionization energy of Mg is similar to that of Na, while the first ionization energy of Ne is much larger. However, the second ionization energy of Mg is relatively low, making it easy to lose the second electron.

8.97 C has an outer shell electron configuration of ns^2np^2; based on this you would expect Si and Ge, which are in the same family, to be most like carbon. Ionization energies for both Si and Ge are similar and tend to be slightly lower than C, but all are intermediate in the range of first ionization energies. The electron affinities of Si and Ge are close to that of C.

8.98 (a) Si and Ga — Ga would be larger than Si because as you trace from Si to Ga on the periodic table you move down a column (radius increases) and then to the left across the period (radius increases). The sum of these two trends would give you a larger radius for Ga.

(b) Si and Ge — Ge would be larger than Si because as you trace from Si to Ge on the periodic table you move down a column and the radius increases.

(c) Si and As — As would be most similar to Si in atomic radius because as you trace from Si to As on the periodic table you move down the column (radius increase) and then to the right across the period (radius decreases). The sum of these two trends would make As smaller than Ga and Ge, and thus closer to the radius of Si.

8.99 (a) N: $[He]2s^22p^3$ Mg: $[Ne]3s^2$ O: $[He]2s^22p^4$
F: $[He]2s^22p^5$ Al: $[Ne]3s^23p^1$

(b) Mg > Al > N > O > F

(c) Al < Mg < O < N < F (from the table)

(d) Mg and Al would have the largest radius because they are in period $n = 3$; Al is smaller than Mg because radius decreases as you move to the right across the period. F is smaller than O, and O is smaller than N because as you move to the right across the period radius decreases.

The first ionization energy of Al is smaller than the first ionization energy of Mg because Al loses the electron from the 3*p* orbital, which is shielded by the electrons in the 3*s* orbital; while Mg loses the electron from the filled 3*s* orbital, which has added stability because it is a filled orbital. The first ionization energy of O is lower than the first ionization energy of N because N has a half-filled 2*p* orbitals, which adds extra stability, thus making it harder to remove the electron. The fourth electron in the O 2*p* orbitals experiences added electron-electron repulsion because it must pair with another electron in the same 2*p* orbital, thus making it easier to remove.

8.100 (a) P: $[Ne]3s^23p^3$ Ca: $[Ar]4s^2$ Si: $[Ne]3s^23p^2$
S: $[Ne]3s^23p^4$ Ga: $[Ar]4s^23d^{10}4p^1$

(b) Ca > Ga > Si > P > S

(c) Ga < Ca < Si < S < P (from table)

(d) Ca and Ga would have the largest radius because they are in period $n = 4$; Ga is smaller than Ca because radius increases as you move to the left across the period. S is smaller than P, and P is smaller than Si because as you move to the right across the period, radius decreases.

The first ionization energy of Ga is smaller than the first ionization energy of Ca because Ga loses the electron from the 4*p* orbital, which is shielded by the electrons in the 4*s* orbital. Ca loses the electron from the filled 4*s* orbital, which has added stability because it is a filled orbital. The first ionization energy of S is lower than the first ionization energy of P because P has a half-filled 3*p* orbital, which adds extra stability, thus making it harder to remove the electron. The fourth electron in the S 3*p* orbitals experiences added electron-electron repulsion because it must pair with another electron in the same 3*p* orbital, thus making it easier to remove.

8.101 As you move to the right across a row in the periodic table for the main-group elements the effective nuclear charge (Z_{eff}) experienced by the electrons in the outermost principal energy level increases, resulting in a stronger attraction between the outermost electrons and the nucleus, and therefore a smaller atomic radii.

Across the row of transition elements the number of electrons in the outermost principal energy level (highest n value) is nearly constant. As another proton is added to the nucleus with each successive element, another electron is added, but that electron goes into an $n_{highest} - 1$ orbital (a core level). The number of outermost electrons stays constant and they experience a roughly constant effective nuclear charge, keeping the radius approximately constant after the first couple of elements in the series.

8.102 Across the row of transition elements, the number of electrons in the outermost principal energy level (highest n value) is nearly constant. As another proton is added to the nucleus with each successive element another electron is added, but the electron goes into an $n_{highest} - 1$ orbital. So, even though the atomic number of Cu is higher than that of V, the outermost electron experiences roughly the same effective nuclear charge and thus the radii of the two elements are nearly the same. Since the radii of the two elements are nearly the same, the volume occupied by the element will be nearly the same. Since the mass increases as the atomic number increases, the mass of Cu is greater than the mass of V; density is mass/volume, so the density of Cu should be greater than the density of V.

We find that the densities are Cu = 8.96 g/cm^3 V = 5.49 g/cm^3 and our prediction was correct.

8.103 The noble gases all have a filled outer quantum level, very high first ionization energies, and positive values for the electron affinity and are thus particularly unreactive. The lighter noble gases will not form any compounds because the ionization energies of He and Ne are both over 2000 kJ/mol. Since ionization energy decreases as you move down a column we find that the heavier noble gases, Ar, Kr, and Xe do form some compounds. They have ionization energies that are close to the ionization energy of H and can thus be forced to lose an electron.

8.104 The halogens will all add an electron to achieve the stability of the noble gas configuration, thus they are all powerful oxidizing agents (they are reduced). F would be the strongest because it adds the electron to the $n = 2$ level achieving the electron configuration of Ne. Since the $n = 2$ level lies lower in energy than the outermost level of the other halogens, it is more energetically favorable for F to gain the noble gas configuration than for the other halogens. This combined with the high ionization energy and relatively exothermic electron affinity makes F very reactive. As you move down the column, the *n* level of the outermost electrons increases, making it less energetically favorable for each of the successive halogens to gain an electron.

8.105 Group 6A: ns^2np^4 Group 7A: ns^2np^5
The electron affinity of the group 7A elements are more negative than the group 6A elements in the same period because group 7A requires only one electron to achieve the noble gas configuration ns^2np^6, while the group 6A elements require two electrons. Adding one electron to the group 6A element will not give them any added stability and leads to extra electron-electron repulsions, so the value of the electron affinity is less negative than that for group 7A.

8.106 Group 5A : ns^2np^3 Group 4A: ns^2np^2
The electron affinity of group 5A elements is more positive than the group 4A elements in the same period because group 5A has a half-filled p sublevel. Adding an electron to this group adds a fourth electron into the p sublevel and increases the electron-electron repulsions. It also eliminates the stability of the half-filled sublevel. Adding an electron to a group 4A element however, adds a third electron into the p sublevel, giving it the added stability of the half-filled sublevel.

8.107 $35 = Br = [Ar]4s^2 3d^{10} 4p^5$ $53 = I = [Kr]5s^2 4d^{10} 5p^5$
Br and I are both halogens with an outermost electron configuration of ns^2np^5; the next element with the same outermost electron configuration is 85, At.

8.108 Begin by writing the electron configuration of the neutral atom. $S = 1s^2 2s^2 2p^6 3s^2 3p^4$
S^+ loses one electron: $1s^2 2s^2 2p^6 3s^2 3p^3$

1s	2s	2p	3s	3p
[↓↑]	[↓↑]	[↓↑][↓↑][↓↑]	[↓↑]	[↑][↑][↑]

S^{2+} loses two electrons: $1s^2 2s^2 2p^6 3s^2 3p^2$

1s	2s	2p	3s	3p
[↓↑]	[↓↑]	[↓↑][↓↑][↓↑]	[↓↑]	[↑][↑][ ]

S^{3+} loses three electrons: $1s^2 2s^2 2p^6 3s^2 3p^1$

1s	2s	2p	3s	3p
[↓↑]	[↓↑]	[↓↑][↓↑][↓↑]	[↓↑]	[↑][ ][ ]

S^{4+} loses four electrons: $1s^2 2s^2 2p^6 3s^2 3p^0$

1s	2s	2p	3s	3p
[↓↑]	[↓↑]	[↓↑][↓↑][↓↑]	[↓↑]	[ ][ ][ ]

S^{5+} loses five electrons: $1s^2 2s^2 2p^6 3s^2 3p^0$

1s	2s	2p	3s	3p
[↓↑]	[↓↑]	[↓↑][↓↑][↓↑]	[↑]	[ ][ ][ ]

S^{6+} loses six electrons: $1s^2 2s^2 2p^6 3s^2 3p^0$

1s	2s	2p	3s	3p
[↓↑]	[↓↑]	[↓↑][↓↑][↓↑]	[ ]	[ ][ ][ ]

8.109 (a) $10 - 2 = 8 \rightarrow$ O; $12 - 2 = 10 \rightarrow$ Ne; $58 - 5 = 53 \rightarrow$ I; $11 - 2 = 9 \rightarrow$ F; $7 - 2 = 5 \rightarrow$ B; $44 - 5 = 39 \rightarrow$ Y; $63 - 6 = 57 \rightarrow$ La; $66 - 6 = 60 \rightarrow$ Nd One If by Land

(b) $9 - 2 = 7 \rightarrow$ N; $99 - 7 = 92 \rightarrow$ U; $30 - 4 = 26 \rightarrow$ Fe; $95 - 7 = 88 \rightarrow$ Ra; $19 - 3 = 16 \rightarrow$ S $47 - 5 = 42 \rightarrow$ Mo; $79 - 6 = 73 \rightarrow$ Ta (backwards) Atoms Are Fun

8.110 The electron affinity of sodium is lower than lithium. Going from lithium to sodium the electron is entering an orbital with a larger principal quantum number and is farther from the nucleus. Since it is farther from the nucleus, the orbital is higher in energy and the addition of the electron is less exothermic.

With chlorine and fluorine, the electron affinity of chlorine is higher. Even though the electron is entering an orbital with a larger principal quantum number, if we look at the atomic radius of the two atoms, we can see that fluorine has a very small radius of 72 pm when compared to chlorine with a radius of 99 pm. Because of the much smaller radius, the repulsive forces between the electrons entering the p orbitals will cause the electron affinity to be less exothermic.

8.111 **Given:** r = 100.00 pm, $q_{proton} = 1.60218 \times 10^{-19}$ C, $q_{electron} = -1.60218 \times 10^{-19}$ C
Find: IE in kJ/mol and λ of ionization
Conceptual Plan: **r, q_{proton}, $q_{electron}$,** $\rightarrow$ **E_{atom}** $\rightarrow$ **E_{mol} and then E_{atom}** $\rightarrow$ λ

$$E = \frac{1}{4\pi\epsilon_o}\frac{q_p q_e}{r} \qquad \frac{1000\text{J}}{\text{kJ}} \qquad \frac{6.022\text{x}0^{23}\text{atom}}{\text{mol}} \qquad \lambda = \frac{hc}{E}$$

Solution:
$$E = \frac{1}{(4)(3.141)\left(8.85 \times 10^{-12}\frac{C^2}{J\,m}\right)} \times \frac{(1.602 \times 10^{-19} C)(-1.602 \times 10^{-19} C)}{(100.00\ pm)\left(\frac{1\ m}{1 \times 10^{12}\ pm}\right)} = -2.30\underline{8} \times 10^{-18}\ J/atom$$

$$-2.30\underline{8} \times 10^{-18}\ J/\ atom \times \frac{6.022 \times 10\ atom}{mol} \times \frac{kJ}{(1000J)} = -1.39 \times 10^3\ kJ/\ mol$$

$$IE = 0 - (-1.39 \times 10^3\ kJ/mol) = 1.39 \times 10^3\ kJ/mol$$

$$\lambda = \frac{(6.626 \times 10^{-34} Js)(3.00 \times 10^8 m/s)\left(\frac{1 \times 10^9\ nm}{m}\right)}{(2.30\underline{8} \times 10^{-18} J)} = 86.1\ nm$$

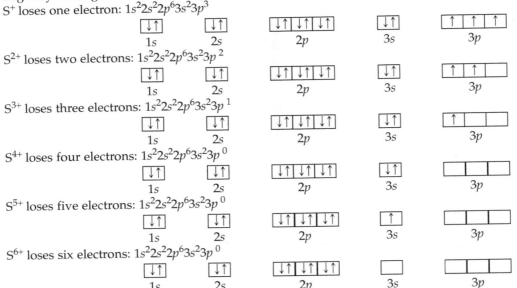

Check: The units of the answer (kJ/mol) are correct. The magnitude of the answer is reasonable since the value is positive and energy must be added to the atom to remove the electron. The units of the wavelength (nm) are correct and the magnitude is reasonable based on the ionization energy.

8.112 **Given:** IE = 496 kJ/mol, $q_{proton} = 1.60218 \times 10^{-19}$ C, $q_{electron} = -1.60218 \times 10^{-19}$ C **Find:** r

Conceptual Plan: kJ/mol → J/mol → J/atom → r

$$\frac{1000\text{J}}{\text{kJ}} \qquad \frac{\text{mol}}{6.022 \times 10^{23}\text{ atom}} \qquad r = \frac{1}{4\pi\epsilon_o}\frac{q_p q_e}{E}$$

Solution: E = - IE = - 496 kJ/mol

$$-496\frac{\text{kJ}}{\text{mol}} \times \frac{1000\text{J}}{\text{kJ}} \times \frac{\text{mol}}{6.022 \times 10^{23}\text{atoms}} = -8.236 \times 10^{-19}\text{ J/ atom}$$

$$r = \frac{1}{(4)(3.141)\left(8.85 \times 10^{-12}\frac{\text{C}^2}{\text{J m}}\right)\left(\frac{1\text{ m}}{1 \times 10^{12}\text{ pm}}\right)} \times \frac{(1.602 \times 10^{-19}\text{C})(-1.602 \times 10^{-19}\text{C})}{(-8.236 \times 10^{-19}\text{ J})} = 280.\text{ pm}$$

The actual atomic radius of sodium is 186 pm. The $3s^1$ electron that is being removed is shielded from the nuclear charge by the inner shell electrons. Thus, the energy of the electron in the 3s orbital is less negative than what would be expected for an electron at a distance of 186 pm. Because the energy is less negative the ionization energy is smaller.

Challenge Problems

8.113 (a) Using Excel, make a table of radius, atomic number, and density. Using xy scatter, make a chart of radius vs. density. With an exponential trendline, estimate the density of argon and xenon. Also, make a chart of atomic number vs. density. With a linear trendline, estimate the density of argon and xenon.

element	radius(pm)	atomic number	density
He	32	2	0.18
Ne	70	10	0.90
Ar	98	18	
Kr	112	36	3.75
Xe	130	54	
Rn		86	9.73
		118	

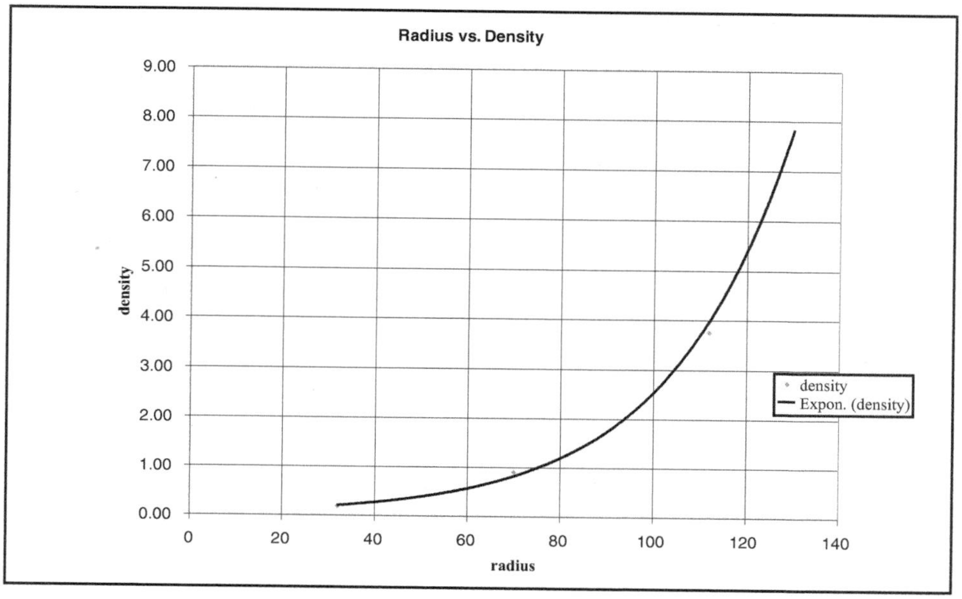

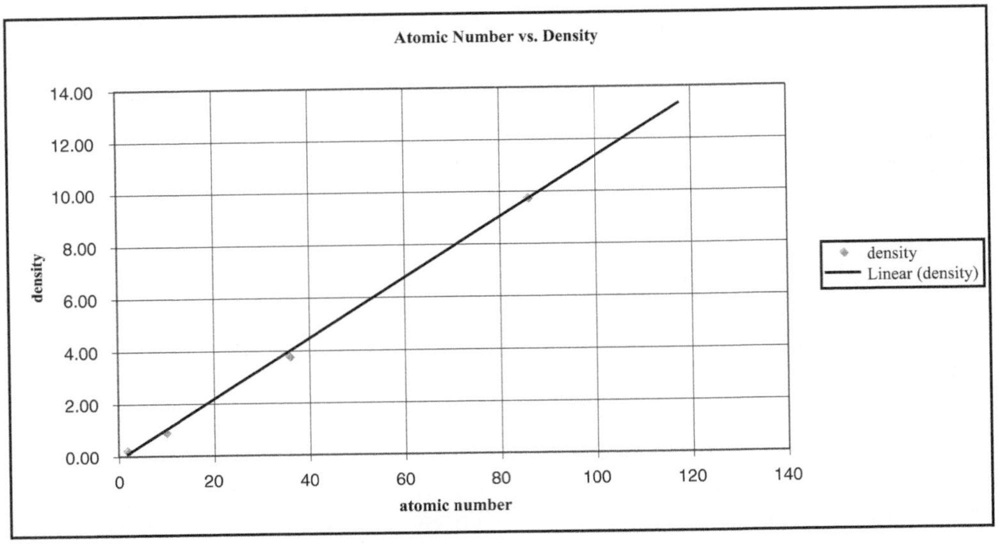

From the radius vs. density chart Ar has a density of ~ 2 g/L and Xe has a density of ~ 7.7 g/L. From the atomic number vs. density chart Ar has a density of ~1.8 g/L and Xe has a density of ~6 g/L.

(b) Using the chart of atomic number vs. density, element 118 would be predicted to have a density of ~ 13 g/L.

(c) **Given:** Ne: M = 20.18 g/mol; r = 70 pm **Find:** mass of neon; d neon
Conceptual Plan: M $\rightarrow$ m_{atom} and then r $\rightarrow$ vol_{atom} and then $\rightarrow$ d

$$\frac{6.022\text{x}10^{23}\text{atoms}}{\text{mol}} \qquad V = \frac{4}{3}\pi r^3 \qquad d = \frac{\text{mass}}{\text{vol}}$$

Solution: $\dfrac{20.18\text{ g}}{\cancel{\text{mol}}} \times \dfrac{\cancel{\text{mol}}}{6.022 \times 10^{23}\text{ atoms}} = 3.35 \times 10^{-23}\text{ g/atom}$

$$V = \frac{4}{3} \times 3.14 \times (70\ \cancel{\text{pm}})^3 \times \left(\frac{\cancel{\text{m}}}{10^{12}\ \cancel{\text{pm}}}\right)^3 \times \frac{\text{L}}{0.0010\ \cancel{\text{m}^3}} = 1.\underline{44} \times 10^{-27}\text{ L}$$

$$d = \frac{3.35 \times 10^{-23}\text{ g}}{1.\underline{44} \times 10^{-27}\text{ L}} = 2.\underline{33} \times 10^4 = 2.3 \times 10^4\text{ g/L}$$

Check: The units of the answer (g/L) are correct. This density is significantly larger than the actual density of neon gas. This suggests that a L of neon is composed of primarily empty space.

(d) **Given:** Ne: M = 20.18 g/ mol, d = 0.90 g/L; Kr: M = 83.30 g/ mol, d = 3.75 g/L; Ar: M = 39.95 g/ mol
Find: d of argon in g/L
Conceptual Plan: d $\rightarrow$ mol/L $\rightarrow$ atoms/L for Kr and Ne and then atoms/L $\rightarrow$ mol/L $\rightarrow$ d for Ar

$$\text{mol} = \frac{\text{mass}}{\text{molar mass}} \qquad \frac{6.022\text{x }10^{23}\text{atoms}}{\text{mol}} \qquad \frac{\text{mol}}{6.022\text{x }10^{23}\text{atoms}} \qquad \frac{39.95\text{ g}}{\text{mol}}$$

Solution: for Ne: $\dfrac{0.90\ \cancel{\text{g}}}{\text{L}} \times \dfrac{\cancel{\text{mol}}}{20.18\ \cancel{\text{g}}} \times \dfrac{6.022 \times 10^{23}\text{ atoms}}{\cancel{\text{mol}}} = 2.69 \times 10^{22}\text{ atoms/ L}$

for Kr: $\dfrac{3.75\ \cancel{\text{g}}}{\text{L}} \times \dfrac{\cancel{\text{mol}}}{83.80\ \cancel{\text{g}}} \times \dfrac{6.022 \times 10^{23}\text{ atoms}}{\cancel{\text{mol}}} = 2.69 \times 10^{22}\text{ atoms/ L}$

for Ar: $\dfrac{2.69 \times 10^{22}\ \cancel{\text{atoms}}}{\text{L}} \times \dfrac{\cancel{\text{mol}}}{6.022 \times 10^{23}\ \cancel{\text{atoms}}} \times \dfrac{39.95\text{ g}}{\cancel{\text{mol}}} = 1.78\text{ g/ L}$

This value is similar to the value calculated in part a. The value of the density calculated from the radius was 2 g/L and the value of the density calculated from the atomic number was 1.8 g/L.
Check: The units of the answer (g/L) are correct. The value of the answer agrees with published value.

8.114 If there were only two p orbitals there would only be 4 p block columns and if there were only three d orbitals there would be only 6 d block columns. So the periodic table would have 12 columns.

H											He
Li	Be							B	C	N	O
F	Ne							Na	Mg	Al	Si
P	S	Cl	Ar	K	Ca	Sc	Ti	V	Cr	Mn	Fe

The noble gas equivalent elements would be He, O, Si, and Fe.
The halogen equivalent elements would be N, Al, and Mn.
The alkali metal equivalent elements would be Li, F, and P.

8.115 The density increases as you move to the right across the first transition series. For the first transition series, the mass increases as you move to the right across the periodic table. However, the radius of the transition series elements stays nearly constant as you move to the right across the periodic table, thus the volume will remain nearly constant. Since density is mass/volume the density of the elements increases.

8.116 If there are three possible spin quantum numbers, there will be three *s* electrons, nine *p* electrons, and fifteen *d* electrons.

(a) Ne(10 e): $1s^3 2s^3 2p^4$

(b) Completed n = 2 level: $1s^3 2s^3 2p^9$ Atomic number = 15

(c) F(9 e): $1s^3 2s^3 2p^3$ There will be 1 unpaired electron in the 1s and 2s and 3 unpaired electrons in the 2p, therefore there are 5 unpaired electrons

8.117 The longest wavelength would be associated with the lowest energy state next to the ground state of carbon, which has two unpaired electrons:
Ground state of carbon:

1s	2s	2p		
↓↑	↓↑	↑	↑	

Longest wavelength: One of the *p* electrons flipped in its orbital, which requires the least amount of energy.

1s	2s	2p		
↓↑	↓↑	↑	↓	

The next wavelength would be associated with the pairing of the two *p* electrons in the same orbital because this requires energy and raises the energy.

1s	2s	2p		
↓↑	↓↑	↓↑		

The next wavelength would be associated with the energy needed to promote one of the *s* electrons to a *p* orbital.

1s	2s	2p		
↓↑	↑	↑	↑	↑

8.118 Element darmstadtium (110) would be in the column with Ni, Pd, and Pt so it might be expected to have an electron configuration similar to Ni or Pd or Pt.
Similar to Ni: $[Rn]7s^2 5f^{14} 6d^8$
Similar to Pd: $[Rn]7s^0 5f^{14} 6d^{10}$
Similar to Pt: $[Rn]\ 7s^1 5f^{14} 6d^9$

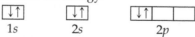

8.119 The element that would fill the 8*s* and 8*p* orbitals would have atomic number 168. The element is in the noble gas family and would have the properties of noble gases. It would have the electron configuration of $[118]8s^2 5g^{18} 6f^{14} 7d^{10} 8p^6$. The outer shell electron (highest *n* level) configuration would be $8s^2 8p^6$. The element would be relatively inert, have a first ionization energy less than 1037 kJ/mol (the first ionization energy of Rn), and have a positive electron affinity. It would be difficult to form compounds with most elements but would be able to form compounds with fluorine.

8.120 To determine the second ionization energies, look at the electron configuration of the 1+ ions.

First write the electron configuration of the atom:		Then write the electron configuration of the 1+ ion:	
Li	$1s^22s^1$	Li^+	$1s^22s^0$
Be	$1s^22s^2$	Be^+	$1s^22s^1$
B	$1s^22s^22p^1$	B^+	$1s^22s^2$
C	$1s^22s^22p^2$	C^+	$1s^22s^22p^1$
N	$1s^22s^22p^3$	N^+	$1s^22s^22p^2$
O	$1s^22s^22p^4$	O^+	$1s^22s^22p^3$
F	$1s^22s^22p^5$	F^+	$1s^22s^22p^4$

Based on the electron configuration of the ions, Li^+ should have the largest second ionization energy since the removal of the second electron involves removing a core electron. The lowest second ionization energy should be Be^+ since removing the second electron takes you to the $1s^2$ (stable) configuration.

O would have the highest second ionization energy because the electron configuration of O^+ has a half-filled p orbital, which is particularly stable and therefore it would require more energy to remove the second electron. N^+ would have the lowest second ionization energy because the size of N^+ would be larger than the radius of the F^+, so the attraction between the outer electron and the nucleus would be less in N^+ than in F^+, making it easier to remove the electron.

8.121 When you move down the column from Al to Ga, the size of the atom actually decreases because not much shielding is contributed by the 3d electrons in the Ga atom, while there is a large increase in the nuclear charge; therefore, the effective nuclear charge is greater for Ga than for Al, so the ionization energy does not decrease. As you go from In to Tl, the ionization energy actually increases because the 4f electrons do not contribute to the shielding of the outermost electrons and there is a large increase in the effective nuclear charge.

8.122 ΔE for the reaction based on the ionization energy and the electron affinity = +147 kJ/ mol

$Na(g) \rightarrow Na^+(g) + e^-$	IE = +496 kJ/mol
$Cl(g) + e^- \rightarrow Cl^-(g)$	EA = - 349 kJ/mol
$Na(g) + Cl(g) \rightarrow Na^+(g) + Cl^-(g)$	ΔE = +147 kJ/mol

8.123 The second electron is added to an ion with a 1 – charge, so there is a large repulsive force that has to be overcome to add the second electron. Thus, it will require energy to add the second electron and the second electron affinity will have a positive value.

8.124 The diagonal relationship between some elements could be explained because the atomic size of the atoms on the diagonal would be about the same. Because on the diagonal, the radius would increase as you go down the column but will decrease as you move to the right across the period. Also, the size of the ion formed would be about the same. Therefore, you might expect the elements to have similar behavior.

8.125 **Given:** Ra, Z = 88 **Find:** Z for next two alkaline earth metals
Solution: The next element would lie in period 8, column 2A. The largest currently known element is 116 in period 7, column 6A. To reach period 8 column 2A you need to add 4 protons, and would have Z = 120.

The alkaline earth metal following 120, would lie in period 9 column 2A. To reach this column, you need to add 18 g-block element protons, 10 d block element protons, 14 f block element protons, 6 p block element protons, and then 2 s block element protons. This would give Z = 170.

8.126 **Given:** Pd = $[Kr]4d^{10}$ **Find:** electron configuration of first two excited states
Solution: The first excited state of Pd would move an electron from a 4d to a 5s orbital. The second excited state would move the electron from a 4d to the 5p orbital.
First excited state: $[Kr]4d^95s^1$
Second excited state: $[Kr]4d^95p^1$

8.127 Francium would have an electron configuration of $[Rn]7s^1$; the atomic radius would be > 265 pm (atomic radius of Cs); the first ionization energy would be less than 376 kJ/mol; the density would be greater than 1.879 g/cm^3; and the melting would be less than 29°C.

(a) $Fr + H_2O \rightarrow Fr^+(aq) + OH^-(aq) + H_2(g)$

(b) $Fr + O_2(g) \rightarrow Fr_2O(s)$

(c) $2Fr + Cl_2(g) \rightarrow FrCl(s)$

8.128 **Given:** Element 165 **Find:** What group would it be in?
Solution: Element 165 would have the electron configuration: [Rn] $7s^26d^{10}5f^{14}7p^68s^25g^{18}7d^{10}6f^{14}8p^3$. The element would behave like nitrogen.

Conceptual Problems

8.129 If six electrons rather than eight electrons led to a stable configuration, the electron configuration of the stable configuration would be ns^2np^4.

(a) A noble gas would have the electron configuration ns^2np^4. This could correspond to the O atom.

(b) A reactive nonmetal would have one less electron than the stable configuration. This would have the electron configuration ns^2np^3. This could correspond to the N atom.

(c) A reactive metal would have one have one more electron than the stable configuration. This would have the electron configuration of ns^1. This could correspond to the Li atom.

8.130 According to Coulomb's law, the potential energy for like charges is positive and the potential energy of opposite charges is negative. So, c would have the highest potential energy since both charges are the same.

For opposite charges, the potential energy increases (becomes less negative) with increasing distance, so d is greater than a.

Since the charge of b is twice the charge of a at the same distance and has opposite charges, it would have the lowest (most negative) potential energy. Ranking from lowest to highest $b < a < d < c$.

8.131 (a) True: An electron in a 3*s* orbital is more shielded than an electron in a 2*s* orbital. This is true since there are more core electrons below a 3s orbital.

(b) True: An electron in a 3*s* orbital penetrates into the region occupied by the core electrons more than electrons in a 3*p* orbital. Examine Figure 8.5, the radial distribution functions for the 3*s*, 3*p*, and 3*d* orbitals. You will see that the 3*s* electrons penetrate more deeply than the 3*p* electrons and more than the 3*d* electrons.

(c) False: An electron in an orbital that penetrates closer to the nucleus will experience less shielding than an electron in an orbital that does not penetrate as far.

(d) True: An electron in an orbital that penetrates close to the nucleus will tend to experience a higher effective nuclear charge than one that does not. Since the orbital penetrates closer to the nucleus, the electron will experience less shielding and, therefore, a higher effective nuclear charge.

8.132 An electron in a 5*p* orbital could have any one of the following combinations of quantum numbers.
5,1, -1,+1/2 5,1,-1,-1/2 5,1,0,+1/2 5,1,0,-1/2 5,1,1,+1/2 5,1,1,-1/2
An electron in a 6*d* orbital could have any one of the following combinations of quantum numbers.
6,2,-2,+1/2 6,2,-2,-1/2 6,2,-1,+1/2 6,2,-1,-1/2 6,2,0,+1/2 6,2,0,-1/2
6,2,1,+1/2 6,2,1,-1/2 6,2,2,+1/2 6,2,2,-1/2

8.133 The 4*s* electrons in calcium have relatively low ionization energies (IE_1 = 590 kJ/mol; IE_2 = 1145 kJ/mol) because they are valence electrons. The energetic cost for calcium to lose a third electron is extraordinarily high because the next electron to be lost is a core electron. Similarly, the electron affinity of fluorine to gain one electron (- 328 kJ/mol) is highly exothermic because the added electron completes fluoride's valence shell. The gain of a second electron by the negatively charged fluoride anion would not be favorable. Therefore, we would expect calcium and fluoride to combine in a 1:2 ratio.

9 Chemical Bonding I: Lewis Theory

Review Questions

9.1 Bonding theories are central to chemistry because they explain how atoms bond together to form molecules. Bonding theories explain why some combinations of atoms are stable and others are not.

9.2 Chemical bonds form because they lower the potential energy between the charged particles that compose the atom. Bonds involve the attraction and repulsion of charged particles.

9.3 The three types of bonds are ionic bonds, which occur between metals and nonmetals and are characterized by the transfer of electrons; covalent bonds, which occur between nonmetals and are characterized by the sharing of electrons; and metallic bonds, which occur between metals and are characterized by electrons being pooled.

9.4 In a Lewis structure, the valence electrons of main-group elements are represented as dots surrounding the symbol for the element. The valence electrons can be determined from the group that they are in on the periodic table.

9.5 Bonds are formed when atoms attain a stable electron configuration. Since the stable configuration usually has eight electrons in the outermost shell; this is known as the octet rule.

9.6 In Lewis theory, a chemical bond is the sharing or transfer of electrons to attain stable electron configurations for the bonding atoms. If electrons are transferred, the bond is an ionic bond. If the electrons are shared, the bond is a covalent bond.

9.7 In Lewis theory, we represent ionic bonding by moving electron dots from the metal to the nonmetal and then allowing the resultant ions to form a crystalline lattice composed of alternating cations and anions. The cation loses its valence electron(s) and is left with an octet in the previous principal energy level; the anion gains electron(s) to form an octet. The Lewis structure of the anion is usually written within brackets with the charge in the upper right-hand corner, outside the brackets. The positive and negative charges attract one another, resulting in the compound.

9.8 To use Lewis theory to determine the formula of an ionic compound, determine the number of valence electrons lost by the metal to form an octet, and the number of electrons gained by the nonmetal to form an octet. Consider the ionic compound formed between sodium and sulfur. The Lewis structures for sodium and sulfur are as follows:

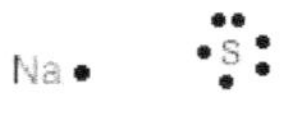

Sodium must lose one electron to achieve an octet, while sulfur must gain two electrons to achieve an octet. So the compound requires two sodium atoms for each sulfur atom giving the formula Na_2S.

9.9 Lattice energy is the energy associated with forming a crystalline lattice of alternating cations and anions from the gaseous ions. Since the cations are positively charged and the anions are negatively charged there is a lowering of potential—as described by Coulomb's law—when the ions come together to form a lattice. That energy is emitted as heat when the lattice forms.

9.10 The formation of the crystalline NaCl lattice from sodium cations and chloride anions is highly exothermic and more than compensates for the endothermicity of the electron transfer process. In other words, the formation of ionic compounds is not exothermic because sodium "wants" to lose electrons and chlorine "wants" to gain them; rather, it is exothermic because of the large amount of heat released when sodium and chlorine ions coalesce to form a crystal lattice.

9.11 The Born–Haber cycle is a hypothetical series of steps that represents the formation of an ionic compound from its constituent elements. The steps are chosen so that the change in enthalpy of each step is known except for the last one, which is the lattice energy. In terms of the formation of NaCl, the steps are as follows:
Step 1: The formation of gaseous sodium from solid sodium (heat of sublimation of sodium)
Step 2: The formation of a chlorine atom from a chlorine molecule (bond energy of chlorine)
Step 3: The ionization of gaseous sodium (ionization energy of sodium)
Step 4: The addition of an electron to gaseous chlorine (the electron affinity of chlorine)
Step 5: The formation of the crystalline solid from the gaseous ions (the lattice energy)

The overall reaction is the formation of NaCl(s), so we can use Hess's law to determine the lattice energy.

$$\Delta H^{\circ}_{f} = \Delta H_{step\ 1} + \Delta H_{step\ 2} + \Delta H_{step\ 3} + \Delta H_{step\ 4} + \Delta H_{step\ 5}$$

$$\Delta H^{\circ}_{f} = \text{heat of sublimation} + \tfrac{1}{2}\ \text{bond energy} + \text{ionization energy} + \text{electron affinity} + \text{lattice energy}$$

Since all the terms are known except the lattice energy, we can calculate the lattice energy.

9.12 As the ionic radii increase as you move down a group, the ions cannot get as close to each other and therefore, do not release as much energy when the lattice forms. Thus, the lattice energy decreases (becomes less negative) as the radius increases.

Since the magnitude of the potential energy of two interacting charges depends not only on the distance between the charges but also on the product of the charges, the lattice energies become more exothermic with increasing magnitude of ionic charge.

9.13 We modeled ionic solids as a lattice of individual ions held together by coulombic forces, which are equal in all directions. To melt the solid, these forces must be overcome, which requires a significant amount of heat. Therefore, the model accounts for the high melting points of ionic solids.

9.14 In the ionic bonding model, electrons are transferred from the metal to the nonmetal, but the transferred electrons remain localized on one atom. The model does not include any free electrons that might conduct electricity, and the ions themselves are fixed in place; therefore, our model accounts for the nonconductivity of ionic solids. When the ionic solid dissolves in water, the cations and anions dissociate, forming free ions in solution. These ions can move in response to electrical forces, creating an electrical current. Thus, our model predicts that solutions of ionic compounds conduct electricity.

9.15 A pair of electrons that is shared between two atoms is called a bonding pair, while a pair of electrons that is associated with only one atom—and therefore, not involved in bonding—is called a lone pair.

9.16 A single bond occurs when one pair of electrons is shared between two atoms. A double bond results when two electron pairs are shared between the same two atoms. Double bonds are shorter and stronger than single bonds. A triple bond results when three electron pairs are shared between the same two atoms. Triple bonds are even shorter and stronger than double bonds.

9.17 Generally, combinations of atoms that can satisfy the octet rule on each atom are stable, while those combinations that do not satisfy the octet rule are not stable.

9.18 Lewis theory shows that covalent bonds are highly directional. The attraction between two covalently bonded atoms is due to the sharing of one or more electron pairs. Thus, each bond links just one specific pair of atoms—in contrast to ionic bonds, which are nondirectional and hold together the entire array of ions. The fundamental units of covalently bonded compounds are individual molecules. These molecules can interact with one another in a number of different ways, however, the interactions between molecules are generally much weaker than the bonding interactions within a molecule. When a molecular compound melts or boils, the molecules themselves remain intact. Only the weak interactions between the molecules must be overcome. Consequently, molecular compounds tend to have lower melting and boiling points than ionic compounds.

9.19 Electronegativity is the ability of an atom to attract electrons to itself in a chemical bond. This results in a polar bond. Electronegativity generally increases across a period in the periodic table. And, electronegativity generally decreases down a column (group) in the periodic table. The most electronegative element is fluorine.

9.20 If two elements with identical electronegativities form a covalent bond, they share the electrons equally, and the bond is purely covalent or nonpolar.

If there is an intermediate electronegativity difference between the two elements, such as between two different nonmetals, then the bond is polar covalent.

If there is a large electronegativity difference between the two elements in a bond, such as normally occurs between a metal and a nonmetal, the electron from the metal is almost completely transferred to the nonmetal, and the bond is ionic.

9.21 Percent ionic character is defined as the ratio of a bond's actual dipole moment to the dipole moment it would have if the electron were completely transferred from one atom to the other, multiplied by 100.

A bond in which an electron is completely transferred from one atom to another would have 100% ionic character. However, no bond is 100% ionic. Percent ionic character generally increases as the electronegativity difference increases. In general, bonds with greater than 50% ionic character are referred to as ionic bonds.

9.22 A dipole moment (μ) occurs anytime there is a separation of positive and negative charge. It is used to quantify the polarity of a bond. The magnitude of the dipole moment created by separating two particles of equal but opposite charges of magnitude (q) by a distance (r) is given by μ = qr.

9.23 To calculate the dipole moment we use μ = qr:

For 100 pm: $\mu = 1.6 \times 10^{-19}\,\cancel{C} \times 100\,\cancel{pm} \times \frac{\cancel{m}}{10^{12}\,\cancel{pm}} \times \frac{D}{3.34 \times 10^{-30}\,\cancel{C}\cdot\cancel{m}} = 4.8\ D$

For 200 pm: $\mu = 1.6 \times 10^{-19}\,\cancel{C} \times 200\,\cancel{pm} \times \frac{\cancel{m}}{10^{12}\,\cancel{pm}} \times \frac{D}{3.34 \times 10^{-30}\,\cancel{C}\cdot\cancel{m}} = 9.6\ D$

9.24 The steps for writing a Lewis structure are as follows:

1. Write the correct skeletal structure for the molecule.
2. Calculate the total number of electrons for the Lewis structure by summing the valence electrons of each atom in the molecule.
3. Distribute the electrons among the atoms, giving octets (or duets for hydrogen) to as many atoms as possible.
4. If any atoms lack an octet, form double or triple bonds as necessary to give them octets.

9.25 The total number of electrons for a Lewis structure of a molecule is the sum of the valence electrons of each atom in the molecule.

The total number of electrons for the Lewis structure of an ion is found by summing the number of valence electrons for each atom and then subtracting 1 electron for each positive charge or adding 1 electron for each negative charge.

9.26 Resonance structures result when you can write two or more Lewis structures for the same molecule. A resonance hybrid is then the weighted average of the resonance structures.

9.27 In some cases we can write resonance structures that are not equivalent. One possible resonance structure may be somewhat better than another. In such cases the true structure may still be represented as an average of the resonance structures, but with the better resonance structure contributing more to the true structure. Multiple nonequivalent resonance structures may be weighted differently in their contributions to the true overall structure of a molecule.

9.28 Formal charge is a fictitious charge assigned to each atom in a Lewis structure that helps us to distinguish among competing Lewis structures. The formal charge of an atom in a Lewis structure is the charge it would have if all bonding electrons were shared equally between the bonded atoms. Formal charge can be calculated simply by taking the number of valence electrons in the atom and subtracting the number of electrons that it "owns" in a Lewis structure. An atom in a Lewis structure "owns" all of its lone pair electrons and 1/2 of its bonding electrons.

Formal charge = number of valence electrons – (number of lone pair electrons + 1/2 number of bonding electrons).

The concept of formal charge is useful because it can help us distinguish between competing skeletal structures or competing resonance structures.

9.29 The octet rule has some exceptions because not all atoms always have eight electrons surrounding them. The three major categories are 1) odd octets—electron species, molecules, or ions with an odd number of electron, for example, NO; 2) incomplete octets—molecules or ions with fewer than eight electrons around an atom, for example, BF_3; and 3) expanded octets—molecules or ions with more than eight electrons around an atom, for example, AsF_5.

9.30 Elements in the third row of the periodic table and beyond often exhibit expanded octets. Elements in the first or second row of the periodic table can never have expanded octets.

9.31 The bond energy of a chemical bond is the energy required to break 1 mole of the bond in the gas phase. Since breaking bonds is endothermic and forming bonds is exothermic we can calculate the overall enthalpy change as a sum of the enthalpy changes associated with breaking the required bonds in the reactants and forming the required bonds in the products.

9.32 A reaction is exothermic when weak bonds break and strong bonds form. A reaction is endothermic when strong bonds break and weak bonds form.

9.33 When metal atoms bond together to form a solid, each metal atom donates one or more electrons to an electron sea.

9.34 Metals conduct electricity because the electrons in a metal are free to move. The movement or flow of electrons in response to an electric potential is an electric current. Metals are also excellent conductors of heat because of the highly-mobile electrons, which help to disperse thermal energy throughout the metal.

The malleability of metals and the ductility of metals are also accounted for by the electron sea model. Since there are no localized or specific "bonds" in a metal, it can be deformed relatively easily by forcing the metal ions to slide past one another. The electron sea can easily accommodate these deformations by flowing into the new shape.

Problems by Topic

Valence Electrons and Dot Structures

9.35 N : $1s^2 2s^2 2p^3$

The electrons included in the Lewis structure are $2s^2 2p^3$.

9.36 Ne : $1s^2 2s^2 2p^6$

The electrons included in the Lewis structure are $2s^2 2p^6$.

9.37 (a) Al: $1s^2 2s^2 2p^6 3s^2 3p^1$

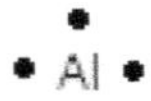

(b) Na^+: $1s^2 2s^2 2p^6$

(c) Cl: $1s^2 2s^2 2p^6 3s^2 3p^5$

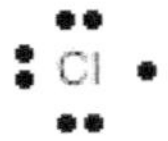

(d)   Cl⁻: $1s^22s^22p^63s^23p^6$

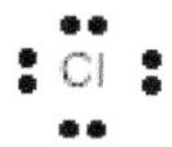

$$:\overset{\bullet\bullet}{\underset{\bullet\bullet}{Cl}}:$$

9.38   (a)   S²⁻ : $1s^22s^22p^63s^23p^6$

$$\left[:\overset{\bullet\bullet}{\underset{\bullet\bullet}{S}}:\right]^{2-}$$

(b)   Mg: $1s^22s^22p^63s^2$

$$Mg:$$

(c)   Mg²⁺: $1s^22s^22p^6$

$$Mg^{2+}$$

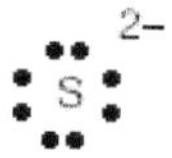

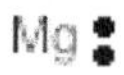

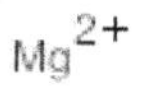

(d)   P: $1s^22s^22p^63s^23p^3$

$$\cdot\overset{\bullet\bullet}{\underset{\bullet}{P}}\cdot$$

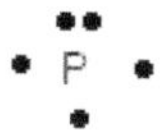

Ionic Lewis Structures and Lattice Energy

9.39   (a)   NaF: Draw the Lewis structures for Na and F based on their valence electrons. Na: $3s^1$ F: $2s^22p^5$

$$Na\bullet \quad :\overset{\bullet\bullet}{\underset{\bullet\bullet}{F}}\bullet$$

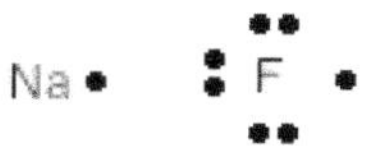

Sodium must lose one electron and be left with the octet from the previous shell, while fluorine needs to gain one electron to get an octet.

$$Na^+ \left[:\overset{\bullet\bullet}{\underset{\bullet\bullet}{F}}:\right]^-$$

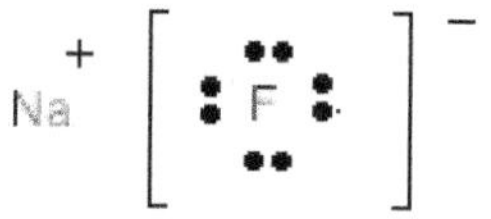

(b)   CaO: Draw the Lewis structures for Ca and O based on their valence electrons. Ca: $4s^2$ O: $2s^22p^4$

$$Ca: \quad :\overset{\bullet\bullet}{\underset{\bullet}{O}}\bullet$$

Calcium must lose two electrons and be left with two 1s electrons from the previous shell, while oxygen needs to gain two electrons to get an octet.

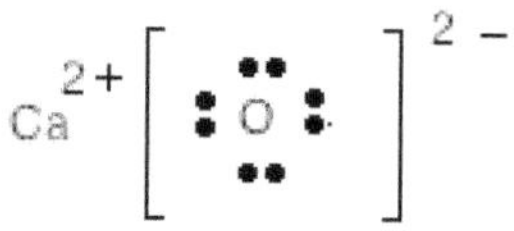

$$Ca^{2+}\left[:\overset{\bullet\bullet}{\underset{\bullet\bullet}{O}}:\right]^{2-}$$

(c)   SrBr₂: Draw the Lewis structures for Sr and Br based on their valence electrons. Sr: $5s^2$ Br: $4s^24p^5$

$$Sr: \quad :\overset{\bullet\bullet}{\underset{\bullet\bullet}{Br}}\bullet$$

Strontium must lose two electrons and be left with the octet from the previous shell, while bromine needs to gain one electron to get an octet.

$$Sr^{2+}\ 2\left[:\overset{\bullet\bullet}{\underset{\bullet\bullet}{Br}}:\right]^-$$

(d) K_2O: Draw the Lewis structures for K and O based on their valence electrons. K: $4s^1$ O: $2s^22p^4$

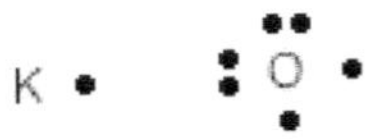

Potassium must lose one electron and be left with the octet from the previous shell, while oxygen needs to gain two electrons to get an octet.

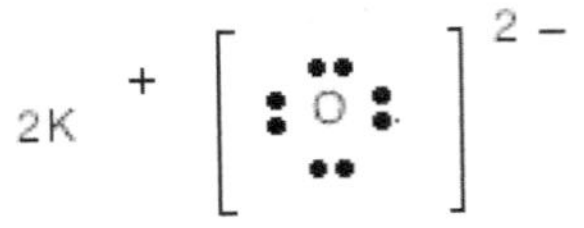

9.40 (a) SrO: Draw the Lewis structures for Sr and O based on their valence electrons. Sr: $5s^2$ O: $2s^22p^4$

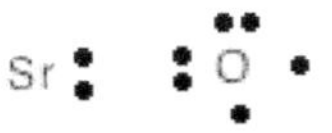

Strontium must lose two electrons and be left with the octet from the previous shell, while oxygen needs to gain two electrons to get an octet.

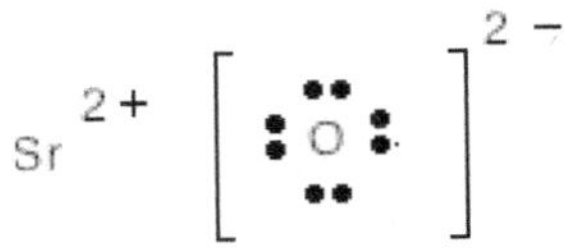

(b) Li_2S: Draw the Lewis structures for Li and S based on their valence electrons. Li: $2s^1$ S: $3s^23p^4$

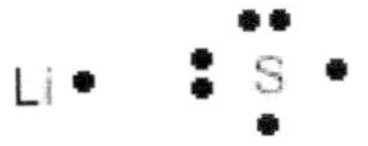

Lithium must lose one electron and be left with two 1s electrons from the previous shell, while sulfur needs to gain two electrons to get an octet.

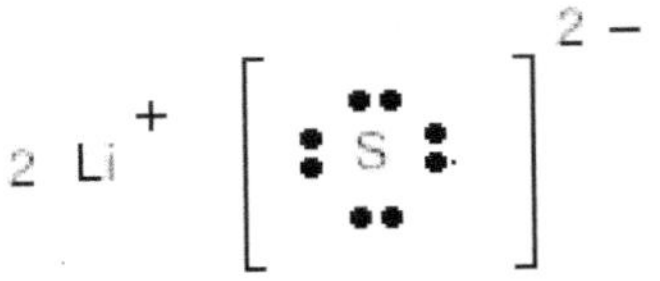

(c) CaI_2: Draw the Lewis structures for Ca and I based on their valence electrons. Ca: $4s^2$ I: $5s^25p^5$

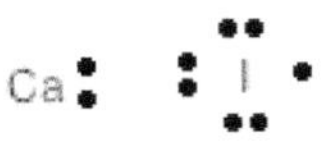

Calcium must lose two electrons and be left with the octet from the previous shell, while iodine needs to gain one electron to get an octet.

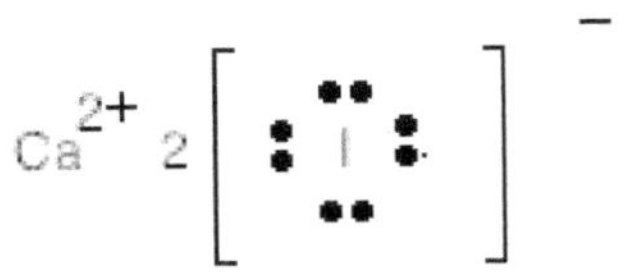

(d) RbF: Draw the Lewis structures for Rb and F based on their valence electrons. Rb: $5s^1$ F: $2s^22p^5$

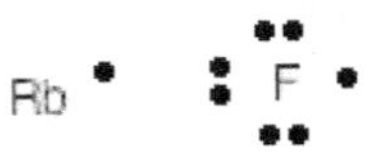

Rubidium must lose one electron and be left with the octet from the previous shell, while fluorine needs to gain one electron to get an octet.

9.41 (a) Sr and Se: Draw the Lewis structures for Sr and Se based on their valence electrons.

Sr: $5s^2$ Se: $4s^24p^4$

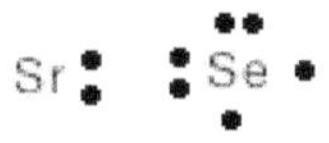

Strontium must lose two electrons and be left with the octet from the previous shell, while selenium needs to gain two electrons to get an octet.

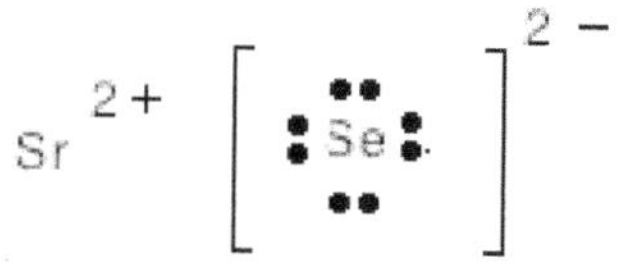

Thus, we need one Sr^{2+} and one Se^{2-}. Write the formula with subscripts (if necessary) to indicate the number of atoms.

SrSe

(b) Ba and Cl: Draw the Lewis structures for Ba and Cl based on their valence electrons.

Ba: $6s^2$ Cl: $3s^23p^5$

Barium must lose two electrons and be left with the octet from the previous shell, while chlorine needs to gain one electron to get an octet.

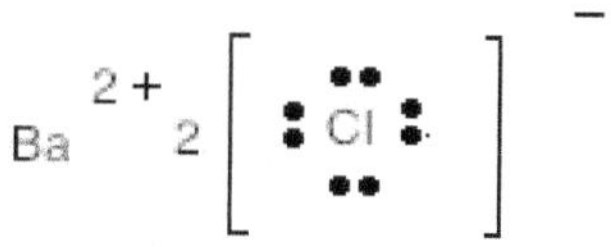

Thus, we need one Ba^{2+} and two Cl^-. Write the formula with subscripts (if necessary) to indicate the number of atoms.

$BaCl_2$

(c) Na and S: Draw the Lewis structures for Na and S based on their valence electrons.

Na: $3s^1$ S: $3s^23p^4$

Sodium must lose one electron and be left with the octet from the previous shell, while sulfur needs to gain two electrons to get an octet.

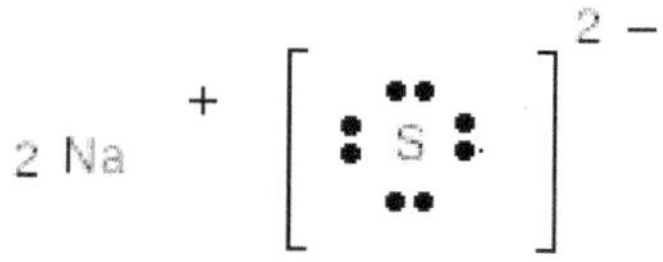

Thus, we need two Na^+ and one S^{2-}. Write the formula with subscripts (if necessary) to indicate the number of atoms.

Na_2S

(d) Al and O: Draw the Lewis structures for Al and O based on their valence electrons.

Al: $3s^23p^1$ O: $2s^22p^4$

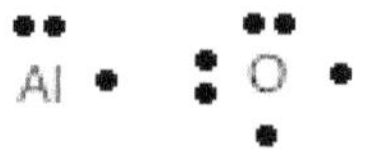

Aluminum must lose three electrons and be left with the octet from the previous shell, while oxygen needs to gain two electrons to get an octet.

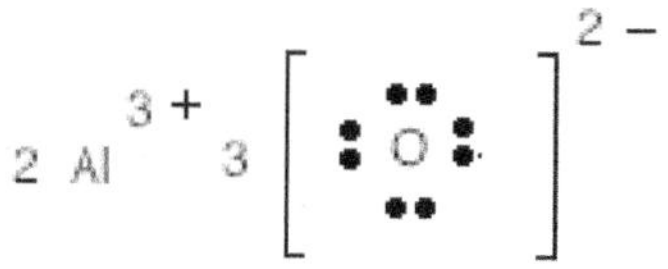

Thus, we need two Al^{3+} and three O^{2-} in order to lose and gain the same number of electrons. Write the formula with subscripts (if necessary) to indicate the number of atoms.

Al_2O_3

9.42 (a) Ca and N: Draw the Lewis structures for Ca and N based on their valence electrons.

Ca: $4s^2$ N: $2s^22p^3$

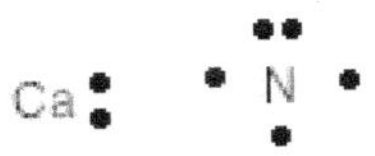

Calcium must lose two electrons and be left with the octet from the previous shell, while nitrogen needs to gain three electrons to get an octet.

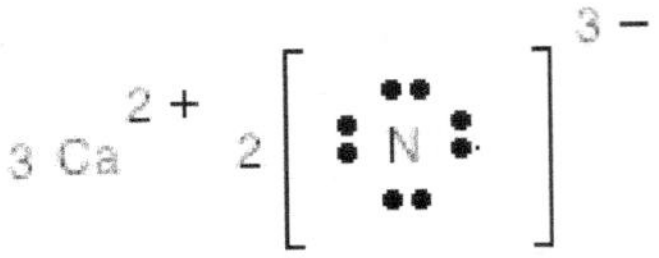

Thus, we need three Ca^{2+} and two N^{3-} in order to lose and gain the same number of electrons. Write the formula with subscripts (if necessary) to indicate the number of atoms.

Ca_3N_2

(b) Mg and I: Draw the Lewis structures for Mg and I based on their valence electrons.

Mg: $3s^2$ I: $5s^25p^5$

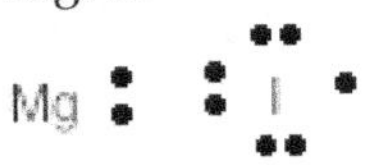

Magnesium must lose two electrons and be left with the octet from the previous shell, while iodine needs to gain one electron to get an octet.

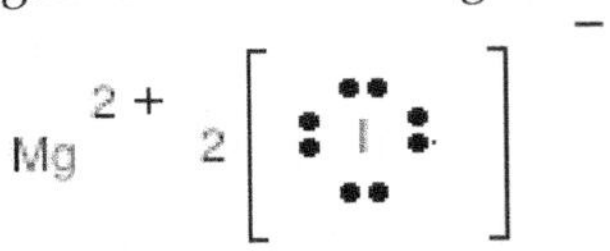

Thus, we need one Mg^{2+} and two I^-. Write the formula with subscripts (if necessary) to indicate the number of atoms.

MgI_2

(c) Ca and S: Draw the Lewis structures for Ca and S based on their valence electrons.

Ca: $4s^2$ S: $3s^23p^4$

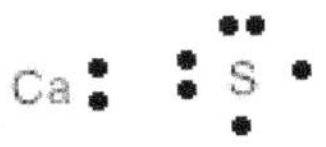

Calcium must lose two electrons and be left with the octet from the previous shell, while sulfur needs to gain two electrons to get an octet.

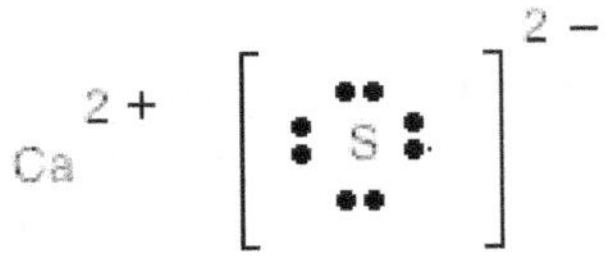

Thus, we need one Ca^{2+} and one S^{2-}. Write the formula with subscripts (if necessary) to indicate the number of atoms.

CaS

(d) Cs and F: Draw the Lewis structures for Cs and F based on their valence electrons.

Cs: $6s^1$ F: $2s^22p^5$

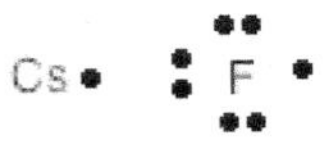

Cesium must lose one electron and be left with the octet from the previous shell, while fluorine needs to gain one electron to get an octet.

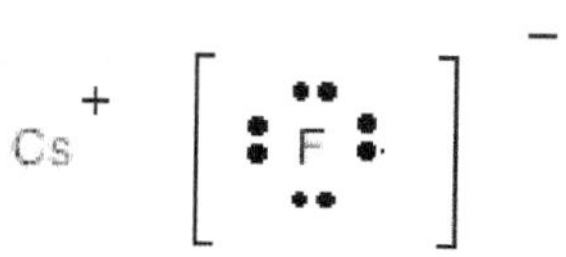

Thus, we need one Cs^+ and one F^-. Write the formula with subscripts (if necessary) to indicate the number of atoms.

CsF

9.43 As the size of the alkaline metal ions increases down the column, so does the distance between the metal cation and the oxide anion. Therefore, the magnitude of the lattice energy of the oxides decreases, making the formation of the oxides less exothermic and the compounds less stable. Since the ions cannot get as close to each other, they therefore do not release as much energy.

9.44 Rubidium is below potassium on the periodic table and iodine is below bromine on the periodic table. Therefore, both the rubidium ion and the iodide ion are larger than the potassium ion and the bromide ion. So, the rubidium ion and the iodide ion cannot get as close to each other as the potassium ion and the bromide ion; thus, they do not release as much energy and the lattice energy of potassium bromide is more exothermic.

9.45 Cesium is slightly larger than barium, but oxygen is slightly larger than fluorine, so we cannot use size to explain the difference in the lattice energy. However, the charge on cesium ion is 1+ and the charge on fluoride ion is 1 –, while the charge on barium ion is 2+ and the charge on oxide ion is 2 –. The coulombic equation states that the magnitude of the potential also depends on the product of the charges. Since the product of the charges for CsF = 1 –, and the product of the charges for BaO = 4 –, the stabilization for BaO relative to CsF should be about four times greater, which is what we see in its much more exothermic lattice energy.

9.46 RbBr < KCl < SrO < CaO. KCl and RbBr both have a product of the charges of 1 –, while SrO and CaO have a product of the charges of 4 –. So, the lattice energies of KCl and RbBr are less than SrO and CaO. Within KCl and RbBr, rubidium ion is larger than potassium ion and bromide ion is larger than chloride ion. Therefore, the rubidium ion and the bromide ion will be farther apart, leading to a smaller lattice energy. Between SrO and CaO, the strontium ion is larger than the calcium ion, so the strontium oxide will have a smaller (less negative) lattice energy.

9.47 **Given:** ΔH_f° KCl = -436.5 kJ/mol; $IE_1(K)$ = 419 kJ/mol; $\Delta H_{sub}(K)$ = 89.0 kJ/mol; $Cl_2(g)$ bond energy = 243 kJ/mol; EA(Cl) = – 349 kJ/mol **Find:** lattice energy

Conceptual Plan:

$$K(s)+1/2Cl_2(g) \xrightarrow{\Delta H_{sub}} K(g)+1/2Cl_2(g) \xrightarrow{IE_1} K^+(g)+1/2Cl_2(g) \xrightarrow{\text{bond energy}} K^+(g)+Cl(g) \xrightarrow{EA} K^+(g)+Cl^-(g) \xrightarrow{\text{lattice energy}} KCl(s)$$

ΔH_f°

Solution: $\Delta H_f^\circ = \Delta H_{sub} + IE_1 + 1/2 \text{ bond energy} + EA + \text{lattice energy}$

$$-436.5\frac{kJ}{mol} = +89.0\frac{kJ}{mol} + 419\frac{kJ}{mol} + \frac{1}{2}(243)\frac{kJ}{mol} + (-349)\frac{kJ}{mol} + \text{lattice energy}$$

lattice energy = – 717 kJ/mol

9.48 **Given:** ΔH_f° CaO = -634.9 kJ/mol; $IE_1(Ca)$ = 590 kJ/mol; $IE_2(Ca)$ = 1145 kJ/mol; $\Delta H_{sub}(Ca)$ = 178 kJ/mol; $O_2(g)$ bond energy = 498 kJ/mol; $EA_1(O)$ = – 141 kJ/mol; $EA_2(O)$ = 744 kJ/mol **Find:** lattice energy

Conceptual Plan:

$$Ca(s)+1/2O_2(g) \xrightarrow{\Delta H_{sub}} Ca(g)+1/2O_2(g) \xrightarrow{IE_1} Ca^+(g)+1/2O_2(g) \xrightarrow{IE_2} Ca^{2+}(g)+1/2O_2(g) \xrightarrow{\text{bond energy}} Ca^{2+}(g)+O(g) \xrightarrow{EA_1} Ca^{2+}(g)+O^-(g)$$

$$\xrightarrow{EA_2} Ca^{2+}(g)+O^{2-}(g) \xrightarrow{\text{lattice energy}} CaBr_2(s)$$

ΔH_f°

Solution: $\Delta H_f^\circ = \Delta H_{sub} + IE_1 + IE_2 + 1/2 \text{ bond energy} + EA_1 + EA_2 + \text{lattice energy}$

$$-634.9\frac{kJ}{mol} = +178\frac{kJ}{mol} + 590\frac{kJ}{mol} + 1145\frac{kJ}{mol} + \frac{1}{2}(498)\frac{kJ}{mol} + (-141)\frac{kJ}{mol} + 744\frac{kJ}{mol} + \text{lattice energy}$$

lattice energy = – 3400 kJ/mol

Simple Covalent Lewis Structures, Electronegativity, and Bond Polarity

9.49 (a) Hydrogen: Write the Lewis structure of each atom based on the number of valence electrons.

When the two hydrogen atoms share their electrons, they each get a duet, which is a stable configuration for hydrogen.

(b) The halogens: Write the Lewis structure of each atom based on the number of valence electrons.

If the two halogens pair together they can each achieve an octet, which is a stable configuration. So, the halogens are predicted to exist as diatomic molecules.

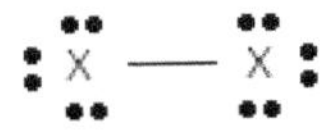

(c) Oxygen: Write the Lewis structure of each atom based on the number of valence electrons.

In order to achieve a stable octet on each oxygen, the oxygen atoms will need to share two electron pairs. So, oxygen is predicted to exist as a diatomic molecule with a double bond.

(d) Nitrogen: Write the Lewis structure of each atom based on the number of valence electrons.

In order to achieve a stable octet on each nitrogen, the nitrogen atoms will need to share three electron pairs. So, nitrogen is predicted to exist as a diatomic molecule with a triple bond.

9.50 Write the Lewis structure for N and H based on the number of valence electrons.

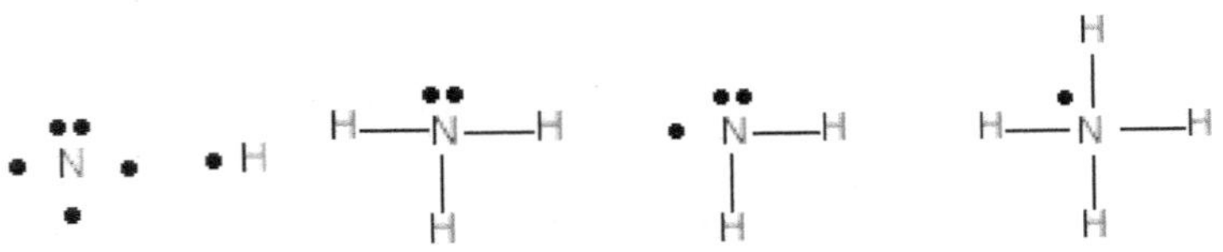

If nitrogen combines with three hydrogen atoms, the nitrogen will achieve a stable octet and each hydrogen will have a duet of electrons. This is a stable configuration. If the nitrogen were to combine with only two hydrogen atoms, the nitrogen could only achieve a seven electron configuration, which is not stable. Also, if the nitrogen were to combine with four hydrogen atoms, the nitrogen would have a nine electron configuration, which is not stable. So, Lewis theory predicts that nitrogen will combine with three hydrogen atoms.

9.51 (a) PH_3: Write the Lewis structure for each atom based on the number of valence electrons.

Phosphorus will share an electron pair with each hydrogen in order to achieve a stable octet.

$$H\!-\!\overset{\bullet\bullet}{\underset{\underset{H}{|}}{P}}\!-\!H$$

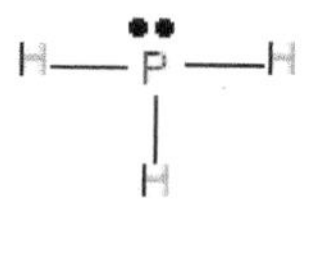

(b) SCl_2:   Write the Lewis structure for each atom based on the number of valence electrons.

$$:\!\overset{\bullet\bullet}{\underset{\bullet}{S}}\!\cdot \qquad :\!\overset{\bullet\bullet}{\underset{\bullet\bullet}{Cl}}\!\cdot$$

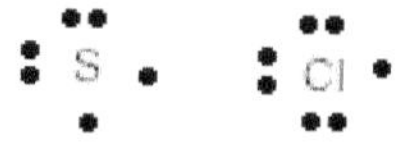

The sulfur will share an electron pair with each chlorine in order to achieve a stable octet.

$$:\!\overset{\bullet\bullet}{\underset{\underset{:\overset{}{\underset{\bullet\bullet}{Cl}}:}{|}}{S}}\!-\!\overset{\bullet\bullet}{\underset{\bullet\bullet}{Cl}}\!:$$

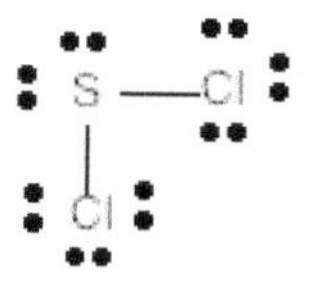

(c)   HI: Write the Lewis structure for each atom based on the number of valence electrons.

$$H\cdot \qquad \cdot\!\overset{\bullet\bullet}{\underset{\bullet\bullet}{I}}\!:$$

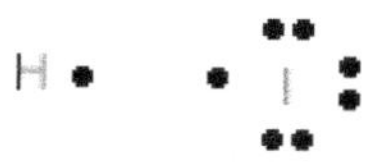

The iodine will share an electron pair with hydrogen in order to achieve a stable octet.

$$H\!-\!\overset{\bullet\bullet}{\underset{\bullet\bullet}{I}}\!:$$

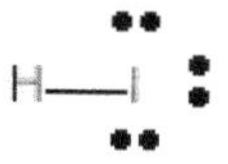

(d) CH_4:   Write the Lewis structure for each atom based on the number of valence electrons.

$$\cdot\!\overset{\bullet\bullet}{C}\!\cdot \qquad H\cdot$$

The carbon will share an electron pair with each hydrogen in order to achieve a stable octet.

$$H\!-\!\overset{\overset{\textstyle H}{|}}{\underset{\underset{\textstyle H}{|}}{C}}\!-\!H$$

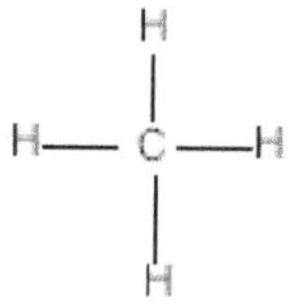

9.52   (a) NF_3:   Write the Lewis structure for each atom based on the number of valence electrons.

$$\cdot\!\overset{\bullet\bullet}{\underset{\bullet}{N}}\!\cdot \qquad \cdot\!\overset{\bullet\bullet}{\underset{\bullet\bullet}{F}}\!:$$

The nitrogen will share an electron pair with each fluorine in order to achieve a stable octet.

$$:\!\overset{\bullet\bullet}{\underset{\bullet\bullet}{F}}\!-\!\overset{\bullet\bullet}{\underset{\underset{:\overset{}{\underset{\bullet\bullet}{F}}:}{|}}{N}}\!-\!\overset{\bullet\bullet}{\underset{\bullet\bullet}{F}}\!:$$

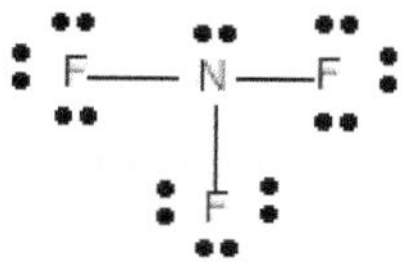

(b) HBr: Write the Lewis structure for each atom based on the number of valence electrons.

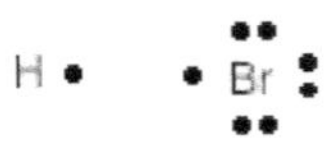

The bromine will share an electron pair with hydrogen in order to achieve a stable octet.

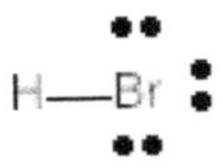

(c) SBr_2: Write the Lewis structure for each atom based on the number of valence electrons.

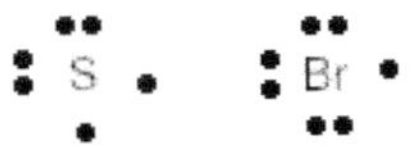

The sulfur will share an electron pair with each bromine in order to achieve a stable octet.

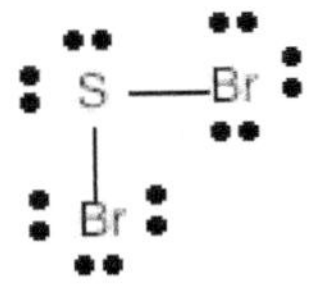

(d) CCl_4: Write the Lewis structure for each atom based on the number of valence electrons.

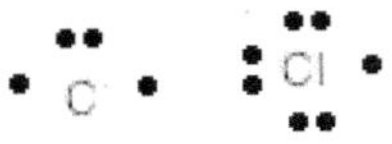

The carbon will share an electron pair with each chlorine in order to achieve a stable octet.

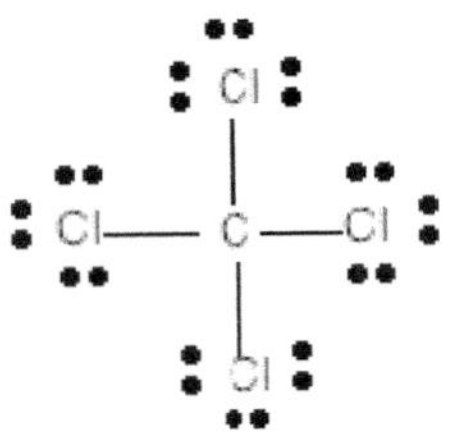

9.53 (a) SF_2: Write the Lewis structure for each atom based on the number of valence electrons.

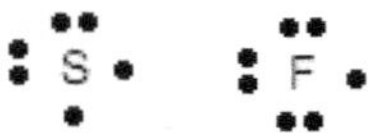

The sulfur will share an electron pair with each fluorine in order to achieve a stable octet.

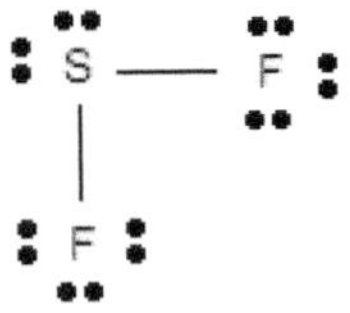

(b) SiH_4: Write the Lewis structure for each atom based on the number of valence electrons.

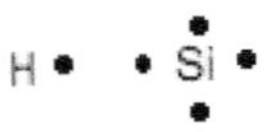

The silicon will share an electron pair with each hydrogen in order to achieve a stable octet.

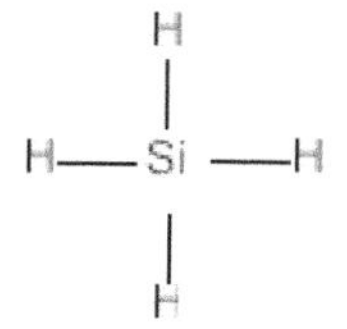

(c) HCOOH Write the Lewis structure for each atom based on the number of valence electrons.

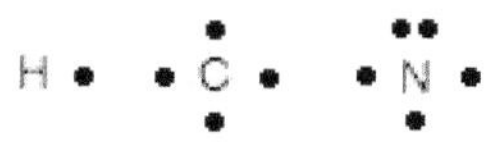

The carbon with share an electron pair with hydrogen, an electron pair with the interior oxygen and 2 electron pair with the terminal oxygen in order to achieve a stable octet. The terminal oxygen will share two electron pairs with carbon in order to achieve a stable octet. The interior oxygen with share an electron pair with carbon and an electron pair with hydrogen in order to achieve a stable octet.

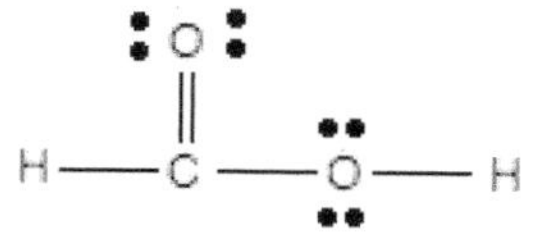

(d) CH_3SH Write the Lewis structure for each atom based on the number of valence electrons.

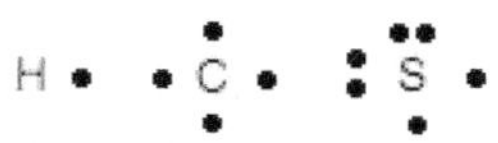

The carbon with share an electron pair with each hydrogen and an electron pair with sulfur in order to achieve a stable octet. The sulfur will share an electron pair with carbon and an electron pair with hydrogen in order to achieve a stable octet.

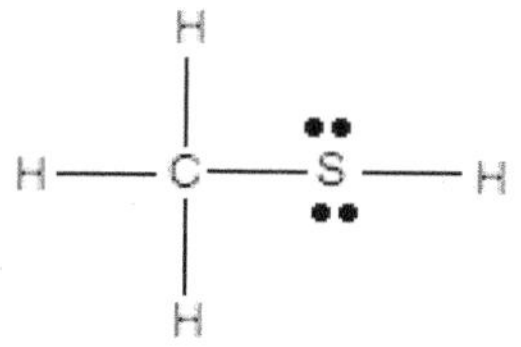

9.54 (a) CH_2O Write the Lewis structure for each atom based on the number of valence electrons.

The carbon will share an electron pair with each hydrogen and two electron pairs with oxygen in order to achieve a stable octet.

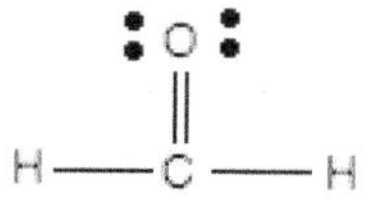

(b) C_2Cl_2 Write the Lewis structure for each atom based on the number of valence electrons.

Each carbon with share three electron pairs with the other carbon and an electron pair with chlorine in order to achieve a stable octet.

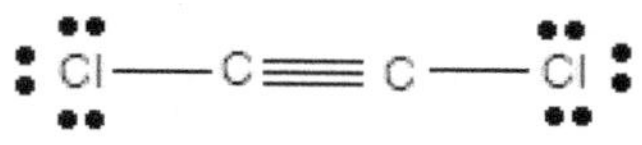

(c) CH_3NH_3 Write the Lewis structure for each atom based on the number of valence electrons.

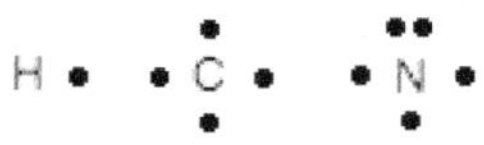

The carbon with share an electron pair with each hydrogen and an electron pair with nitrogen in order to achieve a stable octet. The nitrogen will share an electron pair with carbon and an electron pair with each hydrogen in order to achieve a stable octet.

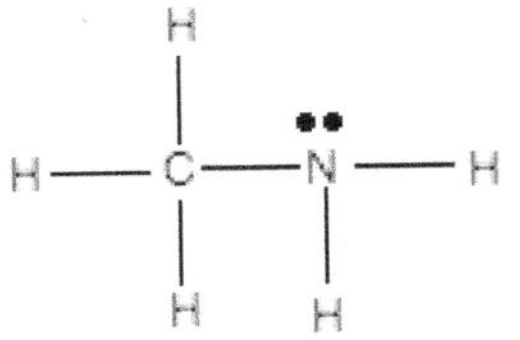

(d) $CFCl_3$ Write the Lewis structure for each atom based on the number of valence electrons.

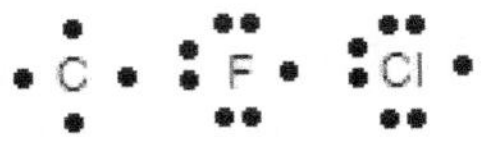

The carbon will share an electron pair with fluorine and with each chlorine in order to achieve a stable octet.

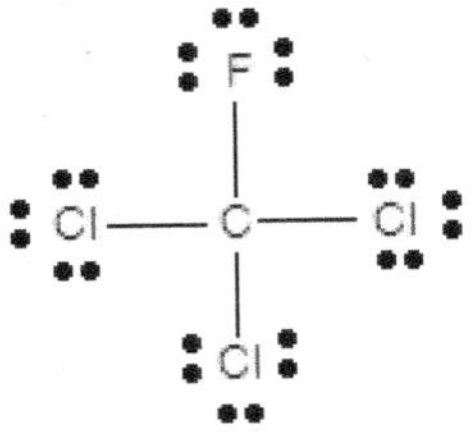

9.55 (a) Br and Br: pure covalent From Figure 9.8 we find the electronegativity of Br is 2.5. Since both atoms are the same, the electronegativity difference (ΔEN) = 0, and using Table 9.1 we classify this bond as pure covalent.

(b) C and Cl: polar covalent From Figure 9.8 we find the electronegativity of C is 2.5 and Cl is 3.0. The electronegativity difference (ΔEN) is $\Delta EN = 3.0 - 2.5 = 0.5$. Using Table 9.1 we classify this bond as polar covalent.

(c) C and S: pure covalent From Figure 9.8 we find the electronegativity of C is 2.5 and S is 2.5. The electronegativity difference (ΔEN) is $\Delta EN = 2.5 - 2.5 = 0$. Using Table 9.1 we classify this bond as pure covalent.

(d) Sr and O: ionic From Figure 9.8 we find the electronegativity of Sr is 1.0 and O is 3.5. The electronegativity difference (ΔEN) is $\Delta EN = 3.5 - 1.0 = 2.5$. Using Table 9.1 we classify this bond as ionic.

9.56 (a) C and N: polar covalent From Figure 9.8 we find the electronegativity of C is 2.5 and N is 3.0. The electronegativity difference (ΔEN) is $\Delta EN = 3.0 - 2.5 = 0.5$. Using Table 9.1 we classify this bond as polar covalent.

(b) N and S: polar covalent From Figure 9.8 we find the electronegativity of S is 2.5 and N is 3.0. The electronegativity difference (ΔEN) is $\Delta EN = 3.0 - 2.5 = 0.5$. Using Table 9.1 we classify this bond as polar covalent.

(c) K and F: ionic From Figure 9.8 we find the electronegativity of K is 0.8 and F is 4.0. The electronegativity difference (ΔEN) is $\Delta EN = 4.0 - 0.8 = 3.2$. Using Table 9.1 we classify this bond as ionic.

(d) N and N: pure covalent From Figure 9.8 we find the electronegativity of N is 3.0. Since both atoms are the same, the electronegativity difference (ΔEN) = 0, and using Table 9.1 we classify this bond as pure covalent.

9.57 CO: Write the Lewis structure for each atom based on the number of valence electrons.

The carbon will share three electron pairs with oxygen in order to achieve a stable octet.
The oxygen atom is more electronegative than the carbon atom, so the oxygen will have a partial negative charge and the carbon will have a partial positive charge.

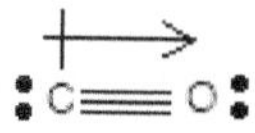

To estimate the percent ionic character, determine the difference in electronegativity between carbon and oxygen.
From Figure 9.8 we find the electronegativity of C is 2.5 and O is 3.5. The electronegativity difference (ΔEN) is $\Delta EN = 3.5 - 2.5 = 1.0$.
From Figure 9.10, we can estimate a percent ionic character of 25%.

9.58 BrF: Write the Lewis structure for each atom based on the number of valence electrons.

The bromine and fluorine will share an electron pair to achieve a stable octet.
The fluorine atom is more electronegative than the bromine atom, so the fluorine will have a partial negative charge and the bromine will have a partial positive charge.

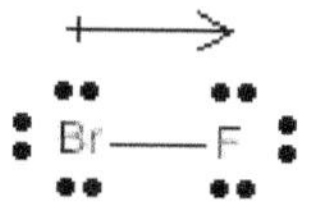

To estimate the percent ionic character, determine the difference in electronegativity between bromine and fluorine.
From Figure 9.8 we find the electronegativity of Br = 2.8 and F = 4.0. The electronegativity difference (ΔEN) is $\Delta EN = 4.0 - 2.8 = 1.2$.
From Figure 9.10, we can estimate a percent ionic character of 30%.

Covalent Lewis Structures, Resonance, and Formal Charge

9.59 (a) CI_4: Write the correct skeletal structure for the molecule.

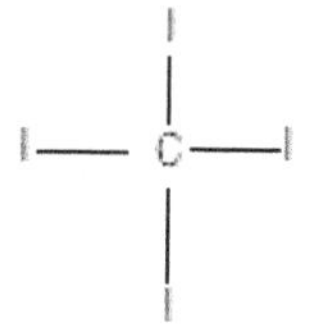

Calculate the total number of electrons for the Lewis structure by summing the number of valence electrons of each atom in the molecule.

(number of valence e^- for C) + 4(number of valence e^- for I) = 4 + 4(7) = 32

Distribute the electrons among the atoms, giving octets to as many atoms as possible. Begin with the bonding electrons, then proceed to lone pairs on terminal atoms and finally to lone pairs on the central atom.

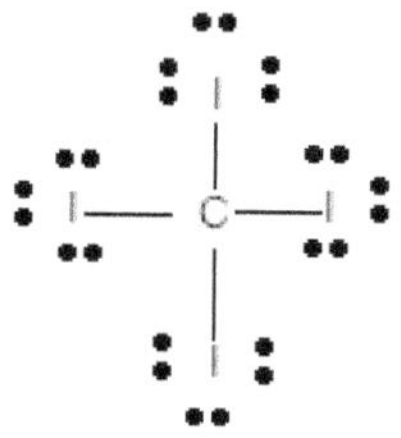

All 32 valence electrons are used.

If any atom lacks an octet, form double or triple bonds as necessary to give them octets.
All atoms have octets; the structure is complete.

(b) N_2O: Write the correct skeletal structure for the molecule.

N is the less electronegative, so it is central.

Calculate the total number of electrons for the Lewis structure by summing the number of valence electrons of each atom in the molecule.

2(number of valence e^- for N) + (number of valence e^- for O) = 2(5) + 6 = 16

Distribute the electrons among the atoms, giving octets to as many atoms as possible. Begin with the bonding electrons, then proceed to lone pairs on terminal atoms and finally to lone pairs on the central atom.

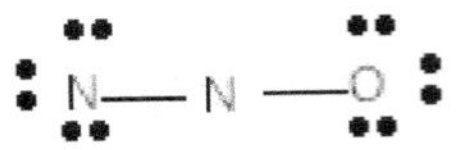

All 16 valence electrons are used.

If any atom lacks an octet, form double or triple bonds as necessary.

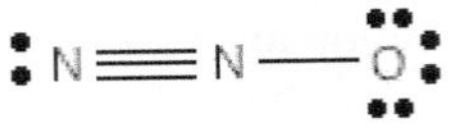

All atoms have octets; the structure is complete.

(c) SiH_4: Write the correct skeletal structure for the molecule.

H is always terminal, so Si is the central atom.

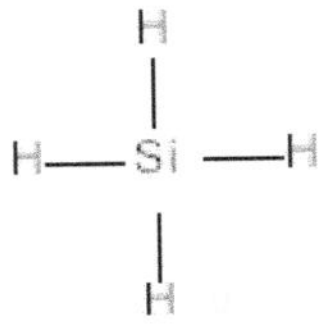

Calculate the total number of electrons for the Lewis structure by summing the number of valence electrons of each atom in the molecule.

(number of valence e^- for Si) + 4(number of valence e^- for H) = 4 + 4(1) = 8

Distribute the electrons among the atoms, giving octets (or duets for H) to as many atoms as possible. Begin with the bonding electrons, then proceed to lone pairs on terminal atoms and finally to lone pairs on the central atom.

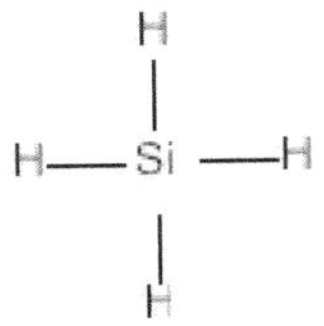

All 8 valence electrons are used.

If any atom lacks an octet, form double or triple bonds as necessary to give them octets.

All atoms have octets; the structure is complete.

(d) Cl_2CO: Write the correct skeletal structure for the molecule.

C is the least electronegative, so it is the central atom.

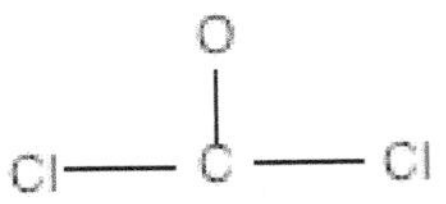

Calculate the total number of electrons for the Lewis structure by summing the number of valence electrons of each atom in the molecule.

(number of valence e^- for C) + 2(number of valence e^- for Cl) + (number of valence e^- for O) = 4 + 2(7) + 6 = 24

Distribute the electrons among the atoms, giving octets to as many atoms as possible. Begin with the bonding electrons, then proceed to lone pairs on terminal atoms and finally to lone pairs on the central atom.

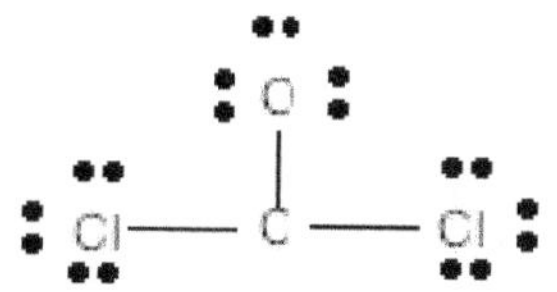

All 24 valence electrons are used.

If any atom lacks an octet, form double or triple bonds as necessary.

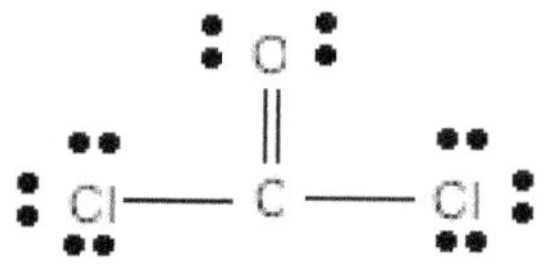

All atoms have octets; the structure is complete.

9.60 (a) H_3COH: Write the correct skeletal structure for the molecule.
C is less electronegative and H is terminal.

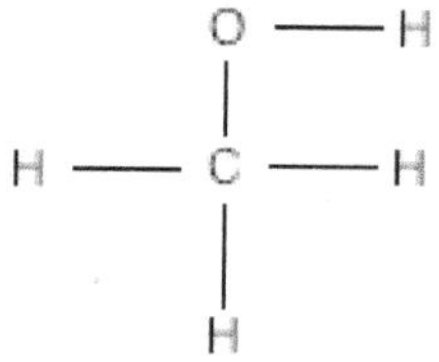

Calculate the total number of electrons for the Lewis structure by summing the number of valence electrons of each atom in the molecule.

(number of valence e^- for C) + 4(number of valence e^- for H) + (number of valence e^- for O) = 4 + 4(1) + 6 = 14

Distribute the electrons among the atoms, giving octets (or duets for H) to as many atoms as possible. Begin with the bonding electrons, then proceed to lone pairs on terminal atoms and finally to lone pairs on the central atoms.

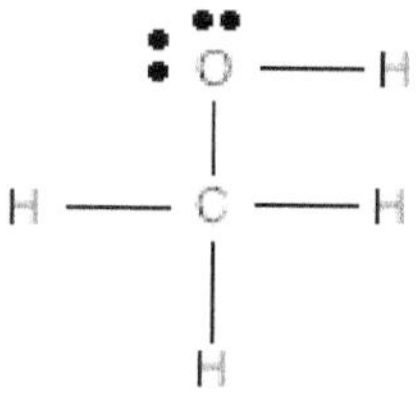

All 14 valence electrons are used.

If any atom lacks an octet, form double or triple bonds as necessary to give them octets.
All atoms have octets (duets for H); the structure is complete.

(b) OH^-: Write the correct skeletal structure for the ion.

Calculate the total number of electrons for the Lewis structure by summing the number of valence electrons of each atom in the ion and adding 1 for the 1 – charge.

(number of valence e^- for O) + (number of valence e^- for H) + 1 = 6 + 1 + 1 = 8

Distribute the electrons among the atoms, giving octets (or duets for H) to as many atoms as possible. Begin with the bonding electrons, then proceed to lone pairs on terminal atoms and finally to lone pairs on the central atom.

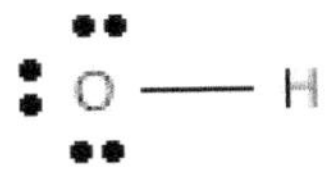

All 8 valence electrons are used.

If any atom lacks an octet, form double or triple bonds as necessary to give them octets. Lastly, write the Lewis structure in brackets with the charge of the ion in the upper right-hand corner.

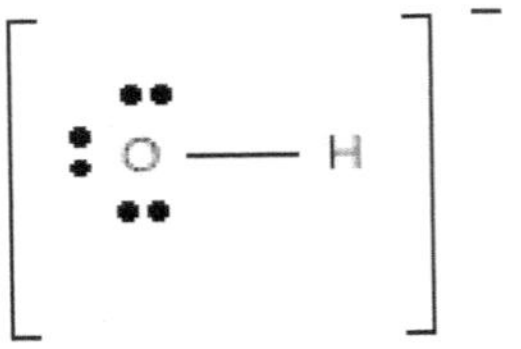

(c) BrO^-: Write the correct skeletal structure for the ion.

Calculate the total number of electrons for the Lewis structure by summing the number of valence electrons of each atom in the ion and adding 1 for the 1 – charge.

(number of valence e^- for O) + (number of valence e^- for Br) + 1 = 6 + 7 + 1 = 14

Distribute the electrons among the atoms, giving octets to as many atoms as possible. Begin with the bonding electrons, then proceed to lone pairs on terminal atoms and finally to lone pairs of the central atom.

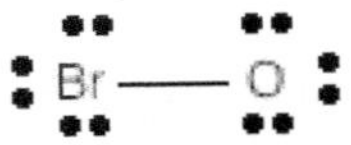

All 14 valence electrons are used.

If any atom lack an octet, form double or triple bonds as necessary to give them octets. Lastly, write the Lewis structure in brackets with the charge of the ion in the upper right-hand corner.

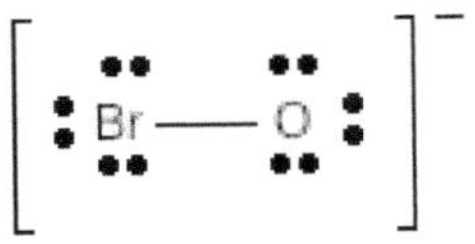

(d) O_2^{2-}: Write the correct skeletal structure for the ion.

Calculate the total number of electrons for the Lewis structure by summing the number of valence electrons of each atom in the ion and adding 2 for the 2 – charge.

2(number of valence e^- for O) + 2 = 2(6)6 + 2 = 14

Distribute the electrons among the atoms, giving octets to as many atoms as possible. Begin with the bonding electrons, then proceed to lone pairs on terminal atoms and finally to lone pairs on the central atom.

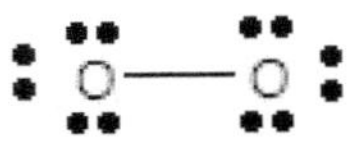

All 14 valence electrons are used.

If any atom lack an octet, form double or triple bonds as necessary to give them octets. Lastly, write the Lewis structure in brackets with the charge of the ion in the upper right-hand corner.

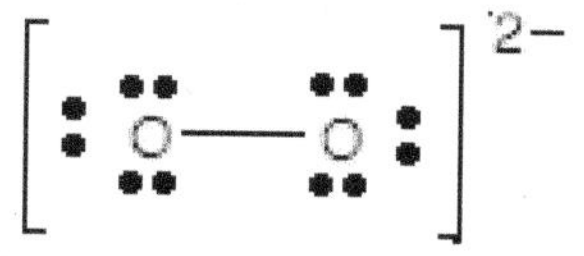

9.61 (a) N_2H_2: Write the correct skeletal structure for the molecule.

Calculate the total number of electrons for the Lewis structure by summing the number of valence electrons of each atom in the molecule.

2(number of valence e^- for N) + 2(number of valence e^- for H) = 2(5) + 2(1) = 12

Distribute the electrons among the atoms, giving octets (or duets for H) to as many atoms as possible. Begin with the bonding electrons, then proceed to lone pairs on terminal atoms and finally to lone pairs on the central atom.

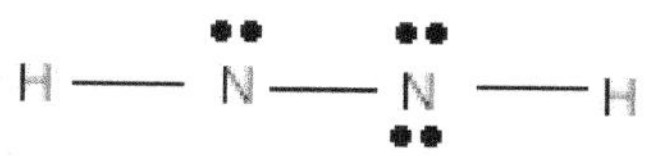

All 12 valence electrons are used.

If any atom lacks an octet, form double or triple bonds as necessary.

All atoms have octets (duets for H); the structure is complete.

(b) N_2H_4: Write the correct skeletal structure for the molecule.

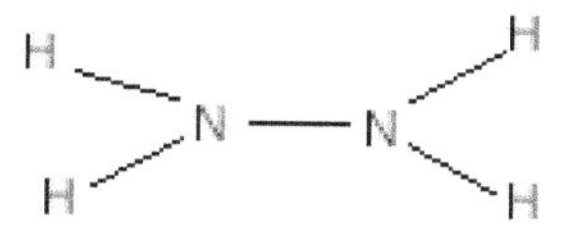

Calculate the total number of electrons for the Lewis structure by summing the valence electrons of each atom in the molecule.

2(number of valence e^- for N) + 4(number of valence e^- for H) = 2(5) + 4(1) = 14

Distribute the electrons among the atoms, giving octets (or duets for H) to as many atoms as possible. Begin with the bonding electrons, then proceed to lone pairs on terminal atoms and finally to lone pairs on the central atom.

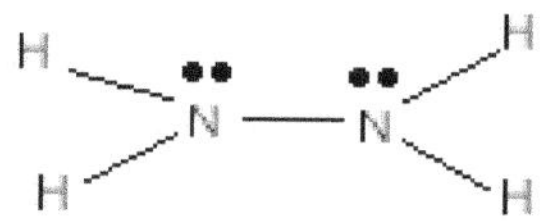

All 14 valence electrons are used.

If any atom lacks an octet, form double or triple bonds as necessary to give them octets. All atoms have octets (duets for H) structure is complete.

(c) C_2H_2: Write the correct skeletal structure for the molecule.

Calculate the total number of electrons for the Lewis structure by summing the number of valence electrons of each atom in the molecule.

2(number of valence e^- for C) + 2(number of valence e^- for H) = 2(4) + 2(1) = 10

Distribute the electrons among the atoms, giving octets (or duets for H) to as many atoms as possible. Begin with the bonding electrons, then proceed to lone pairs on terminal atoms and finally to lone pairs on the central atom.

$$ H \text{---} C \text{---} \overset{\bullet\bullet}{\underset{\bullet\bullet}{C}} \text{---} H $$

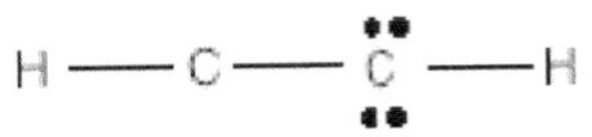

All 10 valence electrons are used.
If any atom lacks an octet, form double or triple bonds as necessary.

$$ H \text{---} C \equiv C \text{---} H $$

All atoms have octets (duets for H); the structure is complete.

(d) C_2H_4:   Write the correct skeletal structure for the molecule.

$$ \begin{array}{ccc} H & & H \\ \diagdown & & \diagup \\ & C \text{---} C & \\ \diagup & & \diagdown \\ H & & H \end{array} $$

Calculate the total number of electrons for the Lewis structure by summing the number of valence electrons of each atom in the molecule.

2(number of valence e⁻ for C) + 4(number of valence e⁻ for H) = 2(4) + 4(1) = 12

Distribute the electrons among the atoms, giving octets (or duets for H) to as many atoms as possible. Begin with the bonding electrons, then proceed to lone pairs on terminal atoms and finally to lone pairs on the central atom.

$$ \begin{array}{ccc} H & & H \\ \diagdown & & \diagup \\ & \overset{\bullet\bullet}{C} \text{---} C & \\ \diagup & & \diagdown \\ H & & H \end{array} $$

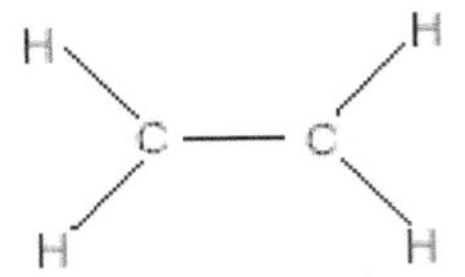

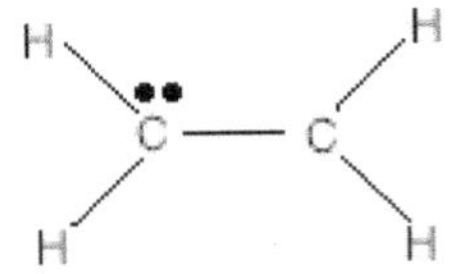

All 12 valence electrons are used.
If any atom lacks an octet, form double or triple bonds as necessary.

$$ \begin{array}{ccc} H & & H \\ \diagdown & & \diagup \\ & C = C & \\ \diagup & & \diagdown \\ H & & H \end{array} $$

All atoms have octets (duets for H) structure is complete.

9.62   (a) H_3COCH_3:   Write the correct skeletal structure for the molecule.

$$ \begin{array}{ccccc} & H & & H & \\ & | & & | & \\ H \text{---} & C & \text{---} O \text{---} & C & \text{---} H \\ & | & & | & \\ & H & & H & \end{array} $$

Calculate the total number of electrons for the Lewis structure by summing the number of valence electrons of each atom in the molecule.

2(number of valence e⁻ for C) + (number of valence e⁻ for O) + 6(number of valence e⁻ for H) = 2(4) + 6 + 6(1) = 20

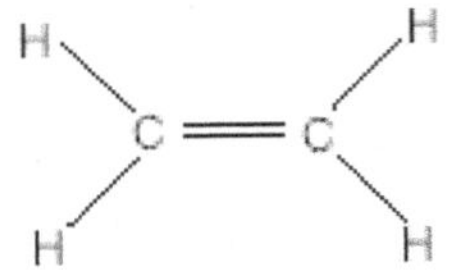

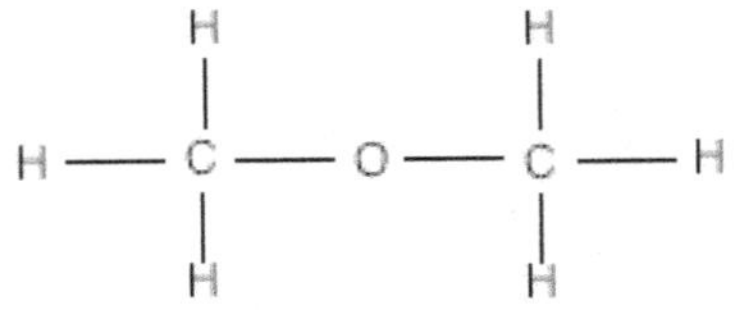

Distribute the electrons among the atoms, giving octets (or duets for H) to as many atoms as possible. Begin with the bonding electrons, then proceed to lone pairs on terminal atoms and finally to lone pairs on the central atom.

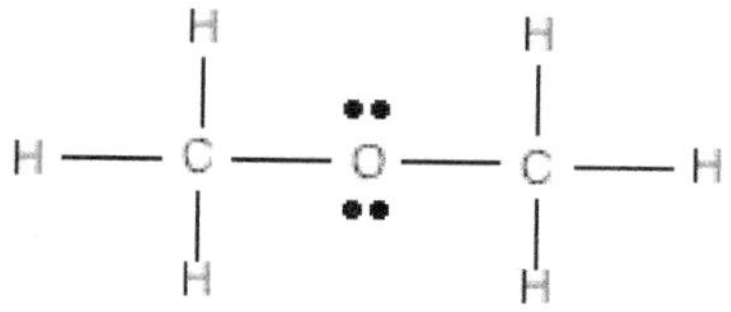

All 20 valence electrons are used.

If any atom lacks an octet, form double or triple bonds as necessary to give them octets. All atoms have octets (duets for H); the structure is complete.

(b) CN^-: Write the correct skeletal structure for the ion.

Calculate the total number of electrons for the Lewis structure by summing the number of valence electrons of each atom in the ion and adding 1 for the 1 – charge.

(number of valence e^- for C) + (number of valence e^- for N) + 1 = 4 + 5 + 1 = 10

Distribute the electrons among the atoms, giving octets to as many atoms as possible. Begin with the bonding electrons, then proceed to lone pairs on terminal atoms and finally to lone pairs on the central atom.

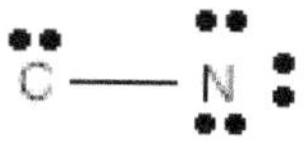

All 10 valence electrons are used.

If any atom lacks an octet, form double or triple bonds as necessary.

Lastly, write the Lewis structure in brackets with the charge of the ion in the upper right-hand corner.

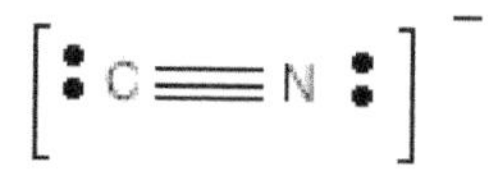

(c) NO_2^-: Write the correct skeletal structure for the ion.

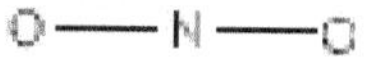

Calculate the total number of electrons for the Lewis structure by summing the number of valence electrons of each atom in the ion and adding 1 for the 1 – charge.

2(number of valence e^- for O) + (number of valence e^- for N) + 1 = 2(6) + 5 + 1 = 18

Distribute the electrons among the atoms, giving octets to as many atoms as possible. Begin with the bonding electrons, then proceed to lone pairs on terminal atoms and finally to lone pairs on the central atom.

All 18 valence electrons are used.

If any atom lacks an octet, form double or triple bonds as necessary.

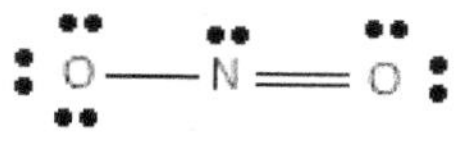

Lastly, write the Lewis structure in brackets with the charge of the ion in the upper right-hand corner.

$$\left[:\ddot{O}—\ddot{N}=\ddot{O}: \right]^{-}$$

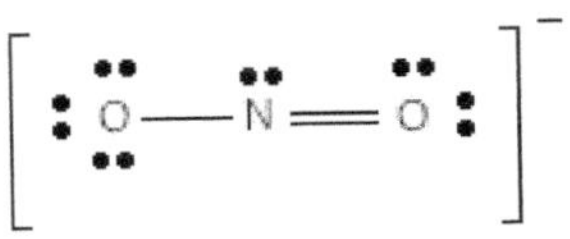

(d)   ClO⁻:   Write the correct skeletal structure for the ion.

Cl — O

Calculate the total number of electrons for the Lewis structure by summing the number of valence electrons of each atom in the ion and adding 1 for the 1 – charge.

(number of valence e⁻ for O) + (number of valence e⁻ for Cl) + 1 = 6 + 7 + 1 = 14

Distribute the electrons among the atoms, giving octets to as many atoms as possible. Begin with the bonding electrons, then proceed to lone pairs on terminal atoms and finally to lone pairs on the central atom.

:Cl̈—Ö:

All 14 valence electrons are used.

If any atom lacks an octet, form double or triple bonds as necessary to give them octets. Lastly, write the Lewis structure in brackets with the charge of the ion in the upper right-hand corner.

$$\left[:\ddot{Cl}—\ddot{O}: \right]^{-}$$

9.63   (a)   SeO₂: Write the correct skeletal structure for the molecule.
Se is the less electronegative, so it is central.

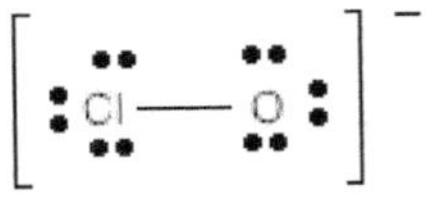

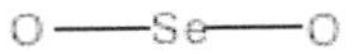

O — Se — O

Calculate the total number of electrons for the Lewis structure by summing the number of valence electrons of each atom in the molecule.

(number of valence e⁻ for Se) + 2(number of valence e⁻ for O) = 6 + 2(6) = 18

Distribute the electrons among the atoms, giving octets to as many atoms as possible. Begin with the bonding electrons, then proceed to lone pairs on terminal atoms and finally to lone pairs on the central atom.

:Ö—Së—Ö:

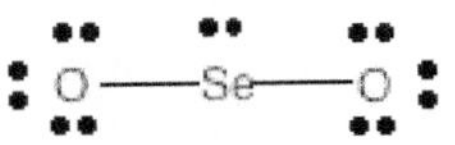

All 18 valence electrons are used.

If any atom lacks an octet, form double or triple bonds as necessary.

:Ö—Së=Ö:

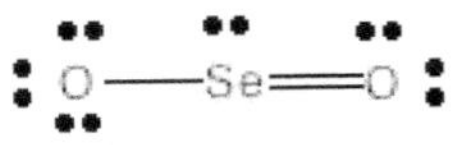

All atoms have octets; the structure is complete. However, the double bond can form from either oxygen atom, so there are two resonance forms.

:Ö—Së=Ö: ⟷ :Ö=Së—Ö:

Calculate the formal charge on each atom by finding the number of valence electrons and subtracting the number of lone pair electrons and one-half the number of bonding electrons.

number of valence electrons	6	6	6	6	6	6
- number of lone pair electrons	6	2	4	4	2	6
- 1/2(number of bonding electrons)	1	3	2	2	3	1
Formal charge	–1	+1	0	0	+1	–1

(b) CO_3^{2-}: Write the correct skeletal structure for the ion.

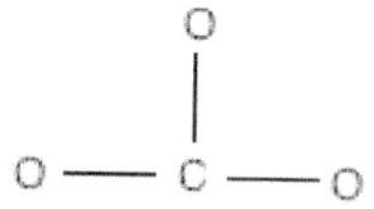

Calculate the total number of electrons for the Lewis structure by summing the number of valence electrons of each atom in the ion and adding 2 for the 2 – charge.

3(number of valence e^- for O) + (number of valence e^- for C) + 2 = 3(6) + 4 + 2 = 24

Distribute the electrons among the atoms, giving octets to as many atoms as possible. Begin with the bonding electrons, then proceed to lone pairs on terminal atoms and finally to lone pairs on the central atom.

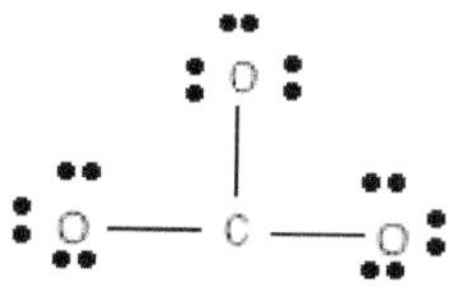

All 24 valence electrons are used.

If any atom lack an octet, form double or triple bonds as necessary.

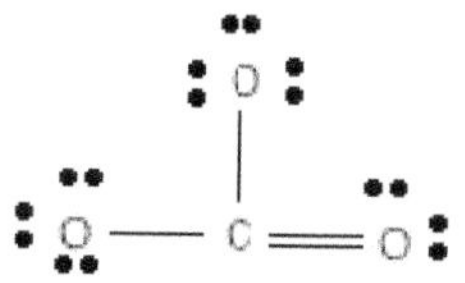

Lastly, write the Lewis structure in brackets with the charge of the ion in the upper right-hand corner.

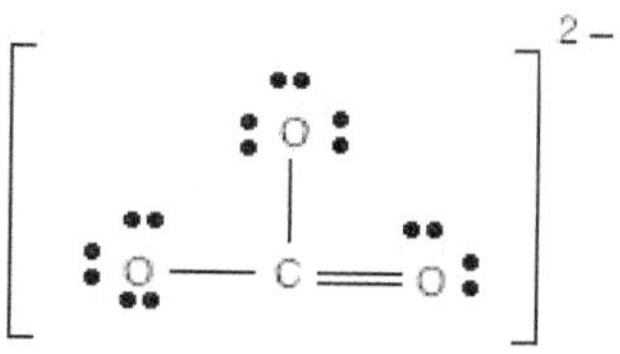

All atoms have octets; the structure is complete. However, the double bond can form from any oxygen atom, so there are three resonance forms.

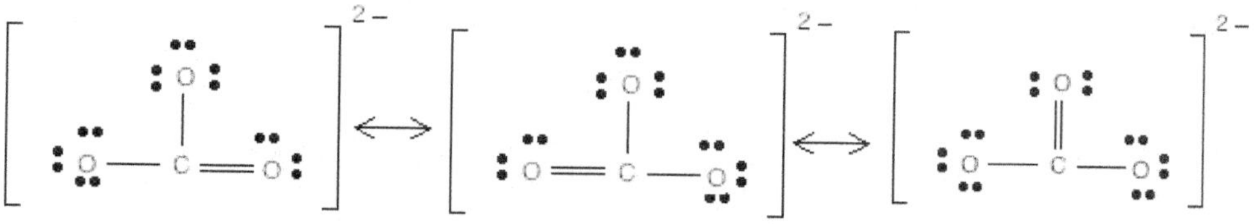

Calculate the formal charge on each atom by finding the number of valence electrons and subtracting the number of lone pair electrons and one-half the number of bonding electrons.

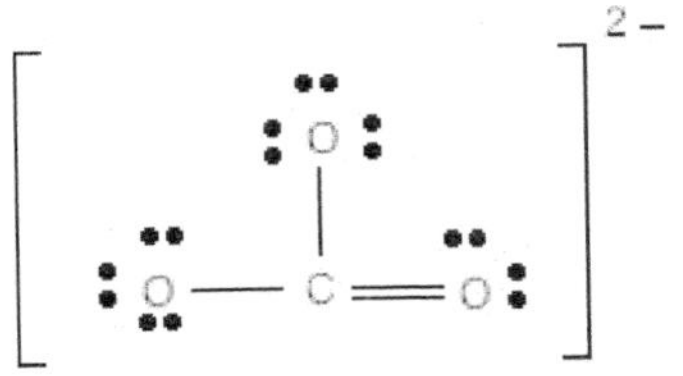

	O_{left}	O_{top}	O_{right}	C
number of valence electrons	6	6	6	4
- number of lone pair electrons	6	6	4	0
- 1/2(number of bonding electrons)	1	1	2	4
Formal charge	–1	–1	0	0

The sum of the formal charges is – 2, which is the overall charge of the ion. The other resonance forms would have the same values for the single and double bonded oxygen atoms.

(c) ClO^-: Write the correct skeletal structure for the ion.

Calculate the total number of electrons for the Lewis structure by summing the number of valence electrons of each atom in the ion and adding 1 for the 1 – charge.

(number of valence e^- for O) + (number of valence e^- for Cl) + 1 = 6 + 7 + 1 = 14

Distribute the electrons among the atoms, giving octets to as many atoms as possible. Begin with the bonding electrons, then proceed to lone pairs on terminal atoms and finally to lone pairs on the central atom.

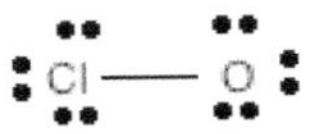

All 14 valence electrons are used.

If any atom lacks an octet, form double or triple bonds as necessary to give them octets. Lastly, write the Lewis structure in brackets with the charge of the ion in the upper right-hand corner.

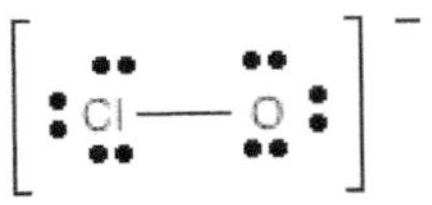

All atoms have octets; the structure is complete.

Calculate the formal charge on each atom by finding the number of valence electrons and subtracting the number of lone pair electrons and one-half the number of bonding electrons.

	Cl	O
number of valence electrons	7	6
- number of lone pair electrons	6	6
- 1/2(number of bonding electrons)	1	1
Formal charge	0	–1

The sum of the formal charges is – 1, which is the overall charge of the ion.

(d) NO_2^-: Write the correct skeletal structure for the ion.

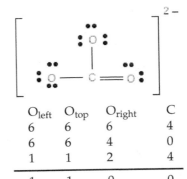

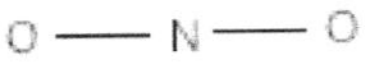

Calculate the total number of electrons for the Lewis structure by summing the number of valence electrons of each atom in the ion and adding 1 for the 1 – charge.

2(number of valence e^- for O) + (number of valence e^- for N) + 1 = 2(6) + 5 + 1 = 18

Distribute the electrons among the atoms, giving octets to as many atoms as possible. Begin with the bonding electrons, then proceed to lone pairs on terminal atoms and finally to lone pairs on the central atom.

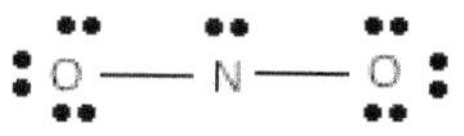

All 14 valence electrons are used.

If any atom lacks an octet, form double or triple bonds as necessary.

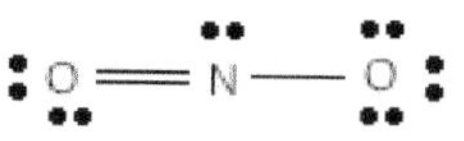

Lastly, write the Lewis structure in brackets with the charge of the ion in the upper right-hand corner.

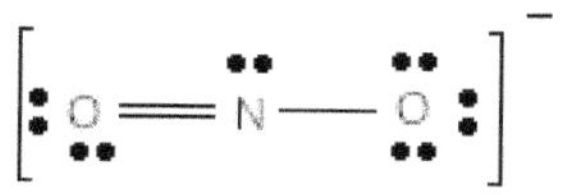

All atoms have octets; the structure is complete. However, the double bond can form from either oxygen atom, so there are two resonance forms.

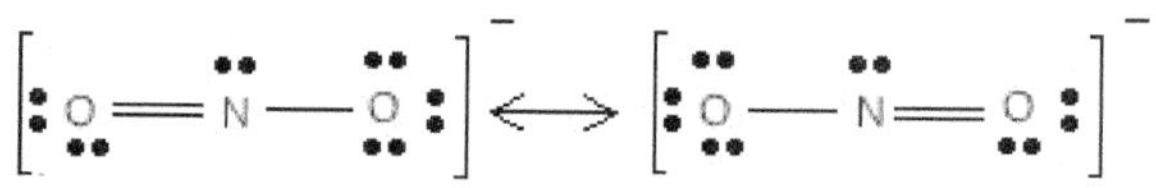

Calculate the formal charge on each atom by finding the number of valence electrons and subtracting the number of lone pair electrons and one-half the number of bonding electrons. Using the left side structure:

	O	N	O
number of valence electrons	6	5	6
- number of lone pair electrons	4	2	6
- 1/2(number of bonding electrons)	2	3	1
Formal charge	0	0	–1

The sum of the formal charges is – 1, which is the overall charge of the ion.

9.64 (a) ClO_3^-: Write the correct skeletal structure for the ion.

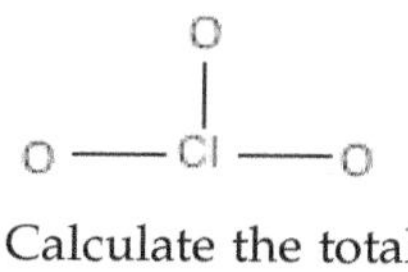

Calculate the total number of electrons for the Lewis structure by summing the number of valence electrons of each atom in the ion and adding 1 for the 1 – charge.

3(number of valence e^- for O) + (number of valence e^- for Cl) + 1 = 3(6) + 7 + 1 = 26

Distribute the electrons among the atoms, giving octets to as many atoms as possible. Begin with the bonding electrons, then proceed to lone pairs on terminal atoms and finally to lone pairs on the central atom.

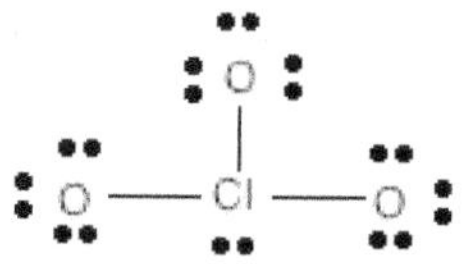

All 26 valence electrons are used.

If any atom lacks an octet, form double or triple bonds as necessary to give them octets. Lastly, write the Lewis structure in brackets with the charge of the ion in the upper right-hand corner.

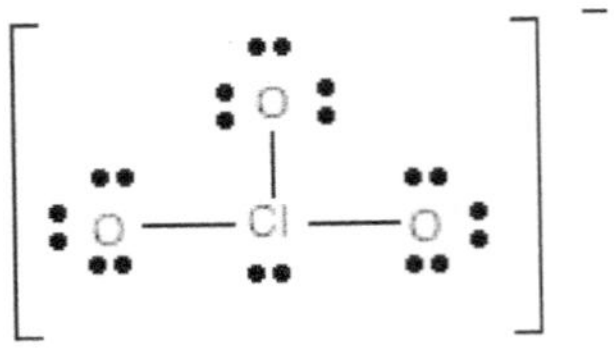

All atoms have octets; the structure is complete.
Calculate the formal charge on each atom by finding the number of valence electrons and subtracting the number of lone pair electrons and one-half the number of bonding electrons.

	O_{left}	O_{top}	O_{right}	Cl
number of valence electrons	6	6	6	7
- number of lone pair electrons	6	6	6	2
- 1/2(number of bonding electrons)	1	1	1	3
Formal charge	–1	–1	–1	+2

The sum of the formal charges is – 1, which is the overall charge of the ion.

(b) ClO_4^-: Write the correct skeletal structure for the ion.

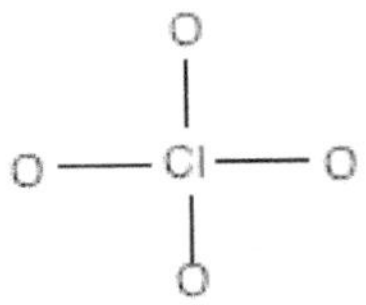

Calculate the total number of electrons for the Lewis structure by summing the number of valence electrons of each atom in the ion and adding 1 for the 1 – charge.

4(number of valence e^- for O) + (number of valence e^- for Cl) + 1 = 4(6) + 7 + 1 = 32

Distribute the electrons among the atoms, giving octets to as many atoms as possible. Begin with the bonding electrons, then proceed to lone pairs on terminal atoms and finally to lone pairs on the central atom.

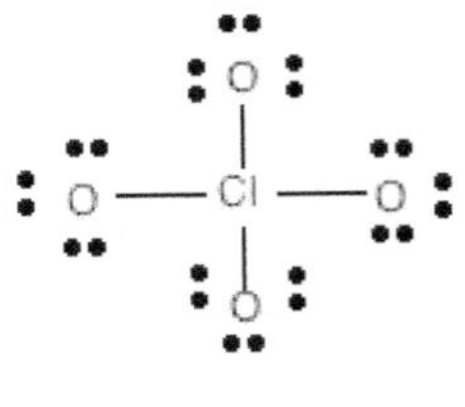

All 26 valence electrons are used.
If any atom lacks an octet, form double or triple bonds as necessary to give them octets. Lastly, write the Lewis structure in brackets with the charge of the ion in the upper right-hand corner.

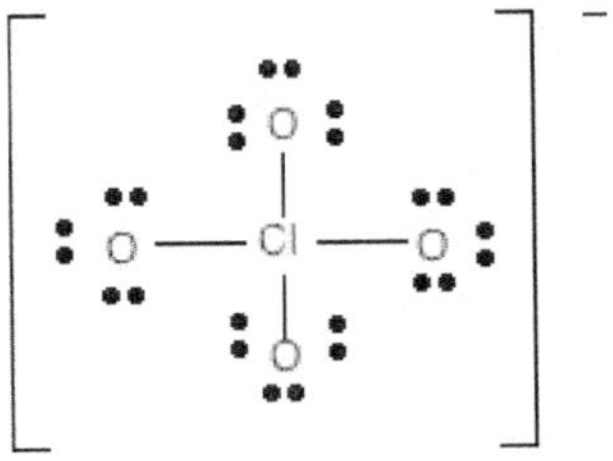

All atoms have octets; the structure is complete.
Calculate the formal charge on each atom by finding the number of valence electrons and subtracting the number of lone pair electrons and one-half the number of bonding electrons.

Using the left side structure:

	O_{left}	O_{top}	O_{right}	O_{bottom}	Cl
number of valence electrons	6	6	6	6	7
- number of lone pair electrons	6	6	6	6	0
- 1/2(number of bonding electrons)	1	1	1	1	4
Formal charge	−1	−1	−1	−1	+3

The sum of the formal charges is – 1, which is the overall charge of the ion.

(c) NO_3^-: Write the correct skeletal structure for the ion.

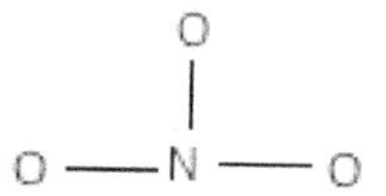

Calculate the total number of electrons for the Lewis structure by summing the number of valence electrons of each atom in the ion and adding 1 for the 1 – charge.

3(number of valence e^- for O) + (number of valence e^- for N) + 1 = 3(6) + 5 + 1 = 24

Distribute the electrons among the atoms, giving octets to as many atoms as possible. Begin with the bonding electrons, then proceed to lone pairs on terminal atoms and finally to lone pairs on the central atom.

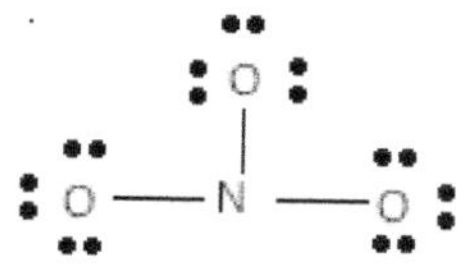

All 24 valence electrons are used.

If any atom lacks an octet, form double or triple bonds as necessary.

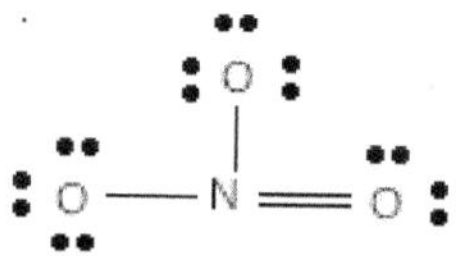

Lastly, write the Lewis structure in brackets with the charge of the ion in the upper right-hand corner.

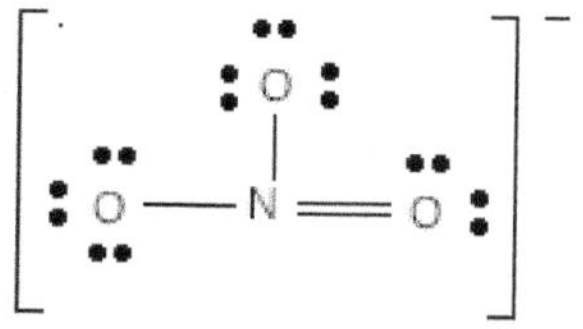

All atoms have octets; the structure is complete. However, the double bond can form from any oxygen atom, so there are three resonance forms.

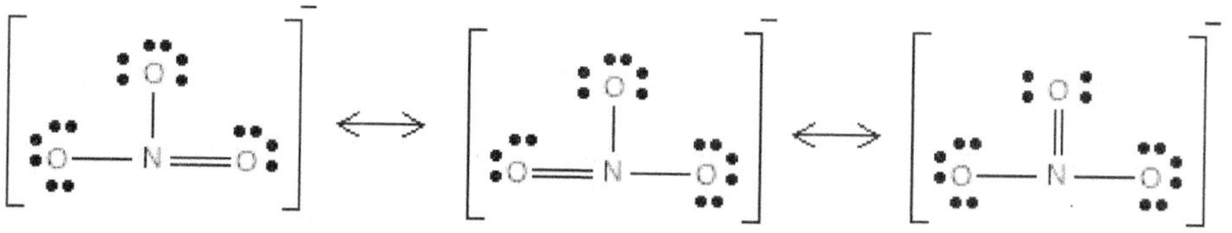

Calculate the formal charge on each atom by finding the number of valence electrons and subtracting the number of lone pair electrons and one-half the number of bonding electrons. Using the left hand structure:

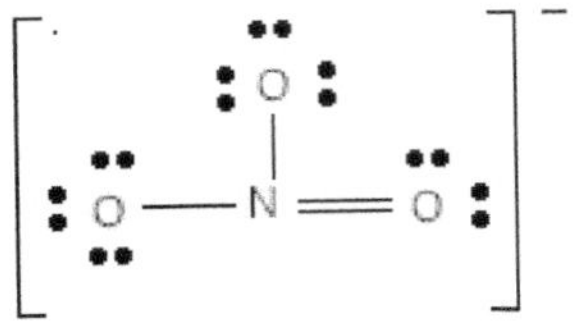

	O_{left}	O_{top}	O_{right}	N
number of valence electrons	6	6	6	5
- number of lone pair electrons	6	6	4	0
- 1/2(number of bonding electrons)	1	1	2	4
Formal charge	–1	–1	0	+1

The sum of the formal charges is – 1, which is the overall charge of the ion. The other resonance forms would have the same values for the single and double bonded oxygen atoms.

(d) NH_4^+: Write the correct skeletal structure for the ion.

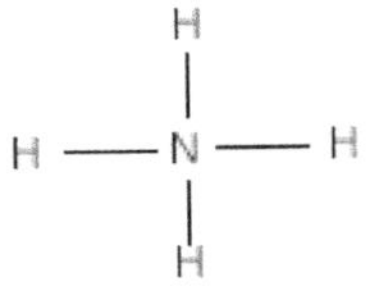

Calculate the total number of electrons for the Lewis structure by summing the valence electrons of each atom in the ion and subtracting 1 for the 1+ charge.

4(number of valence e^- for H) + (number of valence e^- for N) – 1 = 4(1) + 5 – 1 = 8

Distribute the electrons among the atoms, giving octets (or duets for H) to as many atoms as possible. Begin with the bonding electrons, then proceed to lone pairs on terminal atoms and finally to lone pairs on the central atom.

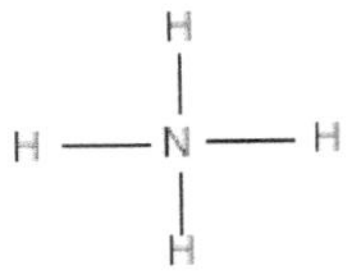

All 8 valence electrons are used.

If any atom lacks an octet, form double or triple bonds as necessary to give them octets. Lastly, write the Lewis structure in brackets with the charge of the ion in the upper right-hand corner.

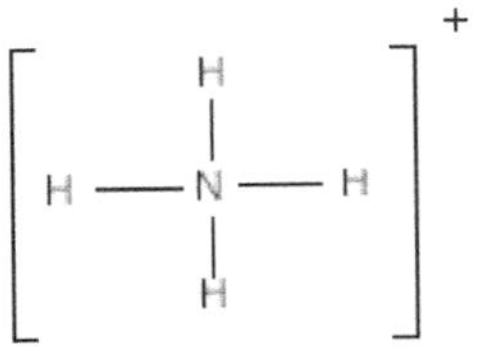

All atoms have octets (duets for H); the structure is complete.

Calculate the formal charge on each atom by finding the number of valence electrons and subtracting the number of lone pair electrons and one-half the number of bonding electrons.

	H_{left}	H_{top}	H_{right}	H_{bottom}	N
number of valence electrons	1	1	1	1	5
- number of lone pair electrons	0	0	0	0	0
- 1/2(number of bonding electrons)	1	1	1	1	4
Formal charge	0	0	0	0	+1

The sum of the formal charges is + 1, which is the overall charge of the ion.

9.65

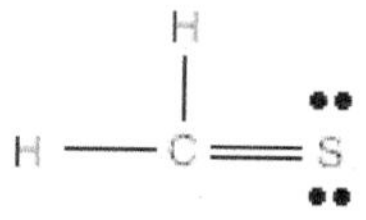

I

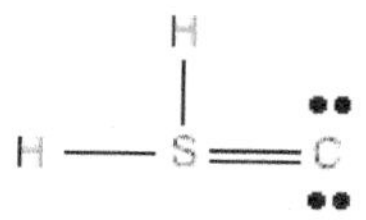

II

Calculate the formal charge on each atom in structure I by finding the number of valence electrons and subtracting the number of lone pair electrons and one-half the number of bonding electrons.

	H_{left}	H_{top}	C	S
number of valence electrons	1	1	4	6
- number of lone pair electrons	0	0	0	4
- 1/2(number of bonding electrons)	1	1	4	2
Formal charge	0	0	0	0

The sum of the formal charges is 0, which is the overall charge of the molecule.

Calculate the formal charge on each atom in structure II by finding the number of valence electrons and subtracting the number of lone pair electrons and one-half the number of bonding electrons.

	H_{left}	H_{top}	S	C
number of valence electrons	1	1	6	4
- number of lone pair electrons	0	0	0	4
- 1/2(number of bonding electrons)	1	1	4	2
Formal charge	0	0	+2	–2

The sum of the formal charges is 0, which is the overall charge of the molecule.

Structure I is the better Lewis structure because it has the least amount of formal charge on each atom.

9.66

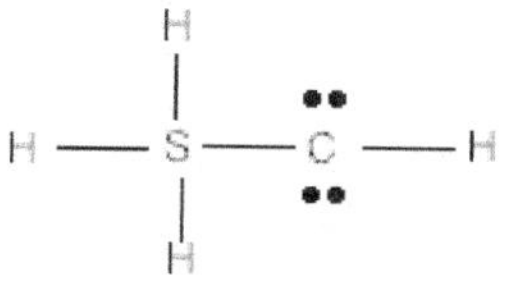

I

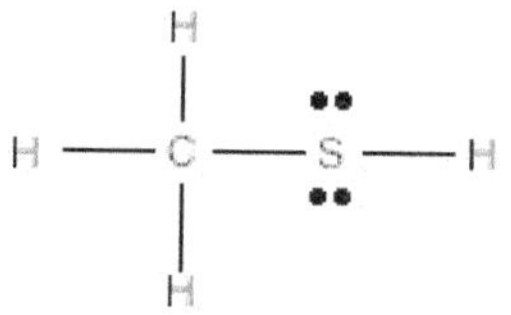

II

Calculate the formal charge on each atom in structure I by finding the number of valence electrons and subtracting the number of lone pair electrons and one-half the number of bonding electrons.

	H_{left}	H_{top}	H_{right}	H_{bottom}	S	C
number of valence electrons	1	1	1	1	6	4
- number of lone pair electrons	0	0	0	0	0	4
- 1/2(number of bonding electrons)	1	1	1	1	4	2
Formal charge	0	0	0	0	+2	–2

The sum of the formal charges is 0, which is the overall charge of the molecule.

Calculate the formal charge on each atom in structure II by finding the number of valence electrons and subtracting the number of lone pair electrons and one-half the number of bonding electrons.

	H_{left}	H_{top}	H_{right}	H_{bottom}	C	S
number of valence electrons	1	1	1	1	4	6
- number of lone pair electrons	0	0	0	0	0	4
- 1/2(number of bonding electrons)	1	1	1	1	4	2
Formal charge	0	0	0	0	0	0

The sum of the formal charges is 0, which is the overall charge of the molecule.

Structure II is the better Lewis structure because it has the least amount of formal charge on each atom.

9.67 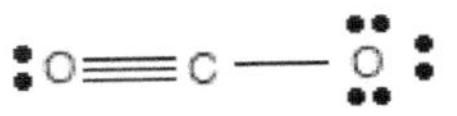 does not provide a significant contribution to the resonance hybrid as it has a +1 formal charge on a very electronegative oxygen.

	O_{left}	O_{right}	C
number of valence electrons	6	6	4
- number of lone pair electrons	2	6	0
- 1/2(number of bonding electrons)	3	1	4
Formal charge	+1	−1	0

9.68 Compare the two forms of each molecule with O as a central atom and a terminal atom. Determine the formal charge on the central atom for all the structures.

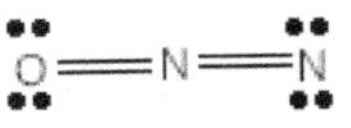
I

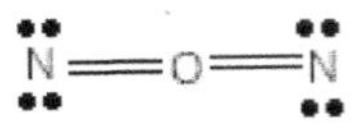
II

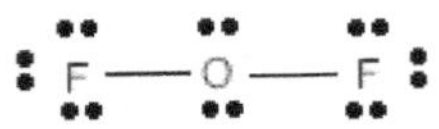
III

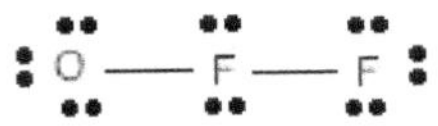
IV

	I	II	III	IV
	N	O	O	F
number of valence electrons	5	6	6	7
- number of lone pair electrons	0	0	4	4
- 1/2(number of bonding electrons)	4	4	4	2
Formal charge	+1	+2	0	+1

From the formal charge on the central atom that O has to be terminal for the N_2O molecule. When O is the central atom it has a +2 formal charge and it is the more electronegative atom. So, this would not be a good structure. For the OF_2 molecule, O has to be the central atom. When O is central it has a formal charge of 0; when the F is central it has a formal charge of +1. This puts a positive formal charge on the most electronegative atom, which is not acceptable.

Odd – Electron Species, Incomplete Octets, and Expanded Octets

9.69 (a) BCl_3: Write the correct skeletal structure for the molecule.
B is the less electronegative, so it is central.

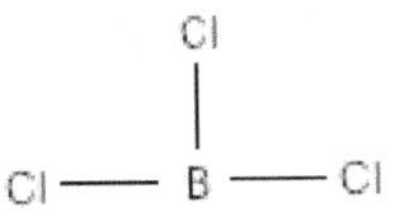

Calculate the total number of electrons for the Lewis structure by summing the number of valence electrons of each atom in the molecule.

(number of valence e^- for B) + 3(number of valence e^- for Cl) = 3 +3(7) = 24

Distribute the electrons among the atoms, giving octets to as many atoms as possible. Begin with the bonding electrons, and then proceed to lone pairs on terminal atoms finally to lone pairs on the central atom.

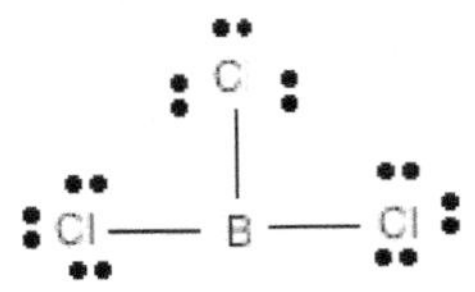

All 24 valence electrons are used.

B has an incomplete octet. If we complete the octet, there is a formal charge of – 1 on the B, which is less electronegative than Cl.

(b) NO_2: Write the correct skeletal structure for the molecule.
N is the less electronegative, so it is central.

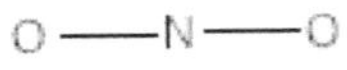

Calculate the total number of electrons for the Lewis structure by summing the number of valence electrons of each atom in the molecule.

(number of valence e^- for N) + 2(number of valence e^- for O) = 5 +2(6) = 17

Distribute the electrons among the atoms, giving octets to as many atoms as possible. Begin with the bonding electrons, then proceed to lone pairs on terminal atoms and finally to lone pairs on the central atom.

All 17 valence electrons are used.

N has an incomplete octet. It has 7 electrons because we have an odd number of valence electrons.

(c) BH_3: Write the correct skeletal structure for the molecule.

B is the less electronegative, so it is central.

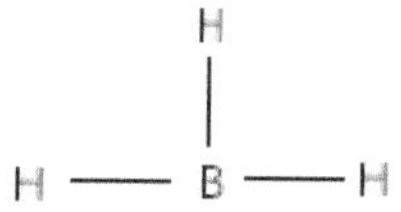

Calculate the total number of electrons for the Lewis structure by summing the number of valence electrons of each atom in the molecule.

(number of valence e^- for B) + 3(number of valence e^- for H) = 3 +3(1) = 6

Distribute the electrons among the atoms, giving octets (or duets for H) to as many atoms as possible. Begin with the bonding electrons, then proceed to lone pairs on terminal atoms and finally to lone pairs on the central atom.

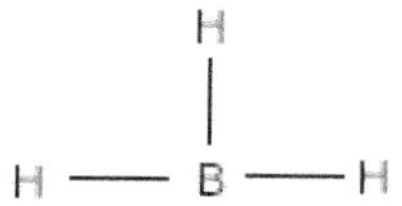

All 6 valence electrons are used.

B has an incomplete octet. H cannot double bond, so it is not possible to complete the octet on B with a double bond.

9.70 (a) BBr_3: Write the correct skeletal structure for the molecule.

B is the less electronegative, so it is central.

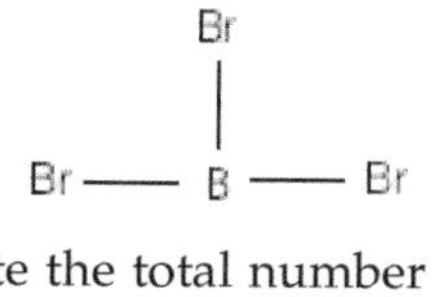

Calculate the total number of electrons for the Lewis structure by summing the number of valence electrons of each atom in the molecule.

(number of valence e^- for B) + 3(number of valence e^- for Br) = 3 +3(7) = 24

Distribute the electrons among the atoms, giving octets to as many atoms as possible. Begin with the bonding electrons, then proceed to lone pairs on terminal atoms and finally to lone pairs on the central atom.

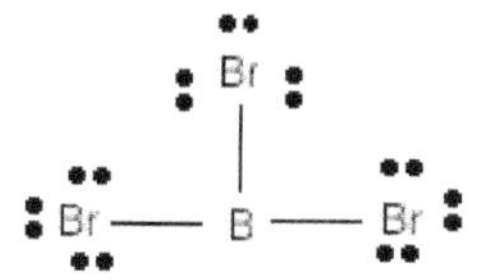

All 24 valence electrons are used.

B has an incomplete octet. If we complete the octet, there is a formal charge of – 1 on the B, which is less electronegative than Br.

(b) NO: Write the correct skeletal structure for the molecule.

Calculate the total number of electrons for the Lewis structure by summing the number of valence electrons of each atom in the molecule.

(number of valence e^- for N) + (number of valence e^- for O) = 5 +6 = 11

Distribute the electrons among the atoms, giving octets to as many atoms as possible. Begin with the bonding electrons, then proceed to lone pairs on terminal atoms, and finally to lone pairs the central atom.

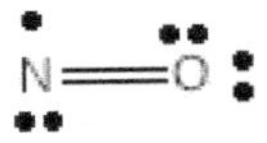

All 11 valence electrons are used.

N has an incomplete octet. It has 7 electrons because we have an odd number of valence electrons.

(c) ClO_2: Write the correct skeletal structure for the molecule.
Cl is less electronegative so it is central.

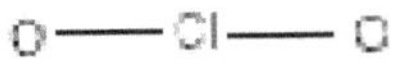

Calculate the total number of electrons for the Lewis structure by summing the number of valence electrons of each atom in the molecule.

(number of valence e^- for Cl) + 2(number of valence e^- for O) = 7 +2(6) = 19

Distribute the electrons among the atoms, giving octets to as many atoms as possible. Begin with the bonding electrons, then proceed to lone pairs on terminal atoms and finally to lone pairs of the central atom.

or

All 19 valence electrons are used.

Cl will have either an incomplete octet or an expanded octet. Because Cl brings 7 electrons, there is an odd number of electrons in the structure.

9.71 (a) PO_4^{3-}: Write the correct skeletal structure for the ion.

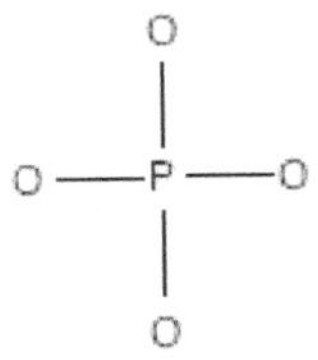

Calculate the total number of electrons for the Lewis structure by summing the number of valence electrons of each atom in the ion and adding 3 for the 3 – charge.

4(number of valence e^- for O) + (number of valence e^- for P) + 3 = 4(6) + 5 + 3 = 32

Distribute the electrons among the atoms, giving octets to as many atoms as possible. Begin with the bonding electrons, then proceed to lone pairs on terminal atoms and finally to lone pairs on the central atom.

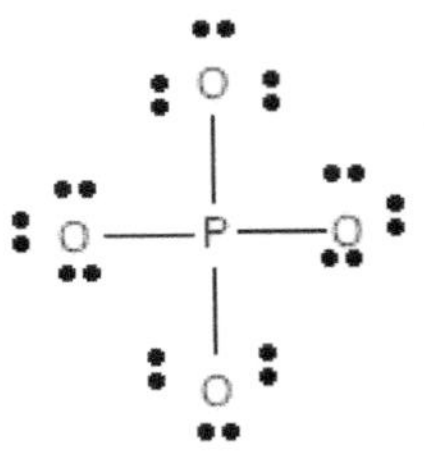

All 32 valence electrons are used.

Lastly, write the Lewis structure in brackets with the charge of the ion in the upper right-hand corner.

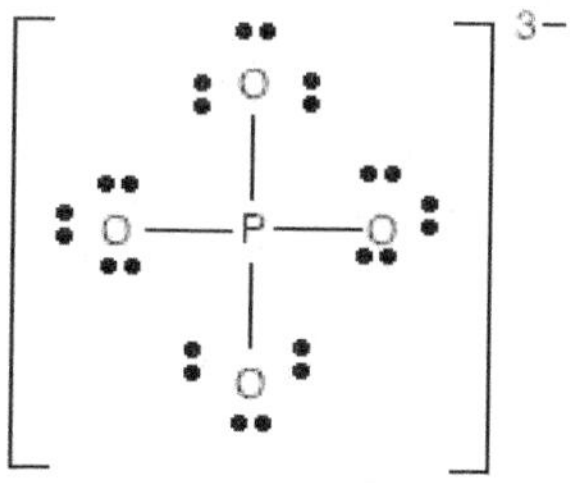

All atoms have octets (duets for H); the structure is complete.

Calculate the formal charge on each atom by finding the number of valence electrons and subtracting the number of lone pair electrons and one-half the number of bonding electrons.

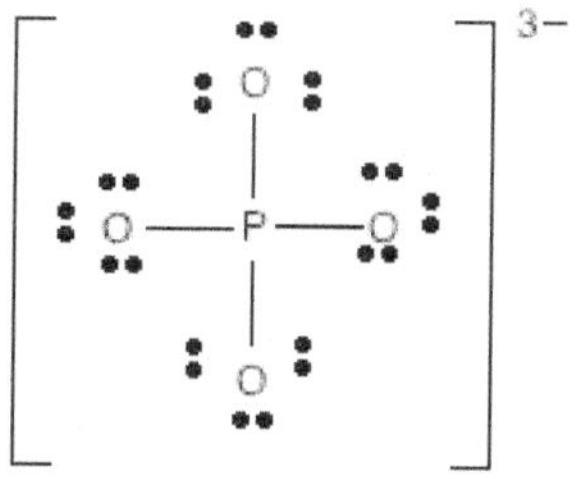

	O_{left}	O_{top}	O_{right}	O_{bottom}	P
number of valence electrons	6	6	6	6	5
- number of lone pair electrons	6	6	6	6	0
- 1/2(number of bonding electrons)	1	1	1	1	4
Formal charge	–1	–1	–1	–1	+1

The sum of the formal charges is –3, which is the overall charge of the ion. However, we can write a resonance structure with a double bond to an oxygen because P can expand its octet. This leads to lower formal charges on P and O.

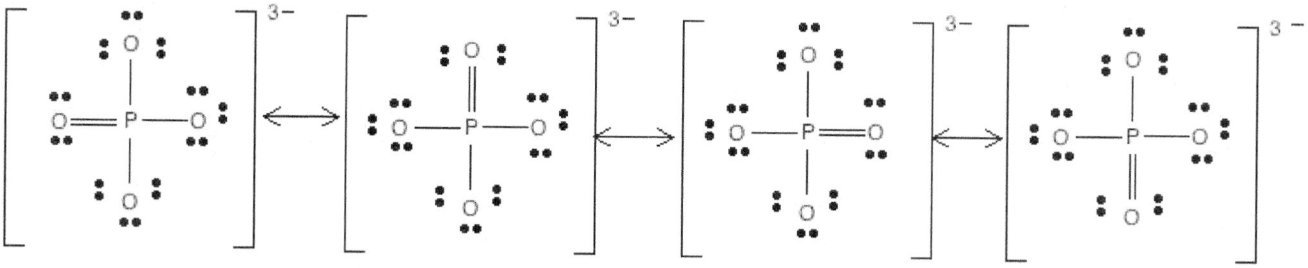

Using the leftmost structure, calculate the formal charge on each atom by finding the number of valence electrons and subtracting the number of lone pair electrons and one-half the number of bonding electrons.

	O_{left}	O_{top}	O_{right}	O_{bottom}	P
number of valence electrons	6	6	6	6	5
- number of lone pair electrons	4	6	6	6	0
- 1/2(number of bonding electrons)	2	1	1	1	5
Formal charge	0	–1	–1	–1	0

The sum of the formal charges is –3, which is the overall charge of the ion. These resonance forms would all have the lower formal charges associated with the double bonded O and P.

(b) CN^-: Write the correct skeletal structure for the ion.

C — N

Calculate the total number of electrons for the Lewis structure by summing the number of valence electrons of each atom in the ion and adding 1 for the 1 – charge.

(number of valence e^- for C) + (number of valence e^- for N) + 1 = 4 + 5 + 1 = 10

Distribute the electrons among the atoms, giving octets \ to as many atoms as possible. Begin with the bonding electrons, then proceed to lone pairs on terminal atoms, and finally to lone pairs on the central atom.

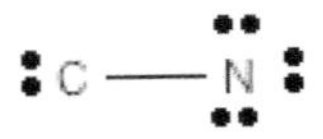

All 10 valence electrons are used.

If any atom lacks an octet, form double or triple bonds as necessary.

Lastly, write the Lewis structure in brackets with the charge of the ion in the upper right-hand corner.

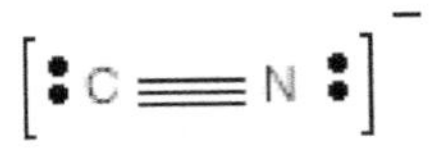

All atoms have octets; the structure is complete.

Calculate the formal charge on each atom by finding the number of valence electrons and subtracting the number of lone pair electrons and one-half the number of bonding electrons.

	C	N
number of valence electrons	4	5
- number of lone pair electrons	2	2
- 1/2(number of bonding electrons)	3	3
Formal charge	–1	0

The sum of the formal charges is – 1, which is the overall charge of the ion.

(c) SO_3^{2-}: Write the correct skeletal structure for the ion.

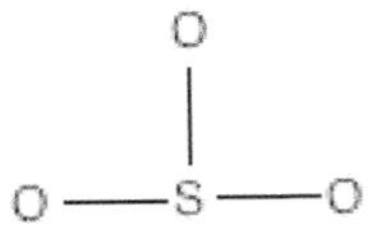

Calculate the total number of electrons for the Lewis structure by summing the valence electrons of each atom in the ion and adding 2 for the 2 – charge.

3(number of valence e^- for O) + (number of valence e^- for S) + 2 = 3(6) + 6 + 2 = 26

Distribute the electrons among the atoms, giving octets to as many atoms as possible. Begin with the bonding electrons, then proceed to lone pairs on terminal atoms and finally to lone pairs on the central atom.

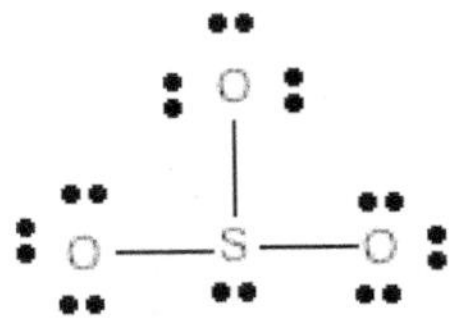

All 26 valence electrons are used.

Lastly, write the Lewis structure in brackets with the charge of the ion in the upper right-hand corner.

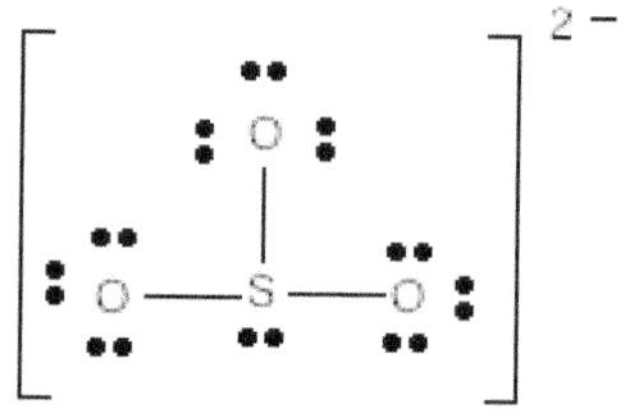

Calculate the formal charge on each atom by finding the number of valence electrons and subtracting the number of lone pair electrons and one-half the number of bonding electrons.

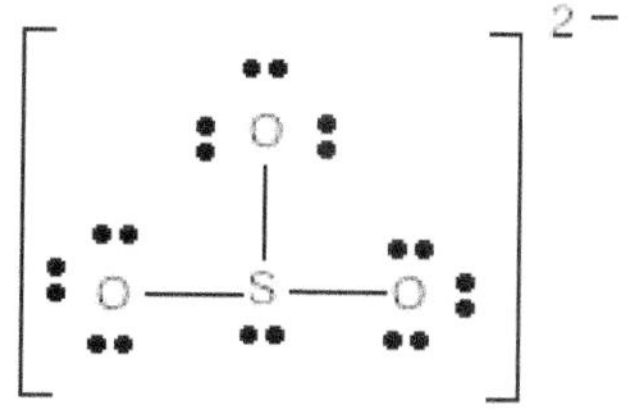

	O_{left}	O_{top}	O_{right}	S
number of valence electrons	6	6	6	6
- number of lone pair electrons	6	6	6	2
- 1/2(number of bonding electrons)	1	1	1	3
Formal charge	–1	–1	–1	+1

The sum of the formal charges is –2, which is the overall charge of the ion. However, we can write a resonance structure with a double bond to an oxygen because S can expand its octet. This leads to a lower formal charge.

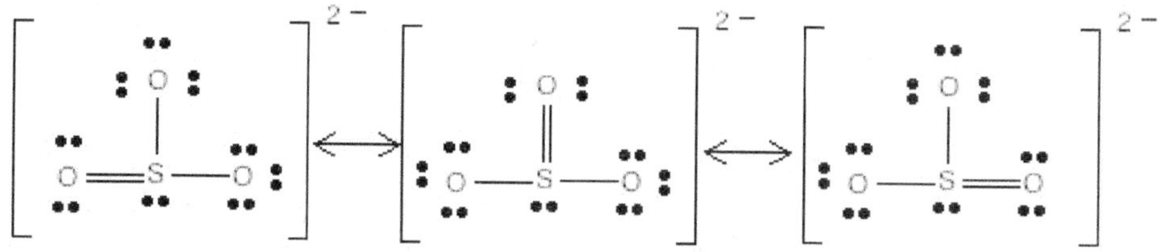

Using the leftmost resonance form, calculate the formal charge on each atom by finding the number of valence electrons and subtracting the number of lone pair electrons and one-half the number of bonding electrons.

	O_{left}	O_{top}	O_{right}	S
number of valence electrons	6	6	6	6
- number of lone pair electrons	4	6	6	2
- 1/2(number of bonding electrons)	2	1	1	4
Formal charge	0	–1	–1	0

The sum of the formal charges is –2, which is the overall charge of the ion. These resonance forms would all have the lower formal charge on the double bonded O and S.

(d) ClO_2^-: Write the correct skeletal structure for the ion.

Calculate the total number of electrons for the Lewis structure by summing the number of valence electrons of each atom in the ion and adding 1 for the 1 – charge.

$$2(\text{number of valence } e^- \text{ for O}) + (\text{number of valence } e^- \text{ for Cl}) + 1 = 2(6) + 7 + 1 = 20$$

Distribute the electrons among the atoms, giving octets (or duets for H) to as many atoms as possible. Begin with the bonding electrons, then proceed to lone pairs on terminal atoms and finally to lone pairs on the central atom.

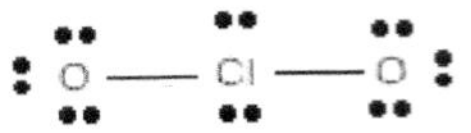

All 20 valence electrons are used.

Lastly, write the Lewis structure in brackets with the charge of the ion in the upper right-hand corner.

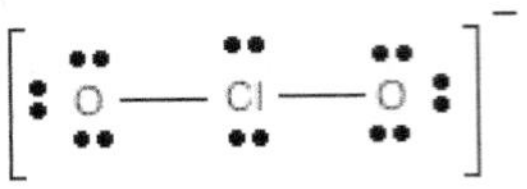

All atoms have octets; the structure is complete.

Calculate the formal charge on each atom by finding the number of valence electrons and subtracting the number of lone pair electrons and one-half the number of bonding electrons.

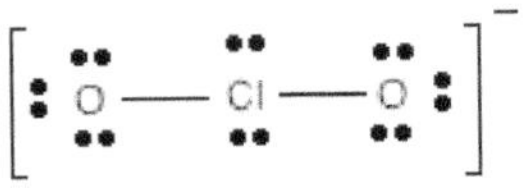

	O_{left}	O_{right}	Cl
number of valence electrons	6	6	7
- number of lone pair electrons	6	6	4
- 1/2(number of bonding electrons)	1	1	2
Formal charge	–1	–1	+1

The sum of the formal charges is –1, which is the overall charge of the ion. However, we can write a resonance structure with a double bond to an oxygen because Cl can expand its octet. This leads to a lower formal charge.

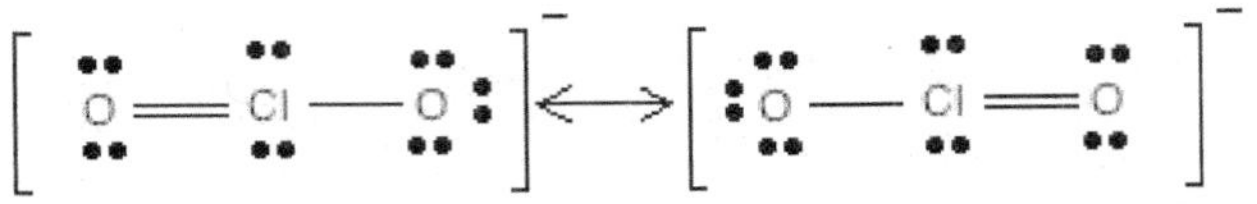

Using the leftmost resonance form, calculate the formal charge on each atom by finding the number of valence electrons and subtracting the number of lone pair electrons and one-half the number of bonding electrons.

	O_{left}	O_{right}	Cl
number of valence electrons	6	6	7
- number of lone pair electrons	4	6	4
- 1/2(number of bonding electrons)	2	1	3
Formal charge	0	–1	0

The sum of the formal charges is –1, which is the overall charge of the ion. These resonance forms would all have the lower formal charge on the double bonded O and Cl.

9.72 (a) SO_4^{2-}: Write the correct skeletal structure for the ion.

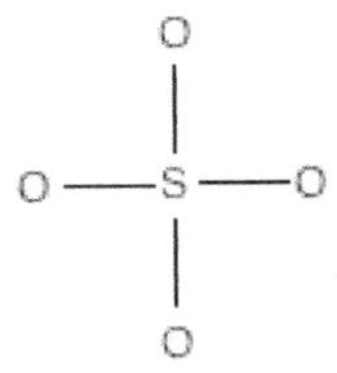

Calculate the total number of electrons for the Lewis structure by summing the valence electrons of each atom in the molecule and adding 2 for the 2 – charge.

4(number of valence e^- for O) + (number of valence e^- for S) + 2 = 4(6) + 6 + 2 = 32

Distribute the electrons among the atoms, giving octets to as many atoms as possible. Begin with the bonding electrons, then proceed to lone pairs on terminal atoms and finally to lone pairs on the central atom.

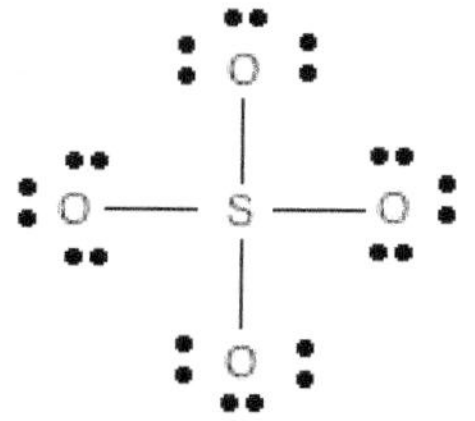

All 32 valence electrons are used.

Lastly, write the Lewis structure in brackets with the charge of the ion in the upper right-hand corner.

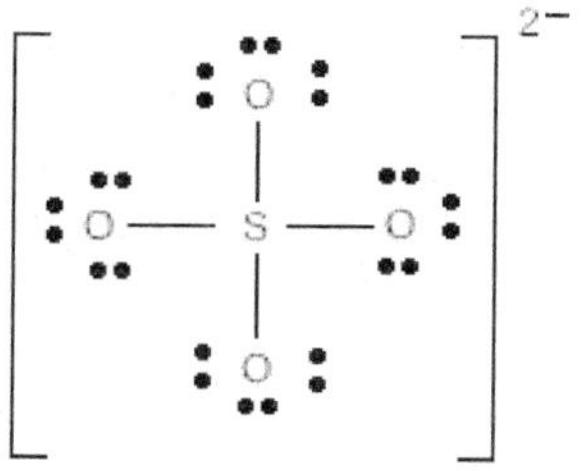

All atoms have octets; the structure is complete.

Calculate the formal charge on each atom by finding the number of valence electrons and subtracting the number of lone pair electrons and one-half the number of bonding electrons.

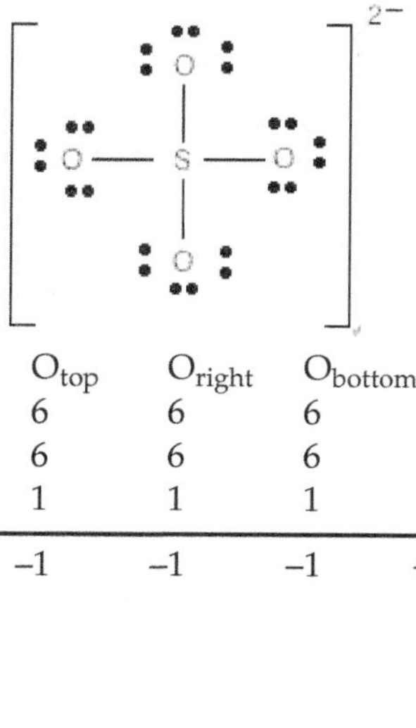

	O_{left}	O_{top}	O_{right}	O_{bottom}	S
number of valence electrons	6	6	6	6	6
- number of lone pair electrons	6	6	6	6	0
- 1/2(number of bonding electrons)	1	1	1	1	4
Formal charge	–1	–1	–1	–1	+2

The sum of the formal charges is – 2, which is the overall charge of the ion. However, we can write a resonance structure with double bonds to two oxygen atoms because S can expand its octet. This leads to lower formal charges.

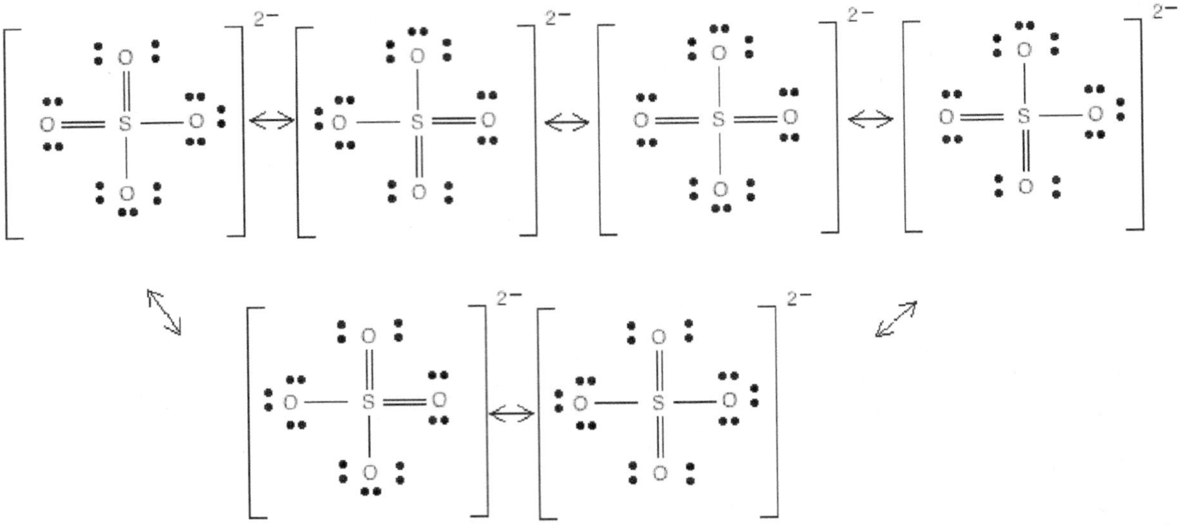

Using the leftmost resonance form, calculate the formal charge on each atom by finding the number of valence electrons and subtracting the number of lone pair electrons and one-half the number of bonding electrons.

	O_{left}	O_{top}	O_{right}	O_{bottom}	S
number of valence electrons	6	6	6	6	6
- number of lone pair electrons	4	4	6	6	0
- 1/2(number of bonding electrons)	2	2	1	1	6
Formal charge	0	0	–1	–1	0

The sum of the formal charges is –2, which is the overall charge of the ion. These resonance forms would all have the lower formal charges on the double bonded O and S.

(b) HSO_4^-: Write the correct skeletal structure for the ion.

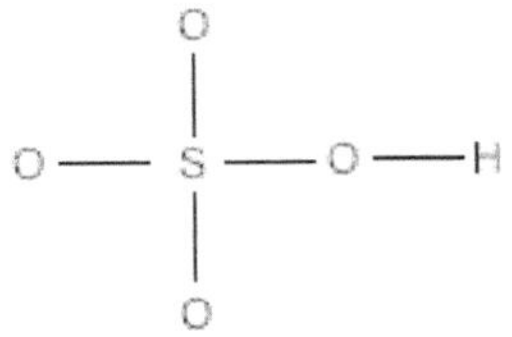

Calculate the total number of electrons for the Lewis structure by summing the valence electrons of each atom in the ion and adding 1 for the 1 – charge.

4(number of valence e^- for O) + (number of valence e^- for S) + (number of valence e^- for H) + 1 = 4(6) + 6 + 1 +1 = 32

Distribute the electrons among the atoms, giving octets (or duets for H) to as many atoms as possible. Begin with the bonding electrons, then proceed to lone pairs on terminal atoms and finally to lone pairs on the central atoms.

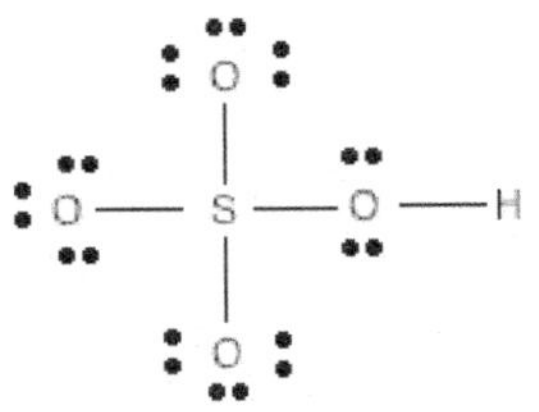

All 32 valence electrons are used.

Lastly, write the Lewis structure in brackets with the charge of the ion in the upper right-hand corner.

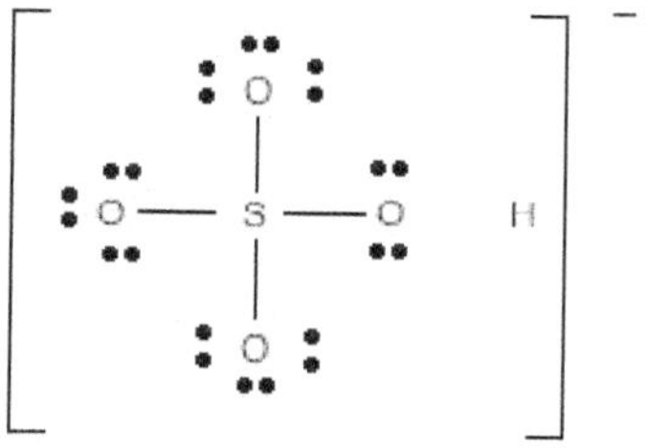

All atoms have octets (duets for H); the structure is complete.
Calculate the formal charge on each atom by finding the number of valence electrons and subtracting the number of lone pair electrons and one-half the number of bonding electrons.

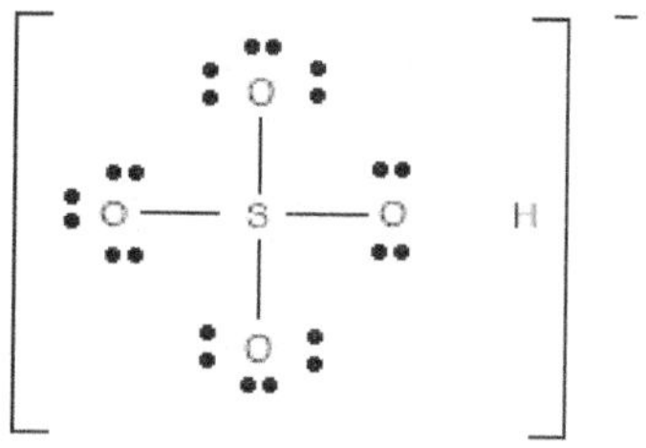

	O_{left}	O_{top}	O_{right}	O_{bottom}	S	H
number of valence electrons	6	6	6	6	6	1
- number of lone pair electrons	6	6	4	6	0	0
- 1/2(number of bonding electrons)	1	1	2	2	4	1
Formal charge	–1	–1	0	–1	+2	0

The sum of the formal charges is – 1, which is the overall charge of the ion. However, we can write a resonance structure with double bonds to two oxygen atoms because S can expand its octet. This leads to a lower formal charges.

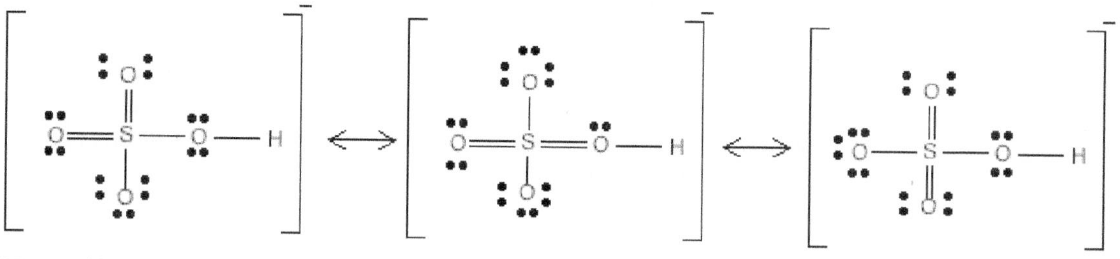

Using the leftmost resonance form, calculate the formal charge on each atom by finding the number of valence electrons and subtracting the number of lone pair electrons and one-half the number of bonding electrons.

	O_{left}	O_{top}	O_{right}	O_{bottom}	S	H
number of valence electrons	6	6	6	6	6	1
- number of lone pair electrons	4	4	4	6	0	0
- 1/2(number of bonding electrons)	2	2	2	2	6	1
Formal charge	0	0	0	–1	0	0

The sum of the formal charges is –1, which is the overall charge of the ion. Each of these resonance forms would all have lower formal charges on O and S.

(c) SO_3: Write the correct skeletal structure for the molecule.

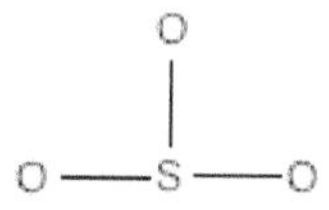

Calculate the total number of electrons for the Lewis structure by summing the number of valence electrons of each atom in the molecule.

3(number of valence e^- for O) + (number of valence e^- for S) = 3(6) + 6 = 24

Distribute the electrons among the atoms, giving octets to as many atoms as possible. Begin with the bonding electrons, then proceed to lone pairs on terminal atoms and finally to lone pairs on the central atom.

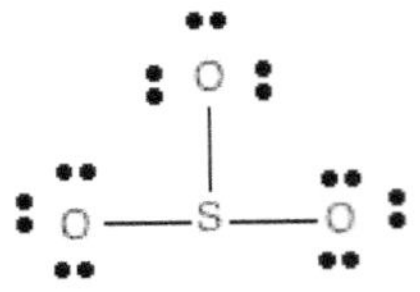

All 24 valence electrons are used.

If any atoms lack an octet, form double or triple bonds as necessary to give them octets.

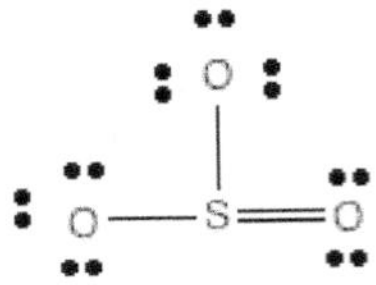

All atoms have octets; the structure is complete.

Calculate the formal charge on each atom by finding the number of valence electrons and subtracting the number of lone pair electrons and one-half the number of bonding electrons.

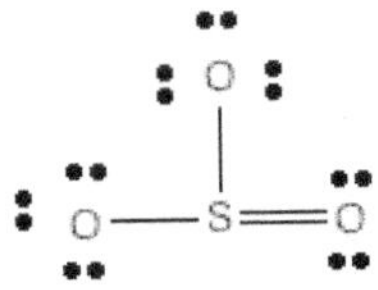

	O_{left}	O_{top}	O_{right}	S
number of valence electrons	6	6	6	6
- number of lone pair electrons	6	6	4	0
- 1/2(number of bonding electrons)	1	1	2	4
Formal charge	−1	−1	0	+2

The sum of the formal charges is 0, which is the overall charge of the molecule. However, we can write a resonance structure with a double bond to all oxygen atoms because S can expand its octet. This leads to lower formal charges.

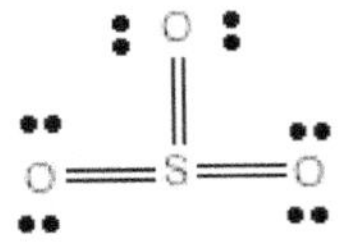

Calculate the formal charge on each atom by finding the number of valence electrons and subtracting the number of lone pair electrons and one-half the number of bonding electrons.

	O_{left}	O_{top}	O_{right}	S
number of valence electrons	6	6	6	6
- number of lone pair electrons	4	4	4	0
- 1/2(number of bonding electrons)	2	2	2	6
Formal charge	0	0	0	0

The sum of the formal charges is 0, which is the overall charge of the molecule. This resonance form would have the lower formal charges on each atom.

(d) BrO_2^-: Write the correct skeletal structure for the ion.

Calculate the total number of electrons for the Lewis structure by summing the number of valence electrons of each atom in the molecule and adding 1 for the 1 – charge.

2(number of valence e^- for O) + (number of valence e^- for Br) + 1 = 2(6) + 7 + 1 = 20

Distribute the electrons among the atoms, giving octets to as many atoms as possible. Begin with the bonding electrons, then proceed to lone pairs on terminal atoms and finally to lone pairs on the central atom.

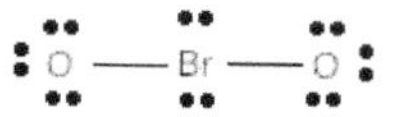

All 20 valence electrons are used.

Lastly, write the Lewis structure in brackets with the charge of the ion in the upper right-hand corner.

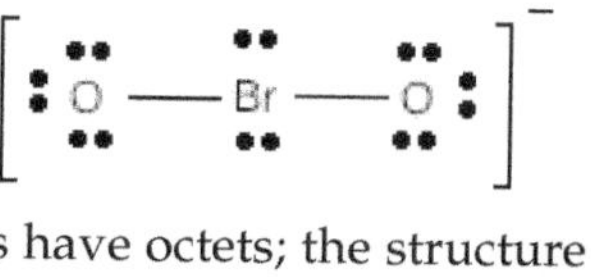

All atoms have octets; the structure is complete.

Calculate the formal charge on each atom by finding the number of valence electrons and subtracting the number of lone pair electrons and one-half the number of bonding electrons.

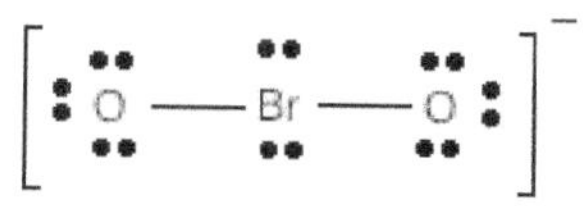

	O_{left}	O_{right}	Br
number of valence electrons	6	6	7
- number of lone pair electrons	6	6	4
- 1/2(number of bonding electrons)	1	1	2
Formal charge	–1	–1	+1

The sum of the formal charges is – 1, which is the overall charge of the ion. However, we can write a resonance structure with a double bond to an oxygen because Br can expand its octet. This leads to a lower formal charge.

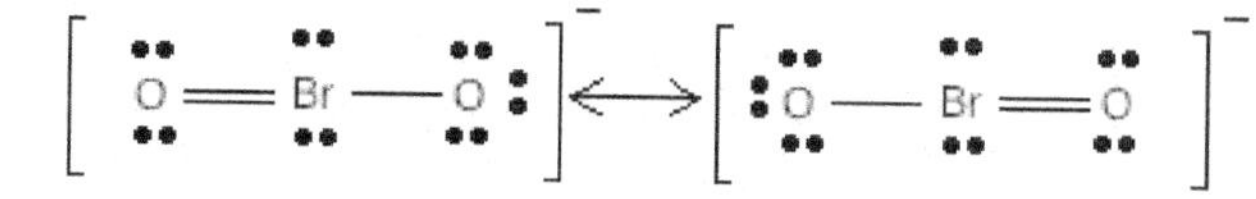

Using the leftmost resonance form, calculate the formal charge on each atom by finding the number of valence electrons and subtracting the number of lone pair electrons and one-half the number of bonding electrons.

	O_{left}	O_{right}	Br
number of valence electron	6	6	7
- number of lone pair electrons	4	6	4
- 1/2(number of bonding electrons)	2	1	3
Formal charge	0	–1	0

The sum of the formal charges is –1, which is the overall charge of the ion. These resonance forms would both have the lower formal charges on the double bonded O and Br.

9.73 (a) PF_5: Write the correct skeletal structure for the molecule.

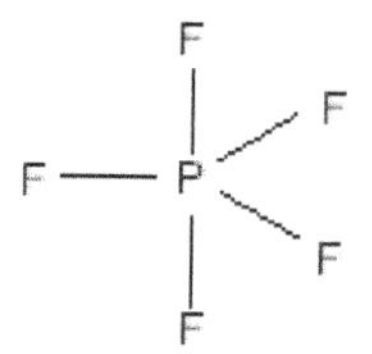

Calculate the total number of electrons for the Lewis structure by summing the number of valence electrons of each atom in the molecule.

(number of valence e^- for P) + 5(number of valence e^- for F) = 5 +5(7) = 40

Distribute the electrons among the atoms, giving octets to as many atoms as possible. Begin with the bonding electrons, then proceed to lone pairs on terminal atoms and finally to lone pairs on the central atom. Arrange additional electrons around the central atom, giving it an expanded octet of up to 12 electrons.

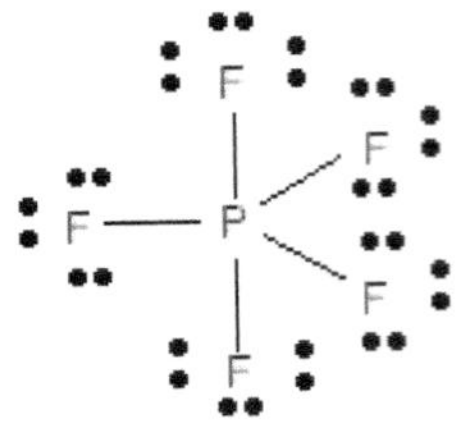

(b) I_3^- : Write the correct skeletal structure for the ion.

Calculate the total number of electrons for the Lewis structure by summing the number of valence electrons of each atom in the ion and adding 1 for the 1 – charge.

$$3(\text{number of valence } e^- \text{ for I}) + 1 = 3(7) + 1 = 22$$

Distribute the electrons among the atoms, giving octets to as many atoms as possible. Begin with the bonding electrons, then proceed to lone pairs on terminal atoms and finally to lone pairs on the central atom. Arrange additional electrons around the central atom, giving it an expanded octet of up to 12 electrons.

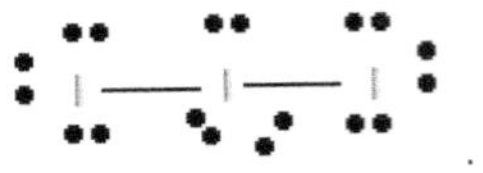

Lastly, write the Lewis structure in brackets with the charge of the ion in the upper right-hand corner.

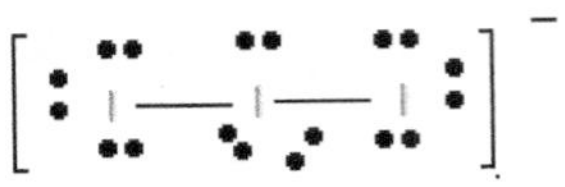

(c) SF_4: Write the correct skeletal structure for the molecule.

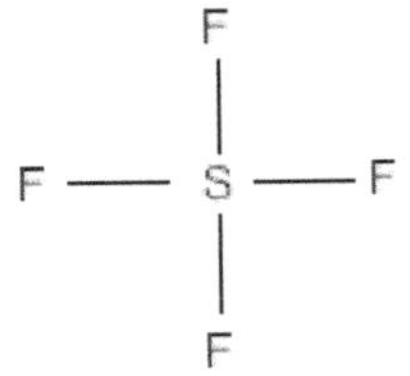

Calculate the total number of electrons for the Lewis structure by summing the number of valence electrons of each atom in the molecule.

$$(\text{number of valence } e^- \text{ for S}) + 4(\text{number of valence } e^- \text{ for F}) = 6 + 4(7) = 34$$

Distribute the electrons among the atoms, giving octets (or duets for H) to as many atoms as possible. Begin with the bonding electrons, and then proceed to lone pairs on terminal atoms and finally to lone pairs on the central atom. Arrange additional electrons around the central atom, giving it an expanded octet of up to 12 electrons.

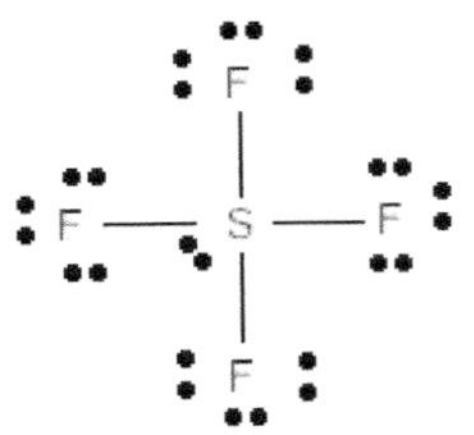

(d) GeF_4: Write the correct skeletal structure for the molecule.

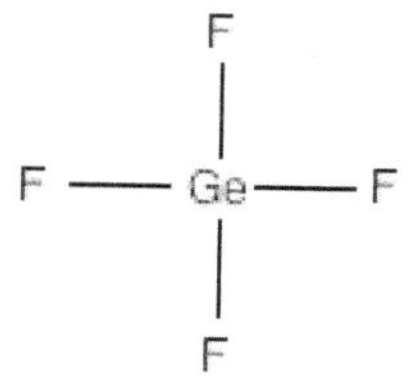

Calculate the total number of electrons for the Lewis structure by summing the number of valence electrons of each atom in the molecule.

(number of valence e^- for Ge) + 4(number of valence e^- for F) = 4 + 4(7) = 32

Distribute the electrons among the atoms, giving octets to as many atoms as possible. Begin with the bonding electrons, then proceed to lone pairs on terminal atoms and finally to lone pairs on the central atom.

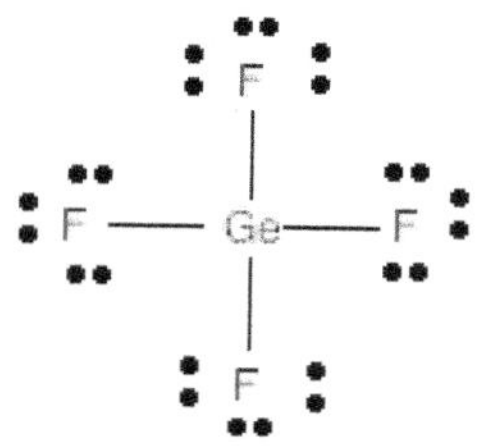

9.74 (a) ClF_5: Write the correct skeletal structure for the molecule.

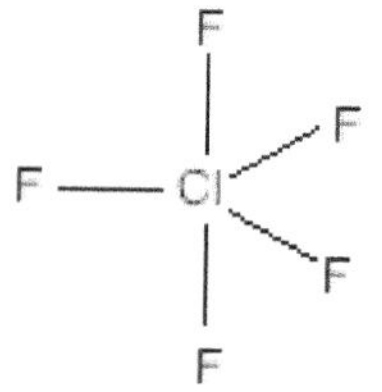

Calculate the total number of electrons for the Lewis structure by summing the valence electrons of each atom in the molecule.

(number of valence e^- for Cl) + 5(number of valence e^- for F) = 7 +5(7) = 42

Distribute the electrons among the atoms, giving octets to as many atoms as possible. Begin with the bonding electrons, then proceed to lone pairs on terminal atoms and finally to lone pairs on the central atom. Arrange additional electrons around the central atom, giving it an expanded octet of up to 12 electrons.

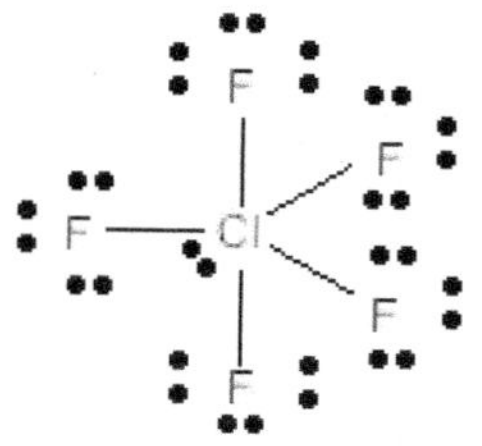

(b) AsF_6^-: Write the correct skeletal structure for the ion.

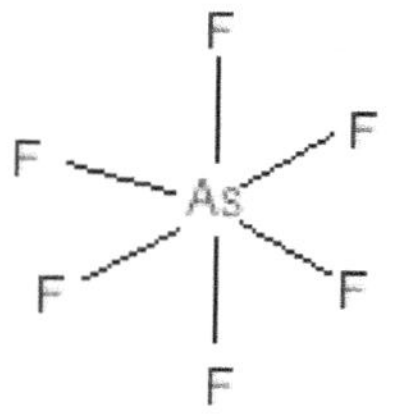

Calculate the total number of electrons for the Lewis structure by summing the valence electrons of each atom in the ion and adding one for the 1 – charge.

(number of valence e^- for As) + 6(number of valence e^- for F) + 1 = 5 +6(7) + 1 = 48

Distribute the electrons among the atoms, giving octets (or duets for H) to as many atoms as possible. Begin with the bonding electrons, then proceed to lone pairs on terminal atoms and finally to lone pairs on the central atom. Arrange additional electrons around the central atom, giving it an expanded octet of up to 12 electrons.

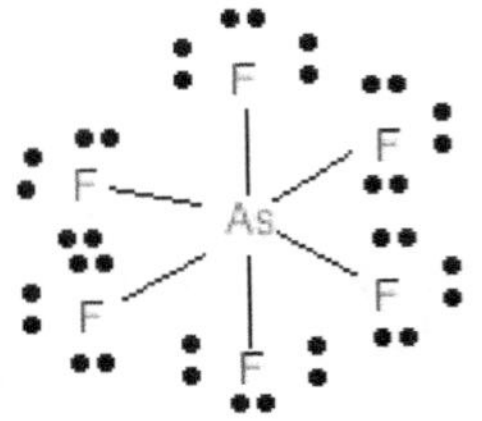

Lastly, write the Lewis structure in brackets with the charge of the ion in the upper right-hand corner.

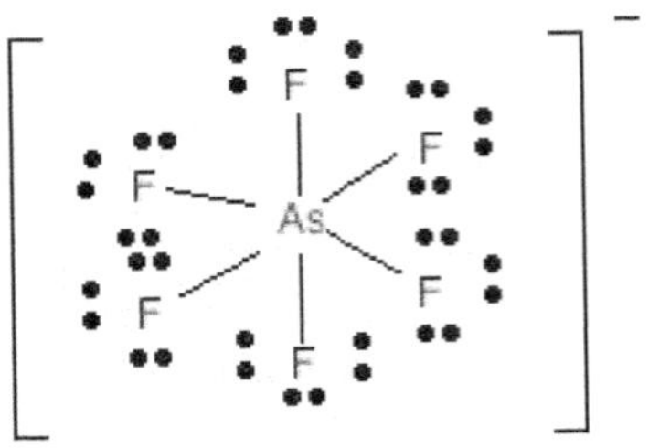

(c) Cl_3PO: Write the correct skeletal structure for the molecule.

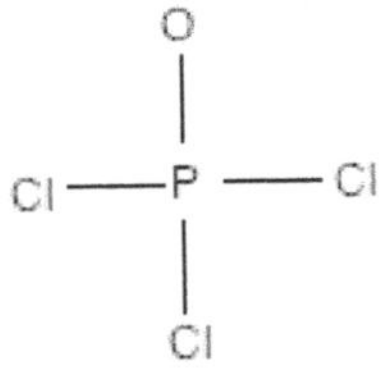

Calculate the total number of electrons for the Lewis structure by summing the valence electron of each atom in the molecule.

(number of valence e^- for P) + (number of valence e^- for O) + 3(number of valence e^- for Cl)= 5 +6 + 3(7) = 32

Distribute the electrons among the atoms, giving octets to as many atoms as possible. Begin with the bonding electrons, then proceed to lone pairs on terminal atoms and finally to lone pairs on the central atom. Arrange additional electrons around the central atom, giving it an expanded octet of up to 12 electrons.

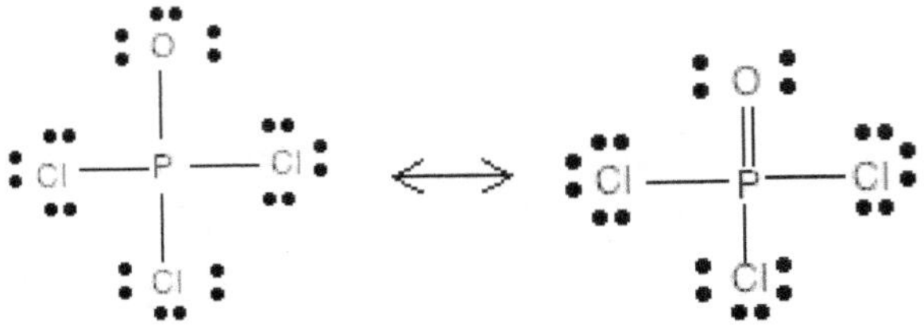

(d) IF_5: Write the correct skeletal structure for the molecule.

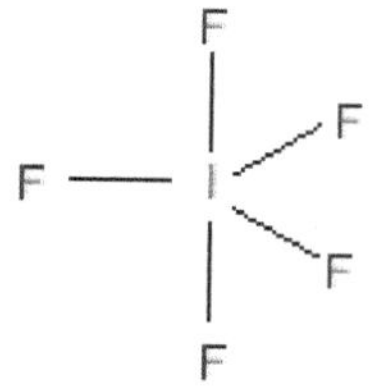

Calculate the total number of electrons for the Lewis structure by summing the valence electrons of each atom in the molecule.

(number of valence e^- for I) + 5(number of valence e^- for F) = 7 +5(7) = 42

Distribute the electrons among the atoms, giving octets to as many atoms as possible. Begin with the bonding electrons, and then proceed to lone pairs on terminal atoms and finally to lone pairs on the central atom. Arrange additional electrons around the central atom, giving it an expanded octet of up to 12 electrons.

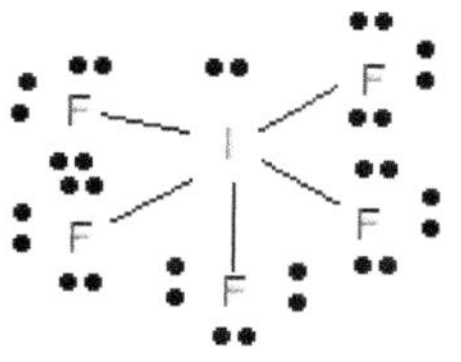

Bond Energies and Bond Lengths

9.75 Bond strength: $H_3CCH_3 < H_2CCH_2 < HCCH$

Bond length: $H_3CCH_3 > H_2CCH_2 > HCCH$

Write the Lewis structures for the three compounds. Compare the C – C bonds. Triple bonds are stronger than double bonds, which are stronger than single bonds. Also, single bonds are longer than double bonds are longer than triple bonds.

HCCH (10 e^-) H_2CCH_2 (12 e^-) H_3CCH_3(14 e^-)

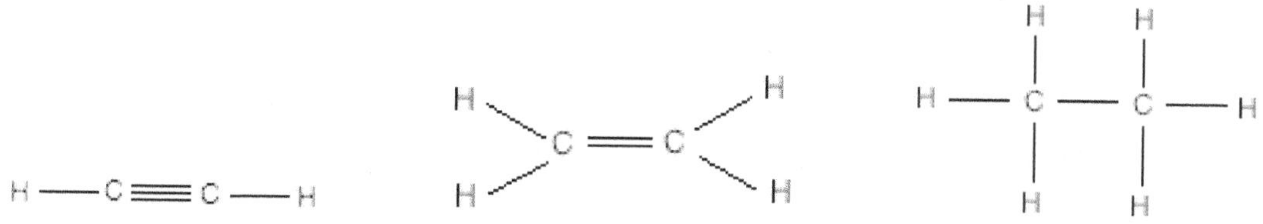

9.76 Stronger bond: HNNH Shorter bond: HNNH

Write the Lewis structures for the three compounds. Compare the N – N bonds. Triple bonds are stronger than double bonds, which are stronger than single bonds. Also, single bonds are longer than double bonds, and double bonds are longer than triple bonds.

H_2NNH_2(14 e^-) HNNH(12 e^-)

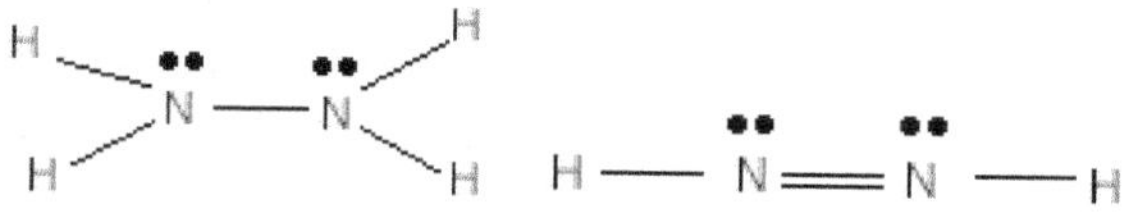

9.77 Rewrite the reaction using the Lewis structures of the molecules involved.

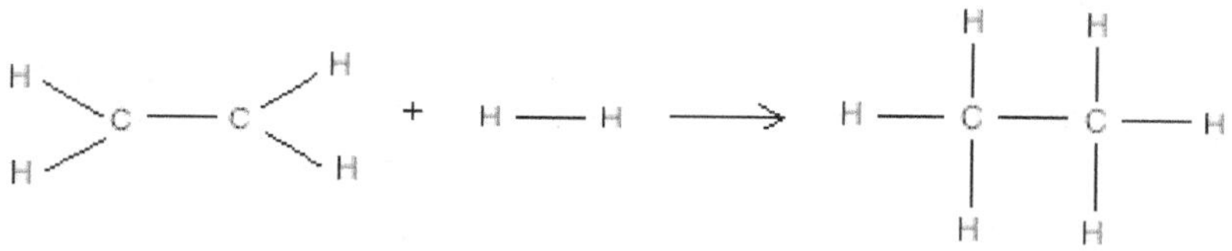

Determine which bonds are broken in the reaction and sum the bond energies of the following:

$\Sigma(\Delta H\text{'s bonds broken})$
$= 4\text{mol}(C - H) + 1\text{mol}(C = C) + 1\text{mol}(H - H)$
$= 4\text{mol}(414 \text{ kJ/mol}) + 1\text{mol}(611 \text{ kJ/mol}) + 1\text{mol}(436 \text{ kJ/mol})$
$= 2703 \text{ kJ/mol}$

Determine which bonds are formed in the reaction and sum the negatives of the bond energies of the following:

$\Sigma(-\Delta H\text{'s bonds formed})$
$= -6\text{mol}(C - H) - 1\text{mol}(C - C)$
$= -6\text{mol}(414 \text{ kJ/mol}) - 1\text{mol}(347 \text{ kJ/mol})$
$= -2831 \text{ kJ/mol}$

Find ΔH_{rxn} by summing the results of the two steps.

$\Delta H_{rxn} = \Sigma(\Delta H\text{'s bonds broken}) + \Sigma(-\Delta H\text{'s bonds formed})$
$= 2703 \text{ kJ/mol} - 2831 \text{ kJ/mol}$
$= -128 \text{ kJ/mol}$

9.78 Rewrite the reaction using the Lewis structures of the molecules involved.

Determine which bonds are broken in the reaction and sum the bond energies of the following:

$\Sigma(\Delta H\text{'s bonds broken})$
$= 5\text{mol}(C - H) + 1\text{mol}(C - C) + 1\text{mol}(C - O) + 1\text{mol}(O - H) + 3\text{mol}(O = O)$
$= 5\text{mol}(414 \text{ kJ/mol}) + 1\text{mol}(347 \text{ kJ/mol}) + 1\text{mol}(350 \text{ kJ/mol}) + 1\text{mol}(464 \text{ kJ/mol}) + 3\text{mol}(498 \text{ kJ/mol})$
$= 4735 \text{ kJ/mol}$

Determine which bonds are formed in the reaction and sum the negatives of the bond energies of the following:

$\Sigma(-\Delta H\text{'s bonds formed})$
$= -4\text{mol}(C = O) - 6\text{mol}(O - H)$
$= -4\text{mol}(799 \text{ kJ/mol}) - 6\text{mol}(464 \text{ kJ/mol})$
$= -5980 \text{ kJ/mol}$

Find ΔH_{rxn} by summing the results of the two steps.

$\Delta H_{rxn} = \Sigma(\Delta H\text{'s bonds broken}) + \Sigma(-\Delta H\text{'s bonds formed})$
$= 4735 \text{ kJ/mol} - 5980 \text{ kJ/mol}$
$= -1245 \text{ kJ/mol}$

9.79 Rewrite the reaction using the Lewis structures of the molecules involved.

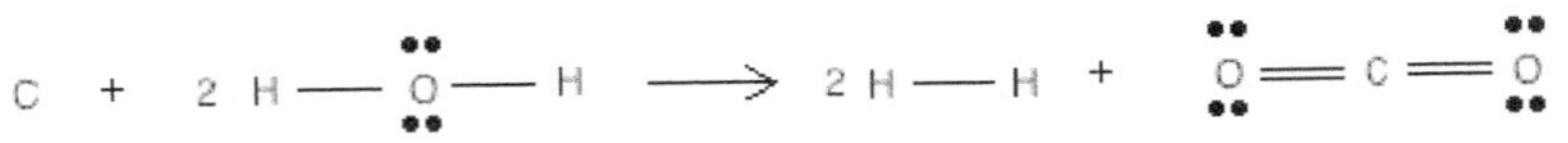

Determine which bonds are broken in the reaction and sum the bond energies of the following:

$\Sigma(\Delta H\text{'s bonds broken})$
$= 4(O - H)$
$= 4(464 \text{ kJ/mol})$
$= 1856 \text{ kJ/mol}$

Determine which bonds are formed in the reaction and sum the negatives of the bond energies of the following:

$\Sigma(-\Delta H\text{'s bonds formed})$
$= -2(C = O) - 2(H - H)$
$= -2(799 \text{ kJ/mol}) - 2(436 \text{ kJ/mol})$
$= -2470 \text{ kJ/mol}$

Find ΔH_{rxn} by summing the results of the two steps.

$\Delta H_{rxn} = \Sigma(\Delta H\text{'s bonds broken}) + \Sigma(-\Delta H\text{'s bonds formed})$
$= 1856 \text{ kJ/mol} - 2470 \text{ kJ/mol}$
$= -614 \text{ kJ/mol}$

9.80 Rewrite the reaction using the Lewis structures of the molecules involved.

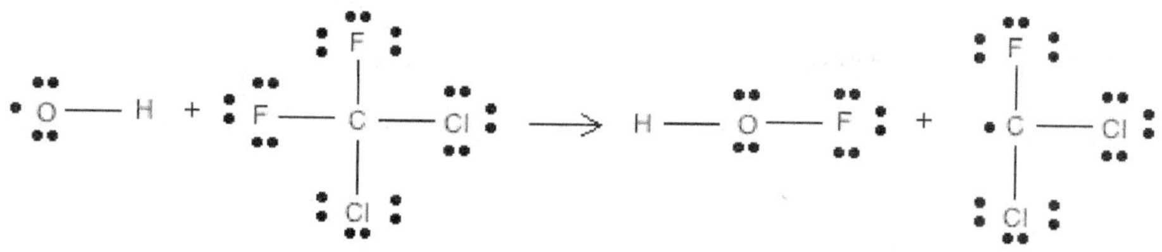

Since the C—F bond energy is not given, it is necessary to look it up (google). The C—F bond energy is 485 kJ.mol.

Determine which bonds are broken in the reaction and sum the bond energies of the following:

$\Sigma(\Delta H\text{'s bonds broken})$
$= (O - H) + 2(C - F) + 2(C - Cl)$
$= (464\ kJ/mol) + 2(485\ kJ/mol) + 2(339\ kJ/mol)$
$= 2112\ kJ/mol$

Determine which bonds are formed in the reaction and sum the negatives of the bond energies of the following:

$\Sigma(-\Delta H\text{'s bonds formed})$
$= -(O - H) - (O - F) - (C - F) - 2(C - Cl)$
$= -(464\ kJ/mol) - (190\ kJ/mol) - (485\ kJ/mol) - 2(339\ kJ/mol)$
$= -1817\ kJ/mol$

Find ΔH_{rxn} by summing the results of the two steps.

$\Delta H_{rxn} = \Sigma(\Delta H\text{'s bonds broken}) + \Sigma(-\Delta H\text{'s bonds formed})$
$= 2112\ kJ/mol - 1817\ kJ/mol$
$= +228\ kJ/mol$

From the bond energies we find the ΔH_{rxn} is positive. Therefore, you need to put more energy into the reaction than you get out of the reaction and this makes the reaction less likely to happen.

Cumulative Problems

9.81 (a) BI_3: This is a covalent compound between two nonmetals.
Write the correct skeletal structure for the molecule.

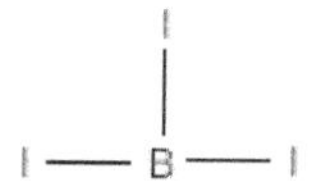

Calculate the total number of electrons for the Lewis structure by summing the number of valence electrons of each atom in the molecule.

(number of valence e^- for B) + (number of valence e^- for I) = 3 +3(7) = 24

Distribute the electrons among the atoms, giving octets to as many atoms as possible. Begin with the bonding electrons, then proceed to lone pairs on terminal atoms and finally to lone pairs on the central atom.

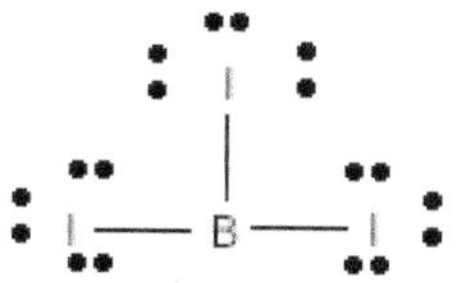

(b) K_2S: This is an ionic compound between a metal and nonmetal.
Draw the Lewis structures for K and S based on their valence electrons. K: $4s^1$ S: $3s^23p^4$

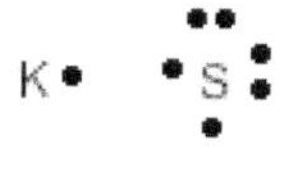

Potassium must lose one electron and be left with the octet from the previous shell, while sulfur needs to gain two electrons to get an octet.

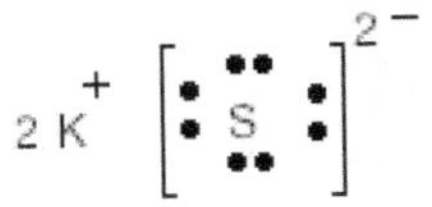

(c) HCFO: This is a covalent compound between nonmetals.
Write the correct skeletal structure for the molecule.

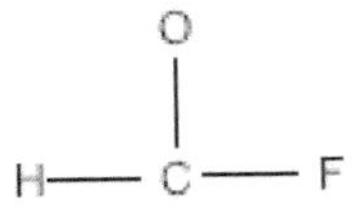

Calculate the total number of electrons for the Lewis structure by summing the number of valence electrons of each atom in the molecule.

(number of valence e^- for H)+(number of valence e^- for C)+(number of valence e^- for F)+(number of valence e^- for O) = 1 + 4 + 7 +6 = 18

Distribute the electrons among the atoms, giving octets to as many atoms as possible. Begin with the bonding electrons, then proceed to lone pairs on terminal atoms and finally to lone pairs on the central atom.

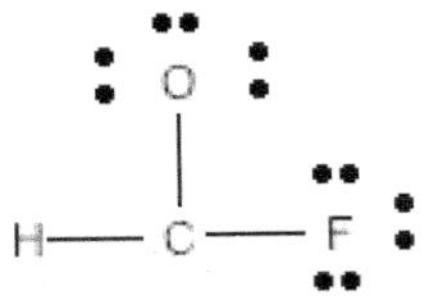

If any atom lacks an octet, form double or triple bonds as necessary to give them octets.

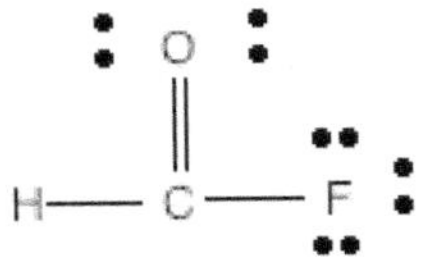

(d) PBr_3: This is a covalent compound between two nonmetals.
Write the correct skeletal structure for the molecule.

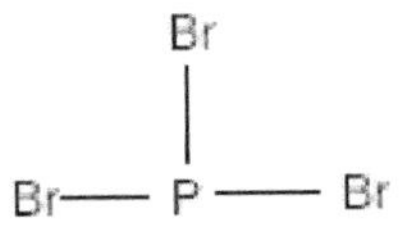

Calculate the total number of electrons for the Lewis structure by summing the number of valence electrons of each atom in the molecule.

(number of valence e^- for P) + 3(number of valence e^- for Br) = 5 + 3(7) = 26.

Distribute the electrons among the atoms, giving octets to as many atoms as possible. Begin with the bonding electrons, and then proceed to lone pairs on terminal atoms and finally to lone pairs on the central atom.

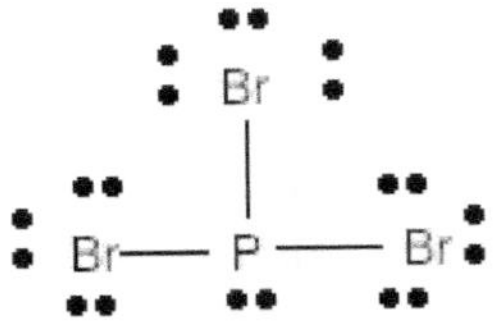

9.82 (a) Al_2O_3: This is an ionic compound between a metal and nonmetal.
Draw the Lewis structures for Al and O based on their valence electrons. Al: $3s^23p^1$ O: $2s^22p^4$

Aluminum must lose three electrons and be left with the octet from the previous shell, while oxygen needs to gain two electrons to get an octet.

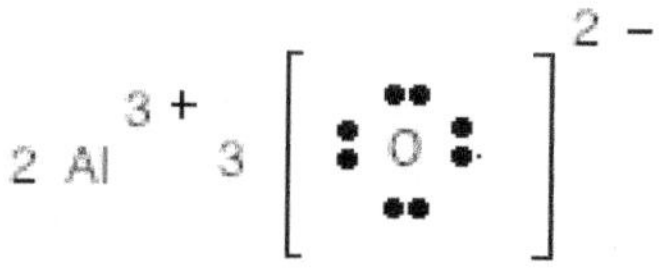

(b) ClF_5: This is a covalent compound between two nonmetals.
Write the correct skeletal structure for the molecule.

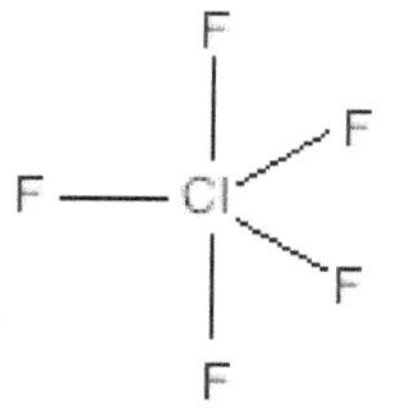

Calculate the total number of electrons for the Lewis structure by summing the number of valence electrons of each atom in the molecule.

(number of valence e^- for Cl) + 5(number of valence e^- for F) = 7 +5(7) = 42

Distribute the electrons among the atoms, giving octets to as many atoms as possible. Begin with the bonding electrons, and then proceed to lone pairs on terminal atoms and finally to lone pairs on the central atom. Arrange additional electrons around the central atom, giving it an expanded octet of up to 12 electrons.

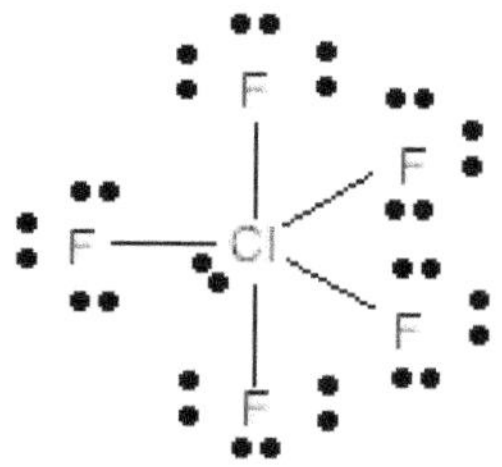

(c) MgI_2: This is an ionic compound between a metal and nonmetal.
Draw the Lewis structures for Mg and I based on their valence electrons. Mg: $3s^2$ I: $5s^25p^5$

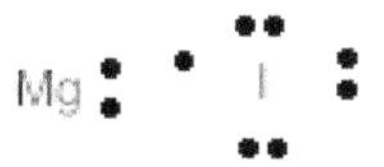

Magnesium must lose two electrons and be left with the octet from the previous shell, while iodine needs to gain one electron to get an octet.

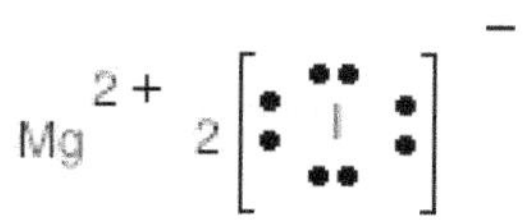

(d) XeO_4: This is a covalent compound between two nonmetals.
Write the correct skeletal structure for the molecule.

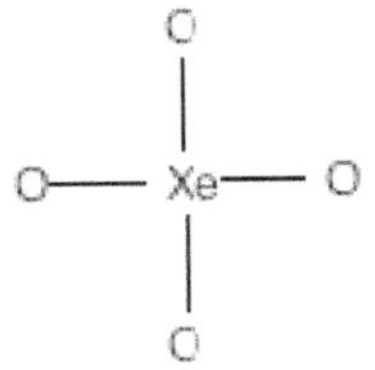

Calculate the total number of electrons for the Lewis structure by summing the valence electrons of each atom in the molecule.

(number of valence e^- for Xe) + 4(number of valence e^- for O) = 8 + 4(6) = 32

Distribute the electrons among the atoms, giving octets (or duets for H) to as many atoms as possible. Begin with the bonding electrons, then proceed to lone pairs on terminal atoms and finally to lone pairs on the central atom.

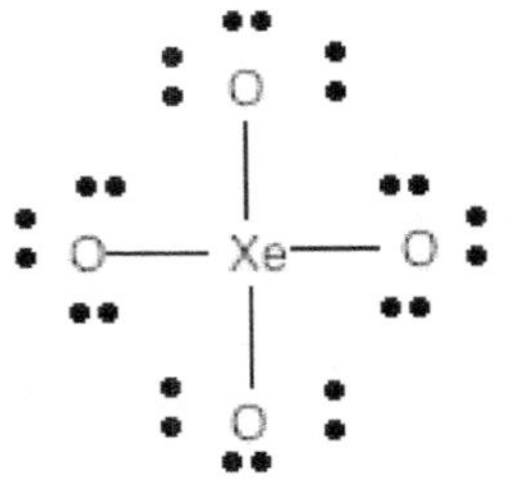

The structure as shown is an appropriate Lewis structure. However, this structure would leave a formal charge on Xe. It can be drawn with all double bonds which would eliminate all the formal charge.

9.83 (a) $BaCO_3$: Ba^{2+}

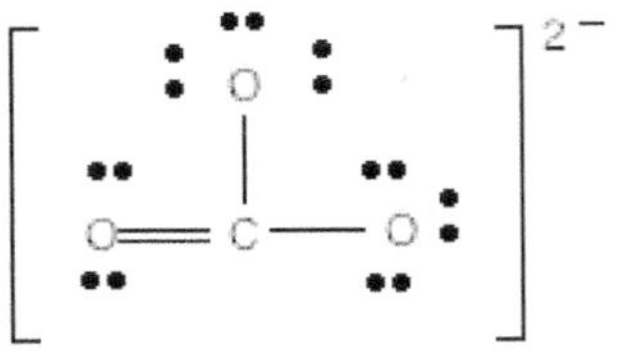

Determine the cation and anion.

Ba^{2+} CO_3^{2-}

Write the Lewis structure for the barium cation based on the valence electrons.

Ba $5s^2$ Ba^{2+} $5s^0$

Ba must lose two electrons and be left with the octet from the previous shell.
Write the Lewis structure for the covalent anion.
Write the correct skeletal structure for the ion.

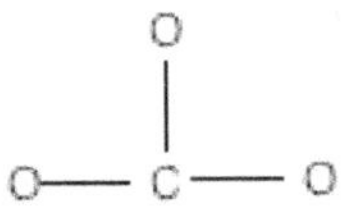

Calculate the total number of electrons for the Lewis structure by summing the number of valence electrons of each atom in the ion and adding two for the 2 – charge.

(number of valence e^- for C) + 3(number of valence e^- for O) = 4 + 3(6) + 2 = 24

Distribute the electrons among the atoms, giving octets to as many atoms as possible. Begin with the bonding electrons, then proceed to lone pairs on terminal atoms and finally to lone pairs on the central atom.

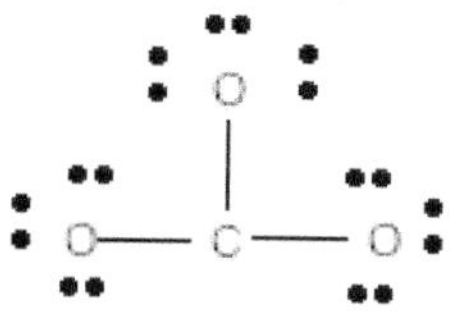

If any atom lacks an octet, form double or triple bonds as necessary.

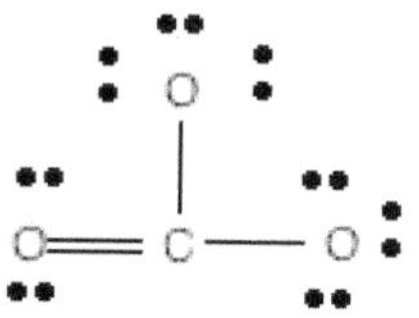

Lastly, write the Lewis structure in brackets with the charge of the ion in the upper right-hand corner.

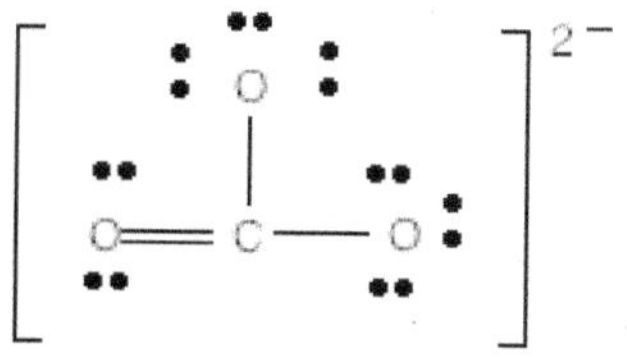

The double bond can be between the C and any of the oxygen atoms, so there are resonance structures.

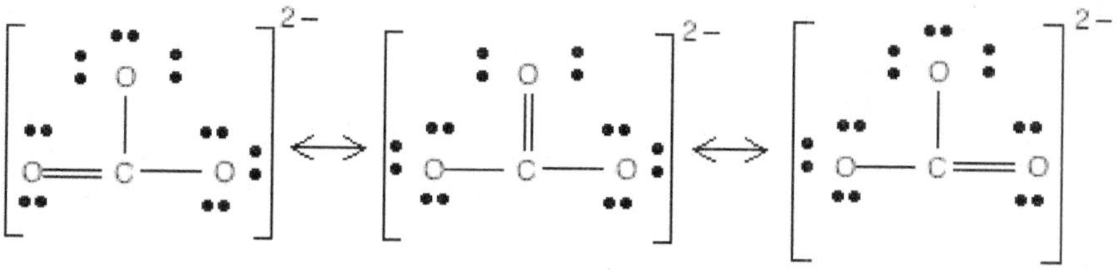

(b) $Ca(OH)_2$: Ca^{2+}

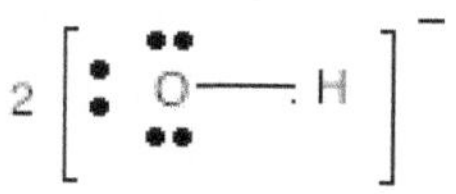

Determine the cation and anion.

Ca^{2+} OH^-

Write the Lewis structure for the calcium cation based on the valence electrons.

Ca $4s^2$ Ca^{2+} $4s^0$

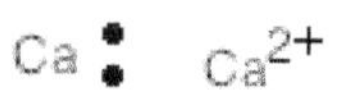

Ca must lose two electrons and be left with the octet from the previous shell.
Write the Lewis structure for the covalent anion.
Write the correct skeletal structure for the ion.

Calculate the total number of electrons for the Lewis structure by summing the valence electrons of each atom in the ion and adding one for the 1 – charge.

(number of valence e^- for H) + (number of valence e^- for O) +1 = 1 + 6 +1 = 8

Distribute the electrons among the atoms, giving octets (or duets for H) to as many atoms as possible. Begin with the bonding electrons, and then proceed to lone pairs on terminal atoms and finally to lone pairs of the central atom.

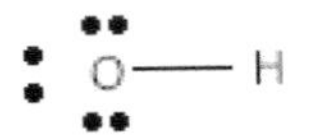

Lastly, write the Lewis structure in brackets with the charge of the ion in the upper right-hand corner.

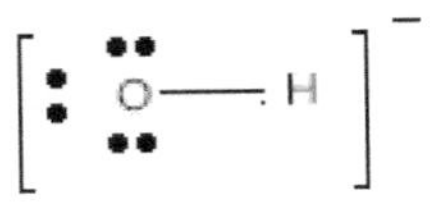

(c) KNO_3: K^+

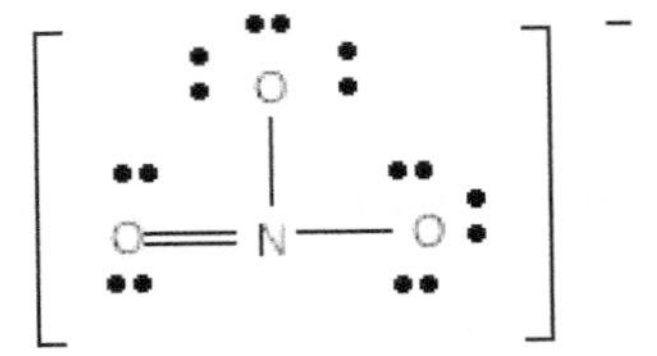

Determine the cation and anion.

K^+ NO_3^-

Write the Lewis structure for the potassium cation based on the valence electrons.

K $4s^1$ K^+ $4s^0$

K• K^+

K must lose one electron and be left with the octet from the previous shell.

Write the Lewis structure for the covalent anion.

Write the correct skeletal structure for the ion.

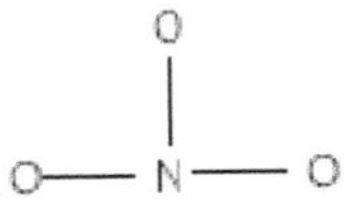

Calculate the total number of electrons for the Lewis structure by summing the valence electrons of each atom in the ion and adding one for the 1 – charge.

(number of valence e^- for N) + (number of valence e^- for O) = 5 + 3(6) +1 = 24

Distribute the electrons among the atoms, giving octets to as many atoms as possible. Begin with the bonding electrons, then proceed to lone pairs on terminal atoms and finally to lone pairs on the central atom.

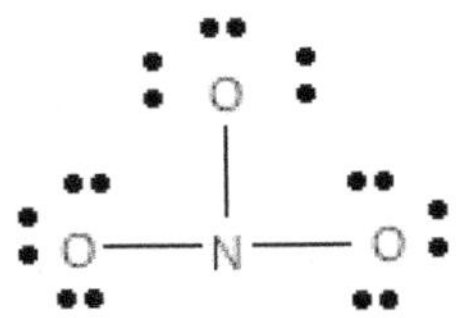

If any atom lacks an octet, form double or triple bonds as necessary.

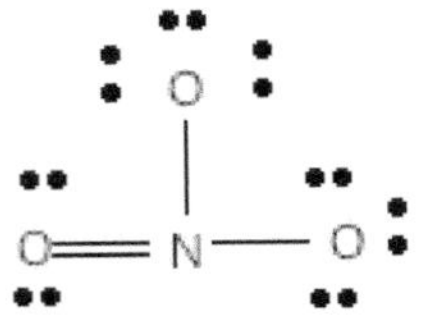

Lastly, write the Lewis structure in brackets with the charge of the ion in the upper right-hand corner.

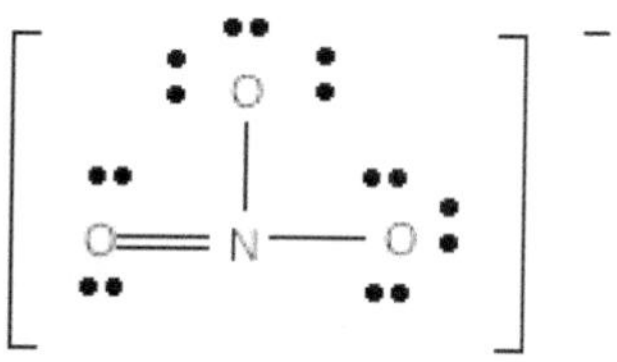

The double bond can be between the N and any of the oxygen atoms, so there are resonance structures.

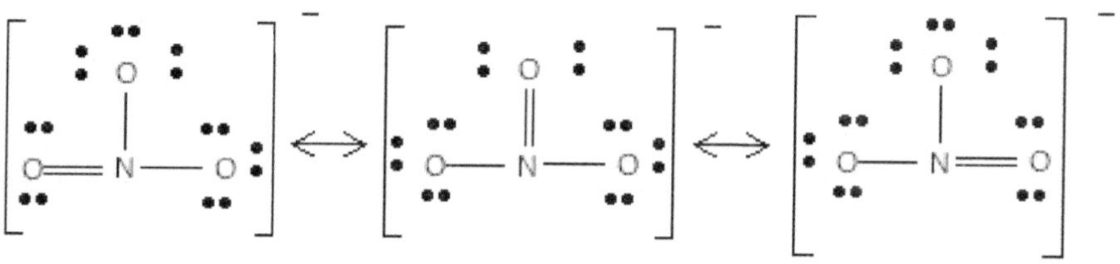

(d) LiIO: Li^+

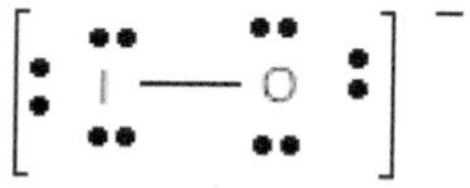

Determine the cation and anion.

Li^+ IO^-

Write the Lewis structure for the lithium cation based on the valence electrons.

Li $2s^1$ Li^+ $2s^0$

Li• Li^+

Li must lose one electron and be left with the octet from the previous shell.
Write the Lewis structure for the covalent anion.
Write the correct skeletal structure for the ion.

Calculate the total number of electron for the Lewis structure by summing the number of valence electrons of each atom in the ion and adding one for the 1 – charge.

(number of valence e^- for I) + (number of valence e^- for O) = 7 +6 + 1 = 14

Distribute the electrons among the atoms, giving octets to as many atoms as possible. Begin with the bonding electrons, then proceed to lone pairs on terminal atoms and finally to lone pairs on the central atom.

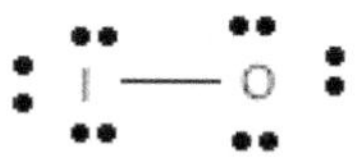

Lastly, write the Lewis structure in brackets with the charge of the ion in the upper right-hand corner.

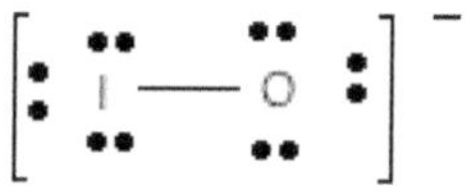

9.84 (a) $RbIO_2$: Rb^+

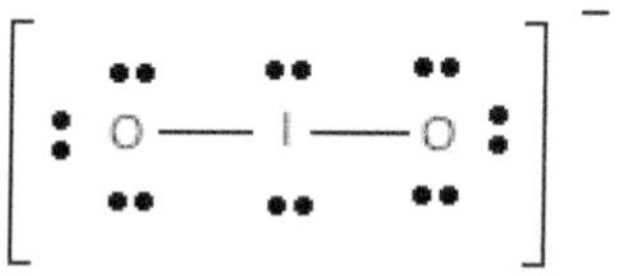

Determine the cation and anion.

Rb^+ IO_2^-

Write the Lewis structure for the Rubidium cation based on the valence electrons.

Rb $5s^1$ Rb^+ $5s^0$

Rb• Rb^+

Rb must lose one electron and be left with the octet from the previous shell.

Write the Lewis structure for the covalent anion.

Write the correct skeletal structure for the ion.

Calculate the total number of electrons for the Lewis structure by summing the valence electrons of each atom in the ion and adding one for the 1 – charge.

(number of valence e^- for I) +2 (number of valence e^- for O) = 7 + 2(6) +1 = 20

Distribute the electrons among the atoms, giving octets to as many atoms as possible. Begin with the bonding electrons, then proceed to lone pairs on terminal atoms and finally to lone pairs on the central atom.

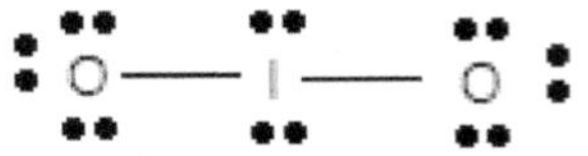

Then form double bond to eliminate formal charge on I.

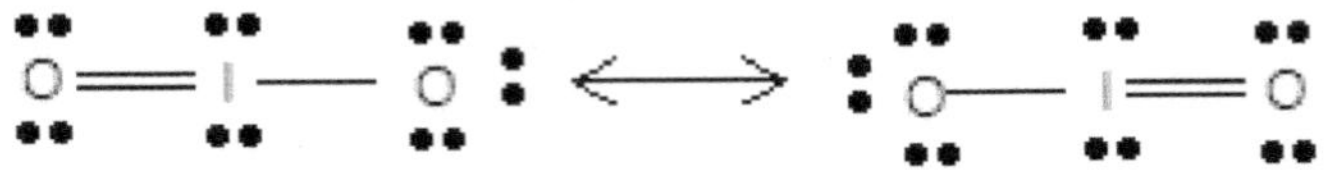

Lastly, write the Lewis structure in brackets with the charge of the ion in the upper right-hand corner.

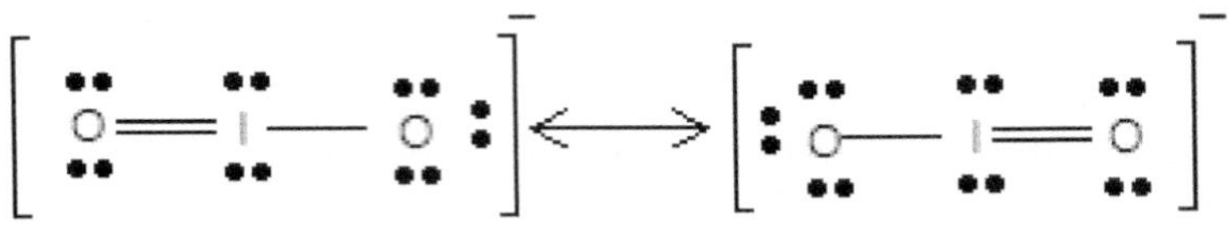

(b) NH_4Cl:

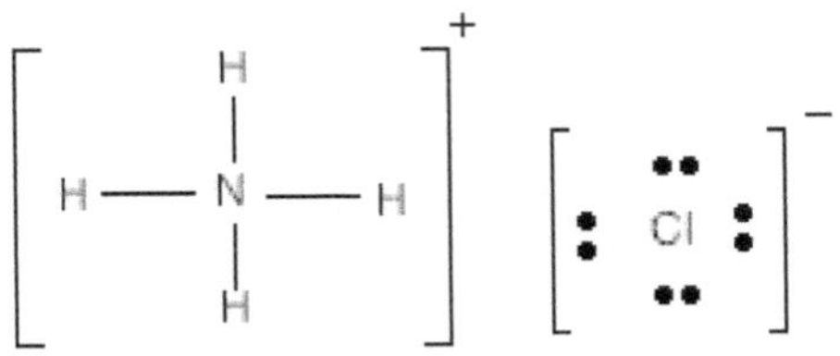

Determine the cation and anion.

NH_4^+ Cl^-

Write the Lewis structure for the covalent cation.

Write the correct skeletal structure for the ion.

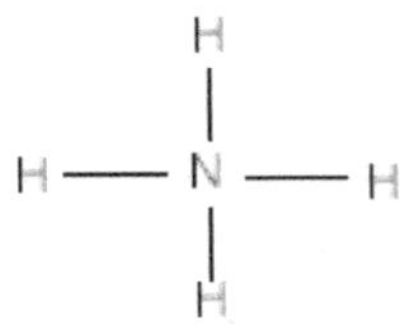

Calculate the total number of electrons for the Lewis structure by summing the number of valence electrons of each atom in the ion and subtracting one for the 1 + charge.

(number of valence e^- for N) + 4(number of valence e^- for H) – 1 = 5 + 4(1) – 1 = 8

Lastly, write the Lewis structure in brackets with the charge of the ion in the upper right-hand corner.

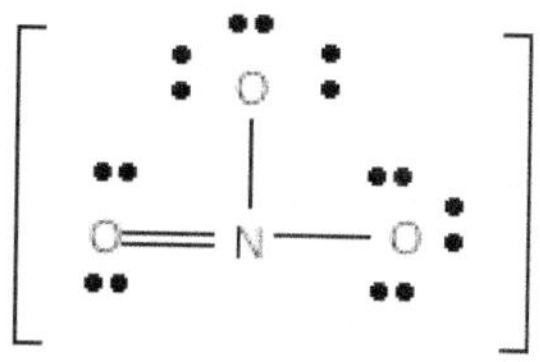

The double bond can be between the N and any of the oxygen atoms, so there are resonance structures.

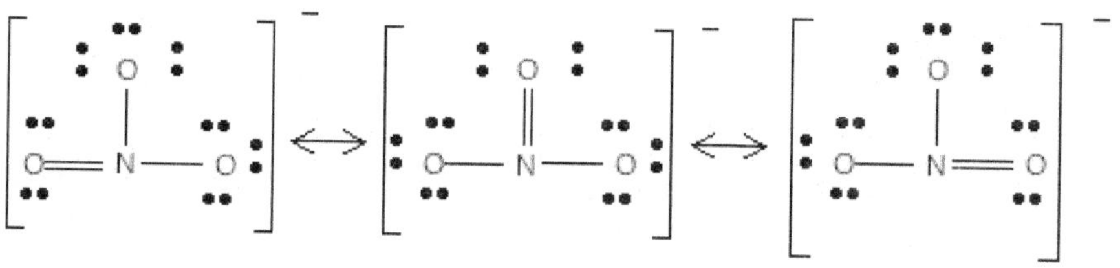

(d) LiIO: Li^+

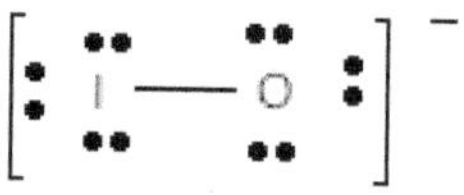

Determine the cation and anion.

Li^+ IO^-

Write the Lewis structure for the lithium cation based on the valence electrons.

Li $2s^1$ Li^+ $2s^0$

Li• Li^+

Li must lose one electron and be left with the octet from the previous shell.
Write the Lewis structure for the covalent anion.
Write the correct skeletal structure for the ion.

Calculate the total number of electron for the Lewis structure by summing the number of valence electrons of each atom in the ion and adding one for the 1 – charge.

(number of valence e^- for I) + (number of valence e^- for O) = 7 +6 + 1 = 14

Distribute the electrons among the atoms, giving octets to as many atoms as possible. Begin with the bonding electrons, then proceed to lone pairs on terminal atoms and finally to lone pairs on the central atom.

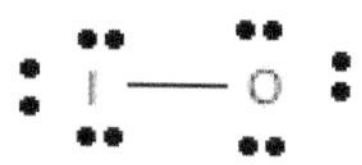

Lastly, write the Lewis structure in brackets with the charge of the ion in the upper right-hand corner.

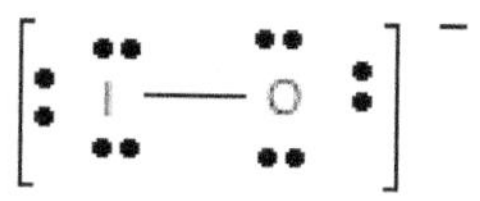

9.84 (a) $RbIO_2$: Rb^+

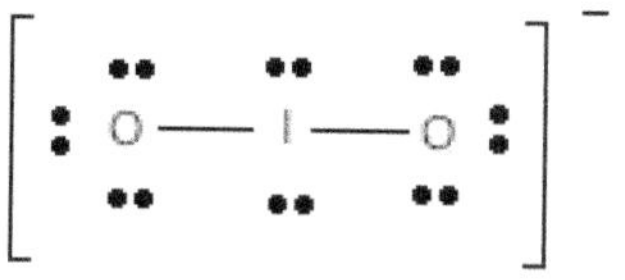

Determine the cation and anion.

Rb^+ IO_2^-

Write the Lewis structure for the Rubidium cation based on the valence electrons.

Rb $5s^1$ Rb^+ $5s^0$

Rb• Rb^+

Rb must lose one electron and be left with the octet from the previous shell.

Write the Lewis structure for the covalent anion.

Write the correct skeletal structure for the ion.

Calculate the total number of electrons for the Lewis structure by summing the valence electrons of each atom in the ion and adding one for the 1 – charge.

(number of valence e^- for I) +2 (number of valence e^- for O) = 7 + 2(6) +1 = 20

Distribute the electrons among the atoms, giving octets to as many atoms as possible. Begin with the bonding electrons, then proceed to lone pairs on terminal atoms and finally to lone pairs on the central atom.

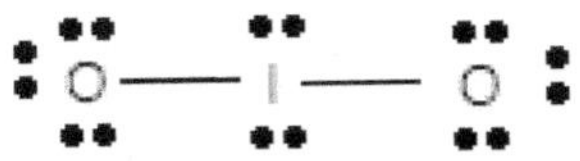

Then form double bond to eliminate formal charge on I.

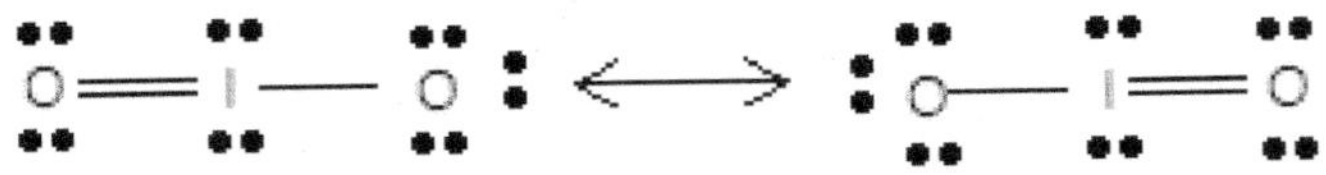

Lastly, write the Lewis structure in brackets with the charge of the ion in the upper right-hand corner.

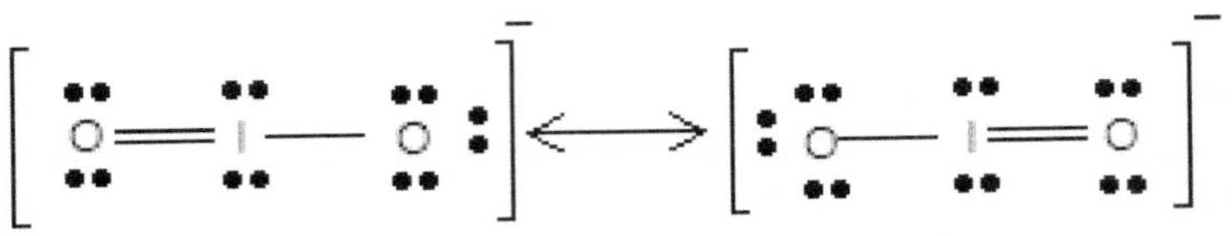

(b) NH_4Cl:

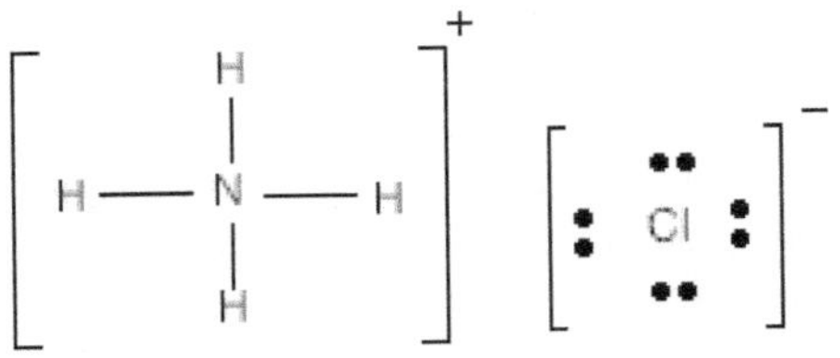

Determine the cation and anion.

NH_4^+ Cl^-

Write the Lewis structure for the covalent cation.

Write the correct skeletal structure for the ion.

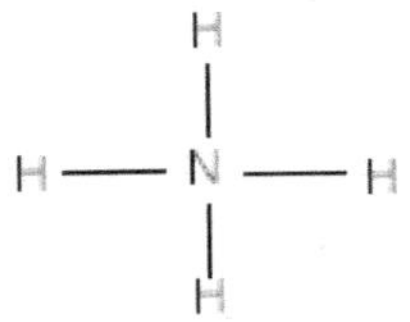

Calculate the total number of electrons for the Lewis structure by summing the number of valence electrons of each atom in the ion and subtracting one for the 1 + charge.

(number of valence e^- for N) + 4(number of valence e^- for H) – 1 = 5 + 4(1) – 1 = 8

Distribute the electrons among the atoms, giving octets (or duets for H) to as many atoms as possible. Begin with the bonding electrons, then proceed to lone pairs on terminal atoms and finally to lone pairs on the central atom.

$$
\begin{array}{c}
\text{H} \\
| \\
\text{H} \!-\! \text{N} \!-\! \text{H} \\
| \\
\text{H}
\end{array}
$$

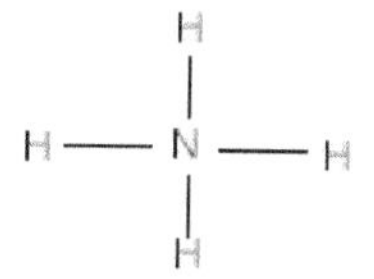

Lastly, write the Lewis structure in brackets with the charge of the ion in the upper right-hand corner.

$$
\left[
\begin{array}{c}
\text{H} \\
| \\
\text{H} \!-\! \text{N} \!-\! \text{H} \\
| \\
\text{H}
\end{array}
\right]^{+}
$$

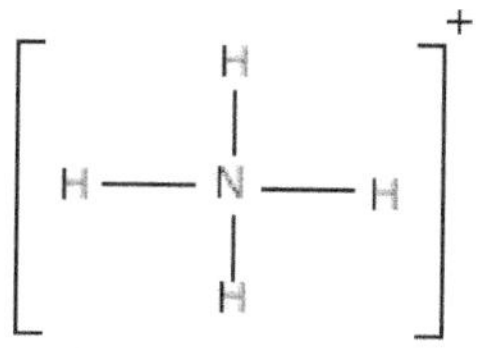

Write the Lewis structure for the chlorine anion based on the valence electrons.
Cl $3s^2 3p^5$

$$\cdot \; \overset{\bullet\bullet}{\underset{\bullet\bullet}{\text{Cl}}} \overset{}{\vphantom{|}} {}_{\bullet}^{\bullet}$$

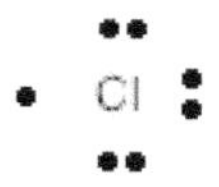

Cl must gain one electron to complete its octet.

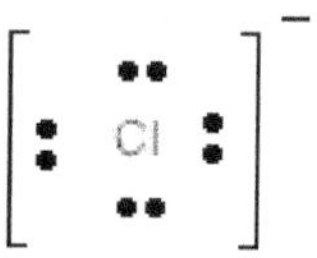

$$
\left[
\; {}_{\bullet}^{\bullet}\; \overset{\bullet\bullet}{\underset{\bullet\bullet}{\text{Cl}}} \; {}_{\bullet}^{\bullet} \;
\right]^{-}
$$

(c)   KOH: K^+

$$
\left[
\; {}_{\bullet}^{\bullet}\; \overset{\bullet\bullet}{\underset{\bullet\bullet}{\text{O}}} \!-\! \text{H} \;
\right]^{-}
$$

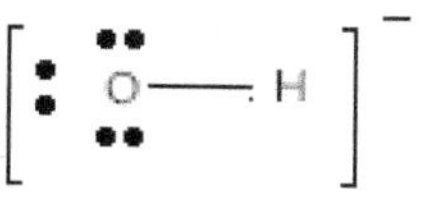

Determine the cation and anion.
      K^+ OH^-
Write the Lewis structure for the potassium cation based on the valence electrons.
      K $4s^1$ K^+ $4s^0$

      K $\bullet$ K^+

K must lose one electron and be left with the octet from the previous shell.
Write the Lewis structure for the covalent anion.
Write the correct skeletal structure for the ion.

$$\text{O} \!-\! \text{H}$$

Calculate the total number of electrons for the Lewis structure by summing the valence electrons of each atom in the ion and adding one for the 1 – charge.
      (number of valence e^- for H) + (number of valence e^- for O) +1 = 1 + 6 +1 = 8
Distribute the electrons among the atoms, giving octets (or duets for H) to as many atoms as possible. Begin with the bonding electrons, then proceed to lone pairs on terminal atoms and finally to lone pairs on the central atom.

$$\; {}_{\bullet}^{\bullet}\; \overset{\bullet\bullet}{\underset{\bullet\bullet}{\text{O}}} \!-\! \text{H}$$

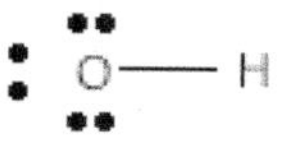

Lastly, write the Lewis structure in brackets with the charge of the ion in the upper right-hand corner.

$$\left[: \overset{\bullet\bullet}{\underset{\bullet\bullet}{O}} \text{---} H \right]^{-}$$

(d) $Sr(CN)_2$: Sr^{2+}

$$\left[: C \equiv N : \right]^{-}$$

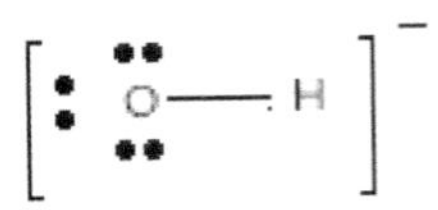

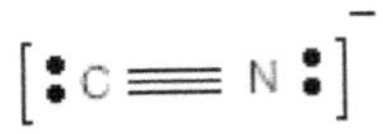

Determine the cation and anion.

Sr^{2+} CN^{-}

Write the Lewis structure for the strontium cation based on the valence electrons.

Sr $5s^2$ Sr^{2+} $5s^0$

$\bullet Sr \bullet$ Sr^{2+}

Sr must lose two electrons and be left with the octet from the previous shell.

Write the Lewis structure for the covalent anion.

Write the correct skeletal structure for the ion.

$$C \text{---} N$$

Calculate the total number of electrons for the Lewis structure by summing the valence electrons of each atom in the ion and adding one for the 1 – charge.

(number of valence e⁻ for N) + (number of valence e⁻ for C) = 5 + 4 + 1 = 10

Distribute the electrons among the atoms, giving octets to as many atoms as possible. Begin with the bonding electrons, then proceed to lone pairs on terminal atoms and finally to lone pairs on the central atom.

$$: C \text{---} \overset{\bullet\bullet}{\underset{\bullet\bullet}{N}} :$$

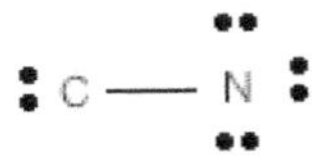

Complete octets on both atoms by forming a triple bond.

$$: C \equiv N :$$

Lastly, write the Lewis structure in brackets with the charge of the ion in the upper right-hand corner.

$$\left[: C \equiv N : \right]^{-}$$

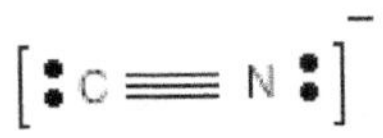

9.85   (a) C_4H_8: Write the correct skeletal structure for the molecule.

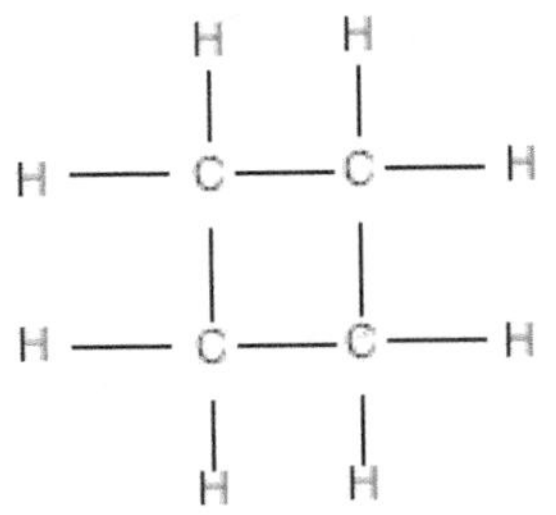

$$
\begin{array}{ccc}
 & H & H \\
 & | & | \\
H \text{---} & C \text{---} C & \text{---} H \\
 & | & | \\
H \text{---} & C \text{---} C & \text{---} H \\
 & | & | \\
 & H & H
\end{array}
$$

Calculate the total number of electrons for the Lewis structure by summing the number of valence electrons of each atom in the molecule.

4 (number of valence e⁻ for C) + 8(number of valence e⁻ for H) = 4(4) + 8(1) = 24

Distribute the electrons among the atoms, giving octets (or duets for H) to as many atoms as possible.

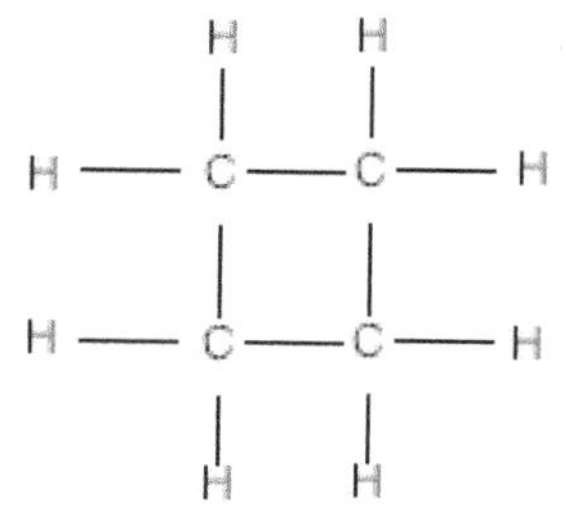

All atoms have octets or duets for H.

(b) C_4H_4: Write the correct skeletal structure for the molecule.

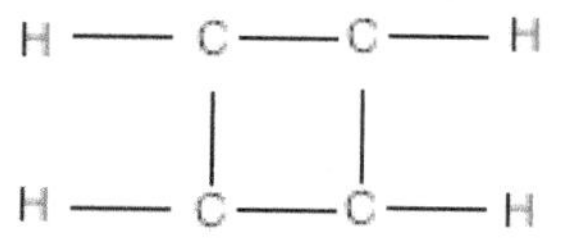

Calculate the total number of electrons for the Lewis structure by summing the number of valence electrons of each atom in the molecule.

$$4\text{ (number of valence e}^-\text{ for C)} + 4\text{(number of valence e}^-\text{ for H)} = 4(4) + 4(1) = 20$$

Distribute the electrons among the atoms, giving octets (or duets for H) to as many atoms as possible.

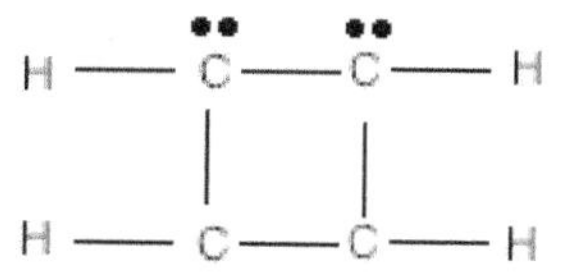

Complete octets by forming double bonds on alternating carbons; draw resonance structures.

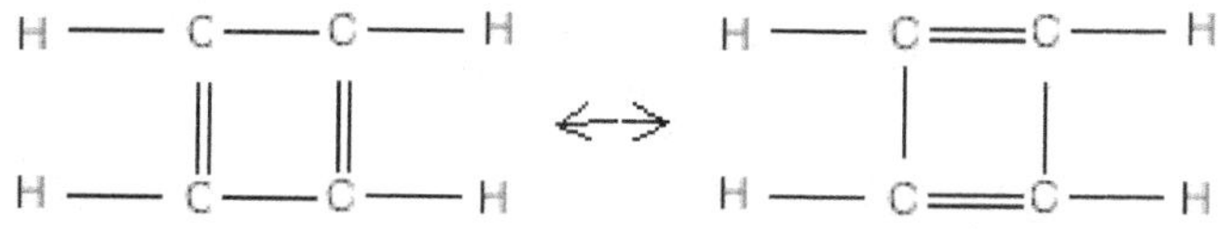

(c) C_6H_{12}: Write the correct skeletal structure for the molecule.

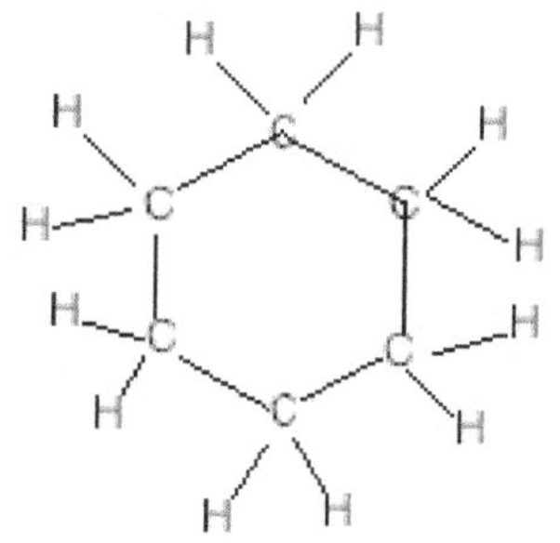

Calculate the total number of electrons for the Lewis structure by summing the valence electrons of each atom in the molecule.

$$6\text{ (number of valence e}^-\text{ for C)} + 12\text{(number of valence e}^-\text{ for H)} = 6(4) + 12(1) = 36$$

Distribute the electrons among the atoms, giving octets (or duets for H) to as many atoms as possible. Begin with the bonding.

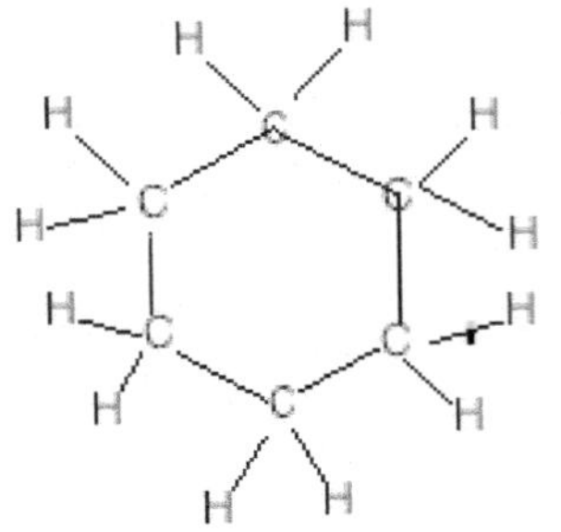

All 36 electrons are used and all atoms have octets or duets for H.

(d) C_6H_6: Write the correct skeletal structure for the molecule.

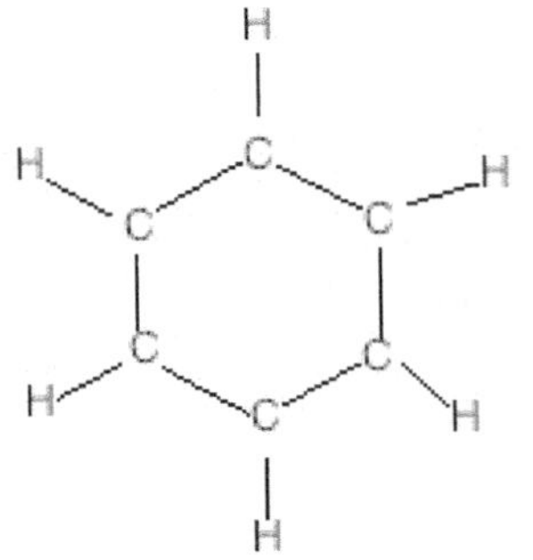

Calculate the total number of electrons for the Lewis structure by summing the number of valence electrons of each atom in the molecule.

6 (number of valence e^- for C) + 6(number of valence e^- for H) = 6(4) + 6(1) = 30

Distribute the electrons among the atoms, giving octets (or duets for H) to as many atoms as possible.

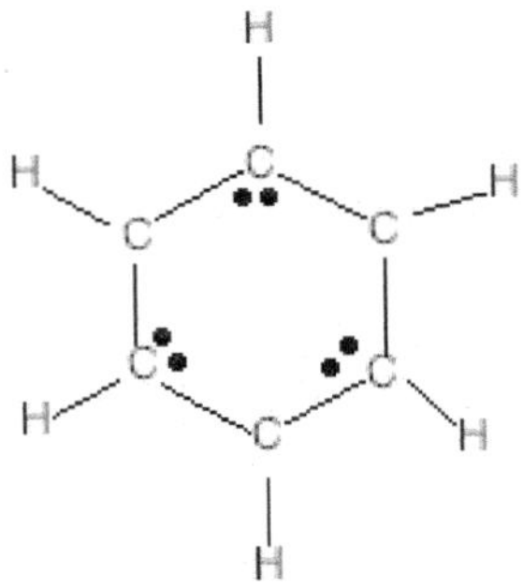

Complete octets by forming double bonds on alternating carbons; draw resonance structures.

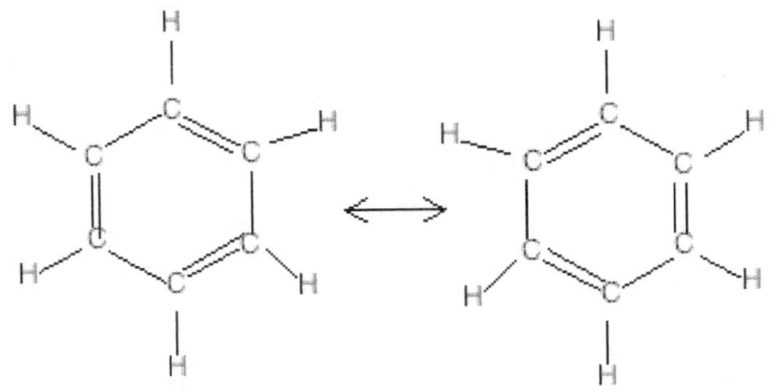

9.86 H_2NCH_2COOH

Write the correct skeletal structure for the molecule.

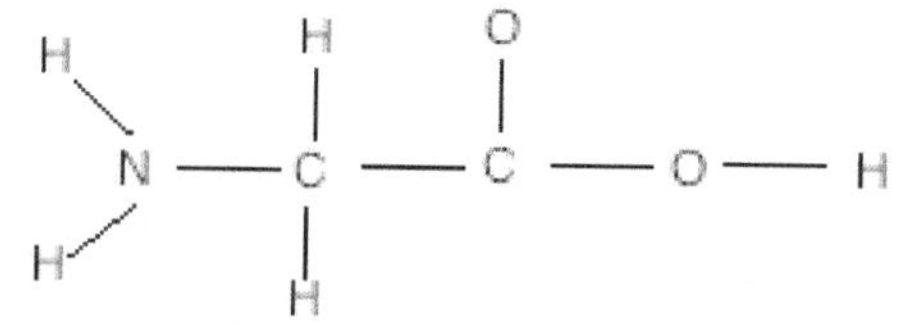

Calculate the total number of electrons for the Lewis structure by summing the number of valence electrons of each atom in the molecule.

2 (number of valence e^- for C) + 2(number of valence e^- for O) + (number of valence e^- for N) + 5(number of valence e^- for H) = 2(4) + 2(6) + 5 + 5(1) = 30

Distribute the electrons among the atoms, giving octets (or duets for H) to as many atoms as possible. Begin with the bonding electrons, and then proceed to lone pairs on terminal atoms and finally to lone pairs on the central atoms.

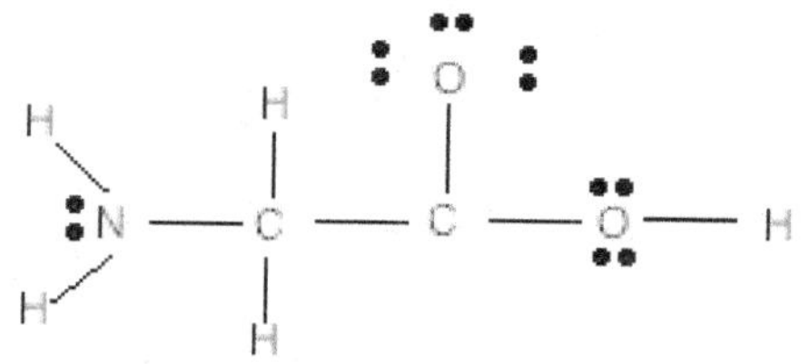

All 30 electrons are used.

Draw a double bond to satisfy the octet on C.

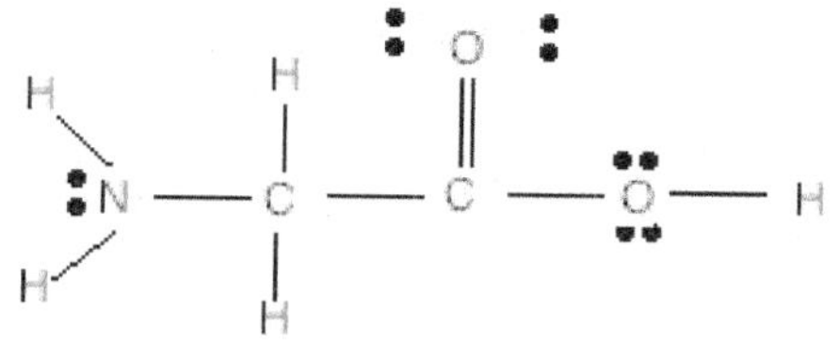

9.87 **Given:** 26.01% C; 4.38 % H; 69.52 % O; molar mass = 46.02 g/mol

Find: molecular formula and Lewis structure

Conceptual Plan: convert mass to mol of each element → pseudoformula → empirical formula

$\frac{1 \text{ mol C}}{12.01 \text{ g C}}$ $\frac{1 \text{ mol H}}{1.008 \text{ g H}}$ $\frac{1 \text{ mol O}}{16.00 \text{ g O}}$ divide by smallest number

→ molecular formula → Lewis structure

empirical formula x n

Solution:

$$26.01 \text{ g C} \times \frac{1 \text{ mol C}}{12.01 \text{ g C}} = 2.166 \text{ mol C}$$

$$4.38 \text{ g H} \times \frac{1 \text{ mol H}}{1.008 \text{ g H}} = 4.3\underline{4}5 \text{ mol H}$$

$$69.52 \text{ g O} \times \frac{1 \text{ mol O}}{16.00 \text{ g O}} = 4.345 \text{ mol O}$$

$$C_{2.166}H_{4.345}O_{4.345}$$

$$C_{\frac{2.166}{2.166}}H_{\frac{4.345}{2.166}}O_{\frac{4.345}{2.166}} \rightarrow CH_2O_2$$

The correct empirical formula is CH_2O_2.

empirical formula mass = (12.01 g/mol) + 2(1.008 g/mol) + 2(16.00 g/mol) = 46.03 g/mol

$$n = \frac{\text{molar mass}}{\text{formula molar mass}} = \frac{46.02 \text{ g/mol}}{46.03 \text{ g/mol}} = 1$$

molecular formula $= CH_2O_2 \times 1$

$= CH_2O_2$

Write the correct skeletal structure for the molecule.

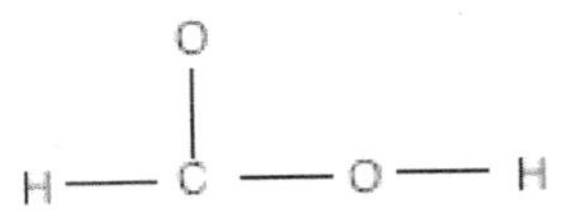

Calculate the total number of electrons for the Lewis structure by summing the number of valence electrons of each atom in the molecule.

(number of valence e^- for C) + 2(number of valence e^- for O) + 2(number of valence e^- for H) = 4 + 2(6) + 2(1) = 18

Distribute the electrons among the atoms, giving octets (or duets for H) to as many atoms as possible. Begin with the bonding electrons, and then proceed to lone pairs on terminal atoms and finally to lone pairs on the central atoms.

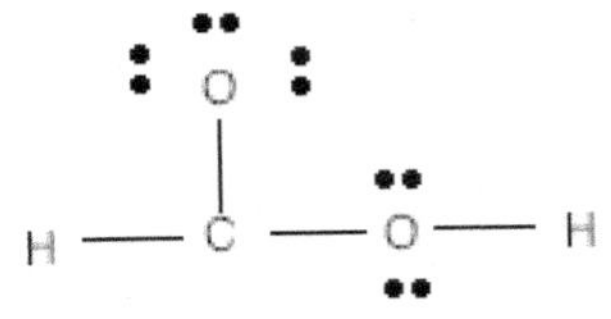

Complete the octet on C by forming a double bond.

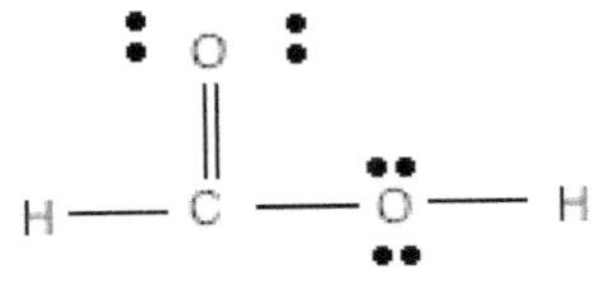

9.88 **Given:** 28.57% C; 4.80 % H; 66.64 % N; molar mass = 42.04 g/mol

Find: molecular formula and Lewis structure

Conceptual Plan: convert mass to mol of each element → pseudoformula → empirical formula

$\frac{1\text{ mol C}}{12.01\text{ g C}}\ \frac{1\text{ mol H}}{1.008\text{ g H}}\ \frac{1\text{ mol N}}{14.00\text{ g N}}$ divide by smallest number

→ molecular formula → Lewis structure

empirical formula x n

Solution:

$$28.57\ \cancel{\text{g C}} \times \frac{1\text{ mol C}}{12.01\ \cancel{\text{g C}}} = 2.380\text{ mol C}$$

$$4.80\ \cancel{\text{g H}} \times \frac{1\text{ mol H}}{1.008\ \cancel{\text{g H}}} = 4.7\underline{6}2\text{ mol H}$$

$$66.64\ \cancel{\text{g N}} \times \frac{1\text{ mol N}}{14.00\ \cancel{\text{g N}}} = 4.760\text{ mol N}$$

$$C_{2.380}H_{4.762}N_{4.762}$$

$$C_{\frac{2.380}{2.380}}H_{\frac{4.762}{2.380}}N_{\frac{4.762}{2.380}} \rightarrow CH_2N_2$$

The correct empirical formula is CH_2N_2.

empirical formula mass = (12.01 g/mol) + 2(1.008 g/mol) + 2(14.00 g/mol) = 42.03 g/mol

$$n = \frac{\text{molar mass}}{\text{formula molar mass}} = \frac{42.04\text{ g/mol}}{42.03\text{ g/mol}} = 1$$

molecular formula $= CH_2N_2 \times 1 = CH_2N_2$

Write the correct skeletal structure for the molecule.

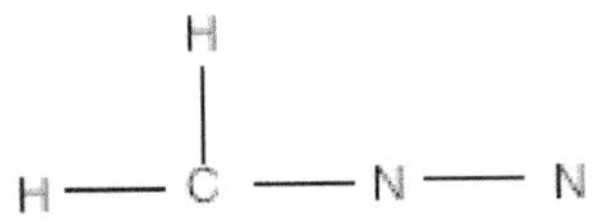

Calculate the total number of electrons for the Lewis structure by summing the number of valence electrons of each atom in the molecule.

(number of valence e^- for C) + 2(number of valence e^- for N) + 2(number of valence e^- for H) = 4 + 2(5) + 2(1) = 16

Distribute the electrons among the atoms, giving octets (or duets for H) to as many atoms as possible. Begin with the bonding electrons, and then proceed to lone pairs on terminal atoms and finally to lone pairs on the central atoms.

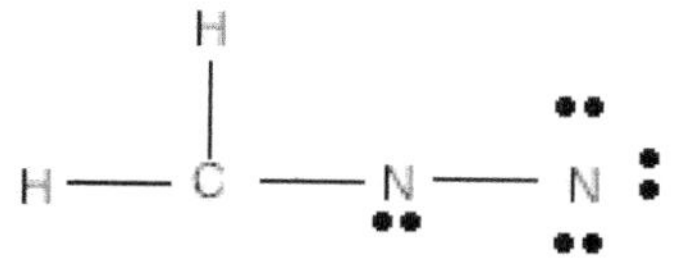

Complete the octet on C and N by forming double bond.

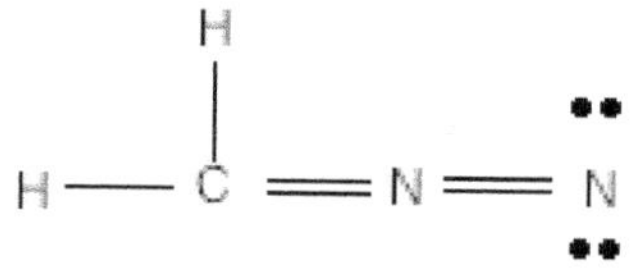

Calculate the formal charge on each atom in the structure by finding the number of valence electrons and subtracting the number of lone pair electrons and one-half the number of bonding electrons.

	H_{left}	H_{top}	C	N_{left}	N_{right}
number of valence electron	1	1	4	5	5
- number of lone pair electrons	0	0	0	0	4
- 1/2(number of bonding electrons)	1	1	4	4	2
Formal charge	0	0	0	+1	-1

The diazomethane molecule has nitrogen atoms next to each other with a +1 and a – 1 charge. Nitrogen is more electronegative than C, which has a 0 formal charge. The nitrogen with the +1 charge is not a very stable configuration for nitrogen, particularly next to the 0 formal charge C atom.

9.89 To determine the values of the lattice energy, it is necessary to look them up online. The lattice energy of Al_2O_3 is –15,916 kJ/mol, the value for Fe_2O_3 is - 14,774 kJ/mol. The thermite reaction is exothermic due to the energy released when the Al_2O_3 lattice forms. The lattice energy of Al_2O_3 is more negative than the lattice energy of Fe_2O_3.

9.90 For NaCl, E is proportional to (1+)(1–) = –1. While for XY, E is proportional to (3+)(3–) = –9. So, the relative stabilization for XY relative to NaCl should be roughly nine times greater. $\Delta H_{lattice}$ (XY) = 9 x $\Delta H_{lattice}$ (NaCl) = 9(–787kJ/mol) = –7083kJ/mol.

9.91 HNO_3 Write the correct skeletal structure for the molecule.

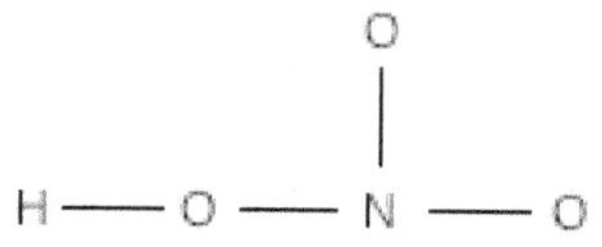

Calculate the total number of electrons for the Lewis structure by summing the number of valence electrons of each atom in the molecule.

3(number of valence e^- for O) + (number of valence e^- for N) + (number of valence e^- for H) = 3(6) + 5 +1 = 24

Distribute the electrons among the atoms, giving octets (or duets for H) to as many atoms as possible. Begin with the bonding electrons, then proceed to lone pairs on terminal atoms and finally to lone pairs on the central atom.

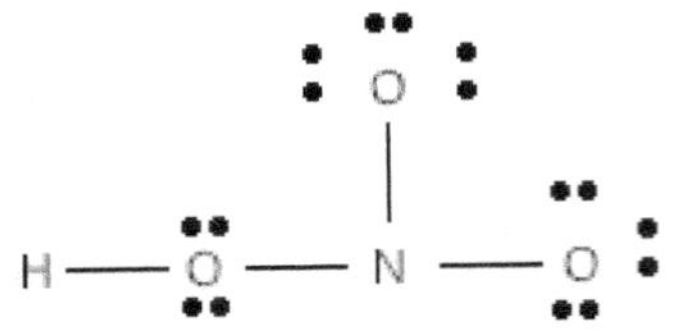

All 24 valence electrons are used.
If any atoms lack an octet, form double or triple bonds as necessary. The double bond can be formed to any of the three oxygen atoms, so there are three resonance forms.

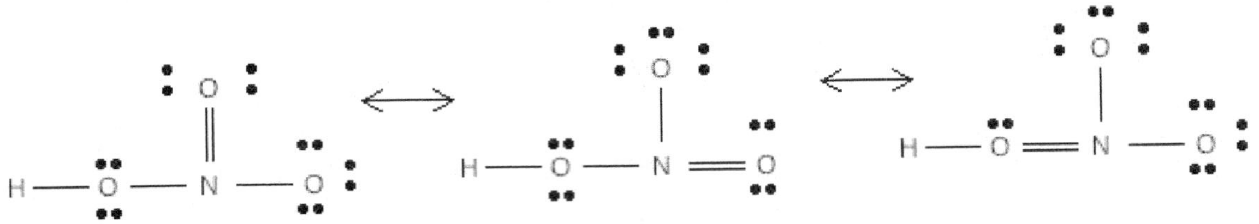

I II III

All atoms have octets (duets for H); the structure is complete.
To determine which resonance hybrid(s) is most important, calculate the formal charge on each atom in each structure by finding the number of valence electrons and subtracting the number of lone pair electrons and one-half the number of bonding electrons.

	Structure I					Structure II				
	O_{left}	O_{top}	O_{right}	N	H	O_{left}	O_{top}	O_{right}	N	H
number of valence electrons	6	6	6	5	1	6	6	6	5	1
- number of lone pair electrons	4	4	6	0	0	4	6	4	0	0
- 1/2(number of bonding electrons)	2	2	1	4	1	2	1	2	4	1
Formal charge	0	0	–1	+1	0	0	–1	0	+1	0

	Structure III				
	O_{left}	O_{top}	O_{right}	N	H
number of valence electrons	6	6	6	5	1
- number of lone pair electrons	2	6	6	0	0
- 1/2(number of bonding electrons)	3	1	1	4	1
Formal charge	+1	–1	–1	+1	0

The sum of the formal charges is 0 for each structure, which is the overall charge of the molecule. However, in structures I and II the individual formal charges are lower. These two forms would contribute equally to the structure of HNO_3. Structure III would be less important since the individual formal charges are higher.

9.92 Cl_2CO Write the correct skeletal structure for the molecule.

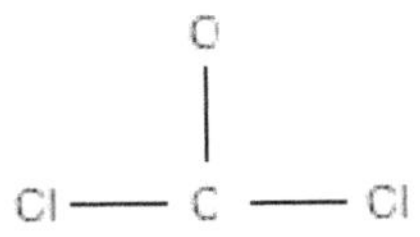

Calculate the total number of electrons for the Lewis structure by summing the number of valence electrons of each atom in the molecule.

1(number of valence e^- for O) + (number of valence e^- for C) + 2(number of valence e^- for Cl) = 6 + 4 + 2(7) = 24

Distribute the electrons among the atoms, giving octets to as many atoms as possible. Begin with the bonding electrons, then proceed to lone pairs on terminal atoms and finally to lone pairs on the central atom.

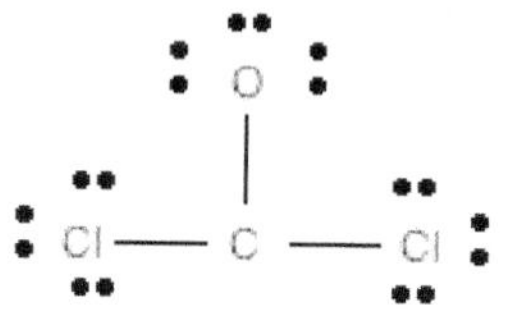

All 24 valence electrons are used.

If any atoms lack an octet, form double or triple bonds as necessary. The double bond can be formed to any of the three terminal atoms, so there are three resonance forms.

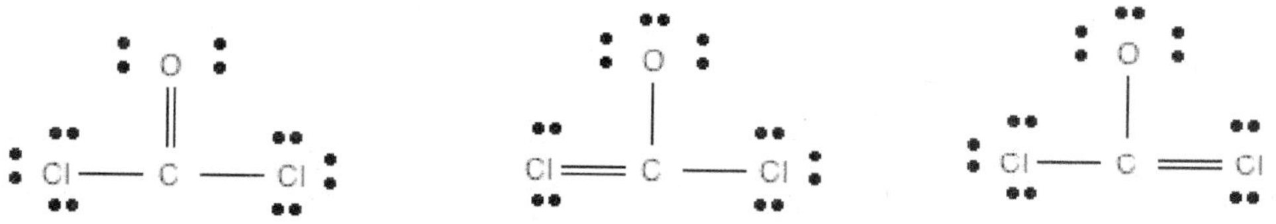

I II III

All atoms have octets; the structures are complete.

To determine which resonance hybrids(s) is most important, calculate the formal charge on each atom in each structure by finding the number of valence electrons and subtracting the number of lone pair electrons and one-half the number of bonding electrons.

	Structure I				Structure II			
	Cl_{left}	Cl_{right}	O	C	Cl_{left}	Cl_{right}	O	C
number of valence electrons	7	7	6	4	7	7	6	4
- number of lone pair electrons	6	6	4	0	4	6	6	0
- 1/2(number of bonding electrons)	1	1	2	4	2	1	1	4
Formal charge	0	0	0	0	+1	0	–1	0

	Structure III			
	Cl_{left}	Cl_{right}	O	C
number of valence electrons	7	7	6	4
- number of lone pair electrons	6	4	6	0
- 1/2(number of bonding electrons)	1	2	1	4
Formal charge	0	+1	–1	0

The sum of the formal charges is 0 for each structure, which is the overall charge of the molecule. However, in structure I the individual formal charges are lower and this form would be more important to Cl_2CO than to structure II and structure III.

9.93 CNO^- Write the skeletal structure:

C – N – O

Determine the number of valence electrons.

(valence e^- from C) + (valence e^- from N) + (valence e^- from O) +1(from the negative charge)

4 + 5 + 6 + 1 = 16

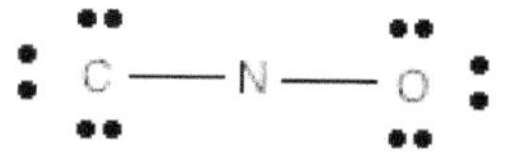

Distribute the electrons to complete octets if possible.

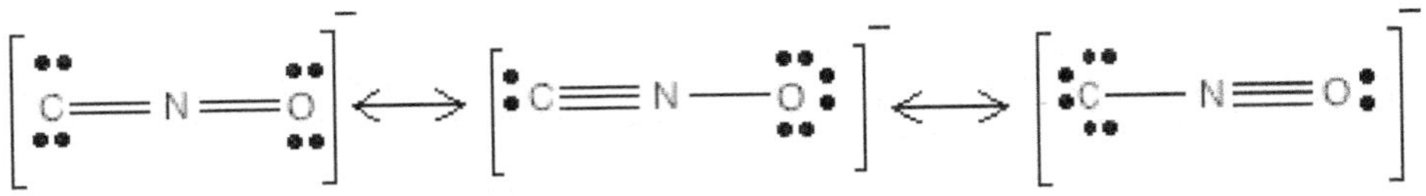

I II III

Determine the formal charge on each atom for each structure.

	Structure I			Structure II		
	C	N	O	C	N	O
number of valence electrons	4	5	6	4	5	6
- number of lone pair electrons	4	0	4	2	0	6
- 1/2(number of bonding electrons)	2	4	2	3	4	1
Formal charge	–2	+1	0	–1	+1	–1

	Structure III		
	C	N	O
number of valence electrons	4	5	6
- number of lone pair electrons	6	0	2
- 1/2(number of bonding electrons)	1	4	3
Formal charge	–3	+1	+1

Structures I, II, and III all follow the octet rule but have varying degrees of negative formal charge on carbon, which is the least electronegative atom. Also the amount of formal charge is very high in all three resonance forms. Although structure II is the best of the resonance forms, none of these resonance forms contribute strongly to the stability of the fulminate ion and the ion is not very stable.

9.94 The Lewis structures for the three ions will be similar. So, we can write the Lewis structure for one ion and use it to determine the other two.

Br_3^-: Write the correct skeletal structure for the ion.

Calculate the total number of electrons for the Lewis structure by summing the number of valence electrons of each atom in the ion and adding 1 for the 1 – charge.

3(number of valence e^- for Br) + 1 = 3(7) +1 = 22

Distribute the electrons among the atoms, giving octets to as many atoms as possible. Begin with the bonding electrons, and then proceed to lone pairs on terminal atoms and finally to lone pairs on the central atom. Assign electrons above 8 to the central atom.

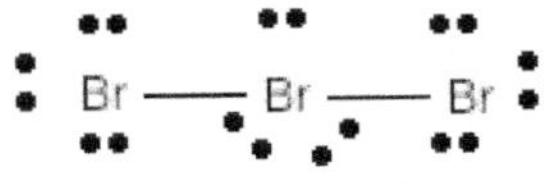

Lastly, place the ion in brackets and place the charge in the upper right-hand corner.

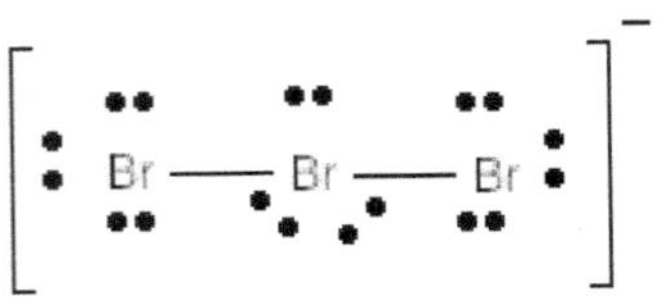

Since Br, I, and F are all in the same family, each of these ions would have 22 electrons and should have the same Lewis structure.

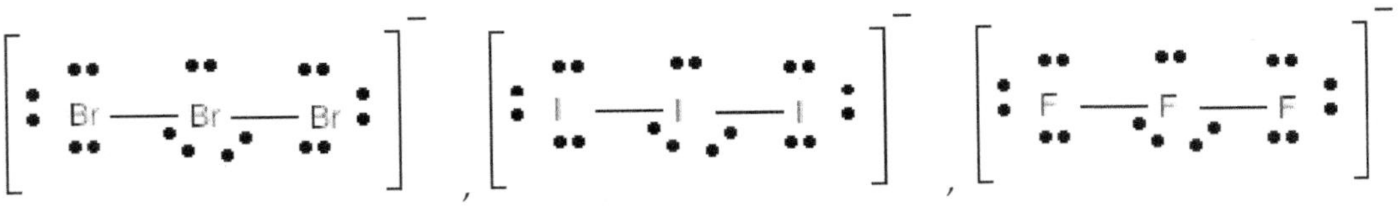

All three ions are written with 5 electron groups around the central atom. Bromine and iodine can accommodate 10 electrons around the central atom, fluorine cannot. Fluorine is in period 2 and can accommodate at most 8 electrons around the central atom because there are no orbitals low enough in energy to hybridize with the 2s and 2p orbitals. Therefore, F_3^- does not exist.

9.95 $HCSNH_2$: Write the correct skeletal structure for the molecule.

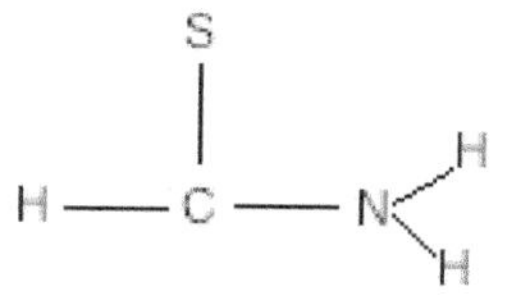

Calculate the total number of electrons for the Lewis structure by summing the number of valence electrons of each atom in the molecule.

(number of valence e^- for N) + (number of valence e^- for S) + (number of valence e^- for C) + 3(number of valence e^- for H) = 5 + 6 + 4 + 3(1) = 18

Distribute the electrons among the atoms, giving octets (or duets for H) to as many atoms as possible. Begin with the bonding electrons, and then proceed to lone pairs on terminal atoms and finally to lone pairs on the central atoms.

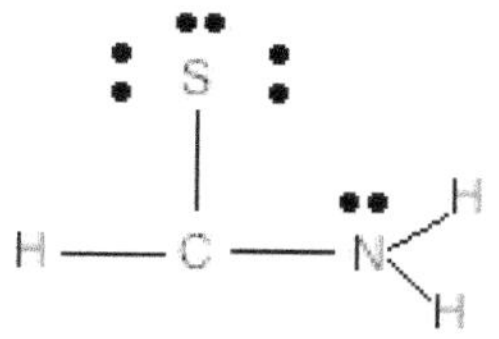

Complete the octet on C by forming a double bond.

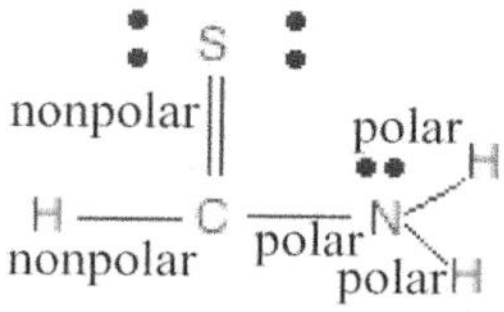

9.96 H_2NCONH_2 Write the correct skeletal structure for the molecule.

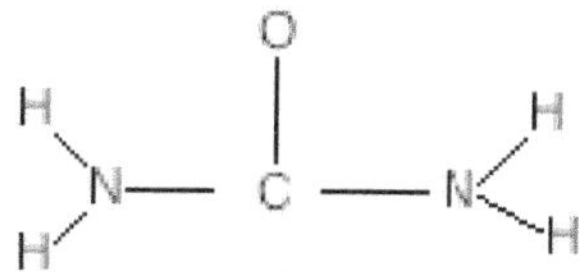

Calculate the total number of electrons for the Lewis structure by summing the number of valence electrons of each atom in the molecule.

2(number of valence e^- for N) + (number of valence e^- for O) + 4(number of valence e^- for H) + (number of valence e^- for C)

= 2(5) + 6 + 2(1) + 4 = 24

Distribute the electrons among the atoms, giving octets (or duets for H) to as many atoms as possible. Begin with the bonding electrons, and then proceed to lone pairs on terminal atoms and finally to lone pairs on the central atoms.

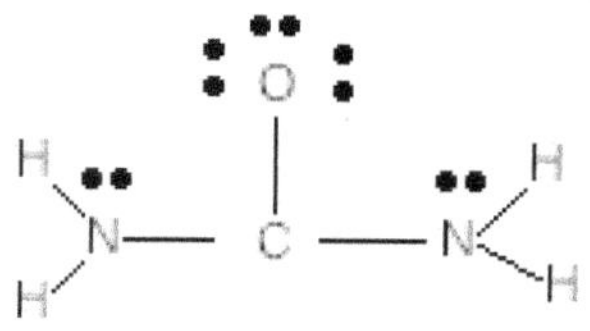

Complete the octet on C with a double bond.

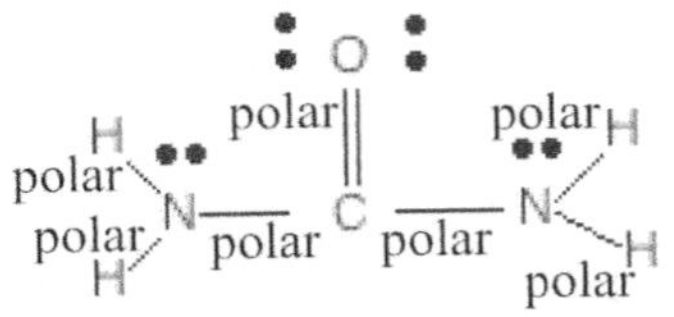

The C – O bond would be the most polar because it has the greater difference in electronegativity. From Figure 9.8,
ΔEN C— O = 1.0 ΔEN C – N = 0.5 ΔEN N – H = 0.9

9.97 (a) O_2^-: Write the correct skeletal structure for the radical.

Calculate the total number of electrons for the Lewis structure by summing the number of valence electrons of each atom in the radical and adding 1 for the 1 – charge.

2(number of valence e^- for O) + 1 = 2(6) + 1 = 13

Distribute the electrons among the atoms, giving octets to as many atoms as possible. Begin with the bonding electrons, then proceed to lone pairs on terminal atoms and finally to lone pairs on the central atom.

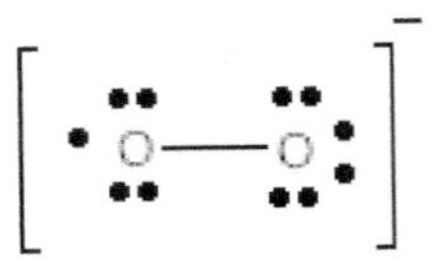

All 13 valence electrons are used.

O has an incomplete octet. It has 7 electrons because we have an odd number of valence electrons.

(b) O^-: Write the Lewis structure based on the valence electrons $2s^2 2p^5$.

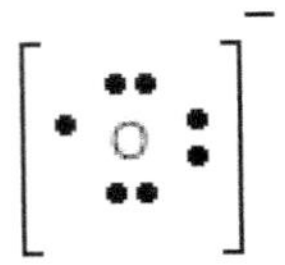

(c) OH: Write the correct skeletal structure for the molecule.

Calculate the total number of electrons for the Lewis structure by summing the number of valence electrons of each atom in the molecule.

(number of valence e^- for O) + (number of valence e^- for H) = 6 + 1 = 7

Distribute the electrons among the atoms, giving octets (or duets for H) to as many atoms as possible. Begin with the bonding electrons, then proceed to lone pairs on terminal atoms and finally to lone pairs on the central atom.

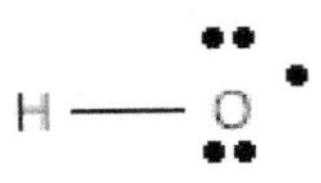

All 7 valence electrons are used.

O has an incomplete octet. It has 7 electrons because we have an odd number of valence electrons.

(d) CH_3OO: Write the correct skeletal structure for the radical.
C is the least electronegative atom, so it is central.

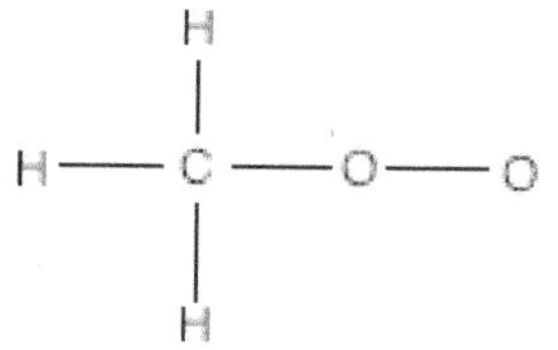

Calculate the total number of electrons for the Lewis structure by summing the number of valence electrons of each atom in the molecule.

3(number of valence e^- for H) + (number of valence e^- for C) + 2(number of valence e^- for O) = 3(1) + 4 +2(6) = 19

Distribute the electrons among the atoms, giving octets (or duets for H) to as many atoms as possible. Begin with the bonding electrons, and then proceed to lone pairs on terminal atoms and finally to lone pairs on the central atoms.

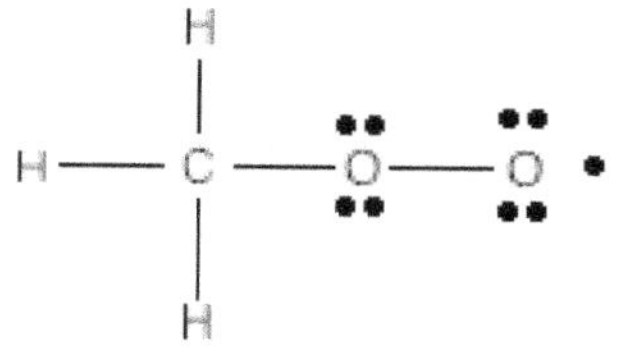

All 19 valence electrons are used.

O has an incomplete octet. It has 7 electrons because we have an odd number of valence electrons.

9.98

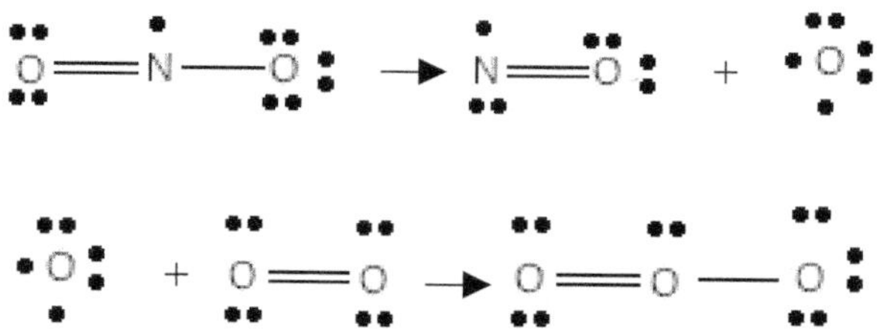

Where NO_2, O, and NO are the free radicals.

9.99 Rewrite the reaction using the Lewis structures of the molecules involved.

$$H-H\,(g) + 1/2\,O=O\,(g) \rightarrow H-O-H$$

Determine which bonds are broken in the reaction and sum the bond energies of the following:

$\Sigma(\Delta H\text{'s bonds broken})$
= 1mol(H – H) + 1/2mol(O = O)
= 1mol(436 kJ/mol) + 1/2mol(498)
= 685 kJ/mol

Determine which bonds are formed in the reaction and sum the negatives of the bond energies of the following:

$\Sigma(-\Delta H\text{'s bonds formed})$
= – 2mol(O – H)
= – 2mol(464 kJ/mol)
= –928 kJ/mol

Find ΔH_{rxn} by summing the results of the two steps.

ΔH_{rxn} = $\Sigma(\Delta H\text{'s bonds broken}) + \Sigma(-\Delta H\text{'s bonds formed})$
= 685 kJ/mol – 928 kJ/mol
= – 243 kJ/mol

$CH_4(g) + 2O_2(g) \rightarrow CO_2(g) + 2H_2O(g)$

Rewrite the reaction using the Lewis structures of the molecules involved.

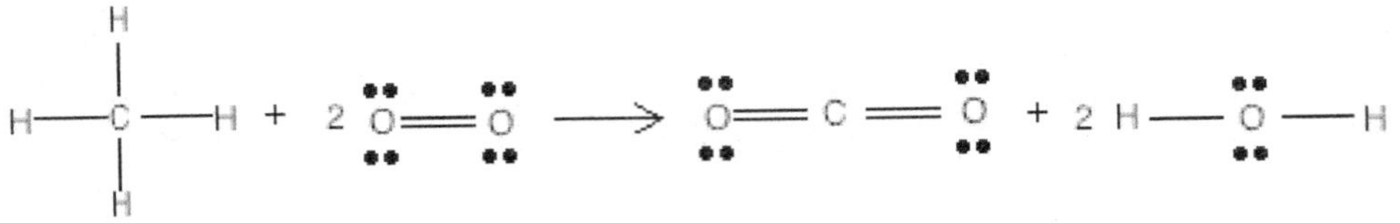

Determine which bonds are broken in the reaction and sum the bond energies of the following:

$\Sigma(\Delta H\text{'s bonds broken})$
$= 4\text{mol}(C - H) + 2\text{mol}(O = O)$
$= 4\text{mol}(414\ \text{kJ/mol}) + 2\text{mol}(498)$
$= 2652\ \text{kJ/mol}$

Determine which bonds are formed in the reaction and sum the negatives of the bond energies of the following:

$\Sigma(-\Delta H\text{'s bonds formed})$
$= -\ 2\text{mol}(C = O) - 4\text{mol}(O - H)$
$= -\ 2\text{mol}(799\ \text{kJ/mol}) - 4\text{mol}(464\ \text{kJ/mol})$
$= -3454\ \text{kJ/mol}$

Find ΔH_{rxn} by summing the results of the two steps.

$\Delta H_{rxn} = \Sigma(\Delta H\text{'s bonds broken}) + \Sigma(-\Delta H\text{'s bonds formed})$
$= 2653\ \text{kJ/mol} - 3454\ \text{kJ/mol}$
$= -\ 802\ \text{kJ/mol}$

Compare the following:

	kJ/mol	kJ/g
H_2	–243	–120
CH_4	–802	–50.1

So, methane yields more energy per mole but hydrogen yields more energy per gram.

9.100 octane = C_8H_{18}

$C_8H_{18}(l) + 25/2O_2(g) \rightarrow 8CO_2(g) + 9H_2O(g)$

Rewrite the reaction using the Lewis structures of the molecules involved.

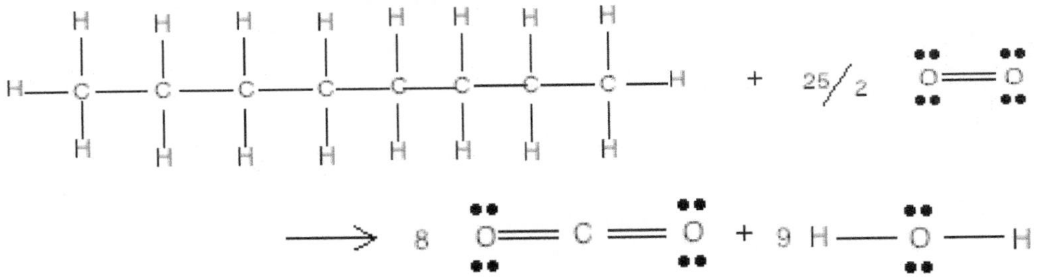

Determine which bonds are broken in the reaction and sum the bond energies of the following:

$\Sigma(\Delta H\text{'s bonds broken})$
$= 18\text{mol}(C - H) + 25/2\ \text{mol}(O = O) + 7\text{mol}(C - C)$
$= 18\text{mol}(414\ \text{kJ/mol}) + 25/2\text{mol}(498) + 7\text{mol}(347)$
$= 16106\ \text{kJ/mol}$

Determine which bonds are formed in the reaction and sum the negatives of the bond energies of the following:

$\Sigma(-\Delta H\text{'s bonds formed})$
$= -\ 16\text{mol}(C = O) - 18\text{mol}(O - H)$
$= -\ 16\text{mol}(799\ \text{kJ/mol}) - 18\text{mol}(464\ \text{kJ/mol})$
$= -21136\ \text{kJ/mol}$

Find ΔH_{rxn} by summing the results of the two steps.

$\Delta H_{rxn} = \Sigma(\Delta H\text{'s bonds broken}) + \Sigma(-\Delta H\text{'s bonds formed})$
$= 16106\ \text{kJ/mol} - 21136\ \text{kJ/mol}$
$= -\ 5030\ \text{kJ/mol}$

You need to look up (google) ΔH_f for octane. $\Delta H_f = -250 kJ/mol$.

$\Delta H_{rxn} = \Sigma(\Delta H_f(products)) - \Sigma(\Delta H_f(reactants))$

$= [8mol \Delta H_f(CO_2(g)) + 9mol \Delta H_f(H_2O(g))] - [1mol \Delta H_f(C_8H_{18}(l)) + 25/2mol \Delta H_f(O_2(g))]$

$= [8mol(- 393.5\ kJ/mol) + 9mol(- 241.8\ kJ/mol)] - [1mol(- 250\ kJ/mol) + 25/2mol(0)]$

$= - 5074\ kJ/mol$

$$\%\ difference = \frac{-5074\ kJ - (-5030\ kJ)}{-5074\ kJ} \times 100 = 0.8672\%$$

You would expect the value calculated from the heats of formation to be more accurate. The bond energy values are average values, not values for a specific molecule. The heats of formation are for specific compounds.

9.101 (a) Cl_2O_7: Write the correct skeletal structure for the molecule.

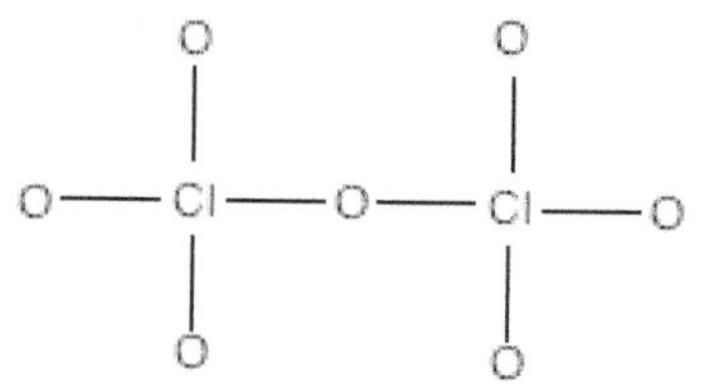

Calculate the total number of electrons for the Lewis structure by summing the valence electrons of each atom in the molecule.

2(number of valence e^- for Cl) + 7(number of valence e^- for O) = 2(7)5 + 7(6) = 56

Distribute the electrons among the atoms, giving octets (or duets for H) to as many atoms as possible. Begin with the bonding electrons, and then proceed to lone pairs on terminal atoms and finally to lone pairs of the central atom.

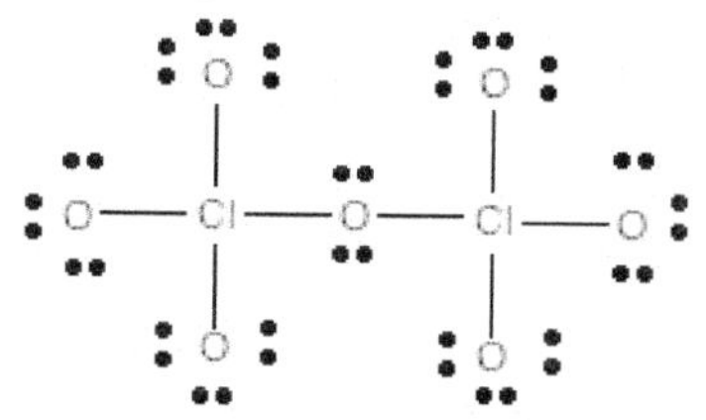

Form double bonds to minimize formal charge.

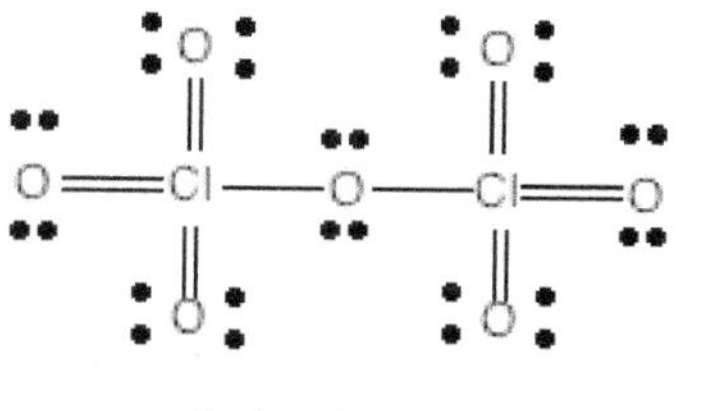

(b) H_3PO_3: Write the correct skeletal structure for the molecule.

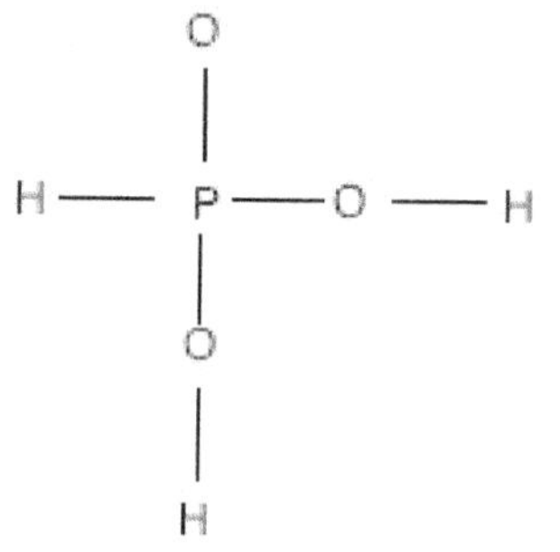

Calculate the total number of electrons for the Lewis structure by summing the valence electrons of each atom in the molecule.

(number of valence e^- for P) + 3(number of valence e^- for O) + 3(number of valence e^- for H) = 5 + 3(6) + 3(1) = 26

Distribute the electrons among the atoms, giving octets (or duets for H) to as many atoms as possible. Begin with the bonding electrons, and then proceed to lone pairs on terminal atoms and finally to lone pairs on central atoms.

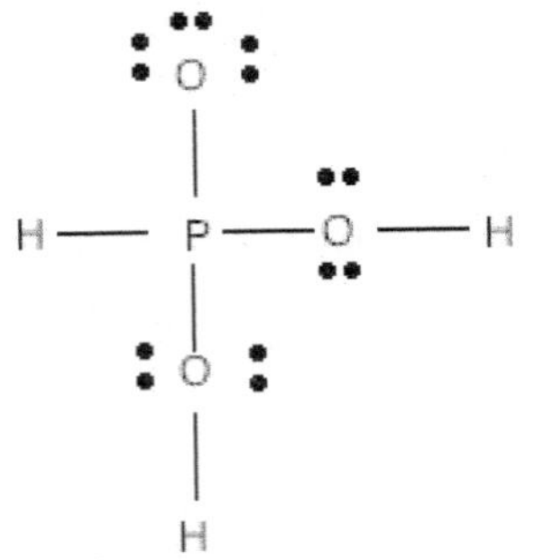

Form a double bond to minimize formal charge.

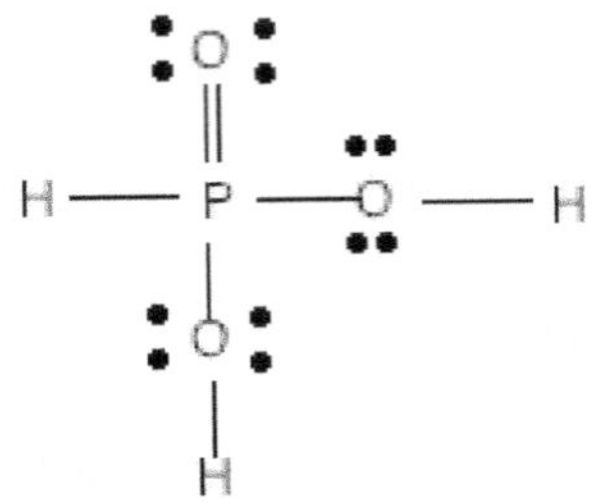

(c) H_3AsO_4: Write the correct skeletal structure for the molecule.

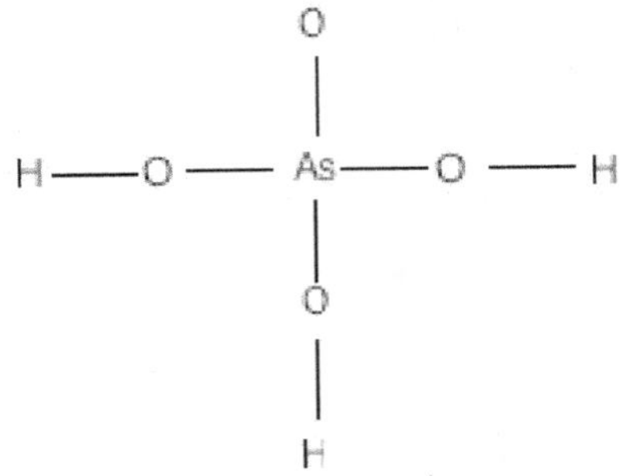

Calculate the total number of electrons for the Lewis structure by summing the valence electrons of each atom in the molecule.

(number of valence e^- for As) + 4(number of valence e^- for O) + 3(number of valence e^- for H) = 5 + 4(6) + 3(1) = 32

Distribute the electrons among the atoms, giving octets (or duets for H) to as many atoms as possible. Begin with the bonding electrons, and then proceed to lone pairs on terminal atoms and finally to lone pairs of the central atom.

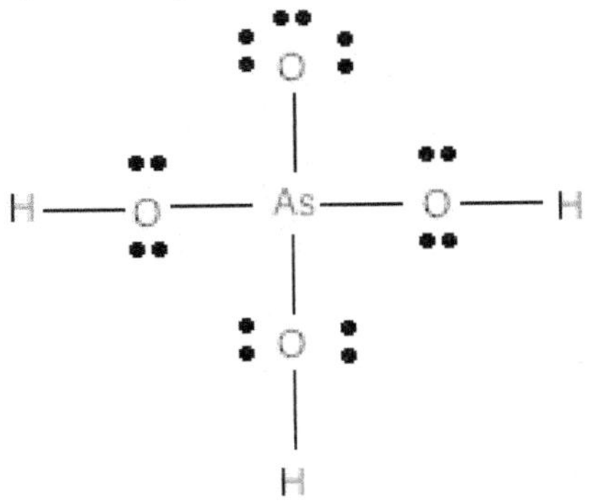

Form a double bond to minimize formal charge.

$$
\begin{array}{c}
\overset{\displaystyle \cdot\cdot}{\underset{\displaystyle \cdot\cdot}{O}} \\
\parallel \\
H - \overset{\cdot\cdot}{\underset{\cdot\cdot}{O}} - As - \overset{\cdot\cdot}{\underset{\cdot\cdot}{O}} - H \\
\mid \\
\overset{\cdot\cdot}{\underset{\cdot\cdot}{O}} \\
\mid \\
H
\end{array}
$$

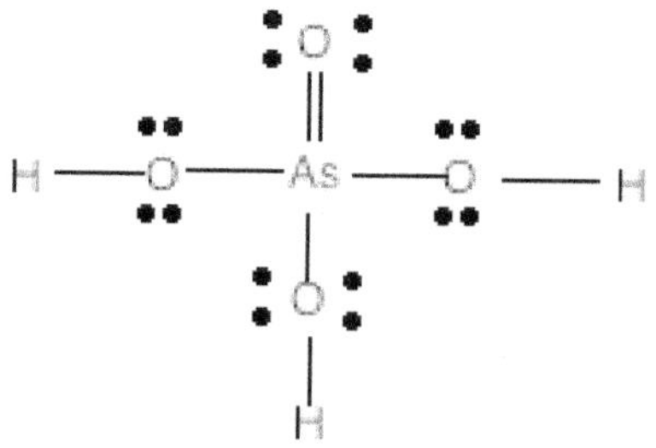

9.102 N_3^-: Write the correct skeletal structure for the ion.

$$ N - N - N $$

Calculate the total number of electrons for the Lewis structure by summing the valence electrons of each atom in the ion and adding 1 for the 1 – charge.

3(number of valence e^- for N) +1 = 3(5) + 1 = 16

Distribute the electrons among the atoms, giving octets to as many atoms as possible. Begin with the bonding electrons, and then proceed to lone pairs on terminal atoms and finally to lone pairs of the central atom.

$$ \overset{\cdot\cdot}{\underset{\cdot\cdot}{:N}} - N - \overset{\cdot\cdot}{\underset{\cdot\cdot}{N:}} $$

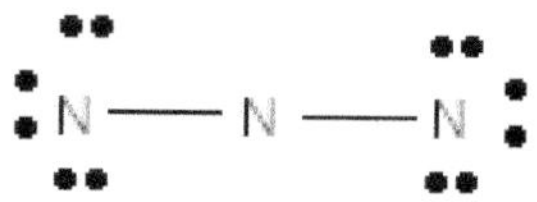

Complete octets with double or triple bonds.

$$ \overset{\cdot\cdot}{\underset{\cdot\cdot}{N}} = N = \overset{\cdot\cdot}{\underset{\cdot\cdot}{N}} $$

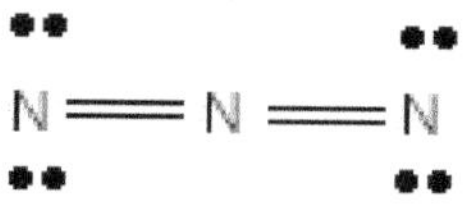

Lastly, write the ion in brackets with the charge in the upper right-hand corner.

$$ \left[\overset{\cdot\cdot}{\underset{\cdot\cdot}{N}} = N = \overset{\cdot\cdot}{\underset{\cdot\cdot}{N}} \right]^- $$

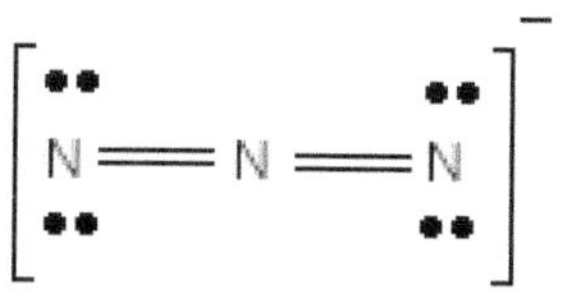

Write the resonance forms.

$$ \left[\overset{\cdot\cdot}{\underset{\cdot\cdot}{N}} = N = \overset{\cdot\cdot}{\underset{\cdot\cdot}{N}} \right]^- \longleftrightarrow \left[:N \equiv N - \overset{\cdot\cdot}{\underset{\cdot\cdot}{N}}: \right]^- \longleftrightarrow \left[\overset{\cdot\cdot}{\underset{\cdot\cdot}{:N}} - N \equiv N: \right]^- $$

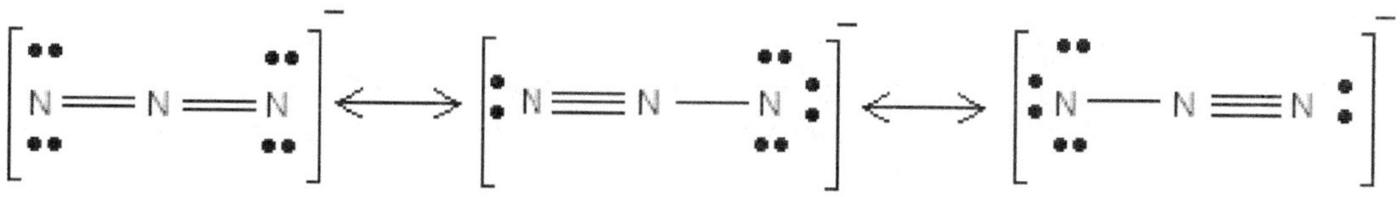

9.103 $Na^+F^- < Na^+O^{2-} < Mg^{2+}F^- < Mg^{2+}O^{2-} < Al^{3+}O^{2-}$

The lattice energy is proportional to the magnitude of the charge and inversely proportional to the distance between the atoms. Na^+F^- would have the smallest lattice energy because the magnitude of the charges on Na and F are the smallest. $Mg^{2+}F^-$ and Na^+O^{2-} both have the same magnitude formal charge, the O^{2-} is larger than F^- in size, and Na^+ is larger than Mg^{2+}, so Na^+O^{2-} should be less than $Mg^{2+}F^-$. The magnitude of the charge makes $Mg^{2+}O^{2-} < Al^{3+}O^{2-}$.

9.104   Rewrite the reaction using the Lewis structures of the molecules involved.

$$ H - H + \overset{\cdot\cdot}{\underset{\cdot\cdot}{:Br}} - \overset{\cdot\cdot}{\underset{\cdot\cdot}{Br}}: \longrightarrow 2 \, H - \overset{\cdot\cdot}{\underset{\cdot\cdot}{Br}}: $$

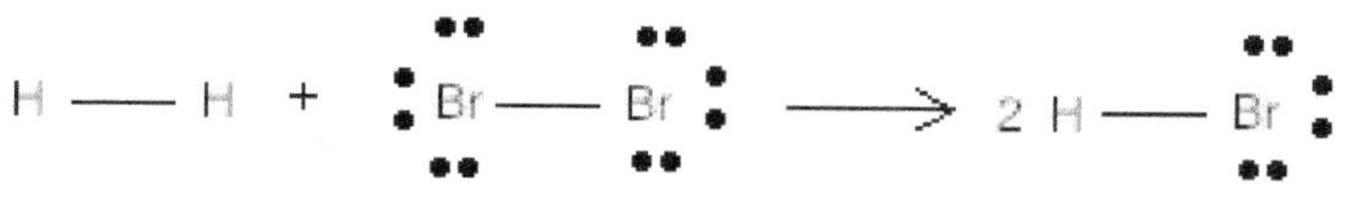

Determine which bonds are broken in the reaction and sum the bond energies of the following:

$\Sigma(\Delta H\text{'s bonds broken})$
$= 1\text{mol}\ (H - H) + 1\text{mol}(Br - Br)$
$= 1\text{mol}(436\ \text{kJ/mol}) + 1\text{mol}(193\ \text{kJ/mol})$
$= 629\ \text{kJ/mol}$

Determine which bonds are formed in the reaction and sum the negatives of the bond energies of the following:

$\Sigma(-\Delta H\text{'s bonds formed})$
$= -2\text{mol}(H - Br)$
$= -2\text{mol}(364\ \text{kJ/mol})$
$= -728\ \text{kJ/mol}$

Find ΔH_{rxn} by summing the results of the two steps.

$\Delta H_{rxn} = \Sigma(\Delta H\text{'s bonds broken}) + \Sigma(-\Delta H\text{'s bonds formed})$
$= 629\ \text{kJ/mol} - 728\ \text{kJ/mol}$
$= -99\ \text{kJ/mol}$

ΔH_f° from the table $= -36.3\ \text{kJ/mol}$

The value for ΔH_f° would be expected to be 1/2 the value calculated from the bond energies but it is not. ΔH_f° is for the formation of HBr from elements in the standard state. The standard state of Br is $Br_2(l)$, while we used bond energies for $Br_2(g)$. If you include the value for the formation of $Br_2(g)$, (–30.9kJ/mol), we obtain a value of – 51.8 kJ/mol for the reaction. This is still not ½ the value of ΔH_f° for the formation of HBr. Since it is not, we can account for the difference by looking at the types of bonds broken and formed. The H_2 and Br_2 bonds are pure covalent bonds, while the HBr bond formed will be polar covalent. The distribution of the electron density will be unequal.

9.105 **Given:** heat atomization CH_4 = 1660 kJ/mol, CH_2Cl_2 = 1495 kJ/mol **Find:** bond energy C – Cl

Write the reaction using the Lewis structure.

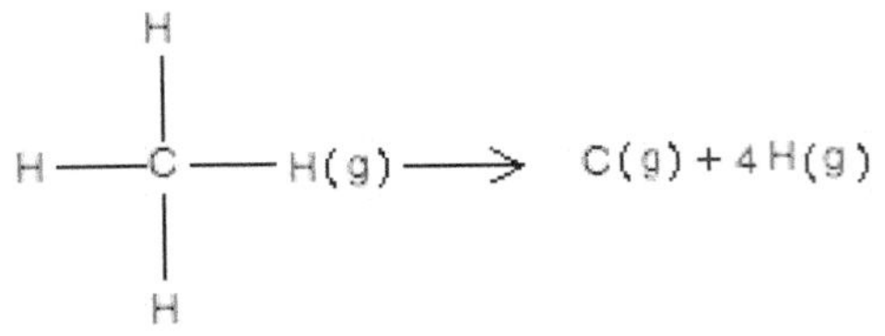

Determine the number and kinds of bonds broken and then ΔH atomization = Σ bonds broken.

ΔH atomization = Σ 4 (C – H) bonds broken

$$\frac{1660\ \text{kJ}}{1\ \text{mol}\ CH_4} \times \frac{1\ \text{mol}\ CH_4}{4\ C - H\ \text{bonds}} = 415\ \text{kJ/C} - \text{H bond}$$

Write the reaction using the Lewis structure.

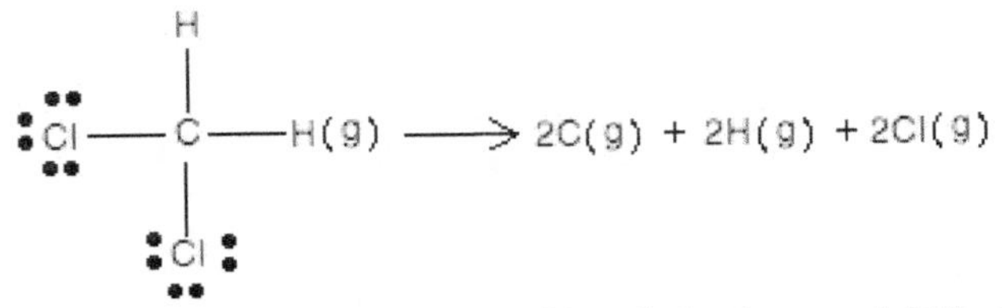

Determine the number and kinds of bonds broken and ΔH atomization = Σ bonds broken.

ΔH atomization = Σ 2 (C – H) bonds broken + 2(C – Cl) bonds broken

1495 kJ/mol = 2(415 kJ/ mol) + 2 (x) x = 333 kJ/mol for the C – Cl bond energy

Check: The bond energy found (333 kJ/mol) is very close to the table value of 339 kJ/mol.

9.106 **Given:** bond energy: C – H = 414 kJ/mol; C – Cl = 339 kJ/mol; C = C = 611 kJ/ mol

Find: Heat of atomization of C_2H_3Cl

Write the reaction using the Lewis structure.

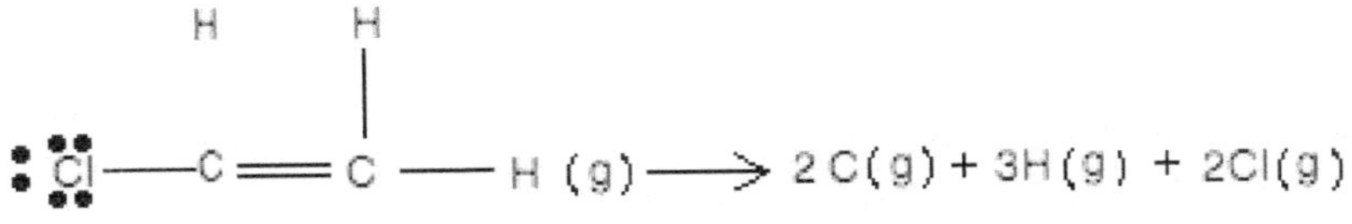

Determine the number and kinds of bonds broken and then ΔH atomization = Σ bonds broken.

$$\begin{aligned}\Delta H \text{ atomization} &= \Sigma\ 3\ (C-H) \text{ bonds broken} + (C-Cl) \text{ bond broken} + (C=C) \text{ bond broken}\\ &= 3(414\ kJ/mol) + (339\ kJ/mol) + (611\ kJ/mol)\\ &= 2192\ kJ/mol\end{aligned}$$

9.107 **Given:** 7.743% H **Find:** Lewis structure

Conceptual Plan: **%H → %C → mass C,H → mol C,H → pseudoformula → empirical formula**

100% − %H; Assume 100 g sample; $\frac{1\ mol\ C}{12.01\ g}$ $\frac{1\ mol\ N}{1.008\ g}$; divide by smallest number

Solution: %C = 100% - 7.743% = 92.568% C

In a 100.00 g sample; 7.743 g H, 92.568 g C

$$7.743\ g\ H \times \frac{1\ mol\ H}{1.008\ g\ H} = 7.682\ mol$$

$$92.568\ g\ C \times \frac{1\ mol\ C}{12.011\ g\ C} = 7.7069\ mol\ C$$

$C_{7.7068}H_{7.682}$

$C_{\frac{7.7068}{7.682}}H_{\frac{7.682}{7.682}} \rightarrow CH$

The smallest molecular formula would be C_2H_2.

Write the correct skeletal structure for the molecule.

Calculate the total number of electrons for the Lewis structure by summing the valence electrons of each atom in the molecule.

2(number of valence e^- for C) + 2(number of valence e^- for H) = 2(4) + 2(1) = 10 e^-

Distribute the electrons among the atoms, giving octets (or duets for H) to as many atoms as possible. Begin with the bonding electrons, then proceed to lone pairs on terminal atoms and finally to lone pairs on the central atom.

Complete the octet on C by forming a triple bond.

9.108 **Given:** 85.5% Cl **Find:** Lewis structure

Conceptual Plan: **%Cl → %C → mass C,Cl → mol C,Cl → pseudoformula → empirical formula**

100% − %Cl; Assume 100 g sample; $\frac{1\ mol\ C}{12.01\ g}$ $\frac{1\ mol\ Cl}{35.45\ g}$; divide by smallest number

Solution: %C = 100% - 85.5% = 14.5% C

In a 100.00 g sample; 85.5 g Cl, 14.5 g C

$$85.5\ g\ Cl \times \frac{1\ mol\ Cl}{35.45\ g\ Cl} = 2.41\ mol$$

$$14.5\ g\ C \times \frac{1\ mol\ C}{12.01\ g\ C} = 1.21\ mol\ C$$

$C_{1.21}Cl_{2.41}$

$C_{\frac{1.21}{1.21}}Cl_{\frac{2.41}{1.21}} \rightarrow CCl_2$

The smallest molecular formula would be C_2Cl_4.

Write the correct skeletal structure for the molecule.

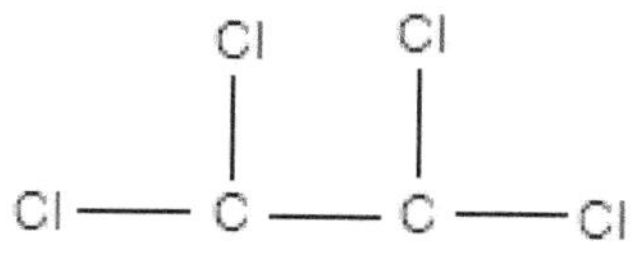

Calculate the total number of electrons for the Lewis structure by summing the valence electrons of each atom in the molecule.

2(number of valence e^- for C) + 4(number of valence e^- for Cl) = 2(4) + 4(7) = 36 e^-

Distribute the electrons among the atoms, giving octets to as many atoms as possible. Begin with the bonding electrons, and then proceed to lone pairs on terminal atoms and finally to lone pairs on the central atoms.

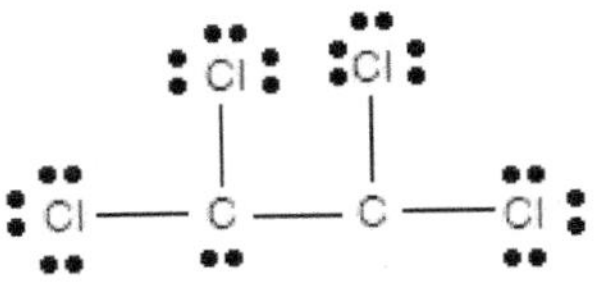

Complete the octet on C by forming a double bond.

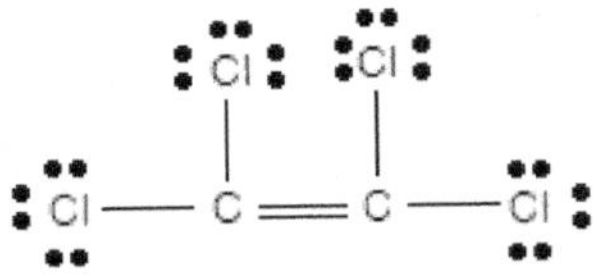

9.109

1 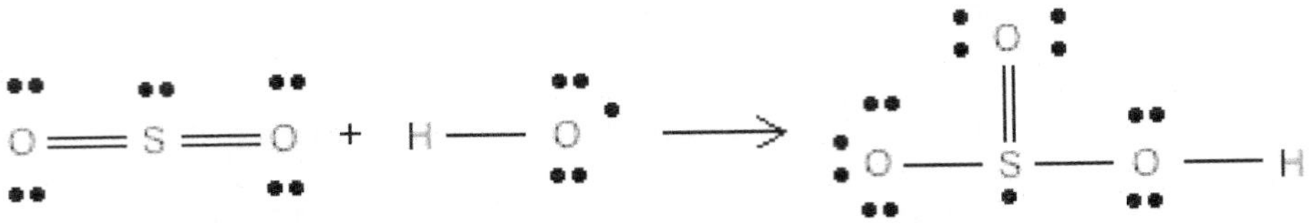

2 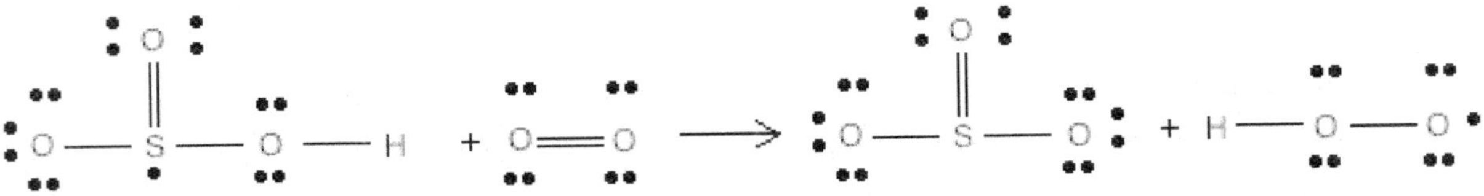

3 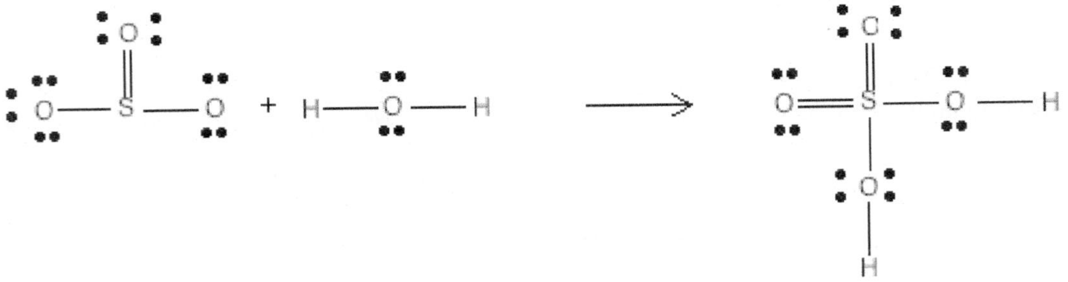

Step 1:

Bonds broken: 2mol(S = O) +1mol(H – O) = 2mol(523kJ/mol) + 1mol(464kJ/mol) = 1510 kJ/mol

Bonds formed: –2mol(S – O) –1mol(S = O) –1mol(O – H) =
–2mol(265 kJ/mol) –1mol(523 kJ/mol) –1mol(464 kJ/mol) = –1517 kJ/mol

ΔH_{step} = –7 kJ/mol

Step 2:

Bonds broken: 2mol(S – O) + 1mol(S = O) + 1mol(O – H) + 1mol(O = O) =
2mol(265 kJ/mol)+1mol(523 kJ/mol)+1mol(464 kJ/mol)+1mol(498 kJ/mol) =
2015 kJ/mol

Bonds formed: $-2mol(S-O) -1mol(S=O) -1mol(O-H) -1mol(O-O) =$
$-2mol(265\ kJ/mol) -1mol(523\ kJ/mol) -1mol(464\ kJ/mol) -1mol(142\ kJ/mol) =$
$-1659\ kJ/mol$
$\Delta H_{step} = +356\ kJ/mol$

Step 3:

Bonds broken: $2mol(S-O) + 1mol(S=O) + 2mol(O-H) =$
$2mol(265\ kJ/mol) + 1mol(523\ kJ/mol) + 2mol(464\ kJ/mol) = 1981\ kJ/mol$

Bonds formed: $-2mol(S-O) - 2mol(S=O) - 2mol(O-H) =$
$-2mol(265\ kJ/mol) + -2mol(523\ kJ/mol) + -2mol(464\ kJ/mol) = -2504\ kJ/mol$
$\Delta H_{step} = -523\ kJ/mol$

Hess's law states that ΔH for the reaction is the sum of ΔH of the steps:
$\Delta H_{rxn} = (-7\ kJ/mol) + (+356\ kJ/mol) + (-523\ kJ/mol) = -174\ kJ/mol$

9.110 **Given:** 0.167 g acid; 27.8 mL 0.100 M NaOH; 40.00% C; 6.71 % H; 53.29 % O
Find: molar mass, molecular formula, Lewis structure
Conceptual Plan: mL → L → mol NaOH → mol acid → molar mass and then:

$\frac{L}{1000\ mL}$ mol = VM mol acid = mol base $\frac{mass}{mol}$

convert mass to mol of each element → pseudoformula → empirical formula → molecular formula

$\frac{1\ mol\ C}{12.01\ g\ C}$ $\frac{1\ mol\ H}{1.008\ g\ H}$ $\frac{1\ mol\ N}{14.00\ g\ N}$ divide by smallest number empirical formula x n

→ Lewis structure

Solution: $27.8\ mL \times \frac{1\ L}{1000\ mL} \times \frac{0.100\ mol\ NaOH}{L} \times \frac{1\ mol\ acid}{1\ mol\ NaOH} = 0.00278\ mol\ acid$

$$\frac{0.167\ g\ acid}{0.00278\ mol\ acid} = 60.1\ g/mol$$

$$40.00\ \cancel{g\,C} \times \frac{1\ mol\ C}{12.01\ \cancel{g\,C}} = 3.331\ mol\ C$$

$$6.71\ \cancel{g\,H} \times \frac{1\ mol\ H}{1.008\ \cancel{g\,H}} = 6.6\underline{5}7\ mol\ H$$

$$53.29\ \cancel{g\,O} \times \frac{1\ mol\ O}{16.00\ \cancel{g\,O}} = 3.331\ mol\ O$$

$C_{3.331}H_{6.657}O_{3.331}$

$C_{\frac{3.331}{3.331}}H_{\frac{6.657}{3.331}}O_{\frac{3.331}{3.331}} \rightarrow CH_2O$

The correct empirical formula is CH_2O.
empirical formula mass = (12.01 g/mol) + 2(1.008 g/mol) + (16.00 g/mol) = 30.03 g/mol

$$n = \frac{molar\ mass}{formula\ molar\ mass} = \frac{60.1\ g/mol}{30.03\ g/mol} = 2$$

molecular formula $= CH_2O \times 2$
$= C_2H_4O_2$

Write the correct skeletal structure for the molecule.

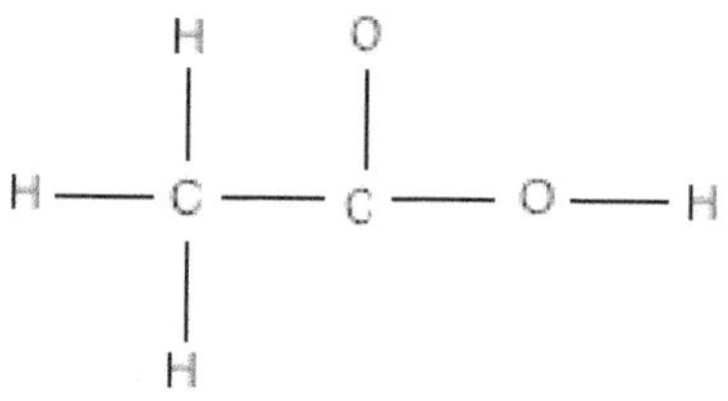

Calculate the total number of electrons for the Lewis structure by summing the number of valence electrons of each atom in the molecule.

2(number of valence e^- for C) + 2(number of valence e^- for O) + 4(number of valence e^- for H)
= 2(4) + 2(6) + 4(1) = 24

Distribute the electrons among the atoms, giving octets (or duets for H) to as many atoms as possible. Begin with the bonding electrons, then proceed to lone pairs on terminal atoms and finally to lone pairs of the central atoms.

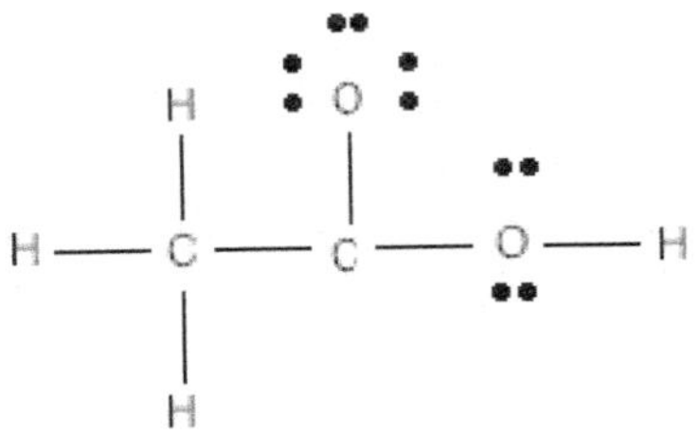

Complete the octet on C by forming a double bond.

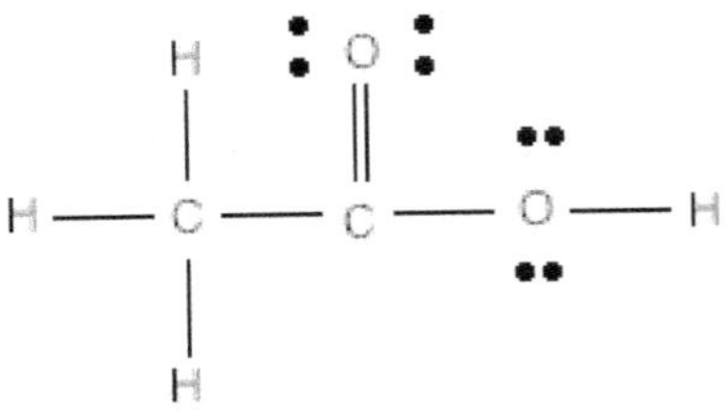

9.111 **Given:** μ = 1.08 D HCl, 20% ionic and μ = 1.82 D HF, 45% ionic **Find:** r
Conceptual Plan: $\mu \rightarrow \mu_{calc} \rightarrow r$

$$\text{\% ionic character} = \frac{\mu}{\mu_{calc}} \times 100$$

Solution: For HCl $\mu_{calc} = \frac{1.08}{0.20} = 5.4\ \text{D}$ $\quad \dfrac{5.4\ \text{D} \times \dfrac{3.34 \times 10^{-30}\ \text{C}\cdot\text{m}}{\text{D}} \times \dfrac{10^{12}\ \text{pm}}{\text{m}}}{1.6 \times 10^{-19}\ \text{C}} = 113\ \text{pm}$

For HF $\mu_{calc} = \frac{1.82}{0.45} = 4.04\ \text{D}$ $\quad \dfrac{4.04\ \text{D} \times \dfrac{3.34 \times 10^{-30}\ \text{C}\cdot\text{m}}{\text{D}} \times \dfrac{10^{12}\ \text{pm}}{\text{m}}}{1.6 \times 10^{-19}\ \text{C}} = 84\ \text{pm}$

From Table 9.4, the bond length of HCl = 127 pm, and HF = 92 pm. Both of these values are slightly higher than the calculated values.

9.112 Formation reaction: $6C(s) + 3H_2(g) \rightarrow C_6H_6(g)$ $\Delta H_f^\circ = 82.9$ kJ/mol
Using bond energies we would have the reaction $6C(g) + 3H_2(g) \rightarrow C_6H_6(g)$, so we have to include in the bond energy calculation the energy needed to convert $C(s) \rightarrow C(g)$ (718.4 kJ/mol).

6molC(s) $\rightarrow$ 6molC(g) 6mol(718.4 kJ/mol) = 4310.4 kJ/mol

Rewrite the reaction with the Lewis structures.

6C(g) + 3 H – H(g)$\rightarrow$ 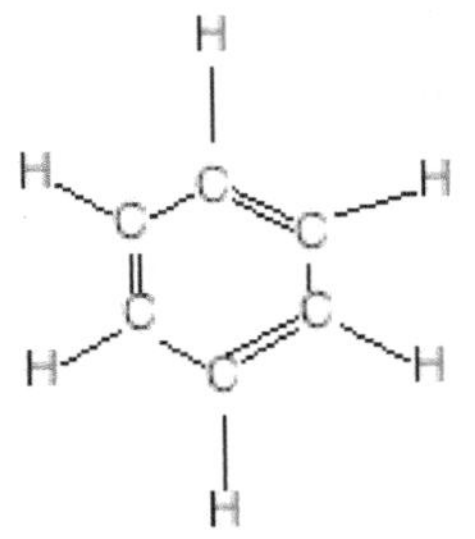 (g)

bonds broken: 3mol(H – H) = 3mol(436 kJ/mol) = 1308 kJ/mol
bonds formed: –3mol(C = C) – 3mol(C – C) – 6mol(C – H) =
–3mol(611kJ/mol) – 3mol(347 kJ/mol) – 6mol(414 kJ/mol) = –5358 kJ/mol

ΔH from bond energies = +(4310 kJ) + (1308 kJ) – 5358 kJ = +260 kJ/mol

The difference between the value calculated from bond energies (260 kJ/mol) and $\Delta H_f^\circ = 82.9$ kJ/mol for benzene leads us to conclude there is a great deal of stabilization from the two resonance forms and that they contribute much to the formation of benzene.

9.113 In order for the four P atoms to be equivalent, they must all be in the same electronic environment. That is, they must all see the same number of bonds and lone pair electrons. The only way to achieve this is with a tetrahedral configuration where the P atoms are at the four points of the tetrahedron.

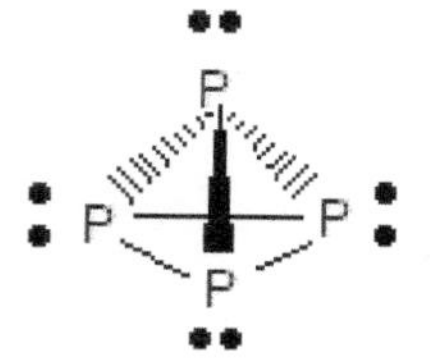

9.114 **Given:** $\Delta H_f^\circ CaBr_2 = -675$ kJ/mol; $IE_1(Ca) = 590$ kJ/mol; $IE_2(Ca) = 1145$ kJ/mol; $\Delta H_{sub}(Ca) = 178$ kJ/mol; $Br_2(g)$ bond energy = 193 kJ/mol; $\Delta H_{vap}(Br_2(l)) = 31$ kJ/mol; EA(Br) = – 325 kJ/mol. **Find:** lattice energy

Conceptual Plan:

$$Ca(s)+Br_2(l) \xrightarrow{\Delta H_{sub}} Ca(g)+Br_2(l) \xrightarrow{IE_1} Ca^+(g)+Br_2(l) \xrightarrow{IE_2} Ca^{2+}(g)+Br_2(l) \xrightarrow{\Delta H_{vap}} Ca^{2+}(g)+Br_2(g) \xrightarrow{\text{bond energy}} Ca^{2+}(g)+2Br(g)$$

$$\xrightarrow{EA} Ca^{2+}(g)+2Br^-(g) \xrightarrow{\text{lattice energy}} CaBr_2(s)$$

$$Ca(s)+Br_2(l) \xrightarrow{\Delta H_f^\circ} CaBr_2(s)$$

Solution: $\Delta H_f^\circ = \Delta H_{sub} + IE_1 + IE_2 + \Delta H_{vap}$ **+ bond energy + 2 EA + lattice energy**

$$-675\frac{kJ}{mol} = +178\frac{kJ}{mol} + 590\frac{kJ}{mol} + 1145\frac{kJ}{mol} + 31\frac{kJ}{mol} + 193\frac{kJ}{mol} + 2(-325)\frac{kJ}{mol} + \text{lattice energy}$$

lattice energy = – 2162 kJ/mol

9.115 **Given:** $\Delta H_f^\circ PI_3(s) = -24.7$kJ/mol; P – I = 184 kJ/mol;I – I = 151kJ/mol; $\Delta H_f^\circ P(g) = 334$ kJ/mol; $\Delta H_f^\circ I_2(g)$ = 62 kJ/mol **Find:** $\Delta H_{sub} PI_3(s)$

Conceptual Plan: $PI_3(s) \rightarrow PI_3(g)$**; use Hess's law**

Solution:

Reaction	ΔH(kJ/mol)	
$PI_3(s) \rightarrow P(s) + 3/2\ I_2(s)$	+ 24.7	(this is the reverse of the formation reaction)
$P(s) \rightarrow P(g)$	+334	(formation of P(g))
$3/2\ I_2(s) \rightarrow 3/2\ I_2(g)$	3/2(62)	(formation of $I_2(g)$)
$3/2\ I_2(g) \rightarrow 3\ I(g)$	3/2(151)	(breaking I – I bond)
$P(g) + 3I(g) \rightarrow PI_3(g)$	– 3(184)	(forming P – I bond)
$PI_3(s) \rightarrow PI_3(g)$	+126	(sublimation of $PI_3(s)$)

9.116 **Given:** C_8H_8 all C's identical, all H's identical **Find:** Lewis structure

In order for the eight C atoms to be equivalent, they must all be in the same electronic environment, and in order for the eight H atoms to be equivalent, they must also all be in the same electronic environment. That is, they must all see the same number and kinds of bonds. One way to achieve this is with a cubic arrangement of the C atoms and then a H atom attached to each C. A second would be a cyclooctatetraene structure.

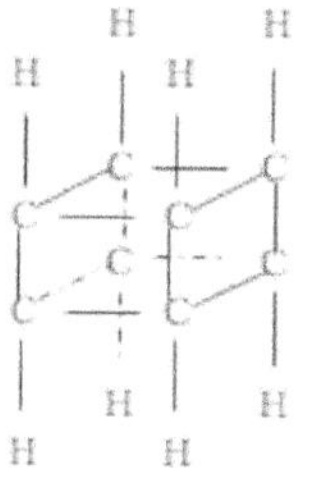

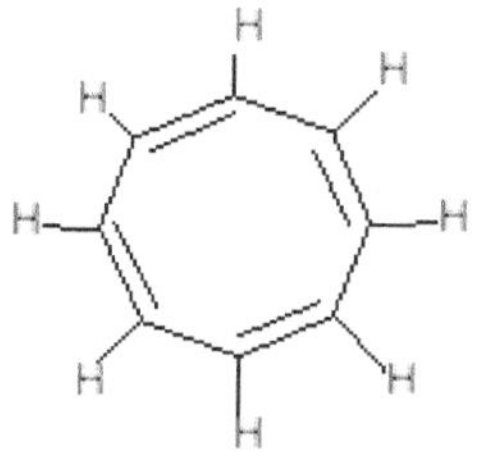

9.117 **Given:** H_2S_4 linear **Find:** oxidation number of each S
Write the correct skeletal structure for the molecule.

Calculate the total number of electrons for the Lewis structure by summing the number of valence electrons of each atom in the molecule.

4(number of valence e^- for S) + 2(number of valence e^- for H) = 4(6) + 2(1) = 26

Distribute the electrons among the atoms, giving octets (or duets for H) to as many atoms as possible.

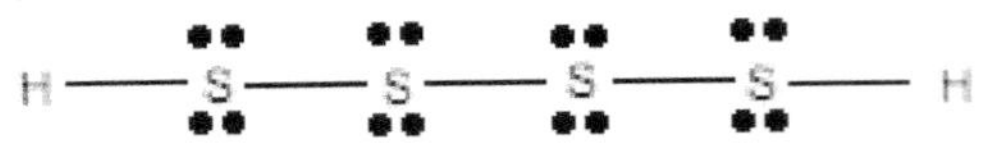

Determine oxidation number on each atom. EN(H) < EN(S), so the electrons in the H – S bond belong to the S atom, while the electrons in the S – S bonds split between the two S atoms.

O. N. = valence electrons – electrons that belong to the atom

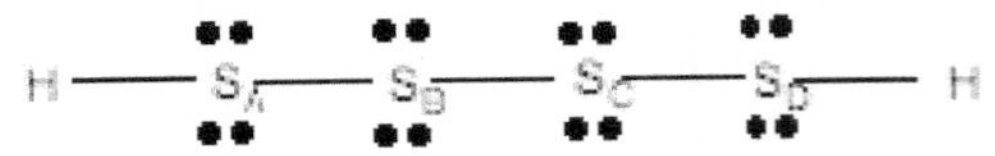

H = 1 – 0 = +1 for each H
S_A = 6 – 7 = –1
S_B = 6 – 6 = 0
S_C = 6 – 6 = 0
S_D = 6 – 7 = –1

9.118 O^{2-} anion has eight electrons and therefore a complete octet, which makes it a stable anion in an ionic solid.
O^- anion has seven electrons. Since it does not have a complete octet, it will not be a stable anion in an ionic solid.
O^{3-} anion has nine electrons. Since O can not accommodate more than eight electrons, this anion will not form.

9.119 **Given:** ΔH_f SO_2 = - 296.8 kJ/mol, S(g) = 277.2 kJ/mol, break O = O bond 498 kJ
Find: S = O bond energy
Conceptual Plan: Use ΔH_f for SO_2 and S(g) and the bond energy of O_2 to determine heat of atomization of SO_2.

Reaction ΔH			(kJ/mol)
$SO_2(g)$	→	~~S(s, rhombic)~~ + ~~$O_2(g)$~~	+296.8
~~S(s, rhombic)~~	→	S(g)	+277.2
~~O=O(g)~~	→	2 O(g)	+498
$SO_2(g)$	→	S(g) + 2 O(g)	+1072

Write the reaction using the Lewis structure.

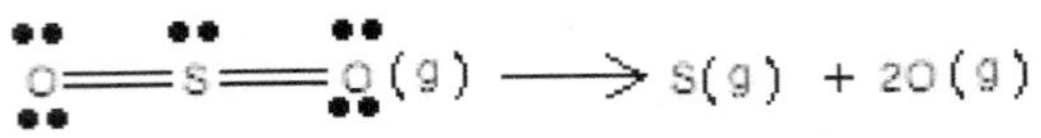

Determine the number and kinds of bonds broken and then ΔH atomization = bonds broken.
ΔH atomization = 2 Σ (S=O) bonds broken.
1072 kJ/mol = 2 (S=O) bonds broken.
S=O bond energy = 536 kJ /mol.
Check: The S=O bond energy is close to the table value of 523 kJ/mol.

Conceptual Problems

9.120 (a) is true: Strong bonds break and weak bonds form. In an endothermic reaction, the energy required to break the bonds is greater than the energy given off when the bonds are formed ($\Delta H > 0$); therefore, in an endothermic reaction the bonds that are breaking are stronger than the bonds that are forming.

9.121 When we say that a compound is "energy rich" we mean that it gives off a great amount of energy when it reacts. It means that there is a lot of energy stored in the compound. This energy is released when the weak bonds in the compound break and much stronger bonds are formed in the product, thereby releasing energy.

9.122 In solid covalent compounds, the electrons in the bonds are shared directly between the atoms involved in the molecule. Each molecule is a distinct unit. Ionic compounds, on the other hand, are not distinct units. Rather, they are composed of alternating positive and negative ions in a three-dimensional crystalline array.

9.123 Lewis theory is successful because it allows us to understand and predict many chemical observations. We can use it to determine the formulae of ionic compounds and to account for the low melting points and boiling points of molecular compounds compared to ionic compounds. Lewis theory allows us to predict what molecules or ions will be stable, which will be more reactive, and which will not exist. Lewis theory, however, does not really tell us anything about how the bonds in the molecules and ions form. It does not give us a way to account for the paramagnetism of oxygen. And, by itself, Lewis theory does not really tell us anything about the shape of the molecule or ion.

10 Chemical Bonding II: Molecular Shapes, Valence Bond Theory, and Molecular Orbital Theory

Review Questions

10.1 The properties of molecules are directly related to their shape. The sensation of taste, immune response, the sense of smell, and many types of drug action all depend on shape-specific interactions between molecules and proteins.

10.2 According to VSEPR theory, the repulsion between electron groups on interior atoms of a molecule determines the geometry of the molecule.

10.3 The five basic electron geometries are
(1) Linear, which has two electron groups.
(2) Trigonal planar, which has three electron groups.
(3) Tetrahedral, which has four electron groups.
(4) Trigonal bipyramid, which has five electron groups.
(5) Octahedral, which has six electron groups.
An electron group is defined as a lone pair of electrons, a single bond, a multiple bond, or even a single electron.

(a) Linear geometry

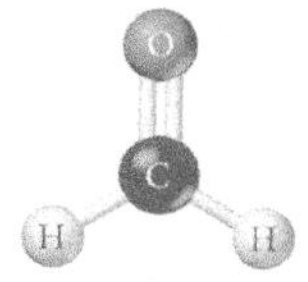

(b) Trigonal planar geometry

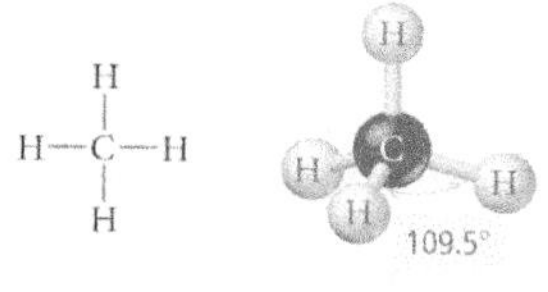

Tetrahedral geometry

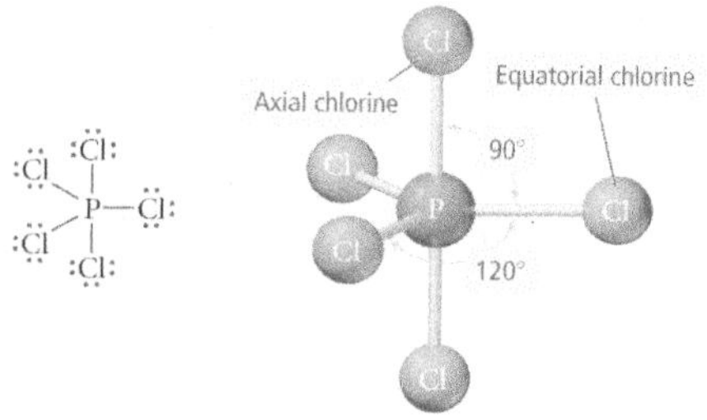

Trigonal bipyramidal geometry

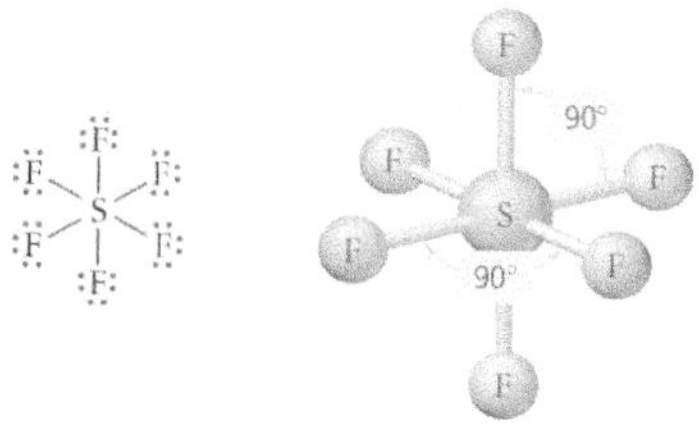

Octahedral geometry

10.4 The electron geometry is the geometrical arrangement of the electron groups around the central atom.

The molecular geometry is the geometrical arrangement of the atoms around the central atom.

The electron geometry and the molecular geometry are the same when every electron group bonds two atoms together. The presence of unbonded lone-pair electrons gives a different molecular geometry and electron geometry.

10.5 (a) Four electron groups give tetrahedral electron geometry, while three bonding groups and one lone pair give a trigonal pyramidal molecular geometry.

(b) Four electron groups give a tetrahedral electron geometry, while two bonding groups and two lone pairs give a bent molecular geometry.

(c) Five electron groups give a trigonal bipyramidal electron geometry, while four bonding groups and one lone pair give a seesaw molecular geometry.

(d) Five electron groups give a trigonal bipyramidal electron geometry, while three bonding groups and two lone pairs give a T-shaped molecular geometry.

(e) Five electron groups gives a trigonal bipyramidal electron geometry, while two bonding groups and three lone pair give a linear geometry.

(f) Six electron groups give an octahedral electron geometry, while five bonding groups and one lone pair give a square pyramidal molecular geometry.

(g) Six electron groups give an octahedral electron geometry, while four bonding groups and two lone pairs gives a square planar molecular geometry.

10.6 Larger molecules may have two or more interior atoms. When predicting the shapes of these molecules, determine the geometry about each interior atom and use these geometries to determine the entire three-dimensional shape of the molecules.

10.7 To determine if a molecule is polar, do the following:

1. Draw the Lewis structure for the molecule and determine the molecular geometry.

2. Determine whether the molecule contains polar bonds.

3. Determine whether the polar bonds add together to form a net dipole moment.

Polarity is important because polar and nonpolar molecules have different properties. Polar molecules interact strongly with other polar molecules, but do not interact with nonpolar molecules, and vice versa.

10.8 According to valence bond theory a chemical bond results from the overlap of two half-filled orbitals with spin-pairing of the two valence electrons.

10.9 According to valence bond theory, the shape of the molecule is determined by the geometry of the overlapping orbitals.

10.10 In valence bond theory, the interaction energy is usually negative (or stabilizing) when the interacting atomic orbitals contain a total of two electrons that can spin-pair.

10.11 Hybridization is a mathematical procedure in which the standard atomic orbitals are combined to form new atomic orbitals called hybrid orbitals. Hybrid orbitals are still localized on individual atoms, but they have different shapes and energies from those of standard atomic orbitals. They are necessary in valence bond theory because they correspond more closely to the actual distribution of electrons in chemically-bonded atoms.

10.12 Hybrid orbitals minimize the energy of the molecule by maximizing the orbital overlap in a bond.

10.13 The number of standard atomic orbitals added together always equals the number of hybrid orbitals formed. The total number of orbitals is conserved.

10.14

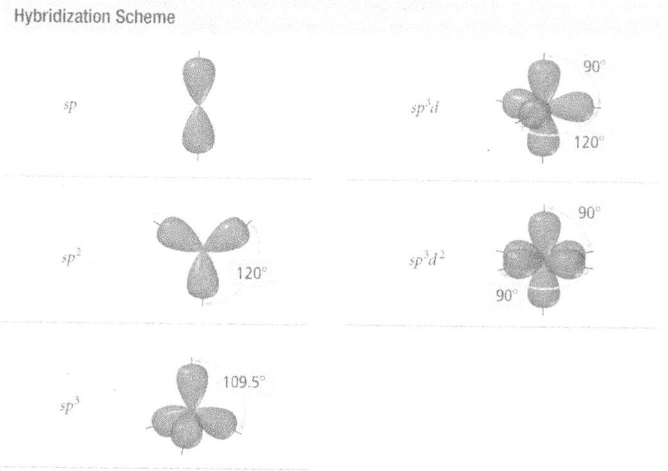

Each sketch indicates the number of hybrid orbitals form.

10.15 The double bond in Lewis theory is simply two pairs of electrons that are shared between the same two atoms. However, in valence bond theory we see that the double bond is made up of two different kinds of bonds. The double bond in valence bond theory consists of one σ bond and one π bond. Valence bond theory shows us that rotation about a double bond is severely restricted. Because of the side-by-side overlap of the *p* orbitals, the π bond must essentially break for rotation to occur. The single bond consists of overlap that results in a σ bond. Since the overlap is linear, rotation is not restricted.

10.16 (a) A linear electron geometry corresponds to *sp* hybridization.

(b) A trigonal planar electron geometry corresponds to sp^2 hybridization.

(c) A tetrahedral electron geometry corresponds to sp^3 hybridization.

(d) A trigonal bipyramidal electron geometry corresponds to sp^3d hybridization.

(e) An octahedral electron geometry corresponds to sp^3d^2 hybridization.

10.17 In molecular orbital theory, atoms will bond when the electrons in the atoms can lower their energy by occupying the molecular orbitals of the resultant molecule.

10.18 In valence bond theory, hybrid orbitals are weighted linear sums of the valence atomic orbitals of a particular atom, and the hybrid orbitals remain localized on that atom. In molecular orbital theory, the molecular orbitals are weighted linear sums of the valence atomic orbitals of all the atoms in a molecule, and many of the molecular orbitals are delocalized over the entire molecule.

10.19 A bonding molecular orbital is lower in energy than the atomic orbitals from which it is formed. There is an increased electron density in the internuclear region.

10.20 An antibonding molecular orbital is higher in energy than the atomic orbitals from which it is formed. There is less electron density in the internuclear region, which results in a node.

10.21 The electrons in orbitals behave like waves. The bonding molecular orbital arises from the constructive interference between the atomic orbitals and is lower in energy than the atomic orbitals. The antibonding molecular orbital arises from the destructive interference between the atomic orbitals and is higher in energy than the atomic orbitals.

10.22 The bond order in a diatomic molecule is the number of electrons in bonding molecular orbitals (MOs) minus the number in antibonding MOs divided by two. The higher the bond order, the stronger the bond. A negative or zero bond order indicates that a bond will not form between the atoms.

10.23 Molecular orbitals can be approximated by a linear combination of atomic orbitals (AOs). The total number of MOs formed from a particular set of AOs will always equal the number of AOs used.

10.24 (a) σ_{2s}

(b) σ^*_{2s}

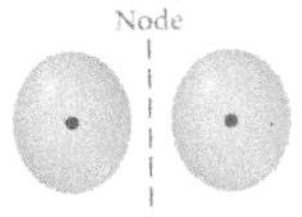

(c) σ_{2p}

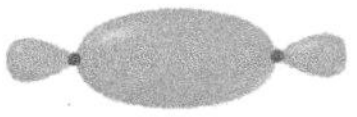

(d) σ^*_{2p}

(e) π_{2p}

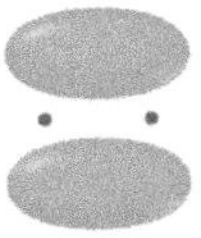

(f) π^*_{2p}

Dashed lines represent nodes.

10.25

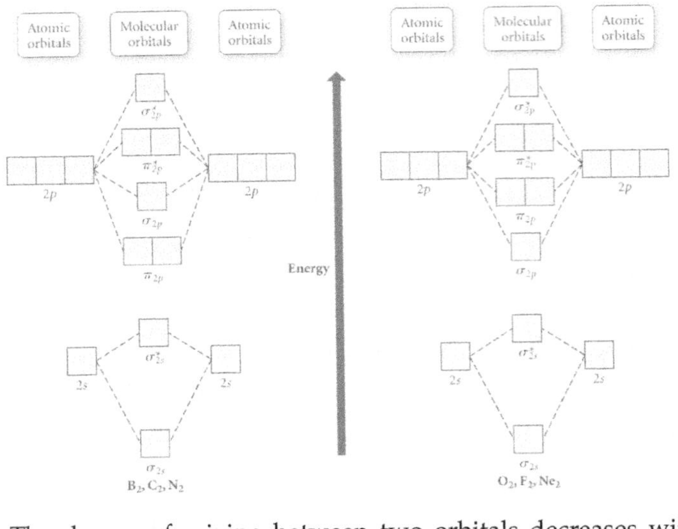

10.26 The degree of mixing between two orbitals decreases with increasing energy difference between them. Mixing of the 2*s* and $2p_x$ orbitals is greater in B_2, C_2, and N_2 than in O_2, F_2, and Ne_2, because in B, C, and N the energy levels of the atomic orbitals are more closely spaced than in O, F, and Ne. This mixing produces a change in energy ordering for the π_{2p} and the σ_{2p} molecular orbitals.

10.27 A paramagnetic species has unpaired electrons in molecular orbitals of equal energy. A paramagnetic species is attracted to a magnetic field. The magnetic property is a direct result of the unpaired electrons. The spin and angular momentum of the electrons generate tiny magnetic fields. A diamagnetic species has all of the electrons paired. The magnetic fields caused by the electron spin and orbital angular momentum tend to cancel each other. A diamagnetic species is not attracted to a magnetic field, and is, in fact, slightly repelled.

10.28 When two atomic orbitals are different, the weighting of each orbital in forming a molecular orbital may be different. When a molecular orbital is approximated as a linear combination of atomic orbitals of different energies, the lower energy atomic orbital makes a greater contribution to the bonding molecular orbital and the higher energy atomic orbital makes a greater contribution to the antibonding molecular orbital. The shape of the molecular orbital shows a greater electron density at the atom that has the lower atomic orbital energy.

10.29 Nonbonding orbitals are atomic orbitals not involved in a bond and will remain localized on the atom.

10.30 In Lewis theory, a chemical bond is the transfer or sharing of electrons represented as dots. Lewis theory allows us to predict the combination of atoms that form stable molecules, and the general shape of a molecule.

Lewis theory is a quick way to predict the stability and shapes of molecules based on the number of valence electrons. However, it does not deal at all with how the bonds that we make are formed. Valence bond theory is a more advanced bonding theory that treats electrons in a quantum-mechanical manner. A quantitative approach is extremely complicated but a qualitative approach allows an understanding of how the bonds are formed. In valence bond theory, electrons reside in quantum-mechanical orbitals localized on individual atoms. When two atoms approach each other, the electrons and nucleus of one atom interact with the electron and nucleus of the other atom. If the energy of the system is lowered, a chemical bond forms. So, valence bond theory portrays a chemical bond as the overlap of two half-filled atomic orbitals. The shape of the molecule can be predicted from the geometry of the overlapping orbitals. Also, valence bond theory explains the rigidity of the double bond. However, valence bond theory falls short in explaining certain phenomenon such as magnetism and certain bond properties. Valence bond theory treats the electrons as if they reside in the quantum-mechanical orbitals that we calculate for an atom. This is an oversimplification that is partially compensated for by introducing the concept of hybridization. An even more complex quantum-mechanical model is molecular orbital theory. In molecular orbital theory, a chemical bond occurs when the electrons in the atoms can lower their energy by occupying the molecular orbitals of the resultant molecule. The chemical bonds in MO theory are not localized between atoms, but spread throughout the entire molecule. Molecular orbital theory uses trial functions to solve the Schrödinger equation for the molecules. In order to determine how well the trial function works, you calculate the energy, trying to minimize the energy. However, no matter how "good" your guess, you can never do better than nature at minimizing energy. These minimum-energy calculations for orbitals must be done by computer.

All three of these models have strengths and weaknesses, none is "correct." What information you need, depends on which approach you use.

Problems by Topic

VSEPR Theory and Molecular Geometry

10.31 Four electron groups: A trigonal pyramidal molecular geometry has three bonding groups and one lone pair of electrons, so there are four electron pairs on atom A.

10.32 Three electron groups: A trigonal planar molecular geometry has three bonding groups and no lone pairs of electrons so there are three electron pairs on atom A.

10.33 (a) 4 total electron groups, 4 bonding groups, 0 lone pairs
A tetrahedral molecular geometry has four bonding groups and no lone pairs. So, there are four total electron groups, four bonding groups, and pairs.

(b) 5 total electron groups, 3 bonding groups, 2 lone pairs
A T-shaped molecular geometry has three bonding groups and two lone pairs. So, there are five total electron groups, three bonding groups, and two lone pairs.

(c) 6 total electron groups, 5 bonding groups, 1 lone pairs
A square pyramidal molecular geometry has five bonding groups and one lone pair. So, there are six total electron groups, five bonding groups, and one lone pairs.

10.34 (a) 6 total electron groups, 6 bonding groups, 0 lone pairs
An octahedral molecular geometry has six bonding groups and no lone pairs. So, there are six total electron groups, six bonding groups, and no lone pairs.

(b) 6 electron groups, 4 bonding groups, 2 lone pairs
A square planar molecular geometry has four bonding groups and two lone pairs. So, there are six total electron groups, four bonding groups, and two lone pairs.

(c) 5 electron groups, 4 bonding groups, 1 lone pair
A seesaw molecular geometry has four bonding groups and one lone pair. So, there are five total electron groups, four bonding groups, and one lone pair.

10.35 (a) PF_3: Electron geometry–tetrahedral; molecular geometry–trigonal pyramidal; bond angle = 109.5°
Because of the lone pair, the bond angle will be less than 109.5°.
Draw a Lewis structure for the molecule:
PF_3 has 26 valence electrons.

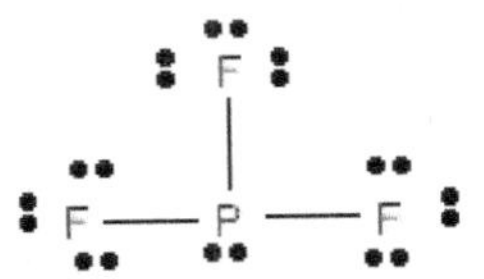

Determine the total number of electron groups around the central atom:
There are four electron groups on P.
Determine the number of bonding groups and the number of lone pairs around the central atom:
There are three bonding groups and one lone pair.
Use Table 10.1 to determine the electron geometry, molecular geometry, and bond angles:
Four electron groups give a tetrahedral electron geometry; three bonding groups and one lone pair give a trigonal pyramidal molecular geometry; the idealized bond angles for tetrahedral geometry are 109.5°. The lone pair will make the bond angle less than idealized.

(b) SBr_2: Electron geometry–tetrahedral; molecular geometry–bent; bond angle = 109.5°
Because of the lone pairs, the bond angle will be less than 109.5°.
Draw a Lewis structure for the molecule:
SBr_2 has 20 valence electrons.

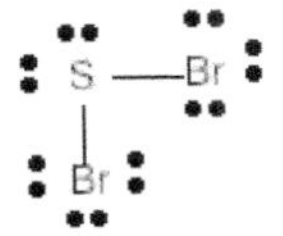

Determine the total number of electron groups around the central atom:
There are four electron groups on S.
Determine the number of bonding groups and the number of lone pairs around the central atom:
There are two bonding groups and two lone pairs.
Use Table 10.1 to determine the electron geometry, molecular geometry, and bond angles:
Four electron groups give a tetrahedral electron geometry; two bonding groups and two lone pair give a bent molecular geometry; the idealized bond angles for tetrahedral geometry are 109.5°. The lone pairs will make the bond angle less than idealized.

(c) $CHCl_3$: Electron geometry–tetrahedral; molecular geometry–tetrahedral; bond angle = 109.5°
Because there are no lone pairs, the bond angle will be 109.5°.
Draw a Lewis structure for the molecule:
$CHCl_3$ has 26 valence electrons.

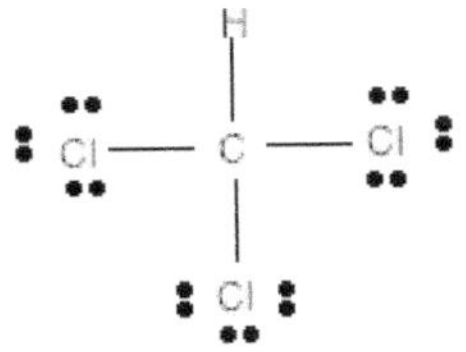

Determine the total number of electron groups around the central atom:
There are four electron groups on C.
Determine the number of bonding groups and the number of lone pairs around the central atom:
There are four bonding groups and no lone pairs.

Use Table 10.1 to determine the electron geometry, molecular geometry, and bond angles: Four electron groups give a tetrahedral electron geometry; four bonding groups and no lone pairs give a tetrahedral molecular geometry; the idealized bond angles for tetrahedral geometry are 109.5°; however, because the attached atoms have different electronegativities the bond angles are less than idealized.

(d) CS_2: Electron geometry–linear; molecular geometry–linear; bond angle = 180°
Because there are no lone pairs, the bond angle will be 180°.
Draw a Lewis structure for the molecule:
CS_2 has 16 valence electrons.

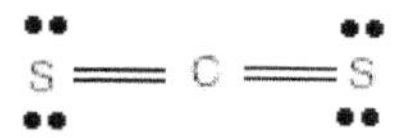

Determine the total number of electron groups around the central atom:
There are two electron groups on C.
Determine the number of bonding groups and the number of lone pairs around the central atom:
There are two bonding groups and no lone pairs.
Use Table 10.1 to determine the electron geometry, molecular geometry, and bond angles:
Two electron groups give a linear geometry; two bonding groups and no lone pairs give a linear molecular geometry; the idealized bond angle is 180°. The molecule will not deviate from this.

10.36 (a) CF_4: Electron geometry–tetrahedral; molecular geometry–tetrahedral; bond angle = 109.5°
Draw a Lewis structure for the molecule:
CF_4 has 32 valence electrons.

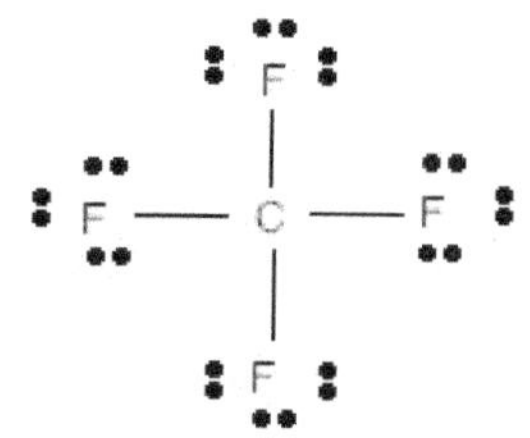

Determine the total number of electron groups around the central atom:
There are four electron groups on C.
Determine the number of bonding groups and the number of lone pairs around the central atom:
There are four bonding groups and no lone pairs.
Use Table 10.1 to determine the electron geometry, molecular geometry, and bond angles:
Four electron groups give a tetrahedral electron geometry; four bonding groups and no lone pairs give a tetrahedral molecular geometry; idealized tetrahedral bond angles for tetrahedral geometry are 109.5°.

(b) NF_3: Electron geometry–tetrahedral; molecular geometry–trigonal pyramidal; bond angle = 109.5°
Because of the lone pair, the bond angle will be less than 109.5°.
Draw a Lewis structure for the molecule:
NF_3 has 26 valence electrons.

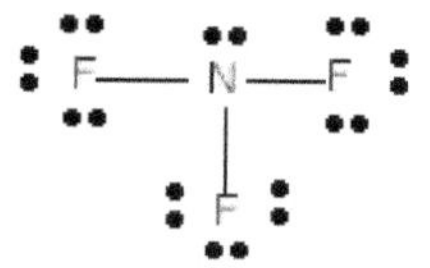

Determine the total number of electron groups around the central atom:
There are four electron groups on N.
Determine the number of bonding groups and the number of lone pairs around the central atom:
There are three bonding groups and one lone pair.
Use Table 10.1 to determine the electron geometry, molecular geometry, and bond angles:

Four electron groups give a tetrahedral electron geometry; three bonding groups and one lone pair give a trigonal pyramidal molecular geometry; the idealized bond angles for tetrahedral geometry are 109.5°. The lone pair will make the bond angles less than idealized.

(c) OF_2: Electron geometry – tetrahedral; molecular geometry – bent; bond angle = 109.5°
Because of the lone pairs, the bond angle will be less than 109.5°.
Draw a Lewis structure for the molecule:
OF_2 has 20 valence electrons.

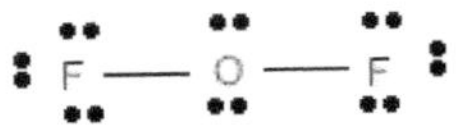

Determine the total number of electron groups around the central atom:
There are four electron groups on O.
Determine the number of bonding groups and the number of lone pairs around the central atom:
There are two bonding groups and two lone pairs.
Use Table 10.1 to determine the electron geometry, molecular geometry, and bond angles:
Four electron groups give a tetrahedral electron geometry; two bonding groups and two lone pairs give a bent molecular geometry; the idealized bond angles for tetrahedral geometry are 109.5°. The lone pairs will make the bond angles less than idealized.

(d) H_2S: Electron geometry – tetrahedral; molecular geometry – bent; bond angle = 109.5°
Because of the lone pair, the bond angle will be less than 109.5°.
Draw a Lewis structure for the molecule:
H_2S has 8 valence electrons.

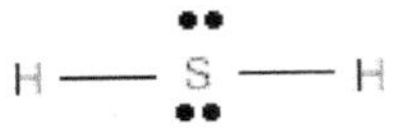

Determine the total number of electron groups around the central atom:
There are four electron groups on S.
Determine the number of bonding groups and the number of lone pairs around the central atom:
There are two bonding groups and two lone pairs.
Use Table 10.1 to determine the electron geometry, molecular geometry, and bond angles:
Four electron groups give a tetrahedral electron geometry; two bonding groups and two lone pairs give a bent molecular geometry; the idealized bond angles for tetrahedral geometry are 109.5°; however, the lone pairs will make the bond angle less than idealized.

10.37 H_2O will have the smaller bond angle because lone pair–lone pair repulsions are greater than lone pair–bonding pair repulsions.

Draw the Lewis structures for both structures:

H_3O^+ has eight valence electrons. H_2O has eight valence electrons.

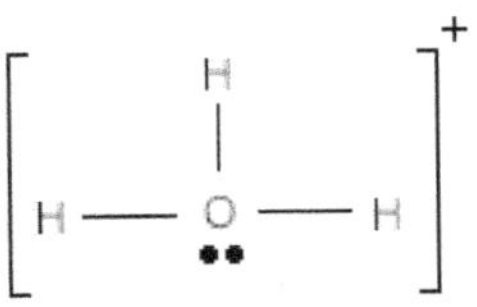

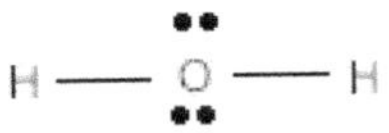

There are three bonding groups and one lone pair. There are two bonding groups and two lone pairs.

Both have 4 electron groups, but the 2 lone pairs in H_2O will cause the bond angle to be smaller because of the lone pair–lone pair repulsions.

10.38 ClO_3^- will have the smaller bond angle because lone pair–bonding pair repulsions are greater than bonding pair–bonding pair repulsions.

Draw the Lewis structures for both structures:

ClO_3^- has 26 valence electrons.

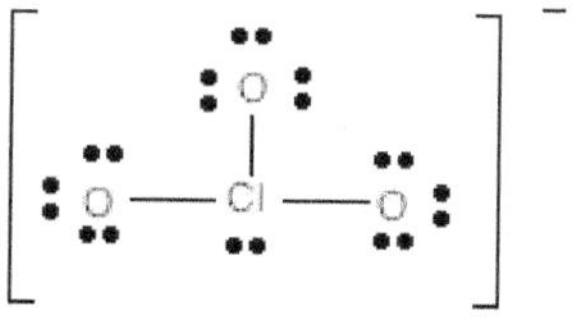

There are three bonding groups and one lone pair.

ClO_4^- has 32 valence electrons.

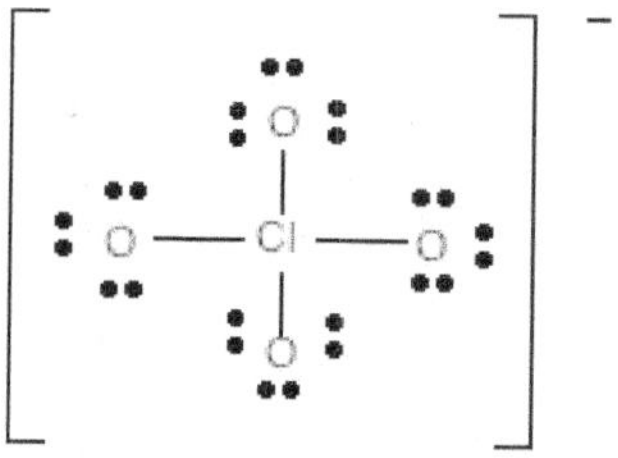

There are four bonding groups and no lone pairs.

Both have four electron groups, but the lone pair in ClO_3^- will cause the bond angle to be smaller because of the lone pair–bonding pair repulsions.

10.39 (a) SF_4 Draw a Lewis structure for the molecule:

SF_4 has 34 valence electrons.

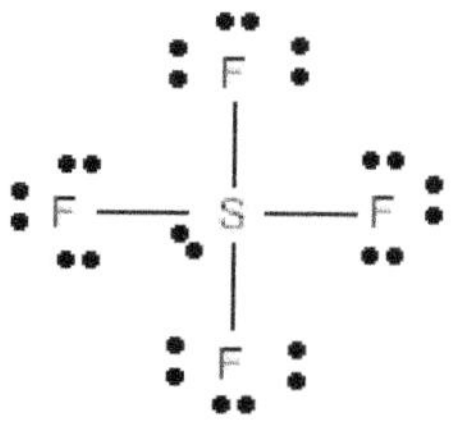

Determine the total number of electron groups around the central atom:
There are five electron groups on S.
Determine the number of bonding groups and the number of lone pairs around the central atom:
There are four bonding groups and one lone pair.
Use Table 10.1 to determine the electron geometry and molecular geometry:
The electron geometry is trigonal bipyramidal so the molecular geometry is seesaw.
Sketch the molecule:

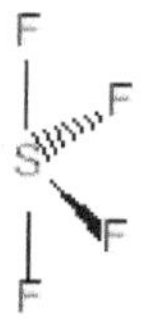

(b) ClF_3 Draw a Lewis structure for the molecule:

ClF_3 has 28 valence electrons.

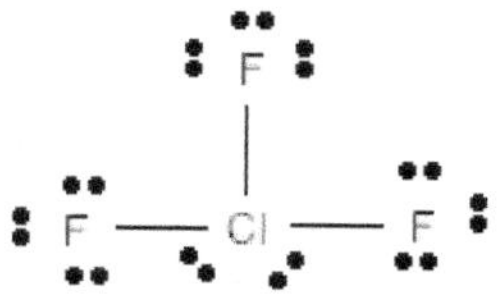

Determine the total number of electron groups around the central atom:
There are five electron groups on Cl.

Determine the number of bonding groups and the number of lone pairs around the central atom:
There are three bonding groups and two lone pairs.
Use Table 10.1 to determine the electron geometry and molecular geometry:
The electron geometry is trigonal bipyramidal so the molecular geometry is T-shaped.
Sketch the molecule:

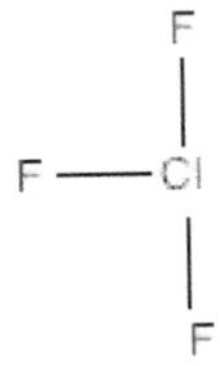

(c) IF_2^- Draw a Lewis structure for the ion:
IF_2^- has 22 valence electrons.

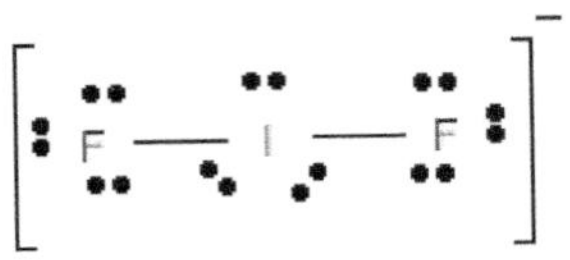

Determine the total number of electron groups around the central atom:
There are five electron groups on I.
Determine the number of bonding groups and the number of lone pairs around the central atom:
There are two bonding groups and three lone pairs.
Use Table 10.1 to determine the electron geometry and molecular geometry:
The electron geometry is trigonal bipyramidal so the molecular geometry is linear.
Sketch the ion:

(d) IBr_4^- Draw a Lewis structure for the ion:
IBr_4^- has 36 valence electrons.

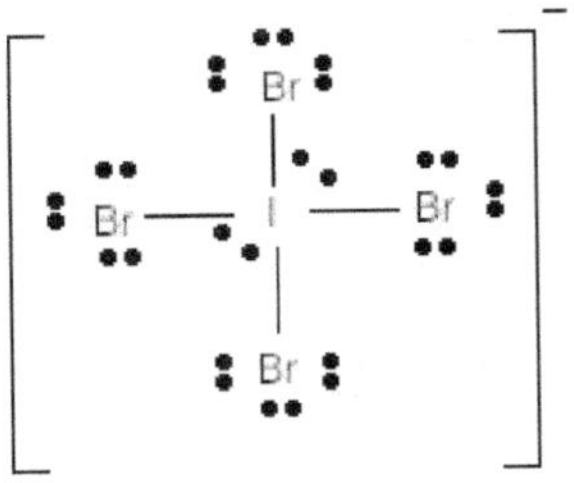

Determine the total number of electron groups around the central atom:
There are six electron groups on I.
Determine the number of bonding groups and the number of lone pairs around the central atom:
There are four bonding groups and two lone pairs.
Use Table 10.1 to determine the electron geometry and molecular geometry:
The electron geometry is octahedral so the molecular geometry is square planar.
Sketch the ion:

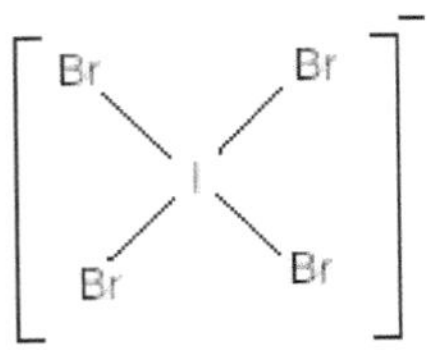

10.40 (a) BrF_5 Draw a Lewis structure for the molecule:
BrF_5 has 42 valence electrons.

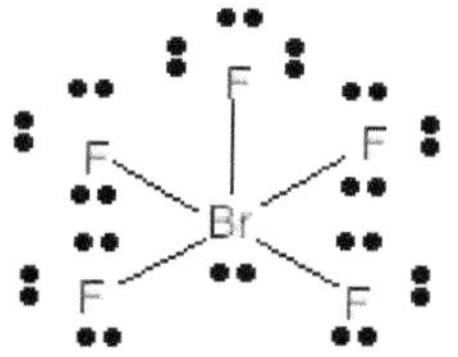

Determine the total number of electron groups around the central atom:
There are six electron groups on Br.
Determine the number of bonding groups and the number of lone pairs around the central atom:
There are five bonding groups and one lone pair.
Use Table 10.1 to determine the electron geometry and molecular geometry:
The electron geometry is octahedral so the molecular geometry is square pyramidal.
Sketch the molecule:

(b) SCl_6 Draw a Lewis structure for the molecule:
SCl_6 has 48 valence electrons.

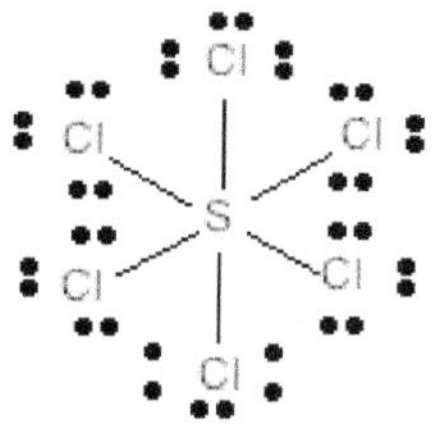

Determine the total number of electron groups around the central atom:
There are six electron groups on S.
Determine the number of bonding groups and the number of lone pairs around the central atom:
There are six bonding groups and no lone pairs.
Use Table 10.1 to determine the electron geometry and molecular geometry:
The electron geometry is octahedral so the molecular geometry is octahedral.
Sketch the molecule:

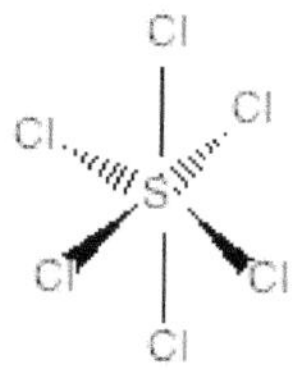

(c) PF_5 Draw a Lewis structure for the molecule:
PF_5 has 40 valence electrons.

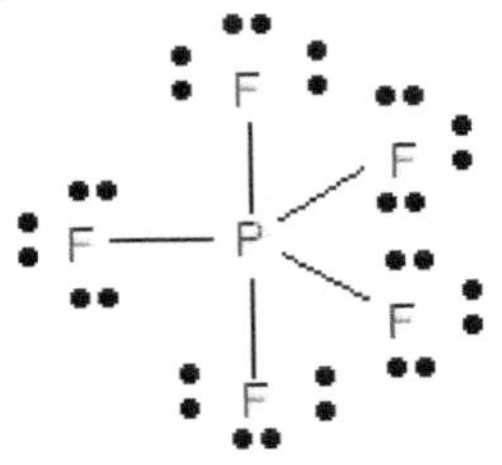

Determine the total number of electron groups around the central atom:
There are five electron groups on P.
Determine the number of bonding groups and the number of lone pairs around the central atom:
There are five bonding groups and no lone pairs.
Use Table 10.1 to determine the electron geometry and molecular geometry:
The electron geometry is trigonal bipyramidal so the molecular geometry is trigonal bipyramidal.
Sketch the molecule:

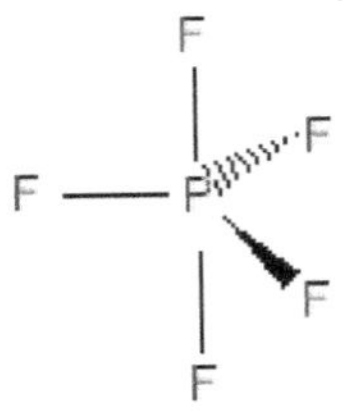

(d) IF_4^+ Draw a Lewis structure for the ion:
IF_4^+ has 34 valence electrons.

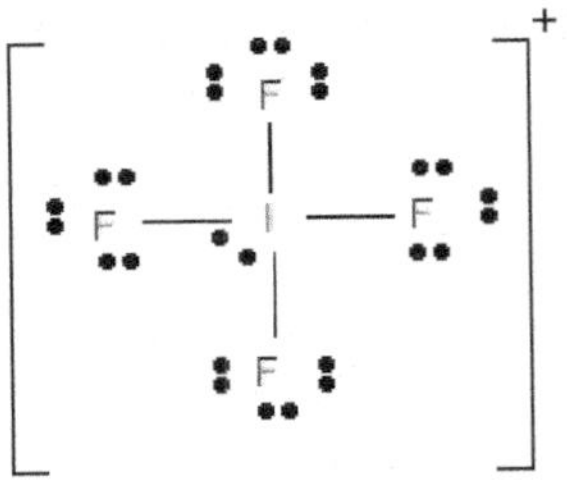

Determine the total number of electron groups around the central atom:
There are five electron groups on I.
Determine the number of bonding groups and the number of lone pairs around the central atom:
There are four bonding groups and one lone pair.
Use Table 10.1 to determine the electron geometry and molecular geometry:
The electron geometry is trigonal bipyramidal so the molecular geometry is seesaw.
Sketch the ion:

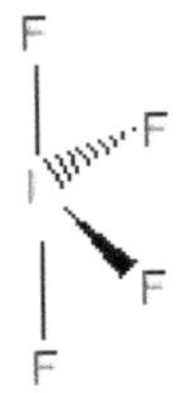

10.41 (a) C_2H_2 Draw the Lewis structure:

Atom	Number of Electron Groups	Number of Lone Pairs	Molecular Geometry
Left C	2	0	Linear
Right C	2	0	Linear

Sketch the molecule:

(b) C_2H_4 Draw the Lewis structure:

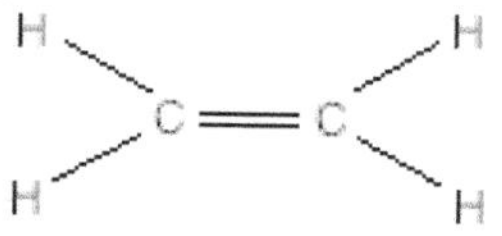

Atom	Number of Electron Groups	Number of Lone Pairs	Molecular Geometry
Left C	3	0	Trigonal planar
Right C	3	0	Trigonal planar

Sketch the molecule:

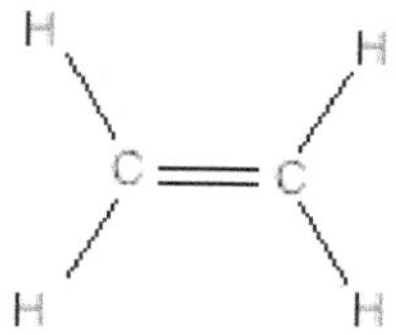

(c) C_2H_6 Draw the Lewis structure:

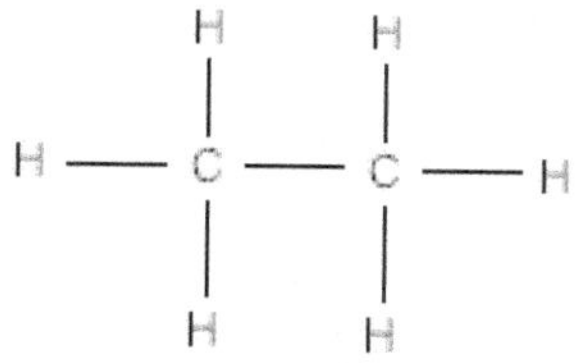

Atom	Number of Electron Groups	Number of Lone Pairs	Molecular Geometry
Left C	4	0	Tetrahedral
Right C	4	0	Tetrahedral

Sketch the molecule:

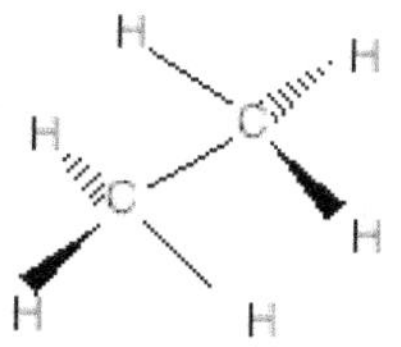

10.42 (a) N_2 Draw the Lewis structure:

Atom	Number of Electron Groups	Number of Lone Pairs	Molecular Geometry
Left N	2	1	Linear
Right N	2	1	Linear

Sketch the molecule:

(b) N_2H_2 Draw the Lewis structure:

Atom	Number of Electron Groups	Number of Lone Pairs	Molecular Geometry
Left N	3	1	Bent
Right N	3	1	Bent

Sketch the molecule:

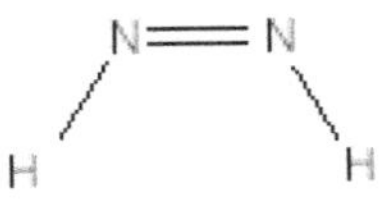

(c) N_2H_4 Draw the Lewis structure:

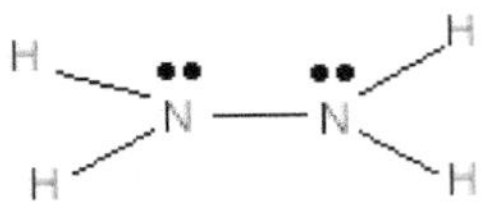

Atom	Number of Electron Groups	Number of Lone Pairs	Molecular Geometry
Left N	4	1	Trigonal pyramidal
Right C	4	1	Trigonal pyramidal

Sketch the molecule:

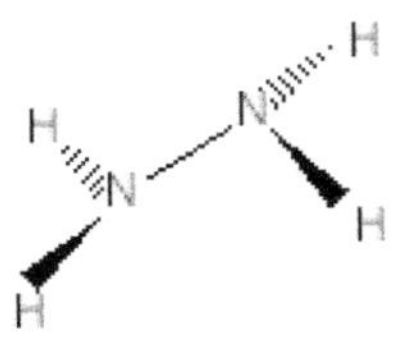

10.43 (a) Four pairs of electrons give a tetrahedral electron geometry. The lone pair would cause lone pair–bonded pair repulsions and would have a trigonal pyramidal molecular geometry.

(b) Five pairs of electrons give a trigonal bipyramidal electron geometry. The lone pair occupies an equatorial position in order to minimize lone pair–bonded pair repulsions and the molecule would have a seesaw molecular geometry.

(c) Six pairs of electrons give an octahedral electron geometry. The two lone pairs would occupy opposite positions in order to minimize lone pair–lone pair repulsions. The molecular geometry would be square planar.

10.44 (a) Four pairs of electrons give a tetrahedral electron geometry. The two lone pairs would cause repulsions that would lead to a bent molecular geometry.

(b) Five pairs of electrons give a trigonal bipyramidal geometry. The three lone pairs would occupy equatorial positions in order to minimize the lone pair–lone pair repulsions. This would give a linear molecular geometry.

(c) Six pairs of electrons give an octahedral electron geometry. The lone pairs would occupy a position to minimize the lone pair–bonded pair repulsions and gives a square pyramidal molecular geometry.

10.45 (a) CH_3OH Draw the Lewis structure and determine the geometry about each interior atom:

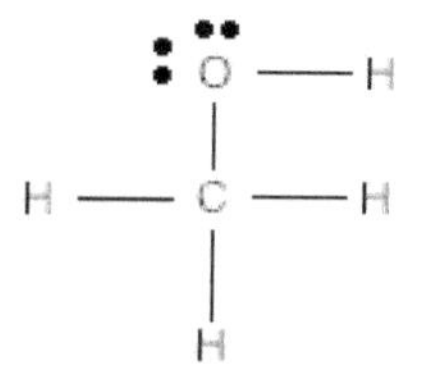

Atom	Number of Electron Groups	Number of Lone Pairs	Molecular Geometry
C	4	0	Tetrahedral
O	4	2	Bent

Sketch the molecule:

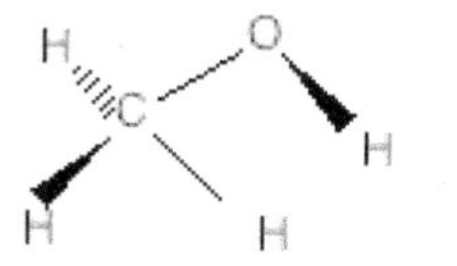

(b) CH_3OCH_3 Draw the Lewis structure and determine the geometry about each interior atom:

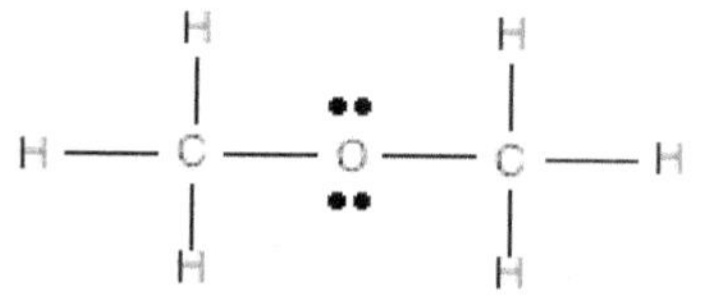

Atom	Number of Electron Groups	Number of Lone Pairs	Molecular Geometry
C	4	0	Tetrahedral
O	4	2	Bent
C	4	0	Tetrahedral

Sketch the molecule:

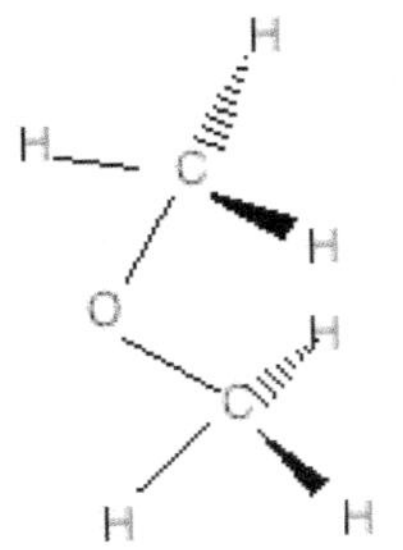

(c) H_2O_2 Draw the Lewis structure and determine the geometry about each interior atom:

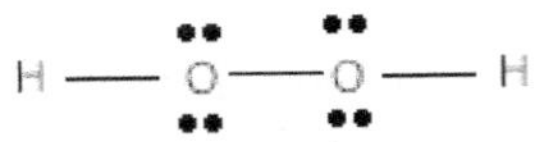

Atom	Number of Electron Groups	Number of Lone Pairs	Molecular Geometry
O	4	2	Bent
O	4	2	Bent

Sketch the molecule:

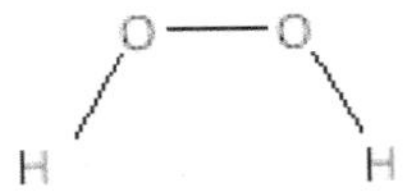

10.46 (a) CH_3NH_2 Draw the Lewis structure and determine the geometry about each interior atom:

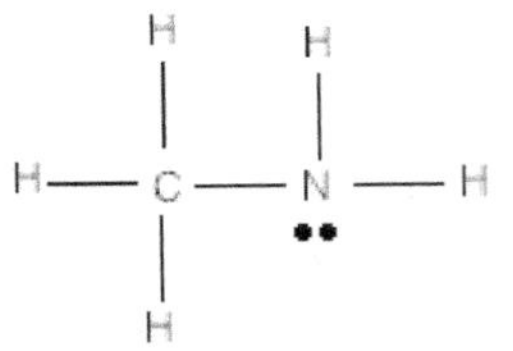

Atom	Number of Electron Groups	Number of Lone Pairs	Molecular Geometry
C	4	0	Tetrahedral
N	4	1	Trigonal Pyramidal

Sketch the molecule:

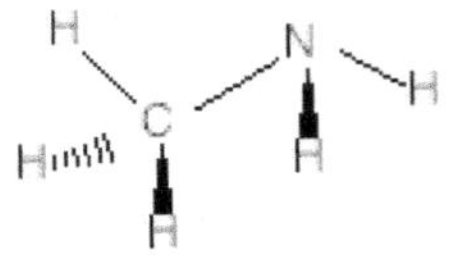

(b) $CH_3CO_2CH_3$ Draw the Lewis structure and determine the geometry about each interior atom:

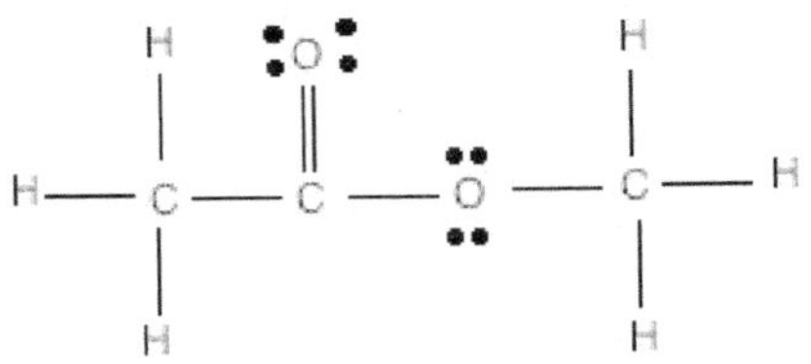

Atom	Number of Electron Groups	Number of Lone Pairs	Molecular Geometry
Left C	4	0	Tetrahedral
Center C	3	0	Trigonal Planar
O	4	2	Bent
Right C	4	0	Tetrahedral

Sketch the molecule:

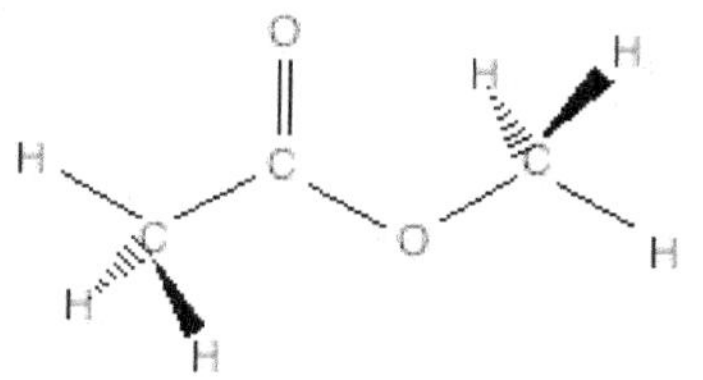

(c) NH_2CO_2H Draw the Lewis structure and determine the geometry about each interior atom:

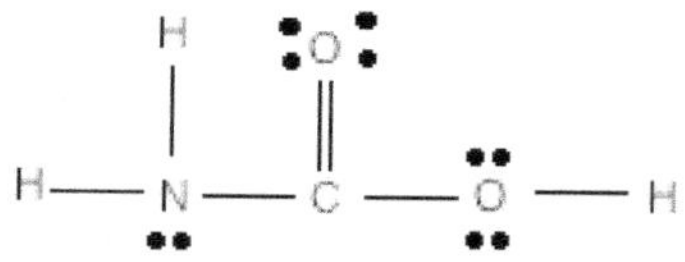

Atom	Number of Electron Groups	Number of Lone Pairs	Molecular Geometry
N	4	1	Trigonal Pyramidal
C	3	0	Trigonal Planar
O	4	2	Bent

Sketch the molecule:

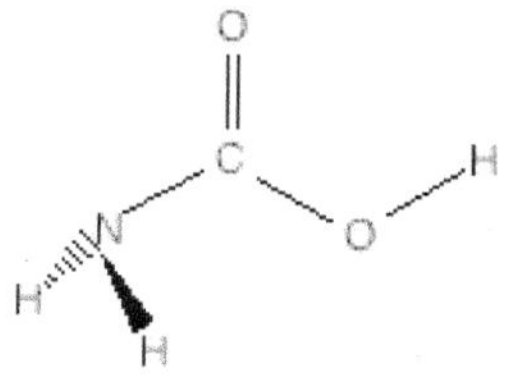

Molecular Shape and Polarity

10.47 Draw the Lewis structure for CO_2 and CCl_4 determine the molecular geometry and then the polarity.

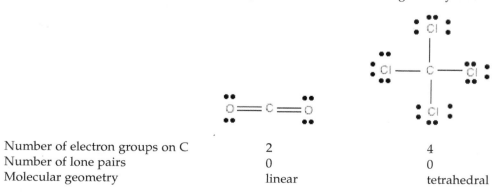

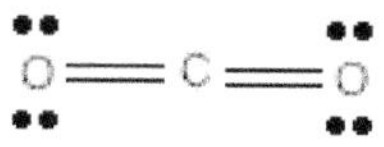

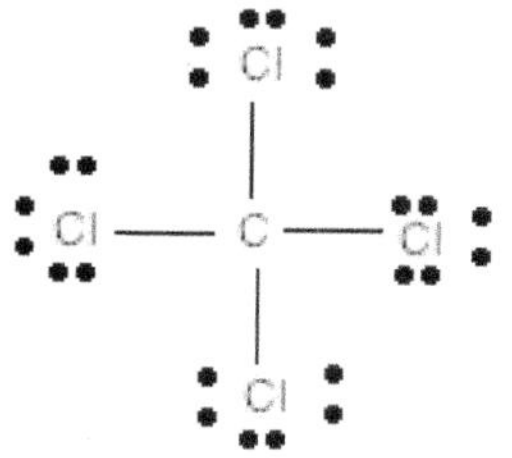

	CO_2	CCl_4
Number of electron groups on C	2	4
Number of lone pairs	0	0
Molecular geometry	linear	tetrahedral

Even though each molecule contains polar bonds, the sum of the bond dipoles gives a net dipole of zero for each molecule.
The linear molecular geometry of CO_2 will have bond vectors that are equal and opposite. 
The tetrahedral molecular geometry of CCl_4 will have bond vectors that are equal and have a net dipole of zero.

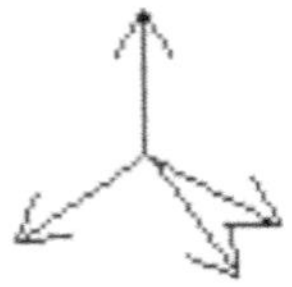

10.48 Draw the Lewis structure of CH_3F determine the molecular geometry and then the polarity.

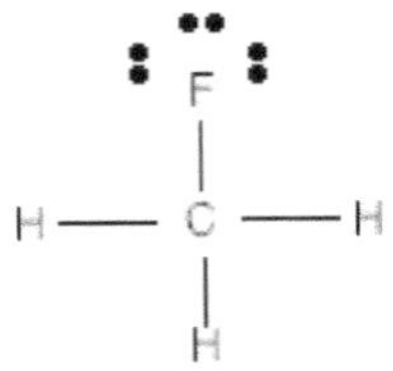

Number of electron groups on C	4
Number of lone pairs	0
Molecular geometry	tetrahedral

The molecule is tetrahedral but is polar because the C – H bond dipoles are different from the C – F bond dipoles. Because the bond dipoles are different, the sum of the bond dipoles is NOT zero. Therefore, the molecule is polar. The tetrahedral molecular geometry of CH_3F will have unequal bond vectors so the molecule will have a net dipole.

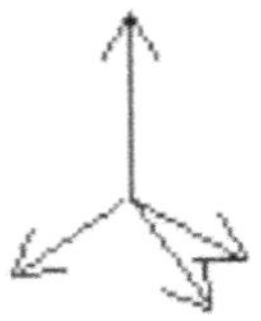

10.49 (a) PF_3 – polar

Draw the Lewis structure and determine the molecular geometry:
The molecular geometry from Exercise 35 is trigonal pyramidal.

Determine if the molecule contains polar bonds:
The electronegativities of P = 2.1 and F = 4. Therefore the bonds are polar.

Determine whether the polar bonds add together to form a net dipole:
Because the molecule is trigonal pyramidal, the three dipole moments sum to a nonzero net dipole moment. The molecule is polar. See Table 10.2 p. 415 in text to see how dipole moments add to determine polarity.

(b) SBr_2 – nonpolar

Draw the Lewis structure and determine the molecular geometry:
The molecular geometry from Exercise 35 is bent.

Determine if the molecule contains polar bonds:
The electronegativities of S = 2.5 and Br = 2.8. Therefore the bonds are nonpolar.

Even though the molecule is bent, since the bonds are nonpolar, the molecule is nonpolar.

(c) $CHCl_3$ – polar

Draw the Lewis structure and determine the molecular geometry:
The molecular geometry from Exercise 35 is tetrahedral.

Determine if the molecule contains polar bonds:
The electronegativities of C = 2.5, H = 2.1, and Cl = 3.0. Therefore the bonds are polar.

Determine whether the polar bonds add together to form a net dipole:
Because the bonds have different dipole moments due to the different atoms involved, the four dipole moments sum to a nonzero net dipole moment. The molecule is polar. See Table 10.2 p. 415 in text to see how dipole moments add to determine polarity.

(d) CS_2 – nonpolar

Draw the Lewis structure and determine the molecular geometry:
The molecular geometry from Exercise 35 is linear.

Determine if the molecule contains polar bonds:
The electronegativities of C = 2.5 and S = 2.5. Therefore the bonds are nonpolar. Also, the molecule is linear, which would result in a zero net dipole even if the bonds were polar.
The molecule is nonpolar. See Table 10.2 p. 415 in text to see how dipole moments add to determine polarity.

10.50 (a) CF_4 – nonpolar

Draw the Lewis structure and determine the molecular geometry:
The molecular geometry from Exercise 36 is tetrahedral.

Determine if the molecule contains polar bonds:
The electronegativities of C = 2.5 and F = 4.0. Therefore the bonds are polar.

Determine whether the polar bonds add together to form a net dipole:
Because the molecular geometry is tetrahedral, the four equal dipole moments sum to a zero net dipole moment. The molecule is nonpolar. See Table 10.2 p. 415 in text to see how dipole moments add to determine polarity.

(b) NF_3 – polar

Draw the Lewis structure and determine the molecular geometry:
The molecular geometry from Exercise 36 is trigonal pyramidal.

Determine if the molecule contains polar bonds:
The electronegativities of N = 3.0 and F = 4.0. Therefore the bonds are polar.

Determine whether the polar bonds add together to form a net dipole:
Because the molecular geometry is trigonal pyramidal, the three dipole moments sum to a nonzero net dipole moment. The molecule is polar. See Table 10.2 p. 415 in text to see how dipole moments add to determine polarity.

(c) OF_2 – polar

Draw the Lewis structure and determine the molecular geometry:
The molecular geometry from Exercise 36 is bent.

Determine if the molecule contains polar bonds:
The electronegativities of O = 3.5 and F = 4.0. Therefore the bonds are polar.

Determine whether the polar bonds add together to form a net dipole:
Because the molecular geometry is bent, the two dipole moments sum to a nonzero net dipole moment. The molecule is polar. See Table 10.2 p. 415 in text to see how dipole moments add to determine polarity.

(d) H_2S – polar

Draw the Lewis structure and determine the molecular geometry:
The molecular geometry from Exercise 36 is bent.

Determine if the molecule contains polar bonds:
The electronegativities of H = 2.1 and S = 2.5. Therefore the bonds are polar.

Determine whether the polar bonds add together to form a net dipole:
Because the molecular geometry is bent, the two dipole moments sum to a nonzero net dipole moment. The molecule is polar. See Table 10.2 p. 415 in text to see how dipole moments add to determine polarity.

10.51 (a) ClO_3^- – polar
Draw the Lewis structure and determine the molecular geometry:

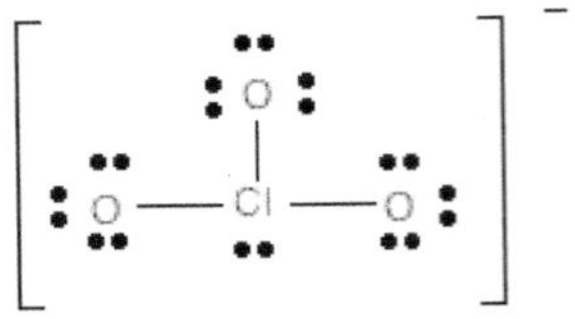

Four electron pairs, with one lone pair give a trigonal pyramidal molecular geometry.

Determine if the molecule contains polar bonds:
The electronegativities of Cl = 3.0 and O = 3.5. Therefore the bonds are polar.

Determine whether the polar bonds add together to form a net dipole:
Because the molecular geometry is trigonal pyramidal, the three dipole moments sum to a nonzero net dipole moment. The molecule is polar. See Table 10.2 p. 415 in text to see how dipole moments add to determine polarity.

(b) SCl_2 – polar
Draw the Lewis structure and determine the molecular geometry:

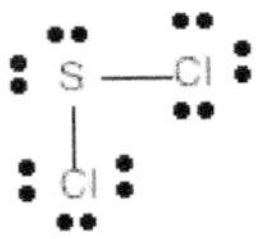

Four electron pairs with two lone pairs give a bent molecular geometry.

Determine if the molecule contains polar bonds:
The electronegativities of S = 2.5 and Cl = 3.0. Therefore the bonds are polar.

Determine whether the polar bonds add together to form a net dipole:
Because the molecular geometry is bent, the two dipole moments sum to a nonzero net dipole moment. The molecule is polar. See Table 10.2 p. 415 in text to see how dipole moments add to determine polarity.

(c) SCl_4 – polar
Draw the Lewis structure and determine the molecular geometry:

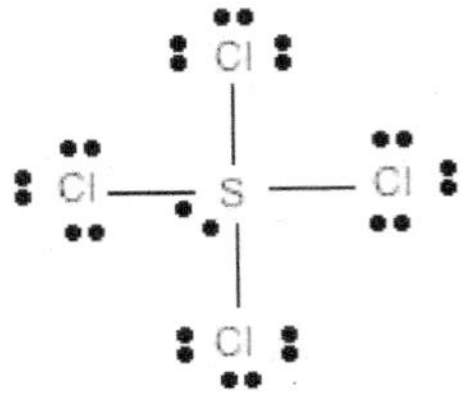

Five electron pairs with one lone pair give a seesaw molecular geometry.

Determine if the molecule contains polar bonds:
The electronegativities of S = 2.5 and Cl = 3.0. Therefore the bonds are polar.

Determine whether the polar bonds add together to form a net dipole:
Because the molecular geometry is seesaw, the four equal dipole moments sum to a nonzero net dipole moment. The molecule is polar.
The seesaw molecular geometry will not have offsetting bond vectors.

(d) $BrCl_5$ – nonpolar
Draw the Lewis structure and determine the molecular geometry.

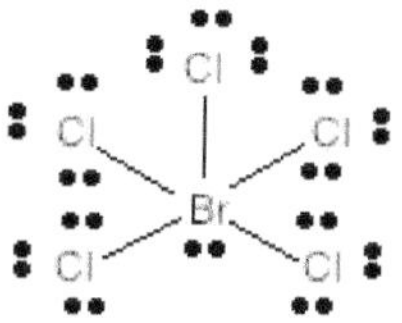

Six electron pairs with one lone pair gives square pyramidal molecular geometry.

Determine if the molecule contains polar bonds:
The electronegativity of Br = 2.8 and Cl = 3.0. The difference is only 0.2, therefore the bonds are nonpolar. Even though the molecular geometry is square pyramidal, the five bonds are nonpolar so there is no net dipole. The molecule is nonpolar.

10.52 (a) $SiCl_4$ – nonpolar
Draw the Lewis structure and determine the molecular geometry:

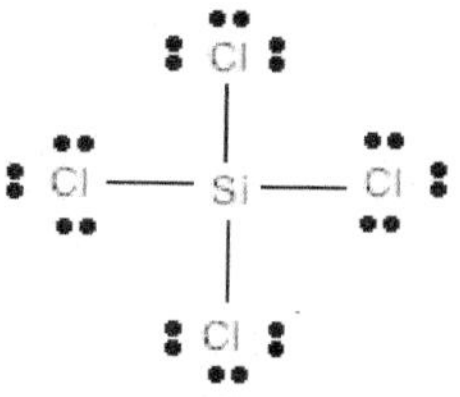

Four electron pairs with no lone pairs give a tetrahedral molecular geometry.

Determine if the molecule contains polar bonds:
The electronegativities of Cl = 3.0 and Si = 1.8. Therefore the bonds are polar.

Determine whether the polar bonds add together to form a net dipole:
Because the molecular geometry is tetrahedral, the four equal dipole moments sum to a zero net dipole moment. The molecule is nonpolar. See Table 10.2 p. 415 in text to see how dipole moments add to determine polarity.

(b) CF_2Cl_2 – polar
Draw the Lewis structure and determine the molecular geometry:

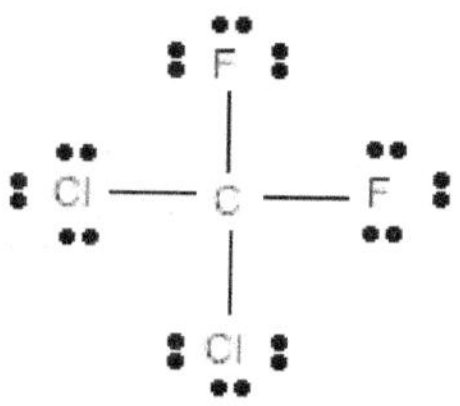

Four electron pairs with no lone pairs give a tetrahedral molecular geometry.

Determine if the molecule contains polar bonds:
The electronegativities of C = 2.5, F = 4.0, and Cl = 3.0. Therefore the bonds are polar.

Determine whether the polar bonds add together to form a net dipole:
Even though the molecular geometry is tetrahedral, which normally yields a nonpolar molecule, the four dipole moments sum to a nonzero net dipole moment because of the different electronegativities of Cl and F. The molecule is polar. See Table 10.2 p. 415 in text to see how dipole moments add to determine polarity.

(c) SeF_6 – nonpolar
Draw the Lewis structure and determine the molecular geometry:

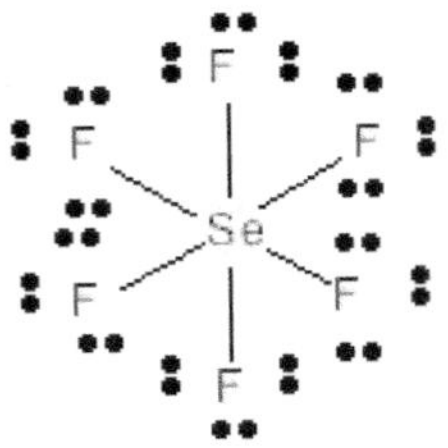

Six electron pairs with no lone pairs give an octahedral molecular geometry.

Determine if the molecule contains polar bonds:
The electronegativities of Se = 3.0 and F = 4.0. Therefore the bonds are polar.

Determine whether the polar bonds add together to form a net dipole:
Because the molecular geometry is octahedral, the six equal dipole moments sum to a zero net dipole moment. The molecule is nonpolar. See Table 10.2 p. 415 in text to see how dipole moments add to determine polarity.

(d) IF_5 – polar
Draw the Lewis structure and determine the molecular geometry:

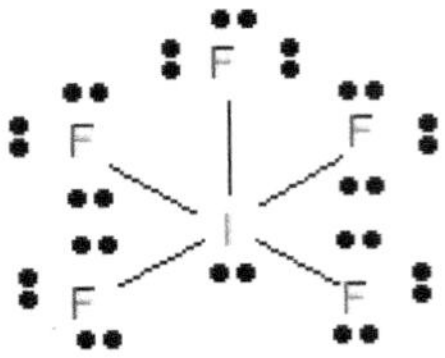

Six electron pairs with one lone pair give square pyramidal molecular geometry.

Determine if the molecule contains polar bonds:
The electronegativities of I = 2.0 and F = 4.0. Therefore the bonds are polar.

Determine whether the polar bonds add together to form a net dipole:
Because the molecular geometry is square pyramidal, the five dipole moments sum to a nonzero net dipole moment. The molecule is polar.
The square pyramid structure has offsetting bond vectors in the equatorial plane, but not in the axial positions.

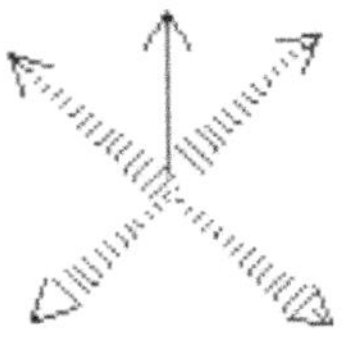

Valence Bond Theory

10.53 (a) Be $2s^2$ No bonds can form. Beryllium contains no unpaired electrons, so no bonds can form without hybridization.

(b) P $3s^23p^3$ Three bonds can form. Phosphorus contains three unpaired electrons, so three bonds can form without hybridization.

(c) F $2s^22p^5$ One bond can form. Fluorine contains one unpaired electron, so one bond can form without hybridization.

10.54 (a) B $2s^22p^1$ One bond can form. Boron contains one unpaired electron, so one bond can form without hybridization.

(b) N $2s^22p^3$ Three bonds can form. Nitrogen contains three unpaired electrons, so three bonds can form without hybridization.

(c) O $2s^22p^4$ Two bonds can form. Oxygen contains two unpaired electrons, so two bonds can form without hybridization.

10.55 PH_3

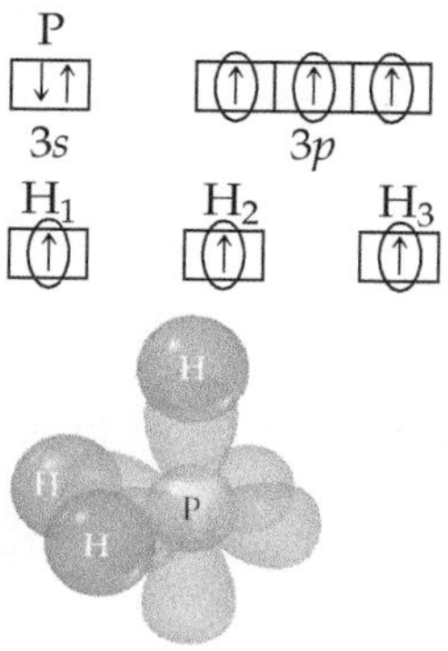

The unhybridized bond angles should be 90°. So, without hybridization, there is good agreement between valence bond theory and the actual bond angle of 93.3°.

10.56 SF_2

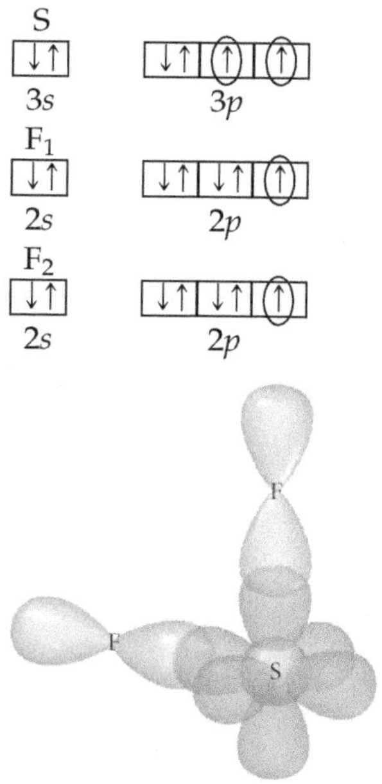

The unhybridized bond angles should be 90°. So, without hybridization, there is not very good agreement between valence bond theory and the actual bond angle of 98.2°.

10.57 C $2s^2 2p^2$

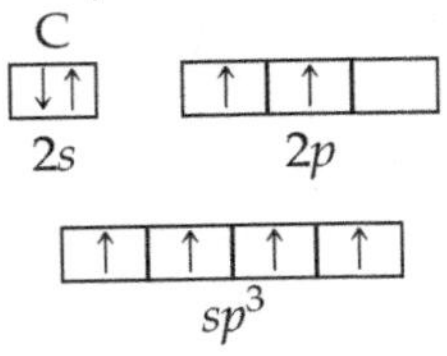

10.58 C $2s^2 2p^2$

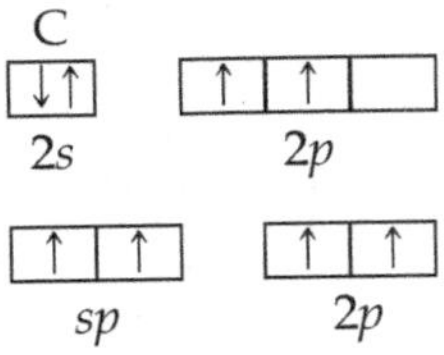

10.59 sp^2 Only sp^2 hybridization of this set of orbitals has a remaining p orbital to form a π bond.
sp^3 hybridization utilizes all 3 p orbitals.
sp^3d^2 hybridization utilizes all 3 p orbitals and 2 d orbitals.

10.60 sp^3d sp^3d hybridization utilizes an s orbital, 3 p orbitals, and d orbital. Since 5 orbitals are used, 5 hybrid orbitals form and 5 bonds can form.
sp^3 Hybridization utilizes an s orbital and 3 p orbitals. Four orbitals are used, so 4 hybrid orbitals form and 4 bonds can form.
sp^2 Hybridization utilizes an s orbital and 2 p orbitals. Three orbitals are used, so 3 hybrid orbitals form. This allows 3 σ and 1 π bond to form for a total of 4 bonds formed.

10.61 (a) CCl_4 Write the Lewis structure for the molecule:

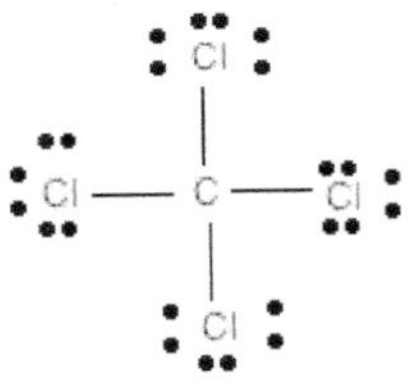

Use VSEPR to predict the electron geometry:
Four electron groups around the central atom give a tetrahedral electron geometry.

Select the correct hybridization for the central atom based on the electron geometry:
Tetrahedral electron geometry has sp^3 hybridization.

Sketch the molecule and label the bonds:

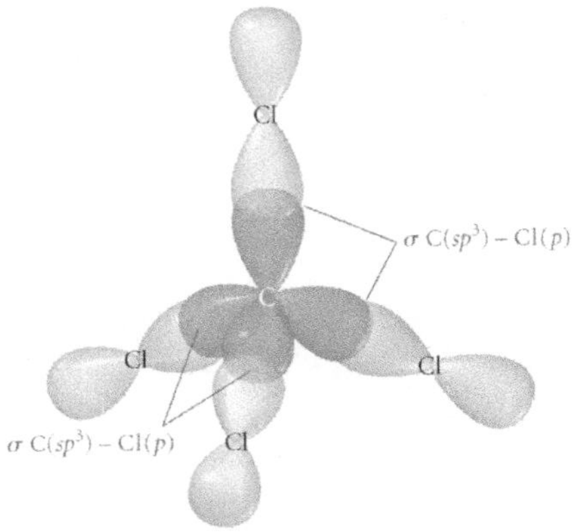

(b) NH_3 Write the Lewis structure for the molecule:

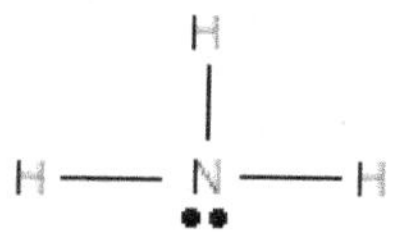

Use VSEPR to predict the electron geometry:
Four electron groups around the central atom give a tetrahedral electron geometry.

Select the correct hybridization for the central atom based on the electron geometry:
Tetrahedral electron geometry has sp^3 hybridization.

Sketch the molecule and label the bonds:

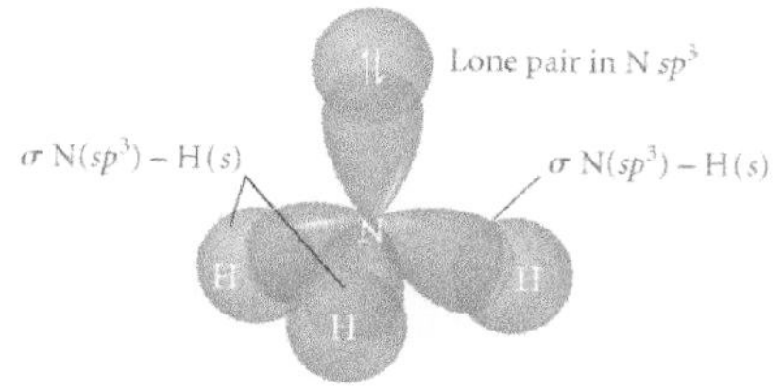

(c) OF_2 Write the Lewis structure for the molecule:

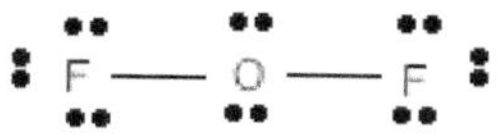

Use VSEPR to predict the electron geometry:
Four electron groups around the central atom give a tetrahedral electron geometry.

Select the correct hybridization for the central atom based on the electron geometry:
Tetrahedral electron geometry has sp^3 hybridization.

Sketch the molecule and label the bonds:

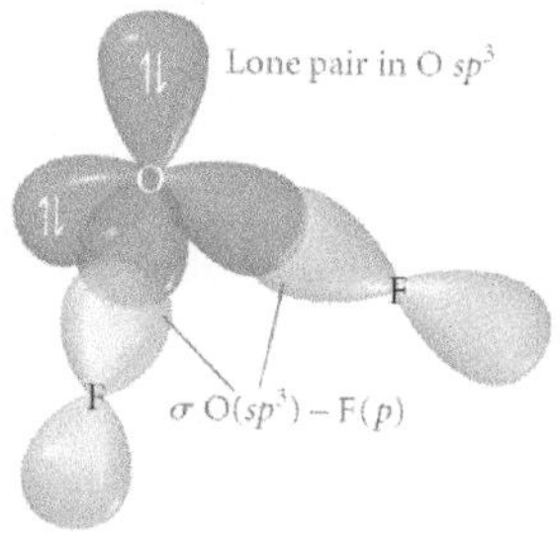

(d) CO_2 Write the Lewis structure for the molecule:

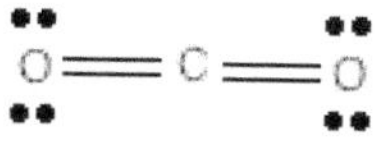

Use VSEPR to predict the electron geometry:
Two electron groups around the central atom give a linear electron geometry.

Select the correct hybridization for the central atom based on the electron geometry:
Linear electron geometry has sp hybridization.

Sketch the molecule and label the bonds:

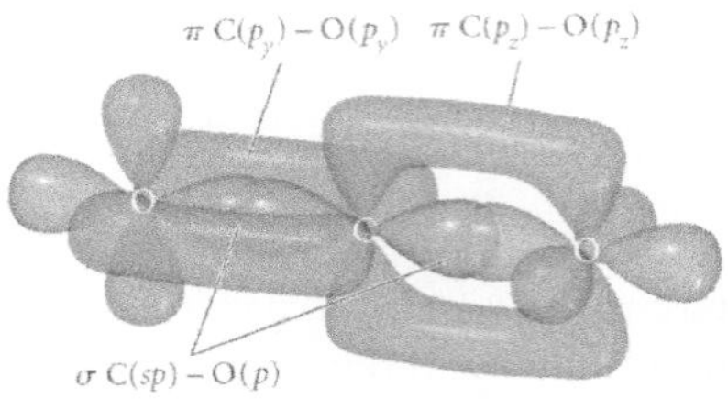

10.62 (a) CH_2Br_2 Write the Lewis structure for the molecule:

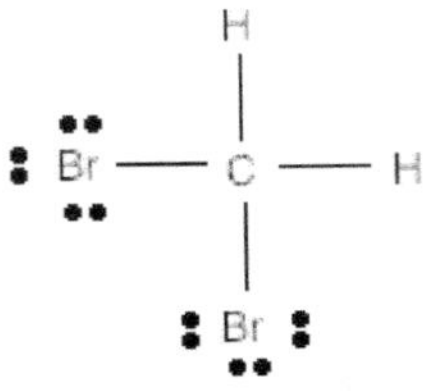

Use VSEPR to predict the electron geometry:
Four electron groups around the central atom give a tetrahedral electron geometry.

Select the correct hybridization for the central atom based on the electron geometry:
Tetrahedral electron geometry has sp^3 hybridization.

Sketch the molecule and label the bonds:

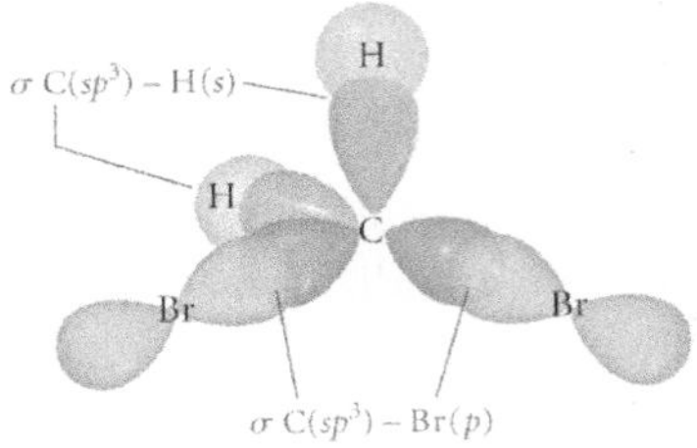

(b) SO_2 Write the Lewis structure for the molecule:

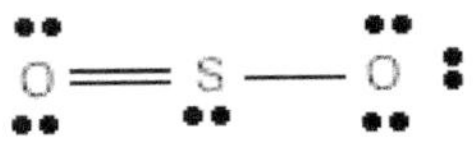

Use VSEPR to predict the electron geometry:
Three electron groups around the central atom give a trigonal planar electron geometry.

Select the correct hybridization for the central atom based on the electron geometry:
Trigonal planar electron geometry has sp^2 hybridization.

Sketch the molecule and label the bonds:

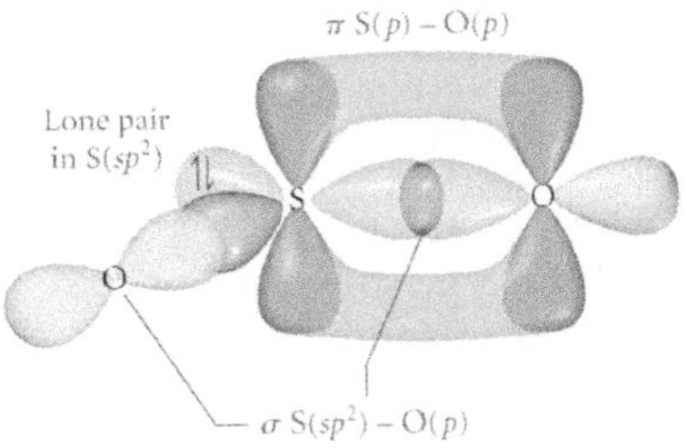

(c) NF_3 Write the Lewis structure for the molecule:

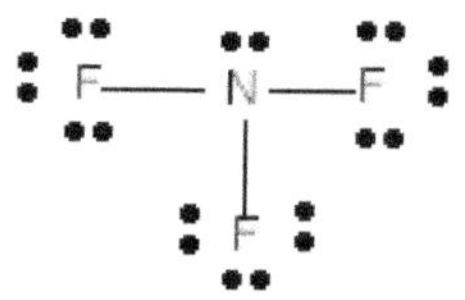

Use VSEPR to predict the electron geometry:
Four electron groups around the central atom give a tetrahedral electron geometry.

Select the correct hybridization for the central atom based on the electron geometry:
Tetrahedral electron geometry has sp^3 hybridization.

Sketch the molecule and label the bonds:

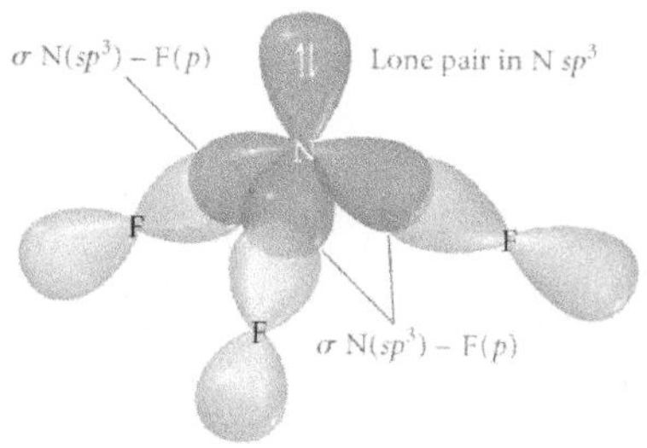

(d) BF_3 Write the Lewis structure for the molecule:

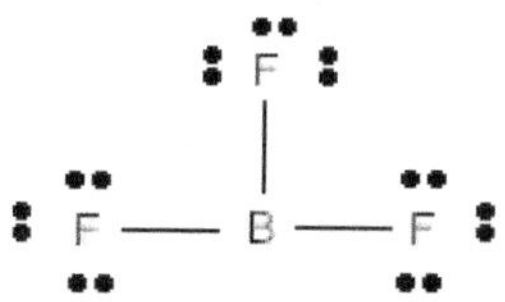

Use VSEPR to predict the electron geometry:
Three electron groups around the central atom give a trigonal planar electron geometry.

Select the correct hybridization for the central atom based on the electron geometry:
Trigonal planar electron geometry has sp^2 hybridization.

Sketch the molecule and label the bonds:

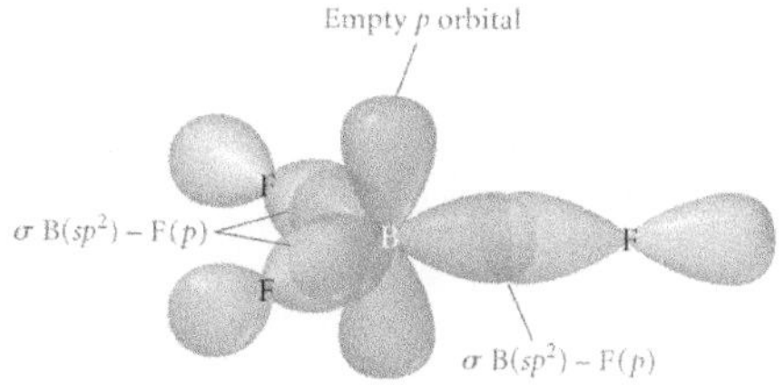

10.63 (a) $COCl_2$ Write the Lewis structure for the molecule:

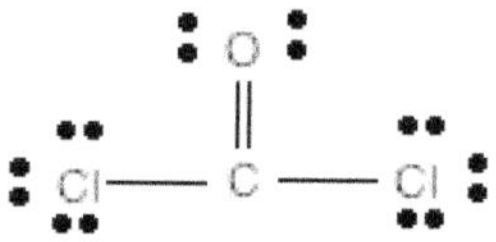

Use VSEPR to predict the electron geometry:
Three electron groups around the central atom give a trigonal planar electron geometry.

Select the correct hybridization for the central atom based on the electron geometry:
Trigonal planar electron geometry has sp^2 hybridization.

Sketch the molecule and label the bonds:

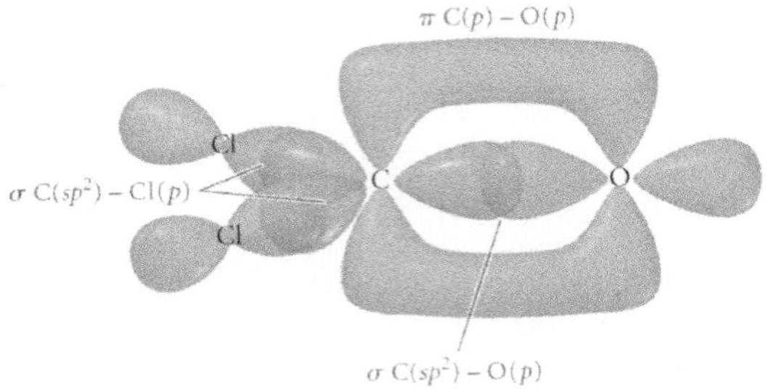

(b) BrF_5 Write the Lewis structure for the molecule:

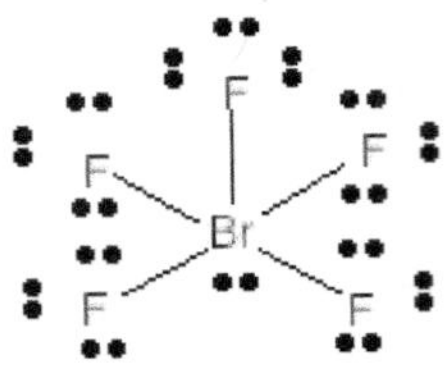

Use VSEPR to predict the electron geometry:
Six electron pairs around the central atoms gives an octahedral electron geometry.

Select the correct hybridization for the central atom based on the electron geometry:
Octahedral electron geometry has sp^3d^2 hybridization.

Sketch the molecule and label the bonds:

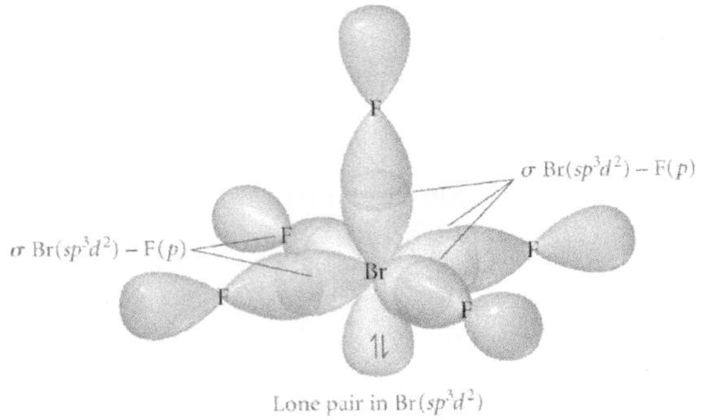

(c) XeF_2 Write the Lewis structure for the molecule:

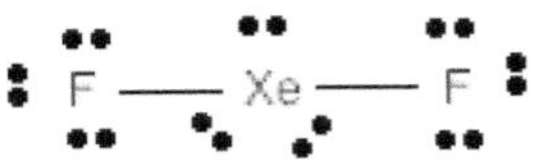

Use VSEPR to predict the electron geometry:
Five electron groups around the central atom give a trigonal bipyramidal geometry.

Select the correct hybridization for the central atom based on the electron geometry:
Trigonal bipyramidal geometry has sp^3d hybridization.

Sketch the molecule and label the bonds:

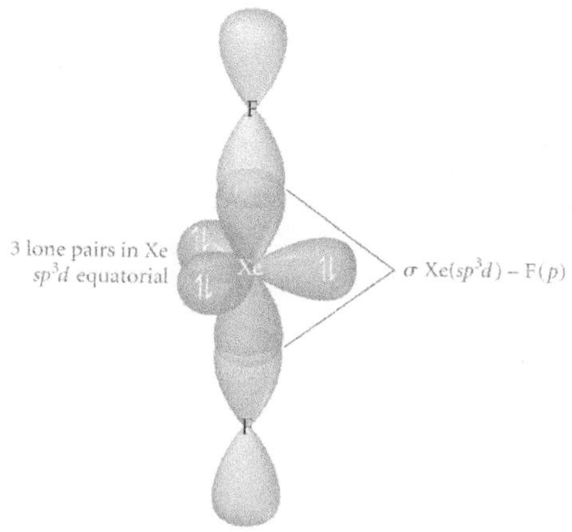

(d) I_3^- Write the Lewis structure for the molecule:

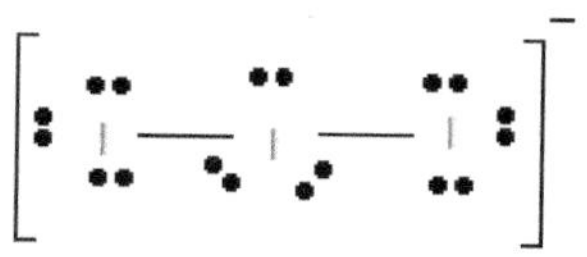

Use VSEPR to predict the electron geometry:
Five electron groups around the central atom give a trigonal bipyramidal geometry.

Select the correct hybridization for the central atom based on the electron geometry:
Trigonal bipyramidal geometry has sp^3d hybridization.

Sketch the molecule and label the bonds:

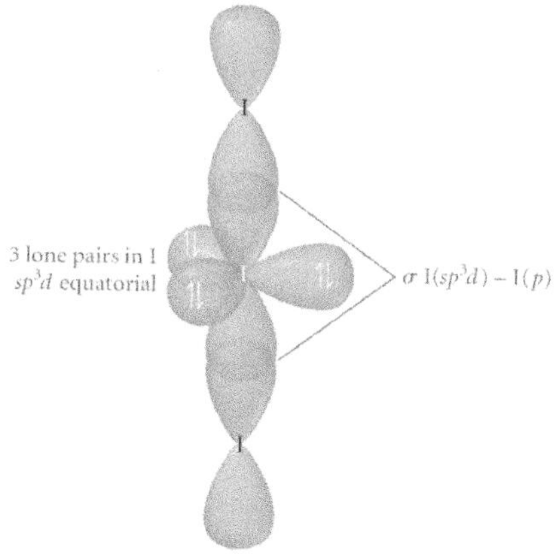

10.64 (a) SO_3^{2-} Write the Lewis structure for the ion:

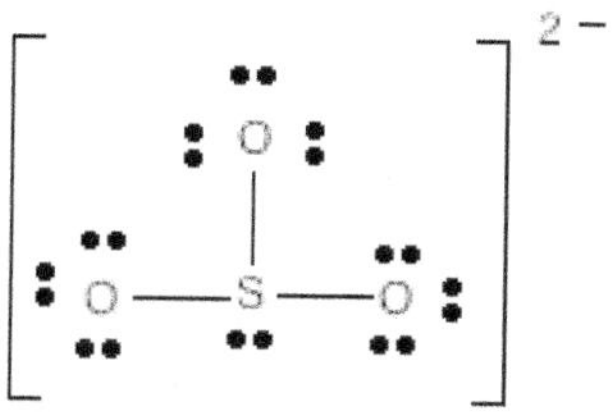

Use VSEPR to predict the electron geometry:
Four electron groups around the central atom give a tetrahedral electron geometry.

Select the correct hybridization for the central atom based on the electron geometry:
Tetrahedral electron geometry has sp^3 hybridization.

Sketch the molecule and label the bonds:

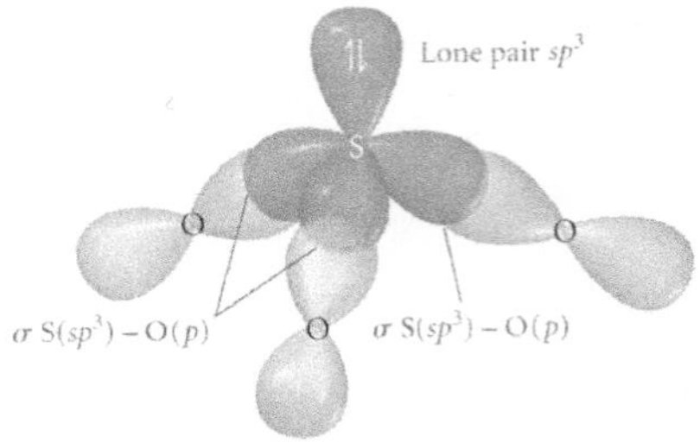

(b) PF_6^- Write the Lewis structure for the ion:

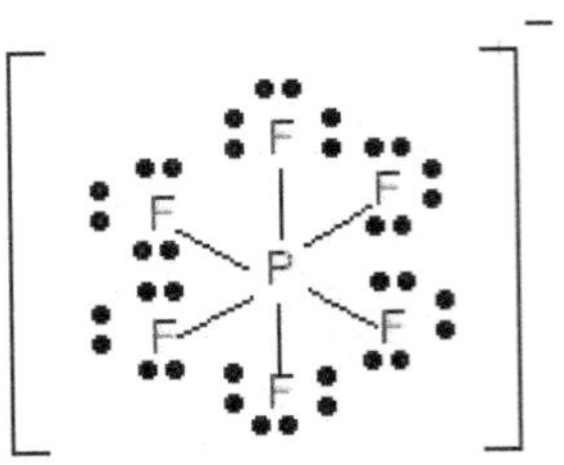

Use VSEPR to predict the electron geometry:
Six electron pairs around the central atoms give an octahedral electron geometry.

Select the correct hybridization for the central atom based on the electron geometry:
Octahedral electron geometry has sp^3d^2 hybridization.

Sketch the molecule and label the bonds:

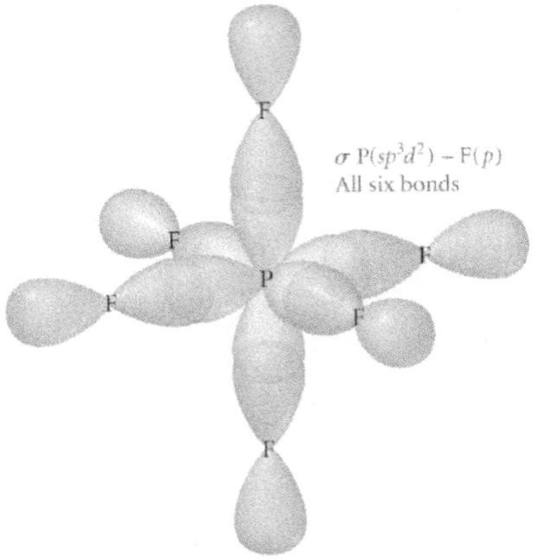

(c) BrF_3 Write the Lewis structure for the molecule:

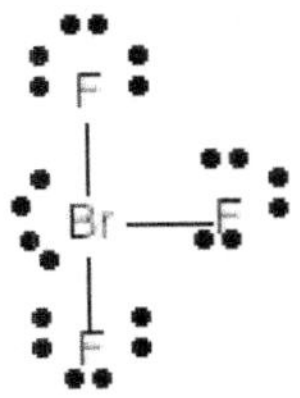

Use VSEPR to predict the electron geometry:
Five electron groups around the central atom give a trigonal bipyramidal geometry.

Select the correct hybridization for the central atom based on the electron geometry:
Trigonal bipyramidal geometry has sp^3d hybridization.

Sketch the molecule and label the bonds:

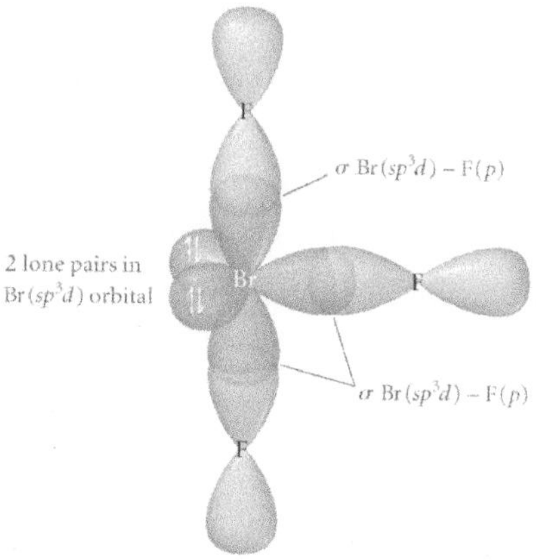

(d) HCN Write the Lewis structure for the molecule:

H — C ≡ N :

Use VSEPR to predict the electron geometry:
Two electron groups around the central atom give a linear electron geometry.

Select the correct hybridization for the central atom based on the electron geometry:
Linear electron geometry has *sp* hybridization.

Sketch the molecule and label the bonds:

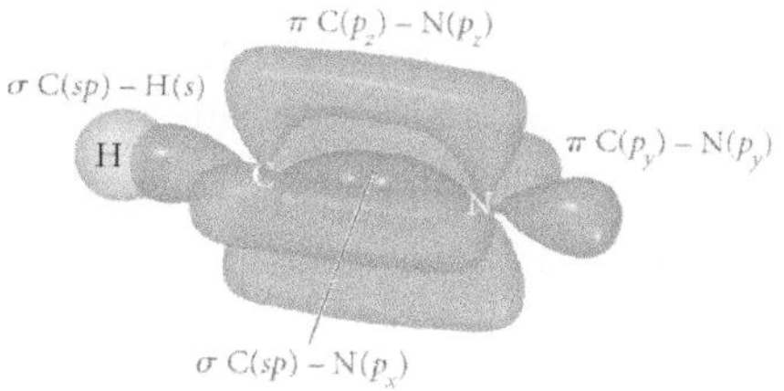

10.65 (a) N_2H_2 Write the Lewis structure for the molecule:

H — N̈ = N̈ — H

Use VSEPR to predict the electron geometry:
Three electron groups around each interior atom give a trigonal planar electron geometry.

Select the correct hybridization for the central atoms based on the electron geometry:
Trigonal planar electron geometry has sp^2 hybridization.

Sketch the molecule and label the bonds:

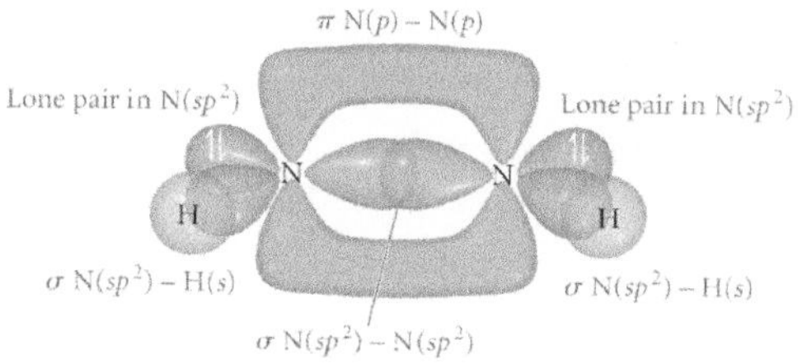

(b) N_2H_4 Write the Lewis structure for the molecule:

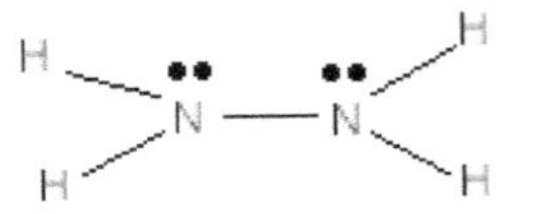

Use VSEPR to predict the electron geometry:
Four electron groups around each interior atom gives tetrahedral electron geometry.

Select the correct hybridization for the central atoms based on the electron geometry:
Tetrahedral electron geometry has sp^3 hybridization.

Sketch the molecule and label the bonds:

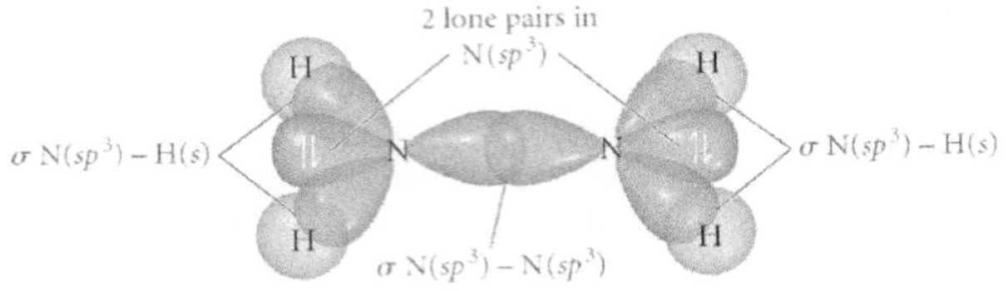

(c) CH_3NH_2 Write the Lewis structure for the molecule:

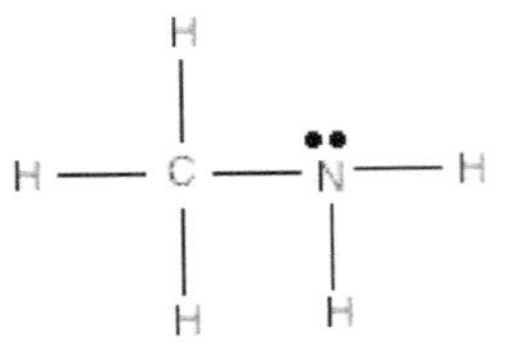

Use VSEPR to predict the electron geometry:
Four electron groups around the C give a tetrahedral electron geometry around the C atom, and four electron groups around the N give a tetrahedral geometry around the N atom.

Select the correct hybridization for the central atoms based on the electron geometry:
Tetrahedral electron geometry has sp^3 hybridization of both C and N.

Sketch the molecule and label the bonds:

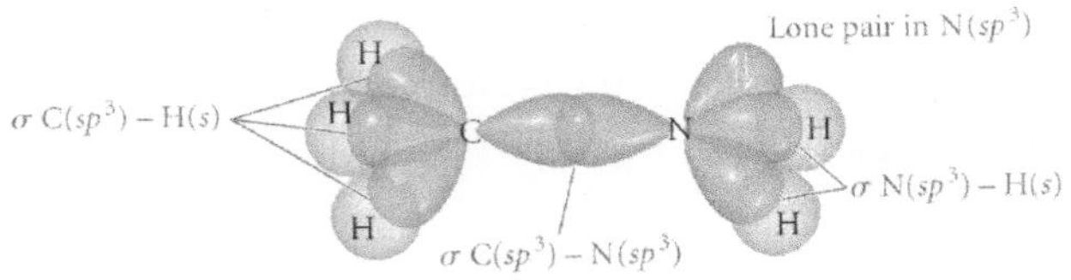

10.66 (a) C_2H_2 Write the Lewis structure for the molecule:

Use VSEPR to predict the electron geometry:
Two electron groups around each interior atom give a linear electron geometry.

Select the correct hybridization for the central atoms based on the electron geometry:
Linear electron geometry has sp hybridization.

Sketch the molecule and label the bonds:

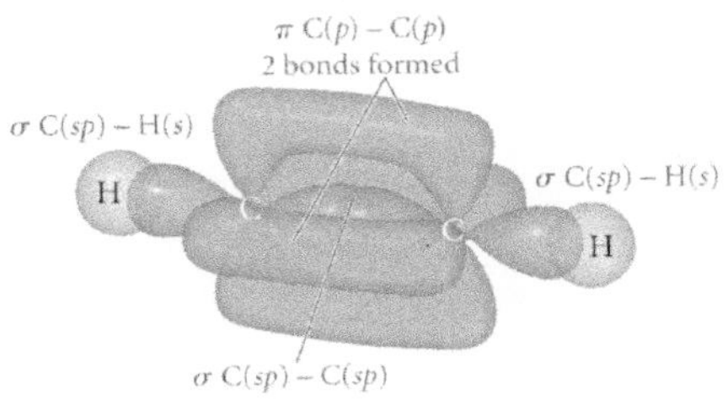

(b) C_2H_4 Write the Lewis structure for the molecule:

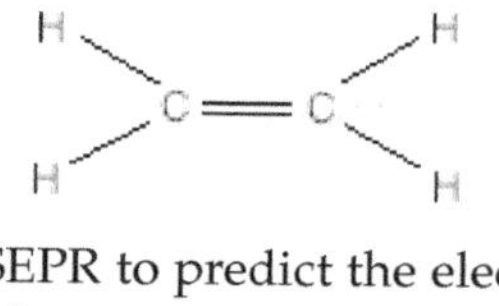

Use VSEPR to predict the electron geometry:
Three electron groups around each interior atom give a trigonal planar electron geometry.

Select the correct hybridization for the central atoms based on the electron geometry:
Trigonal planar electron geometry has sp^2 hybridization.

Sketch the molecule and label the bonds:

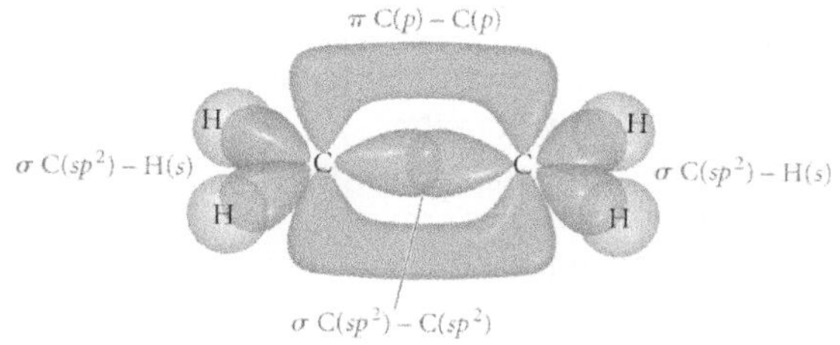

(c) C_2H_6 Write the Lewis structure for the molecule:

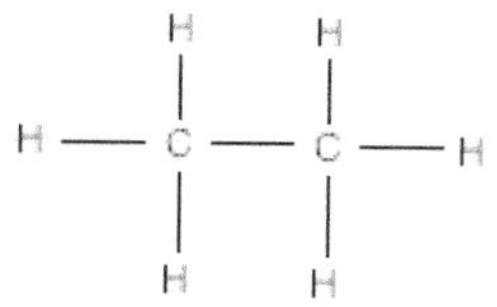

Use VSEPR to predict the electron geometry:
Four electron groups around each interior atoms give a tetrahedral electron geometry.

Select the correct hybridization for the central atoms based on the electron geometry:
Tetrahedral electron geometry has sp^3 hybridization.

Sketch the molecule and label the bonds:

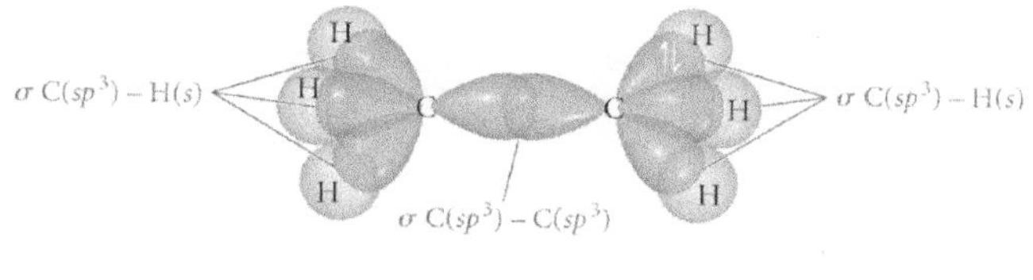

10.67

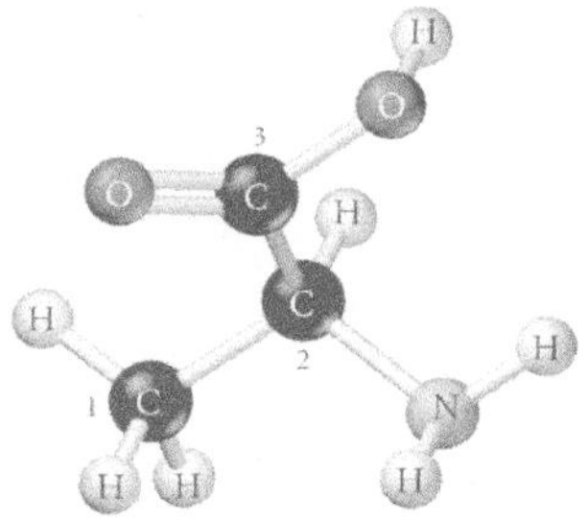

C – 1 and C – 2 each have four electron pairs around the atom, which is tetrahedral electron pair geometry. Tetrahedral electron pair geometry is sp^3 hybridization.
C – 3 has three electron groups around the atom, which is trigonal planar electron pair geometry. Trigonal planar electron pair geometry is sp^2 hybridization.
O has four electron pairs around the atom, which is tetrahedral electron pair geometry. Tetrahedral electron pair geometry is sp^3 hybridization.

N has four electron pairs around the atom, which is tetrahedral electron pair geometry. Tetrahedral electron pair geometry is sp^3 hybridization.

10.68

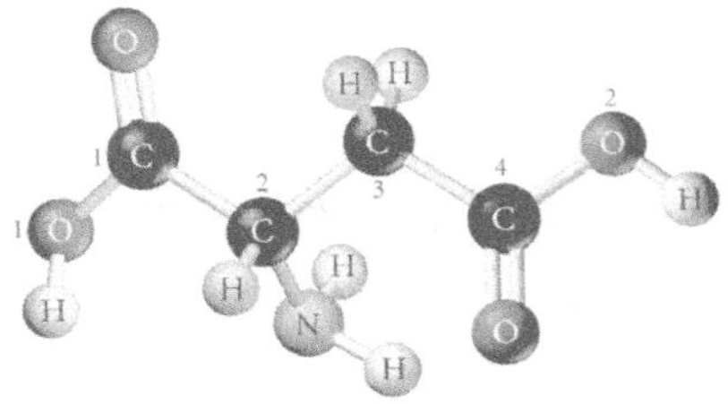

C – 1 and C – 4 each have three electron groups around the atom, which is trigonal planar electron pair geometry. Trigonal planar electron pair geometry is sp^2 hybridization.
C – 2 and C – 3 each have four electron pairs around the atom, which is tetrahedral electron pair geometry. Tetrahedral electron pair geometry is sp^3 hybridization.
O – 1 and O – 2 each have four electron pairs around the atom, which is tetrahedral electron pair geometry. Tetrahedral electron pair geometry is sp^3 hybridization.
N has four electron pairs around the atom, which is tetrahedral electron pair geometry. Tetrahedral electron pair geometry is sp^3 hybridization.

Molecular Orbital Theory

10.69 1*s* + 1*s* constructive interference results in a bonding orbital:

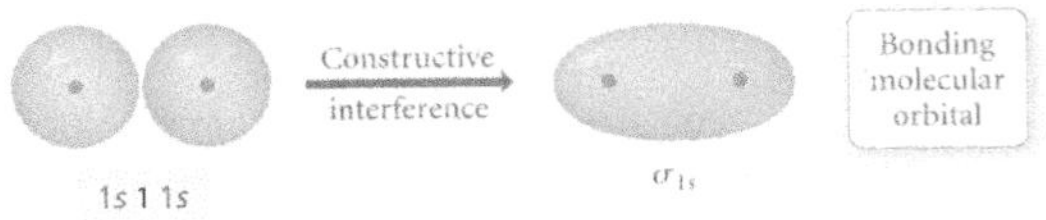

10.70 1*s* – 1*s* destructive interference results in an antibonding orbital:

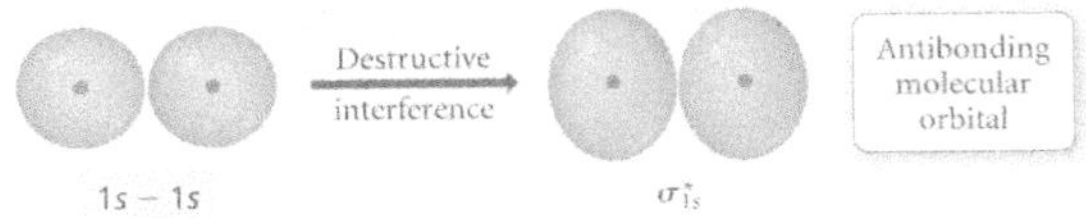

10.71 Be_2^+ has seven electrons.

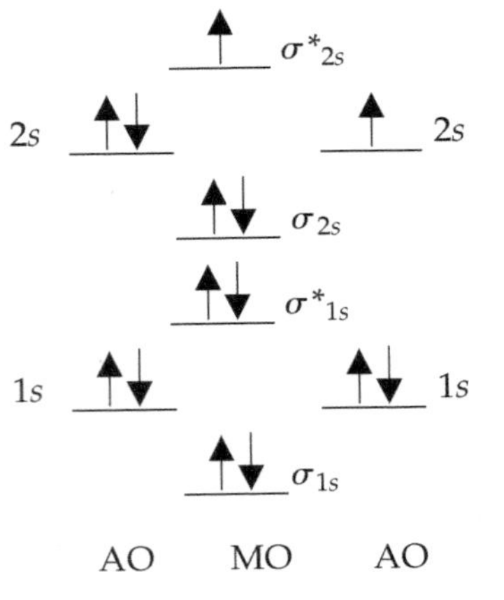

Be_2^- has nine electrons.

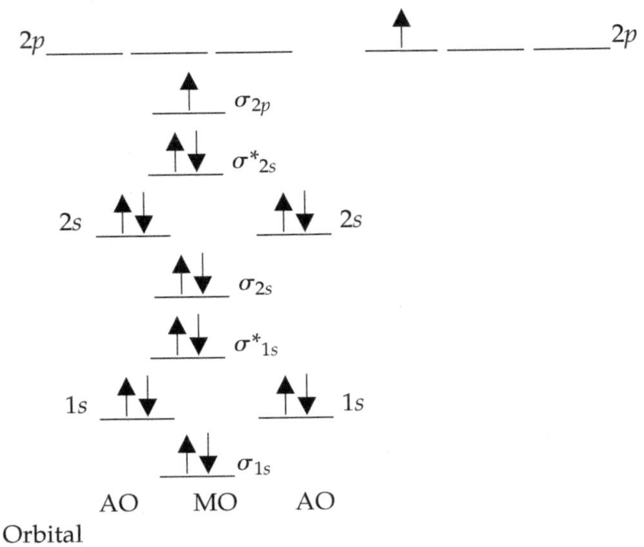

AO = Atomic Orbital; MO = Molecular Orbital

Bond order $= \dfrac{4-3}{2} = \dfrac{1}{2}$ stable

Bond order $= \dfrac{5-4}{2} = \dfrac{1}{2}$ stable

10.72 Li_2^+ has five electrons. Li_2^- has seven electrons.

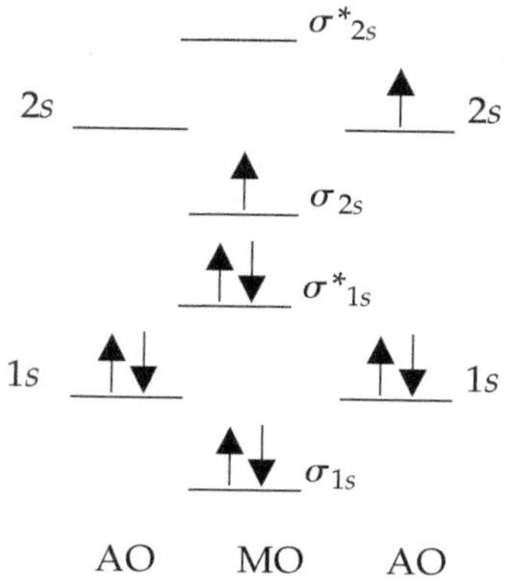

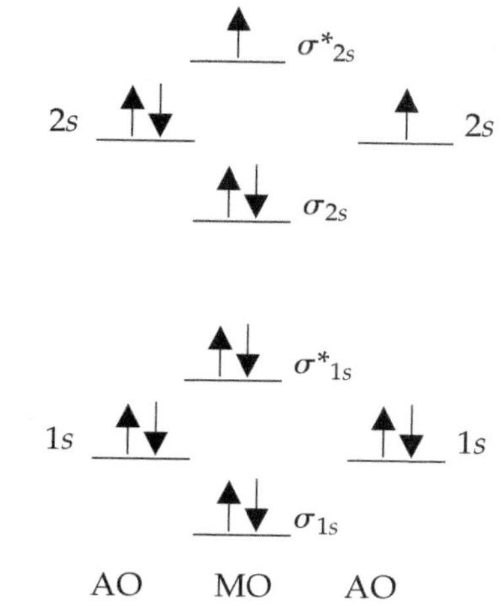

AO = Atomic Orbital; MO = Molecular Orbital

Bond order $= \dfrac{3-2}{2} = \dfrac{1}{2}$ stable   Bond order $= \dfrac{4-3}{2} = \dfrac{1}{2}$ stable

10.73 The bonding and antibonding molecular orbitals from the combination of p_x and p_x atomic orbitals lie along the internuclear axis.

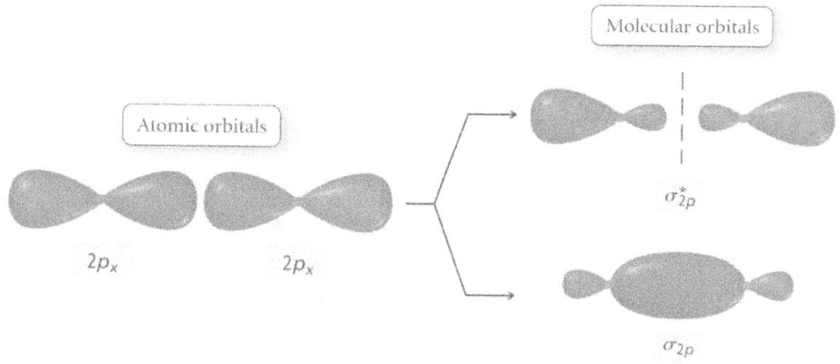

10.74 The bonding and antibonding molecular orbitals from the combination of p_y and p_y atomic orbitals lie above and below the internuclear axis.

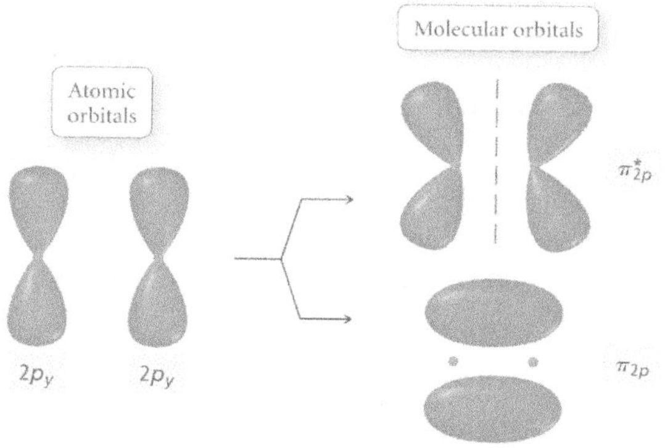

When the p_z and the p_z orbitals combine, similar bonding and antibonding molecular orbitals form. The only difference between the resulting MOs is a rotation about the internuclear axis. The energies and the names

of the bonding and antibonding MOs obtained from the combination of the p_z atomic orbitals are identical to those obtained from the combination of the p_y atomic orbitals, which lie in front and in back of the internuclear axis.

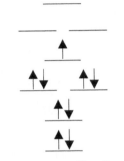

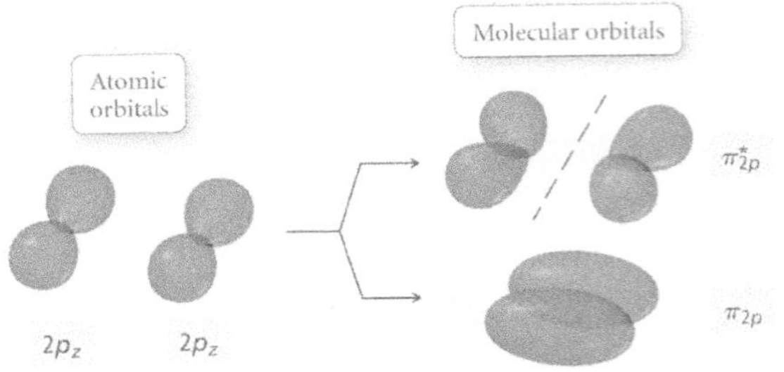

10.75

	(a) 4 valence electrons	(b) 6 valence electrons	(c) 8 valence electrons	(d) 9 valence electrons
σ^*_{2p}	___	___	___	___
σ^*_{2p}	___ ___	___ ___	___ ___	___ ___
σ_{2p}	___	___	___	↑
π_{2p}	___ ___	↑ ↑	↑↓ ↑↓	↑↓ ↑↓
σ^*_{2s}	↑↓	↑↓	↑↓	↑↓
σ_{2s}	↑↓	↑↓	↑↓	↑↓
	Bond order $= \frac{2-2}{2} = 0$	Bond order $= \frac{4-2}{2} = 1$	Bond order $= \frac{6-2}{2} = 2$	Bond order $= \frac{7-2}{2} = 2.5$
	diamagnetic	paramagnetic	diamagnetic	paramagnetic

10.76

	(a) 10 valence electrons	(b) 12 valence electrons	(c) 13 valence electrons	(d) 14 valence electrons
σ^*_{2p}	___	___	___	___
σ^*_{2p}	___ ___	↑ ↑	↑↓ ↑	↑↓ ↑↓
π_{2p}	↑↓ ↑↓	↑↓ ↑↓	↑↓ ↑↓	↑↓ ↑↓
σ_{2p}	↑↓	↑↓	↑↓	↑↓
σ^*_{2s}	↑↓	↑↓	↑↓	↑↓
σ_{2s}	↑↓	↑↓	↑↓	↑↓
	Bond order $= \frac{8-2}{2} = 3$	Bond order $= \frac{8-4}{2} = 2$	Bond order $= \frac{8-5}{2} = 1.5$	Bond order $= \frac{8-6}{2} = 1$
	diamagnetic	paramagnetic	paramagnetic	diamagnetic

10.77 (a) Write an energy level diagram for the molecular orbitals in H_2^{2-}. The ion has four valence electrons. Assign the electrons to the molecular orbitals beginning with the lowest energy orbitals and following Hund's rule.

σ^*_{1s} ↑↓

σ_{1s} ↑↓ Bond order $= \frac{2-2}{2} = 0.$ With a bond order of 0, the ion will not exist.

(b) Write an energy level diagram for the molecular orbitals in Ne_2. The molecule has 16 valence electrons. Assign the electrons to the molecular orbitals beginning with the lowest energy orbitals and following Hund's rule.

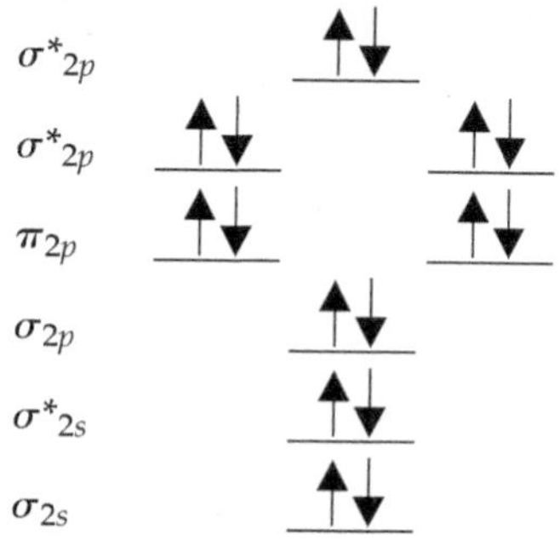

$$\text{Bond order} = \frac{8-8}{2} = 0.$$ With a bond order of 0, the molecule will not exist.

(c) Write an energy level diagram for the molecular orbitals in He_2^{2+}. The ion has two valence electrons. Assign the electrons to the molecular orbitals beginning with the lowest energy orbitals and following Hund's rule.

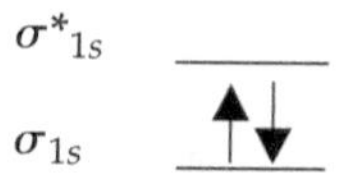

$$\text{Bond order} = \frac{2-0}{2} = 1.$$ With a bond order of 1, the ion will exist.

(d) Write an energy level diagram for the molecular orbitals in F_2^{2-}. The molecule has 16 valence electrons. Assign the electrons to the molecular orbitals beginning with the lowest energy orbitals and following Hund's rule.

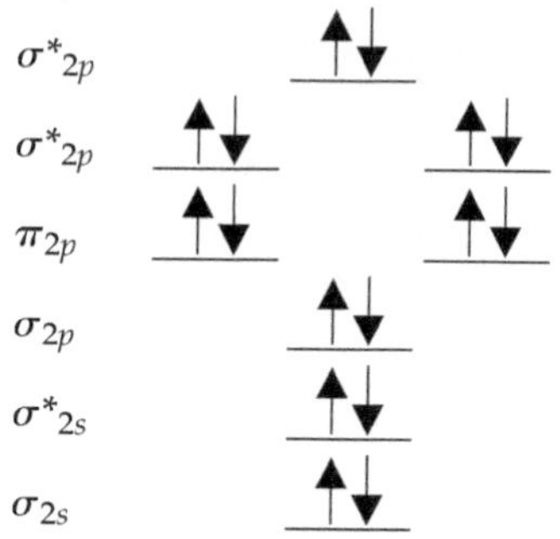

$$\text{Bond order} = \frac{8-8}{2} = 0.$$ With a bond order of 0, the ion will not exist.

10.78 (a) Write an energy level diagram for the molecular orbitals in C_2^{2+}. The ion has six valence electrons. Assign the electrons to the molecular orbitals beginning with the lowest energy orbitals and following Hund's rule.

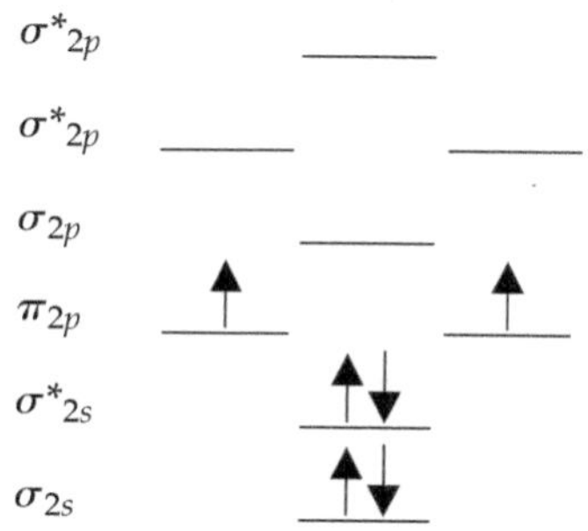

Bond order $= \dfrac{4 - 2}{2} = 1$. With a bond order of 1, the ion will exist.

(b) Write an energy level diagram for the molecular orbitals in Li_2. The ion has two valence electrons. Assign the electrons to the molecular orbitals beginning with the lowest energy orbitals and following Hund's rule.

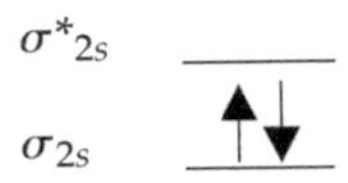

Bond order $= \dfrac{2 - 0}{2} = 1$. With a bond order of 1, the molecule will exist.

(c) Write an energy level diagram for the molecular orbitals in Be_2^{2+}. The ion has two valence electrons. Assign the electrons to the molecular orbitals beginning with the lowest energy orbitals and following Hund's rule.

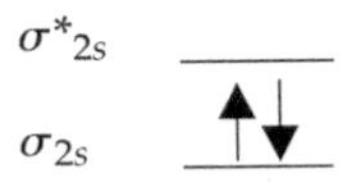

Bond order $= \dfrac{2 - 0}{2} = 1$. With a bond order of 1, the ion will exist.

(d) Write an energy level diagram for the molecular orbitals in Li_2^{2-}. The ion has four valence electrons. Assign the electrons to the molecular orbitals beginning with the lowest energy orbitals and following Hund's rule.

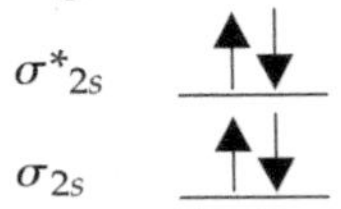

Bond order $= \dfrac{2 - 2}{2} = 0$. With a bond order of 0, the ion will not exist.

10.79 C_2^- has the highest bond order, the highest bond energy, and the shortest bond.
Write an energy level diagram for the molecular orbitals in each of the C_2 species.
Assign the electrons to the molecular orbitals beginning with the lowest energy orbitals and following Hund's rule for each of the species.
C_2 (8 valence electrons); C_2^+ (7 valence electrons): C_2^- (9 valence electrons)

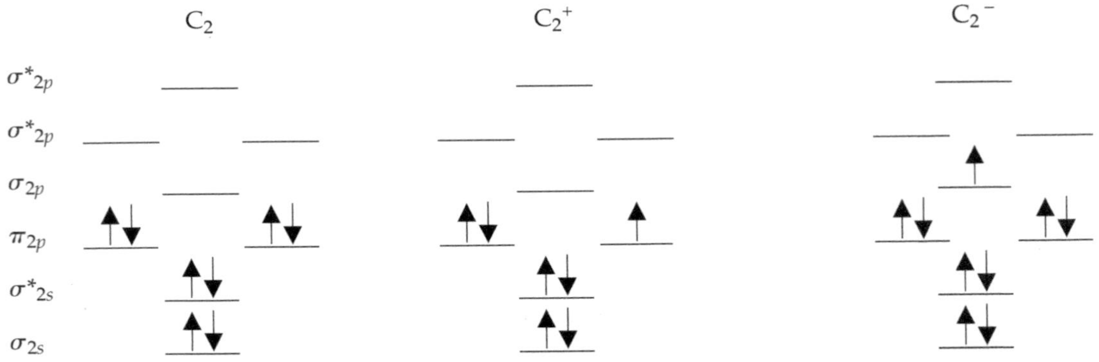

Bond order $= \dfrac{6 - 2}{2} = 2$ Bond order $= \dfrac{5 - 2}{2} = 1.5$ Bond order $= \dfrac{7 - 2}{2} = 2.5$

C_2^- has the highest bond order at 2.5. Bond order is directly related to bond energy, so C_2^- has the largest bond energy and bond order is inversely related to bond length, so C_2^- has the shortest bond length.

10.80 O_2 has the highest bond order, the highest bond energy, and the shortest bond.
Write an energy level diagram for the molecular orbitals in each of the O_2 species.
Assign the electrons to the molecular orbitals beginning with the lowest energy orbitals and following Hund's rule for each of the species.

O_2 (12 valence electrons) O_2^- (13 valence electrons) O_2^{2-} (14 valence electrons)

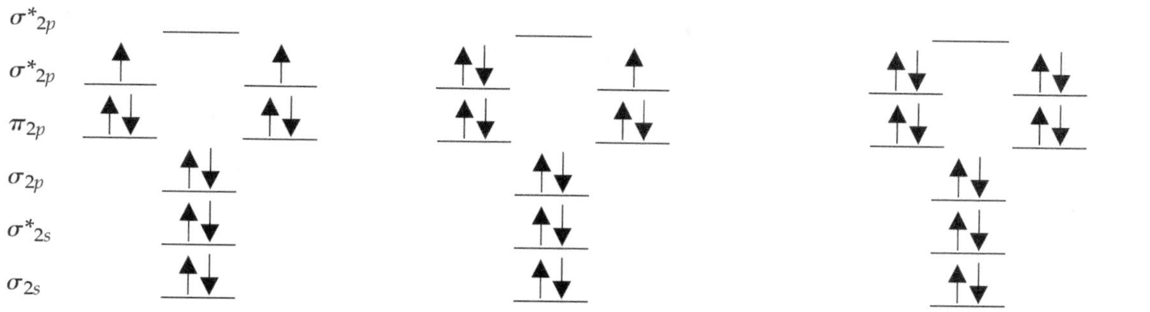

Bond order $= \frac{8-4}{2} = 2$ Bond order $= \frac{8-5}{2} = 1.5$ Bond order $= \frac{8-6}{2} = 1$

O_2 has the highest bond order at 2. Bond order is directly related to bond energy, so O_2 has the largest bond energy and bond order is inversely related to bond length, so O_2 has the shortest bond length.

10.81 Write an energy level diagram for the molecular orbitals in CO using O_2 energy ordering.
Assign the electrons to the molecular orbitals beginning with the lowest energy orbitals and following Hund's rule.
CO has 10 valence electrons.

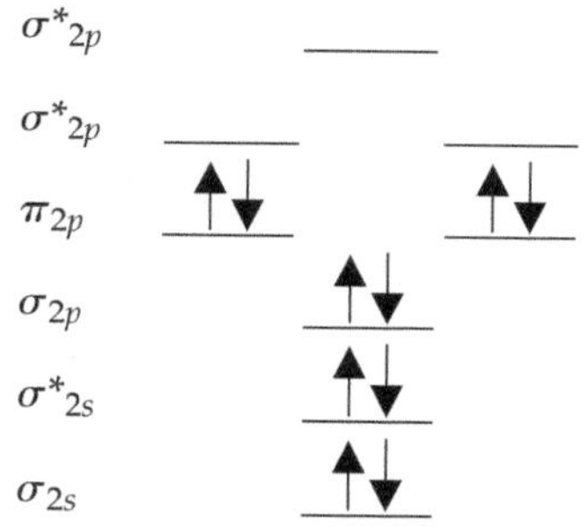

Bond order $= \frac{8-2}{2} = 3$

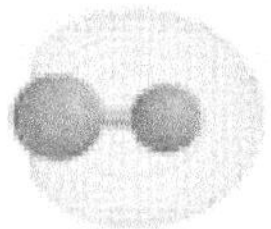

The electron density is toward the O atom since it is more electronegative.

10.82 HCl(8 valence electrons)

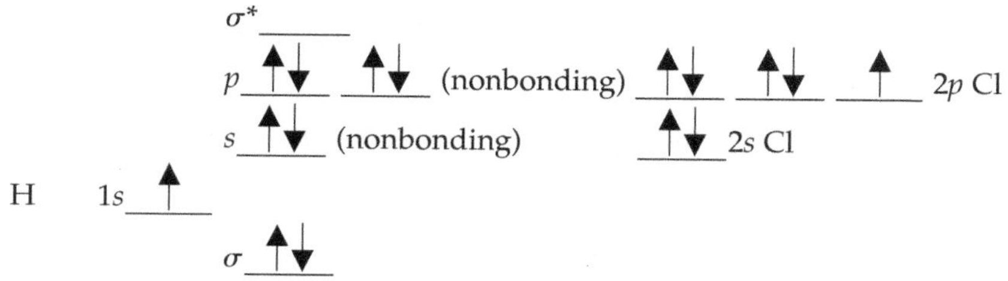

$$\text{Bond order} = \frac{2 - 0}{2} = 1$$

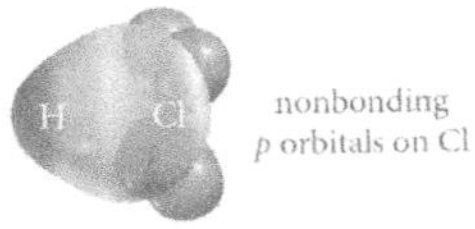

The electron density will be skewed toward the Cl atom since it is more electronegative.

Cumulative Problems

10.83 (a) COF_2 Write the Lewis structure for the molecule:

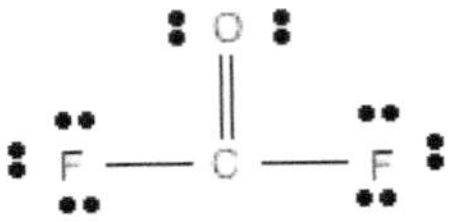

Use VSEPR to predict the electron geometry:
Three electron groups around the central atom give a trigonal planar electron geometry. Three bonding pairs of electrons give a trigonal planar molecular geometry.

Determine if the molecule contains polar bonds:
The electronegativities of C = 2.5, O = 3.5, and F = 4.0 Therefore the bonds are polar.

Determine whether the polar bonds add together to form a net dipole:
Even though a trigonal planar molecular geometry normally is nonpolar, because the bonds have different dipole moments, the sum of the dipole moments is not zero. The molecule is polar. See Table 10.2 p. 415 in text to see how dipole moments add to determine polarity.

Select the correct hybridization for the central atom based on the electron geometry:
Trigonal planar geometry has sp^2 hybridization.

Sketch the molecule and label the bonds:

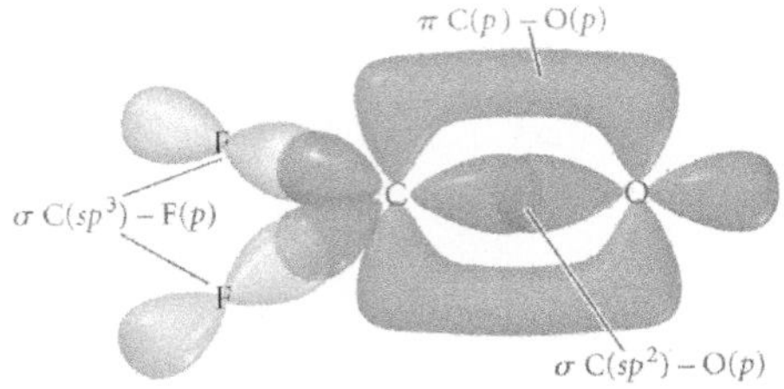

(b) S_2Cl_2 Write the Lewis structure for the molecule:

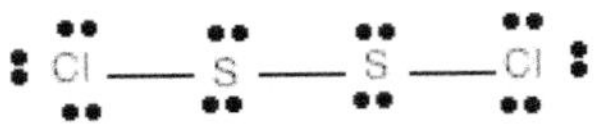

Use VSEPR to predict the electron geometry:
Four electron groups around the central atom give a tetrahedral electron geometry. Two bonding pairs and two lone pairs of electrons give a bent molecular geometry.

Determine if the molecule contains polar bonds:
The electronegativities of S = 2.5 and Cl = 3.0. Therefore the bonds are polar.

Determine whether the polar bonds add together to form a net dipole:
In a bent molecular geometry the sum of the dipole moments is not zero. The molecule is polar. See Table 10.2 p. 415 in text to see how dipole moments add to determine polarity.

Select the correct hybridization for the central atom based on the electron geometry:
Tetrahedral geometry has sp^3 hybridization.

Sketch the molecule and label the bonds:

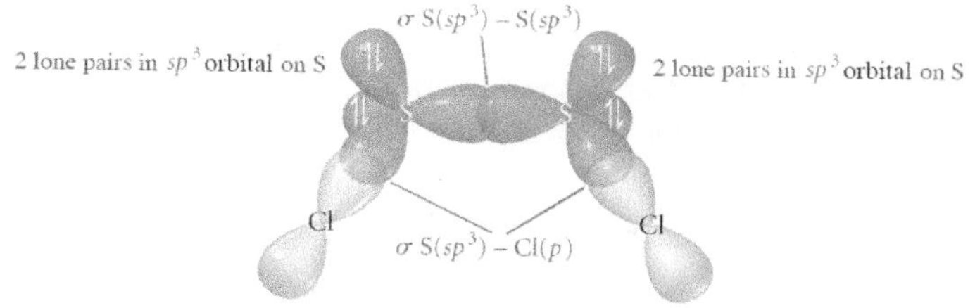

(c) SF_4 Write the Lewis structure for the molecule:

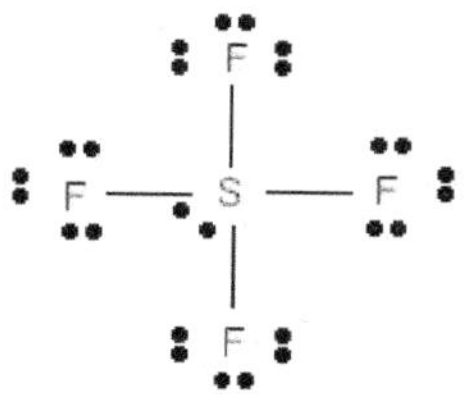

Use VSEPR to predict the electron geometry:
Five electron groups around the central atom give a trigonal bipyramidal electron geometry. Four bonding pairs and one lone pair of electrons give a seesaw molecular geometry.

Determine if the molecule contains polar bonds:
The electronegativities of S = 2.5 and F = 4.0. Therefore the bonds are polar.

Determine whether the polar bonds add together to form a net dipole:
In a seesaw molecular geometry the sum of the dipole moments is not zero. The molecule is polar. See Table 10.2 p. 415 in text to see how dipole moments add to determine polarity.

Select the correct hybridization for the central atom based on the electron geometry:
Trigonal bipyramidal electron geometry has sp^3d hybridization.

Sketch the molecule and label the bonds:

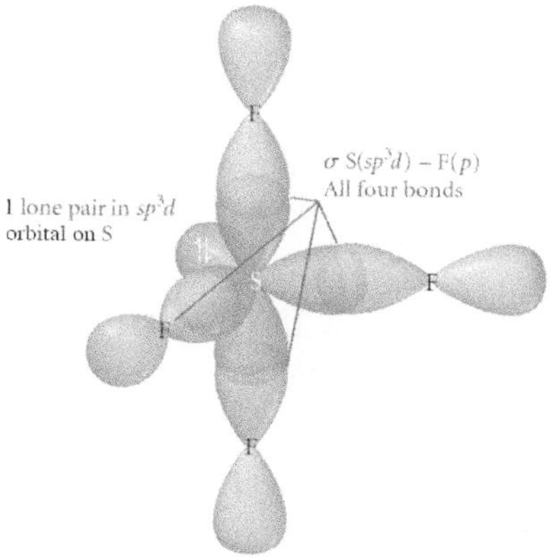

10.84 (a) IF_5 Write the Lewis structure for the molecule:

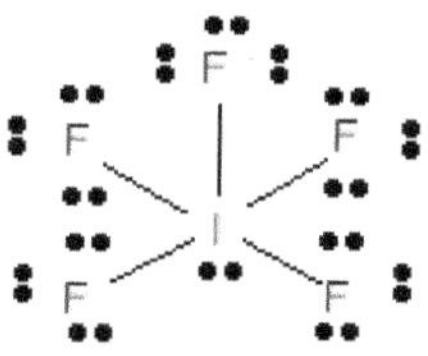

Use VSEPR to predict the electron geometry:
Six electron groups around the central atom give an octahedral electron geometry. Five bonding pairs and one lone pair of electrons give a square pyramidal molecular geometry.
Determine if the molecule contains polar bonds:
The electronegativities of I = 2.5 and F = 4.0. Therefore the bonds are polar.

Determine whether the polar bonds add together to form a net dipole:
In a square pyramidal molecular geometry the sum of the dipole moments is not zero. The molecule is polar. See Table 10.2 p. 415 in text to see how dipole moments add to determine polarity.

Select the correct hybridization for the interior atoms based on the electron geometry:
Octahedral electron geometry has sp^3d^2 hybridization.

Sketch the molecule and label the bonds:

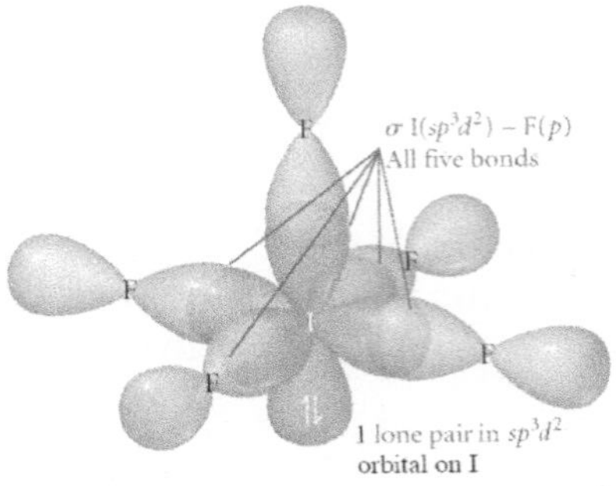

(b) CH_2CHCH_3

Write the Lewis structure for the molecule:

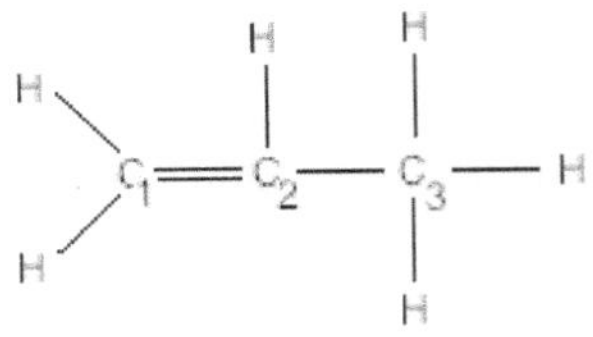

Use VSEPR to predict the electron geometry:
C – 1 and C – 2 each have three electron groups around the atom, which is trigonal planar electron geometry. Three bonding pairs of electrons give a trigonal planar molecular geometry.
C – 3 has four electron groups around the C atom; four electron groups give a tetrahedral electron geometry. Four bonding groups give a tetrahedral molecular geometry.

Determine if the molecule contains polar bonds:
The electronegativities of C = 2.5 and H = 2.1. Therefore the bonds are slightly polar because the difference in electronegativity is less than 0.5.

Determine whether the polar bonds add together to form a net dipole:
The trigonal planar molecular geometry and the tetrahedral molecular geometry give a net dipole moment of zero. The molecule is nonpolar.

Select the correct hybridization for the interior atoms based on the electron geometry:
Trigonal planar electron geometry has sp^2 hybridization and the tetrahedral electron geometry has sp^3 hybridization.

Sketch the molecule and label the bonds:

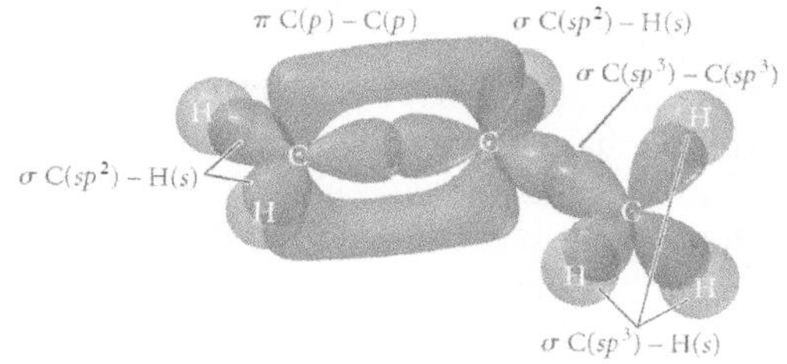

(c) CH_3SH Write the Lewis structure for the molecule:

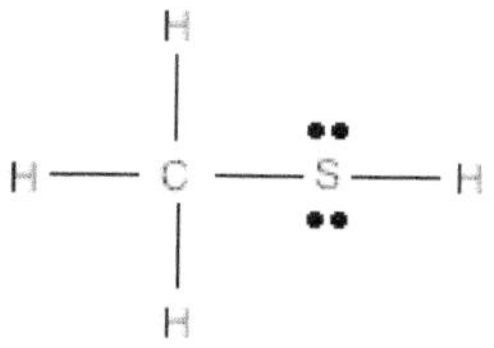

Use VSEPR to predict the electron geometry:
Four electron groups around the C atom and the S atom give a tetrahedral electron geometry. Four bonding pairs of electrons around the C give a tetrahedral molecular geometry and two bonding groups and two lone pairs around the S give a bent molecular geometry.

Determine if the molecule contains polar bonds:
The electronegativities of C = 2.5, S = 2.5, and H = 2.1. The C – H bonds and the S – H bond will be slightly polar, and the C – S bond will be nonpolar.

Determine whether the polar bonds add together to form a net dipole:
In both molecular geometries the sum of the dipole moments is not zero. The molecule is polar.

Select the correct hybridization for the central atom based on the electron geometry:
Tetrahedral electron geometry has sp^3 hybridization on both C and S.

Sketch the molecule and label the bonds:

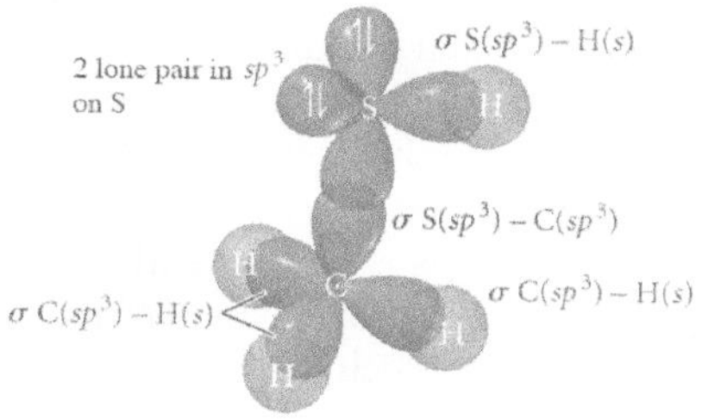

10.85 (a) serine

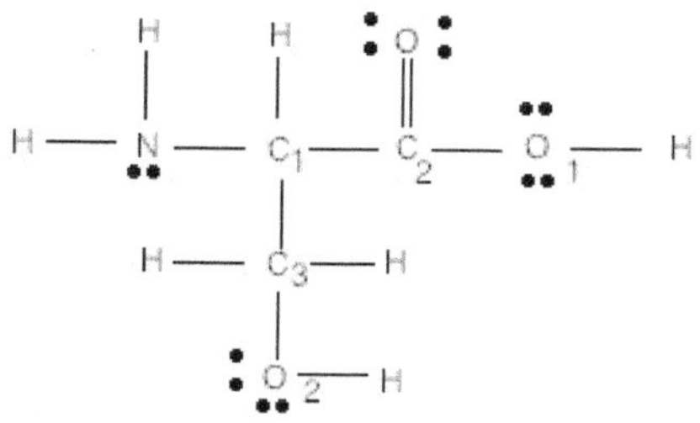

C – 1 and C – 3 each have four electron groups around the atom. Four electron pairs give a tetrahedral electron geometry; tetrahedral electron geometry has sp^3 hybridization. Four bonding pairs and zero lone pairs give a tetrahedral molecular geometry.

C – 2 has three electron groups around the atom. Three electron pairs give a trigonal planar geometry; trigonal planar geometry has sp^2 hybridization. Three bonding pairs and zero lone pairs give a trigonal planar molecular geometry.
N has four electron groups around the atom. Four electron pairs give a tetrahedral electron geometry; tetrahedral electron geometry has sp^3 hybridization. Three bonding pairs and one lone pair give a trigonal pyramidal molecular geometry.
O – 1 and O – 2 each have four electron groups around the atom. Four electron pairs give a tetrahedral electron geometry; tetrahedral electron geometry has sp^3 hybridization. Two bonding pairs and two lone pairs give a bent molecular geometry.

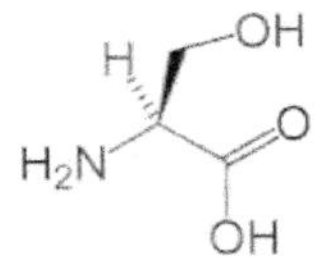

(b) asparagine

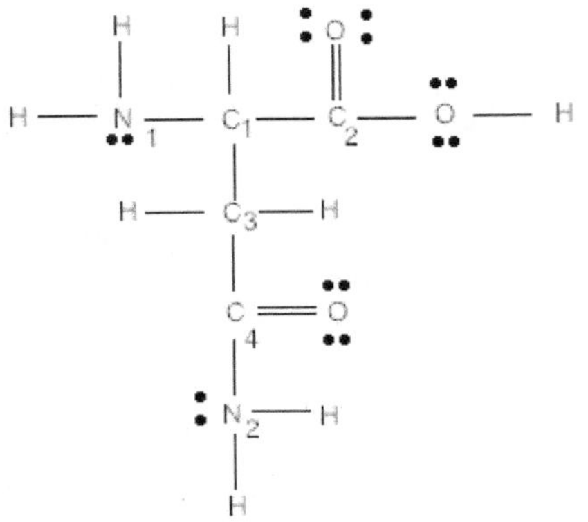

C – 1 and C – 3 each have four electron groups around the atom. Four electron groups give a tetrahedral electron geometry; tetrahedral electron geometry has sp^3 hybridization. Four bonding groups and zero lone pairs give a tetrahedral molecular geometry.
C – 2 and C – 4 each have three electron groups around the atom. Three electron groups give a trigonal planar geometry; trigonal planar geometry has sp^2 hybridization. Three bonding pairs and zero lone groups give a trigonal planar molecular geometry.
N – 1 and N – 2 each have four electron groups around the atom. Four electron groups give a tetrahedral electron geometry; tetrahedral electron geometry has sp^3 hybridization. Three bonding groups and one lone pair give a trigonal pyramidal molecular geometry.
O has four electron groups around the atom. Four electron groups give a tetrahedral electron geometry; tetrahedral electron geometry has sp^3 hybridization. Two bonding groups and two lone pairs give a bent molecular geometry.

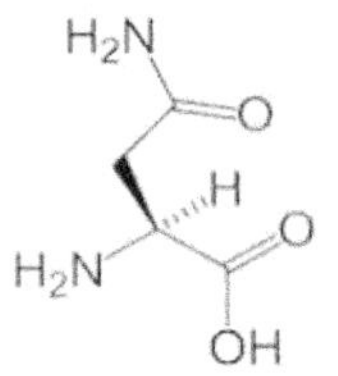

(c) cysteine

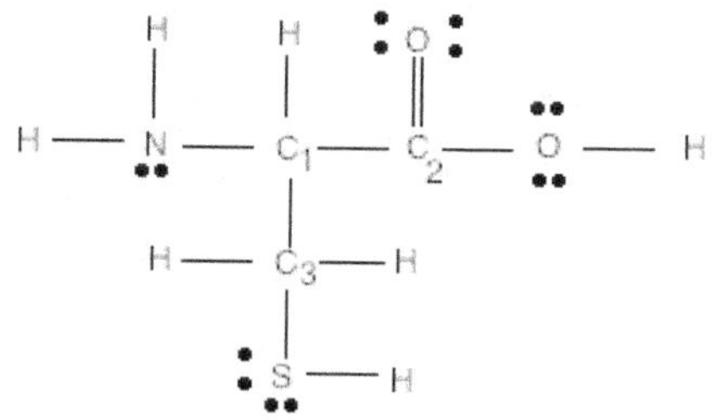

C – 1 and C – 3 each have four electron groups around the atom. Four electron pairs give a tetrahedral electron geometry; tetrahedral electron geometry has *sp*^{3} hybridization. Four bonding pairs and zero lone pairs give a tetrahedral molecular geometry.

C – 2 has three electron groups around the atom. Three electron groups give a trigonal planar geometry; trigonal planar geometry has *sp*^{2} hybridization. Three bonding groups and zero lone pairs give a trigonal planar molecular geometry.

N has four electron groups around the atom. Four electron groups give a tetrahedral electron geometry; tetrahedral electron geometry has *sp*^{3} hybridization. Three bonding groups and one lone pair give a trigonal pyramidal molecular geometry.

O and S have four electron groups around the atom. Four electron groups give a tetrahedral electron geometry; tetrahedral electron geometry has *sp*^{3} hybridization. Two bonding groups and two lone pairs gives bent molecular geometry.

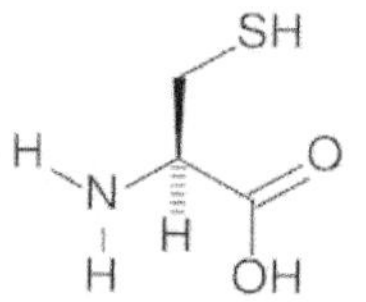

10.86 (a) cytosine

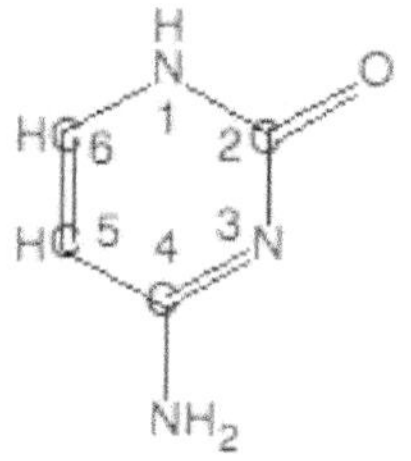

(a)

N – 1 has three bonding pairs of electrons and one lone pair; four electron pairs give a tetrahedral electron geometry and *sp*^{3} hybridization. Three bonding pairs of electrons and one lone pair give a trigonal pyramidal molecular geometry.

C – 2 has three bonding groups of electrons and zero lone pairs; three electron groups give a trigonal planar geometry and *sp*^{2} hybridization. Three bonding pairs of electrons give a trigonal planar molecular geometry.

N – 3 has two bonding groups of electrons and one lone pair; three electron groups give a trigonal planar electron geometry and *sp*^{2} hybridization. Two bonding groups and one lone pair give a bent molecular geometry.

C – 4 has three bonding groups of electrons and zero lone pairs; three electron groups give a trigonal planar geometry and *sp*^{2} hybridization. Three bonding groups of electrons give a trigonal planar molecular geometry.

C – 5 has three bonding groups of electrons and zero lone pairs; three electron groups give a trigonal planar geometry and *sp*^{2} hybridization. Three bonding groups of electrons give a trigonal planar molecular geometry.

C – 6 has three bonding pairs of electrons and zero lone pairs; three electron groups give a trigonal planar geometry and sp^2 hybridization. Three bonding groups of electrons give a trigonal planar molecular geometry.
N outside the ring has three bonding groups of electrons and one lone pair; four electron groups give a tetrahedral electron geometry and sp^3 hybridization. Three bonding groups of electrons give a trigonal pyramidal molecular geometry.

(b) adenine

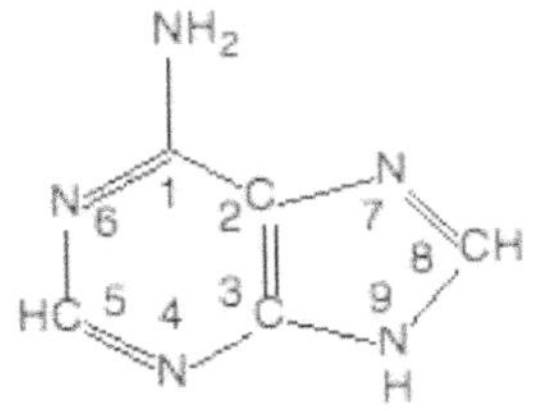

(b)

N – 1 has two bonding groups of electrons and one lone pair; three electron groups give a trigonal planar electron geometry and sp^2 hybridization. Two bonding groups and one lone pair give a bent molecular geometry.
C – 2 has three bonding groups of electrons and zero lone groups; three electron groups give a trigonal planar geometry and sp^2 hybridization. Three bonding groups of electrons give a trigonal planar molecular geometry.
N – 3 has two bonding groups of electrons and one lone pair; three electron groups give a trigonal planar electron geometry and sp^2 hybridization. Two bonding groups and one lone pair give a bent molecular geometry.
C – 4 has three bonding groups of electrons and zero lone groups; three electron groups give a trigonal planar geometry and sp^2 hybridization. Three bonding groups of electrons give a trigonal planar molecular geometry.
C – 5 has three bonding groups of electrons and zero lone groups; three electron groups give a trigonal planar geometry and sp^2 hybridization. Three bonding groups of electrons give a trigonal planar molecular geometry.
C – 6 has three bonding groups of electrons and zero lone groups; three electron groups give a trigonal planar geometry and sp^2 hybridization. Three bonding groups of electrons give a trigonal planar molecular geometry.
N – 7 has two bonding groups of electrons and one lone pair; three electron groups give a trigonal planar electron geometry and sp^2 hybridization. Two bonding groups and one lone pair give a bent molecular geometry.
C – 8 has three bonding groups of electrons and zero lone groups; three electron groups give a trigonal planar geometry and sp^2 hybridization. Three bonding groups of electrons give a trigonal planar molecular geometry.
N – 9 has three bonding groups of electrons and one lone pair; four electron groups give a tetrahedral electron geometry and sp^3 hybridization. Three bonding groups of electrons give a trigonal pyramidal molecular geometry.
N outside the ring has three bonding groups of electrons and one lone pair; four electron groups give a tetrahedral electron geometry and sp^3 hybridization. Three bonding groups of electrons give a trigonal pyramidal molecular geometry.

(c) thymine

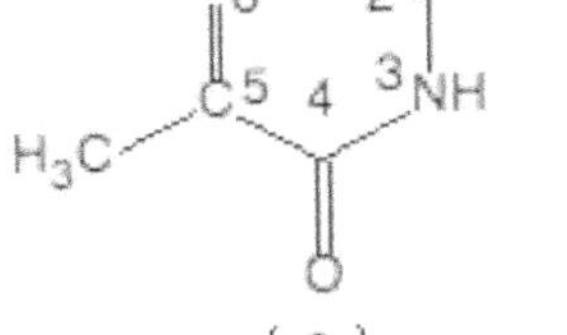

(c)

N – 1 has three bonding pairs of electrons and one lone pair; four electron pairs give a tetrahedral electron geometry and sp^3 hybridization. Three bonding pairs of electrons give a trigonal pyramidal molecular geometry.
C – 2 has three bonding pairs of electrons and zero lone pairs; three electron pairs give a trigonal planar geometry and sp^2 hybridization. Three bonding pairs of electrons give a trigonal planar molecular geometry.
N – 3 has three bonding pairs of electrons and one lone pair; four electron pairs give a tetrahedral electron geometry and sp^3 hybridization. Three bonding pairs and one lone pair give a trigonal pyramidal molecular geometry.
C – 4 has three bonding pairs of electrons and zero lone pairs; three electron pairs give a trigonal planar geometry and sp^2 hybridization. Three bonding pairs of electrons give a trigonal planar molecular geometry.
C – 5 has three bonding pairs of electrons and zero lone pairs; three electron pairs give a trigonal planar geometry and sp^2 hybridization. Three bonding pairs of electrons give a trigonal planar molecular geometry.
C – 6 has three bonding pairs of electrons and zero lone pairs; three electron pairs give a trigonal planar geometry and sp^2 hybridization. Three bonding pairs of electrons give a trigonal planar molecular geometry.
C outside the ring has four bonding pairs of electrons and zero lone pairs; four electron pairs give a tetrahedral electron geometry and sp^3 hybridization. Four bonding pairs of electrons give a tetrahedral molecular geometry.

(d) guanine

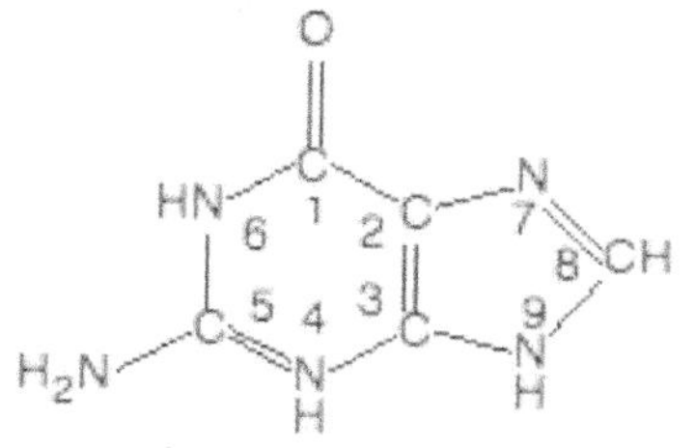

(d)

N – 1 has three bonding pairs of electrons and one lone pair; four electron pairs give a tetrahedral electron geometry and sp^3 hybridization. Three bonding pairs of electrons give a trigonal pyramidal molecular geometry.
C – 2 has three bonding pairs of electrons and zero lone pairs; three electron pairs give a trigonal planar geometry and sp^2 hybridization. Three bonding pairs of electrons give a trigonal planar molecular geometry.
N – 3 has two bonding pairs of electrons and one lone pair; three electron pairs give a trigonal planar electron geometry and sp^2 hybridization. Two bonding pairs and one lone pair give a bent molecular geometry.
C – 4 has three bonding pairs of electrons and zero lone pairs; three electron pairs give a trigonal planar geometry and sp^2 hybridization. Three bonding pairs of electrons give a trigonal planar molecular geometry.
C – 5 has three bonding pairs of electrons and zero lone pairs; three electron pairs give a trigonal planar geometry and sp^2 hybridization. Three bonding pairs of electrons give a trigonal planar molecular geometry.
C – 6 has three bonding pairs of electrons and zero lone pairs; three electron pairs give a trigonal planar geometry and sp^2 hybridization. Three bonding pairs of electrons give a trigonal planar molecular geometry.
N – 7 has two bonding pairs of electrons and one lone pair; three electron pairs give a trigonal planar electron geometry and sp^2 hybridization. Two bonding pairs and one lone pair give a bent molecular geometry.
C – 8 has three bonding pair of electrons and zero lone pair; three electron pairs give a trigonal planar geometry and sp^2 hybridization. Three bonding pairs of electrons give a trigonal planar molecular geometry.

N – 9 has three bonding pairs of electrons and one lone pair; four electron pairs give a tetrahedral electron geometry and sp^3 hybridization. Three bonding pairs of electrons give a trigonal pyramidal molecular geometry.
N outside the ring has three bonding pairs of electrons and one lone pair; four electron pairs give a tetrahedral electron geometry and sp^3 hybridization. Three bonding pairs of electrons give a trigonal pyramidal molecular geometry.

10.87 4 π bonds; 25 σ bonds; the lone pair on the Os and N – 2 occupy sp^2 orbitals; the lone pairs on N – 1, N – 3, and N – 4 occupy sp^3 orbitals.
caffeine

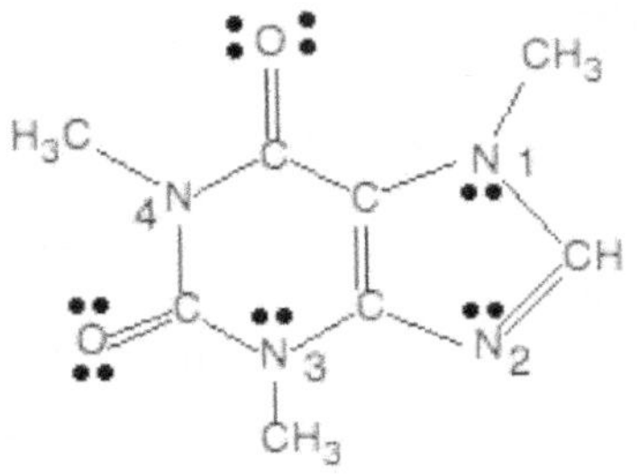

10.88 5 π bonds; 21 σ bonds
aspirin

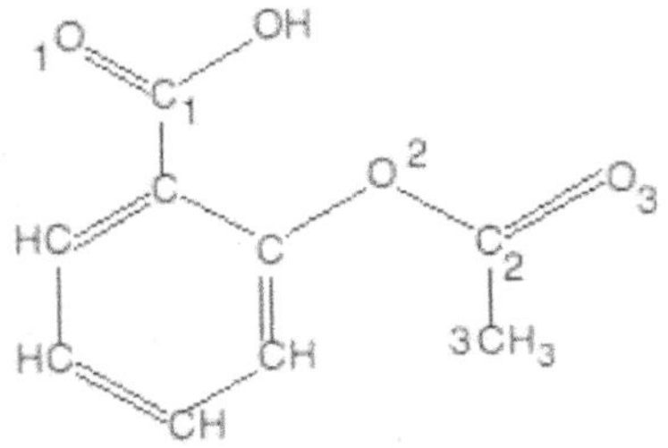

There is rotation around the bond from C – 1 to the ring and from C – 1 to OH bond. There is rotation around the O – 2 to the ring bond and around the O – 2 to C – 2 bond. There is rotation around the C – 2 to C – 3 bond. The C – 1 to O – 1 bond is rigid, the ring structure is rigid, and the C – 2 to O – 3 bond is rigid.

10.89 (a) Water soluble: The 4 C – OH bonds, the C = O bond, and the C – O bonds in the ring, make the molecule polar. Because of the large electronegativity difference between the C and O, each of the bonds will have a dipole moment. The sum of the dipole moments does NOT give a net zero dipole moment, so the molecule is polar. Since it is polar, it will be water soluble.

(b) Fat soluble: There is only one C – O bond in the molecule. The dipole moment from this bond is not enough to make the molecule polar because of all of the nonpolar components of the molecule. The C – H bonds in the structure lead to a net dipole of zero for most of the sites in the molecule. Since the molecule is nonpolar, it is fat soluble.

(c) Water soluble: The carboxylic acid function (COOH group) along with the N atom in the ring make the molecule polar. Because of the electronegativity difference between the C and O and the C and N atoms, the bonds will have a dipole moment and the net dipole moment of the molecule is NOT zero, so the molecule is polar. Since the molecule is polar, it is water soluble.

(d) Fat soluble: The two O atoms in the structure contribute a very small amount to the net dipole moment of this molecule. The majority of the molecule is nonpolar because there is no net dipole moment at the interior C atoms. Because the molecule is nonpolar it is fat soluble.

10.90 The soap molecule has a nonpolar hydrocarbon end and an anionic end when it is dissolved in water. In order to dissolve in water, the sodium stearate congregates to form small spheres (called micelles) with the nonpolar ends on the insides and the anionic ends on the surface. The anionic end interacts with the polar water molecules, while the nonpolar hydrocarbon end can attract and interact with the nonpolar grease. This allows the soapy water to remove the grease by trapping the grease inside the micelle.

10.91 ClF has 14 valence electrons. Assign the electrons to the lowest energy MOs first and then follow Hund's rule. The MOs are formed from the $2s$ and $2p$ orbitals on F and the $3s$ and $3p$ orbitals on Cl.

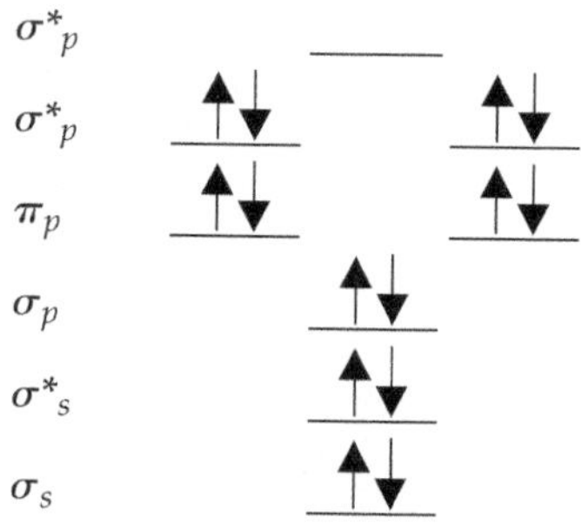

$$\text{Bond order} = \frac{8-6}{2} = 1$$

10.92 CN^+ (8 valence electrons) CN (9 valence electrons) CN^- (10 valence electrons)

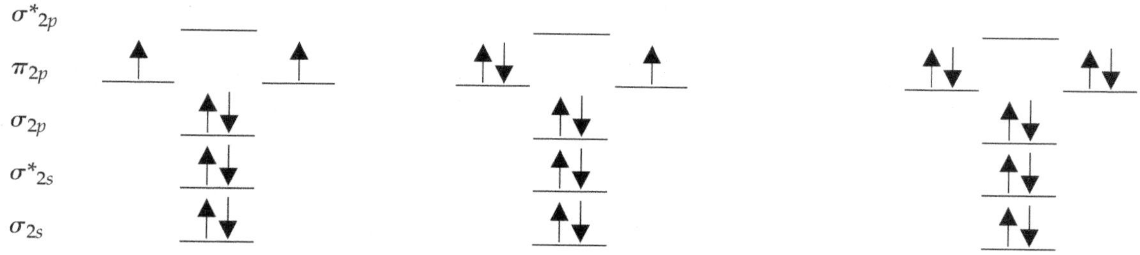

$$\text{Bond order} = \frac{6-2}{2} = 2 \qquad \text{Bond order} = \frac{7-2}{2} = 2.5 \qquad \text{Bond order} = \frac{8-2}{2} = 3$$

According to Lewis theory the CN^- ion would be the most stable because it completes the octet on both atoms. The other two (CN^+ and CN) have an incomplete octet on C.

According to molecular orbital theory, the CN^- ion would be the most stable because it has the highest bond order, 3. The other two species would also exist but would be less stable. Both theories agree that the CN^- ion would be the most stable.

10.93 BrF (14 valence electrons)

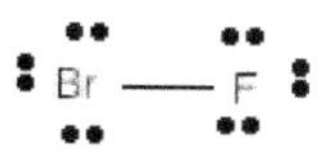

no central atom, no hybridization, no electron structure

BrF_2^- (22 valence electrons)

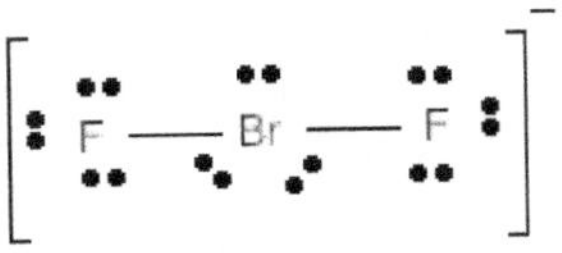

There are five electron pairs on the central atom so the electron geometry is trigonal bipyramidal. The two bonding pairs and three lone pairs give a linear molecular geometry. An electron geometry of trigonal bipyramidal has sp^3d hybridization.

BrF_3 (28 valence electrons)

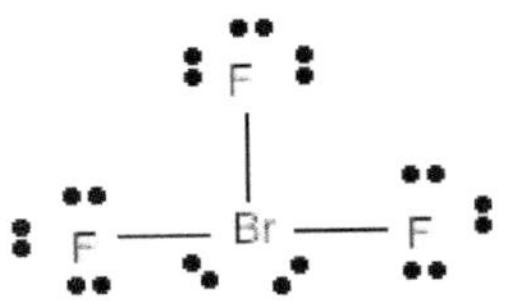

There are five electron pairs on the central atom so the electron geometry is trigonal bipyramidal. The three bonding pairs and two lone pairs give a T-shaped molecular geometry. An electron geometry of trigonal bipyramidal has sp^3d hybridization.

BrF_4^- (36 valence electrons)

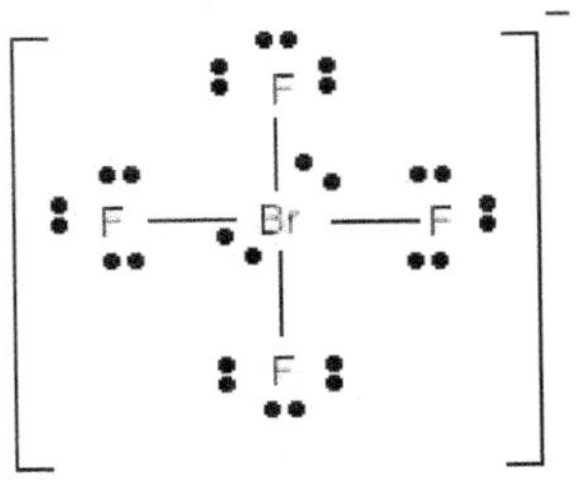

There are six electron pairs on the central atom so the electron geometry is octahedral. The four bonding pairs and two lone pairs give a square planar molecular geometry. An electron geometry of octahedral has sp^3d^2 hybridization.

BrF_5 (42 valence electrons)

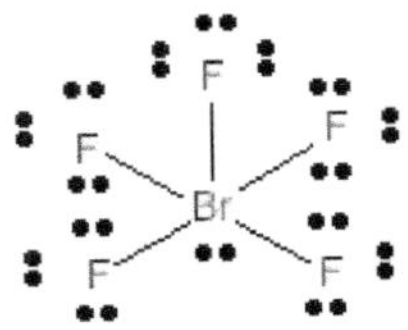

There are six electron pairs on the central atom so the electron geometry is octahedral. The five bonding pairs and one lone pair give a square pyramidal molecular geometry. An electron geometry of octahedral has sp^3d^2 hybridization.

10.94 Write the Lewis structure:

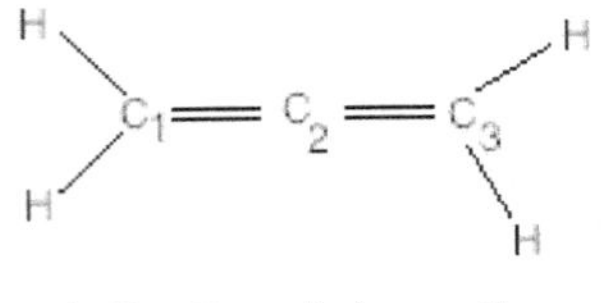

C – 1 and C – 3 each have three groups of electrons and a trigonal planar structure giving sp^2 hybridization on the C with a p orbital left for the π bond. C – 2 has two groups of electrons and is linear, which shows sp hybridization and 2 p orbitals left for the π bonds. According to valence bond theory, the π bonds are formed by the sideways overlap of p orbitals. Since the remaining p orbitals on C – 2 are perpendicular to each other, the π bonds formed between C – 1 and C – 2 and between C – 2 and C – 3 must also be perpendicular to each other. Therefore, the two trigonal planar structures at C –1 and C – 3 will be perpendicular to each other.

10.95 Draw the Lewis structure: $C_4H_6Cl_2$ (36 valence electrons)

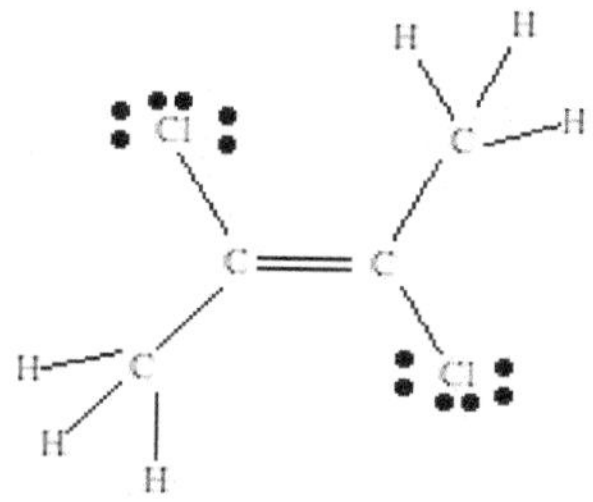

Even though the C –Cl bonds are polar, the net dipole will since the C – Cl bonds and the C – CH_3 bonds are on opposite sides of the double bond. This will result in bond vectors that cancel each other.

10.96 CH_3NO_2 Draw the Lewis structure: (24 valence electrons)

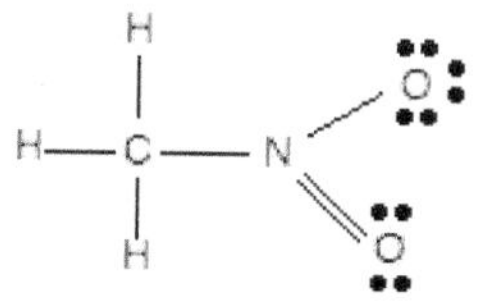

Structure I

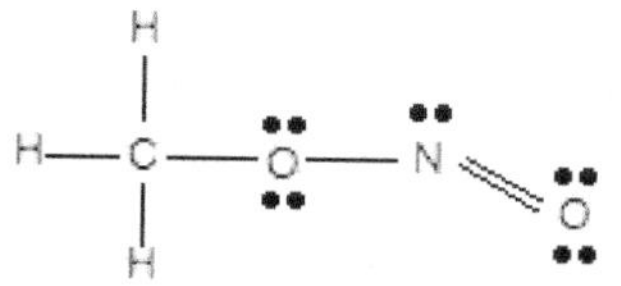

Structure II

In structure I, the N has a trigonal planar electron geometry with three bonds to the N and sp^2 hybridization. This will give an O – N – O bond angle of about 120°. In structure II, the N also has trigonal planar electron geometry and sp^2 hybridization. However, the lone pair of electrons on the N will cause the O – N – O bond angle to be less than 120°.

10.97 (a) N_2O_5 Draw the Lewis structure: (40 valence electrons)

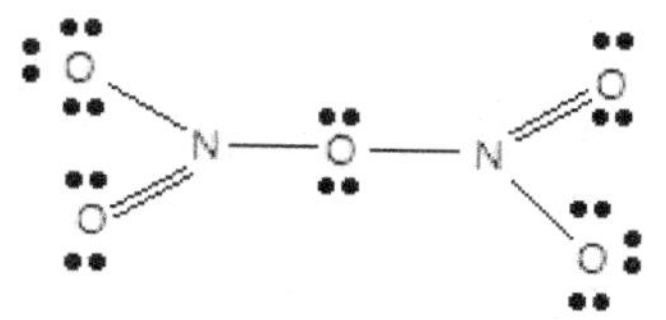

Each N has a trigonal planar electron geometry so there are 3 sp^2 hybrid orbitals on each N. The central O has tetrahedral electron geometry, so there are 4 sp^3 hybrid orbitals. There are a total of 10 hybrid orbitals.

(b) C_2H_5NO Draw the Lewis structure: (24 valence electrons)

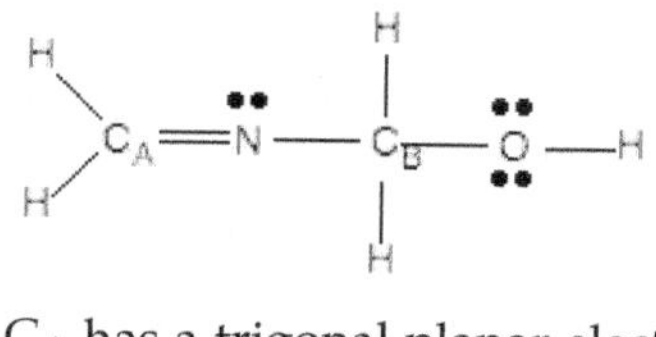

C_A has a trigonal planar electron geometry, so there are 3 sp^2 hybrid orbitals.
N has a trigonal planar electron geometry, so there are 3 sp^2 hybrid orbitals.
C_B has a tetrahedral electron geometry, so there are 4 sp^3 hybrid orbitals.
O has a tetrahedral electron geometry, so there are 4 sp^3 hybrid orbitals.
There are a total of 14 hybrid orbitals.

(c) BrCN Draw the Lewis structure: (16 valence electrons)

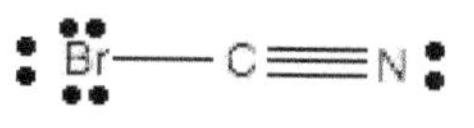

The C has linear electron geometry, so there are 2 *sp* hybrid orbitals.

10.98 (a) $BeBr_2$ Draw the Lewis structure: (16 valence electrons)

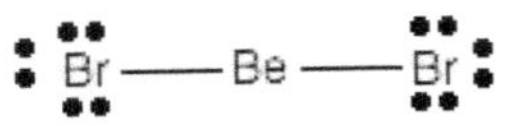

Sketch the molecule.

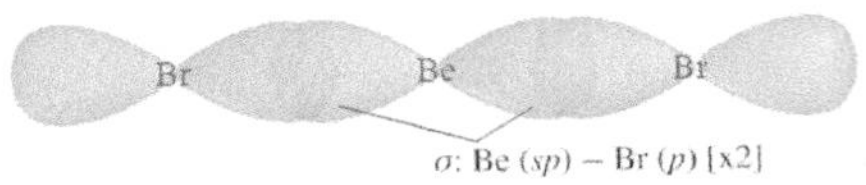

The 2 σ bonds form between a hybrid *sp* orbital on Be and a *p* orbital on Br.

(b) $HgCl_2$ Draw the Lewis structure: (16 valence electrons)

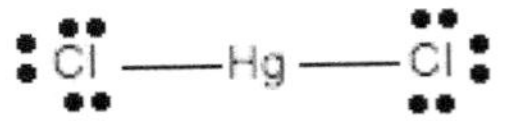

Sketch the molecule.

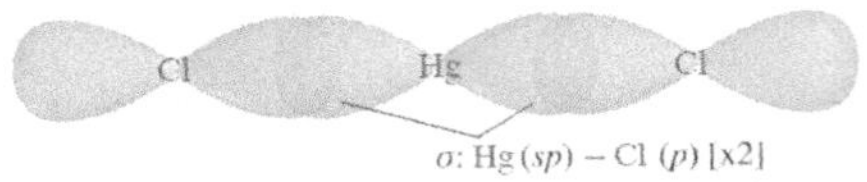

The 2 σ bonds form between a hybrid *sp* orbital on Hg and a *p* orbital on Cl.

(c) ICN Draw the Lewis structure: (16 valence electrons)

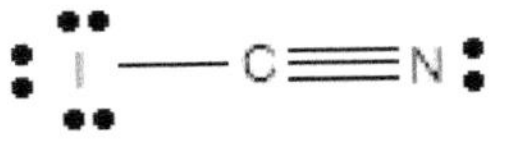

Sketch the molecule.

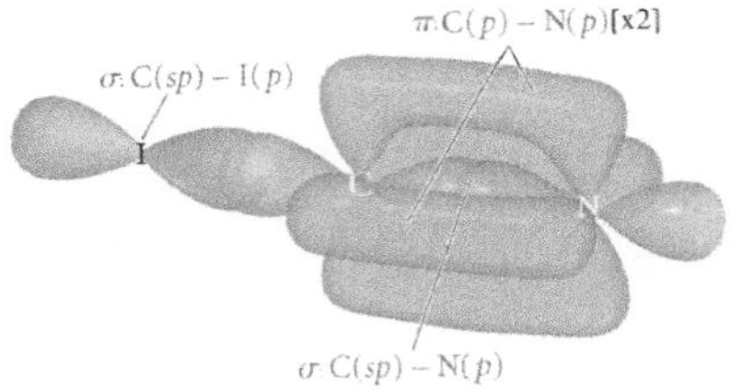

1 σ bond forms between a hybrid *sp* orbital on C and a *p* orbital on I; 1 σ bond forms between a hybrid *sp* orbital on C and a *p* orbital on N; 2 π bonds form between unhybridized *p* orbitals on C and *p* orbitals on N.

Challenge Problems

10.99 According to valence bond theory, CH_4, NH_3, and H_2O are all sp^3 hybridized. This hybridization results in a tetrahedral electron group configuration with a 109.5° bond angle. NH_3 and H_2O deviate from this idealized bond angle because their lone electron pairs exist in their own sp^3 orbitals. The presence of lone pairs lowers the tendency for the central atom's orbitals to hybridize. As a result, as lone pairs are added, the bond angle moves from the 109.5° hybrid angle toward the 90° unhybridized angle.

10.100 Using the MO diagram for H_2O assign the eight valence electrons to the molecular orbitals. Start with the lowest energy orbital first and follow Hund's rule.

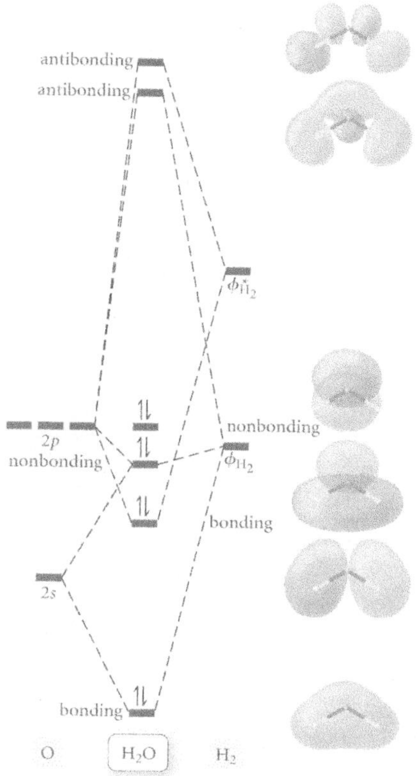

$$\text{Bond order} = \frac{4 - 0}{2} = 2.$$

With a bond order of 2, the molecule is stable.

10.101 Using the MO diagram for NH_3 assign the eight valence electrons to the molecular orbitals. Start with the lowest energy orbital first and follow Hund's rule.

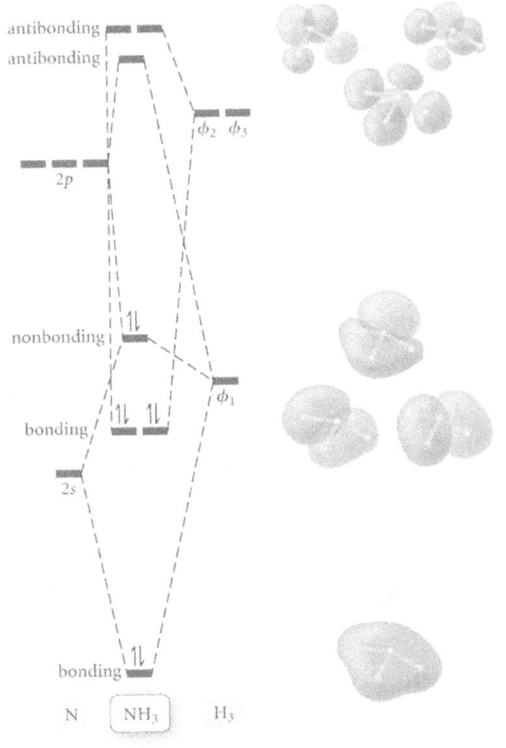

Bond order $= \dfrac{6-0}{2} = 3.$

With a bond order of 3, the molecule is stable.

10.102 (a) In the isomerization, you need to break the C – C π bond but not the σ bond. So the energy needed would be the difference between the bond energy of a C = C bond and a C – C bond.

C = C 611 kJ/mol

C – C 347 kJ/mol

Therefore, the energy needed to break the π bond would be 264 kJ/mol = 2.64×10^5 J/mol

$$\frac{264\text{ kJ}}{\text{mol}} \times \frac{1000\text{ J}}{\text{kJ}} \times \frac{\text{mol}}{6.022 \times 10^{23}\text{ molecules}} = 4.38 \times 10^{-19}\frac{\text{J}}{\text{molecule}}$$

(b) **Given:** 4.38×10^{-19} J/ molecule **Find:** ν and part of the spectrum

Conceptual Plan: $E \rightarrow \nu$

$E = h\nu$

Solution: $\nu = \dfrac{E}{h} = \dfrac{4.38 \times 10^{-19}\text{ J}}{6.626 \times 10^{-34}\text{ J}\cdot\text{s}} = 6.62 \times 10^{14}\text{ s}^{-1}$

This frequency is right near the border of the ultraviolet–visible region of the electromagnetic spectrum.

10.103 For each write the Lewis structure.

Determine electron pair geometry around each central atom.

Determine the molecular geometry, determine idealized bond angles, and predict actual bond angles.

NO_2

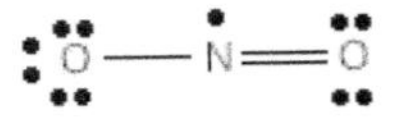

Two bonding groups and a lone electron give a trigonal planar electron geometry; the molecular geometry will be bent. Trigonal planar electron geometry has idealized bond angles of 120°. The bond angle is expected to be slightly less than 120° because of the lone electron occupying the third sp^2 orbital.

NO_2^+

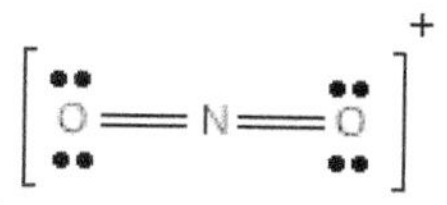

Two bonding groups of electrons and no lone pairs give a linear electron geometry and molecular geometry. Linear electron geometry has a bond angle of 180°.

NO_2^-

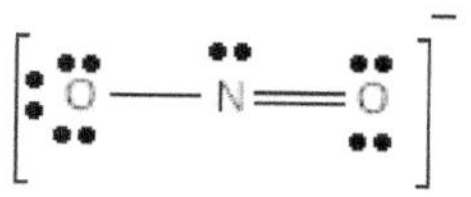

Two bonding groups of electrons and one lone pair give a trigonal planar electron geometry; the molecular geometry will be bent.
Trigonal planar electron geometry has idealized bond angles of 120°. The bond angle is expected to be less than 120° because of the lone pair electrons occupying the third sp^2 orbital. Further, the bond angle should be less than the bond angle in NO_2 because the presence of lone pairs lowers the tendency for the central atom's orbitals to hybridize. As a result, as lone pairs are added, the bond angle moves further from the 120° hybrid angle to the 90° unhybridized angle and the two electrons will increase this tendency.

10.104 As you move down the column from F to Cl to Br to I, the atomic radius of the atoms increases. Because of this, the larger atoms cannot be accommodated with the smaller bond angle. The attached atoms themselves would begin to overlap their orbitals. So, as the size of the attached atom increases, the bond angle becomes larger, approaching the hybridized 109.5° angle.

10.105 CH_5^+ Draw the Lewis structure: (nine valence electrons)

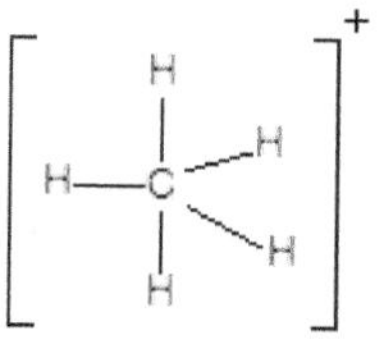

To accommodate the five σ bonds, you need five equal energy hybrid orbitals. So you need to combine five atomic orbitals. The valence electrons on C are in the 2*s* and 2*p* orbitals, so you can combine the *s* and 3 *p* orbitals, but this would only give you four hybrid orbitals. The next lowest energy orbital available on C is the 3*s*, so this would be the next atomic orbital added in. This gives a hybridization of s^2p^3. VSEPR theory would predict that the geometry would be trigonal bipyramid to accommodate the five bonds.

10.106 Both VSEPR theory and hybridization would predict a bond angle of 180°. However, gaseous BaF_2 has a bond angle of 108°. This may be because the 5*d* orbitals are very close in energy to the 6*s* orbitals on the Ba. Thus, these may contribute to the bonding scheme rather than the 6 p orbitals.

Conceptual Problems

10.107 Statement a is the best statement.
Statement b neglects the lowering of potential energy that arises from the interaction of the lone pair electrons with the bonding electrons.
Statement c neglects the interaction of the electrons altogether. The molecular geometries are determined by the number and types of electron groups around the central atom.

10.108 A molecule with four bond groups and one lone pair would need five equivalent positions around the central atom. In two dimensions, this could be accommodated with a pentagon shape around the central atom. The idealized bond angles would be 72°; however, because of the lone pair occupying one of the positions, the bond angles would be less than 72°.

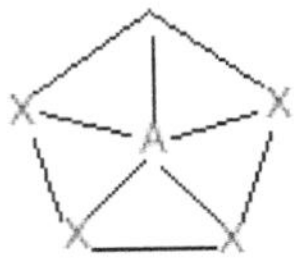

10.109 In Lewis theory, a covalent bond comes from the sharing of electrons.

A single bond shares two electrons (one pair).
A double bond shares four electrons (two pairs).
A triple bond shares six electrons (three pairs).

In valence bond theory, a covalent bond forms when orbitals overlap. The orbitals can be unhybridized or hybridized orbitals.

A single bond forms when a σ bond is formed from the overlap of an *s* orbital with an *s* orbital, an *s* orbital with a *p* orbital, or a *p* orbital and a *p* orbital overlapping end to end. A σ can also form from the overlap of a hybridized orbital on the central atom with an s orbital or with a p orbital overlapping end to end.
A double bond is a combination of a σ bond and a π bond. The π bond forms from the sideways overlap of a *p* orbital on each of the atoms involved in the bond. The *p* orbitals must have the same orientation.
A triple bond is a combination of a σ bond and 2π bonds. The π bonds form from the sideways overlap of a *p* orbital on each of the atoms involved in the bond. The *p* orbitals must have the same orientation so each π bond is formed from a different set of *p* orbitals.

In molecular orbital theory, molecular orbitals form. These are combinations of the atomic orbitals of the atoms involved in the bond. The bonds form when the valence electrons occupy more bonding molecular orbitals than antibonding molecular orbitals. This is calculated by the bond order.

A single bond has a bond order of 1.
A double bond has a bond order of 2.
A triple bond has a bond order of 3.

All three models show the formation of bonds between two atoms. All three models show the formation of the same number of bonds between the atoms involved. Lewis theory tells us only about the number of bonds formed and combined with VSEPR theory allows us to predict the shape of the molecule. It does not, however, tell us anything about how the bonds are formed. Valence bond theory addresses the formation of the different types of bonds, sigma and pi. In valence bond theory the bonds form from the overlap of atomic orbitals on the individual atoms involved in the bonds and the atoms are localized between the two atoms involved in the bond. Molecular orbital theory approaches the formation of bonds by looking at the entire molecule. The electrons are not restricted to any two individual atoms, but treated as belonging to the whole molecule. The electrons reside in molecular orbitals that are part of the entire molecule rather than being restricted to individual atoms. Each model gives us information about the molecule. The amount and type of information that we need determines the model that we choose to use.

10.110 In period 2, the atoms are smaller and they do not have d orbitals available to hybridize, so they cannot accommodate as many atoms around the central atom. In order to complete the octet of electrons multiple bonds must form. In the period 3 and higher atoms, more atoms can surround the central atom, which is larger, and the d orbitals can hybridize with the s and p orbitals. There are now more orbitals available to overlap, and there is space for them to do so. The central atom, therefore, can attain a stable configuration of eight or more electrons without having to multiple bond.

11 Liquids, Solids, and Intermolecular Forces

Review Questions

11.1 The key to the gecko's sticky feet lies in the millions of microhairs, called setae, that line its toes. Each seta is between 30 and 130 μm long and branches out to end in several hundred flattened tips called spatulae. This unique structure allows the gecko's toes to have unusually close contact with the surfaces it climbs. The close contact allows intermolecular forces—which are significant only at short distances—to hold the gecko to the wall.

11.2 Intermolecular forces are important because they are the forces that hold many liquids and solids—such as water and ice, for example—together. These intermolecular forces determine many of the physical properties of a substance. All living organisms depend on intermolecular forces for many physiological processes. Intermolecular forces are responsible for the very existence of the condensed phases.

11.3 The main properties of liquids are that liquids have much higher densities in comparison to gases and generally have lower densities in comparison to solids; liquids have an indefinite shape and assume the shape of their container; liquids have a definite volume; and liquids are not easily compressed.

11.4 The main properties of solids are that solids have much higher densities in comparison to gases, and usually higher densities than liquids; solids have a definite shape; they do not assume the shape of their container; solids have a definite volume; they are not easily compressed; and solids may be crystalline (ordered) or amorphous (disordered).

11.5 Solids may be crystalline, in which case the atoms or molecules that compose them are arranged in a well-ordered three-dimensional array, or they may be amorphous, in which case the atoms or molecules that compose them have no long-range order.

11.6 One phase of matter can be transformed to another by changing the temperature, pressure, or both. A liquid can be converted to a gas by heating, and a gas can be condensed into a liquid by cooling. In general, increases in pressure favor the denser phase, so increasing the pressure of a gas sample can result in a transition to the liquid phase. A solid can be converted to a liquid by heating, and a liquid can be converted to a solid by cooling. In general, increases in pressure favor the denser phase (since atoms are pushed closer together), so increasing the pressure of most liquids can result in a transition to the solid phase.

11.7 Since there is the most molecular motion in the gas phase and the least molecular motion in the solid phase (atoms are pushed closer together), a substance will be converted from a solid then to a liquid and finally to a gas as the temperature increases. The strength of the intermolecular interactions is least in the gas phase, since there are large distances between particles and they are moving very fast. Intermolecular forces are stronger in liquids and solids, where molecules are "touching" one another. The strength of the interactions in the condensed phases will determine at what temperature the substance will melt and boil.

11.8 Intermolecular forces originate from the interactions between charges, partial charges, and temporary charges on molecules (or atoms and ions), much as bonding forces originate from interactions between charged particles in atoms.

11.9 Intermolecular forces, even the strongest ones, are generally much weaker than bonding forces. The reason for the relative weakness of intermolecular forces compared to bonding forces is related to Coulomb's law $\left(E = \frac{1}{4\pi\epsilon_0}\frac{q_1q_2}{r}\right)$. Bonding forces are the result of large charges (the charges on protons and electrons, q_1 and q_2) interacting at very close distances (r). Intermolecular forces are the result of smaller charges (as we shall see in the following discussion) interacting at greater distances.

11.10 Dispersion forces (also called London forces) are the result of fluctuations in the electron distribution within molecules or atoms. Since all atoms and molecules have electrons, they all exhibit dispersion forces. The electrons in an atom or molecule may, at any one instant, be unevenly distributed.

The magnitude of the dispersion force depends on how easily the electrons in the atom or molecule can move or polarize in response to an instantaneous dipole (a temporary change in charge distribution), which in turn depends on the size (or volume) of the electron cloud. A larger electron cloud results in a greater dispersion force because the electrons are held less tightly by the nucleus and can therefore polarize more easily. If all other variables are constant, the dispersion force increases with increasing molar mass because molecules or atoms of higher molar mass generally have more electrons dispersed over a greater volume. The shape of the molecules can also affect the magnitude of the dispersion forces. The larger the area of interaction between two molecules, the larger the dispersion forces.

11.11 The dipole–dipole force exists in all molecules that are polar. Polar molecules have permanent dipoles that interact with the permanent dipoles of neighboring molecules. The positive end of one permanent dipole is attracted to the negative end of another; this attraction is the dipole–dipole force.

11.12 Miscibility is the ability to mix without separating into two phases. In general, polar liquids are miscible with other polar liquids, but are not miscible with nonpolar liquids. Nonpolar liquids are miscible with other nonpolar liquids.

11.13 The hydrogen bond is a sort of super dipole–dipole force. Polar molecules containing hydrogen atoms bonded directly to fluorine, oxygen, or nitrogen exhibit an intermolecular force called hydrogen bonding. The large electronegativity difference between hydrogen and these electronegative elements means that the H atoms will have fairly large partial positive charges ($\delta+$), while the F, O, or N atoms will have fairly large partial negative charges ($\delta-$). In addition, since these atoms are all quite small, they can approach one another very closely. The result is a strong attraction between the hydrogen in each of these molecules and the F, O, or N on its neighbors, an attraction called a hydrogen bond.

11.14 The ion–dipole force occurs when an ionic compound is mixed with a polar compound and is especially important in aqueous solutions of ionic compounds. For example, when sodium chloride is mixed with water, the sodium and chloride ions interact with water molecules via ion–dipole forces. The positive sodium ions interact with the negative poles of water molecules, while the negative chloride ions interact with the positive poles. Ion–dipole forces are the strongest of the types of intermolecular forces discussed here and are responsible for the ability of ionic substances to form solutions with water.

11.15 Surface tension is the tendency of liquids to minimize their surface area. Molecules at the surface have relatively fewer neighbors with which to interact, because there are no molecules above the surface. Consequently, molecules at the surface are inherently less stable—they have higher potential energy—than those in the interior. In order to increase the surface area of the liquid, some molecules from the interior have to be moved to the surface, a process requiring energy. The surface tension of a liquid is the energy required to increase the surface area by a unit amount. Surface tension decreases with decreasing intermolecular forces.

11.16 Viscosity is the resistance of a liquid to flow. Viscosity is measured in a unit called the poise (P), defined as 1 g/cm·s. The centipoise (cP) is a convenient unit because the viscosity of water at room temperature is approximately one centipoise. Viscosity is greater in substances with stronger intermolecular forces because molecules are more strongly attracted to each other, preventing them from flowing around each other as freely. Viscosity also depends on molecular shape, increasing in longer molecules that can interact over a greater area and possibly become entangled. Viscosity increases with increasing molar mass (and therefore increasing magnitude of dispersion forces) and with increasing length (and therefore increasing potential for molecular entanglement). Viscosity also depends on temperature because thermal energy partially overcomes the intermolecular forces, allowing molecules to flow past each other more easily.

11.17 Capillary action is the ability of a liquid to flow against gravity up a narrow tube. Capillary action results from a combination of two forces: the attraction between molecules in a liquid, called cohesive forces, and the attraction between these molecules and the surface of the tube, called adhesive forces. The adhesive forces cause the liquid to spread out over the surface of the tube, while the cohesive forces cause the liquid to stay together. If the adhesive forces are greater than the cohesive forces (as is the case for water in a glass tube), the attraction to the surface draws the liquid up the tube while the cohesive forces pull along those molecules not in direct contact with the tube walls. The liquid rises up the tube until the force of gravity balances the capillary action—the thinner the tube, the higher the rise. If the adhesive forces are smaller than the cohesive forces (as is the case for liquid mercury), the liquid does not rise up the tube at all (and in fact will drop to a level below the level of the surrounding liquid).

11.18 Molecules are in constant motion. The higher the temperature, the greater the average energy of the collection of molecules. However, at any one time, some molecules will have more thermal energy than the average and some will have less. The molecules with the highest thermal energy have enough energy to break free from the surface—where molecules are held less tightly than in the interior due to fewer neighbor–neighbor interactions—and into the gas phase. This process is called vaporization, the phase transition from liquid to gas. The greater the temperature the greater the rate of vaporization. Some of the water molecules in the gas phase, at the low end of the energy distribution curve for the gaseous molecules, can plunge back into the liquid and be captured by intermolecular forces. This process—the opposite of vaporization—is called condensation, the phase transition from gas to liquid.

11.19 The molecules that leave the liquid are the ones at the high end of the energy curve—the most energetic. If no additional heat enters the liquid, the average energy of the entire collection of molecules goes down—much as the class average on an exam goes down if you eliminate the highest-scoring students. So vaporization is an endothermic process; it takes energy to vaporize the molecules in a liquid. Also, vaporization requires overcoming the intermolecular forces that hold liquids together. Since energy must be absorbed to pull the molecules apart, the process is endothermic. Condensation is the opposite process, so it must be exothermic. Also, gas particles have more energy than those in the liquid. It is the least energetic of these that condense, adding energy to the liquid.

11.20 The weaker the intermolecular forces, the more likely it is that molecules are to evaporate at a given temperature, making the liquid more volatile.

11.21 The heat of vaporization (ΔH_{vap}) is the amount of heat required to vaporize one mole of a liquid to a gas. The heat of vaporization of a liquid can be used to calculate the amount of heat energy required to vaporize a given mass of the liquid (or the amount of heat given off by the condensation of a given mass of liquid), and can be used to compare the volatility of two substances.

11.22 Molecules are in constant motion. Molecules leave the liquid for the gas phase and gas phase molecules condense to become a liquid. Dynamic equilibrium has been reached when the rate of condensation and the rate of vaporization become equal. Although condensation and vaporization continue, at equal rates, the concentration of water vapor above the liquid is constant. The pressure of a gas in dynamic equilibrium with its liquid is called its vapor pressure.

11.23 When a system in dynamic equilibrium is disturbed, the system responds so as to minimize the disturbance and return to a state of equilibrium.

11.24 The vapor pressure of a liquid increases with increasing temperature. However, the relationship is not linear, but rather, it is exponential. As the temperature of a liquid increases, the vapor increases more and more quickly. As the temperature is decreased, the vapor pressure decreases following this same relationship.

11.25 The boiling point of a liquid is the temperature at which its vapor pressure equals the external pressure. The normal boiling point of a liquid is the temperature at which its vapor pressure equals 1 atm.

11.26 The Clausius–Clapeyron Equation is the relationship between vapor pressure and temperature. It can be expressed as $\ln P_{vap} = \frac{-\Delta H_{vap}}{R}\left(\frac{1}{T}\right) + \ln \beta$. In this expression P_{vap} is the vapor pressure, β is a constant that depends on the gas, ΔH_{vap} is the heat of vaporization, R is the gas constant (8.314 J/mol K), and T is the temperature in kelvin. The Clausius–Clapeyron equation gives a linear relationship—not between the vapor pressure and the temperature (which have an exponential relationship)—but between the natural log of the vapor pressure and the inverse of temperature. The Clausius–Clapeyron equation leads to a convenient way to measure the heat of vaporization in the laboratory, or to calculate the vapor pressure of a liquid at a temperature (if the heat of vaporization and a vapor pressure at one temperature are known).

11.27 As the temperature rises, more liquid vaporizes and the pressure within the container increases. As more and more gas is forced into the same amount of space, the density of the gas becomes higher and higher. At the same time, the increasing temperature causes the density of the liquid to become lower and lower. At the critical temperature, the meniscus between the liquid and gas disappears and the gas and liquid phases commingle to form a supercritical fluid.

11.28 Sublimation is the phase transition from solid to gas, without going through a liquid phase. A common example of sublimation is the carbon dioxide, where "dry ice" converts from a solid to a gas, without going through a "wet" (or liquid) phase.

11.29 Fusion, or melting, is the phase transition from solid to liquid. The term fusion is used for melting because, if you heat several crystals of a solid, they will fuse into a continuous liquid upon melting. Fusion is endothermic because solids have less kinetic energy than liquids, so energy must be added to a solid to get it to melt.

11.30 The heat of fusion (ΔH_{fus}) is the amount of heat required to melt 1 mol of a solid. The heat of fusion of a solid, which is related to the strength of the intermolecular forces, can be used to calculate the amount of heat energy required to melt a given mass of the solid (or the amount of heat given off by the freezing of a given mass of liquid).

11.31 There are two horizontal lines (i.e. heat is added, but the temperature stays constant) in the heating curve because there are two endothermic phase changes. The heat that is added is used to change the phase from solid to liquid or liquid to gas.

11.32 The slopes indicate how much heat is necessary to increase the temperature of the sample. The slope is proportional to $1/C_s$ (the specific heat capacity of the phase). The amount of molecular motion and the amount of intermolecular interactions is different in each phase, and so the specific heat capacity and the slope is different for each phase and each substance.

11.33 A phase diagram is simply a map of the phase of a substance as a function of pressure (on the y-axis) and temperature (on the x-axis).

Phase Diagram for Water

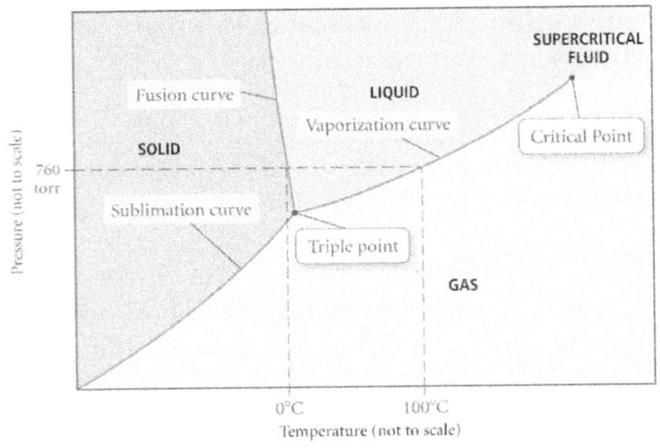

11.34 When a line is crossed in a phase diagram it means that a phase transition has occurred.

11.35 Water has a low molar mass (18.01 g/mol), yet it is a liquid at room temperature. Water's high boiling point for its molar mass can be understood by examining the structure of the water molecule. The bent geometry of the water molecule and the highly polar nature of the O–H bonds result in a molecule with a significant dipole moment. Water's two O–H bonds (hydrogen directly bonded to oxygen) allow a water molecule to form strong hydrogen bonds with four other water molecules, resulting in a relatively high boiling point. Water's high polarity also allows it to dissolve many other polar and ionic compounds, and even a number of nonpolar gases such as oxygen and carbon dioxide (by inducing a dipole moment in their molecules). Water has an exceptionally high specific heat capacity. One significant difference between the phase diagram of water and that of other substances is that the fusion curve for water has a negative slope. The fusion curve within the phase diagrams for most substances has a positive slope because increasing pressure favors the denser phase, which for most substances is the solid phase. This negative slope means that ice is less dense than liquid water and so ice floats. The solid phase sinks in the liquid of most other substances.

11.36 X-ray crystallography is used to examine the structure of crystalline materials (materials that have an ordered array of atoms). The technique is based on the wave nature of X-rays. Atoms within crystal structures have spacings between them on the order of 10^2 pm. When light of similar wavelength (which happens to fall in the X-ray region of the electromagnetic spectrum) interacts with a sample, the waves are diffracted by the atoms. The waves interact with each other to either constructively (they reinforce each other) or destructively (they cancel each other) interfere to form interference patterns or diffraction patterns. The exact pattern of diffraction reveals the spacings between planes of atoms. How the waves interact is dependent on the path that the waves take. Consider two planes of atoms within a crystalline lattice separated by a distance d, as shown in Figure 11.42. If two rays of light with wavelength λ that are initially in phase (that is, the crests of one wave are aligned with the crests of the other) diffract from the two layers, the diffracted rays may interfere with each other constructively or destructively, depending on the difference between the path lengths traveled by each ray. If the difference between the two path lengths ($2a$) is an integral number (n) of wavelengths, then the interference will be constructive or $n\lambda=2a$. Using trigonometry, we can see that the angle of reflection (θ) is related to the distance a and the separation between layers (d) by the following relation: $\sin\theta = a/d$. Rearranging and substituting into $n\lambda=2a$, we get $n\lambda = 2\,d\sin\theta$, known as Bragg's law. For a given wavelength of light incident on atoms arranged in layers, we can then measure the angle that produces constructive interference (which appears as a bright spot on the X-ray diffraction pattern) and then compute d, the distance between the atomic layers.

11.37 A crystalline lattice is the regular arrangements of atoms within a crystalline solid. The crystalline lattice can be represented by a small collection of atoms, ions, or molecules—a fundamental building block called the unit cell. When the unit cell is repeated over and over—like tiles in a floor or the pattern in a wallpaper design, but in three dimensions—the entire lattice can be reproduced.

11.38

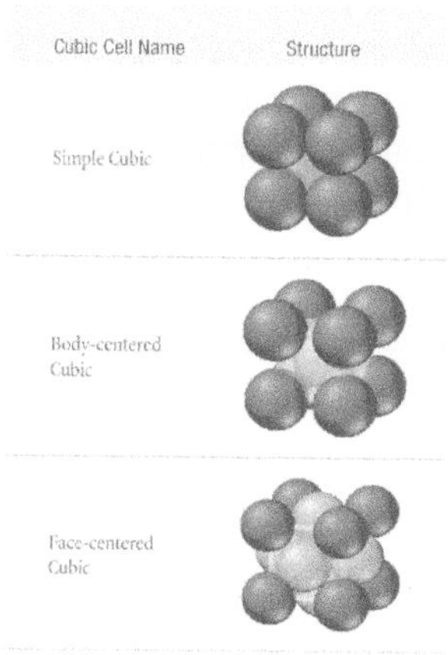

11.39 Atoms in a simple cubic cell structure have a coordination number of 6, an edge length of $2r$, and 1 atom in the unit cell. Atoms in a body-centered cubic cell structure have a coordination number of 8, an edge length of $4r/\sqrt{3}$, and 2 atoms in the unit cell. Atoms in a face-centered cubic cell structure have a coordination number of 12, an edge length of $2\sqrt{2}r$, and 4 atoms in the unit cell.

11.40 In hexagonal closest packing, the third layer of atoms aligns exactly on top of the first. The pattern from one layer to the next is ABAB... with alternating layers aligning exactly on top of one another. The unit cell for this crystal structure is not a cubic unit cell, but a hexagonal one, as shown in Figure 11.48. In cubic closest packing, the third layer of atoms is offset from the first. The pattern from one layer to the next is ABCABC....with every fourth layer aligning with the first. The unit cell for this crystal structure is the face-centered cubic unit cell.

11.41 The three types of solids are molecular solids, ionic solids and atomic solids. Molecular solids are those solids whose composite units are molecules. The lattice sites in a crystalline molecular solid are therefore occupied by molecules. Ice (solid H_2O) and dry ice (solid CO_2) are examples of molecular solids. Molecular solids are held together by the kinds of intermolecular forces—dispersion forces, dipole–dipole forces, and hydrogen bonding. Ionic solids are those solids whose composite units are ions. Table salt (NaCl) and calcium fluoride (CaF_2) are good examples of ionic solids. Ionic solids are held together by the coulombic interactions that occur between the cations and anions occupying the lattice sites in the crystal, which is an ionic bond. Atomic solids are those solids whose composite units are individual atoms. Atomic solids can themselves be divided into three categories—nonbonding atomic solids, metallic atomic solids, and network covalent atomic solids—each held together by a different kind of force. Nonbonding atomic solids, which include only the noble gases in their solid form, are held together by relatively weak dispersion forces. Metallic atomic solids, such as iron or gold, are held together by metallic bonds, which in the simplest model are represented by the interaction of metal cations with a sea of electrons that surround them. Network covalent atomic solids, such as diamond, graphite, and silicon dioxide, are held together by covalent bonds.

11.42 The coordination number of the unit cell for an ionic compound represents the number of close cation–anion interactions. Since these interactions lower potential energy, the crystal structure of a particular ionic compound will be the one that maximizes the coordination number, while accommodating both charge neutrality (each unit cell must be neutral) and the different sizes of the cations and anions that compose the particular compound. In general, the more similar the radii of the cation and the anion, the higher the possible coordination number.

11.43 Cesium chloride (CsCl) is a good example of an ionic compound containing cations and anions of similar size (Cs^+ radius = 167 pm; Cl^- radius = 181 pm). In the cesium chloride structure, the chloride ions occupy the lattice sites of a simple cubic cell and one cesium ion lies in the very center of the cell, as shown in Figure 11.51. Notice that the cesium chloride unit cell contains one chloride anion ($8 \times 1/8 = 1$) and one cesium cation (the cesium ion in the middle belongs entirely to the unit cell) for a ratio of Cs to Cl of 1:1, just as in the formula for the compound.

The crystal structure of sodium chloride must accommodate the more disproportionate sizes of Na^+ (radius = 97 pm) and Cl^- (radius = 181 pm). The larger chloride anion could theoretically fit many of the smaller sodium cations around it, but charge neutrality requires that each sodium cation be surrounded by an equal number of chloride anions. The structure that minimizes the energy is shown in Figure 11.52 and has a coordination number of 6 (each chloride anion is surrounded by six sodium cations and vice versa). You can visualize this structure, called the rock salt structure, as chloride anions occupying the lattice sites of a face-centered cubic structure with the smaller sodium cations occupying the holes between the anions. (Alternatively, you can visualize this structure as the sodium cations occupying the lattice sites of a face-centered cubic structure with the larger chloride anions occupying the spaces between the cations.) Each unit cell contains four chloride anions ($[8 \times 1/8] + [6 \times \frac{1}{2}] = 4$) and four sodium cations ($12 \times \frac{1}{4}$) resulting in a ratio of 1:1, just as in the formula of the compound.

You can visualize this structure (shown in Figure 11.53), called the zinc blende structure, as sulfide anions occupying the lattice sites of a face-centered cubic structure with the smaller zinc cations occupying four of the eight tetrahedral holes located directly beneath each corner atom. A tetrahedral hole is the empty space that lies in the center of a tetrahedral arrangement of four atoms. Each unit cell contains four sulfide anions ($[8 \times 1/8] + [6 \times \frac{1}{2}] = 4$) and four zinc cations (each of the four zinc cations is completely contained within the unit cell), resulting in a ratio of 1:1, just as in the formula of the compound.

11.44 The fluorite (CaF_2) structure shown in Figure 11.54. You can visualize this structure as calcium cations occupying the lattice sites of a face-centered cubic structure with the larger fluoride anions occupying all eight of the tetrahedral holes located directly beneath each corner atom. Each unit cell contains four calcium cations ($[8 \times 1/8] + [6 \times \frac{1}{2}] = 4$) and eight fluoride anions (each of the eight fluoride anions is completely contained within the unit cell), resulting in a cation to anion ratio of 1:2, just as in the formula of the compound.

11.45 Atomic solids can themselves be divided into three categories—nonbonding atomic solids, metallic atomic solids, and network covalent atomic solids. Nonbonding atomic solids, which include only the noble gases in their solid form, are held together by relatively weak dispersion forces. Metallic atomic solids, such as iron or gold, are held together by metallic bonds, which in the simplest model are represented by the interaction of metal cations with a sea of electrons that surround them. Network covalent atomic solids, such as diamond, graphite, and silicon dioxide, are held together by covalent bonds.

11.46 In band theory, bands are the combination atomic orbitals of the atoms within a solid crystal that form orbitals that are not localized on individual atoms, but delocalized over the entire crystal. In band theory, electrons become mobile when they make a transition from the highest occupied molecular orbital into higher-energy empty molecular orbitals. For this reason, the occupied molecular orbitals are often called the valence band and the unoccupied orbitals are called the conduction band.

11.47 The band gap is an energy gap that exists between the valence band and conduction band. In metals, the valence band and conduction band are always energetically continuous—the energy difference between the top of the valence band and the bottom of the conduction band is infinitesimally small. In semiconductors, the band gap is small, allowing some electrons to be promoted at ordinary temperatures resulting in limited conductivity. In insulators, the band gap is large, and electrons are not promoted into the conduction band at ordinary temperatures, resulting in no electrical conductivity.

11.48 Doped semiconductors contain minute amounts of impurities that result in additional electrons in the conduction band or electron "holes" in the valence band. For example, silicon is a group 4A semiconductor. Its valence electrons just fill its valence band. When silicon is doped with phosphorus, a group 5A element with five valence electrons, its conductivity increases. The phosphorus atoms are incorporated into the silicon crystal structure, but each phosphorus atom brings with it one additional electron. Since the valence band is completely full, the additional electrons must go into the conduction band. These electrons are then mobile and can conduct electrical current. This type of semiconductor is called an n-type semiconductor because the charge carriers are negatively charged electrons in the conduction band. Silicon can also be doped with a group 3A element, such as gallium, which has only three valence electrons. When gallium is incorporated into the silicon crystal structure, it results in electron "holes," empty molecular orbitals in the valence band. The presence of holes also allows for the movement of electrical current because electrons in the valence band can move between holes. In this way, the holes move in the opposite direction as the electrons. This type of semiconductor is called a p-type semiconductor because the hole acts as a positive charge.

Intermolecular Forces

11.49 (a) dispersion forces

(b) dispersion forces, dipole–dipole forces, and hydrogen bonding

(c) dispersion forces and dipole–dipole forces

(d) dispersion forces

11.50 (a) dispersion forces

(b) dispersion forces and dipole–dipole forces

(c) dispersion forces

(d) dispersion forces, dipole–dipole forces, and hydrogen bonding

11.51 (a) dispersion forces and dipole–dipole forces

(b) dispersion forces, dipole–dipole forces, and hydrogen bonding

(c) dispersion forces

(d) dispersion forces

11.52 (a) dispersion forces and dipole–dipole forces

(b) dispersion forces and dipole–dipole forces

(c) dispersion forces, dipole–dipole forces, and hydrogen bonding

(d) dispersion forces

11.53 (a) CH_4 < (b) CH_3CH_3 < (c) CH_3CH_2Cl < (d) CH_3CH_2OH. The first two molecules only exhibit dispersion forces, so the boiling point increases with increasing molar mass. The third molecule also exhibits dipole–dipole forces, which are stronger than dispersion forces. The last molecule exhibits hydrogen bonding. Since these are by far the strongest intermolecular forces in this group, the last molecule has the highest boiling point.

11.54 (a) H_2S < (b) H_2Se < (c) H_2O. The first two molecules only exhibit dispersion forces and dipole–dipole forces, so the boiling point increases with increasing molar mass. The third molecule also exhibits hydrogen bonding. Since these are by far the strongest intermolecular forces in this group, the last molecule has the highest boiling point.

11.55 (a) CH_3OH has the higher boiling point since it exhibits hydrogen bonding.

(b) CH_3CH_2OH has the higher boiling point since it exhibits hydrogen bonding.

(c) CH_3CH_3 has the higher boiling point since it has the larger molar mass.

11.56 (a) NH_3 has the higher boiling point since it exhibits hydrogen bonding.

(b) CS_2 has the higher boiling point since it has the larger molar mass.

(c) NO_2 has the higher boiling point since it exhibits dipole–dipole forces.

11.57 (a) Br_2 has the higher vapor pressure since it has the smaller molar mass.

(b) H_2S has the higher vapor pressure since it does not exhibit hydrogen bonding.

(c) PH_3 has the higher vapor pressure since it does not exhibit hydrogen bonding.

11.58 (a) CH_4 has the higher vapor pressure since it has the smaller molar mass and it does not exhibit dipole–dipole forces.

(b) CH_3OH has the higher vapor pressure since it has the smaller molar mass, and both exhibit hydrogen bonding.

(c) H_2CO has the higher vapor pressure since it has the smaller molar mass and it does not exhibit hydrogen bonding.

11.59 (a) This will not form a homogeneous solution, since one is polar and one is nonpolar.

(b) This will form a homogeneous solution. There will be ion–dipole interactions between the K^+ and Cl^- ions and the water molecules. There will also be dispersion forces, dipole–dipole forces, and hydrogen bonding between the water molecules.

(c) This will form a homogeneous solution. There will be dispersion forces present among all of the molecules.

(d) This will form a homogeneous solution. There will be dispersion forces, dipole–dipole forces, and hydrogen bonding among all of the molecules.

11.60 (a) This will form a homogeneous solution. There will only be dispersion forces present.

(b) This will not form a homogeneous solution, since one is polar and one is nonpolar.

(c) This will form a homogeneous solution. There will be ion–dipole interactions between the Li^+ and NO_3^- ions and the water molecules. There will also be dispersion forces, dipole–dipole forces, and hydrogen bonding between the water molecules.

(d) This will not form a homogeneous solution, since one is polar and one is nonpolar.

Surface Tension, Viscosity, and Capillary Action

11.61 Water will have the higher surface tension since it exhibits hydrogen bonding, a strong intermolecular force. Acetone cannot form hydrogen bonds.

11.62 (a) Water "wets" surfaces that are capable of dipole–dipole interactions. The water will form strong adhesive forces with the surface when these dipole–dipole forces are present and so the water will spread to cover as much of the surface as possible. Water does not experience strong intermolecular forces with oil and other nonpolar surfaces. The water will bead up, maximizing the cohesive interactions, which involve strong hydrogen bonds. So water will bead up on surfaces that can only exhibit dispersion forces.

(b) Mercury will bead up on surfaces since it is not capable of forming strong intermolecular interactions (only dispersion forces).

11.63 Compound A will have the higher viscosity since it can interact with other molecules along the entire molecule. The more branched isomer has a smaller surface area allowing for fewer interactions. Also the molecule is very flexible and the molecules can get tangled with each other.

11.64 Multigrade oils contain polymers (long molecules made up of repeating structural units) that coil at low temperatures but unwind at high temperatures. At low temperatures, the coiled polymers—because of their compact shape—do not contribute very much to the viscosity of the oil. As the temperature increases, however, the molecules unwind and their long shape results in intermolecular forces and molecular entanglements that prevent the viscosity from decreasing as much as it would normally. The result is an oil whose viscosity is less temperature-dependent than it would be otherwise, allowing the same oil to be used over a wider range of temperatures.

11.65 In a clean glass tube the water can generate strong adhesive interactions with the glass (due to the dipoles at the surface of the glass). Water experiences adhesive forces with glass that are stronger than its cohesive forces, causing it to climb the surface of a glass tube. When grease or oil coats the glass this interferes with the formation of these adhesive interactions with the glass, since oils are nonpolar and cannot interact strongly with the dipoles in the water. Without experiencing these strong intermolecular forces with oil, the water's cohesive forces will be greater and it will be drawn away from the surface of the tube.

11.66 Water can generate strong adhesive interactions with the glass (due to the dipoles at the surface of the glass), but hexane is nonpolar and cannot interact strongly with the glass surface.

Vaporization and Vapor Pressure

11.67 The water in the 12 cm diameter beaker will evaporate more quickly because there is more surface area for the molecules to evaporate from. The vapor pressure will be the same in the two containers because the vapor pressure is the pressure of the gas when it is in dynamic equilibrium with the liquid (evaporation rate = condensation rate). The vapor pressure is dependent only on the substance and the temperature. The 12 cm diameter container will reach this dynamic equilibrium faster.

11.68 The acetone will evaporate more quickly since it is not capable of forming hydrogen bonds, so the intermolecular forces are much weaker. This will result in a larger vapor pressure at the same temperature as the water.

11.69 The boiling point and higher heat of vaporization of oil are much higher than that of water, so it will not vaporize as quickly as the water. The evaporation of water cools your skin because evaporation is an endothermic process.

11.70 Water molecules have a lower kinetic energy at room temperature than at 100 °C. The heat of vaporization is the energy difference between the molecules in the liquid phase and the gas phase. Since the energy of the liquid is lower at room temperature, then the energy difference that must be overcome to become steam is greater, so the heat of vaporization is greater.

11.71 **Given:** 915 kJ from candy bar, water $d = 1.00$ g/ml **Find:** L(H_2O) vaporized at 100.0 °C
Other: $\Delta H^\circ_{vap} = 40.7$ kJ/mol
Conceptual Plan: $q \rightarrow \text{mol } H_2O \rightarrow \text{g } H_2O \rightarrow \text{mL } H_2O \rightarrow \text{L } H_2O$

$$\frac{1 \text{ mol}}{40.7 \text{ kJ}} \quad \frac{18.01 \text{ g}}{1 \text{ mol}} \quad \frac{1.00 \text{ mL}}{1.00 \text{ g}} \quad \frac{1 \text{ L}}{1000 \text{ mL}}$$

Solution: $915 \text{ kJ} \times \frac{1 \text{ mol}}{40.7 \text{ kJ}} \times \frac{18.02 \text{ g}}{1 \text{ mol}} \times \frac{1.00 \text{ mL}}{1 \text{ g}} \times \frac{1 \text{ L}}{1000 \text{ mL}} = 0.405 \text{ L } H_2O$

Check: The units (L) are correct. The magnitude of the answer (< 1 L) makes physical sense because we are vaporizing about 22 moles of water.

11.72 **Given:** 100.0 mL water, $d = 1.00$ g/ml, heated to 100.0 °C **Find:** heat (kJ) to vaporize at 100.0 °C
Other: $\Delta H^\circ_{vap} = 40.7$ kJ/mol
Conceptual Plan: $\text{mL } H_2O \rightarrow \text{g } H_2O \rightarrow \text{mol } H_2O \rightarrow q$

$$\frac{1.00 \text{ g}}{1.00 \text{ mL}} \quad \frac{1 \text{ mol}}{18.01 \text{ g}} \quad \frac{40.7 \text{ kJ}}{1 \text{ mol}}$$

Solution: $100.0 \text{ mL} \times \frac{1.00 \text{ g}}{1.00 \text{ mL}} \times \frac{1 \text{ mol}}{18.02 \text{ g}} \times \frac{40.7 \text{ kJ}}{1 \text{ mol}} = 226 \text{ kJ}$

Check: The units (kJ) are correct. The magnitude of the answer (226 kJ) makes physical sense because we are vaporizing about 6 moles of water.

11.73 **Given:** 0.95 g water condenses on iron block 75.0 g at $T_i = 22$ °C **Find:** T_f (iron block)
Other: $\Delta H^\circ_{vap} = 44.0$ kJ/mol; $C_{Fe} = 0.449$ J/g · °C from text
Conceptual Plan: $\text{g } H_2O \rightarrow \text{mol } H_2O \rightarrow q_{H_2O} \text{ (kJ)} \rightarrow q_{H_2O} \text{ (J)} \rightarrow q_{Fe}$ **then** $q_{Fe}, m_{Fe}, T_i \rightarrow T_f$

$$\frac{1 \text{ mol}}{18.01 \text{ g}} \quad \frac{-44.0 \text{ kJ}}{1 \text{ mol}} \quad \frac{1000 \text{ J}}{1 \text{ kJ}} \quad -q_{H_2O} = q_{Fe} \quad q = mC_s(T_f - T_i)$$

Solution: $0.95 \text{ g} \times \frac{1 \text{ mol}}{18.02 \text{ g}} \times \frac{-44.0 \text{ kJ}}{1 \text{ mol}} \times \frac{1000 \text{ J}}{1 \text{ kJ}} = -2319.64 \text{ J}$ then $-q_{H_2O} = q_{Fe} = 2319.64$ J then

$q = m\,C_s(T_f - T_i)$. Rearrange to solve for T_f.

$$T_f = \frac{m\,C_s\,T_i + q}{m\,C_s} = \frac{\left(75.0 \text{ g} \times 0.449 \frac{\text{J}}{\text{g} \cdot {}^\circ\text{C}} \times 22\,{}^\circ\text{C}\right) + 2319.64 \text{ J}}{75.0 \text{ g} \times 0.449 \frac{\text{J}}{\text{g} \cdot {}^\circ\text{C}}} = 91\,{}^\circ\text{C}.$$

Check: The units (°C) are correct. The temperature rose, which is consistent with heat being added to the block. The magnitude of the answer (91 °C) makes physical sense because even though we have ~ $\frac{1}{20}$ of a mole, the energy involved in condensation is very large.

11.74 **Given:** 1.15 g rubbing alcohol (C_3H_8O) evaporated from aluminum block 65.0 g at $T_i = 25$ °C
Find: T_f (aluminum block) **Other:** $\Delta H^\circ_{vap} = 45.4$ kJ/mol; $C_{Al} = 0.903$ J/g · °C from text
Conceptual Plan: $\text{g } C_3H_8O \rightarrow \text{mol } C_3H_8O \rightarrow q_{C_3H_8O} \text{ (kJ)} \rightarrow q_{C_3H_8O} \text{ (J)} \rightarrow q_{Al}$ **then** $q_{Al}, m_{Fe}, T_i \rightarrow T_f$

$$\frac{1 \text{ mol}}{60.09 \text{ g}} \quad \frac{-45.4 \text{ kJ}}{1 \text{ mol}} \quad \frac{1000 \text{ J}}{1 \text{ kJ}} \quad -q_{H_2O} = q_{Al} \quad q = m\,C_s(T_f - T_i)$$

Solution: $1.15 \text{ g} \times \frac{1 \text{ mol}}{60.09 \text{ g}} \times \frac{45.4 \text{ kJ}}{1 \text{ mol}} \times \frac{1000 \text{ J}}{1 \text{ kJ}} = 868.8634 \text{ J}$ then $-q_{H_2O} = q_{Al} = -868.8634$ J then

$q = m\,C_s(T_f - T_i)$. Rearrange to solve for T_f.

$$T_f = \frac{m\,C_s\,T_i + q}{m\,C_s} = \frac{\left(65.0\ \text{g} \times 0.903\ \frac{\text{J}}{\text{g}\cdot{}^\circ\text{C}} \times 25\ {}^\circ\text{C}\right) - 868.8634\ \text{J}}{65.0\ \text{g} \times 0.903\ \frac{\text{J}}{\text{g}\cdot{}^\circ\text{C}}} = 10.19698\ {}^\circ\text{C} = 10.\ {}^\circ\text{C}.$$

Check: The units (°C) are correct. The temperature dropped, which is consistent with heat being removed from the block. The magnitude of the answer (10 °C) makes physical sense because even though we have only a fraction of a mole, the energy involved in vaporization is very large.

11.75 **Given:** Temperature (K) / Vapor Pressure (torr) **Find:** ΔH°_{vap} (NH_3) and normal boiling point

Temperature (K)	Vapor Pressure (torr)
200	65.3
210	134.3
220	255.7
230	456.0
235	597.0

Conceptual Plan: To find the heat of vaporization, use Excel or similar software to make a plot of the natural log of vapor pressure (ln *P*) as a function of the inverse of the temperature in K (1/*T*). Then fit the points to a line and determine the slope of the line. Since the slope = – $\Delta H_{vap}/R$, we find the heat of vaporization as follows:

slope = – $\Delta H_{vap}/R$ → ΔH_{vap} = – slope x *R* then J → kJ.

$$\frac{1\ \text{kJ}}{1000\ \text{J}}$$

For the normal boiling point, use the equation of the best fit line, substitute 760 torr for the pressure and calculate the temperature.

Solution: Data was plotted in Excel.

The slope of the best fitting line is – 2969.9 K.

$$\Delta H_{vap} = -\,slope \times R = -(-2969.9\ \text{K}) \times \frac{8.314\ \text{J}}{\text{K mol}} = \frac{2.46917 \times 10^4\ \text{J}}{\text{mol}} \times \frac{1\ \text{kJ}}{1000\ \text{J}} = 24.7\,\frac{\text{kJ}}{\text{mol}}$$

$$\ln P = -\,2969.9\ \text{K}\left(\frac{1}{T}\right) + 19.036 \rightarrow$$

$$\ln 760 = -\,2969.9\ \text{K}\left(\frac{1}{T}\right) + 19.036 \rightarrow$$

$$2969.9\ \text{K}\left(\frac{1}{T}\right) = 19.036 - 6.63332 \rightarrow$$

$$T = \frac{2969.9\ \text{K}}{12.40268} = 239\ \text{K}$$

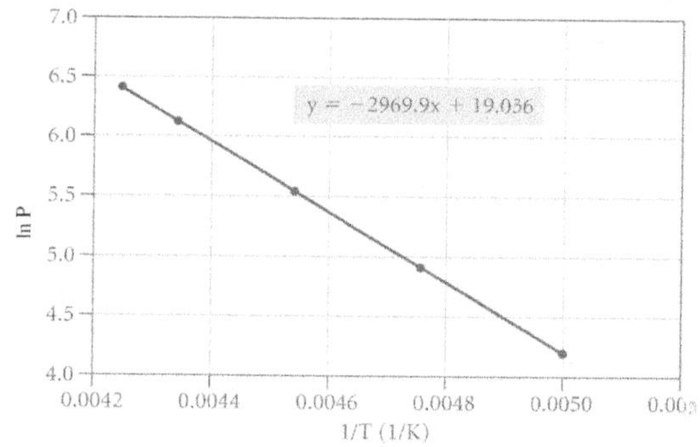

Check: The units (kJ/mol) are correct. The magnitude of the answer (25) is consistent with other values in the text.

11.76 **Given:** Temperature (K) / Vapor Pressure (torr) **Find:** ΔH°_{vap} (N_2) and normal boiling point

Temperature (K)	Vapor Pressure (torr)
65	130.5
70	289.5
75	570.8
80	1028
85	1718

Conceptual Plan: To find the heat of vaporization, use Excel or similar software to make a plot of the natural log of vapor pressure (ln *P*) as a function of the inverse of the temperature in K (1/*T*). Then fit the points to a line and determine the slope of the line. Since the slope = – $\Delta H_{vap}/R$, we find the heat of vaporization as follows:

slope = – $\Delta H_{vap}/R$ → ΔH_{vap} = – slope x *R* then J → kJ.

$$\frac{1\ \text{kJ}}{1000\ \text{J}}$$

For the normal boiling point, use the equation of the best fit line, substitute 760 torr for the pressure, and calculate the temperature.

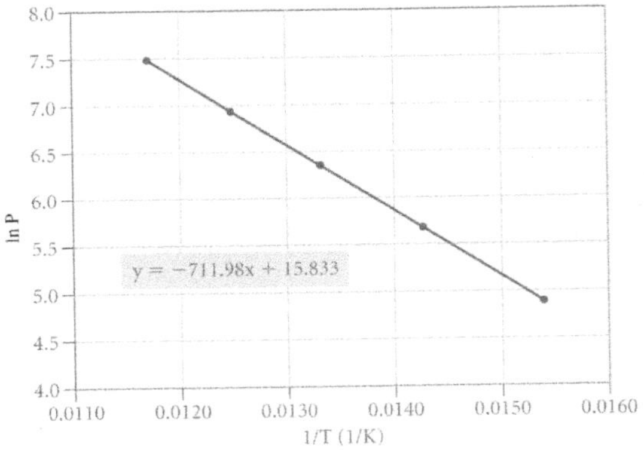

Solution: Data was plotted in Excel.
The slope of the best fitting line is – 711.98 K.

$$\Delta H_{vap} = -\,slope \times R = -(-711.98\ \text{K}) \times \frac{8.314\ \text{J}}{\text{K mol}} = \frac{5.91940 \times 10^3\ \text{J}}{\text{mol}} \times \frac{1\ \text{kJ}}{1000\ \text{J}} = 5.92\ \frac{\text{kJ}}{\text{mol}}$$

$$\ln P = -711.98\ \text{K}\left(\frac{1}{T}\right) + 15.833 \rightarrow$$

$$\ln 760 = -711.98\ \text{K}\left(\frac{1}{T}\right) + 15.833 \rightarrow$$

$$711.98\ \text{K}\left(\frac{1}{T}\right) = 15.833 - 6.63332 \rightarrow$$

$$T = \frac{711.98\ \text{K}}{9.19968} = 77.4\ \text{K}$$

Check: The units (kJ/mol) are correct. The magnitude of the answer is lower than other values quoted in the text. This is consistent with the fact that nitrogen boils at such a low temperature.

11.77 **Given:** ethanol, $\Delta H^\circ_{vap} = 38.56$ kJ/mol; normal boiling point = 78.4 °C **Find:** $P_{Ethanol}$ at 15 °C

Conceptual Plan: °C → K and kJ → J then ΔH°_{vap}, T_1, P_1, T_2 → P_2

$$\text{K} = {^\circ}\text{C} + 273.15 \qquad \frac{1000\ \text{J}}{1\ \text{kJ}} \qquad \ln\frac{P_2}{P_1} = \frac{-\Delta H_{vap}}{R}\left(\frac{1}{T_2} - \frac{1}{T_1}\right)$$

Solution: $T_1 = 78.4\ ^\circ\text{C} + 273.15 = 351.6$ K; $T_2 = 15\ ^\circ\text{C} + 273.15 = 288$ K;

$\frac{38.56\ \text{kJ}}{\text{mol}} \times \frac{1000\ \text{J}}{1\ \text{kJ}} = 3.856 \times 10^4\ \frac{\text{J}}{\text{mol}}$ $P_1 = 760$ torr $\ln\frac{P_2}{P_1} = \frac{-\Delta H_{vap}}{R}\left(\frac{1}{T_2} - \frac{1}{T_1}\right)$. Substitute values in equation.

$$\ln\frac{P_2}{760\ \text{torr}} = \frac{-3.856 \times 10^4\ \frac{\text{J}}{\text{mol}}}{8.314\ \frac{\text{J}}{\text{K}\cdot\text{mol}}}\left(\frac{1}{288\ \text{K}} - \frac{1}{351.6\ \text{K}}\right) = -2.91302 \rightarrow$$

$$\frac{P_2}{760\ \text{torr}} = e^{-2.91302} = 0.054311 \rightarrow P_2 = 0.054311 \times 760\ \text{torr} = 41\ \text{torr}.$$

Check: The units (torr) are correct. Since 15 °C is significantly below the boiling point, we expect the answer to be much less than 760 torr.

11.78 **Given:** benzene, $\Delta H^\circ_{vap} = 30.72$ kJ/mol; normal boiling point = 80.1 °C; $P_2 = 445$ torr **Find:** T_2

Conceptual Plan: °C → K and kJ → J then ΔH°_{vap}, T_1, P_1, T_2 → P_2

$$\text{K} = {^\circ}\text{C} + 273.15 \qquad \frac{1000\ \text{J}}{1\ \text{kJ}} \qquad \ln\frac{P_2}{P_1} = \frac{-\Delta H_{vap}}{R}\left(\frac{1}{T_2} - \frac{1}{T_1}\right)$$

Solution: $T_1 = 80.1\ ^\circ\text{C} + 273.15 = 353.3$ K; $\frac{30.72\ \text{kJ}}{\text{mol}} \times \frac{1000\ \text{J}}{1\ \text{kJ}} = 3.072 \times 10^4\ \frac{\text{J}}{\text{mol}}$; $P_1 = 760$ torr;

$P_2 = 445$ torr $\ln\frac{P_2}{P_1} = \frac{-\Delta H_{vap}}{R}\left(\frac{1}{T_2} - \frac{1}{T_1}\right)$. Substitute values in equation.

$$\ln\frac{445\ \text{torr}}{760\ \text{torr}} = \frac{-3.072 \times 10^4\ \frac{\text{J}}{\text{mol}}}{8.314\ \frac{\text{J}}{\text{K}\cdot\text{mol}}}\left(\frac{1}{T_2} - \frac{1}{353.3\ \text{K}}\right) \rightarrow -0.535244 = -3.694972 \times 10^3\ \text{K}\left(\frac{1}{T_2} - 0.002830456\right)$$

$$\rightarrow \frac{1.44857 \times 10^{-4}}{\text{K}} = \left(\frac{1}{T_2} - \frac{0.002830456}{\text{K}}\right) \rightarrow \frac{1}{T_2} = \frac{2.97531 \times 10^{-3}}{\text{K}} \rightarrow T_2 = 336.0990\ \text{K} = 63\ ^\circ\text{C}.$$

Check: The units (°C) are correct. Since the pressure is over half of 760 torr, we expect a temperature a little lower than the boiling point.

Sublimation and Fusion

11.79 **Given:** 65.8 g water freezes **Find:** energy released **Other:** $\Delta H^\circ_{fus} = 6.02$ kJ/mol from text

Conceptual Plan: g H_2O → mol H_2O → q_{H_2O} (kJ) → q_{H_2O} (J)

$$\frac{1\text{ mol}}{18.01\text{ g}} \quad \frac{-6.02\text{ kJ}}{1\text{ mol}} \quad \frac{1000\text{ J}}{1\text{ kJ}}$$

Solution: $65.8\text{ g} \times \frac{1\text{ mol}}{18.02\text{ g}} \times \frac{-6.02\text{ kJ}}{1\text{ mol}} \times \frac{1000\text{ J}}{1\text{ kJ}} = -21\underline{9}82\text{ J} = 2.20 \times 10^4\text{ J}$ or 2.20×10^4 J released or 22.0 kJ released

Check: The units (J) are correct. The magnitude (22000 J) makes sense since we are freezing about 3 moles of water. Freezing is exothermic, so heat is released.

11.80 **Given:** 50.0 g dry ice(CO_2) sublimation **Find:** heat required **Other:** $\Delta H^\circ_{sub} = 32.3$ kJ/mol

Conceptual Plan: g dry ice → mol dry ice → $q_{dry\ ice}$ (kJ) → $q_{dry\ ice}$ (J)

$$\frac{1\text{ mol}}{44.01\text{ g}} \quad \frac{32.3\text{ kJ}}{1\text{ mol}} \quad \frac{1000\text{ J}}{1\text{ kJ}}$$

Solution: $50.0\text{ g} \times \frac{1\text{ mol}}{44.01\text{ g}} \times \frac{32.3\text{ kJ}}{1\text{ mol}} \times \frac{1000\text{ J}}{1\text{ kJ}} = 36\underline{6}96$ J required $= 36700$ J required or 36.7 kJ absorbed

Check: The units (J) are correct. The magnitude (36700 J) makes sense since we are subliming just over 1 mole of dry ice. Sublimation is endothermic, so heat is required.

11.81 **Given:** 8.5 g ice; 255 g water **Find:** ΔT of water

Other: $\Delta H^\circ_{fus} = 6.0$ kJ/mol; $C_{H_2O} = 4.18$ J/g · °C from text

Conceptual Plan: The first step is to calculate how much heat is removed from the water to melt the ice. $q_{ice} = -q_{water}$ so g (ice) → mol (ice) → q_{fus}(kJ) → q_{fus} (J) → q_{water} (J) then q, m, C_s → ΔT_1

$$\frac{1\text{ mol}}{18.01\text{ g}} \quad \frac{6.0\text{ kJ}}{1\text{ mol}} \quad \frac{1000\text{ J}}{1\text{ kJ}} \quad q_{water} = -q_{ice} \quad q = mC_S\Delta T_1$$

Now we have slightly cooled water (at a temperature of T_1) in contact with 0.0 °C water, and we can calculate a second temperature drop of the water due to mixing of the water that was ice with the initially room temperature water, so $q_{ice} = -q_{water}$ with m, C_s → ΔT_2 with ΔT_1 ΔT_2 → ΔT_{Total}.

$$q = m\,C_s\Delta T_2 \text{ then set } q_{ice} = -q_{water} \quad \Delta T_{Total} = \Delta T_1 + \Delta T_2$$

Solution: $8.5\text{ g} \times \frac{1\text{ mol}}{18.01\text{ g}} \times \frac{6.0\text{ kJ}}{1\text{ mol}} \times \frac{1000\text{ J}}{1\text{ kJ}} = 2.\underline{8}3176 \times 10^3\text{ J}$, $q_{water} = -q_{ice} = -2.\underline{8}3176 \times 10^3$ J

$q = mC_S\Delta T$. Rearrange to solve for ΔT. $\Delta T_1 = \frac{q}{mC_S} = \frac{-2.\underline{8}3176 \times 10^3\text{ J}}{255\text{ g} \times 4.18\frac{\text{J}}{\text{g}\cdot°\text{C}}} = -2.\underline{6}567$ °C.

$q = mC_S\Delta T$ substitute in values and set $q_{ice} = -q_{H_2O}$.

$$q_{ice} = m_{ice}C_{ice}(T_f - T_{icei}) = 8.5\text{ g} \times 4.18\frac{\text{J}}{\text{g}\cdot°\text{C}} \times (T_f - 0.0\text{ °C}) =$$

$$-q_{water} = -m_{water}C_{water}\Delta T_{water2} = -255\text{ g} \times 4.18\frac{\text{J}}{\text{g}\cdot°\text{C}} \times \Delta T_{water2} \rightarrow$$

$8.5\,T_f = -255\Delta T_{water2} = -255(T_f - T_{f1})$. Rearrange to solve for T_f. $8.5\,T_f + 255\,T_f = 255\,T_{f1} \rightarrow$ $26\underline{3}.5\,T_f = 255\,T_{f1} \rightarrow T_f = 0.96\underline{7}74\,T_{f1}$ but $\Delta T_1 = (T_{f1} - T_{i1}) = -2.\underline{6}567$ °C which says that

$T_{f1} = T_{i1} - 2.\underline{6}567$ °C and $\Delta T_{Total} = (T_f - T_{i1})$ so

$\Delta T_{Total} = 0.96\underline{7}74\,T_{f1} - T_{i1} = 0.96\underline{7}74(T_{i1} - 2.\underline{6}567\text{ °C}) - T_{i1} = -2.\underline{6}567\text{ °C} - 0.03\underline{2}26\,T_{i1}$.

This implies that the larger the initial temperature of the water, the larger the temperature drop. If the initial temperature was 90 °C, the temperature drop would be 5.6 °C. If the initial temperature was 25 °C, the temperature drop would be 3.5 °C. If the initial temperature was 5 °C, the temperature drop would be 2.8 °C. This makes physical sense because the lower the initial temperature of the water, the less kinetic energy it initially has and the smaller the heat transfer from the water to the melted ice will be.

Check: The units (°C) are correct. The temperature drop from the melting of the ice is only 2.7 °C because the mass of the water is so much larger than the ice.

11.82 **Given:** 352 mL water, $T_i = 25$ °C, $T_f = 5$ °C, $d = 1.0$ g/mL; ice $T_i = 0$ °C, $T_f = 5$ °C **Find:** g (ice)
Other: $\Delta H^\circ_{fus} = 6.02$ kJ/mol; $C_{H_2O} = 4.18$ J/g·°C from text
Conceptual Plan: mL → g then $m, C_s, T_i, T_f \rightarrow q_{water}$ (J) → q_{ice} (J) then $q_{ice}, \Delta H^\circ_{fus}, C_{H_2O}, T_i, T_f \rightarrow$ g (ice)

$$\frac{1.0\text{ g}}{1.0\text{ mL}} \quad q = m\,C_S(T_f - T_i) \quad q_{ice} = -q_{water} \quad q_{ice} = mC_S(T_f - T_i) + m \times \frac{1\text{ mol}}{18.01\text{ g}} \times \frac{6.02\text{ kJ}}{1\text{ mol}} \times \frac{1000\text{ J}}{1\text{ kJ}}$$

Solution: $352\text{ mL} \times \frac{1.0\text{ g}}{1.0\text{ mL}} = 352\text{ g}$

$$q_{water} = m_{water}\,C_{water}(T_f - T_i) = 352\text{ g} \times 4.18\frac{\text{J}}{\text{g}\cdot°\text{C}} \times (5\,°\text{C} - 25\,°\text{C}) = -2.94272 \times 10^4\text{ J},$$

$$q_{ice} = -q_{water} = 2.94272 \times 10^4\text{ J then } q_{ice} = m\,C_S(T_f - T_i) + m \times \frac{1\text{ mol}}{18.01\text{ g}} \times \frac{6.02\text{ kJ}}{1\text{ mol}} \times \frac{1000\text{ J}}{1\text{ kJ}}$$

Substitute values. $2.94272 \times 10^4\text{ J} = m \times 4.18\frac{\text{J}}{\text{g}\cdot°\text{C}} \times (5\,°\text{C} - 0\,°\text{C}) + m \times \frac{334.26\text{ J}}{1\text{ g}}$. Rearrange to solve for m.

$$m = \frac{2.94272 \times 10^4\text{ J}}{\frac{355.16\text{ J}}{1\text{ g}}} = 83\text{ g}.$$

Check: The units (g) are correct. The temperature drop is large and so is the amount of water we want to cool, so the mass seems reasonable.

11.83 **Given:** 10.0 g ice $T_i = -10.0$ °C to steam at $T_f = 110.0$ °C **Find:** heat required (kJ)
Other: $\Delta H^\circ_{fus} = 6.02$ kJ/mol; $\Delta H^\circ_{vap} = 40.7$ kJ/mol; $C_{ice} = 2.09$ J/g·°C; $C_{water} = 4.18$ J/g·°C; $C_{steam} = 2.01$ J/g·°C
Conceptual Plan: Follow the heating curve in Figure 11.36. $q_{Total} = q_1 + q_2 + q_3 + q_4 + q_5$ where q_1, q_3, and q_5 are heating of a single phase then J → kJ and q_2 and q_4 are phase transitions.

$$q = m\,C_S(T_f - T_i) \quad \frac{1\text{ kJ}}{1000\text{ J}} \quad q = m \times \frac{1\text{ mol}}{18.01\text{ g}} \times \frac{\Delta H}{1\text{ mol}}$$

Solution:

$$q_1 = m_{ice}C_{ice}(T_{icef} - T_{icei}) = 10.0\text{ g} \times 2.09\frac{\text{J}}{\text{g}\cdot°\text{C}} \times (0.0\,°\text{C} - (-10.0\,°\text{C})) = 209\text{ J} \times \frac{1\text{ kJ}}{1000\text{ J}} = 0.209\text{ kJ},$$

$$q_2 = m \times \frac{1\text{ mol}}{18.01\text{ g}} \times \frac{\Delta H_{fus}}{1\text{ mol}} = 10.0\text{ g} \times \frac{1\text{ mol}}{18.01\text{ g}} \times \frac{6.02\text{ kJ}}{1\text{ mol}} = 3.343\text{ kJ},$$

$$q_3 = m_{water}C_{water}(T_{waterf} - T_{wateri}) = 10.0\text{ g} \times 4.18\frac{\text{J}}{\text{g}\cdot°\text{C}} \times (100.0\,°\text{C} - 0.0\,°\text{C}) = 4180\text{ J} \times \frac{1\text{ kJ}}{1000\text{ J}} = 4.18\text{ kJ},$$

$$q_4 = m \times \frac{1\text{ mol}}{18.01\text{ g}} \times \frac{\Delta H_{vap}}{1\text{ mol}} = 10.0\text{ g} \times \frac{1\text{ mol}}{18.01\text{ g}} \times \frac{40.7\text{ kJ}}{1\text{ mol}} = 22.599\text{ kJ},$$

$$q_5 = m_{steam}C_{steam}(T_{steamf} - T_{steami}) = 10.0\text{ g} \times 2.01\frac{\text{J}}{\text{g}\cdot°\text{C}} \times (110.0\,°\text{C} - 100.0\,°\text{C})$$

$$= 201\text{ J} \times \frac{1\text{ kJ}}{1000\text{ J}} = 0.201\text{ kJ}.$$

$q_{Total} = q_1 + q_2 + q_3 + q_4 + q_5 = 0.209\text{ kJ} + 3.343\text{ kJ} + 4.18\text{ kJ} + 22.599\text{ kJ} + 0.201\text{ kJ} = 30.5\text{ kJ}$
Check: The units (kJ) are correct. The total amount of heat is dominated by the vaporization step. Since we have less than 1 mole we expect less than 41 kJ.

11.84 **Given:** 1.00 mole steam $T_i = 145.0$ °C to ice at $T_f = -50.0$ °C **Find:** heat evolved (kJ) **Other:** $\Delta H^\circ_{fus} = 6.02$ kJ/mol; $\Delta H^\circ_{vap} = 40.7$ kJ/mol; $C_{ice} = 2.09$ J/g·°C; $C_{water} = 4.18$ J/g·°C; $C_{steam} = 2.01$ J/g·°C
Conceptual Plan: mol → g Follow the heating curve in Figure 11.36, only in reverse.

$$\frac{18.01\text{ g}}{1\text{ mol}}$$

$q_{Total} = q_1 + q_2 + q_3 + q_4 + q_5$ where q_1, q_3, and q_5 are heating of a single phase then J → kJ

$$q = m\,C_S(T_f - T_i) \quad \frac{1\text{ kJ}}{1000\text{ J}}$$

and q_2 and q_4 are phase transitions.

$$q = mol \times \frac{\Delta H}{1\text{ mol}}$$

Solution: $1.00\ \cancel{\text{mol}} \times \dfrac{18.01\ \text{g}}{1\ \cancel{\text{mol}}} = 18.\underline{0}1\ \text{g}$

$q_1 = m_{\text{steam}}C_{\text{steam}}(T_{\text{steamf}} - T_{\text{steami}}) = 18.\underline{0}1\ \cancel{\text{g}} \times 2.01 \dfrac{\text{J}}{\cancel{\text{g}} \cdot \cancel{^\circ\text{C}}} \times (100.0\ \cancel{^\circ\text{C}} - 145.0\ \cancel{^\circ\text{C}}) = -\ 16\underline{2}9.00\ \cancel{\text{J}} \times \dfrac{1\ \text{kJ}}{1000\ \cancel{\text{J}}}$
$= -\ 1.6\underline{2}9\ \text{kJ}$

$q_2 = mol \times \dfrac{-\Delta H_{\text{vap}}}{1\ \text{mol}} = 1.00\ \cancel{\text{mol}} \times \dfrac{-40.7\ \text{kJ}}{1\ \cancel{\text{mol}}} = -40.7\ \text{kJ},$

$q_3 = m_{\text{water}}C_{\text{water}}(T_{\text{waterf}} - T_{\text{wateri}}) = 18.\underline{0}1\ \cancel{\text{g}} \times 4.18 \dfrac{\text{J}}{\cancel{\text{g}} \cdot \cancel{^\circ\text{C}}} \times (0.0\ \cancel{^\circ\text{C}} - 100.0\ \cancel{^\circ\text{C}}) = -\ 75\underline{2}8.2\ \cancel{\text{J}} \times \dfrac{1\ \text{kJ}}{1000\ \cancel{\text{J}}}$
$= -\ 7.5\underline{2}82\ \text{kJ},$

$q_4 = mol \times \dfrac{-\Delta H_{\text{fus}}}{1\ \text{mol}} = 1.00\ \cancel{\text{mol}} \times \dfrac{-6.02\ \text{kJ}}{1\ \cancel{\text{mol}}} = -6.02\ \text{kJ},$

$q_5 = m_{\text{ice}}C_{\text{ice}}(T_{\text{icef}} - T_{\text{icei}}) = 18.\underline{0}1\ \cancel{\text{g}} \times 2.09 \dfrac{\text{J}}{\cancel{\text{g}} \cdot \cancel{^\circ\text{C}}} \times (-50.0\ \cancel{^\circ\text{C}} - 0.0\ \cancel{^\circ\text{C}}) = -\ 18\underline{8}2.0\ \cancel{\text{J}} \times \dfrac{1\ \text{kJ}}{1000\ \cancel{\text{J}}}$
$= -\ 1.8\underline{8}20\ \text{kJ}$

$q_{\text{Total}} = q_1 + q_2 + q_3 + q_4 + q_5 = -\ 1.6\underline{2}9\ \text{kJ} - 40.7\ \text{kJ} - 7.5\underline{2}82\ \text{kJ} - 6.02\ \text{kJ} - 1.8\underline{8}20\ \text{kJ}$
$= -\ 57.8$ kJ or 57.8 kJ released.

Check: The units (kJ) are correct. The amount of heat is dominated by the vaporization step. Since we have exactly 1 mole we expect more than 41 kJ.

Phase Diagrams

11.85 (a) solid

(b) liquid

(c) gas

(d) supercritical fluid

(e) solid/liquid equilibrium

(f) liquid/gas equilibrium

(g) solid/liquid/gas equilibrium

11.86 (a) 184.4 °C

(b) 113.6 °C

(c) solid

(d) gas

11.87 **Given:** nitrogen, normal boiling point = 77.3 K, normal melting point = 63.1 K, critical temperature = 126.2 K, critical pressure = 2.55×10^4 torr, triple point at 63.1 K and 94.0 torr
Find: Sketch phase diagram. Does nitrogen have a stable liquid phase at 1 atm?

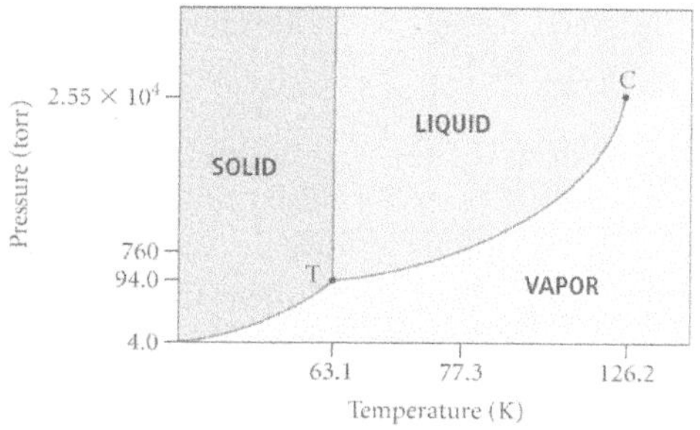

Nitrogen has a stable liquid phase at 1 atm.
Note that the axes are not to scale.

11.88 **Given:** argon, normal boiling point = 87.2 K, normal melting point = 84.1 K, critical temperature = 150.8 K, critical pressure = 48.3 atm, triple point at 83.7 K and 0.68 atm
Find: Sketch phase diagram. Which has the greater density, solid or liquid argon?

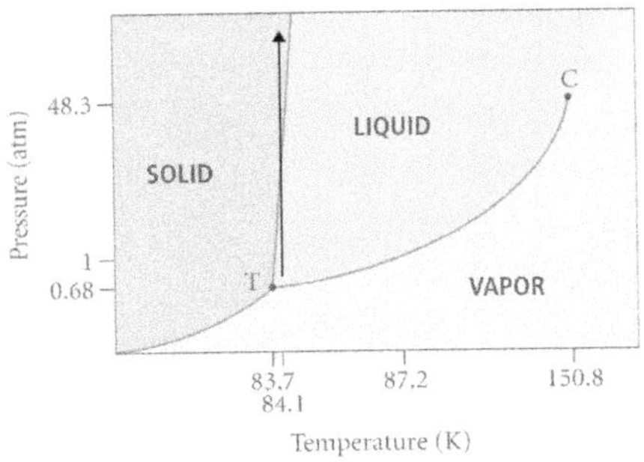

The solid has the higher density because the slope of the solid/liquid equilibrium line is positive. If we start in the liquid and increase the pressure, we will cross into the solid phase, the dense phase.

Note that the axes are not to scale.

11.89 (a) 0.027 mmHg, the higher of the two triple points

(b) The rhombic phase is denser because if we start in the monoclinic phase at 100 °C and increase the pressure, we will cross into the rhombic phase.

11.90 The triple point marked "O" shows the equilibrium of Ice II, Ice III, and Ice V. Ice II is denser than Ice I because you can generate Ice II from Ice I by increasing the pressure (pushing the molecules closer together). Ice III would sink in liquid water. Note that the slope of the Ice III/liquid line has the typical positive slope.

The Uniqueness of Water

11.91 Water has a low molar mass (18.01 g/mol), yet it is a liquid at room temperature. Water's high boiling point for its molar mass can be understood by examining the structure of the water molecule. The bent geometry of the water molecule and the highly polar nature of the O–H bonds result in a molecule with a significant dipole moment. Water's two O–H bonds (hydrogen directly bonded to oxygen) allow a water molecule to form very strong hydrogen bonds with four other water molecules, resulting in a relatively high boiling point.

11.92 Water's high polarity also allows it to dissolve many other polar and ionic compounds, and even a number of nonpolar gases such as oxygen and carbon dioxide (by inducing a dipole moment in their molecules). Consequently, water is the main solvent within living organisms, transporting nutrients and other important compounds throughout the body. Water is also the main solvent of the environment, allowing aquatic animals, for example, to survive by breathing dissolved oxygen and allowing aquatic plants to survive by using dissolved carbon dioxide for photosynthesis.

11.93 Water has an exceptionally high specific heat capacity, which has a moderating effect on the climate of coastal cities. Also, its high ΔH_{vap} causes water evaporation and condensation to have a strong effect on temperature. A tremendous amount of heat can be stored in large bodies of water. Heat will be absorbed or released from large bodies of water preferentially over land around it. In some cities, such as San Francisco, for example, the daily fluctuation in temperature can be less than 10 °C. This same moderating effect occurs over the entire planet, two-thirds of which is covered by water. In other words, without water, the daily temperature fluctuations on our planet might be more like those on Mars, where temperature fluctuations of 63 °C (113 °F) have been measured between early morning and midday.

11.94 One significant difference between the phase diagram of water and that of other substances is the fusion curve for water, which has a negative slope. The fusion curve within the phase diagrams for most substances has a positive slope because increasing pressure favors the denser phase, which for most substances is the solid phase. This negative slope means that ice is less dense than liquid water and so ice floats. The solids sink in the liquids of most other substances. The frozen layer of ice at the surface of a winter lake insulates the water in the lake from further freezing. If this ice layer sank, it would kill bottom-dwelling aquatic life and possibly allow the lake to freeze solid, eliminating virtually all life in the lake.

Types of Solids and Their Structures

11.95 **Given:** X-ray with $\lambda = 154$ pm, maximum reflection angle of $\theta = 28.3°$; assume $n = 1$
Find: distance between layers
Conceptual Plan: $\lambda, \theta, n \rightarrow d$

$n\lambda = 2\,d\,\sin\theta$

Solution: $n\lambda = 2\,d\,\sin\theta$. Rearrange to solve for d. $d = \dfrac{n\,\lambda}{2\sin\theta} = \dfrac{1 \times 154\text{ pm}}{2\sin 28.3°} = 162$ pm.
Check: The units (pm) are correct. The magnitude (164 pm) makes sense since n = 1 and the *sin* is always < 1. The number is consistent with interatomic distances.

11.96 **Given:** distance between layers = 286 pm, maximum reflection angle of $\theta = 7.23°$; assume $n = 1$
Find: λ (X-ray) with
Conceptual Plan: $d, \theta, n \rightarrow \lambda$

$n\lambda = 2\,d\,\sin\theta$

Solution: $n\,\lambda = 2\,d\,\sin\theta$. Rearrange to solve for λ. $\lambda = \dfrac{2\,d\sin\theta}{n} = \dfrac{2 \times 286\text{ pm} \times \sin 7.23°}{1} = 72.0$ pm
Check: The units (pm) are correct. The magnitude (72 pm) makes sense since n = 1 and the *sin* is always < 1. The number is consistent with X-ray wavelengths.

11.97 (a) 8 corner atoms x (1/8 atom / unit cell) = 1 atom / unit cell

(b) 8 corner atoms x (1/8 atom / unit cell) + 1 atom in center = (1 + 1) atoms / unit cell = 2 atoms / unit cell

(c) 8 corner atoms x (1/8 atom / unit cell) + 6 face-centered atoms x (1/2 atom / unit cell) = (1 + 3) atoms / unit cell = 4 atoms / unit cell

11.98 (a) coordination number of 12 since this is a face-centered cubic structure

(b) coordination number of 12 since this is a hexagonal closest packed structure

(c) coordination number of 8 since this is a body-centered cubic structure

11.99 **Given:** platinum, face-centered cubic structure, $r = 139$ pm **Find:** edge length of unit cell and density (g/cm^3)
Conceptual Plan: $r \rightarrow l$ **and** $l \rightarrow V(\text{pm}^3) \rightarrow V(\text{cm}^3)$ **and** $\mathcal{M}$**, FCC structure** $\rightarrow m$ **then** $m, V \rightarrow d$

$l = 2\sqrt{2}\,r$ $\quad V = l^3 \quad \dfrac{(1\text{ cm})^3}{(10^{10}\text{pm})^3} \quad m = \dfrac{4\text{ atoms}}{\text{unit cell}} \times \dfrac{\mathcal{M}}{N_A} \quad d = m/V$

Solution: $l = 2\sqrt{2}\,r = 2\sqrt{2} \times 139\text{ pm} = 39\underline{3}.151\text{ pm} = 393\text{ pm}$ and

$$V = l^3 = (39\underline{3}.151\text{ pm})^3 \times \frac{(1\text{ cm})^3}{(10^{10}\text{ pm})^3} = 6.0\underline{7}682 \times 10^{-23}\text{ cm}^3 \text{ and}$$

$$m = \frac{4\text{ atoms}}{\text{unit cell}} \times \frac{\mathcal{M}}{N_A} = \frac{4\text{ atoms}}{\text{unit cell}} \times \frac{195.09\text{ g}}{1\text{ mol}} \times \frac{1\text{ mol}}{6.022 \times 10^{23}\text{ atoms}} = 1.29\underline{5}848 \times 10^{-21}\,\frac{\text{g}}{\text{unit cell}} \text{ then}$$

$$d = \frac{m}{V} = \frac{1.29\underline{5}848 \times 10^{-21}\,\frac{\text{g}}{\text{unit cell}}}{6.0\underline{7}682 \times 10^{-23}\,\frac{\text{cm}^3}{\text{unit cell}}} = 21.3\,\frac{\text{g}}{\text{cm}^3}$$

Check: The units (pm and g/cm^3) are correct. The magnitude (393 pm) makes sense because it must be larger than the radius of an atom. The magnitude (21 g/ cm^3) is consistent for Pt from Chapter 1.

11.100 **Given:** molybdenum, body-centered cubic structure, $r = 136$ pm
Find: edge length of unit cell and density (g/cm^3)
Conceptual Plan: $r \rightarrow l$ **and** $l \rightarrow V(\text{pm}^3) \rightarrow V(\text{cm}^3)$ **and** $\mathcal{M}$**, BCC structure** $\rightarrow m$ **then** $m, V \rightarrow d$

$l = \dfrac{4\,r}{\sqrt{3}} \quad V = l^3 \quad \dfrac{(1\text{ cm})^3}{(10^{10}\text{pm})^3} \quad m = \dfrac{2\text{ atoms}}{\text{unit cell}} \times \dfrac{\mathcal{M}}{N_A} \quad d = m/V$

Solution: $l = \frac{4\,r}{\sqrt{3}} = \frac{4 \times 136 \text{ pm}}{\sqrt{3}} = 314.079 \text{ pm} = 314 \text{ pm}$ and

$V = l^3 = (314.079 \text{ pm})^3 \times \frac{(1 \text{ cm})^3}{(10^{10} \text{ pm})^3} = 3.09823 \times 10^{-23} \text{ cm}^3$ and

$m = \frac{2 \text{ atoms}}{\text{unit cell}} \times \frac{\mathcal{M}}{N_A} = \frac{2 \text{ atoms}}{\text{unit cell}} \times \frac{95.94 \text{ g}}{1 \text{ mol}} \times \frac{1 \text{ mol}}{6.022 \times 10^{23} \text{ atoms}} = 3.186317 \times 10^{-22} \frac{\text{g}}{\text{unit cell}}$ then

$$d = \frac{m}{V} = \frac{3.186317 \times 10^{-22} \frac{\text{g}}{\text{unit cell}}}{3.09823 \times 10^{-23} \frac{\text{cm}^3}{\text{unit cell}}} = 10.3 \frac{\text{g}}{\text{cm}^3}$$

Check: The units (pm and g/cm^3) are correct. The magnitude (314 pm) makes sense because it must be larger than the radius of an atom. The magnitude (10 g/ cm^3) is reasonable for a metal density.

11.101 **Given:** rhodium, face-centered cubic structure, $d = 12.41 \text{ g/cm}^3$ **Find:** r (Rh)

Conceptual Plan: $\mathcal{M}$, FCC structure → m then m, V → d then V(cm³) → l (cm) → l (pm) then l → r

$m = \frac{4 \text{ atoms}}{\text{unit cell}} \times \frac{\mathcal{M}}{N_A}$; $d = m/V$; $V = l^3$; $\frac{10^{10} \text{ pm}}{1 \text{ cm}}$; $l = 2\sqrt{2}\,r$

Solution: $m = \frac{4 \text{ atoms}}{\text{unit cell}} \times \frac{\mathcal{M}}{N_A} = \frac{4 \text{ atoms}}{\text{unit cell}} \times \frac{102.905 \text{ g}}{1 \text{ mol}} \times \frac{1 \text{ mol}}{6.022 \times 10^{23} \text{ atoms}} = 6.835271 \times 10^{-22} \frac{\text{g}}{\text{unit cell}}$

then $d = \frac{m}{V}$. Rearrange to solve for V. $V = \frac{m}{d} = \frac{6.835271 \times 10^{-22} \frac{\text{g}}{\text{unit cell}}}{12.41 \frac{\text{g}}{\text{cm}^3}} = 5.507873 \times 10^{-23} \frac{\text{cm}^3}{\text{unit cell}}$

then $V = l^3$. Rearrange to solve for l.

$l = \sqrt[3]{V} = \sqrt[3]{5.507873 \times 10^{-23} \text{ cm}^3} = 3.804831 \times 10^{-8} \text{ cm} \times \frac{10^{10} \text{ pm}}{1 \text{ cm}} = 380.4831 \text{ pm}$ then $l = 2\sqrt{2}r$.

Rearrange to solve for r. $r = \frac{l}{2\sqrt{2}} = \frac{380.4831 \text{ pm}}{2\sqrt{2}} = 134.5 \text{ pm}$.

Check: The units (pm) are correct. The magnitude (135 pm) is consistent with an atomic diameter.

11.102 **Given:** barium, body-centered cubic structure, $d = 3.59 \text{ g/cm}^3$ **Find:** r (Ba)

Conceptual Plan: $\mathcal{M}$, BCC structure → m then m, V → d then V(cm³) → l (cm) → l (pm) then l → r

$m = \frac{2 \text{ atoms}}{\text{unit cell}} \times \frac{\mathcal{M}}{N_A}$; $d = m/V$; $V = l^3$; $\frac{10^{10} \text{ pm}}{1 \text{ cm}}$; $l = \frac{4r}{\sqrt{3}}$

Solution: $m = \frac{2 \text{ atoms}}{\text{unit cell}} \times \frac{\mathcal{M}}{N_A} = \frac{2 \text{ atoms}}{\text{unit cell}} \times \frac{137.34 \text{ g}}{1 \text{ mol}} \times \frac{1 \text{ mol}}{6.022 \times 10^{23} \text{ atoms}} = 4.561275 \times 10^{-22} \frac{\text{g}}{\text{unit cell}}$ then

$d = \frac{m}{V}$. Rearrange to solve for V. $V = \frac{m}{d} = \frac{4.561275 \times 10^{-22} \frac{\text{g}}{\text{unit cell}}}{3.59 \frac{\text{g}}{\text{cm}^3}} = 1.270550 \times 10^{-22} \frac{\text{cm}^3}{\text{unit cell}}$

then $V = l^3$. Rearrange to solve for l.

$l = \sqrt[3]{V} = \sqrt[3]{1.270550 \times 10^{-22} \text{ cm}^3} = 5.027336 \times 10^{-8} \text{ cm} \times \frac{10^{10} \text{ pm}}{1 \text{ cm}} = 502.7336 \text{ pm}$

then $l = \frac{4r}{\sqrt{3}}$. Rearrange to solve for r. $r = \frac{l\sqrt{3}}{4} = \frac{502.7336 \text{ pm} \times \sqrt{3}}{4} = 217.7 \text{ pm}$.

Check: The units (pm) are correct. The magnitude (218 pm) is consistent with an atomic diameter.

11.103 **Given:** polonium, simple cubic structure, $d = 9.3 \text{ g/cm}^3$; $r = 167$ pm; $\mathcal{M} = 209$ g/mol **Find:** estimate N_A

Conceptual Plan: r → l and l → V(pm³) → V(cm³) then d, V → m then $\mathcal{M}$, SC structure → m

$l = 2r$; $V = l^3$; $\frac{(1 \text{ cm})^3}{(10^{10} \text{ pm})^3}$; $d = m/V$; $m = \frac{1 \text{ atom}}{\text{unit cell}} \times \frac{\mathcal{M}}{N_A}$

Solution: $l = 2r = 2 \times 167 \text{ pm} = 334 \text{ pm}$ and $V = l^3 = (334 \text{ pm})^3 \times \dfrac{(1 \text{ cm})^3}{(10^{10} \text{ pm})^3} = 3.72597 \times 10^{-23} \text{ cm}^3$ then

$d = \dfrac{m}{V}$. Rearrange to solve for m. $m = d\,V = 9.3 \dfrac{\text{g}}{\text{cm}^3} \times \dfrac{3.72597 \times 10^{-23} \text{ cm}^3}{\text{unit cell}} = 3.46515 \times 10^{-22} \dfrac{\text{g}}{\text{unit cell}}$

then $m = \dfrac{1 \text{ atom}}{\text{unit cell}} \times \dfrac{\mathcal{M}}{N_A}$. Rearrange to solve for N_A.

$N_A = \dfrac{1 \text{ atom}}{\text{unit cell}} \times \dfrac{\mathcal{M}}{m} = \dfrac{1 \text{ atom}}{\text{unit cell}} \times \dfrac{209 \text{ g}}{1 \text{ mol}} \times \dfrac{1 \text{ unit cell}}{3.46515 \times 10^{-22} \text{ g}} = 6.0 \times 10^{23} \dfrac{\text{atom}}{\text{mol}}$.

Check: The units (atoms/mol) are correct. The magnitude (6×10^{23}) is consistent with Avogadro's number.

11.104 **Given:** palladium, face-centered cubic structure, $d = 12.0 \text{ g/cm}^3$; $r = 138$ pm; $\mathcal{M} = 106.42$ g/mol
Find: estimate N_A
Conceptual Plan: $r \rightarrow l$ **and** $l \rightarrow V(\text{pm}^3) \rightarrow V(\text{cm}^3)$ **then** $d, V \rightarrow m$ **then** $\mathcal{M}$**, FCC structure** $\rightarrow m$

$l = 2\sqrt{2}\,r$; $V = l^3$; $\dfrac{(1 \text{ cm})^3}{(10^{10} \text{ pm})^3}$; $d = m/V$; $m = \dfrac{4 \text{ atoms}}{\text{unit cell}} \times \dfrac{\mathcal{M}}{N_A}$

Solution: $l = 2\sqrt{2}\,r = 2\sqrt{2} \times 138 \text{ pm} = 390.323 \text{ pm}$ and

$V = l^3 = (390.323 \text{ pm})^3 \times \dfrac{(1 \text{ cm})^3}{(10^{10} \text{ pm})^3} = 5.94665 \times 10^{-23} \text{ cm}^3$ then $d = \dfrac{m}{V}$. Rearrange to solve for m.

$m = d\,V = 12.0 \dfrac{\text{g}}{\text{cm}^3} \times \dfrac{5.94665 \times 10^{-23} \text{ cm}^3}{\text{unit cell}} = 7.13598 \times 10^{-22} \dfrac{\text{g}}{\text{unit cell}}$ then $m = \dfrac{4 \text{ atoms}}{\text{unit cell}} \times \dfrac{\mathcal{M}}{N_A}$.

Rearrange to solve for N_A. $N_A = \dfrac{4 \text{ atoms}}{\text{unit cell}} \times \dfrac{\mathcal{M}}{m} = \dfrac{4 \text{ atoms}}{\text{unit cell}} \times \dfrac{106.42 \text{ g}}{1 \text{ mol}} \times \dfrac{1 \text{ unit cell}}{7.13598 \times 10^{-22} \text{ g}} = 5.97 \times 10^{23} \dfrac{\text{atom}}{\text{mol}}$.

Check: The units (atoms/mol) are correct. The magnitude (6×10^{23}) is consistent with Avogadro's number.

11.105 (a) atomic, since Ar is an atom

(b) molecular, since water is a molecule

(c) ionic, since K_2O is an ionic solid

(d) atomic, since iron is an atom

11.106 (a) ionic, since $CaCl_2$ is an ionic solid

(b) molecular, since CO_2 is a molecule

(c) atomic, since nickel (Ni) is an atom

(d) molecular, since I_2 is a molecule

11.107 LiCl has the highest melting point since it is the only ionic solid in the group. The other three solids are held together by intermolecular forces, while LiCl is held together by stronger coulombic interactions between the cations and anions of the crystal lattice.

11.108 C (diamond) has the highest melting point (3800 °C). Both covalent network solids and ionic solids have high melting points. NaCl has a melting point of 801 °C. In diamond (Figure 11.57a), each carbon atom forms four covalent bonds to four other carbon atoms in a tetrahedral geometry. This structure extends throughout the entire crystal, so that a diamond crystal can be thought of as a giant molecule, held together by these covalent bonds. Since covalent bonds are very strong, covalent atomic solids have high melting points.

11.109 (a) TiO_2 because it is an ionic solid

(b) $SiCl_4$ because it has a higher molar mass and therefore has stronger dispersion forces

(c) Xe because it has a higher molar mass and therefore has stronger dispersion forces

(d) CaO because the ions have greater charge and therefore stronger dipole–dipole interactions

11.110 (a) Fe because it is an atomic solid held together by metallic bonding

(b) KCl because it is an ionic solid

(c) Ti because it is an atomic solid held together by metallic bonding

(d) H_2O because it is capable of hydrogen bonding

11.111 The Ti atoms occupy the corner positions and the center of the unit cell: 8 corner atoms x (1/8 atom / unit cell) + 1 atom in center = (1 + 1) Ti atoms / unit cell = 2 Ti atoms / unit cell. The O atoms occupy four positions on the top and bottom faces and two positions inside the unit cell: 4 face-centered atoms x (1/2 atom / unit cell) + 2 atoms in the interior = (2 + 2) O atoms / unit cell = 4 O atoms / unit cell. Therefore there are 2 Ti atoms / unit cell and 4 O atoms / unit cell, so the ratio Ti:O is 2:4 or 1:2. The formula for the compound is TiO_2.

11.112 The Re atoms occupy the corner positions and the center of the unit cell: 8 corner atoms x (1/8 atom / unit cell) = 1 Re atom / unit cell. The O atoms occupy twelve edge positions: 12 edge atoms x (1/4 atom / unit cell) = 3 O atoms / unit cell. Therefore there are 1 Re atom / unit cell and 3 O atoms / unit cell, so the ratio Re:O is 1:3. The formula for the compound is ReO_3.

11.113 In CsCl: The Cs atoms occupy the center of the unit cell: 1 atom in center = 1 Cs atom / unit cell. The Cl atoms occupy corner positions of the unit cell: 8 corner atoms x (1/8 atom / unit cell) = 1 Cl atom / unit cell. Therefore there are 1 Cl atom / unit cell and 1 Cl atom / unit cell, so the ratio Cs:Cl is 1:1. The formula for the compound is CsCl, as expected.

In $BaCl_2$: The Ba atoms occupy the corner positions and the face-centered positions of the unit cell: 8 corner atoms x (1/8 atom / unit cell) + 6 face-centered atoms x (1/2 atom / unit cell) = (1 + 3) Ba atoms / unit cell = 4 Ba atoms / unit cell. The Cl atoms occupy eight positions inside the unit cell: 8 Cl atoms / unit cell. Therefore there are 4 Ba atoms / unit cell and 8 Cl atoms / unit cell, so the ratio Ba:Cl is 4:8 or 1:2. The formula for the compound is $BaCl_2$, as expected.

11.114 In Li_2O: The Li atoms occupy eight positions inside the unit cell: 8 Li atoms / unit cell. The O atoms occupy the corner positions and the face-centered positions of the unit cell: 8 corner atoms x (1/8 atom / unit cell) + 6 face-centered atoms x (1/2 atom / unit cell) = (1 + 3) O atoms / unit cell = 4 O atoms / unit cell. Therefore there are 4 O atoms / unit cell and 8 Li atoms / unit cell, so the ratio Li:O is 8:4 or 2:1. The formula for the compound is Li_2O, as expected.

In AgI: The Ag atoms occupy four positions inside the unit cell: 4 Ag atoms / unit cell. The I atoms occupy the corner positions and the face-centered positions of the unit cell: 8 corner atoms x (1/8 atom / unit cell) + 6 face-centered atoms x (1/2 atom / unit cell) = (1+ 3) I atoms / unit cell = 4 I atoms / unit cell. Therefore there are 4 I atoms / unit cell and 4 Ag atoms / unit cell, so the ratio Ag:I is 4:4 or 1:1. The formula for the compound is AgI, as expected.

Band Theory

11.115 (a) Zn should have little or no band gap because it is the only metal in the group.

11.116 **Given:** 5.45 g sodium crystal **Find:** number of molecular orbitals in the valence band

Conceptual Plan: **g → mol → Na_N → number of valence electrons → number of molecular orbitals**

$$\frac{1\text{ mol}}{22.99\text{ g}} \qquad \frac{6.022 \times 10^{23}\text{ atoms}}{1\text{ mol}} \qquad \frac{1\text{ 3s electron}}{1\text{ Na atom}} \qquad \frac{1\text{ molecular orbital}}{1\text{ 3s electron}}$$

Solution: $5.45\ \not{\text{g Na}} \times \frac{1\ \not{\text{mol Na}}}{22.99\ \not{\text{g Na}}} \times \frac{6.022 \times 10^{23}\ \not{\text{Na atoms}}}{1\ \not{\text{mol Na}}} \times \frac{1\ \not{\text{3s electron}}}{1\ \not{\text{Na atom}}} \times \frac{1\text{ molecular orbital}}{1\ \not{\text{3s electron}}}$

$= 1.43 \times 10^{23}$ molecular orbitals

Check: The units (number of molecular orbitals) are correct. The magnitude (10^{23}) is expected since there are so many orbitals because we have about a $\frac{1}{4}$ mole of atoms. Metals can conduct electricity because of these large numbers of orbitals.

11.117 (a) p-type semiconductor: Ge is Group 4A and Ga is Group 3A, so the Ga will generate electron "holes."

(b) n-type semiconductor: Si is Group 4A and As is Group 5A, so the As will add electrons to the conduction band.

11.118 (a) p-type semiconductor: Si is Group 4A and Ga is Group 3A, so the Ga will generate electron "holes."

(b) n-type semiconductor: Ge is Group 4A and Sb is Group 5A, so the Sb will add electrons to the conduction band.

Cumulative Problems

11.119 The general trend is that melting point increases with increasing molar mass. This is due to the fact that the electrons of the larger molecules are held more loosely and a stronger dipole moment can be induced more easily. HF is the exception to the rule. It has a relatively high melting point due to strong intermolecular forces due to hydrogen bonding.

11.120 The general trend is that boiling point increases with increasing molar mass. This is due to the fact that the electrons of the larger molecules are held more loosely and a stronger dipole moment can be induced more easily. H_2O is the exception to the rule. It has a relatively high boiling point due to strong intermolecular forces due to hydrogen bonding.

11.121 **Given:** $P_{H_2O} = 23.76$ torr at 25 °C; 1.25 g water in 1.5 L container **Find:** m (H_2O) as liquid

Conceptual Plan: **°C → K and torr → atm then P, V, T → mol (g) → g (g) then g (g), g (l)$_i$ → g (l)$_f$**

$K = °C + 273.15$; $\frac{1 \text{ atm}}{760 \text{ torr}}$; $PV = nRT$; $\frac{18.01 \text{ g}}{1 \text{ mol}}$; $g(l)_f = g(l)_i - g(g)$

Solution: $T = 25\ °C + 273.15 = 298$ K, $23.76 \text{ torr} \times \frac{1 \text{ atm}}{760 \text{ torr}} = 0.0312\underline{6}32$ atm then $PV = nRT$.

Rearrange to solve for n. $n = \frac{PV}{RT} = \frac{0.0312\underline{6}32 \text{ atm} \times 1.5 \text{ L}}{0.08206 \frac{\text{L} \cdot \text{atm}}{\text{K} \cdot \text{mol}} \times 298 \text{ K}} = 0.001\underline{9}1768$ mol in the gas phase then

$0.001\underline{9}1768 \text{ mol} \times \frac{18.01 \text{ g}}{1 \text{ mol}} = 0.03\underline{4}5375$ g in gas phase then

$g(l)_f = g(l)_i - g(g) = 1.25 \text{ g} - 0.03\underline{4}5375 \text{ g} = 1.22$ g remaining as liquid. Yes, there is 1.22 g of liquid.

Check: The units (g) are correct. The magnitude (1.2 g) is expected since very little material is expected to be in the gas phase.

11.122 **Given:** $P_{CCl_3F} = 856$ torr at 300 K; 11.5 g CCl_3F in 1.0 L container **Find:** m (CCl_3F) as liquid

Conceptual Plan: **torr → atm then P, V, T → mol (g) → g (g) then g (g), g (l)$_i$ → g (l)$_f$**

$\frac{1 \text{ atm}}{760 \text{ torr}}$; $PV = nRT$; $\frac{137.36 \text{ g}}{1 \text{ mol}}$; $g(l)_f = g(l)_i - g(g)$

Solution: $856 \text{ torr} \times \frac{1 \text{ atm}}{760 \text{ torr}} = 1.12\underline{6}32$ atm then $PV = nRT$. Rearrange to solve for n.

$n = \frac{PV}{RT} = \frac{1.12\underline{6}32 \text{ atm} \times 1.0 \text{ L}}{0.08206 \frac{\text{L} \cdot \text{atm}}{\text{K} \cdot \text{mol}} \times 300 \text{ K}} = 0.04\underline{5}7517$ mol in the gas phase then

$0.04\underline{5}7517 \text{ mol} \times \frac{137.36 \text{ g}}{1 \text{ mol}} = 6.\underline{2}845$ g in gas phase then

$g(l)_f = g(l)_i - g(g) = 11.5 \text{ g} - 6.\underline{2}845 \text{ g} = 5.2$ g remaining as liquid. Yes, there is 5.2 g of liquid.

Check: The units (g) are correct. The magnitude (5 g) is expected since even at moderate pressures little material is expected to be in the gas phase.

11.123 Since we are starting at a temperature that is higher and a pressure that is lower than the triple point, the phase transitions will be gas → liquid → solid, or condensation followed by freezing.

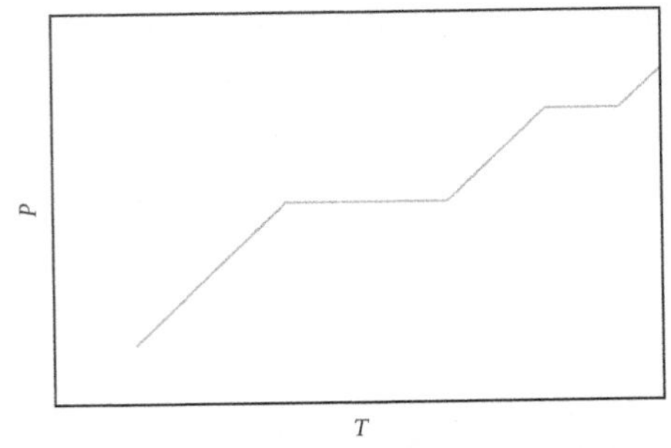

11.124 The solid is denser than the liquid. Since the triple point temperature is lower than the normal melting point, the slope of the fusion curve must be positive. This means that as you start in the liquid phase and increase the pressure you will eventually cross into the solid phase. As pressure increases, the phases get denser, the atoms, molecules, or ions are pushed closer and closer together.

11.125 **Given:** Ice: $T_1 = 0$ °C exactly, $m = 53.5$ g; Water: $T_1 = 75$ °C, $m = 115$ g **Find:** T_f

Other: $\Delta H^\circ_{fus} = 6.0$ kJ/mol; $C_{water} = 4.18$ J/g·°C

Conceptual Plan: $q_{ice} = -q_{water}$ **so g (ice) → mol (ice) →** q_{fus}**(kJ) →** q_{fus} **(J) →** q_{water} **(J) then**

$$\frac{1\text{ mol}}{18.01\text{ g}} \quad \frac{6.02\text{ kJ}}{1\text{ mol}} \quad \frac{1000\text{ J}}{1\text{ kJ}} \quad q_{water} = -q_{ice}$$

$q, m, C_s \rightarrow \Delta T$ **then** $T_i, \Delta T \rightarrow T_2$ **now we have slightly cooled water in contact with 0.0 °C water**

$q = m\,C_S\,\Delta T \qquad \Delta T = T_2 - T_i$

so $q_{ice} = -q_{water}$ **with** $m, C_s, T_i \rightarrow T_f$

$q = mC_s(T_f - T_i)$ then set $q_{ice} = -q_{water}$

Solution: $53.5\text{ g} \times \dfrac{1\text{ mol}}{18.01\text{ g}} \times \dfrac{6.02\text{ kJ}}{1\text{ mol}} \times \dfrac{1000\text{ J}}{1\text{ kJ}} = 1.78828 \times 10^4\text{ J}$, $q_{water} = -q_{ice} = -1.78828 \times 10^4$ J

$q = mC_S\Delta T$. Rearrange to solve for ΔT. $\Delta T = \dfrac{q}{mC_S} = \dfrac{-1.78828 \times 10^4\text{ J}}{115\text{ g} \times 4.18\dfrac{\text{J}}{\text{g}\cdot°\text{C}}} = -37.2017$ °C then

$\Delta T = T_2 - T_i$. Rearrange to solve for T_2. $T_2 = \Delta T + T_i = -37.2017$ °C $+ 75$ °C $= 37.798$ °C

$q = m\,C_s(T_f - T_i)$ substitute in values and set $q_{ice} = -q_{water}$.

$q_{ice} = m_{ice}C_{ice}(T_f - T_{icei}) = 53.5\text{ g} \times 4.18\dfrac{\text{J}}{\text{g}\cdot°\text{C}} \times (T_f - 0.0\text{ °C}) =$

$-q_{water} = -m_{water}\,C_{water}(T_f - T_{water2}) = -115\text{ g} \times 4.18\dfrac{\text{J}}{\text{g}\cdot°\text{C}} \times (T_f - 37.798\text{ °C})$.

Rearrange to solve for T_f.

$53.5T_f = -115(T_f - 37.798\text{ °C}) \rightarrow 53.5\,T_f = -115\,T_f + 4346.8\text{ °C} \rightarrow -4346.8\text{ °C} = -168.5\,T_f$

$\rightarrow T_f = \dfrac{-4346.8\text{ °C}}{-168.5} = 25.8\text{ °C} = 26\text{ °C}.$

Check: The units (°C) are correct. The temperature is between the two initial temperatures. Since the ice mass is about half the water mass, we are not surprised that the temperature is closer to the original ice temperature.

11.126 **Given:** Steam: $T_i = 100$ °C, $m = 0.552$ g; Water: $T_i = 5.0$ °C, $m = 4.25$ g **Find:** T_f

Other: $\Delta H^\circ_{vap} = 40.7$ kJ/mol; $C_{water} = 4.18$ J/g·°C

Conceptual Plan: $q_{steam} = -q_{water}$ **so g (steam) → mol (steam) →** q_{vap}**(kJ) →** q_{fvap} **(J) →** q_{water} **(J) then**

$$\frac{1\text{ mol}}{18.01\text{ g}} \quad \frac{-40.7\text{ kJ}}{1\text{ mol}} \quad \frac{1000\text{ J}}{1\text{ kJ}} \quad q_{steam} = -q_{ice}$$

$q, m, C_s \rightarrow \Delta T$ **then** $T_i, \Delta T \rightarrow T_2$ **now we have slightly warmed water in contact with 100.0 °C water**

$q = mC_S\Delta T \qquad \Delta T = T_2 - T_i$

so $q_{steam} = -q_{water}$ **with** $m, C_s, T_i \rightarrow T_f$

$q = mC_s(T_f - T_i)$ then set $q_{ice} = -q_{water}$

Solution: $0.552\text{ g} \times \dfrac{1\text{ mol}}{18.01\text{ g}} \times \dfrac{-40.7\text{ kJ}}{1\text{ mol}} \times \dfrac{1000\text{ J}}{1\text{ kJ}} = -1.24744 \times 10^3$ J,

$q_{water} = -q_{steam} = -(-1.24744 \times 10^3\text{ J})$ $q = mC_S\Delta T$. Rearrange to solve for ΔT.

$$\Delta T = \frac{q}{mC_S} = \frac{1.24744 \times 10^3 \text{ J}}{4.25 \text{ g} \times 4.18 \frac{\text{J}}{\text{g} \cdot °\text{C}}} = 70.2190 \text{ °C then } \Delta T = T_2 - T_i.$$

Rearrange to solve for T_2. $T_2 = \Delta T + T_i = 70.2190$ °C + 5.0 °C = 75.2190 °C $q = mC_s(T_f - T_i)$ substitute in values and set $q_{steam} = -q_{water}$.

$$q_{steam} = m_{steam}C_{steam}(T_f - T_{steami}) = 0.552 \text{ g} \times 4.18 \frac{\text{J}}{\text{g} \cdot °\text{C}} \times (T_f - 100.0 \text{ °C}) =$$

$$-q_{water} = -m_{water}C_{water}(T_f - T_{water2}) = -4.25 \text{ g} \times 4.18 \frac{\text{J}}{\text{g} \cdot °\text{C}} \times (T_f - 75.2190 \text{ °C}).$$

Rearrange to solve for T_f.

$0.552(T_f - 100.0 \text{ °C}) = -4.25(T_f - 75.2190 \text{ °C}) \rightarrow 0.552\, T_f - 55.2 \text{ °C} = -4.25\, T_f + 319.681 \text{ °C} \rightarrow$

$$-374.881 \text{ °C} = -4.802\, T_f \rightarrow T_f = \frac{-374.881 \text{ °C}}{-4.802} = 78.1 \text{ °C}.$$

Check: The units (°C) are correct. The temperature is between the two initial temperatures. Since there is so much heat involved in the vaporization process, we are not surprised that the temperature is closer to the original steam temperature.

11.127 **Given:** Home: 6.0 m x 10.0 m x 2.2 m; T = 30 °C, P_{H_2O} = 85 % of $P°_{H_2O}$ **Find:** m (H_2O) removed
Other: $P°_{H_2O}$ = 31.86 mmHg from text

Conceptual Plan: $l, w, h \rightarrow V$ **(m³)** $\rightarrow V$ **(cm³)** $\rightarrow V$ **(L) and** $P°_{H_2O} \rightarrow P_{H_2O}$ **(mmHg)** $\rightarrow P_{H_2O}$ **(atm) and**

$V = l\,w\,h$ $\quad \frac{(100 \text{ cm})^3}{(1 \text{ m})^3}$ $\quad \frac{1 \text{ L}}{1000 \text{ cm}^3}$ $\quad P_{H2O} = 0.85\, P°_{H_2O}$ $\quad \frac{1 \text{ atm}}{760 \text{ mmHg}}$

°C $\rightarrow$ **K then** $P, V, T \rightarrow$ **mol (H_2O)** $\rightarrow$ **g (H_2O)**

K = °C + 273.15 $\quad PV = nRT$ $\quad \frac{18.01 \text{ g}}{1 \text{ mol}}$

Solution: $V = l\,w\,h = 6.0 \text{ m} \times 10.0 \text{ m} \times 2.2 \text{ m} = 132 \text{ m}^3 \times \frac{(100 \text{ cm})^3}{(1 \text{ m})^3} \times \frac{1 \text{ L}}{1000 \text{ cm}^3} = 1.32 \times 10^5 \text{ L},$

$P_{H_2O} = 0.85\, P°_{H_2O} = 0.85 \times 31.86 \text{ mmHg} \times \frac{1 \text{ atm}}{760 \text{ mmHg}} = 0.035633 \text{ atm}$, T = 30 °C + 273.15 = 303 K,

then $PV = nRT$. Rearrange to solve for n.

$$n = \frac{PV}{RT} = \frac{0.035633 \text{ atm} \times 1.32 \times 10^5 \text{ L}}{0.08206 \frac{\text{L} \cdot \text{atm}}{\text{K} \cdot \text{mol}} \times 303 \text{ K}} = 189.17 \text{ mol then } 189.17 \text{ mol} \times \frac{18.01 \text{ g}}{1 \text{ mol}} = 3400 \text{ g to remove.}$$

Check: The units (g) are correct. The magnitude of the answer (3400 g) makes sense since the volume of the house is so large. We are removing almost 200 moles of water.

11.128 **Given:** Flask with 0.55 g water at T = 28 °C, $P°_{H_2O}$ = 28.36 mmHg **Find:** minimum V of flask for all vapor
Conceptual Plan: g (H_2O) $\rightarrow$ **mol (H_2O) and** $P°_{H_2O}$ **(mmHg)** $\rightarrow P_{H_2O}$ **(atm) and °C** $\rightarrow$ **K then** $P, n, T \rightarrow V$

$\frac{1 \text{ mol}}{18.01 \text{ g}}$ $\quad \frac{1 \text{ atm}}{760 \text{ mmHg}}$ $\quad$ K = °C + 273.15 $\quad PV = nRT$

Solution: $0.55 \text{ g} \times \frac{1 \text{ mol}}{18.01 \text{ g}} = 0.030539 \text{ mol}$, $P_{H_2O} = 28.63 \text{ mmHg} \times \frac{1 \text{ atm}}{760 \text{ mmHg}} = 0.03767105 \text{ atm},$

T = 28 °C + 273.15 = 301 K, then $PV = nRT$. Rearrange to solve for V.

$$V = \frac{nRT}{P} = \frac{0.030539 \text{ mol} \times 0.08206 \frac{\text{L} \cdot \text{atm}}{\text{K} \cdot \text{mol}} \times 301 \text{ K}}{0.03767105 \text{ atm}} = 20.02 \text{ L} = 2.0 \times 10^1 \text{ L}.$$

Check: The units (L) are correct. The magnitude of the answer (20 L) makes sense since we have about 1/30 mole and a pressure of about 1/30 atm and at STP one mole of a gas occupies 22 L.

11.129 CsCl has a higher melting point than AgI because of its higher coordination number. In CsCl, one anion bonds to eight cations (and vice versa), while in AgI, one anion bonds only to four cations.

11.130 KCl has a higher melting point than copper iodide because of its higher coordination number. In KCl, one anion bonds to six cations (and vice versa). while in copper iodide, one anion bonds only to four cations.

11.131 (a) Atoms are connected across the face diagonal (c), so $c = 4r$.

(b) From the Pythagorean Theorem $c^2 = a^2 + b^2$, from part (a) $c = 4r$, and for a cubic structure $a = l, b = l$ so $(4r)^2 = l^2 + l^2 \rightarrow 16r^2 = 2l^2 \rightarrow 8r^2 = l^2 \rightarrow l = \sqrt{8r^2} \rightarrow l = 2\sqrt{2}r$.

11.132 (a) Atoms are connected across the cube diagonal (c), so $c = 4r$.

(b) Since b forms the diagonal of the face, where each edge length $a = l$ and combining this with the Pythagorean Theorem, $b^2 = l^2 + l^2 \rightarrow b^2 = 2l^2 \rightarrow b = \sqrt{2}l$.

(c) From the Pythagorean Theorem $c^2 = a^2 + b^2$, from part (a) $c = 4r$ and from part (b) $b = \sqrt{2}l$, and for a cubic structure $a = l$ so $(4r)^2 = l^2 + (\sqrt{2}l)^2 \rightarrow 16r^2 = l^2 + 2l^2 \rightarrow 16r^2 = 3l^2 \rightarrow 4r = \sqrt{3}l \rightarrow l = \dfrac{4r}{\sqrt{3}}$.

11.133 **Given:** diamond, V (unit cell) = 0.0454 nm^3; $d = 3.52$ g/cm^3 **Find:** number of carbon atoms / unit cell
Conceptual Plan: $V(\text{nm}^3) \rightarrow V(\text{cm}^3)$ **then** $d, V \rightarrow m \rightarrow$ **mol** $\rightarrow$ **atoms**

$$\frac{(1\text{ cm})^3}{(10^7\text{ nm})^3} \qquad d = m/V \qquad \frac{1\text{ mol}}{12.01\text{ g}} \qquad \frac{6.022 \times 10^{23}\text{ atoms}}{1\text{ mol}}$$

Solution: $0.0454\ \text{nm}^3 \times \dfrac{(1\text{ cm})^3}{(10^7\text{ nm})^3} = 4.54 \times 10^{-23}\text{ cm}^3$ then $d = \dfrac{m}{V}$. Rearrange to solve for m.

$m = d\,V = 3.52\dfrac{\text{g}}{\text{cm}^3} \times 4.54 \times 10^{-23}\text{ cm}^3 = 1.59808 \times 10^{-22}\text{ g}$ then

$$\frac{1.59808 \times 10^{-22}\text{ g}}{\text{unit cell}} \times \frac{1\text{ mol}}{12.01\text{ g}} \times \frac{6.022 \times 10^{23}\text{ atoms}}{1\text{ mol}} = 8.01\frac{\text{C atoms}}{\text{unit cell}} = 8\frac{\text{C atoms}}{\text{unit cell}}$$

Check: The units (atoms) are correct. The magnitude (8) makes sense because it is a fairly small number and our answer is within calculation error of an integer.

11.134 **Given:** metal, $d = 12.3$ g/cm^3; $r = 0.134$ nm, face-centered cubic lattice **Find:** $\mathcal{M}$
Conceptual Plan: $r \rightarrow l \rightarrow V(\text{nm}^3) \rightarrow V(\text{cm}^3)$ **then** $d, V \rightarrow m$ **then** m**, FCC structure** $\rightarrow \mathcal{M}$

$$l = 2\sqrt{2}r \quad V = l^3 \qquad \frac{(1\text{ cm})^3}{(10^7\text{ nm})^3} \qquad d = m/V \qquad m = \frac{4\text{ atoms}}{\text{unit cell}} \times \frac{\mathcal{M}}{N_A}$$

Solution: $l = 2\sqrt{2}r = 2\sqrt{2} \times 0.134\text{ nm} = 0.379009\text{ nm}$,

$V = l^3 = (0.379009\text{ nm})^3 = 0.0544439\text{ nm}^3 \times \dfrac{(1\text{ cm})^3}{(10^7\text{ nm})^3} = 5.44439 \times 10^{-23}\text{ cm}^3$ then $d = \dfrac{m}{V}$. Rearrange to solve for m. $m = d\,V = 12.3\dfrac{\text{g}}{\text{cm}^3} \times 5.44439 \times 10^{-23}\text{ cm}^3 = 6.69660 \times 10^{-22}\text{ g}$ then $m = \dfrac{4\text{ atoms}}{\text{unit cell}} \times \dfrac{\mathcal{M}}{N_A}$.

Rearrange to solve for $\mathcal{M}$.

$$\mathcal{M} = \frac{\text{unit cell}}{4\text{ atoms}} \times N_A \times m = \frac{\text{unit cell}}{4\text{ atoms}} \times \frac{6.022 \times 10^{23}\text{ atoms}}{1\text{ mol}} \times \frac{6.69660 \times 10^{-22}\text{ g}}{\text{unit cell}} = 101\frac{\text{g}}{\text{mol}}\ \text{Ruthenium.}$$

Check: The units (g/mol) are correct. The magnitude (101) makes sense because it is a reasonable atomic mass for a metal and it is close to Ruthenium.

11.135 (a) CO_2 (s) $\rightarrow$ CO_2 (g) at 194.7 K

(b) CO_2 (s) $\rightarrow$ triple point at 216.5 K $\rightarrow$ CO_2 (g) just above 216.5 K

(c) CO_2 (s) $\rightarrow$ CO_2 (l) at somewhat above 216 K $\rightarrow$ CO_2 (g) at around 250 K

(d) CO_2 (s) $\rightarrow$ CO_2 above the critical point where there is no distinction between liquid and gas. This change occurs at about 300 K.

11.136 If atmospheric pressure is 2500 mmHg, water would still be a liquid. At a higher atmospheric pressure water would remain a liquid to a lower temperature than 0 °C; this could reduce the damage done to organisms that are exposed to cold temperatures. At a higher atmospheric pressure there would be more molecules in the gas phase and the atmosphere would not behave as ideally; water might condense more readily, lowering the vapor pressure of water. This could have an adverse effect on living organisms. At higher atmospheric pressures, cell walls would need to be stronger to withstand higher pressures. This would most likely make the cell walls less permeable and affect many biological systems.

11.137 **Given:** metal, $d = 7.8748\ \text{g/cm}^3$; $l = 0.28664$ nm, body-centered cubic lattice **Find:** $\mathcal{M}$
Conceptual Plan: $l \rightarrow V(\text{nm}^3) \rightarrow V(\text{cm}^3)$ **then** $d, V \rightarrow m$ **then** m, **FCC structure** $\rightarrow \mathcal{M}$

$$V = l^3 \qquad \frac{(1\ \text{cm})^3}{(10^7\ \text{nm})^3} \qquad d = m/V \qquad m = \frac{2\ \text{atoms}}{\text{unit cell}} \times \frac{\mathcal{M}}{N_A}$$

Solution: $V = l^3 = (0.28664\ \text{nm})^3 = 0.02355105602\ \text{nm}^3 \times \dfrac{(1\ \text{cm})^3}{(10^7\ \text{nm})^3} = 2.355105602 \times 10^{-23}\ \text{cm}^3$ then $d = \dfrac{m}{V}$.

Rearrange to solve for m. $m = d\,V = 7.8748\ \dfrac{\text{g}}{\text{cm}^3} \times 2.355105602 \times 10^{-23}\ \text{cm}^3 = 1.854598559 \times 10^{-22}\ \text{g}$

then $m = \dfrac{2\ \text{atoms}}{\text{unit cell}} \times \dfrac{\mathcal{M}}{N_A}$. Rearrange to solve for $\mathcal{M}$.

$$\mathcal{M} = \frac{\text{unit cell}}{2\ \text{atoms}} \times N_A \times m = \frac{\text{unit cell}}{2\ \text{atoms}} \times \frac{6.022 \times 10^{23}\ \text{atoms}}{1\ \text{mol}} \times \frac{1.854598559 \times 10^{-22}\ \text{g}}{\text{unit cell}} = 55.842\ \frac{\text{g}}{\text{mol}}$$

$= 55.84\ \dfrac{\text{g}}{\text{mol}}$ iron.

Check: The units (g/mol) are correct. The magnitude (55.8) makes sense because it is a reasonable atomic mass for a metal and it is close to iron.

11.138 There are two spheres in each unit cell. The volume of the unit cell $V = a^3$. Since the spheres occupy 68.0% of the available volume and the volume of a sphere $= \frac{4}{3}\pi r^3$, $0.680V = 0.680a^3 = 2\left(\frac{4}{3}\pi r^3\right)$. Rearranging this to solve for a, we have $a^3 = \dfrac{2\left(\frac{4}{3}\pi r^3\right)}{0.680} \rightarrow a = \sqrt[3]{\dfrac{2\left(\frac{4}{3}\pi\right)}{0.680}}\,r \rightarrow a = 1.58\ \sqrt[3]{\pi}\,r \rightarrow a = 2.31\ r$, which agrees with the solution in Problem 132.

Challenge Problems

11.139 **Given:** KCl, rock salt structure **Find:** density (g/cm^3) **Other:** $r\,(K^+) = 133$ pm; $r\,(Cl^-) = 181$ pm from Chapter 8
Conceptual Plan: Rock salt structure is a face-centered cubic structure with anions at the lattice points and cations in the holes between lattice sites $\rightarrow$ **assume** $r = r(Cl^-)$, **but** $\mathcal{M} = \mathcal{M}(KCl)$
$r(K^+), r(Cl^-) \rightarrow l$ **and** $l \rightarrow V(\text{pm}^3) \rightarrow V(\text{cm}^3)$ **and, FCC structure** $\rightarrow m$ **then** $m, V \rightarrow d$.

$$\text{from Figure 11.52}\ l = 2r(Cl^-) + 2r(K^+) \qquad V = l^3 \qquad \frac{(1\text{cm})^3}{(10^{10}\text{pm})^3} \qquad m = \frac{4\ \text{formula units}}{\text{unit cell}} \times \frac{\mathcal{M}}{N_A} \qquad d = m/V$$

Solution: $l = 2r(Cl^-) + 2r(K^+) = 2(181\ \text{pm}) + 2(133\ \text{pm}) = 628$ pm and

$$V = l^3 = (628\ \text{pm})^3 \times \frac{(1\ \text{cm})^3}{(10^{10}\ \text{pm})^3} = 2.47673 \times 10^{-22}\ \text{cm}^3 \text{ and}$$

$$m = \frac{4\ \text{formula units}}{\text{unit cell}} \times \frac{\mathcal{M}}{N_A} = \frac{4\ \text{formula units}}{\text{unit cell}} \times \frac{74.55\ \text{g}}{1\ \text{mol}} \times \frac{1\ \text{mol}}{6.022 \times 10^{23}\ \text{formula units}}$$

$$= 4.951976 \times 10^{-22}\ \frac{\text{g}}{\text{unit cell}}$$

$$\text{then } d = \frac{m}{V} = \frac{4.951976 \times 10^{-22}\ \frac{\text{g}}{\text{unit cell}}}{2.47673 \times 10^{-22}\ \frac{\text{cm}^3}{\text{unit cell}}} = 1.99940\ \frac{\text{g}}{\text{cm}^3} = 2.00\ \frac{\text{g}}{\text{cm}^3}$$

Check: The units (g/cm^3) are correct. The magnitude (2 g/cm^3) is reasonable for a salt density. The published value is 1.98 g/cm^3. This method of estimating the density gives a value that is close to the experimentally measured density.

11.140 **Given:** butane (C_4H_{10}), ΔH°_{vap} = 22.44 kJ/mol; normal boiling point = – 0.4 °C, 0.55 g; 250 mL flask
Find: amount of butane present as a liquid at – 22 °C, and at 25 °C
Conceptual Plan: at each temperature: °C → K and kJ → J then ΔH°_{vap}, T_1, P_1, T_2 → P_2

$$K = °C + 273.15 \qquad \frac{1000\ J}{1\ kJ} \qquad \ln\frac{P_2}{P_1} = \frac{-\Delta H_{vap}}{R}\left(\frac{1}{T_2} - \frac{1}{T_1}\right)$$

and mL → L then P_2, V, T_2 → mol → g (g) → g (l)

$$\frac{1\ L}{1000\ mL} \qquad PV = nRT \qquad \frac{58.12\ g}{1\ mol} \qquad g(l) = g_{Total} - g(g)$$

Solution: T_1 = – 0.4 °C + 273.15 = 272.8 K; T_2 = – 22 °C + 273.15 = 251 K;

$$\frac{22.44\ kJ}{mol} \times \frac{1000\ J}{1\ kJ} = 2.244 \times 10^4 \frac{J}{mol} \quad P_1 = 1\ atm \quad \ln\frac{P_2}{P_1} = \frac{-\Delta H_{vap}}{R}\left(\frac{1}{T_2} - \frac{1}{T_1}\right)$$

Substitute values in equation.

$$\ln\frac{P_2}{1\ atm} = \frac{-2.244 \times 10^4 \frac{J}{mol}}{8.314 \frac{J}{K \cdot mol}}\left(\frac{1}{251\ K} - \frac{1}{272.8\ K}\right) = -0.859312 \rightarrow \frac{P_2}{1\ atm} = e^{-0.859312} = 0.42345 \rightarrow$$

$$P_2 = 0.42345 \times 1\ atm = 0.42345\ atm \text{ and } 250\ mL \times \frac{1\ L}{1000\ mL} = 0.25\ L \text{ then } PV = nRT.$$

$$\text{Rearrange to solve for } n.\ n = \frac{PV}{RT} = \frac{0.42345\ atm \times 0.25\ L}{0.08206 \frac{L \cdot atm}{K \cdot mol} \times 251\ K} = 0.0051397 \text{ mol then}$$

$$0.0051397\ mol \times \frac{58.12\ g}{1\ mol} = 0.29872 \text{ g in gas phase then}$$

$g(l) = g_{Total} - g(g) = 0.55\ g - 0.29872\ g = 0.25$ gas liquid at – 22°C

$$T_1 = -0.4\ °C + 273.15 = 272.8\ K; \quad T_2 = 25\ °C + 273.15 = 298\ K; \quad \frac{22.44\ kJ}{mol} \times \frac{1000\ J}{1\ kJ} = 2.244 \times 10^4 \frac{J}{mol}$$

$$P_1 = 1\ atm \quad \ln\frac{P_2}{P_1} = \frac{-\Delta H_{vap}}{R}\left(\frac{1}{T_2} - \frac{1}{T_1}\right).$$ Substitute values in equation.

$$\ln\frac{P_2}{1\ atm} = \frac{-2.244 \times 10^4 \frac{J}{mol}}{8.314 \frac{J}{K \cdot mol}}\left(\frac{1}{298\ K} - \frac{1}{272.8\ K}\right) = 0.836667 \rightarrow \frac{P_2}{1\ atm} = e^{0.836667} = 2.30866 \rightarrow$$

$$P_2 = 2.30866 \times 1\ atm = 2.30866\ atm \text{ and } 250\ mL \times \frac{1\ L}{1000\ mL} = 0.25\ L \text{ then } PV = nRT.$$

$$\text{Rearrange to solve for } n.\ n = \frac{PV}{RT} = \frac{2.30866\ atm \times 0.25\ L}{0.08206 \frac{L \cdot atm}{K \cdot mol} \times 298\ K} = 0.023602 \text{ mol then}$$

$0.023602\ mol \times \frac{58.12\ g}{1\ mol} = 1.3718$ g in gas phase since the amount that can be put in the gas phase is greater than the available amount, there is no liquid present at 25 °C.

Check: The units (g) are correct. The magnitude of the answers (0.25 g and 0 g) makes sense since we expect less to be in the liquid phase at a higher temperature. The second temperature is over the boiling point, so we expect a lot in the gas phase.

11.141 Decreasing the pressure will decrease the temperature of liquid nitrogen. Because the nitrogen is boiling, its temperature must be constant at a given pressure. As the pressure decreases, the boiling point decreases, and therefore so does the temperature. Remember that vaporization is an endothermic process, so as the nitrogen vaporizes it will remove heat from the liquid, dropping its temperature. If the pressure drops below the pressure of the triple point, the phase change will shift from vaporization to sublimation and the liquid nitrogen will become solid.

11.142 **Given:** cubic closest packing structure **Find:** fraction of empty space to 5 significant figures
Conceptual Plan: cubic closest packing is the same as face-centered cubic structure so calculate the volume of the atoms and the volume of the unit cell then V_{atoms}, $V_{unit\ cell}$ → % V_{empty}

$$\frac{4\text{ atoms}}{\text{unit cell}} \text{ and } V_{atom} = \frac{\frac{4}{3}\pi r^3}{\text{atom}} \quad V_{unit\ cell} = l^3 \text{ and } l = 2\sqrt{2}r \qquad \%V_{empty} = \frac{V_{unit\ cell} - V_{atoms}}{V_{unit\ cell}} \text{ x } 100\ \%$$

Solution: $V_{atoms} = \frac{4\ \cancel{\text{atoms}}}{\text{unit cell}} \text{ x } \frac{\frac{4}{3}\pi r^3}{\cancel{\text{atom}}} = \frac{\frac{16}{3}\pi r^3}{\text{unit cell}}$ and $V_{unit\ cell} = l^3 = \left(2\sqrt{2}r\right)^3$ so

$$\%\ V_{empty} = \frac{V_{unit\ cell} - V_{atoms}}{V_{unit\ cell}} \text{ x } 100\ \% \text{ or}$$

$$\%\ V_{empty} = \frac{\left(2\sqrt{2}r\right)^3 - \frac{16}{3}\pi r^3}{\left(2\sqrt{2}r\right)^3} \text{ x } 100\ \% = \frac{2^3\,2^{3/2}\,r^3 - \frac{2^4}{3}\pi r^3}{2^3\,2^{3/2}\,r^3} \text{ x } 100\ \% = \frac{\sqrt{2} - \frac{\pi}{3}}{\sqrt{2}} \text{ x } 100\ \% = 25.952\ \%$$

Check: The units (%) are correct. The magnitude (26 %) is consistent with what is stated in the text.

11.143 **Given:** cubic closest packing structure = cube with touching spheres of radius = r on alternating corners of a cube **Find:** body diagonal of cube and radius of tetrahedral hole
Solution: The cell edge length = l and $l^2 + l^2 = (2r)^2 \rightarrow 2l^2 = 4r^2 \rightarrow l^2 = 2r^2$. Since body diagonal = BD is the hypotenuse of the right triangle formed by the face diagonal and the cell edge we have $(BD)^2 = l^2 + (2r)^2 = 2r^2 + 4r^2 = 6r^2 \rightarrow BD = \sqrt{6}r$. The radius of the tetrahedral hole = r_T is half the body diagonal minus the radius of the sphere or

$$r_T = \frac{BD}{2} - r = \frac{\sqrt{6}r}{2} - r = \left(\frac{\sqrt{6}}{2} - 1\right)r = \left(\frac{\sqrt{6} - 2}{2}\right)r = \left(\frac{\sqrt{3}\sqrt{2} - \sqrt{2}\sqrt{2}}{\sqrt{2}\sqrt{2}}\right)r$$

$$= \left(\frac{\sqrt{3} - \sqrt{2}}{\sqrt{2}}\right)r \approx 0.22474r.$$

11.144 **Given:** ΔH°_{fus} = – 6.02 kJ/mol @ 0.0 °C; C_s (liquid water) = 7.52 J/mol · K; C_s (ice) = 37.7 J/mol · K
Find: ΔH_{fus} at –10.0 °C
Conceptual Plan: Assume exactly 1 mol H_2O for all calculations (report answer as kJ/mol). Since K = °C + 273.13, ΔT (°C) = ΔT (K). Construct the following path:

step 2
Liquid @ 0.0 °C → solid @ 0.0 °C
↑ step 1 ↓ step 3
Liquid @ –10.0 °C → solid @ –10.0 °C
step 4

According to Hess's law $\Delta H_1 + \Delta H_2 + \Delta H_3 = \Delta H_4$ = ΔH°_{fus} @ –10.0 °C
at constant P, $\Delta H = q$
for steps 1 and 3 $q = nC_s\Delta T$

for steps 1 and 3 J → kJ

$$\frac{1\text{ kJ}}{1000\text{ J}}$$

Solution:

$$\Delta H_1 = q_1 = nC_S\Delta T = 1\ \cancel{\text{mol}} \text{ x } 75.2\frac{\text{J}}{\cancel{\text{mol}} \cdot \cancel{°\text{C}}} \text{ x } (0.00\ \cancel{°\text{C}} - -10.0\ \cancel{°\text{C}}) = +\ 752\ \cancel{\text{J}} \text{ x } \frac{1\text{ kJ}}{1000\ \cancel{\text{J}}} = +\ 0.752\text{ kJ},$$

$$\Delta H_2 = q_2 = n\Delta H = 1\ \cancel{\text{mol}} \text{ x } -\ 6.02\frac{\text{kJ}}{\cancel{\text{mol}}} = -6.02\text{ kJ},$$

$$\Delta H_3 = q_3 = nC_S\Delta T = 1\ \cancel{\text{mol}} \text{ x } 37.7\frac{\text{J}}{\cancel{\text{mol}} \cdot \cancel{°\text{C}}} \text{ x } (-10.00\ \cancel{°\text{C}} - 0.0\ \cancel{°\text{C}}) = -377\ \cancel{\text{J}} \text{ x } \frac{1\text{ kJ}}{1000\ \cancel{\text{J}}} = -0.377\text{ kJ so}$$

$$\Delta H_4 = \Delta H_1 + \Delta H_2 + \Delta H_3 = 0.752\text{ kJ} - 6.02\text{ kJ} - 0.377\text{ kJ} = -\ 5.65\text{ kJ}$$

Check: The units (kJ/mol) are correct. We expect freezing to release less energy at –10 °C because we are below the normal freezing point.

11.145 **Given:** 1.00 L water, T_i = 298 K, T_f = 373 K - vapor; P_{CH_4} = 1.00 atm **Find:** V (CH_4)
Other: ΔH°_{comb} (CH_4) = 890.4 kJ/mol; C_{water} = 75.2 J/mol · K; ΔH°_{vap} (H_2O) = 40.7 kJ/mol, d = 1.00 g/mL
Conceptual Plan: L → mL → g → mol then heat liquid water: n, C_s, T_i, T_f → q_{1water} (J)

$$\frac{1000\text{ mL}}{1\text{ L}} \quad \frac{1.00\text{ g}}{1.00\text{ mL}} \quad \frac{1\text{ mol}}{18.01\text{ g}} \qquad q = mC_S(T_f - T_i)$$

vaporize water: $n_{water}, \Delta H^\circ_{vap} \rightarrow q_{2water}$ **(J) then calculate total heat** $q_{1water}, q_{2water} \rightarrow q_{water}$ **(J) then**
$q = n\Delta H$ $\qquad$ $q_{1water} + q_{2water} = q_{water}$

q_{water}**(J)** $\rightarrow -q_{CH_4comb}$ **(J)** $\rightarrow n_{CH_4}$ **finally** $n_{CH_4}, P, T \rightarrow V$
$q_{water} = -q_{CH_4comb}$ $\qquad$ $q = n\Delta H$ $\qquad$ $PV = nRT$

Solution: $1.00\ \text{L} \times \dfrac{1000\ \text{mL}}{1\ \text{L}} \times \dfrac{1.00\ \text{g}}{1.00\ \text{mL}} \times \dfrac{1\ \text{mol}}{18.01\ \text{g}} = 55.5247\ \text{mol}\ H_2O$

$q_{1water} = n_{water}C_{water}(T_f - T_i) = 55.5247\ \text{mol} \times 75.2 \dfrac{\text{J}}{\text{mol}\cdot\text{K}} \times (373\ \text{K} - 298\ \text{K}) = 3.1315936 \times 10^5\ \text{J}$
$= 313.15936\ \text{kJ}$,

$q_{2water} = n\Delta H = 55.5247\ \text{mol} \times 40.7 \dfrac{\text{kJ}}{\text{mol}} = 2.259855 \times 10^3\ \text{kJ}$

$q_{1water} + q_{2water} = q_{water} = 313.15936\ \text{kJ} + 2.259855 \times 10^3\ \text{kJ} = 2.57301465 \times 10^3\ \text{kJ}$

$q_{water} = -q_{CH_4comb} = 2.57301465 \times 10^3\ \text{kJ}$ then $q_{CH_4comb} = n\Delta H$. Rearrange to solve for n.

$$n_{CH_4} = \frac{q_{CH_4}}{\Delta H_{CH_4comb}} = \frac{-2.57301465 \times 10^3\ \text{kJ}}{-890.4 \dfrac{\text{kJ}}{\text{mol}}} = 2.8897289\ \text{mol then } PV = nRT.$$

Rearrange to solve for V. $V = \dfrac{nRT}{P} = \dfrac{2.8897289\ \text{mol} \times 0.08206 \dfrac{\text{L}\cdot\text{atm}}{\text{mol}\cdot\text{K}} \times 298\ \text{K}}{1.00\ \text{atm}} = 70.665085\ \text{L} = 70.7\ \text{L}.$

Check: The units (L) are correct. The volume (71 L) is reasonable since we are using about 3 moles of methane.

11.146 $P_{Total} = P_A + P_B$. Looking at the data, we see that as the relative amount of A increases, the pressure decreases, since the vapor pressure of A is less than the vapor pressure of B. Since the solution is almost all A, we expect a vapor pressure just above 24 mmHg. In Chapter 12 we will more fully discuss this relationship and learn that $P_A = \chi_A P^\circ_A$, where $\chi_A = \dfrac{\text{mol A}}{\text{total mol} = \text{mol A} + \text{mol B}}$, $\chi_B = 1 - \chi_A$, and $P_B = \chi_B P^\circ_B$. So

$$P_{Total} = P_A + P_B = \chi_A P^\circ_A + (1 - \chi_A)P^\circ_B = \frac{5\ \text{mol}}{5\ \text{mol} + 1\ \text{mol}} \times 24\ \text{mmHg} + \left(1 - \frac{5\ \text{mol}}{5\ \text{mol} + 1\ \text{mol}}\right) \times 36\ \text{mmHg}$$
$= 26$ mmHg.

11.147 $P_{Total} = P_{N_2} + P_{H_2O} + P_{ethanol}$
P_{N_2}: Use Boyle's law to calculate $P_1V_1 = P_2V_2$. Rearrange to solve for P_2.

$$P_2 = P_1\frac{V_1}{V_2} = 1.0\ \text{atm} \times \frac{1.0\ \text{L}}{3.0\ \text{L}} \times \frac{760\ \text{mmHg}}{1\ \text{atm}} = 253.333\ \text{mmHg}.$$

For water and ethanol, we need to calculate the pressure if all of the liquid were to vaporize in the 3.0 L apparatus. $PV = nRT$. Rearrange to solve for P.

$$P = \frac{nRT}{V} = \frac{2.0\ \text{g} \times \dfrac{1\ \text{mol}}{18.01\ \text{g}} \times 0.08206 \dfrac{\text{L}\cdot\text{atm}}{\text{mol}\cdot\text{K}} \times \dfrac{760\ \text{mmHg}}{1\ \text{atm}} \times 308\ \text{K}}{3.00\ \text{L}} = 71.103\ \text{mmHg}\ H_2O.$$ Since this pressure is greater than the vapor pressure of water at this temperature, then $P_{H_2O} = 42$ mmHg.

$$P = \frac{nRT}{V} = \frac{0.50\ \text{g} \times \dfrac{1\ \text{mol}}{46.07\ \text{g}} \times 0.08206 \dfrac{\text{L}\cdot\text{atm}}{\text{mol}\cdot\text{K}} \times \dfrac{760\ \text{mmHg}}{1\ \text{atm}} \times 308\ \text{K}}{3.00\ \text{L}} = 69.4937\ \text{mmHg ethanol}.$$ Since this pressure is less than the vapor pressure of ethanol at this temperature (102 mmHg), all of the liquid will vaporize and $P_{ethanol} = 69.4937$ mmHg.

Finally, the total pressure is
$P_{Total} = P_{N_2} + P_{H_2O} + P_{ethanol} = 253.333\ \text{mmHg} + 42\ \text{mmHg} + 69.4937\ \text{mmHg} = 364.827\ \text{mmHg}$
$= 360$ mmHg.

Conceptual Problems

11.148 The melting of an ice cube in a glass of water will not raise or lower the level of the liquid in the glass as long as the ice is always floating in the liquid. This is because the ice will displace a volume of water based on its mass. By the same logic, melting floating icebergs will not raise the ocean levels (assuming that the dissolved solids content, and thus the density, will not change when the icebergs melt). Dissolving ice formations that are supported by land will raise the ocean levels, just as pouring more water into the glass will raise the liquid level in the glass.

11.149 The water, a container with a larger surface area will evaporate more quickly because there is more surface area for the molecules to evaporate from. Vapor pressure is the pressure of the gas when it is in dynamic equilibrium with the liquid (evaporation rate = condensation rate). The vapor pressure is dependent only on the substance and the temperature. The larger the surface area, the more quickly it will reach this equilibrium state.

11.150 Substance A will have the larger change in vapor pressure with the same temperature change. To understand this consider the Clausius–Clapeyron equation: $\ln\frac{P_2}{P_1} = \frac{-\Delta H_{\text{vap}}}{R}\left(\frac{1}{T_2} - \frac{1}{T_1}\right)$. If we use the same temperatures we see that $\frac{P_2}{P_1} \, \alpha \, e^{-\Delta H_{\text{vap}}}$. So the smaller the heat of vaporization, the larger the final vapor pressure. We can also consider that the lower the heat of vaporization, the easier it is to convert the substance from a liquid to a gas. This again leads to Substance A having the larger change in vapor pressure.

11.151 The triple point will be at a lower temperature since the fusion equilibrium line has a positive slope. This means that we will be increasing both temperature and pressure as we travel from the triple point to the normal melting point.

11.152 $\Delta H_{\text{sub}} = \Delta H_{\text{fus}} + \Delta H_{\text{vap}}$ as long as the heats of fusion and vaporization are measured at the same temperatures.

11.153 The liquid segment will have the least steep slope because it takes the most kJ/mol to raise the temperature of the phase.

11.154 Water has an exceptionally high specific heat capacity, which has a moderating effect on the temperature of the root cellar. A large amount of heat can be stored in a large vat of water. The heat will be absorbed or released from the large bodies of water preferentially over the area around it. As the temperature of the air drops, the water will release heat, keeping the temperature more constant. If the temperature of the cellar falls enough to begin to freeze the water, the heat given off during the freezing will further protect the food in the cellar.

11.155 The heat of fusion of a substance is always smaller than the heat of vaporization because the number of interactions between particles that are broken is less in fusion than in vaporization. When we melt a solid, the particles have increased mobility, but are still strongly interacting with other liquid particles. In vaporization, all of the interactions between particles must be broken (gas particles have essentially no intermolecular interactions) and the particles must absorb enough energy to move much more rapidly.

12 Solutions

Review Questions

12.1 As seawater moves through the intestine, it flows past cells that line the digestive tract, which consist of largely fluid interiors surrounded by membranes. Although cellular fluids themselves contain dissolved ions, including sodium and chloride, the fluids are more dilute than seawater. Nature's tendency towards mixing (which tends to produce solutions of uniform concentration), together with the selective permeability of the cell membranes (which allow water to flow in and out, but restrict the flow of dissolved solids), cause a flow of solvent out of the body's cells and into the seawater.

12.2 A solution is a homogeneous mixture of two or more substances. A solution has at least two components. The majority component is usually called the solvent and the minority component is usually called the solute.

12.3 A substance is soluble in another substance if they can form a homogeneous mixture. The solubility of a substance is the amount of the substance that will dissolve in a given amount of solvent. Many different units can be used to express solubility, including grams of solute per 100 grams of solvent, grams of solute per liter of solvent, moles of solute per liter of solution, and moles of solute per kilogram of solvent.

12.4 Ideal gases do not interact with each other in any way (that is, there are no significant forces between their constituent particles). When the two gases mix their potential energy remains unchanged, so this does not drive the mixing. The tendency to mix is related, rather, to a concept called entropy. Entropy is a measure of energy randomization or energy dispersal in a system. Recall that a gas at any temperature above 0 K has kinetic energy due to the motion of its atoms. When the gases are separated, their kinetic energies are also confined to those regions. However, when the gases mix the kinetic energy of each gas becomes spread out or dispersed over a larger volume. Therefore, the mixture of the two gases has greater energy dispersal, or greater entropy, than the separated components. The pervasive tendency for all kinds of energy to spread out, or disperse, whenever they are not restrained from doing so is the reason that two ideal gases mix.

12.5 Entropy is a measure of energy randomization or energy dispersal in a system. When two substances mix to form a solution there is an increase in randomness, due to the fact that the components are no longer segregated to separate regions. This makes the formation of a solution energetically favorable, even when it is endothermic.

12.6 Whether two substances will spontaneously mix to form a homogeneous solution is dependent on a number of different types of intermolecular forces including dispersion forces, dipole–dipole forces, hydrogen bonding, and ion–dipole forces.

12.7 A solution always forms if the solvent–solute interactions are comparable to, or stronger than, the solvent–solvent interactions and the solute–solute interactions.

12.8 The statement "like dissolves like" means that similar kinds of solvents dissolve similar kinds of solutes. Polar solvents, such as water, dissolve many polar or ionic solutes, and nonpolar solvents, such as hexane, dissolve many nonpolar solutes.

12.9 Step 1: Separate the solute into its constituent particles. This step is always endothermic (positive ΔH) because energy is required to overcome the forces that hold the solute together.

Step 2: Separate the solvent particles from each other to make room for the solute particles. This step is also endothermic because energy is required to overcome the intermolecular forces among the solvent particles.

Step 3: Mix the solute particles with the solvent particles. This step is exothermic because energy is released as the solute particles interact with the solvent particles through the various types of intermolecular forces.

12.10 The heat of hydration is the enthalpy change that occurs when 1 mol of gaseous solute ions are dissolved in water. In aqueous solutions, $\Delta H_{solvent}$ and ΔH_{mix} can be combined into a single term called the heat of hydration ($\Delta H_{hydration}$). Because the ion–dipole interactions that occur between a dissolved ion and the surrounding water molecules are much stronger than the hydrogen bonds in water, $\Delta H_{hydration}$ is always largely negative (exothermic) for ionic compounds. Using the heat of hydration, we can write the enthalpy of solution as a sum of just two terms, one endothermic and one exothermic: $\Delta H_{soln} = \Delta H_{solute} + \Delta H_{solvent} + \Delta H_{mix} = \Delta H_{solute} + \Delta H_{hydration}$ = endothermic(+) term + exothermic(–) term. For ionic compounds, ΔH_{solute}, the energy required to separate the solute into its constituent particles, is simply the negative of the solute's lattice energy ($\Delta H_{solute} = -\Delta H_{lattice}$), discussed in Section 9.4. For ionic aqueous solutions, then, the overall enthalpy of solution depends on the relative magnitudes of ΔH_{solute} and $\Delta H_{hydration}$, with three possible scenarios (in each case we refer to the magnitude or absolute value of ΔH): (1) If $\Delta H_{solute} < \Delta H_{hydration}$ the amount of energy required to separate the solute into its constituent ions is less than the energy given off when the ions are hydrated. ΔH_{soln} is therefore negative and the solution process is exothermic and the solution feels warm to the touch. (2) If $\Delta H_{solute} > \Delta H_{hydration}$ the amount of energy required to separate the solute into its constituent ions is greater than the energy given off when the ions are hydrated. ΔH_{soln} is therefore positive and the solution process is endothermic (if a solution forms at all) and the resulting solution feels cool to the touch. (3) If $\Delta H_{solute} \approx \Delta H_{hydration}$ the amount of energy required to separate the solute into its constituent ions is about equal to the energy given off when the ions are hydrated. ΔH_{soln} is therefore approximately zero and the solution process is neither appreciably exothermic nor appreciably endothermic and there is no noticeable change in temperature.

12.11 In any solution formation, the initial rate of dissolution far exceeds the rate of deposition. But as the concentration of dissolved solute increases, the rate of deposition also increases. Eventually the rate of dissolution and deposition become equal—dynamic equilibrium has been reached.

A saturated solution is a solution in which the dissolved solute is in dynamic equilibrium with the solid (or undissolved) solute. If you add additional solute to a saturated solution, it will not dissolve.

An unsaturated solution is a solution containing less than the equilibrium amount of solute. If you add additional solute to an unsaturated solution, it will dissolve.

A supersaturated solution is a solution containing more than the equilibrium amount of solute. Such solutions are unstable and the excess solute normally precipitates out of the solution. However, in some cases, if left undisturbed, a supersaturated solution can exist for an extended period of time.

12.12 Although there are exceptions, the solubility of most solids in water increases with increasing temperature. Recrystallization is a common technique to purify a solid. In this technique, the solid is put into water (or some other solvent) at an elevated temperature. Enough solid is added to the solvent to create a saturated solution at the elevated temperature. As the solution cools, it becomes supersaturated and the excess solid begins to come out of solution. If the solution cools slowly, the solid forms crystals as it comes out of solution. The crystalline structure tends to reject impurities, resulting in a purer solid. The solvent is chosen such that the solubility of the impurities is high at the lower temperature reducing the tendency to co-precipitate.

12.13 The solubility of gases in liquids decreases with increasing temperature. The decreasing solubility of gases with increasing temperature results in a lower oxygen concentration available for fish and other aquatic life in warm waters.

12.14 The higher the pressure of a gas above a liquid, the more soluble the gas is in the liquid. In a sealed can of soda pop, for example, the carbon dioxide is maintained in solution by a high pressure of carbon dioxide within the can. When the can is opened, this pressure is released and the solubility of carbon dioxide decreases, resulting in bubbling.

12.15 Henry's law quantifies the solubility of gases with increasing pressure as follows: $S_{gas} = k_H P_{gas}$, where S_{gas} is the solubility of the gas; k_H is a constant of proportionality (called the Henry's law constant) that depends on the specific solute, solvent, and temperature; and P_{gas} is the partial pressure of the gas. The equation simply shows that the solubility of a gas in a liquid is directly proportional to the pressure of the gas above the liquid. If the solubility of a gas is known at a certain temperature, the solubility at another pressure at this temperature can be calculated.

12.16 The common ways of reporting solution concentration include the following:

(a) Molarity: $\text{M} = \dfrac{\text{amount solute (moles)}}{\text{volume solution (L)}}$

(b) molality: $m = \dfrac{\text{amount solute (moles)}}{\text{mass solvent (kg)}}$

(c) parts by mass: $\dfrac{\text{mass solute}}{\text{mass solution}} \times$ multiplication factor, where percent by mass (%) factor = 100, parts per million by mass (ppm) factor = 10^6, and parts per billion by mass (ppb) factor = 10^9

(d) parts by volume (%, ppm, ppb): $\dfrac{\text{volume solute}}{\text{volume solution}} \times$ multiplication factor, where the same factors as in parts by mass are used

(e) mole fraction: $\chi = \dfrac{\text{amount solute (in moles)}}{\text{total amount of solute and solvent (in moles)}}$

(f) mole percent $\chi \times 100\%$

12.17 Parts by mass and parts by volume are ratios of masses and volume, respectively. A parts by mass concentration is the ratio of the mass of the solute to the mass of the solution, all multiplied by a multiplication factor, where percent by mass (%) is the desired unit, the factor = 100; where parts per million by mass (ppm) is the desired unit, the factor = 10^6; and for parts per billion by mass (ppb), the factor = 10^9. The size of the multiplication factor depends on the concentration of the solution. For example, in percent by mass, the multiplication factor is 100 %, so percent by mass $= \dfrac{\text{mass solute}}{\text{mass solution}} \times 100\ \%$. A solution with a concentration of 28 % by mass contains 28 g of solute per 100 g of solution.

12.18 The vapor pressure of the solution is lower than the vapor pressure of the pure solvent. The simplest explanation for the lowering of the vapor pressure of a solution relative to that of the pure solvent is related to the concept of dynamic equilibrium itself. In dynamic equilibrium the rate of vaporization is equal to the rate of condensation. When a nonvolatile solute is added, however, the solute particles interfere with the ability of the solvent particles to vaporize, simply because they occupy some of the surface area formerly occupied by the solvent. The rate of vaporization is therefore diminished compared to that of the pure solvent. The change in the rate of vaporization creates an imbalance in the rates; the rate of condensation is now greater than the rate of vaporization. The net effect is that some of the molecules that were in the gas phase condense into the liquid. As they condense, the reduced number of molecules in the gas phase causes the rate of condensation to decrease. Eventually the two rates become equal again, but only after the concentration of molecules in the gas phase has decreased, which means a lower vapor pressure for the solution compared to the pure solvent.

12.19 Raoult's law quantifies the relationship between the vapor pressure of a solution and its concentration as $P_{solution} = \chi_{solvent} P^{\circ}_{solvent}$, where $P_{solution}$ is the vapor pressure of the solution, $\chi_{solvent}$ is the mole fraction of the solvent, and $P^{\circ}_{solvent}$ is the vapor pressure of the pure solvent. This equation allows you to calculate the vapor pressure of a solution or to calculate the concentration of a solution, given the vapor pressure of the solution.

12.20 An ideal solution is a solution that follows Raoult's law at all concentrations for both the solute and the solvent. A nonideal solution will exhibit deviations from Raoult's law in the vapor pressure of a component as mole fraction of this component decreases from 1 (i.e. the pure component).

12.21 If the solute–solvent interactions are particularly strong (stronger than solvent–solvent interactions), then the solute tends to prevent the solvent from vaporizing as easily as it would otherwise and the vapor pressure of the solution will be less than that predicted by Raoult's law. If the solute–solvent interactions are particularly weak (weaker than solvent-solvent interactions), then the solute tends to allow more vaporization than would occur with just the solvent and the vapor pressure of the solution will be greater than predicted by Raoult's law.

12.22 A nonvolatile solute lowers the vapor pressure of a solution relative to that of the pure solvent. The vapor pressure lowering occurs at all temperatures, which shifts the vaporization curve in the phase diagram. This means that the temperature must be raised above the pure solvent normal boiling point in order for the solution vapor pressures to be raised to 1 atm. This shift also results in a lowering of where the vapor pressure curve intersects the solid-gas curve. The net effect is that the solution has a lower melting point and a higher boiling point than the pure solvent.

12.23 Colligative properties are properties that depend on the amount of solute and not the type of solute. Examples of colligative properties are vapor pressure lowering, freezing point depression, boiling point elevation, and osmotic pressure.

12.24 Osmosis is defined as the flow of solvent from a solution of lower solute concentration to one of higher solute concentration through a semipermeable membrane—a membrane that selectively allows some substances to pass through but not others. The osmotic pressure is the pressure required to stop the osmotic flow and is given by the following equation: $\Pi = MRT$.

12.25 The van't Hoff factor (i) is the ratio of moles of particles in solution to moles of formula units dissolved: $i = \dfrac{\text{moles of particles}}{\text{moles of formula units dissolved}}$. The van't Hoff factor often does not match its theoretical value, due to the fact that the ionic solute is not completely dissolved into the expected number of ions, leaving ion pairs in solution. The result is that the number of particles in the solution is not as high as theoretically expected.

12.26 A colloidal dispersion, or simply a colloid, is a mixture in which a dispersed substance (which is solute-like) is finely divided in a dispersing medium (which is solvent-like). The easiest way to define a colloid is based on the size of the solute-like particles. If the particles are small (for example, individual small molecules), then the mixture is a solution. If the particles have a diameter greater than 1μm (for example, grains of sand), then the mixture is a heterogeneous mixture. If the particles are between 1 nm and 1000 nm in size, the mixture is a colloid. Colloidal particles are small enough to be kept dispersed throughout the dispersing medium by collisions with other molecules or atoms.

12.27 The Tyndall effect is the scattering of light by a colloidal dispersion. The Tyndall effect is often used as a test to determine whether a mixture is a solution or a colloid, since solutions contain completely dissolved solute molecules that are too small to scatter light.

12.28 Colloidal suspensions are kept stable by electrostatic repulsions that occur at their surfaces. These electrostatic repulsions are caused by charges or dipoles on the surface of the particles.

Solubility

12.29 (a) hexane, toluene, or CCl_4; dispersion forces

(b) water, methanol, acetone; dispersion, dipole–dipole, hydrogen bonding

(c) hexane, toluene, or CCl_4; dispersion forces

(d) water, acetone, methanol, ethanol; dispersion, ion–dipole

12.30 (a) water, methanol, ethanol; dispersion, dipole–dipole, hydrogen bonding

(b) water, acetone, methanol, ethanol; dispersion, ion–dipole

(c) hexane, toluene, or CCl_4; dispersion forces

(d) water, acetone, methanol, ethanol; dispersion, ion–dipole

12.31 $HOCH_2CH_2CH_2OH$ would be more soluble in water because it has –OH groups on both ends of the molecule, so it can hydrogen bond on both ends.

12.32 CH_2Cl_2 would be more soluble in water because it is a polar molecule and can exhibit dipole–dipole interactions with the water molecules. CCl_4 is a nonpolar molecule.

12.33 (a) water; dispersion, dipole–dipole, hydrogen bonding

(b) hexane; dispersion forces

(c) water; dispersion, dipole–dipole

(d) water; dispersion, dipole–dipole, hydrogen bonding

12.34 (a) hexane; dispersion forces

(b) water; dispersion, dipole–dipole, hydrogen bonding

(c) hexane; dispersion forces

(d) water; dispersion, dipole–dipole, hydrogen bonding

Energetics of Solution Formation

12.35 (a) endothermic

(b) The lattice energy is greater in magnitude than the heat of hydration.

(c)

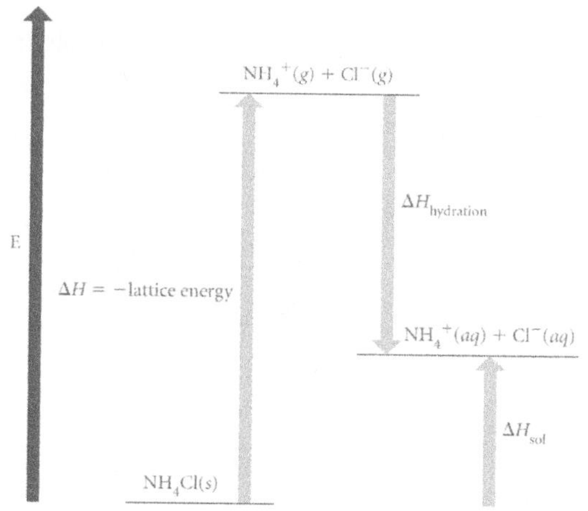

(d) The solution forms because chemical systems tend towards greater entropy.

12.36 (a) exothermic

(b) The lattice energy is smaller in magnitude than the heat of hydration.

(c)

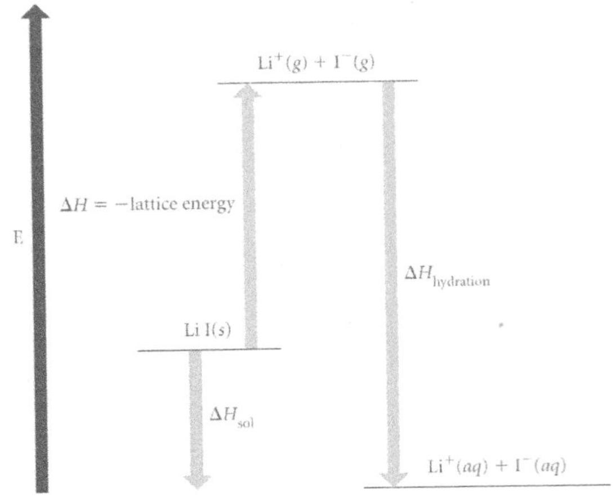

(d) The solution forms because chemical systems tend towards lower energy and greater entropy.

12.37 **Given:** $AgNO_3$: lattice energy = – 820; kJ/mol, ΔH_{soln} = + 22.6 kJ/mol **Find:** $\Delta H_{hydration}$
Conceptual Plan: Lattice Energy, ΔH_{soln} → $\Delta H_{hydration}$

$\Delta H_{soln} = \Delta H_{solute} + \Delta H_{hydration}$ *where* $\Delta H_{solute} = -\Delta H_{lattice}$

Solution: $\Delta H_{soln} = \Delta H_{solute} + \Delta H_{hydration}$ where $\Delta H_{solute} = -\Delta H_{lattice}$ so $\Delta H_{hydration} = \Delta H_{soln} + \Delta H_{lattice}$
$\Delta H_{hydration}$ = 22.6kJ/mol – 820.kJ/mol = – 797kJ/mol
Check: The units (kJ/mol) are correct. The magnitude of the answer (– 800) makes physical sense because the lattice energy is so negative, and thus it dominates the calculation.

12.38 **Given:** LiCl: lattice energy = – 834 kJ/mol, ΔH_{soln} = – 37.0 kJ/mol; NaCl: lattice energy = – 769 kJ/mol, ΔH_{soln} = + 3.88 kJ/mol **Find:** $\Delta H_{hydration}$ and which has stronger ion–dipole interactions
Conceptual Plan: Lattice Energy, ΔH_{soln} → $\Delta H_{hydration}$ then compare values

$\Delta H_{soln} = \Delta H_{solute} + \Delta H_{hydration}$ *where* $\Delta H_{solute} = -\Delta H_{lattice}$

Solution: $\Delta H_{soln} = \Delta H_{solute} + \Delta H_{hydration}$ where $\Delta H_{solute} = -\Delta H_{lattice}$ so $\Delta H_{hydration} = \Delta H_{soln} + \Delta H_{lattice}$
LiCl: $\Delta H_{hydration}$ = – 37.0 kJ/mol – 834 kJ/mol = – 871 kJ/mol

NaCl: $\Delta H_{hydration}$ = + 3.88 kJ/mol – 769 kJ/mol = – 765 kJ/mol

Since $\Delta H_{hydration}$ of LiCl is more negative than for NaCl, LiCl has the stronger ion–dipole interactions.
Check: The units (kJ/mol) are correct. The magnitude of the answer (– 900 and – 800) makes physical sense because the lattice energies are so negative, and thus they dominate the calculation. We expect stronger interactions with lithium, since the Li^+ ion is smaller than the Na^+ ion. Its charge density is higher and it will interact more strongly with the dipoles of the water molecules.

12.39 **Given:** LiI: Lattice Energy = – 7.3 x 10^2 kJ/mol, $\Delta H_{hydration}$ = – 793 kJ/mol; 15.0 g LiI
Find: ΔH_{soln} and heat evolved
Conceptual Plan: Lattice Energy, $\Delta H_{hydration}$ → ΔH_{soln} and g → mol then mol, ΔH_{soln} → q

$\Delta H_{soln} = \Delta H_{solute} + \Delta H_{hydration}$ *where* $\Delta H_{solute} = -\Delta H_{lattice}$ $\qquad \frac{1\ \text{mol}}{133.843\ \text{g}}$ $\qquad q = n\,\Delta H_{soln}$

Solution: $\Delta H_{soln} = \Delta H_{solute} + \Delta H_{hydration}$ where $\Delta H_{solute} = -\Delta H_{lattice}$ so $\Delta H_{soln} = \Delta H_{hydration} - \Delta H_{lattice}$
ΔH_{soln} = – 793 kJ/mol – (–730 kJ/mol) = – 63 kJ/mol = – 6.3 x 10^1 kJ/mol and

$$15.0\ \text{g} \times \frac{1\ \text{mol}}{133.843\ \text{g}} = 0.112072\ \text{mol then}$$

$$q = n\Delta H_{soln} = 0.112072\ \text{mol} \times -6.3 \times 10^1\ \frac{\text{kJ}}{\text{mol}} = -7.0\ \text{kJ or 7 kJ released}$$

Check: The units (kJ/mol and kJ) are correct. The magnitude of the answer (– 60) makes physical sense because the lattice energy and the heat of hydration are about the same. The magnitude of the heat (7) makes physical sense since 15 g is much less than a mole, and thus the amount of heat released is going to be small.

12.40 **Given:** KNO_3: lattice energy = – 163.8 kcal/mol, $\Delta H_{hydration}$ = – 155.5 kcal/mol; 1.00 x 10^2 kJ absorbed
Find: ΔH_{soln} and m (KNO_3)
Conceptual Plan: Lattice Energy, $\Delta H_{hydration}$ → ΔH_{soln} (kcal) → ΔH_{soln} (kcal) then

$\Delta H_{soln} = \Delta H_{solute} + \Delta H_{hydration}$ *where* $\Delta H_{solute} = -\Delta H_{lattice}$

mol, q → ΔH_{soln} then mol → g

$q = n\,\Delta H_{soln}$ $\quad \dfrac{101.11\text{ g}}{1\text{ mol}}$

Solution: $\Delta H_{soln} = \Delta H_{solute} + \Delta H_{hydration}$ where $\Delta H_{solute} = -\Delta H_{lattice}$ so $\Delta H_{soln} = \Delta H_{hydration} - \Delta H_{lattice}$
ΔH_{soln} = [−155.5 kcal/mol − (−163.8 kcal/mol)](4.184 kJ/kcal) = 34.7 kJ/mol then $q = n\,\Delta H_{soln}$.

Rearrange to solve for n. $n = \dfrac{q}{\Delta H_{soln}} = \dfrac{1.00 \times 10^2 \text{ kJ}}{34.7 \dfrac{\text{kJ}}{\text{mol}}}$ = 2.8818 mol then 2.8818 mol x $\dfrac{101.11\text{ g}}{1\text{ mol}}$ = 2.9 x 10^2 g.

Check: The units (kJ/mol and g) are correct. The magnitude of the answer (+ 35) makes physical sense because the lattice energy and the heat of hydration are about the same, with the lattice energy dominating; therefore the answer is positive. The problem hints at a positive heat of solution by saying that heat is absorbed. The magnitude of the mass (290) makes physical sense since 100 kJ will require over 2 moles of salt.

Solution Equilibrium and Factors Affecting Solubility

12.41 The solution is unsaturated since we are dissolving 25 g of NaCl per 100 g of water and the solubility from the figure is ~ 35 g NaCl per 100 g of water at 25° C.

12.42 The solution is almost saturated since we are dissolving 32 g of KNO_3 per 100 g of water and the solubility from the figure is ~ 36 g KNO_3 per 100 g of water at 25° C.

12.43 At 40 °C the solution has 45 g of KNO_3 per 100 g of water and it can contain up to 63 g of KNO_3 per 100 g of water. At 0 °C the solubility from the figure is ~ 14 g KNO_3 per 100 g of water, so ~ 31 g KNO_3 per 100 g of water will precipitate out of solution.

12.44 At 60 °C the solution has 42 g of KCl per 100 g of water and it can contain up to 45 g of KCl per 100 g of water. At 0 °C the solubility from the figure is ~ 26 g KCl per 100 g of water, so ~ 16 g KCl per 100 g of water will precipitate out of solution.

12.45 Since the solubility of gases decreases as the temperature increases boiling will cause dissolved oxygen to be removed from the solution.

12.46 Since the solubility of gases decreases as the temperature increases, dissolved oxygen was removed from the solution and there was no oxygen in the water for the fish to breathe.

12.47 Henry's law says that as pressure increases, nitrogen will more easily dissolve in blood. To reverse this process, divers should ascend to lower pressures.

12.48 Henry's law says that as pressure increases, oxygen will more easily dissolve in blood. To reverse this process, divers should ascend to lower pressures or breathe special gas mixtures with lower oxygen levels.

12.49 **Given:** room temperature, 80.0 L aquarium, P_{Total} = 1.0 atm; χ_{N_2} = 0.78 **Find:** m (N_2)
Other: $k_H(N_2)$ = 6.1 x 10^{-4} M/L at 25 °C
Conceptual Plan: P_{Total}, χ_{N_2} → P_{N_2} then P_{N_2}, $k_H(N_2)$ → S_{N_2} then L → mol → g

$P_{N_2} = \chi_{N_2} P_{Total}$ $\quad S_{N_2} = k_H(N_2) P_{N_2}$ $\quad M = \dfrac{\text{amount solute (moles)}}{\text{volume solution (L)}}$ $\quad \dfrac{28.01\text{ g } N_2}{1\text{ mol } N_2}$

Solution: $P_{N_2} = \chi_{N_2} P_{Total}$ = 0.78 x 1.0 atm = 0.78 atm then

$S_{N_2} = k_H(N_2) P_{N_2}$ = 6.1 x $10^{-4}\dfrac{\text{M}}{\text{atm}}$ x 0.78 atm = 4.758 x 10^{-4} M then

80.0 L x 4.758 x $10^{-4}\dfrac{\text{mol}}{\text{L}}$ x $\dfrac{28.01\text{ g}}{1\text{ mol}}$ = 1.1 g

Check: The units (g) are correct. The magnitude of the answer (1) seems reasonable since we have 80 L of water and expect much less than a mole of nitrogen.

12.50 **Given:** Helium, 25 °C, P_{He} = 1.0 atm **Find:** S_{He} (M) **Other:** $k_H(He)$ = 3.7 x 10^{-4} M/L at 25 °C
Conceptual Plan: $P_{He}, k_H(He) \rightarrow S_{He}$

$$S_{He} = k_H(He)P_{He}$$

Solution: $S_{He} = k_H(He)P_{He} = 3.7 \times 10^{-4} \frac{M}{\cancel{atm}} \times 1.0\ \cancel{atm} = 3.7 \times 10^{-4}\ M$

Check: The units (M) are correct. The magnitude of the answer (10^{-4}) seems reasonable since this is the value of k_H.

Concentrations of Solutions

12.51 **Given:** NaCl and water; 112 g NaCl in 1.00 L solution **Find:** M, *m*, and mass percent
Other: d = 1.08 g/mL
Conceptual Plan: $g_{NaCl} \rightarrow$ **mol and L** $\rightarrow$ **mL** $\rightarrow g_{soln}$ **and** $g_{soln}\ g_{NaCl} \rightarrow g_{H_2O} \rightarrow kg_{H_2O}$ **then**

$$\frac{1\ mol\ NaCl}{58.44\ g\ NaCl} \quad \frac{1000\ mL}{1\ L} \quad \frac{1.08\ g}{1\ mL} \quad g_{H_2O} = g_{soln} - g_{NaCl} \quad \frac{1\ kg}{1000\ g}$$

mol, $V \rightarrow$ **M and mol,** $kg_{H_2O} \rightarrow m$ **and** $g_{soln}\ g_{NaCl} \rightarrow$ **mass percent**

$$M = \frac{\text{amount solute (moles)}}{\text{volume solution (L)}} \quad m = \frac{\text{amount solute (moles)}}{\text{mass solvent (kg)}} \quad \text{mass percent} = \frac{\text{mass solute}}{\text{mass solution}} \times 100\%$$

Solution: $112\ \cancel{g\ NaCl} \times \frac{1\ mol\ NaCl}{58.44\ \cancel{g\ NaCl}} = 1.9\underline{1}64956$ mol NaCl and

$$1.00\ \cancel{L} \times \frac{1000\ \cancel{mL}}{1\ \cancel{L}} \times \frac{1.08\ g}{1\ \cancel{mL}} = 10\underline{8}0\ g\ soln\ and$$

$$g_{H_2O} = g_{soln} - g_{NaCl} = 10\underline{8}0\ g - 112\ g = 9\underline{6}8\ \cancel{g\ H_2O} \times \frac{1\ kg}{1000\ \cancel{g}} = 0.9\underline{6}8\ kg\ H_2O\ then$$

$$M = \frac{\text{amount solute (moles)}}{\text{volume solution (L)}} = \frac{1.9\underline{1}64956\ mol\ NaCl}{1.00\ L\ soln} = 1.92\ M\ and$$

$$m = \frac{\text{amount solute (moles)}}{\text{mass solvent (kg)}} = \frac{1.9\underline{1}64956\ mol\ NaCl}{0.9\underline{6}8\ kg\ H_2O} = 2.0\ m\ and$$

$$\text{mass percent} = \frac{\text{mass solute}}{\text{mass solution}} \times 100\% = \frac{112\ g\ NaCl}{10\underline{8}0\ g\ soln} \times 100\% = 10.4\%\ \text{by mass.}$$

Check: The units (M, *m*, and percent by mass) are correct. The magnitude of the answer (2 M) seems reasonable since we have 112 g NaCl, which is a couple of moles and we have 1 L. The magnitude of the answer (2 *m*) seems reasonable since it is a little higher than the molarity, which we expect since we only use the solvent weight in the denominator. The magnitude of the answer (10%) seems reasonable since we have 112 g NaCl and just over 1000 g of solution.

12.52 **Given:** KNO_3 and water; 72.5 g KNO_3 in 2.00 L solution **Find:** M, *m*, and mass percent
Other: d = 1.05 g/mL
Conceptual Plan: $g_{KNO_3} \rightarrow$ **mol and L** $\rightarrow$ **mL** $\rightarrow g_{soln}$ **and** $g_{soln}\ g_{KNO_3} \rightarrow g_{H_2O} \rightarrow kg_{H_2O}$ **then**

$$\frac{1\ mol\ KNO_3}{101.11\ g\ KNO_3} \quad \frac{1000\ mL}{1\ L} \quad \frac{1.05\ g}{1\ mL} \quad g_{H_2O} = g_{soln} - g_{KNO_3} \quad \frac{1\ kg}{1000\ g}$$

mol, $V \rightarrow$ **M and mol,** $kg_{H_2O} \rightarrow m$ **and** $g_{soln}\ g_{KNO_3} \rightarrow$ **mass percent**

$$M = \frac{\text{amount solute (moles)}}{\text{volume solution (L)}} \quad m = \frac{\text{amount solute (moles)}}{\text{mass solvent (kg)}} \quad \text{mass percent} = \frac{\text{mass solute}}{\text{mass solution}} \times 100\%$$

Solution: $72.5\ \cancel{g\ NaCl} \times \frac{1\ mol\ KNO_3}{101.11\ \cancel{g\ KNO_3}} = 0.71\underline{7}04085$ mol KNO_3 and

$$2.00\ \cancel{L} \times \frac{1000\ \cancel{mL}}{1\ \cancel{L}} \times \frac{1.05\ g}{1\ \cancel{mL}} = 21\underline{0}0\ g\ soln\ and$$

$$g_{H_2O} = g_{soln} - g_{KNO_3} = 21\underline{0}0\ g - 72.5\ g = 202\underline{7}.5\ \cancel{g\ H_2O} \times \frac{1\ kg}{1000\ \cancel{g}} = 2.0\underline{2}75\ kg\ H_2O\ then$$

$$M = \frac{\text{amount solute (moles)}}{\text{volume solution (L)}} = \frac{0.71\underline{7}04085\ mol\ KNO_3}{2.00\ L\ soln} = 0.358\ M\ and$$

$$m = \frac{\text{amount solute (moles)}}{\text{mass solvent (kg)}} = \frac{0.71\underline{7}04085\ mol\ KNO_3}{2.0\underline{2}75\ kg\ H_2O} = 0.354\ m\ and$$

$$\text{mass percent} = \frac{\text{mass solute}}{\text{mass solution}} \times 100\% = \frac{72.5 \text{ g KNO}_3}{21\underline{0}0 \text{ g soln}} \times 100\% = 3.45\% \text{ by mass.}$$

Check: The units (M, *m*, and percent by mass) are correct. The magnitude of the answer (0.358 M) seems reasonable since we have 72.5 g KNO_3, which is less than a mole and we have 2 L. The magnitude of the answer (0.345 *m*) seems reasonable since it is a little higher than the molarity, which we expect since we only use the solvent weight in the denominator. The magnitude of the answer (3.45%) seems reasonable since we have 72.5 g KNO_3 and ~ 2010 g of solution.

12.53 **Given:** initial solution: 50.0 mL of 5.00 M KI; final solution contains: 3.05 g KI in 25.0 mL
Find: final volume to dilute initial solution to
Conceptual Plan: final solution: $g_{KI} \rightarrow$ **mol and mL** $\rightarrow$ **L then mol,** $V \rightarrow M_2$ **then** $M_1, V_1, M_2 \rightarrow V_2$

$$\frac{1 \text{ mol KI}}{166.006 \text{ g KI}} \qquad \frac{1 \text{ L}}{1000 \text{ mL}} \qquad M = \frac{\text{amount solute (moles)}}{\text{volume solution (L)}} \qquad M_1V_1 = M_2V_2$$

Solution: $3.05 \text{ g KI} \times \frac{1 \text{ mol KI}}{166.006 \text{ g KI}} = 0.018\underline{3}7283 \text{ mol KI}$ and $25.0 \text{ mL} \times \frac{1 \text{ L}}{1000 \text{ mL}} = 0.0250 \text{ mL}$

then $M = \frac{\text{amount solute (moles)}}{\text{volume solution (L)}} = \frac{0.018\underline{3}7283 \text{ mol KI}}{0.0250 \text{L soln}} = 0.73\underline{4}9132 \text{ M}$ then $M_1V_1 = M_2V_2$.

Rearrange to solve for V_2. $V_2 = \frac{M_1}{M_2} \times V_1 = \frac{5.00 \text{ M}}{0.73\underline{4}9132 \text{ M}} \times 50.0 \text{ mL} = 340. \text{ mL}$ diluted volume.

Check: The units (mL) are correct. The magnitude of the answer (340 mL) seems reasonable since we are starting with a concentration of 5 M and ending with a concentration of less than 1 M.

12.54 **Given:** initial solution: 125 mL of 8.00 M $CuCl_2$; final solution contains: 4.67 g $CuCl_2$ in 50.0 mL
Find: final volume to dilute initial solution to
Conceptual Plan: final Solution: $g_{CuCl_2} \rightarrow$ **mol and mL** $\rightarrow$ **L then mol,** $V \rightarrow M_2$ **then** $M_1, V_1, M_2 \rightarrow V_2$

$$\frac{1 \text{ mol CuCl}_2}{134.45 \text{ g CuCl}_2} \qquad \frac{1 \text{ L}}{1000 \text{ mL}} \qquad M = \frac{\text{amount solute (moles)}}{\text{volume solution (L)}} \qquad M_1V_1 = M_2V_2$$

Solution: $4.67 \text{ g CuCl}_2 \times \frac{1 \text{ mol CuCl}_2}{134.45 \text{ g CuCl}_2} = 0.034\underline{7}3410 \text{ mol CuCl}_2$ and $50.0 \text{ mL} \times \frac{1 \text{ L}}{1000 \text{ mL}} = 0.0500 \text{ mL}$

then $M = \frac{\text{amount solute (moles)}}{\text{volume solution (L)}} = \frac{0.034\underline{7}3410 \text{ mol CuCl}_2}{0.0500 \text{ L soln}} = 0.69\underline{4}6820 \text{ M}$ then $M_1V_1 = M_2V_2$.

Rearrange to solve for V_2.

$V_2 = \frac{M_1}{M_2} \times V_1 = \frac{8.00 \text{ M}}{0.69\underline{4}6820 \text{ M}} \times 125 \text{ mL} = 1440 \text{ mL}$ diluted volume.

Check: The units (mL) are correct. The magnitude of the answer (1440 mL) seems reasonable since we are starting with a concentration of 8 M and ending with a concentration of less than 1 M.

12.55 **Given:** $AgNO_3$ and water; 3.4% Ag by mass, 4.8 L solution **Find:** *m* (Ag) **Other:** *d* = 1.01 g/mL
Conceptual Plan: **L** $\rightarrow$ **mL** $\rightarrow g_{soln} \rightarrow g_{Ag}$

$$\frac{1000 \text{ mL}}{1 \text{ L}} \qquad \frac{1.01 \text{ g}}{1 \text{ mL}} \qquad \frac{3.4 \text{ g Ag}}{100 \text{ g soln}}$$

Solution: $4.8 \text{ L} \times \frac{1000 \text{ mL}}{1 \text{ L}} \times \frac{1.01 \text{ g}}{1 \text{ mL}} = 4\underline{8}48 \text{ g soln}$ then

$4\underline{8}48 \text{ g soln} \times \frac{3.4 \text{ g Ag}}{100 \text{ g soln}} = 160 \text{ g Ag} = 1.6 \times 10^2 \text{ g Ag}.$

Check: The units (g) are correct. The magnitude of the answer (160 g) seems reasonable since we have almost 5000 g solution.

12.56 **Given:** dioxin and water; 0.085% dioxin by mass, 2.5 L solution **Find:** *m* (dioxin) **Other:** *d* = 1.00 g/mL
Conceptual Plan: **L** $\rightarrow$ **mL** $\rightarrow g_{soln} \rightarrow g_{dioxin}$

$$\frac{1000 \text{ mL}}{1 \text{ L}} \qquad \frac{1.01 \text{ g}}{1 \text{ mL}} \qquad \frac{0.085 \text{ g dioxin}}{100 \text{ g soln}}$$

Solution: $2.5 \text{ L} \times \frac{1000 \text{ mL}}{1 \text{ L}} \times \frac{1.00 \text{ g}}{1 \text{ mL}} = 2\underline{5}00 \text{ g soln}$ then $2\underline{5}00 \text{ g soln} \times \frac{0.085 \text{ g dioxin}}{100 \text{ g soln}} = 2.1 \text{ g dioxin}.$

Check: The units (g) are correct. The magnitude of the answer (2 g) seems reasonable since we have 2500 g solution and a low concentration.

12.57 **Given:** Ca^{2+} and water; 0.0085% Ca^{2+} by mass, 1.2 g Ca **Find:** m (water)

Conceptual Plan: $g_{Ca} \rightarrow g_{soln} \rightarrow g_{H_2O}$

$$\frac{100\text{ g soln}}{0.0085\text{ g Ca}} \qquad g_{H_2O} = g_{soln} - g_{Ca}$$

Solution: $1.2\ \cancel{\text{g Ca}} \times \dfrac{100\text{ g soln}}{0.0085\ \cancel{\text{g Ca}}} = 14\underline{1}18\text{ g soln then}$

$g_{H_2O} = g_{soln} - g_{Ca} = 14\underline{1}18\text{ g} - 1.2\text{ g} = 1.4 \times 10^4\text{ g water.}$

Check: The units (g) are correct. The magnitude of the answer (10^4 g) seems reasonable since we have such a low concentration of Ca.

12.58 **Given:** Pb and water; 0.0011 % Pb by mass, 150 mg Pb **Find:** V (mL) **Other:** d = 1.00 g/mL

Conceptual Plan: $mg_{Pb} \rightarrow g_{Pb} \rightarrow g_{soln} \rightarrow mL$

$$\frac{1000\text{ g}}{1\text{ mg}} \qquad \frac{100\text{ g soln}}{0.0011\text{ g Pb}} \qquad \frac{1\text{ mL}}{1.00\text{ g}}$$

Solution: $150\ \cancel{\text{mg Pb}} \times \dfrac{1\ \cancel{\text{g Pb}}}{1000\ \cancel{\text{mg Pb}}} \times \dfrac{100\ \cancel{\text{g soln}}}{0.0011\ \cancel{\text{g Pb}}} \times \dfrac{1\text{mL}}{1.00\ \cancel{\text{g}}} = 1.4 \times 10^4\text{ mL}$

Check: The units (mL) are correct. The magnitude of the answer (10^4 g) seems reasonable since we have such a low concentration of Pb.

12.59 **Given:** concentrated HNO_3: 70.3% HNO_3 by mass, d = 1.41 g/mL; final solution: 1.15 L of 0.100 M HNO_3

Find: describe final solution preparation

Conceptual Plan: $M_2, V_2 \rightarrow mol_{HNO_3} \rightarrow g_{HNO_3} \rightarrow g_{conc\ acid} \rightarrow mL_{conc\ acid}$ **then describe method**

$$mol = MV \qquad \frac{63.02\text{ g HNO}_3}{1\text{ mol HNO}_3} \qquad \frac{100\text{ g conc acid}}{70.3\text{ g HNO}_3} \qquad \frac{1\text{ mL}}{1.41\text{ g}}$$

Solution: $mol = M\,V = 0.100\dfrac{\text{mol HNO}_3}{1\ \cancel{\text{L soln}}} \times 1.15\ \cancel{\text{L soln}} = 0.115\text{ mol HNO}_3\text{ then}$

$$0.115\ \cancel{\text{mol HNO}_3} \times \frac{63.02\ \cancel{\text{g HNO}_3}}{1\ \cancel{\text{mol HNO}_3}} \times \frac{100\ \cancel{\text{g conc acid}}}{70.3\ \cancel{\text{g HNO}_3}} \times \frac{1\text{ mL conc acid}}{1.41\ \cancel{\text{g conc acid}}} = 7.31\text{ mL conc acid.}$$

Prepare the solution by putting about 1.00 L of distilled water in a container. Carefully pour in the 7.31 mL of the concentrated acid, mix the solution, and allow it to cool. Finally add enough water to generate the total volume of solution (1.15 L). It is important to add acid to water, and not the reverse, since there is such a large amount of heat released upon mixing.

Check: The units (mL) are correct. The magnitude of the answer (7 g) seems reasonable since we are starting with such a very concentrated solution and diluting it to a low concentration.

12.60 **Given:** concentrated HCl: 37.0 % HCl by mass, d = 1.20 g/mL; final solution: 2.85 L of 0.500 M HCl

Find: describe final solution preparation

Conceptual Plan: $M_2, V_2 \rightarrow mol_{HCl} \rightarrow g_{HCl} \rightarrow g_{conc\ acid} \rightarrow mL_{conc\ acid}$ **then describe method**

$$mol = M\,V \qquad \frac{36.46\text{ g HCl}}{1\text{ mol HCl}} \qquad \frac{100\text{ g conc acid}}{37.0\text{ g HCl}} \qquad \frac{1\text{ mL}}{1.20\text{ g}}$$

Solution: $mol = M\,V = 0.500\dfrac{\text{mol HCl}}{1\ \cancel{\text{L soln}}} \times 2.85\ \cancel{\text{L soln}} = 1.4\underline{2}5\text{ mol HCl then}$

$$1.4\underline{2}5\ \cancel{\text{mol HCl}} \times \frac{36.46\ \cancel{\text{g HCl}}}{1\ \cancel{\text{mol HCl}}} \times \frac{100\ \cancel{\text{g conc acid}}}{37.0\ \cancel{\text{g HCl}}} \times \frac{1\text{ mL conc acid}}{1.20\ \cancel{\text{g conc acid}}} = 117\text{ mL conc acid.}$$

Prepare the solution by putting about 2.5 L of distilled water in a container. Carefully pour in the 117 mL of the concentrated acid, mix the solution, and allow it to cool. Finally add enough water to generate the total volume of solution required. It is important to add acid to water, and not the reverse, since there is such a large amount of heat released upon mixing.

Check: The units (mL) are correct. The magnitude of the answer (117 g) seems reasonable since we are starting with such a concentrated solution and diluting it to a low concentration.

12.61 (a) **Given:** 1.00×10^2 mL of 0.500 M KCl **Find:** describe final solution preparation

Conceptual Plan: $mL \rightarrow L$ **then** $M, V \rightarrow mol_{KCl} \rightarrow g_{KCl}$ **then describe method**

$$\frac{1\text{ L}}{1000\text{ mL}} \qquad mol = M\,V \qquad \frac{74.56\text{ g KCl}}{1\text{ mol KCl}}$$

Solution: $1.00 \times 10^2\ \text{mL} \times \dfrac{1\ \text{L}}{1000\ \text{mL}} = 0.100\ \text{L}$

$mol = M\,V = 0.500\,\dfrac{\text{mol KCl}}{1\ \text{L soln}} \times 0.100\ \text{L soln} = 0.0500\ \text{mol KCl}$

then $0.0500\ \text{mol KCl} \times \dfrac{74.56\ \text{g KCl}}{1\ \text{mol KCl}} = 3.73\ \text{g KCl}.$

Prepare the solution by carefully adding 3.73 g KCl to a 100 mL volumetric flask. Add ~ 75 mL of distilled water and agitate the solution until the salt dissolves completely. Finally add enough water to generate a total volume of solution (add water to the mark on the flask).

Check: The units (g) are correct. The magnitude of the answer (4 g) seems reasonable since we are making a small volume of solution and the formula weight of KCl is ~ 75 g/mol.

(b) **Given:** 1.00×10^2 g of 0.500 m KCl **Find:** describe final solution preparation

Conceptual Plan:

$m \rightarrow \textbf{mol}_{\textbf{KCl}}\ \textbf{/1 kg solvent} \rightarrow \textbf{g}_{\textbf{KCl}}\textbf{/1 kg solvent then g}_{\textbf{KCl}}\textbf{/1 kg solvent, g}_{\textbf{soln}} \rightarrow \textbf{g}_{\textbf{KCl}}, \textbf{g}_{\textbf{H}_2\textbf{O}}$

$m = \dfrac{\text{amount solute (moles)}}{\text{mass solvent (kg)}}$ $\quad \dfrac{74.56\ \text{g KCl}}{1\ \text{mol KCl}}$ $\quad g_{soln} = g_{KCl} + g_{H_2O}$

then describe method

Solution: $m = \dfrac{\text{amount solute (moles)}}{\text{mass solvent (kg)}}$ so $0.500\ m = \dfrac{0.500\ \text{mol KCl}}{1\ \text{kg H}_2\text{O}}$ so

$\dfrac{0.500\ \text{mol KCl}}{1\ \text{kg H}_2\text{O}} \times \dfrac{74.56\ \text{g KCl}}{1\ \text{mol KCl}} = \dfrac{37.2\underline{8}\ \text{g KCl}}{1000\ \text{g H}_2\text{O}}$ $\quad g_{soln} = g_{KCl} + g_{H_2O}$ so $g_{soln} - g_{KCl} = g_{H_2O}$

substitute into ratio $\dfrac{37.28\ \text{g KCl}}{1037.28\ \text{g solution}} = \dfrac{x\ \text{g KCl}}{500\ \text{g solution}}$. Cross multiply, and solve for grams KCl.

$0.037\underline{2}8(100\ \text{g soln} - x\ \text{g KCl}) = x\ \text{g KCl} \rightarrow 3.7\underline{2}8 - 0.037\underline{2}8\,(x\ \text{g KCl}) = x\ \text{g KCl} \rightarrow$

$3.7\underline{2}8 = 1.037\underline{2}8\,(x\ \text{g KCl}) \rightarrow \dfrac{3.7\underline{2}8}{1.037\underline{2}8} = x\ \text{g KCl} = 3.59\ \text{g KCl}$ then

$g_{H_2O} = g_{soln} - g_{KCl} = 100.\ \text{g} - 3.59\ \text{g} = 96.41\ \text{g H}_2\text{O}.$

Prepare the solution by carefully adding 3.59 g KCl to a container with 96.41 g of distilled water and agitate the solution until the salt dissolves completely.

Check: The units (g) are correct. The magnitude of the answer (3.6 g) seems reasonable since we are making a small volume of solution and the formula weight of KCl is ~ 75 g/mol.

(c) **Given:** 1.00×10^2 g of 5.0 % KCl by mass **Find:** describe final solution preparation

Conceptual Plan: $\textbf{g}_{\textbf{soln}} \rightarrow \textbf{g}_{\textbf{KCl}}$ **then** $\textbf{g}_{\textbf{KCl}}, \textbf{g}_{\textbf{soln}} \rightarrow \textbf{g}_{\textbf{H}_2\textbf{O}}$

$\dfrac{5.0\ \text{g KCl}}{100\ \text{g soln}}$ $\quad g_{soln} = g_{KCl} + g_{H_2O}$

then describe method

Solution: $1.00 \times 10^2\ \text{g soln} \times \dfrac{5.0\ \text{g KCl}}{100\ \text{g soln}} = 5.0\ \text{g KCl}$ then $g_{soln} = g_{KCl} + g_{H_2O}$.

So $g_{H_2O} = g_{soln} - g_{KCl} = 100.\ \text{g} - 5.0\ \text{g} = 95\ \text{g H}_2\text{O}.$

Prepare the solution by carefully adding 5.0 g KCl to a container with 95 g of distilled water and agitate the solution until the salt dissolves completely.

Check: The units (g) are correct. The magnitude of the answer (5 g) seems reasonable since we are making a small volume of solution and the solution is 5 % by mass KCl.

12.62 (a) **Given:** 125 mL of 0.100 M $NaNO_3$ **Find:** describe final solution preparation

Conceptual Plan: mL $\rightarrow$ L then $M, V \rightarrow \textbf{mol}_{\textbf{NaNO}_3} \rightarrow \textbf{g}_{\textbf{NaNO}_3}$ then describe method

$\dfrac{1\ \text{L}}{1000\ \text{mL}}$ $\quad mol = M\,V$ $\quad \dfrac{85.00\ \text{g NaNO}_3}{1\ \text{mol NaNO}_3}$

Solution: $125\ \text{mL} \times \dfrac{1\ \text{L}}{1000\ \text{mL}} = 0.125\ \text{L}$

$\text{mol} = M\,V = 0.100\,\dfrac{\text{mol NaNO}_3}{1\ \text{L soln}} \times 0.125\ \text{L soln} = 0.0125\ \text{mol NaNO}_3$ then

$0.0125\ \text{mol NaNO}_3 \times \dfrac{85.00\ \text{g NaNO}_3}{1\ \text{mol NaNO}_3} = 1.06\ \text{g NaNO}_3.$

Prepare the solution by carefully adding 1.06 g $NaNO_3$ to a container. Add ~ 100 mL of distilled water and agitate the solution until the salt dissolves completely. Finally add enough water to generate a total volume of solution (125 mL).
Check: The units (g) are correct. The magnitude of the answer (7 g) seems reasonable since we are making a small volume of solution and the formula weight of KCl is ~ 75 g/mol.

(b) **Given:** 125 g of 0.100 m $NaNO_3$ **Find:** describe final solution preparation
Conceptual Plan: $m \rightarrow$ **mol** $_{NaNO_3}$ **/1 kg solvent** $\rightarrow$ **g** $_{NaNO_3}$**/1 kg solvent then**

$$m = \frac{\text{amount solute (moles)}}{\text{mass solvent (kg)}} \qquad \frac{85.00 \text{ g NaNO}_3}{1 \text{ mol NaNO}_3}$$

g $_{NaNO_3}$**/1 kg solvent,** $g_{soln} \rightarrow g_{NaNO_3}, g_{H_2O}$ **then describe method**

$$g_{soln} = g_{NaNO_3} + g_{H_2O}$$

Solution: $m = \dfrac{\text{amount solute (moles)}}{\text{mass solvent (kg)}}$ so $0.100\ m = \dfrac{0.500 \text{ mol NaNO}_3}{1 \text{ kg H}_2\text{O}}$ so

$\dfrac{0.100 \text{ mol NaNO}_3}{1 \text{ kg H}_2\text{O}} \times \dfrac{85.00 \text{ g NaNO}_3}{1 \text{ mol NaNO}_3} = \dfrac{8.5\underline{0} \text{ g NaNO}_3}{1000 \text{ g H}_2\text{O}}$ then $g_{soln} = g_{NaNO_3} + g_{H_2O}$ so

$g_{soln} - g_{NaNO_3} = g_{H_2O}$ substitute into ratio $\dfrac{0.0085\underline{0} \text{ g NaNO}_3}{1 \text{ g H}_2\text{O}} = \dfrac{x \text{ g NaNO}_3}{125 \text{ g soln} - x \text{ g NaNO}_3}$.

Rearrange and solve for x g $NaNO_3$ $0.00850(125 \text{ g soln} - x \text{ g NaNO}_3) = x \text{ g NaNO}_3 \rightarrow$
$1.0625 - 0.00850\,(x \text{ g NaNO}_3) = x \text{ g NaNO}_3 \rightarrow 1.0\underline{6}25 = 1.00850\,(x \text{ g NaNO}_3) \rightarrow$
$\dfrac{1.0\underline{6}25}{1.00850} = x \text{ g NaNO}_3 = 1.05 \text{ g NaNO}_3$ then $g_{H_2O} = g_{soln} - g_{NaNO_3} = 125 \text{ g} - 1.05 \text{ g} = 124 \text{ g H}_2\text{O}$.
Prepare the solution by carefully adding 1.05 g $NaNO_3$ to a container with 124 g of distilled water and agitate the solution until the salt dissolves completely.
Check: The units (g) are correct. The magnitude of the answer (1 g) seems reasonable since we are making a small volume of solution and the formula weight of $NaNO_3$ is 85 g/mol.

(c) **Given:** 125 g of 1.0 % $NaNO_3$ by mass **Find:** describe final solution preparation
Conceptual Plan: $g_{soln} \rightarrow$ **g** $_{NaNO_3}$ **then g** $_{NaNO_3}, g_{soln} \rightarrow g_{H_2O}$

$$\frac{1.0 \text{ g NaNO}_3}{100 \text{ g soln}} \qquad g_{soln} = g_{NaNO_3} + g_{H_2O}$$

then describe method
Solution: $125 \text{ g soln} \times \dfrac{1.0 \text{ g NaNO}_3}{100 \text{ g soln}} = 1.\underline{2}5 \text{ g NaNO}_3$ then $g_{soln} = g_{NaNO_3} + g_{H_2O}$. So

$g_{H_2O} = g_{soln} - g_{NaNO_3} = 125 \text{ g} - 1.25 \text{ g} = 124 \text{ g H}_2\text{O}$.
Prepare the solution by carefully adding 1.3 g $NaNO_3$ to a container with 124 g of distilled water and agitate the solution until the salt dissolves completely.
Check: The units (g) are correct. The magnitude of the answer (1 g) seems reasonable since we are making a small volume of solution and the solution is 1% by mass $NaNO_3$.

12.63 (a) **Given:** 28.4 g of glucose ($C_6H_{12}O_6$) in 355 g water; final volume = 378 mL **Find:** molarity
Conceptual Plan: mL $\rightarrow$ **L and g** $_{C_6H_{12}O_6} \rightarrow$ **mol** $_{C_6H_{12}O_6}$ **then mol** $_{C_6H_{12}O_6}, V \rightarrow$ **M**

$$\frac{1 \text{ L}}{1000 \text{ mL}} \qquad \frac{1 \text{ mol C}_6\text{H}_{12}\text{O}_6}{180.16 \text{ g C}_6\text{H}_{12}\text{O}_6} \qquad M = \frac{\text{amount solute (moles)}}{\text{volume solution (L)}}$$

Solution: $378 \text{ mL} \times \dfrac{1 \text{ L}}{1000 \text{ mL}} = 0.378 \text{ L}$ and

$28.4 \text{ g C}_6\text{H}_{12}\text{O}_6 \times \dfrac{1 \text{ mol C}_6\text{H}_{12}\text{O}_6}{180.16 \text{ g C}_6\text{H}_{12}\text{O}_6} = 0.15\underline{7}638 \text{ mol C}_6\text{H}_{12}\text{O}_6$

$M = \dfrac{\text{amount solute (moles)}}{\text{volume solution (L)}} = \dfrac{0.15\underline{7}638 \text{ mol C}_6\text{H}_{12}\text{O}_6}{0.378 \text{ L}} = 0.417 \text{ M}$

Check: The units (M) are correct. The magnitude of the answer (0.4 M) seems reasonable since we have 1/8 mole in about 1/3 L.

(b) **Given:** 28.4 g of glucose ($C_6H_{12}O_6$) in 355 g water; final volume = 378 mL **Find:** molality
Conceptual Plan: g $_{H_2O} \rightarrow$ **kg** $_{H_2O}$ **and g** $_{C_6H_{12}O_6} \rightarrow$ **mol** $_{C_6H_{12}O_6}$ **then mol** $_{C_6H_{12}O_6}$, **kg** $_{H_2O} \rightarrow m$

$$\frac{1 \text{ kg}}{1000 \text{ g}} \qquad \frac{1 \text{ mol C}_6\text{H}_{12}\text{O}_6}{180.16 \text{ g C}_6\text{H}_{12}\text{O}_6} \qquad m = \frac{\text{amount solute (moles)}}{\text{mass solvent (kg)}}$$

Solution: $355 \text{ g} \times \frac{1 \text{ kg}}{1000 \text{ g}} = 0.355 \text{ kg}$ and

$$28.4 \text{ g } C_6H_{12}O_6 \times \frac{1 \text{ mol } C_6H_{12}O_6}{180.16 \text{ g } C_6H_{12}O_6} = 0.157638 \text{ mol } C_6H_{12}O_6$$

$$m = \frac{\text{amount solute (moles)}}{\text{mass solvent (kg)}} = \frac{0.157638 \text{ mol } C_6H_{12}O_6}{0.355 \text{ kg}} = 0.444\ m$$

Check: The units (m) are correct. The magnitude of the answer (0.4 m) seems reasonable since we have 1/8 mole in about 1/3 kg.

(c) **Given:** 28.4 g of glucose ($C_6H_{12}O_6$) in 355 g water; final volume = 378 mL **Find:** percent by mass
Conceptual Plan: $\mathbf{g}_{C_6H_{12}O_6}, \mathbf{g}_{H_2O} \rightarrow \mathbf{g}_{soln}$ **then** $\mathbf{g}_{C_6H_{12}O_6}, \mathbf{g}_{soln} \rightarrow$ **percent by mass**

$g_{soln} = g_{C_6H_{12}O_6} + g_{H_2O}$ $\quad$ $\text{mass percent} = \frac{\text{mass solute}}{\text{mass solution}} \times 100\%$

Solution: $g_{soln} = g_{C_6H_{12}O_6} + g_{H_2O} = 28.4 \text{ g} + 355 \text{ g} = 383.4 \text{ g soln}$ then

$$\text{mass percent} = \frac{\text{mass solute}}{\text{mass solution}} \times 100\% = \frac{28.4 \text{ g } C_6H_{12}O_6}{383.4 \text{ g soln}} \times 100\% = 7.41 \text{ percent by mass.}$$

Check: The units (percent by mass) are correct. The magnitude of the answer (7%) seems reasonable since we are dissolving 28 g in 355 g.

(d) **Given:** 28.4 g of glucose ($C_6H_{12}O_6$) in 355 g water; final volume = 378 mL **Find:** mole fraction
Conceptual Plan:
$\mathbf{g}_{C_6H_{12}O_6} \rightarrow \mathbf{mol}_{C_6H_{12}O_6}$ **and** $\mathbf{g}_{H_2O} \rightarrow \mathbf{mol}_{H_2O}$ **then mol** $_{C_6H_{12}O_6}, \mathbf{mol}_{H_2O} \rightarrow \chi_{C_6H_{12}O_6}$

$\frac{1 \text{ mol } C_6H_{12}O_6}{180.16 \text{ g } C_6H_{12}O_6}$ $\quad$ $\frac{1 \text{ mol } H_2O}{18.02 \text{ g } H_2O}$ $\quad$ $\chi = \frac{\text{amount solute (in moles)}}{\text{total amount of solute and solvent (in moles)}}$

Solution: $28.4 \text{ g } C_6H_{12}O_6 \times \frac{1 \text{ mol } C_6H_{12}O_6}{180.16 \text{ g } C_6H_{12}O_6} = 0.157638 \text{ mol } C_6H_{12}O_6$ and

$$355 \text{ g } H_2O \times \frac{1 \text{ mol } H_2O}{18.02 \text{ g } H_2O} = 19.7003 \text{ mol } H_2O \text{ then}$$

$$\chi = \frac{\text{amount solute (in moles)}}{\text{total amount of solute and solvent (in moles)}} = \frac{0.157638 \text{ mol}}{0.157638 \text{ mol} + 19.7003 \text{ mol}} = 0.00794$$

Check: The units (none) are correct. The magnitude of the answer (0.008) seems reasonable since we have many more grams of water and water has a much lower molecular weight.

(e) **Given:** 28.4 g of glucose ($C_6H_{12}O_6$) in 355 g water; final volume = 378 mL **Find:** mole percent
Conceptual Plan: use answer from part d) then $\chi_{C_6H_{12}O_6} \rightarrow$ **mole percent**

$\chi \times 100\%$

Solution: mole percent = $\chi \times 100\% = 0.00794 \times 100\% = 0.794$ mole percent
Check: The units (%) are correct. The magnitude of the answer (0.8) seems reasonable since we have many more grams of water, water has a much lower molecular weight, than glucose, and we are increasing the answer from part d) by a factor of 100.

12.64 (a) **Given:** 20.2 mL of methanol (CH_3OH) in 100.0 mL water; final volume = 118 mL **Find:** molarity
Other: d (CH_3OH) = 0.782 g/mL; d (H_2O) = 1.00 g/mL
Conceptual Plan: mL $\rightarrow$ **L and** $\mathbf{mL}_{CH_3OH} \rightarrow \mathbf{g}_{CH_3OH} \rightarrow \mathbf{mol}_{CH_3OH}$ **then mol** $_{CH_3OH}, V \rightarrow$ **M**

$\frac{1 \text{ L}}{1000 \text{ mL}}$ $\quad$ $\frac{0.782 \text{ g}}{1 \text{ mL}}$ $\quad$ $\frac{1 \text{ mol } CH_3OH}{32.04 \text{ g } CH_3OH}$ $\quad$ $M = \frac{\text{amount solute (moles)}}{\text{volume solution (L)}}$

Solution: $118 \text{ mL} \times \frac{1 \text{ L}}{1000 \text{ mL}} = 0.118 \text{ L}$ and

$$20.2 \text{ mL } CH_3OH \times \frac{0.782 \text{ g } CH_3OH}{1 \text{ mL } CH_3OH} \times \frac{1 \text{ mol } CH_3OH}{32.04 \text{ g } CH_3OH} = 0.493021 \text{ mol } CH_3OH$$

$$M = \frac{\text{amount solute (moles)}}{\text{volume solution (L)}} = \frac{0.493021 \text{ mol } CH_3OH}{0.118 \text{ L}} = 4.18 \text{ M}$$

Check: The units (M) are correct. The magnitude of the answer (4 M) seems reasonable since we have 1/2 mole in about 1/8 L.

(b)   **Given:** 20.2 mL of methanol (CH_3OH) in 100.0 mL water; final volume = 118 mL **Find:** molality
Other: d (CH_3OH) = 0.782 g/mL; d (H_2O) = 1.00 g/mL
Conceptual Plan:

$mL_{CH_3OH} \rightarrow g_{CH_3OH} \rightarrow mol_{CH_3OH}$ and $mL_{H_2O} \rightarrow g_{H_2O} \rightarrow kg_{H_2O}$ then mol $_{CH_3OH}$, $kg_{H_2O} \rightarrow m$

$\dfrac{0.782\ g}{1\ mL}$ $\dfrac{1\ mol\ CH_3OH}{32.04\ g\ CH_3OH}$ $\dfrac{1.00\ g}{1\ mL}$ $\dfrac{1\ kg}{1000\ g}$ $m = \dfrac{\text{amount solute (moles)}}{\text{mass solvent (kg)}}$

Solution: $20.2\ \overline{mL\ CH_3OH} \times \dfrac{0.782\ \overline{g\ CH_3OH}}{1\ \overline{mL\ CH_3OH}} \times \dfrac{1\ mol\ CH_3OH}{32.04\ \overline{g\ CH_3OH}} = 0.49\underline{3}021\ mol\ CH_3OH$ and

$100.0\ \overline{mL} \times \dfrac{1.00\ \overline{g}}{1\ \overline{mL}} \times \dfrac{1\ kg}{1000\ \overline{g}} = 0.1000\ kg$ then

$m = \dfrac{\text{amount solute (moles)}}{\text{mass solvent (kg)}} = \dfrac{0.49\underline{3}021\ mol\ CH_3OH}{0.1000\ kg} = 4.93\ m$

Check: The units (m) are correct. The magnitude of the answer (5 m) seems reasonable since we have 1/2 mole in 1/10 kg.

(c)   **Given:** 20.2 mL of methanol (CH_3OH) in 100.0 mL water; final volume = 118 mL **Find:** percent by mass
Other: d (CH_3OH) = 0.782 g/mL; d (H_2O) = 1.00 g/mL
Conceptual Plan: $mL_{CH_3OH} \rightarrow g_{CH_3OH}$ and $mL_{H_2O} \rightarrow g_{H_2O}$ then g $_{CH_3OH}$, $g_{H_2O} \rightarrow g_{soln}$ then

$\dfrac{0.782\ g}{1\ mL}$ $\dfrac{1.00\ g}{1\ mL}$ $g_{soln} = g_{C_6H_{12}O_6} + g_{H_2O}$

g $_{CH_3OH}$, $g_{soln} \rightarrow$ **percent by mass**

mass percent = $\dfrac{\text{mass solute}}{\text{mass solution}} \times 100\%$

Solution: $20.2\ \overline{mL\ CH_3OH} \times \dfrac{0.782\ g\ CH_3OH}{1\ \overline{mL\ CH_3OH}} = 15.\underline{7}964\ g\ CH_3OH$

$100.0\ \overline{mL} \times \dfrac{1.00\ g}{1\ \overline{mL}} = 100.0\ g$. $g_{soln} = g_{CH_3OH} + g_{H_2O} = 15.\underline{7}964\ g + 100.0\ g = 115.\underline{7}964\ g$ soln then

mass percent = $\dfrac{\text{mass solute}}{\text{mass solution}} \times 100\% = \dfrac{15.\underline{7}964\ \overline{g\ CH_3OH}}{115.\underline{7}964\ \overline{g\ soln}} \times 100\% = 13.6$ percent by mass

Check: The units (percent by mass) are correct. The magnitude of the answer (14%) seems reasonable since we are dissolving 16 g in 100 g.

(d)   **Given:** 20.2 mL of methanol (CH_3OH) in 100.0 mL water; final volume = 118 mL **Find:** mole fraction
Other: d (CH_3OH) = 0.782 g/mL; d (H_2O) = 1.00 g/mL
Conceptual Plan: $mL_{CH_3OH} \rightarrow g_{CH_3OH} \rightarrow mol_{CH_3OH}$ and $mL_{H_2O} \rightarrow g_{H_2O} \rightarrow mol_{H_2O}$ then

$\dfrac{0.782\ g}{1\ mL}$ $\dfrac{1\ mol\ CH_3OH}{32.04\ g\ CH_3OH}$ $\dfrac{1.00\ g}{1\ mL}$ $\dfrac{1\ mol\ H_2O}{18.01\ g\ H_2O}$

mol $_{CH_3OH}$, $mol_{H_2O} \rightarrow \chi_{CH_3OH}$

$\chi = \dfrac{\text{amount solute (in moles)}}{\text{total amount of solute and solvent (in moles)}}$

Solution: $20.2\ \overline{mL\ CH_3OH} \times \dfrac{0.782\ \overline{g\ CH_3OH}}{1\ \overline{mL\ CH_3OH}} \times \dfrac{1\ mol\ CH_3OH}{32.04\ \overline{g\ CH_3OH}} = 0.49\underline{3}021\ mol\ CH_3OH$ and

$100.0\ \overline{mL} \times \dfrac{1.00\ \overline{g}}{1\ \overline{mL}} \times \dfrac{1\ mol\ H_2O}{18.01\ \overline{g\ H_2O}} = 5.55\underline{2}471\ mol\ H_2O$ then

$\chi = \dfrac{\text{amount solute (in moles)}}{\text{total amount of solute and solvent (in moles)}} = \dfrac{0.49\underline{3}021\ \overline{mol}}{0.49\underline{3}021\ \overline{mol} + 5.55\underline{2}471\ \overline{mol}} = 0.0815$

Check: The units (none) are correct. The magnitude of the answer (0.08) seems reasonable since we have many more grams of water and water has a lower molecular weight than methanol.

(e)   **Given:** 20.2 mL of methanol (CH_3OH) in 100.0 mL water; final volume = 118 mL **Find:** mole percent
Other: d (CH_3OH) = 0.782 g/mL; d (H_2O) = 1.00 g/mL
Conceptual Plan: use answer from part d) then $\chi_{C_6H_{12}O_6} \rightarrow$ **mole percent**

$\chi \times 100\%$

Solution: mole percent = $\chi \times 100\% = 0.0815 \times 100\% = 8.15$ mole percent
Check: The units (%) are correct. The magnitude of the answer (8) seems reasonable since we have many more grams of water, water has a lower molecular weight than methanol, and we are increasing the answer from part d) by a factor of 100.

12.65   **Given:** 3.0 % H_2O_2 by mass, $d = 1.01$ g/mL   **Find:** molarity
Conceptual Plan:
Assume exactly 100 g of solution; $g_{solution} \rightarrow g_{H_2O_2} \rightarrow mol_{H_2O_2}$ and $g_{solution} \rightarrow mL_{solution} \rightarrow L_{solution}$

$$\frac{3.0 \text{ g } H_2O_2}{100 \text{ g solution}} \quad \frac{1 \text{ mol } H_2O_2}{34.02 \text{ g } H_2O_2} \qquad\qquad \frac{1 \text{ mL}}{1.01 \text{ g}} \quad \frac{1 \text{ L}}{1000 \text{ mL}}$$

then $mol_{H_2O_2}$, $L_{solution} \rightarrow M$

$$M = \frac{\text{amount solute (moles)}}{\text{volume solution (L)}}$$

Solution: $100 \text{ g solution} \times \dfrac{3.0 \text{ g } H_2O_2}{100 \text{ g solution}} \times \dfrac{1 \text{ mol } H_2O_2}{34.02 \text{ g } H_2O_2} = 0.08\underline{8}1834 \text{ mol } H_2O_2$ and

$100 \text{ g solution} \times \dfrac{1 \text{ mL solution}}{1.01 \text{ g solution}} \times \dfrac{1 \text{ L solution}}{1000 \text{ mL solution}} = 0.099\underline{0}099 \text{ L solution}$ then

$M = \dfrac{\text{amount solute (moles)}}{\text{volume solution (L)}} = \dfrac{0.08\underline{8}1834 \text{ mol } H_2O_2}{0.099\underline{0}099 \text{ L solution}} = 0.89 \text{ M } H_2O_2.$

Check: The units (M) are correct. The magnitude of the answer (1) seems reasonable since we are starting with a low concentration solution and pure water is ~ 55.5 M.

12.66   **Given:** 4.55 % NaOCl by mass, $d = 1.02$ g/mL   **Find:** molarity
Conceptual Plan: Assume exactly 100 g of solution; $g_{solution} \rightarrow g_{NaOCl} \rightarrow mol_{NaOCl}$ and $g_{solution} \rightarrow$

$$\frac{4.55 \text{ g NaOCl}}{100 \text{ g solution}} \quad \frac{1 \text{ mol NaOCl}}{74.44 \text{ g NaOCl}} \qquad\qquad \frac{1 \text{ mL}}{1.02 \text{ g}}$$

$mL_{solution} \rightarrow L_{solution}$ then mol_{NaOCl}, $L_{solution} \rightarrow M$

$$\frac{1 \text{ L}}{1000 \text{ mL}} \qquad\qquad M = \frac{\text{amount solute (moles)}}{\text{volume solution (L)}}$$

Solution: $100 \text{ g solution} \times \dfrac{4.55 \text{ g NaOCl}}{100 \text{ g solution}} \times \dfrac{1 \text{ mol NaOCl}}{74.44 \text{ g NaOCl}} = 0.06\underline{1}12305 \text{ mol NaOCl}$ and

$100 \text{ g solution} \times \dfrac{1 \text{ mL solution}}{1.02 \text{ g solution}} \times \dfrac{1 \text{ L solution}}{1000 \text{ mL solution}} = 0.098\underline{0}392 \text{ L solution}$ then

$M = \dfrac{\text{amount solute (moles)}}{\text{volume solution (L)}} = \dfrac{0.06\underline{1}12305 \text{ mol NaOCl}}{0.098\underline{0}392 \text{ L solution}} = 0.623 \text{ M NaOCl}.$

Check: The units (M) are correct. The magnitude of the answer (1) seems reasonable since we are starting with a low concentration solution and pure water is ~ 55.5 M.

12.67   **Given:** 36 % HCl by mass   **Find:** molality and mole fraction
Conceptual Plan: Assume exactly 100 g of solution; $g_{solution} \rightarrow g_{HCl} \rightarrow mol_{HCl}$ and g_{HCl}, $g_{solution} \rightarrow$

$$\frac{36 \text{ g HCl}}{100 \text{ g solution}} \quad \frac{1 \text{ mol HCl}}{36.46 \text{ g HCl}} \qquad\qquad g_{soln} = g_{HCl} + g_{H_2O}$$

$g_{solvent} \rightarrow kg_{solvent}$ then mol_{HCl}, $kg_{solvent} \rightarrow m$ and $g_{solvent} \rightarrow mol_{solvent}$ then mol_{HCl}, $mol_{solvent} \rightarrow \chi_{HCl}$

$$\frac{1 \text{ kg}}{1000 \text{ g}} \qquad m = \frac{\text{amount solute (moles)}}{\text{mass solvent (kg)}} \quad \frac{1 \text{ mol } H_2O}{18.02 \text{ g } H_2O} \quad \chi = \frac{\text{amount solute (in moles)}}{\text{total amount of solute and solvent (in moles)}}$$

Solution: $100 \text{ g solution} \times \dfrac{36 \text{ g HCl}}{100 \text{ g solution}} = 36 \text{ g HCl} \times \dfrac{1 \text{ mol HCl}}{36.46 \text{ g HCl}} = 0.9\underline{8}7383 \text{ mol HCl}$ and

$g_{soln} = g_{HCl} + g_{H_2O}$. Rearrange to solve for $g_{solvent}$. $g_{H_2O} = g_{soln} - g_{HCl} = 100 \text{ g} - 36 \text{ g} = 64 \text{ g } H_2O$

$64 \text{ g } H_2O \times \dfrac{1 \text{ kg } H_2O}{1000 \text{ g } H_2O} = 0.064 \text{ kg } H_2O$ then

$m = \dfrac{\text{amount solute (moles)}}{\text{mass solvent (kg)}} = \dfrac{0.9\underline{8}7383 \text{ mol HCl}}{0.064 \text{ kg}} = 15 \text{ } m \text{ HCl}$ and

$64 \text{ g } H_2O \times \dfrac{1 \text{ mol } H_2O}{18.02 \text{ g } H_2O} = 3.\underline{5}5161 \text{ mol } H_2O$ then

$\chi = \dfrac{\text{amount solvent (in moles)}}{\text{total amount of solute and solvent (in moles)}} = \dfrac{0.9\underline{8}7383 \text{ mol}}{0.9\underline{8}7383 \text{ mol} + 3.\underline{5}5161 \text{ mol}} = 0.22.$

Check: The units (m and unitless) are correct. The magnitudes of the answers (15 and 0.2) seem reasonable since we are starting with a high concentration solution and the molar mass of water is much less than that of HCl.

12.68 **Given:** 5.0 % NaCl by mass **Find:** molality and mole fraction

Conceptual Plan: Assume exactly 100 g of solution; $g_{solution} \rightarrow g_{HCl} \rightarrow mol_{NaCl}$ **and** $g_{NaCl}, g_{solution} \rightarrow$

$\frac{5.0\text{ gNaCl}}{100\text{ g solution}}$ $\frac{1\text{ mol NaCl}}{58.44\text{ g NaCl}}$ $g_{soln} = g_{NaCl} + g_{H_2O}$

$g_{solvent} \rightarrow kg_{solvent}$ **then** $mol_{NaCl}, kg_{solvent} \rightarrow m$ **and** $g_{solvent} \rightarrow mol_{solvent}$ **then** $mol_{NaCl}, mol_{solvent} \rightarrow \chi_{NaCl}$

$\frac{1\text{ kg}}{1000\text{ g}}$ $m = \frac{\text{amount solute (moles)}}{\text{mass solvent (kg)}}$ $\frac{1\text{ mol H}_2\text{O}}{18.02\text{ g H}_2\text{O}}$ $\chi = \frac{\text{amount solute (in moles)}}{\text{total amount of solute and solvent (in moles)}}$

Solution: $100\text{ g solution} \times \frac{5.0\text{ g NaCl}}{100\text{ g solution}} = 5.0\text{ g HCl} \times \frac{1\text{ mol NaCl}}{58.44\text{ g NaCl}} = 0.0855578\text{ mol NaCl}$ and

$g_{soln} = g_{NaCl} + g_{H_2O}$ Rearrange to solve for $g_{solvent}$. $g_{H_2O} = g_{soln} - g_{NaCl} = 100.0\text{ g} - 5.0\text{ g} = 95.0\text{ g H}_2\text{O}$

$95.0\text{ g H}_2\text{O} \times \frac{1\text{ kg H}_2\text{O}}{1000\text{ g H}_2\text{O}} = 0.0950\text{ kg H}_2\text{O}$ then

$m = \frac{\text{amount solute (moles)}}{\text{mass solvent (kg)}} = \frac{0.0855578\text{ mol NaCl}}{0.0950\text{ kg}} = 0.901\ m\text{ NaCl}$ and

$95.0\text{ g H}_2\text{O} \times \frac{1\text{ mol H}_2\text{O}}{18.02\text{ g H}_2\text{O}} = 5.27192\text{ mol H}_2\text{O}$ then

$\chi = \frac{\text{amount solvent (in moles)}}{\text{total amount of solute and solvent (in moles)}} = \frac{0.0855578\text{ mol}}{0.0855578\text{ mol} + 5.27192\text{ mol}} = 0.016.$

Check: The units (m and unitless) are correct. The magnitudes of the answers (1 and 0.02) seem reasonable since we are starting with a low concentration solution and the molar mass of water is much less than that of NaCl.

Vapor Pressure of Solutions

12.69 The level has decreased more in the beaker filled with pure water. The dissolved salt in the seawater decreases the vapor pressure and subsequently lowers the rate of vaporization.

12.70 (b) Assume that the solutions obey Raoult's law ($P_{solution} = \chi_{solvent} P^{\circ}_{solvent}$). Each of the solutions has the same amount of solvent, so we need to compare the number of moles of particles in the solvent. Without doing any calculations we can see that b) will have the lower number of particles than a) because b) has the higher molecular weight. Potassium acetate will generate ~ 2 moles of particles per mole of the salt, so it will generate more than the other two. So solution a) will have the highest vapor pressure.

12.71 **Given:** 24.5 g of glycerin ($C_3H_8O_3$) in 135 mL water at 30 °C; $P^{\circ}_{H_2O} = 31.8$ torr **Find:** P_{H_2O}

Other: d (H_2O) = 1.00 g/mL; glycerin is not ionic solid

Conceptual Plan: $g_{C_3H_8O_3} \rightarrow mol_{C_3H_8O_3}$ **and** $mL_{H_2O} \rightarrow g_{H_2O} \rightarrow mol_{H_2O}$ **then** $mol_{C_3H_8O_3}, mol_{H_2O} \rightarrow \chi_{H_2O}$

$\frac{1\text{ mol C}_3\text{H}_8\text{O}_3}{92.09\text{ g C}_3\text{H}_8\text{O}_3}$ $\frac{1.00\text{ g}}{1\text{ mL}}$ $\frac{1\text{ mol H}_2\text{O}}{18.01\text{ g H}_2\text{O}}$ $\chi = \frac{\text{amount solute (in moles)}}{\text{total amount of solute and solvent (in moles)}}$

then $\chi_{H_2O}, P^{\circ}_{H_2O} \rightarrow P_{H_2O}$

$P_{solution} = \chi_{solvent} P^{\circ}_{solvent}$

Solution: $24.5\text{ g C}_3\text{H}_8\text{O}_3 \times \frac{1\text{ mol C}_3\text{H}_8\text{O}_3}{92.09\text{ g C}_3\text{H}_8\text{O}_3} = 0.2660441\text{ mol C}_3\text{H}_8\text{O}_3$ and

$135\text{ mL} \times \frac{1.00\text{ g}}{1\text{ mL}} \times \frac{1\text{ mol H}_2\text{O}}{18.01\text{ g H}_2\text{O}} = 7.495836\text{ mol H}_2\text{O}$ then

$\chi = \frac{\text{amount solvent (in moles)}}{\text{total amount of solute and solvent (in moles)}} = \frac{7.495836\text{ mol}}{0.2660441\text{ mol} + 7.495836\text{ mol}} = 0.9657243$ then

$P_{solution} = \chi_{solvent} P^{\circ}_{solvent} = 0.9657243 \times 31.8\text{ torr} = 30.7\text{ torr}$

Check: The units (torr) are correct. The magnitude of the answer (31 torr) seems reasonable since it is a drop from the pure vapor pressure. Very few moles of glycerin are added, so the pressure will not drop much.

12.72 **Given:** 12.35 % naphthalene($C_{10}H_8$) by mass in hexane(C_6H_{14}) at 25 °C; $P^{\circ}_{C_6H_{14}} = 151$ torr **Find:** $P_{C_6H_{14}}$

Conceptual Plan: % naphthalene($C_{10}H_8$) by mass $\rightarrow g_{C_{10}H_8}, g_{C_6H_{14}}$ **then** $g_{C_{10}H_8} \rightarrow mol_{C_{10}H_8}$ **and**

$\frac{10.85\text{ g C}_{10}\text{H}_8}{100\text{ g (C}_{10}\text{H}_8 + \text{C}_6\text{H}_{14})}$ $\frac{1\text{ mol C}_{10}\text{H}_8}{128.16\text{ g C}_{10}\text{H}_8}$

g C_6H_{14} → mol C_6H_{14} then mol $C_{10}H_8$, mol C_6H_{14} → χ C_6H_{14} then χ C_6H_{14}, $P^\circ_{C_6H_{14}}$ → P C_6H_{14}

$\frac{1 \text{ mol } C_6H_{14}}{86.17 \text{ g } C_6H_{14}}$ $\quad \chi = \frac{\text{amount solute (in moles)}}{\text{total amount of solute and solvent (in moles)}}$ $\quad P_{\text{solution}} = \chi_{\text{solvent}} P^\circ_{\text{solvent}}$

Solution: $\frac{12.35 \text{ g } C_{10}H_8}{100 \text{ g } (C_{10}H_8 + C_6H_{14})}$ means 12.35 g $C_{10}H_8$ and (100 g – 12.35 g) = 87.65 g C_6H_{14} then

$12.35 \text{ g } C_{10}H_8 \times \frac{1 \text{ mol } C_{10}H_8}{128.16 \text{ g } C_{10}H_8} = 0.096363920 \text{ mol } C_{10}H_8$ and

$87.65 \text{ g } C_6H_{14} \times \frac{1 \text{ mol } C_6H_{14}}{86.17 \text{ g } C_6H_{14}} = 1.0171754 \text{ mol } C_6H_{14}$ then

$\chi = \frac{\text{amount solvent (in moles)}}{\text{total amount of solute and solvent (in moles)}} = \frac{1.0171754 \text{ mol}}{0.096363920 \text{ mol} + 1.0171754 \text{ mol}} = 0.91346159$ then

$P_{\text{solution}} = \chi_{\text{solvent}} P^\circ_{\text{solvent}} = 0.91346159 \times 151 \text{ torr} = 138 \text{ torr } C_6H_{14}$

Check: The units (torr) are correct. The magnitude of the answer (140 torr) seems reasonable since it is a drop from the pure vapor pressure. Only a fraction of a mole of naphthalene is added, so the pressure will not drop much.

12.73 **Given:** 50.0 g of heptane (C_7H_{16}) and 50.0 g of octane (C_8H_{18}) at 25 °C; $P^\circ_{C_7H_{16}} = 45.8$ torr; $P^\circ_{C_8H_{18}} = 10.9$ torr

(a) **Find:** $P_{C_7H_{16}}$, $P_{C_8H_{18}}$

Conceptual Plan: g C_7H_{16} → mol C_7H_{16} and g C_8H_{18} → mol C_8H_{18} then mol C_7H_{16},

$\frac{1 \text{ mol } C_7H_{16}}{100.20 \text{ g } C_7H_{16}}$ $\quad \frac{1 \text{ mol } C_8H_{18}}{114.22 \text{ g } C_8H_{18}}$ $\quad \chi_{C_7H_{16}} = \frac{\text{amount } C_7H_{16} \text{ (in moles)}}{\text{total amount (in moles)}}$

mol C_8H_{18} → χ C_7H_{16}, χ C_8H_{18} then χ C_7H_{16}, $P^\circ_{C_7H_{16}}$ → $P_{C_7H_{16}}$ and χ C_8H_{18}, $P^\circ_{C_8H_{18}}$ → $P_{C_8H_{18}}$

$\chi_{C_8H_{18}} = 1 - \chi_{C_7H_{16}}$ $\quad P_{C_7H_{16}} = \chi_{C_7H_{16}} P^\circ_{C_7H_{16}}$ $\quad P_{C_8H_{18}} = \chi_{C_8H_{18}} P^\circ_{C_8H_{18}}$

Solution: $50.0 \text{ g } C_7H_{16} \times \frac{1 \text{ mol } C_7H_{16}}{100.20 \text{ g } C_7H_{16}} = 0.499002 \text{ mol } C_7H_{16}$ and

$50.0 \text{ g } C_8H_{18} \times \frac{1 \text{ mol } C_8H_{18}}{114.22 \text{ g } C_8H_{18}} = 0.437752 \text{ mol } C_8H_{18}$ then

$\chi_{C_7H_{16}} = \frac{\text{amount } C_7H_{16} \text{ (in moles)}}{\text{total amount (in moles)}} = \frac{0.499002 \text{ mol}}{0.499002 \text{ mol} + 0.437752 \text{ mol}} = 0.532693$ and

$\chi_{C_8H_{18}} = 1 - \chi_{C7H16} = 1 - 0.532693 = 0.467307$ then

$P_{C_7H_{16}} = \chi_{C_7H_{16}} P^\circ_{C_7H_{16}} = 0.532693 \times 45.8 \text{ torr} = 24.4 \text{ torr}$ and

$P_{C_8H_{18}} = \chi_{C_8H_{18}} P^\circ_{C_8H_{18}} = 0.467307 \times 10.9 \text{ torr} = 5.09 \text{ torr}$

Check: The units (torr) are correct. The magnitude of the answer (24 and 5 torr) seems reasonable because we expect a drop in half from the pure vapor pressures since we have roughly a 50:50 mole ratio of the two components.

(b) **Find:** P_{Total}

Conceptual Plan: $P_{C_7H_{16}}$, $P_{C_8H_{18}}$ → P_{Total}

$P_{\text{Total}} = P_{C_7H_{16}} + P_{C_8H_{18}}$

Solution: $P_{\text{Total}} = P_{C_7H_{16}} + P_{C_8H_{18}} = 24.4 \text{ torr} + 5.09 \text{ torr} = 29.5 \text{ torr}$

Check: The units (torr) are correct. The magnitude of the answer (30 torr) seems reasonable considering the two pressures.

(c) **Find:** mass percent composition of the gas phase

Conceptual Plan: since $n \propto P$ and we are calculating a mass percent, which is a ratio of masses, we can simply convert 1 torr to 1 mole so

$P_{C_7H_{16}}$, $P_{C_8H_{18}}$ → $n_{C_7H_{16}}$, $n_{C_8H_{18}}$ then mol C_7H_{16} → g C_7H_{16} and mol C_8H_{18} → g C_8H_{18}

$\frac{100.20 \text{ g } C_7H_{16}}{1 \text{ mol } C_7H_{16}}$ $\quad \frac{114.22 \text{ g } C_8H_{18}}{1 \text{ mol } C_8H_{18}}$

then g C_7H_{16}, g C_8H_{18} → mass percents

$\text{mass percent} = \frac{\text{mass solute}}{\text{mass solution}} \times 100\%$

Solution: so $n_{C_7H_{16}} = 24.4$ mol and $n_{C_8H_{18}} = 5.09$ mol then

$24.4 \cancel{\text{mol } C_7H_{16}} \times \frac{100.20 \text{ g } C_7H_{16}}{1 \cancel{\text{mol } C_7H_{16}}} = 2444.88 \text{ g } C_7H_{16}$ and

$5.09 \cancel{\text{mol } C_8H_{18}} \times \frac{114.22 \text{ g } C_8H_{18}}{1 \cancel{\text{mol } C_8H_{18}}} = 581.380 \text{ g } C_8H_{18}$ then

$\text{mass percent} = \frac{\text{mass solute}}{\text{mass solution}} \times 100\% = \frac{2444.88 \cancel{\text{g } C_7H_{16}}}{2444.88 \cancel{\text{g } C_7H_{16}} + 581.380 \cancel{\text{g } C_8H_{18}}} \times 100\% =$

$= 80.8$ percent by mass C_7H_{16}

then $100\% - 80.8\% = 19.2$ percent by mass C_8H_{18}

Check: The units (%) are correct. The magnitudes of the answers (81% and 19%) seem reasonable considering the two pressures.

(d) The two mass percents are different because the vapor is richer in the more volatile component (the lighter molecule).

12.74 **Given:** pentane(C_5H_{12}) and hexane(C_6H_{14}) $P_{\text{Total}} = 258$ torr; $P^{\circ}_{C_5H_{12}} = 425$ torr; $P^{\circ}_{C_6H_{14}} = 151$ torr at 25°C

Find: $\chi_{C_5H_{12}}$, $\chi_{C_6H_{14}}$

Conceptual Plan: $P_{\text{Total}} = P_{C_5H_{12}} + P_{C_6H_{14}}$ **where** $P_{C_5H_{12}} = \chi_{C_5H_{12}} P^{\circ}_{C_5H_{12}}$ **and** $P_{C_6H_{14}} = \chi_{C_6H_{14}} P^{\circ}_{C_6H_{14}}$ **but** $\chi_{C_6H_{14}} = 1 - \chi_{C_5H_{12}}$ **so** $P_{\text{Total}} = \chi_{C_5H_{12}} P^{\circ}_{C_5H_{12}} + (1 - \chi_{C_5H_{12}}) P^{\circ}_{C_6H_{14}}$ **substitute in values and solve for** $\chi_{C_5H_{12}}$, $\chi_{C_6H_{14}}$

Solution: $P_{\text{Total}} = \chi_{C_5H_{12}} P^{\circ}_{C_5H_{12}} + (1 - \chi_{C_5H_{12}}) P^{\circ}_{C_6H_{14}}$ so

$258 \cancel{\text{torr}} = \chi_{C_5H_{12}} 425 \cancel{\text{torr}} + (1 - \chi_{C_5H_{12}})\, 151 \cancel{\text{torr}} \rightarrow 258 - 151 = \chi_{C_5H_{12}}(425 - 151) \rightarrow$

$\chi_{C_5H_{12}} = \frac{107}{274} = 0.391$ and $\chi_{C_6H_{14}} = 1 - \chi_{C_5H_{12}} = 1 - 0.391 = 0.609$

Check: The units (none) are correct. The magnitudes of the answers (0.4 and 0.6) seem reasonable since the total vapor pressure is closer to the vapor pressure of hexane, so we expect there to be more hexane in the liquid.

12.75 **Given:** 4.08 g of chloroform ($CHCl_3$) and 9.29 g of acetone (CH_3COCH_3); at 35 °C $P^{\circ}_{CHCl_3} = 295$ torr; $P^{\circ}_{CH_3COCH_3} = 332$ torr; assume ideal behavior; $P_{\text{Total measured}} = 312$ torr

Find: P_{CHCl_3}, $P_{CH_3COCH_3}$, P_{Total}, and if the soln is ideal.

Conceptual Plan: **g** $CHCl_3 \rightarrow$ **mol** $CHCl_3$ **and g** $CH_3COCH_3 \rightarrow$ **mol** CH_3COCH_3 **then**

$\frac{1 \text{ mol } CHCl_3}{119.38 \text{ g } CHCl_3}$ $\qquad \frac{1 \text{ mol } CH_3COCH_3}{58.08 \text{ g } CH_3COCH_3}$

$\text{mol}_{CHCl_3}, \text{mol}_{CH_3COCH_3} \rightarrow \chi_{CHCl_3}, \chi_{CH_3COCH_3}$ **then** $\chi_{CHCl_3}, P^{\circ}_{CHCl_3} \rightarrow P_{CHCl_3}$ **and**

$\chi_{CHCl_3} = \frac{\text{amount } CHCl_3 \text{ (in moles)}}{\text{total amount (in moles)}}$ $\quad \chi_{CH_3COCH_3} = 1 - \chi_{CHCl_3}$ $\quad P_{CHCl_3} = \chi_{CHCl_3} P^{\circ}_{CHCl_3}$

$\chi_{CH_3COCH_3}, P^{\circ}_{CH_3COCH_3} \rightarrow P_{CH_3COCH_3}$ **then** $P_{CHCl_3}, P_{CH_3COCH_3} \rightarrow P_{\text{Total}}$ **then compare values**

$P_{CH_3COCH_3} = \chi_{CH_3COCH_3} P^{\circ}_{CH_3COCH_3}$ $\quad P_{\text{Total}} = P_{CHCl_3} + P_{CH_3COCH_{33}}$

Solution:

$4.08 \cancel{\text{g } CHCl_3} \times \frac{1 \text{ mol } CHCl_3}{119.38 \cancel{\text{g } CHCl_3}} = 0.0341766 \text{ mol } CHCl_3$ and

$9.29 \cancel{\text{g } CH_3COCH_3} \times \frac{1 \text{ mol } CH_3COCH_3}{58.08 \cancel{\text{g } CH_3COCH_3}} = 0.159952 \text{ mol } CH_3COCH_3$ then

$\chi_{CHCl_3} = \frac{\text{amount } CHCl_3 \text{ (in moles)}}{\text{total amount (in moles)}} = \frac{0.0341766 \cancel{\text{mol}}}{0.0341766 \cancel{\text{mol}} + 0.159952 \cancel{\text{mol}}} = 0.176052$ and

$\chi_{CH_3COCH_3} = 1 - \chi_{CHCl_3} = 1 - 0.176052 = 0.823948$ then

$P_{CHCl_3} = \chi_{CHCl_3} P^{\circ}_{CHCl_3} = 0.176052 \times 295 \text{ torr} = 51.9 \text{ torr}$ and

$P_{CH_3COCH_3} = \chi_{CH_3COCH_3} P^{\circ}_{CH_3COCH_3} = 0.823948 \times 332 \text{ torr} = 274 \text{ torr}$ then

$P_{\text{Total}} = P_{CHCl_3} + P_{CH_3COCH_3} = 51.9 \text{ torr} + 274 \text{ torr} = 326 \text{ torr}.$

Since 326 torr ≠ 312 torr, the solution is not behaving ideally. The chloroform–acetone interactions are stronger than the chloroform–chloroform and acetone–acetone interactions.

Check: The units (torr) are correct. The magnitude of the answer seems reasonable since each is a fraction of the pure vapor pressure. We are not surprised that the solution is not ideal, since the types of bonds in the two molecules are very different.

12.76 **Given:** methanol (CH_3OH) and water; $\chi_{H_2O} = 0.312$; at 39.9 °C $P_{\text{Total measured}} = 211$ torr; $P^\circ_{CH_3OH} = 256$ torr; $P^\circ_{H_2O} = 55.3$ torr **Find:** is soln ideal?

Conceptual Plan: $\chi_{H_2O} \rightarrow \chi_{CH_3OH}$ **then** $\chi_{H_2O}, P^\circ_{H_2O} \rightarrow P_{H_2O}$ **and** $\chi_{CH_3OH}, P^\circ_{CH_3OH} \rightarrow P_{CH_3OH}$

$\chi_{CH_3OH} = 1 - \chi_{H_2O}$ $\quad P_{H_2O} = \chi_{H_2O} P^\circ_{H_2O}$ $\quad P_{CH_3OH} = \chi_{CH_3OH} P^\circ_{CH_3OH}$

then $P_{H_2O}, P_{CH_3OH} \rightarrow P_{\text{Total}}$ **then compare values**

$P_{\text{Total}} = P_{H_2O} + P_{CH_3OH}$

Solution:

$\chi_{CH_3OH} = 1 - \chi_{H_2O} = 1 - 0.312 = 0.688$ then $P_{H_2O} = \chi_{H_2O} P^\circ_{H_2O} = 0.312 \times 55.3 \text{ torr} = 17.2536$ torr and $P_{CH_3OH} = \chi_{CH_3OH} P^\circ_{CH_3OH} = 0.688 \times 256 \text{ torr} = 176.128$ torr then $P_{\text{Total}} = P_{H_2O} + P_{CH_3OH} = 17.2536 \text{ torr} + 176.128 \text{ torr} = 193$ torr.

Since 193 torr ≠ 211 torr, the solution is not behaving ideally. The methanol–water interactions are weaker than the methanol–methanol and water–water interactions.

Check: The units (torr) are correct. The magnitude of the answer seems reasonable since each is a fraction of the pure vapor pressures. We are not surprised that the solution is not ideal, since the types of bonds in the two molecules are very different.

Freezing Point Depression, Boiling Point Elevation, and Osmosis

12.77 **Given:** 55.8 g of glucose ($C_6H_{12}O_6$) in 455 g water **Find:** T_f and T_b **Other:** $K_f = 1.86$ °C/m; $K_b = 0.512$ °C/m;

Conceptual Plan: $g_{H_2O} \rightarrow kg_{H_2O}$ **and** $g\ C_6H_{12}O_6 \rightarrow mol\ C_6H_{12}O_6$ **then** $mol\ C_6H_{12}O_6, kg_{H_2O} \rightarrow m$

$\frac{1 \text{ kg}}{1000 \text{ g}}$ $\quad \frac{1 \text{ mol } C_6H_{12}O_6}{180.16 \text{ g } C_6H_{12}O_6}$ $\quad m = \frac{\text{amount solute (moles)}}{\text{mass solvent (kg)}}$

$m, K_f \rightarrow \Delta T_f \rightarrow T_f$ **and** $m, K_b \rightarrow \Delta T_b \rightarrow T_b$

$\Delta T_f = K_f m$ $\quad T_f = T^\circ_f - \Delta T_f$ $\quad \Delta T_b = K_b m$ $\quad \Delta T_b = T_b - T^\circ_b$

Solution: $455 \text{ g} \times \frac{1 \text{ kg}}{1000 \text{ g}} = 0.455$ kg and $55.8 \text{ g } C_6H_{12}O_6 \times \frac{1 \text{ mol } C_6H_{12}O_6}{180.16 \text{ g } C_6H_{12}O_6} = 0.309725 \text{ mol } C_6H_{12}O_6$ then

$$m = \frac{\text{amount solute (moles)}}{\text{mass solvent (kg)}} = \frac{0.309725 \text{ mol } C_6H_{12}O_6}{0.455 \text{ kg}} = 0.680714\ m \text{ then}$$

$\Delta T_f = K_f m = 1.86 \frac{°C}{m} \times 0.680714\ m = 1.27$ °C then $T_f = T^\circ_f - \Delta T_f = 0.00 \text{ °C} - 1.27 \text{ °C} = -1.27$ °C and

$\Delta T_b = K_b m = 0.512 \frac{°C}{m} \times 0.680714\ m = 0.349$ °C and $\Delta T_b = T_b - T^\circ_b$ so

$T_b = T^\circ_b + \Delta T_b = 100.000 \text{ °C} + 0.349 \text{ °C} = 100.349$ °C

Check: The units (°C) are correct. The magnitudes of the answers seem reasonable since the molality is ~ 2/3. The shift in boiling point is less than the shift in freezing point because the constant for boiling is smaller than the constant for freezing is smaller than the con.

12.78 **Given:** 21.2 g of ethylene glycol ($C_2H_6O_2$) in 85.4 g water **Find:** T_f and T_b
Other: $K_f = 1.86$ °C/m; $K_b = 0.512$ °C/m;

Conceptual Plan: $g_{H_2O} \rightarrow kg_{H_2O}$ **and** $g\ C_2H_6O_2 \rightarrow mol\ C_2H_6O_2$ **then** $mol\ C_2H_6O_2, kg_{H_2O} \rightarrow m$

$\frac{1 \text{ kg}}{1000 \text{ g}}$ $\quad \frac{1 \text{ mol } C_2H_6O_2}{62.07 \text{ g } C_2H_6O_2}$ $\quad m = \frac{\text{amount solute (moles)}}{\text{mass solvent (kg)}}$

$m, K_f \rightarrow \Delta T_f \rightarrow T_f$ **and** $m, K_b \rightarrow \Delta T_b \rightarrow T_b$

$\Delta T_f = K_f m$ $\quad T_f = T^\circ_f - \Delta T_f$ $\quad \Delta T_b = K_b m$ $\quad \Delta T_b = T_b - T^\circ_b$

Solution: $85.4 \text{ g} \times \frac{1 \text{ kg}}{1000 \text{ g}} = 0.0854$ kg and $21.2 \text{ g } C_2H_6O_2 \times \frac{1 \text{ mol } C_2H_6O_2}{62.07 \text{ g } C_2H_6O_2} = 0.341561 \text{ mol } C_2H_6O_2$ then

$$m = \frac{\text{amount solute (moles)}}{\text{mass solvent (kg)}} = \frac{0.341561 \text{ mol } C_2H_6O_2}{0.0854 \text{ kg}} = 3.99941\ m \text{ then}$$

$\Delta T_f = K_f m = 1.86 \frac{°C}{m} \times 3.99941\ m = 7.43$ °C then $T_f = T^\circ_f - \Delta T_f = 0.00 \text{ °C} - 7.43 \text{ °C} = -7.43$ °C and

$\Delta T_b = K_b m = 0.512 \frac{°C}{m} \times 3.99941\ m = 2.04$ °C and $\Delta T_b = T_b - T^\circ_b$ so

$T_b = T^\circ_b + \Delta T_b = 100.00 \text{ °C} + 2.04 \text{ °C} = 102.04$ °C

Check: The units (°C) are correct. The magnitudes of the answers seem reasonable since the molality is ~ 4. The shift in boiling point is less than the shift in freezing point because the constant for boiling is smaller than the constant for freezing.

12.79 **Given:** 17.5 g of unknown nonelectrolyte in 100.0 g water, $T_f = -1.8\ °C$ **Find:** $\mathcal{M}$

Other: $K_f = 1.86\ °C/m$

Conceptual Plan: $g_{H_2O} \rightarrow kg_{H_2O}$ and $T_f \rightarrow \Delta T_f$ then $\Delta T_f, K_f \rightarrow m$ then $m, kg_{H_2O} \rightarrow mol_{Unk}$

$$\frac{1\ kg}{1000\ g} \qquad T_f = T_f^\circ - \Delta T_f \qquad \Delta T_f = K_f m \qquad m = \frac{\text{amount solute (moles)}}{\text{mass solvent (kg)}}$$

then $g_{Unk}, mol_{Unk} \rightarrow \mathcal{M}$

$$\mathcal{M} = \frac{g_{Unk}}{mol_{Unk}}$$

Solution: $100.0\ g \times \frac{1\ kg}{1000\ g} = 0.1000\ kg$ and $T_f = T_f^\circ - \Delta T_f$ so

$\Delta T_f = T_f^\circ - T_f = 0.00\ °C - (-1.8\ °C) = +1.8\ °C \quad \Delta T_f = K_f m$. Rearrange to solve for m.

$$m = \frac{\Delta T_f}{K_f} = \frac{1.8\ °C}{1.86\ \frac{°C}{m}} = 0.96774\ m \text{ then } m = \frac{\text{amount solute (moles)}}{\text{mass solvent (kg)}} \text{ so}$$

$$mol_{Unk} = m_{Unk} \times kg_{H_2O} = 0.96774\ \frac{mol\ Unk}{kg} \times 0.1000\ kg = 0.096774\ mol\ Unk \text{ then}$$

$$\mathcal{M} = \frac{g_{Unk}}{mol_{Unk}} = \frac{17.5\ g}{0.096774\ mol} = 180\ \frac{g}{mol} = 1.8 \times 10^2\ \frac{g}{mol}.$$

Check: The units (g/mol) are correct. The magnitude of the answer (180 g/mol) seems reasonable since the molality is ~ 0.1 and we have ~18 g. It is a reasonable molecular weight for a solid or liquid.

12.80 **Given:** 35.9 g of unknown nonelectrolyte in 150.0 g water, $T_f = -1.3\ °C$ **Find:** $\mathcal{M}$

Other: $K_f = 1.86\ °C/m$;

Conceptual Plan: $g_{H_2O} \rightarrow kg_{H_2O}$ and $T_f \rightarrow \Delta T_f$ then $\Delta T_f, K_f \rightarrow m$ then $m, kg_{H_2O} \rightarrow mol_{Unk}$

$$\frac{1\ kg}{1000\ g} \qquad T_f = T_f^\circ - \Delta T_f \qquad \Delta T_f = K_f m \qquad m = \frac{\text{amount solute (moles)}}{\text{mass solvent (kg)}}$$

then $g_{Unk}, mol_{Unk} \rightarrow \mathcal{M}$

$$\mathcal{M} = \frac{g_{Unk}}{mol_{Unk}}$$

Solution: $150.0\ g \times \frac{1\ kg}{1000\ g} = 0.1500\ kg$ and $T_f = T_f^\circ - \Delta T_f$ so

$\Delta T_f = T_f^\circ - T_f = 0.00\ °C - -1.3\ °C = +1.3\ °C\ \Delta T_f = K_f m$. Rearrange to solve for m.

$$m = \frac{\Delta T_f}{K_f} = \frac{1.3\ °C}{1.86\ \frac{°C}{m}} = 0.69892\ m \text{ then } m = \frac{\text{amount solute (moles)}}{\text{mass solvent (kg)}} \text{ so}$$

$$mol_{Unk} = m_{Unk} \times kg_{H_2O} = 0.69892\ \frac{mol\ Unk}{kg} \times 0.1500\ kg = 0.104839\ mol\ Unk \text{ then}$$

$$\mathcal{M} = \frac{g_{Unk}}{mol_{Unk}} = \frac{35.9\ g}{0.104839\ mol} = 340\ \frac{g}{mol}.$$

Check: The units (g/mol) are correct. The magnitude of the answer (340 g/mol) seems reasonable since the molality is ~ 0.7 and we have ~36 g. It is a reasonable molecular weight for a solid or liquid.

12.81 **Given:** 24.6 g of glycerin ($C_3H_8O_3$) in 250.0 mL of solution at 298 K **Find:** Π

Conceptual Plan: $mL_{soln} \rightarrow L_{soln}$ and $g_{C_3H_8O_3} \rightarrow mol_{C_3H_8O_3}$ then $mol_{C_3H_8O_3}, L_{soln} \rightarrow$ **M then**

$$\frac{1\ L}{1000\ mL} \qquad \frac{1\ mol\ C_3H_8O_3}{92.09\ g\ C_3H_8O_3} \qquad M = \frac{\text{amount solute (moles)}}{\text{volume solution (L)}}$$

$M, T \rightarrow \Pi$

$$\Pi = M\,RT$$

Solution:

$$250.0\ mL \times \frac{1\ L}{1000\ mL} = 0.2500\ L \text{ and } 24.6\ g\ C_3H_8O_3 \times \frac{1\ mol\ C_3H_8O_3}{92.09\ g\ C_3H_8O_3} = 0.267130\ mol\ C_3H_8O_3 \text{ then}$$

$$M = \frac{\text{amount solute (moles)}}{\text{volume solution (L)}} = \frac{0.267130\ mol\ C_3H_8O_3}{0.2500\ L} = 1.06852\ M \text{ then}$$

$$\Pi = M\,RT = 1.06852\ \frac{mol}{L} \times 0.08206\ \frac{L \cdot atm}{K \cdot mol} \times 298\ K = 26.1\ atm$$

Check: The units (atm) are correct. The magnitude of the answer (26 atm) seems reasonable since the molarity is ~ 1.

12.82 **Given:** sucrose ($C_{12}H_{22}O_{11}$) in 5.00 x 10^2 g water; Π = 8.55 atm at 298 K **Find:** m ($C_{12}H_{22}O_{11}$)
Other: d = 1.0 g/mL
Conceptual Plan: Π, T → M then g H_2O, d, $\mathcal{M}$ → g $C_{12}H_{22}O_{11}$

$$\Pi = M\,RT \qquad M = \frac{\text{amount solute (moles)}}{\text{volume solution (L)}} \text{ with } \frac{1\text{ L}}{1000\text{ mL}}, \frac{342.30\text{ g } C_{12}H_{22}O_{11}}{1\text{ mol } C_{12}H_{22}O_{11}}, \text{ and } \frac{1.0\text{ mL}}{1.0\text{ g}}$$

Solution: $\Pi = M\,RT$ for M. $M = \dfrac{\Pi}{RT} = \dfrac{8.55\text{ atm}}{0.08206\dfrac{\text{L}\cdot\text{atm}}{\text{K}\cdot\text{mol}} \times 298\text{ K}} = 0.349638\dfrac{\text{mol}}{\text{L}}$.

Substitute quantities into the definition of M.

$$M = \frac{\text{amount solute (moles)}}{\text{volume solution (L)}} = \frac{(x\text{ g } C_{12}H_{22}O_{11})\left(\dfrac{1\text{ mol } C_{12}H_{22}O_{11}}{342.30\text{ g } C_{12}H_{22}O_{11}}\right)}{(5.00 \times 10^2\text{ g } H_2O + x\text{ g } C_{12}H_{22}O_{11}) \times \dfrac{1.0\text{ mL}}{1.0\text{ g}} \times \dfrac{1\text{ L}}{1000\text{ mL}}} = 0.349638\frac{\text{mol}}{\text{L}}.$$

Rearrange to solve for x g $C_{12}H_{22}O_{11}$. x g $C_{12}H_{22}O_{11}$ = 0.119681 x (5.00 x 10^2 g H_2O + x g $C_{12}H_{22}O_{11}$) →

$$0.880312 \times (x\text{ g } C_{12}H_{22}O_{11}) = 59.8405 \rightarrow x\text{ g } C_{12}H_{22}O_{11} = \frac{59.8405}{0.880312} = 68.0\text{ g } C_{12}H_{22}O_{11}.$$

Check: The units (g) are correct. The magnitude of the answer (68 g) seems reasonable since the molarity is ~ 1/3 and we have 0.5 L of water.

12.83 **Given:** 27.55 mg unknown protein in 25.0 mL solution; Π = 3.22 torr at 25 °C **Find:** $\mathcal{M}_{\text{unknown protein}}$
Conceptual Plan: °C → K and torr → atm then Π, T → M then mL_{soln} → L_{soln} then

$$K = °C + 273.15 \qquad \frac{1\text{ atm}}{760\text{ torr}} \qquad \Pi = M\,RT \qquad \frac{1\text{ L}}{1000\text{ mL}}$$

L_{soln}, M → mol$_{\text{unknown protein}}$ and mg → g then g$_{\text{unknown protein}}$, mol$_{\text{unknown protein}}$ → $\mathcal{M}_{\text{unknown protein}}$

$$M = \frac{\text{amount solute (moles)}}{\text{volume solution (L)}} \qquad \frac{1\text{ g}}{1000\text{ mg}} \qquad \mathcal{M} = \frac{g_{\text{unknown protein}}}{mol_{\text{unknown protein}}}$$

Solution: 25 °C + 273.15 = 298 K and 3.22 torr x $\dfrac{1\text{ atm}}{760\text{ torr}}$ = 0.00423684 atm $\Pi = M\,RT$ for M.

$$M = \frac{\Pi}{RT} = \frac{0.00423684\text{ atm}}{0.08206\dfrac{\text{L}\cdot\text{atm}}{\text{K}\cdot\text{mol}} \times 298\text{ K}} = 1.73258 \times 10^{-4}\frac{\text{mol}}{\text{L}} \text{ then } 25.0\text{ mL} \times \frac{1\text{ L}}{1000\text{ mL}} = 0.0250\text{ L then}$$

$M = \dfrac{\text{amount solute (moles)}}{\text{volume solution (L)}}$. Rearrange to solve for mol$_{\text{unknown protein}}$.

$$mol_{\text{unknown protein}} = M \times L = 1.73258 \times 10^{-4}\frac{\text{mol}}{\text{L}} \times 0.0250\text{ L} = 4.33146 \times 10^{-6}\text{ mol and}$$

$$27.55\text{ mg} \times \frac{1\text{ g}}{1000\text{ mg}} = 0.02755\text{ g then } \mathcal{M} = \frac{g_{\text{unknown protein}}}{mol_{\text{unknown protein}}} = \frac{0.02755\text{ g}}{4.33146 \times 10^{-6}\text{ mol}} = 6.36 \times 10^3\frac{\text{g}}{\text{mol}}.$$

Check: The units (g/mol) are correct. The magnitude of the answer (6400 g/mol) seems reasonable for a large biological molecule. A small amount of material is put into 0.025 L, so the concentration is very small and the molecular weight is large.

12.84 **Given:** 18.75 mg of hemoglobin in 15.0 mL of solution at 25 °C, $\mathcal{M}_{\text{hemoglobin}}$ = 6.5 x 10^4 g/mol **Find:** Π
Conceptual Plan: mL_{soln} → L_{soln} and mg_H → g_H → mol_H then mol_H, L_{soln} → M then

$$\frac{1\text{ L}}{1000\text{ mL}} \qquad \frac{1\text{ g}}{1000\text{ mg}} \quad \frac{1\text{ mol H}}{6.5 \times 10^4\text{ g H}} \qquad M = \frac{\text{amount solute (moles)}}{\text{volume solution (L)}}$$

***M*, *T* → Π**

$$\Pi = M\,RT$$

Solution:

$$15.0\text{ mL} \times \frac{1\text{ L}}{1000\text{ mL}} = 0.0150\text{ L and } 18.75\text{ mg H} \times \frac{1\text{ g}}{1000\text{ mg}} \times \frac{1\text{ mol H}}{6.5 \times 10^4\text{ g H}} = 2.88465 \times 10^{-7}\text{ mol H then}$$

$$M = \frac{\text{amount solute (moles)}}{\text{volume solution (L)}} = \frac{2.88465 \times 10^{-7}\text{ mol H}}{0.0150\text{ L}} = 1.9231 \times 10^{-5}\text{ M then}$$

$\Pi = M\,RT = 1.9\underline{2}31 \times 10^{-5} \dfrac{\cancel{\text{mol}}}{\cancel{\text{L}}} \times 0.08206 \dfrac{\cancel{\text{L}} \cdot \text{atm}}{\cancel{\text{K}} \cdot \cancel{\text{mol}}} \times 298\,\cancel{\text{K}} = 4.7 \times 10^{-4}\,\text{atm} = 0.36\,\text{torr}$

Check: The units (atm) are correct. The magnitude of the answer (10^{-4} atm) seems reasonable since the molarity is so small.

12.85 (a) **Given:** 0.100 m of K_2S, completely dissociated **Find:** T_f, T_b

Other: $K_f = 1.86$ °C/m; $K_b = 0.512$ °C/m;

Conceptual Plan: $m, i, K_f \rightarrow \Delta T_f$ **then** $\Delta T_f \rightarrow T_f$ **and** $m, i, K_b \rightarrow \Delta T_b$ **then** $\Delta T_b \rightarrow T_b$

$\Delta T_f = K_f\, im_{i=3}$ $\quad T_f = T_f^\circ - \Delta T_f$ $\quad \Delta T_b = K_b\, im_{i=3}$ $\quad T_b = T_b^\circ + \Delta T_b$

Solution: $\Delta T_f = K_f\, im = 1.86 \dfrac{°\text{C}}{\cancel{m}} \times 3 \times 0.100\,\cancel{m} = 0.558\,°\text{C}$ then

$T_f = T_f^\circ - \Delta T_f = 0.000\,°\text{C} - 0.558\,°\text{C} = -0.558\,°\text{C}$ and

$\Delta T_b = K_b\, im = 0.512 \dfrac{°\text{C}}{\cancel{m}} \times 3 \times 0.100\,\cancel{m} = 0.154\,°\text{C}$ then

$T_b = T_b^\circ - \Delta T_b = 100.000\,°\text{C} + 0.154\,°\text{C} = 100.154\,°\text{C}$.

Check: The units (°C) are correct. The magnitude of the answer (– 0.6 °C and 100.2 °C) seems reasonable since the molality of the particles is 0.3. The shift in boiling point is less than the shift in freezing point because the constant for boiling is larger than the constant for freezing.

(b) **Given:** 21.5 g $CuCl_2$ in 4.50×10^2 g water, completely dissociated **Find:** T_f, T_b

Other: $K_f = 1.86$ °C/m; $K_b = 0.512$ °C/m;

Conceptual Plan: $g_{H_2O} \rightarrow kg_{H_2O}$ **and** $g_{CuCl_2} \rightarrow mol_{CuCl_2}$ **then** $mol_{CuCl_2}, kg_{H_2O} \rightarrow m$

$\dfrac{1\,\text{kg}}{1000\,\text{g}}$ $\quad \dfrac{1\,\text{mol CuCl}_2}{134.46\,\text{g CuCl}_2}$ $\quad m = \dfrac{\text{amount solute (moles)}}{\text{mass solvent (kg)}}$

$m, i, K_f \rightarrow \Delta T_f \rightarrow T_f$ **and** $m, i, K_b \rightarrow \Delta T_b \rightarrow T_b$

$\Delta T_f = K_f\, im_{i=3}$ $\quad T_f = T_f^\circ - \Delta T_f$ $\quad \Delta T_b = K_b\, im_{i=3}$ $\quad T_b = T_b^\circ + \Delta T_b$

Solution:

$4.5 \times 10^2\,\cancel{\text{g}} \times \dfrac{1\,\text{kg}}{1000\,\cancel{\text{g}}} = 0.450\,\text{kg}$ and $21.5\,\cancel{\text{g CuCl}_2} \times \dfrac{1\,\text{mol CuCl}_2}{134.46\,\cancel{\text{g CuCl}_2}} = 0.15\underline{9}904\,\text{mol CuCl}_2$ then

$m = \dfrac{\text{amount solute (moles)}}{\text{mass solvent (kg)}} = \dfrac{0.15\underline{9}904\,\text{mol CuCl}_2}{0.450\,\text{kg}} = 0.35\underline{5}341\,m$ then

$\Delta T_f = K_f\, im = 1.86 \dfrac{°\text{C}}{\cancel{m}} \times 3 \times 0.35\underline{5}341\,\cancel{m} = 1.98\,°\text{C}$ then

$T_f = T_f^\circ - \Delta T_f = 0.000\,°\text{C} - 1.98\,°\text{C} = -1.98\,°\text{C}$ and

$\Delta T_b = K_b\, im = 0.512 \dfrac{°\text{C}}{\cancel{m}} \times 3 \times 0.35\underline{5}341\,\cancel{m} = 0.546\,°\text{C}$ then

$T_b = T_b^\circ - \Delta T_b = 100.000\,°\text{C} + 0.546\,°\text{C} = 100.546\,°\text{C}$.

Check: The units (°C) are correct. The magnitude of the answer (– 2 °C and 100.5 °C) seems reasonable since the molality of the particles is ~ 1. The shift in boiling point is less than the shift in freezing point because the constant for boiling is larger than the constant for freezing.

(c) **Given:** 5.5 % by mass $NaNO_3$, completely dissociated **Find:** T_f, T_b

Other: $K_f = 1.86$ °C/m; $K_b = 0.512$ °C/m;

Conceptual Plan: percent by mass $\rightarrow g_{NaNO_3}, g_{H_2O}$ **then** $g_{H_2O} \rightarrow kg_{H_2O}$ **and** $g_{NaNO_3} \rightarrow mol_{NaNO_3}$

$\text{mass percent} = \dfrac{\text{mass solute}}{\text{mass solution}} \times 100\%$ $\quad \dfrac{1\,\text{kg}}{1000\,\text{g}}$ $\quad \dfrac{1\,\text{mol NaNO}_3}{84.99\,\text{g NaNO}_3}$

then $mol_{NaNO_3}, kg_{H_2O} \rightarrow m$ **then** $m, i, K_f \rightarrow \Delta T_f \rightarrow T_f$ **and** $m, i, K_b \rightarrow \Delta T_b \rightarrow T_b$

$m = \dfrac{\text{amount solute (moles)}}{\text{mass solvent (kg)}}$ $\quad \Delta T_f = K_f\, im_{i=2}$ $\quad T_f = T_f^\circ - \Delta T_f$ $\quad \Delta T_b = K_b\, im_{i=2}$ $\quad T_b = T_b^\circ + \Delta T_b$

Solution: $\text{mass percent} = \dfrac{\text{mass solute}}{\text{mass solution}} \times 100\%$ so 5.5 % by mass $NaNO_3$ means 5.5 g $NaNO_3$ and

$100.0\,\text{g} - 5.5\,\text{g} = 94.5\,\text{g}$ water. Then $94.5\,\cancel{\text{g}} \times \dfrac{1\,\text{kg}}{1000\,\cancel{\text{g}}} = 0.0945\,\text{kg}$ and

$5.5\,\cancel{\text{g NaNO}_3} \times \dfrac{1\,\text{mol NaNO}_3}{84.99\,\cancel{\text{g NaNO}_3}} = 0.06\underline{4}713\,\text{mol NaNO}_3$ then

$$m = \frac{\text{amount solute (moles)}}{\text{mass solvent (kg)}} = \frac{0.064713 \text{ mol NaNO}_3}{0.0945 \text{ kg}} = 0.68480 \; m \text{ then}$$

$$\Delta T_f = K_f im = 1.86 \frac{°\text{C}}{m} \times 2 \times 0.68480 \; m = 2.5 \text{ °C then}$$

$$T_f = T_f^{\circ} - \Delta T_f = 0.000 \text{ °C} - 2.3 \text{ °C} = -2.5 \text{ °C and}$$

$$\Delta T_b = K_b im = 0.512 \frac{°\text{C}}{m} \times 2 \times 0.68480 \; m = 0.70 \text{ °C then}$$

$$T_b = T_b^{\circ} - \Delta T_b = 100.000 \text{ °C} + 0.64 \text{ °C} = 100.70 \text{ °C}.$$

Check: The units (°C) are correct. The magnitude of the answer (– 2.5 °C and 100.7 °C) seems reasonable since the molality of the particles is ~ 1. The shift in boiling point is less than the shift in freezing point because the constant for boiling is larger than the constant for freezing.

12.86 (a) **Given:** 10.5 g $FeCl_3$ in 1.50 x 10^2 g water, completely dissociated **Find:** T_f, T_b
Other: $K_f = 1.86$ °C/m; $K_b = 0.512$ °C/m;
Conceptual Plan: $g_{H_2O} \rightarrow kg_{H_2O}$ **and** $g_{FeCl_3} \rightarrow mol_{FeCl_3}$ **then** $mol_{FeCl_3}, kg_{H_2O} \rightarrow m$

$\frac{1 \text{ kg}}{1000 \text{ g}}$ $\quad \frac{1 \text{ mol FeCl}_3}{162.21 \text{ g FeCl}_3}$ $\quad m = \frac{\text{amount solute (moles)}}{\text{mass solvent (kg)}}$

$m, i, K_f \rightarrow \Delta T_f \rightarrow T_f$ **and** $m, i, K_b \rightarrow \Delta T_b \rightarrow T_b$

$\Delta T_f = K_f im_{i=4}$ $\quad T_f = T_f^{\circ} - \Delta T_f$ $\quad \Delta T_b = K_b im_{i=4}$ $\quad T_b = T_b^{\circ} + \Delta T_b$

Solution: $4.5 \times 10^2 \text{ g} \times \frac{1 \text{ kg}}{1000 \text{ g}} = 0.450 \text{ kg and}$

$$10.5 \text{ g FeCl}_3 \times \frac{1 \text{ mol FeCl}_3}{162.21 \text{ g FeCl}_3} = 0.0647325 \text{ mol FeCl}_3 \text{ then}$$

$$m = \frac{\text{amount solute (moles)}}{\text{mass solvent (kg)}} = \frac{0.0647325 \text{ mol FeCl}_3}{0.150 \text{ kg}} = 0.431550 \; m \text{ then}$$

$$\Delta T_f = K_f im = 1.86 \frac{°\text{C}}{m} \times 4 \times 0.431550 \; m = 3.21 \text{ °C then}$$

$$T_f = T_f^{\circ} - \Delta T_f = 0.000 \text{ °C} - 3.21 \text{ °C} = -3.21 \text{ °C and}$$

$$\Delta T_b = K_b im = 0.512 \frac{°\text{C}}{m} \times 4 \times 0.431550 \; m = 0.884 \text{ °C then}$$

$$T_b = T_b^{\circ} - \Delta T_b = 100.000 \text{ °C} + 0.884 \text{ °C} = 100.884 \text{ °C}.$$

Check: The units (°C) are correct. The magnitude of the answer (– 3 °C and 100.9 °C) seems reasonable since the molality of the particles is ~ 2. The shift in boiling point is less than the shift in freezing point because the constant for boiling is smaller than the constant for freezing.

(b) **Given:** 3.5 % by mass KCl, completely dissociated **Find:** T_f, T_b
Other: $K_f = 1.86$ °C/m; $K_b = 0.512$ °C/m;
Conceptual Plan: percent by mass $\rightarrow g_{KCl}, g_{H_2O}$ **then** $g_{H_2O} \rightarrow kg_{H_2O}$ **and** $g_{KCl} \rightarrow mol_{KCl}$ **then**

$\text{mass percent} = \frac{\text{mass solute}}{\text{mass solution}} \times 100\%$ $\quad \frac{1 \text{ kg}}{1000 \text{ g}}$ $\quad \frac{1 \text{ mol KCl}}{74.55 \text{ g KCl}}$

$mol_{NaNO_3}, kg_{H_2O} \rightarrow m$ **then** $m, i, K_f \rightarrow \Delta T_f \rightarrow T_f$ **and** $m, i, K_b \rightarrow \Delta T_b \rightarrow T_b$

$m = \frac{\text{amount solute (moles)}}{\text{mass solvent (kg)}}$ $\quad \Delta T_f = K_f im_{i=2}$ $\quad T_f = T_f^{\circ} - \Delta T_f$ $\quad \Delta T_b = K_b im_{i=2}$ $\quad T_b = T_b^{\circ} + \Delta T_b$

Solution: $\text{mass percent} = \frac{\text{mass solute}}{\text{mass solution}} \times 100\%$ so 3.5% by mass KCl means

3.5 g KCl and 100.0 g – 3.5 g = 96.5 g water. Then $96.5 \text{ g} \times \frac{1 \text{ kg}}{1000 \text{ g}} = 0.0965 \text{ kg and}$

$$3.5 \text{ g KCl} \times \frac{1 \text{ mol KCl}}{74.55 \text{ g KCl}} = 0.046948 \text{ mol KCl}$$

$$\text{then } m = \frac{\text{amount solute (moles)}}{\text{mass solvent (kg)}} = \frac{0.046948 \text{ mol KCl}}{0.0965 \text{ kg}} = 0.48651 \; m \text{ then}$$

$$\Delta T_f = K_f i m = 1.86 \frac{°\text{C}}{m} \times 2 \times 0.48651 \; m = 1.8 \text{ °C then}$$

$T_f = T_f^\circ - \Delta T_f = 0.000\ °C - 1.8\ °C = -1.8\ °C$

and $\Delta T_b = K_b i\, m = 0.512 \frac{°C}{m} \times 2 \times 0.48651\ m = 0.50\ °C$ then

$T_b = T_b^\circ - \Delta T_b = 100.000\ °C + 0.50\ °C = 100.50\ °C.$

Check: The units (°C) are correct. The magnitude of the answer (– 2 °C and 100.5 °C) seems reasonable since the molality of the particles is ~ 1. The shift in boiling point is less than the shift in freezing point because the constant for boiling is smaller than the constant for freezing.

(c) **Given:** 0.150 m of MgF_2, completely dissociated **Find:** T_f, T_b
Other: $K_f = 1.86\ °C/m$; $K_b = 0.512\ °C/m$;
Conceptual Plan: $m, i, K_f \rightarrow \Delta T_f$ **then** $\Delta T_f \rightarrow T_f$ **and** $m, i, K_b \rightarrow \Delta T_b$ **then** $\Delta T_b \rightarrow T_b$

$\Delta T_f = K_f\, i m_{i=3}$ $\quad T_f = T_f^\circ - \Delta T_f$ $\quad \Delta T_b = K_b\, i m_{i=3}$ $\quad T_b = T_b^\circ + \Delta T_b$

Solution: $\Delta T_f = K_f i m = 1.86 \frac{°C}{m} \times 3 \times 0.150\ m = 0.837\ °C$ then

$T_f = T_f^\circ - \Delta T_f = 0.000\ °C - 0.837\ °C = -0.837\ °C$ and

$\Delta T_b = K_b i\, m = 0.512 \frac{°C}{m} \times 3 \times 0.150\ m = 0.230\ °C$ then

$T_b = T_b^\circ - \Delta T_b = 100.000\ °C + 0.230\ °C = 100.230\ °C.$

Check: The units (°C) are correct. The magnitude of the answer (– 0.8 °C and 100.2 °C) seems reasonable since the molality of the particles is 0.5. The shift in boiling point is less than the shift in freezing point because the constant for boiling is smaller than the constant for freezing.

12.87 (a) **Given:** 0.100 m of $FeCl_3$ **Find:** T_f **Other:** $K_f = 1.86\ °C/m$; $i_{measured} = 3.4$
Conceptual Plan: $m, i, K_f \rightarrow \Delta T_f$ **then** $\Delta T_f \rightarrow T_f$

$\Delta T_f = K_f\, i m$ $\quad T_f = T_f^\circ - \Delta T_f$

Solution: $\Delta T_f = K_f i m = 1.86 \frac{°C}{m} \times 3.4 \times 0.100\ m = 0.632\ °C$ then

$T_f = T_f^\circ - \Delta T_f = 0.000\ °C - 0.632\ °C = -0.632\ °C.$

Check: The units (°C) are correct. The magnitude of the answer (– 0.6 °C) seems reasonable since the theoretical molality of the particles is 0.4.

(b) **Given:** 0.085 M of K_2SO_4 at 298 K **Find:** Π **Other:** $i_{measured} = 2.6$
Conceptual Plan: $M, i, T \rightarrow \Pi$

$\Pi = iM\,RT$

Solution: $\Pi = iM\,RT = 2.6 \times 0.085 \frac{mol}{L} \times 0.08206 \frac{L \cdot atm}{K \cdot mol} \times 298\ K = 5.4\ atm$

Check: The units (atm) are correct. The magnitude of the answer (5 atm) seems reasonable since the molarity of particles is ~ 0.2 m.

(c) **Given:** 1.22 % by mass $MgCl_2$ **Find:** T_b **Other:** $K_b = 0.512\ °C/m$; $i_{measured} = 2.7$
Conceptual Plan: percent by mass $\rightarrow g_{MgCl_2}, g_{H_2O}$ **then** $g_{H_2O} \rightarrow kg_{H_2O}$ **and** $g_{MgCl_2} \rightarrow mol_{MgCl_2}$ **then**

$\text{mass percent} = \frac{\text{mass solute}}{\text{mass solution}} \times 100\%$ $\quad \frac{1\ kg}{1000\ g}$ $\quad \frac{1\ mol\ MgCl_2}{95.22\ g\ MgCl_2}$

$mol_{MgCl_2}, kg_{H_2O} \rightarrow m$ **then** $m, i, K_b \rightarrow \Delta T_b \rightarrow T_b$

$m = \frac{\text{amount solute (moles)}}{\text{mass solvent (kg)}}$ $\quad \Delta T_b = K_b\, i m$ $\quad T_b = T_b^\circ + \Delta T_b$

Solution: $\text{mass percent} = \frac{\text{mass solute}}{\text{mass solution}} \times 100\%$ so 1.22 % by mass $MgCl_2$ means 1.22 g $MgCl_2$ and 100.00 g – 1.22 g = 98.78 g water. Then $98.78\ g \times \frac{1\ kg}{1000\ g} = 0.09878\ kg$ and

$1.22\ g\ MgCl_2 \times \frac{1\ mol\ MgCl_2}{95.23\ g\ MgCl_2} = 0.0128110\ mol\ MgCl_2$ then

$m = \frac{\text{amount solute (moles)}}{\text{mass solvent (kg)}} = \frac{0.0128110\ mol\ MgCl_2}{0.09878\ kg} = 0.129693\ m$ then

$\Delta T_b = K_b i m = 0.512 \frac{°C}{m} \times 2.7 \times 0.129706\ m = 0.18\ °C$ then

$T_b = T_b^\circ - \Delta T_b = 100.000\ °C + 0.18\ °C = 100.18\ °C.$

Check: The units (°C) are correct. The magnitude of the answer (100.2 °C) seems reasonable since the molality of the particles is ~ 1/3.

12.88 (a) **Given:** NaCl; 1.50×10^2 g water and $T_f = -1.0$ °C **Find:** m(NaCl)
Other: $K_f = 1.86$ °C/m; $i_{measured} = 1.9$
Conceptual Plan: $T_f \rightarrow \Delta T_f$ **then** $\Delta T_f, i, K_f \rightarrow m$ **then** $g_{H_2O} \rightarrow kg_{H_2O}$ **then** $m, kg_{H_2O} \rightarrow mol_{NaCl}$

$T_f = T_f^\circ - \Delta T_f$ $\quad \Delta T_f = K_f im \quad \frac{1\ kg}{1000\ g} \quad m = \frac{\text{amount solute (moles)}}{\text{mass solvent (kg)}}$

then $mol_{NaCl} \rightarrow g_{NaCl}$

$\frac{58.44\ gNaCl}{1\ mol\ NaCl}$

Solution: $T_f = T_f^\circ - \Delta T_f$ so $\Delta T_f = T_f^\circ - T_f = 0.0\ °C - 1.0\ °C = -1.0\ °C$ then $\Delta T_f = K_f im$.

Rearrange to solve for m. $m = \frac{\Delta T_f}{K_f i} = \frac{1.0\ °C}{1.86 \frac{°C}{m} \times 1.9} = 0.28297 m$ NaCl then

$1.50 \times 10^2\ g \times \frac{1\ kg}{1000\ g} = 0.150\ kg$ then $m = \frac{\text{amount solute (moles)}}{\text{mass solvent (kg)}}$ so

$mol_{NaCl} = m \times kg_{H_2O} = 0.28297 \frac{mol\ NaCl}{kg_{H_2O}} \times 0.150\ kg_{H_2O} = 0.042445\ mol\ NaCl$ then

$0.042445\ mol\ NaCl \times \frac{58.44\ g\ NaCl}{1\ mol\ NaCl} = 2.5\ g\ NaCl.$

Check: The units (g) are correct. The magnitude of the answer (2.5 g) seems reasonable since the temperature change is moderate and NaCl has a low formula mass.

(b) **Given:** $MgSO_4$; 2.50×10^2 mL solution and $\Pi = 3.82$ atm at 298 K **Find:** $m(MgSO_4)$
Other: $i_{measured} = 1.3$
Conceptual Plan: $i, \Pi, T \rightarrow M$ **then** $mL_{soln} \rightarrow L_{soln}$ **then** $L_{soln}, M \rightarrow mol_{MgSO_4} \rightarrow g_{MgSO_4}$

$\Pi = iM RT \quad \frac{1\ L}{1000\ mL} \quad M = \frac{\text{amount solute (moles)}}{\text{volume solution (L)}} \quad \frac{120.38\ g\ MgSO_4}{1\ mol\ MgSO_4}$

Solution: $\Pi = iM RT$. Rearrange to solve for M.

$M = \frac{\Pi}{i RT} = \frac{3.82\ atm}{1.3 \times 0.08206 \frac{L \cdot atm}{K \cdot mol} \times 298\ K} = 0.12016 \frac{mol\ MgSO_4}{L}$ then

$2.50 \times 10^2\ mL \times \frac{1\ L}{1000\ mL} = 0.250\ L$ then $M = \frac{\text{amount solute (moles)}}{\text{volume solution (L)}}$ so

$mol_{MgSO_4} = M \times L_{soln} = 0.12016 \frac{mol\ MgSO_4}{L} \times 0.250\ L = 0.030041\ mol\ MgSO_4$ finally

$0.030041\ mol\ MgSO_4 \times \frac{120.38\ g\ MgSO_4}{1\ mol\ MgSO_4} = 3.6\ g\ MgSO_4.$

Check: The units (g) are correct. The magnitude of the answer (4 g) seems reasonable since the pressure is moderate and $MgSO_4$ has a low formula mass.

(c) **Given:** $FeCl_3$; 2.50×10^2 g water and $T_b = 102$ °C **Find:** $m(FeCl_3)$ **Other:** $K_b = 0.512$ °C/m; $i_{measured} = 3.4$
Conceptual Plan: $T_b \rightarrow \Delta T_b$ **then** $\Delta T_b, i, K_b \rightarrow m$ **then** $g_{H_2O} \rightarrow kg_{H_2O}$ **then** $m, kg_{H_2O} \rightarrow mol_{FeCl_3}$

$T_b = T_b^\circ + \Delta T_b \quad \Delta T_b = K_b im \quad \frac{1\ kg}{1000\ g} \quad m = \frac{\text{amount solute (moles)}}{\text{mass solvent (kg)}}$

then $mol_{FeCl_3} \rightarrow g_{FeCl_3}$

$\frac{162.21\ g\ FeCl_3}{1\ mol\ FeCl_3}$

Solution: $T_b = T_b^\circ + \Delta T_b$ so $\Delta T_b = T_b - T_b^\circ = 102\ °C - 100\ °C = 2\ °C$ then $\Delta T_b = K_b im$.

Rearrange to solve for m. $m = \frac{\Delta T_b}{K_b i} = \frac{2\ °C}{0.512 \frac{°C}{m} \times 3.4} = 1.149\ m\ FeCl_3$ then

$2.50 \times 10^2\ g \times \frac{1\ kg}{1000\ g} = 0.250\ kg$ then $m = \frac{\text{amount solute (moles)}}{\text{mass solvent (kg)}}$ so

$mol_{FeCl_3} = m \times kg_{H_2O} = 1.149 \frac{mol\ FeCl_3}{\cancel{kg_{H_2O}}} \times 0.250\ \cancel{kg_{H_2O}} = 0.2872\ mol\ FeCl_3$ then

$0.2872\ \cancel{mol\ FeCl_3} \times \frac{162.21\ g\ FeCl_3}{1\ \cancel{mol\ FeCl_3}} = 47\ g\ FeCl_3 = 50\ g\ FeCl_3.$

Check: The units (g) are correct. The magnitude of the answer (50 g) seems reasonable since the temperature change is significant and we are making 0.25 L of solution.

12.89 **Given:** 0.100 M of ionic solution, $\Pi = 8.3$ atm at 25 °C **Find:** $i_{measured}$
Conceptual Plan: °C → K then $\Pi, M, T \rightarrow i$

$K = °C + 273.15$ $\qquad \Pi = iMRT$

Solution: 25 °C + 273.15 = 298 K then $\Pi = iMRT$. Rearrange to solve for i.

$$i = \frac{\Pi}{MRT} = \frac{8.3\ \cancel{atm}}{0.100 \frac{\cancel{mol}}{\cancel{L}} \times 0.08206 \frac{\cancel{L} \cdot \cancel{atm}}{\cancel{K} \cdot \cancel{mol}} \times 298\ \cancel{K}} = 3.4.$$

Check: The units (none) are correct. The magnitude of the answer (3) seems reasonable for an ionic solution with a high osmotic pressure.

12.90 **Given:** 8.92 g of KBr in 500.0 mL solution, $\Pi = 6.97$ atm at 25 °C **Find:** $i_{measured}$
Conceptual Plan: °C → K and $mL_{soln} \rightarrow L_{soln}$ and $g_{KBr} \rightarrow mol_{KBr}$ then $mol_{KBr}, L_{soln} \rightarrow$ M then

$K = °C + 273.15$ $\qquad \frac{1\ L}{1000\ mL}$ $\qquad \frac{1\ mol\ KBr}{119.01\ g\ KBr}$ $\qquad M = \frac{amount\ solute\ (moles)}{volume\ solution\ (L)}$

$\Pi, M, T \rightarrow i$

$\Pi = iMRT$

Solution: 25 °C + 273.15 = 298 K and $500.0\ \cancel{mL} \times \frac{1\ L}{1000\ \cancel{mL}} = 0.5000$ L and

$8.93\ \cancel{g\ KBr} \times \frac{1\ mol\ KBr}{119.01\ \cancel{g\ KBr}} = 0.0750357\ mol\ KBr$ then

$M = \frac{amount\ solute\ (moles)}{volume\ solution\ (L)} = \frac{0.0750357\ mol\ KBr}{0.5000\ L} = 0.150071 \frac{mol\ KBr}{L}$ then $\Pi = iMRT$.

Rearrange to solve for i. $i = \frac{\Pi}{MRT} = \frac{6.97\ \cancel{atm}}{0.150071 \frac{\cancel{mol}}{\cancel{L}} \times 0.08206 \frac{\cancel{L} \cdot \cancel{atm}}{\cancel{K} \cdot \cancel{mol}} \times 298\ \cancel{K}} = 1.90.$

Check: The units (none) are correct. The magnitude of the answer (1.9) seems reasonable for KBr since we expect i to be 2 if it completely dissociates. Since both ions are large and have only one charge each, we expect i to be close to the theoretical value.

12.91 **Given:** 5.50 % NaCl by mass in water at 25 °C **Find:** P_{H_2O} **Other:** $P^{\circ}_{H_2O} = 23.78$ torr
Conceptual Plan: % NaCl by mass → g_{NaCl}, g_{H_2O} then $g_{NaCl} \rightarrow mol_{NaCl}$ and

$\frac{5.50\ g\ NaCl}{100\ g\ (NaCl + H_2O)}$ $\qquad \frac{1\ mol\ NaCl}{58.44\ g\ NaCl}$

$g_{H_2O} \rightarrow mol_{H_2O}$ then $mol_{NaCl}, mol_{H_2O} \rightarrow \chi_{H_2O}$ then $\chi_{H_2O}, P^{\circ}_{H_2O} \rightarrow P_{H_2O}$

$\frac{1\ mol\ H_2O}{18.01\ g\ H_2O}$ $\qquad \chi = \frac{amount\ solute\ (in\ moles)}{total\ amount\ of\ solute\ and\ solvent\ (in\ moles)}$ $\qquad P_{solution} = \chi_{solvent} P^{\circ}_{solvent}$

Solution: $\frac{5.50\ g\ NaCl}{100\ g\ (NaCl + H_2O)}$ means 5.50 g NaCl and (100 g – 5.50 g) = 94.5 g H_2O then

$5.50\ \cancel{g\ NaCl} \times \frac{1\ mol\ NaCl}{58.44\ \cancel{g\ NaCl}} = 0.0941136\ mol\ NaCl$ and $94.5\ \cancel{g\ H_2O} \times \frac{1\ mol\ H_2O}{18.01\ \cancel{g\ H_2O}} = 5.24708\ mol\ H_2O$ the

number of moles of solute = $i_{NaCl} \times n_{NaCl}$ so $\chi_{solv} = \frac{amount\ solvent\ (in\ moles)}{total\ amount\ solute\ and\ solvent\ particles\ (in\ moles)} =$

$\frac{5.24708\ \cancel{mol}}{5.24708\ \cancel{mol} + 2(0.0941136\ \cancel{mol})} = 0.96536$ then $P_{soln} = \chi_{solv} P^{\circ}_{solv} = 0.96536 \times 23.78\ torr = 23.0\ torr$

Check: The units (torr) are correct. The magnitude of the answer (23 torr) seems reasonable since it is a drop from the pure vapor pressure. Only a fraction of a mole of NaCl is added, so the pressure will not drop much.

12.92 **Given:** $CaCl_2$ and water; $P^{\circ}_{H_2O} = 92.6$ mm Hg, $P_{H_2O} = 81.6$ mm Hg at 50 °C; **Find:** mass percent $CaCl_2$

Conceptual Plan: $P_{H_2O}, P^{\circ}_{H_2O} \rightarrow \chi_{H_2O}$ **then assume 1 mol water,** $\chi_{H_2O} \rightarrow$ **mol** $_{CaCl_2}$ **then**

$$P_{solution} = \chi_{solvent} P^{\circ}_{solvent} \qquad \chi_{H_2O} = \frac{\text{mol } H_2O}{\text{mol } H_2O + 3 \text{ x mol } CaCl_2}$$

mol $_{CaCl_2} \rightarrow$ **g** $_{CaCl_2}$ **and mol** $_{H_2O} \rightarrow$ **g** $_{H_2O}$ **then g** $_{CaCl_2}$, **g** $_{H_2O} \rightarrow$ **percent by mass** $CaCl_2$

$$\frac{110.99 \text{ g } CaCl_2}{1 \text{ mol } CaCl_2} \qquad \frac{18.01 \text{ g } H_2O}{1 \text{ mol } H_2O} \qquad \text{mass percent} = \frac{\text{mass solute}}{\text{mass solution}} \times 100\%$$

Solution: $P_{solution} = \chi_{solvent} P^{\circ}_{solvent}$. Rearrange to solve for χ_{H_2O}.

$$\chi_{solvent} = \frac{P_{solution}}{P^{\circ}_{solvent}} = \frac{81.6 \text{ mm Hg}}{92.6 \text{ mm Hg}} = 0.881210 \text{ then assume 1 mol water}$$

$$\chi_{H_2O} = \frac{\text{mol } H_2O}{\text{mol } H_2O + 3 \text{ x mol } CaCl_2} \text{ so } 0.881210 = \frac{1 \text{ mol}}{1 \text{ mol} + 3 \text{ x mol } CaCl_2}.$$

Rearrange to solve for mol_{CaCl_2}.

$$0.881210(1 \text{ mol} + 3 \text{ x mol } CaCl_2) = 1 \text{ mol} \rightarrow \text{mol } CaCl_2 = \frac{1 \text{ mol} - 0.881210 \text{ mol}}{2.64363} = 0.0449345 \text{ mol } CaCl_2$$

then $0.0449345 \text{ mol } CaCl_2 \text{ x } \frac{110.99 \text{ g } CaCl_2}{1 \text{ mol } CaCl_2} = 4.98727 \text{ g } CaCl_2$ and $1 \text{ mol } H_2O = 18.01 \text{ g } H_2O$ then

$$\text{mass percent} = \frac{\text{mass solute}}{\text{mass solution}} \times 100\% = \frac{4.98727 \text{ g } CaCl_2}{4.98727 \text{ g} + 18.01 \text{ g}} \text{ x } 100\% = 21.69 \text{ percent by mass } CaCl_2.$$

Check: The units (%) are correct. The magnitude of the answer (22%) seems reasonable since there is a significant drop of the pure vapor pressure and the formula mass of the salt is much larger than water's molar mass.

Cumulative Problems

12.93 Chloroform is polar and has stronger solute–solvent interactions than nonpolar carbon tetrachloride.

12.94 Each molecule has one –OH group that is capable of hydrogen bonding. Since phenol is a smaller molecule than naphthol, the –OH group has a bigger impact on the overall polarity of the molecule.

12.95 **Given:** $KClO_4$: lattice energy = – 599 kJ/mol, $\Delta H_{hydration}$ = – 548 kJ/mol; 10.0 g $KClO_4$ in 100.00 mL solution
Find: ΔH_{soln} and ΔT **Other:** $C_s = 4.05$ J/g °C; $d = 1.05$ g/mL

Conceptual Plan: lattice energy, $\Delta H_{hydration} \rightarrow \Delta H_{soln}$ **and g** $\rightarrow$ **mol then mol,** $\Delta H_{soln} \rightarrow q(\text{kJ}) \rightarrow q(\text{J})$

$$\Delta H_{soln} = \Delta H_{solute} + \Delta H_{hydration} \text{ where } \Delta H_{solute} = -\Delta H_{lattice} \qquad \frac{1 \text{ mol}}{138.56 \text{ g}} \qquad q = n\,\Delta H_{soln} \qquad \frac{1000 \text{ J}}{1 \text{ kJ}}$$

then $\text{mL}_{soln} \rightarrow \text{g}_{soln}$ **then** q, g_{soln}, $C_s \rightarrow \Delta T$

$$\frac{1.05 \text{ g}}{1 \text{ mL}} \qquad q = m\,C_s\,\Delta T$$

Solution: $\Delta H_{soln} = \Delta H_{solute} + \Delta H_{hydration}$ where $\Delta H_{solute} = -\Delta H_{lattice}$ so $\Delta H_{soln} = \Delta H_{hydration} - \Delta H_{lattice}$

$$\Delta H_{soln} = -548 \text{ kJ/mol} - (-599 \text{ kJ/mol}) = +51 \text{ kJ/mol and } 10.0 \text{ g x } \frac{1 \text{ mol}}{138.56 \text{ g}} = 0.0721709 \text{ mol then}$$

$$q = n\,\Delta H_{soln} = 0.0721709 \text{ mol x } 51 \frac{\text{kJ}}{\text{mol}} = +3.6807 \text{ kJ x } \frac{1000 \text{ J}}{1 \text{ kJ}} = +3680.7 \text{ J absorbed then}$$

$100.0 \text{ mL x } \frac{1.05 \text{ g}}{1 \text{ mL}} = 105$ g. Since heat is absorbed when $KClO_4$ dissolves, the temperature will drop or $q = -3680.7$ J and $q = m\,C_s\,\Delta T$. Rearrange to solve for ΔT.

$$\Delta T = \frac{q}{m\,C_s} = \frac{-3680.7 \text{ J}}{105 \text{ g x } 4.05 \frac{\text{J}}{\text{g} \cdot {}^{\circ}\text{C}}} = -8.7\ {}^{\circ}\text{C}.$$

Check: The units (kJ/mol and °C) are correct. The magnitude of the answer (51 kJ/mol) makes physical sense because the lattice energy is larger than the heat of hydration. The magnitude of the temperature change (– 9 °C) makes physical sense since heat is absorbed and the heat of solution is fairly small.

12.96 **Given:** NaOH: lattice energy = – 887 kJ/mol, $\Delta H_{hydration}$ = – 932 kJ/mol; 25.0 g NaOH in solution, T_i = 25.0 °C; T_f = 100.0 °C **Find:** ΔH_{soln} and m (solution) **Other:** $C_s = 4.01$ J/g °C; $d = 1.05$ g/mL

Conceptual Plan: lattice energy, $\Delta H_{hydration}$ → ΔH_{soln} and g → mol then mol, ΔH_{soln} → q(kJ) → q(J)

$\Delta H_{soln} = \Delta H_{solute} + \Delta H_{hydration}$ *where* $\Delta H_{solute} = -\Delta H_{lattice}$ $\quad \frac{1 \text{ mol}}{40.00 \text{ g}}$ $\quad q = n\,\Delta H_{soln}$ $\quad \frac{1000 \text{ J}}{1 \text{ kJ}}$

and T_i, T_f → ΔT then q, ΔT, C_s → g_{soln} then g_{soln} → mL_{soln}

$\Delta T = T_f - T_i$ $\quad q = m\,C_s\,\Delta T$ $\quad \frac{1 \text{ mL}}{1.05 \text{ g}}$

Solution: $\Delta H_{soln} = \Delta H_{solute} + \Delta H_{hydration}$ where $\Delta H_{solute} = -\Delta H_{lattice}$ so $\Delta H_{soln} = \Delta H_{hydration} - \Delta H_{lattice}$

$\Delta H_{soln} = -932 \text{ kJ/mol} - (-887 \text{ kJ/mol}) = -45 \text{ kJ/mol}$ and $25.0 \text{ g} \times \frac{1 \text{ mol}}{40.00 \text{ g}} = 0.625$ mol then

$q = n\,\Delta H_{soln} = 0.625 \text{ mol} \times \left(-45 \frac{\text{kJ}}{\text{mol}}\right) = -28.125 \text{ kJ} \times \frac{1000 \text{ J}}{1 \text{ kJ}} = -28125 \text{ J}$ released then

$\Delta T = T_f - T_i = 100.0\ °\text{C} - 25.0\ °\text{C} = 75.0\ °\text{C}$. Since heat is released when NaOH dissolves the temperature will rise or $q = +28125$ J and $q = m\,C_s\,\Delta T$. Rearrange to solve for m.

$$m = \frac{q}{C_s\,\Delta T} = \frac{+28125 \text{ J}}{4.01 \frac{\text{J}}{\text{g}\cdot °\text{C}} \times 75.0\ °\text{C}} = 93.526 \text{ g soln then } 93.526 \text{ g} \times \frac{1 \text{ mL}}{1.05 \text{ g}} = 89 \text{ mL soln.}$$

Check: The units (kJ/mol and mL) are correct. The magnitude of the answer (– 45 kJ/mol) makes physical sense because the lattice energy is smaller than the heat of hydration. The magnitude of the solution volume (90 mL) makes physical sense since we have 2/3 mole of NaOH and large temperature change. NaOH is a strong base and so we expect heat to be released and need to take precautions in the lab.

12.97 **Given:** Argon, 0.0537 L; 25 °C, $P_{Ar} = 1.0$ atm to make 1.0 L saturated solution **Find:** k_H(Ar)
Conceptual Plan: °C → K and P_{Ar}, V, T → mol_{Ar} then mol_{Ar}, V_{soln}, P_{Ar} → k_H(Ar)

K = °C + 273.15 $\quad PV = nRT$ $\quad S_{Ar} = k_H(\text{Ar})P_{Ar}$ *with* $S_{Ar} = \frac{mol_{Ar}}{L_{soln}}$

Solution: 25 °C + 273.15 = 298 K and $PV = nRT$. Rearrange to solve for n.

$$n = \frac{PV}{RT} = \frac{1.0 \text{ atm} \times 0.0537 \text{ L}}{0.08206 \frac{\text{L}\cdot\text{atm}}{\text{K}\cdot\text{mol}} \times 298 \text{ K}} = 0.00219597 \text{ mol then } S_{Ar} = k_H(\text{Ar})P_{Ar} \text{ with } S_{Ar} = \frac{mol_{Ar}}{L_{soln}}.$$

Substitute in values and rearrange to solve for k_H.

$$k_H(\text{Ar}) = \frac{mol_{Ar}}{L_{soln}\,P_{Ar}} = \frac{0.00219597 \text{ mol}}{1.0\ L_{soln} \times 1.0 \text{ atm}} = 2.2 \times 10^{-3} \frac{\text{M}}{\text{atm}}.$$

Check: The units (M/atm) are correct. The magnitude of the answer (10^{-3}) seems reasonable since it is consistent with other values in the text.

12.98 **Given:** gas: 1.65 L; 25 °C, $P = 725$ torr; and $k_H = 0.112$ M/atm **Find:** volume of saturated solution
Conceptual Plan: °C → K and torr → atm P, V, T → mol_{gas} then mol_{He}, k_H, P → V_{soln}

K = °C + 273.15 $\quad \frac{1 \text{ atm}}{760 \text{ torr}}$ $\quad PV = nRT$ $\quad S_{gas} = k_H(\text{gas})P_{gas}$ *with* $S_{gas} = \frac{mol_{gas}}{L_{soln}}$

Solution: 25 °C + 273.15 = 298 K and $725 \text{ torr} \times \frac{1 \text{ atm}}{760 \text{ torr}} = 0.953947$ atm then $PV = nRT$. Rearrange to solve for n.

$$n = \frac{PV}{RT} = \frac{0.953947 \text{ atm} \times 1.65 \text{ L}}{0.08206 \frac{\text{L}\cdot\text{atm}}{\text{K}\cdot\text{mol}} \times 298 \text{ K}} = 0.0643666 \text{ mol then } S_{gas} = k_H(\text{gas})P_{gas}$$

with $S_{gas} = \frac{mol_{gas}}{L_{soln}}$. Substitute in values and rearrange to solve for V_{soln}.

$$L_{soln} = \frac{mol_{gas}}{k_H(\text{gas})P_{gas}} = \frac{0.0643666 \text{ mol}}{0.112 \frac{\text{mol}}{\text{L}\cdot\text{atm}} \times 0.953947 \text{ atm}} = 0.602 \text{ L soln.}$$

Check: The units (L) are correct. The magnitude of the answer (0.6 L) seems reasonable since the Henry's law constant is so large.

12.99 **Given:** 0.0020 ppm by mass Hg = legal limit; 0.0040 ppm by mass Hg = contaminated water; 50.0 mg Hg ingested **Find:** volume of contaminated water

Conceptual Plan: $mg_{Hg} \rightarrow g_{Hg} \rightarrow g_{H_2O} \rightarrow mL_{H_2O} \rightarrow L_{H_2O}$

$$\frac{1\ g}{1000\ mg} \quad \frac{10^6\ g\ water}{0.0040\ g\ Hg} \quad \frac{1\ mL}{1.00\ g} \quad \frac{1\ L}{1000\ mL}$$

Solution: $50.0\ mg\ Hg \times \frac{1\ g\ Hg}{1000\ mg\ Hg} \times \frac{10^6\ g\ water}{0.0040\ g\ Hg} \times \frac{1\ mL\ water}{1.00\ g\ water} \times \frac{1\ L\ water}{1000\ mL\ water} = 1.3 \times 10^4\ L\ water.$

Check: The units (L) are correct. The magnitude of the answer (10^4 L) seems reasonable since the concentration is so low.

12.100 **Given:** 2.4 g Na ingested/day; 0.050% Na by mass in water; $d = 1.0$ g/mL **Find:** volume of water

Conceptual Plan: $g_{Na} \rightarrow g_{H_2O} \rightarrow mL_{H_2O} \rightarrow L_{H_2O}$

$$\frac{100.000\ g\ water}{0.050\ g\ Na} \quad \frac{1\ mL}{1.0\ g} \quad \frac{1\ L}{1000\ mL}$$

Solution: $2.4\ g\ Na \times \frac{100.000\ g\ solution}{0.050\ g\ Na} \times \frac{1\ mL\ water}{1.0\ g\ solution} \times \frac{1\ L\ water}{1000\ mL\ water} = 4.8\ L\ water$

Check: The units (L) are correct. The magnitude of the answer (5 L) seems reasonable since the concentration is low, but not extremely low.

12.101 **Given:** 12.5% NaCl by mass in water at 55 °C; 2.5 L vapor **Find:** g H_2O in vapor

Other: $P^{\circ}_{H_2O} = 118$ torr, $i_{NaCl} = 2.0$ (complete dissociation)

Conceptual Plan: % NaCl by mass $\rightarrow g_{NaCl}, g_{H_2O}$ then $g_{NaCl} \rightarrow mol_{NaCl}$ and $g_{H_2O} \rightarrow mol_{H_2O}$

$$\frac{12.5\ g\ NaCl}{100\ g\ (NaCl + H_2O)} \quad \frac{1\ mol\ NaCl}{58.44\ g\ NaCl} \quad \frac{1\ mol\ H_2O}{18.01\ g\ H_2O}$$

then $mol_{NaCl}, mol_{H_2O} \rightarrow \chi_{NaCl} \rightarrow \chi_{H_2O}$ then $\chi_{H_2O}, P^{\circ}_{H_2O} \rightarrow P_{H_2O}$

$$\chi = \frac{\text{amount solute (in moles)}}{\text{total amount of solute and solvent (in moles)}} \quad \chi_{H_2O} = 1 - i_{NaCl}\chi_{NaCl} \quad P_{solution} = \chi_{solvent}P^{\circ}_{solvent}$$

then torr $\rightarrow$ atm and °C $\rightarrow$ K $P, V, T \rightarrow mol_{H_2O} \rightarrow g_{H_2O}$

$$\frac{1\ atm}{760\ torr} \quad K = °C + 273.15 \quad PV = nRT \quad \frac{18.01\ g\ H_2O}{1\ mol\ H_2O}$$

Solution: $\frac{12.5\ g\ NaCl}{100\ g\ (NaCl + H_2O)}$ means 12.5 g NaCl and (100 g – 12.5 g) = 87.5 g H_2O then

$12.5\ g\ NaCl \times \frac{1\ mol\ NaCl}{58.44\ g\ NaCl} = 0.213895\ mol\ NaCl$ and $87.5\ g\ H_2O \times \frac{1\ mol\ H_2O}{18.01\ g\ H_2O} = 4.85572\ mol\ H_2O$

then $\chi = \frac{\text{amount solute (in moles)}}{\text{total amount of solute and solvent (in moles)}} = \frac{0.213895\ mol}{0.213895\ mol + 4.85572\ mol} = 0.0421916$

then $\chi_{H_2O} = 1 - i_{NaCl}\chi_{NaCl} = 1 - (2.0 \times 0.0421916) = 0.915617$ then

$P_{solution} = \chi_{solvent}P^{\circ}_{solvent} = 0.915617 \times 118\ torr = 108.043\ torr\ H_2O$ then

$108.043\ torr\ H_2O \times \frac{1\ atm}{760\ torr} = 0.142162\ atm$

and 55 °C + 273.15 = 328 K then $PV = nRT$. Rearrange to solve for n.

$$n = \frac{PV}{RT} = \frac{0.142162\ atm \times 2.5\ L}{0.08206 \frac{L \cdot atm}{K \cdot mol} \times 328\ K} = 0.013204\ mol\ \text{then}$$

$0.013204\ mol\ H_2O \times \frac{18.02\ g\ H_2O}{1\ mol\ H_2O} = 0.24\ g\ H_2O.$

Check: The units (g) are correct. The magnitude of the answer (0.2 g) seems reasonable since there is very little mass in a vapor.

12.102 **Given:** 19.5 mg water in 1 L vapor at 25 °C **Find:** mole percent solute in solution **Other:** $P^{\circ}_{H_2O} = 23.78$ torr

Conceptual Plan: $mg_{H_2O} \rightarrow g_{H_2O} \rightarrow mol_{H_2O}$ and °C $\rightarrow$ K then $V, mol_{H_2O}, T \rightarrow P_{H_2O}$ then

$$\frac{1\ g}{1000\ mg} \quad \frac{1\ mol\ H_2O}{18.01\ g\ H_2O} \quad K = °C + 273.15 \quad PV = nRT$$

then atm $\rightarrow$ torr then $P_{H_2O}, P^{\circ}_{H_2O} \rightarrow \chi_{H_2O} \rightarrow \chi_{solute} \rightarrow$ **mole percent solute**

$$\frac{760\ torr}{1\ atm} \quad P_{H_2O} = \chi_{H_2O}P^{\circ}_{H_2O} \quad \chi_{Solute} = 1 - \chi_{H_2O} \quad \text{mole percent solute} = \chi_{Solute} \times 100\%$$

Solution: $19.5 \text{ mg } H_2O \times \frac{1 \text{ g } H_2O}{1000 \text{ mg } H_2O} \times \frac{1 \text{ mol } H_2O}{18.01 \text{ g } H_2O} = 0.00108273 \text{ mol } H_2O$ and

55 °C + 273.15 = 328 K then $PV = nRT$. Rearrange to solve for P.

$$P = \frac{nRT}{V} = \frac{0.00108273 \text{ mol} \times 0.08206 \frac{\text{L} \cdot \text{atm}}{\text{K} \cdot \text{mol}} \times 328 \text{ K}}{1.00 \text{ L}} = 0.0291424 \text{ atm}$$

$0.0291424 \text{ atm} \times \frac{760 \text{ torr}}{1 \text{ atm}} = 22.1482$ torr and $P_{H_2O} = \chi_{H_2O} P^{\circ}_{H_2O}$. Rearrange to solve for χ_{H_2O}.

$\chi_{H_2O} = \frac{P_{H_2O}}{P^{\circ}_{H_2O}} = \frac{22.1482 \text{ torr}}{23.78 \text{ torr}} = 0.931381$ then $\chi_{\text{solute}} = 1 - \chi_{H_2O} = 1 - 0.931381 = 0.0686192$ then

mole percent solute $= \chi_{\text{solute}} \times 100\% = 0.0686192 \times 100\% = 6.86$ mole percent.

Check: The units (mole percent) are correct. The magnitude of the answer (7 mole percent) seems reasonable since we expect there to be more water than solute.

12.103 **Given:** $T_b = 106.5$ °C aqueous solution **Find:** T_f **Other:** $K_f = 1.86$ °C/m; $K_b = 0.512$ °C/m

Conceptual Plan: $T_b \rightarrow \Delta T_b$ **then** $\Delta T_b, K_b \rightarrow m$ **then** $m, K_f \rightarrow \Delta T_f \rightarrow T_f$

$T_b = T^{\circ}_b + \Delta T_b$ $\quad \Delta T_b = K_b m$ $\quad \Delta T_f = K_f m$ $\quad T_f = T^{\circ}_f - \Delta T_f$

Solution: $T_b = T^{\circ}_b + \Delta T_b$ so $\Delta T_b = T_b - T^{\circ}_b = 106.5 \text{ °C} - 100.0 \text{ °C} = 6.5 \text{ °C}$ then $\Delta T_b = K_b m$.

Rearrange to solve for m. $m = \frac{\Delta T_b}{K_b} = \frac{6.5 \text{ °C}}{0.512 \frac{\text{°C}}{m}} = 12.695\ m$ then

$\Delta T_f = K_f m = 1.86 \frac{\text{°C}}{m} \times 12.695\ m = 23.6 \text{ °C}$ then $T_f = T^{\circ}_f - \Delta T_f = 0.000 \text{ °C} - 23.6 \text{ °C °C} = -24 \text{ °C}$.

Check: The units (°C) are correct. The magnitude of the answer (– 24 °C) seems reasonable since the shift in boiling point is less than the shift in freezing point because the constant for boiling is smaller than the constant for freezing.

12.104 **Given:** $P_{H_2O} = 20.5$ torr at 25 °C aqueous solution **Find:** T_b **Other:** $P^{\circ}_{H_2O} = 23.78$ torr; $K_b = 0.512$ °C/m

Conceptual Plan: $P_{H_2O}, P^{\circ}_{H_2O} \rightarrow \chi_{H_2O}$ **assume 1 kg water kg** $_{H_2O} \rightarrow$ **mol**$_{H_2O}$ **then**

$P_{H_2O} = \chi_{H_2O} P^{\circ}_{H_2O}$ $\quad \frac{1 \text{ mol } H_2O}{18.01 \text{ g } H_2O}$

mol$_{H_2O}$, $\chi_{H_2O} \rightarrow$ **mol** $_{\text{solute}}$ **then mol** $_{\text{solute}}$, **kg** $_{H_2O} \rightarrow m_{\text{solute}}$ **then** $m, K_b \rightarrow \Delta T_b \rightarrow T_b$

$\chi_{H_2O} = \frac{\text{moles } H_2O}{\text{moles } H_2O + \text{moles solute}}$ $\quad m = \frac{\text{amount solute (moles)}}{\text{mass solvent (kg)}}$ $\quad \Delta T_b = K_b m \quad T_b = T^{\circ}_b + \Delta T_b$

Solution: $P_{H_2O} = \chi_{H_2O} P^{\circ}_{H_2O}$. Rearrange to solve for χ_{H_2O}. $\chi_{H_2O} = \frac{P_{H_2O}}{P^{\circ}_{H_2O}} = \frac{20.5 \text{ torr}}{23.78 \text{ torr}} = 0.862069$ then

$1000 \text{ g } H_2O \times \frac{1 \text{ mol } H_2O}{18.01 \text{ g } H_2O} = 55.52470 \text{ mol } H_2O$ then

$\chi_{H_2O} = \frac{\text{moles } H_2O}{\text{moles } H_2O + \text{moles solute}} = \frac{55.52470 \text{ mol}}{55.52470 \text{ mol} + x \text{ mol}} = 0.862069$. Solve for x moles of solute.

$55.52470 \text{ mol} = 0.862069\ (55.52470 \text{ mol} + x \text{ mol}) \rightarrow x = \frac{(55.52470 - 47.8661) \text{ mol}}{0.862069} = 8.88395$ mol then

$m = \frac{\text{amount solute (moles)}}{\text{mass solvent (kg)}} = \frac{8.88395 \text{ mol}}{1 \text{ kg}} = 8.88395\ m$ then $\Delta T_b = K_b m = 0.512 \frac{\text{°C}}{m} \times 8.88395\ m = 4.5 \text{ °C}$

then $T_b = T^{\circ}_b + \Delta T_b = 100.0 \text{ °C} + 4.5 \text{ °C} = 104.5 \text{ °C}$.

Check: The units (°C) are correct. The magnitude of the answer (4.5 °C) seems reasonable since there is a significant lowering of the vapor pressure.

12.105 (a) **Given:** 0.90 % NaCl by mass per volume; isotonic aqueous solution at 25 °C; KCl; $i = 1.9$

Find: % KCl by mass per volume

Conceptual Plan: Isotonic solutions will have the same number of particles. Since i is the same, $\frac{1 \text{ mol KCl}}{1 \text{ mol NaCl}}$ **the new % mass per volume will be the mass ratio of the two salts.**

percent by mass per volume $= \frac{\text{mass solute}}{V} \times 100\%$ $\quad \frac{1 \text{ mol NaCl}}{58.44 \text{ g NaCl}}$ and $\frac{74.56 \text{ g KCl}}{1 \text{ mol KCl}}$

Solution: percent by mass per volume $= \frac{\text{mass solute}}{V} \times 100\% =$

$$= \frac{0.0090 \text{ g NaCl}}{V} \times \frac{1 \text{ mol NaCl}}{58.44 \text{ g NaCl}} \times \frac{1 \text{ mol KCl}}{1 \text{ mol NaCl}} \times \frac{74.56 \text{ g KCl}}{1 \text{ mol KCl}} \times 100\%$$

= 1.1% KCl by mass per volume

Check: The units (% KCl by mass per volume) are correct. The magnitude of the answer (1.1) seems reasonable since the molar mass of KCl is larger than the molar mass of NaCl.

(b) **Given:** 0.90 % NaCl by mass per volume; isotonic aqueous solution at 25 °C; NaBr; $i = 1.9$
Find: % NaBr by mass per volume
Conceptual Plan: Isotonic solutions will have the same number of particles. Since i is the same, $\frac{1 \text{ mol NaBr}}{1 \text{ mol NaCl}}$ **the new % mass per volume will be the mass ratio of the two salts.**

percent by mass per volume $= \frac{\text{mass solute}}{V} \times 100\%$ $\frac{1 \text{ mol NaCl}}{58.44 \text{ g NaCl}}$ and $\frac{102.90 \text{ g NaBr}}{1 \text{ mol NaBr}}$

Solution: percent by mass per volume $= \frac{\text{mass solute}}{V} \times 100\% =$

$$= \frac{0.0090 \text{ g NaCl}}{V} \times \frac{1 \text{ mol NaCl}}{58.44 \text{ g NaCl}} \times \frac{1 \text{ mol NaBr}}{1 \text{ mol NaCl}} \times \frac{102.90 \text{ g NaBr}}{1 \text{ mol NaBr}} \times 100\%$$

= 1.6% NaBr by mass per volume

Check: The units (% NaBr by mass per volume) are correct. The magnitude of the answer (1.6) seems reasonable since the molar mass of NaBr is larger than the molar mass of NaCl.

(c) **Given:** 0.90 % NaCl by mass per volume; isotonic aqueous solution at 25 °C; glucose ($C_6H_{12}O_6$); $i = 1.9$ **Find:** % glucose by mass per volume
Conceptual Plan: Isotonic solutions will have the same number of particles. Since glucose is a nonelectrolyte, the i is not the same, then use the mass ratio of the two compounds.

$\frac{1.9 \text{ mol } C_6H_{12}O_6}{1 \text{ mol NaCl}}$ percent by mass per volume $= \frac{\text{mass solute}}{V} \times 100\%$ $\frac{1 \text{ mol NaCl}}{58.44 \text{ g NaCl}}$ and $\frac{180.16 \text{ g } C_6H_{12}O_6}{1 \text{ mol } C_6H_{12}O_6}$

Solution: percent by mass per volume $= \frac{\text{mass solute}}{V} \times 100\% =$

$$= \frac{0.0090 \text{ g NaCl}}{V} \times \frac{1 \text{ mol NaCl}}{58.44 \text{ g NaCl}} \times \frac{1.9 \text{ mol } C_6H_{12}O_6}{1 \text{ mol NaCl}} \times \frac{180.16 \text{ g } C_6H_{12}O_6}{1 \text{ mol } C_6H_{12}O_6} \times 100\% =$$

= 5.3% $C_6H_{12}O_6$ by mass per volume

Check: The units (% $C_6H_{12}O_6$ by mass per volume) are correct. The magnitude of the answer (1.6) seems reasonable since the molar mass of $C_6H_{12}O_6$ is larger than the molar mass of NaCl and we need more moles of $C_6H_{12}O_6$ since it is a nonelectrolyte.

12.106 **Given:** 28.5 g of magnesium citrate ($Mg_3(C_6H_5O_3)_2$) in 235 mL of solution at 37 °C, complete dissociation
Find: Π
Conceptual Plan: $\text{mL}_{soln} \rightarrow \text{L}_{soln}$ **and** $\text{g}\ Mg_3(C_6H_5O_3)_2 \rightarrow \text{mol}\ Mg_3(C_6H_5O_3)_2$ **then** $\text{mol}\ Mg_3(C_6H_5O_3)_2, \text{L}_{soln} \rightarrow M$

$\frac{1 \text{ L}}{1000 \text{ mL}}$ $\frac{1 \text{ mol } Mg_3(C_6H_5O_3)_2}{323.14 \text{ g } Mg_3(C_6H_5O_3)_2}$ $M = \frac{\text{amount solute (moles)}}{\text{volume solution (L)}}$

then $M, i, T \rightarrow \Pi$

$\Pi = iMRT$ where $i = 5$

Solution: $235 \text{ mL} \times \frac{1 \text{ L}}{1000 \text{ mL}} = 0.235 \text{ L}$ and

$$28.5 \text{ g } Mg_3(C_6H_5O_3)_2 \times \frac{1 \text{ mol } Mg_3(C_6H_5O_3)_2}{323.14 \text{ g } Mg_3(C_6H_5O_3)_2} = 0.08\underline{8}1982 \text{ mol } Mg_3(C_6H_5O_3)_2 \text{ then}$$

$$M = \frac{\text{amount solute (moles)}}{\text{volume solution (L)}} = \frac{0.08\underline{8}1982 \text{ mol } Mg_3(C_6H_5O_3)_2}{0.235 \text{ L}} = 0.37\underline{5}311 \text{ M then}$$

$$\Pi = iMRT = 5 \times 0.37\underline{5}311 \frac{\text{mol}}{\text{L}} \times 0.08206 \frac{\text{L} \cdot \text{atm}}{\text{K} \cdot \text{mol}} \times 310. \text{ K} = 47.7 \text{ atm}$$

Check: The units (atm) are correct. The magnitude of the answer (48 atm) seems reasonable since the molarity is ~ 1.5.

12.107 **Given:** 4.5701 g of $MgCl_2$ and 43.238 g water, $P_{soln} = 0.3624$ atm, $P^\circ_{soln} = 0.3804$ atm at 348.0 K **Find:** $i_{measured}$
Conceptual Plan: $g_{MgCl_2} \rightarrow mol_{MgCl_2}$ and $g_{H_2O} \rightarrow mol_{H_2O}$ then $P_{soln}, P^\circ_{soln}, \rightarrow \chi\ MgCl_2$

$$\frac{1\ \text{mol MgCl}_2}{95.218\ \text{g MgCl}_2} \qquad \frac{1\ \text{mol H}_2\text{O}}{18.015\ \text{g H}_2\text{O}} \qquad P_{Soln} = (1 - \chi_{MgCl_2})P^\circ_{H_2O}$$

then mol $_{MgCl_2}$, mol_{H_2O}, $\chi\ MgCl_2 \rightarrow i$

$$\chi_{MgCl_2} = \frac{i\ (\text{moles MgCl}_2)}{\text{moles H}_2\text{O} + i\ (\text{moles MgCl}_2)}$$

Solution: $4.5701\ \text{g MgCl}_2 \times \dfrac{1\ \text{mol MgCl}_2}{95.218\ \text{g MgCl}_2} = 0.047996177$ mol $MgCl_2$ and

$43.238\ \text{g H}_2\text{O} \times \dfrac{1\ \text{mol H}_2\text{O}}{18.015\ \text{g H}_2\text{O}} = 2.4001110$ mol H_2O then $P_{soln} = (1 - \chi_{MgCl_2})P^\circ_{H_2O}$ so

$\chi_{MgCl_2} = 1 - \dfrac{P_{soln}}{P^\circ_{H_2O}} = 1 - \dfrac{0.3624\ \text{atm}}{0.3804\ \text{atm}} = 0.04731861$. Solve for i.

$i\,(0.047996177) = 0.04731861(2.4001110 + i\,(0.047996177)) \rightarrow$

$i\,(0.047996177 - 0.002271112) = 0.1135699 \rightarrow i = \dfrac{0.1135699}{0.04572506} = 2.484.$

Check: The units (none) are correct. The magnitude of the answer (2.5) seems reasonable for $MgCl_2$ since we expect i to be 3 if it completely dissociates. Since Mg is small and doubly charged, we expect a significant drop from 3.

12.108 **Given:** 7.050 g of HNO_2 and 1.000 kg of water, $T_f = -0.2929$ °C **Find:** fraction dissociated
Other: $K_f = 1.86$ °C/m;
Conceptual Plan: g $_{HNO_2} \rightarrow$ mol $_{HNO_2}$ then mol $_{HNO_2}$, $kg_{H_2O} \rightarrow m$ then m, $\Delta T_{factual}$, $K_f \rightarrow i_{actual}$ then

$$\frac{1\ \text{mol HNO}_2}{47.02\ \text{g HNO}_2} \qquad m = \frac{\text{amount solute (moles)}}{\text{mass solvent (kg)}} \qquad \Delta T_{factual} = i_{actual} m K_f$$

$i_{actual} \rightarrow$ **fraction dissociated**

fraction dissociated = $i_{actual} - 1$

Solution: $7.050\ \text{g HNO}_2 \times \dfrac{1\ \text{mol HNO}_2}{47.02\ \text{g HNO}_2} = 0.1499361$ mol HNO_2 then

$m = \dfrac{\text{amount solute (moles)}}{\text{mass solvent (kg)}} = \dfrac{0.1499361\ \text{mol HNO}_2}{1.000\ \text{kg}} = 0.1499361\ m$ then $\Delta T_{factual} = i_{actual} m K_f \rightarrow$

$0.2929 = i(0.1499361\ m)\left(\dfrac{1.86\ °\text{C}}{m}\right) \rightarrow i = 1.0502$ then fraction dissociated $= i_{actual} - 1 = 1.0502 - 1 = 0.050$

Check: The units (none) are correct. The magnitude of the answer (0.05) seems reasonable since weak acids do not fully dissociate.

12.109 **Given:** $T_b = 375.3$ K aqueous solution **Find:** P_{H_2O} **Other:** $P^\circ_{H_2O} = 0.2467$ atm; $K_b = 0.512$ °C/m
Conceptual Plan: $T_b \rightarrow \Delta T_b$ then $\Delta T_b, K_b \rightarrow m$ assume 1 kg water kg $_{H_2O} \rightarrow mol_{H_2O}$ then

$$T_b = T^\circ_b + \Delta T_b \qquad \Delta T_b = K_b m \qquad \frac{1\ \text{mol H}_2\text{O}}{18.01\ \text{g H}_2\text{O}}$$

$m \rightarrow$ mol $_{Solute}$ then mol_{H_2O}, mol $_{Solute} \rightarrow \chi_{H_2O}$ then $\chi_{H_2O}, P^\circ_{H_2O} \rightarrow P_{H_2O}$

$$m = \frac{\text{amount solute (moles)}}{\text{mass solvent (kg)}} \qquad \chi_{H_2O} = \frac{\text{moles H}_2\text{O}}{\text{moles H}_2\text{O} + \text{moles solute}} \qquad P_{H_2O} = \chi_{H_2O} P^\circ_{H_2O}$$

Solution: $T_b = T^\circ_b + \Delta T_b$ so $\Delta T_b = T_b - T^\circ_b = 375.3\ \text{K} - 373.15\ \text{K} = 2.2\ \text{K} = 2.2$ °C then

$\Delta T_b = K_b m$. Rearrange to solve for m. $m = \dfrac{\Delta T_b}{K_b} = \dfrac{2.2\ °\text{C}}{0.512\ \dfrac{°\text{C}}{m}} = 4.296875\ m$ then

$1000\ \text{g H}_2\text{O} \times \dfrac{1\ \text{mol H}_2\text{O}}{18.01\ \text{g H}_2\text{O}} = 55.49390$ mol H_2O then

$m = \dfrac{\text{amount solute (moles)}}{\text{mass solvent (kg)}} = \dfrac{x\ \text{mol}}{1\ \text{kg}} = 4.296875\ m$ so $x = 4.296875$ mol then

$\chi_{H_2O} = \dfrac{\text{moles H}_2\text{O}}{\text{moles H}_2\text{O} + \text{moles solute}} = \dfrac{55.49390\ \text{mol}}{55.49390\ \text{mol} + 4.296875\ \text{mol}} = 0.9281348$

then $P_{H_2O} = \chi_{H_2O} P^\circ_{H_2O} = 0.9281348 \times 0.2467\ \text{atm} = 0.229$ atm.

Check: The units (atm) are correct. The magnitude of the answer (0.229 atm) seems reasonable since the mole fraction is lowered by ~ 7%.

12.110 **Given:** 0.438 M K_2CrO_4 aqueous solution; d = 1.063 g/mL at 298 K; complete dissociation **Find:** P_{soln}
Other: $P^{\circ}_{H_2O} = 0.0313$ atm

Conceptual Plan: assume 1 L solution, so we have 0.438 $mol_{K_2CrO_4} \rightarrow g_{K_2CrO_4}$ **then** $mL_{soln} \rightarrow g_{soln}$ **then**

$$\frac{194.20\ g\ K_2CrO_4}{1\ mol\ K_2CrO_4} \qquad \frac{1.063\ g}{1\ mL}$$

$g_{K_2CrO_4}, g_{soln} \rightarrow g_{H_2O} \rightarrow mol_{H_2O}$ **then** mol_{H_2O}, $mol_{solute} \rightarrow \chi_{H_2O}$ **then** $\chi_{H_2O}, P^{\circ}_{H_2O} \rightarrow P_{H_2O}$

$$gH_2O = g\ soln - g\ K_2CrO_4 \qquad \frac{1\ mol\ H_2O}{18.01\ g\ H_2O} \qquad \chi_{H_2O} = \frac{moles\ H_2O}{moles\ H_2O + moles\ solute} \qquad P_{soln} = (1 - i\chi_{K_2CrO_4})P^{\circ}_{H_2O}\ \ i = 3$$

Solution: $0.438\ mol\ K_2CrO_4 \times \frac{194.20\ g\ K_2CrO_4}{1\ mol\ K_2CrO_4} = 85.0596\ g\ K_2CrO_4$ then

$1000\ mL \times \frac{1.063\ g}{1\ mL} = 1063$ g soln then

$g\ H_2O = g\ soln - g\ K_2CrO_4 = 1063\ g\ soln - 85.0596\ g\ K_2CrO_4 = 977.9404\ g\ H_2O$ then

$977.9404\ g\ H_2O \times \frac{1\ mol\ H_2O}{18.01\ g\ H_2O} = 54.2999\ mol\ H_2O$ then

$$\chi_{K_2CrO_4} = \frac{moles\ K_2CrO_4}{moles\ H_2O + moles\ K_2CrO_4} = \frac{0.438\ mol}{54.2999\ mol + 0.438\ mol} = 0.00800177 \text{ then}$$

$P_{soln} = (1 - i\chi_{K_2CrO_4})P^{\circ}_{H_2O} = (1 - 3 \times 0.00800177)0.0313\ atm = 0.0305\ atm$

Check: The units (atm) are correct. The magnitude of the answer (0.03 atm) seems reasonable since the mole fraction is lowered by < 1 %.

12.111 **Given:** equal masses of carbon tetrachloride (CCl_4) and chloroform ($CHCl_3$) at 316 K; $P^{\circ}_{CCl_4} = 0.354$ atm; $P^{\circ}_{CHCl_3} = 0.526$ atm **Find:** χ_{CCl_4}, χ_{CHCl_3} in vapor; and P_{CHCl_3} in flask of condensed vapor

Conceptual Plan: assume 100 grams of each $g_{CCl_4} \rightarrow mol_{CCl_4}$ **and** $g_{CHCl_3} \rightarrow mol_{CHCl_3}$ **then**

$$\frac{1\ mol\ CCl_4}{153.82\ g\ CCl_4} \qquad \frac{1\ mol\ CHCl_3}{119.38\ g\ CHCl_3}$$

$mol_{CCl_4}, mol_{CHCl_3} \rightarrow \chi_{CCl_4}, \chi_{CHCl_3}$ **then** $\chi_{CCl_4}, P^{\circ}_{CCl_4} \rightarrow P_{CCl_4}$ **and** $\chi_{CHCl_3}, P^{\circ}_{CHCl_3} \rightarrow P_{CHCl_3}$ **then**

$$\chi_{CCl_4} = \frac{amount\ CCl_4\ (in\ moles)}{total\ amount\ (in\ moles)} \quad \chi_{CHCl_3} = 1 - \chi_{CCl_4} \qquad P_{CCl_4} = \chi_{CCl_4}P^{\circ}_{CCl_4} \qquad P_{CHCl_3} = \chi_{CHCl_3}P^{\circ}_{CHCl_3}$$

$P_{CCl_4}, P_{CHCl_3} \rightarrow P_{Total}$ **then since $n \propto P$ and we are calculating a mass percent, which is a ratio of masses,**

$$P_{Total} = P_{CCl_4} + P_{CHCl_3}$$

we can simply convert 1 atm to 1 mole so $P_{CCl_4}, P_{CHCl_3} \rightarrow n_{CCl_4}, n_{CHCl_3}$ **then**

$$\chi_{CCl_4} = \frac{amount\ CCl_4\ (in\ moles)}{total\ amount\ (in\ moles)}$$

$mol_{CCl_4}, mol_{CHCl_3} \rightarrow \chi_{CCl_4}, \chi_{CHCl_3}$ **then for the second vapor** $\chi_{CHCl_3}, P^{\circ}_{CHCl_3} \rightarrow P_{CHCl_3}$

$$\chi_{CHCl_3} = 1 - \chi_{CCl_4} \qquad P_{CHCl_3} = \chi_{CHCl_3}P^{\circ}_{CHCl_3}$$

Solution: $100.00\ g\ CCl_4 \times \frac{1\ mol\ CCl_4}{153.82\ g\ CCl_4} = 0.65011051\ mol\ CCl_4$ and

$100.00\ g\ CHCl_3 \times \frac{1\ mol\ CHCl_3}{119.38\ g\ CHCl_3} = 0.83766125\ mol\ CHCl_3$ then

$$\chi_{CCl_4} = \frac{amount\ CCl_4\ (in\ moles)}{total\ amount\ (in\ moles)} = \frac{0.65011051\ mol}{0.65011051\ mol + 0.83766125\ mol} = 0.43696925 \text{ and}$$

$\chi_{CHCl_3} = 1 - \chi_{CCl_4} = 1 - 0.43696925 = 0.56303075$ then

$P_{CCl_4} = \chi_{CCl_4}P^{\circ}_{CCl_4} = 0.43696925 \times 0.354\ atm = 0.154687\ atm$ and

$P_{CHCl_3} = \chi_{CHCl_3}P^{\circ}_{CHCl_3} = 0.56303075 \times 0.526\ atm = 0.296154\ atm$ then

$P_{Total} = P_{CCl_4} + P_{CHCl_3} = 0.154687 atm + 0.296154\ atm = 0.450841\ atm$ then

$mol_{CCl_4} = 0.154687$ mol and $mol_{CHCl_3} = 0.296154$ mol then

$$\chi_{CCl_4} = \frac{amount\ CCl_4\ (in\ moles)}{total\ amount\ (in\ moles)} = \frac{0.154687\ mol}{0.154687\ mol + 0.296154\ mol} = 0.343108 = 0.343 \text{ in the first vapor}$$

and $\chi_{CHCl_3} = 1 - \chi_{CCl_4} = 1 - 0.343108 = 0.656892 = 0.657$ in the first vapor; then in the second vapor

$P_{CHCl_3} = \chi_{CHCl_3} P^{\circ}_{CHCl_3} = 0.656892 \times 0.526 \text{ atm} = 0.345525 \text{ atm} = 0.346 \text{ atm}.$

Check: The units (none and atm) are correct. The magnitudes of the answers seem reasonable since it we expect the lighter component to be found preferentially in the vapor phase. This effect is magnified in the second vapor.

12.112 In the previous problem we saw that the original liquid has the $\chi_{CHCl_3} = 0.563$, and when the second vapor is condensed it rose to 0.657. Continue the preceding calculation scheme from Problem 111.

$P_{CCl_4} = \chi_{CCl_4} P^{\circ}_{CCl_4} = 0.343108 \times 0.354 \text{ atm} = 0.121460 \text{ atm}$ converting to moles; mol $_{CCl_4} = 0.121460$ mol and mol $_{CHCl_3} = 0.345525$ mol then

$$\chi_{CCl_4} = \frac{\text{amount } CCl_4 \text{ (in moles)}}{\text{total amount (in moles)}} = \frac{0.121460 \text{ mol}}{0.121460 \text{ mol} + 0.345525 \text{ mol}} = 0.260094 = 0.260 \text{ in the second vapor}$$

and $\chi_{CHCl_3} = 1 - \chi_{CCl_4} = 1 - 0.260094 = 0.739906 = 0.740$ in the second vapor then in the third vapor

$P_{CHCl_3} = \chi_{CHCl_3} P^{\circ}_{CHCl_3} = 0.739906 \times 0.526 \text{ atm} = 0.389191 \text{ atm}$ and

$P_{CCl_4} = \chi_{CCl_4} P^{\circ}_{CCl_4} = 0.260094 \times 0.354 \text{ atm} = 0.0920732 \text{ atm}$ converting to moles

mol $_{CCl_4} = 0.0920732$ mol and mol $_{CHCl_3} = 0.389191$ mol then

$$\chi_{CCl_4} = \frac{\text{amount } CCl_4 \text{ (in moles)}}{\text{total amount (in moles)}} = \frac{0.0920732 \text{ mol}}{0.0920732 \text{ mol} + 0.389191 \text{ mol}} = 0.191315 = 0.191 \text{ in the third vapor}$$

and $\chi_{CHCl_3} = 1 - \chi_{CCl_4} = 1 - 0.191315 = 0.808685 = 0.809$ in the third vapor then in the fourth vapor

$P_{CHCl_3} = \chi_{CHCl_3} P^{\circ}_{CHCl_3} = 0.808685 \times 0.526 \text{ atm} = 0.425368 \text{ atm}$ and

$P_{CCl_4} = \chi_{CCl_4} P^{\circ}_{CCl_4} = 0.191315 \times 0.354 \text{ atm} = 0.0677255 \text{ atm}$ converting to moles

mol $_{CCl_4} = 0.0677255$ mol and mol $_{CHCl_3} = 0.425368$ mol then

$$\chi_{CCl_4} = \frac{\text{amount } CCl_4 \text{ (in moles)}}{\text{total amount (in moles)}} = \frac{0.0677255 \text{ mol}}{0.0677255 \text{ mol} + 0.425368 \text{ mol}} = 0.137348 = 0.137 \text{ in the fourth vapor}$$

and $\chi_{CHCl_3} = 1 - \chi_{CCl_4} = 1 - 0.137348 = 0.862652 = 0.863$ in the fourth vapor. The concentration of the lighter component (chloroform) in the gas phase, increases with each step.

12.113 **Given:** 49.0 % H_2SO_4 by mass, $d = 1.39$ g/cm^3, 25.0 mL diluted to 99.8 cm^3 **Find:** molarity

Conceptual Plan: initial mL$_{solution}$ → g$_{solution}$ → g$_{H_2SO_4}$ → mol$_{H_2SO_4}$ and final mL$_{solution}$ → L$_{solution}$

$$\frac{1.39 \text{ g}}{1 \text{ mL}} \quad \frac{49.0 \text{ g } H_2SO_4}{100 \text{ g solution}} \quad \frac{1 \text{ mol } H_2SO_4}{98.09 \text{ g } H_2SO_4} \quad \frac{1 \text{ L}}{1000 \text{ mL}}$$

then mol$_{H_2SO_4}$, L$_{solution}$ → M

$$M = \frac{\text{amount solute (moles)}}{\text{volume solution (L)}}$$

Solution:

$$25.0 \text{ mL solution} \times \frac{1.39 \text{ g solution}}{1 \text{ mL solution}} \times \frac{49.0 \text{ g } H_2SO_4}{100 \text{ g solution}} \times \frac{1 \text{ mol } H_2SO_4}{98.09 \text{ g } H_2SO_4} = 0.1735906 \text{ mol } H_2SO_4 \text{ and}$$

$$99.8 \text{ mL solution} \times \frac{1 \text{ L solution}}{1000 \text{ mL solution}} = 0.0998 \text{ L solution then}$$

$$M = \frac{\text{amount solute (moles)}}{\text{volume solution (L)}} = \frac{0.1735906 \text{ mol } H_2SO_4}{0.0998 \text{ L solution}} = 1.74 \text{ M } H_2SO_4.$$

Check: The units (M) are correct. The magnitude of the answer (1.74 M) seems reasonable since the solutions is ~ 1/6 surfuric acid.

12.114 **Given:** 50.0 g of solution in water, $\chi_{CH_4N_2O} = 0.0770$ **Find:** mass CH_4N_2O

Conceptual Plan: Set up equations for mass and moles

$$g_{CH_4N_2O} + g_{H_2O} = 50.0 \text{ g} \quad \chi_{CH_4N_2O} = \frac{\text{mol } CH_4N_2O}{\text{mol } CH_4N_2O + \text{mol } H_2O} \quad \frac{1 \text{ mol } H_2O}{18.02 \text{ g } H_2O} \text{ and } \frac{1 \text{ mol } CH_4N_2O}{60.06 \text{ g } CH_4N_2O}$$

Combine relationships and solve for g $_{CH_4N_2O}$

Solution: $g_{CH_4N_2O} + g_{H_2O} = 50.0$ g, $\chi_{CH_4N_2O} = \dfrac{\text{mol } CH_4N_2O}{\text{mol } CH_4N_2O + \text{mol } H_2O}$, $\dfrac{1 \text{ mol } H_2O}{18.02 \text{ g } H_2O}$, and

$\dfrac{1 \text{ mol } CH_4N_2O}{60.06 \text{ g } CH_4N_2O}$. Combine relationships and solve for g $_{CH_4N_2O}$. Start with $g_{H_2O} = 50.0 \text{ g} - g_{CH_4N_2O}$ and substitute into $\chi_{CH_4N_2O}$.

$$\chi_{CH_4N_2O} = 0.0770 = \frac{g\ CH_4N_2O \times \dfrac{1\ mol\ CH_4N_2O}{60.06\ g\ CH_4N_2O}}{g\ CH_4N_2O \times \dfrac{1\ mol\ CH_4N_2O}{60.06\ g\ CH_4N_2O} + (50.0\ g - g\ CH_4N_2O) \times \dfrac{1\ mol\ H_2O}{18.02\ g\ H_2O}}$$ and

solve for $g_{CH_4N_2O}$. $0.0770\left(g\ CH_4N_2O \times \dfrac{1\ mol\ CH_4N_2O}{60.06\ g\ CH_4N_2O} + (50.0\ g - g\ CH_4N_2O) \times \dfrac{1\ mol\ H_2O}{18.02\ g\ H_2O}\right)$

$= g\ CH_4N_2O \times \dfrac{1\ mol\ CH_4N_2O}{60.06\ g\ CH_4N_2O}$

$\rightarrow g\ CH_4N_2O\ (0.001282051) + 0.21365150\ g - g\ CH_4N_2O\ (0.0042730300) = g\ CH_4N_2O(0.01665002)$

$\rightarrow 0.21365150\ g = g\ CH_4N_2O(0.01964100) \rightarrow$

$g\ CH_4N_2O = \dfrac{0.21365150\ g}{0.01964100} = 10.877833\ g\ CH_4N_2O = 10.9\ g\ CH_4N_2O.$

Check: The units (g) are correct. The magnitude of the answer (11 g) seems reasonable since the molar mass of urea is over three times the molar mass of water and the mole fraction is almost 0.1.

12.115 **Given:** 10.05 g of unknown compound in 50.0 g water, $T_f = -3.16\ °C$, mass percent composition of the compound is 60.97% C, 11.94% H, and the rest is O **Find:** molecular formula

Other: $K_f = 1.86\ °C/m$; $d = 1.00\ g/mL$

Conceptual Plan: $g_{H_2O} \rightarrow kg_{H_2O}$ **and** $T_f \rightarrow \Delta T_f$ **then** $\Delta T_f, K_f \rightarrow m$ **then** $m, kg_{H_2O} \rightarrow mol_{Unk}$

$\dfrac{1\ kg}{1000\ g}$ $\quad T_f = T_f^\circ - \Delta T_f \quad \Delta T_f = K_f m \quad m = \dfrac{\text{amount solute (moles)}}{\text{mass solvent (kg)}}$

then $g_{Unk}, mol_{Unk} \rightarrow \mathcal{M} \rightarrow g_C, g_H, g_O \rightarrow mol_C, mol_H, mol_O \rightarrow$ **molecular formula**

$\mathcal{M} = \dfrac{g_{Unk}}{mol_{Unk}}$ $\quad$ mass percents $\quad \dfrac{1\ mol\ C}{12.01\ g\ C}\ \dfrac{1\ mol\ H}{1.008\ g\ H}\ \dfrac{1\ mol\ O}{16.00\ g\ O}$

Solution: $50.0\ \cancel{g} \times \dfrac{1\ kg}{1000\ \cancel{g}} = 0.0500\ kg$ and $T_f = T_f^\circ - \Delta T_f$ so

$\Delta T_f = T_f^\circ - T_f = 0.00\ °C - -3.16\ °C = +3.16\ °C$ $\Delta T_f = K_f m$. Rearrange to solve for m.

$m = \dfrac{\Delta T_f}{K_f} = \dfrac{3.16\ \cancel{°C}}{1.86\ \dfrac{\cancel{°C}}{m}} = 1.69892\ m$ then $m = \dfrac{\text{amount solute (moles)}}{\text{mass solvent (kg)}}$ so

$mol_{Unk} = m_{Unk} \times kg_{H_2O} = 1.69892\dfrac{mol\ Unk}{\cancel{kg}} \times 0.0500\ \cancel{kg} = 0.08494624\ mol\ Unk$ then

$\mathcal{M} = \dfrac{g_{Unk}}{mol_{Unk}} = \dfrac{10.05\ g}{0.08494624\ mol} = 118.3101\ \dfrac{g}{mol}$ then

$\dfrac{118.3101\ \cancel{g\ Unk}}{1\ mol\ Unk} \times \dfrac{60.97\ \cancel{g\ C}}{100\ \cancel{g\ Unk}} \times \dfrac{1\ mol\ C}{12.01\ \cancel{g\ C}} = \dfrac{6.01\ mol\ C}{1\ mol\ Unk}$

$\dfrac{118.3101\ \cancel{g\ Unk}}{1\ mol\ Unk} \times \dfrac{11.94\ \cancel{g\ H}}{100\ \cancel{g\ Unk}} \times \dfrac{1\ mol\ H}{1.008\ \cancel{g\ H}} = \dfrac{14.0\ mol\ H}{1\ mol\ Unk}$ and

$\dfrac{118.3101\ \cancel{g\ Unk}}{1\ mol\ Unk} \times \dfrac{(100 - (60.97 + 11.94))\cancel{g\ O}}{100\ \cancel{g\ Unk}} \times \dfrac{1\ mol\ O}{16.00\ \cancel{g\ O}} = \dfrac{2.00\ mol\ O}{1\ mol\ Unk}.$

So the molecular formula is $C_6H_{12}O_2$.

Check: The units (formula) are correct. The magnitude of the answer (formula with ~ 118 g/mol) seems reasonable since the molality is ~ 1.7 and we have ~10 g. It is a reasonable molecular weight for a solid or liquid. The formula does have the correct molar mass.

12.116 **Given:** 2.10 g unknown compound in 175.0 mL solution; $\Pi = 1.93$ atm at 25 °C; combustion of 24.02 g of the unknown compound produced 28.16 g CO_2 and 8.64 g H_2O **Find:** molecular formula

Conceptual Plan: **°C → K then** $\Pi, T \rightarrow M$ **then** $mL_{soln} \rightarrow L_{soln}$ **then** $L_{soln}, M \rightarrow mol_{unknown}$

$K = °C + 273.15 \quad \Pi = MRT \quad \dfrac{1\ L}{1000\ mL} \quad M = \dfrac{\text{amount solute (moles)}}{\text{volume solution (L)}}$

then $g_{unknown}, mol_{unknown} \rightarrow \mathcal{M}_{unknown}$ **then** $g_{CO_2} \rightarrow mol_C$ **and** $g_{H_2O} \rightarrow mol_H$

$\mathcal{M} = \dfrac{g_{unknown\ protein}}{mol_{unknown\ protein}} \quad \dfrac{1\ mol\ CO_2}{44.01\ g\ CO_2} \quad \dfrac{1\ mol\ H_2O}{18.02\ g\ H_2O}$ and $\dfrac{2\ mol\ H}{1\ mol\ H}$

then g $_{unknown}$, mol $_C$, mol $_H$ → mol $_O$ then mol $_C$, mol $_H$, mol $_O$, $\mathcal{M}$ $_{unknown}$ → molecular formula

$\frac{12.01 \text{ g C}}{1 \text{ mol C}}$ $\frac{1.008 \text{ g H}}{1 \text{ mol H}}$ $\quad$ $\text{g O} = \text{g Total} - \text{g C} - \text{g H} \frac{1 \text{ mol O}}{16.00 \text{ g O}}$

Solution: 25 °C + 273.15 = 298 K and $\Pi = MRT$ for M.

$$M = \frac{\Pi}{RT} = \frac{1.93 \cancel{\text{atm}}}{0.08206 \frac{\text{L} \cdot \cancel{\text{atm}}}{\cancel{\text{K}} \cdot \text{mol}} \times 298 \cancel{\text{K}}} = 0.07892408 \frac{\text{mol}}{\text{L}} \text{ then } 175.0 \cancel{\text{mL}} \times \frac{1 \text{ L}}{1000 \cancel{\text{mL}}} = 0.1750 \text{ L then}$$

$$\text{M} = \frac{\text{amount solute (moles)}}{\text{volume solution (L)}}$$. Rearrange to solve for mol $_{unknown}$.

$$\text{mol}_{\text{unknown}} = M \times L = 0.07892408 \frac{\text{mol}}{\cancel{\text{L}}} \times 0.1750 \cancel{\text{L}} = 0.013811714 \text{ mol then}$$

$$\mathcal{M} = \frac{\text{g}_{\text{unknown}}}{\text{mol}_{\text{unknown}}} = \frac{2.10 \text{ g}}{0.013811714 \text{ mol}} = 152.04485 \frac{\text{g}}{\text{mol}} \text{ then using the combustion data}$$

$$28.16 \cancel{\text{g CO}_2} \times \frac{1 \cancel{\text{mol CO}_2}}{44.01 \cancel{\text{g CO}_2}} \times \frac{1 \text{ mol C}}{1 \cancel{\text{mol CO}_2}} = 0.639854579 \text{ mol C}$$

$$8.64 \cancel{\text{g H}_2\text{O}} \times \frac{1 \cancel{\text{mol H}_2\text{O}}}{18.03 \cancel{\text{g H}_2\text{O}}} \times \frac{2 \text{ mol H}}{1 \cancel{\text{mol H}_2\text{O}}} = 0.95893452 \text{ mol H then g O} = \text{g Total} - \text{g C} - \text{g H} =$$

$$24.02 \text{ g Total} - \left(0.639854579 \cancel{\text{mol C}} \times \frac{12.01 \text{ g C}}{1 \cancel{\text{mol C}}} + 0.95893452 \cancel{\text{mol H}} \times \frac{1.008 \text{ g H}}{1 \cancel{\text{mol H}}}\right) = 15.3687405 \text{ g O then}$$

$$15.3687405 \text{ g O} \times \frac{1 \text{ mol O}}{16.00 \cancel{\text{g O}}} = 0.96054628 \text{ mol O}$$ finally use the molar mass and the moles of each element to get the molecular formula.

$$\frac{152.04485 \cancel{\text{g Unk}}}{1 \text{ mol Unk}} \times \frac{0.639854579 \text{ mol C}}{24.03 \cancel{\text{g Unk}}} = \frac{4.05 \text{ mol C}}{1 \text{ mol Unk}}$$

$$\frac{152.04485 \cancel{\text{g Unk}}}{1 \text{ mol Unk}} \times \frac{0.95893452 \text{ mol H}}{24.03 \cancel{\text{g Unk}}} = \frac{6.07 \text{ mol H}}{1 \text{ mol Unk}}$$

and $$\frac{152.04485 \cancel{\text{g Unk}}}{1 \text{ mol Unk}} \times \frac{0.96054628 \text{ mol O}}{24.03 \cancel{\text{g Unk}}} = \frac{6.08 \text{ mol O}}{1 \text{ mol Unk}}.$$

So the molecular formula is $C_4H_6O_6$.

Check: The units (formula) are correct. The magnitude of the answer (formula with ~ 152 g/mol) seems reasonable since the molarity is ~ 0.08 and we have ~2 g. It is a reasonable molecular weight for a solid or liquid. The formula does have the correct molar mass.

12.117 **Given:** 100.0 mL solution 13.5 % by mass NaCl, d = 1.12 g/mL; T_b = 104.4 °C **Find:** g NaCl or water to add

Other: K_b = 0.512 °C/m; $i_{measured}$ = 1.8

Conceptual Plan: T_b → ΔT_b **then** $\Delta T_b, i, K_b$ → m **then mL$_{solution}$ → g$_{solution}$ → g$_{NaCl}$ → mol$_{NaCl}$ then**

$\Delta T_b = T_b - T_b^\circ$ $\quad$ $\Delta T_b = K_b im$ $\quad$ $\frac{1.12 \text{ g Solution}}{1 \text{ mL Solution}}$ $\frac{13.5 \text{ g NaCl}}{100 \text{ g Solution}}$ $\frac{1 \text{ mol NaCl}}{58.44 \text{ g NaCl}}$

m, mol$_{NaCl}$ → kg$_{H_2O}$ → g$_{H_2O}$ and g$_{solution}$, g$_{NaCl}$ → g$_{H_2O}$ then compare the initial and final g$_{H_2O}$ then

$m = \frac{\text{amount solute (moles)}}{\text{mass solvent (kg)}}$ $\frac{1000 \text{ g}}{1 \text{ kg}}$ $\quad$ $\text{g}_{\text{solution}} = \text{g}_{\text{NaCl}} + \text{g}_{\text{H}_2\text{O}}$

calculate the total NaCl in final solution by scaling-up the amount from the initial solution. Then calculate the difference between the needed and starting amounts of NaCl.

Solution: $\Delta T_b = T_b - T_b^\circ = 104.4 \text{ °C} - 100.0 \text{ °C} = 4.4 \text{ °C}$ then $\Delta T_b = K_b im$.

Rearrange to solve for m. $$m = \frac{\Delta T_b}{K_b i} = \frac{4.4 \cancel{\text{°C}}}{0.512 \frac{\cancel{\text{°C}}}{m} \times 1.8} = 4.774306 \, m \text{ NaCl then}$$

$$100.0 \cancel{\text{mL solution}} \times \frac{1.12 \text{ g solution}}{1 \cancel{\text{mL solution}}} = 112 \cancel{\text{g solution}} \times \frac{13.5 \text{ g NaCl}}{100 \cancel{\text{g solution}}} = 15.13 \cancel{\text{g NaCl}} \times \frac{1 \text{ mol NaCl}}{58.44 \cancel{\text{g NaCl}}}$$

$= 0.2587269$ mol NaCl

then $$m = \frac{\text{amount solute (moles)}}{\text{mass solvent (kg)}}$$. Rearrange to solve for kg$_{H_2O}$.

$$kg_{H_2O} = \frac{mol_{NaCl}}{m} = \frac{0.2587269\ \cancel{mol\ NaCl}}{\frac{4.774306\ \cancel{mol\ NaCl}}{1\ kg_{H_2O}}} = 0.0541915\ \cancel{kg_{H_2O}} \times \frac{1000\ g_{H_2O}}{1\ \cancel{kg_{H_2O}}} = 54.1915\ g_{H_2O} \text{ in final solution}$$

then $g_{solution} = g_{NaCl} + g_{H_2O} = 112$ g solution $- 15.12$ g NaCl $= 96.88$ g H_2O in initial solution. Comparing the initial and final solutions, there is a lot more water in the initial solution so NaCl needs to be added.

In the solution with a boiling point of 104.4 °C, $\frac{15.12\ g\ NaCl}{54.1915\ g\ H_2O} = \frac{x\ g\ NaCl}{96.88\ g\ H_2O}$. Solve for x g NaCl.

$$x\ g\ NaCl = \frac{15.12\ g\ NaCl}{54.1915\ \cancel{g\ H_2O}} \times 96.88\ \cancel{g\ H_2O} = 27.031\ g\ NaCl$$ so the amount to be added is

27.031 g NaCl $-$ 15.12 g NaCl $=$ 11.911 g NaCl $=$ 12 g NaCl.

Check: The units (g) are correct. The magnitude of the answer (12 g) seems reasonable since there is approximately twice as much water as is desired in the initial solution, so the NaCl amount needs to be approximately doubled.

12.118 **Given:** 50.0 mL solution 1.55 % by mass $MgCl_2$, $d = 1.05$ g/mL; add 1.35 g $MgCl_2$ **Find:** T_f
Other: $K_b = 1.86\ °C/m$; $i_{measured} = 2.5$

Conceptual Plan: $mL_{solution} \rightarrow g_{solution} \rightarrow g_{MgCl_2}$ **then calculate final mass of $MgCl_2$** $g_{MgCl_2} \rightarrow mol_{MgCl_2}$ **and**

$\frac{1.05\ g\ solution}{1\ mL\ solution}$ $\frac{1.55\ g\ MgCl_2}{100\ g\ solution}$ add 1.35 g $MgCl_2$ $\frac{1\ mol\ MgCl_2}{95.21\ g\ MgCl_2}$

$g_{solution}, g_{MgCl} \rightarrow g_{H_2O} \rightarrow kg_{H_2O}$ **then** $g_{H_2O}, mol_{MgCl_2} \rightarrow m$ **then** $m, i, K_f \rightarrow \Delta T_f \rightarrow T_f$

$g_{solution} = g_{MgCl_2} + g_{H_2O}$ $\frac{1\ kg}{1000\ g}$ $m = \frac{\text{amount solute (moles)}}{\text{mass solvent (kg)}}$ $\Delta T_f = K_f i m$ $T_f = T_f^{\circ} - \Delta T_f$

Solution: $50.0\ \cancel{mL\ solution} \times \frac{1.05\ g\ solution}{1\ \cancel{mL\ solution}} = 52.5\ \cancel{g\ solution} \times \frac{1.55\ g\ MgCl_2}{100\ \cancel{g\ solution}} = 0.81375\ g\ MgCl_2$

$(0.81375 + 1.35)\ \cancel{g\ MgCl_2} \times \frac{1\ mol\ MgCl_2}{95.21\ \cancel{g\ MgCl_2}} = 0.0227261\ mol\ MgCl_2$ and $g_{solution} = g_{MgCl_2} + g_{H_2O}$ so

$g_{H_2O} = g_{solution} - g_{MgCl_2} = 52.5$ g solution $- 0.81375$ g $MgCl_2 = 51.6863$ g H_2O and

$51.6863\ \cancel{g\ H_2O} \times \frac{1\ kg\ H_2O}{1000\ \cancel{g\ H_2O}} = 0.0516863\ kg\ H_2O$ then $m = \frac{\text{amount solute (moles)}}{\text{mass solvent (kg)}}$

$m = \frac{0.0227261\ mol\ MgCl_2}{0.0516863\ kg\ H_2O} = 0.439693\ m$ then $\Delta T_f = K_f i m = 1.86 \frac{°C}{\cancel{m}} \times 2.5 \times 0.439693\ \cancel{m} = 2.0445\ °C$ then

$T_f = T_f^{\circ} - \Delta T_f = 0.00\ °C - 2.0445\ °C = -2.0\ °C$

Check: The units (°C) are correct. The magnitude of the answer (–2 °C) seems reasonable since the freezing point drops, and almost three particles are generated for each $MgCl_2$.

Challenge Problems

12.119 **Given:** N_2: $k_H(N_2) = 6.1 \times 10^{-4}$ M/L at 25 °C; 14.6 mg/L at 50 °C and 1.00 atm; $P_{N_2} = 0.78$ atm;
O_2: $k_H(O_2) = 1.3 \times 10^{-3}$ M/L at 25 °C; 27.8 mg/L at 50 °C and 1.00 atm; $P_{O_2} = 0.21$ atm; and 1.5 L water
Find: $V\ (N_2)$ and $V\ (O_2)$

Conceptual Plan: at 25 °C: $P_{Total}, \chi_{N_2} \rightarrow P_{N_2}$ **then** $P_{N_2}, k_H(N_2) \rightarrow S_{N_2}$ **then L → mol**

$P_{N_2} = \chi_{N_2} P_{Total}$ $S_{N_2} = k_H(N_2)P_{N_2}$ S_{N_2}

at 50 °C: L → mL → mg → g → mol then $mol_{25\ °C}, mol_{25\ °C} \rightarrow mol_{removed}$ **then °C → K**

$\frac{1000\ mL}{1\ L}$ $\frac{14.6\ mg}{1\ L}$ $\frac{1\ g}{1000\ mg}$ $\frac{1\ mol}{28.01\ g}$ $mol_{removed} = mol_{25\ °C} - mol_{50\ °C}$ K = °C + 273.15

then $P, n, T \rightarrow V$

$PV = nRT$

at 25 °C: $P_{Total}, \chi_{O_2} \rightarrow P_{O_2}$ **then** $P_{O_2}, k_H(O_2) \rightarrow S_{O_2}$ **then L → mol**

$P_{O_2} = \chi_{O_2} P_{Total}$ $S_{O_2} = k_H(O_2)P_{O_2}$ S_{O_2}

at 50 °C: L → mL → mg → g → mol then $mol_{25\ °C}, mol_{25\ °C} \rightarrow mol_{removed}$ **then °C → K**

$\frac{1000\ mL}{1\ L}$ $\frac{27.8\ mg}{1\ L}$ $\frac{1\ g}{1000\ mg}$ $\frac{1\ mol}{32.00\ g}$ $mol_{removed} = mol_{25\ °C} - mol_{50\ °C}$ K = °C + 273.15

then $P, n, T \rightarrow V$

$PV = nRT$

Solution: at 25 °C: $P_{N_2} = \chi_{N_2} P_{Total} = 0.78 \times 1.0 \text{ atm} = 0.78 \text{ atm}$ then

$S_{N_2} = k_H(N_2)P_{N_2} = 6.1 \times 10^{-4} \frac{M}{\text{atm}} \times 0.78 \text{ atm} = 4.758 \times 10^{-4}$ M then

$1.5 \text{ L} \times 4.758 \times 10^{-4} \frac{\text{mol}}{\text{L}} = 0.00071371 \text{ mol}$

at 50 °C: $1.5 \text{ L} \times \frac{14.6 \text{ mg}}{1 \text{ L} \cdot \text{atm}} \times 0.78 \text{ atm} \times \frac{1 \text{ g}}{1000 \text{ mg}} \times \frac{1 \text{ mol}}{28.01 \text{ g}} = 0.00060985 \text{ mol}$ then

$\text{mol}_{\text{removed}} = \text{mol}_{25\,°C} - \text{mol}_{50\,°C} = 0.00071371 \text{ mol} - 0.00060985 \text{ mol} = 1.039 \times 10^{-4} \text{ mol } N_2$

then 50 °C + 273.15 = 323 K then $PV = nRT$. Rearrange to solve for V.

$$V = \frac{nRT}{P} = \frac{1.039 \times 10^{-4} \text{ mol} \times 0.08206 \frac{\text{L} \cdot \text{atm}}{\text{K} \cdot \text{mol}} \times 323 \text{ K}}{1.00 \text{ atm}} = 0.0027539 \text{ L } N_2$$

at 25 °C: $P_{O_2} = \chi_{O_2} P_{Total} = 0.21 \times 1.0 \text{ atm} = 0.21 \text{ atm}$ then

$S_{O_2} = k_H(O_2)P_{O_2} = 1.3 \times 10^{-3} \frac{M}{\text{atm}} \times 0.21 \text{ atm} = 2.73 \times 10^{-4}$ M then

$1.5 \text{ L} \times 2.73 \times 10^{-4} \frac{\text{mol}}{\text{L}} = 0.0004095 \text{ mol}$

at 50 °C: $1.5 \text{ L} \times \frac{27.8 \text{ mg}}{1 \text{ L} \cdot \text{atm}} \times 0.21 \text{ atm} \times \frac{1 \text{ g}}{1000 \text{ mg}} \times \frac{1 \text{ mol}}{32.00 \text{ g}} = 0.00027366 \text{ mol}$ then

$\text{mol}_{\text{removed}} = \text{mol}_{25\,°C} - \text{mol}_{50\,°C} = 0.0004095 \text{ mol} - 0.00027366 \text{ mol} = 1.358 \times 10^{-4} \text{ mol } O_2$

then 50 °C + 273.15 = 323 K then $PV = nRT$. Rearrange to solve for V.

$$V = \frac{nRT}{P} = \frac{1.358 \times 10^{-4} \text{ mol} \times 0.08206 \frac{\text{L} \cdot \text{atm}}{\text{K} \cdot \text{mol}} \times 323 \text{ K}}{1.00 \text{ atm}} = 0.0035994 \text{ L } O_2 \text{ finally}$$

$V_{Total} = V_{N_2} + V_{O_2} = 0.0027526 \text{ L} + 0.0035994 \text{ L} = 0.0064 \text{ L}.$

Check: The units (L) are correct. The magnitude of the answer (0.006 L) seems reasonable since we have so little dissolved gas at room temperature and most is still soluble at 50 °C.

12.120 **Given:** pentane (C_5H_{12}) and hexane (C_6H_{14}): 35.5 percent by mass C_5H_{12} in vapor at 25 °C; $P^{\circ}_{C_5H_{12}}$ = 425 torr; $P^{\circ}_{C_6H_{14}}$ = 151 torr **Find:** percent by mass C_5H_{12} and percent by mass C_6H_{14} in solution

Conceptual Plan: mass percents $\rightarrow$ g$_{C_5H_{12}}$, g $_{C_6H_{14}}$ then g $_{C_5H_{12}}$ $\rightarrow$ mol $_{C_5H_{12}}$ and g $_{C_6H_{14}}$ $\rightarrow$ mol $_{C_6H_{14}}$ then

$\text{mass percent} = \frac{\text{mass solute}}{\text{mass solution}} \times 100\%$ $\qquad \frac{1 \text{ mol } C_5H_{12}}{72.15 \text{ g } C_5H_{12}}$ $\qquad \frac{1 \text{ mol } C_6H_{14}}{86.17 \text{ g } C_6H_{14}}$

mol $_{C_5H_{12}}$, mol $_{C_6H_{14}}$ $\rightarrow$ χ C_5H_{12}vapor then χ C_5H_{12}vapor, $P^{\circ}_{C_5H_{12}}$, $P^{\circ}_{C_6H_{14}}$ $\rightarrow$ χ C_5H_{12}soln then assume

$\chi_{C_5H_{12}} = \frac{\text{amount } C_5H_{12} \text{ (in moles)}}{\text{total amount (in moles)}}$ $\qquad \chi_{C_5H_{12}\text{vapor}} = = \frac{P_{C_5H_{12}}}{P_{Total}} = \frac{\chi_{C_5H_{12}\text{soln}} P^{\circ}_{C_5H_{12}}}{\chi_{C_5H_{12}\text{soln}} P^{\circ}_{C_5H_{12}} + (1 - \chi_{C_5H_{12}\text{soln}})P^{\circ}_{C_6H_{14}}}$

1 total mole of solution $\rightarrow$ mol $_{C_5H_{12}}$, mol $_{C_6H_{14}}$ then mol $_{C_5H_{12}}$ $\rightarrow$ g $_{C_5H_{12}}$ and mol $_{C_6H_{14}}$ $\rightarrow$ g $_{C_6H_{14}}$

$\chi_{C_6H_{14}\text{soln}} = 1 - \chi_{C_5H_{12}\text{soln}}$ $\qquad \frac{72.15 \text{ g } C_5H_{12}}{1 \text{ mol } C_5H_{12}}$ $\qquad \frac{86.17 \text{ g } C_6H_{14}}{1 \text{ mol } C_6H_{14}}$

finally g$_{C_5H_{12}}$, g $_{C_6H_{14}}$ $\rightarrow$ mass percents

$\text{mass percent} = \frac{\text{mass solute}}{\text{mass solution}} \times 100\%$

Solution: mass percent $= \frac{\text{mass solute}}{\text{mass solution}} \times 100\%$ means that 35.5 g C_5H_{12} and 100.0 g – 35.5 g = 64.5 g C_6H_{14}

then $35.5 \text{ g } C_5H_{12} \times \frac{1 \text{ mol } C_5H_{12}}{72.15 \text{ g } C_5H_{12}} = 0.492030 \text{ mol } C_5H_{12}$ and

$64.5 \text{ g } C_6H_{14} \times \frac{1 \text{ mol } C_6H_{14}}{86.17 \text{ g } C_6H_{14}} = 0.748520 \text{ mol } C_6H_{14}$ then

$$\chi_{C_5H_{12}} = \frac{\text{amount } C_5H_{12} \text{ (in moles)}}{\text{total amount (in moles)}} = \frac{0.492030 \text{ mol}}{0.492030 \text{ mol} + 0.748520 \text{ mol}} = 0.396622 \text{ then}$$

$$\chi_{C_5H_{12}\text{vapor}} = = \frac{P_{C_5H_{12}}}{P_{Total}} = \frac{\chi_{C_5H_{12}\text{soln}} P^{\circ}_{C_5H_{12}}}{\chi_{C_5H_{12}\text{soln}} P^{\circ}_{C_5H_{12}} + (1 - \chi_{C_5H_{12}\text{soln}})P^{\circ}_{C_6H_{14}}}.$$

Substitute in values and solve for $\chi_{C_5H_{12}soln}$.

$$0.396622 = \frac{\chi_{C_5H_{12}soln} \times 425\ \cancel{torr}}{\chi_{C_5H_{12}soln} \times 425\ \cancel{torr} + (1 - \chi_{C_5H_{12}soln}) \times 151\ \cancel{torr}} \rightarrow$$

$$0.396622(425\chi_{C_5H_{12}soln} + 151(1 - \chi_{C_5H_{12}soln})) = 425\chi_{C_5H_{12}soln} \rightarrow$$

$$168.564\chi_{C_5H_{12}soln} + 59.8900 - 59.8900\chi_{C_5H_{12}soln} = 425\chi_{C_5H_{12}soln} \rightarrow 316.326\chi_{C_5H_{12}soln} = 59.8900 \rightarrow$$

$$\chi_{C_5H_{12}soln} = \frac{59.8900}{316.326} = 0.189330 \text{ then } \chi_{C_6H_{14}soln} = 1 - \chi_{C_5H_{12}soln} = 1 - 0.189330 = 0.810670 \text{ so}$$

$\text{mol}_{C_5H_{12}} = 0.189330$ mol and $\text{mol}_{C_6H_{14}} = 0.810670$ mol then

$$0.189330\ \cancel{\text{mol } C_5H_{12}} \times \frac{72.15 \text{ g } C_5H_{12}}{1\ \cancel{\text{mol } C_5H_{12}}} = 13.6602 \text{ g } C_5H_{12} \text{ and}$$

$$0.810670\ \cancel{\text{mol } C_6H_{14}} \times \frac{86.17 \text{ g } C_6H_{14}}{1\ \cancel{\text{mol } C_6H_{14}}} = 69.8554 \text{ g } C_6H_{14} \text{ finally}$$

$$\text{mass percent} = \frac{\text{mass solute}}{\text{mass solution}} \times 100\% = \frac{13.6602 \text{ g } C_5H_{12}}{13.6602 \text{ g } C_5H_{12} + 69.8554 \text{ g } C_6H_{14}} \times 100\%$$

$= 16.4$ percent by mass C_5H_{12}

and 100.0 – 16.4 = 83.6 mass percent C_6H_{14}.

Check: The units (mass percent) are correct. We expect the mass percent of C_6H_{14} to be much higher than the mass percent of C_5H_{12} because the vapor is richer in this component and it is the less volatile phase.

12.121 **Given:** 1.10 g glucose ($C_6H_{12}O_6$) and sucrose ($C_{12}H_{22}O_{11}$) mixture in 25.0 mL solution and $\Pi = 3.78$ atm at 298 K **Find:** percent composition of mixture

Conceptual Plan: $\Pi, T \rightarrow M$ **then** $\text{mL}_{soln} \rightarrow \text{L}_{soln}$ **then** $\text{L}_{soln}, M \rightarrow \text{mol}_{mixture}$ **then**

$$\Pi = MRT \qquad \frac{1 \text{ L}}{1000 \text{ mL}} \qquad M = \frac{\text{amount solute (moles)}}{\text{volume solution (L)}}$$

$\text{mol}_{mixture}, \text{g}_{mixture} \rightarrow \text{mol}_{C_6H_{12}O_6}, \text{mol}_{C_{12}H_{22}O_{11}}$ **then**

$$g_{mixture} = \text{mol } C_6H_{12}O_6 \times \frac{180.16 \text{ g } C_6H_{12}O_6}{1 \text{ mol } C_6H_{12}O_6} + \text{mol } C_{12}H_{22}O_{11} \times \frac{342.30 \text{ g } C_{12}H_{22}O_{11}}{1 \text{ mol } C_{12}H_{22}O_{11}} \textit{ with } \text{mol}_{mixture} = \text{mol}_{C_6H_{12}O_6} + \text{mol}_{C_{12}H_{22}O_{11}}$$

$\text{mol}_{C_6H_{12}O_6} \rightarrow \text{g } C_6H_{12}O_6$ **and** $\text{mol}_{C_{12}H_{22}O_{11}} \rightarrow \text{g}_{C_{12}H_{22}O_{11}}$ **and** $\text{g } C_6H_{12}O_6, \text{g}_{C_{12}H_{22}O_{11}} \rightarrow$ **mass percents**

$$\frac{180.16 \text{ g } C_6H_{12}O_6}{1 \text{ mol } C_6H_{12}O_6} \qquad \frac{342.30 \text{ g } C_{12}H_{22}O_{11}}{1 \text{ mol } C_{12}H_{22}O_{11}} \qquad \text{mass percent} = \frac{\text{mass solute}}{\text{mass solution}} \times 100\%$$

Solution: $\Pi = MRT$. Rearrange to solve for M.

$$M = \frac{\Pi}{RT} = \frac{3.78\ \cancel{\text{atm}}}{0.08206 \frac{\text{L} \cdot \cancel{\text{atm}}}{\cancel{\text{K}} \cdot \text{mol}} \times 298\ \cancel{\text{K}}} = 0.154577 \frac{\text{mol mixture}}{\text{L}} \text{ then } 25.0\ \cancel{\text{mL}} \times \frac{1 \text{ L}}{1000\ \cancel{\text{mL}}} = 0.0250 \text{ L}$$

$$\text{then } M = \frac{\text{amount solute (moles)}}{\text{volume solution (L)}} \text{ so}$$

$$mol_{mixture} = M \times L_{soln} = 0.154577 \frac{\text{mol mixture}}{\cancel{\text{L}}} \times 0.0250\ \cancel{\text{L}} = 0.00386442 \text{ mol mixture then}$$

$$g_{mixture} = \cancel{\text{mol } C_6H_{12}O_6} \times \frac{180.16 \text{ g } C_6H_{12}O_6}{1\ \cancel{\text{mol } C_6H_{12}O_6}} + \cancel{\text{mol } C_{12}H_{22}O_{11}} \times \frac{342.30 \text{ g } C_{12}H_{22}O_{11}}{1\ \cancel{\text{mol } C_{12}H_{22}O_{11}}} \text{ with}$$

$$mol_{mixture} = mol\ C_6H_{12}O_6 + mol\ C_{12}H_{22}O_{11} \text{ so}$$

$$1.10 \text{ g} = \text{mol } C_6H_{12}O_6 \times \frac{180.16 \text{ g } C_6H_{12}O_6}{1 \text{ mol } C_6H_{12}O_6} + (0.00386442 \text{ mol} - \text{mol } C_6H_{12}O_6) \times \frac{342.30 \text{ g } C_{12}H_{22}O_{11}}{1 \text{ mol } C_{12}H_{22}O_{11}} \rightarrow$$

$$1.10 = 180.16 \times \text{mol } C_6H_{12}O_6 + 1.32228 - 342.30 \times \text{mol } C_6H_{12}O_6 \rightarrow 162.14\, x \text{ mol } C_6H_{12}O_6 = 0.22228 \rightarrow$$

$$x \text{ mol } C_6H_{12}O_6 = \frac{0.22228}{162.14} = 0.00137091 \text{ mol } C_6H_{12}O_6 \text{ then}$$

$$\text{mol}_{C_{12}H_{22}O_{11}} = \text{mol}_{mixture} - \text{mol}_{C_6H_{12}O_6} = 0.00386442 \text{ mol} - 0.00137091 \text{ mol}$$

$= 0.0024935$ mol $C_{12}H_{22}O_{11}$ then

$$0.00137091\ \cancel{\text{mol } C_6H_{12}O_6} \times \frac{180.16 \text{ g } C_6H_{12}O_6}{1\ \cancel{\text{mol } C_6H_{12}O_6}} = 0.24698 \text{ g } C_6H_{12}O_6 \text{ and}$$

$$0.0024935\ \cancel{\text{mol } C_{12}H_{22}O_{11}} \times \frac{342.30 \text{ g } C_{12}H_{22}O_{11}}{1\ \cancel{\text{mol } C_{12}H_{22}O_{11}}} = 0.85353 \text{ g } C_{12}H_{22}O_{11} \text{ and finally}$$

$$\text{mass percent} = \frac{\text{mass solute}}{\text{mass solution}} \times 100\% = \frac{0.24698\ \cancel{g\ C_6H_{12}O_6}}{0.24698\ \cancel{g\ C_6H_{12}O_6} + 0.85353\ \cancel{g\ C_{12}H_{22}O_{11}}} \times 100\%$$

$= 22.44\%\ C_6H_{12}O_6$ by mass and $100.00\% - 22.44\% = 77.56\%\ C_{12}H_{22}O_{11}$ by mass.

Check: The units (% by mass) are correct. We expect the percent by $C_6H_{12}O_6$ to be larger than that for $C_{12}H_{22}O_{11}$ since the $g_{\text{mixture}}/\text{mol}_{\text{mixture}} = 285$ g/mol, which is closer to $C_{12}H_{22}O_{11}$ than $C_6H_{12}O_6$ and the molar mass of $C_{12}H_{22}O_{11}$ is larger than the molar mass of $C_6H_{12}O_6$. In addition, and most definitively, the masses obtained for sucrose and glucose sum to 1.1g, the initial amount of solid dissolved.

12.122 **Given:** 631 mL methanol (CH_3OH) and 501 mL water; solution = 14.29 M CH_3OH, d (CH_3OH) = 0.792 g/mL
Find: volume change on mixing
Conceptual Plan: $V_{CH_3OH}, V_{H_2O} \rightarrow V_{\text{before mixing}}$ **then** $mL_{CH_3OH} \rightarrow g\ CH_3OH \rightarrow mol_{CH_3OH}$ **then**

$V_{\text{before mixing}} = V_{CH_3OH} + V_{H_2O}$ $\quad \frac{0.792\ g}{1\ mL}$ $\quad \frac{1\ mol\ CH_3OH}{32.04\ g\ CH_3OH}$

$mol_{CH_3OH}, M \rightarrow L_{soln} \rightarrow mL_{soln}$ **then** $V_{\text{before mixing}}, L_{soln} \rightarrow \Delta V_{\text{mixing}}$

$M = \frac{\text{amount solute (moles)}}{\text{volume solution (L)}}$ $\quad \frac{1000\ mL}{1\ L}$ $\quad \Delta V_{\text{mixing}} = V_{\text{before mixing}} - V_{\text{soln}}$

Solution: $V_{\text{before mixing}} = V_{CH_3OH} + V_{H_2O} = 631\ mL + 501\ mL = 1132\ mL$ then

$631\ \cancel{mL} \times \frac{0.793\ \cancel{g}}{1\ \cancel{mL}} \times \frac{1\ mol\ CH_3OH}{32.04\ \cancel{g\ CH_3OH}} = 15.5978\ mol\ CH_3OH$ then $M = \frac{\text{amount solute (moles)}}{\text{volume solution (L)}}$ so

$$L_{\text{soln}} = \frac{mol_{CH_3OH}}{M} = \frac{15.5978\ \cancel{mol\ CH_3OH}}{14.29\ \frac{\cancel{mol\ CH_3OH}}{L}} = 1.09152\ L \text{ then } 1.09152\ \cancel{L} \times \frac{1000\ mL}{1\ \cancel{L}} = 1091.52\ mL \text{ then}$$

$\Delta V_{\text{mixing}} = V_{\text{before mixing}} - V_{\text{soln}} = 1132\ mL - 1091.52\ mL = 40.48\ mL = 4 \times 10^1\ mL$

Check: The units (mL) are correct. Since the intermolecular forces between a methanol molecule and a water molecule are different than between two water molecules or between two methanol molecules, the spacing between molecules changes and thus the volume changes. The amount of the change (~ 4 %) is reasonable.

12.123 **Given:** isopropyl alcohol ($(CH_3)_2CHOH$) and propyl alcohol ($CH_3CH_2CH_2OH$) at 313 K; solution 2/3 by mass isopropyl alcohol $P_{2/3} = 0.110$ atm; solution 1/3 by mass isopropyl alcohol $P_{1/3} = 0.089$ atm;
Find: P°_{iso} and P°_{pro} and explain why they are different
Conceptual Plan: since these are isomers, they have the same molar mass and so the fraction by mass is the same as the mole fraction so mole fractions, P_{soln}s $\rightarrow$ $P°$s

$\chi_{iso} = \frac{\text{amount iso (in moles)}}{\text{total amount (in moles)}}$ $\quad \chi_{pro} = 1 - \chi_{iso}$ $\quad P_{iso} = \chi_{iso}P^\circ_{iso}$ $\quad P_{pro} = \chi_{pro}P^\circ_{pro}$ and $P_{soln} = P_{iso} + P_{pro}$

Solution:

Solution 1: $\chi_{iso} = 2/3$ and $\chi_{iso} = 1/3$ $P_{soln} = P_{iso} + P_{pro}$ so $0.110\ atm = 2/3P^\circ_{iso} + 1/3P^\circ_{pro}$.

Solution 2: $\chi_{iso} = 1/3$ and $\chi_{iso} = 2/3$ $P_{soln} = P_{iso} + P_{pro}$ so $0.089\ atm = 1/3P^\circ_{iso} + 2/3P^\circ_{pro}$. We now have two equations and two unknowns and a number of ways to solve this. One way is to rearrange the first equation for P°_{iso} and then substitute into the other equation. Thus, $P^\circ_{iso} = 3/2(0.110\ atm - 1/3P^\circ_{pro})$ and

$$0.089\ atm = \frac{1}{\cancel{3}}\frac{\cancel{3}}{2}(0.110\ atm - 1/3\ P^\circ_{pro}) + \frac{2}{3}P^\circ_{pro} \rightarrow 0.089\ atm = 0.0550\ atm - \frac{1}{6}P^\circ_{pro} + \frac{2}{3}P^\circ_{pro} \rightarrow$$

$\frac{1}{2}P^\circ_{pro} = 0.0340\ atm \rightarrow P^\circ_{pro} = 0.0680\ atm = 0.068\ atm$ and then

$P^\circ_{iso} = 3/2(0.110\ atm - 1/3P^\circ_{pro}) = 3/2(0.110\ atm - 1/3(0.0680\ atm)) = 0.131\ atm.$

The major intermolecular attractions are between the OH groups. The OH group at the end of the chain in propyl alcohol is more accessible than the one in the middle of the chain in isopropyl alcohol. In addition, the molecular shape of propyl alcohol is a straight chain of carbon atoms, while that of isopropyl alcohol has a branched chain and is more like a ball. The contact area between two ball-like objects is smaller than that of two chain-like objects. The smaller contact area in isopropyl alcohol means the molecules do not attract each other as strongly as do those of propyl alcohol. As a result of both of these factors, the vapor pressure of isopropyl alcohol is higher.

Check: The units (atm) are correct. The magnitude of the answers seems reasonable since the solution partial pressures are both ~0.1 atm.

12.124 **Given:** metal, M, of atomic weight 96 forms MF_x salt; 9.18 g of MF_x completely dissociates in 100.0 g water, $T_b = 374.38$ K **Find:** x and formula unit **Other:** $K_b = 0.512$ °C/m

Conceptual Plan: $g_{H_2O} \rightarrow kg_{H_2O}$ **and** $T_b \rightarrow \Delta T_b$ **then** $\Delta T_f, i, K_f \rightarrow m$ **then** $m, kg_{H_2O} \rightarrow mol_{Unk}$

$\frac{1\ kg}{1000\ g}$ $\quad T_b = T_b^\circ + \Delta T_b \quad \Delta T_b = K_b im$ where $i = 1 + x$ $\quad m = \frac{\text{amount solute (moles)}}{\text{mass solvent (kg)}}$

then $g_{MFx}, mol_{MFx} \rightarrow \mathcal{M} \rightarrow x$

$$\mathcal{M} = \frac{g_{MF_x}}{mol_{MF_x}} \quad \frac{1\ mol\ MF_x}{(96 + 19x)g\ MF_x}$$

Solution: $100.0\ g \times \frac{1\ kg}{1000\ g} = 0.1000\ kg$ and $T_b = T_b^\circ + \Delta T_b$ so

$\Delta T_b = T_b - T_b^\circ = 374.38\ K - 373.15\ K = +1.23\ K = +1.23\ °C$ then $\Delta T_b = K_b im$ where $i = 1 + x$ so

$\Delta T_b = K_b(1 + x)m$. Rearrange to solve for m. $m = \frac{\Delta T_b}{K_b(1 + x)} = \frac{1.23\ °C}{0.512 \frac{°C}{m}(1 + x)} = \frac{2.40234}{(1 + x)} m$ then

$m = \frac{\text{amount solute (moles)}}{\text{mass solvent (kg)}}$ so

$$mol_{MF_x} = m_{MF_x} \times kg_{H_2O} = \frac{2.40234\ mol\ MF_x}{(1 + x)\ kg} \times 0.1000\ kg = \frac{0.240234}{(1 + x)} mol\ MF_x$$

then $\mathcal{M} = \frac{g_{MF_x}}{mol_{MF_x}} = \frac{9.18g}{\frac{0.240234}{(1 + x)} mol\ MF_x} = \frac{1\ mol\ MF_x}{(96 + 19x)\ g\ MF_x}$. Rearrrange and solve for x.

$$(9.18\ g)(1\ mol\ MF_x) = (96 + 19x)(g\ MF_x)\left(\frac{0.240234}{(1 + x)} mol\ MF_x\right) \rightarrow 9.18(1 + x) = 0.240234(96 + 19x)$$

$$\rightarrow 9.18x - 4.5645x = 23.062 - 9.18 \rightarrow 4.6155x = 13.882 \rightarrow x = \frac{13.882}{4.6155} = 3.0 \text{ so the salt is } MF_3.$$

Since molybdenum has an atomic mass ~ 96 amu, the salt is MoF_3.

Check: The units (none) are correct. The answer (3.0) seems reasonable since it is a small integer.

12.125 **Given:** 0.1000 m H_2SO_4 solution; complete dissociation to H^+ and HSO_4^-; limited dissociation to SO_4^{2-}; $T_f = 272.76\ K$ **Find:** $m\ (SO_4^{2-})$ **Other:** $K_f = 1.86\ K/m$

Conceptual Plan: $T_f \rightarrow \Delta T_f$ **then** $m, \Delta T_f, K_f \rightarrow i \rightarrow m\ (SO_4^{2-})$

$T_f = T_f^\circ - \Delta T_f \quad \Delta T_f = K_f im \quad m\ (SO_4^{2-}) = m\ H_2SO_4\ (i - 2.0)/2$

Solution: $T_f = T_f^\circ - \Delta T_f$. Rearrange to solve for ΔT_f. So

$\Delta T_f = T_f^\circ - T_f = 273.15\ K - 272.76\ K = -0.39\ K$ then $\Delta T_f = K_f im$. Rearrange to solve for i.

$$i = \frac{\Delta T_f}{K_f m} = \frac{0.39\ K}{1.86 \frac{K}{m} \times 0.1000\ m} = 2.0968.$$

Remember that when H_2SO_4 completely dissociates, two particles are formed (H^+ and HSO_4^-), so $i = 2$. When HSO_4^- dissociates two particles are generated (SO_4^{2-} and H^+).

$$m(SO_4^{2-}) = m\ H_2SO_4 \frac{i-2}{2} = (0.1000\ m)\frac{2.0968 - 2}{2} = 0.04839\ m = 0.4\ m\ SO_4^{2-}.$$

Check: The units (m) are correct. The magnitude of the answer (0.4 m) seems reasonable since not much of the HSO_4^- dissociates.

12.126 **Given:** 75.0 g of benzene (C_6H_6) and 75.0 g of toluene (C_7H_8) at 303 K $P^\circ_{Total} = 80.9$ mmHg; 100.0 g of benzene (C_6H_6) and 50.0 g of toluene (C_7H_8) at 303 K $P^\circ_{Total} = 93.9$ mmHg **Find:** $P^\circ_{C_6H_6}, P^\circ_{C_8H_8}$

Conceptual Plan: for each solution,

$g_{C_6H_6} \rightarrow mol_{C_7H_8}$ **and** $g_{C_7H_8} \rightarrow mol_{C_7H_8}$ **then** $mol_{C_6H_6}, mol_{C_7H_8} \rightarrow \chi_{C_6H_6}, \chi_{C_7H_8}$ **then**

$\frac{1\ mol\ C_6H_6}{78.11\ g\ C_6H_6} \quad \frac{1\ mol\ C_7H_8}{92.13\ g\ C_7H_8} \quad \chi_{C_6H_6} = \frac{\text{amount } C_6H_6 \text{ (in moles)}}{\text{total amount (in moles)}} \quad \chi_{C_7H_8} = 1 - \chi_{C_6H_6}$

write expressions relating $\chi_{C_6H_6}, P^\circ_{C_6H_6} \rightarrow P_{C_6H_6}$ **and** $\chi_{C_7H_8}, P^\circ_{C_7H_8} \rightarrow P_{C_8H_{18}}$ **and** $P_{C_6H_6}, P_{C_7H_8} \rightarrow P_{Total}$

$P_{C_6H_6} = \chi_{C_6H_6} P^\circ_{C_6H_6} \quad P_{C_7H_8} = \chi_{C_7H_8} P^\circ_{C_7H_8} \quad P_{Total} = P_{C_6H_6} + P_{C_7H_8}$

then solve the two simultaneous equations for $P^\circ_{C_6H_6}$ **and** $P^\circ_{C_7H_8}$.

Solution: For the first solution: $75.0\ g\ C_6H_6 \times \frac{1\ mol\ C_6H_6}{78.11\ g\ C_6H_6} = 0.96018436\ mol\ C_6H_6$ and

$75.0 \cancel{g\,C_7H_8} \times \frac{1 \text{ mol } C_7H_8}{92.13 \cancel{g\,C_7H_8}} = 0.81\underline{4}06708 \text{ mol } C_7H_8$ then

$\chi_{C_6H_6} = \frac{\text{amount } C_6H_6 \text{ (in moles)}}{\text{total amount (in moles)}} = \frac{0.96\underline{0}18436 \cancel{\text{mol}}}{0.96\underline{0}18436 \cancel{\text{mol}} + 0.81\underline{4}06708 \cancel{\text{mol}}} = 0.54\underline{1}17716$ and

$\chi_{C_7H_8} = 1 - \chi_{C_6H_6} = 1 - 0.54\underline{1}17716 = 0.45\underline{8}82284$ then

$P_{\text{Total}} = P_{C_6H_6} + P_{C_7H_8} = \chi_{C_6H_6} P^{\circ}_{C_6H_6} + \chi_{C_7H_8} P^{\circ}_{C_7H_8}$

$= 0.54\underline{1}17716 P^{\circ}_{C_6H_6} + 0.45\underline{8}82284 P^{\circ}_{C_7H_8} = 80.9 \text{ mmHg}.$

For the second solution: $100.0 \cancel{g\,C_6H_6} \times \frac{1 \text{ mol } C_6H_6}{78.11 \cancel{g\,C_6H_6}} = 1.28\underline{0}24581 \text{ mol } C_6H_6$ and

$50.0 \cancel{g\,C_7H_8} \times \frac{1 \text{ mol } C_7H_8}{92.13 \cancel{g\,C_7H_8}} = 0.54\underline{2}71139 \text{ mol } C_7H_8$ then

$\chi_{C_6H_6} = \frac{\text{amount } C_6H_6 \text{ (in moles)}}{\text{total amount (in moles)}} = \frac{1.28\underline{0}24581 \cancel{\text{mol}}}{1.28\underline{0}24581 \cancel{\text{mol}} + 0.54\underline{2}71139 \cancel{\text{mol}}} = 0.70\underline{2}290659$ and

$\chi_{C_7H_8} = 1 - \chi_{C_6H_6} = 1 - 0.70\underline{2}290659 = 0.29\underline{7}709341$ then

$P_{\text{Total}} = P_{C_6H_6} + P_{C_7H_8} = P_{C_7H_{16}} = \chi_{C_6H_6} P^{\circ}_{C_6H_6} + \chi_{C_7H_8} P_{C_7H_8}$

$= 0.70\underline{2}290659 P^{\circ}_{C_6H_6} + 0.29\underline{7}709341 P^{\circ}_{C_7H_8} = 93.9 \text{ mmHg}.$

Solve the the two simultaneous equations for $P^{\circ}_{C_6H_6}$ and $P^{\circ}_{C_7H_8}$

$P^{\circ}_{C_6H_6} = \frac{80.9 \text{ mmHg} - 0.45\underline{8}82284 P^{\circ}_{C_7H_8}}{0.54\underline{1}17716} = 14\underline{9}.48894 \text{ mmHg} - 0.84\underline{7}82373 P^{\circ}_{C_7H_8}$ then

$0.70\underline{2}290659(14\underline{9}.48894 \text{ mmHg} - 0.84\underline{7}82373 P^{\circ}_{C_7H_8}) + 0.29\underline{7}709341 P^{\circ}_{C_7H_8} = 93.9 \text{ mmHg} \rightarrow$

$10\underline{4}.98469 \text{ mmHg} - 0.59\underline{5}41869 P^{\circ}_{C_7H_8} + 0.29\underline{7}709341 P^{\circ}_{C_7H_8} = 93.9 \text{ mmHg} \rightarrow$

$11.\underline{0}8469 \text{ mmHg} = 0.29\underline{7}70935 P^{\circ}_{C_7H_8} \rightarrow$

$P^{\circ}_{C_7H_8} = \frac{11.\underline{0}8469 \text{ mmHg}}{0.29\underline{7}70935} = 37.\underline{2}33261 \text{ mmHg} = 37.2 \text{ mmHg}$ then

$P^{\circ}_{C_6H_6} = 14\underline{9}.48894 \text{ mmHg} - 0.84\underline{7}82373 P^{\circ}_{C_7H_8}$

$= 14\underline{9}.48894 \text{ mmHg} - 0.84\underline{7}82373 \times 37.\underline{2}33261 \text{ mmHg} = 11\underline{7}.9217 \text{ mmHg} = 118 \text{ mmHg}.$

Check: The units (mmHg and mmHg) are correct. The magnitude of the answer (118 mmHg and 37.2 mmHg) seems reasonable since we expect toluene to have a lower vapor pressure than benzene (based on molar mass).

12.127 **Given:** $Na_2CO_3 + NaHCO_3 = 11.60$ g in 1.00 L; treat 300.0 cm^3 of solution with HNO_3 and collect 0.940 L CO_2 at 298 K and 0.972 atm **Find:** M(Na_2CO_3) and M($NaHCO_3$)

Conceptual Plan: *P, V, T* → *n* in 300.0 cm³ then *n* in 300.0 cm³ → *n* in 1.00 L then

$PV = nRT$ take ratio of volumes

set up equations for the total mass and the total moles and solve. Then calculate concentrations.

$g_{Na_2CO_3} + g_{NaHCO_3} = 11.60 \text{ g} \quad \frac{105.99 \text{ g } Na_2CO_3}{1 \text{ mol } Na_2CO_3} \quad \frac{84.01 \text{ g } NaHCO_3}{1 \text{ mol } NaHCO_3} \quad n_{Na_2CO_3} + n_{NaHCO_3} = n.$

Solution: $PV = nRT$. Rearrange to solve for n. $n = \frac{PV}{RT}$

$n_{CO_2} = \frac{0.972 \cancel{\text{atm}} \times 0.940 \cancel{\text{L}}}{0.08206 \frac{\cancel{\text{L}} \cdot \cancel{\text{atm}}}{\text{mol} \cdot \cancel{\text{K}}} \times 298 \cancel{\text{K}}} = 0.03\underline{7}36340 \text{ mol } CO_2$ in 300.0 cm^3 then take ratio of moles to volume to get the moles in 1.00 L

$\frac{0.03\underline{7}36340 \text{ mol } CO_2}{300.0 \text{ cm}^3} \times 1000 \text{ cm}^3 = 0.12\underline{4}5447 \text{ mol } CO_2$ in 1.00 L since one mole of CO_2 is generated for each mole of carbonate. So $n = n_{Na_2CO_3} + n_{NaHCO_3} = 0.12\underline{4}5447$mol and $g_{Na_2CO_3} + g_{NaHCO_3} = 11.60$ g or

$g_{Na_2CO_3} = 11.60 \text{ g} - g_{NaHCO_3}$ using molar masses and substituting

$n_{Na_2CO_3} + n_{NaHCO_3} = 0.12\underline{4}5447\text{mol} = g_{Na_2CO_3} \times \frac{1 \text{ mol } Na_2CO_3}{105.99 \text{ g } Na_2CO_3} + g_{NaHCO_3} \times \frac{1 \text{ mol } NaHCO_3}{84.01 \text{ g } NaHCO_3} =$

$(11.60 \text{ g} - g_{NaHCO_3}) \times \frac{1 \text{ mol } Na_2CO_3}{105.99 \text{ g } Na_2CO_3} + g_{NaHCO_3} \times \frac{1 \text{ mol } NaHCO_3}{84.01 \text{ g } NaHCO_3}$

$$\rightarrow 0.1245447 \text{ mol} = 0.10944429 \text{ mol} - g_{NaHCO_3} \times 0.009434852 \frac{\text{mol}}{\text{g}} + g_{NaHCO_3} 0.011903345 \frac{\text{mol}}{\text{g}}$$

$$\rightarrow 0.01510041 \text{ mol} = g_{NaHCO_3} \times 0.002468493 \frac{\text{mol}}{\text{g}} \rightarrow$$

$$g_{NaHCO_3} = \frac{0.01510041 \cancel{\text{mol}}}{0.002468493 \frac{\cancel{\text{mol}}}{\text{g}}} = 6.117259 \text{ g } NaHCO_3 = 6.1 \text{ g } NaHCO_3 \text{ and then } g_{Na_2CO_3} =$$

$$11.60 \text{ g} - g_{NaHCO_3} = 11.60 \text{ g} - 6.117259 \text{ g } NaHCO_3 = 5.48274 \text{ g } Na_2CO_3 = 5.5 \text{ g } Na_2CO_3 \text{ then M} = \text{mol/L}$$

$$\frac{6.117259 \cancel{\text{g } NaHCO_3} \times \frac{1 \text{ mol } NaHCO_3}{84.01 \cancel{\text{g } NaHCO_3}}}{1.00 \text{ L}} = 0.073 \text{ M } NaHCO_3 \text{ and}$$

$$\frac{5.48274 \cancel{\text{g } Na_2CO_3} \times \frac{1 \text{ mol } Na_2CO_3}{105.99 \cancel{\text{g } Na_2CO_3}}}{1.00 \text{ L}} = 0.052 \text{ M } Na_2CO_3.$$

Check: The units (M and M) are correct. The magnitude of the answer (0.052 M and 0.073 M) makes sense because the number of moles of CO_2 is small (0.12 M). The balance of the two components make sense because if it were all Na_2CO_3 the number of moles would have been 0.109 moles (11.6/105.99) and if it were all $NaHCO_3$ the number of moles would have been 0.138 moles (11.6/84.01)—the actual number of moles is roughly in the middle of these two values.

Conceptual Problems

12.128 (a) The two substances mix because the intermolecular forces among all of the species are roughly equal and there is a pervasive tendency to increase randomness, which happens when the two substances mix.

(b) $\Delta H_{soln} \approx 0$, since the intermolecular forces between themselves are roughly equal to the forces between each other.

(c) ΔH_{solute} and $\Delta H_{solvent}$ are positive, and ΔH_{mix} is negative and equals the sum of ΔH_{solute} and $\Delta H_{solvent}$.

12.129 The warm coolant water should not be put directly into the river without cooling, because it will raise the temperature of the water. When water is warmed, there is less dissolved oxygen in the water and this will be detrimental to aquatic life that depends on this dissolved oxygen.

12.130 (d) More solute particles are found in an ionic solution, since the solute breaks apart into its ions. The vapor pressure is lowered due to fewer solute particles in the vapor phase as more solute particles are present.

12.131 (b) NaCl. If all of the substances have the same cost per kilogram, we need to determine which substance will generate the largest number of particles per kilogram (or gram). $HOCH_2CH_2OH$ generates 1 mol particle / 62.07 g; NaCl generates 2 mol particles / 58.44 g; KCl generates 2 mol particles / 74.56 g; $MgCl_2$ generates 3 mol particles / 95.22 g; and $SrCl_2$ generates 3 particles / 158.53 g. So NaCl will generate 1 mole of particles for each 29 g.

12.132 The balloon not only loses He, it also takes in N_2 and O_2 from the air surrounding the balloon (due to the tendency for mixing), increasing the density of the gas inside the balloon and, thus, increasing the density of the balloon.

13 Chemical Kinetics

Review Questions

13.1 Unlike mammals, which actively regulate their body temperature through metabolic activity, lizards are ectotherms—their body temperature depends on their surroundings. When splashed with cold water, a lizard's body simply gets colder. The drop in body temperature immobilizes the lizard because its movement depends on chemical reactions that occur within its muscles, and the rates of those reactions—how fast they occur—are highly sensitive to temperature. In other words, when the temperature drops, the reactions that produce movement occur more slowly; therefore the movement itself slows down. Cold reptiles are lethargic, unable to move very quickly. For this reason, reptiles try to maintain their body temperature in a narrow range by moving between sun and shade.

13.2 The rates of chemical reactions, and especially the ability to control those rates, are important phenomena in our everyday lives. For example, the human body's ability to switch a specific reaction on or off at a specific time is achieved largely by controlling the rate of that reaction through the use of enzymes. Chemical kinetics is an important subject to chemists and engineers. The launching of a rocket depends on controlling the rate at which fuel burns—too quickly and the rocket can explode, too slowly and it will not leave the ground. The rate of nuclear decay in a nuclear power plant must be carefully controlled in order to provide electricity safely and efficiently. Chemists must always consider reaction rates when synthesizing compounds. No matter how stable a compound might be, its synthesis is impossible if the rate at which it forms is too slow. As we have seen with reptiles, reaction rates are important to life.

13.3 The rate of a chemical reaction is measured as a change in the amounts of reactants or products (usually in terms of concentration) divided by the change in time. Typical units are molarity per second (M/s), molarity per minute (M/min), and molarity per year (M/yr), depending on how fast the reaction proceeds.

13.4 The reaction rate is defined as the negative of the change in concentration of a reactant divided by the change in time, because reactant concentrations decrease as a reaction proceeds; therefore the change in the concentration of a reactant is negative. The negative sign in the definition thus makes the overall rate positive. In other words, the negative sign is the result of the convention that reaction rates are usually reported as positive quantities. Since the product concentrations are increasing, the concentration of a product divided by the change in time is positive.

13.5 The average rate of the reaction can be calculated for any time interval as $\text{Rate} = -\frac{1}{a}\frac{[\text{A}]_{t_2} - [\text{A}]_{t_1}}{t_2 - t_1} = -\frac{1}{b}\frac{[\text{B}]_{t_2} - [\text{B}]_{t_1}}{t_2 - t_1} = \frac{1}{c}\frac{[\text{C}]_{t_2} - [\text{C}]_{t_1}}{t_2 - t_1} = \frac{1}{d}\frac{[\text{D}]_{t_2} - [\text{D}]_{t_1}}{t_2 - t_1}$ for the chemical reaction $a\text{A} + b\text{B} \rightarrow c\text{C} + d\text{D}$. The instantaneous rate of the reaction is the rate at any one point in time, represented by the instantaneous slope of the plot of concentration versus time at that point. We can obtain the instantaneous rate from the slope of the tangent to this curve at the point of interest.

13.6 For a zero order reaction, Rate $= k\,[A]^0 = k$, so doubling the concentration of A does nothing to the reaction rate. For a first order reaction, Rate $= k\,[A]^1 = k\,[A]$, so doubling the concentration of A doubles the reaction rate. For a second order reaction, Rate $= k\,[A]^2$, so doubling the concentration of A quadruples the reaction rate.

13.7 The reaction order cannot be determined by the stoichiometry of the reaction. It can only be determined by running controlled experiments where the concentrations of the reactants are varied and the reaction rates are measured and analyzed.

13.8 When multiple reactants are present, Rate $= k\,[A]^m[B]^n$, where m is the reaction order with respect to A and n is the reaction order with respect to B. The overall order is simply the sum of the exponents $(m + n)$.

13.9 The rate law shows the relationship between the rate of a reaction and the concentrations of the reactants. The integrated rate law for a chemical reaction is a relationship between the concentration of a reactant and time.

13.10 For a zero order reaction, $[A]_t = -\,k\,t + [A]_0$. For a first order reaction, $\ln[A]_t = -\,k\,t + \ln[A]_0$. For a second order reaction, $\dfrac{1}{[A]_t} = k\,t + \dfrac{1}{[A]_0}$.

13.11 The half-life ($t_{1/2}$) of a reaction is the time required for the concentration of a reactant to fall to one-half of its initial value. For a zero order reaction, $t_{1/2} = \dfrac{[A]_0}{2k}$. For a first order reaction, $t_{1/2} = \dfrac{0.693}{k}$. For a second order reaction, $t_{1/2} = \dfrac{1}{k[A]_0}$.

13.12 The rates of chemical reactions are, in general, highly sensitive to temperature. Reaction rates increase as the temperature increases. The temperature dependence of the reaction rate is contained in the rate constant (k) which is actually a constant only when the temperature remains constant.

13.13 The modern form of the Arrhenius equation, which relates the rate constant (k) and the temperature in kelvin (T), is as follows: $k = A\,e^{-E_a/RT}$, where R is the gas constant (8.314 J/mol · K), A is a constant called the frequency factor (or the pre-exponential factor), and E_a is called the activation energy (or activation barrier). The frequency factor is the number of times that the reactants approach the activation barrier per unit time. The exponential factor ($-E_a/RT$) is the fraction of approaches that are successful in surmounting the activation barrier and forming products. The exponential factor increases with increasing temperature, but decreases with an increasing value for the activation energy. As the temperature increases, the number of collisions increases and the number of molecules having enough thermal energy to surmount the activation barrier increases. At any given temperature, a sample of molecules will have a distribution of energies, as shown in Figure 13.14. Under common circumstances, only a small fraction of the molecules have enough energy to make it over the activation barrier. Because of the shape of the energy distribution curve, however, a small change in temperature results in a large difference in the number of molecules having enough energy to surmount the activation barrier.

13.14 An Arrhenius Plot is a plot of the natural log of the rate constant ($\ln k$) versus the inverse of the temperature in Kelvin ($1/T$). It yields a straight line with a slope of $-E_a/R$ and a y-intercept of $\ln A$.

13.15 In the collision model, a chemical reaction occurs after a sufficiently energetic collision between the two reactant molecules. In collision theory, therefore, each approach to the activation barrier is a collision between the reactant molecules. The value of the frequency factor should simply be the number of collisions that occur per second. In the collision model $k = pze^{-E_a/RT}$, where the frequency factor (A) has been separated into two separate parts—p is called the orientation factor and z is the collision frequency. The collision frequency is simply the number of collisions that occur per unit time. The orientation factor says that if two molecules are to react with each other, they must collide in such a way that allows the necessary bonds to break and form. The small orientation factor indicates that the orientational requirements for this reaction are fairly stringent—the molecules must be aligned in a very specific way for the reaction to occur. When two molecules with sufficient energy and the correct orientation collide, something unique happens: The electrons on one of the atoms or molecules are attracted to the nuclei of the other; some bonds begin to weaken while other bonds begin to form and; if all goes well, the reactants go through the transition state and are transformed into the products and a chemical reaction occurs.

13.16 When we write a chemical equation to represent a chemical reaction, we usually represent the overall reaction, not the series of individual steps by which the reaction occurs. The overall equation simply shows the substances present at the beginning of the reaction and the substances formed by the reaction—it does not show the intermediate steps that may be involved. A reaction mechanism is a series of individual chemical steps by which an overall chemical reaction occurs.

13.17 An elementary step is a single step in a reaction mechanism. Elementary steps cannot be broken down into simpler steps—they occur as they are written. Elementary steps are characterized by their molecularity, the number of reactant particles involved in the step. The molecularity of the three most common types of elementary steps are as follows: unimolecular - A $\rightarrow$ products and Rate $= k\,[A]$; bimolecular - A + A $\rightarrow$ products and Rate $= k\,[A]^2$; and bimolecular - A + B $\rightarrow$ products and Rate $= k\,[A][B]$. Elementary steps in which three reactant particles collide, called termolecular steps, are very rare because the probability of three particles simultaneously colliding is small.

13.18 For a proposed reaction mechanism to be valid—mechanisms can only be validated, not proven—two conditions must be met: (1) the elementary steps in the mechanism must sum to the overall reaction; and (2) the rate law predicted by the mechanism must be consistent with the experimentally observed rate law.

13.19 Reaction intermediates are species that are formed in one step of a mechanism and consumed in another step. An intermediate is not found in the balanced equation for the overall reaction, but plays a key role in the mechanism.

13.20 A catalyst is a substance that increases the rate of a chemical reaction but is not consumed by the reaction. A catalyst works by providing an alternative mechanism for the reaction—one in which the rate-determining step has a lower activation energy.

13.21 In homogeneous catalysis, the catalyst exists in the same phase as the reactants. In heterogeneous catalysis, the catalyst exists in a phase different from the reactants. The most common type of heterogenous catalyst is a solid catalyst.

13.22 Heterogeneous catalysis (involving solid catalysts) occurs by the following four-step process: (1) adsorption—the reactants are adsorbed onto the solid surface; (2) diffusion—the reactants diffuse on the surface until they approach each other; (3) reaction—the reactants react to form the products; and (4) desorption—the products desorb from the surface into the gas phase.

13.23 Enzymes are biological catalysts that increase the rates of biochemical reactions. Enzymes are large protein molecules with complex three-dimensional structures. Within that structure is a specific area called the active site. The properties and shape of the active site are just right to bind the reactant molecule, usually called the substrate. The substrate fits into the active site in a manner that is analogous to a key fitting into a lock.

13.24 The general mechanism by which an enzyme (E) binds a substrate (S) and then reacts to form the products (P) is as follows: (1) E + S $\rightleftharpoons$ ES (fast); and (2) ES $\rightarrow$ E + P (slow, rate-limiting).

Reaction Rates

13.25 (a) $\text{Rate} = -\frac{1}{2}\frac{\Delta[\text{HBr}]}{\Delta t} = \frac{\Delta[\text{H}_2]}{\Delta t} = \frac{\Delta[\text{Br}_2]}{\Delta t}$

(b) **Given:** first 25.0 s; 0.600 M to 0.512 M **Find:** average rate

Conceptual Plan: $t_1, t_2, [\text{HBr}]_1, [\text{HBr}]_2 \rightarrow$ **average rate**

$$\text{Rate} = -\frac{1}{2}\frac{\Delta[\text{HBr}]}{\Delta t}$$

Solution:

$$\text{Rate} = -\frac{1}{2}\frac{[\text{HBr}]_{t_2} - [\text{HBr}]_{t_1}}{t_2 - t_1} = -\frac{1}{2}\frac{0.512\text{ M} - 0.600\text{ M}}{25.0\text{ s} - 0.0\text{ s}} = 1.7\underline{6} \times 10^{-3}\,\text{M}\cdot\text{s}^{-1} = 1.8 \times 10^{-3}\,\text{M}\cdot\text{s}^{-1}$$

Check: The units ($\text{M}\cdot\text{s}^{-1}$) are correct. The magnitude of the answer ($10^{-3}\text{M}\cdot\text{s}^{-1}$) makes physical sense because rates are always positive and we are not changing the concentration much in 25 s.

(c) **Given:** 1.50 L vessel, first 15.0 s of reaction, and part (b) data **Find:** mol_{Br_2} formed
Conceptual Plan: average rate, t_1, t_2, → Δ [Br_2] then Δ [Br_2], L → mol_{Br_2} formed

$$\text{Rate} = \frac{\Delta[Br_2]}{\Delta t} \qquad M = \frac{mol_{Br_2}}{L}$$

Solution: $\text{Rate} = 1.76 \times 10^{-3}\,M \cdot s^{-1} = \frac{\Delta[Br_2]}{\Delta t} = \frac{\Delta[Br_2]}{15.0\,s - 0.0\,s}$. Rearrange to solve for $\Delta[Br_2]$.

$\Delta[Br_2] = 1.76 \times 10^{-3}\,\frac{M}{s} \times 15.0\,s = 0.0264\,M$ then $M = \frac{mol_{Br_2}}{L}$. Rearrange to solve for mol_{Br_2}.

$0.264\,\frac{mol\;Br_2}{L} \times 1.50\,L = 0.040\,mol\;Br_2$.

Check: The units (mol) are correct. The magnitude of the answer (0.04 mol) makes physical sense because the time is shorter than in part (b) and we need to divide by 2 and multiply by 1.5 because of the stoichiometric coefficient difference and the volume of the vessel, respectively.

13.26 (a) $\text{Rate} = -\frac{1}{2}\frac{\Delta[N_2O]}{\Delta t} = \frac{1}{2}\frac{\Delta[N_2]}{\Delta t} = \frac{\Delta[O_2]}{\Delta t}$

(b) **Given:** first 15.0 s; 0.015 mol O_2 in 0.500 L **Find:** average rate
Conceptual Plan: mol_{O_2}, L → M then t_1, t_2, $[O_2]_1$, $[O_2]_2$ → average rate

$$M = \frac{mol_{O_2}}{L} \qquad \text{Rate} = \frac{\Delta[O_2]}{\Delta t}$$

Solution: At $t_1 = 0$ s we have no O_2. $M = \frac{mol_{O_2}}{L} = \frac{0.015\,mol\;O_2}{0.500\,L} = 0.030\,M$ then

$\text{Rate} = \frac{[O_2]_{t_2} - [O_2]_{t_1}}{t_2 - t_1} = \frac{0.030\,M - 0.000\,M}{15.0\,s - 0.0\,s} = 2.0 \times 10^{-3}\,M \cdot s^{-1}$.

Check: The units ($M \cdot s^{-1}$) are correct. The magnitude of the answer ($10^{-3}\,M \cdot s^{-1}$) makes physical sense because rates are always positive and we are not changing the concentration much in 15 s.

(c) **Given:** part (b) data **Find:** $\frac{\Delta[N_2O]}{\Delta t}$

Conceptual Plan: average rate → $\frac{\Delta[N_2O]}{\Delta t}$

$$\text{Rate} = -\frac{1}{2}\frac{\Delta[N_2O]}{\Delta t} = \frac{\Delta[O_2]}{\Delta t}$$

Solution: $\text{Rate} = -\frac{1}{2}\frac{\Delta[N_2O]}{\Delta t} = \frac{\Delta[O_2]}{\Delta t}$. Rearrange to solve for $\frac{\Delta[N_2O]}{\Delta t}$.

$\frac{\Delta[N_2O]}{\Delta t} = -2\frac{\Delta[O_2]}{\Delta t} = -2 \times 2.0 \times 10^{-3}\,M \cdot s^{-1} = -0.0040\,M \cdot s^{-1}$.

Check: The units ($M \cdot s^{-1}$) are correct. The magnitude of the answer ($-0.004\,M \cdot s^{-1}$) makes physical sense because we multiply by 2 because of the different stoichiometric coefficients. The change in concentration with time is negative since this is a reactant.

13.27 (a) $\text{Rate} = -\frac{1}{2}\frac{\Delta[A]}{\Delta t} = -\frac{\Delta[B]}{\Delta t} = \frac{1}{3}\frac{\Delta[C]}{\Delta t}$

(b) **Given:** $\frac{\Delta[A]}{\Delta t} = -0.100\,M/s$ **Find:** $\frac{\Delta[B]}{\Delta t}$, and $\frac{\Delta[C]}{\Delta t}$

Conceptual Plan: $\frac{\Delta[A]}{\Delta t}$ → $\frac{\Delta[B]}{\Delta t}$, **and** $\frac{\Delta[C]}{\Delta t}$

$$\text{Rate} = -\frac{1}{2}\frac{\Delta[A]}{\Delta t} = -\frac{\Delta[B]}{\Delta t} = \frac{1}{3}\frac{\Delta[C]}{\Delta t}$$

Solution: $\text{Rate} = -\frac{1}{2}\frac{\Delta[A]}{\Delta t} = -\frac{\Delta[B]}{\Delta t} = \frac{1}{3}\frac{\Delta[C]}{\Delta t}$. Substitute in value and solve for the two desired values. $-\frac{1}{2}\frac{-0.100\,M}{s} = -\frac{\Delta[B]}{\Delta t}$ so $\frac{\Delta[B]}{\Delta t} = -0.0500\,M \cdot s^{-1}$ and $-\frac{1}{2}\frac{-0.100\,M}{s} = \frac{1}{3}\frac{\Delta[C]}{\Delta t}$

so $\frac{\Delta[C]}{\Delta t} = 0.150\,M \cdot s^{-1}$.

Check: The units ($M \cdot s^{-1}$) are correct. The magnitude of the answer ($-0.05\ M \cdot s^{-1}$) makes physical sense because fewer moles of B are reacting for every mole of A and the change in concentration with time is negative since this is a reactant. The magnitude of the answer ($0.15\ M \cdot s^{-1}$) makes physical sense because more moles of C are being formed for every mole of A reacting and the change in concentration with time is positive since this is a product.

13.28 (a) $\text{Rate} = -\frac{\Delta[A]}{\Delta t} = -2\frac{\Delta[B]}{\Delta t} = \frac{1}{2}\frac{\Delta[C]}{\Delta t}$

(b) **Given:** $\frac{\Delta[C]}{\Delta t} = 0.025\ M/s$ **Find:** $\frac{\Delta[B]}{\Delta t}$, and $\frac{\Delta[A]}{\Delta t}$

Conceptual Plan: $\frac{\Delta[C]}{\Delta t} \rightarrow \frac{\Delta[B]}{\Delta t}$, **and** $\frac{\Delta[A]}{\Delta t}$

$$\text{Rate} = -\frac{\Delta[A]}{\Delta t} = -2\frac{\Delta[B]}{\Delta t} = \frac{1}{2}\frac{\Delta[C]}{\Delta t}$$

Solution: $\text{Rate} = -\frac{\Delta[A]}{\Delta t} = -2\frac{\Delta[B]}{\Delta t} = \frac{1}{2}\frac{\Delta[C]}{\Delta t}$. Substitute in value and solve for the two desired values. $-2\frac{\Delta[B]}{\Delta t} = \frac{1}{2}\frac{0.025\ M}{s}$ so $\frac{\Delta[B]}{\Delta t} = -0.0063\ M \cdot s^{-1}$ and $-\frac{\Delta[A]}{\Delta t} = \frac{1}{2}\frac{0.025\ M}{s}$ so $\frac{\Delta[A]}{\Delta t} = -0.013\ M \cdot s^{-1}$.

Check: The units ($M \cdot s^{-1}$) are correct. The magnitude of the answer ($-0.006\ M \cdot s^{-1}$) makes physical sense because fewer moles of B are reacting for every mole of C being formed and the change in concentration with time is negative since this is a reactant. The magnitude of the answer ($-0.01\ M \cdot s^{-1}$) makes physical sense because fewer moles of A are reacting for every mole of C being formed and the change in concentration with time is negative since this is a reactant. B has the smallest stoichiometric coefficient and so its rate of change has the smallest magnitude.

13.29 **Given:** $Cl_2(g) + 3\ F_2(g) \rightarrow 2\ ClF_3(g)$; $\Delta[Cl_2]/\Delta t = -0.012\ M/s$ **Find:** $\Delta[F_2]/\Delta t$; $\Delta[ClF_3]/\Delta t$; and Rate

Conceptual Plan: write the expression for the rate with respect to each species then

$$\text{Rate} = -\frac{\Delta[Cl_2]}{\Delta t} = -\frac{1}{3}\frac{\Delta[F_2]}{\Delta t} = \frac{1}{2}\frac{\Delta[ClF_3]}{\Delta t}$$

rate expression, $\frac{\Delta[Cl_2]}{\Delta t} \rightarrow \frac{\Delta[F_2]}{\Delta t}; \frac{\Delta[ClF_3]}{\Delta t}$**; Rate**

$$\text{Rate} = -\frac{\Delta[Cl_2]}{\Delta t} = -\frac{1}{3}\frac{\Delta[F_2]}{\Delta t} = \frac{1}{2}\frac{\Delta[ClF_3]}{\Delta t}$$

Solution: $\text{Rate} = -\frac{\Delta[Cl_2]}{\Delta t} = -\frac{1}{3}\frac{\Delta[F_2]}{\Delta t} = \frac{1}{2}\frac{\Delta[ClF_3]}{\Delta t}$ so $-\frac{\Delta[Cl_2]}{\Delta t} = -\frac{1}{3}\frac{\Delta[F_2]}{\Delta t}$. Rearrange to solve for $\frac{\Delta[F_2]}{\Delta t}$. $\frac{\Delta[F_2]}{\Delta t} = 3\frac{\Delta[Cl_2]}{\Delta t} = 3(-0.012\ M \cdot s^{-1}) = -0.036\ M \cdot s^{-1}$ and $-\frac{\Delta[Cl_2]}{\Delta t} = \frac{1}{2}\frac{\Delta[ClF_3]}{\Delta t}$. Rearrange to solve for $\frac{\Delta[ClF_3]}{\Delta t}$.

$\frac{\Delta[ClF_3]}{\Delta t} = -2\frac{\Delta[Cl_2]}{\Delta t} = -2(-0.012\ M \cdot s^{-1}) = 0.024\ M \cdot s^{-1}$.

Check: The units ($M \cdot s^{-1}$) are correct. The magnitude of the answers ($-0.036\ M \cdot s^{-1}$ and $0.024\ M \cdot s^{-1}$) makes physical sense because F_2 is being used at three times the rate of Cl_2, ClF_3 is being formed at two times the rate of Cl_2 disappearance, and Cl_2 has a stoichiometric coefficient of 1.

13.30 **Given:** $8\ H_2S(g) + 4\ O_2(g) \rightarrow 8\ H_2O(g) + S_8(g)$; $\Delta[H_2S]/\Delta t = -0.080\ M/s$

Find: $\Delta[O_2]/\Delta t$; $\Delta[H_2O]/\Delta t$; $\Delta[S_8]/\Delta t$; and Rate

Conceptual Plan: write the expression for the rate with respect to each species then

$$\text{Rate} = -\frac{1}{8}\frac{\Delta[H_2S]}{\Delta t} = -\frac{1}{4}\frac{\Delta[O_2]}{\Delta t} = \frac{1}{8}\frac{\Delta[H_2O]}{\Delta t} = \frac{\Delta[S_8]}{\Delta t}$$

rate expression, $\frac{\Delta[H_2S]}{\Delta t} \rightarrow \frac{\Delta[O_2]}{\Delta t}; \frac{\Delta[H_2O]}{\Delta t}; \frac{\Delta[S_8]}{\Delta t}$**; Rate**

$$\text{Rate} = -\frac{1}{8}\frac{\Delta[H_2S]}{\Delta t} = -\frac{1}{4}\frac{\Delta[O_2]}{\Delta t} = \frac{1}{8}\frac{\Delta[H_2O]}{\Delta t} = \frac{\Delta[S_8]}{\Delta t}$$

Solution: Rate $= -\frac{1}{8}\frac{\Delta[H_2S]}{\Delta t} = -\frac{1}{4}\frac{\Delta[O_2]}{\Delta t} = \frac{1}{8}\frac{\Delta[H_2O]}{\Delta t} = \frac{\Delta[S_8]}{\Delta t}$ so

$-\frac{1}{8}\frac{\Delta[H_2S]}{\Delta t} = -\frac{1}{4}\frac{\Delta[O_2]}{\Delta t}$. Rearrange to solve for $\frac{\Delta[O_2]}{\Delta t}$.

$$\frac{\Delta[O_2]}{\Delta t} = \frac{4}{8}\frac{\Delta[H_2S]}{\Delta t} = \frac{1}{2}(-0.080\ \text{M}\cdot\text{s}^{-1}) = -0.040\ \text{M}\cdot\text{s}^{-1}$$

and $-\frac{1}{8}\frac{\Delta[H_2S]}{\Delta t} = \frac{1}{8}\frac{\Delta[H_2O]}{\Delta t}$. Rearrange to solve for $\frac{\Delta[H_2O]}{\Delta t}$.

$$\frac{\Delta[H_2O]}{\Delta t} = -\frac{8}{8}\frac{\Delta[H_2S]}{\Delta t} = -(-0.080\ \text{M}\cdot\text{s}^{-1}) = 0.080\ \text{M}\cdot\text{s}^{-1}$$

and $-\frac{1}{8}\frac{\Delta[H_2S]}{\Delta t} = \frac{\Delta[S_8]}{\Delta t} - \frac{1}{8}\frac{\Delta[H_2S]}{\Delta t} = -\frac{1}{8}(-0.080\ \text{M}\cdot\text{s}^{-1}) = 0.010\ \text{M}\cdot\text{s}^{-1}$.

Check: The units ($\text{M}\cdot\text{s}^{-1}$) are correct. The magnitude of the answers ($-0.040\ \text{M}\cdot\text{s}^{-1}$ – $0.080\ \text{M}\cdot\text{s}^{-1}$, and $0.010\ \text{M}\cdot\text{s}^{-1}$) makes physical sense because O_2 is being used at one-half times the rate of H_2S, H_2O is being formed at two times the rate of H_2S disappearance, S_8 is being formed at one-eighth times the rate of H_2S disappearance, and S_8 has a stoichiometric coefficient of 1.

13.31 (a) **Given:** $[C_4H_8]$ versus time data **Find:** average rate between 0 and 10 s, and between 40 and 50 s
Conceptual Plan: t_1, t_2, $[C_4H_8]_1$, $[C_4H_8]_2$ → **average rate**

$$\text{Rate} = -\frac{\Delta[C_4H_8]}{\Delta t}$$

Solution: For 0 to 10 s Rate $= -\frac{[C_4H_8]_{t_2} - [C_4H_8]_{t_1}}{t_2 - t_1} = -\frac{0.913\ \text{M} - 1.000\ \text{M}}{10.\ \text{s} - 0.\ \text{s}} = 8.7 \times 10^{-3}\ \text{M}\cdot\text{s}^{-1}$ and

for 40 to 50 s: Rate $= -\frac{[C_4H_8]_{t_2} - [C_4H_8]_{t_1}}{t_2 - t_1} = -\frac{0.637\ \text{M} - 0.697\ \text{M}}{50.\ \text{s} - 40.\ \text{s}} = 6.0 \times 10^{-3}\ \text{M}\cdot\text{s}^{-1}$.

Check: The units ($\text{M}\cdot\text{s}^{-1}$) are correct. The magnitude of the answer ($10^{-3}\ \text{M}\cdot\text{s}^{-1}$) makes physical sense because rates are always positive and we are not changing the concentration much in 10 s. Also reactions slow as they proceed because the concentration of the reactants is decreasing.

(b) **Given:** $[C_4H_8]$ versus time data **Find:** $\frac{\Delta[C_2H_4]}{\Delta t}$ between 20 and 30 s

Conceptual Plan: t_1, t_2, $[C_4H_8]_1$, $[C_4H_8]_2$ → $\frac{\Delta[C_2H_4]}{\Delta t}$

$$\text{Rate} = -\frac{\Delta[C_4H_8]}{\Delta t} = \frac{1}{2}\frac{\Delta[C_2H_4]}{\Delta t}$$

Solution: Rate $= -\frac{[C_4H_8]_{t_2} - [C_4H_8]_{t_1}}{t_2 - t_1} = -\frac{0.763\ \text{M} - 0.835\ \text{M}}{30.\ \text{s} - 20.\ \text{s}} = 7.2 \times 10^{-3}\ \text{M}\cdot\text{s}^{-1} = \frac{1}{2}\frac{\Delta[C_2H_4]}{\Delta t}$.

Rearrange to solve for $\frac{\Delta[C_2H_4]}{\Delta t}$. So $\frac{\Delta[C_2H_4]}{\Delta t} = 2(7.2 \times 10^{-3}\ \text{M}\cdot\text{s}^{-1}) = 1.4 \times 10^{-2}\ \text{M}\cdot\text{s}^{-1}$.

Check: The units ($\text{M}\cdot\text{s}^{-1}$) are correct. The magnitude of the answer ($10^{-2}\ \text{M}\cdot\text{s}^{-1}$) makes physical sense because rate of product formation is always positive and we are not changing the concentration much in 10 s. The rate of change of the product is faster than the decline of the reactant because of the stoichiometric coefficients.

13.32 (a) **Given:** $[NO_2]$ versus time data **Find:** average rate between 10 and 20 s, and between 50 and 60 s
Conceptual Plan: t_1, t_2, $[NO_2]_1$, $[NO_2]_2$ → **average rate**

$$\text{Rate} = -\frac{\Delta[NO_2]}{\Delta t}$$

Solution: For 10 to 20 s Rate $= -\dfrac{[NO_2]_{t_2} - [NO_2]_{t_1}}{t_2 - t_1} = -\dfrac{0.904\ M - 0.951\ M}{20.\ s - 10.\ s} = 4.7 \times 10^{-3}\ M \cdot s^{-1}$ and

for 50 to 60 s Rate $= -\dfrac{[NO_2]_{t_2} - [NO_2]_{t_1}}{t_2 - t_1} = -\dfrac{0.740\ M - 0.778\ M}{60.\ s - 50.\ s} = 3.8 \times 10^{-3}\ M \cdot s^{-1}$.

Check: The units ($M \cdot s^{-1}$) are correct. The magnitude of the answer ($10^{-3}\ M \cdot s^{-1}$) makes physical sense because rates are always positive and we are not changing the concentration much in 10 s. Also reactions slow as they proceed because the concentration of the reactants is decreasing.

(b) **Given:** $[NO_2]$ versus time data **Find:** $\dfrac{\Delta[O_2]}{\Delta t}$ between 50 and 60 s

Conceptual Plan: average rate from part a) $\rightarrow \dfrac{\Delta[O_2]}{\Delta t}$

$$\text{Rate} = -\frac{\Delta[NO_2]}{\Delta t} = 2\frac{\Delta[O_2]}{\Delta t}$$

Solution: Rate $= -\dfrac{\Delta[NO_2]}{\Delta t} = 2\dfrac{\Delta[O_2]}{\Delta t}$. Substitute in value and solve for the desired value.

$3.8 \times 10^{-3}\ M \cdot s^{-1} = 2\dfrac{\Delta[O_2]}{\Delta t}$ so $\dfrac{\Delta[O_2]}{\Delta t} = 1.9 \times 10^{-3}\ M \cdot s^{-1}$.

Check: The units ($M \cdot s^{-1}$) are correct. The magnitude of the answer ($10^{-3}\ M \cdot s^{-1}$) makes physical sense because rate of product formation is always positive and we are not changing the concentration much in 10 s. The rate of change of the product is slower than the decline of the reactant because of the stoichiometric coefficients.

13.33 (a) **Given:** $[Br_2]$ versus time plot

Find: (i) average rate between 0 and 25 s; (ii) instantaneous rate at 25 s; and (iii) instantaneous rate of HBr formation at 50 s

Conceptual Plan: (i) t_1, t_2, $[Br_2]_1$, $[Br_2]_2$ $\rightarrow$ **average rate then**

$$\text{Rate} = -\frac{\Delta[Br_2]}{\Delta t}$$

(ii) draw tangent at 25 s and determine slope $\rightarrow$ **instantaneous rate then**

$$\text{Rate} = -\frac{\Delta[Br_2]}{\Delta t}$$

(iii) draw tangent at 50 s and determine slope $\rightarrow$ **instantaneous rate** $\rightarrow \dfrac{\Delta[HBr]}{\Delta t}$

$$\text{Rate} = -\frac{\Delta[Br_2]}{\Delta t} \qquad \text{Rate} = \frac{1}{2}\frac{\Delta[HBr]}{\Delta t}$$

Solution:

(i) Rate $= -\dfrac{[Br_2]_{t_2} - [Br_2]_{t_1}}{t_2 - t_1} = -\dfrac{0.75\ M - 1.00\ M}{25\ s - 0.\ s} =$

$= 1.0 \times 10^{-2}\ M \cdot s^{-1}$

and (ii) at 25 s:

Slope $= \dfrac{\Delta y}{\Delta x} = \dfrac{0.68\ M - 0.85\ M}{35\ s - 15\ s} =$

$- 8.5 \times 10^{-3}\ M \cdot s^{-1}$

since the slope $= \dfrac{\Delta[Br_2]}{\Delta t}$ and Rate $= -\dfrac{\Delta[Br_2]}{\Delta t}$,

then Rate $= -(-8.5 \times 10^{-3}\ M \cdot s^{-1}) = 8.5 \times 10^{-3}\ M \cdot s^{-1}$

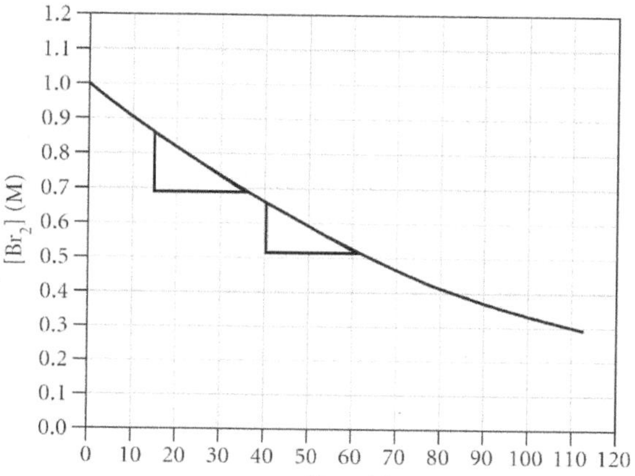

(iii) at 50 s:

Slope $= \dfrac{\Delta y}{\Delta x} = \dfrac{0.53\ M - 0.66\ M}{60.\ s - 40.\ s} =$

$- 6.5 \times 10^{-3}\ M \cdot s^{-1}$

since the slope $= \dfrac{\Delta[Br_2]}{\Delta t}$ and

$$\text{Rate} = -\frac{\Delta[Br_2]}{\Delta t} = \frac{1}{2}\frac{\Delta[HBr]}{\Delta t} \text{ then}$$

$$\frac{\Delta[HBr]}{\Delta t} = -2\frac{\Delta[Br_2]}{\Delta t} = -2(-6.5 \times 10^{-3}\,M \cdot s^{-1}) = 1.3 \times 10^{-2}\,M \cdot s^{-1}$$

Check: The units ($M \cdot s^{-1}$) are correct. The magnitude of the first answer is larger than the second answer because the rate is slowing down and the first answer includes the initial portion of the data. The magnitudes of the answers ($10^{-3}\,M \cdot s^{-1}$) make physical sense because rates are always positive and we are not changing the concentration much.

(b) **Given:** $[Br_2]$ versus time data; and $[HBr]_0 = 0$ M **Find:** plot [HBr] with time

Conceptual Plan: Since Rate $= -\frac{\Delta[Br_2]}{\Delta t} = \frac{1}{2}\frac{\Delta[HBr]}{\Delta t}$. **The rate of change of [HBr] will be twice that of $[Br_2]$. The plot will start at the origin.**

Solution:

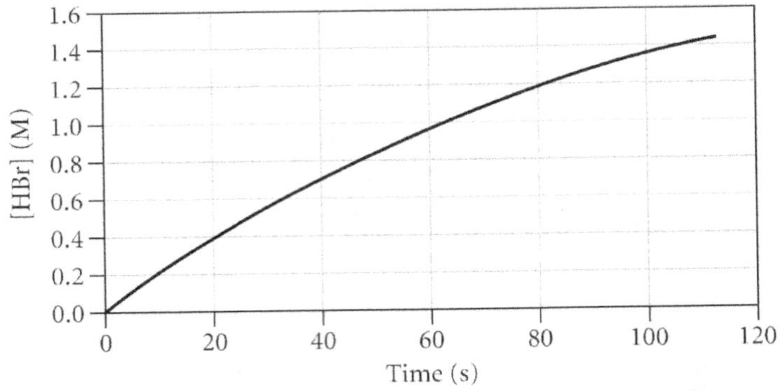

Check: The units (M versus s) are correct. The plot makes sense because the plot has the same general shape of the original plot, only we are increasing instead of decreasing and our concentration axis by a factor of two (to account for the difference in stoichiometric coefficients).

13.34 **Given:** $[H_2O_2]$ versus time plot; and 1.5 L H_2O_2 initially
Find: (a) average rate between 10 and 20 s; (b) instantaneous rate at 30 s; (c) instantaneous rate of O_2 formation at 50 s; and (d) mol_{O_2} formed in first 50 s

Conceptual Plan: (a) $t_1, t_2, [H_2O_2]_1, [H_2O_2]_2 \rightarrow$ **average rate then**

$$\text{Rate} = -\frac{1}{2}\frac{\Delta[H_2O_2]}{\Delta t}$$

(b) **draw tangent at 30 s and determine slope $\rightarrow$ instantaneous rate then**

$$\text{Rate} = -\frac{1}{2}\frac{\Delta[H_2O_2]}{\Delta t}$$

(c) **draw tangent at 50 s and determine slope $\rightarrow$ instantaneous rate $\rightarrow \frac{\Delta[O_2]}{\Delta t}$**

$$\text{Rate} = -\frac{1}{2}\frac{\Delta[H_2O_2]}{\Delta t} \qquad \text{Rate} = \frac{\Delta[O_2]}{\Delta t}$$

(d) $[H_2O_2]_{0\,s}, [H_2O_2]_{50\,s} \rightarrow \Delta[H_2O_2] \rightarrow \Delta[O_2]$ **then** $\Delta[O_2], V \rightarrow mol_{O_2}$

$$\Delta[H_2O_2] = [H_2O_2]_{50\,s} - [H_2O_2]_{0\,s} \qquad \text{Rate} = -\frac{1}{2}\frac{\Delta[H_2O_2]}{\Delta t} = \frac{\Delta[O_2]}{\Delta t} \qquad M = \frac{mol_{O_2}}{L}$$

Solution:

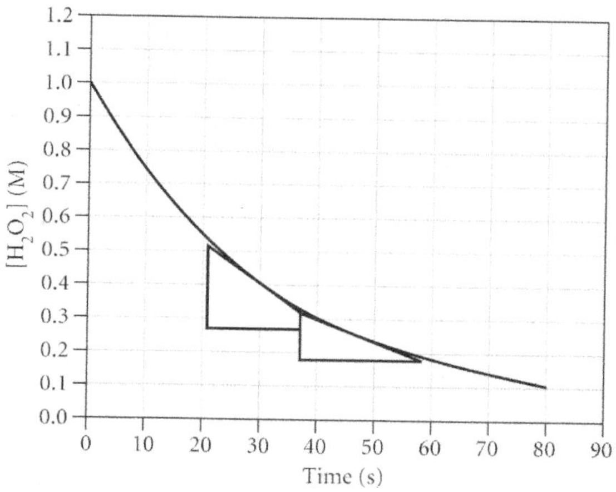

(a) $\text{Rate} = -\dfrac{[H_2O_2]_{t_2} - [H_2O_2]_{t_1}}{t_2 - t_1}$

$= -\dfrac{0.55\text{M} - 0.75\text{ M}}{20.\text{ s} - 10.\text{ s}} =$

$= 2.0 \times 10^{-2}\,\text{M}\cdot\text{s}^{-1}$ and

(b) at 30 s: $\text{Slope} = \dfrac{\Delta y}{\Delta x} = \dfrac{0.28\text{ M} - 0.52\text{ M}}{40.\text{ s} - 20.\text{ s}}$

$= -1.2 \times 10^{-2}\,\text{M}\cdot\text{s}^{-1}$ since the slope $= \dfrac{\Delta[H_2O_2]}{\Delta t}$ and

$\text{Rate} = -\dfrac{1}{2}\dfrac{\Delta[H_2O_2]}{\Delta t}$, then

$\text{Rate} = (-0.5)(-1.2 \times 10^{-2}\,\text{M}\cdot\text{s}^{-1}) = 6.0 \times 10^{-3}\,\text{M}\cdot\text{s}^{-1}$

(c) at 50 s:

$\text{Slope} = \dfrac{\Delta y}{\Delta x} = \dfrac{0.15\text{ M} - 0.28\text{M}}{60.\text{ s} - 40.\text{s}} = -6.5 \times 10^{-3}\,\text{M}\cdot\text{s}^{-1}$ since the slope $= \dfrac{\Delta[H_2O_2]}{\Delta t}$ and

$\text{Rate} = -\dfrac{1}{2}\dfrac{\Delta[H_2O_2]}{\Delta t} = \dfrac{\Delta[O_2]}{\Delta t}$ then $\dfrac{\Delta[O_2]}{\Delta t} = (-0.5)(-6.5 \times 10^{-3}\,\text{M}\cdot\text{s}^{-1}) = 3.3 \times 10^{-3}\,\text{M}\cdot\text{s}^{-1}$

(d) $\Delta[H_2O_2] = [H_2O_2]_{50\text{ s}} - [H_2O_2]_{0\text{ s}} = 0.23\text{ M} - 1.00\text{ M} = 0.77\text{ M}$ since

$\Delta[O_2] = -\dfrac{1}{2}\Delta[H_2O_2] = (-0.5)(0.77\text{M}) = 0.385\text{ M}$ then $\text{M} = \dfrac{\text{mol}_{O_2}}{\text{L}}$ so

$\text{mol}_{O_2} = \text{M}\cdot\text{L} = 0.385\,\dfrac{\text{mol }O_2}{\text{L}} \times 1.5\,\text{L} = 0.58\text{ mol }O_2$

Check: (a) The units ($\text{M}\cdot\text{s}^{-1}$) are correct. The magnitude of the first answer is reasonable considering the concentrations and times involved (1M / 100 s). (b) The units ($\text{M}\cdot\text{s}^{-1}$) are correct. We expect the answer in this part to be less than in the first part because the rate is decreasing as the reaction proceeds. (c) The units ($\text{M}\cdot\text{s}^{-1}$) are correct. We expect the answer in this part to be less than in the first part because the rate is decreasing as the reaction proceeds. (d) The units (mol) are correct. We expect an answer less than 1 mol since the drop in reactant concentration is less than 1 M, we have 1.5 L, and only half as much O_2 is generated as hydrogen peroxide is consumed.

The Rate Law and Reaction Orders

13.35 (a) **Given:** Rate versus [A] plot **Find:** reaction order
Conceptual Plan: Look at shape of plot and match to possibilities.
Solution: The plot is a linear plot, so Rate α [A] or the reaction is first order.
Check: The order of the reaction is a common reaction order.

(b) **Given:** part (a) **Find:** sketch plot of [A] versus time
Conceptual Plan: Using the result from part (a), shape plot of [A] versus time should be curved with [A] decreasing. Use 1.0 M as initial concentration.

Solution:

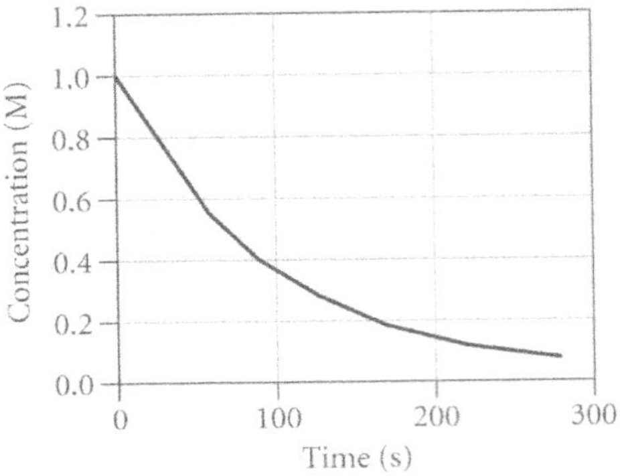

Check: The plot has a shape that matches the one in the text for first order plots.

(c) **Given:** part (a) **Find:** write a rate law and estimate k
Conceptual Plan: Using result from part (a), the slope of the plot is the rate constant.

Solution: Slope $= \dfrac{\Delta y}{\Delta x} = \dfrac{0.010\,\frac{\text{M}}{\text{s}} - 0.00\,\frac{\text{M}}{\text{s}}}{1.0\,\text{M} - 0.0\,\text{M}} = 0.010\ \text{s}^{-1}$ so Rate = $k\,[\text{A}]^1$ or Rate = $k\,[\text{A}]$ or Rate = $0.010\ \text{s}^{-1}\,[\text{A}]$

Check: The units (s^{-1}) are correct. The magnitude of the answer ($10^{-2}\ \text{s}^{-1}$) makes physical sense because of the rate and concentration data. Remember that concentration is in units of M, so plugging the rate constant into the equation has the units of the rate as $\text{M} \cdot \text{s}^{-1}$, which is correct.

13.36 (a) **Given:** Rate versus [A] plot **Find:** reaction order
Conceptual Plan: Look at shape of plot and match to possibilities.
Solution: The plot is a linear plot that is horizontal, so rate is independent of [A] or the reaction is zero order with respect to A.
Check: The order of the reaction is a common reaction order.

(b) **Given:** part (a) **Find:** sketch plot of [A] versus time
Conceptual Plan: Using the result from part (a), shape plot of [A] versus time should be a straight line with [A] decreasing. Use 1.0 M as initial concentration.
Solution:

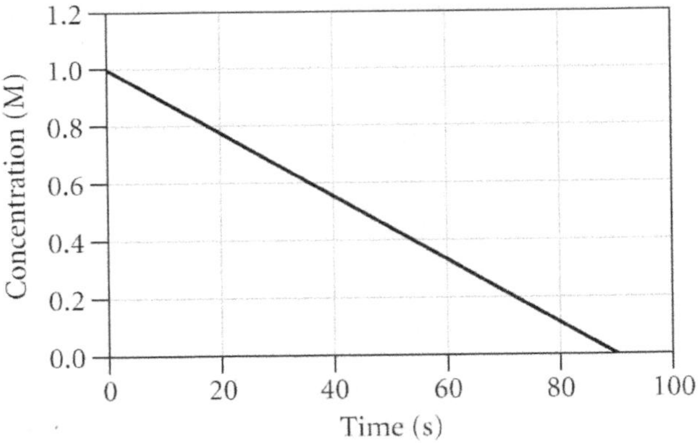

Check: The plot has a shape that matches the one in the text for zero order plots.

(c) **Given:** part (a) **Find:** write a rate law and estimate k
Conceptual Plan: Using result from part (a), the rate is equal to the rate constant.
Solution: Rate = $k\,[\text{A}]^0$ or Rate = k or Rate = $0.011\ \text{M} \cdot \text{s}^{-1}$
Check: The units ($\text{M} \cdot \text{s}^{-1}$) are correct. The magnitude of the answer ($10^{-2}\ \text{M} \cdot \text{s}^{-1}$) makes physical sense because of the rate and concentration data. Plugging the rate constant into the equation, the rate has the units of $\text{M} \cdot \text{s}^{-1}$, which is correct.

13.37 **Given:** reaction order: (a) first-order; (b) second-order; and (c) zero-order **Find:** units of k
Conceptual Plan: Using rate law, rearrange to solve for k.

$$\text{Rate} = k\,[\text{A}]^n \text{, where } n = \text{reaction order}$$

Solution: For all cases rate has units of $M \cdot s^{-1}$ and [A] has units of M

(a) $\text{Rate} = k\,[\text{A}]^1 = k\,[\text{A}] \text{ so } k = \dfrac{\text{Rate}}{[\text{A}]} = \dfrac{\frac{\cancel{M}}{s}}{\cancel{M}} = s^{-1};$

(b) $\text{Rate} = k\,[\text{A}]^2 \text{ so } k = \dfrac{\text{Rate}}{[\text{A}]^2} = \dfrac{\frac{\cancel{M}}{s}}{\cancel{M} \cdot M} = M^{-1} \cdot s^{-1};$

(c) $\text{Rate} = k\,[\text{A}]^0 = k = M \cdot s^{-1}.$

Check: The units (s^{-1}, $M^{-1} \cdot s^{-1}$ and $M \cdot s^{-1}$) are correct. The units for k change with the reaction order so that the units on the rate remain as $M \cdot s^{-1}$.

13.38 **Given:** $k = 0.053/s$ and $[N_2O_5] = 0.055$ M; reaction order: (a) first-order, (b) second-order, and zero-order (change units on k as necessary) **Find:** rate
Conceptual Plan: Using rate law, substitute in values to solve for Rate.

$$\text{Rate} = k\,[N_2O_5]^n \text{, where } n = \text{reaction order}$$

Solution: For all cases Rate has units of $M \cdot s^{-1}$ and [A] has units of M. Use the results from Problem 35 to choose the appropriate units for k.

(a) $\text{Rate} = k\,[N_2O_5]^1 = k\,[N_2O_5] = \dfrac{0.053}{s} \times 0.055\ M = 2.9 \times 10^{-3}\,\dfrac{M}{s};$

(b) $\text{Rate} = k\,[N_2O_5]^2 = k\,[N_2O_5] = \dfrac{0.053}{M\,s} \times (0.055\ M)^2 = 1.6 \times 10^{-4}\,\dfrac{M}{s};$ and

$\text{Rate} = k\,[N_2O_5]^0 = k = 5.3 \times 10^{-2}\,\dfrac{M}{s}$

Check: The units ($M \cdot s^{-1}$) are correct. The magnitude of the rate changes as the order of the reaction changes, because we are multiplying by the concentration a different number of times in each case. The higher the order the lower the rate since the concentration is less than 1 M.

13.39 **Given:** A, B, and C react to form products. Reaction is first order in A, second order in B, and zero order in C **Find:** (a) rate law; (b) overall order of reaction; (c) factor change in rate if [A] doubled; (d) factor change in rate if [B] doubled; (e) factor change in rate if [C] doubled; and (f) factor change in rate if [A], [B], and [C] doubled.
Conceptual Plan:

(a) **Using general rate law form, substitute in values for orders.**

$$\text{Rate} = k\,[\text{A}]^m\,[\text{B}]^n\,[\text{C}]^p \text{, where } m, n, \text{ and } p = \text{reaction orders}$$

(b) **Using rate law in part (a) add up all reaction orders.**

$$\textit{overall reaction order} = m + n + p$$

(c) **through (f) Using rate law from part (a) substitute in concentration changes.**

$$\frac{\text{Rate 2}}{\text{Rate 1}} = \frac{k\,[\text{A}]_2^1\,[\text{B}]_2^2}{k\,[\text{A}]_1^1\,[\text{B}]_1^2}$$

Solution:

(a) $m = 1$, $n = 2$, and $p = 0$ so $\text{Rate} = k\,[\text{A}]^1[\text{B}]^2[\text{C}]^0$ or $\text{Rate} = k\,[\text{A}][\text{B}]^2$.

(b) $\textit{overall reaction order} = m + n + p = 1 + 2 + 0 = 3$ so it is a third order reaction overall.

(c) $\frac{\text{Rate 2}}{\text{Rate 1}} = \frac{k\,[A]_2^1\,[B]_2^2}{k\,[A]_1^1\,[B]_1^2}$ and $[A]_2 = 2\,[A]_1$, $[B]_2 = [B]_1$, $[C]_2 = [C]_1$, so $\frac{\text{Rate 2}}{\text{Rate 1}} = \frac{k\,(2[A]_1)^1\,[B]_1^2}{k\,[A]_1^1\,[B]_1^2} = 2$ so the reaction rate doubles (factor of 2).

(d) $\frac{\text{Rate 2}}{\text{Rate 1}} = \frac{k\,[A]_2^1\,[B]_2^2}{k\,[A]_1^1\,[B]_1^2}$ and $[A]_2 = [A]_1$, $[B]_2 = 2\,[B]_1$, $[C]_2 = [C]_1$, so $\frac{\text{Rate 2}}{\text{Rate 1}} = \frac{k\,[A]_1\,(2\,[B]_1)^2}{k\,[A]_1^1\,[B]_1^2} = 2^2 = 4$ so the reaction rate quadruples (factor of 4).

(e) $\frac{\text{Rate 2}}{\text{Rate 1}} = \frac{k\,[A]_2^1\,[B]_2^2}{k\,[A]_1^1\,[B]_1^2}$ and $[A]_2 = [A]_1$, $[B]_2 = [B]_1$, $[C]_2 = 2\,[C]_1$, so $\frac{\text{Rate 2}}{\text{Rate 1}} = \frac{k\,[A]_1^1\,[B]_1^2}{k\,[A]_1^1\,[B]_1^2} = 1$ so the reaction rate is unchanged (factor of 1).

(f) $\frac{\text{Rate 2}}{\text{Rate 1}} = \frac{k\,[A]_2^1\,[B]_2^2}{k\,[A]_1^1\,[B]_1^2}$ and $[A]_2 = 2\,[A]_1$, $[B]_2 = 2\,[B]_1$, $[C]_2 = 2\,[C]_1$, so

$\frac{\text{Rate 2}}{\text{Rate 1}} = \frac{k\,(2\,[A]_1)^1\,(2\,[B]_1)^2}{k\,[A]_1^1\,[B]_1^2} = 2 \times 2^2 = 8$ so the reaction rate goes up by a factor of 8.

Check: The units (none) are correct. The rate law is consistent with the orders given and the overall order is larger than any of the individual orders. The factors are consistent with the reaction orders. The larger the order, the larger the factor. When all concentrations are changed the rate changes the most. If a reactant is not in the rate law, then changing its concentration has no effect on the reaction rate.

13.40 **Given:** A, B, and C react to form products. Reaction is zero order in A, one-half order in B, and second order in C.

Find: (a) rate law; (b) overall order of reaction; (c) factor change in rate if [A] doubled; (d) factor change in rate if [B] doubled; (e) factor change in rate if [C] doubled; and (f) factor change in rate if [A], [B], and [C] doubled

Conceptual Plan:

(a) **Using general rate law form, substitute in values for orders.**

$$\text{Rate} = k\,[A]^m\,[B]^n\,[C]^p, \text{ where } m, n, \text{ and } p = \text{reaction orders}$$

(b) **Using rate law in part (a) add up all reaction orders.**

$$\textit{overall reaction order} = m + n + p$$

(c) **through (f) Using rate law from part (a) substitute in concentration changes.**

$$\frac{\text{Rate 2}}{\text{Rate 1}} = \frac{k\,[B]_2^{1/2}\,[C]_2^2}{k\,[B]_1^{1/2}\,[C]_1^2}$$

Solution:

(a) $m = 0$, $n = 1/2$, and $p = 2$ so Rate $= k\,[A]^0[B]^{1/2}[C]^2$ or Rate $= k\,[B]^{1/2}[C]^2$.

(b) *overall reaction order* $= m + n + p = 0 + 1/2 + 2 = 5/2 = 2.5$ so it is a two and a half order reaction overall.

(c) $\frac{\text{Rate 2}}{\text{Rate 1}} = \frac{k\,[B]_2^{1/2}\,[C]_2^2}{k\,[B]_1^{1/2}\,[C]_1^2}$ and $[A]_2 = 2\,[A]_1$, $[B]_2 = [B]_1$, $[C]_2 = [C]_1$, so $\frac{\text{Rate 2}}{\text{Rate 1}} = \frac{k\,[B]_1^{1/2}\,[C]_1^2}{k\,[B]_1^{1/2}\,[C]_1^2} = 1$ so the reaction rate is unchanged (factor of 1).

(d) $\frac{\text{Rate 2}}{\text{Rate 1}} = \frac{k\,[B]_2^{1/2}\,[C]_2^2}{k\,[B]_1^{1/2}\,[C]_1^2}$ and $[A]_2 = [A]_1$, $[B]_2 = 2\,[B]_1$, $[C]_2 = [C]_1$, so $\frac{\text{Rate 2}}{\text{Rate 1}} = \frac{k\,(2[B]_1)^{1/2}\,[C]_1^2}{k\,[B]_1^{1/2}\,[C]_1^2} = 2^{1/2}$ so the reaction rate increases by a factor of $2^{1/2}$ or $\sqrt{2}$ or 1.414.

(e) $\frac{\text{Rate 2}}{\text{Rate 1}} = \frac{k\,[B]_2^{1/2}\,[C]_2^2}{k\,[B]_1^{1/2}\,[C]_1^2}$ and $[A]_2 = [A]_1$, $[B]_2 = [B]_1$, $[C]_2 = 2\,[C]_1$, so

$\frac{\text{Rate 2}}{\text{Rate 1}} = \frac{k\,[B]_1^{1/2}\,(2[C]_1)^2}{k\,[B]_1^{1/2}\,[C]_1^2} = 2^2 = 4$ so the reaction rate quadruples (factor of 4).

(f) $\frac{\text{Rate 2}}{\text{Rate 1}} = \frac{k\,[B]_2^{1/2}\,[C]_2^2}{k\,[B]_1^{1/2}\,[C]_1^2}$ and $[A]_2 = 2\,[A]_1, [B]_2 = 2\,[B]_1, [C]_2 = 2\,[C]_1$, so

$\frac{\text{Rate 2}}{\text{Rate 1}} = \frac{\cancel{k}\,(2\cancel{[B]_1})^{1/2}\,(2\cancel{[C]_1})^2}{\cancel{k}\,\cancel{[B]_1^{1/2}}\,\cancel{[C]_1^2}} = 2^{1/2} \times 2^2 = 2^{5/2}$ so the reaction rate goes up by a factor of $2^{5/2}$ or $4\sqrt{2}$ or 5.66.

Check: The units (none) are correct. The rate law is consistent with the orders given and the overall order is larger that any of the individual orders. The factors are consistent with the reaction orders. The larger the order, the larger the factor. When all concentrations are changed the rate changes the most. If a reactant is not in the rate law, then changing its concentration has no effect on the reaction rate.

13.41 **Given:** table of [A] versus initial rate **Find:** rate law and k

Conceptual Plan: Using general rate law form, compare rate ratios to determine reaction order.

$$\frac{\text{Rate 2}}{\text{Rate 1}} = \frac{k\,[A]_2^n}{k\,[A]_1^n}$$

Then use one of the concentration/initial rate pairs to determine k.

$$\text{Rate} = k[A]^n$$

Solution: $\frac{\text{Rate 2}}{\text{Rate 1}} = \frac{k\,[A]_2^n}{k\,[A]_1^n}$ Comparing the first two sets of data $\frac{0.210\,\cancel{M/s}}{0.053\,\cancel{M/s}} = \frac{\cancel{k}\,(0.200\,\cancel{M})^n}{\cancel{k}\,(0.100\,\cancel{M})^n}$ and $3.\underline{9}623 = 2^n$ so n = 2. If we compare the first and the last data sets $\frac{0.473\,\cancel{M/s}}{0.053\,\cancel{M/s}} = \frac{\cancel{k}\,(0.300\,\cancel{M})^n}{\cancel{k}\,(0.100\,\cancel{M})^n}$ and $8.\underline{9}245 = 3^n$ so $n = 2$. This second comparison is not necessary, but it increases our confidence in the reaction order. So Rate $= k\,[A]^2$. Selecting the second data set and rearranging the rate equation

$$k = \frac{\text{Rate}}{[A]^2} = \frac{0.210\,\frac{\text{M}}{\text{s}}}{(0.200\text{ M})^2} = 5.25\text{ M}^{-1}\cdot\text{s}^{-1} \text{ so Rate} = 5.25\text{ M}^{-1}\cdot\text{s}^{-1}[A]^2.$$

Check: The units (none and $M^{-1} \cdot s^{-1}$) are correct. The rate law is a common form. The rate is changing more rapidly than the concentration, so second order is consistent. The rate constant is consistent with the units necessary to get rate as M/s and the magnitude is reasonable since we have a second order reaction.

13.42 **Given:** table of [A] versus initial rate **Find:** rate law and k

Conceptual Plan: Using general rate law form, compare rate ratios to determine reaction order.

$$\frac{\text{Rate 2}}{\text{Rate 1}} = \frac{k\,[A]_2^n}{k\,[A]_1^n}$$

Then use one of the concentration/initial rate pairs to determine k.

$$\text{Rate} = k\,[A]^n$$

Solution: $\frac{\text{Rate 2}}{\text{Rate 1}} = \frac{k\,[A]_2^n}{k\,[A]_1^n}$ Comparing the first two sets of data $\frac{0.016\,\cancel{M/s}}{0.008\,\cancel{M/s}} = \frac{\cancel{k}\,(0.30\,\cancel{M})^n}{\cancel{k}\,(0.15\cancel{M})^n}$ and $2 = 2^n$ so $n = 1$. If we compare the first and the last data sets $\frac{0.032\,\cancel{M/s}}{0.008\,\cancel{M/s}} = \frac{\cancel{k}\,(0.032\,\cancel{M})^n}{\cancel{k}\,(0.008\,\cancel{M})^n}$ and $4 = 4^n$ so $n = 1$. This second comparison is not necessary, but it increases our confidence in the reaction order. So Rate $= k[A]$.

Selecting the second data set and rearranging the rate equation $k = \frac{\text{Rate}}{[A]} = \frac{0.016\,\frac{\cancel{M}}{\text{s}}}{0.30\,\cancel{M}} = 5.3 \times 10^{-2}\,\text{s}^{-1}$ so Rate $= 5.3 \times 10^{-2}\,\text{s}^{-1}[A]$.

Check: The units (none and s^{-1}) are correct. The rate law is a common form. The rate is changing as rapidly as the concentration is consistent with first order. The rate constant is consistent with the units necessary to get rate as M/s and the magnitude is reasonable since we have a first order reaction.

13.43 **Given:** table of $[NO_2]$ and $[F_2]$ versus initial rate **Find:** rate law, k, and overall order

Conceptual Plan: Using general rate law form, compare rate ratios to determine reaction order of each reactant. Be sure to choose data that changes only one concentration at a time.

$$\frac{\text{Rate 2}}{\text{Rate 1}} = \frac{k\,[NO_2]_2^m\,[F_2]_2^n}{k\,[NO_2]_1^m\,[F_2]_1^n}$$

Then use one of the concentration/initial rate pairs to determine k.

$$\text{Rate} = k[NO_2]^m\,[F_2]^n$$

Solution: $\frac{\text{Rate 2}}{\text{Rate 1}} = \frac{k\,[NO_2]_2^m\,[F_2]_2^n}{k\,[NO_2]_1^m\,[F_2]_1^n}$ Comparing the first two sets of data:
$\frac{0.051\ \cancel{M/s}}{0.026\ \cancel{M/s}} = \frac{\cancel{k}\,(0.200\ \cancel{M})^m\,\cancel{(0.100\ M)^n}}{\cancel{k}\,(0.100\ \cancel{M})]^m\,\cancel{(0.100\ M)^n}}$ and $1.9\underline{6}15 = 2^m$ so $m = 1$. If we compare the second and the third data sets: $\frac{0.103\ \cancel{M/s}}{0.051\ \cancel{M/s}} = \frac{\cancel{k}\,\cancel{(0.200\ M)^m}\,(0.200\ \cancel{M})^n}{\cancel{k}\,\cancel{(0.200\ M)^m}\,(0.100\ \cancel{M})^n}$ and $2 = 2^n$ so $n = 1$. Other comparisons can be made, but are not necessary. They should reinforce these values of the reaction orders. So Rate $= k\,[NO_2][F_2]$. Selecting the last data set and rearranging the rate equation $k = \frac{\text{Rate}}{[NO_2][F_2]} = \frac{0.411\ \frac{\cancel{M}}{s}}{(0.400\ \cancel{M})(0.400\ M)} = 2.57\ M^{-1}\cdot s^{-1}$ so Rate $= 2.57\ M^{-1}\cdot s^{-1}\,[NO_2][F_2]$ and the reaction is second order overall.

Check: The units (none and $M^{-1}\cdot s^{-1}$) are correct. The rate law is a common form. The rate is changing as rapidly as each concentration is changing, which is consistent with first order in each reactant. The rate constant is consistent with the units necessary to get rate as M/s and the magnitude is reasonable since we have a second order reaction.

13.44 **Given:** table of $[CH_3Cl]$ and $[Cl_2]$ versus initial rate **Find:** rate law, k, and overall order
Conceptual Plan: Using general rate law form, compare rate ratios to determine reaction order of each reactant. Be sure to choose data that changes only one concentration at a time.

$$\frac{\text{Rate 2}}{\text{Rate 1}} = \frac{k\,[CH_3Cl]_2^m\,[Cl_2]_2^n}{k\,[CH_3Cl]_1^m\,[Cl_2]_1^n}$$

Then use one of the concentration/initial rate pairs to determine k.

$$\text{Rate} = k\,[CH_3Cl]^m\,[Cl_2]^n$$

Solution: $\frac{\text{Rate 2}}{\text{Rate 1}} = \frac{k\,[CH_3Cl]_2^m\,[Cl_2]_2^n}{k\,[CH_3Cl]_1^m\,[Cl_2]_1^n}$. Comparing the first two sets of data:
$\frac{0.029\ \cancel{M/s}}{0.014\ \cancel{M/s}} = \frac{\cancel{k}\,(0.100\ \cancel{M})^m\,\cancel{(0.050\ M)^n}}{\cancel{k}\,(0.050\ \cancel{M})^m\,\cancel{(0.050\ M)^n}}$ and $2.\underline{0}714 = 2^m$ so $m = 1$. If we compare the second and the third data sets: $\frac{0.041\ \cancel{M/s}}{0.029\ \cancel{M/s}} = \frac{\cancel{k}\,\cancel{(0.100\ M)^m}\,(0.100\ \cancel{M})^n}{\cancel{k}\,\cancel{(0.100\ M)^m}\,(0.050\ \cancel{M})^n}$ and $1.4\underline{1}4 = 2^n$ so $n = 1/2$. Other comparisons can be made, but are not necessary. They should reinforce these values of the reaction orders. So Rate $= k\,[CH_3Cl]\,[Cl_2]^{1/2}$. Selecting the last data set and rearranging the rate equation
$k = \frac{\text{Rate}}{[CH_3Cl]\,[Cl_2]^{1/2}} = \frac{0.115\ \frac{\cancel{M}}{s}}{(0.200\ \cancel{M})(0.200\ M)^{1/2}} = 1.29\ M^{-1/2}\cdot s^{-1}$ so Rate $= 1.29\ M^{-1/2}\cdot s^{-1}[CH_3Cl]\,[Cl_2]^{1/2}$ and the reaction is one and a half order overall.

Check: The units (none and $M^{-1/2}\cdot s^{-1}$) are correct. The rate law is not as common as others, but is reasonable. The rate is changing as rapidly as the CH_3Cl concentration is changing, which is consistent with first order in this reactant. The rate is changing a bit more slowly than the Cl_2 concentration, which is consistent with half order in this reactant. The rate constant is consistent with the units necessary to get rate as M/s and the magnitude is reasonable since we have a one and a half order reaction.

The Integrated Rate Law and Half-Life

13.45 (a) The reaction is zero order. Since the slope of the plot is independent of the concentration, there is no dependence of the concentration of the reactant in the rate law.

(b) The reaction is first order. The expression for the half-life of a first order reaction is $t_{1/2} = \frac{0.693}{k}$, which is independent of the reactant concentration.

(c) The reaction is second order. The integrated rate expression for a second order reaction is $\frac{1}{[A]_t} = k\,t + \frac{1}{[A]_0}$, which is linear when the inverse of the concentration is plotted versus time.

13.46 (a) The reaction is second order. The expression for the half-life of a second order reaction, $t_{1/2} = \frac{1}{k[A]_0}$, which shows that the half-life decreases as concentration increases.

(b) The reaction is first order. The integrated rate expression for a first order reaction is $\ln[A]_t = -kt + \ln[A]_0$, which is linear when the natural log of the concentration is plotted versus time.

(c) The reaction is zero order. The expression for the half-life of a zero order reaction, $t_{1/2} = \dfrac{[A]_0}{2k}$, which shows that the half-life increases as concentration increases.

13.47 **Given:** table of [AB] versus time **Find:** reaction order, k, and [AB] at 25 s
Conceptual Plan: Look at the data and see if any common reaction orders can be eliminated. If the data does not show an equal concentration drop with time, then zero order can be eliminated. Look for changes in the half-life (compare time for concentration to drop to one-half of any value). If the half-life is not constant, then the first order can be eliminated. If the half-life is getting longer as the concentration drops, this might suggest second order. Plot the data as indicated by the appropriate rate law. Determine *k* from the slope of the plot. Finally calculate the [AB] at 25 s by using the appropriate integrated rate expression.
Solution: By the preceding logic, we can eliminate both the zero order and the first order reactions. (Alternatively, you could make all three plots and only one should be linear.) This suggests that we should have a second order reaction. Plot 1/[AB] versus time.

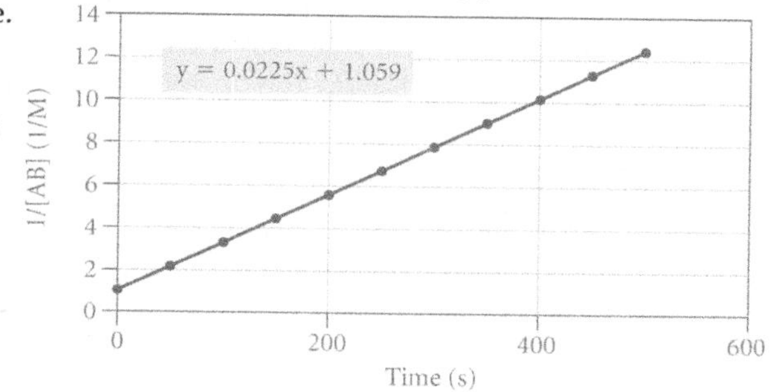

Since $\dfrac{1}{[AB]_t} = kt + \dfrac{1}{[AB]_0}$, the slope will be the rate constant. The slope can be determined by measuring $\Delta y/\Delta x$ on the plot or by using functions, such as "add trendline" in Excel. Thus the rate constant is $0.0225\ M^{-1}\cdot s^{-1}$ and the rate law is Rate $= 0.0225\ M^{-1}\cdot s^{-1}[AB]^2$.
Finally, use $\dfrac{1}{[AB]_t} = kt + \dfrac{1}{[AB]_0}$; substitute in the values of $[AB]_0$, 25 s, and k; and rearrange to solve for [AB] at 25 s. $[AB]_t = \dfrac{1}{kt + \dfrac{1}{[AB]_0}} = \dfrac{1}{(0.0225\ M^{-1}\cdot \cancel{s^{-1}})(25\ \cancel{s}) + \left(\dfrac{1}{0.950\ M}\right)} = 0.619\ M.$

Check: The units (none, $M^{-1}\cdot s^{-1}$, and M) are correct. The rate law is a common form. The plot was extremely linear, confirming second order kinetics. The rate constant is consistent with the units necessary to get rate as M/s and the magnitude is reasonable since we have a second order reaction. The [AB] at 25 s is in between the values at 0 s and 50 s.

13.48 **Given:** table of $[N_2O_5]$ versus time **Find:** reaction order, k, and $[N_2O_5]$ at 250 s
Conceptual Plan: Look at the data and see if any common reaction orders can be eliminated. If the data does not show an equal concentration drop with time, then zero order can be eliminated. Look for changes in the half-life (compare time for concentration to drop to one-half of any value). If the half-life is not constant, then the first order can be eliminated. If the half-life is getting longer as the concentration drops, this might suggest second order. Plot the data as indicated by the appropriate rate law. Determine *k* from the slope of the plot. Finally calculate the $[N_2O_5]$ at 250 s by using the appropriate integrated rate expression.

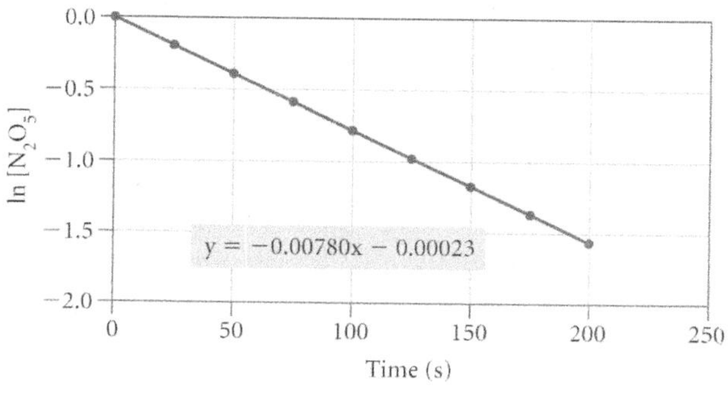

Solution: By the preceding logic, we can see that the reaction is most likely first order. It takes just under 75 s for the concentration to be cut in half for any concentration. Plot ln $[N_2O_5]$ versus time. Since $\ln[A]_t = -kt + \ln[A]_0$, the negative of the slope will be the rate constant. The slope can be determined by measuring $\Delta y/\Delta x$ on the plot or by using functions, such as "add trendline" in Excel. Thus the rate constant is $0.00780\ s^{-1}$ and the rate law is Rate $= 0.00780\ s^{-1}[N_2O_5]$. Finally, use $\ln[N_2O_5]_t = -kt + \ln[N_2O_5]_0$; substitute in the

values of $[N_2O_5]_0$, 250 s, and k; and rearrange to solve for $[N_2O_5]$ at 250 s. $\ln[N_2O_5]_{250\,s} = -(0.00780\ \cancel{s^{-1}})(250\ \cancel{s}) + \cancel{\ln[1.000]_0}$ then $[N_2O_5]_{250\,s} = e^{-1.95} = 0.142M$.
Check: The units (none, s^{-1}, and M) are correct. The rate law is a common form. The plot was extremely linear, confirming first order kinetics. The rate constant is consistent with the units necessary to get rate as M/s and the magnitude is reasonable since we have a first order reaction. The $[N_2O_5]$ at 250 s is less than the value at 200 s.

13.49 **Given:** table of $[C_4H_8]$ versus time **Find:** reaction order, k, and reaction rate when $[C_4H_8] = 0.25$ M
Conceptual Plan: Look at the data and see if any common reaction orders can be eliminated. If the data does not show an equal concentration drop with time, then zero order can be eliminated. Look for changes in half-life (compare time for concentration to drop to one-half of any value). If the half-life is not constant, then the first order can be eliminated. If the half-life is getting longer as the concentration drops, this might suggest second order. Plot the data as indicated by the appropriate rate law. Determine k from the slope of the plot. Finally calculate the reaction rate when $[C_4H_8] = 0.25$ M by using the rate law.
Solution: By the preceding logic, we can see that the reaction is most likely first order. It takes about 60 s for the concentration to be cut in half for any concentration. Plot ln $[C_4H_8]$ versus time. Since $\ln[A]_t = -kt + \ln[A]_0$, the negative of the slope will be the rate constant. The slope can be determined by measuring $\Delta y/\Delta x$ on the plot or by using functions, such as "add trendline" in Excel. Thus the rate constant is 0.0112 s^{-1} and the rate law is Rate = 0.0112 $s^{-1}[C_4H_8]$. Finally, use Rate = 0.0112 $s^{-1}[C_4H_8]$, substitute in the values of $[C_4H_8]$. Rate = 0.0112 $s^{-1}[0.25\ M] = 2.8 \times 10^{-3}\ M \cdot s^{-1}$.

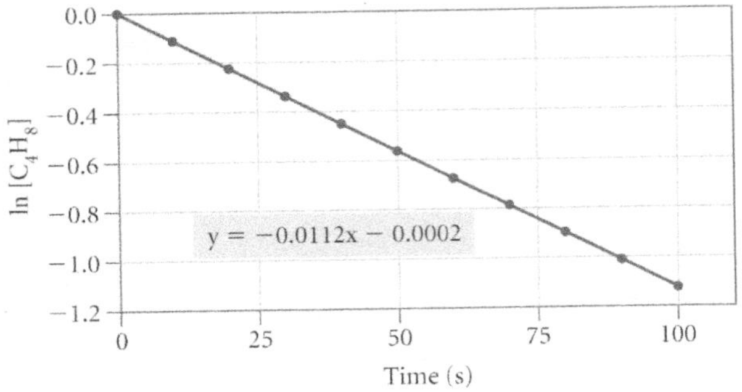

Check: The units (none, s^{-1}, and $M \cdot s^{-1}$) are correct. The rate law is a common form. The plot was extremely linear, confirming first order kinetics. The rate constant is consistent with the units necessary to get rate as M/s and the magnitude is reasonable since we have a first order reaction. The rate when $[C_4H_8] = 0.25$ M is consistent with the average rate using 90 s and 100 s.

13.50 **Given:** table of [A] versus time **Find:** reaction order, k, and reaction rate when [A] = 0.10 M
Conceptual Plan: Look at the data and see if any common reaction orders can be eliminated. If the data does not show an equal concentration drop with time, then zero order can be eliminated. Look for changes in half-life (compare time for concentration to drop to one-half of any value). If the half-life is not constant, then the first order can be eliminated. If the half-life is getting longer as the concentration drops, this might suggest second order. Plot the data as indicated by the appropriate rate law. Determine k from the slope of the plot. Finally calculate the reaction rate when [A] = 0.10 M by using the rate law.
Solution: By the preceding logic, we can see that the reaction is most likely zero order. There is a difference of about 0.085 M between each data point, so the rate is independent of the [A]. Plot [A] versus time. Since $[A]_t = -kt + [A]_0$, the negative of the slope will be the rate constant. The slope can be determined by measuring $\Delta y/\Delta x$ on the plot or by using functions, such as "add trendline" in Excel. Thus the rate constant is $3.41 \times 10^{-3}\ M \cdot s^{-1}$ and the rate law is Rate = $3.41 \times 10^{-3}\ M \cdot s^{-1}$. Finally, since the rate is independent of concentration, Rate = $3.41 \times 10^{-3}\ M \cdot s^{-1}$ at 0.10 M and all other concentrations. NOTE: A plot is not necessary since the kinetics are so simple.

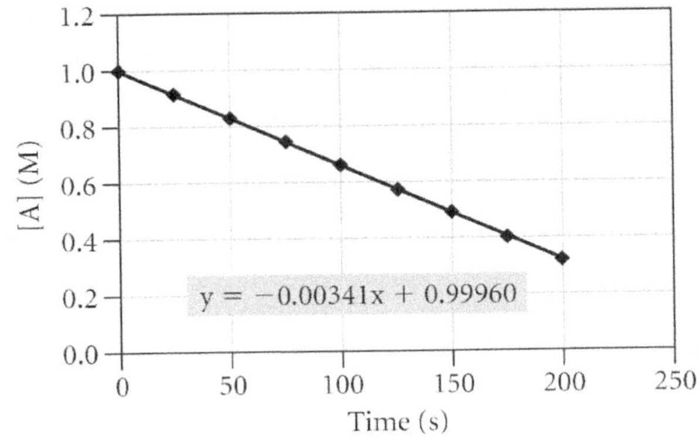

Check: The units (none, $M \cdot s^{-1}$, and $M \cdot s^{-1}$) are correct. The rate law is a common form. The plot was extremely linear, confirming zero order kinetics. The rate constant is consistent with the units necessary to get rate as M/s and the magnitude is reasonable since we have a zero order reaction. The rate is the same as any average rate that can be calculated using the data.

13.51 **Given:** plot of ln [A] versus time has slope = – 0.0045/s; $[A]_0$ = 0.250 M
Find: (a) k; (b) rate law; (c) $t_{1/2}$; and (d) [A] after 225 s
Conceptual Plan:

(a) A plot of ln [A] versus time is linear for a first order reaction. Using $\ln[A]_t = -kt + \ln[A]_0$, the rate constant is the negative of the slope.

(b) Rate law is first order. Add rate constant from part (a).

(c) For a first order reaction, $t_{1/2} = \frac{0.693}{k}$. Substitute in k from part (a).

(d) Use the integrated rate law, $\ln[A]_t = -kt + \ln[A]_0$, and substitute in k and the initial concentration.
Solution:

(a) Since the rate constant is the negative of the slope, $k = 4.5 \times 10^{-3}\ s^{-1}$.

(b) Since the reaction is first order, Rate = $4.5 \times 10^{-3}\ s^{-1}$ [A].

(c) $t_{1/2} = \frac{0.693}{k} = \frac{0.693}{0.0045/s} = 1.5 \times 10^2$ s.

(d) $\ln[A]_t = -kt + \ln[A]_0$, and substitute in k and the initial concentration. So
$\ln[A]_t = -(0.0045/\cancel{s})(225\ \cancel{s}) + \ln 0.250\ M = -2.39879$ and $[A]_{250\ s} = e^{-2.39879} = 0.0908$ M.
Check: The units (s^{-1}, none, s, and M) are correct. The rate law is a common form. The rate constant is consistent with value of the slope. The half-life is consistent with a small value of k. The concentration at 225 s is consistent with being between one and two half-lives.

13.52 **Given:** plot of 1/[AB] versus time has slope = 0.055/M s; $[A]_0$ = 0.250 M
Find: (a) k; (b) rate law; (c) $t_{1/2}$ when $[AB]_0$ = 0.55 M; and (d) [A] and [B] after 75 s
Conceptual Plan:

(a) A plot of 1/ [AB] versus time is linear for a second order reaction. Using $\frac{1}{[AB]_t} = kt + \frac{1}{[AB]_0}$, the rate constant is the slope.

(b) Rate law is second order. Add rate constant from part (a).

(c) For a second order reaction, $t_{1/2} = \frac{1}{k\,[AB]_0}$. Substitute in k from part (a).

(d) Use the integrated rate law, $\frac{1}{[AB]_t} = kt + \frac{1}{[AB]_0}$, and substitute in k, t, and the initial concentration to get the [AB]. Then $[AB]_0$, [AB] → [A], [B].

$\Delta[AB] = [AB]_{0\ s} - [AB]_{75\ s}$ with $\frac{1\ \text{mol A}}{1\ \text{mol AB}}$ and $\frac{1\ \text{mol B}}{1\ \text{mol AB}}$

Solution:

(a) Since the rate constant is the slope, $k = 5.5 \times 10^{-2}\ M^{-1} \cdot s^{-1}$.

(b) Since the reaction is second order, Rate = $5.5 \times 10^{-2}\ M^{-1} \cdot s^{-1}\ [AB]^2$.

(c) $t_{1/2} = \frac{1}{k\,[AB]_0}$ so $t_{1/2} = \frac{1}{(5.5 \times 10^{-2}\ \cancel{M^{-1}} \cdot s^{-1})(0.550\ \cancel{M})} = 33$ s.

(d) $\frac{1}{[AB]_t} = kt + \frac{1}{[AB]_0}$ so $[AB]_t = \frac{1}{kt + \frac{1}{[AB]_0}} = \frac{1}{(5.5 \times 10^{-2}\ M^{-1} \cdot \cancel{s^{-1}})(75\ \cancel{s}) + \left(\frac{1}{0.250\ M}\right)} = 0.12308$ M

then $\Delta[AB] = [AB]_{0\ s} - [AB]_{75\ s} = 0.250\ M - 0.12308\ M = 0.12692$ M AB

so $0.12692 \frac{\cancel{\text{mol AB}}}{L} \times \frac{1\ \text{mol A}}{1\ \cancel{\text{mol AB}}} = 0.13$ M A and $0.12692 \frac{\cancel{\text{mol AB}}}{L} \times \frac{1\ \text{mol B}}{1\ \cancel{\text{mol AB}}} = 0.13$ M B.

Check: The units ($M^{-1} \cdot s^{-1}$, none, s, and M) are correct. The rate law is a common form. The rate constant is consistent with value of the slope. The half-life is consistent with a small value of k. The concentration at 75 s is consistent with being about one half-life.

13.53 **Given:** decomposition of SO_2Cl_2, first order; $k = 1.42 \times 10^{-4}\ s^{-1}$
Find: (a) $t_{1/2}$; (b) t to decrease to 25% of $[SO_2Cl_2]_0$; (c) t to 0.78 M when $[SO_2Cl_2]_0 = 1.00$ M; and (d) $[SO_2Cl_2]$ after 2.00×10^2 s and 5.00×10^2 s when $[SO_2Cl_2]_0 = 0.150$ M
Conceptual Plan:

(a) $k \rightarrow t_{1/2}$

$$t_{1/2} = \frac{0.693}{k}$$

(b) $[SO_2Cl_2]_0$, 25% of $[SO_2Cl_2]_0$, $k \rightarrow t$

$$\ln[A]_t = -kt + \ln[A]_0$$

(c) $[SO_2Cl_2]_0$, $[SO_2Cl_2]_t$, $k \rightarrow t$

$$\ln[A]_t = -kt + \ln[A]_0$$

(d) $[SO_2Cl_2]_0$, t, $k \rightarrow [SO_2Cl_2]_t$

$$\ln[A]_t = -kt + \ln[A]_0$$

Solution:

(a) $$t_{1/2} = \frac{0.693}{k} = \frac{0.693}{1.42 \times 10^{-4}\ s^{-1}} = 4.88 \times 10^3\ s$$

(b) $[SO_2Cl_2]_t = 0.25\ [SO_2Cl_2]_0$. Since $\ln[SO_2Cl_2]_t = -kt + \ln[SO_2Cl_2]_0$ rearrange to solve for t.

$$t = -\frac{1}{k}\ln\frac{[SO_2Cl_2]_t}{[SO_2Cl_2]_0} = -\frac{1}{1.42 \times 10^{-4}\ s^{-1}}\ln\frac{0.25\ \cancel{[SO_2Cl_2]_0}}{\cancel{[SO_2Cl_2]_0}} = 9.8 \times 10^3\ s$$

(c) $[SO_2Cl_2]_t = 0.78$ M; $[SO_2Cl_2]_0 = 1.00$ M. Since $\ln[SO_2Cl_2]_t = -kt + \ln[SO_2Cl_2]_0$ rearrange to solve for t. $t = -\frac{1}{k}\ln\frac{[SO_2Cl_2]_t}{[SO_2Cl_2]_0} = -\frac{1}{1.42 \times 10^{-4}\ s^{-1}}\ln\frac{0.78\ \cancel{M}}{1.00\ \cancel{M}} = 1.7 \times 10^3$ s.

(d) $[SO_2Cl_2]_0 = 0.150$ M and 2.00×10^2 s in

$$\ln[SO_2Cl_2]_t = -\left(1.42 \times 10^{-4}\ \cancel{s^{-1}}\right)\left(2.00 \times 10^2\ \cancel{s}\right) + \ln 0.150\ M = -1.9\underline{2}552 \rightarrow$$

$$[SO_2Cl_2]_t = e^{-1.9\underline{2}552} = 0.146\ M$$

$[SO_2Cl_2]_0 = 0.150$ M and 5.00×10^2 s in

$$\ln[SO_2Cl_2]_t = -\left(1.42 \times 10^{-4}\ \cancel{s^{-1}}\right)\left(5.00 \times 10^2\ \cancel{s}\right) + \ln 0.150\ M = -1.9\underline{6}812 \rightarrow$$

$$[SO_2Cl_2]_t = e^{-1.9\underline{6}812} = 0.140\ M$$

Check: The units (s, s, s, and M) are correct. The rate law is a common form. The half-life is consistent with a small value of k. The time to 25% is consistent with two half-lives. The time to 0.78 M is consistent with being less than one half-life. The final concentrations are consistent with the time being less than one half-life.

13.54 **Given:** decomposition of XY, second order in XY; $k = 7.02 \times 10^{-3}\ M^{-1} \cdot s^{-1}$
Find: (a) $t_{1/2}$ when $[XY]_0 = 0.100$ M; (b) t to decrease to 12.5% of $[XY]_0 = 0.100$ M and 0.200 M; (c) t to 0.062 M when $[XY]_0 = 0.150$ M; and (d) [XY] after 5.0×10^1 s and 5.50×10^2 s when $[XY]_0 = 0.050$ M
Conceptual Plan:

(a) $[XY]_0$, $k \rightarrow t_{1/2}$

$$t_{1/2} = \frac{1}{k\,[A]_0}$$

(b) $[XY]_0$, 12.5 % of $[XY]_0$, $k \rightarrow t$

$$\frac{1}{[A]_t} = kt + \frac{1}{[A]_0}$$

(c) $[XY]_0, [XY]_t, k \rightarrow t$

$$\frac{1}{[A]_t} = kt + \frac{1}{[A]_0}$$

(d) $[XY]_0, t, k \rightarrow [XY]_t$

$$\frac{1}{[A]_t} = kt + \frac{1}{[A]_0}$$

Solution:

(a) $t_{1/2} = \dfrac{1}{k\,[XY]_0} = \dfrac{1}{(7.02 \times 10^{-3}\,\cancel{M^{-1}}s^{-1})\,(0.100\,\cancel{M})} = 1.42 \times 10^3\ s$

(b) $[XY]_t = 0.125\,[XY]_0 = 0.125 \times 0.100\ M = 0.0125\ M$. Since $\dfrac{1}{[XY]_t} = kt + \dfrac{1}{[XY]_0}$ rearrange to solve for t.

$$t = \frac{1}{k}\left(\frac{1}{[XY]_t} - \frac{1}{[XY]_0}\right) = \frac{1}{(7.02 \times 10^{-3}\,\cancel{M^{-1}}\cdot s^{-1})}\left(\frac{1}{0.0125\,\cancel{M}} - \frac{1}{0.100\,\cancel{M}}\right) = 9.97 \times 10^3\ s \text{ and}$$

$[XY]_t = 0.125\,[XY]_0 = 0.125 \times 0.200\ M = 0.0250\ M$. Since $\dfrac{1}{[XY]_t} = kt + \dfrac{1}{[XY]_0}$ rearrange to solve for t.

$$t = \frac{1}{k}\left(\frac{1}{[XY]_t} - \frac{1}{[XY]_0}\right) = \frac{1}{(7.02 \times 10^{-3}\,\cancel{M^{-1}}\cdot s^{-1})}\left(\frac{1}{0.0250\,\cancel{M}} - \frac{1}{0.200\,\cancel{M}}\right) = 4.99 \times 10^3\ s.$$

(c) $[XY]_t = 0.062$; $[XY]_0 = 0.150\ M$. Since $\dfrac{1}{[XY]_t} = kt + \dfrac{1}{[XY]_0}$ rearrange to solve for t.

$$t = \frac{1}{k}\left(\frac{1}{[XY]_t} - \frac{1}{[XY]_0}\right) = \frac{1}{(7.02 \times 10^{-3}\,\cancel{M^{-1}}\cdot s^{-1})}\left(\frac{1}{0.062\,\cancel{M}} - \frac{1}{0.150\,\cancel{M}}\right) = 1.3 \times 10^3\ s.$$

(d) $[XY]_0 = 0.050\ M$ and $5.0 \times 10^1\ s$ in $\dfrac{1}{[XY]_t} = kt + \dfrac{1}{[XY]_0} \rightarrow$

$$\frac{1}{[XY]_t} = (7.02 \times 10^{-3}\,M^{-1}\cdot\cancel{s^{-1}})(5.0 \times 10^1\,\cancel{s}) + \frac{1}{0.050\ M} = \frac{23.\underline{5}1}{M} \text{ so } [XY] = 0.043\ M \text{ and}$$

$[XY]_0 = 0.050\ M$ and $5.50 \times 10^2\ s$ in $\dfrac{1}{[XY]_t} = (7.02 \times 10^{-3}\,M^{-1}\cdot\cancel{s^{-1}})(5.50 \times 10^2\,\cancel{s}) + \dfrac{1}{0.050\ M} = \dfrac{2\underline{3}.861}{M}$

so $[XY] = 0.042\ M$.

Check: The units (s, s, s, s, M, and M) are correct. The rate law is a common form. The half-life is consistent with a small value of k. The time to 12.5% is consistent with three half-lives, where the half-life time is increasing. The next time (5000 s) is shorter because the initial concentration is higher. The last time is the shortest because it is less than a half-life with an intermediate concentration. The final concentrations are consistent with the time being much less than one half-life.

13.55 **Given:** $t_{1/2}$ for radioactive decay of U-238 = 4.5 billion years and independent of $[U\text{-}238]_0$
Find: t to decrease by 10%; number U-238 atoms today, when 1.5×10^{18} atoms formed 13.8 billion years ago
Conceptual Plan: $t_{1/2}$ independent of concentration implies first order kinetics, $t_{1/2} \rightarrow k$ then

$$t_{1/2} = \frac{0.693}{k}$$

90 % of $[U\text{-}238]_0, k \rightarrow t$ and $[U\text{-}238]_0, t, k \rightarrow [U\text{-}238]_t$

$$\ln[A]_t = -kt + \ln[A]_0 \qquad \ln[A]_t = -kt + \ln[A]_0$$

Solution: $t_{1/2} = \dfrac{0.693}{k}$ rearrange to solve for k. $k = \dfrac{0.693}{t_{1/2}} = \dfrac{0.693}{4.5 \times 10^9\ yr} = 1.\underline{5}4 \times 10^{-10}\ yr^{-1}$ then

$[U\text{-}238]_t = 0.10\,[U\text{-}238]_0$. Since $\ln[U\text{-}238]_t = -kt + \ln[U\text{-}238]_0$ rearrange to solve for t.

$$t = -\frac{1}{k}\ln\frac{[U\text{-}238]_t}{[U\text{-}238]_0} = -\frac{1}{1.\underline{5}4 \times 10^{-10}\ yr^{-1}}\ln\frac{0.90\,\cancel{[U\text{-}238]_0}}{\cancel{[U\text{-}238]_0}} = 6.8 \times 10^8\ yr$$

and $[U\text{-}238]_0 = 1.5 \times 10^{18}$ atoms; $t = 13.8 \times 10^9$ yr

$\ln[U\text{-}238]_t = -kt + \ln[U\text{-}238]_0 = -(1.\underline{5}4 \times 10^{-10}\,\cancel{yr^{-1}})(13.8 \times 10^9\,\cancel{yr})$

$+ \ln(1.5 \times 10^{18}\text{atoms}) = 39.7\underline{2}6797 \rightarrow$

$[U\text{-}238]_t = e^{39.7\underline{2}6797} = 1.8 \times 10^{17}\text{atoms}.$

Check: The units (yr and atoms) are correct. The time to 10% decay is consistent with less than one half-life. The final concentration is consistent with the time being about three half-lives.

13.56 **Given:** $t_{1/2}$ for radioactive decay of C-14 = 5730 years
Find: t to decrease by 25%; mmol C-14 atoms left, after 2255 yr in sample initially contains 1.5 mmol C-14
Conceptual Plan: radioactive decay implies first order kinetics, $t_{1/2} \rightarrow k$ then

$$t_{1/2} = \frac{0.693}{k}$$

75% of $[\text{C-14}]_0$, $k \rightarrow t$ and $[\text{C-14}]_0$, t, $k \rightarrow [\text{C-14}]_t$

$$\ln[\text{A}]_t = -kt + \ln[\text{A}]_0 \qquad \ln[\text{A}]_t = -kt + \ln[\text{A}]_0$$

Solution: $t_{1/2} = \frac{0.693}{k}$ rearrange to solve for k. $k = \frac{0.693}{t_{1/2}} = \frac{0.693}{5730 \text{ yr}} = 1.2\underline{0}942 \times 10^{-4} \text{ yr}^{-1}$ then

$[\text{C-14}]_t = 0.75\ [\text{C-14}]_0$. Since $\ln[\text{C-14}]_t = -kt + \ln[\text{C-14}]_0$ rearrange to solve for t.

$$t = -\frac{1}{k}\ln\frac{[\text{C-14}]_t}{[\text{C-14}]_0} = -\frac{1}{1.2\underline{0}942 \times 10^{-4} \text{ yr}^{-1}}\ln\frac{0.75\ \cancel{[\text{C-14}]_0}}{\cancel{[\text{C-14}]_0}} = 2.4 \times 10^3 \text{ yr and } [\text{C-14}]_0 = 1.5 \text{ mmol};$$

$t = 2255$ yr

$\ln[\text{C-14}]_t = -kt + \ln[\text{C-14}]_0 = -(1.2\underline{0}942 \times 10^{-4}\ \cancel{\text{yr}^{-1}})(2255\ \cancel{\text{yr}}) + \ln(1.5 \text{ mmol}) = 0.13\underline{2}741 \rightarrow$

$[\text{C-14}]_t = e^{0.132741} = 1.1$ mmol.

Check: The units (yr and mmol) are correct. The time to 25% decay is consistent with less than one half-life. The final concentration is consistent with the time being less than one half-life.

The Effect of Temperature and the Collision Model

13.57

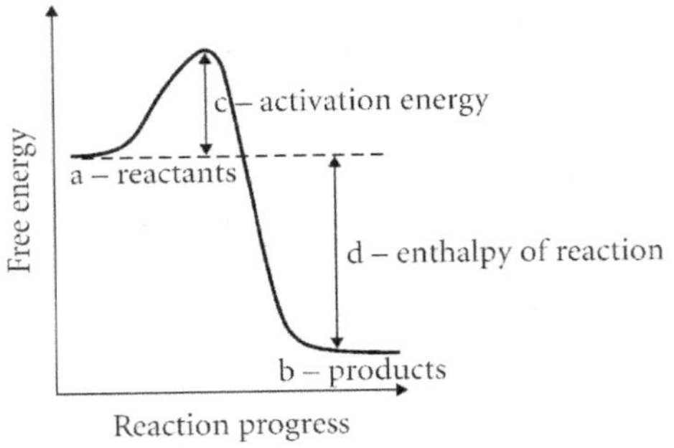

13.58

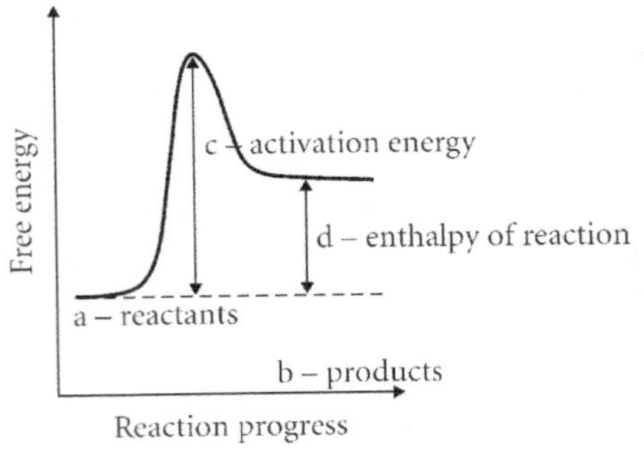

13.59 **Given:** activation energy = 56.8 kJ/mol, frequency factor = 1.5×10^{11} /s, 25 °C **Find:** rate constant
Conceptual Plan: °C $\rightarrow$ K and kJ/mol $\rightarrow$ J/mol then E_a, T, $A \rightarrow k$

$$\text{K} = {}^\circ\text{C} + 273.15 \qquad \frac{1000 \text{ J}}{1 \text{ kJ}} \qquad k = A\,e^{-E_a/RT}$$

Solution: $T = 25°\text{C} + 273.15 = 298$ K and $\frac{56.8\ \cancel{\text{kJ}}}{\text{mol}} \times \frac{1000 \text{ J}}{1\ \cancel{\text{kJ}}} = 5.68 \times 10^4 \frac{\text{J}}{\text{mol}}$ then

$$k = A\,e^{-E_a/RT} = (1.5 \times 10^{11}\,\text{s}^{-1})\,e^{\dfrac{-5.68 \times 10^4\,\frac{\cancel{J}}{\cancel{mol}}}{\left(8.314\,\frac{\cancel{J}}{\cancel{K}\cdot\cancel{mol}}\right)298\,\cancel{K}}} = 17\,\text{s}^{-1}$$

Check: The units (s^{-1}) are correct. The rate constant is consistent with a large activation energy and a large frequency factor.

13.60   **Given:** 32 °C, rate constant = 0.055/s, and frequency factor = 1.2×10^{13} /s   **Find:** activation energy
Conceptual Plan: °C $\rightarrow$ K then E_a, T, A $\rightarrow$ k then J/mol $\rightarrow$ kJ/mol
$$K = °C + 273.15 \qquad k = A\,e^{-E_a/RT} \qquad \frac{1\,\text{kJ}}{1000\,\text{J}}$$

Solution: $T = 32°C + 273.15 = 305$ K then $k = A\,e^{-E_a/RT}$. Rearrange to solve for E_a.

$$E_a = -RT\ln\left(\frac{k}{A}\right) = -8.314\,\frac{\text{J}}{\text{K mol}} \times 305\,\text{K} \times \ln\left(\frac{0.055\,\cancel{s^{-1}}}{1.2 \times 10^{13}\,\cancel{s^{-1}}}\right) = 8.37 \times 10^4\,\frac{\cancel{J}}{\text{mol}} \times \frac{1\,\text{kJ}}{1000\,\cancel{J}} = 83.7\,\frac{\text{kJ}}{\text{mol}}.$$

Check: The units (kJ/mol) are correct. The activation energy is consistent with a modest rate constant and a large frequency factor.

13.61   **Given:** plot of ln k versus 1/T (in K) is linear with a slope of -7445 K   **Find:** E_a
Conceptual Plan: Since $\ln k = \dfrac{-E_a}{R}\left(\dfrac{1}{T}\right) + \ln A$ **a plot of ln k versus 1/T will have a slope** $= -E_a/R$.
Solution: Since the slope $= -7445$ K $= -E_a/R$ then

$$E_a = -(slope)R = -(-7445\,\text{K})\left(8.314\,\frac{\cancel{J}}{\text{K}\cdot\text{mol}}\right)\left(\frac{1\,\text{kJ}}{1000\,\cancel{J}}\right) = 61.90\,\frac{\text{kJ}}{\text{mol}}.$$

Check: The units (kJ/mol) are correct. The activation energy is typical for many reactions.

13.62   **Given:** plot of ln k versus 1/T (in K) is linear with a slope of -1.01×10^4 K   **Find:** E_a
Conceptual Plan: Since $\ln k = \dfrac{-E_a}{R}\left(\dfrac{1}{T}\right) + \ln A$ **a plot of ln k versus 1/T will have a slope** $= -E_a/R$.
Solution: Since the slope $= -1.01 \times 10^4$ K $= -E_a/R$ then

$$E_a = -(slope)R = -(-1.01 \times 10^4\,\text{K})\left(8.314\,\frac{\cancel{J}}{\text{K}\cdot\text{mol}}\right)\left(\frac{1\,\text{kJ}}{1000\,\cancel{J}}\right) = 84.0\,\frac{\text{kJ}}{\text{mol}}.$$

Check: The units (kJ/mol) are correct. The activation energy is typical for many reactions.

13.63   **Given:** table of rate constant versus T **Find:** E_a, and A
Conceptual Plan: Since $\ln k = \dfrac{-E_a}{R}\left(\dfrac{1}{T}\right) + \ln A$ **a plot of ln k versus 1/T will have a slope** $= -E_a/R$ **and an intercept** $= \ln A$.
Solution: The slope can be determined by measuring $\Delta y/\Delta x$ on the plot or by using functions, such as "add trendline" in Excel. Since the slope $= -30189$ K $= -E_a/R$ then
$E_a = -(slope)R =$

$$-(-30189\,\text{K})\left(8.314\,\frac{\cancel{J}}{\text{K}\cdot\text{mol}}\right)\left(\frac{1\,\text{kJ}}{1000\,\cancel{J}}\right) =$$

$$= 251\,\frac{\text{kJ}}{\text{mol}} \text{ and intercept} = 27.399 = \ln A \text{ then}$$

$A = e^{intercept} = e^{27.399} = 7.93 \times 10^{11}\,\text{s}^{-1}$.
Check: The units (kJ/mol and s^{-1}) are correct. The plot was extremely linear, confirming Arrhenius behavior. The activation and frequency factor are typical for many reactions.

y = −30189x + 27.399

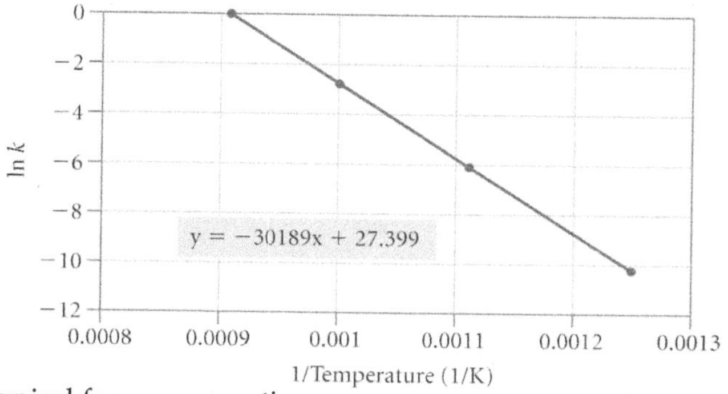

13.64 **Given:** table of rate constant versus T **Find:** E_a, and A

Conceptual Plan: Since $\ln k = \dfrac{-E_a}{R}\left(\dfrac{1}{T}\right) + \ln A$ **a plot of ln k versus $1/T$ will have a slope = $-E_a/R$ and an intercept = ln A.**

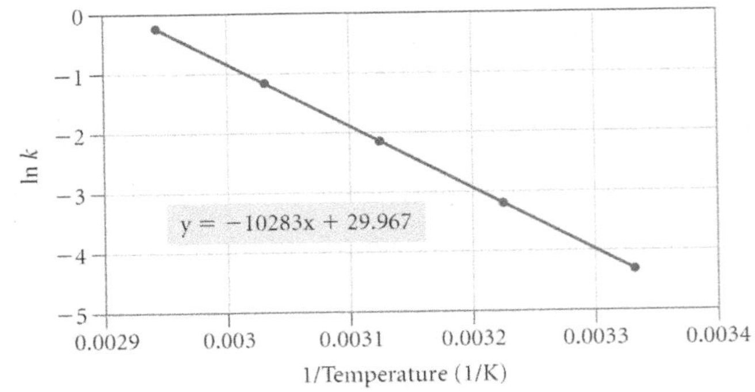

Solution: The slope can be determined by measuring $\Delta y/\Delta x$ on the plot or by using functions, such as "add trendline" in Excel. Since the slope = $-$ 10283 K = $-E_a/R$ then $E_a = -(slope)R =$

$$= -(-10283\ \text{K})\left(8.314\frac{\text{J}}{\text{K}\cdot\text{mol}}\right)\left(\frac{1\ \text{kJ}}{1000\ \text{J}}\right) \text{ and}$$

$$= 85.5\frac{\text{kJ}}{\text{mol}}$$

intercept = 29.967 = ln A then

$A = e^{intercept} = e^{29.967} = 1.03 \times 10^{13}\ \text{s}^{-1}$.

Check: The units (kJ/mol and s^{-1}) are correct. The plot was extremely linear, confirming Arrhenius behavior. The activation and frequency factor are typical for many reactions.

13.65 **Given:** table of rate constant versus T **Find:** E_a and A

Conceptual Plan: Since $\ln k = \dfrac{-E_a}{R}\left(\dfrac{1}{T}\right) + \ln A$ **a plot of ln k versus $1/T$ will have a slope = $-E_a/R$ and an intercept = ln A.**

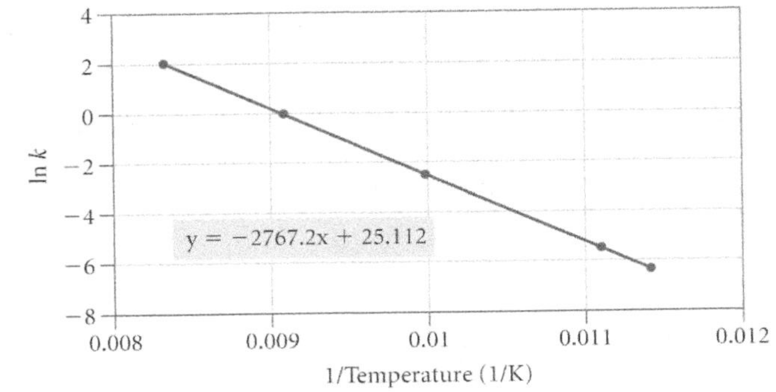

Solution: The slope can be determined by measuring $\Delta y/\Delta x$ on the plot or by using functions, such as "add trendline" in Excel. Since the slope = $-$ 2767.2 K = $-E_a/R$ then $E_a = -(slope)R =$

$$= -(-2767.2\ \text{K})\left(8.314\frac{\text{J}}{\text{K}\cdot\text{mol}}\right)\left(\frac{1\ \text{kJ}}{1000\ \text{J}}\right) =$$

$= 23.0\dfrac{\text{kJ}}{\text{mol}}$ and intercept = 25.112 = ln A then

$A = e^{intercept} = e^{25.112} = 8.05 \times 10^{10}\ \text{s}^{-1}$.

Check: The units (kJ/mol and s^{-1}) are correct. The plot was extremely linear, confirming Arrhenius behavior. The activation and frequency factor are typical for many reactions.

13.66 **Given:** table of rate constant versus T **Find:** E_a and A

Conceptual Plan: Since $\ln k = \dfrac{-E_a}{R}\left(\dfrac{1}{T}\right) + \ln A$ **a plot of ln k versus $1/T$ will have a slope = $-E_a/R$ and an intercept = ln A.**

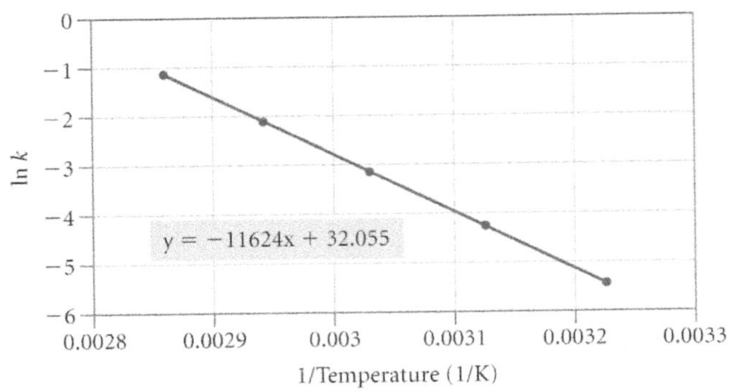

Solution: The slope can be determined by measuring $\Delta y/\Delta x$ on the plot or by using functions, such as "add trendline" in Excel. Since the slope = $-$ 11624 K = $-E_a/R$ then $E_a = -(slope)R =$

$$= -(-11624\ \text{K})\left(8.314\frac{\text{J}}{\text{K}\cdot\text{mol}}\right)\left(\frac{1\ \text{kJ}}{1000\ \text{J}}\right)$$

$= 96.6\dfrac{\text{kJ}}{\text{mol}}$ and intercept = 32.055

= ln A then $A = e^{intercept} = e^{32.055} = 8.34 \times 10^{13}\ \text{s}^{-1}$.

Check: The units (kJ/mol and s^{-1}) are correct. The plot was extremely linear, confirming Arrhenius behavior. The activation and frequency factor are typical for many reactions.

13.67 **Given:** rate constant = 0.0117/s at 400. K, and 0.689/s at 450. K **Find:** (a) E_a and (b) rate constant at 425 K
Conceptual Plan:

(a) $k_1, T_1, k_2, T_2 \rightarrow E_a$ **then J/mol** $\rightarrow$ **kJ/mol**

$$\ln\left(\frac{k_2}{k_1}\right) = \frac{E_a}{R}\left(\frac{1}{T_1} - \frac{1}{T_2}\right) \qquad \frac{1\ \text{kJ}}{1000\ \text{J}}$$

(b) $E_a, k_1, T_1, T_2 \rightarrow k_2$

$$\ln\left(\frac{k_2}{k_1}\right) = \frac{E_a}{R}\left(\frac{1}{T_1} - \frac{1}{T_2}\right)$$

Solution:

(a) $\ln\left(\frac{k_2}{k_1}\right) = \frac{E_a}{R}\left(\frac{1}{T_1} - \frac{1}{T_2}\right)$. Rearrange to solve for E_a.

$$E_a = \frac{R\ln\left(\frac{k_2}{k_1}\right)}{\left(\frac{1}{T_1} - \frac{1}{T_2}\right)} = \frac{8.314\frac{\text{J}}{\text{K}\cdot\text{mol}}\ln\left(\frac{0.689\ \text{s}^{-1}}{0.0117\ \text{s}^{-1}}\right)}{\left(\frac{1}{400.\ \text{K}} - \frac{1}{450.\ \text{K}}\right)} = 1.22 \times 10^5\frac{\text{J}}{\text{mol}} \times \frac{1\ \text{kJ}}{1000\ \text{J}} = 122\frac{\text{kJ}}{\text{mol}}.$$

(b) $\ln\left(\frac{k_2}{k_1}\right) = \frac{E_a}{R}\left(\frac{1}{T_1} - \frac{1}{T_2}\right)$ with k_1, = 0.0117/s, T_1 = 400. K, T_2 = 425 K. Rearrange to solve for k_2.

$$\ln k_2 = \frac{E_a}{R}\left(\frac{1}{T_1} - \frac{1}{T_2}\right) + \ln k_1 = \frac{1.22 \times 10^5\frac{\text{J}}{\text{mol}}}{8.314\frac{\text{J}}{\text{K}\cdot\text{mol}}}\left(\frac{1}{400.\ \text{K}} - \frac{1}{425\ \text{K}}\right) + \ln 0.0117\ \text{s}^{-1} = -2.29\underline{0}2 \rightarrow$$

$$k_2 = e^{-2.29\underline{0}2} = 0.101\ \text{s}^{-1}.$$

Check: The units (kJ/mol and s^{-1}) are correct. The activation energy is typical for a reaction. The rate constant at 425 K is in between the values given at 400 K and 450 K.

13.68 **Given:** rate constant = 0.000122/s at 27 °C, and 0.228/s at 77 °C **Find:** (a) E_a and (b) rate constant at 17 °C
Conceptual Plan:

(a) **°C** $\rightarrow$ **K then** $k_1, T_1, k_2, T_2 \rightarrow E_a$ **then J/mol** $\rightarrow$ **kJ/mol;**

$$\text{K} = °\text{C} + 273.15 \qquad \ln\left(\frac{k_2}{k_1}\right) = \frac{E_a}{R}\left(\frac{1}{T_1} - \frac{1}{T_2}\right) \qquad \frac{1\ \text{kJ}}{1000\ \text{J}}$$

(b) **°C** $\rightarrow$ **K then** $E_a, k_1, T_1, T_2 \rightarrow k_2$

$$\text{K} = °\text{C} + 273.15 \qquad \ln\left(\frac{k_2}{k_1}\right) = \frac{E_a}{R}\left(\frac{1}{T_1} - \frac{1}{T_2}\right)$$

Solution: T_1= 27°C + 273.15 = 300. K and T_2 = 77°C + 273.15 = 350. K then $\ln\left(\frac{k_2}{k_1}\right) = \frac{E_a}{R}\left(\frac{1}{T_1} - \frac{1}{T_2}\right)$

(a) Rearrange to solve for E_a.

$$E_a = \frac{R\ln\left(\frac{k_2}{k_1}\right)}{\left(\frac{1}{T_1} - \frac{1}{T_2}\right)} = \frac{8.314\frac{\text{J}}{\text{K}\cdot\text{mol}}\ln\left(\frac{0.228\ \text{s}^{-1}}{0.000122\ \text{s}^{-1}}\right)}{\left(\frac{1}{300.\ \text{K}} - \frac{1}{350.\ \text{K}}\right)} = 1.32 \times 10^5\frac{\text{J}}{\text{mol}} \times \frac{1\ \text{kJ}}{1000\ \text{J}} = 132\frac{\text{kJ}}{\text{mol}}.$$

(b) $\ln\left(\frac{k_2}{k_1}\right) = \frac{E_a}{R}\left(\frac{1}{T_1} - \frac{1}{T_2}\right)$ with k_1, = 0.000122/s, T_1 = 300. K, T_2 = 17°C + 273.15 = 290 K.
Rearrange to solve for k_2.

$$\ln k_2 = \frac{E_a}{R}\left(\frac{1}{T_1} - \frac{1}{T_2}\right) + \ln k_1 = \frac{1.32 \times 10^5\frac{\text{J}}{\text{mol}}}{8.314\frac{\text{J}}{\text{K}\cdot\text{mol}}}\left(\frac{1}{300.\ \text{K}} - \frac{1}{290.\ \text{K}}\right) + \ln 0.000122\ \text{s}^{-1} = -10.82\underline{9}8$$

$$\rightarrow k_2 = e^{-10.82\underline{9}8} = 0.0000198\ \text{s}^{-1} = 1.98 \times 10^{-5}\ \text{s}^{-1}.$$

Check: The units (kJ/mol and s^{-1}) are correct. The activation energy is typical for a reaction. The rate constant at 17 °C is smaller than the values given at 27 °C.

13.69 **Given:** rate constant doubles from 10.0 °C to 20.0 °C **Find:** E_a

Conceptual Plan: **°C $\rightarrow$ K then $k_1, T_1, k_2, T_2 \rightarrow E_a$ then J/mol $\rightarrow$ kJ/mol;**

$$K = °C + 273.15 \qquad \ln\left(\frac{k_2}{k_1}\right) = \frac{E_a}{R}\left(\frac{1}{T_1} - \frac{1}{T_2}\right) \qquad \frac{1\ \text{kJ}}{1000\ \text{J}}$$

Solution: $T_1 = 10.0\ °C + 273.15 = 283.2\ K$ and $T_2 = 20.0\ °C + 273.15 = 293.2\ K$ and $k_2 = 2\,k_1$ then $\ln\left(\frac{k_2}{k_1}\right) = \frac{E_a}{R}\left(\frac{1}{T_1} - \frac{1}{T_2}\right)$. Rearrange to solve for E_a.

$$E_a = \frac{R\ln\left(\frac{k_2}{k_1}\right)}{\left(\frac{1}{T_1} - \frac{1}{T_2}\right)} = \frac{8.314\frac{\text{J}}{\cancel{\text{K}}\cdot\text{mol}}\ln\left(\frac{2\cancel{k_1}}{\cancel{k_1}}\right)}{\left(\frac{1}{283.2\ \cancel{\text{K}}} - \frac{1}{293.2\ \cancel{\text{K}}}\right)} = 4.7785 \times 10^4 \frac{\cancel{\text{J}}}{\text{mol}} \times \frac{1\ \text{kJ}}{1000\ \cancel{\text{J}}} = 47.79\frac{\text{kJ}}{\text{mol}}.$$

Check: The units (kJ/mol) are correct. The activation energy is typical for a reaction.

13.70 **Given:** rate constant triples from 20.0 °C to 35.0 °C **Find:** E_a

Conceptual Plan: **°C $\rightarrow$ K then $k_1, T_1, k_2, T_2 \rightarrow E_a$ then J/mol $\rightarrow$ kJ/mol;**

$$K = °C + 273.15 \qquad \ln\left(\frac{k_2}{k_1}\right) = \frac{E_a}{R}\left(\frac{1}{T_1} - \frac{1}{T_2}\right) \qquad \frac{1\ \text{kJ}}{1000\ \text{J}}$$

Solution: $T_1 = 20.0\ °C + 273.15 = 293.2\ K$ and $T_2 = 35.0\ °C + 273.15 = 308.2\ K$ and $k_2 = 3\,k_1$ then $\ln\left(\frac{k_2}{k_1}\right) = \frac{E_a}{R}\left(\frac{1}{T_1} - \frac{1}{T_2}\right)$. Rearrange to solve for E_a.

$$E_a = \frac{R\ln\left(\frac{k_2}{k_1}\right)}{\left(\frac{1}{T_1} - \frac{1}{T_2}\right)} = \frac{8.314\frac{\text{J}}{\cancel{\text{K}}\cdot\text{mol}}\ln\left(\frac{3\cancel{k_1}}{\cancel{k_1}}\right)}{\left(\frac{1}{293.2\ \cancel{\text{K}}} - \frac{1}{308.2\ \cancel{\text{K}}}\right)} = 5.502 \times 10^4 \frac{\cancel{\text{J}}}{\text{mol}} \times \frac{1\ \text{kJ}}{1000\ \cancel{\text{J}}} = 55.02\frac{\text{kJ}}{\text{mol}}.$$

Check: The units (kJ/mol) are correct. The activation energy is typical for a reaction.

13.71 Reaction a. would have the faster rate because the orientation factor, p, would be larger for this reaction since the reactants are symmetrical.

13.72 Reaction b. would have the smaller orientation factor, because we are reacting an asymmetric molecule with a homonuclear diatomic molecule (symmetrical) and so the orientation is important. In reaction a both reacting species are symmetrical and so orientation is unimportant.

Reaction Mechanisms

13.73 Since the first reaction is the slow step, it is the rate determining step. Using this first step to determine the rate law, Rate = $k_1\,[AB]^2$. Since this is the observed rate law, this mechanism is consistent with the experimental data.

13.74 (a) The reaction cannot occur in a single step in which X and Y collide, because the rate law would be Rate = $k\,[X]\,[Y]$. This is not consistent with the stated rate law of Rate = $k\,[X]^2\,[Y]$.

(b) Since the second step is the rate determining step, Rate = $k_3\,[X_2]\,[Y]$. X_2 is an intermediate, so its concentration cannot appear in the rate law. Using the fast equilibrium in the first step, we see that $k_1[X]^2 = k_2\,[X_2]$ or $[X_2] = \frac{k_1}{k_2}[X]^2$. Substituting this into the first rate expression we get that Rate = $\frac{k_3\,k_1}{k_2}[X]^2\,[Y]$. Simplifying this expression we see Rate = $k\,[X]^2\,[Y]$, which is consistent with the experimentally derived rate law.

13.75 (a) The overall reaction is the sum of the steps in the mechanism:

$$Cl_2\,(g) \underset{k_2}{\overset{k_1}{\rightleftharpoons}} 2\,\cancel{Cl\,(g)}$$
$$\cancel{Cl\,(g)} + CHCl_3\,(g) \xrightarrow[k_3]{} HCl\,(g) + \cancel{CCl_3\,(g)}$$
$$\cancel{Cl\,(g)} + \cancel{CCl_3\,(g)} \xrightarrow[k_4]{} CCl_4\,(g)$$
$$\overline{Cl_2\,(g) + CHCl_3\,(g) \rightarrow HCl\,(g) + CCl_4\,(g)}$$

(b) The intermediates are the species that are generated by one step and consumed by other steps. These are a Cl (*g*) and CCl_3 (*g*).

(c) Since the second step is the rate determining step, Rate = k_3 [Cl] [$CHCl_3$]. Since Cl is an intermediate, its concentration cannot appear in the rate law. Using the fast equilibrium in the first step, we see that $k_1[Cl_2] = k_2\,[Cl]^2$ or $[Cl] = \sqrt{\frac{k_1}{k_2}}\,[Cl_2]$. Substituting this into the first rate expression we get that Rate = $k_3\sqrt{\frac{k_1}{k_2}}\,[Cl_2]^{1/2}[CHCl_3]$. Simplifying this expression we see Rate = $k\,[Cl_2]^{1/2}\,[CHCl_3]$.

13.76 (a) The overall reaction is the sum of the steps in the mechanism:

$$NO_2\,(g) + Cl_2\,(g) \xrightarrow[k_1]{} ClNO_2\,(g) + \cancel{Cl\,(g)}$$
$$NO_2\,(g) + \cancel{Cl\,(g)} \xrightarrow[k_2]{} ClNO_2\,(g)$$
$$\overline{2\,NO_2\,(g) + Cl_2\,(g) \rightarrow 2\,ClNO_2\,(g)}$$

(b) The intermediates are the species that are generated by one step and consumed by other steps. This is Cl (*g*).

(c) Since the first step is the rate determining step, Rate = k_1 [NO_2] [Cl_2]. Since both of these species are reactants, this is the predicted rate law.

Catalysis

13.77 Heterogeneous catalysts require a large surface area because catalysis can only happen at the active sites on the surface. A greater surface area means greater opportunity for the substrate to react, which results in a speedier reaction.

13.78 The initial and final energies (reactants and products) remain the same. The activation energy drops, from 75 kJ/mol to a smaller value, for example 30 kJ/mol. There are usually more steps in the reaction progress diagram.

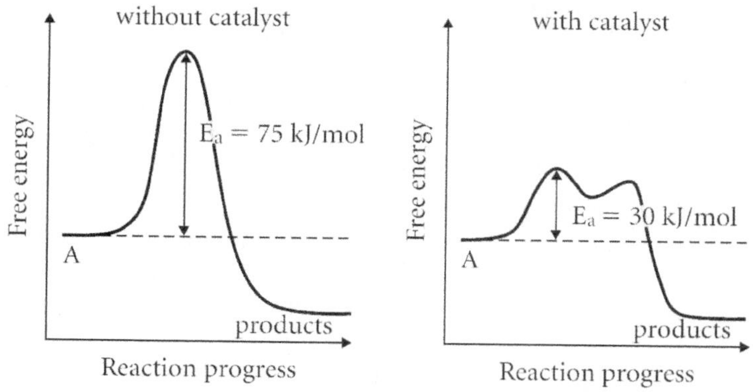

13.79 Assume rate ratio ∝ k ratio (since concentration terms will cancel each other) and $k = A\,e^{-E_a/RT}$. T = 25 °C + 273.15 = 298 K, E_{a_1} = 1.25 x 10^5 J/mol, and E_{a_2} = 5.5 x 10^4 J/mol. Ratio of rates will be

$$\frac{k_2}{k_1} = \frac{\cancel{A}\,e^{-E_{a_2}/RT}}{\cancel{A}\,e^{-E_{a_1}/RT}} = \frac{e^{\frac{-5.5 \times 10^4 \frac{\text{J}}{\text{mol}}}{\left(8.314\frac{\text{J}}{\text{K}\cdot\text{mol}}\right)298\text{ K}}}}{e^{\frac{-1.25 \times 10^5 \frac{\text{J}}{\text{mol}}}{\left(8.314\frac{\text{J}}{\text{K}\cdot\text{mol}}\right)298\text{ K}}}} = \frac{e^{-22.199}}{e^{-50.453}} = 10^{12}.$$

13.80 Assume rate ratio $\propto k$ ratio (since concentration terms will cancel each other) and $k = A\,e^{-E_a/RT}$. $T = 25\ °C + 273.15 = 298$ K. $E_{a_1} = 1.08 \times 10^5$ J/mol. Ratio of rates will be

$$\frac{k_2}{k_1} = 10^6 = \frac{\cancel{A}\,e^{-E_{a_2}/RT}}{\cancel{A}\,e^{-E_{a_1}/RT}} = \frac{e^{\frac{-E_{a_2}}{\left(8.314\frac{\text{J}}{\text{K}\cdot\text{mol}}\right)298\ \text{K}}}}{e^{\frac{-1.08\times10^5\frac{\cancel{\text{J}}}{\cancel{\text{mol}}}}{\left(8.314\frac{\cancel{\text{J}}}{\cancel{\text{K}}\cdot\cancel{\text{mol}}}\right)298\ \cancel{\text{K}}}}} = \frac{e^{\frac{-E_{a_2}}{2.47756\times10^3\frac{\text{J}}{\text{mol}}}}}{1.17\times10^{-19}} \rightarrow e^{\frac{-E_{a_2}}{2.47756\times10^3\frac{\text{J}}{\text{mol}}}} = 1.17\times10^{-13} \rightarrow$$

$$\frac{-E_{a_2}}{2.47756\times10^3\frac{\text{J}}{\text{mol}}} = \ln(1.17\times10^{-13}) = -29.7766 \rightarrow E_{a_2} = 7.38\times10^4\frac{\text{J}}{\text{mol}} = 73.8\frac{\text{kJ}}{\text{mol}}.$$

Cumulative Problems

13.81 **Given:** table of $[CH_3CN]$ versus time **Find:** (a) reaction order, k; (b) $t_{1/2}$; and (c) t for 90% conversion
Conceptual Plan: (a) and (b) Look at the data and see if any common reaction orders can be eliminated. If the data does not show an equal concentration drop with time, then zero order can be eliminated. Look for changes in the half-life (compare time for concentration to drop to one half of any value). If the half-life is not constant, then the first order can be eliminated. If the half-life is getting longer as the concentration drops, this might suggest second order. Plot the data as indicated by the appropriate rate law or if it is first order and there is an obvious half-life in the data, a plot is not necessary. Determine k from the slope of the plot (or using the half-life equation for first order). (c) Finally calculate the time to 90 % conversion using the appropriate integrated rate equation.
Solution: (a) and (b) By the preceding logic, we can see that the reaction is first order. It takes 15.0 h for the concentration to be cut in half for any concentration (1.000 M to 0.501 M; 0.794 M to 0.398 M; and 0.631 M to 0.316 M), so $t_{1/2} = 15.0$ h. Then use $t_{1/2} = \frac{0.693}{k}$ and rearrange to solve for k.

$$k = \frac{0.693}{t_{1/2}} = \frac{0.693}{15.0\ \text{h}} = 0.0462\ \text{h}^{-1}.$$

(c) $[CH_3CN]_t = 0.10\,[CH_3CN]_0$. Since $\ln[CH_3CN]_t = -kt + \ln[CH_3CN]_0$ rearrange to solve for t

$$t = -\frac{1}{k}\ln\frac{[CH_3CN]_t}{[CH_3CN]_0} = -\frac{1}{0.0462\ \text{h}^{-1}}\ln\frac{0.10\,\cancel{[CH_3CN]_0}}{\cancel{[CH_3CN]_0}} = 49.8\ \text{h}.$$

Check: The units (none, h^{-1}, h, and h) are correct. The rate law is a common form. The data showed a constant half-life very clearly. The rate constant is consistent with the units necessary to get rate as M/s and the magnitude is reasonable since we have a first order reaction. The time to 90 % conversion is consistent with a time between three and four half-lives.

13.82 **Given:** table of $[X_2Y]$ versus time
Find: (a) reaction order, k; (b) $t_{1/2}$ at initial concentration; and (c) [X] at 10.0 h
Conceptual Plan: (a) Look at the data and see if any common reaction orders can be eliminated. If the data does not show an equal concentration drop with time, then zero order can be eliminated. Look for changes in the half-life (compare time for concentration to drop to one-half of any value). If the half-life is not constant, then the first order can be eliminated. If the half-life is getting longer as the concentration drops, this might suggest second order. Plot the data as indicated by the appropriate rate law. Determine k from the slope of the plot. (b) Calculate the half-life with the appropriate equation. (c) Finally calculate the $[X_2Y]$ at 10.0 h using the appropriate integrated rate expression and then convert this to a change in $[X_2Y]$ and then to [X] using the reaction stoichiometry.

Solution:

(a) By the preceding logic, we can eliminate both the zero order and the first order reactions. (Alternatively, you could make all three plots and only one should be linear.) This suggests that we should have a second order reaction. Plot $1/[X_2Y]$ versus time. Since $\frac{1}{[X_2Y]_t} = kt + \frac{1}{[X_2Y]_0}$, the slope will be the rate constant. The slope can be determined by measuring $\Delta y/\Delta x$ on the plot or by using functions, such as "add trendline" in Excel. Thus the rate constant is $1.6\underline{8}27\ M^{-1} \cdot h^{-1}$ and the rate law is Rate $= 1.68\ M^{-1} \cdot h^{-1}[X_2Y]^2$.

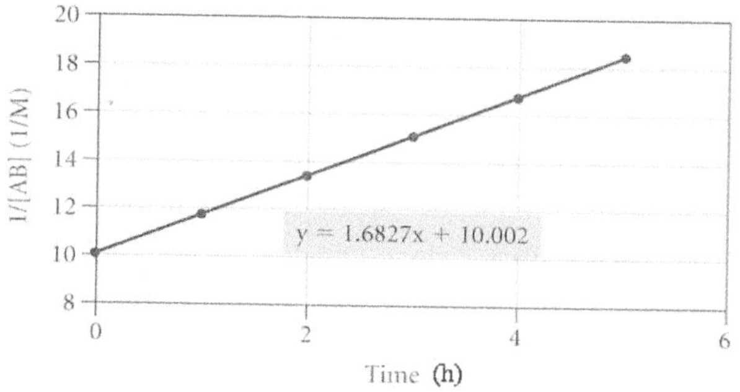

(b) $t_{1/2} = \frac{1}{k\,[X_2Y]_0}$ so $t_{1/2} = \frac{1}{(1.6\underline{8}27\ M^{-1} \cdot h^{-1})\ (0.100\ M)} = 5.94\ h.$

(c) Finally, use $\frac{1}{[X_2Y]_t} = kt + \frac{1}{[X_2Y]_0}$; substitute in the values of $[X_2Y]_0$, 10.0 h, and k; and rearrange to solve for $[X_2Y]$ at 10.0 h.

$$[X_2Y]_t = \frac{1}{kt + \frac{1}{[X_2Y]_0}} = \frac{1}{(1.6\underline{8}27\ M^{-1} \cdot h^{-1})(10.0\ h) + \left(\frac{1}{0.100\ M}\right)} = 0.037\underline{2}759\ M \text{ then}$$

$$\Delta[X_2Y] = [X_2Y]_0 - [X_2Y]_{10.0\,h} = 0.100\ M - 0.037\underline{2}759\ M = 0.06\underline{2}724\ M \text{ then}$$

$$\frac{0.06\underline{2}724\ \text{mol}\ X_2Y}{L} \times \frac{2\ \text{mol X}}{1\ \text{mol}\ X_2Y} = 0.13\ M\ X.$$

Check: The units (none, $M^{-1} \cdot h^{-1}$, h, and M) are correct. The rate law is a common form. The plot was extremely linear, confirming second order kinetics. The rate constant is consistent with the units necessary to get rate as M/s and the magnitude is reasonable since we have a second order reaction. The half-life is consistent with the data table, which indicates that the half-life is a little over 5 h. The [X] at 10 h s is consistent with the changes that we see in the data table through 5 h.

13.83 **Given:** Rate $= k\frac{[A][C]^2}{[B]^{1/2}} = 0.0115$ M/s at certain initial concentrations of A, B and C; double A and C concentration and triple B concentration **Find:** reaction rate

Conceptual Plan: $[A]_1$, $[B]_1$, $[C]_1$, Rate 1, $[A]_2$, $[B]_2$, $[C]_2$ → Rate 2

$$\frac{\text{Rate 2}}{\text{Rate 1}} = \frac{k\frac{[A]_2[C]_2^2}{[B]_2^{1/2}}}{k\frac{[A]_1[C]_1^2}{[B]_1^{1/2}}}$$

Solution: $\frac{\text{Rate 2}}{\text{Rate 1}} = \frac{k\frac{[A]_2[C]_2^2}{[B]_2^{1/2}}}{k\frac{[A]_1[C]_1^2}{[B]_1^{1/2}}}$. Rearrange to solve for Rate 2. Rate 2 $= \frac{k\frac{[A]_2[C]_2^2}{[B]_2^{1/2}}}{k\frac{[A]_1[C]_1^2}{[B]_1^{1/2}}}$,

Rate 1 $[A]_2 = 2[A]_1$, $[B]_2 = 3[B]_1$, $[C]_2 = 2[C]_1$, and Rate 1 = 0.0115 M/s so

$$\text{Rate 2} = \frac{k\frac{2\,[A]_1(2[C]_1)^2}{(3\,[B]_1)^{1/2}}}{k\frac{[A]_1[C]_1^2}{[B]_1^{1/2}}}\ 0.0115\,\frac{M}{s} = \frac{2^3}{3^{1/2}}\,0.0115\,\frac{M}{s} = 0.0531\,\frac{M}{s}.$$

Check: The units ($M \cdot s^{-1}$) are correct. They should increase because we have a factor of eight (2^3) divided by the square root of three (1.73).

13.84 **Given:** Rate $= k\dfrac{[O_3]^2}{[O_2]}$ initially 1.0 mol O_3, and 1.0 mol O_2, in 1.0 L

Find: fraction O_3 reacted when reaction rate is cut in half

Conceptual Plan:

mol, L → M then $[O_3]_1$, $[O_2]_1$, Rate 1, Rate 2 → $[O_3]_2$ then $[O_3]_1$, $[O_3]_2$ → O_3 fraction reacted

$$M = \frac{mol}{L} \qquad \frac{\text{Rate 2}}{\text{Rate 1}} = \frac{k\dfrac{[O_3]_2^2}{[O_2]_2}}{k\dfrac{[O_3]_1^2}{[O_2]_1}} \qquad O_{3\ \text{fraction reacted}} = \frac{[O_3]_1 - [O_3]_2}{[O_3]_1}$$

Solution: $M = \dfrac{mol}{L}$ so $[O_3]_1 = \dfrac{1.0\text{ mol}}{1.0\text{ L}} = 1.0$ M and $[O_2]_1 = \dfrac{1.0\text{ mol}}{1.0\text{ L}} = 1.0$ M. Rate 1 = 2 Rate 2.

Let $x = \Delta[O_3]$ so $[O_3]_2 = [O_3]_1 - x$ and $[O_2]_2 = [O_2]_1 + 3/2\,x$. Substitute values into $\dfrac{\text{Rate 2}}{\text{Rate 1}} = \dfrac{k\dfrac{[O_3]_2^2}{[O_2]_2}}{k\dfrac{[O_3]_1^2}{[O_2]_1}}$ and

rearrange to solve for x. $\dfrac{\cancel{\text{Rate 2}}}{2\,\cancel{\text{Rate 2}}} = \dfrac{\cancel{k}\dfrac{(1.0\text{ M} - x)^2}{(1.0\text{ M} + 3/2\,x)}}{\cancel{k}\dfrac{(1.0\text{ M})^{\cancel{2}}}{\cancel{(1.0\text{ M})}}} \rightarrow 0.50\text{ M}\,(1.0\text{ M} + 3/2\,x) = (1.0\text{ M} - x)^2 \rightarrow$

$0.50 + 0.75\,x = 1.0 - 2.0\,x + x^2 \rightarrow 0 = x^2 - 2.75\,x + 0.50$ solve with quadratic equation

$\left(x = \dfrac{-b \pm \sqrt{b^2 - 4ac}}{2a}\right)$. So

$$x = \frac{2.75 \pm \sqrt{(-2.75)^2 - (4)(1.0)(0.50)}}{2(1.0)} = \frac{2.75 \pm \sqrt{5.5625}}{2.0} = \frac{2.75 \pm 2.3585}{2.0} =$$

= 0.19575 M or 2.55 M. The answer must be 0.19575 M because the other answer is larger than our initial concentration (and is, therefore, impossible).

$$O_{3\ \text{fraction reacted}} = \frac{[O_3]_1 - [O_3]_2}{[O_3]_1} = \frac{x}{[O_3]_1} = \frac{0.19575\ \cancel{M}}{1.0\ \cancel{M}} = 0.2.$$

Check: The units (M) are correct. The concentration is reasonable since there are two forces slowing down the reaction: 1) the decrease in the reactant and 2) the increase of the product (which appears in the rate law). The calculation can be double checked by substituting in the value of x and the resulting rate = 0.5 k.

13.85 **Given:** table of P_{Total} versus time **Find:** rate law, k, and P_{Total} at 2.00 x 10^4 s

Conceptual Plan: Since two moles of gas are generated for each mole of CH_3CHO decomposed, this $P_{CH_3CHO} = P^\circ_{Total} - (P_{Total} - P^\circ_{Total})$. Look at the data and see if any common reaction orders can be eliminated. If the data does not show an equal P_{Total} rise (or P_{CH_3CHO} drop) with time, then zero order can be eliminated. There is not enough data to look for changes in the half-life (compare time for P_{CH_3CHO} to drop to one-half of any value). It does appear that the half-life is getting longer, so the first order can be eliminated. Plot the data as indicated by the appropriate rate law. Determine k from the slope of the plot. Finally calculate the P_{CH_3CHO} at 2.00 x 10^4 s using the appropriate integrated rate expression and then convert this to P_{Total} using the reaction stoichiometry.

Solution: Calculate $P_{CH_3CHO} = P^\circ_{Total} - (P_{Total} - P^\circ_{Total})$.

Time (s)	P_{Total} (atm)	P_{CH_3CHO} (atm)
0	0.22	0.22
1000	0.24	0.20
3000	0.27	0.17
7000	0.31	0.13

By the preceding logic, we can eliminate both the zero order and the first order reactions. (Alternatively, you could make all three plots and only one should be linear.) This suggests that we should have a second order reaction. Plot $1/P_{CH_3CHO}$ versus time. Since $\dfrac{1}{P_{CH_3CHO}} = kt + \dfrac{1}{P^\circ_{CH_3CHO}}$, the slope will be the rate constant. The slope can be determined by measuring $\Delta y/\Delta x$ on the plot or by using functions, such as "add trendline" in Excel. Thus the rate constant is 4.5 x 10^{-4} $atm^{-1} \cdot s^{-1}$ and the rate law is Rate = 4.5 x $10^{-4} atm^{-1} \cdot s^{-1} P_{CH_3CHO}{}^2$.

Finally, use $\frac{1}{P_{CH_3CHO}} = kt + \frac{1}{P^{\circ}_{CH_3CHO}}$; substitute in the values of $P^{\circ}_{CH_3CHO}$, 2.00×10^4 s, and k; and rearrange to solve for $P^{\circ}_{CH_3CHO}$ at 2.00×10^4 s.

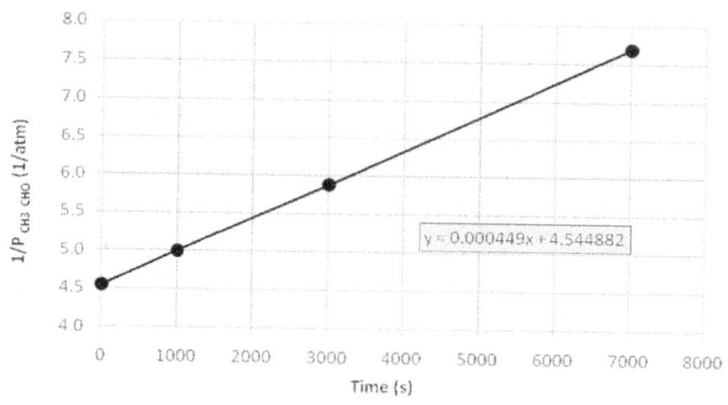

$$P_{CH_3CHO} = \frac{1}{kt + \dfrac{1}{P^{\circ}_{CH_3CHO}}} =$$

$$\frac{1}{(4.5 \times 10^{-4}\,\text{atm}^{-1}\cdot\cancel{\text{s}^{-1}})(2.00 \times 10^4\,\cancel{\text{s}}) + \left(\dfrac{1}{0.22\ \text{atm}}\right)} =$$

$0.07\underline{3}8255\ \text{atm} = 0.074\ \text{atm}$

Finally, from the first equation in the solution $P_{Total} = 2P^{\circ}_{Total} - P_{CH_3CHO} = 2(0.22\ \text{atm}) - 0.07\underline{3}8255\ \text{atm} = 0.3\underline{6}6175\ \text{atm} = 0.37\ \text{atm}$.

Check: The units (none, $\text{atm}^{-1}\cdot\text{s}^{-1}$, and atm) are correct. The rate law is a common form. The plot was extremely linear, confirming second order kinetics. The rate constant is consistent with the units necessary to get rate as atm/s and the magnitude is reasonable since we have a second order reaction. The P_{Total} at 2.00×10^4 s is consistent with the changes that we see in the data table through 7000 s.

13.86 **Given:** table of $P^{\circ}_{H_2C_2O_4}$ versus P_{Total} at 20,000 s **Find:** rate law and k

Conceptual Plan: Since two moles of gas are generated for each mole of $H_2C_2O_4$ decomposed, this $P^{\circ}_{H_2C_2O_4} = P_{H_2C_2O_4} - (P_{Total} - P^{\circ}_{H_2C_2O_4})$ and the Rate = $(P^{\circ}_{H_2C_2O_4} - P_{Total})/20{,}000$ s. Using general rate law form, compare rate ratios to determine reaction order.

$$\frac{\text{Rate 2}}{\text{Rate 1}} = \frac{k\,[A]_2^n}{k\,[A]_1^n}$$

Then use one of the concentration/initial rate pairs to determine k.

$$\text{Rate} = k\,[A]^n$$

Solution: Calculate Rate = $(P^{\circ}_{H_2C_2O_4} - P_{Total})/20{,}000$ s.

Experiment #	**1**	**2**	**3**
$P^{\circ}_{H_2C_2O_4}$ (mmHg)	65.8	92.1	111
P_{Total} at 20000 s (mmHg)	94.6	132	160
Rate (mmHg/s)	0.0014$\underline{4}$	0.001$\underline{9}$95	0.002$\underline{4}$5

$\frac{\text{Rate 2}}{\text{Rate 1}} = \frac{k\,[A]_2^n}{k\,[A]_1^n}$. Comparing the first two sets of data

$\frac{0.001995\ \cancel{\text{mmHg/s}}}{0.00144\ \cancel{\text{mmHg/s}}} = \frac{\cancel{k}\,(92.1\ \cancel{\text{mmHg}})^n}{\cancel{k}\,(65.8\ \cancel{\text{mmHg}})^n}$ and $1.\underline{3}854 = 1.3\underline{9}97^n$ so $n = 1$. If we compare the first and the third data sets $\frac{0.00245\ \cancel{\text{mmHg/s}}}{0.00144\ \cancel{\text{mmHg/s}}} = \frac{\cancel{k}\,(111\ \cancel{\text{mmHg}})^n}{\cancel{k}\,(65.8\ \cancel{\text{mmHg}})^n}$ and $1.\underline{7}0139 = 1.\underline{6}8693^n$ so $n = 1$. This second comparison is not necessary, but it increases our confidence in the reaction order. So Rate $= k\,P_{H_2C_2O_4}$. Selecting the first data set and rearranging the rate equation

$$k = \frac{\text{Rate}}{P_{H_2C_2O_4}} = \frac{0.00144\,\dfrac{\cancel{\text{mmHg}}}{\text{s}}}{65.8\ \cancel{\text{mmHg}}} = 2.19 \times 10^{-5}\,\text{s}^{-1} \text{ so Rate} = 2.19 \times 10^{-5}\,\text{s}^{-1}\,P_{H_2C_2O_4}.$$

Check: The units (none and s^{-1}) are correct. The rate law is a common form. The rate is changing proportionately with the initial pressure, so first order is consistent. The rate constant is consistent with the units necessary to get rate as mmHg/s and the magnitude is reasonable since we have a first order reaction.

13.87 **Given:** N_2O_5 decomposes to NO_2 and O_2, first order in $[N_2O_5]$; $t_{1/2} = 2.81$ h at 25 °C; $V = 1.5$ L, $P^{\circ}_{N_2O_5} = 745$ torr **Find:** P_{O_2} after 215 minutes

Conceptual Plan: Write a balanced reaction. Then $t_{1/2} \rightarrow k$ then °C $\rightarrow$ K and torr $\rightarrow$ atm then

$N_2O_5 \rightarrow 2\,NO_2 + \frac{1}{2}\,O_2$ $\qquad t_{1/2} = \frac{0.693}{k}$ $\qquad$ K = °C + 273.15 $\qquad \frac{1\ \text{atm}}{760\ \text{torr}}$

$P^{\circ}_{N_2O_5}$, $V, T \rightarrow n/V$ **then min** $\rightarrow$ **h then** $[N_2O_5]_0, t, k \rightarrow [N_2O_5]_t$ **then** $[N_2O_5]_0, [N_2O_5]_t \rightarrow [O_2]_t$

$PV = nRT$ $\quad \frac{1\text{ h}}{60\text{ min}}$ $\quad \ln[A]_t = -kt + \ln[A]_0$ $\quad [O_2]_t = ([N_2O_5]_0 - [N_2O_5]_t) \times \frac{1/2 \text{ mol } O_2}{1 \text{ mol } N_2O_5}$

then $[O_2]_t, V, T \rightarrow P^{\circ}_{O_2}$ **and finally atm** $\rightarrow$ **torr**

$PV = nRT$ $\quad \frac{760\text{ torr}}{1\text{ atm}}$

Solution: $t_{1/2} = \frac{0.693}{k}$ and rearrange to solve for k. $k = \frac{0.693}{t_{1/2}} = \frac{0.693}{2.81\text{ h}} = 0.246619\text{ h}^{-1}$. Then

$T = 25\text{ °C} + 273.15 = 298\text{ K}$. $745\text{ torr} \times \frac{1\text{ atm}}{760\text{ torr}} = 0.980263\text{ atm}$ then $PV = nRT$. Rearrange to solve for n/V.

$$\frac{n}{V} = \frac{P}{RT} = \frac{0.980263\text{ atm}}{0.08206 \frac{\text{L} \cdot \text{atm}}{\text{K} \cdot \text{mol}} \times 298\text{ K}} = 0.0400862\text{ M then } 215\text{ min} \times \frac{1\text{ h}}{60\text{ min}} = 3.58333\text{ h}.$$

Since $\ln[N_2O_5]_t = -kt + \ln[N_2O_5]_0 = -(0.246619\text{ h}^{-1})(3.58333\text{h}) + \ln(0.0400862\text{ M}) = -4.10044 \rightarrow$

$[N_2O_5]_t = e^{-4.10044} = 0.0165653\text{ M}$ then

$$[O_2]_t = ([N_2O_5]_0 - [N_2O_5]_t) \times \frac{1/2 \text{ mol } O_2}{1 \text{ mol } N_2O_5} = (0.0400862 \frac{\text{mol } N_2O_5}{\text{L}} - 0.0165653 \frac{\text{mol } N_2O_5}{\text{L}}) \times \frac{1/2 \text{ mol } O_2}{1 \text{ mol } N_2O_5}$$

$= 0.0117605\text{ M } O_2$

then finally $PV = nRT$ and rearrange to solve for P.

$$P = \frac{n}{V}RT = 0.0117605 \frac{\text{mol}}{\text{L}} \times 0.08206 \frac{\text{L atm}}{\text{K} \cdot \text{mol}} \times 298\text{ K} = 0.287589\text{ atm} \times \frac{760\text{ torr}}{1\text{ atm}} = 219\text{ torr}.$$

Check: The units (torr) are correct. The pressure is reasonable because it must be less than one half of the original pressure.

13.88 **Given:** Cyclopropane (C_3H_6) reacts, first order in $[C_3H_6]$; $k = 5.87 \times 10^{-4}$ /s at 485 °C; $V = 2.5$ L, $P^{\circ}_{C_3H_6} = 722$ torr **Find:** t to $P_{C_3H_6} = 100.0$ torr

Conceptual Plan: Since $P \propto$ M we do not need to convert P to M. $P^{\circ}_{C_3H_6}, P_{C_3H_6}, k \rightarrow t$

$\ln[A]_t = -kt + \ln[A]_0$

Solution: $\ln[C_3H_6]_t = -kt + \ln[C_3H_6]_0$ rearrange to solve for t.

$$t = -\frac{1}{k}\ln\frac{[C_3H_6]_t}{[C_3H_6]_0} = -\frac{1}{k}\ln\frac{P_{C_3H_6}}{P^{\circ}_{C_3H_6}} = -\frac{1}{5.87 \times 10^{-4}\text{ s}^{-1}}\ln\frac{100.\text{ torr}}{722\text{ torr}} = 3.37 \times 10^3\text{ s} = 56.1\text{ min}.$$

Check: The units (s or min) are correct. The time is reasonable because it is about three half-lives (pressure dropped to 14% of original pressure).

13.89 **Given:** I_2 formation from I atoms, second order in I; $k = 1.5 \times 10^{10}\text{ M}^{-1} \cdot \text{s}^{-1}$, $[I]_0 = 0.0100$ M

Find: t to decrease by 95%

Conceptual Plan: $[I]_0, [I]_t, k \rightarrow t$

$\frac{1}{[A]_t} = kt + \frac{1}{[A]_0}$

Solution: $[I]_t = 0.05\,[I]_0 = 0.05 \times 0.0100\text{ M} = 0.0005\text{ M}$. Since $\frac{1}{[I]_t} = kt + \frac{1}{[I]_0}$ rearrange to solve for t.

$$t = \frac{1}{k}\left(\frac{1}{[I]_t} - \frac{1}{[I]_0}\right) = \frac{1}{(1.5 \times 10^{10}\text{ M}^{-1} \cdot \text{s}^{-1})}\left(\frac{1}{0.0005\text{ M}} - \frac{1}{0.0100\text{ M}}\right) = 1.267 \times 10^{-7}\text{ s} = 1 \times 10^{-7}\text{ s}.$$

Check: The units (s) are correct. We expect the time to be extremely small because the rate constant is so large.

13.90 **Given:** sucrose hydrolysis, first order in $[C_{12}H_{22}O_{11}]$; $k = 1.8 \times 10^{-4}\text{ s}^{-1}$ at 25 °C; $V = 2.55$ L, $[C_{12}H_{22}O_{11}]_0 = 0.150$ M, and 195 min **Find:** $m(C_{12}H_{22}O_{11})$ hydrolyzed

Conceptual Plan: min $\rightarrow$ **s then** $[C_{12}H_{22}O_{11}]_0, t, k \rightarrow [C_{12}H_{22}O_{11}]_t$ **then**

$\frac{60\text{ s}}{1\text{ min}}$ $\quad \ln[A]_t = -kt + \ln[A]_0$

$V, [C_{12}H_{22}O_{11}]_0, [C_{12}H_{22}O_{11}]_t \rightarrow$ **mol** $C_{12}H_{22}O_{11}$ **hydrolyzed** $\rightarrow$ **g** $C_{12}H_{22}O_{11}$ **hydrolyzed**

$\text{mol } C_{12}H_{22}O_{11} = ([C_{12}H_{22}O_{11}]_0 - [C_{12}H_{22}O_{11}]_t) \times V$ $\quad \frac{342.30\text{ g } C_{12}H_{22}O_{11}}{1\text{ mol } C_{12}H_{22}O_{11}}$

Solution: $195 \text{ min} \times \frac{60 \text{ sec}}{1 \text{ min}} = 11700 \text{ s}$. Since
$\ln [C_{12}H_{22}O_{11}]_t = -kt + \ln [C_{12}H_{22}O_{11}]_0 = -(1.8 \times 10^{-4} \text{ s}^{-1})(11700 \text{ s}) + \ln(0.150 \text{ M}) = -4.00312 \rightarrow$
$[C_{12}H_{22}O_{11}]_t = e^{-4.00312} = 0.0182585 \text{ M}$ then
$\text{mol } C_{12}H_{22}O_{11} = ([C_{12}H_{22}O_{11}]_0 - [C_{12}H_{22}O_{11}]_t) \times V =$

$$\left(0.150 \frac{\text{mol } C_{12}H_{22}O_{11}}{\text{L}} - 0.0182585 \frac{\text{mol } C_{12}H_{22}O_{11}}{\text{L}}\right) \times 2.55 \text{ L} = 0.335941 \text{ mol } C_{12}H_{22}O_{11}$$

$$0.335941 \text{ mol } C_{12}H_{22}O_{11} \times \frac{342.30 \text{ g } C_{12}H_{22}O_{11}}{1 \text{ mol } C_{12}H_{22}O_{11}} = 115 \text{ g } C_{12}H_{22}O_{11}.$$

Check: The units (g) are correct. The mass is reasonable because it must be less than the original amount in solution (131 g). The amount is close to the original amount in solution because the final sucrose concentration is so low, since we have gone over three half-lives.

13.91 **Given:** $AB(aq) \rightarrow A(g) + B(g)$; $k = 0.0118 \text{ M}^{-1} \cdot \text{s}^{-1}$; 250.0 mL of 0.100 M AB; collect gas over water $T = 25.0\ °\text{C}$, $P_{\text{Total}} = 755.1$ mmHg, and $V = 200.0$ mL; $P^{\circ}_{H_2O} = 23.8$ mmHg **Find:** t

Conceptual Plan: $P_{\text{Total}}, P_{H_2O} \rightarrow P_A + P_B$ **then mmHg → atm and mL → L**

$P_{\text{Total}} = P_{H_2O} + P_A + P_B$ $\quad \frac{1 \text{ atm}}{760 \text{ mmHg}}$ $\quad \frac{1 \text{ L}}{1000 \text{ mL}}$

and °C → K $P, V, T \rightarrow n_{A+B} \rightarrow \Delta n_{AB}$ **then** $[AB]_0, V_{AB}, \Delta n_{AB} \rightarrow [AB]$ **then** $k, [AB] \rightarrow t$

$K = °C + 273.15$ $\quad PV = nRT$ $\quad \Delta n_{AB} = \frac{1}{2} n_{A+B}$ $\quad [AB] = [AB]_0 - \frac{\Delta n_{AB}}{V_{AB} \times \frac{1 \text{ L}}{1000 \text{ mL}}}$ $\quad \frac{1}{[AB]_t} = kt + \frac{1}{[AB]_0}$

Solution: $P_{\text{Total}} = P_{H_2O} + P_A + P_B$. Rearrange to solve for $P_A + P_B$. $P_A + P_B = P_{\text{Total}} - P_{H_2O} = 755.1 \text{ mmHg} - 23.8 \text{ mmHg} = 731.3 \text{ mmHg}$

$$P_A + P_B = 731.3 \text{ mmHg} \times \frac{1 \text{ atm}}{760 \text{ mmHg}} = 0.96223684 \text{ atm} \quad V = 200.0 \text{ mL} \times \frac{1 \text{ L}}{1000 \text{ mL}} = 0.2000 \text{ L},$$

$T = 25.0\ °\text{C} + 273.15 = 298.2 \text{ K}$, $PV = nRT$. Rearrange to solve for n. $n = \frac{PV}{RT}$

$$n_{H_2} = \frac{0.96223684 \text{ atm} \times 0.2000 \text{ L}}{0.08206 \frac{\text{L} \cdot \text{atm}}{\text{mol} \cdot \text{K}} \times 298.2 \text{ K}} = 0.0078645309 \text{ mol A + B}.$$ Since one mole each of A and B are generated for each mole of AB reacting $\Delta n_{AB} = \frac{1}{2} n_{A+B} = \frac{1}{2}(0.0078645309 \text{ mol A + B}) = 0.0039322655 \text{ mol AB}$ then

$$[AB] = [AB]_0 - \frac{\Delta n_{AB}}{V_{AB} \times \frac{1 \text{ L}}{1000 \text{ mL}}} = 0.100 \text{ M} - \frac{0.0039322655 \text{ mol AB}}{250.0 \text{ mL} \times \frac{1 \text{ L}}{1000 \text{ mL}}} = 0.100 \text{ M} - 0.015729062 \text{ M}$$
$= 0.0842709$ M.

Since $\frac{1}{[AB]_t} = kt + \frac{1}{[AB]_0}$ rearrange to solve for t.

$$t = \frac{1}{k}\left(\frac{1}{[XY]_t} - \frac{1}{[XY]_0}\right) = \frac{1}{(0.0118 \text{ M}^{-1} \cdot \text{s}^{-1})}\left(\frac{1}{0.0842709 \text{ M}} - \frac{1}{0.100 \text{ M}}\right) = 158.1769 \text{ s} = 160 \text{ s}.$$

Check: The units (s) are correct. The magnitude of the answer (160 s) makes sense because the rate constant is $0.0118 \text{ M}^{-1}\text{s}^{-1}$ and a small volume of gas is generated.

13.92 **Given:** $2\ H_2O_2(aq) \rightarrow 2\ H_2O(l) + O_2(g)$; $k = 0.00752 \text{ s}^{-1}$; 150.0 mL of 30.0% H_2O_2 by mass, $d = 1.11$ g/mL; collect gas over water $T = 20.0\ °\text{C}$, $P_{\text{Total}} = 742.5$ mmHg, and $t = 85.0$ s; $P^{\circ}_{H_2O} = 17.5$ mmHg **Find:** V_{O_2}

Conceptual Plan: $\text{mL}_{\text{solution}} \rightarrow \text{g}_{\text{solution}} \rightarrow \text{g}_{H_2O_2} \rightarrow \text{mol}_{H_2O_2}$ **and** $\text{mL}_{\text{solution}} \rightarrow \text{L}_{\text{solution}}$

$\frac{1.1 \text{ 1g}}{1 \text{ mL}}$ $\quad \frac{30.0 \text{ g } H_2O_2}{100 \text{ g solution}}$ $\quad \frac{1 \text{ mol } H_2O_2}{34.02 \text{ g } H_2O_2}$ $\quad \frac{1 \text{ L}}{1000 \text{ mL}}$

then $\text{mol}_{H_2O_2}, \text{L}_{\text{solution}} \rightarrow \text{M } H_2O_2$ **then** $k, [H_2O_2]_0, t \rightarrow [H_2O_2]_t$ **then**

$M = \frac{\text{amount solute (moles)}}{\text{volume solution (L)}}$ $\quad \ln [A]_t = -kt + \ln [A]_0$

$[H_2O_2]_0, [H_2O_2]_t, \text{L}_{\text{solution}} \rightarrow \Delta n_{H_2O_2} \rightarrow n_{O_2}$ **then** $P_{\text{Total}}, P_{H_2O} \rightarrow P_{O_2}$ **then mmHg → atm**

$\Delta n_{H_2O_2} = ([H_2O_2]_0 - [H_2O_2]) \times V_{H_2O_2}$ $\quad \Delta n_{H_2O_2} = n_{O_2}$ $\quad P_{\text{Total}} = P_{H_2O} + P_{O_2}$ $\quad \frac{1 \text{ atm}}{760 \text{ mmHg}}$

and mL → L and °C → K then $P, n, T \rightarrow V_{O_2}$

$\frac{1 \text{ L}}{1000 \text{ mL}}$ $\quad K = °C + 273.15$ $\quad PV = nRT$

Solution: $150.0 \text{ mL solution} \times \frac{1.11 \text{ g solution}}{1 \text{ mL solution}} \times \frac{30.0 \text{ g } H_2O_2}{100 \text{ g solution}} \times \frac{1 \text{ mol } H_2O_2}{34.02 \text{ g } H_2O_2} = 1.468254 \text{ mol } H_2O_2$ and

$150.0 \text{ mL solution} \times \frac{1 \text{ L solution}}{1000 \text{ mL solution}} = 0.1500 \text{ L solution}$ then

$M = \frac{\text{amount solute (moles)}}{\text{volume solution (L)}} = \frac{1.468254 \text{ mol } H_2O_2}{0.1500 \text{ L solution}} = 9.788360 \text{ M } H_2O_2.$

Since $\ln[H_2O_2]_t = -kt + \ln[H_2O_2]_0 = -(0.00752 \text{ s}^{-1})(85.0 \text{ s}) + \ln(9.788360 \text{ M}) = 1.641994 \rightarrow$

$[H_2O_2]_t = e^{1.641994} = 5.165459 \text{ M}$ then $\Delta n_{H_2O_2} = ([H_2O_2]_0 - [H_2O_2]) \times V_{H_2O_2} \times \frac{1 \text{ L}}{1000 \text{ mL}}$

$\Delta n_{H_2O_2} = (9.788360 \text{ M} - 5.165459 \text{ M}) \times (0.1500 \text{ L}) = 0.6934352 \text{ mol } H_2O_2$

then $\Delta n_{H_2O_2} = 0.5 n_{O_2} = 0.34672 \text{ mol } O_2$ then $P_{Total} = P_{H_2O} + P_{O_2}$. Rearrange to solve for P_{O_2}.

$P_{O_2} = P_{Total} - P_{H_2O} = 742.5 \text{ mmHg} - 17.5 \text{ mmHg} = 725.0 \text{ mmHg}$

$P_{O_2} = 725.0 \text{ mmHg} \times \frac{1 \text{ atm}}{760 \text{ mmHg}} = 0.95394737 \text{ atm}$, $T = 20.0\text{ °C} + 273.15 = 293.2 \text{ K}$, $PV = nRT$.

Rearrange to solve for V. $V = \frac{nRT}{P}$ and

$$V_{O_2} = \frac{0.34672 \text{ mol } O_2 \times 0.08206 \frac{\text{L} \cdot \text{atm}}{\text{mol} \cdot \text{K}} \times 293.2 \text{ K}}{0.95394737 \text{ atm}} = 8.74480 \text{ L } O_2 = 8.75 \text{ L } O_2.$$

Check: The units (L) are correct. The magnitude of the answer (9 L) makes sense because about 0.4 mole of gas is generated (22.4 L = 1 mole gas at STP).

13.93 (a) There are two elementary steps in the reaction mechanism because there are two peaks in the reaction progress diagram.

(b)

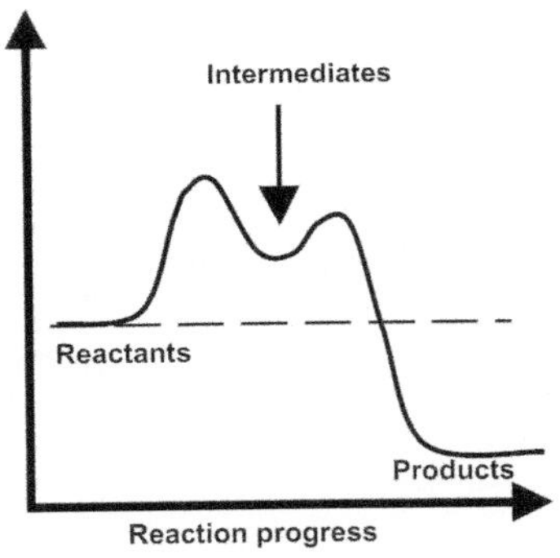

(c) The first step is the rate limiting step because it has the higher activation energy.

(d) The overall reaction is exothermic because the products are at a lower energy than the reactants.

13.94 (a) The first step is the rate limiting step because it has the higher activation energy.

(b) Since the first step is the rate determining step, Rate = k_1 [HCl] [$H_2C{=}CH_2$]. The reaction will be second order overall.

(c) The overall reaction is exothermic because the products are at a lower energy than the reactants.

13.95 **Given:** n-butane desorption from single crystal aluminum oxide, first order; $k = 0.128 \text{ s}^{-1}$ at 150 K; initially completely covered

Find: (a) $t_{1/2}$; (b) t for 25% and for 50% to desorb; (c) fraction remaining after 10 s and 20 s

Conceptual Plan: (a) $k \rightarrow t_{1/2}$ **(b)** $[C_4H_{10}]_0, [C_4H_{10}]_t, k \rightarrow t$ **(c)** $[C_4H_{10}]_0, t, k \rightarrow [C_4H_{10}]_t$

$t_{1/2} = \frac{0.693}{k}$ $\quad \ln[A]_t = -kt + \ln[A]_0$ $\quad \ln[A]_t = -kt + \ln[A]_0$

Solution:

(a) $t_{1/2} = \frac{0.693}{k} = \frac{0.693}{0.128\ s^{-1}} = 5.41\ s.$

(b) $\ln[C_4H_{10}]_t = -kt + \ln[C_4H_{10}]_0$. Rearrange to solve for t. For 25% desorbed $[C_4H_{10}]_t = 0.75\ [C_4H_{10}]_0$ and $t = -\frac{1}{k}\ln\frac{[C_4H_{10}]_t}{[C_4H_{10}]_0} = -\frac{1}{0.128\ s^{-1}}\ln\frac{0.75\ \cancel{[C_4H_{10}]_0}}{\cancel{[C_4H_{10}]_0}} = 2.2\ s.$ For 50% desorbed $[C_4H_{10}]_t = 0.50\ [C_4H_{10}]_0$ and $t = -\frac{1}{k}\ln\frac{[C_4H_{10}]_t}{[C_4H_{10}]_0} = -\frac{1}{0.128\ s^{-1}}\ln\frac{0.50\ \cancel{[C_4H_{10}]_0}}{\cancel{[C_4H_{10}]_0}} = 5.4\ s.$

(c) For 10 s $\ln[C_4H_{10}]_t = -kt + \ln[C_4H_{10}]_0 = -(0.128\cancel{s^{-1}})(10\cancel{s}) + \cancel{\ln(1.00)} = -1.2\underline{8} \rightarrow$
$[C_4H_{10}]_t = e^{-1.2\underline{8}} = 0.28 =$ fraction covered
for 20 s $\ln[C_4H_{10}]_t = -kt + \ln[C_4H_{10}]_0 = -(0.128\ \cancel{s^{-1}})(20\ \cancel{s}) + \cancel{\ln(1.00)} = -2.5\underline{6} \rightarrow$
$[C_4H_{10}]_t = e^{-2.5\underline{6}} = 0.077 =$ fraction covered.

Check: The units (s, s, s, none, and none) are correct. The half-life is reasonable considering the size of the rate constant. The time to 25% desorbed is less than one half-life. The time to 50% desorbed is the half-life. The fraction at 10 s is consistent with about two half-lives. The fraction covered at 20 s is consistent with about four half-lives.

13.96 **Given:** 120 nm film *n*-pentane evaporation from single crystal aluminum oxide, zero order; $k = 1.92 \times 10^{13}$ molecules / cm^2 s at 120 K; initially coverage = 8.9×10^{16} molecules / cm^2
Find: (a) $t_{1/2}$; (b) fraction remaining after 10 s
Conceptual Plan:

(a) $[C_5H_{12}]_0, k \rightarrow t_{1/2}$

$t_{1/2} = \frac{[A]_0}{2k}$

(b) $[C_5H_{12}]_0, t, k \rightarrow [C_5H_{12}]_t$ **then** $[C_5H_{12}]_0, [C_5H_{12}]_t \rightarrow$ **fraction remaining**

$[A]_t = -kt + [A]_0$ fraction remaining $= \frac{[C_5H_{12}]_t}{[C_5H_{12}]_0}$

Solution:

(a) $$t_{1/2} = \frac{[C_5H_{12}]_0}{2k} = \frac{8.9 \times 10^{16}\ \frac{\cancel{molecules}}{\cancel{cm^2}}}{2 \times 1.92 \times 10^{13}\ \frac{\cancel{molecules}}{\cancel{cm^2} \cdot s}} = 2.3 \times 10^3\ s$$

(b) $$[C_5H_{12}]_t = -kt + [C_5H_{12}]_0 = -\left(1.92 \times 10^{13}\ \frac{molecules}{cm^2 \cdot \cancel{s}}\right)(10.\ \cancel{s}) + 8.9 \times 10^{16}\ \frac{molecules}{cm^2}$$
$$= 8.\underline{8}808 \times 10^{16}\ \frac{molecules}{cm^2}$$

$$\text{fraction remaining} = \frac{[C_5H_{12}]_t}{[C_5H_{12}]_0} = \frac{8.\underline{8}808 \times 10^{16}\ \frac{molecules}{cm^2}}{8.9 \times 10^{16}\ \frac{molecules}{cm^2}} = 0.9\underline{9}784 = 1.0$$ so within experimental error, all are remaining on the surface.

Check: The units (s and none) are correct. The half-life is reasonable considering the size of the rate constant. The fraction at 10 s is reasonable given the fact that the time is very, very small compared to the half-life.

13.97 (a) **Given:** table of rate constant versus T **Find:** E_a and A

Conceptual Plan: First convert temperature data into kelvin (°C + 273.15 = K). Since $\ln k = \dfrac{-E_a}{R}\left(\dfrac{1}{T}\right) + \ln A$ **a plot of ln *k* versus 1/*T* will have a slope = $-E_a/R$ and an intercept = ln *A*.**

Solution: The slope can be determined by measuring $\Delta y/\Delta x$ on the plot or by using functions, such as "add trendline" in Excel. Since the slope = – 10759 K = – E_a/R then

$E_a = -(slope)R =$

$$= -(-10759\ \text{K})\left(8.314\ \frac{\text{J}}{\text{K}\cdot\text{mol}}\right)\left(\frac{1\ \text{kJ}}{1000\ \text{J}}\right)$$

$$= 89.5\ \frac{\text{kJ}}{\text{mol}}$$

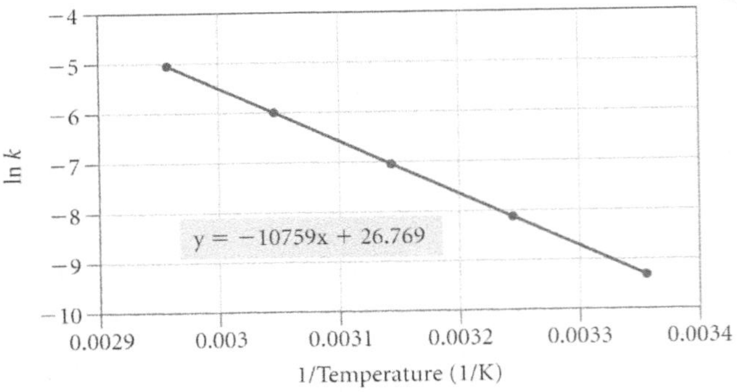

and intercept = 26.769 = ln A then

$A = e^{intercept} = e^{26.769} = 4.22 \times 10^{11}\text{s}^{-1}$.

Check: The units (kJ/mol and s^{-1}) are correct. The plot was extremely linear, confirming Arrhenius behavior. The activation and frequency factor are typical for many reactions.

(b) **Given:** part (a) results **Find:** k at 15 °C

Conceptual Plan: °C → K then *T*, E_a, *A* → *k*

°C + 273.15 = K $\qquad \ln k = \dfrac{-E_a}{R}\left(\dfrac{1}{T}\right) + \ln A$

Solution: 15 °C + 273.15 = 288 K then

$$\ln k = \frac{-E_a}{R}\left(\frac{1}{T}\right) + \ln A = \frac{-89.5\ \frac{\text{kJ}}{\text{mol}} \times \frac{1000\ \text{J}}{1\ \text{kJ}}}{8.314\ \frac{\text{J}}{\text{K}\cdot\text{mol}}}\left(\frac{1}{288\ \text{K}}\right) + \ln(4.22 \times 10^{11}\ \text{s}^{-1}) = -10.610 \rightarrow$$

$k = e^{-10.610} = 2.5 \times 10^{-5}\text{M}^{-1}\cdot\text{s}^{-1}$.

Check: The units ($\text{M}^{-1}\cdot\text{s}^{-1}$) are correct. The value of the rate constant is less than the value at 25 °C.

(c) **Given:** part (a) results, 0.155 M C_2H_5Br and 0.250 M OH^- at 75 °C **Find:** initial reaction rate

Conceptual Plan: °C → K then *T*, E_a, *A* → *k* then *k*, [C_2H_5Br], [OH^-] → initial reaction rate

°C + 273.15 = K $\qquad \ln k = \dfrac{-E_a}{R}\left(\dfrac{1}{T}\right) + \ln A \qquad$ Rate $= k[C_2H_5Br][OH^-]$

Solution: 75 °C + 273.15 = 348 K then

$$\ln k = \frac{-E_a}{R}\left(\frac{1}{T}\right) + \ln A = \frac{-89.5\ \frac{\text{kJ}}{\text{mol}} \times \frac{1000\ \text{J}}{1\ \text{kJ}}}{8.314\ \frac{\text{J}}{\text{K}\cdot\text{mol}}}\left(\frac{1}{348\ \text{K}}\right) + \ln(4.22 \times 10^{11}\ \text{s}^{-1}) = -4.1656 \rightarrow$$

$k = e^{-4.1656} = 1.5521 \times 10^{-2}\text{M}^{-1}\cdot\text{s}^{-1}$.

Rate $= k[C_2H_5Br][OH^-] = (1.5521 \times 10^{-2}\ \text{M}^{-1}\cdot\text{s}^{-1})(0.155\ \text{M})(0.250\ \text{M}) = 6.0 \times 10^{-4}\ \text{M}\cdot\text{s}^{-1}$.

Check: The units ($\text{M}\cdot\text{s}^{-1}$) are correct. The value of the rate is reasonable considering the value of the rate constant (larger than in the table) and the fact that the concentrations are less than 1 M.

13.98 **Given:** $k = 2.35 \times 10^{-4}\ \text{s}^{-1}$ at 293 K and $k = 9.15 \times 10^{-4}\ \text{s}^{-1}$ at 303 K **Find:** A

Conceptual Plan: °C → K then k_1, T_1, k_2, T_2 → E_a then k_2, T_2, E_a → A

K = °C + 273.15 $\qquad \ln k = \dfrac{-E_a}{R}\left(\dfrac{1}{T}\right) + \ln A \qquad k = A\,e^{-E_a/RT}$

Solution: $T_1 = 293$ K, $k_1 = 2.35 \times 10^{-4}\ \text{s}^{-1}$; and $T_2 = 303$ K and $k_2 = 9.15 \times 10^{-4}\ \text{s}^{-1}$ then

$\ln\left(\dfrac{k_2}{k_1}\right) = \dfrac{E_a}{R}\left(\dfrac{1}{T_1} - \dfrac{1}{T_2}\right)$. Rearrange to solve for E_a.

$$E_a = \frac{R\ln\left(\frac{k_2}{k_1}\right)}{\left(\frac{1}{T_1} - \frac{1}{T_2}\right)} = \frac{8.314\ \frac{\text{J}}{\text{K}\cdot\text{mol}}\ln\left(\frac{9.15 \times 10^{-4}\ \text{s}^{-1}}{2.35 \times 10^{-4}\ \text{s}^{-1}}\right)}{\left(\frac{1}{293\ \text{K}} - \frac{1}{303\ \text{K}}\right)} = 1.00334 \times 10^5\ \frac{\text{J}}{\text{mol}}.$$ Since $k = A\,e^{-E_a/RT}$ rearrange

to solve for A. $A = k\,e^{E_a/RT} = 9.15 \times 10^{-4}\,s^{-1}\,e^{\frac{1.00334 \times 10^4 \frac{J}{mol}}{\left(8.314 \frac{J}{K \cdot mol}\right) 303\,K}} = 1.8 \times 10^{14}\,s^{-1}$.

Check: The units (s^{-1}) are correct. The frequency factor is typical for a reaction.

13.99 (a) No, because the activation energy is zero. This means that the rate constant ($k = A\,e^{-E_a/RT}$) will be independent of temperature.

(b) No bond is broken and the two radicals (CH_3) attract each other.

(c) Formation of diatomic gases from atomic gases.

13.100 (a) Nitrogen has a triple bond, so it will take more energy to break the N≡N bond than the H–H bond.

(b) **Given:** E_a = 315 kJ/mol for reaction 1 and E_a = 23 kJ/mol for reaction 2; frequency factor similar; and 25 °C **Find:** ratio of rate constants

Conceptual Plan: °C → K then $T, E_{a_1}, E_{a_2}, A \rightarrow k_1/k_2$

$$°C + 273.15 = K \qquad \frac{k_1}{k_2} = \frac{Ae^{-E_{a_1}/RT}}{Ae^{-E_{a_2}/RT}}$$

Solution: T = 25 °C + 273.15 = 298 K. E_{a_1} = 315 kJ/mol and E_{a_2} = 23 kJ/mol. Ratio of rate constants

will be $\frac{k_1}{k_2} = \frac{Ae^{-E_{a_1}/RT}}{Ae^{-E_{a_2}/RT}} = \frac{e^{\frac{-315 \frac{kJ}{mol} \times \frac{1000\,J}{1\,kJ}}{\left(8.314 \frac{J}{K\,mol}\right) 298\,K}}}{e^{\frac{-23 \frac{kJ}{mol} \times \frac{1000\,J}{1\,kJ}}{\left(8.314 \frac{J}{K\,mol}\right) 298\,K}}} = 6.5 \times 10^{-52}$.

Check: The units (none) are correct. Since there is a large difference between the activation energies, we expect a large difference in the rate constants.

13.101 **Given:** $t_{1/2}$ for radioactive decay of C-14 = 5730 years; bone has 19.5% C-14 in living bone
Find: age of bone
Conceptual Plan: radioactive decay implies first order kinetics, $t_{1/2} \rightarrow k$ then 19.5% of $[C\text{-}14]_0$, $k \rightarrow t$

$$t_{1/2} = \frac{0.693}{k} \qquad \ln[A]_t = -kt + \ln[A]_0$$

Solution: $t_{1/2} = \frac{0.693}{k}$ rearrange to solve for k. $k = \frac{0.693}{t_{1/2}} = \frac{0.693}{5730\,yr} = 1.2\underline{0}942 \times 10^{-4}\,yr^{-1}$ then $[C\text{-}14]_t = 0.195\,[C\text{-}14]_0$. Since $\ln[C\text{-}14]_t = -kt + \ln[C\text{-}14]_0$ rearrange to solve for t.

$$t = -\frac{1}{k}\ln\frac{[C\text{-}14]_t}{[C\text{-}14]_0} = -\frac{1}{1.2\underline{0}942 \times 10^{-4}\,yr^{-1}}\ln\frac{0.195\,\cancel{[C\text{-}14]_0}}{\cancel{[C\text{-}14]_0}} = 1.35 \times 10^4\,yr.$$

Check: The units (yr) are correct. The time to 19.5% decay is consistent with the time being between two and three half-lives.

13.102 **Given:** $t_{1/2}$ for radioactive decay of U-238 = 4.5 billion years; rock has 83.2% of original U-238
Find: age of rock
Conceptual Plan: radioactive decay implies first order kinetics, $t_{1/2} \rightarrow k$ then 82.3% of $[U\text{-}238]_0$, $k \rightarrow t$

$$t_{1/2} = \frac{0.693}{k} \qquad \ln[A]_t = -kt + \ln[A]_0$$

Solution: $t_{1/2} = \frac{0.693}{k}$ rearrange to solve for k. $k = \frac{0.693}{t_{1/2}} = \frac{0.693}{4.5 \times 10^9\,yr} = 1.54 \times 10^{-10}\,yr^{-1}$ then $[U\text{-}238]_t = 0.823\,[U\text{-}238]_0$. Since $\ln[U\text{-}238]_t = -k\,t + \ln[U\text{-}238]_0$ rearrange to solve for t.

$$t = -\frac{1}{k}\ln\frac{[U\text{-}238]_t}{[U\text{-}238]_0} = -\frac{1}{1.54 \times 10^{-10}\,yr^{-1}}\ln\frac{0.832\,\cancel{[U\text{-}238]_0}}{\cancel{[U\text{-}238]_0}} = 1.19 \times 10^9 yr.$$

Check: The units (yr) are correct. The time to 82.3% decay is consistent with the time being less than one half-life.

13.103 (a) For each, check that all steps sum to overall reaction and that the predicted rate law is consistent with experimental data (Rate = $k\,[H_2]\,[I_2]$).
For the first mechanism, the single step is the overall reaction. The rate law is determined by the stoichiometry, so Rate = $k\,[H_2]\,[I_2]$ and the mechanism is valid.
For the second mechanism, the overall reaction is the sum of the steps in the mechanism:

$$I_2\,(g) \underset{k_2}{\overset{k_1}{\rightleftharpoons}} \cancel{2\,I\,(g)}$$

$$H_2\,(g) + \cancel{2\,I\,(g)} \underset{k_3}{\rightarrow} 2\,HI\,(g)$$ So the sum matches the overall reaction.

$$H_2\,(g) + I_2\,(g) \rightarrow 2\,HI(g)$$

Since the second step is the rate determining step, Rate = $k_3\,[H_2]\,[I]^2$. Since I is an intermediate, its concentration cannot appear in the rate law. Using the fast equilibrium in the first step, we see that $k_1[I_2] = k_2\,[I]^2$ or $[I]^2 = \frac{k_1}{k_2}[I_2]$. Substituting this into the first rate expression, we get that

Rate = $k_3\frac{k_1}{k_2}\,[H_2]\,[I_2]$ and the mechanism is valid.

(b) To distinguish between mechanisms, you could look for the buildup of I(g), the intermediate in the second mechanism.

13.104 (a) The overall reaction is the sum of the steps in the mechanism:

$$NH_3\,(aq) + OCl^-\,(aq) \underset{k_2}{\overset{k_1}{\rightleftharpoons}} \cancel{NH_2Cl\,(aq)} + \cancel{OH^-\,(aq)}$$

$$\cancel{NH_2Cl\,(aq)} + NH_3(aq) \underset{k_3}{\rightarrow} \cancel{N_2H_5^+(aq)} + Cl^-(aq)$$

$$\cancel{N_2H_5^+(aq)} + \cancel{OH^-\,(aq)} \underset{k_4}{\rightarrow} N_2H_4\,(aq) + H_2O\,(l)$$

$$2\,NH_3\,(aq) + OCl^-\,(aq) \rightarrow N_2H_4\,(aq) + H_2O(l) + Cl^-\,(aq)$$

So the sum matches the overall reaction.

(b) Since the second step is the rate determining step, Rate = $k_3\,[NH_2Cl]\,[NH_3]$. Since NH_2Cl is an intermediate, its concentration cannot appear in the rate law. Using the fast equilibrium in the first step, we see that $k_1[NH_3]\,[OCl^-] = k_2\,[NH_2Cl]\,[OH^-]$ or $[NH_2Cl] = \frac{k_1}{k_2}\frac{[NH_3]\,[OCl^-]}{[OH^-]}$. Substituting this into the first rate expression, we get that Rate = $k_3\frac{k_1}{k_2}\frac{[NH_3]\,[OCl^-]}{[OH^-]}[NH_3]$ or

Rate = $k_3\frac{k_1}{k_2}\frac{[NH_3]^2\,[OCl^-]}{[OH^-]}$. In a pH neutral solution, $[OH^-] = 10^{-7}$ (see Chapter 15), so that the rate law can be approximated as Rate = $k[NH_3]^2\,[OCl^-]$.

13.105 The steps in the mechanism are as follows:

$$Br_2\,(g) \underset{k_{-1}}{\overset{k_1}{\rightleftharpoons}} 2Br\,(g)$$

$$\cancel{Br\,(g)} + H_2\,(g) \underset{k_2}{\rightarrow} HBr\,(g) + \cancel{H\,(g)}$$

$$\cancel{H\,(g)} + Br_2\,(g) \underset{k_3}{\rightarrow} HBr\,(g) + \cancel{Br\,(g)}$$

Since the second step is the rate determining step, Rate = $k_2\,[H_2]\,[Br]$. Since Br is an intermediate, its concentration cannot appear in the rate law. Using the fast equilibrium in the first step, we see that $k_1[Br_2] = k_{-1}\,[Br]^2$ or $[Br] = \sqrt{\frac{k_1}{k_{-1}}}[Br_2]^{1/2}$. Substituting this into the first rate expression, we get that

Rate = $k_2\sqrt{\frac{k_1}{k_{-1}}}[H_2][Br_2]^{1/2}$. The rate law is 3/2 order overall.

13.106 The sum of the steps in the mechanism are as follows:

$$I_2(g) \underset{k_{-1}}{\overset{k_1}{\rightleftharpoons}} \cancel{2\,I(g)}$$

$$\cancel{I(g)} + H_2(g) \underset{k_{-2}}{\overset{k_2}{\rightleftharpoons}} \cancel{H_2I(g)}$$

$$\cancel{H_2I(g)} + \cancel{I(g)} \xrightarrow[k_3]{} 2\,HI(g)$$

$$H_2(g) + I_2(g) \rightarrow 2\,HI(g)$$

Since the third step is the rate determining step, Rate = k_2 [H_2I] [I]. Since H_2I and I are intermediates, their concentrations cannot appear in the rate law.

Using the fast equilibrium in the first step, we see that $k_1[I_2] = k_{-1}\,[I]^2$ or $[I] = \sqrt{\frac{k_1}{k_{-1}}}\,[I_2]^{1/2}$.

Using the fast equilibrium in the second step, we see that $k_2[H_2]\,[I] = k_{-2}\,[H_2I]^2$ or $[H_2I] = \sqrt{\frac{k_2}{k_{-2}}}\,[H_2]^{1/2}\,[I]$.

Substituting these into the first rate expression, we get that Rate = $k_2\sqrt{\frac{k_2}{k_{-2}}}\,[H_2]^{1/2}[I]\,\sqrt{\frac{k_1}{k_{-1}}}\,[I_2]^{1/2}$. This expression contains I and so another substitution of the first equilibrium expression needs to be done to give Rate = $k_2\sqrt{\frac{k_2}{k_{-2}}}[H_2]^{1/2}\sqrt{\frac{k_1}{k_{-1}}}[I_2]^{1/2}\sqrt{\frac{k_1}{k_{-1}}}[I_2]^{1/2}$. Simplifying we get Rate = $k_2\frac{k_1}{k_{-1}}\sqrt{\frac{k_2}{k_{-2}}}[H_2]^{1/2}[I_2]$.

13.107 (a) For a zero order reaction, the rate is independent of the concentration. If the first half goes in the first 100 minutes, the second half will go in the second 100 minutes. This means that there will be none or 0% left at 200 minutes.

(b) For a first order reaction, the half-life is independent of concentration. This means that if half of the reactant decomposes in the first 100 minutes, then half of this (or another 25% of the original amount) will decompose in the second 100 minutes. This means that at 200 minutes 50% + 25% = 75% has decomposed or 25% remains.

(c) For a second order reaction, $t_{1/2} = \frac{1}{k[A]_0} = 100$ min and the integrated rate expression is $\frac{1}{[A]_t} = kt + \frac{1}{[A]_0}$. We can rearrange the first expression to solve for k as $k = \frac{1}{100\text{ min }[A]_0}$. Substituting this and 200 minutes into the integrated rate expression, we get $\frac{1}{[A]_t} = \frac{200\,\cancel{\text{min}}}{100\,\cancel{\text{min}}\,[A]_0} + \frac{1}{[A]_0} \rightarrow \frac{1}{[A]_t} = \frac{3}{[A]_0} \rightarrow \frac{[A]_t}{[A]_0} = \frac{1}{3}$ or 33% remains.

13.108 **Given:** $t_{1/2}$ for radioactive decay of Pu-239 = 24,000 years; 1 mole initially to 1 atom **Find:** t

Conceptual Plan: radioactive decay implies first order kinetics, $t_{1/2} \rightarrow k$ then [Pu-239]$_0$, [Pu-239]$_t$, $k \rightarrow t$

$$t_{1/2} = \frac{0.693}{k} \qquad \ln[A]_t = -kt + \ln[A]_0$$

Solution: $t_{1/2} = \frac{0.693}{k}$ rearrange to solve for k. $k = \frac{0.693}{t_{1/2}} = \frac{0.693}{24000\text{ yr}} = 2.8875 \times 10^{-5}\text{ yr}^{-1}$ then [Pu-239]$_t$ = 1 and [Pu-239]$_0$ = 6.022×10^{23}. Since ln[Pu-239]$_t$ = $-kt$ + ln[Pu-239]$_0$ rearrange to solve for t. $t = -\frac{1}{k}\ln\frac{[\text{Pu-239}]_t}{[\text{Pu-239}]_0} = -\frac{1}{2.8875 \times 10^{-5}\text{ yr}^{-1}}\ln\frac{1\text{ }\cancel{\text{atom Pu-239}}}{6.022 \times 10^{23}\text{ }\cancel{\text{atom Pu-239}}} = 1.9 \times 10^6$ yr.

Check: The units (yr) are correct. The time to decay to 1 atom is consistent with the time being 79 half-lives, which makes sense since $2^{79} = 6.09 \times 10^{23}$.

13.109 Using the energy diagram shown and using Hess's Law, we can see that the activation energy for the decomposition is equal to the activation energy for the formation reaction plus the heat of formation of 2 moles of HI or

$E_{a\ formation} = E_{a\ decomposition} + 2\Delta H_f^\circ(\text{HI})$. So

$E_{a\ formation} = 185\ \text{kJ} + 2\ \text{mol}(-5.65\ \text{kJ/mol}) = 174\ \text{kJ}$.

Check: Since the reaction is endothermic, we expect the activation energy in the reverse direction to be less in the forward direction.

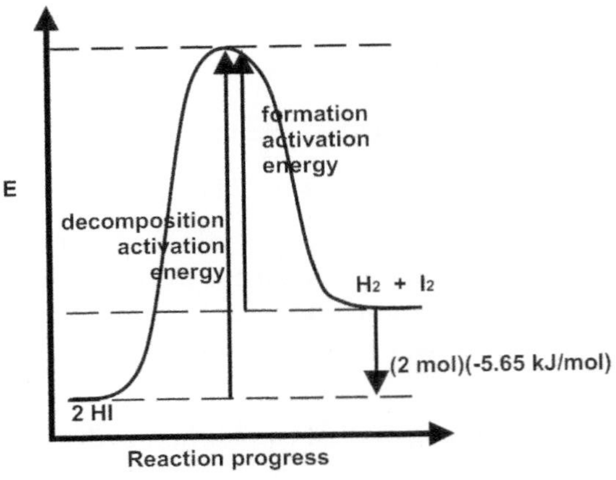

Note: energy axis is not to scale.

13.110 **Given:** first order reaction, $E_a = 249$ kJ/mol, $A = 1.6 \times 10^{14}\ \text{s}^{-1}$, and 710 K
Find: k, fraction decomposed in 15 min and T for double the reaction rate
Conceptual Plan: $T, A, E_a \rightarrow k$ **then min** $\rightarrow$ **s then** $k, t \rightarrow$ **fraction decomposed then** $k_2/k_1, T_1, E_a \rightarrow T_2$

$$k = Ae^{-E_a/RT} \qquad \frac{60\ \text{s}}{1\ \text{min}} \qquad \ln[\text{A}]_t = -kt + \ln[\text{A}]_0 \qquad \ln\left(\frac{k_2}{k_1}\right) = \frac{E_a}{R}\left(\frac{1}{T_1} - \frac{1}{T_2}\right)$$

Solution: Since $k = A\,e^{-E_a/RT} = 1.6 \times 10^{14}\,\text{s}^{-1}\,e^{\frac{-249\frac{\text{kJ}}{\text{mol}} \times \frac{1000\ \text{J}}{1\ \text{kJ}}}{\left(8.314\frac{\text{J}}{\text{K}\cdot\text{mol}}\right)710\ \text{K}}} = 7.6657 \times 10^{-5}\,\text{s}^{-1} = 7.7 \times 10^{-5}\,\text{s}^{-1}$ then

$15\ \text{min} \times \frac{60\ \text{s}}{1\ \text{min}} = 900$ s in $\ln[\text{C}_2\text{H}_5\text{Cl}]_t = -kt + \ln[\text{C}_2\text{H}_5\text{Cl}]_0$. Rearrange to solve for fraction remaining $\rightarrow$

$\frac{[\text{C}_2\text{H}_5\text{Cl}]_t}{[\text{C}_2\text{H}_5\text{Cl}]_0} = e^{-kt} = e^{-(7.6657 \times 10^{-5}\,\text{s}^{-1})(900\ \text{s})} = 0.93333$ thus fraction decomposed $= 1 - 0.93333 = 0.06667 = 0.07$.

$T_1 = 710$ K, $k_2 / k_1 = 2$ and $\ln\left(\frac{k_2}{k_1}\right) = \frac{E_a}{R}\left(\frac{1}{T_1} - \frac{1}{T_2}\right)$. Rearrange to solve for T_2.

$$T_2 = \frac{\frac{E_a}{R}}{\frac{E_a}{RT_1} - \ln\left(\frac{k_2}{k_1}\right)} = \frac{\frac{249\frac{\text{kJ}}{\text{mol}} \times \frac{1000\ \text{J}}{1\ \text{kJ}}}{8.314\frac{\text{J}}{\text{K}\cdot\text{mol}}}}{\left(\frac{249\frac{\text{kJ}}{\text{mol}} \times \frac{1000\ \text{J}}{1\ \text{kJ}}}{8.314\frac{\text{J}}{\text{K}\cdot\text{mol}} \times 710\ \text{K}}\right) - \ln(2)} = 721.86\ K = 720\ K.$$

Check: The units (s^{-1}, none, and K) are correct. The reaction rate is reasonable considering the frequency factor, activation energy, and T. The fraction decomposed is reasonable since 900 s is a small fraction of the half-life. The temperature is reasonable since many reactions double their rate with an increase in temp of 10 K.

Challenge Problems

13.111 (a) Since the rate determining step involves the collision of two molecules, the expected reaction order would be second order.

(b) The proposed mechanism is

$$\text{CH}_3\text{NC} + \text{CH}_3\text{NC} \underset{k_2}{\overset{k_1}{\rightleftharpoons}} \text{CH}_3\text{NC*} + \text{CH}_3\text{NC}\ \text{(fast)}$$

$$\text{CH}_3\text{NC*} \xrightarrow{k_3} \text{CH}_3\text{CN}\ \text{(slow)}$$

So the sum matches the overall reaction.

$$\text{CH}_3\text{NC} \rightarrow \text{CH}_3\text{CN}$$

$\text{CH}_3\text{NC*}$ is the activated molecule. Since the second step is the rate determining step, Rate $= k_3[\text{CH}_3\text{NC*}]$. Since $\text{CH}_3\text{NC*}$ is an intermediate, its concentration cannot appear in the rate law. Using the fast equilibrium in the first step, we see that $k_1[CH_3NC]^2 = k_2[CH_3NC^*][CH_3NC]$ or $[CH_3NC^*] = \frac{k_1}{k_2}[CH_3NC]$. Substituting this into the first rate expression we get that Rate $= k_3\frac{k_1}{k_2}[CH_3NC]$, which simplifies to Rate $= k\,[CH_3NC]$. This matches the experimental observation of first order and the mechanism is valid.

13.112 (a) Rate $= k\,[A]^{1/2}$ and Rate $= -\frac{d\,[A]}{dt}$ so $\frac{d\,[A]}{dt} = -\,k\,[A]^{1/2}$. Moving the A terms to the left and the t and constants to the right we have $\frac{d\,[A]}{[A]^{1/2}} = -\,k\,d\,t$. Integrating we get $\int_{[A]_0}^{[A]}\frac{d\,[A]}{[A]^{1/2}} = -\int_0^t k\,d\,t$. When we evaluate this integral $2[A]^{1/2}\big|_{[A]_0}^{[A]} = -\,k\,t\big|_0^t \rightarrow 2[A]_t^{1/2} - 2[A]_0^{1/2} = -\,k\,t \rightarrow 2[A]_t^{1/2} = -\,kt + 2[A]_0^{1/2}$ which is the desired integrated rate law.

(b) To derive the half-life, set $[A]_t = 1/2[A]_0$. Substituting this into $2[A]_t^{1/2} = -\,kt + 2[A]_0^{1/2}$ we get $2(1/2[A]_0)^{1/2} = -\,k\,t_{1/2} + 2[A]_0^{1/2} \rightarrow t_{1/2} = \frac{2[A]_0^{1/2} - 2\left(1/2[A]_0\right)^{1/2}}{k} \rightarrow t_{1/2} = \frac{\left(2 - 2\sqrt{2}\right)[A]_0^{1/2}}{k}$.

13.113 Rate $= k\,[A]^2$ and Rate $= -\frac{d\,[A]}{dt}$ so $\frac{d[A]}{dt} = -\,k\,[A]^2$. Moving the A terms to the left and the t and constants to the right we have $\frac{d\,[A]}{[A]^2} = -\,k\,d\,t$. Integrating we get $\int_{[A]_0}^{[A]}\frac{d[A]}{[A]^2} = -\int_0^t k\,d\,t$. When we evaluate this integral $-\,[A]^{-1}\big|_{[A]_0}^{[A]} = -\,k\,t\big|_0^t \rightarrow -\,[A]_t^{-1} - (-\,[A]_0^{-1}) = -\,k\,t \rightarrow [A]_t^{-1} = k\,t + [A]_0^{-1}$ or $\frac{1}{[A]_t} = k\,t + \frac{1}{[A]_0}$ which is the desired integrated rate law.

13.114 (a) **Given:** N_2O_5 decomposes to NO_2 and O_2, first order in $[N_2O_5]$; $k = 7.48 \times 10^{-3}\ s^{-1}$; $P^\circ_{N_2O_5} = 0.100$ atm
Find: t to $P_{Total} = 0.145$ atm
Conceptual Plan: Write a balanced reaction. then

$$N_2O_5 \rightarrow 2\,NO_2 + \tfrac{1}{2}\,O_2$$

Then write the expression for P_{Total} in terms of amount reacted then x, $P^\circ_{N_2O_5}$, $k \rightarrow t$

let $x = P_{N_2O_5 reacted}$ $\quad P_{Total} = P_{N_2O_5} + P_{NO_2} + P_{O_2}$ $\qquad \ln[A]_t = -\,k\,t + \ln\,[A]_0$

Solution: $P_{Total} = P_{N_2O_5} + P_{NO_2} + P_{O_2} = (0.100\text{ atm} - x) + (2x) + (1/2x) = 0.100\text{ atm} + 1.5\,x$.
Set $P_{Total} = 0.145\text{ atm} = 0.100\text{ atm} + 1.5\,x$ and solve for x. Note that for every one mole of reactant decomposing there are 2.5 moles of product generated, so the pressure increases by a factor of 1.5.

$$x = \frac{0.145\text{ atm} - 0.100\text{ atm}}{1.5} = 0.030\text{ atm}$$

then $P_{N_2O_5} = 0.100\text{ atm} - x = 0.100\text{ atm} - 0.030\text{ atm} = 0.070$ atm. Since $P \propto n/V$ or M
$\ln[N_2O_5]_t = -\,k\,t + \ln[N_2O_5]_0$ rearrange to solve for t.

$$t = -\frac{\ln\frac{[N_2O_5]_t}{[N_2O_5]_0}}{k} = -\frac{\ln\left(\frac{0.070\ \cancel{atm}}{0.100\ \cancel{atm}}\right)}{7.48 \times 10^{-3}\ s^{-1}} = 4\underline{7}.684\text{ s} = 48\text{ s}.$$

Check: The units (s) are correct. The time is reasonable because it is less than one half-life and the amount decomposing is less that 50%.

(b) **Given:** N_2O_5 decomposes to NO_2 and O_2, first order in $[N_2O_5]$; $k = 7.48 \times 10^{-3}\ s^{-1}$; $P^\circ_{N_2O_5} = 0.100$ atm
Find: t to $P_{Total} = 0.200$ atm
Conceptual Plan: Write a balanced reaction.

$$N_2O_5 \rightarrow 2\,NO_2 + \tfrac{1}{2}\,O_2$$

Then write the expression for P_{Total} in terms of amount reacted then x, $P^\circ_{N_2O_5}$, $k \rightarrow t$

let $x = P_{N_2O_5 reacted}$ $\quad P_{Total} = P_{N_2O_5} + P_{NO_2} + P_{O_2}$ $\qquad \ln[A]_t = -\,k\,t + \ln[A]_0$

Solution: $P_{Total} = P_{N_2O_5} + P_{NO_2} + P_{O_2} = (0.100\text{ atm} - x) + (2\,x) + (1/2\,x) = 0.100\text{ atm} + 1.5\,x$.

$P_{Total} = 0.200 \text{ atm} = 0.100 \text{ atm} + 1.5\,x$. Solve for x. $x = \dfrac{0.200 \text{ atm} - 0.100 \text{ atm}}{1.5} = 0.066\underline{6}67 \text{ atm}$

then $P_{N_2O_5} = 0.100 \text{ atm} - x = 0.100 \text{ atm} - 0.066\underline{6}67 \text{ atm} = 0.03\underline{3}333 \text{ atm}$. Since $P \propto n/V$ or M

$\ln[N_2O_5]_t = -kt + \ln[N_2O_5]_0$ rearrange to solve for t.

$$t = -\frac{\ln\dfrac{[N_2O_5]_t}{[N_2O_5]_0}}{k} = -\frac{\ln\left(\dfrac{0.03\underline{3}333 \text{ atm}}{0.100 \text{ atm}}\right)}{7.48 \times 10^{-3}\text{ s}^{-1}} = 14\underline{6}.873 \text{ s} = 150 \text{ s} = 1.5 \times 10^2 \text{ s}.$$

Check: The units (s) are correct. The time is reasonable because it is between one and two half-lives and the amount decomposing is 67%.

(c) **Given:** N_2O_5 decomposes to NO_2 and O_2, first order in $[N_2O_5]$; $k = 7.48 \times 10^{-3}\text{ s}^{-1}$; $P^{\circ}_{N_2O_5} = 0.100$ atm
Find: P_{Total} after 100 s
Conceptual Plan: $P^{\circ}_{N_2O_5}, k, t \rightarrow P_{N_2O_5}$ then write a balanced reaction. Then $P^{\circ}_{N_2O_5}, P_{N_2O_5} \rightarrow x$ then

$\ln[A]_t = -kt + \ln[A]_0$ $\quad$ $N_2O_5 \rightarrow 2\,NO_2 + \frac{1}{2}\,O_2$ $\quad$ $x = P^{\circ}_{N_2O_5} - P_{N_2O_5}$

Write the expression for P_{Total} in terms of amount reacted.

let $x = P_{N_2O_5 \text{reacted}}$ $\quad$ $P_{Total} = P_{N_2O_5} + P_{NO_2} + P_{O_2}$

Solution: Since $P \propto n/V$ or M

$\ln[N_2O_5]_t = -kt + \ln[N_2O_5]_0 = -(7.48 \times 10^{-3}\text{ s}^{-1})(100\text{ s}) + \ln(0.100\text{ atm}) = -3.0\underline{5}059$

$P_{N_2O_5} = e^{-3.0\underline{5}059} = 0.047\underline{3}312$ atm so

$x = P^{\circ}_{N_2O_5} - P_{N_2O_5} = 0.100 \text{ atm} - 0.047\underline{3}312 \text{ atm} = 0.05\underline{2}669$ atm

finally $P_{Total} = P_{N_2O_5} + P_{NO_2} + P_{O_2} = (0.100 \text{ atm} - x) + (2\,x) + (1/2\,x) = 0.100 \text{ atm} + 1.5\,x =$
$= 0.100 \text{ atm} + 1.5(0.05\underline{2}669 \text{ atm}) = 0.179$ atm

Check: The units (atm) are correct. The pressure is reasonable because the time is between those for parts (a) and (b).

13.115 For this mechanism, the overall reaction is the sum of the steps in the mechanism:

$$Cl_2(g) \underset{k_2}{\overset{k_1}{\rightleftharpoons}} 2Cl(g)$$

$$\cancel{Cl(g)} + CO(g) \underset{k_4}{\overset{k_3}{\rightleftharpoons}} \cancel{ClCO(g)}$$

$$\cancel{ClCO(g)} + Cl_2(g) \xrightarrow[k_5]{} Cl_2CO(g) + \cancel{Cl(g)}$$

$$CO(g) + 2\,Cl_2(g) \rightarrow Cl_2CO(g) + 2\,Cl(g)$$

There is no overall reaction given. Since the third step is the rate determining step, Rate = k_5 [ClCO] [Cl_2]. Since ClCO is an intermediate, its concentration cannot appear in the rate law. Using the fast equilibrium in the second step, we see that k_3[Cl] [CO] = k_4 [ClCO] or [ClCO] = $\dfrac{k_3}{k_4}$[Cl] [CO]. Substituting this expression into the first rate expression we get Rate = $k_5\dfrac{k_3}{k_4}$ [Cl] [CO] [Cl_2]. Since Cl is an intermediate, its concentration cannot appear in the rate law. Using the fast equilibrium in the first step, we see that $k_1[Cl_2] = k_2\,[Cl]^2$ or $[Cl] = \sqrt{\dfrac{k_1}{k_2}[Cl_2]}$. Substituting this expression into last first rate expression we get that

Rate = $k_5\dfrac{k_3}{k_4}\sqrt{\dfrac{k_1}{k_2}[Cl_2]}\,[CO]\,[Cl_2] = k_5\dfrac{k_3}{k_4}\sqrt{\dfrac{k_1}{k_2}}[CO]\,[Cl_2]^{3/2}$. Simplifying this expression we see

Rate = $k\,[CO]\,[Cl_2]^{3/2}$.

13.116 **Given:** N_2O_3 decomposes to NO_2 and NO, first order in $[N_2O_3]$, table of $[NO_2]$ versus time, at 50,000 s = $[N_2O_3] = 0$ **Find:** k
Conceptual Plan: Write a balanced reaction. Then write the expression for $[NO_2]$ in terms $[N_2O_3]$, then

$N_2O_3 \rightarrow NO_2 + NO$ $\quad$ $[N_2O_3] = 0.784\text{ M} - [NO_2]$

plot ln $[N_2O_3]$ versus time. Since $\ln[A]_t = -kt + \ln[A]_0$, the negative of the slope will be the rate constant.
Solution: $[N_2O_3] = 0.784\text{ M} - [NO_2]$.

Plot ln $[N_2O_3]$ versus time. Since $\ln[A]_t = -kt + \ln[A]_0$, the negative of the slope will be the rate constant. The slope can be determined by measuring $\Delta y/\Delta x$ on the plot or by using functions, such as "add trendline" in Excel. The last point (50,000 s) cannot be plotted because the concentration is 0 and the ln 0 is undefined. Thus the rate constant is 3.20 x 10^{-4} s^{-1} and the rate law is Rate = $3.20 \times 10^{-4} s^{-1}[N_2O_3]$.

Check: The units (s^{-1}) are correct. The rate constant is typical for a reaction.

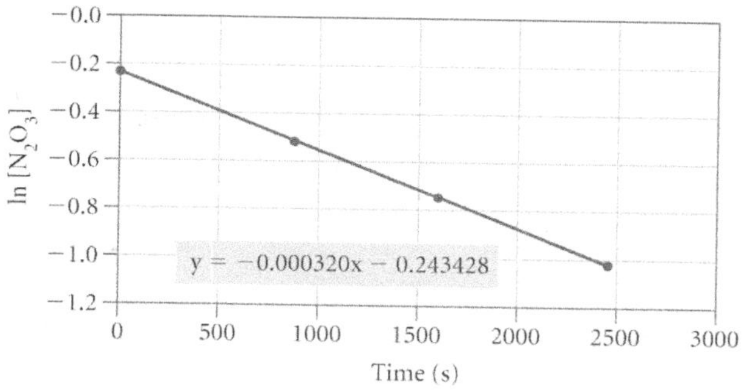

13.117 For the elementary reaction $2\,NOCl(g) \underset{k_{-1}}{\overset{k_1}{\rightleftharpoons}} 2NO(g) + Cl_2(g)$ we see that $k_1\,[NOCl]^2 = k_{-1}\,[NO]^2\,[Cl_2]$. For each mole of NOCl that reacts, one mole of NO and one-half mole of Cl_2 are generated. Since before any reaction only NOCl is present, [NO] = 2 $[Cl_2]$. Substituting this into the first expression, we get that $k_1\,[NOCl]^2 = k_{-1}\,(2[Cl_2])^2\,[Cl_2] \rightarrow k_1\,[NOCl]^2 = 4\,k_{-1}\,[Cl_2]^3$. Rearranging and substituting the specific values into this expression we get

$$[Cl_2] = \sqrt[3]{\frac{k_1}{4k_{-1}}}[NOCl]^{2/3} = \sqrt[3]{\frac{7.8 \times 10^{-2}\frac{L^2}{mol^2 \cdot s}}{4\left(4.7 \times 10^{2}\frac{L^2}{mol^2 \cdot s}\right)}}\left(0.12\,\frac{mol}{L}\right)^{2/3} = 0.00842237\,\frac{mol}{L}\,Cl_2$$

$$= 0.0084\ M\ Cl_2 \text{ and } [Cl_2] = 2\,[NO] = 2\left(0.00842237\,\frac{mol}{L}\right) = 0.0168447\,\frac{mol}{L}\,NO = 0.017\ M\ NO.$$

Conceptual Problems

13.118 Since Rate = $k\,[CHCl_3]\,[Cl_2]^{1/2}$, Rate a = $k\,(3)(3)^{1/2} = 5.2\,k$, Rate b = $k\,(4)(2)^{1/2} = 5.7\,k$, and Rate c = $k\,(2)(4)^{1/2} = 4\,k$. So b has the fastest rate.

13.119 Reaction A is second order. A plot of 1/[A] versus time will be linear $\left(\frac{1}{[A]_t} = kt + \frac{1}{[A]_0}\right)$. Reaction B is first order. A plot of ln [A] versus time will be linear ($\ln[A]_t = -kt + \ln[A]_0$). Reactant concentrations drop more quickly for first order reactions than for second order reactions.

13.120 A reaction that slows down as the reaction proceeds and has a half-life that is dependent on the concentration is a second order reaction. Statement (a) will be false because this describes a first order reaction. Statement (b) is true because it describes a second order reaction. Statements (c) and (d) are false because they describe a zero order reaction.

14 Chemical Equilibrium

Review Questions

14.1 Like adult hemoglobin, fetal hemoglobin is in equilibrium with oxygen. However, the equilibrium constant for fetal hemoglobin is larger than the equilibrium constant for adult hemoglobin, meaning that the reaction tends to go farther in the direction of the product. Consequently, fetal hemoglobin loads oxygen at a lower oxygen concentration than adult hemoglobin. In the placenta, fetal blood flows in close proximity to maternal blood, without the two ever mixing. Because of the different equilibrium constants, the maternal hemoglobin unloads oxygen which the fetal hemoglobin then binds and carries into its own circulatory system. Nature has thus evolved a chemical system through which the mother's hemoglobin can in effect hand off oxygen to the hemoglobin of the fetus.

14.2 Dynamic equilibrium in a chemical reaction is the condition in which the rate of the forward reaction equals the rate of the reverse reaction. Dynamic equilibrium is called dynamic because the forward and reverse reactions are still occurring, however, they are occurring at the same rate.

14.3 The general expression of the equilibrium constant is: $K = \dfrac{[C]^c[D]^d}{[A]^a[B]^b}$

14.4 The equilibrium constant for a reaction is defined as the ratio—at equilibrium—of the concentrations of the products raised to their stoichiometric coefficients divided by the concentrations of the reactants raised to their stoichiometric coefficients. If the equilibrium constant for a reaction is large, the equilibrium point of the reaction lies far to the right—the concentration of products is large and the concentration of reactants is small. If the equilibrium constant for a reaction is small, the equilibrium point of the reaction lies far to the left—the concentration of products is small and the concentration of reactants is large.

14.5 If you reverse the equation, invert the equilibrium constant. $K_{\text{reverse}} = \dfrac{1}{K_{\text{forward}}}$

If you multiply the coefficients in the equation by a factor, raise the equilibrium constant to the same factor. That is, if you multiply the reaction by n, raise the equilibrium constant K to the n. $K' = K^n$

14.6 If you add two or more individual chemical equations to obtain an overall equation, multiply the corresponding equilibrium constants by each other to obtain the overall equilibrium constant. For two reactions with equilibrium constants of K_1 and K_2 the equilibrium constant for the combined reaction $K_3 = K_1K_2$.

14.7 K_c is the equilibrium constant with respect to concentration in molarity. K_p is the equilibrium constant with respect to partial pressures in atmospheres. The two can be related as follows: $K_p = K_c(RT)^{\Delta n}$

14.8 For the equilibrium constant, concentrations are expressed in terms of molarity and partial pressures are expressed in terms of atmospheres. The equilibrium constant usually is written with no units. Formally, the values of concentration or partial pressures that we substitute into the equilibrium constant expressions are ratios of the concentration or pressure to a reference concentration or reference pressure. So, as long as concentration units are expressed in molarity or atmospheres, we simply enter the quantities directly into the equilibrium expression, dropping their corresponding units.

14.9 The concentration of a solid does not change because a solid does not expand to fill its container. Its concentration, therefore, depends only on its density, which is constant as long as some solid is present. Consequently, solids are not included in the equilibrium expression. Similarly, the concentration of a pure liquid does not change, so liquids are also excluded from the equilibrium expression.

14.10 For any reaction, the equilibrium concentrations of the reactants and products will depend on the initial concentration. However, the equilibrium constant will always be the same at a given temperature, regardless of the initial concentrations.

14.11 When we know the initial concentrations of the reactants and products and the equilibrium concentration of one reactant or product, the other equilibrium concentrations can be deduced from the stoichiometry of the reaction. From the initial and equilibrium concentration of the one reactant, we can find the change in concentration for that reactant. Using the stoichiometry of the reaction, we can determine the equilibrium concentrations of the other reactants and products. We generally use an ICE table (I = Initial C = Change E = Equilibrium) to keep track of the changes.

14.12 The definition of the reaction quotient takes the same form as the definition of the equilibrium constant, except that the reaction need not be at equilibrium. So the reaction quotient (Q_c) is the ratio—at any point in the reaction—of the concentrations of the products raised to their stoichiometric coefficients divided by the concentration of the reactants raised to their stoichiometric coefficients. The value of Q relative to K is a measure of the progress of the reaction toward equilibrium. At equilibrium, the reaction quotient is equal to the equilibrium constant.

14.13 Standard states are defined as 1 M concentration, or 1 atm pressure. So the value of K_c and K_p when the reactants and products are in their standard states is 1.

14.14 (a) When $Q < K$ the reaction goes to the right (toward products).

(b) When $Q > K$ the reaction goes to the left (toward reactants).

(c) When $Q = K$ the reaction is at equilibrium.

14.15 To solve a problem given initial concentrations and the equilibrium constant you would prepare an ICE table, calculate Q, compare Q and K_c, predict the direction of the reaction, represent the change with x, sum the table, determine the equilibrium values, put the equilibrium values in the equilibrium expression, and solve for x. Determine the reactant and product concentration.

14.16 When adding or subtracting a small value of x, we can often ignore x because of significant figures. In addition and subtraction, the number of significant figures depends on the number with the fewest decimal places. Therefore, a small value of x would not be significant. In multiplication and division, the number of significant figures depends on the number with the fewest significant figures, therefore, we cannot ignore x in this case.

14.17 According to Le Châtelier's principle, when a chemical system at equilibrium is disturbed, the system shifts in a direction that minimizes the disturbance.

14.18 If a system is at equilibrium,
increasing the concentration of one or more of the reactants causes the reaction to shift to the right.
increasing the concentration of one or more of the products causes the reaction to shift to the left.
decreasing the concentration of one or more of the reactants causes the reaction to shift to the left.
decreasing the concentration of one or more of the products causes the reaction to shift to the right.

14.19 If a chemical system is at equilibrium,
decreasing the volume causes the reaction to shift in the direction that has the fewer moles of gas particles.
increasing the volume causes the reaction to shift in the direction that has the greater number of moles of gas particles.

if a reaction has an equal number of moles of gas on both sides of the chemical equation, then a change in volume produces no effect on the equilibrium.
adding an inert gas to the mixture at a fixed volume has no effect on the equilibrium.

14.20 If the temperature of a system at equilibrium is changed, the system shifts in a direction to counter that change. So, if the temperature is increased, the reaction shifts in the direction that tends to decrease the temperature and vice versa.
In an exothermic chemical reaction,
increasing the temperature causes the reaction to shift left and the value of the equilibrium constant decreases.
decreasing the temperature causes the reaction to shift right and the value of the equilibrium constant increases.
In an endothermic chemical reaction,
increasing the temperature causes the reaction to shift right and the equilibrium constant increases.
decreasing the temperature causes the reaction to shift left and the equilibrium constant decreases.

Problems by Topic

Equilibrium and the Equilibrium Constant

14.21 The equilibrium constant is defined as the concentrations of the products raised to their stoichiometric coefficients divided by the concentrations of the reactants raised to their stoichiometric coefficients.

(a) $K = \dfrac{[SbCl_3][Cl_2]}{[SbCl_5]}$

(b) $K = \dfrac{[NO]^2[Br_2]}{[BrNO]^2}$

(c) $K = \dfrac{[CS_2][H_2]^4}{[CH_4][H_2S]^2}$

(d) $K = \dfrac{[CO_2]^2}{[CO]^2[O_2]}$

14.22 (a) The equilibrium constant is defined as the concentrations of the products **raised to their stoichiometric coefficients** divided by the concentrations of the reactants **raised to their stoichiometric coefficients**.

$K = \dfrac{[H_2]^2[S_2]}{[H_2S]^2}$

(b) The equilibrium constant is defined as the **concentrations of the products** raised to their stoichiometric coefficients **divided by the concentrations of the reactants** raised to their stoichiometric coefficients.

$K = \dfrac{[COCl_2]}{[CO][Cl_2]}$

14.23 With an equilibrium constant of 1.4×10^{-5}, the value of the equilibrium constant is small, therefore, the concentration of reactants will be greater than the concentration of products. This is independent of the initial concentration of the reactants and products.

14.24 Figure a at equilibrium has 8 $C_2H_4Cl_2$, 2 Cl_2, and 2 C_2H_4.
Figure b at equilibrium has 6 $C_2H_4Br_2$, 4 Br_2, and 4 C_2H_4.
Figure c at equilibrium has 3 $C_2H_4I_2$, 7 I_2, and 7 C_2H_4.
Since the equilibrium constant is concentration of products/concentration of reactants, the equilibrium situation which has the largest concentration of products will have the largest equilibrium constant. Therefore, $K_{Cl_2} > K_{Br_2} > K_{I_2}$.

14.25 (i) has 10 H_2 and 10 I_2
(ii) has 7 H_2 and 7 I_2 and 6 HI
(iii) has 5 H_2 and 5 I_2 and 10 HI
(iv) has 4 H_2 and 4 I_2 and 12 HI
(v) has 3 H_2 and 3 I_2 and 14 HI
(vi) has 3 H_2 and 3 I_2 and 14 HI

(a) Concentration of (v) and (vi) are the same, so the system reached equilibrium at (v).

(b) If a catalyst was added to the system, the system would reach the conditions at (v) sooner since a catalyst speeds up the reaction but does not change the equilibrium conditions.

(c) The final figure (vi) would have the same amount of reactants and products since a catalyst speeds up the reaction, but does not change the equilibrium concentrations.

14.26 The equilibrium constant gives us the ratio of products to reactants at equilibrium, it does not say how long it takes to reach equilibrium. So after 15 minutes, if the smaller equilibrium constant has more products, then the kinetics of that reaction are faster.

14.27 (a) If you reverse the reaction, invert the equilibrium constant. So $K' = \frac{1}{K_p} = \frac{1}{2.26 \times 10^4} = 4.42 \times 10^{-5}$.

The reactants will be favored.

(b) If you multiply the coefficients in the equation by a factor, raise the equilibrium constant to the same factor.
So $K' = (K_p)^{1/2} = (2.26 \times 10^4)^{1/2} = 1.50 \times 10^2$. The products will be favored.

(c) Begin with the reverse of the reaction and invert the equilibrium constant.
$K_{reverse} = \frac{1}{K_p} = \frac{1}{2.26 \times 10^4} = 4.42 \times 10^{-5}$
Then multiply the reaction by 2 and raise the value of $K_{reverse}$ to the 2nd power.
$K' = (K_{reverse})^2 = (4.42 \times 10^{-5})^2 = 1.96 \times 10^{-9}$. The reactants will be favored.

14.28 (a) The reaction is multiplied by 1/2, so raise the value of the equilibrium constant to 1/2.
$K' = (K_p)^{1/2} = (2.2 \times 10^6)^{1/2} = 1.5 \times 10^3$. The products will be favored.

(b) The reaction is multiplied by 3, so raise the value of the equilibrium constant to 3.
$K' = (K_p)^3 = (2.2 \times 10^6)^3 = 1.1 \times 10^{19}$. The products will be favored.

(c) Begin with the reverse of the reaction and invert the equilibrium constant.
$K_{reverse} = \frac{1}{K_p} = \frac{1}{2.2 \times 10^6} = 4.5 \times 10^{-7}$
Then multiply the reaction by 2 and raise the value of $K_{reverse}$ to the 2nd power.
$K' = (K_{reverse})^2 = (4.5 \times 10^{-7})^2 = 2.1 \times 10^{-13}$. The reactants will be favored.

14.29 To find the equilibrium constant for reaction 3, you need to combine reactions 1 and 2 to get reaction 3. Begin by reversing reaction 2, then multiply reaction 1 by 2 and add the two new reactions. When you add reactions you multiply the values of K.

$N_2(g) + O_2(g) \rightleftharpoons \cancel{2NO}(g)$ $\qquad K_1 = \frac{1}{K_p} = \frac{1}{2.1 \times 10^{30}} = 4.\underline{7}6 \times 10^{-31}$

$\cancel{2NO}(g) + Br_2(g) \rightleftharpoons 2\,NOBr(g)$ $\qquad K_2 = (K_p)^2 = (5.3)^2 = 2\underline{8}.09$

$N_2(g) + O_2(g) + Br_2(g) \rightleftharpoons 2\,NOBr(g)$ $\qquad K_3 = K_1K_2 = (4.\underline{7}6 \times 10^{-31})(2\underline{8}.09) = 1.3 \times 10^{-29}$

14.30 To find the equilibrium constant for reaction 3, you need to combine reactions 1 and 2 to get reaction 3. Begin by multiplying reaction 1 by 2 and then reverse reaction 2 and add the two new reactions. When you add reactions you multiply the values of *K*.

$$2\,A(s) \rightleftarrows \cancel{B(g)} + \cancel{2C(g)} \qquad K_1 = (K_p)^2 = (0.0334)^2 = 1.1 \times 10^{-3}$$

$$\cancel{B(g)} + \cancel{2C(g)} \leftrightarrows 3\,D(g) \qquad K_2 = \frac{1}{K_p} = \frac{1}{2.35} = 0.425$$

$$2\,A(s) \rightleftarrows 3\,D(g) \qquad K' = K_1 K_2 = (1.1 \times 10^{-3})(0.425) = 4.68 \times 10^{-4}$$

K_p, K_c, and Heterogeneous Equilibria

14.31 (a) **Given:** $K_p = 6.26 \times 10^{-22}$ T = 298K **Find:** K_c

Conceptual Plan: $K_p \rightarrow K_c$

$K_p = K_c(RT)^{\Delta n}$

Solution: Δn = mol product gas – mol reactant gas = 2 – 1 = 1

$$K_c = \frac{K_p}{(RT)^{\Delta n}} = \frac{6.26 \times 10^{-22}}{\left(0.08206 \frac{\text{L} \cdot \text{atm}}{\text{mol} \cdot \cancel{\text{K}}} \times 298\,\cancel{\text{K}}\right)^1} = 2.56 \times 10^{-23}$$

Check: Substitute into the equation and confirm that you get the original value of K_p.

$$K_p = K_c(RT)^{\Delta n} = (2.56 \times 10^{-23})\left(0.08206 \frac{\text{L} \cdot \text{atm}}{\text{mol} \cdot \text{K}} \times 298\right)^1 = 6.26 \times 10^{-22}$$

(b) **Given:** $K_p = 7.7 \times 10^{24}$ T = 298K **Find:** K_c

Conceptual Plan: $K_p \rightarrow K_c$

$K_p = K_c(RT)^{\Delta n}$

Solution: Δn = mol product gas – mol reactant gas = 4 – 2 = 2

$$K_c = \frac{K_p}{(RT)^{\Delta n}} = \frac{7.7 \times 10^{24}}{\left(0.08206 \frac{\text{L} \cdot \text{atm}}{\text{mol} \cdot \cancel{\text{K}}} \times 298\,\cancel{\text{K}}\right)^2} = 1.3 \times 10^{22}$$

Check: Substitute into the equation and confirm that you get the original value of K_p.

$$K_p = K_c(RT)^{\Delta n} = (1.3 \times 10^{22})\left(0.08206 \frac{\text{L} \cdot \text{atm}}{\text{mol} \cdot \text{K}} \times 298\right)^2 = 7.7 \times 10^{24}$$

(c) **Given:** $K_p = 81.9$ T = 298K **Find:** K_c

Conceptual Plan: $K_p \rightarrow K_c$

$K_p = K_c(RT)^{\Delta n}$

Solution: Δn = mol product gas – mol reactant gas = 2 – 2 = 0

$$K_c = \frac{K_p}{(RT)^{\Delta n}} = \frac{81.9}{\left(0.08206 \frac{\text{L} \cdot \text{atm}}{\text{mol} \cdot \cancel{\text{K}}} \times 298\,\cancel{\text{K}}\right)^0} = 81.9$$

Check: Substitute into the equation and confirm that you get the original value of K_p.

$$K_p = K_c(RT)^{\Delta n} = (81.9)\left(0.08206 \frac{\text{L} \cdot \text{atm}}{\text{mol} \cdot \text{K}} \times 298\right)^0 = 81.9$$

14.32 (a) **Given:** $K_c = 5.9 \times 10^{-3}$ T = 298K **Find:** K_p

Conceptual Plan: $K_p \rightarrow K_c$

$K_p = K_c(RT)^{\Delta n}$

Solution: Δn = mol product gas – mol reactant gas = 2 – 1 = 1

$$K_p = K_c(RT)^{\Delta n} = 5.9 \times 10^{-3}\left(0.08206 \frac{\text{L} \cdot \text{atm}}{\text{mol} \cdot \cancel{\text{K}}} \times 298\,\cancel{\text{K}}\right)^1 = 1.4 \times 10^{-1}$$

Check: Substitute into the equation and confirm that you get the original value of K_p.

$$K_c = \frac{K_p}{(RT)^{\Delta n}} = \frac{1.4 \times 10^{-1}}{\left(0.08206 \frac{\text{L} \cdot \text{atm}}{\text{mol} \cdot \cancel{\text{K}}} \times 298\,\cancel{\text{K}}\right)^1} = 0.0059$$

(b) **Given:** $K_c = 3.7 \times 10^8$ T = 298K **Find:** K_p
Conceptual Plan: $K_p \rightarrow K_c$
$K_p = K_c(RT)^{\Delta n}$
Solution: Δn = mol product gas – mol reactant gas = 2 – 4 = – 2

$$K_p = K_c(RT)^{\Delta n} = 3.7 \times 10^8\left(0.08206 \frac{\text{L} \cdot \text{atm}}{\text{mol} \cdot \text{K}} \times 298\ \text{K}\right)^{-2} = 6.2 \times 10^5$$

Check: Substitute into the equation and confirm that you get the original value of K_p.

$$K_c = \frac{K_p}{(RT)^{\Delta n}} = \frac{6.2 \times 10^5}{\left(0.08206 \frac{\text{L} \cdot \text{atm}}{\text{mol} \cdot \text{K}} \times 298\ \text{K}\right)^{-2}} = 3.7 \times 10^8$$

(c) **Given:** $K_c = 4.10 \times 10^{-31}$ T = 298K **Find:** K_p
Conceptual Plan: $K_p \rightarrow K_c$
$K_p = K_c(RT)^{\Delta n}$
Solution: Δn = mol product gas – mol reactant gas = 2 – 2 = 0

$$K_p = K_c(RT)^{\Delta n} = 4.10 \times 10^{-31}\left(0.08206 \frac{\text{L} \cdot \text{atm}}{\text{mol} \cdot \text{K}} \times 298\ \text{K}\right)^0 = 4.10 \times 10^{-31}$$

Check: Substitute into the equation and confirm that you get the original value of K_p.

$$K_c = \frac{K_p}{(RT)^{\Delta n}} = \frac{4.10 \times 10^{-31}}{\left(0.08206 \frac{\text{L} \cdot \text{atm}}{\text{mol} \cdot \text{K}} \times 298\ \text{K}\right)^0} = 4.10\ x\ 10^{-31}$$

14.33 (a) Since H_2O is a liquid, it is omitted from the equilibrium expression. $K_{eq} = \dfrac{[HCO_3^-][OH^-]}{[CO_3^{2-}]}$

(b) Since $KClO_3$ and KCl are both solids, they are omitted from the equilibrium expression. $K_{eq} = [O_2]^3$

(c) Since H_2O is a liquid, it is omitted from the equilibrium expression. $K_{eq} = \dfrac{[H_3O^+][F^-]}{[HF]}$

(d) Since H_2O is a liquid, it is omitted from the equilibrium expression. $K_{eq} = \dfrac{[NH_4^+][OH^-]}{[NH_3]}$

14.34 Since PCl_3 is a liquid, it is omitted from the equilibrium expression. $K_{eq} = \dfrac{[Cl_2]}{[PCl_5]}$

Relating the Equilibrium Constant to Equilibrium Concentrations and Equilibrium Partial Pressures

14.35 **Given:** At equilibrium: [CO] = 0.105M, $[H_2]$ = 0.114M, $[CH_3OH]$ = 0.185M **Find:** K_c
Conceptual Plan: Balanced reaction → equilibrium expression → K_c

Solution: $K_c = \dfrac{[CH_3OH]}{[CO][H_2]^2} = \dfrac{(0.185)}{(0.105)(0.114)^2} = 136$

Check: The answer is reasonable since the concentration of products is greater than the concentration of reactants and the equilibrium constant should be greater than 1.

14.36 **Given:** At equilibrium: $[NH_3]$ = 0.278M, $[H_2S]$ = 0.355M **Find:** K_c
Conceptual Plan: Balanced reaction → equilibrium expression → K_c
Solution: Since NH_4HS is a solid, it is omitted from the equilibrium expression.

$$K_c = [NH_3][H_2S] = (0.278)(0.355) = 0.0987$$

Check: The answer is reasonable since the concentration of products is less than 1M, the equilibrium constant is less than 1.

14.37 At 500K: **Given:** At equilibrium: $[N_2]$ = 0.115M, $[H_2]$ = 0.105M, and $[NH_3]$ = 0.439 **Find:** K_c

Conceptual Plan: Balanced reaction $\rightarrow$ equilibrium expression $\rightarrow$ K_c

Solution: $K_c = \dfrac{[NH_3]^2}{[N_2][H_2]^3} = \dfrac{(0.439)^2}{(0.115)(0.105)^3} = 1.45 \times 10^3$

Check: The value is reasonable since the concentration of products is greater than the concentration of reactants.

At 575K: **Given:** At equilibrium: $[N_2] = 0.110M$, $[NH_3] = 0.128$, $K_c = 9.6$ **Find:** $[H_2]$

Conceptual Plan: Balanced reaction $\rightarrow$ equilibrium expression $\rightarrow$ $[H_2]$

Solution: $K_c = \dfrac{[NH_3]^2}{[N_2][H_2]^3}$ $\quad 9.6 = \dfrac{(0.128)^2}{(0.110)(x)^3}$ $\quad x = 0.249$

Check: Plug the value for x back into the equilibrium expression, and check the value.

$$9.6 = \frac{(0.128)^2}{(0.110)(0.249)^3}$$

At 775K: **Given:** At equilibrium: $[N_2] = 0.120M$, $[H_2] = 0.140$, $K_c = 0.0584$ **Find:** $[NH_3]$

Conceptual Plan: Balanced reaction $\rightarrow$ equilibrium expression $\rightarrow$ $[NH_3]$

Solution: $K_c = \dfrac{[NH_3]^2}{[N_2][H_2]^3}$ $\quad 0.0584 = \dfrac{(x)^2}{(0.120)(0.140)^3}$ $\quad x = 0.00439$

Check: Plug the value for x back into the equilibrium expression, and check the value.

$$0.0584 = \frac{(0.00439)^2}{(0.120)(0.140)^3}$$

14.38 At 25°C: **Given:** At equilibrium: $[H_2] = 0.0355M$, $[I_2] = 0.0388M$, and $[HI] = 0.922$ **Find:** K_c

Conceptual Plan: Balanced reaction $\rightarrow$ equilibrium expression $\rightarrow$ K_c

Solution: $K_c = \dfrac{[HI]^2}{[H_2][I_2]} = \dfrac{(0.922)^2}{(0.0355)(0.0388)} = 617$

Check: The value is reasonable since the concentration of products is greater than the concentration of reactants.

At 340°C: **Given:** At equilibrium: $[I_2] = 0.0455$, and $[HI] = 0.387$, $K_c = 9.6$ **Find:** $[H_2]$

Conceptual Plan: Balanced reaction $\rightarrow$ equilibrium expression $\rightarrow$ $[H_2]$

Solution: $K_c = \dfrac{[HI]^2}{[H_2][I_2]}$ $\quad 9.6 = \dfrac{(0.387)^2}{(x)(0.0455)}$ $\quad x = 0.343$

Check: Plug the value for x back into the equilibrium expression, and check the value.

$$9.6 = \frac{(0.387)^2}{(0.343)(0.0455)}$$

At 445°C: **Given:** At equilibrium: $[H_2] = 0.0485M$, $[I_2] = 0.0468$, $K_c = 50.2$ **Find:** $[HI]$

Conceptual Plan: Balanced reaction $\rightarrow$ equilibrium expression $\rightarrow$ $[HI]$

Solution: $K_c = \dfrac{[HI]^2}{[H_2][I_2]}$ $\quad 50.2 = \dfrac{(x)^2}{(0.0485)(0.0468)}$ $\quad x = 0.338$

Check: Plug the value for x back into the equilibrium expression, and check the value.

$$50.2 = \frac{(0.338)^2}{(0.0485)(0.0468)}$$

14.39 **Given:** $P_{NO} = 108$ torr; $P_{Br_2} = 126$ torr, $K_p = 28.4$ **Find:** P_{NOBr}

Conceptual Plan: **torr $\xrightarrow{\frac{1\ atm}{760\ torr}}$ atm and then balanced reation $\rightarrow$ equilibrium expression $\rightarrow$ P_{NOBr}**

Solution: $P_{NO} = 108 \text{ torr} \times \dfrac{1 \text{ atm}}{760 \text{ torr}} = 0.14\underline{2}1 \text{ atm}$ $\quad P_{Br_2} = 126 \text{ torr} \times \dfrac{1 \text{ atm}}{760 \text{ torr}} = 0.16\underline{5}8$

$K_p = \dfrac{P^2_{NOBr}}{P^2_{NO}P_{Br_2}}$ $\quad 28.4 = \dfrac{x^2}{(0.14\underline{2}1)^2(0.16\underline{5}8)}$ $\quad x = 0.308 \text{ atm} = 234 \text{ torr}$

Check: Plug the value for x back into the equilibrium expression, and check the value.

$$28.3 = \frac{(0.308)^2}{(0.14\underline{2}1)^2(0.16\underline{5}8)}$$

14.40 **Given:** $P_{SO_2} = 137$ torr; $P_{Cl_2} = 285$ torr, $K_p = 2.91 \times 10^3$ **Find:** $P_{SO_2Cl_2}$
Conceptual Plan: torr → atm and then balanced reation → equilibrium expression → $P_{SO_2Cl_2}$

$$\frac{1 \text{ atm}}{760 \text{ torr}}$$

Solution: $P_{SO_2} = 137 \text{ torr} \times \dfrac{1 \text{ atm}}{760 \text{ torr}} = 0.18\underline{0}3 \text{ atm}$ $\quad P_{Cl_2} = 285 \text{ torr} \times \dfrac{1 \text{ atm}}{760 \text{ torr}} = 0.37\underline{5}0$

$$K_p = \frac{P_{SO_2}P_{Cl_2}}{P_{SO_2Cl_2}} \qquad 2.91 \times 10^3 = \frac{(0.18\underline{0}3)(0.37\underline{5}0)}{(x)} \qquad x = 2.32 \times 10^{-5} \text{ atm} = 0.0177 \text{ torr}$$

Check: Plug the value for x back into the equilibrium expression, and check the value.

$$2.91 \times 10^3 = \frac{(0.18\underline{0}3)(0.37\underline{5}0)}{(2.32 \times 10^{-5})}$$

14.41 **Given:** $[Fe^{3+}]_{initial} = 1.0 \times 10^{-3}$ M; $[SCN^-]_{initial} = 8.0 \times 10^{-4}$ M; $[FeSCN^{2+}]_{eq} = 1.7 \times 10^{-4}$M **Find:** K_c
Conceptual Plan:
1. Prepare ICE table
2. Calculate concentration change for known value
3. Calculate concentration changes for other reactants/products
4. Determine equilibrium concentration
5. Write the equilibrium expression and determine K_c

Solution: $Fe^{3+}(aq) + SCN^-(aq) \leftrightarrows FeSCN^{3+}(aq)$

	$[Fe^{3+}]$	$[SCN^-]$	$[FeSCN^{3+}]$
I	1.0×10^{-3}	8.0×10^{-4}	0.00
C	-1.7×10^{-4}	-1.7×10^{-4}	$+1.7 \times 10^{-4}$
E	8.3×10^{-4}	6.3×10^{-4}	1.7×10^{-4}

$$K_c = \frac{[FeSCN^{2+}]}{[Fe^{3+}][SCN^-]} = \frac{(1.7 \times 10^{-4})}{(8.3 \times 10^{-4})(6.3 \times 10^{-4})} = 3.3 \times 10^2$$

14.42 **Given:** $[SO_2Cl_2]_{initial} = 0.020$ M; $[Cl_2]_{eq} = 1.2 \times 10^{-2}$M **Find:** K_c
Conceptual Plan:
1. Prepare ICE table
2. Calculate concentration change for known value
3. Calculate concentration changes for other reactants/products
4. Determine equilibrium concentration
5. Write the equilibrium expression and determine K_c

Solution: $SO_2Cl_2(g) \leftrightarrows SO_2(g) + Cl_2(g)$

	$[SO_2Cl_2]$	$[SO_2]$	$[Cl_2]$
I	0.020	0.00	0.00
C	-1.2×10^{-2}	$+1.2 \times 10^{-2}$	$+1.2 \times 10^{-2}$
E	0.0080	1.2×10^{-2}	1.2×10^{-2}

$$K_c = \frac{[SO_2][Cl_2]}{[SO_2Cl_2]} = \frac{(1.2 \times 10^{-2})(1.2 \times 10^{-2})}{(0.0080)} = 0.018$$

14.43 **Given:** 3.67 L flask, 0.763 g H_2 initial, 96.9 g I_2 initial, 90.4 g HI equilibrium **Find:** K_c
Conceptual Plan: g → mol → M and then

$$n = \frac{g}{\text{molar mass}} \qquad M = \frac{n}{V}$$

1. Prepare ICE table
2. Calculate concentration change for known value
3. Calculate concentration changes for other reactants/products
4. Determine equilibrium concentration
5. Write the equilibrium expression and determine K_c

Solution: $0.763 \text{ g } H_2 \times \dfrac{1 \text{ mol } H_2}{2.016 \text{ g } H_2} = 0.37\underline{8}5 \text{ mol } H_2 \quad \dfrac{0.37\underline{8}5 \text{ mol } H_2}{3.67 \text{ L}} = 0.103$ M. This is an initial concentration

$96.9 \text{ g } I_2 \times \dfrac{1 \text{ mol } I_2}{253.8 \text{ g } I_2} = 0.38\underline{1}8 \text{ mol } I_2 \quad \dfrac{0.38\underline{1}8 \text{ mol } I_2}{3.67 \text{ L}} = 0.104$ M. This is an initial concentration

$90.4 \text{ g HI} \times \dfrac{1 \text{ mol HI}}{127.9 \text{ g } I_2} = 0.70\underline{6}8 \text{ mol HI} \quad \dfrac{0.70\underline{6}8 \text{ mol HI}}{3.67 \text{ L}} = 0.193$ M. This is an equilibrium concentration

	$H_2(g)$ +	$I_2(g)$	$\leftrightarrows$ 2 HI(g)
	$[H_2]$	$[I_2]$	[HI]
I	0.103	0.104	0.00
C	-0.0963	-0.0963	+0.193
E	0.0067	0.0077	0.193

Since HI gained 0.193M, then H_2 and I_2 had to lose 0.193/2 = 0.0963M from the stoichiometry of the balanced reaction.

$$K_c = \frac{[HI]^2}{[H_2][I_2]} = \frac{(0.193)^2}{(0.0065)(0.0075)} = 722$$

14.44 **Given:** 5.19 L flask, 26.9 g CO initial, 2.34 g H_2 initial, 8.65 g CH_3OH equilibrium **Find:** K_c
Conceptual Plan: g → mol → M and then

$n = \frac{g}{\text{molar mass}}$ $M = \frac{n}{V}$

1. **Prepare ICE table**
2. **Calculate concentration change for known value**
3. **Calculate concentration changes for other reactants/products**
4. **Determine equilibrium concentration**
5. **Write the equilibrium expression and determine K_c**

Solution: $26.9 \text{ g CO} \times \frac{1 \text{ mol CO}}{28.01 \text{ g CO}} = 0.9604 \text{ mol CO}$ $\frac{0.9604 \text{ mol CO}}{5.19 \text{ L}} = 0.185 \text{ M}$

$2.34 \text{ g } H_2 \times \frac{1 \text{ mol } H_2}{2.016 \text{ g } H_2} = 1.161 \text{ mol } H_2$ $\frac{1.161 \text{ mol } H_2}{5.19 \text{ L}} = 0.224 \text{ M}$

$8.65 \text{ g } CH_3OH \times \frac{1 \text{ mol } CH_3OH}{32.04 \text{ g } CH_3OH} = 0.2700 \text{ mol } CH_3OH$ $\frac{0.2700 \text{ mol } CH_3OH}{5.19 \text{ L}} = 0.0520 \text{ M}$

	CO(g) +	$2 H_2(g)$	$\leftrightarrows CH_3OH(g)$
	[CO]	$[H_2]$	$[CH_3OH]$
I	0.185	0.224	0.00
C	-0.0520	-0.104	+0.0520
E	0.133	0.120	0.0520

$$K_c = \frac{[CH_3OH]}{[CO][H_2]^2} = \frac{(0.0520)}{(0.133)(0.120)^2} = 27.2$$

Since CH_3OH gained 0.0520 M, CO had to lose 0.0520 M since the stoichiometry is 1:1 and H_2 had to lose 0.104 M since the stoichiometry is 2:1.

The Reaction Quotient and Reaction Direction

14.45 **Given:** $K_c = 8.5 \times 10^{-3}$; $[NH_3] = 0.166M$; $[H_2S] = 0.166M$ **Find:** Will solid form or decompose?
Conceptual Plan: Calculate Q → compare Q and K_c
Solution: $Q = [NH_3][H_2S] = (0.166)(0.166) = 0.0276$
$Q = 0.0276$ and $K_c = 8.5 \times 10^{-3}$ so $Q > K_c$ and the reaction will shift to the left, so more solid will form.

14.46 **Given:** $K_p = 2.4 \times 10^{-4}$; $P_{H_2} = 0.112\text{atm}$; $P_{S_2} = 0.055\text{atm}$; $P_{H_2S} = 0.445\text{atm}$ **Find:** Is the reaction at equilibrium?
Conceptual Plan: Calculate Q → compare Q and K_p

Solution: $Q = \frac{P_{H_2}^2 P_{S_2}}{P_{H_2S}^2} = \frac{(0.112)^2(0.055)}{(0.445)^2} = 3.48 \times 10^{-3}$ $Q = 3.48 \times 10^{-3}$ and $K_p = 2.4 \times 10^{-4}$
so $Q > K_p$, the system is not at equilibrium, and the reaction will shift to the left.

14.47 **Given:** 6.55 g Ag_2SO_4, 1.5 L solution, $K_c = 1.1 \times 10^{-5}$ **Find:** Will more solid dissolve?
Conceptual Plan: g Ag2SO$_4$ → mol Ag2SO$_4$ → [Ag2SO$_4$] → $[Ag^+]$,$[SO_4^{-2}]$ → calculate Q and compare to K_c.

$\frac{1 \text{ mol } Ag_2SO_4}{311.81 \text{ g}}$ $[\,] = \frac{\text{mol } Ag_2SO_4}{\text{vol solution}}$ $Q = [Ag^+]^2[SO_4^{2-}]$

Solution: $6.55 \text{ g } Ag_2SO_4 \left(\frac{1 \text{ mol } Ag_2SO_4}{311.81 \text{ g } Ag_2SO_4}\right) = 0.0210 \text{ mol } Ag_2SO_4$

$\frac{0.0210 \text{ mol } Ag_2SO_4}{1.5 \text{ L solution}} = 0.0140 \text{ M } Ag_2SO_4$

$[Ag^+] = 2[Ag_2SO_4] = 2(0.0140 \text{ M}) = 0.0280 \text{ M}$ $[SO_4^{2-}] = [Ag_2SO_4] = 0.0140 \text{ M}$
$Q = [Ag^+]^2[SO_4^{2-}] = (0.0280)^2(0.0140) = 1.1 \times 10^{-5}$

$Q = K_c$ so the system is at equilibrium and is a saturated solution. Therefore, if more solid is added it will not dissolve.

14.48 **Given:** $K_p = 6.7$ at 298 K; 2.25 L flask; $NO_2 = 0.055$ mol; $N_2O_4 = 0.082$ mol **Find:** Is the reaction at equilibrium?
Conceptual Plan: $K_p \rightarrow K_c$ and mol $\rightarrow$ M and then calculate Q and compare to K_c.

$$K_p = K_c(RT)^{\Delta n} \qquad M = \frac{\text{mol}}{\text{V}}$$

Solution: $$K_c = \frac{K_p}{(RT)^{\Delta n}} = \frac{(6.7)}{\left[\left(.0821\frac{\text{L}\cdot\text{atm}}{\text{mol}\cdot\text{K}}\right)(298\text{ K})\right]^{-1}} = 1\underline{6}4$$

$$Q = \frac{[N_2O_4]}{[NO]^2} = \frac{\left(\frac{0.082\text{ mol}}{2.25\text{ L}}\right)}{\left(\frac{0.055\text{ mol}}{2.25\text{ L}}\right)^2} = 61$$

$Q < K_c$, the reaction is not at equilibrium and will shift to the right.

Finding Equilibrium Concentrations from Initial Concentrations and the Equilibrium Constant

14.49 (a) **Given:** [A] = 1.0 M, [B] = 0.0 $K_c = 4.0$; $a = 1$, $b = 1$ **Find:** [A], [B] at equilibrium
Conceptual Plan: Prepare an ICE table, calculate Q, compare Q and K_c, predict the direction of the reaction, represent the change with x, sum the table, determine the equilibrium values, put the equilibrium values in the equilibrium expression, and solve for x. Determine [A] and [B].
Solution: $A(g) \leftrightarrows B(g)$

	[A]	[B]
I	1.0	0.00
C	$-x$	x
E	$1-x$	x

$$Q = \frac{[B]}{[A]} = \frac{0}{1} = 0$$ $Q < K$ therefore, the reaction will proceed to the right by x.

$$K_c = \frac{[B]}{[A]} = \frac{(x)}{(1-x)} = 4.0 \quad x = 0.80$$

$[A] = 1 - 0.80 = 0.20\text{M} \quad [B] = 0.80\text{M}.$

Check: Plug the values into the equilibrium expression: $K_c = \frac{0.80}{0.20} = 4.0.$

(b) **Given:** [A] = 1.0 M, [B] = 0.0 $K_c = 4.0$; $a = 2$, $b = 2$ **Find:** [A], [B] at equilibrium
Conceptual Plan: Prepare an ICE table, calculate Q, compare Q and K_c, predict the direction of the reaction, represent the change with x, sum the table, determine the equilibrium values, put the equilibrium values in the equilibrium expression, and solve for x. Determine [A] and [B].
Solution: $2\,A(g) \leftrightarrows 2\,B(g)$

	[A]	[B]
I	1.0	0.00
C	$-2x$	$2x$
E	$1-2x$	$2x$

$$Q = \frac{[B]^2}{[A]^2} = \frac{0}{1} = 0$$ $Q < K$ therefore, the reaction will proceed to the right by x.

$$K_c = \frac{[B]^2}{[A]^2} = \frac{(2x)^2}{(1-2x)^2} = 4.0 \quad x = 0.3\underline{3}$$

$[A] = 1 - 2(0.3\underline{3}) = 0.3\underline{3} = 0.33\text{M} \quad [B] = 2(0.3\underline{3}) = 0.66 = 0.66\text{M}$

Check: Plug the values into the equilibrium expression: $K_c = \frac{(0.66)^2}{(0.33)^2} = 4.0.$

(c) **Given:** [A] = 1.0 M, [B] = 0.0 K_c = 4.0; a = 1, b = 2 **Find:** [A], [B] at equilibrium
Conceptual Plan: Prepare an ICE table, calculate Q, compare Q and K_c, predict the direction of the reaction, represent the change with x, sum the table, determine the equilibrium values, put the equilibrium values, in the equilibrium expression, and solve for x. Determine [A] and [B].
Solution: $A(g) \leftrightarrows 2\,B(g)$

	[A]	[B]
I	1.0	0.00
C	$-x$	$2x$
E	$1-x$	$2x$

$Q = \dfrac{[B]^2}{[A]} = \dfrac{0}{1} = 0$ $Q < K$ therefore, the reaction will proceed to the right by x.

$K_c = \dfrac{[B]^2}{[A]} = \dfrac{(2x)^2}{(1-x)} = 4.0$ $4x^2 + 4x - 4 = 0$ Solve using the quadratic equation, Appendix I.

$x = -1.62$ or $x = 0.62$, therefore, $x = 0.62$.

[A] $= 1 - 0.62 = 0.38$M [B] $= 2x = 2(0.62) = 1.\underline{2}4$M $= 1.2$M.

Check: Plug the values into the equilibrium expression: $K_c = \dfrac{(1.24)^2}{0.38} = 4.0$.

14.50 (a) **Given:** [A] = 1.0 M, [B] = 1.0, [C] = 0.0 K_c = 5.0; a = 1, b = 1, c = 2 **Find:**[A],[B],[C] at equilibrium
Conceptual Plan: Prepare an ICE table, calculate Q, compare Q and K_c, predict the direction of the reaction, represent the change with x, sum the table, determine the equilibrium values, put the equilibrium values in the equilibrium expression, and solve for x. Determine [A], [B], and [C].
Solution: $A(g) + B(g) \leftrightarrows 2\,C(g)$

	[A]	[B]	[C]
I	1.0	1.0	0.0
C	$-x$	$-x$	$2x$
E	$1-x$	$1-x$	$2x$

$Q = \dfrac{[C]^2}{[A][B]} = \dfrac{0}{(1)(1)} = 0$ $Q < K$ therefore, the reaction will proceed to the right by x.

$K_c = \dfrac{[C]^2}{[A][B]} = \dfrac{(2x)^2}{(1-x)(1-x)} = 5.0$ $x = 0.53$. Solve by taking the square root of both sides.

[A] $=$ [B] $= 1 - 0.53 = 0.47$ M [C] $= 2x = 1.06$M $= 1.1$M.

Check: Plug the values into the equilibrium expression: $K_c = \dfrac{(1.06)^2}{(0.47)(0.47)} = 5.0$.

(b) **Given:** [A] = 1.0 M, [B] = 1.0, [C] = 0.0 K_c = 5.0; a = 1, b = 1, c = 1 **Find:**[A],[B],[C] at equilibrium
Conceptual Plan: Prepare an ICE table, calculate Q, compare Q and K_c, predict the direction of the reaction, represent the change with x, sum the table, determine the equilibrium values, put the equilibrium values in the equilibrium expression, and solve for x. Determine [A], [B], and [C].
Solution: $A(g) + B(g) \leftrightarrows C(g)$

	[A]	[B]	[C]
I	1.0	1.0	0.0
C	$-x$	$-x$	x
E	$1-x$	$1-x$	x

$Q = \dfrac{[C]}{[A][B]} = \dfrac{0}{(1)(1)} = 0$ $Q < K$ therefore, the reaction will proceed to the right by x.

$K_c = \dfrac{[C]}{[A][B]} = \dfrac{(x)}{(1-x)(1-x)} = 5.0$ $5x^2 - 11x + 5 = 0$ Solve by using the quadratic equation.

$x = 1.56$ or $x = 0.64$, therefore, $x = 0.64$.

[A] $=$ [B] $= 1 - 0.64 = 0.36$ M [C] $= x = 0.64$M.

Check: Plug the values into the equilibrium expression: $K_c = \dfrac{(0.64)}{(0.36)(0.36)} = 4.9$.

(c) **Given:** [A] = 1.0 M, [B] = 1.0, [C] = 0.0 $K_c = 5.0$; $a = 2$, $b = 1$, c = 1 **Find:**[A],[B],[C] at equilibrium
Conceptual Plan: Prepare an ICE table, calculate Q, compare Q and K_c, predict the direction of the reaction, represent the change with x, sum the table, determine the equilibrium values, put the equilibrium values in the equilibrium expression, and solve for x. Determine [A], [B], and [C].
Solution: $2\,A(g) + B(g) \leftrightarrows C(g)$

	[A]	[B]	[C]
I	1.0	1.0	0.0
C	$-2x$	$-x$	x
E	$1-2x$	$1-x$	x

$$Q = \frac{[C]}{[A]^2[B]} = \frac{0}{(1)(1)} = 0$$ $Q < K$ therefore, the reaction will proceed to the right by x.

$$K_c = \frac{[C]}{[A]^2[B]} = \frac{(x)}{(1-2x)^2(1-x)} = 5.0$$

$-20x^3 + 40x^2 - 26x + 5.0 = 0$. Solve by using successive approximations or a cubic equation calculator found on the internet.
$x = 0.3396 = 0.34$
[A] = $1 - 2x$ = 0.32M; [B] = $1 - x$ = 0.66M; [C] = x = 0.34M.

Check: Plug the values into the equilibrium expression: $K_c = \frac{(0.34)}{(0.32)^2(0.66)} = 5.0.$

14.51 **Given:** $[N_2O_4]$ = 0.0500 M, $[NO_2]$ = 0.0 $K_c = 0.513$ **Find:** $[N_2O_4]$, $[NO_2]$ at equilibrium
Conceptual Plan: Prepare an ICE table, calculate Q, compare Q and K_c, predict the direction of the reaction, represent the change with x, sum the table, determine the equilibrium values, put the equilibrium values in the equilibrium expression, and solve for x. Determine $[N_2O_4]$ and $[NO_2]$.
Solution:

$N_2O_4(g) \leftrightarrows 2\,NO_2(g)$

	$[N_2O_4]$	$[NO_2]$
I	0.0500	0.00
C	$-x$	$2x$
E	$0.0500 - x$	$2x$

$$Q = \frac{[NO_2]^2}{[N_2O_4]} = \frac{0}{0.0500} = 0$$ $Q < K$ therefore, the reaction will proceed to the right by x.

$$K_c = \frac{[NO_2]^2}{[N_2O_4]} = \frac{(2x)^2(0.0500 - x)}{= 0.513} \qquad 4x^2 + 0.513x - 0.02565 = 0$$

$$\frac{-b \pm \sqrt{b^2 - 4ac}}{2a} = \frac{-0.513 \pm \sqrt{(0.513)^2 - 4(4)(-0.02565)}}{2(4)} = \frac{-0.513 \pm \sqrt{0.6735}}{2(4)}$$

$x = -0.1667$ or $x = 0.0385$, therefore, $x = 0.0385$.
$[N_2O_4] = 0.0500 - 0.03850 = 0.0115$ M $\quad [NO_2] = 2x = 2(0.03850) = 0.0770$ M.

Check: Plug the values into the equilibrium expression: $K_c = \frac{(0.0770)^2}{0.0115} = 0.515.$

14.52 **Given:** [CO] = 0.1500 M, $[Cl_2]$ = 0.175, $[COCl_2]$ = 0.0 $K_c = 255$ **Find:** [CO], $[Cl_2]$, $[COCl_2]$ at equilibrium
Conceptual Plan: Prepare an ICE table, calculate Q, compare Q and K_c, predict the direction of the reaction, represent the change with x, sum the table, determine the equilibrium values, put the equilibrium values in the equilibrium expression, and solve for x. Determine [CO], $[Cl_2]$. and $[COCl_2]$.
Solution:

$CO(g) + Cl_2(g) \leftrightarrows COCl_2(g)$

	[CO]	$[Cl_2]$	$[COCl_2]$
I	0.1500	0.175	0.0
C	$-x$	$-x$	x
E	$0.1500 - x$	$0.175 - x$	x

$$Q = \frac{[COCl_2]}{[CO][Cl_2]} = \frac{0}{(0.1500)(0.175)} = 0$$ $Q < K$ therefore, the reaction will proceed to the right by x.

$$K_c = \frac{[COCl_2]}{[CO][Cl_2]} = \frac{x}{(0.1500 - x)(0.175 - x)} = 255 \qquad 255x^2 - 83.875x + 6.69375 = 0$$

$\dfrac{-b \pm \sqrt{b^2 - 4ac}}{2a} = \dfrac{-(-83.875) \pm \sqrt{(-83.875)^2 - 4(255)(6.69375)}}{2(255)}$

$x = 0.19\underline{2}7$ or $x = 0.13\underline{6}2$, therefore, $x = 0.13\underline{6}2$.

$[CO] = 0.1500 - 0.13\underline{6}2 = 0.01\underline{3}77$ M

$[Cl_2] = 0.175 - 0.13\underline{6}2 = 0.03\underline{8}78$ M

$[COCl_2] = x = 0.13\underline{6}2$ M

Check: Plug the values into the equilibrium expression: $K_c = \dfrac{(0.1362)}{(0.01377)(0.03878)} = 255.$

14.53 **Given:** [CO] = 0.20 M, $[CO_2]$ = 0.0 $K_c = 4.0 \times 10^3$ **Find:** $[CO_2]$ at equilibrium
Conceptual Plan: Prepare an ICE table, calculate *Q*, compare *Q* and K_c, predict the direction of the reaction, represent the change with *x*, sum the table, determine the equilibrium values, put the equilibrium values in the equilibrium expression, and solve for *x*. Determine [CO], $[Cl_2]$, and $[COCl_2]$.
Solution:

$NiO(s) + CO(g) \leftrightharpoons Ni(s) + CO_2(g)$

	[CO]	$[CO_2]$
I	0.20	0.0
C	$-x$	x
E	$0.10 - x$	x

$Q = \dfrac{[CO_2]}{[CO]} = \dfrac{0}{(0.20)} = 0 \quad Q < K$ therefore, the reaction will proceed to the right by x.

$K_c = \dfrac{[CO_2]}{[CO]} = \dfrac{x}{(0.20 - x)} = 4.0 \times 10^3 \quad 4.0 \times 10^3(0.20 - x) = x$

$x = 0.1\underline{9}9$

$[CO_2] = 0.1\underline{9}9$ M

Check: Since the equilibrium constant is so large, the reaction goes essentially to completion, therefore, it is reasonable that the concentration of product is 0.1$\underline{9}$9 M.

14.54 **Given:** [CO] = 0.110M M, $[H_2O]$ = 0. 110M, $[CO_2]$ = 0.0, $[H_2]$ = 0.0 K_c = 102
Find: [CO], $[H_2O]$, $[CO_2]$, $[H_2]$ at equilibrium
Conceptual Plan: Prepare an ICE table, calculate *Q*, compare *Q* and K_c, predict the direction of the reaction, represent the change with *x*, sum the table, determine the equilibrium values, put the equilibrium values in the equilibrium expression, and solve for *x*. Determine [CO], $[Cl_2]$, and $[COCl_2]$.
Solution:

$CO(g) + H_2O(g) \leftrightharpoons CO_2(g) + H_2(g)$

	[CO]	$[H_2O]$	$[CO_2]$	$[H_2]$
I	0.110	0.110	0.0	0.0
C	$-x$	$-x$	x	x
E	$0.110-x$	$0.110 - x$	x	x

$Q = \dfrac{[CO_2][H_2]}{[CO][H_2O]} = \dfrac{0}{(0.110)(0.110)} = 0 \quad Q < K$ therefore, the reaction will proceed to the right by x.

$K_c = \dfrac{[CO_2][H_2]}{[CO][H_2O]} = \dfrac{(x)(x)}{(0.110 - x)(0.110 - x)} = 102$

$\sqrt{\dfrac{(x)(x)}{(0.110 - x)(0.110 - x)}} = \sqrt{102}$

$\dfrac{x}{0.110 - x} = \pm 10.\underline{0}995$

$\pm 10.\underline{0}995(0.110 - x) = x$

$x = 0.10\underline{0}09$ or $x = 0.12\underline{2}09$, therefore, $x = 0.10\underline{0}$.

$[CO] = [H_2O] = 0.110 - 0.10\underline{0} = 0.010 = 0.010$ M

$[H_2] = [CO_2] = x = 0.10\underline{0} = 0.100$ M

Check: Plug the values into the equilibrium expression: $K_c = \dfrac{(0.100)(0.100)}{(0.010)(0.010)} = 101.2 = 1.0 \times 10^2$; within 1% of true value, answers are valid.

14.55 **Given:** $[HC_2H_3O_2] = 0.210M$, $[H_3O^+] = 0.0$, $[C_2H_3O_2^-] = 0.0$, $K_c = 1.8 \times 10^{-5}$
Find: $[HC_2H_3O2]$, $[H_2O^+]$, $[C_2H_3O_2^-]$ at equilibrium
Conceptual Plan: Prepare an ICE table, calculate Q, compare Q and K_c, predict the direction of the reaction, represent the change with x, sum the table, determine the equilibrium values, put the equilibrium values in the equilibrium expression, and solve for x. Determine [CO], $[Cl_2]$, and $[COCl_2]$.
Solution:

	$HC_2H_3O_2\ (aq)$	$+H_2O(l)$	$\leftrightarrows$	$H_3O^+\ (aq)$ +	$C_2H_3O_2^-(aq)$
	$[HC_2H_3O_2]$	$[H_2O]$		$[H_3O^+]$	$[C_2H_3O_2^-]$
I	0.210			0.0	0.0
C	$-x$			x	x
E	$0.210-x$			x	x

$$Q = \frac{[H_3O^+][C_2H_3O_2^-]}{[HC_2H_3O_2]} = \frac{0}{(0.210)} = 0 \quad Q < K \text{ therefore, the reaction will proceed to the right by } x.$$

$$K_c = \frac{[H_3O^+][C_2H_3O_2^-]}{[HC_2H_3O_2]} = \frac{(x)(x)}{(0.210 - x)} = 1.8 \times 10^{-5}$$

assume x is small compared to 0.210.

$x^2 = 0.210(1.8 \times 10^{-5})$

$x = 0.00194$ check assumption: $\frac{0.00194}{0.210} \times 100 = 0.92\%$; assumption valid.

$[H_3O^+] = [C_2H_3O_2^-] = 0.00194\ M$

$[HC_2H_3O_2] = 0.210 - 0.00194 = 0.20\underline{8}1 = 0.208\ M$

Check: Plug the values into the equilibrium expression: $K_c = \frac{(0.00194)(0.00194)}{(0.208)} = 1.81 \times 10^{-5}$;
the answer is the same to 2 significant figures with the true value, answers are valid.

14.56 **Given:** $[SO_2Cl_2] = 0.175M$ M, $[SO_2] = 0.0$, $[Cl_2] = 0.0$ $K_c = 2.99 \times 10^{-7}$
Find: $[SO_2Cl_2]$, $[SO_2]$, $[Cl_2]$ at equilibrium
Conceptual Plan: Prepare an ICE table, calculate Q, compare Q and K_c, predict the direction of the reaction, represent the change with x, sum the table, determine the equilibrium values, put the equilibrium values in the equilibrium expression, and solve for x. Determine $[SO_2Cl_2]$, $[SO_2]$, and $[Cl_2]$.
Solution:

	$SO_2Cl_2\ (g)$	$\leftrightarrows$	$SO_2\ (g)$ +	$Cl_2(g)$
	$[SO_2Cl_2]$		$[SO_2]$	$[Cl_2]$
I	0.175		0.0	0.0
C	$-x$		x	x
E	$0.175-x$		x	x

$$Q = \frac{[SO_2][Cl_2]}{[SO_2Cl_2]} = \frac{0}{(0.175)} = 0 \quad Q < K \text{ therefore, the reaction will proceed to the right by } x.$$

$$K_c = \frac{[SO_2][Cl_2]}{[SO_2Cl_2]} = \frac{(x)(x)}{(0.175 - x)} = 2.99 \times 10^{-7}$$

assume x is small compared to 0.175.

$x^2 = 2.99 \times 10^{-7}(0.175)$

$x = 2.2\underline{8}7 \times 10^{-4}$ check assumption: $\frac{2.2\underline{8}7 \times 10^{-4}}{0.175} \times 100 = 0.13\%$; assumption valid.

$[SO_2] = [Cl_2] = x = 2.2\underline{8}7 \times 10^{-4} = 2.29 \times 10^{-4}\ M$

$[SO_2Cl_2] = 0.175 - 2.2\underline{8}7 \times 10^{-4} = 0.174\underline{7} = 0.175\ M$

Check: Plug the values into the equilibrium expression:

$$K_c = \frac{(0.2.2\underline{8}7 \times 10^{-4})(2.2\underline{8}7 \times 10^{-4})}{(0.175)} = 2.996 \times 10^{-7} = 3.00 \times 10^{-7};$$

this is within 0.01×10^{-7} of the true value, therefore, answers are valid.

14.57 **Given:** $P_{Br_2} = 755$ torr, $P_{Cl_2} = 735$ torr, $P_{BrCl} = 0.0$, $K_p = 1.11 \times 10^{-4}$ **Find:** P_{BrCl} at equilibrium
Conceptual Plan: Torr → atm and then: Prepare an ICE table, calculate Q, compare Q and K_c, predict the direction of the reaction, represent the change with x, sum the table, determine the equilibrium values, put the equilibrium values in the equilibrium expression, and solve for x. Determine P_{BrCl}
Solution:

$$P_{Br_2} = 755 \text{ torr} \times \frac{1 \text{ atm}}{760 \text{ torr}} = 0.99\underline{3}4 \text{ atm} \quad P_{Cl_2} = 735 \text{ torr} \times \frac{1 \text{ atm}}{760 \text{ torr}} = 0.96\underline{7}1 \text{ atm}$$

$Br_2(g) + Cl_2(g) \leftrightarrows 2\,BrCl(g)$

	P_{Br_2}	P_{Cl_2}	P_{BrCl}
I	0.9934	0.9671	0.0
C	$-x$	$-x$	$2x$
E	$0.9934-x$	$0.9671-x$	$2x$

$$Q = \frac{P^2_{BrCl}}{P_{Br_2}P_{Cl_2}} = \frac{0}{(0.9934)(0.9671)} = 0 \quad Q < K \text{ therefore, the reaction will proceed to the right by } x.$$

$$K_p = \frac{P^2_{BrCl}}{P_{Br_2}P_{Cl_2}} = \frac{(2x)^2}{(0.9934 - x)(0.9671 - x)} = 1.11 \times 10^{-4}$$

assume x is small compared to 0.9934 and 0.9671.

$$\frac{(2x)^2}{(0.9934)(0.9671)} = 1.11 \times 10^{-4} \quad 4x^2 = 1.066 \times 10^{-4}$$

x = 0.00516 atm = 3.92 torr

$P_{BrCl} = 2x = 2(3.92 \text{ torr}) = 7.84$ torr

Check: Plug the values into the equilibrium expression:

$$K_c = \frac{(2(0.00516\,))^2}{(0.9934 - 0.00516)(0.99671 - 0.00516)} = 1.065 \times 10^{-4} = 1.12 \times 10^{-4};$$

this is within 0.01×10^{-4} of the true value, therefore, answers are valid.

14.58 **Given:** $P_{CO} = 1344$ torr, $P_{H_2O} = 1766$ torr, $P_{CO_2} = 0.0$, $P_{H_2} = 0.0$, $K_p = 0.0611$ **Find:** P_{CO_2}, P_{H_2} at equilibrium
Conceptual Plan: Torr → atm and then prepare an ICE table, calculate Q, compare Q and K_c, predict the direction of the reaction, represent the change with x, sum the table, determine the equilibrium values, put the equilibrium values, in the equilibrium expression, and solve for x. Determine P_{CO_2} and P_{H_2}.

Solution: $P_{CO} = 1344 \text{ torr} \times \frac{1 \text{ atm}}{760 \text{ torr}} = 1.76\underline{8}4 \text{ atm} \quad P_{H_2O} = 1766 \text{ torr} \times \frac{1 \text{ atm}}{760 \text{ torr}} = 2.32\underline{3}7 \text{ atm}$

$CO(g) + H_2O(g) \leftrightarrows CO_2(g) + H_2(g)$

	P_{CO}	P_{H_2O}	P_{CO_2}	P_{H_2}
I	1.76\underline{8}4	2.32\underline{3}7	0.0 0.0	
C	$-x$	$-x$	x	x
E	$1.7684-x$	$2.3237-x$	x	x

$$Q = \frac{P_{CO_2}P_{H_2}}{P_{CO}P_{H_2O}} = \frac{0}{(1.7684)(2.3237)} = 0 \quad Q < K \text{ therefore, the reaction will proceed to the right by } x.$$

$$K_p = \frac{P_{CO_2}P_{H_2}}{P_{CO}P_{H_2O}} = \frac{(x)(x)}{(1.7684 - x)(2.3237 - x)} = 0.0611$$

$$x^2 = (0.0611)(4.1092 - 4.0921x + x^2)$$

$$x^2 = (0.25107 - 0.2500x + 0.0611x^2)$$

$$0.9389x^2 + 0.2500\,x - 0.25107 = 0$$

$$\frac{-b \pm \sqrt{b^2 - 4ac}}{2a} = \frac{-0.2500 \pm \sqrt{(0.2500)^2 - 4(0.9389)(-0.25107)}}{2(0.9389)}$$

$x = 0.4008$ *or* -0.6671 so: $x = 0.4008$

$P_{CO_2} = P_{H_2} = x = 0.4008$ atm = 305 torr

Check: Plug the values into the equilibrium expression:

$$K_p = \frac{(0.4008)^2}{(1.7684 - 0.4008)(2.3237 - 0.4008)} = 0.06108 = 0.061;$$

the answers are the same to two significant figures with the true value, therefore, answers are valid.

14.59 (a) **Given:** [A] = 1.0 M, [B] = [C] = 0.0, K_c = 1.0 **Find:** [A], [B], [C] at equilibrium

Conceptual Plan: Prepare an ICE table, calculate Q, compare Q and K_c, predict the direction of the reaction, represent the change with x, sum the table, determine the equilibrium values, put the equilibrium values in the equilibrium expression, and solve for x. Determine [A], [B], and [C].

Solution:

	$A(g)$ $\leftrightarrows$	$B(g)$ +	$C(g)$
	[A]	[B]	[C]
I	1.0	0.0	0.0
C	$-x$	x	x
E	$1.0-x$	x	x

$$Q = \frac{[B][C]}{[A]} = \frac{0}{(1.0)} = 0$$ $Q < K$ therefore, the reaction will proceed to the right by x.

$$K_c = \frac{[B][C]}{[A]} = \frac{(x)(x)}{(1.0 - x)} = 1.0$$

$$x^2 = 1.0(1.0 - x)$$

$$x^2 + x - 1 = 0$$

$$\frac{-b \pm \sqrt{b^2 - 4ac}}{2a} \quad \frac{-1 \pm \sqrt{1^2 - 4(1)(-1)}}{2(1)}$$

$x = 0.6\underline{1}8$ or $x = -1.618$, therefore, $x = 0.6\underline{1}8$.

$[B] = [C] = x = 0.6\underline{1}8 = 0.62$ M

$[A] = 1.0 - 0.6\underline{1}8 = 0.382 = 0.38$ M

Check: Plug the values into the equilibrium expression:

$$K_c = \frac{(0.62)(0.62)}{(0.38)} = 1.01 = 1.0$$; which is the equilibrium constant, so the values are correct.

(b) **Given:** [A] = 1.0 M, [B] = [C] = 0.0, K_c = 0.010 **Find:** [A], [B], [C] at equilibrium

Conceptual Plan: Prepare an ICE table, calculate Q, compare Q and K_c, predict the direction of the reaction, represent the change with x, sum the table, determine the equilibrium values, put the equilibrium values in the equilibrium expression, and solve for x. Determine [A], [B], and [C].

Solution:

	$A(g)$ $\leftrightarrows$	$B(g)$ +	$C(g)$
	[A]	[B]	[C]
I	1.0	0.0	0.0
C	$-x$	x	x
E	$1.0-x$	x	x

$$Q = \frac{[B][C]}{[A]} = \frac{0}{(1.0)} = 0$$ $Q < K$ therefore, the reaction will proceed to the right by x.

$$K_c = \frac{[B][C]}{[A]} = \frac{(x)(x)}{(1.0 - x)} = 0.010$$

$$x^2 = 0.010(1.0 - x)$$

$$x^2 + 0.010x - 0.010 = 0$$

$$\frac{-b \pm \sqrt{b^2 - 4ac}}{2a} \quad \frac{-(0.010) \pm \sqrt{(0.010)^2 - 4(1)(-0.010)}}{2(1)}$$

$x = 0.09\underline{5}12$ *or* $x = -0.1015$, therefore, $x = 0.09\underline{5}12$.

$[B] = [C] = x = 0.09\underline{5}12 = 0.095$ M

$[A] = 1.0 - 0.09\underline{5}12 = 0.90488 = 0.90$ M

Check: Plug the values into the equilibrium expression:

$$K_c = \frac{(0.095)(0.095)}{(0.90)} = 0.01002 = 0.010$$; which is the equilibrium constant, so the values are correct.

(c) **Given:** [A] = 1.0 M, [B] = [C] = 0.0, $K_c = 1.0 \times 10^{-5}$ **Find:** [A], [B], [C] at equilibrium

Conceptual Plan: Prepare an ICE table, calculate Q, compare Q and K_c, predict the direction of the reaction, represent the change with x, sum the table, determine the equilibrium values, put the equilibrium values in the equilibrium expression, and solve for x. Determine [A], [B], and [C].

Solution:

	$A\ (g) \leftrightarrows$	$B\ (g) +$	$C\ (g)$
	[A]	[B]	[C]
I	1.0	0.0	0.0
C	$-x$	x	x
E	$1.0-x$	x	x

$Q = \dfrac{[B][C]}{[A]} = \dfrac{0}{(1.0)} = 0$ $Q < K$ therefore, the reaction will proceed to the right by x.

$K_c = \dfrac{[B][C]}{[A]} = \dfrac{(x)(x)}{(1.0 - x)} = 1.0 \times 10^{-5}$

assume x is small compared to 1.0.

$x^2 = 1.0(1.0 \times 10^{-5})$

$x = 0.00316$ check assumption: $\dfrac{0.00316}{1.0} \times 100 = 0.32\%$, assumption valid.

$[B] = [C] = x = 0.00316 = 0.0032\ M$

$[A] = 1.0 - 0.00316 = 0.9968 = 1.0\ M$

Check: Plug the values into the equilibrium expression:

$K_c = \dfrac{(0.0032)(0.0032)}{(1.0)} = 1.024 \times 10^{-5} = 1.0 \times 10^{-5}$;

which is the equilibrium constant, so the values are correct

14.60 (a) **Given:** $P_B = 1.0$ atm, $P_A = 0.0$ atm, $K_p = 1.0$ **Find:** P_B, P_A at equilibrium

Conceptual Plan: Prepare an ICE table, calculate Q, compare Q and K_p, predict the direction of the reaction, represent the change with x, sum the table, determine the equilibrium values, put the equilibrium values in the equilibrium expression, and solve for x. Determine P_A, P_B.

Solution:

	$A\ (g) \leftrightarrows$	$2\ B\ (g)$
	P_A	P_B
I	0.0	1.0
C	x	$-2x$
E	x	$1.0 - 2x$

$Q = \dfrac{P_B^2}{P_A} =$ since there is no A, the reaction shifts to the left.

$K_p = \dfrac{P_B^2}{P_A} = \dfrac{(1.0 - 2x)^2}{(x)} = 1.0$

$1.0 - 4x + 4x^2 = 1.0x$

$4x^2 - 5x + 1.0 = 0$

$\dfrac{-b \pm \sqrt{b^2 - 4ac}}{2a}$ $\dfrac{-(-5) \pm \sqrt{(-5)^2 - 4(4)(1)}}{2(4)}$

$x = 0.25$ or $x = 1.0x$, therefore, $x = 0.25$.

$P_A = x = 0.25$ atm; $P_B = 1.0 - 2x = 1.0 - 0.50 = 0.50$ atm

Check: Plug the values into the equilibrium expression:

$K_p = \dfrac{(0.50)^2}{(0.25)} = 1.0$; which is the equilibrium constant.

(b) **Given:** $P_B = 1.0$ atm, $P_A = 0.0$ atm, $K_p = 1.0 \times 10^{-4}$ **Find:** P_B, P_A at equilibrium

Conceptual Plan: Prepare an ICE table, calculate Q, compare Q and K_p, predict the direction of the reaction, represent the change with x, sum the table, determine the equilibrium values, put the equilibrium values in the equilibrium expression, and solve for x. Determine P_A, P_B.

Solution:

	A (g) ⇆	2 B (g)
	P_A	P_B
I	0.0	1.0
C	x	$-2x$
E	x	$1.0 - 2x$

$Q = \dfrac{P_B^2}{P_A}$ = since there is no A, the reaction shifts to the left.

$$K_p = \frac{P_B^2}{P_A} = \frac{(1.0 - 2x)^2}{(x)} = 1.0 \times 10^{-4}$$

$1.0 - 4x + 4x^2 = (1.0 \times 10^{-4})x$

$4x^2 - 4.0001\,x + 1.0 = 0$

$$\frac{-b \pm \sqrt{b^2 - 4ac}}{2a} = \frac{-(-4.0001) \pm \sqrt{(-4.0001)^2 - 4(4)(1)}}{2(4)} = \frac{-(-4.0001) \pm \sqrt{8.0 \times 10^{-4}}}{2(4)}$$

$x = 0.50\underline{3}5$ or $x = 0.49\underline{6}5$, therefore, $x = 0.49\underline{6}5$.

$P_A = x = 0.4\underline{9}65 = 0.50$ atm; $P_B = 1.0 - 2x = 1.0 - 2(0.49\underline{6}5) = 0.007$ atm

Check: Plug the values into the equilibrium expression:

$K_p = \dfrac{(0.007)^2}{(0.4\underline{9}65)} = 9.867 \times 10^{-5} = 1.0 \times 10^{-4}$; which is the equilibrium constant.

(c) **Given:** $P_B = 1.0$ atm, $P_A = 0.0$ atm, $K_p = 1.0 \times 10^5$ **Find:** P_B, P_A at equilibrium
Conceptual Plan: Prepare an ICE table, calculate Q, compare Q and K_p, predict the direction of the reaction, represent the change with x, sum the table, determine the equilibrium values, put the equilibrium values in the equilibrium expression, and solve for x. Determine P_A, P_B.
Solution:

	A (g) ⇆	2 B (g)
	P_A	P_B
I	0.0	1.0
C	x	$-2x$
E	x	$1.0 - 2x$

$Q = \dfrac{P_B^2}{P_A}$ = since there is no A, the reaction shifts to the left.

$$K_p = \frac{P_B^2}{P_A} = \frac{(1.0 - 2x)^2}{(x)} = 1.0 \times 10^5$$

assume $2x$ is small compared to 1.0.

$\dfrac{1.0}{x} = 1.0 \times 10^5$

$x = 1.0 \times 10^{-5}$ check assumption: $\dfrac{2(1.0 \times 10^{-5})}{1.0} \times 100\% = 0.002\,\%$; assumption valid.

$P_A = x = 1.0 \times 10^{-5}$ atm; $P_B = 1.0 - 2x = 1.0 - 2(1.0 \times 10^{-5}) = 0.99998$ atm

Check: Plug the values into the equilibrium expression:

$K_p = \dfrac{(0.99998)^2}{(1.0 \times 10^{-5})} = 9.9996 \times 10^4 = 1.0 \times 10^5$; which is the equilibrium constant.

Le Châtelier's Principle

14.61 **Given:** $CO(g) + Cl_2(g) \leftrightarrows COCl_2(g)$ at equilibrium **Find:** What is the effect of each of the following?

(a) $COCl_2$ is added to the reaction mixture: Adding $COCl_2$ increases the concentration of $COCl_2$ and causes the reaction to shift to the left.

(b) Cl_2 is added to the reaction mixture: Adding Cl_2 increases the concentration of Cl_2 and causes the reaction to shift to the right.

(c) $COCl_2$ is removed from the reaction mixture: Removing the $COCl_2$ decreases the concentration of $COCl_2$ and causes the reaction to shift to the right.

14.62 **Given:** $2BrNO(g) \leftrightarrows 2NO(g) + Br_2(g)$ at equilibrium **Find:** What is the effect of each of the following?

(a) NO is added to the reaction mixture: Adding NO increases the concentration of NO and causes the reaction to shift to the left.

(b) BrNO is added to the reaction mixture: Adding BrNO increases the concentration of BrNO and causes the reaction to shift to the right.

(c) Br_2 is removed from the reaction mixture: Removing Br_2 decreases the concentration of Br_2 and causes the reaction to shift to the right.

14.63 **Given:** $2KClO_3(s) \leftrightarrows 2KCl(s) + 3O_2(g)$ at equilibrium **Find:** What is the effect of each of the following?

(a) O_2 is removed from the reaction mixture: Removing the O_2 decreases the concentration of O_2 and causes the reaction to shift to the right.

(b) KCl is added to the reaction mixture: Adding KCl does not cause any change in the reaction. KCl is a solid and the concentration remains constant so the addition of more solid does not change the equilibrium concentration.

(c) $KClO_3$ is added to the reaction mixture: Adding $KClO_3$ does not cause any change in the reaction. $KClO_3$ is a solid and the concentration remains constant so the addition of more solid does not change the equilibrium concentration.

(d) O_2 is added to the reaction mixture: Adding O_2 increases the concentration of O_2 and causes the reaction to shift to the left.

14.64 **Given:** $C(s) + H_2O(g) \leftrightarrows CO(g) + H_2(g)$ **Find:** What is the effect of each of the following?

(a) C is added to the reaction mixture: Adding C does not cause any change in the reaction. C is a solid and the concentration remains constant so the addition of more solid does not change the equilibrium concentration.

(b) H_2O is condensed and removed from the reaction mixture: Removing the H_2O decreases the concentration of H_2O and causes the reaction to shift to the left.

(c) CO is added to the reaction mixture: Adding CO increases the concentration of CO and causes the reaction to shift to the left.

(d) H_2 is removed from the reaction mixture: Removing the H_2 decreases the concentration of H_2 and causes the reaction to shift to the right.

14.65 (a) **Given:** $I_2(g) \leftrightarrows 2I(g)$ at equilibrium **Find:** the effect of increasing the volume.
The chemical equation has 2 moles of gas on the right and 1 mole of gas on the left. Increasing the volume of the reaction mixture decreases the pressure and causes the reaction to shift to the right (toward the side with more moles of gas particles).

(b) **Given:** $2H_2S(g) \leftrightarrows 2H_2(g) + S_2(g)$ **Find:** the effect of decreasing the volume.
The chemical equation has 3 moles of gas on the right and 2 moles of gas on the left. Decreasing the volume of the reaction mixture increases the pressure and causes the reaction to shift to the left (toward the side with fewer moles of gas particles).

(c) **Given:** $I_2(g) + Cl_2(g) \leftrightarrows 2ICl(g)$ **Find:** the effect of decreasing the volume.
The chemical equation has 2 moles of gas on the right and 2 moles of gas on the left. Decreasing the volume of the reaction mixture increases the pressure but causes no shift in the reaction because the moles are equal on both sides.

14.66 (a) **Given:** $CO(g) + H_2O(g) \leftrightarrows CO_2(g) + H_2(g)$ **Find:** the effect of decreasing the volume.
The chemical equation has 2 moles of gas on the right and 2 moles of gas on the left. Decreasing the

volume of the reaction mixture increases the pressure but causes no shift in the reaction because the moles are equal on both sides.

(b) **Given:** $PCl_3(g) + Cl_2(g) \leftrightarrows PCl_5(g)$ **Find:** the effect of increasing the volume.
The chemical equation has 2 moles of gas on the left and 1 mole of gas on the right. Increasing the volume of the reaction mixture decreases the pressure and causes the reaction to shift to the left (toward the side with more moles of gas particles).

(c) **Given:** $CaCO_3(s) \leftrightarrows CaO(s) + CO_2(g)$ **Find:** the effect of increasing the volume.
The chemical equation has 1 mole of gas on the right and 0 moles of gas on the left. Increasing the volume of the reaction mixture decreases the pressure and causes the reaction to shift to the right (toward the side with more moles of gas particles).

14.67 **Given:** $C(s) + CO_2(g) \leftrightarrows 2CO(g)$ is endothermic. **Find:** the effect of increasing the temperature.
Since the reaction is endothermic we can think of the heat as a reactant: Increasing the temperature is equivalent to adding a reactant causing the reaction to shift to the right. This will cause an increase in the concentration of products and a decrease in the concentration of reactant; therefore, the value of K will increase.
Find: the effect of decreasing the temperature
Since the reaction is endothermic we can think of the heat as a reactant: Decreasing the temperature is equivalent to removing a reactant causing the reaction to shift to the left. This will cause a decrease in the concentration of products and an increase in the concentration of reactants; therefore, the value of K will decrease.

14.68 **Given:** $C_6H_{12}O_6(s) + 6\ O_2(g) \leftrightarrows 6CO_2(g) + 6\ H_2O(g)$ is exothermic.
Find: the effect of increasing the temperature
Since the reaction is exothermic we can think of the heat as a product: Increasing the temperature is equivalent to adding a product causing the reaction to shift to the left. This will cause a decrease in the concentration of products and an increase in the concentration of reactant; therefore, the value of K will decrease.
Find: the effect of decreasing the temperature
Since the reaction is exothermic we can think of the heat as a product: Decreasing the temperature is equivalent to removing a product causing the reaction to shift to the right. This will cause an increase in the concentration of products and a decrease in the concentration of reactants; therefore, the value of K will increase.

14.69 **Given:** $C(s) + 2H_2(g) \leftrightarrows CH_4(g)$ is exothermic. **Find:** Determine which will favor CH_4.

(a) Adding more C to the reaction mixture does NOT favor CH_4. Adding C does not cause any change in the reaction. C is a solid and the concentration remains constant so the addition of more solid does not change the equilibrium concentration.

(b) Adding more H_2 to the reaction mixture favors CH_4. Adding H_2 increases the concentration of H_2 causing the reaction to shift to the right.

(c) Raising the temperature of the reaction mixture does NOT favor CH_4. Since the reaction is exothermic we can think of heat as a product, raising the temperature is equivalent to adding a product causing the reaction to shift to the left.

(d) Lowering the volume of the reaction mixture favors CH_4. The chemical equation has 1 mole of gas on the right and 2 moles of gas on the left. Decreasing the volume of the reaction mixture increases the pressure and causes the reaction to shift to the right (toward the side with fewer moles of gas particles).

(e) Adding a catalyst to the reaction mixture does NOT favor CH_4. A catalyst added to the reaction mixture only speeds up the reaction, it does not change the equilibrium concentration.

(f) Adding neon gas to the reaction mixture does NOT favor CH_4. Adding an inert gas to a reaction mixture at a fixed volume has no effect on the equilibrium.

14.70 **Given:** $C(s) + H_2O(g) \leftrightarrows CO(g) + H_2(g)$ is endothermic. **Find:** Determine which will favor H_2.

(a) Adding more C to the reaction mixture does NOT favor H_2. Adding C does not cause any change in the reaction. C is a solid and the concentration remains constant so the addition of more solid does not change the equilibrium concentration.

(b) Adding more H_2O to the reaction mixture favors H_2. Adding H_2O increases the concentration and causes the reaction to shift to the right.

(c) Raising the temperature of the reaction mixture favors H_2. Since the reaction is endothermic we can think of heat as a reactant: Raising the temperature is equivalent to adding a reactant causing the reaction to shift to the right.

(d) Increasing the volume of the reaction mixture favors H_2. The chemical equation has 2 moles of gas on the right and 1 mole of gas on the left. Increasing the volume of the reaction mixture decreases the pressure and causes the reaction to shift to the right (toward the side with more moles of gas particles).

(e) Adding a catalyst to the reaction mixture does NOT favor H_2. A catalyst added to the reaction mixture only speeds up the reaction, it does not change the equilibrium concentration.

(f) Adding an inert gas to the reaction mixture does NOT favor H_2. Adding an inert gas to a reaction mixture at a fixed volume has no effect on the equilibrium.

Cumulative Problems

14.71 (a) To find the value of K for the new equation, combine the two given equations to yield the new equation. Reverse equation 1, and use $1/K_1$ and then add to equation 2. To find K for equation 3 use $(1/K_1)(K_2)$.

$$\begin{array}{llll} HbO_2(aq) & \leftrightarrows & \cancel{Hb(aq)} + O_2(aq) & K_1 = 1/1.8 \\ \cancel{Hb(aq)} + CO(aq) & \leftrightarrows & HbCO(aq) & K_2 = 306 \\ \hline HbO_2(aq) + CO(aq) & \leftrightarrows & HbCO(aq) + O_2(aq) & K_3 = K_1K_2 = (1/1.8)(306) = 170 \end{array}$$

(b) **Given:** O_2 = 20%, CO = 0.10% **Find:** The ratio $\dfrac{[HbCO]}{[HbO_2]}$

Conceptual Plan: Determine the equilibrium expression and then determine $\dfrac{[HbCO]}{[HbO_2]}$

Solution: $K = \dfrac{[HbCO][O_2]}{[HbO_2][CO]}$ $\quad 170 = \dfrac{[HbCO](20.0)}{[HbO_2](0.10)}$ $\quad \dfrac{[HbCO]}{[HbO_2]} = 170\left(\dfrac{0.10}{20.0}\right) = \dfrac{0.85}{1.0}$

Since the ratio is almost 1:1, 0.10% CO will replace about 50% of the O_2 in the blood. The CO blocks the uptake of O_2 by the blood and is therefore highly toxic.

14.72 **Given:** P = 1 atm, T = 298 K, N_2 = 78%, O_2 = 21%, $K_p = 4.1 \times 10^{-31}$ **Find:** [NO] in molecules/cm^3

Conceptual Plan:

%vol $\rightarrow n \rightarrow$ M and then $K_p \rightarrow K_c$ and then prepare an ICE table, represent the change with x, sum the table, determine the equilibrium values, put the equilibrium values in the equilibrium expression, and solve for x. Determine [NO] in mol/L $\rightarrow$ molecules/cm^3.

$PV = nRT \qquad \dfrac{n}{1\text{ L air}} \qquad K_p = K_c(RT)^{\Delta n} \qquad \dfrac{6.022 \times 10^{23}\text{ molecules}}{\text{mole}}\ \dfrac{1\text{ L}}{1000\text{ mL}}\ \dfrac{\text{mL}}{\text{cm}^3}$

Solution: Assume 1 L of air.

$$n_{N_2} = \frac{(1\text{ atm})(0.78\text{ L})}{\left(0.0821\dfrac{\text{L}\cdot\text{atm}}{\text{mol}\cdot\text{K}}\right)(298\text{ K})} = 0.03\underline{1}88\text{ mol} \qquad n_{O_2} = \frac{(1\text{ atm})(0.21\text{ L})}{\left(0.0821\dfrac{\text{L}\cdot\text{atm}}{\text{mol}\cdot\text{K}}\right)(298\text{ K})} = 0.008\underline{5}8\text{ mol}$$

$[N_2] = 0.03\underline{1}88$ mol/L $\quad [O_2] = 0.008\underline{5}8$ mol/L

$$K_p = K_c(RT)^{\Delta n} \quad K_c = \frac{K_p}{(RT)^{\Delta n}} = \frac{4.1 \times 10^{-31}}{\left((0.0821\dfrac{\text{L}\cdot\text{atm}}{\text{mol}\cdot\text{K}})(298\text{K})\right)^0} = 4.1 \times 10^{-31}$$

	$N_2(g)$	$+O_2(g)$ $\leftrightarrows$	$2\,NO(g)$
	$[N_2]$	$[O_2]$	[NO]
I	$0.03\underline{1}9$	$0.008\underline{5}8$	0.0
C	$-x$	$-x$	$2x$
E	$0.03\underline{1}9-x$	$0.008\underline{5}8-x$	$2x$

The reaction will proceed to the right by x.

$$K_C = \frac{[NO]^2}{[N_2][O_2]} = \frac{(2x)^2}{(0.0319 - x)(0.00858 - x)} = 4.1 \times 10^{-31}$$

Assume x is small compared to 0.0085 and to 0.0319.

$x = 5.29 \times 10^{-18}$ check assumption: $\frac{5.29 \times 10^{-18}}{0.00858} \times 100\% = 6.2 \times 10^{-14}\%$

$[NO] = 2x = 2(5.29 \times 10^{-18}) = 1.06 \times 10^{-17}$ M

$$1.06 \times 10^{-17} \frac{\text{mol}}{\text{L}} \times \frac{6.022 \times 10^{23} \text{ molecules}}{\text{mol}} \times \frac{\text{L}}{1000 \text{ mL}} \times \frac{\text{mL}}{\text{cm}^3} = 6.38 \times 10^3 \frac{\text{molecules}}{\text{cm}^3}$$

$$= 6.4 \times 10^3 \frac{\text{molecules}}{\text{cm}^3}$$

Check: The answer is reasonable since the reaction has a small equilibrium constant so you would not expect to produce much product.
The reaction to produce NO is endothermic, so we can think of heat as a reactant. Therefore, raising the temperature (as in an automobile engine) shifts the reaction to the right, producing more NO.

14.73 (a) **Given:** 4.45 g CO_2, 10.0-L, 1200 K, 2.00 g C, $K_p = 5.78$ **Find:** Total pressure

Conceptual Plan: g CO_2 → mol CO_2 and g C → mol C and then determine Limiting Reactant

$\frac{1 \text{ mol } CO_2}{44.01 \text{ g } CO_2}$ $\frac{1 \text{ mol C}}{12.01 \text{ g C}}$

and then mol CO_2 → P CO_2. Prepare an ICE table, represent the change with x, sum the table, determine the equilibrium values, put the equilibrium values in the equilibrium expression, and solve for x.

$PV = nRT$

Solution: $CO_2(g) + C(s) \leftrightarrows 2\,CO(g)$

$$4.45 \text{ g } CO_2 \times \frac{1 \text{ mol}}{44.01 \text{ g } CO_2} = 0.1011 \text{ mol } CO_2 \quad 2.00 \text{ g C} \times \frac{1 \text{ mol}}{12.01 \text{ g C}} = 0.1665 \text{ mol C}$$

Since the stoichiometry is 1:1, the CO_2 is the limiting reactant.

$$P_{CO_2} = \frac{(0.1011 \text{ mol})\left(\frac{0.0821 \text{ L atm}}{\text{mol K}}\right)(1200 \text{ K})}{10.0 \text{ L}} = 0.9960 \text{ atm}$$

	$CO_2(g) + C(s)$	$\leftrightarrows$	$2\,CO(g)$
	P_{CO_2}		P_{CO}
I	0.996		0.0
C	$-x$		$2x$
E	$0.996 - x$		$2x$

The reaction will proceed to the right by x.

$$K_p = \frac{P^2_{CO}}{P_{CO_2}} = \frac{(2x)^2}{(0.996 - x)} = 5.78.$$ Solve using the quadratic equation, found in Appendix I.

$x = 0.678$ atm

$P_{CO_2} = 0.996 \text{ atm} - 0.678 \text{ atm} = 0.318 \text{ atm}$ $P_{CO} = 2(0.678 \text{ atm}) = 1.356 \text{ atm}$

P total = 1.67 atm

Check: Plug the values for the partial pressure into the equilibrium expression. $\frac{(1.356)^2}{0.318} = 5.78$ which is the value of the equilibrium constant.

(b) **Given:** 4.45 g CO_2, 10.0-L, 1200 K, 0.50 g C, $K_p = 5.78$ **Find:** Total pressure

Conceptual Plan: g CO_2 → mol CO_2 and g C → mol C and then determine Limiting Reactant

$\frac{1 \text{ mol } CO_2}{44.01 \text{ g } CO_2}$ $\frac{1 \text{ mol C}}{12.01 \text{ g C}}$

and then mol CO_2 → P_{CO_2}, and mol C → mol CO → P_{CO}

$PV = nRT$ $PV = nRT$

Solution: $CO_2(g) + C(s) \leftrightarrows 2\,CO(g)$

$$4.45 \text{ g } CO_2 \times \frac{1 \text{ mol}}{44.01 \text{ g } CO_2} = 0.1011 \text{ mol } CO_2 \quad 0.50 \text{ g C} \times \frac{1 \text{ mol}}{12.01 \text{ g C}} = 0.0416 \text{ mol C}$$

Since the stoichiometry is 1:1, the C is the limiting reactant; therefore, the moles of CO formed will be determined from the reaction, not the equilibrium.

$$0.0416\ \text{mol C} \times \frac{2\ \text{mol CO}}{1\ \text{mol C}} = 0.0.832\ \text{mol CO}$$

	$CO_2(g)$	$+ C(s)$	$\leftrightarrows 2\,CO(g)$
I	0.1011	0.0416	0.0
C	- 0.0416	-0.0416	2(0.0416)
E	0.0595	0	0.0832

$$P_{CO_2} = \frac{(0.0595\ \text{mol})\left(\frac{0.0821\ \text{L atm}}{\text{mol}\ K}\right)(1200\ \text{K})}{10.0\ \text{L}} = 0.586\ \text{atm}$$

$$P_{CO} = \frac{(0.0832\ \text{mol})\left(\frac{0.0821\ \text{L atm}}{\text{mol K}}\right)(1200\ \text{K})}{10.0\ \text{L}} = 0.820\ \text{atm}$$

$P_{total} = 0.586 + 0.820 = 1.406 = 1.41$ atm

Check: The pressure is less than the equilibrium pressure which is reasonable since the C was the limiting reactant.

14.74 **Given:** At equilibrium: 0.13 mol H_2, 0.13 mol CO, 0.43 mol H_2O, then react all H_2O.
Find: CO at new equilibrium
Conceptual Plan: equilibrium values → K_c, and then new value of H_2O. Prepare an ICE table, represent the change with x, sum the table, determine the equilibrium values, put the equilibrium values in the equilibrium expression, and solve for x.
Solution: $H_2O(g) + C(s) \leftrightarrows H_2(g) + CO(g)$

E 0.43 0.13 0.13 $K_c = \frac{[H_2][CO]}{[H_2O]} = \frac{(0.13)(0.13)}{(0.43)} = 0.0393$

$2\,H_2(g) + O_2(g) \rightarrow 2\,H_2O(g)$ So, 0.13 mol H_2 produces 0.13 mol H_2O, this gives new initial conditions for the equilibrium.

	$H_2O(g) + C(s)$	$\leftrightarrows H_2(g)$	$+ CO(g)$
I	0.56	0	0.13
C	$-x$	$+x$	$+x$
E	$0.56-x$	x	$0.13+x$

$$K_c = \frac{[H_2][CO]}{[H_2O]} = \frac{(x)(0.13 + x)}{(0.56 - x)} = 0.0393 \quad x = 0.086$$

[CO] = 0.13 + 0.086 = 0.216 = 0.22 therefore, 0.22 mol CO. Solve using the quadratic equation, Appendix I.

Check: Determine equilibrium concentration and plug into the equilibrium expression.

$K_c = \frac{[H_2][CO]}{[H_2O]} = \frac{(0.086)(0.22)}{(0.47)} = 0.040$. This is within 0.001 of the equilibrium value so the answer is reasonable.

14.75 **Given:** $V = 10.0$ L, $T = 650$K, 1.0 g MgO, $P_{CO_2} = 0.0260$ atm, $K_p = 0.0260$
Find: mass $MgCO_3$ when volume is 0.100 L
Conceptual Plan: P (10.0L) → P(0.100L). Prepare an ICE table, represent the change with x, sum the table, determine the equilibrium value, put the equilibrium values in the equilibrium expression, and solve for x. Then determine moles CO_2, the limiting reactant, and the mass of $MgCO_3$ formed.

$P_1V_1 = P_2V_2 \quad PV = nRT$

$P_1V_1 = P_2V_2 \quad (0.0260\ \text{atm})(10.0\ \text{L}) = (x)(0.100\ \text{L}) \quad x = 2.60$ atm

	$MgCO_3(s) \leftrightarrows MgO(s) +$	$CO_2(g)$
I		2.60
C		$-x$
E		$2.60 - x$

$K_p = P_{CO_2} = 0.260 = 2.60 - x \quad x = 2.579$ atm

$$n_{CO_2} = \frac{(2.579 \cancel{atm})10.0 \cancel{L}}{\left(\frac{0.0821 \cancel{L\,atm}}{mol \cancel{K}}\right)(650 \cancel{K})} = 0.00483 \text{ mol } CO_2 \quad 1.0 \cancel{g\,MgO} \times \frac{1 \text{ mol}}{40.30 \cancel{g\,MgO}} = 0.0248 \text{ mol MgO}$$

Therefore, CO_2 is the limiting reactant and produces 0.00483 mol $MgCO_3$.

$$0.00483 \cancel{mol\,MgCO_3} \times \frac{84.31 \text{ g } MgCO_3}{1 \cancel{mol\,MgCO_3}} = 0.407 \text{ g } MgCO_3$$

14.76 **Given:** At equilibrium: $P_{I_2} = 0.21$ atm, $P_I = 0.23$ atm.
Find: P of each gas when the volume is compressed to half the initial volume
Conceptual Plan: P at equilibrium to equilibrium constant, determine P at new volume ($P_1V_1=P_2V_2$), prepare an ICE table, represent the change with x, sum the table, determine the equilibrium value, put the equilibrium values in the equilibrium expression, and solve for x.

Solution: $I_2(g) \leftrightarrows 2\,I(g)$ $K_p = \frac{P_I^2}{P_{I_2}} = \frac{(0.23)^2}{(0.21)} = 0.252$

$P_1V_1 = P_2V_2$ For I_2: (0.21 atm)(1) = (x atm)(0.5) $x = 0.42$ atm
For I: (0.23 atm)(1) = (y atm)(0.5) $y = 0.46$ atm

	$I_2(g)$	$\leftrightarrows 2\,I(g)$
I	0.42	0.46
C	$+x$	$-2x$
E	$0.42+x$	$0.46-2x$

$Q = \frac{(0.46)^2}{(0.42)} = 0.50$ Q > K so the reaction shifts to the left.

$K_p = \frac{(0.46 - 2x)^2}{(0.42 + x)} = 0.252$ $x = 0.0567$. Solve using the quadratic equation, Appendix I.

$P_{(I_2)} = 0.42 + 0.057 = 0.477 = 0.48$ atm
$P_{(I)} = 0.46 - 2(0.057) = 0.345 = 0.35$ atm

Check: Plug the equilibrium values into the equilibrium expression: $K_p = \frac{(0.35)^2}{(0.48)} = 0.255 = 0.26$.
The value is within 1 significant figure of the original K_p so the answer is reasonable.

14.77 **Given:** $C_2H_4(g) + Cl_2(g) \leftrightarrows C_2H_4Cl_2v$ is exothermic **Find:** Which of the following will maximize $C_2H_4Cl_2$?

(a) Increasing the reaction volume will not maximize $C_2H_4Cl_2$. The chemical equation has 1 mole of gas on the right and 2 moles of gas on the left. Increasing the volume of the reaction mixture decreases the pressure and causes the reaction to shift to the left (toward the side with more moles of gas particles).

(b) Removing $C_2H_4Cl_2$ as it forms will maximize $C_2H_4Cl_2$. Removing the $C_2H_4Cl_2$ will decrease the concentration of $C_2H_4Cl_2$ and will cause the reaction to shift to the right, producing more $C_2H_4Cl_2$.

(c) Lowering the reaction temperature will maximize $C_2H_4Cl_2$. The reaction is exothermic so we can think of heat as a product. Lowering the temperature will cause the reaction to shift to the right, producing more $C_2H_4Cl_2$.

(d) Adding Cl_2 will maximize $C_2H_4Cl_2$. Adding Cl_2 increases the concentration of Cl_2 so the reaction shifts to the right, which will produce more $C_2H_4Cl_2$.

14.78 **Given:** $C_2H_4(g) + I_2(g) \leftrightarrows C_2H_4I_2(g)$ is endothermic **Find:** Which of the following will maximize $C_2H_4I_2$?

(a) Decreasing the reaction volume will maximize $C_2H_4I_2$. The chemical equation has 1 mole of gas on the right and 2 moles of gas on the left. Decreasing the volume of the reaction mixture increases the pressure and causes the reaction to shift to the right (toward the side with fewer moles of gas particles).

(b) Removing I_2 from the reaction mixture will not maximize $C_2H_4I_2$. Removing I_2 decreases the concentration of I_2 and the reaction will shift to the left to produce more I_2.

(c) Raising the temperature of the reaction will maximize $C_2H_4I_2$. The reaction is endothermic so we can think of heat as a reactant. Raising the temperature will cause the reaction to shift to the right, producing more $C_2H_4I_2$.

(d) Adding C_2H_4 to the reaction mixture will maximize $C_2H_4I_2$. Adding C_2H_4 will increase the concentration of C_2H_4 and cause the reaction to shift to the right to produce more $C_2H_4I_2$.

14.79 **Given:** Reaction 1 at equilibrium: $P_{H_2} = 0.958$ atm; $P_{I_2} = 0.877$ atm; $P_{HI} = 0.0200$ atm: reaction 2: $P_{H_2} = P_{I_2} = 0.621$ atm; $P_{HI} = 0.101$ atm **Find:** Is reaction 2 at equilibrium? If not, what is the P_{HI} at equilibrium?
Conceptual Plan: Use equilibrium partial pressures to determine K_p. Use K_p to determine if reaction 2 is at equilibrium. Prepare an ICE table, calculate Q, compare Q and K_p, predict the direction of the reaction, represent the change with x, sum the table, determine the equilibrium values, put the equilibrium values in the equilibrium expression, and solve for x. Determine P_{HI}.

Solution: $H_2(g) + I_2(g) \leftrightharpoons 2\,HI(g)$

	P_{H_2}	P_{I_2}	P_{HI}
Reaction 1:	0.958	0.877	0.020

$$K_p = \frac{P_{HI}^2}{P_{H_2}P_{I_2}} = \frac{(0.020)^2}{(0.958)(0.877)} = 4.7\underline{6}10 \times 10^{-4}$$

$$Q = \frac{P_{HI}^2}{P_{H_2}P_{I_2}} = \frac{0.101^2}{(0.621)(0.621)} = 0.0264: Q > K \text{ so the reaction shifts to the left.}$$

	$H_2(g)$ +	$I_2(g)$	$\leftrightharpoons 2\,HI(g)$
Reaction 2:	P_{H_2}	P_{I_2}	P_{HI}
I	0.621	0.621	0.101
C	x	x	$-2x$
E	$0.621+x$	$0.621+x$	$0.101 - 2x$

$$K_p = \frac{P_{HI}^2}{P_{H_2}P_{I_2}} = \frac{(0.101 - x)^2}{(0.621 + x)(0.621 + x)} = 4.7\underline{6}10 \times 10^{-4}$$

$$\sqrt{\frac{(0.101 - 2x)^2}{(0.621 + x)(0.621 + x)}} = \sqrt{4.7\underline{6}10 \times 10^{-4}}$$

$$\frac{(0.101 - 2x)}{(0.621 + x)} = 2.1\underline{8}2 \times 10^{-2}$$

$x = 0.04325 = 0.0433$

$P_{H_2} = P_{I_2} = 0.621 + x = 0.621 + 0.0433 = 0.664$ atm;

$P_{HI} = 0.101 - 2x = 0.101 - 2(0.0433) = 0.0144$ atm

Check: Plug the values into the equilibrium expression:

$$K_p = \frac{(0.0144)^2}{(0.664)} = 4.703 \times 10^{-4} = 4.70 \times 10^{-4}$$; this value is close to the original equilbirium constant.

14.80 **Given:** Reaction 1 initial: $H_2S = 0.500$ M; $SO_2 = 0.500$M; H_2O at equilibrium $= 0.0011$ M: reaction 2: $H_2S = 0.250$ M; $SO_2 = 0.325$M; **Find:** $[H_2O]$ at equilibrium in reaction 2
Conceptual Plan: Prepare an ICE table. Determine the equilibrium concentrations in reaction 1 and determine K_c. Use K_c to determine the equilibrium concentrations for reaction 2. Prepare an ICE, calculate Q, compare Q and K_c, predict the direction of the reaction, represent the change with x, sum the table, determine the equilibrium values, put the equilibrium values in the equilibrium expression, and solve for x. Determine $[H_2O]$.

Solution: $2\,H_2S(g) + SO_2(g) \leftrightharpoons 3\,S(s) + 2\,H_2O(g)$

Reaction 1:	$[H_2S]$	$[SO_2]$	$[S]$	$[H_2O]$
I	0.500	0.500	constant	0
C	$-2x$	$-x$		$2x$
E	$0.500-2x$	$0.500-x$		0.0011

$2x = 0.0011$, $x = 5.5 \times 10^{-4}$

$[H_2S] = 0.500 - 0.0011 = 0.4989$ $\quad [SO_2] = 0.500 - 5.5 \times 10^{-4} = 0.49945$

$$K_c = \frac{[H_2O]^2}{[H_2S]^2[SO_2]} = \frac{(0.0011)^2}{(0.4989)^2(0.49945)} = 9.7\underline{3}3 \times 10^{-6}$$

$2\ H_2S(g) + SO_2(g) \leftrightharpoons 3\ S(s) + 2\ H_2O(g)$

Reaction 2:	$[H_2S]$	$[SO_2]$	[S]	$[H_2O]$	
I	0.250	0.325	constant		
C	$-2x$	$-x$		$2x$	Reaction shifts to the right.
E	$0.250-2x$	$0.325-x$		$2x$	

$$K_c = \frac{[H_2O]^2}{[H_2S]^2[SO_2]} = \frac{(2x)^2}{(0.250 - 2x)^2(0.325 - x)} = 9.7\underline{3}3 \times 10^{-6}$$

Assume $2x$ and x are small respectively compared to 0.250 and 0.325.

$4x^2 = 1.9\underline{7}70 \times 10^{-7}$

$x^2 = 4.9\underline{4}25 \times 10^{-8}$

$x = 2.2\underline{2}3 \times 10^{-4}$ check assumption: $\dfrac{2.22 \times 10^{-4}}{0.250} = 8.88 \times 10^{-4} \times 100\% = 0.089\%$; assumption valid

$[H_2O] = 2x = 2(2.22 \times 10^{-4}) = 4.44 \times 10^{-4} M$

$[H_2S] = 0.250 - 2(2.22 \times 10^{-4}) = 0.250 M$

$[SO_2] = 0.325 - 2.22 \times 10^{-4} = 0.325 M$

Check: Plug the values into the equilibrium expression:

$K_c = \dfrac{(4.44 \times 10^{-4})^2}{(0.250)^2(0.325)} = 9.71 \times 10^{-6}$; this value is close to the original equilibrium constant.

14.81 **Given:** 200.0 L container; 1.27 kg N_2; 0.310 kg H_2; 725 K; $K_p = 5.3 \times 10^{-5}$ **Find:** mass in g of NH_3 and % yield
Conceptual Plan: $K_p \rightarrow K_c$ **and then kg → g → mol → M and then prepare an ICE table. Represent the change**

$K_p = K_c(RT)^{\Delta n}$ $\quad \dfrac{1000\text{ g}}{\text{kg}} \quad \dfrac{\text{g}}{\text{molar mass}} \quad \dfrac{\text{mol}}{\text{vol}}$

with x, sum the table, determine the equilibrium values, put the equilibrium values in the equilibrium expression, and solve for x. Determine $[NH_3]$. Then M → mol → g and then determine

M x vol $\quad$ mol x molar mass

theoretical yield NH_3 → % yield.

determine limiting reactant $\quad \dfrac{\text{actual yield}}{\text{theoretical yield}}$

Solution: $K_p = K_c(RT)^{\Delta n}$ $\quad K_c = \dfrac{K_p}{(RT)^{\Delta n}} = \dfrac{5.3 \times 10^{-5}}{\left((0.0821 \frac{\text{L} \cdot \text{atm}}{\text{mol} \cdot \text{K}})(725\text{K})\right)^{-2}} = 0.1\underline{8}77$

$$n_{N_2} = 1.27\ \cancel{\text{kg } N_2} \times \frac{1000\ \cancel{\text{g}}}{\cancel{\text{kg}}} \times \frac{1\text{ mol } N_2}{28.00\ \cancel{\text{g } N_2}} = 45.\underline{3}57\text{ mol } N_2 \quad [N_2] = \frac{45.\underline{3}57\text{ mol}}{200.0\text{ L}} = 0.22\underline{6}78$$

$$n_{H_2} = 0.310\ \cancel{\text{kg } H_2} \times \frac{1000\ \cancel{\text{g}}}{\cancel{\text{kg}}} \times \frac{1\text{ mol } H_2}{2.016\ \cancel{\text{g } H_2}} = 15\underline{3}.77\text{ mol } H_2 \quad [H_2] = \frac{15\underline{3}.77\text{ mol}}{200.0\text{ L}} = 0.76\underline{8}85$$

$N_2(g) + 3\ H_2(g) \leftrightharpoons 2\ NH_3(g)$

Reaction 1:	$[N_2]$	$[H_2]$	$[NH_3]$
I	0.22\underline{6}8	0.76\underline{8}9	0.0
C	$-x$	$-3x$	$2x$
E	$0.2268-x$	$0.7689-3x$	$2x$

Reaction shifts to the right.

$$K_c = \frac{[NH_3]^2}{[N_2][H_2]^3} = \frac{(2x)^2}{(0.2268 - x)(0.7689 - 3x)^3} = 0.1877$$

Assume x is small compared to 0.2268 and $3x$ is small compared to 0.7689.

$\dfrac{(2x)^2}{(0.2268)(0.7689)^3} = 0.1877\ x = 0.06956$ $\qquad x = 0.06956$ is the solution to the problem.

check assumptions: $\dfrac{0.06956}{0.2268} \times 100\% = 30.7$ not valid and $\dfrac{3(0.06956)}{0.7689} \times 100\% = 27.1\%$

Use method of successive substitution to solve for x. This yields $x = 0.0461$.
$[NH_3] = 2x = 2(0.0461) = 0.0922M$
Check: Plug the values into the equilibrium expression:

$$K_c = \frac{(0.0922)^2}{(0.2268 - 0.0461)(0.7689 - 3(0.0461))^3} = 0.1876;$$

this value is close to the original equilibrium constant.

$$\text{Determine grams } NH_3\text{: } 0.0922 \frac{\text{mol } NH_3}{\text{L}} \times \frac{200.0 \text{ L}}{} \times \frac{17.02 \text{ g } NH_3}{\text{mol } NH_3} = 313.8 \text{ g} = 3.1 \times 10^2 \text{ g}$$

Determine the theoretical yield: Determine the limiting reactant:

$$1.27 \text{ kg } N_2 \times \frac{1000 \text{ g}}{\text{kg}} \times \frac{1 \text{ mol } N_2}{28.0 \text{ g } N_2} \times \frac{2 \text{ mol } NH_3}{1 \text{ mol } N_2} \times \frac{17.02 \text{ g } NH_3}{\text{mol } NH_3} = 1544 \text{ g } NH_3$$

$$0.310 \text{ kg } H_2 \times \frac{1000 \text{ g}}{\text{kg}} \times \frac{1 \text{ mol } H_2}{2.016 \text{ g } H_2} \times \frac{2 \text{ mol } NH_3}{3 \text{ mol } H_2} \times \frac{17.02 \text{ g } NH_3}{\text{mol } NH_3} = 1745 \text{ g } NH_3$$

N_2 produces the least amount of NH_3 therefore, it is the limiting reactant and the theoretical yield is 1.54×10^3 g NH_3.

$$\% \text{ yield} = \frac{3.1 \times 10^2 \text{ g}}{1.54 \times 10^3 \text{ g}} \times 100 = 20.\%$$

14.82 **Given:** $V = 85.0$ L, 22.3 kg CH_4, 55.4 kg CO_2, $T = 825$ K, $K_p = 4.5 \times 10^2$ **Find:** g H_2 at equilibrium
Conceptual Plan: kg $\rightarrow$ g $\rightarrow$ mol $\rightarrow$ P and then prepare an ICE table. Represent the change

$\frac{1000 \text{ g}}{\text{kg}}$ $\quad \frac{\text{g}}{\text{molar mass}}$ $\quad PV = nRT$

with x, sum the table, determine the equilibrium values, put the equilibrium values in the equilibrium expression, and solve for x. Determine P_{H_2}. Then $P \rightarrow$ mol $\rightarrow$ g and then determine

$PV = nRT$ $\quad$ mol x molar mass

theoretical yield H_2 $\rightarrow$ % yield.

determine limiting reactant $\quad \frac{\text{actual yield}}{\text{theoretical yield}}$

Solution:

$$n_{CH_4} = 23.3 \text{ kg} \times \frac{1000 \text{ g}}{\text{kg}} \times \frac{1 \text{ mol}}{16.0 \text{ g}} = 1456.2 \text{ mol}$$

$$P_{CH_4} = \frac{nRT}{V} = \frac{(1456 \text{ mol})\left(0.0821 \frac{\text{L} \cdot \text{atm}}{\text{mol} \cdot \text{K}}\right)(825 \text{ K})}{85.0 \text{ L}} = 1160 \text{ atm}$$

$$n_{CO_2} = 55.4 \text{ kg} \times \frac{1000 \text{ g}}{\text{kg}} \times \frac{1 \text{ mol}}{44.0 \text{ g}} = 1259 \text{ mol}$$

$$P_{CO_2} = \frac{nRT}{V} = \frac{(1259 \text{ mol})\left(0.0821 \frac{\text{L} \cdot \text{atm}}{\text{mol} \cdot \text{K}}\right)(825 \text{ K})}{85.0 \text{ L}} = 1003 \text{ atm}$$

	$CH_4(g)$ +	$CO_2(g)$ $\leftrightharpoons$	2 $CO(g)$ +	2 $H_2(g)$
	P_{CH_4}	P_{CO_2}	P_{CO}	P_{H_2}
I	1160	1003	0.00	0.00
C	$-x$	$-x$	$2x$	$2x$
E	$1160-x$	$1003-x$	$2x$	$2x$

$$K_p = \frac{P_{CO}^2 P_{H_2}}{P_{CH_2} P_{CO_2}} = \frac{(2x)^2(2x)^2}{(1160 - x)(1003 - x)} = 4.5 \times 10^2$$

Assume x is small compared to 1003 and 1160.

$x^4 = 3.27 \times 10^7 \quad x = 75.6$

check assumptions: $\frac{75.6}{1003} \times 100\% = 7.54\%$ and $\frac{75.6}{1160} \times 100\% = 6.52\%$ assumptions not valid

Use method of successive substitutions which yields
$x = 73.0$.

Check: Plug into equilibrium expression:

$$K_p = \frac{P_{CO}^2 P_{H_2}}{P_{CH_4} P_{CO_2}} = \frac{(2(73.0))^2(2(73.0))^2}{(1160 - 73.0)(1003 - 73.0)} = 4.49 \times 10^2 = 4.5 \times 10^2$$; which is the equilibrium constant.

Determine the grams of H_2.

$$P_{H_2} = 2(73.0) = 146 \text{ atm} \quad n_{H_2} = \frac{PV}{RT} = \frac{(146 \text{ atm})(85.0 \text{ L})}{\left(0.0821 \frac{\text{L} \cdot \text{atm}}{\text{mol} \cdot \text{K}}\right)(825 \text{ K})} = 18\underline{3}.2 \text{ mol}$$

$$18\underline{3}.2 \text{ mol} \times \frac{2.016 \text{ g } H_2}{\text{mol}} = 369.4 \text{ g} = 369 \text{ g } H_2$$

Determine % yield

$$1456 \text{ mol } CH_4 \times \frac{2 \text{ mol } H_2}{\text{mol } CH_4} = 2912 \text{ mol } H_2$$

$$1259 \text{ mol } CO_2 \times \frac{2 \text{ mol } H_2}{\text{mol } CO_2} = 2518 \text{ mol } H_2$$

CO_2 is limiting reactant.

$$\frac{18\underline{3}.2 \text{ mol } H_2}{2518 \text{ mol } H_2} \times 100 = 7.28\% \text{ yield}$$

14.83 **Given:** At equilibrium: $P_{CO} = 0.30$ atm; $P_{Cl_2} = 0.10$ atm; $P_{COCl_2} = 0.60$ atm, add 0.40 atm Cl_2
Find: P_{CO} when system returns to equilibrium
Conceptual Plan: Use equilibrium partial pressures to determine K_p. For the new conditions prepare an ICE table, represent the change with x, sum the table, determine the equilibrium values, put the equilibrium values in the equilibrium expression, and solve for x. Determine P_{CO}.

Solution: $CO(g) + Cl_2(g) \leftrightarrows COCl_2(g)$

Condition 1:	P_{CO}	P_{Cl_2}	P_{COCl_2}
	0.30	0.10	0.60

$$K_p = \frac{P_{COCl_2}}{P_{CO}P_{Cl_2}} = \frac{(0.60)}{(0.30)(0.10)} = 20.$$

$CO(g) + Cl_2(g) \leftrightarrows COCl_2(g)$

Condition 2:	P_{CO}	P_{Cl_2}	P_{COCl_2}
I	0.30	0.10+0.40	0.60
C	$-x$	$-x$	$+x$
E	$0.30-x$	$0.50-x$	$0.60 + x$

Reaction shifts to the right because the concentration of Cl_2 was increased.

$$K_p = \frac{P_{COCl_2}}{P_{CO}P_{Cl_2}} = \frac{(0.60 + x)}{(0.30 - x)(0.50 - x)} = 20$$

$$20x^2 - 17x + 2.4 = 0$$

$$\frac{-b \pm \sqrt{b^2 - 4ac}}{2a} = \frac{-(-17) \pm \sqrt{(-17)^2 - 4(20)(2.4)}}{2(20)}$$

$x = 0.67$ or 0.18 So, $x = 0.18$.

$P_{CO} = 0.30 - 0.18 = 0.12$ atm; $P_{Cl_2} = 0.50 - 0.18 = 0.32$; $P_{COCl_2} = 0.60 + 0.18 = 0.78$ atm

Check: Plug the values into the equilibrium expression:

$$K_p = \frac{(0.78)}{(0.12)(0.32)} = 20.3 = 20.$$; this is the same as the original equilibrium constant.

14.84 **Given:** $P_{SO_2} = 3.00$ atm; $P_{O_2} = 1.00$ atm; at equilibrium, $P_{total} = 3.75$ atm; $T = 27°C$ **Find:** K_c
Conceptual Plan: Prepare an ICE table, represent the change with x, sum the table, determine the equilibrium values, use the total pressure, and solve for x. Determine partial pressure of each at equilibrium. Determine $K_p \rightarrow K_c$.

$$K_p = K_c(RT)^{\Delta n}$$

Solution: $2\ SO_2(g) + O_2(g) \leftrightharpoons 2\ SO_3(g)$

	P_{SO_2}	P_{O_2}	P_{SO_3}
I	3.00	1.00	0.00
C	$-2x$	$-x$	$+2x$
E	$3.00-2x$	$1.00-x$	$2x$

$P_{Total} = P_{SO_2} + P_{O_2} + P_{SO_3}$ $3.75 = 3.00 - 2x + (1.00 - x) + 2x$

$x = 0.25$ $P_{SO_2} = (3.00 - 2(0.25)) = 2.50$ atm; $P_{O_2} = (1.00 - 0.25) = 0.75$ atm; $P_{SO_3} = 2(0.25) = 0.50$ atm

$$K_p = \frac{P^2_{SO_3}}{P^2_{SO_2}P_{O_2}} = \frac{(0.50)^2}{(2.50)^2(0.75)} = 0.05\underline{3}3 = 0.053$$

Check: The value of the pressure of SO_3 is small compared to the pressures of SO_2 and O_2; therefore, you would expect K_p to be less than 1.

$K_p = K_c(RT)^{\Delta n}$ $0.05\underline{3}3 = K_c((0.0821\frac{\text{L} \cdot \text{atm}}{\text{mol} \cdot \text{K}})(27 + 273\text{K}))^{-1}$

$K_c = 1.\underline{3}12 = 1.3$

14.85 **Given:** $K_p = 0.76$; P_{total} at equilibrium $= 1.00$ **Find:** $P_{initial}$ CCl_4

Conceptual Plan: Prepare an ICE table, represent the P_{CCl_4} with A and the change with x, sum the table, determine the equilibrium values, use the total pressure, and solve for A in terms of x. Determine partial pressure of each at equilibrium, use the equilibrium expression to determine x, and then determine A.

Solution: $CCl_4(g) \leftrightharpoons C(s) + 2\ Cl_2(g)$

	P_{CCl_4}	P_C	P_{Cl_2}
I	A	constant	0.00
C	$-x$		$+2x$
E	$A-x$		$2x$

$P_{Total} = P_{CCl_4} + P_{Cl_2}$ $1.0 = A - x + 2x$ $A = 1 - x$

$P_{CCl_4} = (A - x) = (1 - x) - x = 1 - 2x$; $P_{Cl_2} = (2x)$

$$K_p = \frac{P^2_{Cl_2}}{P_{CCl_4}} = \frac{(2x)^2}{(1 - 2x)} = 0.76$$

$4x^2 + 1.52x - 0.76 = 0$ $x = 0.285$ or -0.665 so $x = 0.2\underline{8}5$

$A = 1 - x = 1.0 - 0.285 = 0.715 = 0.72$ atm

Check: Plug values into equilibrium expression:

$$K_p = \frac{P^2_{Cl_2}}{P_{CCl_4}} = \frac{(2x)^2}{(A - x)} = \frac{(2(0.285))^2}{(0.715 - 0.285)} = 0.755 = 0.76\text{; the original equilibrium constant.}$$

14.86 **Given:** $K = 3.0$; $SO_2 = 2.4$ mol initial; $SO_3 = 1.2$ mol equilibrium **Find:** mol NO_2 initial

Conceptual Plan: Assume 1.0 L, prepare an ICE table, represent the change with x, sum the table, determine the equilibrium values, and determine initial values.

Solution: $SO_2\ (g) + NO_2(g) \leftrightharpoons SO_3(g) + NO(g)$

	$[SO_2]$	$[NO_2]$	$[SO_3]$	$[NO]$
I	2.4	y	0.0	0.0
C	$-x$	$-x$	x	x
E	1.2	$y-1.2$	1.2	1.2

$x = 1.2$, fill in table

$$K = \frac{[SO_3][NO]}{[SO_2][NO_2]} \quad 3.0 = \frac{(1.2)(1.2)}{(1.2)(y - 1.2)} \quad y = 1.6$$

mol NO_2 initial = 1.6 mol

14.87 **Given:** $V = 0.654$ L, $T = 1000$ K, $K_p = 3.9 \times 10^{-2}$ **Find:** mass CaO as equilibrium

Conceptual Plan: $K_p \rightarrow P_{CO_2} \rightarrow n_{(CO_2)} \rightarrow n_{(CaO)} \rightarrow$ g

$PV = nRT$ stoichiometry $\text{g} = \text{n(molar mass)}$

Solution: Since $CaCO_3$ and CaO are solids, they are not included in the equilibrium expression.

$$K_p = P_{CO_2} = 3.9 \times 10^{-2} \quad n = \frac{PV}{RT} = \frac{(3.9 \times 10^{-2}\ \cancel{\text{atm}})(0.654\ \cancel{\text{L}})}{\left(0.0821\ \frac{\cancel{\text{L}} \cdot \cancel{\text{atm}}}{\text{mol} \cdot \cancel{\text{K}}}\right)(1000\ \cancel{\text{K}})} = 3.\underline{1}06 \times 10^{-4}\ \text{mol } CO_2$$

$$3.\underline{1}06 \times 10^{-4}\ \cancel{\text{mol } CO_2} \times \frac{1\ \cancel{\text{mol CaO}}}{1\ \cancel{\text{mol } CO_2}} \times \frac{56.1\ \text{g CaO}}{1\ \cancel{\text{mol CaO}}} = 0.0174\ \text{g} = 0.017\ \text{g CaO}$$

Check: The small value of K would give a small amount of products, so we would not expect to have a large mass of CaO formed.

14.88 **Given:** at equilibrium: N_2O_4, $P = 0.28$ atm; NO_2, $P = 1.1$ atm; $T = 350$ K
Find: equilibrium pressures when volume doubles.
Conceptual Plan: $P_{(N_2O_4)}$, $P_{(NO_2)}$ → K_p and then P when volume doubles. Then prepare an ICE table, represent the change with x, sum the table, and determine the equilibrium values.

Solution: $K_p = \frac{P^2_{NO_2}}{P_{N_2O_4}} = \frac{(1.1)^2}{0.28} = 4.\underline{3}21$

When the volume is doubled, the partial pressure of each gas will decrease by half.

	$N_2O_2(g)$ ⇆	$2\ NO_2(g)$	
	$P_{N_2O_4}$	P_{NO_2}	
I	0.28/2	1.1/2	
C	$-x$	$+2x$	Reaction shifts to the side with more moles, to the right.
E	$0.14-x$	$0.55+2x$	

$$K_p = \frac{P^2_{NO_2}}{P_{N_2O_4}} = \frac{(0.55 + 2x)^2}{(0.14 - x)} = 4.\underline{3}21$$

$$4x^2 + 6.521x - 0.3024 = 0$$

$$\frac{-b \pm \sqrt{b^2 - 4ac}}{2a} = \frac{-(6.521) \pm \sqrt{(6.521)^2 - 4(4)(0.3024)}}{2(4)}$$

$x = 0.0451$ or $- 1.675$ So, $x = 0.0451$

$P_{N_2O_4} = 0.14 - 0.0451 = 0.0949\ \text{atm} = 0.095\ \text{atm}$; $P_{NO_2} = 0.55 + 2(0.0451) = 0.6402 = 0.64\ \text{atm}$

Check: Plug the values into the equilibrium expression:

$$K_p = \frac{(0.6402)^2}{(0.0949)} = 4.31 = 4.3.;$$ this is the same as the original equilibrium constant.

14.89 **Given:** $K_p = 3.10$, Initial $P_{CO} = 215$ torr, $P_{Cl_2} = 245$ torr, **Find:** mole fraction $COCl_2$
Conceptual Plan: P in torr → P in atm. Prepare an ICE table, represent the change with x, sum the table,
$\frac{1\ \text{atm}}{760\ \text{torr}}$
determine the equilibrium values, use the total pressure, and solve for mole fraction.
$\frac{P_{COCl_2}}{P_{Total}}$

Solution: $P_{CO} = (215\ \cancel{\text{torr}})\left(\frac{1\ \text{atm}}{760\ \cancel{\text{torr}}}\right) = 0.28\underline{2}8\ \text{atm}$ $\quad P_{Cl_2} = (245\ \cancel{\text{torr}})\left(\frac{1\ \text{atm}}{760\ \cancel{\text{torr}}}\right) = 0.32\underline{2}3\ \text{atm}$

	$CO(g)$ +	$Cl_2(g)$ ⇆	$COCl_2(g)$	
I	$0.28\underline{2}8$	$0.32\underline{2}3$	0	$Q < K$ so reaction shifts to the right.
C	$-x$	$-x$	$+x$	
E	$0.28\underline{2}8-x$	$0.32\underline{2}3-x$	x	

$$K_p = \frac{P_{COCl_2}}{P_{CO}P_{Cl_2}} = \frac{x}{(0.28\underline{2}8 - x)(0.32\underline{2}3 - x)} = 3.10$$

$x = 0.81\underline{6}1$ or $0.11\underline{1}7$ so $x = 0.117$

$P_{CO} = 0.28\underline{2}8 - 0.11\underline{1}7 = 0.17\underline{1}1$ $\quad P_{Cl_2} = 0.32\underline{2}3 - 0.11\underline{1}7 = 0.21\underline{0}6$ $\quad P_{COCl_2} = 0.11\underline{1}7$

$$\text{mole fraction } COCl_2 = \frac{P_{COCl_2}}{P_{CO} + P_{Cl_2} + P_{COCl_2}} = \frac{0.11\underline{1}7}{0.17\underline{1}1 + 0.21\underline{0}6 + 0.11\underline{1}7} = 0.22\underline{6}3 = 0.226$$

Check: Plug the equilibrium pressures into the equilibrium expression:

$$K_p = \frac{0.11\underline{1}7}{(0.17\underline{1}1)(0.21\underline{0}6)} = 3.0998 = 3.10$$ which is the equilibrium constant so the answer is reasonable.

14.90 **Given:** $K_p = 1.60 \times 10^{-3}$, $T = 700$ K, 1.55 L, $P_{H_2O} = 145$ torr **Find:** % mass H_2 at equilibrium
Conceptual Plan: ***P*(torr) → *P*(atm). Prepare an ICE table, represent the change with *x*, sum the table,**
$\frac{1\text{ atm}}{760\text{ torr}}$
and determine the equilibrium values. *P* → *n* → mass for each → mass %
$PV = nRT$ $\frac{18.02\text{ gl }H_2O}{1\text{ mol }H_2O}$; $\frac{28.01\text{ g CO}}{1\text{ mol CO}}$; $\frac{2.016\text{ g }H_2}{1\text{ mol }H_2}$ $\frac{\text{mass }H_2}{\text{total mass}} \times 100$

Solution: $P_{H_2O} = (145\text{ torr})\left(\frac{1\text{ atm}}{760\text{ torr}}\right) = 0.1908\text{ atm}$

	$H_2O(g)$ + $C(s)$ ⇆	$CO(g)$ +	$H_2(g)$	
I	$0.19\underline{0}8$	0	0	Q < K reaction shifts to the right.
C	$-x$	$+x$	$+x$	
E	$0.19\underline{0}8-x$	x	x	

$$K_p = \frac{P_{CO}P_{H_2}}{P_{H_2O}} = \frac{(x)(x)}{(0.19\underline{0}8 - x)} = 1.60x10^{-3} \quad x = 0.016\underline{6}8 \text{ or } -0.01828 \text{ so } x = 0.016\underline{6}8$$

$P_{CO} = P_{H_2} = 0.016\underline{6}8$ atm $\quad P_{H_2O} = 0.19\underline{0}8 - 0.016\underline{6}8 = 0.17\underline{4}1$ atm

$$n_{CO} = n_{H_2} = \frac{(0.016\underline{6}8\text{ atm})(1.55\text{ L})}{\left(\frac{0.0821\text{ L atm}}{\text{mol K}}\right)(700.0\text{ K})} = 4.4\underline{9}9 \times 10^{-4}\text{ mol}$$

$$n_{H_2O} = \frac{(0.17\underline{4}1\text{ atm})(1.55\text{ L})}{\left(\frac{0.0821\text{ L atm}}{\text{mol K}}\right)(700\text{ K})} = 4.\underline{6}96 \times 10^{-3}\text{ mol}$$

$$(4.4\underline{9}9 \times 10^{-4}\text{ mol CO})\frac{28.01\text{ g CO}}{1\text{ mol CO}} = 0.012\underline{6}0\text{ g CO} \quad (4.4\underline{9}9 \times 10^{-4}\text{ mol }H_2)\frac{2.016\text{ g }H_2}{1\text{ mol}H_2} = 9.0\underline{7}0 \times 10^{-4}\text{ g }H_2$$

$$(4.6\underline{9}5 \times 10^{-3}\text{ mol }H_2O)\frac{18.02\text{ g }H_2O}{1\text{ mol }H_2O} = 0.084\underline{6}1\text{ g }H_2O$$

$$\frac{9.0\underline{7}0 \times 10^{-4}\text{ g }H_2}{(0.012\underline{6}0\text{ g} + 9.0\underline{7}0 \times 10^{-4}\text{ g} + 0.084\underline{6}1\text{ g})} \times 100 = \frac{8.7\underline{7}7 \times 10^{-4}\text{ g }H_2}{(0.09496\text{ g})} \times 100 = 0.92\underline{4}3\% = 0.924\%H_2$$

Check: Plug the equilibrium values into the equilibrium expression:

$$K_p = \frac{(0.016\underline{6}8)(0.016\underline{6}8)}{(0.17\underline{4}1)} = 1.60x10^{-3}$$ which is the equilibrium constant. Thus, the answer is reasonable.

Challenge Problems

14.91 (a) **Given:** $P_{NO} = 522$ torr, $P_{O_2} = 421$ torr; at equilibrium, $P_{total} = 748$ torr **Find:** K_p
Conceptual Plan: Prepare an ICE table, represent the change with *x*, sum the table, determine the equilibrium values, use the total pressure, and solve for *x*. torr → atm → K_p
Solution:

	2 NO(*g*) +	$O_2(g)$ ⇆	2 $NO_2(g)$
	P_{NO}	P_{O_2}	P_{NO_2}
I	522 torr	421 torr	0.00
C	$-2x$	$-x$	$+2x$
E	$522-2x$	$421-x$	$2x$

$P_{Total} = P_{NO} + P_{O_2} + P_{NO_2} \quad 748 = 522 - 2x + (421 - x) + 2x$
$x = 195$ torr $\quad P_{NO} = (522 - 2(195) = 132$ torr;
$P_{O_2} = (421 - 195) = 226$ torr; $\quad P_{NO_2} = 2(195) = 390$ torr

$$P_{NO} = 132\text{ torr} \times \frac{1\text{ atm}}{760\text{ torr}} = 0.17\underline{3}7\text{ atm}; \quad P_{O_2} = 226\text{ torr} \times \frac{1\text{ atm}}{760\text{ torr}} = 0.29\underline{7}4\text{ atm};$$

$$P_{NO_2} = 390\text{ torr} \times \frac{1\text{ atm}}{760\text{ torr}} = 0.51\underline{3}2\text{ atm}$$

$$K_p = \frac{P^2_{NO_2}}{P^2_{NO}P_{O_2}} = \frac{(0.51\underline{3}2)^2}{(0.17\underline{3}7)^2(0.29\underline{7}4)} = 29.34 = 29.3$$

(b) **Given:** = P_{NO} = 255 torr, P_{O_2} = 185 torr, K_p = 29.3 **Find:** equilibrium P_{NO_2}

Conceptual Plan:

torr → atm and then prepare an ICE table. Represent the change with x, sum the table,

$\frac{\text{atm}}{760 \text{ torr}}$

determine the equilibrium values, put the equilibrium values in the equilibrium expression, and solve for x. Determine P_{NO_2}.

Solution: $P_{NO} = 255 \text{ torr} \times \frac{1 \text{ atm}}{760 \text{ torr}} = 0.3355 \text{ atm}$ $\quad P_{O_2} = 185 \text{ torr} \times \frac{1 \text{ atm}}{760 \text{ torr}} = 0.2434 \text{ atm}$

	$2\,NO(g)$ +	$O_2(g)$ ⇆	$2\,NO_2(g)$
	P_{NO}	P_{O_2}	P_{NO_2}
I	0.3355	0.2434	0.00
C	$-2x$	$-x$	$+2x$
E	$0.3355-2x$	$0.2434-x$	$2x$

$$K_p = \frac{P_{NO_2}^2}{P_{NO}^2 P_{O_2}} = \frac{(2x)^2}{(0.3355 - 2x)^2(0.2434 - x)} = 29.3$$

$-117.2x^3 + 63.847x^2 - 12.869x + 0.80272 = 0$. Solve using successive approximations or a cubic equation calculator found on the internet.

$x = 0.1112 \quad P_{NO_2} = 2x = 2(0.1112) = 0.2224 \text{ atm}$

$$0.2224 \text{ atm} \times \frac{760 \text{ torr}}{1 \text{ atm}} = 169.1 \text{ torr} = 169 \text{ torr}$$

Check: Plug the values into the equilibrium expression:

$$K_p = \frac{(0.2224)^2}{(0.1131)^2(0.1322)} = 29.249 = 29.2;$$ this is within 0.1 of the original equilibrium constant.

14.92 **Given:** 2.75 L, 950 K, 0.100 mol SO_2, 0.100 mol O_2; K_p =0.355 **Find:** P_{total} at equilibrium

Conceptual Plan: n → P and then prepare an ICE table. Represent the change with x, sum the table,

$PV = nRT$

determine the equilibrium values, put the equilibrium values in the equilibrium expression, solve for x, and then determine P for each reactant and product → P_{total}.

$P_{total} = P_{SO_2} + P_{O_2} + P_{SO_3}$

Solution: $P = \frac{nRT}{V} \quad P_{O_2} = P_{SO_2} = \frac{(0.100 \text{ mol})\left(0.0821 \frac{\text{L} \cdot \text{atm}}{\text{mol} \cdot \text{K}}\right)(950 \text{ K})}{2.75 \text{ L}} = 2.836 \text{ atm}$

	$2\,SO_2(g)$ +	$O_2(g)$ ⇆	$2\,SO_3(g)$
	P_{SO_2}	P_{O_2}	P_{SO_3}
I	2.836	2.836	0.00
C	$-2x$	$-x$	$+2x$
E	$2.836-2x$	$2.836-x$	$2x$

$$K_p = \frac{P_{SO_3}^2}{P_{SO_2}^2 P_{O_2}} = \frac{(2x)^2}{(2.836 - 2x)^2(2.836 - x)} = 0.355$$

$-1.42x^3 + 8.054x^2 - 14.275x + 8.096 = 0$. Solve using successive approximations or a cubic equation calculator found on the internet.

$x = 0.6629 = 0.663$

$P_{SO_3} = 2x = 2(0.663) = 1.326 = 1.33 \text{ atm}$

$P_{SO_2} = (2.836 - 2x) = (2.836 - 2(0.663)) = 1.510 = 1.51 \text{ atm}$

$P_{O_2} = (2.836 - x) = (2.836 - 0.663) = 2.173 = 2.17 \text{ atm}$

$P_{Total} = 1.33 + 1.51 + 2.17 = 5.01 \text{ atm}$

Check: Plug the values into the equilibrium expression:

$$K_p = \frac{P_{SO_3}^2}{P_{SO_2}^2 P_{O_2}} = \frac{(1.33)^2}{(1.51)^2(2.17)} = 0.3575;$$

this is within 99% of the significant figures of the original equilibrium constant.

14.93 **Given:** P_{NOCl} at equilibrium = 115 torr; $K_p = 0.27$, $T = 700$ K, **Find:** initial pressure NO, Cl_2
Conceptual Plan: torr → atm and then prepare an ICE table. Represent the change with x, sum the table,

$$\frac{\text{atm}}{760 \text{ torr}}$$

determine the equilibrium values, put the equilibrium values in the equilibrium expression, and determine initial pressure.

Solution: $115 \text{ torr} \times \dfrac{1 \text{ atm}}{760 \text{ torr}} = 0.15\underline{1}3 \text{ atm}$

$2\,NO(g) + Cl_2(g) \leftrightharpoons 2\,NOCl(g)$

	P_{NO}	P_{Cl_2}	P_{NOCl}	
I	A	A	0.00	Let A = initial pressure of NO and Cl_2.
C	$-2x$	$-x$	$+2x$	
E	$A-2x$	$A-x$	0.151	$2x = 0.151$, so, $x = 0.0756$
	$A-0.151$	$A-0.0756$		

$$K_p = \frac{P^2_{NOCL}}{P^2_{NO}\,P_{Cl_2}} = \frac{(0.151)^2}{(A-0.151)^2(A-0.0756)} = 0.27$$

$0.27A^3 - 0.1019A^2 + 0.01231A - 0.022336 = 0$. Solve using successive approximations or a cubic equation calculator found on the internet.
$A = 0.565$
$P_{NO} = P_{Cl_2} = A = 0.565 \text{ atm} = 429 \text{ torr}$

Check: Plug the values into the equilibrium expression:

$$K_p = \frac{P^2_{NOCL}}{P^2_{NO}\,P_{Cl_2}} = \frac{(0.151)^2}{(0.565-0.151)^2(0.565-0.0756)}\, 0.2\underline{7}2;$$

this is the same as the original equilibrium constant

14.94 **Given:** $P_{N_2O_4} = 1$ atm, K_p reaction 1 = 1×10^4, K_p reaction 2 = 0.10 **Find:** Which component will have $P > 0.2$atm?
Conceptual Plan: Use reaction 2 to determine P_{NO_2}. Then prepare an ICE table, represent the change with x, sum the table, determine the equilibrium values, put the equilibrium values in the equilibrium expression, and solve for x.
Solution: $2\,NO(g) \leftrightharpoons N_2O_4(g)$

	P_{NO}	$P_{(N_2O_4)}$
I	0.00	1.00
C	$+2x$	$-x$
E	$+2x$	$1.00 - x$

$$K_p = \frac{P_{N_2O_4}}{P^2_{NO}} = \frac{(1.00-x)}{(2x)^2} = 0.10$$

$0.40x^2 + x - 1.00 = 0$

$$\frac{-b \pm \sqrt{b^2-4ac}}{2a} = \frac{-1 \pm \sqrt{1^2 - 4(0.40)(-1.00)}}{2(0.40)}$$

$x = 0.7655 = 0.77$
$P_{NO_2} = 2x = 1.54$
Because K_p for reaction 1 is so large, essentially all of the material are products, so the P_{NO} and P_{O_2} in reaction 1 will be negligible.

14.95 **Given:** $P = 0.750$ atm, density = 0.520 g/L, $T = 337°C$ **Find:** K_c
Conceptual Plan: Prepare an ICE table, represent the P_{CCl_4} with A and the change with x, sum the table, determine the equilibrium values, use the total pressure, and solve for A in terms of x. Determine partial pressure of each at equilibrium in terms of x, use the density to determine

$$d = \frac{PM}{RT}$$

the apparent molar mass, and then use the mole fraction (in terms of P) and the molar mass of each

$$\chi_A = \frac{P_A}{P_{Total}}$$

gas to determine x.

Solution: $2\ NO_2(g) \leftrightarrows 2\ NO(g) + O_2(g)$

	P_{NO_2}	P_{NO}	P_{O_2}
I	A	0.00	0.00
C	$-2x$	$+2x$	$+x$
E	$A-2x$	$2x$	x

$P_{Total} = P_{NO_2} + P_{NO} + P_{O_2} \quad 0.750 = A - 2x + 2x + x \quad A = 0.750 - x$

$P_{NO_2} = (A - 2x) = (0.750 - x) - 2x = (0.750 - 3x);\ P_{NO} = (2x);\ P_{O_2} = x$

$$d = \frac{P\mathcal{M}}{RT} \quad \mathcal{M} = \frac{dRT}{P} = \frac{\left(0.520\,\frac{g}{\cancel{L}}\right)\left(0.0821\,\frac{\cancel{L}\cdot\cancel{atm}}{mol\cdot\cancel{K}}\right)(610\ \cancel{K})}{0.750\ \cancel{atm}} = 34.72\ g/mol$$

$$\mathcal{M} = \chi_{NO_2}\mathcal{M}_{NO_2} + \chi_{NO}\mathcal{M}_{NO} + \chi_{O_2}\mathcal{M}_{O_2} = \frac{P_{NO_2}}{P_{total}}\mathcal{M}_{NO_2} + \frac{P_{NO}}{P_{total}}\mathcal{M}_{NO} + \frac{P_{O_2}}{P_{total}}\mathcal{M}_{O_2}$$

$P_{Total}\mathcal{M} = P_{NO_2}\mathcal{M}_{NO_2} + P_{NO}\mathcal{M}_{NO} + P_{O_2}\mathcal{M}_{O_2}$

$(0.750)(34.7) = (0.750 - 3x)(46.0) + 2x(30.0) + x(32.0)$

$x = 0.184$

$$K_p = \frac{P^2_{NO}P_{O_2}}{P^2_{NO_2}} = \frac{(2x)^2(x)}{(0.750 - 3x)} = \frac{(2(0.184))^2(0.184)}{(0.750 - 3(0.184))^2} = 0.63\underline{5}6$$

$$K_p = K_c(RT)^{\Delta n} \quad 0.63\underline{5}6 = K_c((0.0821\,\frac{L\cdot atm}{mol\cdot K})(610K))^1$$

$K_c = 1.27 \times 10^{-2}$

14.96 **Given:** Reaction 1 $K_c = 7.75$, Reaction 2 $K_c = 4.00$, $[N_2O_5]_{initial} = 4.00M$, $[O_2]_{equil} = 4.50M$
Find: concentration of other species at equilibrium
Conceptual Plan: Combine reaction 1 and reaction 2 to get the overall reaction and then prepare an ICE table. Represent the change with *x*, sum the table, determine the equilibrium values, use the total pressure, and solve for *x*. Use x to determine equilibrium concentration.
Solution: $N_2O_5\ (g) \leftrightarrows \cancel{N_2O_3(g)} + O_2(g) \qquad K_1 = 7.75$

$\cancel{N_2O_3(g)} \leftrightarrows N_2O(g) + O_2(g) \qquad K_2 = 4.00$

$N_2O_5(g) \leftrightarrows N_2O(g) + 2\ O_2(g) \qquad K = K_1K_2 = 31.0$

	N_2O_5	N_2O	O_2
I	4.00	0.00	0.00
C	$-x$	x	$2x$
E	$4.00 - x$	x	4.50

$$K_c = \frac{[N_2O][O_2]^2}{[N_2O_5]} = 31.0 = \frac{(x)(4.50)^2}{(4.00 - x)}$$

$x = 2.42$

$[N_2O_5] = 4.00 - x = 4.00 - 2.42 = 1.58M$

$[N_2O] = x = 2.42M$

$[O_2] = 4.50M$

Use either reaction 1 or reaction 2 and solve for $[N_2O_3]$ represented as y.

$$K_c = \frac{[N_2O_3][O_2]}{[N_2O_5]} = 7.75 = \frac{(y)(4.50)}{(1.58)}$$

$y = 2.72 \quad [N_2O_3] = y = 2.72M$

Check: Plug the values into the equilibrium expression into any of the equilibrium expressions:
e.g., For the overall reaction:

$$K_c = \frac{[N_2O][O_2]^2}{[N_2O_5]} = \frac{(2.42)(4.50)^2}{(1.58)} = 31.0;\ \text{the equilibrium constant}$$

e.g., For reaction 2:

$$K_c = \frac{[N_2O][O_2]}{[N_2O_3]} = \frac{(2.42)(4.50)}{(2.72)} = 4.00$$

14.97 **Given:** $P_{total} = 3.0$ atm, mole fraction $O_2 = 0.12$, $T = 600$ K **Find:** K_p
Conceptual Plan: **mole fraction** $\rightarrow P_{O_2} \rightarrow P_{SO_2} \rightarrow P_{SO_3} \rightarrow K_p$

$$\text{mol fraction} = \frac{P_{O_2}}{P_{Total}} \quad \frac{2P_{SO_2}}{P_{O_2}} \quad P_{SO_3} = P_{Total} - P_{SO_2} - P_{O_2} \quad K_p = \frac{P_{SO_2}P_{O_2}}{P_{SO_3}}$$

Solution: $P_{O_2} = (0.12)(3.0) = 0.36$ atm $\quad P_{SO_2} = 2P_{O_2} = 2(0.36 \text{ atm}) = 0.72$ atm

$$P_{SO_3} = 3.0 - 0.36 - 0.72 = 1.9\underline{2} \quad K_p = \frac{P_{SO_2}P_{O_2}}{P_{SO_3}} = \frac{(0.36)(0.72)^2}{(1.9\underline{2})^2} = 0.01\underline{3}5 = 1.4\text{x}10^{-2}$$

14.98 For reaction mixture d, the x is small approximation is most likely to apply. Since the equilibrium constant is very small, at equilibrium the concentration of products will be small. In mixtures b and c, you would have to lose a large amount of product and the x is small approximation will not apply. In mixture a, the initial concentration is smaller than in mixture d, so while it is a good approximation it is a better approximation for mixture d.

14.99 Yes, the direction will depend on the volume. If the initial moles of A and B are equal, the initial concentrations of A and B are equal regardless of the volume. Since $K_c = \frac{[B]^2}{[A]} = 1$, if the volume is such that the $[A] = [B] < 1.0$, then $Q < K$ and the reaction goes to the right to reach equilibrium. However, if the volume is such that the $[A] = [B] > 1.0$, then $Q > K$ and the reaction goes to the left to reach equilibrium.

14.100 $K_p = 0.50$ means that P(products) < P(reactants). If the reactants and products are in their standard states, then P of each reactant and product = 1.0. So $Q > K$ and to reach equilibrium the reaction will have to shift to the left.

14.101 An examination of the data shows when $P_A = 1.0$ then $P_B = 1.0$, therefore, $K_p = \frac{P_B^b}{P_A^a} = \frac{(1.0)^b}{(1.0)^a} = 1.0$. Therefore, the value of the numerator and denominator must be equal. We see from the data that $P_B = \sqrt{P_A}$, so $P_B^2 = P_A$. Since the stoichiometric coefficients become exponents in the equilibrium expression, $a = 1$ and $b = 2$.

15 Acids and Bases

15.1 The pain of heartburn is caused by hydrochloric acid which is excreted in the stomach to kill microorganisms and activate enzymes that break down food. The hydrochloric acid can sometimes back up out of the stomach and into the esophagus, a phenomenon known as acid reflux. When hydrochloric acid comes in contact with the lining of the esophagus, the H^+ ions irritate the esophageal tissues, resulting in a burning sensation. The simplest way to relieve mild heartburn is to swallow repeatedly. Saliva contains bicarbonate ion (HCO_3^-) that acts as a base and, when swallowed, neutralizes some of the acid in the esophagus. Heartburn can also be treated with antacids such as Tums, milk of magnesia, or Mylanta. These over-the-counter medications contain more base than does saliva and therefore, do a better job of neutralizing the esophageal acid.

15.2 Acids have the following general properties: a sour taste, the ability to dissolve many metals, the ability to turn blue litmus paper red, and the ability to neutralize bases.

Bases have the following general properties: a bitter taste, a slippery feel, the ability to turn red litmus paper blue, and the ability to neutralize acids.

15.3 A carboxylic acid is an organic acid which contains the following group of atoms: $H-O-\overset{\overset{\displaystyle O}{\|}}{C}-$. Carboxylic acids are often found in substances derived from living organisms. Examples include citric acid, malic acid, and acetic acid.

15.4 An Arrhenius acid is a substance that produces H^+ in aqueous solution.

An Arrhenius base is a substance that produces OH^- in aqueous solution.

15.5 The hydronium ion is H_3O^+. In water, H^+ ions always associate with H_2O molecules to form hydronium ions and other associated species with the general formula $H(H_2O)_n^+$.

15.6 A Brønsted–Lowry acid is a proton (H^+) donor.

A Brønsted–Lowry base is a proton (H^+) acceptor.

15.7 According to Huheey, " The differences between the various acid–base concepts are not concerned with which is right, but which is most convenient to use in a particular situation." There is no single correct definition; we use the definition that is best for a particular situation.

15.8 Amphoteric substances are those that can act as acids or bases depending on the circumstances. Some amphoteric substances are H_2O and NH_3.

15.9 A conjugate acid–base pair are two substances related to each other by the transfer of a proton. In the reaction:

$NH_3(aq) + H_2O(l) \leftrightharpoons NH_4^+(aq) + OH^-(aq)$, the conjugate pairs are: NH_3/NH_4^+ and H_2O/OH^-.

15.10 A strong acid completely ionizes in solution. An example is HCl.

A weak acid only partially ionizes in solution. An example is HF.

15.11 A diprotic acid is one that contains two ionizable protons. An example is H_2SO_4.

A triprotic acid is one that contains three ionizable protons. An example is H_3PO_4.

15.12 An acid ionization constant (K_a) is the equilibrium constant for the ionization reaction of a weak acid. The smaller the acid ionization constant, the weaker the acid.

15.13 The autoionization of water is $H_2O(l) + H_2O(l) \leftrightarrows H_3O^+(aq) + OH^-(aq)$ and has the ion product of water $K_w = [H_3O^+][OH^-]$.

It can also be written $H_2O(l) \leftrightarrows H^+(aq) + OH^-(aq)$ and the ion product of water is $K_w = [H^+][OH^-]$. At 25 °C, $K_w = 1.0 \times 10^{-14}$.

15.14 Since $K_w = 1.0 \times 10^{-14}$, the concentration of H_3O^+ times the concentration of OH^- is always 1.0×10^{-14}; therefore, if $[H_3O^+]$ increases, then $[OH^-]$ decreases and if the $[H_3O^+]$ decreases, then $[OH^-]$ increases.

15.15 We define pH as pH = - log$[H_3O^+]$. An acidic solution has a pH < 7, a basic solution has a pH > 7, and a neutral solution has a pH = 7.

15.16 We define pH as pOH = - log$[OH^-]$. An acidic solution has pOH > 7, a basic solution has pOH < 7, and a neutral solution has pOH = 7.

15.17 We can neglect the contribution of the autoionization of water to the H_3O^+ concentration in a solution of a strong or weak acid because it is negligible compared to the concentration from the acid itself. Even the weakest of the weak acids has an ionization constant that is four orders of magnitude larger than that of water.

15.18 The x is small approximation is used when the equilibrium constant is relatively small and the initial concentration is relatively large. We make the assumption that x is small compared to the initial concentration. If the assumption is valid, x is < 5% of the initial concentration.

15.19 The percent ionization is defined as percent ionization $= \dfrac{\text{concentration of ionized acid}}{\text{initial concentration of acid}}\ x\ 100$. The percent ionization of a weak acid decreases with the increasing concentration of the acid.

15.20 The complete ionization of the strong acid produces a significant concentration of H_3O^+ and suppresses the formation of additional H_3O^+ by the ionization of the weak acid. Because of Le Châtelier's principle, the formation of H_3O^+ by the strong acid causes the weak acid to ionize even less than it would in the absence of the strong acid.

15.21 $B(aq) + H_2O(l) \leftrightarrows BH^+(aq) + OH^-(aq)$

15.22 An anion that is the conjugate base of a weak acid is itself a weak base. An anion that is the conjugate base of a strong acid is pH – neutral. $A^-(aq) + H_2O(l) \leftrightarrows HA(aq) + OH^-(aq)$

15.23 At 25 °C, the product of K_a for an acid and K_b for its conjugate base is $K_w = 1.0 \times 10^{-14}$.

15.24 A cation that is the conjugate acid of a weak base such as NH_4^+ is a weak acid. Small highly charged metal cations such as Al^{3+} and Fe^{3+} form weakly acidic solutions.

15.25 For most polyprotic acids, K_{a_1} is much larger than K_{a_2}. Therefore, the amount of H_3O^+ contributed by the first ionization step is much larger than that contributed by the second or third ionization step. In addition, the production of H_3O^+ by the first step inhibits additional production of H_3O^+ by the second step because of Le Châtelier's principle.

15.26 For a weak diprotic acid, $[X^{2-}] = K_{a_2}$. This result is general for all diprotic acids in which the x is small approximation is valid.

15.27 For an H—Y binary acid, the factors affecting the ease with which this hydrogen will be donated are the polarity of the bond and the strength of the bond.

15.28 The factors affecting the ease with which the hydrogen will be donated (and therefore acidic) are the electronegativity of the element Y and the number of oxygen atoms attached to the element Y.

15.29 A Lewis acid is an electron pair acceptor. A Lewis base is an electron pair donor.

15.30 A Lewis acid has an empty orbital (or can rearrange electrons to create an empty orbital) that can accept an electron pair. A Lewis base has a lone pair of electrons it can donate to the Lewis acid.

15.31 The combustion of fossil fuels produces oxides of sulfur and nitrogen, which react with oxygen and water to form sulfuric and nitric acids. These acids then combine with rain to form acid rain. Acid rain is a significant problem in the northeastern United States.

15.32 Acid rain corrodes man-made structures and also damages aquatic environments and forests. Environmental legislation has helped stabilize the amount of acid rain being produced.

Problems by Topic

The Nature and Definitions of Acids and Bases

15.33 (a) acid $HNO_3(aq) \rightarrow H^+(aq) + NO_3^-(aq)$

(b) acid $NH_4^+(aq) \rightarrow H^+(aq) + NH_3(aq)$

(c) base $KOH(aq) \rightarrow K^+(aq) + OH^-(aq)$

(d) acid $HC_2H_3O_2(aq) \rightarrow H^+(aq) + C_2H_3O_2^-(aq)$

15.34 (a) base $NaOH(aq) \rightarrow Na^+(aq) + OH^-(aq)$

(b) acid $H_2SO_4(aq) \rightarrow 2H^+(aq) + SO_4^{2-}(aq)$

(c) acid $HBr(aq) \rightarrow H^+(aq) + Br^-(aq)$

(d) base $Sr(OH)_2(aq) \rightarrow Sr^{2+}(aq) + 2OH^-(aq)$

15.35 (a) Since H_2CO_3 donates a proton to H_2O, it is the acid. After H_2CO_3 donates the proton, it becomes HCO_3^-, the conjugate base. Since H_2O accepts a proton, it is the base. After H_2O accepts the proton, it becomes H_3O^+, the conjugate acid.

(b) Since H_2O donates a proton to NH_3, it is the acid. After H_2O donates the proton, it becomes OH^-, the conjugate base. Since NH_3 accepts a proton, it is the base. After NH_3 accepts the proton, it becomes NH_4^+, the conjugate acid.

(c) Since HNO_3 donates a proton to H_2O, it is the acid. After HNO_3 donates the proton, it becomes NO_3^-, the conjugate base. Since H_2O accepts a proton, it is the base. After H_2O accepts the proton, it becomes H_3O^+, the conjugate acid.

(d) Since H_2O donates a proton to C_5H_5N, it is the acid. After H_2O donates the proton, it becomes OH^-, the conjugate base. Since C_5H_5N accepts a proton, it is the base. After C_5H_5N accepts the proton, it becomes $C_5H_5NH^+$, the conjugate acid.

15.36 (a) Since HI donates a proton to H_2O, it is the acid. After HI donates the proton, it becomes I^-, the conjugate base. Since H_2O accepts a proton, it is the base. After H_2O accepts the proton, it becomes H_3O^+, the conjugate acid.

(b) Since H_2O donates a proton to CH_3NH_2, it is the acid. After H_2O donates the proton, it becomes OH^-, the conjugate base. Since CH_3NH_2 accepts a proton, it is the base. After CH_3NH_2 accepts the proton, it becomes $CH_3NH_3^+$, the conjugate acid.

(c) Since H_2O donates a proton to CO_3^{2-}, it is the acid. After H_2O donates the proton, it becomes OH^-, the conjugate base. Since CO_3^{2-} accepts a proton, it is the base. After CO_3^{2-} accepts the proton, it becomes HCO_3^-, the conjugate acid.

(d) Since HBr donates a proton to H_2O, it is the acid. After HBr donates the proton, it becomes Br^-, the conjugate base. Since H_2O accepts a proton, it is the base. After H_2O accepts the proton, it becomes H_3O^+, the conjugate acid.

15.37 (a) Cl^- $HCl(aq) + H_2O(l) \rightarrow H_3O^+(aq) + Cl^-(aq)$

(b) HSO_3^- $H_2SO_3(aq) + H_2O(l) \leftrightarrows H_3O^+(aq) + HSO_3^-(aq)$

(c) CHO_2^- $HCHO_2(aq) + H_2O(l) \leftrightarrows H_3O^+(aq) + CHO_2^-(aq)$

(d) F^- $HF(aq) + H_2O(l) \leftrightarrows H_3O^+(aq) + F^-(aq)$

15.38 (a) NH_4^+ $NH_3(aq) + H_2O(l) \leftrightarrows NH_4^+(aq) + OH^-(aq)$

(b) $HClO_4$ $HClO_4(aq) + H_2O(l) \rightarrow H_3O^+(aq) + ClO_4^-(aq)$

(c) H_2SO_4 $H_2SO_4(aq) + H_2O(l) \rightarrow H_3O^+(aq) + HSO_4^-(aq)$

(d) HCO^- $HCO_3^-(aq) + H_2O(l) \leftrightarrows H_3O^+(aq) + CO_3^-(aq)$

15.39 $H_2PO_4^-(aq) + H_2O(l) \leftrightarrows H_3O^+(aq) + HPO_4^{2-}(aq)$

$H_2PO_4^-(aq) + H_2O(l) \leftrightarrows H_3PO_4(aq) + OH^-(aq)$

15.40 $HCO_3^-(aq) + HS^-(aq) \leftrightarrows H_2S(aq) + CO_3^{2-}(aq)$

$HCO_3^-(aq) + HS^-(aq) \leftrightarrows H_2CO_3(aq) + S^{2-}(aq)$

Acid Strength and K_a

15.41 (a) HNO_3 is a strong acid.

(b) HCl is a strong acid.

(c) HBr is a strong acid.

(d) H_2SO_3 is a weak acid. $H_2SO_3(aq) + H_2O(l) \leftrightarrows H_3O^+(aq) + HSO_3^-(aq)$

$$K_a = \frac{[H_3O^+][HSO_3^-]}{[H_2SO_3]}$$

15.42 (a) HF is a weak acid. $HF(aq) + H_2O(l) \leftrightarrows H_3O^+(aq) + F^-(aq)$

$$K_a = \frac{[H_3O^+][F^-]}{[HF]}$$

(b) $HCHO_2$ is a weak acid. $HCHO_2(aq) + H_2O(l) \leftrightarrows H_3O^+(aq) + CHO_2^-(aq)$

$$K_a = \frac{[H_3O^+][CHO_2^-]}{[HCHO_2]}$$

(c) H_2SO_4 is a strong acid.

(d) H_2CO_3 is a weak acid. $H_2CO_3(aq) + H_2O(l) \leftrightarrows H_3O^+(aq) + HCO_3^-(aq)$

$$K_{a_1} = \frac{[H_3O^+][HCO_3^-]}{[H_2CO_3]}$$

15.43 (a) contains no HA, 10 H^+, and 10 A^-

(b) contains 3 HA, 3 H^+, and 7 A^-

(c) contains 9 HA, 1 H^+, and 1 A^-

So, solution a > solution b > solution c.

15.44 HCl is a strong acid, $K_a(HF) = 3.5 \times 10^{-4}$, $K_a(HClO) = 2.9 \times 10^{-8}$, $K_a(HC_6H_5O) = 1.3 \times 10^{-10}$.

The larger the value of K_a the stronger the acid and the greater the $[H_3O^+]$.

The order of decreasing $[H_3O^+]$ is HCl > HF > HClO > HC_6H_5O.

15.45 (a) F^- is a stronger base than Cl^-.
F^- is the conjugate base of HF (a weak acid), Cl^- is the conjugate base of HCl (a strong acid), the weaker the acid, the stronger the conjugate base.

(b) NO_2^- is a stronger base than NO_3^-.
NO_2^- is the conjugate base of HNO_2 (a weak acid), NO_3^- is the conjugate base of HNO_3 (a strong acid), the weaker the acid, the stronger the conjugate base.

(c) ClO^- is a stronger base than F^-.
F^- is the conjugate base of HF ($K_a = 3.5 \times 10^{-4}$), ClO^- is the conjugate base of HClO ($K_a = 2.9 \times 10^{-8}$) HClO is the weaker acid, the weaker the acid, the stronger the conjugate base.

15.46 (a) ClO_2^- is a stronger base than ClO_4^-.
ClO_2^- is the conjugate base of $HClO_2$ (a weak acid), ClO_4^- is the conjugate base of $HClO_4$ (a strong acid), the weaker the acid, the stronger the conjugate base.

(b) H_2O is a stronger base than Cl^-.
H_2O is the conjugate base of H_3O^+, Cl^- is the conjugate base of HCl (a strong acid), the weaker the acid, the stronger the conjugate base.

(c) CN^- is stronger base than ClO^-.
CN^- is the conjugate base of HCN ($K_a = 4.9 \times 10^{-10}$), ClO^- is the conjugate base of HClO ($K_a = 2.9 \times 10^{-8}$), the weaker the acid, the stronger the conjugate base.

Autoionization of Water and pH

15.47 (a) **Given:** $K_w = 1.0 \times 10^{-14}$, $[H_3O^+] = 1.2 \times 10^{-8}$ M **Find:** $[OH^-]$
Conceptual Plan: $[H_3O^+] \rightarrow [OH^-]$

$K_w = 1.0 \times 10^{-14} = [H_3O^+][OH^-]$

Solution:

$K_w = 1.0 \times 10^{-14} = (1.2 \times 10^{-8})[OH^-]$

$[OH^-] = 8.3 \times 10^{-7}$M

$[OH^-] > [H_3O^+]$ so the solution is basic.

(b) **Given:** $K_w = 1.0 \times 10^{-14}$, $[H_3O^+] = 8.5 \times 10^{-5}$ M **Find:** $[OH^-]$
Conceptual Plan: $[H_3O^+] \rightarrow [OH^-]$

$K_w = 1.0 \times 10^{-14} = [H_3O^+][OH^-]$

Solution:

$K_w = 1.0 \times 10^{-14} = (8.5 \times 10^{-5})[OH^-]$

$[OH^-] = 1.2 \times 10^{-10}$M

$[H_3O^+] > [OH^-]$ so the solution is acidic.

(c) **Given:** $K_w = 1.0 \times 10^{-14}$, $[H_3O^+] = 3.5 \times 10^{-2}$ M **Find:** $[OH^-]$
Conceptual Plan: $[H_3O^+] \rightarrow [OH^-]$

$K_w = 1.0 \times 10^{-14} = [H_3O^+][OH^-]$

Solution:

$K_w = 1.0 \times 10^{-14} = (3.5 \times 10^{-2})[OH^-]$

$[OH^-] = 2.9 \times 10^{-13}$ M

$[H_3O^+] > [OH^-]$ so the solution is acidic.

15.48 (a) **Given:** $K_w = 1.0 \times 10^{-14}$, $[OH^-] = 1.1 \times 10^{-9}$ M **Find:** $[H_3O^+]$
Conceptual Plan: $[OH^-] \rightarrow [H_3O^+]$

$K_w = 1.0 \times 10^{-14} = [H_3O^+][OH^-]$

Solution:
$K_w = 1.0 \times 10^{-14} = [H_3O^+](1.1 \times 10^{-9})$
$[H_3O^+] = 9.1 \times 10^{-6}$ M
$[H_3O^+] > [OH^-]$ so the solution is acidic.

(b) **Given:** $K_w = 1.0 \times 10^{-14}$, $[OH^-] = 2.9 \times 10^{-2}$ M **Find:** $[H_3O^+]$
Conceptual Plan: $[OH^-] \rightarrow [H_3O^+]$
$K_w = 1.0 \times 10^{-14} = [H_3O^+][OH^-]$
Solution:
$K_w = 1.0 \times 10^{-14} = [H_3O^+](2.9 \times 10^{-2})$
$[H_3O^+] = 3.4 \times 10^{-13}$ M
$[OH^-] > [H_3O^+]$ so the solution is basic.

(c) **Given:** $K_w = 1.0 \times 10^{-14}$, $[OH^-] = 6.9 \times 10^{-12}$ M **Find:** $[H_3O^+]$
Conceptual Plan: $[OH^-] \rightarrow [H_3O^+]$
$K_w = 1.0 \times 10^{-14} = [H_3O^+][OH^-]$
Solution:
$K_w = 1.0 \times 10^{-14} = [H_3O^+](6.9 \times 10^{-12})$
$[H_3O^+] = 1.5 \times 10^{-3}$ M
$[H_3O^+] > [OH^-]$ so the solution is acidic.

15.49 (a) **Given:** $[H_3O^+] = 1.7 \times 10^{-8}$ M **Find:** pH and pOH
Conceptual Plan: $[H_3O^+] \rightarrow pH \rightarrow pOH$
$pH = -\log[H_3O^+]$ $pH + pOH = 14$
Solution: $pH = -\log(1.7 \times 10^{-8}) = 7.77$ $pOH = 14.00 - 7.77 = 6.23$
pH > 7 so the solution is basic.

(b) **Given:** $[H_3O^+] = 1. \times 10^{-7}$ M **Find:** pH and pOH
Conceptual Plan: $[H_3O^+] \rightarrow pH \rightarrow pOH$
$pH = -\log[H_3O^+]$ $pH + pOH = 14$
Solution: $pH = -\log(1.0 \times 10^{-7}) = 7.00$ $pOH = 14.00 - 7.00 = 7.00$
pH = 7 so the solution is neutral.

(c) **Given:** $[H_3O^+] = 2.2 \times 10^{-6}$ M **Find:** pH and pOH
Conceptual Plan: $[H_3O^+] \rightarrow pH \rightarrow pOH$
$pH = -\log[H_3O^+]$ $pH + pOH = 14$
Solution: $pH = -\log(2.2 \times 10^{-6}) = 5.66$ $pOH = 14.00 - 5.66 = 8.34$
pH < 7 so the solution is acidic.

15.50 (a) **Given:** pH = 8.55 **Find:** $[H_3O^+]$, $[OH^-]$
Conceptual Plan: $pH \rightarrow [H_3O^+] \rightarrow [OH^-]$
$pH = -\log[H_3O^+]$ $K_w = 1.0 \times 10^{-14} = [H_3O^+][OH^-]$
Solution: $pH = -\log[H_3O^+]$ $8.55 = -\log[H_3O^+]$
$-8.55 = \log[H_3O^+]$ $10^{-8.55} = 10^{\log[H_3O^+]}$
$10^{-8.55} = [H_3O^+]$ $[H_3O^+] = 2.8 \times 10^{-9}$
$K_w = 1 \times 10^{-14} = (2.8 \times 10^{-9})[OH^-]$
$[OH^-] = 3.6 \times 10^{-6}$ M

(b) **Given:** pH = 11.23 **Find:** $[H_3O^+]$, $[OH^-]$
Conceptual Plan: $pH \rightarrow [H_3O^+] \rightarrow [OH^-]$
$pH = -\log[H_3O^+]$ $K_w = 1.0 \times 10^{-14} = [H_3O^+][OH^-]$
Solution: $pH = -\log[H_3O^+]$ $11.23 = -\log[H_3O^+]$
$-11.23 = \log[H_3O^+]$ $10^{-11.23} = 10^{\log[H_3O^+]}$
$10^{-11.23} = [H_3O^+]$ $[H_3O^+] = 5.9 \times 10^{-12}$
$K_w = 1 \times 10^{-14} = (5.9 \times 10^{-12})[OH^-]$
$[OH^-] = 1.7 \times 10^{-3}$ M

(c) **Given:** pH = 2.87 **Find:** $[H_3O^+]$, $[OH^-]$
Conceptual Plan: **pH → $[H_3O^+]$ → $[OH^-]$**

pH = -log$[H_3O^+]$ $K_w = 1.0 \times 10^{-14} = [H_3O^+][OH^-]$

Solution: $pH = -\log[H_3O^+]$ $2.87 = -\log[H_3O^+]$

$-2.87 = \log[H_3O^+]$ $10^{-2.87} = 10^{\log[H_3O^+]}$

$10^{-2.87} = [H_3O^+]$ $[H_3O^+] = 1.3 \times 10^{-3}$

$K_w = 1 \times 10^{-14} = (1.3 \times 10^{-3})[OH^-]$

$[OH^-] = 7.4 \times 10^{-12}$ M

15.51 pH = -log$[H_3O^+]$ $K_w = 1.0 \times 10^{-14} = [H_3O^+][OH^-]$

$[H_3O^+]$	$[OH^-]$	pH	Acidic or basic
7.1×10^{-4}	1.4×10^{-11}	**3.15**	acidic
3.7×10^{-9}	2.7×10^{-6}	8.43	basic
8×10^{-12}	1×10^{-3}	**11.1**	basic
6.2×10^{-4}	**1.6×10^{-11}**	3.20	acidic

$[H_3O^+] = 10^{-3.15} = 7.1 \times 10^{-4}$ $[OH^-] = \dfrac{1.0 \times 10^{-14}}{7.1 \times 10^{-4}} = 1.4 \times 10^{-11}$

$[OH^-] = \dfrac{1.0 \times 10^{-14}}{3.7 \times 10^{-9}} = 2.7 \times 10^{-6}$ $pH = -\log(3.7 \times 10^{-9}) = 8.43$

$[H_3O^+] = 10^{-11.1} = 8 \times 10^{-12}$ $[OH^-] = \dfrac{1.0 \times 10^{-14}}{8 \times 10^{-12}} = 1 \times 10^{-3}$

$[H_3O^+] = \dfrac{1.0 \times 10^{-14}}{1.6 \times 10^{-11}} = 6.2 \times 10^{-4}$ $pH = -\log(6.2 \times 10^{-4}) = 3.20$

15.52 pH = -log$[H_3O^+]$ $K_w = 1.0 \times 10^{-14} = [H_3O^+][OH^-]$

$[H_3O^+]$	$[OH^-]$	pH	Acidic or basic
3.5×10^{-3}	2.9×10^{-12}	2.46	acidic
2.6×10^{-8}	**3.8×10^{-7}**	7.58	basic
1.8×10^{-9}	5.6×10^{-6}	8.74	basic
7.1×10^{-8}	1.4×10^{-7}	**7.15**	basic

$[OH^-] = \dfrac{1.0 \times 10^{-14}}{3.5 \times 10^{-3}} = 2.9 \times 10^{-12}$ $pH = -\log(3.5 \times 10^{-3}) = 2.46$

$[H_3O^+] = \dfrac{1.0 \times 10^{-14}}{3.8 \times 10^{-7}} = 2.6 \times 10^{-8}$ $pH = -\log(2.6 \times 10^{-8}) = 7.58$

$[OH^-] = \dfrac{1.0 \times 10^{-14}}{1.8 \times 10^{-9}} = 5.6 \times 10^{-6}$ $pH = -\log(1.8 \times 10^{-9}) = 8.74$

$[H_3O^+] = 10^{-7.15} = 7.1 \times 10^{-8}$ $[OH^-] = \dfrac{1.0 \times 10^{-14}}{7.1 \times 10^{-8}} = 1.4 \times 10^{-7}$

15.53 **Given:** $K_w = 2.4 \times 10^{-14}$ at 37°C **Find:** $[H_3O^+]$, pH
Conceptual Plan: **K_w → $[H_3O^+]$ → pH**

$K_w = [H_3O^+][OH^-]$ pH = -log$[H_3O^+]$

Solution: $H_2O(l) + H_2O(l) \leftrightharpoons H_3O^+(aq) + OH^-(aq)$

$K_w = [H_3O^+][OH^-]$

$[H_3O^+] = [OH^-] = \sqrt{K_w} = \sqrt{2.4 \times 10^{-14}} = 1.5 \times 10^{-7}$
$pH = -\log[H_3O^+] = -\log(1.5 \times 10^{-7}) = 6.81$
Check: The value of K_w increased indicating more products formed, so the $[H_3O^+]$ increases and the pH decreases from the values at 25°C.

15.54 The increasing value of K_w indicates more products are formed as the temperature increases. According to Le Châtelier, this means the heat is a reactant. Therefore, the autoionization of water is endothermic.

Acid Solutions

15.55 (a) **Given:** 0.25 M HCl (strong acid) **Find:** $[H_3O^+]$,$[OH^-]$, pH
Conceptual Plan: [HCl] → $[H_3O^+]$ → pH and then $[H_3O^+]$ → $[OH^-]$
[HCl] → $[H_3O^+]$ $pH = -\log[H_3O^+]$ $[H_3O^+][OH^-] = 1.0 \times 10^{-14}$
Solution: 0.25 M HCl = 0.25 M H_3O^+ pH = –log(0.25) = 0.60
$[OH^-] = 1.0 \times 10^{-14}/0.25\ M = 4.0 \times 10^{-14}$
Check: HCl is a strong acid with a relatively high concentration, so we expect the pH to be low and the $[OH^-]$ to be small.

(b) **Given:** 0.015 M HNO_3 (strong acid) **Find:** $[H_3O^+]$,$[OH^-]$, pH
Conceptual Plan: $[HNO_3]$ → $[H_3O^+]$ → pH and then $[H_3O^+]$ → $[OH^-]$
$[HNO_3]$ → $[H_3O^+]$ $pH = -\log[H_3O^+]$ $[H_3O^+][OH^-] = 1.0 \times 10^{-14}$
Solution: 0.015 M HNO_3 = 0.015 M H_3O^+ pH = –log(0.015) = 1.82
$[OH^-] = 1.0 \times 10^{-14}/0.015\ M = 6.7 \times 10^{-13}$
Check: HNO_3 is a strong acid, so we expect the pH to be low and the $[OH^-]$ to be small.

(c) **Given:** 0.052 M HBr and 0.020M HNO_3 (strong acids) **Find:** $[H_3O^+]$,$[OH^-]$, pH
Conceptual Plan: [HBr] + $[HNO_3]$ → $[H_3O^+]$ → pH and then $[H_3O^+]$ → $[OH^-]$
[HBr] + $[HNO_3]$ → $[H_3O^+]$ $pH = -\log[H_3O^+]$ $[H_3O^+][OH^-] = 1.0 \times 10^{-14}$
Solution: 0.052 M HBr = 0.052 M H_3O^+ and 0.020 M HNO_3 = 0.020 M H_3O^+
Total H_3O^+ = 0.052 M + 0.020 M = 0.072 M pH = –log(0.072) = 1.14
$[OH^-] = 1.0 \times 10^{-14}/0.072\ M = 1.4 \times 10^{-13}$
Check: HBr and HNO_3 are both strong acids and completely dissociate. This gives a relatively high concentration, so we expect the pH to be low and the $[OH^-]$ to be small.

(d) **Given:** HNO_3 = 0.655% by mass, $d_{solution}$ = 1.01 g/mL **Find:** $[H_3O^+]$,$[OH^-]$, pH
Conceptual Plan:
% mass HNO_3 → g HNO_3 → mol HNO_3 and then g soln → mL soln → L soln → M HNO_3
$\frac{\%}{100}$ $\frac{\text{mol HNO}_3}{63.018\text{ g HNO}_3}$ $\frac{1.01\text{ g soln}}{\text{mL soln}}$ $\frac{1000\text{ mL soln}}{\text{L soln}}$ $\frac{\text{mol HNO}_3}{\text{L soln}}$
→ M H_3O^+ → pH and then $[H_3O^+]$ → $[OH^-]$
$[HNO_3]$ → $[H_3O^+]$ $pH = -\log[H_3O^+]$ $[H_3O^+][OH^-] = 1.0 \times 10^{-14}$

Solution: $\frac{0.655\ \cancel{\text{g HNO}_3}}{100\ \cancel{\text{g soln}}} \times \frac{1\text{ mol HNO}_3}{63.018\ \cancel{\text{g HNO}_3}} \times \frac{1.01\ \cancel{\text{g soln}}}{\cancel{\text{mL soln}}} \times \frac{1000\ \cancel{\text{mL soln}}}{\text{L soln}} = 0.105\text{ M HNO}_3$

0.105 M HNO_3 = 0.105 M H_3O^+ pH = –log(0.105) = 0.979
$[OH^-] = 1.00 \times 10^{-14}/0.105\ M = 9.52 \times 10^{-14}$
Check: HNO_3 is a strong acid and completely dissociates. This gives a relatively high concentration, so we expect the pH to be low and the $[OH^-]$ to be small.

15.56 (a) **Given:** 0.048 M HI (strong acid) **Find:** $[H_3O^+]$,$[OH^-]$, pH
Conceptual Plan: [HI] → $[H_3O^+]$ → pH and then $[H_3O^+]$ → $[OH^-]$
[HI] → $[H_3O^+]$ $pH = -\log[H_3O^+]$ $[H_3O^+][OH^-] = 1.0 \times 10^{-14}$
Solution: 0.048 M HI = 0.048 M H_3O^+ pH = –log(0.048) = 1.32
$[OH^-] = 1.0 \times 10^{-14}/0.048\ M = 2.1 \times 10^{-13}$
Check: HI is a strong acid with a relatively high concentration, so we expect the pH to be low and the $[OH^-]$ to be small.

(b) **Given:** 0.0895 M $HClO_4$ (strong acid) **Find:** $[H_3O^+]$,$[OH^-]$, pH
Conceptual Plan: $[HClO_4] \rightarrow [H_3O^+] \rightarrow$ **pH and then** $[H_3O^+] \rightarrow [OH^-]$

$[HClO_4] \rightarrow [H_3O^+]$ pH = -log$[H_3O^+]$ $[H_3O^+][OH^-] = 1.0 \times 10^{-14}$

Solution: 0.0895 M $HClO_4$ = 0.0895 M H_3O^+ pH = –log(0.0895) = 1.048
$[OH^-] = 1.0 \times 10^{-14}/0.0895$ M $= 1.1 \times 10^{-13}$
Check: $HClO_4$ is a strong acid, so we expect the pH to be low and the $[OH^-]$ to be small.

(c) **Given:** 0.045 M $HClO_4$ and 0.048 M HCl (strong acids) **Find:** $[H_3O^+]$,$[OH^-]$, pH
Conceptual Plan: $[HCl] + [HClO_4] \rightarrow [H_3O^+] \rightarrow$ **pH and then** $[H_3O^+] \rightarrow [OH^-]$

$[HCl] + [HClO_4] \rightarrow [H_3O^+]$ pH = -log$[H_3O^+]$ $[H_3O^+][OH^-] = 1.0 \times 10^{-14}$

Solution: 0.045 M $HClO_4$ = 0.045 M H_3O^+ and 0.048 M HNO_3 = 0.048 M H_3O^+
Total H_3O^+ = 0.045 M + 0.048 M = 0.093 M pH = –log(0.093) = 1.03
$[OH^-] = 1.0 \times 10^{-14}/0.093$ M $= 1.1 \times 10^{-13}$
Check: $HClO_4$ and HNO_3 are both strong acids and completely dissociate. This gives a relatively high concentration, so we expect the pH to be low and the $[OH^-]$ to be small.

(d) **Given:** HCl = 1.09% by mass, $d_{solution}$ = 1.01 g/mL **Find:** $[H_3O^+]$,$[OH^-]$, pH
Conceptual Plan:
% mass HCl → g HCl → mol HCl and then g soln → mL soln → L soln → M HCl

$\frac{\%}{100}$ $\frac{\text{mol HCl}}{36.46\text{ g HCl}}$ $\frac{1.01\text{ g soln}}{\text{mL soln}}$ $\frac{1000\text{ mL soln}}{\text{L soln}}$ $\frac{\text{mol HCl}}{\text{L soln}}$

→ M H_3O^+ **→ pH and then** $[H_3O^+] \rightarrow [OH^-]$

$[HCl] \rightarrow [H_3O^+]$ pH = -log$[H_3O^+]$ $[H_3O^+][OH^-] = 1 \times 10^{-14}$

Solution: $$\frac{1.09\text{ g HCl}}{100\text{ g soln}} \times \frac{1\text{ mol HCl}}{36.36\text{ g HCl}} \times \frac{1.01\text{ g soln}}{\text{mL soln}} \times \frac{1000\text{ mL soln}}{\text{L soln}} = 0.3019\text{ M} = 0.302\text{ M HCl}$$

0.302 M HCl = 0.302 M H_3O^+ pH = –log(0.302) = 0.520
$[OH^-] = 1.0 \times 10^{-14}/0.302$ M $= 3.31 \times 10^{-14}$
Check: HCl is a strong acid and completely dissociates. This gives a relatively high concentration, so we expect the pH to be low and the $[OH^-]$ to be small.

15.57 (a) **Given:** pH = 1.25, 0.250 L **Find:** g HI
Conceptual Plan: pH → $[H_3O^+]$ **→ [HI] → mol HI → g HI**

pH = -log$[H_3O^+]$ $[H_3O^+] \rightarrow$ [HI] mol = MV g = mol(127.9 g/mol)

Solution: $[H_3O^+] = 10^{-1.25} = 0.056\text{ M} = [HI]$ $\frac{0.056\text{ mol HI}}{\text{L}} \times 0.250\text{ L} \times \frac{127.9\text{ g HI}}{\text{mol HI}} = 1.8\text{ g HI}$

(b) **Given:** pH = 1.75, 0.250 L **Find:** g HI
Conceptual Plan: pH → $[H_3O^+]$ **→ [HI] → mol HI → g HI**

pH = -log$[H_3O^+]$ $[H_3O^+] \rightarrow$ [HI] mol = MV g = mol(127.9 g/mol)

Solution: $[H_3O^+] = 10^{-1.75} = 0.01\underline{7}8\text{ M} = [HI]$ $\frac{0.01\underline{7}8\text{ mol HI}}{\text{L}} \times 0.250\text{ L} \times \frac{127.9\text{ g HI}}{\text{mol HI}} = 0.57\text{ g HI}$

(c) **Given:** pH = 2.85, 0.250 L **Find:** g HI
Conceptual Plan: pH → $[H_3O^+]$ **→ [HI] → mol HI → g HI**

pH = -log$[H_3O^+]$ $[H_3O^+] \rightarrow$ [HI] mol = MV g = mol(127.9 g/mol)

Solution: $[H_3O^+] = 10^{-2.85} = 0.0014\text{ M} = [HI]$ $\frac{0.0014\text{ mol HI}}{\text{L}} \times 0.250\text{ L} \times \frac{127.9\text{ g HI}}{\text{mol HI}} = 0.045\text{ g HI}$

15.58 (a) **Given:** pH = 2.50, 0.500 L **Find:** g $HClO_4$
Conceptual Plan: pH → $[H_3O^+]$ **→** $[HClO_4]$ **→ mol** $HClO_4$ **→ g** $HClO_4$

pH = -log$[H_3O^+]$ $[H_3O^+] \rightarrow [HClO_4]$ mol = MV g = mol(100.46 g/mol)

Solution:
$[H_3O^+] = 10^{-2.50} = 0.003\underline{1}6\text{ M} = [HClO_4]$
$$\frac{0.003\underline{1}6\text{ mol HClO}_4}{\text{L}} \times 0.500\text{ L} \times \frac{100.46\text{ g HClO}_4}{\text{mol HClO}_4} = 0.16\text{ g HClO}_4$$

(b) **Given:** pH = 1.50, 0.500 L **Find:** g $HClO_4$

Conceptual Plan: pH → $[H_3O^+]$ → $[HClO_4]$ → mol $HClO_4$ → g $HClO_4$

pH = -log$[H_3O^+]$ $[H_3O^+]$ → $[HClO_4]$ mol = MV g = mol(100.46 g/mol)

Solution:

$$[H_3O^+] = 10^{-1.50} = 0.03\underline{1}6 \text{ M} = [HClO_4]$$

$$\frac{0.03\underline{1}6 \cancel{\text{mol HClO}_4}}{\cancel{\text{L}}} \times 0.500 \cancel{\text{L}} \times \frac{100.46 \text{ g HClO}_4}{\cancel{\text{mol HClO}_4}} = 1.6 \text{ g HClO}_4$$

(c) **Given:** pH = 0.50, 0.500 L **Find:** g $HClO_4$

Conceptual Plan: pH → $[H_3O^+]$ → $[HClO_4]$ → mol $HClO_4$ → g $HClO_4$

pH = -log$[H_3O^+]$ $[H_3O^+]$ → $[HClO_4]$ mol = MV g = mol(100.46 g/mol)

Solution:

$$[H_3O^+] = 10^{-0.50} = 0.3\underline{1}6\text{M} = [HClO_4]$$

$$\frac{0.3\underline{1}6 \cancel{\text{mol HClO}_4}}{\cancel{\text{L}}} \times 0.500 \cancel{\text{L}} \times \frac{100.46 \text{ g HClO}_4}{\cancel{\text{mol HClO}_4}} = 16 \text{ g HClO}_4$$

15.59 **Given:** 224 mL HCl, 27.2°C, 1.02 atm, 1.5 L solution **Find:** pH

Conceptual Plan: vol HCl → mol HCl → [HCl] → $[H_3O^+]$ → pH

$PV = nRT$ $M = \frac{\text{mol HCl}}{\text{vol soln}}$ $[HCl] = [H_3O^+]$ pH = -log$[H_3O^+]$

$$\textbf{Solution: } n = \frac{(1.02 \cancel{\text{atm}})(224 \cancel{\text{mL}})\left(\frac{\cancel{\text{L}}}{1000 \cancel{\text{mL}}}\right)}{\left(\frac{0.0821 \cancel{\text{L}} \cdot \cancel{\text{atm}}}{\text{mol} \cancel{\text{K}}}\right)((27.2 + 273.15) \cancel{\text{K}})} = 0.0092\underline{7} \text{ mol}$$

$$[HCl] = \frac{0.0092\underline{7} \text{ mol}}{1.5 \text{ L}} = 0.006\underline{1}8 \text{ M} = [H_3O^+] \quad \text{pH} = -\log(0.006\underline{1}8) = 2.21$$

15.60 **Given:** 36.0% HCl, d_{soln} = 1.179 g/mL; 5.00 L pH 1.8 **Find:** vol soln.

Conceptual Plan: % mass HCl → g HCl → mol HCl and then g soln → mL soln → L soln → M HCl

$\frac{\%}{100}$ $\frac{\text{mol HCl}}{36.46 \text{ g HCl}}$ $\frac{1.01 \text{ g soln}}{\text{mL soln}}$ $\frac{1000 \text{ L soln}}{\text{L soln}}$ $\frac{\text{mol HCl}}{\text{L soln}}$

→ M H_3O^+ and then pH → $[H_3O^+]$ and the V_1M_1 → V_2M_2

[HCl] → $[H_3O^+]$ $[H_3O^+] = 10^{-pH}$ $V_1M_1 = V_2M_2$

$$\textbf{Solution: } \frac{36.0 \cancel{\text{g HCl}}}{100 \cancel{\text{g soln}}} \times \frac{1 \text{ mol HCl}}{36.46 \cancel{\text{g HCl}}} \times \frac{1.179 \cancel{\text{g soln}}}{\cancel{\text{mL soln}}} \times \frac{1000 \cancel{\text{mL soln}}}{\text{L soln}} = 11.\underline{6}4 \text{ M HCl}$$

$[H_3O^+] = 10^{-1.8} = 0.0159$ M

$V_1M_1 = V_2M_2$ $V_1(11.\underline{6}4 \text{ M}) = (5.00 \text{ L})(0.0159 \text{ M})$ $V_1 = 0.0068\underline{2}9 \text{ L} = 6.83 \text{ mL}$

15.61 **Given:** 0.100 M benzoic acid. $K_a = 6.5 \times 10^{-5}$ **Find:** $[H_3O^+]$, pH

Conceptual Plan: Write a balanced reaction. Prepare an ICE table, represent the change with x, sum the table, determine the equilibrium values, put the equilibrium values in the equilibrium expression, and solve for x. Determine $[H_3O^+]$ and pH.

Solution: $HC_7H_5O_2(aq) + H_2O(l) \leftrightarrows H_3O^+(aq) + C_7H_5O_2^-(aq)$

I	0.100 M	0.0	0.0
C	$-x$	x	x
E	$0.100 - x$	x	x

$$K_a = \frac{[H_3O^+][C_7H_5O_2^-]}{[HC_7H_5O_2]} = \frac{(x)(x)}{(0.100 - x)} = 6.5 \times 10^{-5}$$

Assume x is small compared to 0.100.

$x^2 = (6.5 \times 10^{-5})(0.100)$ $x = 2.5 \times 10^{-3} \text{ M} = [H_3O^+]$

$$\text{Check assumption: } \frac{2.5 \times 10^{-3}}{0.100} \times 100\% = 2.5\%; \text{ assumption valid.}$$

$\text{pH} = -\log(2.5 \times 10^{-3}) = 2.60$

15.62 **Given:** 0.200 M formic acid. $K_a = 1.8 \times 10^{-4}$ **Find:** $[H_3O^+]$, pH

Conceptual Plan: Write a balanced reaction. Prepare an ICE table, represent the change with x, sum the table, determine the equilibrium values, put the equilibrium values in the equilibrium expression, and solve for x. Determine $[H_3O^+]$ and pH.

Solution: $HCH_2O(aq) + H_2O(l) \rightleftharpoons H_3O^+(aq) + CH_2O^-(aq)$

I	0.200 M	0.0	0.0
C	$-x$	x	x
E	$0.200 - x$	x	x

$$K_a = \frac{[H_3O^+][CH_2O^-]}{[HCH_2O]} = \frac{(x)(x)}{(0.200 - x)} = 1.8 \times 10^{-4}$$

Assume x is small compared to 0.200.

$x^2 = (1.8 \times 10^{-4})(0.200) \quad x = 6.0 \times 10^{-3}\ M = [H_3O^+]$

Check assumption: $\frac{6.0 \times 10^{-3}}{0.200} \times 100\% = 3.0\%$, assumption valid.

$pH = -\log(6.0 \times 10^{-3}) = 2.22$

15.63 (a) **Given:** 0.500 M HNO_2. $K_a = 4.6 \times 10^{-4}$ **Find:** pH

Conceptual Plan: Write a balanced reaction. Prepare an ICE table, represent the change with x, sum the table, determine the equilibrium values, put the equilibrium values in the equilibrium expression, and solve for x. Determine $[H_3O^+]$ and pH.

Solution: $HNO_2(aq) + H_2O(l) \rightleftharpoons H_3O^+(aq) + NO_2^-(aq)$

I	0.500 M	0.0	0.0
C	$-x$	x	x
E	$0.500 - x$	x	x

$$K_a = \frac{[H_3O^+][NO_2^-]}{[HNO_2]} = \frac{(x)(x)}{(0.500 - x)} = 4.6 \times 10^{-4}$$

Assume x is small compared to 0.500.

$x^2 = (4.6 \times 10^{-4})(0.500) \quad x = 0.015\ M = [H_3O^+]$

Check assumption: $\frac{0.015}{0.500} \times 100\% = 3.0\%$ assumption valid.

pH = -log(0.015) = 1.82

(b) **Given:** 0.100 M HNO_2. $K_a = 4.6 \times 10^{-4}$ **Find:** pH

Conceptual Plan: Write a balanced reaction. Prepare an ICE table, represent the change with x, sum the table, determine the equilibrium values, put the equilibrium values in the equilibrium expression, and solve for x. Determine $[H_3O^+]$ and pH.

Solution: $HNO_2(aq) + H_2O(l) \rightleftharpoons H_3O^+(aq) + NO_2^-(aq)$

I	0.100 M	0.0	0.0
C	$-x$	x	x
E	$0.100 - x$	x	x

$$K_a = \frac{[H_3O^+][NO_2^-]}{[HNO_2]} = \frac{(x)(x)}{(0.100 - x)} = 4.6 \times 10^{-4}$$

Assume x is small compared to 0.100.

$x^2 = (4.6 \times 10^{-4})(0.100) \quad x = 0.0068\ M = [H_3O^+]$

Check assumption: $\frac{0.0068}{0.100} \times 100\% = 6.8\%$ assumption not valid, solve using quadratic equation.

$x^2 = (4.6 \times 10^{-4})(0.100 - x) \quad x^2 + 4.6 \times 10^{-4}x - 4.6 \times 10^{-5} = 0$

$x = 0.00656$

$pH = -\log(0.00656) = 2.18$

(c) **Given:** 0.100 M HNO_2. $K_a = 4.6 \times 10^{-4}$ **Find:** pH

Conceptual Plan: Write a balanced reaction. Prepare an ICE table, represent the change with x, sum the table, determine the equilibrium values, put the equilibrium values in the equilibrium expression, and solve for x. Determine $[H_3O^+]$ and pH.

Solution: $HNO_2(aq) + H_2O(l) \leftrightharpoons H_3O^+(aq) + NO_2^-(aq)$

I	0.0100 M	0.0	0.0
C	- x	x	x
E	0.0100 – x	x	x

$$K_a = \frac{[H_3O^+][NO_2^-]}{[HNO_2]} = \frac{(x)(x)}{(0.0100 - x)} = 4.6 \times 10^{-4}$$

Assume x is small compared to 0.100.

$x^2 = (4.6 \times 10^{-4})(0.0100)$ $x = 0.0021$ M = $[H_3O^+]$

Check assumption: $\frac{0.0021}{0.0100} \times 100\% = 21\%$ assumption not valid, solve with quadratic equation.

$x^2 = (4.6 \times 10^{-4})(0.0100 - x)$ $x^2 + 4.6 \times 10^{-4} x - 4.6 \times 10^{-6} = 0$

$x = 0.0019$

pH = $-\log(0.0019) = 2.72$

15.64 (a) **Given:** 0.250 M HF $K_a = 3.5 \times 10^{-4}$ **Find:** pH

Conceptual Plan: Write a balanced reaction. Prepare an ICE table, represent the change with x, sum the table, determine the equilibrium values, put the equilibrium values in the equilibrium expression, and solve for x. Determine $[H_3O^+]$ and pH.

Solution: $HF(aq) + H_2O(l) \leftrightharpoons H_3O^+(aq) + F^-(aq)$

I	0.250 M	0.0	0.0
C	- x	x	x
E	0.250 – x	x	x

$$K_a = \frac{[H_3O^+][F^-]}{[HF]} = \frac{(x)(x)}{(0.250 - x)} = 3.5 \times 10^{-4}$$

Assume x is small compared to 0.250.

$x^2 = (3.5 \times 10^{-4})(0.250)$ $x = 0.00935$ M = $[H_3O^+]$

Check assumption: $\frac{0.00935}{0.250} \times 100\% = 3.7\%$ assumption valid.

pH = $-\log(0.00935) = 2.03$

(b) **Given:** 0.0500 M HF $K_a = 3.5 \times 10^{-4}$ **Find:** pH

Conceptual Plan: Write a balanced reaction. Prepare an ICE table, represent the change with x, sum the table, determine the equilibrium values, put the equilibrium values in the equilibrium expression, and solve for x. Determine $[H_3O^+]$ and pH.

Solution: $HF(aq) + H_2O(l) \leftrightharpoons H_3O^+(aq) + F^-(aq)$

I	0.0500 M	0.0	0.0
C	- x	x	x
E	0.0500 – x	x	x

$$K_a = \frac{[H_3O^+][F^-]}{[HF]} = \frac{(x)(x)}{(0.0500 - x)} = 3.5 \times 10^{-4}$$

Assume x is small compared to 0.0500.

$x^2 = (3.5 \times 10^{-4})(0.0500)$ $x = 0.00418$ M = $[H_3O^+]$

Check assumption: $\frac{0.00418}{0.050} \times 100\% = 8.3\%$ assumption not valid, solve with quadratic equation.

$x^2 + 3.5 \times 10^{-4} x - 1.75 \times 10^{-5} = 0$ $x = 0.0040 = [H_3O^+]$

pH = $-\log(0.0040) = 2.40$

(c) **Given:** 0.0250 M HF $K_a = 3.5 \times 10^{-4}$ **Find:** pH

Conceptual Plan: Write a balanced reaction. Prepare an ICE table, represent the change with x, sum the table, determine the equilibrium values, put the equilibrium values in the equilibrium expression, and solve for x. Determine $[H_3O^+]$ and pH.

Solution: $HF(aq) + H_2O(l) \leftrightharpoons H_3O^+(aq) + F^-(aq)$

I	0.0250 M	0.0	0.0
C	- x	x	x
E	0.0250 – x	x	x

$$K_a = \frac{[H_3O^+][F^-]}{[HF]} = \frac{(x)(x)}{(0.0250 - x)} = 3.5 \times 10^{-4}$$

Assume x is small compared to 0.0250.

$x^2 = (3.5 \times 10^{-4})(0.0250)$ $\quad x = 0.00\underline{2}95\text{ M} = [H_3O^+]$

Check assumption: $\frac{0.00\underline{2}95}{0.0250} \times 100\% = 11.8\%$ assumption not valid, solve with quadratic equation.

$x^2 + 3.5 \times 10^{-4}x - 8.75 \times 10^{-6} = 0$ $\quad x = 0.00\underline{2}79 = [H_3O^+]$

$\text{pH} = -\log(0.00\underline{2}79) = 2.55$

15.65 **Given:** 15.0 mL glacial acetic, $d = 1.05$ g/mL, dilute to 1.50 L, $K_a = 1.8 \times 10^{-5}$ **Find:** pH

Conceptual Plan: mL acetic acid → g acetic acid → mol acetic acid → M and then write a balanced reaction.

$\frac{1.05\text{ g}}{\text{mL}}$ $\quad \frac{\text{mol acetic acid}}{60.05\text{ g}}$ $\quad M = \frac{\text{mol}}{\text{L}}$

Prepare an ICE table, represent the change with x, sum the table, determine the equilibrium values, put the equilibrium values in the equilibrium expression, and solve for x. Determine $[H_3O^+]$ and pH.

Solution: $15.0\text{ mL} \times \frac{1.05\text{ g}}{\text{mL}} \times \frac{1\text{ mol}}{60.05\text{ g}} \times \frac{1}{1.50\text{ L}} = 0.17\underline{4}8\text{ M}$

	$HC_2H_3O_2(aq) + H_2O(l)$ ⇆	$H_3O^+(aq)$ +	$C_2H_3O_2^-(aq)$
I	0.1748 M	0.0	0.0
C	$-x$	x	x
E	$0.1748 - x$	x	x

$$K_a = \frac{[H_3O^+][C_2H_3O_2^-]}{[HC_2H_3O_2]} = \frac{(x)(x)}{(0.1748 - x)} = 1.8 \times 10^{-5}$$

Assume x is small compared to 0.1748.

$x^2 = (1.8 \times 10^{-5})(0.1748)$ $\quad x = 0.001\underline{7}7\text{ M} = [H_3O^+]$

Check assumption: $\frac{0.001\underline{7}7}{0.1748} \times 1005 = 1.0\%$ assumption valid.

$\text{pH} = -\log(0.001\underline{7}7) = 2.75$

15.66 **Given:** 1.35% formic acid, $d = 1.01$ g/mL, $K_a = 1.8 \times 10^{-4}$ **Find:** pH

Conceptual Plan: % formic acid → g formic acid → mol and g soln → mL soln → L soln and then M

$\frac{\text{mol}}{46.03\text{ g}}$ $\quad \frac{1.01\text{ g soln}}{\text{mL soln}}$ $\quad \frac{1000\text{ mL}}{\text{L soln}}$

Write a balanced reaction. Prepare an ICE table, represent the change with x, sum the table, determine the equilibrium values, put the equilibrium values in the equilibrium expression, and solve for x. Determine $[H_3O^+]$ and pH.

Solution: $\frac{1.35\text{ g } HCHO_2}{100\text{ g soln}} \times \frac{\text{mol } HCHO_2}{46.03\text{ g}} \times \frac{1.01\text{ g soln}}{\text{mL soln}} \times \frac{1000\text{ mL soln}}{\text{L soln}} = 0.29\underline{6}2\text{ M}$

	$HCHO_2(aq) + H_2O(l)$ ⇆	$H_3O^+(aq)$ +	$CHO_2^-(aq)$
I	0.2962 M	0.0	0.0
C	$-x$	x	x
E	$0.2962 - x$	x	x

$$K_a = \frac{[H_3O^+][CHO_2^-]}{[HCHO_2]} = \frac{(x)(x)}{(0.2962 - x)} = 1.8 \times 10^{-4}$$

Assume x is small compared to 0.2962.

$x^2 = (1.8 \times 10^{-4})(0.2962)$ $\quad x = 0.007\underline{3}0\text{ M} = [H_3O^+]$

Check assumption: $\frac{0.007\underline{3}0}{0.2962} \times 100\% = 2.5\%$ assumption valid.

$\text{pH} = -\log(0.007\underline{3}0) = 2.14$

15.67 **Given:** 0.185 M HA, pH = 2.95 **Find:** K_a

Conceptual Plan: pH → $[H_3O^+]$ and then write a balanced reaction. Prepare an ICE table, calculate equilibrium concentrations, and then plug into the equilibrium expression to solve for K_a.

Solution: $[H_3O^+] = 10^{-2.95} = 0.00112\ M = [A^-]$

	$HA(aq) + H_2O(l) \leftrightarrows$	$H_3O^+(aq) +$	$A^-(aq)$
I	0.185 M	0.0	0.0
C	$-x$	x	x
E	0.185 – 0.00112	0.00112	0.0011

$$K_a = \frac{[H_3O^+][A^-]}{[HA]} = \frac{(0.00112)(0.00112)}{(0.185 - 0.00112)} = 6.8 \times 10^{-6}$$

15.68 **Given:** 0.115 M HA, pH = 3.29 **Find:** K_a
Conceptual Plan: pH → $[H_3O^+]$ and then write a balanced reaction. Prepare an ICE table, calculate equilibrium concentrations, and then plug into the equilibrium expression to solve for K_a.
Solution: $[H_3O^+] = 10^{-3.29} = 5.\underline{1}3 \times 10^{-4}\ M = [A^-]$

	$HA(aq) + H_2O(l) \leftrightarrows$	$H_3O^+(aq) +$	$A^-(aq)$
I	0.185 M	0.0	0.0
C	$-x$	x	x
E	$0.115 - 5.\underline{1}3 \times 10^{-4}$	$5.\underline{1}3 \times 10^{-4}$	$5.\underline{1}3 \times 10^{-4}$

$$K_a = \frac{[H_3O^+][A^-]}{[HA]} = \frac{(5.\underline{1}3 \times 10^{-4})(5.\underline{1}3 \times 10^{-4})}{(0.115 - 5.\underline{1}3 \times 10^{-4})} = 2.3 \times 10^{-6}$$

15.69 **Given:** 0.125 M HCN $K_a = 4.9 \times 10^{-10}$ **Find:** % ionization
Conceptual Plan: Write a balanced reaction. Prepare an ICE table, represent the change with x, sum the table, determine the equilibrium values, put the equilibrium values in the equilibrium expression, solve for x, and then $x \rightarrow$ % ionization.

$$\%\ \text{ionization} = \frac{x}{[HCN]_{original}} \times 100$$

Solution: $HCN(aq) + H_2O(l) \leftrightarrows H_3O^+(aq) + CN^-(aq)$

I	0.125 M	0.0	0.0
C	$-x$	x	x
E	$0.125 - x$	x	x

$$K_a = \frac{[H_3O^+][CN^-]}{[HCN]} = \frac{(x)(x)}{(0.125 - x)} = 4.9 \times 10^{-10}$$

Assume x is small compared to 0.125.

$x^2 = (4.9 \times 10^{-10})(0.125) \quad x = 7.\underline{8}3 \times 10^{-6}$

$$\%\ \text{ionization} = \frac{7.\underline{8}3 \times 10^{-6}}{0.125} \times 100 = 0.0063\%\ \text{ionized}$$

15.70 **Given:** 0.225 M $HC_7H_5O_2$ $K_a = 6.5 \times 10^{-5}$ **Find:** % ionization
Conceptual Plan: Write a balanced reaction. Prepare an ICE table, represent the change with x, sum the table, determine the equilibrium values, put the equilibrium values in the equilibrium expression, solve for x, and then $x \rightarrow$ % ionization.

$$\%\ \text{ionization} = \frac{x}{[HC_7H_5O_2]_{original}} \times 100$$

Solution: $HC_7H_5O_2(aq) + H_2O(l) \leftrightarrows H_3O^+(aq) + C_7H_5O_2^-(aq)$

I	0.125 M	0.0	0.0
C	$-x$	x	x
E	$0.125 - x$	x	x

$$K_a = \frac{[H_3O^+][C_7H_5O_2^-]}{[HC_7H_5O_2]} = \frac{(x)(x)}{(0.225 - x)} = 6.5 \times 10^{-5}$$

Assume x is small compared to 0.225.

$x^2 = (6.5 \times 10^{-5})(0.1225) \quad x = 0.003\underline{8}2$

$$\%\ \text{ionization} = \frac{0.003\underline{8}2}{0.225} \times 100 = 1.7\%\ \text{ionized}$$

15.71   (a)   **Given:** 1.00 M $HC_2H_3O_2$ $K_a = 1.8 \times 10^{-5}$ **Find:** % ionization
Conceptual Plan: Write a balanced reaction. Prepare an ICE table, represent the change with x, sum the table, determine the equilibrium values, put the equilibrium values in the equilibrium expression, solve for x, and then $x \rightarrow$ % ionization.

$$\% \text{ ionization} = \frac{x}{[HC_2H_3O_2]_{original}} \times 100$$

Solution: $HC_2H_3O_2\ (aq) + H_2O(l) \leftrightarrows H_3O^+(aq) + C_2H_3O_2^-\ (aq)$

I	1.00 M	0.0	0.0
C	$-x$	x	x
E	$1.00 - x$	x	x

$$K_a = \frac{[H_3O^+][C_2H_3O_2^-]}{[HC_2H_3O_2]} = \frac{(x)(x)}{(1.00 - x)} = 1.8 \times 10^{-5}$$

Assume x is small compared to 1.00.

$x^2 = (1.8 \times 10^{-5})(1.00)$ $x = 0.00424$

$$\% \text{ ionization} = \frac{0.00424}{1.00} \times 100 = 0.42\% \text{ ionized}$$

(b)   **Given:** 0.500 M $HC_2H_3O_2$ $K_a = 1.8 \times 10^{-5}$ **Find:** % ionization
Conceptual Plan: Write a balanced reaction. Prepare an ICE table, represent the change with x, sum the table, determine the equilibrium values, put the equilibrium values in the equilibrium expression, solve for x, and then $x \rightarrow$ % ionization.

$$\% \text{ ionization} = \frac{x}{[HC_2H_3O_2]_{original}} \times 100$$

Solution: $HC_2H_3O_2(aq) + H_2O(l) \leftrightarrows H_3O^+(aq) + C_2H_3O_2^-\ (aq)$

I	0.500 M	0.0	0.0
C	$-x$	x	x
E	$0.500 - x$	x	x

$$K_a = \frac{[H_3O^+][C_2H_3O_2^-]}{[HC_2H_3O_2]} = \frac{(x)(x)}{(0.500 - x)} = 1.8 \times 10^{-5}$$

Assume x is small compared to 0.500.

$x^2 = (1.8 \times 10^{-5})(0.500)$ $x = 0.00300$

$$\% \text{ ionization} = \frac{0.00300}{0.500} \times 100 = 0.60\% \text{ ionized}$$

(c)   **Given:** 0.100 M $HC_2H_3O_2$ $K_a = 1.8 \times 10^{-5}$ **Find:** % ionization
Conceptual Plan: Write a balanced reaction. Prepare an ICE table, represent the change with x, sum the table, determine the equilibrium values, put the equilibrium values in the equilibrium expression, solve for x, and then $x \rightarrow$ % ionization.

$$\% \text{ ionization} = \frac{x}{[HC_2H_3O_2]_{original}} \times 100$$

Solution: $HC_2H_3O_2(aq) + H_2O(l) \leftrightarrows H_3O^+(aq) + C_2H_3O_2^-\ (aq)$

I	0.100 M	0.0	0.0
C	$-x$	x	x
E	$0.100 - x$	x	x

$$K_a = \frac{[H_3O^+][C_2H_3O_2^-]}{[HC_2H_3O_2]} = \frac{(x)(x)}{(0.100 - x)} = 1.8 \times 10^{-5}$$

Assume x is small compared to 1.00.

$x^2 = (1.8 \times 10^{-5})(0.100)$ $x = 0.00134$

$$\% \text{ ionization} = \frac{0.00134}{0.100} \times 100 = 1.3\% \text{ ionized}$$

(d)   **Given:** 0.0500 M $HC_2H_3O_2$ $K_a = 1.8 \times 10^{-5}$ **Find:** % ionization
Conceptual Plan: Write a balanced reaction. Prepare an ICE table, represent the change with x, sum the table, determine the equilibrium values, put the equilibrium values in the equilibrium expression, solve for x, and then $x \rightarrow$ % ionization.

$$\% \text{ ionization} = \frac{x}{[HC_2H_3O_2]_{original}} \times 100$$

Solution: $HC_2H_3O_2(aq) + H_2O(l) \leftrightarrows H_3O^+(aq) + C_2H_3O_2^-(aq)$

I	0.0500 M	0.0	0.0
C	$-x$	x	x
E	$0.0500 - x$	x	x

$$K_a = \frac{[H_3O^+][C_2H_3O_2^-]}{[HC_2H_3O_2]} = \frac{(x)(x)}{(0.0500 - x)} = 1.8 \times 10^{-5}$$

Assume x is small compared to 0.0500.

$x^2 = (1.8 \times 10^{-5})(0.0500) \quad x = 9.\underline{4}9 \times 10^{-4}$

$$\% \text{ ionization} = \frac{9.\underline{4}9 \times 10^{-4}}{0.0500} \times 100 = 1.9\% \text{ ionized}$$

15.72 (a) **Given:** 1.00 M $HCHO_2$ $K_a = 1.8 \times 10^{-4}$ **Find:** % ionization

Conceptual Plan: Write a balanced reaction. Prepare an ICE table, represent the change with x, sum the table, determine the equilibrium values, put the equilibrium values in the equilibrium expression, solve for x, and then $x \rightarrow$ % ionization.

$$\% \text{ ionization} = \frac{x}{[HCHO_2]_{original}} \times 100$$

Solution: $HCHO_2(aq) + H_2O(l) \leftrightarrows H_3O^+(aq) + CHO_2^-(aq)$

I	1.00 M	0.0	0.0
C	$-x$	x	x
E	$1.00 - x$	x	x

$$K_a = \frac{[H_3O^+][CHO_2^-]}{[HCHO_2]} = \frac{(x)(x)}{(1.00 - x)} = 1.8 \times 10^{-4}$$

Assume x is small compared to 1.00.

$x^2 = (1.8 \times 10^{-4})(1.00) \quad x = 0.01\underline{3}4$

$$\% \text{ ionization} = \frac{0.01\underline{3}4}{1.00} \times 100 = 1.3\% \text{ ionized}$$

(b) **Given:** 0.500 M $HCHO_2$ $K_a = 1.8 \times 10^{-4}$ **Find:** % ionization

Conceptual Plan: Write a balanced reaction. Prepare an ICE table, represent the change with x, sum the table, determine the equilibrium values, put the equilibrium values in the equilibrium expression, solve for x, and then $x \rightarrow$ % ionization.

$$\% \text{ ionization} = \frac{x}{[HCHO_2]_{original}} \times 100$$

Solution: $HCHO_2(aq) + H_2O(l) \leftrightarrows H_3O^+(aq) + CHO_2^-(aq)$

I	0.500 M	0.0	0.0
C	$-x$	x	x
E	$0.500 - x$	x	x

$$K_a = \frac{[H_3O^+][CHO_2^-]}{[HCHO_2]} = \frac{(x)(x)}{(0.500 - x)} = 1.8 \times 10^{-4}$$

Assume x is small compared to 1.00.

$x^2 = (1.8 \times 10^{-4})(0.500) \quad x = 0.009\underline{4}9$

$$\% \text{ ionization} = \frac{0.009\underline{4}9}{0.500} \times 100 = 1.9\% \text{ ionized}$$

(c) **Given:** 0.100 M $HCHO_2$ $K_a = 1.8 \times 10^{-4}$ **Find:** % ionization

Conceptual Plan: Write a balanced reaction. Prepare an ICE table, represent the change with x, sum the table, determine the equilibrium values, put the equilibrium values in the equilibrium expression, solve for x, and then $x \rightarrow$ % ionization.

$$\% \text{ ionization} = \frac{x}{[HCHO_2]_{original}} \times 100$$

Solution: $HCHO_2(aq) + H_2O(l) \leftrightarrows H_3O^+(aq) + CHO_2^-(aq)$

I	0.100 M	0.0	0.0
C	$-x$	x	x
E	$0.100 - x$	x	x

$$K_a = \frac{[H_3O^+][CHO_2^-]}{[HCHO_2]} = \frac{(x)(x)}{(0.100 - x)} = 1.8 \times 10^{-4}$$

Assume x is small compared to 0.100.

$x^2 = (1.8 \times 10^{-4})(0.100) \quad x = 0.00424$

$$\% \text{ ionization} = \frac{0.00424}{0.100} \times 100 = 4.2\% \text{ ionized}$$

(d) **Given:** 0.0500 M $HCHO_2$ $K_a = 1.8 \times 10^{-4}$ **Find:** % ionization

Conceptual Plan: Write a balanced reaction. Prepare an ICE table, represent the change with x, sum the table, determine the equilibrium values, put the equilibrium values in the equilibrium expression, solve for x, and then $x \rightarrow$ % ionization.

$$\% \text{ ionization} = \frac{x}{[HCHO_2]_{original}} \times 100$$

Solution: $HCHO_2(aq) + H_2O(l) \leftrightarrows H_3O^+(aq) + CHO_2^-(aq)$

	$HCHO_2$	H_3O^+	CHO_2^-
I	0.0500 M	0.0	0.0
C	$-x$	x	x
E	$0.0500 - x$	x	x

$$K_a = \frac{[H_3O^+][CHO_2^-]}{[HCHO_2]} = \frac{(x)(x)}{(0.0500 - x)} = 1.8 \times 10^{-4}$$

Assume x is small compared to 0.0500.

$x^2 = (1.8 \times 10^{-4})(0.0500) \quad x = 0.00300$

$$\% \text{ ionization} = \frac{0.00300}{0.0500} \times 100\% = 6.0\% \text{ ionized}$$

x is small assumption is invalid since 6.0% is greater than the 5.0% limit.

$x^2 + 1.8 \times 10^{-4}x - 9.0 \times 10^{-6} = 0$

Solve for x using the quadratic equation $\quad x = 0.00291$

$$\% \text{ ionization} = \frac{0.00291}{0.0500} \times 100 = 5.8\%$$

15.73 **Given:** 0.148 M HA 1.55% dissociation **Find:** K_a

Conceptual Plan: M $\rightarrow$ $[H_3O^+]$ $\rightarrow$ K_a and then write a balanced reaction, determine equilibrium concentration, and plug into the equilibrium expression.

Solution: (0.148 M HA)(0.0155) = 0.002294 $[H_3O^+] = [A^-]$

$HA(aq) + H_2O(l) \leftrightarrows H_3O^+(aq) + A^-(aq)$

	HA	H_3O^+	A^-
I	0. 148 M	0.0	0.0
C	$-x$	x	x
E	0.148 –0.002294	0.002294	0.002294

$$K_a = \frac{[H_3O^+][A^-]}{[HA]} = \frac{(0.002294)(0.002294)}{(0.148 - 0.002294)} = 3.61 \times 10^{-5}$$

15.74 **Given:** 0.085 M HA 0.59% dissociation **Find:** K_a

Conceptual Plan: M $\rightarrow$ $[H_3O^+]$ $\rightarrow$ K_a and then write a balanced reaction, determine equilibrium concentration, and plug into the equilibrium expression.

Solution: (0.085 M HA)(0.0059) = $5.02 \times 10^{-4}[H_3O^+] = [A^-]$

$HA(aq) + H_2O(l) \leftrightarrows H_3O^+(aq) + A^-(aq)$

	HA	H_3O^+	A^-
I	0. 085 M	0.0	0.0
C	$-x$	x	x
E	$0.085 - 5.02 \times 10^{-4}$	5.02×10^{-4}	5.02×10^{-4}

$$K_a = \frac{[H_3O^+][A^-]}{[HA]} = \frac{(5.02 \times 10^{-4})(5.02 \times 10^{-4})}{(0.085 - 5.02 \times 10^{-4})} = 3.0 \times 10^{-6}$$

15.75 (a) **Given:** 0.250 M HF $K_a = 3.5 \times 10^{-4}$ **Find:** pH, % dissociation

Conceptual Plan: Write a balanced reaction. Prepare an ICE table, represent the change with x, sum the table, determine the equilibrium values, put the equilibrium values in the equilibrium expression, solve for x, and then $x \rightarrow$ % ionization.

$$\% \text{ ionization} = \frac{x}{[HF]_{original}} \times 100$$

Solution: $HF(aq) + H_2O(l) \leftrightharpoons H_3O^+(aq) + F^-(aq)$

I	0.250 M	0.0	0.0
C	$-x$	x	x
E	$0.250 - x$	x	x

$$K_a = \frac{[H_3O^+][F^-]}{[HF]} = \frac{(x)(x)}{(0.250 - x)} = 3.5 \times 10^{-4}$$

Assume x is small compared to 0.250.

$x^2 = (3.5 \times 10^{-4})(0.250)$ $x = 0.00935M = [H_3O^+]$

$$\frac{0.00935}{0.250} \times 100\% = 3.7\%$$

$pH = -\log(0.00935) = 2.03$

(b) **Given:** 0.100 M HF $K_a = 3.5 \times 10^{-4}$ **Find:** pH, % dissociation

Conceptual Plan: Write a balanced reaction. Prepare an ICE table, represent the change with x, sum the table, determine the equilibrium values, put the equilibrium values in the equilibrium expression, solve for x, and then $x \rightarrow$ % ionization.

$$\% \text{ ionization} = \frac{x}{[HF]_{original}} \times 100$$

Solution: $HF(aq) + H_2O(l) \leftrightharpoons H_3O^+(aq) + F^-(aq)$

I	0.1000 M	0.0	0.0
C	$-x$	x	x
E	$0.100 - x$	x	x

$$K_a = \frac{[H_3O^+][F^-]}{[HF]} = \frac{(x)(x)}{(0.100 - x)} = 3.5 \times 10^{-4}$$

Assume x is small compared to 0.100.

$x^2 = (3.5 \times 10^{-4})(0.100)$ $x = 0.00592M = [H_3O^+]$

$$\frac{0.00592}{0.100} \times 100\% = 5.9\%$$

$x > 5.0$ % therefore, assumption invalid, solve using quadratic equation.

$x^2 + 3.5 \times 10^{-4}x - 3.5 \times 10^{-5} = 0$

$x = 0.00574$ or -0.00609

$pH = -\log(0.00574) = 2.24$

$$\% \text{ dissociation} = \frac{0.00574}{0.100} \times 100 = 5.7\%$$

(c) **Given:** 0.050 M HF $K_a = 3.5 \times 10^{-4}$ **Find:** pH, % dissociation

Conceptual Plan: Write a balanced reaction. Prepare an ICE table, represent the change with x, sum the table, determine the equilibrium values, put the equilibrium values in the equilibrium expression, solve for x, and then $x \rightarrow$ % ionization.

$$\% \text{ ionization} = \frac{x}{[HF]_{original}} \times 100$$

Solution: $HF(aq) + H_2O(l) \leftrightharpoons H_3O^+(aq) + F^-(aq)$

I	0.050 M	0.0	0.0
C	$-x$	x	x
E	$0.050 - x$	x	x

$$K_a = \frac{[H_3O^+][F^-]}{[HF]} = \frac{(x)(x)}{(0.050 - x)} = 3.5 \times 10^{-4}$$

Assume x is small compared to 0.050.

$x^2 = (3.5 \times 10^{-4})(0.050)$ $x = 0.00418M = [H_3O^+]$

$$\frac{0.00418}{0.050} \times 100\% = 8.4\%$$

Assumption invalid, solve using quadratic equation.

$x^2 + 3.5 \times 10^{-4} x - 1.75 \times 10^{-5} = 0$

$x = 0.00401$ or -0.00436

$\text{pH} = -\log(0.00401) = 2.40$

$$\% \text{ dissociation} = \frac{0.00401}{0.050} \times 100\% = 8.0\%$$

15.76 (a) **Given:** 0.100 M HA, $K_a = 1.0 \times 10^{-5}$ **Find:** pH, % dissociation

Conceptual Plan: Write a balanced reaction. Prepare an ICE table, represent the change with x, sum the table, determine the equilibrium values, put the equilibrium values in the equilibrium expression, solve for x, and then $x \rightarrow$ % ionization.

$$\% \text{ ionization} = \frac{x}{[\text{HA}]_{\text{original}}} \times 100$$

Solution: $\text{HA}(aq) + \text{H}_2\text{O}(l) \leftrightarrows \text{H}_3\text{O}^+(aq) + \text{A}^-(aq)$

	HA	H_3O^+	A^-
I	0.100 M	0.0	0.0
C	$-x$	x	x
E	$0.100 - x$	x	x

$$K_a = \frac{[\text{H}_3\text{O}^+][\text{A}^-]}{[\text{HA}]} = \frac{(x)(x)}{(0.100 - x)} = 1.0 \times 10^{-5}$$

Assume x is small compared to 0.100.

$x^2 = (1.0 \times 10^{-5})(0.100)$ $\quad x = 0.00100\text{M} = [\text{H}_3\text{O}^+]$

$$\frac{0.00100}{0.100} \times 100\% = 1.0\%$$

$\text{pH} = -\log(0.00100) = 3.00$

(b) **Given:** 0.100 M HA, $K_a = 1.0 \times 10^{-3}$ **Find:** pH, % dissociation

Conceptual Plan: Write a balanced reaction. Prepare an ICE table, represent the change with x, sum the table, determine the equilibrium values, put the equilibrium values in the equilibrium expression, solve for x, and then $x \rightarrow$ % ionization.

$$\% \text{ ionization} = \frac{x}{[\text{HA}]_{\text{original}}} \times 100$$

Solution: $\text{HA}(aq) + \text{H}_2\text{O}(l) \leftrightarrows \text{H}_3\text{O}^+(aq) + \text{A}^-(aq)$

	HA	H_3O^+	A^-
I	0.100 M	0.0	0.0
C	$-x$	x	x
E	$0.100 - x$	x	x

$$K_a = \frac{[\text{H}_3\text{O}^+][\text{A}^-]}{[\text{HA}]} = \frac{(x)(x)}{(0.100 - x)} = 1.0 \times 10^{-3}.$$ Solve using quadratic equation.

$x^2 = (1.0 \times 10^{-3} - x)(0.100)$ $\quad x^2 + 1 \times 10^{-3} x - 1 \times 10^{-4} = 0$

$x = 0.0095 = [\text{H}_3\text{O}^+]$

$$\frac{0.0095}{0.100} \times 100\% = 9.5\%$$

$\text{pH} = -\log(0.0095) = 2.02$

(c) **Given:** 0.100 M HA, $K_a = 1.0 \times 10^{-1}$ **Find:** pH, % dissociation

Conceptual Plan: Write a balanced reaction. Prepare an ICE table, represent the change with x, sum the table, determine the equilibrium values, put the equilibrium values in the equilibrium expression, solve for x, and then $x \rightarrow$ % ionization.

$$\% \text{ ionization} = \frac{x}{[\text{HA}]_{\text{original}}} \times 100$$

Solution: $\text{HA}(aq) + \text{H}_2\text{O}(l) \leftrightarrows \text{H}_3\text{O}^+(aq) + \text{A}^-(aq)$

	HA	H_3O^+	A^-
I	0.100 M	0.0	0.0
C	$-x$	x	x
E	$0.100 - x$	x	x

$$K_a = \frac{[\text{H}_3\text{O}^+][\text{A}^-]}{[\text{HA}]} = \frac{(x)(x)}{(0.100 - x)} = 1.0 \times 10^{-1}$$

$x^2 = (1.0 \times 10^{-1} - x)(0.100)$ $\quad x^2 + 0.10x - 0.01 = 0.$ Solve using quadratic equation.

$x = 0.0616 = [H_3O^+]$

$$\frac{0.0616}{0.100} \times 100\% = 61.6\%$$

$pH = -\log(0.0616) = 1.21$

15.77 (a) **Given:** 0.115 M HBr (strong acid), 0.125 M $HCHO_2$ (weak acid) **Find:** pH
Conceptual Plan: Since the mixture is a strong acid and a weak acid, the strong acid will dominate. Use the concentration of the strong acid to determine $[H_3O^+]$ and then pH.
Solution: 0.115 M HBr = 0.115 M $[H_3O^+]$ pH = -log(0.115) = 0.939

(b) **Given:** 0.150 M HNO_2 (weak acid), 0.085 M HNO_3 (strong acid) **Find:** pH
Conceptual Plan: Since the mixture is a strong acid and a weak acid, the strong acid will dominate. Use the concentration of the strong acid to determine $[H_3O^+]$ and then pH.
Solution: 0.085 M HNO_3 = 0.085 M $[H_3O^+]$ pH = -log(0.085) = 1.07

(c) **Given:** 0.185 M $HCHO_2$, $K_a = 1.8 \times 10^{-4}$; 0.225 M $HC_2H_3O_2$, $K_a = 1.8 \times 10^{-5}$ **Find:** pH
Conceptual Plan: Since the mixture is a weak acid and a weak acid, and the *K* values are only 10^1 apart, you need to find $[H_3O^+]$ from each reaction. Write a balanced reaction. Prepare an ICE table, represent the change with *x*, sum the table, determine the equilibrium values, put the equilibrium values in the equilibrium expression, and solve for *x*.
Solution: $HCHO_2\,(aq) + H_2O(l) \leftrightharpoons H_3O^+(aq) + CHO_2^-\,(aq)$

I	0.185 M	0.0	0.0
C	$-x$	x	x
E	$0.185 - x$	x	x

$$K_a = \frac{[H_3O^+][CHO_2^-]}{[HCHO_2]} = \frac{(x)(x)}{(0.185 - x)} = 1.8 \times 10^{-4}$$

Assume x is small compared to 0.100.

$x^2 = (1.8 \times 10^{-4})(0.185) \quad x = 0.00577$

$HC_2H_3O_2\,(aq) + H_2O(l) \leftrightharpoons H_3O^+(aq) + C_2H_3O_2^-\,(aq)$

I	0.225 M	0.00577	0.0
C	$-x$	x	x
E	$0.225 - x$	x	x

$$K_a = \frac{[H_3O^+][C_2H_3O_2^-]}{[HC_2H_3O_2]} = \frac{(0.00577 + x)(x)}{(0.225 - x)} = 1.8 \times 10^{-5}$$

Assume x is small compared to 0.225.

$x^2 + 0.00602x - 4.05 \times 10^{-6} = 0 \qquad x = 0.00061$

$[H_3O^+] = 0.00577 + x = 0.00577 + 0.00061 = 0.006389$ M

$pH = -\log(0.006389) = 2.19$

(d) **Given:** 0.050 M $HC_2H_3O_2$, $K_a = 1.8 \times 10^{-5}$; 0.050 M HCN, $K_a = 4.9 \times 10^{-10}$ **Find:** pH
Conceptual Plan: Since the values of *K* are more than 10^1 apart, the acid with the larger *K* will dominate the reaction. Write a balanced reaction. Prepare an ICE table, represent the change with *x*, sum the table, determine the equilibrium values, put the equilibrium values in the equilibrium expression, and solve for *x*.
Solution: $HC_2H_3O_2\,(aq) + H_2O(l) \leftrightharpoons H_3O^+(aq) + C_2H_3O_2^-\,(aq)$

I	0.0500 M	0.0	0.0
C	$-x$	x	x
E	$0.0500 - x$	x	x

$$K_a = \frac{[H_3O^+][C_2H_3O_2^-]}{[HC_2H_3O_2]} = \frac{(x)(x)}{(0.0500 - x)} = 1.8 \times 10^{-5}$$

Assume x is small compared to 0.0500.

$x^2 = (1.8 \times 10^{-5})(0.0500) \qquad x = 9.49 \times 10^{-4}$

$pH = -\log(9.49 \times 10^{-4}) = 3.02$

15.78 (a) **Given:** 0.075 M HNO_3 (strong acid), 0.175 M $HC_7H_5O_2$ (weak acid) **Find:** pH
Conceptual Plan: Since the mixture is a strong acid and a weak acid, the strong acid will dominate. Use the concentration of the strong acid to determine [H_3O^+] and then pH.
Solution: 0.075 M HNO_3 = 0.075 M [H_3O^+] pH = - log(0.075) = 1.12

(b) **Given:** 0.020 M HBr (strong acid), 0.015 M $HClO_4$ (strong acid) **Find:** pH
Conceptual Plan: Since the mixture is a strong acid and another strong acid, the [H_3O^+] is the sum of the concentration of both acids. Determine pH.
Solution: 0.020 M HBr = 0.020 [H_3O^+], 0.015 M $HClO_4$ = 0.015 M [H_3O^+]
[H_3O^+] = 0.020 + 0.015 = 0.035 M pH = -log(0.035) = 1.46

(c) **Given:** 0.095M HF, $K_a = 3.5 \times 10^{-4}$; 0.225 M $HC_6H_5O_2$, $K_a = 1.3 \times 10^{-10}$ **Find:** pH
Conceptual Plan: Since the values of *K* are more than 10^1 apart, the acid with the larger *K* will dominate the reaction. Write a balanced reaction. Prepare an ICE table, represent the change with *x*, sum the table, determine the equilibrium values, put the equilibrium values in the equilibrium expression, and solve for *x*.
Solution: $HF(aq) + H_2O(l) \leftrightarrows H_3O^+(aq) + F^-(aq)$

I	0.095 M	0.0	0.0
C	$-x$	x	x
E	$0.095 - x$	x	x

$$K_a = \frac{[H_3O^+][F^-]}{[HF]} = \frac{(x)(x)}{(0.095 - x)} = 3.5 \times 10^{-4}$$

$x^2 = (3.5 \times 10^{-4})(0.095)$ $x = 0.00577\text{ M} = [H_3O^+]$
$(0.00577/0.095) \times 100 = 6.1\%$. Assumption is invalid since 6.1% is greater than the 5.0% limit.
Solve for *x* using the quadratic formula;
$x^2 + 3.5 \times 10^{-4}x - 3.325 \times 10^{-5} = 0$
$x = 0.00559\text{ M} = [H_3O^+]$
$pH = -\log(0.00559) = 2.25$

(d) **Given:** 0.100 M $HCHO_2$, $K_a = 1.8 \times 10^{-4}$; 0.050 M HClO, $K_a = 2.9 \times 10^{-8}$ **Find:** pH
Conceptual Plan: Since the values of *K* are more than 10^1 apart, the acid with the larger *K* will dominate the reaction. Write a balanced reaction. Prepare an ICE table, represent the change with *x*, sum the table, determine the equilibrium values, put the equilibrium values in the equilibrium expression, and solve for *x*.
Solution: $HCHO_2(aq) + H_2O(l) \leftrightarrows H_3O^+(aq) + C_2H_3O_2^-(aq)$

I	0.100 M	0.0	0.0
C	$-x$	x	x
E	$0.100 - x$	x	x

$$K_a = \frac{[H_3O^+][CHO_2^-]}{[HCHO_2]} = \frac{(x)(x)}{(0.100 - x)} = 1.8 \times 10^{-4}$$

Assume *x* is small compared to 0.0500.
$x^2 = (1.8 \times 10^{-4})(0.100)$ $x = 0.00424$
$pH = -\log(0.00424) = 2.37$

Base Solutions

15.79 (a) **Given:** 0.15 M NaOH **Find:** [OH^-], [H_3O^+], pH, pOH
Conceptual Plan: [NaOH] → [OH^-] → [H_3O^+] → pH → pOH
$K_w = [H_3O^+][OH^-]$ $pH = -\log[H_3O^+]$ $pH + pOH = 14$
Solution: [OH^-] = [NaOH] = 0.15M

$$[H_3O^+] = \frac{K_w}{[OH^-]} = \frac{1.0 \times 10^{-14}}{0.15M} = 6.7 \times 10^{-14}\text{ M}$$

$pH = -\log(6.7 \times 10^{-14}) = 13.17$
$pOH = 14.00 - 13.18 = 0.83$

(b) **Given:** 1.5×10^{-3} M $Ca(OH)_2$ **Find:** $[OH^-]$, $[H_3O^+]$, pH, pOH

Conceptual Plan: $[Ca(OH)_2] \rightarrow [OH^-] \rightarrow [H_3O^+] \rightarrow pH \rightarrow pOH$

$K_w = [H_3O^+][OH^-]$ $\quad$ $pH = -\log[H_3O^+]$ $\quad$ $pH + pOH = 14$

Solution: $[OH^-] = 2[Ca(OH)_2] = 2(1.5 \times 10^{-3}) = 0.0030$ M

$$[H_3O^+] = \frac{K_w}{[OH^-]} = \frac{1.0 \times 10^{-14}}{0.0030\ M} = 3.\underline{3}3 \times 10^{-12}\ M$$

$$pH = -\log(3.\underline{3}3 \times 10^{-12}) = 11.48$$

$$pOH = 14.00 - 11.48 = 2.52$$

(c) **Given:** 4.8×10^{-4} M $Sr(OH)_2$ **Find:** $[OH^-]$, $[H_3O^+]$, pH, pOH

Conceptual Plan: $[Sr(OH)_2] \rightarrow [OH^-] \rightarrow [H_3O^+] \rightarrow pH \rightarrow pOH$

$K_w = [H_3O^+][OH^-]$ $\quad$ $pH = -\log[H_3O^+]$ $\quad$ $pH + pOH = 14$

Solution: $[OH^-] = [Sr(OH)_2] = 2(4.8 \times 10^{-4}) = 9.6 \times 10^{-4}$ M

$$[H_3O^+] = \frac{K_w}{[OH^-]} = \frac{1.0 \times 10^{-14}}{9.6 \times 10^{-4}\ M} = 1.\underline{0}4 \times 10^{-11}\ M$$

$$pH = -\log(1.\underline{0}4 \times 10^{-11}) = 10.98$$

$$pOH = 14.00 - 10.98 = 3.02$$

(d) **Given:** 8.7×10^{-5} M KOH **Find:** $[OH^-]$, $[H_3O^+]$, pH, pOH

Conceptual Plan: $[KOH] \rightarrow [OH^-] \rightarrow [H_3O^+] \rightarrow pH \rightarrow pOH$

$K_w = [H_3O^+][OH^-]$ $\quad$ $pH = -\log[H_3O^+]$ $\quad$ $pH + pOH = 14$

Solution: $[OH^-] = [KOH] = 8.7 \times 10^{-5}$ M

$$[H_3O^+] = \frac{K_w}{[OH^-]} = \frac{1.0 \times 10^{-14}}{8.7 \times 10^{-5}\ M} = 1.\underline{1} \times 10^{-10}\ M$$

$$pH = -\log(1.\underline{1} \times 10^{-10}) = 9.94$$

$$pOH = 14.00 - 9.94 = 4.06$$

15.80 (a) **Given:** 8.77×10^{-3} M LiOH **Find:** $[OH^-]$, $[H_3O^+]$, pH, pOH

Conceptual Plan: $[LiOH] \rightarrow [OH^-] \rightarrow [H_3O^+] \rightarrow pH \rightarrow pOH$

$K_w = [H_3O^+][OH^-]$ $\quad$ $pH = -\log[H_3O^+]$ $\quad$ $pH + pOH = 14$

Solution: $[OH^-] = [LiOH] = 8.77 \times 10^{-3}$ M

$$[H_3O^+] = \frac{K_w}{[OH^-]} = \frac{1.0 \times 10^{-14}}{8.77 \times 10^{-3}\ M} = 1.1\underline{4}0 \times 10^{-12}\ M$$

$$pH = -\log(1.1\underline{4}0 \times 10^{-12}) = 11.943$$

$$pOH = 14.00 - 11.943 = 2.057$$

(b) **Given:** 0.0112 M $Ba(OH)_2$ **Find:** $[OH^-]$, $[H_3O^+]$, pH, pOH

Conceptual Plan: $[Ba(OH)_2] \rightarrow [OH^-] \rightarrow [H_3O^+] \rightarrow pH \rightarrow pOH$

$K_w = [H_3O^+][OH^-]$ $\quad$ $pH = -\log[H_3O^+]$ $\quad$ $pH + pOH = 14$

Solution: $[OH^-] = 2[Ba(OH)_2] = 2(0.0112) = 0.0224$ M

$$[H_3O^+] = \frac{K_w}{[OH^-]} = \frac{1.0 \times 10^{-14}}{0.0224\ M} = 4.4\underline{6}4 \times 10^{-13}\ M$$

$$pH = -\log(4.4\underline{6}4 \times 10^{-13}) = 12.350$$

$$pOH = 14.000 - 12.350 = 1.650$$

(c) **Given:** 1.9×10^{-4} M KOH **Find:** $[OH^-]$, $[H_3O^+]$, pH, pOH

Conceptual Plan: $[KOH] \rightarrow [OH^-] \rightarrow [H_3O^+] \rightarrow pH \rightarrow pOH$

$K_w = [H_3O^+][OH^-]$ $\quad$ $pH = -\log[H_3O^+]$ $\quad$ $pH + pOH = 14$

Solution: $[OH^-] = [KOH] = 1.9 \times 10^{-4}$ M

$$[H_3O^+] = \frac{K_w}{[OH^-]} = \frac{1.0 \times 10^{-14}}{1.9 \times 10^{-4}\ M} = 5.\underline{2}6 \times 10^{-11}\ M$$

$$pH = -\log(5.\underline{2}6 \times 10^{-11}) = 10.28$$

$$pOH = 14.00 - 10.28 = 3.72$$

(d) **Given:** 5.0×10^{-4} M $Ca(OH)_2$ **Find:** $[OH^-]$, $[H_3O^+]$, pH, pOH
Conceptual Plan: $[Ca(OH)_2] \rightarrow [OH^-] \rightarrow [H_3O^+] \rightarrow pH \rightarrow pOH$

$K_w = [H_3O^+][OH^-]$ $\quad$ $pH = -\log[H_3O^+]$ $\quad$ $pH + pOH = 14$

Solution: $[OH^-] = [Ca(OH)_2] = 2(5.0 \times 10^{-4}) = 0.0010$ M

$$[H_3O^+] = \frac{K_w}{[OH^-]} = \frac{1.0 \times 10^{-14}}{0.0010\ M} = 1.\underline{0}0 \times 10^{-11}\ M$$

$$pH = -\log(1.\underline{0}0 \times 10^{-11}) = 11.00$$

$$pOH = 14.00 - 11.00 = 3.00$$

15.81 **Given:** 3.85% KOH by mass, $d = 1.01$ g/mL **Find:** pH
Conceptual Plan:
% mass → g KOH → mol KOH and mass soln → mL soln → L soln → M KOH → $[OH^-]$

$\frac{1\ \text{mol KOH}}{56.01\ \text{g KOH}}$ $\quad$ $\frac{1.01\ \text{g soln}}{\text{mL soln}}$ $\quad$ $\frac{1000\ \text{mL soln}}{\text{L soln}}$ $\quad$ $\frac{\text{mol KOH}}{\text{L soln}}$

→ pOH → pH

$pOH = -\log[OH^-]$ $\quad$ $pH + pOH = 14$

Solution:
$$\frac{3.85\ \text{g KOH}}{100.0\ \text{g soln}} \times \frac{1\ \text{mol KOH}}{56.01\ \text{g KOH}} \times \frac{1.01\ \text{g soln}}{\text{mL soln}} \times \frac{1000\ \text{mL soln}}{\text{L soln}} = 0.69\underline{4}2\ \text{M KOH}$$

$[OH^-] = [KOH] = 0.69\underline{4}2$ M $\quad$ $pOH = -\log(0.69\underline{4}2) = 0.159$ $\quad$ $pH = 14.000 - 0.159 = 13.841$

15.82 **Given:** 1.55% NaOH by mass, $d = 1.01$ g/mL **Find:** pH
Conceptual Plan:
% mass → g NaOH → mol NaOH and mass soln → mL soln → L soln → M NaOH → $[OH^-]$

$\frac{1\ \text{mol NaOH}}{40.01\ \text{g NaOH}}$ $\quad$ $\frac{1.01\ \text{g soln}}{\text{mL soln}}$ $\quad$ $\frac{1000\ \text{mL soln}}{\text{L soln}}$ $\quad$ $\frac{\text{mol NaOH}}{\text{L soln}}$

→ pOH → pH

$pOH = -\log[OH^-]$ $\quad$ $pH + pOH = 14$

Solution:
$$\frac{1.55\ \text{g NaOH}}{100.0\ \text{g soln}} \times \frac{1\ \text{mol NaOH}}{40.01\ \text{g KOH}} \times \frac{1.01\ \text{g soln}}{\text{mL soln}} \times \frac{1000\ \text{mL soln}}{\text{L soln}} = 0.39\underline{1}3\ \text{M NaOH}$$

$[OH^-] = [NaOH] = 0.39\underline{1}3$ M $\quad$ $pOH = -\log(0.39\underline{1}3) = 0.407$ $\quad$ $pH = 14.000 - 0.407 = 13.593$

15.83 **Given:** 3.55 L, pH = 12.4; 0.855 M KOH **Find:** Vol
Conceptual Plan: **pH → $[H_3O^+]$ → $[OH^-]$ and then $V_1M_1 = V_2M_2$**

$[H_3O^+] = 10^{-pH}$ $\quad$ $1.0 \times 10^{-14} = [H_3O^+][OH^-]$ $\quad$ $V_1M_1 = V_2M_2$

Solution: $[H_3O^+] = 10^{-12.4} = 3.98 \times 10^{-13}$ $\quad$ $1.0 \times 10^{-14} = 3.98 \times 10^{-13}[OH^-]$
$[OH^-] = 0.025\underline{1}2$
$V_1M_1 = V_2M_2$ $\quad$ $V_1(0.855\ M) = (3.55\ L)(0.0251\ M)$ $\quad$ $V_1 = 0.104$ L

15.84 **Given:** 5.00 L, pH = 10.8; 15.0% NaOH, $d = 1.116$ g/ mL **Find:** Vol
Conceptual Plan:
% mass → g NaOH → mol NaOH and mass soln → mL soln → L soln → M NaOH → $[OH^-]$

$\frac{1\ \text{mol NaOH}}{40.01\ \text{g NaOH}}$ $\quad$ $\frac{1.01\ \text{g soln}}{\text{mL soln}}$ $\quad$ $\frac{1000\ \text{mL soln}}{\text{Lsoln}}$ $\quad$ $\frac{\text{mol NaOH}}{\text{L soln}}$

and then: $V_1M_1 \rightarrow V_2M_2$

$V_1M_1 = V_2M_2$

Solution:
$$\frac{15.0\ \text{g NaOH}}{100.0\ \text{g soln}} \times \frac{1\ \text{mol NaOH}}{40.01\ \text{g KOH}} \times \frac{1.116\ \text{g soln}}{\text{mL soln}} \times \frac{1000\ \text{mL soln}}{\text{L soln}} = 4.1\underline{8}4\ \text{M NaOH}$$

$[OH^-] = [NaOH] = 4.1\underline{8}4$ M
$[H_3O^+] = 10^{-10.8} = 1.58 \times 10^{-11}$ $\quad$ $1.0 \times 10^{-14} = (1.58 \times 10^{-11})[OH^-]$
$[OH^-] = 6.31 \times 10^{-4}$ M
$V_1(4.18\ M) = (5.00\ L)(6.31 \times 10^{-4}\ M)$ $\quad$ $V_1 = 7.55 \times 10^{-4}$ L = 0.8 mL

15.85 (a) $NH_3(aq) + H_2O(l) \leftrightarrows NH_4^+(aq) + OH^-(aq)$ $\quad$ $K_b = \frac{[NH_4^+][OH^-]}{[NH_3]}$

(b) $HCO_3^-(aq) + H_2O(l) \leftrightharpoons H_2CO_3(aq) + OH^-(aq)$ $K_b = \frac{[H_2CO_3][OH^-]}{[HCO_3^-]}$

(c) $CH_3NH_2(aq) + H_2O(l) \leftrightharpoons CH_3NH_3^+(aq) + OH^-(aq)$ $K_b = \frac{[CH_3NH_3^+][OH^-]}{[CH_3NH_2]}$

15.86 (a) $CO_3^{2-}(aq) + H_2O(l) \leftrightharpoons HCO_3^-(aq) + OH^-(aq)$ $K_b = \frac{[HCO_3^-][OH^-]}{[CO_3^{2-}]}$

(b) $C_6H_5NH_2(aq) + H_2O(l) \leftrightharpoons C_6H_5NH_3^+(aq) + OH^-(aq)$ $K_b = \frac{[C_6H_5NH_3^+][OH^-]}{[C_6H_5NH_2]}$

(c) $C_2H_5NH_2(aq) + H_2O(l) \leftrightharpoons C_2H_5NH_3^+(aq) + OH^-(aq)$ $K_b = \frac{[C_2H_5NH_3^+][OH^-]}{[C_2H_5NH_2]}$

15.87 **Given:** 0.15 M NH_3 $K_b = 1.76 \times 10^{-5}$ **Find:** $[OH^-]$, pH, pOH
Conceptual Plan: Write a balanced reaction. Prepare an ICE table, represent the change with x, sum the table, determine the equilibrium values, put the equilibrium values in the equilibrium expression, and solve for x.
$x = [OH^-] \rightarrow$ pOH $\rightarrow$ pH
pOH = -log$[OH^-]$ pH + pOH = 14
Solution: $NH_3(aq) + H_2O(l) \leftrightharpoons NH_4^+(aq) + OH^-(aq)$

	NH_3	NH_4^+	OH^-
I	0.15 M	0.0	0.0
C	$-x$	x	x
E	$0.15 - x$	x	x

$$K_b = \frac{[NH_4^+][OH^-]}{[NH_3]} = \frac{(x)(x)}{(0.15 - x)} = 1.76 \times 10^{-5}$$

Assume x is small.
$x^2 = (1.76 \times 10^{-5})(0.15)$ $x = [OH^-] = 0.00162$ M
pOH $= -\log(0.00162) = 2.79$
pH $= 14.00 - 2.79 = 11.21$

15.88 **Given:** 0.125 M CO_3^{2-} $K_b = 1.8 \times 10^{-4}$ **Find:** $[OH^-]$, pH, pOH
Conceptual Plan: Write a balanced reaction. Prepare an ICE table, represent the change with x, sum the table, determine the equilibrium values, put the equilibrium values in the equilibrium expression, and solve for x.
$x = [OH^-] \rightarrow$ pOH $\rightarrow$ pH
pOH = -log$[OH^-]$ pH + pOH = 14
Solution: $CO_3^{2-}(aq) + H_2O(l) \leftrightharpoons HCO_3^-(aq) + OH^-(aq)$

	CO_3^{2-}	HCO_3^-	OH^-
I	0.125 M	0.0	0.0
C	$-x$	x	x
E	$0.125 - x$	x	x

$$K_b = \frac{[HCO_3^-][OH^-]}{[CO_3^-]} = \frac{(x)(x)}{(0.125 - x)} = 1.8 \times 10^{-4}$$

Assume x is small.
$x^2 = (1.8 \times 10^{-4})(0.125)$ $x = [OH^-] = 0.00474$ M
$\frac{0.00474}{0.125} \times 100\% = 3.8\%$; assumption is valid
pOH $= -\log(0.00474) = 2.32$
pH $= 14.00 - 2.32 = 11.68$

15.89 **Given:** pK_b = 10.4, 455 mg/L caffeine **Find:** pH
Conceptual Plan: pK_b $\rightarrow$ K_b and then mg/L $\rightarrow$ g/L $\rightarrow$ mol/L and then write a balanced reaction. Prepare an ICE table, represent the change with x, sum the table, determine the equilibrium values, put the equilibrium values in the equilibrium expression, and solve for x.
$x = [OH^-] \rightarrow$ pOH $\rightarrow$ pH
pOH = -log$[OH^-]$ pH + pOH = 14

Solution: $K_b = 10^{-10.4} = 3.98 \times 10^{-11}$

$$\frac{455 \text{ mg caffeine}}{\text{L soln}} \times \frac{\text{g caffeine}}{1000 \text{ mg caffeine}} \times \frac{1 \text{ mol caffeine}}{194.19 \text{ g}} = 0.002343 \text{ M caffeine}$$

	$C_8H_{10}N_4O_2(aq) + H_2O(l) \leftrightharpoons$	$HC_8H_{10}N_4O_2^+(aq)$	$+ OH^-(aq)$
I	0.002342	0.0	0.0
C	$-x$	x	x
E	$0.002342 - x$	x	x

$$K_b = \frac{[HC_8H_{10}N_4O_2^+][OH^-]}{[C_8H_{10}N_4O_2]} = \frac{(x)(x)}{(0.002342 - x)} = 3.98 \times 10^{-11}$$

Assume x is small.

$x^2 = (3.98 \times 10^{-11})(0.002342)$ $x = [OH^-] = 3.05 \times 10^{-7}$ M

$\frac{3.05 \times 10^{-7} \text{ M}}{0.002342} \times 100\% = 0.013\%$; assumption is valid

$pOH = -\log(3.05 \times 10^{-7}) = 6.5$

$pH = 14.00 - 6.5 = 7.5$

15.90 **Given:** $pK_b = 4.2$, 225 mg/L amphetamine **Find:** pH

Conceptual Plan: $pK_b \rightarrow K_b$ and then mg/L $\rightarrow$ g/L $\rightarrow$ mol/L and then write a balanced reaction. Prepare an ICE table, represent the change with x, sum the table, determine the equilibrium values, put the equilibrium values in the equilibrium expression, and solve for x.

$x = [OH^-] \rightarrow pOH \rightarrow pH$

$pOH = -\log[OH^-]$ $pH + pOH = 14$

Solution: $K_b = 10^{-4.2} = 6.31 \times 10^{-5}$

$$\frac{225 \text{ mg amphetamine}}{\text{L soln}} \times \frac{\text{g amphetamine}}{1000 \text{ mg amphetamine}} \times \frac{1 \text{ mol amphetamine}}{135.21 \text{ g}} = 0.001664 \text{ M amphetamine}$$

	$C_9H_{13}N(aq) + H_2O(l) \leftrightharpoons$	$C_9H_{13}NH^+(aq)$	$+ OH^-(aq)$
I	0.001664 M	0.0	0.0
C	$-x$	x	x
E	$0.001664 - x$	x	x

$$K_b = \frac{[C_9H_{13}NH^+][OH^-]}{[C_9H_{13}N]} = \frac{(x)(x)}{(0.001664 - x)} = 6.31 \times 10^{-5}$$

Assume x is small.

$x^2 = (6.31 \times 10^{-5})(0.001664)$ $x = [OH^-] = 3.24 \times 10^{-4}$ M

$\frac{3.24 \times 10^{-4}}{0.001664} \times 100\% = 19.4\%$; assumption not valid, solve with quadratic equation.

$x^2 + 6.31 \times 10^{-5} x - 1.05 \times 10^{-7} = 0$

$x = [OH^-] = 2.94 \times 10^{-4}$ M

$pOH = -\log(2.94 \times 10^{-4}) = 3.5$

$pH = 14.00 - 3.5 = 10.5$

15.91 **Given:** 0.150 M morphine, pH = 10.5 **Find:** K_b

Conceptual Plan:

pH $\rightarrow$ pOH $\rightarrow$ $[OH^-]$ and then write a balanced equation, prepare an ICE table, and determine equilibrium concentrations $\rightarrow K_b$.

pH = pOH = 14 $pOH = -\log[OH^-]$

Solution: $pOH = 14.0 - 10.5 = 3.5$ $[OH^-] = 10^{-3.5} = 3.16 \times 10^{-4} = [\text{Hmorphine}^+]$

	morphine$(aq) + H_2O(l) \leftrightharpoons$	Hmorphine$^+(aq)$	$+ OH^-(aq)$
I	0.150 M	0.0	0.0
C	$-x$	x	x
E	$0.150 - x$	3.16×10^{-4}	3.16×10^{-4}

$$K_b = \frac{[\text{Hmorphine}^+][OH^-]}{[\text{morphine}]} = \frac{(3.16 \times 10^{-4})(3.16 \times 10^{-4})}{(0.150 - 3.16 \times 10^{-4})} = 6.68 \times 10^{-7} = 7 \times 10^{-7}$$

15.92 **Given:** 0.135 M base, pH = 11.23 **Find:** K_b
Conceptual Plan:
pH → pOH → [OH⁻] and then write a balanced equation, prepare an ICE table, and determine
$pH = pOH = 14$ $pOH = -\log[OH^-]$
equilibrium concentrations → K_b.
Solution: pOH = 14.00 – 11.23 = 2.77 $[OH^-] = 10^{-2.77} = 1.\underline{6}98 \times 10^{-3} = [HB^+]$

	$B(aq) + H_2O(l) \leftrightharpoons$	$HB^+(aq) +$	$OH^-(aq)$
I	0.135	0.0	0.0
C	$-x$	x	x
E	$0.135 - x$	$1.\underline{6}98 \times 10^{-3}$	$1.\underline{6}98 \times 10^{-3}$

$$K_b = \frac{[HB^+][OH^-]}{[B]} = \frac{(1.\underline{6}98 \times 10^{-3})(1.\underline{6}98 \times 10^{-3})}{(0.135 - 1.\underline{6}98 \times 10^{-3})} = 2.\underline{1}6 \times 10^{-5} = 2.2 \times 10^{-5}$$

Acid – Base Properties of Ions and Salts

15.93 (a) pH neutral: Br^- is the conjugate base of a strong acid; therefore, it is pH neutral.

(b) weak base: ClO^- is the conjugate base of a weak acid; therefore, it is a weak base.
$ClO^-(aq) + H_2O(l) \leftrightharpoons HClO(aq) + OH^-(aq)$

(c) weak base: CN^- is the conjugate base of a weak acid; therefore, it is a weak base.
$CN^-(aq) + H_2O(l) \leftrightharpoons HCN(aq) + OH^-(aq)$

(d) pH neutral: Cl^- is the conjugate base of a strong acid; therefore, it is pH neutral.

15.94 (a) weak base: $C_7H_5O_2^-$ is the conjugate base of a weak acid; therefore, it is a weak base.
$C_7H_5O_2^-(aq) + H_2O(l) \leftrightharpoons HC_7H_5O_2(aq) + OH^-(aq)$

(b) pH neutral: I^- is the conjugate base of a strong acid; therefore, it is pH neutral.

(c) pH neutral: NO_3^- is the conjugate base of a strong acid; therefore, it is pH neutral.

(d) weak base: F^- is the conjugate base of a weak acid; therefore, it is a weak base.
$F^-(aq) + H_2O(l) \leftrightharpoons HF(aq) + OH^-(aq)$

15.95 **Given:** $[F^-] = 0.140$ M, $K_a(HF) = 3.5 \times 10^{-4}$ **Find:** $[OH^-]$, pOH
Conceptual Plan: Determine K_b. Write a balanced reaction. Prepare an ICE table, represent the change
$K_b = \frac{K_w}{K_a}$
with x, sum the table, determine the equilibrium values, put the equilibrium values in the equilibrium expression, and solve for x. Determine [OH⁻] → pOH → pH.
$pOH = -\log[OH^-]$ $pH + pOH = 14$

Solution: $F^-(aq) + H_2O(l) \leftrightharpoons HF(aq) + OH^-(aq)$

	F^-	HF	OH^-
I	0.140 M	0.0	0.0
C	$-x$	x	x
E	$0.140 - x$	x	x

$$K_b = \frac{K_w}{K_a} = \frac{1 \times 10^{-14}}{3.5 \times 10^{-4}} = \frac{(x)(x)}{(0.140 - x)}$$

Assume x is small.
$x = 2.0 \times 10^{-6} = [OH^-]$ $pOH = -\log(2.0 \times 10^{-6}) = 5.70$
$pH = 14.00 - 5.70 = 8.30$

15.96 **Given:** $[HCO_3^-] = 0.250$ M, $K_a(H_2CO_3) = 4.3 \times 10^{-7}$ **Find:** $[OH^-]$, pOH
Conceptual Plan: Determine K_b. Write a balanced reaction. Prepare an ICE table, represent the change
$K_b = \frac{K_w}{K_a}$
with x, sum the table, determine the equilibrium values, put the equilibrium values in the equilibrium expression, and solve for x. Determine [OH⁻] → pOH → pH.
$pOH = -\log[OH^-]$ $pH + pOH = 14$

Solution: $HCO_3^-(aq) + H_2O(l) \leftrightarrows H_2CO_3(aq) + OH^-(aq)$

I	0.250	0.0	0.0
C	$-x$	x	x
E	$0.250 - x$	x	x

$$K_b = \frac{K_w}{K_a} = \frac{1 \times 10^{-14}}{4.3 \times 10^{-7}} = \frac{(x)(x)}{(0.250 - x)}$$

Assume x is small.

$x = 7.6 \times 10^{-5} = [OH^-]$ $pOH = -\log(7.6 \times 10^{-5}) = 4.12$

$pH = 14.00 - 4.12 = 9.88$

15.97 (a) weak acid: NH_4^+ is the conjugate acid of a weak base; therefore, it is a weak acid.
$NH_4^+(aq) + H_2O(l) \leftrightarrows H_3O^+(aq) + NH_3(aq)$

(b) pH neutral: Na^+ is the counterion of a strong base; therefore, it is pH neutral.

(c) weak acid: The Co^{3+} cation is a small, highly charged metal cation; therefore, it is a weak acid.

$Co(H_2O)_6^{3+}(aq) + H_2O(l) \leftrightarrows Co(H_2O)_5(OH)^{2+}(aq) + H_3O^+(aq)$

(d) weak acid: $CH_2NH_3^+$ is the conjugate acid of a weak base; therefore, it is a weak acid.
$CH_2NH_3^+(aq) + H_2O(l) \leftrightarrows H_3O^+(aq) + CH_2NH_2(aq)$

15.98 (a) pH neutral: Sr^{2+} is the counterion of a strong base; therefore, it is pH neutral.

(b) weak acid: The Mn^{3+} cation is a small, highly charged metal cation; therefore, it is a weak acid.
$Mn(H_2O)_6^{3+}(aq) + H_2O(l) \leftrightarrows Mn(H_2O)_5(OH)^{2+}(aq) + H_3O^+(aq)$

(c) weak acid: $C_5H_5NH_3^+$ is the conjugate acid of a weak base; therefore, it is a weak acid.
$C_5H_5NH_3^+(aq) + H_2O(l) \leftrightarrows H_3O^+(aq) + C_5H_5NH_2(aq)$

(d) pH neutral: Li^+ is the counterion of a strong base; therefore, it is pH neutral.

15.99 (a) acidic: $FeCl_3$ Fe^{3+} is a small, highly charged metal cation and is therefore acidic. Cl^- is the conjugate base of a strong acid; therefore, it is pH neutral.

(b) basic: NaF Na^+ is the counterion of a strong base; therefore, it is pH neutral. F^- is the conjugate base of a weak acid; therefore, it is basic.

(c) pH neutral: $CaBr_2$ Ca^{2+} is the counterion of a strong base; therefore, it is pH neutral. Br^- is the conjugate base of a strong acid; therefore, it is pH neutral.

(d) acidic: NH_4Br NH_4^+ is the conjugate acid of a weak base; therefore, it is acidic. Br^- is the conjugate base of a strong acid; therefore, it is pH neutral.

(e) acidic: $C_6H_5NH_3NO_2$ $C_6H_5NH_3^+$ is the conjugate acid of a weak base; therefore, it is a weak acid. NO_2^- is the conjugate base of a weak acid; therefore, it is a weak base. To determine pH, compare K values.

$$K_a(C_6H_5NH_3^+) = \frac{1.0 \times 10^{-14}}{3.9 \times 10^{-10}} = 2.6 \times 10^{-5} \quad K_b(NO_2^-) = \frac{1.0 \times 10^{-14}}{4.6 \times 10^{-4}} = 2.2 \times 10^{-11}$$

$K_a > K_b$; therefore, the solution is acidic.

15.100 (a) acidic: $Al(NO_3)_3$ Al^{3+} is a small, highly charged metal cation and is therefore acidic. NO_3^- is the conjugate base of a strong acid; therefore, it is pH neutral.

(b) acidic: $C_2H_5NH_3NO_3$ $C_2H_5NH_3^+$ is the conjugate acid of a weak base; therefore, it is acidic. NO_3^- is the conjugate base of a strong acid; therefore, it is pH neutral.

(c) basic: K_2CO_3 K^+ is the counterion of a strong base; therefore, it is pH neutral. CO_3^{2-} is the conjugate base of a weak acid; therefore, it is basic.

(d) pH neutral: RbI Rb^+ is the counterion of a strong base; therefore, it is pH neutral. I^- is the conjugate base of a strong acid; therefore, it is pH neutral.

(e) basic NH_4ClO NH_4^+ is the conjugate acid of a weak base; therefore, it is a weak acid. ClO^- is the conjugate base of a weak acid; therefore, it is a weak base. To determine pH, compare K values.

$$K_a(NH_4^+) = \frac{1.0 \times 10^{-14}}{1.8 \times 10^{-5}} = 5.6 \times 10^{-10} \qquad K_b(ClO^-) = \frac{1.0 \times 10^{-14}}{2.9 \times 10^{-8}} = 3.4 \times 10^{-7}$$

$K_b > K_a$; therefore, the solution is basic.

15.101 Identify each species and determine the acid, base, or neutral.

NaCl pH neutral: Na^+ is the counterion of a strong base; therefore, it is pH neutral. Cl^- is the conjugate base of a strong acid; therefore, it is pH neutral.

NH_4Cl acidic: NH_4^+ is the conjugate acid of a weak base; therefore, it is acidic. Cl^- is the conjugate base of a strong acid; therefore, it is pH neutral.

$NaHCO_3$ basic: Na^+ is the counterion of a strong base; therefore, it is pH neutral. HCO_3^- is the conjugate base of a weak acid; therefore, it is basic.

NH_4ClO_2 acidic: NH_4ClO_2 NH_4^+ is the conjugate acid of a weak base; therefore, it is a weak acid. ClO_2^- is the conjugate base of a weak acid; therefore, it is a weak base. $K_a(NH_4^+) = 5.6 \times 10^{-10}$ $K_b(ClO_2^-) = 9.1 \times 10^{-13}$

NaOH strong base

Increasing acidity: $NaOH < NaHCO_3 < NaCl < NH_4ClO_2 < NH_4Cl$

15.102 Identify each species and determine the acid, base, or neutral.

CH_3NH_3Br acidic: $CH_3NH_3^+$ is the conjugate acid of a weak base; therefore, it is acidic. Br^- is the conjugate base of a strong acid; therefore, it is pH neutral.

KOH strong base

KBr pH neutral: K^+ is the counterion of a strong base; therefore, it is pH neutral. Br^- is the conjugate base of a strong acid; therefore, it is pH neutral.

KCN basic: K^+ is the counterion of a strong base; therefore, it is pH neutral. CN^- is the conjugate base of a weak acid; therefore, it is basic.

$C_5H_5NHNO_2$ acidic: $C_5H_5NH^+$ is the conjugate acid of a weak base; therefore, it is acidic. NO_2^- is the conjugate base of a weak acid; therefore, it is basic. $K_a(C_5H_5NH^+) = 5.9 \times 10^{-6}$; $K_b(NO_2^-) = 2.2 \times 10^{-11}$

Increasing basicity: $CH_3NH_3Br < C_5H_5NHNO_2 < KBr < KCN < KOH$

15.103 (a) **Given:** 0.10 M NH_4Cl **Find:** pH

Conceptual Plan: Identify each species and determine which will contribute to pH. Write a balanced reaction. Prepare an ICE table, represent the change with x, sum the table, determine the equilibrium values, put the equilibrium values in the equilibrium expression, and solve for x. Determine $[H_3O^+] \rightarrow$ pH.

Solution: NH_4^+ is the conjugate acid of a weak base; therefore, it is acidic. Cl^- is the conjugate base of a strong acid; therefore, it is pH neutral.

	$NH_4^+(aq) + H_2O(l)$	$\leftrightarrows NH_3(aq)$	$+ H_3O^+(aq)$
I	0.10	0.0	0.0
C	$-x$	x	x
E	$0.10 - x$	x	x

$$K_a = \frac{K_w}{K_b} = \frac{1.0 \times 10^{-14}}{1.8 \times 10^{-5}} = 5.5\underline{6} \times 10^{-10} = \frac{(x)(x)}{(0.10 - x)}$$

Assume x is small.

$x = 7.\underline{4}5 \times 10^{-6} = [H_3O^+]$ $\quad$ pH $= -\log(7.\underline{4}5 \times 10^{-6}) = 5.13$

(b) **Given:** 0.10 M $NaC_2H_3O_2$ **Find:** pH

Conceptual Plan: Identify each species and determine which will contribute to pH. Write a balanced reaction. Prepare an ICE table, represent the change with x, sum the table, determine the equilibrium values, put the equilibrium values in the equilibrium expression, and solve for x. Determine $[OH^-]$ → pOH → pH.

$pOH = -\log[OH^-]$ $pH + pOH = 14$

Solution: Na^+ is the counterion of a strong base; therefore, it is pH neutral. $C_2H_3O_2^-$ is the conjugate base of a weak acid; therefore, it is basic.

$$C_2H_3O_2^-(aq) + H_2O(l) \leftrightarrows HC_2H_3O_2(aq) + OH^-(aq)$$

I	0.10	0.0	0.0
C	$-x$	x	x
E	$0.10 - x$	x	x

$$K_b = \frac{K_w}{K_a} = \frac{1.0 \times 10^{-14}}{1.8 \times 10^{-5}} = 5.56 \times 10^{-10} = \frac{(x)(x)}{(0.10 - x)}$$

Assume x is small.

$x = 7.45 \times 10^{-6} = [OH^-]$ $pOH = -\log(7.45 \times 10^{-6}) = 5.13$

$pH = 14.00 - 5.13 = 8.87$

(c) **Given:** 0.10 M NaCl **Find:** pH

Conceptual Plan: Identify each species and determine which will contribute to pH.

Solution: Na^+ is the counterion of a strong base; therefore, it is pH neutral. Cl^- is the conjugate base of a strong acid; therefore, it is pH neutral.

pH = 7.0

15.104 (a) **Given:** 0.20 M $NaCHO_2$ **Find:** pH

Conceptual Plan: Identify each species and determine which will contribute to pH. Write a balanced reaction. Prepare an ICE table, represent the change with x, sum the table, determine the equilibrium values, put the equilibrium values in the equilibrium expression, and solve for x. Determine $[OH^-]$ → pOH → pH.

$pOH = -\log[OH^-]$ $pH + pOH = 14$

Solution: Na^+ is the counterion of a strong base; therefore, is pH neutral. CHO_2^- is the conjugate base of a weak acid; therefore, it is basic.

$$CHO_2^-(aq) + H_2O(l) \leftrightarrows HCHO_2(aq) + OH^-(aq)$$

I	0.20 M	0.0	0.0
C	$-x$	x	x
E	$0.20 - x$	x	x

$$K_b = \frac{K_w}{K_a} = \frac{1.0 \times 10^{-14}}{1.8 \times 10^{-4}} = 5.56 \times 10^{-11} = \frac{(x)(x)}{(0.20 - x)}$$

Assume x is small.

$x = 3.33 \times 10^{-6} = [OH^-]$ $pOH = -\log(3.33 \times 10^{-6}) = 5.48$

$pH = 14.00 - 5.48 = 8.52$

(b) **Given:** 0.20 M CH_3NH_3I **Find:** pH

Conceptual Plan: Identify each species and determine which will contribute to pH. Write a balanced reaction. Prepare an ICE table, represent the change with x, sum the table, determine the equilibrium values, put the equilibrium values in the equilibrium expression, and solve for x. Determine $[H_3O^+]$ → pH.

Solution: $CH_3NH_4^+$ is the conjugate acid of a weak base; therefore, it is acidic. Cl^- is the conjugate base of a strong acid; therefore, it is pH neutral.

$$CH_3NH_3^+(aq) + H_2O(l) \leftrightarrows CH_3NH_2(aq) + H_3O^+(aq)$$

I	0.20 M	0.0	0.0
C	$-x$	x	x
E	$0.20 - x$	x	x

$$K_a = \frac{K_w}{K_b} = \frac{1.0 \times 10^{-14}}{4.4 \times 10^{-4}} = 2.27 \times 10^{-11} = \frac{(x)(x)}{(0.20 - x)}$$

Assume x is small.
$x = 2.\underline{1}3 \times 10^{-6} = [H_3O^+]$ $pH = -\log(2.\underline{1}3 \times 10^{-6}) = 5.67$

(c) **Given:** 0.20 M KI **Find:** pH
Conceptual Plan: Identify each species and determine which will contribute to pH.
Solution: K^+ is the counterion of a strong base; therefore, it is pH neutral. I^- is the conjugate base of a strong acid; therefore, it is pH neutral.
pH = 7.0

15.105 **Given:** 0.15 M KF **Find:** concentration of all species
Conceptual Plan: Identify each species and determine which will contribute to pH. Write a balanced reaction. Prepare an ICE table, represent the change with x, sum the table, determine the equilibrium values, put the equilibrium values in the equilibrium expression, and solve for x. Then, determine $[OH^-] \rightarrow [H_3O^+]$.

$K_w = [H_3O^+][OH-]$

Solution: K^+ is the counterion of a strong base; therefore, it is pH neutral. F^- is the conjugate base of a weak acid; therefore, it is basic.

$$F^-(aq) + H_2O(l) \leftrightarrows HF(aq) + OH^-(aq)$$

	F^-	HF	OH^-
I	0.15 M	0.0	0.0
C	$-x$	x	x
E	$0.15 - x$	x	x

$$K_b = \frac{K_w}{K_a} = \frac{1.0 \times 10^{-14}}{3.5 \times 10^{-4}} = \frac{(x)(x)}{(0.15 - x)}$$

Assume x is small.

$x = 2.1 \times 10^{-6} = [OH^-] = [HF]$ $[H_3O^+] = \dfrac{K_w}{[OH^-]} = \dfrac{1 \times 10^{-14}}{2.1 \times 10^{-6}} = 4.8 \times 10^{-9}$

$[K^+] = 0.15$ M
$[F^-] = (0.15 - 2.1 \times 10^{-6}) = 0.15$ M
$[HF] = 2.1 \times 10^{-6}$
$[OH^-] = 2.1 \times 10^{-6}$
$[H_3O^+] = 4.8 \times 10^{-9}$

15.106 **Given:** 0.225 M $C_6H_5NH_3Cl$ **Find:** concentration of all species
Conceptual Plan: Identify each species and determine which will contribute to pH. Write a balanced reaction. Prepare an ICE table, represent the change with x, sum the table, determine the equilibrium values, put the equilibrium values in the equilibrium expression, and solve for x. Then, determine $[H_3O^+] \rightarrow [OH^-]$.

$K_w = [H_3O^+][OH-]$

Solution: $C_6H_5NH_3^+$ is the conjugate acid of a weak base; therefore, it is a weak acid. Cl^- is the conjugate base of a strong acid; therefore, it is pH neutral.

$$C_6H_5NH_3^+(aq) + H_2O(l) \leftrightarrows C_6H_5NH_2(aq) + H_3O^+(aq)$$

	$C_6H_5NH_3^+$	$C_6H_5NH_2$	H_3O^+
I	0.225 M	0.0	0.0
C	$-x$	x	x
E	$0.225 - x$	x	x

$$K_a = \frac{K_w}{K_b} = \frac{1.0 \times 10^{-14}}{3.9 \times 10^{-10}} = 2.\underline{5}6 \times 10^{-5} = \frac{(x)(x)}{(0.225 - x)}$$

Assume x is small.

$x = 0.0024 = [H_3O^+] = [CH_5NH_2]$ $[OH^-] = \dfrac{K_w}{[H_3O^+]} = \dfrac{1.0 \times 10^{-14}}{0.0024} = 4.2 \times 10^{-12}$

$[C_6H_5NH_3^+] = 0.225 - 0.0024 = 0.223$ M
$[Cl^-] = 0.225$ M
$[C_6H_5NH_2] = 0.0024$ M
$[H_3O^+] = 0.0024$ M
$[OH^-] = 4.2 \times 10^{-12}$ M

Polyprotic Acids

15.107 $H_3PO_4(aq) + H_2O(l) \leftrightarrows H_3O^+(aq) + H_2PO_4^-(aq)$ $K_{a_1} = \frac{[H_3O^+][H_2PO_4^-]}{[H_3PO_4]}$

$H_2PO_4^-(aq) + H_2O(l) \leftrightarrows H_3O^+(aq) + HPO_4^{2-}(aq)$ $K_{a_2} = \frac{[H_3O^+][HPO_4^{2-}]}{[H_2PO_4^-]}$

$HPO_4^{2-}(aq) + H_2O(l) \leftrightarrows H_3O^+(aq) + PO_4^{3-}(aq)$ $K_{a_3} = \frac{[H_3O^+][PO_4^{3-}]}{[HPO_4^{2-}]}$

15.108 $H_2CO_3(aq) + H_2O(l) \leftrightarrows H_3O^+(aq) + HCO_3^-(aq)$ $K_{a_1} = \frac{[H_3O^+][HCO_3^-]}{[H_2CO_3]}$

$HCO_3^-(aq) + H_2O(l) \leftrightarrows H_3O^+(aq) + CO_3^{2-}(aq)$ $K_{a_2} = \frac{[H_3O^+][CO_3^{2-}]}{[HCO_3^-]}$

15.109 (a) **Given:** 0.350 M H_3PO_4 $K_{a_1} = 7.5 \times 10^{-3}$, $K_{a_2} = 6.2 \times 10^{-8}$ **Find:** $[H_3O^+]$, pH

Conceptual Plan: K_{a_1} is much larger than K_{a_2}, so use K_{a_1} to calculate $[H_3O^+]$. Write a balanced reaction. Prepare an ICE table, represent the change with x, sum the table, determine the equilibrium values, put the equilibrium values in the equilibrium expression, and solve for x.

Solution: $H_3PO_4(aq) + H_2O(l) \leftrightarrows H_3O^+(aq) + H_2PO_4^-(aq)$

	H_3PO_4	H_3O^+	$H_2PO_4^-$
I	0.350 M	0.0	0.0
C	- x	x	x
E	0.350 – x	x	x

$$K_a = \frac{[H_3O^+][H_2PO_4^-]}{[H_3PO_4]} = \frac{(x)(x)}{(0.350 - x)} = 7.3 \times 10^{-3}$$

Assume x is small compared to 0.350.

$x^2 = (7.3\text{x}10^{-3})(0.350)$ $x = 0.0505 \text{ M} = [H_3O^+]$

Check assumption: $\frac{0.0505}{0.350} \times 100\% = 14.4\%$ assumption not valid, solve with quadratic equation.

$x^2 + 7.5 \times 10^{-3} x - 0.002625 = 0$ $x = 0.04\underline{7}62 = [H_3O^+]$

$\text{pH} = -\log(0.04\underline{7}62) = 1.32$

(b) **Given:** 0.350 M $H_2C_2O_4$ $K_{a_1} = 6.0 \times 10^{-2}$, $K_{a_2} = 6.0 \times 10^{-5}$ **Find:** $[H_3O^+]$, pH

Conceptual Plan: K_{a_1} is much larger than K_{a_2}, so use K_{a_1} to calculate $[H_3O^+]$. Write a balanced reaction. Prepare an ICE table, represent the change with x, sum the table, determine the equilibrium values, put the equilibrium values in the equilibrium expression, and solve for x.

Solution: $H_2C_2O_4(aq) + H_2O(l) \leftrightarrows H_3O^+(aq) + HC_2O_4^-(aq)$

	$H_2C_2O_4$	H_3O^+	$HC_2O_4^-$
I	0.350 M	0.0	0.0
C	- x	x	x
E	0.350 – x	x	x

$$K_a = \frac{[H_3O^+][HC_2O_4^-]}{[H_2C_2O_4]} = \frac{(x)(x)}{(0.350 - x)} = 6.0 \times 10^{-2}$$

$x^2 + 6.0 \times 10^{-2} x - 0.021 = 0$ $x = 0.1\underline{1}79 = 0.12 \text{ M } [H_3O^+]$

$\text{pH} = -\log(0.1\underline{1}79) = 0.93$

15.110 (a) **Given:** 0.125 M H_2CO_3 $K_{a_1} = 4.3 \times 10^{-7}$, $K_{a_2} = 5.6 \times 10^{-11}$ **Find:** $[H_3O^+]$, pH

Conceptual Plan: K_{a_1} much larger than K_{a_2}, so use K_{a_1} to calculate $[H_3O^+]$. Write a balanced reaction. Prepare an ICE table, represent the change with x, sum the table, determine the equilibrium values, put the equilibrium values in the equilibrium expression, and solve for x.

Solution: $H_2CO_3(aq) + H_2O(l) \leftrightarrows H_3O^+(aq) + HCO_3^-(aq)$

	H_2CO_3	H_3O^+	HCO_3^-
I	0.125 M	0.0	0.0
C	- x	x	x
E	0.125 – x	x	x

$$K_a = \frac{[H_3O^+][HCO_3^-]}{[H_2CO_3]} = \frac{(x)(x)}{(0.125 - x)} = 4.3 \times 10^{-7}$$

Assume x is small.

$$x^2 = (4.3 \times 10^{-7})(0.125) \quad x = 2.32 \times 10^{-4} = [H_3O^+]$$

$$\frac{2.32 \times 10^{-4}}{0.125} \times 100\% = 0.19\%; \text{ assumption valid}$$

$$pH = -\log(2.32 \times 10^{-4}) = 3.63$$

(b) **Given:** 0.125 M $H_3C_6H_5O_3$ $K_{a_1} = 7.4 \times 10^{-4}$, $K_{a_2} = 1.7 \times 10^{-5}$, $K_{a_3} = 4.0 \times 10^{-7}$ **Find:** $[H_3O^+]$, pH
Conceptual Plan: K_{a_1} and K_{a_2} are only 10^{-1} apart, so use both to calculate $[H_3O^+]$. Write a balanced reaction. Prepare an ICE table, represent the change with x, sum the table, determine the equilibrium values, put the equilibrium values in the equilibrium expression, and solve for x.
Solution: $H_3C_6H_5O_3(aq) + H_2O(l) \leftrightarrows H_3O^+(aq) + H_2C_6H_5O_3^-(aq)$

I	0.125 M	0.0	0.0
C	$-x$	x	x
E	$0.125 - x$	x	x

$$K_{a_1} = \frac{[H_3O^+][H_2C_6H_5O_3^-]}{[H_3C_6H_5O_3]} = \frac{(x)(x)}{(0.125 - x)} = 7.4 \times 10^{-4}$$

Assume x is small.

$$x^2 = (7.4 \times 10^{-4})(0.125) \quad x = 9.62 \times 10^{-3} = [H_3O^+]$$

$$\frac{9.62 \times 10^{-3}}{0.125} \times 100\% = 7.8\%; \text{ assumption not valid, solve with quadratic equation.}$$

$$x^2 + 7.4 \times 10^{-4} x - 9.25 \times 10^{-5} = 0 \quad x = 0.009255 = [H_3O^+] = [H_2C_6H_5O_3^-]$$

and then:

$$H_2C_6H_5O_3^-(aq) + H_2O(l) \leftrightarrows H_3O^+(aq) + HC_6H_5O_3^{2-}(aq)$$

I	0.009255 M	0.009255	0.0
C	$-y$	y	y
E	$0.009255 - y$	$0.009255 + y$	y

$$K_a = \frac{[H_3O^+][HC_6H_5O_3^{2-}]}{[H_2C_6H_5O_3^-]} = \frac{(0.009255 + y)(y)}{(0.009255 - y)} = 1.7 \times 10^{-5}$$

Assume y is small.   Then, $y = 1.7 \times 10^{-5}$

$$\frac{1.7 \times 10^{-5}}{0.009255} \times 100\% = 1.8\%; \text{ assumption valid}$$

$[H_3O^+] = 1.7 \times 10^{-5}$ (from second ionization)
$[H_3O^+] = 0.009255 + 1.7 \times 10^{-5} = 0.00927$ M $pH = -\log(0.00927) = 2.03$

15.111 **Given:** 0.500 M H_2SO_3 $K_{a_1} = 1.6 \times 10^{-2}$, $K_{a_2} = 6.4 \times 10^{-8}$ **Find:** concentration all species
Conceptual Plan: K_{a_1} is much larger than K_{a_2} so, use K_{a_1} to calculate $[H_3O^+]$. Write a balanced reaction. Prepare an ICE table, represent the change with x, sum the table, determine the equilibrium values, put the equilibrium values in the equilibrium expression, and solve for x.
Solution: $H_2SO_3(aq) + H_2O(l) \leftrightarrows H_3O^+(aq) + HSO_3^-(aq)$

I	0.500 M	0.0	0.0
C	$-x$	x	x
E	$0.500 - x$	x	x

$$K_a = \frac{[H_3O^+][HSO_3^-]}{[H_2SO_3]} = \frac{(x)(x)}{(0.500 - x)} = 1.6 \times 10^{-2}$$

$$x^2 + 1.6 \times 10^{-2} x - 0.0080 = 0 \quad x = 0.0818 = 0.082 \text{ M } [H_3O^+] = [HSO_3^-]$$

Use the values from reaction 1 in reaction 2.

$$HSO_3^-(aq) + H_2O(l) \leftrightarrows H_3O^+(aq) + SO_3^{2-}(aq)$$

I	0.0818 M	0.0818	0.0
C	$-y$	y	y
E	$0.0818 - y$	$0.0818 + y$	y

$$K_a = \frac{[H_3O^+][SO_3^{2-}]}{[HSO_3^-]} = \frac{(0.0818 + y)(y)}{(0.0818 - y)} = 6.4 \times 10^{-8}$$

Assume y is small $y = 6.4 \times 10^{-8}$.

$[H_2SO_3] = 0.500 - 0.08\underline{1}8 = 0.418$ M

$[HSO_3^-] = x = 0.08\underline{1}8 = 0.082$ M

$[SO_3^{2-}] = y = 6.4 \times 10^{-8}$ M

$[H_3O^+] = x + y = 0.08\underline{1}8 = 0.082$ M

$$[OH^-] = \frac{K_w}{[H_3O^+]} = \frac{1.0 \times 10^{-14}}{0.0818} = 1.2 \times 10^{-13}\ \text{M}$$

15.112 **Given:** 0.155 M H_2CO_3 $K_{a_1} = 4.3 \times 10^{-7}$, $K_{a_2} = 5.6 \times 10^{-11}$ **Find:** concentration all species

Conceptual Plan: K_{a_1} is much larger than K_{a_2} so, use K_{a_1} to calculate $[H_3O^+]$ and $[HCO_3^-]$. Use K_{a_2} to find $[CO_3^-]$. Write a balanced reaction. Prepare an ICE table, represent the change with x, sum the table, determine the equilibrium values, put the equilibrium values in the equilibrium expression, and solve for x.

Solution: $H_2CO_3(aq) + H_2O(l) \leftrightarrows H_3O^+(aq) + HCO_3^-(aq)$

	H_2CO_3	H_3O^+	HCO_3^-
I	0.125 M	0.0	0.0
C	$-x$	x	x
E	$0.125 - x$	x	x

$$K_a = \frac{[H_3O^+][HCO_3^-]}{[H_2CO_3]} = \frac{(x)(x)}{(0.155 - x)} = 4.3 \times 10^{-7}$$

Assume x is small.

$x^2 = (4.3\times10^{-7})(0.155)$ $x = 2.58 \times 10^{-4}\ \text{M} = [H_3O^+] = [HCO_3^-]$

Reaction 2

$HCO_3^-(aq) + H_2O(l) \leftrightarrows H_3O^+(aq) + CO_3^{2-}(aq)$

Since K_{a_2} is small, $y = [CO_3^{2-}] = K_{a_2}$

$[H_2CO_3] = 0.155 - 2.\underline{5}8 \times 10^{-4} = 0.1547 = 0.155$ M

$[HCO_3^-] = x = 2.\underline{5}8 \times 10^{-4} = 2.6 \times 10^{-4}$ M

$[CO_3^{2-}] = y = 5.6 \times 10^{-11}$ M

$[H_3O^+] = x = 2.\underline{5}8 \times 10^{-4} = 2.6 \times 10^{-4}$ M

$$[OH^-] = \frac{K_w}{[H_3O^+]} = \frac{1.0 \times 10^{-14}}{2.\underline{5}8 \times 10^{-4}} = 3.88 \times 10^{-11}\ \text{M} = 3.9 \times 10^{-11}\ \text{M}$$

15.113 (a) **Given:** $[H_2SO_4] = 0.50$ M $K_{a_2} = 0.012$ **Find:** $[H_3O^+]$, pH

Conceptual Plan: The first ionization step is strong. Use K_{a_2} and reaction 2. Write a balanced reaction. Prepare an ICE table, represent the change with x, sum the table, determine the equilibrium values, put the equilibrium values in the equilibrium expression, and solve for x.

Solution: $H_2SO_4(aq) + H_2O(l) \rightarrow H_3O^+(aq) + HSO_4^-(aq)$ strong

0.50 M

$[H_3O^+] = [HSO_4^-] = 0.50$ M

$HSO_4^-(aq) + H_2O(l) \leftrightarrows H_3O^+(aq) + SO_4^{2-}(aq)$

	HSO_4^-	H_3O^+	SO_4^{2-}
I	0.50 M	0.50	0.0
C	$-x$	x	x
E	$0.500 - x$	$0.50 + x$	x

$$K_a = \frac{[H_3O^+][SO_4^{2-}]}{[HSO_4^-]} = \frac{(0.50 + x)(x)}{(0.50 - x)} = 0.012$$

$x^2 + 0.512\,x - 0.006 = 0$ $x = 0.01\underline{1}5 = [H_3O^+]$ from second ionization step

$[H_3O^+] = 0.50 + 0.012 = 0.51$ M

$\text{pH} = -\log(0.51) = 0.29$

(b) **Given:** $[H_2SO_4] = 0.10$ M $K_{a_2} = 0.012$ **Find:** $[H_3O^+]$, pH

Conceptual Plan: The first ionization step is strong. Use K_{a_2} and reaction 2. Write a balanced reaction. Prepare an ICE table, represent the change with x, sum the table, determine the equilibrium values, put the equilibrium values in the equilibrium expression, and solve for x.

Solution: $H_2SO_4(aq) + H_2O(l) \rightarrow H_3O^+(aq) + HSO_4^-(aq)$ strong

0.10 M

$[H_3O^+] = [HSO_4^-] = 0.10$ M

$HSO_4^-(aq) + H_2O(l) \leftrightarrows H_3O^+(aq) + SO_4^{2-}(aq)$

	HSO_4^-	H_3O^+	SO_4^{2-}
I	0.10 M	0.10	0.0
C	- x	x	x
E	0.10 – x	0.10 + x	x

$$K_a = \frac{[H_3O^+][SO_4^{2-}]}{[HSO_4^-]} = \frac{(0.10 + x)(x)}{(0.10 - x)} = 0.012$$

$x^2 + 0.112x - 0.0012 = 0 \quad x = 0.009848$

$$\frac{0.009848}{0.10} \times 100 = 9.8\%$$ contribution of second ionizations step not negligible

$[H_3O^+] = 0.10 + 0.0085 = 0.1085 = 0.11$M

pH = - log(0.11) = 0.96

(c) **Given:** $[H_2SO_4] = 0.050$ M $K_{a_2} = 0.012$ **Find:** $[H_3O^+]$,pH

Conceptual Plan: The first ionization step is strong. Use K_{a_2} and reaction 2. Write a balanced reaction. Prepare an ICE table, represent the change with x, sum the table, determine the equilibrium values, put the equilibrium values in the equilibrium expression, and solve for x.

Solution: $H_2SO_4(aq) + H_2O(l) \rightarrow H_3O^+(aq) + HSO_4^-(aq)$ strong

0.050 M

$[H_3O^+] = [HSO_4^-] = 0.050$ M

$HSO_4^-(aq) + H_2O(l) \leftrightarrows H_3O^+(aq) + SO_4^{2-}(aq)$

	HSO_4^-	H_3O^+	SO_4^{2-}
I	0.050 M	0.050	0.0
C	- x	x	x
E	0.050 – x	0.050 + x	x

$$K_a = \frac{[H_3O^+][SO_4^{2-}]}{[HSO_4^-]} = \frac{(0.050 + x)(x)}{(0.050 - x)} = 0.012$$

$x^2 + 0.062\,x - 0.006 = 0 \quad x = 0.008509$

$$\frac{0.008509}{0.05} \times 100 = 17\%$$ contribution of second ionizations step not negligible

$[H_3O^+] = 0.050 + 0.0085 = 0.0585 = 0.059$ M pH = - log(0.059) = 1.23

15.114 (a) **Given:** 0.10 M H_2A, $K_{a_1} = 1.0 \times 10^{-4}$, $K_{a_2} = 5.0 \times 10^{-5}$ **Find:** Is the second ionization negligible?

Conceptual Plan: Write a balanced reaction for both ionization steps. Prepare an ICE table, represent the change with x, sum the table, determine the equilibrium values, put the equilibrium values in the equilibrium expression, and solve for x.

$H_2A(aq) + H_2O(l) \rightarrow H_3O^+(aq) + HA^-(aq)$

	H_2A	H_3O^+	HA^-
I	0.10 M	0.0	0.0
C	- x	x	x
E	0.10 – x	x	x

$$K_{a_1} = \frac{[H_3O^+][HA^-]}{[H_2A]} = \frac{(x)(x)}{(0.10 - x)} = 1.0 \times 10^{-4}$$

$x^2 + 1.0 \times 10^{-4}x - 1.0 \times 10^{-5} = 0 \quad x = 0.00311$

$HA^-(aq) + H_2O(l) \leftrightarrows H_3O^+(aq) + A^{2-}(aq)$

	HA^-	H_3O^+	A^{2-}
I	0.00311 M	0.00311 M	0.0
C	- y	y	y
E	0.00311 – y	0.00311 + y	y

$$K_{a_2} = \frac{[H_3O^+][A^{2-}]}{[HA^-]} = \frac{(0.00311 + y)(y)}{(0.00311 - y)} = 5.0 \times 10^{-5}$$

$y^2 + 0.00316\,y - 1.55 \times 10^{-7} = 0 \quad y = 4.83 \times 10^{-5}$

$$\frac{4.83 \times 10^{-5}}{0.00316} \times 100 = 1.5\%$$ contribution of second ionizations step negligible

$[H_3O^+] = 0.00311$ pH = - log(0.00311) = 2.5

(b) **Given:** 0.10 M H_2A, $K_{a_1} = 1.0 \times 10^{-4}$, $K_{a_2} = 1.0 \times 10^{-6}$ **Find:** Is the second ionization negligible?
Conceptual Plan: Write a balanced reaction for both ionization steps. Prepare an ICE table, represent the change with x, sum the table, determine the equilibrium values, put the equilibrium values in the equilibrium expression, and solve for x.

	$H_2A(aq) + H_2O(l)$ $\rightarrow$	$H_3O^+(aq)$ +	$HA^-(aq)$
I	0.10 M	0.0	0.0
C	$-x$	x	x
E	$0.10 - x$	x	x

$$K_{a_1} = \frac{[H_3O^+][HA^-]}{[H_2A]} = \frac{(x)(x)}{(0.10 - x)} = 1.0 \times 10^{-4}$$

$x^2 + 1.0 \times 10^{-4}x - 1.0 \times 10^{-5} = 0 \quad x = 0.003\underline{1}1$

	$HA^-(aq) + H_2O(l) \leftrightarrows$	$H_3O^+(aq)$ +	$A^{2-}(aq)$
I	0.003$\underline{1}$1 M	0.003$\underline{1}$1 M	0.0
C	$-y$	y	y
E	$0.003\underline{1}1 - y$	$0.003\underline{1}1 + y$	y

$$K_{a_2} = \frac{[H_3O^+][A^{2-}]}{[HA^-]} = \frac{(0.003\underline{1}1 + y)(y)}{(0.003\underline{1}1 - y)} = 1.0 \times 10^{-6}$$

$y^2 + 0.00311\,y - 3.11 \times 10^{-9} = 0 \qquad y = 9.\underline{9}8 \times 10^{-7}$

$$\frac{9.\underline{9}8 \times 10^{-7}}{0.00311} \times 100 = 0.032\%$$ contribution of second ionizations step negligible

$[H_3O^+] = 0.003\underline{1}1$ pH = - log(0.003$\underline{1}$1) = 2.5

(c) **Given:** 0.10 M H_2A, $K_{a_1} = 1.0 \times 10^{-4}$, $K_{a_2} = 1.0 \times 10^{-5}$ **Find:** Is the second ionization negligible?
Conceptual Plan: Write a balanced reaction for both ionization steps. Prepare an ICE table, represent the change with x, sum the table, determine the equilibrium values, put the equilibrium values in the equilibrium expression, and solve for x.

	$H_2A(aq) + H_2O(l)$ $\rightarrow$	$H_3O^+(aq)$ +	$HA^-(aq)$
I	0.10 M	0.0	0.0
C	$-x$	x	x
E	$0.10 - x$	x	x

$$K_{a_1} = \frac{[H_3O^+][HA^-]}{[H_2A]} = \frac{(x)(x)}{(0.10 - x)} = 1.0 \times 10^{-4}$$

$x^2 + 1.0 \times 10^{-4}x - 1.0 \times 10^{-5} = 0 \quad x = 0.003\underline{1}1$

	$HA^-(aq) + H_2O(l) \leftrightarrows$	$H_3O^+(aq)$ +	$A^{2-}(aq)$
I	0.003$\underline{1}$1 M	0.003$\underline{1}$1 M	0.0
C	$-y$	y	y
E	$0.003\underline{1}1 - y$	$0.003\underline{1}1 + y$	y

$$K_{a_2} = \frac{[H_3O^+][A^{2-}]}{[HA^-]} = \frac{(0.003\underline{1}1 + y)(y)}{(0.003\underline{1}1 - y)} = 1.0 \times 10^{-5}$$

$y^2 + 0.00311\,y - 3.11 \times 10^{-8} = 0 \qquad y = 9.\underline{9}3 \times 10^{-6}$

$$\frac{9.\underline{9}3 \times 10^{-6}}{0.00311} \times 100 = 0.32\%$$ contribution of second ionizations step negligible

$[H_3O^+] = 0.003\underline{1}1$ pH = -log(0.003$\underline{1}$1) = 2.5

Molecular Structure and Acid Strength

15.115 (a) HCl is the stronger acid. HCl is the weaker bond; therefore, it is more acidic.

(b) HF is the stronger acid. F is more electronegative than O, so the bond is more polar and more acidic.

(c) H_2Se is the stronger acid. The H—Se bond is weaker; therefore, it is more acidic.

15.116 Increasing acid strength: NaH < H_2S < H_2Te < HI

H_2Te is a stronger acid than H_2S because the H—Te bond is weaker. HI is a stronger acid than H_2Te because I is more electronegative than Te. NaH is not acidic because H is more electronegative than Na.

15.117 (a) H_2SO_4 is the stronger acid because it has more oxygen atoms.

(b) $HClO_2$ is the stronger acid because it has more oxygen atoms.

(c) HClO is the stronger acid because Cl is more electronegative than Br.

(d) CCl_3COOH is the stronger acid because Cl is more electronegative than H.

15.118 Increasing acid strength: $HIO_3 < HBrO_3 < HClO_3$.
Cl is more electronegative than Br which is more electronegative than I.

15.119 S^{2-} is the stronger base. Base strength is determined from the corresponding acid. The weaker the acid, the stronger the base. H_2S is the weaker acid because it has a stronger bond.

15.120 AsO_4^{3-} is the stronger base. Base strength is determined from the corresponding acid. The weaker the acid, the stonger the base. H_3AsO_4 is the weaker acid because P is more electronegative than As.

Lewis Acids and Bases

15.121 (a) Lewis acid: Fe^{3+} has an empty *d* orbital and can accept lone pair electrons.

(b) Lewis acid: BH_3 has an empty *p* orbital to accept a lone pair of electrons.

(c) Lewis base: NH_3 has a lone pair of electrons to donate.

(d) Lewis base: F^- has lone pair electrons to donate.

15.122 (a) Lewis acid: $BeCl_2$ has empty *p* orbitals to accept lone pair electrons.

(b) Lewis base: OH^- has lone pair electrons to donate.

(c) Lewis acid: $B(OH)_3$ has an empty *p* orbital to accept a lone pair of electrons.

(d) Lewis base: CN^- has lone pair electrons to donate.

15.123 (a) Fe^{3+} accepts electron pair from H_2O, so Fe^{3+} is the Lewis acid and H_2O is the Lewis base.

(b) Zn^{2+} accepts electron pair from NH_3, so Zn^{2+} is the Lewis acid and NH_3 is the Lewis base.

(c) The empty *p* orbital on B accepts an electron pair from $(CH_3)_3N$, so BF_3 is the Lewis acid and $(CH_3)_3N$ is the Lewis base.

15.124 (a) Ag^+ accepts electron pair from NH_3, so Ag^+ is the Lewis acid and NH_3 is the Lewis base.

(b) The empty *p* orbital on Al accepts an electron pair from NH_3, $AlBr_3$ is the Lewis acid and NH_3 is the Lewis base.

(c) The empty *p* orbital on B accepts an electron pair from F^-, so BF_3 is the Lewis acid and F^- is the Lewis base.

Cumulative Problems

15.125 (a) weak acid. The beaker contains 10 HF molecule, $2H_3O^+$ ions, and $2F^-$ ions. Since both the molecule and the ions exist in solution, the acid is a weak acid.

(b) strong acid. The beaker contains $12H_3O^+$ ions and $2OH^-$ ions. Since the molecule is completely ionized in solution, the acid is a strong acid.

(c) weak acid. The beaker contains 10 $HCHO_2$ molecules, $2H_3O^+$ ions, and $2CHO_2^-$ ions. Since both the molecule and the ions exist in solution, the acid is a weak acid.

(d) strong acid. The beaker contains $12H_3O^+$ ions and $2NO_3^-$ ions. Since the molecule is completely ionized in solution, the acid is a strong acid.

15.126 (a) weak base. The beaker contains 11 NH_3 molecules, 2 NH_4^+ ions, and 2OH^- ions. Since both the molecule and the ions exist in solution, this is a weak base.

(b) strong base. The beaker contains 12 Na^+ ions and 12OH^- ions. Since the molecule is completely ionized in solution, it is a strong base.

(c) weak base. The beaker contains 12 Na^+, 10 H_2CO_3 molecules, 2HCO_3^- ions, and 2OH^- ions. The beaker contains the HCO_3^- ion from the $NaHCO_3$ and H_2CO_3 molecules from the reaction of the salt.

(d) strong base. The beaker contains 12 Sr^{2+} ions and 24 OH^- ions. Since the molecule is completely ionized in solution, it is a strong base.

15.127 $HbH^+(aq) + O_2(aq) \leftrightarrows HbO_2(aq) + H^+(aq)$

Using Le Châtelier's principle, if the $[H^+]$ increases, the reaction will shift left, if the $[H^+]$ decreases, the reaction will shift right. So, if the pH of blood is too acidic (low pH; $[H^+]$ increased), the reaction will shift to the left. This will cause less of the HbO_2 in the blood and decrease the oxygen-carrying capacity of the hemoglobin in the blood.

15.128 $CO_2(g) + H_2O(l) \leftrightarrows H_2CO_3(aq)$

$H_2CO_3(aq) + H_2O(l) \leftrightarrows HCO_3^-(aq) + H_3O^+(aq)$

As the concentration of CO_2 in the atmosphere increases, more will dissolve in H_2O and form H_2CO_3. The H_2CO_3 will then act as a weak acid with H_2O and form HCO_3^- and H_3O^+, causing the water (oceans) to be more acidic. If the pH of the oceans decreases, the added H_3O^+ will react with the CO_3^{2-} ion in the $CaCO_3$ in the limestone structures and decompose the $CaCO_3$.

$2H_3O^+(aq) + CaCO_3(s) \rightarrow Ca^{2+}(aq) + H_2CO_3(aq) + 2H_2O \rightarrow H_2O(l) + CO_2(g)$

15.129 **Given:** 4.00×10^2 mg $Mg(OH)_2$, 2.00×10^2 mL HCl solution, pH = 1.3
Find: volume neutralized, % neutralized.
Conceptual Plan:
mg $Mg(OH)_2$ → g $Mg(OH)_2$ → mol $Mg(OH)_2$ and then pH → $[H_3O^+]$ and then mol $Mg(OH)_2$

$\frac{g\ Mg(OH)_2}{1000\ mg}$ $\frac{mol\ Mg(OH)_2}{58.326g}$ $pH = -\log[H_3O^+]$

mol OH^- → mol H_3O^+ → vol H_3O^+ → % neutralized.

$\frac{2\ OH^-}{Mg(OH)_2}$ $\frac{H_3O^+}{OH^-}$ $\frac{mol\ H_3O^+}{M(H_3O^+)}$ $\frac{vol\ HCl\ neutralized}{total\ vol\ HCl} \times 100$

Solution: $[H_3O^+] = 10^{-1.3} = 0.05011\ M = 0.05\ M$

$$4.00 \times 10^2\ mg\ Mg(OH)_2 \times \frac{g\ Mg(OH)_2}{1000\ mg\ Mg(OH)_2} \times \frac{1\ mol\ Mg(OH)_2}{58.326\ g\ Mg(OH)_2} \times \frac{2\ mol\ OH^-}{1\ mol\ Mg(OH)_2} \times \frac{1\ mol\ H_3O^+}{1\ mol\ OH^-} \times \frac{1\ L}{0.0501\ mol\ H_3O^+} \times \frac{1000\ mL}{L} = 27\underline{3}.7\ mL = 274\ mL\ neutralized$$

Stomach contains 2.00×10^2 mL HCl at pH = 1.3 and 4.00×10^2 mg will neutralize 274 mL of pH 1.3 HCl, so all of the stomach acid will be neutralized.

15.130 **Given:** 4.3 billion L, pH = 5.5 **Find:** mass in kg $CaCO_3$
Conceptual Plan:
pH → $[H_3O^+]$ and then vol lake → mol $[H_3O^+]$ → mol $CaCO_3$ → g $CaCO_3$ → kg $CaCO_3$

$pH = -\log[H_3O^+]$ mol = vol x M $\frac{mol\ CaCO_3}{2\ mol\ H_3O^+}$ $\frac{100.09\ g\ CaCO_3}{mol\ CaCO_3}$ $\frac{kg\ CaCO_3}{1000\ g\ CaCO_3}$

Solution: $[H_3O^+] = 10^{-5.5} = 3.\underline{1}6 \times 10^{-6}$ M

$$4.3 \times 10^9\ L \times \frac{3.\underline{1}6 \times 10^{-6}\ mol\ H_3O^+}{L} \times \frac{1\ mol\ CaCO_3}{2\ mol\ H_3O^+} \times \frac{100.09\ g\ CaCO_3}{mol\ CaCO_3} \times \frac{1\ kg}{1000\ g}$$
$= 680.01\ kg = 6.8 \times 10^2\ kg\ CaCO_3$

15.131 **Given:** pH of Great Lakes acid rain = 4.5, West Coast = 5.4
Find: $[H_3O^+]$ and ratio of Great Lakes/West Coast
Conceptual Plan: pH → $[H_3O^+]$, and then ratio of $[H_3O^+]$ Great Lakes to West Coast.

$pH = -\log[H_3O^+]$

Solution: Great Lakes: $[H_3O^+] = 10^{-4.5} = 3.16 \times 10^{-5}$ M West Coast: $[H_3O^+] = 10^{-5.4} = 3.98 \times 10^{-6}$ M

$$\frac{\text{Great Lakes}}{\text{West Coast}} = \frac{3.16 \times 10^{-5}\text{ M}}{3.98 \times 10^{-6}\text{ M}} = 7.94 = 8 \text{ times more acidic}$$

15.132 **Given:** pH of Sauvignon Blanc = 3.23, Cabernet Sauvignon = 3.64
Find: $[H_3O^+]$ and ratio of Sauvignon Blanc to Cabernet Sauvignon
Conceptual Plan: pH → $[H_3O^+]$, and then ratio of $[H_3O^+]$ Sauvignon Blanc to Cabernet Sauvignon.

$pH = -\log[H_3O^+]$

Solution:

Sauvignon Blanc: $[H_3O^+] = 10^{-3.23} = 5.888 \times 10^{-4}$ M
Cabernet Sauvignon: $[H_3O^+] = 10^{-3.64} = 2.291 \times 10^{-4}$ M

$$\frac{\text{Sauvignon Blanc}}{\text{Cabernet Sauvignon}} = \frac{5.888 \times 10^{-4}\text{ M}}{2.291 \times 10^{-4}\text{ M}} = 2.570 = 2.57 \text{ times more acidic}$$

15.133 **Given:** 6.5×10^2 mg aspirin, 8 ounces water, $pK_a = 3.5$ **Find:** pH of solution
Conceptual Plan:
mg aspirin → g aspirin → mol aspirin and ounces → quart → L and then [aspirin] and pK_a

$\frac{\text{g aspirin}}{1000\text{ mg}}$ $\frac{\text{mol aspirin}}{180.16\text{g}}$ $\frac{1\text{ qt}}{32\text{ ounces}}$ $\frac{1\text{ L}}{1.0567\text{ qt}}$ $\frac{\text{mol aspirin}}{\text{L soln}}$ $pK_a = -\log K_a$

→ K_a. Write a balanced reaction. Prepare an ICE table, represent the change with x, sum the table, determine the equilibrium values, put the equilibrium values in the equilibrium expression, and solve for x. Determine $[H_3O^+]$ → pH.

$pH = -\log[H_3O^+]$

Solution: $$\frac{6.5 \times 10^2 \text{ mg aspirin}}{8 \text{ ounces}} \times \frac{1 \text{ gram aspirin}}{1000 \text{ mg aspirin}} \times \frac{\text{mol aspirin}}{180.16 \text{ g}} \times \frac{32 \text{ ounces}}{\text{qt}} \times \frac{1.0567 \text{ qt}}{1 \text{ L}} = 0.0152 \text{ M}$$

$K_a = 10^{-3.5} = 3.16 \times 10^{-4}$

aspirin(aq) + $H_2O(l)$ ⇆ $H_3O^+(aq)$ + aspirin$^-(aq)$

I	0.0152 M	0.0	0.0
C	$-x$	x	x
E	$0.0152 - x$	x	x

$$K_a = \frac{[H_3O^+][\text{aspirin}^-]}{[\text{aspirin}]} = \frac{(x)(x)}{(0.0152 - x)} = 3.16 \times 10^{-4}$$

$x^2 + 3.16 \times 10^{-4}x - 4.80 \times 10^{-6} = 0$ $x = 2.04 \times 10^{-3}\text{ M} = [H_3O^+]$

$pH = -\log(2.04 \times 10^{-3}) = 2.69 = 2.7$

15.134 **Given:** 565 mg/L ddC, $pK_b = 9.8$ **Find:** % protonated
Conceptual Plan: mg → g → mol → M and then pK_b → K_b then write a balanced reaction. Prepare an ICE table, represent the change with x, sum the table, determine the equilibrium values, put the equilibrium values in the equilibrium expression, and solve for x.

Solution: $$\frac{565 \text{ mg ddC}}{\text{L}} \times \frac{\text{g ddC}}{1000 \text{ mg ddC}} \times \frac{\text{mol ddC}}{224.22 \text{ g ddC}} = 0.0025199 \text{ M}$$

$K_b = 10^{-9.8} = 1.585 \times 10^{-10}$

ddC(aq) + $H_2O(l)$ ⇆ HddC$^+(aq)$ + $OH^-(aq)$

I	0.0025199	0.0	0.0
C	$-x$	x	x
E	$0.0025199 - x$	x	x

$$K_b = \frac{[\text{HddC}^+][OH^-]}{[\text{ddC}]} = \frac{(x)(x)}{(0.0025199 - x)} = 1.585 \times 10^{-10}$$

Assume x is small.

$x^2 = (1.585 \times 10^{-10})(0.0025\underline{1}99)$ $\quad x = [OH^-] = [HddC^+] = 6.32 \times 10^{-7}$ M

$$\% \text{ protonated} = \frac{[HddC^+]_{\text{equilibrium}}}{[ddC]_{\text{original}}} \times 100\% = \frac{(6.32 \times 10^{-7})}{(0.0025\underline{1}99)} \times 100\% = 0.025\ \%$$

15.135 (a) **Given:** 0.0100M $HClO_4$ **Find:** pH

Conceptual Plan: $[HClO_4] \rightarrow [H_3O^+] \rightarrow$ **pH**

$[HClO_4] \rightarrow [H_3O^+]$ $\quad pH = -\log[H_3O^+]$

Solution: 0.0100 M $HClO_4$ = 0.0100 M H_3O^+ $\quad pH = -\log(0.0100) = 2.000$

(b) **Given:** 0.115M $HClO_2$, $K_a = 1.1 \times 10^{-2}$ **Find:** pH

Conceptual Plan: Write a balanced reaction. Prepare an ICE table, represent the change with x, sum the table, determine the equilibrium values, put the equilibrium values in the equilibrium expression, and solve for x. Determine $[H_3O^+]$ and pH.

Solution: $HClO_2\,(aq) + H_2O(l) \leftrightharpoons H_3O^+(aq) + ClO_2^-\,(aq)$

	$HClO_2$	H_3O^+	ClO_2^-
I	0.115 M	0.0	0.0
C	$-x$	x	x
E	$0.115 - x$	x	x

$$K_a = \frac{[H_3O^+][ClO_2^-]}{[HClO_2]} = \frac{(x)(x)}{(0.115 - x)} = 1.1 \times 10^{-2}$$

Assume x is small compared to 0.115.

$x^2 = (1.1 \times 10^{-2})(0.115)$ $\quad x = 0.03\underline{5}6$ M $= [H_3O^+]$

Check assumption: $\frac{0.03\underline{5}6}{0.115} \times 100 = 30.9\%$ assumption not valid, solve with quadratic equation.

$x^2 + 1.1 \times 10^{-2}x - 0.001265 = 0$

$x = 0.03\underline{0}49$ or -0.0415

$pH = -\log(0.03\underline{0}49) = 1.52$

(c) **Given:** 0.045M $Sr(OH)_2$ **Find:** pH

Conceptual Plan: $[Sr(OH)_2] \rightarrow [OH^-] \rightarrow [H_3O^+] \rightarrow$ **pH**

$K_w = [H_3O^+][OH^-]$ $\quad pH = -\log[H_3O^+]$ $\quad pH + pOH = 14$

Solution: $[OH^-] = [Sr(OH)_2] = 2(0.045) = 0.090$ M

$$[H_3O^+] = \frac{K_w}{[OH^-]} = \frac{1.0 \times 10^{-14}}{0.090 \text{ M}} = 1.1\underline{1} \times 10^{-13} \text{ M}$$

$pH = -\log(1.1\underline{1} \times 10^{-13}) = 12.95$

(d) **Given:** 0.0852 KCN, $K_a = 4.9 \times 10^{-10}$ **Find:** pH

Conceptual Plan: Identify each species and determine which will contribute to pH. Write a balanced reaction. Prepare an ICE table, represent the change with x, sum the table, determine the equilibrium values, put the equilibrium values in the equilibrium expression, and solve for x. Determine $[OH^-] \rightarrow$ pOH $\rightarrow$ pH.

$pOH = -\log[OH^-]$ $\quad pH + pOH = 14$

Solution: K^+ is the counterion of a strong base; therefore, is pH neutral. CN^- is the conjugate base of a weak acid; therefore, it is basic.

$CN^-(aq) + H_2O(l) \leftrightharpoons HCN\,(aq) + OH^-(aq)$

	CN^-	HCN	OH^-
I	0.0852 M	0.0	0.0
C	$-x$	x	x
E	$0.0852 - x$	x	x

$$K_b = \frac{K_w}{K_a} = \frac{1.0 \times 10^{-14}}{4.9 \times 10^{-10}} = 2.\underline{0}4 \times 10^{-5} = \frac{(x)(x)}{(0.0852 - x)}$$

Assume x is small.

$x = 1.\underline{3}2 \times 10^{-3}$ M $= [OH^-]$ $\quad pOH = -\log(1.\underline{3}2 \times 10^{-3}) = 2.88$

$pH = 14.00 - 2.88 = 11.12$

(e) **Given:** 0.155 NH_4Cl, K_b (NH_3) = 1.8×10^{-5} **Find:** pH
Conceptual Plan: Identify each species and determine which will contribute to pH. Write a balanced reaction. Prepare an ICE table, represent the change with x, sum the table, determine the equilibrium values, put the equilibrium values in the equilibrium expression, and solve for x. Determine $[H_3O^+]$ → pH.
Solution: NH_4^+ is the conjugate acid of a weak base; therefore, it is acidic. Cl^- is the conjugate base of a strong acid; therefore, it is pH neutral.

	$NH_4^+(aq) + H_2O(l) \leftrightharpoons$	$NH_3(aq)$	$+ H_3O^+(aq)$
I	0.155 M	0.0	0.0
C	$-x$	x	x
E	$0.155 - x$	x	x

$$K_a = \frac{K_w}{K_b} = \frac{1 \times 10^{-14}}{1.8 \times 10^{-5}} = 5.\underline{5}6 \times 10^{-10} = \frac{(x)(x)}{(0.155 - x)}$$

Assume x is small.
$x = 9.\underline{2}8 \times 10^{-6}$ M = $[H_3O^+]$ pH = $-\log(9.\underline{2}8 \times 10^{-6}) = 5.03$

15.136 (a) **Given:** 0.0650 M HNO_3 **Find:** pH
Conceptual Plan: $[HNO_3]$ → $[H_3O^+]$ → **pH**
$[HNO_3] \rightarrow [H_3O^+]$ pH = $-\log[H_3O^+]$
Solution: 0.0650 M HNO_3 = 0.0650 M H_3O^+ pH = $-\log(0.0650) = 1.187$

(b) **Given:** 0.150 M HNO_2, $K_a = 4.6 \times 10^{-4}$ **Find:** pH
Conceptual Plan: Write a balanced reaction. Prepare an ICE table, represent the change with x, sum the table, determine the equilibrium values, put the equilibrium values in the equilibrium expression, and solve for x. Determine $[H_3O^+]$ and pH.
Solution: $HNO_2(aq) + H_2O(l) \leftrightharpoons H_3O^+(aq) + NO_2^-(aq)$

	HNO_2	H_3O^+	NO_2^-
I	0.150 M	0.0	0.0
C	$-x$	x	x
E	$0.150 - x$	x	x

$$K_a = \frac{[H_3O^+][NO_2^-]}{[HNO_2]} = \frac{(x)(x)}{(0.150 - x)} = 4.6 \times 10^{-4}$$

Assume x is small compared to 0.150.
$x^2 = (4.6 \times 10^{-4})(0.150)$ $x = 0.008\underline{3}1$ M = $[H_3O^+]$

Check assumption: $\frac{0.008\underline{3}1}{0.150} \times 100 = 5.54\%$ assumption not valid, solve with quadratic equation.

$x^2 + 4.6 \times 10^{-4}x - 6.9 \times 10^{-5} = 0$
$x = 0.008\underline{0}8$ M = $[H_3O^+]$
pH = $-\log(0.008\underline{0}8) = 2.09$

(c) **Given:** 0.0195 M KOH **Find:** pH
Conceptual Plan: [KOH] → $[OH^-]$ → $[H_3O^+]$ → **pH**
$K_w = [H_3O^+][OH^-]$ pH = $-\log[H_3O^+]$ pH + pOH = 14
Solution: $[OH^-]$ = [KOH] = (0.0195) = 0.0195 M

$$[H_3O^+] = \frac{K_w}{[OH^-]} = \frac{1.0 \times 10^{-14}}{0.0195\ \text{M}} = 5.1\underline{2}8 \times 10^{-13}\ \text{M}$$

pH = $-\log(5.1\underline{2}8 \times 10^{-13}) = 12.290$

(d) **Given:** 0.245 CH_3NH_3I, K_b (CH_3NH_3) = 4.4×10^{-4} **Find:** pH
Conceptual Plan: Identify each species and determine which will contribute to pH. Write a balanced reaction. Prepare an ICE table, represent the change with x, sum the table, determine the equilibrium values, put the equilibrium values in the equilibrium expression, and solve for x. Determine $[H_3O^+]$ → pH.
Solution: $CH_3NH_3^+$ is the conjugate acid of a weak base; therefore, it is acidic. I^- is the conjugate base of a strong acid; therefore, it is pH neutral.

$CH_3NH_4^+\ (aq) + H_2O(l) \leftrightharpoons CH_3NH_2\ (aq) + H_3O^+\ (aq)$

I	0.245 M	0.0	0.0
C	$-x$	x	x
E	$0.245 - x$	x	x

$$K_a = \frac{K_w}{K_b} = \frac{1.0 \times 10^{-14}}{4.4 \times 10^{-4}} = 2.2\underline{7}2 \times 10^{-11} = \frac{(x)(x)}{(0.245 - x)}$$

Assume x is small.

$x = 2.\underline{3}6 \times 10^{-6} = [H_3O^+]$ $\quad pH = -\log(2.\underline{3}6 \times 10^{-6}) = 5.63$

(e) **Given:** 0.318 KC_6H_5O, K_a (HC_6H_5O) = 1.3×10^{-10} **Find:** pH

Conceptual Plan: Identify each species and determine which will contribute to pH. Write a balanced reaction. Prepare an ICE table, represent the change with x, sum the table, determine the equilibrium values, put the equilibrium values in the equilibrium expression, and solve for x. Determine $[OH^-] \rightarrow$ pOH $\rightarrow$ pH.

pOH = -log[OH^-] pH + pOH = 14

Solution: K^+ is the counterion of a strong base; therefore, it is pH neutral. $C_6H_5O^-$ is the conjugate base of a weak acid; therefore, it is basic.

$C_6H_5O^-\ (aq) + H_2O(l) \leftrightharpoons HC_6H_5O\ (aq) + OH^-\ (aq)$

I	0. 318 M	0.0	0.0
C	$-x$	x	x
E	$0.318 - x$	x	x

$$K_b = \frac{K_w}{K_a} = \frac{1.0 \times 10^{-14}}{1.3 \times 10^{-10}} = 7.\underline{6}9 \times 10^{-5} = \frac{(x)(x)}{(0.318 - x)}$$

Assume x is small.

$x = 4.\underline{9}5 \times 10^{-3} = [OH^-]$ $\quad pOH = -\log(4.\underline{9}5 \times 10^{-3}) = 2.31$

pH = 14.00 − 2.31 = 11.69

15.137 (a) **Given:** 0.0550M HI (strong acid), 0.00850M HF (weak acid) **Find:** pH

Conceptual Plan: Since the mixture is a strong acid and a weak acid, the strong acid will dominate. Use the concentration of the strong acid to determine $[H_3O^+]$ and then pH.

Solution: 0.0550M HI = 0.0550 M $[H_3O^+]$ pH = -log(0.0550) = 1.260

(b) **Given:** 0.112 M NaCl (salt), 0.0953 M KF (salt) **Find:** pH

Conceptual Plan: Identify each species and determine which will contribute to pH. Write a balanced reaction. Prepare an ICE table, represent the change with x, sum the table, determine the equilibrium values, put the equilibrium values in the equilibrium expression, and solve for x. Determine $[H_3O^+] \rightarrow$ pH.

Solution: Na^+ is the counterion of a strong base; therefore, it is pH neutral. Cl^- is the conjugate base of a strong acid; therefore, it is pH neutral. K^+ is the counterion of a strong base; therefore, it is pH neutral. F^- is the conjugate base of a weak acid. Therefore, it will produce a basic solution.

$F^-\ (aq) + H_2O(l) \leftrightharpoons HF\ (aq) + OH^-\ (aq)$

I	0.0953 M	0.0	0.0
C	$-x$	x	x
E	$0.0953 - x$	x	x

$$K_b = \frac{K_w}{K_a} = \frac{1.0 \times 10^{-14}}{3.5 \times 10^{-4}} = \frac{(x)(x)}{(0.0953 - x)}$$

Assume x is small.

$x = 1.\underline{6}50 \times 10^{-6} = [OH^-]$ $\quad pOH = -\log(1.\underline{6}50 \times 10^{-6}) = 5.78$

pH = 14.00 − 5.78 = 8.22

(c) **Given:** 0.132 M NH_4Cl (salt), 0.150 M HNO_3 (strong acid) **Find:** pH

Conceptual Plan: Since the mixture is a strong acid and a salt, the strong acid will dominate. Use the concentration of the strong acid to determine $[H_3O^+]$ and then pH.

Solution: 0.150 M HNO_3 = 0.150 M $[H_3O^+]$ pH = - log(0.150) = 0.824

(d) **Given:** 0.0887 M $NaC_7H_5O_2$ (salt) 0.225 M KBr(salt)
Conceptual Plan: Identify each species and determine which will contribute to pH. Write a balanced reaction. Prepare an ICE table, represent the change with *x*, sum the table, determine the equilibrium values, put the equilibrium values in the equilibrium expression, and solve for *x*. Determine $[H_3O^+] \rightarrow$ pH.
Solution: Na^+ is the counterion of a strong base; therefore, it is pH neutral. $C_7H_5O_2^-$ is the conjugate base of a weak acid. Therefore, it will produce a basic solution. K^+ is the counterion of a strong base; therefore, it is pH neutral. Cl^- is the conjugate base of a strong acid; therefore, it is pH neutral.

	$C_7H_5O_2^-(aq) + H_2O(l) \rightleftharpoons$	$HC_7H_5O_2(aq)+$	$OH^-(aq)$
I	0.0887 M	0.0	0.0
C	$-x$	x	x
E	$0.0887 - x$	x	x

$$K_b = \frac{K_w}{K_a} = \frac{1.0 \times 10^{-14}}{6.5 \times 10^{-5}} = \frac{(x)(x)}{(0.0887 - x)}$$

Assume x is small.

$x = 3.\underline{6}94 \times 10^{-6} = [OH^-]$ $pOH = -\log(3.\underline{6}94 \times 10^{-6}) = 5.43$

$pH = 14.00 - 5.43 = 8.57$

(e) **Given:** 0.0450 M HCl (strong acid), 0.0225 M HNO_3 (strong acid) **Find:** pH
Conceptual Plan: Since the mixture is a strong acid and a strong acid, $[H_3O^+]$ is the sum of the concentration of both acids, and then determine pH.
Solution: 0.0450 M HCl = 0.0450 $[H_3O^+]$, 0.0225 M HNO_3 = 0.0225 M $[H_3O^+]$
$[H_3O^+] = 0.0450 + 0.0225 = 0.0675$ M pH = - log(0.0675) = 1.171

15.138 (a) **Given:** 0.050 M KOH (strong base), 0.015 M $Ba(OH)_2$ (strong base) **Find:** pH
Conceptual Plan: Since the mixture is a strong base and a strong base, $[OH^-]$ is the sum of the concentration of both acids. Determine pOH and then pH.
Solution: 0.050 M KOH = 0.050 $[OH^-]$, 0.015 M $Ba(OH)_2$ = 2(0.015 M) $[OH^-]$
$[OH^-] = 0.050 + 0.030 = 0.080$M pOH = - log(0.080) = 1.10, pH = 14.00 – 1.10 = 12.90

(b) **Given:** 0.265 M NH_4NO_3 (salt), 0.102 M HCN(weak acid) **Find:** pH
Conceptual Plan: Identify each species and determine which will contribute to pH. Write a balanced reaction. Prepare an ICE table, represent the change with *x*, sum the table, determine the equilibrium values, put the equilibrium values in the equilibrium expression, and solve for *x*. Determine $[H_3O^+] \rightarrow$ pH.
Solution: NH_4^+ is the conjugate acid of a weak base; therefore, it is acidic. NO_3^- is the conjugate base of a strong acid; therefore, it is pH neutral. HCN is a weak acid and will produce an acidic solution.

$$K_a(NH_4^+) = \frac{1 \times 10^{-14}}{1.8 \times 10^{-5}} = 5.56 \times 10^{-10} \quad K_a(HCN) = 4.9 \times 10^{-10}$$

Solution: $NH_4^+(aq) + H_2O(l) \rightleftharpoons NH_3(aq) + H_3O^+(aq)$

	NH_4^+	NH_3	H_3O^+
I	0.265 M	0.0	0.0
C	$-x$	x	x
E	$0.265 - x$	x	x

$$K_a = \frac{K_w}{K_b} = \frac{1.0 \times 10^{-14}}{1.8 \times 10^{-5}} = 5.\underline{5}6 \times 10^{-10} = \frac{(x)(x)}{(0.265 - x)}$$

Assume x is small.

$x = 1.\underline{2}1 \times 10^{-5} = [H_3O^+]$

	$HCN(aq) + H_2O(l) \rightleftharpoons$	$H_3O^+(aq)$ +	$CN^-(aq)$
I	0.102 M	1.21×10^{-5}	0.0
C	$-x$	x	x
E	$0.102 - x$	$1.21 \times 10^{-5} + x$	x

$$K_a = \frac{[H_3O^+][CN^-]}{[HCN]} = \frac{(1.21 \times 10^{-5} + x)(x)}{(0.102 - x)} = 4.9 \times 10^{-10}$$

Assume x is small compared to 0.102.

$$\frac{(1.21 \times 10^{-5})x + x^2}{0.102} = 4.9 \times 10^{-10}$$
$$(1.21 \times 10^{-5})x + x^2 = 4.998 \times 10^{-11}$$
$$x^2 + (1.21 \times 10^{-5})x - 4.998 \times 10^{-11} = 0$$
$$x = \frac{-1.21 \times 10^{-5} \pm \sqrt{(1.21 \times 10^{-5})^2 - 4(1)(-4.998 \times 10^{-11})}}{2(1)}$$
$x = 3.255 \times 10^{-6}$ or -1.536×10^{-5} Concentration cannot be negative.
$[H_3O^+] = 1.21 \times 10^{-5} + 3.26 \times 10^{-6} = 1.536 \times 10^{-5}$
$pH = -\log(1.536 \times 10^{-5}) = 4.81$

(c) **Given:** 0.075 RbOH (strong base), 0.100 M $NaHCO_3$ (salt)
Conceptual Plan: Since the mixture is a strong base and a salt, the strong base will dominate. Use the concentration of the strong base to determine $[OH^-]$ and then pOH $\rightarrow$ pH.
Solution: 0.075 M RbOH = 0.075 $[OH^-]$ pOH = -log(0.075) = 1.12 pH = 14.00– 1.12 = 12.88

(d) **Given:** 0.088 $HClO_4$ (strong acid), 0.022 KOH (strong base) **Find:** pH
Conceptual Plan: A strong acid and a strong base will neutralize each other. Strong acid is in excess and is used to determine the pH.
Solution: $HClO_4(aq) + KOH(aq) \rightarrow H_2O(l) + KClO_4(aq)$

0.088	0.022
- 0.022	- 0.022
0.066 M	

$[H_3O^+] = 0.066$ pH = -log(0.066) = 1.18

(e) **Given:** 0.115 M NaClO (salt), 0.0500 KI (salt) **Find:** pH
Conceptual Plan: Identify each species and determine which will contribute to pH. Write a balanced reaction. Prepare an ICE table, represent the change with x, sum the table, determine the equilibrium values, put the equilibrium values in the equilibrium expression, and solve for x. Determine $[H_3O^+]$ $\rightarrow$ pH.
Solution: Na^+ is the counterion of a strong base; therefore, it is pH neutral. ClO^- is the conjugate base of a weak acid. Therefore, it will produce a basic solution. K^+ is the counterion of a strong base; therefore, it is pH neutral. I^- is the conjugate base of a strong acid; therefore, it is pH neutral.

	$ClO^-(aq) + H_2O(l)$	$\leftrightarrows$ $HClO(aq)$	$+ OH^-(aq)$
I	0.115 M	0.0	0.0
C	$-x$	x	x
E	$0.115 - x$	x	x

$$K_b = \frac{K_w}{K_a} = \frac{1.0 \times 10^{-14}}{2.9 \times 10^{-8}} = \frac{(x)(x)}{(0.115 - x)}$$
Assume x is small.
$x = 1.99 \times 10^{-4} = [OH^-]$ $pOH = -\log(1.99 \times 10^{-4}) = 3.70$
$pH = 14.00 - 3.70 = 10.30$

15.139 (a) sodium cyanide = NaCN nitric acid = HNO_3
$H^+(aq) + CN^-(aq) \leftrightarrows HCN(aq)$

(b) ammonium chloride = NH_4Cl sodium hydroxide = NaOH
$NH_4^+(aq) + OH^-(aq) \leftrightarrows NH_3(aq) + H_2O(l)$

(c) sodium cyanide = NaCN ammonium bromide = NH_4Br
$NH_4^+(aq) + CN^-(aq) \leftrightarrows NH_3(aq) + HCN(aq)$

(d) potassium hydrogen sulfate = $KHSO_4$ lithium acetate = $LiC_2H_3O_2$
$HSO_4^-(aq) + C_2H_3O_2^-(aq) \leftrightarrows SO_4^{2-}(aq) + HC_2H_3O_2(aq)$

(e) sodium hypochlorite = NaClO ammonia = NH_3
No reaction, both are bases.

15.140 **Given:** 0.682 g opium, 8.92 mL of 0.0116 M H_2SO_4, **Find:** % morphine

Conceptual Plan: vol H_2SO_4 → mol H_2SO_4 → mol H_3O^+ → mol morphine → g morphine → % morphine

$$\text{mol} = VM \qquad \frac{\text{mol } H_3O^+}{H_2SO_4} \qquad \frac{\text{mol morphine}}{\text{mol } H_3O^+} \qquad \frac{285\ 4 \text{ g morphine}}{\text{mol morphine}} \qquad \frac{\text{g morphine}}{\text{g opium}} \times 100$$

Solution:

$$8.92 \cancel{\text{mL } H_2SO_4} \times \frac{1 \cancel{\text{L}}}{1000 \cancel{\text{mL}}} \times \frac{0.0116 \cancel{\text{mol } H_2SO_4}}{\cancel{\text{L}}} \times \frac{2 \cancel{\text{mol } H_3O^+}}{\cancel{\text{mol } H_2SO_4}} \times \frac{\cancel{\text{mol morphine}}}{\cancel{\text{mol } H_3O^+}} \times \frac{285.4 \text{ g morphine}}{\cancel{\text{mol morphine}}}$$

$= 0.05906$ g morphine

$$\frac{0.05906 \text{ g morphine}}{0.682 \text{ g opium}} \times 100 = 8.66\ \%$$

15.141 **Given:** 1.0 M urea, pH = 7.050 **Find:** K_a $Hurea^+$

Conceptual Plan: pH → pOH → [OH⁻] → K_b(urea) → K_a($Hurea^+$). Write a balanced reaction.

$$\text{pH} + \text{pOH} = 14 \quad \text{pOH} = -\log[OH^-]$$

Prepare an ICE table, represent the change with *x*, sum the table, determine the equilibrium values, put the equilibrium values in the equilibrium expression, and determine K_b.

Solution: pOH = 14.000 – 7.050 = 6.950 $[OH^-] = 10^{-6.950} = 1.122 \times 10^{-7}$ M

	urea (*aq*) + $H_2O(l)$ ⇆	$Hurea^+$ (*aq*) +	OH^- (*aq*)
I	1.0 M	0.0	0.0
C	$-x$	x	x
E	$1.0 - 1.122 \times 10^{-7}$	1.122×10^{-7}	1.122×10^{-7}

$$K_b = \frac{[Hurea^+][OH^-]}{[urea]} = \frac{(1.122 \times 10^{-7})(1.122 \times 10^{-7})}{(1.0 - 1.122 \times 10^{-7})} = 1.2589 \times 10^{-14}$$

$$K_a = \frac{K_w}{K_b} = \frac{1.00 \times 10^{-14}}{1.2589 \times 10^{-14}} = 0.7943 = 0.794$$

15.142 **Given:** 0.1 M $HC_2H_3O_2$, $K_a = 1.8 \times 10^{-5}$; 0.10 M NH_4Cl, $K_b = 1.8 \times 10^{-5}$ **Find:** $[NH_3]$

Conceptual Plan: Use $HC_2H_3O_2$ to determine $[H_3O^+]$, then use NH_4Cl to determine $[NH_3]$. Write a balanced reaction. Prepare an ICE table, represent the change with *x*, sum the table, determine the equilibrium values.

Solution:

	$HC_2H_3O_2$ (*aq*) + $H_2O(l)$ ⇆	$H_3O^+(aq)$ +	$C_2H_3O_2^-(aq)$
I	0.10 M	0.0	0.0
C	$-x$	x	x
E	$0.10 - x$	x	x

$$K_a = \frac{[H_3O^+][C_2H_3O_2^-]}{[HC_2H_3O_2]} = \frac{(x)(x)}{(0.10 - x)} = 1.8 \times 10^{-5}$$

Assume x is small compared to 0.10.

$x^2 = (1.8 \times 10^{-5})(0.10)$

$x = [H_3O^+] = 0.00134$ M

	NH_4^+ (*aq*) + $H_2O(l)$ ⇆	NH_3 (*aq*) +	H_3O^+ (*aq*)
I	0.10 M	0.0	0.00134
C -	y	y	y
E	$0.10 - y$	y	$0.00134 + y$

$$K_a = \frac{K_w}{K_b} = \frac{1.0 \times 10^{-14}}{1.8 \times 10^{-5}} = 5.56 \times 10^{-10} = \frac{(y)(0.00134 + y)}{(0.10 - y)}$$

Assume y is small compared to 0.10.

$y^2 + 0.00134\,y - 5.56 \times 10^{-11} = 0$ Solve using the quadratic equation.

$y = [NH_3] = 4.1 \times 10^{-8}$ M

15.143 **Given:** Ca(Lact)$_2$, [Ca^{2+}] = 0.26 M, pH = 8.40 **Find:** K_a lactic acid

Conceptual Plan: [Ca^{2+}] → [$Lact^-$] ; determine K_b lactate ion. Prepare an ICE table, represent the

$$\frac{2 \text{ mol lactate ion}}{1 \text{ mol } Ca^{2+}}$$

change with x, sum the table, and determine the equilibrium constant. K_b → K_a

$$K_a = \frac{K_w}{K_b}$$

Solution: $0.26 \text{ M } \cancel{Ca^{2+}}\left(\frac{2 \text{ mol lact}^-}{1\text{mol } \cancel{Ca^{2+}}}\right) = 0.52 \text{ M lact}^-$

$$Lact^-(aq) + H_2O(l) \rightleftharpoons Hlact(aq) + OH^-(aq)$$

	$Lact^-$	Hlact	OH^-
I	0.52 M	0	0
C	$-x$	$+x$	$+x$
E	$0.52-x$	x	x

pH = 8.40 $[H_3O^+] = 10^{-8.40} = 4.0 \times 10^{-9}$ $[OH^-] = \dfrac{1.0 \times 10^{-14}}{4.0 \times 10^{-9}} = 2.5 \times 10^{-6} = x$

$$K_b = \frac{[Hlact][OH^-]}{[lact^-]} = \frac{(2.5 \times 10^{-6})(2.5 \times 10^{-6})}{(0.52 - 2.5 \times 10^{-6})} = 1.2 \times 10^{-11}$$

$$K_a = \frac{K_w}{K_b} = \frac{(1.0 \times 10^{-14})}{(1.2 \times 10^{-11})} = 8.3 \times 10^{-4}$$

15.144 **Given:** 0.23 mol QHCl, 1.0 L, pH = 4.58 **Find:** K_b quinine

Conceptual Plan: mol QHCl → [QHCl] → [QH^+]; determine K_a QH^+. Prepare an ICE table, represent the

$$M = \frac{\text{mol}}{\text{L}} \qquad \frac{1 \text{ mol } QH^+}{1 \text{ mol QHCl}}$$

change with x, sum the table, and determine the equilibrium constant. K_a → K_b

$$K_b = \frac{K_w}{K_a}$$

Solution: $\dfrac{0.23 \cancel{\text{ mol QHCl}}}{1 \text{ L}}\left(\dfrac{1 \text{ mol } QH^+}{1 \cancel{\text{ mol QHCl}}}\right) = 0.23\text{M } QH^+$

$$QH^+(aq) + H_2O(l) \rightleftharpoons Q(aq) + H_3O^+(aq)$$

	QH^+	Q	H_3O^+
I	0.23 M	0	0
C	$-x$	$+x$	$+x$
E	$0.23 - x$	x	x

pH = 4.58 $[H_3O^+] = 10^{-4.58} = 2.6 \times 10^{-5} = x$

$$K_a = \frac{[Q][H_3O^+]}{[QH^+]} = \frac{(2.6 \times 10^{-5})(2.6 \times 10^{-5})}{(0.23 - 2.6 \times 10^{-5})} = 3.0 \times 10^{-9}$$

$$K_b = \frac{K_w}{K_a} = \frac{(1.0 \times 10^{-14})}{(3.0 \times 10^{-9})} = 3.3 \times 10^{-6}$$

15.145 The calculation is incorrect because it neglects the contribution from the autoionization of water. HI is a strong acid, so $[H_3O^+]$ from HI = 1.0×10^{-7}.

$$H_2O(l) + H_2O(l) \rightleftharpoons H_3O^+(aq) + OH^-(aq)$$

	H_2O	H_3O^+	OH^-
I		1×10^{-7}	0.0
C	$-x$	x	x
E		$1 \times 10^{-7} + x$	x

$K_w = [H_3O^+][OH^-] = 1.0 \times 10^{-14}$

$(1 \times 10^{-7} + x)(x) = 1.0 \times 10^{-14}$ $x^2 + 1 \times 10^{-7}x - 1.0 \times 10^{-14} = 0$

$x = 6.18 \times 10^{-8}$

$[H_3O^+] = (1 \times 10^{-7} + x) = (1 \times 10^{-7} + 6.18 \times 10^{-8}) = 1.618 \times 10^{-7}$

$pH = -\log(1.618 \times 10^{-7}) = 6.79$

15.146 **Given:** 2.55 g HA, molar mass = 85.0 g/mol, 250.0 g H_2O, FP = - 0.257 °C **Find:** K_a

Conceptual Plan:

g HA → mol HA → m HA → i → % ionization and then mol HA → M HA. Then write a

$$\text{mol HA} = \frac{\text{g HA}}{\text{molar mass}} \quad \frac{\text{mol HA}}{\text{kg } H_2O} \quad \Delta T = iK_f m$$

balanced reaction, prepare an ICE table, calculate equilibrium concentrations, and plug into the equilibrium expression to solve for K_a.

Solution: $2.55 \text{ g HA} \times \dfrac{1 \text{ mol}}{85.0 \text{ g HA}} = 0.0300 \text{ mol HA} \qquad \dfrac{0.0300 \text{ mol HA}}{\left(250.0 \text{ g } H_2O \times \dfrac{\text{kg}}{1000 \text{ g}}\right)} = 0.120\ m$

$$\Delta T = iK_f m \quad \Delta T = 0.000\ ^\circ C - (-0.257\ ^\circ C) = 0.257\ ^\circ C$$

$$(0.257\ ^\circ C) = i\left(1.86 \frac{^\circ C}{m}\right)(0.120\ m) \quad i = 1.151 = \text{moles of particles in solution/mol HA}$$

$$HA(aq) + H_2O(l) \leftrightharpoons H_3O^+(aq) + A^-(aq)$$

$$1 - y \qquad y \qquad y$$

So: $(1 - y) + y + y = 1.151$ $\qquad y = 0.151$ = fraction of HA dissociated

$$\text{M HA} = \frac{0.0300 \text{ mol HA}}{(250.0 \text{ g} + 2.55 \text{ g})\left(\dfrac{1.00 \text{ mL}}{1.00 \text{ g}}\right)\left(\dfrac{\text{L}}{1000 \text{ mL}}\right)} = 0.1188 \text{ M}$$

$(0.1188 \text{ M})(0.151) = 0.01794 \text{ M} = [H_3O^+] = [A^-]$ at equilibrium

	$HA(aq) + H_2O(l) \leftrightharpoons$	$H_3O^+(aq) +$	$A^-(aq)$
I	0.1188 M	0.0	0.0
C	$-x$	x	x
E	0. 1188 – 0.01794	0.01794	0.01794

$$K_a = \frac{[H_3O^+][A^-]}{[HA]} = \frac{(0.01794)(0.01794)}{(0.1188 - 0.01794)} = 0.003191 = 3.2 \times 10^{-3}$$

15.147 **Given:** 0.00115 M HCl, 0.01000 M $HClO_2$ $K_a = 1.1 \times 10^{-2}$ **Find:** pH

Conceptual Plan: Use HCl to determine $[H_3O^+]$. Use $[H_3O^+]$ and $HClO_2$ to determine dissociation of $HClO_2$. Write a balanced reaction, prepare an ICE table, calculate equilibrium concentrations, and plug into the equilibrium expression.

Solution: 0.00115 M HCl = 0.00115 M H_3O^+

	$HClO_2(aq) + H_2O(l) \leftrightharpoons$	$H_3O^+(aq) +$	$ClO_2^-(aq)$
I	0.0100 M	0.00115 M	0.0
C	$-x$	x	x
E	$0.01000 - x$	$0.00115 + x$	x

$$K_a = \frac{[H_3O^+][ClO_2^-]}{[HClO_2]} = \frac{(0.00115 + x)(x)}{(0.0100 - x)} = 1.1 \times 10^{-2}$$

$x^2 + 0.01215x - 1.1 \times 10^{-4} = 0 \qquad x = 0.006045$

$[H_3O^+] = 0.00115 + 0.006045 = 0.00719\underline{5}$

$\text{pH} = -\log(0.00719\underline{5}) = 2.14$

15.148 Volume should be increased to 4 L.

$HA(aq) + H_2O(l) \leftrightharpoons H_3O^+(aq) + A^-(aq)$

Initial equilibrium conditions: $[HA] = A$, $[H_3O^+] = [A^-] = x$

$$K_a = \frac{[H_3O^+][A^-]}{[HA]} = \frac{(x)(x)}{(A)}$$

Second equilibrium conditions: $[HA] = A/y$, $[H_3O^+] = [A^-] = x/2$

$$K_a = \frac{[H_3O^+][A^-]}{[HA]} = \frac{(x)(x)}{(A)} = \frac{\left(\dfrac{x}{2}\right)\left(\dfrac{x}{2}\right)}{\left(\dfrac{A}{y}\right)}$$

$\frac{x^2 A}{y} = \frac{x^2 A}{4}$ $y = 4$, so for the concentration of H^+ to be halved, the [A] needs to decrease to 1/4th the original concentration. So, the volume has to increase to 4 L.

15.149 **Given:** 1.0 M HA, $K_a = 1.0 \times 10^{-8}$ $K = 4.0$ for reaction 2 **Find:** $[H^+]$, $[A^-]$, $[HA_2^-]$
Conceptual Plan: Combine reaction 1 and reaction 2 then determine the equilibrium expression and the value of *K*. Prepare an ICE table, calculate equilibrium concentrations, and then plug into the equilibrium expression.
Solution:

$$HA(aq) \leftrightharpoons H^+(aq) + A^-(aq) \qquad K = 1.0 \times 10^{-8}$$
$$HA(aq) + A^-(aq) \leftrightharpoons HA_2^+(aq) \qquad K = 4.0$$
$$2HA(aq) \leftrightharpoons H^+(aq) + HA_2^+(aq) \qquad K = 4.0 \times 10^{-8}$$

	$2HA(aq)$	$H^+(aq)$	$HA_2^+(aq)$
I	1.0 M	0.0	0.0
C	$-2x$	x	x
E	$1.0 - 2x$	x	x

$$K = \frac{[H^+][HA_2^-]}{[HA]^2} = 4.0 \times 10^{-8} = \frac{(x)(x)}{(1.0 - 2x)^2}$$

Take the square root of both sides of the equation. $x = 1.9\underline{9}92 \times 10^{-4}$

$$HA(aq) \leftrightharpoons H^+(aq) + A^-(aq) \qquad K = 1.0 \times 10^{-8}$$

	$HA(aq)$	$H^+(aq)$	$A^-(aq)$
I	1.0 M	1.9992×10^{-4}	0.0
C	$-2y$	y	y
E	$1.0 - 2y$	$1.9992 \times 10^{-4} + y$	y

$$K = \frac{[H^+][A^-]}{[HA]} = 1.0 \times 10^{-8} = \frac{(1.9992 \times 10^{-4} + y)(y)}{(1.0 - 2y)}$$

$y^2 + 1.9992 \times 10^{-4} y - 1 \times 10^{-8} = 0$ $\quad y = 4.\underline{1}4 \times 10^{-5}$

$[H^+] = x + y = 1.\underline{9}992 \times 10^{-4} + 4.\underline{2}9 \times 10^{-5} = 2.4 \times 10^{-4}$
$[A^-] = y = 4.29 \times 10^{-5}$
$[HA_2^-] = x = 2.0 \times 10^{-4}$

15.150 In the gas phase, $(CH_3)_3N$ is a stronger Lewis base than CH_3NH_2 because the N—H bond is more polar than the N—C bond making the lone pair on the N less accessible to the H^+ that needs to be added. In the liquid phase, the steric hindrance from the size of the CH_3 groups becomes more pronounced; therefore, it is harder to add the H^+ ion.

15.151 **Given:** 0.200 mol NH_4CN, 1.00 L, K_b $NH_3 = 1.76 \times 10^{-5}$, K_a HCN $= 4.9 \times 10^{-10}$ **Find:** pH
Conceptual Plan: K_b NH_3 $\rightarrow$ K_a NH_4^+; K_a HCN $\rightarrow$ K_b CN^- **Prepare an ICE table, represent the**
$K_a K_b = K_w$
change with *x*, sum the table, and determine the equilibrium conditions.

Solution: $K_a(NH_4^+) = \frac{1.0 \times 10^{-14}}{1.76 \times 10^{-5}} = 5.68 \times 10^{-10} K_b(CN^-) = \frac{1.0 \times 10^{-14}}{4.9 \times 10^{-10}} = 2.0 \times 10^{-5}$

0.200 M NH_4CN = 0.200 M NH_4^+ and 0.200 M CN^-

Since the value for *K* for CN^- is greater than the *K* for NH_4^+, the CN^- reaction will be larger and the solution will be basic.

$$CN^-(aq) + H_2O(l) \leftrightharpoons HCN(aq) + OH^-(aq)$$

	$CN^-(aq)$	$HCN(aq)$	$OH^-(aq)$
I	0.200 M	0	0
C	$-x$	$+x$	$+x$
E	$0.200 - x$	x	x

$$K_b = \frac{[HCN][OH^-]}{[CN^-]} \; 2.0 \times 10^{-5} = \frac{(x)(x)}{(0.200 - x)}$$ Solve using the quadratic equation.

$x = 0.0020 = [OH^-]$

$$[H_3O^+] = \frac{1.0 \times 10^{-14}}{0.0020} = 5.0 \times 10^{-12} \quad pH = -(5.0 \times 10^{-12}) = 11.30$$

15.152 **Given:** 1.0 L, 0.30 M $HClO_2$, 0.20 mol NaF, K_a $HClO_2 = 1.1 \times 10^{-2}$, K_a HF $= 3.5 \times 10^{-4}$ **Find:** $[HClO_2]$
Conceptual Plan: Determine the products of the reaction of $HClO_2$ and NaF. Prepare an ICE table, represent the change with x, sum the table, and determine the equilibrium conditions.
Solution:

	$HClO_2(aq)$ +	$NaF(aq)$ →	$HF(aq)$ +	$NaClO_2(aq)$
initial	0.30 M	0.20 M		
	-0.20	-0.20	+0.20	+0.20
final	0.10	0	0.20	0.20

Since HF is the weaker acid, the reaction will proceed to the right is the limiting reactant.

The $HClO_2$ has the largest equilibrium constant so it will be the species that contributes to the pH to the largest extent.

	$HClO_2(aq)$ + $H_2O(l)$ ⇆	$ClO_2^-(aq)$ +	$H_3O^+(aq)$
I	0.10 M	0.20	
C	$-x$	$+x$	$+x$
E	$0.10-x$	$0.20+x$	x

$$K_a = \frac{[ClO_2^-][H_3O^+]}{[HClO_2]} 1.1 \times 10^{-2} = \frac{(0.20 + x)(x)}{(0.10 - x)}$$

$x = 0.0051$ $[HClO_2] = 0.10 - 0.0051 = 0.95$ M

15.153 **Given:** mixture Na_2CO_3 and $NaHCO_3 = 82.2$ g, 1.0 L, pH = 9.95, K_a $H_2CO_3 = K_{a_1} = 4.3 \times 10^{-7}$, $K_{a_2} = 5.6 \times 10^{-11}$
Find: mass $NaHCO_3$
Conceptual Plan: Let x = g $NaHCO_3$, y = g Na_2CO_3 → mol $NaHCO_3$, Na_2CO_3 → $[NaHCO_3]$, $[Na_2CO_3]$

$$\frac{1 \text{ mol } NaHCO_3}{84.01\text{g}} \quad \frac{1 \text{ mol } Na_2CO_3}{105.99\text{g}} \qquad M = \frac{\text{mol}}{\text{L}}$$

→ $[HCO_3^-]$, $[CO_3^{2-}]$, K_a (HCO_3^-) → $K_b(CO_3^{2-})$. Prepare an ICE table, represent the change with z,

$$\frac{HCO_3^-}{NaHCO_3} \quad \frac{CO_3^{-2}}{Na_2CO_3} \qquad K_b = \frac{K_w}{K_a}$$

sum the table, and determine the equilibrium conditions.
Solution: Let x = g $NaHCO_3$ and y = g Na_2CO_3 $x + y = 82.2$, so $y = 82.2 - x$

$$\text{mol } NaHCO_3 = x \text{ g } NaHCO_3\left(\frac{1 \text{ mol}}{84.01 \text{ g } NaHCO_3}\right) = \frac{x}{84.01}$$

$$[HCO_3^-] = \left(\frac{\frac{x}{84.01}\text{mol } NaHCO_3}{1\text{L}}\right)\frac{1 \text{ mol } HCO_3^-}{1 \text{ mol } NaHCO_3} = \frac{x}{84.01} \text{ M } HCO_3^-$$

$$\text{mol } Na_2CO_3 = 82.2 - x \text{ g } Na_2CO_3\left(\frac{1 \text{ mol}}{105.99 \text{ g } Na_2CO_3}\right) = \frac{82.2 - x}{105.99} Na_2CO_3$$

$$[CO_3^{-2}] = \left(\frac{\frac{82.2 - x}{105.99}\text{mol } Na_2CO_3}{1\text{L}}\right)\frac{1 \text{ mol } CO_3^{2-}}{1 \text{ mol } Na_2CO_3} = \frac{82.2 - x}{105.99} \text{ M } CO_3^{2-}$$

Since the pH of the solution is basic, it is the hydrolysis of CO_3^{2-} that dominates in the solution.

$$K_b(CO_3^{2-}) = \frac{1.0 \times 10^{-14}}{5.6 \times 10^{-11}} = 1.78 \times 10^{-4} \text{ and: } [H_3O^+] = 10^{-9.95} = 1.12 \times 10^{-10} [OH^-] = \frac{1.0 \times 10^{-14}}{1.12 \times 10^{-10}} = 8.91 \times 10^{-5}$$

	$CO^{2-}(aq)$ + $H_2O(l)$ ⇆	$HCO_3^-(aq)$ +	$OH^-(aq)$
I	$\frac{82.2 - x}{105.99}$	$\frac{x}{84.01}$	
C	$-z$	$+z$	
E	$\left(\frac{82.2 - x}{105.99}\right) - z$	$\left(\frac{x}{84.01}\right) + z$	8.91×10^{-5}

$$K_b(CO_3^{2-}) = 1.78 \times 10^{-4} = \frac{[HCO_3^-][OH^-]}{[CO_3^{2-}]} = \frac{\left(\left(\frac{x}{84.01}\right) - z\right)(8.91 \times 10^{-5})}{\left(\frac{82.2 - x}{105.99}\right) - z}$$ Assume z is small.

$$\frac{1.78 \times 10^{-4}}{8.91 \times 10^{-5}} = \frac{\left(\frac{x}{84.01}\right)}{\left(\frac{82.2 - x}{105.99}\right)} \qquad x = 50.38 = 50.4\text{g } NaHCO_3$$

15.154 **Given:** mixture NaCN and $NaHSO_4$ = 0.60 mol, 1.0 L, pH = 9.9; and $K_a(HCN) = 4.9 \times 10^{-10}$, $K_a(HSO_4^-) = 1.1 \times 10^{-2}$ **Find:** amount NaCN

Conceptual Plan: Determine $[CN^-]$ in solution after the reaction of NaCN and $NaHSO_4$. Then prepare an ICE table, represent the change by x, and determine the equilibrium conditions.

Solution: Since HCN is the weaker acid, we can assume complete reaction between NaCN and $NaHSO_4$. Also, since the solution is basic, the CN^- must be in excess. So, let x = moles of NaCN.

$NaHSO_4(aq)$ +	$NaCN(aq)$ $\rightarrow$	$HCN(aq)$ +	$SO_4^{2-}(aq)$
0.60-x	x	0	0
-(0.60-x)	-(0.60-x)	0.60-x	0.60-x
0	$2x - 0.60$	0.60-x	0.60-x

$[H_3O^+] = 10^{-9.9} = 1.26 \times 10^{-10}$ $\quad [OH^-] = \frac{1.0 \times 10^{-14}}{1.26 \times 10^{-10}} = 7.9 \times 10^{-5}$

	$CN^-(aq) + H_2O(l)$ $\leftrightarrows$	$HCN(aq)$ +	$OH^-(aq)$
I	$2x - 0.60$	$0.60 - x$	0
C	-7.9×10^{-5}	$+7.9 \times 10^{-5}$	$+7.9 \times 10^{-5}$
E	$2x - 0.60 - 7.9 \times 10^{-5}$	$0.60 - x + 7.9 \times 10^{-5}$	7.9×10^{-5}

$$K_b(CN^-) = \frac{K_w}{K_a(HCN)} = \frac{1.0 \times 10^{-14}}{4.9 \times 10^{-10}} = 2.0 \times 10^{-5} = \frac{[HCN][OH^-]}{[CN^-]} = \frac{(0.60 - x)(7.9 \times 10^{-5})}{(2x - 0.60)}$$

$x = 0.50$ = mol NaCN

15.155 Solution b would be most acidic.

(a) 0.0100 M HCl (strong acid) and 0.0100 M KOH (strong base), since the concentrations are equal, the acid and base will completely neutralize each other and the resulting solution will be pH neutral.

(b) 0.0100 M HF (weak acid) and 0.0100 KBr (salt). K_a (HF) = 3.5×10^{-4}. The weak acid will produce an acidic solution. K^+ is the counterion of a strong base and is pH neutral. Br^- is the conjugate base of a strong acid and is pH neutral.

(c) 0.0100 M NH_4Cl (salt) and 0.100 M CH_3NH_3Br. $K_b(NH_3) = 1.8 \times 10^{-5}$, $K_b(CH_3NH_2) = 4.4 \times 10^{-4}$. NH_4^+ is the conjugate acid of a weak base and $CH_3NH_3^+$ is the conjugate acid of a weak base. Cl^- and Br^- are the conjugate bases of strong acids and will be pH neutral. The solution will be acidic. However, because the K_a for the conjugate acids in this solution is smaller K_a for HF, the solution will be acidic, but not as acidic as HF.

(d) 0.100 M NaCN (salt) and 0.100 M $CaCl_2$. Na^+ and Ca^{2+} ion are the counterion of a strong base; therefore, they are pH neutral. Cl^- is the conjugate base of a strong acid and is pH neutral. CN^- is the conjugate base of a weak acid and will produce a basic solution.

15.156 Solution a would be most basic.

(a) 0.100 M NaClO(salt) and 0.100 M NaF(salt). Na^+ is the counterion of a strong base and is pH neutral. ClO^- is the conjugate base of a weak acid (HClO, $K_a = 2.9 \times 10^{-8}$). F^- is the conjugate base of a weak acid (HF, $K_a = 3.5 \times 10^{-4}$). The solution will be basic and ClO^- is a stronger base than F^-.

(b) 0.0100 M KCl(salt) and 0.0100 M $KClO_2$(salt). K^+ is the counterion of a strong base and is pH neutral. Cl^- is the conjugate base of a strong acid and is pH neutral. ClO_2^- is the conjugate base of a weak acid ($HClO_2$, $K_a = 1.1 \times 10^{-2}$) and will produce a basic solution. However, because the ClO_2^- is a weaker conjugate base than ClO^- so solution a will be more basic.

(c) 0.0100 M HNO_3 (strong acid) and 0.0100 M NaOH (strong base), since the concentrations are equal, the acid and base will completely neutralize each other and the resulting solution will be pH neutral.

(d) 0.0100 M NH_4Cl(salt) and 0.0100 M HCN(weak acid). NH_4^+ is the conjugate acid of a weak base and will be acidic. HCN is a weak acid and will be acidic. Cl^- is the conjugate base of a strong acid and is pH neutral.

15.157 $CH_3COOH < CH_2ClCOOH < CHCl_2COOH < CCl_3COOH$

Since Cl is more electronegative than H, as you add Cl you increase the number of electronegative atoms which pulls the electron density away from the O—H group, polarizing the O—H bond, making it more acidic.

16 Aqueous Ionic Equilibrium

Review Questions

16.1 The pH range of human blood is between 7.36 and 7.42. This nearly constant blood pH is maintained by buffers that are chemical systems that resist pH changes, neutralizing an added acid or base. An important buffer system in blood is a mixture of carbonic acid (H_2CO_3) and bicarbonate ion (HCO_3^-).

16.2 A buffer is a chemical system that resists pH changes. The buffer works by neutralizing an added acid or base. Most buffers contain significant amounts of both a weak acid and its conjugate base (or a weak base and its conjugate acid). When additional base is added to a buffer, the weak acid reacts with the base, neutralizing it (generating more of the buffer system conjugate base). When additional acid is added to buffer, the conjugate base reacts with the acid, neutralizing it (generating more of the buffer system conjugate acid). In this way, a buffer can maintain a nearly constant pH.

16.3 The common ion effect occurs when a solution contains two substances ($HC_2H_3O_2$ and $NaC_2H_3O_2$) that share a common ion ($C_2H_3O_2^-$). The presence of the $C_2H_3O_2^-(aq)$ ion causes the acid to ionize even less than it normally would, resulting in a less acidic solution (higher pH). This effect is an example of Le Châtelier's principle shifting an equilibrium, because of the addition (or removal) of the common ion from the solution.

16.4 The Henderson–Hasselbalch equation $\left(\text{pH} = \text{p}K_a + \log\frac{[\text{base}]}{[\text{acid}]}\right)$, allows easy calculation of the pH of a buffer solution from the initial concentrations of the buffer components as long as the "x is small" approximation is valid.

16.5 When the concentration of the conjugate acid and base components of a buffer system are equal the pH is equal to the pK_a of the weak acid of the buffer system. When more of the acid component is present the pH becomes more acidic (pH drops). When more of the base component is present the pH becomes more basic (pH rises). The pH in both cases can be calculates with the Henderson–Hasselbalch equation.

16.6 When the concentration of the conjugate acid and base components of a buffer system are equal the pH is equal to the pK_a of the weak acid of the buffer system. When a small amount of a strong acid is added, it will react with the conjugate base of the buffer system, converting it to the weak acid of the buffer system. Thus the weak acid concentration increases, the conjugate base concentration decreases, and the pH drops slightly at most. When a small amount of a strong base is added, it will react with the weak acid of the buffer system, converting it to the conjugate base of the buffer system. Thus the weak acid concentration decreases, the conjugate base concentration increases, and the pH rises slightly at most.

16.7 To find the pH of this solution, determine which component is the acid, which component is the base, and substitute their concentrations into the Henderson–Hasselbalch equation. The pK_a is the negative of the log of the equilibrium constant of the acid dissociation reaction where the weak acid component and water are the reactants, and the conjugate base and H_3O^+ are the products. At the end, confirm that the "x is small" approximation is valid by calculating the

$[H_3O^+]$ from the pH. Since H_3O^+ is formed by ionization of the acid, the calculated $[H_3O^+]$ has to be less than 0.05 (or 5%) of the initial concentration of the acid in order for the "x is small" approximation to be valid.

16.8 The factors that influence the effectiveness of a buffer are the relative amounts of the acid and conjugate base (the closer they are to each other the more effective the buffer) and the absolute concentrations of the acid and conjugate base (the higher the absolute concentrations the more effective the buffer).

16.9 The relative concentrations of acid and conjugate base should not differ by more than a factor of 10 in order for a buffer to be reasonably effective. Using the Henderson–Hasselbalch equation, this means that the pH should be within one pH unit of the weak acid's pK_a.

16.10 In an acid–base titration, a basic (or acidic) solution of unknown concentration is reacted with an acidic (or basic) solution of known concentration. The known solution is slowly added to the unknown one while the pH is monitored with either a pH meter or an indicator (a substance whose color depends on the pH). As the acid and base combine, they neutralize each other. At the equivalence point—the point in the titration when the number of moles of base is stoichiometrically equal to the number of moles of acid—the titration is complete. When this point is reached, neither reactant is in excess and the number of moles of the reactants are related by the reaction stoichiometry.

16.11 The titration of weak acid by a strong base will always have a basic equivalence point because, at the equivalence point, all of the acid has been converted into its conjugate base, resulting in a weakly basic solution.

16.12 The volume required to get to the equivalence point is only dependent on the concentration and volume of acid or base to be titrated and the base or acid used to do the titration, because the equivalence point is dependent on the stoichiometry of the balanced reaction of the acid and base. The stoichiometry only considers the number of moles involved, not the strength of the reactants involved.

16.13 (a) The initial pH of the solution is simply the pH of the strong acid. Since strong acids completely dissociate, the concentration of H_3O^+ is the concentration of the strong acid and $pH = -\log [H_3O^+]$.

(b) Before the equivalence point, H_3O^+ is in excess. Calculate the $[H_3O^+]$ by subtracting the number of moles of added OH^- from the initial number of moles of H_3O^+ and dividing by the *total* volume. Then convert to pH using $-\log [H_3O^+]$.

(c) At the equivalence point, neither reactant is in excess and the pH = 7.00.

(d) Beyond the equivalence point, OH^- is in excess. Calculate the $[OH^-]$ by subtracting the initial number of moles of H_3O^+ from the number of moles of added OH^- and dividing by the *total* volume. Then convert to pH using $-\log [H_3O^+]$.

16.14 (a) The initial pH is that of the weak acid solution to be titrated. Calculate the pH by working an equilibrium problem (similar to Examples 15.5 and 15.6) using the concentration of the weak acid as the initial concentration.

(b) Between the initial pH and the equivalence point, the solution becomes a buffer. Use the reaction stoichiometry to compute the amounts of each buffer component and then use the Henderson–Hasselbalch equation to compute the pH (as in Example 16.3).

(c) Halfway to the equivalence point, the buffer components are exactly equal and $pH = pK_a$.

(d) At the equivalence point, the acid has all been converted into its conjugate base. Calculate the pH by working an equilibrium problem for the ionization of water by the ion acting as a weak base (similar to Example 15.14). (Compute the concentration of the ion acting as a weak base by dividing the number of moles of the ion by the total volume at the equivalence point.)

(e) Beyond the equivalence point, OH^- is in excess. You can ignore the weak base and calculate the $[OH^-]$ by subtracting the initial number of moles of H_3O^+ from the number of moles of added OH^- and dividing by the total volume, then convert to pH using $-\log [H_3O^+]$.

16.15 When a polyprotic acid is titrated with a strong base, and if K_{a_1} and K_{a_2} are sufficiently different, the pH curve will have two equivalence points because the two acidic protons will be titrated sequentially. The titration of the first acidic proton will be completed before the titration of the second acidic proton.

16.16 The volume required to get to the first equivalence point is identical to the volume between the first and second equivalence points, because the equivalence point is dependent on the stoichiometry of the balanced reaction of the acid and base. The stoichiometry only considers the number of moles involved, not the strength of the reactants involved. There are the same number of moles of the first acidic proton and the second acidic proton.

16.17 The endpoint is the point when the indicator changes color in an acid–base titration. The equivalence point is when stoichiometrically equivalent amounts of acid and base have reacted. With the correct indicator, the endpoint of the titration will occur at the equivalence point.

16.18 An indicator (HIn) is itself a weak organic acid that has a different color than its conjugate base (In^-). The color of a solution containing an indicator depends on the relative concentrations of HIn and In^-. As the $[H_3O^+]$ changes during the titration, the above relative concentrations of HIn and In^- change accordingly. At low pH, the $[H_3O^+]$ is high, the equilibrium favors the acid species, and the color is that of the acid species. As the titration proceeds, the $[H_3O^+]$ decreases, shifting towards higher concentrations of the conjugate base, and the color changes. Because the color of an indicator is intense, only a small amount is required—an amount that will not affect the pH of the solution or the equivalence point of the neutralization reaction.

16.19 The solubility product constant (K_{sp}) is the equilibrium expression for a chemical equation representing the dissolution of an ionic compound. The expression of the solubility product constant of A_mX_n is: $K_{sp} = [A^{n+}]^m [X^{m-}]^n$.

16.20 The molar solubility, S, is simply the solubility in units of moles per liter (mol/L). The molar solubility of a compound, A_mX_n, can be computed directly from K_{sp} by solving for S in the expression: $K_{sp} = (mS)^m (nS)^n = m^m n^n S^{m+n}$.

16.21 In accordance with Le Châtelier's principle, the presence of a common ion in solution causes the equilibrium to shift to the left (compared to its position with pure water as the solvent), which means that less of the ionic compound dissolves. Thus, the solubility of an ionic compound is lower in a solution containing a common ion than in pure water. The exact value of the solubility can be calculated by working an equilibrium problem in which the concentration of the common ion is accounted for in the initial conditions. The molar solubility of a compound, A_mX_n, in a solution with an initial concentration of $A^{n+} = [A^{n+}]_0$ and an initial concentration of $X^{m-} = [X^{m-}]_0$ can be computed directly from K_{sp} by solving for S in the expression: $K_{sp} = ([A^{n+}]_0 + mS)^m ([X^{m-}]_0 + nS)^n$.

16.22 In general, the solubility of an ionic compound with a strongly basic or weakly basic anion increases with increasing acidity (decreasing pH). If the anion is neutralized by reaction with H^+, to form the conjugate acid of the basic anion, Le Châtelier's principle says that the solubility equilibrium will shift to the right, allowing more solid to dissolve. Remember that the K_{sp} expression only has the terms of the cation and the anion concentrations. If the anion is converted to a different species (such as the conjugate acid), the concentration of the anion drops, allowing more solid to dissolve.

16.23 Q is the reaction quotient, the product of the concentrations of the ionic components raised to their stoichiometric coefficients, and K is the product of the concentrations of the ionic components raised to their stoichiometric coefficients at equilibrium. For a solution containing an ionic compound: If $Q < K_{sp}$, the solution is unsaturated. More of the solid ionic compound can dissolve in the solution: If $Q = K_{sp}$, the solution is saturated, the solution is holding the equilibrium amount of the dissolved ions, and additional solid will not dissolve in the solution. If $Q > K_{sp}$, the solution is supersaturated and under most circumstances, the excess solid will precipitate out.

16.24 Selective precipitation, a process for separating metal cations from a solution containing several different dissolved metal cations. In the process, a metal cation can often be separated by the addition of a reagent that forms a precipitate with one of the dissolved cations but not the others. The appropriate reagent must form compounds with both metal cations with sufficiently different K_{sp} values (a difference of a factor of at least 10^3), so that one compound will remains dissolved while the other compound significantly precipitates.

16.25 Qualitative analysis is a systematic way to determine the metal ions present in an unknown solution by the selective precipitation of the ions. The word qualitative means involving quality or kind. So qualitative analysis involves finding the kind of ions present in the solution. Quantitative analysis is concerned with quantity, or the amounts of substances in a solution or mixture.

16.26 A general qualitative analysis scheme involves separating a mixture of the common ions into five groups by sequentially adding five different precipitating agents. After each precipitating agent is added, the mixture is put into a centrifuge to separate the solid from the liquid. The liquid is decanted for the next step, and the solid is set aside for subsequent analysis. Group I removes insoluble chlorides by treating the solution with dilute HCl. Since most chlorides are soluble, the chloride ions do not form a precipitate with the majority of the cations in mixture. However, Ag^+, Pb^{2+}, and Hg_2^{2+} do form insoluble chlorides and will precipitate out. The absence of a precipitate constitutes a negative test for Ag^+, Pb^{2+}, and Hg_2^{2+}. After the solid is separated from the liquid, the solution is ready for the next step, where Group II, acid-insoluble sulfides are removed. This is accomplished by taking the aqueous mixture containing the remaining metal cations and treating it with H_2S, a weak diprotic acid that dissociates to form sulfide ions, S^{2-}. Since the solution is acidic from the first treatment, only the acid-insoluble sulfide metals will precipitate out. These include Hg^{2+}, Cd^{2+}, Bi^{3+}, Cu^{2+}, Sn^{4+}, As^{3+}, and Sb^{3+}. If any of these metal cations are present, they precipitate out as sulfides. After the solid is separated from the liquid, the solution is ready for the next step. In the third step, Group III, the base-insoluble sulfides and hydroxides, are removed by taking the acidic aqueous mixture containing the remaining metal cations and treating it with a base and additional H_2S. The added base reacts with acid, shifting the H_2S ionization equilibria to the right and creating a higher S^{2-} concentration. This causes the precipitation of those sulfides that were too soluble to precipitate out in the previous step, but not soluble enough to prevent precipitation with the higher sulfide ion concentration. The ions that precipitate as sulfides at this point (if they are present) are Co^{2+}, Zn^{2+}, Mn^{2+}, Ni^{2+}, and Fe^{2+}. In addition, the basic solution causes Cr^{3+} and Al^{3+} to precipitate as hydroxides. After the solid is separated from the liquid, the solution is ready for the next step, removing the Group IV, insoluble carbonate, metal ions. At this stage, all of the cations have been precipitated except those belonging to the alkali metal family (group 1A in the periodic table) and the alkaline earth metal family (group 2A in the periodic table). The alkaline earth metal cations can be precipitated by adding sodium carbonate to the solution. The carbonate ion precipitates Mg^{2+}, Ca^{2+}, and Ba^{2+} as metal carbonates, which are separated from the liquid. The only dissolved ions belong to Group V, the alkali metals and NH_4^+. The liquid decanted from the previous step can now contain are Na^+, K^+, and NH_4^+. These cations do not form insoluble compounds with any anions and cannot be precipitated from the solution. Their presence can be tested by other means. Sodium and potassium ions, for example, are usually identified through flame tests. The sodium ion produces a yellow-orange flame and the potassium ion produces a violet flame. By applying the previous procedure, nearly two dozen metal cations can be separated from a solution initially containing all of them. Each of the groups can then be further analyzed to determine the specific ions present from that group.

The Common Ion Effect and Buffers

16.27 The only solution that HNO_2 will ionize less in is d) 0.10 M $NaNO_2$. It is the only solution that generates a common ion NO_2^- with nitrous acid.

16.28 Formic acid is $HCHO_2$ which dissociates to H^+ and CHO_2^-. The only solution that generates a common ion (CHO_2^-) with formic acid is (c) $NaCHO_2$.

16.29 (a) **Given:** 0.20 M $HCHO_2$ and 0.15 M $NaCHO_2$ **Find:** pH **Other:** K_a ($HCHO_2$) = 1.8×10^{-4}

Conceptual Plan: M $NaCHO_2$ → M CHO_2^- then M $HCHO_2$, M CHO_2^- → $[H_3O^+]$ → pH

$NaCHO_2\ (aq) \rightarrow Na^+\ (aq) + CHO_2^-\ (aq)$ *ICE Chart* $pH = -\log[H_3O^+]$

Solution: Since 1 CHO_2^- ion is generated for each $NaCHO_2$, $[CHO_2^-]$ = 0.15 M CHO_2^-.

$$HCHO_2\,(aq) + H_2O\,(l) \rightleftharpoons H_3O^+\,(aq) + CHO_2^-\,(aq)$$

	$[HCHO_2]$	$[H_3O^+]$	$[CHO_2^-]$
Initial	0.20	≈0.00	0.15
Change	$-x$	$+x$	$+x$
Equil	$0.20 - x$	$+x$	$0.15 + x$

$K_a = \dfrac{[H_3O^+][CHO_2^-]}{[HCHO_2]} = 1.8 \times 10^{-4} = \dfrac{x(0.15 + x)}{0.20 - x}$ Assume x is small ($x << 0.15 < 0.20$) so

$\dfrac{x(0.15 + \cancel{x})}{0.20 - \cancel{x}} = 1.8 \times 10^{-4} = \dfrac{x(0.15)}{0.20}$ and $x = 2.4 \times 10^{-4}$ M = $[H_3O^+]$. Confirm that the more stringent assumption is valid.

$\dfrac{2.4 \times 10^{-4}}{0.15} \times 100\% = 0.16\%$ so assumption is valid. Finally,

$pH = -\log [H_3O^+] = -\log (2.4 \times 10^{-4}) = 3.62$

Check: The units (none) are correct. The magnitude of the answer makes physical sense because pH should be greater than $-\log(0.20) = 0.70$ because this is a weak acid and there is a common ion effect.

(b) **Given:** 0.16 M NH_3 and 0.22 M NH_4Cl **Find:** pH **Other:** $K_b\,(NH_3) = 1.79 \times 10^{-5}$

Conceptual Plan: M NH_4Cl → M NH_4^+ then M NH_3, M NH_4^+ → $[OH^-]$ → $[H_3O^+]$ → pH

$NH_4Cl\,(aq) \rightarrow NH_4^+\,(aq) + Cl^-\,(aq)$ *ICE Chart* $K_w = [H_3O^+][OH^-]$ $pH = -\log [H_3O^+]$

Solution: Since 1 NH_4^+ ion is generated for each NH_4Cl, $[NH_4^+] = 0.22$ M NH_4^+.

$$NH_3\,(aq) + H_2O\,(l) \rightleftharpoons NH_4^+\,(aq) + OH^-\,(aq)$$

	$[NH_3]$	$[NH_4^+]$	$[OH^-]$
Initial	0.16	0.22	≈0.00
Change	$-x$	$+x$	$+x$
Equil	$0.16 - x$	$0.22 + x$	$+x$

$K_b = \dfrac{[NH_4^+][OH^-]}{[NH_3]} = 1.79 \times 10^{-5} = \dfrac{(0.22 + x)x}{0.16 - x}$

Assume x is small ($x << 0.16 < 0.22$) so $\dfrac{(0.22 + \cancel{x})x}{0.16 - \cancel{x}} = 1.79 \times 10^{-5} = \dfrac{(0.22)x}{0.16}$ and $x = 1.\underline{3}0182 \times 10^{-5}$ M = $[OH^-]$. Confirm that the more stringent assumption is valid.

$\dfrac{1.\underline{3}0182 \times 10^{-5}}{0.16} \times 100\% = 8.1 \times 10^{-3}\%$ so assumption is valid.

$K_w = [H_3O^+][OH^-]$ so $[H_3O^+] = \dfrac{K_w}{[OH^-]} = \dfrac{1.0 \times 10^{-14}}{1.\underline{3}0182 \times 10^{-5}} = 7.\underline{6}816 \times 10^{-10}$ M.

Finally, $pH = -\log [H_3O^+] = -\log (7.\underline{6}816 \times 10^{-10}) = 9.11$

Check: The units (none) are correct. The magnitude of the answer makes physical sense because pH should be less than $14 + \log(0.16) = 13.2$ because this is a weak base and there is a common ion effect.

16.30 (a) **Given:** 0.195 M $HC_2H_3O_2$ and 0.125 M $KC_2H_3O_2$ **Find:** pH
Other: $K_a\,(HC_2H_3O_2) = 1.8 \times 10^{-5}$

Conceptual Plan: M $KC_2H_3O_2$ → M $C_2H_3O_2^-$ then M $HC_2H_3O_2$, M $C_2H_3O_2^-$ → $[H_3O^+]$ → pH

$KC_2H_3O_2\,(aq) \rightarrow K^+\,(aq) + C_2H_3O_2^-\,(aq)$ *ICE Chart* $pH = -\log [H_3O^+]$

Solution: Since 1 $C_2H_3O_2^-$ ion is generated for each $KC_2H_3O_2$, $[C_2H_3O_2^-] = 0.125$ M $C_2H_3O_2^-$.

$$HC_2H_3O_2\,(aq) + H_2O\,(l) \rightleftharpoons H_3O^+\,(aq) + C_2H_3O_2^-\,(aq)$$

	$[HC_2H_3O_2]$	$[H_3O^+]$	$[C_2H_3O_2^-]$
Initial	0.195	≈0.00	.125
Change	$-x$	$+x$	$+x$
Equil	$0.195 - x$	$+x$	$0.125 + x$

$K_a = \dfrac{[H_3O^+][HC_2H_3O_2^-]}{[HC_2H_3O_2]} = 1.8 \times 10^{-5} = \dfrac{x(0.125 + x)}{0.195 - x}$ Assume x is small ($x << 0.125 < 0.195$) so

$\dfrac{x(0.125 + \cancel{x})}{0.195 - \cancel{x}} = 1.8 \times 10^{-5} = \dfrac{x(0.125)}{0.195}$ and $x = 2.\underline{8}08 \times 10^{-5}$ M = $[H_3O^+]$. Confirm that the more stringent assumption is valid.

$\frac{2.808 \times 10^{-5}}{0.195} \times 100\% = 0.022\%$ so assumption is valid. Finally,

$pH = -\log[H_3O^+] = -\log(2.808 \times 10^{-5}) = 4.55$

Check: The units (none) are correct. The magnitude of the answer makes physical sense because pH should be greater than $-\log(0.125) = 0.90$ because this is a weak acid and there is a common ion effect.

(b) **Given:** 0.255 M CH_3NH_2 and 0.135 M CH_3NH_3Br **Find:** pH

Other: K_b (CH_3NH_2) = 4.4×10^{-4}

Conceptual Plan: M CH_3NH_3Br → M $CH_3NH_3^+$ then

$CH_3NH_3Br\ (aq) \rightarrow CH_3NH_3^+\ (aq) + Br^-\ (aq)$

M CH_3NH_3, M $CH_3NH_3^+$ → $[OH^-]$ → $[H_3O^+]$ → pH

ICE Chart $K_w = [H_3O^+][OH^-]$ $pH = -\log[H_3O^+]$

Solution: Since 1 $CH_3NH_3^+$ ion is generated for each CH_3NH_3Br, $[CH_3NH_3^+] = 0.135$ M $CH_3NH_3^+$.

$$CH_3NH_2\ (aq) + H_2O\ (l) \rightleftharpoons CH_3NH_3^+\ (aq) + OH^-(aq)$$

	$[CH_3NH_2]$	$[CH_3NH_3^+]$	$[OH^-]$
Initial	0.255	0.135	≈0.00
Change	$-x$	$+x$	$+x$
Equil	$0.255 - x$	$0.135 + x$	$+x$

$$K_b = \frac{[CH_3NH_3^+][OH^-]}{[CH_3NH_2]} = 4.4 \times 10^{-4} = \frac{(0.135 + x)x}{0.255 - x}$$

Assume x is small ($x << 0.135 < 0.255$) so $\frac{(0.135 + x)x}{0.255 - x} = 4.4 \times 10^{-4} = \frac{(0.135)x}{0.255}$ and

$x = 8.3111 \times 10^{-4}$ M = $[OH^-]$. Confirm that the more stringent assumption is valid

$\frac{8.3111 \times 10^{-4}}{0.135} \times 100\% = 0.62\%$ so assumption is valid.

$$K_w = [H_3O^+][OH^-] \text{ so } [H_3O^+] = \frac{K_w}{[OH^-]} = \frac{1.0 \times 10^{-14}}{8.3111 \times 10^{-4}} = 1.20321 \times 10^{-11} \text{ M.}$$

Finally, $pH = -\log[H_3O^+] = -\log(1.20321 \times 10^{-11}) = 10.92$.

Check: The units (none) are correct. The magnitude of the answer makes physical sense because pH should be less than $14 + \log(0.255) = 13.4$ because this is a weak base and there is a common ion effect.

16.31 **Given:** 0.15 M $HC_7H_5O_2$ in pure water and in 0.10 M $NaC_7H_5O_2$

Find: % ionization in both solutions **Other:** K_a ($HC_7H_5O_2$) = 6.5×10^{-5}

Conceptual Plan: pure water: M $HC_7H_5O_2$ → $[H_3O^+]$ → % ionization then in $NaC_7H_5O_2$ solution:

ICE Chart $\%\ ionization = \frac{[H_3O^+]_{equil}}{[HC_7H_5O_2]_0} \times 100\%$

M $NaC_7H_5O_2$ → M $C_7H_5O_2^-$ then M $HC_7H_5O_2$, M $C_7H_5O_2^-$ → $[H_3O^+]$ → % ionization

$NaC_7H_5O_2(aq) \rightarrow Na^+\ (aq) + C_7H_5O_2^-\ (aq)$ *ICE Chart* $\%\ ionization = \frac{[H_3O^+]_{equil}}{[HC_7H_5O_2]_0} \times 100\%$

Solution: in pure water:

$$HC_7H_5O_2\ (aq) + H_2O\ (l) \rightleftharpoons H_3O^+\ (aq) + C_7H_5O_2^-(aq)$$

	$[HC_7H_5O_2]$	$[H_3O^+]$	$[C_7H_5O_2^-]$
Initial	0.15	≈0.00	0.00
Change	$-x$	$+x$	$+x$
Equil	$0.15 - x$	$+x$	$+x$

$$K_a = \frac{[H_3O^+][C_7H_5O_2^-]}{[HC_7H_5O_2]} = 6.5 \times 10^{-5} = \frac{x^2}{0.15 - x}$$

Assume x is small ($x << 0.10$) so $\frac{x^2}{0.15 - x} = 6.5 \times 10^{-5} = \frac{x^2}{0.15}$ and $x = 3.1225 \times 10^{-3}$ M = $[H_3O^+]$. Then

$\%\ ionization = \frac{[H_3O^+]_{equil}}{[HC_7H_5O_2]_0} \times 100\% = \frac{3.1225 \times 10^{-3}}{0.15} \times 100\% = 2.1\%$, which also confirms that the assumption is valid (since it is less than 5%). In $NaC_7H_5O_2$ solution: Since 1 $C_7H_5O_2^-$ ion is generated for each $NaC_7H_5O_2$, $[C_7H_5O_2^-] = 0.10$ M $C_7H_5O_2^-$.

$$HC_7H_5O_2\,(aq) + H_2O\,(l) \rightleftharpoons H_3O^+\,(aq) + C_7H_5O_2^-\,(aq)$$

	$[HC_7H_5O_2]$	$[H_3O^+]$	$[C_7H_5O_2^-]$
Initial	0.15	≈0.00	0.10
Change	$-x$	$+x$	$+x$
Equil	$0.15 - x$	$+x$	$0.10 + x$

$K_a = \dfrac{[H_3O^+][C_7H_5O_2^-]}{[HC_7H_5O_2]} = 6.5 \times 10^{-5} = \dfrac{x(0.10 + x)}{0.15 - x}$ Assume x is small ($x << 0.10 < 0.15$) so

$\dfrac{x(0.10 + x)}{0.15 - x} = 6.5 \times 10^{-5} = \dfrac{x(0.10)}{0.15}$ and $x = 9.\underline{7}5 \times 10^{-5}$ M = $[H_3O^+]$, then

$\%\text{ ionization} = \dfrac{[H_3O^+]_{equil}}{[HC_7H_5O_2]_0} \times 100\% = \dfrac{9.\underline{7}5 \times 10^{-5}}{0.15} \times 100\% = 0.065\%$, which also confirms that the assumption is valid (since it is less than 5 %). The percent ionization in the sodium benzoate solution is less than in pure water because of the common ion effect. An increase in one of the products (benzoate ion) shifts the equilibrium to the left, so less acid dissociates.

Check: The units (%) are correct. The magnitude of the answer makes physical sense because the acid is weak and so the percent ionization is low. With a common ion present, the percent ionization decreases.

16.32 **Given:** 0.13 M $HCHO_2$ in pure water and in 0.11 M $KCHO_2$ **Find:** % ionization in both solutions

Other: K_a ($HCHO_2$) = 1.8×10^{-4}

Conceptual Plan: pure water: M $HCHO_2$ → $[H_3O^+]$ → % ionization then in $KCHO_2$ solution:

ICE Chart $\quad \%\text{ ionization} = \dfrac{[H_3O^+]_{equil}}{[HCHO_2]_0} \times 100\%$

M $KCHO_2$ → M CHO_2^- then M $HCHO_2$, M CHO_2^- → $[H_3O^+]$ → % ionization

$KCHO_2\,(aq) \rightarrow K^+\,(aq) + CHO_2^-\,(aq)$ $\quad$ ICE Chart $\quad \%\text{ ionization} = \dfrac{[H_3O^+]_{equil}}{[HCHO_2]_0} \times 100\%$

Solution: in pure water:

$$HCHO_2\,(aq) + H_2O\,(l) \rightleftharpoons H_3O^+\,(aq) + CHO_2^-\,(aq)$$

	$[HCHO_2]$	$[H_3O^+]$	$[CHO_2^-]$
Initial	0.13	≈0.00	0.00
Change	$-x$	$+x$	$+x$
Equil	$0.13 - x$	$+x$	$+x$

$K_a = \dfrac{[H_3O^+][CHO_2^-]}{[HCHO_2]} = 1.8 \times 10^{-4} = \dfrac{x^2}{0.13 - x}$

Assume x is small ($x << 0.10$) so $\dfrac{x^2}{0.13 - x} = 1.8 \times 10^{-4} = \dfrac{x^2}{0.13}$ and $x = 4.\underline{8}374 \times 10^{-3}$ M = $[H_3O^+]$. Then

$\%\text{ ionization} = \dfrac{[H_3O^+]_{equil}}{[HCHO_2]_0} \times 100\% = \dfrac{4.\underline{8}374 \times 10^{-3}}{0.13} \times 100\% = 3.7\%$ which also confirms that the assumption is valid (since it is less than 5%).

In $KCHO_2$ Solution: Since 1 CHO_2^- ion is generated for each $KCHO_2$, $[CHO_2^-]$ = 0.11 M CHO_2^-.

$$HCHO_2\,(aq) + H_2O\,(l) \rightleftharpoons H_3O^+\,(aq) + CHO_2^-\,(aq)$$

	$[HCHO_2]$	$[H_3O^+]$	$[CHO_2^-]$
Initial	0.13	≈0.00	0.11
Change	$-x$	$+x$	$+x$
Equil	$0.13 - x$	$+x$	$0.11 + x$

$K_a = \dfrac{[H_3O^+][CHO_2^-]}{[HCHO_2]} = 1.8 \times 10^{-4} = \dfrac{x(0.11 + x)}{0.13 - x}$

Assume x is small ($x << 0.11 < 0.13$) so $\dfrac{x(0.11 + x)}{0.13 - x} = 1.8 \times 10^{-4} = \dfrac{x(0.11)}{0.13}$ and $x = 2.\underline{1}273 \times 10^{-4}$ M = $[H_3O^+]$.

Then $\%\text{ ionization} = \dfrac{[H_3O^+]_{equil}}{[HCHO_2]_0} \times 100\% = \dfrac{2.\underline{1}273 \times 10^{-4}}{0.13} \times 100\% = 0.16\%$, which also confirms that the assumption is valid (since it is less than 5%). The percent ionization in the potassium formate solution is less than in pure water because of the common ion effect. An increase in one of the products (formate ion) shifts the equilibrium to the left, so less acid dissociates.

Check: The units (%) are correct. The magnitude of the answer makes physical sense because the acid is weak and so the percent ionization is low. With a common ion present, the percent ionization decreases.

16.33 (a) **Given:** 0.15 M HF **Find:** pH **Other:** K_a (HF) = 3.5 x 10^{-4}

Conceptual Plan: M HF → $[H_3O^+]$ → pH

ICE Chart pH = − log $[H_3O^+]$

Solution:

$HF\ (aq) + H_2O\ (l) \rightleftharpoons H_3O^+\ (aq) + F^-(aq)$

	[HF]	$[H_3O^+]$	$[F^-]$
Initial	0.15	≈0.00	0.00
Change	$-x$	$+x$	$+x$
Equil	$0.15 - x$	$+x$	$+x$

$$K_a = \frac{[H_3O^+][F^-]}{[HF]} = 3.5 \times 10^{-4} = \frac{x^2}{0.15 - x}$$ Assume x is small ($x << 0.15$) so

$$\frac{x^2}{0.15 - x} = 3.5 \times 10^{-4} = \frac{x^2}{0.15}$$ and $x = 7.2457 \times 10^{-3}$ M = $[H_3O^+]$. Confirm that

assumption is valid $\frac{7.2457 \times 10^{-3}}{0.15} \times 100\% = 4.8\% < 5\%$ so assumption is valid.

Finally, pH = − log $[H_3O^+]$ = − log (7.2457×10^{-3}) = 2.14.

Check: The units (none) are correct. The magnitude of the answer makes physical sense because pH should be greater than − log (0.15) = 0.82 because this is a weak acid.

(b) **Given:** 0.15 M NaF **Find:** pH **Other:** K_a (HF) = 3.5 x 10^{-4}

Conceptual Plan: M NaF → M F^- and K_a → K_b then M F^- → $[OH^-]$ → $[H_3O^+]$ → pH

$NaF\ (aq) \rightarrow Na^+\ (aq) + F^-\ (aq)$ $K_w = K_a K_b$ *ICE Chart* $K_w = [H_3O^+][OH^-]$ pH = − log $[H_3O^+]$

Solution: Since 1 F^- ion is generated for each NaF, $[F^-]$ = 0.15 M F^-. Since $K_w = K_a K_b$, rearrange to solve for K_b. $$K_b = \frac{K_w}{K_a} = \frac{1.0 \times 10^{-14}}{3.5 \times 10^{-4}} = 2.8571 \times 10^{-11}$$

$F^-\ (aq) + H_2O\ (l) \rightleftharpoons HF\ (aq) + OH^-\ (aq)$

	$[F^-]$	[HF]	$[OH^-]$
Initial	0.15	0.00	≈0.00
Change	$-x$	$+x$	$+x$
Equil	$0.15 - x$	$+x$	$+x$

$$K_b = \frac{[HF][OH^-]}{[F^-]} = 2.8571 \times 10^{-11} = \frac{x^2}{0.15 - x}$$

Assume x is small ($x << 0.15$) so $\frac{x^2}{0.15 - x} = 2.8571 \times 10^{-11} = \frac{x^2}{0.15}$ and $x = 2.0702 \times 10^{-6}$ M = $[OH^-]$.

Confirm that assumption is valid $\frac{2.0702 \times 10^{-6}}{0.15} \times 100\% = 0.0014\% < 5\%$ so assumption is valid.

$$K_w = [H_3O^+][OH^-] \text{ so } [H_3O^+] = \frac{K_w}{[OH^-]} = \frac{1.0 \times 10^{-14}}{2.0702 \times 10^{-6}} = 4.8305 \times 10^{-9}\ M.$$

Finally, pH = − log $[H_3O^+]$ = − log (4.8305×10^{-9}) = 8.32.

Check: The units (none) are correct. The magnitude of the answer makes physical sense because pH should be slightly basic, since the fluoride ion is a very weak base.

(c) **Given:** 0.15 M HF and 0.15 M NaF **Find:** pH **Other:** K_a (HF) = 3.5 x 10^{-4}

Conceptual Plan: M NaF → M F^- then M HF, M F^- → $[H_3O^+]$ → pH

$NaF\ (aq) \rightarrow Na^+\ (aq) + F^-\ (aq)$ *ICE Chart* pH = − log $[H_3O^+]$

Solution: Since 1 F^- ion is generated for each NaF, $[F^-]$ = 0.15 M F^-.

$$HF\,(aq) + H_2O\,(l) \rightleftharpoons H_3O^+\,(aq) + F^-(aq)$$

	$[HF]$	$[H_3O^+]$	$[F^-]$
Initial	0.15	$\approx$0.00	0.15
Change	$-x$	$+x$	$+x$
Equil	$0.15 - x$	$+x$	$0.15 + x$

$$K_a = \frac{[H_3O^+][F^-]}{[HF]} = 3.5 \times 10^{-4} = \frac{x(0.15 + x)}{0.15 - x}$$

Assume x is small ($x << 0.15$) so $\frac{x(0.15 + \cancel{x})}{0.15 - \cancel{x}} = 3.5 \times 10^{-4} = \frac{x(\cancel{0.15})}{\cancel{0.15}}$ and $x = 3.5 \times 10^{-4}$ M $= [H_3O^+]$.

Confirm that assumption is valid $\frac{3.5 \times 10^{-4}}{0.15} \times 100\% = 0.23\% < 5\%$ so assumption is valid.

Finally, $pH = -\log[H_3O^+] = -\log(3.5 \times 10^{-4}) = 3.46$.

Check: The units (none) are correct. The magnitude of the answer makes physical sense because pH should be greater than in part a (2.14) because of the common ion effect suppressing the dissociation of the weak acid.

16.34 (a) **Given:** 0.18 M CH_3NH_2 **Find:** pH **Other:** $K_b\,(CH_3NH_2) = 4.4 \times 10^{-4}$

Conceptual Plan: M CH_3NH_3 → $[OH^-]$ → $[H_3O^+]$ → pH

ICE Chart $\quad K_w = [H_3O^+][OH^-] \quad pH = -\log[H_3O^+]$

Solution:

$$CH_3NH_2\,(aq) + H_2O\,(l) \rightleftharpoons CH_3NH_3^+\,(aq) + OH^-(aq)$$

	$[CH_3NH_2]$	$[CH_3NH_3^+]$	$[OH^-]$
Initial	0.18	0.00	$\approx$0.00
Change	$-x$	$+x$	$+x$
Equil	$0.18 - x$	$+x$	$+x$

$$K_b = \frac{[CH_3NH_3^+][OH^-]}{[CH_3NH_2]} = 4.4 \times 10^{-4} = \frac{x^2}{0.18 - x}$$

Assume x is small ($x << 0.18$) so $\frac{x^2}{0.18 - \cancel{x}} = 4.4 \times 10^{-4} = \frac{x^2}{0.18}$ and $x = 8.\underline{8}994 \times 10^{-3}$ M $= [OH^-]$.

Confirm that assumption is valid $\frac{8.\underline{8}994 \times 10^{-3}}{0.18} \times 100\% = 4.9\% < 5\%$ so assumption is valid.

$K_w = [H_3O^+][OH^-]$ so $[H_3O^+] = \frac{K_w}{[OH^-]} = \frac{1.0 \times 10^{-14}}{8.\underline{8}994 \times 10^{-3}} = 1.\underline{1}237 \times 10^{-12}$ M.

Finally, $pH = -\log[H_3O^+] = -\log(1.\underline{1}237 \times 10^{-12}) = 11.95$.

Check: The units (none) are correct. The magnitude of the answer makes physical sense because pH should be less than 14 + log (0.18) = 13.3 because this is a weak base.

(b) **Given:** 0.18 M CH_3NH_3Cl **Find:** pH **Other:** $K_b\,(CH_3NH_2) = 4.4 \times 10^{-4}$

Conceptual Plan: M CH_3NH_3Cl → M $CH_3NH_3^+$ and K_b → K_a then M $CH_3NH_3^+$ → $[H_3O^+]$ → pH

$CH_3NH_3Cl\,(aq) \rightarrow CH_3NH_3^+\,(aq) + Cl^-\,(aq) \quad K_w = K_a K_b \quad$ *ICE Chart* $\quad pH = -\log[H_3O^+]$

Solution: Since 1 $CH_3NH_3^+$ ion is generated for each CH_3NH_3Cl, $[CH_3NH_3^+] = 0.18$ M $CH_3NH_3^+$.

Since $K_w = K_a K_b$, rearrange to solve for K_a. $\quad K_a = \frac{K_w}{K_b} = \frac{1.0 \times 10^{-14}}{4.4 \times 10^{-4}} = 2.\underline{2}727 \times 10^{-11}$

$$CH_3NH_3^+\,(aq) + H_2O\,(l) \rightleftharpoons H_3O^+\,(aq) + CH_3NH_2(aq)$$

	$[CH_3NH_3^+]$	$[H_3O^+]$	$[CH_3NH_2]$
Initial	0.18	$\approx$0.00	0.00
Change	$-x$	$+x$	$+x$
Equil	$0.18 - x$	$+x$	$+x$

$K_a = \frac{[H_3O^+][CH_3NH_2]}{[CH_3NH_3^+]} = 2.\underline{2}727 \times 10^{-11} = \frac{x^2}{0.18 - x}$. Assume x is small ($x << 0.18$) so

$\frac{x^2}{0.18 - \cancel{x}} = 2.\underline{2}727 \times 10^{-11} = \frac{x^2}{0.18}$ and $x = 2.\underline{0}226 \times 10^{-6}$ M $= [H_3O^+]$.

Confirm that assumption is valid $\frac{2.0\underline{2}26 \times 10^{-6}}{0.18} \times 100\% = 0.0012\% < 5\%$ so assumption is valid.

Finally, pH $= -\log[H_3O^+] = -\log(2.0\underline{2}26 \times 10^{-6}) = 5.69$.

Check: The units (none) are correct. The magnitude of the answer makes physical sense because pH should be slightly acidic, since the methylammonium cation is a very weak acid.

(c) **Given:** 0.18 M CH_3NH_2 and 0.18 M CH_3NH_3Cl **Find:** pH **Other:** K_b (CH_3NH_2) = 4.4 x 10^{-4}

Conceptual Plan: M CH_3NH_3Cl → M $CH_3NH_3^+$ then

$CH_3NH_3Cl\,(aq) \rightarrow CH_3NH_3^+\,(aq) + Cl^-\,(aq)$

M CH_3NH_2, M $CH_3NH_3^+$ → $[OH^-]$ → $[H_3O^+]$ → pH

ICE Chart $K_w = [H_3O^+][OH^-]$ $\quad$ $pH = -\log[H_3O^+]$

Solution: Since 1 $CH_3NH_3^+$ ion is generated for each CH_3NH_3Cl, $[CH_3NH_3^+]$ = 0.105 M $CH_3NH_3^+$.

$$CH_3NH_2\,(aq) + H_2O\,(l) \rightleftharpoons CH_3NH_3^+\,(aq) + OH^-(aq)$$

	$[CH_3NH_2]$	$[CH_3NH_3^+]$	$[OH^-]$
Initial	0.18	0.18	≈0.00
Change	$-x$	$+x$	$+x$
Equil	$0.18 - x$	$0.18 + x$	$+x$

$$K_b = \frac{[CH_3NH_3^+][OH^-]}{[CH_3NH_2]} = 4.4 \times 10^{-4} = \frac{(0.18 + x)x}{0.18 - x}$$

Assume x is small ($x << 0.18$) so $\frac{(0.18 + \cancel{x})x}{0.18 - \cancel{x}} = 4.4 \times 10^{-4} = \frac{(\cancel{0.18})x}{\cancel{0.18}}$ and $x = 4.4 \times 10^{-4}$ M = $[OH^-]$.

Confirm that assumption is valid $\frac{4.4 \times 10^{-4}}{0.18} \times 100\% = 0.24\% < 5\%$ so assumption is valid.

$$K_w = [H_3O^+][OH^-] \text{ so } [H_3O^+] = \frac{K_w}{[OH^-]} = \frac{1.0 \times 10^{-14}}{4.4 \times 10^{-4}} = 2.\underline{2}727 \times 10^{-11}\text{ M.}$$

Finally, pH $= -\log[H_3O^+] = -\log(2.\underline{2}727 \times 10^{-11}) = 10.64$

Check: The units (none) are correct. The magnitude of the answer makes physical sense because pH should be less than 14 + log (0.18) = 13.3 because this is a weak base and there is a common ion effect.

16.35 When an acid (such as HCl) is added it will react with the conjugate base of the buffer system as follows: $HCl + NaC_2H_3O_2 \rightarrow HC_2H_3O_2 + NaCl$. When a base (such as NaOH) is added it will react with the weak acid of the buffer system as follows: $NaOH + HC_2H_3O_2 \rightarrow H_2O + NaC_2H_3O_2$. The reaction generates the other buffer system component.

16.36 When an acid (such as HCl) is added it will react with the conjugate base of the buffer system as follows: $HCl + NH_3 \rightarrow NH_4Cl$. When a base (such as NaOH) is added it will react with the weak acid of the buffer system as follows: $NaOH + NH_4Cl \rightarrow H_2O + NH_3 + NaCl$. The reaction generates the other buffer system component.

16.37 (a) **Given:** 0.20 M $HCHO_2$ and 0.15 M $NaCHO_2$ **Find:** pH **Other:** K_a ($HCHO_2$) = 1.8 x 10^{-4}

Conceptual Plan: Identify acid and base components then M $NaCHO_2$ → M CHO_2^- then

acid = $HCHO_2$ base = CHO_2^- $\qquad$ $NaCHO_2\,(aq) \rightarrow Na^+\,(aq) + CHO_2^-\,(aq)$

K_a, M $HCHO_2$, M CHO_2^- → pH.

$$pH = pK_a + \log\frac{[\text{base}]}{[\text{acid}]}$$

Solution: Acid = $HCHO_2$, so [acid] = $[HCHO_2]$ = 0.20 M. Base = CHO_2^-. Since 1 CHO_2^- ion is generated for each $NaCHO_2$, $[CHO_2^-]$ = 0.15 M CHO_2^- = [base]. Then

$$pH = pK_a + \log\frac{[\text{base}]}{[\text{acid}]} = -\log(1.8 \times 10^{-4}) + \log\frac{0.15\,\cancel{M}}{0.20\,\cancel{M}} = 3.62.$$

Note that in order to use the Henderson–Hasselbalch Equation, the assumption that x is small must be valid. This was confirmed in Problem 29.

Check: The units (none) are correct. The magnitude of the answer makes physical sense because pH should be less than the pK_a of the acid because there is more acid than base. The answer agrees with Problem 29.

(b) **Given:** 0.16 M NH_3 and 0.22 M NH_4Cl **Find:** pH **Other:** K_b (NH_3) = 1.79 x 10^{-5}
Conceptual Plan: Identify acid and base components then M $NH_4Cl \rightarrow$ M NH_4^+ and $K_b \rightarrow pK_b \rightarrow pK_a$

acid = NH_4^+ base = NH_3 $NH_4Cl\ (aq) \rightarrow NH_4^+\ (aq) + Cl^-\ (aq)$ $pK_b = -\log K_b$ $14 = pK_a + pK_b$

then pK_a, M NH_3, M NH_4^+ $\rightarrow$ pH.

$$pH = pK_a + \log\frac{[base]}{[acid]}$$

Solution: Base = NH_3, [base] = [NH_3] = 0.16 M Acid = NH_4^+. Since 1 NH_4^+ ion is generated for each NH_4Cl, [NH_4^+] = 0.18 M NH_4^+ = [acid].
Since K_b (NH_3) = 1.79 x 10^{-5}, $pK_b = -\log K_b = -\log(1.79 \times 10^{-5}) = 4.75$. Since $14 = pK_a + pK_b$,

$$pK_a = 14 - pK_b = 14 - 4.75 = 9.25 \text{ then } pH = pK_a + \log\frac{[base]}{[acid]} = 9.25 + \log\frac{0.16\ \text{M}}{0.22\ \text{M}} = 9.11.$$

Note that in order to use the Henderson–Hasselbalch Equation, the assumption that x is small must be valid. This was confirmed in Problem 29.
Check: The units (none) are correct. The magnitude of the answer makes physical sense because pH should be less than the pK_a of the acid because there is more acid than base. The answer agrees with problem 29, within the error of the value.

16.38 (a) **Given:** 0.195 M $HC_2H_3O_2$ and 0.125 M $KC_2H_3O_2$ **Find:** pH **Other:** K_a ($HC_2H_3O_2$) = 1.8 x 10^{-5}
Conceptual Plan: Identify acid and base components then M $KC_2H_3O_2$ $\rightarrow$ M $C_2H_3O_2^-$ then

acid = $HC_2H_3O_2$ base = $C_2H_3O_2^-$ $KC_2H_3O_2\ (aq) \rightarrow K^+\ (aq) + C_2H_3O_2^-\ (aq)$

M $HC_2H_3O_2$, M $C_2H_3O_2^-$ $\rightarrow$ pH.

$$pH = pK_a + \log\frac{[base]}{[acid]}$$

Solution: Acid = $HC_2H_3O_2$, so [acid] = [$HC_2H_3O_2$] = 0.195 M. Base = $C_2H_3O_2^-$. Since 1 $C_2H_3O_2^-$ ion is generated for each $KC_2H_3O_2$, [$C_2H_3O_2^-$] = 0.125 M $C_2H_3O_2^-$ = [base]. Then

$$pH = pK_a + \log\frac{[base]}{[acid]} = -\log(1.8 \times 10^{-5}) + \log\frac{0.125\ \text{M}}{0.195\ \text{M}} = 4.55.$$

Note that in order to use the Henderson–Hasselbalch Equation, the assumption that x is small must be valid. This was confirmed in Problem 30.
Check: The units (none) are correct. The magnitude of the answer makes physical sense because pH should be less than the pK_a of the acid because there is more acid than base. The answer agrees with Problem 30.

(b) **Given:** 0.255 M CH_3NH_2 and 0.135 M CH_3NH_3Br **Find:** pH **Other:** K_b (CH_3NH_2) = 4.4 x 10^{-4}
Conceptual Plan: Identify acid and base components then M CH_3NH_3Br $\rightarrow$ M $CH_3NH_3^+$ and

acid = $CH_3NH_3^+$ base = CH_3NH_2 $CH_3NH_3Br\ (aq) \rightarrow CH_3NH_3^+\ (aq) + Br^-\ (aq)$

$K_b \rightarrow pK_b \rightarrow pK_a$ then pK_a, M NH_3, M NH_4^+ $\rightarrow$ pH.

$pK_b = -\log K_b$ $14 = pK_a + pK_b$ $pH = pK_a + \log\frac{[base]}{[acid]}$

Solution: Base = CH_3NH_2, [base] = [CH_3NH_2] = 0.255 M Acid = NH_3^+. Since 1 $CH_3NH_3^+$ ion is generated for each CH_3NH_3Br, [$CH_3NH_3^+$] = 0.135 M $CH_3NH_3^+$ = [acid].
Since K_b (CH_3NH_2) = 4.4 x 10^{-4}, $pK_b = -\log K_b = -\log(4.4 \times 10^{-4}) = 3.36$.
Since $14 = pK_a + pK_b$, $pK_a = 14 - pK_b = 14 - 3.36 = 10.64$ then

$$pH = pK_a + \log\frac{[base]}{[acid]} = 10.64 + \log\frac{0.255\ \text{M}}{0.135\ \text{M}} = 10.92.$$

Note that in order to use the Henderson–Hasselbalch Equation, the assumption that x is small must be valid. This was confirmed in Problem 30.
Check: The units (none) are correct. The magnitude of the answer makes physical sense because pH should be greater than the pK_a of the acid because there is more base than acid. The answer agrees with Problem 30.

16.39 (a) **Given:** 0.135 M HClO and 0.155 M KClO **Find:** pH **Other:** K_a (HClO) = 2.9 x 10^{-8}
Conceptual Plan: Identify acid and base components then M KClO $\rightarrow$ M ClO^- then

acid = HClO base = ClO^- $KClO\ (aq) \rightarrow K^+\ (aq) + ClO^-\ (aq)$

M HClO, M ClO^- $\rightarrow$ pH.

$$pH = pK_a + \log\frac{[base]}{[acid]}$$

Solution: Acid = HClO, so [acid] = [HClO] = 0.135 M. Base = ClO^-. Since 1 ClO^- ion is generated for each KClO, $[ClO^-]$ = 0.155 M ClO^- = [base]. Then

$$pH = pK_a + \log\frac{[base]}{[acid]} = -\log(2.9 \times 10^{-8}) + \log\frac{0.155\ \cancel{M}}{0.135\ \cancel{M}} = 7.60.$$

Check: The units (none) are correct. The magnitude of the answer makes physical sense because pH should be greater than the pK_a of the acid because there is more base than acid.

(b) **Given:** 1.05% by mass $C_2H_5NH_2$ and 1.10% by mass $C_2H_5NH_3Br$ **Find:** pH

Other: K_b ($C_2H_5NH_2$) = 5.6 x 10^{-4}

Conceptual Plan: Assume exactly 100 g of solution. Since both components are in the same solution (i.e. the same final volume of solution), the ratio of the moles of each component is the same as the ratio of the molarity of these components and only the relative number of moles needs to be calculated. $g_{Solution} \rightarrow g_{C_2H_5NH_2} \rightarrow mol\ C_2H_5NH_2$ **and** $g_{solution} \rightarrow g\ C_2H_5NH_3Br \rightarrow mol\ C_2H_5NH_3Br$

$$\frac{1.05\ g\ C_2H_5NH_2}{100\ g\ solution} \quad \frac{1\ mol\ C_2H_5NH_2}{45.09\ g\ C_2H_5NH_2} \qquad \frac{1.10\ g\ C_2H_5NH_3Br}{100\ g\ solution} \quad \frac{1\ mol\ C_2H_5NH_3Br}{125.99\ g\ C_2H_5NH_3Br}$$

identify acid and base components then M $C_2H_5NH_3Br$ → M $C_2H_5NH_3^+$ and

acid = $C_2H_5NH_3^+$ base = $C_2H_5NH_2$ $C_2H_5NH_3Br\ (aq) \rightarrow C_2H_5NH_3^+\ (aq) + Br^-\ (aq)$

$K_b \rightarrow pK_b \rightarrow pK_a$ **then** pK_a**, M $C_2H_5NH_2$, M $C_2H_5NH_3^+$ → pH**

$pK_b = -\log K_b \quad 14 = pK_a + pK_b \qquad pH = pK_a + \log\frac{[base]}{[acid]}$

Solution:

$$100\ \cancel{g\ solution} \times \frac{1.05\ \cancel{g\ C_2H_5NH_2}}{100\ \cancel{g\ solution}} \times \frac{1\ mol\ C_2H_5NH_2}{45.09\ \cancel{g\ C_2H_5NH_2}} = 0.02328676\ mol\ C_2H_5NH_2 \text{ and}$$

$$100\ \cancel{g\ solution} \times \frac{1.10\ \cancel{g\ C_2H_5NH_3Br}}{100\ \cancel{g\ solution}} \times \frac{1\ mol\ C_2H_5NH_3Br}{125.99\ \cancel{g\ C_2H_5NH_3Br}} = 0.008730852\ mol\ C_2H_5NH_3Br$$

Then base = $C_2H_5NH_2$, moles of base = mol $C_2H_5NH_2$ = 0.02328676 mol; acid = $C_2H_5NH_3^+$.
Since 1 $C_2H_5NH_3^+$ ion is generated for each $C_2H_5NH_3Br$, mol $C_2H_5NH_3^+$ = 0.008730852 mol.
Since K_b ($C_2H_5NH_2$) = 5.6 x 10^{-4}, $pK_b = -\log K_b = -\log(5.6 \times 10^{-4}) = 3.25$.
Since $14 = pK_a + pK_b$, $pK_a = 14 - pK_b = 14 - 3.25 = 10.75$ then

$$pH = pK_a + \log\frac{mol\ base}{mol\ acid} = 10.75 + \log\frac{0.02328676\ \cancel{mol}}{0.008730852\ \cancel{mol}} = 11.18.$$

Check: The units (none) are correct. The magnitude of the answer makes physical sense because pH should be greater than the pK_a of the acid because there is more base than acid.

(c) **Given:** 10.0 g $HC_2H_3O_2$ and 10.0 g $NaC_2H_3O_2$ in 150.0 mL solution **Find:** pH

Other: K_a ($HC_2H_3O_2$) = 1.8 x 10^{-5}

Conceptual Plan: Identify acid and base components then mL → L and g $HC_2H_3O_2$ → mol $HC_2H_3O_2$

acid = $HC_2H_3O_2$ base = $C_2H_3O_2^-$ $\qquad \frac{1\ L}{1000\ mL} \qquad \frac{1\ mol\ HC_2H_3O_2}{60.05\ g\ HC_2H_3O_2}$

then mol $HC_2H_3O_2$, L → M $HC_2H_3O_2$ and g $NaC_2H_3O_2$ → mol $NaC_2H_3O_2$ then

$M = \frac{mol}{L} \qquad \frac{1\ mol\ NaC_2H_3O_2}{82.04\ g\ NaC_2H_3O_2}$

mol $NaC_2H_3O_2$, L → M $NaC_2H_3O_2$ → M $C_2H_3O_2^-$ then M $HC_2H_3O_2$, M $C_2H_3O_2^-$ → pH.

$M = \frac{mol}{L} \qquad NaC_2H_3O_2\ (aq) \rightarrow Na^+(aq) + C_2H_3O_2^-(aq) \qquad pH = pK_a + \log\frac{[base]}{[acid]}$

Solution: $150.0\ \cancel{mL} \times \frac{1\ L}{1000\ \cancel{mL}} = 0.1500$ L and

$$10.0\ \cancel{g\ HC_2H_3O_2} \times \frac{1\ mol\ HC_2H_3O_2}{60.05\ \cancel{g\ HC_2H_3O_2}} = 0.166528\ mol\ HC_2H_3O_2$$

$$\text{then } M = \frac{mol}{L} = \frac{0.166528\ mol\ HC_2H_3O_2}{0.1500\ L} = 1.11019\ M\ HC_2H_3O_2 \text{ and}$$

$$10.0\ \cancel{g\ NaC_2H_3O_2} \times \frac{1\ mol\ NaC_2H_3O_2}{82.04\ \cancel{g\ NaC_2H_3O_2}} = 0.121892\ mol\ NaC_2H_3O_2 \text{ then}$$

$M = \frac{mol}{L} = \frac{0.121892\ mol\ NaC_2H_3O_2}{0.1500\ L} = 0.812612$ M $NaC_2H_3O_2$. Acid = $HC_2H_3O_2$, so [acid] = $[HC_2H_3O_2]$ = 1.11019 M and base = $C_2H_3O_2^-$. Since 1 $C_2H_3O_2^-$ ion is generated for each $NaC_2H_3O_2$, $[C_2H_3O_2^-]$ = 0.812612 M $C_2H_3O_2^-$ = [base]. Then

$$pH = pK_a + \log\frac{[base]}{[acid]} = -\log(1.8 \times 10^{-5}) + \log\frac{0.812\underline{6}12\ \cancel{M}}{1.1\underline{1}019\ \cancel{M}} = 4.61.$$

Check: The units (none) are correct. The magnitude of the answer makes physical sense because pH should be less than the pK_a of the acid because there is more acid than base.

16.40 (a) **Given:** 0.145 M $HC_3H_5O_2$ (propanoic acid) and 0.115 M $KC_3H_5O_2$ (potassium propanoate) **Find:** pH **Other:** K_a ($HC_3H_5O_2$) = 1.3×10^{-5}

Conceptual Plan: Identify acid and base components then M $KC_3H_5O_2$ → M $C_3H_5O_2^-$ then

acid = $HC_3H_5O_2$ base = $C_3H_5O_2^-$ $KC_3H_5O_2\,(aq) \rightarrow K^+(aq) + C_3H_5O_2^-\,(aq)$

M $HC_3H_5O_2$, M $C_3H_5O_2^-$ → pH.

$$pH = pK_a + \log\frac{[base]}{[acid]}$$

Solution: Acid = $HC_3H_5O_2$, so [acid] = [$HC_3H_5O_2$] = 0.145 M. Base = $C_3H_5O_2^-$. Since 1 $C_3H_5O_2^-$ ion is generated for each $KC_3H_5O_2$, [$C_3H_5O_2^-$] = 0.115 M $C_3H_5O_2^-$ = [base]. Then

$$pH = pK_a + \log\frac{[base]}{[acid]} = -\log(1.3 \times 10^{-5}) + \log\frac{0.115\ \cancel{M}}{0.145\ \cancel{M}} = 4.79.$$

Check: The units (none) are correct. The magnitude of the answer makes physical sense because pH should be less than the pK_a of the acid because there is more acid than base.

(b) **Given:** 0.785% by mass C_2H_5N and 0.985% by mass C_5H_5NHCl **Find:** pH **Other:** K_b (C_5H_5N) = 1.9×10^{-9}

Conceptual Plan: Assume exactly 100 g of solution. Since both components are in the same solution (i.e. the same final volume of solution), the ratio of the moles of each component is the same as the ratio of the molarity of these components and only the relative number of moles needs to be calculated. $g_{solution}$ → $g_{C_5H_5N}$ → mol $_{C_5H_5N}$ and $g_{solution}$ → g $_{C_5H_5NHCl}$ → mol $_{C_5H_5NHCl}$

$$\frac{0.785\ g\ C_5H_5N}{100\ g\ solution} \quad \frac{1\ mol\ C_5H_5N}{79.10\ g\ C_5H_5N} \quad \frac{0.985\ g\ C_5H_5NHCl}{100\ g\ solution} \quad \frac{1\ mol\ C_5H_5NHCl}{115.56\ g\ C_5H_5NHCl}$$

identify acid and base components then M CH_3NH_3Cl → M $CH_3NH_3^+$ and

acid = $C_5H_5NH^+$ base = C_5H_5N $C_5H_5NHCl\,(aq) \longrightarrow C_5H_5NH^+\,(aq) + Cl^-\,(aq)$

K_b → pK_b → pK_a then pK_a, M C_5H_5N, M $C_5H_5NH^+$ → pH

$pK_b = -\log K_b$ $14 = pK_a + pK_b$ $pH = pK_a + \log\frac{[base]}{[acid]}$

Solution:

$$100\ \cancel{g\ solution} \times \frac{0.785\ \cancel{g\ C_5H_5N}}{100\ \cancel{g\ solution}} \times \frac{1\ mol\ C_5H_5N}{79.10\ \cancel{g\ C_5H_5N}} = 0.0099\underline{2}4147\ mol\ C_5H_5N \text{ and}$$

$$100\ \cancel{g\ solution} \times \frac{0.985\ \cancel{g\ C_5H_5NHCl}}{100\ \cancel{g\ solution}} \times \frac{1\ mol\ C_5H_5NHCl}{115.56\ \cancel{g\ C_5H_5NHCl}} = 0.0085\underline{2}3711\ mol\ C_5H_5NHCl$$

Then base = C_5H_5N, moles of base = mol C_5H_5N = 0.0099$\underline{2}$4147 mol; acid = $C_5H_5NH^+$.
Since 1 $C_5H_5NH^+$ ion is generated for each C_5H_5NHCl, mol $C_5H_5NH^+$ = 0.0085$\underline{2}$3711 mol.
Since K_b (C_5H_5N) = 1.7×10^{-9}, $pK_b = -\log K_b = -\log(1.7 \times 10^{-9}) = 8.77$. Since $14 = pK_a + pK_b$, $pK_a = 14 - pK_b = 14 - 8.77 = 5.23$ then

$$pH = pK_a + \log\frac{mol\ base}{mol\ acid} = 5.23 + \log\frac{0.0099\underline{2}4147\ \cancel{mol}}{0.0085\underline{2}3711\ \cancel{mol}} = 5.30.$$

Check: The units (none) are correct. The magnitude of the answer makes physical sense because pH should be greater than the pK_a of the acid because there is more base than acid.

(c) **Given:** 15.0 g HF and 25.0 g NaF in 125 mL solution **Find:** pH **Other:** K_a (HF) = 3.5×10^{-4}

Conceptual Plan: Identify acid and base components then mL → L and g HF → mol HF

acid = HF base = F^- $\frac{1\ L}{1000\ mL}$ $\frac{1\ mol\ HF}{20.01\ g\ HF}$

then mol HF, L → M HF and g NaF → mol NaF then

$M = \frac{mol}{L}$ $\frac{1\ mol\ NaF}{41.99\ g\ NaF}$

mol NaF, L → M NaF → M F^- then M HF, M F^- → pH.

$M = \frac{mol}{L}$ $NaF\,(aq) \rightarrow Na^+\,(aq) + F^-\,(aq)$ $pH = pK_a + \log\frac{[base]}{[acid]}$

Solution: $125\ \cancel{mL} \times \frac{1\ L}{1000\ \cancel{mL}} = 0.125\ L$ and $15.0\ \cancel{g\ HF} \times \frac{1\ mol\ HF}{20.01\ \cancel{g\ HF}} = 0.74\underline{9}625\ mol\ HF$ then

$M = \frac{mol}{L} = \frac{0.749625 \text{ mol HF}}{0.125 \text{ L}} = 5.997 \text{ M HF}$ and $25.0 \text{ g NaF} \times \frac{1 \text{ mol NaF}}{41.99 \text{ g NaF}} = 0.595380 \text{ mol NaF}$

then $M = \frac{mol}{L} = \frac{0.595380 \text{ mol NaF}}{0.125 \text{ L}} = 4.76304 \text{ M NaF}$. Acid = HF, so [acid] = [HF] = 5.997 M and base = F^-. Since $1F^-$ ion is generated for each NaF, $[F^-] = 4.76304 \text{ M } F^-$ = [base]. Then

$pH = pK_a + \log \frac{[base]}{[acid]} = -\log(3.5 \times 10^{-4}) + \log \frac{4.76304 \text{ M}}{5.997 \text{ M}} = 3.36.$

Check: The units (none) are correct. The magnitude of the answer makes physical sense because pH should be less than the pK_a of the acid because there is more acid than base.

16.41 (a) **Given:** 50.0 mL of 0.15 M $HCHO_2$ and 75.0 mL of 0.13 M $NaCHO_2$ **Find:** pH

Other: K_a ($HCHO_2$) = 1.8×10^{-4}

Conceptual Plan: Identify acid and base components then mL $HCHO_2$, mL $NaCHO_2$ → total mL then

acid = $HCHO_2$ base = CHO_2^- total mL = mL $HCHO_2$ + mL $NaCHO_2$

mL $HCHO_2$, M $HCHO_2$, total mL → buffer M $HCHO_2$ and

$M_1 V_1 = M_2 V_2$

mL $NaCHO_2$, M $NaCHO_2$, total mL → buffer M $NaCHO_2$ → buffer M CHO_2^- then

$M_1 V_1 = M_2 V_2$ $NaCHO_2 (aq) \rightarrow Na^+ (aq) + CHO_2^- (aq)$

K_a, M $HCHO_2$, M CHO_2^- → pH.

$pH = pK_a + \log \frac{[base]}{[acid]}$

Solution: total mL = mL $HCHO_2$ + mL $NaCHO_2$ = 50.0 mL + 75.0 mL = 125.0 mL. Then since $M_1 V_1 = M_2 V_2$ rearrange to solve for M_2.

$M_2 = \frac{M_1 V_1}{V_2} = \frac{(0.15 \text{ M})(50.0 \text{ mL})}{125.0 \text{ mL}} = 0.060 \text{ M } HCHO_2$ and

$M_2 = \frac{M_1 V_1}{V_2} = \frac{(0.13 \text{ M})(75.0 \text{ mL})}{125.0 \text{ mL}} = 0.078 \text{ M } NaCHO_2$. Acid = $HCHO_2$, so [acid] = [$HCHO_2$] = 0.060 M. Base = CHO_2^-. Since 1 CHO_2^- ion is generated for each $NaCHO_2$, [CHO_2^-] = 0.078 M CHO_2^- = [base]. Then $pH = pK_a + \log \frac{[base]}{[acid]} = -\log(1.8 \times 10^{-4}) + \log \frac{0.078 \text{ M}}{0.060 \text{ M}} = 3.86.$

Check: The units (none) are correct. The magnitude of the answer makes physical sense because pH should be greater than the pK_a of the acid because there is more base than acid.

(b) **Given:** 125.0 mL of 0.10 M NH_3 and 250.0 mL of 0.10 M NH_4Cl **Find:** pH

Other: K_b (NH_3) = 1.79×10^{-5}

Conceptual Plan: Identify acid and base components then mL NH_3, mL NH_4Cl → total mL then

acid = NH_4^+ base = NH_3 total mL = mL NH_3 + mL NH_4Cl

mL NH_3, M NH_3, total mL → buffer M NH_3 and

$M_1 V_1 = M_2 V_2$

mL NH_4Cl, M NH_4Cl, total mL → buffer M NH_4Cl → buffer M NH_4^+ and K_b → pK_b → pK_a then

$M_1 V_1 = M_2 V_2$ $NH_4Cl (aq) \rightarrow NH_4^+ (aq) + Cl^- (aq)$ $pK_b = -\log K_b$ $14 = pK_a + pK_b$

then pK_a, M NH_3, M NH_4^+ → pH.

$pH = pK_a + \log \frac{[base]}{[acid]}$

Solution: total mL = mL NH_3 + mL NH_4Cl = 125.0 mL + 250.0 mL = 375.0 mL. Then since $M_1 V_1 = M_2 V_2$ rearrange to solve for M_2.

$M_2 = \frac{M_1 V_1}{V_2} = \frac{(0.10 \text{ M})(125.0 \text{ mL})}{375.0 \text{ mL}} = 0.033333 \text{ M } NH_3$ and

$M_2 = \frac{M_1 V_1}{V_2} = \frac{(0.10 \text{ M})(250.0 \text{ mL})}{375.0 \text{ mL}} = 0.066667 \text{ M } NH_4Cl$. Base = NH_3, [base] = [NH_3] = 0.033333 M acid = NH_4^+. Since 1 NH_4^+ ion is generated for each NH_4Cl, [NH_4^+] = 0.0666667 M NH_4^+ = [acid]. Since K_b (NH_3) = 1.79×10^{-5},

$pK_b = -\log K_b = -\log(1.79 \times 10^{-5}) = 4.75$. Since $14 = pK_a + pK_b$,

$pK_a = 14 - pK_b = 14 - 4.75 = 9.25$ then $pH = pK_a + \log \frac{[base]}{[acid]} = 9.25 + \log \frac{0.033333 \text{ M}}{0.066667 \text{ M}} = 8.95.$

Check: The units (none) are correct. The magnitude of the answer makes physical sense because pH should be less than the pK_a of the acid because there is more acid than base.

16.42 (a) **Given:** 150.0 mL of 0.25 M HF and 225.0 mL of 0.30 M NaF **Find:** pH
Other: K_a (HF) = 3.5 x 10^{-4}
Conceptual Plan: Identify acid and base components then mL $HCHO_2$, mL $NaCHO_2$ → total mL then
acid = HF base = F^- total mL = mL HF + mL NaF
mL HF, M HF, total mL → buffer M HF and
$M_1 V_1 = M_2 V_2$
mL NaF, M NaF, total mL → buffer M NaF → buffer M F^-
$M_1 V_1 = M_2 V_2$ NaF (*aq*) → Na^+ (*aq*) + F^- (*aq*)
then K_a, M $HCHO_2$, M CHO_2^- → pH.
$\text{pH} = \text{p}K_a + \log\frac{[\text{base}]}{[\text{acid}]}$

Solution: total mL = mL HF + mL NaF = 150.0 mL + 225.0 mL = 375.0 mL. Then since $M_1 V_1 = M_2 V_2$ rearrange to solve for M_2. $M_2 = \frac{M_1 V_1}{V_2} = \frac{(0.25\text{ M})(150.0\text{ mL})}{375.0\text{ mL}} = 0.10$ M HF and

$M_2 = \frac{M_1 V_1}{V_2} = \frac{(0.30\text{ M})(225.0\text{ mL})}{375.0\text{ mL}} = 0.18$ M NaF. Acid = HF, so [acid] = [HF] = 0.10 M. Base = F^-.
Since 1 F^- ion is generated for each NaF, [F^-] = 0.18 M F^- = [base]. Then
$\text{pH} = \text{p}K_a + \log\frac{[\text{base}]}{[\text{acid}]} = -\log(3.5 \times 10^{-4}) + \log\frac{0.18\text{ M}}{0.10\text{ M}} = 3.71.$

Check: The units (none) are correct. The magnitude of the answer makes physical sense because pH should be greater than the pK_a of the acid because there is more base than acid.

(b) **Given:** 175.0 mL of 0.10 M $C_2H_5NH_2$ and 275.0 mL of 0.20 M $C_2H_5NH_3Cl$ **Find:** pH
Other: K_b ($C_2H_5NH_2$) = 5.6 x 10^{-4}
Conceptual Plan: Identify acid and base components then mL $C_2H_5NH_2$, mL $C_2H_5NH_3Cl$ → total mL
acid = $C_2H_5NH_3^+$ base = $C_2H_5NH_2$ total mL = mL $C_2H_5NH_2$ + mL $C_2H_5NH_3Cl$
then mL NH_3, M $C_2H_5NH_2$, total mL → buffer M $C_2H_5NH_2$ and
$M_1 V_1 = M_2 V_2$
mL NH_4Cl, M $C_2H_5NH_3Cl$, total mL → buffer M $C_2H_5NH_3Cl$ → buffer M $C_2H_5NH_3^+$ and
$M_1 V_1 = M_2 V_2$ $C_2H_5NH_3Cl$ (*aq*) → $C_2H_5NH_3^+$ (*aq*) + Cl^- (*aq*)
K_b → pK_b → pK_a then pK_a, M $C_2H_5NH_2$, M $C_2H_5NH_3^+$ → pH.
$\text{p}K_b = -\log K_b$ $14 = \text{p}K_a + \text{p}K_b$ $\text{pH} = \text{p}K_a + \log\frac{[\text{base}]}{[\text{acid}]}$

Solution: total mL = mL $C_2H_5NH_2$ + mL $C_2H_5NH_3Cl$ = 175.0 mL + 275.0 mL = 450.0 mL.
Then since $M_1 V_1 = M_2 V_2$ rearrange to solve for M_2.
$M_2 = \frac{M_1 V_1}{V_2} = \frac{(0.10\text{ M})(175.0\text{ mL})}{450.0\text{ mL}} = 0.03\underline{8}889$ M $C_2H_5NH_2$ and
$M_2 = \frac{M_1 V_1}{V_2} = \frac{(0.20\text{ M})(275.0\text{ mL})}{450.0\text{ mL}} = 0.1\underline{2}222$ M $C_2H_5NH_3Cl$. Base = $C_2H_5NH_2$,
[base] = [$C_2H_5NH_2$] = 0.03$\underline{8}$889 M. Acid = $C_2H_5NH_3^+$. Since 1 $C_2H_5NH_3^+$ ion is generated for each $C_2H_5NH_3Cl$, [$C_2H_5NH_3^+$] = 0.1$\underline{2}$222 M $C_2H_5NH_3^+$ = [acid]. Since K_b ($C_2H_5NH_2$) = 5.6 x 10^{-4},

$\text{p}K_b = -\log K_b = -\log(5.6 \times 10^{-4}) = 3.25$. Since $14 = \text{p}K_a + \text{p}K_b$,
$\text{p}K_a = 14 - \text{p}K_b = 14 - 3.25 = 10.75$ then
$\text{pH} = \text{p}K_a + \log\frac{[\text{base}]}{[\text{acid}]} = 10.75 + \log\frac{0.03\underline{8}889\text{ M}}{0.1\underline{2}222\text{ M}} = 10.25.$

Check: The units (none) are correct. The magnitude of the answer makes physical sense because pH should be less than the pK_a of the acid because there is more acid than base.

16.43 **Given:** NaF / HF buffer at pH = 4.00 **Find:** [NaF] / [HF] **Other:** K_a (HF) = 3.5 x 10^{-4}
Conceptual Plan: Identify acid and base components then pH, K_a → [NaF] / [HF].
acid = HF base = F^- $\text{pH} = \text{p}K_a + \log\frac{[\text{base}]}{[\text{acid}]}$

Solution: $pH = pK_a + \log\frac{[base]}{[acid]} = -\log(3.5 \times 10^{-4}) + \log\frac{[NaF]}{[HF]} = 4.00$. Solve for [NaF]/[HF].

$\log\frac{[NaF]}{[HF]} = 4.00 - 3.46 = 0.54 \rightarrow \frac{[NaF]}{[HF]} = 10^{0.54} = 3.5.$

Check: The units (none) are correct. The magnitude of the answer makes physical sense because the pH is greater than the pK_a of the acid, so there needs to be more base than acid.

16.44 **Given:** CH_3NH_2 / CH_3NH_3Cl buffer at pH = 10.24 **Find:** $[CH_3NH_2]/[CH_3NH_3Cl]$
Other: K_b $(CH_3NH_2) = 4.4 \times 10^{-4}$
Conceptual Plan: Identify acid and base components and $K_b \rightarrow pK_b \rightarrow pK_a$ then

acid = $CH_3NH_3^+$ base = CH_3N $\quad pK_b = -\log K_b \quad 14 = pK_a + pK_b$

pH, K_a $\rightarrow$ $[CH_3NH_2]/[CH_3NH_3Cl]$.

$pH = pK_a + \log\frac{[base]}{[acid]}$

Solution: Since K_b $(CH_3NH_2) = 4.4 \times 10^{-4}$, $pK_b = -\log K_b = -\log(4.4 \times 10^{-4}) = 3.36$. Since $14 = pK_a + pK_b$, $pK_a = 14 - pK_b = 14 - 3.36 = 10.64$ then

$pH = pK_a + \log\frac{[base]}{[acid]} = 10.64 + \log\frac{[CH_3NH_2]}{[CH_3NH_3Cl]} = 10.24$. Solve for $[CH_3NH_2]/[CH_3NH_3Cl]$.

$\log\frac{[CH_3NH_2]}{[CH_3NH_3Cl]} = 10.24 - 10.64 = -0.40 \rightarrow \frac{[CH_3NH_2]}{[CH_3NH_3Cl]} = 10^{-0.40} = 0.39.$

Check: The units (none) are correct. The magnitude of the answer makes physical sense because the pH is less than the pK_a of the acid, so there needs to be less base than acid.

16.45 **Given:** 150.0 mL buffer of 0.15 M benzoic acid at pH = 4.25 **Find:** mass sodium benzoate
Other: K_a $(HC_7H_5O_2) = 6.5 \times 10^{-5}$
Conceptual Plan: Identify acid and base components then pH, K_a, $[HC_7H_5O_2]$ $\rightarrow$ $[NaC_7H_5O_2]$

acid = $HC_7H_5O_2$ base = $C_7H_5O_2^-$ $\quad pH = pK_a + \log\frac{[base]}{[acid]}$

mL $\rightarrow$ L then $[NaC_7H_5O_2]$, L $\rightarrow$ mol $NaC_7H_5O_2$ $\rightarrow$ g $NaC_7H_5O_2$.

$\frac{1\ L}{1000\ mL} \quad M = \frac{mol}{L} \quad \frac{144.11\ g\ NaC_7H_5O_2}{1\ mol\ NaC_7H_5O_2}$

Solution: $pH = pK_a + \log\frac{[base]}{[acid]} = -\log(6.5 \times 10^{-5}) + \log\frac{[NaC_7H_5O_2]}{0.15\ M} = 4.25$. Solve for $[NaC_7H_5O_2]$.

$\log\frac{[NaC_7H_5O_2]}{0.15\ M} = 4.25 - 4.19 = 0.06291 \rightarrow \frac{[NaC_7H_5O_2]}{0.15\ M} = 10^{0.06291} = 1.1559 \rightarrow$

$[NaC_7H_5O_2] = 0.17338$ M.

Convert to moles using $M = \frac{mol}{L}$.

$\frac{0.17338\ mol\ NaC_7H_5O_2}{1\ L} \times 0.150\ L = 0.026007\ mol\ NaC_7H_5O_2 \times \frac{144.11\ g\ NaC_7H_5O_2}{1\ mol\ NaC_7H_5O_2} = 3.7\ g\ NaC_7H_5O_2$.

Check: The units (g) are correct. The magnitude of the answer makes physical sense because the volume of solution is small and the concentration is low, so much less than a mole is needed.

16.46 **Given:** 2.55 L buffer of 0.155 M NH_3 at pH = 9.55 **Find:** mass ammonium chloride
Other: K_b $(NH_3) = 1.79 \times 10^{-5}$
Conceptual Plan: Identify acid and base components then $K_b \rightarrow pK_b \rightarrow pK_a$ then

acid = NH_4^+ base = NH_3 $\quad pK_b = -\log K_b \quad 14 = pK_a + pK_b$

pH, K_a, $[NH_3]$ $\rightarrow$ $[NH_4Cl]$ then $[NH_4Cl]$, L $\rightarrow$ mol NH_4Cl $\rightarrow$ g NH_4Cl.

$pH = pK_a + \log\frac{[base]}{[acid]} \quad M = \frac{mol}{L} \quad \frac{53.49\ g\ NH_4Cl}{1\ mol\ NH_4Cl}$

Solution: Since K_b $(NH_3) = 1.79 \times 10^{-5}$, $pK_b = -\log K_b = -\log(1.79 \times 10^{-5}) = 4.75$. Since $14 = pK_a + pK_b$,

$pK_a = 14 - pK_b = 14 - 4.75 = 9.25$ then $pH = pK_a + \log\frac{[base]}{[acid]} = 9.25 + \log\frac{0.155\ M}{[NH_4Cl]} = 9.55.$

Solve for $[NH_4Cl]$. $\log\frac{0.155\ M}{[NH_4Cl]} = 9.55 - 9.25 = 0.30 \rightarrow \frac{0.155\ M}{[NH_4Cl]} = 10^{0.30} = 1.99526 \rightarrow$

$[NH_4Cl] = 0.07\underline{7}6841$ M. Convert to moles using $M = \frac{\text{mol}}{\text{L}}$.

$$\frac{0.07\underline{7}6841 \text{ mol } NH_4Cl}{1 \not{L}} \times 2.55 \not{L} = 0.19\underline{8}094 \cancel{\text{mol } NH_4Cl} \times \frac{53.49 \text{ g } NH_4Cl}{1 \cancel{\text{mol } NH_4Cl}} = 10.6 \text{ g } NH_4Cl.$$

Check: The units (g) are correct. The magnitude of the answer makes physical sense because the volume of solution is large and the concentration is low, so less than a mole is needed.

16.47 (a) **Given:** 250.0 mL buffer 0.250 M $HC_2H_3O_2$ and 0.250 M $NaC_2H_3O_2$ **Find:** initial pH
Other: K_a ($HC_2H_3O_2$) = 1.8×10^{-5}

Conceptual Plan: Identify acid and base components then M $NaC_2H_3O_2$ → M $C_2H_3O_2^-$ then

acid = $HC_2H_3O_2$ base = $C_2H_3O_2^-$ $\quad$ $NaC_2H_3O_2\ (aq) \rightarrow Na^+\ (aq) + C_2H_3O_2^-\ (aq)$

M $HC_2H_3O_2$, M $C_2H_3O_2^-$ → pH.

$$pH = pK_a + \log\frac{[\text{base}]}{[\text{acid}]}$$

Solution: Acid = $HC_2H_3O_2$, so [acid] = $[HC_2H_3O_2]$ = 0.250 M. Base = $C_2H_3O_2^-$. Since 1 $C_2H_3O_2^-$ ion is generated for each $NaC_2H_3O_2$, $[C_2H_3O_2^-]$ = 0.250 M $C_2H_3O_2^-$ = [base]. Then

$$pH = pK_a + \log\frac{[\text{base}]}{[\text{acid}]} = -\log(1.8 \times 10^{-5}) + \log\frac{0.250 \cancel{M}}{0.250 \cancel{M}} = 4.74.$$

Check: The units (none) are correct. The magnitude of the answer makes physical sense because pH is equal to the pK_a of the acid because there are equal amounts of acid and base.

(b) **Given:** 250.0 mL buffer 0.250 M $HC_2H_3O_2$ and 0.250 M $NaC_2H_3O_2$, add 0.0050 mol HCl **Find:** pH
Other: K_a ($HC_2H_3O_2$) = 1.8×10^{-5}

Conceptual Plan: Part I: Stoichiometry:

mL → L then $[NaC_2H_3O_2]$, L → mol $NaC_2H_3O_2$ and $[HC_2H_3O_2]$, L → mol $HC_2H_3O_2$

$\frac{1 \text{ L}}{1000 \text{ mL}}$ $\quad$ $M = \frac{\text{mol}}{\text{L}}$ $\quad$ $M = \frac{\text{mol}}{\text{L}}$

write balanced equation then

$HCl + NaC_2H_3O_2 \rightarrow HC_2H_3O_2 + NaCl$

mol $NaC_2H_3O_2$, mol $HC_2H_3O_2$, mol HCl → mol $NaC_2H_3O_2$, mol $HC_2H_3O_2$ then

set up stoichiometry table

Part II: Equilibrium:

mol $NaC_2H_3O_2$, mol $HC_2H_3O_2$, L, K_a → pH

$$pH = pK_a + \log\frac{[\text{base}]}{[\text{acid}]}$$

Solution: $250.0 \cancel{\text{mL}} \times \frac{1 \text{ L}}{1000 \cancel{\text{mL}}} = 0.2500$ L then

$$\frac{0.250 \text{ mol } HC_2H_3O_2}{1 \not{L}} \times 0.250 \not{L} = 0.0625 \text{ mol } HC_2H_3O_2 \text{ and}$$

$$\frac{0.250 \text{ mol } NaC_2H_3O_2}{1 \not{L}} \times 0.250 \not{L} = 0.0625 \text{ mol } NaC_2H_3O_2.$$ Set up a table to track changes:

	$HCl\ (aq)$ +	$NaC_2H_3O_2\ (aq)$ →	$HC_2H_3O_2\ (aq)$ +	$NaCl\ (aq)$
Before addition	≈ 0.00 mol	0.0625 mol	0.0625 mol	0.00 mol
Addition	0.0050 mol	—	—	—
After addition	≈ 0.00 mol	0.0575 mol	0.0675 mol	0.0050 mol

Since the amount of HCl is small, there are still significant amounts of both buffer components, so the Henderson–Hasselbalch equation can be used to calculate the new pH.

$$pH = pK_a + \log\frac{[\text{base}]}{[\text{acid}]} = -\log(1.8 \times 10^{-5}) + \log\frac{\frac{0.0575 \cancel{\text{mol}}}{0.250 \cancel{\text{L}}}}{\frac{0.0675 \cancel{\text{mol}}}{0.250 \cancel{\text{L}}}} = 4.68.$$

Check: The units (none) are correct. The magnitude of the answer makes physical sense because the pH dropped slightly when acid was added.

(c) **Given:** 250.0 mL buffer 0.250 M $HC_2H_3O_2$ and 0.250 M $NaC_2H_3O_2$, add 0.0050 mol NaOH
Find: pH **Other:** K_a ($HC_2H_3O_2$) = 1.8×10^{-5}

Conceptual Plan: Part I: Stoichiometry:

mL → L then $[NaC_2H_3O_2]$, L → mol $NaC_2H_3O_2$ and $[HC_2H_3O_2]$, L → mol $HC_2H_3O_2$

$\frac{1\ L}{1000\ mL}$ $\quad M = \frac{mol}{L}$ $\quad M = \frac{mol}{L}$

write balanced equation then

$NaOH + HC_2H_3O_2 \rightarrow H_2O + NaC_2H_3O_2$

mol $NaC_2H_3O_2$, mol $HC_2H_3O_2$, mol NaOH → mol $NaC_2H_3O_2$, mol $HC_2H_3O_2$ then

set up stoichiometry table

Part II: Equilibrium:

mol $NaC_2H_3O_2$, mol $HC_2H_3O_2$, L, K_a → pH

$$pH = pK_a + \log\frac{[base]}{[acid]}$$

Solution: $250.0\ \cancel{mL} \times \frac{1\ L}{1000\ \cancel{mL}} = 0.2500\ L$ then

$\frac{0.250\ mol\ HC_2H_3O_2}{1\ \cancel{L}} \times 0.2500\ \cancel{L} = 0.0625\ mol\ HC_2H_3O_2$ and

$\frac{0.250\ mol\ NaC_2H_3O_2}{1\ \cancel{L}} \times 0.2500\ \cancel{L} = 0.0625\ mol\ NaC_2H_3O_2$ set up a table to track changes:

	$NaOH\ (aq)$ +	$HC_2H_3O_2\ (aq)$ →	$NaC_2H_3O_2\ (aq)$ +	$H_2O\ (l)$
Before addition	≈ 0.00 mol	0.0625 mol	0.0625 mol	—
Addition	0.0050 mol	—	—	—
After addition	≈ 0.00 mol	0.0575 mol	0.0675 mol	—

Since the amount of NaOH is small, there are still significant amounts of both buffer components, so the Henderson–Hasselbalch equation can be used to calculate the new pH.

$$pH = pK_a + \log\frac{[base]}{[acid]} = -\log(1.8 \times 10^{-5}) + \log\frac{\frac{0.0675\ \cancel{mol}}{\cancel{0.2500\ L}}}{\frac{0.0575\ \cancel{mol}}{\cancel{0.2500\ L}}} = 4.81.$$

Check: The units (none) are correct. The magnitude of the answer makes physical sense because the pH rose slightly when base was added.

16.48 (a) **Given:** 100.0 mL buffer 0.175 M HClO and 0.150 M NaClO **Find:** initial pH

Other: K_a (HClO) = 2.9×10^{-8}

Conceptual Plan: Identify acid and base components then M NaClO → M ClO^- then

acid = HClO base = ClO^- $\quad NaClO\ (aq) \rightarrow Na^+\ (aq) + ClO^-\ (aq)$

M HClO, M ClO^- → pH.

$$pH = pK_a + \log\frac{[base]}{[acid]}$$

Solution: Acid = HClO, so [acid] = [HClO] = 0.175 M. Base = ClO^-. Since 1 ClO^- ion is generated for each NaClO, [ClO^-] = 0.150 M ClO^- = [base].

Then $pH = pK_a + \log\frac{[base]}{[acid]} = -\log(2.9 \times 10^{-8}) + \log\frac{0.150\ \cancel{M}}{0.175\ \cancel{M}} = 7.47.$

Check: The units (none) are correct. The magnitude of the answer makes physical sense because pH is less than the pK_a of the acid because there is more acid than base.

(b) **Given:** 100.0 mL buffer 0.175 M HClO and 0.150 M NaClO, add 150.0 mg HBr **Find:** pH

Other: K_a (HClO) = 2.9×10^{-8}

Conceptual Plan: Part I: Stoichiometry:

mL → L then [NaClO], L → mol NaClO and [HClO], L → mol HClO and

$\frac{1\ L}{1000\ mL}$ $\quad M = \frac{mol}{L}$ $\quad M = \frac{mol}{L}$

mg HBr → g HBr → mol HBr write balanced equation then

$\frac{1\ g\ HBr}{1000\ mg\ HBr}$ $\quad \frac{1\ mol\ HBr}{71.91\ g\ HBr}$ $\quad HBr + NaClO \rightarrow HClO + NaBr$

mol NaClO, mol HClO, mol HBr → mol NaClO, mol HClO then

set up stoichiometry table

Part II: Equilibrium:
mol NaClO, mol HClO, L, K_a → pH

$$pH = pK_a + \log\frac{[base]}{[acid]}$$

Solution: $100.0\ \text{mL} \times \frac{1\ \text{L}}{1000\ \text{mL}} = 0.1000\ \text{L}$ then $\frac{0.175\ \text{mol HClO}}{1\ \text{L}} \times 0.1000\ \text{L} = 0.0175\ \text{mol HClO}$ and $\frac{0.150\ \text{mol NaClO}}{1\ \text{L}} \times 0.1000\ \text{L} = 0.0150\ \text{mol NaClO}$ and

$150.0\ \text{mg HBr} \times \frac{1\ \text{g HBr}}{1000\ \text{mg HBr}} \times \frac{1\ \text{mol HBr}}{80.91\ \text{g HBr}} = 0.001853911\ \text{mol HBr}$ then set up a table to track changes:

	HBr (*aq*) +	NaClO (*aq*) →	HClO (*aq*) +	NaBr (*aq*)
Before addition	≈ 0.00 mol	0.0150 mol	0.0175 mol	0.00 mol
Addition	0.001853911 mol	—	—	—
After addition	≈ 0.00 mol	0.013146 mol	0.015646 mol	0.001853911 mol

Since the amount of HBr is small, there are still significant amounts of both buffer components, so the Henderson–Hasselbalch equation can be used to calculate the new pH.

$$pH = pK_a + \log\frac{[base]}{[acid]} = -\log(2.9 \times 10^{-8}) + \log\frac{\frac{0.013146\ \text{mol}}{0.1000\ \text{L}}}{\frac{0.015646\ \text{mol}}{0.1000\ \text{L}}} = 7.46.$$

Check: The units (none) are correct. The magnitude of the answer makes physical sense because the pH dropped slightly when acid was added. The pH is closer to the pK_a of the acid than at the start.

(c) **Given:** 100.0 mL buffer 0.175 M HClO and 0.150 M NaClO, add 85.0 mg NaOH **Find:** pH
Other: K_a (HClO) = 2.9×10^{-8}
Conceptual Plan: Part I: Stoichiometry:
mL → L then [NaClO], L → mol NaClO and [HClO], L → mol HClO and

$\frac{1\ \text{L}}{1000\ \text{mL}}$ $\quad M = \frac{mol}{L}$ $\quad M = \frac{mol}{L}$

mg NaOH → g NaOH → mol NaOH the write balanced equation then

$\frac{1\ \text{g NaOH}}{1000\ \text{mg NaOH}}$ $\quad \frac{1\ \text{mol NaOH}}{40.00\ \text{g NaOH}}$ $\quad NaOH + HClO \rightarrow H_2O + NaClO$

mol NaClO, mol HClO, mol NaOH → mol NaClO, mol HClO then

set up stoichiometry table

Part II: Equilibrium:
mol NaClO, mol HClO, L, K_a → pH

$$pH = pK_a + \log\frac{[base]}{[acid]}$$

Solution: $100.0\ \text{mL} \times \frac{1\ \text{L}}{1000\ \text{mL}} = 0.1000\ \text{L}$ then $\frac{0.175\ \text{mol HClO}}{1\ \text{L}} \times 0.1000\ \text{L} = 0.0175\ \text{mol HClO}$ and $\frac{0.150\ \text{mol NaClO}}{1\ \text{L}} \times 0.1000\ \text{L} = 0.0150\ \text{mol NaClO}$ and

$85.0\ \text{mg NaOH} \times \frac{1\ \text{g NaOH}}{1000\ \text{mg NaOH}} \times \frac{1\ \text{mol NaOH}}{40.00\ \text{g NaOH}} = 0.00213\ \text{mol NaOH}$

then set up a table to track changes:

	NaOH (*aq*) +	HClO (*aq*) →	NaClO (*aq*) +	H_2O (*l*)
Before addition	≈ 0.00 mol	0.0175 mol	0.0150 mol	—
Addition	0.00213 mol	—	—	—
After addition	≈ 0.00 mol	0.0154 mol	0.0171 mol	—

Since the amount of NaOH is small, there are still significant amounts of both buffer components, so the Henderson–Hasselbalch equation can be used to calculate the new pH.

$$pH = pK_a + \log\frac{[base]}{[acid]} = -\log(2.9 \times 10^{-8}) + \log\frac{\frac{0.0171\ \text{mol}}{0.1000\ \text{L}}}{\frac{0.0154\ \text{mol}}{0.1000\ \text{L}}} = 7.58.$$

Check: The units (none) are correct. The magnitude of the answer makes physical sense because the pH rose slightly when base was added.

16.49 (a) **Given:** 500.0 mL pure water **Find:** initial pH and after adding 0.010 mol HCl

Conceptual Plan: pure water has a pH of 7.00 then mL → L then mol HCl, L → $[H_3O^+]$ → pH

$\frac{1\ L}{1000\ mL}$ $M = \frac{mol}{L}$ $pH = -\log[H_3O^+]$

Solution: Pure water has a pH of 7.00 so initial pH = 7.00, $500.0\ \text{mL} \times \frac{1\ L}{1000\ \text{mL}} = 0.5000\ L$,

then $M = \frac{mol}{L} = \frac{0.010\ mol\ HCl}{0.5000\ L} = 0.020\ M\ HCl$. Since HCl is a strong acid, it dissociates completely, so $pH = -\log[H_3O^+] = -\log(0.020) = 1.70$.

Check: The units (none) are correct. The magnitudes of the answers make physical sense because the pH starts neutral and then drops significantly when acid is added and there is no buffer present.

(b) **Given:** 500.0 mL buffer 0.125 M $HC_2H_3O_2$ and 0.115 M $NaC_2H_3O_2$

Find: initial pH and after adding 0.010 mol HCl **Other:** $K_a\ (HC_2H_3O_2) = 1.8 \times 10^{-5}$

Conceptual Plan: initial pH:

Identify acid and base components then M $NaC_2H_3O_2$ → M $C_2H_3O_2^-$ then

acid = $HC_2H_3O_2$ base = $C_2H_3O_2^-$ $NaC_2H_3O_2\ (aq) \rightarrow Na^+\ (aq) + C_2H_3O_2^-\ (aq)$

M $HC_2H_3O_2$, M $C_2H_3O_2^-$ → pH

$pH = pK_a + \log\frac{[base]}{[acid]}$

pH after HCl addition: Part I: Stoichiometry:

mL → L then $[NaC_2H_3O_2]$, L → mol $NaC_2H_3O_2$ and $[HC_2H_3O_2]$, L → mol $HC_2H_3O_2$

$\frac{1\ L}{1000\ mL}$ $M = \frac{mol}{L}$ $M = \frac{mol}{L}$

write balanced equation then

$HCl + NaC_2H_3O_2 \rightarrow HC_2H_3O_2 + NaCl$

mol $NaC_2H_3O_2$, mol $HC_2H_3O_2$, mol HCl → mol $NaC_2H_3O_2$, mol $HC_2H_3O_2$ then

set up stoichiometry table

Part II: Equilibrium:

mol $NaC_2H_3O_2$, mol $HC_2H_3O_2$, L, K_a → pH

$pH = pK_a + \log\frac{[base]}{[acid]}$

Solution: initial pH: Acid = $HC_2H_3O_2$, so [acid] = $[HC_2H_3O_2]$ = 0.125 M. Base = $C_2H_3O_2^-$. Since 1 $C_2H_3O_2^-$ ion is generated for each $NaC_2H_3O_2$, $[C_2H_3O_2^-]$ = 0.115 M $C_2H_3O_2^-$ = [base]. Then

$$pH = pK_a + \log\frac{[base]}{[acid]} = -\log(1.8 \times 10^{-5}) + \log\frac{0.115\ \text{M}}{0.125\ \text{M}} = 4.71.$$

pH after HCl addition:

$500.0\ \text{mL} \times \frac{1\ L}{1000\ \text{mL}} = 0.5000\ L$ then $\frac{0.125\ mol\ HC_2H_3O_2}{1\ \text{L}} \times 0.5000\ \text{L} = 0.0625\ mol\ HC_2H_3O_2$ and $\frac{0.115\ mol\ NaC_2H_3O_2}{1\ \text{L}} \times 0.5000\ \text{L} = 0.0575\ mol\ NaC_2H_3O_2$. Set up a table to track changes:

	HCl (*aq*) +	$NaC_2H_3O_2$ (*aq*) →	$HC_2H_3O_2$ (*aq*) +	NaCl (*aq*)
Before addition	≈ 0.00 mol	0.0575 mol	0.0625 mol	0.00 mol
Addition	0.010 mol	—	—	—
After addition	≈ 0.00 mol	0.04̲75 mol	0.07̲25 mol	0.10 mol

Since the amount of HCl is small, there are still significant amounts of both buffer components, so the Henderson–Hasselbalch equation can be used to calculate the new pH.

$$pH = pK_a + \log\frac{[base]}{[acid]} = -\log(1.8 \times 10^{-5}) + \log\frac{\frac{0.0475\ \text{mol}}{0.5000\ \text{L}}}{\frac{0.0725\ \text{mol}}{0.5000\ \text{L}}} = 4.56.$$

Check: The units (none) are correct. The magnitudes of the answers make physical sense because the pH started below the pK_a of the acid and it dropped slightly when acid was added.

(c) **Given:** 500.0 mL buffer 0.155 M $CH_3CH_2NH_2$ and 0.145 M $CH_3CH_2NH_3Cl$
Find: initial pH and after adding 0.010 mol HCl **Other:** K_b ($CH_3CH_2NH_2$) = 5.6 x 10^{-4}
Conceptual Plan: initial pH:
Identify acid and base components then M $CH_3CH_2NH_3Cl$ → M $CH_3CH_2NH_3^+$
acid = $C_2H_5NH_3^+$ base = $C_2H_5NH_2$ $C_2H_5NH_3Cl\ (aq) \rightarrow C_2H_5NH_3^+\ (aq) + Cl^-\ (aq)$
and K_b → pK_b → pK_a then pK_a, M $CH_3CH_2NH_2$, M $CH_3CH_2NH_3^+$ → pH
$pK_b = -\log K_b \quad 14 = pK_a + pK_b$ $\quad pH = pK_a + \log\frac{[base]}{[acid]}$
pH after HCl addition: Part I: Stoichiometry:
mL → L then [$CH_3CH_2NH_2$], L → mol $CH_3CH_2NH_2$ and
$\frac{1\ L}{1000\ mL}$ $\quad M = \frac{mol}{L}$
[$CH_3CH_2NH_3Cl$], L → mol $CH_3CH_2NH_3Cl$ write balanced equation then
$M = \frac{mol}{L}$ $\quad HCl + CH_3CH_2NH_2 \rightarrow CH_3CH_2NH_3Cl$
mol $CH_3CH_2NH_2$, mol $CH_3CH_2NH_3Cl$, mol HCl → mol $CH_3CH_2NH_2$, mol $CH_3CH_2NH_3Cl$ then
set up stoichiometry table
Part II: Equilibrium:
mol $CH_3CH_2NH_2$, mol $CH_3CH_2NH_3Cl$, L, K_a → pH
$pH = pK_a + \log\frac{[base]}{[acid]}$

Solution: Base = $CH_3CH_2NH_2$, [base] = [$CH_3CH_2NH_2$] = 0.155 M, acid = $CH_3CH_2NH_3^+$. Since 1 $CH_3CH_2NH_3^+$ ion is generated for each $CH_3CH_2NH_3Cl$, [$CH_3CH_2NH_3^+$] = 0.145 M $CH_3CH_2NH_3^+$ = [acid]. Since K_b ($CH_3CH_2NH_2$) = 5.6 x 10^{-4}, $pK_b = -\log K_b = -\log(5.6 \times 10^{-4}) = 3.25$. Since $14 = pK_a + pK_b$, $pK_a = 14 - pK_b = 14 - 3.25 = 10.75$ then

$$pH = pK_a + \log\frac{[base]}{[acid]} = 10.75 + \log\frac{0.155\ \cancel{M}}{0.145\ \cancel{M}} = 10.78.$$

pH after HCl addition: $500.0\ \cancel{mL} \times \frac{1\ L}{1000\ \cancel{mL}} = 0.5000\ L$ then

$\frac{0.155\ mol\ CH_3CH_2NH_2}{1\ \cancel{L}} \times 0.5000\ \cancel{L} = 0.0775\ mol\ CH_3CH_2NH_2$ and

$\frac{0.145\ mol\ CH_3CH_2NH_3Cl}{1\ \cancel{L}} \times 0.5000\ \cancel{L} = 0.0725\ mol\ CH_3CH_2NH_3Cl$. Set up a table to track changes:

	HCl (*aq*) +	$CH_3CH_2NH_2$ (*aq*) →	$CH_3CH_2NH_3Cl$ (*aq*)
Before addition	≈ 0.00 mol	0.0775 mol	0.0725 mol
Addition	0.010 mol	—	—
After addition	≈ 0.00 mol	0.0675 mol	0.0825 mol

Since the amount of HCl is small, there are still significant amounts of both buffer components, so the Henderson–Hasselbalch equation can be used to calculate the new pH.

$$pH = pK_a + \log\frac{[base]}{[acid]} = 10.75 + \log\frac{\frac{0.0675\ \cancel{mol}}{\cancel{0.5000\ L}}}{\frac{0.0825\ \cancel{mol}}{\cancel{0.5000\ L}}} = 10.66.$$

Check: The units (none) are correct. The magnitudes of the answers make physical sense because the initial pH should be greater than the pK_a of the acid because there is more base than acid and the pH drops slightly when acid is added.

16.50 (a) **Given:** 250.0 mL pure water **Find:** initial pH and after adding 0.010 mol NaOH
Conceptual Plan:
pure water has a pH of 7.00 then mL → L then mol NaOH, L → [OH^-] → [H_3O^+] → pH
$\frac{1\ L}{1000\ mL}$ $\quad M = \frac{mol}{L} \quad K_w = [H_3O^+][OH^-] \quad pH = -\log[H_3O^+]$

Solution: Pure water has a pH of 7.00 so initial pH = 7.00 then $250.0\ \cancel{mL} \times \frac{1\ L}{1000\ \cancel{mL}} = 0.2500\ L$ then

$M = \frac{mol}{L} = \frac{0.010\ mol\ NaOH}{0.2500\ L} = 0.040\ M\ NaOH$. Since NaOH is a strong base, it dissociates completely, so [OH^-] = 0.040 M. $K_w = [H_3O^+][OH^-]$ so

$[H_3O^+] = \frac{K_w}{[OH^-]} = \frac{1.0 \times 10^{-14}}{0.040} = 2.5 \times 10^{-13}$ M and

$pH = -\log [H_3O^+] = -\log (2.5 \times 10^{-13}) = 12.60.$

Check: The units (none) are correct. The magnitudes of the answers make physical sense because the pH started neutral and then rose significantly when base was added and there is no buffer present.

(b) **Given:** 250.0 mL buffer 0.195 M $HCHO_2$ and 0.275 M $KCHO_2$
Find: initial pH and after adding 0.010 mol NaOH **Other:** K_a ($HCHO_2$) = 1.8×10^{-4}
Conceptual Plan: initial pH:
Identify acid and base components then M $KCHO_2$ → M CHO_2^- then

acid = $HCHO_2$ base = CHO_2^- $KCHO_2\ (aq) \rightarrow K^+\ (aq) + CHO_2^-\ (aq)$

M $HCHO_2$, M CHO_2^- → pH

$pH = pK_a + \log \frac{[base]}{[acid]}$

pH after NaOH addition: Part I: Stoichiometry:
mL → L then [$KCHO_2$], L → mol $KCHO_2$ and [$HCHO_2$], L → mol $HCHO_2$

$\frac{1\ L}{1000\ mL}$ $M = \frac{mol}{L}$ $M = \frac{mol}{L}$

write balanced equation then

$NaOH + HCHO_2 \rightarrow NaCHO_2 + H_2O$

mol CHO_2^-, mol $HCHO_2$, mol NaOH → mol $NaCHO_2$, mol $HCHO_2$ then

set up stoichiometry table

Part II: Equilibrium:
mol $NaC_2H_3O_2$, mol $HC_2H_3O_2$, L, K_a → pH

$pH = pK_a + \log \frac{[base]}{[acid]}$

Solution: initial pH: Acid = $HCHO_2$, so [acid] = [$HCHO_2$] = 0.195 M. Base = CHO_2^-.
Since 1 CHO_2^- ion is generated for each $KCHO_2$, [CHO_2^-] = 0.275 M CHO_2^- = [base]. Then

$$pH = pK_a + \log \frac{[base]}{[acid]} = -\log (1.8 \times 10^{-4}) + \log \frac{0.275\ \cancel{M}}{0.195\ \cancel{M}} = 3.89.$$

pH after NaOH addition: $250.0\ \cancel{mL} \times \frac{1\ L}{1000\ \cancel{mL}} = 0.2500$ L then

$\frac{0.195\ mol\ HCHO_2}{1\ \cancel{L}} \times 0.2500\ \cancel{L} = 0.048\underline{7}5$ mol $HCHO_2$ and

$\frac{0.275\ mol\ KCHO_2}{1\ \cancel{L}} \times 0.2500\ \cancel{L} = 0.068\underline{7}5$ mol $KCHO_2$

Set up a table to track changes:

	$NaOH\ (aq)$ +	$HCHO_2\ (aq)$ →	$NaCHO_2\ (aq)$ +	$H_2O\ (l)$
Before addition	≈ 0.00 mol	$0.048\underline{7}5$ mol	$0.068\underline{7}5$ mol	—
Addition	0.010 mol	—	—	—
After addition	≈ 0.00 mol	$0.03\underline{8}75$ mol	$0.07\underline{8}75$ mol	—

Since the amount of NaOH is small, there are still significant amounts of both buffer components, so the Henderson–Hasselbalch equation can be used to calculate the new pH.

$$pH = pK_a + \log \frac{[base]}{[acid]} = -\log (1.8 \times 10^{-4}) + \log \frac{\frac{0.07\underline{8}75\ \cancel{mol}}{\cancel{0.2500\ L}}}{\frac{0.03\underline{8}75\ \cancel{mol}}{\cancel{0.2500\ L}}} = 4.05.$$

Check: The units (none) are correct. The magnitudes of the answers make physical sense because the pH started above the pK_a of the acid and it rose slightly when base was added.

(c) **Given:** 250.0 mL buffer 0.255 M $CH_3CH_2NH_2$ and 0.235 M $CH_3CH_2NH_3Cl$
Find: initial pH and after adding 0.010 mol NaOH **Other:** K_b ($CH_3CH_2NH_2$) = 5.6×10^{-4}
Conceptual Plan: initial pH:
Identify acid and base components then M $CH_3CH_2NH_3Cl$ → M $CH_3CH_2NH_3^+$

acid = $C_2H_5NH_3^+$ base = $C_2H_5NH_2$ $C_2H_5NH_3Cl\ (aq) \rightarrow C_2H_5NH_3^+\ (aq) + Cl^-\ (aq)$

and $K_b \rightarrow pK_b \rightarrow pK_a$ then pK_a, M $CH_3CH_2NH_2$, M $CH_3CH_2NH_3^+ \rightarrow$ pH

$pK_b = -\log K_b \quad 14 = pK_a + pK_b \qquad pH = pK_a + \log\frac{[base]}{[acid]}$

pH after NaOH addition: Part I: Stoichiometry:

mL $\rightarrow$ L then [$CH_3CH_2NH_2$], L $\rightarrow$ mol $CH_3CH_2NH_2$ and

$\frac{1\ L}{1000\ mL} \qquad M = \frac{mol}{L}$

[$CH_3CH_2NH_3Cl$], L $\rightarrow$ mol $CH_3CH_2NH_3Cl$

$M = \frac{mol}{L}$

write balanced equation then

$NaOH + CH_3CH_2NH_3Cl \rightarrow CH_3CH_2NH_2 + NaCl + H_2O$

mol $CH_3CH_2NH_2$, mol $CH_3CH_2NH_3Cl$, mol NaOH $\rightarrow$ mol $CH_3CH_2NH_2$, mol $CH_3CH_2NH_3Cl$

set up stoichiometry table

Part II: Equilibrium:

mol $CH_3CH_2NH_2$, mol $CH_3CH_2NH_3Cl$, L, $K_a \rightarrow$ pH

$pH = pK_a + \log\frac{[base]}{[acid]}$

Solution: Base = $CH_3CH_2NH_2$, [base] = [$CH_3CH_2NH_2$] = 0.255 M Acid = $CH_3CH_2NH_3^+$. Since 1 $CH_3CH_2NH_3^+$ ion is generated for each $CH_3CH_2NH_3Cl$, [$CH_3CH_2NH_3^+$] = 0.235 M $CH_3CH_2NH_3^+$ = [acid]. Since K_b ($CH_3CH_2NH_2$) = 5.6 x 10^{-4}, $pK_b = -\log K_b = -\log(5.6 \times 10^{-4}) = 3.25$. Since $14 = pK_a + pK_b$, $pK_a = 14 - pK_b = 14 - 3.25 = 10.75$ then

$$pH = pK_a + \log\frac{[base]}{[acid]} = 10.75 + \log\frac{0.255\ \cancel{M}}{0.235\ \cancel{M}} = 10.78.$$

pH after HCl addition: $250.0\ \cancel{mL} \times \frac{1\ L}{1000\ \cancel{mL}} = 0.2500$ L then

$\frac{0.255\ mol\ CH_3CH_2NH_2}{1\ \cancel{L}} \times 0.2500\ \cancel{L} = 0.06375$ mol $CH_3CH_2NH_2$ and

$\frac{0.235\ mol\ CH_3CH_2NH_3Cl}{1\ \cancel{L}} \times 0.2500\ \cancel{L} = 0.05875$ mol $CH_3CH_2NH_3Cl$. Set up a table to track changes:

	NaOH (*aq*) +	$CH_3CH_2NH_3Cl$ (*aq*) $\rightarrow$	$CH_3CH_2NH_2$ (*aq*) +	NaCl (*aq*) +	H_2O (*aq*)
Before addition	≈ 0.00 mol	0.05875 mol	0.06375 mol	0.00 mol	—
Addition	0.010 mol	—	—	—	—
After addition	≈ 0.00 mol	0.04875 mol	0.07375 mol		

Since the amount of NaOH is small, there are still significant amounts of both buffer components, so the Henderson–Hasselbalch equation can be used to calculate the new pH.

$$pH = pK_a + \log\frac{[base]}{[acid]} = 10.75 + \log\frac{\frac{0.07375\ \cancel{mol}}{\cancel{0.2500\ L}}}{\frac{0.04875\ \cancel{mol}}{\cancel{0.2500\ L}}} = 10.93.$$

Check: The units (none) are correct. The magnitudes of the answers make physical sense because the initial pH should be greater than the pK_a of the acid because there is more base than acid and the pH rises slightly when base is added.

16.51 **Given:** 350.00 mL 0.150 M HF and 0.150 M NaF buffer
Find: mass NaOH to raise pH to 4.00 and mass NaOH to raise pH to 4.00 with buffer concentrations raised to 0.350 M
Other: K_a (HF) = 3.5 x 10^{-4}
Conceptual Plan: Identify acid and base components. Since [NaF] = [HF] then initial pH = pK_a.

acid = HF base = F^- $\qquad pH = pK_a$

final pH, $pK_a \rightarrow$ [NaF]/[HF] and mL $\rightarrow$ L then [HF], L $\rightarrow$ mol HF and [NaF], L $\rightarrow$ mol NaF

$pH = pK_a + \log\frac{[base]}{[acid]} \qquad \frac{1\ L}{1000\ mL} \qquad M = \frac{mol}{L} \qquad M = \frac{mol}{L}$

then write balanced equation then

$NaOH + HF \rightarrow NaF + H_2O$

mol HF, mol NaF, [NaF]/[HF] → mol NaOH → g NaOH.

set up stoichiometry table $\frac{40.00 \text{ g NaOH}}{1 \text{ mol NaOH}}$

Finally, when the buffer concentrations are raised to 0.350 M, simply multiply the g NaOH by ratio of concentrations (0.350 M / 0.150 M).

Solution: initial pH = $pK_a = -\log(3.5 \times 10^{-4}) = 3.46$ then

$pH = pK_a + \log\frac{[\text{base}]}{[\text{acid}]} = -\log(3.5 \times 10^{-4}) + \log\frac{[\text{NaF}]}{[\text{HF}]} = 4.00$. Solve for [NaF] / [HF].

$\log\frac{[\text{NaF}]}{[\text{HF}]} = 4.00 - 3.46 = 0.54 \rightarrow \frac{[\text{NaF}]}{[\text{HF}]} = 10^{0.54} = 3.5$. $350.0 \text{ mL} \times \frac{1 \text{ L}}{1000 \text{ mL}} = 0.3500 \text{ L}$ then

$\frac{0.150 \text{ mol HF}}{1 \text{ L}} \times 0.3500 \text{ L} = 0.0525 \text{ mol HF}$ and $\frac{0.150 \text{ mol NaF}}{1 \text{ L}} \times 0.3500 \text{ L} = 0.0525 \text{ mol NaF}$

Set up a table to track changes:

	$NaOH\ (aq)$ +	$HF\ (aq)$ →	$NaF\ (aq)$ +	$H_2O\ (aq)$
Before addition	≈ 0.00 mol	0.0525 mol	0.0125 mol	—
Addition	x	—	—	—
After addition	≈ 0.00 mol	$(0.0525 - x)$ mol	$(0.0525 + x)$ mol	—

Since $\frac{[\text{NaF}]}{[\text{HF}]} = 3.5 = \frac{(0.0525 + x) \text{ mol}}{(0.0525 - x) \text{ mol}}$, solve for x. Note that the ratio of moles is the same as the ratio of concentrations, since the volume for both terms is the same. $3.5\,(0.0525 - x) = (0.0525 + x) \rightarrow 0.18375 - 3.5\,x = 0.0525 + x \rightarrow 0.13125 = 4.5\,x \rightarrow x = 0.029167$ mol NaOH then

$0.029167 \text{ mol NaOH} \times \frac{40.00 \text{ g NaOH}}{1 \text{ mol NaOH}} = 1.1667 \text{ g NaOH} = 1.2 \text{ g NaOH}$. Finally multiply the NaOH mass by the ratio of concentrations $1.1667 \text{ g NaOH} \times \frac{0.350 \text{ M}}{0.150 \text{ M}} = 2.7 \text{ g NaOH}$.

Check: The units (g) are correct. The magnitudes of the answers make physical sense because there is much less than a mole of each of the buffer components, so there must be much less than a mole of NaOH. The higher the buffer concentrations, the higher the buffer capacity and the mass of NaOH it can neutralize.

16.52 **Given:** 100.00 mL 0.100 M NH_3 and 0.125 M NH_4Br buffer

Find: mass HCl to lower pH to 9.00 and mass HCl to lower pH to 9.00 with buffer concentrations raised to 0.250 M NH_3 and 0.400 M NH_4Br

Other: $K_b\ (NH_3) = 1.79 \times 10^{-5}$

Conceptual Plan: Identify acid and base components then $K_b \rightarrow pK_b \rightarrow pK_a$ then

acid = NH_4^+ base = NH_3 $\qquad pK_b = -\log K_b \quad 14 = pK_a + pK_b$

final pH, $pK_a \rightarrow [NH_3]/[NH_4^+]$ and mL → L then $[NH_3]$, L → mol NH_3 and

$pH = pK_a + \log\frac{[\text{base}]}{[\text{acid}]} \qquad \frac{1 \text{ L}}{1000 \text{ mL}} \qquad M = \frac{\text{mol}}{\text{L}}$

$[NH_4^+]$, L → mol NH_4^+ then write balanced equation then

$M = \frac{\text{mol}}{\text{L}} \qquad H^+ + NH_3 \rightarrow NH_4^+$

mol NH_3, mol NH_4^+, $[NH_3]/[NH_4^+]$ → mol HCl → g HCl.

set up stoichiometry table $\frac{36.46 \text{ g HCl}}{1 \text{ mol HCl}}$

Solution: Since $K_b\ (NH_3) = 1.79 \times 10^{-5}$, $pK_b = -\log K_b = -\log(1.79 \times 10^{-5}) = 4.75$. Since $14 = pK_a + pK_b$, $pK_a = 14 - pK_b = 14 - 4.75 = 9.25$ then $pH = pK_a + \log\frac{[\text{base}]}{[\text{acid}]} = 9.25 + \log\frac{[NH_3]}{[NH_4^+]} = 9.00$.

Solve for $[NH_4Br]$. $\log\frac{[NH_3]}{[NH_4^+]} = 9.00 - 9.25 = -0.25 \rightarrow \frac{[NH_3]}{[NH_4^+]} = 10^{-0.25} = 0.562341$.

$100.0 \text{ mL} \times \frac{1 \text{ L}}{1000 \text{ mL}} = 0.1000 \text{ L}$ then $\frac{0.100 \text{ mol } NH_3}{1 \text{ L}} \times 0.1000 \text{ L} = 0.0100 \text{ mol } NH_3$ and

$\frac{0.125 \text{ mol } NH_4Br}{1 \text{ L}} \times 0.1000 \text{ L} = 0.0125 \text{ mol } NH_4Br = 0.0125 \text{ mol } NH_4^+$ Since HCl is a strong acid,

$[HCl] = [H^+]$, and set up table to track changes:

	$H^+ (aq)$ +	$NH_3 (aq)$ →	$NH_4^+ (aq)$
Before addition	≈ 0.00 mol	0.0100 mol	0.0125 mol
Addition	x	—	—
After addition	≈ 0.00 mol	$(0.0100 - x)$ mol	$(0.0125 + x)$ mol

Since $\frac{[NH_3]}{[NH_4^+]} = 0.56\underline{2}341 = \frac{(0.0100 - x)\ \text{mol}}{(0.0125 + x)\ \text{mol}}$, solve for x. Note that the ratio of moles is the same as the ratio of concentrations, since the volume for both terms is the same. $0.56\underline{2}341\ (0.0125 + x) = (0.0100 - x) \rightarrow 0.007\underline{0}2926 + 0.56\underline{2}341\ x = 0.0100 - x \rightarrow 1.56\underline{2}341\ x = 0.00\underline{2}9707 \rightarrow x = 0.00\underline{1}9015$ mol HCl then $0.00\underline{1}9015\ \text{mol HCl} \times \frac{36.46\ \text{g HCl}}{1\ \text{mol HCl}} = 0.0\underline{6}932$ g HCl = 0.07 g HCl. For the higher concentration buffer, repeat part of the above calculations. $\frac{0.250\ \text{mol}\ NH_3}{1\ \text{L}} \times 0.1000\ \text{L} = 0.0250$ mol NH_3 and $\frac{0.400\ \text{mol}\ NH_4Br}{1\ \text{L}} \times 0.1000\ \text{L} = 0.0400$ mol NH_4Br = 0.0400 mol NH_4^+.

Since HCl is a strong acid, $[HCl] = [H^+]$, and set up a table to track changes:

	$H^+ (aq)$ +	$NH_3 (aq)$ →	$NH_4^+ (aq)$
Before addition	≈ 0.00 mol	0.0250 mol	0.0400 mol
Addition	x	—	—
After addition	≈ 0.00 mol	$(0.0250 - x)$ mol	$(0.0400 + x)$ mol

Since $\frac{[NH_3]}{[NH_4^+]} = 0.56\underline{2}341 = \frac{(0.0250 - x)\ \text{mol}}{(0.0400 + x)\ \text{mol}}$, solve for x. Note that the ratio of moles is the same as the ratio of concentrations, since the volume for both terms is the same. $0.56\underline{2}341\ (0.0400 + x) = (0.0250 - x) \rightarrow 0.0\underline{2}24936 + 0.56\underline{2}341\ x = 0.0250 - x \rightarrow 1.56\underline{2}341\ x = 0.00\underline{2}50636 \rightarrow x = 0.00\underline{1}6042$ mol HCl then $0.00\underline{1}6042\ \text{mol HCl} \times \frac{36.46\ \text{g HCl}}{1\ \text{mol HCl}} = 0.0\underline{5}8490$ g HCl = 0.06 g HCl.

Check: The units (g) are correct. The magnitudes of the answers make physical sense because there is much less than a mole of each of the buffer components, so there must be much less than a mole of HCl. Also, the pH of the initial buffer is less than the pK_a of the acid, so even less acid is necessary to drop the pH below 9.00. The higher concentration buffer solution requires about the same amount of acid because the initial pH of this buffer is closer to 9.00 than the low concentration buffer.

16.53 (a) Yes, this will be a buffer because NH_3 is a weak base and NH_4^+ is its conjugate acid. The ratio of base to acid is 0.10/0.15 = 0.67, so the pH will be within 1 pH unit of the pK_a.

(b) No, this will not be a buffer solution because HCl is a strong acid and NaOH is a strong base.

(c) Yes, this will be a buffer because HF is a weak acid and the NaOH will convert 20.0/50.0 = 40% of the acid to its conjugate base.

(d) No, this will not be a buffer solution because both components are bases.

(e) No, this will not be a buffer solution because both components are bases.

16.54 (a) Yes, this will be a buffer because HF is a weak acid and F^- is its conjugate base. The ratio of base to acid is (55.0 x 0.15)/(75.0 x 0.10) = 1.1, so the pH will be within 1 pH unit of the pK_a.

(b) No, this will not be a buffer solution because both components are acids.

(c) Yes, this will be a buffer because HF is a weak acid and the KOH will convert (135.0 x 0.050)/(165.0 x 0.10) = 41% of the acid to its conjugate base.

(d) Yes, this will be a buffer because CH_3NH_2 is a weak base and $CH_3NH_3^+$ is its conjugate acid. The ratio of base to acid is (125.0 x 0.15)/(120.0 x 0.25) = 0.63, so the pH will be within 1 pH unit of the pK_a.

(e) Yes, this will be a buffer because CH_3NH_2 is a weak base and the HCl will convert (95.0 x 0.10)/(105.0 x 0.15) = 60% of the base to its conjugate acid.

16.55 (a) **Given:** blood buffer 0.024 M HCO_3^- and 0.0012 M H_2CO_3, $pK_a = 6.1$ **Find:** initial pH

Conceptual Plan: identify acid and base components then M HCO_3^-, M H_2CO_3 → pH

acid = H_2CO_3 base = HCO_3^- $\quad pH = pK_a + \log\frac{[base]}{[acid]}$

Solution: Acid = H_2CO_3, so [acid] = $[H_2CO_3]$ = 0.0012 M. Base = HCO_3^-, so [base] = $[HCO_3^-]$ = 0.024 M HCO_3^-. Then $pH = pK_a + \log\frac{[base]}{[acid]} = 6.1 + \log\frac{0.024\ \cancel{M}}{0.0012\ \cancel{M}} = 7.4$.

Check: The units (none) are correct. The magnitude of the answer makes physical sense because pH is greater than the pK_a of the acid because there is more base than acid.

(b) **Given:** 5.0 L of blood buffer **Find:** mass HCl to lower pH to 7.0

Conceptual Plan: final pH, pK_a → $[HCO_3^-]/[H_2CO_3]$ then $[HCO_3^-]$, L → mol HCO_3^- and

$pH = pK_a + \log\frac{[base]}{[acid]} \quad M = \frac{mol}{L}$

$[H_2CO_3]$, L → mol H_2CO_3 then write balanced equation then

$M = \frac{mol}{L} \quad H^+ + HCO_3^- \rightarrow H_2CO_3$

mol HCO_3^-, mol H_2CO_3, $[HCO_3^-]/[H_2CO_3]$ → mol HCl → g HCl

set up stoichiometry table $\quad \frac{36.46\ g\ HCl}{1\ mol\ HCl}$

Solution: $pH = pK_a + \log\frac{[base]}{[acid]} = 6.1 + \log\frac{[HCO_3^-]}{[H_2CO_3]} = 7.0$. Solve for $[HCO_3^-]/[H_2CO_3]$.

$\log\frac{[HCO_3^-]}{[H_2CO_3]} = 7.0 - 6.1 = 0.9 \rightarrow \frac{[HCO_3^-]}{[H_2CO_3]} = 10^{0.9} = 7.9433$. Then

$\frac{0.024\ mol\ HCO_3^-}{1\ \cancel{L}} \times 5.0\ \cancel{L} = 0.12\ mol\ HCO_3^-$ and $\frac{0.0012\ mol\ H_2CO_3}{1\ \cancel{L}} \times 5.0\ \cancel{L} = 0.0060\ mol\ H_2CO_3$

Since HCl is a strong acid, [HCl] = $[H^+]$, and set up table to track changes:

	$H^+ (aq)$ +	$HCO_3^- (aq)$ →	$H_2CO_3 (aq)$
Before addition	≈ 0.00 mol	0.12 mol	0.0060 mol
Addition	x	—	—
After addition	≈ 0.00 mol	(0.12 – x) mol	(0.0060 + x) mol

Since $\frac{[HCO_3^-]}{[H_2CO_3]} = 7.9433 = \frac{(0.12 - x)\ \cancel{mol}}{(0.0060 + x)\ \cancel{mol}}$, solve for x. Note that the ratio of moles is the same as the ratio of concentrations, since the volume for both terms is the same.

$7.9433\ (0.0060 + x) = (0.12 - x) \rightarrow 0.0476598 + 7.9433\ x = 0.12 - x \rightarrow 8.9433\ x = 0.07234 \rightarrow$

$x = 0.0080888$ mol HCl then $0.0080888\ \cancel{mol\ HCl} \times \frac{36.46\ g\ HCl}{1\ \cancel{mol\ HCl}} = 0.29492\ g\ HCl = 0.3\ g\ HCl$.

Check: The units (g) are correct. The amount of acid needed is small because the concentrations of the buffer components are very low and the buffer starts only 0.4 pH units above the final pH.

(c) **Given:** 5.0 L of blood buffer **Find:** mass NaOH to raise pH to 7.8

Conceptual Plan: final pH, pK_a → $[HCO_3^-]/[H_2CO_3]$ then $[HCO_3^-]$, L → mol HCO_3^- and

$pH = pK_a + \log\frac{[base]}{[acid]} \quad M = \frac{mol}{L}$

$[H_2CO_3]$, L → mol H_2CO_3 then write balanced equation then

$M = \frac{mol}{L} \quad OH^- + H_2CO_3 \rightarrow HCO_3^- + H_2O$

mol HCO_3^-, mol H_2CO_3, $[HCO_3^-]/[H_2CO_3]$ → mol NaOH → g NaOH

set up stoichiometry table $\quad \frac{40.00\ g\ NaOH}{1\ mol\ NaOH}$

Solution: $pH = pK_a + \log\frac{[base]}{[acid]} = 6.1 + \log\frac{[HCO_3^-]}{[H_2CO_3]} = 7.8$.

Solve for $[HCO_3^-]/[H_2CO_3]$. $\log\frac{[HCO_3^-]}{[H_2CO_3]} = 7.8 - 6.1 = 1.7 \rightarrow \frac{[HCO_3^-]}{[H_2CO_3]} = 10^{1.7} = 50.11872$. Then

$\frac{0.024 \text{ mol } HCO_3^-}{1 \text{ L}} \times 5.0 \text{ L} = 0.12 \text{ mol } HCO_3^-$ and $\frac{0.0012 \text{ mol } H_2CO_3}{1 \text{ L}} \times 5.0 \text{ L} = 0.0060 \text{ mol } H_2CO_3$

Since NaOH is a strong base, [NaOH] = [OH^-], and set up table to track changes:

	OH^- (*aq*) +	H_2CO_3 (*aq*) →	HCO_3^- (*aq*) +	H_2O (*l*)
Before addition	≈ 0.00 mol	0.0060 mol	0.12 mol	—
Addition	x	—	—	
After addition	≈ 0.00 mol	$(0.0060 - x)$ mol	$(0.12 + x)$ mol	

Since $\frac{[HCO_3^-]}{[H_2CO_3]} = 50.\underline{1}1872 = \frac{(0.12 + x) \text{ mol}}{(0.0060 - x) \text{ mol}}$, solve for x. Note that the ratio of moles is the same as the ratio of concentrations, since the volume for both terms is the same.

$50.\underline{1}1872(0.0060 - x) = (0.12 + x) \rightarrow 0.3\underline{0}071 - 50.\underline{1}1872x = 0.12 + x \rightarrow 51.\underline{1}1872x = 0.1\underline{8}071$
$\rightarrow x = 0.003\underline{5}351$ mol NaOH then

$0.003\underline{5}351 \text{ mol NaOH} \times \frac{40.00 \text{ g NaOH}}{1 \text{ mol NaOH}} = 0.1\underline{4}141 \text{ g NaOH} = 0.14 \text{ g NaOH}.$

Check: The units (g) are correct. The amount of base needed is small because the concentrations of the buffer components are very low.

16.56 (a) **Given:** $HPO_4^{2-}/H_2PO_4^-$ buffer at pH = 7.1 **Find:** $[HPO_4^{2-}]/[H_2PO_4^-]$
Other: K_{a_2} (H_3PO_4) = 6.2×10^{-8}

Conceptual Plan: identify acid and base components then pH, K_{a_2} → $[HPO_4^{2-}]/[H_2PO_4^-]$

acid = $H_2PO_4^-$ base = HPO_4^{2-} $\qquad$ $pH = pK_a + \log\frac{[\text{base}]}{[\text{acid}]}$

Solution: $pH = pK_a + \log\frac{[\text{base}]}{[\text{acid}]} = -\log(6.2 \times 10^{-8}) + \log\frac{[HPO_4^{2-}]}{[H_2PO_4^-]} = 7.1.$

Solve for $[HPO_4^{2-}]/[H_2PO_4^-]$.

$\log\frac{[HPO_4^{2-}]}{[H_2PO_4^-]} = 7.1 - 7.2 = -0.1 \rightarrow \frac{[HPO_4^{2-}]}{[H_2PO_4^-]} = 10^{-0.1} = 0.\underline{7}9433 = 0.8.$

Check: The units (none) are correct. The magnitude of the answer makes physical sense because the pH is very close, but less than, the pK_a of the acid.

(b) No, H_3PO_4 and $H_2PO_4^-$ cannot be used as a buffer in the cell because the K_{a_1} (H_3PO_4) = 7.5×10^{-3} and so the pK_{a_1} = 2.1. In order to have an effective buffer the pK_a should be within in 1 pH unit of the desired pH (not 5.0 pH units).

16.57 **Given:** $HC_2H_3O_2/KC_2H_3O_2$, $HClO_2/KClO_2$, NH_3/NH_4Cl, and HClO/KClO potential buffer systems to create buffer at pH = 7.20 **Find:** best buffer system and ratio of component masses
Other: K_a ($HC_2H_3O_2$) = 1.8×10^{-5}, K_a ($HClO_2$) = 1.8×10^{-4}, K_b (NH_3) = 1.79×10^{-5}, K_a (HClO) = 2.9×10^{-8}
Conceptual Plan: calculate pK_a of all potential buffer acids for the base K_b → pK_b → pK_a then

$pK_a = -\log K_a$ $\qquad$ $pK_b = -\log K_b$ $\quad$ $14 = pK_a + pK_b$

and choose the pK_a that is closest to 7.20. Then pH, K_a → [base]/[acid] → mass base/mass acid

$pH = pK_a + \log\frac{[\text{base}]}{[\text{acid}]}$ $\qquad$ $\frac{\mathcal{M}\text{ (base)}}{\mathcal{M}\text{ (acid)}}$

Solution: for $HC_2H_3O_2/KC_2H_3O_2$: $pK_a = -\log K_a = -\log(1.8 \times 10^{-5}) = 4.74$; for $HClO_2/KClO_2$:
$pK_a = -\log K_a = -\log(1.8 \times 10^{-4}) = 3.74$; for NH_3/NH_4Cl:

$pK_b = -\log K_b = -\log(1.79 \times 10^{-5}) = 4.75.$

Since $14 = pK_a + pK_b$, $pK_a = 14 - pK_b = 14 - 4.75 = 9.25$; and for HClO/KClO:

$pK_a = -\log K_a = -\log(2.9 \times 10^{-8}) = 7.54$. So the HClO/KClO buffer system has the pK_a that is the closest to 7.20. So, $pH = pK_a + \log\frac{[\text{base}]}{[\text{acid}]} = 7.54 + \log\frac{[KClO]}{[HClO]} = 7.1$. Solve for [KClO]/[HClO].

$\log\frac{[KClO]}{[HClO]} = 7.20 - 7.54 = -0.34 \rightarrow \frac{[KClO]}{[HClO]} = 10^{-0.34} = 0.4\underline{5}7088$. Then convert to mass ratio using

$$\frac{\mathcal{M}\text{ (base)}}{\mathcal{M}\text{ (acid)}},\ 0.45\underline{7}088\ \frac{\frac{\cancel{\text{KClO mol}}}{\cancel{\text{L}}}}{\frac{\cancel{\text{HClO mol}}}{\cancel{\text{L}}}} \times \frac{\frac{90.55\text{ g KClO}}{\cancel{\text{mol KClO}}}}{\frac{52.46\text{ g HClO}}{\cancel{\text{mol HClO}}}} = 0.79\frac{\text{g KClO}}{\text{g HClO}}$$

Check: The units (none and g base/g acid)) are correct. The buffer system with the K_a closest to 10^{-7} is the best choice. The magnitude of the answer makes physical sense because the buffer needs more acid than base (and this fact is not overcome by the heavier molar mass of the base).

16.58 **Given:** HF/KF, HNO_2/KNO_2, NH_3/NH_4Cl, and HClO/KClO potential buffer systems to create buffer at pH = 9.00 **Find:** best buffer system and ratio of component masses
Other: K_a (HF) = 3.5 x 10^{-4}, K_a (HNO_2) = 4.6 x 10^{-4}, K_b (NH_3) = 1.79 x 10^{-5}, K_a (HClO) = 2.9 x 10^{-8}
Conceptual Plan: calculate pK_a of all potential buffer acids for the base K_b → pK_b → pK_a then

$pK_a = -\log K_a$ $\qquad pK_b = -\log K_b \quad 14 = pK_a + pK_b$

and choose the pK_a that is closest to 9.00. Then pH, K_a → [base]/[acid] → mass base/mass acid.

$$pH = pK_a + \log\frac{[\text{base}]}{[\text{acid}]} \qquad \frac{\mathcal{M}\text{ (base)}}{\mathcal{M}\text{ (acid)}}$$

Solution: for HF/KF: $pK_a = -\log K_a = -\log(3.5 \times 10^{-4}) = 3.46$;
for HNO_2/KNO_2 : $pK_a = -\log K_a = -\log(4.6 \times 10^{-4}) = 3.34$;
for NH_3/NH_4Cl: $pK_b = -\log K_b = -\log(1.79 \times 10^{-5}) = 4.75$.
Since $14 = pK_a + pK_b$, $pK_a = 14 - pK_b = 14 - 4.75 = 9.25$;
and for HClO/KClO: $pK_a = -\log K_a = -\log(2.9 \times 10^{-8}) = 7.54$.
So the NH_3/NH_4Cl buffer system has the pK_a that is the closest to 9.00.

So, $pH = pK_a + \log\frac{[\text{base}]}{[\text{acid}]} = 9.25 + \log\frac{[NH_3]}{[NH_4Cl]} = 9.00$. Solve for $[NH_3]/[NH_4Cl]$.

$\log\frac{[NH_3]}{[NH_4Cl]} = 9.00 - 9.25 = -0.25 \rightarrow \frac{[NH_3]}{[NH_4Cl]} = 10^{-0.25} = 0.5\underline{6}2341$. Then convert to mass ratio using

$$\frac{\mathcal{M}\text{ (base)}}{\mathcal{M}\text{ (acid)}},\ 0.5\underline{6}2341\ \frac{\frac{\cancel{NH_3\text{ mol}}}{\cancel{\text{L}}}}{\frac{\cancel{NH_4Cl\text{ mol}}}{\cancel{\text{L}}}} \times \frac{\frac{17.03\text{ g }NH_3}{\cancel{\text{mol }NH_3}}}{\frac{53.49\text{ g }NH_4Cl}{\cancel{\text{mol }NH_4Cl}}} = 0.18\frac{\text{g }NH_3}{\text{g }NH_4Cl}$$

Check: The units (none and g base/g acid) are correct. The buffer system with the K_a closest to 10^{-9} is the best choice. The magnitude of the answer makes physical sense because the buffer needs more acid than base and the acid component has a heavier molar mass, so the mass ratio is small.

16.59 **Given:** 500.0 mL of 0.100 M HNO_2 / 0.150 M KNO_2 buffer and a) 250 mg NaOH, b) 350 mg KOH, c) 1.25 g HBr and d) 1.35 g HI **Find:** if buffer capacity is exceeded
Conceptual Plan: mL → L then [HNO_2], L → mol HNO_2 and [KNO_2], L → mol KNO_2 then

$\frac{1\text{ L}}{1000\text{ mL}} \qquad M = \frac{\text{mol}}{\text{L}} \qquad M = \frac{\text{mol}}{\text{L}}$

then calculate moles of acid or base to be added to the buffer mg → g → mol then

$\frac{1\text{ g}}{1000\text{ mg}} \qquad \mathcal{M}$

compare the added amount to the buffer amount of the opposite component. Ratio of base/acid must be between 0.1 and 10 to maintain the buffer integrity.

Solution: $500.00\ \cancel{\text{mL}} \times \frac{1\text{ L}}{1000\ \cancel{\text{mL}}} = 0.5000$ L then $\frac{0.100\text{ mol }HNO_2}{1\ \cancel{\text{L}}} \times 0.5000\ \cancel{\text{L}} = 0.0500$ mol HNO_2 and

$\frac{0.150\text{ mol }KNO_2}{1\ \cancel{\text{L}}} \times 0.5000\ \cancel{\text{L}} = 0.0750$ mol KNO_2

(a) For NaOH: $250\ \cancel{\text{mg NaOH}} \times \frac{1\ \cancel{\text{g NaOH}}}{1000\ \cancel{\text{mg NaOH}}} \times \frac{1\text{ mol NaOH}}{40.00\ \cancel{\text{g NaOH}}} = 0.006\underline{2}5$ mol NaOH. Since the buffer contains 0.0500 mol acid, the amount of acid is reduced by 0.00625/0.0500 = 12.5% and the ratio of base/acid is still between 0.1 and 10. The buffer capacity is not exceeded.

(b) For KOH: $350 \text{ mg KOH} \times \frac{1 \text{ g KOH}}{1000 \text{ mg KOH}} \times \frac{1 \text{ mol KOH}}{56.11 \text{ g KOH}} = 0.00624 \text{ mol KOH}$. Since the buffer contains 0.0500 mol acid, the amount of acid is reduced by 0.00624/0.0500 = 12.5% and the ratio of base/acid is still between 0.1 and 10. The buffer capacity is not exceeded.

(c) For HBr: $1.25 \text{ g HBr} \times \frac{1 \text{ mol HBr}}{80.91 \text{ g HBr}} = 0.0154496 \text{ mol HBr}$. Since the buffer contains 0.0750 mol base, the amount of acid is reduced by 0.0154/0.0750 = 20.6% and the ratio of base/acid is still between 0.1 and 10. The buffer capacity is not exceeded.

(d) For HI: $1.35 \text{ g HI} \times \frac{1 \text{ mol HI}}{127.91 \text{ g HI}} = 0.0105545 \text{ mol HI}$. Since the buffer contains 0.0750 mol base, the amount of acid is reduced by 0.0106/0.0750 = 14.1% and the ratio of base/acid is still between 0.1 and 10. The buffer capacity is not exceeded.

16.60 **Given:** 1.0 L of 0.125 M HNO_2 / 0.145 M $NaNO_2$ buffer and a) 1.5 g HCl, b) 1.5 g NaOH, c) 1.5 g HI
Find: [HNO_2] and [$NaNO_2$] after addition **Other:** K_a (HNO_2) = 4.6 x 10^{-4}
Conceptual Plan: [HNO_2], L → mol HNO_2 and [$NaNO_2$], L → mol $NaNO_2$ (= mol NO_2^-)

$M = \frac{mol}{L}$ $M = \frac{mol}{L}$

then calculate moles of acid or base to be added to the buffer g → mol

$\mathcal{M}$

then write balanced equation then mol HNO_2, mol NO_2^-, mol added species → mol HNO_2, mol NO_2^-

$H^+ + NO_2^- \rightarrow HNO_2$ *set up stoichiometry table*

$OH^- + HNO_2 \rightarrow NO_2^- + H_2O$

mol HNO_2, L → [HNO_2] and mol NO_2^- (= mol $NaNO_2$), L → [$NaNO_2$]

$M = \frac{mol}{L}$ $M = \frac{mol}{L}$

Solution: $\frac{0.125 \text{ mol } HNO_2}{1 \text{ L}} \times 1.0 \text{ L} = 0.125 \text{ mol } HNO_2$ and $\frac{0.145 \text{ mol } KNO_2}{1 \text{ L}} \times 1.0 \text{ L} = 0.145 \text{ mol } KNO_2$

(a) For HCl: $1.5 \text{ g HCl} \times \frac{1 \text{ mol HCl}}{36.46 \text{ g HCl}} = 0.041141 \text{ mol HCl}$. Since HCl is a strong acid, [HCl] = [H^+], and set up a table to track changes:

	$H^+ (aq)$ +	$NO_2^- (aq)$ →	$HNO_2 (aq)$
Before addition	≈ 0.00 mol	0.145 mol	0.125 mol
Addition	0.041141 mol	—	—
After addition	≈ 0.00 mol	0.104 mol	0.166 mol

Because the concentrations of the acid and base components have not changed much, the buffer is still able to do its job. Finally, since there is 1.0 L of solution, [HNO_2] = 0.17 M and [$NaNO_2$] = 0.10 M.

(b) For NaOH: $1.5 \text{ g NaOH} \times \frac{1 \text{ mol NaOH}}{40.00 \text{ g NaOH}} = 0.0375 \text{ mol NaOH}$. Since NaOH is a strong base, [NaOH] = [OH^-], and set up table to track changes:

	$OH^- (aq)$ +	$HNO_2 (aq)$ →	$NO_2^- (aq)$ +	$H_2O (l)$
Before addition	≈ 0.00 mol	0.125 mol	0.145 mol	—
Addition	0.00375 mol	—	—	—
After addition	≈ 0.00 mol	0.0875 mol	0.1825 mol	—

Because the concentrations of the acid and base components have not changed much, the buffer is still able to do its job. Finally, since there is 1.0 L of solution, [HNO_2] = 0.09 M and [$NaNO_2$] = 0.18 M.

(c) For HI: $1.5 \text{ g HI} \times \frac{1 \text{ mol HI}}{127.91 \text{ g HI}} = 0.011727$ mol HI. Since HI is a strong acid, [HI] = [H^+], and set up a table to track changes:

	$H^+ (aq)$ +	$NO_2^- (aq)$ →	$HNO_2 (aq)$
Before addition	≈ 0.00 mol	0.145 mol	0.125 mol
Addition	0.011727 mol	—	—
After addition	≈ 0.00 mol	0.133 mol	0.137 mol

Because the concentrations of the acid and base components have not changed much, the buffer is still able to do its job. Finally, since there is 1.0 L of solution, [HNO_2] = 0.14 M and [$NaNO_2$] = 0.13 M.
Check: The units (M) are correct. Since the number of moles added is small compared to the buffer components, the buffer still remains active. Adding acid increases the amount of the conjugate base. Adding base increases the amount of the weak acid.

Titrations, pH Curves, and Indicators

16.61 (i) The equivalence point of a titration is where the pH rises sharply as base is added. The pH at the equivalence point is the midpoint of the sharp rise at ~ 50 mL added base. For (a) the pH = ~ 8 and for (b) the pH = ~ 7.

(ii) Graph (a) represents a weak acid and graph (b) represents a strong acid. A strong acid titration starts at a lower pH, has a flatter initial region and a sharper rise at the equivalence point than a weak acid. The pH at the equivalence point of a strong acid is neutral, while the pH at the equivalence point of a weak acid is basic.

16.62 **Given:** 25.0 mL 0.100 M HCl and 0.100 M HF titrated with 0.200 M KOH

(a) **Find:** volume of base to reach equivalence point
Conceptual Plan: The answer for both titrations will be the same since the initial concentration and volumes of the acids are the same and both acids are monoprotic. Write balanced equation

$HCl + KOH \rightarrow KCl + H_2O$ and $HF + KOH \rightarrow KF + H_2O$

then mL → L then [acid], L → mol acid then set mol acid = mol base and

$\frac{1 \text{ L}}{1000 \text{ mL}}$ $\quad M = \frac{\text{mol}}{\text{L}}$ $\quad$ *balanced equation has 1:1 stoichiometry*

[KOH], mol KOH → L KOH → mL KOH

$M = \frac{\text{mol}}{\text{L}}$ $\quad \frac{1000 \text{ mL}}{1 \text{ L}}$

Solution: $25.0 \text{ mL acid} \times \frac{1 \text{ L}}{1000 \text{ mL}} = 0.0250$ L acid then

$\frac{0.100 \text{ mol acid}}{1 \text{ L}} \times 0.0250 \text{ L} = 0.00250$ mol acid. So mol acid = 0.00250 mol = mol KOH then

$0.00250 \text{ mol KOH} \times \frac{1 \text{ L KOH}}{0.200 \text{ mol KOH}} = 0.0125 \text{ L KOH} \times \frac{1000 \text{ mL}}{1 \text{ L}} = 12.5$ mL KOH for both titrations.

Check: The units (mL) are correct. The volume of base is half the volume of acids because the concentration of the base is twice that of the acids. The answer for both titrations is the same because the stoichiometry is the same for both titration reactions.

(b) The pH at the equivalence point will be neutral for HCl (since it is a strong acid) and it will be basic for HF (since it is a weak acid).

(c) The initial pH will be lower for HCl (since it is a strong acid) and so it dissociates completely. The HF (since it is a weak acid) will only partially dissociate and not drop the pH as low as HCl at the same acid concentration.

(d) The titration curves will look like the following:

HCl:

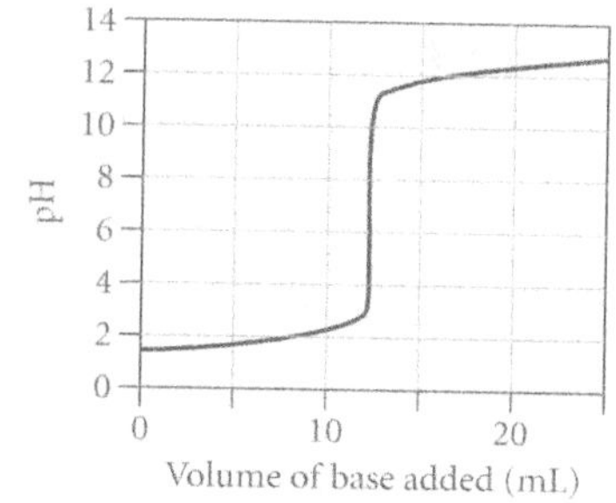

HF:

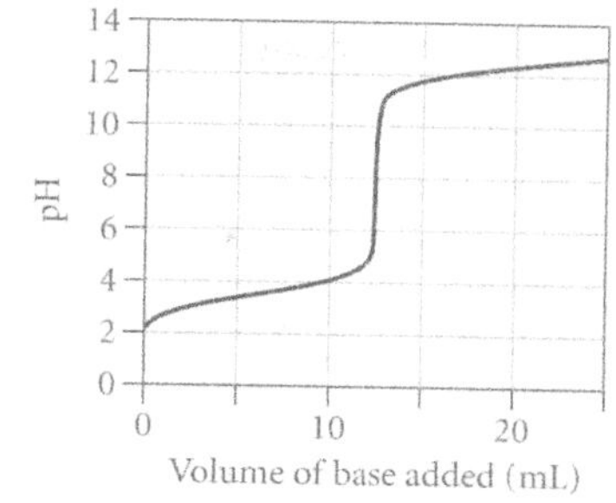

Important features to include are a low initial pH (if strong acid pH is 1 and higher for a weak acid), flat initial region (very flat for strong acid, not as flat for weak acid where pH halfway to equivalence point is the pK_a of the acid), sharp rise at equivalence point, pH at equivalence point (neutral for strong acid and higher for weak acid), and then flatten out at high pH.

16.63 **Given:** 20.0 mL 0.200 M KOH and 0.200 M CH_3NH_2 titrated with 0.100 M HI

(a) **Find:** volume of base to reach equivalence point

Conceptual Plan: The answer for both titrations will be the same since the initial concentration and volumes of the bases are the same. Write balanced equation then mL → L then

$HI + KOH \rightarrow KI + H_2O$ and $HI + KOH \rightarrow CH_3NH_3I$ $\qquad \frac{1\ L}{1000\ mL}$

[base], L → mol base then set mol base = mol acid and [HI], mol HI → L HI → mL HI

$M = \frac{mol}{L}$ *balanced equation has 1:1 stoichiometry* $M = \frac{mol}{L}$ $\frac{1000\ mL}{1\ L}$

Solution: $20.0\ \text{mL base} \times \frac{1\ L}{1000\ mL} = 0.0200\ L$ base then

$\frac{0.200\ \text{mol base}}{1\ L} \times 0.0200\ L = 0.00400$ mol base. So mol base = 0.00400 mol = mol HI then

$0.00400\ \text{mol HI} \times \frac{1\ L\ HI}{0.100\ \text{mol HI}} = 0.0400\ L\ HI \times \frac{1000\ mL}{1\ L} = 40.0$ mL HI for both titrations.

Check: The units (mL) are correct. The volume of acid is twice the volume of bases because the concentration of the base is twice that of the acid in each case. The answer for both titrations is the same because the stoichiometry is the same for both titration reactions.

(b) The pH at the equivalence point will be neutral for KOH (since it is a strong base) and it will be acidic for CH_3NH_2 (since it is a weak base).

(c) The initial pH will be lower for CH_3NH_2 (since it is a weak base and will only partially dissociate and not raise the pH as high as KOH (since it is a strong base and so it dissociates completely) at the same base concentration.

(d) The titration curves will look like the following:

KOH:

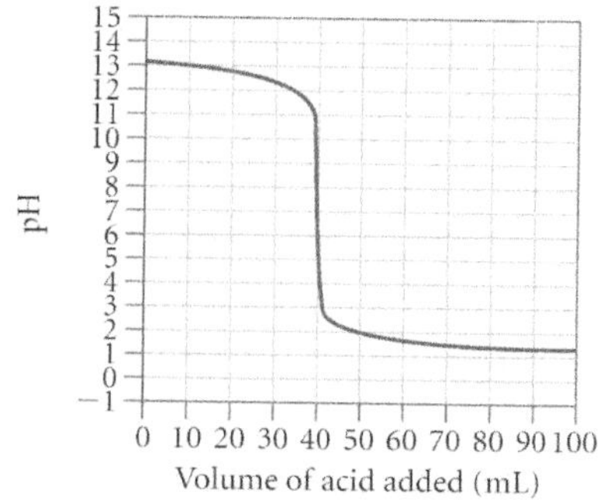

CH_3NH_2:

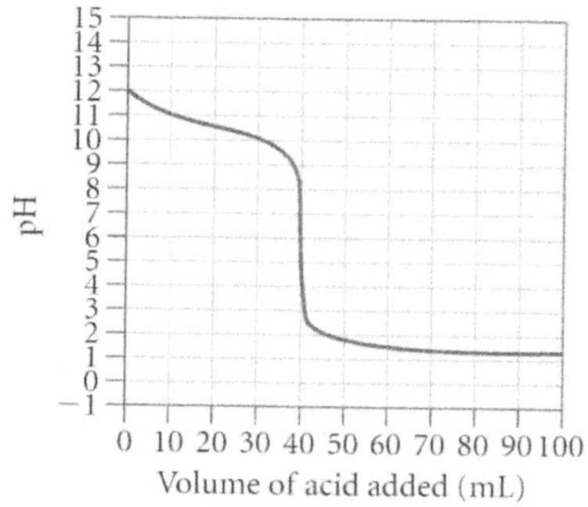

Important features to include are a high initial pH (if strong base pH is over 13 and lower for a weak base), flat initial region (very flat for strong base, not as flat for weak base where pH halfway to equivalence point is the pK_b of the base), sharp drop at equivalence point, pH at equivalence point (neutral for strong base and lower for weak base), and then flatten out at low pH.

16.64 (i) The equivalence point of a titration is where the pH drops sharply as acid is added. The pH at the equivalence point is the midpoint of the sharp drop at ~ 25 mL added acid. For (a) the pH = ~ 7 and for (b) the pH = ~ 5.

(ii) Graph (a) represents a strong base and graph (b) represents a weak base. A strong base titration starts at a higher pH, has a flatter initial region and a sharper drop at the equivalence point than a weak base. The pH at the equivalence point of a strong base is neutral, while the pH at the equivalence point of a weak base is acidic.

16.65 (a) The equivalence point of a titration is where the pH rises sharply as base is added. The volume at the equivalence point is ~ 30 mL. The pH as the equivalence point is the midpoint of the sharp rise at ~ 30 mL added base, which is a pH = ~ 9.

(b) At 0 mL the pH is calculated by doing an equilibrium calculation of a weak acid in water (as done in Chapter 15).

(c) The pH one-half way to the equivalence point is equal to the pK_a of the acid, or ~ 15 mL.

(d) The pH at the equivalence point, or ~ 30 mL, is calculated by doing an equilibrium problem with the K_b of the acid. At the equivalence point, all of the acid has been converted to its conjugate base.

(e) Beyond the equivalence point (30 mL) there is excess base. All of the acid has been converted to its conjugate base and so the pH is calculated by focusing on this excess base concentration.

16.66 (a) The equivalence point of a titration is where the pH drops sharply as acid is added. The volume at the equivalence point is ~ 25 mL. The pH at the equivalence point is the midpoint of the sharp drop at ~ 25 mL added acid, which is a pH = ~ 5.

(b) At 0 mL the pH is calculated by doing an equilibrium calculation of a weak base in water (as done in Chapter 15).

(c) The pH one-half way to the equivalence point is equal to the 14 – pK_b = pK_a of the base, or ~ 12 mL.

(d) The pH at the equivalence point, or ~ 25 mL, is calculated by doing an equilibrium problem with the K_a of the base. At the equivalence point, all of the base has been converted to its conjugate acid.

(e) Beyond the equivalence point (25 mL) there is excess acid. All of the base has been converted to its conjugate acid and so the pH is calculated by focusing on this excess acid concentration.

16.67 **Given:** 35.0 mL of 0.175 M HBr titrated with 0.200 M KOH

(a) **Find:** initial pH
Conceptual Plan: Since HBr is a strong acid, it will dissociate completely, so initial pH = – log $[H_3O^+]$ = – log [HBr].
Solution: pH = – log [HBr] = – log 0.175 = 0.757
Check: The units (none) are correct. The pH is reasonable since the concentration is greater than 0.1 M and the acid dissociates completely, the pH is less than 1.

(b) **Find:** volume of base to reach equivalence point
Conceptual Plan: Write balanced equation then mL → L then [HBr], L → mol HBr then

$HBr + KOH \rightarrow KBr + H_2O$ $\qquad \frac{1\ L}{1000\ mL} \qquad M = \frac{mol}{L}$

set mol acid (HBr) = mol base (KOH) and [KOH], mol KOH → L KOH → mL KOH.

balanced equation has 1:1 stoichiometry $\qquad M = \frac{mol}{L} \qquad \frac{1000\ mL}{1\ L}$

Solution: $35.0\ \cancel{mL\ HBr} \times \frac{1\ L}{1000\ \cancel{mL}} = 0.0350\ L\ HBr$ then

$\frac{0.175\ mol\ HBr}{1\ \cancel{L}} \times 0.0350\ \cancel{L} = 0.0061\underline{2}5\ mol\ HBr.$

So mol acid = mol HBr = 0.006125 mol = mol KOH then

$0.006125 \text{ mol KOH} \times \frac{1 \text{ L}}{0.200 \text{ mol KOH}} = 0.030625 \text{ L KOH} \times \frac{1000 \text{ mL}}{1 \text{ L}} = 30.6 \text{ mL KOH}.$

Check: The units (mL) are correct. The volume of base is a little less than the volume of acid because the concentration of the base is a little greater than that of the acid.

(c) **Find:** pH after adding 10.0 mL of base

Conceptual Plan: Use calculations from part b. Then mL → L then [KOH], L → mol KOH then

$\frac{1 \text{ L}}{1000 \text{ mL}}$ $M = \frac{mol}{L}$

mol HBr, mol KOH → mol excess HBr and L HBr, L KOH → total L then

set up stoichiometry table L HBr + L KOH = total L

mol excess HBr, L → [HBr] → pH.

$M = \frac{mol}{L}$ $pH = -\log[HBr]$

Solution: $10.0 \text{ mL KOH} \times \frac{1 \text{ L}}{1000 \text{ mL}} = 0.0100 \text{ L KOH}$ then

$\frac{0.200 \text{ mol KOH}}{1 \text{ L}} \times 0.0100 \text{ L} = 0.00200 \text{ mol KOH}.$

Since KOH is a strong base, [KOH] = $[OH^-]$, and set up a table to track changes:

	KOH (*aq*) +	HBr (*aq*) →	KBr (*aq*) +	H_2O (*l*)
Before addition	≈ 0.00 mol	0.006125 mol	0.00 mol	—
Addition	0.00200 mol	—	—	—
After addition	≈ 0.00 mol	0.004125 mol	0.00200 mol	—

Then 0.0350 L HBr + 0.0100 L KOH = 0.0450 L total volume.

So mol excess acid = mol HBr = 0.004125 mol in 0.0450 L so

$[HBr] = \frac{0.004125 \text{ mol HBr}}{0.0450 \text{ L}} = 0.0916667 \text{ M}$ and

$pH = -\log[HBr] = -\log 0.0916667 = 1.038.$

Check: The units (none) are correct. The pH is a little higher than the initial pH, which is expected since this is a strong acid.

(d) **Find:** pH at equivalence point

Solution: Since this is a strong acid–strong base titration, the pH at the equivalence point is neutral or 7.

(e) **Find:** pH after adding 5.0 mL of base beyond the equivalence point

Conceptual Plan: Use calculations from parts b & c. Then the pH is only dependent on the amount of excess base and the total solution volumes.

mL excess → L excess then [KOH], L excess → mol KOH excess

$\frac{1 \text{ L}}{1000 \text{ mL}}$ $M = \frac{mol}{L}$

then L HBr, L KOH to equivalence point, L KOH excess → total L then

L HBr + L KOH to equivalence point + L KOH excess = total L

mol excess KOH, total L → [KOH] = $[OH^-]$ → $[H_3O^+]$ → pH

$M = \frac{mol}{L}$ $K_w = [H_3O^+][OH^-]$ $pH = -\log[H_3O^+]$

Solution: $5.0 \text{ mL KOH} \times \frac{1 \text{ L}}{1000 \text{ mL}} = 0.0050 \text{ L KOH}$ excess then

$\frac{0.200 \text{ mol KOH}}{1 \text{ L}} \times 0.0050 \text{ L} = 0.0010$ mol KOH excess. Then 0.0350 L HBr + 0.0306 L KOH + 0.0050 L KOH = 0.0706 L total volume. $[\text{KOH excess}] = \frac{0.0010 \text{ mol KOH excess}}{0.0706 \text{ L}} = 0.014164$ M KOH excess

Since KOH is a strong base, [KOH] excess = $[OH^-]$. $K_w = [H_3O^+][OH^-]$ so

$[H_3O^+] = \frac{K_w}{[OH^-]} = \frac{1.0 \times 10^{-14}}{0.014164} = 7.06 \times 10^{-13}$ M. Finally,

$pH = -\log[H_3O^+] = -\log(7.06 \times 10^{-13}) = 12.15.$

Check: The units (none) are correct. The pH is rising sharply at the equivalence point, so the pH after 5 mL past the equivalence point should be quite basic.

16.68 **Given:** 20.0 mL of 0.125 M HNO_3 titrated with 0.150 M NaOH
Find: pH at five different points and plot titration curve
Conceptual Plan: Choose points to calculate: (i) initial pH, (ii) pH after 5.0 mL, (iii) pH after 10.0 mL, (iv) pH at equivalence point, and (v) pH at 25.0 mL. Points should be on both sides of the equivalence point.

(i) Since HNO_3 is a strong acid, it will dissociate completely, so initial pH = – log [H_3O^+] = – log [HNO_3].
Solution: pH = – log [HNO_3] = – log 0.125 = 0.903
Check: The units (none) are correct. The pH is reasonable since the concentration is greater than 0.1 M and the acid dissociates completely, the pH is less than 1.

(ii) Find: pH after adding 5.0 mL of base
Conceptual Plan: Write balanced equation then mL → L then [HNO_3], L → mol HNO_3 then
$HNO_3 + NaOH \rightarrow NaNO_3 + H_2O$; $\frac{1\text{ L}}{1000\text{ mL}}$; $M = \frac{mol}{L}$
mL → L then [NaOH], L → mol NaOH then mol HNO_3, mol NaOH → mol excess HNO_3
$\frac{1\text{ L}}{1000\text{ mL}}$; $M = \frac{mol}{L}$; *set up stoichiometry table*
and L HNO_3, L NaOH → total L then mol excess HNO_3, L → [HNO_3] → pH.
L HNO_3 + L NaOH = total L ; $M = \frac{mol}{L}$; pH = – log [HNO_3]

Solution: $20.0\ \text{mL HNO}_3 \times \frac{1\text{ L}}{1000\text{ mL}} = 0.0200\text{ L HNO}_3$ then

$\frac{0.125\text{ mol HNO}_3}{1\text{ L}} \times 0.0200\text{ L} = 0.00250\text{ mol HNO}_3$ and $5.0\text{ mL NaOH} \times \frac{1\text{ L}}{1000\text{ mL}} = 0.0050\text{ L NaOH}$

then $\frac{0.150\text{ mol NaOH}}{1\text{ L}} \times 0.0050\text{ L} = 0.00075\text{ mol NaOH}$.

This is a strong acid–strong base titration, so set up a table to track changes:

	NaOH (*aq*) +	HNO_3 (*aq*) →	$NaNO_3$ (*aq*) +	H_2O (*l*)
Before addition	0.00 mol	0.00250 mol	0.00 mol	—
Addition	0.00075 mol	—	—	—
After addition	≈ 0.00 mol	0.00175 mol	0.00075 mol	—

Then 0.0200 L HNO_3 + 0.0050 L NaOH = 0.0250 L total volume. So mol excess acid = mol HNO_3 = 0.00175 mol in 0.0250 L, so $[HNO_3] = \frac{0.00175\text{ mol HNO}_3}{0.0250\text{ L}} = 0.0700\text{ M}$ and

pH = – log [HNO_3] = – log 0.0700 = 1.155.
Check: The units (none) are correct. The pH remains very low in a strong acid–strong base titration before the equivalence point.

(iii) Find: pH after adding 10.0 mL of base
Conceptual Plan: Use calculations for point (ii) then mL → L then [NaOH], L → mol NaOH then
$\frac{1\text{ L}}{1000\text{ mL}}$; $M = \frac{mol}{L}$
mol HNO_3, mol NaOH → mol excess HNO_3 and L HNO_3, L NaOH → total L then
set up stoichiometry table ; L HNO_3 + L NaOH = total L
mol excess HNO_3, L → [HNO_3] → pH.
$M = \frac{mol}{L}$; pH = – log [HNO_3]

Solution: $10.0\text{ mL NaOH} \times \frac{1\text{ L}}{1000\text{ mL}} = 0.0100\text{ L NaOH}$ then

$\frac{0.150\text{ mol NaOH}}{1\text{ L}} \times 0.0100\text{ L} = 0.00150\text{ mol NaOH}$. Set up a table to track changes:

	NaOH (*aq*) +	HNO_3 (*aq*) →	$NaNO_3$ (*aq*) +	H_2O (*l*)
Before addition	0.00 mol	0.00250 mol	0.00 mol	—
Addition	0.00150 mol	—	—	—
After addition	≈ 0.00 mol	0.00100 mol	0.00150 mol	—

Then 0.0200 L HNO_3 + 0.0100 L NaOH = 0.0300 L total volume. So mol excess acid = mol HNO_3 = 0.00100 mol in 0.0300 L, so $[HNO_3] = \frac{0.00100\text{ mol HNO}_3}{0.0300\text{ L}} = 0.03\underline{3}3333\text{ M}$ and

$pH = -\log [HNO_3] = -\log 0.0333333 = 1.477.$

Check: The units (none) are correct. The pH remains very low in a strong acid–strong base titration before the equivalence point.

(iv) **Find:** pH at equivalence point and volume of base to reach equivalence point

Conceptual Plan: Since this is a strong acid–strong base titration, the pH at the equivalence point is neutral or 7. Use calculations for point (ii) then set mol acid (HNO_3) = mol base (NaOH) and

balanced equation has 1:1 stoichiometry

[NaOH], mol NaOH → L NaOH → mL NaOH.

$M = \frac{mol}{L}$ $\quad \frac{1000\ mL}{1\ L}$

Solution: Since this is a strong acid–strong base titration, the pH at the equivalence point is neutral or 7. So mol acid = mol HNO_3 = 0.00250 mol = mol NaOH then

$$0.00250\ \text{mol NaOH} \times \frac{1\ L}{0.150\ \text{mol NaOH}} = 0.0166667\ \text{L NaOH} \times \frac{1000\ mL}{1\ L} = 16.7\ \text{mL NaOH}.$$

Check: The units (none and mL) are correct. The equivalence point pH of a strong acid–strong base titration is neutral. The volume of base is a little less than the volume of acid because the concentration of the base is a little greater than that of the acid.

(v) **Find:** pH after adding 25.0 mL of base

Conceptual Plan: Use calculations for point (ii) then mL → L then [NaOH], L → mol NaOH then

$\frac{1\ L}{1000\ mL}$ $\quad M = \frac{mol}{L}$

mol HNO_3, mol NaOH → mol excess HNO_3 and L HNO_3, L NaOH → total L then

set up stoichiometry table $\quad L\ HNO_3 + L\ NaOH = total\ L$

mol excess NaOH, total L → [NaOH] = [OH^-] → [H_3O^+] → pH.

$M = \frac{mol}{L}$ $\quad K_w = [H_3O^+][OH^-]$ $\quad pH = -\log [H_3O^+]$

Solution: $25.0\ \text{mL NaOH} \times \frac{1\ L}{1000\ mL} = 0.0250\ \text{L NaOH}$ then

$\frac{0.150\ \text{mol NaOH}}{1\ L} \times 0.0250\ L = 0.00375\ \text{mol NaOH}$. Set up table to track changes:

	NaOH (*aq*) +	HNO_3 (*aq*) →	$NaNO_3$ (*aq*) +	H_2O (*l*)
Before addition	0.00 mol	0.00250 mol	0.00 mol	—
Addition	0.00375 mol	—	—	—
After addition	0.00125 mol	≈ 0.00 mol	0.00275 mol	—

Then 0.0200 L HNO_3 + 0.0250 L NaOH = 0.0450 L total volume. So mol excess acid = mol NaOH = 0.00125 mol in 0.0450 L, so

$$[\text{NaOH excess}] = \frac{0.00125\ \text{mol NaOH excess}}{0.0450\ L} = 0.0277778\ \text{M NaOH excess}$$ Since NaOH is a strong base, [NaOH] excess = [OH^-]. $K_w = [H_3O^+][OH^-]$ so

$$[H_3O^+] = \frac{K_w}{[OH^-]} = \frac{1.0 \times 10^{-14}}{0.0277778} = 3.6 \times 10^{-13}\ M.$$ Finally,

$pH = -\log [H_3O^+] = -\log (3.6 \times 10^{-13}) = 12.44.$

Check: The units (none) are correct. The pH is rising sharply at the equivalence point, so the pH over 5 mL past the equivalence point should be quite basic.

Finally plotting these five points, the titration curve looks like the following:

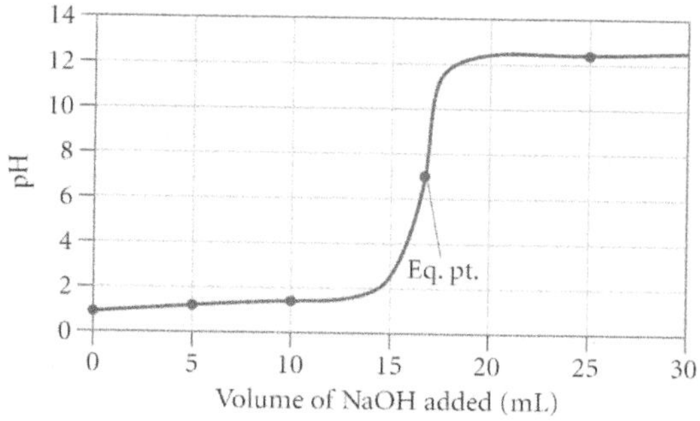

16.69 **Given:** 25.0 mL of 0.115 M RbOH titrated with 0.100 M HCl

(a) **Find:** initial pH

Conceptual Plan: Since RbOH is a strong base, it will dissociate completely, so [RbOH] = [OH⁻] → [H₃O⁺] → pH.

$K_w = [H_3O^+][OH^-]$ $pH = -\log[H_3O^+]$

Solution: Since RbOH is a strong base, [RbOH] excess = $[OH^-]$. $K_w = [H_3O^+][OH^-]$ so

$$[H_3O^+] = \frac{K_w}{[OH^-]} = \frac{1.0 \times 10^{-14}}{0.115} = 8.\underline{6}9565 \times 10^{-14} \text{ M and}$$

$$pH = -\log[H_3O^+] = -\log(8.\underline{6}9565 \times 10^{-14}) = 13.06.$$

Check: The units (none) are correct. The pH is reasonable since the concentration is greater than 0.1 M and the base dissociates completely, the pH is greater than 13.

(b) **Find:** volume of acid to reach equivalence point

Conceptual Plan: Write balanced equation then mL → L then [RbOH], L → mol RbOH then

$HCl + RbOH \rightarrow RbCl + H_2O$ $\frac{1\text{ L}}{1000\text{ mL}}$ $M = \frac{mol}{L}$

set mol base (RbOH) = mol acid (HCl) and [HCl], mol HCl → L HCl → mL HCl.

balanced equation has 1:1 stoichiometry $M = \frac{mol}{L}$ $\frac{1000\text{ mL}}{1\text{ L}}$

Solution: $25.0 \text{ mL RbOH} \times \frac{1\text{ L}}{1000\text{ mL}} = 0.0250 \text{ L RbOH}$ then

$\frac{0.115 \text{ mol RbOH}}{1 \text{ L}} \times 0.0250 \text{ L} = 0.0028\underline{7}5 \text{ mol RbOH}$. So mol base = mol RbOH = $0.0028\underline{7}5$ mol = mol HCl then $0.0028\underline{7}5 \text{ mol HCl} \times \frac{1\text{ L}}{0.100 \text{ mol HCl}} = 0.028\underline{7}5 \text{ L HCl} \times \frac{1000\text{ mL}}{1\text{ L}} = 28.8 \text{ mL HCl}$.

Check: The units (mL) are correct. The volume of acid is greater than the volume of base because the concentration of the base is a little greater than that of the acid.

(c) **Find:** pH after adding 5.0 mL of acid

Conceptual Plan: Use calculations from part (b). Then mL → L then [HCl], L → mol HCl then

$\frac{1\text{ L}}{1000\text{ mL}}$ $M = \frac{mol}{L}$

mol RbOH, mol HCl → mol excess RbOH and L RbOH, L HCl → total L then

set up stoichiometry table L RbOH + L HCl = total L

mol excess RbOH, L → [RbOH] = [OH⁻] → [H₃O⁺] → pH.

$M = \frac{mol}{L}$ $K_w = [H_3O^+][OH^-]$ $pH = -\log[H_3O^+]$

Solution: $5.0 \text{ mL HCl} \times \frac{1\text{ L}}{1000\text{ mL}} = 0.0050 \text{ L HCl}$ then $\frac{0.100 \text{ mol HCl}}{1\text{ L}} \times 0.0050 \text{ L} = 0.00050 \text{ mol HCl}$.

Since HCl is a strong acid, [HCl] = $[H_3O^+]$. Set up a table to track changes:

	$HCl\ (aq)$ +	$RbOH\ (aq)$ →	$RbCl\ (aq)$ +	$H_2O\ (l)$
Before addition	0.00 mol	0.0028$\underline{7}$5 mol	0.00 mol	—
Addition	0.00050 mol	—	—	—
After addition	≈ 0.00 mol	0.0023$\underline{7}$5 mol	0.00050 mol	—

Then 0.0250 L RbOH + 0.0050 L HCl = 0.0300 L total volume. So mol excess base = mol RbOH = $0.0023\underline{7}5$ mol in 0.0300 L so $[RbOH] = \frac{0.0023\underline{7}5 \text{ mol RbOH}}{0.0300 \text{ L}} = 0.079\underline{1}667$ M. Since RbOH is a strong base, [RbOH] excess = $[OH^-]$. $K_w = [H_3O^+][OH^-]$ so $[H_3O^+] = \frac{K_w}{[OH^-]} = \frac{1.0 \times 10^{-14}}{0.079\underline{1}667}$

$= 1.\underline{2}6316 \times 10^{-13}$ M and $pH = -\log[H_3O^+] = -\log(1.\underline{2}6316 \times 10^{-13}) = 12.90$.

Check: The units (none) are correct. The pH is a little lower than the initial pH, which is expected since this is a strong base.

(d) **Find:** pH at equivalence point

Solution: Since this is a strong acid–strong base titration, the pH at the equivalence point is neutral or 7.

(e) **Find:** pH after adding 5.0 mL of acid beyond the equivalence point
Conceptual Plan: Use calculations from parts (b) and (c). Then the pH is only dependent on the amount of excess acid and the total solution volumes. Then
mL excess → L excess then [HCl], L excess → mol HCl excess
$\frac{1\text{ L}}{1000\text{ mL}}$ $M = \frac{\text{mol}}{\text{L}}$
then L RbOH, L HCl to equivalence point, L HCl excess → total L then
L RbOH + L HCl to equivalence point + L HCl excess = total L
mol excess HCl, total L → [HCl] = [H_3O^+] → pH.
$M = \frac{\text{mol}}{\text{L}}$ $pH = -\log[H_3O^+]$

Solution: $5.0\ \text{mL HCl} \times \frac{1\text{ L}}{1000\text{ mL}} = 0.0050\text{ L HCl excess then}$

$\frac{0.100\text{ mol HCl}}{1\text{ L}} \times 0.0050\text{ L} = 0.00050\text{ mol HCl excess}$. Then 0.0250 L RbOH + 0.0288 L HCl + 0.0050 L HCl = 0.0588 L total volume. $[\text{HCl excess}] = \frac{0.00050\text{ mol HCl excess}}{0.0588\text{ L}} = 0.0085034\text{ M HCl excess}$

Since HCl is a strong acid, [HCl] excess = [H_3O^+].
Finally, $pH = -\log[H_3O^+] = -\log(0.0085034) = 2.07$.
Check: The units (none) are correct. The pH is dropping sharply at the equivalence point, so the pH after 5 mL past the equivalence point should be quite acidic.

16.70 **Given:** 15.0 mL of 0.100 M $Ba(OH)_2$ titrated with 0.125 M HCl
Find: pH at five different points and plot titration curve
Conceptual Plan: Choose points to calculate: (i) initial pH, (ii) pH after 10.0 mL, (iii) pH after 20.0 mL, (iv) pH at equivalence point, and (v) pH at 30.0 mL. Points should be on both sides of the equivalence point.

(i) **Find:** initial pH
Conceptual Plan: Since $Ba(OH)_2$ is a strong base, it will dissociate completely, bearing in mind that $Ba(OH)_2 \rightarrow Ba^{2+} + 2\ OH^-$ so 2 hydroxide ions are generated for each barium hydroxide and 2 [$Ba(OH)_2$] = [OH^-] → [H_3O^+] → pH.
$K_w = [H_3O^+][OH^-]$ $pH = -\log[H_3O^+]$
Solution: Since $Ba(OH)_2$ is a strong base, 2 [$Ba(OH)_2$] = [OH^-] = 2 x 0.100 M = 0.200 M.

$K_w = [H_3O^+][OH^-]$ so $[H_3O^+] = \frac{K_w}{[OH^-]} = \frac{1.0 \times 10^{-14}}{0.200} = 5.0 \times 10^{-14}$ M and

$pH = -\log[H_3O^+] = -\log(5.0 \times 10^{-14}) = 13.30$

Check: The units (none) are correct. The pH is reasonable since the concentration is greater than 0.1 M and the base dissociates completely, the pH is greater than 13.

(ii) **Find:** pH after adding 10.0 mL of acid
Conceptual Plan: Write a balanced equation then mL → L then [$Ba(OH)_2$], L → mol $Ba(OH)_2$ then
$2\ HCl + Ba(OH)_2 \rightarrow BaCl_2 + 2\ H_2O$ $\frac{1\text{ L}}{1000\text{ mL}}$ $M = \frac{\text{mol}}{\text{L}}$
mL → L then [HCl], L → mol HCl then mol $Ba(OH)_2$, mol HCl → mol excess $Ba(OH)_2$ and
$\frac{1\text{ L}}{1000\text{ mL}}$ $M = \frac{\text{mol}}{\text{L}}$ set up stoichiometry table
L $Ba(OH)_2$, L HCl → total L then
$M = \frac{\text{mol}}{\text{L}}$
mol excess $Ba(OH)_2$, L → 2 [$Ba(OH)_2$] = [OH^-] → [H_3O^+] → pH.
L $Ba(OH)_2$ + L HCl = total L $K_w = [H_3O^+][OH^-]$ $pH = -\log[H_3O^+]$

Solution: $15.0\ \text{mL Ba(OH)}_2 \times \frac{1\text{ L}}{1000\text{ mL}} = 0.0150\text{ L Ba(OH)}_2$ then

$\frac{0.100\text{ mol Ba(OH)}_2}{1\text{ L}} \times 0.0150\text{ L} = 0.00150\text{ mol Ba(OH)}_2$ and $10.0\ \text{mL HCl} \times \frac{1\text{ L}}{1000\text{ mL}} = 0.0100\text{ L HCl}$

then $\frac{0.125\text{ mol HCl}}{1\text{ L}} \times 0.0100\text{ L} = 0.00125\text{ mol HCl}$. Since HCl is a strong acid, [HCl] = [H_3O^+], and set up a table to track changes:

	2 HCl (*aq*) +	$Ba(OH)_2$ (*aq*) →	$BaCl_2$ (*aq*) +	2 H_2O (*l*)
Before addition	0.00 mol	0.00150 mol	0.00 mol	—
Addition	0.00125 mol	—	—	—
After addition	≈ 0.00 mol	0.000875 mol	0.000625 mol	—

Then 0.0150 L $Ba(OH)_2$ + 0.0100 L HCl = 0.0250 L total volume. So mol excess base = mol $Ba(OH)_2$ = 0.000875 mol in 0.0250 L so $[Ba(OH)_2] = \dfrac{0.000875 \text{ mol } Ba(OH)_2}{0.0250 \text{ L}} = 0.035$ M. Since $Ba(OH)_2$ is a strong base, $2\,[Ba(OH)_2] = [OH^-] = 2 \times 0.035$ M $= 0.070$ M. $K_w = [H_3O^+][OH^-]$ so

$$[H_3O^+] = \frac{K_w}{[OH^-]} = \frac{1.0 \times 10^{-14}}{0.070} = 1.4286 \times 10^{-13} \text{ M and}$$

$pH = -\log [H_3O^+] = -\log(1.4286 \times 10^{-13}) = 12.85.$

Check: The units (none) are correct. The pH is a little lower than the initial pH, which is expected since this is a strong base.

(iii) **Find:** pH after adding 20.0 mL of acid

Conceptual Plan: Use calculations from part (ii) then mL → L then [HCl], L → mol HCl then

$\frac{1 \text{ L}}{1000 \text{ mL}}$ $M = \frac{\text{mol}}{\text{L}}$

mol $Ba(OH)_2$, mol HCl → mol excess $Ba(OH)_2$ and L $Ba(OH)_2$, L HCl → total L then

set up stoichiometry table L $Ba(OH)_2$ + L HCl = total L

mol excess $Ba(OH)_2$, L → 2 $[Ba(OH)_2]$ = $[OH^-]$ → $[H_3O^+]$ → pH.

$M = \frac{\text{mol}}{\text{L}}$ $K_w = [H_3O^+][OH^-]$ $pH = -\log [H_3O^+]$

Solution: $20.0 \cancel{\text{mL HCl}} \times \dfrac{1 \text{ L}}{1000 \cancel{\text{mL}}} = 0.0200$ L HCl then $\dfrac{0.125 \text{ mol HCl}}{1 \cancel{\text{L}}} \times 0.0200 \cancel{\text{L}} = 0.00250$ mol HCl.

Since HCl is a strong acid, $[HCl] = [H_3O^+]$, and set up a table to track changes:

	2 HCl (*aq*) +	$Ba(OH)_2$ (*aq*) →	$BaCl_2$ (*aq*) +	2 H_2O (*l*)
Before addition	0.00 mol	0.00150 mol	0.00 mol	—
Addition	0.00250 mol	—	—	—
After addition	≈ 0.00 mol	0.00025 mol	0.00125 mol	—

Then 0.0150 L $Ba(OH)_2$ + 0.0200 L HCl = 0.0350 L total volume. So mol excess base = mol $Ba(OH)_2$ = 0.00025 mol in 0.0350 L so $[Ba(OH)_2] = \dfrac{0.00025 \text{ mol } Ba(OH)_2}{0.0350 \text{ L}} = 0.0071429$ M. Since $Ba(OH)_2$ is a strong base, $2\,[Ba(OH)_2] = [OH^-] = 2 \times 0.0071429$ M $= 0.014286$ M. $K_w = [H_3O^+][OH^-]$ so

$$[H_3O^+] = \frac{K_w}{[OH^-]} = \frac{1.0 \times 10^{-14}}{0.014286} = 6.99986 \times 10^{-13} \text{ M}$$

and $pH = -\log [H_3O^+] = -\log(6.99986 \times 10^{-13}) = 12.15.$

Check: The units (none) are correct. The pH is a little lower than the initial pH, which is expected since this is a strong base.

(iv) **Find:** pH at equivalence point and volume of acid to reach equivalence point

Solution: Since this is a strong acid–strong base titration, the pH at the equivalence point is neutral or 7.

Conceptual Plan: Use calculations from part (ii) then set 2 mol base ($Ba(OH)_2$) = mol acid (HCl) and

balanced equation has 1:2 stoichiometry

[HCl], mol HCl → L HCl → mL HCl.

$M = \frac{\text{mol}}{\text{L}}$ $\frac{1000 \text{ mL}}{1 \text{ L}}$

Solution: So $0.00150 \text{ mol } Ba(OH)_2 \times \dfrac{2 \text{ mol HCl}}{1 \text{ mol } Ba(OH)_2} = 0.00300$ mol HCl then

$$0.00300 \cancel{\text{mol HCl}} \times \frac{1 \text{ L}}{0.125 \cancel{\text{mol HCl}}} = 0.0240 \cancel{\text{L HCl}} \times \frac{1000 \text{ mL}}{1 \cancel{\text{L}}} = 24.0 \text{ mL HCl.}$$

Check: The units (mL) are correct. The volume of acid is a greater less than the volume of base because two moles of acid are needed for each mole of the base.

(v) **Find:** pH after adding 30.0 mL of acid

Conceptual Plan: Use calculations from earlier parts. Then the pH is only dependent on the amount of excess acid and the total solution volumes.

mL added, mL at equiv. pt. → mL excess → L excess then

$$mL\ excess = mL\ added - mL\ at\ equiv.\ pt. \qquad \frac{1\ L}{1000\ mL}$$

[HCl], L excess → mol HCl excess then L $Ba(OH)_2$, L HCl → total L then

$$M = \frac{mol}{L} \qquad L\ Ba(OH)_2 + L\ HCl = total\ L$$

mol excess HCl, total L → [HCl] = $[H_3O^+]$ → pH

$$M = \frac{mol}{L} \qquad pH = -\log[H_3O^+]$$

Solution: mL HCl excess = mL added – mL to equiv. pt. = 30.0 mL – 24.0 mL = 6.0 mL.

$6.0\ \text{mL HCl} \times \frac{1\ L}{1000\ \text{mL}} = 0.0060$ L HCl excess then

$\frac{0.125\ \text{mol HCl}}{1\ \text{L}} \times 0.0060\ \text{L} = 0.00075$ mol HCl excess. Then 0.0150 L $Ba(OH)_2$ + 0.0300 L HCl =

0.0450 L total volume. $[\text{HCl excess}] = \frac{0.00075\ \text{mol HCl excess}}{0.0450\ \text{L}} = 0.016\underline{6}67$ M HCl excess. Since HCl is a strong acid, [HCl] excess = $[H_3O^+]$. Finally, $pH = -\log[H_3O^+] = -\log(0.01\underline{6}667) = 1.78$.

Check: The units (none) are correct. The pH is dropping sharply at the equivalence point, so the pH after 6 mL past the equivalence point should be quite acidic.

Finally plotting these five points, the titration curve looks like the following:

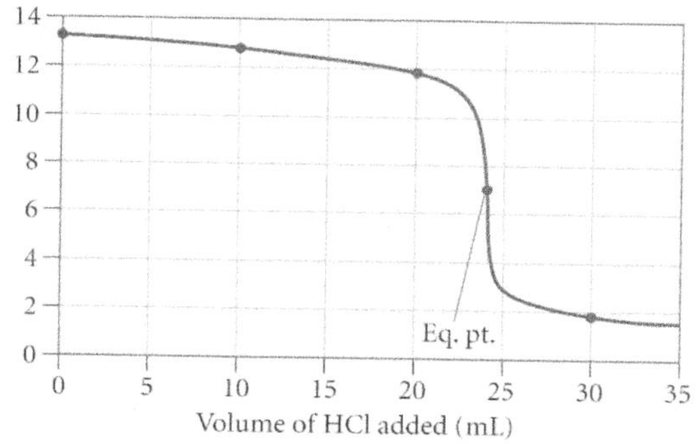

16.71 **Given:** 20.0 mL of 0.105 M $HC_2H_3O_2$ titrated with 0.125 M NaOH **Other:** K_a $(HC_2H_3O_2) = 1.8 \times 10^{-5}$

(a) **Find:** initial pH

Conceptual Plan: Since $HC_2H_3O_2$ is a weak acid, set up an equilibrium problem using the initial concentration.

So M H $C_2H_3O_2$ → $[H_3O^+]$ → pH

ICE Chart $\quad pH = -\log[H_3O^+]$

Solution:

$$HC_3H_3O_2\,(aq) + H_2O\,(l) \rightleftharpoons H_3O^+\,(aq) + C_2H_3O_2^-\,(aq)$$

	$[HC_2H_3O_2]$	$[H_3O^+]$	$[C_2H_3O_2^-]$
Initial	0.105	≈0.00	0.00
Change	$-x$	$+x$	$+x$
Equil	$0.105 - x$	$+x$	$+x$

$K_a = \frac{[H_3O^+][C_2H_3O_2^-]}{[HC_2H_3O_2]} = 1.8 \times 10^{-5} = \frac{x^2}{0.105 - x}$ Assume x is small ($x << 0.105$) so

$\frac{x^2}{0.105 - x} = 1.8 \times 10^{-5} = \frac{x^2}{0.105}$ and $x = 1.\underline{3}748 \times 10^{-3}$ M = $[H_3O^+]$. Confirm that the assumption is valid.

$\frac{1.\underline{3}748 \times 10^{-3}}{0.105} \times 100\% = 1.3\% < 5\%$ so the assumption is valid. Finally,

$pH = -\log[H_3O^+] = -\log(1.\underline{3}748 \times 10^{-3}) = 2.86$.

Check: The units (none) are correct. The magnitude of the answer makes physical sense because pH should be greater than – log (0.105) = 0.98 because this is a weak acid.

(b) **Find:** volume of base to reach equivalence point

Conceptual Plan: Write a balanced equation then mL → L then [$HC_2H_3O_2$], L → mol $HC_2H_3O_2$ then

$HC_2H_3O_2 + NaOH \rightarrow NaC_2H_3O_2 + H_2O$ $\quad \frac{1\ L}{1000\ mL}$ $\quad M = \frac{mol}{L}$

set mol acid($HC_2H_3O_2$) = mol base(NaOH) and [NaOH], mol NaOH → L NaOH → mL NaOH.

balanced equation has 1:1 stoichiometry $\quad M = \frac{mol}{L}$ $\quad \frac{1000\ mL}{1\ L}$

Solution: $20.0\ \text{mL}\ HC_2H_3O_2 \times \frac{1\ L}{1000\ mL} = 0.0200\ L\ HC_2H_3O_2$ then

$\frac{0.105\ mol\ HC_2H_3O_2}{1\ L} \times 0.0200\ L = 0.00210\ mol\ HC_2H_3O_2$.

So mol acid = mol $HC_2H_3O_2$ = 0.00210 mol = mol NaOH then

$0.00210\ mol\ NaOH \times \frac{1\ L}{0.125\ mol\ NaOH} = 0.0168\ L\ NaOH \times \frac{1000\ mL}{1\ L} = 16.8\ mL\ NaOH.$

Check: The units (mL) are correct. The volume of base is a little less than the volume of acid because the concentration of the base is a little greater than that of the acid.

(c) **Find:** pH after adding 5.0 mL of base

Conceptual Plan: Use calculations from part (b). Then mL → L then [NaOH], L → mol NaOH then

$\frac{1\ L}{1000\ mL}$ $\quad M = \frac{mol}{L}$

mol $HC_2H_3O_2$, mol NaOH → mol excess $HC_2H_3O_2$, mol $C_2H_3O_2^-$ and

set up stoichiometry table

L $HC_2H_3O_2$, L NaOH → total L then

L $HC_2H_3O_2$ + L NaOH = total L

mol excess $HC_2H_3O_2$, L → [$HC_2H_3O_2$] and mol excess $C_2H_3O_2^-$, L → [$C_2H_3O_2^-$] then

$M = \frac{mol}{L}$ $\quad M = \frac{mol}{L}$

M $HC_2H_3O_2$, M $C_2H_3O_2^-$ → [H_3O^+] → pH.

ICE Chart $\quad pH = -\log[H_3O^+]$

Solution: $5.0\ mL\ NaOH \times \frac{1\ L}{1000\ mL} = 0.0050\ L\ NaOH$ then

$\frac{0.125\ mol\ NaOH}{1\ L} \times 0.0050\ L = 0.000625\ mol\ NaOH$. Set up a table to track changes:

	NaOH (*aq*) +	$HC_2H_3O_2$ (*aq*) →	$NaC_2H_3O_2$ (*aq*) +	H_2O (*l*)
Before addition	0.00 mol	0.00210 mol	0.00 mol	—
Addition	0.000625mol	—	—	—
After addition	≈ 0.00 mol	0.001475 mol	0.000625 mol	—

Then 0.0200 L $HC_2H_3O_2$ + 0.0050 L NaOH = 0.0250 L total volume. Then

$$[HC_2H_3O_2] = \frac{0.001475\ mol\ HC_2H_3O_2}{0.0250\ L} = 0.0590\ M \text{ and}$$

$$[NaC_2H_3O_2] = \frac{0.000625\ mol\ C_2H_3O_2^-}{0.0250\ L} = 0.025\ M.$$

Since 1 $C_2H_3O_2^-$ ion is generated for each $NaC_2H_3O_2$, [$C_2H_3O_2^-$] = 0.025 M $C_2H_3O_2^-$.

$HC_2H_3O_2\ (aq) + H_2O\ (l) \rightleftharpoons H_3O^+\ (aq) + C_2H_3O_2^-(aq)$

	[$HC_2H_3O_2$]	[H_3O^+]	[$C_2H_3O_2^-$]
Initial	0.0590	≈0.00	0.025
Change	$-x$	$+x$	$+x$
Equil	$0.0590 - x$	$+x$	$0.025 + x$

$K_a = \frac{[H_3O^+][C_2H_3O_2^-]}{[HC_2H_3O_2]} = 1.8 \times 10^{-5} = \frac{x(0.025 + x)}{0.0590 - x}$ Assume x is small ($x << 0.025 < 0.0590$) so

$\frac{x(0.025 + x)}{0.0590 - x} = 1.8 \times 10^{-5} = \frac{x(0.025)}{0.0590}$ and $x = 4.248 \times 10^{-5}$ M = [H_3O^+]. Confirm that the assumption is valid.

$\frac{4.248 \times 10^{-5}}{0.025} \times 100\% = 0.17\% < 5\%$ so the assumption is valid.

Finally, $pH = -\log[H_3O^+] = -\log(4.248 \times 10^{-5}) = 4.37$.

Check: The units (none) are correct. The pH is a little higher than the initial pH, which is expected since some of the acid has been neutralized.

(d) **Find:** pH at one-half of the equivalence point

Conceptual Plan: Since this is a weak acid–strong base titration, the pH at one-half the equivalence point is the pK_a of the weak acid.

Solution: $pH = pK_a = -\log K_a = -\log(1.8 \times 10^{-5}) = 4.74.$

Check: The units (none) are correct. Since this is a weak acid–strong base titration, the pH at one-half the equivalence point is the pK_a of the weak acid, so it should be a little below 5.

(e) **Find:** pH at equivalence point

Conceptual Plan: Use calculations from part (b). Then, since all of the weak acid has been converted to its conjugate base, the pH is only dependent on the hydrolysis reaction of the conjugate base. The mol $C_2H_3O_2^-$ = initial mol $HC_2H_3O_2$ and L $HC_2H_3O_2$, L NaOH to equivalence point $\rightarrow$ total L then

$$\text{L } HC_2H_3O_2 + \text{L NaOH} = \text{total L}$$

mol excess $C_2H_3O_2^-$, L $\rightarrow$ $[C_2H_3O_2^-]$ and K_a $\rightarrow$ K_b then do an equilibrium calculation:

$$M = \frac{\text{mol}}{\text{L}} \qquad K_w = K_a K_b$$

$[C_2H_3O_2^-]$, K_b $\rightarrow$ $[OH^-]$ $\rightarrow$ $[H_3O^+]$ $\rightarrow$ pH.

$$\textit{set up ICE table} \qquad K_w = [H_3O^+][OH^-] \qquad pH = -\log[H_3O^+]$$

Solution: mol $C_2H_3O_2^-$ = initial mol $HC_2H_3O_2$ = 0.00210 mol and total volume = L $HC_2H_3O_2$ + L NaOH = 0.020 L + 0.0168 L = 0.0368 L then

$[C_2H_3O_2^-] = \dfrac{0.00210 \text{ mol } C_2H_3O_2^-}{0.0368 \text{ L}} = 0.05\underline{7}0652$ M and $K_w = K_a K_b$. Rearrange to solve for K_b.

$K_b = \dfrac{K_w}{K_a} = \dfrac{1.0 \times 10^{-14}}{1.8 \times 10^{-5}} = 5.\underline{5}556 \times 10^{-10}$. Set up an ICE table

$$C_2H_3O_2^-(aq) + H_2O(l) \rightleftharpoons HC_2H_3O_2(aq) + OH^-(aq)$$

	$[C_2H_3O_2^-]$	$[HC_2H_3O_2]$	$[OH^-]$
Initial	$0.05\underline{7}0652$	≈ 0.00	≈ 0.00
Change	$-x$	$+x$	$+x$
Equil	$0.05\underline{7}0652 - x$	$+x$	$+x$

$K_b = \dfrac{[HC_2H_3O_2][OH^-]}{[C_2H_3O_2^-]} = 5.\underline{5}556 \times 10^{-10} = \dfrac{x^2}{0.05\underline{7}0652 - x}$ Assume x is small ($x << 0.057$) so

$\dfrac{x^2}{0.05\underline{7}0652 - \cancel{x}} = 5.\underline{5}556 \times 10^{-10} = \dfrac{x^2}{0.05\underline{7}0652}$ and $x = 5.\underline{6}305 \times 10^{-6}$ M = $[OH^-]$.

Confirm that the assumption is valid. $\dfrac{5.\underline{6}305 \times 10^{-6}}{0.05\underline{7}0652} \times 100\% = 0.0099\% < 5\%$ so the assumption is valid.

$K_w = [H_3O^+][OH^-]$ so $[H_3O^+] = \dfrac{K_w}{[OH^-]} = \dfrac{1.0 \times 10^{-14}}{5.\underline{6}305 \times 10^{-6}} = 1.\underline{7}760 \times 10^{-9}$ M.

Finally, $pH = -\log[H_3O^+] = -\log(1.\underline{7}760 \times 10^{-9}) = 8.75.$

Check: The units (none) are correct. Since this is a weak acid–strong base titration, the pH at the equivalence point is basic.

(f) **Find:** pH after adding 5.0 mL of base beyond the equivalence point

Conceptual Plan: Use calculations from parts (b) and (c). Then the pH is only dependent on the amount of excess base and the total solution volumes.

mL excess $\rightarrow$ L excess then [NaOH], L excess $\rightarrow$ mol NaOH excess

$$\frac{1 \text{ L}}{1000 \text{ mL}} \qquad M = \frac{\text{mol}}{\text{L}}$$

then L $HC_2H_3O_2$, L NaOH to equivalence point, L NaOH excess $\rightarrow$ total L then

$$\text{L } HC_2H_3O_2 + \text{L NaOH to equivalence point} + \text{L NaOH excess} = \text{total L}$$

mol excess NaOH, total L $\rightarrow$ [NaOH] = $[OH^-]$ $\rightarrow$ $[H_3O^+]$ $\rightarrow$ pH

$$M = \frac{\text{mol}}{\text{L}} \qquad K_w = [H_3O^+][OH^-] \qquad pH = -\log[H_3O^+]$$

Solution: $5.0\ \cancel{\text{mL NaOH}} \times \frac{1\text{ L}}{1000\ \cancel{\text{mL}}} = 0.0050\text{ L NaOH}$ excess then

$\frac{0.125\text{ mol NaOH}}{1\ \cancel{\text{L}}} \times 0.0050\ \cancel{\text{L}} = 0.000625\text{ mol NaOH excess}$. Then $0.0200\text{ L } HC_2H_3O_2 + 0.0168\text{ L NaOH} + 0.0050\text{ L NaOH} = 0.0418\text{ L}$ total volume.

$[\text{NaOH excess}] = \frac{0.000625\text{ mol NaOH excess}}{0.0418\text{ L}} = 0.0149\underline{5}22\text{ M NaOH}$ excess. Since NaOH is a strong base, [NaOH] excess = $[OH^-]$. The strong base overwhelms the weak base and is insignificant in the calculation. $K_w = [H_3O^+][OH^-]$ so $[H_3O^+] = \frac{K_w}{[OH^-]} = \frac{1.0 \times 10^{-14}}{0.0149\underline{5}22} = 6.\underline{6}88 \times 10^{-13}$ M. Finally,

$pH = -\log[H_3O^+] = -\log(6.\underline{6}88 \times 10^{-13}) = 12.17.$

Check: The units (none) are correct. The pH is rising sharply at the equivalence point, so the pH after 5 mL past the equivalence point should be quite basic.

16.72 **Given:** 30.0 mL of 0.165 M $HC_3H_5O_2$ titrated with 0.300 M KOH **Other:** K_a ($HC_3H_5O_2$) = 1.3×10^{-5}
Find: initial pH
Conceptual Plan: Since $HC_3H_5O_2$ is a weak acid, set up an equilibrium problem using the initial concentration. So M $HC_3H_5O_2$ → $[H_3O^+]$ → pH.
ICE Chart $pH = -\log[H_3O^+]$

Solution:

$$HC_3H_5O_2\,(aq) + H_2O\,(l) \rightleftharpoons H_3O^+\,(aq) + C_3H_5O_2^-\,(aq)$$

	$[HC_3H_5O_2]$	$[H_3O^+]$	$[C_3H_5O_2^-]$
Initial	0.165	≈0.00	0.00
Change	$-x$	$+x$	$+x$
Equil	$0.165 - x$	$+x$	$+x$

$K_a = \frac{[H_3O^+][C_3H_5O_2^-]}{[HC_3H_5O_2]} = 1.3 \times 10^{-5} = \frac{x^2}{0.165 - x}$ Assume x is small ($x << 0.165$) so

$\frac{x^2}{0.165 - \cancel{x}} = 1.3 \times 10^{-5} = \frac{x^2}{0.165}$ and $x = 1.\underline{4}646 \times 10^{-3}$ M = $[H_3O^+]$. Confirm that the assumption is valid.

$\frac{1.\underline{4}646 \times 10^{-3}}{0.165} \times 100\% = 0.89\% < 5\%$ so the assumption is valid. Finally,

$pH = -\log[H_3O^+] = -\log(1.\underline{4}646 \times 10^{-3}) = 2.83.$

Check: The units (none) are correct. The magnitude of the answer makes physical sense because pH should be greater than $-\log(0.165) = 0.78$ because this is a weak acid.
Find: pH after adding 5.0 mL of base
Conceptual Plan: Write a balanced equation then mL → L then $[HC_3H_5O_2]$, L → mol $HC_3H_5O_2$ then
$HC_3H_5O_2 + KOH \rightarrow KC_3H_5O_2 + H_2O$ $\frac{1\text{ L}}{1000\text{ mL}}$ $M = \frac{\text{mol}}{\text{L}}$

mL → L then [KOH], L → mol KOH then
$\frac{1\text{ L}}{1000\text{ mL}}$ $M = \frac{\text{mol}}{\text{L}}$

mol $HC_3H_5O_2$, mol KOH → mol excess $HC_3H_5O_2$, mol $C_3H_5O_2^-$.
set up stoichiometry table

Since there are significant concentrations of both the acid and the conjugate base species, this is a buffer solution and so the Henderson–Hasselbalch equation $\left(pH = pK_a + \log\frac{[\text{base}]}{[\text{acid}]}\right)$ can be used. Also note that the ratio of concentrations is the same as the ratio of moles, since the volume is the same for both species.

Solution: $30.0\ \cancel{\text{mL } HC_3H_5O_2} \times \frac{1\text{ L}}{1000\ \cancel{\text{mL}}} = 0.0300\text{ L } HC_3H_5O_2$ then

$\frac{0.165\text{ mol } HC_3H_5O_2}{1\ \cancel{\text{L}}} \times 0.0300\ \cancel{\text{L}} = 0.00495\text{ mol } HC_3H_5O_2$ and $5.0\ \cancel{\text{mL KOH}} \times \frac{1\text{ L}}{1000\ \cancel{\text{mL}}} = 0.0050\text{ L KOH}$ then

$\frac{0.300 \text{ mol KOH}}{1 \cancel{L}} \times 0.0050 \cancel{L} = 0.0015$ mol KOH. Set up a table to track changes:

	KOH (*aq*) +	$HC_3H_5O_2$ (*aq*) →	$KC_3H_5O_2$ (*aq*) +	H_2O (*l*)
Before addition	0.00 mol	0.00495 mol	0.00 mol	—
Addition	0.0015 mol	—	—	—
After addition	≈ 0.00 mol	0.00345 mol	0.0015 mol	—

Then use the Henderson–Hasselbalch equation since the solution is a buffer.

$$pH = pK_a + \log\frac{[\text{base}]}{[\text{acid}]} = -\log(1.3 \times 10^{-5}) + \log\frac{0.0015}{0.00345} = 4.52$$

Check: The units (none) are correct. The pH is a little higher than the initial pH, which is expected since some of the acid has been neutralized.

Find: pH after adding 10.0 mL of base

Conceptual Plan: Use calculations from above, then mL → L then [KOH], L → mol KOH then

$\frac{1 \text{ L}}{1000 \text{ mL}}$ $M = \frac{\text{mol}}{\text{L}}$

mol $HC_3H_5O_2$, mol KOH → mol excess $HC_3H_5O_2$, mol $C_3H_5O_2^-$.

set up stoichiometry table

Since there are significant concentrations of both the acid and the conjugate base species, this is a buffer solution and so the Henderson–Hasselbalch equation $\left(pH = pK_a + \log\frac{[\text{base}]}{[\text{acid}]}\right)$ can be used. Also note that the ratio of concentrations is the same as the ratio of moles, since the volume is the same for both species.

Solution: $10.0 \cancel{\text{mL KOH}} \times \frac{1 \text{ L}}{1000 \cancel{\text{mL}}} = 0.0100$ L KOH then $\frac{0.300 \text{ mol KOH}}{1 \cancel{L}} \times 0.0100 \cancel{L} = 0.0030$ mol KOH.

Set up a table to track changes:

	KOH (*aq*) +	$HC_3H_5O_2$ (*aq*) →	$KC_3H_5O_2$ (*aq*) +	H_2O (*l*)
Before addition	0.00 mol	0.00495 mol	0.00 mol	—
Addition	0.0030 mol	—	—	—
After addition	≈ 0.00 mol	0.00195 mol	0.0030 mol	—

Then use the Henderson–Hasselbalch equation since the solution is a buffer.

$$pH = pK_a + \log\frac{[\text{base}]}{[\text{acid}]} = -\log(1.3 \times 10^{-5}) + \log\frac{0.0030}{0.00195} = 5.07$$

Check: The units (none) are correct. The pH is a little higher than the last pH, which is expected since some of the acid has been neutralized.

Find: pH at equivalence point

Conceptual Plan: Use calculations from above, then set mol acid ($HC_3H_5O_2$) = mol base (KOH)

balanced equation has 1:1 stoichiometry

and [KOH], mol KOH → L KOH then, since all of the weak acid has been converted to its

$M = \frac{\text{mol}}{\text{L}}$

conjugate base, the pH is only dependent on the hydrolysis reaction of the conjugate base. The mol $C_3H_5O_2^-$ = initial mol $HC_3H_5O_2$ and L $HC_3H_5O_2$, L KOH to equivalence point → total L

L $HC_3H_5O_2$ + L KOH = total L

then mol $C_2H_3O_2^-$, L → [$C_2H_3O_2^-$] and

$M = \frac{\text{mol}}{\text{L}}$

K_a → K_b. Then do an equilibrium calculation: [$C_2H_3O_2^-$], K_b → [OH^-] → [H_3O^+] → pH

$K_w = K_a K_b$ *set up ICE table* $K_w = [H_3O^+][OH^-]$ $pH = -\log[H_3O^+]$

Solution: mol acid = mol $HC_3H_5O_2$ = 0.00495 mol = mol KOH then

$0.00495 \cancel{\text{mol KOH}} \times \frac{1 \text{ L}}{0.300 \cancel{\text{mol KOH}}} = 0.0165$ L KOH. Then total volume = L $HC_3H_5O_2$ + L KOH =

$0.0300 \text{ L} + 0.0165 \text{ L} = 0.0465$ then $[C_3H_5O_2^-] = \frac{0.00495 \text{ mol } C_3H_5O_2^-}{0.0465 \text{ L}} = 0.10\underline{6}452$ M and $K_w = K_a K_b$.

Rearrange to solve for K_b. $K_b = \frac{K_w}{K_a} = \frac{1.0 \times 10^{-14}}{1.3 \times 10^{-5}} = 7.\underline{6}923 \times 10^{-10}$ M. Set up an ICE table:

	$C_3H_5O_2^-\,(aq) + H_2O\,(l)$	$\rightleftharpoons HC_3H_5O_2\,(aq)$	$+\ OH^-(aq)$
	$[C_3H_5O_2^-]$	$[HC_3H_5O_2]$	$[OH^-]$
Initial	0.106452	≈0.00	0.00
Change	$-x$	$+x$	$+x$
Equil	$0.106452 - x$	$+x$	$+x$

$K_b = \dfrac{[HC_3H_5O_2]\,[OH^-]}{[C_3H_5O_2^-]} = 7.6923 \times 10^{-10} = \dfrac{x^2}{0.106452 - x}$ Assume x is small ($x << 0.106$) so

$\dfrac{x^2}{0.106452 - x} = 7.6923 \times 10^{-10} = \dfrac{x^2}{0.106452}$ and $x = 9.0491 \times 10^{-6}$ M = $[OH^-]$.

Confirm that the assumption is valid. $\dfrac{9.0491 \times 10^{-6}}{0.106452} \times 100\% = 0.0085\% < 5\%$ so the assumption is valid.

$K_w = [H_3O^+]\,[OH^-]$ so $[H_3O^+] = \dfrac{K_w}{[OH^-]} = \dfrac{1.0 \times 10^{-14}}{9.0491 \times 10^{-6}} = 1.1051 \times 10^{-9}$ M. Finally,

$pH = -\log [H_3O^+] = -\log (1.1051 \times 10^{-9}) = 8.96.$

Check: The units (none) are correct. Since this is a weak acid–strong base titration, the pH at the equivalence point is basic.

Find: pH at one-half of the equivalence point

Conceptual Plan: Since this is a weak acid–strong base titration, the pH at one-half the equivalence point is the pK_a of the weak acid.

Solution: $pH = pK_a = -\log K_a = -\log (1.3 \times 10^{-5}) = 4.89$ and the volume of added base is 0.5 x 16.5 mL = 8.3 mL.

Check: The units (none) are correct. Since this is a weak acid–strong base titration, the pH at one-half the equivalence point is the pK_a of the weak acid, so it should be a little below 5.

Find: pH after adding 20.0 mL of base

Conceptual Plan: Use calculations from earlier. Then the pH is only dependent on the amount of excess base and the total solution volumes. mL added, mL at equiv. pt. → mL excess → L excess

mL excess = mL added – mL at equiv. pt. $\dfrac{1\text{ L}}{1000\text{ mL}}$

then mL excess → L excess then [KOH], L excess → mol KOH excess

$\dfrac{1\text{ L}}{1000\text{ mL}}$ $M = \dfrac{\text{mol}}{\text{L}}$

then L $HC_3H_5O_2$, L KOH to equivalence point, L KOH excess → total L then

L $HC_2H_3O_2$ + L KOH to equivalence point + L KOH excess = total L

mol excess KOH, total L → [KOH] = $[OH^-]$ → $[H_3O^+]$ → pH

$M = \dfrac{\text{mol}}{\text{L}}$ $K_w = [H_3O^+]\,[OH^-]$ $pH = -\log [H_3O^+]$

Solution: mL KOH excess = mL added – mL to equiv. pt. = 20.0 mL – 16.5 mL = 3.5 mL.

$3.5\text{ mL KOH} \times \dfrac{1\text{ L}}{1000\text{ mL}} = 0.0035$ L KOH excess then

$\dfrac{0.300\text{ mol KOH}}{1\text{ L}} \times 0.0035\text{ L} = 0.00105$ mol KOH excess. Then 0.0300 L $HC_3H_5O_2$ + 0.0165 L KOH + 0.0035 L KOH = 0.0500 L total volume. [KOH excess] $= \dfrac{0.00105\text{ mol KOH excess}}{0.0500\text{ L}} = 0.021$ M KOH excess.

Since KOH is a strong base, [KOH] excess = $[OH^-]$. The strong base overwhelms the weak base and is insignificant in the calculation. $K_w = [H_3O^+]\,[OH^-]$ so $[H_3O^+] = \dfrac{K_w}{[OH^-]} = \dfrac{1.0 \times 10^{-14}}{0.021} = 4.7619 \times 10^{-13}$ M.

Finally, $pH = -\log [H_3O^+] = -\log (4.7619 \times 10^{-13}) = 12.32.$

Check: The units (none) are correct. The pH is rising sharply at the equivalence point, so the pH after 5 mL past the equivalence point should be quite basic.

Find: pH after adding 25.0 mL of base

Conceptual Plan: Use calculations from earlier. Then the pH is only dependent on the amount of excess base and the total solution volumes. mL added, mL at equiv. pt. → mL excess → L excess

mL excess = mL added – mL at equiv. pt. $\dfrac{1\text{ L}}{1000\text{ mL}}$

then mL excess → L excess then [KOH], L excess → mol KOH excess

$\dfrac{1\text{ L}}{1000\text{ mL}}$ $M = \dfrac{\text{mol}}{\text{L}}$

then L $HC_3H_5O_2$, L KOH to equivalence point, L KOH excess → total L then

L $HC_2H_3O_2$ + L KOH to equivalence point + L KOH excess = total L

mol excess KOH, total L → [KOH] = [OH⁻] → [H₃O⁺] → pH

$M = \frac{\text{mol}}{\text{L}}$ $K_w = [H_3O^+][OH^-]$ $pH = -\log[H_3O^+]$

Solution: mL KOH excess = mL added – mL to equiv. pt. = 25.0 mL – 16.5 mL = 8.5 mL.

$8.5 \text{ mL KOH} \times \frac{1 \text{ L}}{1000 \text{ mL}} = 0.0085$ L KOH excess then

$\frac{0.300 \text{ mol KOH}}{1 \text{ L}} \times 0.0085 \text{ L} = 0.00255$ mol KOH excess. Then 0.0300 L $HC_3H_5O_2$ + 0.0165 L KOH +

0.0085 L KOH = 0.0550 L total volume. $[\text{KOH excess}] = \frac{0.00255 \text{ mol KOH excess}}{0.0550 \text{ L}} = 0.046364$ M KOH excess.

Since KOH is a strong base, [KOH] excess = [OH⁻]. The strong base overwhelms the weak base and is insignificant in the calculation. $K_w = [H_3O^+][OH^-]$ So $[H_3O^+] = \frac{K_w}{[OH^-]} = \frac{1.0 \times 10^{-14}}{0.046364} = 2.1569 \times 10^{-13}$ M.

Finally, $pH = -\log[H_3O^+] = -\log(2.1569 \times 10^{-13}) = 12.67$.

Check: The units (none) are correct. The pH is rising sharply at the equivalence point, so the pH after 5 mL past the equivalence point should be quite basic. This pH is higher than the last pH.

Plotting these data points is shown as follows:

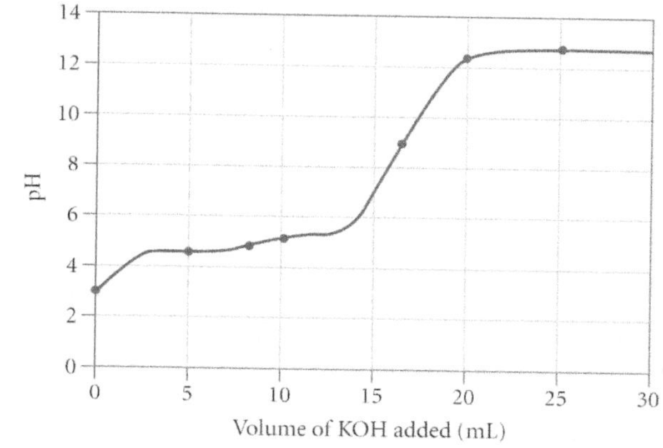

16.73 **Given:** 25.0 mL of 0.175 M CH_3NH_2 titrated with 0.150 M HBr **Other:** K_b (CH_3NH_2) = 4.4×10^{-4}

(a) **Find:** initial pH

Conceptual Plan: Since CH_3NH_2 is a weak base, set up an equilibrium problem using the initial concentration, so M CH_3NH_2 → [OH⁻] → [H₃O⁺] → pH.

ICE Chart $K_w = [H_3O^+][OH^-]$ $pH = -\log[H_3O^+]$

Solution:

$$CH_3NH_2(aq) + H_2O(l) \rightleftharpoons CH_3NH_3^+(aq) + OH^-(aq)$$

	$[CH_3NH_2]$	$[CH_3NH_3^+]$	$[OH^-]$
Initial	0.175	0.00	≈ 0.00
Change	$-x$	$+x$	$+x$
Equil	$0.175 - x$	$+x$	$+x$

$$K_b = \frac{[CH_3NH_3^+][OH^-]}{[CH_3NH_2]} = 4.4 \times 10^{-4} = \frac{x^2}{0.175 - x}$$

Assume x is small ($x << 0.175$) so $\frac{x^2}{0.175 - x} = 4.4 \times 10^{-4} = \frac{x^2}{0.175}$ and $x = 8.7750 \times 10^{-3}$ M = [OH⁻].

Confirm that the assumption is valid. $\frac{8.7750 \times 10^{-3}}{0.175} \times 100\% = 5.0\%$ so the assumption is valid.

$K_w = [H_3O^+][OH^-]$ so $[H_3O^+] = \frac{K_w}{[OH^-]} = \frac{1.0 \times 10^{-14}}{8.7750 \times 10^{-3}} = 1.1396 \times 10^{-12}$ M.

Finally, pH $= -\log [H_3O^+] = -\log(1.1396 \times 10^{-12}) = 11.94$.

Check: The units (none) are correct. The magnitude of the answer makes physical sense because pH should be less than 14 + log (0.175) = 13.2 because this is a weak base.

(b) **Find:** volume of acid to reach equivalence point

Conceptual Plan: Write a balanced equation, then mL → L then $[CH_3NH_2]$, L → mol CH_3NH_2

$HBr + CH_3NH_2 \rightarrow CH_3NH_3Br + H_2O$ $\quad \frac{1\text{ L}}{1000\text{ mL}}$ $\quad M = \frac{\text{mol}}{\text{L}}$

then set mol base (CH_3NH_2) = mol acid (HBr) and [HBr], mol HBr → L HBr → mL HBr.

balanced equation has 1:1 stoichiometry $\quad M = \frac{\text{mol}}{\text{L}}$ $\quad \frac{1000\text{ mL}}{1\text{ L}}$

Solution: $25.0 \text{ mL } CH_3NH_2 \times \frac{1\text{ L}}{1000\text{ mL}} = 0.0250 \text{ L } CH_3NH_2$ then

$\frac{0.175 \text{ mol } CH_3NH_2}{1\text{ L}} \times 0.0250\text{ L} = 0.004375 \text{ mol } CH_3NH_2$. So mol base = mol CH_3NH_2 = 0.004375 mol

= mol HBr then $0.004375 \text{ mol HBr} \times \frac{1\text{ L}}{0.150 \text{ mol HBr}} = 0.0291667 \text{ L HBr} \times \frac{1000\text{ mL}}{1\text{ L}} = 29.2 \text{ mL HBr}$.

Check: The units (mL) are correct. The volume of acid is a greater than the volume of base because the concentration of the base is a little greater than that of the acid.

(c) **Find:** pH after adding 5.0 mL of acid

Conceptual Plan: Use calculations from part (b). Then mL → L then [HBr], L → mol HBr

$\frac{1\text{ L}}{1000\text{ mL}}$ $\quad M = \frac{\text{mol}}{\text{L}}$

then mol CH_3NH_2, mol HBr → mol excess CH_3NH_2 and L CH_3NH_2, L HBr → total L.

set up stoichiometry table $\quad$ L CH_3NH_2 + L HBr = total L

Since there are significant concentrations of both the acid and the conjugate base species, this is a buffer solution and so the Henderson–Hasselbalch equation $\left(pH = pK_a + \log \frac{[base]}{[acid]}\right)$ can be used. Convert K_b to K_a using $K_w = K_a K_b$. Also note that the ratio of concentrations is the same as the ratio of moles, since the volume is the same for both species.

Solution: $5.0 \text{ mL HBr} \times \frac{1\text{ L}}{1000\text{ mL}} = 0.0050 \text{ L HBr}$ then $\frac{0.150 \text{ mol HBr}}{1\text{ L}} \times 0.0050\text{ L} = 0.00075 \text{ mol HBr}$.

Set up a table to track changes:

	HBr (*aq*) +	CH_3NH_2 (*aq*) →	CH_3NH_3Br (*aq*)
Before addition	0.00 mol	0.004375 mol	0.00 mol
Addition	0.00075 mol	—	—
After addition	≈ 0.00 mol	0.003625 mol	0.000750 mol

then $K_w = K_a K_b$ so

$K_a = \frac{K_w}{K_b} = \frac{1.0 \times 10^{-14}}{4.4 \times 10^{-4}} = 2.2727 \times 10^{-11}$ M then use the Henderson–Hasselbalch equation, since the solution is a buffer. $pH = pK_a + \log \frac{[base]}{[acid]} = -\log(2.2727 \times 10^{-11}) + \log \frac{0.003625}{0.000750} = 11.33$

Check: The units (none) are correct. The pH is a little lower than the last pH, which is expected since some of the base has been neutralized.

(d) **Find:** pH at one-half of the equivalence point

Conceptual Plan: Since this is a weak base–strong acid titration, the pH at one-half the equivalence point is the pK_a of the conjugate acid of weak base.

Solution: $pH = pK_a = -\log K_a = -\log(2.2727 \times 10^{-11}) = 10.64$.

Check: The units (none) are correct. Since this is a weak acid–strong base titration, the pH at one-half the equivalence point is the pK_a of the conjugate acid of the weak base, so it should be a little below 11.

(e) **Find:** pH at equivalence point

Conceptual Plan: Use calculations from above. Since all of the weak base has been converted to its conjugate acid, the pH is only dependent on the hydrolysis reaction of the conjugate acid. The mol $CH_3NH_3^+$ = initial mol CH_3NH_2 and

L CH_3NH_2, L HBr to equivalence point → total L then mol $CH_3NH_3^+$, L → $[CH_3NH_3^+]$

L CH_3NH_2 + L HBr = total L $\quad M = \frac{\text{mol}}{\text{L}}$

then do an equilibrium calculation: $[CH_3NH_3^+]$, K_a → $[H_3O^+]$ → pH.

set up ICE table pH = − log $[H_3O^+]$

Solution: mol base = mol acid = mol $CH_3NH_3^+$ = 0.004375 mol. Then total volume = L CH_3NH_2 + L HBr = 0.0250 L + 0.0292 L = 0.0542 then $[CH_3NH_3^+] = \frac{0.004375 \text{ mol } CH_3NH_3^+}{0.0542 \text{ L}} = 0.0807196$ M.

$$CH_3NH_3^+ (aq) + H_2O (l) \rightleftharpoons CH_3NH_2 (aq) + H_3O^+(aq)$$

Set up an ICE table:

	$[CH_3NH_3^+]$	$[CH_3NH_2]$	$[H_3O^+]$
Initial	0.0807196	≈0.00	≈0.00
Change	$-x$	$+x$	$+x$
Equil	$0.0807196 - x$	$+x$	$+x$

$K_a = \frac{[CH_3NH_2][H_3O^+]}{[CH_3NH_3^+]} = 2.2727 \times 10^{-11} = \frac{x^2}{0.0807196 - x}$ Assume x is small ($x << 0.0807$) so

$\frac{x^2}{0.0807196 - x} = 2.2727 \times 10^{-11} = \frac{x^2}{0.0807196}$ and $x = 1.3544 \times 10^{-6} = [H_3O^+]$.

Confirm that the assumption is valid. $\frac{1.3544 \times 10^{-6}}{0.0807106} \times 100\% = 0.0017\% < 5\%$ so the assumption is valid.

Finally, pH = − log $[H_3O^+]$ = − log (1.3544×10^{-6}) = 5.87.

Check: The units (none) are correct. Since this is a weak base–strong acid titration, the pH at the equivalence point is acidic.

(f) **Find:** pH after adding 5.0 mL of acid beyond the equivalence point

Conceptual Plan: Use calculations from parts (b) and (c). Then the pH is only dependent on the amount of excess acid and the total solution volumes.

mL excess → L excess then [HBr], L excess → mol HBr excess

$\frac{1 \text{ L}}{1000 \text{ mL}}$ $M = \frac{\text{mol}}{\text{L}}$

then L CH_3NH_2, L HBr to equivalence point, L HBr excess → total L then

L CH_3NH_2 + L HBr to equivalence point + L HBr excess = total L

mol excess HBr, total L → [HBr] = $[H_3O^+]$ → pH

$M = \frac{\text{mol}}{\text{L}}$ pH = − log $[H_3O^+]$

Solution: $5.0 \text{ mL HBr} \times \frac{1 \text{ L}}{1000 \text{ mL}} = 0.0050$ L HBr excess then

$\frac{0.150 \text{ mol HBr}}{1 \text{ L}} \times 0.0050 \text{ L} = 0.00075$ mol HBr excess. Then 0.0250 L CH_3NH_2 + 0.0292 L HBr + 0.0050 L HBr = 0.0592 L total volume.

$[\text{HBr excess}] = \frac{0.00075 \text{ mol HBr excess}}{0.0592 \text{ L}} = 0.012669$ M HBr excess

Since HBr is a strong acid, [HBr] excess = $[H_3O^+]$. The strong acid overwhelms the weak acid and is insignificant in the calculation. Finally, pH = − log $[H_3O^+]$ = − log (0.012669) = 1.90.

Check: The units (none) are correct. The pH is dropping sharply at the equivalence point, so the pH after 5 mL past the equivalence point should be quite acidic.

16.74 **Given:** 25.0 mL of 0.125 M pyridine (C_5H_5N) titrated with 0.100 M HCl **Other:** K_b (C_5H_5N) = 1.7×10^{-9}

Find: initial pH

Conceptual Plan: Since C_5H_5N is a weak base, set up an equilibrium problem using the initial concentration, so M C_5H_5N → $[OH^-]$ → $[H_3O^+]$ → pH.

ICE Chart $K_w = [H_3O^+][OH^-]$ pH = − log $[H_3O^+]$

Solution:

$$C_5H_5N (aq) + H_2O (l) \rightleftharpoons C_5H_5NH^+ (aq) + OH^-(aq)$$

	$[C_5H_5N]$	$[C_5H_5NH^+]$	$[OH^-]$
Initial	0.125	0.00	≈ 0.00
Change	$-x$	$+x$	$+x$
Equil	$0.125 - x$	$+x$	$+x$

$$K_b = \frac{[C_5H_5NH^+][OH^-]}{[C_5H_5N]} = 1.7 \times 10^{-9} = \frac{x^2}{0.125 - x}$$

Assume x is small ($x << 0.125$) so $\frac{x^2}{0.125 - x} = 1.7 \times 10^{-9} = \frac{x^2}{0.125}$ and $x = 1.4577 \times 10^{-5} = [OH^-]$.

Confirm that the assumption is valid. $\frac{1.4577 \times 10^{-5}}{0.125} \times 100\% = 0.012\% < 5.0\%$ so the assumption is valid.

$K_w = [H_3O^+][OH^-]$ so $[H_3O^+] = \frac{K_w}{[OH^-]} = \frac{1.0 \times 10^{-14}}{1.4577 \times 10^{-5}} = 6.8601 \times 10^{-10}$ M. Finally,

$pH = -\log [H_3O^+] = -\log (6.8601 \times 10^{-10}) = 9.16.$

Check: The units (none) are correct. The magnitude of the answer makes physical sense because pH should be less than 14 + log (0.125) = 13.1 because this is a weak base.

Find: pH after adding 10.0 mL of acid

Conceptual Plan: Write balanced equation then mL → L then $[C_5H_5N]$, L → mol C_5H_5N then

$HCl + C_5H_5N \rightarrow C_5H_5NHCl$; $\frac{1\text{ L}}{1000\text{ mL}}$; $M = \frac{\text{mol}}{\text{L}}$

mL → L then [HCl], L → mol HCl then mol C_5H_5N, mol HCl → mol excess C_5H_5N and

$\frac{1\text{ L}}{1000\text{ mL}}$; $M = \frac{\text{mol}}{\text{L}}$; *set up stoichiometry table*

L C_5H_5N, L HCl → total L then since there are significant concentrations of both the acid and

L C_5H_5N + L HCl = total L

the conjugate base species, this is a buffer solution and so the Henderson–Hasselbalch equation $\left(pH = pK_a + \log\frac{[\text{base}]}{[\text{acid}]}\right)$ can be used. Convert K_b to K_a using $K_w = K_a K_b$. Also note that the ratio of concentrations is the same as the ratio of moles, since the volume is the same for both species.

Solution: $25.0\ \text{mL}\ C_5H_5N \times \frac{1\text{ L}}{1000\text{ mL}} = 0.0250\text{ L } C_5H_5N$ then

$\frac{0.125\text{ mol } C_5H_5N}{1\text{ L}} \times 0.0250\text{ L} = 0.003125\text{ mol } C_5H_5N$ and $10.0\text{ mL HCl} \times \frac{1\text{ L}}{1000\text{ mL}} = 0.0100\text{ L HCl}$ then

$\frac{0.100\text{ mol HCl}}{1\text{ L}} \times 0.0100\text{ L} = 0.00100\text{ mol HCl}$. Set up a table to track changes:

	$HCl\ (aq)$ +	$C_5H_5N\ (aq)$ →	$C_5H_5NHCl\ (aq)$
Before addition	0.00 mol	0.003125 mol	0.00 mol
Addition	0.00100 mol	—	—
After addition	≈ 0.00 mol	0.002125 mol	0.00100 mol

Then $K_w = K_a K_b$ so $K_a = \frac{K_w}{K_b} = \frac{1.0 \times 10^{-14}}{1.7 \times 10^{-9}} = 5.8824 \times 10^{-6}$ M then use the Henderson–Hasselbalch equation since the solution is a buffer.

$$pH = pK_a + \log\frac{[\text{base}]}{[\text{acid}]} = -\log (5.8824 \times 10^{-6}) + \log\frac{0.002125}{0.00100} = 5.56$$

Check: The units (none) are correct. The pH is lower than the last pH, which is expected since some of the base has been neutralized.

Find: pH after adding 20.0 mL of acid

Conceptual Plan: Use calculations from above. Then mL → L then [HCl], L → mol HCl

$\frac{1\text{ L}}{1000\text{ mL}}$; $M = \frac{\text{mol}}{\text{L}}$

then mol C_5H_5N, mol HCl → mol excess C_5H_5N and L C_5H_5N, L HCl → total L.

set up stoichiometry table ; L C_5H_5N + L HCl = total L

Since there are significant concentrations of both the acid and the conjugate base species, this is a buffer solution and so the Henderson–Hasselbalch equation $\left(pH = pK_a + \log\frac{[\text{base}]}{[\text{acid}]}\right)$ can be used. Convert K_b to K_a using $K_w = K_a K_b$. Also note that the ratio of concentrations is the same as the ratio of moles, since the volume is the same for both species.

Solution: $20.0\text{ mL HCl} \times \frac{1\text{ L}}{1000\text{ mL}} = 0.0200\text{ L HCl}$ then $\frac{0.100\text{ mol HCl}}{1\text{ L}} \times 0.0200\text{ L} = 0.00200\text{ mol HCl}$.

Set up a table to track changes:

	$HCl\ (aq)$ +	$C_5H_5N\ (aq)$ →	$C_5H_5NHCl\ (aq)$
Before addition	0.00 mol	0.003125 mol	0.00 mol
Addition	0.00200 mol	—	—
After addition	≈ 0.00 mol	0.001125 mol	0.00200 mol

Then use the Henderson–Hasselbalch equation since the solution is a buffer.

$$pH = pK_a + \log\frac{[\text{base}]}{[\text{acid}]} = -\log(5.8824 \times 10^{-6}) + \log\frac{0.001125}{0.00200} = 4.98$$

Check: The units (none) are correct. The pH is lower than the last pH, which is expected since some of the base has been neutralized.

Find: pH at equivalence point

Conceptual Plan: Use calculations from above. Since all of the weak base has been converted to its conjugate acid, the pH is only dependent on the hydrolysis reaction of the conjugate acid. The mol $C_5H_5NH^+$ = initial mol C_5H_5N then set mol base (C_5H_5N) = mol acid (HCl) and [HCl], mol HCl → L HCl then

balanced equation has 1:1 stoichiometry $\quad M = \frac{\text{mol}}{\text{L}}$

L C_5H_5N, L HCl to equivalence point → total L then mol $C_5H_5NH^+$, L → $[C_5H_5NH^+]$

L C_5H_5N + L HCl = total L $\quad M = \frac{\text{mol}}{\text{L}}$

then do an equilibrium calculation: $[C_5H_5NH^+]$, K_a → $[H_3O^+]$ → pH.

set up ICE table $\quad pH = -\log[H_3O^+]$

Solution: mol base = mol acid = mol $C_5H_5NH^+$ = 0.003125 mol. Then

$$0.003125\ \cancel{\text{mol HCl}} \times \frac{1\ \text{L}}{0.100\ \cancel{\text{mol HCl}}} = 0.03125\ \cancel{\text{L HCl}} \times \frac{1000\ \text{mL}}{1\ \cancel{\text{L}}} = 31.3\ \text{mL HCl then}$$

total volume = L C_5H_5N + L HCl = 0.0250 L + 0.0313 L = 0.05632 L then

$$[C_5H_5NH^+] = \frac{0.003125\ \text{mol}\ C_5H_5NH^+}{0.0563\ \text{L}} = 0.0555062\ \text{M. Set up an ICE table:}$$

	$C_5H_5NH^+\ (aq) + H_2O\ (l) \rightleftharpoons$	$C_5H_5N\ (aq)$ +	$H_3O^+(aq)$
	$[C_5H_5NH^+]$	$[C_5H_5N]$	$[H_3O^+]$
Initial	0.0555062	≈ 0.00	≈ 0.00
Change	$-x$	$+x$	$+x$
Equil	$0.0555062 - x$	$+x$	$+x$

$$K_a = \frac{[C_5H_5N][H_3O^+]}{[C_5H_5NH^+]} = 5.8824 \times 10^{-6} = \frac{x^2}{0.0555062 - x}$$ Assume x is small ($x << 0.0556$) so

$$\frac{x^2}{0.0555062 - \cancel{x}} = 5.8824 \times 10^{-6} = \frac{x^2}{0.0555062}$$ and $x = 5.7141 \times 10^{-4}\ M = [H_3O^+]$. Confirm that the assumption is valid. $\frac{5.7141 \times 10^{-4}}{0.0555062} \times 100\% = 1.0\% < 5\%$ so the assumption is valid.

Finally, $pH = -\log[H_3O^+] = -\log(5.7141 \times 10^{-4}) = 3.24$.

Check: The units (none) are correct. Since this is a weak base–strong acid titration, the pH at the equivalence point is acidic.

Find: pH at one-half of the equivalence point

Conceptual Plan: Since this is a weak base–strong acid titration, the pH at one-half the equivalence point is the pK_a of the conjugate acid of weak base.

Solution: $pH = pK_a = -\log K_a = -\log(5.8824 \times 10^{-6}) = 5.23$ and the volume is 0.5 x 31.3 mL = 15.7 mL.

Check: The units (none) are correct. Since this is a weak base–strong acid titration, the pH at one-half the equivalence point is the pK_a of the conjugate acid of the weak base, so it should be a little below 6.

Find: pH after adding 40.0 mL of acid

Conceptual Plan: Use calculations from above. Then the pH is only dependent on the amount of excess acid and the total solution volumes.

mL added, mL at equiv. pt. → mL excess → L excess then

mL excess = mL added – mL at equiv. pt. $\quad \frac{1\ \text{L}}{1000\ \text{mL}}$

mL excess → L excess then [HCl], L excess → mol HCl excess

$\frac{1\ \text{L}}{1000\ \text{mL}} \quad M = \frac{\text{mol}}{\text{L}}$

then L C_5H_5N, L HCl to equivalence point, L HCl excess $\rightarrow$ total L then

L C_5H_5N + L HCl to equivalence point + L HCl excess = total L

mol excess HCl, total L $\rightarrow$ [HCl] = $[H_3O^+]$ $\rightarrow$ pH

$M = \frac{mol}{L}$ $\quad$ $pH = -\log[H_3O^+]$

Solution: mL excess = mL added – mL at equiv. pt. = 40.0 mL – 31.3 mL = 8.7 mL.

$8.7\ \cancel{mL\ HCl} \times \frac{1\ L}{1000\ \cancel{mL}} = 0.0087$ L HCl excess then $\frac{0.100\ mol\ HCl}{1\ \cancel{L}} \times 0.0087\ \cancel{L} = 0.00087$ mol HCl excess.

Then 0.0250 L C_5H_5N + 0.0313 L HCl + 0.0087 L HCl = 0.0650 L total volume.

$[HCl\ excess] = \frac{0.00087\ mol\ HCl\ excess}{0.0650\ L} = 0.013385$ M HCl excess

Since HCl is a strong acid, [HCl] excess = $[H_3O^+]$. The strong acid overwhelms the weak acid and is insignificant in the calculation. Finally, $pH = -\log[H_3O^+] = -\log(0.013385) = 1.87$.

Check: The units (none) are correct. The pH is dropping sharply at the equivalence point, so the pH after 5 mL past the equivalence point should be quite acidic.

Find: pH after adding 50.0 mL of acid

Conceptual Plan: Use calculations from above. Then the pH is only dependent on the amount of excess acid and the total solution volumes. mL added, mL at equiv. pt. $\rightarrow$ mL excess $\rightarrow$ L excess then

mL excess = mL added – mL at equiv. pt. $\quad$ $\frac{1\ L}{1000\ mL}$

mL excess $\rightarrow$ L excess then [HCl], L excess $\rightarrow$ mol HCl excess

$\frac{1\ L}{1000\ mL}$ $\quad$ $M = \frac{mol}{L}$

then L C_5H_5N, L HCl to equivalence point, L HCl excess $\rightarrow$ total L then

L C_5H_5N + L HCl to equivalence point + L HCl excess = total L

mol excess HCl, total L $\rightarrow$ [HCl] = $[H_3O^+]$ $\rightarrow$ pH

$M = \frac{mol}{L}$ $\quad$ $pH = -\log[H_3O^+]$

Solution: mL excess = mL added – mL at equiv. pt. = 50.0 mL – 31.3 mL = 18.7 mL.

$18.7\ \cancel{mL\ HCl} \times \frac{1\ L}{1000\ \cancel{mL}} = 0.0187$ L HCl excess then

$\frac{0.100\ mol\ HCl}{1\ \cancel{L}} \times 0.0187\ \cancel{L} = 0.00187$ mol HCl excess. Then 0.0250 L C_5H_5N + 0.0313 L HCl + 0.0187 L HBr = 0.0750 L total volume. $[HCl\ excess] = \frac{0.00187\ mol\ HCl\ excess}{0.0750\ L} = 0.024933$ M HCl excess

Since HCl is a strong acid, [HCl] excess = $[H_3O^+]$. The strong acid overwhelms the weak acid and is insignificant in the calculation. Finally, $pH = -\log[H_3O^+] = -\log(0.024933) = 1.60$.

Check: The units (none) are correct. The pH is dropping sharply at the equivalence point, so the pH after 5 mL past the equivalence point should be quite acidic. The pH is lower than the last point.

Plotting these points gives the following:

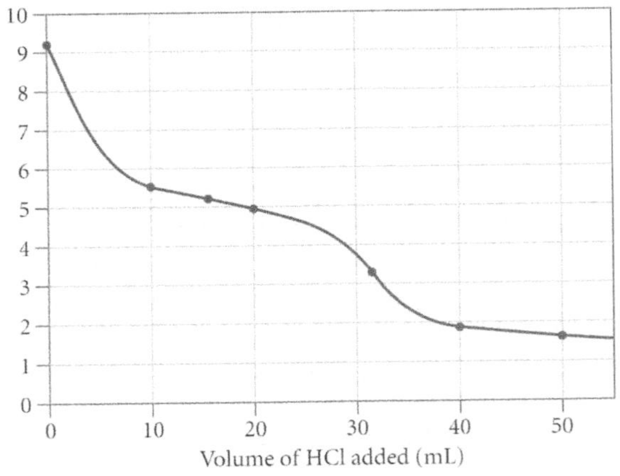

16.75 (i) Acid a is more concentrated, since the equivalence point (where sharp pH rise occurs) is at a higher volume of added base.

(ii) Acid b has the larger K_a, since the pH at a volume of added base equal to half of the equivalence point volume is lower.

16.76 (i) Acid b is more concentrated, since the equivalence point (where sharp pH drop occurs) is at a higher volume of added base.

(ii) Acid b has the larger K_b, since the pH at a volume of added base equal to half of the equivalence point volume is higher.

16.77 **Given:** 0.229 g unknown monoprotic acid titrated with 0.112 M NaOH and curve
Find: molar mass and pK_a of acid
Conceptual Plan: The equivalence point is where sharp pH rise occurs. The pK_a is the pH at a volume of added base equal to half of the equivalence point volume. Then mL NaOH $\xrightarrow{\frac{1\text{ L}}{1000\text{ mL}}}$ L NaOH then [NaOH], L NaOH $\xrightarrow{M = \frac{\text{mol}}{\text{L}}}$ mol NaOH = mol acid then mol NaOH, g acid $\xrightarrow{\frac{\text{g acid}}{\text{mol acid}}}$ molar mass.

Solution: The equivalence point is at 25 mL NaOH. The pH at 0.5 x 25 mL = 13 mL is ~3 = pK_a. Then

$$25 \text{ mL NaOH} \times \frac{1\text{ L}}{1000\text{ mL}} = 0.025 \text{ L NaOH then}$$

$$\frac{0.112 \text{ mol NaOH}}{1 \text{ L}} \times 0.025 \text{ L} = 0.0028 \text{ mol NaOH} = 0.0028 \text{ mol acid then}$$

$$\text{molar mass} = \frac{0.229 \text{ g acid}}{0.0028 \text{ mol acid}} = 82 \text{ g/mol.}$$

Check: The units (none and g/mol) are correct. The pK_a is consistent with a weak acid. The molar mass is reasonable for an acid (>1 g/mol).

16.78 **Given:** 0.446 g unknown monoprotic acid titrated with 0.105 M KOH and curve
Find: molar mass and pK_a of acid
Conceptual Plan: The equivalence point is where sharp pH rise occurs. The pK_a is the pH at a volume of added base equal to half of the equivalence point volume. Then mL KOH $\xrightarrow{\frac{1\text{ L}}{1000\text{ mL}}}$ L KOH then [KOH], L KOH $\xrightarrow{M = \frac{\text{mol}}{\text{L}}}$ mol KOH = mol acid then mol KOH, g acid $\xrightarrow{\frac{\text{g acid}}{\text{mol acid}}}$ molar mass.

Solution: The equivalence point is at 35 mL NaOH. The pH at 0.5 x 35 mL = 18 mL is ~ 4.5 = pK_a. Then

$$35 \text{ mL KOH} \times \frac{1\text{ L}}{1000\text{ mL}} = 0.035 \text{ L KOH then}$$

$$\frac{0.105 \text{ mol KOH}}{1 \text{ L}} \times 0.035 \text{ L} = 0.003\underline{6}75 \text{ mol KOH} = 0.003\underline{6}75 \text{ mol acid then}$$

$$\text{molar mass} = \frac{0.446 \text{ g acid}}{0.003\underline{6}75 \text{ mol acid}} = 120 \text{ g/mol.}$$

Check: The units (none and g/mol) are correct. The pK_a is consistent with a weak acid. The molar mass is reasonable for an acid (>1 g/mol).

16.79 **Given:** 20.0 mL of 0.125 M sulfurous acid (H_2SO_3) titrated with 0.1014 M KOH **Find:** volume of base added
Conceptual Plan: Since this is a diprotic acid, each proton is titrated sequentially. Write balanced equations.

$$H_2SO_3 + OH^- \rightarrow HSO_3^- + H_2O \text{ and } HSO_3^- + OH^- \rightarrow SO_3^{2-} + H_2O$$

Then mL $\xrightarrow{\frac{1\text{ L}}{1000\text{ mL}}}$ L then [H_2SO_3], L $\xrightarrow{M = \frac{\text{mol}}{\text{L}}}$ mol H_2SO_3 then set mol base (H_2SO_3) = mol acid (KOH) and *balanced equation has 1:1 stoichiometry*
[KOH], mol KOH $\xrightarrow{M = \frac{\text{mol}}{\text{L}}}$ L KOH $\xrightarrow{\frac{1000\text{ mL}}{1\text{ L}}}$ mL KOH the volume to the second equivalence point will be double the volume to the first equivalence point.

Solution: $20.0 \text{ mL } H_2SO_3 \times \frac{1\text{ L}}{1000\text{ mL}} = 0.0200 \text{ L } H_2SO_3$ then

$$\frac{0.115 \text{ mol } H_2SO_3}{1 \text{ L}} \times 0.0200 \text{ L} = 0.00230 \text{ mol } H_2SO_3. \text{ So mol base} = \text{mol } H_2SO_3 = 0.00230 \text{ mol} = \text{mol KOH}$$

then $0.00230 \text{ mol KOH} \times \frac{1\text{ L}}{0.1014 \text{ mol KOH}} = 0.022\underline{6}8245 \text{ L KOH} \times \frac{1000\text{ mL}}{1\text{ L}} = 22.7 \text{ mL KOH}$ to first equivalence point. The volume to the second equivalence point is simply twice this amount or 45.4 mL to the second equivalence point.

Check: The units (mL) are correct. The volume of base is a greater than the volume of acid because the concentration of the acid is a little greater that of the base. The volume to the second equivalence point is twice the volume to the first equivalence point.

16.80 **Given:** 20.0 mL of 0.125 M diprotic acid (H_2A) titrated with 0.1019 M KOH **Find:** volume of base added
Conceptual Plan: Since this is a diprotic acid, each proton is titrated sequentially. Write balanced equations.

$$H_2A + OH^- \rightarrow HA^- + H_2O \text{ and } HA^- + OH^- \rightarrow A^{2-} + H_2O$$

Then mL → L then $[H_2A]$, L → mol H_2A then set mol base (H_2A) = mol acid (KOH) and

$\frac{1\ \text{L}}{1000\ \text{mL}}$ $\quad M = \frac{\text{mol}}{\text{L}}$ $\quad$ *balanced equation has 1:1 stoichiometry*

[KOH], mol KOH → L KOH → mL KOH the volume to the second equivalence point will be

$M = \frac{\text{mol}}{\text{L}}$ $\quad \frac{1000\ \text{mL}}{1\ \text{L}}$

double the volume to the first equivalence point.

Solution: $20.0\ \text{mL H}_2\text{A} \times \frac{1\ \text{L}}{1000\ \text{mL}} = 0.0200\ \text{L H}_2\text{A}$ then $\frac{0.125\ \text{mol H}_2\text{A}}{1\ \text{L}} \times 0.0200\ \text{L} = 0.00250\ \text{mol H}_2\text{A}$.

So mol base = mol H_2A = 0.00250 mol = mol KOH then

$0.00250\ \text{mol KOH} \times \frac{1\ \text{L}}{0.1019\ \text{mol KOH}} = 0.024\underline{5}339\ \text{L KOH} \times \frac{1000\ \text{mL}}{1\ \text{L}} = 24.5\ \text{mL KOH}$ to first equivalence point. The volume to the second equivalence point is simply twice this amount or 49.1 mL to the second equivalence point.

Check: The units (mL) are correct. The volume of base is less than the volume of acid because the concentration of the acid is a little greater that of the base. The volume to the second equivalence point is twice the volume to the first equivalence point.

16.81 The indicator will be in its acid form at an acidic pH, so the color in the HCl sample will be red. The color change will occur over the pH range from pH = $pK_a - 1.0$ to pH = $pK_a + 1.0$, so the color will start to change at pH = 5.0 – 1.0 = 4.0 and finish changing by pH = 5.0 + 1.0 = 6.0.

16.82 **Given:** Phenolphthalein $pK_a = 9.7$, acid form = colorless, base form = pink **Find:** $[In^-]/[HIn]$ and color
Conceptual Plan: Calculate [In]/[HIn] using the equation in chapter. If pH < (pK_a – 1.0) then the solution

$$\frac{[In^-]}{[HIn]} = 10^{(pH - pK_a)}$$

is colorless. If pH > pK_a + 1.0 then the solution is pink.
Solution:

(a) $pH = 2.0$ so $\frac{[In^-]}{[HIn]} = 10^{(pH - pK_a)} = 10^{(2.0-9.7)} = 10^{-7.7} = 2 \times 10^{-8}$ and the solution will be colorless.

(b) $pH = 5.0$ so $\frac{[In^-]}{[HIn]} = 10^{(pH - pK_a)} = 10^{(5.0-9.7)} = 10^{-4.7} = 2 \times 10^{-5}$ and the solution will be colorless.

(c) $pH = 8.0$ so $\frac{[In^-]}{[HIn]} = 10^{(pH - pK_a)} = 10^{(8.0-9.7)} = 10^{-1.7} = 2 \times 10^{-2}$ and the solution will be colorless.

(d) $pH = 11.0$ so $\frac{[In^-]}{[HIn]} = 10^{(pH - pK_a)} = 10^{(11.0-9.7)} = 10^{+1.3} = 2 \times 10^{1}$ and the solution will be pink.

Check: The units (none) are correct. The ratio is less than one and the solution is colorless when the solution is more acidic than the pK_a. The ratio is greater than one and the solution is pink when the solution is more basic than the pK_a

16.83 Since the exact conditions of the titration are not given, a rough calculation will suffice. Looking at the pattern of earlier problems, the pH at the equivalence point of a titration of a weak acid and a strong base is the hydrolysis of the conjugate base of the weak acid that has been diluted by a factor of roughly 2 with base. If it is assumed that the initial concentration of the weak acid is ~ 0.1 M, then the conjugate base concentration will be ~ 0.05 M. From earlier calculations it can be seen that the $K_b = \frac{K_w}{K_a} = \frac{[OH^-]^2}{0.05}$ thus

$$[OH^-] = \sqrt{\frac{0.05\ K_w}{K_a}} = \sqrt{\frac{5 \times 10^{-16}}{K_a}} \text{ and the pH} = 14 + \log\sqrt{\frac{5 \times 10^{-16}}{K_a}}.$$

(a) For HF, the $K_a = 3.5 \times 10^{-4}$ and so the above equation approximates the pH at the equivalence point of ~ 8.0. Looking at Table 16.1, phenol red or *m*-nitrophenol will change at the appropriate pH range.

(b) For HCl, the pH at the equivalence point is 7, since HCl is a strong acid. Looking at Table 16.1, alizarin, bromthymol blue, or phenol red will change at the appropriate pH range.

(c) For HCN, the $K_a = 4.9 \times 10^{-10}$ and so the above equation approximates the pH at the equivalence point of ~ 11.0. Looking at Table 16.1, alizarin yellow R will change at the appropriate pH range.

16.84 Since the exact conditions of the titration are not given, a rough calculation will suffice. Looking at the pattern of earlier problems, the pH at the equivalence point of a titration of a weak base and a strong acid is the hydrolysis of the conjugate acid of the weak base that has been diluted by a factor of roughly 2 with acid. If it is assumed that the initial concentration of the weak base is ~ 0.1 M, then the conjugate acid concentration will be ~ 0.05 M. From earlier calculations it can be seen that the $K_a = \frac{K_w}{K_b} = \frac{[H_3O^+]^2}{0.05}$ thus $[H_3O^+] = \sqrt{\frac{0.05\,K_w}{K_b}} = \sqrt{\frac{5 \times 10^{-16}}{K_b}}$ and the pH $= -\log\sqrt{\frac{5 \times 10^{-16}}{K_b}}$.

(a) For CH_3NH_2, the $K_b = 4.4 \times 10^{-4}$ and so the above equation approximates the pH at the equivalence point of ~ 6.0. Looking at Table 16.1, methyl red, Eriochrome Black T, bromocresol purple, alizarin or bromthymol blue will change at the appropriate pH range.

(b) For NaOH, the pH at the equivalence point is 7, since NaOH is a strong base. Looking at Table 16.1, alizarin, bromthymol blue, or phenol red will change at the appropriate pH range.

(c) For $C_6H_5NH_2$, the $K_b = 3.9 \times 10^{-10}$ and so the above equation approximates the pH at the equivalence point of ~ 2.9. Looking at Table 16.1, erythrosin B or 2,4-dinitrophenol will change at the appropriate pH range.

Solubility Equilibria

16.85 For the dissolution reaction, start with the ionic compound as a solid and put it in equilibrium with the appropriate cation and anion, making sure to include the appropriate stoichiometric coefficients. The K_{sp} expression is the product of the concentrations of the cation and anion concentrations raised to their stoichiometric coefficients.

(a) $BaSO_4\,(s) \rightleftharpoons Ba^{2+}\,(aq) + SO_4^{2-}\,(aq)$ and $K_{sp} = [Ba^{2+}]\,[SO_4^{2-}]$.

(b) $PbBr_2\,(s) \rightleftharpoons Pb^{2+}\,(aq) + 2\,Br^-\,(aq)$ and $K_{sp} = [Pb^{2+}]\,[Br^-]^2$.

(c) $Ag_2CrO_4\,(s) \rightleftharpoons 2\,Ag^+\,(aq) + CrO_4^{2-}\,(aq)$ and $K_{sp} = [Ag^+]^2\,[CrO_4^{2-}]$.

16.86 For the dissolution reaction, start with the ionic compound as a solid and put it in equilibrium with the appropriate cation and anion, making sure to include the appropriate stoichiometric coefficients. The K_{sp} expression is the product of the concentrations of the cation and anion concentrations raised to their stoichiometric coefficients.

(a) $CaCO_3\,(s) \rightleftharpoons Ca^{2+}\,(aq) + CO_3^{2-}\,(aq)$ and $K_{sp} = [Ca^{2+}]\,[CO_3^{2-}]$.

(b) $PbCl_2\,(s) \rightleftharpoons Pb^{2+}\,(aq) + 2\,Cl^-\,(aq)$ and $K_{sp} = [Pb^{2+}]\,[Cl^-]^2$.

(c) $AgI\,(s) \rightleftharpoons Ag^+\,(aq) + I^-\,(aq)$ and $K_{sp} = [Ag^+]\,[I^-]$.

16.87 **Given:** ionic compound formula and Table 16.2 of K_{sp} values **Find:** molar solubility (*S*)
Conceptual Plan: The expression of the solubility product constant of A_mX_n is $K_{sp} = [A^{n+}]^m\,[X^{m-}]^n$. The molar solubility of a compound, A_mX_n, can be computed directly from K_{sp} by solving for *S* in the expression $K_{sp} = (mS)^m\,(nS)^n = m^m\,n^n\,S^{m+n}$.
Solution:

(a) For AgBr, $K_{sp} = 5.35 \times 10^{-13}$, $A = Ag^+$, $m = 1$, $X = Br^-$, and $n = 1$ so $K_{sp} = 5.35 \times 10^{-13} = S^2$. Rearrange to solve for *S*. $S = \sqrt{5.35 \times 10^{-13}} = 7.31 \times 10^{-7}$ M.

(b) For $Mg(OH)_2$, $K_{sp} = 2.06 \times 10^{-13}$, $A = Mg^{2+}$, $m = 1$, $X = OH^-$, and $n = 2$ so $K_{sp} = 2.06 \times 10^{-13} = 2^2S^3$.

Rearrange to solve for S. $S = \sqrt[3]{\dfrac{2.06 \times 10^{-13}}{4}} = 3.72 \times 10^{-5}$ M.

(c) For CaF_2, $K_{sp} = 1.46 \times 10^{-10}$, $A = Ca^{2+}$, $m = 1$, $X = F^-$, and $n = 2$ so $K_{sp} = 1.46 \times 10^{-10} = 2^2S^3$. Rearrange to solve for S. $S = \sqrt[3]{\dfrac{1.46 \times 10^{-10}}{4}} = 3.32 \times 10^{-4}$ M.

Check: The units (M) are correct. The molar solubilities are much less than one and dependent not only on the value of the K_{sp}, but also the stoichiometry of the ionic compound. The more ions that are generated, the greater the molar solubility for the same value of the K_{sp}.

16.88 **Given:** ionic compound formula and Table 16.2 of K_{sp} values **Find:** molar solubility (S)
Conceptual Plan: The expression of the solubility product constant of A_mX_n is $K_{sp} = [A^{n+}]^m [X^{m-}]^n$. The molar solubility of a compound, A_mX_n, can be computed directly from K_{sp} by solving for S in the expression $K_{sp} = (mS)^m (nS)^n = m^m n^n S^{m+n}$.
Solution:

(a) For MX, $K_{sp} = 1.27 \times 10^{-36}$, $A = M^+$, $m = 1$, $X = X^-$, and $n = 1$ so $K_{sp} = 1.27 \times 10^{-36} = S^2$. Rearrange to solve for S. $S = \sqrt{1.27 \times 10^{-36}} = 1.13 \times 10^{-18}$ M.

(b) For Ag_2CrO_4, $K_{sp} = 1.12 \times 10^{-12}$, $A = Ag^+$, $m = 2$, $X = CrO_4^{2-}$, and $n = 1$ so $K_{sp} = 1.12 \times 10^{-12} = 2^2S^3$.

Rearrange to solve for S. $S = \sqrt[3]{\dfrac{1.12 \times 10^{-12}}{4}} = 6.54 \times 10^{-5}$ M.

(c) For $Ca(OH)_2$, $K_{sp} = 4.68 \times 10^{-6}$, $A = Ca^{2+}$, $m = 1$, $X = OH^-$, and $n = 2$ so $K_{sp} = 4.68 \times 10^{-6} = 2^2S^3$.

Rearrange to solve for S. $S = \sqrt[3]{\dfrac{4.68 \times 10^{-6}}{4}} = 1.05 \times 10^{-2}$ M.

Check: The units (M) are correct. The molar solubilities are much less than one and dependent not only on the value of the K_{sp}, but also the stoichiometry of the ionic compound. The more ions that are generated, the greater the molar solubility for the same value of the K_{sp}.

16.89 **Given:** ionic compound formula and molar solubility (S) **Find:** K_{sp}
Conceptual Plan: The expression of the solubility product constant of A_mX_n is $K_{sp} = [A^{n+}]^m [X^{m-}]^n$. The molar solubility of a compound, A_mX_n, can be computed directly from K_{sp} by solving for S in the expression $K_{sp} = (mS)^m (nS)^n = m^m n^n S^{m+n}$.
Solution:

(a) For MX, $S = 3.27 \times 10^{-11}$ M, $A = M^+$, m = 1, $X = X^-$, and n = 1 so $K_{sp} = S^2 = (3.27 \times 10^{-11})^2 = 1.07 \times 10^{-21}$.

(b) For PbF_2, $S = 5.63 \times 10^{-3}$ M, $A = Pb^{2+}$, $m = 1$, $X = F^-$, and $n = 2$ so $K_{sp} = 2^2S^3 = 2^2 (5.63 \times 10^{-3})^3 = 7.14 \times 10^{-7}$.

(c) For MgF_2, $S = 2.65 \times 10^{-4}$ M, $A = Mg^{2+}$, $m = 1$, $X = F^-$, and $n = 2$ so $K_{sp} = 2^2S^3 = 2^2 (2.65 \times 10^{-4})^3 = 7.44 \times 10^{-11}$.

Check: The units (none) are correct. The K_{sp} values are much less than one and dependent not only on the value of the solubility, but also the stoichiometry of the ionic compound. The more ions that are generated, the smaller the K_{sp} for the same value of the S.

16.90 **Given:** ionic compound formula and molar solubility (S) **Find:** K_{sp}
Conceptual Plan: The expression of the solubility product constant of A_mX_n is $K_{sp} = [A^{n+}]^m [X^{m-}]^n$. The molar solubility of a compound, A_mX_n, can be computed directly from K_{sp} by solving for S in the expression $K_{sp} = (mS)^m (nS)^n = m^m n^n S^{m+n}$.
Solution:

(a) For $BaCrO_4$, $S = 1.08 \times 10^{-5}$ M, $A = Ba^{2+}$, $m = 1$, $X = CrO_4^{2-}$, and $n = 1$ so $K_{sp} = S^2 = (1.08 \times 10^{-5})^2 = 1.17 \times 10^{-10}$.

(b) For Ag_2SO_3, $S = 1.55 \times 10^{-5}$ M, A = Ag^+, $m = 2$, X = SO_3^{2-}, and $n = 1$ so $K_{sp} = 2^2S^3 = 2^2(1.55 \times 10^{-5})^3 = 1.49 \times 10^{-14}$.

(c) For $Pd(SCN)_2$, $S = 2.22 \times 10^{-8}$ M, A = Pd^{2+}, $m = 1$, X = SCN^-, and $n = 2$ so $K_{sp} = 2^2S^3 = 2^2(2.22 \times 10^{-8}) = 4.38 \times 10^{-23}$.

Check: The units (none) are correct. The K_{sp} values are much less than one and dependent not only on the value of the solubility, but also the stoichiometry of the ionic compound. The more ions that are generated, the smaller the K_{sp} for the same value of the S.

16.91 **Given:** ionic compound formulas AX and AX_2 and $K_{sp} = 1.5 \times 10^{-5}$ **Find:** higher molar solubility (S)
Conceptual Plan: The expression of the solubility product constant of A_mX_n is $K_{sp} = [A^{n+}]^m [X^{m-}]^n$. The molar solubility of a compound, A_mX_n, can be computed directly from K_{sp} by solving for S in the expression $K_{sp} = (mS)^m (nS)^n = m^m n^n S^{m+n}$.
Solution: For AX, $K_{sp} = 1.5 \times 10^{-5}$, $m = 1$, and $n = 1$ so $K_{sp} = 1.5 \times 10^{-5} = S^2$. Rearrange to solve for S. $S = \sqrt{1.5 \times 10^{-5}} = 3.9 \times 10^{-3}$ M. For AX_2, $K_{sp} = 1.5 \times 10^{-5}$, $m = 1$, and $n = 2$ so $K_{sp} = 1.5 \times 10^{-5} = 2^2S^3$.
Rearrange to solve for S. $S = \sqrt[3]{\dfrac{1.5 \times 10^{-5}}{4}} = 1.6 \times 10^{-2}$ M. Since 10^{-2} M > 10^{-3} M, AX_2 has a higher molar solubility.
Check: The units (M) are correct. The more ions that are generated, the greater the molar solubility for the same value of the K_{sp}.

16.92 **Given:** ionic compound formula and molar solubility (S) **Find:** K_{sp}
Conceptual Plan: The expression of the solubility product constant of A_mX_n is $K_{sp} = [A^{n+}]^m [X^{m-}]^n$. The molar solubility of a compound, A_mX_n, can be computed directly from K_{sp} by solving for S in the expression $K_{sp} = (mS)^m (nS)^n = m^m n^n S^{m+n}$.
Solution: AX, $S = 1.35 \times 10^{-4}$ M, $m = 1$, and $n = 1$ so $K_{sp} = S^2 = (1.35 \times 10^{-4})^2 = 1.82 \times 10^{-8}$.
For AX_2, $S = 2.25 \times 10^{-4}$ M, $m = 1$, and $n = 2$ so $K_{sp} = 2^2S^3 = 2^2(2.25 \times 10^{-4})^3 = 4.56 \times 10^{-11}$.
For A_2X, $S = 1.75 \times 10^{-4}$ M, $m = 2$, and $n = 1$ so $K_{sp} = 2^2S^3 = 2^2(1.75 \times 10^{-4})^3 = 2.14 \times 10^{-11}$. So A_2X has the lowest K_{sp}, since it has a lower S than for AX_2.
Check: The units (none) are correct. The K_{sp} values are much less than one and dependent not only on the value of the solubility, but also the stoichiometry of the ionic compound. The more ions that are generated, the smaller the K_{sp} for the same value of the S.

16.93 **Given:** $Fe(OH)_2$ in 100.0 mL solution **Find:** grams of $Fe(OH)_2$ **Other:** $K_{sp} = 4.87 \times 10^{-17}$
Conceptual Plan: The expression of the solubility product constant of A_mX_n is $K_{sp} = [A^{n+}]^m [X^{m-}]^n$. The molar solubility of a compound, A_mX_n, can be computed directly from K_{sp} by solving for S in the expression $K_{sp} = (mS)^m (nS)^n = m^m n^n S^{m+n}$. Then solve for S, then mL → L then ($\frac{1\text{ L}}{1000\text{ mL}}$)

S, L → mol $Fe(OH)_2$ → g $Fe(OH)_2$.
$M = \frac{\text{mol}}{\text{L}}$ $\quad \frac{89.87\text{ g Fe(OH)}_2}{1\text{ mol Fe(OH)}_2}$

Solution: for $Fe(OH)_2$, $K_{sp} = 4.87 \times 10^{-17}$, A = Fe^{2+}, $m = 1$, X = OH^-, and $n = 2$ so $K_{sp} = 4.87 \times 10^{-17} = 2^2S^3$.

Rearrange to solve for S. $S = \sqrt[3]{\dfrac{4.87 \times 10^{-17}}{4}} = 2.30050 \times 10^{-6}$ M. Then $100.0\ \cancel{\text{mL}} \times \dfrac{1\text{ L}}{1000\ \cancel{\text{mL}}} = 0.1000$ L

then $\dfrac{2.30050 \times 10^{-6}\text{ mol Fe(OH)}_2}{1\ \cancel{\text{L}}} \times 0.1000\ \cancel{\text{L}} = 2.30050 \times 10^{-7}\ \cancel{\text{mol Fe(OH)}_2} \times \dfrac{89.87\text{ g Fe(OH)}_2}{1\ \cancel{\text{mol Fe(OH)}_2}}$
$= 2.07 \times 10^{-5}$ g $Fe(OH)_2$.

Check: The units (g) are correct. The solubility rules from Chapter 4 (most hydroxides are insoluble) suggest that very little $Fe(OH)_2$ will dissolve, so the magnitude of the answer is not surprising.

16.94 **Given:** 3.91 mg CuCl in 100.0 mL solution **Find:** K_{sp}
Conceptual Plan: mL → L then mg CuCl → g CuCl → mol CuCl then L, mol CuCl → S
$\frac{1\text{ L}}{1000\text{ mL}}$ $\quad \frac{1\text{ g CuCl}}{1000\text{ mg CuCl}}$ $\quad \frac{1\text{ mol CuCl}}{99.00\text{ g CuCl}}$ $\quad M = \frac{\text{mol}}{\text{L}}$

The expression of the solubility product constant of A_mX_n is $K_{sp} = [A^{n+}]^m [X^{m-}]^n$. The molar solubility of a compound, A_mX_n, can be computed directly from K_{sp} by solving for S in the expression $K_{sp} = (mS)^m (nS)^n = m^m n^n S^{m+n}$.

Solution: $100.0 \text{ mL} \times \dfrac{1 \text{ L}}{1000 \text{ mL}} = 0.1000 \text{ L}$ then

$3.91 \text{ mg CuCl} \times \dfrac{1 \text{ g CuCl}}{1000 \text{ mg CuCl}} \times \dfrac{1 \text{ mol CuCl}}{99.00 \text{ g CuCl}} = 3.94\underline{9}50 \times 10^{-5}$ mol CuCl then

$\dfrac{3.94\underline{9}50 \times 10^{-5} \text{ mol CuCl}}{0.1000 \text{ L}} = 3.94\underline{9}50 \times 10^{-4}$ M CuCl $= S$ then for CuCl A = Cu^+, $m = 1$, X = Cl^-, and $n = 1$ so

$K_{sp} = S^2 = = (3.94\underline{9}50 \times 10^{-4})^2 = 1.56 \times 10^{-7}$.

Check: The units (none) are correct. The value of $K_{sp} << 1$ since only mg dissolve in a liter of solution. The K_{sp} is not too low since CuCl dissociates into only 2 ions and S is 10^{-4}.

16.95 (a) **Given:** BaF_2 **Find:** molar solubility (S) in pure water **Other:** K_{sp} (BaF_2) = 2.45×10^{-5}

Conceptual Plan: The expression of the solubility product constant of A_mX_n is: $K_{sp} = [A^{n+}]^m [X^{m-}]^n$. The molar solubility of a compound, A_mX_n, can be computed directly from K_{sp} by solving for S in the expression: $K_{sp} = (mS)^m (nS)^n = m^m n^n S^{m+n}$.

Solution: BaF_2, $K_{sp} = 2.45 \times 10^{-5}$, A = Ba^{2+}, $m = 1$, X = F^-, and $n = 2$ so $K_{sp} = 2.45 \times 10^{-5} = 2^2S^3$.

Rearrange to solve for S. $S = \sqrt[3]{\dfrac{2.45 \times 10^{-5}}{4}} = 1.83 \times 10^{-2}$ M.

(b) **Given:** BaF_2 **Find:** molar solubility (S) in 0.10 M $Ba(NO_3)_2$ **Other:** K_{sp} (BaF_2) = 2.45×10^{-5}

Conceptual Plan: M $Ba(NO_3)_2$ → M Ba^{2+} then M Ba^{2+}, K_{sp} → S

$Ba(NO_3)_2$ (s) → Ba^{2+} (aq) + 2 NO_3^- (aq) *ICE Chart*

Solution: Since 1 Ba^{2+} ion is generated for each $Ba(NO_3)_2$, $[Ba^{2+}]$ = 0.10 M.

BaF_2 (s) ⇌	Ba^{2+} (aq)	+ 2 F^-(aq)
Initial	0.10	0.00
Change	S	$2S$
Equil	$0.10 + S$	$2S$

K_{sp} (BaF_2) = $[Ba^{2+}][F^-]^2 = 2.45 \times 10^{-5} = (0.10 + S)(2S)^2$.

Assume $S << 0.10$, $2.45 \times 10^{-5} = (0.10)(2S)^2$, and $S = 7.83 \times 10^{-3}$ M. Confirm that the assumption is valid.

$\dfrac{7.83 \times 10^{-3}}{0.10} \times 100\% = 7.8\% > 5\%$ so the assumption is not valid. Since expanding the expression will give a third order polynomial, that is not easily solved directly. Solve by successive approximations. Substitute $S = 7.83 \times 10^{-3}$ M for the S term that is part of a sum (i.e., the one in $(0.10 + S)$). Thus, $2.45 \times 10^{-5} = (0.10 + 7.83 \times 10^{-3})(2S)^2$ and $S = 7.53 \times 10^{-3}$ M. Substitute this new S value again. Thus, $2.45 \times 10^{-5} = (0.10 + 7.53 \times 10^{-3})(2S)^2$ and $S = 7.55 \times 10^{-3}$ M. Substitute this new S value again. Thus, $2.45 \times 10^{-5} = (0.10 + 7.55 \times 10^{-3})(2S)^2$ and $S = 7.55 \times 10^{-3}$ M. So the solution has converged and $S = 7.55 \times 10^{-3}$ M.

(c) **Given:** BaF_2 **Find:** molar solubility (S) in 0.15 M NaF **Other:** K_{sp} (BaF_2) = 2.45×10^{-5}

Conceptual Plan: M NaF → M F^- then M F^-, K_{sp} → S

NaF (s) → Na^+ (aq) + F^- (aq) *ICE Chart*

Solution: Since 1 F^- ion is generated for each NaF, $[F^-]$ = 0.15 M.

BaF_2 (s) ⇌	Ba^{2+} (aq)	+ 2 F^-(aq)
Initial	0.00	0.15
Change	S	$2S$
Equil	S	$0.15 + 2S$

K_{sp} (BaF_2) = $[Ba^{2+}][F^-]^2 = 2.45 \times 10^{-5} = (S)(0.15 + 2S)^2$.

Since $2S << 0.15$, $2.45 \times 10^{-5} = (S)(0.15)^2$, and $S = 1.09 \times 10^{-3}$ M. Confirm that the assumption is valid.

$\dfrac{2(1.09 \times 10^{-3})}{0.15} \times 100\% = 1.5\% < 5\%$ so the assumption is valid.

Check: The units (M) are correct. The solubility of the BaF_2 decreases in the presence of a common ion. The effect of the anion is greater because the K_{sp} expression has the anion concentration squared.

16.96 (a) **Given:** MX **Find:** molar solubility (S) in pure water **Other:** K_{sp} (MX) = 1.27×10^{-36}

Conceptual Plan: The expression of the solubility product constant of A_mX_n is $K_{sp} = [A^{n+}]^m [X^{m-}]^n$.

The molar solubility of a compound, A_mX_n, can be computed directly from K_{sp} by solving for S in the expression $K_{sp} = (mS)^m (nS)^n = m^m n^n S^{m+n}$.
Solution: MX, K_{sp} = 1.27 x 10^{-36}, A = M^{2+}, m = 1, X = X^{2-}, and n = 1. There is a 1:1 ratio of the cation:anion, so K_{sp} = 1.27 x 10^{-36} = S^2. Rearrange to solve for S. S = 1.13 x 10^{-18} M.

(b) **Given:** MX **Find:** molar solubility (S) in 0.25 M MCl_2 **Other:** K_{sp} (MX) = 1.27 x 10^{-36}
Conceptual Plan: M MCl_2 → M M^{2+} then M M^{2+}, K_{sp} → S
$MCl_2(s) \rightarrow M^{2+}(aq) + 2\,Cl^-(aq)$ *ICE Chart*
Solution: Since 1 M^{2+} ion is generated for each MCl_2, $[M^{2+}]$ = 0.25 M.

$MX(s) \rightleftharpoons$	$M^{2+}(aq)$ +	$X^{2-}(aq)$
Initial	0.25	0.00
Change	S	S
Equil	0.25 + S	S

K_{sp} (MX) = $[M^{2+}][X^{2-}]$ = 1.27 x 10^{-36} = (0.25 + S) S.

Assume S << 0.25, 1.27 x 10^{-36} = (0.25) S, and S = 5.08 x 10^{-36} M. Confirm that the assumption is valid.
$\frac{5.08 \times 10^{-36}}{0.25} \times 100\% = 2.0 \times 10^{-33}\% \ll 5\%$ so the assumption is valid.

(c) **Given:** MX **Find:** molar solubility (S) in 0.20 M Na_2S **Other:** K_{sp} (MX) = 1.27 x 10^{-36}
Conceptual Plan: M Na_2X → M X^{2-} then M X^{2-}, K_{sp} → S
$Na_2X(s) \rightarrow 2\,Na^+(aq) + X^{2-}(aq)$ *ICE Chart*
Solution: Since 1 X^{2-} ion is generated for each Na_2X, $[X^{2-}]$ = 0.20 M.

$MX(s) \rightleftharpoons$	$M^{2+}(aq)$ +	$X^{2-}(aq)$
Initial	0.00	0.20
Change	S	S
Equil	S	0.20 + S

K_{sp} (MX) = $[M^{2+}][X^{2-}]$ = 1.27 x 10^{-36} = (S)(0.20 + S).

Since S << 0.20, 1.27 x 10^{-36} = (S)(0.20), and S = 6.35 x 10^{-36} M. Confirm that the assumption is valid.
$\frac{6.35 \times 10^{-36}}{0.20} \times 100\% = 3.2 \times 10^{-33}\% \ll 5\%$ so the assumption is valid.
Check: The units (M) are correct. The solubility of the MX decreases in the presence of a common ion.

16.97 **Given:** $Ca(OH)_2$ **Find:** molar solubility (S) in buffers at a) pH = 4, b) pH = 7, and c) pH = 9
Other: K_{sp} ($Ca(OH)_2$) = 4.68 x 10^{-6}
Conceptual Plan: pH → $[H_3O^+]$ → $[OH^-]$ then M OH^-, K_{sp} → S
$[H_3O^+] = 10^{-pH}$ $K_w = [H_3O^+][OH^-]$ *set up ICE table*
Solution:

(a) pH = 4, so $[H_3O^+] = 10^{-pH} = 10^{-4} = 1 \times 10^{-4}$ M then $K_w = [H_3O^+][OH^-]$ so

$[OH^-] = \frac{K_w}{[H_3O^+]} = \frac{1.0 \times 10^{-14}}{1 \times 10^{-4}} = 1 \times 10^{-10}$ M then

$Ca(OH)_2(s) \rightleftharpoons$	$Ca^{2+}(aq)$ +	$2\,OH^-(aq)$
Initial	0.00	1 x 10^{-10}
Change	S	—
Equil	S	1 x 10^{-10}

K_{sp} ($Ca(OH)_2$) = $[Ca^{2+}][OH^-]^2$ = 4.68 x 10^{-6} = S (1 x $10^{-10})^2$ and S = 5 x 10^{14} M.

(b) pH = 7, so $[H_3O^+] = 10^{-pH} = 10^{-7} = 1 \times 10^{-7}$ M then $K_w = [H_3O^+][OH^-]$ so

$[OH^-] = \frac{K_w}{[H_3O^+]} = \frac{1.0 \times 10^{-14}}{1 \times 10^{-7}} = 1 \times 10^{-7}$ M then

$Ca(OH)_2(s) \rightleftharpoons$	$Ca^{2+}(aq)$ +	$2\,OH^-(aq)$
Initial	0.00	1 x 10^{-7}
Change	S	—
Equil	S	1 x 10^{-7}

K_{sp} ($Ca(OH)_2$) = $[Ca^{2+}][OH^-]^2$ = 4.68 x 10^{-6} = S (1 x $10^{-7})^2$ and S = 5 x 10^{8} M.

(c) pH = 9, so $[H_3O^+] = 10^{-pH} = 10^{-9} = 1 \times 10^{-9}$ M then $K_w = [H_3O^+][OH^-]$ so

$$[OH^-] = \frac{K_w}{[H_3O^+]} = \frac{1.0 \times 10^{-14}}{1 \times 10^{-9}} = 1 \times 10^{-5} \text{ M then}$$

	$Ca(OH)_2\,(s) \rightleftharpoons$	$Ca^{2+}\,(aq)$	$+\ 2\,OH^-(aq)$
Initial		0.00	1×10^{-5}
Change		S	—
Equil		S	1×10^{-5}

$K_{sp}\,(Ca(OH)_2) = [Ca^{2+}][OH^-]^2 = 4.68 \times 10^{-6} = S\,(1 \times 10^{-5})^2$. and $S = 5 \times 10^4$ M.

Check: The units (M) are correct. The solubility of the $Ca(OH)_2$ decreases as the pH increases (and the hydroxide ion concentration increases). Realize that these molar solubilities are not achievable because the saturation point of pure $Ca(OH)_2$ is ~ 30 M. The bottom line is that as long as the hydroxide concentration can be controlled with a buffer, the $Ca(OH)_2$ will be very soluble.

16.98 **Given:** $Mg(OH)_2$ in 1.00×10^2 mL solution **Find:** grams of $Mg(OH)_2$ in pure water and buffer at pH = 10

Other: $K_{sp}\,(Mg(OH)_2) = 2.06 \times 10^{-13}$

Conceptual Plan: For pure water:

The expression of the solubility product constant of A_mX_n is $K_{sp} = [A^{n+}]^m [X^{m-}]^n$. The molar solubility of a compound, A_mX_n, can be computed directly from K_{sp} by solving for S in the expression $K_{sp} = (mS)^m (nS)^n = m^m n^n S^{m+n}$. Then mL → L then S, L → mol $Mg(OH)_2$ → g $Mg(OH)_2$.

$$\frac{1\text{ L}}{1000\text{ mL}} \qquad M = \frac{\text{mol}}{\text{L}} \qquad \frac{58.33\text{ g } Mg(OH)_2}{1\text{ mol } Mg(OH)_2}$$

For buffer Solution: pH → $[H_3O^+]$ → $[OH^-]$ then

$$[H_3O^+] = 10^{-pH} \qquad K_w = [H_3O^+][OH^-]$$

M OH^-, K_{sp} → S then S, L → mol $Mg(OH)_2$ → g $Mg(OH)_2$.

set up ICE table $\qquad M = \frac{\text{mol}}{\text{L}} \qquad \frac{58.33\text{ g } Mg(OH)_2}{1\text{ mol } Mg(OH)_2}$

Solution: For pure water, $K_{sp} = 2.06 \times 10^{-13}$, A = Mg^{2+}, $m = 1$, X = OH^-, and $n = 2$ so $K_{sp} = 2.06 \times 10^{-13} = 2^2S^3$.

Rearrange to solve for S. $S = \sqrt[3]{\dfrac{2.06 \times 10^{-13}}{4}} = 3.7\underline{2}051 \times 10^{-5}$ M. Then

$$1.00 \times 10^2\ \text{mL} \times \frac{1\text{ L}}{1000\text{ mL}} = 0.100\text{ L then}$$

$$\frac{3.7\underline{2}051 \times 10^{-5}\text{ mol } Mg(OH)_2}{1\text{ L}} \times 0.100\text{ L} = 3.7\underline{2}051 \times 10^{-6}\text{ mol } Mg(OH)_2 \times \frac{58.33\text{ g } Mg(OH)_2}{1\text{ mol } Mg(OH)_2} =$$

2.17×10^{-4}g $Mg(OH)_2$

for pH = 10, so $[H_3O^+] = 10^{-pH} = 10^{-10} = 1 \times 10^{-10}$ M then $K_w = [H_3O^+][OH^-]$ so

$$[OH^-] = \frac{K_w}{[H_3O^+]} = \frac{1.0 \times 10^{-14}}{1 \times 10^{-10}} = 1 \times 10^{-4} \text{ M then}$$

	$Mg(OH)_2\,(s) \rightleftharpoons$	$Mg^{2+}\,(aq)$	$+\ OH^-(aq)$
Initial		0.00	1×10^{-4}
Change		S	—
Equil		S	1×10^{-4}

$K_{sp}\,(Mg(OH)_2) = [Mg^{2+}][OH^-]^2 = 2.06 \times 10^{-13} = S\,(1 \times 10^{-4})^2$ and $S = \underline{2}.06 \times 10^{-5}$ M. Then

$$\frac{\underline{2}.06 \times 10^{-5}\text{ mol } Mg(OH)_2}{1\text{ L}} \times 0.100\text{ L} = \underline{2}.06 \times 10^{-6}\text{ mol } Mg(OH)_2 \times \frac{58.33\text{ g } Mg(OH)_2}{1\text{ mol } Mg(OH)_2} = 1 \times 10^{-4}\text{g } Mg(OH)_2.$$

Check: The units (M) are correct. The solubility of the $Mg(OH)_2$ decreases as the pH increases (and the hydroxide ion concentration increases).

16.99 (a) $BaCO_3$ will be more soluble in acidic solutions because CO_3^{2-} is basic. In acidic solutions it can be converted to HCO_3^- and $H_2CO_3^{2-}$. These species are not CO_3^{2-} so they do not appear in the K_{sp} expression.

(b) CuS will be more soluble in acidic solutions because S^{2-} is basic. In acidic solutions it can be converted to HS^- and H_2S^{2-}. These species are not S^{2-} so they do not appear in the K_{sp} expression.

(c) AgCl will not be more soluble in acidic solutions because Cl^- will not react with acidic solutions, because HCl is a strong acid.

(d) PbI_2 will not be more soluble in acidic solutions because I^- will not react with acidic solutions, because HI is a strong acid.

16.100 (a) Hg_2Br_2 will not be more soluble in acidic solutions because Br^- will not react with acidic solutions, because HBr is a strong acid.

(b) $Mg(OH)_2$ will be more soluble in acidic solutions because OH^- is basic. In acidic solutions it can be converted to H_2O. This species is not OH^- and so it does not appear in the K_{sp} expression.

(c) $CaCO_3$ will be more soluble in acidic solutions because CO_3^{2-} is basic. In acidic solutions it can be converted to HCO_3^- and $H_2CO_3^{2-}$. These species are not CO_3^{2-} so they do not appear in the K_{sp} expression.

(d) AgI will not be more soluble in acidic solutions because I^- will not react with acidic solutions, because HI is a strong acid.

Precipitation and Qualitative Analysis

16.101 **Given:** 0.015 M NaF and 0.010 M $Ca(NO_3)_2$ **Find:** Will a precipitate form? If so, identify it.
Other: K_{sp} $(CaF_2) = 1.46 \times 10^{-10}$
Conceptual Plan: Look at all possible combinations and consider the solubility rules from Chapter 4. Salts of alkali metals (Na) are very soluble, so NaF and $NaNO_3$ will be very soluble. Nitrate compounds are very soluble so $NaNO_3$ will be very soluble. The only possibility for a precipitate is CaF_2. Determine if a precipitate will form by determining the concentration of the Ca^{2+} and F^- in solution. Then compute the reaction quotient, *Q*. If $Q > K_{sp}$ then a precipitate will form.
Solution: Since the only possible precipitate is CaF_2, calculate the concentrations of Ca^{2+} and F^-. NaF $(s) \rightarrow Na^+ (aq) + F^- (aq)$. Since 1 F^- ion is generated for each NaF, $[F^-] = 0.015$ M.
$Ca(NO_3)_2 (s) \rightarrow Ca^{2+} (aq) + 2\, NO_3^- (aq)$. Since 1 Ca^{2+} ion is generated for each $Ca(NO_3)_2$, $[Ca^{2+}] = 0.010$ M. Then calculate Q (CaF_2), A = Ca^{2+}, $m = 1$, X = F^-, and $n = 2$. Since $Q = [A^{n+}]^m [X^{m-}]^n$, then $Q\ (CaF_2) = [Ca^{2+}][F^-]^2 = (0.010)(0.015)^2 = 2.3 \times 10^{-6} > 1.46 \times 10^{-10} = K_{sp}\ (CaF_2)$, so a precipitate will form.
Check: The units (none) are correct. The solubility of the CaF_2 is low, and the concentration of ions are extremely large compared to the K_{sp}, so a precipitate will form.

16.102 **Given:** 0.013 M KBr and 0.0035 M $Pb(C_2H_3O_2)_2$ **Find:** Will a precipitate form? If so, identify it.
Other: K_{sp} $(PbBr_2) = 4.67 \times 10^{-6}$
Conceptual Plan: Look at all possible combinations and consider the solubility rules from Chapter 4. Salts of alkali metals (K) are very soluble, so KBr and $KC_2H_3O_2$ will be very soluble. Acetate compounds are very soluble so $Pb(C_2H_3O_2)_2$ and $KC_2H_3O_2$ will be very soluble. The only possibility for a precipitate is $PbBr_2$. Determine if a precipitate will form by determining the concentration of the Pb^{2+} and Br^- in solution. Then compute the reaction quotient, *Q*. If $Q > K_{sp}$ then a precipitate will form.
Solution: Since the only possible precipitate is $PbBr_2$, calculate the concentrations of Pb^{2+} and Br^-.
KBr $(s) \rightarrow K^+ (aq) + Br^- (aq)$. Since 1 Br^- ion is generated for each KBr, $[Br^-] = 0.013$ M. $Pb(C_2H_3O_2)_2 (s) \rightarrow Pb^{2+} (aq) + 2\, C_2H_3O_2^- (aq)$. Since 1 Pb^{2+} ion is generated for each $Pb(C_2H_3O_2)_2$, $[Pb^+] = 0.0035$ M. Then calculate Q $(PbBr_2)$, A = Pb^{2+}, $m = 1$, X = Br^-, and $n = 2$ Since $Q = [A^{n+}]^m [X^{m-}]^n$, then $Q\ (PbBr_2) = [Pb^{2+}][Br^-]^2 = (0.0035)(0.013)^2 = 6.0 \times 10^{-7} < 4.67 \times 10^{-6} = K_{sp}\ (PbBr_2)$, so a precipitate will not form.
Check: The units (none) are correct. The K_{sp} of the $PbBr_2$ is not too low compared to the solution ion concentrations, so a precipitate will not form.

16.103 **Given:** 75.0 mL of NaOH with pOH = 2.58 and 125.0 mL of 0.0018 M $MgCl_2$ **Find:** Will a precipitate form? If so, identify it. **Other:** K_{sp} $(Mg(OH)_2) = 2.06 \times 10^{-13}$
Conceptual Plan: Look at all possible combinations and consider the solubility rules from Chapter 4. Salts of alkali metals (Na) are very soluble, so NaOH and NaCl will be very soluble. Chloride compounds are generally very soluble so $MgCl_2$ and NaCl will be very soluble. The only possibility for a precipitate is $Mg(OH)_2$. Determine if a precipitate will form by determining the concentration of the Mg^{2+} and OH^- in solution. Since pH, not NaOH concentration, is given pOH $\rightarrow$ $[OH^-]$ then

$$[OH^-] = 10^{-pOH}$$

mix solutions and calculate diluted concentrations mL NaOH, mL $MgCl_2$ $\rightarrow$ mL total then

mL NaOH + mL $MgCl_2$ = total mL

mL, initial M $\rightarrow$ final M then compute the reaction quotient, Q.

$M_1 V_1 = M_2 V_2$

If $Q > K_{sp}$ then a precipitate will form.

Solution: Since the only possible precipitate is $Mg(OH)_2$, calculate the concentrations of Mg^{2+} and OH^-. For NaOH at pOH = 2.58, so $[OH^-] = 10^{-pOH} = 10^{-2.58} = 2.\underline{6}3027 \times 10^{-3}$ M and $MgCl_2\ (s) \rightarrow Mg^{2+}\ (aq) + 2\ Cl^-\ (aq)$. Since 1 Mg^{2+} ion is generated for each $MgCl_2$, $[Mg^{2+}] = 0.0018$ M. Then total mL = mL NaOH + mL $MgCl_2$ = 75.0 mL + 125.0 mL = 200.0 mL. Then $M_1 V_1 = M_2 V_2$,

rearrange to solve for M_2. $M_2 = M_1 \dfrac{V_1}{V_2} = 2.\underline{6}3027 \times 10^{-3}\text{ M OH}^- \times \dfrac{75.0\text{ mL}}{200.0\text{ mL}} = 9.\underline{8}635 \times 10^{-4}\text{ M OH}^-$ and

$M_2 = M_1 \dfrac{V_1}{V_2} = 0.0018\text{ M Mg}^+ \times \dfrac{125.0\text{ mL}}{200.0\text{ mL}} = 1.\underline{1}25 \times 10^{-3}\text{ M Mg}^{2+}$. Calculate Q ($Mg(OH)_2$), A = Mg^{2+}, m = 1, X = OH^-, and n = 2. Since $Q = [A^{n+}]^m [X^{m-}]^n$, then $Q\ (Mg(OH)_2) = [Mg^{2+}][OH^-]^2 =$ $(1.\underline{1}25 \times 10^{-3})(9.\underline{8}635 \times 10^{-4})^2 = 1.1 \times 10^{-9} > 2.06 \times 10^{-13} = K_{sp}\ (Mg(OH)_2)$, so a precipitate will form.

Check: The units (none) are correct. The solubility of the $Mg(OH)_2$ is low, and the NaOH (a base) is high enough that the product of the concentration of ions are large compared to the K_{sp}, so a precipitate will form.

16.104 **Given:** 175.0 mL of 0.0055 M KCl and 145.0 mL of 0.0015 M $AgNO_3$

Find: Will a precipitate form? If so, identify it. **Other:** K_{sp} (AgCl) = 1.77×10^{-10}

Conceptual Plan: Look at all possible combinations and consider the solubility rules from Chapter 4. Salts of alkali metals (K) are very soluble, so KCl and KNO_3 will be very soluble. Nitrate compounds are very soluble so KNO_3 and Ag NO_3 will be very soluble. The only possibility for a precipitate is AgCl. Determine if a precipitate will form by determining the concentration of the Ag^+ and Cl^- in solution. Mix solutions and calculate diluted concentrations mL KCl, mL $AgNO_3$ $\rightarrow$ mL total then

mL KCl + mL $AgNO_3$ = total mL

mL, initial M $\rightarrow$ final M then compute the reaction quotient, Q. If $Q > K_{sp}$ then a precipitate will form.

$M_1 V_1 = M_2 V_2$

Solution: Since the only possible precipitate is AgCl, calculate the concentrations of Ag^+ and Cl^-. KCl $(s) \rightarrow K^+\ (aq) + Cl^-\ (aq)$. Since 1 Cl^- ion is generated for each AgCl, $[Cl^-] = 0.0055$ M and $AgNO_3\ (s) \rightarrow Ag^+\ (aq) + NO_3^-\ (aq)$. Since 1 Ag^+ ion is generated for each $AgNO_3$, $[Ag^+] = 0.0015$ M. Then total mL = mL KCl + mL $AgNO_3$ = 175.0 mL + 145.0 mL = 320.0. Then $M_1 V_1 = M_2 V_2$, rearrange to solve for M_2.

$M_2 = M_1 \dfrac{V_1}{V_2} = 0.0055\text{ M Cl}^- \times \dfrac{175.0\text{ mL}}{320.0\text{ mL}} = 0.00300\underline{7}81\text{ M Cl}^-$ and

$M_2 = M_1 \dfrac{V_1}{V_2} = 0.0015\text{ M Ag}^+ \times \dfrac{145.0\text{ mL}}{320.0\text{ mL}} = 0.00067\underline{9}69\text{ M Ag}^+$. Calculate Q (AgCl), A = Ag^+, $m = 1$, X = Cl^-, and $n = 1$. Since $Q = [A^{n+}]^m [X^{m-}]^n$, then Q (AgCl) = $[Ag^+][Cl^-] =$ $(0.00067\underline{9}69)(0.00300\underline{7}81) = 2.0 \times 10^{-6} > 1.77 \times 10^{-10} = K_{sp}$ (AgCl), so a precipitate will form.

Check: The units (none) are correct. The solubility of the AgCl is low, and the concentrations of the ions are high enough that the product of the concentration of ions is very large compared to the K_{sp}, so a precipitate will form.

16.105 **Given:** KOH as precipitation agent in a) 0.015 M $CaCl_2$, b) 0.0025 M $Fe(NO_3)_2$, and c) 0.0018 M $MgBr_2$

Find: concentration of KOH necessary to form a precipitate

Other: $K_{sp}\ (Ca(OH)_2) = 4.68 \times 10^{-6}$, $K_{sp}\ (Fe(OH)_2) = 4.87 \times 10^{-17}$, $K_{sp}\ (Mg(OH)_2) = 2.06 \times 10^{-13}$

Conceptual Plan: The solubility rules from Chapter 4 state that most hydroxides are insoluble, so all precipitates will be hydroxides. Determine the concentration of the cation in solution. Since all metals have an oxidation state of +2 and $[OH^-]$ = [KOH], all of the K_{sp} = [cation] $[KOH]^2$ and so $[KOH] = \sqrt{\dfrac{K_{sp}}{[\text{cation}]}}$.

Solution:

(a) $CaCl_2\ (s) \rightarrow Ca^{2+}\ (aq) + 2\ Cl^-\ (aq)$. Since 1 Ca^{2+} ion is generated for each $CaCl_2$, $[Ca^{2+}] = 0.015$ M.

Then $[KOH] = \sqrt{\dfrac{K_{sp}}{[\text{cation}]}} = \sqrt{\dfrac{4.68 \times 10^{-6}}{0.015}} = 0.018$ M KOH.

(b) $Fe(NO_3)_2\ (s) \rightarrow Fe^{2+}\ (aq) + 2\ NO_3^-\ (aq)$. Since 1 Fe^{2+} ion is generated for each $Fe(NO_3)_2$, $[Fe^{2+}] = 0.0025$ M.

Then $[KOH] = \sqrt{\frac{K_{sp}}{[cation]}} = \sqrt{\frac{4.87 \times 10^{-17}}{0.0025}} = 1.4 \times 10^{-7}$ M KOH.

(c) $MgBr_2\ (s) \rightarrow Mg^{2+}\ (aq) + 2\ Br^-\ (aq)$. Since 1 Mg^{2+} ion is generated for each $MgBr_2$, $[Mg^{2+}] = 0.0018$ M.

Then $[KOH] = \sqrt{\frac{K_{sp}}{[cation]}} = \sqrt{\frac{2.06 \times 10^{-13}}{0.0018}} = 1.1 \times 10^{-5}$ M KOH.

Check: The units (none) are correct. Since all cations have an oxidation state of +2, it can be seen that the [KOH] needed to precipitate the hydroxide is lower the smaller the K_{sp}.

16.106 **Given:** solution and precipitation agent pairs a) 0.035 M $Ba(NO_3)_2$: NaF, b) 0.085 M CaI_2 : K_2SO_4, and c) 0.0018 M $AgNO_3$:RbCl **Find:** concentration of precipitation agent necessary to form a precipitate.
Other: K_{sp} $(BaF_2) = 2.45 \times 10^{-5}$, K_{sp} $(CaSO_4) = 7.10 \times 10^{-5}$, K_{sp} $(AgCl) = 1.77 \times 10^{-10}$
Conceptual Plan: Determine the concentration of the cation in solution. The solubility product constant (K_{sp}) is the equilibrium expression for a chemical equation representing the dissolution of an ionic compound. The expression of the solubility product constant of A_mX_n is $K_{sp} = [A^{n+}]^m [X^{m-}]^n$. Substitute in concentration of cation and solve for concentration of anion.
Solution:

(a) The precipitate is BaF_2. $Ba(NO_3)_2\ (s) \rightarrow Ba^{2+}\ (aq) + 2\ NO_3^-\ (aq)$. Since 1 Ba^{2+} ion is generated for each $Ba(NO_3)_2$, $[Ba^{2+}] = 0.035$ M. Then derive expression for K_{sp} (BaF_2), A = Ba^{2+}, $m = 1$, X = F^-, and $n = 2$ Since $K_{sp} = [Ba^{2+}]\ [F^-]^2$, then K_{sp} $(BaF_2) = 2.45 \times 10^{-5} = 0.035\ [F^-]^2$. Solve for $[F^-]$. $[F^-] = 0.026$ M F^-. Since NaF $(s) \rightarrow Na^+\ (aq) + F^-\ (aq)$, 1 F^- ion is generated for each NaF, [NaF] = 0.026 M NaF.

(b) The precipitate is $CaSO_4$. $CaI_2\ (s) \rightarrow Ca^{2+}\ (aq) + 2\ I^-\ (aq)$. Since 1 Ca^{2+} ion is generated for each CaI_2, $[Ca^{2+}] = 0.085$ M. Then derive expression for K_{sp} $(CaSO_4)$, A = Ca^{2+}, $m = 1$, X = SO_4^{2-}, and $n = 1$ Since $K_{sp} = [Ca^{2+}]\ [SO_4^{2-}]$, then K_{sp} $(CaSO_4) = 7.10 \times 10^{-5} = 0.085\ [SO_4^{2-}]$. Solve for $[SO_4^{2-}]$. $[SO_4^{2-}] = 0.00084$ M SO_4^{2-}. Since $K_2SO_4\ (s) \rightarrow 2\ K^+\ (aq) + SO_4^{2-}\ (aq)$. Since 1 SO_4^{2-} ion is generated for each K_2SO_4, $[K_2SO_4] = 0.00084$ M K_2SO_4.

(c) The precipitate is AgCl. Then $AgNO_3\ (s) \rightarrow Ag^+\ (aq) + NO_3^-\ (aq)$. Since 1 NO_3^- ion is generated for each $AgNO_3$, $[Ag^+] = 0.0018$ M. Then derive expression for K_{sp} (AgCl), A = Ag^+, $m = 1$, X = Cl^-, and $n = 1$ Since $K_{sp} = [Ag^+]\ [Cl^-]$, then K_{sp} (AgCl) $= 1.77 \times 10^{-10} = 0.0018\ [Cl^-]$. Solve for $[Cl^-]$. $[Cl^-] = 9.8 \times 10^{-8}$ M Cl^-. Since RbCl $(s) \rightarrow Rb^+\ (aq) + Cl^-\ (aq)$. Since 1 Cl^- ion is generated for each RbCl, [RbCl] = 9.8×10^{-8} M RbCl.

Check: The units (M) are correct. Comparing part (a) and part (b) the effect of the stoichiometry of the precipitate is seen and the concentration of the precipitation agent is much lower. Looking at part (c) the concentration of the precipitation agent is so low because the K_{sp} is so small.

16.107 **Given:** solution with 0.010 M Ba^{2+} and 0.020 M Ca^{2+} add Na_2SO_4 to form precipitates
Find: (a) which ion precipitates first and minimum $[Na_2SO_4]$ needed; and (b) [first cation] when second cation precipitates **Other:** K_{sp} $(BaSO_4) = 1.07 \times 10^{-10}$, K_{sp} $(CaSO_4) = 7.10 \times 10^{-5}$
Conceptual Plan: (a) The precipitates that will form are $BaSO_4$ and $CaSO_4$.
Use the equation derived in Problem 19 to define K_{sp}. Substitute in concentration of cation and solve for
for ionic compound, A_mX_n, $K_{sp} = [A^{n+}]^m [X^{m-}]^n$
concentration of anion to form precipitate. The cation with the lower anion concentration will precipitate first.

(b) Substitute the higher anion concentration into the K_{sp} expression for the first cation to precipitate and calculate the amount of this first cation to remain in solution.
Solution:

(a) Derive expression for K_{sp} $(BaSO_4)$, A = Ba^{2+}, $m = 1$, X = SO_4^{2-}, and $n = 1$ Since $K_{sp} = [Ba^{2+}]\ [SO_4^{2-}]$, then K_{sp} $(BaSO_4) = 1.07 \times 10^{-10} = 0.010\ [SO_4^{2-}]$. Solve for $[SO_4^{2-}]$. $[SO_4^{2-}] = 1.07 \times 10^{-8}$ M SO_4^{2-}. Since $Na_2SO_4\ (s) \rightarrow 2\ Na^+\ (aq) + SO_4^{2-}\ (aq)$. Since 1 SO_4^{2-} ion is generated for each Na_2SO_4, $[Na_2SO_4] = 1.1 \times 10^{-8}$ M Na_2SO_4 to precipitate $BaSO_4$. Derive expression for K_{sp} $(CaSO_4)$, A = Ca^{2+}, $m = 1$, X = SO_4^{2-}, and $n = 1$ Since $K_{sp} = [Ca^{2+}]\ [SO_4^{2-}]$, then K_{sp} $(CaSO_4) = 7.10 \times 10^{-5} = 0.020\ [SO_4^{2-}]$. Solve for $[SO_4^{2-}]$.

$[SO_4^{\ 2-}] = 0.0036$ M $SO_4^{2-} = 0.0036$ M $Na_2SO_4 = [Na_2SO_4]$ to precipitate $CaSO_4$. Since 1.1×10^{-8} M $Na_2SO_4 << 0.0036$ M Na_2SO_4, the Ba^{2+} will precipitate first.

(b) Since Ca^{2+} will not precipitate until $[Na_2SO_4] = 0.00355$ M Na_2SO_4, substitute this value into the K_{sp} expression for $BaSO_4$. So K_{sp} $(BaSO_4) = [Ba^{2+}]\,[SO_4^{\ 2-}] = 1.07 \times 10^{-10} = [Ba^{2+}]\ 0.0035$. Solve for $[Ba^{2+}] = 3.0 \times 10^{-8}$ M Ba^{2+}.

Check: The units (none, M, and M) are correct. Comparing the two K_{sp} values, it can be seen that the Ba^{2+} will precipitate first since the solubility product is so much lower. Since the K_{sp} value is so low, the concentration of precipitating agent is very low. Since the $CaSO_4$ K_{sp} value is so much higher, the higher $[SO_4^{\ 2-}]$ to precipitate Ca will force the concentration of Ba^{2+} to very low levels.

16.108 **Given:** solution with 0.022 M Fe^{2+} and 0.014 M Mg^{2+} add K_2CO_3 to form precipitates **Find:** (a) which ion precipitates first and minimum $[K_2CO_3]$ needed; and (b) [first cation] when second cation precipitates **Other:** K_{sp} $(FeCO_3) = 3.07 \times 10^{-11}$, K_{sp} $(MgCO_3) = 6.82 \times 10^{-6}$

Conceptual Plan: (a) The precipitates that will form are $FeCO_3$ and $MgCO_3$.

Use the equation derived in Problem 19 to define K_{sp}. Substitute in concentration of cation and solve for

for ionic compound, A_mX_n, $K_{sp} = [A^{n+}]^m\,[X^{m-}]^n$

concentration of anion to form precipitate. The cation with the lower anion concentration will precipitate first.

(b) Substitute the higher anion concentration into the K_{sp} expression for the first cation to precipitate and calculate the amount of this first cation to remain in solution.

Solution:

(a) Derive expression for K_{sp} $(FeCO_3)$, A = Fe^{2+}, $m = 1$, X = $CO_3^{\ 2-}$, and $n = 1$. Since $K_{sp} = [Fe^{2+}]\,[CO_3^{\ 2-}]$, then K_{sp} $(FeCO_3) = 3.07 \times 10^{-11} = 0.022\,[CO_3^{\ 2-}]$. Solve for $[CO_3^{\ 2-}]$. $[CO_3^{\ 2-}] = 1.4 \times 10^{-9}$ M $CO_3^{\ 2-}$. Since K_2CO_3 *(s)* $\rightarrow$ $2\,K^+$ *(aq)* + $CO_3^{\ 2-}$ *(aq)*. Since 1 $CO_3^{\ 2-}$ ion is generated for each K_2CO_3, $[K_2CO_3] = 1.4 \times 10^{-9}$ M K_2CO_3 to precipitate $FeCO_3$. Derive expression for K_{sp} $(MgCO_3)$, A = Mg^{2+}, $m = 1$, X = $CO_3^{\ 2-}$, and $n = 1$. Since $K_{sp} = [Mg^{2+}]\,[CO_3^{\ 2-}]$, then K_{sp} $(MgCO_3) = 6.82 \times 10^{-6} = 0.014\,[CO_3^{\ 2-}]$. Solve for $[CO_3^{\ 2-}]$. $[CO_3^{\ 2-}] = 4.9 \times 10^{-4}$ M $CO_3^{\ 2-} = 4.9 \times 10^{-4}$ M $K_2CO_3 = [K_2CO_3]$ to precipitate $MgCO_3$. Since 1.4×10^{-9} M $K_2CO_3 < 4.9 \times 10^{-4}$ M K_2CO_3, the Fe^{2+} will precipitate first.

(b) Since Mg^{2+} will not precipitate until $[K_2CO_3] = 4.9 \times 10^{-4}$ M K_2CO_3, substitute this value into the K_{sp} expression for $FeCO_3$. So K_{sp} $(FeCO_3) = [Fe^{2+}]\,[CO_3^{\ 2-}] = 3.07 \times 10^{-11} = [Fe^{2+}]\ 4.9 \times 10^{-4}$. Solve for $[Fe^{2+}] = 6.3 \times 10^{-8}$ M Fe^{2+}.

Check: The units (none, M, and M) are correct. Comparing the two K_{sp} values, it can be seen that the Fe^{2+} will precipitate first since the solubility product is so much lower. Since the K_{sp} value is so low, the concentration of precipitating agent is very low. Since the $MgCO_3$ K_{sp} value is so much higher, the higher $[CO_3^{\ 2-}]$ to precipitate Mg will force the concentration of Fe^{2+} to very low levels.

Complex Ion Equilbria

16.109 **Given:** solution with 1.1×10^{-3} M $Zn(NO_3)_2$ and 0.150 M NH_3 **Find:** $[Zn^{2+}]$ at equilibrium **Other:** K_f $(Zn(NH_3)_4^{\ 2+}) = 2.8 \times 10^9$

Conceptual Plan: Write a balanced equation and expression for K_f. Use initial concentrations to set up an ICE table. Since the K_f is so large, assume that reaction essentially goes to completion. Solve for $[Zn^{2+}]$ at equilibrium.

Solution: $Zn(NO_3)_2$ *(s)* $\rightarrow$ Zn^{2+} *(aq)* + $2\,NO_3^-$ *(aq)*. Since 1 Zn^{2+} ion is generated for each $Zn(NO_3)_2$, $[Zn^{2+}] = 1.1 \times 10^{-3}$ M. Balanced equation is:

$$Zn^{2+}\,(aq) + 4\,NH_3\,(aq) \rightleftharpoons Zn(NH_3)_4^{\ 2+}\,(aq)$$

	$[Zn^{2+}]$	$[NH_3]$	$[Zn(NH_3)_4^{\ 2+}]$
Initial	1.1×10^{-3}	0.150	0.00
Change	$\approx 1.1 \times 10^{-3}$	$\approx -4(1.1 \times 10^{-3})$	$\approx 1.1 \times 10^{-3}$
Equil	x	$0.14\underline{5}6$	1.1×10^{-3}

Set up an ICE table with initial concentrations. Since K_f is so large and since initially $[NH_3] > 4\,[Zn^{2+}]$ the reaction essentially goes to completion then write equilibrium expression and solve for x.

$K_f = \frac{[Zn(NH_3)_4^{2+}]}{[Zn^{2+}][NH_3]^4} = 2.8 \times 10^9 = \frac{1.1 \times 10^{-3}}{x\,(0.14\underline{5}6)^4}$ So $x = 8.7 \times 10^{-10}$ M Zn^{2+}. Since x is insignificant compared to the initial concentration, the assumption is valid.

Check: The units (M) are correct. Since K_f is so large, the reaction essentially goes to completion and $[Zn^{2+}]$ is extremely small.

16.110 **Given:** 120.0 mL of 2.8×10^{-3} M $AgNO_3$ mixed with 225.0 mL of 0.10 M NaCN **Find:** $[Ag^+]$ at equilibrium
Other: $K_f\ (Ag(CN)_2^-) = 1 \times 10^{21}$

Conceptual Plan: Mix solutions and calculate diluted concentrations mL $AgNO_3$, mL NaCN → mL total

mL $AgNO_3$ + mL NaCN = total mL

then mL, initial M → final M then write balanced equation and expression for K_f.

$M_1 V_1 = M_2 V_2$

Use initial concentrations to set up an ICE table. Since the K_f is so large, assume that reaction essentially goes to completion. Solve for $[Ag^+]$ at equilibrium.

Solution: $AgNO_3\ (s) \rightarrow Ag^+\ (aq) + NO_3^-\ (aq)$. Since 1 Ag^+ ion is generated for each $AgNO_3$, $[Ag^+] = 2.8 \times 10^{-3}$ M and NaCN $(s) \rightarrow Na^+\ (aq) + CN^-\ (aq)$. Since 1 CN^- ion is generated for each NaCN, $[CN^-] = 0.10$ M. Then total mL = mL $AgNO_3$ + mL NaCN = 120.0 mL + 225.0 mL = 345.0 mL. Then $M_1 V_1 = M_2 V_2$. Rearrange to solve for M_2. $M_2 = M_1 \frac{V_1}{V_2} = 2.8 \times 10^{-3}\text{ M } Ag^+ \times \frac{120.0\text{ mL}}{345.0\text{ mL}} = 0.00097\underline{3}91\text{ M } Ag^+$ and

$M_2 = M_1 \frac{V_1}{V_2} = 0.10\text{ M } CN^- \times \frac{225.0\text{ mL}}{345.0\text{ mL}} = 0.06\underline{5}217\text{ M } CN^-$. The balanced equation is as follows:

$Ag^+\ (aq) + 2\ CN^-\ (aq) \rightleftharpoons Ag(CN)_2^-\ (aq)$

	$[Ag^+]$	$[CN^-]$	$[Ag(CN)_2^-]$
Initial	0.00097391	0.065217	0.00
Change	≈0.00097391	≈ −2(0.00097391)	≈0.00097391
Equil	x	0.063270	0.00097391

Set up an ICE table with initial concentrations. Since K_f is so large and since initially $[CN^-] > 2\,[Ag^+]$ the reaction essentially goes to completion then write equilibrium expression and solve for x.

$K_f = \frac{[Ag(CN)_2^-]}{[Ag^+][CN^-]^2} = 1 \times 10^{21} = \frac{0.00097\underline{3}91}{x\,(0.06\underline{3}270)^2}$ So $x = 2 \times 10^{-22}$ M Ag^+. Since x is insignificant compared to the initial concentration, the assumption is valid.

Check: The units (M) are correct. Since K_f is so large, the reaction essentially goes to completion and $[Ag^+]$ is extremely small.

16.111 **Given:** $FeS\ (s) + 6\ CN^-\ (aq) \rightleftharpoons Fe(CN)_6^{4-}\ (aq) + S^{2-}\ (aq)$ use K_{sp} and K_f values **Find:** K
Other: $K_f\ (Fe(CN)_6^{4-}) = 1.5 \times 10^{35}$, $K_{sp}\ (FeS) = 3.72 \times 10^{-19}$

Conceptual Plan: Identify the appropriate solid and complex ion. Write balanced equations for dissolving the solid and forming the complex ion. Add these two reactions to get the desired overall reaction. Using the rules from Chapter 14, multiply the individual reaction Ks to get the overall K for the sum of these reactions.

Solution: Identify the solid as FeS and the complex ion as $Fe(CN)_6^{4-}$. Write the individual reactions and add them together.

$FeS\ (s) \rightleftharpoons \cancel{Fe^{2+}\ (aq)} + S^{2-}\ (aq)$ $K_{sp} = 1.5 \times 10^{-19}$

$\cancel{Fe^{2+}\ (aq)} + 6\ CN^-\ (aq) \rightleftharpoons Fe(CN)_6^{4-}\ (aq)$ $K_f = 3.72 \times 10^{35}$

$FeS\ (s) + 6\ CN^-(aq) \rightleftharpoons Fe(CN)_6^{4-}(aq) + S^{2-}(aq)$

Since the overall reaction is the simple sum of the two reactions, the overall reaction $K = K_f \times K_{sp} = (1.5 \times 10^{35}) \times (3.72 \times 10^{-19}) = 5.6 \times 10^{16}$.

Check: The units (none) are correct. Since K_f is so large, it overwhelms the K_{sp} and the overall reaction is very spontaneous.

16.112 **Given:** $PbCl_2(s) + 3\ OH^-(aq) \rightleftharpoons Pb(OH)_3^-\ (aq) + 2\ Cl^-\ (aq)$ use K_{sp} and K_f values **Find:** K
Other: $K_f\ (Pb(OH)_3^-) = 8 \times 10^{13}$, $K_{sp}\ (PbCl_2) = 1.17 \times 10^{-5}$

Conceptual Plan: Identify the appropriate solid and complex ion. Write balanced equations for dissolving the solid and forming the complex ion. Add these two reactions to get the desired overall reaction. Using the rules from Chapter 14, multiply the individual reaction *K*s to get the overall *K* for the sum of these reactions.

Solution: Identify the solid as $PbCl_2$ and the complex ion as $Pb(OH)_3^-$. Write the individual reactions and add them together.

$$PbCl_2\,(s) \rightleftharpoons \cancel{Pb^{2+}\,(aq)} + 2\,Cl^-\,(aq) \qquad K_{sp} = 1.17 \times 10^{-5}$$

$$\cancel{Pb^{2+}\,(aq)} + 3\,OH^-\,(aq) \rightleftharpoons Pb(OH)_3^-\,(aq) \qquad K_f = 8 \times 10^{13}$$

$$PbCl_2\,(s) + 3\,OH^-\,(aq) \rightleftharpoons Pb(OH)_3^-\,(aq) + 2\,Cl^-\,(aq)$$

Since the overall reaction is the simple sum of the two reactions, the overall reaction $K = K_f \times K_{sp} = (8 \times 10^{13}) \times (1.17 \times 10^{-5}) = 9 \times 10^{8}$.

Check: The units (none) are correct. Since K_f is so large, it overwhelms the K_{sp} and the overall reaction is very spontaneous.

Cumulative Problems

16.113 **Given:** 150.0 mL solution of 2.05 g sodium benzoate and 2.47 g benzoic acid **Find:** pH

Other: $K_a\,(HC_7H_5O_2) = 6.5 \times 10^{-5}$

Conceptual Plan: g $NaC_7H_5O_2$ → mol $NaC_7H_5O_2$ and g $HC_7H_5O_2$ → mol $HC_7H_5O_2$

$$\frac{1\text{ mol } NaC_7H_5O_2}{144.11\text{ g } NaC_7H_5O_2} \qquad \frac{1\text{ mol } HC_7H_5O_2}{122.13\text{ g } HC_7H_5O_2}$$

Since the two components are in the same solution, the ratio of [base]/[acid] = (mol base)/(mol acid). Then K_a, mol $NaC_7H_5O_2$, mol $HC_7H_5O_2$ → pH.

$$\text{pH} = \text{p}K_a + \log\frac{[\text{base}]}{[\text{acid}]}$$

Solution: $2.05\ \cancel{\text{g } NaC_7H_5O_2} \times \dfrac{1\text{ mol } NaC_7H_5O_2}{144.11\ \cancel{\text{g } NaC_7H_5O_2}} = 0.0142252\text{ mol } NaC_7H_5O_2$ and

$2.47\ \cancel{\text{g } HC_7H_5O_2} \times \dfrac{1\text{ mol } HC_7H_5O_2}{122.13\ \cancel{\text{g } HC_7H_5O_2}} = 0.0202244\text{ mol } HC_7H_5O_2$ then

$$\text{pH} = \text{p}K_a + \log\frac{[\text{base}]}{[\text{acid}]} = \text{p}K_a + \log\frac{\text{mol base}}{\text{mol acid}} = -\log(6.5 \times 10^{-5}) + \log\frac{0.0142252\ \cancel{\text{mol}}}{0.0202244\ \cancel{\text{mol}}} = 4.03.$$

Check: The units (none) are correct. The magnitude of the answer makes physical sense because the pH is a little lower than the pK_a of the acid because there is more acid than base in the buffer solution.

16.114 **Given:** 10.0 mL of 17.5 M acetic acid and 5.54 g sodium acetate diluted to 1.50 L **Find:** pH

Other: $K_a\,(HC_2H_3O_2) = 1.8 \times 10^{-5}$

Conceptual Plan: mL → L then L, initial $HC_2H_3O_2$ M → mol $HC_2H_3O_2$ then

$$\frac{1\text{ L}}{1000\text{ mL}} \qquad M = \frac{\text{mol}}{\text{L}}$$

g $NaC_2H_3O_2$ → mol $NaC_2H_3O_2$ then since the two components are in the same solution,

$$\frac{1\text{ mol } NaC_2H_3O_2}{83.04\text{ g } NaC_2H_3O_2}$$

the ratio of [base]/[acid] = (mol base)/(mol acid). Then K_a, mol $NaC_2H_3O_2$, mol $HC_2H_3O_2$ → pH.

$$\text{pH} = \text{p}K_a + \log\frac{[\text{base}]}{[\text{acid}]}$$

Solution: $10.0\ \cancel{\text{mL}} \times \dfrac{1\text{ L}}{1000\ \cancel{\text{mL}}} = 0.0100\text{ L}$ then

$0.0100\ \cancel{\text{L } HC_2H_3O_2} \times \dfrac{17.5\text{ mol } HC_2H_3O_2}{1\ \cancel{\text{L } HC_2H_3O_2}} = 0.175\text{ mol } HC_2H_3O_2$ then

$5.54\ \cancel{\text{g } NaC_2H_3O_2} \times \dfrac{1\text{ mol } NaC_2H_3O_2}{82.04\ \cancel{\text{g } NaC_2H_3O_2}} = 0.06752803\text{ mol } NaC_2H_3O_2$ then

$$\text{pH} = \text{p}K_a + \log\frac{[\text{base}]}{[\text{acid}]} = \text{p}K_a + \log\frac{\text{mol base}}{\text{mol acid}} = -\log(1.8 \times 10^{-5}) + \log\frac{0.06752803\ \cancel{\text{mol}}}{0.175\ \cancel{\text{mol}}} = 4.33.$$

Check: The units (none) are correct. The magnitude of the answer makes physical sense because the pH is a little lower than the pK_a of the acid because there is more acid than base in the buffer solution.

16.115 **Given:** 150.0 mL of 0.25 M $HCHO_2$ and 75.0 ml of 0.20 M NaOH **Find:** pH **Other:** K_a ($HCHO_2$) = 1.8×10^{-4}
Conceptual Plan: In this buffer, the base is generated by converting some of the formic acid to the formate ion. Part I: Stoichiometry:

mL → L then L, initial $HCHO_2$ M → mol $HCHO_2$ then mL → L then

$\frac{1\text{ L}}{1000\text{ mL}}$ $\quad$ $M = \frac{\text{mol}}{\text{L}}$ $\quad$ $\frac{1\text{ L}}{1000\text{ mL}}$

L, initial NaOH M → mol NaOH then write a balanced equation then

$M = \frac{\text{mol}}{\text{L}}$ $\quad$ $NaOH + HCHO_2 \rightarrow H_2O + NaCHO_2$

mol $HCHO_2$, mol NaOH → mol $NaCHO_2$, mol $HCHO_2$ then

set up stoichiometry table

Part II: Equilibrium:

Since the two components are in the same solution, the ratio of [base]/[acid] = (mol base)/(mol acid). Then K_a, mol $NaCHO_2$, mol $HCHO_2$ → pH.

$$pH = pK_a + \log\frac{[\text{base}]}{[\text{acid}]}$$

Solution: $150.0\text{ mL} \times \frac{1\text{ L}}{1000\text{ mL}} = 0.1500\text{ L}$ then

$0.1500\text{ L } HCHO_2 \times \frac{0.25\text{ mol } HCHO_2}{1\text{ L } HCHO_2} = 0.03\underline{7}5\text{ mol } HCHO_2.$

Then $75.0\text{ mL} \times \frac{1\text{ L}}{1000\text{ mL}} = 0.0750\text{ L}$ then $0.0750\text{ L NaOH} \times \frac{0.20\text{ mol NaOH}}{1\text{ L NaOH}} = 0.015\text{ mol NaOH}$ then set up a table to track changes:

	NaOH (*aq*) +	$HCHO_2$ (*aq*) →	$NaCHO_2$ (*aq*) +	H_2O (*l*)
Before addition	0.00 mol	0.03$\underline{7}$5 mol	0.00 mol	—
Addition	0.015 mol	—	—	—
After addition	≈0.00 mol	0.02$\underline{2}$5 mol	0.015 mol	—

Since the amount of NaOH is small, there are significant amounts of both buffer components, so the Henderson–Hasselbalch equation can be used to calculate the pH.

$$pH = pK_a + \log\frac{[\text{base}]}{[\text{acid}]} = pK_a + \log\frac{\text{mol base}}{\text{mol acid}} = -\log(1.8 \times 10^{-4}) + \log\frac{0.015\text{ mol}}{0.02\underline{2}5\text{ mol}} = 3.57.$$

Check: The units (none) are correct. The magnitude of the answer makes physical sense because the pH is a little lower than the pK_a of the acid because there is more acid than base in the buffer solution.

16.116 **Given:** 750.0 mL solution of 3.55 g NH_3 and 4.78 g HCl **Find:** pH **Other:** K_b (NH_3) = 1.79×10^{-5}
Conceptual Plan: In this buffer, the acid is generated by converting some of the ammonia to the ammonium ion. Part I: Stoichiometry:

g NH_3 → mol NH_3 and g HCl → mol HCl write a balanced equation then

$\frac{1\text{ mol } NH_3}{17.03\text{ g } NH_3}$ $\quad$ $\frac{1\text{ mol HCl}}{36.46\text{ g HCl}}$ $\quad$ $NH_3 + HCl \rightarrow NH_4Cl$

mol NH_3, mol HCl → mol NH_3, mol NH_4Cl then

set up stoichiometry table

Part II: Equilibrium:

K_b → pK_b → pK_a then since the two components are in the same solution,

$pK_b = -\log K_b$ $\quad$ $14 = pK_a + pK_b$

the ratio of [base]/[acid] = (mol base)/(mol acid). Then pK_a, mol NH_3, mol NH_4Cl → pH.

$$pH = pK_a + \log\frac{[\text{base}]}{[\text{acid}]}$$

Solution: $3.55\text{ g } NH_3 \times \frac{1\text{ mol } NH_3}{17.03\text{ g } NH_3} = 0.20\underline{8}456\text{ mol } NH_3$ and

$4.78 \text{ g HCl} \times \frac{1 \text{ mol HCl}}{36.46 \text{ g HCl}} = 0.13\underline{1}103 \text{ mol HCl}$ then set up a table to track changes:

	$HCl\,(aq)$ +	$NH_3\,(aq)$ →	$NH_4Cl\,(aq)$
Before addition	0.00 mol	0.20$\underline{8}$456 mol	0.00 mol
Addition	0.13$\underline{1}$103 mol	—	—
After addition	≈0.00 mol	0.07$\underline{7}$353 mol	0.13$\underline{1}$103 mol

Since the amount of HCl is small, there are significant amounts of both buffer components, so the Henderson–Hasselbalch equation can be used to calculate the pH.

Since $K_b\,(NH_3) = 1.79 \times 10^{-5}$, $pK_b = -\log K_b = -\log(1.79 \times 10^{-5}) = 4.75$. Since $14 = pK_a + pK_b$, $pK_a = 14 - pK_b = 14 - 4.75 = 9.25$ then

$$pH = pK_a + \log\frac{[base]}{[acid]} = pK_a + \log\frac{\text{mol base}}{\text{mol acid}} = 9.25 + \log\frac{0.07\underline{7}353 \text{ mol}}{0.13\underline{1}103 \text{ mol}} = 9.02.$$

Check: The units (none) are correct. The magnitude of the answer makes physical sense because the pH is a little lower than the pK_a of the acid because there is more acid than base in the buffer solution.

16.117 **Given:** 1.0 L of buffer of 0.25 mol NH_3 and 0.25 mol NH_4Cl; adjust to pH = 8.75
Find: mass NaOH or HCl **Other:** $K_b\,(NH_3) = 1.79 \times 10^{-5}$

Conceptual Plan: To decide which reagent needs to be added to adjust pH, calculate the initial pH. Since the mol NH_3 = mol NH_4Cl, the pH = pK_a so $K_b \rightarrow pK_b \rightarrow pK_a$ then

acid = NH_4^+ base = NH_3 $\qquad pK_b = -\log K_b \quad 14 = pK_a + pK_b$

final pH, pK_a → $[NH_3]/[NH_4^+]$ then $[NH_3]$, L → mol NH_3 and $[NH_4^+]$, L → mol NH_4^+

$pH = pK_a + \log\frac{[base]}{[acid]} \qquad M = \frac{mol}{L} \qquad M = \frac{mol}{L}$

then write a balanced equation then

$H^+ + NH_3 \rightarrow NH_4^+$

mol NH_3, mol NH_4^+, $[NH_3]/[NH_4^+]$ → mol HCl → g HCl.

set up stoichiometry table $\qquad \frac{36.46 \text{ g HCl}}{1 \text{ mol HCl}}$

Solution: Since $K_b\,(NH_3) = 1.79 \times 10^{-5}$, $pK_b = -\log K_b = -\log(1.79 \times 10^{-5}) = 4.75$. Since $14 = pK_a + pK_b$, $pK_a = 14 - pK_b = 14 - 4.75 = 9.25$. Since the desired pH is lower (8.75) HCl (a strong acid) needs to be added. Then $pH = pK_a + \log\frac{[base]}{[acid]} = 9.25 + \log\frac{[NH_3]}{[NH_4^+]} = 8.75$. Solve for $\frac{[NH_3]}{[NH_4^+]}$.

$$\log\frac{[NH_3]}{[NH_4^+]} = 8.75 - 9.25 = -0.50 \rightarrow \frac{[NH_3]}{[NH_4^+]} = 10^{-0.50} = 0.3\underline{1}623. \text{ Then}$$

$\frac{0.25 \text{ mol } NH_3}{1 \text{ L}} \times 1.0 \text{ L} = 0.25 \text{ mol } NH_3$ and

$\frac{0.25 \text{ mol } NH_4Cl}{1 \text{ L}} \times 1.0 \text{ L} = 0.25 \text{ mol } NH_4Cl = 0.25 \text{ mol } NH_4^+$. Since HCl is a strong acid, $[HCl] = [H^+]$, and set up a table to track changes:

	$H^+\,(aq)$ +	$NH_3\,(aq)$ →	$NH_4^+\,(aq)$
Before addition	≈0.00 mol	0.25 mol	0.25 mol
Addition	x	—	—
After addition	≈0.00 mol	$(0.25 - x)$ mol	$(0.25 + x)$ mol

Since $\frac{[NH_3]}{[NH_4^+]} = 0.3\underline{1}623 = \frac{(0.25 - x) \text{ mol}}{(0.25 + x) \text{ mol}}$, solve for x. Note that the ratio of moles is the same as the ratio of concentrations, since the volume for both terms is the same. $0.3\underline{1}623\,(0.25 + x) = (0.25 - x) \rightarrow 0.07\underline{9}0575 + 0.3\underline{1}623\,x = 0.25 - x \rightarrow 1.3\underline{1}623\,x = 0.1\underline{7}094 \rightarrow x = 0.1\underline{2}987$ mol HCl then

$$0.1\underline{2}987 \text{ mol HCl} \times \frac{36.46 \text{ g HCl}}{1 \text{ mol HCl}} = 4.7 \text{ g HCl}.$$

Check: The units (g) are correct. The magnitude of the answer makes physical sense because there is much less than a mole of each of the buffer components, so there must be much less than a mole of HCl.

16.118 **Given:** 250.0 mL of buffer of 0.025 mol $HCHO_2$ and 0.025 mol $NaCHO_2$; adjust to pH = 4.10
Find: mass NaOH or HCl **Other:** K_a ($HCHO_2$) = 1.8 x 10^{-4}
Conceptual Plan: To decide which reagent needs to be added to adjust pH, calculate the initial pH. Since the mol $HCHO_2$ = mol $NaCHO_2$, the pH = pK_a then final pH, pK_a → [$NaCHO_2$]/[$HCHO_2$]

acid = $HCHO_2$ base = $HCHO_2^-$ $\quad pK_a = -\log K_a \quad pH = pK_a + \log\frac{[base]}{[acid]}$

then mL → L then write a balanced equation then

$\frac{1\ L}{1000\ mL}$ $\quad NaOH + HCHO_2 \rightarrow NaCHO_2 + H_2O$

mol $NaCHO_2$, mol $HCHO_2$, [$NaCHO_2$]/[$HCHO_2$] → mol NaOH → g NaOH.

set up stoichiometry table $\quad \frac{40.00\ g\ NaOH}{1\ mol\ NaOH}$

Solution: Since K_a ($HCHO_2$) = 1.8 x 10^{-4}, $pK_a = -\log K_a = -\log(1.8 \times 10^{-4}) = 3.74$. Since the desired pH (4.10) is higher NaOH (a strong base) needs to be added. Then

$pH = pK_a + \log\frac{[base]}{[acid]} = 3.74 + \log\frac{[NaCHO_2]}{[HCHO_2]} = 4.10$. Solve for $\frac{[NaCHO_2]}{[HCHO_2]}$.

$\log\frac{[NaCHO_2]}{[HCHO_2]} = 4.10 - 3.74 = 0.36 \rightarrow \frac{[NaCHO_2]}{[HCHO_2]} = 10^{+0.36} = 2.2\underline{9}087$. Then, since NaOH is a strong base, [NaOH] = [OH^-], and set up a table to track changes:

	$NaOH\ (aq)$ +	$HCHO_2\ (aq)$ →	$NaCHO_2\ (aq)$ +	$H_2O\ (l)$
Before addition	≈0.00 mol	0.025 mol	0.025 mol	—
Addition	x	$-x$	$+x$	—
After addition	≈0.00 mol	(0.025 – x) mol	(0.025 + x) mol	—

Since $pH = pK_a + \log\frac{[A^-]}{[HA]}$ so $4.10 = 3.74 + \log\frac{0.025\ mol + x}{0.025\ mol - x}$ solve for x. Note that the ratio of moles is the same as the ratio of concentrations, since the volume for both terms is the same

$0.360 = \log\frac{0.025\ mol + x}{0.025\ mol - x} \rightarrow 2.29 = \frac{0.025\ mol + x}{0.025\ mol - x} \rightarrow 0.05\underline{7}3 - 2.29x = 0.025 + x \rightarrow 3.29x = 0.03\underline{2}3 \rightarrow$

$x = 0.00\underline{9}81$ mol then $0.00981\ \cancel{mol\ NaOH} \times \frac{40.00\ g\ NaOH}{1\ \cancel{mol\ NaOH}} = 0.39\ g\ NaOH$.

Check: The units (g) are correct. The magnitude of the answer makes physical sense because there is much less than a mole of each of the buffer components, so there must be much less than a mole of NaOH.

16.119 (a) **Given:** potassium hydrogen phthalate = KHP = $KHC_8H_4O_4$ titration with NaOH
Find: balanced equation
Conceptual Plan: The reaction will be a titration of the acid proton, leaving the phthalate ion intact. The K will not be titrated since it is basic.
Solution: $NaOH\ (aq) + KHC_8H_4O_4\ (aq) \rightarrow Na^+\ (aq) + K^+\ (aq) + C_8H_4O_4^{2-}\ (aq) + H_2O\ (l)$
Check: An acid–base reaction generates a salt (soluble here) and water. There is only one acidic proton in KHP.

(b) **Given:** 0.5527 g KHP titrated with 25.87 mL of NaOH solution **Find:** [NaOH]
Conceptual Plan:
g KHP → mol KHP → mol NaOH and mL → L then mol NaOH and mL → M NaOH

$\frac{1\ mol\ KHP}{204.22\ g\ KHP}$ *1:1 from balance equation* $\quad \frac{1\ L}{1000\ mL} \quad M = \frac{mol}{L}$

Solution: $0.5527\ \cancel{g\ KHP} \times \frac{1\ mol\ KHP}{204.22\ \cancel{g\ KHP}} = 0.0027\underline{0}6395$ mol KHP; mol KHP = mol acid = mol base =

$0.0027\underline{0}6395$ mol NaOH then $25.87\ \cancel{mL} \times \frac{1\ L}{1000\ \cancel{mL}} = 0.02587$ L then

$[NaOH] = \frac{0.0027\underline{0}6395\ mol\ NaOH}{0.02587\ L} = 0.1046\ M\ NaOH$.

Check: The units (M) are correct. The magnitude of the answer makes physical sense because there is much less than a mole of acid. The magnitude of the moles of acid and base are smaller than the volume of base in liters.

16.120 **Given:** 0.5224 g monoprotic acid titrated with 23.82 mL of 0.0998 M NaOH solution
Find: molar mass of acid
Conceptual Plan: mL → L then M NaOH, L → mol NaOH → mol acid then mol acid, g acid → $\mathcal{M}$

$\frac{1\ L}{1000\ mL}$ $\qquad$ $M = \frac{mol}{L}$ $\qquad$ *1:1 for monoprotic acid* $\qquad$ $\mathcal{M} = \frac{g\ acid}{mol\ acid}$

Solution: $23.82\ \text{mL} \times \frac{1\ L}{1000\ \text{mL}} = 0.02382\ L$ then

$0.02382\ \text{L NaOH} \times \frac{0.0998\ mol\ NaOH}{1\ \text{L NaOH}} = 0.00237724\ mol\ NaOH;$ 0.00237724 mol NaOH = mol base =

mol acid = 0.00237724 mol acid then $M = \frac{g\ acid}{mol\ acid} = \frac{0.5224\ g\ acid}{0.00237724\ mol\ acid} = 220.\ g/mol.$

Check: The units (g/mol) are correct. The magnitude of the answer makes physical sense because there is much less than a mole of acid and about a half a gram of acid, so the molar mass will be high. The number is reasonable for an acid (must be > 20 g/mol – lightest acid is HF).

16.121 **Given:** 0.25 mol weak acid with 10.0 mL of 3.00 M KOH diluted to 1.5000 L has pH = 3.85 **Find:** pK_a of acid
Conceptual Plan: mL → L then M KOH, L → mol KOH then write a balanced reaction

$\frac{1\ L}{1000\ mL}$ $\qquad$ $M = \frac{mol}{L}$ $\qquad$ $KOH + HA \rightarrow NaA + H_2O$

added mol KOH, initial mol acid → equil. mol KOH, equil. mol acid then

set up stoichiometry table

equil. mol KOH, equil. mol acid, pH → pK_a.

$pH = pK_a + \log\frac{[base]}{[acid]}$

Solution: $10.00\ \text{mL} \times \frac{1\ L}{1000\ \text{mL}} = 0.01000\ L$ then $0.01000\ \text{L KOH} \times \frac{3.00\ mol\ KOH}{1\ \text{L KOH}} = 0.0300\ mol\ KOH$ then

Since KOH is a strong base, [KOH] = [OH$^-$], and set up a table to track changes:

	KOH (*aq*) +	HA (*aq*) →	KA (*aq*) +	H_2O (*l*)
Before addition	≈0.00 mol	0.25 mol	0.00 mol	—
Addition	0.0300 mol	—	—	—
After addition	≈0.00 mol	0.22 mol	0.0300 mol	—

Since the ratio of base to acid is between 0.1 and 10, it is a buffer solution. Note that the ratio of moles is the same as the ratio of concentrations, since the volume for both terms is the same.

$pH = pK_a + \log\frac{[base]}{[acid]} = pK_a + \log\frac{0.0300\ mol}{0.22\ mol} = 3.85.$ Solve for pK_a.

$pK_a = 3.85 - \log\frac{0.0300\ mol}{0.22\ mol} = 4.72.$

Check: The units (none) are correct. The magnitude of the answer makes physical sense because there is more acid than base at equilibrium, so the pK_a is higher than the pH of the solution.

16.122 **Given:** 5.55 g weak acid with $K_a = 1.3 \times 10^{-4}$ with 5.00 mL of 6.00 M NaOH diluted to 750 mL has pH = 4.25
Find: molar mass of acid
Conceptual Plan: mL → L then M NaOH, L → mol NaOH then write a balanced reaction

$\frac{1\ L}{1000\ mL}$ $\qquad$ $M = \frac{mol}{L}$ $\qquad$ $NaOH + HA \rightarrow NaA + H_2O$

added mol NaOH, initial mol acid → equil. mol NaOH, equil. mol acid then

set up stoichiometry table

added mol NaOH, equil. mol acid, pH, pK_a → equil. mol NaOH, equil. mol acid then

$pH = pK_a + \log\frac{[base]}{[acid]}$

mol acid, g acid → $\mathcal{M}$.

$\mathcal{M} = \frac{g\ acid}{mol\ acid}$

Solution: $5.00\ \text{mL} \times \frac{1\ L}{1000\ \text{mL}} = 0.00500\ L$ then $0.00500\ \text{L NaOH} \times \frac{6.00\ mol\ NaOH}{1\ \text{L NaOH}} = 0.0300\ mol\ NaOH.$

Since NaOH is a strong base, [NaOH] = [OH^-], and set up a table to track changes:

	$NaOH\,(aq)$ +	$HA\,(aq)$ →	$NaA\,(aq)$ +	$H_2O\,(l)$
Before addition	≈0.00 mol	x mol	0.00 mol	—
Addition	0.0300 mol	—	—	—
After addition	≈0.00 mol	x – 0.0300 mol	0.0300 mol	—

Since the pH is within 1 unit of the pK_a, it is a buffer solution. Note that the ratio of moles is the same as the ratio of concentrations, since the volume for both terms is the same.

$$\text{pH} = \text{p}K_a + \log\frac{[\text{base}]}{[\text{acid}]} = -\log(1.3 \times 10^{-4}) + \log\frac{0.0300\text{ mol}}{(x - 0.0300)\text{ mol}} = 4.25.$$

Solve for x. $\log 0.0300 - \log(x - 0.0300) = 4.25 - 3.89 \rightarrow -\log(x - 0.0300) = 1.8\underline{8}288 \rightarrow$

$x - 0.0300 = 10^{-1.8\underline{8}288} = 0.013\underline{0}955 \rightarrow x = 0.043\underline{0}855$ mol. Finally,

$$M = \frac{\text{g acid}}{\text{mol acid}} = \frac{5.55\text{ g acid}}{0.043\underline{0}855\text{ mol acid}} = 129\text{ g/mol}$$

Check: The units (g/mol) are correct. The magnitude of the answer makes physical sense because there is much less than a mole of acid and about 6 grams of acid, so the molar mass will be high. The number is reasonable for an acid (must be > 20 g/mol – lightest acid is HF).

16.123 **Given:** 0.552 g ascorbic acid dissolved in 20.00 mL and titrated with 28.42 mL of 0.1103 M KOH solution; pH = 3.72 when 10.0 mL KOH added **Find:** molar mass and K_a of acid

Conceptual Plan: mL → L then M KOH, L → mol KOH → mol acid then mol acid, g acid → $\mathcal{M}$

$\frac{1\text{ L}}{1000\text{ mL}}$ $M = \frac{\text{mol}}{\text{L}}$ 1:1 for monoprotic acid $\mathcal{M} = \frac{\text{g acid}}{\text{mol acid}}$

For the second part of the problem:

mL → L then M KOH, L → mol KOH then write a balanced reaction

$\frac{1\text{ L}}{1000\text{ mL}}$ $M = \frac{\text{mol}}{\text{L}}$ $KOH + HA \rightarrow NaA + H_2O$

added mol KOH, initial mol acid → equil. mol KOH, equil. mol acid then

set up stoichiometry table

equil. mol KOH, equil. mol acid, pH → pK_a → K_a.

$\text{pH} = \text{p}K_a + \log\frac{[\text{base}]}{[\text{acid}]}$ $\text{p}K_a = -\log K_a$

Solution: $28.42\text{ mL} \times \frac{1\text{ L}}{1000\text{ mL}} = 0.02842\text{ L}$ then

$0.02842\text{ L KOH} \times \frac{0.1103\text{ mol KOH}}{1\text{ L KOH}} = 0.0031\underline{3}4726\text{ mol KOH} = \text{mol base} = \text{mol acid} = 0.0031\underline{3}4726\text{ mol}$

ascorbic acid then $M = \frac{\text{g acid}}{\text{mol acid}} = \frac{0.552\text{ g acid}}{0.0031\underline{3}4726\text{ mol acid}} = 176\text{ g/mol}$. For the second part of the problem,

$10.00\text{ mL} \times \frac{1\text{ L}}{1000\text{ mL}} = 0.01000\text{ L}$ then $0.01000\text{ L KOH} \times \frac{0.1103\text{ mol KOH}}{1\text{ L KOH}} = 0.001103\text{ mol KOH}$ then

Since KOH is a strong base, [KOH] = [OH^-], and set up a table to track changes:

	$KOH\,(aq)$ +	$HA\,(aq)$ →	$KA\,(aq)$ +	$H_2O\,(l)$
Before addition	≈0.00 mol	0.0031$\underline{3}$4726 mol	0.00 mol	—
Addition	0.001103 mol	—	—	—
After addition	≈0.00 mol	0.0020$\underline{3}$1726 mol	0.001103 mol	—

Since the ratio of base to acid is between 0.1 and 10, it is a buffer solution. Note that the ratio of moles is the same as the ratio of concentrations, since the volume for both terms is the same.

$$\text{pH} = \text{p}K_a + \log\frac{[\text{base}]}{[\text{acid}]} = \text{p}K_a + \log\frac{0.001103\text{ mol}}{0.0020\underline{3}1726\text{ mol}} = 3.72.$$ Solve for pK_a.

$$\text{p}K_a = 3.72 - \log\frac{0.001103}{0.0020\underline{3}1726} = 3.9\underline{8}529 \text{ and so } \text{p}K_a = -\log K_a$$

or $K_a = 10^{-\text{p}K_a} = 10^{-3.9\underline{8}529} = 1.0 \times 10^{-4}$.

Check: The units (g/mol and none) are correct. The magnitude of the answer makes physical sense because there is much less than a mole of acid and about a half a gram of acid, so the molar mass will be high. The number is reasonable for an acid (must be > 20 g/mol – lightest acid is HF). The K_a is reasonable because the pK_a is within 1 unit of the pH when the titration solution is behaving as a buffer.

16.124   **Given:** titration data in Problem 123   **Find:** initial pH
Conceptual Plan: Since ascorbic acid is a weak acid, set up an equilibrium problem using the initial concentration. so mL $\rightarrow$ L then mol HA, L $\rightarrow$ M HA $\rightarrow$ $[H_3O^+]$ $\rightarrow$ pH

$$\frac{1\ L}{1000\ mL} \qquad M = \frac{mol}{L} \quad ICE\ Chart \quad pH = -\log [H_3O^+]$$

Solution: $20.00\ \cancel{mL} \times \dfrac{1\ L}{1000\ \cancel{mL}} = 0.02000\ L$ then $\dfrac{0.003134726\ mol\ HA}{0.02000\ L\ HA} = 0.156\underline{7}363\ mol\ HA$ then

$$HA\ (aq) + H_2O\ (l) \rightleftharpoons H_3O^+\ (aq) + A^-\ (aq)$$

	[HA]	$[H_3O^+]$	$[A^-]$
Initial	0.156$\underline{7}$363	≈ 0.00	0.00
Change	$-x$	$+x$	$+x$
Equil	0.156$\underline{7}$363 $- x$	$+x$	$+x$

and $K_a = \dfrac{[H_3O^+]\,[A^-]}{[HA]} = 1.0 \times 10^{-4} = \dfrac{x^2}{0.1567363 - x}$

Assume x is small ($x \ll 0.1567$) so $\dfrac{x^2}{0.1567363 - x} = 1.0 \times 10^{-4} = \dfrac{x^2}{0.1567363}$ and $x = 3.\underline{9}590 \times 10^{-3} =$

$= [H_3O^+]$. Confirm that the assumption the is valid. $\dfrac{3.\underline{9}590 \times 10^{-3}}{0.1567363} \times 100\% = 2.5\% < 5\%$ so the assumption is valid.

Finally, pH $= -\log [H_3O^+] = -\log (3.\underline{9}590 \times 10^{-3}) = 2.40$
Check: The units (none) are correct. The magnitude of the answer makes physical sense because pH should be greater than $-\log (0.1567) = 0.80$ because this is a weak acid.
Find: pH at one-half of the equivalence point
Conceptual Plan: Since this is a weak acid–strong base titration, the pH at one-half the equivalence point is the pK_a of the weak acid.
Solution: pH $= pK_a = -\log K_a = -\log (1.0 \times 10^{-4}) = 4.00$ and the volume of added base is 0.5×28.42 mL $= 14.21$ mL.
Check: The units (none) are correct. Since this is a weak acid–strong base titration, the pH at one-half the equivalence point is the pK_a of the weak acid, so it should be 4.
Find: pH at equivalence point
Conceptual Plan: Use the calculations from above, then since all of the weak acid has been converted to its conjugate base, the pH is only dependent on the hydrolysis reaction of the conjugate base. The mol A^- = initial mol HA and L HA, L KOH to equivalence point $\rightarrow$ total L then mol A^-, L $\rightarrow$ $[A^-]$

$$L\ HA + L\ KOH = total\ L \qquad M = \frac{mol}{L}$$

and $K_a \rightarrow K_b$ **then do equilibrium calculation:** $[A], K_b \rightarrow [OH^-] \rightarrow [H_3O^+] \rightarrow$ pH.

$$K_w = K_a K_b \qquad\qquad set\ up\ ICE\ table \qquad K_w = [H_3O^+][OH^-] \quad pH = -\log [H_3O^+]$$

Solution: total volume = L HA + L KOH = 0.0200 L + 0.02842 L = 0.048$\underline{4}$2 L then

$[A^-] = \dfrac{0.003134726\ mol\ A^-}{0.048\underline{4}2\ L} = 0.0647403\ M$ and $K_w = K_a K_b$. Rearrange to solve for K_b.

$K_b = \dfrac{K_w}{K_a} = \dfrac{1.0 \times 10^{-14}}{1.0 \times 10^{-4}} = 1.0 \times 10^{-10}$. Set up an ICE table:

$$A^-\ (aq) + H_2O\ (l) \rightleftharpoons HA\ (aq) + OH^-\ (aq)$$

	$[A^-]$	[HA]	$[OH^-]$
Initial	0.064$\underline{7}$403	≈ 0.00	≈ 0.00
Change	$-x$	$+x$	$+x$
Equil	0.064$\underline{7}$403 $- x$	$+x$	$+x$

$K_b = \dfrac{[HA]\,[OH^-]}{[A^-]} = 1.0 \times 10^{-10} = \dfrac{x^2}{0.0647403 - x}$ Assume x is small ($x \ll 0.0647$) so

$\frac{x^2}{0.0647403 - x} = 1.0 \times 10^{-10} = \frac{x^2}{0.0647403}$ and $x = 2.5444 \times 10^{-6} = [OH^-]$. Confirm that the assumption is valid.

$\frac{2.5444 \times 10^{-6}}{0.0647403} \times 100\% = 0.0039\% < 5\%$ so the assumption is valid. $K_w = [H_3O^+][OH^-]$ so

$[H_3O^+] = \frac{K_w}{[OH^-]} = \frac{1.0 \times 10^{-14}}{2.5444 \times 10^{-6}} = 3.9302 \times 10^{-9}$ M. Finally,

$pH = -\log[H_3O^+] = -\log(3.9302 \times 10^{-9}) = 8.41$.

Check: The units (none) are correct. Since this is a weak acid–strong base titration, the pH at the equivalence point is basic.

Find: pH after adding 5.0 mL of excess base

Conceptual Plan: Use calculations from earlier. Then the pH is only dependent on the amount of excess base and the total solution volumes. mL excess → L excess then [KOH], L excess → mol KOH excess

$\frac{1\ L}{1000\ mL}$ $\qquad M = \frac{mol}{L}$

then L HA, L KOH to equivalence point, L KOH excess → total L then

L HA + L NaOH to equivalence point + L NaOH excess = total L

mol excess KOH, total L → [KOH] = [OH⁻] → [H₃O⁺] → pH.

$M = \frac{mol}{L}$ $\qquad K_w = [H_3O^+][OH^-]$ $\qquad pH = -\log[H_3O^+]$

Solution: $5.0\ \text{mL KOH} \times \frac{1\ L}{1000\ mL} = 0.0050$ L KOH excess then

$\frac{0.1103\ mol\ KOH}{1\ L} \times 0.0050\ L = 0.0005515$ mol KOH excess. then

0.020 L HA + 0.02842 L KOH + 0.0050 L KOH = 0.05342 L total volume.

$[KOH\ excess] = \frac{0.0005515\ mol\ KOH\ excess}{0.05342\ L} = 0.010324$ M KOH excess. Since KOH is a strong base,

[KOH] excess = [OH⁻]. The strong base overwhelms the weak base and is insignificant in the calculation.

$K_w = [H_3O^+][OH^-]$ so $[H_3O^+] = \frac{K_w}{[OH^-]} = \frac{1.0 \times 10^{-14}}{0.010324} = 9.6863 \times 10^{-13}$ M. Finally,

$pH = -\log[H_3O^+] = -\log(9.6863 \times 10^{-13}) = 12.01$.

Check: The units (none) are correct. The pH is rising sharply at the equivalence point, so the pH after 5 mL past the equivalence point should be quite basic.

Given: above data

Find: titration curve and suitable indicator

Solution: Plotting these data points is shown as follows:

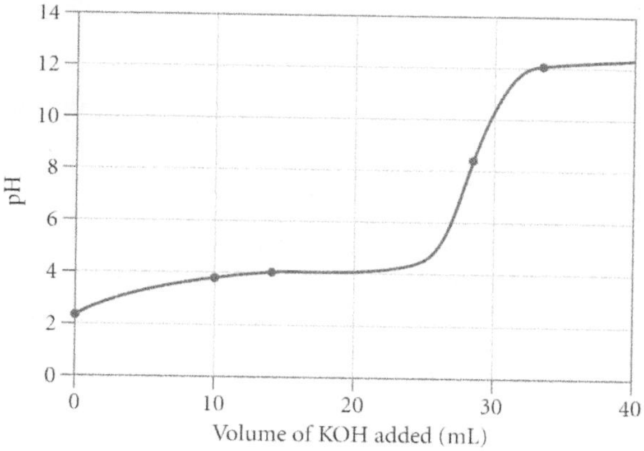

Since the pH at the equivalence point is 8.42, appropriate indicator a are *m*-Nitrophenol or Thymol Blue.

16.125 **Given:** saturated $CaCO_3$ solution; precipitate 1.00×10^2 mg $CaCO_3$ **Find:** volume of solution evaporated

Other: $K_{sp}(CaCO_3) = 4.96 \times 10^{-9}$

Conceptual Plan: mg $CaCO_3$ → g $CaCO_3$ → mol $CaCO_3$

$\frac{1\ g\ CaCO_3}{1000\ mg\ CaCO_3}$ $\qquad \frac{1\ mol\ CaCO_3}{100.09\ g\ CaCO_3}$

The expression of the solubility product constant of A_mX_n is $K_{sp} = [A^{n+}]^m [X^{m-}]^n$. The molar solubility of a compound, A_mX_n, can be computed directly from K_{sp} by solving for S in the expression $K_{sp} = (mS)^m (nS)^n = m^m n^n S^{m+n}$. Then mol $CaCO_3$, $S \rightarrow$ L.

$$M = \frac{mol}{L}$$

Solution: $1.00 \times 10^2 \text{ mg } CaCO_3 \times \frac{1 \text{ g } CaCO_3}{1000 \text{ mg } CaCO_3} \times \frac{1 \text{ mol } CaCO_3}{100.09 \text{ g } CaCO_3} = 9.99101 \times 10^{-4}$ mol $CaCO_3$ then $K_{sp} = 4.96 \times 10^{-9}$, $A = Ca^{2+}$, $m = 1$, $X = CO_3^{2-}$, and $n = 1$ so $K_{sp} = 4.96 \times 10^{-9} = S^2$. Rearrange to solve for S. $S = \sqrt{4.96 \times 10^{-9}} = 7.04273 \times 10^{-5}$ M. Finally,

$$9.99101 \times 10^{-4} \text{ mol } CaCO_3 \times \frac{1 \text{ L}}{7.04273 \times 10^{-5} \text{ mol } CaCO_3} = 14.2 \text{ L}.$$

Check: The units (L) are correct. The volume should be large since the solubility is low.

16.126 **Given:** $[Na^+] = 0.140$ M and K_{sp} ($NaC_5H_3N_4$) $= 5.76 \times 10^{-8}$ **Find:** $[C_5H_3N_4^-]$ to form precipitate
Conceptual Plan: Write a balanced equation and expression for K_{sp}. Then $[Na^+]$, $K_{sp} \rightarrow [C_5H_3N_4^-]$.
Solution: $NaC_5H_3N_4$ (*s*) $\rightarrow Na^+$ (*aq*) + $C_5H_3N_4^-$(*aq*). So $K_{sp} = [Na^+] [C_5H_3N_4^-] = 5.76 \times 10^{-8} = (0.140) [C_5H_3N_4^-]$. Solve for $[C_5H_3N_4^-]$ then $[C_5H_3N_4^-] = 4.11 \times 10^{-7}$ M.
Check: The units (M) are correct. Since K_{sp} is so small and the sodium concentration is fairly high, the urate concentration is driven to a very low level.

16.127 **Given:** $[Ca^{2+}] = 9.2$ mg/dL and K_{sp} ($Ca_2P_2O_7$) $= 8.64 \times 10^{-13}$ **Find:** $[P_2O_7^{4-}]$ to form precipitate
Conceptual Plan: mg Ca^{2+} /dL $\rightarrow$ g Ca^{2+} /dL $\rightarrow$ mol Ca^{2+}/dL $\rightarrow$ mol Ca^{2+}/L then

$$\frac{1 \text{ g } Ca^{2+}}{1000 \text{ mg } Ca^{2+}} \qquad \frac{1 \text{ mol } Ca^{2+}}{40.08 \text{ g } Ca^{2+}} \qquad \frac{10 \text{ dL}}{1 \text{ L}}$$

Write a balanced equation and expression for K_{sp}. Then $[Ca^{2+}]$, $K_{sp} \rightarrow [P_2O_7^{4-}]$.

Solution: $9.2 \frac{\text{mg } Ca^{2+}}{\text{dL}} \times \frac{1 \text{ g } Ca^{2+}}{1000 \text{ mg } Ca^{2+}} \times \frac{1 \text{ mol } Ca^{2+}}{40.08 \text{ g } Ca^{2+}} \times \frac{10 \text{ dL}}{1 \text{ L}} = 2.29541 \times 10^{-3}$ M Ca^{2+} then write equation $Ca_2P_2O_7$ (*s*) $\rightarrow 2\ Ca^{2+}$ (*aq*) + $P_2O_7^{4-}$ (*aq*). So $K_{sp} = [Ca^{2+}]^2 [P_2O_7^{4-}] = 8.64 \times 10^{-13} =$
$= (2.29541 \times 10^{-3})^2 [P_2O_7^{4-}]$. Solve for $[P_2O_7^{4-}]$ then $[P_2O_7^{4-}] = 1.6 \times 10^{-7}$ M.
Check: The units (M) are correct. Since K_{sp} is so small and the calcium concentration is relatively high, the diphosphate concentration required is at a very low level.

16.128 **Given:** AgCl in 0.100 M NH_3 **Find:** molar solubility (S)
Other: K_f ($Ag(NH_3)_2^+$) $= 1.7 \times 10^7$, K_{sp} (AgCl) $= 1.77 \times 10^{-10}$
Conceptual Plan: Identify the appropriate solid and complex ion. Write balanced equations for dissolving the solid and forming the complex ion. Add these two reactions to get the desired overall reaction. Using the rules from Chapter 14, multiply the individual reaction Ks to get the overall K for the sum of these reactions. Then M NH_3, $K \rightarrow S$.

ICE Chart

Solution: Identify the solid as AgCl and the complex ion as $Ag(NH_3)_2^+$. Write the individual reactions and add them together.

AgCl (*s*) $\rightleftharpoons$ ~~Ag^+ (*aq*)~~ + Cl^- (aq)	$K_{sp} = 1.77 \times 10^{-10}$
~~Ag^+ (*aq*)~~ + 2 NH_3 (*aq*) $\rightleftharpoons$ $Ag(NH_3)_2^+$ (*aq*)	$K_f = 1.7 \times 10^7$
AgCl (*s*) + 2 NH_3 (*aq*) $\rightleftharpoons$ $Ag(NH_3)_2^+$ (*aq*) + Cl^- (*aq*)	

Since the overall reaction is the simple sum of the two reactions, the overall reaction $K = K_f K_{sp} =$
$= (1.7 \times 10^7) \times (1.77 \times 10^{-10}) = 3.009 \times 10^{-3}$. Then set up an ICE table:

AgCl (*s*) + 2 NH_3 (*aq*) $\rightleftharpoons$ $Ag(NH_3)_2^+$ (*aq*) + Cl^- (*aq*)

	$[NH_3]$	$[Ag(NH_3)_2^+]$	$[Cl^-]$
Initial	0.100	0.00	0.00
Change	$-2S$	$+S$	$+S$
Equil	$0.100 - 2S$	$+S$	$+S$

$K = \frac{[Ag(NH_3)_2^+][Cl^-]}{[NH_3]^2} = 3.\underline{0}09 \times 10^{-3} = \frac{S^2}{(0.100 - 2S)^2}$. Simplify by taking the square root of the expression. $\sqrt{3.\underline{0}09 \times 10^{-3}} = 5.\underline{4}854 \times 10^{-2} = \frac{S}{(0.100 - 2S)}$ Solve for S. $(5.\underline{4}854 \times 10^{-2})(0.100 - 2S) = S$ $\rightarrow 5.\underline{4}854 \times 10^{-3} = (1.1\underline{0}971)\,S \rightarrow S = 4.\underline{9}431 \times 10^{-3} = 4.9 \times 10^{-3}$ M.

Check: The units (M) are correct. Since K_f is large, the overall K is larger than the original K_{sp} and the solubility of AgCl increases over that of pure water ($\sqrt{1.77 \times 10^{-10}} = 1.33 \times 10^{-5}$ M).

16.129 **Given:** MX in 0.150 M NaCN **Find:** molar solubility (S)
Other: $K_f\ (M(CN)_4^{2-}) = 1.0 \times 10^{25}$, $K_{sp}\ (MX) = [M^{2+}][X^{2-}] = 1.27 \times 10^{-36}$
Conceptual Plan: Identify the appropriate solid and complex ion. Write balanced equations for dissolving the solid and forming the complex ion. Add these two reactions to get the desired overall reaction. Using the rules from Chapter 14, multiply the individual reaction *K*s to get the overall *K* for the sum of these reactions. Then M NaCN, *K* → *S*.

ICE Chart

Solution: Identify the solid as MX and the complex ion as $M(CN)_4^{2-}$. Write the individual reactions and add them together.

$MX(s) \rightleftharpoons \cancel{M^{2+}(aq)} + X^{2-}(aq)$ $\quad K_{sp} = 1.27 \times 10^{-36}$

$\cancel{M^{2+}(aq)} + 4\,CN^-(aq) \rightleftharpoons M(CN)_4^{2-}(aq)$ $\quad K_f = 1.0 \times 10^{25}$

$MX(s) + 4\,CN^-(aq) \rightleftharpoons M(CN)_4^{2-}(aq) + X^{2-}(aq)$

Since the overall reaction is the simple sum of the two reactions, the overall reaction $K = K_f\,K_{sp} = (1.0 \times 10^{25}) \times (1.27 \times 10^{-36}) = 1.\underline{2}7 \times 10^{-11}$. NaCN ($s$) → $Na^+(aq) + CN^-(aq)$. Since 1 CN^- ion is generated for each NaCN, $[CN^-] = 0.150$ M. Set up an ICE table:

$MX(s) + 4\,CN^-(aq) \rightleftharpoons M(CN)_4^{2-}(aq) + X^{2-}(aq)$

	$[CN^-]$	$[M(CN)_4^{2-}]$	$[X^{2-}]$
Initial	0.150	0.00	0.00
Change	$-4\,S$	$+S$	$+S$
Equil	$0.150 - 4S$	$+S$	$+S$

$K = \frac{[M(CN)_4^{2-}][X^{2-}]}{[CN^-]^4} = 1.\underline{2}7 \times 10^{-11} = \frac{S^2}{(0.150 - 4\,S)^4}$.

Assume S is small ($4S << 0.150$) so $\frac{S^2}{(0.150 - \cancel{4S})^4} = 1.\underline{2}7 \times 10^{-11} = \frac{S^2}{(0.150)^4}$ and $S = 8.\underline{0}183 \times 10^{-8} = 8.0 \times 10^{-8}$ M. Confirm that the assumption is valid. $\frac{4(8.\underline{0}183 \times 10^{-8})}{0.150} \times 100\% = 0.00021\% \ll 5\%$ so the assumption is valid.

Check: The units (M) are correct. Since K_f is large, the overall K is larger than the original K_{sp} and the solubility of MX increases over that of pure water ($\sqrt{1.27 \times 10^{-36}} = 1.13 \times 10^{-18}$ M).

16.130 **Given:** 0.10 M ϕNH_2, keep $[\phi NH_3^+] < 1.0 \times 10^{-9}$ and $K_b\ (\phi NH_2) = 4.3 \times 10^{-10}$ **Find:** [NaOH]
Conceptual Plan: M ϕNH_2, maximum M ϕNH_3^+ → $[OH^-]$ = [NaOH]

ICE Chart $\quad K_w = [H_3O^+][OH^-] \quad pH = -\log[H_3O^+]$

Solution: Set up an ICE table. Since the amount of the conjugate acid is set so small, the concentration of the weak base is not significantly changing.

$\phi NH_2(aq) + H_2O(l) \rightleftharpoons \phi NH_3^+(aq) + OH^-(aq)$

	$[\phi NH_3]$	$[\phi NH_4^+]$	$[OH^-]$
Initial	0.10	0.00	≈ 0.00
Change	—	—	$+x$
Equil	≈ 0.10	1.0×10^{-9}	$+x$

$$K_b = \frac{[\phi NH_4^+][OH^-]}{[\phi NH_2]} = 4.3 \times 10^{-10} = \frac{(1.0 \times 10^{-9})x}{\approx 0.10}$$

Solve for x. So $x = 0.043$ M = $[OH^-]$. NaOH $(aq) \rightarrow Na^+ (aq) + OH^- (aq)$. Since 1 OH^- ion is generated for each NaOH, [NaOH] = 0.043 M NaOH.

Check: The units (M) are correct. The magnitude of the answer makes physical sense because $[OH^-]$ needs to be about one order of magnitude lower than the aniline concentration (comparing K_b with maximum conjugate acid concentrations).

16.131 **Given:** 100.0 mL of 0.36 M NH_2OH and 50.0 mL of 0.26 M HCl and K_b (NH_2OH) = 1.10×10^{-8} **Find:** pH

Conceptual Plan: Identify acid and base components mL → L then $[NH_2OH]$, L → mol NH_2OH

acid = NH_3OH^+ base = NH_2OH $\quad \frac{1 \text{ L}}{1000 \text{ mL}} \quad M = \frac{\text{mol}}{\text{L}}$

then mL → L then [HCl], L → mol HCl then write balanced equation then

$\frac{1 \text{ L}}{1000 \text{ mL}} \quad M = \frac{\text{mol}}{\text{L}} \quad HCl + NH_2OH \rightarrow NH_3OHCl$

mol NH_2OH, mol HCl → mol excess NH_2OH, mol NH_3OH^+.

set up stoichiometry table

Since there are significant amounts of both the acid and the conjugate base species, this is a buffer solution and so the Henderson–Hasselbalch equation $\left(\text{pH} = \text{p}K_a + \log \frac{[\text{base}]}{[\text{acid}]}\right)$ can be used. Convert K_b to K_a using $K_w = K_a K_b$. Also note that ratio of concentrations is the same as the ratio of moles, since the volume is the same for both species.

Solution: $100 \cancel{\text{mL } NH_2OH} \times \frac{1 \text{ L}}{1000 \cancel{\text{mL}}} = 0.1 \text{ L } NH_2OH$ then

$\frac{0.36 \text{ mol } NH_2OH}{1 \cancel{\text{L}}} \times 0.1000 \cancel{\text{L}} = 0.036 \text{ mol } NH_2OH$. $50.0 \cancel{\text{mL HCl}} \times \frac{1 \text{ L}}{1000 \cancel{\text{mL}}} = 0.0500 \text{ L HCl}$ then

$\frac{0.26 \text{ mol HCl}}{1 \cancel{\text{L}}} \times 0.0500 \cancel{\text{L}} = 0.013 \text{ mol HCl}$. Set up a table to track changes:

	HCl (aq) +	NH_2OH (aq) →	NH_3OHCl (aq)
Before addition	0.00 mol	0.036 mol	0.00 mol
Addition	0.013 mol	—	—
After addition	≈0.00 mol	0.023 mol	0.013 mol

Then $K_w = K_a K_b$ so $K_a = \frac{K_w}{K_b} = \frac{1.0 \times 10^{-14}}{1.10 \times 10^{-8}} = 9.0\underline{9}09 \times 10^{-7}$ M then use Henderson–Hasselbalch equation, since the solution is a buffer. Note that the ratio of moles is the same as the ratio of concentrations, since the volume for both terms is the same.

$$\text{pH} = \text{p}K_a + \log \frac{[\text{base}]}{[\text{acid}]} = -\log(9.0\underline{9}09 \times 10^{-7}) + \log \frac{0.023 \cancel{\text{mol}}}{0.013 \cancel{\text{mol}}} = 6.2\underline{8}918 = 6.29.$$

Check: The units (none) are correct. The magnitude of the answer makes physical sense because pH should be more than the pK_a of the acid because there is more base than acid.

16.132 **Given:** 0.867 g diprotic acid titrated with 32.2 mL of 0.182 M $Ba(OH)_2$ solution **Find:** molar mass of acid

Conceptual Plan: Write a balanced reaction then mL → L then M $Ba(OH)_2$, L → mol $Ba(OH)_2$ → mol acid

$H_2A + Ba(OH)_2 \rightarrow BaA + 2\,H_2O \quad \frac{1 \text{ L}}{1000 \text{ mL}} \quad M = \frac{\text{mol}}{\text{L}} \quad 1:1$

then mol acid, g acid → $\mathcal{M}$.

$\mathcal{M} = \frac{\text{g acid}}{\text{mol acid}}$

Solution: $32.2 \cancel{\text{mL}} \times \frac{1 \text{ L}}{1000 \cancel{\text{mL}}} = 0.0322 \text{ L}$ then

$0.0322 \cancel{\text{L } Ba(OH)_2} \times \frac{0.182 \text{ mol } Ba(OH)_2}{1 \cancel{\text{L } Ba(OH)_2}} = 0.0058\underline{6}04 \cancel{\text{mol } Ba(OH)_2} \times \frac{1 \text{ mol } H_2A}{1 \cancel{\text{mol } Ba(OH)_2}} = 0.0058\underline{6}04 \text{ mol } H_2A$

then $\mathcal{M} = \frac{\text{g acid}}{\text{mol acid}} = \frac{0.867 \text{ g } H_2A}{0.0058\underline{6}04 \text{ mol } H_2A} = 148 \text{ g/mol}.$

Check: The units (g/mol) are correct. The magnitude of the answer makes physical sense because there is much less than a mole of acid and about a half a gram of acid, so the molar mass will be high. The number is reasonable for an acid (must be > 20 g/mol – lightest acid is HF).

16.133 **Given:** 25.0 mL of NaOH titrated with 19.6 mL of 0.189 M HCl solution; 10.0 mL of H_3PO_4 titrated with 34.9 mL NaOH **Find:** concentration of H_3PO_4 solution

Conceptual Plan: Write the first balanced reaction then mL → L then M HCl, L → mol HCl → mol NaOH

$HCl + NaOH \rightarrow NaCl + H_2O$ $\quad \frac{1\ L}{1000\ mL}$ $\quad M = \frac{mol}{L}$ $\quad$ 1:1

then mL → L then mol NaOH, L → M NaOH then write 2nd balanced reaction then mL → L

$\frac{1\ L}{1000\ mL}$ $\quad H_3PO_4 + 3\ NaOH \rightarrow Na_3PO_4 + 3\ H_2O$ $\quad \frac{1\ L}{1000\ mL}$

then M NaOH, L → mol NaOH → mol H_3PO_4 then mL → L then mol H_3PO_4, L → M H_3PO_4.

$M = \frac{mol}{L}$ $\quad$ 3:1 $\quad \frac{1\ L}{1000\ mL}$ $\quad M = \frac{mol}{L}$

Solution: In the first titration, $19.6\ \cancel{mL} \times \frac{1\ L}{1000\ \cancel{mL}} = 0.0196\ L$ then

$0.0196\ \cancel{L\ HCl} \times \frac{0.189\ mol\ HCl}{1\ \cancel{L\ HCl}} = 0.0037\underline{0}44\ \cancel{mol\ HCl} \times \frac{1\ mol\ NaOH}{1\ \cancel{mol\ HCl}} = 0.0037\underline{0}44\ mol\ NaOH$ then

$25.0\ \cancel{mL} \times \frac{1\ L}{1000\ \cancel{mL}} = 0.0250\ L$ then $\frac{0.0037\underline{0}44\ mol\ NaOH}{0.0250\ L\ NaOH} = 0.148\underline{1}76\ M\ NaOH$. In the second titration,

$34.9\ \cancel{mL} \times \frac{1\ L}{1000\ \cancel{mL}} = 0.0349\ L$ then

$0.0349\ \cancel{L\ NaOH} \times \frac{0.148\underline{1}76\ mol\ NaOH}{1\ \cancel{L\ NaOH}} = 0.005\underline{1}7134\ \cancel{mol\ NaOH} \times \frac{1\ mol\ H_3PO_4}{3\ \cancel{mol\ NaOH}} = 0.00172\underline{3}78\ mol\ H_3PO_4$

then $10.0\ \cancel{mL} \times \frac{1\ L}{1000\ \cancel{mL}} = 0.0100\ L$ then $\frac{0.00172\underline{3}78\ mol\ H_3PO_4}{0.0100\ L\ H_3PO_4} = 0.172\ M\ H_3PO_4$.

Check: The units (M) are correct. The magnitude of the answer makes physical sense because the concentration of NaOH is a little lower than the HCl (because the volume of NaOH is greater than HCl) and the concentration of H_3PO_4 is more than the NaOH (because the ratio of the volume of NaOH to volume of H_3PO_4 is just over 3 and H_3PO_4 is a triprotic acid).

16.134 **Given:** 250.0 cm^3 of 1.4 M HCOOH; adjust to pH = 3.36 **Find:** mass NaCOOH

Other: K_a (HCOOH) = 1.8×10^{-4}

Conceptual Plan: cm^3 → L and K_a → pK_a then [HCOOH], pH, pK_a → [NaCOOH]

$\frac{1\ L}{1000\ mL}$ $\quad pK_a = -\log K_a$ $\quad$ acid = HCOOH base = NaCOOH $\quad pH = pK_a + \log\frac{[base]}{[acid]}$

then [NCOOH], L → mol NaCOOH → g NaCOOH

$M = \frac{mol}{L}$ $\quad \frac{68.01\ g\ NaCOOH}{1\ mol\ NaCOOH}$

Solution: $250.0\cancel{mL} \times \frac{1\ L}{1000\ \cancel{mL}} = 0.2500\ L$ since K_a (HCOOH) = 1.8×10^{-4},

$pK_a = -\log K_a = -\log(1.8 \times 10^{-4}) = 3.74$. Since acid = HCOOH base = NaCOOH

$pH = pK_a + \log\frac{[base]}{[acid]} = 3.74 + \log\frac{[NaCOOH]}{1.4\ M} = 3.36$. Solve for [NaCOOH].

$\log\frac{[NaCOOH]}{1.4\ M} = 3.36 - 3.74 = -0.38 \rightarrow \frac{[NaCOOH]}{1.4\ M} = 10^{-0.38} = 0.4\underline{1}6869 \rightarrow$

$[NaCOOH] = 0.4\underline{1}6869 \times 1.4\ M = 0.5\underline{8}3617\ M\ NaCOOH$. Then

$\frac{0.5\underline{8}3617\ mol\ NaCOOH}{1\ \cancel{L}} \times 0.2500\cancel{L} = 0.1\underline{4}590\ \cancel{mol\ NaCOOH} \times \frac{68.01\ g\ NaCOOH}{1\ \cancel{mol\ NaCOOH}} = 9.\underline{9}230\ g\ NaCOOH$

= 9.9 g NaCOOH.

Check: The units (g) are correct. The magnitude of the answer makes physical sense because there is more acid in the buffer than base (pH < pK_a) and there is less than a mole of acid in buffer, so there must be less than a mole of NaCOOH.

16.135 **Given:** $(CH_3)_2NH/(CH_3)_2NH_2Cl$ buffer at pH = 10.43 **Find:** relative masses of $(CH_3)_2NH$ and $(CH_3)_2NH_2Cl$
Other: $K_b((CH_3)_2NH) = 5.4 \times 10^{-4}$
Conceptual Plan: $K_b \rightarrow pK_b \rightarrow pK_a$ **then pH,** $pK_a \rightarrow [(CH_3)_2NH] / [(CH_3)_2NH_2^+]$ **then**

$pK_b = -\log K_b \quad 14 = pK_a + pK_b \quad \text{acid} = (CH_3)_2NH_2^+ \text{ base} = (CH_3)_2NH \qquad pH = pK_a + \log\frac{[\text{base}]}{[\text{acid}]}$

$[(CH_3)_2NH]/[(CH_3)_2NH_2^+] \rightarrow$ **g** $(CH_3)_2NH$ / **g** $(CH_3)_2NH_2^+$

$\frac{45.09 \text{ g } (CH_3)_2NH}{1 \text{ mol } (CH_3)_2NH} \quad \frac{81.54 \text{ g } (CH_3)_2NH_2Cl}{1 \text{ mol } (CH_3)_2NH_2Cl}$

Solution: Since $K_b((CH_3)_2NH) = 5.4 \times 10^{-4}$, $pK_b = -\log K_b = -\log(5.4 \times 10^{-4}) = 3.27$.
Since $14 = pK_a + pK_b$, $pK_a = 14 - pK_b = 14 - 3.27 = 10.73$. Since $[\text{acid}] = [(CH_3)_2NH_2^+] = [(CH_3)_2NH_2Cl]$ and $[\text{base}] = [(CH_3)_2NH]$ then $pH = pK_a + \log\frac{[\text{base}]}{[\text{acid}]} = 10.73 + \log\frac{[(CH_3)_2NH]}{[(CH_3)_2NH_2Cl]} = 10.43$. Solve for $\frac{[(CH_3)_2NH]}{[(CH_3)_2NH_2Cl]}$. $\log\frac{[(CH_3)_2NH]}{[(CH_3)_2NH_2Cl]} = 10.43 - 10.73 = -0.30 \rightarrow \frac{[(CH_3)_2NH]}{[(CH_3)_2NH_2Cl]} = 10^{-0.30} = 0.5\underline{0}1187$.

Then $\frac{0.501187 \text{ mol } (CH_3)_2NH}{1 \text{ mol } (CH_3)_2NH_2Cl} \times \frac{45.09 \text{ g } (CH_3)_2NH}{1 \text{ mol } (CH_3)_2NH} \times \frac{1 \text{ mol } (CH_3)_2NH_2Cl}{81.54 \text{ g } (CH_3)_2NH_2Cl} = \frac{0.2\underline{7}7147 \text{ g } (CH_3)_2NH}{\text{g } (CH_3)_2NH_2Cl}$

$= \frac{0.28 \text{ g } (CH_3)_2NH}{\text{g } (CH_3)_2NH_2Cl}$ or $\frac{3.6 \text{ g } (CH_3)_2NH_2Cl}{\text{g } (CH_3)_2NH}$.

Check: The units (g/g) are correct. The magnitude of the answer makes physical sense since there are more moles of acid than base in the buffer (pH < pK_a) and the molar mass of the acid is greater than the molar mass of the base. Thus, the ratio of the mass of the base to the mass of the acid is expected to be less than 1.

16.136 **Given:** 2.0 L HCN / NaCN buffer at pH = 9.8, complete dissociation of NaCN; osmotic pressure = 1.35 atm at 298 K **Find:** masses of HCN and NaCN **Other:** $K_a(HCN) = 4.9 \times 10^{-10}$
Conceptual Plan: $K_a \rightarrow pK_a$ **then pH,** $pK_a \rightarrow [CN^-] / [HCN]$ **then** $\Pi, T \rightarrow$ **M then**

$pK_a = -\log K_a \quad \text{acid} = HCN \text{ base} = CN^- \qquad pH = pK_a + \log\frac{[\text{base}]}{[\text{acid}]} \qquad \Pi = MRT$

Assume that HCN does not dissociate and NaCN completely dissociates, then M = [HCN] +2[NaCN]. Use [NaCN] / [HCN] and M = [HCN] +2[NaCN] to solve for [HCN] and [NaCN]. Then [HCN], L → g HCN and [HCN], L → g HCN.

$M = \frac{\text{amount solute (moles)}}{\text{volume solution (L)}} \quad \frac{27.03 \text{ g HCN}}{1 \text{ mol HCN}} \quad \frac{49.01 \text{ g NaCN}}{1 \text{ mol NaCN}}$

Solution: Since $K_a(HCN) = 4.9 \times 10^{-10}$, $pK_a = -\log K_a = -\log(4.9 \times 10^{-10}) = 9.31$. Since [acid] = [HCN] and $[\text{base}] = [CN^-] = [NaCN]$ then $pH = pK_a + \log\frac{[\text{base}]}{[\text{acid}]} = 9.31 + \log\frac{[NaCN]}{[HCN]} = 9.8$. Solve for $\frac{[NaCN]}{[HCN]}$.

$\log\frac{[NaCN]}{[HCN]} = 9.8 - 9.31 = 0.\underline{4}9 \rightarrow \frac{[NaCN]}{[HCN]} = 10^{-0.49} = 3.\underline{0}9169$.

Then $\Pi = MRT$ Rearrange to solve for M.

$$M = \frac{\Pi}{RT} = \frac{1.35 \text{ atm}}{0.08206 \frac{\text{L} \cdot \text{atm}}{\text{K} \cdot \text{mol}} \times 298 \text{ K}} = 0.055\underline{2}0596 \frac{\text{mol particles}}{\text{L}}$$

Assume that HCN does not dissociate and NaCN completely dissociates, then M = [HCN] +2[NaCN]. Use [NaCN] / [HCN] = 3.$\underline{0}$9169 and M = [HCN] +2[NaCN] to solve for [HCN] and [NaCN]. So, [NaCN] = 3.$\underline{0}$9169[HCN] → $M = 0.055\underline{2}0596 \frac{\text{mol particles}}{\text{L}} = [HCN] + 2(3.\underline{0}9169[HCN]) \rightarrow$

$0.055\underline{2}0596 \frac{\text{mol particles}}{\text{L}} = 7.\underline{1}8338[HCN] \rightarrow [HCN] = 0.007\underline{6}8523$ M and

$[NaCN] = 3.\underline{0}9169[HCN] = 3.\underline{0}9169 \times 0.007\underline{6}8523 \text{ M} = 0.02\underline{3}7604$ M. Finally,

$\frac{0.007\underline{6}8523 \text{ mol HCN}}{\text{L solution}} \times 2.0 \text{ L solution} \times \frac{27.03 \text{ g HCN}}{1 \text{ mol HCN}} = 0.4\underline{1}546 \text{ g HCN} = 0.42 \text{ g HCN}$ and

$\frac{0.02\underline{3}7604 \text{ mol NaCN}}{\text{L solution}} \times 2.0 \text{ L solution} \times \frac{49.01 \text{ g NaCN}}{1 \text{ mol NaCN}} = 2.\underline{3}304 \text{ g NaCN} = 2.3 \text{ g NaCN}$.

Check: The units (g and g) are correct. The magnitude of the answer makes physical sense since there are more moles of base than acid in the buffer (pH > pK_a) and the molar mass of the base is greater than the molar mass of the acid.

16.137 **Given:** $HC_7H_5O_2$ / $C_7H_5O_2Na$ buffer at pH = 4.55, complete dissociation of $C_7H_5O_2Na$, d = 1.01 g/mL; T_f = –2.0 °C **Find:** [$HC_7H_5O_2$] and [$C_7H_5O_2Na$] **Other:** K_a ($HC_7H_5O_2$) = 6.5 x 10^{-5}, K_f = 1.86 °C/m

Conceptual Plan: $K_a \rightarrow$ pK_a then pH, p$K_a \rightarrow$ [$C_7H_5O_2Na$] / [$HC_7H_5O_2$] and $T_f \rightarrow \Delta T_f$ then

$$pK_a = -\log K_a \quad \text{acid} = HC_7H_5O_2 \quad \text{base} = C_7H_5O_2^- \quad pH = pK_a + \log\frac{[\text{base}]}{[\text{acid}]} \qquad T_f = T_f^\circ - \Delta T_f$$

ΔT_f, i, K_f $\rightarrow$ m then assume 1 kg water (or 1000 g water).

$$\Delta T_f = K_f m \qquad m = \frac{\text{amount solute (moles)}}{\text{mass solvent (kg)}}$$

Assume that $HC_7H_5O_2$ does not dissociate and $C_7H_5O_2Na$ completely dissociates, then mol particles = mol $HC_7H_5O_2$ +2(mol $C_7H_5O_2Na$). Use [$C_7H_5O_2Na$] / [$HC_7H_5O_2$] and total mol particles = mol [$HC_7H_5O_2$] +2(mol $C_7H_5O_2Na$) to solve for mol $HC_7H_5O_2$ and mol $C_7H_5O_2Na$. Then

mol $HC_7H_5O_2$ $\rightarrow$ g mol $HC_7H_5O_2$ and mol $C_7H_5O_2Na$ $\rightarrow$ g $C_7H_5O_2Na$ then

$$\frac{122.12 \text{ g } HC_7H_5O_2}{1 \text{ mol } HC_7H_5O_2} \qquad \frac{143.94 \text{ g } C_7H_5O_2Na}{1 \text{ mol } HC_7H_5O_2Na}$$

g mol $HC_7H_5O_2$, g $C_7H_5O_2Na$, g water $\rightarrow$ g solution $\rightarrow$ mL solution $\rightarrow$ L solution then

$$\text{g mol } HC_7H_5O_2 + \text{g } C_7H_5O_2Na + \text{g water} = \text{g solution} \qquad d = \frac{1 \text{ mL}}{1.01 \text{ g}} \qquad \frac{1 \text{ L}}{1000 \text{ mL}}$$

mol $HC_7H_5O_2$, L $\rightarrow$ M $HC_7H_5O_2$ and mol $C_7H_5O_2Na$, L $\rightarrow$ M $C_7H_5O_2$ Na.

$$M = \frac{\text{mol}}{\text{L}} \qquad M = \frac{\text{mol}}{\text{L}}$$

Solution: Since K_a ($HC_7H_5O_2$) = 6.5 x 10^{-5}, pK_a = $-\log K_a$ = $-\log(6.5 \times 10^{-5})$ = 4.19. Since [acid] = [$HC_7H_5O_2$] and [base] = [$C_7H_5O_2^-$] = [$C_7H_5O_2Na$] then

$$pH = pK_a + \log\frac{[\text{base}]}{[\text{acid}]} = 4.19 + \log\frac{[C_7H_5O_2Na]}{[HC_7H_5O_2]} = 4.55. \text{ Solve for } \frac{[C_7H_5O_2Na]}{[HC_7H_5O_2]}.$$

$$\log\frac{[C_7H_5O_2Na]}{[HC_7H_5O_2]} = 4.55 - 4.19 = 0.36 \rightarrow \frac{[C_7H_5O_2Na]}{[HC_7H_5O_2]} = 10^{0.36} = 2.2\underline{9}087. \text{ Then } T_f = T_f^\circ - \Delta T_f \text{ so}$$

$\Delta T_f = T_f^\circ - T_f$ = 0.0 °C – (–2.0 °C) = 2.0 °C then $\Delta T_f = K_f\, m$. Rearrange to solve for m.

$$m = \frac{\Delta T_f}{K_f} = \frac{2.0\ \cancel{°C}}{1.86\,\frac{\cancel{°C}}{m}} = 1.\underline{0}7527\,\frac{\text{mol particles}}{\text{kg solvent}}$$ Assume 1 kg water, so we have 1.$\underline{0}$7527 mol particles.

Assume that $HC_7H_5O_2$ does not dissociate and $C_7H_5O_2Na$ completely dissociates, then 1.$\underline{0}$7527 mol particles = mol $HC_7H_5O_2$ +2(mol $C_7H_5O_2Na$). Use [$C_7H_5O_2Na$] / [$HC_7H_5O_2$] = 2.2$\underline{9}$087 and 1.$\underline{0}$7527 mol particles = mol [$HC_7H_5O_2$] +2(mol $C_7H_5O_2Na$) to solve for mol $HC_7H_5O_2$ and mol $C_7H_5O_2Na$. So, mol $C_7H_5O_2Na$ = 2.2$\underline{9}$087(mol $HC_7H_5O_2$) $\rightarrow$ 1.$\underline{0}$7527 mol particles = mol $HC_7H_5O_2$ + 2 (2.2$\underline{9}$087 mol $HC_7H_5O_2$) $\rightarrow$ 1.$\underline{0}$7527 mol particles = 5.$\underline{5}$8174 mol $HC_7H_5O_2$ $\rightarrow$ mol $HC_7H_5O_2$ = 0.1$\underline{9}$2641 mol and mol $C_7H_5O_2Na$ = 2.29087 x mol $HC_7H_5O_2$ = 2.2$\underline{9}$087 x 0.1$\underline{9}$2641 mol $HC_7H_5O_2$ = 0.4$\underline{4}$1315 mol $C_7H_5O_2Na$

$$0.1\underline{9}2641\ \cancel{\text{mol } HC_7H_5O_2} \times \frac{122.12 \text{ g } HC_7H_5O_2}{1\ \cancel{\text{mol } HC_7H_5O_2}} = 2\underline{3}.5253 \text{ g } HC_7H_5O_2 \text{ and}$$

$$0.4\underline{4}1315\ \cancel{\text{mol } C_7H_5O_2Na} \times \frac{143.94 \text{ g } C_7H_5O_2Na}{1\ \cancel{\text{mol } C_7H_5O_2Na}} = 6\underline{3}.5229 \text{ g } C_7H_5O_2Na \text{ then}$$

2$\underline{3}$.5253 g mol $HC_7H_5O_2$ + 6$\underline{3}$.5229 g $C_7H_5O_2Na$ + 1000 g water = 108$\underline{7}$.048 g solution then

$$108\underline{7}.048\ \cancel{\text{g solution}} \times \frac{1\ \cancel{\text{mL}}}{1.01\ \cancel{\text{g}}} \times \frac{1 \text{ L}}{1000\ \cancel{\text{mL}}} = 1.0\underline{7}6285 \text{ L. Finally,}$$

$$\frac{0.1\underline{9}2641 \text{ mol } HC_7H_5O_2}{1.0\underline{7}6285 \text{ L}} = 0.1\underline{7}8987 \text{ M } HC_7H_5O_2 = 0.18 \text{ M } HC_7H_5O_2 \text{ and}$$

$$\frac{0.4\underline{4}1315 \text{ mol } C_7H_5O_2Na}{1.0\underline{7}6285 \text{ L}} = 0.4\underline{1}0035 \text{ M } C_7H_5O_2Na = 0.41 \text{ M } C_7H_5O_2Na.$$

Check: The units (M and M) are correct. The magnitude of the answer makes physical sense since there are more moles of base than acid in the buffer (pH > pK_a).

Challenge Problems

16.138 The Henderson–Hasselbalch equation is $pH = pK_a + \log\frac{[base]}{[acid]}$. Remember that $14 = pH + pOH$ and $14 = pK_a + pK_b$. Substituting these into the Henderson–Hasselbalch equation: $14 - pOH = 14 - pK_b + \log\frac{[base]}{[acid]}$. Simplifying the expression gives: $pOH = pK_b - \log\frac{[base]}{[acid]}$.

16.139 **Given:** 10.0 L of 75 ppm $CaCO_3$ and 55 ppm $MgCO_3$ (by mass)
Find: mass Na_2CO_3 to precipitate 90.0% of ions
Other: K_{sp} ($CaCO_3$) = 4.96×10^{-9} and K_{sp} ($MgCO_3$) = 6.82×10^{-6}
Conceptual Plan: Assume that the density of water is 1.00 g/mL. L water → mL water → g water then

$\frac{1000\text{ mL}}{1\text{ L}}$ $\frac{1.00\text{ g water}}{1\text{ mL}}$

g water → g $CaCO_3$ → mol $CaCO_3$ → mol Ca^{2+} and g water → g $MgCO_3$ → mol $MgCO_3$ then

$\frac{75\text{ g }CaCO_3}{10^6\text{ g water}}$ $\frac{1\text{ mol }CaCO_3}{100.09\text{ g }CaCO_3}$ $\frac{1\text{ mol }Ca^{2+}}{1\text{ mol }CaCO_3}$ $\frac{55\text{ g }MgCO_3}{10^6\text{ g water}}$ $\frac{1\text{ mol }MgCO_3}{84.32\text{ g }MgCO_3}$

mol $MgCO_3$ → mol Mg^{2+} then comparing the two K_{sp} values, essentially all of the Ca^{2+} will

$\frac{1\text{ mol }Mg^{2+}}{1\text{ mol }MgCO_3}$

precipitate before the Mg^{2+} will begin to precipitate. Since 90.0% of the ions are to be precipitates, there will be 10.0 % of the ions left in solution (all will be Mg^{2+}).

$(0.100)(\text{mol }Ca^{2+} + \text{mol }Mg^{2+})$

Calculate the moles of ions remaining in solution. Then mol Mg^{2+}, L → M Mg^{2+}.

$M = \frac{mol}{L}$

The solubility product constant (K_{sp}) is the equilibrium expression for a chemical equation representing the dissolution of an ionic compound. The expression of the solubility product constant of A_mX_n is $K_{sp} = [A^{n+}]^m [X^{m-}]^n$. Use this equation to M Mg^{2+}, K_{sp} → M CO_3^{2-} then M CO_3^{2-}, L → mol CO_3^{2-}

for ionic compound, A_mX_n, $K_{sp} = [A^{n+}]^m [X^{m-}]^n$. $M = \frac{mol}{L}$

then mol CO_3^{2-} → mol Na_2CO_3 → g Na_2CO_3.

$\frac{1\text{ mol }CO_3^{2-}}{1\text{ mol }Na_2CO_3}$ $\frac{105.99\text{ g }Na_2CO_3}{1\text{ mol }Na_2CO_3}$

Solution: $10.0\text{ L} \times \frac{1000\text{ mL}}{1\text{ L}} \times \frac{1.00\text{ g water}}{1\text{ mL}} = 1.00 \times 10^4$ g water then

$1.00 \times 10^4\text{ g water} \times \frac{75\text{ g }CaCO_3}{10^6\text{ g water}} \times \frac{1\text{ mol }CaCO_3}{100.09\text{ g }CaCO_3} \times \frac{1\text{ mol }Ca^{2+}}{1\text{ mol }CaCO_3} = 0.0074933\text{ mol }Ca^{2+}$ and

$1.00 \times 10^4\text{ g water} \times \frac{55\text{ g }MgCO_3}{10^6\text{ g water}} \times \frac{1\text{ mol }MgCO_3}{84.32\text{ g }MgCO_3} \times \frac{1\text{ mol }Mg^{2+}}{1\text{ mol }MgCO_3} = 0.0065228\text{ mol }Mg^{2+}$ so the ions remaining in solution after 90.0% precipitate out = $(0.100)(\text{mol }Ca^{2+} + \text{mol }Mg^{2+})$
$= (0.100)(0.0074933\text{ mol }Ca^{2+} + 0.0065228\text{ mol }Mg^{2+}) = 0.00140161$ mol ions

so $\frac{0.00140607\text{ mol }Mg^{2+}}{10.0\text{ L}} = 0.000140161\text{ M }Mg^{2+}$. Then $K_{sp} = 6.82 \times 10^{-6}$, $A = Mg^{2+}$, $m = 1$, $X = CO_3^{2-}$, and $n = 1$, so $K_{sp} = 6.82 \times 10^{-6} = [Mg^{2+}][CO_3^{2-}] = (0.00140161)[CO_3^{2-}]$. Rearrange to solve for $[CO_3^{2-}]$.
So $[CO_3^{2-}] = 0.0486583$ M. Then

$\frac{0.0486583\text{ mol }CO_3^{2-}}{1\text{ L}} \times 10.0\text{ L} \times \frac{1\text{ mol }Na_2CO_3}{1\text{ mol }CO_3^{2-}} \times \frac{105.99\text{ g }Na_2CO_3}{1\text{ mol }Na_2CO_3} = 51.6\text{ g }Na_2CO_3$.

Check: The units (g) are correct. The mass is reasonable to put in a washing machine load.

16.140 **Given:** 0.558 g diprotic acid with molar mass = 255.8 g/mol dissolved in 25.00 mL water and titrated saturated $Ca(OH)_2$ solution **Other:** K_{sp} ($Ca(OH)_2$) = 4.68×10^{-6}

(a) **Find:** volume of base to the first and second equivalence points
Conceptual Plan:
Calculate the [$Ca(OH)_2$] by using the equation derived in Problem 20 and solve for S.

for ionic compound, A_mX_n, $K_{sp} = m^m n^n S^{m+n}$.

Then write a balanced reaction for titration of both protons. (Volume to the first equivalence point will

$H_2A + Ca(OH)_2 \rightarrow CaA + 2\ H_2O$

be half of this.) Then g H_2A, $\mathcal{M} \rightarrow$ mol $H_2A \rightarrow$ mol $Ca(OH)_2$ then

$\mathcal{M} = \frac{\text{g acid}}{\text{mol acid}}$ 1:1

M $Ca(OH)_2$, mol $Ca(OH)_2 \rightarrow$ L $Ca(OH)_2 \rightarrow$ mL $Ca(OH)_2$. Finally, divide the volume to

$M = \frac{\text{mol}}{\text{L}}$ $\frac{1000\text{ mL}}{1\text{ L}}$

the second equivalence point by 2 to get the volume to the first equivalence point.

Solution: for $Ca(OH)_2$, $K_{sp} = 4.68 \times 10^{-6}$, A = Ca^{2+}, $m = 1$, X = OH^-, and $n = 2$ so $K_{sp} = 4.68 \times 10^{-6} = 2^2S^3$.

Rearrange to solve for S. $S = \sqrt[3]{\frac{4.68 \times 10^{-6}}{4}} = 1.05 \times 10^{-2}$ M.

$0.558 \text{ g } H_2A \times \frac{1 \text{ mol } H_2A}{255.8 \text{ g } H_2A} = 0.00218139 \text{ mol } H_2A$. Since the stoichiometry of the overall titration reaction is 1:1 then 0.00218139 mol H_2A = 0.00218139 mol $Ca(OH)_2$.

Then $0.00218139 \text{ mol } Ca(OH)_2 \times \frac{1 \text{ L } Ca(OH)_2}{0.0105 \text{ mol } Ca(OH)_2} \times \frac{1000 \text{ mL } Ca(OH)_2}{1 \text{ L } Ca(OH)_2} = 208 \text{ mL } Ca(OH)_2$ to reach the second equivalence point. Then $\frac{1}{2}$ (208 mL $Ca(OH)_2$) = 104 mL $Ca(OH)_2$ to reach the first equivalence point.

Check: The units (mL and mL) are correct. The magnitude of the answer makes physical sense because the concentration of the $Ca(OH)_2$ solution is so low.

(b) **Given:** after adding 25.0 mL of $Ca(OH)_2$ solution pH = 3.82 **Find:** pK_{a_1} of acid
Conceptual Plan:
mL $\rightarrow$ L then M $Ca(OH)_2$, L $\rightarrow$ mol $Ca(OH)_2 \rightarrow$ mol OH^- then write a balanced reaction

$\frac{1\text{ L}}{1000\text{ mL}}$ $M = \frac{\text{mol}}{\text{L}}$ $Ca(OH)_2 \rightarrow Ca^{2+} + 2\ OH^-$ $OH^- + H_2A \rightarrow HA^- + H_2O$

added mol OH^-, initial mol acid $\rightarrow$ equil. mol HA^-, equil. mol H_2A then

set up stoichiometry table

equil. mol HA^-, equil. mol H_2A, pH $\rightarrow$ pK_{a_1}

$pH = pK_a + \log \frac{[\text{base}]}{[\text{acid}]}$

Solution: $25.0 \text{ mL} \times \frac{1 \text{ L}}{1000 \text{ mL}} = 0.0250 \text{ L}$ then

$0.0250 \text{ L } Ca(OH)_2 \times \frac{0.0105 \text{ mol } Ca(OH)_2}{1 \text{ L } Ca(OH)_2} = 0.0002625 \text{ mol } Ca(OH)_2 \times \frac{2 \text{ mol } OH^-}{1 \text{ mol } Ca(OH)_2}$

= 0.000525 mol OH^- then set up a table to track changes:

	OH^- (*aq*) +	H_2A (*aq*) $\rightarrow$	HA^- (*aq*) +	H_2O (*l*)
Before addition	≈0.00 mol	0.00218139 mol	0.00 mol	—
Addition	0.000525 mol	—	—	—
After addition	≈0.00 mol	0.00165639 mol	0.000525 mol	—

Since the ratio of base to acid is between 0.1 and 10, so it is a buffer solution. Note that the ratio of moles is the same as the ratio of concentrations, since the volume for both terms is the same.

$pH = pK_a + \log \frac{[\text{base}]}{[\text{acid}]} = pK_{a_1} + \log \frac{0.000525 \text{ mol}}{0.00165639 \text{ mol}} = 3.82$. Solve for pK_{a_1}.

$pK_{a_1} = 3.82 - \log \frac{0.000525}{0.00165639} = 4.32.$

Check: The units (none) are correct. The magnitude of the answer makes physical sense because there is more acid than base at equilibrium, so the pK_{a_1} is higher than the pH of the solution.

(c) **Given:** after adding 20.0 mL of $Ca(OH)_2$ solution after first equivalence point pH = 8.25
Find: pK_{a_2} of acid
Conceptual Plan:
mL → L then M $Ca(OH)_2$, L → mol $Ca(OH)_2$ → mol OH^- then write balanced reaction

$\frac{1\ L}{1000\ mL}$ $M = \frac{mol}{L}$ $Ca(OH)_2 \rightarrow Ca^{2+} + 2\ OH^-$ $OH^- + HA^- \rightarrow A^{2-} + H_2O$

added mol OH^-, initial mol acid → equil. mol HA^-, equil. mol A^{2-} then

set up stoichiometry table

equil. mol HA^-, equil. mol A^{2-}, pH → pK_{a_2}

$pH = pK_a + \log\frac{[base]}{[acid]}$

Solution: $20.0\ \text{mL} \times \frac{1\ L}{1000\ \text{mL}} = 0.0200\ L$ then

$0.0200\ \text{L Ca(OH)}_2 \times \frac{0.0105\ \text{mol Ca(OH)}_2}{1\ \text{L Ca(OH)}_2} = 0.000210\ \text{mol Ca(OH)}_2 \times \frac{2\ \text{mol OH}^-}{1\ \text{mol Ca(OH)}_2}$

$= 0.000420$ mol OH^- then set up a table to track changes:

	OH^- (aq)	+ HA^- (aq)	→ A^{2-} (aq)	+ H_2O (l)
Before addition	≈0.00 mol	$0.0021\underline{8}139$ mol	0.00 mol	—
Addition	0.000420 mol	—	—	—
After addition	≈0.00 mol	$0.0017\underline{6}139$ mol	0.000420 mol	—

Since the ratio of base to acid is between 0.1 and 10 it is a buffer solution. Note that the ratio of moles is the same as the ratio of concentrations, since the volume for both terms is the same.

$pH = pK_a + \log\frac{[base]}{[acid]} = pK_{a_2} + \log\frac{0.000420\ \text{mol}}{0.0017\underline{6}139\ \text{mol}} = 8.25$. Solve for pK_{a_2}.

$pK_{a_2} = 8.25 - \log\frac{0.000420}{0.0017\underline{6}139} = 8.87.$

Check: The units (none) are correct. The magnitude of the answer makes physical sense because there is more acid than base at equilibrium, so the pK_{a_2} is higher than the pH of the solution.

16.141 **Given:** excess $Mg(OH)_2$ in 1.00 L of 1.0 M NH_4Cl has pH = 9.00 **Find:** K_{sp} ($Mg(OH)_2$)
Other: K_b (NH_3) = 1.76 x 10^{-5}
Conceptual Plan: M NH_4Cl → M NH_4^+ and K_b → K_a then final pH → $[H_3O^+]$ then

$NH_4Cl\ (aq) \rightarrow NH_4^+\ (aq) + Cl^-\ (aq)$ $K_w = K_a K_b$ $[H_3O^+] = 10^{-pH}$

M NH_4^+, M H_3O^+, K_a → x. Since x is significant compared to initial M NH_4^+ this is a buffer solution.

ICE Chart

The NH_4^+ is neutralized with $Mg(OH)_2$. Since $Mg(OH)_2\ (s) \rightleftharpoons Mg^{2+}\ (aq) + 2\ OH^-(aq)$ there are 2 moles of OH^- generated for each mole of $Mg(OH)_2$ dissolved. Thus $\frac{1}{2}$ (x mol OH^-) = mol $Mg(OH)_2$ was dissolved in 1.00 L of solution. Since there is 1.00 L solution mol $Mg(OH)_2$ = $[Mg^{2+}]$ and $[H_3O^+]$ → $[OH^-]$.

$K_w = [H_3O^+][OH^-]$

Finally, write an expression for K_{sp} ($Mg(OH)_2$) and substitute in values for $[Mg^{2+}]$ and $[OH^-]$.
Solution: Since 1 NH_4^+ ion is generated for each NH_4Cl, $[NH_4^+]$ = 1.0 M NH_4^+. Since $K_w = K_a K_b$, rearrange to solve for K_a. $K_a = \frac{K_w}{K_b} = \frac{1.0 \times 10^{-14}}{1.76 \times 10^{-5}} = 5.\underline{6}818 \times 10^{-10}$. Final pH = 9.00, so

$[H_3O^+] = 10^{-pH} = 10^{-9.00} = 1.0 \times 10^{-9}$ M. Set up an ICE Chart:

$NH_4^+\ (aq) + H_2O\ (l) \rightleftharpoons H_3O^+\ (aq) + NH_3\ (aq)$

	$[NH_4^+]$	$[H_3O^+]$	$[NH_3]$
Initial	1.0	≈0.00	0.00
Change	$-x$	$+x$	$+x$
Equil	$1.0 - x$	1.0 x	$10^{-9} + x$

$K_a = \frac{[H_3O^+][NH_3]}{[NH_4^+]} = 5.\underline{6}818 \times 10^{-10} = \frac{(1.0 \times 10^{-9})x}{1.0 - x}.$

Solve for x. $5.\underline{6}818 \times 10^{-10}(1.0 - x) = (1.0 \times 10^{-9})x \rightarrow 5.\underline{6}818 \times 10^{-10} = (1.0 \times 10^{-9} + 5.\underline{6}818 \times 10^{-10})x$

$\rightarrow x = 0.36\underline{2}318$, so this is a buffer solution. Since there is 1.00 L of solution, 0.36$\underline{2}$318 mol of NH_4^+ is neutralized with $Mg(OH)_2$. Since $Mg(OH)_2\ (s) \rightleftharpoons Mg^{2+}\ (aq) + 2\ OH^-\ (aq)$ there are 2 moles of OH^- generated for each mole of $Mg(OH)_2$ dissolved. Thus $\frac{1}{2}$ (0.36$\underline{2}$318 mol OH^-) = 0.1$\underline{8}$1159 mol $Mg(OH)_2$ was dissolved in 1.00 L of solution. Thus the $[Mg^{2+}]$ = 0.1$\underline{8}$1159 M. Since $K_w = [H_3O^+][OH^-]$ so

$$[OH^-] = \frac{K_w}{[H_3O^+]} = \frac{1.0 \times 10^{-14}}{1.0 \times 10^{-9}} = 1.0 \times 10^{-5}\text{ M then}$$

$K_{sp}\ (Mg(OH)_2) = [Mg^{2+}][OH^-]^2 = (0.1\underline{8}1159)(1.0 \times 10^{-5})^2 = 1.8 \times 10^{-11}$.

Check: The units (none) are correct. The magnitude of the answer makes physical sense because the concentration of NH_4Cl is high and so it took a significant amount of $Mg(OH)_2$ to raise the pH to 9.00. Note that this number disagrees with the accepted value for the K_{sp} ($Mg(OH)_2$). This is most likely due to errors in the measurements in this experiment.

16.142 **Given:** 1.0 L of 0.10 M H_2CO_3 titrated with NaOH to $[H^+] = 3.2 \times 10^{-11}$ M (assume no volume change) **Find:** mass NaOH **Other:** K_{a_1} (H_2CO_3) = 4.3×10^{-7}, K_{a_2} (H_2CO_3) = 5.6×10^{-11}

Conceptual Plan: Comparing the $[H^+]$ to the K_as it can be seen that the pH is just below the pK_{a_2} so the final solution is a buffer solution where the acid is HCO_3^- and the base is CO_3^{2-}. The total NaOH will be the amount needed to get to the first equivalence point and then what is needed to get to final pH. To first equivalence point,

L, M CO_3^{2-} → mol CO_3^{2-} → mol NaOH then use the Henderson-Hasselbalch equation to calculate

$M = \frac{mol}{L}$ *1:1 ratio*

the $[CO_3^{2-}]/[HCO_3^-]$. Then solve for $[CO_3^{2-}]$ knowing that $[CO_3^{2-}] + [HCO_3^-]$ = initial $[H_2CO_3]$.

$pH = pK_a + \log\frac{[base]}{[acid]}$

Then L, M CO_3^{2-} → mol CO_3^{2-} → mol NaOH beyond first equivalence point then add two NaOH

$M = \frac{mol}{L}$ *1:1 ratio*

moles and finally total mol NaOH → g NaOH.

$\frac{40.00\text{ g NaOH}}{1\text{ mol NaOH}}$

Solution: To the first equivalence point,

$$1.0\ \text{L } H_2CO_3 \times \frac{0.10\ \text{mol } H_2CO_3}{1\ \text{L } H_2CO_3} \times \frac{1\ \text{mol } HCO_3^-}{1\ \text{mol } H_2CO_3} \times \frac{1\ \text{mol NaOH}}{1\ \text{mol } HCO_3^-} = 0.10\ \text{mol NaOH}.$$

To the final pH, $pH = pK_a + \log\frac{[base]}{[acid]}$ so $-\log[H^+] = -\log K_{a_2} + \log\frac{[CO_3^{2-}]}{[HCO_3^-]} \rightarrow$

$$-\log(3.2 \times 10^{-11}) = -\log(5.6 \times 10^{-11}) + \log\frac{[CO_3^{2-}]}{[HCO_3^-]} \rightarrow 10.49 = 10.25 + \log\frac{[CO_3^{2-}]}{[HCO_3^-]}$$

$$\rightarrow 0.24 = \log\frac{[CO_3^{2-}]}{[HCO_3^-]} \rightarrow \frac{[CO_3^{2-}]}{[HCO_3^-]} = 10^{+0.24} = 1.7\underline{3}780 \text{ and } [CO_3^{2-}] + [HCO_3^-] = \text{initial } [H_2CO_3] = 0.10\text{ M}.$$

Thus $[HCO_3^-] = 0.10[CO_3^{2-}]$, and $\frac{[CO_3^{2-}]}{0.10\text{ M} - [CO_3^{2-}]} = 1.7\underline{3}780 \rightarrow [CO_3^{2-}] = 1.7\underline{3}780\,(0.10\text{ M} - [CO_3^{2-}])$

$\rightarrow [CO_3^{2-}] = 0.17\underline{3}780\text{ M} - 1.7\underline{3}780\,[CO_3^{2-}] \rightarrow 2.7\underline{3}780\,[CO_3^{2-}] = 0.17\underline{3}780\text{ M} \rightarrow$

$$[CO_3^{2-}] = 0.0634743\text{ M then } 1.0\ \text{L } CO_3^{2-} \times \frac{0.0634743\ \text{mol } CO_3^{2-}}{1\ \text{L } CO_3^{2-}} \times \frac{1\ \text{mol NaOH}}{1\ \text{mol } CO_3^{2-}} = 0.0634743\ \text{mol NaOH}.$$

So, the total mole NaOH = 0.10 mol + 0.0634743 mol = 0.1634743 mol NaOH. Finally,

$$0.1634743\ \text{mol NaOH} \times \frac{40.00\text{ g NaOH}}{1\ \text{mol NaOH}} = 6.5\text{ g NaOH}.$$

Check: The units (g) are correct. The magnitude of the answer makes physical sense because if all of the acid were fully titrated 0.20 mol of NaOH (or 8 g) would be required. The pH indicates that the titration is most of the way there.

16.143 (a) **Given:** $Au(OH)_3$ in pure water **Find:** molar solubility (S) **Other:** $K_{sp} = 5.5 \times 10^{-46}$

Conceptual Plan: Use equations derived in Problems 19 and 20 and solve for S. Then

for ionic compound, A_mX_n, $K_{sp} = [A^{n+}]^m [X^{m-}]^n = m^m n^n S^{m+n}$.

check answer for validity.
Solution: For $Au(OH)_3$, $K_{sp} = 5.5 \times 10^{-46}$, A = Au^{3+}, $m = 1$, X = OH^-, and $n = 3$ so $K_{sp} = [Au^{3+}][OH^-]^3$ $= 5.5 \times 10^{-46} = 3^3S^4$. Rearrange to solve for S. $S = \sqrt[4]{\dfrac{5.5 \times 10^{-46}}{27}} = 2.1 \times 10^{-12}$ M. This answer suggests that the $[OH^-] = 3(2.1 \times 10^{-12}\text{ M}) = 6.3 \times 10^{-12}$ M. This result is lower than found in pure water (1.0×10^{-7} M), so substitute this value for $[OH^-]$, and solve for $S = [Au^{3+}]$. So $K_{sp} = [Au^{3+}][OH^-]^3$ $= 5.5 \times 10^{-46} = S\,(1.0 \times 10^{-7}\text{ M})^3$ and solving for S gives $S = 5.5 \times 10^{-25}$ M.
Check: The units (M) are correct. Since K_{sp} is so small the autoionization of water must be considered and the solubility is smaller than normally anticipated.

(b) **Given:** $Au(OH)_3$ in 1.0 M HNO_3 **Find:** molar solubility (S) **Other:** $K_{sp} = 5.5 \times 10^{-46}$
Conceptual Plan: Since HNO_3 is a strong acid, it will neutralize the gold(III) hydroxide (through the reaction of H^+ with OH^- to form water (the reverse of the autoionization of water equilibrium). Write balanced equations for dissolving the solid and for the neutralization reaction. Add these two reactions to get the desired overall reaction. Using the rules from Chapter 14, multiply the individual reaction Ks to get the overall K for the sum of these reactions. then M HNO_3, $K \rightarrow S$.

ICE Chart

Solution: Identify the solid as $Au(OH)_3$. Write the individual reactions and add them together.

$Au(OH)_3\,(s) \rightleftharpoons Au^{3+}\,(aq) + \cancel{3\,OH^-\,(aq)}$ $\qquad K_{sp} = 5.5 \times 10^{-46}$

$3\,H^+\,(aq) + \cancel{3\,OH^-\,(aq)} \rightleftharpoons 3\,H_2O\,(l)$ $\qquad \left(\dfrac{1}{K_w}\right)^3 = \left(\dfrac{1}{1.0 \times 10^{-14}}\right)^3$

$Au(OH)_3\,(s) + 3\,H^+\,(aq) \rightleftharpoons Au^{3+}\,(aq) + 3\,H_2O\,(l)$

Since the overall reaction is the sum of the dissolution reaction and three times the reverse of the autoionization of water reaction, the overall reaction

$K = K_{sp}\left(\dfrac{1}{K_w}\right)^3 = (5.5 \times 10^{-46})\left(\dfrac{1}{1.0 \times 10^{-14}}\right)^3 = 5.5 \times 10^{-4} = \dfrac{[Au^{3+}]}{[H^+]^3}$ then since HNO_3 is a strong acid, it will completely dissociate to H^+ and NO_3^-. Set up an ICE table.

$Au(OH)_3\,(s) + 3\,H^+\,(aq) \rightleftharpoons Au^{3+}\,(aq) + 3\,H_2O\,(l)$

	$[H^+]$	$[Au^{3+}]$
Initial	1.0	0.00
Change	$-3S$	$+S$
Equil	$1.0 - 3S$	$+S$

$K = \dfrac{[Au^{3+}]}{[H^+]^3} = 5.5 \times 10^{-4} = \dfrac{S}{(1.0 - 3S)^3}$.

Assume S is small ($3S << 1.0$) so $\dfrac{S}{(1.0 - \cancel{3S})^3} = 5.5 \times 10^{-4}\text{ M} = \dfrac{S}{(1.0)^3} = S$. Confirm that the assumption is valid. $\dfrac{3(5.5 \times 10^{-4})}{1.0} \times 100\% = 0.017\% \ll 5\%$ so the assumption is valid.
Check: The units (M) are correct. K is much larger than the original K_{sp} so the solubility of $Au(OH)_3$ increases over that of pure water.

16.144 **Given:** excess AgCl in 0.10 M KI **Find:** $[I^-]$ **Other:** K_{sp} (AgCl) $= 1.77 \times 10^{-10}$, K_{sp} (AgI) $= 8.51 \times 10^{-17}$
Conceptual Plan:
Since the KI does not generate a common ion with AgCl, use equations derived in Problems 19 and 20 and solve for S. So S(AgCl) = $[Ag^+]$ then use the equation derived in Problem 19 to get K_{sp} (KI)

for ionic compound, A_mX_n, $K_{sp} = [A^{n+}]^m[X^{m-}]^n = m^m n^n S^{m+n}$.

for ionic compound, A_mX_n, $K_{sp} = [A^{n+}]^m[X^{m-}]^n$.

expression. Substitute value for $[Ag^+]$ into K_{sp} (KI) expression and solve for $[I^-]$.
Solution: For AgCl, K_{sp} (AgCl) $= 1.77 \times 10^{-10}$, A = Ag^+, $m = 1$, X = Cl^-, and $n = 1$ so $K_{sp} = [Ag^+][Cl^-] = 1.77 \times 10^{-10} = S^2$. Rearrange to solve for S. $S = 1.33 \times 10^{-5}$ M. then, K_{sp} (AgI) $= 8.51 \times 10^{-17}$, A = Ag^+, $m = 1$, X = I^-, and $n = 1$ so $K_{sp} = [Ag^+][I^-] = 8.51 \times 10^{-17}$. Substitute value for $[Ag^+]$ into K_{sp} (KI) expression and solve for $[I^-]$. $8.51 \times 10^{-17} = (1.33 \times 10^{-5})[I^-]$, so $[I^-] = 6.40 \times 10^{-12}$ M.

Check: The units (M) are correct. Since there are silver ions generated from the excess AgCl in solution, the iodide ions are converted to AgI and the concentration of remaining iodide ions is controlled by the solubility of the AgCl.

16.145 **Given:** 1.00 L of 0.100 M $MgCO_3$ **Find:** volume of 0.100 M Na_2CO_3 to precipitate 99% of Mg^{2+} ions
Other: K_{sp} ($MgCO_3$) = 6.82×10^{-6}
Conceptual Plan:
Since 99% of the Mg^{2+} ions are to be precipitated, there will be 1% of the ions left in solution.

$(0.01)(0.100 \text{ M } Mg^{2+})$

Let x = required volume (in L). Calculate the amount of CO_3^{2-} added and the amount of Mg^{2+} that does not precipitate and remains in solution. Use these to calculate the $[Mg^{2+}]$ and $[CO_3^{2-}]$. The solubility product constant (K_{sp}) is the equilibrium expression for a chemical equation representing the dissolution of an ionic compound. The expression of the solubility product constant of A_mX_n is $K_{sp} = [A^{n+}]^m [X^{m-}]^n$. Substitute these expressions in this equation to $[Mg^{2+}]$, $[CO_3^{2-}]$, K_{sp} $\rightarrow x$

for ionic compound, A_mX_n, $K_{sp} = [A^{n+}]^m [X^{m-}]^n$.

Solution: Since 99% of the Mg^{2+} ions are to be precipitated, there will be 1% of the ions left in solution or $(0.01)(0.100 \text{ M } Mg^{2+}) = 0.001 \text{ M } Mg^{2+}$. Let x = required volume (in L). The volume of the solution after precipitation is $(1.00 + x)$. The amount of CO_3^{2-} added = $(0.100\text{M})(x \text{ L}) = 0.100x$ mol CO_3^{2-}. The amount of Mg^{2+} that does not precipitate and remains in solution is $(0.100 \text{ M})(1.00 \text{ L})(0.001) = 1.00 \times 10^{-3}$ mol and the amount that precipitates = 0.099 mol, which is also equal to the amount of CO_3^{2-} used. The amount of CO_3^{2-} remaining in solution is $(0.10x - 0.099)$. Thus, $[Mg^{2+}] = 1.00 \times 10^{-3}$ mol/$(1.00 + x)$ L and $[CO_3^{2-}] = (0.10x - 0.099)$ mol/$(1.00 + x)$ L. Then $K_{sp} = 6.82 \times 10^{-6}$, A = Mg^{2+}, m = 1, X = CO_3^{2-}, and n = 1, so $K_{sp} = 6.82 \times 10^{-6}$

$$= [Mg^{2+}][CO_3^{2-}] = \frac{(1.00 \times 10^{-3})(0.10x - 0.099)}{(1.00 + x)^2}.$$ Rearrange to solve for x.

$$1.00 + 2.00x + x^2 = \frac{1.0 \times 10^{-4}x - 9.9 \times 10^{-5}}{6.82 \times 10^{-6}} \rightarrow 0 = x^2 - 1\underline{2}.6628x + 1\underline{5}.4526$$ Using quadratic equation,

$x = 1.\underline{3}68 \text{ L} = 1.4 \text{ L}$

Check: The units (L) are correct. The necessary concentration is very low, so the volume fairly large.

16.146 **Given:** solution with 0.40 M HCN **Find:** solubility of CuI
Other: K_{sp} (CuI) = 1.1×10^{-12}, K_f ($Cu(CN)_2^-$) = 1×10^{24}
Conceptual Plan: Write balanced equations for the solubility of CuI and reaction with CN^- and expressions for K_{sp} and K_f. Use initial concentrations to set up an ICE table. Since the K is so large, assume that reaction essentially goes to completion. Solve for $[I^-]$ at equilibrium.
Solution: Write two reactions and combine.

$CuI(s) \rightleftharpoons \cancel{Cu^+(aq)} + I^-(aq)$ with $K_{sp} = [Cu^+][I^-] = 1.1 \times 10^{-12}$

$\cancel{Cu^+(aq)} + 2\,CN^-(aq) \rightleftharpoons Cu(CN)_2^-(aq)$ with $K_f = \dfrac{[Cu(CN)_2^-]}{[Cu^+][CN^-]^2} = 1 \times 10^{24}$

$CuI(s) + 2\,CN^-(aq) \rightleftharpoons Cu(CN)_2^-(aq) + I^-(aq)$

with $K = K_{sp}K_f = \cancel{[Cu^+]}[I^-]\dfrac{[Cu(CN)_2^-]}{\cancel{[Cu^+]}[CN^-]^2} = (1.1 \times 10^{-12})(1 \times 10^{24})$

$$K = \frac{[Cu(CN)_2^-][I^-]}{[CN^-]^2} = \underline{1}.1 \times 10^{12}$$

Since $K_{sp} = [Cu^+][I^-] = 1.1 \times 10^{-12}$ without HCN present

$[Cu^+] = [I^-] = \sqrt{1.1 \times 10^{-12}} = 1.\underline{0}48 \times 10^{-6}$ M. Set up an ICE table with initial concentrations. Since K is so large and since initially $[CN^-] > 2\,[I^-]$ the reaction essentially goes to completion then write equilibrium expression and solve for x.

$CuI\ (s) + 2\,CN^-\ (aq) \rightleftharpoons Cu(CN)_2^-\ (aq) + I^-\ (aq)$

	$[CN^-]$	$[Cu(CN)_2^-]$	$[I^-]$
Initial	0.40	0.00	$1.\underline{0}48 \times 10^{-6}$
Change	≈ -0.40	$\approx 1/2\,(0.40)$	$\approx 1/2\,(0.40)$
Equil	$0.40 - 2x$	x	$1.\underline{0}48 \times 10^{-6} + x$

$K = \dfrac{[Cu(CN)_2^-][I^-]}{[CN^-]^2} = \dfrac{(x)(1.\underline{0}48 \times 10^{-6} + x)}{(0.40 - 2x)^2} = \underline{1}.1 \times 10^{12}$. Assume that $x >> 1.\underline{0}48 \times 10^{-6}$ M so

$\dfrac{(x)(x)}{(0.40 - 2x)^2} = \underline{1}.1 \times 10^{12} = \dfrac{(x)^2}{(0.40 - 2x)^2} \rightarrow \sqrt{\underline{1}.1 \times 10^{12}} = \dfrac{x}{0.40 - 2x} = \underline{1}.049 \times 10^6 \rightarrow$

$x = 0.\underline{1}9995$. So $[I^-] = x = 0.\underline{1}9995$ M $=$ 0.2 M I^-. Since $1.\underline{0}48 \times 10^{-6}$ M is insignificant compared to x, the assumption is valid. The solubility of CuI is 0.2 M or one-half the initial concentration of HCN.

Check: The units (M) are correct. Since K is so large, the reaction essentially goes to completion and the solubility of CuI is dramatically increased.

16.147 **Given:** 1.0 L solution with 0.10 M $Ba(OH)_2$ and excess $Zn(OH)_2$ **Find:** pH

Other: $K_{sp}\ (Zn(OH)_2) = 3 \times 10^{-15}$, $K_f\ (Zn(OH)_4^{2-}) = 2 \times 10^{15}$

Conceptual Plan: Since $[Ba(OH)_2]$ = 0.10 M then $[OH^-]$ = 0.20 M. Write balanced equations for the solubility of $Zn(OH)_2$ and reaction with excess OH^- and expressions for K_{sp} and K_f. Use initial concentrations to set up an ICE table. Solve for $[OH^-]$ at equilibrium. Then $[OH^-] \rightarrow [H_3O^+] \rightarrow$ pH.

$K_w = [H_3O^+][OH^-]$ $\quad pH = -\log[H_3O^+]$

Solution: Write two reactions and combine.

$Zn(OH)_2(s) \rightleftharpoons \cancel{Zn^{2+}(aq)} + \cancel{2}\,OH^-\ (aq)$ with $K_{sp} = [Zn^{2+}][OH^-]^2 = 3 \times 10^{-15}$

$\cancel{Zn^{2+}(aq)} + \cancel{4}2\,OH^-\ (aq) \rightleftharpoons Zn(OH)_4^{2-}\ (aq)$ with $K_f = \dfrac{[Zn(OH)_4^{2-}]}{[Zn^{2+}][OH^-]^4} = 2 \times 10^{15}$

$Zn(OH)_2\ (s) + 2\,OH^-\ (aq) \rightleftharpoons Zn(OH)_4^{2-}\ (aq)$

with $K = K_{sp}\,K_f = \cancel{[Zn^{2+}][OH^-]^2}\,\dfrac{[Zn(OH)_4^{2-}]}{\cancel{[Zn^{2+}]}[OH^-]^{\cancel{4}2}} = (3 \times 10^{-15})(2 \times 10^{15})$

$K = \dfrac{[Zn(OH)_4^{2-}]}{[OH^-]^2} = 6$. Set up an ICE table with initial concentration and solve for x.

$Zn(OH)_2\ (s) + 2\,OH^-\ (aq) \rightleftharpoons Zn(OH)_4^{2-}\ (aq)$

	$[OH^-]$	$[Zn(OH)_4^{2-}]$
Initial	0.20	0.00
Change	$-2x$	x
Equil	$0.20 - 2x$	x

$K = \dfrac{[Zn(OH)_4^{2-}]}{[OH^-]^2} = \dfrac{x}{(0.20 - 2x)^2} = 6$

$x = 6\,(0.20 - 2x)^2 \rightarrow x = 6\,(4x^2 - 0.80x + 0.040) \rightarrow x = 24x^2 - 4.8x + 0.24 \rightarrow$

$0 = 24x^2 - 5.8x + 0.24$ Using quadratic equation, $x = 0.0530049 \rightarrow$

So $[OH^-] = 0.20 - 2x = 0.20 - 2(0.05\underline{3}0049) = 0.0\underline{9}3990$ M OH^-. then $K_w = [H_3O^+][OH^-]$ so

$[H_3O^+] = \dfrac{K_w}{[OH^-]} = \dfrac{1.0 \times 10^{-14}}{0.0\underline{9}3990} = 1.\underline{0}6394 \times 10^{-13}$ M. Finally,

$pH = -\log[H_3O^+] = -\log(1.\underline{0}6394 \times 10^{-13}) = 12.97$.

Check: The units (none) are correct. Since the pH of the solution before the addition of the $Zn(OH)_2$ is 13.30, the reaction decreases the $[OH^-]$ and the pH drops.

16.148 **Given:** 1.00 L of 2.0 M $HC_2H_3O_2$ and 1.0 M $C_2H_3O_2^-$ **Find:** amount of HCl to pH= 4.00

Other: $K_a\ (HC_2H_3O_2) = 1.8 \times 10^{-5}$

Conceptual Plan: Identify acid and base components then final pH, pK_a $\rightarrow$ $[C_2H_3O_2^-]/[HC_2H_3O_2]$ then

acid = $HC_2H_3O_2$ base = $C_2H_3O_2^-$ $\quad pH = pK_a + \log\dfrac{[base]}{[acid]}$

$[C_2H_3O_2^-]$, L → mol $C_2H_3O_2^-$ and $[HC_2H_3O_2]$, L → mol $HC_2H_3O_2$ then write balanced equation then

$M = \frac{mol}{L}$ $M = \frac{mol}{L}$ $HCl + C_2H_3O_2^- \rightarrow HC_2H_3O_2 + Cl^-$

initial mol $NaC_2H_3O_2$, initial mol $HC_2H_3O_2$, final $[C_2H_3O_2^-]/[HC_2H_3O_2]$ → mol HCl → g HCl.

set up stoichiometry table $\frac{36.46 \text{ g HCl}}{1 \text{ mol HCl}}$

Solution: Since K_a ($HC_2H_3O_2$) = 1.8×10^{-5}, $pK_a = -\log K_a = -\log(1.8 \times 10^{-5}) = 4.74$.

Then $pH = pK_a + \log\frac{[base]}{[acid]} = 4.74 + \log\frac{[C_2H_3O_2^-]}{[HC_2H_3O_2]} = 4.00$. Solve for $\frac{[C_2H_3O_2^-]}{[HC_2H_3O_2]}$.

$\log\frac{[C_2H_3O_2^-]}{[HC_2H_3O_2]} = 4.00 - 4.74 = -0.74 \rightarrow \frac{[C_2H_3O_2^-]}{[HC_2H_3O_2]} = 10^{-0.74} = 0.1\underline{8}1970.$

Then $\frac{2.0 \text{ mol } HC_2H_3O_2}{1 \text{ L}} \times 1.00 \text{ L} = 2.0 \text{ mol } HC_2H_3O_2$ and

$\frac{1.0 \text{ mol } C_2H_3O_2^-}{1 \text{ L}} \times 1.00 \text{ L} = 1.0 \text{ mol } C_2H_3O_2^-$ set up a table to track changes:

	HCl (*aq*) +	$C_2H_3O_2^-$ (*aq*) →	$HC_2H_3O_2$ (*aq*) +	Cl^- (*aq*)
Before addition	0.0 mol	1.0 mol	2.0 mol	0.0 mol
Addition	$-x$ mol	$-x$ mol	x mol	x mol
After addition	≈0.00 mol	$(1.0 - x)$ mol	$(2.0 + x)$ mol	x mol

Combine the final line of table with $\frac{[C_2H_3O_2^-]}{[HC_2H_3O_2]} = 0.1\underline{8}1970.$

So $\frac{[C_2H_3O_2^-]}{[HC_2H_3O_2]} = 0.1\underline{8}1970 = \frac{(1.0 - x)}{(2.0 + x)}$ Solve for x. $0.1\underline{8}1970(2.0 + x) = 1.0 - x \rightarrow$

$x + 0.1\underline{8}1970x = 1.0 - 0.3\underline{6}394 \rightarrow 1.1\underline{8}1970x = 0.6\underline{3}606 \rightarrow x = 0.5\underline{3}8135 \text{ mol HCl} = 0.54 \text{ mol HCl}$

then $0.5\underline{3}8135 \text{ mol HCl} \times \frac{36.46 \text{ g HCl}}{1 \text{ mol HCl}} = 1\underline{9}.6204 \text{ g HCl} = 20. \text{ g HCl}.$

Check: The units (mol or g) are correct. The magnitude of the answer make physical sense because the initial $[C_2H_3O_2^-]/[HC_2H_3O_2] = 0.50$ and it is reduced to ~0.18 and the starting number of moles of base = 1.0 mol, so there must be much less than a mole of HCl added.

Conceptual Problems

16.149 If the concentration of the acid is greater than the concentration of the base, then the pH will be less than the pK_a. If the concentration of the acid is equal to the concentration of the base, then the pH will be equal to the pK_a. If the concentration of the acid is less than the concentration of the base, then the pH will be greater than the pK_a.

(a) $pH < pK_a$

(b) $pH > pK_a$

(c) $pH = pK_a$, the OH^- will convert half of the acid to base

(d) $pH > pK_a$, the OH^- will convert more than half of the acid to base

16.150 As long as the [base]/[acid] is between 0.1 and 10, the buffer will still be active and the buffer capacity will not have been exceeded.

(a) No, the buffer capacity is not exceeded because [base]/[acid] = 0.22/0.08.

(b) No, the buffer capacity is not exceeded because [base]/[acid] = 0.18/0.12.

(c) Yes, the buffer capacity will be exceeded because all of the acid is converted to base.

(d) No, the buffer capacity is not exceeded because [base]/[acid] = 0.19/0.11.

16.151 Only (b) is correct. The volume to the first equivalence point will be the same since the number of moles of acid is the same. The pH profiles of the two titrations will be different.

16.152 Only (c) is correct. If the volume of base is twice as high, then the acid concentration is twice as high and the weaker acid has the higher pH at the equivalence point.

16.153 (a) The solubility will be unchanged since the pH is constant and there are no common ions added.

(b) The solubility will be less because extra fluoride ions are added, suppressing the solubility of the fluoride ionic compound.

(c) The solubility will increase because some of the fluoride ion will be converted to HF, and so more of the ionic compound can be dissolved.

17 Free Energy and Thermodynamics

Review Questions

17.1 The first law of thermodynamics states that energy is conserved in chemical processes. When we burn gasoline to run a car, for example, the amount of energy produced by the chemical reaction does not vanish, nor does any new energy appear that was not present before the combustion. Some of the energy from the combustion reaction goes toward driving the car forward (about 20%), and the rest is dissipated into the surroundings as heat (just feel the engine). However, the total energy given off by the combustion reaction exactly equals the sum of the amount of energy driving the car forward and the amount dissipated as heat—energy is conserved. In other words, when it comes to energy, you can't win; you cannot create energy that was not there to begin with.

17.2 The second law of thermodynamics implies that, not only can we not win in an energy transaction, but we cannot break even. In every process that involves energy, some of the energy is lost to the surroundings as heat. This means that no process is perfectly efficient. This amount of energy that must be lost to the surroundings in order for the process to occur at all is nature's heat tax, an unavoidable cut of every energy transaction.

17.3 A perpetual motion machine is a machine that perpetually moves without any energy input. This machine is not possible because if the machine is to be in motion, it must pay the heat tax with each cycle of its motion—over time, it will therefore run down and stop moving.

17.4 It is more efficient to heat your home with a natural gas furnace because you are burning the fuel in your home and using the heat from the combustion to heat the air that is circulated in your home. When you use an electric furnace, fuel is burned at the electric company's power plant, then converted to electricity. This electricity is transmitted to your home through wires and through power substations. Once it reaches your home, the electricity then needs to be converted to heat to warm the air that circulates in your home. Each step must pay a heat tax. Using a natural gas furnace has fewer steps and so it pays a much lower tax.

17.5 A spontaneous process is one that occurs without ongoing outside intervention (such as the performance of work by some external force). For example, when you drop a book in a gravitational field, the book spontaneously drops to the floor.

17.6 In thermodynamics, the spontaneity of a reaction is the direction in which and extent to which a chemical reaction proceeds. Kinetics is the speed of the reaction—how fast a reaction takes place. A reaction may be thermodynamically spontaneous, but kinetically slow at a given temperature. For example, the conversion of diamond to graphite is thermodynamically spontaneous. But your diamonds will not become worthless anytime soon because the process is extremely slow kinetically. Although the rate of a spontaneous process can be increased by the use of a catalyst, a nonspontaneous process cannot be made spontaneous by the use of a catalyst. Catalysts affect only the rate of a reaction, not the spontaneity.

17.7 Entropy (S) is a thermodynamic function that is proportional to the number of energetically equivalent ways to arrange the components of a system to achieve a particular state. Entropy, like enthalpy, is a state function—its value depends only on the state of the system, not on how the system got to that state. Therefore, for any process, the change in entropy is just the entropy of the final state minus the entropy of the initial state or $\Delta S = S_{final} - S_{initial}$.

17.8 The entropy of a gas increases when it expands into a vacuum because the number of possible states increases (such as where the particle is located).

17.9 Microstates are the number of internal arrangements. These microstates give rise to the same external arrangement, or macrostate. If I have three gas particles (A, B and C) and two containers, the fact that the first container has two particles and the other container has one particle is a macrostate. The fact that particles A and C are in the first container and particle B is in the other container is a microstate. There are at least as many microstates as there are macrostates.

17.10 The entropy of a state is proportional to the number of energetically equivalent ways to arrange the components of the system to achieve a particular state. This implies the state with the highest entropy also has the greatest dispersal of energy.

17.11 The second law of thermodynamics states that for any spontaneous process, the entropy of the universe increases ($\Delta S_{univ} > 0$). The criterion for spontaneity is the entropy of the universe. Processes that increase the entropy of the universe—those that result in greater dispersal or randomization of energy—occur spontaneously. Processes that decrease the entropy of the universe do not occur spontaneously. Heat travels from a substance at higher temperature to one at lower temperature because the process disperses thermal energy. The cooler object has less thermal energy, so transferring heat from the warmer object results in greater energy randomization—the energy that was concentrated in the hot substance becomes dispersed between the two substances.

17.12 The entropy of a sample of matter increases as it changes state from a solid to a liquid and then to a gas, because the amount of molecular motion and the amount of thermal energy is the greatest in the gas phase and is least in the solid phase.

17.13 When water freezes at temperatures below 0 °C, the entropy of the water decreases, yet the process is spontaneous because the entropy of the universe increases ($\Delta S_{univ} > 0$). The entropy of the system can decrease ($\Delta S_{sys} < 0$) as long as the entropy of the surroundings increases by a greater amount ($\Delta S_{surr} > -\Delta S_{sys}$) so that the overall entropy of the universe undergoes a net increase. For liquid water freezing, the change in entropy for the system (ΔS_{sys}) is negative because the water becomes more ordered. For ΔS_{univ} to be positive, ΔS_{surr} must be positive and greater in absolute value (or magnitude) than ΔS_{sys}. We learned in Chapter 6 that freezing is an exothermic process: it gives off heat to the surroundings. If we think of entropy as the dispersal or randomization of energy, then the release of heat energy by the system disperses that energy into the surroundings, increasing the entropy of the surroundings. The freezing of water below 0 °C increases the entropy of the universe because the heat given off to the surroundings increases the entropy of the surroundings to a sufficient degree to overcome the entropy decrease in the water. The freezing of water becomes nonspontaneous above 0 °C because the magnitude of the increase in the entropy of the surroundings due to the dispersal of energy into the surroundings is temperature dependent. The higher the temperature, the smaller the percent increase in entropy for a given rise in temperature. Therefore, the impact of the heat released to the surroundings by the freezing of water depends on the temperature of the surroundings—the higher the temperature, the smaller the impact.

17.14 Exothermic processes ($-\Delta H_{sys}$) tend to be spontaneous at low temperatures because they increase the entropy of the surroundings ($+\Delta S_{surr}$). Since $\Delta S_{surr} = \dfrac{-\Delta H_{sys}}{T}$, as temperature increases a given negative ΔH produces a smaller positive ΔS_{surr}; therefore, exothermicity becomes less of a determining factor for spontaneity as temperature increases.

17.15 The change in Gibbs free energy for a process is proportional to the negative of ΔS_{univ}. Since ΔS_{univ} is a criterion for spontaneity, ΔG is also a criterion for spontaneity (although opposite in sign).

17.16 (a) ΔH negative, ΔS positive. If a reaction is exothermic ($\Delta H < 0$), and if the change in entropy for the reaction is positive ($\Delta S > 0$), then the change in free energy will be negative at all temperatures and the reaction will therefore be spontaneous at all temperatures.

(b) ΔH positive, ΔS negative. If a reaction is endothermic ($\Delta H > 0$), and if the change in entropy for the reaction is negative ($\Delta S < 0$), then the change in free energy will be positive at all temperatures and the reaction will therefore be nonspontaneous at all temperatures.

(c) ΔH negative, ΔS negative. If a reaction is exothermic ($\Delta H < 0$), and if the change in entropy for the reaction is negative ($\Delta S < 0$), then the change in free energy will depend on temperature. The reaction will be spontaneous at low temperature, but nonspontaneous at high temperature.

(d) ΔH positive, ΔS positive. If a reaction is endothermic ($\Delta H > 0$), and if the change in entropy for the reaction is positive ($\Delta S > 0$), then the change in free energy will also depend on temperature. The reaction will be nonspontaneous at low temperature, but spontaneous at high temperature.

17.17 The third law of thermodynamics states that the entropy of a perfect crystal at absolute zero (0 K) is zero. For enthalpy we defined a standard state, so that we could define a "zero" for the scale. This is not necessary for entropy because there is an absolute zero.

17.18 Gases have much greater standard entropy because they have more energetically equivalent ways to arrange their components, which in turn results in greater energy dispersal at 25 °C.

17.19 The larger the molar mass, the greater the entropy at 25 °C. For a given state of matter, entropy generally increases with increasing molecular complexity.

17.20 To calculate ΔS°_{rxn}, subtract the standard entropies of the reactants multiplied by their stoichiometric coefficients from the standard entropies of the products multiplied by their stoichiometric coefficients or $\Delta S^\circ_{rxn} = \sum n_p S^\circ(\text{products}) - \sum n_r S^\circ(\text{reactants})$ where, n_p represents the stoichiometric coefficients of the products, n_r represents the stoichiometric coefficients of the reactants, and S° represents the standard entropies. Keep in mind when using this equation that, unlike enthalpies of formation, which are equal to zero for elements in their standard states, standard entropies are always nonzero at 25 °C.

17.21 The three ways of calculating the ΔG_{rxn} are to

- use tabulated values of standard enthalpies of formation to calculate ΔH°_{rxn} and use tabulated values of standard entropies to calculate ΔS°_{rxn}; then use the values of ΔH°_{rxn} and ΔS°_{rxn} calculated in these ways to calculate the standard free energy change for a reaction by using the equation $\Delta G^\circ_{rxn} = \Delta H^\circ_{rxn} - T\,\Delta S^\circ_{rxn}$.
- use tabulated values of the standard free energies of formation to calculate ΔG°_{rxn} using an equation similar to that used for standard enthalpy of a reaction $\Delta G^\circ_{rxn} = \sum n_p \Delta G^\circ_f(\text{products}) - \sum n_r \Delta G^\circ_f(\text{reactants})$.
- use a reaction pathway or stepwise reaction to sum the changes in free energy for each of the steps in a manner similar to that used in Chapter 6 for enthalpy of stepwise reactions.

The method to calculate the free energy of a reaction at temperatures other than at 25°C is the first method. The second method is only applicable at 25°C. The third method is only applicable at the temperature of the individual reactions, generally 25°C.

17.22 The change in free energy of a chemical reaction represents the maximum amount of energy available, or free, to do work (if ΔG°_{rxn} is negative).

17.23 The standard free energy change for a reaction (ΔG°_{rxn}) applies only to standard conditions. For a gas, standard conditions are those in which the pure gas is present at a partial pressure of 1 atmosphere. For nonstandard conditions, we need to calculate ΔG_{rxn} (not ΔG°_{rxn}) to predict spontaneity.

17.24 Even though ΔG°_{vap} is positive at room temperature, liquid water is in equilibrium with water vapor at a pressure of 0.0313 atm. The vapor pressure of water is just not as high as 1 atm, the standard conditions of a gas. This means that some water will evaporate.

17.25 The free energy of reaction under nonstandard conditions (ΔG_{rxn}) can be calculated from ΔG°_{rxn} using the relationship $\Delta G_{rxn} = \Delta G^\circ_{rxn} + RT \ln Q$, where Q is the reaction quotient (defined in Section 14.7), T is the temperature in K, and R is the gas constant in the appropriate units (8.314 J/mol K).

17.26 The relationship between ΔG°_{rxn} and K is $\Delta G^\circ_{rxn} = -RT \ln K$. When ΔG°_{rxn} is positive this means that the log of K is negative and $K < 1$. Under standard conditions (when $Q = 1$) the reaction is spontaneous in the reverse direction. When ΔG°_{rxn} is zero this means that the log of K is zero and $K = 1$. The reaction happens to be at equilibrium under standard conditions. When ΔG°_{rxn} is negative the log of K is positive and $K > 1$. Under standard conditions (when $Q = 1$) the reaction is spontaneous in the forward direction.

Entropy, the Second Law of Thermodynamics, and the Direction of Spontaneous Change

17.27 a and c are spontaneous processes.

17.28 a and c are nonspontaneous processes. Nonspontaneous processes are not impossible. Work of some form must be added to make the process proceed.

17.29 System B has the greatest entropy. There is only one energetically equivalent arrangement for System A. However, the particles of System B may exchange positions for a second energetically equivalent arrangement.

17.30 There is only one energetically equivalent arrangement for System A. There are 3! or 6 energetically equivalent arrangements for System B. System B has the greatest entropy, since there are more energetically equivalent arrangements for System B.

17.31 (a) $\Delta S > 0$ because a gas is being generated.

(b) $\Delta S < 0$ because 2 moles of gas are being converted to 1 mole of gas.

(c) $\Delta S < 0$ because a gas is being converted to a solid.

(d) $\Delta S < 0$ because 4 moles of gas are being converted to 2 moles of gas.

17.32 (a) $\Delta S < 0$ because a gas is being converted to a solid.

(b) $\Delta S < 0$ because 5 moles of gas are being converted to 4 moles of gas.

(c) $\Delta S > 0$ because 2 moles of gas are being converted to 3 moles of gas.

(d) $\Delta S < 0$ because 2 moles of gas are being converted to a solid.

17.33 (a) $\Delta S_{sys} > 0$, because 6 moles of gas are being converted to 7 moles of gas. Since $\Delta H < 0$ and $\Delta S_{surr} > 0$, the reaction is spontaneous at all temperatures.

(b) $\Delta S_{sys} < 0$ because 2 moles of different gases are being converted to 2 moles of one gas. Since $\Delta H > 0$ and $\Delta S_{surr} < 0$, the reaction is nonspontaneous at all temperatures.

(c) $\Delta S_{sys} < 0$, because 3 moles of gas are being converted to 2 moles of gas. Since $\Delta H > 0$ and $\Delta S_{surr} < 0$, the reaction is nonspontaneous at all temperatures.

(d) $\Delta S_{sys} > 0$, because 9 moles of gas are being converted to 10 moles of gas. Since $\Delta H < 0$ and $\Delta S_{surr} > 0$, the reaction is spontaneous at all temperatures.

17.34 (a) $\Delta S_{sys} < 0$, because 3 moles of gas are being converted to 2 moles of gas. Since $\Delta H < 0$ and $\Delta S_{surr} > 0$, the reaction is spontaneous at low temperatures.

(b) $\Delta S_{sys} > 0$ because 2 moles of gas are being converted to 3 moles of gas. Since $\Delta H > 0$ and $\Delta S_{surr} < 0$, the reaction is spontaneous at high temperatures.

(c) $\Delta S_{sys} < 0$, because 3 moles of gas are being converted to 2 moles of gas. Since $\Delta H < 0$ and $\Delta S_{surr} > 0$, the reaction is spontaneous at low temperatures.

(d) $\Delta S_{sys} < 0$, because 1 mole of a complicated gas is being converted to 1 mole of gas and a solid. Since $\Delta H > 0$ and $\Delta S_{surr} > 0$, the reaction is nonspontaneous at all temperatures.

17.35 (a) **Given:** $\Delta H^{\circ}_{rxn} = -385$ kJ, $T = 298$ K **Find:** ΔS_{surr}

Conceptual Plan: kJ → J then ΔH°_{rxn}, T → ΔS_{surr}

$\frac{1000\ J}{1\ kJ}$ $\Delta S_{surr} = \frac{-\Delta H_{sys}}{T}$

Solution: $-385\ \text{kJ} \times \frac{1000\ J}{1\ \text{kJ}} = -385{,}000$ J then

$$\Delta S_{surr} = \frac{-\Delta H_{sys}}{T} = \frac{-(-385{,}000\ J)}{298\ K} = 1290\ J/K = 1.29 \times 10^3\ J/K$$

Check: The units (J/K) are correct. The magnitude of the answer (10^3 J/K) makes sense because the kJ and the temperature started with very similar values and then a factor of 10^3 was applied.

(b) **Given:** $\Delta H^{\circ}_{rxn} = -385$ kJ, $T = 77$ K **Find:** ΔS_{surr}

Conceptual Plan: kJ → J then ΔH°_{rxn}, T → ΔS_{surr}

$\frac{1000\ J}{1\ kJ}$ $\Delta S_{surr} = \frac{-\Delta H_{sys}}{T}$

Solution: $-385\ \text{kJ} \times \frac{1000\ J}{1\ \text{kJ}} = -385{,}000$ J then $\Delta S_{surr} = \frac{-\Delta H_{sys}}{T} = \frac{-(-385{,}000\ J)}{77\ K} = 5.00 \times 10^3\ J/K$

Check: The units (J/K) are correct. The magnitude of the answer (5×10^3 J/K) makes sense because the temperature is much lower than in part (a), so the answer should increase.

(c) **Given:** $\Delta H^{\circ}_{rxn} = +114$ kJ, $T = 298$ K **Find:** ΔS_{surr}

Conceptual Plan: kJ → J then ΔH°_{rxn}, T → ΔS_{surr}

$\frac{1000\ J}{1\ kJ}$ $\Delta S_{surr} = \frac{-\Delta H_{sys}}{T}$

Solution: $+114\ \text{kJ} \times \frac{1000\ J}{1\ \text{kJ}} = +114{,}000$ J then $\Delta S_{surr} = \frac{-\Delta H_{sys}}{T} = \frac{-114{,}000\ J}{298\ K} = -383\ J/K$

Check: The units (J/K) are correct. The magnitude of the answer (– 400 J/K) makes sense because the kJ are less and of the opposite sign than part (a) so the answer should decrease.

(d) **Given:** $\Delta H^{\circ}_{rxn} = +114$ kJ, $T = 77$ K **Find:** ΔS_{surr}

Conceptual Plan: kJ → J then ΔH°_{rxn}, T → ΔS_{surr}

$\frac{1000\ J}{1\ kJ}$ $\Delta S_{surr} = \frac{-\Delta H_{sys}}{T}$

Solution: $+114\ \text{kJ} \times \frac{1000\ J}{1\ \text{kJ}} = +114{,}000$ J then

$$\Delta S_{surr} = \frac{-\Delta H_{sys}}{T} = \frac{-114{,}000\ J}{77\ K} = -1480\ \frac{J}{K} = -1.48 \times 10^3\ J/K$$

Check: The units (J/K) are correct. The magnitude of the answer (-2×10^3 J/K) makes sense because the temperature is much lower than in part (c), so the answer should increase.

17.36 **Given:** $\Delta H^{\circ}_{rxn} = -112$ kJ, $\Delta S_{rxn} = 354$ J/K **Find:** T when $\Delta S^{\circ}_{rxn} = \Delta S_{surr}$

Conceptual Plan: kJ → J then set $\Delta S^{\circ}_{rxn} = \Delta S_{surr}$ then ΔH°_{rxn}, ΔS_{surr} → T

$\frac{1000\ J}{1\ kJ}$ $\Delta S_{surr} = \frac{-\Delta H_{sys}}{T}$

Solution: $-112\ \text{kJ} \times \frac{1000\ J}{1\ \text{kJ}} = -112{,}000$ J then set $\Delta S^{\circ}_{rxn} = 354$ J/K $= \Delta S_{surr}$ then

$$T = \frac{-\Delta H_{sys}}{\Delta S_{surr}} = \frac{-(-112{,}000\ \text{J})}{354\ \frac{\text{J}}{K}} = +316\ K.$$

Check: The units (K) are correct. The magnitude of the answer (316 K) makes sense because there is almost a factor of 300 between the enthalpy and the entropy.

17.37 (a) **Given:** $\Delta H^{\circ}_{rxn} = +115$ kJ, $\Delta S_{rxn} = -263$ J/K, $T = 298$ K **Find:** ΔS_{univ} and spontaneity

Conceptual Plan: kJ → J then ΔH°_{rxn}, T → ΔS_{surr} then ΔS_{rxn}, ΔS_{surr} → ΔS_{univ}

$\frac{1000\ J}{1\ kJ}$ $\Delta S_{surr} = \frac{-\Delta H_{sys}}{T}$ $\Delta S_{univ} = \Delta S_{sys} + \Delta S_{surr}$

Solution: $115\ \cancel{kJ} \times \frac{1000\ J}{1\ \cancel{kJ}} = 115{,}000\ J$ then $\Delta S_{surr} = \frac{-\Delta H_{sys}}{T} = \frac{-(115{,}000\ J)}{298\ K} = -38\underline{5}.906\ J/K$ then $\Delta S_{univ} = \Delta S_{sys} + \Delta S_{surr} = -263\ J/K - 38\underline{5}.906\ J/K = -649\ J/K$ so the reaction is nonspontaneous.
Check: The units (J/K) are correct. The magnitude of the answer (–650 J/K) makes sense because both terms were negative, so the reaction is nonspontaneous.

(b) **Given:** $\Delta H^\circ_{rxn} = -115$ kJ, $\Delta S_{rxn} = +263$ J/K, $T = 298$ K **Find:** ΔS_{univ} and spontaneity
Conceptual Plan: kJ → J then ΔH°_{rxn}, T → ΔS_{surr} then ΔS_{rxn}, ΔS_{surr} → ΔS_{univ}

$\frac{1000\ J}{1\ kJ}$ $\qquad \Delta S_{surr} = \frac{-\Delta H_{sys}}{T}$ $\qquad \Delta S_{univ} = \Delta S_{sys} + \Delta S_{surr}$

Solution: $-115\ \cancel{kJ} \times \frac{1000\ J}{1\ \cancel{kJ}} = -115{,}000\ J$ then $\Delta S_{surr} = \frac{-\Delta H_{sys}}{T} = \frac{-(-115{,}000\ J)}{298\ K} = 38\underline{5}.906\ J/K$ then $\Delta S_{univ} = \Delta S_{sys} + \Delta S_{surr} = +263\ J/K + 38\underline{5}.906\ J/K = +649\ J/K$ so the reaction is spontaneous.
Check: The units (J/K) are correct. The magnitude of the answer (+650 J/K) makes sense because both terms were positive, so the reaction is spontaneous.

(c) **Given:** $\Delta H^\circ_{rxn} = -115$ kJ, $\Delta S_{rxn} = -263$ J/K, $T = 298$ K **Find:** ΔS_{univ} and spontaneity
Conceptual Plan: kJ → J then ΔH°_{rxn}, T → ΔS_{surr} then ΔS_{rxn}, ΔS_{surr} → ΔS_{univ}

$\frac{1000\ J}{1\ kJ}$ $\qquad \Delta S_{surr} = \frac{-\Delta H_{sys}}{T}$ $\qquad \Delta S_{univ} = \Delta S_{sys} + \Delta S_{surr}$

Solution: $-115\ \cancel{kJ} \times \frac{1000\ J}{1\ \cancel{kJ}} = -115{,}000\ J$ then $\Delta S_{surr} = \frac{-\Delta H_{sys}}{T} = \frac{-(-115{,}000\ J)}{298\ K} = +38\underline{5}.906\ J/K$ then $\Delta S_{univ} = \Delta S_{sys} + \Delta S_{surr} = -263\ J/K + 38\underline{5}.906\ J/K = +123\ J/K$ so the reaction is spontaneous.
Check: The units (J/K) are correct. The magnitude of the answer (120 J/K) makes sense because the larger term was positive, so the reaction is spontaneous.

(d) **Given:** $\Delta H^\circ_{rxn} = -115$ kJ, $\Delta S_{rxn} = -263$ J/K, $T = 615$ K **Find:** ΔS_{univ} and spontaneity
Conceptual Plan: kJ → J then ΔH°_{rxn}, T → ΔS_{surr} then ΔS_{rxn}, ΔS_{surr} → ΔS_{univ}

$\frac{1000\ J}{1\ kJ}$ $\qquad \Delta S_{surr} = \frac{-\Delta H_{sys}}{T}$ $\qquad \Delta S_{univ} = \Delta S_{sys} + \Delta S_{surr}$

Solution: $-115\ \cancel{kJ} \times \frac{1000\ J}{1\ \cancel{kJ}} = -115{,}000\ J$ then $\Delta S_{surr} = \frac{-\Delta H_{sys}}{T} = \frac{-(-115{,}000\ J)}{615\ K} = +18\underline{6}.992\ J/K$ then $\Delta S_{univ} = \Delta S_{sys} + \Delta S_{surr} = -263\ J/K + 18\underline{6}.992\ J/K = -76\ J/K$ so the reaction is nonspontaneous.
Check: The units (J/K) are correct. The magnitude of the answer (– 80 J/K) makes sense because the larger term was negative, so the reaction is nonspontaneous.

17.38 (a) **Given:** $\Delta H^\circ_{rxn} = -95$ kJ, $\Delta S_{rxn} = -157$ J/K, $T = 298$ K **Find:** ΔS_{univ} and spontaneity
Conceptual Plan: kJ → J then ΔH°_{rxn}, T → ΔS_{surr} then ΔS_{rxn}, ΔS_{surr} → ΔS_{univ}

$\frac{1000\ J}{1\ kJ}$ $\qquad \Delta S_{surr} = \frac{-\Delta H_{sys}}{T}$ $\qquad \Delta S_{univ} = \Delta S_{sys} + \Delta S_{surr}$

Solution: $-95\ \cancel{kJ} \times \frac{1000\ J}{1\ \cancel{kJ}} = +95{,}000\ J$ then $\Delta S_{surr} = \frac{-\Delta H_{sys}}{T} = \frac{-(-95{,}000\ J)}{298\ K} = +3\underline{1}8.79\ J/K$ then

$\Delta S_{univ} = \Delta S_{sys} + \Delta S_{surr} = -157\ J/K + 3\underline{1}8.79\ J/K = +1\underline{6}2\ J/K = +1.6 \times 10^2\ J/K$ so the reaction is spontaneous.

Check: The units (J/K) are correct. The magnitude of the answer (+ 160 J/K) makes sense because the surroundings gain more entropy than the system loses, so the reaction is spontaneous.

(b) **Given:** $\Delta H^\circ_{rxn} = -95$ kJ, $\Delta S_{rxn} = -157$ J/K, $T = 855$ K **Find:** ΔS_{univ} and spontaneity
Conceptual Plan: kJ → J then ΔH°_{rxn}, T → ΔS_{surr} then ΔS_{rxn}, ΔS_{surr} → ΔS_{univ}

$\frac{1000\ J}{1\ kJ}$ $\qquad \Delta S_{surr} = \frac{-\Delta H_{sys}}{T}$ $\qquad \Delta S_{univ} = \Delta S_{sys} + \Delta S_{surr}$

Solution: $-95\ \text{kJ} \times \dfrac{1000\ \text{J}}{1\ \text{kJ}} = +95{,}000\ \text{J}$ then $\Delta S_{surr} = \dfrac{-\Delta H_{sys}}{T} = \dfrac{-(-95{,}000\ \text{J})}{855\ \text{K}} = +111.11\ \text{J/K}$ then $\Delta S_{univ} = \Delta S_{sys} + \Delta S_{surr} = -157\ \text{J/K} + 111.11\ \text{J/K} = -46\ \text{J/K} = -5 \times 10^{1}\ \text{J/K}$ so the reaction is nonspontaneous.

Check: The units (J/K) are correct. The magnitude of the answer (–50 J/K) makes sense because at a higher temperature, the entropy of the surroundings is reduced, so that the entropy reduction of the system dominates and the reaction is nonspontaneous.

(c) **Given:** $\Delta H^\circ_{rxn} = +95$ kJ, $\Delta S_{rxn} = -157$ J/K, $T = 298$ K **Find:** ΔS_{univ} and spontaneity

Conceptual Plan: kJ → J then ΔH°_{rxn}, T → ΔS_{surr} then ΔS_{rxn}, ΔS_{surr} → ΔS_{univ}

$\dfrac{1000\ \text{J}}{1\ \text{kJ}}$ $\quad \Delta S_{surr} = \dfrac{-\Delta H_{sys}}{T} \quad \Delta S_{univ} = \Delta S_{sys} + \Delta S_{surr}$

Solution: $+95\ \text{kJ} \times \dfrac{1000\ \text{J}}{1\ \text{kJ}} = +95{,}000\ \text{J}$ then $\Delta S_{surr} = \dfrac{-\Delta H_{sys}}{T} = \dfrac{-95{,}000\ \text{J}}{298\ \text{K}} = -318.79\ \text{J/K}$ then

$\Delta S_{univ} = \Delta S_{sys} + \Delta S_{surr} = -157\ \text{J/K} - 318.79\ \text{J/K} = -476\ \text{J/K} = -4.8 \times 10^{2}\ \text{J/K}$ so the reaction nonspontaneous.

Check: The units (J/K) are correct. The magnitude of the answer (− 480 J/K) makes sense because both terms are negative, so the sum is negative and the reaction is nonspontaneous.

(d) **Given:** $\Delta H^\circ_{rxn} = -95$ kJ, $\Delta S_{rxn} = +157$ J/K, $T = 398$ K **Find:** ΔS_{univ} and spontaneity

Conceptual Plan: kJ → J then ΔH°_{rxn}, T → ΔS_{surr} then ΔS_{rxn}, ΔS_{surr} → ΔS_{univ}

$\dfrac{1000\ \text{J}}{1\ \text{kJ}}$ $\quad \Delta S_{surr} = \dfrac{-\Delta H_{sys}}{T} \quad \Delta S_{univ} = \Delta S_{sys} + \Delta S_{surr}$

Solution: $-95\ \text{kJ} \times \dfrac{1000\ \text{J}}{1\ \text{kJ}} = -95{,}000\ \text{J}$ then $\Delta S_{surr} = \dfrac{-\Delta H_{sys}}{T} = \dfrac{-(-95{,}000\ \text{J})}{398\ \text{K}} = +238.69\ \text{J/K}$

then $\Delta S_{univ} = \Delta S_{sys} + \Delta S_{surr} = +157\ \text{J/K} + 238.69\ \text{J/K} = +396\ \text{J/K} = +4.0 \times 10^{2}\ \text{J/K}$ so the reaction is spontaneous.

Check: The units (J/K) are correct. The magnitude of the answer (400 J/K) makes sense because both terms are positive, so the sum is positive and the reaction is spontaneous.

Standard Entropy Changes and Gibbs Free Energy

17.39 (a) **Given:** $\Delta H^\circ_{rxn} = +115$ kJ, $\Delta S_{rxn} = -263$ J/K, $T = 298$ K **Find:** ΔG and spontaneity

Conceptual Plan: J/K → kJ/K then ΔH°_{rxn}, ΔS_{rxn}, T → ΔG

$\dfrac{1000\ \text{J}}{1\ \text{kJ}}$ $\quad \Delta G = \Delta H_{rxn} - T\Delta S_{rxn}$

Solution: $-263\ \dfrac{\text{J}}{\text{K}} \times \dfrac{1\ \text{kJ}}{1000\ \text{J}} = -0.263\ \text{kJ/K}$ then

$$\Delta G = \Delta H_{rxn} - T\Delta S_{rxn} = +115\ \text{kJ} - (298\ \text{K})\left(-0.263\ \frac{\text{kJ}}{\text{K}}\right) = +1.93 \times 10^{2}\ \text{kJ} = +1.93 \times 10^{5}\ \text{J}$$

so the reaction is nonspontaneous.

Check: The units (kJ) are correct. The magnitude of the answer (+ 190 kJ) makes sense because both terms were positive, so the reaction is nonspontaneous.

(b) **Given:** $\Delta H^\circ_{rxn} = -115$ kJ, $\Delta S_{rxn} = +263$ J/K, $T = 298$ K **Find:** ΔG and spontaneity

Conceptual Plan: J/K → kJ/K then ΔH°_{rxn}, ΔS_{rxn}, T → ΔG

$\dfrac{1000\ \text{J}}{1\ \text{kJ}}$ $\quad \Delta G = \Delta H_{rxn} - T\Delta S_{rxn}$

Solution: $+263\ \dfrac{\text{J}}{\text{K}} \times \dfrac{1\ \text{kJ}}{1000\ \text{J}} = +0.263\ \text{kJ/K}$ then

$$\Delta G = \Delta H_{rxn} - T\Delta S_{rxn} = -115\ \text{kJ} - (298\ \text{K})\left(0.263\ \frac{\text{kJ}}{\text{K}}\right) = -193\ \text{kJ} = -1.93 \times 10^{2}\ \text{kJ} = -1.93 \times 10^{5}\ \text{J}$$

so the reaction is spontaneous.

Check: The units (kJ) are correct. The magnitude of the answer (–190 kJ) makes sense because both terms were negative, so the reaction is spontaneous.

(c) **Given:** $\Delta H^{\circ}_{rxn} = -115$ kJ, $\Delta S_{rxn} = -263$ J/K, $T = 298$ K **Find:** ΔG and spontaneity

Conceptual Plan: **J/K → kJ/K then ΔH°_{rxn}, ΔS_{rxn}, T → ΔG**

$$\frac{1000\text{ J}}{1\text{ kJ}} \qquad \Delta G = \Delta H_{rxn} - T\Delta S_{rxn}$$

Solution: $-263\frac{\text{J}}{\text{K}} \times \frac{1\text{ kJ}}{1000\text{ J}} = -0.263$ kJ/K then $\Delta G = \Delta H_{rxn} - T\Delta S_{rxn} =$

$$-115\text{ kJ} - (298\text{ K})\left(-0.263\frac{\text{kJ}}{\text{K}}\right) = -36.626\text{ kJ} = -3.7 \times 10^{1}\text{ kJ} = -3.7 \times 10^{4}\text{ J}$$ so the reaction is spontaneous.

Check: The units (kJ) are correct. The magnitude of the answer (–40 kJ) makes sense because the larger term was negative, so the reaction is spontaneous.

(d) **Given:** $\Delta H^{\circ}_{rxn} = -115$ kJ, $\Delta S_{rxn} = -263$ J/K, $T = 615$ K **Find:** ΔG and spontaneity

Conceptual Plan: **J/K → kJ/K then ΔH°_{rxn}, ΔS_{rxn}, T → ΔG**

$$\frac{1000\text{ J}}{1\text{ kJ}} \qquad \Delta G = \Delta H_{rxn} - T\Delta S_{rxn}$$

Solution: $-263\frac{\text{J}}{\text{K}} \times \frac{1\text{ kJ}}{1000\text{ J}} = -0.263$ kJ/K then

$$\Delta G = \Delta H_{rxn} - T\Delta S_{rxn} = -115\text{ kJ} - (615\text{ K})\left(-0.263\frac{\text{kJ}}{\text{K}}\right) = +47\text{ kJ} = +4.7 \times 10^{4}\text{ J}$$ so the reaction is nonspontaneous.

Check: The units (J/K) are correct. The magnitude of the answer (+ 47 kJ) makes sense because the larger term was positive, so the reaction is nonspontaneous.

17.40 (a) **Given:** $\Delta H^{\circ}_{rxn} = -95$ kJ, $\Delta S_{rxn} = -157$ J/K, $T = 298$ K **Find:** ΔG and spontaneity

Conceptual Plan: **J/K → kJ/K then ΔH°_{rxn}, ΔS_{rxn}, T → ΔG**

$$\frac{1\text{ kJ}}{1000\text{ J}} \qquad \Delta G = \Delta H_{rxn} - T\Delta S_{rxn}$$

Solution: $-157\frac{\text{J}}{\text{K}} \times \frac{1\text{ kJ}}{1000\text{ J}} = -0.157$ kJ/K then

$$\Delta G = \Delta H_{rxn} - T\Delta S_{rxn} = -95\text{ kJ} - (298\text{ K})\left(-0.157\frac{\text{kJ}}{\text{K}}\right) = -48\text{ kJ}$$ so the reaction is spontaneous.

Check: The units (kJ) are correct. The magnitude of the answer (– 50 kJ) makes sense because the negative enthalpy dominates over the entropy term, so the reaction is spontaneous.

(b) **Given:** $\Delta H^{\circ}_{rxn} = -95$ kJ, $\Delta S_{rxn} = -157$ J/K, $T = 855$ K **Find:** ΔG and spontaneity

Conceptual Plan: **J/K → kJ/K then ΔH°_{rxn}, ΔS_{rxn}, T → ΔG**

$$\frac{1\text{ kJ}}{1000\text{ J}} \qquad \Delta G = \Delta H_{rxn} - T\Delta S_{rxn}$$

Solution: $-157\frac{\text{J}}{\text{K}} \times \frac{1\text{ kJ}}{1000\text{ J}} = -0.157$ kJ/K then

$$\Delta G = \Delta H_{rxn} - T\Delta S_{rxn} = -95\text{ kJ} - (855\text{ K})\left(-0.157\frac{\text{kJ}}{\text{K}}\right) = +39\text{ kJ}$$ so the reaction is nonspontaneous.

Check: The units (kJ) are correct. The magnitude of the answer (+ 40 kJ) makes sense because at a higher temperature, the entropy term now dominates and the reaction is nonspontaneous.

(c) **Given:** $\Delta H^{\circ}_{rxn} = +95$ kJ, $\Delta S_{rxn} = -157$ J/K, $T = 298$ K **Find:** ΔG and spontaneity

Conceptual Plan: **J/K → kJ/K then ΔH°_{rxn}, ΔS_{rxn}, T → ΔG**

$$\frac{1\text{ kJ}}{1000\text{ J}} \qquad \Delta G = \Delta H_{rxn} - T\Delta S_{rxn}$$

Solution: $-157\frac{\text{J}}{\text{K}} \times \frac{1\text{ kJ}}{1000\text{ J}} = -0.157$ kJ/K then

$$\Delta G = \Delta H_{rxn} - T\Delta S_{rxn} = +95\text{ kJ} - (298\text{ K})\left(-0.157\frac{\text{kJ}}{\text{K}}\right) = +142\text{ kJ}$$ so the reaction is nonspontaneous.

Check: The units (kJ) are correct. The magnitude of the answer (+ 140 kJ) makes sense because both terms are positive, so the sum is positive and the reaction is nonspontaneous.

(d) **Given:** $\Delta H^\circ_{rxn} = -95$ kJ, $\Delta S_{rxn} = +157$ J/K, $T = 398$ K **Find:** ΔG and spontaneity
Conceptual Plan: **J/K → kJ/K then $\Delta H^\circ_{rxn}, \Delta S_{rxn}, T \rightarrow \Delta G$**

$\frac{1\text{ kJ}}{1000\text{ J}}$ $\qquad$ $\Delta G = \Delta H_{rxn} - T\Delta S_{rxn}$

Solution: $+157\frac{\text{J}}{\text{K}} \times \frac{1\text{ kJ}}{1000\text{ J}} = +0.157\frac{\text{kJ}}{\text{K}}$ then

$$\Delta G = \Delta H_{rxn} - T\Delta S_{rxn} = -95\text{ kJ} - (398\text{ K})\left(0.157\frac{\text{kJ}}{\text{K}}\right) = -157\text{ kJ}$$ so the reaction is spontaneous.

Check: The units (kJ) are correct. The magnitude of the answer (– 160 kJ) makes sense because both terms are negative, so the sum is negative and the reaction is spontaneous.

17.41 **Given:** $\Delta H^\circ_{rxn} = -2217$ kJ, $\Delta S_{rxn} = +101.1$ J/K, $T = 25$ °C **Find:** ΔG and spontaneity
Conceptual Plan: **°C → K then J/K → kJ/K then $\Delta H^\circ_{rxn}, \Delta S_{rxn}, T \rightarrow \Delta G$**

$K = 273.15 + °C$ $\qquad$ $\frac{1\text{ kJ}}{1000\text{ J}}$ $\qquad$ $\Delta G = \Delta H_{rxn} - T\Delta S_{rxn}$

Solution: $T = 273.15 + 25\text{ °C} = 298$ K then $+101.1\frac{\text{J}}{\text{K}} \times \frac{1\text{ kJ}}{1000\text{ J}} = +0.1011\frac{\text{kJ}}{\text{K}}$ then

$$\Delta G = \Delta H_{rxn} - T\Delta S_{rxn} = -2217\text{ kJ} - (298\text{ K})\left(0.1011\frac{\text{kJ}}{\text{K}}\right) = -2247\text{ kJ} = -2.247 \times 10^6\text{ J}$$

so the reaction is spontaneous.

Check: The units (kJ) are correct. The magnitude of the answer (– 2250 kJ) makes sense because both terms are negative, so the reaction is spontaneous.

17.42 **Given:** $\Delta H^\circ_{rxn} = -1269{,}8$ kJ, $\Delta S_{rxn} = -364.6$ J/K, $T = 25$ °C **Find:** ΔG and spontaneity
Conceptual Plan: **°C → K then J/K → kJ/K then $\Delta H^\circ_{rxn}, \Delta S_{rxn}, T \rightarrow \Delta G$**

$K = 273.15 + °C$ $\qquad$ $\frac{1\text{ kJ}}{1000\text{ J}}$ $\qquad$ $\Delta G = \Delta H_{rxn} - T\Delta S_{rxn}$

Solution: $T = 273.15 + 25\text{ °C} = 298$ K then $-364.6\frac{\text{J}}{\text{K}} \times \frac{1\text{ kJ}}{1000\text{ J}} = -0.3646\frac{\text{kJ}}{\text{K}}$ then

$$\Delta G = \Delta H_{rxn} - T\Delta S_{rxn} = -1269.8\text{ kJ} - (298\text{ K})\left(-0.3646\frac{\text{kJ}}{\text{K}}\right) = -1161.1\text{ kJ} = -1.161 \times 10^6\text{ J}$$

so the reaction is spontaneous.

Check: The units (kJ) are correct. The magnitude of the answer (– 1200 kJ) makes sense because the negative enthalpy term dominates over the positive entropy term, so the reaction is spontaneous.

17.43

ΔH	ΔS	ΔG	**Low Temp.**	**High Temp.**
–	+	–	Spontaneous	Spontaneous
–	–	Temp. dependent	Spontaneous	Nonspontaneous
+	+	Temp. dependent	Nonspontaneous	Spontaneous
+	–	+	Nonspontaneous	Nonspontaneous

17.44 (a) ΔH°_{rxn} for a condensation is negative and ΔS_{rxn} is negative, so the reaction will be spontaneous at low temperatures (< 100 °C).

(b) ΔH°_{rxn} for a sublimation is positive and ΔS_{rxn} is positive, so the reaction will be spontaneous at high temperatures (> – 78.5 °C).

(c) ΔH°_{rxn} for a bond breaking is positive and ΔS_{rxn} is positive, so the reaction will be spontaneous at high temperatures.

(d) ΔH°_{rxn} is positive and ΔS_{rxn} is positive, so the reaction will be spontaneous at high temperatures.

17.45 The molar entropy of a substance increases with increasing temperatures. The kinetic energy and the molecular motion increases. The substance will have access to an increased number of energy levels.

17.46 The third law of thermodynamics states that the entropy of a perfect crystal at absolute zero (0 K) is zero. For enthalpy we defined a standard state so that we could define a "zero" for the scale. This is not necessary for entropy because there is an absolute zero for the entropy scale.

17.47 (a) CO_2 (*g*) because it has greater molar mass/complexity.

(b) CH_3OH (*g*) because it is in the gas phase.

(c) CO_2 (*g*) because it has greater molar mass/complexity.

(d) SiH_4 (*g*) because it has greater molar mass.

(e) $CH_3CH_2CH_3$ (*g*) because it has greater molar mass/complexity.

(f) NaBr (*aq*) because a solution has more entropy than a solid crystal.

17.48 (a) $NaNO_3$ (*aq*) because a solution has more entropy than a solid crystal.

(b) CH_3CH_3 (*g*) because it has greater molar mass/complexity.

(c) Br_2 (*g*) because it is in the gas phase.

(d) Br_2 (*g*) because it has greater molar mass.

(e) PCl_5 (*g*) because it has greater molar mass/complexity.

(f) $CH_3CH_2CH_2CH_3$ (*g*) because it has greater complexity.

17.49 (a) He (*g*) < Ne (*g*) < SO_2 (*g*) < NH_3 (*g*) < CH_3CH_2OH (*g*). All are in the gas phase. From He to Ne there is an increase in molar mass, beyond that, the molecules increase in complexity.

(b) H_2O (*s*) < H_2O (*l*) < H_2O (*g*). Entropy increases as we go from a solid to a liquid to a gas.

(c) CH_4 (*g*) < CF_4 (*g*) < CCl_4 (*g*). Entropy increases as the molar mass increases.

17.50 (a) F_2 (*g*) < Cl_2 (*g*) < Br_2 (*g*) < I_2 (*g*). All are in the gas phase. Entropy increases as the molar mass increases.

(b) H_2O (*g*) < H_2S (*g*) < H_2O_2 (*g*). Entropy increases as the molar mass and the complexity of the molecules increases.

(c) C (*s*, diamond) < C (*s*, graphite) < C (*s*, amorphous). Entropy increases as the complexity increases. The diamond structure is ordered in all three dimensions. Graphite has ordered sheets that can slide with respect to each other. The amorphous carbon has no long range order.

17.51 (a) **Given:** C_2H_4 (*g*) + H_2 (*g*) → C_2H_6 (*g*) **Find:** ΔS°_{rxn}

Conceptual Plan: $\Delta S^\circ_{rxn} = \sum n_p S^\circ(\text{products}) - \sum n_r S^\circ(\text{reactants})$

Solution:

Reactant/Product	S°(J/mol K from Appendix IIB)
C_2H_4 (*g*)	219.3
H_2 (*g*)	130.7
C_2H_6 (*g*)	229.2

Be sure to pull data for the correct formula and phase.

$$\begin{aligned}\Delta S^\circ_{rxn} &= \sum n_p S^\circ(\text{products}) - \sum n_r S^\circ(\text{reactants})\\ &= [1(S^\circ(C_2H_6\,(g))] - [1(S^\circ(C_2H_4\,(g)) + 1(S^\circ(H_2\,(g))]\\ &= [1(229.2\text{ J/K})] - [1(219.3\text{ J/K}) + 1(130.7\text{ J/K})]\\ &= [229.2\text{ J/K}] - [350.0\text{ J/K}]\\ &= -120.8\text{ J/K}\end{aligned}$$

The moles of gas are decreasing.

Check: The units (J/K) are correct. The answer is negative, which is consistent with 2 moles of gas going to 1 mole of gas.

(b) **Given:** $C(s) + H_2O(g) \rightarrow CO(g) + H_2(g)$ **Find:** ΔS°_{rxn}
Conceptual Plan: $\Delta S^\circ_{rxn} = \sum n_p S^\circ(\text{products}) - \sum n_r S^\circ(\text{reactants})$
Solution:

Reactant/Product	S°(J/mol K from Appendix IIB)
$C(s)$	5.7
$H_2O(g)$	188.8
$CO(g)$	197.7
$H_2(g)$	130.7

Be sure to pull data for the correct formula and phase.

$$\begin{aligned}\Delta S^\circ_{rxn} &= \sum n_p S^\circ(\text{products}) - \sum n_r S^\circ(\text{reactants})\\ &= [1(S^\circ(CO(g)) + 1(S^\circ(H_2(g))] - [1(S^\circ(C(s)) + 1(S^\circ(H_2O(g))]\\ &= [1(197.7\ J/K) + 1(130.7\ J/K)] - [1(5.7\ J/K) + 1(188.8\ J/K)]\\ &= [328.4\ J/K] - [194.5\ J/K]\\ &= +133.9\ J/K\end{aligned}$$

The moles of gas are increasing.

Check: The units (J/K) are correct. The answer is positive, which is consistent with 1 mole of gas going to 1 mole of gas.

(c) **Given:** $CO(g) + H_2O(g) \rightarrow H_2(g) + CO_2(g)$ **Find:** ΔS°_{rxn}
Conceptual Plan: $\Delta S^\circ_{rxn} = \sum n_p S^\circ(\text{products}) - \sum n_r S^\circ(\text{reactants})$
Solution:

Reactant/Product	S°(J/mol K from Appendix IIB)
$CO(g)$	197.7
$H_2O(g)$	188.8
$H_2(g)$	130.7
$CO_2(g)$	213.8

Be sure to pull data for the correct formula and phase.

$$\begin{aligned}\Delta S^\circ_{rxn} &= \sum n_p S^\circ(\text{products}) - \sum n_r S^\circ(\text{reactants})\\ &= [1(S^\circ(H_2(g)) + 1(S^\circ(CO_2(g))] - [1(S^\circ(CO(g)) + 1(S^\circ(H_2O(g))]\\ &= [1(130.7\ J/K) + 1(213.8\ J/K)] - [1(197.7\ J/K) + 1(188.8\ J/K)]\\ &= [344.5\ J/K] - [386.5\ J/K]\\ &= -42.0\ J/K\end{aligned}$$

The change is small because the number of moles of gas is constant.
Check: The units (J/K) are correct. The answer is small and negative, which is consistent with a constant number of moles of gas. Water molecules are bent and carbon dioxide molecules are linear, so the water has more complexity. Also, carbon monoxide is more complex than hydrogen gas.

(d) **Given:** $2\ H_2S(g) + 3\ O_2(g) \rightarrow 2\ H_2O(l) + 2\ SO_2(g)$ **Find:** ΔS°_{rxn}
Conceptual Plan: $\Delta S^\circ_{rxn} = \sum n_p S^\circ(\text{products}) - \sum n_r S^\circ(\text{reactants})$
Solution:

Reactant/Product	S°(J/mol K from Appendix IIB)
$H_2S(g)$	205.8
$O_2(g)$	205.2
$H_2O(l)$	70.0
$SO_2(g)$	248.2

Be sure to pull data for the correct formula and phase.

$$\begin{aligned}\Delta S^\circ_{rxn} &= \sum n_p S^\circ(\text{products}) - \sum n_r S^\circ(\text{reactants})\\ &= [2(S^\circ(H_2O(l)) + 2(S^\circ(SO_2(g))] - [2(S^\circ(H_2S(g)) + 3(S^\circ(O_2(g))]\\ &= [2(70.0\ J/K) + 2(248.2\ J/K)] - [2(205.8\ J/K) + 3(205.2\ J/K)]\\ &= [636.4\ J/K] - [1027.2\ J/K]\\ &= -390.8\ J/K\end{aligned}$$

The number of moles of gas is decreasing.
Check: The units (J/K) are correct. The answer is negative, which is consistent with a decrease in the number of moles of gas.

17.52 (a) **Given:** $3\ NO_2\ (g) + H_2O\ (l) \rightarrow 2\ HNO_3\ (aq) + NO\ (g)$ **Find:** ΔS°_{rxn}

Conceptual Plan: $\Delta S^\circ_{rxn} = \sum n_p S^\circ(\text{products}) - \sum n_r S^\circ(\text{reactants})$

Solution:

Reactant/Product	S°(J/mol K from Appendix IIB)
$NO_2\ (g)$	240.1
$H_2O\ (l)$	70.0
$HNO_3\ (aq)$	146
$NO\ (g)$	210.8

Be sure to pull data for the correct formula and phase.

$$\begin{aligned}\Delta S^\circ_{rxn} &= \sum n_p S^\circ(\text{products}) - \sum n_r S^\circ(\text{reactants})\\ &= [2(S^\circ(HNO_3\ (aq)) + 1(S^\circ(NO\ (g))] - [3(S^\circ(NO_2\ (g)) + 1(S^\circ(H_2O\ (l))]\\ &= [2(146\ J/K) + 1(210.8\ J/K)] - [3(240.1\ J/K) + 1(70.0\ J/K)]\\ &= [50\underline{2}.8\ J/K] - [790.3\ J/K]\\ &= -288\ J/K\end{aligned}$$

The number of moles of gas is decreasing.

Check: The units (J/K) are correct. The answer is negative, which is consistent with a decrease in the number of moles of gas.

(b) **Given:** $Cr_2O_3\ (s) + 3\ CO\ (g) \rightarrow 2\ Cr\ (s) + 3\ CO_2\ (g)$ **Find:** ΔS°_{rxn}

Conceptual Plan: $\Delta S^\circ_{rxn} = \sum n_p S^\circ(\text{products}) - \sum n_r S^\circ(\text{reactants})$

Solution:

Reactant/Product	S°(J/mol K from Appendix IIB)
$Cr_2O_3\ (s)$	81.2
$CO\ (g)$	197.7
$Cr\ (s)$	23.8
$CO_2\ (g)$	213.8

Be sure to pull data for the correct formula and phase.

$$\begin{aligned}\Delta S^\circ_{rxn} &= \sum n_p S^\circ(\text{products}) - \sum n_r S^\circ(\text{reactants})\\ &= [2(S^\circ(Cr\ (s)) + 3(S^\circ(CO_2\ (g))] - [1(S^\circ(Cr_2O_3\ (s)) + 3(S^\circ(CO\ (g))]\\ &= [2(23.8\ J/K) + 3(213.8\ J/K)] - [1(81.2\ J/K) + 3(197.7\ J/K)]\\ &= [689.0\ J/K] - [674.3\ J/K]\\ &= +14.7\ J/K\end{aligned}$$

The change is small because the number of moles of gas is constant.

Check: The units (J/K) are correct. The answer is small and positive, which is consistent with a constant number of moles of gas. Carbon dioxide molecules have more complexity than carbon monoxide molecules, but the chromium oxide is more complex than chromium metal.

(c) **Given:** $SO_2\ (g) + \frac{1}{2}\ O_2\ (g) \rightarrow SO_3\ (g)$ **Find:** ΔS°_{rxn}

Conceptual Plan: $\Delta S^\circ_{rxn} = \sum n_p S^\circ(\text{products}) - \sum n_r S^\circ(\text{reactants})$

Solution:

Reactant/Product	S°(J/mol K from Appendix IIB)
$SO_2\ (g)$	248.2
$O_2\ (g)$	205.2
$SO_3\ (g)$	256.8

Be sure to pull data for the correct formula and phase.

$$\begin{aligned}\Delta S^\circ_{rxn} &= \sum n_p S^\circ(\text{products}) - \sum n_r S^\circ(\text{reactants})\\ &= [1(S^\circ(SO_3\ (g))] - [1(S^\circ(SO_2\ (g)) + 1/2(S^\circ(O_2\ (g))]\\ &= [1(256.8\ J/K)] - [1(248.2\ J/K) + 1/2(205.2\ J/K)]\\ &= [256.8\ J/K] - [350.8\ J/K]\\ &= -94.0\ J/K\end{aligned}$$

The number of moles of gas is decreasing.

Check: The units (J/K) are correct. The answer is negative, which is consistent with a decrease in the number of moles of gas.

(d) **Given:** N_2O_4 (*g*) + 4 H_2 (*g*) → N_2 (*g*) + 4 H_2O (*g*) **Find:** ΔS°_{rxn}
Conceptual Plan: $\Delta S^\circ_{rxn} = \sum n_p S^\circ(\text{products}) - \sum n_r S^\circ(\text{reactants})$
Solution:

Reactant/Product	S°(J/mol K from Appendix IIB)
N_2O_4 (*g*)	304.4
H_2 (*g*)	130.7
N_2 (*g*)	191.6
H_2O (*g*)	188.8

Be sure to pull data for the correct formula and phase.

$$\begin{aligned}\Delta S^\circ_{rxn} &= \sum n_p S^\circ(\text{products}) - \sum n_r S^\circ(\text{reactants})\\ &= [1(S^\circ(N_2\ (g)) + 4(S^\circ(H_2O\ (g))] - [1(S^\circ(N_2O_4\ (g)) + 4(S^\circ(H_2\ (g))]\\ &= [1(191.6\ \text{J/K}) + 4(188.8\ \text{J/K})] - [1(304.4\ \text{J/K}) + 4(130.7\ \text{J/K})]\\ &= [946.8\ \text{J/K}] - [827.2\ \text{J/K}]\\ &= +119.6\ \text{J/K}\end{aligned}$$

The change is small because the number of moles of gas is constant.
Check: The units (J/K) are correct. The answer is positive, which is consistent with 1 mole of a complex gas and 4 moles of a simple gas going to 1 mole of a simple gas and 4 moles of a complex gas.

17.53 **Given:** CH_2Cl_2 (*g*) formed from elements in standard states **Find:** ΔS° and rationalize sign
Conceptual Plan: Write a balanced reaction, then $\Delta S^\circ_{rxn} = \sum n_p S^\circ(\text{products}) - \sum n_r S^\circ(\text{reactants})$
Solution: C (*s*) + H_2 (*g*) + Cl_2 (*g*) → CH_2Cl_2 (*g*)

Reactant/Product	S°(J/mol K from Appendix IIB)
C (*s*)	5.7
H_2 (*g*)	130.7
Cl_2 (*g*)	223.1
CH_2Cl_2 (*g*)	270.2

Be sure to pull data for the correct formula and phase.

$$\begin{aligned}\Delta S^\circ_{rxn} &= \sum n_p S^\circ(\text{products}) - \sum n_r S^\circ(\text{reactants})\\ &= [1(S^\circ(CH_2Cl_2\ (g))] - [1(S^\circ(C\ (s)) + 1(S^\circ(H_2\ (g)) + 1(S^\circ(Cl_2\ (g))]\\ &= [1(270.2\ \text{J/K})] - [1(5.7\ \text{J/K}) + 1(130.7\ \text{J/K}) + 1(223.1\ \text{J/K})]\\ &= [270.2\ \text{J/K}] - [359.5\ \text{J/K}]\\ &= -89.3\ \text{J/K}\end{aligned}$$

The moles of gas are decreasing.
Check: The units (J/K) are correct. The answer is negative, which is consistent with 2 moles of gas going to 1 mole of gas.

17.54 **Given:** NF_3 (*g*) formed from elements in standard states **Find:** ΔS° and rationalize sign
Conceptual Plan: Write balanced reaction, then $\Delta S^\circ_{rxn} = \sum n_p S^\circ(\text{products}) - \sum n_r S^\circ(\text{reactants})$.
Solution: $\frac{1}{2}$ N_2 (*g*) + 3/2 F_2 (*g*) → NF_3 (*g*)

Reactant/Product	S°(J/mol K from Appendix IIB)
N_2 (*g*)	191.6
F_2 (*g*)	202.79
NF_3 (*g*)	260.8

Be sure to pull data for the correct formula and phase.

$$\begin{aligned}\Delta S^\circ_{rxn} &= \sum n_p S^\circ(\text{products}) - \sum n_r S^\circ(\text{reactants})\\ &= [1(S^\circ(NF_3\ (g))] - [1/2(S^\circ(N_2\ (g)) + 3/2(S^\circ(F_2\ (g))]\\ &= [1(260.8\ \text{J/K})] - [1/2(191.6\ \text{J/K}) + 3/2(202.79\ \text{J/K})]\\ &= [260.8\ \text{J/K}] - [399.\underline{9}85\ \text{J/K}]\\ &= -139.2\ \text{J/K}\end{aligned}$$

The moles of gas are decreasing.

Check: The units (J/K) are correct. The answer is negative, which is consistent with 2 moles of simple gases going to 1 mole of a complex gas.

17.55 **Given:** methanol (CH_3OH) combustion at 25 °C **Find:** ΔH°_{rxn}, ΔS°_{rxn}, ΔG°_{rxn}, and sponteneity
Conceptual Plan: Write a balanced reaction then $\Delta H^\circ_{rxn} = \sum n_p H^\circ_f(\text{products}) - \sum n_r H^\circ_f(\text{reactants})$ **then** $\Delta S^\circ_{rxn} = \sum n_p S^\circ(\text{products}) - \sum n_r S^\circ(\text{reactants})$ **then °C → K then J/K → kJ/K then**

K = 273.15 + °C $\quad \frac{1\ kJ}{1000\ J}$

$\Delta H^\circ_{rxn}, \Delta S^\circ_{rxn}, T \rightarrow \Delta G^\circ$.

$\Delta G = \Delta H_{rxn} - T\Delta S_{rxn}$

Solution: Combustion is combined with oxygen to form carbon dioxide and water.
$2\ CH_3OH\ (l) + 3\ O_2\ (g) \rightarrow 2\ CO_2\ (g) + 4\ H_2O\ (g)$

Reactant/Product	ΔH°_f(kJ/mol from Appendix IIB)
CH_3OH (*l*)	− 238.6
O_2 (*g*)	0.0
CO_2 (*g*)	− 393.5
H_2O (*g*)	− 241.8

Be sure to pull data for the correct formula and phase.

$$\begin{aligned}\Delta H^\circ_{rxn} &= \Sigma n_p \Delta H^\circ_f(\text{products}) - \Sigma n_r \Delta H^\circ_f(\text{reactants})\\ &= [2(\Delta H^\circ_f(CO_2(g))) + 4(\Delta H^\circ_f(H_2O(g)))] - [2(\Delta H^\circ_f(CH_3OH(l))) + 3(\Delta H^\circ_f(O_2(g)))]\\ &= [2(-393.5\ kJ) + 4(-241.8\ kJ)] - [2(-238.6\ kJ) + 3(0.0\ kJ)]\\ &= [-1754.2\ kJ] - [-477.2\ kJ]\\ &= -1277\ kJ \text{ then}\end{aligned}$$

Reactant/Product	S°(J/mol K from Appendix IIB)
CH_3OH (*l*)	126.8
O_2 (*g*)	205.2
CO_2 (*g*)	213.8
H_2O (*g*)	188.8

Be sure to pull data for the correct formula and phase.

$$\begin{aligned}\Delta S^\circ_{rxn} &= \Sigma n_p S^\circ(\text{products}) - \Sigma n_r S^\circ(\text{reactants})\\ &= [2(S^\circ(CO_2(g))) + 4(S^\circ(H_2O(g)))] - [2(S^\circ(CH_3OH(l))) + 3(S^\circ(O_2(g)))]\\ &= [2(213.8\ J/K) + 4(188.8\ J/K)] - [2(126.8\ J/K) + 3(205.2\ J/K)]\\ &= [1182.8\ J/K] - [869.2\ J/K]\\ &= 313.6\ J/K\end{aligned}$$

then $T = 273.15 + 25\ °C = 298\ K$ then $+313.6 \frac{J}{K} \times \frac{1\ kJ}{1000\ J} = +0.3136\ kJ/K$ then

$\Delta G = \Delta H_{rxn} - T\Delta S_{rxn} = -1277\ kJ - (298\ K)\left(+0.3136 \frac{kJ}{K}\right) = -1370.\ kJ = -1.370 \times 10^6\ J$ so the reaction is spontaneous.

Check: The units (kJ, J/K, and kJ) are correct. Combustion reactions are exothermic and we see a large negative enthalpy. We expect a large positive entropy because we have an increase in the number of moles of gas. The free energy is the sum of two negative terms so we expect a large negative free energy and the reaction is spontaneous.

17.56 **Given:** form glucose ($C_6H_{12}O_6$) and oxygen from sunlight, carbon dioxide, and water at 25 °C
Find: ΔH°_{rxn}, ΔS°_{rxn}, ΔG°_{rxn}, and sponteneity
Conceptual Plan: Write a balanced reaction then $\Delta H^\circ_{rxn} = \sum n_p H^\circ_f(\text{products}) - \sum n_r H^\circ_f(\text{reactants})$ **then** $\Delta S^\circ_{rxn} = \sum n_p S^\circ(\text{products}) - \sum n_r S^\circ(\text{reactants})$ **then °C → K then J/K → kJ/K then** $\Delta H^\circ_{rxn}, \Delta S^\circ_{rxn}, T \rightarrow \Delta G^\circ$.

K = 273.15 + °C $\quad \frac{1\ kJ}{1000\ J} \quad \Delta G = \Delta H_{rxn} - T\Delta S_{rxn}$

Solution: $6\ CO_2\ (g) + 6\ H_2O\ (l) \rightarrow C_6H_{12}O_6\ (s) + 6\ O_2\ (g)$

Reactant/Product	ΔH°_f(kJ/mol from Appendix IIB)
CO_2 (*g*)	− 393.5
H_2O (*l*)	− 285.8
$C_6H_{12}O_6$ (*s*)	− 1273.3
O_2 (*g*)	0.0

Be sure to pull data for the correct formula and phase.

$$\Delta H^\circ_{rxn} = \sum n_p \Delta H^\circ_f(\text{products}) - \sum n_r \Delta H^\circ_f(\text{reactants})$$
$$= [1(\Delta H^\circ_f(C_6H_{12}O_6\ (s))) + 6(\Delta H^\circ_f(O_2\ (g)))\ ] - [6(\Delta H^\circ_f(CO_2\ (g))) + 6(\Delta H^\circ_f(H_2O\ (l)))]$$
$$= [\ 1(-1273.3\text{ kJ}) + 6(0.0\text{ kJ})\ ] - [6(-393.5\text{ kJ}) + 6(-285.8\text{ kJ})]$$
$$= [-1273.3\text{ kJ}] - [-4075.8\text{ kJ}]$$
$$= +2802.5\text{ kJ then}$$

Reactant/Product	S°(J/mol K from Appendix IIB)
$CO_2\ (g)$	213.8
$H_2O\ (l)$	70.0
$C_6H_{12}O_6\ (s)$	212.1
$O_2\ (g)$	205.2

Be sure to pull data for the correct formula and phase.

$$\Delta S^\circ_{rxn} = \sum n_p S^\circ(\text{products}) - \sum n_r S^\circ(\text{reactants})$$
$$= [1(S^\circ(C_6H_{12}O_6\ (s))) + 6(S^\circ(O_2\ (g)))\ ] - [6(S^\circ(CO_2\ (g))) + 6(S^\circ(H_2O\ (l)))]$$
$$= [1(212.1\text{ J/K}) + 6(205.2\text{ J/K})\ ] - [6(213.8\text{ J/K}) + 6(70.0\text{ J/K})]$$
$$= [1443.3\text{ J/K}] - [1702.8\text{ J/K}]$$
$$= -259.5\text{ J/K}$$

then $T = 273.15 + 25\text{ °C} = 298\text{ K}$ then $-259.5\frac{\text{J}}{\text{K}} \times \frac{1\text{ kJ}}{1000\text{ J}} = -0.2595\text{ kJ/K}$ then

$\Delta G = \Delta H_{rxn} - T\Delta S_{rxn} = +2802.5\text{ kJ} - (298\text{ K})\left(-0.2595\frac{\text{kJ}}{\text{K}}\right) = +2879.8\text{ kJ} = +2.8798 \times 10^6\text{ J}$ so the reaction is nonspontaneous.

Check: The units (kJ, J/K, and kJ) are correct. The reaction requires the input of light energy, so we expect that this will be an endothermic reaction. We expect a negative entropy change because we are going from 6 moles of a gas and 6 moles of a liquid to 6 moles of a gas and 1 mole of a solid. The free energy is the sum of two positive terms so we expect a large positive free energy and the reaction is non-spontaneous. Photosynthesis does not happen on its own; light energy must be added to make the process move forward.

17.57 (a) **Given:** $N_2O_4\ (g) \rightarrow 2\ NO_2\ (g)$ at 25 °C

Find: ΔH°_{rxn}, ΔS°_{rxn}, ΔG°_{rxn}, spontaneity. Can temperature be changed to make it spontaneous?

Conceptual Plan: $\Delta H^\circ_{rxn} = \sum n_p H^\circ_f(\text{products}) - \sum n_r H^\circ_f(\text{reactants})$ **then**

$\Delta S^\circ_{rxn} = \sum n_p S^\circ(\text{products}) - \sum n_r S^\circ(\text{reactants})$ **then °C → K then J/K → kJ/K then**

$K = 273.15 + \text{°C}$ $\quad \frac{1\text{ kJ}}{1000\text{ J}}$

$\Delta H^\circ_{rxn}, \Delta S_{rxn}, T \rightarrow \Delta G$

$\Delta G = \Delta H_{rxn} - T\Delta S_{rxn}$

Solution:

Reactant/Product	ΔH°_f(kJ/mol from Appendix IIB)
$N_2O_4\ (g)$	11.1
$NO_2\ (g)$	33.2

Be sure to pull data for the correct formula and phase.

$$\Delta H^\circ_{rxn} = \sum n_p \Delta H^\circ_f(\text{products}) - \sum n_r \Delta H^\circ_f(\text{reactants})$$
$$= [2(\Delta H^\circ_f(NO_2\ (g)))\ ] - [1(\Delta H^\circ_f(N_2O_4\ (g)))]$$
$$= [\ 2(33.2\text{ kJ})\ ] - [1(11.1\text{ kJ})]$$
$$= [66.4\text{ kJ}] - [11.1\text{ kJ}]$$
$$= +55.3\text{ kJ then}$$

Reactant/Product	S°(J/mol K from Appendix IIB)
$N_2O_4\ (g)$	304.4
$NO_2\ (g)$	240.1

Be sure to pull data for the correct formula and phase.

$\Delta S^\circ_{rxn} = \sum n_p S^\circ(\text{products}) - \sum n_r S^\circ(\text{reactants})$
$= [2(S^\circ(NO_2\ (g)))] - [1(S^\circ(N_2O_4\ (g)))]$
$= [2(240.1\ J/K)] - [1(304.4\ J/K)]$
$= [480.2\ J/K] - [304.4\ J/K]$
$= +175.8\ J/K$ then $T = 273.15 + 25\ °C = 298\ K$ then

$+175.8 \frac{J}{K} \times \frac{1\ kJ}{1000\ J} = +0.1758\ kJ/K$ then

$\Delta G^\circ = \Delta H^\circ_{rxn} - T\Delta S^\circ_{rxn} = +55.3\ kJ - (298\ K)\left(+0.1758 \frac{kJ}{K}\right) = +2.9\ kJ = +2.9 \times 10^3\ J$ so

the reaction is nonspontaneous. It can be made spontaneous by raising the temperature.
Check: The units (kJ, J/K, and kJ) are correct. The reaction requires the breaking of a bond, so we expect that this will be an endothermic reaction. We expect a positive entropy change because we are increasing the number of moles of gas. Since the positive enthalpy term dominates at room temperature, the reaction is nonspontaneous. The second term can dominate if we raise the temperature high enough.

(b) **Given:** $NH_4Cl\ (s) \rightarrow HCl\ (g) + NH_3\ (g)$ at 25 °C
Find: ΔH°_{rxn}, ΔS°_{rxn}, ΔG°_{rxn}, spontaneity. Can temperature be changed to make it spontaneous?
Conceptual Plan: $\Delta H^\circ_{rxn} = \sum n_p H^\circ_f(\text{products}) - \sum n_r H^\circ_f(\text{reactants})$ **then**
$\Delta S^\circ_{rxn} = \sum n_p S^\circ(\text{products}) - \sum n_r S^\circ(\text{reactants})$ **then °C → K then J/K → kJ/K then**
$K = 273.15 + °C$ $\quad \frac{1\ kJ}{1000\ J}$

$\Delta H^\circ_{rxn}, \Delta S_{rxn}, T \rightarrow \Delta G$
$\Delta G = \Delta H_{rxn} - T\Delta S_{rxn}$

Solution:

Reactant/Product	ΔH°_f(kJ/mol from Appendix IIB)
$NH_4Cl\ (s)$	− 314.4
$HCl\ (g)$	− 92.3
$NH_3\ (g)$	− 45.9

Be sure to pull data for the correct formula and phase.
$\Delta H^\circ_{rxn} = \sum n_p \Delta H^\circ_f(\text{products}) - \sum n_r \Delta H^\circ_f(\text{reactants})$
$= [1(\Delta H^\circ_f(HCl\ (g))) + 1(\Delta H^\circ_f(NH_3\ (g)))] - [1(\Delta H^\circ_f(NH_4Cl\ (g)))]$
$= [1(-92.3\ kJ) + 1(-45.9\ kJ)] - [1(-314.4\ kJ)]$
$= [-138.2\ kJ] - [-314.4\ kJ]$
$= +176.2\ kJ$ then

Reactant/Product	S°(J/mol K from Appendix IIB)
$NH_4Cl\ (s)$	94.6
$HCl\ (g)$	186.9
$NH_3\ (g)$	192.8

Be sure to pull data for the correct formula and phase.
$\Delta S^\circ_{rxn} = \sum n_p S^\circ(\text{products}) - \sum n_r S^\circ(\text{reactants})$
$= [1(S^\circ(HCl\ (g))) + 1(S^\circ(NH_3\ (g)))] - [1(S^\circ(NH_4Cl\ (g)))]$
$= [1(186.9\ J/K) + 1(192.8\ J/K)] - [1(94.6\ J/K)]$
$= [379.7\ J/K] - [94.6\ J/K]$
$= +285.1\ J/K$

then $T = 273.15 + 25\ °C = 298\ K$ then $+285.1 \frac{J}{K} \times \frac{1\ kJ}{1000\ J} = +0.2851\ kJ/K$ then

$\Delta G^\circ = \Delta H^\circ_{rxn} - T\Delta S^\circ_{rxn} = +176.2\ kJ - (298\ K)\left(+0.2851 \frac{kJ}{K}\right) = +91.2\ kJ = +9.12 \times 10^4\ J$

so the reaction is nonspontaneous. It can be made spontaneous by raising the temperature.
Check: The units (kJ, J/K, and kJ) are correct. The reaction requires the breaking of a bond, so we expect that this will be an endothermic reaction. We expect a positive entropy change because we are increasing the number of moles of gas. Since the positive enthalpy term dominates at room temperature, the reaction is nonspontaneous. The second term can dominate if we raise the temperature high enough.

(c) **Given:** $3\ H_2\ (g) + Fe_2O_3\ (s) \rightarrow 2\ Fe\ (s) + 3\ H_2O\ (g)$ at 25 °C **Find:** ΔH°_{rxn}, ΔS°_{rxn}, ΔG°_{rxn}, spontaneity. Can temperature be changed to make it spontaneous?

Conceptual Plan: $\Delta H^\circ_{rxn} = \sum n_p H^\circ_f(\text{products}) - \sum n_r H^\circ_f(\text{reactants})$ **then**

$\Delta S^\circ_{rxn} = \sum n_p S^\circ(\text{products}) - \sum n_r S^\circ(\text{reactants})$ **then °C → K then J/K → kJ/K then**

$K = 273.15 + °C$ $\quad \frac{1\ kJ}{1000\ J}$

$\Delta H^\circ_{rxn}, \Delta S_{rxn}, T \rightarrow \Delta G$

$\Delta G = \Delta H_{rxn} - T\Delta S_{rxn}$

Solution:

Reactant/Product	ΔH°_f(kJ/mol from Appendix IIB)
$H_2\ (g)$	0.0
$Fe_2O_3\ (s)$	− 824.2
$Fe\ (s)$	0.0
$H_2O\ (g)$	− 241.8

Be sure to pull data for the correct formula and phase.

$$\begin{aligned}\Delta H^\circ_{rxn} &= \sum n_p \Delta H^\circ_f(\text{products}) - \sum n_r \Delta H^\circ_f(\text{reactants})\\ &= [2(\Delta H^\circ_f(Fe\ (s))) + 3(\Delta H^\circ_f(H_2O\ (g)))] - [3(\Delta H^\circ_f(H_2\ (g))) + 1(\Delta H^\circ_f(Fe_2O_3\ (s)))]\\ &= [2(0.0\ kJ) + 3(-241.8\ kJ)] - [3(0.0\ kJ) + 1(-824.2\ kJ)]\\ &= [-725.4\ kJ] - [-824.2\ kJ]\\ &= +98.8\ kJ \text{ then}\end{aligned}$$

Reactant/Product	S°(J/mol K from Appendix IIB)
$H_2\ (g)$	130.7
$Fe_2O_3\ (s)$	87.4
$Fe\ (s)$	27.3
$H_2O\ (g)$	188.8

Be sure to pull data for the correct formula and phase.

$$\begin{aligned}\Delta S^\circ_{rxn} &= \sum n_p S^\circ(\text{products}) - \sum n_r S^\circ(\text{reactants})\\ &= [2(S^\circ(Fe\ (s))) + 3(S^\circ(H_2O\ (g)))] - [3(S^\circ(H_2\ (g))) + 1(S^\circ(Fe_2O_3\ (s)))]\\ &= [2(27.3\ J/K) + 3(188.8\ J/K)] - [3(130.7\ J/K) + 1(87.4\ J/K)]\\ &= [621.0\ J/K] - [479.5\ J/K]\\ &= +141.5\ J/K\end{aligned}$$

then $T = 273.15 + 25\ °C = 298\ K$ then $+141.5 \frac{J}{K} \times \frac{1\ kJ}{1000\ J} = +0.1415\ kJ/K$ then

$$\Delta G^\circ = \Delta H^\circ_{rxn} - T\Delta S^\circ_{rxn} = +98.8\ kJ - (298\ K)\left(+0.1415 \frac{kJ}{K}\right) = +56.6\ kJ = +5.66 \times 10^4\ J$$

so the reaction is nonspontaneous. It can be made spontaneous by raising the temperature.

Check: The units (kJ, J/K, and kJ) are correct. The reaction requires the breaking of a bond, so we expect that this will be an endothermic reaction. We expect a positive entropy change because there is no change in the number of moles of gas, but the product gas is more complex. Since the positive enthalpy term dominates at room temperature, the reaction is nonspontaneous. The second term can dominate if we raise the temperature high enough. This process is the opposite of rusting, so we are not surprised that it is nonspontaneous.

(d) **Given:** $N_2\ (g) + 3\ H_2\ (g) \rightarrow 2\ NH_3\ (g)$ at 25 °C

Find: ΔH°_{rxn}, ΔS°_{rxn}, ΔG°_{rxn}, spontaneity. Can temperature be changed to make it spontaneous?

Conceptual Plan: $\Delta H^\circ_{rxn} = \sum n_p H^\circ_f(\text{products}) - \sum n_r H^\circ_f(\text{reactants})$ **then**

$\Delta S^\circ_{rxn} = \sum n_p S^\circ(\text{products}) - \sum n_r S^\circ(\text{reactants})$ **then °C → K then J/K → kJ/K then**

$K = 273.15 + °C$ $\quad \frac{1\ kJ}{1000\ J}$

$\Delta H^\circ_{rxn}, \Delta S_{rxn}, T \rightarrow \Delta G$

$\Delta G = \Delta H_{rxn} - T\Delta S_{rxn}$

Solution:

Reactant/Product	ΔH_f°(kJ/mol from Appendix IIB)
N_2 (g)	0.0
H_2 (g)	0.0
NH_3 (g)	− 45.9

Be sure to pull data for the correct formula and phase.

$$\begin{aligned}\Delta H^\circ_{rxn} &= \sum n_p \Delta H_f^\circ(\text{products}) - \sum n_r \Delta H_f^\circ(\text{reactants})\\ &= [\,2(\Delta H_f^\circ(NH_3\ (g)))\,] - [1(\Delta H_f^\circ(N_2\ (g))) + 3(\Delta H_f^\circ(H_2\ (g)))]\\ &= [2(-45.9\text{ kJ})] - [1(0.0\text{ kJ}) + 3(0.0\text{ kJ})]\\ &= [-91.8\text{ kJ}] - [0.0\text{ kJ}]\\ &= -91.8\text{ kJ then}\end{aligned}$$

Reactant/Product	S°(J/mol K from Appendix IIB)
N_2 (g)	191.6
H_2 (g)	130.7
NH_3 (g)	192.8

Be sure to pull data for the correct formula and phase.

$$\begin{aligned}\Delta S^\circ_{rxn} &= \sum n_p S^\circ(\text{products}) - \sum n_r S^\circ(\text{reactants})\\ &= [\,2(S^\circ(NH_3\ (g)))\,] - [1(S^\circ(N_2\ (g))) + 3(S^\circ(H_2\ (g)))]\\ &= [2(192.8\text{ J/K})] - [1(191.6\text{ J/K}) + 3(130.7\text{ J/K})]\\ &= [385.6\text{ J/K}] - [583.7\text{ J/K}]\\ &= -198.1\text{ J/K}\end{aligned}$$

then $T = 273.15 + 25\ °\text{C} = 298\text{ K}$ then $-198.1\frac{\text{J}}{\text{K}} \times \frac{1\text{ kJ}}{1000\text{ J}} = -0.1981\text{ kJ/K}$ then

$$\Delta G^\circ = \Delta H^\circ_{rxn} - T\Delta S^\circ_{rxn} = -91.8\text{ kJ} - (298\text{ K})\left(-0.1981\frac{\text{kJ}}{\text{K}}\right) = -32.8\text{ kJ} = -3.28 \times 10^4\text{ J so}$$

the reaction is spontaneous.

Check: The units (kJ, J/K, and kJ) are correct. The reaction requires the breaking of a bond, so we expect that this will be an endothermic reaction. We expect a positive entropy change because are increasing the number of moles of gas. Since the negative enthalpy term dominates at room temperature, the reaction is spontaneous. The second term can dominate if we raise the temperature high enough.

17.58 (a) **Given:** 2 CH_4 (g) → C_2H_6 (g) + H_2 (g) at 25 °C **Find:** ΔH°_{rxn}, ΔS°_{rxn}, ΔG°_{rxn}, spontaneity. Can temperature be changed to make it spontaneous?

Conceptual Plan: $\Delta H^\circ_{rxn} = \sum n_p H_f^\circ(\text{products}) - \sum n_r H_f^\circ(\text{reactants})$ **then**

$\Delta S^\circ_{rxn} = \sum n_p S^\circ(\text{products}) - \sum n_r S^\circ(\text{reactants})$ **then °C → K then J/K → kJ/K then**

$\text{K} = 273.15 + °\text{C}$ $\qquad \frac{1\text{ kJ}}{1000\text{ J}}$

$\Delta H^\circ_{rxn}, \Delta S_{rxn}, T \rightarrow \Delta G$

$\Delta G = \Delta H_{rxn} - T\Delta S_{rxn}$

Solution:

Reactant/Product	ΔH_f°(kJ/mol from Appendix IIB)
CH_4 (g)	− 74.6
C_2H_6 (g)	− 84.6
H_2 (g)	0.0

Be sure to pull data for the correct formula and phase.

$$\begin{aligned}\Delta H^\circ_{rxn} &= \sum n_p \Delta H_f^\circ(\text{products}) - \sum n_r \Delta H_f^\circ(\text{reactants})\\ &= [\,1(\Delta H_f^\circ(C_2H_6\ (g))) + 1(\Delta H_f^\circ(H_2\ (g)))] - [2(\Delta H_f^\circ(CH_4\ (g)))]\\ &= [1(-84.6\text{ kJ}) + 1(0.0\text{ kJ})] - [2(-74.6\text{ kJ})]\\ &= [-84.6\text{ kJ}] - [-149.2\text{ kJ}]\\ &= +64.6\text{ kJ then}\end{aligned}$$

Reactant/Product	S°(J/mol K from Appendix IIB)
CH_4 (*g*)	186.3
C_2H_6 (*g*)	229.2
H_2 (*g*)	130.7

Be sure to pull data for the correct formula and phase.

$$\begin{aligned}\Delta S^\circ_{rxn} &= \sum n_p S^\circ(\text{products}) - \sum n_r S^\circ(\text{reactants}) \\ &= [1(S^\circ(C_2H_6\ (g))) + 1(S^\circ(H_2\ (g)))] - [2(S^\circ(CH_4\ (g)))] \\ &= [1(229.2\ \text{J/K}) + 1(130.7\ \text{J/K})] - [2(186.3\ \text{J/K})] \\ &= [359.9\ \text{J/K}] - [372.6\ \text{J/K}] \\ &= -12.7\ \text{J/K}\end{aligned}$$

then $T = 273.15 + 25\ °C = 298$ K then $-12.7\frac{\text{J}}{\text{K}} \times \frac{1\ \text{kJ}}{1000\ \text{J}} = -0.0127$ kJ/K then

$$\Delta G^\circ = \Delta H^\circ_{rxn} - T\Delta S^\circ_{rxn} = +64.6\ \text{kJ} - (298\ \text{K})\left(-0.0127\frac{\text{kJ}}{\text{K}}\right) = +68.4\ \text{kJ} = +6.84 \times 10^4\ \text{J}$$

so the reaction is nonspontaneous. Since both terms are positive, this reaction cannot be spontaneous at any temperature.

Check: The units (kJ, J/K, and kJ) are correct. The 2 moles of methane have a lower enthalpy than 1 mole of ethane, so we expect that this will be an endothermic reaction. We expect a very small entropy change because the number of moles of gas is unchanged. Since both terms are positive, the reaction is nonspontaneous. Since both terms are positive, this reaction cannot be spontaneous at any temperature.

(b) **Given:** $2\ NH_3\ (g) \rightarrow N_2H_4\ (g) + H_2\ (g)$ at 25 °C

Find: ΔH°_{rxn}, ΔS°_{rxn}, ΔG°_{rxn}, spontaneity and can temperature be changed to make it spontaneous?

Conceptual Plan: $\Delta H^\circ_{rxn} = \sum n_p H^\circ_f(\text{products}) - \sum n_r H^\circ_f(\text{reactants})$ **then**

$\Delta S^\circ_{rxn} = \sum n_p S^\circ(\text{products}) - \sum n_r S^\circ(\text{reactants})$ **then °C → K then J/K → kJ/K then**

$K = 273.15 + °C$ $\qquad \frac{1\ \text{kJ}}{1000\ \text{J}}$

$\Delta H^\circ_{rxn}, \Delta S_{rxn}, T \rightarrow \Delta G$

$\Delta G = \Delta H_{rxn} - T\Delta S_{rxn}$

Solution:

Reactant/Product	ΔH°_f(kJ/mol from Appendix IIB)
NH_3 (*g*)	− 45.9
N_2H_4 (*g*)	95.4
H_2 (*g*)	0.0

Be sure to pull data for the correct formula and phase.

$$\begin{aligned}\Delta H^\circ_{rxn} &= \sum n_p \Delta H^\circ_f(\text{products}) - \sum n_r \Delta H^\circ_f(\text{reactants}) \\ &= [1(\Delta H^\circ_f(N_2H_4\ (g))) + 1(\Delta H^\circ_f(H_2\ (g)))] - [2(\Delta H^\circ_f(NH_3\ (g)))] \\ &= [1(95.4\ \text{kJ}) + 1(0.0\ \text{kJ})] - [2(-45.9\ \text{kJ})] \\ &= [95.4\ \text{kJ}] - [-91.8\ \text{kJ}] \\ &= +187.2\ \text{kJ then}\end{aligned}$$

Reactant/Product	S°(J/mol K from Appendix IIB)
NH_3 (*g*)	192.8
N_2H_4 (*g*)	238.5
H_2 (*g*)	130.7

Be sure to pull data for the correct formula and phase.

$$\begin{aligned}\Delta S^\circ_{rxn} &= \sum n_p S^\circ(\text{products}) - \sum n_r S^\circ(\text{reactants}) \\ &= [1(S^\circ(N_2H_4\ (g))) + 1(S^\circ(H_2\ (g)))] - [2(S^\circ(NH_3\ (g)))] \\ &= [1(238.5\ \text{J/K}) + 1(130.7\ \text{J/K})] - [2(192.8\ \text{J/K})] \\ &= [369.2\ \text{J/K}] - [385.6\ \text{J/K}] \\ &= -16.4\ \text{J/K then}\end{aligned}$$

$T = 273.15 + 25\ °C = 298\ K$ then $-16.4 \frac{J}{K} \times \frac{1\ kJ}{1000\ J} = -0.0164\ kJ/K$ then

$$\Delta G^\circ = \Delta H^\circ_{rxn} - T\Delta S^\circ_{rxn} = +187.2\ kJ - (298\ K)\left(-0.0164 \frac{kJ}{K}\right) = +192.1\ kJ = +1.921 \times 10^5\ J$$

so the reaction is nonspontaneous. Both terms are positive and so the reaction is not spontaneous at any temperature.

Check: The units (kJ, J/K, and kJ) are correct. N_2H_4 has such a high enthalpy of formation compared to ammonia, that we expect that this will be an endothermic reaction. We expect a very small entropy change because the number of moles of gas is unchanged. Since both terms are positive, the reaction is nonspontaneous. Since both terms are positive, this reaction cannot be spontaneous at any temperature.

(c) **Given:** $N_2\ (g) + O_2\ (g) \rightarrow 2\ NO\ (g)$ at 25 °C

Find: ΔH°_{rxn}, ΔS°_{rxn}, ΔG°_{rxn}, spontaneity. Can temperature be changed to make it spontaneous?

Conceptual Plan: $\Delta H^\circ_{rxn} = \sum n_p H^\circ_f(\text{products}) - \sum n_r H^\circ_f(\text{reactants})$ **then**

$\Delta S^\circ_{rxn} = \sum n_p S^\circ(\text{products}) - \sum n_r S^\circ(\text{reactants})$ **then °C → K then J/K → kJ/K then**

$K = 273.15 + °C$ $\qquad \frac{1\ kJ}{1000\ J}$

$\Delta H^\circ_{rxn}, \Delta S_{rxn}, T \rightarrow \Delta G$

$\Delta G = \Delta H_{rxn} - T\Delta S_{rxn}$

Solution:

Reactant/Product	ΔH°_f(kJ/mol from Appendix IIB)
$N_2\ (g)$	0.0
$O_2\ (g)$	0.0
$NO\ (g)$	91.3

Be sure to pull data for the correct formula and phase.

$$\begin{aligned}\Delta H^\circ_{rxn} &= \sum n_p \Delta H^\circ_f(\text{products}) - \sum n_r \Delta H^\circ_f(\text{reactants})\\ &= [2(\Delta H^\circ_f(NO\ (g)))] - [1(\Delta H^\circ_f(N_2\ (g))) + 1(\Delta H^\circ_f(O_2\ (g)))]\\ &= [2(91.3\ kJ)] - [1(0.0\ kJ) + 1(0.0\ kJ)]\\ &= [182.6\ kJ] - [0.0\ kJ]\\ &= +182.6\ kJ \text{ then}\end{aligned}$$

Reactant/Product	S°(J/mol K from Appendix IIB)
$N_2\ (g)$	191.6
$O_2\ (g)$	205.2
$NO\ (g)$	210.8

Be sure to pull data for the correct formula and phase.

$$\begin{aligned}\Delta S^\circ_{rxn} &= \sum n_p S^\circ(\text{products}) - \sum n_r S^\circ(\text{reactants})\\ &= [2(S^\circ(NO\ (g)))] - [1(S^\circ(N_2\ (g))) + 1(S^\circ(O_2\ (g)))]\\ &= [2(210.8\ J/K)] - [1(191.6\ J/K) + 1(205.2\ J/K)]\\ &= [421.6\ J/K] - [396.8\ J/K]\\ &= +24.8\ J/K\end{aligned}$$

then $T = 273.15 + 25\ °C = 298\ K$ then $+24.8 \frac{J}{K} \times \frac{1\ kJ}{1000\ J} = +0.0248\ kJ/K$ then

$$\Delta G^\circ = \Delta H^\circ_{rxn} - T\Delta S^\circ_{rxn} = +182.6\ kJ - (298\ K)\left(0.0248 \frac{kJ}{K}\right) = +175.2\ kJ = +1.752 \times 10^5\ J$$ so

the reaction is nonspontaneous. It can be spontaneous at high temperatures.

Check: The units (kJ, J/K, and kJ) are correct. The enthalpy is twice the enthalpy of formation of NO. We expect a very small entropy change because the number of moles of gas is unchanged. Since the positive enthalpy term dominates at room temperature, the reaction is nonspontaneous. The second term can dominate if we raise the temperature high enough.

(d) **Given:** $2\ KClO_3\ (s) \rightarrow 2\ KCl\ (s) + 3\ O_2\ (g)$ at 25 °C
Find: ΔH°_{rxn}, ΔS°_{rxn}, ΔG°_{rxn}, spontaneity. Can temperature be changed to make it spontaneous?
Conceptual Plan: $\Delta H^\circ_{rxn} = \sum n_p H^\circ_f(\text{products}) - \sum n_r H^\circ_f(\text{reactants})$ **then**
$\Delta S^\circ_{rxn} = \sum n_p S^\circ(\text{products}) - \sum n_r S^\circ(\text{reactants})$ **then °C → K then J/K → kJ/K then**

$K = 273.15 + °C$ $\qquad \dfrac{1\ kJ}{1000\ J}$

$\Delta H^\circ_{rxn}, \Delta S^\circ_{rxn}, T \rightarrow \Delta G$

$\Delta G = \Delta H_{rxn} - T\Delta S_{rxn}$

Solution:

Reactant/Product	ΔH°_f(kJ/mol from Appendix IIB)
$KClO_3\ (s)$	− 397.7
$KCl\ (s)$	− 436.5
$O_2\ (g)$	0.0

Be sure to pull data for the correct formula and phase.

$$\begin{aligned}\Delta H^\circ_{rxn} &= \sum n_p \Delta H^\circ_f(\text{products}) - \sum n_r \Delta H^\circ_f(\text{reactants})\\ &= [2(\Delta H^\circ_f(KCl\ (s))) + 3(\Delta H^\circ_f(O_2\ (g)))] - [2(\Delta H^\circ_f(KClO_3\ (s)))]\\ &= [2(-436.5\ kJ) + 3(0.0\ kJ)] - [2(-397.7\ kJ)]\\ &= [-873.0\ kJ] - [-795.4\ kJ]\\ &= -77.6\ kJ \text{ then}\end{aligned}$$

Reactant/Product	S°(J/mol K from Appendix IIB)
$KClO_3\ (s)$	143.1
$KCl\ (s)$	82.6
$O_2\ (g)$	205.2

Be sure to pull data for the correct formula and phase.

$$\begin{aligned}\Delta S^\circ_{rxn} &= \sum n_p S^\circ(\text{products}) - \sum n_r S^\circ(\text{reactants})\\ &= [2(S^\circ(KCl\ (s))) + 3(S^\circ(O_2\ (g)))] - [2(S^\circ(KClO_3\ (s)))]\\ &= [2(82.6\ J/K) + 3(205.2\ J/K)] - [2(143.1\ J/K)]\\ &= [780.8\ J/K] - [286.2\ J/K]\\ &= +494.6\ J/K \text{ then}\end{aligned}$$

$T = 273.15 + 25\ °C = 298\ K$ then $+494.6\ \dfrac{J}{K} \times \dfrac{1\ kJ}{1000\ J} = +0.4946\ kJ/K$ then

$\Delta G^\circ = \Delta H^\circ_{rxn} - T\Delta S^\circ_{rxn} = -77.6\ kJ - (298\ K)\left(0.4946\ \dfrac{kJ}{K}\right) = -225.0\ kJ = -2.250 \times 10^6\ J$ so the reaction is spontaneous. Since both terms are negative, the reaction is spontaneous at all temperatures.
Check: The units (kJ, J/K, and kJ) are correct. The reaction is exothermic because the enthalpy of formation of KCl is less than that for $KClO_3$. We expect a positive entropy change because the number of moles of gas is increasing. Since both terms are negative, the reaction is spontaneous at all temperatures.

17.59 (a) **Given:** $N_2O_4\ (g) \rightarrow 2\ NO_2\ (g)$ at 25 °C **Find:** ΔG°_{rxn}, spontaneity and compare to Problem 57. Determine which method would show how free energy changes with temperature.
Conceptual Plan: $\Delta G^\circ_{rxn} = \sum n_p \Delta G^\circ_f(\text{products}) - \sum n_r \Delta G^\circ_f(\text{reactants})$ **then compare to Problem 57**
Solution:

Reactant/Product	ΔG°_f(kJ/mol from Appendix IIB)
$N_2O_4\ (g)$	99.8
$NO_2\ (g)$	51.3

Be sure to pull data for the correct formula and phase.

$\Delta G^\circ_{rxn} = \sum n_p \Delta G^\circ_f(\text{products}) - \sum n_r \Delta G^\circ_f(\text{reactants})$
$= [2(\Delta G^\circ_f(NO_2\ (g)))] - [1(\Delta G^\circ_f(N_2O_4\ (g)))]$
$= [\ 2(51.\ 3\ kJ)\ ] - [1(99.8\ kJ)]$
$= [102.6\ kJ] - [99.8\ kJ]$
$= +\ 2.8\ kJ$
so the reaction is nonspontaneous. The value is similar to Problem 57.
Check: The units (kJ) are correct. The free energy of the products is greater than the reactants, so the answer is positive and the reaction is nonspontaneous. The answer is the same as in Problem 57 within the error of the calculation.

(b) **Given:** $NH_4Cl\ (s) \rightarrow HCl\ (g) + NH_3\ (g)$ at 25 °C
Find: ΔG°_{rxn}, spontaneity and compare to Problem 57
Conceptual Plan: $\Delta G^\circ_{rxn} = \sum n_p \Delta G^\circ_f(\text{products}) - \sum n_r \Delta G^\circ_f(\text{reactants})$ **then compare to Problem 57**
Solution:

Reactant/Product	ΔG°_f(kJ/mol from Appendix IIB)
$NH_4Cl\ (s)$	− 202.9
$HCl\ (g)$	− 95.3
$NH_3\ (g)$	− 16.4

Be sure to pull data for the correct formula and phase.
$\Delta G^\circ_{rxn} = \sum n_p \Delta G^\circ_f(\text{products}) - \sum n_r \Delta G^\circ_f(\text{reactants})$
$= [1(\Delta G^\circ_f(HCl\ (g))) + 1(\Delta G^\circ_f(NH_3\ (g)))\ ] - [1(\Delta G^\circ_f(NH_4Cl\ (g)))]$
$= [1(-\ 95.3\ kJ) + 1(-\ 16.4\ kJ)\ ] - [1(-\ 202.9\ kJ)]$
$= [-\ 111.7\ kJ] - [-\ 202.9\ kJ]$
$= +\ 91.2\ kJ$
so the reaction is nonspontaneous.
The result is the same as in Problem 57.
Check: The units (kJ) are correct. The answer matches Problem 57.

(c) **Given:** $3\ H_2\ (g) + Fe_2O_3\ (s) \rightarrow 2\ Fe\ (s) + 3\ H_2O\ (g)$ at 25 °C
Find: ΔG°_{rxn}, spontaneity and compare to Problem 57
Conceptual Plan: $\Delta G^\circ_{rxn} = \sum n_p \Delta G^\circ_f(\text{products}) - \sum n_r \Delta G^\circ_f(\text{reactants})$ **then compare to Problem 57**
Solution:

Reactant/Product	ΔG°_f(kJ/mol from Appendix IIB)
$H_2\ (g)$	0.0
$Fe_2O_3\ (s)$	− 742.2
$Fe\ (s)$	0.0
$H_2O\ (g)$	− 228.6

Be sure to pull data for the correct formula and phase.
$\Delta G^\circ_{rxn} = \sum n_p \Delta G^\circ_f(\text{products}) - \sum n_r \Delta G^\circ_f(\text{reactants})$
$= [2(\Delta G^\circ_f(Fe\ (s))) + 3(\Delta G^\circ_f(H_2O\ (g)))] - [3(\Delta G^\circ_f(H_2\ (g))) + 1(\Delta G^\circ_f(Fe_2O_3\ (s)))]$
$= [2(\ 0.0\ kJ) + 3(-\ 228.6\ kJ\ )\ ] - [3(0.0\ kJ) + 1(-\ 742.2\ kJ)]$
$= [-\ 685.8\ kJ] - [-\ 742.2\ kJ]$
$= +\ 56.4\ kJ$
so the reaction is nonspontaneous. The value is similar to that in Problem 57.
Check: The units (kJ) are correct. The answer is the same as in Problem 57 within the error of the calculation.

(d) **Given:** $N_2\ (g) + 3\ H_2\ (g) \rightarrow 2\ NH_3\ (g)$ at 25 °C
Find: ΔG°_{rxn}, spontaneity and compare to Problem 57
Conceptual Plan: $\Delta G^\circ_{rxn} = \sum n_p \Delta G^\circ_f(\text{products}) - \sum n_r \Delta G^\circ_f(\text{reactants})$ **then compare to Problem 57**
Solution:

Reactant/Product	ΔG°_f(kJ/mol from Appendix IIB)
$N_2\ (g)$	0.0
$H_2\ (g)$	0.0
$NH_3\ (g)$	− 16.4

Be sure to pull data for the correct formula and phase.

$\Delta G^\circ_{rxn} = \sum n_p \Delta G^\circ_f(\text{products}) - \sum n_r \Delta G^\circ_f(\text{reactants})$

$= [\,2(\Delta G^\circ_f(NH_3\ (g)))\,] - [1(\Delta G^\circ_f(N_2\ (g))) + 3(\Delta G^\circ_f(H_2\ (g)))]$

$= [2(-16.4\text{ kJ})] - [1(0.0\text{ kJ}) + 3(0.0\text{ kJ})]$

$= [-32.8\text{ kJ}] - [0.0\text{ kJ}]$

$= -32.8\text{ kJ}$

so the reaction is spontaneous. The result is the same as in Problem 57.

Check: The units (kJ) are correct. The answer matches Problem 57.

Values calculated by the two methods are comparable. The method using ΔH° and ΔS° is longer, but it can be used to determine how ΔG° changes with temperature.

17.60 (a) **Given:** $2\ CH_4\ (g) \rightarrow C_2H_6\ (g) + H_2\ (g)$ at 25 °C **Find:** ΔG°_{rxn}, spontaneity and compare to Problem 58

Determine which method would show how free energy changes with temperature.

Conceptual Plan: $\Delta G^\circ_{rxn} = \sum n_p \Delta G^\circ_f(\text{products}) - \sum n_r \Delta G^\circ_f(\text{reactants})$ **then compare to Problem 58**

Solution:

Reactant/Product	ΔG°_f(kJ/mol from Appendix IIB)
$CH_4\ (g)$	− 50.5
$C_2H_6\ (g)$	− 32.0
$H_2\ (g)$	0.0

Be sure to pull data for the correct formula and phase.

$\Delta G^\circ_{rxn} = \sum n_p \Delta G^\circ_f(\text{products}) - \sum n_r \Delta G^\circ_f(\text{reactants})$

$= [\,1(\Delta G^\circ_f(C_2H_6\ (g))) + 1(\Delta G^\circ_f(H_2\ (g)))] - [2(\Delta G^\circ_f(CH_4\ (g)))]$

$= [1(-32.0\text{ kJ}) + 1(0.0\text{ kJ})\,] - [2(-50.5\text{ kJ})]$

$= [-32.0\text{ kJ}] - [-101.0\text{ kJ}]$

$= +69.0\text{ kJ}$

so the reaction is spontaneous. The value is similar to that in Problem 58.

Check: The units (kJ) are correct. The answer is the same as in Problem 58 within the error of the calculation.

(b) **Given:** $2\ NH_3\ (g) \rightarrow N_2H_4\ (g) + H_2\ (g)$ at 25 °C

Find: ΔG°_{rxn}, spontaneity and compare to Problem 58

Conceptual Plan: $\Delta G^\circ_{rxn} = \sum n_p \Delta G^\circ_f(\text{products}) - \sum n_r \Delta G^\circ_f(\text{reactants})$ **then compare to Problem 58**

Solution:

Reactant/Product	ΔG°_f(kJ/mol from Appendix IIB)
$NH_3\ (g)$	− 16.4
$N_2H_4\ (g)$	159.4
$H_2\ (g)$	0.0

Be sure to pull data for the correct formula and phase.

$\Delta G^\circ_{rxn} = \sum n_p \Delta G^\circ_f(\text{products}) - \sum n_r \Delta G^\circ_f(\text{reactants})$

$= [1(\Delta G^\circ_f(N_2H_4\ (g))) + 1(\Delta G^\circ_f(H_2\ (g)))] - [\,2(\Delta G^\circ_f(NH_3\ (g)))]$

$= [1(159.4\text{ kJ}) + 1(0.0\text{ kJ})] - [2(-16.4\text{ kJ})]$

$= [159.4\text{ kJ}] - [-32.8\text{ kJ}]$

$= +192.2\text{ kJ}$

so the reaction is nonspontaneous. The value is similar to in Problem 58.

Check: The units (kJ) are correct. The answer is the same as in Problem 58 within the error of the calculation.

(c) **Given:** $N_2\ (g) + O_2\ (g) \rightarrow 2\ NO\ (g)$ at 25 °C

Find: ΔG°_{rxn}, spontaneity and compare to Problem 58

Conceptual Plan: $\Delta G^\circ_{rxn} = \sum n_p \Delta G^\circ_f(\text{products}) - \sum n_r \Delta G^\circ_f(\text{reactants})$ **then compare to Problem 58**

Solution:

Reactant/Product	ΔG°_f(kJ/mol from Appendix IIB)
$N_2\ (g)$	0.0
$O_2\ (g)$	0.0
$NO\ (g)$	87.6

Be sure to pull data for the correct formula and phase.

$\Delta G^\circ_{rxn} = \sum n_p \Delta G^\circ_f(\text{products}) - \sum n_r \Delta G^\circ_f(\text{reactants})$
$= [2(\Delta G^\circ_f(\text{NO}\ (g)))] - [1(\Delta G^\circ_f(\text{N}_2\ (g))) + 1(\Delta G^\circ_f(\text{O}_2\ (g)))]$
$= [2(87.6\text{ kJ})] - [1(0.0\text{ kJ}) + 1(0.0\text{ kJ})]$
$= [175.2\text{ kJ}] - [0.0\text{ kJ}]$
$= +175.2\text{ kJ}$

so the reaction is nonspontaneous. The result is the same as in Problem 58.

Check: The units (kJ) are correct. The answer matches Problem 58.

(d) **Given:** $2\ \text{KClO}_3\ (s) \rightarrow 2\ \text{KCl}\ (s) + 3\ \text{O}_2\ (g)$ at 25 °C
Find: ΔG°_{rxn}, spontaneity and compare to Problem 58
Conceptual Plan: $\Delta G^\circ_{rxn} = \sum n_p \Delta G^\circ_f(\text{products}) - \sum n_r \Delta G^\circ_f(\text{reactants})$ **then compare to Problem 58**
Solution:

Reactant/Product	ΔG°_f(kJ/mol from Appendix IIB)
$\text{KClO}_3\ (s)$	−296.3
$\text{KCl}\ (s)$	−408.5
$\text{O}_2\ (g)$	0.0

Be sure to pull data for the correct formula and phase.

$\Delta G^\circ_{rxn} = \sum n_p \Delta G^\circ_f(\text{products}) - \sum n_r \Delta G^\circ_f(\text{reactants})$
$= [2(\Delta G^\circ_f(\text{KCl}\ (s))) + 1(\Delta G^\circ_f(\text{O}_2\ (g)))] - [2(\Delta G^\circ_f(\text{KClO}_3\ (s)))]$
$= [2(-408.5\text{ kJ}) + 3(0.0\text{ kJ})] - [2(-296.3\text{ kJ})]$
$= [-817.0\text{ kJ}] - [-592.6\text{ kJ}]$
$= -224.4\text{ kJ}$

so the reaction is spontaneous. The value is similar to Problem 58.

Check: The units (kJ) are correct. The answer is the same as in Problem 58 within the error of the calculation.

Values calculated by the two methods are comparable. The method using ΔH° and ΔS° is longer, but it can be used to determine how ΔG° changes with temperature.

17.61 **Given:** $2\ \text{NO}\ (g) + \text{O}_2\ (g) \rightarrow 2\ \text{NO}_2\ (g)$ **Find:** ΔG°_{rxn} and spontaneity at (a) 298 K, (b) 715 K, and (c) 855 K
Conceptual Plan: $\Delta H^\circ_{rxn} = \sum n_p H^\circ_f(\text{products}) - \sum n_r H^\circ_f(\text{reactants})$ **then**
$\Delta S^\circ_{rxn} = \sum n_p S^\circ(\text{products}) - \sum n_r S^\circ(\text{reactants})$ **then J/K → kJ/K then** $\Delta H^\circ_{rxn}, \Delta S_{rxn}, T \rightarrow \Delta G$

$\frac{1\text{ kJ}}{1000\text{ J}}$ $\qquad \Delta G = \Delta H_{rxn} - T\Delta S_{rxn}$

Solution:

Reactant/Product	ΔH°_f(kJ/mol from Appendix IIB)
$\text{NO}\ (g)$	91.3
$\text{O}_2\ (g)$	0.0
$\text{NO}_2\ (g)$	33.2

Be sure to pull data for the correct formula and phase.

$\Delta H^\circ_{rxn} = \sum n_p \Delta H^\circ_f(\text{products}) - \sum n_r \Delta H^\circ_f(\text{reactants})$
$= [2(\Delta H^\circ_f(\text{NO}_2\ (g)))] - [2(\Delta H^\circ_f(\text{NO}\ (g))) + 1(\Delta H^\circ_f(\text{O}_2\ (g)))]$
$= [2(33.2\text{ kJ})] - [2(91.3\text{ kJ}) + 1(0.0\text{ kJ})]$
$= [66.4\text{ kJ}] - [182.6\text{ kJ}]$
$= -116.2\text{ kJ}$ then

Reactant/Product	S°(J/mol K from Appendix IIB)
$\text{NO}\ (g)$	210.8
$\text{O}_2\ (g)$	205.2
$\text{NO}_2\ (g)$	240.1

Be sure to pull data for the correct formula and phase.

$$\begin{aligned}\Delta S^\circ_{rxn} &= \sum n_p S^\circ(\text{products}) - \sum n_r S^\circ(\text{reactants})\\ &= [2(S^\circ(NO_2\ (g)))] - [2(S^\circ(NO\ (g))) + 1(S^\circ(O_2\ (g)))]\\ &= [2(240.1\ J/K)] - [2(210.8\ J/K) + 1(205.2\ J/K)] \quad \text{then } -146.6\frac{J}{K} \times \frac{1\ kJ}{1000\ J} = -0.1466\ kJ/K \text{ then}\\ &= [480.2\ J/K] - [626.8\ J/K]\\ &= -146.6\ J/K\end{aligned}$$

(a) $\Delta G^\circ = \Delta H^\circ_{rxn} - T\Delta S^\circ_{rxn} = -116.2\ kJ - (298\ K)\left(-0.1466\frac{kJ}{K}\right) = -72.5\ kJ = -7.25 \times 10^4\ J$ so the reaction is spontaneous.

(b) $\Delta G^\circ = \Delta H^\circ_{rxn} - T\Delta S^\circ_{rxn} = -116.2\ kJ - (715\ K)\left(-0.1466\frac{kJ}{K}\right) = -11.4\ kJ = -1.14 \times 10^4\ J$ so the reaction is spontaneous.

(c) $\Delta G^\circ = \Delta H^\circ_{rxn} - T\Delta S^\circ_{rxn} = -116.2\ kJ - (855\ K)\left(-0.1466\frac{kJ}{K}\right) = +9.1\ kJ = +9.1 \times 10^3\ J$ so the reaction is nonspontaneous.

Check: The units (kJ) are correct. The enthalpy term dominates at low temperatures, making the reaction spontaneous. As the temperature increases, the decrease in entropy starts to dominate and in the last case the reaction is nonspontaneous.

17.62 **Given:** $CaCO_3\ (s) \rightarrow CaO\ (s) + CO_2\ (g)$ **Find:** ΔG°_{rxn} and spontaneity at (a) 298 K, (b) 1055 K, and (c) 1455 K
Conceptual Plan: $\Delta H^\circ_{rxn} = \sum n_p H^\circ_f(\text{products}) - \sum n_r H^\circ_f(\text{reactants})$ **then**
$\Delta S^\circ_{rxn} = \sum n_p S^\circ(\text{products}) - \sum n_r S^\circ(\text{reactants})$ **then J/K → kJ/K then** $\Delta H^\circ_{rxn}, \Delta S_{rxn}, T \rightarrow \Delta G$

$\frac{1\ kJ}{1000\ J}$ $\Delta G = \Delta H_{rxn} - T\Delta S_{rxn}$

Solution:

Reactant/Product	ΔH°_f(kJ/mol from Appendix IIB)
$CaCO_3\ (s)$	− 1207.6
$CaO\ (s)$	− 634.9
$CO_2\ (g)$	− 393.5

Be sure to pull data for the correct formula and phase.

$$\begin{aligned}\Delta H^\circ_{rxn} &= \sum n_p \Delta H^\circ_f(\text{products}) - \sum n_r \Delta H^\circ_f(\text{reactants})\\ &= [1(\Delta H^\circ_f(CaO\ (g))) + 1(\Delta H^\circ_f(CO_2\ (g)))] - [1(\Delta H^\circ_f(CaCO_2\ (g)))]\\ &= [1(-634.9\ kJ) + 1(-393.5\ kJ)] - [1(-1207.6\ kJ)]\\ &= [-1028.4\ kJ] - [-1207.6\ kJ]\\ &= +179.2\ kJ \text{ then}\end{aligned}$$

Reactant/Product	S°(J/mol K from Appendix IIB)
$CaCO_3\ (s)$	91.7
$CaO\ (s)$	38.1
$CO_2\ (g)$	213.8

Be sure to pull data for the correct formula and phase.

$$\begin{aligned}\Delta S^\circ_{rxn} &= \sum n_p S^\circ(\text{products}) - \sum n_r S^\circ(\text{reactants})\\ &= [1(S^\circ(CaO\ (g))) + 1(S^\circ(CO_2\ (g)))] - [1(S^\circ(CaCO_2\ (g)))]\\ &= [1(38.1\ J/K) + 1(213.8\ J/K)] - [1(91.7\ J/K)]\\ &= [251.9\ J/K] - [91.7\ J/K]\\ &= +160.2\ J/K \text{ then } 160.2\frac{J}{K} \times \frac{1\ kJ}{1000\ J} = +0.1602\ kJ/K \text{ then}\end{aligned}$$

(a) $\Delta G^\circ = \Delta H^\circ_{rxn} - T\Delta S^\circ_{rxn} = +179.2\ kJ - (298\ K)\left(+0.1602\frac{kJ}{K}\right) = +131.5\ kJ = +1.315 \times 10^5\ J$ so the reaction is nonspontaneous.

(b) $\Delta G^\circ = \Delta H^\circ_{rxn} - T\Delta S^\circ_{rxn} = +179.2\text{ kJ} - (1055\text{ K})\left(+0.1602\frac{\text{kJ}}{\text{K}}\right) = +10.2\text{ kJ} = +1.02 \times 10^4\text{ J}$

so the reaction is nonspontaneous.

(c) $\Delta G^\circ = \Delta H^\circ_{rxn} - T\Delta S^\circ_{rxn} = +179.2\text{ kJ} - (1455\text{ K})\left(+0.1602\frac{\text{kJ}}{\text{K}}\right) = -53.9\text{ kJ} = -5.39 \times 10^4\text{ J}$

so the reaction is spontaneous.

Check: The units (kJ) are correct. The enthalpy term dominates at low temperatures, making the reaction nonspontaneous. As the temperature increases, the increase in entropy starts to dominate and in the last case the reaction is spontaneous.

17.63 Since the first reaction has Fe_2O_3 as a product and the reaction of interest has it as a reactant, we need to reverse the first reaction. When the reaction direction is reversed, ΔG changes.

$Fe_2O_3\,(s) \rightarrow 2\,Fe\,(s) + 3/2\,O_2\,(g)$ $\quad \Delta G^\circ = +742.2\text{ kJ}$

Since the second reaction has 1 mole CO as a reactant and the reaction of interest has 3 moles of CO as a reactant, we need to multiply the second reaction and the ΔG by 3.

$3\,[CO\,(g) + 1/2\,O_2\,(g) \rightarrow CO_2\,(g)]$ $\quad \Delta G^\circ = 3(-257.2\text{ kJ}) = -771.6\text{ kJ}$

Hess's law states the ΔG of the net reaction is the sum of the ΔG of the steps.

The rewritten reactions are:

$Fe_2O_3\,(s) \rightarrow 2\,Fe\,(s) + \cancel{3/2\,O_2\,(g)}$ $\quad \Delta G^\circ = +742.2\text{ kJ}$

$3\,CO\,(g) + \cancel{3/2\,O_2\,(g)} \rightarrow 3\,CO_2\,(g)$ $\quad \Delta G^\circ = -771.6\text{ kJ}$

$Fe_2O_3\,(s) + 3\,CO\,(g) \rightarrow 2\,Fe\,(s) + 3\,CO_2\,(g)$ $\quad \Delta G_{rxn} = -29.4\text{ kJ}$

17.64 Since the first reaction has $CaCO_3$ as a product and the reaction of interest has it as a reactant, we need to reverse the first reaction. When the reaction direction is reversed, ΔG changes.

$CaCO_3\,(s) \rightarrow Ca\,(s) + CO_2(g) + 1/2\,O_2\,(g)$ $\quad \Delta G^\circ = +734.4\text{ kJ}$

Since the second reaction has 2 moles CaO as a product and the reaction of interest has 1 mole of CaO as a product, we need to multiply it by $\frac{1}{2}$. The ΔG of the second reaction is multiplied by $\frac{1}{2}$.

$1/2[\,2\,Ca\,(s) + O_2\,(g) \rightarrow 2\,CaO\,(s)\,]$ $\quad \Delta G^\circ = 1/2(-1206.6\text{ kJ}) = -603.3\text{ kJ}$

Hess's law states the ΔH of the net reaction is the sum of the ΔH of the steps.

The rewritten reactions are:

$CaCO_3\,(s) \rightarrow \cancel{Ca\,(s)} + CO_2\,(g) + \cancel{1/2\,O_2\,(g)}$ $\quad \Delta G^\circ = +734.4\text{ kJ}$

$1/2[\,\cancel{2\,Ca\,(s)} + \cancel{O_2\,(g)} \rightarrow 2\,CaO\,(s)\,]$ $\quad \Delta G^\circ = -603.3\text{ kJ}$

$CaCO_3\,(s) \rightarrow CaO\,(s) + CO_2\,(g)$ $\quad \Delta G_{rxn} = +131.1\text{ kJ}$

Free Energy Changes, Nonstandard Conditions, and the Equilibrium Constant

17.65 (a) **Given:** $I_2\,(s) \rightarrow I_2\,(g)$ at 25.0 °C **Find:** ΔG°_{rxn}

Conceptual Plan: $\Delta G^\circ_{rxn} = \sum n_p \Delta G^\circ_f(\text{products}) - \sum n_r \Delta G^\circ_f(\text{reactants})$

Solution:

Reactant/Product	ΔG°_f(kJ/mol from Appendix IIB)
$I_2\,(s)$	0.0
$I_2\,(g)$	19.3

Be sure to pull data for the correct formula and phase.

$\Delta G^\circ_{rxn} = \sum n_p \Delta G^\circ_f(\text{products}) - \sum n_r \Delta G^\circ_f(\text{reactants})$

$= [1(\Delta G^\circ_f(I_2\,(g)))] - [1(\Delta G^\circ_f(I_2\,(s)))]$

$= [1(19.3\text{ kJ})] - [1(0.0\text{ kJ})]$

$= +19.3\text{ kJ}$ so the reaction is nonspontaneous.

Check: The units (kJ) are correct. The answer is positive because gases have higher free energy than solids and the free energy change of the reaction is the same as free energy of formation of gaseous iodine.

(b) **Given:** $I_2\ (s) \rightarrow I_2\ (g)$ at 25.0 °C (i) $P_{I_2} = 1.00$ mmHg; (ii) $P_{I_2} = 0.100$ mmHg **Find:** ΔG_{rxn}
Conceptual Plan: °C → K and mmHg → atm then $\Delta G^\circ_{rxn}, P_{I_2}, T \rightarrow \Delta G_{rxn}$

$$K = 273.15 + °C \qquad \frac{1\ \text{atm}}{760\ \text{mmHg}} \qquad \Delta G_{rxn} = \Delta G^\circ_{rxn} + RT \ln Q \ \textit{where}\ Q = P_{I_2}$$

Solution: $T = 273.15 + 25.0\ °C = 298.2$ K and (i) $1.00\ \text{mmHg} \times \dfrac{1\ \text{atm}}{760\ \text{mmHg}} = 0.00131579$ atm

then $\Delta G_{rxn} = \Delta G^\circ_{rxn} + RT \ln Q = \Delta G^\circ_{rxn} + RT \ln P_{I_2} =$

$+19.3\ \text{kJ} + \left(8.314 \dfrac{\text{J}}{\text{K} \cdot \text{mol}}\right)\left(\dfrac{1\ \text{kJ}}{1000\ \text{J}}\right)(298.2\ \text{K}) \ln (0.00131579) = +2.9$ kJ so the reaction is nonspontaneous.

Then (ii) $0.100\ \text{mmHg} \times \dfrac{1\ \text{atm}}{760\ \text{mmHg}} = 0.000131579$ atm then

$\Delta G_{rxn} = \Delta G^\circ_{rxn} + RT \ln Q = \Delta G^\circ_{rxn} + RT \ln P_{I_2} =$

$+19.3\ \text{kJ} + \left(8.314 \dfrac{\text{J}}{\text{K} \cdot \text{mol}}\right)\left(\dfrac{1\ \text{kJ}}{1000\ \text{J}}\right)(298.2\ \text{K}) \ln (0.000131579) = -2.9$ kJ so the reaction is spontaneous.

Check: The units (kJ) are correct. The answer is positive at higher pressure because the pressure is higher than the vapor pressure of iodine. Once the desired pressure is below the vapor pressure (0.31 mmHg at 25.0 °C), the reaction becomes spontaneous.

(c) Iodine sublimes at room temperature because there is an equilibrium between the solid and the gas phases. The vapor pressure is low (0.31 mmHg at 25.0 °C), so a small amount of iodine can remain in the gas phase, which is consistent with the free energy values.

17.66 (a) **Given:** $CH_3OH\ (l) \rightarrow CH_3OH\ (g)$ at 25.0 °C **Find:** ΔG°_{rxn}
Conceptual Plan: $\Delta G^\circ_{rxn} = \sum n_p \Delta G^\circ_f(\text{products}) - \sum n_r \Delta G^\circ_f(\text{reactants})$
Solution:

Reactant/Product	ΔG°_f(kJ/mol from Appendix IIB)
$CH_3OH\ (l)$	− 166.6
$CH_3OH\ (g)$	− 162.3

Be sure to pull data for the correct formula and phase.

$$\begin{aligned}\Delta G^\circ_{rxn} &= \sum n_p \Delta G^\circ_f(\text{products}) - \sum n_r \Delta G^\circ_f(\text{reactants}) \\ &= [1(\Delta G^\circ_f(CH_3OH\ (g)))] - [1(\Delta G^\circ_f(CH_3OH\ (l)))] \\ &= [1(-162.3\ \text{kJ})] - [1(-166.6\ \text{kJ})] \\ &= +4.3\ \text{kJ}\end{aligned}$$

so the reaction is nonspontaneous.

Check: The units (kJ) are correct. The answer is positive because gases have higher free energy than liquids.

(b) **Given:** $CH_3OH\ (l) \rightarrow CH_3OH\ (g)$ at 25.0 °C (i) $P_{CH_3OH} = 150.0$ mmHg; (ii) $P_{CH_3OH} = 100.0$ mmHg and (ii) $P_{CH_3OH} = 10.0$ mmHg **Find:** ΔG_{rxn}
Conceptual Plan: °C → K and mmHg → atm then $\Delta G^\circ_{rxn}, P_{CH_3OH}, T \rightarrow \Delta G_{rxn}$

$$K = 273.15 + °C \qquad \frac{1\ \text{atm}}{760\ \text{mmHg}} \qquad \Delta G_{rxn} = \Delta G^\circ_{rxn} + RT \ln Q \ \textit{where}\ Q = P_{CH_3OH}$$

Solution: $T = 273.15 + 25.0\ °C = 298.2$ K and (i) $150.0\ \text{mmHg} \times \dfrac{1\ \text{atm}}{760\ \text{mmHg}} = 0.1973684$ atm then

$\Delta G_{rxn} = \Delta G^\circ_{rxn} + RT \ln Q = \Delta G^\circ_{rxn} + RT \ln P_{CH_3OH} =$

$+4.3\ \text{kJ} + \left(8.314 \dfrac{\text{J}}{\text{K} \cdot \text{mol}}\right)\left(\dfrac{1\ \text{kJ}}{1000\ \text{J}}\right)(298.2\ \text{K}) \ln (0.1973684) = +0.3$ kJ so the reaction is nonspontaneous.

Then (ii) $100.0\ \text{mmHg} \times \dfrac{1\ \text{atm}}{760\ \text{mmHg}} = 0.131579$ atm then

$\Delta G_{rxn} = \Delta G^\circ_{rxn} + RT \ln Q = \Delta G^\circ_{rxn} + RT \ln P_{CH_3OH} =$

$+4.3\ \text{kJ} + \left(8.314 \dfrac{\text{J}}{\text{K} \cdot \text{mol}}\right)\left(\dfrac{1\ \text{kJ}}{1000\ \text{J}}\right)(298.2\ \text{K}) \ln (0.131579) = -0.7$ kJ so the reaction is spontaneous.

Then (iii) $10.0 \text{ mmHg} \times \frac{1 \text{ atm}}{760 \text{ mmHg}} = 0.013\underline{1}579 \text{ atm}$ then

$\Delta G_{rxn} = \Delta G^\circ_{rxn} + RT \ln Q = \Delta G^\circ_{rxn} + RT \ln P_{CH_3OH} =$

$+4.3 \text{ kJ} + \left(8.314 \frac{\text{J}}{\text{K} \cdot \text{mol}}\right)\left(\frac{1 \text{ kJ}}{1000 \text{ J}}\right)(298.2 \text{ K}) \ln (0.013\underline{1}579) = -6.4 \text{ kJ}$ so the reaction is spontaneous.

Check: The units (kJ) are correct. The answer is positive at high pressures because the pressure is higher than the vapor pressure of methanol. Once the desired pressure is below the vapor pressure (143 mmHg at 25.0 °C), the reaction becomes spontaneous.

(c) Methanol evaporates at room temperature because there is an equilibrium between the liquid and the gas phases. The vapor pressure is moderate (143 mmHg at 25.0 °C), so a moderate amount of methanol can remain in the gas phase, which is consistent with the free energy values.

17.67 **Given:** $CH_3OH\ (g) \rightleftharpoons CO\ (g) + 2\ H_2\ (g)$ at 25 °C, $P_{CH_3OH} = 0.855$ atm, $P_{CO} = 0.125$ atm, $P_{H_2} = 0.183$ atm
Find: ΔG
Conceptual Plan:
$\Delta G^\circ_{rxn} = \sum n_p \Delta G^\circ_f(\text{products}) - \sum n_r \Delta G^\circ_f(\text{reactants})$ **then °C → K then** $\Delta G^\circ_{rxn}, P_{CH_3OH}, P_{CO}, P_{H_2}, T \rightarrow \Delta G$

$K = 273.15 + °C \quad \Delta G_{rxn} = \Delta G^\circ_{rxn} + RT \ln Q$ *where* $Q = \frac{P_{CO}P^2_{H_2}}{P_{CH_3OH}}$

Solution:

Reactant/Product	ΔG°_f(kJ/mol from Appendix IIB)
$CH_3OH\ (g)$	− 162.3
$CO\ (g)$	− 137.2
$H_2\ (g)$	0.0

Be sure to pull data for the correct formula and phase.

$$\begin{aligned}\Delta G^\circ_{rxn} &= \sum n_p \Delta G^\circ_f(\text{products}) - \sum n_r \Delta G^\circ_f(\text{reactants})\\ &= [1(\Delta G^\circ_f(CO\ (g))) + 2(\Delta G^\circ_f(H_2\ (g)))] - [1(\Delta G^\circ_f(CH_3OH\ (g)))]\\ &= [1(-137.2 \text{ kJ}) + 2(0.0 \text{ kJ})] - [1(-162.3 \text{ kJ})]\\ &= [-137.2 \text{ kJ}] - [-162.3 \text{ kJ}]\\ &= +25.1 \text{ kJ}\end{aligned}$$

$T = 273.15 + 25\ °C = 298$ K then $Q = \frac{P_{CO}P^2_{H_2}}{P_{CH_3OH}} = \frac{(0.125)(0.183)^2}{0.855} = 0.0048\underline{9}605$ then

$\Delta G_{rxn} = \Delta G^\circ_{rxn} + RT \ln Q = +25.1 \text{ kJ} + \left(8.314 \frac{\text{J}}{\text{K} \cdot \text{mol}}\right)\left(\frac{1 \text{ kJ}}{1000 \text{ J}}\right)(298 \text{ K}) \ln (0.0048\underline{9}605) = +11.9 \text{ kJ}$

so the reaction is nonspontaneous.
Check: The units (kJ) are correct. The standard free energy for the reaction was positive and the fact that Q was less than one made the free energy smaller, but the reaction at these conditions is still not spontaneous.

17.68 **Given:** $CO_2\ (g) + CCl_4\ (g) \rightleftharpoons 2\ COCl_2\ (g)$ at 25 °C, $P_{CO_2} = 0.112$ atm, $P_{CCl_4} = 0.174$ atm, $P_{COCl_2} = 0.744$ atm
Find: ΔG
Conceptual Plan:
$\Delta G^\circ_{rxn} = \sum n_p \Delta G^\circ_f(\text{products}) - \sum n_r \Delta G^\circ_f(\text{reactants})$ **then °C → K then** $\Delta G^\circ_{rxn}, P_{CO_2}, P_{CCl_4}, P_{COCl_2}, T \rightarrow \Delta G$

$K = 273.15 + °C \quad \Delta G_{rxn} = \Delta G^\circ_{rxn} + RT \ln Q$ *where* $Q = \frac{P^2_{COCl_2}}{P_{CO_2}P_{CCl_4}}$

Solution:

Reactant/Product	ΔG°_f(kJ/mol from Appendix IIB)
$CO_2\ (g)$	− 394.4
$CCl_4\ (g)$	− 62.3
$COCl_2\ (g)$	− 204.9

Be sure to pull data for the correct formula and phase.

$$\begin{aligned}\Delta G^\circ_{rxn} &= \sum n_p \Delta G^\circ_f(\text{products}) - \sum n_r \Delta G^\circ_f(\text{reactants})\\ &= [2(\Delta G^\circ_f(COCl_2\ (g)))] - [1(\Delta G^\circ_f(CO_2\ (g))) + 1(\Delta G^\circ_f(CCl_4\ (g)))]\\ &= [2(-204.9 \text{ kJ})] - [1(-394.4 \text{ kJ}) + 1(-62.3 \text{ kJ})]\\ &= [-409.8 \text{ kJ}] - [-456.7 \text{ kJ}]\\ &= +46.9 \text{ kJ}\end{aligned}$$

$T = 273.15 + 25\ °C = 298\ K$ then $Q = \dfrac{P^2_{COCl_2}}{P_{CO_2}P_{CCl_4}} = \dfrac{(0.744)^2}{(0.112)(0.174)} = 28.\underline{4}039$ then

$$\Delta G_{rxn} = \Delta G^{\circ}_{rxn} + RT \ln Q = +46.9\ kJ + \left(8.314 \frac{J}{K \cdot mol}\right)\left(\frac{1\ kJ}{1000\ J}\right)(298\ K) \ln(28.\underline{4}039) = +55.2\ kJ$$

so the reaction is nonspontaneous.

Check: The units (kJ) are correct. The standard free energy for the reaction was positive and the fact that Q was greater than one made the free energy larger, so the reaction is less spontaneous in the forward direction at these conditions than at standard conditions.

17.69 (a) **Given:** $2\ CO\ (g) + O_2\ (g) \rightleftharpoons 2\ CO_2\ (g)$ at 25 °C **Find:** K

Conceptual Plan:

$\Delta G^{\circ}_{rxn} = \sum n_p \Delta G^{\circ}_f(\text{products}) - \sum n_r \Delta G^{\circ}_f(\text{reactants})$ **then °C → K then** $\Delta G^{\circ}_{rxn}, T \rightarrow K$

$K = 273.15 + °C \qquad \Delta G^{\circ}_{rxn} = -RT \ln K$

Solution:

Reactant/Product	ΔG°_f(kJ/mol from Appendix IIB)
$CO\ (g)$	− 137.2
$O_2\ (g)$	0.0
$CO_2\ (g)$	− 394.4

Be sure to pull data for the correct formula and phase.

$$\begin{aligned}\Delta G^{\circ}_{rxn} &= \sum n_p \Delta G^{\circ}_f(\text{products}) - \sum n_r \Delta G^{\circ}_f(\text{reactants}) \\ &= [2(\Delta G^{\circ}_f(CO_2\ (g)))] - [2(\Delta G^{\circ}_f(CO\ (g))) + 1(\Delta G^{\circ}_f(O_2\ (g)))] \\ &= [2(-394.4\ kJ)] - [2(-137.2\ kJ) + 1(0.0\ kJ)] \\ &= [-788.8\ kJ] - [-274.4\ kJ] \\ &= -514.4\ kJ\end{aligned}$$

$T = 273.15 + 25\ °C = 298\ K$ then

$\Delta G^{\circ}_{rxn} = -RT \ln K$. Rearrange to solve for K.

$$K = e^{\frac{-\Delta G^{\circ}_{rxn}}{RT}} = e^{\frac{-(-514.4\ kJ) \times \frac{1000\ J}{1\ kJ}}{\left(8.314 \frac{J}{K \cdot mol}\right)(298\ K)}} = e^{207.\underline{6}23} = 1.48 \times 10^{90}.$$

Check: The units (none) are correct. The standard free energy for the reaction was very negative and so we expect a very large K. The reaction is spontaneous, so mostly products are present at equilibrium.

(b) **Given:** $2\ H_2S\ (g) \rightleftharpoons 2\ H_2\ (g) + S_2\ (g)$ at 25 °C **Find:** K

Conceptual Plan:

$\Delta G^{\circ}_{rxn} = \sum n_p \Delta G^{\circ}_f(\text{products}) - \sum n_r \Delta G^{\circ}_f(\text{reactants})$ **then °C → K then** $\Delta G^{\circ}_{rxn}, T \rightarrow K$

$K = 273.15 + °C \qquad \Delta G^{\circ}_{rxn} = -RT \ln K$

Solution:

Reactant/Product	ΔG°_f(kJ/mol from Appendix IIB)
$H_2S\ (g)$	− 33.4
$H_2\ (g)$	0.0
$S_2\ (g)$	79.7

Be sure to pull data for the correct formula and phase.

$$\begin{aligned}\Delta G^{\circ}_{rxn} &= \sum n_p \Delta G^{\circ}_f(\text{products}) - \sum n_r \Delta G^{\circ}_f(\text{reactants}) \\ &= [2(\Delta G^{\circ}_f(H_2\ (g))) + 1(\Delta G^{\circ}_f(S_2\ (g)))] - [2(\Delta G^{\circ}_f(H_2S\ (g)))] \\ &= [2(0.0\ kJ)] + 1(79.7\ kJ)] - [2(-33.4\ kJ)] \\ &= [79.7\ kJ] - [-66.8\ kJ] \\ &= +146.5\ kJ\end{aligned}$$

$T = 273.15 + 25\ °C = 298\ K$ then

$\Delta G^{\circ}_{rxn} = -RT \ln K$. Rearrange to solve for K.

$$K = e^{\frac{-\Delta G^{\circ}_{rxn}}{RT}} = e^{\frac{-146.5\ kJ \times \frac{1000\ J}{1\ kJ}}{\left(8.314 \frac{J}{K \cdot mol}\right)(298\ K)}} = e^{-59.\underline{1}305} = 2.09 \times 10^{-26}.$$

Check: The units (none) are correct. The standard free energy for the reaction was positive and so we expect a small K. The reaction is nonspontaneous and so mostly reactants are present at equilibrium.

17.70 (a) **Given:** $2\ NO_2\ (g) \rightleftharpoons N_2O_4\ (g)$ at 25 °C **Find:** K

Conceptual Plan:

$\Delta G^\circ_{rxn} = \sum n_p \Delta G^\circ_f(\text{products}) - \sum n_r \Delta G^\circ_f(\text{reactants})$ **then °C → K then** $\Delta G^\circ_{rxn}, T \rightarrow K$

$K = 273.15 + °C$ $\qquad \Delta G^\circ_{rxn} = -RT \ln K$

Solution:

Reactant/Product	ΔG°_f(kJ/mol from Appendix IIB)
$NO_2\ (g)$	51.3
$N_2O_4\ (g)$	99.8

Be sure to pull data for the correct formula and phase.

$$\begin{aligned}\Delta G^\circ_{rxn} &= \sum n_p \Delta G^\circ_f(\text{products}) - \sum n_r \Delta G^\circ_f(\text{reactants})\\ &= [1(\Delta G^\circ_f(N_2O_4\ (g)))] - [2(\Delta G^\circ_f(NO_2\ (g)))]\\ &= [1(99.8\text{ kJ})] - [2(51.3\text{ kJ})]\\ &= [99.8\text{ kJ}] - [102.6\text{ kJ}]\\ &= -2.8\text{ kJ}\end{aligned}$$

$T = 273.15 + 25\ °C = 298\ K$ then

$\Delta G^\circ_{rxn} = -RT \ln K$ Rearrange to solve for K.

$$K = e^{\frac{-\Delta G^\circ_{rxn}}{RT}} = e^{\frac{-(-2.8\text{ kJ}) \times \frac{1000\text{ J}}{1\text{ kJ}}}{\left(8.314\frac{\text{J}}{\text{K}\cdot\text{mol}}\right)(298\text{ K})}} = e^{1.1301} = 3.1.$$

Check: The units (none) are correct. The standard free energy for the reaction was very slightly negative, so we expect a K just over 1. The reaction is spontaneous and so mostly products are present at equilibrium.

(b) **Given:** $Br_2\ (g) + Cl_2\ (g) \rightleftharpoons 2\ BrCl\ (g)$ at 25 °C **Find:** K

Conceptual Plan:

$\Delta G^\circ_{rxn} = \sum n_p \Delta G^\circ_f(\text{products}) - \sum n_r \Delta G^\circ_f(\text{reactants})$ **then °C → K then** $\Delta G^\circ_{rxn}, T \rightarrow K$

$K = 273.15 + °C$ $\qquad \Delta G^\circ_{rxn} = -RT \ln K$

Solution:

Reactant/Product	ΔG°_f(kJ/mol from Appendix IIB)
$Br_2\ (g)$	3.1
$Cl_2\ (g)$	0.0
$BrCl\ (g)$	− 1.0

Be sure to pull data for the correct formula and phase.

$$\begin{aligned}\Delta G^\circ_{rxn} &= \sum n_p \Delta G^\circ_f(\text{products}) - \sum n_r \Delta G^\circ_f(\text{reactants})\\ &= [2(\Delta G^\circ_f(BrCl\ (g)))] - [1(\Delta G^\circ_f(Br_2\ (g))) + 1(\Delta G^\circ_f(Cl_2\ (g)))]\\ &= [2(-1.0\text{ kJ})] - [1(3.1\text{ kJ}) + 1(0.0\text{ kJ})]\\ &= [-2.0\text{ kJ}] - [3.1\text{ kJ}]\\ &= -5.1\text{ kJ}\end{aligned}$$

$T = 273.15 + 25\ °C = 298\ K$ then $\Delta G^\circ_{rxn} = -RT \ln K$

Rearrange to solve for K. $K = e^{\frac{-\Delta G^\circ_{rxn}}{RT}} = e^{\frac{-(-5.1\text{ kJ}) \times \frac{1000\text{ J}}{1\text{ kJ}}}{\left(8.314\frac{\text{J}}{\text{K}\cdot\text{mol}}\right)(298\text{ K})}} = e^{2.0585} = 7.8.$

Check: The units (none) are correct. The standard free energy for the reaction was very slightly negative, so we expect a K just over 1. The reaction is spontaneous.

17.71 **Given:** $CO\ (g) + 2\ H_2\ (g) \rightleftharpoons CH_3OH\ (g)$ $K_p = 2.26 \times 10^4$ at 25 °C

Find: ΔG°_{rxn} at (a) standard conditions, (b) at equilibrium, and (c) $P_{CH_3OH} = 1.0$ atm, $P_{CO} = P_{H_2} = 0.010$ atm

Conceptual Plan: °C $\rightarrow$ K then (a) $K, T \rightarrow \Delta G^\circ_{rxn}$ then (b) at equilibrium $\Delta G_{rxn} = 0$ then

$K = 273.15 + °C$ $\quad \Delta G^\circ_{rxn} = -RT \ln K$

(c) $\Delta G^\circ_{rxn}, P_{CH_3OH}, P_{CO}, P_{H_2}, T \rightarrow \Delta G$

$$\Delta G_{rxn} = \Delta G^\circ_{rxn} + RT \ln Q \text{ where } Q = \frac{P_{CH_3OH}}{P_{CO}P^2_{H_2}}$$

Solution: $T = 273.15 + 25\ °C = 298$ K then

(a) $$\Delta G^\circ_{rxn} = -RT \ln K = -\left(8.314 \frac{J}{K \cdot mol}\right)\left(\frac{1\ kJ}{1000\ J}\right)(298\ K) \ln(2.26 \times 10^4) = -24.8\ kJ$$

(b) at equilibrium $\Delta G_{rxn} = 0$

(c) $$Q = \frac{P_{CH_3OH}}{P_{CO}P^2_{H_2}} = \frac{1.0}{(0.010)(0.010)^2} = 1.0 \times 10^6 \text{ then}$$

$$\Delta G_{rxn} = \Delta G^\circ_{rxn} + RT \ln Q = -24.8\ kJ + \left(8.314 \frac{J}{K \cdot mol}\right)\left(\frac{1\ kJ}{1000\ J}\right)(298\ K) \ln(1.0 \times 10^6) = +9.4\ kJ$$

Check: The units (kJ) are correct. The K was greater than one so we expect a negative standard free energy for the reaction. At equilibrium, by definition, the free energy change is zero. Since the conditions give a $Q > K$ then the reaction needs to proceed in the reverse direction, which means that the reaction is spontaneous in the reverse direction.

17.72 **Given:** $I_2(g) + Cl_2(g) \rightleftharpoons 2\,ICl(g)$ $K_p = 81.9$ at 25 °C **Find:** ΔG°_{rxn} at (a) standard conditions, (b) at equilibrium, and (c) $P_{ICl} = 2.55$ atm, $P_{I_2} = 0.325$ atm, $P_{Cl_2} = 0.221$ atm

Conceptual Plan: °C $\rightarrow$ K then (a) $K, T \rightarrow \Delta G^\circ_{rxn}$ then (b) at equilibrium $\Delta G_{rxn} = 0$ then

$K = 273.15 + °C$ $\quad \Delta G^\circ_{rxn} = -RT \ln K$

(c) $\Delta G^\circ_{rxn}, P_{ICl}, P_{I_2}, P_{Cl_2}, T \rightarrow \Delta G$

$$\Delta G_{rxn} = \Delta G^\circ_{rxn} + RT \ln Q \text{ where } Q = \frac{P^2_{ICl}}{P_{I_2}P_{Cl_2}}$$

Solution: $T = 273.15 + 25\ °C = 298$ K then

(a) $$\Delta G^\circ_{rxn} = -RT \ln K = -\left(8.314 \frac{J}{K \cdot mol}\right)\left(\frac{1\ kJ}{1000\ J}\right)(298\ K) \ln(81.9) = -10.9\ kJ$$

(b) at equilibrium $\Delta G_{rxn} = 0$

(c) $$Q = \frac{P^2_{ICl}}{P_{I_2}P_{Cl_2}} = \frac{(2.55)^2}{(0.325)(0.221)} = 90.5\underline{3}25 \text{ then}$$

$$\Delta G_{rxn} = \Delta G^\circ_{rxn} + RT \ln Q = -10.9\ kJ + \left(8.314 \frac{J}{K \cdot mol}\right)\left(\frac{1\ kJ}{1000\ J}\right)(298\ K) \ln(90.5\underline{3}25) = +0.3\ kJ$$

Check: The units (kJ) are correct. The K was greater than one so we expect a negative standard free energy for the reaction. At equilibrium, by definition, the free energy change is zero. Since the conditions give a Q just greater than K, the reaction needs to proceed in the reverse direction, which means that the reverse reaction is slightly spontaneous.

17.73 (a) **Given:** $2\,CO(g) + O_2(g) \rightleftharpoons 2\,CO_2(g)$ at 25 °C **Find:** K at 525 K

Conceptual Plan: $\Delta H^\circ_{rxn} = \sum n_p H^\circ_f(\text{products}) - \sum n_r H^\circ_f(\text{reactants})$ then

$\Delta S^\circ_{rxn} = \sum n_p S^\circ(\text{products}) - \sum n_r S^\circ(\text{reactants})$ then J/K $\rightarrow$ kJ/K then $\Delta H^\circ_{rxn}, \Delta S_{rxn}, T \rightarrow \Delta G$

$\frac{1\ kJ}{1000\ J}$ $\quad \Delta G = \Delta H_{rxn} - T\Delta S_{rxn}$

then $\Delta G^\circ_{rxn}, T \rightarrow K$

$\Delta G^\circ_{rxn} = -RT \ln K$

Solution:

Reactant/Product	ΔH°_f(kJ/mol from Appendix IIB)
$CO(g)$	− 110.5
$O_2(g)$	0.0
$CO_2(g)$	− 393.5

Be sure to pull data for the correct formula and phase.

$$\Delta H^\circ_{rxn} = \sum n_p \Delta H^\circ_f(\text{products}) - \sum n_r \Delta H^\circ_f(\text{reactants})$$
$$= [2(\Delta H^\circ_f(CO_2\ (g)))] - [2(\Delta H^\circ_f(CO\ (g))) + 1(\Delta H^\circ_f(O_2\ (g)))]$$
$$= [2(-393.5\text{ kJ})] - [2(-110.5\text{ kJ}) + 1(0.0\text{ kJ})] \quad \text{then}$$
$$= [-787.0\text{ kJ}] - [-221.0\text{ kJ}]$$
$$= -566.0\text{ kJ}$$

Reactant/Product	S°(J/mol K from Appendix IIB)
CO (g)	197.7
O_2 (g)	205.2
CO_2 (g)	213.8

Be sure to pull data for the correct formula and phase.

$$\Delta S^\circ_{rxn} = \sum n_p S^\circ(\text{products}) - \sum n_r S^\circ(\text{reactants})$$
$$= [2(S^\circ(CO_2\ (g)))] - [2(S^\circ(CO\ (g))) + 1(S^\circ(O_2\ (g)))]$$
$$= [2(213.8\text{ J/K})] - [2(197.7\text{ J/K}) + 1(205.2\text{ J/K})] \quad \text{then}$$
$$= [427.6\text{ J/K}] - [600.6\text{ J/K}]$$
$$= -173.0\text{ J/K}$$

$$-173.0\frac{\text{J}}{\text{K}} \times \frac{1\text{ kJ}}{1000\text{ J}} = -0.1730\text{ kJ/K then}$$

$$\Delta G^\circ = \Delta H^\circ_{rxn} - T\Delta S^\circ_{rxn} = -566.0\text{ kJ} - (525\text{ K})\left(-0.1730\frac{\text{kJ}}{\text{K}}\right) = -475.2\text{ kJ} = -4.752 \times 10^5\text{ J then}$$

$\Delta G^\circ_{rxn} = -RT\ln K$. Rearrange to solve for K.

$$K = e^{\frac{-\Delta G^\circ_{rxn}}{RT}} = e^{\frac{-(-4.752\times10^5\text{ J})}{\left(8.314\frac{\text{J}}{\text{K}\cdot\text{mol}}\right)(525\text{ K})}} = e^{108.864} = 1.90 \times 10^{47}.$$

Check: The units (none) are correct. The free energy change is very negative, indicating a spontaneous reaction. This results in a very large K.

(b) **Given:** $2\ H_2S\ (g) \rightleftharpoons 2\ H_2\ (g) + S_2\ (g)$ at 25 °C **Find:** K at 525 K

Conceptual Plan: $\Delta H^\circ_{rxn} = \sum n_p H^\circ_f(\text{products}) - \sum n_r H^\circ_f(\text{reactants})$ **then**

$\Delta S^\circ_{rxn} = \sum n_p S^\circ(\text{products}) - \sum n_r S^\circ(\text{reactants})$ **then J/K → kJ/K then** $\Delta H^\circ_{rxn}, \Delta S_{rxn}, T \rightarrow \Delta G$

$\frac{1\text{ kJ}}{1000\text{ J}}$ $\qquad \Delta G = \Delta H_{rxn} - T\Delta S_{rxn}$

then $\Delta G^\circ_{rxn}, T \rightarrow K$

$\Delta G^\circ_{rxn} = -RT\ln K$

Solution:

Reactant/Product	ΔH°_f(kJ/mol from Appendix IIB)
H_2S (g)	−20.6
H_2 (g)	0.0
S_2 (g)	128.6

Be sure to pull data for the correct formula and phase.

$$\Delta H^\circ_{rxn} = \sum n_p \Delta H^\circ_f(\text{products}) - \sum n_r \Delta H^\circ_f(\text{reactants})$$
$$= [2(\Delta H^\circ_f(H_2\ (g))) + 1(\Delta H^\circ_f(S_2\ (g)))] - [2(\Delta H^\circ_f(H_2S\ (g)))]$$
$$= [2(0.0\text{ kJ}) + 1(128.6\text{ kJ})] - [2(-20.6\text{ kJ})]$$
$$= [128.6\text{ kJ}] - [-41.2\text{ kJ}]$$
$$= +169.8\text{ kJ then}$$

Reactant/Product	S°(J/mol K from Appendix IIB)
H_2S (g)	205.8
H_2 (g)	130.7
S_2 (g)	228.2

Be sure to pull data for the correct formula and phase.

$$\Delta S^\circ_{rxn} = \sum n_p S^\circ(\text{products}) - \sum n_r S^\circ(\text{reactants})$$
$$= [2(S^\circ(H_2\ (g))) + 1(S^\circ(S_2\ (g)))] - [2(S^\circ(H_2S\ (g)))]$$
$$= [2(130.7\ \text{J/K}) + 1(228.2\ \text{J/K})] - [2(205.8\ \text{J/K})]$$
$$= [489.6\ \text{J/K}] - [411.6\ \text{J/K}]$$
$$= +78.0\ \text{J/K}$$

then $+\ 78.0 \frac{\text{J}}{\text{K}} \times \frac{1\ \text{kJ}}{1000\ \text{J}} = +\ 0.0780\ \text{kJ/K}$ then

$$\Delta G^\circ = \Delta H^\circ_{rxn} - T\Delta S^\circ_{rxn} = +169.8\ \text{kJ} - (525\ \text{K})\left(+0.0780\frac{\text{kJ}}{\text{K}}\right) = +128.\underline{8}5\ \text{kJ} = +1.28\underline{8}5 \times 10^5\ \text{J then}$$

$\Delta G^\circ_{rxn} = -RT \ln K$. Rearrange to solve for K.

$$K = e^{\frac{-\Delta G^\circ_{rxn}}{RT}} = e^{\frac{-1.2885 \times 10^5\ \text{J}}{\left(8.314\frac{\text{J}}{\text{K}\cdot\text{mol}}\right)(525\ \text{K})}} = e^{-29.\underline{5}199} = 1.51 \times 10^{-13}.$$

Check: The units (none) are correct. The free energy change is positive, indicating a nonspontaneous reaction. This results in a very small K.

17.74 (a) **Given:** $2\ NO_2\ (g) \rightleftharpoons N_2O_4\ (g)$ at 25 °C **Find:** K at 655 K

Conceptual Plan: $\Delta H^\circ_{rxn} = \sum n_p H^\circ_f(\text{products}) - \sum n_r H^\circ_f(\text{reactants})$ **then**

$\Delta S^\circ_{rxn} = \sum n_p S^\circ(\text{products}) - \sum n_r S^\circ(\text{reactants})$ **then J/K → kJ/K then** $\Delta H^\circ_{rxn}, \Delta S_{rxn}, T \rightarrow \Delta G$

$\frac{1\ \text{kJ}}{1000\ \text{J}}$ $\qquad \Delta G = \Delta H_{rxn} - T\Delta S_{rxn}$

then $\Delta G^\circ_{rxn}, T \rightarrow K$

$\Delta G^\circ_{rxn} = -RT \ln K$

Solution:

Reactant/Product	ΔH°_f(kJ/mol from Appendix IIB)
$NO_2\ (g)$	33.2
$N_2O_4\ (g)$	11.1

Be sure to pull data for the correct formula and phase.

$$\Delta H^\circ_{rxn} = \sum n_p \Delta H^\circ_f(\text{products}) - \sum n_r \Delta H^\circ_f(\text{reactants})$$
$$= [1(\Delta H^\circ_f(N_2O_4\ (g)))] - [2(\Delta H^\circ_f(NO_2\ (g)))]$$
$$= [1(11.1\ \text{kJ})] - [2(33.2\ \text{kJ})]$$
$$= [11.1\ \text{kJ}] - [66.4\ \text{kJ}]$$
$$= -55.3\ \text{kJ then}$$

Reactant/Product	S°(J/mol K from Appendix IIB)
$NO_2\ (g)$	240.1
$N_2O_4\ (g)$	304.4

Be sure to pull data for the correct formula and phase.

$$\Delta S^\circ_{rxn} = \sum n_p S^\circ(\text{products}) - \sum n_r S^\circ(\text{reactants})$$
$$= [1(S^\circ(N_2O_4\ (g)))] - [2(S^\circ(NO_2\ (g)))]$$
$$= [1(304.4\ \text{J/K})] - [2(240.1\ \text{J/K})]$$
$$= [304.4\ \text{J/K}] - [480.2\ \text{J/K}]$$
$$= -175.8\ \text{J/K}$$

then $-\ 175.8 \frac{\text{J}}{\text{K}} \times \frac{1\ \text{kJ}}{1000\ \text{J}} = -\ 0.1758\ \text{kJ/K}$ then

$$\Delta G^\circ = \Delta H^\circ_{rxn} - T\Delta S^\circ_{rxn} = -55.3\ \text{kJ} - (655\ \text{K})\left(-0.1758\frac{\text{kJ}}{\text{K}}\right) = +59.\underline{8}\ \text{kJ} = +5.9\underline{8}49 \times 10^4\ \text{J then}$$

$\Delta G^\circ_{rxn} = -RT \ln K$. Rearrange to solve for K.

$$K = e^{\frac{-\Delta G^\circ_{rxn}}{RT}} = e^{\frac{-5.9849 \times 10^4\ \text{J}}{\left(8.314\frac{\text{J}}{\text{K}\cdot\text{mol}}\right)(655\ \text{K})}} = e^{-10.\underline{9}902} = 1.69 \times 10^{-5}.$$

Check: The units (none) are correct. The free energy change is positive, indicating a nonspontaneous reaction. This results in a very small K.

(b) **Given:** Br_2 (*g*) + Cl_2 (*g*) $\rightleftharpoons$ 2 BrCl (*g*) at 25 °C **Find:** *K* at 655 K

Conceptual Plan: $\Delta H^\circ_{rxn} = \sum n_p H^\circ_f(\text{products}) - \sum n_r H^\circ_f(\text{reactants})$ **then**

$\Delta S^\circ_{rxn} = \sum n_p S^\circ(\text{products}) - \sum n_r S^\circ(\text{reactants})$ **then J/K → kJ/K then** $\Delta H^\circ_{rxn}, \Delta S_{rxn}, T \rightarrow \Delta G$

$\frac{1\ \text{kJ}}{1000\ \text{J}}$ $\qquad \Delta G = \Delta H_{rxn} - T\Delta S_{rxn}$

then $\Delta G^\circ_{rxn}, T \rightarrow K$

$\Delta G^\circ_{rxn} = -RT \ln K$

Solution:

Reactant/Product	ΔH°_f(kJ/mol from Appendix IIB)
Br_2 (*g*)	30.9
Cl_2 (*g*)	0.0
BrCl (*g*)	14.6

Be sure to pull data for the correct formula and phase.

$$\begin{aligned}\Delta H^\circ_{rxn} &= \sum n_p \Delta H^\circ_f(\text{products}) - \sum n_r \Delta H^\circ_f(\text{reactants})\\ &= [2(\Delta H^\circ_f(\text{BrCl}\ (g)))] - [1(\Delta H^\circ_f(\text{Br}_2\ (g))) + 1(\Delta H^\circ_f(\text{Cl}_2\ (g)))]\\ &= [2(14.6\ \text{kJ})] - [1(30.9\ \text{kJ}) + 1(0.0\ \text{kJ})]\\ &= [29.2\ \text{kJ}] - [30.9\ \text{kJ}]\\ &= -1.7\ \text{kJ then}\end{aligned}$$

Reactant/Product	S°(J/mol K from Appendix IIB)
Br_2 (*g*)	245.5
Cl_2 (*g*)	223.1
BrCl (*g*)	240.0

Be sure to pull data for the correct formula and phase.

$$\begin{aligned}\Delta S^\circ_{rxn} &= \sum n_p S^\circ(\text{products}) - \sum n_r S^\circ(\text{reactants})\\ &= [2(S^\circ(\text{BrCl}\ (g)))] - [1(S^\circ(\text{Br}_2\ (g))) + 1(S^\circ(\text{Cl}_2\ (g)))]\\ &= [2(240.0\ \text{J/K})] - [1(245.5\ \text{J/K}) + 1(223.1\ \text{J/K})]\\ &= [480.0\ \text{J/K}] - [468.6\ \text{J/K}]\\ &= +11.4\ \text{J/K}\end{aligned}$$

then $+\ 11.4\frac{\text{J}}{\text{K}} \times \frac{1\ \text{kJ}}{1000\ \text{J}} = +\ 0.0114\ \text{kJ/K}$ then

$$\Delta G^\circ = \Delta H^\circ_{rxn} - T\Delta S^\circ_{rxn} = -1.7\ \text{kJ} - (655\ \text{K})\left(+0.0114\frac{\text{kJ}}{\text{K}}\right) = -9.\underline{1}67\ \text{kJ} = -9.\underline{1}67 \times 10^3\ \text{J then}$$

$\Delta G^\circ_{rxn} = -RT \ln K$. Rearrange to solve for *K*.

$$K = e^{\frac{-\Delta G^\circ_{rxn}}{RT}} = e^{\frac{-(-9.\underline{1}67 \times 10^3\ \text{J})}{\left(8.314\frac{\text{J}}{\text{K}\cdot\text{mol}}\right)(655\ \text{K})}} = e^{1.\underline{6}834} = 5.38.$$

Check: The units (none) are correct. The free energy change is positive, indicating a nonspontaneous reaction. This results in a small *K*.

17.75 **Given:** table of K_p versus temperature **Find:** $\Delta H^\circ_{rxn}, \Delta S^\circ_{rxn}$

Conceptual Plan: Plot ln *K* verus 1/*T*. The slope will be –$\Delta H^\circ_{rxn}/R$ and the intercept will be $\Delta S^\circ_{rxn}/R$.

Solution: Plot ln *K* verus 1/*T*. Since $\ln K = -\frac{\Delta H^\circ_{rxn}}{R}\frac{1}{T} + \frac{\Delta S^\circ_{rxn}}{R}$, the negative of the slope will be $-\frac{\Delta H^\circ_{rxn}}{R}$ and the intercept will be $\frac{\Delta S^\circ_{rxn}}{R}$. The slope can be determined by measuring $\Delta y/\Delta x$ on the plot or by using functions, such as "add trendline" in Excel. Since the slope is – 60$\underline{9}$2.2 K,

$$\Delta H^\circ_{rxn} = -\ slope\ R = -\ (-60\underline{9}2.2\ \text{K})\left(8.314\frac{\text{J}}{\text{K}\cdot\text{mol}}\right)\left(\frac{1\ \text{kJ}}{1000\ \text{J}}\right) = 50.\underline{6}1\ \text{kJ/mol} = 50.6\ \text{kJ/mol}.$$ Since the intercept is 27.$\underline{1}$36 K^{-1}, $\Delta S^\circ_{rxn} = intercept\ R = \left(\frac{27.136}{\text{K}}\right)\left(8.314\frac{\text{J}}{\text{K}\cdot\text{mol}}\right) = 22\underline{5}.609\ \text{J/K} = 226\ \text{J/K}$.

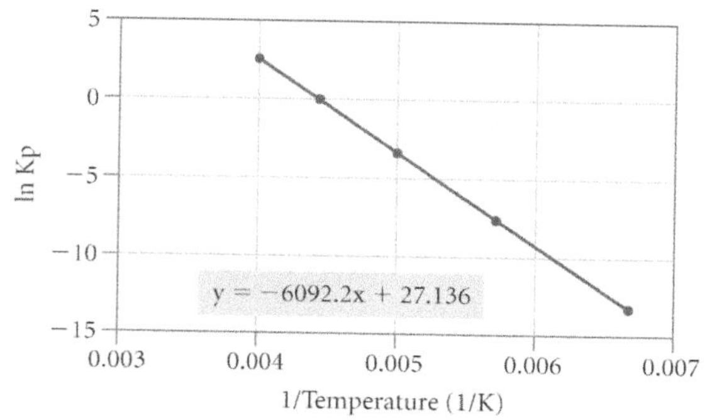

Check: The units are correct (kJ/mole and J/K). The plot is very linear. The numbers are typical for reactions. Since the slope is negative, the enthalpy change must be positive.

17.76 **Given:** table of K_p versus temperature **Find:** ΔH°_{rxn}, ΔS°_{rxn}

Conceptual Plan: Plot ln *K* verus 1/*T*. The slope will be $-\Delta H^\circ_{rxn}/R$ and the intercept will be $\Delta S^\circ_{rxn}/R$.

Solution: Plot ln *K* verus 1/*T*. Since $\ln K = -\frac{\Delta H^\circ_{rxn}}{R}\frac{1}{T} + \frac{\Delta S^\circ_{rxn}}{R}$, the negative of the slope will be $-\frac{\Delta H^\circ_{rxn}}{R}$ and the intercept will be $\frac{\Delta S^\circ_{rxn}}{R}$. The slope can be determined by measuring $\Delta y/\Delta x$ on the plot or by using functions, such as "add trendline" in Excel. Since the slope is – 13704 K,

$\Delta H^\circ_{rxn} = -\ slope\ R =$

$$= -(-13\underline{7}04\ \text{K})\left(8.314\frac{\text{J}}{\text{K}\cdot\text{mol}}\right)\left(\frac{1\ \text{kJ}}{1000\ \text{J}}\right) = .$$

$= 11\underline{3}.935$ kJ/mol $=$ 114 kJ/mol

Since the intercept is 75.$\underline{0}$42 K^{-1}, $\Delta S^\circ_{rxn} = intercept\ R = \left(\frac{75.0\underline{4}2}{\text{K}}\right)\left(8.314\frac{\text{J}}{\text{K}\cdot\text{mol}}\right) = 62\underline{3}.899\ \text{J/K} = 624\ \text{J/K}.$

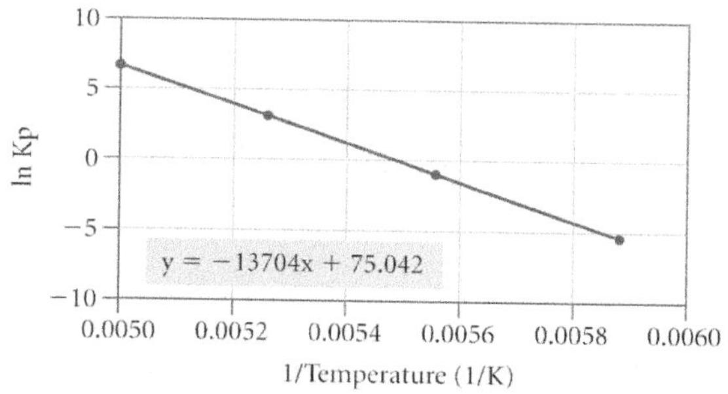

Check: The units are correct (kJ/mole and J/K). The plot is very linear. The numbers are typical for reactions. Since the slope is negative, the enthalpy change must be positive.

17.77 **Given:** $\Delta H^\circ_{rxn} = -25.8$ kJ/mol, $K = 1.4 \times 10^3$ at 298 K **Find:** K at 655 K

Conceptual Plan: $\Delta H^\circ_{rxn}, K_1, T_1, T_2 \rightarrow K_2$

$$\ln K = -\frac{\Delta H^\circ_{rxn}}{R}\frac{1}{T} + \frac{\Delta S^\circ_{rxn}}{R}$$

Solution: Since $\ln K = -\frac{\Delta H^\circ_{rxn}}{R}\frac{1}{T} + \frac{\Delta S^\circ_{rxn}}{R}$, $\ln K_1 + \frac{\Delta H^\circ_{rxn}}{R}\frac{1}{T_1} = \frac{\Delta S^\circ_{rxn}}{R} = \ln K_2 + \frac{\Delta H^\circ_{rxn}}{R}\frac{1}{T_2}$.

Rearrange to solve for K_2.

$$\ln K_2 = \ln K_1 + \frac{\Delta H^\circ_{rxn}}{R}\left(\frac{1}{T_1} - \frac{1}{T_2}\right) = \ln(1.4 \times 10^3) + \frac{\frac{-25.8\ \text{kJ}}{\text{mol}} \times \frac{1000\ \text{J}}{1\ \text{kJ}}}{8.314\frac{\text{J}}{\text{K}\cdot\text{mol}}}\left(\frac{1}{298\ \text{K}} - \frac{1}{655\ \text{K}}\right) = 1.\underline{5}6852 \text{ and so}$$

$K_2 = e^{1.\underline{5}6852} = 4.\underline{7}9954 = 4.8$

Check: The units are correct (none). Since the reaction is exothermic we expect the *K* to decrease with increasing temperature.

17.78 **Given:** $K_1 = 8.5 \times 10^3$ at 298 K, $K_2 = 0.65$ at 755 K **Find:** ΔH°_{rxn}

Conceptual Plan: $K_1, K_2, T_1, T_2 \rightarrow \Delta H^\circ_{rxn}$

$$\ln K = -\frac{\Delta H^\circ_{rxn}}{R}\frac{1}{T} + \frac{\Delta S^\circ_{rxn}}{R}$$

Solution: Since $\ln K = -\frac{\Delta H^\circ_{rxn}}{R}\frac{1}{T} + \frac{\Delta S^\circ_{rxn}}{R}$, $\ln K_1 + \frac{\Delta H^\circ_{rxn}}{R}\frac{1}{T_1} = \frac{\Delta S^\circ_{rxn}}{R} = \ln K_2 + \frac{\Delta H^\circ_{rxn}}{R}\frac{1}{T_2}$. Rearrange to solve for ΔH°_{rxn}.

$$\Delta H^\circ_{rxn} = \frac{\ln\frac{K_2}{K_1}}{\left(\frac{1}{T_1} - \frac{1}{T_2}\right)} R = \frac{\ln\left(\frac{0.65}{8.5 \times 10^3}\right)}{\left(\frac{1}{298\ \text{K}} - \frac{1}{755\ \text{K}}\right)} \times 8.314 \frac{\text{J}}{\text{K} \cdot \text{mol}} \times \frac{1\ \text{kJ}}{1000\ \text{J}} = -38.7973\ \text{kJ/mol} = -38.8\ \text{kJ/mol}$$

Check: The units are correct (kJ/mol). Since K decreases with increasing temperature the reaction is expected to be exothermic.

Cumulative Problems

17.79 (a) +, since vapors have higher entropy than liquids.

(b) –, since solids have less entropy than liquids.

(c) –, since there is only one microstate for the final macrostate and there are six microstates for the initial macrostate.

17.80 (a) +, since vapors have higher entropy than solids.

(b) –, since liquids have less entropy than vapors.

(c) +, since there are twenty microstates for the final macrostate and there are only six microstates for the initial macrostate.

17.81 (a) **Given:** $N_2\ (g) + O_2\ (g) \rightarrow 2\ NO\ (g)$ **Find:** ΔG°_{rxn}, and K_p at 25 °C

Conceptual Plan: $\Delta H^\circ_{rxn} = \sum n_p H^\circ_f(\text{products}) - \sum n_r H^\circ_f(\text{reactants})$ **then**

$\Delta S^\circ_{rxn} = \sum n_p S^\circ(\text{products}) - \sum n_r S^\circ(\text{reactants})$ **then °C → K then J/K → kJ/K then**

$K = 273.15 + °C$ $\qquad \frac{1\ \text{kJ}}{1000\ \text{J}}$

$\Delta H^\circ_{rxn}, \Delta S_{rxn}, T \rightarrow \Delta G$ **then** $\Delta G^\circ_{rxn}, T \rightarrow K$

$\Delta G = \Delta H_{rxn} - T\Delta S_{rxn}$ $\qquad \Delta G^\circ_{rxn} = -RT \ln K$

Solution:

Reactant/Product	ΔH°_f(kJ/mol from Appendix IIB)
$N_2\ (g)$	0.0
$O_2\ (g)$	0.0
$NO\ (g)$	91.3

Be sure to pull data for the correct formula and phase.

$$\begin{aligned}\Delta H^\circ_{rxn} &= \sum n_p \Delta H^\circ_f(\text{products}) - \sum n_r \Delta H^\circ_f(\text{reactants}) \\ &= [2(\Delta H^\circ_f(NO\ (g)))] - [1(\Delta H^\circ_f(N_2\ (g))) + 1(\Delta H^\circ_f(O_2\ (g)))] \\ &= [2(91.3\ \text{kJ})] - [1(0.0\ \text{kJ}) + 1(0.0\ \text{kJ})] \\ &= [182.6\ \text{kJ}] - [0.0\ \text{kJ}] \\ &= +182.6\ \text{kJ then}\end{aligned}$$

Reactant/Product	S°(J/mol K from Appendix IIB)
$N_2\ (g)$	191.6
$O_2\ (g)$	205.2
$NO\ (g)$	210.8

Be sure to pull data for the correct formula and phase.

$$\Delta S^\circ_{rxn} = \sum n_p S^\circ(\text{products}) - \sum n_r S^\circ(\text{reactants})$$
$$= [2(S^\circ(NO\ (g)))] - [1(S^\circ(N_2\ (g))) + 1(S^\circ(O_2\ (g)))]$$
$$= [2(210.8\ J/K)] - [1(191.6\ J/K) + 1(205.2\ J/K)]$$
$$= [421.6\ J/K] - [396.8\ J/K]$$
$$= +24.8\ J/K$$

then $T = 273.15 + 25\ °C = 298\ K$ then $+24.8 \frac{J}{K} \times \frac{1\ kJ}{1000\ J} = +0.0248\ kJ/K$ then

$$\Delta G^\circ = \Delta H^\circ_{rxn} - T\Delta S^\circ_{rxn} = +182.6\ kJ - (298\ K)\left(0.0248 \frac{kJ}{K}\right) = +175.2\ kJ = +1.752 \times 10^5\ J$$

then $\Delta G^\circ_{rxn} = -RT \ln K$. Rearrange to solve for K.

$K = e^{\frac{-\Delta G^\circ_{rxn}}{RT}} = e^{\frac{-1.752 \times 10^5 J}{\left(8.314 \frac{J}{K \cdot mol}\right)(298\ K)}} = e^{-70.7144} = 1.95 \times 10^{-31}$ so the reaction is nonspontaneous and at equilibrium mostly reactants are present.

Check: The units (kJ and none) are correct. The enthalpy is twice the enthalpy of formation of NO. We expect a very small entropy change because the number of moles of gas is unchanged. Since the positive enthalpy term dominates at room temperature, the free energy change is very positive and the reaction in the forward direction is nonspontaneous. This results in a very small K.

(b) **Given:** $N_2\ (g) + O_2\ (g) \rightarrow 2\ NO\ (g)$ **Find:** ΔG°_{rxn} at 2000 K

Conceptual Plan: Use results from part (a) $\Delta H^\circ_{rxn}, \Delta S_{rxn}, T \rightarrow \Delta G$ **then** $\Delta G^\circ_{rxn}, T \rightarrow K$

$\Delta G = \Delta H_{rxn} - T\Delta S_{rxn}$ $\Delta G^\circ_{rxn} = -RT \ln K$

Solution: $\Delta G = \Delta H_{rxn} - T\Delta S_{rxn} = +182.6\ kJ - (2000\ K)\left(0.0248 \frac{kJ}{K}\right) = +133.0\ kJ = +1.330 \times 10^5\ J$

then $\Delta G^\circ_{rxn} = -RT \ln K$. Rearrange to solve for K.

$K = e^{\frac{-\Delta G^\circ_{rxn}}{RT}} = e^{\frac{-1.330 \times 10^5 J}{\left(8.314 \frac{J}{K \cdot mol}\right)(2000\ K)}} = e^{-7.998557} = 3.36 \times 10^{-4}$ so the forward reaction is becoming more spontaneous.

Check: The units (kJ and none) are correct. As the temperature rises, the entropy term becomes more significant. The free energy change is reduced and the K increases. The reaction is still nonspontaneous.

17.82 **Given:** $3\ NO_2\ (g) + H_2O\ (l) \rightarrow 2\ HNO_3\ (aq) + NO\ (g)$ **Find:** ΔG°_{rxn}, and K_p at 25 °C

Conceptual Plan: $\Delta G^\circ_{rxn} = \sum n_p \Delta G^\circ_f(\text{products}) - \sum n_r \Delta G^\circ_f(\text{reactants})$ **then** $\Delta G^\circ_{rxn}, T \rightarrow K$

$\Delta G^\circ_{rxn} = -RT \ln K$

Solution:

Reactant/Product	ΔG°_f(kJ/mol from Appendix IIB)
$NO_2\ (g)$	51.3
$H_2O\ (l)$	− 237.1
$HNO_3\ (aq)$	− 110.9
$NO\ (g)$	87.6

Be sure to pull data for the correct formula and phase.

$$\Delta G^\circ_{rxn} = \sum n_p \Delta G^\circ_f(\text{products}) - \sum n_r \Delta G^\circ_f(\text{reactants})$$
$$= [2(\Delta G^\circ_f(HNO_3\ (g))) + 1(\Delta G^\circ_f(NO\ (g)))] - [3(\Delta G^\circ_f(NO_2\ (g))) + 1(\Delta G^\circ_f(H_2O\ (l)))]$$
$$= [2(-110.9\ kJ) + 1(87.6\ kJ)] - [3(51.3\ kJ) + 1(-237.1\ kJ)]$$
$$= [-134.2\ kJ] - [-83.2\ kJ]$$
$$= -51.0\ kJ = -5.10 \times 10^4\ J$$

then $\Delta G^\circ_{rxn} = -RT \ln K$

Rearrange to solve for K. $K = e^{\frac{-\Delta G^\circ_{rxn}}{RT}} = e^{\frac{-(-5.10 \times 10^4 J)}{\left(8.314 \frac{J}{K \cdot mol}\right)(298\ K)}} = e^{20.5847} = 8.71 \times 10^8$ so the reaction is spontaneous.

Check: The units (kJ and none) are correct. The free energy change is negative and the reaction is spontaneous. This results in a large K.

17.83 **Given:** $C_2H_4\ (g) + X_2\ (g) \rightarrow C_2H_4X_2\ (g)$ where X = Cl, Br, and I
Find: ΔH°_{rxn}, ΔS°_{rxn}, ΔG°_{rxn} and K at 25 °C and spontaneity trends with X and temperature
Conceptual Plan: $\Delta H^\circ_{rxn} = \sum n_p H^\circ_f(\text{products}) - \sum n_r H^\circ_f(\text{reactants})$ **then**

$\Delta S^\circ_{rxn} = \sum n_p S^\circ(\text{products}) - \sum n_r S^\circ(\text{reactants})$ **then °C → K then J/K → kJ/K then**

$K = 273.15 + °C$ $\quad \frac{1\ kJ}{1000\ J}$

$\Delta H^\circ_{rxn}, \Delta S_{rxn}, T \rightarrow \Delta G$

$\Delta G = \Delta H_{rxn} - T\Delta S_{rxn}$

Solution:

Reactant/Product	ΔH°_f(kJ/mol from Appendix IIB)
$C_2H_4\ (g)$	52.4
$Cl_2\ (g)$	0.0
$C_2H_4Cl_2\ (g)$	− 129.7

Be sure to pull data for the correct formula and phase.

$$\begin{aligned}\Delta H^\circ_{rxn} &= \sum n_p \Delta H^\circ_f(\text{products}) - \sum n_r \Delta H^\circ_f(\text{reactants})\\ &= [1(\Delta H^\circ_f(C_2H_4Cl_2\ (g)))] - [1(\Delta H^\circ_f(C_2H_4\ (g))) + 1(\Delta H^\circ_f(Cl_2\ (g)))]\\ &= [1(-129.7\ kJ)] - [1(52.4\ kJ) + 1(0.0\ kJ)]\\ &= [-129.7\ kJ] - [52.4\ kJ]\\ &= -182.1\ kJ \text{ then}\end{aligned}$$

Reactant/Product	S°(J/mol K from Appendix IIB)
$C_2H_4\ (g)$	219.3
$Cl_2\ (g)$	223.1
$C_2H_4Cl_2\ (g)$	308.0

Be sure to pull data for the correct formula and phase.

$$\begin{aligned}\Delta S^\circ_{rxn} &= \sum n_p S^\circ(\text{products}) - \sum n_r S^\circ(\text{reactants})\\ &= [1(S^\circ(C_2H_4Cl_2\ (g)))] - [1(S^\circ(C_2H_4\ (g))) + 1(S^\circ(Cl_2\ (g)))]\\ &= [1(308.0\ J/K)] - [1(219.3\ J/K) + 1(223.1\ J/K)]\\ &= [308.0\ J/K] - [442.4\ J/K]\\ &= -134.4\ J/K\end{aligned}$$

then $T = 273.15 + 25\ °C = 298\ K$ then $-134.4 \frac{J}{K} \times \frac{1\ kJ}{1000\ J} = -0.1344\ kJ/K$ then

$$\Delta G^\circ = \Delta H^\circ_{rxn} - T\Delta S^\circ_{rxn} = -182.1\ kJ - (298\ K)\left(-0.1344 \frac{kJ}{K}\right) = -142.0\ kJ = -1.420 \times 10^5\ J \text{ then}$$

$\Delta G^\circ_{rxn} = -RT \ln K$. Rearrange to solve for K.

$$K = e^{\frac{-\Delta G^\circ_{rxn}}{RT}} = e^{\frac{-(-1.420 \times 10^5\ J)}{\left(8.314 \frac{J}{K \cdot mol}\right)(298\ K)}} = e^{57.334} = 7.94 \times 10^{24}$$ so the reaction is spontaneous.

Reactant/Product	ΔH°_f(kJ/mol from Appendix IIB)
$C_2H_4\ (g)$	52.4
$Br_2\ (g)$	30.9
$C_2H_4Br_2\ (g)$	38.3

Be sure to pull data for the correct formula and phase.

$$\begin{aligned}\Delta H^\circ_{rxn} &= \sum n_p \Delta H^\circ_f(\text{products}) - \sum n_r \Delta H^\circ_f(\text{reactants})\\ &= [1(\Delta H^\circ_f(C_2H_4Br_2\ (g)))] - [1(\Delta H^\circ_f(C_2H_4\ (g))) + 1(\Delta H^\circ_f(Br_2\ (g)))]\\ &= [1(38.3\ kJ)] - [1(52.4\ kJ) + 1(30.9\ kJ)]\\ &= [38.3\ kJ] - [83.3\ kJ]\\ &= -45.0\ kJ \text{ then}\end{aligned}$$

Reactant/Product	S°(J/mol K from Appendix IIB)
C_2H_4 (g)	219.3
Br_2 (g)	245.5
$C_2H_4Br_2$ (g)	330.6

Be sure to pull data for the correct formula and phase.

$$\begin{aligned}\Delta S^\circ_{rxn} &= \sum n_p S^\circ(\text{products}) - \sum n_r S^\circ(\text{reactants})\\ &= [1(S^\circ(C_2H_4Br_2\ (g)))] - [1(S^\circ(C_2H_4\ (g))) + 1(S^\circ(Br_2\ (g)))]\\ &= [1(330.6\ J/K)] - [1(219.3\ J/K) + 1(245.5\ J/K)]\\ &= [330.6\ J/K] - [464.8\ J/K]\\ &= -\ 134.2\ J/K\end{aligned}$$

then $-134.2\frac{J}{K} \times \frac{1\ kJ}{1000\ J} = -\ 0.1342\ kJ/K$

then $\Delta G^\circ = \Delta H^\circ_{rxn} - T\Delta S^\circ_{rxn} = -45.0\ kJ - (298\ K)\left(-0.1342\frac{kJ}{K}\right) = -5.0\ kJ = -5.0 \times 10^3\ J$

then $\Delta G^\circ_{rxn} = -\ RT\ \ln\ K$

Rearrange to solve for K. $K = e^{\frac{-\Delta G^\circ_{rxn}}{RT}} = e^{\frac{-(-5.0008 \times 10^3\ J)}{\left(8.314\frac{J}{K \cdot mol}\right)(298\ K)}} = e^{2.021495} = 7.5$ so the reaction is spontaneous.

Reactant/Product	ΔH°_f(kJ/mol from Appendix IIB)
C_2H_4 (g)	52.4
I_2 (g)	62.42
$C_2H_4I_2$ (g)	66.5

Be sure to pull data for the correct formula and phase.

$$\begin{aligned}\Delta H^\circ_{rxn} &= \sum n_p \Delta H^\circ_f(\text{products}) - \sum n_r \Delta H^\circ_f(\text{reactants})\\ &= [1(\Delta H^\circ_f(C_2H_4I_2\ (g)))] - [1(\Delta H^\circ_f(C_2H_4\ (g))) + 1(\Delta H^\circ_f(I_2\ (g)))]\\ &= [1(66.5\ kJ)] - [1(52.4\ kJ) + 1(62.42\ kJ)]\\ &= [66.5\ kJ] - [114.82\ kJ]\\ &= -\ 48.32\ kJ\ \text{then}\end{aligned}$$

Reactant/Product	S°(J/mol K from Appendix IIB)
C_2H_4 (g)	219.3
I_2 (g)	260.69
$C_2H_4I_2$ (g)	347.8

Be sure to pull data for the correct formula and phase.

$$\begin{aligned}\Delta S^\circ_{rxn} &= \sum n_p S^\circ(\text{products}) - \sum n_r S^\circ(\text{reactants})\\ &= [1(S^\circ(C_2H_4I_2\ (g)))] - [1(S^\circ(C_2H_4\ (g))) + 1(S^\circ(I_2\ (g)))]\\ &= [1(347.8\ J/K)] - [1(219.3\ J/K) + 1(260.69\ J/K)]\\ &= [347.8\ J/K] - [479.99\ J/K]\\ &= -132.2\ J/K\end{aligned}$$

then $-\ 132.2\frac{J}{K} \times \frac{1\ kJ}{1000\ J} = -\ 0.1322\ kJ/K$

then $\Delta G^\circ = \Delta H^\circ_{rxn} - T\Delta S^\circ_{rxn} = -48.32\ kJ - (298\ K)\left(-0.1322\frac{kJ}{K}\right) = -8.9244\ kJ = -8.9244 \times 10^3\ J$

then $\Delta G^\circ_{rxn} = -\ RT\ \ln\ K$. Rearrange to solve for K.

$K = e^{\frac{-\Delta G^\circ_{rxn}}{RT}} = e^{\frac{-(-8.9244 \times 10^3\ J)}{\left(8.314\frac{J}{K \cdot mol}\right)(298\ K)}} = e^{3.6021} = 37$ and the reaction is spontaneous.

Cl_2 is the most spontaneous in the forward direction; I_2 is the least. The entropy change in the reactions is very constant. The spontaneity is determined by the standard enthalpy of formation of the dihalogenated ethane. Higher temperatures make the forward reactions less spontaneous.
Check: The units (kJ and none) are correct. The enthalpy change becomes less negative as we move to larger halogens. The enthalpy term dominates at room temperature, the free energy change is the same sign as the enthalpy change. The more negative the free energy change, the larger the *K*.

17.84 **Given:** $H_2(g) + X_2(g) \rightarrow 2\,HX(g)$ where X = Cl, Br, and I
Find: ΔH°_{rxn}, ΔS°_{rxn}, ΔG°_{rxn} and *K* at 25 °C and spontaneity trends with X and temperature
Conceptual Plan: $\Delta H^\circ_{rxn} = \sum n_p H^\circ_f(\text{products}) - \sum n_r H^\circ_f(\text{reactants})$ **then**
$\Delta S^\circ_{rxn} = \sum n_p S^\circ(\text{products}) - \sum n_r S^\circ(\text{reactants})$ **then °C → K then J/K → kJ/K then**

$K = 273.15 + °C$ $\quad \frac{1\text{ kJ}}{1000\text{ J}}$

$\Delta H^\circ_{rxn}, \Delta S_{rxn}, T \rightarrow \Delta G$

$\Delta G = \Delta H_{rxn} - T\Delta S_{rxn}$

Solution:

Reactant/Product	ΔH°_f(kJ/mol from Appendix IIB)
$H_2(g)$	0.0
$Cl_2(g)$	0.0
$HCl(g)$	− 92.3

Be sure to pull data for the correct formula and phase.

$$\begin{aligned}\Delta H^\circ_{rxn} &= \sum n_p \Delta H^\circ_f(\text{products}) - \sum n_r \Delta H^\circ_f(\text{reactants})\\ &= [2(\Delta H^\circ_f(HCl(g)))] - [1(\Delta H^\circ_f(H_2(g))) + 1(\Delta H^\circ_f(Cl_2(g)))]\\ &= [2(-92.3\text{ kJ})] - [1(0.0\text{ kJ}) + 1(0.0\text{ kJ})]\\ &= [-184.6\text{ kJ}] - [0.0]\\ &= -184.6\text{ kJ} \text{ then}\end{aligned}$$

Reactant/Product	S°(J/mol K from Appendix IIB)
$H_2(g)$	130.7
$Cl_2(g)$	223.1
$HCl(g)$	186.9

Be sure to pull data for the correct formula and phase.

$$\begin{aligned}\Delta S^\circ_{rxn} &= \sum n_p S^\circ(\text{products}) - \sum n_r S^\circ(\text{reactants})\\ &= [2(S^\circ(HCl(g)))] - [1(S^\circ(H_2(g))) + 1(S^\circ(Cl_2(g)))]\\ &= [2(186.9\text{ J/K})] - [1(130.7\text{ J/K}) + 1(223.1\text{ J/K})]\\ &= [373.8\text{ J/K}] - [353.8\text{ J/K}]\\ &= +20.0\text{ J/K}\end{aligned}$$

then $T = 273.15 + 25\text{ °C} = 298\text{ K}$ then $+20.0\frac{\text{J}}{\text{K}} \times \frac{1\text{ kJ}}{1000\text{ J}} = +0.0200\text{ kJ/K}$ then

$\Delta G^\circ = \Delta H^\circ_{rxn} - T\Delta S^\circ_{rxn} = -184.6\text{ kJ} - (298\text{ K})\left(+0.0200\frac{\text{kJ}}{\text{K}}\right) = -190.6\text{ kJ} = -1.906 \times 10^5\text{ J}$ then

$\Delta G^\circ_{rxn} = -RT\ln K$. Rearrange to solve for *K*.

$$K = e^{\frac{-\Delta G^\circ_{rxn}}{RT}} = e^{\left(\frac{-(-1.906 \times 10^5\text{ J})}{\left(8.314\frac{\text{J}}{\text{K}\cdot\text{mol}}\right)(298\text{ K})}\right)} = e^{76.9140} = 2.53 \times 10^{33}$$ so the reaction is spontaneous.

Reactant/Product	ΔH°_f(kJ/mol from Appendix IIB)
$H_2(g)$	0.0
$Br_2(g)$	30.9
$HBr(g)$	− 36.3

Be sure to pull data for the correct formula and phase.

$$\Delta H^\circ_{rxn} = \sum n_p \Delta H^\circ_f(\text{products}) - \sum n_r \Delta H^\circ_f(\text{reactants})$$
$$= [2(\Delta H^\circ_f(HBr\ (g)))] - [1(\Delta H^\circ_f(H_2\ (g))) + 1(\Delta H^\circ_f(Br_2\ (g)))]$$
$$= [2(-36.3\text{ kJ})] - [1(0.0\text{ kJ}) + 1(30.9\text{ kJ})]$$
$$= [-72.6\text{ kJ}] - [30.9\text{ kJ}]$$
$$= -103.5\text{ kJ} \text{ then}$$

Reactant/Product	S°(J/mol K from Appendix IIB)
H_2 (*g*)	130.7
Br_2 (*g*)	245.5
HBr (*g*)	198.7

Be sure to pull data for the correct formula and phase.

$$\Delta S^\circ_{rxn} = \sum n_p S^\circ(\text{products}) - \sum n_r S^\circ(\text{reactants})$$
$$= [2(S^\circ(HBr\ (g)))] - [1(S^\circ(H_2\ (g))) + 1(S^\circ(Br_2\ (g)))]$$
$$= [2(198.7\text{ J/K})] - [1(130.7\text{ J/K}) + 1(245.5\text{ J/K})] \quad \text{then } +21.2\frac{\text{J}}{\text{K}} \times \frac{1\text{ kJ}}{1000\text{ J}} = +0.0212\text{ kJ/K}$$
$$= [397.4\text{ J/K}] - [376.2\text{ J/K}]$$
$$= +21.2\text{ J/K}$$

then $\Delta G^\circ = \Delta H^\circ_{rxn} - T\Delta S^\circ_{rxn} = -103.5\text{ kJ} - (298\text{ K})(+0.0212\frac{\text{kJ}}{\text{K}}) = -109.8176\text{ kJ} = -1.098176 \times 10^5\text{ J}$

then $\Delta G^\circ_{rxn} = -RT \ln K$. Rearrange to solve for K.

$$K = e^{\frac{-\Delta G^\circ_{rxn}}{RT}} = e^{\frac{-(-1.098176 \times 10^5\text{ J})}{\left(8.314\frac{\text{J}}{\text{K}\cdot\text{mol}}\right)(298\text{ K})}} = e^{44.3247} = 1.78 \times 10^{19}$$ so the reaction is spontaneous.

Reactant/Product	ΔH°_f(kJ/mol from Appendix IIB)
H_2 (*g*)	0.0
I_2 (*g*)	62.42
HI (*g*)	26.5

Be sure to pull data for the correct formula and phase.

$$\Delta H^\circ_{rxn} = \sum n_p \Delta H^\circ_f(\text{products}) - \sum n_r \Delta H^\circ_f(\text{reactants})$$
$$= [2(\Delta H^\circ_f(HI\ (g)))] - [1(\Delta H^\circ_f(H_2\ (g))) + 1(\Delta H^\circ_f(I_2\ (g)))]$$
$$= [2(26.5\text{ kJ})] - [1(0.0\text{ kJ}) + 1(62.42\text{ kJ})]$$
$$= [53.0\text{ kJ}] - [62.42\text{ kJ}]$$
$$= -9.42\text{ kJ} \text{ then}$$

Reactant/Product	S°(J/mol K from Appendix IIB)
H_2 (*g*)	130.7
I_2 (*g*)	260.69
HI (*g*)	206.6

Be sure to pull data for the correct formula and phase.

$$\Delta S^\circ_{rxn} = \sum n_p S^\circ(\text{products}) - \sum n_r S^\circ(\text{reactants})$$
$$= [2(S^\circ(HI\ (g)))] - [1(S^\circ(H_2\ (g))) + 1(S^\circ(I_2\ (g)))]$$
$$= [2(206.6\text{ J/K})] - [1(130.7\text{ J/K}) + 1(260.69\text{ J/K})]$$
$$= [413.2\text{ J/K}] - [391.39\text{ J/K}]$$
$$= +21.8\text{ J/K}$$

then $21.8\frac{\text{J}}{\text{K}} \times \frac{1\text{ kJ}}{1000\text{ J}} = +0.0218\text{ kJ/K}$

then $\Delta G^\circ = \Delta H^\circ_{rxn} - T\Delta S^\circ_{rxn} = -9.42\text{ kJ} - (298\text{ K})\left(+0.0218\frac{\text{kJ}}{\text{K}}\right) = -15.9164\text{ kJ} = -1.59164 \times 10^4\text{ J}$ then

$\Delta G^\circ_{rxn} = -RT \ln K$. Rearrange to solve for K.

$$K = e^{\frac{-\Delta G^\circ_{rxn}}{RT}} = e^{\frac{-(-1.59164 \times 10^4\text{ J})}{\left(8.314\frac{\text{J}}{\text{K}\cdot\text{mol}}\right)(298\text{ K})}} = e^{6.42419} = 6.17 \times 10^2 = 617.$$ The reaction is spontaneous.

Cl_2 is the most spontaneous, I_2 is the least. The entropy change in the reactions is very constant. The spontaneity is determined by the standard enthalpy of formation of the acid. Higher temperatures make the reactions more spontaneous.
Check: The units (kJ and none) are correct. The enthalpy is twice the enthalpy of formation of the acid. We expect a very small entropy change because the number of moles of gas is unchanged. Since both terms are negative, the free energy change is negative and the reaction is spontaneous. The more negative the free energy change, the larger the *K*.

17.85 (a) **Given:** $N_2O\ (g) + NO_2\ (g) \rightleftharpoons 3\ NO\ (g)$ at 298 K **Find:** ΔG°_{rxn}
Conceptual Plan: $\Delta G^\circ_{rxn} = \sum n_p \Delta G^\circ_f(\text{products}) - \sum n_r \Delta G^\circ_f(\text{reactants})$
Solution:

Reactant/Product	ΔG°_f(kJ/mol from Appendix IIB)
$N_2O\ (g)$	103.7
$NO_2\ (g)$	51.3
$NO\ (g)$	87.6

Be sure to pull data for the correct formula and phase.

$$\begin{aligned}\Delta G^\circ_{rxn} &= \sum n_p \Delta G^\circ_f(\text{products}) - \sum n_r \Delta G^\circ_f(\text{reactants})\\ &= [3(\Delta G^\circ_f(NO\ (g)))] - [1(\Delta G^\circ_f(N_2O\ (g))) + 1(\Delta G^\circ_f(NO_2\ (g)))]\\ &= [3(87.6\text{ kJ})] - [1(103.7\text{ kJ}) + 1(51.3\text{ kJ})]\\ &= [262.8\text{ kJ}] - [155.0\text{ kJ}]\\ &= +107.8\text{ kJ}\end{aligned}$$

The reaction is nonspontaneous.
Check: The units (kJ) are correct. The standard free energy for the reaction was positive and so the reaction is nonspontaneous.

(b) **Given:** $P_{N_2O} = P_{NO_2} = 1.0$ atm initially **Find:** P_{N_2O} when reaction ceases to be spontaneous
Conceptual Plan: Reaction will no longer be spontaneous when $Q = K$, so $\Delta G^\circ_{rxn}, T \rightarrow K$.

$$\Delta G^\circ_{rxn} = -RT\ln K$$

Then solve the equilibrium problem to get gas pressures, since $K << 1$ the amount of NO generated will be very, very small compared to 1.0 atm, so, within experimental error, $P_{N_2O} = P_{NO_2} = 1.0$ atm. Simply solve for P_{NO}.

$$K = \frac{P^3_{NO}}{P_{N_2O}P_{NO_2}}$$

Solution: $\Delta G^\circ_{rxn} = -RT\ln K$. Rearrange to solve for *K*.

$$K = e^{\frac{-\Delta G^\circ_{rxn}}{RT}} = e^{\frac{-(+107.8\text{ kJ}) \times \frac{1000\text{ J}}{1\text{ kJ}}}{\left(8.314\frac{\text{J}}{\text{K}\cdot\text{mol}}\right)(298\text{ K})}} = e^{-43.5103} = 1.27 \times 10^{-19}.$$ Since $K = \frac{P^3_{NO}}{P_{N_2O}P_{NO_2}}$, rearrange to solve for P_{NO}. $P^3_{NO} = \sqrt[3]{K\,P_{N_2O}P_{NO_2}} = \sqrt[3]{(1.27 \times 10^{-19})(1.0)(1.0)} = 5.0 \times 10^{-7}$ atm.
Note that the assumption that P_{N_2O} was very, very small was valid.
Check: The units (atm) are correct. Since the free energy change was positive, the *K* was very small. This leads us to expect that very little NO will be formed.

(c) **Given:** $N_2O\ (g) + NO_2\ (g) \rightleftharpoons 3\ NO\ (g)$ **Find:** temperature for spontaneity
Conceptual Plan: $\Delta H^\circ_{rxn} = \sum n_p H^\circ_f(\text{products}) - \sum n_r H^\circ_f(\text{reactants})$ **then**
$\Delta S^\circ_{rxn} = \sum n_p S^\circ(\text{products}) - \sum n_r S^\circ(\text{reactants})$ **then J/K $\rightarrow$ kJ/K then $\Delta H^\circ_{rxn}, \Delta S_{rxn} \rightarrow T$**

$$\frac{1\text{ kJ}}{1000\text{ J}} \qquad \Delta G = \Delta H_{rxn} - T\Delta S_{rxn}$$

Solution:

Reactant/Product	ΔH°_f(kJ/mol from Appendix IIB)
$N_2O\ (g)$	81.6
$NO_2\ (g)$	33.2
$NO\ (g)$	91.3

Be sure to pull data for the correct formula and phase.

$\Delta H^\circ_{rxn} = \sum n_p \Delta H^\circ_f(\text{products}) - \sum n_r \Delta H^\circ_f(\text{reactants})$
$= [3(\Delta H^\circ_f(NO\ (g)))\ ] - [1(\Delta H^\circ_f(N_2O\ (g))) + 1(\Delta H^\circ_f(NO_2\ (g)))]$
$= [\ 3(\ 91.3\text{ kJ})\ ] - [1(81.6\text{ kJ}) + 1(33.2\text{ kJ})]$
$= [273.9\text{ kJ}] - [114.8\text{ kJ}]$
$= +\ 159.1\text{ kJ}$ then

Reactant/Product	S°(J/mol K from Appendix IIB)
N_2O (g)	220.0
NO_2 (g)	240.1
NO (g)	210.8

Be sure to pull data for the correct formula and phase.

$\Delta S^\circ_{rxn} = \sum n_p S^\circ(\text{products}) - \sum n_r S^\circ(\text{reactants})$
$= [3(S^\circ(NO\ (g)))\ ] - [1(S^\circ(N_2O\ (g))) + 1(S^\circ(NO_2\ (g)))]$
$= [3(210.8\text{ J/K})] - [1(220.0\text{ J/K}) + 1(240.1\text{ J/K})]$
$= [632.4\text{ J/K}] - [460.1\text{ J/K}]$
$= +\ 172.3\text{ J/K}$

then $+\ 172.3\frac{\text{J}}{\text{K}} \times \frac{1\text{ kJ}}{1000\text{ J}} = +\ 0.1723\text{ kJ/K}$. Since $\Delta G = \Delta H_{rxn} - T\Delta S_{rxn}$, set $\Delta G = 0$ and rearrange to solve for T. $T = \frac{\Delta H_{rxn}}{\Delta S_{rxn}} = \frac{+\ 159.1\text{ kJ}}{0.1723\frac{\text{kJ}}{\text{K}}} = +\ 923.4\text{ K}.$

Check: The units (K) are correct. The reaction can be made more spontaneous by raising the temperature, because the entropy change is positive (increase in the number of moles of gas).

17.86 (a) **Given:** $BaCO_3\ (s) \rightleftharpoons BaO\ (s) + CO_2\ (g)$ at 298 K **Find:** ΔG°_{rxn}
Conceptual Plan: $\Delta G^\circ_{rxn} = \sum n_p \Delta G^\circ_f(\text{products}) - \sum n_r \Delta G^\circ_f(\text{reactants})$
Solution:

Reactant/Product	ΔG°_f(kJ/mol from Appendix IIB)
$BaCO_3$ (s)	− 1134.4
BaO (s)	− 520.3
CO_2 (g)	− 394.4

Be sure to pull data for the correct formula and phase.

$\Delta G^\circ_{rxn} = \sum n_p \Delta G^\circ_f(\text{products}) - \sum n_r \Delta G^\circ_f(\text{reactants})$
$= [1(\Delta G^\circ_f(BaO\ (s))) + 1(\Delta G^\circ_f(CO_2\ (g)))] - [1(\Delta G^\circ_f(BaCO_3\ (s)))]$
$= [1(-\ 520.3\text{ kJ}) + 1(-\ 394.4\text{ kJ})] - [1(-\ 1134.4\text{ kJ})]$
$= [-\ 914.7\text{ kJ}] - [-\ 1134.4\text{ kJ}]$
$= +\ 219.7\text{ kJ}$

The reaction is nonspontaneous.

Check: The units (kJ) are correct. The standard free energy for the reaction was positive and so the reaction is nonspontaneous.

(b) **Given:** $BaCO_3$ (s) initially in container **Find:** P_{CO_2} at equilibrium
Conceptual Plan: Reaction will be at equilibrium when Q = K, so $\Delta G^\circ_{rxn}, T \rightarrow K \rightarrow P_{CO_2}$.

$\Delta G^\circ_{rxn} = -\ RT\ln K \qquad K = P_{CO_2}$

Solution: $\Delta G^\circ_{rxn} = -\ RT\ln K$. Rearrange to solve for K.

$$K = e^{\frac{-\Delta G^\circ_{rxn}}{RT}} = e^{\frac{-(-\ 219.7\text{ kJ}) \times \frac{1000\text{ J}}{1\text{ kJ}}}{\left(8.314\frac{\text{J}}{\text{K}\cdot\text{mol}}\right)(298\text{ K})}} = e^{-88.6755} = 3.08 \times 10^{-39}.$$ So $P_{CO_2} = 3.08 \times 10^{-39}$ atm.

Check: The units (atm) are correct. Since the free energy change was very positive, the K was very, very small. This leads us to expect that very little carbon dioxide will be formed.

(c) **Given:** $BaCO_3\ (s) \rightleftharpoons BaO\ (s) + CO_2\ (g)$ **Find:** temperature for $P_{CO_2} = 1.0$ atm
Conceptual Plan: $\Delta H^\circ_{rxn} = \sum n_p H^\circ_f(\text{products}) - \sum n_r H^\circ_f(\text{reactants})$ **then**
$\Delta S^\circ_{rxn} = \sum n_p S^\circ(\text{products}) - \sum n_r S^\circ(\text{reactants})$ **then J/K → kJ/K then** $\Delta H^\circ_{rxn}, \Delta S_{rxn} \rightarrow T$

$$\frac{1\text{ kJ}}{1000\text{ J}} \qquad \Delta G = \Delta H_{rxn} - T\Delta S_{rxn}$$

Solution:

Reactant/Product	ΔH°_f(kJ/mol from Appendix IIB)
$BaCO_3\ (s)$	− 1213.0
$BaO\ (s)$	− 548.0
$CO_2\ (g)$	− 393.5

Be sure to pull data for the correct formula and phase.

$$\begin{aligned}\Delta H^\circ_{rxn} &= \sum n_p \Delta H^\circ_f(\text{products}) - \sum n_r \Delta H^\circ_f(\text{reactants})\\ &= [1(\Delta H^\circ_f(BaO\ (s))) + 1(\Delta H^\circ_f(CO_2\ (g)))] - [1(\Delta H^\circ_f(BaCO_3\ (s)))]\\ &= [1(-548.0\text{ kJ}) + 1(-393.5\text{ kJ})] - [1(-1213.0\text{ kJ})]\\ &= [-941.5\text{ kJ}] - [-1213.0\text{ kJ}]\\ &= +271.5\text{ kJ then}\end{aligned}$$

Reactant/Product	S°(J/mol K from Appendix IIB)
$BaCO_3\ (s)$	112.1
$BaO\ (s)$	72.1
$CO_2\ (g)$	213.8

Be sure to pull data for the correct formula and phase.

$$\begin{aligned}\Delta S^\circ_{rxn} &= \sum n_p S^\circ(\text{products}) - \sum n_r S^\circ(\text{reactants})\\ &= [1(S^\circ(BaO\ (s))) + 1(S^\circ(CO_2\ (g)))] - [1(S^\circ(BaCO_3\ (s)))]\\ &= [1(72.1\text{ J/K}) + 1(213.8\text{ J/K})] - [1(112.1\text{ J/K})]\\ &= [285.9\text{ J/K}] - [112.1\text{ J/K}]\\ &= +173.8\text{ J/K then}\end{aligned}$$

$+173.8\dfrac{\text{J}}{\text{K}} \times \dfrac{1\text{ kJ}}{1000\text{ J}} = +0.1738$ kJ/K. Since $\Delta G = \Delta H_{rxn} - T\Delta S_{rxn}$, set $\Delta G = 0$ and rearrange to solve for T. $T = \dfrac{\Delta H_{rxn}}{\Delta S_{rxn}} = \dfrac{+271.5\text{ kJ}}{0.1738\dfrac{\text{kJ}}{\text{K}}} = +1562$ K. When $\Delta G = 0$ and $K = 1$, so at 1562 K $P_{CO_2} = 1.0$ atm.

Check: The units (K) are correct. The reaction can be made more spontaneous by raising the temperature, because the entropy change is positive (increase in the number of moles of gas). We expect a high temperature because the enthalpy change is so positive.

17.87 (a) **Given:** $ATP\ (aq) + H_2O\ (l) \rightarrow ADP\ (aq) + P_i\ (aq)$ $\Delta G^\circ_{rxn} = -30.5$ kJ at 298 K **Find:** K
Conceptual Plan: $\Delta G^\circ_{rxn}, T \rightarrow K$

$$\Delta G^\circ_{rxn} = -RT\ln K$$

Solution: $\Delta G^\circ_{rxn} = -RT\ln K$. Rearrange to solve for K.

$$K = e^{\frac{-\Delta G^\circ_{rxn}}{RT}} = e^{\frac{-(-30.5\text{ kJ})\times\frac{1000\text{ J}}{1\text{ kJ}}}{\left(8.314\frac{\text{J}}{\text{K}\cdot\text{mol}}\right)(298\text{ K})}} = e^{12.3104} = 2.22\times10^5.$$

Check: The units (none) are correct. The free energy change is negative and the reaction is spontaneous. This results in a large K.

(b) **Given:** oxidation of glucose drives reforming of ATP
Find: ΔG°_{rxn} of oxidation of glucose and moles ATP formed per mole of glucose
Conceptual Plan: Write a balanced reaction for glucose oxidation then
$\Delta G^\circ_{rxn} = \sum n_p \Delta G^\circ_f(\text{products}) - \sum n_r \Delta G^\circ_f(\text{reactants})$ **then** ΔG°_{rxn}**s → moles ATP/ mole glucose.**

$$\frac{\Delta G^\circ_{rxn}\text{ glucose oxidation}}{\Delta G^\circ_{rxn}\text{ ATP hydrolysis}}$$

Solution: $C_6H_{12}O_6\ (s)\ +\ 6\ O_2\ (g)\ \rightarrow\ 6\ CO_2\ (g)\ +6\ H_2O\ (l)$

Reactant/Product	ΔG_f°(kJ/mol from Appendix IIB)
$C_6H_{12}O_6\ (s)$	− 910.4
$O_2\ (g)$	0.0
$CO_2\ (g)$	− 394.4
$H_2O\ (l)$	− 237.1

Be sure to pull data for the correct formula and phase.

$$\begin{aligned}\Delta G^\circ_{rxn} &= \sum n_p \Delta G_f^\circ(\text{products}) - \sum n_r \Delta G_f^\circ(\text{reactants})\\ &= [6(\Delta G_f^\circ(CO_2\ (g))) + 6(\Delta G_f^\circ(H_2O\ (l)))] - [1(\Delta G_f^\circ(C_6H_{12}O_6\ (s))) + 6(\Delta G_f^\circ(O_2\ (g)))]\\ &= [6(-394.4\text{ kJ}) + 6(-237.1\text{ kJ})] - [1(-910.4\text{ kJ}) + 6(0.0\text{ kJ})]\\ &= [-3789.0\text{ kJ}] - [-910.4\text{ kJ}]\\ &= -2878.6\text{ kJ}\end{aligned}$$

So the reaction is very spontaneous.
$$\frac{2878.6\dfrac{\cancel{\text{kJ generated}}}{\text{mole glucose oxidized}}}{30.5\dfrac{\cancel{\text{kJ needed}}}{\text{mole ATP reformed}}} = 94.4\frac{\text{mole ATP reformed}}{\text{mole glucose oxidized}}$$

Check: The units (mol) are correct. The free energy change for the glucose oxidation is large compared to the ATP hydrolysis, so we expect to reform many moles of ATP.

17.88 **Given:** $ATP\ (aq) + H_2O\ (l) \rightarrow ADP\ (aq) + P_i\ (aq)$ $\Delta G^\circ_{rxn} = -30.5$ kJ at 298 K
Find: ΔG_{rxn} when [ATP] = 0.0031 M, [ADP] = 0.0014 M and $[P_i]$ = 0.0048 M
Conceptual Plan: ΔG°_{rxn}**, [ATP], [ADP], $[P_i]$, $T \rightarrow \Delta G$**

$$\Delta G_{rxn} = \Delta G^\circ_{rxn} + RT\ln Q \text{ where } Q = \frac{[ADP]\,[P_i]}{[ATP]}$$

Solution: $Q = \dfrac{[ADP]\,[P_i]}{[ATP]} = \dfrac{(0.0014)(0.0048)}{0.0031} = 0.00216774$ then

$$\Delta G_{rxn} = \Delta G^\circ_{rxn} + RT\ln Q = -30.5\text{ kJ} + \left(8.314\frac{\cancel{\text{J}}}{\cancel{\text{K}}\cdot\text{mol}}\right)\left(\frac{1\text{ kJ}}{1000\ \cancel{\text{J}}}\right)(298\ \cancel{\text{K}})\ln(0.00216774) = -45.7\text{ kJ}$$

Check: The units (kJ) are correct. The Q is less than one so we expect a free energy more negative than at standard conditions.

17.89 (a) **Given:** $2\ CO\ (g) + 2\ NO\ (g) \rightarrow N_2\ (g) + 2\ CO_2\ (g)$ **Find:** ΔG°_{rxn} and effect of increasing T on ΔG
Conceptual Plan: $\Delta G^\circ_{rxn} = \sum n_p \Delta G_f^\circ$**(products)** $- \sum n_r \Delta G_f^\circ$**(reactants)**

Solution:

Reactant/Product	ΔG_f°(kJ/mol from Appendix IIB)
$CO\ (g)$	− 137.2
$NO\ (g)$	87.6
$N_2\ (g)$	0.0
$CO_2\ (g)$	− 394.4

Be sure to pull data for the correct formula and phase.

$$\begin{aligned}\Delta G^\circ_{rxn} &= \sum n_p \Delta G_f^\circ(\text{products}) - \sum n_r \Delta G_f^\circ(\text{reactants})\\ &= [1(\Delta G_f^\circ(N_2\ (g))) + 2(\Delta G_f^\circ(CO_2\ (g)))] - [2(\Delta G_f^\circ(CO\ (g))) + 2(\Delta G_f^\circ(NO\ (g)))]\\ &= [1(0.0\text{ kJ}) + 2(-394.4\text{ kJ})] - [2(-137.2\text{ kJ}) + 2(87.6\text{ kJ})]\\ &= [-788.8\text{ kJ}] - [-99.2\text{ kJ}]\\ &= -689.6\text{ kJ}\end{aligned}$$

Since the number of moles of gas is decreasing, the entropy change is negative and so ΔG will become less negative with increasing temperature.
Check: The units (kJ) are correct. The free energy change is negative since the carbon dioxide has such a low free energy of formation.

(b) **Given:** $5\ H_2\ (g) + 2\ NO\ (g) \rightarrow 2\ NH_3\ (g) + 2\ H_2O\ (g)$ **Find:** ΔG°_{rxn} and effect of increasing T on ΔG
Conceptual Plan: $\Delta G^\circ_{rxn} = \sum n_p \Delta G_f^\circ$**(products)** $- \sum n_r \Delta G_f^\circ$**(reactants)**

Solution:

Reactant/Product	ΔG_f°(kJ/mol from Appendix IIB)
H_2 (*g*)	0.0
NO (*g*)	87.6
NH_3 (*g*)	− 16.4
H_2O (*g*)	− 228.6

Be sure to pull data for the correct formula and phase.

$$\begin{aligned}\Delta G^\circ_{rxn} &= \sum n_p \Delta G_f^\circ(\text{products}) - \sum n_r \Delta G_f^\circ(\text{reactants})\\ &= [2(\Delta G_f^\circ(NH_3\ (g))) + 2(\Delta G_f^\circ(H_2O\ (g)))] - [5(\Delta G_f^\circ(H_2\ (g))) + 2(\Delta G_f^\circ(NO\ (g)))]\\ &= [2(-16.4\text{ kJ}) + 2(-228.6\text{ kJ})] - [5(0.0\text{ kJ}) + 2(87.6\text{ kJ})]\\ &= [-490.0\text{ kJ}] - [175.2\text{ kJ}]\\ &= -665.2\text{ kJ}\end{aligned}$$

Since the number of moles of gas is decreasing, the entropy change is negative and so ΔG will become less negative with increasing temperature.

Check: The units (kJ) are correct. The free energy change is negative since ammonia and water have such a low free energy of formation.

(c) **Given:** 2 H_2 (*g*) + 2 NO (*g*) → N_2 (*g*) + 2 H_2O (*g*) **Find:** ΔG°_{rxn} and effect of increasing *T* on ΔG
Conceptual Plan: $\Delta G^\circ_{rxn} = \sum n_p \Delta G_f^\circ(\textbf{products}) - \sum n_r \Delta G_f^\circ(\textbf{reactants})$

Solution:

Reactant/Product	ΔG_f°(kJ/mol from Appendix IIB)
H_2 (*g*)	0.0
NO (*g*)	87.6
N_2 (*g*)	0.0
H_2O (*g*)	− 228.6

Be sure to pull data for the correct formula and phase.

$$\begin{aligned}\Delta G^\circ_{rxn} &= \sum n_p \Delta G_f^\circ(\text{products}) - \sum n_r \Delta G_f^\circ(\text{reactants})\\ &= [1(\Delta G_f^\circ(N_2\ (g))) + 2(\Delta G_f^\circ(H_2O\ (g)))] - [2(\Delta G_f^\circ(H_2\ (g))) + 2(\Delta G_f^\circ(NO\ (g)))]\\ &= [1(0.0\text{ kJ}) + 2(-228.6\text{ kJ})] - [2(0.0\text{ kJ}) + 2(87.6\text{ kJ})]\\ &= [-457.2\text{ kJ}] - [175.2\text{ kJ}]\\ &= -632.4\text{ kJ}\end{aligned}$$

Since the number of moles of gas is decreasing, the entropy change is negative and so ΔG will become less negative with increasing temperature.

Check: The units (kJ) are correct. The free energy change is negative since water has such a low free energy of formation.

(d) **Given:** 2 NH_3 (*g*) + 2 O_2 (*g*) → N_2O (*g*) + 3 H_2O (*g*) **Find:** ΔG°_{rxn} and effect of increasing *T* on ΔG
Conceptual Plan: $\Delta G^\circ_{rxn} = \sum n_p \Delta G_f^\circ(\textbf{products}) - \sum n_r \Delta G_f^\circ(\textbf{reactants})$

Solution:

Reactant/Product	ΔG_f°(kJ/mol from Appendix IIB)
NH_3 (*g*)	− 16.4
O_2 (*g*)	0.0
N_2O (*g*)	103.7
H_2O (*g*)	− 228.6

Be sure to pull data for the correct formula and phase.

$$\begin{aligned}\Delta G^\circ_{rxn} &= \sum n_p \Delta G_f^\circ(\text{products}) - \sum n_r \Delta G_f^\circ(\text{reactants})\\ &= [1(\Delta G_f^\circ(N_2O\ (g))) + 3(\Delta G_f^\circ(H_2O\ (g)))] - [2(\Delta G_f^\circ(NH_3\ (g))) + 2(\Delta G_f^\circ(O_2\ (g)))]\\ &= [1(103.7\text{ kJ}) + 3(-228.6\text{ kJ})] - [2(-16.4\text{ kJ}) + 2(0.0\text{ kJ})]\\ &= [-582.1\text{ kJ}] - [-32.8\text{ kJ}]\\ &= -549.3\text{ kJ}\end{aligned}$$

Since the number of moles of gas is constant the entropy change will be small and slightly negative, so the magnitude of ΔG will decrease with increasing temperature.

Check: The units (kJ) are correct. The free energy change is negative since water has such a low free energy of formation. The entropy change is negative once the S° values are reviewed ($\Delta S_{rxn} = -9.6$ J/K).

17.90 (a) **Given:** $NH_3\ (g) + HBr\ (g) \rightarrow NH_4Br\ (s)$ **Find:** ΔG°_{rxn} effect of decreasing T on ΔG

Conceptual Plan: $\Delta G^\circ_{rxn} = \sum n_p \Delta G^\circ_f(\text{products}) - \sum n_r \Delta G^\circ_f(\text{reactants})$

Solution:

Reactant/Product	ΔG°_f(kJ/mol from Appendix IIB)
$NH_3\ (g)$	− 16.4
$HBr\ (g)$	− 53.4
$NH_4Br\ (s)$	− 175.2

Be sure to pull data for the correct formula and phase.

$$\begin{aligned}\Delta G^\circ_{rxn} &= \sum n_p \Delta G^\circ_f(\text{products}) - \sum n_r \Delta G^\circ_f(\text{reactants})\\ &= [1(\Delta G^\circ_f(NH_4Br\ (s)))] - [1(\Delta G^\circ_f(NH_3\ (g))) + 1(\Delta G^\circ_f(HBr\ (g)))]\\ &= [1(-175.2\text{ kJ})] - [1(-16.4\text{ kJ}) + 1(-53.4\text{ kJ})]\\ &= [-175.2\text{ kJ}] - [-69.8\text{ kJ}]\\ &= -105.4\text{ kJ}\end{aligned}$$

Since the number of moles of gas decreases, the entropy change will be negative and ΔG will become more negative with decreasing temperature.

Check: The units (kJ) are correct. The free energy change is negative since ammonium bromide has such a low free energy of formation.

(b) **Given:** $CaCO_3\ (s) \rightarrow CaO\ (s) + CO_2\ (g)$ **Find:** ΔG°_{rxn} effect of decreasing T on ΔG

Conceptual Plan: $\Delta G^\circ_{rxn} = \sum n_p \Delta G^\circ_f(\text{products}) - \sum n_r \Delta G^\circ_f(\text{reactants})$

Solution:

Reactant/Product	ΔG°_f(kJ/mol from Appendix IIB)
$CaCO_3\ (s)$	− 1129.1
$CaO\ (s)$	− 603.3
$CO_2\ (g)$	− 394.4

Be sure to pull data for the correct formula and phase.

$$\begin{aligned}\Delta G^\circ_{rxn} &= \sum n_p \Delta G^\circ_f(\text{products}) - \sum n_r \Delta G^\circ_f(\text{reactants})\\ &= [1(\Delta G^\circ_f(CaO\ (s))) + 1(\Delta G^\circ_f(CO_2\ (g)))] - [1(\Delta G^\circ_f(CaCO_3\ (s)))]\\ &= [1(-603.3\text{ kJ}) + 1(-394.4\text{ kJ})] - [1(-1129.1\text{ kJ})]\\ &= [-997.7\text{ kJ}] - [-1129.1\text{ kJ}]\\ &= +131.4\text{ kJ}\end{aligned}$$

Since the number of moles of gas increases, the entropy change will be positive and ΔG will become more positive with decreasing temperature.

Check: The units (kJ) are correct. The free energy change is positive since calcium carbonate has such a large free energy of formation.

(c) **Given:** $CH_4\ (g) + 3\ Cl_2\ (g) \rightarrow CHCl_3\ (g) + 3\ HCl\ (g)$ **Find:** ΔG°_{rxn} effect of decreasing T on ΔG

Conceptual Plan: $\Delta G^\circ_{rxn} = \sum n_p \Delta G^\circ_f(\text{products}) - \sum n_r \Delta G^\circ_f(\text{reactants})$

Solution:

Reactant/Product	ΔG°_f(kJ/mol from Appendix IIB)
$CH_4\ (g)$	− 50.5
$Cl_2\ (g)$	0.0
$CHCl_3\ (g)$	− 70.4
$HCl\ (g)$	− 95.3

Be sure to pull data for the correct formula and phase.

$$\begin{aligned}\Delta G^\circ_{rxn} &= \sum n_p \Delta G^\circ_f(\text{products}) - \sum n_r \Delta G^\circ_f(\text{reactants})\\ &= [1(\Delta G^\circ_f(CHCl_3\ (g))) + 3(\Delta G^\circ_f(HCl\ (g)))] - [1(\Delta G^\circ_f(CH_4\ (g))) + 3(\Delta G^\circ_f(Cl_2\ (g)))]\\ &= [1(-70.4\text{ kJ}) + 3(-95.3\text{ kJ})] - [1(-50.5\text{ kJ}) + 3(0.0\text{ kJ})]\\ &= [-356.3\text{ kJ}] - [-50.5\text{ kJ}]\\ &= -305.8\text{ kJ}\end{aligned}$$

Since the number of moles of gas is constant, the entropy change will be small. The entropy change is so small that the magnitude of ΔG will remain constant with decreasing temperature.

Check: The units (kJ) are correct. The free energy change is negative since chloroform and hydrogen chloride have such low free energies of formation. The entropy change is slightly positive once the S° values are reviewed ($\Delta S_{rxn} = + 0.7$ J/K).

17.91 With one exception, the formation of any oxide of nitrogen at 298 K requires more moles of gas as reactants than are formed as products. For example 1 mole of N_2O requires 0.5 moles of O_2 and 1 mole of N_2; 1 mole of N_2O_3 requires 1 mole of N_2 and 1.5 moles of O_2, and so on. The exception is NO, where 1 mole of NO requires 0.5 moles of O_2 and 0.5 moles of N_2: $\frac{1}{2}N_2(g) + \frac{1}{2}O_2(g) \rightarrow NO(g)$. This reaction has a positive ΔS because what is essentially mixing of the N and O has taken place in the product.

17.92 ΔG°_f becomes less negative as the atomic number increases because the bond length increases and the bond strength decreases. There is less chemical energy stored in the longer bonds. The ΔS°_f increases as the atomic number increases because of the halides in the hydrogen halides. This is because the hydrogen halide has a low entropy component (hydrogen) and a high entropy component (the halide, which increases as the atomic number of the halide increases).

17.93 **Given:** $X_2\,(g) \rightarrow 2\,X\,(g)$; $P_{\text{initial }X_2} = 755$ torr, $P_{\text{final X}} = 103$ torr at 298 K; $P_{\text{initial }X_2} = 748$ torr, $P_{\text{final X}} = 532$ torr at 755 K **Find:** ΔH°_{rxn}

Conceptual Plan: at each temperature $P_{\text{initial }X_2}, P_{\text{final X}} \rightarrow K$ then $K_1, K_2, T_1, T_2 \rightarrow \Delta H^\circ_{rxn}$

Use stoichiometry to calculate $[X_2]_{\text{final}}$ *and* $K = \frac{P_X^2}{P_{X_2}}$ $\qquad \ln K = -\frac{\Delta H^\circ_{rxn}}{R}\frac{1}{T} + \frac{\Delta S^\circ_{rxn}}{R}$

Solution: Use stoichiometry of $X_2\,(g) \rightarrow 2\,X\,(g)$; $P_{\text{final }X_2} = P_{\text{initial }X_2} - \frac{1}{2}P_{\text{final X}}$ so that at $T_1 = 298$ K

$P_{\text{final }X_2} = P_{\text{initial }X_2} - \frac{1}{2}P_{\text{final X}} = 755\text{ torr} - \frac{1}{2}(103\text{ torr}) = 703.5$ torr and at $T_{12} = 755$ K $P_{\text{final }X_2} = P_{\text{initial }X_2} - \frac{1}{2}$ $P_{\text{final X}} = 748\text{ torr} - \frac{1}{2}(532\text{ torr}) = 482$ torr. Then $K = \frac{P_X^2}{P_{X_2}}$ so that at $T_1 = 298$ K

$$K_1 = \frac{P_X^2}{P_{X_2}} = \frac{(103)^2}{703.5} = 15.08031 \text{ and at } T_2 = 755\text{ K } K_2 = \frac{P_X^2}{P_{X_2}} = \frac{(532)^2}{482} = 587.1867.$$

Since $\ln K = -\frac{\Delta H^\circ_{rxn}}{R}\frac{1}{T} + \frac{\Delta S^\circ_{rxn}}{R}$, $\ln K_1 + \frac{\Delta H^\circ_{rxn}}{R}\frac{1}{T_1} = \frac{\Delta S^\circ_{rxn}}{R} = \ln K_2 + \frac{\Delta H^\circ_{rxn}}{R}\frac{1}{T_2}$.

Rearrange to solve for ΔH°_{rxn}.

$$\Delta H^\circ_{rxn} = \frac{\ln\frac{K_2}{K_1}}{\left(\frac{1}{T_1} - \frac{1}{T_2}\right)}R = \frac{\ln\left(\frac{587.1867}{15.08031}\right)}{\left(\frac{1}{298\text{ K}} - \frac{1}{755\text{ K}}\right)} \times 8.314\frac{\text{J}}{\text{K}\cdot\text{mol}} \times \frac{1\text{ kJ}}{1000\text{ J}} = 14.9889\text{ kJ/mol} = 15.0\text{ kJ/mol}$$

Check: The units are correct (kJ/mol). Since K increases with increasing temperature the reaction is expected to be endothermic.

17.94 **Given:** $N_2O_4\,(g) \rightarrow 2\,N_2O\,(g)$; $P_{\text{initial }N_2O_4} = 0.100$ atm, at equilibrium 58% decomposed at 298 K; $\Delta H^\circ_{rxn} =$ 55.3 kJ/mol **Find:** percent decomposed at 388 K

Conceptual Plan: at 298 K $P_{\text{initial }N_2O_4}$, percent decomposed $\rightarrow K_1$ then $\Delta H^\circ_{rxn}, K_1, T_1, T_2 \rightarrow K_2$

Use stoichiometry to calculate $[N_2O_4]_{\text{final}}$ *and* $[NO_2]_{\text{final}}$ *and* $K = \frac{P_{NO_2}^2}{P_{N_2O_4}}$ $\qquad \ln K = -\frac{\Delta H^\circ_{rxn}}{r}\frac{1}{T} + \frac{\Delta S^\circ_{rxn}}{r}$

then $K_2, P_{\text{initial }N_2O_4} \rightarrow$ percent decomposed

Use stoichiometry to calculate $[N_2O_4]_{\text{final}}$ *and* $[NO_2]_{\text{final}}$ *and* $K = \frac{P_{NO_2}^2}{P_{N_2O_4}}$

Solution: $K_1 = \frac{P_{NO_2}^2}{P_{N_2O_4}} = \frac{(2 \times 0.100 \times (0.58))^2}{0.100 \times (1 - 0.58)} = 0.320381$. Since $\ln K = -\frac{\Delta H^\circ_{rxn}}{r}\frac{1}{T} + \frac{\Delta S^\circ_{rxn}}{r}$,

$\ln K_1 + \frac{\Delta H^\circ_{rxn}}{r}\frac{1}{T_1} = \frac{\Delta S^\circ_{rxn}}{r} = \ln K_2 + \frac{\Delta H^\circ_{rxn}}{r}\frac{1}{T_2}$. Rearrange to solve for K_2.

$$\ln K_2 = \ln K_1 + \frac{\Delta H^\circ_{rxn}}{r}\left(\frac{1}{T_1} - \frac{1}{T_2}\right) = \ln(0.320381) + \frac{\frac{55.3\text{ kJ}}{\text{mol}} \times \frac{1000\text{ J}}{1\text{ kJ}}}{8.314\frac{\text{J}}{\text{K}\cdot\text{mol}}}\left(\frac{1}{298\text{ K}} - \frac{1}{388\text{ K}}\right) = 4.03913 \text{ so}$$

$K_2 = e^{4.03913} = 56.77693$ then

Let $x = \left(\frac{\%\ \text{decomposed}}{100}\right)$ then $K_2 = \frac{P^2_{NO_2}}{P_{N_2O_4}} = \frac{(2x)^2}{0.100 - x} = 56.77693$. Rearrange to solve for x.

$(2\,x)^2 = 56.77693\,(0.100 - x) \rightarrow$

$x^2 = 5.677693 - 56.77693x) \rightarrow$

$x^2 + 56.77693\,x - 56.77693 = 0$. Using quadratic equation, $x = 0.099$ or $\frac{0.099}{0.100} \times 100\% = 99\%$ decomposed.

Check: The units are correct (% decomposed). Since the reaction is endothermic we expect the K to increase with increasing temperature. If we plug the % decomposed into the equation for K_2 we get the correct value for K_2.

17.95 (a) $\Delta S_{univ} > 0$. The process is spontaneous. It is slow unless a spark is applied.

(b) $\Delta S_{univ} > 0$. Although the change in the system is not spontaneous; the overall change, which includes such processes as combustion or water flow to generate electricity, is spontaneous.

(c) ΔS_{univ} 0, The acorn oak/tree system is becoming more ordered, so the processes associated with growth are not spontaneous. But they are driven by spontaneous processes such as the generation of heat by the sun and the reactions that produce energy in the cell.

17.96 The Haber process is carried out at high temperature, because the reaction rate is so much larger at higher temperatures. In the Haber process the ammonia product is continually removed via condensation, so the decreasing value of K is not very important to the overall process.

17.97 At equilibrium ($P_{H_2O} = 18.3$ mmHg), $\Delta G_{rxn} = 0$.

$$Q = P^6_{H_2O} = \left(\frac{\frac{18.3\ \text{mmHg}}{760\ \text{mmHg}}}{1\ \text{atm}}\right)^6 = (0.02407894\ \text{atm})^6 = 1.949059 \times 10^{-10} \text{ and}$$

$\Delta G_{rxn} = \Delta G^\circ_{rxn} + R\,T \ln Q = 0$ Rearrange to solve for ΔG°_{rxn}(at $P_{H_2O} = 760$ mmHg = standard conditions)

$$\Delta G^\circ_{rxn} = \Delta G_{rxn} - R\,T \ln Q = 0 - \left(8.314 \frac{\text{J}}{\text{K} \cdot \text{mol}}\right)\left(\frac{1\ \text{kJ}}{1000\ \text{J}}\right)(298\ \text{K}) \ln(1.949059 \times 10^{-10}) = 55.3948 \frac{\text{kJ}}{\text{mol}}$$

$$= 55.4 \frac{\text{kJ}}{\text{mol}}.$$

17.98 **Given:** AgCl, $\Delta H^\circ_{rxn} = 65.7$ kJ/mol, $S_1 = 1.33 \times 10^{-5}$ M at 25 °C (298 K) **Find:** S at 50.0 °C

Conceptual Plan: **°C $\rightarrow$ K then $S_1 \rightarrow K_1$ then $\Delta H^\circ_{rxn}, K_1, T_1, T_2 \rightarrow K_2 \rightarrow S_2$**

$K = 273.15 + °C$ $K_{sp} = [Ag^+][Cl^-] = S^2$ $\ln K = -\frac{\Delta H^\circ_{rxn}}{R}\frac{1}{T} + \frac{\Delta S^\circ_{rxn}}{R}$ $K_{sp} = S^2$

Solution: $T_1 = 273.15 + 25 = 298$ K, and $T_2 = 273.15 + 50.0 = 323.2$ K, then

$K_{sp} = [Ag^+][Cl^-] = S^2 = (1.33 \times 10^{-5})^2 = 1.7689 \times 10^{-10}$. Since $\ln K = -\frac{\Delta H^\circ_{rxn}}{R}\frac{1}{T} + \frac{\Delta S^\circ_{rxn}}{R}$,

$\ln K_1 + \frac{\Delta H^\circ_{rxn}}{R}\frac{1}{T_1} = \frac{\Delta S^\circ_{rxn}}{R} = \ln K_2 + \frac{\Delta H^\circ_{rxn}}{R}\frac{1}{T_2}$. Rearrange to solve for K_2.

$$\ln K_2 = \ln K_1 + \frac{\Delta H^\circ_{rxn}}{R}\left(\frac{1}{T_1} - \frac{1}{T_2}\right) = \ln(1.7689 \times 10^{-10}) + \frac{\frac{65.7\ \text{kJ}}{\text{mol}} \times \frac{1000\ \text{J}}{1\ \text{kJ}}}{8.314 \frac{\text{J}}{\text{K} \cdot \text{mol}}}\left(\frac{1}{298\ \text{K}} - \frac{1}{323.2\ \text{K}}\right)$$

$= -2.038032$ and so $K_2 = e^{-2.038032} = 1.409089 \times 10^{-9}$. Since $K_{sp} = [Ag^+][Cl^-] = S^2 = 1.409089 \times 10^{-9}$

so $S = 3.75378 \times 10^{-5}$ M $= 3.8 \times 10^{-5}$ M

Check: The units are correct (M). Since the reaction is endothermic we expect the K (and S) to increase with increasing temperature.

Challenge Problems

17.99 (a) **Given:** glutamate (aq) + NH_3 (aq) $\rightarrow$ glutamine (aq) + H_2O (l) $\Delta G^{\circ}_{rxn} = +14.2$ kJ at 298 K **Find:** K

Conceptual Plan: $\Delta G^{\circ}_{rxn}, T \rightarrow K$

$\Delta G^{\circ}_{rxn} = -RT \ln K$

Solution: $\Delta G^{\circ}_{rxn} = -RT \ln K$. Rearrange to solve for K.

$$K = e^{\frac{-\Delta G^{\circ}_{rxn}}{RT}} = e^{\frac{-(+14.2\ \text{kJ}) \times \frac{1000\ \text{J}}{1\ \text{kJ}}}{\left(8.314 \frac{\text{J}}{\text{K}\cdot\text{mol}}\right)(298\ \text{K})}} = e^{-5.73142} = 3.24 \times 10^{-3}.$$

Check: The units (none) are correct. The free energy change is positive and the reaction is nonspontaneous. This results in a small K.

(b) **Given:** pair ATP hydrolysis with glutamate/NH_3 reaction **Find:** show coupled reactions, ΔG°_{rxn} and K

Conceptual Plan: Use the reaction mechanism shown, where A = NH_3 and B = glutamate ($C_5H_8O_4N^-$), then calculate ΔG°_{rxn} by adding free energies of reactions then $\Delta G^{\circ}_{rxn}, T \rightarrow K$.

$\Delta G^{\circ}_{rxn} = -RT \ln K$

Solution:

$NH_3\ (aq) + ATP\ (aq) + \cancel{H_2O\ (l)} \rightarrow \cancel{NH_3 - P_i(aq)} + ADP\ (aq)$ $\quad \Delta G^{\circ}_{rxn} = -30.5$ kJ

$\cancel{NH_3 - P_i(aq)} + C_5H_8O_4N^-\ (aq) \rightarrow C_5H_9O_3N_2^-\ (aq) + \cancel{H_2O\ (l)} + P_i(aq)$ $\quad \Delta G^{\circ}_{rxn} = +14.2$ kJ

$NH_3\ (aq) + C_5H_8O_4N^-(aq) + ATP\ (aq) \rightarrow C_5H_9O_3N_2^-\ (aq) + ADP\ (aq) + P_i(aq)$ $\quad \Delta G^{\circ}_{rxn} = -16.3$ kJ

then $\Delta G^{\circ}_{rxn} = -RT \ln K$. Rearrange to solve for K.

$$K = e^{\frac{-\Delta G^{\circ}_{rxn}}{RT}} = e^{\frac{-(-16.3\ \text{kJ}) \times \frac{1000\ \text{J}}{1\ \text{kJ}}}{\left(8.314 \frac{\text{J}}{\text{K}\cdot\text{mol}}\right)(298\ \text{K})}} = e^{6.57902} = 7.20 \times 10^{2}.$$

Check: The units (none) are correct. The free energy change is negative and the reaction is spontaneous. This results in a large K.

17.100 **Given:** flask configurations **Find:** entropy and rank as increasing entropy

Conceptual Plan: Calculate the number of possible states then W $\rightarrow$ S then rank.

$W = \frac{n!}{(n-r!)\,r!}$ *where n = # particles and r = # particle in one flask* $S = k \ln W$

Solution:

(a) $W = \frac{n!}{(n-r)!\,r!} = \frac{5!}{(0)!\,5!} = 1$ then $S = k \ln W = \left(1.38 \times 10^{-23} \frac{\text{J}}{\text{K}}\right) \ln 1 = 0;$

(b) $W = \frac{n!}{(n-r)!\,r!} = \frac{5!}{(2)!\,3!} = 10$ then $S = k \ln W = \left(1.38 \times 10^{-23} \frac{\text{J}}{\text{K}}\right) \ln 10 = 3.18 \times 10^{-23}$ J/K; and

(c) $W = \frac{n!}{(n-r)!\,r!} = \frac{5!}{(1)!\,4!} = 5$ then $S = k \ln W = \left(1.38 \times 10^{-23} \frac{\text{J}}{\text{K}}\right) \ln 5 = 2.22 \times 10^{-23}$ J/K.

So (a) < (c) < (b).

Check: The units (J/K) are correct. The more possibilities for rearranging particles the higher the entropy.

17.101 (a) **Given:** $\frac{1}{2} H_2\ (g) + \frac{1}{2} Cl_2\ (g) \rightarrow HCl\ (g)$, define standard state as 2 atm **Find:** ΔG°_f

Conceptual Plan: $\Delta G^{\circ}_f, P_{H_2}, P_{Cl_2}, P_{HCl}, T \rightarrow$ new ΔG°_f

$\Delta G_{rxn} = \Delta G^{\circ}_{rxn} + RT \ln Q$ *where* $Q = \frac{P_{HCl}}{P_{H_2}^{1/2} P_{Cl_2}^{1/2}}$

Solution: $\Delta G^{\circ}_f = -95.3$ kJ/mol and $Q = \frac{P_{HCl}}{P_{H_2}^{1/2} P_{Cl_2}^{1/2}} = \frac{2}{2^{1/2}\,2^{1/2}} = 1$ then

$$\Delta G_{rxn} = \Delta G^{\circ}_{rxn} + RT \ln Q = -95.3 \frac{\text{kJ}}{\text{mol}} + \left(8.314 \frac{\text{J}}{\text{K}\cdot\text{mol}}\right)\left(\frac{1\ \text{kJ}}{1000\ \text{J}}\right)(298\ \text{K}) \ln(1) =$$

-95.3 kJ/mol $= -95{,}300$ J/mol

Since the number of moles of reactants and products are the same, the decrease in volume affects the entropy of both equally, so there is no change in ΔG_f°.

Check: The units (kJ) are correct. The Q is one so ΔG_f° is unchanged under the new standard conditions.

(b) **Given:** $N_2\,(g) + \frac{1}{2}\,O_2\,(g) \rightarrow N_2O\,(g)$, define standard state as 2 atm **Find:** ΔG_f°

Conceptual Plan: $\Delta G_f^\circ, P_{N_2}, P_{O_2}, P_{N_2O}, T \rightarrow$ **new** ΔG_f°

$$\Delta G_{rxn} = \Delta G_{rxn}^\circ + RT\ln Q \text{ where } Q = \frac{P_{N_2O}}{P_{N_2}\,P_{O_2}^{1/2}}$$

Solution: $\Delta G_f^\circ = +\,103.7$ kJ/mol and $Q = \dfrac{P_{N_2O}}{P_{N_2}\,P_{O_2}^{1/2}} = \dfrac{2}{2\,2^{1/2}} = \dfrac{1}{\sqrt{2}}$ then

$$\Delta G_{rxn} = \Delta G_{rxn}^\circ + RT\ln Q = +\,103.7\frac{\text{kJ}}{\text{mol}} + \left(8.314\frac{\text{J}}{\text{K}\cdot\text{mol}}\right)\left(\frac{1\text{ kJ}}{1000\text{ J}}\right)(298\text{ K})\ln\left(\frac{1}{\sqrt{2}}\right) =$$

$+\,102.8$ kJ/mol $= +\,102{,}800$ J/mol

The entropy of the reactants (1.5 mol) is decreased more than the entropy of the product (1 mol). Since the product is relatively more favored at lower volume, ΔG_f° is less positive.

Check: The units (kJ) are correct. The Q is less than one so ΔG_f° is reduced under the new standard conditions.

(c) **Given:** $\frac{1}{2}\,H_2\,(g) \rightarrow H\,(g)$, define standard state as 2 atm **Find:** ΔG_f°

Conceptual Plan: $\Delta G_f^\circ, P_{H2}, P_H, T \rightarrow$ **new** ΔG_f°

$$\Delta G_{rxn} = \Delta G_{rxn}^\circ + RT\ln Q \text{ where } Q = \frac{P_H}{P_{H_2}^{1/2}}$$

Solution: $\Delta G_f^\circ = +\,203.3$ kJ/mol and $Q = \dfrac{P_H}{P_{H_2}^{1/2}} = \dfrac{2}{2^{1/2}} = \sqrt{2}$ then

$$\Delta G_{rxn} = \Delta G_{rxn}^\circ + RT\ln Q = +\,203.3\frac{\text{kJ}}{\text{mol}} + \left(8.314\frac{\text{J}}{\text{K}\cdot\text{mol}}\right)\left(\frac{1\text{ kJ}}{1000\text{ J}}\right)(298\text{ K})\ln\left(\sqrt{2}\right) =$$

$+\,204.2$ kJ/mol $= +\,204{,}200$ J/mol

The entropy of the product (1 mol) is decreased more than the entropy of the reactant (1/2 mol). Since the product is relatively less favored, ΔG_f° is more positive.

Check: The units (kJ) are correct. The Q is greater than one so ΔG_f° is increased under the new standard conditions.

17.102 **Given:** $H_2O\,(l) \rightarrow H_2O\,(s)$ at $-\,10$ °C $\Delta G_{freezing} = -\,210$ J/mol, $\Delta H_{fusion} = +\,5610$ J/mol **Find:** ΔS_{univ} at $-\,10$ °C

Conceptual Plan: **°C $\rightarrow$ K then** $\Delta G_{freezing}, \Delta H_{fus}, T \rightarrow \Delta S_{univ}$

$$K = 273.15 + °C \qquad \Delta G = \Delta H_{rxn} - T\Delta S_{rxn} \quad \Delta S_{univ} = \Delta S_{sys} + \Delta S_{surr}$$

Solution: $T = -\,10$ °C $+ 273.15 = 263$ K, $\Delta H_{freezing} = -\,5610$ J/mol $= -\,\Delta H_{fusion}$ then $\Delta G = \Delta H_{rxn} - T\Delta S_{rxn}$.

Rearrange to solve for ΔS. $\Delta S_{freezing} = \dfrac{\Delta H_{freezing} - \Delta G_{freezing}}{T} = \Delta S_{sys}$. Then

$$\Delta S_{univ} = \Delta S_{sys} + \Delta S_{surr} = \frac{\Delta H_{freezing} - \Delta G_{freezing}}{T} - \frac{\Delta H_{freezing}}{T} = -\frac{\Delta G_{freezing}}{T} = \frac{-(-\,210\text{ J})}{263\text{ K}}$$

$= +\,0.798$ J/K.

Check: The units (J/K) are correct. The entropy for freezing should be negative since the solid has a more ordered structure.

17.103 **Given:** $K = 3.9 \times 10^5$ at 300 K and $K = 1.2 \times 10^{-1}$ at 500 K **Find:** ΔH_{rxn}°, ΔS_{rxn}°

Conceptual Plan: Plot ln K verus $1/T$. The slope will be $-\Delta H_{rxn}^\circ/R$ and the intercept will be $\Delta S_{rxn}^\circ/R$.

Solution: Plot ln K verus $1/T$. Since $\ln K = -\dfrac{\Delta H_{rxn}^\circ}{R}\dfrac{1}{T} + \dfrac{\Delta S_{rxn}^\circ}{R}$, the negative of the slope will be $-\dfrac{\Delta H_{rxn}^\circ}{R}$ and the intercept will be $\dfrac{\Delta S_{rxn}^\circ}{R}$. The slope can be determined by measuring $\Delta y/\Delta x$ on the plot or by using functions, such as "add trendline" in Excel. Since the slope is $+\,1\underline{1}246$ K,

$\Delta H^\circ_{rxn} = -\, slope\ R =$

$= -(+11246\ \text{K})\left(8.314 \frac{\text{J}}{\text{K} \cdot \text{mol}}\right)\left(\frac{1\ \text{kJ}}{1000\ \text{J}}\right) =$

$= -93.499\ \text{kJ/mol} = -93\ \text{kJ/mol}$

Since the intercept is $-24.612\ \text{K}^{-1}$,

$\Delta S^\circ_{rxn} = intercept\ R = \left(\frac{-24.612}{\text{K}}\right)\left(8.314 \frac{\text{J}}{\text{K} \cdot \text{mol}}\right)$

$= -204.62\ \text{J/K} = -2.0 \times 10^2\ \text{J/K}.$

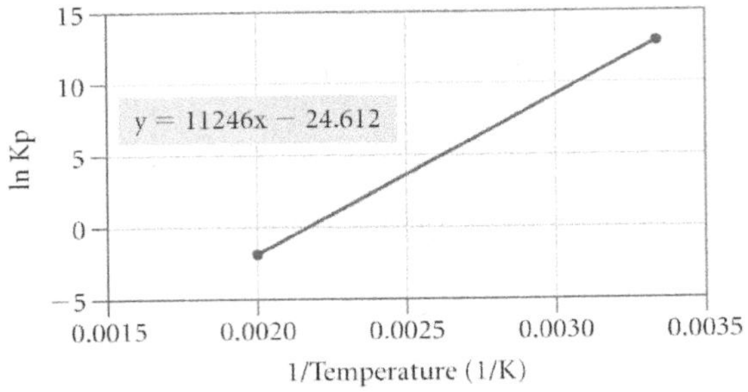

Note: This problem can also be solved using the mathematically equivalent equation in Problems 93 and 94.
Check: The units are correct (kJ/mole and J/K mol). The numbers are typical for reactions. Since the slope is positive, the enthalpy change must be negative. The entropy change is expected to be negative since the number of moles of gas is decreasing.

17.104 (a) **Given:** $NH_4NO_3\ (s) \rightarrow HNO_3\ (g) + NH_3\ (g)$ **Find:** ΔG°_{rxn}

Conceptual Plan: $\Delta G^\circ_{rxn} = \sum n_p \Delta G^\circ_f(\text{products}) - \sum n_r \Delta G^\circ_f(\text{reactants})$

Solution:

Reactant/Product	ΔG°_f(kJ/mol from Appendix IIB)
$NH_4NO_3\ (s)$	− 183.9
$HNO_3\ (g)$	− 73.5
$NH_3\ (g)$	− 16.4

Be sure to pull data for the correct formula and phase.

$\Delta G^\circ_{rxn} = \sum n_p \Delta G^\circ_f(\text{products}) - \sum n_r \Delta G^\circ_f(\text{reactants})$

$= [1(\Delta G^\circ_f(HNO_3\ (g))) + 1(\Delta G^\circ_f(NH_3\ (g)))] - [1(\Delta G^\circ_f(NH_4NO_3\ (s)))]$

$= [1(-73.5\ \text{kJ}) + 1(-16.4\ \text{kJ})] - [1(-183.9\ \text{kJ})]$

$= [-89.9\ \text{kJ}] - [-183.9\ \text{kJ}]$

$= +94.0\ \text{kJ}$

Check: The units (kJ) are correct. The free energy change is positive since ammonium nitrate has such a low free energy of formation.

(b) **Given:** $NH_4NO_3\ (s) \rightarrow N_2O\ (g) + 2\ H_2O\ (g)$ **Find:** ΔG°_{rxn}

Conceptual Plan: $\Delta G^\circ_{rxn} = \sum n_p \Delta G^\circ_f(\text{products}) - \sum n_r \Delta G^\circ_f(\text{reactants})$

Solution:

Reactant/Product	ΔG°_f(kJ/mol from Appendix IIB)
$NH_4NO_3\ (s)$	− 183.9
$N_2O\ (g)$	103.7
$H_2O\ (g)$	− 228.6

Be sure to pull data for the correct formula and phase.

$\Delta G^\circ_{rxn} = \sum n_p \Delta G^\circ_f(\text{products}) - \sum n_r \Delta G^\circ_f(\text{reactants})$

$= [1(\Delta G^\circ_f(N_2O\ (g))) + 2(\Delta G^\circ_f(H_2O\ (g)))] - [1(\Delta G^\circ_f(NH_4NO_3\ (s)))]$

$= [1(103.7\ \text{kJ}) + 2(-228.6\ \text{kJ})] - [1(-183.9\ \text{kJ})]$

$= [-353.5\ \text{kJ}] - [-183.9\ \text{kJ}]$

$= -169.6\ \text{kJ}$

Check: The units (kJ) are correct. The free energy change is negative since water has such a low free energy of formation.

(c) **Given:** $NH_4NO_3\ (s) \rightarrow N_2\ (g) + \frac{1}{2}\ O_2\ (g) + 2\ H_2O\ (g)$ **Find:** ΔG°_{rxn}

Conceptual Plan: $\Delta G^\circ_{rxn} = \sum n_p \Delta G^\circ_f(\text{products}) - \sum n_r \Delta G^\circ_f(\text{reactants})$

Solution:

Reactant/Product	ΔG°_f(kJ/mol from Appendix IIB)
$NH_4NO_3\ (s)$	− 183.9
$N_2\ (g)$	0.0
$O_2\ (g)$	0.0
$H_2O\ (g)$	− 228.6

Be sure to pull data for the correct formula and phase.

$$\Delta G^\circ_{rxn} = \sum n_p \Delta G^\circ_f(\text{products}) - \sum n_r \Delta G^\circ_f(\text{reactants})$$
$$= [1(\Delta G^\circ_f(N_2\ (g))) + 1/2(\Delta G^\circ_f(O_2\ (g))) + 2(\Delta G^\circ_f(H_2O\ (g)))] - [1(\Delta G^\circ_f(NH_4NO_3\ (s)))]$$
$$= [1(0.0\ \text{kJ}) + 1/\ 2(0.0\ \text{kJ}) + 2(-228.6\ \text{kJ})] - [1(-183.9\ \text{kJ})]$$
$$= [-457.2\ \text{kJ}] - [-183.9\ \text{kJ}]$$
$$= -273.3\ \text{kJ}$$

Check: The units (kJ) are correct. The free energy change is negative since water has such a low free energy of formation.

The second and third reactions are spontaneous, so we would expect decomposition products of N_2O, N_2, O_2, and H_2O in the gas phase. It is still possible for ammonium nitrate to remain as a solid because the thermodynamics of the reaction say nothing of the kinetics of the reaction (reaction can be extremely slow). Since all of the products are gases, the decomposition of ammonium nitrate will result in a large increase in volume (explosion). Some of the products aid in combustion, which could facilitate the combustion of materials near the ammonium nitrate. Also, N_2O is known as laughing gas, which has anesthetic and toxic effects on humans. The solid should not be kept in tightly sealed containers.

17.105 **Given:** ΔH°_{vap} table **Find:** ΔS_{vap} then compare values

Conceptual Plan: **°C → K then $\Delta H^\circ_{vap}, T \rightarrow \Delta S_{vap}$**

$$K = 273.15 + °C \qquad \Delta S_{vap} = \frac{-\Delta H_{vap}}{T}$$

Solution:

Diethyl ether: $T = 273.15 + 34.6 = 307.8\ \text{K}$ then $\Delta S_{vap} = \dfrac{\Delta H_{vap}}{T} = \dfrac{26.5\ \text{kJ}}{307.8\ \text{K}} = 0.0861\ \text{kJ/K} = 86.1\ \text{J/K}$

Acetone: $T = 273.15 + 56.1 = 329.3\ \text{K}$ then $\Delta S_{vap} = \dfrac{\Delta H_{vap}}{T} = \dfrac{29.1\ \text{kJ}}{329.3\ \text{K}} = 0.0884\ \text{kJ/K} = 88.4\ \text{J/K}$

Benzene: $T = 273.15 + 79.8 = 353.0\ \text{K}$ then $\Delta S_{vap} = \dfrac{\Delta H_{vap}}{T} = \dfrac{30.8\ \text{kJ}}{353.0\ \text{K}} = 0.0873\ \text{kJ/K} = 87.3\ \text{J/K}$

Chloroform: $T = 273.15 + 60.8 = 334.0\ \text{K}$ then $\Delta S_{vap} = \dfrac{\Delta H_{vap}}{T} = \dfrac{29.4\ \text{kJ}}{334.0\ \text{K}} = 0.0880\ \text{kJ/K} = 88.0\ \text{J/K}$

Ethanol: $T = 273.15 + 77.8 = 351.0\ \text{K}$ then $\Delta S_{vap} = \dfrac{\Delta H_{vap}}{T} = \dfrac{38.6\ \text{kJ}}{351.0\ \text{K}} = 0.110\ \text{kJ/K} = 110.\ \text{J/K}$

Water: $T = 273.15 + 100 = 373.15\ \text{K}$ then $\Delta S_{vap} = \dfrac{\Delta H_{vap}}{T} = \dfrac{40.7\ \text{kJ}}{373.15\ \text{K}} = 0.109\ \text{kJ/K} = 109\ \text{J/K}$

The first four values are very similar, because they have similar intermolecular forces between molecules (dispersion forces and/or dipole-dipole interactions). The values for ethanol and water are higher, because the intermolecular forces between molecules are stronger, due to hydrogen bonding. Because of this, more energy is dispersed when these interactions are broken.

Conceptual Problems

17.106 A butane lighter is more efficient than an electric lighter since the butane lighter process is accomplished in one step. When you use an electric lighter, fuel is burned to generate electricity. This electricity is transmitted to the lighter through wires. Once it reaches the lighter, the electricity then needs to be converted to heat. Each step must pay a heat tax. Using a butane lighter has fewer steps and so it pays a much lower tax.

17.107 (c) The spontaneity of a reaction says nothing about the speed of a reaction. It only states which direction the reaction will go as it approaches equilibrium.

17.108 (a) and (c) will both increase the entropy of the surroundings because they are both exothermic reactions (adding thermal energy to the surroundings).

17.109 (b) has the largest decrease in the number of microstates from the initial to the final state. In (a) there are initially $\frac{9\,!}{4!\,4!\,1!} = 90$ microstates and $\frac{9\,!}{3!\,3!\,3!} = 1680$ microstates at the end, so $\Delta S > 0$. In (b) there are initially $\frac{9\,!}{4!\,2!\,3!} = 1260$ microstates and $\frac{9\,!}{6!\,3!\,0!} = 84$ microstates at the end, so $\Delta S < 0$. In (c) there are initially $\frac{9\,!}{3!\,4!\,2!} = 1260$ microstates and $\frac{9\,!}{3!\,4!\,2!} = 1260$ microstates at the end, so $\Delta S = 0$. Also the final state in (b) has the least entropy.

17.110 (c) If the entropy of a system is increasing, the enthalpy of a reaction can be overcome (if necessary) by the entropy change as long as the temperature is high enough. If the entropy change of the system is decreasing, the reaction must be exothermic in order to be spontaneous since the entropy is working against spontaneity.

17.111 (c) Since the vapor pressure of water at 298 K is 23.78 mmHg or 0.03129 atm. As long as the desired pressure (0.010 atm) is less than the equilibrium vapor pressure of water, the reaction will be spontaneous.

17.112 (a) and (b) are both true. Since $\Delta G_{rxn} = \Delta G^{\circ}_{rxn} + RT \ln Q$ and $\Delta G^{\circ}_{rxn} = -42.5$ kJ, in order for $\Delta G_{rxn} = 0$ the second term must be positive. This necessitates that $Q > 1$ or that we have more product than reactant. Any reaction at equilibrium has $\Delta G_{rxn} = 0$.

18 Electrochemistry

Review Questions

18.1 Electrochemistry uses spontaneous redox reactions to generate electrical energy.

18.2 Electricity can be used to drive non-spontaneous redox reactions, such as those that occur in gold or silver plating.

18.3 Oxidation is the loss of electrons and corresponds to an increase in oxidation state. Reduction is the gain of electrons and corresponds to a decrease in oxidation state. Balancing redox reactions can be more complicated than balancing other types of reactions because both the mass (or number of each type of atom) and the charge must be balanced. Redox reactions occurring in aqueous solutions can be balanced by using a special procedure called the half-reaction method of balancing. In this procedure, the overall equation is broken down into two half-reactions: one for oxidation and one for reduction. The half-reactions are balanced individually and then added together so that the number of electrons generated in the oxidation half-reaction is the same as the number of electrons consumed in the reduction half-reaction.

18.4 A voltaic (or galvanic) cell produces electrical current from a spontaneous chemical reaction. An electrochemical cell, called an eletrolytic cell, uses electrical current to drive a nonspontaneous chemical reaction.

18.5 In all electrochemical cells, the electrode where oxidation occurs is called the anode. In a voltaic cell, the anode is labeled with a negative (–) sign. The anode is negative because the oxidation reaction that occurs at the anode releases electrons. Electrons flow from the anode to the cathode (from negative to positive) through the wires connecting the electrodes.

18.6 In all electrochemical cells, the electrode where reduction occurs is called the cathode. The cathode of a voltaic cell is labeled with a (+) sign. The cathode is positive because the reduction reaction that occurs at the cathode takes up electrons. Electrons flow from the anode to the cathode (from negative to positive) through the wires connecting the electrodes.

18.7 A salt bridge is a pathway by which ions can flow between the half-cells and complete an electrical circuit and maintaining electroneutrality, without the solutions in the half-cells totally mixing.

18.8 Electrical current is measured in units of amperes (A). One ampere, or amp, represents the flow of one coulomb (a measure of electrical charge) per second: 1 A = 1 C/s. Potential difference is a measure of the difference in potential energy (usually in joules) per unit of charge (coulombs). The SI unit of potential difference is the volt (V), which is equal to one joule per coulomb: 1 V = 1 J/C. The potential difference is the drop in potential energy and the current is a measure of how many electrons travel across this potential difference.

18.9 The standard cell potential E°_{cell} or standard emf is the cell potential under standard conditions (1 M concentration for reactants in solution and 1 atm pressure for gaseous reactants). The cell potential is a measure of the overall tendency of the redox reaction to occur spontaneously. The more positive the cell potential, the more spontaneous the reaction. A negative cell potential indicates a nonspontaneous reaction.

18.10 Electrochemical cells are often represented with a compact notation called a cell diagram or line notation. In this representation, the oxidation half-reaction is always written on the left and the reduction on the right. A double vertical line (||), indicating the salt bridge, separates the two half-reactions. Substances in different phases are separated by a single vertical line (|), which represents the boundary between the phases. For some redox reactions, the reactants and products of one or both of the half-reactions may be in the same phase. In these cases, the reactants and products are simply separated from each other with a comma in the line diagram. Such cells use an inert electrode, such as platinum (Pt) or graphite, as the anode or cathode (or both).

18.11 Inert electrodes, such as platinum (Pt) or graphite, are used as the anode or cathode (or both) when the reactants and products of one or both of the half-reactions are in the same phase.

18.12 The standard hydrogen electrode (SHE) half-cell is the half-cell that is normally chosen to have a potential of zero. This cell consists of an inert platinum electrode immersed in 1 M HCl with hydrogen gas at 1 atm bubbling through the solution. When the SHE acts as the cathode, the following half-reaction occurs: $2\ H^+\ (aq) + 2\ e^- \rightarrow H_2\ (g)\ E^\circ_{red} = 0.00$ V. If we combine the standard hydrogen electrode half-cell with another half-cell of interest, we can measure the voltage and assign it to the half-cell of interest.

18.13 The overall cell potential for any electrochemical cell will always be the sum of the half-cell potential for the oxidation reaction and the half-cell potential for the reduction reaction or $E^\circ_{cell} = E^\circ_{cathode} - E^\circ_{anode}$.

18.14 Half-reactions with large positive reduction half-cell potentials have a strong tendency to have the reduction reaction occur in the forward direction and the reactants are therefore excellent oxidzing agents. Half-reactions with large negative reduction half-cell potentials have a strong tendency for the reduction reaction to occur in the reverse direction and so they have a strong tendency to be oxidized. These are excellent reducing agents.

18.15 In general, any reduction half-reaction will be spontaneous when paired with the reverse of a half-reaction below it in the table.

18.16 In general, metals whose reduction half-reactions lie below the reduction of H^+ to H_2 in Table 18.1 will dissolve in acids, while metals above it will not. An important exception to this rule is nitric acid (HNO_3) which can oxidize metals through the following reduction half-reaction: $NO_3^-(aq) + 4\ H^+\ (aq) + 3\ e^- \rightarrow NO\ (g) + 2\ H_2O\ (l)\ E^\circ_{red} = 0.96$ V. Since this half-reaction is above the reduction of H^+ in Table 18.1, HNO_3 can oxidize metals (such as copper, for example) that can't be oxidizied by HCl.

18.17 We have seen that a positive standard cell potential (E°_{cell}) corresponds to a spontaneous oxidation-reduction reaction. We also know (from Chapter 17) that the spontaneity of a reaction is determined by the sign of ΔG^o. Therefore, E°_{cell} and ΔG^o must be related. We also know from Section 17.9 that ΔG^o for a reaction is related to the equilibrium constant *(K)* for the reaction. Since E°_{cell} and ΔG^o are related, then E°_{cell} and K must also be related. The equation that relates the three quantities is: $\Delta G^\circ_{rxn} = -RT \ln K = -nFE^\circ_{cell}$.

18.18 A redox reaction with a small equilibrium constant ($K < 1$) will not be spontaneous and so will have a negative E°_{cell} and a positive ΔG°_{rxn}.

18.19 The Nernst equation relates concentration and cell potential as follows: $E_{cell} = E^\circ_{cell} - \dfrac{0.0592\ \text{V}}{n} \log Q$, where E_{cell} is the cell potential in V, E°_{cell} is the standard cell potential in V, n is the number of moles of electrons transferred in the redox reaction, and Q is the reaction quotient. Increasing the concentration of the reactants decreases the value of Q and so it increases the cell potential. Increasing the concentration of the products increases the value of Q and so it decreases the cell potential.

18.20 The Nernst equation states that: $E_{cell} = E^\circ_{cell} - \dfrac{0.0592\ \text{V}}{n} \log Q$. Under standard conditions, $Q = 1$, and (since $\log 1 = 0$) the second term drops out and $E_{cell} = E^\circ_{cell}$.

18.21 A concentration cell is a voltaic cell in which both half reactions are the same, but in which a difference in concentration drives the current flow (since the cell potential depends, not only on the half-reactions occurring in the cell, but also on the concentrations of the reactants and products in those half-reactions). Therefore $E_{cell} = -\dfrac{0.0592\ \text{V}}{n} \log Q$.

18.22 In an inexpensive dry-cell battery zinc is oxidized at the anode according to the following reaction: $Zn\ (s) \rightarrow Zn^{2+}\ (aq) + 2\ e^-$. The cathode is a carbon rod immersed in a moist paste of MnO_2 that also contains NH_4Cl. The MnO_2 is reduced to Mn_2O_3 according to the following reaction: $2\ MnO_2\ (s) + 2\ NH_4^+\ (aq) + 2\ e^- \rightarrow Mn_2O_3\ (s) + 2\ NH_3\ (aq) + H_2O\ (l)$. These two half-reactions produce a voltage of about 1.5 volts.

The more common alkaline batteries employ slightly different half-reactions that use a base (therefore the name alkaline). The anode reaction is: $Zn\ (s) + 2\ OH^-\ (aq) \rightarrow Zn(OH)_2\ (s) + 2\ e^-$. The cathode reaction is: $2\ MnO_2\ (s) + 2\ H_2O\ (l) + 2\ e^- \rightarrow 2\ MnO(OH)\ (s) + 2\ OH^-\ (aq)$.

18.23 Lead-acid storage batteries consist of six electrochemical cells wired in series, in which each cell produces 2 V for a total of 12 V. Each cell contains a porous lead anode where oxidation occurs according to: $Pb\ (s) + HSO_4^-\ (aq) \rightarrow PbSO_4\ (s) + H^+\ (aq) + 2\ e^-$ and a lead(IV) oxide cathode where reduction occurs according to: $PbO_2\ (s) + HSO_4^-\ (aq) + 3\ H^+\ (aq) + 2\ e^- \rightarrow PbSO_4\ (s) + 2\ H_2O\ (l)$. As electrical current is drawn from the battery, both the anode and the cathode become coated with $PbSO_4\ (s)$ and the solution becomes depleted of $HSO_4^-\ (aq)$. If the battery is run for a long time without recharging, too much $PbSO_4\ (s)$ develops on the surface of the electrodes and the battery goes dead. The lead-acid storage battery can be recharged, however, by running electrical current through it in reverse. The electrical current, which must come from an external source such as an alternator in a car, causes the preceding reaction to occur in reverse, converting the $PbSO_4\ (s)$ back to $Pb\ (s)$ and $PbO_2\ (s)$, recharging the battery.

18.24 The most common types of portable rechargeable batteries include the nickel-cadmium (NiCad) battery, the nickel metal hydride (NiMH) battery, and the lithium ion battery.

The nickel-cadmium (NiCad) battery consists of an anode composed of solid cadmium and a cathode composed of $NiO(OH)(s)$. The electrolyte is usually $KOH(aq)$. During operation, the cadmium is oxidized and the NiO(OH) is reduced according to the following equations:

Anode reaction: $Cd\ (s) + 2\ OH^-\ (aq) \rightarrow Cd(OH)_2\ (s) + 2\ e^-$

Cathode reaction: $2NiO(OH)\ (s) + 2\ H_2O\ (l) + 2e^- \rightarrow 2\ Ni(OH)_2\ (s) + 2\ OH^-\ (aq)$

The overall reaction produces about 1.30 V. As current is drawn from the NiCad battery, solid cadmium hydroxide accumulates on the anode and solid nickel(II) hydroxide accumulates on the cathode. By running current in the opposite direction, the reactants can be regenerated from the products.

The NiMH battery uses the same cathode reaction as the NiCad battery but a different anode reaction. In the anode of a NiMH battery, hydrogen atoms held in a metal alloy are oxidized. If we let M represent the metal alloy, we can write the half-reactions as follows:

Anode reaction: $M \cdot H\ (s) + OH^-\ (aq) \rightarrow M\ (s) + H_2O\ (l) + e^-$

Cathode reaction: $NiO(OH)\ (s) + H_2O\ (l) + e^- \rightarrow Ni(OH)_2\ (s) + OH^-\ (aq)$.

The lithium-ion battery is the newest and most expensive common type of rechargeable battery. The lithium battery works differently than the other batteries we have examined so far, and the details of its operation are beyond our current scope. Briefly, we can think of the operation of the lithium battery as being due primarily to the motion of lithium ions from the anode to the cathode. The anode is composed of graphite into which lithium ions are incorporated between layers of carbon atoms. Upon discharge, the lithium ions spontaneously migrate to the cathode, which consists of a lithium transition metal oxide such as $LiCoO_2$ or $LiMn_2O_4$. The transition metal is reduced during this process. Upon recharging, the transition metal is oxidized, forcing the lithium to migrate back into the graphite. The flow of lithium ions from the anode to the cathode causes a corresponding flow of electrons in the external circuit.

18.25 Fuel cells are like batteries, but the reactants must be constantly replenished. Normal batteries lose their ability to generate voltage with use because the reactants become depleted as electrical current is drawn from the battery. In a fuel cell, the reactants—the fuel—constantly flow through the battery, generating electrical current as they undergo a redox reaction.

The most common fuel cell is the hydrogen–oxygen fuel cell. In the cell, hydrogen gas flows past the anode (a screen coated with a platinum catalyst) and undergoes oxidation: $2\ H_2\ (g) + 4\ OH^-\ (aq) \rightarrow 4\ H_2O\ (l) + 4\ e^-$. Oxygen gas flows past the cathode (a similar screen) and undergoes reduction: $O_2\ (g) + 2\ H_2O\ (l) + 4\ e^- \rightarrow 4\ OH^-\ (aq)$. The half-reactions sum to the following overall reaction: $2\ H_2\ (g) + O_2\ (g) \rightarrow 2\ H_2O\ (l)$. Notice that the only product is water.

18.26 Breathalyzers work because the quantity of ethyl alcohol (CH_3CH_2OH) in the breath is proportional to the quantity of ethyl alcohol in the bloodstream. One type of breathalyzer employs a fuel cell to measure the quantity of alcohol in the breath. When a suspect blows into the breathalyzer, ethyl alcohol is oxidized to acetic acid ($HC_2H_3O_2$) at the anode according to the following reaction: $CH_3CH_2OH\ (g) + 4OH^-\ (aq) \rightarrow HC_2H_3O_2\ (g) + 3\ H_2O\ (l) + 4\ e^-$. At the cathode, oxygen is reduced according to the following reaction: $O_2\ (g) + 2\ H_2O\ (l) + 4\ e^- \rightarrow 4\ OH^-\ (aq)$. The overall reaction is simply the oxidation of ethyl alcohol to acetic acid and water as follows: $CH_3CH_2OH\ (g) + O_2\ (g) \rightarrow HC_2H_3O_2\ (g) + H_2O\ (l)$. The magnitude of electrical current produced depends on the quantity of alcohol in the breath. A higher current reveals a higher blood alcohol level. When calibrated correctly, the fuel-cell breathalyzer can precisely measure the blood alcohol level of a suspected drunk driver.

18.27 Applications of electrolysis include breaking water into hydrogen and oxygen, converting metal oxides to pure metals, production of sodium from molten sodium chloride, and plating metals onto other metals (for example, silver can be plated onto a less expensive metal).

18.28 In an electrolytic cell, the source of the electrons is the external power source. The external power source must draw electrons away from the anode; thus, the anode must be connected to the positive terminal of the battery (as shown in Figure 18.22). Similarly, the power source drives electrons towards the cathode (where they will be used in reduction), so the cathode must be connected to the negative terminal of the battery. The charge labels (+ and –) on an electrolytic cell are therefore opposite of what they are in a voltaic cell.

18.29 The anion is oxidized. The cation is reduced to the metal.

18.30 In the electrolysis of a mixture of ions, the cation that is most easily reduced (the one with the least negative, or most positive, reduction half-cell potential) is reduced first and the anion that is most easily oxidized (the one that has the least negative, or most positive, oxidation half-cell potential) will be oxidized first.

18.31 In the electrolysis of aqueous NaCl solutions, two different reduction half-reactions are possible at the cathode, the reduction of Na^+ and the reduction of water.

$2\ Na^+\ (l) + 2\ e^- \rightarrow 2\ Na\ (s)$ $\quad E^\circ_{red} = -2.71\ V$

$2\ H_2O\ (l) + 2\ e^- \rightarrow H_2\ (g) + 2\ OH^-\ (aq)$ $\quad E_{red} = -0.41\ V\ ([OH^-] = 10^{-7}\ M)$

The half-reaction that occurs most easily (the one with the least negative, or most positive, half-cell potential) will be the one that actually occurs.

18.32 An overvoltage is an additional voltage that must be applied in order to get some non-spontaneous reactions to occur. Overvoltages are important because the desired reaction may not occur at all, and the overvoltage can control what products are produced.

18.33 We can determine the number of moles of electrons that have flowed in a given electrolysis cell by measuring the total charge that has flowed through cell, which in turn depends on the magnitude of current and the time that the current has run. Since 1 ampere = 1 C/s, if we multiply the amount of current (in A) flowing through the cell by the time (in s) that the current flowed, we can find the total charge that passed through the cell in that time: current (C/s) × time (s) = charge (C). The relationship between charge and the number of moles of electrons is given by Faraday's constant, which corresponds to the charge in coulombs of 1 mol of electrons, so $F = 96{,}485\ C/mole\ e^-$. These relationships can be used to solve problems involving the stoichiometry of electrolytic cells.

18.34 Corrosion is the (usually) gradual nearly always undesired oxidation of metals that occurs when they are exposed to oxidizing agents in the environment. This metal oxidation will be spontaneous when the half-reaction for the reduction of the metal ion lies below the half-reactions for the reduction of oxygen (+ 1.23 V) in Table 18.1. Many metals, such as aluminum, form oxides that coat the surface of the metal and prevent further corrosion.

18.35 Moisture must be present for many corrosion reactions to occur. The presence of water is necessary because water is a reactant in many oxidation reactions (such as $4\ Fe^{2+}\ (aq) + O_2\ (g) + (4 + 2n)\ H_2O\ (l) \rightarrow 2\ Fe_2O_3 \cdot n\ H_2O\ (s) + 8\ H^+\ (aq)$), and also because charge (either electrons or ions) must be free to flow between the anodic and cathodic regions.

Additional electrolytes promote more corrosion. The presence of an electrolyte (such as sodium chloride) on the surface of iron promotes rusting because it enhances current flow. This is why cars rust so quickly in cold climates where roads are salted, or in areas directly adjacent to beaches where salt-water mist is present.

The presence of acids promotes corrosion. Since H^+ ions are involved as a reactant in the reduction of oxygen, lower pH enhances the cathodic reaction and leads to faster corrosion.

18.36 The most obvious way to prevent rust formation is to keep iron dry. Without water, the redox reaction cannot occur. Another way of preventing rust formation is to coat the iron with a substance that is impervious to water. Cars, for example, are painted and sealed to prevent rust. A scratch in the paint, however, can lead to rusting of the underlying iron. Rust can also be prevented by placing a sacrificial electrode in electrical contact with the iron. The sacrificial electrode must be composed of a metal that oxidizes more easily than iron (that is, it must be below iron in Table 18.1). The sacrificial electrode then oxidizes in place of the iron (just as the more easily oxidizable species in a mixture will be the one to oxidize), protecting the iron from oxidation. Another way to protect iron from rusting is to coat it with a metal that oxidizes more easily than iron. Galvanized nails, for example, are coated with a thin layer of zinc. Since zinc has a more positive half-cell potential for oxidation, it will oxidize in place of the underlying iron (just as a sacrificial electrode does). The oxide of zinc is not crumbly and remains on the nail as a protective coating.

Balancing Redox Reactions

18.37 **Conceptual Plan: Separate the overall reaction into two half-reactions: one for oxidation and one for reduction. → Balance each half-reaction with respect to mass in the following order: 1) balance all elements other than H and O, 2) balance O by adding H_2O, and 3) balance H by adding H^+. → Balance each half-reaction with respect to charge by adding electrons. (The sum of the charges on both sides of the equation should be made equal by adding electrons as necessary.) → Make the number of electrons in both half-reactions equal by multiplying one or both half-reactions by a small whole number. → Add the two half-reactions together, canceling electrons and other species as necessary. → Verify that the reaction is balanced both with respect to mass and with respect to charge.**

Solution:

(a)

Separate:	$K(s) \rightarrow K^+(aq)$	and	$Cr^{3+}(aq) \rightarrow Cr(s)$
Balance elements:	$K(s) \rightarrow K^+(aq)$	and	$Cr^{3+}(aq) \rightarrow Cr(s)$
Add electrons:	$K(s) \rightarrow K^+(aq) + e^-$	and	$Cr^{3+}(aq) + 3e^- \rightarrow Cr(s)$
Equalize electrons:	$3K(s) \rightarrow 3K^+(aq) + 3e^-$	and	$Cr^{3+}(aq) + 3e^- \rightarrow Cr(s)$

Add half-reactions: $3K(s) + Cr^{3+}(aq) + \cancel{3e^-} \rightarrow 3K^+(aq) + \cancel{3e^-} + Cr(s)$

Cancel electrons: $3K(s) + Cr^{3+}(aq) \rightarrow 3K^+(aq) + Cr(s)$

Check:

Reactants	Products
3 K atoms	3 K atoms
1 Cr atom	1 Cr atom
+3 charge	+3 charge

(b)

Separate:	$Al(s) \rightarrow Al^{3+}(aq)$	and	$Fe^{2+}(aq) \rightarrow Fe(s)$
Balance elements:	$Al(s) \rightarrow Al^{3+}(aq)$	and	$Fe^{2+}(aq) \rightarrow Fe(s)$
Add electrons:	$Al(s) \rightarrow Al^{3+}(aq) + 3e^-$	and	$Fe^{2+}(aq) + 2e^- \rightarrow Fe(s)$
Equalize electrons:	$2Al(s) \rightarrow 2Al^{3+}(aq) + 6e^-$	and	$3Fe^{2+}(aq) + 6e^- \rightarrow 3Fe(s)$

Add half-reactions: $2Al(s) + 3Fe^{2+}(aq) + \cancel{6e^-} \rightarrow 2Al^{3+}(aq) + \cancel{6e^-} + 3Fe(s)$

Cancel electrons: $2Al(s) + 3Fe^{2+}(aq) \rightarrow 2Al^{3+}(aq) + 3Fe(s)$

Check:

Reactants	Products
2 Al atoms	2 Al atoms
3 Fe atom	3 Fe atom
+6 charge	+6 charge

(c)

Separate:	$BrO_3^-(aq) \rightarrow Br^-(aq)$	and	$N_2H_4(g) \rightarrow N_2(g)$
Balance non H & O elements:	$BrO_3^-(aq) \rightarrow Br^-(aq)$	and	$N_2H_4(g) \rightarrow N_2(g)$
Balance O with H_2O:	$BrO_3^-(aq) \rightarrow Br^-(aq) + 3H_2O(l)$	and	$N_2H_4(g) \rightarrow N_2(g)$

Balance H with H^+: $BrO_3^-(aq) + 6H^+(aq) \rightarrow Br^-(aq) + 3H_2O(l)$ and $N_2H_4(g) \rightarrow N_2(g) + 4H^+(aq)$

Add electrons:

BrO_3^- (aq) + 6 H^+ (aq) + 6 e^- → Br^- (aq) + 3 H_2O (l) and N_2H_4 (g) → N_2 (g) + 4 H^+ (aq) + 4 e^-

Equalize electrons:

2 BrO_3^- (aq) + 12 H^+ (aq) + 12 e^- → 2 Br^- (aq) + 6 H_2O (l) and 3 N_2H_4 (g) → 3 N_2 (g) + 12 H^+ (aq) + 12 e^-

Add half-reactions: 2 BrO_3^- (aq) + ~~12 H^+ (aq)~~ + 3 N_2H_4 (g) + ~~12 e^-~~ → 2 Br^- (aq) + 6 H_2O (l) + 3 N_2 (g) + ~~12 H^+ (aq)~~ + ~~12 e^-~~

Cancel electrons & others: 2 BrO_3^- (aq) + 3 N_2H_4 (g) → 2 Br^- (aq) + 6 H_2O (l) + 3 N_2 (g)

Check:

Reactants	Products
2 Br atoms	2 Br atoms
6 O atoms	6 O atoms
12 H atoms	12 H atoms
6 N atoms	6 N atoms
–2 charge	–2 charge

18.38 **Conceptual Plan: Separate the overall reaction into two half-reactions: one for oxidation and one for reduction. → Balance each half-reaction with respect to mass in the following order: 1) balance all elements other than H and O, 2) balance O by adding H_2O, and 3) balance H by adding H^+. → Balance each half-reaction with respect to charge by adding electrons. (The sum of the charges on both sides of the equation should be made equal by adding electrons as necessary.) → Make the number of electrons in both half-reactions equal by multiplying one or both half-reactions by a small whole number. → Add the two half-reactions together, canceling electrons and other species as necessary. → Verify that the reaction is balanced both with respect to mass and with respect to charge.**

Solution:

(a)
Separate: Zn (s) → Zn^{2+} (aq) and Sn^{2+} (aq) → Sn (s)
Balance elements: Zn (s) → Zn^{2+} (aq) and Sn^{2+} (aq) → Sn (s)
Add electrons: Zn (s) → Zn^{2+} (aq) + 2 e^- and Sn^{2+} (aq) + 2 e^- → Sn (s)
Equalize electrons: Zn (s) → Zn^{2+} (aq) + 2 e^- and Sn^{2+} (aq) + 2 e^- → Sn (s)
Add half-reactions: Zn (s) + Sn^{2+} (aq) + ~~2 e^-~~ → Zn^{2+} (aq) + ~~2 e^-~~ + Sn (s)
Cancel electrons: Zn (s) + Sn^{2+} (aq) → Zn^{2+} (aq) + Sn (s)

Check:

Reactants	Products
1 Zn atom	1 Zn atom
1 Sn atom	1 Sn atom
+2 charge	+2 charge

(b)
Separate: Mg (s) → Mg^{2+} (aq) and Cr^{3+} (aq) → Cr (s)
Balance elements: Mg (s) → Mg^{2+} (aq) and Cr^{3+} (aq) → Cr (s)
Add electrons: Mg (s) → Mg^{2+} (aq) + 2 e^- and Cr^{3+} (aq) + 3 e^- → Cr (s)
Equalize electrons: 3 Mg (s) → 3 Mg^{2+} (aq) + 6 e^- and 2 Cr^{3+} (aq) + 6 e^- → 2 Cr (s)
Add half-reactions: 3 Mg (s) + 2 Cr^{3+} (aq) + ~~6 e^-~~ → 3 Mg^{2+} (aq) + ~~6 e^-~~ + 2 Cr (s)
Cancel electrons: 3 Mg (s) + 2 Cr^{3+} (aq) → 3 Mg^{2+} (aq) + 2 Cr (s)

Check:

Reactants	Products
3 Mg atoms	3 Mg atoms
2 Cr atoms	2 Cr atoms
+6 charge	+6 charge

(c)
Separate: MnO_4^- (aq) → Mn^{2+} (aq) and Al (s) → Al^{3+} (aq)
Balance non H & O elements: MnO_4^- (aq) → Mn^{2+} (aq) and Al (s) → Al^{3+} (aq)
Balance O with H_2O: MnO_4^- (aq) → Mn^{2+} (aq) + 4 H_2O (l) and Al (s) → Al^{3+} (aq)
Balance H with H^+: MnO_4^- (aq) + 8 H^+ (aq) → Mn^{2+} (aq) + 4 H_2O (l) and Al (s) → Al^{3+} (aq)
Add electrons: MnO_4^- (aq) + 8 H^+ (aq) + 5 e^- → Mn^{2+} (aq) + 4 H_2O (l) and Al (s) → Al^{3+} (aq) + 3 e^-
Equalize electrons:
3 MnO_4^- (aq) + 24 H^+ (aq) + 15 e^- → 3 Mn^{2+} (aq) + 12 H_2O (l) and 5 Al (s) → 5 Al^{3+} (aq) + 15 e^-
Add half-reactions:
3 MnO_4^- (aq) + 24 H^+ (aq) + ~~15 e^-~~ + 5 Al (s) → 3 Mn^{2+} (aq) + 12 H_2O (l) + 5 Al^{3+} (aq) + ~~15 e^-~~
Cancel electrons: 3 MnO_4^- (aq) + 24 H^+ (aq) + 5 Al (s) → 3 Mn^{2+} (aq) + 12 H_2O (l) + 5 Al^{3+} (aq)

Check:

Reactants	Products
3 Mn atoms	3 Mn atoms
12 O atoms	12 O atoms
24 H atoms	24 H atoms
5 Al atoms	5 Al atoms
+21 charge	+21 charge

18.39 **Conceptual Plan: Separate the overall reaction into two half-reactions: one for oxidation and one for reduction. → Balance each half-reaction with respect to mass in the following order: 1) balance all elements other than H and O, 2) balance O by adding H_2O, and 3) balance H by adding H^+. → Balance each half-reaction with respect to charge by adding electrons. (The sum of the charges on both sides of the equation should be made equal by adding electrons as necessary.) → Make the number of electrons in both half-reactions equal by multiplying one or both half-reactions by a small whole number. → Add the two half-reactions together, canceling electrons and other species as necessary. → Verify that the reaction is balanced both with respect to mass and with respect to charge.**

Solution:

(a) Separate: PbO_2 (*s*) → Pb^{2+} (*aq*) and I^- (*aq*) → I_2 (*s*)

Balance non H & O elements: PbO_2 (*s*) → Pb^{2+} (*aq*) and 2 I^- (*aq*) → I_2 (*s*)

Balance O with H_2O: PbO_2 (*s*) → Pb^{2+} (*aq*) + 2 H_2O (*l*) and 2 I^- (*aq*) → I_2 (*s*)

Balance H with H^+: PbO_2 (*s*) + 4 H^+ (*aq*) → Pb^{2+} (*aq*) + 2 H_2O (*l*) and 2 I^- (*aq*) → I_2 (*s*)

Add electrons: PbO_2 (*s*) + 4 H^+ (*aq*) + 2 e^- → Pb^{2+} (*aq*) + 2 H_2O (*l*) and 2 I^- (*aq*) → I_2 (*s*) + 2 e^-

Equalize electrons: PbO_2 (*s*) + 4 H^+ (*aq*) + 2 e^- → Pb^{2+} (*aq*) + 2 H_2O (*l*) and 2 I^- (*aq*) → I_2 (*s*) + 2 e^-

Add half-reactions: PbO_2 (*s*) + 4 H^+ (*aq*) + ~~2 e^-~~ + 2 I^- (*aq*) → Pb^{2+} (*aq*) + 2 H_2O (*l*) + I_2 (*s*) + ~~2 e^-~~

Cancel electrons & others: PbO_2 (*s*) + 4 H^+ (*aq*) + 2 I^- (*aq*) → Pb^{2+} (*aq*) + 2 H_2O (*l*) + I_2 (*s*)

Check:

Reactants	Products
1 Pb atom	1 Pb atom
2 O atoms	2 O atoms
4 H atoms	4 H atoms
2 I atoms	2 I atoms
+2 charge	+2 charge

(b) Separate: MnO_4^- (*aq*) → Mn^{2+} (*aq*) and SO_3^{2-} (*aq*) → SO_4^{2-} (*aq*)

Balance non H & O elements: MnO_4^- (*aq*) → Mn^{2+} (*aq*) and SO_3^{2-} (*aq*) → SO_4^{2-} (*aq*)

Balance O with H_2O: MnO_4^- (*aq*) → Mn^{2+} (*aq*) + 4 H_2O (*l*) and SO_3^{2-} (*aq*) + H_2O (*l*) → SO_4^{2-} (*aq*)

Balance H with H^+:

MnO_4^- (*aq*) +8 H^+ (*aq*) → Mn^{2+} (*aq*) + 4 H_2O (*l*) and SO_3^{2-} (*aq*)+ H_2O (*l*) → SO_4^{2-} (*aq*)+ 2 H^+ (*aq*)

Add electrons: MnO_4^- (*aq*) + 8 H^+ (*aq*) + 5 e^- → Mn^{2+} (*aq*) + 4 H_2O (*l*) and

SO_3^{2-} (*aq*)+ H_2O (*l*) → SO_4^{2-} (*aq*)+ 2 H^+ (*aq*) + 2 e^-

Equalize electrons: 2 MnO_4^- (*aq*) + 16 H^+ (*aq*) + 10 e^- → 2 Mn^{2+} (*aq*) + 8 H_2O (*l*) and

5 SO_3^{2-} (*aq*) + 5 H_2O (*l*) → 5 SO_4^{2-} (*aq*) + 10 H^+ (*aq*) + 10 e^-

Add half-reactions: 2 MnO_4^- (*aq*) + 6 ~~16~~ H^+(*aq*) + ~~10 e^-~~ + 5 SO_3^{2-} (*aq*) + ~~5 H_2O (*l*)~~ →

2 Mn^{2+} (*aq*) + 3 ~~8~~ H_2O (*l*) + 5 SO_4^{2-} (*aq*) + ~~10 H^+(*aq*)~~ + ~~10 e^-~~

Cancel electrons: 2 MnO_4^- (*aq*) + 6 H^+ (*aq*) + 5 SO_3^{2-} (*aq*) → 2 Mn^{2+} (*aq*) + 3 H_2O (*l*) + 5 SO_4^{2-} (*aq*)

Check:

Reactants	Products
2 Mn atoms	2 Mn atoms
23 O atoms	23 O atoms
6 H atoms	6 H atoms
5 S atoms	5 S atoms
–6 charge	–6 charge

(c) Separate: $S_2O_3^{2-}$ (*aq*) → SO_4^{2-} (*aq*) and Cl_2 (*g*) → Cl^- (*aq*)

Balance non H & O elements: $S_2O_3^{2-}$ (*aq*) → 2 SO_4^{2-} (*aq*) and Cl_2 (*g*) → 2 Cl^- (*aq*)

Balance O with H_2O: $S_2O_3^{2-}$ (*aq*) + 5 H_2O (*l*) → 2 SO_4^{2-} (*aq*) and Cl_2 (*g*) → 2 Cl^- (*aq*)

Balance H with H^+: $S_2O_3^{2-}$ (*aq*) + 5 H_2O (*l*) → 2 SO_4^{2-} (*aq*) + 10 H^+ (*aq*) and Cl_2 (*g*) → 2 Cl^- (*aq*)

Add electrons:

$S_2O_3^{2-}$ (*aq*) + 5 H_2O (*l*) → 2 SO_4^{2-} (*aq*) + 10 H^+ (*aq*) + 8 e^- and Cl_2 (*g*) + 2 e^- → 2 Cl^- (*aq*)

Equalize electrons:
$S_2O_3^{2-}$ (*aq*) + 5 H_2O (*l*) → 2 SO_4^{2-} (*aq*) + 10 H^+ (*aq*) + 8 e^- and 4 Cl_2 (*g*) + 8 e^- → 8 Cl^- (*aq*)

Add half-reactions:
$S_2O_3^{2-}$ (*aq*) + 5 H_2O (*l*) + 4 Cl_2 (*g*) + ~~8 e^-~~ → 2 SO_4^{2-} (*aq*) + 10 H^+ (*aq*) + ~~8 e^-~~ + 8 Cl^- (*aq*)

Cancel electrons: $S_2O_3^{2-}$ (*aq*) + 5 H_2O (*l*) + 4 Cl_2 (*g*) → 2 SO_4^{2-} (*aq*) + 10 H^+ (*aq*) + 8 Cl^- (*aq*)

Check:

Reactants	Products
2 S atoms	2 S atoms
8 O atoms	8 O atoms
10 H atoms	10 H atoms
8 Cl atoms	8 Cl atoms
–2 charge	–2 charge

18.40 **Conceptual Plan: Separate the overall reaction into two half-reactions: one for oxidation and one for reduction. → Balance each half-reaction with respect to mass in the following order: 1) balance all elements other than H and O, 2) balance O by adding H_2O, and 3) balance H by adding H^+. → Balance each half-reaction with respect to charge by adding electrons. (The sum of the charges on both sides of the equation should be made equal by adding electrons as necessary.) → Make the number of electrons in both half-reactions equal by multiplying one or both half-reactions by a small whole number. → Add the two half-reactions together, canceling electrons and other species as necessary. → Verify that the reaction is balanced both with respect to mass and with respect to charge.**

Solution:

(a) Separate: NO_2^- (*aq*) → NO (*g*) and I^- (*aq*) → I_2 (*s*)

Balance non H & O elements: NO_2^- (*aq*) → NO (*g*) and 2 I^- (*aq*) → I_2 (*s*)

Balance O with H_2O: NO_2^- (*aq*) → NO (*g*) + H_2O (*l*) and 2 I^- (*aq*) → I_2 (*s*)

Balance H with H^+: NO_2^- (*aq*) + 2 H^+ (*aq*) → NO (*g*) + H_2O (*l*) and 2 I^- (*aq*) → I_2 (*s*)

Add electrons: NO_2^- (*aq*) + 2 H^+ (*aq*) + e^- → NO (*g*) + H_2O (*l*) and 2 I^- (*aq*) → I_2 (*s*) + 2 e^-

Equalize electrons: 2 NO_2^- (*aq*) + 4 H^+ (*aq*) + 2 e^- → 2 NO (*g*) + 2 H_2O (*l*) and 2 I^- (*aq*) → I_2 (*s*) + 2 e^-

Add half-reactions: 2 NO_2^- (*aq*) + 4 H^+ (*aq*) + ~~2 e^-~~ + 2 I^- (*aq*) → 2 NO (*g*) + 2 H_2O (*l*) + I_2 (*s*) + ~~2 e^-~~

Cancel electrons: 2 NO_2^- (*aq*) + 4 H^+ (*aq*) + 2 I^- (*aq*) → 2 NO (*g*) + 2 H_2O (*l*) + I_2 (*s*)

Check:

Reactants	Products
2 N atoms	2 N atoms
4 O atoms	4 O atoms
4 H atoms	4 H atoms
2 I atoms	2 I atoms
0 charge	0 charge

(b) Separate: ClO_4^- (*aq*) → ClO_3^- (*aq*) and Cl^- (*aq*) → Cl_2 (*g*)

Balance non H & O elements: ClO_4^- (*aq*) → ClO_3^- (*aq*) and 2 Cl^- (*aq*) → Cl_2 (*g*)

Balance O with H_2O: ClO_4^- (*aq*) → ClO_3^- (*aq*) + H_2O (*l*) and 2 Cl^- (*aq*) → Cl_2 (*g*)

Balance H with H^+: ClO_4^- (*aq*) + 2 H^+ (*aq*) → ClO_3^- (*aq*) + H_2O (*l*) and 2 Cl^- (*aq*) → Cl_2 (*g*)

Add electrons: ClO_4^- (*aq*) + 2 H^+ (*aq*) + 2 e^- → ClO_3^- (*aq*) + H_2O (*l*) and 2 Cl^- (*aq*) → Cl_2 (*g*) + 2 e^-

Equalize electrons: ClO_4^- (*aq*) + 2 H^+ (*aq*) + 2 e^- → ClO_3^- (*aq*) + H_2O (*l*) and 2 Cl^- (*aq*) → Cl_2 (*g*) + 2 e^-

Add half-reactions: ClO_4^- (*aq*) + 2 H^+ (*aq*) + ~~2 e^-~~ + 2 Cl^- (*aq*) → ClO_3^- (*aq*) + H_2O (*l*) + Cl_2 (*g*) + ~~2 e^-~~

Cancel electrons: ClO_4^- (*aq*) + 2 H^+ (*aq*) + 2 Cl^- (*aq*) → ClO_3^- (*aq*) + H_2O (*l*) + Cl_2 (*g*)

Check:

Reactants	Products
3 Cl atoms	3 Cl atoms
4 O atoms	4 O atoms
2 H atoms	2 H atoms
–1 charge	–1 charge

(c) Separate: NO_3^- (*aq*) → NO (*g*) and Sn^{2+} (*aq*) → Sn^{4+} (*aq*)

Balance non H & O elements: NO_3^- (*aq*) → NO (*g*) and Sn^{2+} (*aq*) → Sn^{4+} (*aq*)

Balance O with H_2O: NO_3^- (*aq*) → NO (*g*) + 2 H_2O (*l*) and Sn^{2+} (*aq*) → Sn^{4+} (*aq*)

Balance H with H^+: NO_3^- (*aq*) + 4 H^+ (*aq*) → NO (*g*) + 2 H_2O (*l*) and Sn^{2+} (*aq*) → Sn^{4+} (*aq*)

Add electrons: NO_3^- (*aq*) + 4 H^+ (*aq*) + 3 e^- → NO (*g*) + 2 H_2O (*l*) and Sn^{2+} (*aq*) → Sn^{4+} (*aq*) + 2 e^-

Equalize electrons:

$2\ NO_3^-\ (aq) + 8\ H^+\ (aq) + 6\ e^- \rightarrow 2\ NO\ (g) + 4\ H_2O\ (l)$ and $3\ Sn^{2+}\ (aq) \rightarrow 3\ Sn^{4+}\ (aq) + 6\ e^-$

Add half-reactions:

$2\ NO_3^-\ (aq) + 8\ H^+\ (aq) + \cancel{6\ e^-} + 3\ Sn^{2+}\ (aq) \rightarrow 2\ NO\ (g) + 4\ H_2O\ (l) + 3\ Sn^{4+}\ (aq) + \cancel{6\ e^-}$

Cancel electrons: $2\ NO_3^-\ (aq) + 8\ H^+\ (aq) + 3\ Sn^{2+}\ (aq) \rightarrow 2\ NO\ (g) + 4\ H_2O\ (l) + 3\ Sn^{4+}\ (aq)$

Check:

Reactants	Products
2 N atoms	2 N atoms
6 O atoms	6 O atoms
8 H atoms	8 H atoms
3 Sn atoms	3 Sn atoms
+12 charge	+12 charge

18.41 **Conceptual Plan: Separate the overall reaction into two half-reactions: one for oxidation and one for reduction. → Balance each half-reaction with respect to mass in the following order: 1) balance all elements other than H and O, 2) balance O by adding H_2O, 3) balance H by adding H^+, and 4) neutralize H^+ by adding enough OH^- to neutralize each H^+. Add the same number of OH^- ions to each side of the equation. → Balance each half-reaction with respect to charge by adding electrons. (The sum of the charges on both sides of the equation should be made equal by adding electrons as necessary.) → Make the number of electrons in both half-reactions equal by multiplying one or both half-reactions by a small whole number. → Add the two half-reactions together, canceling electrons and other species as necessary. → Verify that the reaction is balanced both with respect to mass and with respect to charge.**

Solution:

(a) Separate: $ClO_2\ (aq) \rightarrow ClO_2^-\ (aq)$ and $H_2O_2\ (aq) \rightarrow O_2\ (g)$

Balance non H & O elements: $ClO_2\ (aq) \rightarrow ClO_2^-\ (aq)$ and $H_2O_2\ (aq) \rightarrow O_2\ (g)$

Balance O with H_2O: $ClO_2\ (aq) \rightarrow ClO_2^-\ (aq)$ and $H_2O_2\ (aq) \rightarrow O_2\ (g)$

Balance H with H^+: $ClO_2\ (aq) \rightarrow ClO_2^-\ (aq)$ and $H_2O_2\ (aq) \rightarrow O_2\ (g) + 2\ H^+\ (aq)$

Neutralize H^+ with OH^-:

$ClO_2\ (aq) \rightarrow ClO_2^-\ (aq)$ and $H_2O_2\ (aq) + 2\ OH^-\ (aq) \rightarrow O_2\ (g) + \underbrace{2\ H^+\ (aq) + 2\ OH^-\ (aq)}_{2\ H_2O\ (l)}$

Add electrons: $ClO_2\ (aq) + e^- \rightarrow ClO_2^-\ (aq)$ and $H_2O_2\ (aq) + 2\ OH^-\ (aq) \rightarrow O_2\ (g) + 2\ H_2O\ (l) + 2\ e^-$

Equalize electrons:

$2\ ClO_2\ (aq) + 2\ e^- \rightarrow 2\ ClO_2^-\ (aq)$ and $H_2O_2\ (aq) + 2\ OH^-\ (aq) \rightarrow O_2\ (g) + 2\ H_2O\ (l) + 2\ e^-$

Add half-reactions:

$2\ ClO_2\ (aq) + \cancel{2\ e^-} + H_2O_2\ (aq) + 2\ OH^-\ (aq) \rightarrow 2\ ClO_2^-\ (aq) + O_2\ (g) + 2\ H_2O\ (l) + \cancel{2\ e^-}$

Cancel electrons: $2\ ClO_2\ (aq) + H_2O_2\ (aq) + 2\ OH^-\ (aq) \rightarrow 2\ ClO_2^-\ (aq) + O_2\ (g) + 2\ H_2O\ (l)$

Check:

Reactants	Products
2 Cl atoms	2 Cl atoms
8 O atoms	8 O atoms
4 H atoms	4 H atoms
–2 charge	–2 charge

(b) Separate: $MnO_4^-\ (aq) \rightarrow MnO_2\ (s)$ and $Al\ (s) \rightarrow Al(OH)_4^-\ (aq)$

Balance non H & O elements: $MnO_4^-\ (aq) \rightarrow MnO_2\ (s)$ and $Al\ (s) \rightarrow Al(OH)_4^-\ (aq)$

Balance O with H_2O: $MnO_4^-\ (aq) \rightarrow MnO_2\ (s) + 2\ H_2O\ (l)$ and $Al\ (s) + 4\ H_2O\ (l) \rightarrow Al(OH)_4^-\ (aq)$

Balance H with H^+:

$MnO_4^-\ (aq) + 4\ H^+\ (aq) \rightarrow MnO_2\ (s) + 2\ H_2O\ (l)$ and $Al\ (s) + 4\ H_2O\ (l) \rightarrow Al(OH)_4^-\ (aq) + 4\ H^+\ (aq)$

Neutralize H^+ with OH^-: $MnO_4^-\ (aq) + \underbrace{4\ H^+\ (aq) + 4\ OH^-\ (aq)}_{2\ \cancel{4}\ H_2O\ (l)} \rightarrow MnO_2\ (s) + \cancel{2\ H_2O\ (l)} + 4\ OH^-\ (aq)$

and $Al\ (s) + \cancel{4\ H_2O\ (l)} + 4\ OH^-\ (aq) \rightarrow Al(OH)_4^-\ (aq) + \underbrace{4\ H^+\ (aq) + 4\ OH^-\ (aq)}_{\cancel{4\ H_2O\ (l)}}$

Add electrons: $MnO_4^-\ (aq) + 2\ H_2O\ (l) + 3\ e^- \rightarrow MnO_2\ (s) + 4\ OH^-\ (aq)$ and

$Al\ (s) + 4\ OH^-\ (aq) \rightarrow Al(OH)_4^-\ (aq) + 3\ e^-$

Equalize electrons: $MnO_4^-\ (aq) + 2\ H_2O\ (l) + 3\ e^- \rightarrow MnO_2\ (s) + 4\ OH^-\ (aq)$ and

$Al\ (s) + 4\ OH^-\ (aq) \rightarrow Al(OH)_4^-\ (aq) + 3\ e^-$

Add half-reactions:

$MnO_4^-\ (aq) + 2\ H_2O\ (l) + \cancel{3\ e^-} + Al\ (s) + \cancel{4\ OH^-\ (aq)} \rightarrow MnO_2\ (s) + \cancel{4\ OH^-\ (aq)} + Al(OH)_4^-\ (aq) + \cancel{3\ e^-}$

Cancel electrons: $MnO_4^-\ (aq) + 2\ H_2O\ (l) + Al\ (s) \rightarrow MnO_2\ (s) + Al(OH)_4^-\ (aq)$

Check:

Reactants	Products
1 Mn atom	1 Mn atom
6 O atoms	6 O atoms
4 H atoms	4 H atoms
1 Al atom	1 Al atom
–1 charge	–1 charge

(c) Separate: $Cl_2\ (g) \rightarrow Cl^-\ (aq)$ and $Cl_2\ (g) \rightarrow ClO^-\ (aq)$

Balance non H & O elements: $Cl_2\ (g) \rightarrow 2\ Cl^-\ (aq)$ and $Cl_2\ (g) \rightarrow 2\ ClO^-\ (aq)$

Balance O with H_2O: $Cl_2\ (g) \rightarrow 2\ Cl^-\ (aq)$ and $Cl_2\ (g) + 2\ H_2O\ (l) \rightarrow 2\ ClO^-\ (aq)$

Balance H with H^+: $Cl_2\ (g) \rightarrow 2\ Cl^-\ (aq)$ and $Cl_2\ (g) + 2\ H_2O\ (l) \rightarrow 2\ ClO^-\ (aq) + 4\ H^+\ (aq)$

Neutralize H^+ with OH^-:

$Cl_2\ (g) \rightarrow 2\ Cl^-\ (aq)$ and $Cl_2\ (g) + \cancel{2\ H_2O\ (l)} + 4\ OH^-\ (aq) \rightarrow 2\ ClO^-\ (aq) + \underbrace{4\ H^+\ (aq) + 4\ OH^-\ (aq)}_{2\ \cancel{4}\ H_2O\ (l)}$

Add electrons: $Cl_2\ (g) + 2\ e^- \rightarrow 2\ Cl^-\ (aq)$ and $Cl_2\ (g) + 4\ OH^-\ (aq) \rightarrow 2\ ClO^-\ (aq) + 2\ H_2O\ (l) + 2\ e^-$

Equalize electrons: $Cl_2\ (g) + 2\ e^- \rightarrow 2\ Cl^-\ (aq)$ and $Cl_2\ (g) + 4\ OH^-\ (aq) \rightarrow 2\ ClO^-\ (aq) + 2\ H_2O\ (l) + 2\ e^-$

Add half-reactions: $Cl_2\ (g) + \cancel{2\ e^-} + Cl_2\ (g) + 4\ OH^-\ (aq) \rightarrow 2\ Cl^-\ (aq) + 2\ ClO^-\ (aq) + 2\ H_2O\ (l) + \cancel{2\ e^-}$

Cancel electrons: $2\ Cl_2\ (g) + 4\ OH^-\ (aq) \rightarrow 2\ Cl^-\ (aq) + 2\ ClO^-\ (aq) + 2\ H_2O\ (l)$

Simplify: $Cl_2\ (g) + 2\ OH^-\ (aq) \rightarrow Cl^-\ (aq) + ClO^-\ (aq) + H_2O\ (l)$

Check:

Reactants	Products
2 Cl atoms	2 Cl atoms
2 O atoms	2 O atoms
2 H atoms	2 H atoms
–2 charge	–2 charge

18.42 **Conceptual Plan: Separate the overall reaction into two half-reactions: one for oxidation and one for reduction. → Balance each half-reaction with respect to mass in the following order: 1) balance all elements other than H and O, 2) balance O by adding H_2O, 3) balance H by adding H^+, and 4) neutralize H^+ by adding enough OH^- to neutralize each H^+. Add the same number of OH^- ions to each side of the equation. → Balance each half-reaction with respect to charge by adding electrons. (The sum of the charges on both sides of the equation should be made equal by adding electrons as necessary.) → Make the number of electrons in both half-reactions equal by multiplying one or both half-reactions by a small whole number. → Add the two half-reactions together, canceling electrons and other species as necessary. → Verify that the reaction is balanced both with respect to mass and with respect to charge.**

Solution:

(a) Separate: $MnO_4^-\ (aq) \rightarrow MnO_2\ (s)$ and $Br^-\ (aq) \rightarrow BrO_3^-\ (aq)$

Balance non H & O elements: $MnO_4^-\ (aq) \rightarrow MnO_2\ (s)$ and $Br^-\ (aq) \rightarrow BrO_3^-\ (aq)$

Balance O with H_2O: $MnO_4^-\ (aq) \rightarrow MnO_2\ (s) + 2\ H_2O\ (l)$ and $Br^-\ (aq) + 3\ H_2O\ (l) \rightarrow BrO_3^-\ (aq)$

Balance H with H^+:

$MnO_4^-\ (aq) + 4\ H^+\ (aq) \rightarrow MnO_2\ (s) + 2\ H_2O\ (l)$ and $Br^-\ (aq) + 3\ H_2O\ (l) \rightarrow BrO_3^-\ (aq) + 6\ H^+\ (aq)$

Neutralize H^+ with OH^-: $MnO_4^-\ (aq) + \underbrace{4\ H^+\ (aq) + 4\ OH^-\ (aq)}_{2\ \cancel{4}\ H_2O\ (l)} \rightarrow MnO_2\ (s) + \cancel{2\ H_2O\ (l)} + 4\ OH^-\ (aq)$

and $Br^-\ (aq) + \cancel{3\ H_2O\ (l)} + 6\ OH^-\ (aq) \rightarrow BrO_3^-\ (aq) + \underbrace{6\ H^+\ (aq) + 6\ OH^-\ (aq)}_{3\ \cancel{6}\ H_2O\ (l)}$

Add electrons: $MnO_4^-\ (aq) + 2\ H_2O\ (l) + 3\ e^- \rightarrow MnO_2\ (s) + 4\ OH^-\ (aq)$ and

$Br^-\ (aq) + 6\ OH^-\ (aq) \rightarrow BrO_3^-\ (aq) + 3\ H_2O\ (l) + 6\ e^-$

Equalize electrons: $2\ MnO_4^-\ (aq) + 4\ H_2O\ (l) + 6\ e^- \rightarrow 2\ MnO_2\ (s) + 8\ OH^-\ (aq)$ and

$Br^-\ (aq) + 6\ OH^-\ (aq) \rightarrow BrO_3^-\ (aq) + 3\ H_2O\ (l) + 6\ e^-$

Add half-reactions: $2\ MnO_4^-\ (aq) + 1\ \cancel{4}\ H_2O\ (l) + \cancel{6\ e^-} + Br^-\ (aq) + \cancel{6\ OH^-\ (aq)} \rightarrow$

$2\ MnO_2\ (s) + 2\ \cancel{8}\ OH^-\ (aq) + BrO_3^-\ (aq) + \cancel{3\ H_2O\ (l)} + \cancel{6\ e^-}$

Cancel electrons & others: $2\ MnO_4^-\ (aq) + H_2O\ (l) + Br^-\ (aq) \rightarrow 2\ MnO_2\ (s) + 2\ OH^-\ (aq) + BrO_3^-\ (aq)$

Check:

Reactants	Products
2 Mn atoms	2 Mn atoms
9 O atoms	9 O atoms
2 H atoms	2 H atoms
1 Br atom	1 Br atom
–3 charge	–3 charge

(b) Separate: $Ag\ (s) + CN^-\ (aq) \rightarrow Ag(CN)_2^-\ (aq)$ and $O_2\ (g) \rightarrow$

Balance non H & O elements: $Ag\ (s) + 2\ CN^-\ (aq) \rightarrow Ag(CN)_2^-\ (aq)$ and $O_2\ (g) \rightarrow$

Balance O with H_2O: $Ag\ (s) + 2\ CN^-\ (aq) \rightarrow Ag(CN)_2^-\ (aq)$ and $O_2\ (g) \rightarrow 2\ H_2O\ (l)$

Balance H with H^+: $Ag\ (s) + 2\ CN^-\ (aq) \rightarrow Ag(CN)_2^-\ (aq)$ and $O_2\ (g) + 4\ H^+\ (aq) \rightarrow 2\ H_2O\ (l)$

Neutralize H^+ with OH^-:

$Ag\ (s) + 2\ CN^-\ (aq \rightarrow Ag(CN)_2^-\ (aq)$ and $O_2\ (g) + \underbrace{4\ H^+\ (aq) + 4\ OH^-\ (aq)}_{2\ \not{4}\ H_2O\ (l)} \rightarrow \cancel{2\ H_2O\ (l)} + 4\ OH^-\ (aq)$

Add electrons: $Ag\ (s) + 2\ CN^-\ (aq) \rightarrow Ag(CN)_2^-\ (aq) + e^-$ and $O_2\ (g) + 2\ H_2O\ (l)\ ) + 4\ e^- \rightarrow 4\ OH^-\ (aq)$

Equalize electrons:

$4\ Ag\ (s) + 8\ CN^-\ (aq) \rightarrow 4\ Ag(CN)_2^-\ (aq) + 4\ e^-$ and $O_2\ (g) + 2\ H_2O\ (l) + 4\ e^- \rightarrow 4\ OH^-\ (aq)$

Add half-reactions:

$4\ Ag\ (s) + 8\ CN^-\ (aq) + O_2\ (g) + 2\ H_2O\ (l) + \cancel{4\ e^-} \rightarrow 4\ Ag(CN)_2^-\ (aq) + \cancel{4\ e^-} + 4\ OH^-\ (aq)$

Cancel electrons: $4\ Ag\ (s) + 8\ CN^-\ (aq) + O_2\ (g) + 2\ H_2O\ (l) \rightarrow 4\ Ag(CN)_2^-\ (aq) + 4\ OH^-\ (aq)$

Check:

Reactants	Products
4 Ag atoms	4 Ag atoms
8 C atoms	8 C atoms
8 N atoms	8 N atoms
4 O atoms	4 O atoms
4 H atoms	4 H atoms
–8 charge	–8 charge

(c) Separate: $NO_2^-\ (aq) \rightarrow NH_3\ (g)$ and $Al\ (s) \rightarrow AlO_2^-\ (aq)$

Balance non H & O elements: $NO_2^-\ (aq) \rightarrow NH_3\ (g)$ and $Al\ (s) \rightarrow AlO_2^-\ (aq)$

Balance O with H_2O: $NO_2^-\ (aq) \rightarrow NH_3\ (g) + 2\ H_2O\ (l)$ and $Al\ (s) + 2\ H_2O\ (l) \rightarrow AlO_2^-\ (aq)$

Balance H with H^+: $NO_2^-\ (aq) + 7\ H^+\ (aq) \rightarrow NH_3\ (g) + 2\ H_2O\ (l)$ and

$Al\ (s) + 2\ H_2O\ (l) \rightarrow AlO_2^-\ (aq) + 4\ H^+\ (aq)$

Neutralize H^+ with OH^-: $NO_2^-\ (aq) + \underbrace{7\ H^+\ (aq) + 7\ OH^-\ (aq)}_{5\ \not{7}\ H_2O\ (l)} \rightarrow NH_3\ (g) + \cancel{2\ H_2O\ (l)} + 7\ OH^-\ (aq)$ and

$Al\ (s) + \cancel{2\ H_2O\ (l)} + 4\ OH^-\ (aq) \rightarrow AlO_2^-\ (aq) + \underbrace{4\ H^+\ (aq) + 4\ OH^-\ (aq)}_{2\ \not{4}\ H_2O\ (l)}$

Add electrons: $NO_2^-\ (aq) + 5\ H_2O\ (l) + 6\ e^- \rightarrow NH_3\ (g) + 7\ OH^-\ (aq)$ and

$Al\ (s) + 4\ OH^-\ (aq) \rightarrow AlO_2^-\ (aq) + 2\ H_2O\ (l) + 3\ e^-$

Equalize electrons: $NO_2^-\ (aq) + 5\ H_2O\ (l) + 6\ e^- \rightarrow NH_3\ (g) + 7\ OH^-\ (aq)$ and

$2\ Al\ (s) + 8\ OH^-\ (aq) \rightarrow 2\ AlO_2^-\ (aq) + 4\ H_2O\ (l) + 6\ e^-$

Add half-reactions: $NO_2^-\ (aq) + 1\ \not{5}\ H_2O\ (l) + \cancel{6\ e^-} + 2\ Al\ (s) + 1\ \not{8}\ OH^-\ (aq) \rightarrow$

$NH_3\ (g) + \cancel{7\ OH^-\ (aq)} + 2\ AlO_2^-\ (aq) + \cancel{4\ H_2O\ (l)} + \cancel{6\ e^-}$

Cancel electrons & others: $NO_2^-\ (aq) + H_2O\ (l) + 2\ Al\ (s) + OH^-\ (aq) \rightarrow NH_3\ (g) + 2\ AlO_2^-\ (aq)$

Check:

Reactants	Products
1 N atom	1 N atom
4 O atoms	4 O atoms
3 H atoms	3 H atoms
2 Al atoms	2 Al atoms
–2 charge	–2 charge

Voltaic Cells, Standard Cell Potentials, and Direction of Spontaneity

18.43 **Given:** voltaic cell overall redox reaction
Find: Sketch voltaic cell, labeling anode, cathode, all species, and direction of electron flow
Conceptual Plan: Separate the overall reaction into two half-cell reactions and add electrons as needed to balance reactions. Put the anode reaction on the left (oxidation = electrons as product) and the cathode reaction on the right (reduction = electrons as reactant). Electrons flow from anode to cathode.
Solution:

(a) $2\ Ag^+\ (aq) + Pb\ (s) \rightarrow 2\ Ag\ (s) + Pb^{2+}\ (aq)$ separates to $2\ Ag^+\ (aq) \rightarrow 2\ Ag\ (s)$ and $Pb\ (s) \rightarrow Pb^{2+}\ (aq)$ then add electrons to balance to get the cathode reaction: $2\ Ag^+\ (aq) + 2\ e^- \rightarrow 2\ Ag\ (s)$ and the anode reaction: $Pb\ (s) \rightarrow Pb^{2+}\ (aq) + 2\ e^-$.

Since we have Pb (*s*) as the reactant for the oxidation, it will be our anode. Since we have Ag (*s*) as the product for the reduction, it will be our cathode. Simplify the cathode reaction, dividing all terms by 2.

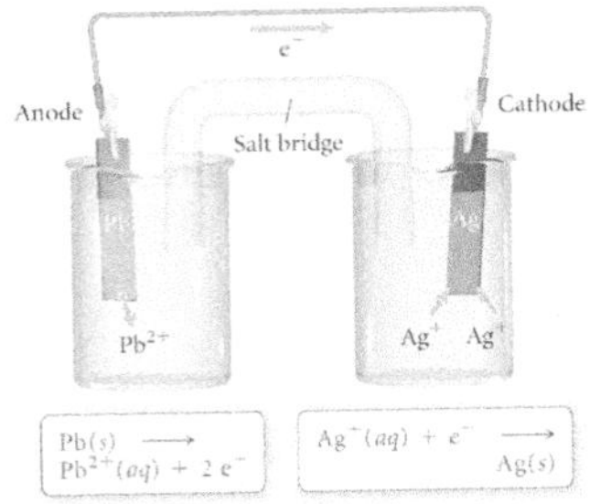

(b) $2\ ClO_2\ (g) + 2\ I^-\ (aq) \rightarrow 2\ ClO_2^-\ (aq) + I_2\ (s)$ separates to $2\ ClO_2\ (g) \rightarrow 2\ ClO_2^-\ (aq)$ and $2\ I^-\ (aq) \rightarrow I_2\ (s)$ then add electrons to balance to get the cathode reaction: $2\ ClO_2\ (g) + 2\ e^- \rightarrow 2\ ClO_2^-\ (aq)$ and the anode reaction: $2\ I^-\ (aq) \rightarrow I_2\ (s) + 2\ e^-$.

Since we have I^- (*aq*) as the reactant for the oxidation, we will need to use Pt as our anode. Since we have ClO_2^- (*aq*) as the product for the reduction, we will need to use Pt as our cathode. Since ClO_2 (*g*) is our reactant for the reduction, we need to use an electrode assembly like that used for a SHE. Simplify the cathode reaction, dividing all terms by 2.

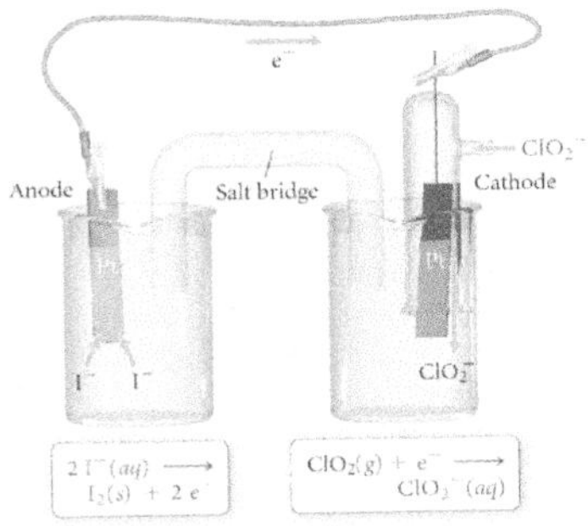

(c) $O_2\ (g) + 4\ H^+\ (aq) + 2\ Zn\ (s) \rightarrow 2\ H_2O\ (l) + 2\ Zn^{2+}\ (aq)$ separates to $O_2\ (g) + 4\ H^+\ (aq) \rightarrow 2\ H_2O\ (l)$ and $2\ Zn\ (s) \rightarrow 2\ Zn^{2+}\ (aq)$ then add electrons to balance to get the cathode reaction: $O_2\ (g) + 4\ H^+\ (aq) + 4\ e^- \rightarrow 2\ H_2O\ (l)$ and the anode reaction: $2\ Zn\ (s) \rightarrow 2\ Zn^{2+}\ (aq) + 4\ e^-$.

Since we have Zn (*s*) as the reactant for the oxidation, it will be our anode. Since we have H_2O (*l*) as the product for the reduction, we will need to use Pt as our cathode. Since O_2 (*g*) is our reactant for the reduction, we need to use an electrode assembly like the one that is used for a SHE. Simplify the anode reaction, dividing all terms by 2.

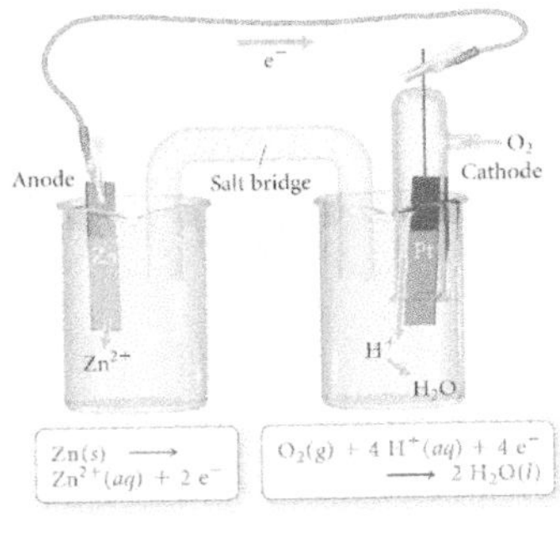

18.44 **Given:** voltaic cell overall redox reaction
Find: Sketch voltaic cell, labeling anode, cathode, all species, and direction of electron flow
Conceptual Plan: Separate the overall reaction into two half-cell reactions and add electrons as needed to balance reactions. Put the anode reaction on the left (oxidation = electrons as product) and the cathode reaction on the right (reduction = electrons as reactant). Electrons flow from anode to cathode.
Solution:

(a) $Ni^{2+}\ (aq) + Mg\ (s) \rightarrow Ni\ (s) + Mg^{2+}\ (aq)$ separates to $Ni^{2+}\ (aq) \rightarrow Ni\ (s)$ and $Mg\ (s) \rightarrow Mg^{2+}\ (aq)$ then add electrons to balance to get the cathode reaction: $Ni^{2+}\ (aq) + 2\ e^- \rightarrow Ni\ (s)$ and the anode reaction: $Mg\ (s) \rightarrow Mg^{2+}\ (aq) + 2\ e^-$.

Since we have Mg (*s*) as the reactant for the oxidation, it will be our anode. Since we have Ni (*s*) as the product for the reduction, it will be our cathode.

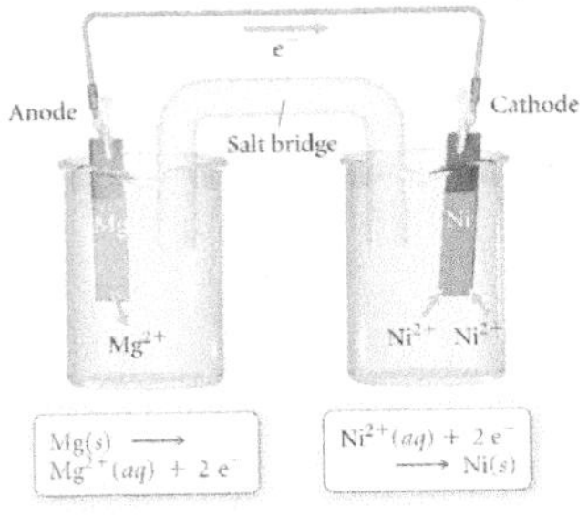

(b) $2\ H^+\ (aq) + Fe\ (s) \rightarrow H_2\ (g) + Fe^{2+}\ (aq)$ separates to $2\ H^+\ (aq) \rightarrow H_2\ (g)$ and $Fe\ (s) \rightarrow Fe^{2+}\ (aq)$ then add electrons to balance to get the cathode reaction: $2\ H^+\ (aq) + 2\ e^- \rightarrow H_2\ (g)$ and the anode reaction: $Fe\ (s) \rightarrow Fe^{2+}\ (aq) + 2\ e^-$.

Since we have Fe (*s*) as the reactant for the oxidation, it will be our anode. Since we have H_2 (*g*) as the product for the reduction, we will need to use Pt as our cathode and the product can leave using an electrode assembly like that used for a SHE.

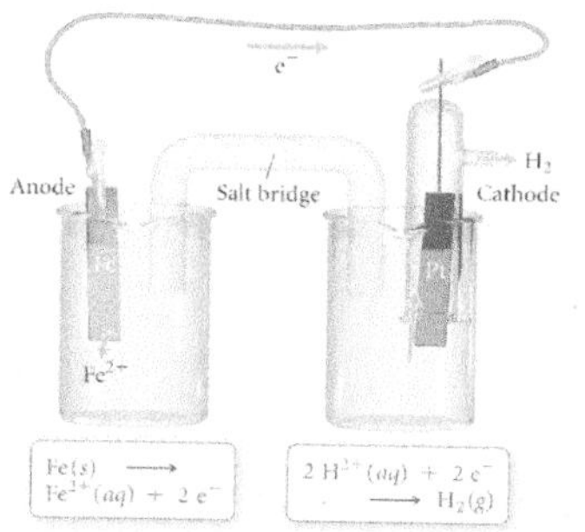

(c) $2\ NO_3^-\ (aq) + 8\ H^+\ (aq) + 3\ Cu\ (s) \rightarrow 2\ NO\ (g) + 4\ H_2O\ (l) + 3\ Cu^{2+}\ (aq)$ separates to $2\ NO_3^-\ (aq) + 8\ H^+\ (aq) \rightarrow 2\ NO\ (g) + 4\ H_2O\ (l)$ and $3\ Cu\ (s) \rightarrow 3\ Cu^{2+}\ (aq)$ then add electrons to balance to get the cathode reaction: $2\ NO_3^-\ (aq) + 8\ H^+\ (aq) + 6\ e^- \rightarrow 2\ NO\ (g) + 4\ H_2O\ (l)$ and the anode reaction: $3\ Cu\ (s) \rightarrow 3\ Cu^{2+}\ (aq) + 6\ e^-$.

Since we have Cu (*s*) as the reactant for the oxidation, it will be our anode. Since we have H_2O (*l*) and NO (*g*) as the products for the reduction, we will need to use Pt as our cathode and the gaseous product can leave using an electrode assembly like that used for a SHE.

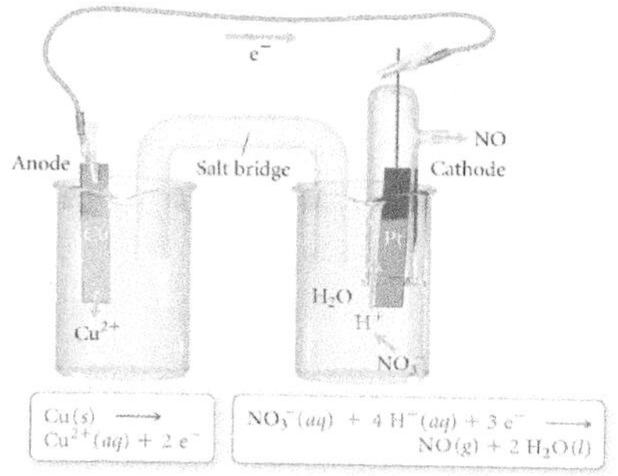

18.45 **Given:** overall reactions from Problem 43 **Find:** E°_{cell}
Conceptual Plan: Look up half-reactions from the solution of Problem 43 in Table 18.1. Calculate the standard cell potential by subtracting the electrode potential of the anode from the electrode potential of the cathode: $E^\circ_{cell} = E^\circ_{cathode} - E^\circ_{anode}$.
Solution:

(a) $Ag^+\ (aq) + e^- \rightarrow Ag\ (s)$ $E^\circ_{red} = 0.80\ V = E^\circ_{cathode}$ and $Pb\ (s) \rightarrow Pb^{2+}\ (aq) + 2\ e^-$ $E^\circ_{red} = -\ 0.13\ V = E^\circ_{anode}$. Then $E^\circ_{cell} = E^\circ_{cathode} - E^\circ_{anode} = 0.80\ V - (-\ 0.13\ V) = 0.93\ V$.

(b) $ClO_2\ (g) + e^- \rightarrow ClO_2^-\ (aq)$ $E^\circ_{red} = 0.95\ V = E^\circ_{cathode}$ and $2\ I^-\ (aq) \rightarrow I_2\ (s) + 2\ e^-$ $E^\circ_{red} = +\ 0.54\ V = E^\circ_{anode}$. Then $E^\circ_{cell} = E^\circ_{cathode} - E^\circ_{anode} = 0.95\ V - 0.54\ V = 0.41\ V$.

(c) $O_2\ (g) + 4\ H^+\ (aq) + 4\ e^- \rightarrow 2\ H_2O\ (l)$ $E^\circ_{red} = 1.23\ V$ and $Zn\ (s) \rightarrow Zn^{2+}\ (aq) + 2\ e^-$ $E^\circ_{red} = -\ 0.76\ V = E^\circ_{anode}$. Then $E^\circ_{cell} = E^\circ_{cathode} - E^\circ_{anode} = 1.23\ V - (-\ 0.76\ V) = 1.99\ V$.

Check: The units (V) are correct. All of the voltages are positive, which is consistent with a voltaic cell.

18.46 **Given:** overall reactions from Problem 44 **Find:** E°_{cell}
Conceptual Plan: Look up half-reactions from the solution of Problem 44 in Table 18.1. Calculate the standard cell potential by subtracting the electrode potential of the anode from the electrode potential of the cathode: $E^\circ_{cell} = E^\circ_{cathode} - E^\circ_{anode}$.
Solution:

(a) $Ni^{2+}\ (aq) + 2\ e^- \rightarrow Ni\ (s)$ $E^\circ_{red} = -\ 0.23\ V = E^\circ_{cathode}$ and $Mg\ (s) \rightarrow Mg^{2+}\ (aq) + 2\ e^-$ $E^\circ_{red} = -\ 2.37\ V = E^\circ_{anode}$. Then $E^\circ_{cell} = E^\circ_{cathode} - E^\circ_{anode} = -\ 0.23\ V - (-\ 2.37\ V) = 2.14\ V$.

(b) $2\ H^+\ (aq) + 2\ e^- \rightarrow H_2\ (g)$ $E^\circ_{red} = 0.00\ V = E^\circ_{cathode}$ and $Fe\ (s) \rightarrow Fe^{2+}\ (aq) + 2\ e^-$ $E^\circ_{red} = -\ 0.45\ V = E^\circ_{anode}$. Then $E^\circ_{cell} = E^\circ_{cathode} - E^\circ_{anode} = 0.00\ V - (-\ 0.45\ V) = 0.45\ V$.

(c) $NO_3^-\ (aq) + 4\ H^+\ (aq) + 3\ e^- \rightarrow NO\ (g) + 2\ H_2O\ (l)$ $E^\circ_{red} = 0.96\ V = E^\circ_{cathode}$ and $Cu\ (s) \rightarrow Cu^{2+}\ (aq) + 2\ e^-$ $E^\circ_{red} = -\ 0.34\ V = E^\circ_{anode}$. Then $E^\circ_{cell} = E^\circ_{cathode} - E^\circ_{anode} = 0.96\ V - 0.34\ V = 0.62\ V$.

Check: The units (V) are correct. All of the voltages are positive, which is consistent with a voltaic cell.

18.47 **Given:** voltaic cell drawing
Find: (a) determine electron flow direction, anode, and cathode; (b) write balanced overall reaction and calculate E°_{cell}; (c) label electrodes as + and –; and (d) directions of anions and cations from salt bridge

Conceptual Plan: Look at each half-cell and write a reduction reaction by using electrode and solution composition and adding electrons to balance. Look up half-reactions and standard reduction potentials in Table 18.1. Since this is a voltaic cell, the cell potentials must be assigned to give a positive E°_{cell}. Calculate the standard cell potential by subtracting the electrode potential of the anode from the electrode potential of the cathode: $E^\circ_{cell} = E^\circ_{cathode} - E^\circ_{anode}$, choosing the electrode assignments to give a positive E°_{cell}.

(a) Label the electrode where the oxidation occurs as the anode. Label the electrode where the reduction occurs as the cathode. Electrons flow from anode to cathode.

(b) Take two half-cell reactions and multiply the reactions as necessary to equalize the number of electrons transferred. Add the two half-cell reactions and cancel electrons and any other species.

(c) Label anode as (–) and cathode as (+).

(d) Cations will flow from the salt bridge towards the cathode and the anions will flow from the salt bridge towards the anode.

Solution:
left side: Fe^{3+} (aq) → Fe (s) and right side: Cr^{3+} (aq) → Cr (s) add electrons to balance Fe^{3+} (aq) + 3 e^- → Fe (s) and right side: Cr^{3+} (aq) + 3 e^- → Cr (s). Look up cell standard reduction potentials: Fe^{3+} (aq) + 3 e^- → Fe (s) E°_{red} = – 0.036 V and Cr^{3+} (aq) + 3 e^- → Cr (s) E°_{red} = – 0.73 V. In order to get a positive cell potential, the second reaction is the oxidation reaction (anode). $E^\circ_{cell} = E^\circ_{cathode} - E^\circ_{anode}$ = – 0.036 V – (– 0.73 V) = + 0.69 V. (a, c, and d)

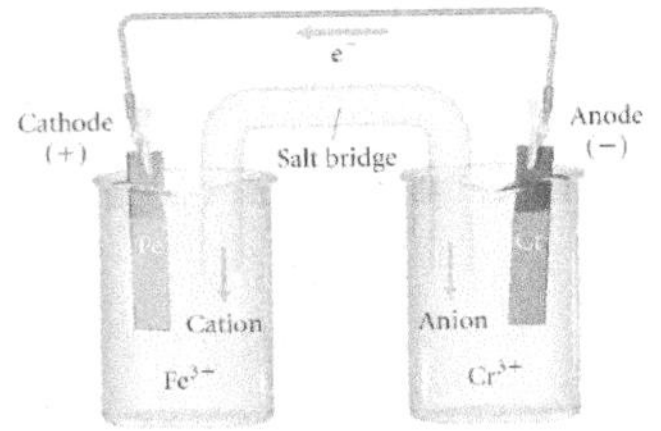

(b) Add two half-reactions with the second reaction reversed.
Fe^{3+} (aq) + ~~3 e^-~~ + Cr (s) → Fe (s) + Cr^{3+} (aq) + ~~3 e^-~~.
Cancel electrons to get: Fe^{3+} (aq) + Cr (s) → Fe (s) + Cr^{3+} (aq).
Check: All atoms and charge are balanced. The units (V) are correct. The cell potential is positive which is consistent with a voltaic cell.

18.48 **Given:** voltaic cell drawing
Find: (a) determine electron flow direction, anode, and cathode; (b) write balanced overall reaction and calculate E°_{cell}; (c) label electrodes as + and –; and (d) directions of anions and cations from salt bridge
Conceptual Plan: Look at each half-cell and write a reduction reaction by using electrode and solution composition and adding electrons to balance. Look up half-reactions and standard reduction potentials in Table 18.1. Since this is a voltaic cell, the cell potentials must be assigned to give a positive E°_{cell}. Calculate the standard cell potential by subtracting the electrode potential of the anode from the electrode potential of the cathode: $E^\circ_{cell} = E^\circ_{cathode} - E^\circ_{anode}$, choosing the electrode assignments to give a positive E°_{cell}.

(a) Label the electrode where the oxidation occurs as the anode. Label the electrode where the reduction occurs as the cathode. Electrons flow from anode to cathode.

(b) Take two half-cell reactions and multiply the reactions as necessary to equalize the number of electrons transferred. Add the two half-cell reactions and cancel electrons and any other species.

(c) Label anode as (–) and cathode as (+).

(d) Cations will flow from the salt bridge towards the cathode and the anions will flow from salt bridge towards the anode.

Solution: left side: Pb^{2+} (aq) → Pb (s) and right side: Cl_2 (g) → 2 Cl^- (aq) add electrons to balance Pb^{2+} (aq) + 2 e^- → Pb (s) and right side: Cl_2 (g) + 2 e^- → 2 Cl^- (aq). Look up cell standard reduction potentials: Pb^{2+} (aq) + 2 e^- → Pb (s) E°_{red} = – 0.13 V and Cl_2 (g) + 2 e^- → 2 Cl^- (aq) E°_{red} = 1.36 V. In order to get a positive cell potential, the first reaction is the oxidation reaction (anode). $E^\circ_{cell} = E^\circ_{cathode} - E^\circ_{anode}$ = 1.36 V– (– 0.13 V) = + 1.49 V. (a, c, and d)

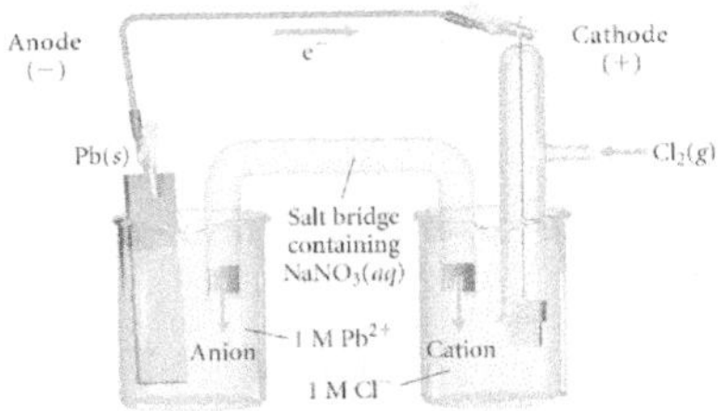

(b) Add two half-reactions with the first reaction reversed.
$Pb\ (s) + Cl_2\ (g) + \cancel{2e^-} \rightarrow Pb^{2+}\ (aq) + \cancel{2e^-} + 2\ Cl^-\ (aq)$.
Cancel electrons to get: $Pb\ (s) + Cl_2\ (g) \rightarrow Pb^{2}+\ (aq) + 2\ Cl^-\ (aq)$.
Check: All atoms and charge are balanced. The units (V) are correct. The cell potential is positive which is consistent with a voltaic cell.

18.49 **Given:** overall reactions from Problem 43 **Find:** line notation
Conceptual Plan: Use the solution from Problem 43. Write the oxidation half-reaction components on the left and the reduction on the right. A double vertical line (||), indicating the salt bridge, separates the two half-reactions. Substances in different phases are separated by a single vertical line (|), which represents the boundary between the phases. For some redox reactions, the reactants and products of one or both of the half-reactions may be in the same phase. In these cases, the reactants and products are simply separated from each other with a comma in the line diagram. Such cells use an inert electrode, such as platinum (Pt) or graphite, as the anode or cathode (or both).
Solution:

(a) Reduction reaction: $Ag^+\ (aq) + e^- \rightarrow Ag\ (s)$ and the oxidation reaction: $Pb\ (s) \rightarrow Pb^2 + (aq) + 2\ e^-$ so $Pb\ (s)\,|\,Pb^{2+}\ (aq)\,||\,Ag^+\ (aq)\,|\,Ag\ (s)$

(b) Reduction reaction: $ClO_2\ (g) + e^- \rightarrow ClO_2^-\ (aq)$ and the oxidation reaction: $2\ I^-\ (aq) \rightarrow I_2\ (s) + 2\ e^-$ so $Pt\ (s)\,|\,I^-\ (aq)\,|\,I_2\ (s)\,||\,ClO_2\ (g)\,|\,ClO_2^-\ (aq)\,|\,Pt\ (s)$

(c) Reduction reaction: $O_2\ (g) + 4\ H^+\ (aq) + 4\ e^- \rightarrow 2\ H_2O\ (l)$ and the oxidation reaction: $Zn\ (s) \rightarrow Zn^{2+}\ (aq) + 2\ e^-$ so $Zn\ (s)\,|\,Zn^{2+}\ (aq)\ ||\,O_2\ (g)\,|\,H^+\ (aq),\ H_2O\ (l)\,|\,Pt\ (s)$

18.50 **Given:** overall reactions from Problem 44 **Find:** line notation
Conceptual Plan: Use the solution from Problem 44. Write the oxidation half-reaction components on the left and the reduction on the right. A double vertical line (||), indicating the salt bridge, separates the two half-reactions. Substances in different phases are separated by a single vertical line (|), which represents the boundary between the phases. For some redox reactions, the reactants and products of one or both of the half-reactions may be in the same phase. In these cases, the reactants and products are simply separated from each other with a comma in the line diagram. Such cells use an inert electrode, such as platinum (Pt) or graphite, as the anode or cathode (or both).
Solution:

(a) Reduction reaction: $Ni^{2+}\ (aq) + 2\ e^- \rightarrow Ni\ (s)$ and the oxidation reaction: $Mg\ (s) \rightarrow Mg^{2+}\ (aq) + 2\ e^-$ so $Mg\ (s)\,|\,Mg^{2+}\ (aq)\,||\,Ni^{2+}\ (aq)\ |\,Ni\ (s)$

(b) Reduction reaction: $2\ H^+\ (aq) + 2\ e^- \rightarrow H_2\ (g)$ and the oxidation reaction: $Fe\ (s) \rightarrow Fe^{2+}\ (aq) + 2\ e^-$ so $Fe\ (s)\,|\,Fe^{2+}\ (aq)\,||\,H^+\ (aq)\,|\,H_2\ (g)\,|\,Pt\ (s)$

(c) Reduction reaction: $NO_3^-\ (aq) + 4\ H^+\ (aq) + 3\ e^- \rightarrow NO\ (g) + 2\ H_2O\ (l)$ and the oxidation reaction: $Cu\ (s) \rightarrow Cu^{2+}\ (aq) + 2\ e^-$ so $Cu\ (s)\,|\,Cu^{2+}\ (aq)\ ||\,NO_3^-\ (aq),\ H^+\ (aq)\ ),\ H_2O\ (l)\,|\,NO\ (g)\,|\,Pt\ (s)$

18.51 **Given:** $Sn\ (s)\,|\,Sn^{2+}\ (aq)\ ||\,NO_3^-\ (aq),\ H^+\ (aq)\ ),\ H_2O\ (l)\,|\,NO\ (g)\,|\,Pt\ (s)$
Find: Sketch voltaic cell, labeling anode, cathode, all species, direction of electron flow, and E°_{cell}
Conceptual Plan: Separate overall reaction into two half-cell reactions knowing that the oxidation half-reaction components are on the left and the reduction half-reaction components are on the right. Add electrons as needed to balance reactions. Multiply the half-reactions by the appropriate factors to have an equal number of electrons transferred. Add the half-cell reactions and cancel electrons. Put anode reaction on the left (oxidation = electrons as product) and cathode reaction on the right (reduction = electrons as reactant). Electrons flow from anode to cathode. Look up half-reactions in Table 18.1. Calculate the standard cell potential by subtracting the electrode potential of the anode from the electrode potential of the cathode: $E^\circ_{cell} = E^\circ_{cathode} - E^\circ_{anode}$.

Solution: Oxidation reaction (anode): Sn (*s*) $\rightarrow$ Sn^{2+} (*aq*) + 2 e^- $E^\circ_{red} = -0.14$ V and reduction reaction (cathode): NO_3^- (*aq*) + 4 H^+ (*aq*) + 3 e^- $\rightarrow$ NO (*g*) + 2 H_2O (*l*) $E^\circ_{red} = 0.96$ V. $E^\circ_{cell} = E^\circ_{cathode} - E^\circ_{anode} = 0.96\text{ V} - (-0.14\text{ V}) = 1.10$ V. Multiply first reaction by 3 and the second reaction by 2 so that 6 electrons are transferred. 3 Sn (*s*) $\rightarrow$ 3 Sn^{2+} (*aq*) + 6 e^- and 2 NO_3^- (*aq*) + 8 H^+ (*aq*) + 6 e^- $\rightarrow$ 2 NO (*g*) + 4 H_2O (*l*). Add the two half-reactions and cancel electrons 3 Sn (*s*) + 2 NO_3^- (*aq*) + 8 H^+ (*aq*) + $\cancel{6\,e^-}$ $\rightarrow$ 3 Sn^{2+} (*aq*) + $\cancel{6\,e^-}$ + 2 NO (*g*) + 4 H_2O (*l*). So balanced reaction is: 3 Sn (*s*) + 2 NO_3^- (*aq*) + 8 H^+ (*aq*) $\rightarrow$ 3 Sn^{2+} (*aq*) + 2 NO (*g*) + 4 H_2O (*l*).

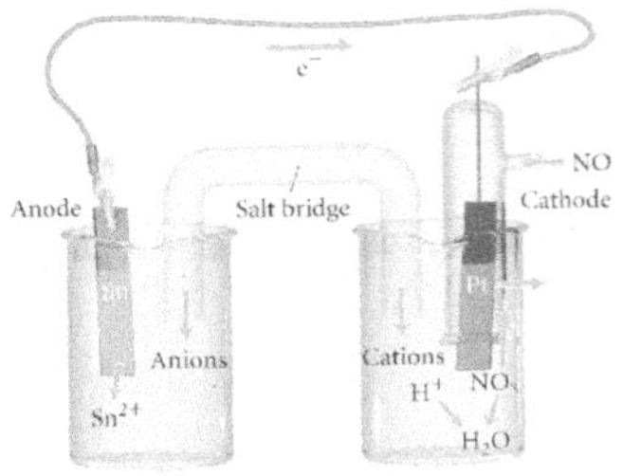

Check: All atoms and charge are balanced. The units (V) are correct. The cell potential is positive which is consistent with a voltaic cell.

18.52 **Given:** Mn (*s*) | Mn^{2+} (*aq*) || ClO_2 (*g*) | ClO_2^- (*aq*) | Pt (*s*)
Find: Sketch voltaic cell, labeling anode, cathode, all species, direction of electron flow, and E°_{cell}
Conceptual Plan: Separate the overall reaction into two half-cell reactions knowing that the oxidation half-reaction components are on the left and the reduction half-reaction components are on the right. Add electrons as needed to balance reactions. Multiply the half-reactions by the appropriate factors to have an equal number of electrons transferred. Add the half-cell reactions and cancel electrons. Put the anode reaction on the left (oxidation = electrons as product) and the cathode reaction on the right (reduction = electrons as reactant). Electrons flow from anode to cathode. Look up half-reactions in Table 18.1. Calculate the standard cell potential by subtracting the electrode potential of the anode from the electrode potential of the cathode: $E^\circ_{cell} = E^\circ_{cathode} - E^\circ_{anode}$.
Solution: Oxidation reaction (anode): Mn (*s*) $\rightarrow$ Mn^{2+} (*aq*) + 2 e^- $E^\circ_{red} = -1.18$ V and reduction reaction (cathode): ClO_2 (*g*) + e^- $\rightarrow$ ClO_2^- (*aq*) $E^\circ_{red} = 0.95$ V. $E^\circ_{cell} = E^\circ_{cathode} - E^\circ_{anode} = 0.95\text{ V} - (-1.18\text{ V}) = 2.13$ V. Multiply the second reaction by 2 so that 2 electrons are transferred. Mn (*s*) $\rightarrow$ Mn^{2+} (*aq*) + 2 e^- and 2 ClO_2 (*g*) + 2 e^- $\rightarrow$ 2 ClO_2^- (*aq*). Add the two half-reactions and cancel electrons Mn (*s*) + 2 ClO_2 (*g*) + $\cancel{2\,e^-}$ $\rightarrow$ Mn^{2+} (*aq*) + $\cancel{2\,e^-}$ + 2 ClO_2^- (*aq*). So balanced reaction is: Mn (*s*) + 2 ClO_2 (*g*) $\rightarrow$ Mn^{2+} (*aq*) + 2 ClO_2^- (*aq*).
Check: All atoms and charge are balanced. The units (V) are correct. The cell potential is positive which is consistent with a voltaic cell.

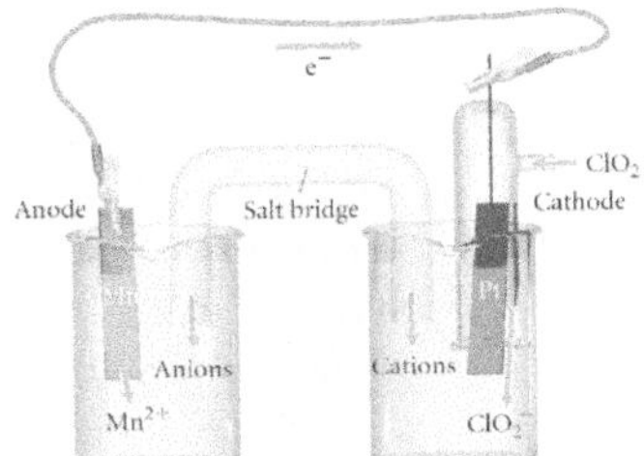

18.53 **Given:** overall reactions **Find:** spontaneity in forward direction
Conceptual Plan: Separate the overall reaction into two half-cell reactions and add electrons as needed to balance reactions. Look up half-reactions in Table 18.1. Calculate the standard cell potential by subtracting the electrode potential of the anode from the electrode potential of the cathode: $E^\circ_{cell} = E^\circ_{cathode} - E^\circ_{anode}$. If $E^\circ_{cell} > 0$ the reaction is spontaneous in the forward direction.
Solution:

(a) Ni (*s*) + Zn^{2+} (*aq*) $\rightarrow$ Ni^{2+} (*aq*) + Zn (*s*) separates to Ni (*s*) $\rightarrow$ Ni^{2+} (*aq*) and Zn^{2+} (*aq*) $\rightarrow$ Zn (*s*) add electrons Ni (*s*) $\rightarrow$ Ni^{2+} (*aq*) + 2 e^- and Zn^{2+} (*aq*) + 2 e^- $\rightarrow$ Zn (*s*). Look up cell potentials. Ni is oxidized so $E^\circ_{red} = -0.23\text{ V} = E^\circ_{anode}$. Zn^{2+} is reduced so $E^\circ_{cathode} = -0.76$ V. Then $E^\circ_{cell} = E^\circ_{cathode} - E^\circ_{anode} = -0.76\text{ V} - (-0.23\text{ V}) = -0.53$ V and so the reaction is nonspontaneous.

(b) Ni (*s*) + Pb^{2+} (*aq*) $\rightarrow$ Ni^{2+} (*aq*) + Pb (*s*) separates to Ni (*s*) $\rightarrow$ Ni^{2+} (*aq*) and Pb^{2+} (*aq*) $\rightarrow$ Pb (*s*) add electrons Ni (*s*) $\rightarrow$ Ni^{2+} (*aq*) + 2 e^- and Pb^{2+} (*aq*) + 2 e^- $\rightarrow$ Pb (*s*). Look up cell potentials. Ni is oxidized so $E^\circ_{red} = -0.23\text{ V} = E^\circ_{anode}$. Pb^{2+} is reduced so $E^\circ_{red} = -0.13\text{ V} = E^\circ_{cathode}$. Then $E^\circ_{cell} = E^\circ_{cathode} - E^\circ_{anode} = -0.13\text{ V} - (-0.23\text{ V}) = +0.10$ V and so the reaction is spontaneous.

(c) Al (*s*) + 3 Ag^+ (*aq*) $\rightarrow$ Al^{3+} (*aq*) + 3 Ag (*s*) separates to Al (*s*) $\rightarrow$ Al^{3+} (*aq*) and 3 Ag^+ (*aq*) $\rightarrow$ 3 Ag (*s*) add electrons Al (*s*) $\rightarrow$ Al^{3+} (*aq*) + 3 e^- and 3 Ag^+ (*aq*) + 3 e^- $\rightarrow$ 3 Ag (*s*). Simplify the Ag reaction to: Ag^+ (*aq*) + e^- $\rightarrow$ Ag (*s*). Look up cell potentials. Al is oxidized so $E^\circ_{red} = -1.66\text{ V} = E^\circ_{anode}$. Ag^+ is reduced so $E^\circ_{red} = 0.80\text{ V} = E^\circ_{cathode}$. Then $E^\circ_{cell} = E^\circ_{cathode} - E^\circ_{anode} = 0.80\text{ V} - (-1.66\text{ V}) = +2.46$ V and so the reaction is spontaneous.

(d) Pb (*s*) + Mn^{2+} (*aq*) $\rightarrow$ Pb^{2+} (*aq*) + Mn (*s*) separates to Pb (*s*) $\rightarrow$ Pb^{2+} (*aq*) and Mn^{2+} (*aq*) $\rightarrow$ Mn (*s*) add electrons Pb (*s*) $\rightarrow$ Pb^{2+} (*aq*) + 2 e^- and Mn^{2+} (*aq*) + 2 e^- $\rightarrow$ Mn (*s*). Look up cell potentials. Pb is oxidized so $E^\circ_{red} = -0.13$ V $= E^\circ_{anode}$. Mn^{2+} is reduced so $E^\circ_{red} = -1.18$ V $= E^\circ_{cathode}$. Then $E^\circ_{cell} = E^\circ_{cathode} - E^\circ_{anode} = -1.18$ V $- (-0.13$ V$) = -1.05$ V and so the reaction is nonspontaneous.

Check: The units (V) are correct. If the voltage is positive, the reaction is spontaneous. If the voltage is negative, the reaction is nonspontaneous.

18.54 **Given:** overall reactions **Find:** spontaneity in reverse direction

Conceptual Plan: Separate the overall reaction into two half-cell reactions and add electrons as needed to balance reactions. Look up half-reactions in Table 18.1. Calculate the standard cell potential by subtracting the electrode potential of the anode from the electrode potential of the cathode: $E^\circ_{cell} = E^\circ_{cathode} - E^\circ_{anode}$. If $E^\circ_{cell} < 0$ the reaction is spontaneous in the reverse direction.

Solution:

(a) Ca^{2+} (*aq*) + Zn (*s*) $\rightarrow$ Ca (*s*) + Zn^{2+} (*aq*) separates to Ca^{2+} (*aq*) $\rightarrow$ Ca (*s*) and Zn (*s*) $\rightarrow$ Zn^{2+} (*aq*) add electrons Ca^{2+} (*aq*) + 2 e^- $\rightarrow$ Ca (*s*) and Zn (*s*) $\rightarrow$ Zn^{2+} (*aq*) + 2 e^-. Look up cell potentials. Zn is oxidized so $E^\circ_{red} = -0.76$ V $= E^\circ_{anode}$. Ca^{2+} is reduced so $E^\circ_{red} = -2.76$ V $= E^\circ_{cathode}$. Then $E^\circ_{cell} = E^\circ_{cathode} - E^\circ_{anode} = -2.76$ V $- (-0.76$ V$) = -2.00$ V and so the reaction is spontaneous in the reverse direction.

(b) 2 Ag^+ (*aq*) + Ni (*s*) $\rightarrow$ 2 Ag (*s*) + Ni^{2+} (*aq*) separates to 2 Ag^+ (*aq*) $\rightarrow$ 2 Ag (*s*) and Ni (*s*) $\rightarrow$ Ni^{2+} (*aq*) add electrons 2 Ag^+ (*aq*) + 2 e^- $\rightarrow$ 2 Ag (*s*) and Ni (*s*) $\rightarrow$ Ni^{2+} (*aq*) + 2 e^-. Simplify the Ag reaction to: Ag^+ (*aq*) + e^- $\rightarrow$ Ag (*s*). Look up cell potentials. Ni is oxidized so $E^\circ_{red} = -0.23$ V $= E^\circ_{anode}$. Ag^+ is reduced so $E^\circ_{red} = 0.80$ V $= E^\circ_{cathode}$. Then $E^\circ_{cell} = E^\circ_{cathode} - E^\circ_{anode} = 0.80$ V $- (-0.23$ V$) = +1.03$ V and so the reaction is nonspontaneous in the reverse direction.

(c) Fe (*s*) + Mn^{2+} (*aq*) $\rightarrow$ Fe^{2+} (*aq*) + Mn (*s*) separates to Fe (*s*) $\rightarrow$ Fe^{2+} (*aq*) and Mn^{2+} (*aq*) $\rightarrow$ Mn (*s*) add electrons Fe (*s*) $\rightarrow$ Fe^{2+} (*aq*) + 2 e^- and Mn^{2+} (*aq*) + 2 e^- $\rightarrow$ Mn (*s*). Look up cell potentials. Fe is oxidized so $E^\circ_{red} = -0.45$ V $= E^\circ_{anode}$. Mn^{2+} is reduced so $E^\circ_{red} = -1.18$ V $= E^\circ_{cathode}$. Then $E^\circ_{cell} = E^\circ_{cathode} - E^\circ_{anode} = -1.18$ V $- (-0.45$ V$) = -0.73$ V and so the reaction is spontaneous in the reverse direction.

(d) 2 Al (*s*) + 3 Pb^{2+} (*aq*) $\rightarrow$ 2 Al^{3+} (*aq*) + 3 Pb (*s*) separates to 2 Al (*s*) $\rightarrow$ 2 Al^{3+} (*aq*) and 3 Pb^{2+} (*aq*) $\rightarrow$ 3 Pb (*s*) add electrons 2 Al (*s*) $\rightarrow$ 2 Al^{3+} (*aq*) + 6 e^- and 3 Pb^{2+} (*aq*) + 6 e^- $\rightarrow$ 2 Pb (*s*). Simplify the reactions to Al (*s*) $\rightarrow$ Al^{3+} (*aq*) + 3 e^- and Pb^{2+} (*aq*) + 2 e^- $\rightarrow$ Pb (*s*). Look up cell potentials. Al is oxidized so $E^\circ_{red} = -1.66$ V $= E^\circ_{anode}$. Pb^{2+} is reduced so $E^\circ_{red} = -0.13$ V$= E^\circ_{cathode}$. Then $E^\circ_{cell} = E^\circ_{cathode} - E^\circ_{anode} = -0.13$ V $- (-1.66$ V$) = +1.53$ V and so the reaction is nonspontaneous in the reverse direction.

Check: The units (V) are correct. If the voltage is negative, the reaction is spontaneous in the reverse direction.

18.55 In order for a metal to be able to reduce an ion, it must be below it in Table 18.1 (need positive $E^\circ_{cell} = E^\circ_{cathode} - E^\circ_{anode}$). So we need a metal that is below Mn^{2+}, but above Mg^{2+}. Aluminum is the only one in the table that meets these criteria.

18.56 In order for a metal to be oxidized into an ion by another species, it must be below it in Table 18.1 (need positive $E^\circ_{cell} = E^\circ_{cathode} - E^\circ_{anode}$). So we need a metal that is above Fe^{2+}, but below Sn^{2+}. Nickel and cadmium meet these criteria.

18.57 In general, metals whose reduction half-reactions lie below the reduction of H^+ to H_2 in Table 18.1 will dissolve in acids, while metals above it will not. (a) Al and (c) Pb meet this criterion. To write the balanced redox reactions, pair the oxidation of the metal with the reduction of H^+ to H_2 (2 H^+ (*aq*) + 2 e^- $\rightarrow$ H_2 (*g*)). For Al, Al (*s*) $\rightarrow$ Al^{3+} (*aq*) + 3 e^-. In order to balance the number of electrons transferred we need to multiply the Al reaction by 2 and the H^+ reaction by 3. So, 2 Al (*s*) $\rightarrow$ 2 Al^{3+} (*aq*) + 6 e^- and 6 H^+ (*aq*) + 6 e^- $\rightarrow$ 3 H_2 (*g*). Adding the two reactions: 2 Al (*s*) + 6 H^+ (*aq*) + ~~6 e^-~~ $\rightarrow$ 2 Al^{3+} (*aq*) + ~~6 e^-~~ + 3 H_2 (*g*). Simplify to 2 Al (*s*) + 6 H^+(*aq*) $\rightarrow$ 2 Al^{3+} (*aq*) + 3 H_2 (*g*). For Pb, Pb (*s*) $\rightarrow$ Pb^{2+} (*aq*) + 2 e^-. Since each reaction involves 2 electrons we can add the two reactions. Pb (*s*) + 2 H^+ (*aq*) + ~~2 e^-~~ $\rightarrow$ Pb^{2+} (*aq*) + ~~2 e^-~~ + H_2 (*g*). Simplify to Pb (*s*) + 2 H^+ (*aq*) $\rightarrow$ Pb^{2+} (*aq*) + H_2 (*g*).

18.58 In general, metals whose reduction half-reactions lie below the reduction of H^+ to H_2 in Table 18.1 will dissolve in acids, while metals above it will not. Only (b) Fe meets this criterion. To write the balanced redox reactions, pair the oxidation of the metal with the reduction of H^+ to H_2 (2 H^+(*aq*) + 2 e^- $\rightarrow$ H_2 (*g*)). For Fe there are two possible reactions, Fe (*s*) $\rightarrow$ Fe^{3+} (*aq*) + 3 e^- and Fe (*s*) $\rightarrow$ Fe^{2+} (*aq*) + 2 e^-. Since the second reaction is lower in Table 18.1, the cell potential will be more positive. This means that this reaction will be more spontaneous and thus preferred. Since each reaction involves two electrons we can add the two reactions. $Fe\ (s) + 2\ H^+\ (aq) + \cancel{2\ e^-} \rightarrow Fe^{2+}\ (aq) + \cancel{2\ e^-} + H_2\ (g)$. Simplify to $Fe\ (s) + 2\ H^+\ (aq) \rightarrow Fe^{2+}\ (aq) + H_2\ (g)$.

18.59 Nitric acid (HNO_3) oxidizes metals through the following reduction half-reaction: $NO_3^-\ (aq) + 4\ H^+\ (aq) + 3\ e^- \rightarrow NO\ (g) + 2\ H_2O\ (l)\ E^\circ_{red} = 0.96$ V. Since this half-reaction is above the reduction of H^+ in Table 18.1, HNO_3 can oxidize metals (such as copper, for example) that cannot be oxidized by HCl. (a) Cu, which is below nitric acid in the table, will be oxidized, but (b) Au, which is above nitric acid in the table, (which has a reduction potential of 1.50 V) will not be oxidized. To write the balanced redox reactions, pair the oxidation of the metal with the reduction of nitric acid ($NO_3^-\ (aq) + 4\ H^+\ (aq) + 3\ e^- \rightarrow NO\ (g) + 2\ H_2O\ (l)$). For Cu, $Cu\ (s) \rightarrow Cu^{2+}\ (aq) + 2\ e^-$. In order to balance the number of electrons transferred we need to multiply the Cu reaction by 3 and the nitric acid reaction by 2. So, $3\ Cu\ (s) \rightarrow 3\ Cu^{2+}\ (aq) + 6\ e^-$ and $2\ NO_3^-\ (aq) + 8\ H^+\ (aq) + 6\ e^- \rightarrow 2\ NO\ (g) + 4\ H_2O\ (l)$. Adding the two reactions: $3\ Cu\ (s) + 2\ NO_3^-\ (aq) + 8\ H^+\ (aq) + \cancel{6\ e^-} \rightarrow 3\ Cu^{2+}\ (aq) + \cancel{6\ e^-} + 2\ NO\ (g) + 4\ H_2O\ (l)$. Simplify to $3\ Cu\ (s) + 2\ NO_3^-\ (aq) + 8\ H^+\ (aq) \rightarrow 3\ Cu^{2+}\ (aq) + 2\ NO\ (g) + 4\ H_2O\ (l)$.

18.60 Iodic acid (HIO_3) oxidizes metals through the following reduction half-reaction: $IO_3^-\ (aq) + 6\ H^+\ (aq) + 5\ e^- \rightarrow \frac{1}{2}\ I_2\ (aq) + 3\ H_2O\ (l)\ E^\circ_{red} = 1.20$ V. Since this half-reaction is above the reduction of H^+ in Table 18.1, HIO_3 can oxidize metals (such as copper, for example) that cannot be oxidized by HCl. (a) Au (which has a reduction potential of 1.50 V) will not be oxidized, but (b) Cr (which has a reduction potential of – 0.73 V) will be oxidized by both HCl and HIO_3. To write the balanced redox reactions, pair the oxidation of the metal with the reduction of iodic acid ($IO_3^-\ (aq) + 6\ H^+\ (aq) + 5\ e^- \rightarrow \frac{1}{2}\ I_2\ (aq) + 3\ H_2O\ (l)$). For Cr, $Cr\ (s) \rightarrow Cr^{3+}\ (aq) + 3\ e^-$. In order to balance the number of electrons transferred we need to multiply the Cr reaction by 5 and the iodic acid reaction by 3. So, $5\ Cr\ (s) \rightarrow 5\ Cr^{3+}\ (aq) + 15\ e^-$ and $3\ IO_3^-\ (aq) + 18\ H^+\ (aq) + 15\ e^- \rightarrow 3/2\ I_2\ (aq) + 9\ H_2O\ (l)$. Adding the two reactions: $5\ Cr\ (s) + 3\ IO_3^-\ (aq) + 18\ H^+\ (aq) + \cancel{15\ e^-} \rightarrow 5\ Cr^{3+}\ (aq) + \cancel{15\ e^-} + 3/2\ I_2\ (aq) + 9\ H_2O\ (l)$. Simplify to $5\ Cr\ (s) + 3\ IO_3^-\ (aq) + 18\ H^+\ (aq) \rightarrow 5\ Cr^{3+}\ (aq) + 3/2\ I_2\ (aq) + 9\ H_2O\ (l)$.

18.61 **Given:** overall reactions **Find:** E°_{cell} and spontaneity in forward direction
Conceptual Plan: Separate the overall reaction into two half-cell reactions and add electrons as needed to balance reactions. Look up half-reactions in Table 18.1. Calculate the standard cell potential by subtracting the electrode potential of the anode from the electrode potential of the cathode: $E^\circ_{cell} = E^\circ_{cathode} - E^\circ_{anode}$. If $E^\circ_{cell} > 0$ the reaction is spontaneous in the forward direction.
Solution:

(a) $2\ Cu\ (s) + Mn^{2+}\ (aq) \rightarrow 2\ Cu^+\ (aq) + Mn\ (s)$ separates to $2\ Cu\ (s) \rightarrow 2\ Cu^+\ (aq)$ and $Mn^{2+}\ (aq) \rightarrow Mn\ (s)$ add electrons $2\ Cu\ (s) \rightarrow 2\ Cu^+\ (aq) + 2\ e^-$ and $Mn^{2+}\ (aq) + 2\ e^- \rightarrow Mn\ (s)$. Simplify the Cu reaction to: $Cu\ (s) \rightarrow Cu^+\ (aq) + e^-$. Look up cell potentials. Cu is oxidized so $E^\circ_{red} = +\ 0.52\ V = E^\circ_{anode}$. Mn^{2+} is reduced so $E^\circ_{red} = -\ 1.18\ V = E^\circ_{cathode}$. Then $E^\circ_{cell} = E^\circ_{cathode} - E^\circ_{anode} = -\ 1.18\ V - 0.52\ V = -\ 1.70$ V and so the reaction is nonspontaneous.

(b) $MnO_2\ (s) + 4\ H^+(aq) + Zn\ (s) \rightarrow Mn^{2+}\ (aq) + 2\ H_2O\ (l) + Zn^{2+}\ (aq)$ separates to $MnO_2\ (s) + 4\ H^+(aq) \rightarrow Mn^{2+}\ (aq) + 2\ H_2O\ (l)$ and $Zn\ (s) \rightarrow Zn^{2+}\ (aq)$ add electrons $MnO_2\ (s) + 4\ H^+(aq) + 2\ e^- \rightarrow Mn^{2+}\ (aq) + 2\ H_2O\ (l)$ and $Zn\ (s) \rightarrow Zn^{2+}\ (aq) + 2\ e^-$. Look up cell potentials. Zn is oxidized so $E^\circ_{red} = -\ 0.76\ V = E^\circ_{anode}$. Mn is reduced so $E^\circ_{red} = 1.21\ V = E^\circ_{cathode}$. Then $E^\circ_{cell} = E^\circ_{cathode} - E^\circ_{anode} = 1.21\ V - (-\ 0.76\ V) = +\ 1.97$ V and so the reaction is spontaneous.

(c) $Cl_2\ (g) + 2\ F^-\ (aq) \rightarrow 2\ Cl^-\ (aq) + F_2\ (g)$ separates to $Cl_2\ (g) \rightarrow 2\ Cl^-\ (aq)$ and $2\ F^-\ (aq) \rightarrow F_2\ (g)$ add electrons $Cl_2\ (g) + 2\ e^- \rightarrow 2\ Cl^-\ (aq)$ and $2\ F^-\ (aq) \rightarrow F_2\ (g) + 2\ e^-$. Look up cell potentials. F^- is oxidized so $E^\circ_{red} = 2.87\ V = E^\circ_{anode}$. Cl is reduced so $E^\circ_{red} = 1.36\ V = E^\circ_{cathode}$. Then $E^\circ_{cell} = E^\circ_{cathode} - E^\circ_{anode} = 1.36\ V - 2.87\ V = -\ 1.51$ V and so the reaction is nonspontaneous.

Check: The units (V) are correct. If the voltage is positive, the reaction is spontaneous.

18.62 **Given:** overall reactions **Find:** E°_{cell} and spontaneity in forward direction
Conceptual Plan: Separate the overall reaction into two half-cell reactions and add electrons as needed to balance reactions. Look up half-reactions in Table 18.1. Calculate the standard cell potential by subtracting the electrode potential of the anode from the electrode potential of the cathode: $E^\circ_{cell} = E^\circ_{cathode} - E^\circ_{anode}$. If $E^\circ_{cell} > 0$ the reaction is spontaneous in the forward direction.

Solution:

(a) $O_2\ (g) + 2\ H_2O\ (l) + 4\ Ag\ (s) \rightarrow 4\ OH^-\ (aq) + 4\ Ag^+\ (aq)$ separates to $O_2\ (g) + 2\ H_2O\ (l) \rightarrow 4\ OH^-\ (aq)$ and $4\ Ag\ (s) \rightarrow 4\ Ag^+\ (aq)$ add electrons $O_2\ (g) + 2\ H_2O\ (l) + 4\ e^- \rightarrow 4\ OH^-\ (aq)$ and $4\ Ag\ (s) \rightarrow 4\ Ag^+\ (aq) + 2\ e^-$. Simplify the Ag reaction to: $Ag\ (s) \rightarrow Ag^+\ (aq) + e^-$. Look up cell potentials. Ag is oxidized so $E^\circ_{red} = +\ 0.80\ V = E^\circ_{anode}$. O is reduced so $E^\circ_{red} = 0.40\ V = E^\circ_{cathode}$. Then $E^\circ_{cell} = E^\circ_{cathode} - E^\circ_{anode} = 0.40\ V - 0.80\ V = -\ 0.40\ V$ and so the reaction is nonspontaneous.

(b) $Br_2\ (l) + 2\ I^-\ (aq) \rightarrow 2\ Br^-\ (aq) + I_2\ (g)$ separates to $Br_2\ (g) \rightarrow 2\ Br^-\ (aq)$ and $2\ I^-\ (aq) \rightarrow I_2\ (g)$ add electrons $Br_2\ (g) + 2\ e^- \rightarrow 2\ Br^-\ (aq)$ and $2\ I^-\ (aq) \rightarrow I_2\ (g) + 2\ e^-$. Look up cell potentials. I is oxidized so $E^\circ_{red} = 0.54\ V = E^\circ_{anode}$. Br is reduced so $E^\circ_{red} = 1.09\ V = E^\circ_{cathode}$. Then $E^\circ_{cell} = E^\circ_{cathode} - E^\circ_{anode} = 1.09\ V - 0.54\ V = +\ 0.55\ V$ and so the reaction is spontaneous.

(c) $PbO_2\ (s) + 4\ H^+(aq) + Sn\ (s) \rightarrow Pb^{2+}\ (aq) + 2\ H_2O\ (l) + Sn^{2+}\ (aq)$ separates to $PbO_2\ (s) + 4\ H^+(aq) \rightarrow Pb^{2+}\ (aq) + 2\ H_2O\ (l)$ and $Sn\ (s) \rightarrow Sn^{2+}\ (aq)$ add electrons $PbO_2\ (s) + 4\ H^+(aq) + 2\ e^- \rightarrow Pb^{2+}\ (aq) + 2\ H_2O\ (l)$ and $Sn\ (s) \rightarrow Sn^{2+}\ (aq) + 2\ e^-$. Look up cell potentials. Sn is oxidized so $E^\circ_{red} = -\ 0.14\ V = E^\circ_{anode}$. Pb is reduced so $E^\circ_{red} = 1.46\ V = E^\circ_{cathode}$. Then $E^\circ_{cell} = E^\circ_{cathode} - E^\circ_{anode} = 1.46\ V - (-\ 0.14\ V) = +\ 1.60\ V$ and so the reaction is spontaneous.

Check: The units (V) are correct. If the voltage is positive, the reaction is spontaneous.

18.63 (a) Pb^{2+}. The strongest oxidizing agent is the one with the reduction reaction that is closest to the top of Table 18.1 (most positive, least negative reduction potential).

18.64 (b) Al. The strongest reducing agent is the one with the reduction reaction that yields the metal that is closest to the bottom of Table 18.1 (most negative, least positive reduction potential).

Cell Potential, Free Energy, and the Equilibrium Constant

18.65 **Given:** overall reactions **Find:** ΔG°_{rxn} and spontaneity in forward direction

Conceptual Plan: Separate the overall reaction into two half-cell reactions and add electrons as needed to balance reactions. Look up half-reactions in Table 18.1. Calculate the standard cell potential by subtracting the electrode potential of the anode from the electrode potential of the cathode: $E^\circ_{cell} = E^\circ_{cathode} - E^\circ_{anode}$, then calculate ΔG°_{rxn} using $\Delta G^\circ_{rxn} = -\ n\ F\ E^\circ_{cell}$.

Solution:

(a) $Pb^{2+}\ (aq) + Mg\ (s) \rightarrow Pb\ (s) + Mg^{2+}\ (aq)$ separates to $Pb^{2+}\ (aq) \rightarrow Pb\ (s)$ and $Mg\ (s) \rightarrow Mg^{2+}\ (aq)$. Add electrons. $Pb^{2+}\ (aq) + 2\ e^- \rightarrow Pb\ (s)$ and $Mg\ (s) \rightarrow Mg^{2+}\ (aq) + 2\ e^-$. Look up cell potentials. Mg is oxidized so $E^\circ_{red} = -\ 2.37\ V = E^\circ_{anode}$. Pb^{2+} is reduced so $E^\circ_{red} = -\ 0.13\ V = E^\circ_{cathode}$. Then $E^\circ_{cell} = E^\circ_{cathode} - E^\circ_{anode} = -\ 0.13\ V - (-\ 2.37\ V) = +\ 2.24\ V$. $n = 2$ so $\Delta G^\circ_{rxn} = -\ n\ F\ E^\circ_{cell}$

$$= -2\ \text{mol e}^- \times \frac{96{,}485\ C}{\text{mol e}^-} \times 2.24\ V = -\ 2 \times 96{,}485\ C \times 2.24\ \frac{J}{C} = -\ 4.32 \times 10^5\ J = -\ 432\ kJ.$$

(b) $Br_2\ (l) + 2\ Cl^-\ (aq) \rightarrow 2\ Br^-\ (aq) + Cl_2\ (g)$ separates to $Br_2\ (g) \rightarrow 2\ Br^-\ (aq)$ and $2\ Cl^-\ (aq) \rightarrow Cl_2\ (g)$. Add electrons. $Br_2\ (g) + 2\ e^- \rightarrow 2\ Br^-\ (aq)$ and $2\ Cl^-\ (aq) \rightarrow Cl_2\ (g) + 2\ e^-$. Look up cell potentials. Cl is oxidized so $E^\circ_{red} = 1.36\ V = E^\circ_{anode}$. Br is reduced so $E^\circ_{red} = 1.09\ V = E^\circ_{cathode}$. Then $E^\circ_{cell} = E^\circ_{cathode} - E^\circ_{anode} = 1.09\ V - 1.36\ V = -\ 0.27\ V$. $n = 2$ so $\Delta G^\circ_{rxn} = -\ n\ F\ E^\circ_{cell}$

$$= -2\ \text{mol e}^- \times \frac{96{,}485\ C}{\text{mol e}^-} \times -\ 0.27\ V = -\ 2 \times 96{,}485\ C \times -\ 0.27\ \frac{J}{C} = 5.2 \times 10^4\ J = 52\ kJ.$$

(c) $MnO_2\ (s) + 4\ H^+(aq) + Cu\ (s) \rightarrow Mn^{2+}\ (aq) + 2\ H_2O\ (l) + Cu^{2+}\ (aq)$ separates to $MnO_2\ (s) + 4\ H^+(aq) \rightarrow Mn^{2+}\ (aq) + 2\ H_2O\ (l)$ and $Cu\ (s) \rightarrow Cu^{2+}\ (aq)$. Add electrons. $MnO_2\ (s) + 4\ H^+(aq) + 2\ e^- \rightarrow Mn^{2+}\ (aq) + 2\ H_2O\ (l)$ and $Cu\ (s) \rightarrow Cu^{2+}\ (aq) + 2\ e^-$. Look up cell potentials. Cu is oxidized so $E^\circ_{red} = 0.34\ V = E^\circ_{anode}$. Mn is reduced so $E^\circ_{red} = 1.21\ V = E^\circ_{cathode}$. Then $E^\circ_{cell} = E^\circ_{cathode} - E^\circ_{anode}$ $= 1.21\ V - 0.34\ V = +\ 0.87\ V$. $n = 2$ so $\Delta G^\circ_{rxn} = -n\ F\ E^\circ_{cell} = -2\ \text{mol e}^- \times \frac{96{,}485\ C}{\text{mol e}^-} \times 0.87\ V =$

$$-\ 2 \times 96{,}485\ C \times 0.87\ \frac{J}{C} = -1.7 \times 10^5\ J = -1.7 \times 10^2\ kJ.$$

Check: The units (kJ) are correct. If the voltage is positive, the reaction is spontaneous and the free energy change is negative.

18.66 **Given:** overall reactions **Find:** ΔG°_{rxn} and spontaneity in forward direction
Conceptual Plan: Separate the overall reaction into two half-cell reactions and add electrons as needed to balance reactions. Look up half-reactions in Table 18.1. Calculate the standard cell potential by subtracting the electrode potential of the anode from the electrode potential of the cathode: $E^\circ_{cell} = E^\circ_{cathode} - E^\circ_{anode}$, then calculate ΔG°_{rxn} using $\Delta G^\circ_{rxn} = -nFE^\circ_{cell}$.
Solution:

(a) $2\ Fe^{3+}(aq) + 3\ Sn(s) \rightarrow 2\ Fe(s) + 3\ Sn^{2+}(aq)$ separates to $2\ Fe^{3+}(aq) \rightarrow 2\ Fe(s)$ and $3\ Sn(s) \rightarrow 3\ Sn^{2+}(aq)$ add electrons $2\ Fe^{3+}(aq) + 6\ e^- \rightarrow 2\ Fe(s)$ and $3\ Sn(s) \rightarrow 3\ Sn^{2+}(aq) + 6\ e^-$. Simplify reactions to $Fe^{3+}(aq) + 3\ e^- \rightarrow Fe(s)$ and $Sn(s) \rightarrow Sn^{2+}(aq) + 2\ e^-$. Look up cell potentials. Sn is oxidized so $E^\circ_{red} = -0.14\ V = E^\circ_{anode}$. Fe^{3+} is reduced so $E^\circ_{red} = -0.036\ V = E^\circ_{cathode}$. Then $E^\circ_{cell} = E^\circ_{cathode} - E^\circ_{anode} = -0.036\ V - (-0.14\ V) = +0.1\underline{0}4\ V$. $n = 6$ so $\Delta G^\circ_{rxn} = -nFE^\circ_{cell}$

$$= -6\ \text{mol e}^- \times \frac{96{,}485\ C}{\text{mol e}^-} \times 0.1\underline{0}4\ V = -6 \times 96{,}485\ C \times 0.1\underline{0}4\ \frac{J}{C} = -6.0 \times 10^4\ J = -6.0 \times 10^1\ kJ.$$

(b) $O_2(g) + 2\ H_2O(l) + 2\ Cu(s) \rightarrow 4\ OH^-(aq) + 2\ Cu^{2+}(aq)$ separates to $O_2(g) + 2\ H_2O(l) \rightarrow 4\ OH^-(aq)$ and $2\ Cu(s) \rightarrow 2\ Cu^{2+}(aq)$ add electrons $O_2(g) + 2\ H_2O(l) + 4\ e^- \rightarrow 4\ OH^-(aq)$ and $2\ Cu(s) \rightarrow 2\ Cu^{2+}(aq) + 4\ e^-$. Simplify the Cu reaction to: $Cu(s) \rightarrow Cu^{2+}(aq) + 2\ e^-$. Look up cell potentials. Cu is oxidized so $E^\circ_{red} = 0.34\ V = E^\circ_{anode}$. O is reduced so $E^\circ_{red} = 0.40\ V = E^\circ_{cathode}$. Then $E^\circ_{cell} = E^\circ_{cathode} - E^\circ_{anode} = 0.40\ V - 0.34\ V = +0.06\ V$. $n = 4$ so $\Delta G^\circ_{rxn} = -nFE^\circ_{cell} = -4\ \text{mol e}^- \times \frac{96{,}485\ C}{\text{mol e}^-} \times 0.06\ V$

$$= -4 \times 96{,}485\ C \times 0.06\ \frac{J}{C} = -2 \times 10^4\ J = -2 \times 10^1\ kJ.$$

(c) $Br_2(l) + 2\ I^-(aq) \rightarrow 2\ Br^-(aq) + I_2(g)$ separates to $Br_2(g) \rightarrow 2\ Br^-(aq)$ and $2\ I^-(aq) \rightarrow I_2(g)$ add electrons $Br_2(g) + 2\ e^- \rightarrow 2\ Br^-(aq)$ and $2\ I^-(aq) \rightarrow I_2(g) + 2\ e^-$. Look up cell potentials. I is oxidized so $E^\circ_{red} = -0.54\ V = E^\circ_{anode}$. Br is reduced so $E^\circ_{red} = 1.09\ V = E^\circ_{cathode}$. Then $E^\circ_{cell} = E^\circ_{cathode} - E^\circ_{anode} = 1.09\ V - 0.54\ V = +0.55\ V$. $n = 2$ so $\Delta G^\circ_{rxn} = -nFE^\circ_{cell} = -2\ \text{mol e}^- \times \frac{96{,}485\ C}{\text{mol e}^-} \times 0.55\ V$

$$= -2 \times 96{,}485\ C \times 0.55\ \frac{J}{C} = -1.1 \times 10^5\ J = -1.1 \times 10^2\ kJ.$$

Check: The units (kJ) are correct. If the voltage is positive, the reaction is spontaneous and the free energy change is negative.

18.67 **Given:** overall reactions from Problem 65 **Find:** K
Conceptual Plan: °C $\rightarrow$ K then ΔG°_{rxn}, $T \rightarrow K$

$K = 273.15 + °C$ $\qquad$ $\Delta G^\circ_{rxn} = -RT\ln K$

Solution: $T = 273.15 + 25\ °C = 298\ K$ then

(a) $\Delta G^\circ_{rxn} = -RT\ln K$. Rearrange to solve for K.

$$K = e^{\frac{-\Delta G^\circ_{rxn}}{RT}} = e^{\frac{-(-432\ kJ) \times \frac{1000\ J}{1\ kJ}}{\left(8.314\frac{J}{K\cdot mol}\right)(298\ K)}} = e^{17\underline{4}.364} = 5.31 \times 10^{75}.$$

(b) $\Delta G^\circ_{rxn} = -RT\ln K$. Rearrange to solve for K.

$$K = e^{\frac{-\Delta G^\circ_{rxn}}{RT}} = e^{\frac{-52\ kJ \times \frac{1000\ J}{1\ kJ}}{\left(8.314\frac{J}{K\cdot mol}\right)(298\ K)}} = e^{-2\underline{0}.988} = 7.7 \times 10^{-10}.$$

(c) $\Delta G^\circ_{rxn} = -RT\ln K$. Rearrange to solve for K.

$$K = e^{\frac{-\Delta G^\circ_{rxn}}{RT}} = e^{\frac{-(-170\ kJ) \times \frac{1000\ J}{1\ kJ}}{\left(8.314\frac{J}{K\cdot mol}\right)(298\ K)}} = e^{6\underline{8}.616} = 6.3 \times 10^{29}.$$

Check: The units (none) are correct. If the voltage is positive, the reaction is spontaneous and the free energy change is negative and the equilibrium constant is large.

18.68 **Given:** overall reactions from Problem 66 **Find:** K

Conceptual Plan: °C → K then $\Delta G^\circ_{rxn}, T \rightarrow K$

K = 273.15 + °C $\qquad \Delta G^\circ_{rxn} = -RT\ln K$

Solution: T = 273.15 + 25 °C = 298 K then

(a) $\Delta G^\circ_{rxn} = -RT\ln K$. Rearrange to solve for K.

$$K = e^{\frac{-\Delta G^\circ_{rxn}}{RT}} = e^{\frac{-(-60\ \text{kJ}) \times \frac{1000\ \text{J}}{1\ \text{kJ}}}{\left(8.314\frac{\text{J}}{\text{K}\cdot\text{mol}}\right)(298\ \text{K})}} = e^{24.217} = 3.3 \times 10^{10}.$$

(b) $\Delta G^\circ_{rxn} = -RT\ln K$. Rearrange to solve for K.

$$K = e^{\frac{-\Delta G^\circ_{rxn}}{RT}} = e^{\frac{-(-20\ \text{kJ}) \times \frac{1000\ \text{J}}{1\ \text{kJ}}}{\left(8.314\frac{\text{J}}{\text{K}\cdot\text{mol}}\right)(298\ \text{K})}} = e^{8.072} = 3 \times 10^{3}.$$

(c) $\Delta G^\circ_{rxn} = -RT\ln K$. Rearrange to solve for K.

$$K = e^{\frac{-\Delta G^\circ_{rxn}}{RT}} = e^{\frac{-(-110\ \text{kJ}) \times \frac{1000\ \text{J}}{1\ \text{kJ}}}{\left(8.314\frac{\text{J}}{\text{K}\cdot\text{mol}}\right)(298\ \text{K})}} = e^{44.398} = 1.9 \times 10^{19}.$$

Check: The units (none) are correct. If the voltage is positive, the reaction is spontaneous and the free energy change is negative and the equilibrium constant is large.

18.69 **Given:** Ni^{2+} (aq) + Cd (s) → **Find:** K

Conceptual Plan: Write two half-cell reactions and add electrons as needed to balance the reactions. Look up half-reactions in Table 18.1. Calculate the standard cell potential by subtracting the electrode potential of the anode from the electrode potential of the cathode: $E^\circ_{cell} = E^\circ_{cathode} - E^\circ_{anode}$, then °C → K then $E^\circ_{cell}, n, T \rightarrow K$.

K = 273.15 + °C $\qquad \Delta G^\circ_{rxn} = -RT\ln K = -nFE^\circ_{cell}$

Solution: Ni^{2+} (aq) + 2 e⁻ → Ni (s) and Cd (s) → Cd^{2+} (aq) + 2 e⁻. Look up cell potentials. Cd is oxidized so E°_{red} = – 0.40 V = E°_{anode}. Ni^{2+} is reduced so E°_{red} = – 0.23 V = $E^\circ_{cathode}$. Then $E^\circ_{cell} = E^\circ_{cathode} - E^\circ_{anode}$ = – 0.23 V – (– 0.40 V) = + 0.17 V. The overall reaction is Ni^{2+} (aq) + Cd (s) → Ni (s) + Cd^{2+} (aq). n = 2 and T = 273.15 + 25 °C = 298 K then $\Delta G^\circ_{rxn} = -RT\ln K = -nFE^\circ_{cell}$. Rearrange to solve for K.

$$K = e^{\frac{nFE^\circ_{cell}}{RT}} = e^{\frac{2\ \text{mol e}^- \times \frac{96{,}485\ \text{C}}{\text{mol e}^-} \times 0.17\ \frac{\text{J}}{\text{C}}}{\left(8.314\frac{\text{J}}{\text{K}\cdot\text{mol}}\right)(298\ \text{K})}} = e^{13.241} = 5.6 \times 10^{5}.$$

Check: The units (none) are correct. If the voltage is positive, the reaction is spontaneous and the equilibrium constant is large.

18.70 **Given:** Fe^{2+} (aq) + Zn (s) → **Find:** K

Conceptual Plan: Write two half-cell reactions and add electrons as needed to balance the reactions. Look up half-reactions in Table 18.1. Calculate the standard cell potential by subtracting the electrode potential of the anode from the electrode potential of the cathode: $E^\circ_{cell} = E^\circ_{cathode} - E^\circ_{anode}$, then °C → K then $E^\circ_{cell}, n, T \rightarrow K$.

K = 273.15 + °C $\qquad \Delta G^\circ_{rxn} = -RT\ln K = -nFE^\circ_{cell}$

Solution: Fe^{2+} (aq) + 2 e⁻ → Fe (s) and Zn (s) → Zn^{2+} (aq) + 2 e⁻. Look up cell potentials. Zn is oxidized so E°_{red} = – 0.76 V = E°_{anode}. Fe^{2+} is reduced so E°_{red} = – 0.45 V= $E^\circ_{cathode}$. Then $E^\circ_{cell} = E^\circ_{cathode} - E^\circ_{anode}$ = – 0.45 V – (– 0.76 V) = + 0.31 V. The overall reaction is Fe^{2+} (aq) + Zn (s) → Fe (s) + Zn^{2+} (aq). n = 2 and T = 273.15 + 25 °C = 298 K then $\Delta G^\circ_{rxn} = -RT\ln K = -nFE^\circ_{cell}$. Rearrange to solve for K.

$$K = e^{\frac{n F E^\circ_{cell}}{R T}} = e^{\frac{2\ \text{mol e}^- \times \frac{96{,}485\ \text{C}}{\text{mol e}^-} \times 0.31\ \frac{\text{J}}{\text{C}}}{\left(8.314\frac{\text{J}}{\text{K}\cdot\text{mol}}\right)(298\ \text{K})}} = e^{24.145} = 3.1 \times 10^{10}.$$

Check: The units (none) are correct. If the voltage is positive, the reaction is spontaneous and the equilibrium constant is large.

18.71 **Given:** $n = 2$ and $K = 25$ **Find:** ΔG°_{rxn} and E°_{cell}

Conceptual Plan: $K, T \rightarrow \Delta G^\circ_{rxn}$ **and** $\Delta G^\circ_{rxn}, n \rightarrow E^\circ_{cell}$

$\Delta G^\circ_{rxn} = -R T \ln K$ $\qquad \Delta G^\circ_{rxn} = -n F E^\circ_{cell}$

Solution: $\Delta G^\circ_{rxn} = -R T \ln K = -\left(8.314\frac{\text{J}}{\text{K}\cdot\text{mol}}\right)(298\ \text{K}) \ln 25 = -7.97500 \times 10^3\ \text{J} = -8.0\ \text{kJ}$ and

$\Delta G^\circ_{rxn} = -n F E^\circ_{cell}$. Rearrange to solve for E°_{cell}.

$$E^\circ_{cell} = \frac{\Delta G^\circ_{rxn}}{-n F} = \frac{-7.97500 \times 10^3\ \text{J}}{-2\ \text{mol e}^- \times \frac{96{,}485\ \text{C}}{\text{mol e}^-}} = 0.041\ \frac{\text{V}\cdot\text{C}}{\text{C}} = 0.041\ \text{V}.$$

Check: The units (kJ and V) are correct. If $K > 1$ then the voltage is positive, the free energy change is negative.

18.72 **Given:** $n = 3$ and $K = 0.050$ **Find:** ΔG°_{rxn} and E°_{cell}

Conceptual Plan: $K, T \rightarrow \Delta G^\circ_{rxn}$ **and** $\Delta G^\circ_{rxn}, n \rightarrow E^\circ_{cell}$

$\Delta G^\circ_{rxn} = -R T \ln K$ $\qquad \Delta G^\circ_{rxn} = -n F E^\circ_{cell}$

Solution: $\Delta G^\circ_{rxn} = -R T \ln K = -\left(8.314\frac{\text{J}}{\text{K}\cdot\text{mol}}\right)(298\ \text{K}) \ln 0.050 = 7.4221 \times 10^3\ \text{J} = 7.4\ \text{kJ}$ and

$\Delta G^\circ_{rxn} = -n F E^\circ_{cell}$. Rearrange to solve for E°_{cell}.

$$E^\circ_{cell} = \frac{\Delta G^\circ_{rxn}}{-n F} = \frac{7.4221 \times 10^3\ \text{J}}{-3\ \text{mol e}^- \times \frac{96{,}485\ \text{C}}{\text{mol e}^-}} = -0.026\ \frac{\text{V}\cdot\text{C}}{\text{C}} = -0.026\ \text{V}.$$

Check: The units (kJ and V) are correct. If $K < 1$ then the voltage is negative, the free energy change is positive.

Non-Standard Conditions and the Nernst Equation

18.73 **Given:** $Sn^{2+}\ (aq) + Mn\ (s) \rightarrow Sn\ (s) + Mn^{2+}\ (aq)$

Find: (a) E°_{cell}; (b) E_{cell} when $[Sn^{2+}] = 0.0100$ M; $[Mn^{2+}] = 2.00$ M; and (c) E_{cell} when $[Sn^{2+}] = 2.00$ M; $[Mn^{2+}] = 0.0100$ M

Conceptual Plan: (a) Separate the overall reaction into two half-cell reactions and add electrons as needed to balance the reactions. Look up half-reactions in Table 18.1. Calculate the standard cell potential by subtracting the electrode potential of the anode from the electrode potential of the cathode: $E^\circ_{cell} = E^\circ_{cathode} - E^\circ_{anode}$. (b) and (c) E°_{cell}, $[Sn^{2+}]$, $[Mn^{2+}]$, $n \rightarrow E_{cell}$

$$E_{cell} = E^\circ_{cell} - \frac{0.0592\ V}{n} \log Q \text{ where } Q = \frac{[Mn^{2+}]}{[Sn^{2+}]}$$

Solution:

(a) Separate the overall reaction to: $Sn^{2+}\ (aq) \rightarrow Sn\ (s)$ and $Mn\ (s) \rightarrow Mn^{2+}\ (aq)$. Add electrons $Sn^{2+}\ (aq) + 2\ e^- \rightarrow Sn\ (s)$ and $Mn\ (s) \rightarrow Mn^{2+}\ (aq) + 2\ e^-$. Look up cell potentials. Mn is oxidized so $E^\circ_{red} = -1.18\ V = E^\circ_{anode}$. Sn^{2+} is reduced so $E^\circ_{red} = -0.14\ V = E^\circ_{cathode}$. Then $E^\circ_{cell} = E^\circ_{cathode} - E^\circ_{anode} = -0.14\ V - (-1.18\ V) = +1.04\ V$.

(b) $Q = \frac{[Mn^{2+}]}{[Sn^{2+}]} = \frac{2.00\ \text{M}}{0.0100\ \text{M}} = 200.$ and $n = 2$ then

$$E_{cell} = E^\circ_{cell} - \frac{0.0592\ V}{n} \log Q = 1.04\ V - \frac{0.0592\ V}{2} \log 200. = +0.97\ V$$

(c) $Q = \frac{[Mn^{2+}]}{[Sn^{2+}]} = \frac{0.0100\text{ M}}{2.00\text{ M}} = 0.00500$ and $n = 2$ then

$$E_{cell} = E^\circ_{cell} - \frac{0.0592\text{ V}}{n}\log Q = 1.04\text{ V} - \frac{0.0592\text{ V}}{2}\log 0.00500 = +1.11\text{ V}$$

Check: The units (V, V, and V) are correct. The Sn^{2+} reduction reaction is above the Mn^{2+} reduction reaction, so the standard cell potential will be positive. Having more products than reactants reduces the cell potential. Having more reactants than products raises the cell potential.

18.74 **Given:** $2\ Fe^{3+}\ (aq) + 3\ Mg\ (s) \rightarrow 2\ Fe\ (s) + 3\ Mg^{2+}\ (aq)$ **Find:** (a) E°_{cell}; (b) E_{cell} when $[Fe^{3+}] = 1.0 \times 10^{-3}$ M; $[Mg^{2+}] = 2.50$ M; and (c) E_{cell} when $[Fe^{3+}] = 2.00$ M; $[Mg^{2+}] = 1.5 \times 10^{-3}$ M

Conceptual Plan: (a) Separate the overall reaction into two half-cell reactions and add electrons as needed to balance reactions. Look up half-reactions in Table 18.1. Calculate the standard cell potential by subtracting the electrode potential of the anode from the electrode potential of the cathode: $E^\circ_{cell} = E^\circ_{cathode} - E^\circ_{anode}$. (b) and (c) E°_{cell}, $[Fe^{3+}]$, $[Mg^{2+}]$, $n \rightarrow E_{cell}$

$$E_{cell} = E^\circ_{cell} - \frac{0.0592\ V}{n}\log Q \text{ where } Q = \frac{[Mg^{2+}]^3}{[Fe^{3+}]^2}$$

Solution:

(a) Separate the overall reaction to: $2\ Fe^{3+}\ (aq) \rightarrow 2\ Fe\ (s)$ and $3\ Mg\ (s) \rightarrow 3\ Mg^{2+}\ (aq)$. Add electrons $2\ Fe^{3+} + 6\ e^-\ (aq) \rightarrow 2\ Fe\ (s)$ and $3\ Mg\ (s) \rightarrow 3\ Mg^{2+}\ (aq) + 6\ e^-$. Look up cell potentials. Mg is oxidized so $E^\circ_{red} = -2.37\text{ V} = E^\circ_{anode}$. Fe^{3+} is reduced so $E^\circ_{red} = -0.036\text{ V} = E^\circ_{cathode}$. Then $E^\circ_{cell} = E^\circ_{cathode} - E^\circ_{anode} = -0.036\text{ V} - (-2.37\text{ V}) = +2.3\underline{3}4\text{ V} = +2.33\text{ V}$.

(b) $Q = \frac{[Mg^{2+}]^3}{[Fe^{3+}]^2} = \frac{(2.50)^3}{(1.0 \times 10^{-3})^2} = 1.\underline{5}625 \times 10^7$ and $n = 6$ then

$$E_{cell} = E^\circ_{cell} - \frac{0.0592\text{ V}}{n}\log Q = 2.3\underline{3}4\text{ V} - \frac{0.0592\text{ V}}{6}\log 1.\underline{5}625 \times 10^7 = +2.26\text{ V}$$

(c) $Q = \frac{[Mg^{2+}]^3}{[Fe^{3+}]^2} = \frac{(1.5 \times 10^{-3})^3}{(2.00)^2} = 8.\underline{4}375 \times 10^{-10}$ and $n = 6$ then

$$E_{cell} = E^\circ_{cell} - \frac{0.0592\text{ V}}{n}\log Q = 2.3\underline{3}4\text{ V} - \frac{0.0592\text{ V}}{6}\log 8.\underline{4}375 \times 10^{-10} = +2.42\text{ V}$$

Check: The units (V, V, and V) are correct. The Fe^{3+} reduction reaction is above the Mg^{2+} reduction reaction, so the standard cell potential will be positive. Having more products than reactants reduces the cell potential. Having more reactants than products raises the cell potential.

18.75 **Given:** $Pb\ (s) \rightarrow Pb^{2+}\ (aq,\ 0.10\text{ M}) + 2\ e^-$ and $MnO_4^-\ (aq,\ 1.50\text{ M}) + 4\ H^+\ (aq,\ 2.0\text{ M}) + 3\ e^- \rightarrow MnO_2\ (s) + 2\ H_2O\ (l)$ **Find:** E_{cell}

Conceptual Plan: Look up half-reactions in Table 18.1. Calculate the standard cell potential by subtracting the electrode potential of the anode from the electrode potential of the cathode: $E^\circ_{cell} = E^\circ_{cathode} - E^\circ_{anode}$. Equalize the number of electrons transferred by multiplying the first reaction by 3 and the second reaction by 2. Add the two half-cell reactions and cancel the electrons. Then E°_{cell}, $[Pb^{2+}]$, $[MnO_4^-]$, $[H^+]$, $n \rightarrow E_{cell}$

$$E_{cell} = E^\circ_{cell} - \frac{0.0592\ V}{n}\log Q \text{ where } Q = \frac{[Pb^{2+}]^3}{[MnO_4^-]^2[H^+]^8}$$

Solution: Pb is oxidized so $E^\circ_{red} = -0.13\text{ V} = E^\circ_{anode}$. Mn is reduced so $E^\circ_{red} = 1.68\text{ V} = E^\circ_{cathode}$. Then $E^\circ_{cell} = E^\circ_{cathode} - E^\circ_{anode} = 1.68\text{ V} - (-0.13\text{ V}) = +1.81$ V. Equalizing the electrons: $3\ Pb\ (s) \rightarrow 3\ Pb^{2+}\ (aq) + 6\ e^-$ and $2\ MnO_4^-\ (aq) + 8\ H^+\ (aq) + 6\ e^- \rightarrow 2\ MnO_2\ (s) + 4\ H_2O\ (l)$. Adding the two reactions: $3\ Pb\ (s) + 2\ MnO_4^-\ (aq) + 8\ H^+\ (aq) + \cancel{6\ e^-} \rightarrow 3\ Pb^{2+}\ (aq) + \cancel{6\ e^-} + 2\ MnO_2\ (s) + 4\ H_2O\ (l)$. Cancel the electrons: $3\ Pb\ (s) + 2\ MnO_4^-\ (aq) + 8\ H^+\ (aq) \rightarrow 3\ Pb^{2+} + (aq) + 2\ MnO_2\ (s) + 4\ H_2O\ (l)$. So $n = 6$ and $Q = \frac{[Pb^{2+}]^3}{[MnO_4^-]^2[H^+]^8} = \frac{(0.10)^3}{(1.50)^2(2.0)^8}$

$= 1.\underline{7}361 \times 10^{-6}$ then $E_{cell} = E^\circ_{cell} - \frac{0.0592\text{ V}}{n}\log Q = 1.81\text{ V} - \frac{0.0592\text{ V}}{6}\log 1.\underline{7}361 \times 10^{-6} = +1.87$ V.

Check: The units (V) are correct. The MnO_4^- reduction reaction is above the Pb^{2+} reduction reaction, so the standard cell potential will be positive. Having more reactants than products raises the cell potential.

18.76 **Given:** Sn (*s*) $\rightarrow$ Sn^{2+} (*aq*, 2.00 M) + 2 e^- and ClO_2 (*g*, 0.100 atm) + e^- $\rightarrow$ ClO_2^- (*aq*, 2.00 M) **Find:** E_{cell}
Conceptual Plan: Look up half-reactions in Table 18.1. Calculate the standard cell potential by subtracting the electrode potential of the anode from the electrode potential of the cathode: $E^\circ_{cell} = E^\circ_{cathode} - E^\circ_{anode}$. Equalize the number of electrons transferred by multiplying the second reaction by 2. Add the two half-cell reactions and cancel the electrons. Then E°_{cell}, $[Sn^{2+}]$, P_{ClO_2}, $[ClO_2^-]$, n $\rightarrow$ E_{cell}

$$\text{Ecell} = E^\circ_{cell} - \frac{0.0592\ V}{n}\log Q \text{ where } Q = \frac{[Sn^{2+}][ClO_2^-]^2}{P_{ClO_2}{}^2}$$

Solution: Sn is oxidized so $E^\circ_{red} = -0.14\ V = E^\circ_{anode}$. ClO_2 is reduced so $E^\circ_{red} = 0.95\ V = E^\circ_{cathode}$. Then $E^\circ_{cell} = E^\circ_{cathode} - E^\circ_{anode} = 0.95\ V - (-0.14\ V) = +1.09\ V$. Equalizing the electrons: Sn (*s*) $\rightarrow$ Sn^{2+} (*aq*) + 2 e^- and 2 ClO_2 (*g*) + 2 e^- $\rightarrow$ 2 ClO_2^- (*aq*). Adding the two reactions: Sn (*s*) + 2 ClO_2 (*g*) + ~~2 e^-~~ $\rightarrow$ Sn^{2+} (*aq*) + ~~2 e^-~~ + 2 ClO_2^- (*aq*). Cancel the electrons: Sn (*s*) + 2 ClO_2 (*g*) $\rightarrow$ Sn^{2+} (*aq*) + 2 ClO_2^- (*aq*). So $n = 2$ and

$$Q = \frac{[Sn^{2+}][ClO_2^-]^2}{P_{ClO_2}{}^2} = \frac{(2.00)(2.00)^2}{(0.100)^2} = 800. \text{ Then}$$

$$E_{cell} = E^\circ_{cell} - \frac{0.0592\ V}{n}\log Q = 1.09\ V - \frac{0.0592\ V}{2}\log 800. = +1.00\ V.$$

Check: The units (V) are correct. The ClO_2 reduction reaction is above the Sn^{2+} reduction reaction, so the standard cell potential will be positive. Having more products than reactants lowers the cell potential.

18.77 **Given:** Zn/Zn^{2+} and Ni/Ni^{2+} half-cells in voltaic cell; initially $[Ni^{2+}] = 1.50$ M, and $[Zn^{2+}] = 0.100$ M
Find: (a) initial E_{cell}; (b) E_{cell} when $[Ni^{2+}] = 0.500$ M; and (c) $[Ni^{2+}]$ and $[Zn^{2+}]$ when $E_{cell} = 0.45$ V
Conceptual Plan:

(a) **Write two half-cell reactions and add electrons as needed to balance reactions. Look up half-reactions in Table 18.1. Calculate the standard cell potential by subtracting the electrode potential of the anode from the electrode potential of the cathode: $E^\circ_{cell} = E^\circ_{cathode} - E^\circ_{anode}$. Choose the direction of the half-cell reactions so that E°_{cell} . 0. Add two half-cell reactions and cancel electrons to generate overall reaction. Define Q based on overall reaction. Then E°_{cell}, [Ni2+], [Zn2+], n $\rightarrow$ E_{cell}**

$$E_{cell} = E^\circ_{cell} - \frac{0.0592\ V}{n}\log Q$$

(b) **When $[Ni^{2+}] = 0.500$ M, then $[Zn^{2+}] = 1.100$ M (since the stoichiometric coefficients for Ni^{2+}: Zn^{2+} are 1:1, and the $[Ni^{2+}]$ drops by 1.00 M, the other concentration must rise by 1.00 M). Then E°_{cell}, $[Ni^{2+}]$, $[Zn^{2+}]$, n $\rightarrow$ E_{cell}**

$$E_{cell} = E^\circ_{cell} - \frac{0.0592\ V}{n}\log Q$$

(c) **E°_{cell}, E_{cell}, n $\rightarrow$ $[Zn^{2+}]/[Ni^{2+}]$ $\rightarrow$ $[Ni^{2+}]$, $[Zn^{2+}]$**

$$E_{cell} = E^\circ_{cell} - \frac{0.0592\ V}{n}\log Q \qquad [Ni^{2+}] + [Zn^{2+}] = 1.50\ M + 0.100\ M = 1.60\ M$$

Solution:

(a) Zn^{2+} (*aq*) + 2 e^- $\rightarrow$ Zn (*s*) and Ni^{2+} (*aq*) + 2 e^- $\rightarrow$ Ni (*s*). Look up cell potentials. For Zn, $E^\circ_{red} = -0.76$ V. For Ni, $E^\circ_{red} = -0.23$ V. In order to get a positive E°_{cell} Zn is oxidized so $E^\circ_{red} = -0.76\ V = E^\circ_{anode}$. Ni^{2+} is reduced so $E^\circ_{red} = -0.23\ V = E^\circ_{cathode}$. Then $E^\circ_{cell} = E^\circ_{cathode} - E^\circ_{anode} = -0.23\ V - (-0.76\ V) = +0.53\ V$. Adding the two half-cell reactions: Zn (*s*) + Ni^{2+} (*aq*) + ~~2 e^-~~ $\rightarrow$ Zn^{2+} (*aq*) + ~~2 e^-~~ + Ni (*s*). The overall reaction is: Zn (*s*) + Ni^{2+} (*aq*) $\rightarrow$ Zn^{2+} (*aq*) + Ni (*s*). Then $Q = \frac{[Zn^{2+}]}{[Ni^{2+}]} = \frac{0.100}{1.50} = 0.06\underline{6}6667$ and $n = 2$

then $E_{cell} = E^\circ_{cell} - \frac{0.0592\ V}{n}\log Q = 0.53\ V - \frac{0.0592\ V}{2}\log 0.06\underline{6}6667 = +0.56\ V.$

(b) $$Q = \frac{[Zn^{2+}]}{[Ni^{2+}]} = \frac{1.100}{0.500} = 2.20 \text{ then}$$

$$E_{cell} = E^\circ_{cell} - \frac{0.0592\ V}{n}\log Q = 0.53\ V - \frac{0.0592\ V}{2}\log 2.20 = +0.52\ V.$$

(c) $E_{cell} = E^\circ_{cell} - \frac{0.0592\ V}{n} \log Q$ so $0.45\ V = 0.53\ V - \frac{0.0592\ V}{2} \log Q \rightarrow 0.08\ \cancel{V} = \frac{0.0592\ \cancel{V}}{2} \log Q \rightarrow$

$\log Q = 2.\underline{7}0270 \rightarrow Q = 10^{2.\underline{7}0270} = 5\underline{0}4.32$ then $Q = 5\underline{0}4.32 = \frac{[Zn^{2+}]}{1.60\ M - [Zn^{2+}]}$ solving for $[Zn^{2+}]$

$(5\underline{0}4.32)(1.60\ M - [Zn^{2+}] = [Zn^{2+}] \rightarrow [Zn^{2+}] = \frac{8\underline{0}6.906\ M}{5\underline{0}5.32} = 1.\underline{5}9628\ M = 1.60\ M$ then

$[Ni^{2+}] = 1.60\ M - 1.\underline{5}9628\ M = 0.003\ M.$

Check: The units (V, V, and M) are correct. The standard cell potential is positive and since there are more reactants than products this raises the cell potential. As the reaction proceeds, reactants are converted to products so the cell potential drops for parts (b) and (c).

18.78 **Given:** Pb/Pb^{2+} and Cu/Cu^{2+} half-cells in voltaic cell; initially $[Pb^{2+}] = 0.0500\ M$, and $[Cu^{2+}] = 1.50\ M$
Find: (a) initial E_{cell}; (b) E_{cell} when $[Cu^{2+}] = 0.200\ M$; and (c) $[Pb^{2+}]$ and $[Cu^{2+}]$ when $E_{cell} = 0.35\ V$
Conceptual Plan:

(a) **Write two half-cell reactions and add electrons as needed to balance reactions. Look up half-reactions in Table 18.1. Calculate the standard cell potential by subtracting the electrode potential of the anode from the electrode potential of the cathode: $E^\circ_{cell} = E^\circ_{cathode} - E^\circ_{anode}$. Choose the direction of the half-cell reactions so that $E^\circ_{cell} > 0$. Add two half-cell reactions and cancel electrons to generate overall reaction. Define Q based on overall reaction. Then E°_{cell}, $[Pb^{2+}]$, $[Cu^{2+}]$, $n \rightarrow E_{cell}$**

$$E_{cell} = E^\circ_{cell} - \frac{0.0592\ V}{n} \log Q$$

(b) **When $[Cu^{2+}] = 0.200\ M$, then $[Pb^{2+}] = 1.35\ M$ (since the stoichiometric coefficients for Pb^{2+}: Cu^{2+} are 1:1, and the $[Cu^{2+}]$ drops by 1.30 M, the other concentration must rise by 1.30 M). Then E°_{cell}, $[Pb^{2+}]$, $[Cu^{2+}]$, $n \rightarrow E_{cell}$**

$$E_{cell} = E^\circ_{cell} - \frac{0.0592\ V}{n} \log Q$$

(c) **E°_{cell}, E_{cell}, $n \rightarrow [Pb^{2+}] / [Cu^{2+}] \rightarrow [Pb^{2+}]$, $[Cu^{2+}]$**

$$E_{cell} = E^\circ_{cell} - \frac{0.0592\ V}{n} \log Q \qquad [Pb^{2+}] + [Cu^{2+}] = 0.0500\ M + 1.50\ M = 1.55\ M$$

Solution:

(a) $Pb^{2+}\ (aq) + 2\ e^- \rightarrow Pb\ (s)$ and $Cu^{2+}\ (aq) + 2\ e^- \rightarrow Cu\ (s)$. Look up cell potentials. For Pb, $E^\circ_{red} = -0.13\ V$. For Cu, $E^\circ_{red} = +0.34\ V$. In order to get a positive E°_{cell} Pb is oxidized so $E^\circ_{red} = -0.13\ V = E^\circ_{anode}$. Cu^{2+} is reduced so $E^\circ_{red} = 0.34\ V = E^\circ_{cathode}$. Then $E^\circ_{cell} = E^\circ_{cathode} - E^\circ_{anode} = 0.34\ V - (-0.13\ V) = +0.47\ V$. Adding the two half-cell reactions: $Pb\ (s) + Cu^{2+}\ (aq) + \cancel{2e^-} \rightarrow Pb^{2+}\ (aq) + \cancel{2e^-} + Cu\ (s)$. The overall reaction is: $Pb\ (s) + Cu^{2+}\ (aq) \rightarrow Pb^{2+}\ (aq) + Cu\ (s)$. Then $Q = \frac{[Pb^{2+}]}{[Cu^{2+}]} = \frac{0.050}{1.50} = 0.03\underline{3}333$ and $n = 2$

then $E_{cell} = E^\circ_{cell} - \frac{0.0592\ V}{n} \log Q = 0.47\ V - \frac{0.0592\ V}{2} \log 0.03\underline{3}333 = +0.51\ V.$

(b) $Q = \frac{[Pb^{2+}]}{[Cu^{2+}]} = \frac{1.35}{0.200} = 6.75$ then

$E_{cell} = E^\circ_{cell} - \frac{0.0592\ V}{n} \log Q = 0.47\ V - \frac{0.0592\ V}{2} \log 6.75 = +0.45\ V.$

(c) $E_{cell} = E^\circ_{cell} - \frac{0.0592\ V}{n} \log Q$ so $0.35\ V = 0.47\ V - \frac{0.0592\ V}{2} \log Q \rightarrow 0.12\ \cancel{V} = \frac{0.0592\ \cancel{V}}{2} \log Q \rightarrow$

$\log Q = 4.\underline{0}540 \rightarrow Q = 10^{4.\underline{0}540} = 1.\underline{1}325 \times 10^4$ then $Q = 1.\underline{1}325 \times 10^4 = \frac{[Pb^{2+}]}{1.55\ M - [Pb^{2+}]}$ solving for

$[Pb^{2+}]$. $(1.\underline{1}325 \times 10^4)(1.55\ M - [Pb^{2+}]) = [Pb^{2+}] \rightarrow [Pb^{2+}] = \frac{1.\underline{7}554 \times 10^4\ M}{1.\underline{1}326 \times 10^4} = 1.\underline{5}487\ M = 1.5\ M$

then $[Cu^{2+}] = 1.55\ M - 1.\underline{5}487\ M = 0.\underline{0}01345\ M = 0.0\ M.$

Check: The units (V, V, and M) are correct. The standard cell potential is positive and since there are more reactants than products this raises the cell potential. As the reaction proceeds, reactants are converted to products so the cell potential drops for parts (b) and (c).

18.79 **Given:** Zn/Zn^{2+} concentration cell, with $[Zn^{2+}] = 2.0$ M in one half-cell and $[Zn^{2+}] = 1.0 \times 10^{-3}$ M in other half-cell **Find:** Sketch a voltaic cell, labeling the anode, the cathode, the reactions at electrodes, all species, and the direction of electron flow.
Conceptual Plan: In a concentration cell, the half-cell with the higher concentration is always the half-cell where the reduction takes place (contains the cathode). The two half-cell reactions are the same, only reversed. Put anode reaction on the left (oxidation = electrons as product) and cathode reaction on the right (reduction = electrons as reactant). Electrons flow from anode to cathode.
Solution:

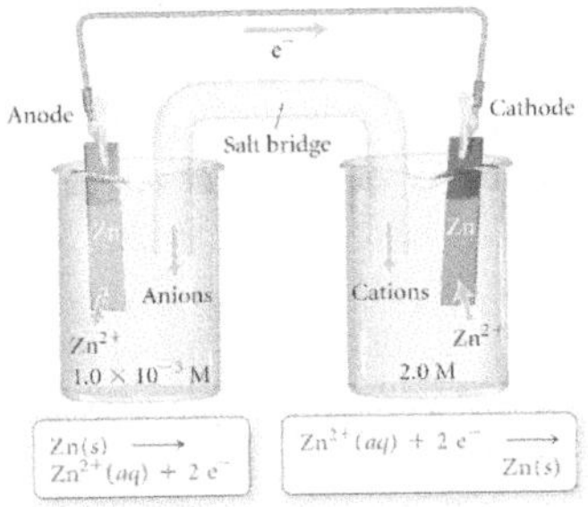

Check: The figure looks similar to the right side of Figure 18.10.

18.80 **Given:** Pb/Pb^{2+} concentration cell sketch
Find: (a) Label the anode and cathode, (b) indicate direction of electron flow, and (c) indicate what happens to $[Pb^{2+}]$ in each half-cell with time.
Conceptual Plan: (a) In a concentration cell, the half-cell with the higher concentration is always the half-cell where the reduction takes place (contains the cathode). (b) Electrons flow from anode to cathode. (c) Each half-cell reaction moves forward, so the direction of the concentration changes in each half-cell can be determined.
Solution:

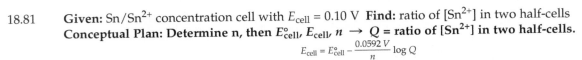

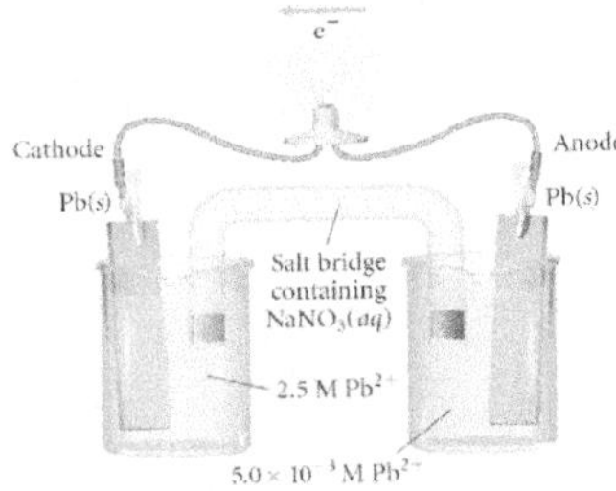

(c) As the reaction proceeds, the left half-cell (cathode = reduction reaction) will decrease in concentration, and the right half-cell (anode = oxidation reaction) will increase in concentration. Eventually the two concentrations will be the same and the flow of electrons will stop.

Check: The figure looks similar to the right side of Figure 18.10.

18.81 **Given:** Sn/Sn^{2+} concentration cell with $E_{cell} = 0.10$ V **Find:** ratio of $[Sn^{2+}]$ in two half-cells
Conceptual Plan: Determine n, then E°_{cell}, E_{cell}, $n \rightarrow Q$ = ratio of $[Sn^{2+}]$ in two half-cells.

$$E_{cell} = E^\circ_{cell} - \frac{0.0592\ V}{n} \log Q$$

Solution: Since $Sn^{2+}(aq) + 2\,e^- \rightarrow Sn(s)$, $n = 2$. In a concentration cell, $E^\circ_{cell} = 0$ V. So

$$E_{cell} = E^\circ_{cell} - \frac{0.0592\ V}{n} \log Q \text{ so } 0.10\ V = 0.00\ V - \frac{0.0592\ V}{2} \log Q \rightarrow 0.10\ V = -\frac{0.0592\ V}{2} \log Q \rightarrow$$

$$\log Q = -3.3784 \rightarrow Q = 10^{-3.3784} = 4.2 \times 10^{-4} = \frac{[Sn^{2+}](ox)}{[Sn^{2+}](red)}.$$

Check: The units (none) are correct. Since the concentration in the reduction reaction half-cell is always greater than the concentration in the oxidation half-cell in a voltaic concentration cell, the Q or ratio of two cells is less than 1.

18.82 **Given:** Cu/Cu^{2+} concentration cell with $E_{cell} = 0.22$ V; and $[Cu^{2+}] = 1.5 \times 10^{-3}$ M **Find:** $[Cu^{2+}]$ in other half-cell
Conceptual Plan: Determine n, then E°_{cell}, E_{cell}, $n \rightarrow Q$ = ratio of $[Cu^{2+}]$ in two half-cells then

$$E_{cell} = E^\circ_{cell} - \frac{0.0592\ V}{n} \log Q$$

$[Cu^{2+}]$ one side, $Q \rightarrow [Cu^{2+}]$ other side.

$$Q = \frac{[Cu^{2+}](ox)}{[Cu^{2+}](red)}$$

Solution: Since Sn^{2+} (*aq*) + 2 e^- $\rightarrow$ Sn (*s*), $n = 2$. In a concentration cell, $E^\circ_{cell} = 0$ V. So

$$E_{cell} = E^\circ_{cell} - \frac{0.0592\text{ V}}{n}\log Q \text{ so } 0.22\text{ V} = 0.00\text{ V} - \frac{0.0592\text{ V}}{2}\log Q \rightarrow 0.22\cancel{\text{V}} = -\frac{0.0592\cancel{\text{V}}}{2}\log Q \rightarrow$$

$$\log Q = -7.4324 \rightarrow Q = 10^{-7.4324} = 3.6946 \times 10^{-8} = \frac{[Cu^{2+}](ox)}{[Cu^{2+}](red)}.$$

$$[Cu^{2+}](red) = \frac{[Cu^{2+}](ox)}{Q} = \frac{1.5 \times 10^{-3}\text{ M}}{3.6946 \times 10^{-8}} = 4.0 \times 10^4\text{ M}$$ The problem states that the given concentration is the higher concentration, so

$[Cu^{2+}](ox) = [Cu^{2+}](red) \times Q = (1.5 \times 10^{-3}\text{ M})(3.6946 \times 10^{-8}) = 5.5 \times 10^{-11}$ M, which is low, but possible.

Check: The units (M) are correct. Since the voltage is fairly high for a concentration cell, there must be a very small Q, which leads to an extremely low concentration on the oxidation side.

Batteries, Fuel Cells, and Corrosion

18.83 **Given:** alkaline battery **Find:** optimum mass ratio of Zn to MnO_2

Conceptual Plan: Look up alkaline battery reactions. Use stoichiometry to get mole ratio. Then

$Zn\ (s) + 2\ OH^-\ (aq) \rightarrow Zn(OH)_2\ (s) + 2\ e^-$ $\qquad \frac{1\text{ mol Zn}}{2\text{ mol}MnO_2}$

$2\ MnO_2\ (s) + 2\ H_2O\ (l) + 2\ e^- \rightarrow 2\ MnO(OH)\ (s) + 2\ OH^-\ (aq)$.

mol Zn $\rightarrow$ g Zn then mol MnO_2 $\rightarrow$ g MnO_2.

$\frac{65.41\text{ g Zn}}{1\text{ mol Zn}} \qquad \frac{1\text{ mol }MnO_2}{86.94\text{ g }MnO_2}$

Solution: $$\frac{1\ \cancel{\text{mol Zn}}}{2\ \cancel{\text{mol }MnO_2}} \times \frac{65.41\text{ g Zn}}{1\ \cancel{\text{mol Zn}}} \times \frac{1\ \cancel{\text{mol }MnO_2}}{86.94\text{ g }MnO_2} = 0.3762\frac{\text{g Zn}}{\text{g }MnO_2}.$$

Check: The units (mass ratio) are correct. Since more moles of MnO_2 are needed and the molar mass is larger, the ratio is less than 1.

18.84 **Given:** lead storage battery, 1.00 g Pb oxidizes **Find:** mass $PbSO_4$

Conceptual Plan: Look up lead acid battery reactions. Then g Pb $\rightarrow$ mol Pb $\rightarrow$ mol $PbSO_4$ $\rightarrow$ g $PbSO_4$.

$Pb\ (s) + HSO_4^-\ (aq) \rightarrow PbSO_4\ (s) + H^+\ (aq) + 2\ e^-$ $\qquad \frac{1\text{ mol Pb}}{207.2\text{ g Pb}} \quad \frac{2\text{ mol }PbSO_4}{1\text{ mol Pb}} \quad \frac{303.27\text{ g }PbSO_4}{1\text{ mol }PbSO_4}$

$PbO_2\ (s) + HSO_4^-\ (aq) + 3\ H^+\ (aq) + 2\ e^- \rightarrow PbSO_4\ (s) + 2\ H_2O\ (l)$.

Solution: $$1.00\ \cancel{\text{g Pb}} \times \frac{1\ \cancel{\text{mol Pb}}}{207.2\ \cancel{\text{g Pb}}} \times \frac{2\ \cancel{\text{mol }PbSO_4}}{1\ \cancel{\text{mol Pb}}} \times \frac{303.27\text{ g }PbSO_4}{1\ \cancel{\text{mol }PbSO_4}} = 2.93\text{ g }PbSO_4.$$

Check: The units (g) are correct. Since more moles of $PbSO_4$ are generated and the molar mass is larger, the mass is larger.

18.85 **Given:** $CH_4\ (g) + 2\ O_2\ (g) \rightarrow CO_2\ (g) + 2\ H_2O\ (g)$ **Find:** E°_{cell}

Conceptual Plan: $\Delta G^\circ_{rxn} = \sum n_p \Delta G^\circ_f(\text{products}) - \sum n_r \Delta G^\circ_f(\text{reactants})$ **and determine n then $\Delta G^\circ_{rxn}, n \rightarrow E^\circ_{cell}$**

$\Delta G^\circ_{rxn} = -nFE^\circ_{cell}$

Solution:

Reactant/Product	ΔG°_f (kJ/mol from Appendix IIB)
CH_4 (*g*)	− 50.5
O_2 (*g*)	0.0
CO_2 (*g*)	− 394.4
H_2O (*g*)	− 228.6

Be sure to pull data for the correct formula and phase.

$\Delta G^\circ_{rxn} = \sum n_p \Delta G^\circ_f(\text{products}) - \sum n_r \Delta G^\circ_f(\text{reactants})$

$= [1(\Delta G^\circ_f(CO_2\ (g))) + 2(\Delta G^\circ_f(H_2O\ (g)))] - [1(\Delta G^\circ_f(CH_4\ (g))) + 2(\Delta G^\circ_f(O_2\ (g)))]$

$= [1(-394.4\text{ kJ}) + 2(-228.6\text{ kJ})] - [1(-50.5\text{ kJ}) + 2(0.0\text{ kJ})]$

$= [-851.6\text{ kJ}] - [-50.5\text{ kJ}]$

$= -801.1\text{ kJ} = -8.011 \times 10^5\text{ J}$

Also, since one C atom goes from an oxidation state of – 4 to + 4 and 4 O atoms are going from 0 to –2, then $n = 8$ and $\Delta G^\circ_{rxn} = -nFE^\circ_{cell}$. Rearrange to solve for E°_{cell}.

$$E^\circ_{cell} = \frac{\Delta G^\circ_{rxn}}{-nF} = \frac{-8.011 \times 10^5\text{ J}}{-8\ \cancel{\text{mol e}^-} \times \dfrac{96{,}485\text{ C}}{\cancel{\text{mol e}^-}}} = 1.038\ \frac{\text{V}\cdot\cancel{\text{C}}}{\cancel{\text{C}}} = 1.038\text{ V}.$$

Check: The units (V) are correct. The cell voltage is positive which is consistent with a spontaneous reaction.

18.86 **Given:** $CH_3CH_2OH\ (g) + O_2\ (g) \rightarrow HC_2H_3O_2\ (g) + H_2O\ (g)$ **Find:** E°_{cell}

Conceptual Plan: $\Delta G^\circ_{rxn} = \sum n_p \Delta G^\circ_f(\text{products}) - \sum n_r \Delta G^\circ_f(\text{reactants})$ **and determine** n **then**

$\Delta G^\circ_{rxn}, n \rightarrow E^\circ_{cell}$

$\Delta G^\circ_{rxn} = -nFE^\circ_{cell}$

Solution:

Reactant/Product	ΔG°_f (kJ/mol from Appendix IIB)
$CH_3CH_2OH\ (g)$	– 167.9
$O_2\ (g)$	0.0
$HC_2H_3O_2\ (g)$	– 374.2
$H_2O\ (g)$	– 228.6

Be sure to pull data for the correct formula and phase.

$\Delta G^\circ_{rxn} = \sum n_p \Delta G^\circ_f(\text{products}) - \sum n_r \Delta G^\circ_f(\text{reactants})$

$= [1(\Delta G^\circ_f(HC_2H_3O_2\ (g))) + 1(\Delta G^\circ_f(H_2O\ (g)))] - [1(\Delta G^\circ_f(CH_3CH_2OH\ (g))) + 1(\Delta G^\circ_f(O_2\ (g)))]$

$= [1(-374.2\text{ kJ}) + 1(-228.6\text{ kJ})] - [1(-167.9\text{ kJ}) + 1(0.0\text{ kJ})]$

$= [-602.8\text{ kJ}] - [-167.9\text{ kJ}]$

$= -434.9\text{ kJ} = -4.349 \times 10^5\text{ J}$

Also, since two O atoms are going from 0 to – 2 so $n = 4$ then $\Delta G^\circ_{rxn} = -nFE^\circ_{cell}$. Rearrange to solve for E°_{cell}.

$$E^\circ_{cell} = \frac{\Delta G^\circ_{rxn}}{-nF} = \frac{-4.349 \times 10^5\text{ J}}{-4\ \cancel{\text{mol e}^-} \times \dfrac{96{,}485\text{ C}}{\cancel{\text{mol e}^-}}} = 1.127\ \frac{\text{V}\cdot\cancel{\text{C}}}{\cancel{\text{C}}} = 1.127\text{ V}.$$

Check: The units (V) are correct. The cell voltage is positive which is consistent with a spontaneous reaction.

18.87 When iron corrodes or rusts, it oxidizes to Fe^{2+}. In order for a metal to be able to protect iron, it must be more easily oxidized than iron or be below it in Table 18.1. (a) Zn and (c) Mn meet this criterion.

18.88 When iron corrodes or rusts, it oxidizes to Fe^{2+}. In order for a metal to be able to protect iron, it must be more easily oxidized than iron or be below it in Table 18.1. (a) Mg and (b) Cr meet this criterion.

Electrolytic Cells and Electrolysis

18.89 **Given:** electrolytic cell sketch

Find: (a) Label the anode and cathode and indicate half-reactions, (b) indicate direction of electron flow, and (c) Label battery terminals and calculate minimum voltage to drive reaction

Conceptual Plan: (a) Write two half-cell reactions and add electrons as needed to balance reactions. Look up half-reactions in Table 18.1. Calculate the standard cell potential by subtracting the electrode potential of the anode from the electrode potential of the cathode: $E^\circ_{cell} = E^\circ_{cathode} - E^\circ_{anode}$. Choose the direction of the half-cell reactions so that $E^\circ_{cell} < 0$. (b) Electrons flow from anode to cathode. (c) Each half-cell reaction moves forward, so direction of the concentration changes can be determined.

Solution:

(a) Ni^{2+} *(aq)* + 2 e^- $\longrightarrow$ Ni *(s)* and Cd^{2+} *(aq)* + 2 e^- $\longrightarrow$ Cd *(s)*. Look up cell potentials. For Ni, E°_{red} = – 0.23 V. For Cd, E°_{red} = – 0.40 V. In order to get a negative cell potential, Ni is oxidized so E°_{red} = – 0.23 V = E°_{anode}. Cd^{2+} is reduced so E°_{red} = – 0.23 V = $E^\circ_{cathode}$. Then E°_{cell} = $E^\circ_{cathode}$ – E°_{anode} = – 0.40 V – (– 0.23 V) = – 0.17 V. Since oxidation occurs at the anode, the Ni is the anode and the reaction is Ni *(s)* $\longrightarrow$ Ni^{2+} *(aq)* + 2 e^-. Since reduction takes place at the cathode, Cd is the cathode and the reaction is Cd^{2+} *(aq)* + 2 e^- $\longrightarrow$ Cd *(s)*.

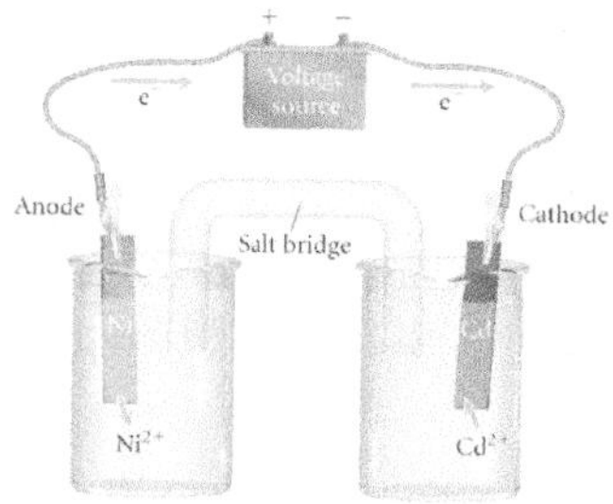

(c) Since reduction is occurring at the cathode, the battery terminal closest to the cathode is the negative terminal. Since the cell potential from part (a) is = – 0.17 V, a minimum of 0.17 V must be applied by the battery.

Check: The reaction is nonspontaneous, since the reduction of Ni^{2+} is above Cd^{2+}. Electrons still flow from the anode to the cathode. The reaction can be made spontaneous with the application of electrical energy.

18.90 **Given:** electrolytic cell Mn^{2+} reduced to Mn and Sn oxidized to Sn^{2+}

Find: Draw a cell and label the anode and cathode, write half-reactions, indicate the direction of electron flow, and calculate the minimum voltage to drive reaction.

Conceptual Plan: Write two half-cell reactions and add electrons as needed to balance reactions. Look up half-reactions in Table 18.1. Calculate the standard cell potential by subtracting the electrode potential of the anode from the electrode potential of the cathode: E°_{cell} = $E^\circ_{cathode}$ – E°_{anode}. Anode is where oxidation occurs, so Sn is anode and Mn is cathode. Electrons flow from anode to cathode. The minimum potential needed is E°_{cell}.

Solution: Mn^{2+} *(aq)* + 2 e^- $\longrightarrow$ Mn *(s)* and Sn^{2+} *(aq)* + 2 e^- $\longrightarrow$ Sn *(s)*. Look up cell potentials. For Mn^{2+}, E°_{red} = – 1.18 V. For Sn, E°_{red} = – 0.14 V. Since Sn is oxidized, E°_{red} = – 0.14 V = E°_{anode}. Then E°_{cell} = $E^\circ_{cathode}$ – E°_{anode} = – 1.18 V – (– 0.14 V) = – 1.04 V. Since oxidation occurs at the anode, the Sn is the anode and the reaction is Sn *(s)* $\longrightarrow$ Sn^{2+} *(aq)* + 2 e^-. Since reduction takes place at the cathode, Mn is the cathode and the reaction is Mn^{2+} *(aq)* + 2 e^- $\longrightarrow$ Mn *(s)*. Electrons flow from the anode to the cathode. Since the cell potential is – 1.04 V, a minimum of 1.04 V must be applied by the battery.

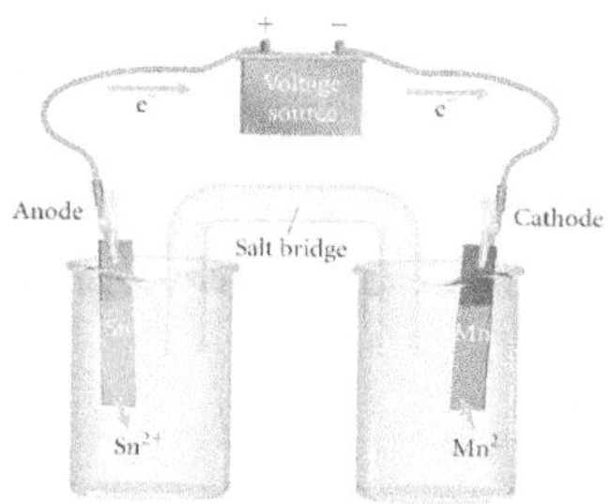

Check: The reaction is nonspontaneous, since the reduction of Sn^{2+} is above Mn^{2+}. Electrons still flow from the anode to the cathode. The reaction can be made spontaneous with the application of electrical energy.

18.91 **Given:** electrolysis of molten KBr **Find:** write half-reactions

Conceptual Plan: Write two half-cell reactions, taking the cation and the anion to their elemental forms at high temperatures and adding electrons as needed to balance reactions.

Solution: KBr breaks apart to K^+ and Br^-. K^+ *(l)* + e^- $\longrightarrow$ K *(l)* and 2 Br^- *(l)* $\longrightarrow$ Br_2 *(g)* + 2 e^-.

Check: The cation is reduced and the anion is oxidized. Mass and charge are balanced in the reactions.

18.92 **Given:** electrolysis of molten NaI **Find:** products

Conceptual Plan: The products are the cation and the anion in their elemental forms at high temperatures.

Solution: NaI breaks apart to Na^+ and I^-, so the elemental forms are Na *(l)* and I_2 *(g)*.

Check: The cation is reduced and the anion is oxidized.

18.93 **Given:** electrolysis of mixture of molten KBr and molten LiBr **Find:** write half-reactions

Conceptual Plan: Write two half-cell reactions, taking the cation and the anion to their elemental forms at high temperatures and adding electrons as needed to balance reactions. Look up cation cell potentials to see which one generates the more spontaneous reaction.

Solution: KBr breaks apart to K^+ and Br^-. K^+ *(l)* + e^- $\longrightarrow$ K *(l)* and 2 Br^- *(l)* $\longrightarrow$ Br_2 *(g)* + 2 e^-. LiBr breaks apart to Li^+ and Br^-. Li^+ *(l)* + e^- $\longrightarrow$ Li *(l)* and 2 Br^- *(l)* $\longrightarrow$ Br_2 *(g)* + 2 e^-. The anions are the same so the anode reaction is 2 Br^- *(l)* $\longrightarrow$ Br_2 *(g)* + 2 e^-. Looking up the cation reduction potentials, for K^+ E°_{red} = – 2.92 V and for Li^+ E°_{red} = – 3.04 V. Since the reduction potential is more positive for K^+, the reaction at the cathode is K^+ *(l)* + e^- $\longrightarrow$ K *(l)*.

Check: The cation is reduced and the anion is oxidized. Mass and charge are balanced in the reactions. The cation that is higher in Table 18.1 will be the reaction at the cathode.

18.94 **Given:** electrolysis of mixture of molten KI and molten KBr **Find:** products
Conceptual Plan: Write two half-cell reactions, taking the cation and the anion to their elemental forms at high temperatures and adding electrons as needed to balance reactions. Look up anion cell potentials to see which one generates the more spontaneous reaction.
Solution: KI breaks apart to K^+ and I^-. $K^+ (l) + e^- \rightarrow K (l)$ and $2 I^- (l) \rightarrow I_2 (g) + 2 e^-$. KBr breaks apart to K^+ and Br^-. $K^+ (l) + e^- \rightarrow K (l)$ and $2 Br^- (l) \rightarrow Br_2 (g) + 2 e^-$. The cations are the same so the cathode reaction is $K^+ (l) + e^- \rightarrow K (l)$ and the product will be K (*l*). Looking up the anion reduction potentials, for Br^- $E^\circ_{anode} = E^\circ_{red} = +1.09$ V and for I^- $E^\circ_{anode} = E^\circ_{red} = +0.54$ V. Since the anode (oxidation) potential is smaller for I^- the cell potential will be larger, the reaction at the anode is $2 I^- (l) \rightarrow I_2 (g) + 2 e^-$ and the product will be I_2 (*g*).
Check: The cation is reduced and the anion is oxidized. The anion that is lower in Table 18.1 will be the reaction at the anode.

18.95 **Given:** electrolysis of aqueous solutions **Find:** write half-reactions
Conceptual Plan: Write two half-cell reactions, taking the cation and the anion to their elemental forms at standard conditions and adding electrons as needed to balance reactions. Look up cell potentials and compare to the cell potentials for the electrolysis of water to see which one generates the more spontaneous reaction.
Solution: The hydrolysis of water reactions are: At a neutral pH, $2 H_2O (l) \rightarrow O_2 (g) + 4 H^+ (aq) + 4 e^-$ where $E = -0.82$ V; and when $[OH^-] = 10^{-7}$ M $2 H_2O (l) + 2 e^- \rightarrow H_2 (g) + OH^- (aq)$ where $E = -0.41$ V.

(a) NaBr breaks apart to Na^+ and Br^-. $Na^+ (aq) + e^- \rightarrow Na (s)$ and $2 Br^- (aq) \rightarrow Br_2 (l) + 2 e^-$. Looking up the half-cell potentials, for Na^+ $E^\circ_{red} = -2.71$ V and for Br^- $E^\circ_{anode} = E^\circ_{red} = +1.09$ V. Since -0.82 V is more positive than $E^\circ_{anode} = -1.09$ V, the oxidation reaction will be: $2 H_2O (l) \rightarrow O_2 (g) + 4 H^+ (aq) + 4 e^-$ at the anode. Since -0.41 V is more positive than $= -2.71$ V, the reduction reaction will be: $2 H_2O (l) + 2 e^- \rightarrow H_2 (g) + OH^- (aq)$ at the cathode.

(b) PbI_2 breaks apart to Pb^{2+} and I^-. $Pb^{2+} (aq) + 2 e^- \rightarrow Pb (s)$ and $2 I^- (aq) \rightarrow I_2 (s) + 2 e^-$. Looking up the half-cell potentials, for Pb^{2+} $E^\circ_{red} = -0.13$ V and for I^- $E^\circ_{anode} = E^\circ_{red} = -0.54$ V. Since $E^\circ_{anode} = -0.54$ V is more positive than $= -0.82$ V, the oxidation reaction will be: $2 I^- (aq) \rightarrow I_2 (s) + 2 e^-$ at the anode. Since -0.13 V is more positive than $= -0.41$ V, the reduction reaction will be: $Pb^{2+} (aq) + 2 e^- \rightarrow Pb (s)$ at the cathode.

(c) Na_2SO_4 breaks apart to Na^+ and SO_4^{2-}. $Na^+ (aq) + e^- \rightarrow Na (s)$ and $SO_4^{2-} (aq) + 4 H^+ (aq) + 2 e^- \rightarrow H_2SO_3 (aq) + H_2O (l)$. Notice that both of these are reductions. Since S is in such a high oxidation state (+6) it can not be oxidized. Looking up the half-cell potentials, for Na^+ $E^\circ_{red} = -2.71$ V and for SO_4^{2-} $E^\circ_{red} = 0.20$ V. Since sodium sulfate solutions are neutral and not acidic, even though 0.20 V is more positive than -0.41 V and -2.71 V, the reduction reaction will not be: $SO_4^{2-} (aq) + 4 H^+ (aq) + 2 e^- \rightarrow H_2SO_3 (aq) + H_2O (l)$ at the cathode, which only occurs in acidic solutions. Thus, the reduction reaction will be $Na^+ (aq) + e^- \rightarrow Na (s)$. Since only one oxidation reaction is possible, the oxidation reaction will be: $2 H_2O (l) \rightarrow O_2 (g) + 4 H^+ (aq) + 4 e^-$ at the anode.

Check: The most positive reactions are the reactions that will occur.

18.96 **Given:** electrolysis of aqueous solutions **Find:** write half-reactions
Conceptual Plan: Write two half-cell reactions, taking the cation and the anion to their elemental forms at standard conditions and adding electrons as needed to balance reactions. Look up cell potentials and compare to the cell potentials for the electrolysis of water to see which one generates the more spontaneous reaction.
Solution: The hydrolysis of water reactions are: At a neutral pH, $2 H_2O (l) \rightarrow O_2 (g) + 4 H^+ (aq) + 4 e^-$ where $E = -0.82$ V; and when $[OH^-] = 10^{-7}$ M $2 H_2O (l) + 2 e^- \rightarrow H_2 (g) + 2 OH^- (aq)$ where $E = -0.41$ V.

(a) $Ni(NO_3)_2$ breaks apart to Ni^{2+} and NO_3^-. $Ni^{2+} (aq) + 2 e^- \rightarrow Ni (s)$ and $NO_3^- (aq) + 4 H^+ (aq) + 3 e^- \rightarrow NO (g) + 2 H_2O (l)$. Notice that both of these are reductions. Since N is in such a high oxidation state (+5) it can not be oxidized. Looking up the half-cell potentials, for Ni^{2+} $E^\circ_{red} = -0.23$ V and for NO_3^- $E^\circ_{red} = +0.96$ V. Since 0.96 V is more positive than -0.23 V and -0.41 V, the reduction reaction will be: $NO_3^- (aq) + 4 H^+ (aq) + 3 e^- \rightarrow NO (g) + 2 H_2O (l)$ at the cathode. Since only one oxidation reaction is possible, the oxidation reaction will be: $2 H_2O (l) \rightarrow O_2 (g) + 4 H^+ (aq) + 4 e^-$ at the anode.

(b) KCl breaks apart to K^+ and Cl^-. K^+ (*aq*) + e^- $\rightarrow$ K (*s*) and 2 Cl^- (*aq*) $\rightarrow$ Cl_2 (*s*) + 2 e^-. Looking up the half-cell potentials, for K^+ $E^\circ_{cathode} = E^\circ_{red} = -2.92$ V and for Cl^- $E^\circ_{anode} = E^\circ_{red} = +1.36$ V. Since – 0.82 V is more positive than = – 1.36 V, the oxidation reaction will be: 2 H_2O (*l*) $\rightarrow$ O_2 (*g*) + 4 H^+ (*aq*) + 4 e^- at the anode. Since $E^\circ_{anode} = -0.41$ V is more positive than $E^\circ_{cathode} = -2.92$ V, the reduction reaction will be: 2 H_2O (*l*) + 2 e^- $\rightarrow$ H_2 (*g*) + OH^- (*aq*) at the cathode.

(c) $CuBr_2$ breaks apart to Cu^{2+} and Br^-. Cu^{2+} (*aq*) + 2 e^- $\rightarrow$ Cu (*s*) and 2 Br^- (*aq*) $\rightarrow$ Br_2 (*l*) + 2 e^-. Looking up the half-cell potentials, for Cu^{2+} $E^\circ_{cathode} = E^\circ_{red} = +0.34$ V and for Br^- $E^\circ_{anode} = E^\circ_{red} = -1.09$ V. Since – 0.82 V is more positive than = – 1.09 V, the oxidation reaction will be: 2 H_2O (*l*) $\rightarrow$ O_2 (*g*) + 4 H^+ (*aq*) + 4 e^- at the anode. Since + 0.34 V is more positive than = – 0.41 V, the reduction reaction will be: Cu^{2+} (*aq*) + 2 e^- $\rightarrow$ Cu (*s*) at the cathode.

Check: The most positive reactions are the reactions that will occur.

18.97 **Given:** electrolysis cell to electroplate Cu onto a metal surface
Find: Draw a cell and label the anode and cathode and write half-reactions.
Conceptual Plan: Write two half-cell reactions and add electrons as needed to balance reactions. The cathode reaction will be the reduction of Cu^{2+} to the metal. The anode will be the reverse reaction.
Solution:

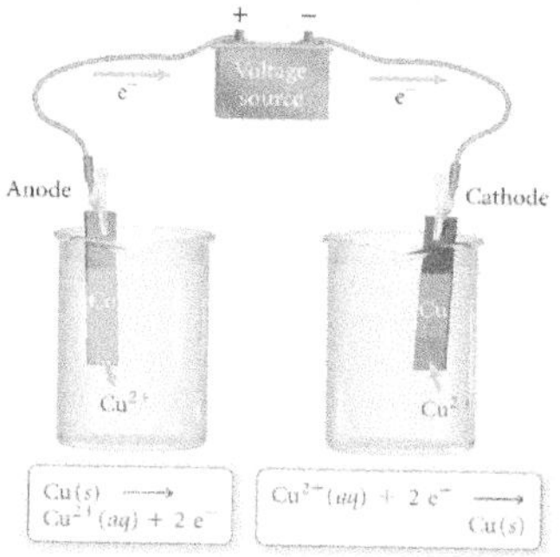

Check: The metal to be plated is the cathode, since metal ions are converted to Cu (*s*) on the surface of the metal.

18.98 **Given:** electrolysis cell to electroplate Ni onto a metal surface
Find: Draw a cell and label the anode and cathode and write half-reactions.
Conceptual Plan: Write two half-cell reactions and add electrons as needed to balance reactions. The cathode reaction will be the reduction of Ni^{2+} to the metal. The anode will be the reverse reaction.
Solution:

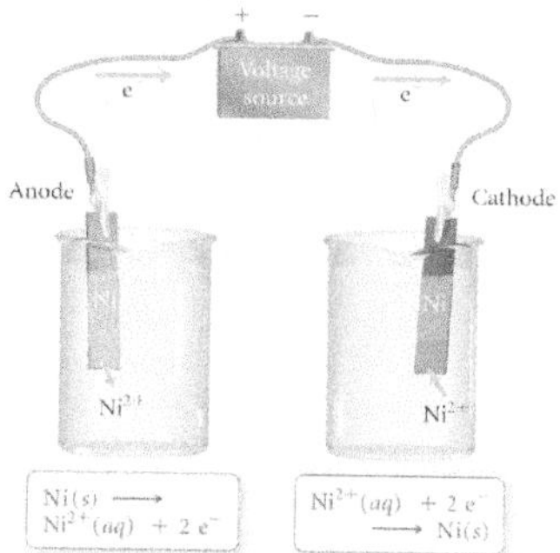

Check: The metal to be plated is the cathode, since metal ions are converted to Ni (*s*) on the surface of the metal.

18.99 **Given:** Cu electroplating of 325 mg Cu at a current of 5.6 A; Cu^{2+} (*aq*) + 2 e^- $\rightarrow$ Cu (*s*) **Find:** time
Conceptual Plan: mg Cu $\rightarrow$ g Cu $\rightarrow$ mol Cu $\rightarrow$ mol e^- $\rightarrow$ C $\rightarrow$ s

$$\frac{1\text{ g}}{1000\text{ mg}} \quad \frac{1\text{ mol Cu}}{63.55\text{ g Cu}} \quad \frac{2\text{ mol e}^-}{1\text{ mol Cu}} \quad \frac{96{,}485\text{ C}}{1\text{ mol e}^-} \quad \frac{1\text{ s}}{5.6\text{ C}}$$

Solution: $325\ \cancel{\text{mg Cu}} \times \frac{1\ \cancel{\text{g Cu}}}{1000\ \cancel{\text{mg Cu}}} \times \frac{1\ \cancel{\text{mol Cu}}}{63.55\ \cancel{\text{g Cu}}} \times \frac{2\ \cancel{\text{mol e}^-}}{1\ \cancel{\text{mol Cu}}} \times \frac{96{,}485\ \cancel{\text{C}}}{1\ \cancel{\text{mol e}^-}} \times \frac{1\text{ s}}{5.6\ \cancel{\text{C}}} = 180\text{ s.}$

Check: The units (s) are correct. Since far less than a mole of Cu is electroplated, the time is short.

18.100 **Given:** Ag electroplating at a current of 6.8 A for 72 min; $Ag^+ (aq) + e^- \rightarrow Ag (s)$ **Find:** mass of Ag

Conceptual Plan: min → s → C → mol e⁻ → mol Ag → g Ag

$$\frac{60 \text{ s}}{1 \text{ min}} \quad \frac{5.8 \text{ C}}{1 \text{ s}} \quad \frac{1 \text{ mol e}^-}{96{,}485 \text{ C}} \quad \frac{1 \text{ mol Ag}}{1 \text{ mol e}^-} \quad \frac{107.87 \text{ g Ag}}{1 \text{ mol Ag}}$$

Solution: $72 \text{ min} \times \frac{60 \text{ s}}{1 \text{ min}} \times \frac{6.8 \text{ C}}{1 \text{ s}} \times \frac{1 \text{ mol e}^-}{96{,}485 \text{ C}} \times \frac{1 \text{ mol Ag}}{1 \text{ mol e}^-} \times \frac{107.87 \text{ g Ag}}{1 \text{ mol Ag}} = 33 \text{ g Ag}$

Check: The units (g) are correct. Since less than a mole of electrons is used, the mass is less than the molar mass of Ag.

18.101 **Given:** Na electrolysis, 1.0 kg in one hour **Find:** current

Conceptual Plan: $Na^+ (l) + e^- \rightarrow Na (l)$ $\frac{\text{kg Na}}{\text{h}} \rightarrow \frac{\text{g Na}}{\text{h}} \rightarrow \frac{\text{mol Na}}{\text{h}} \rightarrow \frac{\text{mol e}^-}{\text{h}} \rightarrow \frac{\text{C}}{\text{h}} \rightarrow \frac{\text{C}}{\text{min}} \rightarrow \frac{\text{C}}{\text{s}}$

$$\frac{1000 \text{ g}}{1 \text{ kg}} \quad \frac{1 \text{ mol Na}}{22.99 \text{ g Na}} \quad \frac{1 \text{ mol e}^-}{1 \text{ mol Na}} \quad \frac{96{,}485 \text{ C}}{1 \text{mol e}^-} \quad \frac{1 \text{ h}}{60 \text{ min}} \quad \frac{1 \text{ min}}{60 \text{ s}}$$

Solution:

$$\frac{1.0 \text{ kg Na}}{1 \text{ h}} \times \frac{1000 \text{ g Na}}{1 \text{ kg Na}} \times \frac{1 \text{ mol Na}}{22.99 \text{ g Na}} \times \frac{1 \text{ mol e}^-}{1 \text{ mol Na}} \times \frac{96{,}485 \text{ C}}{1 \text{ mol e}^-} \times \frac{1 \text{ h}}{60 \text{ min}} \times \frac{1 \text{ min}}{60 \text{ s}} = 1.2 \times 10^3 \frac{\text{C}}{\text{s}} = 1.2 \times 10^3 \text{ A}$$

Check: The units (A) are correct. Since the amount per hour is so large we expect a very large current.

18.102 **Given:** Al electrolysis at a current of 25 A for 1 hour; $Al^{3+} (aq) + 3 e^- \rightarrow Al (s)$ **Find:** mass of Al

Conceptual Plan: h → min → s → C → mol e⁻ → mol Al → g Al

$$\frac{60 \text{ min}}{1 \text{ h}} \quad \frac{60 \text{ s}}{1 \text{ min}} \quad \frac{25 \text{ C}}{1 \text{ s}} \quad \frac{1 \text{ mol e}^-}{96{,}485 \text{ C}} \quad \frac{1 \text{ mol Al}}{3 \text{ mol e}^-} \quad \frac{26.98 \text{ g Al}}{1 \text{ mol Al}}$$

Solution: $1 \text{ h} \times \frac{60 \text{ min}}{1 \text{ h}} \times \frac{60 \text{ s}}{1 \text{ min}} \times \frac{25 \text{ C}}{1 \text{ s}} \times \frac{1 \text{ mol e}^-}{96{,}485 \text{ C}} \times \frac{1 \text{ mol Al}}{3 \text{ mol e}^-} \times \frac{26.98 \text{ g Al}}{1 \text{ mol Al}} = 8.4 \text{ g Al.}$

Check: The units (g) are correct. Since three moles of electrons are used per mole of Al^{3+}, the mass is less than the molar mass of Al.

Cumulative Problems

18.103 **Given:** $MnO_4^- (aq) + Zn (s) \rightarrow Mn^{2+} (aq) + Zn^{2+} (aq)$ 0.500 M $KMnO_4$ and 2.85 g Zn

Find: balance equation and volume $KMnO_4$ solution

Conceptual Plan: Separate the overall reaction into two half-reactions: one for oxidation and one for reduction. → Balance each half-reaction with respect to mass in the following order: 1) balance all elements other than H and O, 2) balance O by adding H_2O, and 3) balance H by adding H^+. → Balance each half-reaction with respect to charge by adding electrons. (The sum of the charges on both sides of the equation should be made equal by adding electrons as necessary.) → Make the number of electrons in both half-reactions equal by multiplying one or both half-reactions by a small whole number. → Add the two half-reactions together, canceling electrons and other species as necessary. → Verify that the reaction is balanced both with respect to mass and with respect to charge. Then

g Zn → mol Zn → mol MnO_4^- → L MnO_4^- → mL MnO_4^-.

$$\frac{1 \text{ mol Zn}}{65.41 \text{ g Zn}} \quad \frac{2 \text{ mol MnO}_4^-}{5 \text{ mol Zn}} \quad \frac{1 \text{ L MnO}_4^-}{0.500 \text{ mol MnO}_4^-} \quad \frac{1000 \text{ mL MnO}_4^-}{1 \text{ L MnO}_4^-}$$

Solution:

Separate: $MnO_4^- (aq) \rightarrow Mn^{2+} (aq)$ and $Zn (s) \rightarrow Zn^{2+} (aq)$

Balance non H & O elements: $MnO_4^- (aq) \rightarrow Mn^{2+} (aq)$ and $Zn (s) \rightarrow Zn^{2+} (aq)$

Balance O with H_2O: $MnO_4^- (aq) \rightarrow Mn^{2+} (aq) + 4 H_2O (l)$ and $Zn (s) \rightarrow Zn^{2+} (aq)$

Balance H with H^+: $MnO_4^- (aq) + 8 H^+ (aq) \rightarrow Mn^{2+} (aq) + 4 H_2O (l)$ and $Zn (s) \rightarrow Zn^{2+} (aq)$

Add electrons: $MnO_4^- (aq) + 8 H^+ (aq) + 5 e^- \rightarrow Mn^{2+} (aq) + 4 H_2O (l)$ and $Zn (s) \rightarrow Zn^{2+} (aq) + 2 e^-$

Equalize electrons:

$2 MnO_4^- (aq) + 16 H^+ (aq) + 10 e^- \rightarrow 2 Mn^{2+} (aq) + 8 H_2O (l)$ and $5 Zn (s) \rightarrow 5 Zn^{2+} (aq) + 10 e^-$

Add half-reactions:

$2 MnO_4^- (aq) + 16 H^+ (aq) + 10 e^- + 5 Zn (s) \rightarrow 2 Mn^{2+} (aq) + 8 H_2O (l) + 5 Zn^{2+} (aq) + 10 e^-$

Cancel electrons: $2 MnO_4^- (aq) + 16 H^+ (aq) + 5 Zn (s) \rightarrow 2 Mn^{2+} (aq) + 8 H_2O (l) + 5 Zn^{2+} (aq)$

$$2.85 \text{ g Zn} \times \frac{1 \text{ mol Zn}}{65.41 \text{ g Zn}} \times \frac{2 \text{ mol MnO}_4^-}{5 \text{ mol Zn}} \times \frac{1 \text{ L MnO}_4^-}{0.500 \text{ mol MnO}_4^-} \times \frac{1000 \text{ mL MnO}_4^-}{1 \text{ L MnO}_4^-} = 34.9 \text{ mL MnO}_4^- =$$

$= 34.9 \text{ mL KMnO}_4$.

Check:

Reactants	Products
2 Mn atoms	2 Mn atoms
8 O atoms	8 O atoms
16 H atoms	16 H atoms
5 Zn atoms	5 Zn atoms
+14 charge	+14 charge

The units (mL) are correct. Since far less than a mole of zinc is used, less than a mole of permanganate is consumed, so the volume is less than a liter.

18.104 **Given:** $Cr_2O_7^{2-}$ (*aq*) + Cu (*s*) $\rightarrow$ Cr^{3+} (*aq*) + Cu^{2+} (*aq*) 0.850 M $K_2Cr_2O_7$ and 5.25 g Zn
Find: balance equation and volume $K_2Cr_2O_7$ solution
Conceptual Plan: Separate the overall reaction into two half-reactions: one for oxidation and one for reduction. → Balance each half-reaction with respect to mass in the following order: 1) balance all elements other than H and O, 2) balance O by adding H_2O, and 3) balance H by adding H^+. → Balance each half-reaction with respect to charge by adding electrons. (The sum of the charges on both sides of the equation should be made equal by adding electrons as necessary.) → Make the number of electrons in both half-reactions equal by multiplying one or both half-reactions by a small whole number. → Add the two half-reactions together, canceling electrons and other species as necessary. → Verify that the reaction is balanced both with respect to mass and with respect to charge.
then g Cu → mol Cu → mol $Cr_2O_7^{2-}$ → L $Cr_2O_7^{2-}$ → mL $Cr_2O_7^{2-}$

$$\frac{1 \text{ mol Cu}}{63.55 \text{ g Cu}} \quad \frac{1 \text{ mol } Cr_2O_7^{2-}}{3 \text{ mol Cu}} \quad \frac{1 \text{ L } Cr_2O_7^{2-}}{0.850 \text{ mol } Cr_2O_7^{2-}} \quad \frac{1000 \text{ mL } Cr_2O_7^{2-}}{1 \text{ L } Cr_2O_7^{2-}}$$

Solution:

Separate: $Cr_2O_7^{2-}$ (*aq*) → Cr^{3+} (*aq*) and Cu (*s*) → Cu^{2+} (*aq*)
Balance non H & O elements: $Cr_2O_7^{2-}$ (*aq*)→ 2 Cr^{3+} (*aq*) and Cu (*s*) → Cu^{2+} (*aq*)
Balance O with H_2O: $Cr_2O_7^{2-}$ (*aq*) → 2 Cr^{3+} (*aq*) + 7 H_2O (*l*) and Cu (*s*) → Cu^{2+} (*aq*)
Balance H with H^+: $Cr_2O_7^{2-}$ (*aq*) + 14 H^+ (*aq*) → 2 Cr^{3+} (*aq*) + 7 H_2O (*l*) and Cu (*s*) → Cu^{2+} (*aq*)
Add electrons: $Cr_2O_7^{2-}$ (*aq*) + 14 H^+ (*aq*) + 6 e^- → 2 Cr^{3+} (*aq*) + 7 H_2O (*l*) and Cu (*s*) → Cu^{2+} (*aq*) + 2e^-
Equalize electrons:
$Cr_2O_7^{2-}$ (*aq*) + 14 H^+ (*aq*) + 6 e^- → 2 Cr^{3+} (*aq*) + 7 H_2O (*l*) and 3 Cu (*s*) → 3 Cu^{2+} (*aq*) + 6 e^-
Add half-reactions:
$Cr_2O_7^{2-}$ (*aq*) + 14 H^+ (*aq*) + ~~6 e^-~~ + 3 Cu (*s*) → 2 Cr^{3+} (*aq*) + 7 H_2O (*l*) + 3 Cu^{2+} (*aq*) + ~~6 e^-~~
Cancel electrons: $Cr_2O_7^{2-}$ (*aq*) + 14 H^+ (*aq*) + 3 Cu (*s*) → 2 Cr^{3+} (*aq*) + 7 H_2O (*l*) + 3 Cu^{2+} (*aq*)

$$5.25 \text{ g Cu} \times \frac{1 \text{ mol Cu}}{63.55 \text{ g Cu}} \times \frac{1 \text{ mol } Cr_2O_7^{2-}}{3 \text{ mol Cu}} \times \frac{1 \text{ L } Cr_2O_7^{2-}}{0.850 \text{ mol } Cr_2O_7^{2-}} \times \frac{1000 \text{ mL } Cr_2O_7^{2-}}{1 \text{ L } Cr_2O_7^{2-}} = 32.4 \text{ mL } Cr_2O_7^{2-} =$$
$= 32.4$ mL $K_2Cr_2O_7$.

Check:

Reactants	Products
2 Cr atoms	2 Cr atoms
7 O atoms	7 O atoms
14 H atoms	14 H atoms
3 Cu atoms	3 Cu atoms
+12 charge	+12 charge

The units (mL) are correct. Since far less than a mole of copper is used, less than a mole of dichromate is consumed, so the volume is less than a liter.

18.105 **Given:** beaker with Al strip and Cu^{2+} ions **Find:** draw sketch after Al is submerged for a few minutes
Conceptual Plan: Write two half-cell reactions and add electrons as needed to balance reactions. Look up half-reactions in Table 18.1. Calculate the standard cell potential by subtracting the electrode potential of the anode from the electrode potential of the cathode: $E^\circ_{cell} = E^\circ_{cathode} - E^\circ_{anode}$. If $E^\circ_{cell} > 0$ the reaction is spontaneous in the forward direction and Al will dissolve and Cu will deposit.
Solution: Al (*s*) → Al^{3+} (*aq*) and Cu^{2+} (*aq*) → Cu (*s*) add electrons Al (*s*) → Al^{3+} (*aq*) + 3 e^- and Cu^{2+} (*aq*) + 2 e^- → Cu (*s*). Look up cell potentials. Al is oxidized so $E^\circ_{anode} = E^\circ_{red} = -1.66$ V Cu^{2+} is reduced so $E^\circ_{cathode} = E^\circ_{red} = 0.34$ V. Then $E^\circ_{cell} = E^\circ_{cathode} - E^\circ_{anode} = 0.34 \text{ V} - (-1.66 \text{ V}) = +2.00$ V and so the reaction is spontaneous. Al will dissolve to generate Al^{3+} (*aq*) and Cu (*s*) will deposit.
Check: The units (V) are correct. If the voltage is positive, the reaction is spontaneous so Al will dissolve and Cu will deposit.

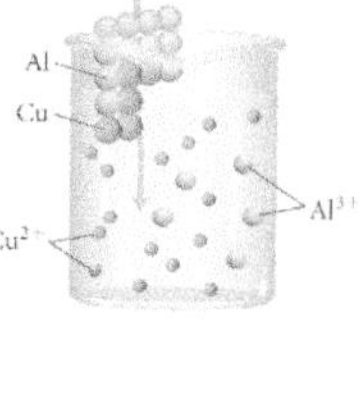

18.106 **Given:** Zn/Zn^{2+} and Ni/Ni^{2+} half-cells in voltaic cell
Find: draw sketch after substantial amount of current generated
Conceptual Plan: Write two half-cell reactions and add electrons as needed to balance reactions. Look up half-reactions in Table 18.1. Calculate the standard cell potential by subtracting the electrode potential of the anode from the electrode potential of the cathode: $E^\circ_{cell} = E^\circ_{cathode} - E^\circ_{anode}$. Choose the direction of the half-cell reactions so that E°_{cell} . 0. Add two half-cell reactions and cancel electrons to generate overall reaction. Since reaction is spontaneous it will move forward.
Solution: Zn^{2+} (*aq*) + 2 e^- $\rightarrow$ Zn (*s*) and Ni^{2+} (*aq*) + 2 e^- $\rightarrow$ Ni (*s*). Look up cell potentials. For Zn, E°_{red} = – 0.76 V. For Ni, E°_{red} = – 0.23 V. In order to get a positive E°_{cell} the sign of the Zn potential must be reversed. Zn is oxidized so $E^\circ_{anode} = E^\circ_{red}$ = – 0.76 V. Ni^{2+} is reduced so $E^\circ_{cathode} = E^\circ_{red}$ = – 0.23 V. Then $E^\circ_{cell} = E^\circ_{cathode} + E^\circ_{anode}$ = – 0.23 V – (– 0.76 V) V = + 0.53 V. Adding the two half-cell reactions: Zn (*s*) + Ni^{2+} (*aq*) + $\cancel{2e^-}$ $\rightarrow$ Zn^{2+} (*aq*) + $\cancel{2e^-}$ + Ni (*s*). The overall reaction is: Zn (*s*) + Ni^{2+} (*aq*) $\rightarrow$ Zn^{2+} (*aq*) + Ni (*s*). Zn will dissolve to generate Zn^{2+} (*aq*) and Ni (*s*) will deposit.

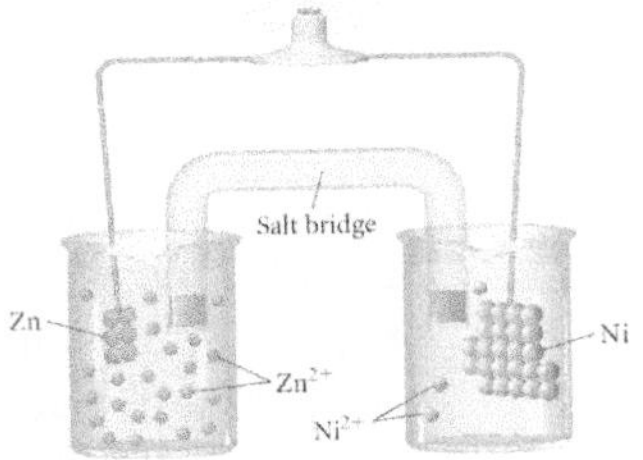

Check: The units (V) are correct. Since Ni is above Zn in Table 18.1, Ni is reduced. If the voltage is positive, the reaction is spontaneous so Zn will dissolve and Ni will deposit.

18.107 **Given:** (a) 2.15 g Al; (b) 4.85 g Cu; and (c) 2.42 g Ag in 3.5 M HI
Find: If metal dissolves, write a balanced reaction and the minimum amount of HI needed to dissolve the metal.
Conceptual Plan: In general, metals whose reduction half-reactions lie below the reduction of H^+ to H_2 in Table 18.1 will dissolve in acids, while metals above it will not. Stop here if metal does not dissolve. To write the balanced redox reactions, pair the oxidation of the metal with the reduction of H^+ to H_2 (2 H^+(*aq*) + 2 e^- $\rightarrow$ H_2(*g*)). Balance the number of electrons transferred. Add the two reactions. Cancel electrons. Then g metal $\rightarrow$ mol metal $\rightarrow$ mol H^+ $\rightarrow$ L HI $\rightarrow$ mL HI

$$\mathcal{M} \qquad \frac{x \text{ mol H}^+}{y \text{ mol metal}} \qquad \frac{1 \text{ L HI}}{3.5 \text{ mol HI}} \qquad \frac{1000 \text{ mL HI}}{1 \text{ L HI}}$$

Solution:

(a) Al meets this criterion. For Al, Al (*s*) $\rightarrow$ Al^{3+} (*aq*) + 3 e^-. We need to multiply the Al reaction by 2 and the H^+ reaction by 3. So, 2 Al (*s*) $\rightarrow$ 2 Al^{3+} (*aq*) + 6 e^- and 6 H^+ (*aq*) + 6 e^- $\rightarrow$ 3 H_2 (*g*). Adding the half-reactions together: 2 Al (*s*) + 6 H^+ (*aq*) + $\cancel{6e^-}$ $\rightarrow$ 2 Al^{3+} (*aq*) + $\cancel{6e^-}$+ 3 H_2 (*g*). Simplify to 2 Al (*s*) + 6 H^+ (*aq*) $\rightarrow$ 2 Al^{3+} (*aq*) + 3 H_2 (*g*). Then

$$2.15 \cancel{\text{g Al}} \times \frac{1 \cancel{\text{mol Al}}}{26.98 \cancel{\text{g Al}}} \times \frac{6 \cancel{\text{mol H}^+}}{2 \cancel{\text{mol Al}}} \times \frac{1 \cancel{\text{L HI}}}{3.5 \cancel{\text{mol HI}}} \times \frac{1000 \text{ mL HI}}{1 \cancel{\text{L HI}}} = 68.3 \text{ mL HI.}$$

(b) Cu does not meet this criterion, so it will not dissolve in HI.

(c) Ag does not meet this criterion, so it will not dissolve in HI.
Check: Only metals with negative reduction potentials will dissolve. The volume of acid needed is fairly small since the amount of metal is much less than 1 mole and the concentration of acid is high.

18.108 **Given:** (a) 5.90 g Au; (b) 2.55 g Cu; and (c) 4.83 g Sn in 6.0 M HNO_3
Find: If the metal dissolves, write the balanced reaction and minimum amount of HNO_3 needed to dissolve the metal.
Conceptual Plan: Nitric acid (HNO_3) oxidizes metals through the following reduction half-reaction: NO_3^- (*aq*) + 4 H^+ (*aq*) + 3 e^- $\rightarrow$ NO (*g*) + 2 H_2O (*l*) E°_{red} = 0.96 V. Since this half-reaction is above the reduction of H^+ in Table 18.1, HNO_3 can oxidize metals that can't be oxidizied by HCl.
Solution:

(a) Au (which has a reduction potential of 1.50 V) will not be oxidized, so it will not dissolve in HNO_3.

(b) Cu will be oxidized (which has a reduction potential of 0.34 V). To write the balanced redox reactions, pair the oxidation of the copper (Cu (*s*) $\rightarrow$ Cu^{2+} (*aq*) + 2 e^-) with the reduction of nitric acid (NO_3^- (*aq*) + 4 H^+ (*aq*) + 3 e^- $\rightarrow$ NO (*g*) + 2 H_2O (*l*)). In order to balance the number of electrons transferred we need to multiply the Cu reaction by 3 and the nitric acid reaction by 2. So, 3 Cu (*s*) $\rightarrow$ 3 Cu^{2+} (*aq*) + 6 e^- and 2 NO_3^- (*aq*) + 8 H^+ (*aq*) + 6 e^- $\rightarrow$ 2 NO (*g*) + 4 H_2O (*l*). Adding the two reactions: 3 Cu (*s*)

$+ 2 NO_3^- (aq) + 8 H^+ (aq) + \cancel{6 e^-} \rightarrow 3 Cu^{2+} (aq) + \cancel{6 e^-} + 2 NO (g) + 4 H_2O (l)$. Simplify to $3 Cu (s) + 2 NO_3^- (aq) + 8 H^+ (aq) \rightarrow 3 Cu^{2+} (aq) + 2 NO (g) + 4 H_2O (l)$. Then

$$2.55 \cancel{g\ Cu} \times \frac{1 \cancel{mol\ Cu}}{63.55 \cancel{g\ Cu}} \times \frac{8 \cancel{mol\ H^+}}{3 \cancel{mol\ Cu}} \times \frac{1 \cancel{L\ HNO_3}}{6.0 \cancel{mol\ HNO_3}} \times \frac{1000\ mL\ HNO_3}{1 \cancel{L\ HNO_3}} = 18\ mL\ HNO_3.$$

Use stoichiometric coefficient of H^+ since it is larger than the NO_3^- stoichiometric coefficient.

(c) Sn will be oxidized (which has a reduction potential of – 0.14 V). To write the balanced redox reactions, pair the oxidation of the tin ($Sn (s) \rightarrow Sn^{2+} (aq) + 2 e^-$) with the reduction of nitric acid ($NO_3^- (aq) + 4 H^+ (aq) + 3 e^- \rightarrow NO (g) + 2 H_2O (l)$). In order to balance the number of electrons transferred we need to multiply the Sn reaction by 3 and the nitric acid reaction by 2. So, $3 Sn (s) \rightarrow 3 Sn^{2+} (aq) + 6 e^-$ and $2 NO_3^- (aq) + 8 H^+ (aq) + 6 e^- \rightarrow 2 NO (g) + 4 H_2O (l)$. Adding the two reactions: $3 Sn (s) + 2 NO_3^- (aq) + 8 H^+ (aq) + \cancel{6 e^-} \rightarrow 3 Sn^{2+} (aq) + \cancel{6 e^-} + 2 NO (g) + 4 H_2O (l)$. Simplify to $3 Sn (s) + 2 NO_3^- (aq) + 8 H^+ (aq) \rightarrow 3 Sn^{2+} (aq) + 2 NO (g) + 4 H_2O (l)$. Then

$$4.83 \cancel{g\ Sn} \times \frac{1 \cancel{mol\ Sn}}{118.71 \cancel{g\ Sn}} \times \frac{8 \cancel{mol\ H^+}}{3 \cancel{mol\ Sn}} \times \frac{1 \cancel{L\ HNO_3}}{6.0 \cancel{mol\ HNO_3}} \times \frac{1000\ mL\ HNO_3}{1 \cancel{L\ HNO_3}} = 18\ mL\ HNO_3.$$

Use stoichiometric coefficient of H^+ since it is larger than the NO_3^- stoichiometric coefficient.

Check: Only metals with reduction potentials less than 0.96 V will dissolve. The volume of acid needed is fairly small since the amount of metal is much less than 1 mole and the concentration of acid is high.

18.109 **Given:** $Pt (s) | H_2 (g, 1\ atm) | H^+ (aq, ?\ M) || Cu^{2+} (aq, 1.0\ M) | Cu (s)$, $E_{cell} = 355$ mV **Find:** pH

Conceptual Plan: Write half-reactions from line notation. Look up half-reactions in Table 18.1. Calculate the standard cell potential by subtracting the electrode potential of the anode from the electrode potential of the cathode: $E^\circ_{cell} = E^\circ_{cathode} - E^\circ_{anode}$. Add the two half-cell reactions and cancel the electrons. Then mV $\rightarrow$ V then E°_{cell}, E_{cell}, P_{H_2}, $[Cu^{2+}]$, $n \rightarrow [H^+] \rightarrow$ pH.

$$\frac{1\ V}{1000\ mV} \qquad E_{cell} = E^\circ_{cell} - \frac{0.0592\ V}{n} \log Q \qquad pH = -\log [H^+]$$

Solution: The half-reactions are: $H_2 (g) \rightarrow 2 H^+(aq) + 2 e^-$ and $Cu^{2+} (aq) + 2 e^- \rightarrow Cu (s)$. H is oxidized so $E^\circ_{red} = 0.00\ V = E^\circ_{anode}$. Cu is reduced so $E^\circ_{red} = 0.34\ V = E^\circ_{cathode}$. Then $E^\circ_{cell} = E^\circ_{cathode} - E^\circ_{anode} = 0.34\ V - 0.00\ V = +0.34\ V$. Adding the two reactions: $H_2 (g) + Cu^{2+} (aq) + \cancel{2 e^-} \rightarrow 2 H^+ (aq) + \cancel{2 e^-} + Cu (s)$. Cancel the electrons: $H_2 (g) + Cu^{2+} (aq) \rightarrow 2 H^+ (aq) + Cu (s)$. Then $355 \cancel{mV} \times \frac{1\ V}{1000 \cancel{mV}} = 0.355$ V. So $n = 2$ and $Q = \frac{[H^+]^2}{P_{H_2}[Cu^{2+}]} = \frac{(x)^2}{(1)(1.0)} = x^2$ then $E_{cell} = E^\circ_{cell} - \frac{0.0592\ V}{n} \log Q$ substitute in values and solve for x.

$$0.355\ V = 0.34\ V - \frac{0.0592\ V}{2} \log x^2 \rightarrow 0.015 \cancel{V} = -\frac{0.0592 \cancel{V}}{2} \log x^2 \rightarrow -0.50676 = \log x^2 \rightarrow$$

$$x^2 = 10^{-0.50676} = 0.31135 \rightarrow x = 0.55798 \text{ then pH} = -\log [H^+] = -\log [0.55798] = 0.25338 = 0.3.$$

Check: The units (none) are correct. The pH is acidic, which is consistent with dissolving a metal in acid.

18.110 **Given:** $Pt (s) | H_2 (g, 1\ atm) | H^+ (aq, 1.0\ M) || Au^{3+} (aq, ?\ M) | Au (s)$, $E_{cell} = 1.22$ V **Find:** $[Au^{3+}]$

Conceptual Plan: Write half-reactions from line notation. Look up half-reactions in Table 18.1. Calculate the standard cell potential by subtracting the electrode potential of the anode from the electrode potential of the cathode: $E^\circ_{cell} = E^\circ_{cathode} - E^\circ_{anode}$. Equalize the number of electrons transferred and then add the two half-cell reactions and cancel the electrons.

Then E°_{cell}, E_{cell}, P_{H_2}, $[H^+]$, $n \rightarrow [Au^{3+}]$.

$$E_{cell} = E^\circ_{cell} - \frac{0.0592\ V}{n} \log Q$$

Solution: The half-reactions are: $H_2 (g) \rightarrow 2 H^+(aq) + 2 e^-$ and $Au^{3+} (aq) + 3 e^- \rightarrow Au (s)$. H is oxidized so $E^\circ_{red} = 0.00\ V = E^\circ_{anode}$. Au is reduced so $E^\circ_{red} = 1.50\ V = E^\circ_{cathode}$. Then $E^\circ_{cell} = E^\circ_{cathode} - E^\circ_{anode} = 1.50\ V - 0.00\ V = +1.50\ V$. Equalize the number of electrons transferred by multiplying the first reaction by 3 and the second reaction by 2 so $3 H_2 (g) \rightarrow 6 H^+(aq) + 6 e^-$ and $2 Au^{3+} (aq) + 6 e^- \rightarrow 2 Au (s)$. Adding the two reactions: $3 H_2 (g) + 2 Au^{3+} (aq) + \cancel{6 e^-} \rightarrow 6 H^+ (aq) + \cancel{6 e^-} + 2 Au (s)$. Cancel the electrons: $3 H_2 (g) + 2 Au^{3+} (aq) \rightarrow 6 H^+(aq) + 2 Au (s)$. So $n = 6$ and $Q = \frac{[H^+]^6}{P^3_{H_2}[Au^{3+}]^2} = \frac{(1.0)^6}{(1)^3(x)^2} = x^{-2}$ then $E_{cell} = E^\circ_{cell} - \frac{0.0592\ V}{n} \log Q$ substitute in values and solve for x. $1.22\ V = 1.50\ V - \frac{0.0592\ V}{6} \log x^{-2} \rightarrow$

$0.28 \text{ V} = \frac{0.0592 \text{ V}}{6} \log x^{-2} \rightarrow 28.3784 = \log x^{-2} \rightarrow x^{-2} = 10^{28.3784} = 2.3899 \times 10^{28} \rightarrow$

$x = 6.4686 \times 10^{-15}$ M.

Check: The units (none) are correct. The concentration is expected to be low because the cell potential must be reduced.

18.111 You should be wary of the battery because the most a pairing of half-cell reactions can generate is 5 to 6 V, not 24 V.

18.112 **Given:** lithium oxidizing and fluorine gas reducing **Find:** $E°_{cell}$ and why is the battery hard to produce?
Conceptual Plan: Write two half-cell reactions, taking the elemental forms to cations and anions and adding electrons as needed to balance reactions. Look up half-reactions in Table 18.1. Calculate the standard cell potential by subtracting the electrode potential of the anode from the electrode potential of the cathode: $E°_{cell} = E°_{cathode} - E°_{anode}$.
Solution: Li $(l) \rightarrow$ Li$^+$ (l) + e$^-$ and F_2 (g) + 2 e$^-$ $\rightarrow$ 2 F$^-$ (l). Looking up the reduction potentials, for Li $E°_{anode} = E°_{red} = -3.04$ V and for F_2 $E°_{cathode} = E°_{red} = -2.87$ V. So $E°_{cell} = E°_{cathode} - E°_{anode} = 2.87 \text{ V} - (-3.04 \text{ V}) = 5.92$ V. One of the problems with using this system is getting a high concentration of F_2, since it is a gas and gases have low densities.
Check: The units (V) are correct. The metal is oxidized and the nonmetal is reduced, so we expect a high cell potential.

18.113 **Given:** Mg oxidation and Cu^{2+} reduction; initially $[Mg^{2+}] = 1.0 \times 10^{-4}$ M and $[Cu^{2+}] = 1.5$ M in 1.0 L half-cells
Find: (a) initial E_{cell}; (b) E_{cell} after 5.0 A for 8.0 h; and (c) how long can battery deliver 5.0 A
Conceptual Plan:

(a) **Write the two half-cell reactions and add electrons as needed to balance reactions. Look up half-reactions in Table 18.1. Calculate the standard cell potential by subtracting the electrode potential of the anode from the electrode potential of the cathode: $E°_{cell} = E°_{cathode} - E°_{anode}$. Add the two half-cell reactions, cancel electrons, and determine n. Then $E°_{cell}$, $[Mg^{2+}]$, $[Cu^{2+}]$, $n \rightarrow E_{cell}$.**

$$E_{cell} = E°_{cell} - \frac{0.0592 \text{ V}}{n} \log Q$$

(b) **h $\rightarrow$ min $\rightarrow$ s $\rightarrow$ C $\rightarrow$ mol e$^-$ $\rightarrow$ mol Cu reduced $\rightarrow$ $[Cu^{2+}]$ and**

$$\frac{60 \text{ min}}{1 \text{ h}} \quad \frac{60 \text{ s}}{1 \text{ min}} \quad \frac{5.0 \text{ C}}{1 \text{ s}} \quad \frac{1 \text{ mol e}^-}{96{,}485 \text{ C}} \quad \frac{1 \text{ mol Cu}^{2+}}{2 \text{ mol e}^-} \quad \text{since } V = 1.0\text{L} \quad [Cu^{2+}] = [Cu^{2+}] - \frac{\text{mol Cu}^{2+} \text{ reduced}}{1.0 \text{ L}}$$

mol Cu reduced $\rightarrow$ mol Mg oxidized $\rightarrow$ $[Mg^{2+}]$

$$\frac{1 \text{ mol Mg oxidized}}{1 \text{ mol Cu}^{2+} \text{reduced}} \quad \text{since } V = 1.0\text{L} \quad [Mg^{2+}] = [Mg^{2+}] + \frac{\text{mol Mg oxidized}}{1.0 \text{ L}}$$

(c) **$[Cu^{2+}]$ $\rightarrow$ mol e$^-$ $\rightarrow$ C $\rightarrow$ s $\rightarrow$ min $\rightarrow$ h**

$$\frac{1 \text{ mol e}^-}{2 \text{ mol Cu}^{2+}} \quad \frac{96{,}485 \text{ C}}{1 \text{ mol e}^-} \quad \frac{1 \text{ s}}{5.0 \text{ C}} \quad \frac{1 \text{ min}}{60 \text{ s}} \quad \frac{1 \text{ h}}{60 \text{ min}}$$

Solution:

(a) Write half-reactions and add electrons Cu^{2+} (aq) + 2 e$^-$ $\rightarrow$ Cu (s) and Mg (s) $\rightarrow$ Mg^{2+} (aq) + 2 e$^-$. Look up cell potentials. Mg is oxidized so $E°_{red} = -2.37 \text{ V} = E°_{anode}$. Cu^{2+} is reduced so $E°_{red} = 0.34 \text{ V} = E°_{cathode}$. Then $E°_{cell} = E°_{cathode} - E°_{anode} = 0.34 \text{ V} - (-2.37 \text{ V}) = +2.71$ V. Add the two half-cell reactions: Cu^{2+} (aq) + $\cancel{2 e^-}$ + Mg (s) $\rightarrow$ Cu (s) + Mg^{2+} (aq) + $\cancel{2 e^-}$. Simplify to Cu^{2+} (aq) + Mg (s) $\rightarrow$ Cu (s) + Mg^{2+} (aq). So $Q = \frac{[Mg^{2+}]}{[Cu^{2+}]} = \frac{1.0 \times 10^{-4}}{1.5} = 6.6667 \times 10^{-5}$ and $n = 2$ then

$$E_{cell} = E°_{cell} - \frac{0.0592 \text{ V}}{n} \log Q = 2.71 \text{ V} - \frac{0.0592 \text{ V}}{2} \log 6.6667 \times 10^{-5} = +2.83361 \text{ V} = +2.83 \text{ V}.$$

(b) $$8.0 \cancel{\text{h}} \times \frac{60 \cancel{\text{min}}}{1 \cancel{\text{h}}} \times \frac{60 \cancel{\text{s}}}{1 \cancel{\text{min}}} \times \frac{5.0 \cancel{\text{C}}}{1 \cancel{\text{s}}} \times \frac{1 \cancel{\text{mol e}^-}}{96{,}485 \cancel{\text{C}}} \times \frac{1 \text{ mol Cu}^{2+}}{2 \cancel{\text{mol e}^-}} = 0.74623 \text{ mol Cu}^{2+} \text{ and}$$

$$[Cu^{2+}] = [Cu^{2+}] - \frac{\text{mol Cu}^{2+} \text{ reduced}}{1.0 \text{ L}} = 1.5 \text{ M} - \frac{0.74623 \text{ mol Cu}^{2+}}{1.0 \text{ L}} = 0.75377 \text{ M Cu}^{2+} \text{ and}$$

$$0.74623 \cancel{\text{mol Cu}^{2+}} \times \frac{1 \text{ mol Mg oxidized}}{1 \cancel{\text{mol Cu}^{2+} \text{reduced}}} = 0.74623 \text{ mol Mg oxidized and}$$

$$[Mg^{2+}] = [Mg^{2+}] + \frac{\text{mol Mg oxidized}}{1.0\text{ L}} = 1.0 \times 10^{-4}\text{ M} + \frac{0.74\underline{6}23\text{ mol Mg oxidized}}{1.0\text{ L}}$$

$$= 0.74\underline{6}33\text{ M } Mg^{2+}$$

$$Q = \frac{[Mg^{2+}]}{[Cu^{2+}]} = \frac{0.74\underline{6}33}{0.75\underline{3}77} = 0.99\underline{0}13 \text{ and } n = 2 \text{ then}$$

$$E_{cell} = E^{\circ}_{cell} - \frac{0.0592\text{ V}}{n}\log Q = 2.71\text{ V} - \frac{0.0592\text{ V}}{2}\log 0.99\underline{0}13 = +2.7\underline{1}013\text{ V} = +2.71\text{ V}.$$

(c) In 1.0 L there are initially 1.5 moles of Cu^{2+}. So

$$1.5\ \cancel{\text{mol } Cu^{2+}} \times \frac{2\ \cancel{\text{mol e}^-}}{1\ \cancel{\text{mol } Cu^{2+}}} \times \frac{96{,}485\ \cancel{\text{C}}}{1\ \cancel{\text{mol e}^-}} \times \frac{1\ \cancel{\text{s}}}{5.0\ \cancel{\text{C}}} \times \frac{1\ \cancel{\text{min}}}{60\ \cancel{\text{s}}} \times \frac{1\text{ h}}{60\ \cancel{\text{min}}} = 16\text{ h}$$

Check: The units (V, V, and h) are correct. The Cu^{2+} reduction reaction is above the Mg^{2+} reduction reaction, so the standard cell potential will be positive. Having more reactants than products increases the cell potential. As the reaction proceeds the potential drops. The concentrations drop by $\frac{1}{2}$ in 8 hours (part (b)), so it is all consumed in 16 hours.

18.114 **Given:** Ag/Ag^+ concentration cell; initially $[Ag^+] = 1.25$ M and 1.0×10^{-3} M in 2.0 L half-cells
Find: (a) how long can battery deliver 2.5A; (b) mass of Ag plated after 3.5 A for 5.5 h; and (c) how long can battery deliver 5.0 A to redissolve 1.00×10^2 g Ag with 10.0 A
Conceptual Plan:

(a) **Write the two half-cell reactions and add electrons as needed to balance reactions. Then $[Ag^+]$, V → mol Ag^+ → mol e^- → C → s → min → h**

$$M = \frac{\text{mol } Ag^+}{\text{L}} \qquad \frac{1\text{ mol e}^-}{1\text{ mol } Ag^+} \qquad \frac{96{,}485\text{ C}}{1\text{ mol e}^-} \quad \frac{1\text{ s}}{2.5\text{ C}} \quad \frac{1\text{ min}}{60\text{ s}} \quad \frac{1\text{ h}}{60\text{ min}}$$

(b) **h → min → s → C → mol e^- → mol Ag → g Ag**

$$\frac{60\text{ min}}{1\text{ h}} \quad \frac{60\text{ s}}{1\text{ min}} \quad \frac{3.5\text{ C}}{1\text{ s}} \quad \frac{1\text{ mol e}^-}{96{,}485\text{ C}} \quad \frac{1\text{ mol Ag}}{1\text{ mol e}^-} \quad \frac{107.87\text{ g Ag}}{1\text{ mol Ag}}$$

(c) **g Ag → mol Ag → mol e^- → C → s → min → h**

$$\frac{1\text{ mol Ag}}{107.87\text{ g Ag}} \quad \frac{1\text{ mol e}^-}{1\text{ mol Ag}} \quad \frac{96{,}485\text{ C}}{1\text{ mol e}^-} \quad \frac{1\text{ s}}{10.0\text{ C}} \quad \frac{1\text{ min}}{60\text{ s}} \quad \frac{1\text{ h}}{60\text{ min}}$$

Solution:

(a) Write half-reactions and add electrons $Ag+ (aq) + e^- \rightarrow Ag\ (s)$. $M = \frac{\text{mol } Ag^+}{\text{L}}$ so

$$\text{mol } Ag^+ = M \times L = 1.25 \frac{\text{mol } Ag^+}{\cancel{\text{L}}} \times 2.0\ \cancel{\text{L}} = 2.50\text{ mol } Ag^+ \text{ then}$$

$$2.50\ \cancel{\text{mol } Ag^+} \times \frac{1\ \cancel{\text{mol e}^-}}{1\ \cancel{\text{mol } Ag^+}} \times \frac{96{,}485\ \cancel{\text{C}}}{1\ \cancel{\text{mol e}^-}} \times \frac{1\ \cancel{\text{s}}}{2.5\ \cancel{\text{C}}} \times \frac{1\ \cancel{\text{min}}}{60\ \cancel{\text{s}}} \times \frac{1\text{ h}}{60\ \cancel{\text{min}}} = 27\text{ h.}$$

(b) $$5.5\ \cancel{\text{h}} \times \frac{60\ \cancel{\text{min}}}{1\ \cancel{\text{h}}} \times \frac{60\ \cancel{\text{s}}}{1\ \cancel{\text{min}}} \times \frac{3.5\ \cancel{\text{C}}}{1\ \cancel{\text{s}}} \times \frac{1\ \cancel{\text{mol e}^-}}{96{,}485\ \cancel{\text{C}}} \times \frac{1\ \cancel{\text{mol Ag}}}{1\ \cancel{\text{mol e}^-}} \times \frac{107.87\text{ g Ag}}{1\ \cancel{\text{mol Ag}}} = 77\text{ g Ag}$$

(c) $$1.00 \times 10^2\ \cancel{\text{g Ag}} \times \frac{1\ \cancel{\text{mol Ag}}}{107.87\ \cancel{\text{g Ag}}} \times \frac{1\ \cancel{\text{mol e}^-}}{1\ \cancel{\text{mol Ag}}} \times \frac{96{,}485\ \cancel{\text{C}}}{1\ \cancel{\text{mol e}^-}} \times \frac{1\text{ s}}{10.0\ \cancel{\text{C}}} \times \frac{1\ \cancel{\text{min}}}{60\ \cancel{\text{s}}} \times \frac{1\text{ h}}{60\ \cancel{\text{min}}} = 2.48\text{ h}$$

Check: The units (h, g, and h) are correct. Since 2.5 moles need to be plated, we expect it to take a long time. The time is shorter by a factor of ~30 and the current is larger by about 1.5 so we expect less Ag to be plated in part (b) as compared to part (a). We expect a shorter time in part (c) than in part (b) because the current is so much larger. In parts (b) and (c) we are not exhausting the 2.5 moles initially in the half-cell.

18.115 **Given:** water electrolysis at 7.8 A; H_2 (*g*): $V = 25.0$ L, $P = 25.0$ atm; $T = 25$ °C **Find:** time
Conceptual Plan: °C → K then *V*, *P*, *T* → *n* then write half-reactions

$$K = °C + 273.15 \qquad PV = nRT$$

mol H_2 → mol e^- → C → s → min → h

$$\frac{2\text{ mol e}^-}{1\text{ mol } H_2} \quad \frac{96{,}485\text{ C}}{1\text{ mol e}^-} \quad \frac{1\text{ s}}{7.8\text{ C}} \quad \frac{1\text{ min}}{60\text{ s}} \quad \frac{1\text{ h}}{60\text{ min}}$$

Solution: $T = 25\,°C + 273.15 = 298\,K$, then $PV = nRT$ Rearrange to solve for n.

$$n = \frac{PV}{RT} = \frac{25.0\;\text{atm} \times 25.0\;\text{L}}{0.08206\;\dfrac{\text{L} \cdot \text{atm}}{\text{mol} \cdot \text{K}} \times 298\;\text{K}} = 25.\underline{5}583\;\text{mol}\;H_2.$$ The hydrolysis of water reactions are:

$2\,H_2O\,(l) \rightarrow O_2\,(g) + 4\,H^+\,(aq) + 4\,e^-$ and $2\,H_2O\,(l) + 2\,e^- \rightarrow H_2\,(g) + OH^-\,(aq)$.

$25.5583\;\text{mol}\;H_2 \times \dfrac{2\;\text{mol}\;e^-}{1\;\text{mol}\;H_2} \times \dfrac{96{,}485\;\text{C}}{1\;\text{mol}\;e^-} \times \dfrac{1\;\text{s}}{7.8\;\text{C}} \times \dfrac{1\;\text{min}}{60\;\text{s}} \times \dfrac{1\;\text{h}}{60\;\text{min}} = 176\;\text{h}.$

Check: The units (h) are correct. Since we have 25 L of gas at 25 atm and 25 °C we expect ~25 moles of gas (remember 1 mole of gas at STP = 22.4 L). A very long time is expected since we have so many moles of gas to generate.

18.116 **Given:** A fuel-cell breathalyzer test; 188 mL yields 324 mA for 10 s; $P = 1.0\,atm$, $T = 25\,°C$
Find: percent by volume ethanol in breath
Conceptual Plan: Write the reaction and determine n, and mA $\rightarrow$ A then

$$\frac{1\;\text{A}}{1000\;\text{mA}}$$

$\mathbf{s \rightarrow C \rightarrow mol\;e^- \rightarrow mol\;CH_3CH_2OH}$ and $\mathbf{°C \rightarrow K}$ and $\mathbf{mL \rightarrow L}$ then $\mathbf{V, n, T \rightarrow P_{CH_3CH_2OH}}$

$\dfrac{0.324\;\text{C}}{1\;\text{s}}\;\dfrac{1\;\text{mol}\;e^-}{96{,}485\;\text{C}}\;\dfrac{1\;\text{mol}\;CH_3CH_2OH}{4\;\text{mol}\;e^-}\qquad\qquad K = °C + 273.15 \qquad \dfrac{1\;\text{L}}{1000\;\text{mL}} \qquad\quad PV = nRT$

then $P_{CH_3CH_2OH}$, P_{Total}, $\rightarrow$ percent by volume CH_3CH_2OH.

$$\text{percent by volume}\;CH_3CH_2OH = \frac{P_{CH_3CH_2OH}}{P_{Total}} \times 100\%$$

Solution: $CH_3CH_2OH\,(g) + O_2\,(g) \rightarrow HC_2H_3O_2\,(g) + H_2O\,(g)$ since 2 O atoms are going from 0 to

-2 so $n = 4$ and $324\;\text{mA} \times \dfrac{1\;\text{A}}{1000\;\text{mA}} = 0.324\;\text{A}$ then

$10\;\text{s} \times \dfrac{0.324\;\text{C}}{1\;\text{s}} \times \dfrac{1\;\text{mol}\;e^-}{96{,}485\;\text{C}} \times \dfrac{1\;\text{mol}\;CH_3CH_2OH}{4\;\text{mol}\;e^-} = 8.\underline{3}951 \times 10^{-6}\;\text{mol}\;CH_3CH_2OH$ and

$T = 25\,°C + 273.15 = 298\,K$, and $188\;\text{mL} \times \dfrac{1\;\text{L}}{1000\;\text{mL}} = 0.188\;\text{L}$ then $PV = nRT$. Rearrange to solve for P.

$$P = \frac{nRT}{V} = \frac{8.\underline{3}951 \times 10^{-6}\;\text{mol} \times 0.08206\;\dfrac{\text{L} \cdot \text{atm}}{\text{mol} \cdot \text{K}} \times 298\;\text{K}}{0.188\;\text{L}} = 1.\underline{0}9198 \times 10^{-3}\;\text{atm}\;CH_3CH_2OH$$ then

$$\text{percent by volume}\;CH_3CH_2OH = \frac{P_{CH_3CH_2OH}}{P_{Total}} \times 100\% = \frac{1.\underline{0}9198 \times 10^{-3}\;\text{atm}}{1.0\;\text{atm}} \times 100\%$$

$= 0.\underline{1}09198\% = 0.1\%$.
Check: The units (%) are correct. Since the volume and current are so low we expect a small percent by volume. This number is typical for a failing blood alcohol test.

18.117 **Given:** $Cu\,(s)\,|\,CuI\,(s)\,|\,I^-\,(aq,\,1.0\,M)\,||\,Cu^+\,(aq,\,1.0\,M)\,|\,Cu\,(s)$, $K_{sp}\,(CuI) = 1.1 \times 10^{-12}$ **Find:** E_{cell}
Conceptual Plan: Write half-reactions from line notation. Since this is a concentration cell $E°_{cell} = 0.00\,V$.
Then K_{sp}, $[I^-] \rightarrow [Cu^+](ox)$ then $E°_{cell}$, $[Cu^+](ox)$, $[Cu^+](red)$, $n \rightarrow E_{cell}$.

$K_{sp} = [Cu^+]\,[I^-]$ $\qquad\qquad\qquad\qquad\qquad E_{cell} = E°_{cell} - \dfrac{0.0592\;V}{n}\log Q$

Solution: The half-reactions are: $Cu\,(s) \rightarrow Cu^+(aq) + e^-$ and $Cu^+\,(aq) + e^- \rightarrow Cu\,(s)$. Since this is a concentration cell $E°_{cell} = 0.00\,V$ and $n = 1$. Since $K_{sp} = [Cu^+]\,[I^-]$, rearrange to solve for $[Cu^+](ox)$.

$[Cu^+]\,(ox) = \dfrac{K_{sp}}{[I^-]} = \dfrac{1.1 \times 10^{-12}}{1.0} = 1.1 \times 10^{-12}\;M$ then

$Q = \dfrac{[Cu^+](ox)}{[Cu^+](red)} = \dfrac{1.1 \times 10^{-12}}{1.0} = 1.1 \times 10^{-12}$ then

$E_{cell} = E°_{cell} - \dfrac{0.0592\;V}{n}\log Q = 0.00\,V - \dfrac{0.0592\;V}{1}\log\,(1.1 \times 10^{-12}) = 0.71\,V.$
Check: The units (V) are correct. Since $[Cu^+](ox)$ is so low and $[Cu^+](red)$ is high, the Q is very small so the voltage increase compared to the standard value is significant.

18.118 **Given:** $Zn(OH)_2\ (s) + 2\ e^- \rightarrow Zn\ (s) + 2\ OH^-\ (aq)$, $K_{sp}\ (Zn(OH)_2) = 1.8 \times 10^{-14}$ **Find:** E for half-cell
Conceptual Plan: Look up the half-reaction for the Zn reduction (E°_{red}) in Table 18.1, determine n, then $K_{sp} \rightarrow [OH^-]$ then E°_{cell}, $[OH^-]$, $n \rightarrow E_{cell}$.

$K_{sp} = [Zn^{2+}][OH^-]^2$ $\qquad E_{cell} = E^\circ_{cell} - \frac{0.0592\ V}{n} \log Q$

Solution: The reduction half-reaction is: $Zn^{2+}\ (aq) + 2\ e^- \rightarrow Zn\ (s)$ and $E^\circ_{red} = -0.76$ V and $n = 2$. Since $K_{sp} = [Zn^{2+}][OH^-]^2 = S\ (2S)^2 = 4\ S^3$, rearrange to solve for $S = [OH^-]$.

$$S = [OH^-] = \sqrt[3]{\frac{K_{sp}}{4}} = \sqrt[3]{\frac{1.8 \times 10^{-14}}{4}} = 1.\underline{6}5096 \times 10^{-5}\ \text{M then}$$

$$Q = [OH^-]^2 = (1.\underline{6}5096 \times 10^{-5})^2 = 2.\underline{7}257 \times 10^{-10}\ \text{then}$$

$$E_{cell} = E^\circ_{cell} - \frac{0.0592\ V}{n} \log Q = -0.76\ V - \frac{0.0592\ V}{2} \log (2.\underline{7}257 \times 10^{-10}) = -0.48\ V.$$

Check: The units (V) are correct. Since $[OH^-]$ is so low, the Q is very small so the voltage increase is significant, but the half-reaction is nonspontanous.

18.119 **Given:** (a) disproportionation of $Mn^{2+}\ (aq)$ to Mn (s) and $MnO_2\ (s)$; and (b) disproportionation of $MnO_2\ (s)$ to $Mn^{2+}\ (aq)$ and $MnO_4^-\ (s)$ in acidic solution **Find:** ΔG°_{rxn} and K
Conceptual Plan: Separate the overall reaction into two half-reactions: one for oxidation and one for reduction. → Balance each half-reaction with respect to mass in the following order: 1) balance all elements other than H and O, 2) balance O by adding H_2O, and 3) balance H by adding H^+. → Balance each half-reaction with respect to charge by adding electrons. (The sum of the charges on both sides of the equation should be made equal by adding electrons as necessary.) → Make the number of electrons in both half-reactions equal by multiplying one or both half-reactions by a small whole number. → Add the two half-reactions together, canceling electrons and other species as necessary. → Verify that the reaction is balanced both with respect to mass and with respect to charge. Look up half-reactions in Table 18.1. Calculate the standard cell potential by subtracting the electrode potential of the anode from the electrode potential of the cathode: $E^\circ_{cell} = E^\circ_{cathode} - E^\circ_{anode}$.
Then calculate ΔG°_{rxn} using $\Delta G^\circ_{rxn} = -n\ F\ E^\circ_{cell}$. Finally °C → K then ΔG°_{rxn}, $T \rightarrow K$.

$K = 273.15 + °C$ $\qquad \Delta G^\circ_{rxn} = -R\ T \ln K$

Solution:

(a) Separate: $Mn^{2+}\ (aq) \rightarrow MnO_2\ (s)$ and $Mn^{2+}\ (aq) \rightarrow Mn\ (s)$
Balance non H & O elements: $Mn^{2+}\ (aq) \rightarrow MnO_2\ (s)$ and $Mn^{2+}\ (aq) \rightarrow Mn\ (s)$
Balance O with H_2O: $Mn^{2+}\ (aq) + 2\ H_2O\ (l) \rightarrow MnO_2\ (s)$ and $Mn^{2+}\ (aq) \rightarrow Mn\ (s)$
Balance H with H^+: $Mn^{2+}\ (aq) + 2\ H_2O\ (l) \rightarrow MnO_2\ (s) + 4\ H^+\ (aq)$ and $Mn^{2+}\ (aq) \rightarrow Mn\ (s)$
Add electrons: $Mn^{2+}\ (aq) + 2\ H_2O\ (l) \rightarrow MnO_2\ (s) + 4\ H^+\ (aq) + 2\ e^-$ and $Mn^{2+}\ (aq) + 2\ e^- \rightarrow Mn\ (s)$
Equalize electrons: $Mn^{2+}\ (aq) + 2\ H_2O\ (l) \rightarrow MnO_2\ (s) + 4\ H^+\ (aq) + 2\ e^-$ and $Mn^{2+}\ (aq) + 2\ e^- \rightarrow Mn\ (s)$
Add half-reactions: $Mn^{2+}\ (aq) + 2\ H_2O\ (l) + Mn^{2+}\ (aq) + \cancel{2\ e^-} \rightarrow MnO_2\ (s) + 4\ H^+\ (aq) + \cancel{2\ e^-} + Mn\ (s)$
Cancel electrons: $2\ Mn^{2+}\ (aq) + 2\ H_2O\ (l) \rightarrow MnO_2\ (s) + 4\ H^+\ (aq) + Mn\ (s)$
Look up cell potentials. Mn is oxidized in the first half-cell reaction so $E^\circ_{anode} = E^\circ_{red} = +1.21$ V. Mn is reduced in the second half-cell reaction so $E^\circ_{cathode} = E^\circ_{red} = -1.18$ V. Then $E^\circ_{cell} = E^\circ_{cathode} - E^\circ_{anode} = -1.18\ V - 1.21\ V = -2.39$ V. $n = 2$ so

$$\Delta G^\circ_{rxn} = -n\ F\ E^\circ_{cell} = -2\ \cancel{\text{mol e}^-} \times \frac{96{,}485\ C}{\cancel{\text{mol e}^-}} \times -2.39\ V = -2 \times 96{,}485\ \cancel{C} \times -2.39\ \frac{J}{\cancel{C}} =$$

$4.\underline{6}1198 \times 10^5$ J $= 461$ kJ and $T = 273.15 + 25$ °C $= 298$ K then
$\Delta G^\circ_{rxn} = -R\ T \ln K$. Rearrange to solve for K.

$$K = e^{\frac{-\Delta G^\circ_{rxn}}{RT}} = e^{\frac{-4.\underline{6}1198 \times 10^5\ \cancel{J}}{\left(8.314 \frac{\cancel{J}}{\cancel{K} \cdot mol}\right)(298\ \cancel{K})}} = e^{-1\underline{8}6.149} = 1.43 \times 10^{-81}$$

Check:

Reactants	Products
2 Mn atoms	2 Mn atoms
2 O atoms	2 O atoms
4 H atoms	4 H atoms
+4 charge	+4 charge

The units (kJ and none) are correct. If the voltage is negative, the reaction is nonspontaneous and the free energy change is very positive and the equilibrium constant is extremely small.

(b) Separate: $MnO_2\ (s) \rightarrow Mn^{2+}\ (aq)$ and $MnO_2\ (s) \rightarrow MnO_4^-\ (aq)$

Balance non H & O elements: $MnO_2\ (s) \rightarrow Mn^{2+}\ (aq)$ and $MnO_2\ (s) \rightarrow MnO_4^-\ (aq)$

Balance O with H_2O: $MnO_2\ (s) \rightarrow Mn^{2+}\ (aq) + 2\ H_2O\ (l)$ and $MnO_2\ (s) + 2\ H_2O\ (l) \rightarrow MnO_4^-\ (aq)$

Balance H with H^+:

$MnO_2\ (s) + 4\ H^+\ (aq) \rightarrow Mn^{2+}\ (aq) + 2\ H_2O\ (l)$ and $MnO_2\ (s) + 2\ H_2O\ (l) \rightarrow MnO_4^-\ (aq) + 4\ H^+\ (aq)$

Add electrons: $MnO_2\ (s) + 4\ H^+(aq) + 2\ e^- \rightarrow Mn^{2+}\ (aq) + 2\ H_2O\ (l)$ and $MnO_2\ (s) + 2\ H_2O\ (l) \rightarrow MnO_4^-\ (aq) + 4\ H^+\ (aq) + 3e^-$

Equalize electrons: $3\ MnO_2\ (s) + 12\ H^+\ (aq) + 6\ e^- \rightarrow 3\ Mn^{2+}\ (aq) + 6\ H_2O\ (l)$ and $2\ MnO_2\ (s) + 4\ H_2O\ (l) \rightarrow 2\ MnO_4^-\ (aq) + 8\ H^+\ (aq) + 6\ e^-$

Add half-reactions: $3\ MnO_2\ (s) + 4\ \cancel{12\ H^+\ (aq)} + \cancel{6\ e^-} + 2\ MnO_2\ (s) + \cancel{4\ H_2O\ (l)} \rightarrow$
$3\ Mn^{2+}\ (aq) + 2\ \cancel{6}\ H_2O\ (l) + 2\ MnO_4^-\ (aq) + \cancel{8\ H^+\ (aq)} + \cancel{6\ e^-}$

Cancel electrons & species: $5\ MnO_2\ (s) + 4\ H^+\ (aq) \rightarrow 3\ Mn^{2+}\ (aq) + 2\ H_2O\ (l) + 2\ MnO_4^-\ (aq)$

Look up cell potentials. Mn is reduced in the first half-cell reaction so $E^\circ_{cathode} = E^\circ_{red} = 1.21$ V. Mn is oxidized in the second half-cell reaction so $E^\circ_{anode} = E^\circ_{red} = +\ 1.68$ V. Then $E^\circ_{cell} = E^\circ_{cathode} - E^\circ_{anode}$ $= 1.21\ V - 1.68\ V = -\ 0.47$ V. $n = 6$ so

$$\Delta G^\circ_{rxn} = -\ n\ F\ E^\circ_{cell} = -\ 6\ \cancel{mol\ e^-} \times \frac{96{,}485\ C}{\cancel{mol\ e^-}} \times -\ 0.47\ V = -\ 6 \times 96{,}485\ \cancel{C} \times -\ 0.47 \frac{J}{\cancel{C}}$$

$= 2.7\underline{2}09 \times 10^5\ J = 270\ kJ = 2.7 \times 10^2$ kJ. $T = 273.15 + 25\ °C = 298$ K then $\Delta G^\circ_{rxn} = -\ R\ T \ln K$.

Rearrange to solve for K. $K = e^{\frac{-\Delta G^\circ_{rxn}}{RT}} = e^{\frac{-2.7\underline{2}09 \times 10^5\ \cancel{J}}{\left(8.314 \frac{\cancel{J}}{\cancel{K} \cdot mol}\right)(298\ \cancel{K})}} = e^{-10\underline{9}.82} = 2.0 \times 10^{-48}$

Check:

Reactants	Products
5 Mn atoms	5 Mn atoms
10 O atoms	10 O atoms
4 H atoms	4 H atoms
+4 charge	+4 charge

The units (kJ and none) are correct. If the voltage is negative, the reaction is nonspontaneous, the free energy change is very positive, and the equilibrium constant is extremely small. The voltage is less than in part (a) so the free energy change is not as large and the equilibrium constant is not as small.

18.120 **Given:** (a) reaction of $Cr^{2+}\ (aq)$ with $Cr_2O_7^{2-}\ (aq)$ in acidic solution to form $Cr^{3+}\ (aq)$; and (b) reaction of $Cr^{3+}\ (aq)$ with Cr (s) to form $Cr^{2+}\ (aq)$ **Find:** ΔG°_{rxn} and K

Conceptual Plan: Separate the overall reaction into two half-reactions: one for oxidation and one for reduction. → Balance each half-reaction with respect to mass in the following order: 1) balance all elements other than H and O, 2) balance O by adding H_2O, and 3) balance H by adding H^+. → Balance each half-reaction with respect to charge by adding electrons. (The sum of the charges on both sides of the equation should be made equal by adding electrons as necessary.) → Make the number of electrons in both half-reactions equal by multiplying one or both half-reactions by a small whole number. → Add the two half-reactions together, canceling electrons and other species as necessary. → Verify that the reaction is balanced both with respect to mass and with respect to charge. Look up half-reactions in Table 18.1. Calculate the standard cell potential by subtracting the electrode potential of the anode from the electrode potential of the cathode: $E^\circ_{cell} = E^\circ_{cathode} - E^\circ_{anode}$.

Then calculate ΔG°_{rxn} using $\Delta G^\circ_{rxn} = -\ n\ F\ E^\circ_{cell}$. Finally°C → K then ΔG°_{rxn}, T → K.

$K = 273.15 + °C$ $\qquad$ $\Delta G^\circ_{rxn} = -\ R\ T \ln K$

Solution:

(a) Separate: $Cr^{2+}(aq) \rightarrow Cr^{3+}(aq)$ and $Cr_2O_7^{2-}(aq) \rightarrow Cr^{3+}(aq)$
Balance non H & O elements: $Cr^{2+}(aq) \rightarrow Cr^{3+}(aq)$ and $Cr_2O_7^{2-}(aq) \rightarrow 2\,Cr^{3+}(aq)$
Balance O with H_2O: $Cr^{2+}(aq) \rightarrow Cr^{3+}(aq)$ and $Cr_2O_7^{2-}(aq) \rightarrow 2\,Cr^{3+}(aq) + 7\,H_2O\,(l)$
Balance H with H^+: $Cr^{2+}(aq) \rightarrow Cr^{3+}(aq)$ and $Cr_2O_7^{2-}(aq) + 14\,H^+(aq) \rightarrow 2\,Cr^{3+}(aq) + 7\,H_2O\,(l)$
Add electrons: $Cr^{2+}(aq) \rightarrow Cr^{3+}(aq) + e^-$ and $Cr_2O_7^{2-}(aq) + 14\,H^+(aq) + 6\,e^- \rightarrow 2\,Cr^{3+}(aq) + 7\,H_2O\,(l)$
Equalize electrons:
$6\,Cr^{2+}(aq) \rightarrow 6\,Cr^{3+}(aq) + 6\,e^-$ and $Cr_2O_7^{2-}(aq) + 14\,H^+(aq) + 6\,e^- \rightarrow 2\,Cr^{3+}(aq) + 7\,H_2O\,(l)$
Add half-reactions:
$6\,Cr^{2+}(aq) + Cr_2O_7^{2-}(aq) + 14\,H^+(aq) + \cancel{6\,e^-} \rightarrow 6\,Cr^{3+}(aq) + \cancel{6\,e^-} + 2\,Cr^{3+}(aq) + 7\,H_2O\,(l)$
Cancel electrons: $6\,Cr^{2+}(aq) + Cr_2O_7^{2-}(aq) + 14\,H^+(aq) \rightarrow 8\,Cr^{3+}(aq) + 7\,H_2O\,(l)$
Look up cell potentials. Cr is oxidized in the first half-cell reaction so $E^\circ_{red} = -0.50\text{ V} = E^\circ_{anode}$. Cr is reduced in the second half-cell reaction so $E^\circ_{red} = 1.33\text{ V} = E^\circ_{cathode}$. Then $E^\circ_{cell} = E^\circ_{cathode} - E^\circ_{anode} =$
$1.33\text{ V} - (-0.50\text{ V}) = +1.83\text{ V}$. $n = 6$ so $\Delta G^\circ_{rxn} = -n\,F\,E^\circ_{cell} = -6\,\cancel{\text{mol e}^-} \times \frac{96{,}485\text{ C}}{\cancel{\text{mol e}^-}} \times 1.83\text{ V}$

$= -6 \times 96{,}485\,\cancel{\text{C}} \times 1.83\frac{\text{J}}{\cancel{\text{C}}} = -1.0\underline{5}941 \times 10^6\text{ J} = -1.06 \times 10^3\text{ kJ}$ and $T = 273.15 + 25\text{ °C} = 298\text{ K}$ then

$\Delta G^\circ_{rxn} = -R\,T\ln K$. Rearrange to solve for K.

$$K = e^{\frac{-\Delta G^\circ_{rxn}}{RT}} = e^{\frac{-(-1.05941 \times 10^6\,\cancel{\text{J}})}{\left(8.314\frac{\cancel{\text{J}}}{\cancel{\text{K}}\cdot\text{mol}}\right)(298\,\cancel{\text{K}})}} = e^{42\underline{7}.598} = 5.05 \times 10^{185}.$$

Check:

Reactants	Products
8 Cr atoms	8 Cr atoms
7 O atoms	7 O atoms
14 H atoms	14 H atoms
+24 charge	+24 charge

The units (kJ and none) are correct. If the voltage is positive, the reaction is spontaneous, the free energy change is very negative, and the equilibrium constant is extremely large.

(b) Separate: $Cr^{3+}(aq) \rightarrow Cr^{2+}(aq)$ and $Cr\,(s) \rightarrow Cr^{2+}(aq)$
Balance: $Cr^{3+}(aq) \rightarrow Cr^{2+}(aq)$ and $Cr\,(s) \rightarrow Cr^{2+}(aq)$
Add electrons: $Cr^{3+}(aq) + e^- \rightarrow Cr^{2+}(aq)$ and $Cr\,(s) \rightarrow Cr^{2+}(aq) + 2\,e^-$
Equalize electrons: $2\,Cr^{3+}(aq) + 2\,e^- \rightarrow 2\,Cr^{2+}(aq)$ and $Cr\,(s) \rightarrow Cr^{2+}(aq) + 2\,e^-$
Add half-reactions: $2\,Cr^{3+}(aq) + \cancel{2\,e^-} + Cr\,(s) \rightarrow 2\,Cr^{2+}(aq) + Cr^{2+}(aq) + \cancel{2\,e^-}$
Cancel electrons & species: $2\,Cr^{3+}(aq) + Cr\,(s) \rightarrow 3\,Cr^{2+}(aq)$
Look up cell potentials. Cr is reduced in the first half-cell reaction so $E^\circ_{red} = -0.50\text{ V} = E^\circ_{cathode}$. Cr is oxidized in the second half-cell reaction so $E^\circ_{red} = -0.91\text{ V} = E^\circ_{anode}$. Then $E^\circ_{cell} = E^\circ_{cathode} - E^\circ_{anode} =$
$-0.50\text{ V} - (-0.91\text{ V}) = +0.41\text{ V}$. $n = 2$ so $\Delta G^\circ_{rxn} = -n\,F\,E^\circ_{cell} = -2\,\cancel{\text{mol e}^-} \times \frac{96{,}485\text{ C}}{\cancel{\text{mol e}^-}} \times 0.41\text{ V}$

$= -2 \times 96{,}485\,\cancel{\text{C}} \times 0.41\frac{\text{J}}{\cancel{\text{C}}} = -7.\underline{9}118 \times 10^4\text{ J} = -79\text{ kJ}$. $T = 273.15 + 25\text{ °C} = 298\text{ K}$

then $\Delta G^\circ_{rxn} = -R\,T\ln K$. Rearrange to solve for K.

$$K = e^{\frac{-\Delta G^\circ_{rxn}}{RT}} = e^{\frac{-(-7.9118 \times 10^4\,\cancel{\text{J}})}{\left(8.314\frac{\cancel{\text{J}}}{\cancel{\text{K}}\cdot\text{mol}}\right)(298\,\cancel{\text{K}})}} = e^{3\underline{1}.934} = 7.4 \times 10^{13}.$$

Check:

Reactants	Products
3 Cr atoms	3 Cr atoms
+6 charge	+6 charge

The units (kJ and none) are correct. If the voltage is positive, the reaction is spontaneous, the free energy change is negative, and the equilibrium constant is large. The voltage and n are less than in part (a) so the free energy change is not as negative and the equilibrium constant is not as large.

18.121 **Given:** Metal, M, 50.9 g/mol, 1.20 g of metal reduced in 23.6 minutes at 6.42 A from molten chloride
Find: empirical formula of chloride
Conceptual Plan: min → s → C → mol e^- and g M → mol M then mol e^-, mol M → charge → MCl_x

$$\frac{60\ s}{1\ min}\ \frac{6.42\ C}{1\ s}\ \frac{1\ mol\ e^-}{96{,}485\ C}\qquad \frac{1\ mol\ M}{50.9\ g\ M}\qquad \frac{1\ mol\ e^-}{1\ mol\ M}$$

Solution: $23.6\ \cancel{min} \times \frac{60\ \cancel{s}}{1\ \cancel{min}} \times \frac{6.42\ \cancel{C}}{1\ \cancel{s}} \times \frac{1\ mol\ e^-}{96{,}485\ \cancel{C}} = 0.0942190\ mol\ e^-$ and

$1.20\ \cancel{g\ M} \times \frac{1\ mol\ M}{50.9\ \cancel{g\ M}} = 0.0235756\ mol\ M$ then $\frac{0.0942190\ mol\ e^-}{0.02357561\ mol\ M} = 3.99646\ \frac{e^-}{M}$

so the empirical formula is MCl_4.

Check: The units (none) are correct. The result was an integer within the error of the measurements. The formula is typical for a metal salt. It could be vanadium, which has a +4 oxidation state.

18.122 **Given:** molten MF_3 electrolysis, 1.25 g of metal reduced in 16.2 minutes at 3.86 A **Find:** molar mass of metal
Conceptual Plan: min → s → C → mol e^- → mol M then g M, mol M → molar mass

$$\frac{60\ s}{1\ min}\ \frac{6.42\ C}{1\ s}\ \frac{1\ mol\ e^-}{96{,}485\ C}\ \frac{1\ mol\ M}{3\ mol\ e^-}\qquad \mathcal{M} = \frac{g\ M}{mol\ M}$$

Solution: $16.2\ \cancel{min} \times \frac{60\ \cancel{s}}{1\ \cancel{min}} \times \frac{3.86\ \cancel{C}}{1\ \cancel{s}} \times \frac{1\ \cancel{mol\ e^-}}{96{,}485\ \cancel{C}} \times \frac{1\ mol\ M}{3\ \cancel{mol\ e^-}} = 0.0129620\ mol\ M$ then

$\mathcal{M} = \frac{1.25\ g\ M}{0.0129620\ mol\ M} = 96.4\ \frac{g}{mol}$.

Check: The units (g/mol) are correct. The result was a number typical for metals and it could be niobium, which is known to have a +3 oxidation state.

18.123 **Given:** 0.535g impure Sn; dissolve to form Sn^{2+} and titrate with 0.0344 L of 0.0448 M NO_3^- to generate NO
Find: percent by mass Sn
Conceptual Plan: use balanced reaction from Problem 40(c) then
L → mol NO_3^- → mol Sn → g Sn → percent by mass Sn

$$M = \frac{mol}{L}\qquad \frac{3\ mol\ Sn}{2\ mol\ NO_3^-}\qquad \frac{118.71\ g\ Sn}{1\ mol\ Sn}\qquad \text{percent by mass Sn} = \frac{g\ Sn}{g\ sample} \times 100\%$$

Solution: $2\ NO_3^-\ (aq) + 8\ H^+\ (aq) + 3\ Sn^{2+}\ (aq) \rightarrow 2\ NO\ (g) + 4\ H_2O\ (l) + 3\ Sn^{4+}\ (aq)$

$0.0344\ \cancel{L} \times \frac{0.0448\ \cancel{mol\ NO_3^-}}{1\ \cancel{L}} \times \frac{3\ \cancel{mol\ Sn}}{2\ \cancel{mol\ NO_3^-}} \times \frac{118.71\ g\ Sn}{1\ \cancel{mol\ Sn}} = 0.2744195\ g\ Sn$ then

percent by mass Sn $= \frac{g\ Sn}{g\ sample} \times 100\% = \frac{0.2744195\ \cancel{g\ Sn}}{0.535\ \cancel{g\ sample}} \times 100\% = 51.3\%$ by mass Sn.

Check: The units (% by mass) are correct. The result was a number less than 100%.

18.124 **Given:** 0.0251 L Cu^+ solution titrated with 0.0322 L of 0.129 M $KMnO_4$ to generate Cu^{2+} and Mn^{2+}
Find: concentration of Cu solution
Conceptual Plan: Use the balanced reaction from Problem 103, except change metal and stoichiometry by a factor of 2 then L MnO_4^- → mol MnO_4^- → mol Cu^+ → $[Cu^+]$.

$$M = \frac{mol}{L}\qquad \frac{5\ mol\ Cu^+}{2\ mol\ MnO_4^-}\qquad M = \frac{mol}{L}$$

Solution: $MnO_4^-\ (aq) + 8\ H^+\ (aq) + 5\ Cu^+\ (aq) \rightarrow Mn^{2+}\ (aq) + 4\ H_2O\ (l) + 5\ Cu^{2+}\ (aq)$

$0.0322\ \cancel{L\ MnO_4^-} \times \frac{0.129\ \cancel{mol\ MnO_4^-}}{1\ \cancel{L\ MnO_4^-}} \times \frac{5\ mol\ Cu^+}{1\ \cancel{mol\ MnO_4^-}} = 0.020769\ mol\ Cu^+$ then

$[Cu^{2+}] = \frac{0.020769\ mol\ Cu^{2+}}{0.0251\ L} = 0.827\ M\ Cu^{2+}$

Check: The units (M) are correct. The Cu concentration is much higher than the $KMnO_4$ concentration because of the reaction stoichiometry.

18.125 **Given:** 1.25 L of a 0.552 M HBr solution, convert H^+ to $H_2(g)$ for 73 minutes at 11.32 A **Find:** pH
Conceptual Plan: min → s → C → mol e^- → mol H^+ consumed and L, M → mol H^+ initially then

$$\frac{60\ s}{1\ min}\ \frac{11.32\ C}{1\ s}\ \frac{1\ mol\ e^-}{96{,}485\ C}\ \frac{2\ mol\ H^+}{2\ mol\ e^-}\qquad M = \frac{mol}{L}$$

mol H+ initially, mol H^+ consumed → mol H^+ remaining then mol H^+ remaining, L → $[H^+]$ → pH

$$\text{mol } H^+ \text{ initially} - \text{mol } H^+ \text{ consumed} = \text{mol } H^+ \text{ remaining}\qquad M = \frac{mol}{L}\qquad pH = -\log[H^+]$$

Solution: $2\ H^+\ (aq) + 2\ e^- \rightarrow H_2\ (g)$

$$73\ \text{min} \times \frac{60\ \text{s}}{1\ \text{min}} \times \frac{11.32\ \text{C}}{1\ \text{s}} \times \frac{1\ \text{mol e}^-}{96{,}485\ \text{C}} \times \frac{2\ \text{mol H}^+}{2\ \text{mol e}^-} = 0.51\underline{3}879\ \text{mol H}^+ \text{ consumed and}$$

$$1.25\ \text{L H}^+ \times \frac{0.552\ \text{mol H}^+}{1\ \text{L H}^+} = 0.690\ \text{mol H}^+ \text{ initially then mol H}^+ \text{ initially} - \text{mol H}^+ \text{ consumed} =$$

mol H^+ remaining = 0.690 mol H^+ initially − 0.51$\underline{3}$879 mol H^+ consumed = 0.1$\underline{7}$612 mol H^+ remaining

$$\text{then } [H^+] = \frac{0.1\underline{7}612\ \text{mol H}^+}{1.25\ \text{L}} = 0.1\underline{4}0897\ \text{M H}^+ \text{ then pH} = -\log [H^+] = = -\log 0.1\underline{4}0897 = 0.85.$$

Check: The units (none) are correct. The result is a pH higher than the initial pH (− log (0.552) = 0.258), as is expected.

18.126 **Given:** 215 mL of a 0.500 M NaCl solution, initially at pH = 7.00; after 15 minutes a 10.0 mL aliquot is titrated with 22.8 mL 0.100 M HCl **Find:** current (A)

Conceptual Plan: titration is neutralizing base generated in the hydrolysis so
mL HCl, mL HCl, mL aliquot → mol OH⁻ in aliquot → mol OH⁻ in solution then min → s then

$M_{Acid}V_{Acid} = M_{Base}V_{Base}$ $M_1V_1 = M_2V_2$ $\frac{60\ \text{s}}{1\ \text{min}}$

mol OH⁻ in solution, s → mol e⁻/s → C/s

$\frac{2\ \text{mol e}^-}{2\ \text{mol OH}^-}$ $\frac{96{,}485\ \text{C}}{1\ \text{mol e}^-}$

Solution: $2\ NaCl\ (aq) + 2\ H_2O\ (l) \rightarrow H_2\ (g) + Cl_2\ (g) + 2\ Na^+\ (aq) + 2\ OH^-\ (aq)$

$M_{Acid}V_{Acid} = M_{Base}V_{Base}$ so

$$22.8\ \text{mL HCl} \times \frac{0.100\ \text{mol HCl}}{1000\ \text{mL HCl}} \times \frac{1\ \text{mol OH}^-}{1\ \text{mol HCl}} = 0.00228\ \text{mol OH}^-$$

$$0.00228\ \text{mol OH}^- \text{ in aliquot} \times \frac{215\ \text{mL}}{10.0\ \text{mL}} = 0.049\underline{0}2\ \text{mol OH}^- \text{ in solution}$$

$$\frac{0.049\underline{0}2\ \text{mol OH}^- \text{ in solution}}{15\ \text{min}} \times \frac{1\ \text{min}}{60\ \text{s}} \times \frac{2\ \text{mol e}^-}{2\ \text{mol OH}^-} \times \frac{96{,}485\ \text{C}}{1\ \text{mol e}^-} = 5.\underline{2}552\ \frac{\text{C}}{\text{s}} = 5.3\ \text{A}$$

Check: The units (A) are correct. The current is reasonable for an electrolysis process.

18.127 **Given:** MnO_2/Mn^{2+} electrode at pH 10.24 **Find:** $[Mn^{2+}]$ to get half-cell potential = 0.00 V

Conceptual Plan: pH → [H⁺] then

$pH = -\log [H^+]$

Write half-cell reactions and look up half-reactions in Table 18.1. Define *Q* based on half-cell reaction. Then $E^\circ_{half\text{-}cell}$, *n*, [H⁺] → [Mn²⁺].

$$E_{half\text{-}cell} = E^\circ_{half\text{-}cell} - \frac{0.0592\ V}{n} \log Q$$

Solution: Since pH = − log [H⁺] so $[H^+] = 10^{-pH} = 10^{-10.24} = 5.\underline{7}5440 \times 10^{-11}$ M

$$MnO_2\ (s) + 4\ H^+(aq) + 2\ e^- \rightarrow Mn^{2+}\ (aq) + 2\ H_2O\ (l)\ E^\circ_{half\text{-}cell} = 1.21\ V,\ n = 2, \text{ and } Q = \frac{[Mn^{2+}]}{[H^+]^4}.$$

$$E_{half\text{-}cell} = E^\circ_{half\text{-}cell} - \frac{0.0592\ V}{n} \log Q \text{ so } 0.00\ V = 1.21\ V - \frac{0.0592\ V}{2} \log \frac{[Mn^{2+}]}{(5.\underline{7}5440 \times 10^{-11})^4} \rightarrow$$

$$1.21\ V = \frac{0.0592\ V}{2} \log \frac{[Mn^{2+}]}{(5.\underline{7}5440 \times 10^{-11})^4} \rightarrow 40.8\underline{7}84 = \log \frac{[Mn^{2+}]}{(5.\underline{7}5440 \times 10^{-11})^4} \rightarrow$$

$$\frac{[Mn^{2+}]}{(5.\underline{7}5440 \times 10^{-11})^4} = 10^{40.8\underline{7}84} = 7.\underline{5}5750 \times 10^{40} \rightarrow [Mn^{2+}] = 0.8\underline{2}8664\ M = 0.83\ M\ Mn^{2+}$$

Check: The units (M) are correct. The standard half-cell potential is very large and positive. Most of the shift towards 0.00 V is due to the fourth-order dependence in [H⁺] at a high pH, so the [Mn²⁺] is close to 1 M. So the concentration is reasonable.

18.128 **Given:** SHE **Find:** pH to get half-cell potential = − 0.122 V

Conceptual Plan: Write the half-cell reaction. The standard half-cell potential is 0.00 V. Define *Q* based on half-cell reaction. Then $E^\circ_{half\text{-}cell}$, *n* → [H⁺] → pH.

$$E_{half\text{-}cell} = E^\circ_{half\text{-}cell} - \frac{0.0592\ V}{n} \log Q \qquad pH = -\log [H^+]$$

Solution: $2\ H^+\ (aq) + 2\ e^- \rightarrow H_2\ (g)$ $E^\circ_{\text{half-cell}} = 0.00$ V, $n = 2$, and $Q = \frac{1}{[H^+]^2}$.

$E_{\text{half-cell}} = E^\circ_{\text{half-cell}} - \frac{0.0592\ \text{V}}{n} \log Q$ so $-0.122\ \text{V} = 0.00\ \text{V} - \frac{0.0592\ \text{V}}{2} \log [H^+]^{-2} \rightarrow$
$4.12162 = \log [H^+]^{-2} \rightarrow [H^+]^{-2} = 10^{4.12162} = 1.32319 \times 10^4 \rightarrow [H^+] = 0.00869339$ M
Since pH = – log [H⁺] = = – log (0.00869339) = 2.06081 = 2.06.
Check: The units (none) are correct. There is an inverse second-order dependence in $[H^+]$ and so we expect an acidic pH.

Challenge Problems

18.129 **Given:** hydrogen–oxygen fuel cell; 1.2×10^3 kWh of electricity/month **Find:** V of $H_2\ (g)$ at STP/month
Conceptual Plan: Write half-reactions. Look up half-reactions at pH 7. The reaction on the left is the oxidation. Calculate the standard cell potential by subtracting the electrode potential of the anode from the electrode potential of the cathode: $E^\circ_{\text{cell}} = E^\circ_{\text{cathode}} - E^\circ_{\text{anode}}$. Add the two half-cell reactions and cancel the electrons. Then kWh → J → C → mol e⁻ → mol H_2 → V.

$$\frac{3.60 \times 10^6\ \text{J}}{1\ \text{kWh}} \quad \frac{1\ \text{C}}{0.41\ \text{J}} \quad \frac{1\ \text{mol e}^-}{96{,}485\ \text{C}} \quad \frac{2\ \text{mol H}_2}{4\ \text{mol e}^-} \quad \text{at STP}\ \frac{22.414\ \text{L}}{1\ \text{mol H}_2}$$

Solution: $2\ H_2\ (g) + 4\ OH^-\ (aq) \rightarrow 4\ H_2O\ (l) + 4\ e^-$ where $E^\circ_{\text{red}} = -0.83\ \text{V} = E^\circ_{\text{anode}}$; and $O_2\ (g) + 2\ H_2O\ (l) + 4\ e^- \rightarrow 4\ OH^-\ (aq)$ where $E^\circ_{\text{red}} = 0.40\ \text{V} = E^\circ_{\text{cathode}}$. $E^\circ_{\text{cell}} = E^\circ_{\text{cathode}} - E^\circ_{\text{anode}} = 0.40\ \text{V} - (-0.83\ \text{V}) = 1.23\ \text{V}$ = 1.23 J/C and $n = 4$. Net reaction is: $2\ H_2\ (g) + O_2\ (g) \rightarrow 2\ H_2O\ (l)$. Then

$$1.2 \times 10^3\ \text{kWh} \times \frac{3.60 \times 10^6\ \text{J}}{1\ \text{kWh}} \times \frac{1\ \text{C}}{1.23\ \text{J}} \times \frac{1\ \text{mol e}^-}{96{,}485\ \text{C}} \times \frac{2\ \text{mol H}_2}{4\ \text{mol e}^-} \times \frac{22.414\ \text{L}}{1\ \text{mol H}_2} = 4.1 \times 10^5\ \text{L}.$$

Check: The units (L) are correct. A large volume is expected since we are trying to generate a large amount of electricity.

18.130 **Given:** voltaic cell to measure $[Cu^{2+}]$; SHE electrode paired with Cu^{2+}/Cu cell
Find: parameters to plot for a calibrations curve and what is the slope of the curve
Conceptual Plan: Write the two half-cell reactions and add electrons as needed to balance reactions. Look up half-reactions in Table 18.1. Calculate the standard cell potential by subtracting the electrode potential of the anode from the electrode potential of the cathode: $E^\circ_{\text{cell}} = E^\circ_{\text{cathode}} - E^\circ_{\text{anode}}$. Add the two half-cell reactions and cancel electrons and determine n. Then E°_{cell}, P_{H_2}, $[H^+]$, $[Cu^{2+}]$, n → E_{cell}.

$$E_{\text{cell}} = E^\circ_{\text{cell}} - \frac{0.0592\ V}{n} \log Q$$

Solution: Write half-reactions and add electrons $H_2\ (g) \rightarrow 2\ H^+\ (aq) + 2\ e^-$ and $Cu^{2+}\ (aq) + 2\ e^- \rightarrow Cu\ (s)$. Look up cell potentials. H is oxidized so $E^\circ_{\text{red}} = 0.00\ \text{V} = E^\circ_{\text{anode}}$. Cu^{2+} is reduced so $E^\circ_{\text{red}} = 0.34\ \text{V} = E^\circ_{\text{cathode}}$. Then $E^\circ_{\text{cell}} = E^\circ_{\text{cathode}} - E^\circ_{\text{anode}} = 0.34\ \text{V} - 0.00\ \text{V} = +0.34$ V. Add the two half-cell reactions: $H_2\ (g) + Cu^{2+}\ (aq) + 2e^- \rightarrow 2\ H^+\ (aq) + 2e^- + Cu\ (s)$. Simplify to $H_2\ (g) + Cu^{2+}\ (aq) \rightarrow 2\ H^+\ (aq) + Cu\ (s)$. So $Q = \frac{[H^+]^2}{P_{H_2}[Cu^{2+}]}$ and $n = 2$ then $E_{\text{cell}} = E^\circ_{\text{cell}} - \frac{0.0592\ \text{V}}{n} \log Q = 0.34\ \text{V} - \frac{0.0592\ \text{V}}{2} \log \frac{[H^+]^2}{P_{H_2}[Cu^{2+}]}$. If the anode half-cell is buffered at a constant pH and a constant P_{H_2} is used then two of the terms in Q are constant and can be pulled out of the expression so that

$$E_{\text{cell}} = 0.34\ \text{V} - \frac{0.0592\ \text{V}}{2}\left(\log \frac{[H^+]^2}{P_{H_2}} - \log [Cu^{2+}]\right)$$

$$= \left(0.34\ \text{V} - \frac{0.0592\ \text{V}}{2} \log \frac{[H^+]^2}{P_{H_2}}\right) + (0.0296\ \text{V}) \log [Cu^{2+}].$$

If we plot $\log [Cu^{2+}]$ versus E°_{cell}, the slope will be 0.0296 V. Note: the value of the both the slope and the y-intercept are needed to calculated the copper concentration.

18.131 **Given:** Au^{3+}/Au electroplating; surface area = 49.8 cm², Au thickness = 1.00×10^{-3} cm, density = 19.3 g/cm³; at 3.25 A **Find:** time
Conceptual Plan: Write the half-cell reaction and add electrons as needed to balance reactions. Then surface area, thickness → V → g Au → mol Au → mol e⁻ → C → s.

$$V = \textit{surface area} \times \textit{thickness} \quad \frac{19.3\ \text{g Au}}{1\ \text{cm}^3\ \text{Au}} \quad \frac{1\ \text{mol Au}}{196.97\ \text{g Au}} \quad \frac{3\ \text{mol e}^-}{1\ \text{mol Au}} \quad \frac{96{,}485\ \text{C}}{1\ \text{mol e}^-} \quad \frac{1\ \text{s}}{3.25\ \text{C}}$$

Solution: Write the half-reaction and add electrons Au^{3+} *(aq)* + 3 e^- $\rightarrow$ Au *(s)*.

V = *surface area* x *thickness* = $(49.8\ cm^2)(1.00 \times 10^{-3}\ cm) = 0.0498\ cm^3$ then

$$0.0498\ \cancel{cm^3\ Au} \times \frac{19.3\ \cancel{g\ Au}}{1\ \cancel{cm^3\ Au}} \times \frac{1\ \cancel{mol\ Au}}{196.97\ \cancel{g\ Au}} \times \frac{3\ \cancel{mol\ e^-}}{1\ \cancel{mol\ Au}} \times \frac{96{,}485\ \cancel{C}}{1\ \cancel{mol\ e^-}} \times \frac{1\ s}{3.25\ \cancel{C}} = 435\ s.$$

Check: The units (*s*) are correct. Since the layer is so thin there is far less than a mole of gold, so the time is not very long. In order to be an economical process, it must be fairly quick.

18.132 **Given:** electrodeposit mixture Cu and Cd with 1.20 F (1 F = 1 mol e^-); total mass = 50.36 g
Find: mass of $CuSO_4$

Conceptual Plan: Write the half-cell reaction and add electrons as needed to balance reactions. Then F $\rightarrow$ mol e^- $\rightarrow$ mol (Cu + Cd) then let x = g Cu so that (50.36 g − x g) = g Cd then g Cu $\rightarrow$ mol Cu

$\frac{1\ mol\ e^-}{1\ F}$ $\quad \frac{1\ mol\ (Cu + Cd)}{2\ mol\ e^-}$ $\quad \frac{1\ mol\ Cu}{63.55\ g\ Cu}$

and g Cd $\rightarrow$ mol Cd then solve for x = g Cu $\rightarrow$ g $CuSO_4$.

$\frac{1\ mol\ Cd}{112.41\ g\ Cd}$ $\quad \frac{159.62\ g\ CuSO_4}{63.55\ g\ Cu}$

Solution: Cu^{2+} *(aq)* + 2 e^- $\rightarrow$ Cu *(s)* and Cd^{2+} *(aq)* + 2 e^- $\rightarrow$ Cd *(s)*, so n = 2 for both metals.

$$1.20\ \cancel{F} \times \frac{1\ \cancel{mol\ e^-}}{1\ \cancel{F}} \times \frac{1\ mol\ (Cu + Cd)}{2\ \cancel{mol\ e^-}} = 0.600\ mol\ (Cu + Cd)$$ then let x = g Cu so that (50.36 g − x g) = g Cd

then $x\ \cancel{g\ Cu} \times \frac{1\ mol\ Cu}{63.55\ \cancel{g\ Cu}} = \frac{x}{63.55}$ mol Cu and $(50.36 - x)\ \cancel{g\ Cd} \times \frac{1\ mol\ Cd}{112.41\ \cancel{g\ Cd}} = \frac{(50.36 - x)}{112.41}$ mol Cd

then 0.600 mol (Cu + Cd) = $\frac{x}{63.55}$ mol Cu + $\frac{(50.36 - x)}{112.41}$ mol Cd. Solve for x.

$0.600 = 0.01573564\ x + 0.4480028 - 0.008896006\ x \rightarrow x = 22.\underline{2}2300\ g\ Cu \rightarrow$

$$22.\underline{2}2300\ \cancel{g\ Cu} \times \frac{159.62\ g\ CuSO_4}{63.55\ \cancel{g\ Cu}} = 55.8\ g\ CuSO_4.$$

Check: The units (*g*) are correct. The result is reasonable since 0.600 mol Cu = 38.1 g and 0.600 mol Cd = 67.4 g and the amount deposited is in between the two values.

18.133 **Given:** $C_2O_4^{2-} \rightarrow CO_2$ and MnO_4^- *(aq)* $\rightarrow$ Mn^{2+} *(aq)*; 50.1 mL of MnO_4^- to titrate 0.339 g $Na_2C_2O_4$; and 4.62 g U sample titrated by 32.3 mL MnO_4^-; and $UO^{2+} \rightarrow UO_2^{2+}$ **Find:** percent U in sample

Conceptual Plan: Separate the overall reaction into two half-reactions: one for oxidation and one for reduction. $\rightarrow$ Balance each half-reaction with respect to mass in the following order: 1) balance all elements other than H and O, 2) balance O by adding H_2O, and 3) balance H by adding H^+. $\rightarrow$ Balance each half-reaction with respect to charge by adding electrons. (The sum of the charges on both sides of the equation should be made equal by adding electrons as necessary.) $\rightarrow$ Make the number of electrons in both half-reactions equal by multiplying one or both half-reactions by a small whole number. $\rightarrow$ Add the two half-reactions together, canceling electrons and other species as necessary. $\rightarrow$ Verify that the reaction is balanced both with respect to mass and with respect to charge. Then mL MnO_4^- $\rightarrow$ LMnO_4^- and g $Na_2C_2O_4$ $\rightarrow$ mol $Na_2C_2O_4$ $\rightarrow$ mol MnO_4^- then

$\frac{1\ L\ MnO_4^-}{1000\ mL\ MnO_4^-}$ $\quad \frac{1\ mol\ Na_2C_2O_4}{134.00\ g\ Na_2C_2O_4}$ $\quad \frac{2\ mol\ MnO_4^-}{5\ mol\ Zn}$ $\quad \frac{1\ L\ MnO_4^-}{0.500\ mol\ MnO_4^-}$

L MnO_4^-, mol MnO_4^- $\rightarrow$ M MnO_4^- then write U half-reactions and balance as above. $\rightarrow$

$$M = \frac{mol\ MnO_4^-}{L}$$

Make the number of electrons in both half-reactions equal by multiplying one or both half-reactions by a small whole number. $\rightarrow$ Add the two half-reactions together, canceling electrons and other species as necessary. $\rightarrow$ Verify that the reaction is balanced both with respect to mass and with respect to charge. Then mL MnO_4^-, M MnO_4^- $\rightarrow$ mol MnO_4^- $\rightarrow$ mol U $\rightarrow$ g U then g U, g sample $\rightarrow$ % U.

$M = \frac{mol\ MnO_4^-}{L}$ $\quad \frac{5\ mol\ U}{2\ mol\ MnO_4^-}$ $\quad \frac{238.03\ g\ U}{1\ mol\ U}$ $\quad$ percent U = $\frac{g\ U}{g\ sample} \times 100\%$

Solution:

Separate: MnO_4^- *(aq)* $\rightarrow$ Mn^{2+} *(aq)* and $C_2O_4^{2-}$ *(aq)* $\rightarrow$ CO_2 *(g)*
Balance non H & O elements: MnO_4^- *(aq)* $\rightarrow$ Mn^{2+} *(aq)* and $C_2O_4^{2-}$ *(aq)* $\rightarrow$ 2 CO_2 *(g)*
Balance O with H_2O: MnO_4^- *(aq)* $\rightarrow$ Mn^{2+} *(aq)* + 4 H_2O *(l)* and $C_2O_4^{2-}$ *(aq)* $\rightarrow$ 2 CO_2 *(g)*
Balance H with H^+: MnO_4^- *(aq)* + 8 H^+ *(aq)* $\rightarrow$ Mn^{2+} *(aq)* + 4 H_2O *(l)* and $C_2O_4^{2-}$ *(aq)* $\rightarrow$ 2 CO_2 *(g)*

Add electrons: $MnO_4^-\ (aq) + 8\ H^+\ (aq) + 5\ e^- \rightarrow Mn^{2+}\ (aq) + 4\ H_2O\ (l)$ and $C_2O_4^{2-}\ (aq) \rightarrow 2\ CO_2\ (g) + 2\ e^-$
Equalize electrons:
$2\ MnO_4^-\ (aq) + 16\ H^+\ (aq) + 10\ e^- \rightarrow 2\ Mn^{2+}\ (aq) + 8\ H_2O\ (l)$ and $5\ C_2O_4^{2-}\ (aq) \rightarrow 10\ CO_2\ (g) + 10\ e^-$
Add half-reactions:
$2\ MnO_4^-\ (aq) + 16\ H^+\ (aq) + \cancel{10\ e^-} + 5\ C_2O_4^{2-}\ (aq) \rightarrow 2\ Mn^{2+}\ (aq) + 8\ H_2O\ (l) + 10\ CO_2\ (g) + \cancel{10\ e^-}$
Cancel electrons: $2\ MnO_4^-\ (aq) + 16\ H^+\ (aq) + 5\ C_2O_4^{2-}\ (aq) \rightarrow 2\ Mn^{2+}\ (aq) + 8\ H_2O\ (l) + 10\ CO_2\ (g)$

then $50.1\ \cancel{\text{ml } MnO_4^-} \times \dfrac{1\text{L } MnO_4^-}{1000\ \cancel{\text{mL } MnO_4^-}} = 0.0501\ \text{L } MnO_4^-$

$$0.399\ \cancel{\text{g } Na_2C_2O_4} \times \frac{1\ \cancel{\text{mol } Na_2C_2O_4}}{134.00\ \cancel{\text{g } Na_2C_2O_4}} \times \frac{2\ \text{mol } MnO_4^-}{5\ \cancel{\text{mol } Na_2C_2O_4}} = 0.0011\underline{9}10448\ \text{mol } MnO_4^-$$

$$M = \frac{0.0011\underline{9}10448\ \text{mol } MnO_4^-}{0.0501\ \text{L}} = 0.023\underline{7}73345\ \text{M } MnO_4^-$$

Separate: $MnO_4^-\ (aq) \rightarrow Mn^{2+}\ (aq)$ and $UO^{2+}\ (aq) \rightarrow UO_2^{2+}\ (aq)$
Balance non H & O elements: $MnO_4^-\ (aq) \rightarrow Mn^{2+}\ (aq)$ and $UO^{2+}\ (aq) \rightarrow UO_2^{2+}\ (aq)$
Balance O with H_2O: $MnO_4^-\ (aq) \rightarrow Mn^{2+}\ (aq) + 4\ H_2O\ (l)$ and $UO^{2+}\ (aq) + H_2O\ (l) \rightarrow UO_2^{2+}\ (aq)$
Balance H with H^+:
$MnO_4^-\ (aq) + 8\ H^+\ (aq) \rightarrow Mn^{2+}\ (aq) + 4\ H_2O\ (l)$ and $UO^{2+}\ (aq) + H_2O\ (l) \rightarrow UO_2^{2+}\ (aq) + 2\ H^+\ (aq)$
Add electrons: $MnO_4^-\ (aq) + 8\ H^+\ (aq) + 5\ e^- \rightarrow Mn^{2+}\ (aq) + 4\ H_2O\ (l)$ and
$UO^{2+}\ (aq) + H_2O\ (l) \rightarrow UO_2^{2+}\ (aq) + 2\ H^+\ (aq) + 2\ e^-$
Equalize electrons: $2\ MnO_4^-\ (aq) + 16\ H^+\ (aq) + 10\ e^- \rightarrow 2\ Mn^{2+}\ (aq) + 8\ H_2O\ (l)$ and
$5\ UO^{2+}\ (aq) + 5\ H_2O\ (l) \rightarrow 5\ UO_2^{2+}\ (aq) + 10\ H^+\ (aq) + 10\ e^-$
Add half-reactions: $2\ MnO_4^-\ (aq) + 6\ \cancel{16}\ H^+(aq) + \cancel{10\ e^-} + 5\ UO^{2+}\ (aq) + \cancel{5\ H_2O\ (l)} \rightarrow$
$2\ Mn^{2+}\ (aq) + 3\ \cancel{8}\ H_2O\ (l) + 5\ UO_2^{2+}\ (aq) + \cancel{10\ H^+ (aq)} + \cancel{10\ e^-}$

Cancel electrons & species:
$2\ MnO_4^-\ (aq) + 6\ H^+\ (aq) + 5\ UO^{2+}\ (aq) \rightarrow 2\ Mn^{2+}\ (aq) + 3\ H_2O\ (l) + 5\ UO_2^{2+}\ (aq)$

$$32.3\ \cancel{\text{mL } MnO_4^-} \times \frac{0.023\underline{7}73345\ \cancel{\text{mol } MnO_4^-}}{1000\ \cancel{\text{mL } MnO_4^-}} \times \frac{5\ \cancel{\text{mol U}}}{2\ \cancel{\text{mol } MnO_4^-}} \times \frac{238.03\ \text{g U}}{1\ \cancel{\text{mol U}}} = 0.45\underline{6}9457\ \text{g U then}$$

$$\text{percent U} = \frac{\text{g U}}{\text{g sample}} \times 100\% = \frac{0.45\underline{6}9457\ \text{g U}}{4.63\ \text{g sample}} \times 100\% = 9.87\%.$$

Check: first reaction

Reactants	Products
2 Mn atoms	2 Mn atoms
28 O atoms	28 O atoms
16 H atoms	16 H atoms
10 C atoms	10 C atoms
+4 charge	+4 charge

second reaction

Reactants	Products
2 Mn atoms	2 Mn atoms
13 O atoms	13 O atoms
6 H atoms	6 H atoms
5 U atoms	5 U atoms
+14 charge	+14 charge

The reactions are balanced. The units (%) are correct. The percentage is between 0 and 100%.

18.134 **Given:** 2.33 A applied to Cu electroplating of 1.74 g; also electroplate Au and Ag
Find: time, g Au, and g Ag
Conceptual Plan: **g Cu → mol Cu → mol e⁻ → C → s then**

$\dfrac{1\ \text{mol Cu}}{63.55\ \text{g Cu}}$ $\dfrac{2\ \text{mol } e^-}{1\ \text{mol Cu}}$ $\dfrac{96{,}485\ \text{C}}{1\ \text{mol } e^-}$ $\dfrac{1\ \text{s}}{2.33\ \text{C}}$

s → C → mol e⁻ → mol Au → g Au and s → C → mol e⁻ → mol Ag → g Ag

$\dfrac{2.33\ \text{C}}{1\ \text{s}}$ $\dfrac{1\ \text{mol } e^-}{96{,}485\ \text{C}}$ $\dfrac{1\ \text{mol Au}}{3\ \text{mol } e^-}$ $\dfrac{196.97\ \text{g Au}}{1\ \text{mol Au}}$ $\dfrac{2.33\ \text{C}}{1\ \text{s}}$ $\dfrac{1\ \text{mol } e^-}{96{,}485\ \text{C}}$ $\dfrac{1\ \text{mol Ag}}{1\ \text{mol } e^-}$ $\dfrac{107.87\ \text{g Ag}}{1\ \text{mol Ag}}$

Solution: $Cu^{2+}\ (aq) + 2\ e^- \rightarrow Cu\ (s)$

$$1.74\ \cancel{\text{g Cu}} \times \frac{1\ \cancel{\text{mol Cu}}}{63.55\ \cancel{\text{g Cu}}} \times \frac{2\ \cancel{\text{mol } e^-}}{1\ \cancel{\text{mol Cu}}} \times \frac{96{,}485\ \cancel{\text{C}}}{1\ \cancel{\text{mol } e^-}} \times \frac{1\ \text{s}}{2.33\ \cancel{\text{C}}} = 22\underline{6}7.61\ \text{s} = 2270\ \text{s or } 37.8\ \text{min.}$$

$Au^{3+}(aq) + 3e^- \rightarrow Au(s)$

$$2267.61\ \text{s} \times \frac{2.33\ \text{C}}{1\ \text{s}} \times \frac{1\ \text{mol e}^-}{96{,}485\ \text{C}} \times \frac{1\ \text{mol Au}}{3\ \text{mol e}^-} \times \frac{196.97\ \text{g Au}}{1\ \text{mol Au}} = 3.59536\ \text{g Au} = 3.60\ \text{g Au}$$

$Ag^+(aq) + e^- \rightarrow Ag(s)$

$$2267.61\ \text{s} \times \frac{2.33\ \text{C}}{1\ \text{s}} \times \frac{1\ \text{mol e}^-}{96{,}485\ \text{C}} \times \frac{1\ \text{mol Ag}}{1\ \text{mol e}^-} \times \frac{107.87\ \text{g Ag}}{1\ \text{mol Ag}} = 5.906975\ \text{g Ag} = 5.91\ \text{g Ag}$$

Check: The units (s, g, and g) are correct. Since far less than a mole of Cu is electroplated, the time is short. The mass of Au is higher because of the relatively higher molar mass of Au (even taking into account the moles of electrons needed). The mass of Ag is the highest since the molar mass is less than twice as high as Cu, but takes only half the electrons per mole of metal.

18.135 The overall cell reaction for the first cell is $2Cu^+(aq) \rightarrow Cu^{2+}(aq) + Cu(s)$. The overall cell reaction for the second cell is $Cu^+(aq) \rightarrow Cu^{2+}(aq)$. The biggest difference in $E°$ is because $n = 1$ for the first cell and $n = 2$ for the second cell. Since $\Delta G°_{rxn} = -\, n\, F\, E°_{cell}$ for the first cell

$$\Delta G°_{rxn} = -1\ \text{mol e}^- \times \frac{96{,}485\ \text{C}}{\text{mol e}^-} \times 0.364\ \text{V} = -1 \times 96{,}485\ \text{C} \times 0.364\frac{\text{J}}{\text{C}} = -35.1\ \text{kJ}$$ and for the second cell

$$\Delta G°_{rxn} = -2\ \text{mol e}^- \times \frac{96{,}485\ \text{C}}{\text{mol e}^-} \times 0.182\ \text{V} = -2 \times 96{,}485\ \text{C} \times 0.182\frac{\text{J}}{\text{C}} = -35.1\ \text{kJ}$$. Thus $\Delta G°_{rxn}$ is the same.

Conceptual Problems

18.136 (b) If $E°_{cell} > 0$ and $E_{cell} = E°_{cell} - \frac{0.0592\ V}{n}\log Q < 0$ this means that the second term dominates and is negative. This means that $Q > 1$. If $E_{cell} < 0$ then $K, 1$, since the reaction is nonspontaneous or $Q > K$.

18.137 (a) Looking for anion reductions that are in between the reduction potentials of Cl_2 and Br_2. The only one that meets this criterion is the dichromate ion.

18.138 (b) If the free energy change is negative this is a spontaneous reaction. This translates to a positive cell potential and a large equilibrium constant.

19 Radioactivity and Nuclear Chemistry

Review Questions

19.1 Radioactivity is the emission of subatomic particles or high-energy electromagnetic radiation by the nuclei of certain atoms. Radioactivity was discovered in 1896 by a French scientist named Antoine-Henri Becquerel (1852–1908). Becquerel placed crystals—composed of potassium uranyl sulfate, a compound known to phosphoresce—on top of a photographic plate wrapped in black cloth. The photographic plate showed a bright exposure spot where the crystals had been. Becquerel, Marie Curie, and Pierre Curie received the Nobel Prize for the discovery of radioactivity.

19.2 Marie Curie discovered that elements besides uranium emitted radiation, such as polonium and radium. She changed the name uranic rays to radiation.

19.3 A is the mass number (number of protons + neutrons); Z is the atomic number (number of protons) and X is the chemical symbol of the element.

19.4 A proton is described as ${}^{1}_{1}\text{p}$, a neutron as ${}^{1}_{0}\text{n}$, and an electron as ${}^{0}_{-1}\text{e}$.

19.5 An alpha particle has the same symbol as a helium nucleus, ${}^{4}_{2}\text{He}$. When an element emits an alpha particle, the number of protons in its nucleus decreases by two and the mass number decreases by four, transforming it into a different element.

19.6 An beta particle has the same symbol as an electron, ${}^{0}_{-1}\text{e}$. When an atom emits a beta particle, its atomic number increases by one because it now has an additional proton. The mass number is unchanged.

19.7 Gamma rays are high-energy (short-wavelength) photons and have a symbol of ${}^{0}_{0}\gamma$. A gamma ray has no charge and no mass. When a gamma-ray photon is emitted from a radioactive atom, it does not change the mass number or the atomic number of the element. Gamma rays, however, are usually emitted in conjunction with other types of radiation.

19.8 A positron is the anti-particle of the electron: that is, it has the same mass, but opposite charge. It has a symbol of ${}^{0}_{+1}\text{e}$. When an atom emits a positron, its atomic number decreases by one because it now has one fewer protons, but the mass number remains unchanged.

19.9 Electron capture occurs when a nucleus assimilates an electron from an inner orbital of its electron cloud. Like positron emission, the net effect of electron capture is the conversion of a proton into a neutron: ${}^{1}_{1}\text{p} + {}^{0}_{-1}\text{e} \rightarrow {}^{1}_{0}\text{n}$. When an atom undergoes electron capture, its atomic number decreases by one because it has one less proton, and its mass number is unchanged.

19.10 (a) Ionizing power: gamma rays < beta particles ~ positrons < alpha particles

(b) Penetrating power: alpha particles < beta particles ~ positrons < gamma rays

19.11 For the lighter elements, the N/Z ratio of stable isotopes is about one (equal numbers of neutrons and protons). However, beyond about $Z = 20$, the N/Z ratio of stable nuclei begins to get larger (reaching about 1.5). Above $Z = 83$, stable nuclei do not exist.

19.12 Magic numbers are certain numbers of nucleons (N or $Z = 2, 8, 20, 28, 50, 82$, and $N = 126$) that have unique stability. Nuclei containing a magic number of protons or neutrons are particularly stable.

19.13 (a) Film-badge dosimeters consist of photographic film held in a small case that is pinned to clothing and are standard for most people working with or near radioactive substances. These badges are collected and processed (or developed) regularly as a way to monitor a person's exposure. The more exposed the film has become in a given period of time, the more radioactivity the person has been exposed to.

(b) A Geiger-Müller counter (commonly referred to as a Geiger counter) is an instrument that can detect radioactivity instantaneously. Particles emitted by radioactive nuclei pass through an argon-filled chamber. The energetic particles create a trail of ionized argon atoms. An applied high voltage between a wire within the chamber and the chamber itself causes these newly formed ions to produce an electrical signal that can be detected on a meter or turned into an audible click. Each click corresponds to a radioactive particle passing through the argon gas chamber. This clicking is the stereotypical sound most people associate with a radiation detector.

(c) A scintillation counter is another instrument that can detect radioactivity instantaneously. In this device, the radioactive emissions pass through a material (such as NaI or CsI) that emits ultraviolet or visible light in response to excitation by energetic particles. The radioactivity excites the atoms to a higher energy state. The atoms release this energy as light, which is then detected and turned into an electrical signal that can be read on a meter.

19.14 The half-life is the time it takes for one-half of the parent nuclides in a radioactive sample to decay to the daughter nuclides, and is identical to the concept of half-life for chemical reactions that we covered in Chapter 13. Thus, the relationship between the half-life of a nuclide and its rate constant is given by the same expression (Equation 13.19) that we derived for a first-order reaction in Section 13.4: $t_{1/2} = \dfrac{0.693}{k}$. Nuclides that decay quickly have short half-lives and large rate constants—they are considered very active (many decay events per unit time). Nuclides that decay slowly have long half-lives and are less active (fewer decay events per unit time).

19.15 Radiocarbon dating, a technique devised in 1949 by Willard Libby at the University of Chicago, is used by archeologists, geologists, anthropologists, and other scientists to estimate the ages of fossils and artifacts. Carbon-14 is constantly formed in the upper atmosphere by the neutron bombardment of nitrogen and then decays back to nitrogen by beta emission with a half-life of 5,730 years. The continuous formation of carbon-14 in the atmosphere and its continuous decay back to nitrogen-14 produces a nearly constant equilibrium amount of atmospheric carbon-14, which is oxidized to carbon dioxide and incorporated into plants by photosynthesis. The C-14 then makes its way up the food chain and ultimately into all living organisms. As a result, all living plants, animals, and humans contain the same ratio of carbon-14 to carbon-12 (^{14}C:^{12}C) as is found in the atmosphere. When a living organism dies, however, it stops incorporating new carbon-14 into its tissues. The ^{14}C:^{12}C ratio then decreases with a half-life of 5,730 years. The accuracy of carbon-14 dating can be checked against objects whose ages are known from historical sources.

In order to make C-14 dating more accurate, scientists have studied the carbon-14 content of western bristlecone pine trees, which can live up to 5,000 years. The tree trunk contains growth rings corresponding to each year of the tree's life, and the wood laid down in each ring incorporates carbon derived from the carbon dioxide in the atmosphere at that time. The rings thus provide a record of the historical atmospheric carbon-14 content and allow for corrections to carbon-14 concentrations due to atmospheric changes.

The maximum age that can be estimated from carbon-14 dating is about 50,000 years—beyond that, the amount of carbon-14 becomes too low to measure accurately.

19.16 The ratio of uranium-238 to lead-206 within igneous rocks (rocks of volcanic origin) measures the time that has passed since the rock solidified (at which point the "radiometric clock" was reset). Since U-238 decays into Pb-206 with a half-life of 4.5×10^9 years, the relative amounts of U-238 and Pb-206 in a uranium-containing rock reveal its age. The method uses similar half-life calculations as the carbon dating method, only the half-life is much longer, so much older materials can be dated. The oldest rocks have an age of approximately 4.0 billion years, establishing a lower boundary for the age of the Earth (the Earth must be at least as old as its oldest rocks). The ages of about 70 meteorites that have struck the earth have also been extensively studied and have been found to be about 4.5 billion years old. Since the meteorites were formed at the same time as our solar system (which includes the Earth), the best estimate for the age of the Earth is therefore about 4.5 billion years.

19.17 Nuclear fission is the splitting of an atom into smaller products. The process emits enormous amounts of energy. Three researchers in Germany—Lise Meitner (1878–1968), Fritz Strassmann (1902–1980), and Otto Hahn (1879–1968), repeating uranium bombardment experiments by Fermi, performed careful chemical analysis of the products. The nucleus of the neutron-bombarded uranium atom is split into barium, krypton, and other smaller products. A nuclear equation for a fission reaction, showing how uranium breaks apart into the daughter nuclides, is ${}^{235}_{92}\mathrm{U} + {}^{1}_{0}\mathrm{n} \rightarrow {}^{140}_{56}\mathrm{Ba} + {}^{93}_{36}\mathrm{Kr} + 3\,{}^{1}_{0}\mathrm{n}$ + energy. The process produces three neutrons, which have the potential to initiate fission in three other U-235 atoms. Scientists quickly realized that a sample rich in U-235 could undergo a chain reaction in which neutrons produced by the fission of one uranium nucleus would induce fission in other uranium nuclei. The result would be a self-amplifying reaction capable of producing an enormous amount of energy—an atomic bomb. However, to make a bomb, a critical mass of U-235—enough U-235 to produce a self-sustaining reaction—would be necessary. Since an enormous amount of energy is produced, it can be used to produce steam to drive turbines (as shown in Figure 19.11).

19.18 The Manhattan Project was a top-secret endeavor with the main goal of building an atomic bomb before the Germans did. The project was led by physicist J.R. Oppenheimer (1904–1967) at a high-security research facility in Los Alamos, New Mexico. Four years later, on July 16, 1945, the world's first nuclear weapon was successfully detonated at a test site in New Mexico. The first atomic bomb exploded with a force equivalent to 18,000 tons of dynamite. Ironically, the Germans—who had not made a successful nuclear bomb—had already been defeated by this time. Instead, the atomic bomb was used on Japan. One bomb was dropped on Hiroshima and a second bomb was dropped on Nagasaki. Together, the bombs killed approximately 200,000 people and forced Japan to surrender.

19.19 The advantages of using fission to generate electricity are: 1) a typical nuclear power plant generates enough electricity for a city of about 1 million people and uses about 50 kg of fuel per day as opposed to a coal-burning power plant using about 2,000,000 kg of fuel to generate the same amount of electricity); and 2) a nuclear power plant generates no air pollution and no greenhouse gases. (Coal-burning power plants also emit carbon dioxide, a greenhouse gas.) The disadvantages are: 1) the danger of nuclear accidents, such as overheating and the release of radiation; and 2) waste disposal, since the products of the reaction are radioactive and have long half-lives.

19.20 The mass of the products is usually different than the mass of the reactants because in nuclear reactions, matter can be converted to energy. The relationship between the amount of matter that is lost and the amount of energy formed is given by Einstein's famous equation relating the two quantities, $E = mc^2$, where E is the energy produced, m is the mass lost, and c is the speed of light.

19.21 This difference in mass between the products and the reactants is known as the mass defect. The energy corresponding to the mass defect, obtained by substituting the mass defect into the equation $E = mc^2$, is known as the nuclear binding energy, the amount of energy that would be required to break apart the nucleus into its component nucleons. The nuclear binding energy per nucleon peaks at a mass number of 60. The significance of this is that the nuclides with mass numbers of about 60 are among the most stable.

19.22 Nuclear fusion is the combination of two light nuclei to form a heavier one. Both fusion and fission emit large amounts of energy because they both form daughter nuclides with greater binding energies per nucleon than the parent nuclides.

19.23 An extremely high temperature is required for fusion to occur. To date no material can withstand these temperatures. The U.S. Congress has reduced funding for these projects so that it is less likely that a viable process will be developed.

19.24 Transmutation is a process that results in the transformation of one element into another. Examples are: ${}^{14}_{7}\mathrm{N} + {}^{4}_{2}\mathrm{He} \rightarrow {}^{17}_{8}\mathrm{O} + {}^{1}_{1}\mathrm{H}$ and ${}^{27}_{13}\mathrm{Al} + {}^{4}_{2}\mathrm{He} \rightarrow {}^{30}_{15}\mathrm{P} + {}^{1}_{0}\mathrm{n}$.

19.25 In a single-stage linear accelerator, a charged particle such as a proton is accelerated in an evacuated tube. The accelerating force is provided by a potential difference between the ends of the tube. In multi-stage linear accelerators, such as the Stanford Linear Accelerator (SLAC) at Stanford University (Figure 19.14), a series of tubes of increasing length are connected to a source of alternating voltage, as shown in Figure 19.15. The voltage alternates in such a way that, as a positively charged particle leaves a particular tube, that tube becomes positively charged, repelling the particle to the next tube. At the same time, the tube the particle is now approaching becomes negatively charged, pulling the particle towards it. This continues throughout the linear accelerator, allowing the particle to be accelerated to velocities up to 90% of the speed of light. Linear accelerators can be used to conduct nuclear transmutations, making nuclides that don't normally exist in nature.

19.26 In a cyclotron, a similarly alternating voltage as used in linear accelerators is used to accelerate a charged particle, only this time the alternating voltage is applied between the two semi-circular halves of the cyclotron (Figure 19.16). A charged particle originally in the middle of the two semi-circles is accelerated back and forth between them. Additional magnets cause the particle to move in a spiral path. As the charged particle spirals out from the center, it gains speed and eventually exits the cyclotron aimed at the target.

19.27 The energy associated with radioactivity can ionize molecules. When radiation ionizes important molecules in living cells, problems can develop. The ingestion of radioactive materials, especially alpha and beta emitters, is particularly dangerous because the radioactivity is then inside the body and can do even more damage. The effects of radiation can be divided into three different types: acute radiation damage, increased cancer risk, and genetic effects.

19.28 Different type of radiation have different ionizing power (gamma rays $<$ beta particles ~ positrons $<$ alpha particles) and different penetrating power (alpha particles $<$ beta particles ~ positrons $<$ gamma rays).

19.29 The biological effectiveness factor, or RBE, (for relative biological effectiveness), corrects the dosage (in rads) for the type of radiation. It is a correction factor that is usually multiplied by the dose in rads to obtain the dose in a unit called the rem for roentgen equivalent man. So, dose in rads $\times$ biological effectiveness factor = dose in rem. The biological effectiveness factor for alpha radiation for example, is much higher than for gamma radiation.

19.30 The use of radioactivity in diagnosis usually involves a radiotracer, a radioactive nuclide that has been attached to a compound or introduced into a mixture in order to track the movement of the compound or mixture within the body. Tracers are useful in the diagnosis of disease because of two main factors: 1) the sensitivity with which radioactivity can be detected, and 2) the identical chemical behavior of a radioactive nucleus and its non-radioactive counterpart. Since different elements are taken up preferentially by different organs or tissues, various radiotracers can be used to monitor metabolic activity and image a variety of organs and structures, including the kidneys, heart, brain, gallbladder, bones, and arteries. Radiotracers can also be used to locate infections or cancer within the body. Cancerous tumors can be detected because they naturally concentrate phosphorus. When a patient is given phosphorus-32 (a radioactive isotope of phosphorus), the tumors concentrate the radioactive phosphorous and become sources of radioactivity that can be detected.

Because radiation kills cells, and because it is particularly effective at killing rapidly dividing cells, it is often used as a therapy for cancer (cancer cells reproduce much faster than normal cells). Gamma rays are focused on internal tumors to kill them.

Radioactive Decay and Nuclide Stability

19.31 **Conceptual Plan: Begin with the symbol for a parent nuclide on the left side of the equation and the symbol for a particle on the right side (except for electron capture). → Equalize the sum of the mass numbers and the sum of the atomic numbers on both sides of the equation by writing the appropriate mass number and atomic number for the unknown daughter nuclide. → Using the periodic table, deduce the identity of the unknown daughter nuclide from the atomic number and write its symbol.**
Solution:

(a) U-234 (alpha decay) ${}^{234}_{92}\text{U} \rightarrow {}^{?}_{?}? + {}^{4}_{2}\text{He}$ then ${}^{234}_{92}\text{U} \rightarrow {}^{230}_{90}? + {}^{4}_{2}\text{He}$ then ${}^{234}_{92}\text{U} \rightarrow {}^{230}_{90}\text{Th} + {}^{4}_{2}\text{He}$

(b) Th-230 (alpha decay) ${}^{230}_{90}\text{Th} \rightarrow {}^{?}_{?}? + {}^{4}_{2}\text{He}$ then ${}^{230}_{90}\text{Th} \rightarrow {}^{226}_{88}? + {}^{4}_{2}\text{He}$ then ${}^{230}_{90}\text{Th} \rightarrow {}^{226}_{88}\text{Ra} + {}^{4}_{2}\text{He}$

(c) Pb-214 (beta decay) ${}^{214}_{82}\text{Pb} \rightarrow {}^{?}_{?}? + {}^{0}_{-1}\text{e}$ then ${}^{214}_{82}\text{Pb} \rightarrow {}^{214}_{83}? + {}^{0}_{-1}\text{e}$ then ${}^{214}_{82}\text{Pb} \rightarrow {}^{214}_{83}\text{Bi} + {}^{0}_{-1}\text{e}$

(d) N-13 (positron emission) ${}^{13}_{7}\text{N} \rightarrow {}^{?}_{?}? + {}^{0}_{+1}\text{e}$ then ${}^{13}_{7}\text{N} \rightarrow {}^{13}_{6}? + {}^{0}_{+1}\text{e}$ then ${}^{13}_{7}\text{N} \rightarrow {}^{13}_{6}\text{C} + {}^{0}_{+1}\text{e}$

(e) Cr-51 (electron capture) ${}^{51}_{24}\text{C} + {}^{0}_{-1}\text{e} \rightarrow {}^{?}_{?}?$ then ${}^{51}_{24}\text{Cr} + {}^{0}_{-1}\text{e} \rightarrow {}^{51}_{23}?$ then ${}^{51}_{24}\text{Cr} + {}^{0}_{-1}\text{e} \rightarrow {}^{51}_{23}\text{V}$

Check: (a) 234 = 230 + 4, 92 = 90 + 2, and thorium is atomic number 90. (b) 230 = 226 + 4, 90 = 88 + 2, and radium is atomic number 88. (c) 214 = 214 + 0, 82 = 83 – 1, and bismuth is atomic number 83. (d) 13 = 13 + 0, 7 = 6 + 1, and carbon is atomic number 6. (e) 51 + 0 = 51, 24 – 1 = 23, and vanadium is atomic number 23.

19.32 **Conceptual Plan: Begin with the symbol for a parent nuclide on the left side of the equation and the symbol for a particle on the right side (except for electron capture). → Equalize the sum of the mass numbers and the sum of the atomic numbers on both sides of the equation by writing the appropriate mass number and atomic number for the unknown daughter nuclide. → Using the periodic table, deduce the identity of the unknown daughter nuclide from the atomic number and write its symbol.**
Solution:

(a) Po-210 (alpha decay) ${}^{210}_{84}\text{Po} \rightarrow {}^{?}_{?}? + {}^{4}_{2}\text{He}$ then ${}^{210}_{84}\text{Po} \rightarrow {}^{206}_{82}? + {}^{4}_{2}\text{He}$ then ${}^{210}_{84}\text{Po} \rightarrow {}^{206}_{82}\text{Pb} + {}^{4}_{2}\text{He}$

(b) Ac-227 (beta decay) ${}^{227}_{89}\text{Ac} \rightarrow {}^{?}_{?}? + {}^{0}_{-1}\text{e}$ then ${}^{227}_{89}\text{Ac} \rightarrow {}^{227}_{90}? + {}^{0}_{-1}\text{e}$ then ${}^{227}_{89}\text{Ac} \rightarrow {}^{227}_{90}\text{Th} + {}^{0}_{-1}\text{e}$

(c) Tl-207 (beta decay) ${}^{207}_{81}\text{Tl} \rightarrow {}^{?}_{?}? + {}^{0}_{-1}\text{e}$ then ${}^{207}_{81}\text{Tl} \rightarrow {}^{207}_{82}? + {}^{0}_{-1}\text{e}$ then ${}^{207}_{81}\text{Tl} \rightarrow {}^{207}_{82}\text{Pb} + {}^{0}_{-1}\text{e}$

(d) O-15 (positron emission) ${}^{15}_{8}\text{O} \rightarrow {}^{?}_{?}? + {}^{0}_{+1}\text{e}$ then ${}^{15}_{8}\text{O} \rightarrow {}^{15}_{7}? + {}^{0}_{+1}\text{e}$ then ${}^{15}_{8}\text{O} \rightarrow {}^{15}_{7}\text{N} + {}^{0}_{+1}\text{e}$

(e) Pd-103 (electron capture) ${}^{103}_{46}\text{Pd} + {}^{0}_{-1}\text{e} \rightarrow {}^{?}_{?}?$ then ${}^{103}_{46}\text{Pd} + {}^{0}_{-1}\text{e} \rightarrow {}^{103}_{45}?$ then ${}^{103}_{46}\text{Pd} + {}^{0}_{-1}\text{e} \rightarrow {}^{103}_{45}\text{Rh}$

Check: (a) 210 = 210 + 4, 84 = 82 + 2, and lead is atomic number 82. (b) 227 = 227 + 0, 89 = 90 – 1, and thorium is atomic number 90. (c) 207 = 207 + 0, 81 = 82 – 1, and lead is atomic number 82. (d) 15 = 15 + 0, 8 = 7 + 1, and nitrogen is atomic number 7. (e) 103 + 0 = 103, 46 – 1 = 45, and rhodium is atomic number 45.

19.33 **Given:** Th-232 decay series: $\alpha, \beta, \beta, \alpha$ **Find:** balanced decay reactions
Conceptual Plan: Begin with the symbol for a parent nuclide on the left side of the equation and the symbol for a particle on the right side (except for electron capture). → Equalize the sum of the mass numbers and the sum of the atomic numbers on both sides of the equation by writing the appropriate mass number and atomic number for the unknown daughter nuclide. → Using the periodic table, deduce the identity of the unknown daughter nuclide from the atomic number and write its symbol. → Use the product of this reaction to write the next reaction.
Solution:
Th-232 (alpha decay) ${}^{232}_{90}\text{Th} \rightarrow {}^{?}_{?}? + {}^{4}_{2}\text{He}$ then ${}^{232}_{90}\text{Th} \rightarrow {}^{228}_{88}? + {}^{4}_{2}\text{He}$ then ${}^{232}_{90}\text{Th} \rightarrow {}^{228}_{88}\text{Ra} + {}^{4}_{2}\text{He}$
Ra-228 (beta decay) ${}^{228}_{88}\text{Ra} \rightarrow {}^{?}_{?}? + {}^{0}_{-1}\text{e}$ then ${}^{228}_{88}\text{Ra} \rightarrow {}^{228}_{89}? + {}^{0}_{-1}\text{e}$ then ${}^{228}_{88}\text{Ra} \rightarrow {}^{228}_{89}\text{Ac} + {}^{0}_{-1}\text{e}$
Ac-228 (beta decay) ${}^{228}_{89}\text{Ac} \rightarrow {}^{?}_{?}? + {}^{0}_{-1}\text{e}$ then ${}^{228}_{89}\text{Ac} \rightarrow {}^{228}_{90}? + {}^{0}_{-1}\text{e}$ then ${}^{228}_{89}\text{Ac} \rightarrow {}^{228}_{90}\text{Th} + {}^{0}_{-1}\text{e}$
Th-228 (alpha decay) ${}^{228}_{90}\text{Th} \rightarrow {}^{?}_{?}? + {}^{4}_{2}\text{He}$ then ${}^{228}_{90}\text{Th} \rightarrow {}^{224}_{88}? + {}^{4}_{2}\text{He}$ then ${}^{228}_{90}\text{Th} \rightarrow {}^{224}_{88}\text{Ra} + {}^{4}_{2}\text{He}$
Thus the decay series is: ${}^{232}_{90}\text{Th} \rightarrow {}^{228}_{88}\text{Ra} + {}^{4}_{2}\text{He}$, ${}^{228}_{88}\text{Ra} \rightarrow {}^{228}_{89}\text{Ac} + {}^{0}_{-1}\text{e}$, ${}^{228}_{89}\text{Ac} \rightarrow {}^{228}_{90}\text{Th} + {}^{0}_{-1}\text{e}$, ${}^{228}_{90}\text{Th} \rightarrow {}^{224}_{88}\text{Ra} + {}^{4}_{2}\text{He}$.
Check: 232 = 228 + 4, 90 = 88 + 2, and radium is atomic number 88. 228 = 228 + 0, 88 = 89 – 1, and actinium is atomic number 89. 228 = 228 + 0, 89 = 90 – 1, and thorium is atomic number 90. 228 = 224 + 4, 90 = 88 + 2, and radium is atomic number 88.

19.34 **Given:** Rn-220 decay series: $\alpha, \alpha, \beta, \alpha$ **Find:** balanced decay reactions
Conceptual Plan: Begin with the symbol for a parent nuclide on the left side of the equation and the symbol for a particle on the right side (except for electron capture). → Equalize the sum of the mass numbers and the sum of the atomic numbers on both sides of the equation by writing the appropriate mass number and atomic number for the unknown daughter nuclide. → Using the periodic table, deduce the identity of the unknown daughter nuclide from the atomic number and write its symbol. → Use the product of this reaction to write the next reaction.

Solution:
Rn-220 (alpha decay) $^{220}_{86}Rn \rightarrow ^{?}_{?}? + ^{4}_{2}He$ then $^{220}_{86}Rn \rightarrow ^{216}_{84}? + ^{4}_{2}He$ then $^{220}_{86}Rn \rightarrow ^{216}_{84}Po + ^{4}_{2}He$
Po-216 (alpha decay) $^{216}_{84}Po \rightarrow ^{?}_{?}? + ^{4}_{2}He$ then $^{216}_{84}Po \rightarrow ^{212}_{82}? + ^{4}_{2}He$ then $^{216}_{84}Po \rightarrow ^{212}_{82}Pb + ^{4}_{2}He$
Pb-212 (beta decay) $^{212}_{82}Pb \rightarrow ^{?}_{?}? + ^{0}_{-1}e$ then $^{212}_{82}Pb \rightarrow ^{212}_{83}? + ^{0}_{-1}e$ then $^{212}_{82}Pb \rightarrow ^{212}_{83}Bi + ^{0}_{-1}e$
Bi-212 (alpha decay) $^{212}_{83}Bi \rightarrow ^{?}_{?}? + ^{4}_{2}He$ then $^{212}_{83}Bi \rightarrow ^{208}_{81}? + ^{4}_{2}He$ then $^{212}_{83}Bi \rightarrow ^{208}_{81}Tl + ^{4}_{2}He$
Thus the decay series is: $^{220}_{86}Rn \rightarrow ^{216}_{84}Po + ^{4}_{2}He$, $^{216}_{84}Po \rightarrow ^{212}_{82}Pb + ^{4}_{2}He$, $^{212}_{82}Pb \rightarrow ^{212}_{83}Bi + ^{0}_{-1}e$, $^{212}_{83}Bi \rightarrow ^{208}_{81}Tl + ^{4}_{2}He$.
Check: 220 = 216 + 4, 86 = 84 + 2, and polonium is atomic number 84. 216 = 212 + 4, 84 = 82 + 2, and lead is atomic number 82. 212 = 212 + 0, 82 = 83 – 1, and bismuth is atomic number 83. 220 = 208 + 4, 83 = 81 + 2, and thallium is atomic number 81.

19.35 **Conceptual Plan: Equalize the sum of the mass numbers and the sum of the atomic numbers on both sides of the equation by writing the appropriate mass number and atomic number for the unknown species. → Using the periodic table and the list of particles, deduce the identity of the unknown species from the atomic number and write its symbol.**
Solution:

(a) $^{?}_{?}? \rightarrow ^{217}_{85}At + ^{4}_{2}He$ becomes $^{221}_{87}? \rightarrow ^{217}_{85}At + ^{4}_{2}He$ then $^{221}_{87}Fr \rightarrow ^{217}_{85}At + ^{4}_{2}He$

(b) $^{241}_{94}Pu \rightarrow ^{241}_{95}Am + ^{?}_{?}?$ becomes $^{241}_{94}Pu \rightarrow ^{241}_{95}Am + ^{0}_{-1}?$ then $^{241}_{94}Pu \rightarrow ^{241}_{95}Am + ^{0}_{-1}e$

(c) $^{19}_{11}Na \rightarrow ^{19}_{10}Ne + ^{?}_{?}?$ becomes $^{19}_{11}Na \rightarrow ^{19}_{10}Ne + ^{0}_{1}?$ then $^{19}_{11}Na \rightarrow ^{19}_{10}Ne + ^{0}_{+1}e$

(d) $^{75}_{34}Se + ^{?}_{?}? \rightarrow ^{75}_{33}As$ becomes $^{75}_{34}Se + ^{0}_{-1}? \rightarrow ^{75}_{33}As$ then $^{75}_{34}Se + ^{0}_{-1}e \rightarrow ^{75}_{33}As$
Check: (a) 221 = 217 + 4, 87 = 85 + 2, and francium is atomic number 87. (b) 241 = 241 + 0, 94 = 95 – 1, and the particle is a beta particle. (c) 19 = 19 + 0, 11 = 10 + 1, and the particle is a positron. (d) 75 = 75 + 0, 34 – 1 = 33, and the particle is an electron.

19.36 **Conceptual Plan: Equalize the sum of the mass numbers and the sum of the atomic numbers on both sides of the equation by writing the appropriate mass number and atomic number for the unknown species. → Using the periodic table and the list of particles, deduce the identity of the unknown species from the atomic number and write its symbol.**
Solution:

(a) $^{241}_{95}Am \rightarrow ^{237}_{93}Np + ^{?}_{?}?$ becomes $^{241}_{95}Am \rightarrow ^{237}_{93}Np + ^{4}_{2}?$ then $^{241}_{95}Am \rightarrow ^{237}_{93}Np + ^{4}_{2}He$

(b) $^{?}_{?}? \rightarrow ^{233}_{92}U + ^{0}_{-1}e$ becomes $^{233}_{91}? \rightarrow ^{233}_{92}U + ^{0}_{-1}e$ then $^{233}_{91}Pa \rightarrow ^{233}_{92}U + ^{0}_{-1}e$

(c) $^{237}_{93}Np \rightarrow ^{?}_{?}? + ^{4}_{2}He$ becomes $^{237}_{93}Np \rightarrow ^{233}_{91}? + ^{4}_{2}He$ then $^{237}_{93}Np \rightarrow ^{233}_{91}Pa + ^{4}_{2}He$

(d) $^{75}_{35}Br \rightarrow ^{?}_{?}? + ^{0}_{+1}e$ becomes $^{75}_{35}Br \rightarrow ^{75}_{34}? + ^{0}_{+1}e$ then $^{75}_{35}Br \rightarrow ^{75}_{34}Se + ^{0}_{+1}e$
Check: (a) 241 = 237 + 4, 95 = 93 + 2, and the particle is an alpha particle. (b) 233 = 233 + 0, 91 = 92 – 1, and protactinium is atomic number 91. (c) 237 = 233 + 4, 93 = 91 + 2, and protactinium is atomic number 91. (d) 75 = 75 + 0, 35 = 34 + 1, and selenium is atomic number 34.

19.37 (a) Mg-26: stable, N/Z ratio is close to 1, acceptable for low Z atoms

(b) Ne-25: not stable, N/Z ratio much too high for low Z atom

(c) Co-51: not stable, N/Z ratio is less than 1, much too low

(d) Te-124: stable, N/Z ratio is acceptable for this Z

19.38 (a) Ti-48: stable, N/Z ratio is acceptable for this Z

(b) Cr-63: not stable, N/Z ratio much too high for this Z

(c) Sn-102: not stable, N/Z ratio is close to 1, much too low for this Z

(d) Y-88: stable, N/Z ratio is acceptable for this Z

19.39 Sc, V, and Mn, each have odd numbers of protons. Atoms with an odd number of protons typically have fewer stable isotopes than those with an even number of protons.

19.40 Aluminum and sodium both have an odd Z, which have fewer stable isotopes. These atoms are both small Z atoms and so the N/Z should be close to 1. There is only one option that meets both criteria for aluminum and sodium. Neon and magnesium have an even Z and so they have more options for stable isotopes.

19.41 (a) Mo-109, $N = 67$, $Z = 42$, $N/Z = 1.6$, beta decay, since N/Z is too high

(b) Ru-90, $N = 46$, $Z = 44$, $N/Z = 1.0$, positron emission, since N/Z is too low

(c) P-27, $N = 15$, $Z = 12$, $N/Z = 0.8$, positron emission, since N/Z is too low

(d) Rn-196, $N = 110$, $Z = 86$, $N/Z = 1.3$, positron emission, since N/Z is too low

19.42 (a) Sb-132, $N = 81$, $Z = 51$, $N/Z = 1.6$, beta decay, since N/Z is too high

(b) Te-139, $N = 87$, $Z = 52$, $N/Z = 1.7$, beta decay, since N/Z is too high

(c) Fr-202, $N = 115$, $Z = 87$, $N/Z = 1.3$, positron emission, since N/Z is too low

(d) Ba-123, $N = 67$, $Z = 56$, $N/Z = 1.2$, positron emission, since N/Z is too low

19.43 (a) Cs-125, $N/Z = 70/55 = 1.3$; Cs-113, $N/Z = 58/55 = 1.1$; Cs-125 will have the longer half-life, since it is closer to the proper N/Z

(b) Fe-62, $N/Z = 36/26 = 1.4$; Fe-70, $N/Z = 44/26 = 1.7$; Fe-62 will have the longer half-life, since it is closer to the proper N/Z

19.44 (a) Cs-149, $N/Z = 94/55 = 1.7$; Cs-139, $N/Z = 84/55 = 1.5$; Cs-139 will have the longer half-life, since it is closer to the proper N/Z

(b) Fe-52, $N/Z = 26/26 = 1.0$; Fe-45, $N/Z = 19/26 = 0.7$ Fe-52 will have the longer half-life, since it is closer to the proper N/Z

The Kinetics of Radioactive Decay and Radiometric Dating

19.45 **Given:** U-235, $t_{1/2}$ for radioactive decay = 703 million years **Find:** t to 10.0% of initial amount
Conceptual Plan: radioactive decay implies first order kinetics, $t_{1/2} \rightarrow k$ then

$$t_{1/2} = \frac{0.693}{k}$$

$m_{\text{U-235 }0}, m_{\text{U-235 }t}, k \rightarrow t$

$$\ln N_t = -kt + \ln N_0$$

Solution: $t_{1/2} = \dfrac{0.693}{k}$ rearrange to solve for k. $k = \dfrac{0.693}{t_{1/2}} = \dfrac{0.693}{703 \times 10^6 \text{ yr}} = 9.8\underline{5}7752 \times 10^{-10} \text{ yr}^{-1}$. Since $\ln m_{\text{U-235 }t} = -kt + \ln m_{\text{U-235 }0}$ rearrange to solve for t

$$t = -\frac{1}{k} \ln \frac{m_{\text{U-235 }t}}{m_{\text{U-235 }0}} = -\frac{1}{9.8\underline{5}7752 \times 10^{-10} \text{ yr}^{-1}} \ln \frac{10.0\%}{100.0\%} = 2.34 \times 10^9 \text{ yr}.$$

Check: The units (yr) are correct. The time is just over 3 half-lives, when 1/8 of the original amount will be left.

19.46 **Given:** initially 0.050 mg Tc-99m, $t_{1/2}$ for radioactive decay = 6.0 h **Find:** t to 1.0×10^{-3} mg
Conceptual Plan: radioactive decay implies first order kinetics, $t_{1/2} \rightarrow k$ then

$$t_{1/2} = \frac{0.693}{k}$$

$m_{\text{Tc-99m }0}, m_{\text{Tc-99m }t}, k \rightarrow t$

$$\ln N_t = -kt + \ln N_0$$

Solution: $t_{1/2} = \dfrac{0.693}{k}$ rearrange to solve for k. $k = \dfrac{0.693}{t_{1/2}} = \dfrac{0.693}{6.0 \text{ h}} = 0.1\underline{1}55 \text{ h}^{-1}$. Since

$\ln m_{\text{Tc-99m }t} = -kt + \ln m_{\text{Tc-99m }0}$ rearrange to solve for t

$$t = -\frac{1}{k}\ln\frac{m_{\text{Tc-99m t}}}{m_{\text{Tc-99m 0}}} = -\frac{1}{0.11\underline{5}5\ \text{h}^{-1}}\ln\frac{1.0\times10^{-3}\ \cancel{\text{mg}}}{0.050\ \cancel{\text{mg}}} = 34\ \text{h}.$$

Check: The units (h) are correct. The time is just over 5 half-lives and the amount is under 1/32 or $1/2^5$ of the original amount.

19.47 **Given:** $t_{1/2}$ for isotope decay = 3.8 days; 1.55 g isotope initially **Find:** mass of isotope after 5.5 days
Conceptual Plan: radioactive decay implies first order kinetics, $t_{1/2} \rightarrow k$ then

$t_{1/2} = \frac{0.693}{k}$

$m_{\text{isotope }0}$**, t, k** $\rightarrow$ $m_{\text{isotope }t}$

$\ln N_t = -kt + \ln N_0$

Solution: $t_{1/2} = \dfrac{0.693}{k}$ rearrange to solve for k. $k = \dfrac{0.693}{t_{1/2}} = \dfrac{0.693}{3.8\ \text{days}} = 0.1\underline{8}237\ \text{day}^{-1}$. Since

$\ln N_t = -kt + \ln N_0 = -(0.1\underline{8}237\ \cancel{\text{day}^{-1}})(5.5\ \cancel{\text{day}}) + \ln(1.55\ \text{g}) = -0.5\underline{6}478 \rightarrow N_t = e^{-0.5\underline{6}478} = 0.57\ \text{g}.$

Check: The units (g) are correct. The amount is consistent with a time between one and two half-lives.

19.48 **Given:** $t_{1/2}$ for I-131 = 8 days; 58 mg dose at 8:00 am **Find:** mass of I-131 at 5:00 pm next day
Conceptual Plan: radioactive decay implies first order kinetics, $t_{1/2} \rightarrow k$ and determine days since dose

$t_{1/2} = \frac{0.693}{k}$

then $m_{\text{I-131 }0}$, t, k $\rightarrow$ $m_{\text{I-131 }t}$

$\ln N_t = -kt + \ln N_0$

Solution: $t_{1/2} = \dfrac{0.693}{k}$ rearrange to solve for k. $k = \dfrac{0.693}{t_{1/2}} = \dfrac{0.693}{8\ \text{days}} = 0.0\underline{8}6625\ \text{day}^{-1}$. The time since the dose is one day plus 9 hours or (1 + 9/24) days = 1.375 days. Since $\ln m_{\text{I-131 }t} = -kt + \ln m_{\text{I-131 }0}$
$= -(0.0\underline{8}6625\ \cancel{\text{day}^{-1}})(1.375\ \cancel{\text{day}}) + \ln(58\ \text{mg}) = 3.\underline{9}413 \rightarrow m = e^{3.\underline{9}413} = 51\ \text{mg}.$

Check: The units (mg) are correct. The amount is consistent with a time less than one half-life.

19.49 **Given:** F-18 initial decay rate = 1.5×10^5 /s, $t_{1/2}$ for F-18 = 1.83 h **Find:** t to decay rate of 2.5×10^3 /s
Conceptual Plan: radioactive decay implies first order kinetics, $t_{1/2} \rightarrow k$ then Rate$_0$, Rate$_t$, $k \rightarrow t$

$t_{1/2} = \frac{0.693}{k}$ $\qquad \ln\frac{\text{Rate}_t}{\text{Rate}_0} = -kt$

Solution: $t_{1/2} = \dfrac{0.693}{k}$ rearrange to solve for k. $k = \dfrac{0.693}{t_{1/2}} = \dfrac{0.693}{1.83\ \text{h}} = 0.3\underline{7}8689\ \text{h}^{-1}$. Since

$\ln\dfrac{\text{Rate}_t}{\text{Rate}_0} = -kt$ rearrange to solve for t

$$t = -\frac{1}{k}\ln\frac{\text{Rate}_t}{\text{Rate}_0} = -\frac{1}{0.3\underline{7}8689\ \text{h}^{-1}}\ln\frac{2.5\times10^3\ \cancel{/\text{s}}}{1.5\times10^5\ \cancel{/\text{s}}} = 10.8\ \text{h}.$$

Check: The units (h) are correct. The time is between 5 and 6 half-lives and the rate is just over $1/2^6$ of the original amount.

19.50 **Given:** Tl-201 initial decay rate = 5.88×10^4 /s, $t_{1/2}$ for Tl-201 = 3.042 days **Find:** t to decay rate of 287 /s
Conceptual Plan: radioactive decay implies first order kinetics, $t_{1/2} \rightarrow k$ then Rate$_0$, Rate$_t$, $k \rightarrow t$

$t_{1/2} = \frac{0.693}{k}$ $\qquad \ln\frac{\text{Rate}_t}{\text{Rate}_0} = -kt$

Solution: $t_{1/2} = \dfrac{0.693}{k}$ rearrange to solve for k. $k = \dfrac{0.693}{t_{1/2}} = \dfrac{0.69315}{3.042\ \text{days}} = 0.227\underline{8}590\ \text{day}^{-1}$. Since

$\ln\dfrac{\text{Rate}_t}{\text{Rate}_0} = -kt$ rearrange to solve for t

$$t = -\frac{1}{k}\ln\frac{\text{Rate}_t}{\text{Rate}_0} = -\frac{1}{0.227\underline{8}590\ \text{day}^{-1}}\ln\frac{287\ \cancel{/\text{s}}}{5.88\times10^4\ \cancel{/\text{s}}} = 2\underline{3}.358\ \text{days} = 23\ \text{days}.$$

Check: The units (days) are correct. The time is between 7 and 8 half-lives and the rate is just over $1/2^8$ of the original amount.

19.51 **Given:** boat analysis, C-14/C-12 = 72.5% of living organism **Find:** t
Other: $t_{1/2}$ for decay of C-14 = 5730 years
Conceptual Plan: radioactive decay implies first order kinetics, $t_{1/2} \rightarrow k$ then 72.5 % of $m_{\text{C-14 }0}$, $k \rightarrow t$

$$t_{1/2} = \frac{0.693}{k} \qquad \ln N_t = -kt + \ln N_0$$

Solution: $t_{1/2} = \dfrac{0.693}{k}$ rearrange to solve for k. $k = \dfrac{0.693}{t_{1/2}} = \dfrac{0.693}{5730 \text{ yr}} = 1.2\underline{0}942 \times 10^{-4} \text{ yr}^{-1}$ then
$[\text{C-14}]_t = 0.725\,[\text{C-14}]_0$. Since $\ln m_{\text{C-14 }t} = -kt + \ln m_{\text{C-14 }0}$ rearrange to solve for t.

$$t = -\frac{1}{k}\ln\frac{m_{\text{C-14 }t}}{m_{\text{C-14 }0}} = -\frac{1}{1.2\underline{0}942 \times 10^{-4} \text{ yr}^{-1}}\ln\frac{0.725\,\cancel{m_{\text{C-14 }0}}}{\cancel{m_{\text{C-14 }0}}} = 2.66 \times 10^3 \text{ yr.}$$

Check: The units (yr) are correct. The time to 72.5% decay is consistent a time less than one half-life.

19.52 **Given:** peat analysis, C-14/C-12 = 22.8% of living organism **Find:** t
Other: $t_{1/2}$ for decay of C-14 = 5730 years
Conceptual Plan: radioactive decay implies first order kinetics, $t_{1/2} \rightarrow k$ then 72.5% of $[\text{C-14}]_0$, $k \rightarrow t$

$$t_{1/2} = \frac{0.693}{k} \qquad \ln N_t = -kt + \ln N_0$$

Solution: $t_{1/2} = \dfrac{0.693}{k}$ rearrange to solve for k. $k = \dfrac{0.693}{t_{1/2}} = \dfrac{0.693}{5730 \text{ yr}} = 1.2\underline{0}942 \times 10^{-4} \text{ yr}^{-1}$ then
$[\text{C-14}]_t = 0.228\,[\text{C-14}]_0$. Since $\ln m_{\text{C-14 }t} = -kt + \ln m_{\text{C-14 }0}$, rearrange to solve for t.

$$t = -\frac{1}{k}\ln\frac{m_{\text{C-14 }t}}{m_{\text{C-14 }0}} = -\frac{1}{1.2\underline{0}942 \times 10^{-4} \text{ yr}^{-1}}\ln\frac{0.228\,\cancel{m_{\text{C-14 }0}}}{\cancel{m_{\text{C-14 }0}}} = 1.22 \times 10^4 \text{ yr.}$$

Check: The units (yr) are correct. The time to 22.8% decay is consistent a time just more than two half-lives.

19.53 **Given:** skull analysis, C-14 decay rate = 15.3 dis/min · gC in living organisms and 0.85 dis/min · gC in skull
Find: t **Other:** $t_{1/2}$ for decay of C-14 = 5730 years
Conceptual Plan: radioactive decay implies first order kinetics, $t_{1/2} \rightarrow k$ then Rate_0, Rate_t, $k \rightarrow t$

$$t_{1/2} = \frac{0.693}{k} \qquad \ln\frac{\text{Rate}_t}{\text{Rate}_0} = -kt$$

Solution: $t_{1/2} = \dfrac{0.693}{k}$ rearrange to solve for k. $k = \dfrac{0.693}{t_{1/2}} = \dfrac{0.693}{5730 \text{ yr}} = 1.2\underline{0}942 \times 10^{-4} \text{ yr}^{-1}$

Since $\ln\dfrac{\text{Rate}_t}{\text{Rate}_0} = -kt$, rearrange to solve for t.

$$t = -\frac{1}{k}\ln\frac{\text{Rate}_t}{\text{Rate}_0} = -\frac{1}{1.2\underline{0}942 \times 10^{-4} \text{ yr}^{-1}}\ln\frac{0.85\,\cancel{\text{dis/min}\cdot\text{gC}}}{15.3\,\cancel{\text{dis/min}\cdot\text{gC}}} = 2.39 \times 10^4 \text{ yr.}$$

Check: The units (yr) are correct. The rate is 6% of initial value and the time is consistent a time just more than four half-lives.

19.54 **Given:** mammoth analysis, C-14 decay rate = 15.3 dis/min · gC in living organisms and 0.48 dis/min · gC in mammoth **Find:** When did the mammoth live? **Other:** $t_{1/2}$ for decay of C-14 = 5730 years
Conceptual Plan: radioactive decay implies first order kinetics, $t_{1/2} \rightarrow k$ then Rate_0, Rate_t, $k \rightarrow t$

$$t_{1/2} = \frac{0.693}{k} \qquad \ln\frac{\text{Rate}_t}{\text{Rate}_0} = -kt$$

Solution: $t_{1/2} = \dfrac{0.693}{k}$ rearrange to solve for k. $k = \dfrac{0.693}{t_{1/2}} = \dfrac{0.693}{5730 \text{ yr}} = 1.2\underline{0}942 \times 10^{-4} \text{ yr}^{-1}$

Since $\ln\dfrac{\text{Rate}_t}{\text{Rate}_0} = -kt$, rearrange to solve for t.

$$t = -\frac{1}{k}\ln\frac{\text{Rate}_t}{\text{Rate}_0} = -\frac{1}{1.2\underline{0}942 \times 10^{-4} \text{ yr}^{-1}}\ln\frac{0.48\,\cancel{\text{dis/min}\cdot\text{gC}}}{15.3\,\cancel{\text{dis/min}\cdot\text{gC}}} = 2.9 \times 10^4 \text{ yr ago.}$$

Check: The units (yr) are correct. The rate is 3% of initial value and the time is consistent a time just more than five half-lives.

19.55 **Given:** rock analysis, 0.438 g Pb-206 to every 1.00 g U-238, no Pb-206 initially **Find:** age of rock
Other: $t_{1/2}$ for decay of U-238 to Pb-206 = 4.5×10^9 years

Conceptual Plan: radioactive decay implies first order kinetics, $t_{1/2}$ → k then

$t_{1/2} = \frac{0.693}{k}$

g Pb-206 → mol Pb-206 → mol U-238 → g U-238 then $m_{U\text{-}238\ 0}$, $m_{U\text{-}238\ t}$, k → t

$\frac{1 \text{ mol Pb-206}}{206 \text{ g Pb-206}}$ $\frac{1 \text{ mol U-238}}{1 \text{ mol Pb-206}}$ $\frac{238 \text{ g U-238}}{1 \text{ mol U-238}}$ $\ln N_t = -kt + \ln N_0$

Solution: $t_{1/2} = \frac{0.693}{k}$ rearrange to solve for k. $k = \frac{0.693}{t_{1/2}} = \frac{0.693}{4.5 \times 10^9 \text{yr}} = 1.54 \times 10^{-10} \text{ yr}^{-1}$ then

$0.438 \cancel{\text{g Pb-206}} \times \frac{1 \cancel{\text{mol Pb-206}}}{206 \cancel{\text{g Pb-206}}} \times \frac{1 \cancel{\text{mol U-238}}}{1 \cancel{\text{mol Pb-206}}} \times \frac{238 \text{ g U-238}}{1 \cancel{\text{mol U-238}}} = 0.506039 \text{ g U-238}$. Since

$\ln \frac{m_{U\text{-}238\ t}}{m_{U\text{-}238\ 0}} = -kt$, rearrange to solve for t.

$$t = -\frac{1}{k} \ln \frac{m_{U\text{-}238\ t}}{m_{U\text{-}238\ 0}} = -\frac{1}{1.54 \times 10^{-10} \text{ yr}^{-1}} \ln \frac{1.00 \cancel{\text{g U-238}}}{(1.00 + 0.506039) \cancel{\text{g U-238}}} = 2.7 \times 10^9 \text{ yr.}$$

Check: The units (yr) are correct. The amount of Pb-206 is less than half of the initial U-238 amount and time is less than one half-life.

19.56 **Given:** meteor analysis, 0.855 g Pb-206 : 1.00 g U-238, no Pb-206 initially **Find:** age of meteor
Other: $t_{1/2}$ for decay of U-238 to Pb-206 = 4.5×10^9 years
Conceptual Plan: radioactive decay implies first order kinetics, $t_{1/2}$ → k then

$t_{1/2} = \frac{0.693}{k}$

g Pb-206 → mol Pb-206 → mol U-238 → g U-238 then $m_{U\text{-}238\ 0}$, $m_{U\text{-}238\ t}$, k → t

$\frac{1 \text{ mol Pb-206}}{206 \text{ g Pb-206}}$ $\frac{1 \text{ mol U-238}}{1 \text{ mol Pb-206}}$ $\frac{238 \text{ g U-238}}{1 \text{ mol U-238}}$ $\ln N_t = -kt + \ln N_0$

Solution: $t_{1/2} = \frac{0.693}{k}$ rearrange to solve for k. $k = \frac{0.693}{t_{1/2}} = \frac{0.693}{4.5 \times 10^9 \text{ yr}} = 1.54 \times 10^{-10} \text{ yr}^{-1}$ then

$0.855 \cancel{\text{g Pb-206}} \times \frac{1 \cancel{\text{mol Pb-206}}}{206 \cancel{\text{g Pb-206}}} \times \frac{1 \cancel{\text{mol U-238}}}{1 \cancel{\text{mol Pb-206}}} \times \frac{238 \text{ g U-238}}{1 \cancel{\text{mol U-238}}} = 0.987816 \text{ g U-238}$. Since

$\ln \frac{m_{U\text{-}238\ t}}{m_{U\text{-}238\ 0}} = -kt$, rearrange to solve for t.

$$t = -\frac{1}{k} \ln \frac{m_{U\text{-}238\ t}}{m_{U\text{-}238\ 0}} = -\frac{1}{1.54 \times 10^{-10} \text{ yr}^{-1}} \ln \frac{1.00 \cancel{\text{g U-238}}}{(1.00 + 0.987816) \cancel{\text{g U-238}}} = 4.5 \times 10^9 \text{ yr.}$$

Check: The units (yr) are correct. The amount of Pb-206 is just less than the initial U-238 amount and time is just under one half-life.

Fission, Fusion, and Transmutation

19.57 **Given:** U-235 fission induced by neutrons to Xe-144 and Sr-90 **Find:** number of neutrons produced
Conceptual Plan: Write the species given on the appropriate side of the equation. → Equalize the sum of the mass numbers and the sum of the atomic numbers on both sides of the equation by writing the stoichiometric coefficient in front of the desired species.
Solution: ${}^{235}_{92}\text{U} + {}^{1}_{0}\text{n} \rightarrow {}^{144}_{54}\text{Xe} + {}^{90}_{38}\text{Sr} + ?\,{}^{1}_{0}\text{n}$ becomes ${}^{235}_{92}\text{U} + {}^{1}_{0}\text{n} \rightarrow {}^{144}_{54}\text{Xe} + {}^{90}_{38}\text{Sr} + 2\,{}^{1}_{0}\text{n}$ so two neutrons are produced.
Check: 235 + 1 = 144 + 90 + 2, 92 + 0 = 54 + 38 + 0, and no other particle is necessary to balance the equation.

19.58 **Given:** U-235 fission to Te-137 and Zr-97 **Find:** number of neutrons produced
Conceptual Plan: Write the species given on the appropriate side of the equation. → Equalize the sum of the mass numbers and the sum of the atomic numbers on both sides of the equation by writing the stoichiometric coefficient in front of the desired species.
Solution: ${}^{235}_{92}\text{U} + {}^{1}_{0}\text{n} \rightarrow {}^{137}_{52}\text{Te} + {}^{97}_{40}\text{Zr} + ?\,{}^{1}_{0}\text{n}$ becomes ${}^{235}_{92}\text{U} + {}^{1}_{0}\text{n} \rightarrow {}^{137}_{52}\text{Te} + {}^{97}_{40}\text{Zr} + 2\,{}^{1}_{0}\text{n}$ so two neutrons are produced.
Check: 235 + 1 = 137 + 97 + 2, 92 + 0 = 52 + 40 + 0, and no other particle is necessary to balance the equation.

19.59 **Given:** fusion of two H-2 atoms to form He-3 and one neutron **Find:** balanced equation
Conceptual Plan: Write the species given on the appropriate side of the equation. → Equalize the sum of the mass numbers and the sum of the atomic numbers on both sides of the equation by writing the stoichiometric coefficient in front of the desired species.
Solution: $2\,{}^{2}_{1}\text{H} \rightarrow {}^{3}_{2}\text{He} + {}^{1}_{0}\text{n}$.
Check: 2(2) = 3 + 1, 2(1) = 2 + 0, and no other particle is necessary to balance the equation.

19.60 **Given:** fusion of H-3 and H-1 atoms to form He-4 **Find:** balanced equation
Conceptual Plan: Write the species given on the appropriate side of the equation. → Equalize the sum of the mass numbers and the sum of the atomic numbers on both sides of the equation by writing the stoichiometric coefficient in front of the desired species.
Solution: ${}^{3}_{1}\text{H} + {}^{1}_{1}\text{H} \rightarrow {}^{4}_{2}\text{He}$.
Check: 3 + 1 = 4, 1 + 1 = 2, and no other particle is necessary to balance the equation.

19.61 **Given:** U-238 bombarded by neutrons to form U-239 which undergoes two beta decays to form Pu-239
Find: balanced equations
Conceptual Plan: Write the species given on the appropriate side of the equation. → Equalize the sum of the mass numbers and the sum of the atomic numbers on both sides of the equation by writing the stoichiometric coefficient in front of the desired species. → Use the product of this reaction to write the next reaction until the process is complete.
Solution: ${}^{238}_{92}\text{U} + ?\,{}^{1}_{0}\text{n} \rightarrow {}^{239}_{92}\text{U}$ becomes ${}^{238}_{92}\text{U} + {}^{1}_{0}\text{n} \rightarrow {}^{239}_{92}\text{U}$ then
beta decay ${}^{239}_{92}\text{U} \rightarrow {}^{?}_{?}? + {}^{0}_{-1}\text{e}$ becomes ${}^{239}_{92}\text{U} \rightarrow {}^{239}_{93}? + {}^{0}_{-1}\text{e}$ then ${}^{239}_{92}\text{U} \rightarrow {}^{239}_{93}\text{Np} + {}^{0}_{-1}\text{e}$ then
beta decay ${}^{239}_{93}\text{Np} \rightarrow {}^{?}_{?}? + {}^{0}_{-1}\text{e}$ becomes ${}^{239}_{93}\text{Np} \rightarrow {}^{239}_{94}? + {}^{0}_{-1}\text{e}$ then ${}^{239}_{93}\text{Np} \rightarrow {}^{239}_{94}\text{Pu} + {}^{0}_{-1}\text{e}$.
The entire process is ${}^{238}_{92}\text{U} + {}^{1}_{0}\text{n} \rightarrow {}^{239}_{92}\text{U}$, ${}^{239}_{92}\text{U} \rightarrow {}^{239}_{93}\text{Np} + {}^{0}_{-1}\text{e}$, ${}^{239}_{93}\text{Np} \rightarrow {}^{239}_{94}\text{Pu} + {}^{0}_{-1}\text{e}$.
Check: 238 + 1 = 239, 92 + 0 = 92, and no other particle is necessary to balance the equation. 239 = 239 + 0, 92 = 93 – 1, and neptunium is atomic number 93. 239 = 239 + 0, 93 = 94 – 1, and plutonium is atomic number 94.

19.62 **Given:** Al-27 bombarded by a neutron and then undergoes an alpha decay and a beta decay
Find: balanced equations
Conceptual Plan: Write the species given on the appropriate side of the equation. → Equalize the sum of the mass numbers and the sum of the atomic numbers on both sides of the equation by writing the stoichiometric coefficient in front of the desired species. → Use the product of this reaction to write the next reaction until the process is complete.
Solution: ${}^{27}_{13}\text{Al} + {}^{1}_{0}\text{n} \rightarrow {}^{?}_{?}?$ becomes ${}^{27}_{13}\text{Al} + {}^{1}_{0}\text{n} \rightarrow {}^{28}_{13}?$ then ${}^{27}_{13}\text{Al} + {}^{1}_{0}\text{n} \rightarrow {}^{28}_{13}\text{Al}$ then
alpha decay ${}^{28}_{13}\text{Al} \rightarrow {}^{?}_{?}? + {}^{4}_{2}\text{He}$ becomes ${}^{28}_{13}\text{Al} \rightarrow {}^{24}_{11}? + {}^{4}_{2}\text{He}$ then ${}^{28}_{13}\text{Al} \rightarrow {}^{24}_{11}\text{Na} + {}^{4}_{2}\text{He}$ then
beta decay ${}^{24}_{11}\text{Na} \rightarrow {}^{?}_{?}? + {}^{0}_{-1}\text{e}$ becomes ${}^{24}_{11}\text{Na} \rightarrow {}^{24}_{12}? + {}^{0}_{-1}\text{e}$ then ${}^{24}_{11}\text{Na} \rightarrow {}^{24}_{12}\text{Mg} + {}^{0}_{-1}\text{e}$.
The entire process is ${}^{27}_{13}\text{Al} + {}^{1}_{0}\text{n} \rightarrow {}^{28}_{13}\text{Al}$, ${}^{28}_{13}\text{Al} \rightarrow {}^{24}_{11}\text{Na} + {}^{4}_{2}\text{He}$, ${}^{24}_{11}\text{Na} \rightarrow {}^{24}_{12}\text{Mg} + {}^{0}_{-1}\text{e}$.
Check: 27 + 1 = 28, 13 + 0 = 13, and aluminum is atomic number 13. 28 = 24 + 4, 13 = 11 + 2, and sodium is atomic number 11. 24 = 24 + 0, 11 = 12 – 1, and magnesium is atomic number 12.

19.63 **Given:** Rf-257 synthesized by bombarding Cf-249 with C-12 **Find:** balanced equation
Conceptual Plan: Write the species given on the appropriate side of the equation. → Equalize the sum of the mass numbers and the sum of the atomic numbers on both sides of the equation by writing the stoichiometric coefficient in front of the desired species. → Use the product of this reaction to write the next reaction until the process is complete.
Solution: ${}^{249}_{98}\text{Cf} + {}^{12}_{6}\text{C} \rightarrow {}^{257}_{?}\text{Rf} + ?\,{}^{?}_{?}?$ becomes ${}^{249}_{98}\text{Cf} + {}^{12}_{6}\text{C} \rightarrow {}^{257}_{104}\text{Rf} + 4\,{}^{1}_{0}\text{n}$.
Check: 249 + 12 = 257 – 4, 98 + 6 = 104 + 0, and rutherfordium is atomic number 104, four neutrons are needed to balance the equation.

19.64 **Given:** Bi-209 bombarded by Cr-54 to form Bh and one neutron **Find:** balanced equations
Conceptual Plan: Write the species given on the appropriate side of the equation. → Equalize the sum of the mass numbers and the sum of the atomic numbers on both sides of the equation by writing the stoichiometric coefficient in front of the desired species. → Use the product of this reaction to write the next reaction until the process is complete.
Solution: ${}^{209}_{83}\text{Bi} + {}^{54}_{24}\text{Cr} \rightarrow {}_{107}^{?}\text{Bh} + {}^{1}_{0}\text{n}$ becomes ${}^{209}_{83}\text{Bi} + {}^{54}_{24}\text{Cr} \rightarrow {}^{262}_{107}\text{Bh} + {}^{1}_{0}\text{n}$.

Check: 209 + 54 = 262 + 1, 83 + 24 = 107 + 0, bhorium is atomic number 107 and no other particles are needed to balance the equation.

Energetics of Nuclear Reactions, Mass Defect, and Nuclear Binding Energy

19.65 **Given:** 1.0 g of matter converted to energy **Find:** energy

Conceptual Plan: **g → kg → *E***

$\frac{1\text{ kg}}{1000\text{ g}}$ $\quad E = mc^2$

Solution: $1.0\,\cancel{\text{g}} \times \frac{1\text{ kg}}{1000\,\cancel{\text{g}}} = 0.0010\text{ kg}$ then $E = mc^2 = (0.0010\text{ kg})\left(2.9979 \times 10^8\ \frac{\text{m}}{\text{s}}\right)^2 = 9.0 \times 10^{13}\text{ J}$

Check: The units (J) are correct. The magnitude of the answer makes physical sense because we are converting a large quantity of amus to energy.

19.66 **Given:** 1.0×10^3 kWh of electricity/month from nuclear reaction **Find:** mass converted to energy / year

Conceptual Plan: **kWh → J → kg → g then g/month → g/year**

$\frac{3.60 \times 10^6\text{ J}}{1\text{ kWh}}$ $\quad E = mc^2$ $\quad \frac{1000\text{ g}}{1\text{ kg}}$ $\quad \frac{12\text{ months}}{1\text{ year}}$

Solution: $1.0 \times 10^3\,\cancel{\text{kWh}} \times \frac{3.60 \times 10^6\text{ J}}{1\,\cancel{\text{kWh}}} = 3.6 \times 10^9\text{ J}$. Since $E = mc^2$, rearrange to solve for m.

$$m = \frac{E}{c^2} = \frac{3.6 \times 10^9\text{ kg}\frac{\cancel{\text{m}^2}}{\cancel{\text{s}^2}}}{\left(2.9979 \times 10^8\frac{\cancel{\text{m}}}{\cancel{\text{s}}}\right)^2} = 4.0 \times 10^{-8}\,\cancel{\text{kg}} \times \frac{1000\text{ g}}{1\,\cancel{\text{kg}}} = 4.0 \times 10^{-5}\text{ g. Then}$$

$$\frac{4.0 \times 10^{-5}\text{ g}}{1\,\cancel{\text{month}}} \times \frac{12\,\cancel{\text{months}}}{1\text{ year}} = \frac{4.8 \times 10^{-4}\text{ g}}{1\text{ year}}$$

Check: The units (g) are correct. A small mass is expected since nuclear reactions generate a large amount of energy.

19.67 **Given:** (a) O-16 = 15.9949145 amu; (b) Ni-58 = 57.935346 amu; and (c) Xe-129 = 128.904780 amu

Find: mass defect and nuclear binding energy per nucleon

Conceptual Plan: **^A_ZX, isotope mass → mass defect → nuclear binding energy per nucleon**

mass defect = $Z(\text{mass }^1_1\text{H}) + (A - Z)(\text{mass }^1_0\text{n}) - \text{mass of isotope}$ $\quad \frac{931.5\text{ MeV}}{(1\text{ amu})(A\text{ nucleons})}$

Solution: mass defect $= Z(\text{mass }^1_1\text{H}) + (A - Z)(\text{mass }^1_0\text{n}) - \text{mass of isotope}$.

(a) O-16 mass defect $= 8(1.00783\text{ amu}) + (16 - 8)(1.00866\text{ amu}) - 15.9949145\text{ amu}$

$= 0.137\underline{0}055\text{ amu} = 0.13701\text{ amu}$ and $0.137\underline{0}055\,\cancel{\text{amu}} \times \frac{931.5\text{ MeV}}{(1\,\cancel{\text{amu}})(16\text{ nucleons})} = 7.976\frac{\text{MeV}}{\text{nucleon}}$.

(b) Ni-58 mass defect $= 28(1.00783\text{ amu}) + (58 - 28)(1.00866\text{ amu}) - 57.935346\text{ amu}$

$= 0.5436\underline{9}4\text{ amu} = 0.54369\text{ amu}$ and $0.5436\underline{9}4\,\cancel{\text{amu}} \times \frac{931.5\text{ MeV}}{(1\,\cancel{\text{amu}})(58\text{ nucleons})} = 8.732\frac{\text{MeV}}{\text{nucleon}}$.

(c) Xe-129 mass defect $= 54(1.00783\text{ amu}) + (129 - 54)(1.00866\text{ amu}) - 128.904780\text{ amu}$

$= 1.16754\text{ amu}$ and $1.16754\,\cancel{\text{amu}} \times \frac{931.5\text{ MeV}}{(1\,\cancel{\text{amu}})\,(129\text{ nucleons})} = 8.431\frac{\text{MeV}}{\text{nucleon}}$.

Check: The units (amu and MeV/nucleon) are correct. The mass defect increases with an increasing number of nucleons, but the MeV/nucleon does not change by as much (on a relative basis).

19.68 **Given:** (a) Li-7 = 7.016003 amu; (b) Ti-48 = 47.947947 amu; and (c) Ag-107 = 106.905092 amu

Find: mass defect and nuclear binding energy per nucleon

Conceptual Plan: **^A_ZX, isotope mass → mass defect → nuclear binding energy per nucleon**

mass defect = $Z(\text{mass }^1_1\text{H}) + (A - Z)(\text{mass }^1_0\text{n}) - \text{mass of isotope}$ $\quad \frac{931.5\text{ MeV}}{(1\text{ amu})(A\text{ nucleons})}$

Solution: mass defect $= Z(\text{mass }^1_1\text{H}) + (A - Z)(\text{mass }^1_0\text{n}) - \text{mass of isotope}$.

(a) Li-7 mass defect = 3(1.00783 amu) + (7 − 3)(1.00866 amu) − 7.016003 amu

$= 0.042127 \text{ amu} = 0.04213 \text{ amu and } 0.042127 \text{ amu} \times \frac{931.5 \text{ MeV}}{(1 \text{ amu})(7 \text{ nucleons})} = 5.602 \frac{\text{MeV}}{\text{nucleon}}$.

(b) Ti-48 mass defect = 22(1.00783 amu) + (48 − 22)(1.00866 amu) − 47.947947 amu

$= 0.449473 \text{ amu} = 0.44947 \text{ amu and } 0.449473 \text{ amu} \times \frac{931.5 \text{ MeV}}{(1 \text{ amu})(48 \text{ nucleons})} = 8.723 \frac{\text{MeV}}{\text{nucleon}}$.

(c) Ag-107 mass defect = 47(1.00783 amu) + (107 − 47)(1.00866 amu) − 106.905092 amu

$= 0.982518 \text{ amu} = 0.98252 \text{ amu and } 0.982518 \text{ amu} \times \frac{931.5 \text{ MeV}}{(1 \text{ amu})(107 \text{ nucleons})} = 8.553 \frac{\text{MeV}}{\text{nucleon}}$.

Check: The units (amu and MeV/nucleon) are correct. The mass defect increases with an increasing number of nucleons, but the MeV/nucleon does not change by as much (on a relative basis).

19.69 **Given:** ${}^{235}_{92}\text{U} + {}^{1}_{0}\text{n} \rightarrow {}^{144}_{54}\text{Xe} + {}^{90}_{38}\text{Sr} + 2\,{}^{1}_{0}\text{n}$, U-235 = 235.043922 amu, Xe-144 = 143.9385 amu, and Sr-90 = 89.907738 amu **Find:** energy per g of U-235

Conceptual Plan: mass of products & reactants → mass defect → mass defect / g of U-235 then

mass defect = $\sum$mass of reactants − $\sum$mass of products $\quad \frac{\text{mass defect}}{235.043922 \text{ g U-235}}$

g → kg → *E*

$\frac{1 \text{ kg}}{1000 \text{ g}} \quad E = mc^2$

Solution: mass defect = $\sum$mass of reactants − $\sum$mass of products notice that we can cancel a neutron from each side to get: ${}^{235}_{92}\text{U} \rightarrow {}^{144}_{54}\text{Xe} + {}^{90}_{38}\text{Sr} + {}^{1}_{0}\text{n}$ and

mass defect = 235.043922 g − (143.9385 g + 89.907738 g + 1.00866 g) = 0.189024 g

then $\frac{0.189024 \text{ g}}{235.043922 \text{ g U-235}} \times \frac{1 \text{ kg}}{1000 \text{ g}} = 8.04207 \times 10^{-7} \frac{\text{kg}}{\text{g U-235}}$ then

$$E = mc^2 = \left(8.04207 \times 10^{-7} \frac{\text{kg}}{\text{g U-235}}\right)\left(2.9979 \times 10^8 \frac{\text{m}}{\text{s}}\right)^2 = 7.228 \times 10^{10} \frac{\text{J}}{\text{g U-235}}.$$

Check: The units (J) are correct. A large amount of energy is expected per gram of fuel in a nuclear reactor.

19.70 **Given:** ${}^{235}_{92}\text{U} + {}^{1}_{0}\text{n} \rightarrow {}^{137}_{52}\text{Te} + {}^{97}_{40}\text{Zr} + 2\,{}^{1}_{0}\text{n}$, U-235 = 235.043922 amu, Te-137 = 136.9253 amu, and Zr-97 = 96.910950 amu **Find:** energy per mol of U-235

Conceptual Plan: mass of products & reactants → mass defect → mass defect / mol of U-235 then

mass defect = $\sum$mass of reactants − $\sum$mass of products $\quad \frac{\text{mass defect}}{235.043922 \text{ g U-235}}$

g → kg → *E*

$\frac{1 \text{ kg}}{1000 \text{ g}} \quad E = mc^2$

Solution: mass defect = $\sum$mass of reactants − $\sum$mass of products, notice that we can cancel a neutron from each side to get: ${}^{235}_{92}\text{U} \rightarrow {}^{137}_{52}\text{Te} + {}^{97}_{40}\text{Zr} + {}^{1}_{0}\text{n}$ and

mass defect = 235.043922 g − (136.9253 g + 96.910950 g + 1.00866 g) = 0.199012 g/mol U-235

then $\frac{0.199012 \text{ g}}{\text{mol U-235}} \times \frac{1 \text{ kg}}{1000 \text{ g}} = 1.99012 \text{ g} \times 10^{-4} \frac{\text{kg}}{\text{mol U-235}}$ then

$$E = mc^2 = \left(1.99012 \text{ g} \times 10^{-4} \frac{\text{kg}}{\text{mol U-235}}\right)\left(2.9979 \times 10^8 \frac{\text{m}}{\text{s}}\right)^2 = 1.789 \times 10^{13} \frac{\text{J}}{\text{mol U-235}}.$$

Check: The units (J) are correct. A large amount of energy is expected per gram of fuel in a nuclear reactor.

19.71 **Given:** $2\,{}^{2}_{1}\text{H} \rightarrow {}^{3}_{2}\text{He} + {}^{1}_{0}\text{n}$, H-2 = 2.014102 amu, and He-3 = 3.016029 amu **Find:** energy per g reactant

Conceptual Plan: mass of products & reactants → mass defect → mass defect / g of H-2 then

mass defect = $\sum$mass of reactants − $\sum$mass of products $\quad \frac{\text{mass defect}}{2(2.014102 \text{ g H-2})}$

g → kg → *E*

$\frac{1 \text{ kg}}{1000 \text{ g}} \quad E = mc^2$

Solution: mass defect = $\sum$mass of reactants − $\sum$mass of products and

mass defect = 2(2.014102 g) − (3.016029 g + 1.00866 g) = 0.003515 g then $\frac{0.003515 \text{ g}}{2(2.014102 \text{ g H-2})} \times \frac{1 \text{ kg}}{1000 \text{ g}} = 8.72597 \times 10^{-7} \frac{\text{kg}}{\text{g H-2}}$ then

$E = m c^2 = \left(8.72597 \times 10^{-7} \frac{\text{kg}}{\text{g H-2}}\right)\left(2.9979 \times 10^8 \frac{\text{m}}{\text{s}}\right)^2 = 7.84 \times 10^{10} \frac{\text{J}}{\text{g H-2}}$.

Check: The units (J) are correct. A large amount of energy is expected per gram of fuel in a fusion reaction.

19.72 **Given:** ${}^3_1\text{H} + {}^1_1\text{H} \rightarrow {}^4_2\text{He}$, H-3 = 3.016049 amu, H-1 = 1.007825 amu, and He-4 = 4.002603 amu
Find: energy per g reactant
Conceptual Plan: mass of products & reactants → mass defect → mass defect / g reactant then

mass defect $= \sum$mass of reactants $- \sum$mass of products; $\frac{\text{mass defect}}{\text{g reactant}}$

g → kg → *E*

$\frac{1 \text{ kg}}{1000 \text{ g}}$; $E = m c^2$

Solution: mass defect $= \sum$mass of reactants $- \sum$mass of products and
mass defect = (3.016049 g + 1.007825 g) − 4.002603 g = 4.023874 g − 4.002603 g = 0.021271 g

then $\frac{0.021271 \text{ g}}{4.023874 \text{ g reactants}} \times \frac{1 \text{ kg}}{1000 \text{ g}} = 5.2861993 \times 10^{-6} \frac{\text{kg}}{\text{g reactants}}$ then

$E = m c^2 = \left(5.2861993 \times 10^{-6} \frac{\text{kg}}{\text{g reactants}}\right)\left(2.9979 \times 10^8 \frac{\text{m}}{\text{s}}\right)^2 = 4.7509 \times 10^{11} \frac{\text{J}}{\text{g reactants}}$.

Check: The units (J) are correct. A large amount of energy is expected per gram of fuel in a fusion reaction.

Effects and Applications of Radioactivity

19.73 **Given:** 75 kg human exposed to 32.8 rad and falling from chair **Find:** energy absorbed in each case
Conceptual Plan: rad, kg → J and assume *d* = 0.50 m chair height then mass, *d* → J

$1 \text{ rad} = \frac{0.01 \text{ J}}{1 \text{ kg body tissue}}$; $E = F \cdot d = m g d$

Solution: $32.8 \text{ rad} = 32.8 \frac{0.01 \text{ J}}{1 \text{ kg body tissue}} \times 75 \text{ kg} = 25 \text{ J}$ and

$E = F \cdot d = m g d = 75 \text{ kg} \times 9.8 \frac{\text{m}}{\text{s}^2} \times 0.50 \text{ m} = 370 \text{ kg} \frac{\text{m}^2}{\text{s}^2} = 370 \text{ J}$.

Check: The units (J and J) are correct. Allowable radiation exposures are low, since the radiation is very ionizing and, thus, damaging to tissue. Falling may have more energy, but it is not ionizing.

19.74 **Given:** 55 g mouse exposed to 20.5 rad **Find:** energy absorbed
Conceptual Plan: g → kg then rad, kg → J

$\frac{1 \text{ kg}}{1000 \text{ g}}$; $\frac{0.01 \text{ J}}{1 \text{ kg body tissue}}$

Solution: $55 \text{ g} \times \frac{1 \text{ kg}}{1000 \text{ g}} = 0.055 \text{ kg}$ then $20.5 \text{ rad} = 20.5 \frac{0.01 \text{ J}}{1 \text{ kg body tissue}} \times 0.055 \text{ kg} = 0.011 \text{ J}$.

Check: The units (J) are correct. Allowable radiation exposures are low, since the radiation is very ionizing and, thus, damaging to tissue.

19.75 **Given:** $t_{1/2}$ for F-18 = 1.83 h, 65% of F-18 makes it to the hospital traveling at 60.0 miles/hour
Find: distance between hospital and cyclotron
Conceptual Plan: $t_{1/2}$ → *k* then $m_{\text{F-18 } 0}$, $m_{\text{F-18 } t}$, *k* → *t* then h → mi

$t_{1/2} = \frac{0.693}{k}$; $\ln \frac{m_{\text{F-18 } t}}{m_{\text{F-18 } 0}} = -k t$; $\frac{60.0 \text{ mi}}{1 \text{ h}}$

Solution: $t_{1/2} = \frac{0.693}{k}$ rearrange to solve for k. $k = \frac{0.693}{t_{1/2}} = \frac{0.693}{1.83 \text{ h}} = 0.378689 \text{ h}^{-1}$. Since

$\ln \frac{m_{\text{F-18 } t}}{m_{\text{F-18 } 0}} = -k t$ rearrange to solve for t

$t = -\frac{1}{k} \ln \frac{m_{\text{F-18 } t}}{m_{\text{F-18 } 0}} = -\frac{1}{0.378689 \text{ h}^{-1}} \ln \frac{0.65 \, m_{\text{F-18 } 0}}{m_{\text{F-18 } 0}} = 1.1376 \text{ h}$. Then

$1.1376\ \cancel{h} \times \frac{60.0\ \text{mi}}{1\ \cancel{h}} = 68\ \text{mi.}$

Check: The units (mi) are correct. The time is less than one half-life, so the distance is less than 1.83 times the speed of travel.

19.76 **Given:** I-131, 155 mg, $t_{1/2} = 8.0$ days **Find:** exposure (in Ci) after 4.0 h

Conceptual Plan: $\textbf{h} \rightarrow \textbf{day and } t_{1/2} \rightarrow k \textbf{ then } m_{\text{I-131 }0}, t, k \rightarrow m_{\text{I-131 }t}$

$\frac{1\ \text{day}}{24\ \text{hr}}$ $\quad t_{1/2} = \frac{0.693}{k}$ $\quad \ln N_t = -kt + \ln N_0$

then $\textbf{mg}_0, \textbf{mg}_t \rightarrow$ **mg decayed** $\rightarrow$ **g decayed** $\rightarrow$ **mol decayed** $\rightarrow$ **beta decays then h** $\rightarrow$ **min** $\rightarrow$ **s**

$\text{mg}_0 - \text{mg}_t = \text{mg decayed}$ $\quad \frac{1\ \text{g}}{1000\ \text{mg}}$ $\quad \frac{1\ \text{mol I-131}}{131\ \text{g I-131}}$ $\quad \frac{6.022 \times 10^{23}\ \text{beta decays}}{1\ \text{mol I-131}}$ $\quad \frac{60\ \text{min}}{1\ \text{h}}$ $\quad \frac{60\ \text{s}}{1\ \text{min}}$

then beta decays, s $\rightarrow$ **beta decays / s** $\rightarrow$ **Ci**

take ratio $\quad \frac{1\ \text{Ci}}{\frac{3.7 \times 10^{10}\ \text{decays}}{\text{s}}}$

Solution: $4.0\ \cancel{h} \times \frac{1\ \text{day}}{24\ \cancel{h}} = 0.1\underline{6}667\ \text{day then } t_{1/2} = \frac{0.693}{k}$ rearrange to solve for k.

$k = \frac{0.693}{t_{1/2}} = \frac{0.693}{8.0\ \text{days}} = 0.08\underline{6}625\ \text{day}^{-1}$. Since

$\ln m_{\text{I-131 }t} = -kt + \ln m_{\text{I-131 }0} = -(0.08\underline{6}625\ \cancel{\text{day}^{-1}})(0.1\underline{6}667\ \cancel{\text{day}}) + \ln(155\ \text{mg}) = 5.02\underline{8}99 \rightarrow$

$m_{\text{I-131 }t} = e^{5.02\underline{8}99} = 152.\underline{7}78\ \text{mg}$. Then

$\text{mg}_0 - \text{mg}_t = \text{mg decayed} = 155\ \text{mg} - 152.\underline{7}78\ \text{mg} = \underline{2}.222\ \text{mg I-131 then}$

$\underline{2}.222\ \cancel{\text{mg I-131}} \times \frac{1\ \cancel{\text{g I-131}}}{1000\ \cancel{\text{mg I-131}}} \times \frac{1\ \cancel{\text{mol I-131}}}{131\ \cancel{\text{g I-131}}} \times \frac{6.022 \times 10^{23}\ \text{beta decays}}{1\ \cancel{\text{mol I-131}}} = \underline{1}.0213 \times 10^{19}\ \text{beta decays}$

$\text{then } 4.0\ \cancel{h} \times \frac{60\ \cancel{\text{min}}}{1\ \cancel{h}} \times \frac{60\ \text{s}}{1\ \cancel{\text{min}}} = 1.44 \times 10^4\ \text{s then}$

$\frac{\underline{1}.0213 \times 10^{19}\ \cancel{\text{beta decays}}}{1.44 \times 10^4\ \cancel{\text{s}}} \times \frac{1\ \text{Ci}}{\frac{3.7 \times 10^{10}\ \cancel{\text{decays}}}{\cancel{\text{s}}}} = \underline{1}.9169 \times 10^4\ \text{Ci} = 2 \times 10^4\ \text{Ci}$

Check: The units (Ci) are correct. The amount that decays is large since the half-life is fairly short and so the dose is high.

Cumulative Problems

19.77 **Given:** Incomplete reactions **Find:** balanced reaction and energy (in J/mol reactant)

Conceptual Plan: Equalize the sum of the mass numbers and the sum of the atomic numbers on both sides of the equation by writing the appropriate mass number and atomic number for the unknown species. $\rightarrow$ **Using the periodic table and the list of particles, deduce the identity of the unknown species from the atomic number and write its symbol. then**

mass of products & reactants $\rightarrow$ **mass defect in g** $\rightarrow$ **mass defect in kg** $\rightarrow$ $\boldsymbol{E}$

$\text{mass defect} = \sum \text{mass of reactants} - \sum \text{mass of products}$ $\quad \frac{1\ \text{kg}}{1000\ \text{g}}$ $\quad E = mc^2$

Solution:

(a) ${}^{?}_{?}? + {}^{9}_{4}\text{Be} \rightarrow {}^{6}_{3}\text{Li} + {}^{4}_{2}\text{He}$ becomes ${}^{1}_{1}? + {}^{9}_{4}\text{Be} \rightarrow {}^{6}_{3}\text{Li} + {}^{4}_{2}\text{He}$ then ${}^{1}_{1}\text{H} + {}^{9}_{4}\text{Be} \rightarrow {}^{6}_{3}\text{Li} + {}^{4}_{2}\text{He}$

$\text{mass defect} = \sum \text{mass of reactants} - \sum \text{mass of products}$ and

$\text{mass defect} = (1.00783\ \text{g} + 9.012182\ \text{g}) - (6.015122\ \text{g} + 4.002603\ \text{g}) = 0.0022\underline{8}7\ \text{g}$

$\text{then } \frac{0.0022\underline{8}7\ \cancel{\text{g}}}{2\ \text{mol reactants}} \times \frac{1\ \text{kg}}{1000\ \cancel{\text{g}}} = 1.14\underline{3}5 \times 10^{-6} \frac{\text{kg}}{\text{mol reactants}}$ then

$E = mc^2 = \left(1.14\underline{3}5 \times 10^{-6} \frac{\text{kg}}{\text{mol reactants}}\right)\left(2.9979 \times 10^8 \frac{\text{m}}{\text{s}}\right)^2 = 1.03 \times 10^{11} \frac{\text{J}}{\text{mol reactants}}.$

Check: 1 + 9 = 6 + 4, 1 + 4 = 3 + 2. The units (J) are correct.

(b) $^{209}_{83}Bi + ^{64}_{28}Ni \rightarrow ^{272}_{111}Rg + ^{?}_{?}?$ becomes $^{209}_{83}Bi + ^{64}_{28}Ni \rightarrow ^{272}_{111}Rg + ^{1}_{0}?$ then $^{209}_{83}Bi + ^{64}_{28}Ni \rightarrow ^{272}_{111}Rg + ^{1}_{0}n$
mass defect = (208.980384 g + 63.927969 g) − (272.1535 g + 1.00866 g) = − 0.253807 g
(Note: Since this is negative, energy must be put in.)
then $\frac{0.253807\ \cancel{g}}{2\ \text{mol reactants}} \times \frac{1\ \text{kg}}{1000\ \cancel{g}} = 1.269035 \times 10^{-4} \frac{\text{kg}}{\text{mol reactants}}$ then

$$E = mc^2 = \left(1.269035 \times 10^{-4} \frac{\text{kg}}{\text{mol reactants}}\right)\left(2.9979 \times 10^8 \frac{\text{m}}{\text{s}}\right)^2 = 1.141 \times 10^{13} \frac{\text{J}}{\text{mol reactants}}$$

Check: 209 + 64 = 272 + 1, 83 + 28 = 111 + 0. The units (J) are correct.

(c) $^{179}_{74}W + ^{?}_{?}? \rightarrow ^{179}_{73}Ta$ becomes $^{179}_{74}W + ^{0}_{-1}? \rightarrow ^{179}_{73}Ta$ then $^{179}_{74}W + ^{0}_{-1}e \rightarrow ^{179}_{73}Ta$
mass defect = (178.94707 g + 0.00055 g) − 178.94593 g = 0.00169 g then
$\frac{0.00169\ \cancel{g}}{2\ \text{mol reactants}} \times \frac{1\ \text{kg}}{1000\ \cancel{g}} = 8.45 \times 10^{-7} \frac{\text{kg}}{\text{mol reactants}}$ then

$$E = mc^2 = \left(8.45 \times 10^{-7} \frac{\text{kg}}{\text{mol reactants}}\right)\left(2.9979 \times 10^8 \frac{\text{m}}{\text{s}}\right)^2 = 7.59 \times 10^{10} \frac{\text{J}}{\text{mol reactants}}$$

Check: 179 + 0 = 179, 74 – 1 = 73. The units (J) are correct.

19.78 **Given:** Incomplete reactions **Find:** balanced reaction and energy (in J/mol reactant)
Conceptual Plan: Equalize the sum of the mass numbers and the sum of the atomic numbers on both sides of the equation by writing the appropriate mass number and atomic number for the unknown species. → Using the periodic table and the list of particles, deduce the identity of the unknown species from the atomic number and write its symbol. then
mass of products & reactants → mass defect in g → mass defect in kg → *E*
mass defect = $\sum$mass of reactants − $\sum$mass of products $\quad \frac{1\ \text{kg}}{1000\ \text{g}} \quad E = mc^2$
Solution:

(a) $^{27}_{13}Al + ^{4}_{2}He \rightarrow ^{30}_{15}P + ^{?}_{?}?$ becomes $^{27}_{13}Al + ^{4}_{2}He \rightarrow ^{30}_{15}P + ^{1}_{0}?$ then $^{27}_{13}Al + ^{4}_{2}He \rightarrow ^{30}_{15}P + ^{1}_{0}n$
mass defect = $\sum$mass of reactants − $\sum$mass of products and
mass defect = (26.981538 g + 4.002603 g) − (29.981801g + 1.00866 g) = − 0.00632 g
(Note: Since this is negative, energy must be put in.) then
$\frac{0.00632\ \cancel{g}}{2\ \text{mol reactants}} \times \frac{1\ \text{kg}}{1000\ \cancel{g}} = 3.16 \times 10^{-6} \frac{\text{kg}}{\text{mol reactants}}$ then

$$E = mc^2 = \left(3.16 \times 10^{-6} \frac{\text{kg}}{\text{mol reactants}}\right)\left(2.9979 \times 10^8 \frac{\text{m}}{\text{s}}\right)^2 = 2.84 \times 10^{11} \frac{\text{J}}{\text{mol reactants}}.$$

Check: 27 + 4 = 30 + 1, 13 + 2 = 15 + 0. The units (J) are correct.

(b) $^{32}_{16}S + ^{?}_{?}? \rightarrow ^{29}_{14}Si + ^{4}_{2}He$ becomes $^{32}_{16}S + ^{1}_{0}? \rightarrow ^{29}_{14}Si + ^{4}_{2}He$ then $^{32}_{16}S + ^{1}_{0}n \rightarrow ^{29}_{14}Si + ^{4}_{2}He$
mass defect = (31.972071 g + 1.00866 g) − (28.976495 g + 4.002603 g) = 0.001633 g
then $\frac{0.001633\ \cancel{g}}{2\ \text{mol reactants}} \times \frac{1\ \text{kg}}{1000\ \cancel{g}} = 8.165 \times 10^{-7} \frac{\text{kg}}{\text{mol reactants}}$ then

$$E = mc^2 = \left(8.165 \times 10^{-7} \frac{\text{kg}}{\text{mol reactants}}\right)\left(2.9979 \times 10^8 \frac{\text{m}}{\text{s}}\right)^2 = 7.34 \times 10^{10} \frac{\text{J}}{\text{mol reactants}}$$

Check: 32 + 1 = 29 + 4, 16 + 0 = 14 + 2. The units (J) are correct.

(c) $^{241}_{95}Am \rightarrow ^{237}_{93}Np + ^{?}_{?}?$ becomes $^{241}_{95}Am \rightarrow ^{237}_{93}Np + ^{4}_{2}?$ then $^{241}_{95}Am \rightarrow ^{237}_{93}Np + ^{4}_{2}He$
mass defect = 241.056822 g − (237.048166 g + 4.002603 g) = 0.006053 g then
$\frac{0.006053\ \cancel{g}}{1\ \text{mol reactants}} \times \frac{1\ \text{kg}}{1000\ \cancel{g}} = 6.053 \times 10^{-6} \frac{\text{kg}}{\text{mol reactants}}$ then

$$E = mc^2 = \left(6.053 \times 10^{-6} \frac{\text{kg}}{\text{mol reactants}}\right)\left(2.9979 \times 10^8 \frac{\text{m}}{\text{s}}\right)^2 = 5.440 \times 10^{11} \frac{\text{J}}{\text{mol reactant}}$$

Check: 241 = 237 + 4, 95 = 93 + 2. The units (J) are correct.

19.79 **Given:** (a) Ru-114, (b) Ra-216, (c) Zn-58, and (d) Ne-31 **Find:** Write a nuclear equation for the most likely decay.
Conceptual Plan: Referring to the Valley of Stability graph in Figure 19.5, decide on the most likely decay mode depending on *N/Z* (too large = beta decay, too low = positron emission). → Write the symbol for the parent nuclide on the left side of the equation and the symbol for a particle on the right side. → Equalize the sum of the mass numbers and the sum of the atomic numbers on both sides of the equation by writing the appropriate mass number and atomic number for the unknown daughter nuclide. → Using the periodic table, deduce the identity of the unknown daughter nuclide from the atomic number and write its symbol.
Solution:

(a) Ru-114 ($N/Z = 1.6$) will undergo beta decay ${}^{114}_{44}\text{Ru} \rightarrow {}^{?}_{?}? + {}^{0}_{-1}\text{e}$ then ${}^{114}_{44}\text{Ru} \rightarrow {}^{114}_{45}? + {}^{0}_{-1}\text{e}$ then ${}^{114}_{44}\text{Ru} \rightarrow {}^{114}_{45}\text{Rh} + {}^{0}_{-1}\text{e}$

(b) Ra-216 ($N/Z = 1.4$) will undergo positron emission ${}^{216}_{88}\text{Ra} \rightarrow {}^{?}_{?}? + {}^{0}_{+1}\text{e}$ then ${}^{216}_{88}\text{Ra} \rightarrow {}^{216}_{87}? + {}^{0}_{+1}\text{e}$ then ${}^{216}_{88}\text{Ra} \rightarrow {}^{216}_{87}\text{Fr} + {}^{0}_{+1}\text{e}$

(c) Zn-58 ($N/Z = 0.9$) will undergo positron emission ${}^{58}_{30}\text{Zn} \rightarrow {}^{?}_{?}? + {}^{0}_{+1}\text{e}$ then ${}^{58}_{30}\text{Zn} \rightarrow {}^{58}_{29}? + {}^{0}_{+1}\text{e}$ then ${}^{58}_{30}\text{Zn} \rightarrow {}^{58}_{29}\text{Cu} + {}^{0}_{+1}\text{e}$

(d) Ne-31 ($N/Z = 2$) will undergo beta decay ${}^{31}_{10}\text{Ne} \rightarrow {}^{?}_{?}? + {}^{0}_{-1}\text{e}$ then ${}^{31}_{10}\text{Ne} \rightarrow {}^{31}_{11}? + {}^{0}_{-1}\text{e}$ then ${}^{31}_{10}\text{Ne} \rightarrow {}^{31}_{11}\text{Na} + {}^{0}_{-1}\text{e}$

Check: (a) 114 = 114 + 0, 44 = 45 – 1, and rhodium is atomic number 45. (b) 216 = 216 + 0, 88 = 87 + 1, and francium is atomic number 87. (c) 58 = 58 + 0, 30 = 29 + 1, and copper is atomic number 29. (d) 31 = 31 + 0, 10 = 11 – 1, and sodium is atomic number 11.

19.80 **Given:** (a) Kr-74, (b) Th-221, (c) Ar-44, and (d) Nb-85 **Find:** Write a nuclear equation for the most likely decay.
Conceptual Plan: Referring to the Valley of Stability graph in Figure 19.5, decide on the most likely decay mode depending on *N/Z* (too large = beta decay, too low = positron emission). → Write the symbol for the parent nuclide on the left side of the equation and the symbol for a particle on the right side. → Equalize the sum of the mass numbers and the sum of the atomic numbers on both sides of the equation by writing the appropriate mass number and atomic number for the unknown daughter nuclide. → Using the periodic table, deduce the identity of the unknown daughter nuclide from the atomic number and write its symbol.
Solution:

(a) Kr-74 ($N/Z = 1$) will undergo positron emission ${}^{74}_{36}\text{Kr} \rightarrow {}^{?}_{?}? + {}^{0}_{+1}\text{e}$ then ${}^{74}_{36}\text{Kr} \rightarrow {}^{74}_{35}? + {}^{0}_{+1}\text{e}$ then ${}^{74}_{36}\text{Kr} \rightarrow {}^{74}_{35}\text{Br} + {}^{0}_{+1}\text{e}$

(b) Th-221 ($N/Z = 1.5$) will undergo positron emission ${}^{221}_{90}\text{Th} \rightarrow {}^{?}_{?}? + {}^{0}_{+1}\text{e}$ then ${}^{221}_{90}\text{Th} \rightarrow {}^{221}_{89}? + {}^{0}_{+1}\text{e}$ then ${}^{221}_{90}\text{Th} \rightarrow {}^{221}_{89}\text{Ac} + {}^{0}_{+1}\text{e}$

(c) Ar-44 ($N/Z = 1.4$) will undergo beta decay ${}^{44}_{18}\text{Ar} \rightarrow {}^{?}_{?}? + {}^{0}_{-1}\text{e}$ then ${}^{44}_{18}\text{Ar} \rightarrow {}^{44}_{19}? + {}^{0}_{-1}\text{e}$ then ${}^{44}_{18}\text{Ar} \rightarrow {}^{44}_{19}\text{K} + {}^{0}_{-1}\text{e}$

(d) Nb-85 ($N/Z = 1.1$) will undergo positron emission ${}^{85}_{41}\text{Nb} \rightarrow {}^{?}_{?}? + {}^{0}_{+1}\text{e}$ then ${}^{85}_{41}\text{Nb} \rightarrow {}^{85}_{40}? + {}^{0}_{+1}\text{e}$ then ${}^{85}_{41}\text{Nb} \rightarrow {}^{85}_{40}\text{Zr} + {}^{0}_{+1}\text{e}$

Check: (a) 74 = 74 + 0, 36 = 35 + 1, and bromine is atomic number 35. (b) 221 = 221 + 0, 90 = 89 + 1, and actinium is atomic number 89. (c) 44 = 44 + 0, 18 = 19 – 1, and potassium is atomic number 19. (d) 85 = 85 + 0, 41 = 40 + 1, and zirconium is atomic number 40.

19.81 **Given:** Bi-210, $t_{1/2} = 5.0$ days, 1.2 g Bi-210, 209.984105 amu, 5.5% absorbed
Find: beta emissions in 15.5 days and dose (in Ci)
Conceptual Plan: $t_{1/2} \rightarrow k$ **then** $m_{\text{Bi-210 }0}, t, k \rightarrow m_{\text{Bi-210 }t}$ **then**

$$t_{1/2} = \frac{0.693}{k} \qquad \ln N_t = -kt + \ln N_0$$

g_0, g_t → g decayed → mol decayed → beta decays then day → h → min → s then

$g_0 - g_t$ = g decayed $\frac{1 \text{ mol Bi-210}}{209.984105 \text{ g Bi-210}}$ $\frac{6.022 \times 10^{23} \text{ beta decays}}{1 \text{ mol Bi-210}}$ $\frac{1 \text{ day}}{24 \text{ h}}$ $\frac{60 \text{ min}}{1 \text{ h}}$ $\frac{60 \text{ s}}{1 \text{ min}}$

beta decays, s → beta decays / s → Ci available → Ci absorbed

take ratio $\frac{1 \text{ Ci}}{3.7 \times 10^{10} \frac{\text{decays}}{\text{s}}}$ $\frac{5.5 \text{ Ci absorbed}}{100 \text{ Ci emitted}}$

Solution: $t_{1/2} = \frac{0.693}{k}$ rearrange to solve for k. $k = \frac{0.693}{t_{1/2}} = \frac{0.693}{5.0 \text{ days}} = 0.1386 \text{ day}^{-1}$. Since

$\ln m_{\text{Bi-210 t}} = -kt + \ln m_{\text{Bi-210 0}} = -(0.1386 \text{ day}^{-1})(13.5 \text{ day}) + \ln(1.2 \text{ g}) = -1.6888 \rightarrow$

$m_{\text{Bi-210 } t} = e^{-1.6888} = 0.18475$ g. then $g_0 - g_t$ = g decayed = 1.2 g − 0.18475 g = 1.0153 g Bi-210

then $1.0153 \text{ g Bi-210} \times \frac{1 \text{ mol Bi-210}}{209.984105 \text{ g Bi-210}} \times \frac{6.022 \times 10^{23} \text{ beta decays}}{1 \text{ mol Bi-210}} = 2.9116 \times 10^{21}$ beta decays

$= 2.9 \times 10^{21}$ beta decays then $13.5 \text{ day} \times \frac{24 \text{ h}}{1 \text{ day}} \times \frac{60 \text{ min}}{1 \text{ h}} \times \frac{60 \text{ s}}{1 \text{ min}} = 1.1664 \times 10^6$ s then

$$\frac{2.9116 \times 10^{21} \text{ beta decays}}{1.1664 \times 10^6 \text{ s}} \times \frac{1 \text{ Ci}}{3.7 \times 10^{10} \frac{\text{decays}}{\text{s}}} = 6.7466 \times 10^4 \text{ Ci emitted} \times \frac{5.5 \text{ Ci absorbed}}{100 \text{ Ci emitted}} = 3700 \text{ Ci.}$$

Check: The units (decays and Ci) are correct. The amount that decays is large since the time is over 3 half-lives and we have a relatively large amount of the isotope. Since the decay is large, the dosage is large.

19.82 **Given:** Po-218, $t_{1/2}$ = 3.0 minutes, 55 mg Po-218, 218.008965 amu
Find: alpha emissions in 25.0 min and dose (in Ci)
Conceptual Plan: $t_{1/2}$ → k then $m_{\text{Po-218 } 0}$, t, k → $m_{\text{Po-218 } t}$ then

$t_{1/2} = \frac{0.693}{k}$ $\ln N_t = -kt + \ln N_0$

mg_0, mg_t → mg decayed → g decayed → mol decayed → alpha decays then min → s

$mg_0 - mg_t$ = mg decayed $\frac{1 \text{ g}}{1000 \text{ mg}}$ $\frac{1 \text{ mol Po-218}}{218.008965 \text{ g Po-218}}$ $\frac{6.022 \times 10^{23} \text{ beta decays}}{1 \text{ mol Po-218}}$ $\frac{60 \text{ s}}{1 \text{ min}}$

then beta decays, s → beta decays / s → Ci

take ratio $\frac{1 \text{ Ci}}{3.7 \times 10^{10} \frac{\text{decays}}{\text{s}}}$

Solution: $t_{1/2} = \frac{0.693}{k}$ rearrange to solve for k. $k = \frac{0.693}{t_{1/2}} = \frac{0.693}{3.0 \text{ min}} = 0.231 \text{ min}^{-1}$. Since

$\ln m_{\text{Po-218 } t} = -kt + \ln m_{\text{Po-218 } 0} = -(0.231 \text{ min}^{-1})(25.0 \text{ min}) + \ln(55 \text{ mg}) = -1.7677 \rightarrow$

$m_{\text{Po-218 } t} = e^{-1.7677} = 0.17073$ mg. then

$mg_0 - mg_t$ = mg decayed = 55 mg − 0.17073 mg = 54.829 mg Po-218 then 54.829 mg Po-218

$$54.829 \text{ mg Po-218} \times \frac{1 \text{ g Po-218}}{1000 \text{ mg Po-218}} \times \frac{1 \text{ mol Po-218}}{218.008965 \text{ g Po-218}} \times \frac{6.022 \times 10^{23} \text{ alpha decays}}{1 \text{ mol Po-218}} =$$

1.5145×10^{20} alpha decays $= 1.5 \times 10^{20}$ alpha decays then $25.0 \text{ min} \times \frac{60 \text{ s}}{1 \text{ min}} = 1.5 \times 10^3$ s then

$$\frac{1.5145 \times 10^{20} \text{ alpha decays}}{1.5 \times 10^3 \text{ s}} \times \frac{1 \text{ Ci}}{3.7 \times 10^{10} \frac{\text{decays}}{\text{s}}} = 2.7 \times 10^6 \text{ Ci.}$$

Check: The units (decays and Ci) are correct. The amount that decays is large since the time is over 8 half-lives, so almost the entire isotope has decayed. Since the decay rate is large (small half-life), the dosage is large.

19.83 **Given:** Ra-226 (226.05402 amu) decays to Rn-224, $t_{1/2} = 1.6 \times 10^3$ yr, 25.0 g Ra-226, T = 25.0 °C, P = 1.0 atm
Find: V of Rn-224 gas produced in 5.0 day
Conceptual Plan: day → yr then $t_{1/2}$ → k then $m_{\text{Ra-226 } 0}$, t, k → $m_{\text{Ra-226 } t}$

$\frac{1 \text{ yr}}{365.24 \text{ day}}$ $t_{1/2} = \frac{0.693}{k}$ $\ln N_t = -kt + \ln N_0$

then g_0, g_t → g decayed → mol decayed → mol Rn-224 formed then °C → K then then P, n, T → V

$g_0 - g_t$ = g decayed $\frac{1 \text{ mol Ra-226}}{226.05402 \text{ g Ra-226}}$ $\frac{1 \text{ mol Rn-224}}{1 \text{ mol Ra-226}}$ K = °C + 273.15 $PV = nRT$

Solution: $5.0 \cancel{\text{day}} \times \frac{1 \text{ yr}}{365.24 \cancel{\text{day}}} = 0.013690 \text{ yr}$ then $t_{1/2} = \frac{0.693}{k}$ rearrange to solve for k.

$k = \frac{0.693}{t_{1/2}} = \frac{0.693}{1.6 \times 10^3 \text{ yr}} = 4.33125 \times 10^{-4} \text{ yr}^{-1}$. Since

$\ln m_{\text{Ra-226 } t} = -kt + \ln m_{\text{Ra-226 } 0} = -(4.33125 \times 10^{-4} \cancel{\text{yr}^{-1}})(0.013690 \cancel{\text{yr}}) + \ln(25.0 \text{ g}) = 3.21887$

$\rightarrow m_{\text{Ra-226 } t} = e^{3.21887} = 24.9999 \text{ g}$. Then

$mg_0 - mg_t = \text{mg decayed} = 25.0 \text{ g} - 24.9999 \text{ g} = 0.000148 \text{ g Ra-226}$ then

$0.000148 \cancel{\text{g Ra-226}} \times \frac{1 \cancel{\text{mol Ra-226}}}{226.05402 \cancel{\text{g Ra-226}}} \times \frac{1 \text{ mol Rn-224}}{1 \cancel{\text{mol Ra-226}}} = 6.5576 \times 10^{-7} \text{ mol Rn-224}$ then

and $T = 25.0\ °\text{C} + 273.15 = 298.2 \text{ K}$, then $PV = nRT$ Rearrange to solve for V.

$$V = \frac{nRT}{P} = \frac{6.5576 \times 10^{-7} \cancel{\text{mol}} \times 0.08206 \frac{\text{L} \cdot \cancel{\text{atm}}}{\cancel{\text{mol}} \cdot \cancel{\text{K}}} \times 298.2 \cancel{\text{K}}}{1.0 \cancel{\text{atm}}} = 1.6047 \times 10^{-5} \text{ L} = 1.6 \times 10^{-5} \text{ L}.$$ Two

significant figures are reported as requested in the problem.

Check: The units (L) are correct. The amount of gas is small since the time is so small compared to the half-life.

19.84 **Given:** U-235 (235.043922 amu) neutron- induced fission to Ba-140 and Kr-93, 1.00 g U-235, $T = 25.0\ °\text{C}$, $P = 1.0$ atm **Find:** V of Kr-93 gas produced

Conceptual Plan: Write the species given on the appropriate side of the equation. → Equalize the sum of the mass numbers and the sum of the atomic numbers on both sides of the equation by writing the stoichiometric coefficient in front of the desired species. Then

g U-235 → mol U-235 → mol Kr-93 formed then °C → K then $P, n, T \rightarrow V$

$\frac{1 \text{ mol U-235}}{235.043922 \text{ g U-235}}$ $\quad \frac{1 \text{ mol Kr-93}}{1 \text{ mol U-235}}$ $\quad K = °\text{C} + 273.15$ $\quad PV = nRT$

Solution: ${}^{235}_{92}\text{U} + {}^{1}_{0}\text{n} \rightarrow {}^{140}_{56}\text{Ba} + {}^{93}_{36}\text{Kr} + ?{}^{1}_{0}\text{n}$ becomes ${}^{235}_{92}\text{U} + {}^{1}_{0}\text{n} \rightarrow {}^{140}_{56}\text{Ba} + {}^{93}_{36}\text{Kr} + 3{}^{1}_{0}\text{n}$. then

$1.00 \cancel{\text{g U-235}} \times \frac{1 \cancel{\text{mol U-235}}}{235.043922 \cancel{\text{g U-235}}} \times \frac{1 \text{ mol Kr-93}}{1 \cancel{\text{mol U-235}}} = 4.25452 \times 10^{-3} \text{mol Kr-93}$ then

and $T = 25.0\ °\text{C} + 273.15 = 298.2 \text{ K}$, then $PV = nRT$. Rearrange to solve for V.

$$V = \frac{nRT}{P} = \frac{4.25452 \times 10^{-3} \cancel{\text{mol}} \times 0.08206 \frac{\text{L} \cdot \cancel{\text{atm}}}{\cancel{\text{mol}} \cdot \cancel{\text{K}}} \times 298.2 \cancel{\text{K}}}{1.0 \cancel{\text{atm}}} = 0.104109 \text{ L} = 0.10 \text{ L}.$$

Check: 235 + 1 = 140 + 93 + 3(1), 92 + 0 = 56 + 36 + 3(0), and no other particle is necessary to balance the equation. The units (L) are correct. About 1/200 mole of gas is generated so we expect the volume to be about 22/200 L.

19.85 **Given:** ${}^{0}_{+1}\text{e} + {}^{0}_{-1}\text{e} \rightarrow 2\,{}^{0}_{0}\gamma$ **Find:** energy (in kJ/mol)

Conceptual Plan:

mass of products & reactants → mass defect (g) → kg → kg/mol → E (J/mol) → E (kJ/mol)

$\text{mass defect} = \sum \text{mass of reactants} - \sum \text{mass of products}$ $\quad \frac{1 \text{ kg}}{1000 \text{ g}}$ $\quad 2 \text{ mol}$ $\quad E = mc^2$ $\quad \frac{1 \text{ kJ}}{1000 \text{ J}}$

Solution: $\text{mass defect} = \sum \text{mass of reactants} - \sum \text{mass of products} = (0.00055 \text{ g} + 0.00055 \text{ g}) - 0 \text{ g}$

$= 0.00110 \text{ g}$ then $\frac{0.00110 \cancel{\text{g}}}{2 \text{ mol}} \times \frac{1 \text{ kg}}{1000 \cancel{\text{g}}} = 5.50 \times 10^{-7} \frac{\text{kg}}{\text{mol}}$ then

$$E = mc^2 = \left(5.50 \times 10^{-7} \frac{\text{kg}}{\text{mol}}\right)\left(2.9979 \times 10^8 \frac{\text{m}}{\text{s}}\right)^2 = 4.94307 \times 10^{10} \frac{\cancel{\text{J}}}{\text{mol}} \times \frac{1 \text{ kJ}}{1000 \cancel{\text{J}}} = 4.94 \times 10^7 \frac{\text{kJ}}{\text{mol}}.$$

Check: The units (kJ/mol and pm) are correct. A large amount of energy is expected per mole of mass lost. The photon is in the gamma ray region of the electromagnetic spectrum.

19.86 **Given:** 1.0 MW power/day **Find:** minimum rate of mass loss required

Conceptual Plan: MW → MWh → kWh → J → kg → g

$\frac{24 \text{ h}}{1 \text{ day}}$ $\quad \frac{1000 \text{ kWh}}{1 \text{ MWh}}$ $\quad \frac{3.60 \times 10^6 \text{ J}}{1 \text{ kWh}}$ $\quad E = mc^2$ $\quad \frac{1000 \text{ g}}{1 \text{ kg}}$

Solution: $1.0 \cancel{\text{MW}} \times \frac{24 \cancel{\text{h}}}{1 \text{ day}} \times \frac{1000 \cancel{\text{kWh}}}{1 \cancel{\text{MWh}}} \times \frac{3.60 \times 10^6 \text{ J}}{1 \cancel{\text{kWh}}} = 8.64 \times 10^{10} \frac{\text{J}}{\text{day}}$. Since $E = mc^2$, rearrange to solve

$$\text{for } m.\ m = \frac{E}{c^2} = \frac{8.64 \times 10^{10}\ \frac{\text{kg}}{\text{day}}\ \frac{\cancel{\text{m}^2}}{\cancel{\text{s}^2}}}{\left(2.9979 \times 10^8\ \frac{\cancel{\text{m}}}{\cancel{\text{s}}}\right)^2} = 9.6 \times 10^{-7}\ \frac{\cancel{\text{kg}}}{\text{day}} \times \frac{1000\ \text{g}}{1\ \cancel{\text{kg}}} = 9.6 \times 10^{-4}\ \frac{\text{g}}{\text{day}}.$$

Check: The units (g/day) are correct. A large amount of energy is expected per gram of mass lost.

19.87 **Given:** ^{3}He = 3.016030 amu **Find:** nuclear binding energy per atom
Conceptual Plan: $^A_Z X$**, isotope mass → mass defect → nuclear binding energy per nucleon**

mass defect $= Z(\text{mass } ^1_1\text{H}) + (A - Z)(\text{mass } ^1_0\text{n}) -$ mass of isotope $\quad \frac{931.5\ \text{MeV}}{1\ \text{amu}}$

Solution: mass defect $= Z(\text{mass } ^1_1\text{H}) + (A - Z)(\text{mass } ^1_0\text{n}) -$ mass of isotope.
He-3 mass defect = 2(1.00783 amu) + (3 − 2)(1.00866 amu) − 3.016030 amu = 0.00829 amu

and $0.00829\ \cancel{\text{amu}} \times \frac{931.5\ \text{MeV}}{1\ \cancel{\text{amu}}} = 7.72\ \text{MeV}$.

Check: The units (MeV) are correct. The number of nucleons is small, so the MeV is not that large.

19.88 **Given:** $4\ ^1_1\text{H} \rightarrow\ ^4_2\text{He}$ **Find:** energy (in J/mol reactant)
Conceptual Plan: mass of products & reactants → mass defect in g → mass defect in kg → E

mass defect $= \sum$mass of reactants $- \sum$mass of products $\quad \frac{1\ \text{kg}}{1000\ \text{g}} \quad E = mc^2$

Solution:
mass defect $= \sum$mass of reactants $- \sum$mass of products = 4(1.00783 g) − 4.002603 g = 0.028717 g

then $\frac{0.028717\ \cancel{\text{g}}}{4\ \text{mol reactants}} \times \frac{1\ \text{kg}}{1000\ \cancel{\text{g}}} = 7.17925 \times 10^{-6}\ \frac{\text{kg}}{\text{mol reactants}}$ then

$$E = mc^2 = \left(7.17925 \times 10^{-6}\ \frac{\text{kg}}{\text{mol reactants}}\right)\left(2.9979 \times 10^8\ \frac{\text{m}}{\text{s}}\right)^2 = 6.4523 \times 10^{11}\ \frac{\text{J}}{\text{mol reactants}}.$$

Check: The units (J/mol) are correct.

19.89 **Given:** ^{247}Es and 5 neutrons made by bombarding ^{238}U **Find:** identity of bombarding particle
Conceptual Plan: Begin with the symbols for the nuclides given. → Equalize the sum of the mass numbers and the sum of the atomic numbers on both sides of the equation by writing the appropriate mass number and atomic number for the unknown daughter nuclide. → Using the periodic table, deduce the identity of the unknown nuclide from the atomic number and write its symbol.
Solution:
$^{238}_{92}\text{U} + ^{?}_{?}? \rightarrow\ ^{247}_{99}\text{Es} + 5\ ^1_0\text{n}$ then $^{238}_{92}\text{U} + ^{14}_{7}? \rightarrow\ ^{247}_{99}\text{Es} + 5\ ^1_0\text{n}$ then $^{238}_{92}\text{U} + ^{14}_{7}\text{N} \rightarrow\ ^{247}_{99}\text{Es} + 5\ ^1_0\text{n}$
Check: 238 + 14 = 247 + 5(1), 92 + 7 = 99 + 5(0), and nitrogen is atomic number 7.

19.90 **Given:** ^{6}Li reacts with ^{2}H to form 2 identical particles **Find:** identity of product particles
Conceptual Plan: Begin with the symbols for the nuclides given. → Equalize the sum of the mass numbers and the sum of the atomic numbers on both sides of the equation by writing the appropriate mass number and atomic number for the unknown daughter nuclide. → Using the periodic table, deduce the identity of the unknown nuclide from the atomic number and write its symbol.
Solution:
$^6_3\text{Li} + ^2_1\text{H} \rightarrow 2\ ^?_??$ then $^6_3\text{Li} + ^2_1\text{H} \rightarrow 2\ ^4_2?$ then $^6_3\text{Li} + ^2_1\text{H} \rightarrow 2\ ^4_2\text{He}$ or two alpha particles.
Check: 6 + 2 = 2(4), 3 + 1 = 2(2), and helium is atomic number 2.

19.91 **Given:** $t_{1/2}$ for decay of ^{238}U = 4.5 x 10^9 years, 1.6 g rock, 29 dis/s all radioactivity from U-238
Find: percent by mass ^{238}U in rock
Conceptual Plan: $t_{1/2}$ **→** k **and s → min → h → day → yr then Rate,** k **→** N **→ mol ^{238}U → g ^{238}U**

$t_{1/2} = \frac{0.693}{k} \quad \frac{1\ \text{min}}{60\ \text{s}} \quad \frac{1\ \text{h}}{60\ \text{min}} \quad \frac{1\ \text{day}}{24\ \text{h}} \quad \frac{1\ \text{yr}}{365.24\ \text{day}} \quad \text{Rate} = kN \quad \frac{1\ \text{mol dis}}{6.022 \times 10^{23}\ \text{dis}} \quad \frac{238\ \text{g}\ ^{238}\text{U}}{1\ \text{mol}\ ^{238}\text{U}}$

then g ^{238}U, g rock → percent by mass ^{238}U

percent by mass $^{238}\text{U} = \frac{\text{g}\ ^{238}\text{U}}{\text{g rock}} \times 100\%$

Solution: $t_{1/2} = \frac{0.693}{k}$ rearrange to solve for k. $k = \frac{0.693}{t_{1/2}} = \frac{0.693}{4.5 \times 10^9\ \text{yr}} = 1.54 \times 10^{-10}\ \text{yr}^{-1}$ and

$1\ \text{s} \times \frac{1\ \text{min}}{60\ \text{s}} \times \frac{1\ \text{h}}{60\ \text{min}} \times \frac{1\ \text{day}}{24\ \text{h}} \times \frac{1\ \text{yr}}{365.24\ \text{day}} = 3.16889554 \times 10^{-8}\ \text{yr}$. Rate $= k\,N$. Rearrange to solve for N.

$$N = \frac{\text{Rate}}{k} = \frac{29\ \frac{\text{dis}}{3.16889554 \times 10^{-8}\ \text{yr}}}{1.54 \times 10^{-10}\ \text{yr}^{-1}} = 5.9425 \times 10^{18}\ \text{dis then}$$

$$5.9425 \times 10^{18}\ \text{dis} \times \frac{1\ \text{mol dis}}{6.022 \times 10^{23}\ \text{dis}} \times \frac{238\ \text{g}\ ^{238}\text{U}}{1\ \text{mol}\ ^{238}\text{U}} = 2.3486 \times 10^{-3}\ \text{g}\ ^{238}\text{U then}$$

$$\text{percent by mass}\ ^{238}\text{U} = \frac{\text{g}\ ^{238}\text{U}}{\text{g rock}} \times 100\% = \frac{2.3486 \times 10^{-3}\ \text{g}\ ^{238}\text{U}}{1.6\ \text{g rock}} \times 100\% = 0.15\%.$$

Check: The units (%) are correct. The mass percent is low because the dis/s is low.

19.92 **Given:** $t_{1/2}$ for decay of ^{232}Th = 1.4×10^{10} years **Find:** number of dis emitted by 1.0 mol ^{232}Th in 1 min

Conceptual Plan: $t_{1/2} \rightarrow k$ **then** $N, k \rightarrow$ **Rate (dis/yr)** $\rightarrow$ **dis/day** $\rightarrow$ **dis/h** $\rightarrow$ **dis/min**

$t_{1/2} = \frac{0.693}{k}$ Rate $= k\,N$ $\frac{1\ \text{yr}}{365.24\ \text{day}}$ $\frac{1\ \text{day}}{24\ \text{h}}$ $\frac{1\ \text{h}}{60\ \text{min}}$

Solution: $t_{1/2} = \frac{0.693}{k}$ rearrange to solve for k. $k = \frac{0.693}{t_{1/2}} = \frac{0.693}{1.4 \times 10^{10}\ \text{yr}} = 4.95 \times 10^{-11}\ \text{yr}^{-1}$ then

$$\text{Rate} = k\,N = (4.95 \times 10^{-11}\ \text{yr}^{-1})(6.022 \times 10^{23}\ \text{dis}) \times \frac{1\ \text{yr}}{365.24\ \text{day}} \times \frac{1\ \text{day}}{24\ \text{h}} = 3.4 \times 10^{9}\ \text{dis/h}$$

$$3.4 \times 10^{9}\ \text{dis/h} \times \frac{1\ \text{h}}{60\ \text{min}} = 5.7 \times 10^{7}\ \text{dis/min}$$

Check: The units (dis/h and dis/min) are correct. The rate is high since the amount of ^{232}Th is high.

19.93 **Given:** $V = 1.50$ L, $P = 745$ mmHg, $T = 25.0$ °C, 3.55% Ra-220 by volume, $t_{1/2} = 55.6$ s

Find: number of alpha particles emitted in 5.00 min

Conceptual Plan: **mmHg** $\rightarrow$ **atm and °C** $\rightarrow$ **K then** $P, V, T \rightarrow n_{\text{Total}} \rightarrow n_{\text{Ra-220}}$ **and min** $\rightarrow$ **s**

$\frac{1\ \text{atm}}{760\ \text{mmHg}}$ K = °C + 273.15 $PV = nRT$ $\frac{3.55\ \text{Ra-220 particles}}{100\ \text{gas particles}}$ $\frac{60\ \text{s}}{1\ \text{min}}$

then $t_{1/2} \rightarrow k$ **then** $n_{\text{Ra-220 0}}, t, k \rightarrow n_{\text{Ra-220}\ t} \rightarrow$ **number of particles remaining** $\rightarrow$ **particles emitted**

$t_{1/2} = \frac{0.693}{k}$ $\ln N_t = -k\,t + \ln N_0$ $\frac{6.022 \times 10^{23}\ \text{particles}}{1\ \text{mol}}$

Solution: $745\ \text{mmHg} \times \frac{1\ \text{atm}}{760\ \text{mmHg}} = 0.9802632\ \text{atm}$ and $T = 25.0\ °\text{C} + 273.15 = 298.2$ K, then

$PV = nRT$ Rearrange to solve for n.

$$n = \frac{PV}{RT} = \frac{0.9802632\ \text{atm} \times 1.50\ \text{L}}{0.08206\ \frac{\text{L} \cdot \text{atm}}{\text{mol} \cdot \text{K}} \times 298.2\ \text{K}} = 0.06008897\ \text{mol gas particles}$$

$$\text{then } 0.06008897\ \text{mol gas particles} \times \frac{3.55\ \text{mol Ra-220 particles}}{100\ \text{mol gas particles}} = 0.002133158\ \text{mol Ra-220 particles}$$

$5.00\ \text{min} \times \frac{60\ \text{s}}{1\ \text{min}} = 300.\ \text{s}$ then $t_{1/2} = \frac{0.693}{k}$ and rearrange to solve for k.

$k = \frac{0.693}{t_{1/2}} = \frac{0.693}{55.6\ \text{s}} = 0.01246403\ \text{s}^{-1}$. Since

$$\ln m_{\text{Ra-220}\ t} = -k\,t + \ln m_{\text{Ra-220 0}} = -(0.01246403\ \text{s}^{-1})(300.\ \text{s}) + \ln(0.002133158\ \text{mol}) = -9.889361 \rightarrow$$

$m_{\text{Ra-220}\ t} = e^{-9.889361} = 5.071136 \times 10^{-5}$ mol alpha particles remaining.

The number of alpha particles emitted would be the difference between this and the initial number of moles.

0.002133158 mol – 0.00005071136 mol = 0.002082446 mol

$$0.002082446 \ \cancel{mol} \times \frac{6.022 \times 10^{23} \text{ particles}}{1 \ \cancel{mol}} = 1.254062 \times 10^{21} \text{ particles} = 1.25 \times 10^{21} \text{ particles.}$$

Check: The units (particles) are correct. The amount of particles is far less than a mole, since we have far less than a mole of gas.

19.94 **Given:** 228 mL of 2.35 by mass $MgCl_2$; exactly $\frac{1}{2}$ of Mg is Mg-28, $t_{1/2} = 21$ h, $d = 1.02$ g/mL

Find: decay rate after 4.00 days

Conceptual Plan: mL $\rightarrow$ g solution $\rightarrow$ g $MgCl_2$ $\rightarrow$ mol Mg $\rightarrow$ atoms Mg $\rightarrow$ atoms Mg-28 and

$$\frac{1.02 \text{ g}}{1 \text{ mL}} \qquad \frac{2.35 \text{ g } MgCl_2}{100 \text{ g solution}} \qquad \frac{1 \text{ mol Mg}}{95.21 \text{ g } MgCl_2} \qquad \frac{6.022 \times 10^{23} \text{ Mg atoms}}{1 \text{ mol Mg}} \qquad \frac{1 \text{ Mg-28 atom}}{2 \text{ Mg atoms}}$$

days $\rightarrow$ h then $t_{1/2} \rightarrow k$ then $N_{\text{Mg-28 } 0}, t, k \rightarrow N_{\text{Mg-28 } t} \rightarrow$ **Rate**

$$\frac{24 \text{ h}}{1 \text{ day}} \qquad t_{1/2} = \frac{0.693}{k} \qquad \ln N_t = -kt + \ln N_0 \quad \text{Rate} = kN$$

Solution: $228 \ \cancel{\text{mL solution}} \times \dfrac{1.02 \ \cancel{\text{g solution}}}{1 \ \cancel{\text{mL solution}}} \times \dfrac{2.35 \ \cancel{\text{g } MgCl_2}}{100 \ \cancel{\text{g solution}}} \times \dfrac{1 \ \cancel{\text{mol Mg}}}{95.21 \ \cancel{\text{g } MgCl_2}} \times \dfrac{6.022 \times 10^{23} \ \cancel{\text{Mg atoms}}}{1 \ \cancel{\text{mol Mg}}}$

$\times \dfrac{1 \text{ Mg-28 atom}}{2 \ \cancel{\text{Mg atoms}}} = 1.728348 \times 10^{22}$ Mg-28 atoms

and $21 \ \cancel{h} \times \dfrac{1 \text{ day}}{24 \ \cancel{h}} = 0.875$ day then $t_{1/2} = \dfrac{0.693}{k}$ rearrange to solve for k.

$k = \dfrac{0.693}{t_{1/2}} = \dfrac{0.693}{0.875 \text{ day}} = 0.792 \text{ day}^{-1}$. Since

$\ln N_{\text{Mg-28 } t} = -kt + \ln N_{\text{Mg-28 } 0} = -(0.792 \ \cancel{\text{day}^{-1}})(4.00 \ \cancel{\text{day}}) + \ln(1.728348 \times 10^{22}) = 48.03604$

$\rightarrow N_{\text{Mg-28 } t} = e^{48.03604} = 7.2742 \times 10^{20}$ Mg-28 atoms. Finally, Rate $= kN$, so

Rate $= 0.792/\text{day} \times 7.2742 \times 10^{20} = 5.8 \times 10^{20}$ atoms/day.

Check: The units (atoms) are correct. The amount of particles is far less than a mole, since we have a dilute solution.

19.95 **Given:** $_{+1}^0 e + _{-1}^0 e \rightarrow 2_0^0 \gamma$ **Find:** wavelength of gamma ray photons

Conceptual Plan:

mass of products & reactants $\rightarrow$ mass defect (g) $\rightarrow$ kg $\rightarrow$ kg/mol $\rightarrow$ E (J/mol) $\rightarrow$ E (kJ/mol)

$$\text{mass defect} = \sum \text{mass of reactants} - \sum \text{mass of products} \quad \frac{1 \text{ kg}}{1000 \text{ g}} \quad 2 \text{ mol} \quad E = mc^2 \quad \frac{1 \text{ kJ}}{1000 \text{ J}}$$

This energy is for 2 moles of γ, so E (J/2 mol γ) $\rightarrow$ E (J/ γ photon) $\rightarrow$ λ.

$$\frac{1 \text{ mol photons}}{6.022 \times 10^{23} \text{ photons}} \qquad E = \frac{hc}{\lambda}$$

Solution: mass defect $= \sum \text{mass of reactants} - \sum \text{mass of products} = (0.00055 \text{ g} + 0.00055 \text{ g}) - 0 \text{ g}$

$= 0.00110$ g then $\dfrac{0.00110 \ \cancel{g}}{2 \text{ mol}} \times \dfrac{1 \text{ kg}}{1000 \ \cancel{g}} = 5.50 \times 10^{-7} \dfrac{\text{kg}}{\text{mol}}$ then

$E = mc^2 = \left(5.50 \times 10^{-7} \dfrac{\text{kg}}{\text{mol}}\right)\left(2.9979 \times 10^8 \dfrac{\text{m}}{\text{s}}\right)^2 = 4.94307 \times 10^{10} \dfrac{\cancel{J}}{\text{mol}} \times \dfrac{1 \text{ kJ}}{1000 \ \cancel{J}} = 4.94 \times 10^7 \dfrac{\text{kJ}}{\text{mol}}.$

$E = 4.94307 \times 10^{10} \dfrac{J}{\cancel{\text{mol }\gamma}} \times \dfrac{1 \ \cancel{\text{mol }\gamma}}{6.022 \times 10^{23} \gamma \text{ photons}} = 8.20835 \times 10^{-14} \dfrac{J}{\gamma \text{ photons}}$. Then $E = \dfrac{hc}{\lambda}$. Rearrange

to solve for λ. $\lambda = \dfrac{hc}{E} = \dfrac{(6.626 \times 10^{-34} \ \cancel{J} \cdot \cancel{s})\left(2.9979 \times 10^8 \dfrac{\text{m}}{\cancel{s}}\right)}{8.20835 \times 10^{-14} \dfrac{\cancel{J}}{\gamma \text{ photons}}} = 2.42 \times 10^{-12}$ m $= 2.42$ pm.

Check: The units (m or pm) are correct. A large amount of energy is expected per mole of mass lost. The photon is in the gamma ray region of the electromagnetic spectrum.

19.96 **Given:** 1.0 mg U-235, $t_{1/2} = 7.1 \times 10^8$ yr **Find:** alpha particles emitted in 1.0 min

Conceptual Plan: Since the time is so small compared to the half-life, use Rate = kN_0 and calculate the number of particles emitted based on the initial rate.

mg → g → mol → atoms (N_0) and

$$\frac{1\text{ g}}{1000\text{ mg}} \quad \frac{1\text{ mol}}{235\text{ g}} \quad \frac{6.022 \times 10^{23}\text{atoms}}{1\text{ mol}}$$

min → h → days → yr then $t_{1/2}$ → k then $N_{\text{U-235 }0}$, t, k → alpha particles emitted

$$\frac{1\text{ h}}{60\text{ min}} \quad \frac{1\text{ day}}{24\text{ h}} \quad \frac{1\text{ yr}}{365.24\text{ days}} \quad t_{1/2} = \frac{0.693}{k} \quad \text{Rate} = kN_0$$

Solution: $1.0\text{ mg} \times \frac{1\text{ g}}{1000\text{ mg}} \times \frac{1\text{ mol}}{235\text{ g}} \times \frac{6.022 \times 10^{23}\text{ atoms}}{1\text{ mol}} = 2.56255 \times 10^{18}$ atoms and

$1.0\text{ min} \times \frac{1\text{ h}}{60\text{ min}} \times \frac{1\text{ day}}{24\text{ h}} \times \frac{1\text{ yr}}{365.24\text{ day}} = 1.901337 \times 10^{-6}$ yr then $t_{1/2} = \frac{0.693}{k}$ rearrange to solve for k.

$k = \frac{0.693}{t_{1/2}} = \frac{0.693}{7.1 \times 10^8\text{yr}} = 9.76056 \times 10^{-10}\text{ yr}^{-1}$. then

Rate $= -k\,N_{\text{U-235 }0} = (9.76056 \times 10^{-10}\text{ yr}^{-1})(2.56255 \times 10^{18}\text{ particles}) = 2.501192 \times 10^9$particles/yr then →

$\frac{2.501192 \times 10^9\text{ particles}}{1\text{ yr}} \times 1.901337 \times 10^{-6}\text{ yr} = 4755.6$ particles $=$ 4800 particles emitted.

Check: The units (particles) are correct. The amount of particles is small because the half-life is long and the observation time is small.

19.97 **Given:** ${}^2_1\text{H} + {}^2_1\text{H} \rightarrow {}^3_2\text{He} + {}^1_0\text{n}$ releases 3.3 MeV; ${}^2_1\text{H} + {}^2_1\text{H} \rightarrow {}^3_1\text{H} + {}^1_1\text{p}$ releases 4.0 MeV;

Find: The energy change for ${}^3_2\text{He} + {}^1_0\text{n} \rightarrow {}^3_1\text{H} + {}^1_1\text{p}$ and explain why this can happen at a much lower temperature.

Conceptual Plan: Use Hess's law to calculate the energy change, and give the two reactions.

Solution:

${}^3_2\text{He} + {}^1_0\text{n} \rightarrow {}^2_1\text{H} + {}^2_1\text{H} \quad \Delta E = 3.3$ MeV

${}^2_1\text{H} + {}^2_1\text{H} \rightarrow {}^3_1\text{H} + {}^1_1\text{p} \quad \Delta E = -4.0$ MeV

${}^3_2\text{He} + {}^1_0\text{n} \rightarrow {}^3_1\text{H} + {}^1_1\text{p} \quad \Delta E = -0.7$ MeV

The energy change is much less and there is no coulombic barrier for collision with a neutron, so the process can occur at lower temperatures.

Check: The units (MeV) are correct. Since one reaction releases energy and one requires energy, the resulting energy change is much smaller in magnitude.

19.98 **Given:** ${}^{18}_9\text{F} + {}^0_{-1}\text{e} \rightarrow {}^{18}_8\text{O}$ and ${}^{18}_9\text{F} \rightarrow {}^{18}_8\text{O} + {}^0_{+1}\text{e}$ **Find:** difference in energy released

Other: ${}^{18}_9\text{F} = 18.000950$ g and ${}^{18}_8\text{O} = 17.9991598$ g

Conceptual Plan: For each reaction calculate: mass of products & reactants → mass defect in amu then

mass defect $= \sum$mass of reactants $- \sum$mass of products

calculate the difference between the two mass defects in amu → E.

$$\frac{931.5\text{ MeV}}{1\text{ amu}}$$

Solution: Since mass defect $= \sum$mass of reactants $- \sum$mass of products

for ${}^{18}_9\text{F} + {}^0_{-1}\text{e} \rightarrow {}^{18}_8\text{O}$

mass defect = (18.000950 amu + 0.0005486 amu) − (17.9991598 amu) = +0.0023388 amu and for

${}^{18}_9\text{F} \rightarrow {}^{18}_8\text{O} + {}^0_{+1}\text{e}$ mass defect = (18.000950 amu) − (17.9991598 amu + 0.0005486) = +0.0012416 amu

The mass defect difference between the two reactions is 0.0010972 amu = mass of two electrons

then $0.0010972\text{ amu} \times \frac{931.5\text{ MeV}}{1\text{ amu}} = 1.022$ MeV

Check: The units (MeV) are correct. The energy is smaller than most nuclear reactions because the mass difference is small.

Challenge Problems

19.99 (a) **Given:** 72,500 kg Al *(s)* and 10 Al *(s)* + 6 NH_4ClO_4 *(s)* → 4 Al_2O_3 *(s)* + 2 $AlCl_3$ *(s)* + 12 H_2O *(g)* + 3 N_2 *(g)* and 608,000 kg O_2 *(g)* that reacts with hydrogen to form gaseous water
Find: energy generated (ΔH°_{rxn})
Conceptual Plan: Write a balanced reaction for O_2 *(g)* then
$\Delta H^\circ_{rxn} = \sum n_p \Delta H^\circ_f(\text{products}) - \sum n_r \Delta H^\circ_f(\text{reactants})$ then
kg → g → mol → energy then add the results from the two reactions.
$\frac{1000\text{ g}}{1\text{ kg}}$ $\mathcal{M}$ ΔH°_{rxn}

Solution:

Reactant/Product	ΔH°_f(kJ/mol from Appendix IIB)
Al *(s)*	0.0
NH_4ClO_4 *(s)*	– 295
Al_2O_3 *(s)*	– 1675.7
$AlCl_3$ *(s)*	– 704.2
H_2O *(g)*	– 241.8
N_2 *(g)*	0.0

Be sure to pull data for the correct formula and phase.

$$\Delta H^\circ_{rxn} = \sum n_p \Delta H^\circ_f(\text{products}) - \sum n_r \Delta H^\circ_f(\text{reactants})$$
$$= [4(\Delta H^\circ_f(Al_2O_3\,(s))) + 2(\Delta H^\circ_f(AlCl_3\,(s))) + 12(\Delta H^\circ_f(H_2O\,(g))) + 3(\Delta H^\circ_f(N_2\,(g)))] + - [10(\Delta H^\circ_f(Al\,(s))) + 6(\Delta H^\circ_f(NH_4ClO_4\,(s)))]$$
$$= [4(-1675.7\text{ kJ}) + 2(-704.2\text{ kJ}) + 12(-241.8\text{ kJ}) + 3(0.0\text{ kJ})] - [10(0.0\text{ kJ}) + 6(-295\text{ kJ})]$$
$$= [-11012.8\text{ kJ}] - [-1770.\text{ kJ}]$$
$$= -9242.8\text{ kJ}$$

then $72{,}500\ \cancel{\text{kg Al}} \times \frac{1000\ \cancel{\text{g Al}}}{1\ \cancel{\text{kg Al}}} \times \frac{1\ \cancel{\text{mol Al}}}{26.98\ \cancel{\text{g Al}}} \times \frac{9242.8\text{ kJ}}{10\ \cancel{\text{mol Al}}} = 2.483703 \times 10^9\text{ kJ}.$

balanced reaction: $H_2\,(g) + \frac{1}{2}O_2\,(g) \rightarrow H_2O\,(g)$ $\Delta H^\circ_{rxn} = \Delta H^\circ_f(H_2O\,(g)) = -241.8$ kJ/mol then

$608{,}000\ \cancel{\text{kg O}_2} \times \frac{1000\ \cancel{\text{g O}_2}}{1\ \cancel{\text{kg O}_2}} \times \frac{1\ \cancel{\text{mol O}_2}}{32.00\ \cancel{\text{g O}_2}} \times \frac{241.8\text{ kJ}}{0.5\ \cancel{\text{mol O}_2}} = 9.1884 \times 10^9\text{ kJ}.$ So the total is

$2.483703 \times 10^9\text{ kJ} + 9.1884 \times 10^9\text{ kJ} = 1.1672103 \times 10^{10}\text{ kJ} = 1.167 \times 10^{10}\text{ kJ}.$

Check: The units (kJ) are correct. The answer is very large because the reactions are very exothermic and the weight of reactants is so large.

(b) **Given:** ${}^1_1H + {}^{-1}_{-1}p + {}^{0}_{+1}e \rightarrow {}^0_0\gamma$ **Find:** mass of antimatter to give same energy as part (a)
Conceptual Plan: Since the reaction is an annihilation reaction, no matter will be left, so the mass of antimatter is the same as the mass of the hydrogen. so kJ → J → kg → g
$\frac{1000\text{ J}}{1\text{ kJ}}$ $E = mc^2$ $\frac{1000\text{ g}}{1\text{ kg}}$

Solution: $1.1672103 \times 10^{10}\ \cancel{\text{kJ}} \times \frac{1000\text{ J}}{1\ \cancel{\text{kJ}}} = 1.1672103 \times 10^{13}$ J. Since $E = mc^2$, rearrange to solve for m.

$$m = \frac{E}{c^2} = \frac{1.1672103 \times 10^{13}\text{ kg}\frac{\cancel{m^2}}{\cancel{s^2}}}{\left(2.9979 \times 10^8\frac{\cancel{m}}{\cancel{s}}\right)^2} = 1.299 \times 10^{-4}\ \cancel{\text{kg}} \times \frac{1000\text{ g}}{1\ \cancel{\text{kg}}} = 0.1299\text{ g total matter, 0.649 g each}$$

of matter and antimatter.

Check: The units (g) are correct. A small mass is expected since nuclear reactions generate a large amount of energy.

19.100 **Given:** 85.0 g animal, ingests 10.0 mg of substance with 2.55% by mass Pu-239, alpha emitter, $t_{1/2}$ = 24,110 years
Find: (a) initial exposure in Ci, and (b) all radiation absorbed and 7.77×10^{-12} J/emission, RBE = 20, dose in rads in the first 4.0 hours and dose in rems in the first 4.0 hours

Conceptual Plan:

(a) **$t_{1/2}$ → k and mg → g → g Pu-239 → mol Pu-239 → atoms Pu-239**

$t_{1/2} = \frac{0.693}{k}$ $\frac{1\text{ g}}{1000\text{ mg}}$ $\frac{2.22\text{ g Pu-239}}{100\text{ g substance}}$ $\frac{1\text{ mol Pu-239}}{239\text{ g Pu-239}}$ $\frac{6.022 \times 10^{23}\text{ Pu-239 atoms}}{1\text{ mol Pu-239}}$

then N, k → Rate (dis/yr) → dis/day → dis/h → dis/min → dis/s → Ci

Rate $= kN$ $\frac{1\text{ yr}}{365.24\text{ day}}$ $\frac{1\text{ day}}{24\text{ h}}$ $\frac{1\text{ h}}{60\text{ min}}$ $\frac{1\text{ min}}{60\text{ s}}$ $\frac{1\text{ Ci}}{\frac{3.7 \times 10^{10}\text{ decays}}{\text{s}}}$

(b) **h → min → s then dis/s, s → alpha decays → J and g → kg then J, animal mass → rad → rem**

$\frac{60\text{ min}}{1\text{ h}}$ $\frac{1\text{ s}}{60\text{ min}}$ multiply terms $\frac{7.77 \times 10^{-12}\text{ J}}{\text{decay}}$ $\frac{1\text{ kg}}{1000\text{ g}}$ $\frac{1\text{ rad}}{\frac{0.01\text{ J}}{\text{kg animal}}}$ rem = RBE x rad

Solution:

(a) $t_{1/2} = \frac{0.693}{k}$ rearrange to solve for k. $k = \frac{0.693}{t_{1/2}} = \frac{0.693}{24{,}110\text{ yr}} = 2.874326 \times 10^{-5}\text{ yr}^{-1}$ then

$$10.0\text{ mg} \times \frac{1\text{ g}}{1000\text{ mg}} \times \frac{2.55\text{ g Pu-239}}{100\text{ g substance}} \times \frac{1\text{ mol Pu-239}}{239\text{ g Pu-239}} \times \frac{6.022 \times 10^{23}\text{ Pu-239 atoms}}{1\text{ mol Pu-239}}$$

$= 6.425146 \times 10^{17}$ Pu-239 atoms

Rate $= kN =$

$$(2.874326 \times 10^{-5}\text{ yr}^{-1})(6.425146 \times 10^{17}\text{ Pu-239 atoms}) \times \frac{1\text{ yr}}{365.24\text{ day}} \times \frac{1\text{ day}}{24\text{ h}} \times \frac{1\text{ h}}{60\text{ min}} \times \frac{1\text{ min}}{60\text{ s}}$$

$$= 5.85230 \times 10^{5}\,\frac{\text{dis}}{\text{s}} \times \frac{1\text{ Ci}}{\frac{3.7 \times 10^{10}\text{ decays}}{\text{s}}} = 1.58170 \times 10^{-5}\text{ Ci}$$

(b) $4.0\text{ h} \times \frac{1\text{ day}}{24\text{ h}} \times \frac{1\text{ yr}}{365.24\text{ day}} = 4.5632 \times 10^{-4}$ yr Since the time is so much less than the $t_{1/2}$ (10^{-6}%) the concentration is essentially constant. Use dis/s and time to get dose,

so $4.0\text{ h} \times \frac{60\text{ min}}{1\text{ h}} \times \frac{60\text{ s}}{1\text{ min}} = 1.44 \times 10^{4}\text{ s}$

$$5.85230 \times 10^{5}\,\frac{\text{dis}}{\text{s}} \times 1.44 \times 10^{4}\text{ s} = 8.42731 \times 10^{9}\text{ decays} \times \frac{7.77 \times 10^{-12}\text{ J}}{\text{decay}} = 6.54802 \times 10^{-2}\text{ J and}$$

$$85.0\text{ g} \times \frac{1\text{ kg}}{1000\text{ g}} = 0.0850\text{ kg then } \frac{6.54802 \times 10^{-2}\text{ J}}{0.0850\text{ kg}} \times \frac{1\text{ rad}}{\frac{0.01\text{ J}}{\text{kg animal}}} = 77\text{ rad and}$$

rem = RBE x rad = 20 x 77 rad = 1.5×10^{3} rem and the animal will die.

Check: The units (Ci, rem, and rad) are correct. The number of Curies is small because of the conversion factor. The dose in rems and rad are high because it is an alpha emitter and the isotope was ingested.

19.101 **Given:** ${}^{235}_{92}\text{U} \rightarrow {}^{206}_{82}\text{Pb}$ and ${}^{232}_{90}\text{Th} \rightarrow {}^{206}_{82}\text{Pb}$ **Find:** decay series

Conceptual Plan: Write the species given on the appropriate side of the equation. → Equalize the sum of the mass numbers and the sum of the atomic numbers on both sides of the equation by writing the stoichiometric coefficient in front of the desired species.

Solution: ${}^{235}_{92}\text{U} \rightarrow {}^{?}_{82}\text{Pb} + ?\,{}^{4}_{2}\text{He} + ?\,{}^{0}_{-1}\text{e}$ becomes ${}^{235}_{92}\text{U} \rightarrow {}^{207}_{82}\text{Pb} + 7\,{}^{4}_{2}\text{He} + 4\,{}^{0}_{-1}\text{e}$.

${}^{232}_{90}\text{Th} \rightarrow {}^{?}_{82}\text{Pb} + ?\,{}^{4}_{2}\text{He} + ?\,{}^{0}_{-1}\text{e}$ becomes ${}^{232}_{90}\text{Th} \rightarrow {}^{208}_{82}\text{Pb} + 6\,{}^{4}_{2}\text{He} + 4\,{}^{0}_{-1}\text{e}$.

U-235 forms Pb-207 in 7 α-decays and 4 β-decays and Th-232 forms Pb-208 in 6 α-decays and 4 β-decays.

Check: 235 = 207 + 7(4) + 4(0), and 92 = 82 + 7(2) + 4(–1). 232 = 208 + 6(4) + 4(0), and 90 = 82 + 6(2) + 4(–1). The mass of the Pb can be determined because alpha particles are large and need to be included as integer values. To make the masses balance requires more alpha particles than can be supported by the number of protons in the total equation. To account for this, an appropriate number of beta decays are added.

19.102 **Given:** $MH_2 \rightarrow He(g) + X(\text{noble gas})(g) + H_2(g)$, 0.025 mol MH_2; $V = 2.0$ L, $P = 0.55$ atm, $T = 298$ K, 82 min
Find: $t_{1/2}$
Conceptual Plan: $P, V, T \rightarrow n_{gas} \rightarrow n_{M\,t}$ **then** $n_{M\,0}, n_{M\,t}, t \rightarrow k \rightarrow t_{1/2}$

$PV = nRT$ $\quad n_{M\,t} = 0.025\text{ mol} - 1/3\, n_{H_2}$ $\quad \ln N_t = -kt + \ln N_0$ $\quad t_{1/2} = \frac{0.693}{k}$

Solution: $PV = nRT$ Rearrange to solve for n. $n = \frac{PV}{RT} = \frac{0.55\ \text{atm} \times 2.0\ \text{L}}{0.08206\ \frac{\text{L}\cdot\text{atm}}{\text{mol}\cdot\text{K}} \times 298\ \text{K}} = 0.0449826$ mol gas

then $n_{M\,t} = 0.025\text{ mol} - 1/3\, n_{gas} = 0.025\text{ mol} - 1/3(0.0449826\text{ mol}) = 0.01000579$ mol then

$\ln N_{M\,t} = -kt + \ln N_{M\,0}$ Rearrange to solve for k. $k = \frac{\ln \frac{N_{M\,0}}{N_{M\,t}}}{t} = \frac{\ln \frac{0.025\ \text{mol}}{0.01000579\ \text{mol}}}{82\text{ min}} = 0.011672\ \text{min}^{-1}$

then $t_{1/2} = \frac{0.693}{k} = \frac{0.693}{0.011672\ \text{min}^{-1}} = 62.05664\text{ min} = 62\text{ min}$

Check: The units (min) are correct. The half-life is reasonable since most of the hydride decomposes in the 82 minutes.

19.103 **Given:** $H^{38}_{17}Cl\,(g) \rightarrow {}^{38}_{18}Ar\,(g) + {}^{0}_{-1}e + 1/2\, H_2\,(g)$, 0.40 mol $H^{38}_{17}Cl\,(g)$; $V = 6.24$ L, $P = 1650$ mmHg, $t_{1/2} = 80.0$ min **Find:** T
Conceptual Plan: Since $t = 2\, t_{1/2}$ **then** $N_{Cl\text{-}38\ t} = \frac{1}{4} N_{Cl\text{-}38\ 0} \rightarrow n_{gas\ t}$ **then mmHg** $\rightarrow$ **atm and**

$n_{gas\ t} = 3/2\, n_{HCl\ 0} - 1/2\, n_{HCl\ t}$ $\quad \frac{1\ \text{atm}}{760\ \text{mmHg}}$

$P, V, n_{gas\ t} \rightarrow T$

$PV = nRT$

Solution: Since $t = 2\, t_{1/2}$ then $N_{Cl\text{-}38\ t} = \frac{1}{4} N_{Cl\text{-}38\ 0} = \frac{1}{4}(0.40\text{ mol}) = 0.10$ mol. As the HCl disintegrates, it produces argon gas, beta particles and hydrogen gas, with a ratio of 3 particles produced (2 Ar, 1 H_2) for every 2 HCl molecules that decay. There were initially 0.40 mole of undisintegrated gas, and now there are 0.10 mole HCl remaining. So the total number of gas particles now in the container is:
$n_{gas\ t} = 3/2\, n_{HCl\ 0} - 1/2\, n_{HCl\ t} = 3/2(0.40\text{ mol}) - 1/2\,(0.10\text{ mol}) = 0.55$ mol gas then $PV = nRT$. Rearrange to solve for T. $T = \frac{PV}{nR} = \frac{1650\ \text{mmHg} \times \frac{1\ \text{atm}}{760\ \text{mmHg}} \times 6.24\ \text{L}}{0.55\ \text{mol} \times 0.08206\ \frac{\text{L}\cdot\text{atm}}{\text{mol}\cdot\text{K}}} = 300.17\text{ K} = 3.0 \times 10^2\text{ K}$

Check: The units (K) are correct. The temperature is reasonable considering the volume of a gas at STP and most of the initial 0.40 mol has decomposed.

19.104 **Given:** ${}^{x}_{5}BF_3\,(g) + {}^{1}_{0}n \rightarrow {}^{x-3}_{3}LiF\,(s) + {}^{4}_{2}He\,(g) + F_2\,(g)$, 0.20 mol BF_3, react half of BF_3, $V = 3.0$ L, $T = 298$ K
Find: P
Conceptual Plan: Since one half of BF_3 is reacted, $N_{B\ t} = \frac{1}{2} N_{B\ 0} \rightarrow n_{gas\ t}$ **then** $V, n_{gas\ t}, T \rightarrow P$.

$n_{gas\ t} = 1/2\, n_{BF_3\ 0} + 2\,(n_{BF_3\ 0} - n_{BF_3\ t})$ $\quad PV = nRT$

Solution: Since one half of BF_3 is reacted, $N_{B\ t} = \frac{1}{2} N_{B\ 0} = \frac{1}{2}(0.20\text{ mol}) = 0.10$ mol BF_3 then $n_{gas\ t} = 1/2\, n_{BF_3\ 0} + 2\,(n_{BF_3\ 0} - n_{BF_3\ t}) = \frac{1}{2}(0.20\text{ mol}) + 2(0.20\text{ mol} - 0.10\text{ mol}) = 0.30$ mol then $PV = nRT$

Rearrange to solve for P. $P = \frac{nRT}{V} = \frac{0.30\ \text{mol} \times 0.08206\ \frac{\text{L}\cdot\text{atm}}{\text{mol}\cdot\text{K}} \times 298\ \text{K}}{3.0\ \text{L}} = 2.44539\text{ atm} = 2.4\text{ atm}$

Check: The units (atm) are correct. The pressure is reasonable considering the conditions of a gas at STP and half of the initial 0.20 mol has decomposed.

Conceptual Problems

19.105 **Given:** ${}^{21}_{9}F \rightarrow {}^{?}_{?}? + {}^{0}_{-1}e$ **Find:** missing nucleus
Conceptual Plan: Write the species given on the appropriate side of the equation. $\rightarrow$ **Equalize the sum of the mass numbers and the sum of the atomic numbers on both sides of the equation by writing the stoichiometric coefficient in front of the desired species.**

Solution: ${}^{21}_{9}\text{F} \rightarrow {}^{?}_{?}? + {}^{0}_{-1}\text{e}$ becomes ${}^{21}_{9}\text{F} \rightarrow {}^{21}_{10}\text{Ne} + {}^{0}_{-1}\text{e}$.

Check: 21 = 21 + 0, and 9 = 10 + −1. Neon is atomic number 10 and no other species are needed to balance the equation.

19.106 7. Since $1/2^6 = 1.6\%$ and $1/2^7 = 0.8\%$.

19.107 Nuclide A is more dangerous because the half-life is shorter (18.5 days) and so it decays faster.

19.108 The gamma emitter is a greater threat while you sleep because it can penetrate more tissue. The alpha particles will not penetrate the wall to enter your bedroom. The alpha emitter is a greater threat if you ingest it since it is more ionizing.

19.109 Iodine is used by the thyroid gland to make hormones. Normally we ingest iodine in foods, especially iodized salt. The thyroid gland cannot tell the difference between stable and radioactive iodine and will absorb both. KI tables work by blocking radioactive iodine from entering the thyroid. When a person takes KI, the stable iodine in the tablet gets absorbed by the thyroid. Because KI contains so much stable iodine, the thyroid gland becomes "full" and cannot absorb any more iodine—either stable or radioactive—for the next 24 hours.